FINANCIAL ACCOUNTING STANDARDS BOARD (FASB): 1973 TO PRESENT

(CONTINUED INSIDE BACK COVER)

INTERMEDIATE ACCOUNTING

RANDOM HOUSE ACCOUNTING SERIES ADVISOR:

CHARLES H. SMITH

Peat, Marwick, Mitchell Professor of Accounting
The Pennsylvania State University

INTERMEDIATE

ACCOUNTING

SECOND EDITION

LANNY G. CHASTEEN
Oklahoma State University

RICHARD E. FLAHERTY
Arizona State University

MELVIN C. O'CONNOR
Michigan State University

**RANDOM HOUSE
BUSINESS DIVISION**
NEW YORK

Permissions Acknowledgments

Material from Uniform CPA Examination Questions and Unofficial Answers, copyright © 1951, 1952, 1953, 1954, 1957, 1959, 1961, 1962, 1963, 1964, 1965, 1966, 1967, 1968, 1969, 1970, 1971, 1972, 1973, 1974, 1975, 1976, 1977, 1978, 1979, 1980, 1981, 1982, 1983, 1984 by the American Institute of Certified Public Accountants, Inc., is adapted with permission.

Material from the Certificate in Management Accounting Examination, copyright © 1977, 1978, 1981 by the National Association of Accountants, is reprinted and/or adapted with permission.

Material is reprinted, with permission, from the 1975 Chartered Accounts Examination, published by the Canadian Institute of Chartered Accountants, Toronto, Canada.

Materials issued by the FASB are copyright by Financial Accounting Standards Board, High Ridge Park, Stamford, Connecticut, 06905, U.S.A., and reprinted with permission. Copies of the complete document are available from the FASB.

Second Edition

98765432

Library of Congress Cataloging in Publication Data

Chasteen, Lanny G., 1942–
    Intermediate accounting.

    Includes index.
    1. Accounting.   I. Flaherty, Richard E., 1944–
II. O'Connor, Melvin C.   III. Title.
HF5635.C474   1986   657'.044   86-29865
ISBN 0-394-35802-3

Manufactured in the United States of America by Rand McNally & Co., Taunton, MA

Designed by Betty Binns Graphics/Martin Lubin

To our parents

and to

Jane
Jamie
Joey

Ricci
Kristin
Erin

Darlene
Kevin

ABOUT THE SERIES ADVISOR
CHARLES H. SMITH

Peat, Marwick, Mitchell Professor of Accounting
The Pennsylvania State University

Charles Smith, Consulting Editor for Random House's Accounting Series, is Chairman of the Department of Accounting and Management Information Systems at The Pennsylvania State University. He earned his undergraduate degree at the University of Cape Town and his M.S. and Ph.D. degrees at The Pennsylvania State University. His research interests are in various financial accounting issues and the international dimensions of accounting. His publications have appeared in many U.S. and foreign journals, including *The Accounting Review,* the *Journal of Accounting Research,* and the *Journal of Accountancy.* Professor Smith has served on the editorial boards of *The Accounting Review,* the *Journal of Accountancy, The Accounting Journal,* and the *Quarterly Review of Economics and Business.* Professor Smith has served on numerous national professional committees, including the American Accounting Association's Financial Accounting Standards Committee (as chairperson). He is currently the chairman of the American Accounting Association's Operational Review Task Force. Professor Smith has taught at the University of Washington, the University of Texas at Austin, Arizona State University, the University of Illinois at Urbana-Champaign, and the University of Cape Town.

ABOUT THE AUTHORS

Lanny G. Chasteen, Ph.D., CPA, is professor of accounting in the School of Accounting at Oklahoma State University. He holds a bachelors degree from the University of Texas at Austin, and masters and doctorate degrees from the University of Arkansas. Professor Chasteen has published articles in *The Accounting Review,* the *Journal of Accounting Education,* the *Journal of Accountancy, Abacus,* and other professional journals. The articles have dealt with such topics as alternative inventory valuation methods, changing prices, leases, and revenue recognition. Professor Chasteen has received the Outstanding Teacher Award in the College of Business Administration at OSU; additionally he has taught at the University of Texas at Austin, Texas Tech University, the University of Texas at Arlington, and the University of Tulsa. Since 1979, he has taught courses in IBM's Continuing Professional Education Program. His public accounting experience was with Deloitte, Haskins, and Sells. Professor Chasteen is a member of the American Institute of Certified Public Accountants, the American Accounting Association, Beta Gamma Sigma, and Beta Alpha Psi, and he has served on committees of the American Accounting Association (AAA).

Richard E. Flaherty, Ph.D., CPA, is professor of accounting at Arizona State University. He received his B.S., M.S., and Ph.D. degrees from the University of Kansas. Professor Flaherty previously taught at Oklahoma State University and the University of Illinois. He also served as a research associate for the Financial Accounting Standards Board. He has served as a consultant on financial reporting issues to a number of businesses and has taught in numerous professional development programs. Professor Flaherty has published articles on financial accounting theory and practice in such journals as *The Accounting Review, The CPA Journal,* and the *Journal of Accounting, Auditing & Finance.* Also, Professor Flaherty is the author of Accounting Education Research Monograph No. 3, *The Core of the Curriculum for Accounting Majors,* published by the American Accounting Association. He is a member of the American Accounting Association, the American Institute of Certified Public Accounts (AICPA), Beta Alpha Psi, Beta Gamma Sigma, and Delta Sigma Pi. He has served the AAA as chairman of its Committee to Nominate Notable Contributions to the Accounting Literature. He is currently serving on the Board of Examiners of the AICPA and on the Theory Subcommittee of the Board of Examiners.

Melvin C. O'Connor, Ph.D., CPA, is a professor of accounting and chairperson of the Department of Accounting in the Graduate School of Business Administration at Michigan State University. He earned his B.S., M.S., and Ph.D. degrees at the University of Kansas. Professor O'Connor has been Director of the Accounting Doctoral Program at Michigan State and was Michigan State's Beta Alpha Psi Professor of the Year in 1980–81. Professor O'Connor has published articles on financial accounting theory and practice in *The Accounting Review,* the *Journal of Accountancy, Management Accounting,* and the *Financial Analysts Journal.* His publications are in the areas of financial statement analysis, materiality standards, replacement cost accounting, and accounting in the oil and gas industries. Also, Professor O'Connor is coauthor of two monographs published by the National Association of Accountants, *Replacement Costing: Complying with Disclosure Requirements* and *Replacement Cost Disclosures: A Study of Compliance with the SEC Requirement.* He has served on AAA committees, including the Committee on Financial Accounting Standards. Professor O'Connor is a member of the American Accounting Association, the American Institute of Certified Public Accountants, the Michigan Association of Certified Public Accountants, Phi Kappa Phi, Beta Gamma Sigma, and Beta Alpha Psi.

PREFACE

The extremely favorable response to our first edition indicates that our view of accounting education and of the role of intermediate accounting within the education process is shared by many instructors. Therefore, this edition represents a fine tuning and strengthening of the first edition, rather than a major departure. As we stated in the first edition, we believe that accounting education should prepare students both to do accounting and to understand and critically evaluate accounting. Intermediate accounting should reflect this dual objective. While most of the intermediate accounting textbooks attempt to achieve these two objectives, and are organized in a similar fashion, our text and supporting materials do have several distinctive characteristics.

ORGANIZATION AND COVERAGE

The chapter sequence is unchanged from the first edition. We describe the environment of financial accounting in Chapter 1 and present a conceptual framework for financial accounting and reporting in Chapter 2. The accounting process and the resulting financial statement are discussed in Chapters 3, 4, and 5. Revenue recognition is the subject in Chapter 6, which may be covered at any point in the course. Chapter 7 presents the time value of money concepts and sample applications. Asset accounting and reporting are covered in Chapters 8 through 14. Current liabilities and contingencies are discussed in Chapter 15, and accounting for bonds, both as investments and as liabilities, is covered in Chapter 16. The special topics of leases, pensions, and income taxes are presented in Chapters 17, 18, and 19, respectively. Chapters 20 and 21 cover contributed capital and retained earnings, respectively. Chapter 22 discusses accounting changes and error corrections. In Chapter 23, the statement of cash flows is explained. Earnings per share is the subject of Chapter 24. Accounting for price changes is presented in Chapter 25, and financial statement analysis is described in Chapter 26.

FASB pronouncements and other FASB actions through October 1986 have been incorporated into the text. The major changes resulting from FASB activities are in Chapters 5 and 23 (which discuss the statement of cash flows), 18 (accounting for pensions, which has been totally revised), and 19 (which includes an overview of the proposed changes in accounting for income taxes). Other significant changes in coverage and presentation are outlined below.

CONCEPTUAL INTEGRATION WITH A STRONG PROCEDURAL ORIENTATION

We introduce and discuss in detail the conceptual framework of accounting in Chapters 1 and 2. This framework is used throughout the text to explain and evaluate accounting procedures. To further our objective of integrating the conceptual framework throughout the text, we have added a new feature to this edition—a summary of important topics and concept applications at the end of each chapter. These summaries reinforce the relationship between the conceptual framework and the procedures discussed in the chapter, in addition to providing a review of chapter highlights. Also, alternative accounting procedures and disclosure alternatives are evaluated routinely in terms of their usefulness in predicting and assessing cash flows to the firm.

PRESENTATION AND READABILITY

Most intermediate accounting textbooks do an adequate job of describing accounting procedures for the straightforward accounting topics, such as inventory cost flows, depreciation accounting, and accounting for receivables. However, our coverage of even these relatively simple topics stands out when compared to competing texts, because we do more than merely describe accounting procedures. Our presentation of procedures is amply illustrated, with many exhibits and references to real-world situations. Moreover, references to the conceptual framework are woven through our procedural discussions to emphasize the relationship between accounting concepts and procedures.

Users of the first edition have reinforced our belief that we present the more complex accounting topics in a clear, concise, and thorough manner. Rather than shying away from controversial and difficult problem areas, we attack them head-on, using the conceptual framework to critically evaluate the accounting alternatives. We have added summary exhibits and illustrations of several key topics to clarify the issues discussed. In addition, we have increased our use of margin notes in this edition.

SUBSTANTIAL INCREASE IN END-OF-CHAPTER MATERIAL

Our end-of-chapter material is unusually extensive and diverse. There are over 900 cases, exercises and problems in the text. There are 8 percent more questions, 25 percent more cases, and 20 percent more exercises and problems than there were in our first edition. Furthermore, most of the problem material that appeared in the first edition has been revised. Much of the new end-of-chapter problem material is of moderate difficulty. Also, the new material has been class-tested and the solutions to all end-of-chapter material have been thoroughly reviewed by the authors and by outside reviewers.

OTHER IMPORTANT FEATURES

EARLY PRESENTATION OF REVENUE RECOGNITION A thorough understanding of revenue recognition criteria as a means of dealing with uncertainty regarding future cash flows is essential to understanding specific accounting procedures. Therefore, revenue recognition is presented early in the text (Chapter 6). This placement also reflects the authors' preference for introducing conceptual material early in the course. However, this chapter may be covered at any time after Chapter 2.

COMPLEX ISSUES TREATED IN A FLEXIBLE MANNER A building block approach is used for topics such as leases (Chapter 17), pensions (Chapter 18), earnings per share (Chapter 24), and price changes (Chapter 25). A conceptual introduction is followed by explanations of progressively more complex procedural issues. These chapters are organized so that they may be covered in varying degrees of detail.

SHORT-TERM AND LONG-TERM INVESTMENTS COVERED IN ONE CHAPTER Because there are more similarities than differences between accounting for short-term and long-term investments, coverage within a single chapter is pedagogically sound and efficient.

PRESENT AND FUTURE VALUE COVERAGE Concepts of present and future value are discussed early in the text (Chapter 7) and are used frequently throughout the chapters thereafter, beginning with some examples of accounting applications in Chapter 7. Time diagrams are used extensively to clarify the concepts of present and future value.

RELATIONSHIP BETWEEN ACCOUNTING AND THE ENVIRONMENT Accounting issues are frequently evaluated in terms of their historical development and economic consequences. For example, the oil and gas accounting controversy is discussed in Chapter 13, the politics of accounting for leases is discussed in Chapter 17, and political influences on pension accounting are described in Chapter 18.

EXTENSIVE USE OF REAL-WORLD EXAMPLES   Extensive excerpts from actual financial statements are presented to relate the text coverage to the practice of accounting. For example, a complete set of financial statements for the Coca-Cola Company is included in the appendix to Chapter 5. In Chapter 9, excerpts from the financial statements of Bethlehem Steel Corporation and Sears, Roebuck and Company are used to demonstrate the reporting of inventories. Financial statement disclosures for property, plant, and equipment for Raytheon Company and Subsidiaries are reproduced in Chapter 12. In Chapter 15, the liabilities and shareholders' investment section of the 1984 financial statements of Abbot Laboratories are presented, along with a footnote related to litigation contingencies. The pensions disclosures in the annual report of Phillips Petroleum Company are presented in Chapter 18. We have drawn on the published financial statements of many other companies to demonstrate reporting practices.

MAJOR CHANGES IN SECOND EDITION

Innumerable changes have been made throughout the text. The following changes, discussed by chapter, significantly distinguish this edition from the first edition:

- In Chapter 1, the discussion of the role, organization, and reporting requirements of the SEC has been expanded.

- *Statements of Financial Accounting Concepts* through *Statement No. 6* have been integrated into our discussion of the conceptual framework in Chapter 2.

- Two significant improvements were made in Chapter 4. The discussion of discontinued operations has been expanded substantially and now includes two new illustrations of how measurement guidelines are applied and an exhibit displaying the calculation of the gain or loss from discontinued operations (Exhibit 4–7). Also, the addition of a comprehensive income statement illustration at the end of Chapter 4 integrates the various items discussed in the chapter.

- In Chapter 5, the new statement of cash flows is introduced, the discussion of subsequent events has been expanded and clarified, and a section on the evaluation of financial statements has been added at the end of the chapter.

- In Chapter 7, annuities due are presented in an improved and simplified manner.

- Product financing arrangements are covered in more detail in Chapter 9. Also, Chapter 9 now includes a thorough treatment of the development of indexes (double-extension method and chain-link method) for applying dollar-value LIFO. The dollar-value LIFO exhibit (Exhibit 9–12) has been revised and clarified by a new exhibit (Exhibit 9–13).

- In Chapter 10, firm purchase commitments are discussed more thoroughly. The dollar-value retail LIFO illustration (summarized in Exhibit 10–16) has been revised and shortened to a three-year period.

- A flow chart (Exhibit 11–1) has been added in Chapter 11 to describe the accounting process for nonmonetary exchanges. Also, the coverage of interest capitalization has been expanded substantially, and several illustrations and supporting problem material have been added.

- A new section on impairment of value of plant assets has been added to Chapter 12.

- A summary matrix (Exhibit 13–1) of the accounting requirements for intangibles has been added to Chapter 13. Also, we have added a section on accounting for computer software, along with supporting end-of-chapter material.

- A summary of the accounting requirements for security investments has been added to Chapter 14 (Exhibit 14–3). Also in Chapter 14, the equity method presentation is now tied to the Chapter 13 illustration of goodwill.

- Chapter 16 includes a more extensive discussion of debt extinguishment, including in-substance defeasance and instantaneous defeasance.

- Chapter 18 has been completely rewritten to reflect *FASB Statement Nos. 87* and *88*. As a result, this chapter provides the most complete, up-to-date coverage of pension plan accounting available, yet it retains the conceptual emphasis of the first edition. Substantial new problem material and an actual illustration from the 1985 annual report of Phillips Petroleum Company are included. The chapter, end-of-chapter material, and solutions to the end-of-chapter material all were class-tested at several universities during the spring and summer of 1986.

- In Chapter 19, an overview of the FASB's proposed changes in accounting for income taxes has been added.

- At the end of Chapter 21, there is a new section that discusses some conceptual issues in reporting stockholders' equity.

- Chapter 23 has been revised thoroughly to emphasize the statement of cash flows. The working capital approach has been relegated to an appendix.

- The earnings per share presentation (Chapter 24) has been streamlined. Quarterly computations have been relegated to a footnote, the effective yield test for common stock equivalency status has been incorporated, and the coverage of the ranking of dilutive securities and the effect of actual dilution has been expanded.

- Accounting for price changes (Chapter 25) has been shortened and updated. In particular, the coverage of constant dollar accounting has been condensed.

SUPPLEMENTARY MATERIALS

SUPPLEMENTARY LEARNING AIDS

STUDENT MASTERY GUIDE—by John Cumming and Clayton Hock (both of Miami University, Oxford, Ohio). The study guide is available in two volumes: Vol. I covers Chapters 1–15 and 25; Vol. II covers Chapters 12–26. Each chapter contains a list of chapter objectives and a detailed chapter review. The Self-Study Learning section includes a review of key terms and concepts, true-false questions, multiple-choice questions, and extended problems—all with solutions. A final section discusses common errors.

COMPUTERIZED STUDENT MASTERY GUIDE—The *Computerized Student Mastery Guide* enables students to devise a personal method of study using the materials written by Professors Cumming and Hock. The purpose of this study guide is to provide an efficient system of study, adaptable to students' individual needs or preferences. The study options for the student include selection of a starting point by chapter or topic, self-assessment on mastery via pre- and post-tests, record-keeping on progress and areas to review, and choice of question type (multiple-choice, true-false, or fill-in-the-blanks). The *Computerized Student Mastery Guide* is available for the IBM PC/PC-XT, true compatibles, and Apple IIe/IIc computers.

WORKING PAPERS—This supplement provides students with the necessary forms to work the problems and exercises at the ends of chapters in the text.

MANUAL PRACTICE SET—by Donald Tang and Nancy O'Rourke Tang (both of Portland State University). Based on a combined wholesaling, retailing and service concern, the *Practice Set* is designed to provide students with a comprehensive review of the accounting process, and practice in the application of concepts and skills. Students are given the opportunity to assess a series of complex events to determine year-end accrual, disclosure, or adjustment, and to complete a full set of financial statements, including all related footnotes.

COMPUTER-ASSISTED PRACTICE SET—by Louis F. Biagioni (Indiana State University). *Gemco-II,* now in its second edition, is a challenging computer-assisted practice available for use in the intermediate accounting course. Classroom-tested by the author, it teaches students the accounting cycle while familiarizing them with computer accounting systems. *Gemco-II* requires students to record transactions, make adjusting entries, and generate the reports of the General Microcomputer Corporation. The package includes extensive HELP screens and tutorials that make the programs educational and unique. Available for use with the IBM PC/PC-XT and true compatibles.

SPREADSHEET EXERCISES AND PROBLEMS—This spreadsheet package will help students advance their accounting proficiency while gaining critical hands-on exposure to the workings of spreadsheet software. The package contains exercises and problems from the text in template format. The easy-to-learn spreadsheet program is also provided. An on-line tutorial is supplied that will teach the basics of using the spreadsheet programs. Available for the IBM PC/PC-XT, true compatibles, and the Apple IIe/IIC.

TEMPLATES AND PROBLEMS FOR LOTUS 1-2-3®—by George F. Hanks and Paul W. Parkison (Ball State University). The package is a collection of 40 spreadsheet templates for the widely accepted business package, Lotus 1-2-3. A student book with problems and worksheets for each spreadsheet and a Lotus 1-2-3 tutorial are included in each package. The adopter's desk set includes an instructor's manual with solutions to the problems and worksheets. Available for the IBM PC/PC-XT and true compatibles.

MCBS GENERAL LEDGER ACCOUNTING SYSTEM—The *MCBS General Ledger Accounting System* is a real-world package currently used by small businesses to meet their accounting needs. Students will benefit from exposure to these essentials of computerized accounting systems. This system is available for the IBM PC/PC-XT and true compatibles.

STARCALC: THE UNIVERSITY SPREADSHEET—by Joseph A. Russo, Jr. (Pace University). *StarCalc, The Students' Tool for Analysis and Reporting,* is a powerful and sophisticated, yet inexpensive, spreadsheet program designed for academic use. Featuring the most commonly used functions in the popular commercial package Lotus 1-2-3, including graphs, macros, sophisticated report printing, on-line help, a diagnostic error-detection system, and a command structure similar to 1-2-3, *StarCalc* provides the students with a tool they will use throughout their careers. *StarCalc*'s accompanying text is self-teaching and includes problems and exercises covering basic accounting principles. An instructor's manual provides solutions to the problems. Available for the IBM PC/PC-XT and true compatibles.

DECISION-BASED CASE PROBLEMS—These 15 computerized cases provide students with the experience of analysis and interaction as they solve and work through each case. The program provides real accounting environments in which students must determine from all the material that is available to them what is relevant information. As students proceed through the cases, they determine their own paths and sequences of requesting information and doing the computations. The program provides genuine diagnosis and remediation using a sophisticated error-detection and tracking scheme. A memory-resident financial calculator is available for students' use in computations. Available for the IBM PC/PC-XT and true compatibles.

TEACHING AIDS   INSTRUCTOR'S RESOURCE MANUAL—by Janet Kimbrell (Oklahoma State University). This manual increases the breadth of teaching materials available to professors. Each chapter begins with a restatement of the chapter objective from the *Student Mastery Guide*. This is followed by a detailed lecture outline and a point-by-point chapter review. Procedural and conceptual extensions are provided, as are issues for reflection and discussion. An annotated bibliography suggests extra reading materials. Assignment characteristics and classification tables also are provided. Much of the material is accompanied by detailed illustrations that expand the extensive visual exhibits in the text.

SOLUTIONS MANUAL—This volume provides fully worked solutions to all questions, cases, exercises, and problems in the text. The solutions are thoroughly explained and each step is illustrated to enhance discussion of assignment and other materials.

CHECK FIGURES—This booklet provides key figures in the solutions to the materials at the ends of the chapters. These figures allow students to check the accuracy of their progress in attaining the solutions.

TRANSPARENCIES—Approximately 400 acetate transparencies are reproduced from the *Solutions Manual* as a classroom aid in reviewing homework assignments. Forty exhibits from the text also are reproduced.

TEST BANK—by Alan A. Cherry and Alan H. Falcon (both of Loyola Marymount University). The *Test Bank* includes approximately 1,000 questions and problems. Each chapter offers multiple-choice questions, extended problems, and, in most chapters, essay questions.

COMPUTERIZED TEST BANK: THE RANDOM HOUSE TESTMAKER—The *Random House Testmaker* allows access to a broad range of testmaking functions. With it, you can prepare tests quickly and easily. This powerful program allows you to view questions as you select them for a test, scramble questions to create different versions of the test; add your own questions; edit questions; sort/select questions by type (multiple-choice, true-false, matching, essay, or short answer), objective, and difficulty; and view and save a test. It includes all the questions available in the printed test bank. Available for the IBM PC/PC-XT, true compatibles, and the Apple IIe/IIc computers.

ACKNOWLEDGMENTS

Many individuals have contributed generously of their time and expertise in the development of the second edition. Their comments and suggestions on accounting teaching matters as well as on technical issues have been invaluable. They are:

Stephen L. Buzby	*Michigan State University*
Alan A. Cherry	*Loyola Marymount University*
Dennis H. Hudson	*University of Tulsa*
Wallace R. Leese	*California State University, Chico*
Fred Mittelstaedt	*Arizona State University*
Brock Murdock	*California State University, Chico*
William R. Pasewark	*University of Georgia*
Philip Regier	*Arizona State University*

Richard L. Rogers	*Indiana University*
Anwar Y. Salimi	*California State University, Sacramento*
Richard H. Simpson	*University of Massachusetts*
Paul Solomon	*San Jose State University*
Mary S. Stone	*University of Alabama*
Donald Tang	*Portland State University*
James H. Thompson	*University of Mississippi*

We are doubly grateful to Richard Simpson, James Thompson, Anwar Salimi, and William Pasewark for also reviewing the end-of-chapter assignment material. They carefully checked the questions, cases, exercises, and problems for consistency with text discussions and painstakingly reworked our solutions examining them for accuracy, completeness, and clarity of presentation.

Others who contributed to this edition include Careen Blyle and Kathie Rogos, who assisted in the preparation of the *Solutions Manual*. Tanie Jacobs and Michael Yost helped to create the *Working Papers*. Their efforts are appreciated.

We appreciate the cooperation of the American Institute of Certified Public Accountants and the Financial Accounting Standards Board for allowing us to draw on their pronouncements for much of the text discussion. We also acknowledge permission from the American Institute of Certified Public Accountants, the Canadian Institute of Chartered Accountants, the Certified General Accountants Association of Canada, and the Institute of Management Accounting of the National Association of Accountants to adapt materials from their professional examinations.

Finally, we are most grateful for the excellent assistance provided by the professionals at Random House—June Smith, Paul Shensa, Diana Merritt, Barbara DiPanni, Cele Gardner, and last, but certainly not least, Judith Kromm. As was true for the first edition, the contributions of Random House staff made a tremendous difference in the quality of this text.

LANNY G. CHASTEEN
Oklahoma State University

RICHARD E. FLAHERTY
Arizona State University

MELVIN C. O'CONNOR
Michigan State University

November 1986

CONTENTS

INTERMEDIATE ACCOUNTING

1 FINANCIAL ACCOUNTING AND REPORTING: AN INTRODUCTION AND HISTORICAL DEVELOPMENT

Accounting provides a service through measurement of and communication about economic activities.

Accounting is a service activity. Its function is to provide useful financial information about economic entities to interested parties, such as managers, investors, and creditors. Accounting also may be described as a measurement-communication activity. The usefulness of accounting information depends on effective measurement of the economic activities of entities and on effective communication of those measurements to users of that information.

Accounting information can be divided into two broad categories, according to the type of decision maker who uses it: **Management accounting** provides information to decision makers who are inside the economic entity. These internal users of accounting information are managers at various organizational levels of the entity. **Financial accounting** provides information to those decision makers who are outside the economic entity, such as investors, creditors, and governmental agencies. Financial accounting information also is used by managers inside the economic entity.

We use the term **financial accounting and reporting** to describe the dual role of the accountant in (1) measuring and recording the economic activities of an entity and (2) communicating the recorded data to external users. This text focuses on the accounting and reporting practices used by a business firm to provide financial information to decision makers outside the firm.

THE ENVIRONMENT AND ROLE OF FINANCIAL ACCOUNTING AND REPORTING

Financial accounting and reporting are products of the economic environment in which they are practiced. Therefore, we shall begin by examining the economic environment in which financial accounting and reporting take place and discussing who uses financial accounting information and how it is used.

ECONOMIC ENVIRONMENT

The United States has a highly developed exchange economy. Most business firms do not consume the goods and services they produce. Instead, firms exchange goods and services produced for money or claims to money (e.g., accounts receivable) with the objective of maximizing the economic welfare of the owners of the firm. Money is the basis of exchange in the economy, and people make decisions relating to consumption, saving, and investment on the basis of allocations of their present and expected money resources.

In today's economy, the production and marketing of goods and services are long and costly processes that require continuous access to large amounts of money capital. The corporate form of business has eased the task of raising large amounts of needed capital by enabling firms to issue stocks and bonds in organized securities markets. The owners (stockholders) of corporations usually expect to receive dividends from their investments and expect that the market value of their shares of stock will increase. Stockholders prefer to leave direct management of the firm to professional managers—the stewards who have been delegated the authority to serve the best interests of the firm and who are directly accountable to the stockholders. Bondholders and other creditors who lend money to the firm expect to receive interest on the amounts loaned to the firm and to have the principal amount of the loan returned to them at the due date of the loan.

Organized securities markets, such as the New York Stock Exchange, allow investors to buy and sell securities with relative ease. Most transactions in securities markets occur after the securities are originally issued by business firms. Except for the initial issue of securities by a firm, securities are transferred from one investor to another, and no part of the exchange price goes to the business that originally issued the securities. These exchanges are referred to as secondary market transactions because they do not involve the firm that originally issued the securities.

Even though no additional resources flow directly to the firm that originally issued the securities, secondary market transactions are important to the firm because these transactions help to set market prices for securities that it may choose to issue at a later date. In addition, security prices have an important impact on the economic welfare of investors. While many factors, such as worldwide, national, or industry-level economic conditions, may affect the market prices of securities, security prices are largely dependent on the cash flows that firms generate from earnings and other operating activities.

Because most investors and creditors are far removed from the firm's day-to-day activities, they rely on financial accounting data as a principal source of information when they make decisions about buying, selling, or holding investments in the firm. There is considerable evidence that securities markets react to financial accounting information in quite a sophisticated manner. Securities markets are ''efficient'' with respect to published financial accounting information; that is, security prices react to published financial accounting information quickly and without bias. Because securities markets are efficient, no investor can expect to use published accounting information to earn abnormal or above-average returns on security investments. Rather, each investor can expect to earn a return on investment in a particular security that is commensurate with the risk associated with that investment. Many people believe that the publishing of financial accounting information is an important factor in the efficiency of securities markets, and that financial reporting serves a preemptive role—that is, publishing financial accounting information helps to prevent abnormal returns from accruing to individuals who trade on inside information (information not available to the public).[1]

Financial accounting information influences resource allocation.

In addition to its use in investor and creditor decisions, financial accounting information also plays a role in other decisions about resource allocation. For example, financial accounting information is used in employee wage negotiations, in the establishment of management compensation and bonus agreements, and in pension funding decisions.

Various government units, especially those of the federal government, are significant components of the environment of financial accounting and reporting. The United States government plays a major role in resource allocation by levying and collecting taxes and by borrowing and spending money. In addition, the federal government regulates activities of businesses and individuals through legislation and federal commissions, such as the Federal Trade Commission and the Securities and Exchange Commission. Government

---

[1] Beaver, William H., ''What Should Be the FASB's Objective?,'' *Journal of Accountancy,* August 1973, pp. 49–56.

regulation is intended to promote the public welfare. Federal commissions often use financial accounting information to monitor the activities of regulated companies and to assist in policy making.

USES AND USERS OF FINANCIAL ACCOUNTING INFORMATION

Users and potential users of financial accounting information may have either a direct or indirect economic interest in a particular business. People or groups with indirect interest in a business advise, represent, or otherwise influence those who have or contemplate having direct interests in it.

Among the users of financial accounting information who have **direct** interests in a business are:

Examples of users with direct economic interests in a business.

1. Investors or potential investors, who make decisions about whether to obtain, retain, increase, or decrease investments.

2. Creditors and suppliers, who must decide whether to extend credit, and, if so, must determine credit terms.

3. Employees engaged in negotiations to increase wages or fringe benefits, who must evaluate the extent to which employees (as a group) have contributed to increased productivity, and therefore what increases in compensation the business can afford.

4. Employees or potential employees, who may want to consider the possibility of terminating or seeking employment in the business.

5. Management and directors of the business, who assess the firm's financing needs, evaluate results of past economic decisions, and project the firm's future financial position and earnings.

Among the users of financial accounting information with **indirect** interests in a business are:

Examples of users with indirect economic interests in a business.

1. Financial analysts and advisers, who help investors and potential investors evaluate investments in particular businesses (financial accounting information aids in the selection of appropriate investments for their clients).

2. Stock exchanges, which consider financial accounting information when they accept stocks for listing or cancellation, when they suspend trading in a particular stock, and when they make judgments about proper accounting practices and the need for additional disclosures about business activities in financial reports.

3. Regulatory authorities, such as the Federal Power Commission, which use accounting information when they make decisions about requested price increases or rate increases for the products or services of regulated businesses.

Role of financial accounting and reporting.

As you can see from the preceding examples, accounting information helps investors, creditors, managers, and other users make resource allocation decisions. Thus, the role of financial accounting and reporting is to provide evenhanded (neutral or unbiased) financial information, which, in conjunction with information from other sources, assists in the efficient allocation of scarce resources in our economy. Financial information that is neutral or unbiased means that the information is not intended to influence a user's behavior in a particular direction.

THE ECONOMIC ENVIRONMENT AND FINANCIAL ACCOUNTING AND REPORTING

The economic environment and thus the needs of users of accounting information change continuously. As these changes occur, financial accounting and reporting practices also change to provide information useful for decision making. For example, the growth of multinational corporations has increased the importance of the way financial statements of foreign subsidiaries, which are denominated in a foreign currency, are translated into U.S. dollars for financial reporting purposes. As another example, persistent inflation, especially since 1973, has caused both accountants and users of financial accounting information to address the issue of financial reporting in periods of inflation. If a company purchased merchandise for $100, then sold it for $200 at a time when continued operation required the firm to pay $180 to replace it, what is the amount of income on the sale? Is it $100? Is it $20? This issue is discussed more thoroughly in Chapters 2 and 25.

Just as financial accounting and reporting practices are affected by the economic environment, so also the economic environment is affected by financial accounting and reporting practices. Financial accounting and reporting influence the behavior of users of accounting information. Therefore, many accountants, businesses, and users of accounting information believe that the potential economic consequences or economic impact of a required accounting or reporting practice should be considered by authoritative bodies, such as the Financial Accounting Standards Board (FASB) or the Securities and Exchange Commission (SEC), when accounting or reporting requirements are established.

That accounting has an economic impact was made clear by opponents of the FASB's position regarding accounting and reporting practices for oil and gas exploration. In 1978 the FASB required that the costs of exploration activities be expensed currently if the exploration did not result in a successful well (i.e., discovery of oil or gas). Small, exploratory oil and gas companies, which had been recording exploration costs as assets and expensing these costs over several years, argued (unsuccessfully) that the FASB's accounting requirement would reduce their reported income, make them less attractive to investors and creditors, and thus reduce their ability to raise the capital necessary to continue exploratory activities. They argued further that the FASB's position would have an adverse impact on society because it would reduce efforts to find new energy reserves.

The economic environment and financial accounting and reporting thus impact on each other. Financial accounting and reporting practices are influenced by environmental changes. At the same time, financial accounting and reporting practices affect the behavior of users in the economic environment.

The economic environment and financial accounting and reporting impact on each other.

THE NATURE AND CONTENT OF FINANCIAL ACCOUNTING AND REPORTING

Financial accounting and reporting provide "a continual history, quantified in money terms, of economic resources and obligations of a business enterprise, and economic activities that change those resources and obligations."[2] But what does the expression "financial accounting and reporting" in fact encompass? It encompasses the financial statements and supplementary information that are required to be published externally under generally accepted accounting principles (GAAP). In this section we discuss the nature of financial accounting and reporting under GAAP, why financial accounting and reporting standards are important, and how financial accounting information relates to other information used in decision making.

GENERALLY ACCEPTED ACCOUNTING PRINCIPLES (GAAP)

Generally accepted accounting principles consist of the financial accounting and reporting assumptions, standards, and practices that a business firm must use in preparing external financial statements. Generally accepted accounting principles or standards, as they are sometimes called, are prescribed by authoritative bodies, such as the FASB, and are based on theoretical as well as practical considerations. They represent a consensus among accountants as to what is considered acceptable practice at a given time. Generally accepted accounting principles provide financial statement users with confidence that the

---

[2] "Basic Concepts and Accounting Principles Underlying Financial Statements of Business Enterprises," *Statement of the Accounting Principles Board No. 4* (New York: AICPA, October 1970), para. 41.

statements are representationally faithful, provide firms and accountants who prepare financial statements with guidance on how to account for and report economic activities, and provide independent auditors of financial statements with a basis for evaluating the fairness and completeness of the statements. As we pointed out earlier, generally accepted accounting principles, and practices based on these principles, evolve and change over time in response to changes in the economic environment. Since current accounting practice is based on GAAP, we shall sometimes refer to GAAP as the "conventional system." Later in this chapter we shall discuss the historical development of GAAP in more detail.

FINANCIAL ACCOUNTING AND REPORTING STANDARDS

Financial accounting and reporting require many estimates, assumptions, and professional judgments by management and by accountants. Calculations of depreciation and estimates of uncollectible accounts receivable are two examples. As a result, personal bias, misassessments of facts, errors in estimation, and ambiguity may affect the measurement and communication of economic events. The potential for such influences on accounting information is not surprising when one considers, for example, the significance of accounting information to wage negotiations, management bonuses, bank lending decisions, and so on.

Financial statements should have credibility to external users. In addition, given accounting's service nature, it is essential that the information in financial reports be useful in decision making. Standards or principles for financial accounting and reporting contribute to the credibility and usefulness of financial data. Without standards to guide accounting and reporting practice, each accountant would, in effect, have to develop his or her own financial accounting theory, practices, and procedures. Under these circumstances, users of financial accounting information would find that reported information offered little help when they had to make comparisons among competing uses of scarce resources. Historically, standard setting has been in the public interest.

FINANCIAL REPORTING IN RELATION TO OTHER INFORMATION USED IN DECISION MAKING

In our earlier discussion of the role of financial accounting and reporting, we pointed out that financial information, in conjunction with other information, assists in resource allocation. Thus, financial reporting is not the only information source used in decision making. Exhibit 1–1 shows the total set of information that may be used in making investment, credit, and similar decisions. Reading from the left side of the exhibit, notice that the financial information subject to an independent auditor's opinion includes not only the financial statements, but also the notes to the financial statements. The financial statements required under GAAP are:

1. The *balance sheet* or *statement of financial position*.
2. The *income statement*.
3. The *statement of retained earnings* or the *statement of other changes in owners'* or *stockholders' equity*.
4. The *statement of changes in financial position*. In a recent *Exposure Draft,* the FASB proposed that this statement be replaced by *a statement of cash flows*.

Financial statements are a central component of financial reporting and serve as a principal means of communicating the effects of transactions and other economic events to decision makers outside an economic entity. (A transaction is the transfer of something of value between two or more entities.) A financial statement is a formal tabulation of account names and dollar amounts derived from accounting records maintained by an economic entity. Financial statements display either the financial position of the entity at a point in time or one or more kinds of changes in financial position of the entity during a period of time. The financial statements of an entity are a fundamentally related set that articulate (interrelate) with each other and that are derived from the same underlying

The financial statements of an entity interrelate.

EXHIBIT 1–1 INFORMATION USED IN INVESTMENT, CREDIT, AND SIMILAR DECISIONS

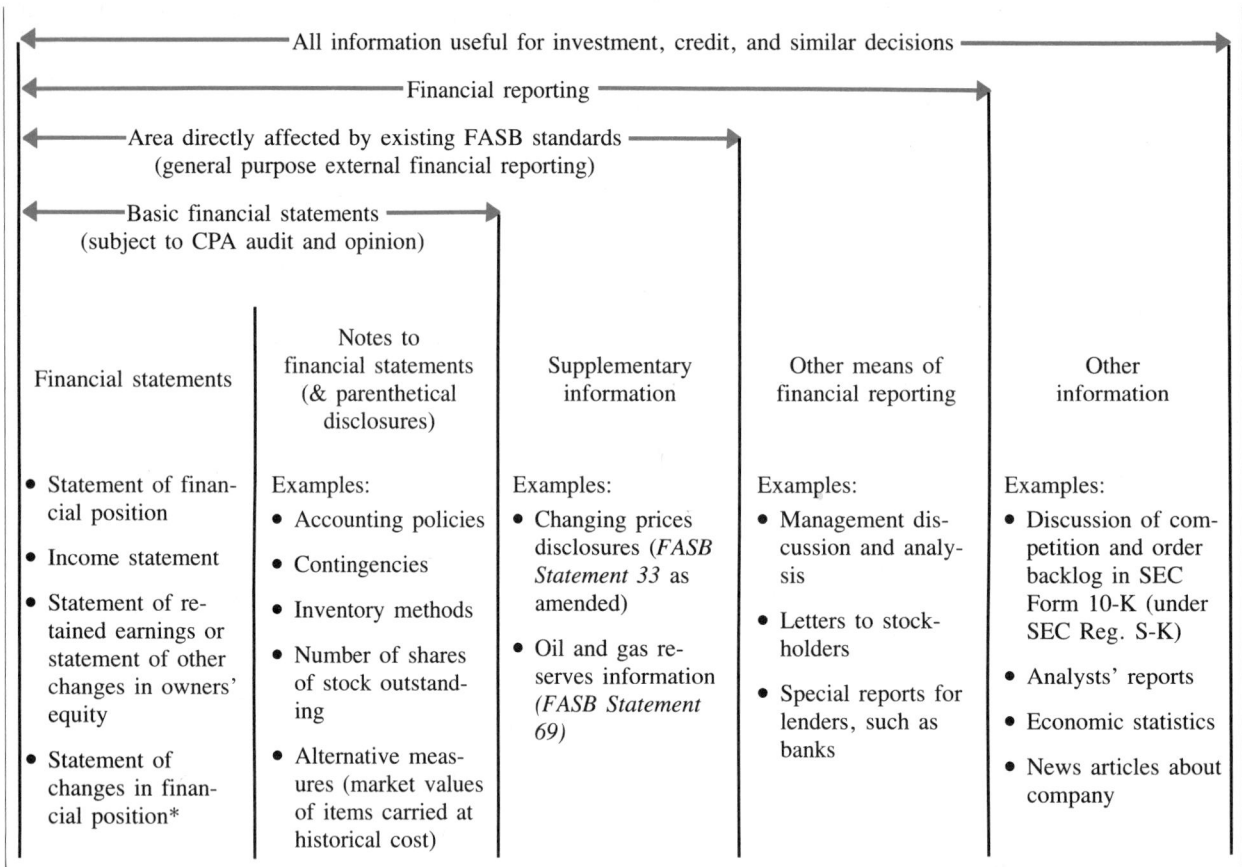

* In a recent *Exposure Draft,* the FASB proposed that this statement be replaced by a statement of cash flows.

Based on ''Recognition and Measurement in Financial Statements of Business Enterprises,'' *Statement of Financial Accounting Concepts No. 5* (Stamford, Conn.: FASB, 1984), p. 5.

economic data. Financial statements interrelate because they report different aspects of the same transactions or other economic events affecting an entity. Although each financial statement presents information that is different from the others, no individual statement is likely to serve a single purpose or provide all the financial information necessary for a particular decision.

Information provided in notes to the financial statements or parenthetically on the face of the financial statements, such as significant accounting policies, pension plan description, or segmented financial data, enhances or explains information reported in the financial statements. In addition, supplementary information, such as disclosures of the effects of changing prices on the firm's financial statements, along with voluntary management discussion and analysis, adds support and explanation to the financial statements and notes to the financial statements.

Supplementary information is not subject to an independent auditor's opinion but must be disclosed as either the FASB or the SEC requires. For example, supplementary disclosure of the effects of changing prices on a firm's financial statements is required by the FASB. The SEC requires interim financial statements to be filed and requires numerous other disclosures, such as information about auditor changes. While many SEC filings may not appear in a firm's annual report, they are available to the public on request. Many

Notes to the financial statements enhance or explain the statements.

firms voluntarily disclose other financial information, such as expenditures for research and development, expenditures for employee training, and social welfare expenditures.

As Exhibit 1–1 shows, the FASB's area of interest is **general purpose external financial reporting.** General purpose financial reporting is designed to serve the needs of external users of financial information in general, rather than the needs of particular user groups. Specifically, general purpose external financial reporting is directed toward what appears to be a common interest among external users of financial information—a firm's ability to generate positive net cash flows from operating activities. This common interest in information about cash flows forms the basis for the financial reporting objectives and other concepts of financial accounting theory discussed in Chapter 2.

As Exhibit 1–1 further indicates, financial reporting may go beyond what is included in general purpose external financial reporting. Financial reporting sometimes involves the preparation of special reports for specific users who are in a position to request special information. For example, a potential lender, such as a bank, often can demand additional financial information before making a lending decision.

Finally, as Exhibit 1–1 shows, information other than financial reporting information may be used in investment, credit, and similar decisions. For example, prospective investors often use market tips, analysts' reports, and special news releases as inputs to investment decisions.

In the remainder of this chapter we shall discuss briefly how historical events have influenced current accounting principles, standards, and practices. This brief perspective will help you to see how accounting has developed historically. In addition, it will familiarize you with attempts by the accounting profession to establish principles or standards for financial accounting and reporting. Finally, once you have some understanding of the history of the accounting profession, you will be in a better position to understand and appreciate future developments in accounting.

> External users are interested in a firm's ability to generate positive net cash flows.

THE HISTORICAL DEVELOPMENT OF FINANCIAL ACCOUNTING AND REPORTING

Exhibit 1–2 shows that the development of financial accounting and reporting can be divided into three time periods:

1. Pre-formal-theory era: the period from the beginning of the fifteenth century through 1929.

2. Problem-solving era: the period from 1930 through 1972.

3. Conceptual-framework era: the period from 1972 to the present.

We have designated 1930 as the end of the pre-formal-theory era and the beginning of the problem-solving era because that was the year in which the first meaningful efforts were made by the accounting profession, through what is now called the American Institute of Certified Public Accountants (AICPA),[3] to develop an underlying cohesive theory or rationale for financial accounting and reporting. Even though theory continued to develop from 1930 to 1972, most of the work of the AICPA dealt with the resolution of particular current accounting problems, such as accounting for intangible assets or inventories, rather than with the formulation of a general theoretical framework for financial accounting and reporting.

[3] The AICPA is the professional organizational body for CPAs. The AICPA is similar to the American Bar Association in law and the American Medical Association in medicine.

EXHIBIT 1—2 IMPORTANT EVENTS IN THE DEVELOPMENT OF FINANCIAL ACCOUNTING AND REPORTING, BY ERA

1. PRE-FORMAL-THEORY ERA

15th century–1930

15th century:	origin of double-entry bookkeeping
1400–1800:	emphasis on accounting information for internal uses
19th century:	growth in financial accounting for external uses
Early 20th century:	introduction of business taxation; increased need for accounting records
To 1930:	most accounting practices based on judgments of individual accountants

2. PROBLEM-SOLVING ERA

1930–1972

1930:	first American Institute of Accountants standing committee on accounting procedures
1933:	Securities Act
1934:	Securities Exchange Act; Securities & Exchange Commission (SEC) established
1938:	formation of American Institute of Accountants Committee on Accounting Procedures; the SEC delegates standard setting to the private sector
1957:	American Institute of Accountants (AIA) becomes American Institute of Certified Public Accountants (AICPA)
1959:	Accounting Principles Board (APB) begins operations
1964:	AICPA Rule 203
1970:	*APB Statement No. 4*
1971:	AICPA appoints Study Group on Establishment of Accounting Principles and Study Group on the Objectives of Financial Statements
1972:	Report of Study Group on Establishment of Accounting Principles submitted to AICPA

3. CONCEPTUAL-FRAMEWORK ERA

1973–present

1973:	Financial Accounting Standards Board (FASB) begins operations
	Report of Study Group on the Objectives of Financial Statements completed
1974:	FASB publishes a *Discussion Memorandum (DM)* on conceptual framework
1976:	FASB publishes documents related to conceptual framework:

1. Tentative conclusions on objectives of financial statements
2. Scope of conceptual framework
3. *DM* on elements of financial statements

1978:	FASB publishes *Statement of Financial Accounting Concepts (SFAC) No. 1,* ''Objectives of Financial Reporting by Business Enterprises''
1980:	FASB publishes:

1. *SFAC No. 2,* ''Qualitative Characteristics of Accounting Information''
2. *SFAC No. 3,* ''Elements of Financial Statements of Business Enterprises''
3. *SFAC No. 4,* ''Objectives of Financial Reporting by Nonbusiness Organizations''

1984:	FASB publishes *SFAC No. 5,* ''Recognition and Measurement in Financial Statements of Business Enterprises''
1985:	FASB publishes *SFAC No. 6,* ''Elements of Financial Statements, a Replacement of *FASB Concepts Statement No. 3.*''

Note: There may be names and terms in this exhibit with which you are not familiar. They are introduced later in this chapter. This exhibit can be used as an overview of developments in financial accounting and reporting.

The conceptual-framework era began in 1973, when the FASB became the authoritative standard-setting body for financial accounting and reporting. The FASB immediately began work on a long-term project aimed at developing cohesive theoretical concepts that can be used as general guidelines for future financial accounting and reporting standards. This project is known as the **conceptual framework project.** We shall have more to say about it at the end of this chapter.

THE PRE-FORMAL-THEORY ERA: BEFORE 1930

The origins of accounting date at least as far back as the Roman Empire and double-entry bookkeeping originated in Italy in the early fifteenth century.[4] However, the period that began with the Industrial Revolution and continued through the early twentieth century probably is an appropriate starting point in the development of financial accounting and reporting. Before that time, businesses were small single proprietorships or small partnerships, and accounting was used primarily for internal purposes only. Large-scale credit was not widespread, and there was little, if any, need for external reporting. From the early nineteenth century, however, financial accounting and reporting grew tremendously as businesses became larger and more complex, capital requirements increased, companies began to obtain external financing by issuing stock, and the corporate form of business flourished.

Many institutional factors during this period contributed to the development of financial accounting and reporting. The Industrial Revolution and the growth of railroads stimulated thought about depreciation concepts because of the significance of long-lived assets. In addition, the distinction between contributed, or invested, capital and retained earnings became important as companies began to pay dividends to investors. Many abuses occurred and investors were sometimes misled because of the lack of accounting standards for cash distributions that were returns *of* invested capital (investment recovery) versus cash distributions that were returns *on* invested capital (earnings). The introduction of business taxation stimulated discussion about what should be included in income, and it also caused many companies to begin to keep accounting records.

The period before 1930 sometimes is called a period of laissez-faire accounting because accountants used their own judgment in determining the most useful practice in a given situation. Although accounting became a recognized profession during this period, accounting practices varied and fell far short of the standards of GAAP today. For example, many companies did not disclose sales revenues or record depreciation. The latter was especially true in less prosperous years.

THE PROBLEM-SOLVING ERA: 1930–72

Because of criticism of financial accounting and reporting practices from both inside and outside the accounting profession, in 1930, in the aftermath of the 1929 stock market crash, the American Institute of Accountants (AIA)[5] appointed (1) a committee to work with the New York Stock Exchange on issues of common interest to stock exchanges, investors, and accountants and (2) a committee to address accounting issues and procedures. These appointments were in response to a change in accounting objectives: whereas earlier financial information had been intended strictly for management and creditors, it was now intended to meet the needs of investors and stockholders also.

Securities and Exchange Commission

The stock market crash and the events that preceded and contributed to it not only influenced the activities of the AIA, but also influenced federal legislation related to security exchanges. During the 23 years prior to 1934, all but one state enacted legislation to

[4] The first published description of double-entry bookkeeping appeared in 1494, in a book by Luca Pacioli titled *Summa de arithmetica, geometria, proportioni et proportionalita.*

[5] The American Institute of Accountants was renamed the American Institute of Certified Public Accountants in 1957.

regulate the purchase and sale of corporate securities. Commonly called **blue sky laws,** these laws vary widely among the states and apply only to intrastate transactions. From an overall standpoint of protecting the public against misrepresentations, manipulations, and other fraudulent acts in connection with the purchase and sale of securities, the blue sky laws have proven to be relatively ineffective. The stock market crash is indicative of the inadequacy of state-by-state legislation.

In an effort to restore investor confidence, to reestablish integrity in the capital markets, and to supplement the intrastate regulation provided by the blue sky laws, Congress passed the Securities Act of 1933 and the Securities Exchange Act of 1934. The 1933 act sets forth accounting and disclosure requirements for initial offerings of securities; the 1934 act applies to subsequent trading in outstanding securities and sets forth periodic reporting requirements for companies listed on organized stock exchanges and in the over-the-counter markets. The Securities and Exchange Commission (SEC) is a federal regulatory agency that was established in 1934 to administer the Securities Act of 1933, the Securities Exchange Act of 1934, and several other federal acts.

The SEC is composed of five commissioners, who are appointed by the President of the United States. One commissioner is designated by the President to serve as chairman of the SEC. The commissioners serve five-year terms, with the term of one commissioner expiring each year. No more than three commissioners can be from the same political party. The SEC is supported by an extensive professional staff, consisting primarily of lawyers, accountants, and financial analysts. Headquartered in Washington, D.C., the SEC has nine regional offices and eight branch offices located in major cities throughout the country. It is organized into several separate offices, such as the Office of the Chief Accountant, and five divisions: Corporate Regulation, Investment Management, Corporation Finance, Enforcement, and Market Regulation.

The Office of the Chief Accountant and the Division of Corporation Finance are particularly important to the accounting profession. The Chief Accountant is the primary accounting officer of the SEC and is responsible for all accounting and auditing matters in connection with the administration of the various acts. The Chief Accountant advises the SEC regarding accounting problems and recommends courses of action. The Chief Accountant also drafts rules and regulations governing the form and content of financial statements that must be filed with the SEC. The Division of Corporation Finance reviews the registration statements and the reports that registrants file with the SEC. The Division's review is intended to ensure that all required financial statements and supporting schedules have been included in SEC filings, and that financial statements that are filed have been prepared in accordance with GAAP, as well as with the rules, regulations, and policies issued by the SEC. The SEC does not perform audits of registrants' financial statements. Instead, it relies on the audit reports of registrants' independent CPAs to establish whether financial statements have been prepared in accordance with GAAP. Thus, the work of accountants is very important in SEC reporting. Accountants prepare and review the financial statements, supporting schedules, and reports that are filed with the SEC, and accountants conduct the independent audits of registrants' financial statements.

The SEC has the legal authority to prescribe accounting and reporting standards.

The SEC is a powerful force in financial accounting and reporting because it has the legal authority to prescribe accounting principles and procedures for companies under its jurisdiction, and to prescribe the form and content of financial reports filed with the SEC. However, in recognition of the expertise, experience, and activity of the accounting profession in the area of establishing accounting principles and procedures, the SEC delegated the responsibility to prescribe accounting principles and procedures to the private sector in 1938. The SEC adopted the policy of generally relying on GAAP, as established by the accounting profession, for evaluating reports and statements filed with the Commission. This policy was reaffirmed by the SEC in 1973 in *Accounting Series Release No. 150,* which states that

> principles, standards and practices promulgated by the FASB will be considered by the Commission as having substantial authoritative support, and those contrary to such FASB promulgations will be considered to have no support.[6]

The SEC's policy of relying on the private sector to set standards does not mean that the SEC has relinquished either its responsibilities or its authority. The SEC has influenced financial accounting and reporting practices through its comments to the AICPA and, more recently, to the FASB. On those occasions when the SEC concluded that the profession's standard-setting bodies were moving too slowly or in the wrong direction, it established its own financial reporting requirements, imposed a moratorium on accounting practices, or overruled a private sector pronouncement. For example, the SEC began to require certain large companies to disclose replacement cost data three years before the FASB issued *Statement No. 33,* "Financial Reporting and Changing Prices," in 1979. In 1974 the SEC issued *Accounting Series Release No. 163,* which imposed a moratorium on the capitalization of interest cost. This moratorium was lifted after the FASB issued *Statement No. 34,* "Capitalization of Interest Cost," in 1979. The only time the SEC overruled a pronouncement of the FASB was in 1978, when the SEC rejected the standards prescribed by *FASB Statement No. 19,* "Financial Accounting and Reporting for Oil and Gas Producing Companies." As a result, the FASB issued *Statement No. 25,* "Suspension of Certain Accounting Requirements for Oil and Gas Producing Companies," which suspended the effective dates of most of the requirements of *Statement No. 19.* Finally, in 1982 the FASB amended *Statements Nos. 19* and *25* with *Statement No. 69,* "Disclosures about Oil and Gas Producing Activities." Shortly thereafter, the SEC amended its disclosure requirements for oil and gas producers to require compliance with the provisions of *FASB Statement No. 69.*

The SEC has influenced financial accounting and reporting practices through its own filing requirements, *Regulation S-X, Regulation S-K, Accounting Series Releases (ASRs), Financial Reporting Releases (FRRs), Accounting and Auditing Enforcement Releases (AAERs),* and *Staff Accounting Bulletins (SABs). Regulation S-X* lists the specific financial statements that must be filed by SEC registrants and also prescribes the form and content of those financial statements, notes to the financial statements, and schedules supporting the financial statements. *Regulation S-K* is concerned with nonfinancial statement disclosure requirements, including a description of the company's business, a description of the company's properties, a description of the company's legal proceedings, information about the company's directors and management, and management's discussion and analysis of financial condition and results of operation. *Accounting Series Releases* primarily explain accounting procedures and set forth accounting and reporting guidelines. *ASRs* were discontinued in 1982. Those *ASRs* that had continuing relevance to financial reporting were codified by topic and issued as *Financial Reporting Release No. 1.* Since 1982, several additional *FRRs* have been issued. *Accounting and Auditing Enforcement Releases* announce accounting and auditing matters related to the SEC's enforcement activities, and are organized alphabetically by topic. All *ASRs* related to enforcement proceedings and issued prior to May 1982 were codified into *AAER No. 1. Staff Accounting Bulletins* present interpretations and practices followed by departments of the SEC that are responsible for reviewing the disclosure requirements of federal securities

---

[6] "Statement of Policy on the Establishment and Improvement of Accounting Principles and Standards," *Accounting Series Release No. 150* (Washington, D.C.: SEC, December 20, 1973).

laws. Much of the subject matter of *SAB*s arises from specific questions raised by registrants on various matters contained in GAAP or *Regulation S-X*. *SAB*s do not constitute official rules or regulations, nor do they have the official approval of the SEC. Although SEC pronouncements are very important, they affect GAAP only indirectly because only those business firms regulated by the SEC must comply with SEC rules. Firms not registered with the SEC need to comply only with GAAP.

American Institute of Certified Public Accountants

Until 1973, the AICPA provided the private sector leadership in developing financial accounting and reporting principles and practices. The AICPA acted primarily through its Committee on Accounting Procedure (CAP) from 1938 through 1959 and through the Accounting Principles Board (APB) from 1959 through 1973. When the FASB was established in 1973 as an independent standards-setting body, the AICPA established the Accounting Standards Executive Committee (AcSEC) as the senior technical committee to speak for the AICPA on matters of financial accounting and reporting. AcSEC frequently advises the FASB on agenda items and also provides guidance to AICPA members on issues not resolved by existing pronouncements.

COMMITTEE ON ACCOUNTING PROCEDURE (CAP)   From 1938 to 1959, the Committee on Accounting Procedure (CAP), a committee of the AICPA which had 21 members, issued 51 *Accounting Research Bulletins (ARBs)* on matters of financial accounting and reporting practice. The CAP devoted most of its time to resolving specific accounting and reporting problems rather than to developing either general accounting principles or a theoretical framework that could be used to resolve future accounting and reporting problems.

ACCOUNTING PRINCIPLES BOARD (APB) In 1959 the Accounting Principles Board (APB) replaced the CAP. The objectives of the APB were (1) to establish broad accounting principles; (2) to set up rules or guidelines for applying these principles to specific situations; and (3) to conduct research on which those principles, rules, and guidelines would be based. An Accounting Research Division with a permanent research staff also was established.

The APB operated from 1959 through June 1973. The Board's membership ranged from 18 to 21; all of the members belonged to the AICPA. Members were selected primarily from the accounting profession but were chosen also from industry, the academic community, and government. During its existence the APB issued 31 *Opinions* and four *Statements*. *APB Opinions* are authoritative pronouncements that set forth GAAP; *APB Statements* are primarily informative and basically serve to enhance interested parties' understanding of accounting matters.

Before 1964, enforcement of *APB Opinions* and effective *Accounting Research Bulletins* depended almost entirely on the prestige of the AICPA and the APB. A major factor in the APB's prestige was the SEC's delegation of authority to it.

In 1964 the AICPA adopted a requirement (now Rule 203 of the Code of Professional Ethics of the AICPA) that no member of the AICPA may express an opinion that financial statements are presented in conformity with GAAP if those statements contain any material departures from effective *ARB*s, *APB Opinions,* or, now, *FASB Statements of Financial Accounting Standards*. This requirement must be met unless the member can demonstrate that, because of unusual circumstances, the financial statements would otherwise be misleading. Even if such circumstances can be demonstrated, departures from official pronouncements must be disclosed in the financial statements along with the reasons for departure.

Almost from the beginning of its existence the APB was criticized for its inability to reduce the areas of difference and inconsistency in financial accounting and reporting. There were specific complaints about the lack of research underlying *APB Opinions,* the lack of output from the APB, the tendency of *APB Opinions,* like the *ARBs,* to be concerned with specific problems, and the failure of the Board to develop a theoretical framework for financial accounting and reporting. The APB's major effort toward a theoretical framework was *APB Statement No. 4,* "Basic Concepts and Accounting Principles Underlying Financial Statements of Business Enterprises." *Statement No. 4,* however, was descriptive ("what is"), not prescriptive ("what ought to be").

Much criticism focused on the APB's structure, specifically: (1) its large size (18 to 21 members); (2) the part-time status of all APB members (all were full-time employees of CPA firms, universities, or companies); (3) the lack of compensation for Board members; (4) their brief meeting times, only a few days each month; (5) the inability of the Accounting Research Division to provide timely research for *APB Opinions;* and (6) the excessive influence of CPA firms and, by implication, their clients on *APB Opinions.*

As a result of the dissatisfaction with the system for developing accounting principles, the AICPA appointed two committees in 1971: the Study Group on Establishment of Accounting Principles and the Study Group on the Objectives of Financial Statements. The Study Group on Establishment of Accounting Principles was established to examine the organization and operation of the Accounting Principles Board and to determine necessary improvements. Its recommendations led to the creation of the Financial Accounting Standards Board and its supporting structure. The Study Group on the Objectives of Financial Statements attempted to identify the objectives of financial accounting and reporting. The report, published in 1973, was an important input to the FASB's work on the conceptual framework for financial accounting and reporting.

THE CONCEPTUAL FRAMEWORK ERA: 1973 TO THE PRESENT

Dissatisfied with the APB's standard-setting effort, the Study Group on Establishment of Accounting Principles recommended that the APB be abolished and that an autonomous Financial Accounting Standards Board with seven full-time, remunerated members, only four of whom must be CPAs, become the standard-setting body in the accounting profession. This recommendation, along with the following supporting recommendations, was readily accepted by the AICPA:

1. There should be a nine-member Financial Accounting Foundation responsible for (a) appointing members of the Financial Accounting Standards Board, (b) appointing approximately 35 members to a Financial Accounting Standards Advisory Council, (c) securing adequate financing for the new standard-setting structure, and (d) periodically reviewing the structure.

2. There should be a Financial Accounting Standards Advisory Council to work with the FASB in identifying accounting issues, establishing priorities, and reacting to proposed standards.

3. There should be research activities within the FASB structure in support of its activities.

Financial Accounting Standards Board (FASB)

The FASB sets accounting and reporting standards.

The FASB began operations in July 1973 with the objective of developing financial accounting and reporting standards that would help to maintain user confidence in, and the credibility of, externally reported financial data. The FASB is responsible to the entire economic community, not just to the public accounting profession. The structure of the

FASB organization, as well as its supporting structure, are presented in Exhibit 1–3. The FASB issues four types of official pronouncements:

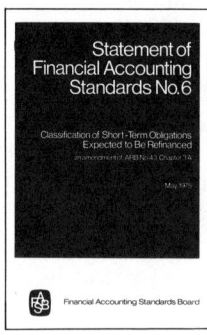

1. *Statements of Financial Accounting Standards (SFAS). Statements of Standards,* along with *APB Opinions* and *CAP Accounting Research Bulletins* that remain effective, are considered to be GAAP and are binding in accounting practice.

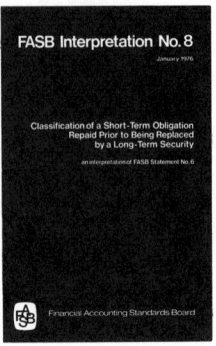

2. *Interpretations of ARBs, APB Opinions,* and *FASB Statements of Standards. FASB Interpretations* modify or extend existing *Statements of Standards* and predecessor documents and have the same authority as *Statements of Standards.*

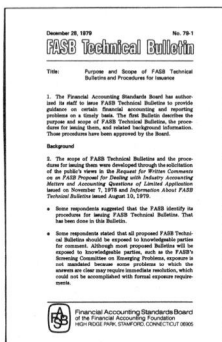

3. *Technical Bulletins. Technical Bulletins* provide guidance in the application of *FASB Statements of Standards* or *Interpretations, APB Opinions,* and *CAP Accounting Research Bulletins.*

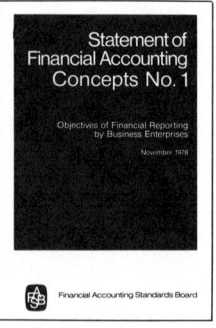

4. *Statements of Financial Accounting Concepts (SFAC). Statements of Concepts* present the conceptual framework of financial accounting and reporting. *Statements of Concepts* differ from *Statements of Standards* in that a *Statement of Concepts* does not establish GAAP.

EXHIBIT 1–3 THE FASB AND ITS SUPPORTING STRUCTURE

FINANCIAL ACCOUNTING FOUNDATION (FAF)

6 organizations that sponsor the FASB

15 trustees, 13 of whom are named by the sponsoring organizations and 2 of whom are at-large members elected by FASB Board of Trustees

3-year renewable terms, 2 terms maximum

Appoints members of FASB and Financial Accounting Standards Advisory Council

Raises and manages funds for FASB operations

Oversees operations of the FASB, but does not get involved in standard setting

FINANCIAL ACCOUNTING STANDARDS ADVISORY COUNCIL (FASAC)

Salaried chairman and executive director

Approximately 38 volunteer members

One-year terms; 3 renewals permitted

Advises FASB on policy matters, agenda items, and technical issues

EMERGING ISSUES TASK FORCE

Chaired by FASB's Director of Research and Technical Activities

15 members: 11 directors of accounting and auditing of CPA firms; 2 FEI representatives; 1 NAA representative; 1 Business Roundtable representative. Participation by SEC Chief Accountant.

Identifies, investigates, and reviews emerging issues, and advises FASB whether the issues merit Board attention.

FINANCIAL ACCOUNTING STANDARDS BOARD (FASB)

FASB Chairman and 6 other Board members

Executive Assistant———— Public Relations Council

————— Government Relations Manager

Director of Research and Technical Activities

Research and technical activities staff

☐ 40–50 professional staff plus support staff

☐ Project team for each agenda project

☐ Research

☐ Drafting of *Discussion Memoranda, Exposure Drafts*, and *Statements*

☐ Leading of task forces

☐ Analysis of comments

☐ Leading of Board discussion

☐ Public communication

☐ Response to technical inquiries

Director of Administration

Administrative Staff

☐ Controller, Accounting

☐ Personnel

☐ Publications production

☐ Publications distribution

☐ Word processing

☐ Office services

☐ Public Relations Counsel

☐ Government Relations Manager

☐ Information Systems

☐ Library

Issues official pronouncements:

Statements of Financial Accounting Standards

Interpretations

Technical Bulletins

Statements of Financial Accounting Concepts

Since June of 1985, all of the above types of pronouncements, as well as several other FASB documents, have been published under a single title, *Financial Accounting Series*. Each document included in the *Financial Accounting Series* continues to be subtitled as a *Statement of Financial Accounting Standards, Technical Bulletin,* and so on, as appropriate. All existing standards, based on *FASB Statements* and *Interpretations, APB Opinions* and *Accounting Research Bulletins,* are integrated and published by the FASB in its *Current Text.* The *Current Text* is in two volumes, one for general standards and one for industry standards. *Original Pronouncements,* also published by the FASB, contains all *FASB Statements* and *APB Opinions* in chronological order.

In an effort to be responsive to public opinion, the FASB goes through a lengthy process of preparation and review before issuing either a *Statement of Financial Accounting Standards* or a *Statement of Financial Accounting Concepts*. The usual steps of this process are as follows:

The steps in issuing an FASB Statement.

1. An accounting or reporting problem is identified and placed on the FASB's agenda. For a *Statement of Financial Accounting Concepts* the problem is at a conceptual level.

2. Research and analysis are conducted by the FASB technical staff and a select task force of experts from outside the FASB structure. Occasionally *Research Reports* are issued.

3. A *Discussion Memorandum,* presenting a detailed analysis of all identified aspects of the problem, is prepared and distributed to any interested party.

4. A public hearing is held to discuss the issues raised by the *Discussion Memorandum*.

5. The public response to the *Discussion Memorandum* (from the public hearing and letters of response sent to the FASB) is analyzed carefully by the FASB and its staff.

6. A preliminary draft of a proposed *Statement,* called an *Exposure Draft,* is issued.

7. All responses to the *Exposure Draft* that are received by a specified date at least 30 days after the issuing of the *Exposure Draft* are analyzed.

8. The FASB decides whether to issue a *Statement*. Support of a majority of the seven members is required to issue a *Statement*.

9. A *Statement* is issued.

As shown by the list of accounting pronouncements reproduced inside the covers of this text, the FASB has been very productive. Although many *Statements of Financial Accounting Standards* and *Interpretations* are directed toward specific problems and are similar to the outputs of the CAP and APB, the FASB also has made significant strides in its **conceptual framework project.** The conceptual framework project deals with theoretical and conceptual issues and is intended to provide an underlying structure for future *Statements of Standards*. It has been described as

Description of the FASB's conceptual framework.

> a constitution, a coherent system of interrelated objectives and fundamentals that can lead to consistent standards and that prescribes the nature, function, and limits of financial accounting and reporting. The fundamentals are the underlying concepts of accounting, concepts that guide the selection of events to be accounted for, the measurement of those events, and the means of summarizing and communicating them to interested parties.[7]

Much of the theoretical foundation underlying financial accounting and reporting, which is the subject of Chapter 2, is based on the conceptual framework.

---

[7] "Conceptual Framework for Financial Accounting and Reporting: Elements of Financial Statements and Their Measurement," *Discussion Memorandum* (Stamford, Conn.: FASB, 1976), p. 2.

OTHER GROUPS THAT INFLUENCE THEORY AND PRACTICE

In addition to the SEC, the AICPA, and the FASB, a number of other groups have had various degrees of influence on financial accounting and reporting. Among the more prominent are the American Accounting Association (AAA), the National Association of Accountants (NAA), the Financial Executives Institute (FEI), the Internal Revenue Service (IRS), and the Congress of the United States.

The AAA is an organization primarily for accounting educators, although many independent, industrial, and governmental accountants also are members. Its broad objectives are to contribute to the development of accounting theory, to encourage and sponsor accounting research, and to improve the quality of accounting education. The AAA's influence on financial accounting and reporting has been greatest at the conceptual rather than the practice level. The academic members of the AAA are the source of much of the research on accounting issues, and many of their research findings are published in the AAA's quarterly journal, *The Accounting Review*.

The NAA was organized in 1919 and is oriented toward managerial accounting issues. In 1968, however, the NAA broadened its research interests to include all information needed by business managers and investors. In addition to publishing the periodical *Management Accounting*, the NAA has funded several major accounting research projects and it tends to provide a broad perspective on standard setting.

The FEI was founded in 1931. Through its Financial Executives Research Foundation, the FEI has undertaken and published several studies related to financial accounting and reporting issues. The FEI has contributed to the development of financial accounting and reporting standards through the cooperation of its technical committee on corporate reporting with both the APB and the FASB. The FEI also publishes a monthly journal, *FE: The Magazine for Financial Executives*.

The Internal Revenue Service (IRS) has influenced financial accounting and reporting practices because of the willingness of the accounting profession to accept tax accounting requirements as generally accepted accounting principles in many instances.

Recently Congress has become an active and powerful force in the setting of accounting and reporting standards. In 1976 and 1977 the U.S. Senate and the House of Representatives formed separate subcommittees that concurrently studied the accounting profession. The Senate subcommittee, known as the Metcalf Committee, and the House subcommittee, known as the Moss Committee, reached very similar conclusions. The subcommittees recommended that the setting of accounting and reporting standards should remain in the private sector. They also made it clear, however, that the accounting profession, working in cooperation with the SEC, must act in a timely manner to implement the policy goals recommended in the subcommittee reports. In the area of financial accounting and reporting, for example, the subcommittees recommended that (1) uniformity in the development and application of accounting standards should be a major goal, and (2) the concepts of fairness and independence should be fundamental in the development and application of accounting standards. In response to the subcommittees' concerns, the FASB reorganized its operations to increase due process, openness, and consistency in its actions. Reorganization also occurred within the AICPA, which established a public board to oversee peer reviews of CPA firms that perform audits of business firms registered with the SEC.

In 1985, the House Subcommittee on Oversight and Investigation, known as the Dingall Committee, initiated hearings on the SEC's effectiveness in overseeing the accounting profession's progress since the mid-1970s in improving the usefulness, integrity, and credibility of financial reporting by public companies. The Dingall Committee hearings were a follow-up to the Metcalf Committee hearings and covered quality control, independence, enforcement, and standard setting in the accounting profession. At the time of writing of this edition of *Intermediate Accounting*, the Dingall Committee conclusions have not yet been made public. We anticipate, however, that the committee will conclude that more government regulation of the accounting profession is in the public interest and that the SEC needs more authority in support of its role of overseeing the accounting profession.

Pressure groups, such as corporate interest groups, business organizations, financial analysts, and the press, also have an influence on financial accounting and reporting standards. Naturally, any institution that may be affected by financial accounting and reporting practices will act in what it considers to be its own interest. Accounting and reporting policy making is a political process as well as a technical process. Choices must be made among alternatives, and the alternatives selected are unlikely to satisfy everyone who will be affected by them. Pressure may be brought to bear on those who set standards, and compromises are sometimes necessary to make a proposed financial accounting or reporting practice generally acceptable. Political influences on financial accounting and reporting will be illustrated throughout the text as specific accounting or reporting topics are presented.

Pressure groups influence accounting and reporting standards.

SUMMARY OF IMPORTANT TOPICS AND CONCEPT APPLICATIONS

1. Accounting provides a service by **measuring, recording,** and **communicating** financial information about economic entities to interested persons.

2. The financial accountant has a dual role: (1) measuring and recording the economic activities of an entity and (2) communicating the recorded data to external users.

3. The purpose of financial accounting and reporting is to provide **unbiased** financial information that can be used in the efficient allocation of scarce resources.

4. Generally accepted accounting principles (GAAP) consist of the financial accounting and reporting assumptions, standards, and practices that a business firm must use when preparing external financial statements that are subject to audit by an independent certified public accountant.

5. The financial statements required under GAAP are (1) the balance sheet, (2) the income statement, (3) the statement of retained earnings or the statement of other changes in owners' or stockholders' equity, and (4) the statement of changes in financial position. (The FASB has proposed a statement of cash flows.)

6. The financial statements of an entity **interrelate (articulate)** with each other.

7. General purpose external financial statements are directed toward providing information about a firm's ability to generate positive **net cash flows,** which is the common point of interest among external users of financial information.

8. The Securities and Exchange Commission (SEC) has the legal authority to prescribe accounting and reporting standards for business firms under its jurisdiction.

9. The SEC relies on the private sector, in particular the FASB, to set standards, but retains its responsibilities and authority with respect to accounting standards.

10. The Financial Accounting Standards Board (FASB) sets accounting and reporting standards. Other major groups influencing the standard-setting process include the SEC, AICPA, AAA, NAA, FEI, IRS, and the Congress of the United States.

11. The FASB issues four types of official pronouncements: *Statements of Financial Accounting Standards, Interpretations, Technical Bulletins,* and *Statements of Financial Accounting Concepts.*

12. Pressure groups, such as corporate interest groups, business organizations, financial analysts, and the press, also influence financial accounting and reporting standards. Standard setting is in large part a political process.

QUESTIONS

Q1-1. Distinguish between management accounting and financial accounting.

Q1-2. What is the dual role of the financial accountant?

Q1-3. What is the role of financial accounting and reporting?

Q1-4. List the financial statements most frequently provided to external users of accounting information.

Q1-5. What is meant by the term "general purpose financial statements"?

Q1-6. What does it mean to say that the securities markets are efficient with respect to published financial accounting information?

Q1-7. List some users of financial accounting information who have "direct" interests in a business.

Q1-8. List some users of financial accounting information who have "indirect" interests in a business.

Q1-9. Distinguish between users of financial accounting information who have "direct" interests in a business and those who have "indirect" interests in a business.

Q1-10. What are "generally accepted accounting principles"?

Q1-11. How do generally accepted accounting principles help users, preparers, and auditors of financial statements, respectively?

Q1-12. What does it mean to say that the financial statements of an entity articulate with each other?

Q1-13. Why are "standards" or "principles" of financial accounting and reporting important?

Q1-14. Financial reporting is not the only source of information needed for decision making by people outside a firm. Give some examples of information sources other than a firm's financial reports.

Q1-15. Explain how the SEC influences financial accounting and reporting.

Q1-16. Discuss the specific congressional activities that have influenced the accounting profession since the beginning of the 1970s.

Q1-17. Distinguish between *APB Opinions* and *APB Statements*.

Q1-18. Explain the important change that occurred in 1964 with respect to the force or status of *ARB*s and *APB Opinions,* and which subsequently applied to *FASB Statements of Financial Accounting Standards.*

Q1-19. What does Rule 203 of the Code of Professional Ethics of the AICPA state?

Q1-20. What were some of the specific criticisms made about the APB?

Q1-21. In what respects did the initial FASB structure, as recommended by the Study Group on Establishment of Accounting Principles, respond to criticisms of the APB?

Q1-22. Describe the FASB organization, including its supporting structure.

Q1-23. Identify and characterize the types of final official pronouncements issued by the FASB.

Q1-24. How does an *FASB Statement of Financial Accounting Concepts* differ from a *Statement of Financial Accounting Standards?*

Q1-25. Explain how the FASB's overall approach to policy making differs from the APB's approach.

Q1-26. Discuss why it might be appropriate to describe financial accounting and reporting standard setting as a political process.

Q1-27. What steps usually are followed by the FASB in issuing a *Statement of Financial Accounting Standards?*

Q1-28. Explain, using an example or two, how the economic environment and financial accounting and reporting impact on each other.

CASES

C1-1. THE ENVIRONMENT OF FINANCIAL ACCOUNTING AND REPORTING Assume that you are one of several individuals being considered for membership on the FASB. As part of the interview process, you will be asked to identify and briefly comment on a few aspects of the environment in which financial accounting and reporting standards must be established.

REQUIRED

Prepare an outline of the comments you plan to make in regard to the environment question.

C1-2. THE DEVELOPMENT OF ACCOUNTING PRACTICE Because you are a CPA, you have been asked by a local community interest group to be a guest at its monthly dinner meeting and to make a few after-dinner remarks on the effects of recent government investigations of the public accounting profession. During dinner the person sitting next to you, having read that double-entry accounting may have originated in Italy, comments, ''It's a good thing government has stepped in, because accounting hasn't changed since the Italians invented it.''

REQUIRED

What response would you make regarding changes in financial accounting and reporting since the fifteenth century in Italy?

C1-3. FACTORS AFFECTING EARLY DEVELOPMENT OF ACCOUNTING Discuss how the following factors affected accounting theory and practice during the period 1800–1929:

1. The Industrial Revolution.
2. The growth of railroads.
3. The taxation of income.
4. The development of the corporate form of business.

C1-4. USE OF FINANCIAL ACCOUNTING INFORMATION Financial accounting information often plays a role in the decisions and actions of investors, creditors, employees, and government units, among others.

REQUIRED

Discuss how financial accounting information may be useful to investors, creditors, employees, and government units, respectively.

C1-5. INTERRELATION OF ACCOUNTING AND ITS ENVIRONMENT Assume that as a member of the FASB you know there has been considerable negative reaction by corporations to a recently issued tentative *Statement of Financial Accounting Standards* on accounting for leases. The essence of most of the negative reaction is that ''if the proposed *Standard* is implemented, it will change the types of lease agreements into which corporations will enter. In effect, the *Standard* will *cause* certain lease agreements to be made even though such agreements are economically unsound.''

In an effort to reduce the level of negativism surrounding the proposed lease accounting *Standard* and to enlighten the business community, you have been selected by the FASB to attend a forthcoming national corporate seminar on the lease accounting issue. Your specific responsibility at the seminar, however, is not to discuss lease accounting but rather to present some brief comments, including examples, regarding the interrelation between financial accounting and reporting and the economic environment.

REQUIRED

Prepare a rough draft of the comments you plan to make at the seminar.

C1-6. THE NATURE OF FINANCIAL STATEMENTS Your daughter has been assigned the task of providing her seventh-grade class with an ''expert'' presentation on some aspect of a profession the students might choose to enter for their careers. She has come to you for help. As a practicing accountant, you wonder if a career in the accounting profession might be of interest to your daughter's classmates and you ask if she would like you to make a presentation on external financial statements and the accountant's role in preparing those statements. In particular, you intend to concentrate your remarks on the nature of external financial statements and the notes and supplementary information that often accompany the financial statements.

REQUIRED

Prepare a two- or three-paragraph discussion of financial statements, notes, and supplementary information to take with you as a ''handout'' for your daughter's class.

C1-7. THE PROBLEM-SOLVING ERA As part of a history class you are taking, you have been asked to select a profession and to discuss policy and practice development in that profession during the twentieth century. Since you are an accounting major, you have decided to discuss policy and practice development in financial accounting and reporting. You plan to emphasize the time period from 1930 to the present and to center your discussion on the roles and activities of the SEC, the AICPA, and the FASB.

REQUIRED

Write several paragraphs in response to the history assignment outlined above.

C1-8. APPROACHES TO POLICY MAKING Suppose that you have been called to testify before a U.S. Senate subcommittee studying the development of accounting standards. The specific question put to you by the subcommittee is: "What are the similarities and differences among the Committee on Accounting Procedures, the Accounting Principles Board, and the Financial Accounting Standards Board with respect to their organizational structures, their output of principles or standards, and their approaches to policy making?"

REQUIRED

Draft a response to this question.

C1-9. POLITICAL PRESSURES AND POLICY MAKING In the early 1970s, a noted academician and former member of the APB stated: "My hypothesis is that the setting of accounting standards is as much a product of political action as of flawless logic or empirical findings" (C. T. Horngren, "Statements in Quotes," *Journal of Accountancy,* October 1973, p. 61). Today this view is more widely held than ever before.

REQUIRED

Identify and comment on the influence on accounting policy making of some of the groups, agencies, and so on which exist in the current environment of financial accounting and reporting.

EXERCISES

E1-1. SOURCES OF ACCOUNTING PRONOUNCEMENTS Several organizations and documents that have or might influence or establish financial accounting and reporting practices are listed below.

ORGANIZATIONS	DOCUMENTS
A. Securities and Exchange Commission	1. Opinions
B. Accounting Principles Board	2. Statements of Concepts
C. Financial Accounting Standards Board	3. Financial Reporting Releases
D. Committee on Accounting Procedure	4. Technical Bulletins
	5. Statements of Standards
	6. Accounting Series Releases
	7. Regulation S-X
	8. Staff Accounting Bulletins
	9. Accounting Research Bulletins
	10. Discussion Memoranda

REQUIRED

Identify (by number) all documents related to each organization listed above.

E1-2. CONCEPTUAL FRAMEWORK Important developments in the FASB's conceptual framework project occurred in the following years: 1974, 1976, 1978, 1980, 1984, and 1985.

REQUIRED

List the particular conceptual framework action or actions taken by the FASB in each of the above years.

2 FINANCIAL ACCOUNTING AND REPORTING: A THEORETICAL STRUCTURE

Accounting theory has been defined as "logical reasoning in the form of a set of broad principles that (1) provide a general frame of reference by which accounting practices can be evaluated and (2) guide the development of new practices and procedures."[1] As the business environment becomes more complex, firms engage in increasingly complex transactions. An accountant must be able to analyze these transactions and resolve accounting and reporting issues. Furthermore, an accountant needs to be able to analyze accounting and reporting issues in order to participate in the development of new financial accounting and reporting standards.

Chapter 1 demonstrated how accounting practice combines generally accepted accounting principles (GAAP) and theoretical concepts. In this chapter we shall present a theoretical structure for financial accounting and reporting.[2]

Before we begin our study of accounting theory, it will be instructive to see how theory can help in the resolution of accounting issues.[3] As an example, assume that CBS Television has entered into a noncancelable agreement with the National Basketball Association (NBA) for the exclusive right to televise all NBA games during the next 20 years and that CBS has agreed to pay the NBA $10 million annually, plus 1 percent of all revenues derived from the telecasts of NBA games.

This agreement raises several accounting issues for both CBS and the NBA:

1. Is the exclusive right to televise the games an *asset* to CBS? If so, how should this asset be measured and reported in CBS's financial statements?

2. Has CBS incurred a *liability* to the NBA as a result of this 20-year noncancelable agreement? If so, how should the obligation ($10 million annually plus 1 percent of *future* revenues) be measured and reported?

3. Should the NBA report the cash inflows to be received as *revenue*? If so, at what point or points in time should this revenue be reported?

---

[1] Eldon Hendriksen, *Accounting Theory,* 4th ed. (Homewood, Ill.: Richard D. Irwin, 1982), p. 1.

[2] The accounting discipline at present is based not on one particular theory, but rather on a collection of theories. The approach taken in this chapter focuses on financial reporting objectives and is similar to that used by the FASB in the conceptual framework project. In this chapter we discuss financial accounting theory, but we often refer simply to "accounting theory."

[3] As we pointed out in Chapter 1, political considerations also play a role in the resolution of accounting issues. Thus theory may *assist,* rather than dictate, resolution.

4. Should this agreement be disclosed in the financial statements of CBS and the NBA? If so, what is the most *useful* method of disclosing this agreement?

Financial accounting theory can be of assistance in answering these questions.

Exhibit 2–1 presents the financial accounting theory structure that will be discussed in this chapter. As we pointed out in Chapter 1, financial accounting and reporting are

EXHIBIT 2–1   THE STRUCTURE OF FINANCIAL ACCOUNTING THEORY

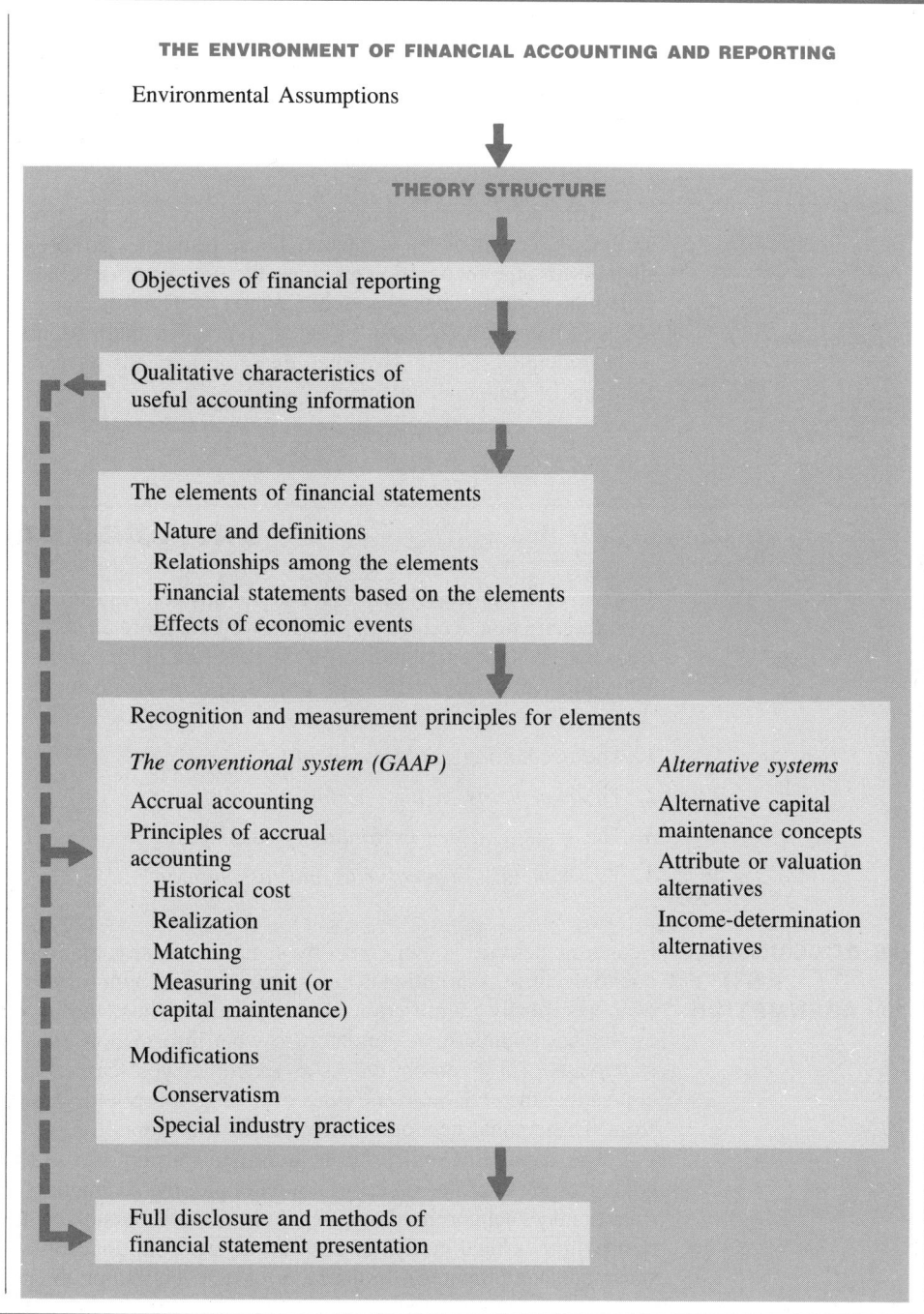

affected by the economic environment. Correspondingly, the structure of financial accounting theory is affected by the environment of financial accounting and reporting. Financial reporting objectives, which focus on providing useful information to users of financial reports and which comprise the first level in our accounting theory structure, are derived from environmental influences. Characteristics of useful accounting information, called qualitative characteristics, make up the next level of the accounting theory structure and provide a basis for choosing among accounting and reporting alternatives in light of the objectives. These qualitative characteristics are pervasive, and as Exhibit 2–1 shows, they influence the manner in which elements of financial statements are defined, measured, and reported.

The elements of financial statements.

Financial statement elements are the building blocks with which financial statements are constructed; they include assets, liabilities, equity, revenues, expenses, gains, losses, and net income or loss. In this chapter we shall define each element, discuss the relationships among the elements, and introduce the financial statements that are based on these elements.

After defining the elements, we shall examine the broad principles for recognition and measurement of the elements. These principles are presented in two parts. First we shall discuss the recognition and measurement principles that underlie GAAP, or what we called the conventional system in Chapter 1. Then, because the conventional system has received increased criticism in recent years, we shall discuss some alternative measurement principles. Finally, we shall examine methods of disclosing information about the elements of financial statements.

ENVIRONMENTAL ASSUMPTIONS

In Chapter 1 we described the economic environment in which financial accounting and reporting are practiced. In this section we look more closely at the environmental assumptions that provide a foundation for the structure of financial accounting theory and explain why financial information is presented in a given manner. These assumptions are:

1. The *accounting entity assumption*.
2. The *periodicity* or *time period assumption*.
3. The *going concern* or *continuity assumption*.
4. The *monetary* or *measuring unit assumption*.

THE ACCOUNTING ENTITY ASSUMPTION

Economic activity is carried on by specific business enterprises. The essence of the accounting entity assumption is that accountants account for and report financial information of a specifically identified accounting entity. Thus, the **accounting entity assumption** establishes boundaries or limits as to what information may be included in the financial statements of a given entity. As an example, you learned in your accounting principles course that the economic activities of a single proprietorship are accounted for separately from the personal economic activities of the proprietor.

The accounting entity that is identified for purposes of financial reports may or may not correspond to a legal entity. For example, the accounting entity under certain circumstances may be a corporation (a legal entity) or a division or department within a corporation (within a legal entity) or a group of legal entities (for which consolidated financial statements are prepared). In the latter case, even though the parent company and subsidiary companies are separate legal entities, they are combined as a single accounting entity for financial reporting purposes.

THE PERIODICITY OR TIME PERIOD ASSUMPTION

Another characteristic of the economic environment is that investors, creditors, and other parties make resource allocation decisions on a continuing basis and need timely financial information to assist them in decision making. Thus, those parties who are served by externally reported financial data impose periodicity on an accounting entity. The **periodicity** or **time period assumption** means that the economic activities of an accounting entity are divided into various artificial time periods for financial reporting purposes. The time period used in financial reporting generally is one year, although financial reports often are prepared on a monthly or quarterly basis.

THE GOING CONCERN OR CONTINUITY ASSUMPTION

Our economic environment is characterized by business entities that continue in operation on a relatively permanent basis. Although some businesses may encounter financial difficulties and may cease operations, such occurrences are not the normal expectation. The **going concern** or **continuity assumption** means that in the absence of evidence to the contrary, it is assumed that the business will continue to operate indefinitely, at least long enough to carry out existing plans, commitments, and contracts. Perhaps the going concern assumption can best be explained by analogy to the way people conduct their own lives. Most people have no reason to expect death in the near future, and so conduct their affairs as if they have an indefinite, but not infinite, future life. Although people do not expect to live forever, until they have strong evidence of imminent death, such as very old age or serious illness, they continue to act and think as if their lives will continue. Similarly, the accountant assumes that the accounting entity has a future life of undetermined length, unless there is evidence of imminent failure.

When an entity appears not to be a going concern, a change may be made in its method of accounting and reporting. For example, it may be proper to report liquidation values in the financial statements. This consideration arose prior to Braniff International Corporation's bankruptcy, when in 1980 the external auditors expressed doubt about Braniff's ability to continue as a going concern because of continuing net losses and a deteriorating financial position. Accounting for entities that are not considered to be going concerns usually is studied in advanced accounting courses.

THE MONETARY OR MEASURING UNIT ASSUMPTION

Exchanges in our society are measured in dollars. Therefore, we assume that the number of dollars or dollar equivalents (in noncash transactions) should be the measure of the results of the economic activities of the accounting entity, and that they should be reported in those units. This **monetary** or **measuring unit assumption** implies that the dollar has the same characteristic—stability over time—as all generally accepted measuring units, such as the inch or the pound. Just as an inch in 1957 is the same as an inch in 1987, so a dollar in 1957 should be the same as a dollar in 1987. Here lies the critical weakness of the assumption of measurement in monetary units. That is, in terms of general purchasing power, a 1987 dollar is not the same as a 1957 dollar. When inflation in the United States causes a decline in the purchasing power of the dollar, many people question the use of the dollar as the appropriate measuring unit for financial reporting purposes. One suggested alternative is that the general purchasing power of the dollar should be the measuring unit for financial reporting. *FASB Statement No. 33,* issued in 1979 and amended in 1984, requires supplementary disclosures of the impact of inflation and changing prices on certain financial statement numbers of many companies. At the time this textbook was published, the FASB was seriously considering making *Statement No. 33* disclosures voluntary.

OBJECTIVES OF FINANCIAL REPORTING

As we saw in Chapter 1, financial accounting and reporting are influenced by the economic environment in which they are practiced. Similarly, the objectives of financial reporting are affected by the economic environment, including the uses and users of financial accounting information that were discussed in Chapter 1. In addition, the objectives of financial reporting are affected by the characteristics and limitations of the information that is provided by financial statements. Therefore, before turning our attention to the objectives of financial reporting, we briefly discuss some of the **characteristics** and **limitations** of financial statement information prepared under existing accounting practices.

CHARACTERISTICS AND LIMITATIONS OF FINANCIAL STATEMENT INFORMATION

Financial statements provide information that is primarily financial in nature and that generally is quantified and expressed in units of money. While other information can be disclosed in financial statements, most of the contents of financial statements involve adding, subtracting, multiplying, and dividing numbers and thus require common units of measure, which, under GAAP, are units of money. Hence, *one limitation of the information reported in financial statements is that measurements are made only in units of money.*

The numbers reported in financial statements often are the results of approximate, rather than exact, measures. Reported numbers commonly involve estimates, allocations, summarizations, classifications, and judgments. Thus, despite the measurement precision that may be implied by financial statements, we must remember that *a second limitation of financial statement information is that, with few exceptions, accounting measures actually are approximations, based on accounting rules and conventions.* For example, the depreciation expense reported in the income statement for a period is based on an accounting convention, such as the straight-line depreciation method, and is not necessarily a measure of the amount of depreciable asset service potential that was used up during the period.

Financial statements provide information primarily reflecting the financial effects of transactions and events that already have occurred, rather than expectations and projections about the future. Even though estimates based on expectations about the future may be used in financial reporting, they normally are used in assessing the financial effects of past transactions or events or in determining the present status of an asset or liability. For example, in the case of a depreciable asset, estimates of future economic life and salvage value are used in calculating depreciation expense associated with the just completed accounting period. The fact that *financial statements provide information that is largely historical, while financial statement users are interested in the future,* is still another limitation of financial statement information.

THE ROLE AND OBJECTIVES OF FINANCIAL ACCOUNTING AND REPORTING

In Chapter 1 we stated that the role of financial accounting and reporting is to provide evenhanded (neutral or unbiased) information that helps promote the efficient allocation of scarce resources in capital and other markets. Also, financial statements are based on general purpose external financial reporting, which is directed toward financial statement users' common interest in a firm's ability to generate positive net cash flows from operations. The **objectives of financial reporting** are concerned with fulfilling the role of financial accounting and reporting and are directed at general purpose financial reporting by business firms.

The three basic financial reporting objectives set forth in *Statement of Financial Accounting Concepts No. 1* are:

1. Financial reporting should provide information that is useful to present and potential investors and creditors and other users in making rational investment, credit, and similar decisions. The information should be comprehensible to those who have a reasonable understanding of business and economic activities and are willing to study the information with reasonable diligence.

2. Financial reporting should provide information to help present and potential investors and creditors and other users to assess the amounts, timing, and uncertainty of prospective cash receipts from dividends or interest and the proceeds from the sale, redemption, or maturity of securities or loans. Since investors' and creditors' cash flows are related to enterprise cash flows, financial reporting should provide information to help investors, creditors, and others assess the amounts, timing, and uncertainty of prospective net cash inflows to the related enterprise.

3. Financial reporting should provide information about the economic resources of an enterprise, which are sources, direct or indirect, of future cash inflows; the claims to those resources (obligations of the enterprise to transfer resources to other entities and owners' equity), which are sources, direct or indirect, of future cash outflows; and the effects of transactions, events, and circumstances that cause changes in resources and claims to those resources.[4]

Because the objectives of financial reporting need a focus so that they are not too vague or abstract, the objectives emphasize information that is useful for investment and credit decisions. Investors and creditors and their advisers are the most easily identified and prominent groups of external users of financial statement information who normally lack the authority to specifically prescribe the information that they want. In addition, information provided to meet investors' and creditors' needs is likely to have general utility to other groups of external users who are interested in essentially the same financial aspects of a business as are investors and creditors.

The three basic objectives of financial reporting are important because they provide a perspective that is helpful in resolving specific financial accounting and reporting issues. The objectives are those of financial reporting rather than goals for investors, creditors, or others who use financial statement information. Thus, they are consistent with the role of providing financial information that is useful in making economic decisions, and are not aimed at determining what those decisions should be.

The first objective is broad and focuses on information that is useful in investor and creditor decision making. This objective encompasses information useful to those with either direct or indirect interest in the firm. Investors, creditors, and others who may use financial information have varying degrees of understanding of financial information, and the way and extent to which they rely on and use the information also may vary greatly. Since financial information is a tool, it cannot be of much use to those who do not understand it, to those who are unable or unwilling to use it, or to those who misuse it. As a result, the first objective specifies that financial reporting should provide information that can be used by all who have a reasonable understanding of business and economic activities and who are willing to learn to use the information properly.

The second objective is somewhat narrower than the first and relates to investors' and creditors' interests in receiving cash flows from investments in or loans to firms. The second objective also relates investors' and creditors' cash flow prospects to the cash flow prospects of the firm. The firm's ability to pay dividends and interest, as well as the market prices of the firm's securities, is affected by the firm's ability to generate favorable cash flows. Thus, in assessing their own cash flow prospects, investors, creditors, and

---

[4] "Objectives of Financial Reporting by Business Enterprises," *Statement of Financial Accounting Concepts No. 1* (Stamford, Conn.: FASB, 1978).

others can benefit from information that is helpful in assessing the amounts, timing, and uncertainty of prospective net cash inflows to the related firm.

The third objective emphasizes the provision of information about scarce economic resources that are needed to carry on economic activity, claims to economic resources, and changes in economic resources and obligations brought about by earnings activities and other operating activities. Such information helps investors, creditors, and others identify the firm's financial strengths and weaknesses and assess its liquidity and solvency. Moreover, it provides direct indications of the cash flow potentials of some resources and of the cash needed to satisfy many, if not most, obligations. However, many cash flows cannot be linked with specific resources and obligations but, instead, are the result of combining resources in the operating activities of the firm. For this reason, financial reporting should provide information about the firm's financial performance, which is summarized by earnings, during a period. According to the FASB, ''the primary focus of financial reporting is information about an enterprise's performance provided by measures of earnings and its components.''[5] Investors and creditors may use evaluations of the firm's past earnings performance to develop expectations about future earnings performance, which, in turn, lead to expectations about cash flows related to investing in or lending to the firm.

QUALITATIVE CHARACTERISTICS OF USEFUL ACCOUNTING INFORMATION

Financial reporting objectives focus on **decision usefulness;** that is, on providing information that will be useful for decision making. Therefore, the qualities or characteristics of useful information are the next stage in our accounting theory structure. These qualitative characteristics provide a basis for choosing among accounting and reporting alternatives, such as alternative depreciation methods, alternative methods of valuing assets, and alternative methods of disclosure. The qualitative characteristics thus help to provide an answer to the question, What characteristics of accounting information make it useful for decision making?

Exhibit 2–2 presents a hierarchy of qualitative characteristics. The boxes representing decision makers and decision usefulness relate the qualitative characteristics to the previously discussed financial reporting objectives, which stress usefulness of information to decision makers. **Understandability** means that the user must understand the information presented if the information is to be useful in decision making. Understandability is designated as a user-specific quality because information that has the other qualities may be useful to some users but not to others, depending on how well the specific users understand the information presented. Remember that the first financial reporting objective is that information should be comprehensible to those who have a reasonable understanding of business and economic activities and who are willing to study the information. Therefore, the understandability characteristic implies that financial reporting should not exclude useful information simply because it is difficult to understand. Special effort, such as additional education, may be needed to increase a user's understanding of financial information.

PRIMARY QUALITATIVE CHARACTERISTICS

The primary qualities that make accounting information useful are **relevance** and **reliability.** They are called primary qualities because information *must* possess these two qualities to be useful. Relevance and reliability, and their components, are discussed below.

[5] Ibid., para. 43.

EXHIBIT 2–2   A HIERARCHY OF ACCOUNTING QUALITIES

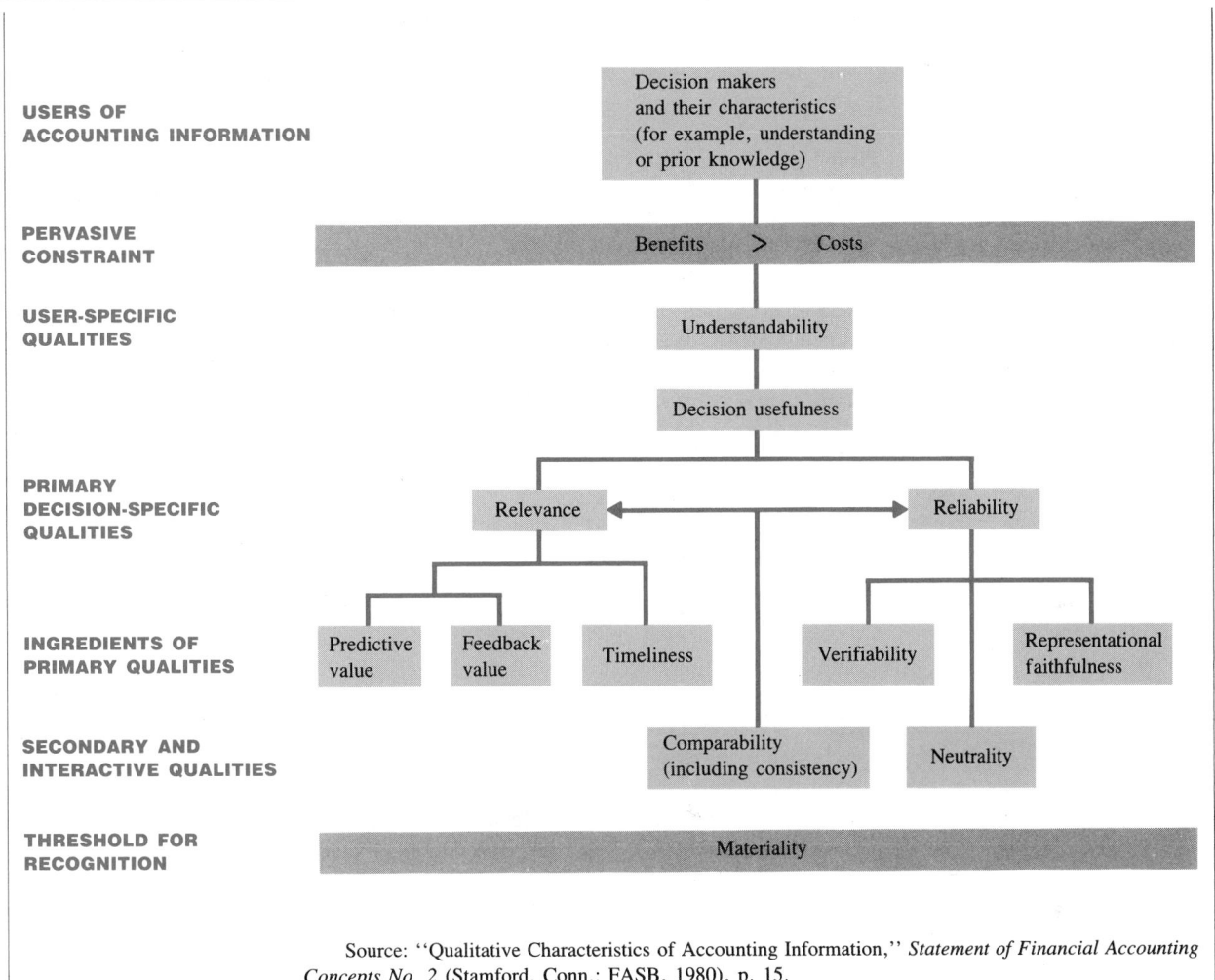

Source: "Qualitative Characteristics of Accounting Information," *Statement of Financial Accounting Concepts No. 2* (Stamford, Conn.: FASB, 1980), p. 15.

Relevance

Relevance means that the accounting information is capable of making a difference in a decision. To be relevant, information must either confirm or change the decision maker's expectations. If information confirms expectations, it increases the probability that the results will be as expected. If it changes expectations, it changes the perceived probabilities of previously identified possible outcomes. Either way, relevant information makes a difference to a decision maker. Relevance of information, however, does not mean that a decision already made must be changed or that a course of action already taken must be altered. If someone decides to hold an investment rather than sell it, information that supports that decision is relevant, just as information that led the investor to sell would be relevant.

    Predictive value and **feedback value** are two components of relevance. Information can affect a decision by improving the decision maker's ability to predict—predictive value—or by confirming or correcting the decision maker's earlier expectation—

feedback value. Often information does both at once, because knowledge about the outcomes of actions already taken will generally improve the decision maker's ability to predict outcomes of similar future actions. Predictive value and feedback value are consistent with the second financial reporting objective of providing information to help users predict and assess cash flows.

Timeliness is the third component of relevance. If accounting information is to be capable of affecting a decision, the information must be available at the time the decision is to be made. Timeliness alone cannot make information relevant, but information that is not timely is not relevant. There are many situations in which it may be necessary to trade off some of the precision of accounting information in order to make the information timely. For example, although interim (e.g., quarterly) financial statements normally are less complete and less precise than annual statements, they are more timely. Notice the relationship of timeliness to the time period assumption and periodic reporting. The need for timely financial information is a major reason why the economic activities of a firm are divided into artificial time periods for financial reporting purposes.

Reliability

Reliability means that a user can depend on or have confidence in the reported information. Accounting information is considered reliable when it actually represents what it purports to represent and when the information can be verified.

Representational faithfulness is agreement between a measure and the item being measured.

Representational faithfulness means that there is agreement between a financial measure or description and the underlying economic phenomenon being measured or described. In accounting, economic resources and obligations and events that change those resources and obligations are represented in financial reports. Let us return to the hypothetical agreement between CBS and the NBA. CBS acquired the exclusive right to televise NBA games over a 20-year period and agreed to make payments to the NBA over this same period. Therefore, many people believe that CBS should report on its balance sheet the right acquired as an asset and the related obligation as a liability. This disclosure would make CBS's financial statements representationally faithful regarding the benefit obtained and obligation incurred when it entered into the agreement with the NBA.

Verifiability increases the assurance that accounting measures represent what they purport to represent. *Statement of Financial Accounting Concepts No. 2* states that "verifiable financial accounting information provides results that would be substantially duplicated by independent measurers using the same measurement methods."[6] That is, verification implies a consensus among accountants on the measurement of an economic event and on the way it is reported. For example, the amount of cash reported on a balance sheet is highly verifiable. The book value of a depreciable asset, however, may have low verifiability because accountants may use different methods to determine cost, salvage value, and the estimated life of the asset. **Objectivity** often is used as a synonym for verifiability.

Relevance versus Reliability

Accounting information must have some degree of both relevance and reliability if it is to be useful for decision making. Relevance and reliability often conflict with each other, however. It may be necessary in some situations to sacrifice some degree of relevance in order to increase reliability or to sacrifice some degree of reliability in order to increase relevance. For example, there has been much controversy over the inclusion of financial forecasts in annual reports. Many people believe that forecasts provide users with information that is *relevant* to efforts to assess a firm's future cash flows. Other people,

---

[6] "Qualitative Characteristics of Accounting Information," *Statement of Financial Accounting Concepts No. 2* (Stamford, Conn.: FASB, 1980), para. 82.

however, believe that the information contained in a forecast is too *unreliable* because of the subjectivity of the estimates entailed in efforts to assess future events. As another example of the trade-off between relevance and reliability, information about the current values of a company's assets may be more *relevant* than historical cost information, but the historical cost information may be much more *reliable* than current value information.

SECONDARY QUALITATIVE CHARACTERISTICS

Although information must be relevant and reliable to be useful, other characteristics also are desirable. The secondary characteristics shown in Exhibit 2–2 are neutrality and comparability. They are classified as secondary because they are desirable qualities of accounting information, but they are not so important as relevance and reliability. **Neutrality** means that accounting information should be neutral, or evenhanded, with respect to the impact of the information on users' behavior. Notice the relationship of neutrality to the discussion of economic consequences in Chapter 1. Since accounting information affects the economic environment, it is important that accounting information be neutral, or unbiased. While financial reporting is aimed at the one general economic consequence, that is, resource allocation, it should be neutral with respect to all other consequences. For example, financial reporting should not be aimed at accomplishing a specific economic goal, such as increasing research and development.

Comparability enhances the usefulness of accounting information.

Comparability means that the usefulness of accounting information in decision making is enhanced if that information is comparable with similar information about other accounting entities and with similar information about the same accounting entity over time. **Interfirm comparability** is achieved when firms use similar accounting procedures when they are faced with similar economic circumstances. An example of interfirm comparability would be Chrysler's and Ford's use of, say, LIFO in accounting for automobile inventories. **Interperiod comparability,** or **consistency,** requires consistent application of accounting procedures through time. Consistency is referred to in the standard opinion rendered by an independent auditor:

> In our opinion, the aforementioned financial statements present fairly the financial position of XYZ Corporation at December 31, 19xx, and the results of its operations and the changes in its financial position for the year then ended, in conformity with generally accepted accounting principles applied on a basis *consistent with that of the preceding year.* [Emphasis added.]

Consistency does not mean that an entity can never make a change in its accounting practices, such as a change from FIFO to LIFO in accounting for inventories. If a change is made, however, it should result from a change in economic circumstances. In addition, the nature of the change and its effect on the financial statements should be disclosed. In practice, the entity must also be able to demonstrate that the new accounting practice is preferable to the old practice, given the change in economic circumstances.

OTHER CONSIDERATIONS AND CONSTRAINTS

Two other concepts, **information benefits versus information costs** and **materiality,** also appear in Exhibit 2–2. On occasion, application of these concepts may modify the choice of an accounting or reporting practice that might have been made based on only a strict consideration of the qualitative characteristics.

Information Benefits versus Information Costs

Since the preparation of accounting information is not costless, accounting standard-setters must consider whether the benefits derived from a particular accounting disclosure are greater than the costs of generating that disclosure. For example, is a requirement that companies disclose current value information cost-effective? Many people would say no, because the costs of preparing current value disclosures are thought to be greater than the benefits obtained by users of those disclosures.

What makes accounting information different from commodities that are traded in the marketplace? Commodities traded in the marketplace are private goods; the associated benefits and costs of a private good can be traced to a particular buyer or seller. Accounting information, on the other hand, is a public good, and the benefits of accounting information cannot always be confined to those who "pay" for it. Furthermore, the costs of providing the information may be widely diffused. Because it is difficult to assess the benefits versus the costs of a public good such as accounting information, application of the "benefit must exceed cost" rule to the problem of choosing among alternative accounting and reporting practices is at best very subjective. Nevertheless, the benefits and costs associated with accounting and reporting choices should be evaluated so far as possible.

Materiality

Information is considered to be material if it is likely to have a significant effect on a user's decision. Materiality implies that generally accepted accounting principles need to be strictly followed only in accounting for and reporting material items. Lack of materiality does not justify the omission of or failure to report an item; it simply justifies expedient, cost-effective treatment of immaterial items.

Materiality is an important consideration that has an impact on financial accounting and reporting practices, as is illustrated by the statement that appears at the end of each of the FASB's *Statements of Financial Accounting Standards:* "The provisions of this Statement need not be applied to immaterial items." Materiality considerations have been cited in court cases. In one case, the judge ruled that a material fact was one "which if it had been correctly stated or disclosed would have deterred or tended to deter the average prudent investor from purchasing the securities in question."[7]

Materiality is a somewhat elusive concept because it is dependent on (1) the relative dollar amount of an item, (2) the nature of an item (e.g., a legal payment versus an illegal payment), or (3) some combination of the relative amount and nature of an item. For example, a decision by Exxon to record the purchase of a $10 wastebasket as an expense instead of as an asset (the wastebasket has future service potential) may be based on the immateriality of the $10 in comparison with the dollar amount of Exxon's total assets. A decision to disclose a small loan to an officer of a company in the external financial statements, on the other hand, is likely to be based on the nature of the transaction rather than the dollar amount of the loan. Finally, the materiality threshold may vary from company to company. For example, a $70,000 loss from a lawsuit would be material for many companies, but might not be material for a company as large as Exxon. Because materiality judgments often involve factors peculiar to a particular situation, the FASB has not yet found it feasible to develop a set of general materiality guidelines.

THE ELEMENTS OF FINANCIAL STATEMENTS

The elements of financial statements are "the building blocks with which financial statements are constructed—the classes of items that financial statements comprise."[8] The basic elements—assets, liabilities, equity, revenues, expenses, gains, losses, and net

[7] Escott et al. v. BarChris Construction Corporation et al., 283 Fed. Supp. (District Court S.D., New York, 1968), p. 681.

[8] "Elements of Financial Statements of Business Enterprises," *Statement of Financial Accounting Concepts No. 3* (Stamford, Conn.: FASB, 1980), para. 5. *SFAC No. 3* was replaced in 1985 by *SFAC No. 6. SFAC No. 6* is expanded in scope to encompass not-for-profit organizations. Otherwise, the wording is essentially the same as in *SFAC No. 3.*

income or loss—are financial representations or expressions of an entity's economic resources, claims to or interests in its resources, and the financial effects of transactions or other economic events that cause changes in economic resources or claims to them.

DEFINITIONS AND RELATIONSHIPS OF ELEMENTS

Definitions of the elements of financial statements are important because they provide guidance in determining how a transaction or other economic event should be reported in financial statements. For example, assume that a manufacturing company suddenly discovers that the land which it owns and on which its plant is located contains several thousand tons of valuable minerals. Should the minerals be recorded as an asset? Does this discovery create revenue? As another example, assume that a large corporation establishes a pension plan for its employees. The firm agrees to give its employees credit for services rendered before the plan was adopted in determining their pension benefits when they retire. Is the obligation to pay these benefits based on past services a liability at the date the pension plan is established? These examples and related questions illustrate the importance of definitions for the various financial statement elements.

Assets

Three essential characteristics of an asset.

Assets are probable future economic benefits obtained or controlled by a particular entity as a result of past transactions or events. Three essential characteristics are present in the definition of an asset. First, an asset has future economic benefit or future service potential in the form of positive cash flows.[9] Second, an entity can obtain the future economic benefit from use of the asset and can control other entities' access to that benefit. For example, an interstate highway in front of a company's factory, while probably beneficial to the company, is not an asset of the company, because other entities also have free use of the highway. On the other hand, an access road built by a company to its factory is an asset. Finally, the transaction that gives rise to the future economic benefit has already occurred; that is, the asset's existence is not dependent on a future transaction or event. To illustrate, a contract may call for the purchase by one firm of specific goods to be delivered by a second firm in the future. The firm that buys those goods does not yet consider them assets, however, because the actual delivery of the goods has not taken place. This kind of event is an exchange of promises called an **executory contract.**

Liabilities

Three essential characteristics of a liability.

Liabilities are probable future sacrifices of economic benefits arising from present obligations of a particular entity to transfer assets or provide services to other entities in the future as a result of past transactions or events. Three characteristics of liabilities can be seen in this definition. First, a liability obligates a company to transfer cash or other assets or provide services at some future time. For example, a dividend payable in cash is a liability because the declaration of a cash dividend obligates the company to transfer cash to stockholders on the payment date. A dividend distributable in stock of the declaring company, however, is not a liability because the obligation is to distribute the company's own stock, instead of cash or other assets, to stockholders. Second, the obligation to transfer assets or to provide services must pertain to a particular entity. For example, if Company *A* guarantees to pay a note issued by Company *B* in the event that Company *B* is unable to pay the debt at maturity, Company *A* does not incur a liability as a result of the guarantee. Company *A*'s obligation as a guarantor becomes a liability only if Company *B* defaults on the note. Finally, the transaction or event that obligates the entity to transfer assets or provide services must already have taken place. To return to the example

---

[9] These positive cash flows may be direct or indirect. For example, an account receivable has a direct future cash flow benefit. On the other hand, the future cash inflow associated with a machine is indirect, if the machine is used to produce a product that is then sold for cash.

in our definition of assets, the agreement to purchase goods in the future does not give rise to a liability. A liability to pay for the goods arises only when the goods are received at a future date.

Equity

Equity, or net assets, is the residual interest in the assets of an entity after its liabilities have been deducted. Because equity is a residual interest, it cannot be measured independently of assets and liabilities. The relationship between assets, liabilities, and equity is the basis for the accounting equation:

$$\text{Assets} = \text{Liabilities} + \text{Equity}$$

or rearranged to emphasize equity:

$$\text{Equity} = \text{Assets} - \text{Liabilities}$$

Equity is sometimes called **stockholders' equity** or **owners' equity.**

Investments by owners and distributions to owners are called **equity transactions** or **capital transactions.** A company's sale (issuance) of its own common stock is an investment by the owners. A cash dividend declared and paid by a company to holders of its common stock is a distribution to the owners. Both the issuance of stock and the payment of a cash dividend are equity transactions.

Revenues

Revenues are inflows of assets or settlements of liabilities, or both, during a period as a result of the delivery or production of goods, the rendering of services, or other earnings activities that constitute an entity's major or primary operations. Two essential characteristics of revenues are that revenues (1) arise from a company's primary earnings activities and (2) are recurring or continuing in nature. For example, a supermarket's sales of groceries each year constitute revenues, whereas an isolated sale of land the supermarket owns adjacent to the store is not revenue, but, instead, might yield a gain or loss. (Gains and losses will be defined and contrasted with revenues and expenses later.) Accounting theorists sometimes describe revenue as ''entity accomplishments'' or as ''the product of the enterprise.''

Two essential characteristics of revenues.

Expenses

Expenses are outflows of assets or the incurrence of liabilities, or both, during a period as a result of the delivery or production of goods, the rendering of services, or other earnings activities that constitute an entity's major or primary operations. The essential characteristic of expenses is that they are incurred in the generation of revenue. Referring to the supermarket example we considered earlier, salaries of checkers and other personnel are expenses. Expenses are sometimes described as ''entity efforts'' or ''entity sacrifices'' associated with the earning of revenue.

The essential characteristic of expenses.

Gains and Losses

Gains are increases in equity or net assets from peripheral or incidental transactions of an entity. Gains arise from transactions and economic events that do not result in revenues or owner investments. **Losses** are decreases in equity or net assets from peripheral or incidental transactions of an entity. Losses arise from transactions and economic events that do not result in expenses or distributions to owners.

There are some important distinctions between revenues and gains and between expenses and losses. First, revenues and expenses relate to the major or primary operating activities of a company, whereas gains and losses relate to peripheral activities. Conse-

Revenues and expenses contrasted with gains and losses.

quently, revenues and expenses provide different cash flow signals from those provided by gains and losses. To illustrate, because revenues are ongoing and are associated with a company's primary operating activity, users of financial statements should assess and predict cash flows associated with revenues and make predictions of future revenues differently than they would cash flows associated with gains.

Second, revenues and expenses refer to *gross* inflows and outflows, whereas gains and losses refer to *net* inflows and outflows. For example, sales revenue is a major revenue item for a merchandising company and represents a gross inflow of resources resulting from its sales activity. In contrast, a gain on a sale of a firm's plant, property, or equipment is the difference between the book value of the plant, property, or equipment and the cash or other resources received from the sale.

Net Income or Net Loss

Under GAAP, **net income** or **net loss** refers to the change in equity (i.e., the change in net assets) of an entity during the period as a result of transactions and other economic events that result in revenues, expenses, gains, and losses. Thus, net income or net loss includes all changes in equity during a period except for investments by and distributions to owners, and certain other changes in net assets (such as changes in market values of investments in noncurrent marketable equity securities). Mathematically, net income or net loss is determined by revenues, expenses, gains, and losses as follows:

$$\text{Net income or net loss} = \text{Revenues} - \text{Expenses} + \text{Gains} - \text{Losses}$$

In this text, as in current practice, the term **earnings** sometimes will be used as a synonym for *net income* or as a way of capturing the elements (i.e., revenues, expenses, gains, losses) that comprise income.

It is important that you know, however, that the use of *earnings* as a synonym for *income* differs from the conceptual position taken by the FASB in its *Statement of Financial Accounting Concepts No. 5* (1984). In *Statement of Financial Accounting Concepts No. 5,* the FASB suggested that earnings be a measure of performance for a period and, to the extent feasible, exclude items that are extraneous to that period, that is, items belonging primarily to other periods. Specifically, the FASB proposed that earnings should not include the following two classes of items:

1. "Effects of certain accounting adjustments of earlier periods that are recognized in the period, such as the principal example in present practice—cumulative effects of changes in accounting principles—which are included in present net income but are excluded from earnings as set forth in this Statement."[10] (Reporting cumulative effects of changes in accounting principles is introduced in Chapter 4 of this text and is discussed in detail in Chapter 22.)

2. "Certain other changes in net assets (principally certain holding gains and losses) that are recognized in the period, such as some changes in market values of investments in marketable equity securities classified as noncurrent assets, some changes in market values of investments in industries having specialized accounting practices for marketable securities, and foreign currency translation adjustments."[11] (Accounting for marketable equity securities is discussed in Chapter 14 of this text.)

The FASB proposed a new term, **comprehensive income,** which would include

---

[10] "Recognition and Measurement in Financial Statements of Business Enterprises," *Statement of Financial Accounting Concepts No. 5* (Stamford, Conn.: FASB, 1984), para. 42a.

[11] Ibid., para. 42b.

items not includable in its new concept of earnings. The relationship between earnings and comprehensive income described in *Statement of Concepts No. 5* is as follows:[12]

Comprehensive income includes all changes in equity except transactions with owners.

+ Revenues

− Expenses

+ Gains

− Losses

= **Earnings**

+/− Cumulative accounting adjustments

+/− Other nonowner changes in equity

= **Comprehensive income**

While it is important for you to be aware of the views expressed by the FASB in its *Statements of Concepts,* you should remember that *Statements of Concepts* do not prescribe GAAP. Therefore, even though the FASB has adopted the conceptual view that the term *comprehensive income* should be used, in this text we follow existing practice, using the term **net income** to describe the ''bottom line'' of the income statement. Furthermore, we will sometimes use the term *earnings* in place of *net income,* a practice that also is consistent with current accounting practice.

FINANCIAL STATEMENTS BASED ON ELEMENTS

In our discussion of the objectives of financial reporting, we pointed out that financial reporting should provide information about economic resources, claims to or interests in resources, and changes in resources and obligations from earnings and other activities which are helpful in assessing a company's cash flows. Economic resources, claims to or interests in resources, and changes in resources and obligations are represented by the elements of financial statements that were defined in the preceding section. These elements are the basis for a company's financial statements.

The **balance sheet,** also called the **statement of financial position,** reports an entity's assets, liabilities, and equity at the end of each accounting period. The **income statement** reports revenues, expenses, gains, losses, and the resulting net income or loss, and thus summarizes a company's earnings performance during an accounting period. The **statement of changes in owners' equity** summarizes the transactions that affect owners' equity during an accounting period. Finally, the **statement of cash flows** summarizes cash inflows and outflows from operating activities, investing activities, and financing activities during the accounting period.

EFFECTS OF ECONOMIC EVENTS

An **economic event** is an occurrence or happening that has a consequence to an entity. Economic events may be external or internal to the entity. An **external event** occurs when an entity is affected by something in its environment, such as the activity of another entity, an increase in the cost of materials purchased by the entity, or a natural disaster. An **internal event** occurs within an entity, such as the use of raw materials in production.

External economic events may be classified as either transactions or events other than transactions. A **transaction** is the transfer of something of value between two or more entities. If an entity both receives and sacrifices something of value, the transaction is an **exchange** or **reciprocal transfer** to the entity. A company's purchase of merchandise for cash or on account is an exchange transaction. On the other hand, if the transaction is such that an entity either receives something of value or sacrifices something of value but not both, the transaction is called a **nonreciprocal transfer.** A city's donation of land to a company for company operating purposes is a nonreciprocal transfer to the company.

[12] Based on para. 44 of *FASB Statement of Concepts No. 5*.

External events other than transactions include price changes, changes in market interest rates, and natural disasters.

Economic events have various effects on a company's financial statement elements. These effects are shown in Exhibit 2–3. As Exhibit 2–3 illustrates, all economic events that are recognized have a dual effect on the financial statement elements. That is, if a transaction or other economic event causes an increase or decrease in one element, another element also is increased or decreased. This duality is the basis for double-entry bookkeeping, which is discussed in Chapter 3. Some examples of the dual effect of economic events on the financial statement elements are shown below.

ECONOMIC EVENT	EXAMPLE
Exchange of assets for assets	Acquisition of inventory for cash. Inventory is increased, cash is decreased.
Acquisition of assets by incurring liabilities	Acquisition of land by issuing a note. Land is increased, notes payable is increased.
Change in assets accompanied by change in equity	A consulting firm earns revenue by performing consulting services for cash. Cash is increased, equity is increased.
Change in assets accompanied by change in equity	A company issues its own stock for cash. Cash is increased, equity is increased.

Under present accounting practice, not all economic events are captured and reported in financial statements. Only those economic events that can be both identified with the accounting entity and quantified in dollars are recorded and reported.

EXHIBIT 2–3   EFFECTS OF ECONOMIC EVENTS ON FINANCIAL STATEMENT ELEMENTS

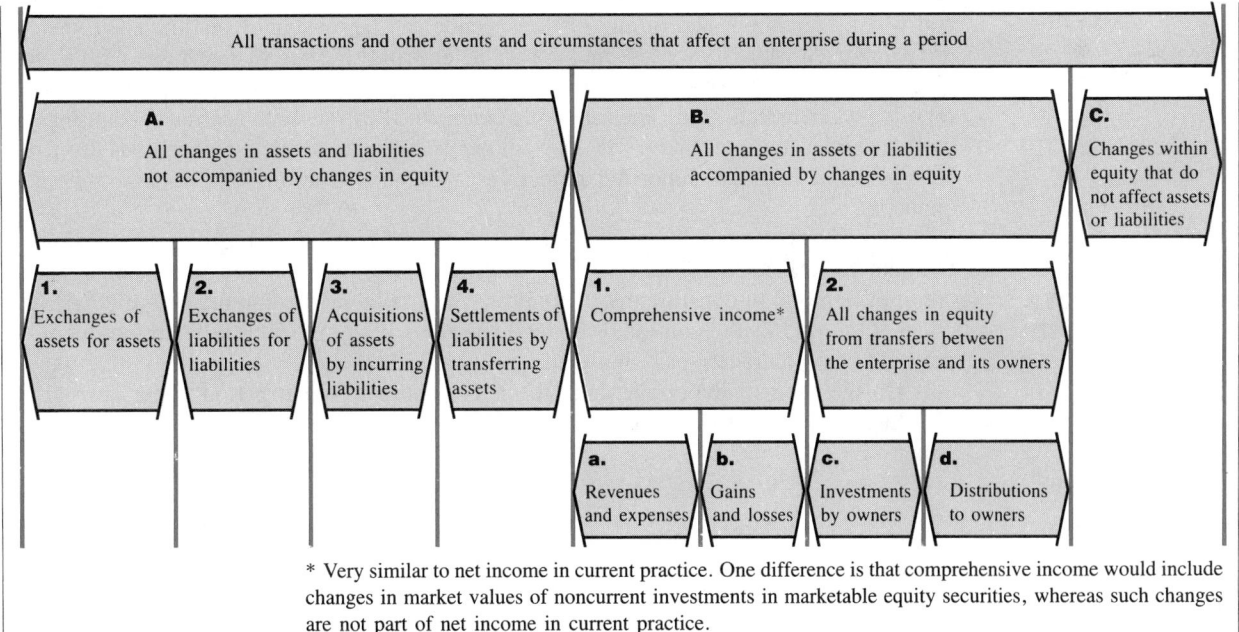

* Very similar to net income in current practice. One difference is that comprehensive income would include changes in market values of noncurrent investments in marketable equity securities, whereas such changes are not part of net income in current practice.

Source: "Elements of Financial Statements," *Statement of Financial Accounting Concepts No. 3* (Stamford, Conn.: FASB, 1980).

RECOGNITION AND MEASUREMENT PRINCIPLES FOR ELEMENTS

In the preceding section we defined the elements of financial statements, pointed out relationships among them, introduced the financial statements that are based on the elements, and discussed how transactions and other economic events affect the elements. Notice that nothing was said about either *when* the elements are recorded or *how* they are measured. The recognition and measurement principles for the elements provide guidance on these issues. Our discussion of these principles is divided into two parts: those principles that underlie the conventional system (GAAP) and those that underlie alternatives to the conventional system.

BASIC PRINCIPLES UNDERLYING THE CONVENTIONAL SYSTEM

Accrual Accounting

Although a company's earnings and related operating activities are continuous, they are reported for specific intervals of time in order to provide useful information for decision making on a timely basis. Some activities may begin and end during the accounting period, while other activities may require two or more accounting periods for completion. An automobile dealer, for example, may spend cash for an inventory of automobiles, sell the automobiles, and also collect cash from the buyers in one accounting period. Or the dealer may spend cash for an inventory of cars in one accounting period, sell the cars in the second period, and collect cash from the buyers in the third period. In addition, the dealer's showroom was purchased in one period but it will provide economic benefits over several accounting periods. In measuring earnings, which provide signals about cash flows, how should revenues and expenses be reported? Should they be reported on the basis of cash inflows and outflows or on the basis of transactions that have present and future cash consequences?

Accrual vs. cash-basis accounting.

Accrual accounting focuses on transactions and other economic events that have cash consequences rather than strictly on transactions involving only cash receipts or cash disbursements. Under accrual accounting, transactions and other economic events are recorded when they occur. Revenues are recognized and reported when they are earned and when the amount and timing of the revenue can be reasonably estimated. Expenses are recognized when they occur and are deducted from revenue to determine net income. Under **cash-basis accounting,** revenues are reported when cash is received; expenses are reported when cash is paid. The following examples illustrate both accrual accounting and cash-basis accounting. They will also allow us to contrast the two methods from the standpoint of financial reporting objectives and the definitions of financial statement elements.

Suppose that a contractor begins business in period 1 and agrees to construct a building for a local bank for $60,000. During period 1, the contractor incurs costs on credit of $35,000 in constructing the building, and delivers the completed building to the client. In period 2, the contractor collects the sales price of $60,000 from the client. In period 3, the contractor pays his creditors the $35,000 due.

On the basis of the above data, the net incomes for each period under accrual accounting and cash-basis accounting are as follows:

	PERIOD			
	1	2	3	TOTAL
Cash-basis accounting				
Cash receipts	$ –0–	$60,000	—	$60,000
Cash disbursements	–0–	—	$(35,000)	(35,000)
Net income	$ –0–	$60,000	$(35,000)	$25,000

| | PERIOD | | | |
	1	2	3	TOTAL
Accrual accounting				
Revenues	$60,000	—	—	$60,000
Expenses	(35,000)	—	—	(35,000)
Net income	$25,000	$ –0–	$ –0–	$25,000

Notice that for the three periods combined, both methods result in the same total net income. The difference between accrual accounting and cash-basis accounting lies in the *timing* of net income.

Under *cash-basis accounting,* net income is zero in period 1, since the sale of the building and purchase of materials, labor, and other assets or services used in constructing the building are on credit. Net income is $60,000 in period 2, and in period 3 there is a net loss of $35,000.

Under *accrual accounting,* because the contractor constructs and delivers the building to the bank in period 1 and because the net cash consequences (net cash flows) of this earnings activity are known with a high degree of certainty at the end of period 1, net income of $25,000 is reported. In periods 2 and 3, however, since no earnings activities take place, no income or loss is reported.

Let us modify the situation slightly. If the contracting company were a publicly held company and constructed several buildings on an ongoing basis, its profitability ultimately would affect the dividends paid to its stockholders and the market value of its outstanding shares. Thus, in making decisions to purchase or sell shares, owners and potential investors would need timely information about present and future cash flows to the firm to assist them in evaluating the firm and in making assessments and predictions about cash flows to them. Accrual accounting provides this information by reporting the net cash flows associated with earnings activities as soon as these cash flows can be estimated with some acceptable level of confidence. In our earlier example, these net cash effects are known and reported in period 1 on an accrual basis, whereas on a cash basis the cash effects are spread out over several periods and are misleading. For example, at the end of period 1, cash-basis accounting indicates that the contractor has not engaged in any profitable construction activity during the period. At the end of the second period a user would assume, on the basis of the income statement data, that net cash flows on the contract are or ultimately will be $60,000. The user would not know until the end of the third period that net income and net cash flow on the project were only $25,000.

In summary, accrual accounting is grounded in cash flows but reports transactions and other events with cash consequences at the time the transactions occur instead of when cash is received and paid. Accrual accounting also is superior to cash-basis accounting from the standpoint of the definitions of financial statement elements, as our next illustration shows.

Suppose that on January 1, 1987, C. J. Isuki formed a used car company by investing $20,000 cash. A summary of the company's transactions during January is as follows:

1. Purchased four cars for cash at $6,000 each.

2. Rented a building for an office and showroom and paid three months' rent in advance— $3,000.

3. Sold three cars for $9,000 each. Two sales were for cash. The third was on a deferred payment plan; collections on this sale were $1,000 during January.

4. Salesmen earned a $300 commission on each car sold. At the end of January, commissions were paid on the two cars sold for cash, and the company owed a salesman the commission on the third sale.

5. Office salaries incurred and paid totaled $800.

Cash-basis and accrual-basis financial statements for January based on this illustration appear in Exhibit 2–4. There are several things that make cash-basis accounting inconsistent with the theory underlying the financial statement elements:

1. The cash approach understates the amount of revenue and inflows of assets in January from the sale of the three cars. The $8,000 receivable is a future cash inflow that is ignored in cash-basis accounting.

2. The expense associated with the cost of cars sold in January is overstated because only three cars were sold. The fourth car is an asset in the form of inventory. This car has future cash inflow potential because it can be sold later.

3. The cash approach ignores part of the commissions that have been earned by the salesmen. Since three cars were sold, salesmen have earned $900 in commissions. Also the company is obligated to pay a salesman an additional $300, which is a liability.

4. Rent expense for January is overstated under the cash approach because the $3,000 payment for rent provides economic benefits over three months. The right to use the building for two more months, represented financially as prepaid rent, is an asset.

In accrual accounting, cash flows that precede the related earnings activities are called **prepayments** (from cash outflows) or **unearned** (from cash inflows). For example, prepaid rent of $2,000 shown in the balance sheet in Exhibit 2–4 is a prepayment. Earnings activities that precede the related cash flows are called **accruals.** The receivable of $8,000 shown on the balance sheet in Exhibit 2–4 is accrued revenue and the commission payable of $300 is an accrued expense.

The Historical Cost Principle

Under the **historical cost principle,** the exchange price established or cost incurred at the time a transaction occurs is the basis for initially recording assets and liabilities. This principle is used for initial recording because cost usually is the best estimate of an asset's or liability's fair market value.[13] When a cost is not incurred at the acquisition date, such as when a company acquires a machine by issuing shares of its stock, the exchange price is determined by reference to the fair market value of what is received or given, whichever is more clearly determinable.

After the acquisition or exchange date, the continued use of historical cost for an asset, less depreciation, if applicable, often results in reported data that are based on out-of-date prices. Asset prices may change because of inflation, changes in supply and demand, technology, and other factors. Thus, historical cost may become irrelevant for decision-making purposes. Under GAAP, the carrying value of an asset is occasionally written down or reduced to the current market value if current market is below cost, but an asset is rarely written up and reported above historical cost. Many accountants believe that the merit of reporting verifiable, actual transaction costs in the financial statement exceeds the possible disadvantage of reporting out-of-date data. In other words, many accountants would prefer to trade off some relevance in order to increase the reliability of the reported data.

[13] Conceptually, the cost and fair market value of an asset are equal at the acquisition date.

EXHIBIT 2—4   FINANCIAL STATEMENTS BASED ON
CASH-BASIS AND ACCRUAL ACCOUNTING

Isuki Used Cars

INCOME STATEMENT
FOR THE MONTH ENDED JANUARY 31, 1987

	CASH BASIS	ACCRUAL
Revenues	$ 19,000*	$ 27,000†
Expenses		
Cost of cars: Purchased (4 @ $6,000)	$ 24,000	
Sold (3 @ $6,000)		$ 18,000
Commissions	600	900
Salaries	800	800
Rent	3,000	1,000
Total expenses	$(28,400)	$(20,700)
Net income (loss)	$ (9,400)	$ 6,300

BALANCE SHEET
AS OF JANUARY 31, 1987

ASSETS	CASH BASIS	ACCRUAL
Cash	$10,600‡	$10,600‡
Receivable from customer ($9,000 − $1,000)		8,000
Inventory		6,000
Prepaid rent		2,000
Total assets	$10,600	$26,600

LIABILITIES AND EQUITY		
Commissions payable		$ 300
C. J. Isuki, equity	$10,600§	26,300¶
Total liabilities and equity	$10,600	$26,600

* ($9,000 × 2) + $1,000.

† $9,000 × 3.

‡ Original investment	$ 20,000
Cash sales (2 @ $9,000)	18,000
Collection on deferred payment sale	1,000
Cars purchased (4 @ $6,000)	(24,000)
Rent payment	(3,000)
Sales commission paid	(600)
Office salaries paid	(800)
Current cash balance	$ 10,600

§ Beginning investment less net loss: $20,000 − $9,400.

¶ Beginning investment plus net income: $20,000 + $6,300.

The Realization Principle

Realization vs. recognition of revenue.

The **realization principle** is used to determine when revenue should be recognized and reported in the income statement. Although the terms *realization* and *recognition* sometimes are used interchangeably, they have different meanings in accounting. **Recognition** is the act of *recording* revenue in the accounting records and reporting it in the financial statements. **Realization** is a more abstract concept used to determine *when* revenue should be recognized. Realization thus relates to the timing of revenue recognition. A more robust definition of realization is that realization describes the occurrence of an event that reduces uncertainty about future cash flows to an acceptable level to justify recognition of revenue.[14] This is the same definition of realization that is conveyed by the FASB in its *Statement of Financial Accounting Concepts No. 5.*[15]

The realization principle sets two criteria for revenue recognition.

When the realization principle is applied under GAAP, two criteria are used to determine when revenue should be recognized and reported in the income statement: (1) when the amount and timing of revenue to be received are reasonably determinable and (2) when the earnings process is virtually complete. The first of these two criteria is broader in scope than the old *APB Statement No. 4* criterion that an exchange must have taken place.[16] Current GAAP, as well as theory, places more emphasis on the reduction of uncertainty about cash flows than on the occurrence of a specific transaction or event as a requisite for realization. Even if the criteria for recognition have been met, subject to a cost/benefit constraint and a materiality requirement, recognition should occur only if:

1. The item meets the definition of an element of financial statements,

2. the item has a relevant attribute, measurable with sufficient reliability,

3. information about the item is capable of making a difference in user decisions (it is relevant), and

4. information about the item is reliable (it is representationally faithful, verifiable, and neutral).[17]

Another way of interpreting the realization principle is that revenue should be considered for recognition in the income statement when the particular event that is critical to the earning of the revenue has occurred and when the amount and timing of revenue to be received are reasonably determinable. For example, for the most common type of revenue transaction, a sale of goods, the critical event normally is the sale rather than the acquisition or production of the goods or collection of the sales price from the customer. Thus, revenue normally is reported in the income statement in the period of the sale.

THE EARNINGS PROCESS   Although the earnings activity or process that produces revenue is different for a manufacturing firm than for a merchandising firm, and varies from firm to firm, certain aspects of the process may be generalized across firms. We have identified these common aspects of the earnings process on the time line in Exhibit 2–5.

Exhibit 2–5 illustrates a firm's earnings process on a conceptual basis and is equally applicable to a manufacturing firm and a merchandising firm. A manufacturing firm acquires the components of production, manufactures the product, sells it, then collects

[14] "Report of the Committee on Concepts and Standards—External Reporting," *Accounting Review* 49 (1974), supplement.

[15] *FASB Statement of Financial Accounting Concepts No. 5,* para. 50.

[16] "Basic Concepts and Accounting Principles Underlying Financial Statements of Business Enterprises," *Statement of the Accounting Principles Board No. 4* (New York: AICPA, 1970), para. 150.

[17] *FASB Statement of Financial Accounting Concepts No. 5,* para. 63.

EXHIBIT 2–5   THE EARNINGS PROCESS

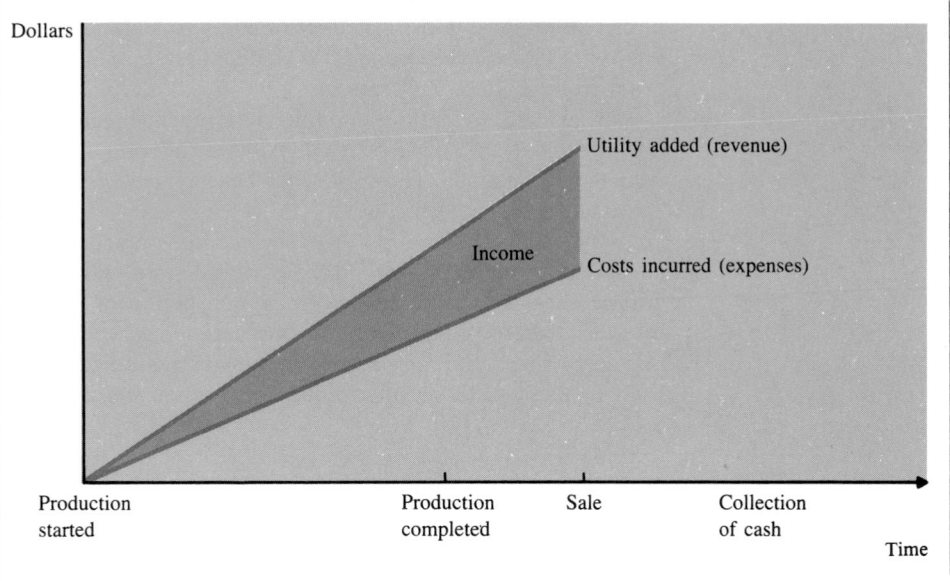

cash from the sale. The period between the sale and associated cash collection may be of zero duration, as in a cash sale, or quite long, as in a sale in exchange for a long-term receivable. The earnings process of a merchandising firm differs in that inventory is acquired and then held until the time of sale. From the point of sale on, the earnings process of a merchandising firm is the same as that for a manufacturing firm.

The earnings process of a firm that provides services is essentially the same as that shown in Exhibit 2–5, except that the production period is replaced by the period of providing services, and the point of sale is the point at which the service performance is complete.

Conceptually, the earnings process is continuous, as utility or value is constantly being added to the service or good. For example, value is added to goods as inputs, such as raw materials and labor, are transformed into finished products. In a given situation, the two realization criteria set forth earlier *could* be met, and revenue recognized, at any point during the earnings process. In the following paragraphs we shall discuss briefly recognition of revenue at the time of sale, the most common point of revenue recognition, as well as at other points during the earnings process—during production, at the completion of production, and at the time cash is collected.

REVENUE RECOGNITION AT THE POINT OF SALE   The sale is the most critical event in most companies' earnings processes. Thus, revenue normally is recognized at the point of sale. The sale event normally occurs when (1) ownership of goods is transferred to a buyer; (2) services are performed; or (3) asset services (e.g., apartment rentals) have been provided (e.g., the apartment has been occupied during the period).

REVENUE RECOGNITION DURING PRODUCTION   Contractual arrangements between the producer or seller and the buyer sometimes specify and guarantee selling prices to an extent sufficient to meet the criteria of revenue recognition before sale and delivery. Revenue may be recognized during production if (1) the contract price is fixed or determinable, (2) total production cost can be reasonably estimated, and (3) the cost incurred during the current accounting period or the percentage of production completion is known or can be reasonably estimated. Revenue is sometimes recognized during production on long-term construction contracts. Under these circumstances, production is the critical event in the earnings process.

Note that if these three conditions for revenue recognition during production are met, it is possible to determine with a high degree of certainty the net cash flows that will result from the transactions. Thus, users can be provided with information that will help them to assess and predict cash flows.

The accounting method used to recognize revenue during production on long-term construction contracts is called the **percentage-of-completion method.** When the above criteria are not met during the production period of a long-term construction contract, revenue is not recognized until the production has been completed. This method of recognizing revenue at the completion of production is called the **completed-contract method.** Both of these methods of revenue recognition are discussed thoroughly in Chapter 6.

REVENUE RECOGNITION AT THE COMPLETION OF PRODUCTION   Revenue may be recognized before sale in other than long-term construction contracts as long as the revenue recognition criteria are met. Precious minerals, such as gold and silver, and some agricultural commodities, such as wheat and corn, are not produced under long-term contracts, but the two criteria for recognition of revenue are often met at the completion of production. The ready marketability of such goods results in a reasonably certain market price; that is, the amount and timing of revenue to be received is reasonably determinable. Furthermore, marketing or selling costs are zero or minimal, so the earnings process is virtually complete. When there is a ready market for a product at a known market price and the marketing costs are immaterial, the critical event in the earnings process is the completion of production, not the sale of the product. In these cases, it is appropriate to recognize revenue when production is completed.

REVENUE RECOGNITION WHEN CASH IS COLLECTED   When sales are made on account and when reasonable estimates of uncollectible accounts cannot be made, revenue is recognized as cash is collected. Under these circumstances, even though a sale has occurred, there is too much uncertainty about the amount of cash to be received to warrant recognition of revenue before the cash is collected. When sales are made under a deferred payment plan, revenue is sometimes recognized as cash is collected. Two methods of revenue recognition when sales are made on account are the **installment method** and the **cost-recovery method.** Under the *installment method,* part of each dollar collected is assumed to represent a recovery of cost and part is assumed to represent income. Under the *cost-recovery method,* no income is recognized until after the amount of cash collected equals the cost of the asset sold; subsequent cash collections are reported as income.

The Matching Principle

The **matching principle** means that revenues generated and expenses incurred in generating those revenues should be reported in the same income statement. Revenues for an accounting period are recognized in accordance with the realization principle. Then the expenses incurred in generating those revenues are determined in accordance with the matching principle. Thus, expenses are reported in the income statement for the accounting period in which the related revenues are recognized.

The matching principle emphasizes the cause-and-effect association or relationship between expense and revenue. This association, however, is sometimes difficult to identify. For example, an expense that is incurred may not generate any obvious revenue. Such a situation occurs when an interior decorator employed by a company that sells furniture provides free advice to customers about wallpaper, paint, or room arrangements.

While little or no revenue can be associated directly with the interior decorator's service, there is no doubt that the expense of employing the decorator is incurred by the furniture store in the expectation that such a service contributes to revenues.

Because of the difficulty of associating expenses with revenues, general guidelines are used to apply the matching principle:

Three guidelines for applying the matching principle.

1. Associating cause and effect.

2. Systematic and rational allocation.

3. Immediate recognition.

ASSOCIATING CAUSE AND EFFECT   The most obvious matching of expenses and revenues occurs when the cost of goods sold is related to or associated with revenues generated from the sale of the goods. In this instance there is a clear and direct relationship between the revenue recognized and the associated cost of goods sold. For example, the cost of an electronic TV game sold by a hardware store can be determined easily and can be matched with the revenue from its sale. Any sales commissions on the sale can also be matched against the associated revenue.

SYSTEMATIC AND RATIONAL ALLOCATION   Some costs are incurred to acquire assets that provide benefits to the entity over several years. A typical example is the cost of a depreciable plant asset. Even though there is no clear-cut relationship to specific revenues during each year in which the asset is used, the asset contributes to revenues over its useful life. Therefore, a *systematic and rational allocation method* of matching the cost of using the asset with the revenues generated is employed. If the asset is expected to provide equal benefits toward revenue each year, for example, an equal amount of cost should be expensed each year. This cost allocation method is called straight-line depreciation or amortization of the cost of the asset.

IMMEDIATE RECOGNITION   Finally, some costs may be incurred when there is no ascertainable future benefit or when the future benefits are highly uncertain. These costs, such as advertising, the salaries of supervisors, and the salary of the interior decorator mentioned earlier, are recorded as expenses in the period in which they are incurred.

Measuring Unit or Capital Maintenance Concept

At the beginning of this chapter we discussed the measuring unit assumption that the dollar does not fluctuate in purchasing power. The measuring unit assumption concept may also be described as the general **capital maintenance concept** underlying the conventional system.

Capital maintenance requires a return of capital before there is a return on capital.

Capital maintenance means that the net assets or investments of an entity must be maintained, or recovered through revenues, before a company has earnings. Under the conventional system, the capital maintenance concept generally used in income determination is *originally invested dollars* or *nominal dollars,* and income results if a company recovers more dollars from revenues than it originally invested in the asset sold. If you bought shares of RCA common stock for $1,000 some years ago, for example, and if you sell those shares for $1,500, your income is $500.

However, persistent inflation in the United States in the 1970s caused many people to question the usefulness of the monetary assumption or the nominal dollar capital maintenance concept that underlies the conventional system. Later in this chapter we shall examine some income determination alternatives that may provide more useful information about earnings in periods of changing prices.

Modifications of the Basic Principles

Under GAAP, the recognition and measurement principles underlying accrual accounting are used to record transactions that then are reported in the financial statements. In some circumstances, however, accountants depart from a strict application of the principles of accrual accounting.

CONSERVATISM Many accounting and reporting practices require judgment and estimates because future economic events are uncertain. **Conservatism** is an effort to ensure that the risk or uncertainty inherent in business situations is adequately considered. Under conservatism, when two or more accounting alternatives appear to be equally capable of fulfilling financial reporting objectives, the alternative that has the least favorable impact on net income and financial position is chosen. Conservatism does not imply deliberate, consistent understatement of net assets and income; it is a method of dealing with uncertainty about future cash flows.

SPECIAL INDUSTRY PRACTICES **Special industry accounting or reporting practices** are used in many industries, such as utilities, railroads, oil and gas companies, and investment companies. Investment companies, for example, often report securities at market value instead of cost, because users evaluate these companies' operations in terms of changes in the market values of their investment portfolios. If the special accounting practices are followed by all firms in the industry, comparability is improved.

ALTERNATIVE SYSTEMS OF DETERMINING INCOME

The conventional system for determining income under GAAP is only one of many possible systems. Alternative income determination systems are based on (1) alternative concepts of capital maintenance and (2) alternative methods of valuing assets and liabilities. Both a capital maintenance concept and a method of valuing assets and liabilities are necessary in order to measure a company's net income for a given accounting period.

Alternative Capital Maintenance Concepts

As we stated earlier, capital maintenance means that the net assets or investments must be recovered through revenues before a company has earnings or income. Stated another way, as a company generates cash inflows from its earnings activities, a concept of capital maintenance is necessary to determine the portion of the cash inflows that represents a return *of* capital or investment recovery and the portion that represents a return *on* capital or earnings. Three concepts of capital maintenance are discussed below.

MAINTAINING CAPITAL IN UNITS OF MONEY Under the **nominal dollar concept of capital maintenance,** earnings arise as long as a company recovers more from revenues than the nominal dollar investment in the asset sold. For example, if a retail clothing company purchases a shirt at a cost of $20 and later sells it for $50, income on the sale is $30:

Revenue (cash inflow from sale)............ $50
Investment to be recovered
   (return *of* capital) .... (20)
Income (return *on* capital) $30

As indicated earlier, the nominal dollar concept of capital maintenance underlies the conventional accounting and reporting system. This concept of capital maintenance is sometimes called financial capital maintenance, as is the case in *FASB Statement of Concepts No. 5.*

MAINTAINING CAPITAL IN UNITS OF GENERAL PURCHASING POWER   Many accountants believe that in periods of inflation, nominal dollars are not useful for measuring a company's income. They feel that because the dollar loses general purchasing power in a period of inflation, more useful financial statement data are provided with a **general purchasing power concept of capital maintenance.** Under this concept, income arises only if a company is able to recover more from revenues than the general purchasing power equivalent of its investment. If the general price level, such as the consumer price index, doubled from the time the company in the previous example purchased the inventory until the inventory was sold, income from the sale would be only $10:

Revenue (cash inflow from sale)............. $ 50
Investment of general purchasing
  power to be recovered (return
  of capital): $20 × 2 .... (40)
Income (return *on* capital) $10

Because the general price level has doubled since the inventory was purchased, the company would have to sell the shirt for at least $40 to maintain the same level of general purchasing power as it invested in the shirt inventory. Thus income under the general purchasing power concept of capital maintenance is only $10, as compared to the $30 calculated when the nominal dollar capital maintenance concept is used.

The general purchasing power concept of capital maintenance is also called **constant dollar accounting.** The significant feature of this method is the change in the measuring unit from nominal dollars to general purchasing power units or constant dollars.

MAINTAINING CAPITAL IN PHYSICAL UNITS   Another concept of capital maintenance that has received much support in inflationary periods is the **physical capital maintenance concept.** Under this concept, income arises only if a company can recover in revenues more than the current or replacement cost of the item sold. In the clothing store example, if the shirt that originally cost $20 was sold for $50 at a time when the current cost of replacement was $45, income would be $5:

Revenue (cash inflow from sales)............. $50
Current cost of replacement
  (return *of* capital) .... (45)
Income (return *on* capital) $5

If the company plans to continue its operations by replacing the shirt and repeating the earnings activity, income will be only $5, because $45 of the $50 cash inflow is necessary to replace the shirt sold.

Alternative Attributes to Be Measured

Another necessary concept in periodic income determination is measurement of an attribute for an asset or liability. Examples of an asset's attributes include its volume, its color, and its weight. Users of financial statements, however, are interested in financial attributes, which are more useful in making economic decisions. These measured attributes are sometimes called asset and liability valuation methods.

Five alternative attributes to be measured or valuation methods that can be used for assets are: (1) historical cost, (2) current cost, (3) current exit value, (4) expected exit value, and (5) present value of expected cash flows. The generic term **current value** sometimes is used to describe the last four valuation methods.

The **historical cost** method of valuing assets underlies the conventional system discussed earlier in this chapter. **Current cost,** on the other hand, is the amount of cash that would have to be paid if an asset or equivalent asset service were to be acquired currently. Although historical cost and current cost are the same on the date that an asset is acquired, these attributes can be quite different later on. Assume that one of your relatives bought a home in 1977 for $60,000. Because costs have continually increased in the home building industry, it is likely that the current cost of replacing this home in 1987 would be more than $150,000, even though the historical cost of the home is $60,000.

Current exit value is the amount of cash that would be received currently if an asset were sold under conditions of orderly liquidation. Assume that you own 100 shares of AT&T stock. The quoted price of an AT&T share on the New York Stock Exchange times the 100 shares that you own, less brokerage commission, is the current exit value of your investment on the date of the quoted price. When assets are to be sold in the normal course of business, current exit value sometimes is called **current market selling price.**

Expected exit value is the nondiscounted cash flow associated with the expected sale or conversion of an asset at some future date. **Present value of expected cash flows** is similar to expected exit value except that the cash flows are discounted at an appropriate rate of interest to reflect risk and the time value of money.

Assume that you hold a $1,000 noninterest-bearing note that was issued by Paramount Pictures and is payable one year from now. Assume further that the current market rate of interest is 10 percent on notes of similar risk. The expected exit value of the note (what you expect to receive on the maturity date) is $1,000, but the present value of the note is only $909 ($1,000 ÷ 1.10). The present value of $909 means that the cash inflow to be received in one year is not worth $1,000 now because of the time value of money.

These five attributes or valuation methods also may be applied to liabilities as follows:

Historical proceeds: the amount recorded at the exchange date equal to the amount of cash or cash equivalent received.

Current proceeds: the amount that would be received if the same liability were incurred currently.

Current exit value: the amount of cash that would have to be paid currently to eliminate or settle the liability.

Expected exit value: the amount of cash expected to be paid to eliminate or settle the liability in the due course of business.

Present value of expected cash flows: same as expected exit value, except that the cash flows are discounted at an appropriate rate of interest.

The conventional financial accounting and reporting system is best described as a modified historical cost system.

The conventional system underlying GAAP often is called the *historical cost system,* meaning that assets and liabilities generally are measured and recorded at historical cost (historical exchange price). In addition to historical cost, however, other attributes of assets and liabilities also are measured and may be reported under GAAP. For example, *current cost* is used in lower-of-cost-or-market procedures for inventories, *current exit value* is used in lower-of-cost-or-market procedures for marketable equity securities, *expected exit value* is used for accounts receivable and accounts payable, and *present value of expected cash flows* is used for long-term receivables and payables. Moreover, some assets are acquired, and some liabilities are incurred, without exchanges. For example, an asset might be found or might be contributed to the firm. In these circumstances, there is no exchange price and some attribute other than historical cost must be measured. Therefore, rather than using the misleading ''historical cost system'' to characterize the conventional system underlying GAAP, it is more appropriate to characterize the conventional system as a *modified historical cost system.*

Capital Maintenance, Asset Valuation, and Income Determination

Both a concept of capital maintenance and an asset valuation method are necessary to determine a company's income during a period. From a balance sheet standpoint, asset and liability valuation methods or measured attributes are used to determine the total dollar amount of net assets at the end of an accounting period. A specified capital maintenance concept determines how much of this dollar total is necessary to maintain the beginning-of-period invested capital and how much of the dollar total represents income:

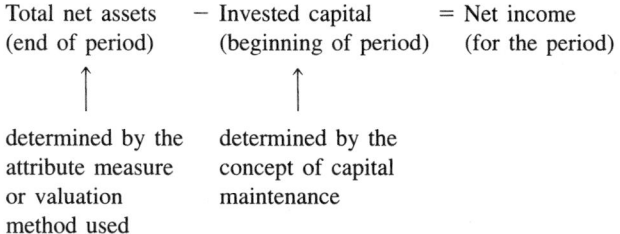

Exhibit 2–6 demonstrates how capital maintenance and asset valuation interact in income determination. Under alternative 1 in Exhibit 2–6, income for 1987 is zero, because the land is valued at historical cost and capital is maintained in nominal dollars. This approach is the one used under GAAP. Under alternative 2, the land is valued at its current exit value of $1,500. Because invested capital is to be maintained in nominal dollars, income of $500 results. This value change of $500 recognized as income under alternative 2 sometimes is called a **holding gain.** Under alternative 3 the land also is valued at $1,500, but because the general price level has increased 20 percent during the year, invested capital in end-of-1987 constant dollars is $1,200, and income for 1987 is only $300. Notice that under alternative 3, if the land's current exit value had been $1,200 at the end of 1987, income would have been zero because the $200 increase in the value of the land would have allowed the company to maintain a constant amount of general purchasing power during the year.

EXHIBIT 2–6   INTERACTION OF CAPITAL MAINTENANCE AND ASSET VALUATION IN INCOME DETERMINATION

FACTS:

1. Company X organized at the beginning of 1987 with only one asset, land, acquired at a cost of $1,000. The company did not sell the land during 1987.

2. The current exit value of the land increased during 1987 by $500 and was $1,500 at the end of 1987.

3. The general price level increased 20 percent during 1987.

Net income for 1987 under the following alternatives:

ASSET VALUATION METHOD/ CAPITAL MAINTENANCE CONCEPT	1 HISTORICAL COST/NOMINAL DOLLARS	2 CURRENT EXIT VALUE/NOMINAL DOLLARS	3 CURRENT EXIT VALUE/ GENERAL PURCHASING POWER OR CONSTANT DOLLARS
TOTAL ASSETS AT THE END OF 1987	$1,000	$1,500	$1,500
AMOUNT NEEDED TO MAINTAIN INVESTED CAPITAL	(1,000)	(1,000)	(1,200)
NET INCOME FOR 1987	$ –0–	$ 500	$ 300

FULL DISCLOSURE AND METHODS OF
FINANCIAL STATEMENT PRESENTATION

The final stage in our discussion of an accounting theory framework deals with full disclosure and methods of financial presentation. These concepts are very important in deciding how information should be displayed in financial statements and related notes in order to satisfy the financial reporting objectives discussed at the beginning of this chapter.

FULL DISCLOSURE   In Chapter 1 we pointed out that securities markets are efficient with respect to *publicly available* data, including financial statement data. The implication for financial reporting is that disclosure is an important issue in financial accounting and reporting.

Full disclosure means that published financial statements and related notes should include any economic information related to the accounting entity that is significant enough to affect the decisions of an informed and prudent user of the financial statements. Full disclosure is important for the following reasons:

1. Under GAAP, alternative accounting procedures, such as depreciation methods, inventory methods, and methods of revenue recognition, are used under differing circumstances.

2. Companies occasionally make changes in accounting or reporting procedures which affect the comparability of financial statements (e.g., a company may change from FIFO to LIFO in accounting for inventories).

3. Full disclosure facilitates the functioning of an efficient capital market by providing additional information about items included in basic financial statements. This additional information may be useful in making investment decisions.

As we indicated when we discussed the qualitative characteristics of useful accounting information, generally accepted accounting principles permit a great variety of accounting practices. Because of the variety of acceptable accounting practices, users of the financial statements must be informed about the accounting methods employed by a particular entity when they evaluate and assess the company's earnings performance, financial position, and present and future cash flows. Hence, full disclosure increases the relevance and reliability of accounting information.

Common methods of providing disclosure include reporting the various accounts and account balances of the entity in its financial statements, using clarifying parenthetical comments and explanatory footnotes, and presenting supplementary information related to such items as lease commitments, pension obligations, the impact of inflation on earnings, and contingencies. You may want to refer back to Exhibit 1–1 (page 6) for a summary of forms of disclosure and for examples of items typically disclosed. In conclusion, full disclosure is aimed at improving the clarity, quality, and quantity of economic data disclosed by the accounting entity.

METHODS OF   Methods of financial statement presentation, especially information about earnings, have
PRESENTATION   generated much discussion and research. The following questions illustrate some considerations in regard to methods of disclosing data to help users assess and predict future cash flows, evaluate a company's earnings performance, and in general make intelligent investment decisions necessary for efficient allocation of scarce resources:

1. What guidelines are necessary to distinguish between normal, recurring earnings activities and those that are unusual and nonrecurring?

2. Is information about earnings activities on a segment basis (e.g., product segments and geographical segments) useful? If so, how should segments be defined?

3. Should distinctions be made between costs that vary with volume and costs that remain fixed regardless of changes in volume?

4. Are distinctions between committed and discretionary expenditures helpful in assessing future cash flows?

5. How can financial statement information be presented to reveal a company's liquidity and ability to adapt financially to a changing environmental situation?

6. What level of aggregation or disaggregation of income statement data is necessary to allow users to analyze and assess the components of income?

7. Is a single net income number desirable, or should multiple income measures be disclosed?

8. What type of reporting should be required for economic events that relate to operations of earlier periods?

Conceptually, these questions must be answered by reference to the financial reporting objectives. Chapters 4, 5, and 23, which examine financial statements in some detail, discuss the manner in which many of these issues are resolved under generally accepted accounting principles.

SUMMARY OF IMPORTANT TOPICS AND CONCEPT APPLICATIONS

1. Accounting theory provides a general frame of reference by which accounting principles can be evaluated and guides the development of new practices and procedures.

2. The structure of financial accounting and reporting theory is comprised of (1) objectives of financial reporting, (2) qualitative characteristics of useful accounting information, (3) elements of financial statements, (4) recognition and measurement principles for the elements, and (5) full disclosure.

3. The four environmental assumptions underlying the structure of financial accounting theory are (1) the accounting entity assumption, (2) the periodicity assumption, (3) the going concern assumption, and (4) the monetary assumption.

4. The three basic objectives of financial reporting are directed at general purpose financial reporting by business firms.

5. The qualitative characteristics of useful accounting information are pervasive and provide a basis for choosing among accounting and reporting alternatives.

6. The overriding criterion for choosing among accounting and reporting alternatives is **decision usefulness. Understandability** is an important ingredient of useful information.

7. The primary characteristics that make accounting information useful are **relevance** and **reliability. Predictive value, feedback value,** and **timeliness** are the three components of relevance. **Representational faithfulness** and **verifiability** are the components of reliability.

8. **Neutrality, comparability,** and **consistency** are secondary characteristics of useful accounting information.

9. **Information benefits versus information costs** and **materiality** may result in modification of accounting or reporting choices.

10. The basic elements of financial statements of business entities are assets, liabilities, equity, revenues, expenses, gains, losses, and net income or loss.

11. Comprehensive income, a term proposed by the FASB in *Statement of Financial Accounting Concepts No. 5,* is a broader concept than earnings. Comprehensive income includes all changes in equity except transactions with owners.

12. Recognition and measurement principles for the elements of financial statements are (1) **accrual accounting,** (2) the **historical cost principle,** (3) the **realization principle,** (4) the **matching principle,** and (5) **capital maintenance.** The basic principles sometimes are modified by conservatism and special industry accounting or reporting practices.

13. Alternatives to GAAP that have been proposed for determining income are based on (1) alternative capital maintenance concepts and (2) alternative methods of valuing assets and liabilities.

14. **Full disclosure** in financial reporting is important to providing useful information.

QUESTIONS

Q2-1. List the four environmental assumptions that underlie financial accounting and reporting.

Q2-2. Discuss the accounting entity assumption.

Q2-3. Can there be a distinction between a legal entity and an accounting entity? Explain.

Q2-4. What is meant by the periodicity assumption?

Q2-5. What is the going concern assumption?

Q2-6. What is assumed under the monetary or measuring unit assumption?

Q2-7. What is the role of financial accounting and reporting?

Q2-8. Discuss the characteristics and limitations of financial statement information.

Q2-9. List and discuss the objectives of financial reporting.

Q2-10. Given the need for accounting information that is useful for decision making, what are the two primary qualities of useful accounting information?

Q2-11. What does it mean for accounting information to be relevant? What are the components of relevant information?

Q2-12. What is the nature of reliable accounting information?

Q2-13. What does it mean to say that information has representational faithfulness?

Q2-14. In the context of accounting, what does verifiability mean?

Q2-15. Why does the fact that accounting information is a public good cause a problem in operationalizing the traditional cost versus benefit rule for choosing among alternatives?

Q2-16. Why is materiality important in financial accounting and reporting? What does materiality mean in financial accounting and reporting practice?

Q2-17. What is an asset? A liability?

Q2-18. Distinguish between revenues and gains, and between expenses and losses.

Q2-19. Explain the distinction between *net income,* as the term is used in current accounting practice, and *earnings,* as the term is suggested for use by the FASB in *Statement of Concepts No. 5.*

Q2-20. Economic events may be classified by the nature of the event and by the effect of the event on the financial statement elements. Discuss each classification.

Q2-21. What are the basic principles underlying the conventional financial accounting and reporting system?

Q2-22. Distinguish between accrual accounting and cash-basis accounting.

Q2-23. Explain the historical cost principle.

Q2-24. How is the historical cost principle modified when assets are acquired at zero cost to an entity?

Q2-25. Distinguish between revenue realization and revenue recognition.

Q2-26. What is meant by the phrase ''the earnings process'' and what are the components of the earnings process for (1) a merchandising firm, (2) a manufacturing firm, and (3) a service organization?

Q2-27. Why is the revenue realization principle important?

Q2-28. What are the two criteria of the revenue realization principle?

Q2-29. Even if the recognition criteria have been met, according to *FASB Statement of Concepts No. 5,* what additional conditions should exist for recognition to occur?

Q2-30. Under what circumstances might revenue be recognized at the completion of production?

Q2-31. Under what circumstances should revenue recognition be deferred until cash has been collected?

Q2-32. Explain the matching principle. Describe the general guidelines that are used in matching expenses and revenues.

Q2-33. Discuss the following concepts of capital maintenance: (1) maintaining capital in units of money, (2) maintaining capital in units of general purchasing power, and (3) maintaining capital in physical units.

Q2-34. Explain the concept of conservatism within the context of financial accounting and reporting.

Q2-35. To what does the phrase ''attributes to be measured'' refer?

Q2-36. List and discuss five attributes of elements of financial statements that could be measured.

Q2-37. Why might the conventional financial accounting and reporting system best be referred to as a *modified* historical cost system?

Q2-38. What is required under full disclosure in financial statements and related notes?

CASES

C2-1. ENVIRONMENTAL ASSUMPTIONS   In Chapters 1 and 2 you learned something about the economic environment of financial accounting and reporting. In addition to seeing the interrelationships between financial accounting and reporting and the economic environment, you saw some evidence of the complexity of the economic environment. As often is the case in complex situations, some simplifying assumptions about the business and economic environment are needed as a foundation for the theory and practice of financial accounting and reporting.

REQUIRED

Briefly discuss each of the four environmental assumptions that underlie the theory and practice of financial accounting and reporting. Be sure that each discussion includes both a clear statement of the nature of the assumption and an indication of how the assumption affects financial accounting and reporting.

C2-2. FINANCIAL REPORTING OBJECTIVES   Recently a potential investor entered your brokerage office and inquired about investing in common stocks. He said he was interested in returns through dividends and market price appreciation of the stock, and had concluded that financial statements of publicly held firms were of absolutely no use to him in evaluating investment alternatives. In fact, he was of the opinion that financial statements published in annual reports were of little or no value to society's allocation of scarce resources among competing investments.

REQUIRED

Draft a response to the potential investor outlining (1) the role of financial reporting, (2) how financial reporting objectives meet that role, and (3) how published financial statement information may be useful in evaluating possible cash flows to individual investors.

C2-3. FINANCIAL REPORTING OBJECTIVES   Assume that you belong to a country club that is the ''in'' place for young professionals in your community. In addition to a number of CPAs, such as yourself, the club's membership includes doctors, dentists, lawyers, and members of several other professions. One day you and a few other club members, none of whom is an accountant but you, are discussing the purposes served by your respective professions. A lawyer member of the group asserts that ''accountants are only in it for the money'' and that ''everyone knows that financial statements are useless because financial reporting is intended to help management keep the stockholders in the dark about what's going on.'' Being offended by the lawyer's assertion and mildly amused by what seems to you to be a case of the ''pot calling the kettle black,'' you are determined to convince the rest of the group that the lawyer is wrong.

REQUIRED

For the benefit of the lawyer and the others who are discussing their professions' roles and purposes, list the three objectives of financial reporting. Explain why the objectives are important and go into some detail regarding the intent of each objective and how the three objectives are related to each other.

C2-4. THE ACCOUNTING ENTITY ASSUMPTION   The concept of the accounting entity often is considered to be the most fundamental of the accounting concepts, one that pervades all of accounting.

REQUIRED

1. a) What is an accounting entity?

b) Explain why the accounting entity concept is so fundamental that it pervades all of accounting.

2. For each of the following, indicate whether the concept of accounting entity is applicable; discuss and give illustrations.

a) A unit created by or under law.

b) The product-line segment of an enterprise.

c) A combination of legal units and/or product-line segments.

d) All of the activities of an owner or a group of owners.

e) An industry.

f) The economy of the United States.

(AICPA, adapted)

C2-5. QUALITATIVE CHARACTERISTICS   Assume that you are a member of the FASB technical staff. You have been assigned to provide corporate accountants with guidance on how to choose between alternative financial accounting and reporting practices. You have decided to schedule several free regional seminars for this purpose and to answer any questions the participants may have about particular accounting or reporting choices they face.

REQUIRED

Draft some opening comments for the seminars, discussing the qualitative characteristics of useful accounting information and indicating the importance of these characteristics to choices among alternative accounting and reporting practices.

C2-6. QUALITATIVE CHARACTERISTICS   You are engaged in the audit of Darlene, Inc., which opened its first branch office in 1987. During the audit Ricci Darlene, president, raises the question of the accounting treatment of the operating loss of the branch office for its first year, an amount that is material.

The president proposes to capitalize the operating loss as a start-up expense to be amortized over a five-year period. She states that branch offices of other firms in the same field generally suffer a first-year operating loss that is invariably capitalized, and you are aware of this practice. She argues, therefore, that the loss should be capitalized so that the accounting will be ''conservative''; further, she argues that the accounting must be ''consistent'' with established industry practice.

REQUIRED

Discuss the president's use of the words ''conservative'' and ''consistent'' from the standpoint of accounting terminology. Discuss the accounting treatment you would recommend.

(AICPA, adapted)

C2-7. QUALITATIVE CHARACTERISTICS The Financial Accounting Standards Board (FASB) has been working on a conceptual framework for financial accounting and reporting. The FASB has issued six *Statements of Financial Accounting Concepts*. These statements are intended to set forth objectives and fundamentals that will be the basis for developing financial accounting and reporting standards. The objectives identify the goals and purposes of financial reporting. The fundamentals are the underlying concepts of financial accounting—concepts that guide the selection of transactions, events, and circumstances to be accounted for; their recognition and measurement; and the means of summarizing and communicating them to interested parties.

The purpose of *Statement of Financial Accounting Concepts No. 2*, ''Qualitative Characteristics of Accounting Information,'' is to examine the characteristics that make accounting information useful. The characteristics or qualities of information discussed in *Statement of Financial Accounting Concepts No. 2* are the ingredients that make information useful and are the qualities to be sought when accounting choices are made.

REQUIRED

1. Identify and discuss the benefits which can be expected to be derived from the FASB's conceptual framework study.

2. What is the most important quality for accounting information as identified in *Statement of Financial Accounting Concepts No. 2*? Explain why it is the most important.

3. *Statement of Financial Accounting Concepts No. 2* describes a number of key characteristics or qualities for accounting information. Briefly discuss the importance of any three of these qualities for financial reporting purposes.

(IMA, adapted)

C2-8. THE MATERIALITY CONCEPT Some accountants believe that the materiality concept is the most important concept of financial accounting and reporting.

REQUIRED

1. Discuss the meaning of the materiality concept, indicating its essential characteristics.

2. Why might materiality be considered the most important concept in financial accounting and reporting?

C2-9. FINANCIAL STATEMENT ELEMENTS Dual Corporation requests your advice on determining how the items below should be classified as financial statement elements.

a) Dual wishes to know if its own stock, which has not yet been issued, should be considered an asset.
b) Several years ago Dual issued long-term bonds for financing purposes. The bond contract specifies that two years hence Dual must issue 10 shares of its common stock for each $1,000 bond outstanding. Dual wonders if the obligation for the common shares should be considered a liability.
c) During the current year Dual sold land that had been purchased for speculative purposes. The company is unsure whether to classify the sale as revenue or as a gain.
d) The state in which Dual operates recently made some improvements to a state-owned bridge that provides access to Dual's property. Dual wishes to show the fair value of these improvements as an intangible asset.

REQUIRED

On the basis of the definitions and relevant characteristics of the financial statement elements, draft a brief response for each of the four items above.

C2-10. FINANCIAL STATEMENT ELEMENTS: ASSETS   The general ledger of Pleasure-Vision, a corporation engaged in the development and production of television programs for commercial sponsorship, contains the following accounts before amortization at the end of the current year:

ACCOUNT	DEBIT BALANCE
Sealing Wax & Kings	$51,000
The Messenger	36,000
The Desperado	17,500
Shin Bone	8,000
Studio rearrangement	5,000

An examination of contracts and records revealed the following information:

a) The first two accounts listed above represent the total cost of completed programs that were televised during the accounting period just ended. Under the terms of an existing contract, *Sealing Wax & Kings* will be rerun during the next accounting period, at a fee equal to 50 percent of the fee for the first televising of the program. The contract for the first run produced $300,000 of revenue. The contract with the sponsor of *The Messenger* provides that he may, at his option, rerun the program during the next season at a fee of 75 percent of the fee for the first televising of the program.

b) The balance in the *Desperado* account is the cost of a new program that has just been completed and is being considered by several companies for commercial sponsorship.

c) The balance in the *Shin Bone* account represents the cost of a partially completed program for a projected series that has been abandoned.

d) The balance of the studio rearrangement account consists of payments made to a firm of engineers that prepared a report relative to the more efficient use of existing studio space and equipment.

REQUIRED

1. Which of the above accounts should be considered assets? Give reasons for your answers.

2. How would you report each of the accounts in the financial statements of Pleasure-Vision? Explain.

(AICPA, adapted)

C2-11. CONCEPT OF EARNINGS   In *Statement of Concepts No. 5,* the FASB suggested a concept of earnings that differs from current practice, in which *earnings* often is used as a synonym for *net income* or the "bottom line" on the income statement. The FASB stated that its proposed concepts of earnings would "be subject to the process of gradual change or evolution that has characterized the development of net income."

REQUIRED

Explain in as much detail as you can the difference(s) between net income or earnings, as the terms are used in current practice, and earnings and comprehensive income, as the terms are defined in *Statement of Concepts No. 5.* Your explanation should include an example income statement showing how earnings and comprehensive income relate to each other according to the FASB's proposal.

C2-12. ACCRUAL VS. CASH-BASIS ACCOUNTING   Generally accepted accounting principles require the use of accruals and deferrals or prepayments in the determination of income.

REQUIRED

1. How does accrual accounting affect the determination of income? Include in your discussion what constitutes an accrual and a deferral, and give appropriate examples of each.

2. Contrast accrual accounting with cash-basis accounting.

(AICPA, adapted)

C2-13. CASH-BASIS VS. ACCRUAL ACCOUNTING   Mr. Jacobs, owner of Jacobs' Retail Hardware, states that he computes income on a cash basis. At the end of each year he takes a physical inventory and computes the cost of all merchandise on hand. To this amount he adds the ending balance of accounts receivable, because he considers this to be a part of inventory on the cash basis. He deducts from this total the ending balance of accounts payable for merchandise to arrive at what he calls inventory (net).

The following information has been taken from Mr. Jacobs' cash-basis income statements for the years indicated:

	1989	1988	1987
Cash received	$ 173,000	$ 164,000	$ 150,000
Cost of goods sold			
Inventory (net), Jan. 1	$ 8,000	$ 11,000	$ 3,000
Total purchases	109,000	102,000	95,000
Goods available for sale	$ 117,000	$ 113,000	$ 98,000
Inventory (net), Dec. 31	(1,000)	(8,000)	(11,000)
Cost of goods sold	$(116,000)	$(105,000)	$ (87,000)
Gross margin	$ 57,000	$ 59,000	$ 63,000

Additional information is as follows for the years indicated:

	1989	1988	1987
Cash sales	$151,000	$147,000	$141,000
Credit sales	24,000	18,000	14,000
Accounts receivable, Dec. 31	8,000	6,000	5,000
Accounts payable for merchandise,			
Dec. 31	33,000	20,000	13,000

REQUIRED

1. Without reference to the specific situation described above, discuss cash-basis and accrual accounting and indicate their conceptual merits.

2. Is the gross margin for Jacobs' Retail Hardware being computed on a cash basis? Evaluate and explain the approach used with illustrative computations of the cash-basis gross margin for 1988.

3. Explain why the gross margin for Jacobs' Retail Hardware shows a decrease while sales and cash receipts are increasing.

(AICPA, adapted)

C2-14. ASSUMPTIONS AND PRINCIPLES   The current financial reporting practices followed by business organizations reflect the growth and development of the United States and world economies and the informational needs of today's sophisticated users of financial reports. Since the Middle Ages, when simple reports of stewardship were prepared, the scope of accounting information has been increasing, as has the responsibility for its content. From the beginning of the Industrial Revolution, when businesses became separate legal entities and the emphasis on financial position began to emerge, accounting information has evolved to meet the objectives of those supplying and relying on capital to fulfill the needs of society. Today the concept of income has taken on greater importance and the measurement of earnings is more closely scrutinized in both the public and private sectors. Thus, the evolution of financial reporting has witnessed a shift from an emphasis on financial position to an emphasis on income, changes in financial position, and the details of these items, which often are disclosed in the notes accompanying the financial statements.

REQUIRED

1. Identify the external users of general purpose financial statements and describe how the statements are used.

2. Basic assumptions are critical to the development of accounting. If a user does not understand the basic assumptions made by accountants, the user cannot understand why the information is presented as it is. Explain each of the following basic assumptions of accounting and indicate its effect on general purpose financial statements.

    a) Accounting entity assumption.

    b) Periodicity assumption.

    c) Going concern assumption.

    d) Monetary unit assumption.

3. Basic principles of accounting relate to how assets, liabilities, revenues, and expenses are to be identified, measured, and reported. Explain each of the following basic principles of accounting and indicate its impact on the presentation of general purpose financial statements.

    a) Historical cost principle.

    b) Realization principle.

    c) Matching principle.

(IMA, adapted)

C2-15. REVENUE RECOGNITION The earning of revenue by a business enterprise is recognized for accounting purposes when the transaction is recorded. In some situations, revenue is recognized approximately as it is earned in the economic sense. In other situations, however, accountants have developed guidelines for recognizing revenue by other criteria, such as at the point of sale.

REQUIRED

1. Explain why revenue is often recognized as earned at time of sale, and justify the practice.

2. Explain in what situations it would be appropriate to recognize revenue as the productive activity takes place.

3. At what times, other than those included in parts 1 and 2 above, may it be appropriate to recognize revenue? Explain.

(AICPA, adapted)

C2-16. REVENUE RECOGNITION Bidders, Inc., was organized in 1987 to bid on natural gas leases. Bidders resells the leases on which it bids to gas exploration companies. Because considerable time, effort, and costs are incurred in gathering information for purposes of submitting bids, Bidders sells the leases before it actually acquires them. It collects the sale price shortly after a sale is made. If Bidders is unable to obtain the lease, it refunds 95 percent of the sale price to the buyer and keeps the other 5 percent to cover the cost, time, and effort of gathering information associated with the bidding process.

Bidders' management is uncertain about when to recognize revenue in connection with its bidding operation and has asked you to evaluate the following recognition alternatives and to make a recommendation as to when revenue should be recognized. The alternatives are:

    a) When the lease is sold to the exploration company, subject to Bidders' obtaining the lease.

    b) When the cash is collected from the exploration company.

    c) When Bidders incurs the costs associated with the bidding process.

    d) When the lease is obtained by Bidders.

REQUIRED

Evaluate the above alternatives and select the appropriate point for revenue recognition. Give reasons for your recommendation.

C2-17. REVENUE RECOGNITION After you present your report on your examination of the Norris Publishing Company's financial statements to its board of directors, one of the new directors expresses surprise that the income statement assumes that an equal proportion of the revenue is earned with the publication of every issue of the company's magazine. He feels that the "crucial event" in the process of earning revenue in the magazine business is the cash sale of a subscription. He says that he does not understand why most of the revenue cannot be "realized" in the period of the sale.

REQUIRED

1. List the various accepted methods for recognizing revenue in the accounts and explain when the methods are appropriate.

2. Discuss the propriety of timing the realization of revenue in the Norris Publishing Company's account with:
  a) The cash sale of a magazine subscription.
  b) The publication of the magazine every month.
  c) Both events, by realizing a portion of the revenue with cash sale of a magazine subscription and a portion of the revenue with the publication of the magazine every month.

(AICPA, adapted)

C2-18. REVENUE REALIZATION AND RECOGNITION

1. Distinguish among earning revenue, recognition of revenue, and realization of revenue.

2. Revenue is normally recognized at the time of sale. Sometimes, however, revenue is recognized at other times, such as *(a)* during production, *(b)* at the completion of production, or *(c)* during cash collection. What circumstances justify the alternative recognition times? Discuss each alternative separately.

3. The above alternatives are sometimes characterized as exceptions to the realization of revenue at the time of sale. Formulate a definition of realization that encompasses all the alternatives in such a way that they are not considered exceptions. Justify your definition with respect to each alternative.

C2-19. EXPENSE RECOGNITION Construct-A-Shell sells and erects shell houses—frame structures that are completely finished on the outside but are unfinished on the inside except for flooring, partition studding, and ceiling joists. Shell houses are sold chiefly to customers who are handy with tools and who have time to do the interior wiring, plumbing, wall completion and finishing, and other work necessary to make the shell houses livable dwellings.

Construct-A-Shell buys shell houses from a manufacturer in unassembled packages consisting of all lumber, roofing, doors, windows, and similar materials necessary to complete a shell house. Upon commencing operations in a new area, Construct-A-Shell buys or leases land as a site for its local warehouse, field office, and display houses. Sample display houses are erected at a total cost of from $9,000 to $14,000, including the cost of the unassembled packages. The chief cost element of the display houses is the unassembled packages, since erection is a short, low-cost operation. Old sample models are torn down or altered into new models every three to seven years. Sample display houses have little salvage value because dismantling and moving costs amount to nearly as much as the cost of an unassembled package.

REQUIRED

1. A choice must be made between *(a)* expensing the costs of sample display houses in the period in which the expenditure is made and *(b)* spreading the costs over more than one period. Discuss the advantages of each method.

2. For 1*b*, discuss amortizing cost on the basis of time versus number of shell houses sold.

(AICPA, adapted)

C2-20. EXPENSE RECOGNITION An accountant must be familiar with the concepts involved in determining earnings of a business entity. The amount of earnings reported for a business entity is dependent on the proper recognition, in general, of revenue and expense for a given time period. In some situations, costs are recognized as expenses at the time of product sale; in other situations, guidelines have been developed for recognizing costs as expenses or losses by other criteria.

REQUIRED

1. Explain the rationale for recognizing costs as expenses at the time of product sale.

2. What is the rationale for treating costs as expenses of a period rather than assigning the costs to an asset? Explain.

3. In what general circumstances would it be appropriate to treat a cost as an asset instead of as an expense? Explain.

4. Some expenses are assigned to specific accounting periods on the basis of systematic and rational allocation of asset cost. Explain the underlying rationale for recognizing expenses on the basis of systematic and rational allocation of asset cost.

5. Identify the necessary conditions in which it would be appropriate to treat a cost as a loss.

(AICPA, adapted)

C2-21.   CAPITAL MAINTENANCE

1. *A* and *B* both invested $1,000 in a nightclub operation. *C* invested $1,000 in common stock of *X* Corporation in the hope that the price of the stock would rise so that he could buy a piece of land that was for sale for $1,200. After two years, *A*, *B*, and *C* cashed in their investments for $1,500. In talking with them you find that *A* considers that he earned a profit over the two-year period, *B* considers that he broke even, and *C* considers that he lost money because the owner of the land now wants $2,000 for it. The general price level increased 50 percent over the two-year period.

REQUIRED

Discuss the capital maintenance concepts apparently employed by *A*, *B*, and *C*.

2. Assume that you purchased a home for $40,000 in 1974 by paying $10,000 down and signing a 30-year mortgage at an interest rate of 8 percent. Today your house has an estimated selling price of $100,000, interest rates are now 10 percent, and the general level of prices has increased 50 percent since 1974.

REQUIRED

What factors should you consider in determining whether your capital has been maintained during this time period and whether you are better off as a result of making this home investment in 1974?

C2-22.   EXIT VALUE   Your boss wants to learn more about several concepts of current value that were introduced during a recent seminar he attended. He has asked you to prepare brief written comments about the concept of exit value.

REQUIRED

1. Discuss the meaning of "exit value."

2. Distinguish between current exit value and expected exit value.

3. Explain how exit values may be useful in meeting financial reporting objectives.

C2-23.   FINANCIAL STATEMENT ELEMENTS   The Baccus Corporation purchased $180,000 of computer equipment for $120,000 cash and an obligation to deliver an indeterminate number of shares of its $10 par common stock, with a market value of $15,000, on January 1 of each year for the next five years. Hence $75,000 in market value of shares will be required to discharge the $60,000 balance due on the equipment.

The corporation immediately acquired 3,000 shares of its own stock for $45,000, expecting the market value of the stock to increase substantially before the delivery dates. A total of 2,500 of these shares, costing $37,500, were subsequently issued in settlement of the equipment contract.

REQUIRED

1. Discuss the propriety of recording the cost of the equipment as
  a) $120,000 (the cash payment).
  b) $180,000 (the cash equivalent price of the equipment).
  c) $195,000 (the $120,000 cash payment plus the $75,000 market value of the stock that must be issued in order to settle the obligation in accordance with the terms of the agreement).

d) $157,500 (the $120,000 cash payment plus the $37,500 cost of the 2,500 shares issued for the equipment).

2. Discuss the arguments for treating the obligation as
   a) A liability.
   b) Common stock subscribed (part of stockholders' equity).

3. Would any of your answers to part 2 be different if previously unissued shares had been used to settle the obligation?

4. Discuss the arguments for treating the corporation's repurchased shares as *(a)* an asset; *(b)* a reduction in stockholders' equity.

5. Has the corporation earned revenue or made a gain by holding its own shares while their market value increased?

EXERCISES

E2-1. QUALITATIVE CHARACTERISTICS Identify by letter the qualitative characteristic or characteristics of useful accounting information that best relate to each concept or phrase below. A characteristic may be used more than once.

a) Understandability	**f)** Feedback value	**k)** Neutrality
b) Decision usefulness	**g)** Materiality	**l)** Comparability
c) Relevance	**h)** Timeliness	**m)** Consistency
d) Reliability	**i)** Verifiability	**n)** Benefit exceeds cost
e) Predictive value	**j)** Representational faithfulness	

_____ **1.** Accounting information may confirm the decision maker's earlier expectation.

_____ **2.** A primary qualitative characteristic.

_____ **3.** Expedient, cost-effective treatment of some items is justified by this concept.

_____ **4.** Essential for interperiod comparisons.

_____ **5.** Characteristic dealing with consensus of a group.

_____ **6.** Agreement between a measure and the thing being measured.

_____ **7.** Essential for interfirm comparisons.

_____ **8.** Periodic reporting, especially interim reporting, relates to this characteristic.

_____ **9.** Balancing relevant disclosures with resources required to generate such disclosures.

_____ **10.** This characteristic implies that standards do not favor a particular user group.

_____ **11.** Accounting information should be capable of making a difference in a decision.

_____ **12.** To be useful, accounting information must be available to the decision maker when the decision is being made.

E2-2. QUALITATIVE CHARACTERISTICS Listed below are statements that relate to the qualitative characteristics of useful accounting information and to modifications of the basic principles underlying GAAP.
   a) Companies usually record as expenses all expenditures for supplies that do not exceed a specified amount.
   b) All companies in the utility industry disclose interest expense, but do not include the expense in the operating section of the income statement.
   c) The SEC requires that the 10-K report include comparative statement data.
   d) When a company adopts LIFO, a change cannot be made to FIFO unless economic circumstances change.
   e) Although the cost of polluting the environment may be relevant information for inclusion in annual reports, few companies provide such disclosures.

f) Most accountants, if asked to determine the cost of K-Mart's inventory by using, say, FIFO, would probably reach similar conclusions.

g) Ace Trucking Company made an expenditure of $350,000 to remodel and improve its warehouse facilities. The company's manager could not decide whether to expense this amount. After discussing the matter with the company's accountant and external auditor, he expensed the amount.

h) Before the 1930s, many companies did not disclose the amount of sales revenue. Today all companies disclose such items.

i) The use of footnotes and supplementary disclosures in annual reports has increased dramatically in recent years.

j) Real estate investment trust companies report their real estate investments at market value, while other companies generally use either cost or lower of cost or market.

REQUIRED

What concept is described or relates to each of the above statements?

E2-3. CASH-BASIS VS. ACCRUAL ACCOUNTING The data below pertain to the operating activities of Dale Wholesale for the years 1987, 1988, and 1989:

	1987	1988	1989
Cash sales	$10,000	$ 8,000	$ 8,000
Credit sales	15,000	19,000	24,000
Expenses (cash)	9,000	12,000	6,000
Accrued expenses	12,000	14,000	20,000

REQUIRED

1. Calculate the income for each year under cash-basis accounting.

2. Calculate the income for each year under accrual accounting.

E2-4. CASH-BASIS VS. ACCRUAL ACCOUNTING The following cash-basis income statements pertain to the Strike-Out Company's operations:

	1987	1988
Cash receipts from customers	$150,000	$140,000
Cash disbursements to creditors, employees, etc.	(100,000)	(120,000)
Cash-basis income	$ 50,000	$ 20,000

Additional data are as follows:

Accounts receivable		
Beginning of year	$20,000	$60,000
End of year	60,000	30,000
Payables		
Beginning of year	$19,000	$ 3,000
End of year	3,000	6,000

REQUIRED

Calculate the accrual-basis income for 1987 and 1988.

E2-5. CASH-BASIS VS. ACCRUAL ACCOUNTING The Hagler Company reported net income of $30,000 for the year just ended. Since Hagler uses cash-basis accounting, the following items were excluded from the determination of net income:

Cost of sales

Beginning inventory	$ 5,000
Purchases	5,000
Ending inventory	4,000
Bad debts expense	2,500
Write-down of damaged equipment	1,000
Depreciation expense	2,000
Interest accrued on bonds held	3,000
Sales on account	15,000

REQUIRED

On the basis of the above data and assuming that the $30,000 reported net income included *(a)* a $4,000 payment to a creditor for purchases made the previous year and *(b)* $3,000 in customer payments for goods that will be completed and delivered next year, calculate the accrual-basis net income for the Hagler Company.

E2-6.   CAPITAL MAINTENANCE CONCEPTS   Haka Shoe Company purchased two pairs of shoes at the beginning of 1987 for $75 per pair. At the end of 1987, both pairs were sold for $120 per pair. During the year, the general level of prices increased by 40 percent; if Haka Shoe plans to operate in 1988, however, the shoes must be replaced at a cost of $120 per pair.

REQUIRED

Calculate the earnings for Haka Shoe Company for 1987 under the following capital maintenance concepts:

1. Nominal dollars.

2. General purchasing power units at the end of 1987.

3. Physical capital.

E2-7.   CAPITAL MAINTENANCE CONCEPTS   In Chapter 2, three capital maintenance concepts were discussed and illustrated. Assume that the president of a small business knows the following facts regarding a particular inventory item (Item A) and regarding the general level of prices in the economy:

a) Five units of Item A were bought at the beginning of the current year and were sold at the end of the current year.

b) Each unit was purchased for $92 and was sold for $110.

c) The general level of prices rose by 30 percent during the year.

d) Each item could be replaced for $103 at the end of the year.

REQUIRED

In order that she may better understand the alternative concepts of capital maintenance, the president asks you to calculate income related to inventory of item A under each of the capital maintenance concepts discussed in the chapter. Be sure to identify clearly each concept as you use it.

E2-8.   BASIC ASSUMPTIONS AND PRINCIPLES UNDERLYING CONVENTIONAL FINANCIAL REPORTING   Several statements related to financial reporting practice appear below. Describe the assumption or principle applicable to each statement.

a) Annual reports usually cover a one-year period.

b) Liquidation values usually are not reported in financial statements filed with the SEC and other agencies.

c) IBM Corporation reports revenue associated with computer sales at the point of sale.

d) Rockwell International depreciates equipment over its estimated useful life.

e) Allman Corporation bought the assets of a failing competitor at a price substantially below estimated fair value, but recorded the assets acquired at the cash price paid.

f) Companies record goodwill only when goodwill is purchased in a merger transaction.

g) Hromas operates a grocery store. During 1987 he withdrew $2,000 in cash for personal use at the local dog track. The amount was not expensed on the books of the grocery store.

h) Polly Darton, Inc., owns a controlling stock interest in several music publishing companies. Financial statements for Polly Darton, Inc., include the dollar amounts of relevant financial data pertaining to these (legally separate) companies.

i) Costs incurred to improve the efficiency of the Car Wash Company are recorded as assets and expensed as revenue from washing cars is earned and reported in Car Wash's income statement.

j) A company may not continually switch or change the method of computing depreciation on long-lived assets.

k) In addition to the basic financial statements, most companies include extensive footnotes and other supplementary data in their published financial statements.

l) *APB Opinion No. 22* requires that a statement of accounting policies (inventory pricing methods used, depreciation policies, revenue recognition policies, lease commitments, etc.) be included as an integral part of published financial statements.

m) The city of Slick, Oklahoma, recently donated a tract of land to Yamasaki Motorcycle Corporation in connection with a manufacturing plant to be built in Slick. Yamasaki recorded the land at its fair market value of $780,000.

n) For the past thirteen years, Booker Corporation has used the installment method of revenue recognition because of an inability to estimate uncollectible accounts.

o) Jamie Exploration Company depletes (depreciates) its mineral deposits on a cost-per-ton basis but depreciates its mine shafts on a straight-line basis.

E2-9. REVIEW OF CONCEPTS   Describe the concept, principle, or assumption that appears to be violated in each independent situation outlined below.

a) Included among the liabilities in the balance sheet for Conservative Cutter Corporation is this item: "Obligation for fees related to consulting services to be received, $35,000."

b) During 1987 Floyd Masters, Inc., paid a customer $300,000 in settlement of a lawsuit stemming from a golf-cart accident. The company recorded the event as follows:

Intangibles	300,000	
Cash		300,000

c) In 1986 McConnell Watercraft received a government contract for 300 hang gliders. The contract was recorded as revenue in 1987, although work on the contract did not begin until mid-1987.

d) Jim Jones Antiques recently purchased an antique Volkswagen at an auction for $4,000. Jones, the owner, felt that the car was worth at least $7,000 and directed his controller to record the purchase as follows:

Merchandise	7,000	
Cash		4,000
Gain on bargain purchase		3,000

e) When the corporation that owned the Half-Mile Island nuclear plant was assessed a stiff penalty from a governmental unit for a nuclear accident, the corporation recorded the penalty as a "deferred charge," arguing that future revenues would easily cover the penalty.

f) In 1987, Sott Railroad Company entered into a 100-year noncancelable agreement to lease railroad cars at an annual lease payment of $4 million. Sott excluded information about this transaction from its 1987 financial statements since technically it was not considered a liability (the amount is material).

g) Recently the Dead Sea Oil Company built a pipeline to carry petroleum products from the oil field to its refinery. The cost of the pipeline, which was $30 million, was expensed. Dead Sea's net assets have averaged $50 million over the past 15 years.

h) Jasper Discount House sells microwave ovens on a deferred payment plan. The company recognizes revenue on a cash-collection (i.e., installment) basis even though no uncollectible accounts have occurred since the company began operating twenty years ago.

i) The Gulf Airport Authority (a governmental unit) constructed two new runways at the municipal airport it owns and operates. One common carrier, Tex-Lou Airlines, recognized the benefits that the construction would have on its ability to increase the number of flights into the airport, and accordingly made the following entry on its books:

Runway improvements (intangibles) 300,000
    Contributed capital   300,000

j) Smoother, Inc., adopted a depreciation policy by which the depreciation method (e.g., accelerated, straight-line, units of production, etc.) used each year would be selected in accordance with its ability to permit the firm to maintain (and thus report) a 20 percent rate of return on beginning owners' equity.

k) Byers Corporation recently reported a dividend distributable in its own shares as a liability.

l) In 1987 the Timpkins Company resold shares of its own stock that it had previously purchased in the open market for more than it had paid for previous purchases. The excess was reported as a gain on Timpkins' 1987 income statement.

E2-10. ENVIRONMENTAL ASSUMPTIONS, QUALITATIVE CHARACTERISTICS, RECOGNITION, AND MEASUREMENT PRINCIPLES   Several widely used financial accounting and reporting practices are listed below.

a) The costs of assets are capitalized and charged to expense over the periods benefited.

b) Revenues are recorded when earned and expenses are recorded when incurred.

c) The exchange price established in a transaction actually entered into by the accounting entity is the proper basis for initially recording assets.

d) Revenue is recorded in the accounting records and reported in the financial statements.

e) Revenue normally is reported in the income statement in the period of sale.

f) Inventories and marketable equity securities are valued on the basis of lower of cost or market.

g) The assets and liabilities of stockholders are not included with the assets and liabilities of the corporation whose stock they hold.

h) Income results when the number of dollars of revenue earned exceeds the number of dollars of expenses incurred. (Do not use the matching principle.)

i) All economic information that is significant enough to affect users' decisions is reported in financial statements.

j) The financial statements of a company usually are prepared on a consolidated basis, with the financial data of the various activities of the parent company aggregated with those of its subsidiaries.

k) Financial reports issued between the dates of annual financial statements, which are called interim reports, are available from many companies.

l) Financial statements are issued at regular intervals, such as annually.

m) When the useful economic life of a plant asset is determined, it is assumed that the business that owns the asset will continue operations indefinitely.

n) In order for a company's financial statements to be comparable from year to year, changes in accounting practices should be made only when economic circumstances change.

o) Current values are not generally reported, and one argument supporting continuation of this practice is that it is very costly to prepare current value disclosures.

REQUIRED

Identify the environmental assumption, qualitative characteristic, or recognition and measurement principle that best supports each of the above accounting and reporting practices.

3 THE ACCOUNTING PROCESS: A REVIEW

The size of an accounting entity determines the complexity of its operations and financial reports. General Motors, as you might expect, has more complex operations and financial reports than a small department store because it has larger markets, more products, greater management information needs, more interaction with government agencies, and a larger volume of business transactions. Despite differences in size and complexity of operations, the accounting systems and related procedures of most accounting entities share several common features:

Common features of accounting systems.

1. The types of economic events captured by the system.

2. The accounting model used to express the financial effects of economic events.

3. The accounting process or cycle used to record and process data.

These features are discussed in this chapter as we review the process by which economic events affecting a firm are captured, processed, summarized, and reported in the financial statements. The financial statements produced by the process are examined in more detail in Chapters 4 and 5.

The information provided by financial accounting and reporting enables managers and external users to answer such questions as:

Was a profit made this past year?

What is the trend in profits over the past several years?

Should a dividend be paid this year?

Are cash flows being generated according to expectations?

Is the firm becoming too heavily in debt?

Are sales keeping in step with a growing market?

What is the rate of return on capital invested?

Accounting systems generate the economic information needed to answer these and other similar questions. Before we examine how information is collected, processed, and presented to users, we must review the nature of economic events whose financial effects appear in financial reports.

ECONOMIC EVENTS CAPTURED BY AN ACCOUNTING SYSTEM

An **economic event** is an occurrence or happening that has a consequence to an entity. Economic events may be classified in two ways:

1. By the nature of the event. In Chapter 2 we distinguished between *external events,* such as exchanges and nonreciprocal transfers, and *internal events,* such as the use of raw materials within the firm.

2. By the effect of the economic event on the financial statement elements. The effects of events on the financial statement elements were illustrated in Exhibit 2–3 in Chapter 2.

In Chapter 2 we pointed out that not all economic events are captured and reported in the financial statements. To be recognized the event must fit the definition of a financial statement element, it must have a relevant attribute that is measurable with sufficient reliability, and information about the economic event must be both relevant and reliable. For example, a sale to a customer is recognized because it satisfies the above criteria. On the other hand, a tax cut that may increase consumers' spendable income and ultimately result in increased sales is not recognized because the tax cut does not meet the definition of an asset, revenue, or any other element, nor is the effect on sales measurable with sufficient reliability.

THE ACCOUNTING EQUATION USED TO EXPRESS FINANCIAL EFFECTS OF ECONOMIC EVENTS

In its most simplified form, the accounting equation used to express financial effects of economic events is as follows:

Assets = Liabilities + Equity

Assets are probable future economic benefits obtained or controlled by a particular accounting entity as a result of past transactions or events. **Liabilities** are probable future sacrifices of economic benefits arising from present obligations of a particular accounting entity to transfer assets or provide services to other entities in the future as a result of past transactions or events. **Equity** is the residual interest in the assets of an entity that remains after deducting its liabilities—in other words, Assets − Liabilities = Equity. In a business enterprise, equity is the ownership interest and is called **owners' equity.**

Economic events have a dual effect on the accounting equation.

We saw in Chapter 2 that each economic event affecting a business has a dual effect on the accounting equation. The five transactions below illustrate this dual effect:

1. A dentist invested $10,000 cash in a dental practice.

Assets = Liabilities + Owners' equity
+$10,000   +$10,000

2. The dental practice purchased supplies on account at a cost of $800.

Assets = Liabilities + Owners' equity
+$800   +$800

3. Dental services were performed for patients on account, $1,000.

$$\text{Assets} = \text{Liabilities} + \text{Owners' equity}$$
$$+\$1,000 \qquad\qquad\qquad +\$1,000$$

4. Supplies costing $300 were used.

$$\text{Assets} = \text{Liabilities} + \text{Owners' equity}$$
$$-\$300 \qquad\qquad\qquad -\$300$$

5. The dental practice paid $600 on accounts payable.

$$\text{Assets} = \text{Liabilities} + \text{Owners' equity}$$
$$-\$600 \quad -\$600$$

The first transaction is a capital transaction and increases assets and owners' equity. The second transaction is an asset and liability transaction because both assets and liabilities are increased. The third and fourth transactions are revenue and expense transactions, respectively, and are examples of the types of transactions that meet the definitions of revenues and expenses discussed in Chapter 2. The final transaction is an asset and liability transaction because both assets and liabilities are decreased.

For a corporation, the accounting equation may be expanded as shown in Exhibit 3–1. For corporate entities, owners' equity is called **stockholders' equity.** Stockholders' interests in the assets of a corporation arise from two sources—investments in the entity and earnings or net income of the entity. **Contributed capital** represents the investments by stockholders, and **retained earnings** equals the corporation's cumulative net income retained in the corporation and not distributed as dividends to stockholders. **Dividends** represent distributions of assets resulting from profitable operations to stockholders as a return on their investment.

In order to provide relevant and timely financial information to users, financial statements are prepared periodically in accordance with the *time period assumption*. The accounting equation shown in Exhibit 3–1 may be interpreted within a time period context. The first two equations in Exhibit 3–1 apply at the *end* of an accounting period. The third equation shows that retained earnings at the end of a period equals the beginning-of-period retained earnings plus net income for the period less dividends declared during the period. The last equation shows that net income for the period equals revenues less expenses plus gains less losses.

EXHIBIT 3–1 THE ACCOUNTING EQUATION FOR A CORPORATION

$$\text{Assets} = \text{Liabilities} + \text{Stockholders' equity}$$

$$\text{Stockholders' equity} = \text{Contributed capital} + \text{Retained earnings}$$

$$\text{Retained earnings} = \text{Beginning retained earnings} + \text{Net income for the period} - \text{Dividends}$$

$$\text{Net income} = \text{Revenues} - \text{Expenses} + \text{Gains} - \text{Losses}$$

ACCOUNTS A company may have many assets and liabilities, and many revenues, expenses, gains, and losses. The effects of transactions that cause changes in the various financial statement elements are summarized in **accounts.** Accounts are used to accumulate the effects of transactions and other economic events on each financial statement item. An account, in ''T-account'' form, appears below.

Account title	Account no.
Debit side	Credit side

The vertical portion of the T divides the account into two sides. The left side is called the **debit** side and the right side is called the **credit** side.[1] A dollar amount is said to be *debited* to an account when it is entered on the left side and *credited* to an account when it is entered on the right side. The **account title** is the name of the account (e.g., cash or inventory). The **account number** is simply the number assigned to the account for record-keeping purposes and is helpful in processing data, especially in computerized accounting systems. To illustrate how accounts may be numbered, a corporation might use the following three-digit account numbers for the financial statement elements:

Asset accounts	100–199
Liability accounts	200–299
Stockholders' equity accounts	300–399
Revenue and gain accounts	400–499
Expense and loss accounts	500–599

The relationship between increases and decreases in account balances and the principle of debit and credit is shown in Exhibit 3–2 and is summarized below:

DEBITS INDICATE	CREDITS INDICATE
Asset increases	Asset decreases
Liability decreases	Liability increases
Stockholders' equity decreases	Stockholders' equity increases
Expenses	Revenues
Losses	Gains
Revenue reductions	Expense reductions
Gain reductions	Loss reductions

Principle of debit and credit.

The principle of debit and credit is related to the accounting equation so that memorized rules can be avoided. Assets appear on the left side of the accounting equation and are debited for increases. Liabilities and stockholders' equity appear on the right side of the accounting equation and are credited for increases. As Exhibit 3–2 shows, revenues increase stockholders' equity and are credited for increases. Also, expenses decrease stockholders' equity and are debited for increases. At any time, the balance in an account may be determined as the difference between the debit and credit entries in the account. Asset, expense, and loss accounts normally have debit balances; liability, stockholders' equity, revenue, and gain accounts normally have credit balances.

[1] The words ''debit'' and ''credit'' are derived from the Latin words *debitum* (debt) and *creditum* (loan). The terms arose because early records were kept initially to show amounts due to and from individual merchants. In modern accounting, however, ''debit'' and ''credit'' simply mean the left side and right side, respectively, of an account.

EXHIBIT 3–2 RELATIONSHIP BETWEEN THE FINANCIAL STATEMENT ELEMENTS AND THE PRINCIPLE OF DEBIT AND CREDIT

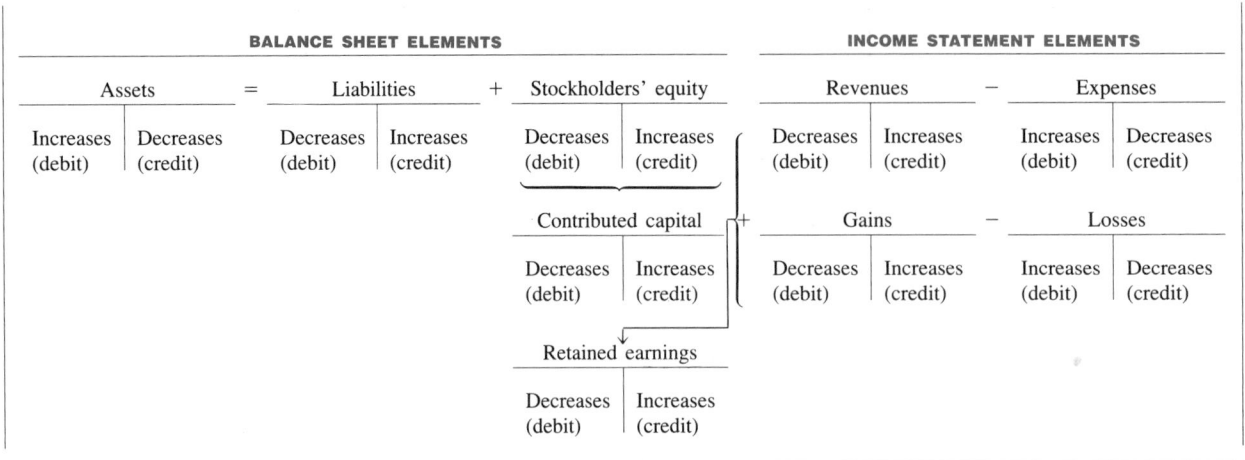

BALANCE SHEET ELEMENTS			**INCOME STATEMENT ELEMENTS**	

Assets	=	Liabilities	+	Stockholders' equity		Revenues	−	Expenses
Increases (debit) · Decreases (credit)		Decreases (debit) · Increases (credit)		Decreases (debit) · Increases (credit)		Decreases (debit) · Increases (credit)		Increases (debit) · Decreases (credit)

Contributed capital + Gains − Losses

| Decreases (debit) · Increases (credit) | | Decreases (debit) · Increases (credit) | | Increases (debit) · Decreases (credit) |

Retained earnings

| Decreases (debit) · Increases (credit) |

EFFECTS OF TRANSACTIONS ON THE ACCOUNTING EQUATION

The dual effect of transactions on the accounting equation and the rules for debit and credit are illustrated in Exhibit 3–3 for the dental practice example used earlier. Several points about Exhibit 3–3 are important:

Double-entry book-keeping.

1. Each transaction is analyzed first in terms of the effect on the elements of the accounting equation. Notice that each transaction has a dual effect on the accounting equation.

2. The dollar amounts of the transactions are entered into the appropriate accounts as increases and decreases in accordance with the rules of debit and credit.

3. For every debit made to an account, a corresponding credit is made to another account. Thus for every transaction, the dollar amounts of debits and credits are equal. Because at least two accounts are affected by each transaction, this practice sometimes is described as a *double-entry* system.

4. The effects of the transactions on the accounting equation are shown on the right side of Exhibit 3–3. Notice that the equality of the accounting equation, Assets = Liabilities + Owners' equity, is maintained after each transaction.

REAL AND NOMINAL ACCOUNTS

Accounts for the balance sheet elements are called **real** or **permanent accounts,** because these accounts provide an ongoing record of assets, liabilities, and owners' equity. Income statement accounts are called **nominal** or **temporary accounts** because these accounts are used to accumulate changes in assets and liabilities that arise from earnings activities during each accounting period. The nominal account balances are reduced to zero (closed) at the end of each accounting period in order to ready them for recording the next period's transactions.

THE ACCOUNTING PROCESS OR CYCLE

Description of the accounting cycle.

Now that we have discussed the accounting equation, the nature of accounts, and the principle of debit and credit which is used to show the effect of transactions and other economic events on a business, we are ready to discuss how financial information is accumulated. The accounting process or cycle consists of the procedures used to collect,

EXHIBIT 3–3   TRANSACTION ANALYSIS, RULES FOR DEBIT AND CREDIT, AND THE ACCOUNTING EQUATION

ECONOMIC EVENT	ANALYSIS OF EVENT	ACCOUNTING ENTRY	CUMULATIVE BALANCES IN THE ACCOUNTING EQUATION
			ASSETS = LIABILITIES + OWNERS' EQUITY
1. A dentist invested $10,000 in a dental practice.	Assets (cash) increased by $10,000. Owners' equity increased by $10,000.	**Cash** — Debit 10,000 / Credit — **Owners' Equity** — Debit — / Credit 10,000	+10,000 = 0 + +10,000 10,000 = 0 + 10,000
2. The dental practice purchased dental supplies on account at a cost of $800.	Assets (supplies) increased by $800. Liabilities (accounts payable) increased by $800.	**Supplies** — Debit 800 / Credit — **Accounts Payable** — Debit — / Credit 800	+800 = +800 + 10,800 = 800 + 10,000
3. Dental services were performed for patients on account, $1,000.	Assets (accounts receivable) increased by $1,000. Owners' equity (revenue) increased by $1,000.	**Accounts Receivable** — Debit 1,000 / Credit — **Revenues** — Debit — / Credit 1,000	+1,000 = + +1,000 11,800 = 800 + 11,000
4. Supplies costing $300 were used.	Assets (supplies) decreased by $300. Owners' equity (expenses) decreased (increased) by $300.	**Supplies Expense** — Debit 300 / Credit — **Supplies** — Debit — / Credit 800* , 300	−300 = + −300 11,500 = 800 + 10,700
5. The practice paid $600 on account payable.	Assets (cash) decreased by $600. Liabilities (accounts payable) decreased by $600.	**Accounts Payable** — Debit 600 / Credit 800* **Cash** — Debit 10,000† / Credit 600	−600 = −600 + 10,900 = 200 + 10,700

* From transaction #2.
† From transaction #1.

EXHIBIT 3—4   THE ACCOUNTING CYCLE

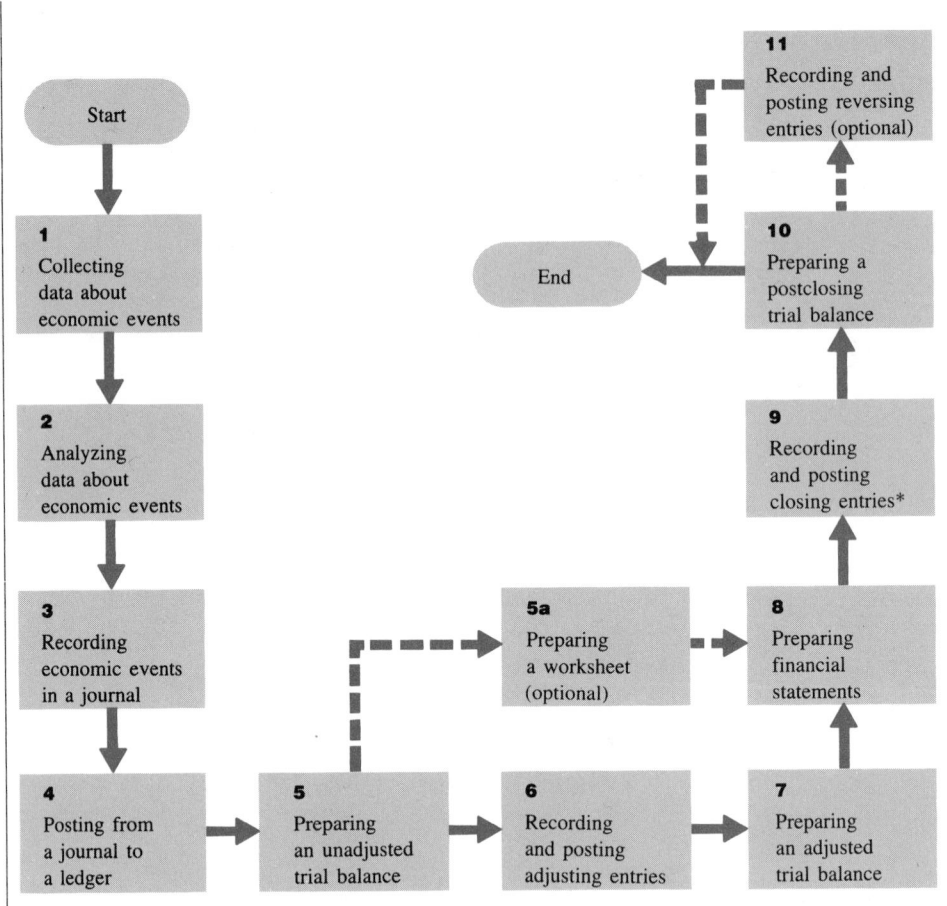

Note: Steps 1–4 occur during the accounting period. Steps 5–10 occur at the end of the accounting period. Step 11 (optional) occurs at the beginning of the following accounting period.

* At this time, adjusting entries also must be recorded and posted if a worksheet is used.

EXHIBIT 3—5   SOME SOURCE DOCUMENTS FOR SELECTED ECONOMIC EVENTS

ECONOMIC EVENT	SOURCE DOCUMENT
Cash sales	Cash register tapes
Credit sales	Sales invoices
Purchases of merchandise, supplies, and other assets	Purchase orders, purchase invoices, freight bills
Purchases of labor services (e.g., salaries and wages)	Time tickets, clock cards
Depreciation of long-lived assets	Depreciation schedules
Interest on notes held as investments	Note contract
Interest on savings accounts; service charges on checking accounts	Monthly bank statements
Customer defaults on accounts	Letters from customer or from customer's attorney
Warranty claims on merchandise sold	Warranty claim forms

process, and report the effects of economic events that affect an entity during the accounting period. As Exhibit 3–4 shows, this process begins with collecting or capturing economic data and ends with reporting these data in the financial statements. Each step is described and illustrated in the remainder of this chapter.

COLLECTING DATA ABOUT ECONOMIC EVENTS

The first step in the accounting cycle is to collect data about those economic events that will enter a company's accounting system. Data about economic events are collected from source documents. A **source document** provides evidence that an economic event has occurred. Some examples of source documents that provide verification about the occurrence of economic events are shown in Exhibit 3–5.

ANALYZING DATA ABOUT ECONOMIC EVENTS

Once economic data have been collected through source documents, the next step is to analyze the data to determine the effects of relevant economic events on the company's financial statement elements. This step is mental, but is very important because analysis of the effects will determine how the event is to be entered into the accounting system in the recording step, which follows. Notice that we analyzed the effects of the economic events in the examples in Exhibit 3–3 and that the entries in the T-accounts were based on this analysis.

Accounting theory assists in data analysis.

Analysis can be very difficult in more complex business transactions, and therefore can become a significant activity. Accounting theory helps the accountant to determine the impact of a transaction on the financial statement elements of a business and to record these events. For example, the realization principle is used to determine when a sale transaction should be recorded. The definition of an asset must be applied to determine whether a particular economic event gives rise to an asset. If an asset is recorded, expense recognition principles provide guidelines for determining how the asset should be expensed as its service potential expires. Objectivity and verifiability govern whether or not particular economic events will be recorded. Consistency ensures that similar events will be recorded in a similar manner. These examples are not meant to be exhaustive, but they do illustrate the importance of accounting theory in analyzing transactions.

RECORDING ECONOMIC EVENTS IN A JOURNAL

The recording process is the first step in entering the economic data previously collected and analyzed into a firm's accounting records. The device that is used to record these transactions is called a book of original entry, or a **journal.** A journal simply provides a chronological record of the firm's transactions and other economic events that have taken place.

Advantages of a journal.

In Exhibit 3–3 the effects (increase and decrease or debit and credit) of the economic events were shown directly in the related T-accounts. This approach was used for illustration only. In practice, the transactions are first entered into a journal, then transferred (posted) to the appropriate accounts. The advantages of initial recording in a journal are that it provides a chronological record of the economic events recognized during the period and that all information about the entire transaction appears in one place. For example, notice in Exhibit 3–3 that when the events were recorded directly into the T-accounts, no record of the entire transaction appeared in one place (i.e., the debit part of the transaction appeared in one account, whereas the credit appeared in another). Thus, if a question about the original transaction arises, the journal information can be used for verification.

The General Journal

One method of recording transactions makes use of a single journal, called a **general journal.** To illustrate recording in a general journal, assume that the transactions listed below for The Hardware Corporation took place in May 1987, during its first month of operations:

May 1 Corporate charter was received authorizing the issuance of 100,000 shares of $5 par common stock. Issued 16,250 shares at $8 per share.

May 1 Borrowed $30,000 from City Bank by issuing a $30,000 note due in two years. Interest at 10% is payable annually.

May 1 Purchased the assets of Zenith Hardware Corporation for $75,000 in cash. The assets consisted of inventory of $60,000, supplies of $4,000, and fixtures and equipment of $11,000.

May 2 Paid rent on a building for 12 months in advance, $7,200. Debited rent expense.

May 3 Purchased display equipment for $10,000 from Northern Supply Company. Paid $2,000 cash, the balance to be paid in 60 days.

May 4 Purchased merchandise on account from Quik Wholesale. Cost of the merchandise was $45,000.

May 4 Paid $1,800 cash for supplies, which were recorded as an asset.

May 5 Sold miscellaneous hardware totaling $25,000 to Ace Builders on account.

May 9 Purchased merchandise costing $30,000 from Nails, Inc., on account. The transportation cost on the merchandise totaled $250 and was paid in cash.

May 11 Received $12,000 of the amount due from Ace Builders.

May 12 Paid sales salaries totaling $3,000.

May 20 Cash sales of hardware, $15,000.

May 20 Subleased the top floor of the building rented on May 2 for $300 per month. Credited rent revenue.

May 22 Received $5,000 from sale of gift certificates. Credited unearned revenue—gift certificates.

May 24 Purchased temporary investments for cash at a cost of $3,600.

May 25 Returned defective merchandise costing $1,200 to Nails, Inc.

May 26 Sold miscellaneous hardware totaling $24,000 to Rite-Way Construction. Rite-Way paid $6,000 cash, and the balance was on account.

May 28 Paid the amount due to Quik Wholesale. Received a 2 percent discount for prompt payment.

May 29 Purchased merchandise on account from Handy Dandy Supply at a cost of $6,000.

May 30 Cash sales of hardware, $18,000.

These transactions will be used as the underlying data for illustrating and discussing the remaining steps of the accounting cycle. We shall assume that The Hardware Corporation prepares monthly financial statements; therefore, the cycle will be illustrated for an accounting period of one month.

The above transactions are recorded in general journal form in Exhibit 3–6 (pages 78–79). Notice the format of the general journal and of the journal entries. The first column in the journal shows the date of the transaction. Next, the accounts debited and credited and a brief explanation of the transaction are shown. The ''folio'' column is also called a ''posting reference column.'' When the journal entries are posted to the individual accounts during the next step of the accounting cycle, the account numbers of the related accounts affected by the entries will be entered in this column to indicate that the amounts have been transferred to the appropriate accounts. Finally, the last two columns are for the dollar amounts of the debits and credits.

For instructional purposes, transaction analysis and a brief explanation of each entry appear below:

May 1	Cash 130,000	
	Common stock	81,250
	Contributed capital in excess of par	48,750

This transaction (a nonreciprocal transfer) increases the asset, cash, and stockholders' equity by $130,000. Cash is debited since increases in assets are recorded as debits. Stockholders' equity accounts are credited because increases in equity are recorded as credits. When common stock is sold above par value, the difference between the issue price and par is credited to contributed capital in excess of par, which is part of contributed capital.

| May 1 | Cash .... 30,000 | |
| | Notes payable .... | 30,000 |

The issuance of the note increases both an asset, cash, and a liability, notes payable. Cash is debited, because asset increases are recorded as debits. Notes payable is credited, because liability increases are recorded as credits.

May 1	Inventory 60,000	
	Supplies 4,000	
	Fixtures and equipment....................... 11,000	
	Cash	75,000

This exchange transaction increases the assets, inventory, supplies, and fixtures and equipment, and decreases the asset, cash, by $75,000. The assets purchased are recorded as debits to the individual accounts, and cash is credited.

| May 2 | Rent expense .... 7,200 | |
| | Cash .... | 7,200 |

The payment of $7,200 provides the company with the use of the building for 12 months. While this expenditure gives rise to an asset, it is recorded temporarily in an expense account. More will be said about this entry later.

May 3	Fixtures and equipment....................... 10,000	
	Cash	2,000
	Accounts payable	8,000

This exchange transaction increases total assets and total liabilities by $8,000. Fixtures and equipment is debited (increased) for $10,000, cash is credited for $2,000, and accounts payable is credited for $8,000.

| May 4 | Purchases .... 45,000 | |
| | Accounts payable .... | 45,000 |

This exchange transaction increases the asset, inventory, and the liability, accounts payable, by $45,000. The purchase of merchandise is recorded *temporarily,* however, in a purchases account. This procedure is a feature of the periodic inventory system assumed to be used by The Hardware Corporation. Under the **periodic inventory system,** purchases of inventory are not recorded in the inventory account. Instead, the inventory account is adjusted at the end of the accounting period to record the cost of the merchandise still on hand at that time. Also, when sales are made (see the May 5 transaction), the related cost of the goods sold is not recorded. The cost of the goods sold is determined and accounted for at the end of the accounting period on the basis of the following relationship:[2]

$$\begin{matrix} \text{Beginning} \\ \text{inventory} \end{matrix} + \begin{matrix} \text{Net cost of} \\ \text{purchases} \end{matrix} - \begin{matrix} \text{Ending} \\ \text{inventory} \end{matrix} = \begin{matrix} \text{Cost of} \\ \text{goods sold} \end{matrix}$$

May 4	Supplies 1,800		
	Cash		1,800

The purchase of supplies increases the asset, supplies, and decreases the asset, cash. Supplies is debited and cash is credited for the amount of the purchase.

May 5	Accounts receivable 25,000		
	Sales......................................		25,000

The sale of merchandise on account increases the asset, accounts receivable, and stockholders' equity. As illustrated in Exhibit 3–3, this increase in stockholders' equity is temporarily recorded in the revenue account, sales. At the end of the accounting period, revenues less expenses (net income or loss) will be transferred to stockholders' equity in the closing step of the accounting cycle.

May 9	Purchases 30,000		
	Transportation in 250		
	Accounts payable		30,000
	Cash		250

We analyzed a purchase of merchandise in the May 4 entry. The transportation cost on the May 9 purchase represents an additional cost of the merchandise and is recorded temporarily in a separate account. At the end of the period, transportation in will be closed to cost of goods sold in a manner similar to the closing of the purchases account.

May 11	Cash 12,000		
	Accounts receivable		12,000

Collections from customers increase the asset, cash, and decrease the asset, accounts receivable. Cash is debited and accounts receivable is credited for $12,000.

May 12	Salaries expense 3,000		
	Cash		3,000

This entry recognizes the labor services received through May 12. Since these services already have been beneficial in generating revenue through May 12, an expense results.

---

[2] An alternative inventory system is a perpetual system. Under a **perpetual inventory system,** the cost of merchandise purchased for resale is debited to (recorded directly in) the inventory account. When merchandise is sold, in addition to the sales entry, the cost of goods sold is recorded at that time by debiting cost of goods sold and crediting inventory. Periodic and perpetual inventory systems are examined in more detail in Chapter 9.

Salaries expense is debited (which decreases stockholders' equity) and cash is credited.

May 20	Cash	15,000	
	Sales		15,000

This transaction is similar to the sale transaction on May 5 except that it is a cash sale rather than a credit sale. The analysis is the same as that discussed for the credit sale on May 5.

May 20	Cash	300	
	Rent revenue		300

Because The Hardware Corporation received $300 in exchange for an obligation to permit a tenant to use a portion of its building for a month, both assets and liabilities are increased by $300. The $300 will not be fully earned until June 20. For *bookkeeping purposes,* however, a revenue account is temporarily credited. Rent revenue and a liability account, unearned rent, will be adjusted at the end of May for the portion of the rent earned as of May 31. More will be said about this entry later.

May 22	Cash	5,000	
	Unearned revenue—gift certificates		5,000

The receipt of cash for sales of gift certificates increases assets and liabilities (unearned revenue) because the company has an obligation to deliver merchandise to customers who redeem the certificates. As the gift certificates are redeemed and the merchandise is transferred to the gift certificate holders, the obligation will be satisfied and revenue will be earned.

May 24	Investments	3,600	
	Cash		3,600

In this transaction, The Hardware Corporation exchanged one asset, cash, for another asset, investments. Investments is increased (debited) and cash is decreased (credited) for $3,600.

May 25	Accounts payable	1,200	
	Purchase returns		1,200

The return of defective merchandise decreases liabilities and reduces merchandise available for sale. Because a periodic inventory system is being used, however, this decrease is recorded as purchase returns (a reduction in purchases) and will be considered further when the inventory adjustments are made at the end of the accounting period.

May 26	Cash	6,000	
	Accounts receivable	18,000	
	Sales		24,000

The above entry records the partial cash and partial credit sale. This transaction can be analyzed in the same manner as previous cash sales and credit sales transactions.

May 28	Accounts payable	45,000	
	Purchase discounts		900
	Cash		44,100

EXHIBIT 3—6

The Hardware Corporation

GENERAL JOURNAL   PAGE 1

DATE	ACCOUNT TITLE AND EXPLANATION	FOLIO	DEBIT	CREDIT
1987				
May 1	Cash		130,000	
	Common stock			81,250
	Contributed capital in excess of par			48,750
	To record sale of common stock.			
May 1	Cash		30,000	
	Notes payable			30,000
	To record issuance of note payable.			
May 1	Inventory....................................		60,000	
	Supplies....................................		4,000	
	Fixtures and equipment		11,000	
	Cash			75,000
	To record acquisition of assets of Zenith Hardware.			
May 2	Rent expense................................		7,200	
	Cash			7,200
	To record advance payment of rent.			
May 3	Fixtures and equipment		10,000	
	Cash			2,000
	Accounts payable			8,000
	To record purchase of equipment.			
May 4	Purchases		45,000	
	Accounts payable			45,000
	To record purchase of merchandise.			
May 4	Supplies....................................		1,800	
	Cash			1,800
	To record purchase of supplies.			
May 5	Accounts receivable		25,000	
	Sales			25,000
	To record sales on account.			
May 9	Purchases		30,000	
	Transportation in...........................		250	
	Accounts payable			30,000
	Cash			250
	To record purchases of merchandise and related freight costs.			

The company's supplier granted a purchase discount of $900 (.02 × $45,000) for prompt payment. Liabilities are decreased by $45,000 and assets are decreased by $45,000. Because a periodic inventory system is being used, however, the cost of the inventory is not reduced by the amount of the discount. This $900 reduction will be considered in the cost of goods sold and ending inventory adjustments later in the accounting cycle.

May 29	Purchases	6,000	
	Accounts payable		6,000

The Hardware Corporation

GENERAL JOURNAL   PAGE 1

DATE	ACCOUNT TITLE AND EXPLANATION	FOLIO	DEBIT	CREDIT
May 11	Cash		12,000	
	Accounts receivable			12,000
	To record collections from customers.			
May 12	Salaries expense		3,000	
	Cash			3,000
	To record salaries expense.			
May 20	Cash		15,000	
	Sales			15,000
	To record cash sales of merchandise.			
May 20	Cash		300	
	Rent revenue................................			300
	To record receipt of rent in advance for sublease.			
May 22	Cash		5,000	
	Unearned revenue—gift certificates			5,000
	To record receipt of cash for gift certificates.			
May 24	Investments		3,600	
	Cash			3,600
	To record purchase of investments.			
May 25	Accounts payable		1,200	
	Purchase returns			1,200
	To record return of defective merchandise.			
May 26	Cash		6,000	
	Accounts receivable		18,000	
	Sales			24,000
	To record cash sales and sales on account.			
May 28	Accounts payable		45,000	
	Purchase discounts			900
	Cash			44,100
	To record payment of amount due less discount.			
May 29	Purchases		6,000	
	Accounts payable			6,000
	To record purchases on account.			
May 30	Cash		18,000	
	Sales			18,000
	To record cash sales.			

This purchase transaction can be analyzed in the same manner as the credit purchase made on May 4.

May 30	Cash 18,000	
	Sales....................................	18,000

This transaction can be analyzed in the same way as previous cash sales.

Special Journals

Many companies use **special journals** to record economic events of a similar nature. For example, if a company has many sales of merchandise for cash (e.g., cash sales made by a department store), a **cash receipts journal** may be used to facilitate the recording of all of these repetitive transactions. A **cash disbursements journal** may be used to record all transactions involving cash disbursements. The use of special journals also may lead to more efficient use of labor services because the work may be divided. For example, one employee may be assigned to record cash sales in the cash receipts journal, while another employee may have responsibility for recording cash payments in a cash disbursements journal.

The most commonly used special journals, in addition to the general journal, are as follows:

SPECIAL JOURNAL	TRANSACTIONS RECORDED
Cash receipts	Cash receipts from all sources
Cash disbursements	Cash disbursements for all purposes
Sales	Sales on account
Purchases	Purchases of merchandise on account

The use of special journals is discussed and illustrated in Appendix 3–1.

Physical Forms of Journals

Journals may take many forms. A journal in which entries are made by hand may take the form shown in Exhibit 3–6. In a highly sophisticated computerized accounting system, the journal may consist of a document that authorizes a computer operator to enter data into the computerized accounting system. An example of such a document appears in Exhibit 3–7. In practice, an actual journal may not exist. Data for entry into the accounts may consist of business source documents, such as sales invoices.

Regardless of the nature and form of the journal, the journalizing process is the first step in entering financial data about economic events into the company's accounting system. Journalizing not only provides a chronological record of economic events recognized by a company, but also summarizes in one place all relevant information about such events (e.g., date, accounts debited and credited, amounts, and explanations).

POSTING FROM A JOURNAL TO LEDGER ACCOUNTS

Once the transactions have been recorded in the journal, the next step in the accounting cycle is to transfer the journalized information to ledger accounts, as indicated in Exhibit 3–4 (Step 4).

Ledger Accounts

Physically, accounts are kept in a **ledger.** In a manual system, the ledger may consist of a notebook containing a sheet of paper for each account. In a computerized system, the ledger may consist of tracks on a tape or a floppy disk.

The Posting Process

Posting of the journal entries shown in Exhibit 3–6 to the ledger accounts is presented in Exhibit 3–8. In order to illustrate the posting of journal data to ledger accounts, some of the original journal entries, with the folio column completed, are also shown. The numbers in the folio column indicate the account numbers to which the data are posted. In each account, ''GJ 1'' indicates the page number in the general journal from which the data were posted. To understand the posting process thoroughly, you should trace each journal entry's debit and credit to the appropriate account.

EXHIBIT 3—7   A TYPICAL JOURNAL VOUCHER

AUTHORIZATION TO DEBIT OR CREDIT THE ACCOUNTS AS INDICATED BELOW IN THE AMOUNTS AND FOR THE PURPOSES SHOWN:

OSU Journal Entry   Please Type   WRITTEN BY   DATE WRITTEN

Entry Code*	Account Number				Object Source	Description (20)	Amount	P/F	FY	Requisition # Order #	I.D. # Invoice #
	A	L	Dept.	Subcode							

(Form rows, each with DR / CR entries, Req/Ord and ID/Inv sub-columns — repeated nine times.)

EXPLANATION: _____

_____

_____

Authorizing Officer   Number

* Entry Code explanation on reverse side   Date of Record

Source: Office of the Comptroller, Oklahoma State University.

General and Subsidiary Ledgers

The composite of all the accounts shown in Exhibit 3–8 is known as a company's **general ledger.** Notice that additional detail about items included in an account balance is not provided in the general ledger. For example, the balance in the accounts receivable account represents the sum of amounts due from various customers. Likewise, the balance in the accounts payable account represents amounts owed to several suppliers. In order to provide detailed information about the composition of an account balance, some companies use **subsidiary ledgers.** For example, The Hardware Corporation might use a subsidiary ledger to show amounts owed to individual suppliers. The relationship between The Hardware Corporation's accounts payable balance and the amounts due to individual creditors is shown in Exhibit 3–9.

When subsidiary ledgers are used, the general ledger account that contains a balance equal to the sum of the balances of the subsidiary ledger accounts is called a **controlling account.** In practice, companies often use subsidiary ledgers and controlling accounts for such accounts as accounts receivable, plant and equipment, accounts payable, and expenses. The use of subsidiary ledgers reduces the need for several general ledger accounts related to similar transactions. Subsidiary ledgers are discussed further in Appendix 3–1.

EXHIBIT 3—8 POSTING OF JOURNAL ENTRIES TO LEDGER ACCOUNTS

The Hardware Corporation
SELECTED JOURNAL ENTRIES

DATE	ACCOUNT TITLE AND EXPLANATION	FOLIO	DEBIT	CREDIT
May 1	Cash	100	130,000	
	Common stock	310		81,250
	Contributed capital in excess of par	320		48,750
1	Inventory	140	60,000	
	Supplies	120	4,000	
	Fixtures and equipment......................	150	11,000	
	Cash	100		75,000
2	Rent expense	560	7,200	
	Cash	100		7,200

ACCOUNTS AFTER POSTING OF JOURNAL ENTRIES FROM EXHIBIT 3–6

Cash   100

May 1	GJ 1	130,000	May 1	GJ 1	75,000	
1	GJ 1	30,000	2	GJ 1	7,200	
11	GJ 1	12,000	3	GJ 1	2,000	
20	GJ 1	15,000	4	GJ 1	1,800	
20	GJ 1	300	9	GJ 1	250	
22	GJ 1	5,000	12	GJ 1	3,000	
26	GJ 1	6,000	24	GJ 1	3,600	
30	GJ 1	18,000	28	GJ 1	44,100	
31 Balance		79,350				

Supplies   120

May 1	GJ 1	4,000
4	GJ 1	1,800
31 Balance		5,800

Accounts receivable   110

May 5	GJ 1	25,000	May 11	GJ 1	12,000
26	GJ 1	18,000			
31 Balance		31,000			

Investments   130

May 24	GJ 1	3,600

Inventory   140

May 1	GJ 1	60,000

Fixtures and equipment   150

May 1	GJ 1	11,000
3	GJ 1	10,000
31 Balance		21,000

EXHIBIT 3—9 ACCOUNTS PAYABLE IN GENERAL
LEDGER AND IN SUBSIDIARY LEDGER

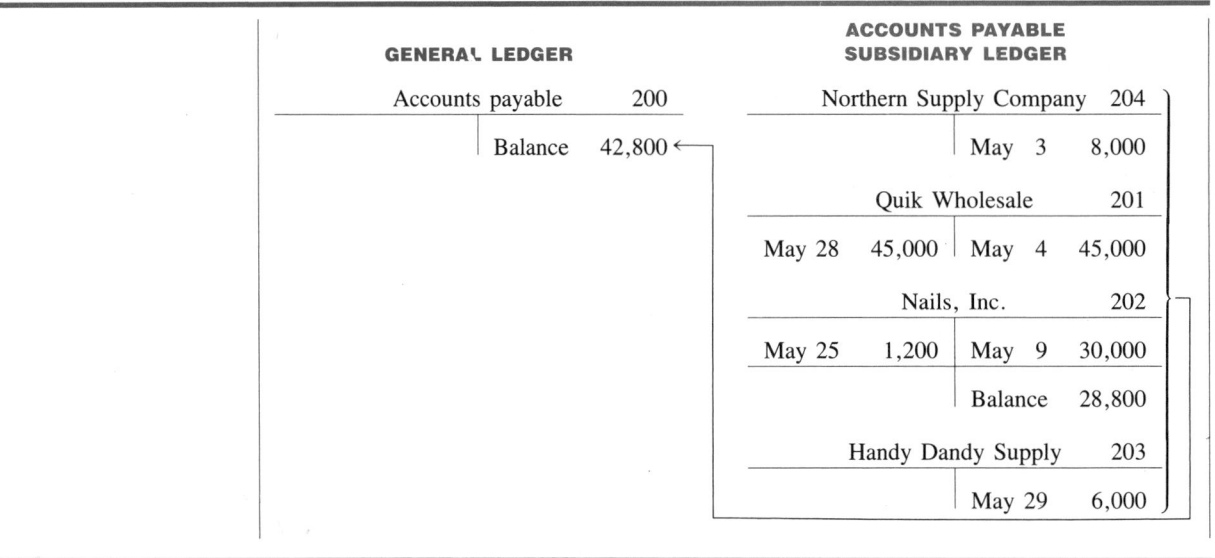

Accounts payable						200
May 25	GJ 1	1,200	May 3	GJ 1	8,000	
28	GJ 1	45,000	4	GJ 1	45,000	
			9	GJ 1	30,000	
			29	GJ 1	6,000	
			31 Balance		42,800	

Notes payable				205
	May 1	GJ 1	30,000	

Unearned revenue—gift certificates				210
	May 22	GJ 1	5,000	

Common stock				310
	May 1	GJ 1	81,250	

Contributed capital in excess of par				320
	May 1	GJ 1	48,750	

Sales				400
	May 5	GJ 1	25,000	
	20	GJ 1	15,000	
	26	GJ 1	24,000	
	30	GJ 1	18,000	
	31 Balance		82,000	

Rent revenue				420
	May 20	GJ 1	300	

Purchases				510
May 4	GJ 1	45,000		
9	GJ 1	30,000		
29	GJ 1	6,000		
31 Balance		81,000		

Purchase returns				520
	May 25	GJ 1	1,200	

Purchase discounts				530
	May 28	GJ 1	900	

Transportation in				540
May 9	GJ 1	250		

Salaries expense				550
May 12	GJ 1	3,000		

Rent expense				560
May 2	GJ 1	7,200		

PREPARING AN UNADJUSTED TRIAL BALANCE

Once the transactions and other economic events have been recorded in the journal and posted to the appropriate ledger accounts, the next step in the accounting cycle is to prepare an unadjusted trial balance. The **unadjusted trial balance** is prepared at the end of the accounting period and is a listing of each account and account balance in the general ledger, before any adjusting entries are made. Exhibit 3–10 presents the unadjusted trial balance for The Hardware Corporation on May 31, 1987. The accounts shown in this trial balance are listed in the following order: assets, liabilities, stockholders' equity, revenues, and expenses. The unadjusted trial balance is a useful step in the accounting process for the following reasons:

1. The unadjusted trial balance verifies the equality of the debits and credits posted to the ledger accounts before adjusting entries are made. Although it does not prove that all transactions have been recorded and posted correctly (e.g., if a purchase of supplies is debited to revenue, the transaction has been incorrectly recorded, but the debits and credits are still equal), it does reveal errors such as posting a debit as a credit, or posting a debit but failing to post the related credit.

2. The unadjusted trial balance facilitates preparing adjusting entries because it provides a listing of each account's debit or credit balance.

EXHIBIT 3—10

The Hardware Corporation
UNADJUSTED TRIAL BALANCE
MAY 31, 1987

ACCOUNT	DR	CR
Cash	$ 79,350	
Accounts receivable	31,000	
Supplies	5,800	
Investments	3,600	
Inventory	60,000	
Fixtures and equipment	21,000	
Accounts payable		$ 42,800
Notes payable		30,000
Unearned revenue—gift certificates		5,000
Common stock		81,250
Contributed capital in excess of par		48,750
Sales		82,000
Rent revenue		300
Purchases	81,000	
Purchase returns		1,200
Purchase discounts		900
Transportation in	250	
Salaries expense	3,000	
Rent expense	7,200	
	$292,200	$292,200

PREPARING ADJUSTING ENTRIES

Reasons for adjusting entries.

To this point, all of The Hardware Corporation's external transactions have been recorded in the accounts. However, additional transactions and internal events may have occurred but may not have yet been recorded. For example, salary expenses may have accrued since the last payday but have not yet been recorded. Or supplies may have been used but not recorded as expenses. Under accrual accounting and the related principles of matching and of revenue and expense recognition, these events must be recorded to permit proper measurement of The Hardware Corporation's net income for May and to facilitate the preparation of financial statements at the end of the month. The recording of these additional transactions and internal events is called **preparing adjusting entries** and is the next step in the accounting cycle.

The following information for unrecorded transactions and internal events is provided as the basis for adjusting entries at the end of May:

1. Prepaid rent, end of May, $6,600.

2. Supplies used during May, $1,300.

3. Rent revenue from sublease earned during May, $100.

4. Sales from redemptions of gift certificates, $3,500.

5. Interest accrued on notes payable, $250.

6. Salaries accrued, end of May, $2,500.

7. Depreciation on fixtures and equipment, $350. The Hardware Corporation uses straight-line depreciation on its assets, which have an estimated useful life of five years and no salvage value.

8. Estimated uncollectible accounts receivable, $215. The company estimates uncollectible accounts to be approximately .5 percent of credit sales.

9. Ending inventory, based on a physical count of merchandise on hand and priced at cost, $72,000.

Adjusting entries may be classified as follows:

1. Prepayments—cash flows *precede* earnings activities.
   a) Prepaid expenses.
   b) Unearned revenues.
2. Accruals—cash flows *follow* earnings activities.
   a) Accrued expenses.
   b) Accrued revenues.
3. Estimated items.
4. Inventory adjustments.

We shall examine each type of adjustment using the data for The Hardware Corporation.

Prepayments

Prepayments are transactions in which assets have been acquired in advance of their use or in which obligations to deliver goods or services result from assets received. For prepayments, *the cash flows precede the earnings activity*. For example, a company may acquire supplies for cash, and later use the supplies in the process of earning revenue. Prepayments have been recorded and thus necessitate allocation between asset and expense accounts or between liability and revenue accounts at the end of the accounting period.

PREPAID EXPENSES **Prepaid expenses** are the costs of assets acquired when a company makes an expenditure that gives rise to future economic benefits. For example, a company may acquire insurance protection by purchasing an insurance policy. Or it may acquire the potential future services of a factory building by making an advance rental payment. These two examples are commonly categorized as prepaid insurance and prepaid rent. Other prepaid expenses include prepaid advertising and supplies. As the economic benefits are received, these prepayments are transferred to expense accounts.

Companies acquire assets, not expenses. Even though prepaid expenses represent assets, however, some companies initially *record* prepaid expenses by debiting an expense account instead of an asset account. This bookkeeping procedure is often followed for several reasons:

1. The company expects to receive the benefits from the asset during the current accounting period. Thus, this procedure avoids the necessity of making an end-of-period adjusting entry.
2. The company's practice is to record all prepayments as expenses, then make the appropriate adjustments at the end of the accounting period.
3. The dollar amount of the prepayment, which should be recorded as an asset, may be immaterial.

Adjustments for prepaid expenses are designed to expense the cost of asset services used while leaving in the asset account the cost of asset services applicable to future accounting periods. The adjusting entry necessary for prepaid expenses depends on whether the initial expenditure was recorded as an asset or as an expense. This point is illustrated below for two types of prepaid expenses of The Hardware Corporation.

The first prepaid expense requiring adjustment is prepaid rent. The company paid $7,200 for twelve months' rent on a building. Assuming equal services are received each month, the rent expense for May (one month) is $600. Since the company originally recorded the rent payment in the rent expense account, the following adjusting entry is required on May 31:

Prepaid rent. 6,600
    Rent expense.   6,600

After this adjusting entry has been posted to the appropriate ledger accounts, the prepaid rent account has a balance of $6,600, and the rent expense account has a balance of $600:

Prepaid rent			Rent expense			
May 31			May 3	7,200	May 31	
Adjusting	6,600				Adjusting	6,600
			Balance	600		

The second prepaid expense to be adjusted is supplies. The company made two purchases of supplies at a total cost of $5,800 and recorded both transactions in the asset account, supplies. Supplies costing $1,300 were used during May, and thus the following adjusting entry is necessary:

Supplies expense 1,300
    Supplies.   1,300

After posting, the supplies and supplies expense accounts appear as follows:

Supplies				Supplies expense		
May 1	4,000	May 31		May 31		
May 4	1,800	Adjusting	1,300	Adjusting	1,300	
Balance	4,500					

The first adjusting entry required the debiting of an asset account (prepaid rent) and crediting of an expense account (rent expense) and the second required the debiting of an expense account (supplies expense) and crediting of an asset account (supplies). However, the purpose of both entries is the same—to record the cost of assets used or asset services received in an expense account while leaving the cost of assets on hand or the cost of services to be received in the future in an asset account. The portion of prepaid expenses applicable to future periods is known as **unexpired costs** and the portion of prepaid expenses that is expensed during the current period is called **expired costs.**

UNEARNED REVENUE **Unearned revenues** are obligations to provide goods or services arising from receipts of assets (usually cash) before the goods are sold or services are rendered. As the company provides the goods or services, the related revenues are earned, recorded in the accounts, and reported in the income statement. End-of-period adjustments apportion the amounts earned as revenues; the amounts unearned are reported as liabilities. The two adjustments related to unearned revenue are illustrated below for The Hardware Corporation.

The first adjustment is for rent revenue. On May 20, 1987, the company subleased the upper floor of the building at a monthly rental of $300. If we assume that the rent is earned evenly each month, only one-third of the rent has been earned between the sublease date, May 20, and the end of May. Because the company credited rent revenue when the cash was received, the following adjustment is necessary:

Rent revenue 200
    Unearned rent revenue   200

Once the adjustment has been posted to the ledger accounts, the rent revenue account will have a credit balance of $100, which is the amount of rent earned during May.[3] The unearned rent revenue account has a balance of $200, which is the amount that is unearned at the end of May (and will be earned in June):

Rent revenue				Unearned rent revenue		
May 31 Adjusting	200	May 20	300		May 31 Adjusting	200
		Balance	100			

The other adjustment is for sales and redemptions of gift certificates. On May 22, 1987, The Hardware Corporation sold gift certificates totaling $5,000. The $5,000 was credited to unearned revenue from gift certificates because the company is obligated to deliver goods to those customers who redeem the certificates. By the end of May, gift certificates totaling $3,500 have been redeemed. Therefore, the following adjusting entry is required:[4]

Unearned revenue—gift certificates 3,500
    Sales   3,500

After the adjustment is posted to the ledger accounts, unearned revenue—gift certificates will have a credit balance of $1,500, which is the sales value of the gift certificates still outstanding at the end of May.

Sales		Unearned revenue—gift certificates		
	May 31 Adjusting 3,500	May 31 Adjusting 3,500	May 22	5,000
			Balance	1,500

In the prepaid expense adjustments above, The Hardware Corporation initially recorded some prepayments as expenses and others as assets when cash was paid. Likewise, in the unearned revenue adjustments, one cash receipt initially was offset by a credit to revenue and the other cash receipt was offset by a credit to a liability. Although these bookkeeping procedures appear to be inconsistent, they were made this way *for illustra-*

---

[3] Since the company leased the building and is now subleasing a part of it, the rent received for subleasing could be viewed as a reduction in rent expense. If this approach were used, the following adjustment would be made:

Rent revenue 300
    Rent expense   100
    Unearned rent revenue   200

[4] Because a periodic inventory system is in use, the cost of the goods related to redemptions of gift certificates will be included in the cost of goods sold when the end-of-year inventory and purchases adjustments are made.

tion only to show the various forms that adjusting entries might take. In practice, it is unlikely that a company would follow such a policy; it would probably record all prepayments as either expenses or assets and all unearned items as either revenues or liabilities. The end-of-period adjusting entries would depend on the particular policy used.

Accruals

Accruals arise from earnings activities that precede the related cash flows, and are transactions and internal events that have occurred but have not been recorded. Accruals necessitate adjustments that affect either (1) expense and liability accounts or (2) asset and revenue accounts. Revenues that are earned before their collection are called accrued revenues, and expenses that are incurred before they are paid are called accrued expenses. Revenue accruals always increase assets (receivables) and owners' equity (revenue). Expense accruals always decrease owners' equity (by increasing expenses) and increase liabilities (payables).

The first adjusting entry for the May transactions of The Hardware Corporation is made to record interest of $250 accrued on notes payable:

Interest expense 250
  Interest payable   250
($30,000 × .10 × 1/12)

If The Hardware Corporation continues to prepare monthly statements, this adjusting entry will be made each month, and on May 1, 1988, the balance in the interest payable account will be $3,000 ($250 × 12). When the interest is paid on May 1, 1988, interest payable will be debited and cash will be credited for $3,000.

The second adjustment is for accrued salary expense. The Hardware Corporation has received employee services from the last payday (May 12) to the end of May but has neither recorded nor paid for these services. Therefore, the following adjusting entry is necessary:

Salaries expense 2,500
  Salaries payable   2,500

Assuming that salaries of $5,500 are paid in June at the end of the regular payment period, $3,000 constitutes payment for employee services received in June (salaries expense in June), and $2,500 is payment of the liability, salaries payable, existing at the end of May.

Distinction between Prepayments and Accruals

At this point it is important to distinguish between prepayments and accruals. In accrual accounting and under the matching principle, adjustments for these two groups of items are necessary for opposite reasons:

1. *Prepayments* have been recorded but necessitate end-of-period allocations between asset and expense accounts and between liability and revenue accounts.

2. *Accruals* have occurred but have not been recorded and necessitate end-of-period adjustments of either expense and liability accounts or asset and revenue accounts.

In addition, prepayments and accruals may be distinguished on the basis of the relationship between earnings activities and related cash flow. For prepayments, the cash flow occurs before (leads) the related earnings activity, whereas for accruals, the cash flow follows (lags) the related earnings activity. These "leads and lags" are summarized in Exhibit 3–11, where the balance sheet elements are shown in the rows and the income statement elements are shown in the columns. The intersection of each row and column represents an adjustment involving either a prepayment or an accrual.

EXHIBIT 3–11 ADJUSTMENTS FOR PREPAYMENTS AND ACCRUALS

| | INCOME STATEMENT | |
BALANCE SHEET	REVENUE	EXPENSE
ASSETS	Accrued revenues*	Prepaid expenses†
	Asset Dr	Expense Dr
	Revenue Cr	Asset Cr
LIABILITIES	Unearned revenue†	Accrued expenses*
	Liability Dr	Expense Dr
	Revenue Cr	Liability Cr

* Earnings activity occurs before the related cash flow.

† Cash flow occurs before the related earnings activity.

Estimated Items

Two of the three remaining adjustments required in The Hardware Corporation accounts for May 1987 are for expenses that must be **estimated** at the end of the accounting period in order to match revenues and expenses in determining net income for the month of May. These two estimated expenses are depreciation expense and uncollectible accounts expense. Although estimates are an inherent part of the accounting process and are also necessary in making adjustments for prepayments and accruals, it is accepted practice to use the term ''estimated items'' to describe adjustments for depreciation and uncollectible accounts.

DEPRECIATION EXPENSE **Depreciation expense** is the estimated cost of services received (or potential services expired) during the period from the use of plant and equipment in the earnings process. Services of plant and equipment cannot generally be purchased in small amounts, as can, for example, labor services or raw materials. When a company purchases an asset that provides economic benefits which extend over several accounting periods, the estimated cost of the services that are beneficial to the generation of revenue in a given accounting period must be deducted from the revenue recognized in that period in accordance with the matching principle. Under GAAP, depreciation is a cost allocation process in which an asset's cost, less salvage value, if any, is allocated over the asset's estimated useful economic life in a systematic and rational manner.[5]

On the basis of the adjustment information on pages 84–85, the following adjusting entry would be made to record The Hardware Corporation's depreciation expense for the month of May:

```
Depreciation expense . . . . . . . . . . . . . . . . . . . . . . . . . . . . . . . . . . . . . 350
    Accumulated depreciation—fixtures and equipment . . . . . . . . . . . . .        350
```

The $350 is calculated as follows:

$$\frac{\text{Cost minus salvage}}{\text{Useful life}} = \text{Annual depreciation, assuming the use of the straight-line method}$$

$$\frac{\$21,000 - \$0}{5} = \$4,200 \text{ annual depreciation expense}$$

$$\frac{\$4,200}{12} = \$350 \text{ monthly depreciation expense}$$

[5] The cost of plant and equipment may be viewed as a long-term prepayment.

Accumulated depreciation is shown on the balance sheet as a deduction from fixtures and equipment and is called a **contra asset** or **valuation** account. Accounting for depreciation of plant and equipment is discussed in more detail in Chapter 12.

UNCOLLECTIBLE ACCOUNTS EXPENSE   **Uncollectible accounts expense,** or **bad debt expense,** describes receivables that are expected to be uncollectible.[6] Under some circumstances, uncollectible accounts are not recorded as expenses until it is known for certain that the accounts are uncollectible. However, these expenses usually are estimated and recorded in the period in which sales are made to match revenue and expense on the income statement and to provide future cash flow signals on a timely basis.

The Hardware Corporation estimates that the dollar amount of uncollectible accounts will approximate 1/2 of 1 percent of credit sales each month. Thus, the following entry would be made to record this expense:

```
Uncollectible accounts expense ................................ 215
    Allowance for uncollectible accounts .........................          215
```

The $215 is calculated as follows:

```
Credit sales May 5 ................................ $25,000
            May 26 ............................   18,000
            Total ................................ $43,000
                                              × .005
            Uncollectible accounts expense............ $   215
```

The allowance for uncollectible accounts is reported on the balance sheet as a deduction from accounts receivable and is called a contra asset or valuation account. Because the receivables are reported net of the allowance, the net receivables balance is the amount of cash that is expected to be collected in the near future and thus better satisfies the financial reporting objective of providing information about future cash inflows to the company. As individual customers' accounts become uncollectible, the allowance account is debited and accounts receivable is credited for the amount of each customer's account written off.

Adjusting entries for uncollectible accounts expense are similar to accruals. That is, the entry to record uncollectible accounts expense may be viewed as an adjustment of a previously recorded accrual of sales on account. Accounting and reporting for accounts receivable and uncollectible accounts are covered in detail in Chapter 8.

Inventory Adjustments

Recall that The Hardware Corporation uses a periodic inventory system. Under this system, merchandise purchases and such related items as transportation costs on merchandise, returned merchandise, and cash discounts from early payments on purchases are not recorded in the inventory account. Temporary accounts are used to record these transactions. The use of temporary accounts provides the management of The Hardware Corporation with information about the costs of current purchases, the amount of transportation costs incurred, and the dollar amount of purchase returns without having this information buried in the inventory account. In addition, no entries are made to record the cost of merchandise sold.

In order to determine the cost of goods sold during May, which is deducted, along with other expenses, from sales for the purpose of determining income, we must compare the cost of merchandise on hand on May 31 with the total cost of merchandise available for sale during May.

At the end of the accounting period, a physical inventory of merchandise on hand is taken, and the cost of this merchandise is determined. The inventory account must then be

---

[6] Some accountants consider classification of uncollectible accounts as a reduction in sales rather than as an expense to be conceptually appealing.

adjusted to show the cost of the merchandise on hand at the end of the period. Also, it is necessary to make an adjustment to record the cost of goods sold during the period. The cost of goods sold by The Hardware Corporation during May may be calculated, on the basis of the account balances in Exhibit 3–8, as follows:

Beginning inventory		$ 60,000
Purchases	$81,000	
Transportation in	250	
Purchase returns	(1,200)	
Purchase discounts	(900)	
Net cost of purchases		79,150
Cost of goods available for sale during May		$139,150
Ending inventory (from page 85)		(72,000)
Cost of goods sold		$ 67,150

As shown above, The Hardware Corporation had $60,000 of merchandise at the beginning of May and purchased merchandise costing $79,150 during May. Therefore, merchandise costing $139,150 was available for sale during the month. Since the company has merchandise costing $72,000 remaining on May 31, the cost of goods sold is $67,150.

Before we illustrate the adjusting entries to record the ending inventory and cost of goods sold, two hypothetical questions should make the above calculation clearer:

1. If *no* inventory remained on May 31, what would be the cost of goods sold?

2. If *no* sales were made during May, what would be the cost of goods sold and the cost of the ending inventory?

It should be clear that the answer to the first question is $139,150 and that the answer to the second question is $0 for the cost of goods sold and $139,150 for the cost of the ending inventory.[7] In summary, the following equation sets forth the relationship between inventories, purchases, and cost of goods sold:

$$\underset{(BI)}{\underset{\text{inventory}}{\text{Beginning}}} + \underset{(P)}{\underset{\text{purchases}}{\text{Net cost of}}} - \underset{(EI)}{\underset{\text{inventory}}{\text{Ending}}} = \underset{(CGS)}{\underset{\text{goods sold}}{\text{Cost of}}}$$

Although the equation is intuitively obvious, you should memorize it, as you will use it throughout much of your study of accounting.

The adjusting entries to record the cost of goods sold are as follows:

Cost of goods sold	60,000	
Inventory (beginning)		60,000
To transfer the beginning inventory balance to cost of goods sold.		

Cost of goods sold	79,150	
Purchase returns	1,200	
Purchase discounts	900	
Purchases		81,000
Transportation in		250
To transfer the net cost of purchases to cost of goods sold.		

Inventory (ending)	72,000	
Cost of goods sold		72,000
To record the ending inventory in the accounts as an asset.		

[7] These hypothetical questions ignore the possibility of shrinkage (i.e., theft, breakage, or spoilage) and errors in recording purchase transactions and in taking inventory. Technically, these factors should be considered. Here, however, they unnecessarily complicate and detract from the conceptual discussion.

EXHIBIT 3–12   COST OF GOODS SOLD AND RELATED
INVENTORY ACCOUNTS AFTER POSTING

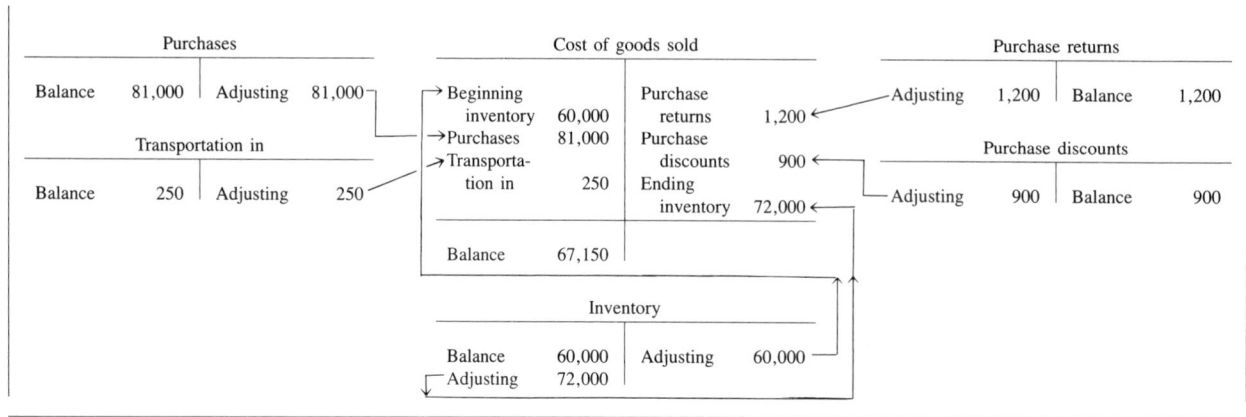

Alternatively, one compound entry could be made as follows:

Inventory (ending)	72,000	
Purchase returns	1,200	
Purchase discounts	900	
Cost of goods sold	67,150	
Inventory (beginning)		60,000
Purchases		81,000
Transportation in		250

When these adjustments have been posted, the accounts affected will appear as shown in Exhibit 3–12.

Inventory and cost of goods sold adjusting entries sometimes are made in the closing step of the accounting cycle. Under this approach, the ending inventory is recorded in the accounts when the income statement accounts are closed. This alternative approach is illustrated later in the chapter when we describe the use of a worksheet.

Adjusting Entries: A Summary

Once the adjustments have been recorded in the general journal, they are posted to the general ledger. The general ledger is reproduced with the adjustments posted at a later point in this chapter. Some important points about the reason for and purpose of adjusting entries are summarized below.

1. Adjusting entries are necessary under accrual accounting to record economic events related to the company's earnings activities that have occurred but have not been recorded at the end of the accounting period.

2. The adjustments are necessary to match revenues earned and expenses incurred in order to determine net income for the period. In addition, assets and liabilities are properly measured after the adjusting entries are made.

3. Each adjusting entry affects a real (balance sheet) account and a nominal (income statement) account.

4. For prepayments and unearned items, the form of the adjusting entry depends on how the prepaid expense or unearned revenue item was recorded initially. However, the purpose of the adjustment is the same. For prepaid expenses, that portion of the cost of

asset services that represents future economic benefits appears on the balance sheet as an asset, and that portion of the cost of asset services that provided benefits during the current year appears on the income statement as an expense. For unearned revenues, the portion earned during the period is shown on the income statement as revenue, whereas the portion that will be earned in a subsequent period is reported on the balance sheet as a liability.

5. In short, this step in the accounting cycle is necessary to make the resulting financial statements representationally faithful and thus more useful to investors, creditors, management, and other users of the statements.

PREPARING THE ADJUSTED TRIAL BALANCE

The **adjusted trial balance** for The Hardware Corporation appears in Exhibit 3–13. It is called an *adjusted* trial balance because it lists the ledger accounts and their balances after the adjusting entries have been posted. The adjusted trial balance is useful because it tests the accuracy of the account balances after the adjusting entries have been posted. In addition, it contains all the information necessary to complete the next step in the accounting cycle—preparation of financial statements.

EXHIBIT 3–13

The Hardware Corporation
ADJUSTED TRIAL BALANCE
MAY 31, 1987

ACCOUNT	DR	CR
Cash	$ 79,350	
Accounts receivable	31,000	
Allowance for uncollectible accounts		$ 215
Supplies	4,500	
Prepaid rent	6,600	
Investments	3,600	
Inventory	72,000	
Fixtures and equipment	21,000	
Accumulated depreciation—fixtures and equipment		350
Accounts payable		42,800
Notes payable		30,000
Salaries payable		2,500
Interest payable		250
Unearned revenue—gift certificates		1,500
Unearned rent		200
Common stock		81,250
Contributed capital in excess of par		48,750
Sales		85,500
Rent revenue		100
Cost of goods sold	67,150	
Depreciation expense	350	
Interest expense	250	
Salaries expense	5,500	
Rent expense	600	
Supplies expense	1,300	
Uncollectible accounts expense	215	
	$293,415	$293,415

EXHIBIT 3–14

The Hardware Corporation

INCOME STATEMENT FOR THE MONTH OF MAY 1987

Sales		$85,500
Cost of goods sold		(67,150)
Gross margin		$18,350
Rent revenue		100
		$18,450
Other expenses:		
Depreciation	$ 350	
Interest	250	
Salaries	5,500	
Rent	600	
Supplies	1,300	
Uncollectible accounts	215	
Total other expenses		(8,215)
Net income		$10,235

PREPARING THE FINANCIAL STATEMENTS

Now that we have recorded and posted the many transactions of The Hardware Corporation, we are ready to prepare the financial statements. These statements are the end product of the accounting process. The financial statements for The Hardware Corporation appear in Exhibits 3–14 through 3–17. We discuss each exhibit briefly.

The Income Statement

The **income statement** presents a summary of a company's earnings activities for the accounting period. The income statement reports the revenues earned and the expenses incurred in earning the revenues. Net income or loss equals revenues less expenses. The income statement allows users to determine whether a company made a profit during the accounting period covered by the statement and also may help them to assess the company's future cash flows, and thus to assess future cash flows to themselves.

The Hardware Corporation's income statement for the month of May appears in Exhibit 3–14. Net income for May is $10,235, which is the difference between total revenues and total expenses. Since the income statement elements are a part of stockholders' equity, the net income for May will be added to stockholders' equity on the May 31, 1987, balance sheet. The format, classification, and other aspects of the income statement are discussed in more detail in Chapter 4.

The Balance Sheet or Statement of Financial Position

The **balance sheet** or **statement of financial position** reports a company's financial position at a point in time. The elements of the balance sheet—assets, liabilities, and equity—correspond to the elements of the accounting equation discussed earlier in this chapter.

The Hardware Corporation's balance sheet at May 31, 1987, appears in Exhibit 3–15. Assets are listed on the balance sheet according to the traditional classifications of current and noncurrent. **Current assets** are those that are expected to be converted into cash or used or consumed within a relatively short period of time, generally within one year or the company's operating cycle, whichever is longer. Assets whose benefits extend over longer periods include plant and equipment, intangibles, and long-term investments,

EXHIBIT 3—15

The Hardware Corporation
BALANCE SHEET
MAY 31, 1987

ASSETS		
Current assets		
Cash.....................		$79,350
Accounts receivable	$31,000	
Less: Allowance for uncollectible accounts...	(215)	30,785
Investments		3,600
Inventory		72,000
Supplies..................		4,500
Prepaid rent..............		6,600
Total current assets ...		$196,835
Plant and equipment		
Fixtures and equipment	$21,000	
Less: Accumulated depreciation...........	(350)	$ 20,650
Total assets		$217,485

LIABILITIES AND STOCKHOLDERS' EQUITY	
Current liabilities	
Accounts payable	$ 42,800
Interest payable.........................	250
Salaries payable	2,500
Unearned revenue from gift certificates	1,500
Unearned rent	200
Total current liabilities	$ 47,250
Long-term liabilities	
Notes payable (due in 1989)	30,000
Total liabilities	$ 77,250
Stockholders' equity	
Common stock ($5 par, 100,000 shares authorized, 16,250 shares issued)	81,250
Contributed capital in excess of par	48,750
Retained earnings	10,235
Total stockholders' equity	$140,235
Total liabilities and stockholders' equity	$217,485

and are classified accordingly. For example, accounts receivable are classified as current since they are expected to be collected shortly after the balance sheet date; investments are classified as current because it is assumed that The Hardware Corporation does not plan to hold these investments over a long period of time.

Liabilities also are classified as current or noncurrent (long-term). **Current liabilities** are those that will require the use of current assets or that will be discharged within a relatively short period of time, usually within one year. For example, interest payable is classified as current since it will be paid within one year. Notes payable, on the other hand, are classified as noncurrent or long-term, since they will not be paid until 1989. These current and noncurrent classifications increase the usefulness of the financial statements by providing information about the timing of future cash inflows and outflows.

Since net income increases stockholders' equity, the net income for May is reported on the balance sheet in the stockholders' equity section under retained earnings. In the closing step of the accounting cycle, the balances in the income statement accounts are transferred to the retained earnings account. The format, classification, and other related aspects of balance sheet reporting are discussed at greater length in Chapter 5.

The Statement of Retained Earnings

The statement of retained earnings for The Hardware Corporation is shown in Exhibit 3–16. This statement is designed to reconcile the beginning and ending retained earnings balances. Income for the period increases retained earnings and dividends decrease retained earnings. The only item affecting The Hardware Corporation's retained earnings in May was the net income for the month.

EXHIBIT 3–16

The Hardware Corporation
STATEMENT OF RETAINED EARNINGS
FOR THE MONTH OF MAY 1987

Retained earnings, May 1, 1987	$ –0–
Net income for May	10,235
Retained earnings, May 31, 1987	$10,235

Assume that The Hardware Corporation declared and paid a cash dividend of $7,500 in June, 1987. The entry to record the dividend would be as follows:

Dividends declared	7,500	
Cash		7,500

This dividend would appear as a deduction on the statement of retained earnings for the month of June, 1987, and the dividends declared account would be closed to retained earnings at the end of June.[8] The statement of retained earnings is covered in more detail in Chapters 5 and 21.

The Statement of Cash Flows

The statement of cash flows is another financial statement that The Hardware Corporation would prepare. This statement discloses the amount of cash generated by and used in a company's operating, financing, and investing activities during the accounting period. The Hardware Corporation's statement of cash flows appears in Exhibit 3–17. Notice that because the company spent more cash in its operating activities than it received, there was a net outflow of cash from operations.

The source of the information presented in Exhibit 3–17 is the company's cash ledger account, which appears in Exhibit 3–8 on page 82. Alternatively, the information may be obtained from The Hardware Corporation's cash receipts and cash disbursements journals (Exhibits 3–25 and 3–26, respectively) in Appendix 3–1, at the end of the chapter. When these sources are not available in a problem or in practice, other approaches must be used to prepare this statement. These approaches are discussed in detail in Chapter 23.

PREPARING CLOSING ENTRIES

Closing entries are needed to reduce revenue and expense accounts to zero to begin the next accounting period.

After the financial statements have been prepared, it is necessary to reduce the income statement (nominal) account balances in the ledger to zero so that these accounts can be used to collect the revenue and expense transaction data for the following accounting period. This procedure is called **closing the accounts.** To facilitate the closing process, one new nominal account, income summary, is opened, and the revenue and expense account balances are transferred to this account. The income summary account balance is then transferred to owners' equity or, in the case of The Hardware Corporation, to retained earnings. Three steps are necessary to close the income statement accounts and to transfer the resulting balance in the income summary account to retained earnings:

---

[8] Many companies record dividends directly in the retained earnings account, as follows:

Retained earnings	xx	
Cash		xx

EXHIBIT 3–17

The Hardware Corporation
STATEMENT OF CASH FLOWS
FOR THE MONTH OF MAY, 1987

Cash flows from operating activities:

Cash sales and collections on credit sales	$ 51,000	
Revenue collected in advance	5,000	
Purchases of merchandise	(106,350)	
Purchases of supplies	(5,800)	
Payment of salaries	(3,000)	
Payment of rent (net of $300 sublease)	(6,900)	
Net cash used by operating activities		$(66,050)
Cash flows from investing activities:		
Purchases of fixtures and equipment	$(11,000)	
Purchases of investments	(3,600)	
Net cash used by investing activities		(14,600)
Cash flows from financing activities:		
Issued common stock	$130,000	
Issued notes payable	30,000	
Net cash provided by financing activities		160,000
Net increase in cash		$ 79,350

1. All income statement accounts with *credit* balances are *debited* and the income summary account is credited in an amount equal to the total debits.

2. All income statement accounts with *debit* balances are *credited,* and the income summary account is debited in an amount equal to the total credits.

3. The balance in the income summary account is transferred to retained earnings. If earnings activities result in net income, income summary is debited and retained earnings is credited. If instead a net loss results, retained earnings is debited and income summary is credited.

Closing entries for The Hardware Corporation are shown below:

Sales	85,500	
Rent revenue	100	
Income summary		85,600
To close revenues to income summary.		

Income summary	75,365	
Cost of goods sold		67,150
Depreciation expense		350
Salaries expense		5,500
Rent expense		600
Supplies expenses		1,300
Uncollectible accounts expense		215
Interest expense		250
To close expenses to income summary.		

Income summary	10,235	
Retained earnings		10,235
To close net income to retained earnings.		

The general ledger accounts for The Hardware Corporation, after the above closing entries have been posted, are shown in Exhibit 3–18. The adjusting entries that were

EXHIBIT 3—18

The Hardware Corporation
GENERAL LEDGER ACCOUNTS AFTER POSTING OF CLOSING ENTRIES

Cash — 100

May 1	GJ 1	130,000	May 1	GJ 1	75,000
1	GJ 1	30,000	2	GJ 1	7,200
11	GJ 1	12,000	3	GJ 1	2,000
20	GJ 1	15,000	4	GJ 1	1,800
20	GJ 1	300	9	GJ 1	250
22	GJ 1	5,000	12	GJ 1	3,000
26	GJ 1	6,000	24	GJ 1	3,600
26	GJ 1	6,000	24	GJ 1	3,600
30	GJ 1	18,000	28	GJ 1	44,100
		216,300			136,950
			Balance		79,350
		216,300			216,300
31 Balance		79,350			

Accounts receivable — 110

May 5	GJ 1	25,000	May 11	GJ 1	12,000
26	GJ 1	18,000			
		43,000			12,000
			Balance		31,000
		43,000			43,000
31 Balance		31,000			

Allowance for uncollectible accounts — 111

			May 31	GJ 2	215

Supplies — 120

May 1	GJ 1	4,000	May 31	GJ 2	1,300
4	GJ 1	1,800			
		5,800			1,300
			Balance		4,500
		5,800			5,800
31 Balance		4,500			

Prepaid rent — 121

May 31	GJ 2	6,600

Investments — 130

May 24	GJ 1	3,600

Inventory — 140

May 1	GJ 1	60,000	May 31	GJ 2	60,000
31	GJ 2	72,000			
		132,000			60,000
			Balance		72,000
		132,000			132,000
31 Balance		72,000			

Fixtures and equipment — 150

May 1	GJ 1	11,000			
3	GJ 1	10,000			
31 Balance		21,000			

Accumulated depreciation— fixtures and equipment — 151

			May 31	GJ 2	350

Accounts payable — 200

May 25	GJ 1	1,200	May 3	GJ 1	8,000
28	GJ 1	45,000	4	GJ 1	45,000
			9	GJ 1	30,000
			29	GJ 1	6,000
		46,200			89,000
31 Balance		42,800			
		89,000			89,000
			31 Balance		42,800

Notes payable — 205

			May 31	GJ 1	30,000

Unearned revenue—gift certificates — 210

May 31	GJ 2	3,500	May 22	GJ 1	5,000
Balance		1,500			
		5,000			5,000
			31 Balance		1,500

Unearned rent — 211

			May 31	GJ 2	200

Salaries payable			212
	May 31	GJ 2	2,500

Interest payable			213
	May 31	GJ 2	250

Common stock			310
	May 1	GJ 1	81,250

Contributed capital in excess of par			320
	May 1	GJ 1	48,750

Retained earnings			321
	May 31	GJ 3	10,235

Sales						400
May 31	GJ 3	85,500	May 5	GJ 1	25,000
			20	GJ 1	15,000
			26	GJ 1	24,000
			30	GJ 1	30,000
			31	GJ 2	3,500
		85,500			85,500

Rent revenue						420
May 31	GJ 2	200	May 20	GJ 1	300
31	GJ 3	100			
		300			300

Cost of goods sold						500
May 31	GJ 2	67,150	May 31	GJ 3	67,150

Purchases						510
May 4	GJ 1	45,000	May 31	GJ 2	81,000
9	GJ 1	30,000			
29	GJ 1	6,000			
		81,000			81,000

Purchase returns						520
May 31	GJ 2	1,200	May 25	GJ 1	1,200

Purchase discounts						530
May 31	GJ 2	900	May 28	GJ 1	900

Transportation in						540
May 9	GJ 1	250	May 31	GJ 2	250

Depreciation expense						541
May 31	GJ 2	350	May 31	GJ 3	350

Salaries expense						550
May 12	GJ 1	3,000	May 31	GJ 3	5,500
31	GJ 2	2,500			
		5,500			5,500

Rent expense						560
May 2	GJ 1	7,200	May 31	GJ 2	6,600
			31	GJ 3	600
		7,200			7,200

Interest expense						565
May 31	GJ 2	250	May 31	GJ 3	250

Supplies expense						570
May 31	GJ 2	1,300	May 31	GJ 3	1,300

Uncollectible accounts expense						580
May 31	GJ 2	215	May 31	GJ 3	215

Income summary						590
May 31	GJ 3	75,365	May 31	GJ 3	85,600
31	GJ 3	10,235			
		85,600			85,600

recorded earlier also have been posted to these accounts. In Exhibit 3–18 we have assumed that all of the transactions *during* the period were recorded on page 1 of The Hardware Corporation's general journal, that *adjusting* entries were recorded on page 2, and that *closing* entries were recorded on page 3.

PREPARING A POSTCLOSING TRIAL BALANCE

Once the income statement accounts have been closed, a company prepares a **postclosing trial balance.** The postclosing trial balance lists the real accounts and their respective balances in the general ledger after closing entries have been posted. Preparation of a postclosing trial balance tests the equality of the debits and credits in the ledger after the closing entries have been posted. This trial balance shows the real accounts and their balances, which will be carried forward to the next accounting period. The postclosing trial balance for The Hardware Corporation, based on the account balances presented in Exhibit 3–18, appears in Exhibit 3–19 (page 101).

At this point the accounting cycle has been completed. The nominal accounts have been closed. The real account balances have been determined, and the ledger accounts are now ready to accumulate transaction data and other economic events in the next accounting period.

REVERSING ENTRIES

Reversing entries are optional, not mandatory.

Some companies make reversing entries at the beginning of an accounting period. A **reversing entry** is a reversal of an adjusting entry that was made at the end of the previous accounting period. As we shall see below, the purpose of a reversing entry is to simplify the recording of transactions in the next accounting period. Keep in mind that reversing entries are optional, not mandatory. To illustrate reversing entries, we shall assume that companies choose to make reversing entries as of the beginning of the accounting period.

Prepayments and Unearned Items

Reversing entries should be made for prepayments and unearned items if the original transactions involving them were recorded in nominal accounts. This procedure assumes that prepayments and unearned items will be recorded in nominal accounts during the following accounting period and thus increases bookkeeping consistency.

To illustrate, assume that on October 1, 1987, XYZ Company purchased a two-year insurance policy on its buildings, paid the annual premium of $2,400 in advance, and recorded the transaction as follows:

Insurance expense..2,400
   Cash... 2,400

If the company closes its books on December 31, 1987, the adjusting entry required at the end of the year is as follows:

Prepaid insurance 2,100
   Insurance expense....................................... 2,100
(21/24 × $2,400)
To adjust insurance expense to the correct expense for 1987 and to record the unexpired insurance as an asset.

Once the closing entries are made, the prepaid insurance account has a balance of $2,100 and the $300 balance in the insurance expense account ($2,400 − $2,100) has been closed to income summary. Because the company recorded the original transaction as an expense and presumably will do so for future insurance coverage, the following reversing entry is appropriate on January 1, 1988:

Insurance expense..2,100
   Prepaid insurance 2,100

EXHIBIT 3–19

The Hardware Corporation
POSTCLOSING TRIAL BALANCE
MAY 31, 1987

ACCOUNT	DR	CR
Cash.	$ 79,350	
Accounts receivable	31,000	
Allowance for uncollectible accounts		$ 215
Supplies.	4,500	
Prepaid rent.	6,600	
Investments	3,600	
Inventory	72,000	
Fixtures and equipment	21,000	
Accumulated depreciation—fixtures and equipment		350
Interest payable.		250
Accounts payable		42,800
Notes payable		30,000
Unearned revenue—gift certificates		1,500
Unearned rent		200
Salaries payable		2,500
Common stock		81,250
Contributed capital in excess of par		48,750
Retained earnings		10,235
	$218,050	$218,050

After the reversing entry is posted at the beginning of 1988, the prepaid insurance account balance is zero and the insurance expense account has a debit balance of $2,100. An adjusting entry, similar to the one just shown but in the amount of $900 ($2,100 − $1,200), would be required at the end of 1988. Reversal of this amount at the beginning of 1989 eliminates the necessity of an adjusting entry at the end of 1989, because coverage will expire on October 1, 1989.

Accruals

Reversing entries for accruals simplify recording transactions in the following period.

Reversing entries often are made for accrued revenue and expense adjustments in order to simplify the accounting procedures for these items in the following period, when the revenue is collected or the expense is paid. To illustrate, assume that a company pays its employees' salaries of $30,000 every other Friday (based on ten working days). The company's fiscal year ends on December 31, which in 1986 falls on a Wednesday. The adjusting entry required on December 31, 1986, to record the accrued salaries, assuming three working days have elapsed since the last payday, is as follows:

Salaries expense	9,000	
Salaries payable		9,000
(3/10 × $30,000)		

After all closing entries are made on December 31, this adjusting entry will be reversed on January 1, 1987:

Salaries payable	9,000	
Salaries expense		9,000

The reversing entry reduces the salaries payable account to zero and places a credit balance of $9,000 in salaries expense. When the salaries of $30,000 are paid on the next payday, the following entry is made:

```
Salaries expense .......................................30,000
    Cash.............................................          30,000
```

When the $30,000 is posted to the salaries expense account, the account will show a debit balance of $21,000, which will be the correct amount of salaries expense thus far in 1987. These concepts are further illustrated in the following T-accounts:

Accounts after adjustment:

Salaries expense		Salaries payable	
Assumed balance before adjustment	153,000		Adjusting 9,000
Adjusting	9,000		

Accounts after closing:

Salaries expense		Salaries payable	
162,000	Closing 162,000		Adjusting 9,000

Accounts after reversing:

Salaries expense		Salaries payable	
162,000	162,000	Reversing 9,000	9,000
	Reversing 9,000		

EXHIBIT 3–20   TO REVERSE OR NOT TO REVERSE?

ADJUSTING ENTRY	REVERSE?	REASON
Prepaid rent ....xx Rent expense xx	Yes	Adjusting entry increases an asset account
Unearned revenue .....xx Revenue xx	No	Adjusting entry does not increase a liability account

Depreciation
    expense...........xx
    Accumulated
        depreciation   xx
	No	Adjusting entry does not increase an asset account; accumulated depreciation is a contra-asset account

Interest expense ......xx Interest payable xx	Yes	Adjusting entry increases a liability account

Salaries expense account after the first pay period in the following accounting period:

Salaries expense			
	162,000		162,000
	30,000	Reversing	9,000
Balance	21,000		

Without the use of reversing entries, when salaries are paid for the first time in 1987, it would be necessary to determine what portion of the $30,000 payment relates to 1987 expense and what portion represents payment of the beginning-of-year liability. This determination is unnecessary and is automatically shown in the accounts when reversing entries are used.

Reversing Entries: Summary

Reversing entries are not mandatory, but may help to simplify bookkeeping. If a company chooses to make reversing entries, the following rule is a reminder of which adjustments should and should not be reversed: If the adjusting entry increases an asset or liability account, reverse the adjusting entry; otherwise, do not reverse. This rule is illustrated in Exhibit 3–20.

If The Hardware Corporation chose to use reversing entries, the following adjusting entries should be reversed:

ADJUSTING ENTRY	PAGE
Prepaid rent	86
Unearned rent	86
Accrued interest	88
Accrued salaries	88

USE OF A WORKSHEET

A worksheet facilitates financial statement preparation.

A worksheet sometimes is used in the accounting cycle to facilitate the work of making adjusting entries and preparing financial statements. As Exhibit 3–4 on page 72 indicates, the preparation of a worksheet is an optional but sometimes very useful step in the accounting cycle. A worksheet permits the accountant to assemble all the ledger account balances and adjustment information together on one schedule. In addition, a worksheet permits a company to prepare interim (e.g., monthly or quarterly) statements even though the company may close its books only once a year. The worksheet is not a formal statement, but merely a working paper.

A 10-column worksheet for The Hardware Corporation is presented in Exhibit 3–21, and its preparation is outlined below.

1. The unadjusted trial balance (see Exhibit 3–10) is recorded in the first two columns of the worksheet.

2. The worksheet adjusting entries, prepared from and keyed to the adjustments information on pages 84–85, are entered into the second pair of columns. If a new account is needed for an adjustment, it is added at the bottom of the worksheet (e.g., prepaid rent or supplies expense).

Notice that, in contrast to the adjusting entries made earlier for cost of goods sold on pages 91–92, no worksheet adjusting entries are made to transfer the purchases and

EXHIBIT 3–21

The Hardware Corporation
WORKSHEET FOR THE MONTH OF MAY 1987

ACCOUNT	UNADJUSTED TRIAL BALANCE DR	CR	ADJUSTMENTS DR	CR	ADJUSTED TRIAL BALANCE DR	CR	INCOME STATEMENT DR	CR	BALANCE SHEET DR	CR
Cash	79,350				79,350				79,350	
Accounts receivable	31,000				31,000				31,000	
Supplies	5,800			(2)1,300	4,500				4,500	
Investments	3,600				3,600				3,600	
Inventory	60,000				60,000		60,000	72,000	72,000	
Fixtures and equipment	21,000				21,000				21,000	
Accounts payable		42,800				42,800				42,800
Notes payable		30,000				30,000				30,000
Unearned revenue—gift certificates		5,000	(4)3,500			1,500				1,500
Common stock		81,250				81,250				81,250
Contributed capital in excess of par		48,750				48,750				48,750
Sales		82,000		(4)3,500		85,500		85,500		
Rent revenue		300	(3) 200			100		100		
Purchases	81,000				81,000		81,000			
Purchase returns		1,200				1,200		1,200		
Purchase discounts		900				900		900		
Transportation in	250				250		250			
Salaries expense	3,000		(6)2,500		5,500		5,500			
Rent expense	7,200			(1)6,600	600		600			
	292,200	292,200								
Prepaid rent			(1)6,600		6,600				6,600	
Supplies expense			(2)1,300		1,300		1,300			
Unearned rent				(3) 200		200				200
Interest expense			(5) 250		250		250			
Interest payable				(5) 250		250				250
Salaries payable				(6)2,500		2,500				2,500
Depreciation expense			(7) 350		350		350			
Accumulated depreciation				(7) 350		350				350
Uncollectible accounts expense			(8) 215		215		215			
Allowance for uncollectible accounts				(8) 215		215				215
			14,915	14,915	295,515	295,515	149,465	159,700		
Income tax expense			4,094				4,094*			
Income tax payable				4,094						4,094
Net income							6,141			6,141
							159,700	159,700	218,050	218,050

* .40($159,700 − $149,465)

inventory data to cost of goods sold. The reason we have not done so is to illustrate an alternative method for handling the inventory and cost of goods sold adjustments. We shall have more to say about this alternative method later.

3. On the basis of the trial balance and adjustments columns, the adjusted trial balance is constructed by extending the trial balance and adjustments data into the third pair of columns. This third pair of columns is often omitted, and the unadjusted trial balance and adjustment data are combined and extended directly into the income statement and balance sheet columns. In this case, the worksheet consists of only eight columns.

4. The data in the adjusted trial balance columns (or the trial balance and adjustments columns, if an eight-column worksheet is being prepared) are extended into the income statement and balance sheet columns, as appropriate. The nominal account balances are extended into the appropriate income statement columns (preserving the previous debit or credit balances), and the real account balances are extended into the balance sheet columns.

   The beginning inventory of $60,000 is entered into the *debit* column of the income statement (remember that on page 91 this amount was *debited* to cost of goods sold). The ending inventory of $72,000 is entered on the worksheet in *two* columns, as a *credit* in the income statement column and as a *debit* in the balance sheet column (remember that on page 91 the inventory was *debited* and cost of goods sold *credited* for the cost of the ending inventory).

   The cost of goods sold data appear in the worksheet although these data are not transferred to a cost of goods sold account. To illustrate, partial data from the worksheet income statement columns are as follows:

ACCOUNT	DR	CR
Inventory	60,000	72,000
Purchases	81,000	
Purchase returns		1,200
Purchase discounts		900
Transportation in	250	
	141,250	74,100

   The difference between these debits and credits is cost of goods sold ($141,250 − $74,100 = $67,150).

5. In order to introduce income taxes, the worksheet illustration assumes that The Hardware Corporation's income tax rate is 40 percent. Net income before taxes is $10,235, which is the difference between the income statement credit and debit column totals ($159,700 − $149,465 = $10,235). Thus, one more adjusting entry is made in the adjustments columns to record the tax. Income tax expense is debited and income tax payable is credited for $4,094 (.40 × $10,235). Income tax expense is then extended to the income statement debit column, and income tax payable is extended to the balance sheet credit column as a liability. Finally, the net income of $6,141 is shown as a debit to balance the income statement columns and as a credit to balance the balance sheet columns. (If the adjustment for taxes were not made, net income for May would have been $10,235, per the income statement in Exhibit 3–14; this amount would have been the balancing debit and credit in the income statement and balance sheet columns, respectively.)

   Now the income statement and balance sheet for The Hardware Corporation may be prepared right from the income statement and balance sheet columns of the worksheet. The adjusting entries (including taxes) can be transferred directly from the worksheet to the general journal and posted to the appropriate accounts. Closing entries also can be made on the basis of the income statement columns of the worksheet. Income summary would be debited for the total debits in the income statement column, and the individual accounts would be credited. Likewise, income summary would be credited for the total credits in the income statement column and the individual accounts would be debited. Thus the inventory and purchases data are treated as closing entries instead of as adjustments, as in our earlier illustration.

Since The Hardware Corporation began operations in May, the worksheet shown in Exhibit 3–21 did not incorporate a retained earnings account at the beginning of May. Exhibit 3–22 illustrates how a worksheet would be prepared for The Hardware Corporation at the end of June 1987. Several points are important about this worksheet.

1. While the worksheet has 12 columns, the first two pairs of columns have been omitted to avoid repetition. It differs from the 10-column worksheet shown in Exhibit 3–21 only in the addition of a pair of columns for retained earnings.

2. Many of the accounts shown in the adjusted trial balance carry over from the May 31 postclosing trial balance (e.g., the prepaid rent account balance has been reduced by $600 for the rent expense for June, and accumulated depreciation has been increased by $350 for the depreciation expense for June).

3. The retained earnings account balance of $6,141 represents the beginning of June balance and is the same amount as shown on the worksheet in Exhibit 3–21.

4. The Hardware Corporation declared and paid dividends of $5,000 during June. Note that the beginning retained earnings, the net income of $10,800, and the dividends of $5,000 are entered into the retained earnings column of the worksheet. The balancing debit in this column is the retained earnings balance at the end of June and is extended to the balance sheet credit column.

The presence of beginning retained earnings does not necessitate the use of a 12-column worksheet. An 8- or 10-column worksheet can be prepared by extending beginning retained earnings (and also dividends declared, if appropriate) on the adjusted trial balance directly to the balance sheet columns. For balance sheet reporting purposes, the ending retained earnings figure would be determined as follows:

$$\begin{matrix} \text{Beginning} \\ \text{retained earnings} \end{matrix} + \begin{matrix} \text{Net} \\ \text{income} \end{matrix} - \text{Dividends} = \begin{matrix} \text{Ending} \\ \text{retained earnings} \end{matrix}$$

PROPRIETORSHIP AND PARTNERSHIP ACCOUNTING ENTITIES

In the accounting cycle illustration just completed, we have used a corporation as the accounting entity. As a result, owners' (stockholders') equity was subdivided into the following accounts: common stock, contributed capital in excess of par, and retained earnings. The first two accounts were used to record the issuance of stock. The corporation's net income for the accounting period was transferred to retained earnings at the end of the accounting period. In a single proprietorship, one real account (e.g., owners' equity

EXHIBIT 3–22

The Hardware Corporation
PARTIAL WORKSHEET FOR THE MONTH OF JUNE 1987

ACCOUNT	ADJUSTED TRIAL BALANCE DR	CR	INCOME STATEMENT DR	CR	RETAINED EARNINGS DR	CR	BALANCE SHEET DR	CR
Cash	52,041						52,041	
Accounts receivable	54,000						54,000	
Allowance for uncollectible accounts		500						500
Supplies	7,000						7,000	
Investments	3,600						3,600	
Prepaid rent	6,000						6,000	
Inventory	72,000		72,000	65,000			65,000	
Fixtures and equipment	21,000						21,000	
Accumulated depreciation		700						700
Accounts payable		54,000						54,000
Interest payable		500						500
Salaries payable		3,800						3,800
Common stock		81,250						81,250
Contributed capital in excess of par		48,750						48,750
Retained earnings		6,141				6,141		
Sales		104,000		104,000				
Rent revenue		200		200				
Purchases	70,000		70,000					
Purchase returns		300		300				
Purchase discounts		450		450				
Transportation in	300		300					
Salaries expense	6,300		6,300					
Rent expense	600		600					
Interest expense	250		250					
Depreciation expense	350		350					
Uncollectible accounts expense	400		400					
Supplies expense	1,750		1,750					
Dividends declared	5,000				5,000			
	300,591	300,591	151,950	169,950				
Income tax expense			7,200					
Income tax payable								7,200
Net income (to retained earnings)			10,800			10,800		
			169,950	169,950	5,000	16,941		
Retained earnings (to balance sheet)					11,941			11,941
					16,941	16,941	208,641	208,641

or J. Smith, capital) replaces the stockholders' equity accounts. In a partnership, an owner's equity account is established for each partner. In addition, if the owner or owners withdraw assets for personal use during an accounting period, a nominal or **drawing account** is established to record these withdrawals. The drawing account is closed to the capital account at the end of the accounting period.

To illustrate, assume that Michael Krull began a single proprietorship. Transactions and other events that affect owner's equity would be recorded as follows:
Initial investment by owner:

Assets (detailed) . . . . *xx*
    M. Krull, capital . . . .   *xx*

Withdrawals by owner:

M. Krull, drawings . . . . *xx*
    Assets (detailed) . . . .   *xx*

Closing of income summary account (assuming a profit):

Income summary . . . . *xx*
    M. Krull, capital . . . .   *xx*

Closing of withdrawals to capital account:

M. Krull, capital . . . . *xx*
    M. Krull, drawings . . . .   *xx*

SUMMARY OF IMPORTANT TOPICS AND CONCEPT APPLICATIONS

1. All accounting systems share the following common features—types of economic events captured by the system, the double-entry bookkeeping model, and procedures used to record and process data.
2. The accounting equation (A = L + OE) expresses the financial effects of economic events. The **financial statement elements** that make up financial statements are related as follows:

$$\text{Assets} = \text{Liabilities} + \text{Owners' equity}$$
$$\text{Net income} = \text{Revenues} - \text{Expenses} + \text{Gains} - \text{Losses}$$
$$\text{Equity} = \text{Net income} + \text{Investments by owners} - \text{Distributions to owners}$$

3. Only economic events that meet certain **recognition** criteria are recorded in a company's accounts and reported in its financial statements.
4. The accounting cycle consists of the procedures used to capture, measure, process, and report the financial effects of economic events affecting an entity during an accounting period. Under the **periodicity** assumption, the cycle begins with collecting data about economic events and recording the data in either a general journal or special journals. The remaining steps in the accounting cycle include posting from the journal (or journals) to the general ledger accounts (and perhaps also subsidiary ledgers), preparing an unadjusted trial balance, recording and posting adjusting entries, preparing an adjusted trial balance, preparing the financial statements, recording and posting closing entries, and preparing a post-closing trial balance. Recording and posting reversing entries is an additional, but optional, step.

5. Under **accrual accounting,** adjusting entries are made at the end of each accounting period. Adjusting entries made for revenues and expenses are of two types—accruals and prepayments. Accrual adjusting entries are made to record revenues earned and expenses incurred in advance of cash receipt or payment. Adjusting entries for prepayments apportion to ''revenue'' amounts of earned revenue and to ''expense'' assets used to generate revenue. Adjusting entries thus **match** revenues and expenses to the accounting period benefited.

6. A worksheet often is used to facilitate the preparation of adjusting entries and financial statements.

7. For **accounting entities** other than corporations, an **equity** account is established for each owner. For corporate entities, owners' equity usually is subdivided into three categories—capital stock, contributed capital in excess of par, and retained earnings.

APPENDIX 3-1

SUBSIDIARY LEDGERS AND SPECIAL JOURNALS; METHODS OF PROCESSING FINANCIAL DATA

The daily transactions for The Hardware Corporation were recorded in one book of original entry, the general journal. Transactions were posted from this journal to the ledger accounts at the end of the month. In practice, transactions recorded daily may be posted to the ledger accounts daily, weekly, or monthly, depending on company policy.

The use of one journal and one ledger works very well for small companies, and it was helpful in our review of the accounting cycle. In practice, however, the use of only one journal and one ledger may be inefficient, because even moderate-sized businesses may have a large number of similar or identical transactions in an accounting period, and special journals may increase recording efficiency. In this appendix we illustrate how the more common special journals and subsidiary ledgers contribute to efficient collection and processing of accounting information.

SUBSIDIARY LEDGERS

Many companies use subsidiary ledgers to provide detailed information about the composition of an account balance. Subsidiary ledgers are especially helpful in determining amounts owed to individual creditors or receivables due from individual customers. Subsidiary ledgers for receivables and payables are used extensively in accounting practice because so many business transactions are made on credit. A large company, such as a large department store, may have thousands of credit customers. Manufacturing firms use subsidiary ledgers for their many suppliers and also for accumulating cost information related to complex manufacturing processes.

The relationship between the controlling accounts in the general ledger and subsidiary ledgers was illustrated in Exhibit 3-9. In the next section, we explore subsidiary ledgers further as we illustrate the recording and posting steps of the accounting cycle with the use of special journals.

SPECIAL JOURNALS

Many companies use special journals to increase the speed and efficiency of recording transactions. Similar transactions, such as a credit sale, can be recorded in one journal, while other similar transactions, such as a credit purchase, can be recorded in another journal. Special journals thus permit the recording of different types of transactions by different employees, dividing the labor needed to maintain accounting records. Furthermore, posting is more efficient. Instead of posting every single transaction from the general journal, one may combine similar transactions, and the totals can be posted less frequently.

The more common types of special journals are as follows:

1. The **purchases journal** is used to record all credit purchases of merchandise. (Cash purchases of merchandise are recorded in the cash disbursements journal.) A **multi-column purchases journal** is used to record all credit purchases of supplies, equipment, and other assets as well as merchandise.

2. The **sales journal** is used to record all credit sales of merchandise. (Cash sales are recorded in the cash receipts journal.)

3. The **cash receipts journal** is used to record all cash received, regardless of its source.

4. The **cash disbursements journal** is used to record all cash payments by a company.

5. The **general journal** is used to record transactions that are not recorded in any of the special journals.

In the following sections, we illustrate and discuss recording in and posting from the special journals. The general ledger accounts and the accounts receivable and accounts payable subsidiary ledger accounts to which the data are posted appear in Exhibits 3-28 through 3-30. As each journal is discussed, you should trace the recording and posting from the journal to the affected ledger accounts. Also, three-column ledger accounts, which are used in practice, are illustrated here instead of the T-account form, which was used previously for illustration purposes.

Purchases Journal

The purchases journal provides a record of the credit purchases of merchandise. When subsidiary ledgers are used, the purchases journal is designed so that postings can be made not only to the accounts payable subsidiary ledger but also to the controlling account, accounts payable, in the general ledger.

RECORDING IN THE PURCHASES JOURNAL   Listed below are the transactions for The Hardware Corporation for May 1987 that would be recorded in the purchases journal.

    May 4 Purchased merchandise on account from Quik Wholesale. Cost of the merchandise was $45,000.

    May 9 Purchased merchandise costing $30,000 from Nails, Inc., on account. Transportation cost on the merchandise totaled $250 and was paid in cash. (Transportation costs are recorded in the cash disbursements journal.)

    May 29 Purchased merchandise on account from Handy Dandy Supply at a cost of $6,000.

These transactions would be recorded daily in the purchases journal as shown in Exhibit 3–23.

This type of journal is called a one-column purchases journal because only one column is provided for money amounts. Two general ledger accounts, however, are affected by each line entry in the journal. Each line entry increases purchases and accounts payable. The numbers in the folio (posting reference) column will be explained shortly.

The *multiple-column* purchases journal is more versatile and can accommodate many more types of credit transactions. The multiple-column journal, sometimes called an **invoice register,** allows a business to record not only credit purchases of merchandise but also credit purchases of supplies, equipment, and other assets.

EXHIBIT 3—23

The Hardware Corporation

PURCHASES JOURNAL   PAGE 1

DATE	ACCOUNT CREDITED	FOLIO	AMOUNT
1987			
May 4	Quik Wholesale	201	45,000
9	Nails, Inc.	202	30,000
29	Handy Dandy Supply	203	6,000
		510/200	81,000

POSTING FROM THE PURCHASES JOURNAL   The individual creditor amounts are posted daily to the creditors' accounts in the subsidiary ledger. For example, at the close of business on May 4, the $45,000 amount payable to Quik Wholesale is posted as a credit to Quik Wholesale's account in the accounts payable subsidiary ledger. ''P 1'' under the folio or posting reference column in the Quik Wholesale account indicates that the amount was posted from page 1 of the purchases journal. The ''201'' under the posting reference column in the purchases journal means that $45,000 was posted to account number 201. These same procedures would be followed each day.

At the end of the month, the amount column in the purchases journal is totaled, and the total is posted to the general ledger accounts. For example, $81,000 is posted as a debit to purchases (account number 510) in the general ledger, and $81,000 is also posted as a credit to accounts payable (account number 200). Posting in this fashion keeps the debits and credits in the general ledger equal, and at the same time keeps the sum of the individual accounts in the accounts payable subsidiary ledger equal to the balance of the accounts payable controlling account in the general ledger.

Sales Journal

The sales journal is used to record credit sales of merchandise. The sales journal must be designed so that postings can be made not only to the accounts receivable subsidiary ledger but also to the controlling account, accounts receivable, in the general ledger.

RECORDING IN THE SALES JOURNAL   The credit sales for The Hardware Corporation were as follows:

May 5 Sold miscellaneous hardware totaling $25,000 to Ace Builders on account.

May 26 Sold miscellaneous hardware totaling $24,000 to Rite-Way Construction. Rite-Way paid $6,000 cash and the balance was on open account. (The cash received is recorded in the cash receipts journal.)

These credit sales would be recorded in the sales journal as illustrated in Exhibit 3–24.

POSTING FROM THE SALES JOURNAL   As Exhibit 3–24 shows, credit sales for the month of May totaled $49,000. This total is posted as a debit to the controlling account, accounts receivable, and as a credit to the sales account in the general ledger at the end of the month. Because both of these accounts are maintained in the general ledger, the debits and credits are equal. The individual items in the sales journal are posted daily to the corresponding customers' accounts in the accounts receivable subsidiary ledger, as shown in

EXHIBIT 3–24

The Hardware Corporation

SALES JOURNAL   PAGE 1

DATE	ACCOUNT DEBITED	FOLIO	AMOUNT
1987			
May 5	Ace Builders	112	25,000
26	Rite-Way Construction	113	24,000
		110/400	49,000

Exhibit 3–29. Posting in this fashion, as with the purchases journal, keeps the debits and credits equal in the general ledger and also causes the sum of the customers' accounts in the accounts receivable subsidiary ledger to be equal to the balance of the accounts receivable controlling account in the general ledger. As you study the posting process, note that the abbreviation "S" is used in the ledger as a posting reference to identify items posted from the sales journal. The numbers in the posting reference column in the sales journal refer to the account numbers of individual customers in the accounts receivable subsidiary ledger and to the account numbers for accounts receivable and sales in the general ledger.

Cash Receipts Journal

The number of columns in a cash receipts journal varies from company to company. Most companies, however, require a journal that includes at least a cash debit column, a sales discount debit column (if sales discounts are allowed), an accounts receivable credit column, a sales credit column, and a general ledger credit column.

RECORDING IN THE CASH RECEIPTS JOURNAL   The cash receipt transactions for The Hardware Corporation are listed below and recorded in the cash receipts journal in Exhibit 3–25.

May 1 Sold for cash 16,250 shares of $5 par common stock at $8 per share.

May 1 Borrowed $30,000 from City Bank by issuing a $30,000 note due in two years. Interest at 10% is payable annually.

May 11 Received $12,000 of the amount due from Ace Builders.

May 20 Cash sales of hardware, $15,000.

May 20 Subleased for $300 per month the top floor of the building previously rented. Received cash of $300 and credited rent revenue.

May 22 Received $5,000 from the sale of gift certificates. Credited unearned revenue— gift certificates.

May 26 Sold miscellaneous hardware totaling $24,000 to Rite-Way Construction. Rite-Way paid $6,000 cash, and the balance was on open account. (The total sales were recorded in the sales journal.)

May 30 Cash sales of hardware, $18,000.

The account credited column shows the general ledger accounts and individual customer accounts in the accounts receivable subsidiary ledger that are affected by the various transactions. In cases where a general ledger account, other than those provided for in the journal columns, is listed under the account credited column, the dollar amount of the credit appears in the general ledger column. Because The Hardware Corporation did not allow sales discounts, no amounts appear in this column. If, however, Ace Builders were allowed a 2 percent discount for prompt payment, cash would be debited for $11,760

EXHIBIT 3—25

The Hardware Corporation

CASH RECEIPTS JOURNAL   PAGE 1

| | | | DEBIT | | CREDIT | | |
| | | | CASH | SALES DISCOUNTS | ACCOUNTS RECEIVABLE | SALES | GENERAL LEDGER |
DATE	ACCOUNT CREDITED	FOLIO					
1987							
May 1	Common stock	310	81,250				81,250
	Contributed capital in excess of par	320	48,750				48,750
1	Notes payable	205	30,000				30,000
11	Ace Builders	112	12,000		12,000		
20	Sales	✓	15,000			15,000	
20	Rent revenue	420	300				300
22	Unearned revenue	210	5,000				5,000
26	Rite-Way Construction	113	6,000		6,000		
30	Sales	✓	18,000			18,000	
	Total		216,300		18,000	33,000	165,300
			(100)		(110)	(400)	(✓)

[$12,000 − .02($12,000)], $240 would be entered in the sales discount debit column, and $12,000 would be entered in the accounts receivable credit column.

POSTING FROM THE CASH RECEIPTS JOURNAL   Line amounts in the general ledger credit column of the cash receipts journal are posted daily to the corresponding general ledger account name shown in the account credited column. The total of the general ledger credit column is not posted, because the amounts that make up the total have all been posted daily directly to the general ledger. The total is checked (✓) to show that it has already been posted.

Each amount in the accounts receivable credit column is posted daily to the credit side of the corresponding customer's account in the accounts receivable subsidiary ledger. The total of the accounts receivable credit column ($18,000 in this example) is posted at the end of the month as a credit to the accounts receivable account in the general ledger. After this posting, the balance in the controlling account, accounts receivable, will equal the sum of the customer balances in the subsidiary accounts receivable ledger. The total in the cash debit column is posted at the end of the month as a debit to the cash account in the general ledger. Likewise, the total in the sales credit column is posted periodically (e.g., monthly) to the sales account in the general ledger.

The use of posting references in the cash receipts journal also should be noted. For example, the number "310" in the folio column opposite "Common stock" indicates that the $81,250 amount in the cash debit column was posted to account number 310 in the general ledger. Likewise, the "100" below the total of the cash debit column indicates that $216,300 was posted to account number 100 in the general ledger. In the ledger accounts, the posting reference "CR" means that this amount was posted from the cash receipts journal.

Cash Disbursements Journal

If a company engages in relatively few cash transactions, the general journal is usually adequate. When there are many cash transactions, however, it may become necessary to use a multiple-column journal designed to handle many varied cash transactions in a systematic and routine fashion. The number and types of columns contained in a cash disbursements journal vary from company to company. Most companies, however, will

EXHIBIT 3–26

The Hardware Corporation
CASH DISBURSEMENTS JOURNAL

PAGE 1

			DEBIT		CREDIT	
DATE	ACCOUNT DEBITED	FOLIO	ACCOUNTS PAYABLE	GENERAL LEDGER	PURCHASE DISCOUNTS	CASH
1987						
May 1	Inventory	140		60,000		60,000
	Supplies	120		4,000		4,000
	Fixtures and equipment	150		11,000		11,000
2	Rent expense	560		7,200		7,200
3	Northern Supply	204	2,000			2,000
4	Supplies	120		1,800		1,800
9	Transportation in	540		250		250
12	Salaries expense	550		3,000		3,000
24	Investments	130		3,600		3,600
28	Quik Wholesale	201	45,000		900	44,100
	Total		47,000	90,850	900	136,950
			(200)	(✔)	(530)	(100)

require a journal that contains at least a general ledger debit column, an accounts payable debit column, a purchase discount credit column, and a cash credit column.

RECORDING IN THE CASH DISBURSEMENTS JOURNAL   The transactions involving disbursements for The Hardware Corporation are listed below and recorded in the cash disbursements journal in Exhibit 3–26.

May 1 Purchased the assets of Zenith Hardware Corporation for $75,000 cash. The assets consisted of inventory of $60,000, supplies of $4,000, and fixtures of $11,000.

May 2 Paid rent on a building for 12 months in advance, $7,200. Debited rent expense.

May 3 Purchased display equipment for $10,000 from Northern Supply Company. Paid $2,000 cash, the balance to be paid in 60 days. (The purchase of equipment will be recorded in the general journal rather than in the purchases journal, since this purchase is not for merchandise.)

May 4 Paid $1,800 cash for supplies, which were recorded as an asset.

May 9 Paid transportation cost of $250 on merchandise purchased from Nails, Inc.

May 12 Paid sales salaries totaling $3,000.

May 24 Purchased temporary investments at a cost of $3,600.

May 28 Paid the $45,000 amount due to Quik Wholesale. Received a 2% discount for prompt payment.

POSTING FROM THE CASH DISBURSEMENTS JOURNAL   Each individual amount in the accounts payable debit column is posted daily to the individual creditor's account in the accounts payable subsidiary ledger. The total of the accounts payable debit column ($47,000) is posted at the end of the month as a debit to the accounts payable account in the general ledger. After these postings, the controlling account and the subsidiary ledger will be in agreement.

EXHIBIT 3–27

The Hardware Corporation
GENERAL JOURNAL
PAGE 1

DATE	ACCOUNT TITLE AND EXPLANATION	FOLIO	DR	CR
1987				
May 3	Fixtures and equipment	150	10,000	
	Accounts payable			
	(Northern Supply)	200/204		10,000
	To record purchase of fixtures and equipment.			
25	Accounts payable			
	(Nails, Inc.)	200/202	1,200	
	Purchase returns	520		1,200
	To record return of defective merchandise.			

Each amount in the general ledger debit column is posted daily from the cash disbursements journal to the corresponding general ledger account. For example, $60,000 is posted as a debit to the inventory account in the general ledger, and $4,000 is posted as a debit to the supplies account in the general ledger. The total of the general ledger debit column is not posted, since the individual amounts that make up the total have been posted directly to the general ledger. The total general ledger debit of $90,850 is checked (✔) to show that it has already been posted.

The total amount in the purchase discounts credit column is posted at the end of the month as a credit to purchase discounts in the general ledger. The amounts in the cash credit column are not posted individually, but the total is posted at the end of the month as a credit to the cash account in the general ledger.

Posting references are employed in the cash disbursements journal in the same way as in the cash receipts journal. The abbreviation "CD" is used in the ledger to indicate that posting was made from the cash disbursements journal.

General Journal

Even when special journals are used, transactions arise that cannot be recorded in the special journals. These transactions, along with adjusting and closing entries, are recorded in the general journal. In the case of The Hardware Corporation, two transactions are recorded in the general journal, as shown in Exhibit 3–27, since they cannot be recorded in any of the special journals.

As illustrated previously with controlling accounts, amounts are posted not only to the controlling account in the general ledger but also to the individual customers' and creditors' accounts in the subsidiary ledgers. Since totals are not posted from the general journal, each item must be posted individually. Thus only individual items may be posted from the general journal to a controlling account (either accounts receivable or accounts payable). Since we must also post the same item to the subsidiary ledger, the item is posted twice. This procedure is called **double posting.** For example, the $10,000 credit in the first entry is posted to the accounts payable controlling account and also to Northern Supply in the accounts payable subsidiary ledger.

All of the transactions for The Hardware Corporation for the month of May have now been recorded and posted. The ledger accounts in Exhibits 3–28 through 3–30 represent the balances in the various general ledger and subsidiary ledger accounts after all transactions, including those in the general journal, have been posted. These results should be compared with the ledger accounts in Exhibit 3–8. Notice that whether or not special journals are used, the final ledger account balances are the same.

EXHIBIT 3—28

The Hardware Corporation
GENERAL LEDGER ACCOUNTS

CASH   ACCOUNT NO. 100

DATE	EXPLANATION	FOLIO	DEBIT	CREDIT	BALANCE
1987					
May 31		CR 1	216,300		216,300
31		CD 1		136,950	79,350

ACCOUNTS RECEIVABLE   ACCOUNT NO. 110

DATE	EXPLANATION	FOLIO	DEBIT	CREDIT	BALANCE
1987					
May 31		S 1	49,000		49,000
31		CR 1		18,000	31,000

SUPPLIES   ACCOUNT NO. 120

DATE	EXPLANATION	FOLIO	DEBIT	CREDIT	BALANCE
1987					
May 1		CD 1	4,000		4,000
4		CD 1	1,800		5,800

INVESTMENTS   ACCOUNT NO. 130

DATE	EXPLANATION	FOLIO	DEBIT	CREDIT	BALANCE
1987					
May 24		CD 1	3,600		3,600

INVENTORY   ACCOUNT NO. 140

DATE	EXPLANATION	FOLIO	DEBIT	CREDIT	BALANCE
1987					
May 1		CD 1	60,000		60,000

FIXTURES AND EQUIPMENT   ACCOUNT NO. 150

DATE	EXPLANATION	FOLIO	DEBIT	CREDIT	BALANCE
1987					
May 1		CD 1	11,000		11,000
3		GJ 1	10,000		21,000

ACCOUNTS PAYABLE   ACCOUNT NO. 200

DATE	EXPLANATION	FOLIO	DEBIT	CREDIT	BALANCE
1987					
May 3		GJ 1		10,000	10,000
25		GJ 1	1,200		8,800
31		P 1		81,000	89,800
31		CD 1	47,000		42,800

NOTES PAYABLE   ACCOUNT NO. 205

DATE	EXPLANATION	FOLIO	DEBIT	CREDIT	BALANCE
1987					
May 1		CR 1		30,000	30,000

UNEARNED REVENUE   ACCOUNT NO. 210

DATE	EXPLANATION	FOLIO	DEBIT	CREDIT	BALANCE
1987					
May 22		CR 1		5,000	5,000

COMMON STOCK — ACCOUNT NO. 310

DATE	EXPLANATION	FOLIO	DEBIT	CREDIT	BALANCE
1987					
May 1		CR 1		81,250	81,250

CONTRIBUTED CAPITAL IN EXCESS OF PAR — ACCOUNT NO. 320

DATE	EXPLANATION	FOLIO	DEBIT	CREDIT	BALANCE
1987					
May 1		CR 1		48,750	48,750

SALES — ACCOUNT NO. 400

DATE	EXPLANATION	FOLIO	DEBIT	CREDIT	BALANCE
1987					
May 31		S 1		49,000	49,000
31		CR 1		33,000	82,000

RENT REVENUE — ACCOUNT NO. 420

DATE	EXPLANATION	FOLIO	DEBIT	CREDIT	BALANCE
1987					
May 20		CR 1		300	300

PURCHASES — ACCOUNT NO. 510

DATE	EXPLANATION	FOLIO	DEBIT	CREDIT	BALANCE
1987					
May 31		P 1	81,000		81,000

PURCHASE RETURNS — ACCOUNT NO. 520

DATE	EXPLANATION	FOLIO	DEBIT	CREDIT	BALANCE
1987					
May 25		GJ 1		1,200	1,200

PURCHASE DISCOUNTS — ACCOUNT NO. 530

DATE	EXPLANATION	FOLIO	DEBIT	CREDIT	BALANCE
1987					
May 31		CD 1		900	900

TRANSPORTATION IN — ACCOUNT NO. 540

DATE	EXPLANATION	FOLIO	DEBIT	CREDIT	BALANCE
1987					
May 9		CD 1	250		250

SALARIES EXPENSE — ACCOUNT NO. 550

DATE	EXPLANATION	FOLIO	DEBIT	CREDIT	BALANCE
1987					
May 12		CD 1	3,000		3,000

RENT EXPENSE — ACCOUNT NO. 560

DATE	EXPLANATION	FOLIO	DEBIT	CREDIT	BALANCE
1987					
May 2		CD 1	7,200		7,200

EXHIBIT 3—29

The Hardware Corporation
ACCOUNTS RECEIVABLE SUBSIDIARY LEDGER

ACE BUILDERS   ACCOUNT NO. 112

DATE	EXPLANATION	FOLIO	DEBIT	CREDIT	BALANCE
1987					
May 5		S 1	25,000		25,000
11		CR 1		12,000	13,000

RITE-WAY CONSTRUCTION   ACCOUNT NO. 113

DATE	EXPLANATION	FOLIO	DEBIT	CREDIT	BALANCE
1987					
May 26		S 1	24,000		24,000
26		CR 1		6,000	18,000

EXHIBIT 3—30

The Hardware Corporation
ACCOUNTS PAYABLE SUBSIDIARY LEDGER

QUIK WHOLESALE   ACCOUNT NO. 201

DATE	EXPLANATION	FOLIO	DEBIT	CREDIT	BALANCE
1987					
May 4		P 1		45,000	45,000
28		CD 1	45,000		0

NAILS, INC.   ACCOUNT NO. 202

DATE	EXPLANATION	FOLIO	DEBIT	CREDIT	BALANCE
1987					
May 9		P 1		30,000	30,000
25		GJ 1	1,200		28,800

HANDY DANDY SUPPLY   ACCOUNT NO. 203

DATE	EXPLANATION	FOLIO	DEBIT	CREDIT	BALANCE
1987					
May 29		P 1		6,000	6,000

NORTHERN SUPPLY   ACCOUNT NO. 204

DATE	EXPLANATION	FOLIO	DEBIT	CREDIT	BALANCE
1987					
May 3		GJ 1		10,000	10,000
3		CD 1	2,000		8,000

The remaining steps in the accounting cycle for The Hardware Corporation are not illustrated in this appendix, since these steps are identical to those covered in the chapter. The formal adjusting, closing, and reversing (if appropriate) entries would be recorded in the general journal and posted to the appropriate general ledger accounts.

VOUCHER SYSTEM

A voucher system is used by many companies to strengthen control over cash disbursements. Under this system, a voucher is prepared for *every* disbursement of cash. Vouchers are numbered consecutively, and information about what is purchased, the account to be debited, and the amount of the purchase is entered on each voucher. In addition, the voucher must be approved for payment by the person given authority to approve payment.

Under a voucher system, a **voucher register** replaces the purchases journal. A voucher register for The Hardware Corporation in which selected transactions have been entered appears in Exhibit 3–31. Notice that *all* transactions requiring cash disbursements are entered in the voucher register. While the voucher register illustrated has debit columns only for purchases and the general ledger, in practice a voucher register may have debit columns for many accounts.

The cash disbursements journal is simplified when a voucher register is used. Since all transactions that require a cash payment must be vouchered and a credit made to the vouchers payable account, a one-column cash disbursement journal called a **check register** may be used. A two-column check register with a purchase discounts column may be required if cash discounts are applicable. The check register also shows the voucher number for each check. As Exhibit 3–31 indicates, the check number is entered in the voucher register when the voucher is paid.

METHODS OF PROCESSING FINANCIAL DATA

At the beginning of this chapter we pointed out that an entity's accounting system should be tailored to the characteristics and complexities of that entity. For a small company, an information-processing system in which entries are made by hand on paper, as previously illustrated, may be sufficient.

EXHIBIT 3–31

The Hardware Corporation
VOUCHER REGISTER
PAGE 1

DATE	VOUCHER NUMBER	CREDITOR	PAYMENT DATE	PAYMENT NUMBER	VOUCHERS PAYABLE CREDIT	PUR-CHASES DEBIT	GENERAL LEDGER DEBIT ACCOUNT	GENERAL LEDGER DEBIT AMOUNT
1987								
May 1	100	Zenith Hardware	May 1	001	75,000		Inventory	60,000
							Supplies	4,000
							Fixtures	11,000
May 2	101	Realty, Inc.	May 2	002	7,200		Rent expense	7,200
May 4	103	Quik Wholesale	May 28	011	45,000	45,000		
May 9	105	Nails, Inc.	June 5	021	30,000	30,000		
May 9	106	Fast Freight	May 9	016	250		Transportation in	250
May 12	107	Employees	May 12	017	3,000		Salaries expense	3,000

Computers are used in many accounting systems. A computer can process information much faster and more efficiently than any of the other data-processing methods. In addition, it can be programmed to accomplish a wide variety of processing tasks—bookkeeping, inventory control, payroll accounting, and so on. In recent years, **time-sharing arrangements** make it possible for even smaller businesses to use the services of a computer. For example, a large bank may own a large computer and sell computer time to small hardware stores, clothing stores, and record shops. These businesses may use the computer for inventory control, customer billings, and accounts payable record keeping. Finally, **microcomputers** make it possible for small businesses to take advantage of the speed, accuracy, and efficiency of a computer at comparatively low cost. In addition to offering programming capabilities, such as BASIC, these computers run a wide variety of software programs, such as spreadsheets, word processing, data bases, and graphics.

QUESTIONS

Questions marked with an asterisk (*) refer to Appendix 3–1.

Q3-1. What are the features common to accounting and reporting systems, regardless of the complexity of the entity?

Q3-2. A) Give an example of each of the following types of economic events.

1. External event—exchange.

2. External event—nonreciprocal transfer.

3. Internal event.

B) What is the distinguishing characteristic of an exchange?

Q3-3. This chapter discussed the dual nature of transactions on the accounting equation. For each transaction below, indicate the effect on the accounting equation. Use + for increase, − for decrease, and N for no effect.

| | EFFECT ON | | |
TRANSACTION	ASSETS	LIABILITIES	OWNERS' EQUITY
a) Purchased a machine with cash			
b) Borrowed cash by issuing a note			
c) Net income for the period			
d) Owner investment in the business			
e) Owner withdrawal from the business			
f) Paid the note in *b*			
g) Sold a building at a gain			
h) Sold a building at a loss			
i) Purchased supplies on account			

Q3-4. What are source documents? What is their role in the accounting cycle?

Q3-5. Explain the process and purpose of journalizing transactions.

Q3-6. Why is the posting step in the accounting cycle useful?

Q3-7. The steps in the accounting cycle are listed below, but not necessarily in the proper order. Number these steps in the proper order.

____ Financial statement preparation
____ Collection of data about economic events
____ Analysis of effects of transactions and other events
____ Reversing entries
____ Unadjusted trial balance preparation
____ Adjusted trial balance preparation
____ Recording transactions during the period
____ Postclosing trial balance preparation
____ Posting transactions during the period
____ Recording and posting closing entries
____ Recording and posting adjusting entries

*Q3-8. How are subsidiary ledgers related to general ledger controlling accounts?

*Q3-9. Many companies use special journals to record transactions. What are some of the advantages of using special journals?

Q3-10. Why might a company elect to make reversing entries? What guidelines may be used to determine when an adjusting entry should be reversed?

Q3-11. What is the purpose of adjusting entries?

Q3-12. An unadjusted trial balance is prepared at the end of the accounting period as a step in the accounting cycle. Why is this step important? Which of the following errors would be revealed by an unadjusted trial balance? Why?

    1. A debit item was posted twice from the journal to the ledger.

    2. Debit and credit items in equal amounts were not posted.

    3. A purchase of merchandise was recorded as an expense.

    4. A purchase of merchandise was recorded as a debit to sales.

    5. An error was made in totaling the cash account, which resulted in an overstatement of the account.

Q3-13. Where would each of the following items appear on a 10-column worksheet?

    1. Balance, before adjustment, of the salaries expense account

    2. Adjusting entry for depreciation expense

    3. Ending inventory

    4. Dividends declared and paid during the period

    5. Beginning inventory

    6. Sales discounts

    7. Beginning retained earnings

Q3-14. Classify each of the following as a real or nominal account:

1. Allowance for doubtful accounts	**5.** Cost of goods sold
2. Ending inventory	**6.** Mr. *X*, withdrawals
3. Purchase returns	**7.** Mr. *X*, capital
4. Interest receivable	**8.** Prepaid insurance

*Q3-15. What is meant by ''double posting''?

*Q3-16. What types of transactions would be recorded in the following special journals?

    1. Purchases journal (one-column)

    2. Cash receipts journal

    3. General journal

    4. Purchases journal (multicolumn)

    5. Sales journal

    6. Cash disbursements journal

*Q3-17. A company recorded the following transaction in general journal form:

Notes receivable	12,000	
Cash	24,000	
Sales		36,000
To record sales of merchandise.		

Assume that the company uses special journals such as those illustrated in Appendix 3–1. How would this transaction be recorded?

Q3-18. A company's ledger accounts showed a debit of $2,600 posted to interest revenue at the beginning of 1988. What kind of account is this (e.g., revenue, expense, etc.) and how did it arise?

Q3-19. Why are closing entries necessary? What accounts are affected by closing entries?

Q3-20. How is a worksheet used in the accounting cycle? What are the advantages of preparing a worksheet?

Q3-21. The bookkeeper for Work, Inc., made the following errors in extending items in the adjusted trial balance columns to the income statement and balance sheet columns of a worksheet. What effect would each error have on the affected columns? Also state why the error would or would not be automatically detected.

    1. A revenue item was extended into the balance sheet credit column.

    2. An asset item was extended into the income statement credit column.

    3. An expense item was extended into the balance sheet debit column.

    4. A revenue item was extended into the income statement debit column.

*Q3-22. What is the purpose of a voucher system?

CASES

C3-1. DOUBLE-ENTRY BOOKKEEPING For some time Mr. Friend has operated a small grocery. He has limited his accounts to single-entry records and has engaged outside assistance only for preparation of his tax return. He has never needed to obtain credit and does not expect to do so. Mr. Friend approaches you with the statement that he has heard of double-entry bookkeeping and would like to know what benefits, if any, he would derive from the use of such a system.

REQUIRED

    1. Prepare a brief statement of the advantages and disadvantages of double-entry bookkeeping.

2. Mr. Friend has maintained a record of the grocery store's cash receipts and disbursements. The cash records for April of the current year appear as follows:

Balance, April 1		$ 6,500
Receipts		
Cash sales	$19,650	
Customer collections	23,960	
Additional investment by Mr. Friend	5,000	48,610
Disbursements		
Grocery purchases	$11,900	
Withdrawals by Mr. Friend	2,000	
Purchases of grocery bags, string, etc.............	459	
Clerical salaries	14,600	
Other	750	(29,709)
Balance, April 30		$25,401

Explain to Mr. Friend how the above cash transactions would be recorded in a double-entry system.

C3-2. ACCRUAL ACCOUNTING CONCEPTS On January 1, 1987, Slim Hudson opened a western wear shop in a neighborhood shopping center. Recently he came to you for advice in connection with a bank loan. The bank has requested financial statements for the six months ending June 30, 1987. Slim has kept limited records and has asked how the following items should be considered in the preparation of financial statements.

a) No records have been maintained for merchandise purchases, although the company's checkbook indicates that $42,000 has been paid to creditors since January 1. You also determine that there are purchase invoices outstanding at June 30 which total $8,000.

b) During the six-month period, the company has returned unsalable merchandise that was purchased for $2,000. Since the merchandise was paid for, the manufacturer issued the company a credit to be used against future purchases.

c) The company took a physical inventory on June 30. The merchandise on hand had a cost of $16,000. On June 30, immediately after the inventory, Slim's ex-wife took clothing with a cost of $1,200 and sales value of $2,000 as a draw against Slim's personal child-support check.

d) The owner of the shop next door told Slim that prepayments and accruals must be considered in preparing the financial statements on June 30. Slim is confused about these terms and considers them irrelevant, arguing that a banker once said, "all that really matters is cash flows."

e) The western store borrowed $10,000 from a savings and loan company shortly after commencing operations. By June 30, $6,000 has been repaid, as has interest of $600. The company's records show revenue of $10,000 and expenses of $6,600 in connection with these events.

f) Fixtures and display equipment costing $9,000 were acquired on a deferred payment plan. As of June 30, $3,200 of this amount has been repaid. Slim's uncle has advised him that this should be considered depreciation on the fixtures and equipment, since "things wash out eventually."

g) Slim has inquired about what financial statements should be prepared for the bank in addition to the statement of cash receipts and disbursements, which he thinks measures the western store's earnings for the first six months of operation.

h) Just before your arrival at the western store, Slim glanced at a trade association manual that described a system of record keeping in terms of the accounting cycle. He is confused about the meaning of the accounting cycle and the steps involved in it.

REQUIRED

Draft a brief response to each of the items above.

EXERCISES	The exercise marked with an asterisk (*) refers to Appendix 3–1.

E3-1. RULES OF DEBIT AND CREDIT: RECORDING TRANSACTIONS IN ACCOUNTS   Below is a list of accounts, with each account name preceded by a letter. Indicate the account debited and credited to record each transaction below by placing the letter corresponding to the correct account to the right of each transaction.

a) Cash   **f)** Rent expense
b) Pat Bone, capital   **g)** Accounts payable
c) Accounts receivable   **h)** Agency revenue
d) Office equipment   **i)** Salaries expense
e) Supplies   **j)** Unearned revenue

	DEBIT	CREDIT
Example: Pat Bone started an advertising agency by investing cash.	*a*	*b*
1. Purchased office equipment and office supplies on account.		
2. Rented a building and paid the monthly rent.		
3. Completed layout work on a magazine for a client and received cash.		
4. Returned a portion of the office equipment purchased in transaction 1.		
5. Placed a TV advertisement for a client on account.		
6. Paid the balance due on the equipment and supplies purchased in transaction 1.		
7. Paid the salary of her secretary.		
8. Withdrew supplies for her personal use.		
9. Received cash as an advance payment for art and layout work to be completed next year.		
10. Collected cash from client in transaction 5.		

E3-2. TRIAL BALANCE PREPARATION   The unadjusted trial balance below was prepared by your client and does not balance. Additional information relating to the trial balance also appears below.

Razor Racquet Club
TRIAL BALANCE
DECEMBER 31, 1987

ACCOUNT	DEBIT	CREDIT
Cash	$ 3,300	
Receivables from club members	41,600	
Supplies	400	
Building	75,000	
Accumulated depreciation—building		$ 33,000
Land	61,000	
Accounts payable		38,200
Notes payable		10,000
D. Razor, capital		50,000
Club member advances		5,400
Club revenues		110,400
Salaries expense	46,500	
Advertising expense	12,000	
Tournament expense	19,000	
	$258,800	$247,000

a) D. Razor withdrew supplies totaling $180 for personal use. The withdrawal was not recorded.

b) Salaries expense for November was $5,000 and was recorded correctly in the journal. However, the debit was posted twice to the salaries expense account.

c) Advertising expenses of $3,000 were incorrectly debited to the land account.

d) Club revenues for the month of May 1987 totaled $3,400. When the transaction was posted from the journal to the ledger, the club revenue account was debited instead of credited for $3,400.

e) On December 5, 1987, the company received a bill for $750 for newspaper advertising for November. The transaction had not been recorded nor had the bill been paid at the end of 1987.

REQUIRED

1. Prepare a corrected trial balance.

2. Give appropriate entries required to correct the accounts. Also, explain how the remaining accounts would be corrected if a formal entry is not required.

E3-3. ADJUSTING ENTRIES Prepare adjusting entries for the data below:

a) Unearned revenue of $1,000 was recorded during the year. By the end of the year, $800 was earned.

b) Office salaries of $700 have accrued since the last payment period.

c) Interest revenue of $500 has been earned but is unrecorded at the end of the year.

d) Uncollectible accounts expense is determined by adjusting the allowance for doubtful accounts to 4 percent of the ending accounts receivable balance. At the end of the year, the balance in the accounts receivable account was $55,000, and the credit balance in the allowance account was $700.

e) Assets are depreciated by the straight-line method. Assets subject to depreciation had a cost of $30,000, estimated useful life of five years, and estimated salvage value of $3,000.

f) Included among the accounts on the unadjusted trial balance were supplies expense with a debit balance of $8,000, and supplies with a debit balance of $4,000. Supplies on hand at the end of the year totaled $4,500.

E3-4. ADJUSTING AND REVERSING ENTRIES The following transactions and other data relate to operating activities of A & R Company, which closes its books each December 31.

a) A & R purchased $1,000 in office supplies on March 1, 1987. On December 31, 1987, $600 in office supplies were on hand.

b) A & R received $6,000 on November 1, 1987, which represented an advance payment for six months' rent on a building owned by A & R.

c) A & R holds a $2,000 note, dated November 1, 1987. The note and interest of $240 are due on February 1, 1988. Interest accrued at December 31, 1987, totals $160.

d) At the end of 1987, A & R had accrued salaries of $3,200. Salary payments of $10,000 are made during the first week of each month.

REQUIRED

1. Prepare the adjusting entries for the above four items, assuming that the original debits or credits for prepayments and unearned items were recorded in real accounts.

2. Repeat the requirement in part 1, this time assuming that the original debits or credits for prepaid and unearned items were recorded in nominal accounts.

3. Prepare any reversing entries appropriate for part 1.

4. Prepare any reversing entries appropriate for part 2.

E3-5. COMPUTING COST OF GOODS SOLD Roth, Inc., uses a periodic inventory system for merchandise transactions. The following partial data relate to operating activities for the current year:

Sales	$160,000	Purchase discounts	$ 3,600
Transportation in	16,000	Ending inventory	33,000
Purchase returns	5,000	Sales discounts	2,000
Beginning inventory	42,000	Purchases	90,000

REQUIRED

Calculate Roth's cost of goods sold.

E3-6. ADJUSTING ENTRIES For each of the independent situations below, prepare the proper adjusting entry. Assume that the accounting period for each company ends on December 31, 1987.

1. In December of 1987, a consulting firm started and completed a project with a sales price of $25,000. The project has not been recorded on the books of the consulting firm, and the firm will not receive payment from the client until mid-January of 1988. Costs incurred on the project were $8,500 and have been recorded in a prepaid expense account.

2. A company always debits prepaid insurance when it purchases or renews an insurance policy. An expiring policy was renewed on July 31, 1987, and was debited to the asset account. The three-year renewal cost $63,000, which was $27,000 more than the policy had cost three years earlier.

3. At the end of 1986, a company reported salaries payable of $25,000 on its balance sheet. Salary payments to employees during 1987 were $210,000 and this amount was debited to salaries expense. At the end of 1987, the balance in salaries payable is still $25,000, and salaries of $23,000 for services rendered in December 1987 remained unpaid.

4. On April 1, 1987, a company rented a building for a two-year period and paid $30,000 rent in advance; this amount was debited to rent expense. During November and December, the company subleased one floor of the building for $2,000 per month. The sublease revenue was credited to rent revenue. The company wishes to show sublease revenue as a reduction in rent expense.

5. A company began the 1987 fiscal year with a balance of $12,000 in the supplies asset account. During the year, supplies were purchased at a cost of $22,000 and this amount was debited to the supplies expense account. An inventory on December 31, 1987, showed supplies of $20,000 on hand.

E3-7. ADJUSTING AND REVERSING ENTRIES The unadjusted and adjusted trial balances for Manhattan Fishery appear below.

TRIAL BALANCES, DECEMBER 31, 1987

ACCOUNT	UNADJUSTED DR	UNADJUSTED CR	ADJUSTED DR	ADJUSTED CR
Cash.............................	$ 30,000		$ 30,000	
Accounts receivable	29,000		29,000	
Allowance for uncollectible accounts........		$ 3,600		$ 4,000
Investments	36,000		36,000	
Inventory	115,000		50,000	
Interest receivable.............			3,600	
Prepaid insurance	6,400		3,000	
Supplies.....................	12,000		1,200	
Plant and equipment...........	94,000		94,000	
Accumulated depreciation		26,000		36,000
Accounts payable		50,000		50,000
Unearned rent revenue				20,000
Salaries payable				10,500
M. Hattan, capital		58,800		58,800
Sales		200,000		200,000
Rent revenue..................		56,000		36,000
Interest revenue				3,600
Purchases....................	50,000			
Supplies expense			10,800	
Cost of goods sold			115,000	
Insurance expense.............			3,400	
Salaries expense	22,000		32,500	
Uncollectible accounts expense			400	
Depreciation expense			10,000	
	$394,400	$394,400	$418,900	$418,900

THE ACCOUNTING PROCESS: A REVIEW

REQUIRED

1. Prepare the adjusting entries at December 31, 1987.

2. Assuming that Manhattan uses reversing entries, which of the entries in part 1 should be reversed?

E3-8. ADJUSTING, CLOSING, AND REVERSING ENTRIES Armstrong Company's interest expense account on June 30, 1987, the close of its fiscal year, appeared as follows:

Interest expense	
October 31, 1986	6,300
December 21, 1986	12,000
March 5, 1987	15,000
May 7, 1987	7,700

Interest expense of $4,000 has accrued, but is unrecorded, at June 30, 1987.

REQUIRED

1. Set up the following T-accounts: interest expense, interest payable, and income summary.

2. Record any adjusting entries directly in the T-accounts.

3. Close all appropriate accounts (except income summary).

4. Reverse the June 30, 1987, adjusting entry.

5. What is the nature of the interest expense account immediately after the reversing entry has been made?

6. Interest payments of $8,500 were made on July 10, 1987. Record this transaction.

7. What portion of the $8,500 interest payment made on July 10, 1987, represents interest expense thus far for July 1987?

E3-9. COST OF GOODS SOLD RELATIONSHIPS For each of the situations below, determine the missing amounts.

	BEGINNING INVENTORY	ENDING INVENTORY	PURCHASES	PURCHASE RETURNS	COST OF GOODS SOLD
1.	$12,000	$14,000	$36,000	$7,000	?
2.	10,000	?	61,000	3,000	$42,000
3.	12,000	–0–	?	–0–	40,000
4.	?	4,000	40,000	5,000	41,000

E3-10. CLOSING ENTRIES From the data below, prepare the appropriate closing entries.

Sales	$150,000
Merchandise inventory, 1/1/87	30,000
Sales discounts	5,000
Other expenses	20,000
Dividends	10,000
Purchases	120,000
Merchandise inventory, 12/31/87	40,000
Purchase returns	8,000
Stockholders' equity	180,000
Other revenue	9,000

E3-11. INCOME STATEMENT Refer to the data in Exercise 3–10.

REQUIRED

Prepare an income statement for the year ending December 31, 1987.

E3-12. PREPARATION OF A WORKSHEET   An unadjusted trial balance at January 31, 1987, for the Homer Marcus Department Store is as follows:

Cash	$ 12,000	
Accounts receivable	36,000	
Allowance for uncollectible accounts		$ 4,800
Supplies	4,500	
Other prepaid expenses	6,000	
Inventory, 1/31/86	94,000	
Fixtures and equipment	50,000	
Accumulated depreciation		10,000
Accounts payable		25,000
Notes payable		8,000
H. Marcus, capital		198,500
Sales		270,000
Sales returns	20,000	
Purchases	160,000	
Purchase returns		3,200
Rent expense	60,000	
Salaries expense	50,000	
Advertising expense	20,000	
Other expenses	7,000	
Total	$519,500	$519,500

Information for adjustments for the fiscal year ending January 31, 1987, is as follows:

a) Estimated uncollectible accounts expense: 1/2 of 1 percent of net sales.

b) Supplies on hand at January 31, 1987, $600.

c) Included in other prepaid expenses is prepaid insurance, of which $560 expired during the year ending January 31, 1987.

d) Ending inventory on January 31, 1987, $80,000.

e) Fixtures and equipment are depreciated at the rate of 5 percent per year.

f) Interest accrued on notes payable, $400 (include in other expenses).

g) H. Marcus pays $36,000 in rent on October 1 of each year, which represents the rent for the next twelve months.

h) Sales salaries accrued on January 31, 1987, $3,200.

i) On January 27, 1987, H. Marcus paid Byrd Advertising $10,000 in connection with a white-sale promotion to be conducted during February 1987.

REQUIRED

Prepare a 10-column worksheet for Homer Marcus Department Store.

E3-13. PREPARING FINANCIAL STATEMENTS FROM WORKSHEET DATA   Refer to the worksheet that was prepared in Exercise 3-12.

REQUIRED

Prepare the income statement and balance sheet for Homer Marcus Department Store for the year ending January 31, 1987.

E3-14. PREPARING CLOSING AND REVERSING ENTRIES FROM WORKSHEET DATA   Refer to the worksheet that was prepared in Exercise 3-12.

REQUIRED

1. Prepare the closing entries for Homer Marcus Department Store.

2. Assuming that Homer Marcus desires to make reversing entries to simplify the accounting procedures in the following year, indicate by letter which of the adjusting entries should be reversed as of February 1, 1987.

E3-15. COST OF GOODS SOLD; ADJUSTING AND CLOSING ENTRIES The following data relate to the cost of goods sold for Dupree's Sporting Goods:

Beginning inventory	$ 7,000
Transportation in	500
Purchases	12,500
Purchase returns	750
Purchase discounts	250
Ending inventory	9,000

REQUIRED

1. Set up T-accounts for the above items (use only one T-account for inventory).

2. Assuming that the cost of goods sold is determined and recorded through the use of adjusting entries, transfer the above data to a cost of goods sold T-account.

3. Assuming that the T-accounts in part 1 are reduced to zero in the closing step of the accounting process, prepare general journal entries to close the merchandising transactions to income summary.

4. Verify that the balance in the cost of goods sold account in part 2 equals the balance in the income summary account in part 3.

* E3-16. SPECIAL JOURNALS A business uses the following special journals: cash receipts (CR), cash disbursements (CD), single-column sales (S), single-column purchases (P), and general journal (GJ). Indicate, by inserting CR, CD, S, P, or GJ in the space provided, in which journal each of the following transactions would be recorded.

_____ **a)** Purchase of office equipment for cash

_____ **b)** Payment to a creditor for merchandise previously purchased on account

_____ **c)** Return of a cash sale (cash was refunded)

_____ **d)** Purchase of merchandise on credit

_____ **e)** Sale of merchandise on credit

_____ **f)** Adjusting entries

_____ **g)** Sale of office equipment on credit

_____ **h)** Return on a credit purchase

_____ **i)** Return of a credit sale

_____ **j)** Purchase of office supplies on credit

_____ **k)** Customer collections

_____ **l)** Payment of monthly salaries

_____ **m)** Cash sales

_____ **n)** Closing entries

_____ **o)** Purchase of land by issuance of common stock

PROBLEMS

Problems marked with an asterisk (*) refer to Appendix 3–1.

P3-1. JOURNAL ENTRIES, POSTING, TRIAL BALANCE The following transactions occurred for the Von Erich Music Corporation during its first year of operations:

a) Sold 10,000 shares of $5 par common stock for $12 per share.

b) Purchased a building at a cost of $60,000. Paid $20,000 down with the balance due in 120 days.

c) Purchased record display equipment for $25,000 cash.

d) Purchases on account, $100,000. The periodic inventory system is used.

e) Sales: on account, $60,000; for cash, $80,000.

f) Paid clerical salaries totaling $18,000.

g) Collected $45,000 from credit customers.

h) Paid the balance due on the record display equipment.

i) Paid $25,000 on accounts payable.

j) Borrowed $30,000 by issuing a short-term note.

REQUIRED

1. Record the above transactions in general journal form.

2. Set up T-accounts for the necessary accounts. Post the journal entries to the T-accounts.

3. Prepare an unadjusted trial balance.

P3-2. JOURNAL ENTRIES; ACCOUNTING CYCLE The May 31, 1987, postclosing trial balance for Mitchell Wholesale Grocery appeared as follows:

Cash...	$ 2,500	
Accounts receivable	12,000	
Allowance for uncollectible accounts		$ 2,400
Dividends receivable	150	
Supplies..	4,000	
Inventories......................................	29,500	
Investment in common stock (noncurrent)	5,000	
Buildings and equipment	50,000	
Accumulated depreciation		15,000
Accounts payable		3,300
Salaries payable		600
Interest payable..................................		250
15% notes payable		20,000
Common stock		40,000
Retained earnings		21,600
Total	$103,150	$103,150

The following transactions and other economic events took place during June 1987 on the dates indicated:

1   Made reversing entries for dividends receivable, supplies, salaries payable, and interest payable.

2   Paid the monthly interest on the notes payable, $250 ($20,000 × .15 × 1/12).

3   Purchased groceries on account at a cost of $17,500 (assume a periodic inventory system).

6   Grocery sales: on account, $13,500; for cash, $8,000.

8   Paid salaries totaling $2,400.

9   Cash collections from customers, $11,600.

10   Purchased groceries for cash at a cost of $13,000.

12   Wrote off a customer's account of $300 as uncollectible.

16   Grocery sales: on account, $6,500; for cash, $10,000.

19   Made payment on accounts payable of $18,000. Received a 2% purchases discount.

21   One customer returned $150 in groceries that were purchased on account.

24   Paid sales salaries totaling $3,600.

25   Purchased groceries on account at a cost of $5,400.

29   Grocery sales: on account, $12,000; for cash, $5,400.

30   Received dividends on investments, $150.

30   Cash collections from customers, $8,000.

30   Declared a cash dividend of $5,000 to be paid in July.

REQUIRED

1. Open T-accounts and enter the May 31 postclosing trial balance information in the various T-accounts.

2. Record the June transactions in general journal form.

3. Post the journal entries in part 2 to the appropriate T-accounts.

4. Prepare the end-of-June adjusting entries in journal form. Information for adjustments:
  a) Uncollectible accounts expense, 1 percent of net credit sales.
  b) Supplies used, $2,800.
  c) Depreciation expense, $650.
  d) Salaries accrued, end of June, $740.
  e) Interest accrued on notes payable, $250.

5. Post the adjusting entries to the ledger accounts.

6. Prepare the income statement and balance sheet for the month of June. The ending inventory was $39,000.

P3-3.   CLOSING ENTRIES   Refer to the data in Problem 3-2. Prepare the journal entries to close the nominal accounts. Close the purchases accounts and the inventory accounts directly to income summary.

P3-4.   ADJUSTING ENTRIES   Adjustment data for the Banner Corporation for the year ending December 31, 1987, are as follows:
  a) Banner holds a $10,000 note receivable dated April 1, 1987. The note is a one-year note with interest payable at 12 percent.
  b) During 1987 Banner purchased supplies at a cost of $35,000. The transactions were originally recorded as expenses. On December 31, 1987, there were supplies on hand costing $21,000.
  c) Banner depreciates its assets on a straight-line basis and records one-half of a year's depreciation on acquisitions made during the year. The plant and equipment account appears as follows:

DATE OF ACQUISITION	ITEM	USEFUL LIFE	SALVAGE	COST
4/1/83	Building	30	$5,000	$50,000
12/10/86	Machinery	10	–0–	24,000
6/3/87	Equipment	4	3,000	33,000

  d) Banner leases the land on which its plant and equipment are located. At the beginning of 1987, Banner made a lease payment covering 1987 and 1988. The annual lease payments are $10,000 and were debited to rent expense.
  e) In 1987 Banner received $38,000 in advance fees for consulting to be performed over the next two years. Banner accounted for the receipt as consulting revenue earned, but only $20,000 had been earned at the end of 1987.
  f) In 1982 Banner issued 10-year, $100,000, 10 percent bonds payable at par. Interest is payable each March 1 and September 1.
  g) Banner calculates uncollectible accounts expense as 3 percent of net credit sales. During 1987 sales were $300,000, of which 40 percent were credit sales. Credit sale returns totaled $5,000.
  h) At the end of 1987, Banner had accrued salaries payable of $18,000.
  i) On December 1, 1986, Banner purchased a three-year fire insurance policy at a cost of $10,800. The acquisition was recorded in the prepaid insurance account.

j) On December 31, 1987, Banner had warranty service contracts outstanding on 2,000 soft drink machines that it sold to customers during 1987. Banner estimated that the cost of servicing the machines would average $3 per machine during the warranty period. During 1984, warranty costs incurred were recorded as follows:

Warranty expense 1,470
Cash   1,470

REQUIRED

Prepare adjusting entries for the above data.

P3-5.   ADJUSTING ENTRIES   Information for making the year-end adjusting entries for the Trishway Skating Rink appears below.

a) On March 1, 1987, Trishway purchased a three-year liability insurance policy at a cost of $4,800. Trishway's accounting policy is to record prepaid insurance transactions as expenses, to make appropriate year-end adjusting entries, and to reverse the adjustments at the beginning of the following year.

b) On November 30, 1987, Trishway renewed the annual lease on the skating rink by making a $6,000 lease payment, which was recorded as prepaid rent.

c) On July 1, 1986, Trishway purchased 10, $1,000 bonds of the local city at a cost of $10,000 plus accrued interest from May 1. The stated annual interest rate on the bonds is 12 percent, payable quarterly on May 1, August 1, November 1, and February 1.

d) Trishway's depreciable assets have a cost of $25,000 and are being depreciated on a straight-line basis with an estimated 20-year useful life and estimated salvage value of $3,000.

e) At the end of 1987, Trishway's concession and skating revenue account had a credit balance of $320,000. During 1987, Trishway received $43,000 in advances for private skating parties; $10,000 of the proceeds was credited to unearned skating revenue, and the remainder was credited to concession and skating revenue. At the end of 1987, advances of $16,000 were still unearned, since these parties had not been held.

f) Salary transactions during 1987 appear as follows:

Salaries payable

Salary payments in January 1987	9,400	Beginning of 1987	$7,500

Salaries expense

Salary payments February 1 through December 26	$106,000		

Salaries of $3,200 have accrued from December 26 to the end of the year.

g) The following information concerning advertising accounts was taken from Trishway's ledger:

BALANCE

Advertising expense (January 1, 1987) . . . . $3,600 credit
Prepaid advertising (January 1, 1987) . . . . $2,900 debit

Total disbursements made for advertising in 1987 were $25,000 and were debited to advertising expense. The correct amount of advertising expense for 1987 is $22,500.

h) On the unadjusted trial balance, a suspense account with a debit balance of $32,000 was composed of the following:

Withdrawals by H. Trishway, owner $19,000
Miscellaneous postage expense   4,000
Contributions to YMCA Swim Fund   6,000
Cost of having skating rink cleaned and fumigated 15,000
Proceeds from sale of fully depreciated skates and jukebox
    with an original cost of $30,000 . . . . (12,000)
                                                                                                          $32,000

i) At the beginning of 1987 the skate supplies account had a debit balance of $2,800. Purchases of supplies during 1987 were debited to the supplies account and totaled $11,300. Supplies on hand at the end of 1987 totaled $5,000.

j) On December 28, 1987, Trishway received a bill for $3,000 from Stronglatch Security, Inc., for night security services rendered during December. This transaction has not been recorded.

REQUIRED

Prepare the necessary December 31, 1987, adjusting entries from the above information.

P3-6. JOURNAL ENTRIES; FINANCIAL STATEMENTS   The January 1, 1987, balance sheet and combined statement of income and retained earnings for the year ending December 31, 1987, and additional information for the Cowboy Cable Communications Corporation are shown below.

Cowboy Cable Communications Corporation
BALANCE SHEET
AS OF JANUARY 1, 1987

ASSETS		LIABILITIES AND STOCKHOLDERS' EQUITY	
Cash	$121,000	Accounts payable	$164,000
Receivables (net of allowance for uncollectible accounts)	88,000	Salaries payable	8,000
		Bonds payable (at par)	200,000
Prepaid expenses	46,000	Income taxes payable	130,000
Inventory of communication supplies	146,000	Common stock	150,000
Plant and equipment	340,000	Contributed capital in excess of par	50,000
Accumulated depreciation	(100,000)	Retained earnings	56,000
Land	75,000		
Long-term investments	42,000		
	$758,000		$758,000

Cowboy Cable Communications Corporation
STATEMENT OF INCOME AND RETAINED EARNINGS
FOR THE YEAR ENDED DECEMBER 31, 1987

Revenues and gains	
Cable service revenues	$640,000
Investment and dividend revenues	8,400
Gain on sale of land	20,000
Expenses	
Communication supplies expense	(375,000)
Depreciation expense	(68,000)
Expiration of prepaid expenses	(46,000)
Salaries expense	(190,000)
Uncollectible accounts expense	(10,000)
Interest expense	(20,000)
Income tax expense (credit)	30,000
Net loss	$ (10,600)
Retained earnings, January 1, 1987	56,000
Cash dividends	(24,000)
Retained earnings, December 31, 1987	$ 21,400

a) All cable revenues are initially recorded on account.

b) The land that was sold had a cost of $30,000.

c) Of the interest and dividend revenues, $6,000 were end-of-year accruals.

d) Because of the net loss before taxes, the company received a $30,000 tax credit against previous years' taxes. As a result, the company paid the beginning tax liability less the $30,000 credit.

e) Customers' accounts aggregating $17,500 were written off as uncollectible.

f) Collections on accounts receivable, $625,000.

g) Purchases of communications supplies on account totaled $400,000.

h) The ending accounts payable balance was $225,000.

i) Accrued salaries payable, December 31, 1987, $18,000.

j) There was no interest payable at the end of 1987.

REQUIRED

1. Prepare, in summary form, journal entries to record CCCC's transactions for 1987.

2. Prepare CCCC's balance sheet on December 31, 1987.

P3-7. THE ACCOUNTING CYCLE   Milton's Campus Clothing Store was organized on September 1, 1987. Below are the summary transactions for the store's first two months of operations:

September

a) Milton invested $120,000 cash and a building and land in the business. The building had a fair market value of $60,000, and the fair market value of the land was $20,000.

b) The business acquired the clothing inventory of Dona Company for $75,000. Dona was going out of business. Assume Milton uses the periodic inventory method.

c) Supplies were purchased for cash at a cost of $6,000.

d) Clothing purchases on account, $45,000.

e) Clothing sales for cash, $36,000; on account, $40,000.

f) Salary expenses paid in cash, $26,000.

g) Accounts receivable collections, $35,000.

h) Payments on accounts payable, $28,000.

i) Other expenses paid in cash, $5,600.

j) Owner withdrawals of cash, $3,500.

k) End-of-month adjustment data:

Depreciation	$ 1,000
Uncollectible accounts expense	250
Supplies used	1,200
Ending inventory	90,000
Accrued salaries	1,200

October

a) Purchases of clothing on account, $65,000.

b) Supplies purchased for cash, $3,000.

c) Write-off of customer accounts, $100.

d) Clothing sales for cash, $50,000; on account, $72,000.

e) Salaries paid in cash, $31,000.

f) Accounts receivable collections, $48,000.

g) Payments on accounts payable, $70,000.

h) Milton invested additional cash of $35,000 in the business.

i) Other expenses paid in cash, $6,000.

j) End-of-month adjustment data:

Depreciation	$ 1,000
Uncollectible accounts expense	600
Supplies used	6,000
Ending inventory	80,000

REQUIRED

1. Record the September transactions in general journal form and post the transactions to the necessary T-accounts.

2. Prepare an 8-column worksheet at September 30 using the following format:

UNADJUSTED TRIAL BALANCE		ADJUSTMENTS		INCOME STATEMENT		BALANCE SHEET	
DR	CR	DR	CR	DR	CR	DR	CR

3. Post the adjusting entries from the worksheet directly to the T-accounts.

4. Prepare closing entries for September and post to the T-accounts.

5. Record the October transactions in general journal form and post the transactions to the necessary T-accounts. Milton does not make reversing entries.

6. Record the adjusting entries at October 31 in general journal form and post to the T-accounts.

7. Prepare the income statement for October and the balance sheet at the end of October.

P3-8.   PREPARATION OF A 12-COLUMN WORKSHEET   Unadjusted trial balance data and adjustment information for the Jennings Corporation for the year ended December 31, 1987, appear below.
Unadjusted trial balance data:

Cash	$ 4,000
Accounts receivable (net of allowance)	5,200
Supplies	2,900
Investments	3,000
Prepaid insurance	2,500
Inventory	10,000
Plant and equipment (net of accumulated depreciation)	15,000
Accounts payable	6,000
Notes payable	3,000
Common stock	20,000
Retained earnings	15,000
Dividends declared	2,000
Interest revenue	500
Sales	60,300
Sales returns	4,000
Purchases	44,000
Salaries expense	9,000
Insurance expense	3,000
Interest expense	200

Adjustment information:

Uncollectible accounts expense	$ 300
Depreciation expense	1,500
Supplies on hand	900
Insurance expense for the period	2,400
Accrued interest revenue	200
Ending inventory	23,000
Accrued salaries payable	400
Accrued interest payable	100
Unearned revenue (offsetting credit to cash was recorded in the sales account)	280
Accrued property taxes	150
Income tax expense equals 30% of income before taxes.	

REQUIRED

Prepare a 12-column worksheet similar to the worksheet illustrated in Exhibit 3–22.

P3-9. WORKSHEET PREPARATION On the worksheet below, certain data are missing.

	TRIAL BALANCE		ADJUST-MENTS		INCOME STATEMENT		BALANCE SHEET	
	DR	CR	DR	CR	DR	CR	DR	CR
Cash..................	45						45	
Receivables	70		25				95	
Prepaid insurance				5			10	
Plant and equipment......	80						80	
Accumulated depreciation .		20						
Accounts payable		40						40
Unearned revenue........			20					5
Salaries payable		0						
Common stock		20						
Contributed capital in excess of par..........		20						
Retained earnings		45						
Revenues..............		100						
Salaries expense			15		40			
Depreciation expense	0				10			
Insurance expense........								
Other expenses	35				35			
Total								
Net income (loss)								
Total								

REQUIRED

Determine the missing data and complete the worksheet.

P3-10. RECORDING TRANSACTIONS; LEDGERS You have been given the following trial balances of the Sandmeyer Company. The trial balance as of December 31, 1987, was taken on a gross basis; that is, the totals of the debits and of the credits in each of the ledger accounts, including any balance from the postclosing trial balance as of June 30, 1987, rather than the final balance, have been included. You are advised that the company records disbursements for expense items through liability accounts before making payment.

The books are not available. The trial balance is out of balance by $270, which is shown as "unlocated difference." You are told that cash in bank of $28,044 has been verified.

The Sandmeyer Company

TRIAL BALANCES

ACCOUNT	JUNE 30, 1987		DECEMBER 31, 1987	
Cash in bank..............	$ 21,849		$ 275,016	$ 246,972
Investments	30,500		40,712	5,000
Accounts receivable	47,420		301,425	248,979
Merchandise inventory	55,542		208,856	153,495
Office furniture and fixtures ..	8,663		11,164	635
Accumulated depreciation		$ 4,967	176	5,940
Note payable..............		30,000	10,000	30,000
Accounts payable		15,879	211,658	233,986
Income taxes payable		7,350	5,658	11,050
Common stock		50,000		50,000
Retained earnings		55,778	10,000	55,778
Sales			481	254,005

ACCOUNT	JUNE 30, 1987		DECEMBER 31, 1987	
Cost of goods sold			151,914	
Salaries expense			15,500	
Other administrative expense . .			21,567	
Selling expense			25,348	
Uncollectible accounts expense			665	
Writedown of obsolete merchandise			1,025	
Gain on sale of investment . . .				168
Loss on sale of fixtures			23	
Interest expense			850	
Income tax expense			3,700	
Unlocated difference			270	
	$163,974	$163,974	$1,296,008	$1,296,008

REQUIRED

Reconstruct the ledger accounts as they probably appear by recording the transactions for the period in journal form and posting to the ledger accounts. You need not prepare financial statements, but you should state where you think the error occurred in the books and give reasons to support your conclusion.

(AICPA, adapted)

P3-11. RECORDING TRANSACTIONS; FINANCIAL STATEMENTS   The Computer Shop (a sole proprietorship) does not have complete records on a double-entry basis. From your investigation of its records, however, you have established the information shown below.

a) The assets and liabilities as of December 31, 1986, were:

	DR	CR
Cash	$ 5,175	
Accounts receivable	10,556	
Allowance, uncollectible accounts		$ 740
Fixtures	3,130	
Accumulated depreciation		1,110
Prepaid insurance	158	
Supplies	79	
Accounts payable		4,244
Miscellaneous payables		206
Taxes payable		202
Merchandise inventory	19,243	
Notes payable		5,000
Roberts, capital		26,839

b) A summary of The Computer Shop's transactions for 1987 as recorded in the checkbook shows:

Deposits for the year (including the redeposit of $304 of checks charged back by the bank)	$83,187
Checks written during the year	84,070
Customers' checks charged back by the bank	304
Bank service charges	22

c) The following information is available as to accounts payable:

Purchases of merchandise on account during year	$57,789
Purchase returns	1,418
Payments on account by check	55,461

d) Information as to accounts receivable shows the following:

Accounts written off	$ 812
Accounts collected	43,083
Balance of accounts, December 31, 1987 (of this balance, $700 is estimated to be uncollectible)	11,921

e) Checks written during the year include checks for the following items:

Salaries	$10,988
Rent	3,600
Heat, lights, telephone	394
Supplies	280
Insurance	341
Taxes and licenses	1,017
Withdrawals by Roberts	6,140
Miscellaneous expense	769
Merchandise purchases	2,080
Notes payable	3,000
	$28,609

f) Merchandise inventory as of December 31, 1987, was $17,807. Prepaid insurance amounted to $122 and supplies on hand totaled $105 as of December 31, 1987. Accrued taxes payable were $216, and miscellaneous accrued expenses were $73 at the year's end.

g) Cash sales for the year are assumed to account for all cash received other than that collected on accounts. Fixtures are to be depreciated at the rate of 10 percent per year.

REQUIRED

Using the above data, prepare an income statement for 1987 and a balance sheet as of December 31, 1987. Before preparing these statements, you may find it useful to prepare journal entries for the information in parts *b* through *g* above.

(AICPA, adapted)

* P3-12. SPECIAL JOURNALS AND SUBSIDIARY LEDGERS   The following information shows the accounts receivable of the Mary Day Company:

ACCOUNTS RECEIVABLE (CONTROL)

DEBITS

Balance	$ 58,000
Sales journal	130,000

CREDITS

Cash receipts journal	$50,000
General journal	2,300
General journal	1,400

ACCOUNTS RECEIVABLE SUBSIDIARY LEDGER

	DEBIT	CREDIT	BALANCE
P. Presley:			
Balance			$20,000
Sales	$60,000		80,000
General journal		$ 3,200	76,800
Cash receipts journal		50,000	26,800
K. Rodgers:			
Balance			13,000
Sales journal	30,000		43,000
General journal		1,400	41,600
R. Leftwich:			
Balance			25,000
Sales journal	40,000		65,000
Cash receipts journal		20,000	45,000

REQUIRED

Determine whether the controlling account agrees with the subsidiary ledger. Also determine the causes of any lack of agreement (explain fully, showing all computations).

* P3-13. SPECIAL JOURNALS AND SUBSIDIARY LEDGERS   Heartache Company recorded some transactions in the general and special journals shown below.

GENERAL JOURNAL				PURCHASES JOURNAL	
Mar 11	Accts pay—Y	1,000		Mar 5 X	6,000
	Pur returns		1,000	10 Y	4,000
14	Office supplies	600		15 Z	2,000
	Accts pay—W		600		

CASH DISBURSEMENTS JOURNAL

		MISCEL-LANEOUS	ACCOUNTS PAYABLE	PURCHASE DISCOUNTS	CASH
Mar 5	Purchases	1,000			1,000
10	X (in full settlement)				5,880
22	Y (in full settlement)		3,000		
27	Transportation in (on purchase from X)				200

REQUIRED

1. Set up T-accounts for the following general ledger and subsidiary ledger accounts. General ledger: Purchases, transportation in, cash, purchase discounts, purchase returns, office supplies, and accounts payable. Accounts payable subsidiary ledger: Mr. *W*, Mr. *X*, Mr. *Y*, and Ms. *Z*.

2. Post the general journal entries.

3. Post all appropriate data from the purchases journal.

4. Complete the missing numbers in the cash disbursements journal, then post all appropriate data.

*P3-14. SPECIAL JOURNALS Klaus Garage entered into the following transactions for the month of December 1987:

1   Revenue from car repairs, $700 (on account).

3   Purchased supplies on account, $300.

9   Purchased a winch (equipment) from Zee Foundry on credit, $1,200.

10   Cash revenue from car repairs, $950.

16   Paid salaries for first half of December, $600.

19   Customer collections, $350.

21   Cash revenue from car repairs, $1,100.

21   Ran an advertisement wishing the general public "Season's Greetings." Paid the newspaper $20.

22   Returned defective supplies of $50 purchased on December 3, and paid the balance due.

24   Paid rent on the garage for January 1985, $200.

27   Revenue from toy repairs, $150 (on account).

29   Customer collections, $600.

31   Paid salaries for remainder of December, $600.

31   S. Klaus withdrew $100 in cash for personal use.

The garage uses special journals in which entries are made on the following pages as of November 30, 1987:

JOURNAL	PAGE
Sales	3
Purchases (with columns headed Supplies and Equipment)	6
Cash disbursements	12
Cash receipts	16
General	4

The following ledger accounts and balances are appropriate:

ACCOUNT	BALANCE, NOVEMBER 30	ACCOUNT NUMBER
Cash	$ 3,600	100
Customer receivables	1,000	101
Supplies	900	102
Equipment	13,000	103
Prepaid rent	200	104
Accounts payable	4,700	201
S. Klaus, capital	14,000	300
Revenues	–0–	400
Supplies expense	–0–	510
Advertising expense	–0–	511
Salaries expense	–0–	512

REQUIRED

1. Open ledger accounts in T-account form and enter the November 30, 1987, balances.

2. Record the December transactions in the appropriate journals. (You may construct your journals in a manner similar to those illustrated in the chapter.)

3. Post the journal entries to the appropriate ledger accounts using posting references.

4. Prepare an unadjusted trial balance from the ledger account balances after the posting in part 3.

P3-15. TRANSACTION ANALYSIS; FINANCIAL STATEMENTS Morrow Wholesale has kept limited records and has never had an audit until 1987. As the senior auditor in charge of the audit, you have been presented with the following information:

a) Morrow was incorporated in 1982 and sold 11,000 shares of its $10 par common stock for $25 per share. There have been no other common stock transactions.

b) Cash balance in checkbook, December 31, 1986 . . . . $24,000

Deposits
Cash sales	$250,000
Proceeds of $5,000 note issued on July 1 and	
bearing interest at 12%, payable annually	5,000
Customer collections	146,000
Proceeds on sale of fully depreciated	
equipment (original cost, $20,000)	5,000
Total deposits	$406,000

Checks written
Purchases of merchandise	$120,000
Payments to creditors	60,000
Salaries	10,000
Advertising (to be run in 1988)	10,000
Miscellaneous expenses	5,500
Total checks written	$205,500

c) Morrow had no outstanding payables at the beginning of 1987 but owes creditors $36,000 for unpaid purchases on December 31, 1987.

d) In 1987 Morrow began selling on a cash-only basis. Receivables at the beginning of 1987 totaled $155,000. The uncollected receivables were written off as miscellaneous expenses in 1987.

e) Morrow's cost of goods sold is 80 percent of sales. The inventory at the beginning of 1987 was $80,000.

f) At the beginning of 1987, equipment with a cost and accumulated depreciation of $80,000 and $20,000, respectively, was on hand. All equipment is depreciated on a straight-line basis over 10 years with no estimated salvage value. The sale of equipment was made on December 30, 1987.

g) Retained earnings at the beginning of 1987 totaled $63,000. During the fourth quarter of 1987, a cash dividend of $10,000 was declared and is to be paid in January 1988.

h) Morrow's only other asset at the beginning of 1987 was an investment in Honeydew Common Stock. During 1987 this stock was exchanged for land and a gain of $4,000 was recognized.

i) The income tax rate is 35 percent.

j) At the end of 1987, sales salaries of $2,000 have accrued but have not been paid.

REQUIRED

Prepare an income statement for the year ended December 31, 1987, and a balance sheet at December 31, 1987, for Morrow Wholesale.

4 THE INCOME STATEMENT AND STATEMENT OF RETAINED EARNINGS

Financial statements are the end product of the accounting process. The income statement reports the net income or net loss from operating activities and forms the basis of investment and other decisions. For example, net income per share, called earnings per share, is used extensively in security investment decision making. Because of the complexities surrounding the many events and transactions that affect a firm, and because of the information needs of financial statement users, constructing the income statement is much more difficult than it was a few years ago.

Suppose that a department store that is short of cash sells its building for more than the book value. The department store then signs a long-term lease with the purchaser to rent the building for the remainder of its useful life. The present value of the rental payments provided for in the lease equals the selling price of the building. Does this transaction give rise to a gain for the department store? In addition to income measurement, income statement presentation also can be difficult. For example, financial analysts are interested not only in the "bottom line" net income number, but also in the many elements or components of net income. The only way to evaluate a firm's performance properly and to assess and predict its future cash flows is to analyze these components.

Two basic income statement issues: measurement issue and format issue.

Thus the two basic issues that confront the producers of an income statement are (1) determination of net income—the *measurement issue*—and (2) reporting of income information—the *format issue*.

In this chapter we shall briefly review the theory underlying the measurement of accounting income. The major portion of the chapter, however, will be devoted to an analysis of the way income information is reported—the format issue. We shall identify and discuss the significant components of income and present alternative reporting format possibilities. Additional income disclosures, such as earnings per share, interim reporting, and segment reporting, also are presented. The chapter concludes with an examination of the statement of retained earnings, which explains the change in retained earnings from the beginning to the end of the accounting period.

We have excerpted many of the illustrations of statement presentations in this and other chapters from actual financial statements. You can gain a better perspective, however, by looking at such presentations within the context of the total set of financial statements. Thus the financial statements, notes, and auditor's report from the 1985 annual report of The Coca-Cola Company are reproduced in their entirety in Appendix 5–1. You may wish to scan the income statement and related notes at this point. Also, you may find it helpful to refer to these statements as we discuss presentations related to various items in this chapter and throughout the book.

INCOME MEASUREMENT

Income measurement requires both a capital maintenance concept and the measurement of an attribute.

One of the objectives of financial accounting and reporting is to provide information regarding the effects of transactions, events, and circumstances related to a firm's earnings activities that change its resources and claims to those resources. This information appears in the income statement and related notes and supplementary information. As we pointed out in Chapter 2, income determination or measurement requires the measurement of a particular asset and liability attribute, in conjunction with a particular capital maintenance concept. Under the modified historical cost system comprising GAAP, historical cost is the primary attribute measured, although other attributes of many assets and liabilities also are measured. The predominant capital maintenance concept underlying the determination of income in the modified historical cost accounting system is the maintenance of original invested dollars (nominal dollars). That is, an entity earns income when it generates revenues in excess of the historical cost of resources consumed in producing the revenue. Further, the accrual accounting principles of realization and matching govern the timing of recognition of changes in the amounts of resources and obligations as a result of the entity's earnings activities. In summary, income determination is an attempt to match effort and accomplishment; revenues are the accomplishments and expenses are the efforts expended in attaining revenues.

Net income or net loss is the change in equity or net assets resulting from transactions and other economic events related to an entity's primary and peripheral operating activities. Net income equals revenues minus expenses plus gains minus losses. Two approaches may be used to calculate net income, both based on these definitions of income.

Under the **net assets approach,** the net assets of an entity are compared at two points in time. Assuming no investments or withdrawals of assets by owners during the period, an increase in net assets represents net income; a decrease in net assets represents a net loss.

Assume that a company's net assets were as follows at the beginning and end of 1987.

Net assets, January 1, 1987. . . . . $50,000
Net assets, December 31, 1987 . . . . $55,000

Since no assets were invested or withdrawn by the owners during the period, the increase in net assets of $5,000 is the net income for the period.

Now assume instead that the owners invested assets of $2,000 during 1987 and withdrew assets of $5,000 during 1987. Net income can be computed as follows:

Ending net assets $55,000
Add: Asset withdrawals by owners 5,000
Deduct: Asset investments by owners . . . . (2,000)
Ending net assets excluding effect
   of capital transactions $58,000
Deduct: Beginning net assets . . . . (50,000)
Net income . . . . $ 8,000

Transactions with owners affect net assets but they are not related to the earnings activities of the firm. Thus, owners' withdrawals must be added back and owners' investments must be deducted to determine accounting income under the net assets approach.

A significant weakness of the net assets approach is that no information is provided to explain why net income was $8,000. In order to provide this information, accountants have adopted a **transactions approach** to measuring income, and this approach underlies the income statement.

The transactions approach reports revenues and expenses related to the primary earning activities of an entity and gains and losses from peripheral activities within the accounting period. For example, the net income of $8,000 could be measured by listing the revenues, expenses, gains, and losses for the period (amounts assumed):

> *The transactions approach is used to report income information.*

Revenues	$180,000
Expenses	(160,000)
Gains	10,000
Losses	(22,000)
Net income	$ 8,000

To summarize, although it is feasible to determine net income by either the net assets approach or the transactions approach, the transactions approach is used in practice to prepare the income statement. The transactions approach discloses the component transactions and events that give rise to net income or net loss. Disclosure of these components allows users to evaluate a company's performance better and thus provides better information for decision making.

REPORTING INCOME INFORMATION

Although accountants use a transactions approach to measure income and to construct the income statement, several reporting issues still remain:

Should the income statement distinguish between recurring and nonrecurring income items?

How much detail should be presented on the income statement?

Would some information be better presented in the notes to the income statement?

In this section we shall discuss how information must be reported on the income statement under generally accepted accounting principles. After discussing these reporting requirements, we shall examine briefly some unresolved reporting issues.

CURRENT OPERATING PERFORMANCE VERSUS ALL-INCLUSIVE INCOME STATEMENTS

The vast majority of a firm's transactions relate to its current or primary operating activities. However, certain types of gains and losses and other economic events that affect income are not related to current operations or are ambiguous in their relationship to operations. For example, a firm may dispose of a major product line, or sell a company it owns, or incur an unusual loss as a result of a catastrophe, such as a storm. These events have significantly different cash flow implications from the firm's ongoing earnings activities. For some time, controversy existed over how firms should report the income effect of events and transactions that were not directly related to current operating activities. Thus historically, two approaches to presenting income information evolved—the current operating performance approach and the all-inclusive approach.

Current Operating Performance Approach

An income statement prepared under the **current operating performance approach** would include only regularly recurring operating revenues and expenses. Unusual or nonrecurring items would be reported directly in the statement of retained earnings. Accountants who support the current operating performance approach argue that an earnings figure should be useful for predicting future earnings, and that the inclusion of irregular, unusual, or nonrecurring gains and losses may cause users to draw misleading conclusions. They argue further that users cannot adequately distinguish between recurring and nonrecurring items, and that statement preparers are in a better position to make this distinction. Finally, they maintain that, even if nonrecurring items are clearly identified in arriving at net income, users may focus solely on income and fail to study its components. To avoid this possibility, they say, firms should include only items that are expected to recur regularly in the income statement.

The current operating performance approach is of interest primarily from a historical standpoint, because under the elements definitions in Chapter 2 and under GAAP, virtually all components of net income must be included in the income statement. This approach to reporting income and its components is called the **all-inclusive approach**.

All-Inclusive Approach

Advocates of the all-inclusive approach maintain that the sum of periodic net income over the life of an entity ought to equal the net income of the entity for the total period of its existence. Thus all revenues, expenses, gains, and losses should be reported in the income statement. Advocates argue that there is the possibility of manipulation of earnings if a firm is allowed to omit the effects of some transactions from the income statement and to report them directly in retained earnings. For example, assume that unusual and nonrecurring transactions and events are excluded from the income statement and entered directly into retained earnings. Assume further that management must decide which items are unusual and nonrecurring. In the absence of specific, detailed criteria, management could choose to include gains in the income statement as regular and recurring items and to exclude losses as unusual and nonrecurring items.

The FASB, in *Statement of Financial Accounting Concepts No. 3* and again in *Statement of Concepts No. 5*, distinguishes between earnings and comprehensive income. *Earnings,* as the term is used by the FASB, is a measure of entity performance: the extent to which asset inflows (revenues and gains) exceed asset outflows (expenses and losses) for substantially completed cash-to-cash cycles during the period. *Comprehensive income* is a broad measure of the effects of all recognized changes in net assets during a period except those resulting from investments by owners and distributions to owners. For example, the cumulative effect of a change in accounting principle would be included in comprehensive income, but not in earnings. In the context of our discussion of the current operating performance and all-inclusive approaches to income determination, comprehensive income is comparable to net income as determined under the all-inclusive approach.

The all-inclusive approach underlies income reporting.

The current operating performance approach and the all-inclusive approach are extremes, the former supporting the inclusion of the effects of only regularly recurring events in the income statement and the latter supporting the inclusion of all revenues, expenses, gains, and losses in the income statement. The all-inclusive approach comes closest to describing current reporting practices under GAAP, because virtually all revenues, expenses, gains, and losses are included in net income. The required manner of disclosure of the components of net income, however, also accomplishes most of the objectives of the current operating performance approach. In the following section we shall describe and illustrate the components of net income and the associated reporting requirements.

EXHIBIT 4–1   INCOME STATEMENT FORMAT REQUIRED BY *OPINION NO. 30*

Income from continuing operations	$xxx
Discontinued operations	xx
Extraordinary gains and losses	xx
Cumulative effect of change in accounting principle	xx
Net income	$xxx

EXHIBIT 4–2   EXTRACT FROM *THE WALL STREET JOURNAL*'S "DIGEST OF EARNINGS REPORTS"

CARLSBERG CORP. (O)

Year May 31:	1985	1984
Revenues	$33,535,000	$33,921,000
Inco cnt op	1,054,000	4,881,000
Loss dis op	2,049,000	1,985,000
Net loss	d995,000	c2,896,000
Shr earns (primary):		
Inco cnt op	.23	1.36
Net loss	....	c.81
Shr earns (fully diluted):		
Inco cnt op	.23	1.13
Net loss	....	c.67
Quarter:		
Revenues	13,737,000	12,088,000
Inco cnt op	165,000	1,999,000
Loss dis op	910,000	1,345,000
Net loss	d745,000	c654,000
Shr earns:		
Inco cnt op	.04	.44
Net loss	....	c.14

c-Income, d-Includes a net charge of $1,647,000 from the write-down of assets.

LAM RESEARCH CORP. (O)

Year June 30:	1985	1984
Sales	$34,447,000	$19,135,000
Income	5,169,000	1,416,000
aExtrd cred	198,000	1,222,000
Net income	5,367,000	2,638,000
Shr earns:		
Income	.69	.25
Net income	.71	.46
Quarter:		
Sales	9,135,000	6,296,000
Income	1,199,000	641,000
aExtrd cred	....	446,000
Net income	1,199,000	1,087,000
Shr earns:		
Income	.16	.10
Net income	.16	.16

a-Tax benefit from tax loss carryforward.

Source: *The Wall Street Journal*, August 28, 1985, p. 12.

INCOME STATEMENT FORMAT UNDER GAAP

The income statement reports revenues, expenses, gains, and losses related to transactions and events occurring during a specified time period. *APB Opinion No. 30* provides the format requirements for reporting earnings information,[1] which are summarized in Exhibit 4–1. The order of presentation in Exhibit 4–1 is inflexible: the income components must be presented in the order shown. Furthermore, all revenues, expenses, gains, and losses must fit into one of the categories depicted in Exhibit 4–1.

When the financial news media publish corporate earnings results, they also give very careful attention to the reporting format requirements of *Opinion No. 30*. For example, Exhibit 4–2 shows how data from the "Digest of Earnings Reports" published daily by *The Wall Street Journal* closely follows the income statement format. Note that Carlsberg Corp. provided separate disclosure of the results of discontinued operations. Lam Research reported the tax benefit of the loss carryforward as an extraordinary gain.

Before examining the components of income in more detail, we briefly discuss intraperiod tax allocation, which affects the reporting of earnings information.

Intraperiod Tax Allocation

In reporting income tax expense, or income tax savings associated with a tax-deductible loss, firms must follow the process of **intraperiod tax allocation.** Stated simply, intraperiod tax allocation means that the income tax effect of an item should be reported

---

[1] "Reporting the Results of Operations," *Opinions of the Accounting Principles Board No. 30* (New York: AICPA, 1973).

with the item to which the tax is related. For example, if a company incurred a tax-deductible extraordinary loss of $100,000 as a result of a catastrophe when its tax rate was 40 percent, the loss would be reported as $60,000 [$100,000 − (.40 × $100,000)]. Since the loss is tax-deductible, income taxes otherwise payable are reduced by $40,000 and the $40,000 tax saving is reported as a reduction in the amount of the loss.

Intraperiod tax allocation contributes to the objectives of financial reporting by presenting income statement information that permits users to evaluate, assess, and predict net cash flows to the firm. The following illustration provides data to demonstrate how intraperiod tax allocation accomplishes this objective. Adam Corporation's revenues and operating expenses for 1987 were $160,000 and $60,000, respectively. In addition, the corporation had an extraordinary gain of $40,000 in 1987. The income tax rate was 40 percent, and the revenues, expenses, and extraordinary gain also appeared on the corporation's tax return, resulting in an income tax liability of $56,000 [.40($160,000 − $60,000 + $40,000)]. Thus net income for 1987 was $84,000:

$160,000 − $60,000 + $40,000 − $56,000 = $84,000
revenues   expenses   gain   taxes   net income

Two versions of the corporation's income statement, one with and one without intraperiod tax allocation, are shown in Exhibit 4–3. Which one better depicts the net cash flow effects of Adam Corporation's primary and peripheral operating activities? The income statement prepared with intraperiod tax allocation is the better presentation because had the gain *not* occurred, net income would have been $60,000 instead of $44,000. Which of the two presentations provides the better basis for users to predict *future* net income and cash flows? The income statement prepared with intraperiod tax allocation provides a better basis. Since the extraordinary gain is, by its nature, unusual and nonrecurring, the income before extraordinary gain of $60,000 probably is a better predictor of future income than the $44,000. As a matter of fact, if 1988 operations were identical to those of 1987 except for the extraordinary item, net income would be $60,000.

In summary, intraperiod tax allocation allows the user to assess the after-tax impact of the events and transactions that affect net income. Income tax expense or income tax

EXHIBIT 4–3

Adam Corporation

INCOME STATEMENT FOR 1987

	WITHOUT TAX ALLOCATION	WITH TAX ALLOCATION
Revenues	$160,000	$160,000
Operating expenses	(60,000)	(60,000)
Income from operations before taxes	$100,000	$100,000
Income tax expense	(56,000)	(40,000)
Income before extraordinary gain	$ 44,000	$ 60,000
Extraordinary gain	40,000	
Extraordinary gain (net of $16,000 taxes)		24,000
Net income	$ 84,000	$ 84,000

EXHIBIT 4–4

Georgia-Pacific Corporation

STATEMENT OF CONSOLIDATED INCOME
FOR THE YEAR ENDED DECEMBER 31, 1984
(millions of dollars)

Net sales		$ 6,682
Costs and expenses		
Cost of sales	5,441	
Selling, general and administrative	426	
Depreciation and depletion	282	
Interest	156	
		$(6,305)
Income from continuing operations before unusual items and income taxes		$ 377
Unusual items, net		19
Income from continuing operations before income taxes		$ 396
Provision for income taxes		(143)
Income from continuing operations		$ 253
Discontinued operations:		
Operating income, net of taxes		$ 26
(Loss) on disposal, net of taxes		(160)
Income (loss) from discontinued operations		$ (134)
Net income		$ 119

Five items require intraperiod tax allocation.

savings must be reported separately for (1) income from continuing operations, (2) discontinued operations, (3) extraordinary items, (4) cumulative effect adjustments, and (5) prior period adjustments. Prior period adjustments are reported as an addition to or subtraction from the balance of retained earnings at the beginning of the period. They are described in detail in the section of this chapter dealing with the statement of retained earnings. Items affecting income from continuing operations are reported at their gross amount and then one amount for income taxes is related to income from continuing operations. Each of the items included in the income statement after income from continuing operations should be reported net of any related tax expense or tax savings.

Exhibit 4–4 shows how intraperiod tax allocation appeared in a recent income statement of Georgia-Pacific Corporation.

Income from Continuing Operations

Several alternatives exist for reporting the individual revenues, expenses, gains, and losses that enter into the determination of income from continuing operations. Two distinct approaches, however, are in general use: the single-step approach and the multiple-step approach.

Under the **single-step approach,** income from continuing operations consists of two categories: (1) revenues and gains and (2) expenses and losses. As Exhibit 4–5 illustrates, this statement format matches total revenues against total expenses to determine the net income or loss from continuing operations for the period. The primary advantage of the single-step approach is its simplicity.

EXHIBIT 4–5   SINGLE-STEP INCOME STATEMENT

Pacter Company
INCOME STATEMENT
FOR THE YEAR ENDED DECEMBER 31, 1987

Revenues		
Net sales	$400,800	
Service revenue	25,600	
Interest	12,200	
Dividends	5,000	
Gains on sale of equipment	2,400	
Total revenues		$446,000
Expenses		
Cost of goods sold	$244,000	
Selling and administrative	121,700	
Interest	16,300	
Income taxes	29,900	
Loss on sale of securities	2,700	
Total expenses		(414,600)
Income from continuing operations		$ 31,400

EXHIBIT 4–6   MULTIPLE-STEP INCOME STATEMENT

Jerome Company
INCOME STATEMENT
FOR THE YEAR ENDED DECEMBER 31, 1987

Net sales	$1,675,900
Cost of goods sold	(1,276,500)
Gross profit	$ 399,400
Selling, general, and administrative expenses	(151,000)
Operating profit	$ 248,400
Other income, net	18,800
	$ 267,200
Interest expense	(34,200)
Income from continuing operations before taxes	$ 233,000
Income taxes	(64,900)
Income from continuing operations	$ 168,100

The multiple-step approach is illustrated in Exhibit 4–6. An advantage of the **multiple-step approach** is that it provides for a number of subtotals that are not shown in a single-step income statement. For example, cost of goods sold is deducted from net sales to obtain gross profit on sales. A comparison of period-to-period gross profit rates is useful in assessing performance and in predicting future cash flows from the sale of products. Separate identification of operating income also is useful for predictive purposes because of its recurring nature. Likewise, nonoperating revenues, expenses, gains, and losses are reported separately from operating items in a multiple-step approach. Because financing expenses are often fixed, segregation of these costs from variable and discretionary costs is useful for prediction of future earnings. As Exhibit 4–6 shows, income tax expense typically is deducted separately as the last item before income from continuing operations.

Regardless of the particular format a company adopts, it is important to maintain consistency from year to year, because users of financial statements need comparative data. The format adopted should be one that management believes is most useful. Also, regardless of the format used, companies must report separately the effects of discontinued operations, extraordinary items, and the cumulative effect of changes in accounting principles.

Discontinued Operations

Discontinuing the operations of a segment of a business (for example, by selling a major line of business) has an impact on a firm's ability to generate future cash flows. Thus, in order to facilitate users' predictions of cash flows, discontinued operations must be adequately disclosed. The three major issues associated with discontinued operations are (1) identification of discontinued operations, (2) measurement of gain or loss, and (3) disclosure requirements. We shall discuss the requirements for each of these issues, as specified by *APB Opinion No. 30,* in the remainder of this section.

IDENTIFICATION OF DISCONTINUED OPERATIONS   The term **discontinued operations** is used to describe ''the operations of a segment of a business . . . that has been sold, abandoned, spun off, or otherwise disposed of or, although still operating, is the subject of a formal plan for disposal.''[2] Thus, discontinued operations may include both actual dispositions during the period and planned dispositions. Only those discontinued business segments that constitute (1) separate major lines of business or (2) separate classes of customer qualify for treatment as discontinued operations. Also, the assets, operating results, and activities must be clearly distinguishable, both physically and operationally. Disposals of assets in the normal course of evolution of an entity's business, such as disposal of part of a line of business, the phasing out of a product line, and changes occasioned by technological improvements, do not constitute discontinued operations.

Events that are classified as disposals of a segment include the following:

1. A sale by a diversified company of a major division that represents the company's only activities in the electronics industry.

2. A sale by a meat packing company of a 25 percent interest in a professional football team which has been accounted for under the equity method. All other activities of the company are in the meat packing business.

3. A sale by a communications company of all its radio stations, which represent 30 percent of gross revenues. The company's remaining activities are three television stations and a publishing company. The radio station's assets and operating results are clearly distinguishable.

4. A sale by a food distributor of one of its two divisions. One division sells food at wholesale, primarily to supermarket chains, and the other division sells food through its chain of fast-food restaurants, some of which are franchised and some of which are company-owned. Both divisions are in the business of distribution of food. The nature of selling food through fast-food outlets, however, is vastly different from that of wholesaling food to supermarket chains.

[2] *APB Opinion No. 30,* para. 8.

In situations 1, 2, and 3, assets and results of operations are segmented and clearly distinguishable physically, operationally, and for reporting purposes. In situation 4, two major classes of customers exist.

Events that are *not* disposals of a segment include the following:

1. The sale by a mining company of a major foreign subsidiary engaged in silver mining, which represents all of the company's activities in that particular country.

2. The sale by a petrochemical company of a 25 percent interest in a petrochemical plant which is accounted for as an investment in a corporate joint venture under the equity method. The remaining activities of the company are in the same line of business as the 25 percent interest that has been sold.

3. The discontinuance by a manufacturer of children's wear of all of its operations in Italy, which consisted of designing and selling children's wear for the Italian market.

4. The sale by a diversified company of a subsidiary that manufactures furniture. The company has retained its other furniture manufacturing subsidiary.

5. The sale of all the assets (including the plant) related to the manufacture of men's woolen suits by an apparel manufacturer in order to concentrate activities in the manufacture of men's suits from synthetic products.

In situations 1, 2, and 4 there has been a sale of only part of a line of business. In situation 3, the nationality of customers is not a determining factor, and in situation 5 the firm is disposing of a product line rather than a major line of business.

MEASUREMENT OF GAIN OR LOSS   In order to describe the procedure for measuring a gain or loss arising from discontinued operations, it is first necessary to define the measurement date and the disposal date. The **measurement date** is the date on which management commits itself to a formal plan to dispose of a segment. At a minimum, such a plan must include identification of major assets to be disposed of, the expected method of disposal, the period expected to be required for disposal (usually not more than one year from the measurement date), an active program to find a buyer if disposal is by sale, the estimated results of operations from the measurement date to the disposal date, and the estimated proceeds upon disposal. The **disposal date** is the date the sale is closed if disposal is by sale or the date when operations cease if disposal is by abandonment.[3]

Two components of gain or loss on discontinued operations.

The gain or loss on disposal must be estimated as of the measurement date. In the period in which the measurement date occurs, the gain or loss consists of two parts: (1) the operating income or loss (net of taxes) for the discontinued segment from the beginning of the period to the measurement date; and (2) the operating income or loss during the phase-out period (net of taxes) and the gain or loss on disposal of the segment (net of taxes). If a loss is expected, it should be recognized at the measurement date. If a gain is expected, it should be recognized when it is realized, usually on the disposal date. Note that if the measurement date and the disposal date are in the same accounting period, the second part consists of gains and losses actually realized during the period.

When the disposal date occurs in a period subsequent to the period of the measurement date, the measurement problem becomes more complex. In this case, the second part of the gain or loss described in the preceding paragraph must be separated into two components: (1) the *realized* gain or loss between the measurement date and the end of the accounting period, and (2) the *estimated* gain or loss from the end of the accounting period to the disposal date. Remember that each of these two components consists of operating income or loss and gain or loss on disposal. If there is an *estimated loss* from the end of

---

[3] Ibid., para. 14.

the accounting period to the disposal date, the estimated loss should be added to the realized loss or deducted from the realized gain. If there is an *estimated gain,* the estimated gain may be recognized only to the extent of realized losses between the measurement date and the end of the accounting period. Thus, this is a rare accounting situation in which anticipated gains may be recognized, but only to the extent of realized losses.

To illustrate the application of these measurement guidelines, assume the following:

	CASE 1	CASE 2
Income from continuing operations...................	$500,000	$500,000
Operating income (loss) for discontinued operation during period prior to measurement date (net of taxes)................	(30,000)	30,000
Operating income (loss) for discontinued operation during period from measurement date to end of period (net of taxes).................................	(10,000)	10,000
Gain (loss) on disposal prior to end of period (net of taxes)...........................	40,000	(40,000)
Estimated operating income (loss) during subsequent period (net of taxes)	(20,000)	(10,000)
Estimated gain (loss) on disposal during subsequent period (net of taxes)	(80,000)	80,000

In Case 1, the loss from discontinued operations in the year of the measurement period would be $100,000, consisting of the $30,000 operating loss prior to the measurement date and the $70,000 realized and estimated loss after the measurement date. The $70,000 is a combination of the realized gain of $30,000 ($40,000 − $10,000) and the estimated loss of $100,000 ($80,000 + $20,000). In Case 2, the gain from discontinued operations in the year of the measurement period would be $30,000, which is the $30,000 operating income prior to the measurement date. The realized loss of $30,000 ($40,000 − $10,000) is offset by $30,000 of the $70,000 ($80,000 − $10,000) estimated gain, producing a net effect of zero for the phase-out period during the current year. In effect, $30,000 of the $70,000 estimated gain is recognized in the current accounting period. The remainder of the gain will be recognized when it is actually realized in the subsequent period. The solutions to Cases 1 and 2 are shown in time-line format in Exhibit 4–7.

DISCLOSURE REQUIREMENTS   Exhibit 4–8 illustrates the required format for reporting discontinued operations, using the figures from Case 1 and assuming a 50 percent tax rate on all items. Note the two components of the discontinued operations presentation: (1) operating loss up to the measurement date, and (2) realized and estimated loss on disposal, including operating loss, from the measurement date to the disposal date. As Exhibit 4–1 indicates, this information must be presented after income from continuing operations and before extraordinary items. All components are to be shown on a net of tax basis. The income taxes applicable to the components must be disclosed either in the income statement or in the notes that accompany the financial statements. Also, revenues from the discontinued operations must be disclosed in the related notes. In addition, for prior periods presented currently on a comparative basis, the net operating results of the discontinued segment should be reported separately in the income statements for the prior periods. Data on earnings per share must be presented in the income statement for income from continuing operations and for net income, but per share data are optional for results of the discontinued operations and for the gain or loss on disposal. As a result of all these disclosures, income from continuing operations is kept clean for predictive purposes.

| **EXHIBIT 4–7** | CALCULATION OF GAIN/LOSS FROM DISCONTINUED OPERATIONS |

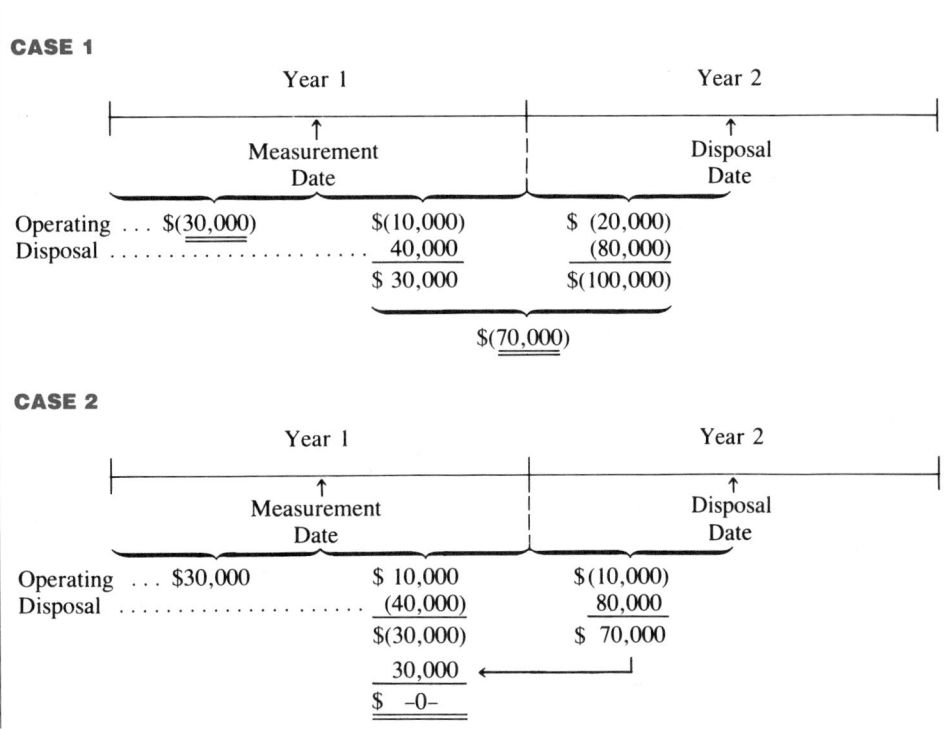

CASE 1

	Year 1		Year 2
	↑ Measurement Date		↑ Disposal Date
Operating ... $(30,000)	$(10,000)	$ (20,000)
Disposal	40,000	(80,000)
	$ 30,000	$(100,000)
		$(70,000)

CASE 2

	Year 1		Year 2
	↑ Measurement Date		↑ Disposal Date
Operating ... $30,000	$ 10,000	$(10,000)
Disposal	(40,000)	80,000
	$(30,000)	$ 70,000
	30,000 ←	
	$ –0–	

| **EXHIBIT 4–8** | REQUIRED INCOME STATEMENT FORMAT FOR REPORTING DISCONTINUED OPERATIONS |

Income from continuing operations before income taxes	$1,000,000	
Provision for income taxes	(500,000)	
Income from continuing operations...................		$500,000
Discontinued operations		
Loss from operations of discontinued Division X (less applicable income tax savings of $30,000)	$ (30,000)	
Loss on disposal of Division X, including provision of $60,000 for operating losses during phase-out period (less applicable income tax savings of $70,000) ...	(70,000)	(100,000)
Net income		$400,000

The following additional information should be disclosed in the notes for the year in which the measurement date occurs:

1. The identity of the discontinued segment.

2. The expected disposal date, if known.

3. The expected manner of disposal.

4. A description of the remaining assets and liabilities of the discontinued segment at the balance sheet date.

5. The operating income or loss and any disposal proceeds during the period from the measurement date to the balance sheet date.[4]

In summary, the objective is to disclose fully the impact of the disposal on the entity by separate disclosure of the remaining net assets of the segment and by *purifying* income from continuing operations.

Extraordinary Items

In 1966 the Accounting Principles Board issued *APB Opinion No. 9,* ''Reporting the Results of Operations,'' which required that the income statement should include extraordinary items and that they should be reported separately in the income statement. The objectives of this requirement were to separate the effect of extraordinary events on earnings from income generated from ordinary operations, and to show in the income statement all items of income and loss that occurred during the period, except those items that clearly relate to prior periods. Criteria for identifying extraordinary items were also specified in the *Opinion*. The application of the criteria in the late 1960s and early 1970s, however, did not result in the uniformity of classification and reporting expected by the APB. Many firms tended to include gains in ordinary income and to report losses as extraordinary items, so that investor and creditor expectations regarding future cash flows would be maximized. The APB therefore reexamined the problem and issued *Opinion No. 30.*

In *Opinion No. 30* the APB narrowed the criteria for extraordinary items and made them more specific, so that fewer items would qualify as extraordinary. According to *Opinion No. 30, both* of the following criteria must be met for an item to be classified as extraordinary:

1. *Unusual nature*—the underlying event or transaction should possess a high degree of abnormality and be of a type clearly unrelated to, or only incidentally related to, the ordinary and typical activities of the entity, *taking into account the environment in which the entity operates*. [Emphasis added.]

2. *Infrequency of occurrence*—the underlying event or transaction should be of a type that would not reasonably be expected to recur in the foreseeable future, *taking into account the environment in which the entity operates*.[5] [Emphasis added.]

> Extraordinary items must be material, unusual, and infrequent in occurrence, considering the entity's operating environment.

The presumption underlying *Opinion No. 30* is that items are ordinary and usual unless the available evidence clearly indicates that *both* of the above criteria are met. The following events typically do not qualify as extraordinary items, according to the *Opinion*, because they are not unusual or because they may be expected to recur regularly:

1. Write-down or write-off of receivables, inventories, equipment leased to others, or intangible assets.

2. Gains or losses from exchange or translation of foreign currencies, including those relating to major devaluations and revaluations.

3. Gains or losses on disposal of a segment of a business.

4. Other gains or losses from sale or abandonment of property, plant, or equipment used in the business.

5. Effects of a strike, including those against competitors and major suppliers.

6. Adjustment of accruals on long-term contracts.[6]

---

[4] *APB Opinion No. 30*, para. 18.

[5] *APB Opinion No. 30*, para. 20.

[6] *APB Opinion No. 30*, para. 23.

Occasionally one of these items may be part of an event or transaction that gives rise to an extraordinary item. In these rare instances, the portion of the above items that is "the direct result of a major casualty (such as an earthquake), an expropriation, or a prohibition under a newly enacted law or regulation that clearly meets both criteria" for an extraordinary item should be reported as an extraordinary gain or loss.

Note that both criteria conclude with the phrase "taking into account the environment in which the entity operates." Thus what is extraordinary for one entity may not be extraordinary for another entity because of environmental differences. For example, a casualty loss from earthquake damage to a company's plant in Kansas may constitute an extraordinary item, whereas a casualty loss from earthquake damage in California may not qualify as an extraordinary item. Likewise, classification of similar events as extraordinary or ordinary may differ from one year to another for the same entity as environmental conditions change. The environment includes such factors as the characteristics of the industry or industries in which the entity operates, geographical location, and the extent of government regulation.

Examples of transactions that meet both criteria (unusual in nature and infrequent in occurrence) for qualification as an extraordinary item are as follows:

1. A large portion of a tobacco manufacturer's crops are destroyed by a hailstorm. Severe damage from hailstorms in the locality where the manufacturer grows tobacco is rare.

2. A steel fabricating company sells the only land it owns. The land was acquired ten years ago for future expansion, but shortly thereafter the company abandoned all plans for expansion and held the land for appreciation.

3. A company sells a block of common stock of a publicly traded company. The block of shares, which represents less than 10 percent of the publicly held company, is the only security investment the company has ever owned.

4. An earthquake destroys one of the oil refineries owned by a large multinational oil company.

Examples of transactions that do *not* meet both criteria are the following:

1. A Florida citrus grower's crop is damaged by frost. Frost damage is normally experienced every three or four years in the grower's area.

2. A company that operates a chain of warehouses sells the excess land surrounding one of its warehouses. When the company buys property to establish a new warehouse, it usually buys more land than it expects to use with the expectation that the land will appreciate in value. In the past five years the company has twice sold such excess land.

3. A large diversified company sells a block of shares from its portfolio of securities which it has acquired for investment purposes. This is the first sale from its portfolio of securities. The company owns several securities for investment purposes.

4. A textile manufacturer with only one plant moves to another location. It has not relocated a plant in 20 years and has no plans to do so in the foreseeable future.

For 1 and 2 above, the events are not infrequent, and given the environment in which the companies operate, they may be expected to recur. The activities in 3 and 4 represent ordinary and typical activities for the companies involved, and are therefore not unusual. Even though the textile manufacturer in 4 has no plans to relocate again, relocations are not an infrequent occurrence.

Reporting firms must include descriptive captions and amounts for individual extraordinary items where practicable, along with disclosure of the nature of the items involved and the applicable amount of income taxes. Also, when extraordinary items

EXHIBIT 4—9 INCOME STATEMENT PRESENTATION OF EXTRAORDINARY ITEM

Varlen Corporation and Subsidiaries
PARTIAL INCOME STATEMENT
FOR THE YEAR ENDED JANUARY 31, 1984

Income before extraordinary item	$5,984,893
Extraordinary item	
(less applicable income taxes of $398,000) (note 10)	(379,289)
Net income	$5,605,604

(10) EXTRAORDINARY ITEM

The extraordinary item results from the settlement in 1984 of an action which had been initiated in 1979 by David A. Clark against the Company seeking to recover profits resulting from an invention which he claimed to have disclosed to a representative of Unit Rail Anchor Company, Inc.'s Beall Manufacturing Division, (a predecessor of the Company) in 1961, which was prior to the formation of the Company. The estimated net cost (including certain legal fees and expenses) of the settlement to the Company was $379,000 (net of a related tax benefit of $398,000), or $.09 per share, all of which was recognized in the fiscal year ended January 31, 1984. The Company believes the settlement to be unusual and nonrecurring, and, accordingly, its cost has been reflected as an extraordinary item.

---

exist, earnings per share must be disclosed in the income statement for both (1) income before extraordinary items and (2) net income. Since earnings per share for extraordinary items can then be determined by subtraction, disclosure of that figure is not required.

Exhibit 4–9, excerpted from a recent annual report of Varlen Corporation, demonstrates the income statement presentation of extraordinary items. As Varlen Corporation explains in the accompanying footnote, the event that caused the loss, the settlement of litigation related to a patent infringement charge, was unusual and nonrecurring. Therefore, the loss was classified as an extraordinary item.

ITEMS ALWAYS REPORTED AS EXTRAORDINARY ITEMS   Current practice requires the impact of two types of transactions always to be reported as extraordinary items, whether or not the two criteria set forth in *Opinion No. 30* are met. First, *material gains and losses from extinguishment of debt,* whether early or at maturity, are required to be reported, net of the tax effect, as extraordinary items.[7] Also, the per share amount of the net gain or loss must be disclosed either in the income statement or in the notes to the financial statements. Second, the *tax benefit of income tax loss carryforwards recognized in periods subsequent to the loss* always must be reported as an extraordinary item.[8]

We should point out that the reporting of these two transactions as extraordinary items does not appear to be supportable from an accounting theory standpoint. For gains and losses on early extinguishment of debt, it appears that the FASB wished to "flag" the huge gains resulting from debt retirement when the market values of companies' debts were driven down below book value because of high interest rates in the inflation of the 1970s. For income tax loss carryforwards, the tax benefit, if it materializes, always has a favorable effect on income. The APB simply decided that this effect should be labeled extraordinary.

[7] "Reporting Gains and Losses from Extinguishment of Debt: An amendment of *APB Opinion No. 30,*" *Statement of Financial Accounting Standards No. 4* (Stamford, Conn.: FASB, 1975), para. 8.

[8] "Accounting for Income Taxes," *Opinions of the Accounting Principles Board No. 11* (New York: AICPA, 1967), para. 45. Chapter 19 contains a detailed discussion of tax loss carryforwards.

UNUSUAL OR INFREQUENT ITEMS Some items meet one, but not both, of the criteria for classification as extraordinary items. That is, some events or transactions result in material gains and losses that are unusual or infrequent, but not both. *Opinion No. 30* specifies that these items should be reported as components of income from continuing operations at their gross amounts (that is, *not* net of taxes). The items should be listed separately in the income statement or the characteristics and effects of the item may be disclosed in the notes to the financial statements. They should not be reported in any manner that implies that they are extraordinary items.

For example, Georgia-Pacific Corporation included in its 1983 income statement, under "Unusual items, net," $38,000,000 from the settlement of a gas dispute and a loss of $156,000,000 from facility disposals and asset write-downs. Even though these items do not constitute extraordinary items, financial statement users making predictions regarding the cash-generating ability of Georgia-Pacific should recognize the unusual nature of these items.

Changes in Accounting Principle

In our discussion of the qualities of useful information, we pointed out the importance of consistency in the use of accounting principles through time. Occasionally, however, a company may adopt a different accounting principle from the one used in previous periods. For example, a company may change from FIFO to average cost in accounting for inventories, or from the straight-line method to the accelerated method of depreciation of plant and equipment.

APB Opinion No. 20 requires that the cumulative effect of most changes in accounting principle be disclosed in the income statement in the period in which the company makes the change.[9] The cumulative effect is the difference between (1) the carrying value of the affected asset or liability under the previously used principle and (2) what the carrying value would have been if the newly adopted principle had been used in previous periods. The cumulative effect must be reported in the income statement net of applicable taxes. Accounting for the asset or liability in the current period is based on the new principle. The case of the Thompson Corporation provides an example of a change in accounting principle. At the beginning of 1985, the Thompson Corporation purchased equipment costing $30,000. The equipment was being depreciated by the sum-of-the-years'-digits method, on the basis of an estimated five-year life and zero salvage value. In 1987 Thompson changed to straight-line depreciation with no changes in the estimated useful life or salvage value. The sum-of-the-years'-digits method will be continued for tax purposes, and the applicable tax rate is 40 percent. The cumulative effect of this change is calculated as follows:

	DEPRECIATION UNDER				
YEAR	SUM-OF-THE-YEARS'-DIGITS	STRAIGHT LINE	DIFFER-ENCE	TAX ON DIFFER-ENCE	DIFFER-ENCE NET OF TAX
1985	5/15 × $30,000 = $10,000	$6,000	$4,000	$1,600	$2,400
1986	4/15 × 30,000 = 8,000	6,000	2,000	800	1,200
	Cumulative effect, net of tax......................................				$3,600

[9] "Accounting Changes," *Opinions of the Accounting Principles Board No. 20* (New York: AICPA, 1971). *Opinion No. 20* requires that the cumulative effect of changes in certain accounting principles be disclosed by restating prior period financial statements instead of reporting the cumulative effect in the current period income statements. Additionally, many FASB transition rules require restatement of prior period financial statements. These types of changes and disclosure are discussed in Chapter 22.

EXHIBIT 4–10 | REPORTING A CHANGE IN ACCOUNTING PRINCIPLE

Thompson Corporation

PARTIAL INCOME STATEMENT
FOR THE YEAR ENDED DECEMBER 31, 1987

Income before extraordinary item and change in accounting principle	$19,200
Extraordinary gain on early extinguishment of debt, net of applicable taxes of $4,000	6,000
Cumulative effect of change in accounting principle, net of applicable taxes of $2,400 (Note A)	3,600
Net income	$28,800

Note A: In 1987 the company changed its method of depreciating equipment from sum-of-the-years'-digits to straight line. The change was made in order better to match against revenue the cost of services received from use of the equipment. The cumulative effect of the change, net of taxes, was $3,600, and is reported in the income statement for 1987. Depreciation of $6,000 in 1987 is based on the newly adopted straight-line method.

Exhibit 4–10 shows how the change in accounting principle is disclosed in Thompson's income statement for 1987. Notice that Note A describes the change, sets forth the reason for it, and points out that depreciation expense for 1987 is based on the newly adopted method.

A change in accounting principle is one type of **accounting change** that occurs in practice. Other types of accounting changes include changes in accounting estimates and changes in the reporting entity. A change in the estimated useful life of depreciable assets and a change in the estimated percentage of uncollectible accounts are examples of changes in accounting estimates. A change in the composition of a group of companies under common control and issuing combined financial statements, called **consolidated financial statements,** is an example of a change in reporting entity. Accounting for and disclosure of these types of accounting changes are covered in depth in Chapter 22.

ADDITIONAL DISCLOSURES OF INCOME INFORMATION

In addition to the information requirements of *Opinion No. 30,* firms must also report certain additional information about income and its components. The reporting requirements for earnings per share, interim reporting, and segment reporting are discussed briefly here and are covered in greater depth in Chapters 24 and 26.

Earnings per Share

Perhaps the most often quoted figure related to a company's performance is earnings per share (EPS). Users find earnings on a per share basis easier to understand than net income. The popularity of EPS and the increased complexity of corporate capital structures that include convertible securities and stock options led the APB to issue reporting and computational guidelines for EPS in *Opinion No. 15* in 1969. We discuss the detailed computational guidelines in Chapter 24.[10]

EPS information, which usually appears on the face of the income statement, must be disclosed by publicly held companies. If discontinued operations, an extraordinary item, and a change in accounting principle all exist within a particular reporting period, firms must report EPS for income from continuing operations, income before extraordinary items, the cumulative effect of a change in accounting principle, and net income. Since income statement users may then compute per share amounts for discontinued operations

---

[10] "Earnings per Share," *Opinions of the Accounting Principles Board No. 15* (New York: AICPA, 1969).

EXHIBIT 4–11 | DUAL PRESENTATION OF EARNINGS PER SHARE

Georgia-Pacific Corporation

SCHEDULE OF PRIMARY AND FULLY-DILUTED EPS
FOR THE YEAR ENDED DECEMBER 31, 1984

Per common share—primary
Income from continuing operations $2.28
Income (loss) from discontinued operations . . . . (1.31)

Net income . . . . $ .97
Per common share—fully diluted
Income from continuing operations $2.24
Income (loss) from discontinued operations . . . . (1.27)

Net income . . . . $ .97

and extraordinary items by subtraction, disclosure of the EPS effect of discontinued operations and extraordinary items is optional. However, most entities do disclose the per share effect of these items.

Many complexities may arise in computing and reporting EPS. If a company has debt or preferred stock outstanding which is convertible into common stock, or has options outstanding which permit the holder to acquire common stock, *Opinion No. 15* generally requires a dual presentation of EPS in the income statement. The two presentations are called **primary EPS** and **fully diluted EPS,** respectively. Exhibit 4–11 illustrates a dual presentation of EPS by Georgia-Pacific Corporation.

Interim Reporting

As we said in Chapter 2, information, to be useful, must be disclosed on a timely basis. Because investment decisions, credit decisions, and other decisions affecting entities are made frequently, a significant demand exists for **interim reporting** of operating information; that is, reporting of information covering periods of less than one year. As a result, *quarterly* reporting of selected financial information has become quite common.

Companies whose stock is traded on an organized exchange must issue quarterly financial information. Quarterly reports must be filed with the Securities and Exchange Commission on Form 10-Q. *APB Opinion No. 28* governs quarterly reports to stockholders.[11] Quarterly reports are much less detailed than annual reports, often containing only condensed earnings information.

Segment Reporting

Many companies operate in more than one industry or transact a major share of their business in foreign countries. Because of the different levels of risk and return associated with operations in various industries and countries, users interested in evaluating the cash flow potential of the total entity require information on major **segments.** *FASB Statement No. 14* requires companies to report certain information for industry segments that contribute 10 percent or more of the entity's total revenue, operating profit or loss, or identifiable assets.[12] Earnings information required for reportable segments includes (1) revenues and (2) pretax operating profit or loss.

[11] ''Interim Financial Reporting,'' *Opinions of the Accounting Principles Board No. 28* (New York: AICPA, 1973). We examine interim reporting requirements in detail in Chapter 26.

[12] ''Financial Reporting for Segments of a Business Enterprise,'' *Statement of Financial Accounting Standards No. 14* (Stamford, Conn.: FASB, 1976). Chapter 26 includes a detailed discussion of segment reporting requirements.

UNRESOLVED ISSUES
The development of rules for reporting income and its components has not been related to a set of basic concepts because there has been no general agreement on concepts. Thus the accounting profession has developed reporting rules piecemeal, and the rules have often been criticized for their inadequacies and inconsistencies.

Users complain that existing income statements do not provide enough information about past income activities to enable them to assess future income and cash flows. Specifically, it is argued that there is inadequate disclosure of the effects of unusual events or transactions and economic changes that affect the relationship between recurring revenues and expenses, such as a large price change in an important resource. Further, recent professional pronouncements, such as the requirement that research and development costs be recorded as expenses as they are incurred, may increase the variability of income without disclosing the reasons for the increased variability. Also, users have historically focused on the final net income number rather than on the components of income.

Some income components are reasonably stable over time. Disclosure of the stable components of income assists users to predict future amounts of these items. Reporting of historical data on the *volume* of goods and services sold, selling *prices,* and the *range* of goods and services provided further helps users to project future cash flows. Historical reporting of the fixed and variable components of such expenses and of changes in prices of major resources also helps users to predict cash flows.

Other income components may be highly volatile. Information about these irregular components should be reported so that users may separate the effects of these items from those that are more stable. Examples of relatively volatile income components are discontinued operations, extraordinary items, and the effects of accounting changes.

Despite efforts over the last few years to make income statements more informative, many income statement users are still dissatisfied with current practice. As we said in Chapter 1, financial information is disclosed (1) in the main body of the statements, (2) in notes accompanying the statements, and (3) as supplementary information. Thus information about income and its components could appear in any of these places. Additional decisions about displaying income information include the amount of detail to be reported and the manner in which it should be presented. Accountants currently lack definitive guidance for these decisions.

Partially in response to the above criticisms, as we discussed earlier in this chapter, the FASB has devoted several paragraphs of *Statement of Financial Accounting Concepts No. 5* to a discussion of the statement of earnings and comprehensive income. This discussion does not appear to suggest radical departures from current practice in reporting income information. However, it does emphasize the need for information about the various components of earnings and comprehensive income that differ in risk, stability, and predictability. With improved reporting, users would find present and future income and cash flows easier to assess, and preparers would benefit from increased credibility of financial statements.

STATEMENT OF RETAINED EARNINGS

As described in Chapter 3, net income increases retained earnings and net loss decreases retained earnings. Thus, retained earnings reflects the cumulative earnings experience of an entity. Also, dividend payments decrease retained earnings. The statement of retained earnings highlights this relationship between net income and dividends. Corporations typically present a statement of retained earnings in their annual reports to stockholders. The primary purpose of the statement of retained earnings is to explain the change in the retained earnings balance from the beginning to the end of the accounting period. Re-

EXHIBIT 4—12

Colt Industries, Inc., and Subsidiaries
STATEMENT OF RETAINED EARNINGS
FROM 1984 ANNUAL REPORT
(in thousands of dollars)

Balance, beginning of period	$420,939
Net earnings (loss) for the period	132,229
Dividends	(48,766)
Balance, end of period	$504,402

tained earnings available for dividends may be restricted by contractual arrangements, managerial decisions, or legal requirements. For example, management may decide to retain assets arising from profitable operations to finance a plant expansion. Such restrictions should be disclosed in the retained earnings statement or related notes.

Exhibit 4–12 provides an example of a statement of retained earnings from the 1984 annual report of Colt Industries. Companies often include such a presentation in a **statement of stockholders' equity,** which analyzes changes in all stockholders' equity accounts, rather than only changes in retained earnings. Also, since companies must present comparative income statements for at least the last three years in their annual report, the statement of retained earnings typically includes columns in which amounts from the two immediately preceding years are listed beside the amounts for the current year.

PRIOR PERIOD ADJUSTMENTS

As we said earlier in this chapter, the all-inclusive income statement, in which all revenues, expenses, gains, and losses appear, typifies current accounting practice. *FASB Statement No. 16* led to an even greater emphasis on the all-inclusive income statement by requiring that the effects of all revenues, expenses, gains, and losses except the following must be included in the determination of net income:

1. Correction of an error in the financial statement of a prior period.

2. Adjustments that result from realization of income tax benefits of preacquisition operating loss carryforwards of purchased subsidiaries.[13]

The effect of either of these two events must be reported as a direct addition to or deduction from the beginning retained earnings balance in the period in which the error correction or adjustment occurs.

Before the issuance of *FASB Statement No. 16,* guidance was lacking for the treatment of error corrections. Errors may occur as a result of mathematical mistakes, misapplication of accounting principles, or misuse of facts. Companies could, and many did, include the effects of corrections that would increase net income in the income statement, often buried in operating income. The effects of error corrections that would decrease net income if they were included in the income statement often were reported directly in retained earnings. Under *Statement No. 16,* firms must exclude the effects of error corrections related to prior periods from the determination of current net income because the errors have no relationship to current operations.

[13] "Prior Period Adjustments," *Statement of Financial Accounting Standards No. 16* (Stamford, Conn.: FASB, 1977).

The following illustration provides an example of an error correction. Assume that a firm acquired a depreciable asset with an estimated four-year life at the beginning of 1987 at a cost of $4,000, and at the end of 1988 discovered that no depreciation had been recorded for the asset during 1987. Assuming no salvage value, straight-line depreciation, and ignoring income taxes, the firm must make the following entry at the end of 1988 to correct for the overstatement of 1987 net income:

Retained earnings	1,000	
Accumulated depreciation		1,000

The normal entry for depreciation expense would be made at the end of 1988. The $1,000 correction would be deducted from the beginning balance of retained earnings to arrive at the adjusted beginning balance (the balance that would have been reported had the error not occurred), as indicated below.

Beginning retained earnings (as originally stated)	$x,xxx
Deduct: Adjustment for failure to record depreciation in year 1	(1,000)
Restated beginning retained earnings	$x,xxx

In addition, prior period financial statements reported currently for comparative purposes must be restated to reflect the correction. That is, they must be restated to report the amounts that would have been reported had the error not occurred. This process is illustrated in Chapter 22.

The second type of prior period adjustment prohibits companies from increasing earnings by acquiring companies with unused loss carryforwards. When a company incurs a net loss, under certain circumstances it may claim a refund for taxes previously paid or a reduction in taxes otherwise payable in future periods. The circumstances and procedures for these ''carrybacks'' and ''carryforwards'' of operating losses are discussed in detail in Chapter 19.

EXHIBIT 4–13

Oakite Products, Inc., and Subsidiaries

COMBINED STATEMENT OF INCOME
AND RETAINED EARNINGS
FROM 1984 ANNUAL REPORT
(in thousands of dollars, except per share amounts)

Net sales	$83,272
Cost of sales	(45,383)
Gross profit..	$37,889
Selling, general and administrative expenses	(28,553)
Operating income	$ 9,336
Other deductions, net......................................	(153)
Income before provision for income taxes	$ 9,183
Provision for income taxes	(4,392)
Net income ($2.88 per share)	$ 4,791
Retained earnings at beginning of year	25,665
Dividends paid ($1.52 per share)	(2,532)
Retained earnings at end of year...	$27,924

COMBINED STATEMENT OF INCOME AND RETAINED EARNINGS

Some companies combine their income statement and statement of retained earnings into one statement. An advantage of this approach is that it clearly demonstrates the relationship between net income and retained earnings. A disadvantage is that the net income figure is buried in the statement rather than appearing as a total at the bottom. A combined statement of income and retained earnings is presented in Exhibit 4–13, which is excerpted from a recent annual report of Oakite Products, Inc.

SUMMARY PRESENTATION OF INCOME INFORMATION

In order to summarize the format requirements discussed in this chapter, we have included Exhibit 4–14 (pp. 164–165). This exhibit not only shows how items following income from continuing operations are displayed, but also demonstrates a detailed, multiple-step presentation of income from continuing operations. Although this amount of detail would seldom be found in financial statements prepared for external users, the exhibit does show where the various revenues, expenses, gains and losses typically are included.

SUMMARY OF IMPORTANT TOPICS AND CONCEPT APPLICATIONS

1. The income statement assists in achieving financial reporting objectives by providing information regarding the effects of transactions, events, and circumstances related to earnings activities that change a firm's resources and claims to those resources.

2. Income measurement requires both a capital maintenance concept and the measurement of a particular asset and liability attribute. Under GAAP, historical cost is the primary attribute measured, and the capital maintenance concept used is original invested dollars.

3. Two approaches to calculating net income are the **net assets approach** and the **transactions approach.**

4. The **current operating performance approach** and the **all-inclusive approach** reflect two different views about the role of the income statement. The all-inclusive approach, which requires that all revenues, expenses, gains, and losses must be included in the income statement, best describes current practice.

5. **Intraperiod tax allocation,** which requires that the income tax effect of an item must be reported with the item, contributes to the objectives of financial reporting by assisting users in evaluating, assessing, and predicting net cash flows to the firm.

6. Income statements prepared according to GAAP must report three items separately from income from continuing operations: (1) discontinued operations; (2) extraordinary items; and (3) cumulative effect of change in accounting principle. All of these items must be reported on a net-of-tax basis.

7. Separate reporting of **discontinued operations, extraordinary gains and losses,** and the **cumulative effect of changes in accounting principles** facilitates user predictions of cash flows.

8. In order to be reported as a discontinued operation, a segment must be a separate major line of business or a separate class of customer. Also, the assets, operating results, and activities of the segment must be clearly distinguishable. The gain or loss on discontinued operations consists of (1) the operating income or loss from the beginning of the period to the **measurement date** and (2) the operating income or loss during the phase-out period and the disposal gain or loss.

EXHIBIT 4—14   DETAILED PRESENTATION OF INCOME INFORMATION

WRL Company, Inc.

INCOME STATEMENT
FOR THE YEAR ENDED DECEMBER 31, 1987

Sales			$300,000
Less: Sales returns and allowances	$ 3,000		
Sales discounts	2,000	(5,000)	$295,000
Cost of goods sold:			
Beginning inventory		$30,000	
Purchases	$200,000		
Less: Returns and allowances $10,000			
Discounts taken 15,000	(25,000)	175,000	
Freight-in		5,000	
Cost of goods available for sale		$210,000	
Less: Ending inventory		(20,000)	190,000
Gross profit on sales			$105,000
Less: Operating expenses			
Selling expenses:			
Sales salaries	$ 11,000		
Advertising and promotion	19,000		
Freight-out	7,000		
Depreciation	23,000		
Bad debts expense	4,000		
Other selling expenses	1,000	$65,000	
General and administrative expenses:			
Administrative salaries	$ 20,000		
Property taxes	1,000		
Depreciation	4,000		
Insurance expense	900		
Research and development	1,100		
Other general and administrative	500	27,500	(92,500)
Operating income			$ 12,500
Other revenues and gains:			
Interest revenue	$ 600		
Dividend revenue	1,400		
Gain on sale of land	3,500		
Gain on sale of fixed assets	4,200	$ 9,700	

9. Extraordinary items, which take into account the environment in which the entity operates, are unusual and infrequent in occurrence.

10. Additional income information that must be reported includes earnings per share data, interim reports, and segment information.

11. The income statement format is continually evolving to meet the needs of users interested in assessing future income and cash flows. *Statement of Concepts No. 5* emphasizes the need for information about the various components of **earnings and**

Other expenses and losses:			
Interest on long-term debt	$ 700		
Loss on valuation of current marketable securities	1,800		
Loss on disposal of part of a division	4,000		
Unusual charge—loss on sale of investments	2,200	(8,700)	1,000
Income from continuing operations before income taxes			$ 13,500
Income tax expense			(2,100)
Income from continuing operations.........................			$ 11,400
Discontinued operations:			
Income from operations of discontinued segment *X*			
(less related tax of $4,000)		$ 8,000	
Loss on disposal of segment *X*, including provision			
of $10,000 for operating losses during phase-out			
period (less related tax savings of $5,000)..............		(12,000)	(4,000)
Income before extraordinary items and cumulative effect			
of a change in an accounting principle...................			$ 7,400
Extraordinary items:			
Loss due to earthquake (net of $2,000 tax savings)		$ (3,000)	
Gain on debt extinguishment (net of $1,600 tax)		4,400	
Gain on forced sale of assets to state municipality			
(net of $1,800 tax).................................		3,000	4,400
Cumulative effect on prior years of retroactive application			
of new depreciation method (net of $7,000 tax)			6,000
Net income			$ 17,800
Earnings per common share*:			
Income from continuing operations.....................			$1.14
Income from discontinued segment *X*....................			.80
Loss on disposal of segment *X*			(1.20)
Income before extraordinary items and cumulative effect.....			$ .74
Extraordinary items			.44
Cumulative effect of change in an accounting principle			.60
Net income			$1.78

*Assuming 10,000 shares outstanding.

comprehensive income that differ in risk, stability, and predictability. **Decision usefulness** can be enhanced only by providing more **timely** and more **reliable** information.

12. The statement of retained earnings reconciles the beginning and ending retained earnings balances. **Prior period adjustments** must be reported as an addition to or deduction from the beginning balance of retained earnings in the period in which the adjustment is made.

QUESTIONS

Q4-1. Why is it necessary to measure a particular attribute and to adopt a particular capital maintenance concept in order to determine accounting income?

Q4-2. What are the advantages to a transaction approach to reporting of accounting income as opposed to a net assets approach?

Q4-3. What is the periodicity assumption, and what is its relationship to income determination?

Q4-4. What is the revenue realization principle, and what is its role in income determination?

Q4-5. What is the matching principle, and what is its role in income determination?

Q4-6. What are the advantages and disadvantages of (1) the current operating approach and (2) the all-inclusive approach to income determination? Which approach is more descriptive of current practice? Explain.

Q4-7. What are (1) the single-step approach and (2) the multiple-step approach to the presentation of earnings information? Describe the advantages and disadvantages of each approach.

Q4-8. What is intraperiod tax allocation? How is the objective of intraperiod tax allocation related to the assessment of past and future cash flows?

Q4-9. What are discontinued operations, and how are they required to be reported?

Q4-10. What is meant by "measurement date" and "disposal date" with respect to discontinued operations?

Q4-11. What are the two criteria that must be met in order for an item to qualify as extraordinary? What two items must always be reported as extraordinary items?

Q4-12. How should extraordinary items be reported in the financial statements?

Q4-13. How should material items that meet one, but not both, of the criteria for extraordinary items be reported in the financial statements?

Q4-14. What are the three basic types of accounting changes covered by *APB Opinion No. 20?*

Q4-15. How are changes in accounting principle generally required to be reported in financial statements? What is the rationale underlying this treatment?

Q4-16. Give two examples of a change in accounting estimate.

Q4-17. Give an example of a change in reporting entity.

Q4-18. According to *FASB Statement No. 16,* what are the only two types of items that should be treated as prior period adjustments?

Q4-19. How should the effect of a prior period adjustment be reported in the financial statements?

Q4-20. Where should earnings per share data be disclosed in the financial statements? For which reported figures are earnings per share data required?

Q4-21. What is meant by the terms "interim reporting" and "segment reporting"?

Q4-22. In what ways have current reporting practices been criticized as inadequate with respect to stable and volatile components of earnings?

Q4-23. What is the purpose of the statement of retained earnings? What are the advantages and disadvantages of a combined statement of income and retained earnings?

CASES

C4-1. CONCEPTS UNDERLYING INCOME DETERMINATION   Several underlying concepts have particular relevance to the existing process of income determination. An understanding of these ideas helps greatly to explain current practice regarding income determination. Of particular relevance are the following four concepts:

    a) Periodicity assumption.
    b) Accrual approach.
    c) Revenue realization principle.
    d) Matching principle.

REQUIRED

Discuss the meaning of each of these concepts and describe their roles in the existing process of income determination.

C4-2. CURRENT OPERATING PERFORMANCE VIEW VS. ALL-INCLUSIVE VIEW   As the controller of Diversified Company, you have been asked by the president of the company to explain to him why certain items are included in the current period income statement. Specifically, he does not understand why a casualty loss (classified as an extraordinary item) and an item referred to as ''cumulative effect of change from straight line to accelerated depreciation'' are included in the determination of current period earnings. The president believes that the purpose of presenting the current year's earnings is to enable investors to project future earnings and future cash flows.

REQUIRED

Draft a memorandum to the president explaining the general view underlying the existing process of income determination. Your memorandum should distinguish between the current operating performance view and the all-inclusive view of income determination.

C4-3. INTRAPERIOD TAX ALLOCATION   The income tax effect of the various items that enter into the determination of net income and the tax effect of items taken directly to retained earnings must be reported according to the concept of intraperiod tax allocation.

REQUIRED

    1. What is the purpose of intraperiod tax allocation?

    2. Describe how intraperiod tax allocation is applied to:
      a) Income from continuing operations.
      b) Items that appear on the income statement after income from continuing operations.
      c) Prior period adjustments.

    3. Describe how earnings information would be reported for the items in part 2 if intraperiod tax allocation were not required. What problems do you see with such an approach?

C4-4. EXTRAORDINARY ITEMS   Certain items are required to be classified as extraordinary items. Two criteria must be met in order for an item to be classified as extraordinary.

REQUIRED

    1. Describe the two criteria that must be met in order for an item to be classified as extraordinary.

    2. Develop two examples that you believe constitute extraordinary items. Be specific.

    3. Describe the financial statement presentation of extraordinary items. What is the rationale for this treatment?

    4. Describe the financial statement presentation of items that meet one but not both of the criteria for extraordinary items.

C4-5. INCOME STATEMENT CLASSIFICATION   Chewning Company is engaged primarily in commercial and agricultural land sales, but also makes some retail land sales and condominium sales. Chewning recently acquired a retail land sales project with the agreement that it could return the property with no liability to Chewning if it did not desire to pursue the project. Chewning invested considerable money in the project before deciding, because of a declining economy, to return the project to the original owner before any sales were made.

REQUIRED

Describe the appropriate income statement presentation of the amount invested in the retail land sales project in the period in which the project was abandoned and returned to the original owner. Cite authoritative literature to support your answer.

(AICPA, adapted)

C4-6. EXTRAORDINARY ITEMS A textile manufacturer entered into firm purchase commitments for cotton at a very favorable price. The company currently has a very long position of purchase commitments at a low fixed price. Some of these contracts may be sold at a tremendous profit, as the cost of raw cotton has increased tremendously in recent months. The profit that might be realized from the sale of these contracts is extremely material in relation to normal operating income. The company has not sold such commitment contracts in the past, nor does it anticipate selling such contracts in the future.

REQUIRED

Should the sale of cotton futures commitment contracts be considered an extraordinary item? Explain your answer.

(AICPA, adapted)

C4-7. INCOME STATEMENT PRESENTATION The following events and transactions are to be considered independently. Assume that each item is material.

> **1.** The U.S. government exercises its right of eminent domain on some land owned by a rancher. This land is then designated as a wilderness area. The transaction results in a gain to the rancher.

> **2.** As a result of a court decision, James Brothers must write off the cost of its trademark on a board game that has been quite profitable.

> **3.** A company discovers that it has been misapplying the guidelines for accounting for leases. The company begins to apply the guidelines correctly in the current year.

> **4.** As a result of the Penn Square bank failure, a company loses part of its cash balance in excess of the $100,000 FDIC guarantee.

> **5.** A company suffers a loss on the value of its investment in ABC Corporation after it is disclosed that ABC issued false and misleading financial statements that materially overstated income.

> **6.** A major customer declares bankruptcy, causing a write-off of that customer's receivable.

> **7.** A company incurs a loss on the abandonment of some equipment formerly used in the business. This is the only time in the company's history that it has had such an abandonment.

REQUIRED

Determine the effect of each of the above items on the income statement in the period in which the event occurred. Include in your answer the appropriate classification of the income statement effect.

C4-8. ACCOUNTING CHANGES The various types of accounting changes may significantly affect the presentation of both financial position and results of operations for an accounting period and the trends shown in comparative financial statements and historical summaries.

REQUIRED

> **1.** Describe a change in accounting principle and how it should be reported in the income statement of the period when the change occurred.

> **2.** Other types of accounting changes are changes in accounting estimates and changes in reporting entity. Describe and give an example of each of these types of accounting changes.

(AICPA, adapted)

C4-9. INCOME STATEMENT PRESENTATION David Company's income statements for the years ended December 31, 1987, and December 31, 1986, were as follows:

David Company
STATEMENT OF INCOME

	YEAR ENDED DECEMBER 31	
	1987	1986
	(000 OMITTED)	
Net sales	$ 900,000	$ 750,000
Costs and expenses:		
Cost of goods sold	$ 720,000	$ 600,000
Selling, general and administrative expenses	112,000	90,000
Other, net	11,000	9,000
Total costs and expenses	$(843,000)	$(699,000)
Income from continuing operations before income taxes	$ 57,000	$ 51,000
Income taxes	(23,000)	(24,000)
Income from continuing operations	$ 34,000	$ 27,000
Loss on disposal of Dex Division, including provision of $1,500,000 for operating losses during phase-out period, less applicable income tax savings of $8,000,000	(8,000)	
Cumulative effect on prior years of change in depreciation method, less applicable income taxes of $1,500,000		3,000
Net income	$ 26,000	$ 30,000
Earnings per share of common stock:		
Income before cumulative effect of change in depreciation method	$ 2.60	$ 2.70
Cumulative effect on prior years of change in depreciation method, less applicable income taxes		.30
Net income	$ 2.60	$ 3.00

Additional facts are as follows:

a) On January 1, 1986, David Company changed its depreciation method for previously recorded plant machinery from the double-declining balance method to the straight-line method. The effect of applying the straight-line method for the year of and year after the change is included in David Company's income statements for the two years in cost of goods sold.

b) The loss from operations of the discontinued Dex Division from January 1, 1987, to September 30, 1987 (the portion of the year prior to the measurement date), and from January 1, 1986, to December 31, 1986, is included in David Company's income statements for the two years in "Other, net."

c) David Company has a simple capital structure with only common stock outstanding. The net income per share of common stock was based on the weighted average number of common shares outstanding during each year.

REQUIRED

Determine from the additional facts above whether the presentation of those facts in David Company's income statements is appropriate. If the presentation is appropriate, discuss the theoretical rationale for the presentation. If the presentation is not appropriate, specify the appropriate presentation and discuss its theoretical rationale.

(AICPA, adapted)

EXERCISES

E4-1. NET ASSETS APPROACH TO INCOME DETERMINATION The records of Cooper Company disclosed the following information:

Total assets, 1/1/87	$623,000
Total liabilities, 1/1/87	472,000
Total assets, 12/31/87	761,500
Total liabilities, 12/31/87	527,400
Cash dividends declared and paid during 1987	32,100
Additional investments of cash by stockholders in exchange for common stock	84,000
Fair market value of land donated to Cooper during 1987 (also amount at which recorded)	10,700

REQUIRED

1. Compute net income for Cooper Company for 1987.

2. What weakness do you see in presenting earnings information as computed in part 1?

E4-2. TRANSACTIONS APPROACH TO INCOME DETERMINATION The following account balances were taken from the ledger of T. J.'s Discount Store at the end of the year:

Sales revenue	$978,500
Purchases	496,300
Beginning inventory	73,000
Ending inventory	68,800
Selling expenses	106,400
Lease revenues	48,000
Interest expense	19,200
Income tax expense	74,900
Investment revenue	9,800
Purchase discounts	8,900
Freight in	16,600
Administrative expenses	91,700
Dividends declared	36,300
Sales discounts	23,900

REQUIRED

1. Compute net income for the current year.

2. What advantage does the transactions approach have over the net assets approach to presenting earnings information?

E4-3. SINGLE-STEP INCOME STATEMENT The following items relate to the current year's operations of Johnson Equipment Company:

Inventory, beginning of year	$ 69,126,500
Depreciation	5,032,200
Sales	293,621,000
Purchases	198,735,600
Inventory, end of year	63,433,500
Sales returns and allowances	4,111,700
Freight in	33,007,200
Income taxes	11,813,000
Purchase discounts, returns, and allowances	27,234,500
Miscellaneous revenue	2,364,000
Selling, general, and administrative expenses	46,045,300
Interest expense	4,952,200
Other expenses	670,100

There were 4.5 million shares of common stock outstanding during the period.

REQUIRED

1. Prepare in good form a single-step income statement, including EPS.

2. Discuss the advantages and disadvantages of the single-step income statement.

E4-4. SINGLE-STEP INCOME STATEMENT Wetotum Railroad Corporation has the following revenue and expense items at the end of the current year (in thousands of dollars):

State and local taxes	$ 54,097
Sales	849,722
Crude oil and other raw materials used	468,727
Depreciation, depletion, and amortization	129,716
Transportation revenues	1,174,544
Other operating costs	216,661
Salaries, wages, and employee benefits	614,351
Interest expense	60,672
Materials and supplies used	273,559
Other revenue	40,698
Federal income taxes	59,506

In addition to the above items, Wetotum made a material adjustment at the end of the current year to an accrued liability account established eight years earlier. The company elected eight years ago to participate in Amtrak, which assumed responsibilities for providing intercity rail passenger service from participating railroads. The liability account was established to reflect accruals to provide for severance payments to employees affected by the discontinuance of passenger services and the write-off of passenger facilities. A review during the current year indicated an excess accrual. Therefore, the balance of the accrued liability has been reduced and the adjustment of $7.5 million is to be reflected in the financial statements for the current period. Also, 4 million shares of common stock were outstanding during the period.

REQUIRED

Prepare in good form a single-step income statement, including EPS.

E4-5. SINGLE-STEP AND MULTIPLE-STEP INCOME STATEMENT The following income statement items were taken from the accounts of Comfy Computer Corporation (in millions of dollars):

Sales	$2,845.7
Interest expense	39.3
Research and development costs	187.2
Gain on sale of fixed assets	16.7
Cost of sales	2,239.3
Computer rental and service revenue	702.1
Income taxes	140.7
Tax benefit from carryforward of prior year's operating loss	19.9
Selling, general, and administrative expenses	794.0
Interest revenue	17.5

There were 21 million shares of common stock outstanding during the year.

REQUIRED

1. Prepare a single-step income statement, including EPS.

2. Prepare a multiple-step income statement, including EPS.

3. Which format do you prefer? Why?

E4-6. SINGLE-STEP AND MULTIPLE-STEP INCOME STATEMENT   Olive's Oil Company had the following items to be reported in the current period financial statements (in thousands of dollars):

Interest expense	$ 29,771
Cost of sales	2,722,954
Income taxes	58,500
Depreciation, depletion, and amortization	80,146
Sales	3,451,224
Excise taxes on petroleum products	235,557
Interest revenue	51,043
Selling, administrative, and general expenses	254,016
Gain from extinguishment of debt (net of tax effect)	13,008
Exploration costs of nonproductive wells (expensed as incurred)	21,329

In addition, 25 million shares of common stock were outstanding during the period.

REQUIRED

  1. Prepare a single-step income statement, including EPS.

  2. Prepare a multiple-step income statement, including EPS.

  3. Which format do you prefer? Why?

E4-7. DISCONTINUED OPERATIONS, INCOME STATEMENT PREPARATION   Accountants for Food Specialties, Inc., obtained the following information from the accounting records of the company for 1987 (in thousands of dollars):

Selling, general, and administrative expenses	$ 52,555
Sales	660,486
Depreciation and amortization	7,952
Cost of sales	582,265
Interest expense	11,631
Provision for uncollectible note	1,135
Other revenue	2,162
Income taxes	2,414

   The "provision for uncollectible note" relates to a mortgage note receivable from Bungling Bakery, a company that has filed for the protection of the court under Chapter XI of the federal bankruptcy act. During the year, Food Specialties disposed of its apparel segment. The operating loss from segment operations during the year prior to the measurement date was $3,020,000, net of taxes of $990,000. After the measurement date, the combined operating loss and loss on disposal of the segment was an additional $3,290,000, net of tax benefits of $2,212,000.

REQUIRED

Prepare the income statement for Food Specialties, Inc., for 1987.

E4-8. DISCONTINUED OPERATIONS, INCOME STATEMENT PRESENTATION   As chief accountant for the Rocky Point Fish Company, you have received the following information regarding 1987 activities (in thousands of dollars):

Advertising expense	$ 825
Gain on disposition of fixed assets	1,003
Gross sales	175,453
General, selling, and administrative expenses	11,297
Sales discounts	5,556
Cost of sales	140,109
Reduction of income taxes arising from carryforward of prior years' operating losses	1,310
Miscellaneous expenses	187
Interest revenue	590
Interest expense	4,736
Income taxes	4,574

During the year the company decided to discontinue its pet food division, which produces pet food from residuals of the company's seafood processing operations. The operating income from the discontinued division during the year prior to the measurement date was $35,000 net of taxes of $10,000. The company is continuing to operate the division until a buyer is found. It is anticipated that a buyer will be found within the first few months of the next year and that a loss of $1,270,000 (net of tax benefits of $934,000) will result from the disposal.

In addition, several unusual operations were being phased out during the year, including tropical shrimp product lines, frozen retail products, a fleet of scallop fishing vessels, and a crabmeat processing operation. The loss during the year from these operations, which do not qualify as discontinued operations according to *APB Opinion No. 30,* was $3,184,000. The number of common shares outstanding during the year was 500,000.

REQUIRED

Prepare a multiple-step income statement for Rocky Point Fish Company for the year ended December 31, 1987.

E4-9. DISCONTINUED OPERATIONS

A) On May 1, 1987, the board of directors of Edgewood, Inc., approved a formal plan to sell its electronics division. The division is considered a segment of the business. It is expected that the actual sale will occur in the first three months of 1988. During 1987 the electronics division had a loss from operations, before any tax effect, of $1.2 million, which was incurred evenly throughout the year. Edgewood's effective tax rate for 1987 is 40 percent.

REQUIRED

Calculate the amount that Edgewood should report as loss from operations of the discontinued electronics division for the year ended December 31, 1987.

B) On April 30, 1987, Empire Corporation, whose fiscal year-end is September 30, adopted a plan to discontinue the operations of Bello Division on November 30, 1987. Bello contributed a major portion of Empire's sales volume. Empire estimated that Bello would sustain a loss of $460,000 from May 1, 1987, through September 30, 1987, and would sustain an additional loss of $220,000 from October 1, 1987, to November 30, 1987. Empire estimated that it would realize a gain of $600,000 on the sale of Bello's assets. At September 30, 1987, Empire determined that Bello had actually lost $1,120,000 for the fiscal year, of which $420,000 represented the loss from May 1 to September 30, 1987.

REQUIRED

Ignoring income tax effects, how much should Empire report in its income statement for the year ending September 30, 1987, as gain or loss on disposal of Bello?

(AICPA, adapted)

E4-10. INCOME STATEMENT PREPARATION   Husky Corporation calculated after-tax income of $800,000 from continuing operations for 1987. The following information was not considered in arriving at the $800,000:

a) During 1987, Husky sold its headquarters building for an after-tax gain of $1 million.
b) In 1987, Husky sold its Doz Division, a major segment of its business. Husky realized a gain of $650,000 after taxes on the disposal of the assets of Doz. Operating losses of Doz in 1987 prior to the decision to dispose of the division were $710,000 (net of tax benefits).
c) In 1987, Husky adopted the double-declining balance method of depreciation. Previously, the straight-line method had been used. The change decreased 1987 income by $20,000 (before taxes). The cumulative effect on prior periods' income was a $130,000 decrease (before taxes).

REQUIRED

Present in good form the 1987 income statement for Husky Corporation, beginning with income from continuing operations. Assume an income tax rate of 40 percent on all items for all years. There were 100,000 shares of common stock outstanding throughout 1987.

E4-11. INCOME STATEMENT PRESENTATION OF ACCOUNTING CHANGES AND DISCONTINUED OPERATIONS Scientific Innovators, Inc., reported income from continuing operations for 1987 of $2,950,000. In addition, the following information relates to 1987:

a) The company disposed of its heat treating equipment division during the year at a loss (net of $131,000 tax benefit) of $68,000. The loss from operations of this division during the year prior to the measurement date (net of tax benefit of $170,000) was $152,000.

b) The company changed its accounting policy for commission revenues at the beginning of 1987 in order better to match marketing expenses and commission revenues within the same accounting period. The company adopted the policy of recognizing commission revenues when all of its marketing services are completed and the order is accepted by the supplier; previously, commissions were recognized at the time the supplier shipped the product. The effect of this change was to increase income from continuing operations by $11,000 for 1987. The cumulative effect of the change on previous years' income (net of income tax of $120,000) was an increase of $130,000.

c) There were 1 million shares of common stock outstanding during the period.

REQUIRED

Prepare the income statement for Scientific Innovators for 1987, beginning with "Income from continuing operations."

E4-12. CHANGE IN ACCOUNTING PRINCIPLE; ERROR CORRECTION; COMBINED STATEMENT OF INCOME AND RETAINED EARNINGS Quenchum, Inc., a soft-drink company, has the following items to be reflected in its 1987 financial statements (in thousands of dollars):

Net sales	$271,008
Administrative, marketing, and general expenses	88,969
Federal and state income taxes	18,845
Uninsured casualty loss, net of tax benefit of $1,100 (extraordinary)	1,464
Cost of sales	141,093
Other revenue	1,945

In addition, you determine that Quenchum changed its method of inventory costing from FIFO to average cost as of the beginning of 1987. The effect of this change was to decrease current earnings (net of applicable taxes of $894,000) by $986,000. The cumulative effect on prior years was a decrease in net income (net of taxes of $2,849,000) of $3,178,000.

Also, it was discovered that depreciation expense had been understated by $1,245,000 in last year's income statement. The marginal tax rate was 45 percent in 1986. Dividends of $12,300,000 were paid during 1987. The retained earnings balance at January 1, 1987, was $42,371,000.

REQUIRED

1. Prepare a combined multiple-step statement of income and retained earnings for Quenchum, Inc., for the year ended December 31, 1987.

2. Describe the advantages and disadvantages of the combined statement of income and retained earnings.

E4-13. COMBINED STATEMENT OF INCOME AND RETAINED EARNINGS Sun Devil Company accumulated the following items during 1987 (in thousands of dollars):

Interest expense	$ 1,350
Net sales	326,846
Depreciation and amortization	2,791
Cost of sales	226,758
Provision for income taxes	12,665
Bad debt expense	1,177
Other revenue	160
Contribution to employees' profit-sharing plan	2,695
Advertising, selling, administrative, and general expenses	26,681
Cash dividends	1,017
Beginning retained earnings	33,913
Average number of common shares outstanding	18,474,000

REQUIRED

Prepare a combined single-step statement of income and retained earnings for Sun Devil Company for the year ended December 31, 1987.

PROBLEMS

P4-1. SINGLE-STEP INCOME STATEMENT   You are charged with the responsibility of preparing the income statement for Crooch Exploration Corporation for the year ended March 31, 1988. Pertinent information for accomplishing this task is set forth below (in thousands of dollars):

	DR	CR
Provision for income taxes	$ 460	
Production expenses	424	
Well supervisory fees		$ 187
Drilling program marketing expenses	139	
Commissions and drilling arrangements revenue		946
Interest expense	301	
Tax benefit from carryforward of prior years' net operating losses (extraordinary)		267
General and administrative expenses	1,467	
Oil and gas sales		2,560
Management fees		322
Provision for losses on advances	91	
Depreciation, depletion, and amortization	358	
Cumulative effect on prior years of change in method of allocating administrative overhead (net of tax effect)		152

On average, there were 3,904,000 shares of stock outstanding during the year.

REQUIRED

1. Prepare a single-step income statement for the year ended March 31, 1988, including EPS.

2. What disclosures are necessary with respect to the change in method of overhead allocation?

P4-2. COMBINED STATEMENT OF INCOME AND RETAINED EARNINGS   Goodyear Van Lines, Inc., presents its results of operations and retained earnings reconciliation in a combined statement. Selected information from the accounts for 1987 is as follows (in thousands of dollars):

Communications and utilities expense	$ 445
Rent expense	327
Operating revenues	22,309
Salaries, wages, and fringe benefits	2,883
Depreciation and amortization	215
Leasing revenues	123
Interest expense	271
Loss on disposal of equipment	23
Supplies expense	286
Purchased transportation costs (current expense)	13,970
Administrative and general expenses	1,589
Miscellaneous revenue	131
Insurance expense	969
Agent commission fees	2,663
Taxes and licenses	90
Retained earnings *deficit,* beginning of year	694

On average, 880,000 shares of stock were outstanding during the year.

REQUIRED

Prepare a combined single-step statement of income (loss) and retained earnings (deficit) for 1987, including net income (loss) per share.

P4-3. SINGLE-STEP INCOME STATEMENT   Dew Drop Inns, Inc., is in the process of preparing financial statements for 1987. Relevant data are as follows (in thousands of dollars):

	DR	CR
Food and beverage revenues		$ 78,895
Medical revenues		39,883
Room and related services expense	$65,859	
Construction expense	4,798	
License sales and royalties		11,545
General and administrative expense	42,373	
Room and related services revenue		171,462
Medical expenses	31,497	
Construction revenue		6,064
Interest and dividend revenue		8,540
Depreciation	16,752	
Provision for income taxes	5,367	
Other revenue		5,877
Other operating expenses	49,192	
Gain on extinguishment of debt (net of taxes of $9,946)		8,659
Loss from expropriation of Jamaican resort facilities (net of tax benefit of $496)	1,396	
Loss from discontinuance of furniture manufacturing division (net of tax benefits of $518)	636	

There were 25 million shares of common stock outstanding during the year.

REQUIRED

1. Prepare a single-step income statement, including EPS, for the year ended December 31, 1987.

2. Describe the disclosures required for any items presented after income from continuing operations.

P4-4. MULTIPLE-STEP INCOME STATEMENT; DISCONTINUED OPERATIONS   Accounts of Jayhawk Drugs Corporation showed the following balances at the end of 1987 (in thousands of dollars):

Inventory, 1/1/87	$14,767
Purchase discounts, returns, and allowances	5,280
Sales	98,197
Inventory, 12/31/87	9,519
Purchases	71,650
Sales discounts, returns, and allowances	7,480
Freight in	2,321
Interest expense	1,395
Other revenue	119
Selling, general, and administrative expenses	12,486
Provision for loss on closed facilities	168

a) The provision for loss on closed facilities was established to cover the estimated loss on the disposal of certain facilities associated with the company's wholesale drug operation, which have been or are in the process of being closed. This item does not qualify for treatment as a discontinued operation.

b) In December 1987 the board of directors determined that the company's wholesale surgical supply operations were to be discontinued. In connection with this planned disposition, realized and estimated losses from disposal of assets are expected to total $111,342 (net of tax benefit of $74,232). The loss from operations of the discontinued segment (net of tax benefit of $678,245) was $1,948,990 in 1987.

c) The income tax rate on all items except discontinued operations is 35 percent.

d) There were 7 million shares of common stock outstanding during the year.

REQUIRED

Prepare a multiple-step income statement for 1987, including EPS.

P4-5. DISCONTINUED OPERATIONS Condensed income statements for Zola Corporation, a diversified company, were as follows for the two years ended December 31, 1987 and 1986:

	1987	1986
Net sales	$10,000,000	$9,600,000
Cost of sales	(6,200,000)	(6,000,000)
Gross profit	$ 3,800,000	$3,600,000
Operating expenses	(2,200,000)	(2,400,000)
Operating income	$ 1,600,000	$1,200,000
Gain on sale of division	900,000	—
	$ 2,500,000	$1,200,000
Provision for income taxes	(1,250,000)	(600,000)
Net income	$ 1,250,000	$ 600,000

On January 1, 1987, Zola entered into an agreement to sell for $3,200,000 the assets and product line of one of its separate operating divisions. The sale was consummated on December 31, 1987, and resulted in a gain of $900,000. This division's contribution to Zola's reported income before income taxes for each year was as follows:

1987 .... $640,000 loss
1986 .... $500,000 loss

REQUIRED

Assuming an income tax rate of 50 percent, prepare revised comparative income statements for 1987 and 1986, properly reporting the effect of the discontinued operation.

(AICPA, adapted)

P4-6. DISCONTINUED OPERATIONS Assume the following notation (all figures net of tax effect) related to a segment disposal:

o = operating income (loss) from beginning of period to measurement date
r_1 = realized operating income (loss) from measurement date to end of fiscal year
r_2 = realized gain (loss) on disposal of segment assets to end of fiscal year
e_1 = estimated operating income (loss) from end of fiscal year to disposal date
e_2 = estimated gain (loss) on disposal of segment assets from end of fiscal year to disposal date

Now assume the following amounts:

	CASE 1	CASE 2	CASE 3	CASE 4
o	$80,000	$(80,000)	$80,000	$80,000
r_1	20,000	20,000	20,000	20,000
r_2	50,000	(50,000)	(50,000)	50,000
e_1	10,000	10,000	10,000	10,000
e_2	(90,000)	(90,000)	90,000	90,000

REQUIRED

For each case, calculate the amount that should be reported as discontinued operations in the income statement.

P4-7. REPORTING EARNINGS INFORMATION   Houston Corporation has tentatively computed income from continuing operations before taxes as $8,400,000 for 1987. The following items have *not* been considered in arriving at income from continuing operations:

   a) It was discovered during 1987 that depreciation of $86,800 on a plant facility had inadvertently been omitted in the previous year.

   b) The company sold investments from its portfolio during the year for $623,000. The cost of the securities disposed of was $767,000.

   c) During the year, a patent with an original cost of $221,000 and book value of $84,000 was written off as worthless because a competitor marketed a slightly modified but significantly improved product at a similar price.

   d) As the result of a strike by union employees which lasted 45 days, the company incurred excess labor costs of $318,000 associated with the employment of short-term nonunion laborers and additional security forces during the strike.

   e) In July 1987 the company purchased and retired a portion of its long-term debt in the open market at a price of $1,281,000. The carrying value of the debt at the date of purchase was $1,549,000 (applicable tax rate 25 percent).

   f) In December 1987 the company decided to change its method of inventory costing effective as of January 1, 1987, for a major portion of its inventories from average cost to FIFO. This change decreased cost of goods sold for 1987 by $148,000. Prior years' income would have been $861,000 more (net of taxes of $427,000) if the company had been using FIFO during those years.

   g) Except as specified in *e*, the applicable tax rate was 40 percent.

   h) There were 3.5 million shares of stock outstanding during the year.

REQUIRED

   1. Prepare an income statement for 1987, including EPS, beginning with income from continuing operations before taxes.

   2. Describe the required disclosures for items *a–f*.

P4-8. REPORTING EARNINGS INFORMATION   Warren Communication Corporation computed income from continuing operations before taxes as $34,850,000 for 1987. The accountant who prepared the tentative income statement, however, had some doubts about the appropriate treatment of certain items that appeared to be nonroutine, and did not consider the following items:

   a) Warren had invested $4,988,000 over a three-year period in the production of a television show. At the time the expenditures were made, there was little doubt about the ability to recover these costs through the sale of commercial time. Thus Warren deferred these costs, to be matched against future revenues. During 1987, however, the National Television Viewing Board issued a regulation that effectively prohibited the televising of the show to the general public. Warren determined that revenues of approximately $800,000 could be generated through the sale of rights to the show to various pay television operations. Accordingly, the deferral was reduced to $800,000.

   b) During the year, fixed assets with a book value of $1,321,000 were sold for $589,000.

   c) A major production facility in Los Angeles was totally destroyed by an earthquake. The book value of the property, which was insured for $2,000,000, was $4,523,000.

   d) The applicable tax rate was 40 percent.

   e) There were 28 million shares of stock outstanding during the year.

REQUIRED

   1. Prepare an income statement for 1987, beginning with income from operations before taxes and including EPS.

   2. Describe the required disclosures for items *a–c*.

P4-9. STATEMENT OF RETAINED EARNINGS; ERROR CORRECTION   Bedford Corporation had a retained earnings balance of $394,000 on December 31, 1986. Net income for 1987 was $72,000. During 1987 cash dividends of $10,000 were declared and paid on preferred shares and cash dividends of $23,000 were declared on the no-par common shares, to be paid in January 1988. It was discovered during 1987 that a machine that had been acquired at the beginning of 1982 for $15,000 had been erroneously expensed upon acquisition. Total estimated useful life was 15 years. In addition, a 5 percent stock dividend was declared and issued during 1987. The fair market value of the shares issued, $41,000, was transferred from retained earnings to capital stock. The tax rate for all periods was 40 percent. Bedford uses straight-line depreciation for its machinery.

REQUIRED

Prepare a statement of retained earnings for Bedford Corporation for the year ended December 31, 1987.

P4-10. PREPARATION OF INCOME STATEMENT AND STATEMENT OF RETAINED EARNINGS FirTree Corporation is accumulating financial data needed to prepare the financial statements for the year ended December 31, 1987. The retained earnings totaled $1,700,000 at January 1, 1987. Cash dividends of $36,000 were declared during 1987. The 1987 estimated income before taxes without considering the five items described below is $870,000. The information regarding the following activities has been taken from the company's records:

a) A lawsuit arising from a 1985 claim was settled by the company during 1987 for $70,000. The loss has not been accrued and is due for payment in March 1988.

b) The company sold one of several buildings in its Finishing Division at a gain of $20,000.

c) FirTree experienced a $200,000 loss of timber in 1987 due to a flood resulting from the eruption of a volcano that had been inactive for over 50 years. The loss was not covered by insurance.

d) The company changed its method for depreciating its buildings in 1987 from an accelerated method to straight-line. Total depreciation on the buildings through the end of 1986 would have been $260,000 lower if the straight-line method had been used. The change was made for both book and tax purposes.

e) Office equipment purchased in January 1986 for $45,000 was incorrectly debited to office supplies expense. The straight-line method is used to depreciate office equipment for book and tax purposes. The office equipment was estimated to have a three-year life with no expected scrap value. This error has not been corrected.

Assume that FirTree Corporation is subject to a 40 percent income tax rate on all items.

REQUIRED

A) 1. Calculate the 1987 income from operations before income taxes for FirTree Corporation, identifying adjustments, if any, that need to be made to the estimated income of $870,000.

2. Prepare a partial income statement for FirTree Corporation for the year ended December 31, 1987, beginning with the amount for adjusted income from operations before income taxes as calculated in requirement A.1.

B) Prepare a statement of retained earnings for FirTree Corporation for the year ended December 31, 1987.

(AICPA, adapted)

5 THE BALANCE SHEET AND STATEMENT OF CASH FLOWS

Historically, investors and other financial statement users generally concentrated their analysis on the income statement, focusing specifically on net income and earnings per share as a basis for decision making. However, in recent years users have become increasingly concerned about liquidity and financial flexibility. These characteristics of a firm can be evaluated properly only by studying the balance sheet, also called the statement of financial position, and the statement of cash flows. Many investors discovered the hard way that reasonable expectations regarding future cash flows require the study of *all* of the basic financial statements.

In this chapter we describe and illustrate the purpose, format, and content of the balance sheet and of the statement of cash flows. The balance sheet coverage in this chapter will provide the background you need to understand later chapters. The uses of the balance sheet are discussed in the next section, followed by an analysis of classification and valuation of items included in the balance sheet. Next we describe and illustrate notes and supplementary information. These notes and supplementary disclosures may relate to the income statement or statement of cash flows as well as to the balance sheet. The last section of the chapter presents a brief introduction to the statement of cash flows.

USES OF THE BALANCE SHEET

As transactions and events occur during the period, we record the effects in the appropriate accounts according to generally accepted accounting principles, always maintaining the equality in the accounting equation: Assets = Liabilities + Owners' equity. The balance sheet is a summary of assets, liabilities, and owners' equity accounts and their related account balances at a specific date. One may think of the balance sheet as a statement of the economic resources (assets) available to an entity and of the claims to, or interests in, those resources (liabilities and owners' equity) at the statement date.

Another way to think of the information contained in the balance sheet is to view it as a still photograph of a dynamic process. In preparing a balance sheet, we are halting momentarily the inflows and outflows associated with earnings and other activities in order to assess the entity's resources and claims to those resources. This set of resources and obligations represents the results of all past activities, and it likewise represents the base with which the entity enters the next period.

The balance sheet is a primary source of information about a firm's liquidity and financial flexibility. **Liquidity** depends on the amount of time expected to lapse until an asset is converted into cash or until a liability is paid. For example, analysis of a firm's current assets, which represent short-term sources of cash, in relation to current liabilities, which represent short-term obligations to pay cash, permits an assessment of a firm's ability to meet financial obligations as they mature and of short-term dividend-paying ability. **Financial flexibility** is a firm's ability to alter future cash flows by responding to unexpected needs and opportunities. Thus, financial flexibility is a measure of a firm's adaptability. The balance sheet, by reporting available resources and the amounts and timing of claims on those resources, provides information useful for assessing a firm's financial flexibility. For example, a firm's ratio of long-term debt to owners' equity may be so high as to indicate that the firm has no additional long-term borrowing capacity. Thus, to raise additional capital the firm may be forced to issue additional capital stock, which could dilute the earnings per share. Such information is relevant to present and prospective investors.

In addition to providing information on liquidity and financial flexibility, the balance sheet is useful in assessing a firm's profitability. By relating net income to assets or to owners' equity, investors can determine the firm's return on invested resources. Also, a comparison of certain balance sheet items with related income statement items provides users with a measure of the efficiency with which resources are being employed by the firm. For example, cost of goods sold, an income statement item, divided by inventory, a balance sheet item, provides a measure of the firm's ability to generate sales by maintaining a given amount of inventory.

There are limitations to what the balance sheet conveys, however. Under generally accepted accounting principles, current market values are not disclosed for most balance sheet items. The accounting process underlying the balance sheet is based on the historical cost principle. Further, some resources that are used to generate future cash flows are not recorded in the accounts because the accounting process is based on transactions. For example, the value of a superior management group is not recorded in the accounts even though future cash flows are enhanced by the superior management team. The balance sheet does not portray the fair market value of the total entity. Because some resources are not recorded, and because most resources that are recorded are not reported at current market value, the amount of the recorded assets minus liabilities is not likely to be representative of the entity's fair market value. The information reported in the balance sheet, however, should be useful to those interested in assessing the fair market value of the entity.

CLASSIFICATION AND VALUATION IN THE BALANCE SHEET

As we have noted, a balance sheet summarizes the balances of assets, liabilities, and owners' equity accounts. These accounts are grouped together in classes to assist users. In general, the classifications should indicate the amounts and liquidity of available resources, management's intent with respect to the use of the resources, and the amounts and timing of obligations that require liquid resources for settlement.

Assets that differ in their expected function should be reported separately. For example, inventories generate cash flows through sales, whereas property, plant, and equip-

EXHIBIT 5–1	TYPICAL BALANCE SHEET CLASSIFICATIONS

ASSETS	**LIABILITIES AND OWNERS' EQUITY**
Current assets	Current liabilities
Noncurrent assets	Long-term liabilities
Investments and funds	Owners' equity
Property, plant, and equipment	Contributed capital
Intangible assets	Retained earnings
Other assets	

ment assets generate cash flows through internal use in operations. Thus these two categories of assets should be reported separately.

Assets and liabilities with different implications for financial flexibility should be reported separately. For example, because operating assets, such as property, plant, and equipment, afford a firm less financial flexibility than assets held for investment purposes, such as investments in the capital stock of other companies, these two categories of assets should be reported separately.

The format depicted in Exhibit 5–1 for the balance sheet is the most common in current use. (See pages 204–205, in Appendix 5–1, where we present the balance sheet of an actual firm.) The classification scheme shown in Exhibit 5–1 is based primarily on liquidity. Within the assets category, current assets are more liquid than noncurrent assets. Within the liabilities category, current liabilities are more liquid than long-term liabilities. The items under owners' equity in Exhibit 5–1 are those that appear in the reports of corporations. In the report of a proprietorship or partnership, the owners' equity section would consist only of the capital accounts of the owners.

There are two common statement formats for the balance sheet: the **account form** and the **report form.** A balance sheet presented under the *account form* lists assets on the left side of the balance sheet and presents liabilities and owners' equity items on the right side, as in Exhibit 5–1. In the *report form,* assets are listed first and then liabilities and owners' equity items are presented below the assets.

In the remainder of this section, we describe the content of each balance sheet classification and summarize the basic valuation guidelines for the balance sheet items. This chapter provides a useful overview before the detailed study of individual balance sheet items in subsequent chapters.

CURRENT ASSETS Assets are divided into two broad categories in the balance sheet: current assets and noncurrent assets. **Current assets** are cash and other assets that can reasonably be expected to be converted to cash or consumed during one year or during the normal operating cycle of the business, whichever is longer.[1] The **operating cycle** is the time between the acquisition of inventory and the conversion of that inventory back into cash. For example, the operating cycle of a distillery making good whiskey may extend 10 years, whereas the operating cycle of a grocery store may be no more than several days. The distinction between current and noncurrent assets for the distiller is based on the 10-year period, whereas the distinction for the grocery store is based on a one-year period. Any asset whose use is restricted for purposes other than current operations must be excluded from current assets. For example, cash set aside in a special fund to repay long-term debt would not be classified as a current asset.

[1] Committee on Accounting Procedure, "Restatement and Revision of Accounting Research Bulletins," *Accounting Research Bulletin No. 43* (New York: AICPA, 1953), chap. 3, sec. A.

EXHIBIT 5–2   PRESENTATION OF CURRENT ASSETS

International Business Machines Corporation and Subsidiary Companies

FROM 1984 ANNUAL REPORT
(in millions of dollars)

CURRENT ASSETS

Cash...	$ 600
Marketable securities, at cost, which approximates market	3,762
Notes and accounts receivable-trade, net of allowances	7,393
Other accounts receivable	718
Inventories..	6,598
Prepaid expenses and other current assets	1,304
	$20,375

The current asset presentation in Exhibit 5–2 is reproduced from a recent annual report of IBM Corporation. Note that the current assets are ordered according to their liquidity.

CASH   Cash is the most common current asset. It is listed first under current assets because it is the most liquid asset. All cash balances on hand and on deposit that are readily available for current operating purposes should be included in the balance sheet in the cash category under current assets.

TEMPORARY INVESTMENTS   The next most liquid asset, and thus the next category presented under current assets, consists of temporary investments of idle cash. These investments are sometimes described as **short-term investments** or, as in Exhibit 5–2, **marketable securities.** In order to qualify for inclusion in the current asset section, the investment must be readily marketable *and* the intent of management must be to convert the asset into cash for operating purposes within one year or the operating cycle, whichever is longer. Examples of temporary investments include U.S. treasury bills and capital stock of other companies acquired as a temporary investment of idle cash. The objective in holding temporary investments is to have a pool of resources available for conversion to cash on very short notice. Thus, the most relevant basis for valuation of temporary investments is current market value, because that amount is the cash inflow that would result from the sale of the securities at the balance sheet date. *FASB Statement No. 12,* issued in 1975, requires that temporary investments in marketable securities representing ownership shares in a corporation must be reported at the lower of aggregate cost or market value at the balance sheet date.[2] Thus, marketable **equity** securities are reported at market value only if the aggregate market value is below cost. If market value exceeds cost, the investment is reported at cost, but market value must be disclosed.

Temporary investments in marketable **debt** securities, such as government or corporate bonds, are reported either at cost or at lower of cost or market. The authoritative literature requires that such investments must be reported at cost.[3] However, since the publication of *Statement No. 12,* many companies have extended the *Statement*'s requirement that marketable *equity* securities must be reported at the lower of aggregate cost or market to marketable *debt* securities as well. Thus, two different valuation methods are being used in practice for marketable debt securities. Also, when a significant and perma-

[2] "Accounting for Certain Marketable Securities," *Statement of Financial Accounting Standards No. 12* (Stamford, Conn.: FASB, 1975).

[3] *Accounting Research Bulletin No. 43,* chap. 3, sec. A.

nent decline in market value below cost occurs, such securities must be reported at market value.

SHORT-TERM RECEIVABLES   Short-term receivables are claims to cash which are expected to be exercised within one year or the operating cycle, whichever is longer. They often constitute a significant portion of current assets. In our credit society, a firm's credit and collection policies have a strong influence on profitability. **Trade receivables** result from sales of goods or services on account. For example, a routine credit sale of inventory to a customer creates a trade receivable. That is, a firm sells goods or services in exchange for a promise to pay according to specified terms. **Nontrade receivables** arise when a firm lends money on a short-term basis. For example, a firm may lend cash to a company officer on a short-term basis. Usually these nontrade receivables are supported by a formal contractual agreement specifying the terms of repayment and are called **notes receivable.** Short-term receivables are reported at **net realizable value,** which is the amount of cash expected to be collected. Because anticipated uncollectible accounts, discounts, and returns and allowances reduce the expected cash flow from receivables, these expected cash flow reductions should be disclosed.

INVENTORIES   In manufacturing and in wholesale and retail merchandising, a large percentage of a firm's resources is tied up in inventory. **Inventories** are those assets that merchandising firms acquire for resale or that manufacturers produce for sale to customers in the ordinary course of business. Inventories are one step further removed from cash than receivables. Thus, inventories follow receivables in the current asset section of the balance sheet. Inventories generally are accounted for in accordance with the historical cost principle. However, when the revenue-producing ability of inventory falls below its cost, the inventory is valued at the lower market value, as we discuss more fully in Chapter 10. Furthermore, inventories occasionally are valued at net realizable value when selling prices are known, the sale is not a critical event in the earning process, and selling costs are minimal. This method is discussed more fully in Chapter 6.

A manufacturing concern has four kinds of inventory: (1) raw materials, which are goods acquired for use in the production process and which ultimately become the finished product; (2) work in process, which consists of partially completed goods; (3) finished goods, which are goods ready for sale to customers; and (4) miscellaneous supplies, which are items consumed in the production process but are not primary materials. The balance sheet for a manufacturing concern should include these four categories. In a merchandising concern there are no raw materials or work-in-process inventories since there is no production process.

PREPAID EXPENSES   Prepaid expenses included under current assets are expenditures made in exchange for benefits, usually in the form of services, not yet received but expected to be received within one year or the operating cycle, whichever is longer. For example, payment in advance for a one-year insurance policy should be classified as a prepaid expense at the time of the expenditure because the payment precedes the receipt of the benefits. Companies often include premium prepayments for two, three, or more years in current assets even though part of the advance payment applies to periods beyond the current operating cycle or one year, whichever is longer. Such a presentation is acceptable only if the amounts included are not material. Other common prepaid expenses include prepaid rent, office supplies, and taxes. Prepaid expenses are reported at cost.

CURRENT LIABILITIES   **Current liabilities** are obligations that are expected to be eliminated either through the use of existing current assets or by the creation of other current liabilities. In order to be classified as a current liability, (1) the obligation must mature within one year or the operating cycle, whichever is longer, and (2) management must *intend* to use existing current assets or to create other current liabilities to satisfy the obligation. For example, accounts payable resulting from short-term credit purchases from a supplier should be classified as a current liability because of the expectation that existing current assets will be used to eliminate the obligation. Likewise, if a firm borrows cash in exchange for a 90-day note and expects to eliminate the note by replacing it with another short-term note, the original note should be classified as a current liability because it is expected to be eliminated by the creation of another current liability.

Working capital analysis.   Users pay particular attention to the relationship between current assets and current liabilities. The difference between current assets and current liabilities, called **working capital,** is an approximation of the pool of resources available to management to conduct daily operations. Likewise, current assets divided by current liabilities, called the **current ratio,** provides a rough indication of the short-term debt-paying ability of the firm. For example, if a firm has a 2 to 1 current ratio, that means that current assets are twice as large as current liabilities. In most circumstances, a firm with a 2 to 1 current ratio will have little difficulty paying its debts as they become due. More specifically, a comparison of cash, temporary investments, and receivables to current liabilities provides information about a firm's solvency and short-term dividend-paying potential.

In general, the valuation of current liabilities is straightforward because most current liabilities are monetary obligations; that is, obligations to pay a fixed amount of cash in the near future. Thus, we report current liabilities at the number of dollars expected to be required to eliminate the obligations. Exhibit 5–3 illustrates a typical presentation of current liabilities.

NOTES PAYABLE   **Notes payable** are short-term promises to pay cash which are supported by written promissory notes. Notes payable may be **trade payables** or **nontrade payables,** as described earlier in our discussion of short-term receivables. Such notes are usually reported at their face amount.

ACCOUNTS PAYABLE   **Accounts payable** are the counterpart of accounts receivable. Accounts payable arise when a firm purchases goods, supplies, or services on credit. They are recorded at the amount expected to be paid to eliminate the obligation.

ACCRUED EXPENSES (ACCRUED LIABILITIES)   During any accounting period, firms incur certain expenses that have not been paid by the end of the accounting period. For example, interest on indebtedness accrues as time passes. When interest payment dates do not

---

EXHIBIT 5–3   PRESENTATION OF CURRENT LIABILITIES

Masco Corporation and Consolidated Subsidiaries
FROM 1984 ANNUAL REPORT

CURRENT LIABILITIES

Notes payable	$ 8,740,000
Accounts payable	39,820,000
Income taxes	17,430,000
Accrued liabilities	37,980,000
Total current liabilities	$103,970,000

coincide with the end of an accounting period, a liability exists at year's end for the interest that has accrued but has not been paid. Likewise, obligations for wages and salaries that have been earned by employees but not paid as of the end of the period are **accrued expenses (accrued liabilities).** Other examples include property taxes, payroll taxes, and income taxes. Income taxes often are reported separately, since they typically constitute a significant liability, as indicated in Exhibit 5–3.

Items previously classified as long-term debt that will mature within the next operating cycle or one year, whichever is longer, *and* that will require the use of existing current assets for elimination, should be reported as current liabilities. For example, if a bond obligation that will mature during the next year is going to be eliminated by use of cash generated from operations, the obligation should be classified as a current liability. If, however, a special fund that is classified as a noncurrent asset is the source of the debt elimination, then the portion of the debt maturing currently should not be reported as a current liability.

NONCURRENT ASSETS

Assets are classified as noncurrent if they are not expected to be converted into cash or consumed during one year or during the operating cycle, whichever is longer. Noncurrent assets include investments and special-purpose funds, property, plant, and equipment, and intangible assets.

INVESTMENTS AND SPECIAL-PURPOSE FUNDS   Most large companies own a variety of nonoperating assets. That is, a firm purchases assets that are not used to produce the goods or services that comprise its ongoing operations. For example, a firm may invest in securities of other companies with the intention of holding the investment for a long period of time. A company may make long-term loans to other companies, to corporate officers, or to others. Special-purpose funds may be set up to accumulate resources to accomplish certain long-term objectives, such as a plant expansion or elimination of a long-term debt. A manufacturing concern may purchase land for speculative purposes. These assets and others like them are classified as **investments** and **funds.** Although they appear to be quite diverse, they are all **noncurrent nonoperating assets.** These assets all generate future cash flows to the firm. Investments in other companies produce dividends and stock appreciation. Long-term loans create a claim for cash. Cash set aside in special-purpose funds is invested in securities to earn a return. Investment in land creates an expectation of future cash flows when the property is sold.

Investments and funds are reported after current assets on the balance sheet. Although historical cost is the primary basis for valuation of investments and funds, significant exceptions exist. Departures from historical cost will be discussed later in the book as the appropriate topics are covered. The methods used to assign values to assets included in investments and special-purpose funds must be disclosed. Knowledge of these methods is necessary for an understanding of the cash flow implications of the various assets.

PROPERTY, PLANT, AND EQUIPMENT   The next major category on the balance sheet is **property, plant, and equipment.** Most business entities have a substantial investment in physical property that generates cash flows over several accounting periods as the assets are used in operations. The major assets included in this category are land, buildings, machinery and equipment, furniture and fixtures, leasehold improvements, and land improvements. Inclusion of an asset within the property, plant, and equipment section implies that the firm is using the asset to generate revenues from operations. Thus, if any of these assets are not being used actively in operations, they should be excluded from the property, plant, and equipment category and reported as other assets.

At acquisition, property, plant, and equipment assets are recorded at cost. Because the benefit period for most types of property, plant, and equipment assets is limited, a firm transfers the cost of these assets to an expense account systematically over the periods in which the firm uses the assets to generate cash flows from operations. The amount transferred to expense each period is called **depreciation.** The objective of the depreciation process is to match the costs invested in plant and equipment with the benefits derived in the form of revenues. Depreciable assets are reported in the balance sheet at cost less accumulated depreciation up to the balance sheet date. However, firms continue to report land at cost unless there has been a substantial and permanent decline in market value below cost, in which case the land must be reported at market value, and a loss equal to the difference between cost and market value must be recognized.

INTANGIBLE ASSETS   Like property, plant, and equipment, **intangible assets** produce benefits over several time periods. The major distinction between property, plant, and equipment and intangible assets is that intangibles lack physical substance. They are valuable because of the rights and privileges that they convey to their owner. Examples of intangible assets are patents, copyrights, trademarks, franchises, and goodwill.

Intangible assets are recorded initially at cost. After acquisition, their cost is matched systematically against the related revenues. Intangible assets are reported at cost less accumulated **amortization,** which is the term used to describe the amount of cost transferred to expense each period. The cost of an intangible asset must be amortized over the asset's expected useful life or forty years, whichever is less.[4]

OTHER ASSETS   The balance sheet category **other assets** includes assets that do not logically fit in some other category. For example, many companies include costs associated with beginning the business, such as attorney fees and the costs of printing and engraving stock certificates, in this category. Also, the book value of idle plant often is included in this category. Because of the vagueness of the term "other assets," any significant items within this category should be adequately described in the footnotes to the financial statements.

LONG-TERM LIABILITIES   **Long-term liabilities** are obligations that will be settled beyond the operating cycle or one year, whichever is longer. The most common long-term liabilities are long-term notes, bonds, deferred taxes, pension obligations, and lease obligations. For balance sheet users to understand fully the impact of these commitments on a company's future operations, the terms of repayment of principal, interest payments, conversion features, and restrictions on dividend payments and borrowing must be disclosed. For bonds payable, the premium or discount should be separately disclosed. Generally, these obligations are reported at the present value of the future cash payments.

One of the more controversial issues in accounting currently is what is called *off balance sheet financing*. This term refers to forms of financing that are not reported in the balance sheet, such as certain long-term lease commitments and other obligations. One particularly controversial technique, referred to as *defeasance*, allows a firm to reduce debt on its balance sheet by creating a trust to service the debt. These issues are discussed more fully in connection with the related topics throughout the text.

OWNERS' EQUITY   Rearranging the accounting equation, we know that Assets − Liabilities = **Owners' equity.** In a sole proprietorship, owner's equity is a single account. In a partnership there are multiple owners, and a separate amount is reported in owners' equity for each partner. Reporting for the owners' equity of a corporation, called stockholders' equity, is considerably more complex. Legal constraints, accounting guidelines, and the separation of

---

[4] "Intangible Assets," *Opinions of the Accounting Principles Board No. 17* (New York: AICPA, August 1970).

EXHIBIT 5—4 PRESENTATION OF STOCKHOLDERS' EQUITY

STOCKHOLDERS' EQUITY

Contributed capital	
Common stock	$ 17,896
Other contributed capital	501,038
Total contributed capital	$518,934
Retained earnings	318,398
Total stockholders' equity	$837,332

corporate ownership and management interact to produce substantial information requirements for the equity interests in a corporation. Stockholders' equity consists of two common categories: (1) contributed capital and (2) retained earnings. This dichotomy of the equity in a corporation represents two distinct sources of or claims to an entity's assets—contributions by owners, called **contributed capital,** and earnings reinvested in the business, known as **retained earnings.** An illustration of the stockholders' equity section of a corporate balance sheet is presented in Exhibit 5–4.[5]

CONTRIBUTED CAPITAL   When a corporation issues stock, assets increase by the amount of cash contributed. This increase in assets also is recorded as *contributed capital,* indicating that the addition to assets came from the owners. Contributed capital is divided into the par or stated value and other contributed capital. **Legal capital,** which is defined by state law, usually is the par or stated value of the shares issued and outstanding. **Par value** or **stated value** is an arbitrary amount per share specified in the corporate charter and printed on the stock certificate. Other contributed capital results from the issuance of shares of stock at an amount in excess of par or stated value. If a firm has more than one class of stock issued and outstanding, such as preferred stock and common stock, a further subdivision within contributed capital informs users what portion of contributed capital came from each class of stock.

A variety of terms are used to describe components of contributed capital. Balance sheet users must become familiar with such terms as capital surplus, additional contributed capital, and other capital related to shares.

RETAINED EARNINGS   *Retained earnings* is the account used to record net income or net loss and dividend distributions. Net income increases retained earnings; net losses and dividends decrease retained earnings. The balance of the retained earnings account, which is reported in the balance sheet, is the amount by which total net income exceeds total dividends since the firm began operations. As we saw in Chapter 4, prior period adjustments also are recorded in retained earnings. Many companies include a **statement of retained earnings** in their financial statements, which explains the change in the balance of retained earnings from the beginning to the end of the accounting period.

UNCLASSIFIED BALANCE SHEETS   Companies in certain industries do not prepare balance sheets according to the format of Exhibit 5–1. In general, regulated industries, such as banks, insurance companies, and utilities, follow somewhat different formats because of regulatory requirements. In the

---

[5] Net unrealized losses on long-term marketable equity securities, treasury stock and foreign currency translation adjustments also are reported in stockholders' equity. These disclosures appear in Chapters 14, 20 and 21, respectively.

development of these special formats and of the accounting principles underlying these balance sheets, the information requirements of users seldom have been given significant attention. Regulatory authorities often have been unaware of or not sufficiently concerned about the information needs of users. Thus, the financial reports generated according to regulatory requirements are not likely to be as useful as those that give primary consideration to the information needs of users.

NOTES AND SUPPLEMENTARY INFORMATION

In reporting financial information to assist users in decision making, a firm faces two decisions: a placement decision and a display decision. The **placement decision** governs whether information should be reported in the main body of financial statements, in the notes to the financial statements, or as supplementary information. As we illustrated in Exhibit 1–1 in Chapter 1, financial reporting encompasses all three of these possibilities. The **display decision** governs the amount of detail to be reported and the manner of presentation. Note that display and placement are pertinent to all financial statements, not just the balance sheet.

Two general criteria are useful in deciding where information should be reported. To be reported in the main body of financial statements, information must be a financial statement element and must meet other recognition criteria as described in Chapter 2. For items that meet the criteria, disclosure by other means is not an acceptable substitute. The notes should amplify or explain items presented in the main body of financial statements. For example, the notes may include a schedule of lease payments to amplify a lease liability in the balance sheet. Supplementary information, on the other hand, may provide a different perspective from that adopted in the financial statements. For example, supplementary information may include current market values of assets or information about the effects of inflation on operating activities. Also, management's discussion of the financial reports may be included as supplementary information. Second, because different users may require different levels of detail, the notes should present detail that cannot reasonably be included in the main body of the financial statements. Supplementary information can provide even more detailed data useful only for specialized analyses. When this guideline is followed, users can minimize the cost of using the information and, if supplementary information need not be audited, preparers can lower their audit cost.

CONTINGENCIES At the balance sheet date, certain conditions or circumstances may make it uncertain whether the firm should report a gain or a loss. The outcome will be determined by the occurrence or nonoccurrence of some future event. These conditions are called **contingencies.** Accounting for and reporting of loss contingencies is prescribed by *FASB Statement No. 5*.[6]

A **loss contingency** represents a possible reduction in future net cash flows of an entity. For example, if a firm sells its product on credit, it creates the possibility that a portion of the receivables generated will not be collected. The possible loss due to uncollectible receivables is a loss contingency. The three possible treatments of a loss contingency are (1) accrual of an estimated loss, (2) disclosure but not accrual of the potential loss, and (3) no disclosure at all.

---

[6] "Accounting for Contingencies," *Statement of Financial Accounting Standards No. 5* (Stamford, Conn.: FASB, 1975).

EXHIBIT 5–5 DISCLOSURE OF CONTINGENCIES

Rockwell International Corporation and Consolidated Subsidiaries
FROM 1984 ANNUAL REPORT

CONTINGENT LIABILITIES

As of September 30, 1984 the company, under contracts with agencies of the Iranian Government, had receivables and inventories outstanding of approximately $33 million, had cash advances (not yet applied) from these agencies of approximately $20 million, and was contingently liable with respect to an aggregate of approximately $46 million under bank letters of credit and guarantees (all of which were called several years ago) of the cash advances and of company performance. The company has been involved in litigation since 1980 and in arbitration before the Iran-United States Claims Tribunal since 1982 regarding disputes relating to these matters. The ultimate outcome of this litigation and arbitration is not determinable presently. Management believes, however, that an adverse resolution of the foregoing matters would not have a material effect on the financial position of the company.

Various other lawsuits and claims are pending or have been asserted against the company. Although the outcome of such matters cannot be predicted with certainty and some lawsuits or claims may be disposed of unfavorably to the company, management believes their disposition will not have a material adverse effect on the consolidated financial statements of the company.

Rockwell International Corporation made the contingency disclosures shown in Exhibit 5–5. Note that the contingencies relate to both various assets and possible claims against Rockwell as a result of litigation.

A **gain contingency** represents a possible increase in future net cash flows of an entity, such as a claim against others for patent infringement. Gain contingencies usually should not be accrued. They typically are reported in the financial statements only when they are realized. We discuss the accounting for loss contingencies and gain contingencies in detail in Chapter 15.

LONG-TERM COMMITMENTS

Many companies finance expansion by incurring **long-term commitments,** such as notes, bonds, or leases. In order for the statement user to understand fully the impact of such commitments on a company's future cash flows, supporting schedules are often necessary. Exhibit 5–6 illustrates the types of disclosure typically made with respect to such commitments. Users can determine the amount and timing of future cash flows for long-term obligations by analyzing these notes, because due dates and amounts are reported.

PROPERTY, PLANT, AND EQUIPMENT

Because the balance sheet condenses financial information, the presentation of **property, plant, and equipment** is a summary of many separate assets. For most companies, property, plant, and equipment includes several major categories, such as land, buildings, machinery and equipment, leasehold improvements, and perhaps construction in progress. So that users may assess the ability of a firm to generate cash with plant and equipment items and the possibility of future cash outflows for additional plant and equipment, entities must disclose, either in the balance sheet or in the notes, major categories and accumulated depreciation.[7] The disclosure of accumulated depreciation, along with

---

[7] Additional disclosures related to plant and equipment are required by ''Financial Reporting and Changing Prices,'' *Statement of Financial Accounting Standards No. 33* (Stamford, Conn.: FASB, 1979). These requirements are described in Chapter 25.

EXHIBIT 5–6   DISCLOSURE OF LONG-TERM COMMITMENTS

R. J. Reynolds Industries, Inc.
FROM 1984 ANNUAL REPORT

Note 10: Long-term Debt

	DECEMBER 31, 1984	
	DUE WITHIN ONE YEAR	**DUE AFTER ONE YEAR**[2]
Long-term debt consisted of the following:		
7 7/8% Debentures, with annual sinking fund payments through 1994 (reduced by $5 million and $9 million of such debentures held by the Company on December 31, 1984 and 1983, respectively, for future sinking fund requirements)	$ —	$ 45
7 3/8% Debentures, due February 1, 2001, annual sinking fund payments began in 1982 (reduced by $60 million and $65 million of such debentures held by the Company on December 31, 1984 and 1983, respectively, for future sinking fund requirements)[1]	—	25
8 % Debentures, due January 15, 2007, with semiannual sinking fund payments beginning in 1988 (reduced by $28 million of such debentures held by the Company on December 31, 1984 and 1983, for future sinking fund requirements)[1] . . .	—	122
13.35% Sinking fund debentures, due October 1, 2012, with annual sinking fund payments beginning in 1993	—	200
9 5/8% Notes, due January 15, 1985	100	—
8 3/8% Notes, due February 15, 1985	90	—
9 3/4% Notes, due January 15, 1986	—	100
10 7/8% Notes, due October 15, 1988	—	100
12 3/4% Guaranteed notes, due October 1, 1989	—	100
10.45% Notes, due May 15, 1990	—	150
Zero coupon guaranteed notes, due February 19, 1992, net of discount of $249 million at December 31, 1984, effective interest rate of 14.64%	—	151
8.9% Notes, due October 1, 1996, annual prepayments began in 1981	6	69
Capitalized lease obligations and other indebtedness	31	195
	$227	$1,257

[1] In August 1983, the Company acquired $49 million of its 7 3/8% debentures and $28 million of its 8% debentures prior to scheduled maturity in exchange for cash of $29 million and 591,296 shares of common stock (see Note 13). This transaction resulted in a $19 million gain which was included in "Other income (expense), net."

[2] The payment schedule of debt due through 1989 is as follows (in millions): 1986—$140; 1987—$36; 1988—$136; and 1989—$129.

knowledge of depreciation methods used, permits users to estimate the timing of future cash outflows to replace existing plant and equipment. Exhibit 5–7 illustrates the disclosures related to property, plant, and equipment.

STOCKHOLDERS' EQUITY

Legal requirements and complex stock agreements complicate the reporting of *stockholders' equity*. Supporting schedules in the notes to the financial statements are used to report changes in capital stock accounts and changes in retained earnings during the period. Corporations must disclose the number of shares of each class of stock authorized, issued,

EXHIBIT 5–7   DISCLOSURES OF PROPERTY, PLANT, AND EQUIPMENT

Holiday Inns, Inc.
FROM 1984 ANNUAL REPORT
(in thousands of dollars)

FROM BALANCE SHEET:

Property and equipment, at cost

Land, buildings, improvements and equipment	$2,129,000
Accumulated depreciation and amortization	(455,570)
	$1,673,430

FROM NOTES:

Owned property

Land and land rights	$ 239,328
Buildings, improvements and other	1,228,446
Furniture, fixtures and equipment	609,150
	$2,076,924
Accumulated depreciation and amortization	(434,383)
	$1,642,541

Property under capital leases

Land	—
Buildings, improvements and other	$ 42,302
Furniture, fixtures and equipment	9,774
	$ 52,076
Accumulated amortization	(21,187)
	$ 30,889
Total property and equipment, net	$1,673,430

Land held for future development or disposition is included in the land account and amounted to $54,842,000 and $53,132,000 in 1984 and 1983, respectively.

A portion of property and equipment is pledged as security for certain long-term debt.

Depreciation and amortization are calculated on the straight-line method. Lease amortization is included in depreciation expense.

Interest capitalized during construction in 1984, 1983 and 1982, was $15,424,000, $22,180,000, and $8,401,000, respectively.

---

outstanding, and held in the treasury, and the characteristics of each class of stock, such as par or stated value, dividend rate, liquidation preference, call price, and conversion terms. Exhibit 5–8 illustrates typical disclosures related to stockholders' equity.

ACCOUNTING POLICIES

The accounting policies summary provides information regarding choices among accounting alternatives.

Since 1972, companies issuing financial statements prepared in accordance with generally accepted accounting principles must include as an integral part of the financial statements a summary of significant accounting policies.[8] **Accounting policies** are the specific accounting principles and methods of applying them that have been adopted by the firm's management for preparation of the financial statements. In *Opinion No. 22* the APB recognized that despite the efforts of all involved parties to reduce the number of accepta-

---

[8] "Disclosure of Accounting Policies," *Opinions of the Accounting Principles Board No. 22* (New York: AICPA, 1972).

EXHIBIT 5—8   DISCLOSURES OF STOCKHOLDERS' EQUITY

International Business Machines Corporation and Subsidiary Companies

FROM 1984 ANNUAL REPORT
(in millions of dollars)

FROM BALANCE SHEET:

Stockholders' equity
Capital stock, par value $1.25 per share .... $ 5,998
   Shares authorized: 750,000,000
   Issued: 1984—613,076,500; 1983—610,724,641
Retained earnings 23,486
Translation adjustments .... (2,948)
                                                           $26,536
Less: Treasury stock, at cost .... (47)
   Shares: 1984—390,961 .... $26,489

FROM CONSOLIDATED STATEMENT OF STOCKHOLDERS' EQUITY:

		CAPITAL STOCK	RETAINED EARNINGS	TRANSLATION ADJUSTMENTS	TREASURY STOCK	TOTAL
1982	Stockholders' equity, January 1, 1982	$4,389	$13,909	$ (622)	$ —	$17,676
	Net earnings		4,409			4,409
	Cash dividends declared...............		(2,053)			(2,053)
	Capital stock issued under employee and stockholder plans (10,112,504 shares) ..	602				602
	Treasury stock (391,743 shares) acquired and sold under employee plans		(6)			(6)
	Tax reductions applicable to stock related to employee plans	17				17
	Translation adjustments			(685)		(685)
	Stockholders' equity, December 31, 1982 ...	$5,008	$16,259	$(1,307)	—	$19,960
1983	Net earnings		5,485			5,485
	Cash dividends declared...............		(2,251)			(2,251)
	Capital stock issued under employee and stockholder plans (8,318,513 shares)	741				741
	Treasury stock (221,508 shares) acquired and sold under employee plans		(4)			(4)
	Tax reductions applicable to stock related to employee plans	51				51
	Translation adjustments			(763)		(763)
	Stockholders' equity, December 31, 1983 ...	$5,800	$19,489	$(2,070)	—	$23,219
1984	Net earnings		6,582			6,582
	Cash dividends declared...............		(2,507)			(2,507)
	Capital stock issued under employee plans (2,351,859 shares)	154				154
	Purchases (6,711,522 shares) and sales (6,320,561 shares) of treasury stock under employee and stockholder plans—net....................		(78)		(47)	(125)
	Tax reductions applicable to stock related to employee plans	44				44
	Translation adjustments			(878)		(878)
	Stockholders' equity, December 31, 1984 ...	$5,998	$23,486	$(2,948)	$(47)	$26,489

ble alternatives, there are still many areas where choices exist and where management must exercise judgment in the selection and application of accounting policies. If financial statement users know and understand the accounting principles used and the methods of applying them, the comparability of financial data is improved. In order for information to be useful, it must be comparable and it must be understandable.

The summary of significant accounting policies should include, where applicable, such information as the basis of consolidation, depreciation methods, inventory pricing, amortization of intangibles, and foreign currency translation practices. The footnote describing policies should not duplicate details provided elsewhere in the financial statements. *Opinion No. 22,* while recognizing the need for flexibility with respect to format, expresses a preference for placement of the summary of significant accounting policies before the notes or as the initial note to the financial statements. An illustration of a summary of significant accounting policies is included in the appendix to this chapter. Throughout the text, we describe specific required disclosures.

SUBSEQUENT EVENTS

Because of the time required to complete the year-end closing and to perform the audit, firms usually issue financial statements several weeks after the end of the accounting period. Certain events other than normal operating activities may occur between the statement date (the end of the accounting period) and the date of issuance of the financial statements. Because timeliness is an important characteristic of accounting information, it is essential that management inform investors and other users of significant events occurring during this period. This information might alter cash flow projections for the firm, and thus for individuals relying upon the firm for cash flows. Such events, referred to as **poststatement events** or **subsequent events,** are of two types: (1) events that provide further evidence of conditions that existed at the statement date and (2) events that provide evidence with respect to conditions that did not exist at the balance sheet date.

Events in the first category require adjustment of the amounts reported in the financial statements because they relate to existing conditions at the statement date. All available information should be used to make the amounts reported in the financial statements as accurate as possible. For example, an accrued liability related to litigation may require adjustment if the firm settles the litigation after the statement date and before the financial statements are issued for an amount significantly different from the accrued amount. Because the event that gave rise to the liability occurred prior to the statement date, all available evidence, including that arising after the statement date but before the issue date, should be reflected in the financial statement amounts.

Events in the second category do not require adjustment of amounts in the financial statements. Footnotes, schedules, and pro forma statements (supplementary statements reflecting the impact of the new information) are common methods of disclosure for these events. For example, if a firm engages in major new debt or equity financing during the poststatement period, disclosure is necessary to enable users to make meaningful cash flow projections. Other common events in this category include casualty losses (for example, due to fires or floods), litigation settlements related to events occurring after the balance sheet date, and the sale of part of the firm or purchase of another firm.

Note that the effect of events in both categories discussed above can be isolated and quantified on the financial statements. Other subsequent events that may affect the firm require neither statement adjustment nor disclosure in the financial statements or notes. Examples include changes in management, new or pending legislation that might alter the entity's expectations, and changes in product emphasis. While such events clearly are important in assessing future cash flows from an entity, the effect of such items on the financial statements is not readily quantifiable. As *Statement of Concepts No. 5* discusses, recognition involves reporting an item in the financial statements in both words and

EXHIBIT 5—9   DISCLOSURE OF SUBSEQUENT EVENT

Holiday Inns, Inc.

FROM ANNUAL REPORT
FOR THE FISCAL YEAR ENDED DECEMBER 28, 1984

SUBSEQUENT EVENT

On January 10, 1985, a subsidiary of the company and Hotel Corporation, a privately held company based in Wichita, Kansas, formed a 50/50 joint venture which acquired the rights and license agreements of the Brock Residence Inn franchise system from the Brock Hotel Corporation. These rights and agreements were acquired for $20 million in cash and assumption of $2.1 million in existing notes payable; no other obligations or liabilities of either Brock Residence Inns or Brock Hotel Corporation were assumed in connection with this transaction. The company advanced the cash to the joint venture to make the acquisition.

numbers. When such reporting is not feasible, the management letter to stockholders is the appropriate location for disclosure.

Exhibit 5–9 illustrates the disclosure of a subsequent event. Note that this event is relevant to the assessment of future cash flows to the firm.

THE STATEMENT OF CASH FLOWS

An income statement reports the effect of operations on a firm's financial position. The balance sheet reports the aggregate effect of revenues, expenses, gains, and losses on an entity's financial position. However, many other events and transactions occur during an accounting period that affect a firm's financial position and thus its cash flow prospects. That is, the income statement alone is not adequate to assess a firm's cash flows. For example, a firm may use resources to expand its plant or may generate additional resources by issuing long-term debt or capital stock. How does a financial statement user determine the impact of this transaction? The **statement of cash flows** summarizes the cash inflows and cash outflows for a period related to a firm's operating, financing, and investing activities, thus providing information useful in assessing future cash flows. We introduce the statement of cash flows in this section and we discuss preparation techniques and additional complexities in Chapter 23.

The relationship among the income statement, balance sheet, statement of retained earnings, and statement of cash flows is shown in Exhibit 5–10. The balance sheet is a static statement, analogous to a snapshot of a business at a point in time. The income statement, statement of retained earnings or stockholders' equity, and statement of cash flows are statements of flows during a period of time; these statements are more comparable to movies than to snapshots. As we mentioned above, however, the statement of cash flows is a much broader flow statement than the income statement.

EXHIBIT 5—10 RELATIONSHIP OF STATEMENT OF CASH FLOWS TO OTHER FINANCIAL STATEMENTS

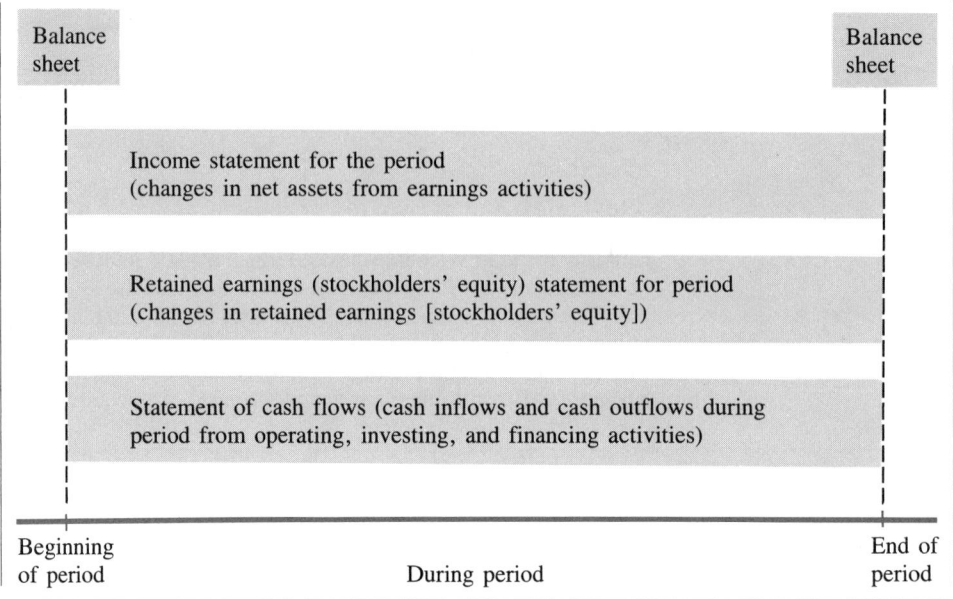

BACKGROUND The usefulness of "funds flow" information has been recognized for many years by statement preparers and users. Since 1971, companies preparing financial statements in accordance with GAAP have been required to include a funds flow statement, also called a **statement of changes in financial position,** in their annual reports to shareholders for each year for which an income statement is presented. However, several different definitions of "funds" (for example, cash, cash and cash equivalents, and working capital) have been used as the focus of the statement. Also, the format of the statement has varied considerably in practice.

In recent years, the significance of cash flow information about entities has been increasingly recognized. The FASB has stated in *Statement of Concepts No. 5* that a complete set of financial statements should show cash flows during the period. As a result of the recognized need for cash flow information, the FASB has issued an *Exposure Draft* of a *Statement of Financial Accounting Standards.*[9] If the *Exposure Draft* is issued as a *Statement,* a statement of cash flows would replace the statement of changes in financial position. Because it is highly likely that the proposed *Statement,* perhaps with minor modifications, will have been issued by the time this text is published or shortly thereafter, the discussion in the remainder of this section will focus on the statement of cash flows as presented in the *Exposure Draft.* A discussion of the statement of changes in financial position prepared under the working capital concept of funds is included in Appendix 23–1.

USES OF STATEMENT OF CASH FLOWS The statement of cash flows reports inflows and outflows of **cash** for a firm during the accounting period. The common transactions and events that provide cash are as follows:

1. Operating activities that result in cash inflows.

2. Issuance of long-term debt.

[9] "Statement of Cash Flows," *Proposed Statement of Financial Accounting Standards* (Stamford, Conn.: FASB, 1986).

3. Issuance of capital stock.

4. Sale of noncurrent assets.

Common transactions and events that result in cash outflows are as follows:

1. Operating activities that result in funds outflows.

2. Retirement of long-term debt.

3. Retirement of capital stock.

4. Purchase of noncurrent assets.

5. Dividends on capital stock.

These common inflows and outflows of cash are illustrated in Exhibit 5–11.

One measure of a company's profitability is net income. Over the life of the company, total reported net income or net loss equals net cash inflow or outflow.[10] Since income determination is based on *accrual accounting,* however, the equality of income and cash flows rarely holds for short time periods, such as annual accounting periods. For example, a company may operate for several years because its annual cash inflows exceed

[10] This relationship ignores capital transactions and assumes a nominal dollar (units of money) concept of capital maintenance.

EXHIBIT 5–11   INFLOWS AND OUTFLOWS OF CASH

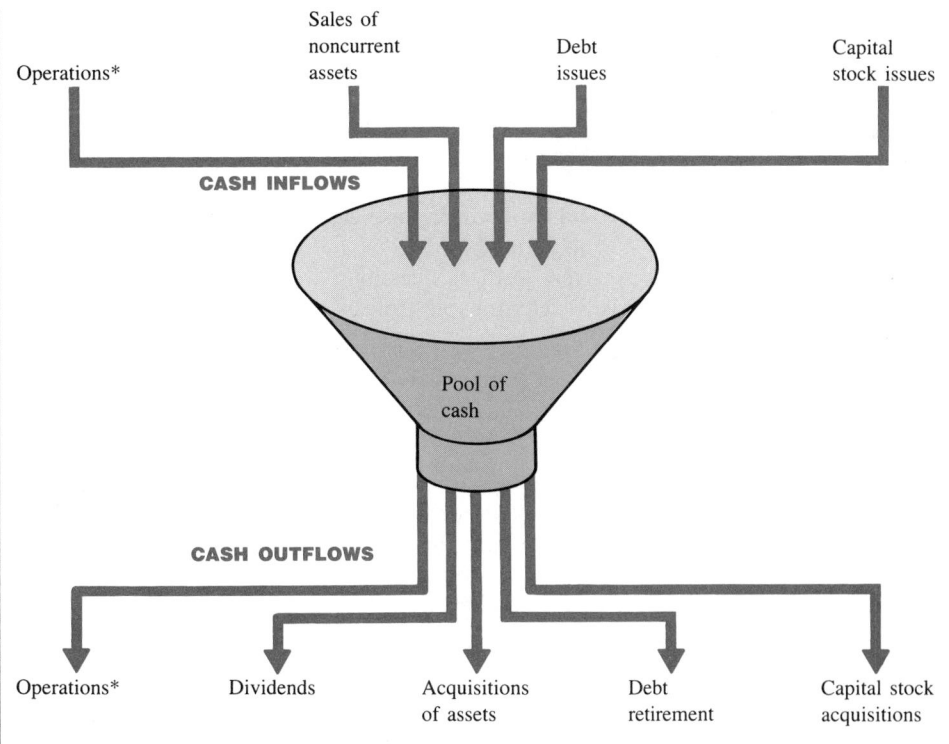

* Generally, operations represent a net cash inflow if revenues exceed expenses. If expenses exceed revenues, a net cash outflow from operations usually results.

The statement of cash flows complements the income statement and other financial statements.

its required annual cash payments even though the company may not be profitable in the long run. Or, a profitable company may experience severe short-run cash problems.

The statement of cash flows complements the income statement by disclosing the amount of cash generated by the company's operating activities. It also complements the balance sheet by disclosing cash flow transactions which cause changes in assets, liabilities, and stockholders' equity. For example, the amount of cash used to purchase long-lived assets during an accounting period is reported on the statement of cash flows.

Thus, the statement of cash flows provides information about the following activities and company characteristics:

1. *Cash provided by or used by operating activities.* While income as reported in the income statement is of primary importance to users in evaluating performance, many revenues and expenses result from accruals and allocations that do not affect cash. For example, depreciation expense does not cause an outflow of cash, although it appears on the income statement. Thus, the statement of cash flows provides useful information about the cash generated from a company's primary operating activities and may help to answer the following types of questions:
   a) If a company operates at a profit, why is it continually short of cash?
   b) How can a company operate at a loss and still generate huge inflows of cash from operations?

2. *Cash provided by or used by investing activities.* The statement of cash flows can provide information needed to answer the following questions about investing activities:
   a) Is the company making capital expenditures to modernize, expand, or replace worn-out or obsolete plant and equipment?
   b) Did the company acquire any long-term investments or other income-producing assets?
   c) Did the company obtain cash from disposals of long-lived assets? If so, in what amounts?

3. *Cash provided by or used by financing activities.* The statement of cash flows can provide answers to the following types of questions about a company's financing activities:
   a) Was financing obtained during the period through the issuance of debt or equity securities? If so, what were the amounts of cash obtained?
   b) Did the company use cash to retire any long-term debt or equity securities during the period?
   Answers to these questions do not appear on the income statement and may not be easily determinable from successive balance sheets.

4. *The "quality" of earnings.* The **quality of earnings** refers to how closely income is correlated with cash flows—the higher the correlation, the higher the earnings quality. A comparison of net income with cash generated from operating activities may provide information for assessing the quality of earnings.

5. *Evaluation of solvency, liquidity, and financial flexibility.* **Solvency** is the ability of a firm to pay its debts as they mature. **Liquidity** is the ability to generate adequate amounts of cash for specific purposes and also refers to assets' and liabilities' "nearness to cash." **Financial flexibility** refers to a firm's ability to adapt during a period of financial adversity, to obtain financing, to liquidate nonoperating assets for cash, and to modify operations to increase short-run cash inflows. The statement of cash flows disclosures help users evaluate solvency, liquidity, and financial flexibility.

The statement of cash flows helps to satisfy the qualitative characteristics of financial reporting.

Many users believe that the statement of cash flows presented in conjunction with an income statement better satisfies many of the qualitative characteristics discussed in Chapter 2 than the income statement alone can satisfy. For example, in addition to *relevance,* which underlies the five points enumerated above, the statement of cash flows may be more *reliable* than the income statement, because the information presented in the statement of cash flows avoids many of the arbitrary allocations and estimates (for example, depreciation expense) which are necessary in income determination. Furthermore, *comparability* among firms may be enhanced through the statement of cash flows. Because GAAP permits the use of many alternative accounting procedures to determine income, interfirm comparisons often are difficult. Finally, a statement of cash flows is readily *understandable*.

   None of this is meant to lessen the importance of the income statement and balance sheet as reports on performance and as sources of information to users who wish to assess cash flows in connection with their investment decisions. When investment decisions are made, many factors must be assessed. The income statement and balance sheet provide information about some, but not all, of these factors. The statement of cash flows provides information about other factors. Furthermore, a significant body of empirical research suggests that cash flow information is useful.[11]

ILLUSTRATION OF STATEMENT OF CASH FLOWS

A hypothetical statement of cash flows is presented in Exhibit 5–12. Note that the first item under cash flows from operating activities is net income. However, net income must be adjusted to get cash provided by operating activities by (1) adding back those amounts

[11] See, for example, David Hawkins and Walter Campbell, *Equity Valuation: Models, Analysis, and Implications* (New York: Financial Executives Research Foundation, 1978); Morton Backer and Martin Gosman, *Financial Reporting and Business Liquidity* (New York: National Association of Accountants, 1978).

EXHIBIT 5–12

Applegate Corporation
STATEMENT OF CASH FLOWS
FOR THE YEAR ENDED DECEMBER 31, 1987

Cash flows from operating activities:		
Operations: Net income	$130,000	
Add (deduct) noncash expenses, revenues, losses, and gains included in income:		
Depreciation expense	50,000	
Amortization of goodwill	24,000	
Gain on sale of fixed assets	(10,000)	
Increase in accounts receivable	(10,000)	
Decrease in inventories	45,000	
Increase in accounts payable	20,000	
Decrease in salaries payable	(10,000)	
Net cash provided by operating activities		$239,000
Cash flows from investing activities:		
Sale of plant assets	$ 40,000	
Purchase of equipment	(120,000)	
Purchase of land	(76,000)	
Net cash used by investing activities		(156,000)
Cash flows from financing activities:		
Issuance of common stock	$ 80,000	
Retire long-term debt	(50,000)	
Acquire common stock	(5,000)	
Pay dividends	(60,000)	
Net cash used by financing activities		(35,000)
Net increase in cash		$ 48,000

that did not require cash but were deducted in determining net income and (2) adjusting net income for operating cash flows that were not reflected in determining net income. As an example of the first type of adjustment, depreciation expense does not require a cash outflow in the period in which the expense is recorded. Therefore, the amount deducted as depreciation expense in determining net income must be added back to get cash provided by operating activities.

The second category of adjustments is a bit more complex. Because accrual accounting is used to determine net income, the amounts included in revenues and expenses are not perfectly correlated with cash flows during the period. For example, because the accounts receivable balance increased by $10,000 during the period, we know the amount of cash generated from sales is $10,000 less than the amount recorded for sales on an accrual basis. That is, $10,000 of the amount recorded as sales is reflected in the balance sheet as an increase in receivables rather than as an increase in cash. Thus, the increase in receivables must be deducted from net income to adjust net income to cash provided by operations. This same approach must be followed to adjust all other revenues and expenses to a cash basis. Also, the gain on sale of fixed assets of $10,000 must be deducted so that the cash generated from the sale ($40,000) may be shown separately as an investing activity. The final result is that net income from operations is converted to cash provided by operating activities.

The statement clearly distinguishes the cash flows related to operating, investing, and financing activities. This format would be required under the FASB's proposed *Statement*.

EVALUATION OF FINANCIAL STATEMENTS

In Chapters 4 and 5 we have described the objectives and content of the basic financial statements. These statements, individually and as a set, are designed to meet the objectives of financial reporting. The statements are interrelated. Both statements reflect the results of the same events or transactions, but from different viewpoints. Thus, the statements complement each other. No one statement is likely to be adequate to meet the accounting information needs for a particular decision. For example, the income statement provides profitability information, but rate of return calculations also require information found in the balance sheet. Also, the statement of cash flows provides useful cash flow information, but the income statement and balance sheet generally must be used in conjunction with the statement of cash flows to assess future cash flows meaningfully.

The financial statements are intended to meet the needs of investors, creditors, and other users who have a common interest in the amount, timing, and uncertainty of firm cash flows. The fact that the financial statements are general purpose statements means that they do not satisfy all users equally well and that they are not all-purpose statements.

The processes of classification and aggregation are necessary to simplify the vast amount of data that an accounting system generates. Classification into groups that are homogeneous in terms of some important characteristics, such as risk, stability, and liquidity, enhances predictive value. Aggregation is necessary to convey information that would be obscure, at best, if great amounts of detail were reported in the financial statements. If aggregation is carried to an extreme, however, meaningful information may be buried and users may tend to focus on a few simplified, condensed figures, such as net income or earnings per share. One of the most difficult tasks in accounting is to strike a balance between the need to simplify and the need to retain in the financial statements the information required to make decisions about complex business enterprises.

SUMMARY OF IMPORTANT TOPICS AND CONCEPT APPLICATIONS

1. The balance sheet, also called the statement of financial position, summarizes the resources, obligations, and residual ownership interests in an entity at a point in time. It is a source of information about a firm's **liquidity** and its **financial flexibility,** as well as providing information useful in assessing a firm's **profitability** and **efficiency.**

2. Classification in the balance sheet assists users in evaluating a firm's liquidity and financial flexibility. **Current assets and current liabilities** are reported separately from noncurrent assets and liabilities.

3. Owners' equity is the residual interest of the owners in a business enterprise. In a corporation, owners' (stockholders') equity consists of **contributed capital** (investments by owners) and retained earnings (net income reinvested in the business).

4. Reporting financial information involves both a **placement decision** (determining whether information should be reported in the body of the financial statements, in the notes, or as supplementary information) and a **display decision** (determining how much detail should be provided for an item and the manner of presentation). Only items that meet the definition of a financial statement **element** and that meet **recognition criteria** may be reported in the body of the financial statements.

5. A summary of **significant accounting policies** must be included as an integral part of the financial statements. This summary informs users of a firm's choices among accounting alternatives, and thus enhances the **comparability** of financial statements.

6. **Subsequent events,** events that occur after the statement date and before the statements are issued, may require adjustment of the statement amounts if they relate to conditions that existed at the statement date.

7. The **statement of cash flows** reports inflows and outflows of cash during a period. The statement of cash flows provides information about cash flows from operating, investing, and financing activities. The statement is useful for decision-making because it provides **relevant** and **reliable** information for predicting cash flows.

8. **Classification** and **aggregation** are necessary to meet the objective of **decision usefulness.** A constant difficulty in accounting is striking the proper balance between the need to simplify to make the information understandable and the need for relevant, reliable information as a basis for informed decision-making.

APPENDIX 5–1

ACTUAL FINANCIAL STATEMENTS

Appendix 5–1 contains a complete set of financial statements for The Coca-Cola Company. You should review these statements now. We discuss statement presentation issues and disclosure issues throughout the text. These statements should serve as a constant reference throughout your study of intermediate accounting. As you learn more about the principles underlying financial statements and gain an appreciation of the types of information required to be disclosed, these financial statements will become more comprehensible and informative.

SELECTED FINANCIAL DATA
(In millions except per share data)

Year Ended December 31,		1985	1984	1983
Summary of Operations (a,b)	Net operating revenues	$7,904	$ 7,152	$6,641
	Cost of goods and services	4,194	3,823	3,618
	Gross profit	3,710	3,329	3,023
	Selling, administrative and general expenses	2,665	2,287	2,041
	Operating income	1,045	1,042	982
	Interest income	148	129	83
	Interest expense	168	123	72
	Other income (deductions)—net	68	7	(2)
	Income from continuing operations before income taxes	1,093	1,055	991
	Income taxes	415	433	438
	Income from continuing operations	$ 678	$ 622	$ 553
	Net income	$ 722	$ 629	$ 559
Per Share Data (d)	Income from continuing operations	$ 5.17	$ 4.70	$ 4.06
	Net income	5.51	4.76	4.10
	Dividends	2.96	2.76	2.68
Year-End Position	Cash and marketable securities	$ 865	$ 782	$ 611
	Property, plant and equipment—net	1,884	1,623	1,561
	Total assets	6,898	5,958	5,228
	Long-term debt	889	740	513
	Total debt	1,315	1,363	620
	Shareholders' equity	2,979	2,778	2,921
	Total capital (e)	4,294	4,141	3,541
Financial Ratios	Income from continuing operations to net operating revenues	8.6%	8.7%	8.3%
	Income from continuing operations to average shareholders' equity	23.5%	21.8%	19.4%
	Total debt to total capital	30.6%	32.9%	17.5%
	Dividend payout	53.7%	58.0%	65.3%
Other Data	Average shares outstanding (d)	131	132	136
	Capital expenditures	$ 542	$ 391	$ 384
	Depreciation	178	159	147
	Market price per share at December 31 (d)	84.50	62.375	53.50

Notes: (a) Operating results for 1975-1984 have been restated to exclude the results of Presto Products, Incorporated, and Winkler/Flexible Products, Inc., which were sold in December 1985 and accounted for as discontinued operations.
(b) In June 1982, the Company acquired Columbia Pictures Industries, Inc., in a purchase transaction.

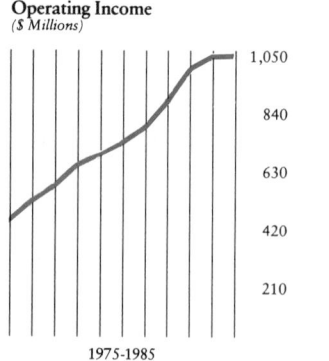

Operating Income
($ Millions)

1,050
840
630
420
210

1975-1985

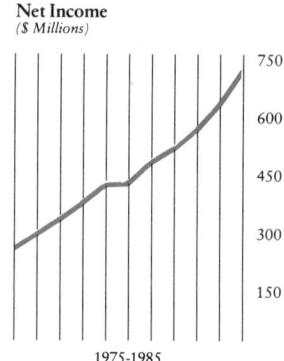

Net Income
($ Millions)

750
600
450
300
150

1975-1985

The Coca-Cola Company and Subsidiaries

	1982(c)	1981	1980	1979	1978	1977	1976	1975
	$5,862	$5,540	$ 5,327	$4,472	$ 3,938	$3,265	$2,877	$ 2,726
	3,189	3,062	2,988	2,431	2,148	1,790	1,574	1,598
	2,673	2,478	2,339	2,041	1,790	1,475	1,303	1,128
	1,810	1,706	1,620	1,367	1,159	915	802	689
	863	772	719	674	631	560	501	439
	106	70	40	36	35	29	29	22
	74	38	35	10	7	6	6	6
	7	(23)	(10)	(2)	(14)	(10)	(4)	(8)
	902	781	714	698	645	573	520	447
	408	349	320	312	294	263	242	214
	$ 494	$ 432	$ 394	$ 386	$ 351	$ 310	$ 278	$ 233
	$ 512	$ 482	$ 422	$ 420	$ 375	$ 331	$ 294	$ 249
	$ 3.81	$ 3.50	$ 3.19	$ 3.13	$ 2.84	$ 2.52	$ 2.25	$ 1.89
	3.95	3.90	3.42	3.40	3.03	2.68	2.38	2.02
	2.48	2.32	2.16	1.96	1.74	1.54	1.325	1.15
	$ 261	$ 340	$ 231	$ 149	$ 321	$ 350	$ 364	$ 389
	1,539	1,409	1,341	1,284	1,065	887	738	647
	4,923	3,565	3,406	2,938	2,583	2,254	2,007	1,801
	462	137	133	31	15	15	11	16
	583	232	228	139	69	57	52	42
	2,779	2,271	2,075	1,919	1,740	1,578	1,434	1,302
	3,362	2,503	2,303	2,058	1,809	1,635	1,486	1,344
	8.4%	7.8%	7.4%	8.6%	8.9%	9.5%	9.7%	8.5%
	19.6%	19.9%	19.7%	21.1%	21.2%	20.6%	20.3%	18.7%
	17.3%	9.3%	9.9%	6.8%	3.8%	3.5%	3.5%	3.1%
	62.8%	59.5%	63.2%	57.6%	57.4%	57.5%	55.7%	56.9%
	130	124	124	124	124	123	123	123
	$ 382	$ 330	$ 293	$ 381	$ 306	$ 264	$ 191	$ 145
	138	128	123	103	86	76	66	63
	52.00	34.75	33.375	34.50	43.875	37.25	39.50	41.125

(c) In 1982, the Company adopted Statement of Financial Accounting Standards No. 52, "Foreign Currency Translation."

(d) Adjusted for a two-for-one stock split in 1977.
(e) Includes shareholders' equity and total debt.

Income Per Share From Continuing Operations *($)*

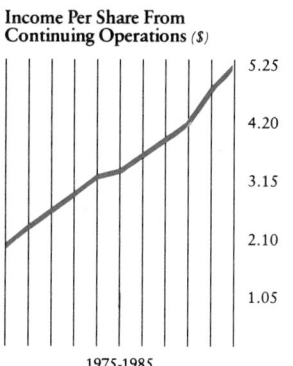

1975-1985

Return on Shareholders' Equity (%)

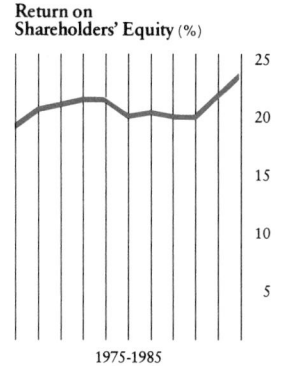

1975-1985

CONSOLIDATED BALANCE SHEETS
(In thousands except share data)

Assets		December 31, 1985	December 31, 1984
Current	Cash	$ 495,672	$ 307,564
	Marketable securities, at cost (approximates market)	369,491	474,575
		865,163	782,139
	Trade accounts receivable, less allowances of $19,479 in 1985 and $20,670 in 1984	897,200	872,332
	Inventories and film costs	913,293	740,063
	Prepaid expenses and other assets	294,628	241,326
	Total Current Assets	2,970,284	2,635,860
Investments, Film Costs and Other Assets	Investments (principally investments in affiliates)	470,575	334,220
	Film costs	536,112	341,662
	Receivables and other assets	364,581	408,324
		1,371,268	1,084,206
Property, Plant and Equipment	Land	139,450	130,883
	Buildings and improvements	771,088	645,150
	Machinery and equipment	1,742,118	1,518,264
	Containers	358,354	337,993
		3,011,010	2,632,290
	Less allowances for depreciation	1,127,301	1,009,715
		1,883,709	1,622,575
Goodwill and Other Intangible Assets		672,445	615,428
		$6,897,706	$5,958,069

The Coca-Cola Company and Subsidiaries

		December 31,	
Liabilities and Shareholders' Equity		1985	1984
Current	Accounts payable and accrued expenses	$1,108,964	$1,020,807
	Loans and notes payable	391,629	502,216
	Current maturities of long-term debt	34,495	120,300
	Entertainment obligations	215,249	192,537
	Accrued taxes—including income taxes	253,507	186,942
	Total Current Liabilities	2,003,844	2,022,802
Entertainment Obligations		270,676	175,234
Long-Term Debt		889,201	740,001
Deferred Income Taxes		320,832	241,966
Deferred Entertainment Revenue		434,096	—
Shareholders' Equity	Common stock, no par value— Authorized: 180,000,000 shares in 1985 and 1984; Issued: 137,699,566 shares in 1985 and 137,263,936 shares in 1984	69,227	69,009
	Capital surplus	602,617	532,186
	Reinvested earnings	3,092,255	2,758,895
	Foreign currency translation adjustment	(181,440)	(234,811)
		3,582,659	3,125,279
	Less treasury stock, at cost (9,039,031 shares in 1985; 6,438,873 shares in 1984)	603,602	347,213
		2,979,057	2,778,066
		$6,897,706	$5,958,069

See Notes to Consolidated Financial Statements.

CONSOLIDATED STATEMENTS OF INCOME

The Coca-Cola Company and Subsidiaries

(In thousands except per share data)

Year Ended December 31,	1985	1984	1983
Net Operating Revenues	$7,903,904	$7,151,826	$6,640,759
Cost of goods and services	4,193,557	3,822,637	3,617,699
Gross Profit	3,710,347	3,329,189	3,023,060
Selling, administrative and general expenses	2,664,945	2,287,041	2,041,257
Operating Income	1,045,402	1,042,148	981,803
Interest income	147,523	128,823	82,877
Interest expense	167,822	122,983	72,145
Other income (deductions)—net	67,746	6,841	(2,025)
Income From Continuing Operations			
Before Income Taxes	1,092,849	1,054,829	990,510
Income taxes	415,283	433,071	437,566
Income From Continuing Operations	677,566	621,758	552,944
Income from discontinued operations (net of applicable income taxes of $7,870 in 1985, $6,144 in 1984 and $4,920 in 1983)	9,000	7,060	5,843
Gain on disposal of discontinued operations (net of applicable income taxes of $20,252)	35,733	—	—
Net Income	$ 722,299	$ 628,818	$ 558,787
Per Share			
Continuing operations	$ 5.17	$ 4.70	$ 4.06
Discontinued operations	.34	.06	.04
Net income	$ 5.51	$ 4.76	$ 4.10
Average Shares Outstanding	131,118	132,210	136,222

See Notes to Consolidated Financial Statements.

CONSOLIDATED STATEMENTS OF SHAREHOLDERS' EQUITY

The Coca-Cola Company and Subsidiaries

(In thousands except per share data)

Three Years Ended December 31, 1985	Number of Shares		Amount				
	Common Stock	Treasury Stock	Common Stock	Capital Surplus	Reinvested Earnings	Foreign Currency Translation	Treasury Stock
Balance January 1, 1983	136,100	359	$68,427	$478,308	$2,300,217	$ (54,486)	$ (13,812)
Sales to employees exercising stock options and appreciation rights	387	—	194	13,327	—	—	—
Tax benefit from sale of option shares by employees	—	—	—	1,616	—	—	—
Translation adjustments (net of income taxes of $13,346)	—	—	—	—	—	(76,154)	—
Treasury stock issued in connection with an acquisition	—	(58)	—	(1,847)	—	—	2,258
Stock issued under Restricted Stock Award Plan	167	—	83	8,627	—	—	—
Net income	—	—	—	—	558,787	—	—
Dividends (per share—$2.68)	—	—	—	—	(364,789)	—	—
Balance December 31, 1983	136,654	301	68,704	500,031	2,494,215	(130,640)	(11,554)
Sales to employees exercising stock options and appreciation rights	316	—	158	10,931	—	—	—
Tax benefit from sale of option shares by employees	—	—	—	2,557	—	—	—
Translation adjustments (net of income taxes of $2,950)	—	—	—	—	—	(104,171)	—
Stock issued under Restricted Stock Award Plan	294	—	147	18,667	—	—	—
Treasury stock purchased	—	6,138	—	—	—	—	(335,659)
Net income	—	—	—	—	628,818	—	—
Dividends (per share—$2.76)	—	—	—	—	(364,138)	—	—
Balance December 31, 1984	137,264	6,439	69,009	532,186	2,758,895	(234,811)	(347,213)
Sales to employees exercising stock options and appreciation rights	342	(41)	171	13,647	—	—	1,552
Tax benefit from sale of option shares by employees	—	—	—	3,492	—	—	—
Translation adjustments (net of income taxes of $841)	—	—	—	—	—	53,371	—
Treasury stock issued in connection with an acquisition	—	(2,359)	—	46,653	—	—	121,989
Stock issued under Restricted Stock Award Plan	94	—	47	6,639	—	—	—
Treasury stock purchased	—	5,000	—	—	—	—	(379,930)
Net income	—	—	—	—	722,299	—	—
Dividends (per share—$2.96)	—	—	—	—	(388,939)	—	—
Balance December 31, 1985	137,700	9,039	$69,227	$602,617	$3,092,255	$(181,440)	$(603,602)

See Notes to Consolidated Financial Statements.

CONSOLIDATED STATEMENTS OF CHANGES
IN FINANCIAL POSITION (In thousands)

The Coca-Cola Company and Subsidiaries

Year Ended December 31,		1985	1984	1983
Operations	Income from continuing operations	$ 677,566	$ 621,758	$ 552,944
	Depreciation	178,123	159,083	147,129
	Amortization			
	Goodwill	17,740	16,705	16,056
	Noncurrent film costs	138,965	136,714	57,167
	Deferred income taxes	94,790	84,473	11,643
	Other	14,222	18,381	25,258
	Discontinued operations	53,573	15,222	21,779
	Working capital provided by operations	1,174,979	1,052,336	831,976
	Decrease (increase) in working capital	24,429	(45,504)	32,635
	Net additions to noncurrent film costs	(155,405)	(225,764)	(98,319)
	Cash provided by operations	1,044,003	781,068	766,292
	Increase in deferred entertainment revenue	434,096	—	—
	Decrease (increase) in investments and other assets	122,466	(259,953)	(19,361)
	Additions to property, plant and equipment	(496,994)	(338,929)	(376,197)
	Disposals of property, plant and equipment	35,929	67,161	34,972
	Increase (decrease) in noncurrent entertainment obligations	32,378	(50,895)	35,721
	Other	27,256	(22,241)	(2,595)
	Net cash invested in operations	(278,965)	(604,857)	(327,460)
	Net cash available from operations	1,199,134	176,211	438,832
Financing Activities	Increase (decrease) in loans and notes payable and current portion of long-term debt	(196,097)	510,260	(15,220)
	Increase in long-term debt	186,502	347,099	71,181
	Decrease in long-term debt	(34,495)	(120,300)	(20,783)
	Common stock issued (includes treasury)	194,190	32,460	22,000
	Repurchase of common stock	(379,930)	(335,659)	—
	Cash provided by (used for) financing activities	(229,830)	433,860	57,178
Acquisitions and Discontinued Operations	Acquisitions of purchased companies			
	Net working capital	(127,899)	32,070	(1,847)
	Property, plant and equipment—net	(44,994)	(51,829)	(7,439)
	Other assets, net of other liabilities	(320,817)	69	583
	Goodwill	(60,611)	(55,573)	(7,480)
	Discontinued operations			
	Net working capital	29,209	—	145,530
	Net long-term assets (including property, plant and equipment)	27,771	—	89,990
	Resources provided by (used for) acquisitions and discontinued operations	(497,341)	(75,263)	219,337
Dividends		(388,939)	(364,138)	(364,789)
Cash and Current Marketable Securities	Net increase during the year	83,024	170,670	350,558
	Balance at beginning of year	782,139	611,469	260,911
	Balance at end of year	$ 865,163	$ 782,139	$ 611,469

See Notes to Consolidated Financial Statements.

NOTES TO CONSOLIDATED FINANCIAL STATEMENTS

The Coca-Cola Company and Subsidiaries

1. Accounting Policies. The major accounting policies and practices followed by the Company and its subsidiaries are as follows:

Consolidation: The consolidated financial statements include the accounts of the Company and its majority-owned subsidiaries except for Coca-Cola Financial Corporation (CCFC). All significant intercompany accounts and transactions are eliminated in consolidation. CCFC, a wholly owned finance subsidiary, initiated operations in 1984 and is accounted for under the equity method. CCFC's operations for 1985 and 1984 were not significant to the consolidated financial statements.

Inventories and Film Costs: Inventories are valued at the lower of cost or market. In general, inventories are valued on the basis of average cost or first-in, first-out (FIFO) methods. However, certain soft drink and citrus inventories are valued on the last-in, first-out (LIFO) method. The excess of current costs over LIFO stated values amounted to approximately $38 million and $54 million at December 31, 1985 and 1984, respectively.

Film costs include film production, print, pre-release and other advertising costs expected to benefit future periods, accrued profit participations and capitalized interest. The individual film forecast method is used to amortize these costs based on the revenues recognized in proportion to management's estimate of ultimate revenues to be received. Based on the Company's estimate of revenues as of December 31, 1985, approximately 72% of unamortized film costs are expected to be amortized over the next three years.

The costs of feature and television films are classified as current assets to the extent such costs are expected to be recovered through the respective primary markets; remaining costs relating to film production are classified as noncurrent.

Revenues from theatrical exhibition of feature films are recognized on the dates of exhibition. Revenues from television licensing agreements are recognized when films are available for telecasting. Cash collected in advance of the time of availability is recorded as deferred entertainment revenue. Motion picture revenues are derived from the following markets: domestic and foreign theater, home video, pay television, network television and independent broadcast television. The Company's average revenue recognition cycle for motion pictures is approximately seven years.

Property, Plant and Equipment: Property, plant and equipment is stated at cost, less allowance for depreciation, except that foreign subsidiaries carry bottles and shells in service at amounts (less than cost) which generally correspond with deposit prices obtained from customers. Approximately 95% of depreciation expense was determined by the straight-line method for the year ended December 31, 1985, and approximately 92% for the years ended December 31, 1984 and 1983. The annual rates of depreciation are 2% to 10% for buildings and improvements and 7% to 34% for machinery and equipment. Investment tax credits are accounted for by the flow-through method.

Capitalized Interest: Interest capitalized as part of the cost of acquisition, construction or production of major assets (including film costs) was $35 million, $26 million and $18 million in 1985, 1984 and 1983, respectively.

Goodwill and Other Intangible Assets: Goodwill and other intangible assets are stated on the basis of cost and, if acquired subsequent to October 31, 1970, are being amortized, principally on a straight-line basis, over the estimated future periods to be benefited (not exceeding 40 years). Accumulated amortization amounted to $73 million and $57 million at December 31, 1985 and 1984, respectively.

2. Inventories and Film Costs are comprised of the following (in thousands):

	December 31,	
	1985	1984
Finished goods	$318,153	$284,711
Work in process	17,374	17,154
Raw materials and supplies	366,797	341,098
Film costs (includes in process costs of $51,901 in 1985 and $31,043 in 1984)	210,969	97,100
	$913,293	$740,063
Noncurrent—Film costs		
Completed	$411,110	$192,877
In process	125,002	148,785
	$536,112	$341,662

3. Short-Term Borrowings and Credit Arrangements. Loans and notes payable consist of commercial paper and notes payable to banks and other financial institutions of $392 million and $502 million at December 31, 1985 and 1984, respectively.

Under lines of credit and other credit facilities for short-term debt with various financial institutions, the Company, including CCFC, may borrow up to $671 million. These lines of credit are subject to normal banking terms and conditions. At December 31, 1985, the unused portion of the credit lines was $560 million. Some of the financial arrangements require compensating balances which are not material.

4. Accounts Payable and Accrued Expenses are composed of the following amounts (in thousands):

	December 31,	
	1985	1984
Trade accounts payable	$ 969,150	$ 878,564
Deposits on bottles and shells	51,472	47,848
Other	88,342	94,395
	$1,108,964	$1,020,807

NOTES TO CONSOLIDATED FINANCIAL STATEMENTS

5. Accrued Taxes are composed of the following amounts (in thousands):

	December 31,	
	1985	1984
Income taxes	$191,742	$128,372
Sales, payroll and miscellaneous taxes	61,765	58,570
	$253,507	$186,942

6. Long-Term Debt consists of the following amounts (in thousands):

	December 31,	
	1985	1984
9⅞% notes due June 1, 1985	$ —	$ 99,988
10⅜% notes due June 1, 1988	99,198	98,866
11⅜% notes due November 28, 1988	100,000	100,000
12¾% notes due August 1, 1989	99,821	99,771
11¾% notes due October 1, 1989 (redeemable after September 30, 1986)	98,641	98,279
11¾% notes due October 16, 1991 (redeemable after October 16, 1988)	99,793	99,757
9⅞% notes due August 1, 1992 (redeemable after July 31, 1989)	98,562	98,345
9⅞% notes due November 26, 1992 (redeemable after November 26, 1989)	100,000	—
Other	227,681	165,295
	923,696	860,301
Less current portion	34,495	120,300
	$889,201	$740,001

Notes outstanding at December 31, 1985, were issued outside the United States and are redeemable at the Company's option under certain limited conditions related to United States and foreign tax laws. The 11⅜% notes and the 9⅞% notes due November 26, 1992, were issued with detachable warrants which grant the holder the right to purchase additional notes bearing the same interest rate and maturing in 1991 and 1992, respectively. The warrants expire November 28, 1988, and November 26, 1989, respectively.

Other long-term debt consists of various mortgages and notes with maturity dates ranging from 1986 to 2011. Interest on a portion of this debt varies with the changes in the prime rate, and the weighted average interest rate applicable to the remainder is approximately 10.3%.

Maturities of long-term debt for the five years succeeding December 31, 1985, are as follows (in thousands):

1986	$ 34,495
1987	62,829
1988	225,613
1989	218,002
1990	16,773

The above notes include various restrictions, none of which are presently significant to the Company. The Company is contingently liable for guarantees of indebtedness owed by some of its independent bottling companies ($115 million), CCFC ($119 million), and others, totalling approximately $257 million at December 31, 1985.

7. Pension Plans. The Company and its subsidiaries sponsor and/or contribute to various pension plans covering substantially all United States employees and certain employees in non-United States locations. Pension expense for continuing operations determined under various actuarial cost methods, principally the aggregate level cost method, amounted to approximately $42 million in 1985, $35 million in 1984 and $39 million in 1983. Pension costs are generally funded currently.

The actuarial present value of accumulated benefits, as estimated by consulting actuaries, and net assets available for benefits of Company and subsidiary-sponsored plans in the United States are presented below (in thousands):

	January 1,	
	1985	1984
Actuarial present value of accumulated plan benefits		
Vested	$236,943	$217,558
Nonvested	24,549	17,527
	$261,492	$235,085
Net assets available for benefits	$351,283	$334,357

The weighted average assumed rate of return used in determining the actuarial present value of accumulated plan benefits was approximately 9% for 1985 and 1984.

The Company has various pension plans in locations outside the United States. These locations are not required to report to United States governmental agencies and do not determine the actuarial present value of accumulated plan benefits or net assets available for benefits as calculated and disclosed above. For such plans, the value of the pension funds and balance sheet accruals exceeded the actuarially computed value of benefits as of January 1, 1985 and 1984, as estimated by consulting actuaries.

The Company also has a plan which provides post-retirement health care and life insurance benefits to virtually all employees who retire with a minimum of five years of service; the aggregate cost of these benefits is not significant.

8. Income Taxes. The components of income before income taxes for both continuing and discontinued operations consist of the following (in thousands):

	Year Ended December 31,		
	1985	1984	1983
United States	$ 548,411	$ 457,260	$ 409,613
Foreign	617,293	610,773	591,660
	$1,165,704	$1,068,033	$1,001,273

The Coca-Cola Company and Subsidiaries

Income taxes for continuing and discontinued operations consist of the following amounts (in thousands):

Year Ended December 31,	United States	State & Local	Foreign	Total
1985				
Current	$ 42,275	$17,295	$288,051	$347,621
Deferred	65,115	7,897	22,772	95,784
1984				
Current	$ 45,411	$23,085	$285,788	$354,284
Deferred	67,891	3,403	13,637	84,931
1983				
Current	$114,195	$25,615	$287,846	$427,656
Deferred	4,493	1,068	9,269	14,830

A reconciliation of the statutory United States federal rate and effective rates is as follows:

	1985	1984	1983
Statutory rate	**46.0%**	46.0%	46.0%
State income taxes—net of federal benefit	**1.2**	1.3	1.4
Earnings in jurisdictions taxed at lower rates (principally Puerto Rico)	**(5.1)**	(3.0)	(1.9)
Investment tax credits	**(3.3)**	(2.9)	(2.0)
Other—net	**(.8)**	(.3)	.7
	38.0%	41.1%	44.2%
Investment tax credits included in determination of above rates (in millions)	**$38**	$34	$20

Deferred taxes are provided principally for depreciation, film costs and television and other licensing income which are recognized in different years for financial statement and income tax purposes. The Company has manufacturing facilities in Puerto Rico that operate under a Puerto Rican tax exemption which expires in 1995. In 1984, the Company completed an organizational restructuring in the Entertainment Business Sector which resulted in an increase in the tax bases of certain assets.

Appropriate United States and foreign income taxes have been provided for earnings of subsidiary companies which are expected to be remitted to the parent company in the near future. Accumulated unremitted earnings of foreign subsidiaries which are expected to be required for use in the foreign operations were approximately $67 million at December 31, 1985, exclusive of amounts which if remitted would result in little or no tax.

9. Stock Options and Other Stock Plans. The amended 1983 Restricted Stock Award Plan provides that 1,000,000 shares of restricted common stock may be granted to certain officers and key employees of the Company. The shares are subject to forfeiture if the employee leaves the Company for reasons other than death, disability or retirement and may not be transferred by the employee prior to death, disability or retirement. The employee receives dividends on the shares and may vote the shares. The market value of the shares at the date of grant is charged to operations over the vesting periods. Shares granted were 94,000 shares, 294,500 shares and 166,500 shares, in 1985, 1984 and 1983, respectively. At December 31, 1985, 445,000 shares were available to be granted under this Plan.

The Company's 1983 Stock Option Plan covers 2,000,000 shares of the Company's common stock. The Plan provides for the granting of stock appreciation rights and stock options to certain officers and employees. Stock appreciation rights permit the holder, upon surrendering all or part of the related stock option, to receive cash, common stock or a combination thereof, in an amount up to 100% of the difference between the market price and the option price. Included in options outstanding at December 31, 1985, were various options granted under previous plans and other options granted not as a part of an option plan.

Further information relating to options is as follows:

	1985	1984	1983
Options outstanding at January 1	**1,866,445**	1,713,222	1,507,162
Options granted in the year	**481,450**	454,650	487,900
Options exercised in the year	**(360,646)**	(264,845)	(203,361)
Options cancelled in the year	**(99,864)**	(36,582)	(78,479)
Options outstanding at December 31	**1,887,385**	1,866,445	1,713,222
Options exercisable at December 31	**1,064,326**	868,596	750,026
Shares available at December 31 for options which may be granted	**709,421**	1,131,950	1,577,858
Option prices per share Exercised in the year	**$31-$64**	$25-$52	$25-$50
Unexercised at year-end	**$31-$71**	$31-$64	$25-$52

Not reflected above are options assumed in connection with the acquisition of Columbia Pictures Industries, Inc., covering 6,000 shares of the Company's common stock at December 31, 1985. The option price for these options is $37. During 1985, options for 21,400 such shares were exercised, and no options were cancelled.

In 1985, the Company entered into Performance Unit Agreements, whereby certain officers will be granted cash awards based upon the difference in the market value of 185,000 shares of the Company's common stock at the measurement dates and the base price of $61.875, the market value as of January 2, 1985. Under these agreements, the cost will be charged to operations over the vesting period.

NOTES TO CONSOLIDATED FINANCIAL STATEMENTS

10. Acquisitions. In 1985, 1984 and 1983, the Company purchased various bottling companies to operate. The operating results for these companies have been included in the consolidated statements of income from the dates of acquisition and do not have a significant effect on operating results for those respective years.

In August 1985, the Company purchased certain assets and properties of Embassy Communications and Affiliates (Embassy) and Tandem Productions (Tandem). The purchase price for the assets of Tandem was approximately $178 million in cash and the assumption of certain ordinary course trade liabilities. The purchase price for Embassy was approximately $267 million, comprised of approximately 2.4 million shares of the Company's common stock and the payment of existing debt. Embassy and Tandem are engaged principally in the production and distribution of television programs. The operating results for these companies have been included in the consolidated statement of income from the date of acquisition. Embassy Pictures and certain receivables and contract rights, which were acquired in conjunction with the above acquisitions, were subsequently sold.

In December 1985, the Company acquired Nutri-Foods Int'l., Inc., a manufacturer of juice-based frozen desserts. The total purchase price was comprised of approximately $30 million in cash at closing, plus participation in Nutri-Foods' earnings through December 31, 1989. Such earnings will be paid to former principal owners who continue as employees of Nutri-Foods Int'l., Inc.

In 1984, the Company purchased a substantial equity interest in The Mid-Atlantic Coca-Cola Bottling Company, Inc., at a cost of more than $60 million. This investment was made with the intent of selling it to other purchasers as part of the bottler restructuring efforts. Accordingly, the investment is accounted for as temporary under the cost method of accounting.

Included in current marketable securities at December 31, 1985, is $161 million on deposit with an escrow agent. It is anticipated that most of this amount will be used to acquire Louisiana Coca-Cola Bottling Co.

11. Divestitures and Discontinued Operations. In December 1985, the Company sold Presto Products, Incorporated, and Winkler/Flexible Products, Inc., manufacturers of plastic products, for approximately $112 million. In November 1983, the Company sold its wine business for book value plus advances, amounting to approximately $230 million. Operating results for these companies have been reported as discontinued operations. Net revenues of discontinued operations were $235 million, $212 million and $350 million in 1985, 1984 and 1983, respectively. In 1984, the Company sold Ronco Enterprises, Inc., a manufacturer and distributor of pasta products, for cash. This transaction had no significant effect on consolidated operating results.

In 1985, the Company sold capital stock of several United States bottling operations; these disposals resulted in gains of approximately $67 million. In conjunction with its continuing bottler restructuring efforts in 1984, the Company sold bottling interests in Australia and Japan and provided for possible losses in Guatemala, where an independent bottler ceased operations. Such efforts resulted in net pretax gains of approximately $18 million in 1984.

12. Receivable and Contract Right Conversions. During 1985, the Company sold its rights to cash payments under contracts related to certain films and television programs not presently available for telecast. Approximately $31 million of such rights were acquired by CCFC, the Company's wholly owned finance subsidiary. These transactions resulted in deferred revenue which is recognized as operating revenue as the respective materials become available for telecast. The differences between the present value of the contracts and the amounts to be recognized as revenue are being reported as non-operating deductions. Certain entertainment and other accounts receivable, totalling $465 million, were also sold during the year. These transactions are subject to recourse. The uncollected balance of receivables, including unearned interest, was approximately $413 million at December 31, 1985.

13. Working Capital. Decreases (increases) in working capital (excluding cash, marketable securities, loans and notes payable and current portion of long-term debt), by component, were:

	1985	1984	1983
Trade accounts receivable	$ 63,459	$(72,127)	$(69,107)
Inventories and film costs	(137,873)	18,070	(57,776)
Prepaid expenses and other assets	(52,974)	(45,737)	55,663
Accounts payable and accrued expenses	78,299	47,472	143,957
Entertainment obligations	8,648	38,324	(590)
Accrued taxes	64,870	(31,506)	(39,512)
Decrease (increase)	$ 24,429	$(45,504)	$ 32,635

14. Subsequent Events. On January 27, 1986, the Company announced an agreement in principle to merge its United States bottling operations with JTL Corporation, the Company's largest independent bottler. The combined entity will account for approximately 25% of the Company's domestic soft drink unit volume.

On February 18, 1986, the Company announced an agreement in principle to acquire for cash Merv Griffin Enterprises, which produces and distributes television game shows. On February 20, 1986, the Company announced an agreement in principle to acquire Dr Pepper Company, the fourth largest soft drink maker, for approximately $470 million, which includes the assumption of $170 million in debt. These proposed acquisitions are subject to the execution of definitive agreements and the receipt of consents and approvals by governmental authorities and regulatory agencies.

The Coca-Cola Company and Subsidiaries

15. Lines of Business. The Company operates principally in the soft drink industry. The Entertainment Business Sector is engaged in the production and distribution of motion picture and television products and other entertainment related activities. Citrus, fruit drinks, coffee and other products are included in the Foods Business Sector. Intercompany transfers between sectors are not material. Information concerning operations in different lines of business is as follows (in millions):

Year Ended December 31,		1985	1984	1983
Net Operating Revenues*	Soft drinks	$5,510.0	$5,014.9	$4,694.6
	Entertainment	1,072.1	884.7	849.5
	Foods	1,321.8	1,252.2	1,096.7
	Consolidated net operating revenues	$7,903.9	$7,151.8	$6,640.8
Operating Income*	Soft drinks	$ 880.7	$ 879.6	$ 858.6
	Entertainment	160.6	121.1	90.6
	Foods	117.5	122.3	110.5
	General expenses	(113.4)	(80.9)	(77.9)
	Consolidated operating income	$1,045.4	$1,042.1	$ 981.8
Identifiable Assets at Year-End	Soft drinks	$3,679.5	$3,009.6	$2,670.6
	Entertainment	1,802.4	1,615.4	1,394.0
	Foods	473.5	369.1	340.1
	Corporate assets (principally marketable securities, investments and fixed assets)	942.3	873.1	731.3
	Discontinued operations	—	90.9	91.8
	Consolidated assets	$6,897.7	$5,958.1	$5,227.8
Capital Expenditures (including fixed assets of purchased companies)	Soft drinks	$ 326.2	$ 294.6	$ 237.6
	Entertainment	22.4	31.2	72.9
	Foods	113.8	39.9	45.1
	Corporate	79.6	25.1	28.0
	Consolidated capital expenditures	$ 542.0	$ 390.8	$ 383.6
Depreciation and Amortization of Goodwill*	Soft drinks	$ 140.9	$ 127.0	$ 120.4
	Entertainment	19.7	17.6	15.7
	Foods	21.2	20.3	18.7
	Corporate	14.1	10.9	8.4
	Consolidated depreciation and amortization of goodwill	$ 195.9	$ 175.8	$ 163.2

*Operating results for 1983 and 1984 have been restated to exclude the results of Presto Products, Incorporated, and Winkler/Flexible Products, Inc., subsidiaries of the Company which were sold in December 1985 and accounted for as discontinued operations.

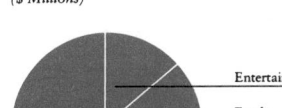

Net Operating Revenues
($ Millions)

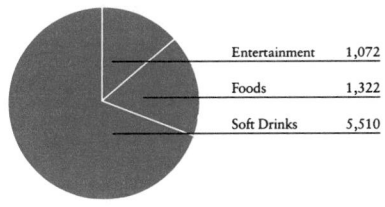

Entertainment	1,072
Foods	1,322
Soft Drinks	5,510

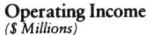

Operating Income
($ Millions)

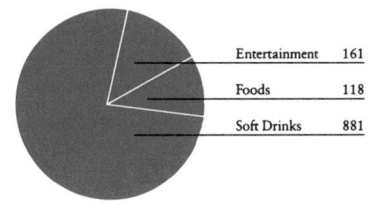

Entertainment	161
Foods	118
Soft Drinks	881

16. Operations in Geographic Areas. Information about the Company's operations in different geographic areas is pre-sented below (in millions). Intercompany transfers between geographic areas are not material.

Year Ended December 31,		1985	1984	1983
Net Operating Revenues*	United States	$4,908.4	$4,354.2	$3,883.2
	Latin America	452.4	429.6	401.3
	Europe and Africa	1,240.6	1,183.8	1,225.6
	Pacific and Canada	1,302.5	1,184.2	1,130.7
	Consolidated net operating revenues	$7,903.9	$7,151.8	$6,640.8
Operating Income*	United States	$ 548.3	$ 534.8	$ 487.9
	Latin America	87.3	89.6	69.4
	Europe and Africa	284.3	272.5	295.4
	Pacific and Canada	238.9	226.1	207.0
	General expenses	(113.4)	(80.9)	(77.9)
	Consolidated operating income	$1,045.4	$1,042.1	$ 981.8
Identifiable Assets at Year-End	United States	$4,228.0	$3,484.6	$2,904.7
	Latin America	380.8	409.8	420.9
	Europe and Africa	805.0	636.4	606.5
	Pacific and Canada	541.6	463.3	472.6
	Corporate assets (principally marketable securities, investments and fixed assets)	942.3	873.1	731.3
	Discontinued operations	—	90.9	91.8
	Consolidated assets	$6,897.7	$5,958.1	$5,227.8
Identifiable Liabilities of Operations Outside the United States		$ 742.6	$ 714.5	$ 652.0

*Operating results for 1983 and 1984 have been restated to exclude the results of Presto Products, Incorporated, and Winkler/Flexible Products, Inc., subsidiaries of the Company which were sold in December 1985 and accounted for as discontinued operations.

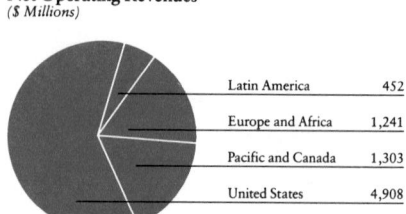

Net Operating Revenues
($ Millions)

Latin America	452
Europe and Africa	1,241
Pacific and Canada	1,303
United States	4,908

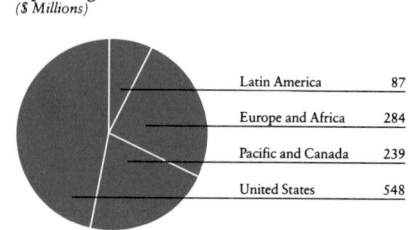

Operating Income
($ Millions)

Latin America	87
Europe and Africa	284
Pacific and Canada	239
United States	548

REPORT OF INDEPENDENT ACCOUNTANTS

The Coca-Cola Company and Subsidiaries

Board of Directors and Shareholders
The Coca-Cola Company
Atlanta, Georgia

We have examined the consolidated balance sheets of The Coca-Cola Company and subsidiaries as of December 31, 1985 and 1984, and the related consolidated statements of income, shareholders' equity and changes in financial position for each of the three years in the period ended December 31, 1985. Our examinations were made in accordance with generally accepted auditing standards and, accordingly, included such tests of the accounting records and such other auditing procedures as we considered necessary in the circumstances.

In our opinion, the financial statements referred to above present fairly the consolidated financial position of The Coca-Cola Company and subsidiaries at December 31, 1985 and 1984, and the consolidated results of their operations and changes in their financial position for each of the three years in the period ended December 31, 1985, in conformity with generally accepted accounting principles applied on a consistent basis.

Ernst & Whinney

Atlanta, Georgia
January 31, 1986, except for Note 14,
as to which the date is February 20, 1986

REPORT OF MANAGEMENT

Management is responsible for the preparation and integrity of the consolidated financial statements appearing in this Annual Report. The financial statements were prepared in conformity with generally accepted accounting principles appropriate in the circumstances and, accordingly, include some amounts based on management's best judgments and estimates. Financial information in this Annual Report is consistent with that in the financial statements.

Management is responsible for maintaining a system of internal accounting controls and procedures to provide reasonable assurance, at an appropriate cost/benefit relationship, that assets are safeguarded and that transactions are authorized, recorded and reported properly. The internal accounting control system is augmented by a program of internal audits and appropriate reviews by management, written policies and guidelines, careful selection and training of qualified personnel and a written Code of Business Conduct adopted by the Board of Directors, applicable to all employees of the Company and its subsidiaries. Management believes that the Company's internal accounting controls provide reasonable assurance that assets are safeguarded against material loss from unauthorized use or disposition and that the financial records are reliable for preparing financial statements and other data and maintaining accountability for assets.

The Audit Committee of the Board of Directors, composed solely of Directors who are not officers of the Company, meets with the independent accountants, management and internal auditors periodically to discuss internal accounting controls, auditing and financial reporting matters. The Committee reviews with the independent accountants the scope and results of the audit effort. The Committee also meets with the independent accountants without management present to ensure that the independent accountants have free access to the Committee.

The independent accountants, Ernst & Whinney, are recommended by the Audit Committee of the Board of Directors, selected by the Board of Directors and ratified by the shareholders. Ernst & Whinney is engaged to examine the consolidated financial statements of The Coca-Cola Company and subsidiaries and conduct such tests and related procedures as they deem necessary in conformity with generally accepted auditing standards. The opinion of the independent accountants, based upon their examination of the consolidated financial statements, is contained in this Annual Report.

Roberto C. Goizueta
Chairman, Board of Directors,
and Chief Executive Officer

M. Douglas Ivester
Senior Vice President
and Chief Financial Officer

January 31, 1986, except for Note 14,
as to which the date is February 20, 1986

Supplemental Information on the Effects of Changing Prices (Unaudited)

General. The following unaudited disclosures were prepared in accordance with standards issued by the Financial Accounting Standards Board and are intended to quantify the impact of inflation on earnings and production facilities. The inflation-adjusted data is presented under the specific price changes method (current cost). Only those items most affected by inflation have been adjusted; i.e., inventories, property, plant and equipment, the related costs of goods and services sold and depreciation and amortization expense. Although the resulting measurements cannot be used as precise indicators of the effects of inflation, they do provide an indication of the effect of increases in specific prices of the Company's inventories and properties.

The adjustments for specific price changes involve a substantial number of judgments as well as the use of various estimating techniques employed to control the cost of accumulating the data. The data reported should not be thought of as precise measurements of the assets and expenses involved, or of the amount at which the assets could be sold. Rather, they represent reasonable approximations of the price changes that have occurred in the business environment in which the Company operates.

A brief explanation of the current cost method is presented below.

The current cost method attempts to measure the effect of increases in the specific prices of the Company's inventories and properties. It is intended to estimate what it would cost in 1985 dollars to replace the Company's inventories and existing properties.

Under this method, cost of goods sold valued on the average method is adjusted to reflect the current cost of inventories at the date of sale. That portion of cost of goods sold valued on the LIFO method approximates the current cost of inventory at the date of sale and generally remains unchanged from the amounts presented in the primary financial statements.

Current cost depreciation expense is based on the average current cost of properties in the year. The depreciation methods, salvage values and useful lives are the same as those used in the primary statements.

The current cost of finished products inventory was approximated by adjusting historical amounts to reflect current costs for material, labor and overhead expenses as well as current cost depreciation, where applicable. The current cost for inventories other than finished products was determined on the basis of price lists or appropriate supplier quotations and by other managerial estimates consistent with established purchasing and production procedures.

Statement of Income Adjusted for Changing Prices
(In millions except per share data)

Year Ended December 31, 1985	As Reported in the Primary Statements	Adjusted for Changes in Specific Prices (Current Costs)
Net operating revenues	$7,903.9	$7,903.9
Cost of goods and services (excluding depreciation)	4,125.2	4,165.5
Depreciation and amortization	181.7	255.2
Other operating expenses	2,549.4	2,549.4
Other (income) deductions—net	(45.2)	2.0
Income from continuing operations before income taxes	1,092.8	931.8
Income taxes	415.2	415.2
Income from continuing operations	$ 677.6	$ 516.6
Income per share from continuing operations	$ 5.17	$ 3.94
Effective income tax rate	38.0%	44.6%
Purchasing power gain from holding net monetary liabilities in the year		$ 42.6
Increase in specific prices of inventories and property, plant and equipment held in the year		$ 84.4
Less effect of increase in general price level		129.9
Increase in specific prices over increase in the general price level		$ (45.5)
Estimated translation adjustment		$ 50.0
Inventory and film costs	$1,449.4	$1,489.9
Property, plant and equipment—net	$1,883.7	$2,428.8

A significant part of the Company's operations is measured in functional currencies other than the United States dollar. Adjustments to reflect the effects of general inflation were determined on the translate-restate method using the United States Consumer Price Index—Urban.

The Coca-Cola Company and Subsidiaries

Since motion picture films are the result of a unique blending of the artistic talents of many individuals and are produced under widely varying circumstances, it is not feasible to develop the current cost of film inventories, particularly since the Company would rarely, if ever, attempt to duplicate an existing film property. In view of these considerations and as permitted by Statement of Financial Accounting Standards No. 46, film inventories have been valued on the basis of constant dollar equivalents. Direct supplier quotations, published price lists, engineering estimates, construction quotations, appraisals and published and internally developed indexes were the methods used to determine the current cost of property, plant and equipment.

Under current cost accounting, increases in specific prices (current cost) of inventories and properties held during the year are not included in income from continuing operations.

Income Taxes. Taxes on income included in the supplementary statement of income are the same as reported in the primary financial statements. In most countries, present tax laws do not allow deductions for the effects of inflation.

Purchasing Power Gain. During periods of inflation, monetary assets, such as cash, marketable securities and accounts receivable, lose purchasing power since they will buy fewer goods when the general price level increases. The holding of monetary liabilities, such as accounts payable, accruals and debt, results in a gain of purchasing power because cheaper dollars will be used to repay the obligations. The Company has benefited from a net monetary liability position in recent years, resulting in a net gain in purchasing power. This gain does not represent an increase in funds available for distribution to shareholders and does not necessarily imply that incurring more debt would be beneficial to the Company.

Increase in Specific Prices. Shown separately are the total changes in current costs for inventories and properties, that component of the total change due to general inflation and that component of the change attributable to fluctuations in exchange rates.

Five-Year Comparison of Selected Supplemental Financial Data Adjusted for Effects of Changing Prices (In Average 1985 Dollars)
(In millions except per share data)

Year Ended December 31,	1985	1984	1983	1982	1981
Net operating revenues	$7,903.9	$7,404.9	$7,168.5	$6,531.1	$6,550.8
Current cost information					
Income from continuing operations	516.6	560.0	518.6	432.2	397.9
Income per share from continuing operations	3.94	4.24	3.81	3.32	3.21
Increase in specific prices over (under) increase in the general price level, including translation adjustments	4.5	(258.6)	(248.5)	(206.1)	(244.7)
Net assets at year-end	3,553.4	3,545.4	3,890.2	4,029.4	3,708.3
Purchasing power gain on net monetary items	42.6	27.0	30.0	19.7	28.9
Cash dividends declared per share					
As reported	2.96	2.76	2.68	2.48	2.32
Adjusted for general inflation	2.96	2.86	2.89	2.76	2.74
Market price per common share at year-end					
Historical amount	84.50	62.375	53.50	52.00	34.75
Adjusted for general inflation	84.50	64.58	57.75	57.94	41.09
Average Consumer Price Index — Urban CPI(U) (1967 = 100)	322.1	311.1	298.4	289.1	272.4

QUESTIONS

Q5-1. What is the relationship between the fundamental accounting equation, the balance sheet, and cash flows of an entity?

Q5-2. What are liquidity and financial flexibility, and how does the balance sheet provide information useful for the assessment of liquidity and financial flexibility?

Q5-3. Does a balance sheet show the fair market value of an entity? Explain.

Q5-4. Why is a reasonably standard classification system, consistently applied, important in financial statements?

Q5-5. What typical classifications are presented in a classified balance sheet? Describe them briefly.

Q5-6. What are current assets, current liabilities, and working capital, and what are their roles in an economic entity?

Q5-7. Current assets are valued variously at their face amount, cost, net realizable value, and lower of cost or market. Why?

Q5-8. What is the typical basis for ordering current assets for statement presentation purposes? Why?

Q5-9. How do inventories in a manufacturing concern differ from inventories for a wholesale or retail concern?

Q5-10. What is the justification for classifying prepaid expenses as current assets?

Q5-11. What is the theoretically correct valuation of a monetary obligation? Why are current liabilities typically not recorded at their theoretically correct valuation?

Q5-12. Under what circumstances might currently maturing long-term debt properly be excluded from current liabilities?

Q5-13. What are accrued liabilities? Give three examples.

Q5-14. How does management's intent affect the classification of marketable equity securities?

Q5-15. What are four major categories within the property, plant, and equipment classification?

Q5-16. How do tangible assets differ from intangible assets?

Q5-17. Why is the classification ''other assets'' necessary?

Q5-18. Does the valuation approach for long-term liabilities differ from that for current liabilities? Explain.

Q5-19. What are the two basic categories of owners' equity in a corporation? Describe each category and explain the rationale for the distinction.

Q5-20. Why do companies in certain industries (for example, financial institutions and public utilities) either present balance sheets that are unclassified or follow a classification scheme different from the one presented in Chapter 5?

Q5-21. Why do footnotes and supplementary schedules always accompany financial statements?

Q5-22. What are the three possible treatments of a loss contingency?

Q5-23. What are accounting policies? Why is it important that they be disclosed?

Q5-24. What are three balance sheet items for which the accounting policies would probably be disclosed in the summary of significant accounting policies?

Q5-25. What is a poststatement event? Under what conditions would a poststatement event require accrual as of the statement date?

Q5-26. What is the purpose of the statement of cash flows? Explain.

Q5-27. What information does the statement of cash flows convey that cannot be obtained from the income statement or the balance sheet?

Q5-28. What are four major categories of inflows and four major categories of outflows of cash?

CASES

C5-1. ENTITY VALUATION VERSUS ASSET VALUATION   The following statement has been taken with some modification from the accounting literature:

> If the value of an entity were to be determined by computing the sum of the present values of the marginal (or incremental) expected net receipts of individual tangible and intangible assets, the resulting valuation would tend to be less than if the value were determined by computing the present value of total expected net receipts for the entire entity (that is, the resulting valuation of parts would yield a sum that was less than that for the whole). This would be true even if the same pattern of interest or discount rates were used for both valuations.

REQUIRED

Evaluate the above statement, indicating and explaining your agreement or disagreement with each point made.

(AICPA, adapted)

C5-2. FINANCIAL STATEMENT PRESENTATION   The following is the complete set of financial statements prepared by Oberlin Corporation:

Oberlin Corporation

STATEMENT OF EARNINGS AND
RETAINED EARNINGS
FOR THE FISCAL YEAR ENDED AUGUST 31, 1987

Sales		$3,500,000
Less returns and allowances		(35,000)
Net sales		$3,465,000
Less cost of goods sold		(1,039,000)
Gross margin		$2,426,000
Less:		
Selling expenses	$1,000,000	
General and administrative expense (Note 1)	1,079,000	(2,079,000)
Operating earnings		$ 347,000
Add other revenue:		
Purchase discounts	$ 10,000	
Gain on increased value of investments in real estate	100,000	
Gain on sales of treasury stock	200,000	
Correction of error in last year's statement	90,000	400,000
Ordinary earnings		$ 747,000
Add extraordinary item—gain on sale of fixed asset		53,000
Earnings before income tax		$ 800,000
Less income tax expense		(380,000)
Net earnings		$ 420,000
Add beginning retained earnings		2,750,000
		$3,170,000
Less:		
Contingent liability (Note 3)		(300,000)
Ending unappropriated retained earnings		$2,870,000

Oberlin Corporation
STATEMENT OF FINANCIAL POSITION
AS OF AUGUST 31, 1987

ASSETS

Current assets		
Cash..	$ 80,000	
Accounts receivable, net	110,000	
Inventory	130,000	
Total current assets........................		$ 320,000
Other assets		
Land and building, net.........................	$4,000,000	
Investments in real estate (current value)..........	1,668,000	
Goodwill (Note 2)	250,000	
Discount on bonds payable	42,000	
Total other assets		5,960,000
Total assets		$6,280,000

LIABILITIES AND STOCKHOLDERS' EQUITY

Current liabilities		
Accounts payable	$ 140,000	
Income taxes payable	320,000	
Total current liabilities		$ 460,000
Other liabilities		
Due to Grant, Inc. (Note 3)	$ 300,000	
Liability under employee pension plan	450,000	
Bonds payable (including portion due within		
one year)................................	1,000,000	
Deferred taxes...............................	58,000	
Total other liabilities		1,808,000
Total liabilities		$2,268,000
Stockholders' equity		
Common stock	$1,000,000	
Contributed capital in excess of par	142,000	
Unappropriated retained earnings	2,870,000	
Total stockholders' equity		4,012,000
Total liabilities and stockholders' equity		$6,280,000

FOOTNOTES TO THE FINANCIAL STATEMENTS

1. Depreciation expense is included in general and administrative expenses. During the fiscal year, the Company changed from the straight-line method of depreciation to the sum-of-the-years'-digits method.

2. As per federal income tax laws, goodwill is not amortized. The goodwill was "acquired" in 1984.

3. The amount due to Grant, Inc., is contingent upon the outcome of a lawsuit which is currently pending. The amount of loss, if any, is not expected to exceed $300,000.

REQUIRED

Identify and explain the deficiencies in the presentation of Oberlin's financial statements. There are *no* arithmetical errors in the statements. Organize your answer as follows:

1. Deficiencies in the income statement and retained earnings.

2. Deficiencies in the statement of financial position.

3. General comments.

If an item appears on both statements, identify the deficiencies for each statement separately.

(AICPA, adapted)

C5-3. FINANCIAL STATEMENT PRESENTATION In 1972 a new partnership purchased land on the edge of the town of Midville, erected a building, and opened a furniture and appliance store under the name of Furniture Fair. The partnership agreement specified that profits or losses would be shared equally after the allocation of partners' salary allowances and interest on average capital balances. Midville has grown considerably and the store is now the most prominent in a fashionable suburban area. Good management, imaginative merchandising, and the general growth of the economy have made Furniture Fair the leading and most profitable firm of its type in Midville's trade area.

Now the partners want to admit an investor and incorporate the business and have obtained a charter for Furniture Fair, Inc. Each partner will purchase at par an amount of preferred stock equal to the book value of his interest in the partnership and common stock equal to that portion of the fair market value that exceeds the book value. The investor will purchase at a 10 percent premium over par value common and preferred stock equal to one-third the number of shares of each class of stock purchased by the partners. The corporation will then purchase the Furniture Fair partnership at its fair market value from the partners. After the consummation of the partners' plan, the corporation will own the partnership's assets, assume its liabilities, and employ the partners as the management of the corporation.

REQUIRED

1. Identify and explain the differences in items and valuations that you would expect to find between the assets to appear on the balance sheet of the proposed corporation and the assets that appear on the partnership's balance sheet.

2. Identify and explain the differences that would be expected between an income statement prepared for the proposed corporation and an income statement prepared for the partnership.

(AICPA, adapted)

C5-4. FINANCIAL STATEMENT PRESENTATION The following year-end financial statements were prepared by the Jackson Corporation's bookkeeper. The Jackson Corporation operates a chain of retail stores.

Jackson Corporation
BALANCE SHEET
AS OF JUNE 30, 1987
ASSETS

Current assets		
Cash..........................		$ 100,000
Notes receivable		90,000
Accounts receivable, less reserve		
for doubtful accounts		75,000
Inventories......................		395,500
Investment securities (at cost)		100,000
Total current assets		$ 760,500
Property, plant, and equipment		
Land (at cost) (Note 1)	$175,000	
Buildings, at cost less accumulated		
depreciation of $350,000	500,000	
Equipment at cost less accumulated		
depreciation of $180,000	400,000	1,075,000
Intangibles.......................		450,000
Other assets		
Prepaid expenses		6,405
Total assets		$2,291,905

LIABILITIES AND OWNERS' EQUITY

Current liabilities			
Accounts payable			$ 100,500
Estimated income taxes payable			160,000
Total current liabilities			$ 260,500
Long-term liabilities			
9% serial bonds, $50,000 due annually on December 31			
Maturity value		$850,000	
Less unamortized discount		(35,000)	815,000
Total liabilities			$1,075,500
Owners' equity			
Common stock, stated value $10 (authorized and issued, 75,000 shares)		$750,000	
Retained earnings			
Appropriated (Note 2)	$110,000		
Free	356,405	466,405	1,216,405
Total liabilities and owners' equity			$2,291,905

Jackson Corporation

INCOME STATEMENT
FOR THE YEAR ENDED JUNE 30, 1987

Sales			$2,500,000
Interest income			6,000
Total revenue			$2,506,000
Cost of goods sold			(1,780,000)
Gross margin			$ 726,000
Operating expenses			
Selling expenses			
Salaries	$95,000		
Advertising	85,000		
Sales returns and allowances	50,000	$230,000	
General and administrative expenses			
Salaries	$84,000		
Property taxes	38,000		
Depreciation and amortization	86,000		
Rent	75,000		
Interest on serial bonds	48,000	331,000	(561,000)
Income before income taxes			$ 165,000
Income taxes			(160,000)
Net income			$ 5,000

NOTES TO FINANCIAL STATEMENTS

Note 1. Includes a future store site acquired during the year at a cost of $75,000.
Note 2. Retained earnings in the amount of $110,000 have been set aside to finance expansion.

REQUIRED

Identify and discuss the defects in the financial statements above with respect to terminology, disclosures, and classification. Your discussion should explain why you consider them to be defects.

(AICPA, adapted)

C5-5. CURRENT ASSET AND CURRENT LIABILITY CLASSIFICATION   Below are the account titles of a number of debit and credit accounts as they might appear on the balance sheet of the Carlton Corporation as of October 31, 1987.

DEBITS

Cash in bank	Goodwill
Land	Inventory of finished goods
Inventory of operating parts and supplies	Inventory of work in process
Inventory of raw materials	Deficit
Patents	Interest accrued on U.S. government securities
Cash and U.S. government bonds set aside for property additions	Notes receivable
Investment in subsidiary	Petty cash fund
Accounts receivable	U.S. government securities
U.S. government contracts	Treasury stock
Regular	Unamortized bond discount
Installments, due in 1987	
Installments, due in 1988–89	

CREDITS

Accrued payroll	9 1/2% first mortgage bonds due in 1994
Provision for renegotiation of U.S. government contracts	Cash dividend on preferred stock, payable 11/1/87
Notes payable	Allowance for doubtful accounts receivable
Accrued interest on bonds	
Accumulated depreciation	Provision for federal income taxes
Accounts payable	Customers' advances (on contracts to be completed in 1988)
Capital in excess of par	
Accrued interest on notes payable	Appropriation for possible decline in value of raw materials inventory
8% first mortgage bonds to be redeemed in 1987 out of current assets	Premium on bonds redeemable in 1987
Capital stock, preferred	Officers' 1987 bonus accrued

REQUIRED

Select the current asset and current liability items from among these debits and credits. If there appear to be certain borderline cases that you are unable to classify without further information, mention them and explain your difficulty, or give your reasons for making questionable classifications, if any.

(AICPA, adapted)

C5-6. SUBSEQUENT EVENTS   The following events and transactions related to Mock Company occurred after the balance sheet date of December 31, 1987, and before the financial statements were issued in 1988. None of the items are reflected in the financial statements as of December 31, 1987.

1. A supplier to whom Mock owes $10,000 declared bankruptcy on February 2, 1988.

2. A warehouse containing a substantial portion of Mock's inventory was destroyed by fire on February 7, 1988.

3. On March 1, 1988, Mock issued bonds at an interest rate 2 percentage points above the prime rate.

4. On March 3, 1988, the IRS assessed Mock an additional $100,000 for the 1985 tax year. However, both the tax attorneys for Mock and the tax accountants have indicated that it is likely that the IRS will agree to a $75,000 settlement.

5. On November 31, 1987, Mock initiated a lawsuit seeking $300,000 in damages from a firm that Mock claims infringed on one of its patents. Mock's attorneys have stated that the chances of winning and of getting the $300,000 are "excellent."

6. In order to secure a bank loan of $50,000, Mock pledged as collateral certain fixed assets with a net book value of $100,000. Mock applied for the loan on December 20, 1987, and the bank approved the loan on January 10, 1988.

REQUIRED

Describe the appropriate accounting and reporting for each of the above items in the financial statements and related notes as of December 31, 1987. Treat each item independently.

C5-7. SUBSEQUENT EVENTS There are three types of reporting available for subsequent (poststatement) events:

1. Adjust amounts in financial statements.

2. Disclosure, but no adjustment.

3. Neither disclosure nor adjustment.

The following subsequent events must fit into one of the three categories listed above:
  a) Retirement of the company treasurer.
  b) Issuance of a significant amount of common stock.
  c) Settlement of litigation against the company when the event giving rise to the claim took place prior to the balance sheet date.
  d) Material loss on the sale of marketable securities.
  e) Material loss on a receivable due to a customer's bankruptcy.
  f) Employee strike.
  g) Loss of a warehouse and contents due to fire.
  h) Introduction of a new product line.
  i) Sale of a significant portion of the company's assets.
  j) Settlement of a federal income tax obligation at considerably more than anticipated at year-end.

REQUIRED

Describe the appropriate treatment of each item.

C5-8. DISCLOSURES The preliminary draft of the statement of financial position at the end of the current fiscal year for Jebec Industries is presented below. The statement will be incorporated into the annual report to stockholders and will present the dollar amounts at the end of both the current and prior years in a side-by-side comparative basis. The accounts in the statement are properly classified, and the dollar amounts have been determined in accordance with generally accepted accounting principles. The company does not intend to provide any more detailed information in the body of the statement.

Jebec Industries

STATEMENT OF FINANCIAL POSITION
NOVEMBER 30, 1987
(millions of dollars)

ASSETS

Current assets
Cash	$ 9.0
Marketable equity securities	4.5
Accounts receivable-trade (net)	75.3
Inventories	152.0
Prepayments and other	3.2
Total current assets	$244.0
Investments in equity securities	36.8
Plant, property, and equipment (net)	524.7
Total assets	$805.5

LIABILITIES AND STOCKHOLDERS' EQUITY

Current liabilities
    Current maturities on long-term debt .... $ 24.3
    Notes payable 53.0
    Accounts payable 93.2
    Accrued taxes 28.2
    Accrued interest 7.3
    Other 2.9

        Total current liabilities $208.9
Long-term debt 318.1

        Total liabilities $527.0
Stockholders' equity
    Preferred stock .... $ 20.0
    Common stock 51.3
    Paid in capital on common stock 43.6
    Retained earnings-appropriated 27.2
    Retained earnings-unappropriated 136.4

        Total stockholders' equity $278.5

        Total liabilities and stockholders' equity $805.5

REQUIRED

Identify the accounts which most likely would require further disclosure in the notes to the financial statements and describe what information would have to be disclosed in those notes by Jebec Industries before the statement can be included as part of the annual report for presentation to its stockholders.

(IMA, adapted)

C5-9.   STATEMENT OF CASH FLOWS As a professor of accounting at a major university, you have agreed to participate in an executive development course for selected management personnel of a large corporation. The students in the course have no accounting background. Your function is to introduce them to the fundamentals of financial accounting. As a part of your presentation, you must explain what the statement of cash flows is and how it relates to the other basic financial statements.

REQUIRED

Draft a handout to be used in the executive development course to explain the purpose and uses of the statement of cash flows. Include an explanation of its relationship to the other basic financial statements. Remember that you are dealing with people who have just been introduced to accounting formally in this course. However, they are bright, successful managers in a major corporation.

EXERCISES

E5-1. BALANCE SHEET CLASSIFICATION The following classification scheme typically is used in the preparation of a balance sheet:

a) Current assets
b) Investments and funds
c) Property, plant, and equipment
d) Intangible assets
e) Other assets

f) Current liabilities
g) Long-term liabilities
h) Contributed capital
i) Retained earnings

Indicate by inserting the appropriate letter the category in which an entity typically would place each of the following items. Indicate a contra-account by inserting a dash before the letter.

_____ Goodwill

_____ Bonds payable (due in 8 years)

_____ Petty cash

_____ Trade accounts receivable

_____ Investment in subsidiary

_____ Accrued wages

_____ Patents

_____ Raw materials inventory

_____ Mortgage payable

_____ Preferred stock

_____ Income taxes payable

_____ Organization costs

_____ Premium on common stock

_____ Buildings

_____ Bond sinking fund

_____ Cash

_____ Deferred rearrangement costs

_____ Accumulated depreciation

_____ Discount on bonds payable

_____ Land (held for speculative purposes)

_____ Prepaid expenses

_____ Accounts payable

E5-2. BALANCE SHEET CLASSIFICATION The following classification scheme typically is employed in the preparation of a balance sheet.

a) Current assets
b) Investments and funds
c) Property, plant, and equipment
d) Intangible assets
e) Other assets

f) Current liabilities
g) Long-term liabilities
h) Contributed capital
i) Retained earnings

Indicate by inserting the appropriate letter the category in which an entity typically would place each of the following items. Indicate a contra-account by inserting a dash before the letter.

_____ Additional paid-in capital

_____ Work-in-process inventory

_____ Notes receivable (short-term)

_____ Copyrights

_____ Machinery

_____ Allowance for uncollectible accounts

_____ Premium on bonds payable

_____ Supplies inventory

_____ Unearned revenue (long-term)

_____ Inventory

_____ Marketable securities (short-term)

_____ Notes payable (short-term)

_____ Accrued payroll taxes

_____ Leasehold improvements

_____ Retained earnings appropriated for plant expansion

_____ Long-term receivables

_____ Accumulated amortization

_____ Current maturities of long-term debt

_____ Donated capital

_____ Deferred income taxes (long-term credit)

E5-3. BALANCE SHEET CLASSIFICATION Answer each of the following multiple-choice questions related to balance sheet items and justify your answer.

1. An example of an item that is not an element of working capital is:
   a) Accrued interest on notes receivable.
   b) Treasury stock.
   c) Goods in process.
   d) Temporary investments.

2. The test of marketability must be met before an entity can classify securities owned as:
   a) Debentures.
   b) Treasury stock.
   c) Long-term investments.
   d) Current assets.

3. An example of an item that is not a liability is:
   a) Dividends payable in the corporation's own stock.
   b) Advances from customers on contracts.
   c) Accrued estimated warranty costs.
   d) The portion of long-term debt due within one year.

E5-4. EFFECT OF ERRORS ON FINANCIAL STATEMENTS Your employer approaches you for assistance regarding the financial statements prepared in 1987 and 1988. The employer is not completely satisfied with the previous accountant's work and has asked you to check on the accuracy of the statements prepared. Your examination reveals the following:

a) An invoice for a $3,000 shipment of goods was received and the purchase recorded on December 26, 1987. The goods were shipped f.o.b. destination (which means they belonged to the seller until they arrived at the buyer's place of business), did not arrive until January 3, 1988, and were not included in the December 31, 1987, inventory count.

b) A three-year insurance policy was purchased for $1,500 on June 30, 1987, and the full amount was expensed at that time.

c) Accrued wages at the end of 1987 and 1988 amounted to $1,000 and $800, respectively. The accountant did not make the necessary year-end adjustments.

d) On October 1, 1987, the company purchased at par $10,000 of 9 percent corporate bonds. The bonds were dated October 1, 1987, and paid interest semiannually. The accountant recorded interest earned when received.

e) Depreciation was not recorded in either 1987 or 1988. The amounts were $900 for 1987 and $1,200 for 1988.

REQUIRED

Assuming a December 31 fiscal year-end, indicate the amount of the understatement *(U)* and overstatement *(O)* of each of the above, for 1987 *and* 1988, on:

1. Total assets.
2. Total liabilities.
3. Net income.

E5-5. BALANCE SHEET PREPARATION Following is a list of items taken from the December 31, 1987, balance sheet of Loma Vista Company (amounts omitted):

Allowance for depreciation—buildings	Machinery and equipment
Deferred income taxes (credit, noncurrent)	Finished products inventory
Current portion of long-term debt	Trade accounts receivable
Work-in-process inventory	Prepaid expenses
Buildings	Accrued expenses
Cash	Income taxes payable

Notes payable to banks (short-term)
Raw materials
Land
Marketable securities (short-term)
Deferred charges
Retained earnings
Accounts payable
Common stock

Preferred stock
Contributed capital in excess of par
Bonds payable
Allowance for depreciation—machinery and
  equipment
Investment in subsidiary
Goodwill

REQUIRED

Using the above information, prepare a balance sheet in good form.

E5-6. BALANCE SHEET PREPARATION Snappy Photo, Inc., had the following balance sheet items at December 31, 1987 (amounts omitted):

Inventories
Accumulated depreciation
Deferred expenses
Current maturities of notes payable
Preferred stock
Automobiles and trucks
Accrued income taxes
Prepaid expenses
Accounts receivable
Life insurance loans payable
  (long-term)
Leasehold improvements
Refundable federal income taxes
Machinery and equipment
Accounts payable
Allowance for bad debts
Land

Notes payable (noncurrent)
Picture island kiosks (film drop
  centers)
Goodwill
Notes receivable (noncurrent)
Accrued liabilities
Amounts payable under noncompetition
  agreements (noncurrent)
Additional paid-in capital
Furniture and fixtures
Retained earnings
Cash
Buildings
Deferred revenues (current)
Notes receivable (current)
Notes payable (short-term)
Common stock

REQUIRED

Using the above information, prepare a balance sheet in good form.

E5-7. EFFECT OF TRANSACTIONS ON BALANCE SHEET Indicate in the space provided below the effect on assets, liabilities, and stockholders' equity of the items set forth below. For no change, indicate 0; for increase, +; for decrease, −.

	ASSETS	LIABILITIES	STOCKHOLDERS' EQUITY
a) Issuance of shares for cash.			
b) Declaration of a cash dividend.			
c) Issuance of shares for land to be held as an investment.			
d) Retirement of bond liability by issuance of stock.			
e) Payment of cash dividend in *b*.			

E5-8. BALANCE SHEET FORMAT   The following balance sheet has been submitted to you for review:

Emmy Lou Company

BALANCE SHEET
FOR THE PERIOD 1/1/87 TO 12/31/87
(in thousands of dollars)

ASSETS

Fixed assets–tangible		
Land	$300	
Buildings and equipment	120	
Less: Reserve for depreciation	(40)	$380
Factory supplies		10
Current assets		
Inventory	$ 97	
Accounts receivable	52	
Cash	43	192
Fixed assets–intangibles		
Patents	$ 37	
Goodwill	26	63
Deferred charges		
Discount on bonds payable	$ 5	
Returnable containers	21	26
Total Assets		$671

LIABILITIES

Current liabilities		
Accounts payable	$ 80	
Allowance for doubtful accounts	6	
Wages payable	100	$186
Long-term liabilities		
Bonds payable	$200	
Reserve for contingencies	50	250
Equity		
Capital stock, $5 par value,		
10,000 shares issued and outstanding	$ 50	
Capital surplus	34	
Earned surplus	176	
Dividends paid	(25)	235
Total liabilities		$671

REQUIRED

Prepare a balance sheet in good form.

E5-9. EFFECT OF ERRORS ON FINANCIAL STATEMENTS   Certain errors were made by the Gibson Manufacturing Company. Indicate in the space provided below the effects of the errors on the company's statements by inserting *O* to indicate an overstatement, *U* to indicate an understatement, and *N* to indicate no effect.

	TOTAL REVENUE	TOTAL EXPENSE	TOTAL ASSETS	TOTAL LIABILITIES	OWNERS' EQUITY
a)					
b)					
c)					
d)					

a) Failed to accrue year-end interest on bonds payable.
b) Failed to adjust prepaid insurance (recorded initially as insurance expense).
c) Recorded the payment of an account payable by a debit to cash and a credit to accounts payable.
d) Failed to record the purchase of a fixed asset on credit.

E5-10. STATEMENT OF CASH FLOWS   Rocky Road Corporation had net income of $450,000 for 1987. However, cash provided by operations was $680,000. Cash also was affected during 1987 by the following events:
   a) Issued capital stock for $63,000.
   b) Received $26,000 in long-term loan.
   c) Paid dividends of $212,000.
   d) Received $54,000 from disposition of assets.
   e) Retired long-term debt for $43,000.
   f) Acquired treasury stock for $82,000.
   g) Acquired plant assets for $127,000.

REQUIRED

Prepare a statement of cash flows.

E5-11. STATEMENT OF CASH FLOWS   An income statement and comparative balance sheets for Hawk, Inc., appear below.

Hawk, Inc.

COMPARATIVE BALANCE SHEETS

	12/31/86	12/31/87
Assets		
Cash..	$ 24,000	$ 60,000
Receivables	19,000	15,000
Inventory	31,000	59,000
Plant and equipment............................	48,000	72,000
Accumulated depreciation	(12,000)	(24,000)
Land	20,000	4,000
Total	$130,000	$186,000
Liabilities and stockholders' equity		
Accounts payable	$ 16,000	$ 18,000
Notes payable (short-term)......................	7,000	2,000
Bonds payable	–0–	30,000
Common stock (no par)	80,000	92,000
Retained earnings	27,000	44,000
Total	$130,000	$186,000

INCOME STATEMENT
FOR THE YEAR ENDED DECEMBER 31, 1987

Revenues	$150,000
Cost of goods sold	(80,000)
Depreciation	(12,000)
Other expenses	(16,000)
Loss on sale of land	(10,000)
Net income	$ 32,000

REQUIRED

Prepare a statement of cash flows for 1987.

PROBLEMS The problem marked with an asterisk (*) refers to Appendix 5–1.

P5-1. BALANCE SHEET PREPARATION The Continental Company had the following account balances at December 31, 1987 (in millions of dollars):

	DEBIT	CREDIT
Common stock		$ 480.1
Accounts payable		4,612.4
Machinery and equipment	$14,434.1	
Cash	177.3	
Retained earnings		?
Accounts receivable	1,624.3	
Accumulated depreciation—land improvements		430.6
Land	268.0	
Income taxes payable		944.8
Notes receivable	4,007.2	
Buildings	4,975.4	
Accrued liabilities		5,013.3
Allowance for bad debts		7.2
Inventories	7,576.7	
Furniture and office equipment	317.9	
Investments (noncurrent)	2,812.1	
Notes payable (long-term)		300.0
Additional paid-in capital		792.0
Prepaid expenses	729.3	
Short-term investments	3,877.5	
Accumulated depreciation—buildings		3,014.2
Unearned revenues (long-term)		1,384.4
Bonds payable		684.7
Land improvements	719.3	
Accumulated depreciation—furniture and office equipment		161.7
Unamortized discount on bonds	5.8	
Leasehold improvements (net of amortization)	22.3	
Accumulated depreciation—machinery and equipment		9,832.3
Construction in progress	1,315.0	
Special tools	992.4	
Incentive program fund	181.1	
Preferred stock		283.6
Unearned revenues (current)		94.6

REQUIRED

Prepare a balance sheet in good form.

P5-2. BALANCE SHEET AND INCOME STATEMENT PREPARATION The accounts of Lone Pine Industries, Inc., at December 31, 1987, disclose the following information (credits in parentheses; all amounts in thousands of dollars):

Trucks, tractors, trailers	$ 95,749
Accounts payable	(148,663)
Net sales	(1,643,364)
Income taxes payable	(18,393)
Interest expense	34,172
Allowance for doubtful accounts	(6,363)
Inventories	169,198
Accrued liabilities	(60,316)
Cost of goods sold	1,383,978
Notes payable (current)	(11,241)
Terminals and improvements	39,490
Bonds payable (long-term)	(223,258)
Income tax expense	26,523
Buildings and improvements	88,034
Prepaid expenses	8,294
Notes receivable (noncurrent)	21,536
Deferred income taxes	(11,761)
Current portion of long-term debt	(27,768)
Land (used in operations)	21,499
Other assets	18,029
Other expense (net of other revenue)	5,323
Machinery and equipment	110,955
Preferred stock	(1,980)
Accumulated depreciation (combined)	(129,759)
Common stock	(13,628)
Goodwill	44,986
Contributed capital in excess of par	(90,967)
Capitalized lease obligations (long-term)	(39,036)
Selling, general, and administrative expenses	174,126
Accounts receivable	182,879
Investment property	19,110
Treasury stock	13,280
Allowance for doubtful notes	(7,007)
Operating rights	24,572
Cash	60,351
Retained earnings	(127,822)

REQUIRED

1. Prepare a single-step income statement.

2. Prepare a balance sheet in good form.

P5-3. PREPARATION OF CORRECTED BALANCE SHEET Chewning Forest Products, Inc., drafted the balance sheet shown on the following page. In addition, in reviewing the information underlying the balance sheet, you discover the following:

    a) The refundable income taxes relate to income taxes paid in prior years by the company. Although the item is still being contested by the IRS, the company believes there is a reasonable possibility that the amount will be refunded. Therefore, at the end of 1987 it accrued the receivable with a corresponding credit to retained earnings, since the item related to prior years' operations.

    b) Of the amount reported as bonds payable, $14,874,000 is due within the next year.

Chewning Forest Products, Inc.

BALANCE SHEET
FOR THE YEAR ENDED DECEMBER 31, 1987
(in thousands of dollars)

ASSETS

Refundable income taxes	$ 4,110
Timber and timberlands	14,397
Prepaid expenses	9,113
Construction in progress	5,253
Cash	14,247
Inventories	86,723
Investments (long-term)	6,530
Receivables	48,394
Machinery and equipment	220,413
Assets held for disposal	2,955
Marketable securities (short-term, at cost, which approximates market)	482
Land	6,956
Long-term receivables	20,101
Buildings	49,670
	$489,344

EQUITIES

Accounts payable	$ 25,612
Bonds payable	171,988
Allowance for doubtful accounts	1,127
Preferred stock	1,149
Common stock	5,533
Accumulated depreciation	76,868
Notes payable (short-term)	41,000
Contributed capital in excess of par	78,550
Retained earnings	60,257
Deferred income taxes	7,807
Accrued payables	19,453
	$489,344

REQUIRED

Prepare a corrected balance sheet in good form.

P5-4. CONTINGENCIES   Consider the following independent situations:

a) Before the year's financial statements are issued, a firm learns that by the end of its fiscal year it probably will have incurred a liability for obligations related to product warranties. The firm can reasonably estimate the amount of the loss involved.

b) Ajax Company is being sued for negligence in permitting the local residents to be exposed to highly toxic chemicals from its plant and thereby causing numerous illnesses among them. Ajax's lawyer states that, as of December 31, 1987, it is probable that Ajax will lose the suit and be found liable for a judgment, but the amount of the expected judgment is not determinable.

c) Splatter Corporation, a manufacturer of household paints, is preparing annual financial statements. Because of a recently proven health hazard in one of its paints, the government clearly has indicated its intent to order Splatter to recall all cans of this paint sold in the last six months. Splatter's management estimates that this recall will cost $800,000.

d) In January 1984 Consumer Corporation purchased a patent for a new consumer product for $180,000. At the time of purchase, the patent was valid for fifteen years. Owing to the competitive nature of the product, however, Consumer Corporation estimated that the patent would have a useful life of only ten years. During 1987, Consumer permanently removed the product from the market because of a potential health hazard present in the product. Consumer records amortization in each year, and did so in 1987.

e) Tackle Company sells football helmets. In 1987 Tackle discovered a defect in the helmets which has produced lawsuits that are reasonably estimated to result in losses of $900,000. On the basis of its own experience and the experience of other enterprises in the business, Tackle considers it probable that additional lawsuits will result in material losses, but the amount of additional losses cannot be reasonably estimated.

REQUIRED

Indicate the appropriate accounting and disclosure requirements for each of the above situations.

P5-5. BALANCE SHEET AND INCOME STATEMENT PREPARATION The Track and Field Company, a partnership, was organized on January 1, 1987, with each partner investing $25,000 in cash. The partners failed to provide an adequate system of records, and when asked to present financial statements as of December 31, 1987, were unable to do so. You were called in to prepare the required statements. Your investigation of available data and your discussions with the partners revealed the following:

a) Total cash receipts (including partners' investments) from January 1 to December 31, 1987, were $109,840. Included in receipts was a bank loan of $2,000, on which $120 of interest had accrued on December 31, 1987.

b) An analysis of cash disbursements showed the following:

Payment for land ($5,000) and building ($30,000)	$35,000
Payment for furniture and fixtures	8,000
Payment of salaries and wages	2,850
Payment of other expenses	825
Payment of accounts payable	51,165

c) On December 31 you ascertained the following account balances:

Accounts payable	$2,160
Accounts receivable	5,680
Inventory	8,920
Prepaid expenses	180
Accrued payables other than interest	210

d) You also learned that goods costing $500 were purchased during the year and paid for by the company, but were found to be for the personal use of Field, who had not reimbursed the company.

e) You determined that recognition of the following was required: depreciation of building at a rate of 10 percent; depreciation of furniture and fixtures at a rate of 20 percent; estimated uncollectible accounts receivable, $350.

REQUIRED

Prepare in good form:

1. A balance sheet as of December 31, 1987.

2. An income statement for the year ended December 31, 1987.

(CGAA, adapted)

P5-6. EQUITY TRANSACTIONS AND STATEMENT OF STOCKHOLDERS' EQUITY At December 31, 1986, the stockholders' equity of the Shank Golf Club Company totaled $2,207,500. The balances of various accounts at that date were as follows:

4% preferred stock, par $100 (10,000 shares authorized, 5,000 shares issued)	$500,000
Premium on preferred stock	7,500
Common stock, $15 par (100,000 shares authorized, 50,000 shares issued)	750,000
Appropriation for plant expansion	150,000
Appropriation for bond retirement	200,000
Retained earnings (unappropriated)	600,000

The following transactions occurred during 1987:

March 20 The regular semiannual preferred dividend was declared, payable April 1.

April 1 Payment of previously declared dividend.

June 15 The regular semiannual common dividend of 40 cents per share was declared, payable July 10.

July 10 Payment of the previously declared dividend.

Sept. 20 Regular semiannual preferred dividend was declared, payable October 1.

Oct. 1 Payment of previously declared dividend.

Nov. 15 The board of directors met and appropriated an additional $50,000 of retained earnings for plant expansion, another $50,000 for bond retirement, and $25,000 for contingencies related to a pending court case.

Dec. 15 The regular semiannual dividend of 40 cents per common share was declared payable January 10. In addition, a 10 percent stock dividend (5,000 shares) was declared to common stockholders of record as of December 20, to be issued January 20. The market price of the stock was $20 per share (which is the amount that should be transferred from retained earnings to contributed capital).

REQUIRED

1. Prepare all journal entries necessary to reflect the above transactions during 1987.

2. Prepare a statement of stockholders' equity at December 31, 1987, assuming net income for 1987 amounted to $165,000.

(CGAA, adapted)

P5-7. BALANCE SHEET PREPARATION AND ANALYSIS DeBerg Co. began business as a corporation on December 3, 1985. The accounting for the business since its inception has been done by Bill Miles. Miles' primary responsibilities are in the purchasing area and his previous experience in accounting was limited. Sam Cray, a qualified accountant, was hired to perform the company's accounting functions in December of 1987. The first task he was assigned was to review the accounting for the company's first two years, and to make any corrections that might be necessary to ensure that the company's 1986–87 financial statements were proper. The pre-closing trial balance as of November 30, 1987, that is presented below includes year-end adjustments that were prepared by Miles.

DeBerg Co.
PRECLOSING TRIAL BALANCE
NOVEMBER 30, 1987

	DEBIT	CREDIT
Cash	$ 1,150	
Accounts receivable	9,350	
Note receivable	3,000	
Inventory	10,500	
Land	8,000	
Furniture and fixtures	20,000	
Unexpired insurance	600	
Accounts payable		$ 4,950
Notes payable		5,000
Common stock, $10 par		25,000
Additional paid-in capital		2,700
Retained earnings		8,950
Sales		103,800
Purchases	78,750	
Purchase returns		450
Selling expenses	12,000	
Administrative expenses	7,500	
Total	$150,850	$150,850

Cray's review of the accounting records and other records uncovered the following additional information.

1. Checks totaling $2,350 had been written to vendors and recorded in the November 1987 cash disbursements journal but were still in the vault on December 7.

2. All receivables from 1985–86 credit sales either had been collected or written off. The estimate for bad debts arising from 1986–87 sales was $2,000 and the following entry was made to recognize this fact.

Selling expense	2,000	
Accounts receivable		2,000

3. The note receivable for $3,000 is from a customer. This three-month note is dated November 1, 1987, and has an annual interest rate of 18%.

4. The physical inventory on November 30, 1987, includes $9,900 of product on hand and $2,100 of inventory issued to Apex Co. on a consignment basis.

5. The furniture and fixtures were acquired on December 3, 1985. These fixed assets are being depreciated on a straight-line basis over a ten-year life with no salvage value. The following adjusting entry was made by Miles in November 1987 to recognize depreciation.

Selling expense	2,000	
Administrative expense	500	
Furniture and fixtures		2,500

The same adjusting entry was made for the 1985–86 fiscal year.

6. The company has one prepaid insurance policy. The policy covers a one-year period and was purchased for $1,200 on June 1, 1987.

7. The notes payable were issued on November 1, 1987, with an annual interest rate of 12%. The principal and interest are payable on August 1, 1988.

8. On November 20, 1987, the Board of Directors declared a cash dividend of $2,500 payable on December 14, 1987. The dividend is payable to stockholders of record as of December 3, 1987.

9. The tax return for the 1986–87 fiscal year appears to be properly prepared and shows no tax liability.

REQUIRED

1. Prepare a statement of financial position, in good form, for the DeBerg Co. as of November 30, 1987.

2. Discuss the information value of a statement of financial position alone as compared to a full set of financial statements (income statement, statement of changes in financial position, and statement of financial position).

3. Contrast the information value of a set of current year financial statements to a set of comparative financial statements. (IMA, adapted)

P5-8. STATEMENT OF CASH FLOWS The balance sheets of Tahoe Ski Company showed the following:

	12/31/87	**12/31/86**
Cash	$ 10,000	$ 12,000
Accounts receivable (net)	18,000	10,000
Inventory	24,000	20,000
Long-term investments	10,000	24,000
Plant and equipment	104,000	60,000
	$166,000	$126,000
Accumulated depreciation	$ 14,000	$ 10,000
Accounts payable	16,000	12,000
Notes payable—long-term	40,000	32,000
Capital stock	60,000	50,000
Retained earnings	36,000	22,000
	$166,000	$126,000

The income statement for 1987 appears below:

Sales	$320,000
Cost of sales	(200,000)
Gross margin	$120,000
Expenses	
Expenses, including income taxes, paid in cash $96,000	
Depreciation 6,000	(102,000)
Loss on disposal of investments	(4,000)
Gain on disposal of fixed assets	2,000
Net income	$ 16,000

Additional data concerning changes in the noncurrent accounts:
   a) Cash dividends paid, $2,000
   b) Issue of common stock for cash, $10,000
   c) Machinery disposed of during the year cost $6,000

REQUIRED

Prepare a statement of cash flows for 1987.

(CGAA, adapted)

*P5-9.   REVIEW OF CHAPTERS 4 AND 5   Answer the following questions related to the financial statements and related information of The Coca-Cola Company presented in Appendix 5–1. Your answers should relate to 1985 only, unless otherwise indicated.

REQUIRED

   1. What is the nature of The Coca-Cola Company's (Coke's) business?

   2. How does Coke's revenue pattern compare to its net income trend from 1983 through 1985?

   3. What proportion of net income was paid to stockholders as cash dividends in 1985? Is this comparable to 1983 and 1984?

   4. Are there any special charges or credits in *(a)* the 1985 income statement and *(b)* the other income statement? Explain.

   5. What depreciation methods does Coke use?

   6. Why do income taxes differ from 46 percent (the statutory tax rate) of income before income taxes? What are the components of the provision for income taxes?

   7. What are the earnings per share? Does Coke report a dual presentation of EPS? Explain.

   8. How much of Coke's operating income came from outside the U.S.?

   9. Based on the discussion in Chapter 4, how would you characterize the form of the income statement? Comment on format and terminology strengths and weaknesses.

   10. What is Coke's largest current asset? largest current liability?

   11. What is the current ratio (current assets divided by current liabilities) for *(a)* 1985 and *(b)* 1984?

   12. What is the basis for valuing inventories?

   13. What are the components of accrued liabilities?

   14. What is Coke's most significant noncurrent liability?

   15. What are the major components of Coke's long-term debt?

   16. Does Coke have any unused lines of credit?

   17. Did Coke have any contingencies at the end of 1985? Explain.

   18. What types of stock does Coke have authorized? issued?

19. What caused the capital surplus to increase during 1985?

20. Based on the discussion in Chapter 5, how would you characterize Coke's balance sheet? Comment on format and terminology strengths and weaknesses.

21. What definition of funds does Coke employ in its statement of changes in financial position?

22. What were the major sources and uses of funds during 1985?

23. What adjustments to net income were made to arrive at funds provided by operations?

24. Which line of business contributed the most to sales and other revenues during 1985?

25. Which line of business has the greatest asset investment?

26. How did Coke's current cost income from continuing operations compare to its historical cost income from continuing operations?

6 REVENUE RECOGNITION AND INCOME DETERMINATION

Under accrual accounting, accountants measure the net cash flow effects of earnings activities by recording and reporting transactions that have cash consequences as the transactions take place, rather than waiting until the cash is received or paid. In accrual accounting, the realization principle governs the recognition of revenue, and expenses are matched against revenues to determine income. As we discussed in Chapter 2, accrual accounting generally provides better signals about future cash flows than does cash basis accounting, and thus better satisfies the objectives of financial reporting.

For many years, revenue recognition and income determination have been among the most controversial areas in accounting. Numerous lawsuits have stemmed from "premature" recognition of revenue, especially in the building and construction industry. In many of these cases, either the reported revenue was not collectible or the net income or net cash flow effect of the earnings activity could not be estimated reliably. In addition, many financial institutions have been accused of "accounting gimmickry" because of their revenue recognition methods:

> Many thrifts are also increasing their profits with fees from mortgages sales that they haven't actually received. When an S&L (savings and loan) sells a mortgage to another company, it often continues to service the mortgage by accepting delivery of the monthly payments. After deducting a service fee, it passes on the money to the new owner of the mortgage. Many thrifts immediately book all their expected fee income as profit when they sell a mortgage. Such income can be a significant portion of a thrift's profits.
>
> At City Federal Savings & Loan Association in Elizabeth, N.J., $64.2 million of the thrift's $66.8 million in 1984 pre-tax earnings came from fee income associated with mortgage sales.[1]

Because revenue recognition and income determination are of such importance and so closely related to the objectives of financial accounting, we examine these concepts in detail in this chapter. An overview, based on our discussion of revenue and income in Chapters 2 and 4, is presented first. Next we discuss and illustrate the recording and reporting of revenue and income at various points in a company's earnings cycle. Then we present some specialized industry applications of revenue recognition. Accounting for consignment transactions concludes the chapter.

[1] "Accounting at Thrifts Provokes Controversy as Gimmickry Mounts," *The Wall Street Journal*, March 21, 1985, p. 23.

AN OVERVIEW OF REVENUE CONCEPTS

It is important to distinguish among (1) the nature or definition of revenue, (2) the measurement of revenue, and (3) the realization of revenue. Revenues were *defined* in Chapter 2 as increases in net assets from delivery or production of goods, rendering of services, or other activities that constitute a company's major or primary operations. Revenues are *measured* at the fair value or cash equivalent price of assets received. *Realization* is a technical accounting term that governs the *timing* of revenue recognition—when should revenue be *recognized* (recorded) and reported in the income statement?

THE REVENUE EARNING PROCESS

Exhibit 6–1 is a time line, reproduced from Chapter 2, which illustrates the company's earnings process. Revenue is *earned* throughout this process as value—in the form of time, place, and form utility—is added to the costs of productive inputs. For example, a company may acquire raw materials and transform these materials and labor inputs into a final product. Earnings activities may overlap; that is, some goods may be sold while other goods are being produced. In addition, the economic resources used to generate revenue and income may benefit one product in one accounting period (for example, cost of merchandise sold) or many products over several accounting periods (for example, long-lived depreciable assets). While the economic events pictured in Exhibit 6–1 may not represent the sequence of earnings activities for all companies, the exhibit allows us to focus on the nature of the earnings process.

RECOGNITION AND THE REALIZATION PRINCIPLE

Even though revenue is earned continuously, it is impractical to recognize it on a continuous basis and it is infeasible to associate portions of total revenue with each activity that contributes to revenue. Therefore, accountants select a point or points in the earnings process at which to recognize revenue. There are many points at which revenue could be recognized. Revenue could be recognized during production, at the completion of production, while the completed product is awaiting sale, at the point of sale, or, for credit sales, when cash is collected. As we pointed out in Chapter 2, accountants use the realization principle as a guideline for determining when revenue should be recognized. **Realization**

EXHIBIT 6–1   THE EARNINGS PROCESS

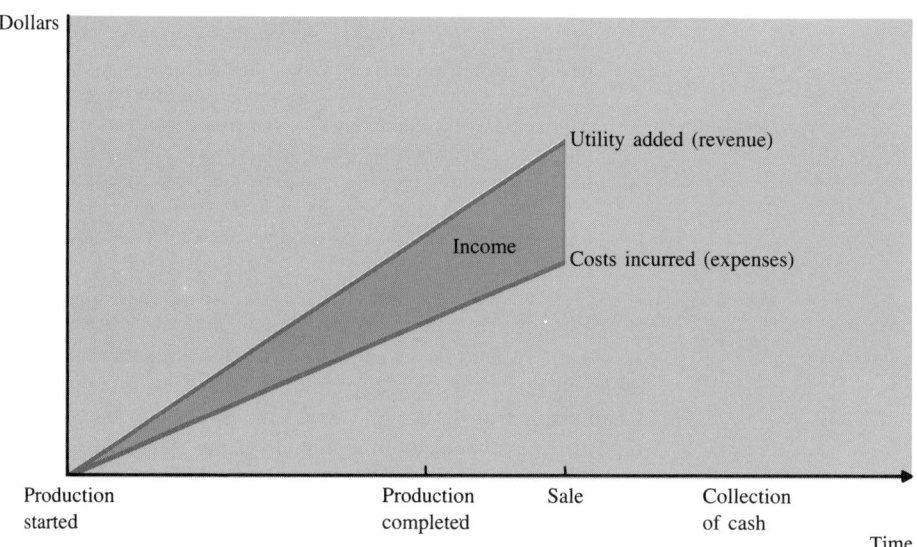

Realization refers to the reduction of uncertainty about future cash flows.

refers, conceptually, to the occurrence of an event or events that reduce the uncertainty about the net cash flow effect of an earnings activity to an acceptable level. In practice, the realization principle sets forth the criteria or guidelines used to determine when to recognize revenue. Revenues should be recognized and reported in the income statement when:

1. The amount and timing of revenue to be received are reasonably determinable.

2. The earnings process is complete or virtually complete.

Notice that these criteria are consistent with, but are more operational than, the general *recognition* criteria for the financial statement elements presented in Chapter 2.

The first criterion means that the expected cash inflows must be objectively determinable before revenue can be recorded. The second criterion means that until the earnings process is complete or virtually complete, the company has not fulfilled all of its economic obligations related to the transaction. Thus the second criterion considers the sacrifices (expenses) or *expected cash outflows* associated with the transaction. In summary, revenues are recorded on the basis of the realization principle. Expenses, which are incurred in the earnings process, are matched against revenues on the basis of one or more of the expense recognition guidelines presented in Chapter 2. Revenues minus expenses equal net income or net loss for the accounting period.

The revenue recognition criteria illustrate how accountants must balance *relevance* and *reliability* in achieving the financial reporting objective of providing information that assists users in predicting, evaluating, and assessing cash flows. On the one hand, *timely* information about revenue, income, and cash flows increases the relevance of the reported information. On the other hand, the information also must be reliable—*verifiable* and *representationally faithful*—in order to be useful. Notice how the above criteria or guidelines incorporate both qualitative characteristics.

Revenue recognition criteria meet qualitative characteristics of accounting information.

In the following sections, we discuss revenue recognition at various points in companies' earnings processes. As you read and study this material, which covers revenue from sales of products as well as from services, you should remember that the specific practices discussed and illustrated are applications of the above conceptual considerations.

REVENUE RECOGNITION AT THE POINT OF SALE

Most merchandising and manufacturing companies recognize revenue at the point of sale because the two recognition criteria usually are met at this point.[2] The amount of revenue recognized is established by the exchange price at the time of sale. If the sale is for cash or on short-term account, there usually is no uncertainty about the amount or the timing of the cash flows. In addition, the point of sale represents the completion of the earnings process because the merchandise has been transferred to the buyer. Thus, the seller usually has fulfilled all obligations to the buyer at this point.

[2] In practice, liquidity or nearness to cash often plays a role in revenue and income recognition. Revenues and income usually are recognized when an exchange results in an increase in liquidity. Interestingly, the change in liquidity (more liquidity or less liquidity) resulting from an exchange may be the primary distinction between a purchase and a sale. When an asset received in an exchange transaction is less liquid than the asset sacrificed, the transaction is classified as a purchase. When the asset received is more liquid than the asset sacrificed, the transaction is classified as a sale.

Revenue recognition at the point of sale, however, is often complicated by the following factors:

1. Sales made on credit, trade and cash discounts, uncollectible accounts, and interest on receivables that are collectible over extended periods of time.

2. Costs related to the sale that are incurred after the date of sale.

3. Return privileges on merchandise sold.

SALES MADE ON CREDIT

Accounting for receivables arising from credit sales is discussed in detail in Chapter 8. Only an overview is presented here. Since revenue is measured at the fair value or cash equivalent price of the assets received in exchange, revenue from credit sales should be recorded net of any trade and sales discounts and at the present value of the amount of cash to be received. Because it is desirable to report on the income statement the amount of cash expected from the sale, it is also necessary to allow for any sales which are estimated to be uncollectible. This procedure also results in reporting accounts receivable on the balance sheet at the amount of cash expected to be collected from customers. Methods of estimating uncollectible accounts were introduced in our discussion of the accounting cycle in Chapter 3 and are discussed at length in Chapter 8.

COSTS INCURRED AFTER THE POINT OF SALE

Although the earnings process may be virtually complete at the date of sale, occasionally sale-related costs are incurred subsequent to the sale date. For example, a hardware store that sells television sets may offer a two-year warranty on the sets. According to the theory underlying accrual accounting, the cost of servicing the warranty should be estimated and accrued at the date of sale or at the end of the accounting period in which the sale is made so that expenses are properly matched against the revenue recognized.

Suppose that Margie Hardware sold 100 television sets. On the basis of past experience, the company estimates that warranty costs will average about $7 per set. The following entry would be made to record the costs estimated to arise after the sale date:

```
Warranty expense . . . . . . . . . . . . . . . . . . . . . . . . . . . . . . . . . . . . . . . . . . 700
    Estimated warranty obligations . . . . . . . . . . . . . . . . . . . . . . . . . . . . . . .    700
```

Actual costs incurred during the warranty period would be recorded as a debit to the liability account, estimated warranty obligations, and as a credit to the appropriate asset accounts. Accounting for warranty obligations is covered in more depth in Chapter 15.

RETURN PRIVILEGES

In some industries, such as newspaper publishing, book publishing, perishable food sales, and record and tape sales, customers are given the right to return goods under certain circumstances. Goods may be returned for a refund, for a credit to be applied to other purchases or amounts owed, or for exchange for other merchandise. In determining the amount of revenue to be recognized at the point of sale, the seller must consider that some goods may be returned. If possible returns are not considered, the amount of revenue reported may not measure the expected inflow of cash.

If returns are infrequent, are small in dollar amount, and occur over a fairly short time period following the sale, sales returns should be debited and accounts receivable or cash should be credited as goods are returned. Even though the sale may be recorded in a different accounting period than the related sales return, the mismatching of sales and returns is probably immaterial in these circumstances.

When the return privilege covers a longer period of time and when a significant dollar amount of returns is experienced, an allowance for expected returns should be established at the sale date or at the end of the accounting period in order to measure the expected cash flows resulting from the sale. Assume, for example, that Penn Limited sells goods on account and allows its customers very lenient return privileges. Past experience indicates that sales returns generally average about 15 percent of sales. During 1987, sales were $200,000 and actual returns were $18,000. The entries based on the allowance method for sales returns are as follows:

Accounts receivable	200,000	
Allowance for sales returns ($200,000 × .15)		30,000
Sales		170,000
To record 1987 sales on account and estimated returns.		
Allowance for sales returns	18,000	
Accounts receivable		18,000
To record actual returns during 1987.		

The balance of $12,000 in the allowance for sales returns account at the end of 1987 is a contra asset account to accounts receivable. It is deducted from accounts receivable on the balance sheet at the end of 1987 so that the expected net realizable value of accounts receivable is reported. Any returns in 1988 resulting from 1987 sales will be debited to the allowance account.

Assuming a periodic inventory system, for actual sales returns occurring in 1987, cost of goods sold will be adjusted automatically in the physical count of the ending inventory, since any returned goods that are not resold will be included in the ending inventory. For the remaining sales returns of $12,000 that are expected to occur in 1988, inventory should be increased and cost of goods sold decreased for cost, or net realizable value less a normal profit, associated with the goods that are expected to be returned. For example, if the cost associated with the $12,000 of remaining expected sales returns is $8,000, the following entry would be appropriate:

Inventory	8,000	
Cost of goods sold		8,000

Under a perpetual inventory system, the above adjusting entry would not be necessary if the original entry to record cost of goods sold were based on sales less expected returns. Disclosure of the nature of and reasons for the allowance for sales returns and related adjustments should be made in the notes to the financial statements.

In some circumstances, the seller's risk associated with customers' return privileges may be so great that a sale should *not* be recorded initially. Circumstances that increase the level of uncertainty about future net cash flows related to return privileges include (1) the lack of a fixed or determinable sales price, (2) the purchaser's lack of obligation to pay the seller if the merchandise cannot be sold or is stolen or damaged, (3) an obligation on the part of the seller to assist the purchaser in product resale, and (4) an inability to reasonably estimate the future returns. Thus, until the two revenue recognition criteria are met, any customer collections should be recorded as deposits or as unearned revenue.[3]

REVENUE RECOGNITION DURING PRODUCTION

Some companies engage in earnings activities in which production of the goods to be sold extends over several accounting periods. For example, bridges, airplanes, office buildings, and oil refineries all require several years to complete. A timber company may plant pine seedlings that require a number of years of growth before the timber can be cut,

---

[3] "Revenue Recognition When Right of Return Exists," *Statement of Financial Accounting Standards No. 48* (Stamford, Conn.: FASB, 1981).

processed, and sold as lumber. Should some revenue and income be recognized each year during the progress of these types of production in order to provide timely information about earnings and future cash flows to investors and other users? If the net cash flows from these earnings activities can be estimated with a high degree of certainty, the answer is yes.

LONG-TERM CONSTRUCTION CONTRACTS

There are two methods of accounting for revenues, expenses, and income under long-term construction contracts (such as those for buildings, bridges, airplanes, and ships):

1. The percentage-of-completion method.
2. The completed-contract method.

Although the completed-contract method does not lead to revenue recognition during production, it is presented here so that we may compare these two accounting methods.

The Percentage-of-Completion Method

When contractual arrangements and production processes extend over several accounting periods, the producer-seller should recognize revenue and income during production if:

1. The total price of the contract—the price that the buyer will pay—is known or is determinable.
2. The total cost of the construction project to the producer-seller is reasonably estimable.
3. The cost incurred by the producer-seller during the current accounting period, or the percentage of production completed, is known or is reasonably estimable. Stated another way, the producer-seller can measure reliably the extent of completion of production during each accounting period.

Under these circumstances, the net cash flow effects of the construction activity are reasonably determinable through time. That is, the amount of revenue can be estimated with reasonable certainty because the contract price usually is known; the percentage of the project completed during a period is assumed to represent the portion of the earnings process completed during that period. The accounting method that is used to recognize revenue during the production process is the **percentage-of-completion method.**

APPLYING THE PERCENTAGE-OF-COMPLETION METHOD At the end of each accounting period, the total contract price is compared with estimated total construction costs, and the estimated total income on the project is determined. In some instances the estimated income may change from period to period because the estimated total construction costs may change as construction progresses. Once the estimated total income on the project is determined, the portion of the total income that should be recognized to date (the period between the start of the project and the end of the current accounting period) is calculated. This calculation is based on some measure of the percentage of completion of the total project. Assume, for example, that at the end of year 2 of a long-term contract to construct a bridge at a contract price of $5 million, the total cost of construction is estimated to be $4.5 million. Therefore, at the end of year 2 the estimated total income on the project is $500,000. If the bridge is estimated to be 80 percent complete at the end of year 2, then 80 percent of $500,000, or $400,000, is the amount of income that should be recognized for the period between the start of the project and the end of year 2.

Once the amount of income that should be recognized on the project through the end of the current accounting period is determined, it is necessary to deduct any income that has been recognized on the project in prior accounting periods in order to calculate the amount of income that should be recognized in the current accounting period. If $240,000 of income had been recognized on the construction of the bridge in year 1, then $160,000 (the $400,000 total income-to-date less the $240,000 income recognized in year 1) should be recognized as income in year 2.

MEASURING THE PERCENTAGE OF COMPLETION The percentage of completion of a project may be based on the relationship between costs incurred up to the current date and total estimated construction costs; that is, any new information about estimated costs necessary to complete the project is included in the latest total cost estimates. Alternatively, the percentage of completion may be based on some physical measure of completion. For example, units of input, such as the number of hours of labor used to date compared with estimated total labor hours needed on the project, or units of output, such as the number of miles of road completed as compared with the total contract miles, might be an appropriate measure of the extent of completion.

The components of construction costs are similar to those of other types of manufacturing costs—direct material costs, direct labor costs, and overhead costs. With respect to direct materials, an interesting question arises: Should the cost of direct materials *purchased* be included in the calculation of the completion percentage? This question is important for two reasons: (1) Construction companies typically acquire a large portion of their construction materials early in the construction phase in order to avoid price increases and to take advantage of quantity discounts, and (2) larger amounts of income will be recognized in the early years of the contract if the cost of these material purchases is included in the completion percentage. As a practical example, in the 1970s, Frigitemp, a diversified corporation that manufactured custom-made refrigeration equipment for ships and hotels, decorated hotels and casinos, and built food-service systems, declared bankruptcy. The company used the percentage-of-completion method in many of its construction contracts. One factor that caused the company financial stress was the ''front-end loading'' of income orchestrated by the inclusion of materials *purchased* in its percentage-of-completion calculations. In one instance, the company issued promissory notes to a supplier who in turn invoiced the company for $4.2 million in deck planking, most of which was still in the form of trees growing on the West Coast. Frigitemp even billed its customer for this amount.

Costs of material *purchases* should not be included in the percentage-of-completion calculation. Instead, these material costs should be included only as the materials are used, for the following reasons:

1. The materials are assets until they are used.

2. The earnings activity consists of conversion of these inputs into a final product. Except for possible place utility, such as getting the materials to the construction site, no utility has been added to these materials purchased.

3. Since the construction process is lengthy, it is not certain that all of the materials purchased will be used on the particular project.

ACCOUNTING AND REPORTING In accounting for long-term construction contracts, an inventory account, construction in progress, is debited for the costs incurred in completing the project. In addition, the construction in progress account is debited and construction income is credited for income that is recognized on the project. Thus, under the percentage-of-completion method, the construction in progress inventory account is composed of costs incurred to date plus income recognized to date on the project. At any balance sheet date, the account balance may be interpreted as the market value of the resource being constructed. If the project continues to be profitable, the balance in the construction in progress account at the end of each accounting period will equal the contract price times the percentage of completion. When the project is completed, the balance in the construction in progress inventory account will equal the contract price.

Because of the extended construction period related to a long-term contract and the need to finance continuing construction costs, a construction contract typically specifies that the contractor may periodically bill the purchaser for part of the contract price. These billings are recorded by debiting accounts receivable and crediting billings on construction contract. The billings on construction contract account and the construction in progress account are reported as offsets against each other on the balance sheet. If the sum of construction in progress and income to date exceeds the billings on the construction to date, the net amount is reported on the balance sheet as an asset and represents an amount to be recovered from future billings. If the reverse relationship exists, the net amount is reported on the balance sheet as a liability and represents unfulfilled obligations to customers. We shall present a detailed illustration of accounting for and reporting of long-term construction projects after the next section.

The Completed-Contract Method

The **completed-contract method** of accounting for long-term construction contracts should be used when it is not possible to make reasonably dependable estimates of the extent of completion. Conceptually, the completed-contract method is similar to revenue recognition at the completion of production or at the date of sale since the product is delivered to the purchaser at completion.

As the name implies, under the completed-contract method no income is recognized until the project is completed. During the course of construction, costs incurred on the project are debited to construction in progress. Billings to the customer are recorded by debiting accounts receivable and crediting billings on construction contract. In this respect and in terms of reporting these accounts on the balance sheet, the completed-contract method is like the percentage-of-completion method. From a balance sheet standpoint, the essential difference between the two methods is that since no income is recognized under the completed-contract method until construction is completed, the construction in progress inventory account includes only construction costs incurred. At the completion date, the construction in progress account balance will be less than the contract price by the amount of the income on the project.

The percentage-of-completion method and the completed-contract method are not alternatives available under the same set of circumstances. When the contract price or revenue is known and when future construction costs can be reasonably estimated, the percentage-of-completion method provides better signals about net cash flows and therefore provides more relevant and useful data. If these two conditions are not met, however, the completed-contract method must be used to avoid reporting data that may not be reliable.

The percentage-of-completion method and the completed-contract method are not alternatives.

Accounting for Long-Term Construction Contracts

Assume that at the beginning of 1987, Breezmore Corporation entered into a contract to construct a revolutionary electricity-generating windmill for the city of Washita Falls. The contract price was $1 million. Information related to construction activity from the beginning of 1987 through the end of 1989, when construction was completed, is as follows:

	1987	1988	1989
Construction costs incurred to date	$200,000	$500,000	$875,000
Estimated cost to complete construction	600,000	350,000	–0–
Estimated total construction costs	$800,000	$850,000	$875,000
Billings on contract	180,000	490,000	330,000
Cash payments by purchaser	170,000	240,000	590,000

EXHIBIT 6–2   GROSS PROFIT (INCOME) TO BE RECOGNIZED
UNDER THE PERCENTAGE-OF-COMPLETION METHOD

	1987	1988	1989
Construction costs incurred to date	$200,000	$500,000	$875,000
Estimated cost to complete construction	600,000	350,000	–0–
Estimated total cost of construction	$800,000	$850,000	$875,000
Estimated percentage of completion to date (construction costs incurred to date ÷ estimated total cost of construction)	25%	59%*	100%
Estimated total income ($1,000,000 contract price less estimated total cost of construction)	$200,000	$150,000	$125,000
Income recognized to date (estimated percentage of completion × estimated total income)	$ 50,000	$ 88,500	$125,000
Income recognized in current year (income recognized to date less income recognized in previous years)	$ 50,000	$ 38,500†	$ 36,500‡

* Rounded.

† $88,500 − $50,000.

‡ $125,000 − $88,500.

Observe that the estimated *total* cost of construction (construction costs incurred to date plus estimated costs to complete) changes from year to year. Such changes are common in long-term contracts because the future is never predictable with certainty. Estimates of total construction costs become more certain, however, as time passes.

The amount of income to be recognized each year under the percentage-of-completion method is illustrated in Exhibit 6–2. The journal entries under the two methods appear in Exhibit 6–3.

The following points about the journal entries in Exhibit 6–3 are important. First, in all years other than the year in which the project is completed and accepted by the purchaser, the percentage-of-completion method and the completed-contract method require the same journal entries, except for the annual income recognition entry under the percentage-of-completion method. Second, when income is recognized each accounting period under the percentage-of-completion method, it results in an increase in the inventory account, construction in progress. Third, because construction in progress under the percentage-of-completion method includes costs incurred as well as income recognized to date, by the time the project is completed the construction in progress account and the billings on construction contract account are both equal to the contract price. Hence under the percentage-of-completion method, the two accounts are closed out against each other. Finally, because no income is recognized during the course of the construction period under the completed-contract method, the difference between construction in progress and billings on construction contract in the year the project is completed and accepted is equal to the total income to be recognized on the project. Hence under the completed-contract method, closing construction in progress out against billings on construction contract yields the total income on the project, which is recognized in the year of completion.

EXHIBIT 6—3   JOURNAL ENTRIES FOR PERCENTAGE-OF-COMPLETION AND COMPLETED-CONTRACT METHODS OF ACCOUNTING FOR LONG-TERM CONSTRUCTION CONTRACTS

	PERCENTAGE-OF-COMPLETION METHOD		COMPLETED-CONTRACT METHOD	
1987				
To record construction costs:				
Construction in progress	200,000		200,000	
Materials, wages payable, cash, etc.		200,000		200,000
To record billings:				
Accounts receivable	180,000		180,000	
Billings on construction contract...................		180,000		180,000
To record cash collections:				
Cash...	170,000		170,000	
Accounts receivable		170,000		170,000
*To record income recognized:**				
Construction in progress	50,000		No entry	
Income on long-term construction contract		50,000		
1988				
To record construction costs:				
Construction in progress	300,000		300,000	
Materials, wages payable, cash, etc.		300,000		300,000
To record billings:				
Accounts receivable	490,000		490,000	
Billings on construction contract...................		490,000		490,000
To record cash collections:				
Cash...	240,000		240,000	
Accounts receivable		240,000		240,000
*To record income recognized:**				
Construction in progress	38,500		No entry	
Income on long-term construction contract		38,500		
1989				
To record construction costs:				
Construction in progress	375,000		375,000	
Materials, wages payable, cash, etc.		375,000		375,000
To record billings:				
Accounts receivable	330,000		330,000	
Billings on construction contract...................		330,000		330,000
To record cash collections:				
Cash...	590,000		590,000	
Accounts receivable		590,000		590,000
To record income recognized and to close construction contract accounts:				
Percentage-of-completion method:*				
Construction in progress	36,500			
Income on long-term construction contract		36,500		
Billings on construction contract....................1,000,000				
Construction in progress		1,000,000		
Completed-contract method:				
Billings on construction contract....................			1,000,000	
Construction in progress				875,000
Income on long-term construction contract				125,000

      * Equivalent entries to show the amounts of *revenue* and *expense* recognized each year under the percentage-of-completion method would be:

	1987	1988	1989
Construction in progress	50,000	38,500	36,500
Costs of construction revenue ...200,000		300,000	375,000
Construction revenue	250,000	338,500	411,500

Since construction income is based on the percentage of completion, construction revenue equals the costs incurred in the current period plus the amount of income recognized in the current period. Construction expenses, then, equal the costs incurred in generating the revenue.

Reporting Long-Term Construction Contracts

As indicated earlier, if construction in progress exceeds billings on construction contract, the difference is reported on the balance sheet as a *current asset*. If the amount in the billings on construction contract account exceeds the amount in the construction in progress account, the difference is reported as a *current liability*. The difference is reported as a current item because the contractor's operating cycle covers the length of the construction period.

Footnote disclosures that are unique to companies with long-term construction contracts include the accounting method used, the basis for assessing completion, the basis for recognizing income, and the basis of classifying assets and liabilities. Exhibit 6–4, which is based on the data in the Breezmore illustration and the journal entries in Exhibit 6–3, illustrates these disclosures.

Losses on Long-Term Construction Contracts

To this point we have assumed that the construction contract was profitable, in terms of the income recognized each period as well as total income on the contract. In this section we shall consider accounting for and reporting losses on long-term construction contracts.

When cost estimates indicate that a loss should be expected, the loss should be immediately recognized, under both the percentage-of-completion method and the completed-contract method. There can be either of two types of losses. First, when the percentage-of-completion method is used, the periodic calculation of income to be recognized may indicate that although the overall contract is expected to be profitable, a loss must be reported for the current period. This situation will occur when the income recognized in previous accounting periods exceeds the income that should have been recognized to date, given income and percentage-of-completion calculations for the current accounting period. For example, assume that at the end of the third year of a four-year contract for construction that is 80 percent complete, total income on the contract is estimated to be $50,000, and $45,000 of income has been recognized through the end of the second year. In this case, income recognized to date should be $40,000 ($50,000 × 80 percent). Therefore, it is necessary to recognize a $5,000 loss for the third year:

Loss on long-term construction contract 5,000
    Construction in progress   5,000

> Losses on long-term construction contracts are recognized in full under both methods as soon as the losses occur.

This type of loss is the result of a **change in accounting estimate** and must be recorded in the current period. Changes in accounting estimates are discussed in detail in Chapter 22. Given the conditions that justify the use of the percentage-of-completion method, this type of loss should occur only infrequently and will not arise under the completed-contract method because no income is recognized until the construction project is completed.

The second type of loss arises when it is expected that total construction costs will exceed the contract price and can arise with either the completed-contract method or the percentage-of-completion method. Such a loss arises because of unexpected increases in construction costs. Assume, for example, that Apple Corporation uses the percentage-of-completion method in accounting for its long-term construction contracts. Through the end of the second year of a four-year contract, it has recognized $30,000 of income. At the end of the third year, Apple estimates that total construction costs on a $250,000 contract will be $260,000.

At the end of the third year, Apple Corporation must recognize a loss of $40,000, which consists of the $10,000 loss expected on the contract plus the $30,000 income previously recognized that must be removed from the construction in progress account. The entry to record the loss is:

Loss on long-term construction contract 40,000
    Construction in progress   40,000

EXHIBIT 6–4   ILLUSTRATIVE FINANCIAL STATEMENT REPORTING
AND FOOTNOTE DISCLOSURES FOR A COMPANY
WITH A LONG-TERM CONSTRUCTION CONTRACT

PERCENTAGE-OF-COMPLETION METHOD

	1987	1988	1989
PARTIAL INCOME STATEMENT			
Revenue from long-term construction contracts	$250,000	$338,500	$411,500
Costs of construction revenue	(200,000)	(300,000)	(375,000)
Income (gross profit) on long-term construction contracts	$ 50,000	$ 38,500	$ 36,500
PARTIAL BALANCE SHEET			
Current assets			
Accounts receivable	$ 10,000	$260,000	
Inventories			
Construction in progress $250,000			
Less: Billings . . . . (180,000)	70,000		
Current liabilities			
Billings on construction contract		$670,000	
Less: Construction in progress		(588,500)	81,500

NOTE 1 SIGNIFICANT ACCOUNTING POLICIES (in part)

Long-term construction contracts: The company recognizes profit on long-term construction contracts by using the percentage-of-completion method of accounting. The percentage of completion is based on the ratio of cost incurred to date as compared to estimated total construction cost. When costs incurred plus profits recognized to date exceed amounts billed, a current asset equal to the difference and classified as inventory is reported on the balance sheet. In 1987 this amount equaled $70,000. When amounts billed exceed costs incurred plus profits recognized to date, a current liability equal to the difference is reported on the balance sheet. In 1988 this amount was $81,500. Construction costs include direct materials, direct labor, and overhead costs associated with the project.

If at the end of the fourth year the actual total construction costs equal $260,000, the $40,000 reduction of construction in progress for the previously recognized $30,000 income plus the $10,000 overall loss on the contract will yield a final construction in progress balance that is equal to the contract price. Thus, the loss and the unfavorable net cash flow effect will have been reported on a timely basis in the third year, the year in which it first became known. In addition, the construction in progress account will be reported at the amount expected to be recoverable on the contract. If Apple had used the completed-contract method, the amount of loss recorded in the previous entry would be only $10,000 ($260,000 − $250,000), because no income would have been recognized in the two previous years.

Recognition of losses on long-term construction contracts is an application of recoverable value.

The recognition of losses on long-term construction contracts when those losses first become known is an example of how conservatism deals with uncertainty about future cash flows under generally accepted accounting principles. It also illustrates an application of *recoverable value* in balance sheet valuation.

COMPLETED-CONTRACT METHOD

	1987	1988	1989
PARTIAL INCOME STATEMENT			
Completed-contract method:			
Revenue from long-term construction contracts	—	—	$1,000,000
Costs of construction revenue	—	—	(875,000)
Income (gross profit) on long-term construction			
contracts	—	—	$ 125,000
PARTIAL BALANCE SHEET			
Current assets			
Accounts receivable	$10,000	$260,000	
Inventories			
Construction in progress $200,000			
Less: Billings . . . . (180,000)	20,000		
Current liabilities			
Billings on construction contract		$670,000	
Less: Construction in progress		(500,000)	170,000

NOTE 1 SIGNIFICANT ACCOUNTING POLICIES (in part)

Long-term construction contracts: The company uses the completed-contract method of accounting for long-term construction contracts. Under this method, no profit is recognized until the construction project is either complete or substantially complete. During the period of construction, construction costs are accumulated in a construction in progress account and customer billings are accumulated in a billings on construction contract account. Construction costs include direct materials, direct labor, and overhead costs associated with the project. Any excess of costs incurred to date over billings is reported among inventories as a current asset. In 1987 this amount was $20,000. Any excess of billings over costs incurred to date is reported as a current liability. In 1988 this amount was $170,000.

PRODUCTS REQUIRING AGING

Many products require several accounting periods of preparation before they are in their intended salable form. Timber companies, for example, may plant seedlings, which require care—fertilizing, watering, thinning, insect treatment—for a number of years before they are sold. Distilleries allow fine whiskies to age several years before they are marketed and sold. Thus, these types of products become more valuable through time. Should this *accretion* in value be recognized as income on a periodic basis? Even though these products do increase in value through time, future economic conditions, such as consumer demand, technological change, future selling prices, and future costs, are so uncertain that the net cash flow effects of this accretion in value cannot be reasonably estimated. As a result, income is not recognized on an accretion basis. An exception may arise when a contract to age a specific product for a customer is agreed upon before the aging process begins. If future costs can be estimated and if the seller is relieved of any future obligation in the event that the purchaser is dissatisfied with the product, the percentage-of-completion method would appear to be appropriate.

REVENUE RECOGNITION AT COMPLETION OF PRODUCTION

As Exhibit 6–1 indicates, revenue could be recognized when production is completed. The circumstances that justify revenue recognition at this point are as follows:

1. The product is sold in a market with a reasonably assured selling price.

2. The costs of selling and distributing the product are insignificant and can be reasonably estimated.

3. Production, rather than sale, is considered to be the most **critical** event in the earnings process. For example, whereas the most crucial event in earning revenue for a farm implement manufacturer probably is *selling* wheat combines and other farm implements, the most crucial event for a wheat farmer probably is *harvesting* the mature wheat.

Revenue often is recognized at the completion of production for such products as agricultural products and some precious metals. To illustrate this method, assume that at the beginning of 1987 Collins Farms started operations. During 1987 the company planted and harvested 10,000 bushels of corn. Eight thousand bushels were sold in 1987, and the remaining bushels were sold in 1988. Additional data are as follows:

Selling price of corn, per bushel		$3.00
Variable production cost (paid in cash), per bushel		$1.00
Depreciation on production equipment		$6,000
Selling cost, per bushel (incurred and paid at time of sale)		$.20
Cash collected on sales:		
1987	$18,000	
1988	10,000	
1989	2,000	$30,000

Financial position of Collins Farms at the beginning of 1987:
Equipment $60,000; Contributed capital $60,000

Exhibit 6–5 presents the financial statements for Collins Farms for 1987 and 1988 when revenue is recognized at the completion of production. For comparative purposes, the financial statements when revenue is recognized at the point of sale also appear in Exhibit 6–5. Some important points about revenue recognition at the completion of production and about the exhibit are summarized below:

1. As Exhibit 6–5 indicates, both methods show the same amount of total net income once all of the corn has been sold. The difference between the two methods lies only in the *timing* of the recognition of net income.

2. When revenue and income are recognized at completion of production, inventory is reported at *net realizable value* or *expected exit value*. Notice that at the end of 1987, the carrying value of the corn inventory is $5,600, which represents the future selling price of $6,000 (2,000 × $3) less the future selling costs of $400 (2,000 × $.20). This $5,600 amount represents the *future net cash flows* associated with the sale of the corn.

3. When the sales price is assured and when future selling costs can be estimated, revenue and income recognition at completion of production provides earlier signals about future net cash flows than does the point-of-sale method. In Exhibit 6–5, notice that the net income of $12,000 is reported in 1987 under the completed-production method, but it is reported partially in 1987 ($9,600) and partially in 1988 ($2,400) under the point-of-sale method.

EXHIBIT 6–5 REVENUE RECOGNITION AT COMPLETION OF PRODUCTION AND AT POINT OF SALE

	AT COMPLETION OF PRODUCTION		AT POINT OF SALE	
INCOME STATEMENT	1987	1988	1987	1988
Revenues	$ 30,000	—	$ 24,000	$ 6,000
Expenses				
Cost of goods produced/sold				
Variable production costs	$(10,000)	—	$ (8,000)	$(2,000)
Depreciation	(6,000)	—	(4,800)*	(1,200)
Total cost of goods produced/sold	$(16,000)	—	$(12,800)	$ (3,200)
Selling expenses	(2,000)		(1,600)	(400)
Net income	$ 12,000	—	$ 9,600	$ 2,400
BALANCE SHEET				
Cash	$ 6,400	$16,000	$ 6,400	$16,000
Accounts receivable	6,000†	2,000‡	6,000†	2,000‡
Inventory of corn	5,600§	—	3,200¶	—
Equipment (net of accumulated depreciation)	54,000	54,000	54,000	54,000
	$ 72,000	$72,000	$ 69,600	$72,000
Contributed capital	$ 60,000	$60,000	$ 60,000	$60,000
Retained earnings	12,000	12,000	9,600	12,000
	$ 72,000	$72,000	$ 69,600	$72,000

* .80 × $6,000.		
† Sales in 1987	$24,000	
Collections in 1987	(18,000)	
	$ 6,000	
‡ Beginning balance	$ 6,000	
Sales in 1988	6,000	
Collections in 1988	(10,000)	
	$ 2,000	

§ $6,000 (sales price) − $400 (future selling costs).
¶ .20 × $16,000 production costs.

How would Collins incorporate this method of revenue recognition into its accounts? Although many procedures are possible, one approach would be to record the corn at its selling price as production is completed and the corn is placed in inventory. The summary entries below illustrate this approach:

Inventory	16,000	
Cash		10,000
Accumulated depreciation		6,000
To record cost of corn harvested in 1987.		

Inventory	14,000	
Cost of goods produced	16,000	
Revenue		30,000
To record revenue, costs to be matched against revenue, and inventory at selling price for 1987.		

Sales would be recorded by debiting accounts receivable and crediting inventory, and collections would be recorded in the usual manner:

```
Accounts receivable ................................... 24,000
    Inventory .........................................          24,000
To record sales made in 1987.

Cash................................................. 18,000
    Accounts receivable ................................          18,000
To record collections in 1987.
```

During 1987, selling expenses would be recorded as the sales are made. In addition, an adjusting entry would be necessary at the end of 1987 to accrue selling expenses to be paid when the remaining inventory is sold in 1988:

```
Selling expenses ....................................... 1,600
    Cash...............................................          1,600
To record selling expenses on 1987 sales.

Selling expenses .......................................   400
    Inventory .........................................            400
To accrue selling expenses on unsold inventory (2,000 × $.20).
```

Notice that the selling expense accrual reduces the carrying value of inventory to its net realizable value of $5,600 ($6,000 − $400).

When Collins Farms sells the remaining inventory in 1988, the following entry would be made:

```
Accounts receivable (2,000 × $3)........................... 6,000
    Inventory .........................................          5,600
    Cash (2,000 × $.20) ...............................            400
```

Accounts receivable is debited for the dollar amount of sales, inventory is credited for its net realizable (carrying) value, and cash is credited for the costs incurred in selling the remaining bushels. Since revenue and income were recognized when production was completed in 1987, revenue and expense accounts are not affected in 1988. The entry to record 1988 cash collections from customers is the same under both the point-of-sale method and the completed-production method.

Notice that Collins Farms, by recognizing income at the completion of production becomes something of a grain speculator during the holding period from production to sale. If grain prices fluctuate during this holding period, holding gains and losses on the inventory, similar to those discussed on page 49 in Chapter 2, result and should be recognized. However, if the holding gains and losses are frequent and material, one might argue that Collins Farms should not be using this revenue recognition method because the net cash flow uncertainty is too great to warrant revenue and income recognition before the sale occurs.

In the 1970s, a variation of this method of revenue recognition, **reserve recognition accounting** (RRA) was proposed for oil and gas exploration companies. Many people felt that discovery of proven oil and gas reserves was the critical event in the earnings process. They asserted further that more relevant and timely financial reporting information resulted from basing income on discovery of these energy resources rather than on their sale. Under RRA, income is measured at the present value of the estimated future sales of the discovered reserves less the exploration costs incurred in finding the reserves and less the present value of the cost of extracting them.[4] Opponents of RRA felt that although

---

[4] Other components of RRA income include (1) interest on the carrying value of reserves and (2) revisions of previously reported income due to changes in estimated selling prices, costs, and quantities of proven reserves.

RRA provided relevant information, its usefulness was impaired by its lack of reliability. RRA was a very controversial concept for theoretical, practical, and political reasons. Certain disclosures, similar to RRA, are required for oil and gas companies by the FASB. These disclosures are discussed in Chapter 13.

REVENUE RECOGNITION DURING CASH COLLECTION

We indicated earlier that when the revenue recognition criteria are met before or at the point of sale, revenue should be recognized and reported in the income statement. Further, under the matching concept, expenses incurred in earning the revenue should be recognized and matched against revenue to measure net income. If sales are made on account, the allowance (accrual) method of accounting for uncollectible accounts should be used to estimate the dollar amount of receivables expected to be uncollectible.

Recognition of revenue during cash collection is appropriate when uncollectibles cannot be estimated.

Under certain circumstances, uncertainty about the ultimate cash collection of a credit sale may be so great that revenue should not be recognized at the point of sale. For example, the company may have no basis for estimating the dollar amount of uncollectibles. Thus, the net cash flow effect of the earnings activity may be so uncertain that revenue and income should be recognized only when cash is collected. Two methods of revenue recognition after the point of sale are the installment method and the cost recovery method.

THE INSTALLMENT METHOD

A sale of an item such as a television set, a refrigerator, or an automobile on an installment or deferred payment plan does not in itself justify the use of the installment method. If the criteria for revenue recognition are met on the date that an installment sale occurs, revenue and related expenses, including uncollectible accounts expense, should be recognized at that point. As a practical example, Sears, Inc., has annual installment sales in the millions of dollars, but it recognizes revenue and income at the point of sale. However, when the collection period on a credit sale extends over a long period of time and there is no reasonable basis for estimating uncollectible accounts, the **installment method** of accounting is appropriate. Under the installment method, gross profit (sales less cost of goods sold) arising from the sale is deferred and recognized as cash collections take place.

Income Recognition under the Installment Method

Let us assume that Jay Electronics sells home computers for $250 on a deferred payment plan—$50 down, the balance payable in four equal quarterly installments of $50. The computers are manufactured by Jay at a cost of $150 each. On October 1, 1987, Jay sells two computers under the above terms. Jay's accounting period ends on December 31. (Jay also charges interest on the outstanding unpaid balance of the installment. Although the interest payments are due each quarter in addition to the quarterly installments, to simplify the illustration we shall ignore interest.)

In applying the installment method, we must calculate the gross profit percentage on the sale. The gross profit percentage on Jay's 1987 sales is 40 percent:

$$\frac{\text{Gross profit}}{\text{percentage}} = \frac{\text{Sales} - \text{Cost of goods sold}}{\text{Sales}} = \frac{\$500 - \$300}{\$500} = \frac{\$200}{\$500} = 40\%$$

As cash collections are made, 40 cents of each dollar of cash collected is assumed to represent profit, and 60 cents of each dollar of cash collected is assumed to represent a recovery of cost. Thus, the income recognized each year by Jay Electronics is as follows:

	1987	1988	TOTAL
Cash collections	$200	$300	$500
Gross profit percentage	40%	40%	40%
Gross profit recognized	$ 80	$120	$200

Jay Electronics would make the following entries in 1987:

10/1/87

1. Cash 100
   Installment receivables 400
       Installment sales 500
   To record installment sales.

2. Cost of installment sales................................. 300
       Inventory 300
   To record the cost of installment sales.

12/31/87

3. Cash 100
       Installment receivables 100
   To record collection of the first quarterly installments.

4. Installment sales 500
       Cost of installment sales.............................. 300
       Deferred gross profit.................................. 200
   To close the sales and cost of goods sold accounts and defer the gross profit.

5. Deferred gross profit..................................... 80
       Realized gross profit.................................. 80
   To record realized gross profit based on cash collections.

The first two entries are to record the two installment sales ($250 × 2) and related cost of goods sold ($150 × 2), and entry 3 is to record the first installment payments received from the two customers ($50 × 2). Entries 4 and 5 represent the year-end adjustments necessary under the installment method. Because profit is to be recognized on the basis of cash collections, the entire gross profit applicable to the installment sales made in 1987 is deferred initially. This deferral is accomplished in the fourth entry. Entry 5 records the amount of gross profit realized in 1987.

Financial statement data applicable to these transactions would appear as follows:

INCOME STATEMENT FOR 1987

Sales (based on cash collections)	$200
Cost of sales (.60 × $200)	(120)
Realized gross profit	$ 80
Expenses	(xx)
Net income	$ xx

BALANCE SHEET, END OF 1987

Installment receivables	$300
Less: Deferred gross profit	(120)
Installment receivables (net)	$180

The income statement reports the $80 gross profit and the usual expenses that are deducted from gross profit to arrive at net income. Also, total sales of $500 for 1987, along with the related cost of goods sold and deferred gross profit, could be disclosed in a footnote to provide users with information about the company's sales activities and related gross profit that are not recognized because of uncertainty about collection of the installment receivables arising from sales. On the balance sheet the deferred gross profit should be reported as a contra asset account to installment receivables. The net receivable balance of $180 may be interpreted as the unrecovered cost of the computers sold:

Cost of computers sold $300
Less: Cash collections ($200) × cost percentage (.60) . . . . (120)
    Unrecovered cost, end of 1987 . . . . $180

The installment receivables are classified as current assets if collection will occur within one year or within the company's operating cycle; otherwise they are classified as noncurrent assets.

At this point it should be clear why a *gross profit percentage,* rather than a net profit percentage, is used to recognize income under the installment method. Since the installment receivables balance, net of the deferred gross profit, represents the unrecovered cost of the assets sold, only those costs that normally would be considered inventoriable costs are included in the calculation of deferred gross profit.

Varying Gross Profit Rates through Time

Changes in costs, selling prices, and the mix of merchandise sold may cause the gross profit rate on merchandise sales to vary from year to year. Therefore, it is necessary to segregate in the accounting records the installment receivables by the year in which the sales that generated the receivables were made. This segregation is necessary in order to determine the amount of gross profit to be recognized on cash collections in a given year.

Assume that May Hardware sells merchandise on a deferred payment plan and uses the installment method of accounting. Information related to sales and customer collections for 1987 and 1988 is as follows:

	1987	1988
Sales	$140,000	$160,000
Cost of goods sold	84,000	112,000
Gross profit rate	40%	30%
Customer collections		
On 1987 sales	100,000	25,000
On 1988 sales		150,000

Summary journal entries and related financial statement data for 1987 and 1988 under the installment method are shown in Exhibit 6–6. Notice that separate accounts for installment receivables are used for each year's sales and cash collections. Alternatively, the company might maintain only one controlling installment receivables account and use a subsidiary installment receivables ledger to distinguish between the sales of the two years. If desirable, a separate deferred gross profit account also could be maintained for each year's installment receivables.

Accounting for Credit Defaults

When a customer defaults on a credit sale contract, the merchandise normally is repossessed by the seller. The seller usually requires installment payments large enough so that if the buyer defaults, the fair value of the merchandise repossessed is at least equal to the

EXHIBIT 6—6

May Hardware

JOURNAL ENTRIES, 1987 AND 1988,
UNDER THE INSTALLMENT METHOD

	1987		1988	
Installment receivables, 1987	140,000			
Installment receivables, 1988			160,000	
Sales		140,000		160,000
To record sales on account.				
Cost of goods sold	84,000		112,000	
Inventory		84,000		112,000
To record cost of sales.				
Cash	100,000		175,000	
Installment receivables, 1987		100,000		25,000
Installment receivables, 1988				150,000
To record customer collections.				
Sales	140,000		160,000	
Cost of goods sold		84,000		112,000
Deferred gross profit		56,000		48,000
To close nominal accounts and record deferred gross profit.				
Deferred gross profit	40,000		55,000	
Realized gross profit		40,000		55,000
To record gross profit realized in:				

1987: $100,000 \times .4 = \$40,000$

1988: on 1987 sales, $\$25,000 \times .4 = \$10,000$
      on 1988 sales, $\$150,000 \times .3 = \underline{45,000}$
                        $\underline{\underline{\$55,000}}$

INCOME STATEMENT FOR THE YEAR

	1987	1988
Sales (based on cash collections)	$100,000	$175,000
Cost of sales	(60,000)	
($175,000 sales − $55,000 realized gross profit above)		(120,000)
Realized gross profit	$ 40,000	$ 55,000

BALANCE SHEET, END OF YEAR

	1987	1988
Installment receivables	$ 40,000	$ 25,000
Less: Deferred gross profit	(16,000)	(9,000)
Installment receivables, net	$ 24,000	$ 16,000

unpaid receivable balance, net of any deferred gross profit. In accounting for defaults under the installment method, the unpaid receivable balance and related deferred gross profit are removed from the accounts. The difference between the net receivable balance (unpaid balance less applicable deferred gross profit) and the fair value of the repossessed merchandise is the gain or loss on repossession.

To illustrate, refer to the Jay Electronics example and assume that one of Jay's customers defaulted shortly after making the second (March 31, 1988) installment. Assuming that the repossessed computer had a fair value of $50, the following entry would be made to record the default:

Inventory of repossessed merchandise	50	
Deferred gross profit (.4 × $100)	40	
Loss on repossession	10	
Installment receivables ($250 − $150)		100

The fair value of the repossessed merchandise represents its selling price in its present condition. If the merchandise must be reworked or reconditioned before being resold, it should be recorded at its expected selling price after reconditioning less estimated reconditioning costs.

THE COST RECOVERY METHOD

Under the **cost recovery method,** no income is recognized on credit sales until the cost of the merchandise sold has been *fully* recovered through cash collections. After the cost of the merchandise sold has been recovered from cash collections, all remaining cash collections are reported as income in the period in which they are collected. Let us refer to Jay Electronics again. Because the costs of $300 were not fully recovered until the second installment on March 31, 1988 (only $200 was collected in 1987—$100 on the two down payments and $100 from the first installments), no income is recognized in 1987 under the cost recovery method. As the final two payments of $100 each are received, the entire $200 is recognized as income.

The cost recovery method also is used by many companies when there is significant uncertainty about the profitability associated with a new or specific venture or contract. For example, aircraft manufacturers, such as Boeing, sometimes use the cost recovery method when they are uncertain whether revenues will be sufficient to produce a profit on a plane construction or modification project.

EVALUATION OF CASH COLLECTION METHODS

In practice, the installment method is used more frequently than the cost recovery method. One reason for this is that the installment method is acceptable, under specified conditions, for income tax purposes. The cost recovery method is acceptable for tax purposes only under very restrictive conditions. In spite of the greater popularity of the installment method, we prefer the cost recovery method on theoretical grounds. Postponement of revenue (gross profit) recognition until cash collection occurs is justified only when reasonable estimates of uncollectible accounts cannot be made. Yet the installment method assumption—that is, for each dollar of cash collected, one portion is cost recovery and another portion is profit—is valid only if it is expected that the entire receivable arising from the sale will be collected. This expectation, however, is counter to the circumstances under which the installment method is normally used. For this reason we prefer the cost recovery method when there is any significant uncertainty about future cash inflows from receivables.

DISCLOSURE OF BASES OF REVENUE RECOGNITION

Many companies disclose in the summary of significant accounting policies the basis on which revenues are recognized. An example of such a disclosure appeared in the notes to the financial statements of IBM Corporation.

Gross income is recognized from sales when the product is shipped or in certain cases upon customer acceptance, from rentals in the month in which they accrue, and from services over the contractual period or as the services are performed. Rental plans include maintenance service and contain discontinuance and purchase option provisions. Rental terms are predominantly monthly or for a two-year period, with some covering periods up to five years.

SUMMARY OF REVENUE AND INCOME RECOGNITION CONCEPTS

We have pointed out that under accrual accounting the net cash flow effects of earnings activities are reported when they can be measured at an acceptable level of certainty. Professional judgment is often necessary to make this determination. The realization principle establishes criteria for recognizing revenue and income. While these criteria generally are met at the point of sale, they sometimes are met before a sale occurs or even after a sale occurs.

The *amount* of revenue and income *ultimately* recognized is the same under all of the revenue recognition methods. The differences among the various methods relate to *timing—when* revenue and income are recognized. Timing differences are not trivial, however, given our financial reporting objectives of providing useful and timely information to help users to predict and assess cash flows.

Exhibit 6–7 provides a summary illustration of the effects on periodic income for some of the revenue and income recognition approaches discussed in this chapter. The data in Exhibit 6–7 are based on the Collins Farms example on page 252 and Exhibit 6–5.

Before discussing some specialized industry applications of revenue recognition concepts, we should point out that the realization principle also is applied in practice to gains and losses, although in slightly different ways. Gains generally are not recognized under generally accepted accounting principles until an exchange takes place. Thus for gains, realization, or the reduction of cash flow uncertainty, presumably does not occur until the *exchange* occurs. Losses, however, frequently are recognized *before* an exchange takes place (for example, lower of cost or market for inventories and marketable securities). These losses generally are described as *unrealized,* either because an exchange has not occurred or because there is uncertainty regarding the net cash flow effect of the loss. Occasionally, reported losses are described as *realized* even in the absence of an exchange if the net cash flow effect of the loss can be estimated with reasonable certainty.

SPECIALIZED INDUSTRY APPLICATIONS

Revenue recognition in specialized industries is based on concepts previously discussed.

Authoritative accounting bodies have issued somewhat detailed and procedural standards for revenue and income recognition in certain industries because of these industries' specialized economic circumstances and practices. Detailed coverage of these specific accounting and reporting requirements does not appear in this text since these requirements are simply applications of the concepts already discussed. However, an overview is presented in the remainder of this chapter.

SERVICE INDUSTRIES

The United States is rapidly becoming a service economy, and the types of services offered in our society are continually increasing. Some examples of services currently being provided are:

Accounting	Entertainment
Advertising and public relations	Health care
Architecture	Legal services
Automobile repairs	Management consulting and executive placement
Business and home security	Real estate brokerage services
Computer services	Recreational and physical fitness
Employment agencies	Travel agencies

EXHIBIT 6-7   SUMMARY OF REVENUE AND INCOME RECOGNITION
APPROACHES FOR COLLINS FARMS (BASED ON EXHIBIT 6–5)

REVENUE RECOGNITION METHOD	INCOME REPORTED	
At completion of production:	1987	$12,000
	1988	—
	1989	—
	Total	$12,000
At point of sale:	1987	$ 9,600
	1988	2,400
	1989	—
	Total	$12,000
During cash collection:		
Installment method	1987 $18,000 cash collected × .4 =	$ 7,200
Profit rate is 40%	1988 $10,000 cash collected × .4 =	4,000
$\left(\dfrac{\$12,000}{\$30,000} = .4\right)$*	1989 $ 2,000 cash collected × .4 =	800
	Total	$12,000
Cost recovery method	1987 $18,000 − $14,400† =	$ 3,600
	1988 $10,000 − $3,600‡ =	6,400
	1989 $ 2,000 − $0 =	2,000
	Total	$12,000

* For instructional purposes only, we have included the selling expenses in the computation of the profit rate.

† $12,800 (cost of goods sold) + $1,600 (selling costs).

‡ $3,200 (cost of goods sold) + $400 (selling costs).

In these and other service industries, revenue results from the performance of a service rather than from production and sale of a product. The revenue recognition criteria for service companies are identical, conceptually, to those discussed at the beginning of the chapter. Revenue should be recognized when (1) the amount and timing of the service fee are reasonably determinable and (2) the services have been performed. In practice, these two criteria are applied by service companies under one of four methods. When performance of a service consists of a single act, the **specific performance method** should be used. Under this method, revenue is recognized when the act has been completed. When performance consists of a number of similar acts, the **proportional performance method** should be used. This method is applied, conceptually, in the same manner as the percentage-of-completion method for long-term construction contracts. When more than one act is required and the final act is considered the "critical event" in the earnings process, the **completed performance method** should be used. This method is applied in a manner similar to the completed-production method and also should be used when the number of acts, which may extend over an indeterminable period of time, is not determinable, so that the extent of performance cannot be determined. For example, a computer service company that contracts to assist a retailer in installing, testing, and debugging sophisticated software programs for inventory control should not recognize revenue until the system is operational. Finally, the **collection method** should be used in those circumstances where there is significant uncertainty regarding the collectibility of service revenue.[5]

Sales of franchises occur in the restaurant, fast foods, motel, auto rental, and similar businesses. In a typical franchise arrangement, the buyer, or **franchisee,** obtains the right to sell the **franchisor's** products and to use the franchisor's name for a specified length of time in a specified location. In addition, the franchisor often promises to assist the franchisee in selecting a business site, constructing facilities, training employees, establishing and maintaining a record-keeping system, sales promotion and advertising, and other business activities. In return, the franchisor earns revenue from (1) an *initial franchise fee* related to the sale of the franchise and services performed and (2) *continuing periodic fees* paid by the franchisee for services provided on a continuing basis. The periodic fee usually is based on a percentage of the franchisee's sales.

Accounting for the Initial Franchise Fee

There is no difficulty in accounting for the *continuing periodic fees* received by the franchisor as revenue in the accounting periods in which they are received. Accounting for the *initial franchise fee,* however, raises a difficult revenue recognition issue. In the 1960s and early 1970s it was common practice for the franchisor to "front-end" income. That is, the entire franchise fee was reported as revenue in the period in which the franchise contract was signed, regardless of the fact that the fee was to be collected in installments over an extended number of future accounting periods, and regardless of the remaining services to be performed. In terms of the revenue recognition criteria presented earlier, this practice is inappropriate if there is no basis for estimating the collectibility of future installments of the fee, or if the franchisor must perform in the future a significant number of the services promised in the franchise arrangement. *FASB Statement No. 45* requires that the initial franchise fee should be recognized as revenue when the franchisor has substantially performed the services promised in the franchise arrangement and when the collectibility of the initial franchise fee is reasonably assured.[6]

Assume, for instance, that Burger Boy sells restaurant franchises for $20,000, payable 10 percent down with the balance due in four annual installments plus interest on the unpaid balance. In return for the initial franchise fee of $20,000, Burger Boy will assist the franchisee in selecting a location, obtaining financing, and installing an accounting system, and will provide expert advice over a specified period on such matters as employee motivation, advertising, planning, and financing. In addition to the initial franchise fee, Burger Boy will receive 1 percent of each restaurant's monthly sales in return for permitting each franchisee to purchase meal ingredients below normal market prices.

There are several methods of accounting for the initial franchise fee, depending on the circumstances.

1. If no services have been provided by the franchisor at the time the initial payment is received, but if collectibility of the receivable is assured, the following entry would be appropriate:

Cash	2,000	
Receivable from franchisee	18,000	
Unearned franchise fee		20,000

---

[5] "Accounting for Certain Service Transactions," *FASB Invitation to Comment* (Stamford, Conn.: FASB, 1978).

[6] "Accounting for Franchise Fee Revenue," *Statement of Financial Accounting Standards No. 45* (Stamford, Conn.: FASB, 1981).

Despite the receipt of $2,000 in cash, the franchise fee is recorded as unearned because no services have been provided. As the franchisor provides services to the franchisee, the following entry would be made by the franchisor to record the franchise fee earned (the *amounts* to be debited and credited would depend on the amount of the services provided relative to the total estimated services to be provided):

Unearned franchise fee	*xx*	
Franchise fee revenue		*xx*

2. If substantially all services have been provided by the franchisor, and if collectibility of the receivable is reasonably assured, the following entry would be appropriate:

Cash	2,000	
Receivable from franchisee	18,000	
Franchise fee revenue		20,000

3. If substantially all services have been provided but there is no basis for estimating uncollectibles (i.e., uncertainty exists about ultimate cash inflows), the following entry would be appropriate:

Cash	2,000	
Receivable from franchisee	18,000	
Deferred franchise fee		18,000
Franchise fee revenue		2,000

In entry 3 we credited deferred franchise fee, whereas we credited unearned franchise fee in entry 1, above. This distinction may appear subtle, but it is very important. In the first entry, the franchise fee was not yet earned. Here the fee has been earned—that is, all of the services have been provided—but there is uncertainty about collecting the receivable. Thus, the deferred franchise fee account is similar to the deferred gross profit account under the installment method of accounting. The installment method or cost recovery method could be used to recognize franchise fee revenue as cash collections occur. Other approaches are possible, depending on the circumstances. Professional accounting judgment is necessary in applying the revenue recognition guidelines in a given situation.

Some franchise agreements stipulate that any payments made to the franchisor will be refunded if for any reason the franchisee fails to open. Since this stipulation may create uncertainty about net cash inflows to the franchisor, it should be considered in determining the amount of revenue to be recognized before the franchisee's opening date.

Continuing Periodic Fees

Burger Boy would make the following entry each month to record the continuing service fees:

Cash (or accounts receivable)	*xx*	
Service revenue		*xx*

Expenses incurred by the franchisor in providing the continuing services would be deducted from service revenue in order to determine periodic income from these service activities.

REAL ESTATE SALES AND RETAIL LAND SALES   *Real estate sales* often involve relatively small down payments, perhaps 20 percent or less, and an extended period of time, perhaps 25 years or more, for payment of the balance due. Because of the lengthy payment period, uncertainty about the collectibility of payments on a real estate sale may be greater than is typical for many other types of sales transactions. Also, the seller may be required by the contract to perform significant services after the sale, such as managing or maintaining the property.

Thus, many real estate sales may not meet the revenue recognition criteria at the time of the sale. There may be a substantial number of services to be performed by the seller after the sale, and it may be difficult to estimate related costs yet to be incurred. In addition, uncertainty about the collectibility of payments due may make it difficult to estimate the amount of revenue that will be received. Hence, it may be necessary to postpone recognition of all or part of the revenue until the revenue recognition criteria are met. Until the services are performed, collections should be recorded as a deposit (unearned revenue). Even after the seller has performed the required services, the installment sales method or the cost recovery method may be appropriate for recognizing revenue if estimates of uncollectibles are not possible. The FASB has established detailed rules to be used in deciding whether revenue on a real estate sale should be recognized at the time of sale or later, as cash is collected.[7]

Retail sales of undeveloped land are similar to real estate sales except that the volume of sales usually is much greater, the size of the down payment usually is a smaller percentage of the sales price, and the seller usually agrees to develop the land by subdividing the property, obtaining regulatory approvals, selling the lots, and making improvements such as grading, landscaping, paving, and other property enhancements. Furthermore, the sales contract generally is unenforceable (the seller's only recourse is repossession of the property), and the purchaser may have refund privileges for a specified period of time.

Under rules established by the FASB,[8] revenue should be recognized on retail land sales only when the following conditions are met: (1) the refund period has expired, (2) the cumulative payments equal or exceed 10 percent of the sales price, (3) the receivables are collectible and are not subordinate to new loans on the property, and (4) the seller either is not obligated to make improvements on the lots sold or has made progress on improvements promised. Cash received before the above conditions are met should be recorded as a deposit (unearned revenue). Notice how these conditions are specific applications of the two revenue recognition criteria discussed earlier.

As an example of a similar transaction, Thousand Trails, Inc., an outdoor recreation company, develops campgrounds for use by people willing to pay a membership fee of several thousand dollars. The fee gives members access to well-maintained campgrounds in various parts of the country; Thousand Trails calls them ''the poor man's country club.'' Some people have raised questions about the company's revenue recognition methods. Thousand Trails records the entire membership fee as revenue shortly after a member's contract is signed, despite the fact that members pay only about 10 percent down, with the balance payable over a period of up to seven years. The company has little recourse against contract defaults other than suspension of membership privileges. The other aspect of income recognition that has been questioned is the method the company uses to match costs with revenues. Thousand Trails pro-rates its actual and projected costs to revenue on the basis of the number of members who will eventually use the facilities. For example, if a campground can support 5,000 members, 1/5,000th of current and projected costs are matched against revenue from each new member. In 1984 the company was pro-rating costs on the basis of 240,000 estimated members although there were only 70,000 actual members. As a result of the company's methods of revenue recognition, reported earnings were positive ($16.2 million, or $1.51 per share through the first nine

---

[7] ''Accounting for Sales of Real Estate,'' *Statement of Financial Accounting Standards No. 66* (Stamford, Conn.: FASB, 1982).

[8] Ibid.

months of 1984), despite the fact that cash flows were negative (estimated to be $40 million for 1984).[9]

BARTER TRANSACTIONS

Inflation and other economic circumstances have caused many companies to engage in barter transactions. For example, an automobile dealer may enter into an agreement with a cleaning service company to sell a truck in exchange for cleaning services to be received over an extended period of time. Some companies derive a major portion of their revenues from barter transactions that result in inflows of nonfinancial assets or services instead of cash. Since revenue transactions normally result in cash inflows, some interesting questions arise: Should revenue be recognized on these barter transactions? If so, how is it to be measured? From another perspective, if revenue recognition is deferred until an expected cash inflow materializes, what effect does this delay, which may extend over several periods, have on the timeliness of earnings reporting?

No specific revenue recognition guidelines currently exist specifically for barter transactions, although *APB Opinion No. 29,* on nonmonetary exchanges, addresses some transactions that are similar. It appears, however, that since the nature of a barter transaction differs little from that of a sales transaction, perhaps revenue should be recognized and measured at the exchange price (called a **trading unit** in barter transactions) established in the transaction. This suggestion is not inconsistent with *APB Opinion No. 29.* Accounting for barter transactions presents some real challenges to accountants and raises some interesting theory questions. It is likely that we will see growing numbers of these types of transactions, which may prompt FASB involvement.

CONSIGNMENT SALES

Many manufacturers and distributors arrange for their products to be sold by retailers or dealers on a **consignment** basis. Under such an arrangement, the seller, or consignor, retains title to the merchandise, and the dealer, or consignee, acts as a selling agent. The dealer accepts and agrees to sell the merchandise. The dealer earns a commission on the products sold and periodically remits the cash from sales, less the commission earned, to the manufacturer or distributor. For example, grocery stores often do not wish to make a substantial investment in cosmetics and drugs. Therefore, these items may be sold on consignment, with the grocery store earning a commission on sales of these products.

Assume that Looking Good, Inc., sells wigs on a consignment basis. The company ships 800 wigs to Mitchell Discount Center for sale at $60 each and pays $1,600 in transportation costs. The wigs cost Looking Good $20 each. Mitchell Discount Center is allowed a commission of 20 percent on each wig sold; during the year Mitchell sells 300 wigs and spends $2,400 for 800 plastic storage boxes, which Looking Good has agreed to reimburse. At the end of the year, Mitchell remits the sales proceeds, net of commissions and reimbursable costs, to Looking Good.

Journal entries for the consignment activity appear in Exhibit 6–8. Several points about these journal entries are pertinent:

1. The shipment of merchandise on a consignment is *not* a sale because the two revenue recognition criteria are not satisfied. Inventory is simply being transferred to another location. Another inventory account, inventory on consignment, is established so that the consignor knows the cost of goods on consignment.

2. The transportation costs represent an additional cost of the inventory on consignment and are recorded accordingly.

[9] "A Look at Thousand Trails Raises Question about Viability of Its Plan," *The Wall Street Journal,* November 11, 1984, pp. 35, 63.

EXHIBIT 6–8 ACCOUNTING FOR CONSIGNMENTS

1. Consignor ships 800 wigs costing $20 each to consignee.

CONSIGNOR			**CONSIGNEE**	
(LOOKING GOOD, INC.)			**(MITCHELL DISCOUNT CENTER)**	
Inventory on consignment	16,000		No entry	
Inventory		16,000		

2. Consignor pays $1,600 in transportation costs ($2 per wig).

CONSIGNOR			**CONSIGNEE**	
Inventory on consignment	1,600		No entry	
Cash		1,600		

3. Consignee spends $2,400 for wig storage boxes ($2,400/800 wigs = $3 per wig).

CONSIGNOR			**CONSIGNEE**	
No entry			Payable to consignor	2,400
			Cash	2,400

4. Consignee sells 300 wigs at $60 each and earns a 20% commission on wigs sold.

CONSIGNOR			**CONSIGNEE**	
No entry			Cash	18,000
			Commission revenue	3,600
			Payable to consignor	14,400

5. Consignee notifies consignor of wigs sold and remits sales proceeds, less commissions earned and reimbursable costs.

CONSIGNOR			**CONSIGNEE**	
Cash	12,000		Payable to consignor	12,000
Inventory on consignment	2,400		Cash	12,000
Commission expense	3,600		($14,400 − $2,400)	
Consignment sales		18,000		
Cost of consignment sales	7,500			
Inventory on consignment		7,500		
(300 × $25*)				

6. Reconstruction of the inventory on consignment account:

Inventory on consignment			
Initial shipment	16,000	Cost of sales	7,500
Transportation costs	1,600	Balance	12,500
Wig storage boxes	2,400		
	20,000		20,000
Balance (500 wigs at $25 each)	$12,500		

*$20 + $2 transportation costs + $3 cost of storage boxes.

3. As the consignee records the wigs sold, the commissions earned and the liability to the consignor are recorded.

4. The consignee notifies the consignor of the wigs sold through the use of an *account sales* document. This document, which summarizes the consignment activities and the net proceeds from sale, is forwarded to the consignor. The consignor records the sales, cost of goods sold, commissions expense, and the cost of the storage boxes.

5. The balance in the inventory account represents the cost of the merchandise remaining on consignment.

SUMMARY OF IMPORTANT TOPICS AND CONCEPT APPLICATIONS

1. Revenues are increases in net assets from delivery or production of goods, rendering of services, or other activities that constitute a company's major or primary operations. Revenues are measured at the **fair value** or **cash equivalent exchange price** of assets received.

2. Although the earning of revenue and income is a continuous process as form, place, and time utility (and thus value) are added to input costs, accountants select a point (or points) in time at which to recognize revenue and income in the accounts and in the financial statements.

3. The **realization principle** establishes criteria for determining when revenue should be recognized. **Recognition** is the act of recording and reporting revenue.

4. The two **revenue recognition criteria**—(1) reasonable determination of the amount and timing of revenue to be received and (2) completion or virtual completion of an earnings process—establish guidelines for measuring the **net cash flow effect** of earnings activities as soon as the effect can be measured at an acceptable level of certainty. Thus, the criteria relate to the qualitative characteristics of **relevance** and **reliability,** the two primary qualities of **decision usefulness.**

5. The most common revenue recognition point is the point of sale, because the two revenue recognition criteria usually are satisfied at that point.

6. Revenue may be recognized during production if the sales price and estimated completion costs are measurable with sufficient reliability. This method of revenue recognition often is used in accounting for long-term construction contracts and is called the **percentage-of-completion method.**

7. Revenue may be recognized at the completion of production but before the sale, if the sales price is reasonably assured and if the cost of selling and distributing the product is insignificant and can be reasonably estimated. Under these circumstances, production, rather than sale, is considered the most critical event in the earnings process.

8. When sales are made on credit and there is no reasonable basis for estimating uncollectibility, revenue may be recognized as collections take place. Two methods of revenue recognition—the **installment method** and the **cost recovery method**—may be used to recognize revenue under these circumstances.

9. Authoritative bodies, such as the FASB, have issued specific accounting rules and requirements for revenue recognition in various industries. These requirements can be quite detailed, but they represent applications of the conceptual criteria.

10. Consignment transactions do not meet the revenue recognition criteria and therefore are not accounted for as sales. Since the consignee is acting as an agent for the consignor, the consignor recognizes revenue and related expenses as the consignment goods are sold by the consignee.

QUESTIONS

Q6-1. How is accrual accounting related to the measurement of cash flows?

Q6-2. Distinguish among *earning* revenue, revenue *recognition,* and revenue *realization.*

Q6-3. Realization has nothing to do with the income concept but does determine the timing of income recognition. Explain.

Q6-4. What two criteria must be met to recognize revenue?

Q6-5. Methods of revenue recognition are also methods of recognizing income. Briefly explain.

Q6-6. What factors must be considered when revenue is recognized at the point of sale?

Q6-7. Under what circumstances is it proper to recognize revenue as productive activity takes place?

Q6-8. Distinguish between the percentage-of-completion method and the completed-contract method of accounting for long-term construction contracts in terms of the following:
1) Income recognition.
2) Valuation of construction in progress.
3) Recognition of losses on construction contracts.

Q6-9. Discuss two methods that may be used to estimate the percentage of completion of long-term construction contracts.

Q6-10. **1)** What is meant by accretion?
2) Why is value accretion generally not recognized under GAAP?

Q6-11. **1)** Discuss the critical event concept in revenue recognition.
2) Briefly discuss the following statement: ''The critical event in a bank's loan activity is the making of a loan; therefore interest on a loan should be recognized when the loan is made.''

Q6-12. Under what circumstances is it preferable to recognize revenue at the completion of production?

Q6-13. Explain how inventories are reported at net realizable value when income is recognized at the completion of production.

Q6-14. Discuss some acceptable methods of accounting for initial franchise fee revenue.

Q6-15. Why is revenue usually not recognized when a sale is made in connection with retail land sales?

Q6-16. Briefly explain the nature of a consignment arrangement.

Q6-17. How are the revenue recognition concepts explained in this chapter related to the objectives of financial reporting?

Q6-18. In accounting for long-term construction contracts (those taking longer than one year to complete), the two methods commonly followed are the percentage-of-completion method and the completed-contract method.
1) Discuss how earnings on long-term construction contracts are recognized and computed under these two methods.
2) Under what circumstances is it preferable to use one method rather than the other?

CASES

C6-1. REVENUE RECOGNITION METHODS   DVS Industries has four operating divisions—Queenswood Construction Division, Paperback Publishing Division, Protection Securities Division, and DVS Barter Division. Each division maintains its own accounting system and method of revenue recognition.

Queenswood Construction Division. During the fiscal year ended November 30, 1987, Queenswood Construction Division had one construction project in process. A $24,000,000 contract for construction of a civic center was granted on June 19, 1987, and construction began on August 1, 1987. Estimated costs of completion at the contract date were $20,000,000 over a two-year time period from the date of the contract. On November 30, 1987, construction costs of $6,000,000 had been incurred and progress billings of $6,600,000 had been made. The construction costs to complete the remainder of the project were reviewed on November 30, 1987, and were estimated to amount to only $12,000,000 due to an expected decline in raw materials costs. Revenue recognition is based upon the percentage of completion method.

Paperback Publishing Division. The Paperback Publishing Division sells large volumes of novels to a few book distributors which in turn sell to several national chains of bookstores. Paperback allows distributors to return up to 30 percent of sales, and distributors give the same terms to bookstores. While returns from individual titles fluctuate greatly, the returns from distributors have averaged 20 percent in each of the past five years. A total of $8,000,000 of paperback novel sales were made to distributors during fiscal 1987. On November 30, 1987, $3,000,000 of fiscal 1987 sales were still subject to return privileges over the next six months. The remaining $5,000,000 of fiscal 1987 sales had actual returns of 21 percent. Sales from fiscal 1986 totaling $2,000,000 were collected in fiscal 1987 less 18 percent returns. This division records revenue according to the method referred to as revenue recognition when the right of return exists.

Protection Securities Division. Protection Securities Division works through manufacturers' agents in various cities. Orders for alarm systems and down payments are forwarded from agents, and the Division ships the goods f.o.b. factory directly to customers (usually police departments and security guard companies). Customers are billed directly for the balance due plus actual shipping costs. The firm received orders for $6,000,000 of goods during the fiscal year ended November 30, 1987. Down payments of $600,000 were received and $5,000,000 of goods were billed and shipped. Actual freight costs of $100,000 were also billed. Commissions of 10 percent on product price are paid manufacturing agents after goods are shipped to customers. Such goods are warranted for 90 days after shipment, and warranty returns have been about one percent of sales. Revenue is recognized at the point of sale by this Division.

DVS Barter Division. The DVS Barter Division was organized to distribute products and services from the other three divisions to users in exchange for goods and services needed in the primary operating activities of these divisions. As examples, during the past year, DVS acquired alarm systems from the Protection Securities Division. These systems were exchanged with a security guard firm for security protection at the other divisions' plants. DVS also arranged for the construction division to build a showroom for a local automobile dealer in exchange for a fleet of cars to be used by the various divisions.

REQUIRED

1. Define and describe each of the following methods of revenue recognition and indicate the circumstances under which each is in accordance with generally accepted accounting principles:

    a) Point of sale.
    b) Completion of production.
    c) Percentage of completion.
    d) Installment.

2. Calculate the revenue to be recognized in fiscal year 1987 for DVS Industries' construction division, the publishing division, and the protection securities division.

3. Discuss how the barter division might recognize revenue.

(IMA, adapted)

C6-2.   CONSIGNMENTS   Heaven Chocolates was organized early this year and decided to sell its chocolate candy on a consignment basis. During the year several thousand boxes costing $6 per box were shipped to candy stores across the country. The chocolates are marked to sell for $10 per box, and the candy dealers are paid a commission of $1 for each box sold.

The president of the company argues that revenue and income should be recognized when the boxes are shipped, because *(a)* the selling price, cost, and commission are known; *(b)* the candy dealers have stated their intentions to sell the chocolates they have accepted on consignment; *(c)* the chocolates have left the company headquarters; and *(d)* shipping the chocolates is the critical event in the company's earning process.

REQUIRED

1. Draft a response to the president's statements, indicating the nature of a consignment and when revenue should be recognized on the chocolates.

2. Using the information below, determine the amount of income earned by Heaven Chocolates and the proper amount of inventory to be reported on the company's end-of-year balance sheet:

Boxes shipped...	80,000
Boxes sold by consignees as reported on account sales	49,500
Boxes destroyed in shipment or returned by consignee because of spoilage	500
Transportation costs	
On shipments to consignees	$12,000
On returned goods	$ 250

C6-3. FRANCHISES Southern Fried Shrimp sells franchises to independent operators throughout the southeastern United States. The contract with the franchisee includes the following provisions:

The franchisee is charged an initial fee of $25,000. Of this amount, $5,000 is payable when the agreement is signed and a $4,000 noninterest-bearing note is payable at the end of each of the five subsequent years.

All of the initial franchise fee collected by Southern Fried Shrimp is to be refunded and the remaining obligation canceled if for any reason the franchisee fails to open his store.

In return for the initial franchise fee, Southern Fried Shrimp agrees *(a)* to assist the franchisee in selecting the location for the business, *(b)* to negotiate the lease for the land, *(c)* to obtain financing and assist with building design, *(d)* to supervise construction, *(e)* to establish accounting and tax records, and *(f)* to provide expert advice over a five-year period on such matters as employee and management training, quality control, and promotion.

In addition to the initial franchise fee, the franchisee is required to pay to Southern Fried Shrimp a monthly fee of 2 percent of sales for menu planning, recipe innovations, and the privilege of purchasing ingredients from Southern Fried Shrimp at or below prevailing prices.

Management of Southern Fried Shrimp estimates that the value of the services rendered to the franchisee at the time the contract is signed amounts to at least $5,000. All franchisees to date have opened their stores at the scheduled time and none has defaulted on any of the notes receivable.

The credit ratings of all franchisees would entitle them to borrow at the current interest rate of 10 percent. The present value of an ordinary annuity of five annual receipts of $4,000 each discounted at 10 percent is $15,163.

REQUIRED

1. Discuss the alternatives that Southern Fried Shrimp might use to account for the initial franchise fee, evaluate each by applying generally accepted accounting principles to this situation, and prepare illustrative entries for each alternative.

2. Given the nature of Southern Fried Shrimp's agreement with its franchisees, when should revenue be recognized? Discuss the question of revenue recognition for both the initial franchise fee and the additional monthly fee of 2 percent of sales, and give illustrative entries for both types of revenue.

3. Assuming that Southern Fried Shrimp sells some franchises for $35,000, which includes a charge of $10,000 for the rental of equipment for its useful life of 10 years, that $15,000 of the fee is payable immediately and the balance on noninterest-bearing notes at $4,000 per year, that no portion of the $10,000 rental payment is refundable in case the franchisee goes out of business, and that title to the equipment remains with the franchisor, what would be the preferable method of accounting for the rental portion of the initial franchise fee? Explain.

(AICPA, adapted)

C6-4. REVENUE RECOGNITION AT POINT OF SALES ORDER You are chief accountant for Shook, Inc., a manufacturer of 40-channel CB radios. The company has a very aggressive marketing organization throughout the country and a very sophisticated standard cost system in its manufacturing division.

Recently Linda Marak, head of the marketing division, suggested to you that the company should begin recognizing revenue (and resulting income) on the basis of *sales orders received* instead of in the traditional manner, on the basis of delivery of CBs to customers. (There is a time lag between receipt of an order and delivery of the CB to the customer.)

REQUIRED

1. Briefly discuss the arguments for and against Marak's proposal.

2. Assume that the firm implemented Marak's proposal. The CBs sell for $100 per unit and the standard cost per unit is $80. Prepare entries to record the following events (the firm's fiscal year ends December 31).

December 30	Received order for 50 radios. Sales commissions, 5% of sales price.
January 10	Completed production of 50 radios at a cost of $85 per unit.
January 20	Shipped radios to customers (customers pay transportation costs).
February 1	Received cash from customers.

C6-5. REVENUE RECOGNITION ON TRADING STAMPS Odessa Stamps, Inc., was formed early this year to sell trading stamps throughout the Southwest. Retailers distribute the stamps free to their customers. Books for accumulating the stamps and catalogs illustrating the merchandise for which the stamps may be exchanged are given free to retailers for distribution to stamp recipients. Centers with inventories of merchandise to be exchanged for the stamps have been established. Retailers may not return unused stamps to Odessa.

The following schedule expresses Odessa's expectations as to percentages of a normal month's activity that will be attained after various periods of time. For this purpose, a normal month's activity is defined as the level of operations expected when expansion of activities ceases or tapers off to a stable rate. The company expects that this level will be attained in the third year and that sales of stamps will average $2 million per month throughout the third year.

MONTH	ACTUAL STAMP SALES (PERCENT)	MERCHANDISE PREMIUM PURCHASES (PERCENT)	STAMP REDEMPTIONS (PERCENT)
6	30%	40%	10%
12	60	60	45
18	80	80	70
24	90	90	80
30	100	100	95

Odessa plans to adopt an annual closing date at the end of each 12 months of operation.

REQUIRED

1. Discuss the factors to be considered in determining when revenue should be recognized in measuring the income of a business enterprise.

2. Discuss the accounting alternatives that should be considered by Odessa Stamps, Inc., for the recognition of its revenues and related expenses.

3. For each accounting alternative discussed in part 2, give balance sheet accounts that should be used and indicate how each should be classified.

(AICPA, adapted)

C6-6. REVENUE RECOGNITION ALTERNATIVES At the beginning of 1986, Cowboy Company began a business to manufacture and sell an imitation of Rubic's Cube. Near the end of 1986, a sales order was received which called for delivery of 100,000 cubes on October 1, 1987. Production was started late in 1986 but was not completed until mid-1987.

REQUIRED

For each independent situation below, discuss whether revenue (and income) should be recognized at the point in time indicated. Your answers should be brief but comprehensive.

1. Recognize revenue when the sales order is received. Cowboy is able to predict manufacturing costs perfectly. The purchaser pays in full on the date of the sales order and the purchase price is not refundable.

2. Same as 1, except that Cowboy will not receive the cash from the sale until December 31, 1987. The purchaser has a history of defaulting on purchase agreements.

3. Recognize revenue on October 1, 1987. Cowboy agrees to allow the purchaser to pay in monthly installments beginning on November 1, 1987. While some possibility of noncollection is present, Cowboy can make reasonable estimates of such amounts.

4. Recognize revenue on October 1, 1987. The purchaser will pay cash on that date, but has the right to return any unsold cubes for refund (or credit against future purchases) on or before December 1, 1987. Cowboy can make reasonable estimates of returns.

5. Recognize revenue when production is complete. Substantial delivery costs may be incurred upon delivery. These costs cannot be estimated before actual delivery.

EXERCISES

E6-1. PERCENTAGE-OF-COMPLETION METHOD The Shuford Construction Corporation uses the percentage-of-completion method of accounting. In 1987 Shuford began work on a contract for construction of a hotel at a contract price of $16 million. Other details follow:

Costs incurred during the year	$2,400,000
Estimated costs to complete as of 12/31/87	9,600,000
Billings during the year	3,440,000
Collections during the year	2,000,000

REQUIRED

Calculate the income that should be recognized in 1987.

E6-2. PERCENTAGE-OF-COMPLETION METHOD In 1987 Costello Nuclear Corporation began construction work under a three-year contract. The contract price was $800,000. Costello uses the percentage-of-completion method for financial accounting purposes. The income to be recognized each year is based on the proportion of cost incurred to total estimated costs for completing the contract. The financial statement presentations related to this contract at December 31, 1987, follow:

BALANCE SHEET

Accounts receivable—construction contract billings		$15,000
Construction in progress	$50,000	
Less contract billings	(47,000)	
Cost of uncompleted contract in excess of billings		3,000

INCOME STATEMENT

Income (before tax) on the contract recognized in 1987	$10,000

REQUIRED

1. How much cash was collected in 1987 on this contract?

2. What was the initial estimated total income before tax on this contract?

(AICPA, adapted)

E6-3. INCOME RECOGNITION ON LONG-TERM CONTRACTS Daytime Construction Company began operating on January 1, 1987, and during the year the company contracted with the city of Dallas to build a dome over the Cotton Bowl. Daytime Construction estimated that it would take four years to complete the facility at a total cost of $9.6 million. The total contract price was $12 million. During 1987 the company incurred $2.56 million in construction costs related to the dome construction, including $60,000 in materials purchased but not used in 1987. The estimated cost to complete the contract was $7.5 million as of December 31, 1987. The city of Dallas was billed for 25 percent of the contract price.

REQUIRED

Prepare schedules to compute the amount of income to be recognized for the year ended December 31, 1987, using each of the following methods:

1. Completed-contract method.

2. Percentage-of-completion method.

E6-4. INCOME RECOGNITION ON LONG-TERM CONTRACTS Homer Construction Corporation contracted to construct a building for $400,000. Construction began in 1987 and was completed in 1988. End-of-year data related to the contract are summarized below:

	12/31/87	12/31/88
Costs incurred	$200,000	$110,000
Estimated costs to complete	100,000	–0–

Homer used the percentage-of-completion method as the basis for income recognition.

REQUIRED

1. What income should Homer report on the contract for 1987 and 1988, respectively?

2. Prepare all necessary journal entries for 1987 and 1988.

3. If Homer used the completed-contract method to account for the above contract, what income would be reported for 1987 and 1988, respectively?

E6-5. PERCENTAGE-OF-COMPLETION METHOD In 1987 Veek Builders agreed to construct an apartment house for $750,000. Information relating to costs, billings, and collections for this contract is as follows:

	1987	1988	1989
Costs incurred to date	$180,000	$330,000	$770,000
Estimated costs yet to be incurred	420,000	450,000	–0–
Customer billings to date	75,000	270,000	750,000
Customer collections to date	60,000	225,000	675,000

Veek Builders uses the percentage-of-completion method of accounting for long-term construction contracts.

REQUIRED

1. Calculate the amount of income (loss) to be recognized in 1987 and 1988.

2. Prepare all necessary journal entries for 1987 and 1988.

E6-6. COMPLETED-CONTRACT METHOD Refer to E6-5 and assume that Veek Builders used the completed-contract method of accounting for long-term construction contracts. Prepare all necessary journal entries for 1987 and 1988.

E6-7. CASH COLLECTION METHODS Gibson, Inc., appropriately uses the installment sales method of accounting. The following information is taken from Gibson's accounting records for 1987 and 1988.

	1987	1988
Installment sales	$500,000	$580,000
Cost of installment sales	400,000	493,000
Cash collected on 1987 sales	280,000	100,000
Cash collected on 1988 sales	–0–	310,000

REQUIRED

1. Compute the income recognized in 1987 and 1988, respectively.

2. What is the aggregate balance of the deferred gross profit account at the end of 1988?

3. Assume now that Gibson uses the cost recovery method. Compute the amount of income recognized in 1987 and 1988.

E6-8. REVENUE RECOGNITION METHODS   The Aim Company, a farm corporation, produced the following in its first year of operations:

	SELLING PRICE PER BUSHEL
9,000 bushels of wheat	$2.40
6,000 bushels of oats	1.40

During the year it sold two-thirds of the grain produced and collected three-fourths of the selling price on the grain sold; the balance is to be collected in equal amounts during each of the two following years.

Additional data for the first year:

Wealth at beginning of year 1	$100,000
Wealth at end of year 1	115,000
Depreciation on productive plant and equipment	3,000
Other production costs (cash)	4,500
Miscellaneous administrative costs (cash)	3,600
Selling and delivery costs (incurred and paid at time of sale), per bushel . .	.10
Dividends paid to stockholders during year 1	10,000

The Aim Company is enthusiastic about the accountant's concept of matching expenses and revenues; it wishes to carry the idea to the extreme and to match with revenues not only all direct expenses but also all indirect expenses, such as those for administration.

REQUIRED

1. If revenues were recognized when production is complete (i.e., inventory is carried at net selling price), what would be Aim's income for year 1, computed in accordance with the company's matching objective?

2. If revenue were recognized on the sales basis, Aim's income for year 1 would be what amount?

3. If revenue were recognized on the installment basis, Aim's income for year 1 would be what amount?

4. Recently the company's president was introduced to a noted British economist who convinced him that the accountant's accrual approach to measuring income in fact was merely a partial accrual, and that full accrual would require consideration of changes in "wealth," which he defined as "the present value of expected net future receipts." He suggested that full accrual income for a period would be determined to be the amount that could be spent during a period while wealth remained unchanged. Aim's income, measured in this way for year 1, would be what amount?

(AICPA, adapted)

E6-9. REVENUE RECOGNITION METHODS   We-G-Board, Inc., manufactures and sells a special device for finding oil, and the company has experienced much success with the product. In 1987 the company manufactured 400 devices at a cost of $100 each. Each device has a selling price of $175.

During 1987 the company sold 300 devices and collected $32,000 from customers on such sales. During 1988, the company sold 100 devices, and total cash collections were $28,000. The remainder of the receivables was collected in 1989.

REQUIRED

1. Compute the amount of income (revenue less expense) to be recognized for 1987, 1988, and 1989 under the following revenue recognition alternatives:
   a) Revenue is recognized when production is completed.
   b) Revenue is recognized when a sale is made.
   c) Revenue is recognized under the installment method.
   d) Revenue is recognized under the cost recovery method.

2. Prepare journal entries for 1987 under each alternative. The company uses a perpetual inventory system.

E6-10. REVENUE RECOGNITION WITH RIGHT OF RETURN   Pfonk Company is a distributor of paperback books. The books are sold to retail stores with the stipulation that up to 25 percent of the books can be returned within three months. Actual returns have averaged 20 percent in each of the last eight years.

Pfonk shipped 9 million books to retail stores during the current fiscal year ending May 31, 1987. All books have a unit sales price of $2.00 and a unit cost of $1.50. A total of 2 million books shipped during the current year are still subject to the 25 percent return privilege during the first three months of the 1987–88 fiscal year. Actual returns on 1986–87 shipments have been 19 percent to date.

As of May 31, 1986, a total of 1.8 million books shipped during the 1985–86 fiscal year still had a right of return. Collections on these shipments during the 1986–87 fiscal year totaled $2,844,000, and 378,000 books were returned for credit.

REQUIRED

1. Determine the net sales revenue to be recognized for the year ending May 31, 1987, from shipments made during this fiscal year.

2. Prepare journal entries to record the following transactions related to Pfonk's operations (Pfonk uses the allowance method for returns):
   a) Shipments made during the current year and associated costs.
   b) Actual returns from current year shipments.
   c) Collections on shipments made during the previous year.
   d) Actual returns from the shipments made during the previous year.

(IMA, adapted)

E6-11. INSTALLMENT METHOD   During Pay 'n' Pay Company's first year of operations, it made sales of $200,000 (all on installment) at an average gross profit on sales of 45 percent. Collections during the year from down payments and installment payments totaled $50,000. Inventory purchases during the year were $150,000, and the cost of inventory on hand at year-end was $40,000. Pay 'n' Pay uses a periodic inventory system.

REQUIRED

Using the installment method, make summary journal entries to record each of the following:

1. The ending inventory and cost of installment sales.

2. The installment sales and cash collections.

3. The deferred gross profit.

4. The realized gross profit.

E6-12. FRANCHISES   Racquet Court Corporation sells franchises. The initial franchise fee is $50,000, payable 10 percent down with the balance in five equal annual installments plus interest at 12 percent on the unpaid balance. In return for the initial fee, the corporation agrees to assist in designing and constructing a clubhouse, to help the franchisee to obtain financing, to help train a club pro, and to provide management advice to the franchisee over a five-year period.

REQUIRED

Prepare the franchisor's entry to record (1) the initial franchise fee, (2) the first annual installment, and (3) interest under the following independent assumptions:

1. At the time the franchise is signed, none of the services promised have been provided; however, at least 90 percent of the services have been provided on the date of the first installment. Collectibility of the franchise fee is assured.

2. Same as 1, except that collectibility of the remaining installments cannot be estimated.

3. At the time the franchise is signed, the value of the services rendered is estimated to be at least $5,000. The remaining services are performed equally over the five-year period, and collectibility of the franchise fee is assured.

4. At the time the franchise is signed, all of the services promised have been provided, and collection of the franchise fee is assured.

5. Same as 4, except that collectibility of the remaining installments cannot be estimated.

E6-13. CONSIGNMENTS Tea and Me sells special blends of coffee and tea on a consignment basis. During 1987 the following transactions, given in summary form, occurred:

a) Shipped merchandise costing $18,000 to various dealers on a consignment basis.

b) Transportation costs incurred on consignment shipments totaled $3,200.

c) Account sales documents submitted by consignees indicated that 85 percent of the consignment merchandise had been sold for $22,000. Commissions amounted to $2,200, and the balance of $19,800 was received from various consignees.

d) Tea and Me recorded the consignment sales and related expenses upon receipt of the account sales.

REQUIRED

Prepare all necessary entries to record the above transactions.

E6-14. RETAIL SALES OF UNDEVELOPED LAND On January 1, 1987, Speculative Ideas, Ltd., was organized to purchase raw land for development into residential housing lots. The following transactions occurred during 1987:

January 15	Acquired 10 acres of land at a cost of $100,000. The company plans to subdivide the land into 10 building sites.
January 31	Obtained sales contracts for all 10 sites at a sales price of $25,000 per site, payable $5,000 down with the balance in 10 quarterly installments. Purchasers can void their sales contracts and receive refunds of all previous payments up until the due date of the third installment.
March 10	Subcontracted grading and paving of the development area and advanced the subcontractor $8,000.
May 1	Received first installment from all purchasers.
August 1	Received second installment from all purchasers.
August 30	The paving and grading work was completed, and the subcontractor was paid the remaining $12,000 due.
October 19	Two purchasers decided to cancel the sales contract and were given refunds of amounts previously paid.
November 1	Received third installment from the remaining purchasers.
November 30	Performed landscaping and all other services promised to purchasers at a cost of $16,000.

Until all services have been performed by Speculative Ideas, customer payments are to be recorded as unearned revenue. In addition, no receivables should be recorded until the refund privilege has expired. Costs should be deferred and not recognized as expenses until the related revenue is recognized. Once the services have been performed, the sales method is appropriate.

REQUIRED

Prepare entries to record the 1987 transactions for Speculative Ideas, Ltd.

E6-15. CONSIGNMENTS   Sadler Artistics sells paintings on a consignment basis. During 1987, Sadler shipped 6,250 paintings to Hobby Lobby Hardware. Each painting had a cost of $15 and a selling price of $50. Freight on the shipments totaled $25,000. Hobby Lobby receives a 10 percent commission on each painting sold and is reimbursed for all expenses it incurs in selling the paintings. During 1987, Hobby Lobby sold 5,100 paintings and incurred reimbursable expenses of $11,750. The consignee remitted cash to Sadler Artistics for the units sold less commissions and expenses.

REQUIRED

1. Calculate the amount of cash remitted to Sadler Artistics from Hobby Lobby.
2. Calculate Sadler Artistics' income from consignment sales made by Hobby Lobby.
3. Calculate Hobby Lobby's income from the sale of paintings on a consignment basis.

E6-16. CONSIGNMENTS   Brusewitz Company sells three-wheel motorbikes on a consignment basis. During the current year the following transactions occurred:

a) Shipped 100 bikes on a consignment basis. The cost of each bike was $800, and each was to be sold for $1,200.

b) Freight on the consignment shipment was $1,500 and was paid by Brusewitz.

c) Brusewitz received the following account sales from the consignee at the end of the year:

Bikes received		100	
Bikes unsold		(40)	
Bikes sold		60 × $1,200	$72,000
Less:			
Commissions	$10,800		
Advertising	500		(11,300)
Amount due to Brusewitz			$60,700
Amount remitted			$50,000

REQUIRED

Prepare the journal entries for the above transactions for Brusewitz Company.

PROBLEMS

P6-1. REVENUE RECOGNITION AT THE POINT OF SALE   Video Cassette sells video discs and recognizes revenue at the point of sale. At the beginning of 1987 it had the following balance sheet:

Cash	$15,000	Contributed capital	$55,000
Video disc inventory		Retained earnings	10,000
(2,000 units)	20,000		
Plant and equipment	30,000		
Total	$65,000		$65,000

During 1987 the following transactions occurred:

a) Sales of video discs at $30 each on account:

1st quarter, 150 units
2nd quarter, 500 units
3rd quarter, 300 units
4th quarter, 200 units

b) The company allows unlimited sales returns for one quarter *following* the sale and estimates that 10 percent of all discs sold on account will be returned. Actual returns were as follows:

1st quarter sales, 14 units
2nd quarter sales, 60 units
3rd quarter sales, 21 units
4th quarter sales, 5 units

c) A one-year warranty on the discs is offered. Warranty costs generally average about $2 per disc. Actual warranty costs incurred during 1987 totaled $600.

d) Cash collections during 1987 totaled $22,000 and customer accounts totaling $1,200 were written off as uncollectible during the year.

e) The company estimates that 6 percent of the accounts receivable balance, net of estimated returns, at the end of 1987 will prove uncollectible.

f) Depreciation expense for 1987 was $1,500, and operating expenses of $3,000 were paid in cash.

REQUIRED

1. Prepare journal entries to record the above transactions and end-of-year adjustments.

2. Prepare an income statement for the year ended December 31, 1987.

3. Prepare Video Cassette's balance sheet at December 31, 1987.

P6-2. LONG-TERM CONSTRUCTION CONTRACTS The board of directors of DeWitt Construction Company is meeting to choose between the completed-contract method and the percentage-of-completion method of accounting for long-term contracts in the company's financial statements. You have been engaged to assist DeWitt's controller in the preparation of a presentation to be given at the board meeting. The controller provides you with the following information:

a) DeWitt commenced doing business on January 1, 1987.

b) Construction activities for the year ended December 31, 1987, were as follows:

PROJECT	TOTAL CONTRACT PRICE	BILLINGS THROUGH 12/31/87	CASH COLLECTIONS THROUGH 12/31/87
A	$ 520,000	$ 350,000	$ 310,000
B	670,000	210,000	210,000
C	475,000	475,000	395,000
D	200,000	70,000	50,000
E	460,000	400,000	400,000
	$2,325,000	$1,505,000	$1,365,000

PROJECT	CONTRACT COSTS INCURRED THROUGH 12/31/87	ESTIMATED ADDITIONAL COSTS TO COMPLETE CONTRACTS
A	$ 424,000	$106,000
B	126,000	504,000
C	315,000	–0–
D	112,750	92,250
E	370,000	30,000
	$1,347,750	$732,250

c) Each contract is with a different customer.

d) Any work remaining to be done on the contracts is expected to be completed in 1988.

REQUIRED

1. Prepare a schedule by project, computing the amount of income (or loss) before selling, general, and administrative expenses for the year ended December 31, 1987, which would be reported under:

a) The completed-contract method.
b) The percentage-of-completion method (based on estimated costs).

2. Following is a balance sheet that compares balances resulting from the use of the two methods of accounting for long-term contracts. For each numbered blank space on the statement, supply the correct balance (indicating DR or CR as appropriate). Disregard income taxes.

DeWitt Construction Company
BALANCE SHEET
DECEMBER 31, 1987

	COMPLETED-CONTRACT METHOD	PERCENTAGE-OF-COMPLETION METHOD
Assets		
Cash..............................	$x,xxx	$x,xxx
Accounts (contracts) receivable..........	1	2
Cost of uncompleted contracts in excess of billings..................	3	—
Costs and estimated earnings in excess of billings on uncompleted contracts.........................	—	4
Property, plant, and equipment, net......	x,xxx	x,xxx
Other assets.........................	x,xxx	x,xxx
	$x,xxx	$x,xxx
Liabilities and stockholders' equity		
Accounts payable and accrued liabilities........................	$x,xxx	$x,xxx
Billings on uncompleted contracts in excess of cost....................	5	—
Billings in excess of costs and estimated earnings on uncompleted contracts.........................	—	6
Notes payable......................	x,xxx	x,xxx
Common stock......................	x,xxx	x,xxx
Retained earnings....................	x,xxx	x,xxx
	$x,xxx	$x,xxx

(AICPA, adapted)

P6-3. INCOME DETERMINATION FOR VARIOUS METHODS OF REVENUE RECOGNITION The following information relates to a five-year period for OFC Corporation, a manufacturer and distributor of long-range television antenna dishes made to sell for $400 each.

1987	Began production of 1,000 dishes and incurred costs of $150 per dish. Estimated cost to complete dishes, $90 per dish.
1988	Completed the dishes started in 1987. Completion costs were $100 per dish.
1989	Sold 400 dishes on account; collected $100,000 in cash from customers.
1990	Sold 500 dishes on account; collected cash from customers as follows: on 1989 sales, $40,000; on 1990 sales, $160,000.
1991	Sold the remaining 100 dishes for cash; collected the remaining cash due on previous years' sales.

REQUIRED

Calculate the amount of income to be recognized each year under each of the following revenue recognition methods:

1. Percentage-of-completion method.

2. Completed-contract method (when production is complete).

3. Sales method.

4. Installment method.

5. Cost recovery method.

P6-4. THE INSTALLMENT METHOD   Karen Corporation sells pianos on an installment basis. Summary information appears below:

	1987	1988	1989
Sales	$100,000	$120,000	$250,000
Cost of sales	(70,000)	(90,000)	(180,000)
Gross profit	$ 30,000	$ 30,000	$ 70,000
Customer collections on:			
1987 sales	$ 30,000	$ 55,000	$ 15,000
1988 sales		60,000	30,000
1989 sales			120,000

REQUIRED

1. Calculate the amount of gross profit that would be recognized each year under the installment method.

2. Prepare all journal entries required in 1989 under the installment method.

3. Calculate the amount of gross profit that would be recognized each year under the cost recovery method.

P6-5. THE INSTALLMENT METHOD OF ACCOUNTING   The following information relates to activities of Landry Auto Mart, which sells imported cars on an installment plan and uses the installment method of accounting:

	1987	1988
Installment sales	$800,000	$900,000
Cost of installment sales	600,000	630,000
Operating expenses	70,000	110,000
Cash collections		
on 1987 sales	450,000	300,000
on 1988 sales	—	640,000

REQUIRED

1. Prepare all required journal entries for Landry Auto Mart for 1987 and 1988.

2. Show how the above information would appear on Landry Auto Mart's balance sheet at the end of 1987 and 1988.

3. In early 1989 a customer defaults on a 1987 installment sale. The automobile, with a fair market value of $3,500, is repossessed. The unpaid balance on the installment is $6,000. Prepare the entry to record the repossession.

P6-6. REVENUE RECOGNITION ALTERNATIVES   At the beginning of 1987, Leroy Lansing began a business manufacturing and selling a high-demand carburation device designed to increase the performance of 4-cylinder automobiles. Financial data related to production costs, sales price, and sales commissions are given below (the devices are sold through auto parts houses and a commission is allowed on all units sold):

Production costs . . . . $25 per device
Selling price . . . . $80 per device
Sales commission . . . . 15% of sales per device

To encourage sales, Lansing agreed that the parts houses could sell the devices on credit, and that they could remit all cash collections annually after deducting the 15 percent commission on all units sold during the year.

Production, sales, and cash remittance data for 1987, 1988, and 1989 are as follows:

	1987	1988	1989
Units produced and delivered			
to parts houses	30,000	44,000	–0–
Units sold	18,000	50,000	6,000
Cash remittances			
Collections	$1,000,000	$3,600,000	$1,320,000
Sales commissions	(216,000)	(600,000)	(72,000)
Net remittances	$ 784,000	$3,000,000	$1,248,000

REQUIRED

1. Compute the income to be recognized each year under the following alternatives:
   a) Production basis.
   b) Sales basis.
   c) Installment basis. Do not include sales commissions in calculating the gross profit ratio.

   Use the following format for alternatives *a* and *b*:
   Revenues . . . . *xxx*
   Production costs matched against revenue . . . . (*xxx*)
   Sales commissions . . . . (*xxx*)
   Income . . . . *xxx*

2. Verify that each of the above alternatives gives identical results for the three years combined.

3. Do any of the above alternatives give results similar to that of a consignment? Explain.

P6-7. THE INSTALLMENT METHOD   Aichele Sales Company sells goods and accounts for such sales on the installment basis. At the end of each year it takes up gross profit on the basis of the year(s) of collection rather than the year of sale; accordingly, each collection consists of cost and gross profit elements.

The balances of the control accounts for installment accounts receivable at the beginning and end of 1987 were:

	1/1/87	12/31/87
Installment accounts receivable, 1985	$ 24,020	$ –0–
Installment accounts receivable, 1986	344,460	67,440
Installment accounts receivable, 1987		410,090

As collections are made, the company debits cash and credits installment accounts receivable. During 1987, upon default in payment by customers, the company repossesses merchandise having an estimated wholesale value of $1,400. The sales were made in 1986 for $5,400, and $3,200 has been collected before default. The company records the default and repossession by a debit to inventory of repossessed merchandise and a credit to installment accounts receivable, 1986, for the uncollected receivable balance.

The company's sales and cost of sales for the applicable three years are summarized below:

	1985	1986	1987
Net sales	$380,000	$432,000	$602,000
Cost of sales	247,000	285,120	379,260

REQUIRED

Prepare journal entries to record at December 31, 1987, (1) the recognition of profits and (2) any other adjustments arising from the above data. Give complete explanations in support of your entries.

(AICPA, adapted)

P6-8. SERVICE REVENUE At the beginning of 1987, Pay-Only-Once, Ltd. (POO) began offering, at ten regional locations, a CPA review course for prospective CPA examination candidates. POO set the tuition fee at $800, which covered a review of all four parts of the Uniform CPA Examination. The tuition fee was payable in cash at the first review session and permitted the candidate to take one or more parts of POO's review course as many times as necessary to pass the exam.

POO's statement of financial position at the beginning of 1987 consisted of cash, $50,000; notes payable, $48,000; and partners' capital, $2,000.

The following information applies to POO's review course and other activities for 1987 and 1988:

	1987	1988
Number of first-time candidates:		
May examination	600	1,200
November examination.	900	1,600
Number of retake candidates:		
May examination	—	70
November examination.	45	95
Direct cost per candidate . . . . $	175	$ 195
Instructional costs $200,000		$450,000
Overhead costs (including facilities, administrative,		
and miscellaneous costs) . . . . $ 35,000		$ 45,000
Payments on note . . . . $ 10,000		$ 20,000
Partners' cash withdrawals.	–0–	$ 25,000

In addition to the above information, a 1986 study by AASBA (American Association of State Boards of Accountancy) showed that, on the average, 8 percent of unsuccessful candidates who have taken a CPA review course take it a second time. After the first retake, the percentage of unsuccessful candidates who repeat the review course is almost zero.

POO's fiscal year ends each year on December 31. The November exam results are announced the following February.

REQUIRED

1. Prepare summary general journal entries for Pay-Only-Once, Ltd. for the company's operating activities for 1987 and 1988. Assume that all expenses are paid in cash.

2. Prepare income statements for Pay-Only-Once, Ltd. for 1987 and 1988.

3. Prepare balance sheets for Pay-Only-Once, Ltd. at the end of 1987 and 1988.

P6-9. INSTALLMENT SALES OF REAL ESTATE   On January 1, 1987, Lau Realty Company sold a plot of real estate to a developer for $320,000. The property had cost Lau Realty $100,000, and subsequent drainage and paving cost an additional $140,000. Selling expenses on the real estate totaled $5,000. The terms of sale were as follows: 20 percent down, with the balance due in 10 annual payments, beginning on December 31, 1987. Interest at 10 percent on the unpaid balance also was to be paid at the end of the year.

REQUIRED

1. Prepare all entries through the end of 1989, assuming that Lau Realty uses the installment method.

2. Show how the above data would appear on a balance sheet at the end of 1989, assuming that Lau Realty's accounting period ends immediately after the third installment is received.

P6-10. LONG-TERM CONSTRUCTION CONTRACTS

A) Curtiss Construction Company, Inc., entered into a firm fixed-price contract with Axelrod Associates on July 1, 1987, to construct a four-story office building. At that time, Curtiss estimated that it would take between two and three years to complete the project. The total contract price for construction of the building is $4 million. Curtiss appropriately accounts for this contract under the completed-contract method in its financial statements and in figuring its income tax. The building was deemed substantially completed on December 31, 1989. Estimated percentage of completion, accumulated contract costs incurred, estimated costs to complete the contract, and accumulated billings to Axelrod under the contract were as follows:

	12/31/87	12/31/88	12/31/89
Percentage of completion......	10%	60%	100%
Contract costs incurred........$	350,000	$2,500,000	$4,250,000
Estimated costs to complete the contract.......	3,150,000	1,700,000	—
Billings to Axelrod..........	720,000	2,160,000	3,600,000

REQUIRED

1. Prepare schedules to compute the amount to be shown as ''cost of uncompleted contract in excess of related billings'' or ''billings on uncompleted contract in excess of related costs'' at December 31, 1987, 1988, and 1989. Ignore income taxes. Show supporting computations in good form.

2. Prepare schedules to compute the profit or loss to be recognized as a result of this contract for the years ended December 31, 1987, 1988, and 1989. Ignore income taxes. Show supporting computations in good form.

B) On April 1, 1987, Butler, Inc., entered into a cost-plus-fixed-fee contract to construct an electric generator for Dalton Corporation. At the contract date, Butler estimated that it would take two years to complete the project, at a cost of $2 million. The fixed fee stipulated in the contract is $300,000. Butler appropriately accounts for this contract under the percentage-of-completion method. During 1987 Butler incurred costs of $700,000 related to the project, and the estimated cost at December 31, 1987, to complete the contract is $1.4 million. Dalton was billed $500,000 under the contract and remitted $300,000 to Butler.

REQUIRED

1. Prepare a schedule to compute the amount of gross profit to be recognized by Butler under the contract for the year ended December 31, 1987. Show supporting computations in good form.

2. Prepare Butler's journal entries for the above data.

(AICPA, adapted)

P6-11. REVENUE RECOGNITION FOR FRANCHISES   Hit and Putt is a nationwide seller of the Hit and Putt franchise. Two types of franchises are offered for sale, and the terms of each are given below:

FRANCHISE	TYPE	FRANCHISE FEE	DETAILS
A	Use of name only	$ 50,000	The franchisee may use the Hit and Putt name for an unlimited period of time; no services are required by the franchisor
B	Use of name and access to franchisor services	$100,000	Same as A except that, for an additional $50,000, the franchisor also agrees to provide financial and managerial advice to franchisee over a five-year period

Both types of franchises require a 50 percent down payment, with the balance payable in four equal annual installments. Interest is also received on the outstanding balance, but can be ignored in this problem.

Information related to franchise sales and operating costs for the franchisor for 1987 and 1988 is summarized below.

	1987	1988
a) Number of Type A franchises sold (collectibility of the installments could not be estimated for 4 franchises sold in 1987 and 6 franchises sold in 1988; for the remaining franchises, it is estimated that 1% will not be collected)	20	24
b) Number of Type B franchises sold (for these franchises, it is estimated that 1% will not be collected)	8	12
c) For Type B franchises, it is estimated that the financial and managerial services are provided equally over the five-year period.		
d) As of 12/31/88, all installments have been received on schedule.		
e) For simplicity, assume that all franchises are sold on the first day of each year		
f) Cash operating expenses (exclusive of any uncollectible accounts provisions)	$136,000	$170,000

REQUIRED

1. Prepare income statements for 1987 and 1988 for Hit and Putt and show supporting computations in good form.

2. Assume that Hit and Putt's balance sheet at the beginning of 1987 consisted of cash of $20,000 and owners' equity of $20,000. Prepare balance sheets at the end of 1987 and 1988.

P6-12. THE INSTALLMENT METHOD OF ACCOUNTING   The EZ Mart Appliance Store started business on January 1, 1987. Separate accounts were set up for installment and cash sales, but no perpetual inventory record was maintained. On the installment sales, a down payment of one-third was required, with the balance payable in 18 equal monthly installments. A deferred gross profit account was created at each year's end for the current year's installment sales. When contracts were defaulted, the unpaid balances were debited to bad debt expense, and sales of repossessed merchandise were credited to this account. The expense account was adjusted at year's end to reflect the actual loss.

A summary of the transactions of the EZ Mart Appliance Store for 1987 and 1988 follows:

	1987	1988
Sales		
New merchandise for cash	$ 21,348	$ 29,180
New merchandise on installment (including 1/3		
cash down payment)	188,652	265,320
Sales of repossessed merchandise	600	700
Purchases	154,000	173,585
Physical inventories at 12/31		
New merchandise at cost	36,400	48,010
Repossessions at realizable (market) value	150	160
Unpaid balances of installment contracts defaulted		
1987 sales	2,865	3,725
1988 sales		3,010
Cash collections on installment contracts,		
exclusive of down payments		
1987 sales	42,943	61,385
1988 sales		55,960

REQUIRED

1. Calculate the gross profit rates for the years 1987 and 1988.

2. In T-account form, reproduce the ledger accounts for installment accounts receivable.

3. Calculate the net loss on defaulted accounts for the year 1987. It is assumed that realizable value is an appropriate basis for recording repossessed merchandise.

4. Prepare a schedule showing the gross profit recognized for the year 1988 which would be reported on the income statement.

(AICPA, adapted)

P6-13.   LONG-TERM CONTRACTS; INSTALLMENT ACCOUNTING   The Roof Corporation sells road graders and also uses some of its graders in highway construction. Its trial balance at the end of 1987 is as follows:

	DEBIT	CREDIT
Cash	$ 106,000	
Accounts receivable (net of uncollectible accounts)	124,000	
Construction in progress	470,000	
Inventory of graders	250,000	
Plant and equipment	185,000	
Accumulated depreciation		$ 40,000
Accounts payable		188,000
Billings on contracts		400,000
Deferred gross profit		18,000
Common stock		250,000
Retained earnings		187,000
Sales of graders		330,000
Cost of graders sold	231,000	
Operating expenses	47,000	
	$1,413,000	$1,413,000

Additional information about 1987 operations is given below:

1. The gross profit rate on graders has remained constant for many years.

2. Roof has two long-term highway construction projects in progress on which the percentage-of-completion method is used. Financial data about these projects are as follows:

	PROJECT #101	PROJECT #102
Project started . . . . January 1, 1986		January 1, 1987
Contract price	$800,000	$200,000
Costs incurred		
During 1986	100,000	—
During 1987	200,000	110,000
Estimated completion costs		
At the end of 1986.	400,000	—
At the end of 1987.	300,000	100,000
Billings on contract		
1986.	150,000	—
1987.	300,000	110,000
Cash collections		
Through the end of 1987	150,000	10,000

No adjusting entries have been made for 1987.

3. During 1987, a grader that was previously used for construction was sold for $15,000, and the proceeds were credited to the plant and equipment account. The grader's original cost was $50,000, and it was 60 percent depreciated.

4. Roof uses the accrual (sales) method of accounting for sales of graders and has not recorded uncollectible accounts expense for 1987, which should be based on 2 percent of sales. During 1986, two sales were made to customers *S* and *T* and, because collectibility could not be estimated on these two isolated sales, the installment method was used. Customer *S* has an account balance of $25,000 at the end of 1987. In August of 1987, customer *T* defaulted on the remaining $10,000 owed. Since the repossessed grader was worthless, the company wrote off customer *T*'s account to operating expenses.

REQUIRED

1. Prepare any necessary adjusting and correcting entries at the end of 1987.

2. Prepare the income statement for 1987 for Roof Corporation.

3. Prepare the balance sheet at the end of 1987 for Roof Corporation.

P6-14. POINT OF SALE: BARTER Columbus Trading Corporation was organized on January 1, 1987, to act as a bartering agent for companies and individuals who wished to trade assets under a bartering arrangement. The corporation's initial pool of assets, contributed by three partners who share profits and losses equally, consisted of $30,000 in cash, a warehouse with a fair market value of $60,000, and goods to be bartered with a fair market value of $150,000.

The bartering arrangements are as follows:

1. A membership fee of $100 is required of each customer. This fee is payable "up front" and is not refundable. However, $50 of this amount may be applied to barter transactions in which the customers' goods sacrificed are valued at less than the goods received (see item 2, below). No portion of the fee may be applied toward agent commissions (see item 3, below). Industry experience indicates that a member uses the services of a bartering agent for approximately four years.

2. Customers bring to the warehouse any goods that they wish to barter. The corporation determines the fair value of the goods by consulting a nationally distributed "black barter book." Customers either pay cash or are paid cash for the difference between the fair market values of the bartered goods.

3. The corporation charges a service fee equal to 10 percent of the established value of each barter transaction. This fee is payable in cash at the time the barter transaction takes place.

The following information pertains to Columbus Trading Corporation's operating activities for 1987:

Membership fees	$400,000
Portion of membership fees applied to bartering	140,000
Fair value of goods accepted from customers	450,000
Fair value of goods delivered to customers	560,000
Concessions revenue (soft drinks, candy, etc)	18,000
Operating expenses	
Depreciation expense	6,000
Costs of concessions	2,500
Salaries	24,000
Miscellaneous (includes telephone, electricity, supplies, and advertising)	8,800

REQUIRED

1. Calculate Columbus Trading Corporation's service fees for 1987.

2. Prepare journal entries for Columbus Trading Corporation's operations for 1987.

3. Prepare the income statement for 1987 and the statement of financial position for Columbus Trading Corporation at the end of 1987.

P6-15. INSTALLMENT METHOD OF ACCOUNTING   The following trial balance consists of the beginning account balances and the total debits and credits to the accounts of McAlister Company, which sells merchandise on a deferred payment plan and uses the installment method of accounting:

ACCOUNT	DEBIT	CREDIT
Cash	$ 333,000	$ 142,000
Installment accounts receivable	310,000	285,000
Inventory of new merchandise	244,000	120,000
Inventory of repossessed merchandise	800	
Accounts payable	120,000	220,000
Deferred gross profit	95,800	104,000
Common stock		100,000
Retained earnings		50,000
Sales	300,000	300,000
Interest earned on installment receivables		10,000
Purchases	200,000	200,000
Expenses	22,000	
Loss on repossession	400	
Realized gross profit		95,000
	$1,626,000	$1,626,000

Additional information:

1. Interest collected during the year was $8,000.

2. During the year, a customer defaulted on an installment contract, and the merchandise was repossessed. The amount debited to deferred gross profit was $800, which represented a 40 percent gross profit on the uncollected amount.

REQUIRED

1. Prepare, in summary form, all journal entries made by McAlister Company during the year.

2. Construct McAlister Company's balance sheet at the beginning of the year.

P6-16. CONSIGNMENTS   The Aron Manufacturing Company closes its books annually on December 31. In investigating the accounts of the company for 1987, you discover the following facts:

a) During November and December, the company shipped stoves to two dealers, *P* and *Q*, on a consignment basis. The consignment agreements provided that each stove was to be sold by the consignee for $180 each. The consignee was to be allowed a 25 percent commission on each sale and was to be reimbursed for all expenses paid in connection with the stoves. Sales on account are at the consignee's risk.

b) At the time of shipment, the consignor debited accounts receivable and credited sales $120 for each stove, this amount being the usual sale price received by the consignor; on this basis a gross profit of 20 percent on cost is realized.

c) All cash received from these two consignees was credited to accounts receivable. No other entries have been made in respect to these accounts.

d) Information as to all of the transactions with the consignees is as follows:
   Stoves shipped out: to *P*, 100; to *Q*, 40.
   Stoves unsold by consignees as of 12/31/87: *P*, 35; *Q*, 25.
   Crating and shipping cost to consignor, $84.
   Freight paid by consignees: *P*, $130; *Q*, $100.
   Cash advanced by *P* at date of receipt of the first 100 stoves, $4,000; cash subsequently remitted by *P*, $5,395.
   Cash remitted by *Q*, $575.

REQUIRED

1. Prepare journal entries for the transactions completed and the adjustments required by the Aron Company.

2. Prepare a trial balance of the accounts affected by these transactions and adjustments.

(AICPA, adapted)

7 CONCEPTS OF PRESENT AND FUTURE VALUE

Concepts of present and future value are useful in decision making.

Money has a time value. **Time value** means that a dollar is worth more now than a dollar one year hence because the dollar held today can be invested to earn interest or some other form of return and thus will be more than one dollar one year hence.[1] In this chapter, we will examine the concepts of **present value**—the present worth of an amount to be paid or received at some future date—and **future value**—the future worth of an amount invested today. Although you may be familiar with the concepts of present and future value, you may not be aware of the impact of these concepts on accounting theory and practice, as well as on your personal financial activities. Accountants use the concepts of present and future value to measure and record economic events, to interpret accounting data, and to provide managers and external users of accounting information with relevant data for decision making.

For example, specific accounting topics that incorporate present and future value concepts are:

1. **Capital budgeting.** In planning long-range capital expenditures, managers of a company evaluate the profitability of alternative capital projects. Capital budgeting techniques are used to compare the present value of future cash inflows with current cash outflows to determine if a project is desirable.

2. **Valuation of financial statement elements.** Present value concepts are used to value notes, bonds, and lease obligations, to determine interest expense, and to measure a company's pension obligations. In Chapter 2 we pointed out that under the historical cost or initial recording principle, historical cost is at least a *minimum* estimate of the present value of the future cash flows associated with an asset or liability.

In your personal activities, present and future value concepts help you to answer questions such as the following:

[1] "A bird in the hand is worth two in the bush," the old saying goes; but it may be worth three or more in inflationary periods. In periods of inflation, investors demand higher rates of return on their investments. We assume in this chapter either that inflation is minimal or that interest rates include an adjustment for its effects.

If I purchase a home and finance the purchase price at an interest rate of 14 percent, what are my monthly payments?

If I can invest my savings at 12 percent, how much should I save each year in order to be able to retire at some future date and receive a specified monthly retirement benefit?

What will my rate of return be if I purchase this investment and receive a specified cash flow each year over some specified time period?

What is the net cost of this life insurance policy as compared to another life insurance policy?

As another illustration of how present value concepts are applied in practice, in 1980 a fire killed 84 people at the MGM Grand Hotel in Las Vegas. Shortly after the fire, MGM purchased a liability insurance policy, which the insuring company *backdated* twenty days before the fire.[2] Evidently the insurer calculated that the premium charged MGM would allow a profit and would be sufficient to cover the **present value** of final liability judgments, which sometimes are litigated over a quite lengthy period of time.

The examples that we shall use in this chapter cover only a few of the many applications of present and future value. As we examine new topics in later chapters, we shall employ many of the fundamentals presented here.

INTEREST AND THE TIME VALUE OF MONEY

Interest is the *cost* of borrowing money or the *return* from lending money. If you lend someone $5 today and you receive $6 one year from today, the difference of $1 represents interest that you earned on the amount lent. From the borrower's standpoint, the $1 difference also represents interest paid on the amount borrowed. Interest rates usually are stated as, or understood to be, annual rates. If you borrow $100 from a bank at 6 percent per annum (year), you must pay the bank $100 plus $6 [(.06) ($100) = $6] or $106 at the end of the year. The interest rate applicable in an economic transaction is affected by the perceived risk or probability of nonpayment in the transaction. To illustrate, a bank may lend money to customer *A*, a low-risk customer, at a 10 percent rate of interest while charging customer *B*, a high-risk customer, 16 percent interest. Firms and individuals attempt to balance risk and return in their investment decisions and undertake more risky investments only if the prospective rates of return are higher. For example, a money-market certificate of deposit that pays 12 percent interest is less risky than an investment in an oil drilling venture that may pay a 100 percent rate of return *if* the well is successful.

In theory, as well as in practice, an interest rate is comprised of three components:

More risky investments require higher expected rates of return.

1. A *pure* rate of interest based on an economic concept called the marginal productivity of capital. In a risk-free and inflation-free environment, many economists believe that this rate is about 3 percent or 4 percent.

2. A *risk* factor to compensate for uncertainty. As we illustrated above, the higher the perceived risk, the higher the rate of interest.

3. An *inflation* factor applicable in periods of inflation. In periods of inflation, lenders demand higher rates of return to compensate for the decline in purchasing power between the time money is loaned and the time it is repaid.

[2] M. Smith and R. Witt, "Retroactive Liability Insurance—the Economics of Insuring a Known Loss," *CPCU Journal*, September 1983, pp. 147–153.

The *dollar* amount of interest in a given situation is a function of three variables:

1. The *amount* borrowed or invested. This amount sometimes is called the **principal.** The larger the principal, the larger the dollar amount of interest.

2. The *rate of interest.* The higher the rate of interest on a given principal, the larger will be the dollar amount of interest.

3. The *time period* covered by the loan. The longer the period of time for which money is borrowed, the larger the dollar amount of interest.[3]

SIMPLE INTEREST   **Simple interest** is interest that is earned only on the original principal. The formula for computing simple interest is as follows:

$$I = (p)(i)(n)$$

where I = simple interest

p = principal (amount borrowed or lent)

i = interest rate per year

n = number of years (or fractional portion of a year)

If you borrow $100 for one year at 10 percent, the interest for the year is $10:

$$\begin{aligned} I &= (p)(i)(n) \\ &= (\$100)(.10)(1) \\ &= \$10 \end{aligned}$$

If you borrow $100 for 3 months at 10 percent, the interest is $2.50:

$$I = (\$100)(.10)(.25) \qquad \left(\frac{3 \text{ months}}{12 \text{ months}} = .25 \text{ of a year} \right)$$

$$= \$2.50$$

Banks often deduct interest in advance at the time the loan is made. Interest that is deducted in advance is called **discount.** In the first example, if the interest is deducted at the time of the loan, the borrower will receive only $90 and must repay $100. Obviously, if the borrower must pay $10 interest when $90 is borrowed, the *effective* interest cost is higher than if the borrower must pay $10 on $100. We shall say more about effective interest rates in the following section.

COMPOUND INTEREST   **Compound interest** is interest that is earned on both principal *and* interest. Under simple interest, interest is earned only on the original principal. When interest is compounded, however, interest is earned each period on the original principal *and* on the interest accumulated for the preceding periods. Stated another way, the principal increases each period as interest earned for that period is added to it. For example, assume that you deposited $1,000 today in a bank savings account that paid 10 percent interest compounded annually (i.e., interest is computed and added to your account once a year). The

---

[3] In this text, time periods will be specified as years, months, or days. A month will be considered as 1/12 of a year, and a day will be considered as 1/360 of a year. When banks compute interest, however, they consider a day to be 1/365 of a year.

EXHIBIT 7–1   AMOUNT EARNED OVER FOUR YEARS AT SIMPLE
AND COMPOUND INTEREST OF 10 PERCENT

END OF YEAR	INTEREST EARNED	CUMULATIVE INTEREST EARNED	INVESTMENT BALANCE
	SIMPLE INTEREST		
1	$1,000(.10) = $100	$100	$1,100
2	$1,000(.10) = 100	200	1,200
3	$1,000(.10) = 100	300	1,300
4	$1,000(.10) = 100	400	1,400
	COMPOUND INTEREST		
1	$1,000(.10) = $100.00	$100.00	$1,100.00
2	$1,100(.10) = 110.00	210.00	1,210.00
3	$1,210(.10) = 121.00	331.00	1,331.00
4	$1,331(.10) = 133.10	464.10	1,464.10

amount of interest earned over a four-year period under compound interest as compared to simple interest is shown in Exhibit 7–1.

Interest rates normally are stated as annual rates. When interest is compounded for periods of less than a year, the following steps are necessary before compound interest can be calculated:

1. Divide the annual rate by the number of compounding periods per year to determine the interest rate per compounding period.

2. Multiply the number of years involved by the number of compounding periods per year to obtain the total number of interest compounding periods.

Notice that the applicable periods no longer refer to years but to *interest periods*. The four examples in Exhibit 7–2 illustrate these two steps. These steps will be used in later examples in this chapter.

EXHIBIT 7–2   CALCULATION OF COMPOUND INTEREST AT FOUR
INTEREST RATES AND COMPOUNDING PERIODS

EXAMPLE	ANNUAL INTEREST RATE	INTEREST COMPOUNDED	INTEREST RATE PER COM- POUNDING PERIOD	NUMBER OF COMPOUNDING PERIODS
1	12%	Annually for 3 years	.12 ÷ 1 = .12	3 years × 1 compounding period = 3 periods
2	6%	Semiannually for 4 years	.06 ÷ 2 = .03	4 years × 2 compounding periods = 8 periods
3	6%	Quarterly for 5 years	.06 ÷ 4 = .015	5 years × 4 compounding periods = 20 periods
4	18%	Monthly for 9 years	.18 ÷ 12 = .015	9 years × 12 compounding periods = 108 periods

When interest is compounded more frequently than once a year, the *effective annual interest rate* can be calculated as follows:

$$\text{Effective annual rate} = \left(1 + \frac{i}{c}\right)^c - 1$$

where i = annual interest rate

c = number of compoundings per year

In terms of the four examples in Exhibit 7–2:

EXAMPLE		EFFECTIVE ANNUAL RATE
1	$\left(1 + \frac{.12}{1}\right)^1 - 1 = 1.12 - 1 \quad =$	12.00%
2	$\left(1 + \frac{.06}{2}\right)^2 - 1 = 1.0609 - 1 =$	6.09%
3	$\left(1 + \frac{.06}{4}\right)^4 - 1 = 1.0614 - 1 =$	6.14%
4	$\left(1 + \frac{.18}{12}\right)^{12} - 1 = 1.1956 - 1 =$	19.56%

These calculations are made easily with a microcomputer or with a hand calculator.[4]

Some banks offer daily or even *continuous* compounding on money deposited in savings accounts. Continuous compounding requires the use of natural logarithms. Since the underlying concepts are complex mathematically, they are not discussed in this text.

PRESENT AND FUTURE VALUES OF SINGLE AMOUNTS

We are now ready to discuss present and future values based on the principle of compound interest. Time diagrams are used to help you visualize the cash flows associated with present and future value concepts.

TIME DIAGRAMS   Since cash flows have a time value, a **time diagram** is a convenient way to visualize these cash flows over time. A typical time diagram appears below:

Point 0 on the diagram represents the present date in a problem situation. The horizontal line is divided into equal time periods, which represent the interest or compounding periods. The time diagram above contains five interest periods. In this chapter we shall use time diagrams often, since they are useful in visualizing the cash flows in our examples. You will also find them a valuable aid in solving any problems that deal with the time value of money.

[4] The effective annual rate for many combinations of annual interest rates and compoundings per year also can be found by using Table A in Appendix 7–1. Table A is discussed in the next section.

FUTURE VALUE OF A SINGLE AMOUNT

When an amount is invested for several interest periods at a specified rate of interest, it will accumulate to a larger amount because of compounding. At the end of the last interest period, this larger amount is called the **future value of a single amount** and is represented by the symbol *a*. To illustrate, if $354.60 is invested today, what is the *future value* of this amount in four years at an interest rate of 5 percent compounded annually? We may plot this problem on a time diagram, as follows:

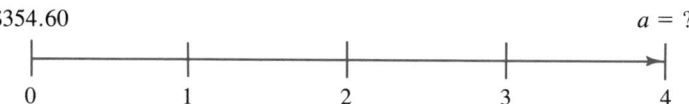

One way to solve this problem is to calculate how much has been accumulated at the end of each period:

	AMOUNT	CALCULATION
Beginning principal (year 0)	$354.60	
Interest (year 1)	17.73	($354.60)(.05)
Amount (end of year 1)	$372.33	($354.60)(1.05)
Interest (year 2)	18.62	($372.33)(.05)
Amount (end of year 2)	$390.95	($372.33)(1.05)
Interest (year 3)	19.55	($390.95)(.05)
Amount (end of year 3)	$410.50	($390.95)(1.05)
Interest (year 4)	20.52	($410.50)(.05)
Amount (end of year 4)	$431.02	($410.50)(1.05)

A general formula for the future value of a single amount can be developed from the calculations in the right-hand column above:

$$a = p\,(a_{\overline{n}|\,i})$$

where a = future value of a single amount

p = beginning principal

$a_{\overline{n}|\,i}$ (read "small a angle n at i") = $(1 + i)^n$

i = interest rate per period

n = number of interest periods

The symbols a and $a_{\overline{n}|\,i}$ should not be confused. The symbol $a_{\overline{n}|\,i}$ is simply a shorthand notation for the formula $(1 + i)^n$. The symbol a represents the future value of a single amount and is determined by multiplying *any* principal (p) times the appropriate interest factor, $(1 + i)^n$, when i and n are given. In the above example:

$$a = \$354.60(a_{\overline{4}|\,5\%})$$
$$= \$354.60(1.05)^4$$
$$= \$354.60(1.2155)$$
$$= \$431.02$$

While we can calculate $(1.05)^4$ by hand or with a calculator, tables have been constructed for these future value factors ($a_{\overline{n}|\,i}$) for various interest rates and time periods. Table A in Appendix 7–1 contains these future value factors. A portion of Table A appears in Exhibit 7–3. To use Table A, simply multiply the principal amount by the appropriate interest factor in the table to obtain the future value.

| **EXHIBIT 7–3** | FUTURE VALUE OF 1 (TABLE A) | | | $a_{\overline{n}|\,i} = (1 + i)^n$ | |

			i		
n	**2%**	**3%**	**4%**	**5%**	**6%**
1	1.0200	1.0300	1.0400	1.0500	1.0600
2	1.0404	1.0609	1.0816	1.1025	1.1236
3	1.0612	1.0927	1.1249	1.1576	1.1910
4	1.0824	1.1255	1.1699	1.2155	1.2625
5	1.1041	1.1593	1.2167	1.2763	1.3382
6	1.1262	1.1941	1.2653	1.3401	1.4185
7	1.1487	1.2299	1.3159	1.4071	1.5036
8	1.1717	1.2668	1.3686	1.4775	1.5938
9	1.1951	1.3048	1.4233	1.5513	1.6895
10	1.2190	1.3439	1.4802	1.6289	1.7908

To illustrate how a future value table is used, assume you borrow $10,000 today from a bank. How much will you owe the bank at the end of five years if the rate of interest is 12 percent compounded semiannually? The solution is as follows:

$$a = \$10,000(a_{\overline{10}|\,6\%})$$
$$= \$10,000(1.7908)$$
$$= \$17,908$$

Note that because we are compounding semiannually, the number of periods is 10 and the interest rate per period is 6 percent. Reading the table in Exhibit 7–3 indicates that the factor corresponding to 10 periods at 6 percent is 1.7908. Thus, if we borrow $10,000 today from a bank, we will owe the bank $17,908 at the end of the fifth year if the bank charges interest at 12 percent compounded semiannually.[5]

PRESENT VALUE OF A SINGLE AMOUNT

Determining future values of single amounts is important in many investing and lending situations. The concept of the **present value of a single amount,** however, has more applications in financial accounting. The present value concept provides an answer to the following general question: What is the value today (the present value) of an amount to be received or paid at some future date? To illustrate, assume that in five years you wish to purchase a motorcycle which will sell for $4,000 at that point. If the interest rate you can earn is 10 percent compounded annually, how much must you invest today so that your original investment and interest will accumulate to $4,000 at the end of the fifth year?

A time diagram for this problem is as follows:

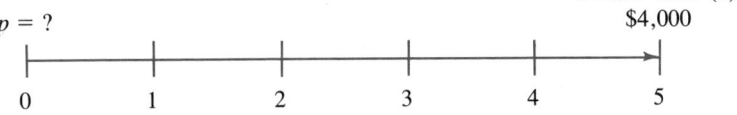

Future value (a)
$4,000

$p = ?$

0   1   2   3   4   5

Notice that we wish to find the *present value* of a future amount when the future amount is known, whereas before we wished to find the *future value* when the present value was known.

Since $a = p(a_{\overline{n}|\,i}) = p(1 + i)^n$,

$$p = \frac{a}{a_{\overline{n}|\,i}} = \frac{a}{(1 + i)^n}$$

[5] The effective annual rate in this example is 12.36% $[(1 + .12/2)^2 - 1]$. This amount is found in Exhibit 7–3 under the 6% column (12% ÷ 2) and the $n = 2$ row (two compoundings per year).

This relationship means that to find the present value of a future amount, we can divide the known future amount by the appropriate factor in Table A. Therefore, our problem can be solved as follows:

$$
\begin{aligned}
p &= \frac{a}{a\,\overline{n}\mid i} \\
&= \frac{\$4,000}{a\,\overline{5}\mid 10\%} \\
&= \frac{\$4,000}{1.6105} \\
&= \$2,483.70
\end{aligned}
$$

The $2,483.70 represents the present value of $4,000 *discounted* for five years at 10 percent. In other words, if you invest $2,483.70 at 10 percent interest compounded annually, the investment will grow to $4,000 at the end of year 5. This result is shown in Exhibit 7–4. Notice the pattern in which the interest of $1,516.30 ($4,000.00 − $2,483.70) is earned over the five-year period. This pattern is characteristic of the *effective interest method* of calculating interest. Under the effective interest method, the dollar amount of periodic interest increases (decreases) as the investment increases (decreases).

Although we can always use Table A to calculate present values, tables have been constructed to provide these present value factors directly. Table B in Appendix 7–1 contains factors for the present value of 1 at various interest rates and time periods. A portion of Table B appears in Exhibit 7–5.

The present value factors in Table B are reciprocals of the future value factors in Table A.

The present value factors in Table B are **reciprocals** of the future value factors in Table A, as Exhibit 7–6 illustrates. Thus, the present value of a single amount is:

$$
p = a(p\,\overline{n}\mid i)
$$

where p = present value of a single future amount

a = the future amount

$p\,\overline{n}\mid i$ (read "small p angle n at i") = $\dfrac{1}{(1 + i)^n}$

i = interest rate per period

n = number of periods

To illustrate the use of the present value formula and table, assume we have the opportunity to purchase a zero-coupon bond that will pay us $13,000 at its maturity date at the end of six years. (A zero-coupon bond pays no periodic interest.) What is the present value of this investment at a rate of return of 8 percent? That is, if the required rate of return is 8 percent, how much would we be willing to invest now in order to receive $13,000 at the end of six years?

$$
\begin{aligned}
p &= a(p\,\overline{n}\mid i) \\
&= \$13,000(p\,\overline{6}\mid 8\%) \\
&= \$13,000(.6302) \\
&= \$8,192.60
\end{aligned}
$$

The present value factor is determined by finding the amount in Table B that corresponds to 6 periods at 8 percent interest. Multiplying this factor, .6302, by the future amount gives us the present value of $8,192.60.

EXHIBIT 7–4   GROWTH OF INITIAL INVESTMENT (PRESENT VALUE) OF $2,483.70 TO $4,000 IN FIVE YEARS AT 10 PERCENT INTEREST COMPOUNDED ANNUALLY

YEAR	(a) BEGINNING INVESTMENT	(b) INTEREST FOR YEAR $(a \times .10)$	(c) ENDING INVESTMENT $(a + b)$
1	$2,483.70	$248.37	$2,732.07
2	2,732.07	273.21	3,005.28
3	3,005.28	300.53	3,305.81
4	3,305.81	330.58	3,636.39
5	3,636.39	363.61*	4,000.00
		$1,516.30	

* Rounded down by $.03.

EXHIBIT 7–5   PRESENT VALUE OF 1 (TABLE B) $$p_{\overline{n}|\,i} = \frac{1}{a_{\overline{n}|\,i}} = \frac{1}{(1+i)^n}$$

			i		
n	2%	3%	4%	5%	6%
1	0.9804	0.9709	0.9615	0.9524	0.9434
2	0.9612	0.9426	0.9246	0.9070	0.8900
3	0.9423	0.9151	0.8890	0.8638	0.8396
4	0.9238	0.8885	0.8548	0.8227	0.7921
5	0.9057	0.8626	0.8219	0.7835	0.7423

EXHIBIT 7–6   RELATIONSHIP BETWEEN TABLE A AND TABLE B
(10% INTEREST COLUMN, FROM APPENDIX 7–1)

n	1 ÷ TABLE A FACTOR	= TABLE B FACTOR
1	1 ÷ 1.1000	= .9091
2	1 ÷ 1.2100	= .8264
3	1 ÷ 1.3310	= .7513
⋮	⋮	⋮
12	1 ÷ 3.1384	= .3186
⋮	⋮	⋮
20	1 ÷ 6.7275	= .1486

OTHER VALUES RELATED TO SINGLE AMOUNTS   So far in this chapter we have illustrated future and present values of single amounts when the number of periods and the rate of interest were given. In this section we shall look at some different but related problems. Our purpose here is to demonstrate that if we know the values of any three of the four variables (p, a, i, and n), we can determine the value of the fourth variable.

Finding n When p, a, and i Are Known

Assume that your client needs $25,000 for major construction expenditures in the future. At the present time he has only $11,580 in funds. How many years will it take him to accumulate $25,000 if $11,580 is invested at 8 percent?

In this example, both the present and future values are known ($11,580 and $25,000, respectively). The interest rate also is known, and we are trying to determine the number of periods (n) required for $11,580 invested at 8 percent to accumulate to $25,000. A time diagram is as follows:

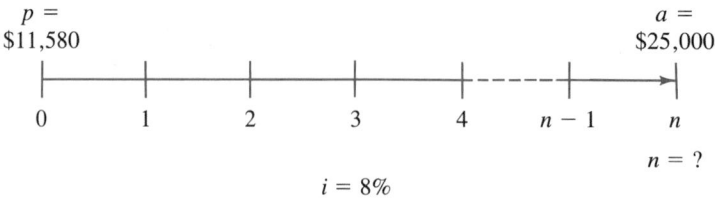

Since both the present and future values are known, we can approach the problem from the viewpoint of either present value or future value.

From the viewpoint of present value:

$$p = a(p_{\overline{n}|\,8\%})$$

$$\$11{,}580 = \$25{,}000(p_{\overline{n}|\,8\%})$$

$$p_{\overline{n}|\,8\%} = \frac{\$11{,}580}{\$25{,}000} = .4632$$

We need to find how many interest periods correspond to the present value factor of .4632 when $i = 8$ percent. Using Table B and reading down the 8 percent column, we find that the number of periods (n) corresponding to .4632 is 10. Thus, it will take 10 years for $11,580 to accumulate to $25,000 at an earnings rate of 8 percent.

From the viewpoint of future value:

$$a = p(a_{\overline{n}|\,8\%})$$

$$\$25{,}000 = \$11{,}580(a_{\overline{n}|\,8\%})$$

$$a_{\overline{n}|\,8\%} = \frac{\$25{,}000}{\$11{,}580} = 2.1589$$

Using Table A and reading down the 8 percent column, we find that 2.1589 corresponds to 10 periods, as we would expect after our previous calculation from the viewpoint of present value.

Finding i When p, a, and n Are Known

What interest rate is necessary in order for a single amount of $5,645 invested today to accumulate to $10,000 in six years?

A time diagram and the solution appear below. While the problem can be approached as either a present value or future value problem, we have presented the solution in terms of present value only:

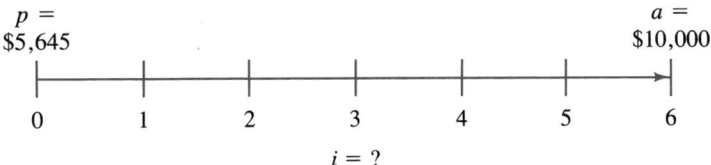

$$p = a(p_{\overline{n}|\,i})$$

$$\$5,645 = \$10,000(p_{\overline{6}|i})$$

$$p_{\overline{6}|i} = .5645$$

Using Table B and reading across the $n = 6$ row, we find that .5645 corresponds to an interest rate of 10 percent. Thus, if \$5,645 is invested at 10 percent, it will accumulate to \$10,000 at the end of the sixth year.

Changing Interest Rates

In our economy interest rates change because of inflation, fluctuations in supply and demand, investors' perceptions of risk, and other factors. To illustrate a situation with changing interest rates, assume that Polly Frank deposited \$15,000 in a savings account on January 1, 1987. What is the amount in her savings account at the end of 16 years if the rate of interest is 6 percent for the first 10 years and 10 percent for the remaining six years?

The solution is fairly straightforward if we visualize the problem in two parts, as illustrated in the time diagram below:

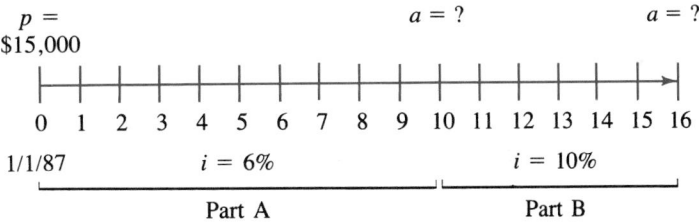

Part A: Future value at the end of year 10:

$$a = \$15,000(a_{\overline{10}|\,6\%})$$
$$= \$15,000(1.7908)$$
$$= \$26,862$$

Part B: Future value at the end of year 16:

$$a = \$26,862(a_{\overline{6}|\,10\%})$$
$$= \$26,862(1.7716)$$
$$= \$47,588.72$$

The \$15,000 will earn interest at 6 percent for 10 years and will accumulate to \$26,862 at the end of the tenth year. Beginning in the eleventh year, the \$26,862 will earn interest at 10 percent and will accumulate to \$47,588.72 at the end of the sixteenth year.

ANNUITIES

An annuity is a series of equal periodic cash flows.

In the previous section, we discussed the concepts of present and future values of single amounts. In this section we shall discuss present and future value concepts related to a series of equal cash flows, called an annuity. An **annuity** is a series of equal cash flows occurring at equal intervals over a period of time.[6] If the first cash flow occurs at the *end* of the first interest period, the annuity is an **ordinary annuity** (or an annuity in arrears). If the first cash flow occurs at the *beginning* of the first interest period, the annuity is called an **annuity due** (or an annuity in advance). The difference between an ordinary annuity and an annuity due is illustrated in Exhibit 7–7.

As with single amounts, the basic concepts for annuities are determining (1) to what amount the periodic cash flows (i.e., an annuity) will accumulate at some future point, and (2) the present value of a series of equal, periodic future cash flows (i.e., an annuity).

The first part of this section deals with ordinary annuities; annuities due will be discussed later. Annuities have many applications in accounting because many of the cash flows related to bonds, notes, leases, and pensions, for example, may be thought of as annuities.

FUTURE VALUE OF AN ORDINARY ANNUITY

To illustrate how the future value of an ordinary annuity is determined, assume that you deposit $100 in a savings account at the end of each year for four years. What will be the amount in your savings account at the end of the fourth year if the interest rate is 5 percent compounded annually?[7] A time diagram is as follows:

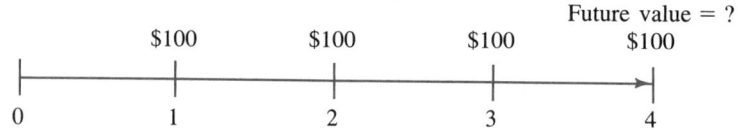

[6] These cash flows are often called **rents.**

[7] In all of the examples in this book, we shall assume that the periodic rents (e.g., $100 each year in this example) coincide with the compounding period (e.g., annually in this example). Cases in which the compounding period differs from the timing of the cash flows are beyond the scope of this textbook.

EXHIBIT 7–7 TIME DIAGRAMS OF AN ORDINARY ANNUITY AND AN ANNUITY DUE

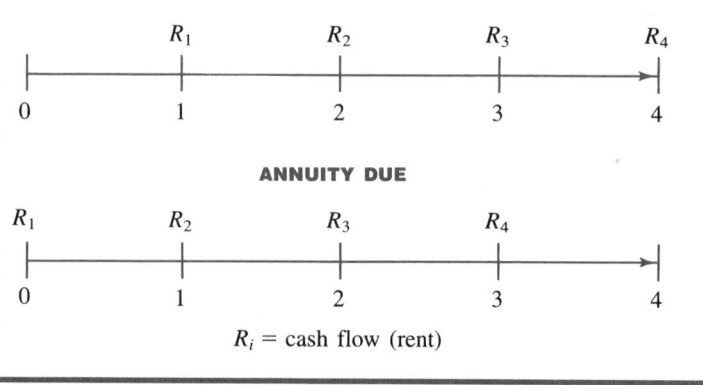

To find this future value, we can treat each cash flow as a single amount and calculate the future value of each single amount as shown below:

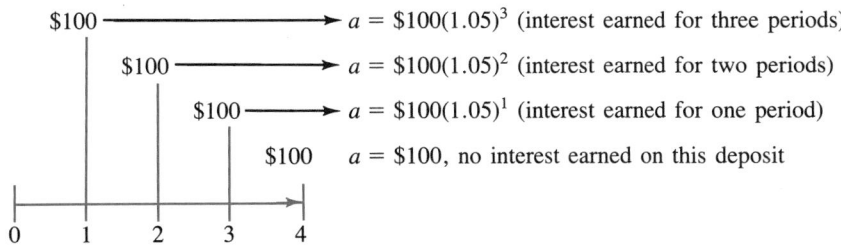

Thus, we have:

Future value of an
ordinary annuity $= \$100(1.05)^3 + \$100(1.05)^2 + \$100(1.05)^1 + \$100$
$= \$100[(1.05)^3 + (1.05)^2 + (1.05)^1 + 1]$
$= \$100(1.1576 + 1.1025 + 1.05 + 1)$
$= \$100(4.3101)$
$= \$431.01$

Therefore, if you deposit $100 in a savings account at the end of each year for four years, your balance will be $431.01 at the end of the fourth year. Exhibit 7–8 illustrates how your savings will grow during the four-year period.

This approach can become tedious and time consuming as the number of rents increases. The calculation above is based on a geometric progression and, while not derived here, can be summed to obtain $\$100\left[\dfrac{(1 + .05)^4 - 1}{.05}\right]$. Thus, the formula for the future value of an ordinary annuity is as follows:

$$A = R(A_{\overline{n}|\,i})$$

where A = future value of an ordinary annuity

R = periodic cash flows (rents)

$A_{\overline{n}|\,i}$ (read "capital A angle n at i") $= \dfrac{(1 + i)^n - 1}{i}$

n = number of rents

i = interest rate per period

EXHIBIT 7–8 GROWTH IN INVESTMENT FROM AN ORDINARY ANNUITY OF $100 EACH YEAR FOR FOUR YEARS AT 5 PERCENT

YEAR	(a) BEGINNING INVESTMENT BALANCE	(b) INTEREST EARNED (a × .05)	(c) ANNUAL DEPOSIT AT YEAR END	(d) ENDING INVESTMENT BALANCE (a + b + c)
1	–0–	–0–	$100	$100.00
2	$100.00	$ 5.00	100	205.00
3	205.00	10.25	100	315.25
4	315.25	15.76	100	431.01

EXHIBIT 7–9 | FUTURE VALUE OF AN ORDINARY ANNUITY OF 1 (TABLE C) | $A_{\overline{n}|\,i} = \dfrac{(1-i)^n - 1}{i}$

			i		
n	2%	3%	4%	5%	6%
1	1.0000	1.0000	1.0000	1.0000	1.0000
2	2.0200	2.0300	2.0400	2.0500	2.0600
3	3.0604	3.0909	3.1216	3.1525	3.1836
4	4.1216	4.1836	4.2465	4.3101	4.3746
5	5.2040	5.3091	5.4163	5.5256	5.6371
6	6.3081	6.4684	6.6330	6.8019	6.9753
7	7.4343	7.6625	7.8983	8.1420	8.3938
8	8.5830	8.8923	9.2142	9.5491	9.8975
9	9.7546	10.1591	10.5828	11.0266	11.4913
10	10.9497	11.4639	12.0061	12.5779	13.1808

Table C in Appendix 7–1 gives the future value of ordinary annuity factors for various values of i and n. A portion of Table C appears in Exhibit 7–9. To use the Table C factors in the formula, simply multiply the periodic rent by the annuity factor that corresponds to the appropriate i and n to obtain the future value of the ordinary annuity.

To illustrate the use of the future value of an annuity formula and Table C, assume that Goody Corporation must accumulate a pension fund for retiring employees. If today is January 1, 1987, how much will be accumulated by January 1, 1992, if $200 is deposited each six months in a savings account that earns 12 percent compounded semiannually? The first deposit will be made on July 1, 1987. A time diagram and the solution appear below:

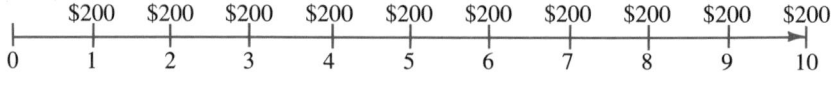

$A = R(A_{\overline{n}|\,i})$
  $= \$200(A_{\overline{10}|\,6\%})$
  $= \$200(13.1808)$
  $= \$2,636.16$

Thus, if Goody makes the 10 semiannual deposits on the indicated dates, funds totaling $2,636.16 will be available on January 1, 1992.

It should be apparent that Table C (future value of an ordinary annuity of 1) and Table A (future value of 1) are related, since, as we stated earlier, we can treat each cash flow of an annuity as a single amount, find the future value of each cash flow, then add the individual future values of all of the cash flows to obtain the future value of an ordinary annuity. This relationship is shown in Exhibit 7–10. As Exhibit 7–10 demonstrates, the Table C factors may be derived from the Table A factors by subtracting 1 from the Table A factor, then dividing the result by the interest rate (i).

PRESENT VALUE OF AN ORDINARY ANNUITY

Accountants also use the concept of the **present value of an ordinary annuity** in solving many accounting problems. For example, assume that your client Tim Dubois is considering investing in a solar energy unit that will provide annual cash savings of $1,200 each year for five years. The first cash saving will occur at the end of the current year. What is the present value of this investment at an interest rate, or rate of return, of 10 percent? That is, how much should your client be willing to invest in order to save $1,200 per year for five years if he expects to earn a 10 percent rate of return?

EXHIBIT 7–10   RELATIONSHIP BETWEEN TABLE A AND TABLE C

n	TABLE A: FUTURE VALUE OF 1 AT 5% $a_{\overline{n}|\,i} = (1+i)^n$	$(1+i)^n - 1$	$\div$	i	$=$	TABLE C: FUTURE VALUE OF AN ORDINARY ANNUITY OF 1 AT 5% $A_{\overline{n}|\,i} = \dfrac{(1+i)^n - 1}{i}$
1	1.0500	.0500	.05			1.0000
2	1.1025	.1025	.05			2.0500
3	1.1576	.1576	.05			3.1520
5	1.2763	.2763	.05			5.5260
10	1.6289	.6289	.05			12.5780
20	2.6533	1.6533	.05			33.0660

A time diagram would look like this:

Present value = ? $1,200 $1,200 $1,200 $1,200 $1,200

0   1   2   3   4   5

To determine the present value of this ordinary annuity, we may treat each $1,200 cash flow as a single amount, find the present value of each single amount, then add the individual present values to obtain the total present value:

$$\text{Present value of ordinary annuity} = \frac{\$1,200}{(1.10)} + \frac{\$1,200}{(1.10)^2} + \frac{\$1,200}{(1.10)^3} + \frac{\$1,200}{(1.10)^4} + \frac{\$1,200}{(1.10)^5}$$

or

$$\text{Present value of ordinary annuity} = \$1,200\left[\frac{1}{(1.10)} + \frac{1}{(1.10)^2} + \frac{1}{(1.10)^3} + \frac{1}{(1.10)^4} + \frac{1}{(1.10)^5}\right]$$
$$= \$1,200(.9091 + .8264 + .7513 + .6830 + .6209)$$
$$= \$1,200(3.7908)$$
$$= \$4,548.95$$

The solution may be interpreted as follows: If your client invests $4,548.95 in a solar unit that provides cash savings of $1,200 each year for five years, the rate of return earned on the investment is 10 percent per year.

The calculation above can become cumbersome when an annuity covers several periods. Therefore, the use of a formula is more efficient. The formula for the present value of an ordinary annuity is as follows:

$$P = R(P_{\overline{n}|\,i})$$

where P = present value of an ordinary annuity

R = ordinary annuity (periodic cash flow or rent)

$$P_{\overline{n}|\,i} \text{ (read ``capital } P \text{ angle } n \text{ at } i\text{'')} = \frac{1 - \dfrac{1}{(1+i)^n}}{i}$$

n = number of rents

i = interest (discount) rate per period

EXHIBIT 7–11 PRESENT VALUE OF AN ORDINARY ANNUITY OF 1 (TABLE D)

$$P_{\overline{n}|i} = \frac{1 - \dfrac{1}{(1+i)^n}}{i}$$

			i			
n	2%	3%	4%	5%	$\cdots$	10%
1	0.9804	0.9709	0.9615	0.9524	$\cdots$	0.9091
2	1.9416	1.9135	1.8861	1.8594	$\cdots$	1.7355
3	2.8839	2.8286	2.7751	2.7232	$\cdots$	2.4869
4	3.8077	3.7171	3.6299	3.5460	$\cdots$	3.1699
5	4.7135	4.5797	4.4518	4.3295	$\cdots$	3.7908
6	5.6014	5.4172	5.2421	5.0757	$\cdots$	4.3553
7	6.4720	6.2303	6.0021	5.7864	$\cdots$	4.8684
8	7.3255	7.0197	6.7327	6.4632	$\cdots$	5.3349
9	8.1622	7.7861	7.4353	7.1078	$\cdots$	5.7590
10	8.9826	8.5302	8.1109	7.7217	$\cdots$	6.1946

Table D in Appendix 7–1 gives the factors for the present value of an ordinary annuity for various values of i and n. A portion of Table D appears in Exhibit 7–11. To use the Table D factors in the formula, simply multiply the periodic rents by the annuity factor that corresponds to the appropriate i and n to obtain the present value of the ordinary annuity.

Applying the formula and Table D to the solar energy unit example, we have:

$$P = R(P_{\overline{n}|i})$$
$$= \$1,200(P_{\overline{5}|10\%})$$
$$= \$1,200(3.7908)$$
$$= \$4,548.95$$

To further illustrate the calculations for the present value of an ordinary annuity, assume that Penny Lane, Inc., wishes to deposit, in a financial institution, an amount that will enable the company to withdraw cash of $1,250 per year for 10 years, with the first withdrawal to be made on December 31, 1987. How much should be deposited on January 1, 1987, if the deposit earns 10 percent compounded annually? The problem can be solved as follows:

$$P = R(P_{\overline{n}|i})$$
$$= \$1,250(P_{\overline{10}|10\%})$$
$$= \$1,250(6.1446)$$
$$= \$7,680.75$$

Thus, if the company deposits $7,680.75 on January 1, 1987, it will be able to withdraw $1,250 each year for 10 years, the first withdrawal to be made on December 31, 1987. The schedule in Exhibit 7–12 shows how the amount on deposit gradually decreases to zero during the 10-year period. Notice that the annual interest earnings in column 2 *increase* the amount on deposit, while the annual withdrawals in column 3 *decrease* the amount on deposit. Another way to interpret Exhibit 7–12 is to view each periodic withdrawal as consisting of two distinct elements: (1) withdrawal of the interest earned during the period and (2) withdrawal of a portion of the principal. For example, in 1991, the $1,250 withdrawal consists of interest in the amount of $544.41 and principal in the

EXHIBIT 7–12   SCHEDULE OF DECLINE IN DEPOSIT FROM ANNUAL WITHDRAWALS

YEAR	(1) BEGINNING BALANCE	+	(2) INTEREST AT 10%*	−	(3) WITHDRAWAL	=	(4) ENDING BALANCE
1987	$7,680.75		$768.08		$1,250.00		7,198.83
1988	7,198.83		719.88		1,250.00		6,668.71
1989	6,668.71		666.87		1,250.00		6,085.58
1990	6,085.58		608.56		1,250.00		5,444.14
1991	5,444.14		544.41		1,250.00		4,738.55
1992	4,738.55		473.86		1,250.00		3,962.41
1993	3,962.41		396.24		1,250.00		3,108.65
1994	3,108.65		310.86		1,250.00		2,169.51
1995	2,169.51		216.95		1,250.00		1,136.46
1996	1,136.46		113.64		1,250.00		0.00†

* 10% of the beginning balance on deposit.

† Rounding error of $.10.

amount of $705.59 ($1,250.00 − $544.41). The principal withdrawal causes the amount on deposit to decrease from $5,444.14 to $4,738.55, or a reduction of $705.59.

> The table factors in Table D are cumulative summations of the table factors in Table B.

As with the two future value tables there is a relationship between the two present value tables discussed so far. This relationship between Table B and Table D is shown in Exhibit 7–13. Notice that the present value factors in Table D are the cumulative summations of the present value factors in Table B.

OTHER VALUES RELATED TO ORDINARY ANNUITIES

Earlier in this chapter we discussed how other variables (e.g., the interest rate or the number of periods) related to single amounts can be determined when both the present and future values of single amounts are known. These same concepts also apply to annuities and are illustrated in this section.

Finding n When R, P or A, and i Are Known

Accountants frequently need to determine the annuity payments necessary to accumulate a certain dollar amount. For example, a company may need to accumulate funds to retire a debt at some point in the future. To illustrate, if today is January 1, 1987, how many year-end deposits of $10,000, the first to be made at the end of 1987, are necessary to accumulate $61,051, if the interest rate is 10 percent compounded annually?

EXHIBIT 7–13   RELATIONSHIP BETWEEN TABLE B AND TABLE D

n	TABLE B: PRESENT VALUE OF 1 AT 5%	TABLE D: PRESENT VALUE OF ORDINARY ANNUITY OF 1 AT 5%
1	.9524	.9524
2	.9070	.9524 + .9070 = 1.8594
3	.8638	.9524 + .9070 + .8638 = 2.7232
4	.8227	.9524 + .9070 + .8638 + .8227 = 3.5460
5	.7835	.9524 + .9070 + .8638 + .8227 + .7835 = 4.3295

Notice that $61,051 represents the *future value* of n (to be determined) $10,000 year-end cash flows, at an interest rate of 10 percent. Thus,

$$A = R(A_{\overline{n}|\,i})$$

$$\$61,051 = \$10,000(A_{\overline{n}|\,10\%})$$

$$A_{\overline{n}|\,10\%} = \frac{\$61,051}{\$10,000} = 6.1051$$

Consulting Table C (future value of an ordinary annuity) and reading down the 10 percent column, we find that the number of periods (n) corresponding to 6.1051 is five. Thus, it will take five $10,000 year-end deposits (or five years) to accumulate $61,051 at an interest rate (rate of return) of 10 percent.

Finding i When R, P or A, and n Are Known

Accountants often are called upon to determine the rate of interest that is implicit, or implied, in a loan agreement. In these cases the interest rate must be calculated from other variables. For example, assume that on January 1, 1988, Kathy Dorr borrows $10,170 from Good National Bank. The bank requires her to repay the loan in 10 equal annual payments of $1,800. The first payment is due on December 31, 1988. What rate of interest is the bank charging on the loan?

The $10,170 borrowed represents the present value of 10 end-of-year cash payments of $1,800 at an interest rate of i percent (to be determined). Using the formula for the present value of an ordinary annuity, we can determine the interest rate as follows:

$$P = R(P_{\overline{n}|\,i})$$

$$\$10,170 = \$1,800(P_{\overline{10}|\,i})$$

$$P_{\overline{10}|\,i} = 5.6500$$

Reading across the $n = 10$ row in Table D, we find that the interest rate that corresponds to the factor of 5.6500 is 12 percent. Thus, the bank is charging Kathy Dorr an interest rate of 12 percent on the unpaid balance of the loan.

Finding R When P or A, i, and n Are Known

Many present value problems require calculating either the periodic cash payments necessary to liquidate a current debt or the periodic cash investment necessary to accumulate a given future amount. Assume, for example, that on January 1, 1987, Jobe Corporation owes $35,000 to a creditor. If Jobe decides to liquidate the debt by making 15 equal payments at the end of each year beginning on December 31, 1987, what periodic payment is required if the creditor charges 12 percent interest on the unpaid balance?

Here we are trying to find the periodic payments (rents) that will liquidate a debt that has a present value of $35,000. We use the formula for the present value of an ordinary annuity:

$$P = R(P_{\overline{15}|\,12\%})$$

$$\$35,000 = R(6.8109)$$

$$R = \$5,138.82$$

Thus, Jobe must make 15 annual end-of-year payments of $5,138.82 in order to liquidate its $35,000 debt.

ANNUITIES DUE   Up to this point we have discussed ordinary annuities, in which the periodic cash flows occur at the *end* of each interest period. In many business transactions, such as lease payments, the annuity payment occurs at the *beginning* of each interest period and is called an *annuity due.*

Table C and Table D provide the future value and present value factors corresponding to ordinary annuities. For annuity due problems, a formula modification must be made before Tables C and D can be used.

Future Value of an Annuity Due

We will begin by illustrating how the future value of an annuity due is calculated. Assume that beginning on July 1, 1987, JoAnn Hugh makes four annual deposits of $100 to a savings account. How much does she have in the account on July 1, 1991, if the savings account pays 12 percent interest compounded annually?

As the time diagram below illustrates, these deposits represent an annuity due, since they are made at the *beginning* of each interest period instead of at the end, as in an ordinary annuity.

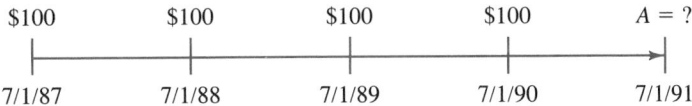

In order to make the situation represented by the time diagram appear as an ordinary annuity, we can extend the time line back one period (one year in this example). Also, if we temporarily ignore the last interest period, the time diagram represents an ordinary annuity of four rents for four periods ending on July 1, 1990.

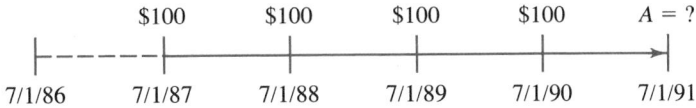

Once we have calculated the future value of the ordinary annuity on July 1, 1990, we can treat this future value as a single amount and compound the amount for one period from July 1, 1990, to July 1, 1991. This final calculation will give us the future value at July 1, 1991.

We can combine these two steps by modifying the formula for the future value of an ordinary annuity to obtain the formula for the future value of an annuity due as follows:

Future value of:	*Formula:*
Ordinary annuity (A)	$A = R(A_{\overline{n}|\,i})$
Annuity due (A_D)	$A_D = R(A_{\overline{n}|\,i})(1 + i)$

The future value of the annuity due in the numerical example is calculated as follows:

$$
\begin{aligned}
A_D &= \$100(A_{\overline{4}|\,12\%})(1.12) \\
&= \$100(4.7793)(1.12) \\
&= \$100(5.3528) \\
&= \$535.28
\end{aligned}
$$

Thus, if JoAnn Hugh makes four $100 deposits each year beginning on July 1, 1987, her savings account will have a balance of $535.28 on July 1, 1991.

Present Value of an Annuity Due

To demonstrate the modifications for the present value of an annuity due, assume that on March 1, 1987, Denise Company leases a building for six years and agrees to make six annual lease payments of $600 each, the first of which is due on March 1, 1987. What is the *present value* of the obligation if the interest rate is 8 percent? In other words, what equivalent lump-sum amount should the building owner agree to take if Denise agrees to pay the entire lease obligation on March 1, 1987?

Here is the corresponding time diagram:

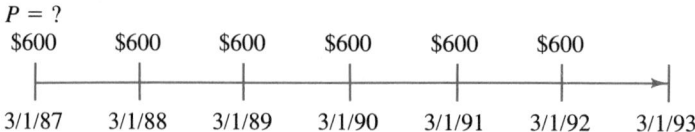

Because we are calculating the present value, there is no interest for the sixth period. After making the last lease payment, Denise has no further cash flow obligations, although the company will use the building through March 1, 1993. If we extend the time diagram back one period, it appears as follows:

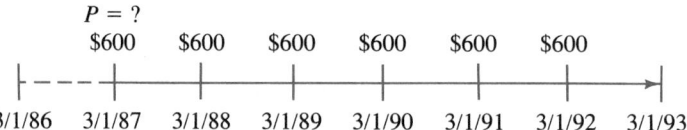

The diagram now appears as an ordinary annuity that begins on March 1, 1986, and ends with the last rent on March 1, 1992. Thus, we can find the present value of this annuity on March 1, 1986, then compound this amount for one period (to March 1, 1987). These adjustments modify the formula for the present value of an ordinary annuity to the present value of an annuity due, as shown below:

Present value of:	*Formula:*
Ordinary annuity (P)	$P = R(P_{\overline{n}|\,i})$
Annuity due (P_D)	$P_D = R(P_{D\,\overline{n}|\,i})$ where $P_{D\,\overline{n}|\,i} = (P_{\overline{n}|\,i})(1 + i)$

In terms of the numerical example:

$$P_D = \$600(P_{\overline{6}|\,8\%})(1.08)$$

$$= \$600(4.6229)(1.08)$$

$$= \$600(4.9927)$$

$$= \$2,995.62$$

So the present value of the lease obligation is $2,995.62. At an interest rate of 8 percent, Denise could pay this amount on March 1, 1987, and obtain the right to use the building for the six-year period. In our theory discussion in Chapter 2, we pointed out that business transactions are recorded at the *exchange price* established in the transaction. The present value of $2,995.62 may be thought of as the exchange price established in the leasing transaction. In Chapter 17 we discuss the circumstances under which Denise Company would record an asset and a related liability at $2,995.62.

EXHIBIT 7–14   RELATIONSHIP BETWEEN TABLE D (PRESENT
VALUE OF AN ORDINARY ANNUITY) AND TABLE E
(PRESENT VALUE OF AN ANNUITY DUE)

INTEREST RATE (i) = 10%

n	TABLE D FACTORS $P_{\overline{n}|\,10\%}$	×	$(1 + i)$	=	TABLE E FACTORS $(P_{\overline{n}|\,10\%})(1.10)$
1	.9091		1.10		1.0000
2	1.7355		1.10		1.9091
3	2.4869		1.10		2.7355
4	3.1699		1.10		3.4869
5	3.7908		1.10		4.1699
6	4.3553		1.10		4.7908

Because many problems in practice require the calculation of the present value of an annuity due, we have included Table E in Appendix 7–1, which shows the factors for the present value of an annuity due. Table E is related to Table D as shown in Exhibit 7–14. Table D always can be used in problems that deal with the present value of an annuity due providing that the modifications discussed above are made. However, Table E provides these factors directly. Table E also will prove useful in solving many of the problems that appear in Chapter 17 on leases.

**DEFERRED
ANNUITIES**
The final type of annuity that we wish to discuss is called a deferred annuity. A **deferred annuity** is an annuity in which the first rent occurs after at least two interest periods have expired. A time diagram depicting a five-year ordinary annuity deferred for three periods appears below:

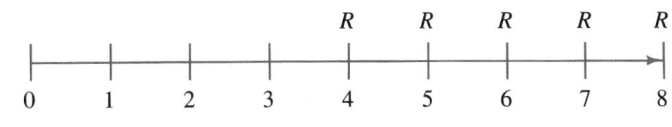

Present date

In this case, notice that four interest periods elapse before the cash flows begin. Notice also that from an end-of-period-three vantage point, the annuity appears as an ordinary annuity. To illustrate how to determine the *future value of a deferred annuity,* assume that at the end of 1987 you decide to make five $1,000 annual deposits in a savings account, the first deposit to be made at the end of 1991. How much will be in the account at the end of 1995 if the savings account earns interest at 10 percent?

The corresponding time diagram is as follows:

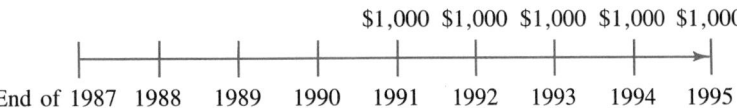

Since no deposits are made before the end of 1991, we can view the deferred annuity as the future value of a $1,000 ordinary annuity for five years at 10 percent.

$$A = \$1,000(A_{\overline{5}|10\%})$$
$$= \$1,000(6.1051)$$
$$= \$6,105.10$$

The future value of a deferred annuity is identical to the future value of an ordinary annuity.

Notice that the future value of a deferred annuity is exactly the same as the future value of an ordinary annuity. The three-year deferral has no effect on the future value, because the first cash flow does not occur until the end of 1991.

Many problems in practice deal with the *present value of a deferred annuity*. Accountants often are required to find the present value of a stream of cash flows that will begin several years in the future. Determining the present value of future retirement benefits from a pension plan is an example. As another example, assume that you wished to make five annual withdrawals of $1,000 from a savings account, the first withdrawal to be made at the end of 1991. How much must you deposit at the end of 1987 if the savings account will earn interest at 10 percent?

To find the present value of this deferred annuity, we can treat the problem in two parts as demonstrated by the time diagram and calculations below:

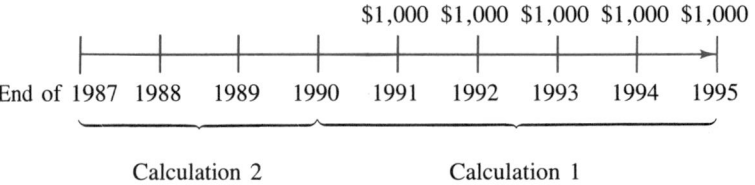

Calculations:

1. Find the present value of the ordinary annuity at the end of 1990.

    1. $P = \$1,000(P_{\overline{5}|10\%})$
           $= \$1,000(P_{\overline{5}|10\%})$
           $= \$1,000(3.7908)$
           $= \$3,790.80$

2. Consider the answer in part 1 as a single amount at the end of 1990. Find the present value of this amount at the end of 1987.

    2. $p = \$3,790.80(p_{\overline{3}|10\%})$
           $= \$3,790.80(.7513)$
           $= \$2,848.00$

If desired, the above two calculations can be combined into one calculation as follows:

$$P = \$1,000(P_{\overline{5}|10\%})(p_{\overline{3}|10\%})$$
$$= \$1,000(3.7908)(.7513)$$
$$= \$2,848.00$$

An equivalent approach for finding the present value of this deferred annuity is as follows:

1. Add fictitious rents for the first three periods.

2. Find the present value of the resulting ordinary annuity with eight rents.

3. Subtract the present value of an ordinary annuity with the three fictitious rents.

Applying these steps to our problem:

$$P = \$1,000(P_{\overline{8}|\ 10\%}) - \$1,000(P_{\overline{3}|\ 10\%})$$
$$= \$1,000[(P_{\overline{8}|10\%}) - (P_{\overline{3}|\ 10\%})]$$
$$= \$1,000(5.3349 - 2.4869)$$
$$= \$1,000(2.8480)$$
$$= \$2,848.00$$

In summary, if $2,848.00 is deposited at the end of 1987 in a savings account that earns 10 percent interest, the account will total $3,790.80 at the end of 1990, which will allow annual withdrawals of $1,000 beginning at the end of 1991. After the fifth withdrawal at the end of 1995, the savings account balance will be zero. Exhibit 7–15 is based on this problem and shows that the savings account will be exhausted at the end of 1995. Notice that the amount on deposit at the end of 1990 corresponds, except for rounding, to the first calculation in the first approach for determining the present value of the deferred annuity above.

TABLE INTERPOLATION

Interpolation is necessary when exact table factors, not found in the tables in Appendix 7–1, are required.

To this point all of our illustrations have been constructed so that the interest rate and corresponding present value and future value factors could be found exactly in the tables in Appendix 7–1. Frequently, however, interpolation must be used to find a required interest rate. If, for instance, Lance Byrd invests $3,000 today and it accumulates to $5,000 at the end of 10 years, what rate of return does he earn on his investment?

If we solve this problem by finding the future value of a single amount, we have the following:

$$a = p(a_{\overline{n}|\ i})$$

$$\$5,000 = \$3,000(a_{\overline{10}|\ i})$$

$$a_{\overline{10}|\ i} = 1.6667$$

EXHIBIT 7–15   SCHEDULE OF INTEREST AND WITHDRAWALS FOR A DEFERRED ANNUITY

YEAR	BEGINNING BALANCE	+	INTEREST AT 10%*	–	WITHDRAWALS	=	ENDING BALANCE
1988	$2,848.00		$284.80		—		$3,132.80
1989	3,132.80		313.28		—		3,446.08
1990	3,446.08		344.61		—		3,790.69
1991	3,790.69		379.07		$1,000		3,169.76
1992	3,169.76		316.98		1,000		2,486.74
1993	2,486.74		248.68		1,000		1,735.42
1994	1,735.42		173.54		1,000		908.96
1995	908.96		90.90		1,000		–0– †

* 10% times the beginning balance.

† Rounding error of $.14.

Using Table A and reading across the $n = 10$ row, we find that this future value factor of 1.6667 corresponds to a rate of interest between 5 and 6 percent. If a more precise answer is needed, we can interpolate as shown below:

INTEREST RATE	TABLE FACTOR
.05	1.6289
i = ?	1.6667
.06	1.7908

.0378   .1619

$$i = .05 + \left[\left(\frac{.0378}{.1619}\right) \times (.06 - .05)\right]$$

$$= .05 + (.23 \times .01)$$
$$= .05 + .0023$$
$$= 5.23\%$$

The factor corresponding to the desired rate is closer to 5 percent than 6 percent. Interpolation allows us to calculate how far between the two table factors the factor corresponding to the unknown rate lies. Notice that the factor of 1.6667 is approximately one-fourth (.0378/.1619) of the way between 5 percent and 6 percent. As shown, the rate of return is approximately 5.23 percent.

Now assume that on January 1, 1987, County Bank accepts a deposit of $10,000 and allows the depositor to make 15 annual withdrawals of $950, the first withdrawal to be made on December 31, 1987. What rate of interest on the remaining balance is the bank paying the depositor?

This problem requires us to find the rate of interest corresponding to the present value of an ordinary annuity:

$$P = R(P_{\overline{n}|\,i})$$
$$\$10,000 = \$950(P_{\overline{15}|\,i})$$
$$P_{\overline{15}|\,i} = 10.5263$$

Using Table D and reading across the $n = 15$ row, we find that the factor of 10.5263 corresponds to an interest rate between 4 and 5 percent. Applying the interpolation procedure, we have:

INTEREST RATE	TABLE FACTOR
.04	11.1184
i = ?	10.5263
.05	10.3797

.5921   .7387

$$i = .04 + \left[\left(\frac{.5921}{.7387}\right) \times (.05 - .04)\right]$$

$$= .04 + (.80 \times .01)$$
$$= .04 + .008$$
$$= 4.8\%$$

Notice that 10.5263 is about 80 percent (.5921/.7387) of the way between 4 percent and 5 percent. Thus the rate of interest earned on the deposit is approximately 4.8 percent.

In summary, interpolation can be used when problems require a more precise answer than the tables provide. In most situations, however, this added precision is not necessary.

Before we illustrate some additional applications of present and future value in accounting, the present and future value concepts discussed in this chapter are summarized in Exhibit 7–16. As you study the exhibit, use the time diagram to visualize the cash flows. Some problems use all of the cash flows shown in the time diagram while others use one or more.

EXHIBIT 7–16   REPRESENTATIVE PROBLEMS BASED ON
CONCEPTS OF PRESENT AND FUTURE VALUE

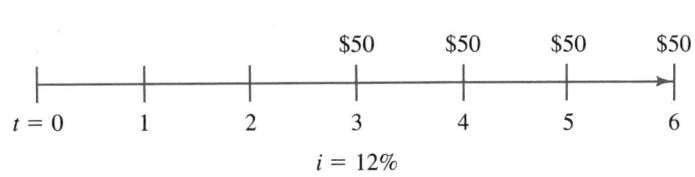

$i = 12\%$

PROBLEM	CONCEPT	SOLUTION
1. What is the future value at $t = 6$ of the $50 cash flow occurring at $t = 3$?	Future value of a single amount	$a = p(a_{\overline{3}\mid 12\%})$ $= \$50(1.4049)$ $= \$70.25$
2. What is the present value at $t = 2$ of the $50 cash flow occurring at $t = 6$?	Present value of a single amount	$p = a(p_{\overline{4}\mid 12\%})$ $= \$50(.6355)$ $= \$31.78$
3. At $t = 2$, what is the future value at the end of period 6 of the $50 cash flows occurring at $t = 3$ through 6?	Future value of an ordinary annuity	$A = R(A_{\overline{4}\mid 12\%})$ $= \$50(4.7793)$ $= \$238.97$
4. At $t = 3$, what is the future value at the end of period 6 of the $50 cash flows occurring at $t = 3$ through 5?	Future value of an annuity due	$A_D = R(A_{\overline{3}\mid 12\%})(1.12)$ $= \$50(3.7793)$ $= \$188.97$
5. What is the present value at $t = 2$ of the $50 cash flows occurring at $t = 3$ through 6?	Present value of an ordinary annuity	$P = R(P_{\overline{4}\mid 12\%})$ $= \$50(3.0373)$ $= \$151.87$
6. What is the present value at $t = 3$ of the $50 cash flows occurring at $t = 3$ through 5?	Present value of an annuity due	$P_D = R(P_{D\overline{3}\mid 12\%})$ $= \$50(2.6901)$ $= \$134.51$
7. At $t = 0$, what is the future value at the end of period 6 of the $50 cash flows occurring at $t = 3$ through 6?	Future value of a deferred annuity	$A = R(A_{\overline{4}\mid 12\%})$ $= \$50(4.7793)$ $= \$238.97$
8. What is the present value at $t = 0$ of the $50 cash flows occurring at $t = 3$ through 6?	Present value of a deferred annuity	$P = R(P_{\overline{4}\mid 12\%})$ $= \$50(3.0373)$ $= \$151.87$ and $p = \$151.87(p_{\overline{2}\mid 12\%})$ $= \$151.87(.7972)$ $= \$121.07$ or equivalently, $P = R(P_{\overline{6}\mid 12\%} - P_{\overline{2}\mid 12\%})$ $= \$50(4.1114 - 1.6901)$ $= \$50(2.4213)$ $= \$121.07$

ACCOUNTING APPLICATIONS OF PRESENT AND FUTURE VALUE

We are now ready to consider some specific accounting applications of present and future value concepts. These illustrations are by no means exhaustive, and other applications of present and future values appear throughout this text.

VALUING LONG-TERM BONDS

A company that issues a long-term bond usually incurs *two* obligations: (1) the obligation to pay interest periodically during the life of the bond, and (2) the obligation to pay the maturity value or face value of the bond at maturity. Concepts of present value are used to calculate the selling price of the bond given the face amount, the market interest rate, the stated interest rate on the bond, and the bond's maturity date.

Assume, for example, that Foster Corporation plans to issue bonds that have a maturity value of $100,000, pay annual interest at 6 percent, and mature in 10 years. What is the selling price of the bonds if at the date of sale the current market rate of interest for bonds of similar risk is *(a)* 6 percent? *(b)* 10 percent? and *(c)* 4 percent?

Intuitively, you probably suspect that if the stated interest rate on the bonds equals the market rate of 6 percent, the bonds will sell at par or at the face amount of $100,000, and you are correct. You also may suspect that if the current market rate of interest is 10 percent but the stated rate on the bonds is only 6 percent, no one will pay par value, because paying the par value will provide a rate of return each year of only 6 percent (rate of return = interest ÷ principal = $6,000 ÷ $100,000). Economic theory tells us that under these circumstances, the demand for these bonds will not support a selling price of $100,000. A buyer will pay no more than a price that provides an *effective yield* equal to the current market rate of interest. A similar statement can be made where the market rate of interest of 4 percent is less than the stated rate. In this instance, the price will be bid up over the par value until the effective yield equals the current market rate of interest.

A bond's cash flows are a combination of a single amount and an annuity.

Notice that a bond's cash flows for interest payments are an annuity and the principal payment is a single amount. The selling price of the bond can be calculated by finding the present values of the interest annuity and of the principal amount due on the bond's maturity date. The selling price calculations appear in Exhibit 7–17, and the time diagram depicting the cash flows appears on page 315.

EXHIBIT 7–17 USING PRESENT VALUE CONCEPTS IN BOND VALUATION

	SELLING PRICE OF BONDS TO PROVIDE AN EFFECTIVE YIELD OF		
	4%	6%	10%
Present value of principal:			
$100,000(.6756)*	$ 67,560		
100,000(.5584)†		$ 55,840	
100,000(.3855)‡			$38,550
plus			
Present value of interest:			
$6,000(8.1109)§	48,665		
6,000(7.3601)¶		44,160	
6,000(6.1446)**			36,868
Selling price	$116,225	$100,000	$75,418

* $p_{\overline{10}|\,4\%} = .6756$ ‡ $p_{\overline{10}|\,10\%} = .3855$ ¶ $P_{\overline{10}|\,6\%} = 7.3601$

† $p_{\overline{10}|\,6\%} = .5584$ § $P_{\overline{10}|\,4\%} = 8.1109$ ** $P_{\overline{10}|\,10\%} = 6.1446$

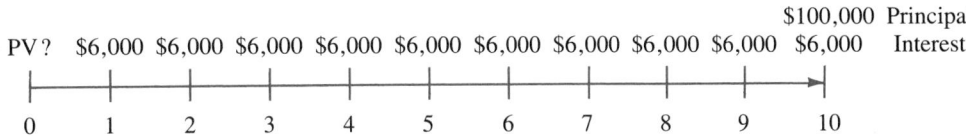

If the bonds sell at $116,225 to yield 4 percent, they are said to sell at a *premium* of $16,225 over par value. On the other hand, if the bonds sell for $75,418 to yield 10 percent, they are said to sell at a *discount* of $24,582 ($100,000 par value minus $75,418). Accounting for bond premium and discount is discussed in depth in Chapter 16.

OBLIGATIONS ARISING UNDER EMPLOYER PENSION PLANS

Many employers establish pension plans for their employees. Accountants often are required to determine the present value of pension obligations for financial reporting. To illustrate, assume that on January 1, 1987, Funding Corporation initiated a pension plan under which each of its employees would receive a pension annuity of $1,000 per year beginning one year after retirement and continuing until death. Employee A will retire at the end of 1993 and, according to mortality tables, is expected to live long enough to receive eight pension payments. What is the present value of Funding Corporation's pension obligation for employee A at the beginning of 1987 if the interest rate is 10 percent? As Exhibit 7–18 indicates, these pension payments represent a *deferred annuity*. The present value of this deferred annuity is calculated in Exhibit 7–18.

We find that $2,737.87 is the amount of Funding Corporation's pension obligation at the beginning of 1987. While pension plans are much more complicated in practice, our purpose here is to show how present value concepts apply to the determination of pension obligations. Accounting for pensions is discussed in more detail in Chapter 18.

EQUIPMENT REPLACEMENT FUNDS

Many companies periodically invest cash in an equipment replacement fund to ensure that adequate cash will be available when a fixed asset needs to be replaced. To illustrate, assume that on January 1, 1987, Firesweep acquires a piece of machinery that has an expected life of 10 years. When the machine is replaced at the end of 10 years, Firesweep expects the replacement cost to be $125,000. Firesweep wishes to establish a fund by investing cash at the end of each year beginning December 31, 1987, so that adequate funds will be available for replacement of the machine. If the investment earns 8 percent compounded annually, how much money must be invested each year?

EXHIBIT 7–18   USING PRESENT VALUE CONCEPTS TO DETERMINE PENSION OBLIGATIONS

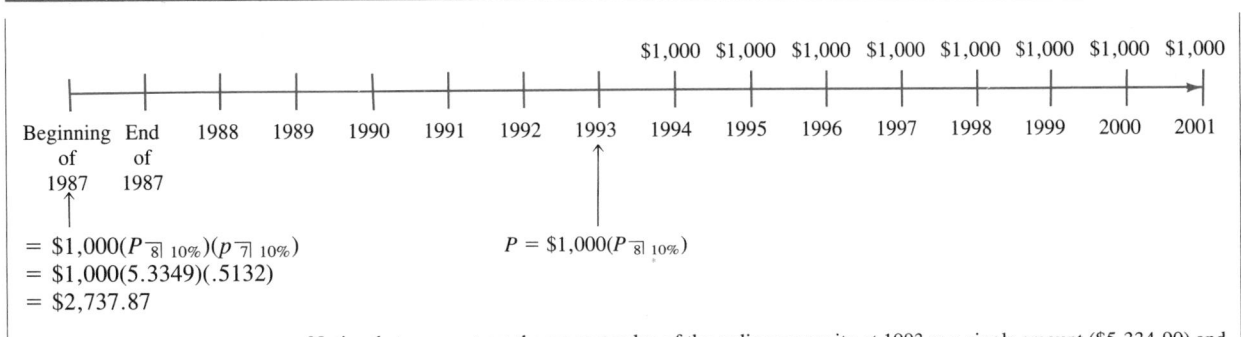

$= \$1,000(P\,\overline{\,_{8|}\,}\,_{10\%})(p\,\overline{\,_{7|}\,}\,_{10\%})$
$= \$1,000(5.3349)(.5132)$
$= \$2,737.87$

$P = \$1,000(P\,\overline{\,_{8|}\,}\,_{10\%})$

Notice that we can treat the present value of the ordinary annuity at 1993 as a single amount ($5,334.90) and then find its present value at the beginning of 1987.

This problem requires us to find the periodic amount (rent) necessary to accumulate $125,000 at the end of 10 years. Since $125,000 is a future value and the deposits are to be made at the end of each year, we must calculate the periodic rents that correspond to the future value of an ordinary annuity:

$$A = R(A_{\overline{10}|\,8\%})$$

$$\$125,000 = R(14.4866)$$

$$R = \$8,628.66$$

Therefore, if Firesweep invests $8,628.66 each year in an investment which earns 8 percent each year, the company will have $125,000 at the end of 10 years to replace the machine.

LEASE OBLIGATIONS

Many companies lease rather than purchase property for use in their business. For example, on July 1, 1987, Sneaky, Inc., signed a 25-year noncancelable lease agreement with Royalty Real Estate for a building. The lease term covered the remaining life of the building. The annual lease payments were $12,000 payable each July 1, and the first lease payment was due July 1, 1987. What is the present value of the lease obligation at a discount rate of 10 percent?

Because the first lease payment is due on the date of the lease agreement, we are calculating the present value of an annuity due:

$$P_D = R(P_{\overline{n}|\,i})(1 + i)$$
$$= \$12,000(P_{\overline{25}|\,10\%})(1.10)$$
$$= \$12,000(9.9847)$$
$$= \$119,816$$

The present value of the lease obligation is $119,816. Many accountants and users believe that present values of lease obligations should be disclosed on financial statements in order to satisfy the financial reporting objectives discussed in Chapter 2. The $119,816 also may be thought of as the cash equivalent price of the building. Disclosure of this information may increase comparability between Sneaky, Inc., and other companies that purchase their buildings outright. This leasing issue and others are discussed in Chapter 17.

SUMMARY OF IMPORTANT TOPICS AND CONCEPT APPLICATIONS

1. Present and future value concepts have many theoretical and practical applications in accounting.
2. Four basic concepts of present and future value are:
   a) The **future value of a single amount**—the amount to which a single sum will accumulate at a future date, given an interest rate.
   b) The **present value of a single amount**—the worth today of a single amount to be paid or received at some future date, given an interest (discount) rate.
   c) The **future value of an ordinary annuity**—the amount to which a series of equal, end-of-period cash flows (rents) will accumulate at a future date, given an interest rate.

d) The **present value of an ordinary annuity**—the worth today of a series of equal, end-of-period future cash flows (rents), given an interest (discount) rate.

Tables have been developed to provide present and future value factors for these concepts. Appendix 7–1 contains a set of these tables.

3. An **annuity due** differs from an ordinary annuity in that the cash flows in an annuity due occur at the beginning of the period, rather than at the end of the period. The table factors for ordinary annuities can be converted to factors for an annuity due by compounding the table factors for one interest period at the given interest rate.

4. A **deferred annuity** is one in which the first rent occurs after at least two interest periods have expired.

APPENDIX 7–1

PRESENT AND FUTURE VALUE TABLES

The tables used to determine the future and present values of 1, the future and present values of an ordinary annuity of 1, and the present value of an annuity due of 1 are presented on pages 318–22.

TABLE A — FUTURE VALUE OF 1 (a)

$$a = a_{\overline{n}|i} = (1 + i)^n$$

This table shows the compound amount of \$1 at various interest rates and for various time periods. The table may be used to find the future value of *any* dollar amount by multiplying the dollar amount by the factor below corresponding to the appropriate interest rate (i) and number of periods (n).

i

n	1%	1.5%	2%	2.5%	3%	4%	5%	6%	8%	10%	12%	16%	20%
1	1.0100	1.0150	1.0200	1.0250	1.0300	1.0400	1.0500	1.0600	1.0800	1.1000	1.1200	1.1600	1.2000
2	1.0201	1.0302	1.0404	1.0506	1.0609	1.0816	1.1025	1.1236	1.1664	1.2100	1.2544	1.3456	1.4400
3	1.0303	1.0457	1.0612	1.0769	1.0927	1.1249	1.1576	1.1910	1.2597	1.3310	1.4049	1.5609	1.7280
4	1.0406	1.0614	1.0824	1.1038	1.1255	1.1699	1.2155	1.2625	1.3605	1.4641	1.5735	1.8106	2.0736
5	1.0510	1.0773	1.1041	1.1314	1.1593	1.2167	1.2763	1.3382	1.4693	1.6105	1.7623	2.1003	2.4883
6	1.0615	1.0934	1.1262	1.1597	1.1941	1.2653	1.3401	1.4185	1.5869	1.7716	1.9738	2.4364	2.9860
7	1.0721	1.1098	1.1487	1.1887	1.2299	1.3159	1.4071	1.5036	1.7138	1.9487	2.2107	2.8262	3.5832
8	1.0829	1.1265	1.1717	1.2184	1.2668	1.3686	1.4775	1.5938	1.8509	2.1436	2.4760	3.2784	4.2998
9	1.0937	1.1434	1.1951	1.2489	1.3048	1.4233	1.5513	1.6895	1.9990	2.3579	2.7731	3.8030	5.1598
10	1.1046	1.1605	1.2190	1.2801	1.3439	1.4802	1.6289	1.7908	2.1589	2.5937	3.1058	4.4114	6.1917
11	1.1157	1.1779	1.2434	1.3121	1.3842	1.5395	1.7103	1.8983	2.3316	2.8531	3.4786	5.1173	7.4301
12	1.1268	1.1956	1.2682	1.3449	1.4258	1.6010	1.7959	2.0122	2.5182	3.1384	3.8960	5.9360	8.9161
13	1.1381	1.2136	1.2936	1.3785	1.4685	1.6651	1.8856	2.1329	2.7196	3.4523	4.3635	6.8858	10.6993
14	1.1495	1.2318	1.3195	1.4130	1.5126	1.7317	1.9799	2.2609	2.9372	3.7975	4.8871	7.9875	12.8392
15	1.1610	1.2502	1.3459	1.4483	1.5580	1.8009	2.0789	2.3966	3.1722	4.1772	5.4736	9.2655	15.4070
16	1.1726	1.2690	1.3728	1.4845	1.6047	1.8730	2.1829	2.5404	3.4259	4.5950	6.1304	10.7480	18.4884
17	1.1843	1.2880	1.4002	1.5216	1.6528	1.9479	2.2920	2.6928	3.7000	5.0545	6.8660	12.4677	22.1861
18	1.1961	1.3073	1.4282	1.5597	1.7024	2.0258	2.4066	2.8543	3.9960	5.5599	7.6900	14.4625	26.6233
19	1.2081	1.3270	1.4568	1.5987	1.7535	2.1068	2.5270	3.0256	4.3157	6.1159	8.6128	16.7765	31.9480
20	1.2202	1.3469	1.4859	1.6386	1.8061	2.1911	2.6533	3.2071	4.6610	6.7275	9.6463	19.4608	38.3376
21	1.2324	1.3671	1.5157	1.6796	1.8603	2.2788	2.7860	3.3996	5.0338	7.4002	10.8039	22.5745	46.0051
22	1.2447	1.3876	1.5460	1.7216	1.9161	2.3699	2.9253	3.6035	5.4365	8.1403	12.1003	26.1864	55.2061
23	1.2572	1.4084	1.5769	1.7646	1.9736	2.4647	3.0715	3.8198	5.8715	8.9543	13.5523	30.3762	66.2474
24	1.2697	1.4295	1.6084	1.8087	2.0328	2.5633	3.2251	4.0489	6.3412	9.8497	15.1786	35.2364	79.4969
25	1.2824	1.4509	1.6406	1.8539	2.0938	2.6658	3.3864	4.2919	6.8485	10.8347	17.0001	40.8742	95.3962
30	1.3478	1.5631	1.8114	2.0976	2.4273	3.2434	4.3219	5.7435	10.0627	17.4494	29.9599	85.8499	237.3763
50	1.6446	2.1052	2.6916	3.4371	4.3839	7.1067	11.4674	18.4202	46.9016	117.3909	289.0022	1670.7038	9100.4382

PRESENT VALUE OF 1 (p)

This table shows the present value of $1 discounted at various rates of interest and for various time periods. The table may be used to find the present value of *any* future dollar amount by multiplying the future dollar amount by the table factor corresponding to the appropriate interest rate (i) and number of periods (n).

$$p = p_{\overline{n}|i} = \frac{1}{(1+i)^n}$$

n	1%	1.5%	2%	2.5%	3%	4%	5%	6%	8%	10%	12%	16%	20%
1	0.9901	0.9852	0.9804	0.9756	0.9709	0.9615	0.9524	0.9434	0.9259	0.9091	0.8929	0.8621	0.8333
2	0.9803	0.9707	0.9612	0.9518	0.9426	0.9246	0.9070	0.8900	0.8573	0.8264	0.7972	0.7432	0.6944
3	0.9706	0.9563	0.9423	0.9286	0.9151	0.8890	0.8638	0.8396	0.7938	0.7513	0.7118	0.6407	0.5787
4	0.9610	0.9422	0.9238	0.9060	0.8885	0.8548	0.8227	0.7921	0.7350	0.6830	0.6355	0.5523	0.4823
5	0.9515	0.9283	0.9057	0.8839	0.8626	0.8219	0.7835	0.7473	0.6806	0.6209	0.5674	0.4761	0.4019
6	0.9420	0.9145	0.8880	0.8623	0.8375	0.7903	0.7462	0.7050	0.6302	0.5645	0.5066	0.4104	0.3349
7	0.9327	0.9010	0.8706	0.8413	0.8131	0.7599	0.7107	0.6651	0.5835	0.5132	0.4523	0.3538	0.2791
8	0.9235	0.8877	0.8535	0.8207	0.7894	0.7307	0.6768	0.6274	0.5403	0.4665	0.4039	0.3050	0.2326
9	0.9143	0.8746	0.8368	0.8007	0.7664	0.7026	0.6446	0.5919	0.5002	0.4241	0.3606	0.2630	0.1938
10	0.9053	0.8617	0.8203	0.7812	0.7441	0.6756	0.6139	0.5584	0.4632	0.3855	0.3220	0.2267	0.1615
11	0.8963	0.8489	0.8043	0.7621	0.7224	0.6496	0.5847	0.5268	0.4289	0.3505	0.2875	0.1954	0.1346
12	0.8874	0.8364	0.7885	0.7436	0.7014	0.6246	0.5568	0.4970	0.3971	0.3186	0.2567	0.1685	0.1122
13	0.8787	0.8240	0.7730	0.7254	0.6810	0.6006	0.5303	0.4688	0.3677	0.2897	0.2292	0.1452	0.0935
14	0.8700	0.8118	0.7579	0.7077	0.6611	0.5775	0.5051	0.4423	0.3405	0.2633	0.2046	0.1252	0.0779
15	0.8613	0.7999	0.7430	0.6905	0.6419	0.5553	0.4810	0.4173	0.3152	0.2394	0.1827	0.1079	0.0649
16	0.8528	0.7880	0.7284	0.6736	0.6232	0.5339	0.4581	0.3936	0.2919	0.2176	0.1631	0.0930	0.0541
17	0.8444	0.7764	0.7142	0.6572	0.6050	0.5134	0.4363	0.3714	0.2703	0.1978	0.1456	0.0802	0.0451
18	0.8360	0.7649	0.7002	0.6412	0.5874	0.4936	0.4155	0.3503	0.2502	0.1799	0.1300	0.0691	0.0376
19	0.8277	0.7536	0.6864	0.6255	0.5703	0.4746	0.3957	0.3305	0.2317	0.1635	0.1161	0.0596	0.0313
20	0.8195	0.7425	0.6730	0.6103	0.5537	0.4564	0.3769	0.3118	0.2145	0.1486	0.1037	0.0514	0.0261
21	0.8114	0.7315	0.6598	0.5954	0.5375	0.4388	0.3589	0.2942	0.1987	0.1351	0.0926	0.0443	0.0217
22	0.8034	0.7207	0.6468	0.5809	0.5219	0.4220	0.3418	0.2775	0.1839	0.1228	0.0826	0.0382	0.0181
23	0.7954	0.7100	0.6342	0.5667	0.5067	0.4057	0.3256	0.2618	0.1703	0.1117	0.0738	0.0329	0.0151
24	0.7876	0.6995	0.6217	0.5529	0.4919	0.3901	0.3101	0.2470	0.1577	0.1015	0.0659	0.0284	0.0126
25	0.7798	0.6892	0.6095	0.5394	0.4776	0.3751	0.2953	0.2330	0.1460	0.0923	0.0588	0.0245	0.0105
30	0.7419	0.6398	0.5521	0.4767	0.4120	0.3083	0.2314	0.1741	0.0994	0.0573	0.0334	0.0116	0.0042
50	0.6080	0.4750	0.3715	0.2909	0.2281	0.1407	0.0872	0.0543	0.0213	0.0085	0.0035	0.0006	0.0001

TABLE C

FUTURE VALUE OF AN ORDINARY ANNUITY OF 1 (A)

$$A = A_{\overline{n}|i} = \frac{(1+i)^n - 1}{i}$$

This table shows the future value of an ordinary annuity of $1 at various rates of interest and for various rents. The table may be used to find the future value of an ordinary annuity of *any* dollar amount by multiplying the dollar amount of the rents by the factor corresponding to the appropriate interest rate (i) and number of rents (n).

n	1%	1.5%	2%	2.5%	3%	4%	5%	6%	8%	10%	12%	16%	20%
1	1.0000	1.0000	1.0000	1.0000	1.0000	1.0000	1.0000	1.0000	1.0000	1.0000	1.0000	1.0000	1.0000
2	2.0100	2.0150	2.0200	2.0250	2.0300	2.0400	2.0500	2.0600	2.0800	2.1000	2.1200	2.1600	2.2000
3	3.0301	3.0452	3.0604	3.0756	3.0909	3.1216	3.1525	3.1836	3.2464	3.3100	3.3744	3.5056	3.6400
4	4.0604	4.0909	4.1216	4.1525	4.1836	4.2465	4.3101	4.3746	4.5061	4.6410	4.7793	5.0665	5.3680
5	5.1010	5.1523	5.2040	5.2563	5.3091	5.4163	5.5256	5.6371	5.8666	6.1051	6.3528	6.8771	7.4416
6	6.1520	6.2296	6.3081	6.3877	6.4684	6.6330	6.8019	6.9753	7.3359	7.7156	8.1152	8.9775	9.9299
7	7.2135	7.3230	7.4343	7.5474	7.6625	7.8983	8.1420	8.3938	8.9228	9.4872	10.0890	11.4139	12.9159
8	8.2857	8.4328	8.5830	8.7361	8.8923	9.2142	9.5491	9.8975	10.6366	11.4359	12.2997	14.2401	16.4991
9	9.3685	9.5593	9.7546	9.9545	10.1591	10.5828	11.0266	11.4913	12.4876	13.5795	14.7757	17.5185	20.7989
10	10.4622	10.7027	10.9497	11.2034	11.4639	12.0061	12.5779	13.1808	14.4866	15.9374	17.5487	21.3215	25.9587
11	11.5668	11.8633	12.1687	12.4835	12.8078	13.4864	14.2068	14.9716	16.6455	18.5312	20.6546	25.7329	32.1504
12	12.6825	13.0412	13.4121	13.7956	14.1920	15.0258	15.9171	16.8699	18.9771	21.3843	24.1331	30.8502	39.5805
13	13.8093	14.2368	14.6803	15.1404	15.6178	16.6268	17.7130	18.8821	21.4953	24.5227	28.0291	36.7862	48.4966
14	14.9474	15.4504	15.9739	16.5190	17.0863	18.2919	19.5986	21.0151	24.2149	27.9750	32.3926	43.6720	59.1959
15	16.0969	16.6821	17.2934	17.9319	18.5989	20.0236	21.5786	23.2760	27.1521	31.7725	37.2797	51.6595	72.0351
16	17.2579	17.9324	18.6393	19.3802	20.1569	21.8245	23.6575	25.6725	30.3243	35.9497	42.7533	60.9250	87.4421
17	18.4304	19.2014	20.0121	20.8647	21.7616	23.6975	25.8404	28.2129	33.7502	40.5447	48.8837	71.6730	105.9306
18	19.6148	20.4894	21.4123	22.3864	23.4144	25.6454	28.1324	30.9057	37.4502	45.5992	55.7497	84.1407	128.1167
19	20.8109	21.7967	22.8406	23.9460	25.1169	27.6712	30.5390	33.7600	41.4463	51.1591	63.4397	98.6032	154.7400
20	22.0190	23.1237	24.2974	25.5447	26.8704	29.7781	33.0660	36.7856	45.7620	57.2750	72.0524	115.3797	186.6880
21	23.2392	24.4705	25.7833	27.1833	28.6765	31.9692	35.7193	39.9927	50.4229	64.0025	81.6987	134.8405	225.0256
22	24.4716	25.8376	27.2990	28.8629	30.5368	34.2480	38.5052	43.3923	55.4568	71.4027	92.5026	157.4150	271.0307
23	25.7163	27.2251	28.8450	30.5844	32.4529	36.6179	41.4305	46.9958	60.8933	79.5430	104.6029	183.6014	326.2369
24	26.9735	28.6335	30.4219	32.3490	34.4265	39.0826	44.5020	50.8156	66.7648	88.4973	118.1552	213.9776	392.4842
25	28.2432	30.0630	32.0303	34.1578	36.4593	41.6459	47.7271	54.8645	73.1059	98.3471	133.3339	249.2140	471.9811
30	34.7849	37.5387	40.5681	43.9027	47.5754	56.0849	66.4389	79.0582	113.2832	164.4940	241.3327	530.3117	1181.8816
50	64.4632	73.6828	84.5794	97.4844	112.7969	152.6671	209.3480	290.3359	573.7702	1163.9085	2400.0183	10435.6488	45497.1910

TABLE D

PRESENT VALUE OF AN ORDINARY ANNUITY OF 1 (P)

This table shows the present value of an ordinary annuity of $1 at various interest rates and for various rents. The table may be used to find the present value of an ordinary annuity of *any* dollar amount by multiplying the dollar amounts of the rents by the factor corresponding to the appropriate interest rate (i) and number of rents (n).

$$P = P_{\overline{n}|i} = \frac{1 - \dfrac{1}{(1+i)^n}}{i}$$

n	1%	1.5%	2%	2.5%	3%	4%	5%	6%	8%	10%	12%	16%	20%
1	0.9901	0.9852	0.9804	0.9756	0.9709	0.9615	0.9524	0.9434	0.9259	0.9091	0.8929	0.8621	0.8333
2	1.9704	1.9559	1.9416	1.9274	1.9135	1.8861	1.8594	1.8334	1.7833	1.7355	1.6901	1.6052	1.5278
3	2.9410	2.9122	2.8839	2.8560	2.8286	2.7751	2.7232	2.6730	2.5771	2.4869	2.4018	2.2459	2.1065
4	3.9020	3.8544	3.8077	3.7620	3.7171	3.6299	3.5460	3.4651	3.3121	3.1699	3.0373	2.7982	2.5887
5	4.8534	4.7826	4.7135	4.6458	4.5797	4.4518	4.3295	4.2124	3.9927	3.7908	3.6048	3.2743	2.9906
6	5.7955	5.6972	5.6014	5.5081	5.4172	5.2421	5.0757	4.9173	4.6229	4.3553	4.1114	3.6847	3.3755
7	6.7282	6.5982	6.4720	6.3494	6.2303	6.0021	5.7864	5.5824	5.2064	4.8684	4.5638	4.0386	3.6046
8	7.6517	7.4859	7.3255	7.1701	7.0197	6.7327	6.4632	6.2098	5.7466	5.3349	4.9676	4.3436	3.8372
9	8.5660	8.3605	8.1622	7.9709	7.7861	7.4353	7.1078	6.8017	6.2469	5.7590	5.3283	4.6065	4.0310
10	9.4713	9.2222	8.9826	8.7521	8.5302	8.1109	7.7217	7.3601	6.7101	6.1446	5.6502	4.8332	4.1925
11	10.3676	10.0711	9.7868	9.5142	9.2526	8.7605	8.3064	7.8869	7.1390	6.4951	5.9377	5.0286	4.3271
12	11.2551	10.9075	10.5753	10.2578	9.9540	9.3851	8.8633	8.3838	7.5361	6.8137	6.1944	5.1971	4.4392
13	12.1337	11.7315	11.3484	10.9832	10.6350	9.9856	9.3936	8.8527	7.9038	7.1034	6.4235	5.3423	4.5327
14	13.0037	12.5434	12.1063	11.6909	11.2961	10.5631	9.8986	9.2950	8.2442	7.3667	6.6282	5.4675	4.6106
15	13.8651	13.3432	12.8493	12.3814	11.9379	11.1184	10.3797	9.7122	8.5595	7.6061	6.8109	5.5755	4.6755
16	14.7179	14.1313	13.5777	13.0550	12.5611	11.6523	10.8378	10.1059	8.8514	7.8237	6.9740	5.6685	4.7296
17	15.5623	14.9077	14.2919	13.7122	13.1661	12.1657	11.2741	10.4773	9.1216	8.0216	7.1196	5.7487	4.7746
18	16.3983	15.6726	14.9920	14.3534	13.7535	12.6593	11.6896	10.8276	9.3719	8.2014	7.2497	5.8178	4.8122
19	17.2260	16.4262	15.6785	14.9789	14.3238	13.1339	12.0853	11.1581	9.6036	8.3649	7.3658	5.8775	4.8435
20	18.0456	17.1686	16.3514	15.5892	14.8775	13.5903	12.4622	11.4699	9.8181	8.5136	7.4694	5.9288	4.8696
21	18.8570	17.9001	17.0112	16.1846	15.4150	14.0292	12.8212	11.7641	10.0168	8.6487	7.5620	5.9731	4.8913
22	19.6604	18.6208	17.6581	16.7654	15.9369	14.4511	13.1630	12.0416	10.2007	8.7715	7.6446	6.0113	4.9094
23	20.4558	19.3309	18.2922	17.3321	16.4436	14.8568	13.4886	12.3034	10.3711	8.8832	7.7184	6.0442	4.9245
24	21.2434	20.0304	18.9139	17.8850	16.9355	15.2470	13.7986	12.5504	10.5288	8.9847	7.7843	6.0726	4.9371
25	22.0232	20.7196	19.5235	18.4244	17.4132	15.6221	14.0939	12.7834	10.6748	9.0770	7.8431	6.0971	4.9476
30	25.8077	24.0158	22.3965	20.9303	19.6004	17.2920	15.3725	13.7648	11.2578	9.4269	8.0552	6.1772	4.9789
50	39.1961	34.9997	31.4236	28.3623	25.7298	21.4822	18.2559	15.7619	12.2335	9.9148	8.3045	6.2463	4.9995

TABLE E

PRESENT VALUE OF AN ANNUITY DUE OF $1 ($P_D$)

This table shows the present value of an annuity due of $1 at various rates of interest and for various numbers of rents. The table may be used to find the present value of an annuity due of *any* dollar amount by multiplying the dollar amount of the rents by the appropriate factors corresponding to the interest rate (i) and number of rents (n).

$$P_D = P_{D\,\overline{n}|i} = (P_{\overline{n}|i})(1 + i) = \left[\frac{1 - \frac{1}{(1+i)^n}}{i} \right][1 + i]$$

n	1%	1.5%	2%	2.5%	3%	4%	5%	6%	8%	10%	12%	16%	20%
1	1.0000	1.0000	1.0000	1.0000	1.0000	1.0000	1.0000	1.0000	1.0000	1.0000	1.0000	1.0000	1.0000
2	1.9901	1.9852	1.9804	1.9756	1.9709	1.9615	1.9524	1.9434	1.9259	1.9091	1.8929	1.8621	1.8333
3	2.9704	2.9559	2.9416	2.9274	2.9135	2.8861	2.8594	2.8334	2.7833	2.7355	2.6901	2.6052	2.5278
4	3.9410	3.9122	3.8839	3.8560	3.8286	3.7751	3.7232	3.6730	3.5771	3.4869	3.4018	3.2459	3.1065
5	4.9020	4.8544	4.8077	4.7620	4.7171	4.6299	4.5460	4.4651	4.3121	4.1699	4.0373	3.7982	3.5887
6	5.8534	5.7826	5.7135	5.6458	5.5797	5.4518	5.3295	5.2124	4.9927	4.7908	4.6048	4.2743	3.9906
7	6.7955	6.6972	6.6014	6.5081	6.4172	6.2421	6.0757	5.9173	5.6229	5.3553	5.1114	4.6847	4.3255
8	7.7282	7.5982	7.4720	7.3494	7.2303	7.0021	6.7864	6.5824	6.2064	5.8684	5.5638	5.0386	4.6046
9	8.6517	8.4859	8.3255	8.1701	8.0197	7.7327	7.4632	7.2098	6.7466	6.3349	5.9676	5.3436	4.8372
10	9.5660	9.3605	9.1622	8.9709	8.7861	8.4353	8.1078	7.8017	7.2469	6.7590	6.3283	5.6065	5.0310
11	10.4713	10.2222	9.9826	9.7521	9.5302	9.1109	8.7217	8.3601	7.7101	7.1446	6.6502	5.8332	5.1925
12	11.3676	11.0711	10.7869	10.5142	10.2526	9.7605	9.3064	8.8869	8.1390	7.4951	6.9377	6.0286	5.3271
13	12.2551	11.9075	11.5753	11.2578	10.9540	10.3851	9.8633	9.3838	8.5361	7.8137	7.1944	6.1971	5.4392
14	13.1337	12.7315	12.3484	11.9832	11.6350	10.9857	10.3936	9.8527	8.9038	8.1034	7.4235	6.3423	5.5327
15	14.0037	13.5434	13.1063	12.6909	12.2961	11.5631	10.8986	10.2950	9.2442	8.3667	7.6282	6.4675	5.6106
16	14.8651	14.3432	13.8493	13.3814	12.9379	12.1184	11.3797	10.7123	9.5595	8.6061	7.8109	6.5755	5.6755
17	15.7179	15.1313	14.5777	14.0550	13.5611	12.6523	11.8378	11.1059	9.8514	8.8237	7.9740	6.6685	5.7296
18	16.5623	15.9077	15.2919	14.7122	14.1661	13.1657	12.2741	11.4773	10.1216	9.0216	8.1196	6.7487	5.7746
19	17.3983	16.6726	15.9920	15.3534	14.7535	13.6593	12.6896	11.8276	10.3719	9.2014	8.2497	6.8178	5.8122
20	18.2260	17.4262	16.6785	15.9789	15.3238	14.1339	13.0853	12.1581	10.6036	9.3649	8.3658	6.8775	5.8435
21	19.0456	18.1686	17.3514	16.5892	15.8775	14.5903	13.4622	12.4699	10.8182	9.5136	8.4694	6.9288	5.8696
22	19.8570	18.9001	18.0112	17.1846	16.4150	15.0292	13.8212	12.7641	11.0168	9.6487	8.5620	6.9731	5.8913
23	20.6604	19.6208	18.6581	17.7654	16.9369	15.4511	14.1630	13.0416	11.2007	9.7715	8.6446	7.0113	5.9094
24	21.4558	20.3309	19.2922	18.3321	17.4436	15.8568	14.4886	13.3034	11.3711	9.8832	8.7184	7.0442	5.9245
25	22.2434	21.0304	19.9139	18.8850	17.9355	16.2470	14.7986	13.5504	11.5288	9.9847	8.7843	7.0726	5.9371
30	26.0658	24.3761	22.8444	21.4536	20.1885	17.9837	16.1411	14.5907	12.1584	10.3696	9.0218	7.1656	5.9747
50	39.5881	35.5247	32.0521	29.0714	26.5017	22.3415	19.1687	16.7076	13.2122	10.9063	9.3010	7.2457	5.9993

QUESTIONS

Q7-1. How are present and future value concepts used by the professional accountant?

Q7-2. Define interest.

Q7-3. Distinguish between simple interest and compound interest, and between interest and discount.

Q7-4. **A)** Since interest rates usually are stated as annual rates, what adjustments must be made when compounding or discounting occurs more often than once each year?

B) Given an interest rate of 12 percent, compute the interest rate per period and the number of compounding periods for each of the following situations:

    1. Semiannual compounding for 4 years.

    2. Annual compounding for 10 years.

    3. Quarterly compounding for 6 years.

    4. Monthly compounding for 12 years.

Q7-5. **A)** Define an annuity.

B) Distinguish between an ordinary annuity and an annuity due.

Q7-6. Construct a time diagram for the present value of an ordinary annuity of cash flows of $R for three years if the interest rate is 10 percent compounded semiannually.

Q7-7. **A)** How is the future value of an ordinary annuity related to the future value of a single amount?

B) How is the present value of an ordinary annuity related to the present value of a single amount?

C) How is the future value of a single amount related to the present value of a single amount?

Q7-8. What is a deferred annuity?

Q7-9. **A)** What formula modification must be made to use Table C to find future values of annuities due?

B) What formula modification must be made to use Table D to find present values of annuities due?

Q7-10. For each of the lettered amounts, select the numbered concept that applies to the problem and name the table from Appendix 7–1 that should be used to solve the problem.

    1. Future value of a single amount.   **5.** Future value of an annuity due.

    2. Present value of a single amount.   **6.** Present value of an annuity due.

    3. Future value of an ordinary annuity.   **7.** Future value of a deferred annuity.

    4. Present value of an ordinary annuity.   **8.** Present value of a deferred annuity.

    a) The amount owed today if a debt of $x is due in 10 years.

    b) The amount that will accumulate if $x is deposited at the beginning of each year for 10 years.

    c) The annual periodic payment required to liquidate a debt due today. The payments will be made at the end of each year and will be made for 10 years.

    d) The amount to which $x deposited today will accumulate in 15 years.

    e) The present value of 10 semiannual payments of $x, the first of which is to be received in 2 1/2 years.

    f) The annual periodic deposit required to accumulate $x at the end of 15 years. The deposits are made at the beginning of each year, beginning today.

    g) Same as *f,* except that the first payment is made at the beginning of the fourth year.

    h) The amount of proceeds if an interest-bearing bond maturing in 10 years is sold today.

    i) The amount of proceeds if a noninterest-bearing note maturing in five years is issued today.

    j) The amount required to liquidate a debt 10 years before maturity. The debt is due 15 years from today.

Q7-11. Using Appendix 7–1, find the appropriate table factors for the following present value and future value concepts, where i = annual interest rate and n = number of years.

1. Present value of 1 when $i = 10$ percent compounded annually, $n = 10$.

2. Future value of 1 when $i = 12$ percent compounded quarterly, $n = 4$.

3. Future value of an ordinary annuity when $i = 10$ percent compounded semiannually, $n = 10$.

4. Present value of annuity due when $i = 6$ percent compounded annually, $n = 10$.

5. Present value of an ordinary annuity when $i = 12$ percent compounded monthly, $n = 2$.

6. Future value of annuity due when $i = 8$ percent compounded annually, $n = 15$.

7. Present value of a deferred annuity when $i = 6$ percent compounded annually, $n = 10$. The first cash flow occurs at the end of year 3.

EXERCISES

E7-1. FUTURE VALUES AND PRESENT VALUES OF SINGLE AMOUNTS

A) Calculate the future value of the following amounts for the indicated interest rates and years:

	AMOUNT INVESTED	i	COMPOUNDED	YEARS
1.	$1,200	10%	Semiannually	5
2.	3,600	8	Annually	4
3.	900	12	Quarterly	4

B) Calculate the present value of the following future amounts for the indicated interest rates and years:

	FUTURE VALUE	i	COMPOUNDED	YEARS
1.	$15,000	6%	Annually	8
2.	7,000	8	Semiannually	5
3.	12,000	12	Monthly	2

E7-2. FUTURE VALUES AND PRESENT VALUES OF ANNUITIES

A) Calculate the future value of the following ordinary annuities at the indicated interest rates and interest periods:

	PERIODIC CASH FLOW	i	COMPOUNDED	YEARS
1.	$400	10%	Annually	4
2.	600	12	Quarterly	4
3.	800	10	Semiannually	5

B) Use the same instructions as in part A but now assume that the annuities are annuities due.

C) Calculate the present value of the following ordinary annuities at the indicated interest rates and interest periods:

	PERIODIC CASH FLOW	i	COMPOUNDED	YEARS
1.	$5,000	4%	Annually	10
2.	5,850	8	Semiannually	6
3.	5,850	8	Quarterly	4

D) Use the same instructions as in part C but now assume that the annuities are annuities due.

E7-3. FINDING UNKNOWN VARIABLES RELATED TO PRESENT AND FUTURE VALUES   For each situation below, all of which deal with single amounts, find the unknown variable (x). Assume that interest is compounded annually.

	FUTURE VALUE	PRESENT VALUE	i	n (YEARS)
1.	$24,000	x	10%	10
2.	16,000	$ 4,988.80	x	20
3.	31,722	10,000.00	8	x
4.	16,098	8,000.00	x	12
5.	25,000	17,624.00	6	x

E7-4. FINDING UNKNOWN VARIABLES RELATED TO PRESENT AND FUTURE VALUES   For each situation below, all of which deal with annuities, find the unknown variable (x). Assume that each cash flow occurs at the end of each year and that interest is compounded annually. Do not interpolate.

	FUTURE VALUE (A) OR PRESENT VALUE (P)	R	i	n
1.	$12,000 (A)	x	8%	6
2.	10,000 (P)	x	10	15
3.	8,000 (A)	$1,500	4	x
4.	18,000 (A)	1,000	x	13
5.	16,500 (P)	2,000	10	x
6.	20,000 (P)	2,000	x	24

E7-5. SINGLE AMOUNTS

A) On December 25, 1987, Ms. Christmas received for her twenty-first birthday the sum of $10,000, the result of an investment her father made on the date of her birth.

REQUIRED

Calculate the amount of the original investment at an earnings rate of 10 percent compounded annually.

B) On January 1, 1988, Mr. New Year deposited $3,500 in a savings account that earns interest at the rate of 12 percent compounded semiannually.

REQUIRED

Calculate the balance in the account at the end of 1994.

E7-6. ANNUITIES   Mr. Zee wishes to accumulate $100,000 by investing $10,000 at the beginning of each year in a sinking fund that yields 10 percent compounded annually.

REQUIRED

1. Find the year in which the sinking fund will reach $100,000.

2. As you discovered in part 1, fewer than 15 payments will be required for the fund to reach $100,000. Therefore, calculate the annuity payments that Mr. Zee could make under this plan to ensure that he had $100,000 at the end of the fifteenth year.

(CGAA, adapted)

E7-7. VALUATION OF BONDS   Patrick Company is planning to issue $400,000 (par value) of bonds that mature in 12 years and pay interest at the rate of 8 percent at the end of each year.

REQUIRED

Find the selling price of the bonds at the following market (effective) rates of interest:

1. 4%

2. 10%

E7-8. ANNUITIES—PRESENT AND FUTURE VALUES   On March 1, 1987, Mr. Keys makes the first of 10 equal annual deposits in a sinking fund. Beginning on March 1, 2003, Mr. Keys will make the first of 10 annual withdrawals of $1,000 from the fund, after which the fund will be exhausted. The interest rate is 8 percent compounded annually.

REQUIRED

Calculate the amount of the annual deposits.   (CGAA, adapted)

E7-9. CONCEPTS OF PRESENT AND FUTURE VALUE   For each amount below, state which present or future value concept applies, then solve the problem.

1. The amount to which $1,000 will accumulate in five years at 6 percent compounded annually.

2. The present value of $1,500 due in eight years at 6 percent, compounded semiannually.

3. The present value of an ordinary annuity of $500 every six months for 10 years at 8 percent, compounded semiannually.

4. The amount of an annuity due of $600 every three months for four years at 12 percent, compounded quarterly.

5. The present value of an ordinary annuity of $3,000 per year for 15 years at 3 percent, compounded annually.

6. The present value of $1,000 due in six years at 8 percent, compounded quarterly.

E7-10. INTEREST SCHEDULES FOR ANNUITIES

A) Calculate the semiannual, end-of-period deposit necessary to accumulate a $20,000 fund at the end of six years, if the fund earns interest at the annual rate of 8 percent compounded semiannually. Prepare a schedule showing the accumulation for the six-year period.

B) If $10,000 is invested at the beginning of year 1 at 6 percent, what amount can be withdrawn at the end of each year for five years? Construct a schedule showing that the fund balance will be zero at the end of the fifth year.

C) If $50,000 is invested today to earn an annual return of 10 percent, what equal amounts can be withdrawn at the end of the fourth year and each of the next four years? Construct a schedule showing that the fund balance will be zero at the end of the eighth year.

E7-11. ORDINARY ANNUITIES; DETERMINING RENTS AND OTHER VARIABLES

A) You borrow $10,000 and wish to repay it in 10 equal annual installments, the first being payable one year following the date on which the money was borrowed. The debt bears interest at 12 percent.

REQUIRED

Calculate the annual installment required.

B) A man is allowed $800 for his old half-ton truck on the purchase of an $8,000 camper. He makes a down payment of $x and retires the debt with 24 monthly payments of $300. Money is worth 12 percent per annum compounded monthly.

REQUIRED

Calculate the amount of the down payment.   (CGAA, adapted)

E7-12. ORDINARY ANNUITY   You wish to accumulate $10,000 in a trust fund over a period ending five years from today's date. The trust pays interest at 6 percent semiannually. You intend to make a series of equal successive semiannual payments. The first payment will be made six months from today and the last one five years from today's date.

REQUIRED

Calculate the amount of each semiannual payment that will be necessary to meet your objective.

(CGAA, adapted)

E7-13. ANNUITIES DUE   On May 1, 1987, Mr. Ries opens a new savings account with an initial deposit of $100. He continues to deposit $100 on the first of each month, provided that the accumulated value just before the deposit is less than $2,600; otherwise he makes no further deposits. The account earns interest at 12 percent compounded monthly.

REQUIRED

Find the amount in the account on July 1, 1990.

(CGAA, adapted)

E7-14. ANNUITIES   Mr. Cie's mortgage of $100 per month on the first of each month will finally be paid in full on November 1, 1987. The interest rate is 12 percent compounded monthly. After his payment on June 1, 1987, Mr. Cie wishes to know the present value of the remaining payments.

REQUIRED

Find the present value of the remaining payments on June 1, 1987.

(CGAA, adapted)

E7-15. IMPLICIT INTEREST RATES   A car can be purchased for either $10,000 cash or $2,070 cash plus 12 successive monthly payments of $750 each.

REQUIRED

Calculate the effective rate of interest implicit in the deferred payments.

E7-16. ANNUITIES—CHANGING RENTS   Tommy and Judy Dossey have a 10 percent mortgage on their new home, which at the current rate of payment will be fully paid off in 20 years. If they decide to double their annual payments on the mortgage, how long will it take them to pay it off? Assume that mortgage payments are made once a year, at the end of the year.

E7-17. COMPUTING RENTS   Mr. Lee has obligations of $5,000 due August 1, 1989, and $6,000 due August 1, 1990. He and his creditor agree to settle the debt with two equal payments on August 1, 1987, and August 1, 1988. The interest rate is 12 percent compounded annually.

REQUIRED

Find the size of the two equal payments.

E7-18. PRESENT AND FUTURE VALUES; TABLE SELECTION   Reproduced below are the first three lines from the 2 percent columns of each of several present and future value tables. For each of the following items, you are to select from among these fragmentary tables the one from which the amount required can be obtained *most directly* (assuming that the complete table is available in each instance):

1. The amount to which a single sum would accumulate at compound interest by the end of a specified period (interest compounded annually).

2. The amount that must be appropriated at the end of each of a specific number of years to provide for the accumulation, at annually compounded interest, of a certain sum.

3. The amount that must be deposited in a fund that will earn interest at a specified rate, compounded annually, in order to make possible the withdrawal of certain equal sums annually over a specified period starting one year from date of deposit.

4. The amount of interest that will accumulate on a single deposit by the end of a specified period (interest compounded semiannually).

5. The amount, net of compound discount, which if paid now would settle a debt of larger amount due at a specified future date.

PERIODS	TABLE A	TABLE B	TABLE C	TABLE D	TABLE E	TABLE F
0	1.0000		1.0000			
1	0.9804	1.0200	1.0200	1.0000	0.9804	1.0200
2	0.9612	2.0604	1.0404	0.4950	1.9416	0.5150
3		3.1216		0.3268	2.8839	0.3468

(AICPA, adapted)

PROBLEMS

P7-1. ORDINARY ANNUITIES AND PRESENT VALUES

A) The city of Wetwater wishes to accumulate $100,000 by making equal successive payments into a fund at the end of each six months for five years. The fund bears interest at 5 percent, compounded semiannually.

REQUIRED

Calculate the amount of each of the payments.

B) Assume instead that the city desires to make one lump-sum payment immediately which would accumulate to $100,000 by the end of the fifth year.

REQUIRED

Calculate the amount of the payment.

P7-2. SOLVING FOR UNKNOWN VARIABLES—SINGLE AMOUNTS Mark Sharp made a deposit of $60,000 in a savings account. After he had left the amount on deposit for 12 years at 8 percent interest, the resultant accumulation was $151,092.

REQUIRED

1. Show how the accumulated amount could be determined.

2. Assume that the number of interest periods is unknown but that the other three values are known. Show how the number of periods could be determined.

3. Assume that the interest rate is unknown but that the other three values are known. Show how the interest rate could be determined.

P7-3. SOLVING FOR UNKNOWN VARIABLES—ANNUITIES Lynn Quick received $1,200 per year for nine years, beginning at the end of year 1. At an interest rate of 10 percent, the value of this annuity at the beginning of year 1 was $6,910.82.

REQUIRED

1. Show how the amount received could be determined.

2. Assume that the number of interest periods is unknown but that the other three values are known. Show how the number of periods could be determined.

3. Assume that the interest rate is unknown but that the other three values are known. Show how the interest rate could be determined.

P7-4. ANNUITIES

A) Exactly eight years ago the Hammers bought a summer cottage for $10,000. They paid $1,000 down and $1,000 on each subsequent anniversary date. Rather than paying the usual $1,000, which is due today, they have decided to pay off the entire debt. The agreement permits them to pay off any part of the debt without penalty.

REQUIRED

Calculate the amount of cash the Hammers will need to pay off the entire debt if the interest rate on the debt is 8 percent.

B) Today a corporation sold the rights to a secret process to the Canadian government and received a cash payment of $10,000. The government has undertaken to pay an additional $1,000 five years from today's date and at the end of each succeeding year forever.

REQUIRED

Find the present value of these payments at a 6 percent annual rate of return.

(CGAA, adapted)

P7-5. DEFERRED ANNUITIES

A) A firm wishes to know how much must be deposited today ($t = 0$) in a savings account at 8 percent compounded annually in order to make the following withdrawals:

t	AMOUNT WITHDRAWN AT END OF PERIOD
7	$3,000
8	3,000
9	6,000
10	6,000

REQUIRED

Calculate the amount that must be deposited.

B) Charlie Smith, Jr., will begin attending college 10 years from today. Charlie's father estimates his son's expenses to be $15,000 per year for each of the five years that he will attend school. His father plans to invest an equal amount each year, beginning one year from today, for 10 years and estimates that the investment will earn 10 percent compounded annually. Assume that each year's investment will be made at the end of the year and that the son's expenses occur at the beginning of each school year.

REQUIRED

Calculate how much the father must invest each year.

P7-6. CALCULATING RENTS AND PRESENT VALUES Tang Corporation acquires an asset with a fair market value of $100,000 by issuing a $100,000 note payable. The asset will generate end-of-year cash flows of $41,635 each year for three years and will have zero salvage value at the end of the third year. The note payable bears interest at 8 percent and will be amortized (paid off) with three equal end-of-year payments.

The company's president disagrees with the controller on how to account for the asset, liability, and net income over the three-year period. The president feels that, in order to smooth income and to assist users in making predictions about future cash flows, net income each year should be the difference between the cash flows from the investment and the cash paid to amortize the note. The controller believes that net income should be the difference between the earnings on the asset (based on the asset's effective rate of return) and the interest expense on the note, calculated using the effective interest method.

REQUIRED

1. Calculate *(a)* the effective rate of return on the asset and *(b)* the annual end-of-year payments on the note.

2. Using the president's approach, calculate each year's net income and the total net income over the three-year period.

3. Using the controller's approach, calculate each year's net income and the total net income over the three-year period.

4. Do you prefer the president's approach or the controller's approach? Give reasons for your answer.

P7-7. PRESENT VALUE APPLICATIONS Several years ago, Quasar Financial Services issued at par (face value) $100,000 of 10 percent bonds. The bonds pay interest annually and mature in six years. Since the market rate of interest for similar bonds currently is above 10 percent, Quasar would like to retire these bonds and report a retirement gain on its income statement. However, state regulatory authorities will not permit the retirement.

At the advice of counsel, Quasar has decided to invest cash in a certificate of deposit issued by Superbankamerica, which is currently paying 12 percent on six-year certificates. The amount to be deposited will be the present value of Quasar's bond obligation, discounted at 12 percent. This amount will be sufficient to service the interest on the debt and to retire the debt at maturity. If Quasar signs a written agreement to leave the certificate of deposit at Superbankamerica during the six-year period, regulatory authorities will permit Quasar to report a gain equal to the difference between the $100,000 carrying value of the bonds and the amount of the certificate of deposit.

REQUIRED

1. Calculate the amount of the Superbankamerica certificate of deposit and the amount of the gain.

2. Prepare a schedule that demonstrates that the cash flows from the certificate of deposit will be sufficient to service the debt. Assume that interest on the certificate of deposit is paid annually and that Quasar can adjust the principal amount of the certificate at the end of each year; i.e., interest is added to the principal at the end of each year.

P7-8. CHANGING INTEREST RATES

A) A company deposited $20,000 in a savings account on January 1, 1987, and left it on deposit for eight years.

REQUIRED

1. How much had accumulated on December 31, 1994, if the savings account earned 8 percent for each of the first two years, 10 percent for each of the next three years, and 12 percent for each of the last three years?

2. Prepare a schedule showing the growth in the savings account from January 1, 1987, through December 31, 1994.

B) A company deposited $2,000 at the end of each year in a savings account. Six deposits were made over a six-year period.

REQUIRED

1. How much had accumulated at the end of the sixth year if the account earned 8 percent each of the first three years and 10 percent each of the last three years?

2. Prepare a schedule showing the growth in the savings account during the six-year period.

P7-9. DEFERRED ANNUITIES Stimudent, Inc. is contemplating making a tender offer for the common stock of Action Corporation. Although Action presently is not generating any net cash inflows, Stimudent estimates that Action's average annual net cash flows will be $300,000 beginning six years from now and continuing for 30 years. Stimudent desires a 12 percent rate of return on its investments.

REQUIRED

Calculate the amount that Stimudent should offer for Action's stock using the following approaches:

1. Find the future value of Action's cash flows at the end of year 35; then find the present value at the beginning of the first year.

2. Find the present value of Action's cash flows at the end of year 5; then find the present value at the beginning of the first year.

P7-10. EFFECTIVE INTEREST RATES AND RENTS You recently have inherited $50,000 from a rich uncle and are comparing savings accounts at four banks. You plan to deposit the $50,000 inheritance in one of the banks for a two-year period, after which you will use the proceeds to buy either a new Porsche Targa or a deluxe tent trailer. The following savings plans apply at the four banks:

BANK	INTEREST PAID ON DEPOSITS
City Trust	13% compounded annually
Mercantile Merchants	12% compounded semiannually
Friendly American	12% compounded quarterly
Bankers Group	12% compounded monthly

REQUIRED

1. Calculate the effective annual interest rate (yield) for each bank.

2. Assume that you deposited $12,500 (1/4 × $50,000) in each bank at the beginning of year one. Calculate the total amount of your investment at the end of the second year. (*Note:* You must calculate the amount in City Trust by hand or with a calculator because the tables in Appendix 7–1 do not contain a 13 percent interest rate.)

3. Assume instead that you decided to make your $50,000 deposit in Bankers Group (this bank gave green stamps). After making the deposit at the beginning of year 1, you decided to make 12 equal monthly withdrawals, beginning at the end of the first month of year 2. Calculate the amount of each withdrawal.

4. Refer to requirement 3. Assume that you decided to withdraw $3,000 at the end of each month for 12 months, beginning at the end of the first month of year 2. Calculate your deposit balance at the end of the second year.

P7-11. ORDINARY ANNUITY APPLICATIONS

A) Your client has agreed to sell property for $60,000. He is to receive $20,000 cash at the date of sale and 20 notes of equal amount which will not bear interest. The notes are due serially, one each six months, starting six months from the date of sale. It is agreed that the notes will include on their face an amount that will equal 6 percent interest compounded semiannually.

REQUIRED

Calculate the amount of each note.

B) Peter Jones, an employee of the Union Company, asks your advice on the following matter: He is eligible to participate in a company insurance and retirement plan. His payment into the company plan would amount to $500 each six months for the next ten years; and starting with the eleventh year, he would receive an annual payment of $1,080 for life. He does not need insurance protection and states that he can save and invest each six months the amounts to be paid into the company plan so that he will earn 6 percent compounded semiannually. Also, he can continue to earn the same rate on his capital after retirement. He would like to have an equal amount of funds *per year* for 15 years after retirement.

REQUIRED

Assuming that he can carry out his personal saving and investing plan, how much can he expect to have available *each six months* for the 15 years following his retirement?

(AICPA, adapted)

P7-12. PRESENT AND FUTURE VALUES; MISCELLANEOUS

A) Jeff Ungerer will owe $10,000 at the end of 1991. The interest rate is 8 percent compounded annually. Compute the four equal annual payments necessary to retire the debt, the first payment to be made at the end of 1988.

B) On May 1, 1987, Erik Millington purchased a used car on a one-year installment contract that required payments of $100 on May 1, 1987, and $100 on the first day of each month thereafter, with the last payment due on April 1, 1988. The annual interest rate is 12 percent compounded monthly. Compute the apparent cash price for the car at May 1, 1987.

C) Trish Houston has an investment that will be worth $4,000 at the end of year 10. If the interest rate is 8 percent compounded annually, what is the present value of the investment at the beginning of year 1?

P7-13. ANNUITIES; MISCELLANEOUS APPLICATIONS

A) Anne Strickland is considering an investment that promises annual cash flows of $600 at the end of each year for six years starting at the end of year 4. If the interest rate is 6 percent, what is the present value of the investment at the beginning of year 1?

B) Prepare a schedule for part A which demonstrates that the present value is sufficient to allow six cash flows of $600 beginning at the end of year 4.

C) If Huey Louis deposits $1,000 in a savings account at the beginning of 1987, what is the approximate number of quarterly $150 withdrawals that he can make if the interest rate is 8 percent compounded quarterly? The first withdrawal will be made at the end of the first quarter of 1988.

P7-14. APPLICATIONS OF ANNUITY AND SINGLE AMOUNT CONCEPTS

A) Your client has made annual payments of $2,500 into a fund at the close of each year for the past nine years. The fund balance immediately after the ninth payment totaled $26,457. She has asked you how many more $2,500 annual payments will be required to bring the fund to $50,000, assuming that the fund continues to earn interest at 4 percent compounded annually. Calculate the number of full payments required and the amount of the final payment if the entire $2,500 is not required.

B) Your client wishes to provide for the payment of an obligation of $200,000 due on July 1, 1995. She plans to deposit $20,000 in a special fund each July 1 for eight years, starting July 1, 1988. She also wishes to make an initial deposit on July 1, 1987, of an amount which, with its accumulated interest, will bring the fund up to $200,000 at the maturity of the obligation. She expects that the fund will earn interest at the rate of 4 percent compounded annually. Compute the amount to be deposited July 1, 1987. (AICPA, adapted)

P7-15. BOND VALUATION   On January 1, 1987, MyKoo Corporation issued $1 million in five-year, 5 percent serial bonds to be repaid in the amount of $200,000 on January 1, 1988, 1989, 1990, 1991, and 1992. Interest is payable at the end of each year. The bonds were sold to yield a rate of 6 percent.

REQUIRED

1. Construct a time diagram showing the cash flow obligations for MyKoo Corporation in connection with the bonds payable.

2. Prepare a schedule showing the computation of the total amount received from the issuance of the serial bonds.

(AICPA, adapted)

P7-16. TABLE RELATIONSHIPS; ANNUITIES   In computing the present value of an ordinary annuity, we used the table factor from Table D, which is based on the formula

$$P_{\overline{n}|\,i} = \frac{1 - \dfrac{1}{(1 + i)^n}}{i}$$

REQUIRED

1. Assuming that $i = 10$ percent, calculate the present value of an ordinary annuity of $10 each period for (a) 25 periods; (b) 50 periods.

2. Is your answer to part 1 fairly close to $100? If so, what might you conclude about present values of annuities that extend over *very* long periods of time? (*Hint:* Notice that the table factors under the 10 percent column get closer and closer to the factor of 10.000 and that the $10 cash flow ÷ .10 = $100.)

P7-17. ANNUITIES—PRESENT AND FUTURE VALUES   A bank in Oklahoma City advertised the following proposal in order to attract deposits: "If you will deposit $1,000 per year (at the end of each year for 10 years) in our bank, at the end of 10 years you may begin withdrawing $1,594 annually for the rest of *your* life, for the rest of your *children's* lives, for the rest of your *grandchildren's* lives. These annual withdrawals may continue forever and ever!"

REQUIRED

1. Assume that the bank pays 10 percent interest on deposits. Explain and demonstrate how the bank could make such an attractive proposal.

2. Assume that the amount withdrawn each year was $1,774, beginning at the end of the eleventh year. Approximately how many years could these withdrawals continue?

8 CASH AND RECEIVABLES

We have looked at the financial statements in Chapters 4 and 5 and have studied the concepts and principles that underlie their preparation. Now let us turn to a closer examination of the specific balance sheet accounts that comprise assets, liabilities, and stockholders' equity. We will begin with assets, examining the major asset categories in the order in which they are presented in the balance sheet. Cash and receivables, which are claims to cash, are highly liquid assets and are the subject of this chapter. Marketable securities, another group of highly liquid assets, are discussed in Chapter 14.

The term **liquidity** is used to indicate the ease with which an asset can be converted into cash, and a company's liquidity provides an indication of its ability to pay obligations as they become due. Other things being equal, a highly liquid company may be less likely to experience financial difficulties than a less liquid company. Chrysler Corporation's financial difficulties in the late 1970s, for example, stemmed in part from a lack of cash and other liquid assets needed to finance its operations. Thus, liquidity is important to investors who want to assess a company's prospective future cash flows. In accounting for cash and receivables, the accountant is concerned with measuring these elements and with providing disclosures that will facilitate an assessment of a firm's liquidity.

CASH

Cash, the most liquid of all assets, is a medium of exchange used to purchase goods and services and to discharge obligations. Cash is so widely accepted that there are almost no restrictions on its use in business transactions. Cash includes U.S. currency and coins, personal checks, money orders, demand deposits, cashiers' checks, bank drafts, petty cash, change funds, and most savings deposits (banks seldom enforce the requirement that depositors give prior notice before withdrawing funds from savings accounts). Foreign currencies are included in cash if they are freely convertible into the domestic currency. Sums of money held as an asset but restricted for specific uses should not be categorized as cash, because they are not available as a medium of exchange in any transaction. Restricted deposits, postdated checks, IOUs, stamps, and certificates of deposit are not included in cash because they are not readily exchangeable and are not freely available for

| **EXHIBIT 8–1** | BALANCE SHEET CLASSIFICATION OF NONCASH ITEMS |

ITEM	CLASSIFICATION	REASON FOR CLASSIFICATION
Deposits with a trustee (e.g., construction funds advanced)	Noncurrent assets	Cannot be used to discharge current obligations because they are earmarked for a specific purpose
Postdated checks	Receivables	Generally, banks do not accept such checks for deposit
IOUs	Receivables	Generally, banks do not accept IOUs for deposit
Postage stamps	Supplies	Not an accepted medium of exchange
Certificates of deposit	Investments	Not available for immediate withdrawal without a substantial penalty

purchasing goods and services or discharging obligations. These items should be classified as shown in Exhibit 8–1.

CONTROL OF CASH Although cash control does not affect financial reporting directly, we shall review the principles of control over cash because effective control is a part of management's overall responsibility to stockholders and other parties who have an interest in the business. Cash management and control are important for the following reasons:

1. Since cash is used as a medium of exchange, management must ensure, through proper planning, that needed cash will be on hand to meet obligations as they arise. A cash budget is one vehicle for quantifying plans of management.

2. Because cash can be invested to earn income, a well-managed firm should keep idle cash balances to a minimum.

3. Cash is a universal medium of exchange, and proper controls are needed to prevent its theft, loss, and misappropriation.

Control over Receipts and Disbursements of Cash

To achieve proper control over cash, cash receipts should be recorded and deposited promptly, usually daily. The responsibilities for recording and depositing cash should be assigned to different individuals. Control over cash disbursements is designed to ensure that only proper cash payments are made. A firm can control its disbursements by separating the responsibility of recording cash disbursements from that of making payments, such as writing checks. Furthermore, no cash disbursement should be made without proper support for the expenditure, such as an invoice, a purchase order, or a labor time ticket.

A firm's internal control procedures are designed to safeguard its assets and to reduce the possibility of errors and fraud. Internal control encompasses accounting controls and administrative controls:

1. **Accounting controls** consist of the plan of organization and all methods and procedures that are concerned mainly with, and relate directly to, the safeguarding of assets and the reliability of the financial records. They generally include the systems of authorization and approval, separation of duties concerned with record keeping and accounting reports from duties concerned with operations or custody of assets, physical controls over assets, and internal auditing.

2. **Administrative controls** consist of the plan of organization and all methods and procedures that are concerned mainly with operational efficiency and adherence to managerial policies, and usually relate only indirectly to the financial records. They generally include statistical analyses, time and motion studies, performance reports, employee training programs, and quality controls.[1]

A strong internal control system increases the reliability of financial reports.

A strong system of internal control increases the reliability—and consequently the usefulness—of financial reports. More and more business entities are therefore engaging CPAs to issue opinions on their internal control systems. The accounting profession has established detailed procedures to be applied in the auditing of internal control systems.[2]

Petty Cash

Many firms establish petty cash funds of a fixed amount for small expenditures that do not justify a formal authorization and disbursement procedure. The individual placed in charge of the petty cash fund is responsible for making payments for expenditures that are supported by proper vouchers. Periodically, a check, payable to petty cash, is written on the firm's regular checking account to replenish the fund. At this point the expenditures made from petty cash and the related disbursement are recorded in the accounts.

Assume, for example, that on June 1 The Bike Shop established a $300 petty cash fund for small expenditures. On June 16 the petty cash trustee submitted vouchers for several miscellaneous disbursements made through June 16 and requested replenishment of the fund. On June 16 the petty cash fund contained the following vouchers and cash balance:

Postage expenditures	$ 75
Freight paid on merchandise	110
Supplies purchased and used	30
Cash on hand	85
Total	$300

The entries to record the establishment of the fund, the expenditures, and the fund replenishment are:

June 1	Petty cash	300	
	Cash		300
	To record the establishment of the petty cash fund.		
June 16	Supplies expense ($75 + $30)	105	
	Transportation in	110	
	Cash		215
	To record replenishment of the fund.		

Occasionally the amount of cash on hand will not equal the amount that should be on hand because of errors made in payments or unaccounted-for expenditures. When this occurs, cash short-and-over should be debited or credited, and the offsetting debit or credit should be made to cash. The cash short-and-over account should be closed to miscellaneous expenses at the end of the accounting period.

Petty cash on hand is an asset because it is part of the firm's cash balance. The petty

---

[1] Auditing Standards Board, ''The Auditor's Study and Evaluation of Internal Control,'' *Statement on Auditing Standards No. 1* (New York: AICPA, 1973), sec. 320.

[2] Auditing Standards Board, ''Reporting on Internal Accounting Control,'' *Statement on Auditing Standards No. 30* (New York: AICPA, 1980).

cash fund should always be replenished at the end of an accounting period so that expenses will be properly recorded and cash will be correctly stated.

The size of a petty cash fund occasionally may be increased or decreased. An increase in the size of the fund is recorded by debiting petty cash and crediting cash. A decrease is recorded by debiting cash and crediting petty cash.

RECONCILIATION OF CASH BALANCES

Banks send depositors monthly statements of their checking account activities. Each month the depositors should reconcile these statements with the cash balances shown in their accounting records as a part of the overall control over cash. The purpose of the bank reconciliation is to ensure that entries in the cash account agree with the bank's independent records of the depositing firm's cash receipt and disbursement activities.

The ending balance of cash shown on the monthly bank statement seldom will agree with the ending cash balance in the firm's records for one or more of the following reasons:

1. The bank may show deposits to the customer's account that have not been entered as cash receipts in the customer's books. An example of this type of transaction is a note receivable collected by the bank for the benefit of the customer. The customer may have no knowledge of the collection until the bank statement is received.

2. The bank may have debited (reduced) the customer's account balance for transactions not known to the customer until the bank statement is received. For example, a bank normally credits (increases) a customer's cash balance immediately for checks deposited. If the maker of the check does not have adequate funds deposited, the bank then reduces the customer's cash balance. These checks are sometimes called NSF (not sufficient funds) checks and are returned to the customer depositor. Other items that reduce depositor balances include service charges, charges for safe deposit boxes, and charges for printing checks.

3. A customer may have recorded cash receipts that have not yet been recorded by the bank as deposits. For example, if near the end of the month the customer makes a deposit, it may not appear in the bank statement as a deposit until the following month.

4. A customer may have recorded cash disbursements that have not yet been paid by the bank at the bank statement date. For example, a customer may have written checks in payment for goods and services but these checks have not been presented to and paid by the bank at the time the bank statement is prepared and mailed to the customer. These checks are called outstanding checks and will appear on the monthly bank statement in the month when they are paid by the bank. (Outstanding *certified* checks are not included here, since the bank reduces the customer's account balance when the certified check is prepared by the bank.)

5. Finally, errors on the part of the bank or the customer can cause the bank balance to disagree with the customer's book balance.

In preparing the bank reconciliation, notice that items 1 and 2 have been recorded by the bank but not by the firm, and therefore these items will affect the *firm's* ending cash balance. Since items 3 and 4 have been recorded by the firm but not by the bank, these items will alter the reported cash balance on the *bank statement*. Finally, the errors in item 5 will affect the reported balance of the firm or the bank, depending on which party made the error. Obviously, any bank error should be called to the bank's attention promptly.

As an illustration, assume that Wezzel Corporation's accounting records show a cash balance of $8,672.89 on February 28, 1987. The bank statement for February reported an ending balance in Wezzel Corporation's bank account of $1,768.22. On examining the monthly transactions on the bank statement and comparing the statement with the cash account, Wezzel discovered the following:

1. Checks written during the month but not appearing on the bank statement and not returned with the statement:

CHECK NUMBER	AMOUNT
94	$ 400.00
107	1,870.00
112	500.00
113	870.00
	$3,640.00

2. A deposit of $400 was made on February 26 but did not appear on the bank statement.

3. On February 27, Wezzel Corporation redeemed a two-month certificate of deposit at the bank's suburban branch. The face amount was $10,000 and interest totaled $600. The cash proceeds were deposited at the branch bank but the information did not reach the main bank for processing until March 2.

4. Bank service charges for February, $2.30, had not been recorded by Wezzel.

5. One of Wezzel's customers' checks was returned with the bank statement. The check, totaling $26.37, was marked "NSF."

6. The bank collected a note for Wezzel on February 19 totaling $214, of which $14 was interest revenue.

7. On February 25, Wezzel Corporation made a deposit totaling $630, which represented receivable collections. Wezzel's bookkeeper made a transposition error in recording the deposit in the cash account and recorded the deposit as $360.

Exhibit 8–2 shows how the bank statement ending balance of $1,768.22 may be reconciled with Wezzel's ending cash balance of $8,672.89. Note that items 2 and 3 are added to the bank balance, item 1 is deducted from the bank balance, items 6 and 7 are added to the book balance, and items 4 and 5 are deducted from the book balance.

EXHIBIT 8–2

Wezzel Corporation
BANK RECONCILIATION
FEBRUARY 28, 1987

Balance per bank statement		$ 1,768.22
Add: Deposit in transit.	$ 400.00	
Proceeds from matured CD	10,600.00	11,000.00
		$12,768.22
Deduct: Outstanding checks.		(3,640.00)
Corrected cash balance.		$ 9,128.22
Balance per books		$ 8,672.89
Add: Understatement of deposit from transposition error . . . . . $	270.00	
Proceeds of note collected by bank	214.00	484.00
		$ 9,156.89
Deduct: Service charge . . . . $	2.30	
NSF check	26.37	(28.67)
Corrected cash balance.		$ 9,128.22

The bank reconciliation shown in Exhibit 8–2 is useful for several reasons. First, the reconciliation arrives at the correct cash balance of $9,128.22 for financial statement purposes.[3] Second, items that increase and decrease the balance per books to arrive at the correct cash balance provide the necessary information to adjust Wezzel Corporation's cash account in the general ledger.

The entries required to adjust and correct Wezzel Corporation's books at February 28, 1987, are as follows:

Cash...	484.00	
Accounts receivable		270.00
Notes receivable		200.00
Interest revenue		14.00
Accounts receivable	26.37	
Miscellaneous expense	2.30	
Cash...		28.67

Notice that the adjusting entries shown above consist of reconciling items in the lower section of the bank reconciliation shown in Exhibit 8–2.

Another form of reconciliation often used in practice is a cash receipts and disbursements reconciliation (sometimes called a **comprehensive reconciliation** or a **proof of cash**). The comprehensive reconciliation provides not only a reconciliation of the ending bank balance with the ending book balance but also a reconciliation of beginning cash balances and all cash receipts and disbursements during the period. The comprehensive reconciliation is a frequently used auditing procedure and is discussed in Appendix 8–1.

CASH DISCLOSURES: OVERDRAFTS AND COMPENSATING BALANCES

Disclosures related to balance sheet presentation of cash are important to users in assessing liquidity. Two important cash disclosures are overdrafts and compensating balances.

Overdrafts

Occasionally a firm will write checks that cause an **overdraft** in its bank account at a balance sheet date. If the firm has other unrestricted checking account balances at the same bank which are greater than the amount of the overdraft, the overdraft may be offset against these positive cash balances; otherwise, the overdraft should be classified as a current liability, similar to a temporary loan.

Compensating Balances

Recently, many banks have required borrowers to maintain compensating balances on loans made to those borrowers. A **compensating balance** is the portion of the loan that must remain on deposit during the period of the loan. If, for example, a company borrows $50,000 from a bank and is required to maintain a 10 percent compensating balance, $5,000 of the amount loaned must remain on deposit at the bank during the loan period. Since a compensating balance requirement reduces liquidity by restricting the use of a portion of the reported cash balance at a statement date, disclosure of such compensating balance requirements is necessary to enable users to assess future cash flows and liquidity. *SEC Financial Reporting Release No. 1* requires that companies disclose information related to compensating balance arrangements in connection with short-term debt and

A compensating balance requirement restricts the use of a portion of a firm's cash balance.

[3] A variation of the format shown in Exhibit 8–2 begins with the bank balance, adds and deducts the reconciling items as appropriate, and reconciles to the book balance. This approach, however, does not clearly indicate the correct ending cash balance.

lines of credit. The following compensating balance disclosure appeared in the annual report of Public Service Company of Colorado:

Arrangements for bank lines of credit totaled $65,000,000 at December 31, 1984, and were maintained entirely by fee payments in lieu of compensating balances. These lines of credit were reduced at the Company's request effective July 1, 1984, from $111,849,000 at December 31, 1983, consisting of $17,549,000 maintained by compensating balances and $94,300,000 maintained by fee payments in lieu of balances. The compensating bank balance arrangements provided that the Company maintain average compensating balances in the amount of $877,450 for the six-month period ending June 30, 1984, $877,450 for the six-month period ending December 31, 1983 and $1,806,200 for the six-month period ending June 30, 1983. These bank lines of credit are also used to support the Company's issuance of commercial paper. At the Company's request, confirmed uncommitted bank lines of credit totalling $53,000,000 at December 31, 1983 were discontinued during 1984. The Company generally may borrow under uncommitted preapproved lines of credit upon request, however, the banks have no firm commitment to make such loans.

RECEIVABLES

Receivables arise when a firm sells goods or services on credit and obtains the right to receive cash in the future, or when it lends money to another firm and receives a note in exchange. Receivables are **monetary assets** because they represent claims to receive fixed amounts of cash. In theory, receivables should be valued at the present value of future cash flows to be received. In practice, however, many short-term receivables are valued at face amount or at net realizable value instead of present value because the discount or interest factor is not material.

The two most common types of receivables are account, or trade, receivables and notes receivable. Other receivables include those from employees and officers, advances made to affiliated companies (such as a branch office or a subsidiary), receivables from governmental units for tax refunds, those arising from long-term leasing agreements, and those arising from accruals such as interest.

In recent years the use of bank credit cards (for example, Visa or Mastercard) for consumer purchases has increased dramatically. When a retailer's customers purchase goods with bank credit cards, the retailer deposits the credit card slips in its bank checking account. Periodically the bank deducts from the retailer's account a credit card or service fee for processing the slips. The customers make credit card payments directly to the bank that is acting as a clearing agent; therefore, credit card sales do not result in receivables from the retailer's standpoint.

ACCOUNTS RECEIVABLE

Accounts receivable arise from the sale of goods or services on account. In our economic system, many exchanges take place on credit, especially among wholesalers and manufacturers. Firms expect that by selling on credit, they will achieve greater sales and profits than they would if their sales were on a cash-only basis. Even though a firm runs the risk of not being able to collect some receivables, it expects that these uncollectible accounts and the associated costs of credit sales will be sufficiently offset by an increase in sales to generate greater earnings.

A sale made on open account is an informal contract between the buyer and seller, and the terms of sale can vary depending on the business or industry. The accounting considerations associated with sales of goods and services on account are as follows:

1. Determining the amount of the receivable due from the customer.
2. Determining when the receivable should be recognized as an asset.
3. Determining what recognition should be given to the possibility that the amount owed may not be collected.

These considerations were introduced briefly in Chapter 6. Whereas our discussion in Chapter 6 focused on the revenue side of the transaction and the resulting income statement effect, our discussion here will focus primarily on the accounts receivable side of the transaction and the resulting balance sheet effect.

Determining Amounts Due on Receivables

Because revenue arises from the sale of goods or services, the determination of the amount due from sales transactions on account is precisely the same problem as determining the amount of revenue to be recognized from the transaction. Conceptually, the **amount due** is equal to the *current cash equivalent exchange price* as a result of the transaction between the buyer and seller. Although the exchange price may be blurred sometimes in practice because of trade and cash discounts, customer returns of goods previously sold on credit, and the length of the collection period, the amount to be recognized is clear conceptually: *it is the exchange price established in the transaction.* This amount is the initial recorded amount for accounts receivable; it is also the amount of revenue recorded in the transaction.

TRADE DISCOUNTS Some manufacturing companies publish suggested retail prices or list prices for their products and quote **trade discounts** applicable to various groups of buyers, such as distributors, wholesalers, and retailers. By quoting list prices and trade discounts, manufacturers are able to price their products differently to different groups by varying the trade discount instead of publishing a separate price list for each group. Trade discounts applicable to a list price also enable manufacturers to adjust selling prices to compensate for changing costs simply by adjusting the trade discount, thus avoiding the cost of publishing new price lists as costs change. Thus, trade discounts are a convenient pricing mechanism and are never recorded. For example, if a manufacturer sold goods with a list price of $700 at a trade discount of 40 percent, the selling price and the amount to be recorded as a receivable would be $700 \times (1 - .40)$ or $420, which represents the exchange price of the asset sold.

SALES DISCOUNTS Many companies grant customers cash or sales discounts to encourage prompt payment for purchases made on account. For example, a company may offer the following cash discount terms: "2%/10, net 30." If a customer who purchases supplies on account at a sales price of $1,000 pays within 10 days of the invoice date, the customer may deduct 2 percent of $1,000, or $20, from the sales price and remit $980. If the customer pays after 10 days, however, the entire $1,000 is owed.[4] Although many customers may not take advantage of cash discounts, rational customers should do so even if they must borrow the money to pay within the 10-day period. The loss of the 2 percent discount in exchange for an additional 20 days to make payment is roughly equivalent to a 36 percent annual rate of interest (.02 times 18, 20-day periods in a year).

---

[4] Another common type of sales discount is "2%/10 EOM," where EOM means "end of the month." The customer is allowed a 2 percent discount if payment is received within 10 days following the end of the month. For example, if a purchase is made any time in March, the discount is allowed if payment is made before April 10.

EXHIBIT 8-3   TWO METHODS OF ACCOUNTING FOR SALES DISCOUNTS

NET METHOD: RECEIVABLE AND SALE RECORDED NET OF SALES DISCOUNT

SITUATION	ENTRY	
At the time of sale, the receivable and sale are recorded net of the cash discount	Accounts receivable........980	
	Sales.................	980
and		
if the customer pays within the discount period and remits $980	Cash 980	
	Accounts receivable......	980
or		
if the customer does not pay within the discount period and thus remits $1,000	Cash 1,000	
	Accounts receivable......	980
	Interest revenue	20

GROSS METHOD: RECEIVABLE AND SALE RECORDED AT GROSS AMOUNT

SITUATION	ENTRY	
At the time of sale, the receivable and sale are recorded at the gross sales price	Accounts receivable......1,000	
	Sales...............	1,000
and		
if the customer pays within the discount period, the discount is recorded in a contra-sales account and reported on the income statement as a reduction from sales	Cash 980	
	Sales discounts........... 20	
	Accounts receivable	1,000
or		
if the customer does not pay within the discount period, the full amount is received.	Cash 1,000	
	Accounts receivable	1,000

If most customers take advantage of cash discounts, $980 provides the best measure of the cash inflow to be realized from the sale. The sale thus should be recorded at $980, since that amount represents the ''cash equivalent price'' at the exchange date. This method is called the net method. In practice, another method, the gross method, often is used to account for sales discounts. Both methods are illustrated in Exhibit 8–3.

Under the net method, if the seller's fiscal period ends after the discount period has elapsed but before the customer has made full remittance, an adjusting entry debiting accounts receivable and crediting interest revenue for $20 is necessary to adjust the receivable to the full amount to be received and to record the interest revenue.[5]

Both the net method and the gross method give the same results if customers take the cash discount. The amount of revenue reported is the same because sales discounts are deducted from sales in the income statement. However, if customers do not take the cash discounts, the gross method overstates sales and understates interest revenue even though there is no effect on net income. While we believe that the net method is more consistent with the accounting theory concepts discussed in Chapter 2, the gross method probably is more widely used in practice, perhaps because of materiality considerations and simplicity.

[5] Under a variation of the net method, the receivable is recorded at the gross amount, the sale at the net amount, and a receivable valuation account—allowance for sales discount—is established for the amount of the discount. When payment is received, the receivable is credited for the gross amount, and the allowance is reduced either because of the amount of cash received or because of the interest revenue.

SALES RETURNS In Chapter 6 we discussed accounting for sales returns in connection with measuring the amount of revenue to be reported on the income statement. When goods are sold on account, consideration of sales returns is necessary because otherwise the entire amount reported as receivables at a balance sheet date may not ultimately result in an inflow of cash.

The following accounting procedures for sales returns were presented in Chapter 6:

1. If returns are infrequent and small in dollar amount, they may be recorded as they occur. Even though mismatching may occur, it should not be material.

2. When companies experience a significant dollar amount of returns and can make reasonable estimates of expected returns, the allowance method should be used.

3. Under certain circumstances, the seller's risk from customer return privileges may be so great that a sale should not be recorded until the return period has expired.

INTEREST ON RECEIVABLES Most accounts receivable do not bear interest if the customer pays the amount owed within the period set forth in the terms of sale. However, the purchaser must pay interest or a finance charge on the unpaid balance if payment is not made within this time period. For example, Sears, Inc., offers a revolving credit plan whereby customers must pay a finance charge of 1 1/2 percent per month on the average unpaid balance unless the credit purchases are paid for within approximately 20 days from the date that a statement is received.[6]

Many companies sell consumer durables, such as television sets, refrigerators, and dishwashers, on an installment or deferred payment plan. Because the installment payments are made over an extended period of time, the seller charges the customer interest on the unpaid balance. The interest charges may be included implicitly in the periodic payments required, or they may be calculated and paid separately.

Because the total amount received by the seller over the life of the installment contract includes both interest and the exchange price of the item sold that would have been charged had the purchaser paid cash, the receivable should be recorded initially at its present value—the cash equivalent exchange value of the item sold. Part of the cash that is collected on the receivables after the date of sale represents interest on the unpaid balance of the receivable, and part represents a reduction of the receivable balance.

Assume that on January 1, Cerf Plumbing Corporation sells a deluxe heat pump on an installment plan. The heat pump has a cash price of $1,500 and a deferred payment price of $1,688.68, which is payable as follows: $100 down with 12 monthly payments of $132.39, the first payment due at the end of January. Interest at an effective rate of 2 percent per month is included in the deferred payment price.[7]

---

[6] There are many methods of calculating the finance charge. This finance charge is similar in concept to interest charged by credit card companies, such as Visa and Mastercard.

[7] Cerf calculated the monthly payments as follows:

Cash price $1,500
Less: Down payment . . . . (100)
   Balance to be financed $1,400

$1,400 is the present value of an ordinary annuity of x (to be determined) for 12 months at 2 percent per period:

$$\$1,400 = xP_{\overline{12}|2\%}$$
$$\$1,400 = x(10.5750) \qquad \text{(from Table D in Appendix 7–1)}$$
$$x = \frac{\$1,400}{10.5750}$$
$$x = \$132.39$$

Recording the transaction at $1,688.68 overstates both receivables and sales, because (1) the exchange price of the heat pump is $1,500 and (2) $188.68 represents interest that will be earned over the life of the installment contract. The receivable should be recorded at $1,500, and the monthly interest revenue should be based on the **effective interest method,** introduced in Chapter 7. Under this method, the interest earned each period (each month in this example) equals 2 percent of the receivable balance at the beginning of the period. The receivable balance at any date is the present value of the remaining payments. Entries to record the sale on January 1 and the first installment receipt on January 31 appear below.

January 1	Cash..................................	100.00	
	Accounts receivable	1,400.00	
	Sales		1,500.00
	To record the sale.		
January 31	Cash..................................	132.39	
	Interest revenue (.02 × $1,400)..........		28.00
	Accounts receivable ($132.39 − $28.00) ...		104.39
	To record the first installment receipt and interest for January.		

The entries to record the cash collection and interest for the remaining months would be identical to those above except for the amounts of interest revenue. The schedule that appears in Exhibit 8–4 shows the amounts that would be recorded as interest revenue for January and for the remaining months. As Exhibit 8–4 indicates, the amount of interest revenue becomes smaller each period as the receivable balance decreases, because each

EXHIBIT 8–4   SCHEDULE OF INTEREST REVENUE AND RECEIVABLE BALANCE UNDER THE EFFECTIVE INTEREST METHOD

MONTH	(1) CASH	(2) INTEREST*	(3) RECEIVABLE BALANCE†
			$1,400.00
January	$ 132.39	$ 28.00	1,295.61
February	132.39	25.91	1,189.13
March	132.39	23.78	1,080.52
April	132.39	21.61	969.74
May	132.39	19.40	856.75
June	132.39	17.14	741.50
July	132.39	14.83	623.94
August	132.39	12.48	504.03
September	132.39	10.08	381.71
October	132.39	7.63	256.95
November	132.39	5.14	129.70
December	132.39	2.68‡	–0–
	$1,588.68	$188.68	

* 2% of previous receivable balance.

† Previous receivable balance plus col. 2 minus col. 1.

‡ Rounded by $.09.

period the interest earned represents 2 percent of the receivable balance at the beginning of the period. Notice also that interest increases the receivable balance and that the cash receipts decrease the receivable balance: Monthly change in receivable balance = Interest earned − Cash receipt.

Some companies sell goods on account and allow customers an extended period of time for payment without any *explicit* mention of interest. Since a rational seller would not forgo interest when the cash collection period is very long, the seller would most likely increase the selling price to compensate for the "lost" interest. Failure to recognize the interest implicit in such transactions, however, can be misleading because the seller includes in sales revenue the implicit interest, which should be recognized over the period of collection.

To illustrate, assume that Nerf Corporation sells mobile homes for either $15,000 cash or $18,096 payable as follows: no down payment, with $6,032 payable at the end of each year for three years. The present value of the three $6,032 cash payments equals $15,000, and the $3,096 increase over the three-year period is interest.

Since the fair market value or cash equivalent exchange price of the mobile homes is $15,000, the sale should be recorded as follows:

Accounts receivable	15,000	
Sales		15,000

Interest revenue should be recognized over the three-year period by means of the effective interest method, illustrated in Exhibit 8–4.[8]

Determining When Receivables Should Be Recognized as Assets

In the previous section we discussed determination of the amount due on receivables. We pointed out that this problem is precisely the same as that of determining the amount of revenue arising from a company's earnings activities. Similarly, the issue of *when* the receivable should be recorded as an asset is directly related to *when* revenue should be recognized from an exchange transaction.

Recognition of receivables as assets parallels revenue recognition.

In Chapters 2 and 6 we discussed the realization principle, which governs the recognition of revenue. Under this principle, revenue should be recognized when (1) the earnings process is complete or virtually complete and (2) the amount and timing of cash to be received can be reasonably estimated. Until these criteria have been met, there is too much uncertainty about the transaction's ultimate net cash flow effect to justify recognition of revenue and net income. We also pointed out in Chapters 2 and 6 that in many cases these criteria are met at the point of sale, but that occasionally revenue should be recognized at other times. Where receivables are concerned, revenue is recognized on the basis of cash collections from customers under certain circumstances. The two methods of revenue recognition under a cash-collection basis—the installment method and the cost recovery method—and the circumstances justifying a cash-collection basis were discussed in Chapter 6.

---

[8] The interest rate implicit in this example is 10 percent, determined as follows:

$$\$15,000 = \$6,032(P_{\overline{3}|x\%})$$
$$P_{\overline{3}|x\%} = 2.4867$$

From Table D in Appendix 7–1 we find that the interest rate that corresponds to 2.4867 for three periods is approximately 10 percent. The first year's cash receipt would be recorded as follows:

Cash	6,032	
Interest revenue (.10 × $15,000)		1,500
Accounts receivable ($6,032 − $1,500)		4,532

Estimating Uncollectible Accounts

As we said earlier, companies that sell on account generally expect that most, but perhaps not all, of their credit sales will be collected in cash. They assume, moreover, that the increased sales and earnings will more than offset any increased costs associated with credit sales.

In accordance with the matching principle and the financial reporting objective of providing information to help users to predict future cash flows, estimates of uncollectible accounts expense (sometimes called bad debts expense) should be made and recorded in the accounts in the period in which the sale takes place when (1) it is highly probable that some accounts will prove uncollectible and (2) the dollar amount of uncollectible accounts reasonably can be estimated.[9] Two methods of accounting for uncollectible accounts are used in practice—the allowance (or accrual) method and the direct write-off method.

ALLOWANCE OR ACCRUAL METHOD   When it is highly probable that some accounts receivable will not be collected and the seller can make reasonable estimates of the dollar amounts, the **allowance method** should be used for uncollectible accounts. Under this method, an estimate of uncollectible accounts is made each period and reported in the income statement as an expense.[10] On the balance sheet, estimated uncollectible receivables are represented by an accounts receivable valuation or contra-account—allowance for uncollectible accounts. The valuation account is used because it is not known *which* customers' accounts will prove uncollectible. There are three generally accepted procedures that may be used in applying the allowance method. Each is discussed below.

Percentage of credit sales.   Under this procedure, the estimate of uncollectible accounts expense is based on a historically determined percentage of each period's *credit* sales. Total sales can be used instead of credit sales provided there is a relatively stable relationship between credit sales and total sales. Assume, for instance, that Bennet Corporation's past experience indicated that ultimate uncollectible accounts averaged about 2 percent of current credit sales. If credit sales in 1987 were $110,000, the uncollectible accounts expense for 1987 would be $2,200 ($110,000 × .02). The end-of-year adjusting entry would be as follows:

Uncollectible accounts expense 2,200		
Allowance for uncollectible accounts		2,200

The uncollectible accounts expense of $2,200 would be reported on the income statement, and the allowance account balance would be reported as a deduction from accounts receivable. It should be noted that this procedure emphasizes matching uncollectible accounts expense with sales revenue. The ending balance in the allowance account is the balance before the adjusting entry plus the amount of the adjustment.

Percentage of ending accounts receivable.   Under this procedure, the percentage of the ending balance of accounts receivable not expected to be collected is determined. The allowance account is then adjusted to equal this percentage.

Assume, for example, that past experience indicates that approximately 3 percent of Seibert Corporation's ending accounts receivable balance is estimated to be uncollectible.

---

[9] "Accounting for Contingencies," *Statement of Financial Accounting Standards No. 5* (Stamford, Conn.: FASB, 1975).

[10] Some accountants prefer to report uncollectible accounts expense as a deduction from sales, since it represents that portion of reported sales not expected to be collected. In practice, however, the tendency is to consider uncollectibles expense as an administrative expense, since granting of credit and collection are management responsibilities.

Assume further that Seibert's accounts receivable balance at the end of 1987 is $240,000, and that the credit balance in the allowance account before adjustment is $5,100. On the basis of the 3 percent estimate, the desired ending balance in the allowance account would be $7,200 ($240,000 × .03). Since the balance before adjustment is $5,100, the adjusting entry to record the uncollectible accounts expense for 1987 would be:

```
Uncollectible accounts expense ............................. 2,100
    Allowance for uncollectible accounts ......................        2,100
    ($7,200 − $5,100)
```

Whereas the first procedure emphasizes matching on the income statement, this procedure emphasizes valuation of the receivables at net realizable value on the balance sheet. The expense is the amount necessary to adjust the ending allowance account balance to the desired level.

Aging of accounts receivable. Aging of the accounts receivable balance is similar to, but is a more precise variation of, the second procedure. Aging considers that the longer a receivable is outstanding, the less likely it is to be collected. In the aging procedure, the individual account balances are classified according to the number of days outstanding. Once the aging schedule has been completed, a separate percentage is applied to each age classification group instead of applying an overall percentage, as in the second procedure. Hence, the aging procedure also stresses the reporting of receivables at net realizable value. The aging procedure is illustrated in Exhibit 8–5 for the Creed Corporation.

EXHIBIT 8–5   ACCOUNTS RECEIVABLE AGING SCHEDULE

Creed Corporation

CUSTOMER	BALANCE 12/31/87	LESS THAN 30	30–60	61–90	OVER 90
Bird Corporation	$ 300	$ 300			
Johnson Company	1,400	900	$500		
McHale, Inc.	400				$400
Fringe, Ltd.	400			$400	
Casey Jones	1,000	1,000			
Parrish, Ltd.	700	400	200	100	
Total	$4,200	$2,600	$700	$500	$400

AGE (DAYS)	AMOUNT	PERCENT ESTIMATED UNCOLLECTIBLE	REQUIRED ENDING BALANCE IN ALLOWANCE ACCOUNT
Less than 30	$2,600	2%	$ 52
30–60	700	4	28
61–90	500	16	80
Over 90	400	40	160
Total	$4,200		$320

If the ending balance in the allowance account had a *debit* balance of $100,[11] the adjusting entry to record the uncollectible accounts expense for 1987 would be:

Uncollectible accounts expense 420
   Allowance for uncollectible accounts   420
[$320 (from Exhibit 8–5) + $100]

Under all three procedures, an actual write-off of a customer's account has no effect on the net carrying value or book value of accounts receivable. Refer to Exhibit 8–5 and note that accounts receivable and the related allowance would appear on the balance sheet as follows:

Accounts receivable $4,200
Less: Allowance for uncollectible accounts . . . .   (320)
   Accounts receivable (net). $3,880

Assume that in early January 1988 it was determined that Parrish, Ltd., could pay $600 of the $700 owed; the balance of $100 was determined to be uncollectible. The following entry would be made to record the write-off of the balance of Parrish's account:

Allowance for uncollectible accounts 100
   Accounts receivable   100

After the write-off, the net carrying value of the receivables would still be $3,880:

Accounts receivable ($4,200 − $100) $4,100
Less: Allowance for uncollectible accounts ($320 − $100) . . . .   (220)
   Accounts receivable, net $3,880

In practice, write-offs of uncollectible accounts can be significant. For example, a few years ago Montgomery Ward wrote off uncollectible accounts totaling $118.4 million, or 3.05 percent of its credit sales.

Occasionally a customer, whose account has been written off, will pay all or a portion of the amount previously owed. When this occurs, the customer's account should first be restored by debiting accounts receivable and crediting the allowance account for the amount to be received. Then, cash should be debited and accounts receivable credited for the amount received.

The percentage of credit sales procedure sometimes is called an **income statement approach** because it emphasizes matching uncollectible accounts expense against current revenues. The two procedures that adjust the allowance account to a desired ending balance are sometimes called **balance sheet approaches** because both emphasize valuation of the receivables at net realizable value on the balance sheet. Also, aging often is used as an auditing procedure to verify the reasonableness of the other two procedures. Regardless of the procedure followed, if experience indicates that the percentages used in making the accruals are too low or too high, they should be adjusted accordingly. These

---

[11] A debit balance, before adjustment, is possible because the entry to record uncollectible accounts expense is made at the *end* of the period, while actual write-offs of accounts are made periodically *during* the period. In other words, the expense of $420 in the example above includes $100 of receivables *known* to be uncollectible plus $320 of receivables *estimated* to be uncollectible.

adjustments represent changes in estimates and their impact on income should be disclosed in the financial statements in the period of the change.[12]

DIRECT WRITE-OFF METHOD   Under the **direct write-off method,** no entries are made until a customer actually defaults on payment, at which time the expense is recognized and the uncollectible account receivable is written off. For example, if Barq Corporation made sales of $120 on account to Mr. Izuzu, and if subsequently it was determined that Mr. Izuzu was unable to pay the balance owed of $80, the following entry would be made to record the uncollectible account:

Uncollectible accounts expense 80
    Accounts receivable   80

The use of the direct write-off method may result in an overstatement of accounts receivable because there may be receivables carried on the books that are not collectible and thus will not result in cash inflows. In addition, the direct write-off method violates the matching concept when sales are made in one accounting period and the uncollectible expense is recorded in a subsequent period. Support for the direct write-off method rests on lack of material differences between this method and the allowance method and on cost/benefit considerations.

NOTES RECEIVABLE

Notes receivable are rights to receive a specified amount of cash in the future. They may arise from sales transactions, but most notes receivable originate from lending transactions. In contrast to an account receivable, which arises from an informal agreement between buyer and seller, a note receivable is a written contractual agreement in which the maker, the party who must pay the note at maturity, agrees to pay a specified sum of money to the payee under the terms of the contract.

If a note bears interest, the maker agrees to pay interest at a specified rate during the term of the note and to pay the face amount or principal at maturity. If a note is noninterest-bearing, the maker agrees to pay only the face amount at maturity.

A business may accept a note for several reasons:

1. A customer who desires more time to pay for a purchase on open account may issue a note.

2. A business may lend money and accept a note in exchange for the cash sacrificed.

3. Companies that sell higher-priced merchandise may accept a note in exchange for the merchandise sold so that the purchaser may defer payment beyond the customary short-term terms of trade.

4. A note is a negotiable instrument and is transferable by endorsement.

Valuation of Notes Receivable

Notes receivable are valued at present value.

Notes receivable, like accounts receivable and other monetary assets, should be valued at the present value of future cash flows to be received. Since the cash flows, which consist of principal and perhaps interest payments, are specified in the contract, there is little uncertainty about their amount or timing.[13] When uncollectible notes are expected, the

---

[12] ''Accounting Changes,'' *Opinions of the Accounting Principles Board No. 20* (New York: AICPA, 1971).

[13] In periods of inflation, many lenders make modifications in traditional note, bond, and mortgage contracts. Instead of accepting notes with fixed interest rates and fixed maturity values, they may demand variable rate notes, notes whose maturity value may increase with inflation, or notes that are payable in goods whose prices may increase with inflation. We discuss these types of debt instruments in Appendix 16–1.

allowance method of estimating uncollectibles, similar to the method discussed earlier for accounts receivable, should be used.

Since exchanges are measured at exchange prices on the exchange date, the present value of a note received in exchange for cash or goods or services equals the fair market value of the cash or goods or services sacrificed. However, the face or maturity amount of a note may or may not equal its present value. Three situations will illustrate these concepts.

FACE VALUE EQUALS PRESENT VALUE   The present value of a note receivable will equal the face value if the rate of interest stated in the note equals the market rate of interest for notes of similar risk. Assume, for example, that Curl Finance Corporation lent $10,000 in exchange for a three-year $10,000 note bearing interest at 8 percent annually. The cash flows from the note appear in the time diagram below. If the current market rate of interest is also 8 percent, the present value of the note would be $10,000, calculated as follows:

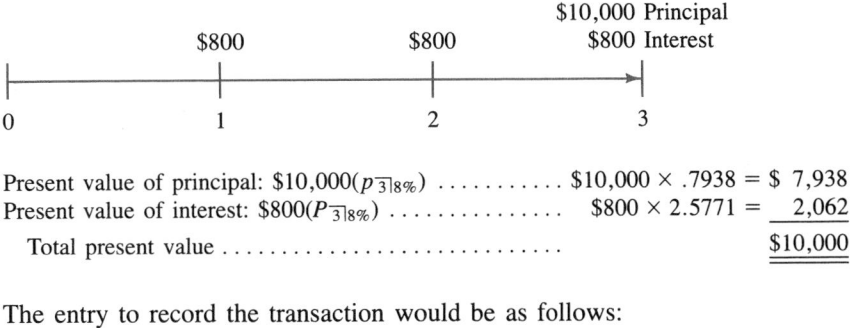

Present value of principal: $10,000($p_{\overline{3}|8\%}$) . . . . $10,000 × .7938 = $ 7,938
Present value of interest: $800($P_{\overline{3}|8\%}$) . . . . $800 × 2.5771 = 2,062

  Total present value $10,000

The entry to record the transaction would be as follows:

Notes receivable 10,000
  Cash.   10,000

The effective rate of interest earned on the note receivable is thus 8 percent, since that is the rate that equates the present value of the note with the amount of cash sacrificed. The effective rate also can be thought of as the **historical rate of interest** since this is the rate established in the transaction. Each year Curl would record the interest earned by debiting cash and crediting interest revenue for $800.

FACE VALUE GREATER THAN PRESENT VALUE FOR AN INTEREST-BEARING NOTE   Companies often accept notes in which the stated interest rate is less than the market rate at the date of exchange. When the stated rate of interest specified in a note is less than the market rate of interest, the present value of the note and the amount of cash sacrificed will be less than the face value. Assume, for example, that Curl Finance accepted a three-year 8 percent note with a maturity value of $10,000 when the current rate of interest was 12 percent. Since Curl could thus earn 12 percent on other investments of similar risk in the market, the company would not sacrifice $10,000 for the right to receive annual cash flows of $800 (.08 × $10,000) plus $10,000 at maturity. The present value of the note receivable would be less than $10,000, because the market rate of 12 percent exceeds the stated rate of 8 percent:

Present value of principal: $10,000($p_{\overline{3}|12\%}$). . . . . $10,000 × .7118 = $7,118
Present value of interest: $800($P_{\overline{3}|12\%}$) . . . . $800 × 2.4018 = 1,922

  Total present value $9,040

Thus, Curl would sacrifice only $9,040 in exchange for the right to receive three annual cash flows of $800 plus $10,000 at maturity if the market rate at the exchange date was 12 percent. The entry to record the transaction would be as follows:

Notes receivable 10,000
    Discount on notes receivable 960
    Cash 9,040

The discount on notes receivable represents unearned interest and is a contra-asset account to the notes receivable account. For example, if Curl prepared a balance sheet immediately after this transaction was recorded, the note receivable would be reported at $10,000 less the discount of $960, or $9,040.

At the end of year 1, the entry to record the receipt of cash and interest revenue would be as follows:

Cash 800
Discount on notes receivable ($1,085 − $800) 285
    Interest revenue (.12 × $9,040) 1,085

Interest is recognized and the discount is amortized or reduced each year by the effective interest method. A discount amortization and interest revenue schedule for this example appears in Exhibit 8–6.

There is an important relationship between (1) the use of the present value attribute for valuation of monetary assets after the date of an exchange and (2) the use of the effective interest method of amortizing discounts on notes and accounts receivable. The use of the effective interest method of amortizing a discount each period gives precisely the same results as discounting the remaining cash flows at any point in time at the historical rate (or effective rate) of interest implicit in the original exchange transaction. Notice that in Exhibit 8–6, the carrying values of the note receivable at the beginning of year 1 and at the end of years 1, 2, and 3 were $9,040, $9,325, $9,644, and $10,000, respectively. Except for slight rounding errors, these carrying values are exactly the same as we would obtain if we discounted the remaining cash flows associated with the note at the end of years 1, 2, and 3 at the historical (or effective rate) of 12 percent. The time diagrams and computations shown in Exhibit 8–7 illustrate this important relationship.

The effective interest method results in valuing monetary assets at present value when the discount rate is the historical or effective rate.

EXHIBIT 8–6   AMORTIZATION OF A DISCOUNT ON NOTES RECEIVABLE

YEAR	(1) INTEREST REVENUE (CR)*	(2) CASH (DR)	(3) DISCOUNT (DR)†	(4) NOTES RECEIVABLE BALANCE (NET OF UNAMORTIZED DISCOUNT)‡
				$ 9,040
1	$1,085	$800	$285	9,325
2	1,119	800	319	9,644
3	1,157	800	357	10,000
	$3,361	$2,400	$961	

* .12 × previous balance in col. 4.

† Col. 1 minus col. 2.

‡ Previous balance in col. 4 plus col. 3.

EXHIBIT 8–7 | VALUATION OF NOTES RECEIVABLE AT PRESENT VALUE

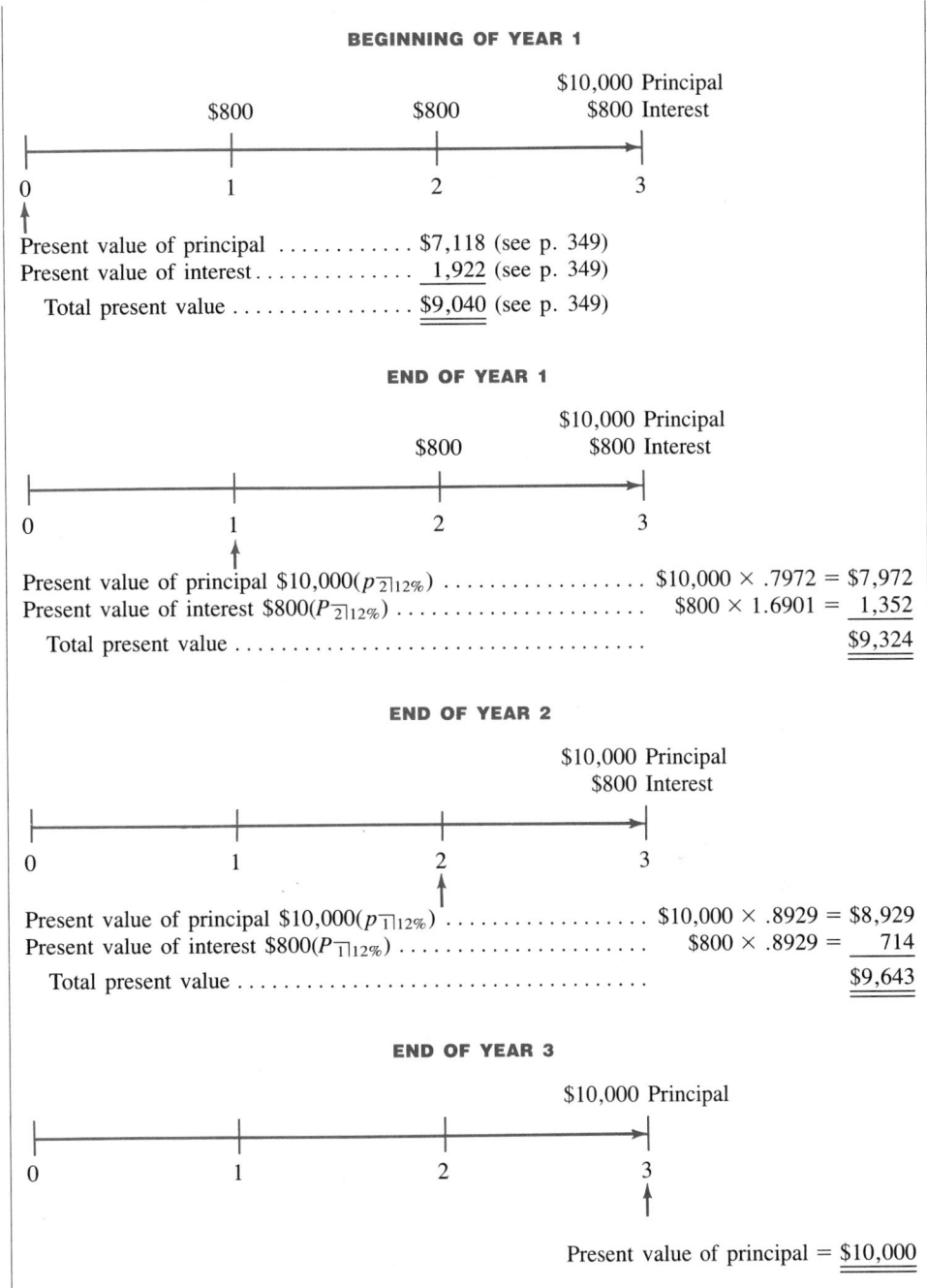

In Chapter 2 we also discussed the asset attributes of current exit value and current cost. Since market rates of interest change over time with changes in supply and demand, varying expectations, and inflation, the use of a *current market rate* instead of the historical rate at the end of each period to discount remaining cash flows associated with receivables gives results approximating the current exit value (what the receivable could be sold for) or current cost (what it would require to replace the receivable).[14] While such a departure from historical cost is not currently acceptable under GAAP, many accountants believe that this approach would provide useful cash flow signals if a company planned to sell the receivable in the very near future.

FACE VALUE GREATER THAN PRESENT VALUE FOR A NONINTEREST-BEARING NOTE   It should be clear from the previous discussion that interest is implicit in note transactions, whether or not the note bears a stated rate of interest. Therefore, the face amount of a noninterest-bearing note always will exceed its present value (assuming any positive market rate of interest).

To illustrate, if Curl Finance Corporation accepted a $10,000 noninterest-bearing note due in three years when the current market rate of interest was 12 percent, the present value of the note would be $7,118 (see the example on p. 349). Curl would be willing to sacrifice only $7,118 in order to receive a cash flow of $10,000 at the end of three years. The entry to record the exchange would be:

Notes receivable	10,000	
Discount on notes receivable		2,882
Cash		7,118

Interest revenue would be recognized over the three-year period and the discount would be amortized by the effective interest method. For example, interest revenue for the first year would be recorded as follows:

Discount on note receivable	854	
Interest revenue		854

IMPLICIT OR IMPUTED INTEREST IN PRACTICE: *APB OPINION NO. 21*   For many years, no authoritative guidelines existed for valuing notes with unrealistic rates of interest. In practice, some companies were able to "front-end" or overstate revenue by accepting noninterest-bearing notes in exchange for goods or services and recording the notes at their face amount. In addition, companies used a variety of methods to compute interest on notes. While some companies used the effective interest method, many others used the straight-line method. Thus, comparability and usefulness suffered because many firms were trying to impact net income in a desired direction. Accounting Principles Board *Opinion No. 21,* "Interest on Receivables and Payables," issued in 1971, applies to bonds, mortgage notes, secured notes (those issued with assets pledged as security), unsecured notes, notes issued for equipment purchases, and accounts receivable and payables that arise from trade terms exceeding one year.[15] The essence of *Opinion No. 21* can be illustrated by three situations similar to the cases previously discussed.

Notes received for cash.   When a note is *exchanged for cash,* the present value of the note equals the amount of cash sacrificed, as illustrated in our earlier examples. The interest rate implicit in the transaction is the rate that equates the present value of the cash flows to be received with the cash sacrificed. Any discount is amortized over the life of the note by the effective interest method.

---

[14] The use of current values for notes receivable also gives rise to **holding gains and losses.** A holding gain (loss) arises if interest rates fall (rise). Over the life of the note, however, the holding gain plus interest revenue calculated at current market rates will equal interest revenue at the historical rate.

[15] Receivables and payables that arise from customary trade terms not exceeding one year are excluded from coverage by *Opinion No. 21* for reasons of materiality.

Notes received for nonmonetary assets or services. Occasionally, a company will sell merchandise or other assets or perform services and accept a note in exchange. Although the present value of the note and the fair value of the asset sacrificed or service provided are assumed to be equal, circumstances may be such that one of these values is uncertain or unknown. *Opinion No. 21* provides that in these circumstances, the present value of the note or the fair value of the sacrifice, whichever is more clearly evident, should be used to value the exchange.

Assume, for example, that at the beginning of year 1, Carl, Inc., sold a tract of land that originally cost $9,000, and accepted a $15,000 note that was payable as follows: end of year 1, $5,000; end of year 2, $5,000; end of year 3, $5,000. The note paid interest at the rate of 2 percent each year. The fair market value of the land was not objectively determinable because five appraisers had given five widely different figures. The applicable current market rate of interest at the beginning of year 1 was 10 percent. The present value of the note and imputed fair market value of the land would be determined as follows:[16]

Present value of principal:
(present value of a $5,000 annuity for
three years at 10%):
$5,000(P_{\overline{3}|10\%})$ . . . . $5,000 × 2.4869 = $12,435

Present value of interest:
$300(p_{\overline{1}|10\%})$. . . . . $300 × .9091 =   273
$200(p_{\overline{2}|10\%})$. . . . . 200 × .8264 =   165
$100(p_{\overline{3}|10\%})$. . . . . 100 × .7513 =   75

Total present value $12,948

The entry to record the sale would be:

Notes receivable 15,000		
Discount on notes receivable ($15,000 − $12,948).	2,052	
Land	9,000	
Gain on sale of land ($12,948 − $9,000)	3,948	

At the end of each year, interest revenue would be calculated under the effective interest method. For example, for year 1 the entry to record the interest and note maturity would be as follows:

Cash. 300		
Discount on notes receivable ($1,295 − $300) 995		
Interest revenue (.10 × $12,948)	1,295	

Cash. 5,000		
Notes receivable	5,000	

[16] A time diagram would appear as follows:

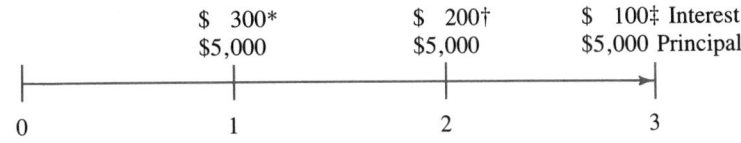

	$ 300*	$ 200†	$ 100‡ Interest
	$5,000	$5,000	$5,000 Principal
0	1	2	3

* $15,000 × .02.
† $10,000 × .02.
‡ $5,000 × .02.

If the fair market value of the land were known with a high degree of certainty, it could be used to establish the exchange price. The implicit interest rate in the exchange would then be calculated for purposes of recording interest revenue.[17]

Notes and other rights or privileges received in exchange for cash. Occasionally a company may lend money and receive, in addition to a note, the *right to buy assets,* such as merchandise, at a discount from the borrower's regular selling prices. The lender may be willing to accept a noninterest-bearing note or a note with an unreasonably low rate of interest and sacrifice cash equal to the face amount of the note because of the additional right to buy at a discount. Thus, the cash sacrificed represents a loan as well as a prepayment on assets to be purchased. Before *Opinion No. 21* was issued, many companies ignored the right acquired and recorded the note at its face value. *Opinion No. 21* requires that the right acquired should be recorded as an asset at an amount equal to the discount on the note, determined by discounting the cash flows associated with the note at the then current rate of interest.

Assume, for example, that at the beginning of year 1 Gibco Discount accepts a two-year $6,000 noninterest-bearing note from a supplier plus the right to purchase 200 cases of oil at a discount price in exchange for $6,000. If the current market rate of interest is 10 percent, the transaction should be recorded as follows:

Notes receivable	6,000	
Prepaid purchases	1,042	
Discount on notes receivable		1,042
Cash		6,000

Present value of note: $6,000 times present value of $1 for two years at 10% [from Table B]: $6,000 × .8264 = $4,958; $6,000 − $4,958 = $1,042

Notice that the right to buy at a discount meets all of the characteristics of an asset that we discussed in Chapter 2.

Interest revenue would be recognized by amortizing the discount over the two-year period under the effective interest method. The asset, prepaid purchases, is allocated to purchases or inventory in proportion to the number of cases of oil purchased each year as compared to the total purchases to be made. For example, if 100 cases were purchased in year 1, the following entry would be made:

Purchases	521	
Prepaid purchases		521

(100/200 × $1,042)

In accordance with the cost principle, the $521 addition to purchases in year 1 is part of the cost of these purchases, since a portion of the right to purchase at a discount has been sacrificed.

USING RECEIVABLES TO SECURE IMMEDIATE CASH

Companies often use accounts and notes receivable to obtain immediate cash rather than wait to collect the amount due under the terms of the original exchange. Some years ago, for example, J. C. Penney sold several million dollars of its credit card receivables to Citicorp. Citicorp received as income a service charge from Penney's and interest on the purchased receivables. In 1985 Coca-Cola sold approximately $750 million in receivables from its entertainment division. The proceeds from the receivables, which normally are collected over a 6- to 30-month period, were to be used either to buy back Coca-Cola

---

[17] The implicit rate could be determined by the procedure discussed on pp. 305–307. Here it would be necessary to use a trial-and-error method to find the effective interest rate, because the cash flows are not uniform.

common stock, to liquidate short-term debt, or to reinvest at a higher rate of return.

Many methods may be used to generate cash from receivables. These methods range from using the receivables as collateral for a loan to selling the receivables outright. In practice, a desire on the part of many companies to engage in "off balance sheet financing" has created a gray area between these two extremes. That is, is a transfer of receivables in exchange for cash a *sale* transaction or a *borrowing* transaction? This distinction is important because in a sale transaction, the receivables are removed from the seller's books and a gain or loss on sale is recorded. On the other hand, a borrowing transaction results in the recording of a liability on the books of the transferor; the receivables merely serve as collateral for the loan.

Conceptually, a sale transaction results if the ownership risks and benefits associated with the receivables are transferred from the transferor to the transferee or if the net cash flow effects of the transfer can be reasonably estimated by the transferor; otherwise, the transfer of receivables represents a borrowing transaction to the transferor. The methods of generating cash from receivables and the appropriate accounting methods are discussed in the following paragraphs.

Discounting Notes Receivable

Occasionally a company may sell notes receivable to a third party, usually a bank, in order to obtain cash. If the sale is *without recourse,* the seller has no further obligations in case the maker of the note fails to pay the bank on the note's maturity date. Most notes, however, are sold *with recourse,* which means that the transferor is contingently liable and must pay the amount due in the event the debtor defaults on payment at maturity. The process of selling notes is known as **discounting,** and the interest that the purchaser of the note earns from holding the note to maturity is the discount. This discount is the difference between the proceeds paid to the seller of the note and the amount due on the note at maturity. The discount usually is computed on the note's maturity value; this practice increases the effective return earned by the purchaser.

Selling a note to secure cash is called discounting a note.

Assume that Cleo Corporation accepted a 9 percent 60-day note for $20,000 from a customer in settlement of an account. After holding the note for 24 days, Cleo discounted the note, with recourse, to a bank. The bank used a discount rate of 10 percent.

The bank would calculate the discount and proceeds as follows:

Face amount of note	$20,000
Interest to maturity ($20,000 × .09 × 60/360)	300
Maturity value	$20,300
Discount, calculated on maturity value ($20,300 × .10 × 36/360)	(203)
Proceeds to Cleo..	$20,097

The discount of $203 represents the interest to be earned by the bank from holding the note for the remaining 36 days until maturity.

Conceptually, Cleo should recognize interest revenue of $120 for the 24 days that the note has been held ($20,000 × .09 × 24/360 = $120), and recognize as a loss from sale the difference between the note's carrying value plus accrued interest ($20,000 + $120) at the date of discounting and the proceeds of $20,097:

Cash...	20,097	
Loss on sale of note...................................	23	
Notes receivable discounted...........................		20,000
Interest revenue		120

In practice, the $120 and $23 sometimes are netted and recorded as interest revenue if the proceeds exceed the carrying value of the note or interest expense if the proceeds are less than the carrying value of the note. Under this approach, the entry would be:

Cash..	20,097	
Notes receivable discounted............................		20,000
Interest revenue ($120 − $23)...........................		97

The notes receivable discounted account should be reported as a contra-asset account to notes receivable. The contingent liability also should be disclosed in the financial statements.

When the maker of the note pays the bank at maturity, Cleo would make the following entry:

Notes receivable discounted..............................	20,000	
Notes receivable		20,000

On the other hand, if the maker defaults at maturity, Cleo must pay the bank the maturity value of $20,300 and would make the following entry:

Receivable from customer	20,300	
Notes receivable discounted..............................	20,000	
Notes receivable		20,000
Cash..		20,300

If Cleo were unable to collect the account, it would be written off as uncollectible.

Using Receivables as Security for a Loan

Receivables are often pledged or assigned when money is borrowed.

Companies often borrow money by using receivables as security or collateral for a loan. Under an informal **pledging** arrangement, the receivables serve as security for the loan. In case of default, the lender has legal rights to the receivables in satisfaction of the debt.

Another arrangement for using receivables to collateralize a loan is called an **assignment**. Under an assignment, one company, called the assignor, borrows money from another company, called the assignee. The assignor agrees that the proceeds from the collection of receivables will be used to retire the loan. Legally, the assignment gives the assignee the same right to collect the note as the assignor had before the assignment. Customers' payments sometimes are made to the assignor, but normally they are remitted directly to the assignee. The assignee lends less than the face amount of the receivables assigned in order to provide some additional security or "cushion" for the loan agreement. The assignee usually deducts a finance fee or service charge in advance on the amount loaned and also charges interest on the unpaid loan balance.

Assume that on March 1, Ruth, Inc., assigns $75,000 in accounts receivable to House Finance as security for a loan. House Finance lends cash equal to 80 percent of the accounts assigned and charges a finance fee equal to 4 percent of the face amount of the loan plus interest on the unpaid loan balance at the rate of 1 percent per month. The entries below illustrate recording of the assignment, as well as subsequent collection and payment transactions.

March 1 Assigned receivables of $75,000. Received cash equal to 80% of the receivables assigned, less a 4% finance charge.

Cash ($75,000 × .80 × .96)	57,600	
Finance fee expense (.04 × $60,000)	2,400	
Payable to House Finance		60,000
Accounts receivable assigned.....................	75,000	
Accounts receivable		75,000

The first entry is to record the loan, and the second entry is to reclassify the accounts receivable assigned since they are restricted specifically for repayment of the loan to House Finance.

March 31 Collected receivables totaling $40,000. Paid this amount to House Finance as interest and a reduction in the payable.

Cash..	40,000	
Accounts receivable assigned.................		40,000
Interest expense (.01 × $60,000)	600	
Payable to House Finance	39,400	
Cash....................................		40,000

April 30 Collected receivables totaling $30,000. Paid the interest and balance due to House Finance.

Cash..	30,000	
Accounts receivable assigned..................		30,000
Interest expense [.01 × ($60,000 − $39,400)].......	206	
Payable to House Finance	20,600	
Cash....................................		20,806

April 30 Reclassified remaining assigned receivables.

Accounts receivable	5,000	
Accounts receivable assigned..................		5,000

The balance sheet presentation of the assignment is shown in Exhibit 8–8. For instructional purposes, presentation is shown for each month during the period of the assignment. Note that the amount payable is offset against the assigned receivables, and the difference is the assignor's **equity in the assigned receivables.** This presentation is proper because the receivables are restricted specifically for retirement of the loan.

Factoring of Accounts Receivable

In many manufacturing industries, such as clothing and textiles, companies historically have transferred their receivables to financial institutions known as factors. By transferring the receivables to a factor in exchange for cash, a company is able to accelerate the receivables-to-cash portion of its operating cycle. In addition, under certain transfer agreements, collection risks may be shifted to the factor. A factoring company earns income by paying the transferor less than the expected realizable value of the receivables. This discount is composed of a factoring fee, which may be quite high if the transfer is without recourse, and interest, which reflects the waiting period before the receivables are

---

EXHIBIT 8–8   AN ASSIGNOR'S PRESENTATION OF AN ASSIGNMENT IN THE BALANCE SHEET

	MARCH 1	MARCH 31	APRIL 30
Accounts receivable	—	—	$5,000
Accounts receivable assigned	$75,000	$35,000	—
Less: Payable to House Finance	(60,000)	(20,600)	—
Equity in assigned receivables...........	$15,000	$14,400	

collected. In some cases, factors may hold back a portion of the amount to be paid to the transferor to allow for subsequent reductions in the amount due from the debtors. Customers of the transferor usually are notified of the factoring arrangement and make payments directly to the factor.

Receivables may be transferred with recourse or without recourse. Receivables transferred *without recourse* should be recorded as a *sale* because (1) ownership risks and benefits are transferred from the transferor to the transferee (the factoring company) and (2) the net cash flow effect of the transfer is known at the date of transfer. To illustrate, assume that Cummings Corporation transfers receivables with a face value of $100,000 to Hock Factoring. Estimated uncollectible accounts of $2,000 have been accrued by Cummings. The factoring company charges a 9 percent factoring fee plus interest of $3,000 to compensate for the waiting period before the receivables are collected. Cummings' entry to record the sale is as follows:

```
Cash [$100,000 − (.09 × $100,000) − $3,000] ............. 88,000
Allowance for uncollectible accounts ...................... 2,000
Loss on sale of receivables ($98,000 − $88,000) ............ 10,000
    Accounts receivable ..................................            100,000
```

When receivables are transferred *with recourse,* the transferor agrees to make good any receivables that are not collectible. Even though ownership risks and benefits are not shifted completely to the transferee, the transfer should be recorded as a *sale* if the net cash flow effect of the transfer can be reasonably estimated;[18] otherwise the transfer of receivables is a borrowing and a *liability* should be recorded. Conditions that affect this determination, *all* of which must be met in order for the tranferor to record a sale, include the transferor's surrender of control of the economic benefits associated with the receivables, the transferor's ability to make a reasonable estimate of its obligations to the transferee under the recourse provisions, and the transferee's inability to require the transferor to repurchase the receivables, except in accordance with the recourse provisions.[19]

To illustrate accounting for transfers of receivable with recourse, refer to the data for Cummings Corporation and Hock Factoring and assume the following changes and additional information:

1. The transfer is with recourse, and thus the factoring fee is 2 percent instead of 9 percent.

2. Cummings estimates that customer sales discounts will equal 6 percent of the receivables' face value.

3. The factoring agreement provides that Hock Factoring may hold back $10,000 to allow for reductions in the amounts to be collected.

The transfer still represents a sale because Cummings is able to estimate the net cash flow effect of the transaction. Cummings' entry to record the sale of receivables is as follows:

[18] This situation is somewhat analogous to accruing estimated warranty obligations in measuring the net cash flow effect of a sale, which we discussed briefly in Chapter 6. In the case of a warranty, the selling firm retains the risk associated with defective merchandise but may be able to make a reasonable estimate of its obligation under the warranty.

[19] "Reporting by Transferors for Transfers of Receivables with Recourse," *Statement of Financial Accounting Standards No. 77* (Stamford, Conn: FASB, 1983).

Cash [$100,000 − (.02 × $100,000) − $3,000 − $10,000] .. 85,000
Due from Hock Factoring ($10,000 − $2,000 − $6,000).... 2,000
Allowance for uncollectible accounts 2,000
Sales discounts 6,000
Loss on sale of receivables ($92,000 − $87,000) 5,000
    Accounts receivable   100,000

Notice that the $10,000 amount due from Hock has been reduced by the estimated uncollectibles and sales discounts and that the loss on sale is the difference between the receivables' net carrying value of $92,000 ($100,000 − $2,000 allowance − $6,000 estimated sales discounts) and the assets received from Hock ($85,000 cash + $2,000 receivable).

If the transfer did not meet the sale criteria—if, for example, Cummings could not estimate the amount of sales discounts and agreed to repurchase the receivables on Hock's demand—the transfer would be recorded as a liability, and the following entry would be appropriate:

Cash..85,000
Due from Hock Factoring 10,000
Interest expense 5,000
    Payable to Hock Factoring   100,000

Interest expense of $5,000 should be allocated over the term of the loan. As customers' remittances were received by Hock, Cummings would debit the payable and credit accounts receivable. Cummings would record uncollectible accounts and sales discounts in the normal manner, as illustrated earlier in the chapter. Assuming that $1,800 of the $100,000 in receivables were written off as uncollectible, sales discounts totaled $7,300, and the remaining receivables of $90,900 ($100,000 − $1,800 − $7,300) were collected, the following entry would be made by Cummings for final settlement with Hock:

Cash... 900
Payable to Hock Factoring ($100,000 − $90,900) 9,100
    Due from Hock Factoring   10,000

CASH AND RECEIVABLES PRESENTATION IN THE BALANCE SHEET

As we stated in Chapter 5, unrestricted cash balances are reported on the balance sheet as current assets. Cash that is restricted for a certain purpose—for example, for retirement of long-term debt—is reported as an investment. Receivables that are expected to be collected within one year or the operating cycle, whichever is longer, are reported as current assets in the balance sheet. These receivables include accounts receivable, installment receivables, short-term notes receivable, and receivables from governmental units. Receivables from employees and officers should be disclosed separately. Unearned interest and discounts on receivables and allowances for doubtful accounts should be reported as contra-asset accounts to the appropriate receivables. Any receivables pledged as security for loans also should be disclosed. Exhibit 8–9 illustrates these disclosures.

EXHIBIT 8—9   PRESENTATION OF CASH AND RECEIVABLES IN THE BALANCE SHEET

Current assets
Cash (including savings deposits)		$128,500
Accounts receivable (net of allowance for doubtful		
accounts of $16,000)		175,000
Accounts receivable assigned	$45,000	
Less: Notes payable (Note 1)	(22,000)	
Equity in assigned receivables......................		23,000
Installment receivables (net of unearned interest of		
$10,000 and deferred gross profit of $36,000)		80,000
Notes receivable	$65,000	
Less: Allowance for doubtful accounts...................	(13,000)	
Unearned interest	(10,000)	
	$42,000	
Less: Notes receivable discounted (Note 2)	(8,000)	34,000
Receivables from officers		10,000

.
.
.

Note 1. The company has assigned a portion of its accounts receivable in connection with the issuance of a note. Such receivables are restricted specifically to retirement of the note.

Note 2. During the current year the company discounted some notes receivable to a bank. The company is contingently liable to the bank for these notes and must pay the bank the maturity value of $8,500 in the event that the makers of the notes default on payment.

SUMMARY OF IMPORTANT TOPICS AND CONCEPT APPLICATIONS

1. Accounting procedures for cash include bank reconciliations and the four-column proof of cash, the use of a petty cash fund, and insuring that adequate balance sheet disclosures are made regarding cash that is restricted as its use. These procedures are designed to provide proper internal control of cash and to make cash disclosures **representationally faithful.**

2. The three accounting considerations for accounts receivable include determining (measuring) the amounts of receivables due from customers, determining when receivables should be recognized as assets (a revenue recognition issue), and estimating the amount of receivables that will not be collected. These considerations relate to providing useful signals about **present and future cash flows** to assist investors in **decision making.**

3. Receivables are measured at **net realizable value,** which means net of trade and cash discounts and net of estimated sales returns. Net realizable value assumes that the returns can be estimated in a reliable manner. Receivables that are collectible over a period of time are measured at **present value** if interest is a material amount. Interest on long-term receivables is calculated by the **effective interest method.**

4. When it is probable that some accounts receivable will not be collected and the amounts can be estimated, uncollectible accounts expense should be accrued in the period in which the credit sales are made. The objective of this procedure is to report the **estimated net cash flow effects of the sale** during the period of sale and to report receivables at **net realizable value.** In practice, this expense is calculated as a percent-

age of sales, as a percentage of ending accounts receivable, or by aging the receivables. When reliable estimates of uncollectible accounts cannot be made, an expense is recorded only as accounts prove uncollectible (the direct write-off method).

5. Notes receivable are valued at the **present value** of the cash flows to be received. The **effective interest method** is used to record interest revenue during the period over which the note is outstanding. The interest rate used in applying the effective interest method is that rate which is implicit in the exchange price established when the note is received. This exchange price may be based on either the fair value of the note received or the fair value of the asset or assets received in exchange for the note.

6. In order to accelerate cash flows, companies often transfer notes and accounts receivable prior to their maturity dates or use them as borrowing collateral. Determining whether a transfer of receivables is a sale or a borrowing is important so that the resulting accounting procedures and financial statements are **representationally faithful.** When the net cash flow effects of the transfer of receivables can be estimated with some degree of **reliability,** the transaction should be recorded as a sale. Otherwise, the transfer should be accounted for as a borrowing.

APPENDIX 8–1

COMPREHENSIVE CASH RECONCILIATION

As we stated earlier in this chapter, a comprehensive reconciliation or proof of cash not only provides a reconciliation of the ending balance of the firm's cash account with the bank statement but also reconciles the beginning cash balance and all receipts and disbursements shown in the bank statement and in the firm's books.

Assume that the following information for March is a continuation of the Wezzel Corporation example on pages 336–38.

1. Reproduction of cash account from general ledger (T-account form):

	Cash		
Balance 2/28/87	8,672.89	March disbursements	97,469.33
March receipts	94,050.75	Balance 3/31/87	5,254.31
	102,723.64		102,723.64
Balance 3/31/87	5,254.31		

2. Summary totals of deposits and other credits and checks written and other debits from the March bank statement:

Beginning balance	$ 1,768.22
Deposits and other credits	104,290.38
Checks and other debits	(99,335.46)
Ending balance	$ 6,723.14

3. The February bank reconciliation below is reproduced from Exhibit 8–2:

Balance per bank statement		$ 1,768.22
Add: Deposit in transit	$ 400.00	
Proceeds from matured CD	10,600.00	11,000.00
		$12,768.22
Deduct: Outstanding checks		(3,640.00)
Corrected cash balance		$ 9,128.22
Balance per books		$ 8,672.89
Add: Understatement of deposit from		
transposition error	$ 270.00	
Proceeds of note collected by bank	214.00	484.00
		$ 9,156.89
Deduct: Service charge	$ 2.30	
NSF check	26.37	(28.67)
Corrected cash balance		$ 9,128.22

4. Deposits in transit, March 31: $250.00.

5. Outstanding checks, March 31: $1,870.00.

6. The customer's check that was returned with the February bank statement was redeposited on March 30 at the customer's request. The bank did not process the check until April 3. (This redeposit is not included in item 4 above.)

7. A check for $90.00 was recorded in the cash disbursements journal as $9.00.

8. Miscellaneous bank charges for March:

Service charge	$ 3.40
Charge for printing checks	15.40
Safety deposit box charge for 1987	25.00

The comprehensive cash reconciliation for Wezzel Corporation for March appears in Exhibit 8–10. The format of the reconciliation and the explanation of the reconciling items follow.

1. The four columns in Exhibit 8–10 are for entering the beginning balance (February 28), total March cash receipts, total March cash disbursements, and the ending balance (March 31) per the bank statement (top part of statement) and per the firm's cash account (bottom part of statement).

2. The reconciliation of the beginning balances per bank and per books is exactly the same as the bank reconciliation for February presented in Exhibit 8–2 and reproduced in this appendix. The illustration assumes that the firm did not make adjusting entries at the end of the previous month. If adjusting entries had been made in February (as discussed in the chapter and as would usually be the case), the beginning balance per books would be $9,128.22 at February 28 and there would be no reconciling items under the first column for the beginning balance per books.

3. The column numbers not in parentheses represent *additions* in arriving at the column totals while the column numbers in parentheses represent *deductions* in arriving at column totals.

EXHIBIT 8–10

Wezzel Corporation

COMPREHENSIVE CASH RECONCILIATION
MARCH 1987

	(1) FEBRUARY 28 RECONCILIATION	(2) MARCH RECEIPTS	(3) MARCH DISBURSEMENTS	(4) MARCH 31 RECONCILIATION
Balance per bank	$ 1,768.22	$104,290.38	$99,335.46	$6,723.14
Add:				
Deposit in transit, 2/28/87	400.00	(400.00)		
Deposit in transit, 3/31/87		250.00		250.00
Redeposit of NSF check		26.37		26.37
Proceeds from matured CD	10,600.00	(10,600.00)		
Deduct:				
Outstanding checks, 2/28/87	(3,640.00)		(3,640.00)	
Outstanding checks, 3/31/87			1,870.00	(1,870.00)
Corrected bank balance	$ 9,128.22	$ 93,566.75	$97,565.46	$5,129.51
Balance per books	$ 8,672.89	$ 94,050.75	$97,469.33	$5,254.31
Add:				
Error in deposit................	270.00	(270.00)		
Proceeds from note.............	214.00	(214.00)		
Deduct:				
Service charge, February	(2.30)		(2.30)	
Service charge, March			3.40	(3.40)
Check printing charge			15.40	(15.40)
Safety deposit charge			25.00	(25.00)
NSF check	(26.37)		(26.37)	
Error in recording check			81.00	(81.00)
Corrected book balance	$ 9,128.22	$ 93,566.75	$97,565.46	$5,129.51

4. The reconciliation may be explained as follows:

a) Beginning and ending balances (cols. 1 and 4). Reconciliation of the beginning balances per books and per bank has been covered in the chapter, and reconciliation of the ending balances per books and per bank is exactly the same. Notice that the corrected beginning and ending balances per bank and per books represent the correct cash balance to be reported on the balance sheet at February 28 and March 31, respectively.

b) Reconciliation of March receipts (col. 2).

i. Per bank statement: Since the $400 deposit in transit and the CD proceeds of $10,600 were actually February cash receipts (although they were not recorded by the bank until early in March), these amounts are *deducted* from March receipts per bank. Likewise, since the $250 deposit in transit and the redeposited NSF check at the end of March were actually March receipts (although they were not recorded by the bank until April), the amounts are *added* to March receipts per bank. The $250 deposit in transit and the $26.37 redeposited NSF check also are extended to column 4, as the items increase the bank balance on the ending reconciliation.

ii. Per books: Since we assumed that the firm did not make adjusting entries at the end of February, the deposit error and the note proceeds represent February receipts and must be deducted from March receipts. (Notice that if the firm did make adjusting entries at the end of February, there would be no reconciling items to March receipts, as the beginning balance would be properly stated at $9,128.22.)

c) Reconciliation of March disbursements (col. 3).

i. Per bank: Since the outstanding checks totaling $3,640 at the end of February represent February expenditures, they must be deducted from March disbursements. Likewise, since outstanding checks at the end of March totaling $1,870 represent March expenditures, this amount must be added to March disbursements. The $1,870 outstanding checks at the end of March must also be extended to column 4, as these outstanding checks decrease the bank balance on the ending reconciliation.

ii. Per books: Since the firm did not make adjusting entries at the end of February, the February service charge ($2.30) and the NSF check ($26.37) must be deducted from March disbursements. The March service charge ($3.40), the charge for printing checks ($15.40), the safety deposit box charge ($25.00), and the error ($81.00) increase March disbursements. These items must be added to March disbursements and also deducted from the March 31 ending cash balance.

When the comprehensive cash reconciliation is completed, the beginning and ending cash balances per bank and per books have been reconciled to the correct cash balance. Also, cash control is strengthened, since all cash receipts and disbursements per books have been reconciled with the bank statement.

QUESTIONS

The question marked with an asterisk (*) refers to Appendix 8–1.

Q8-1. What is cash and what items normally are included in the cash account?

Q8-2. Why is control of cash important?

Q8-3. Identify some internal control procedures designed to achieve better control over cash receipts and disbursements.

Q8-4. What is a petty cash fund, and what purposes are served by the use of such a fund?

Q8-5. How should a bank overdraft at the end of the fiscal year be classified on the balance sheet?

Q8-6. In what numbered space in the following bank reconciliation format should each of the items listed below appear? If an item should not appear, so indicate by marking it 5.

Balance, per bank statement xx	Balance, per books xx
Add: .... (1)	Add: .... (3)
Deduct: .... (2)	Deduct: .... (4)
Corrected bank balance xx	Corrected book balance xx

a) Note collected by bank on behalf of firm.
b) Service charge for month.
c) NSF check returned to firm by bank.
d) Outstanding checks.
e) An outstanding certified check.
f) Deposits in transit.
g) A deposit the firm failed to record.

Q8-7. Given the following information, compute the balance per books (before adjustment):

Balance, per bank statement $3,000.00
Service charge for month... 4.00
Outstanding checks, end of month 129.00
Deposit in transit 400.00
Deposit of $120 recorded by the firm as a deposit of $12.

*Q8-8. What are the advantages of a comprehensive cash reconciliation statement?

Q8-9. Identify three considerations that arise in accounting for accounts receivable.

Q8-10. **A)** Distinguish between trade discounts and cash discounts offered by sellers of merchandise and discuss the purpose of each type of discount.

B) Explain the procedures and rationale underlying the ''gross'' vs. the ''net'' method of accounting for cash discounts.

Q8-11. Under what circumstances is the installment method of accounting appropriate for receivables that are collectible over an extended period of time?

Q8-12. Company A follows the practice of *factoring* receivables, company B uses receivables as *pledges,* while company C *assigns* receivables periodically. How do these practices differ?

Q8-13. The following items appear as receivables for Joelle Corporation:

	DR	CR
Accounts receivable	$45,000	
Allowance for doubtful accounts..........................		$4,400
Receivable from officer	1,200	
Notes receivable	16,000	
Unearned interest		2,700
Receivables with credit balances—customers		400
Allowance for loan losses		1,600
Notes receivable discounted.............................		1,000
Interest on notes receivable	600	
Purchase advances	1,500	

How should each item be presented on a classified balance sheet?

Q8-14. Big Apple, Inc., assigned $35,000 of accounts receivable as a basis for a loan. The assignee advanced $32,000 to Big Apple. What accounts of Big Apple would be affected by the transaction? How would the accounts be presented on a balance sheet?

Q8-15. What is the nature of the account, notes receivable discounted?

Q8-16. **A)** What effect does ''fair market value at exchange date'' have on the valuing of notes at present value?

B) Construct a transaction in which the face amount of a note equals its present value.

C) Construct a transaction in which the face amount of a note exceeds its present value.

Q8-17. How is the effective interest method related to the valuing of notes at present value?

CASES

C8-1. ESTIMATING UNCOLLECTIBLE ACCOUNTS During the audit of accounts receivable, your client asks why the current year's income statement reports bad debt expense when some accounts may become uncollectible *next* year. He then said that he had read that financial statements should be based on verifiable, objective evidence, and that it seemed to him to be much more objective to wait until individual accounts receivable were actually determined to be uncollectible before recording them as expenses.

REQUIRED

1. Discuss the theoretical justification of the allowance method as contrasted with the direct write-off method of accounting for bad debts.

2. Describe the percentage of sales method and the aging method of estimating bad debts. Explain how well each method accomplishes the objectives of the allowance method of accounting for bad debts.

3. Of what merit is your client's contention that the allowance method lacks the objectivity of the direct write-off method? Discuss in terms of accounting's measurement function.

(AICPA, adapted)

C8-2. ALLOWANCES; RECEIVABLE VALUATION   The president and the controller of Betterdata Corporation were discussing the merits of the use of allowances in connection with accounts receivable. The controller suggested that the following allowances be used in connection with the company's receivables: an allowance for sales discounts, an allowance for bad debts, and an allowance for sales returns.

The president strongly opposed the controller's suggestion on the basis that (1) too much subjectivity is introduced into the statements, (2) the resulting data are hypothetical, and (3) the resulting statements are not useful or reliable.

REQUIRED

1. What are the objectives underlying the use of allowances in connection with accounts receivable?

2. Under what circumstances would the allowances suggested by the controller be appropriate?

C8-3. EXCHANGES INVOLVING VALUATION OF NOTES   Business transactions often involve the exchange of property, goods, or services for notes or similar instruments that may stipulate no interest rate or an interest rate that varies from prevailing rates.

REQUIRED

1. When a note is received in exchange for property, goods, or services, what value should be placed on the note if it bears interest at a reasonable rate and is issued in a bargained transaction? If it bears no interest or is not issued in a bargained transaction? Explain.

2. If the recorded value of a note differs from the face value, how should the difference be accounted for? How should this difference be presented in the financial statements? Explain.

(AICPA, adapted)

C8-4. VALUING NOTES; INTEREST   Luxury Limousine Services purchases luxury automobiles from the Cadillac Division of General Motors, cuts them in half, adds a middle section, and finishes out the cars as limousines. The sales price of a limousine, which varies with the extent of interior furnishing, averages about $100,000. Because the limousines usually are sold in New York City to private individuals who operate transportation services, the company requires a small down payment and accepts a note, payable in 10 annual installments, for the balance of the sales price. The notes bear interest at 2 percent per year; the buyers would normally have to finance the purchases at a much higher rate of interest.

During your audit of Luxury Limousine Services, you discover that the company has been recording the notes receivable at face value and crediting sales revenue for the notes' face value. Interest revenue on the notes then is calculated on the basis of the 2 percent stated interest rate.

REQUIRED

1. Discuss the impact on the financial statements of the company's methods of accounting for notes receivable and interest revenue. In the course of your discussion, indicate the proper method of accounting.

2. Assume that the prevailing rate of interest applicable to the notes accepted by Luxury Limousine Services is 10 percent. On the basis of an average sales price per limousine of $100,000 and an average down payment of $5,000, calculate the amount of misstatement of the following items in the company's financial statements (for simplicity, assume that the sale is made at the beginning of the year and that each installment payment is received at the end of the year):

a) Sales revenue in the year of sale.

b) Interest revenue for the first and second years that the note is outstanding.

c) Notes receivable at the end of the first and second years.

C8-5. CASH GENERATION FROM RECEIVABLES   Slippery Kitchens, Inc., is a nationwide distributor of no-wax vinyl kitchen floors. At the beginning of the current year, its accounts and notes receivable appeared as follows:

Accounts receivable $2,500,000
Notes receivable   400,000

During the current year, the company continually has found itself without the necessary cash to conduct its day-to-day operations. Slippery Kitchens has considered borrowing $2 million from a local bank, but the company president is concerned about the effect of such a loan on the company's balance sheet. Recently, during a lunch at the local country club, a friend of the president's suggested that Slippery Kitchens use its accounts and notes receivable as a way to generate the necessary cash needed for operations. The president was intrigued by this suggestion and has asked you to analyze the effects of the following alternatives on the company's income statement, the statement of cash flows, and the statement of financial position:

1. Pledge the accounts receivable as security for a $2 million loan.

2. Sell the receivables, without recourse, to a factor. Factors normally pay only about 80 percent of face value for receivables on a nonrecourse basis.

3. Same as part 2, except that the sale is with recourse. Slippery Kitchens cannot estimate its obligation to the factor and will receive cash approximating 95 percent of the receivables' face value on a recourse basis.

4. Discount the notes receivable at the local bank. The notes have a maturity value of $450,000, and the bank's discount will be approximately $65,000.

5. Assign both the notes and the accounts receivable to a bank in another state. This bank will advance 85 percent of the face value of the receivables, less a service charge and periodic interest on the uncollected receivables. The president's friend favors this alternative and points out that it is the most attractive way of obtaining needed funds without "loading up the debt section of the company's balance sheet."

REQUIRED

Draft a response to each alternative. In your responses, indicate what the effects would be on each financial statement mentioned. You may indicate the effects in general terms.

EXERCISES

E8-1. PETTY CASH FUND   On May 1, 1987, Vernon Company installed a petty cash fund of $200. On May 20, 1987, the fund custodian presented for reimbursement vouchers for the following expenditures:

Supplies purchased and used $29.00
Postage 48.00
Withdrawal of money by Vernon for personal use 50.00
Freight paid on purchases 35.00

The fund was replenished on May 20, 1987. On May 27, 1987, the petty cash fund was increased by $100.

REQUIRED

Prepare entries to record:

1. Establishment of the fund.
2. Replenishment of the fund.
3. Increase in the balance of the fund.

E8-2. BANK RECONCILIATION   The following data apply to the cash records of the Holly Company:

Ending cash balance, per books $5,120
Ending cash balance, per bank statement 4,000
Outstanding checks 910
Service charge for month 3
Proceeds from bank collection of note (including interest of $8) 108
Deposits in transit 2,000
In error, Holly Company recorded a deposit of $15 for cash sales as $150.

REQUIRED

1. Prepare a bank reconciliation for the month.
2. Prepare the journal entry to adjust Holly's accounts.

E8-3. DETERMINING A CASH SHORTAGE THROUGH A BANK RECONCILIATION   As auditor for May Charnes, you are attempting to determine an apparent cash shortage that Charnes believes resulted from an employee's theft. You have assembled the following information for the month of October:

Cash balance per books, 10/1 .... $10,196.37
Cash receipts for October, per books 24,647.50
Cash disbursements for October, per books 33,470.91
Cash balance, per bank statement, 10/31 .... 534.14
Deposit in transit, 10/31 .... 700.00
Outstanding checks, 10/31 .... 270.38
Service charge for month 9.20

You have reason to believe that a customer's cash payment on account was entered in the books as a cash receipt but was not deposited in the bank.

REQUIRED

Calculate the amount of the apparent cash shortage.

E8-4. BANK RECONCILIATION   The following data are available for the *Texarkana Daily News*:
a) The newspaper's bank statement shows a balance of $63,834.87 at September 30, 1987.
b) The bank balance per the *Daily News*'s records is $51,732.06.
c) Deposits in transit, September 30, $6,025.50.
d) Checks outstanding as of September 30, $9,540.84.
e) On September 29, the bank collected a note for the *Daily News* for $8,889.00, including interest of $89.00. The bank charged a collection fee of $25.20.
f) In recording a check from an advertiser in the amount of $480.00, the *Daily News*'s bookkeeper recorded the amount of $48.00.
g) Bank service charges for the month, $15.93.
h) Included in the bank statement was a check from a customer in the amount of $558.00 which was marked NSF by the bank.
i) Included in the bank statement was a debit memo for $134.40 which the bank had erroneously charged to the *Daily News*.

REQUIRED

    1. Prepare a bank reconciliation for the *Texarkana Daily News* on September 30, 1987.

    2. Prepare the necessary journal entries for the newspaper on September 30, 1987.

E8-5. ESTIMATING UNCOLLECTIBLE ACCOUNTS EXPENSE   Nike Cup Corporation had the following accounts receivable and allowance for uncollectible accounts balances at the end of 1987 before any expense adjustment:

Accounts receivable . . . . $66,000 Dr
Allowance for uncollectible accounts . . . .   3,000 Cr

Sales in 1987 totaled $530,000 (10 percent of sales were for cash), and write-offs of customer accounts totaled $3,200.

REQUIRED

    1. Calculate the balance in the allowance account at the beginning of 1987.

    2. Prepare the adjusting entry to record uncollectible accounts expense under the following assumptions:
      a) 1 percent of credit sales will prove uncollectible.
      b) 10 percent of ending accounts receivable are uncollectible.
      c) Aging of the receivables indicates that $6,400 is probably uncollectible.

E8-6. UNCOLLECTIBLE ACCOUNTS EXPENSE; CUSTOMER COLLECTIONS   The following year-end information relates to Shawnee Corporation's credit sales for 1987, 1988, and 1989:

YEAR	ACCOUNTS RECEIVABLE	ALLOWANCE FOR UNCOLLECTIBLE ACCOUNTS	ACCOUNTS WRITTEN OFF
1987	$78,000	$3,400	$1,600
1988	83,000	3,600	1,900
1989	74,000	3,000	1,200

REQUIRED

    1. Calculate the uncollectible accounts expense for 1988 and 1989.

    2. Assume that in 1988 and 1989, sales (all credit) total $250,000 each year. Calculate the customer collections for these years.

E8-7. UNCOLLECTIBLE ACCOUNTS EXPENSE   During your audit of Crystal Beaches, Inc., you discover that the company used the direct write-off method in accounting for uncollectible accounts. You have convinced management that the allowance method should have been used, and this method will be used for the current year, ending December 31, 1987. Your supervisor has agreed to make the necessary year-end entries; however, you have been asked to analyze the three years of records since Crystal Beaches began operations. Your analysis indicates that the following accounts have been written off to expense:

	1985	1986	1987
1985 accounts receivable	$2,000	$2,400	—
1986 accounts receivable	—	800	$4,000
1987 accounts receivable	—	—	3,200

Estimated uncollectible accounts as of December 31, 1987, were as follows:

1986 accounts receivable $1,400
1987 accounts receivable   3,000

REQUIRED

1. Calculate the amount of overstatement or understatement of net income for 1985 and 1986 from using the direct write-off method instead of the preferred allowance method.

2. Calculate the uncollectible accounts expense for 1987 under the allowance method.

3. Calculate the correct balance in the allowance account at December 31, 1987.

E8-8. JOURNAL ENTRIES FOR SALES AND UNCOLLECTIBLE ACCOUNTS At the beginning of December, 1987, Maxima Enterprises had a debit balance in accounts receivable of $504,000 and a credit balance of $26,400 in allowance for doubtful accounts. During December, the following transactions occurred:
   a) Sales on account, $360,000.
   b) Sales returns and allowances, $7,200.
   c) Cash payments on account by customers, $355,200.
   d) Write-off of the Nisson account, $7,680.
On December 31, 1987, Maxima decided that the allowance account balance should be adjusted to $29,280 to reflect the net realizable value of the receivables.

REQUIRED

1. Prepare journal entries for items *a* through *d* and for the adjusting entry to the allowance account.

2. Calculate the balance in accounts receivable and the allowance account at December 31, 1987.

3. In July, 1988, Nisson paid to Maxima the amount previously written off. Prepare Maxima's journal entry to record this receipt.

E8-9. DISCOUNTING NOTES RECEIVABLE The following notes are held by a firm:
   a) A two-month 10 percent note receivable for $8,000 dated November 1, 1987.
   b) A six-month noninterest-bearing note for $20,000 dated October 1, 1987. The market rate of interest was 12 percent on October 1.
   c) A one-month 12 percent note receivable for $500,000 dated December 1, 1987.
   d) A one-year 4 percent note receivable for $160,000 dated September 1, 1987. The market rate of interest on September 1 was 10 percent.

REQUIRED

Prepare the appropriate entries to record the above transactions, assuming that the notes were discounted at a bank on December 1, 1987, that no interest accruals were made before discounting, and that the discount rate was 12 percent. Use monthly intervals, not days.

E8-10. TRANSFERS OF RECEIVABLES On March 1, Mayberry Corporation transferred receivables with a face value of $250,000 to Gomer Factors. By the end of May, receivables with a face value of $240,000 had been collected, $9,820 were determined to be uncollectible, and cash discounts of $7,030 had been taken by Mayberry's customers.

REQUIRED

Prepare Mayberry's March 1 entry to record the transfer of receivables under the following three independent assumptions:

1. The transfer was without recourse. Gomer Factors charged a $15,000 factoring fee plus interest of $5,000 during the three-month period. On March 1, Mayberry estimated uncollectible accounts to be $9,800 and cash discounts to be $7,000 and made appropriate accruals for these estimates.

2. Same facts as in part 1, except that the transfer was with recourse and the factor fee was $8,000.

3. Same facts as in part 2, except that Mayberry agreed to purchase up to $100,000 in receivables on Gomer's demand. During the three-month period, Mayberry purchased receivables with a face value of $40,000 from Gomer.

E8-11. ACCOUNTS RECEIVABLE CLASSIFICATION   The December 31, 1987 balance sheet of Brumfield Company contained an accounts receivable balance of $50,000. An examination revealed that accounts receivable were composed of the following items:

Customers' accounts	$40,750
Employees' accounts, current	2,000
Equity in $10,000 of uncollected accounts receivable assigned with recourse	4,000
Selling price of merchandise sent by Brumfield on consignment at 125% of cost and not sold by consignee	6,250
Allowance for uncollectible accounts	(3,000)
	$50,000

REQUIRED

What is the correct balance of accounts receivable at December 31, 1987?

(AICPA, adapted)

E8-12. DETERMINING SALES FROM RECEIVABLES DATA   For the month of December 1987 the records of Lance Corporation show the following information:

Cash received on accounts receivable	$35,000
Cash sales	30,000
Accounts receivable, 12/1/87	80,000
Accounts receivable, 12/31/87	74,000
Accounts receivable written off as uncollectible	1,000

The corporation uses the direct write-off method in accounting for uncollectible accounts receivable.

REQUIRED

What are the gross sales for the month of December 1987?

(AICPA, adapted)

E8-13. SALES RETURNS   Fracas Tape Distributors sells tapes and records to record shops and discount stores. These retailers have the privilege of returning to Fracas any unsold merchandise for full credit or for other merchandise in exchange. Because of obsolescence, returned goods are normally resold overseas for 30 percent of the original selling price. Fracas uses a perpetual inventory system and records returned merchandise at net realizable value less a normal profit.

The following transactions occurred during the year:

a) Sold, on account, 20,000 record albums of "Cold Winter Day" for $100,000. The cost per album was $1.

b) Customers returned 4,000 albums for credit.

c) The returned albums were sold (no return privilege) for cash to an overseas discount shop for $1.50 per album.

REQUIRED

1. Prepare the entries to record the above transactions, assuming that Fracas does not use an allowance for sales returns account.

2. Prepare the entries to record the above transactions, assuming that Fracas uses an allowance for sales returns account and that it is estimated that 35 percent of the albums originally sold will be returned.

E8-14. VALUATION OF NOTES   Given below are three independent situations that relate to the valuation of notes:

a) Accepted a three-year noninterest-bearing note for $10,000 and gave up cash of $7,118.

b) Accepted a three-year, $8,000, 6 percent note in exchange for a piece of land that had a cost of $2,000. The land's fair market value was not objectively determinable; the market rate of interest for notes of similar risk was 10 percent.

c) Accepted a $10,000, two-year noninterest-bearing note in exchange for a building with a fair market value of $8,260. The building was carried at $10,000 cost less $3,000 accumulated depreciation.

REQUIRED

For each of the situations above:

1. Prepare the entry to record the transaction.

2. Prepare a schedule showing interest revenue earned each year under the effective interest method.

E8-15. NOTES AND PRIVILEGES EXCHANGED FOR CASH On January 1, 1987, Red Gas and Supply lent an oil supplier $10,000 and accepted a $10,000 two-year note with interest at 4 percent payable annually. Red Gas also obtained the right to purchase oil lubricants during 1987 at a discount as a part of the note transaction, since the oil supplier would normally have to pay 12 percent interest to borrow money.

REQUIRED

1. Prepare the entry required by Red Gas to record the note transaction.

2. Calculate the interest earned by Red Gas in 1987 and 1988.

3. Assume that Red Gas paid for purchases totaling $8,000 in 1987. Prepare the entry Red Gas would make to record these purchases.

E8-16. VALUING NOTES RECEIVABLE On December 31, 1987, Kyle Corporation sold for $15,000 an old machine having an original cost of $50,000 and a book value of $6,000. The terms of the sale were as follows:

a) $5,000 down payment.

b) $5,000 payable on December 31 for each of the next two years.

The agreement of sale made no mention of interest; however, 10 percent would be a fair rate for this type of transaction.

REQUIRED

1. Prepare the entry to record the sale on December 31, 1987.

2. Prepare the entry to record the receipt of $5,000 on December 31, 1988.

(AICPA, adapted)

E8-17. GROSS AND NET METHOD FOR SALES DISCOUNTS Majestic, Inc., sells washers to appliance stores with credit terms of 2%/10 EOM. The washers have a sales price of $300 each. During March and April the following transactions occurred:

March 3   Sold three washers on account to Discount Services, Inc.

March 17   Sold four washers on account to Big Top Stores.

March 26   Big Top returned one washer because of paint defects.

April 6   Received payment in full from Discount Services, Inc.

April 15   Received payment in full from Big Top Stores.

REQUIRED

Prepare entries for Majestic to record the transactions for March and April under (a) the gross method and (b) the net method for sales discounts.

E8-18. ASSIGNMENT OF ACCOUNTS RECEIVABLE   On March 1, Usry Corporation assigned accounts receivable of $100,000 and received $80,000 less a 2 percent finance fee. On April 1, $40,000 was collected on receivables and forwarded to the finance company; $400 of that amount represented interest. Also during April, $10,000 of the assigned accounts were written off as uncollectible under the allowance method, and $10,000 additional receivables were assigned. On May 1, $50,000 was collected, and the loan was paid in full plus $202 in interest.

REQUIRED

Prepare the appropriate entries.

PROBLEMS

Problems marked with an asterisk (*) refer to Appendix 8-1.

P8-1. RECONCILING A BANK STATEMENT   The information below pertains to the cash account and bank account of L. Hefner Corporation for the month of December.

a) Bank checking account balance, December 31, $271.90.

b) Cash balance per books, December 31, $54.50.

c) A customer's check for $60 was returned with the November bank statement. The check was redeposited in December, but was returned with the December bank statement marked NSF. Hefner decided to forgo the possibility of trying to collect on the check.

d) Deposits in transit on December 31:

#1246	$200.00
#1247	49.70
#1248	20.00

e) The bank charged Hefner's account in December for $21 for a check written by the M. Heffing Company.

f) Outstanding checks at December 31:

#64	$ 26.25
#73	128.00
#75	53.50
#79	94.85
#82	560.00

(Check #64 was also outstanding at the end of November.)

g) Bank charges for the month of December:

Service charge, $2.70
Charge for note collections (see part *h*), $9

h) Notes collected by bank but not recorded in Hefner's records:

Principal $360.00
Interest. 7.20

i) Deposit #1230 in the amount of $78 was recorded by Hefner in the cash account as $478.

j) Check #70 in the amount of $250 was written to establish a petty cash fund. Hefner failed to record the check.

REQUIRED

1. Construct a bank reconciliation for the month of December.

2. Prepare the entries necessary to adjust and correct the accounts of Hefner Corporation.

P8-2. RECONCILING A BANK STATEMENT   The cash account and bank statement for Rona Sumers Company for the month of July appear below.

Cash

July 1 Bal.	4,829	Check #216	July 3	140
3	480	217	5	316
5	629	218	5	219
9	780	219	9	160
9	79	221	14	80
12	810	222	14	68
14	635	223	15	104
23	90	224	16	394
28	14	225	19	175
31	220	226	20	175
31	165	227	21	314
	8,731	228	24	48
		229	29	96
		230	30	112
				2,401

Rona Sumers Account #HL241

CHECKS				DEPOSITS	DATE	BALANCE
					July 1	6,077
48		1,040		165	2	5,154
325				480	3	5,309
140				692	5	5,861
219	316	160		79	9	5,245
1,260				780	10	4,765
79DM				1,445	14	6,131
80	68	394	104		18	5,485
				110NC	20	5,595
175	314			90	23	5,196
48					25	5,148
				14	29	5,162
96	4SC			165	31	5,227

DM: debit memo (NSF check)   SC: service charge   NC: note collection

Additional information:

a) The bank statement is correct in all respects.

b) Rona Sumers failed to record check #220, which was written on July 9 to acquire equipment.

c) The interest on the note collected by the bank was $10.

d) Check #225, written to a supplier, was destroyed in the check-writing machine, and check #226 was issued as a replacement.

REQUIRED

1. Prepare a bank reconciliation statement for the months of June and July.

2. Prepare the entries at July 31 to adjust the accounts of Rona Sumers.

P8-3. RECONCILING A BANK STATEMENT   You are engaged in the audit of Watkins, Inc., and have gathered the following information about the firm's cash account balance at December 31, 1987.

a) The cash account (in summary form) is as follows:

Cash

Balance, 12/1/87	7,173	Disbursements during	
Receipts for December	35,620	December	38,920

b) The bank statement for December contained the following:

11/30 balance	$ 6,844
Total deposits and other credits	35,962
Checks and other debits	39,029

(including a service charge of $7, an NSF check of $48, and a safety deposit charge of $20)

c) Deposit in transit, December 31, $300.

d) On December 10 the company failed to record a deposit made to the bank totaling $214.

e) The only check outstanding at December 31 was check #1046, which was also outstanding at November 30.

f) The November 30 bank reconciliation was as follows:

Balance per bank		$6,844
Add:		
Deposit in transit		680
Service charge for November		13
Error made by Watkins in recording check for $180;		
check was recorded at $18		162
Deduct:		
Outstanding checks		
#1043	$100	
#1044	70	
#1046	65	
#1048	39	(274)
Note collected by bank (including interest)		(252)
Balance per books		$7,173

REQUIRED

1. Calculate the correct cash balance at November 30.

2. Prepare a bank reconciliation statement for December which arrives at the correct cash balance per books and per bank.

*P8-4. COMPREHENSIVE CASH RECONCILIATION Use the information in Problem 8-3 to prepare a comprehensive bank reconciliation (four-column "proof of cash").

*P8-5. COMPREHENSIVE CASH RECONCILIATION You have completed your examination of the cash on hand and in banks in your audit of the Hoosier Company's financial statement for the year ended December 31, 1987, and noted the following:

a) The company maintains a general bank account at the National Bank and a payroll bank account at the City Bank. All checks are signed by the company president, Douglas Hoosier.

b) Data and reconciliations prepared by Donald Hume, the company bookkeeper, at November 30, 1987, indicated that the payroll account had a $1,000 general ledger and bank balance with no in-transit or outstanding items, and the general bank account had a $12,405 general ledger balance with checks outstanding aggregating $918 (#1202 for $575 and #1205 for $343) and one deposit of $492 in transit.

c) Your surprise cash count on Thursday, January 2, 1988, revealed that customers' checks totaling $540 and a National Bank deposit slip for that amount dated December 29, 1987, were in the company safe and that no cash was in transit to the bank at that time. Your examination of the general account checkbook revealed check #1216 to be the first unused check.

d) Company general ledger accounts are prepared on a posting machine and all transactions are posted in chronological sequence. The ledger card for the general bank account is reproduced below:

General Ledger

GENERAL BANK ACCOUNT
(NATIONAL BANK)

REF.	DEBITS	CREDITS	BALANCE
Bal.			12,405
12/1	496		12,901
1206		1,675	11,226
1207		645	10,581
12/6	832		11,413
1208		1,706	9,707
12/8	975		10,682
1209		2,062	8,620
1210		3,945	4,675
1211		6,237	1,562*
12/12	8,045		6,483
12/15	9,549		16,032
1212		1,845	14,187
RT		241	13,946
1213		350	13,596
D		2,072	11,524
12/22	1,513		13,037
1214		2,597	10,440
1215		1,739	8,701
12/29	540		9,241
12/31	942		10,183
1216		1,120	9,063
	22,892	26,234	

RT: returned check   D: draft   *credit balance

e) The December statements from both banks were delivered unopened to you. The City Bank statement contained deposits for $1,675, $1,706, $1,845, and $2,597, and 72 paid checks totaling $7,823. The National Bank statement is reproduced below:

The National Bank

ACCOUNT: HOOSIER COMPANY (GENERAL ACCOUNT)

DATE	CHARGES		CREDITS	BALANCE
11/30/87				12,831
12/1/87			492	13,323
12/5/87	1,675	267RT	496	11,877
12/8/87	575		832	12,134
12/11/87	1,706	654	975	10,749
12/14/87	1,987D	2,062	8,045	14,745
12/18/87	6,237	1,845	9,949	16,612
12/21/87	241RT	546RT	546CM	16,371
12/22/87	2,072D		1,513	15,812
12/26/87	2,597			13,215
12/28/87	362	4DM	1,010CM	13,859
12/29/87	12DM		362	14,209

Total charges—$24,842   Total credits—$24,220

CM: credit memo   D: draft
RT: returned check   DM: debit memo

f) Cutoff statements were secured by you personally from both banks on January 8, 1988, and the National Bank statement is reproduced below:

The National Bank

ACCOUNT: HOOSIER COMPANY (GENERAL ACCOUNT)

DATE	CHARGES		CREDITS	BALANCE
12/29/87				14,209
1/2/88	1,739	3,945	540	9,065
1/5/88	350		942	9,657

g) You determine that the bank statements are correct except that the National Bank incorrectly charged a returned check on December 21 but credited the account the same day.
h) The $362 check charged by the National Bank on December 28 was check #2000, drawn payable to Hoosier Company and endorsed "Hoosier Company by Donald Hume." Your investigation shows that the amount credited by the National Bank on December 29 was an unauthorized transfer from the City Bank payroll account to the National Bank general account by the company's bookkeeper, who made no related entry in the company's records. The check was charged to Hoosier Company on January 2, 1988, on the cutoff statement received by you from the City Bank.
i) Drafts charged against the National Bank account were for trade acceptances that were signed by Douglas Hoosier and issued to a supplier.
j) On December 28 a 60-day, 6 percent $1,000 note was collected by the National Bank for Hoosier for a $4 collection fee.
k) The $12 debit memo from the National Bank was a charge for printed checks.
l) Check #1213 was issued to replace check #1205 when the latter was reported not received by a vendor. Because of the delay in paying this account, Hoosier Company was no longer entitled to the 2 percent cash discount it had taken in preparing the original check.

REQUIRED

Prepare a comprehensive reconciliation for December 1987 for Hoosier's general bank account in the National Bank. Your proof of cash should show the calculation of the adjusted balances for both the bank statement and the general ledger account of the National Bank for cash in the bank November 30, December receipts, December disbursements, and cash in the bank December 31. Use the format presented on page 363 of the text.

(AICPA, adapted)

P8-6. PETTY CASH The following transactions for J & L Trucking took place in June and July:

June 1   Established a petty cash fund in the amount of $300.

June 19   The custodian of the fund requested replenishment of the fund and submitted the following vouchers:

Postage stamps and envelopes ....$ 26.00
Warehouse supplies 27.00
Cash withdrawal by owner 50.00
Miscellaneous garage repairs 37.00
Cash in fund 160.00

July 3   Decreased the amount of the fund by $100.

July 20   The custodian requested replenishment of the fund and submitted the following vouchers:

Garage repairs $44.00
Warehouse supplies 39.00
Miscellaneous expenditures 14.00
Cash in fund 90.00

REQUIRED

1. Prepare the entries to record the above petty cash transactions.

2. How would the petty cash fund appear on a June 30 balance sheet?

P8-7. ESTIMATING UNCOLLECTIBLE RECEIVABLES   The balance sheet presentation for Mumps Company at the end of 1986 was as follows:

Accounts receivable	$140,000
Allowance for uncollectible accounts	13,000

During 1987 the following transactions occurred:

Cash sales	$694,000
Credit sales	878,000
Returns on credit sales	3,500
Cash collections from customers:	
Within the cash discount period (credit terms provide for a	
2% discount)	313,600
After the discount period had expired	640,000
Accounts written off as uncollectible	14,000

REQUIRED

1. Prepare the entries to record the 1987 transactions. Mumps uses the gross method for cash discounts.

2. Prepare the adjusting entry to record uncollectible accounts expense for 1987 under the following assumptions:
   a) The expense is based on 1 percent of net credit sales.
   b) The expense is based on adjustment of the allowance account to equal 12 percent of the ending accounts receivable balance.
   c) Aging of the accounts indicates that receivables totaling $6,400 are uncollectible.

P8-8. ACCOUNTS RECEIVABLE AND ALLOWANCE TRANSACTIONS AND RELATIONSHIPS   The following information is available for the Fouke Company (in thousands of dollars):

	1986	1987	1988
Charge sales	$ 900	$1,100	$1,000
Cash sales	600	800	700
Total	$1,500	$1,900	$1,700
Accounts receivable (end of year)	$ 170	$ 230	$ 220
Allowance for doubtful accounts (end of year)	47	30	56
Accounts written off as uncollectible (during year)	2	50	4

REQUIRED

Assuming there was no change in the method used to estimate doubtful accounts during 1986, 1987, and 1988, what was the balance in the allowance for doubtful accounts at the beginning of 1986?

(AICPA, adapted)

P8-9. UNCOLLECTIBLE ACCOUNTS EXPENSE; AGING   Redford Corporation uses the allowance method of accounting for bad debts and has used a historical rate of 1.25 percent of credit sales to estimate this expense. The aging schedule of Redford's accounts receivable at the end of the current year appears as follows:

DAYS OUTSTANDING	AMOUNT	PROBABILITY OF COLLECTION
0–30 days	$350,000	.98
31–60 days	90,000	.90
61–90 days	40,000	.75
Over 90 days	20,000	.50

Total credit sales for the current year were $3,200,000. The allowance account had a credit balance of $29,400 at the beginning of the current year, and accounts totaling $27,500 were written off during the current year.

REQUIRED

> **1.** Calculate the expense for the current year if Redford continues to use the percentage of sales method to estimate its bad debt expense.
>
> **2.** Calculate the expense for the current year if bad debt expense is based on an aging of the accounts receivable.
>
> **3.** Refer to requirement 2. Calculate the balance in the allowance account at the end of the current year.

P8-10. NOTES WITH BELOW-MARKET RATES OF INTEREST   Sparkplug sold a parcel of land to Fan Belt Company and accepted, in lieu of cash, a three-year $20,000 promissory note bearing interest at 6 percent. Sparkplug had acquired the land several years ago for $4,000. At the sale date, the rate of interest for notes of similar risk was 12 percent.

REQUIRED

> **1.** Prepare Sparkplug's journal entry to record the sale of land.
>
> **2.** Prepare the journal entries to record interest revenue each year.
>
> **3.** Assume that Sparkplug recorded the sale at the face value of the note and that interest revenue each year has been calculated on the basis of the 6 percent stated rate in the note. Calculate the amount of overstatement or understatement that this procedure would have on net income for each of the three years.

P8-11. INSTALLMENT METHOD OF ACCOUNTING; INTEREST ON INSTALLMENTS   Cola Land Realty sells land on a deferred payment plan. At the beginning of 1987 the company sold a tract of land that had cost $294,383 for $500,000, payable as follows: $100,000 down, with the balance payable in five equal end-of-year installments of $80,000 each. Interest at 10 percent is implicit in the installment payments.

REQUIRED

> **1.** Calculate the sales price of the land.
>
> **2.** Prepare a schedule that shows the interest revenue to be recognized each year under the effective interest method.
>
> **3.** Calculate the profit from the sale to be recognized each year from 1987 through 1991 under (a) the sales or accrual method; (b) the installment method.

P8-12. VALUATION OF NOTES; DISCOUNTING NOTES RECEIVABLE   The notes receivable and related accounts at December 31, 1986, for Bel-Air Corporation appear as follows:

Notes receivable	$18,200
Less: Notes receivable discounted	(5,000)
Unearned interest	(1,200)
	$12,000

The note account consists of two notes. The note not discounted is a noninterest-bearing note due at the end of 1987 and accepted at a 10 percent effective rate of interest.

During 1987 the following note transactions occurred:

March 1   Bel-Air was notified that the maker of the note discounted by Bel-Air paid the note at maturity.

April 1   Sold a machine with a fair market value of $15,000 by accepting a two-year $15,000 note with an interest rate of 12 percent. The book value of the machine sold was $12,000.

July 1   Sold land by accepting a one-year 6 percent note with a face value of $10,000. The market rate of interest for notes of similar risk was 12 percent, and the cost of the land sold was $7,000.

Nov. 1   Loaned $20,000 to a truck supplier by accepting a $20,000 noninterest-bearing note due in four years. Bel-Air also received an option to acquire a truck at a discount any time during the four-year period. The market rate of interest on November 1 was 12 percent.

Dec. 31   Discounted the note accepted in April, receiving proceeds of $15,900.

Dec. 31   Recorded interest on the remaining notes held.

REQUIRED

Prepare journal entries to record the above transactions.

P8-13.   CORRECTING ERRORS INVOLVING IMPROPER VALUATION OF NOTES RECEIVABLE   On January 1, 1987, Sacks sold a piece of land that had an original cost of $50,000 by accepting four 8 percent notes for $20,000 each. The notes are due as follows:

12/31/87 ....$20,000
12/31/88 20,000
12/31/89 40,000

While the fair market value of the land could not be determined objectively by appraisers, the current rate of interest on January 1, 1987, was 12 percent. Sacks recorded the sale on January 1, 1987, and the cash interest and note collected on December 31, 1987, as follows:

Jan. 1	Notes receivable 80,000		
	Land	50,000	
	Gain on sale of land	30,000	
Dec. 31	Cash 6,400		
	Interest revenue	6,400	
	(.08 × $80,000)		
	Cash 20,000		
	Notes receivable	20,000	

REQUIRED

1. Prepare the entries at December 31, 1987, to correct the errors made by Sacks with respect to the gain and the interest revenue.

2. Prepare the entries to record interest revenue and note collections at the end of 1988 and 1989.

P8-14.   ASSIGNMENT OF ACCOUNTS RECEIVABLE   Bee Company finances some of its current operations by assigning accounts receivable to a finance company. On July 1, 1987, it assigned accounts amounting to $60,000, and the finance company lent 80 percent of the accounts assigned less a commission charge of 1/2 of 1 percent of the total accounts assigned.

On July 31 the Bee Company received a statement that the finance company had collected $30,000 of these accounts and had made an additional charge of 1/2 of 1 percent of the total accounts outstanding as of July 31. This charge was to be deducted at the time of the first remittance due Bee Company from the finance company. On August 31 the Bee Company received a second statement from the finance company, together with a check for the amount due. The statement indicated that the finance company had collected an additional $20,000 and had made a further charge of 1/2 of 1 percent of the balance outstanding as of August 31.

REQUIRED

1. Prepare the entry to record the assignment of the accounts.

2. Prepare Bee's entry to record the data from the first report from the finance company (July 31).

3. Prepare Bee's entry to record the data in the report of August 31.

4. Explain how the items should be reported on the financial statements of Bee Company at July 31 and August 31.

P8-15. AGING RECEIVABLES Abbott Company sells office equipment and supplies to many organizations in the city and surrounding area on contract terms of 2/10, n/30. In the past, over 75 percent of the credit customers have taken advantage of the discount by paying within 10 days of the invoice date.

The number of customers taking the full 30 days to pay has increased within the last year. Current indications are that less than 60 percent of the customers are now taking the discount. Bad debts as a percentage of gross credit sales have risen from the 1.5 percent provided in past years to about 4 percent in the current year.

The controller has responded to a request for more information on the deterioration in collections of accounts receivable with the report reproduced below.

Abbott Company

FINANCE COMMITTEE REPORT
ACCOUNTS RECEIVABLE COLLECTIONS
MAY 31, 1987

The fact that some credit accounts will prove uncollectible is normal. Annual bad debt write-offs have been 1.5 percent of gross credit sales over the past five years. During the last fiscal year, this percentage increased to slightly less than 4 percent. The current accounts receivable balance is $1.2 million. The condition of this balance in terms of age and probability of collection is as follows:

PROPORTION OF TOTAL	AGE CATEGORY	PROBABILITY OF COLLECTION
68.0%	Not yet due	99.0%
15.0	Less than 30 days past due	96.5
8.0	30 to 60 days past due	95.0
5.0	61 to 120 days past due	91.0
2.5	121 to 180 days past due	75.0
1.5	Over 180 days past due	20.0

The allowance for doubtful accounts had a credit balance of $30,250 on June 1, 1986. Abbott has provided for a monthly bad debts expense accrual during the current fiscal year based on the assumption that 4 percent of gross credit sales will be uncollectible. Total gross credit sales for the 1986–87 fiscal year amounted to $3 million. Write-offs of bad accounts during the year totaled $108,750.

REQUIRED

1. Prepare an accounts receivable aging schedule for the Abbott Company using the age categories identified in the controller's report to the Finance Committee, showing:
  a) The amount of accounts receivable outstanding for each age category and in total.
  b) The estimated amount that is uncollectible for each category and in total.

2. Compute the amount of the year-end adjustment necessary to bring allowance for doubtful accounts to the balance indicated by the aging analysis. Then prepare the necessary journal entry to adjust the accounting records.

(IMA, adapted)

P8-16. LONG-TERM RECEIVABLES; INTEREST Linden, Inc., had the following long-term receivable account balances at December 31, 1986:

Note receivable from sale of division $1,500,000
Note receivable from officer 400,000

Transactions during 1987 and other information relating to Linden's long-term receivables were as follows:

a) The $1.5 million note receivable is dated May 1, 1986, bears interest at 9 percent, and represents the balance of the consideration received from the sale of Linden's electronics division to Pitt Company. Principal payments of $500,000 plus appropriate interest are due on May 1, 1987, 1988, and 1989. The first principal and interest payment was made on May 1, 1987. Collection of the note installments is reasonably assured.

b) The $400,000 note receivable is dated December 31, 1984, bears interest at 8 percent, and is due on December 31, 1989. The note is due from Robert Finley, president of Linden, Inc., and is collateralized by 10,000 shares of Linden's common stock. Interest is payable annually on December 31 and all interest payments were paid on their due dates through December 31, 1987. The quoted market price of Linden's common stock was $45 per share on December 31, 1987.

c) On April 1, 1987, Linden sold a patent to Bell Company in exchange for a $100,000 non-interest-bearing note due on April 1, 1989. There was no established exchange price for the patent, and the note had no ready market. The prevailing rate of interest for a note of this type at April 1, 1987, was 15 percent. The present value of $1 for two periods at 15 percent is 0.756. The patent had a carrying value of $40,000 at January 1, 1987, and the amortization for the year ended December 31, 1987, would have been $8,000. The collection of the note receivable from Bell is reasonably assured.

d) On July 1, 1987, Linden sold a parcel of land to Carr Company for $200,000 under an installment sale contract. Carr made a $60,000 cash down payment on July 1, 1987, and signed a four-year 16 percent note for the $140,000 balance. The equal annual payments of principal and interest on the note will be $50,000 payable on July 1, 1988, through July 1, 1991. The land could have been sold at an established cash price of $200,000. The cost of the land to Linden was $150,000. Circumstances are such that the collection of the installments on the note is reasonably assured.

REQUIRED

1. Prepare the long-term receivables section of Linden's balance sheet at December 31, 1987.

2. Prepare a schedule showing the current portion of the long-term receivables and accrued interest receivable that would appear in Linden's balance sheet at December 31, 1987.

3. Prepare a schedule showing interest revenue from the long-term receivables and gains recognized on sale of assets that would appear on Linden's income statement for the year ended December 31, 1987.

(AICPA, adapted)

P8-17. COMPREHENSIVE REVIEW OF ACCOUNTS RECEIVABLE AND UNCOLLECTIBLE ACCOUNTS The following T-accounts show transactions affecting accounts receivable for the year ending December 31, 1987. All sales were on credit.

Accounts receivable

Beginning balance	100,000	Sales returns	5,000
Sales	60,000	Collections	29,400

Allowance for doubtful accounts

Write-offs	3,000	Beginning balance	5,000
		Notes receivable	1,000

Additional information:

a) Credit sales amounted to $90,000 but were recorded in accounts receivable at cost.

b) A customer gave a note in full settlement of his account. The entry was recorded as follows:

Notes receivable 1,000
Allowance for doubtful accounts   1,000

c) Customers are given a 2 percent cash discount for prompt payment. All cash collections were within the discount period, and the amount credited to accounts receivable was net of the discount. Sales discounts should be recorded under the gross method.

REQUIRED

1. Calculate the uncollectible accounts expense for the year under the assumption that the expense is determined by adjusting the allowance account to equal 5 percent of ending accounts receivable.

2. Prepare the entries to record the uncollectible accounts expense for 1987 and to correct any errors in the above transactions.

P8-18. ACCOUNTS RECEIVABLE; UNCOLLECTIBLE ACCOUNTS   Sam Wholesale Company has been in business for five years but has never had an audit of its financial statements. Engaged to make an audit for 1987, you find that the company's balance sheet carries no allowance for uncollectible accounts; instead, uncollectible accounts have been expensed as written off with recoveries credited to income as collected. The company's policy is to write off at December 31 of each year those accounts on which no collections have been received for three months. The installment contracts provide for uniform monthly payments over a two-year period.

On your recommendation, the company agrees to revise its accounts for 1987 according to the allowance method. The allowance is to be based on a percentage of sales derived from the experience of prior years.

Statistics for the past five years appear below:

YEAR	CREDIT SALES	ACCOUNTS WRITTEN OFF AND YEAR OF SALE			RECOVERIES AND YEAR OF SALE
1983	$100,000	1983 $ 550			
1984	250,000	1983 1,500	1984 $1,000		1983 $100
1985	300,000	1983 500	1984 4,000	1985 $1,300	1984 400
1986	325,000	1984 1,200	1985 4,500	1986 1,500	1985 500
1987	275,000	1985 2,700	1986 5,000	1987 1,400	1986 600

Accounts receivable at December 31, 1987, are as follows:

1986 sales	$ 15,000
1987 sales	135,000
	$150,000

REQUIRED

Prepare the adjusting entry or entries with appropriate explanations to set up the allowance for uncollectible accounts.

(AICPA, adapted)

P8-19. UNCOLLECTIBLE ACCOUNTS, ASSIGNMENTS, FACTORING, VALUATION OF NOTES

A) At January 1, 1987, the credit balance in the allowance for doubtful accounts of the Master Company was $400,000. For 1987 the provision for doubtful accounts is based on a percentage of net sales. Net sales for 1987 were $50 million. The 1987 provision for doubtful accounts, based on the latest available facts, is estimated to be .7 percent of net sales. During 1987 uncollectible receivables amounting to $410,000 were written off against the allowance for doubtful accounts.

REQUIRED

Prepare a schedule computing the balance in Master's allowance for doubtful accounts at December 31, 1987.

B) The Guide Company requires additional cash for its business. Guide has decided to use its accounts receivable to raise the additional cash as follows:

    a) On July 1, 1987, Guide assigned $200,000 of accounts receivable to the Cell Finance Company. Guide received an advance from Cell of 85 percent of the assigned accounts receivable less a commission on the advance of 3 percent. Before December 31, 1987, Guide collected $150,000 on the assigned accounts receivable, and remitted $160,000 to Cell, $10,000 of which represented interest on the advance from Cell.

    b) On December 1, 1987, Guide sold $300,000 of net accounts receivable to the Factoring Company for $260,000. The receivables were sold outright on a nonrecourse basis.

    c) On December 31, 1987, Guide received an advance of $100,000 from the Domestic Bank by pledging $120,000 of its accounts receivable. Guide's first payment to Domestic is due on January 30, 1988.

REQUIRED

Prepare a schedule showing the income statement effect for the year ended December 31, 1987, as a result of the above facts.

C) On January 1, 1986, the Lock Company sold to the Key Company property that originally cost Lock $600,000. Key gave Lock a $900,000 noninterest-bearing note payable in six equal annual installments of $150,000, with the first payment due and paid on January 1, 1986. There was no established exchange price for the property and the note has no ready market. The prevailing rate of interest for a note of this type is 12 percent.

REQUIRED

Prepare a schedule computing the balance in Lock's net receivables from Key at December 31, 1987, based on the above facts. Also, prepare a schedule showing the income or loss before income taxes for the years ended December 31, 1986 and 1987, which Lock should record as a result of the above facts.

D) Allen Corporation transfers receivables with a face value of $80,000 to Ford Factors. The transfer is with recourse, and Allen has recorded allowances for sales discounts and uncollectible accounts totaling $3,000, which are reasonable estimates of these amounts. Ford Factors pays Allen $76,500 for the receivables, less a $20,000 hold-back pending final collection of Allen's receivables.

REQUIRED

Prepare Allen Corporation's entry to record the transfer.

                                                    (AICPA, adapted)

P8-20. COMPREHENSIVE REVIEW OF CASH AND RECEIVABLES   You are conducting an audit of the Presley & Parker Company for the year ending December 31, 1987. Below are several transactions engaged in by the company from January 1985, the date it began operations, through 1987.

    a) While P&P uses the allowance method of accounting for uncollectible accounts, recoveries of previously written-off amounts are credited to miscellaneous revenues. Past recoveries are as follows:

1985	None
1986	$3,800
1987	4,700

    b) On January 2, 1986, P&P made an installment sale for $12,000. The installment contract called for 24 monthly payments of $500 plus 1 percent interest on the unpaid balance beginning January 31, 1986. The item sold had cost P&P $9,000. Since collectibility of the installment could not be estimated, P&P used the installment method of accounting for the transaction. After making the payment on June 30, 1987, the customer defaulted on the contract and P&P repossessed the item sold, which had an estimated fair value of $1,200.

P&P recorded the default and repossession as follows:

```
Repossessed merchandise...........................1,000
    Installment receivables ...........................          1,000
```

c) On July 1, 1986, P&P sold a tract of land that cost $30,000 by accepting a three-year 4 percent note receivable for $60,000. Interest is payable each July 1. At the date of sale, the market rate of interest for similar notes was 10 percent. P&P recorded the sale and related interest as follows:

```
7/1/86   Notes receivable ..........................60,000
             Land ................................          30,000
             Gain on sale .........................          30,000

12/31/86   No entry because P&P's bookkeeper decided the interest revenue
           accrual would even out in 1987 when the cash was collected.

7/1/87   Cash ...................................2,400
             Interest revenue ......................          2,400

12/31/87   No entry because P&P's bookkeeper decided the interest revenue
           accrual would even out in 1988 when the cash was collected.
```

d) On November 1, 1987, P&P discounted a 6 percent 90-day $4,000 customer's note dated September 1, 1987. The bank discounted the note at 10 percent, and P&P received proceeds of $4,026.67. P&P recorded the transaction as follows:

```
Cash.........................................4,026.67
    Notes receivable ...............................          4,026.67
```

e) On December 1, 1987, P&P assigned $30,000 in accounts receivable to a finance company with recourse, receiving 90 percent of the accounts assigned less a service charge of 1 percent of the advance. Customers were directed to remit directly to the finance company. The assignment was recorded as follows:

```
Cash ($27,000 − $270) ..........................26,730
Interest expense ................................ 3,270
    Accounts receivable ...........................          30,000
```

At the end of December, P&P was notified by the finance company that $20,000 of receivables assigned had been collected and that $300 of such collections should be considered interest. No entry had been made for the collections and interest.

f) P&P's bank reconciliation for the month of December 1987 was as follows:

```
Balance per bank ......................................  $16,023
Deposit in transit ......................................    2,000
Service charge ........................................       12
Error by P&P bookkeeper on check #166..................      300
Outstanding checks.....................................   (2,630)
Balance per books .....................................  $15,705
```

P&P made the following adjusting entry for the above:

```
Cash.........................................2,630
    Accounts payable .............................          2,630
```

g) P&P has a petty cash fund of $350. When the cash fund was replenished in September for expenditures of $178, the following entry was made:

```
Petty cash ........................................ 178
    Cash.........................................          178
```

h) On December 31, 1987, P&P transferred receivables with a face value of $25,000 to a finance company and received $22,000 in cash. P&P has agreed to take back a maximum of $15,000 of these receivables should the finance company need the funds. P&P could not make a reasonable estimate of customer bad debts and other deductions because these receivables arose from a new sales market. P&P recorded the transfer as follows:

```
Cash........................................22,000
Loss on sale of receivables .....................  3,000
    Accounts receivable ...........................        25,000
```

REQUIRED

For each transaction you are to prepare an adjusting or correcting entry, as necessary. All errors that affect years prior to 1987 should be corrected through the partners' capital accounts. Presley and Parker share profits and losses in a 3:2 ratio, respectively.

9 INVENTORY VALUATION: DETERMINING COST AND USING COST FLOW ASSUMPTIONS

Inventory is the term used to describe the assets of a company that are intended for sale in the ordinary course of business, are in the process of being produced for sale, or are to be used currently in producing goods to be sold. What constitutes inventory for a particular company depends on the normal operating activities of that company. For example, marketable securities would be inventory for a securities dealer, but a manufacturer of drill presses would classify them as an investment. A road grader would be inventory to a manufacturer of road graders, but would be classified as property, plant, and equipment by a road construction company.

Proper identification of inventory items and valuation of inventory are important because inventory can have a material effect on both the balance sheet and the income statement. The inventory of manufacturing and merchandising companies often is one of the most significant assets, in dollar amount, reported on the balance sheet. In addition, the cost of inventory sold, normally called cost of goods sold, is a major expense for many companies. Inventory on hand at the end of an accounting period is reported as a current asset on the balance sheet because it is expected to be sold or used to produce goods for sale within one year or one operating cycle, whichever is longer.

The basic issues raised in accounting for and reporting inventory are:

Inventory accounting and reporting issues.

1. Classifying inventories.
2. Selecting an inventory accounting system.
3. Identifying items to be included in inventory.
4. Determining the expenditures and cost allocations to be included in inventory cost.
5. Making assumptions about inventory cost flow, when necessary.
6. Choosing among alternatives to the cost basis of valuing inventory, when necessary.
7. Estimating inventory costs when a physical count of inventory items is not practicable or possible.

Issues 1 through 5 are discussed in this chapter; alternatives to the cost basis of valuing inventory and methods of estimating inventory costs are discussed in Chapter 10.

MAJOR INVENTORY CLASSIFICATIONS

The inventory classifications reported on the balance sheet and the costs included in those inventory classifications depend on the normal operating activities of the company. A **merchandising company** ordinarily purchases goods for resale to customers, either at wholesale or at retail. As consumers, most of us are more familiar with retail merchandising companies than we are with wholesale merchandising companies. For example, Sears, Montgomery Ward, the local Oldsmobile dealership, and the local grocery store are primarily retailers in that most, if not all, of their sales are to consumers. All merchandising companies, whether wholesalers or retailers, have only one general class of inventory— **merchandise inventory,** or simply **inventory.** The merchandise inventory account, however, often consists of several specific inventories of goods intended for sale. For example, the merchandise inventory of an Oldsmobile dealership might consist of inventories of several car models, such as Omegas, Cutlasses, Delta 88s, and Toronados. Merchandise inventory costs normally include the purchase price of the inventory plus any other costs incurred to get the inventory items in location and condition for sale to customers.

A **manufacturing company** produces the goods that it sells, rather than purchasing completed goods for resale. As a result, manufacturing companies normally have three types of inventory, each of which is associated with a stage of the production process: raw materials inventory, work-in-process inventory, and finished goods inventory.

Raw materials inventory consists of goods and materials that ultimately will become part of the manufactured product, but that have not yet entered the production process. For example, the raw materials inventory of an automobile manufacturer might include sheet metal, nuts, bolts, and paint. The cost of raw materials inventory generally includes the purchase price of the materials plus shipping and similar costs necessary to get the materials into place for use in the production process.

Work-in-process inventory consists of units in the production process that require additional work before becoming finished goods. The costs normally included in the work-in-process inventory are the costs of the raw materials incorporated in the product and the cost of labor applied directly to the completion of the product to date, plus manufacturing overhead costs incurred before the date when the amount of work-in-process inventory is determined. Manufacturing overhead costs include the cost of supplies used in the production process, such as machine oil; the cost of labor necessary to support the production process; insurance and utilities expense; and depreciation on property, plant, and equipment employed in the production process.

EXHIBIT 9–1	INVENTORY ACCOUNT AND INVENTORY COST FLOWS FOR A MERCHANDISING COMPANY

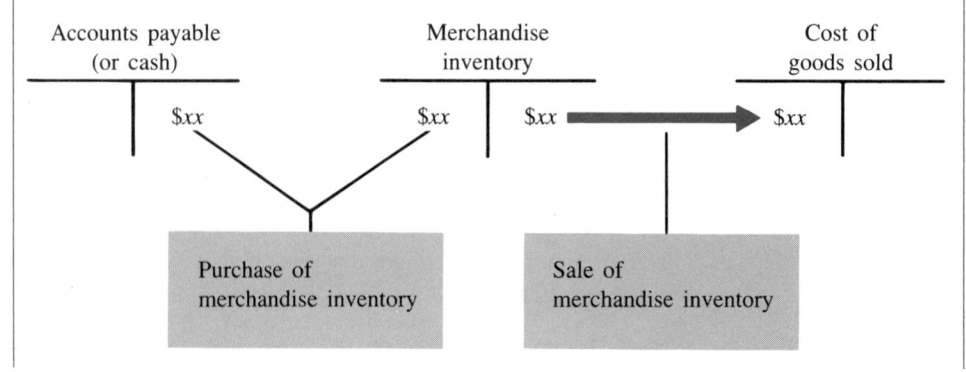

EXHIBIT 9–2 INVENTORY ACCOUNTS AND INVENTORY COST
FLOWS FOR A MANUFACTURING COMPANY

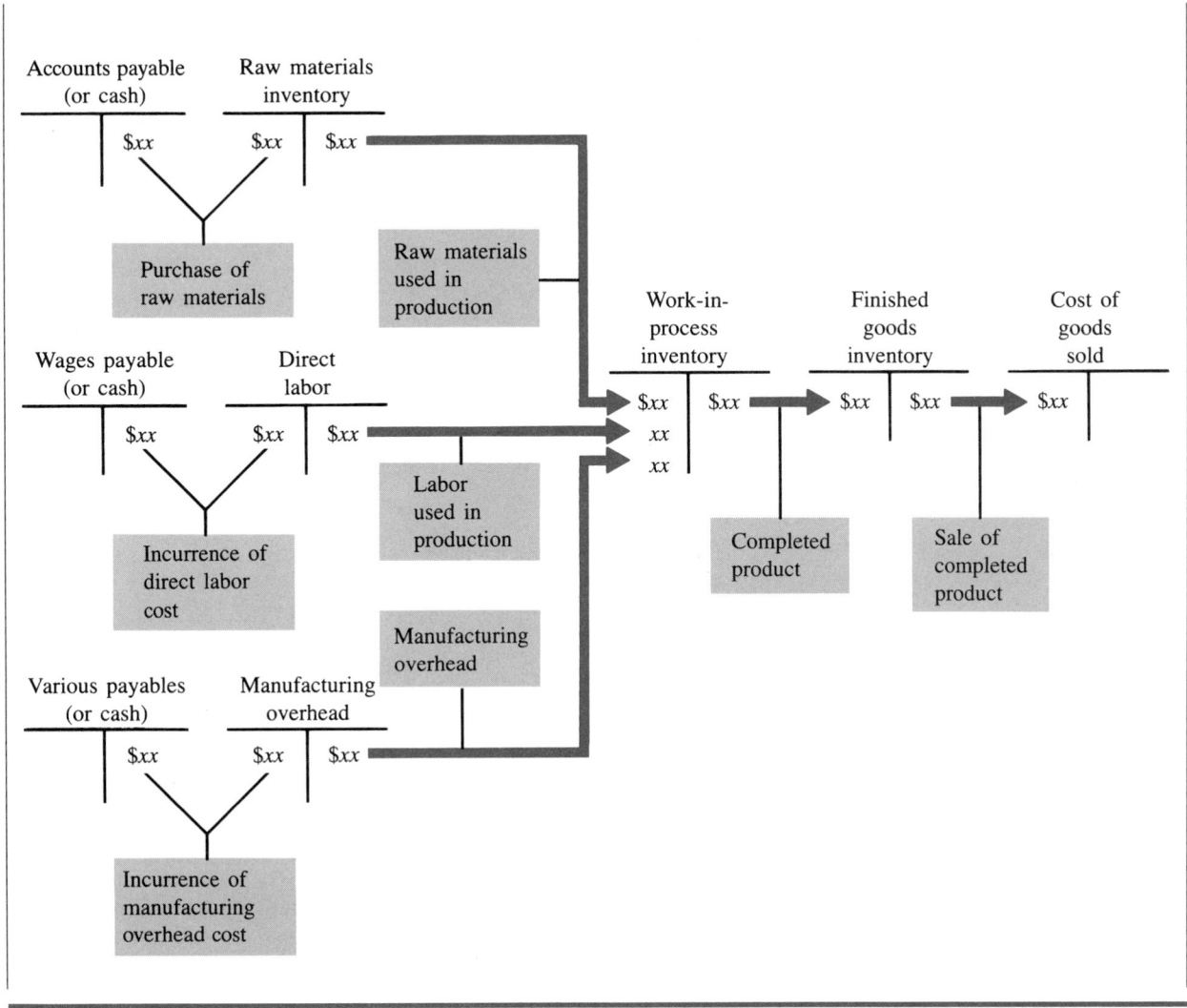

Finished goods inventory consists of units that have been completed and are available for sale at the end of the accounting period. The cost of finished goods includes the costs of raw materials and labor that can be traced directly to the completed product as well as manufacturing overhead costs incurred during the production process.

The inventory accounts and the costs flowing into and out of those accounts for a merchandising company and a manufacturing company are presented in Exhibits 9–1 and 9–2, respectively. Additional inventory accounts are sometimes found on a balance sheet as well. For example, there may be an inventory of office supplies or an inventory of supplies to be used in a production process. These minor inventories and the more significant merchandise inventory, raw materials inventory, work-in-process inventory, and finished goods inventory all are accounted for in accordance with either a periodic inventory system or a perpetual inventory system.

INVENTORY ACCOUNTING SYSTEMS

In accounting for inventory we need to determine both the amount of inventory on hand at the end of the accounting period, which is to be reported as a current asset on the balance sheet, and the cost of inventory sold during the accounting period, which is to be reported as an expense on the income statement. The amount of inventory on hand and the cost of inventory sold can be determined by either the periodic inventory system or the perpetual inventory system.

THE PERIODIC INVENTORY SYSTEM

As the name implies, when the **periodic inventory system** is used, the amount of inventory on hand is determined only periodically. All inventory acquisitions during an accounting period are recorded by debiting a purchases account. The dollar amount in the purchases account at the end of the accounting period is added to the cost of the inventory on hand at the beginning of the period to determine the total cost of goods available for sale. The inventory on hand at the end of the accounting period is determined by a physical count, and the cost of this ending inventory is deducted from the cost of goods available for sale to determine the cost of goods sold. As a result, when the periodic inventory system is used, a physical inventory count is essential, and cost of goods sold is a *residual* amount that is dependent on ending inventory:

Beginning inventory	$100,000
Plus: Net inventory purchases during the period	80,000
Cost of goods available for sale	$180,000
Less: Ending inventory	(15,000)
Cost of goods sold	$165,000

The balance in the inventory account is not adjusted until a physical count is made. Once the inventory on hand has been determined by physical count at the end of an accounting period, the inventory account is credited for the beginning inventory balance and the purchases account is closed with a credit. The sum of the dollar amounts of beginning inventory and purchases is the cost of merchandise that was available for sale during the accounting period. This merchandise either has been sold during the period or is still on hand at the end of the period. Therefore, the inventory account is debited for the dollar amount of ending inventory, based on the physical count, and cost of goods sold is debited for the dollar amount of inventory that was available for sale and that is not included in the ending inventory balance. The usual entries made under the periodic inventory system are illustrated in the left-hand column of Exhibit 9–3 (p. 392).

THE PERPETUAL INVENTORY SYSTEM

When the **perpetual inventory system** is used, there is a continuous record of changes in inventory and the inventory account balance. The inventory account is debited to record inventory acquisitions. Sales of inventory are recorded by debiting the cost of goods sold account and crediting the inventory account for the cost of merchandise sold. Thus, the perpetual inventory system provides a *continuous record* of the balances in both the inventory account and the cost of goods sold account. If the company has a computerized bookkeeping system, it is possible to record additions to and withdrawals from inventory almost instantaneously. Moreover, development and growth of computerized bookkeeping systems have made the perpetual inventory system cost-effective for an increasing number of companies.

Even though a physical inventory count is not required in order to report inventory on hand when the perpetual inventory system is used, all inventory items should be counted at least once each year in order to verify the amount reported as inventory. Since the purpose of this physical count is simply to verify the perpetual inventory records, however, the count need not be made at a single point in time and it need not take place only at or near the end of the accounting period. Counts of the various inventory items can be staggered throughout the accounting period, thus reducing the inconvenience and cost that often are associated with a shutdown of operations for a complete inventory count.

The physical inventory count may yield an inventory balance that differs from the balance in the perpetual inventory records because of accounting or counting errors or because of inventory shrinkages resulting from losses, thefts, or waste. Should a difference occur, the balance of the inventory account should be adjusted to agree with the physical count. If the physical count was *greater* than the perpetual records by $500, adjustment of the inventory account would be as follows:

Inventory	500	
Inventory overage		500

If the physical count was *less* than the perpetual records by $300, the following entry would be made:

Inventory shortage	300	
Inventory		300

Any inventory overage or shortage recorded as shown above should be closed to the income summary. Although an inventory overage or shortage usually is reported as a separate line item in income statements prepared for internal use, as an aid in management's efforts to control inventory, these accounts often are combined with cost of goods sold for external reporting purposes. Illustrative entries for the perpetual inventory system are shown in the right-hand column of Exhibit 9–3.

THE PERIODIC AND PERPETUAL INVENTORY SYSTEMS COMPARED

The essential distinction between the periodic inventory system and the perpetual inventory system is that under the periodic system, the cost of inventory sold is determined by deducting the cost of the ending inventory from the cost of inventory available for sale during the period. In contrast, under the perpetual system, the cost of inventory sold is subtracted from the cost of inventory available for sale to give the cost of the ending inventory. In addition, the periodic system *requires* a physical inventory count before ending inventory and cost of goods sold can be recorded, whereas a physical inventory count serves only to verify the inventory records if a perpetual system is used. The periodic inventory system is best suited to companies with large varieties of low-cost inventory items, such as a hardware store. The perpetual system is better suited to high-cost inventory items for which continuous monitoring of inventory is important, as in the case of the inventory of an automobile dealership.

The periodic inventory system has several disadvantages as compared to the perpetual inventory system. One disadvantage is the periodic system's dependence on a complete physical inventory count at the end of each accounting period. Physical inventory counts can be time-consuming, inconvenient, and costly, and may interfere with the company's normal operation. As a result, physical inventory counts seldom are made more often than once a year, at the end of the company's fiscal year. In practice, most companies' fiscal years are set to end at whatever time of year inventories tend to be at comparatively low levels.

A second disadvantage of the periodic system is that cost of goods sold is computed by deducting ending inventory from goods available for sale. The underlying assumption is that inventory that is not on hand at the end of the accounting period must have been sold. This assumption ignores the possibility that various inventory shrinkages, such as breakage, theft, losses, and waste, may have occurred during the period. Generally, no information about these matters is provided by the periodic inventory system. Therefore, the periodic system is not a good system for effective management control of inventory. The perpetual system, on the other hand, does provide records that are desirable for effective control of inventory. With the help of computers, especially mini- and micro-computers (IBMs, Apples, etc.), both small and large businesses are able to maintain perpetual records of inventory quantities and costs, plus other data, such as supplier, location, and reorder points. Perpetual inventory records not only help management to keep track of costly inventory items but also increase its ability to avoid customer dissatisfaction because a particular inventory item is out of stock.

Finally, when the periodic system is used it is difficult to report a reasonably accurate interim inventory figure unless some sort of supplementary perpetual inventory records are available or interim physical inventory counts are made. For this reason, the perpetual inventory system is likely to be much more cost-effective than the periodic system when interim (e.g., monthly or quarterly) financial statements must be prepared.

As an illustration of the accounting differences between the periodic and perpetual inventory systems, consider the following data for 1987 and the related comparative entries presented in Exhibit 9–3 for the Jacobs Television Shop.

Beginning inventory (25 units @ $400) $10,000
Purchases (80 units @ $400) 32,000
Ending inventory (30 units @ $400) 12,000
Sales (74 units @ $500 selling price) 37,000
Inventory shortage (1 unit @ $400)   400

Observe that both inventory systems produce a $30,000 debit to the income summary for 1987. Under the periodic system, however, the $400 inventory shortage is not separately identifiable because of the assumption that all television sets not included in the physical inventory count must have been sold.

EXHIBIT 9–3   ENTRIES UNDER THE PERIODIC AND PERPETUAL INVENTORY SYSTEMS

PERIODIC INVENTORY SYSTEM		PERPETUAL INVENTORY SYSTEM	
To record purchase of television sets for sale:			
Purchases 32,000		Inventory 32,000	
Accounts payable	32,000	Accounts payable	32,000
(80 × $400)		(80 × $400)	
Entries made as sales occur:			
Accounts receivable 37,000		Accounts receivable 37,000	
Sales revenue	37,000	Sales revenue	37,000
(74 × $500)		(74 × $500)	
(No entry for inventory withdrawal or to record cost of goods sold)		Cost of goods sold 29,600	
		Inventory	29,600
		(74 × $400)	
Year-end adjusting and closing entries:			
Cost of goods sold (residual) 30,000		Inventory shortage 400	
Ending inventory (30 × $400) 12,000		Inventory	400
Beginning inventory (25 × $400)	10,000	(1 × $400)	
Purchases (80 × $400)	32,000		
Income summary 30,000		Income summary 30,000	
Cost of goods sold	30,000	Inventory shortage	400
		Cost of goods sold	29,600

ITEMS TO BE INCLUDED IN INVENTORY

Generally it is not difficult to identify most items that should be included in inventory because the company has the items in its possession and holds legal title to them. In some situations, however, identification of items properly included in inventory is more difficult. For example, a company may hold goods that it does not own or own goods that it does not hold, such as when goods are in transit from a supplier but title already has passed to the company purchasing the goods.

When it is difficult to determine which items should be included in the current period's inventory, several factors should be considered, including legal title, physical possession, contractual terms, special industry practices, and intentions of the parties involved. In addition, when inventory identification problems must be resolved there is no substitute for sound professional judgment by the accountant.

GOODS IN TRANSIT
Purchases of inventory should be recorded by the buyer when legal title passes to the buyer. Often, however, it is not easy to determine exactly when title passes. Because the financial statements normally are not materially affected, companies usually record inventory purchases as goods are received. When a company follows this practice, the purchases account (when a periodic system is used) or the inventory account (when a perpetual system is used) and related accounts payable must be adjusted for any goods in transit and for which title has passed to the buyer as of the end of the accounting period.

When considering goods in transit for possible inclusion in inventory, the company must review the terms of the shipping agreement. If goods are shipped "F.O.B. [free on board] shipping point," legal title and the responsibilities of ownership, such as insurance, pass to the buyer when the seller delivers the goods to the shipping agent. For example, if goods are shipped from Kansas City "F.O.B. Kansas City," title passes to the buyer when the goods are transferred to the shipping agent in Kansas City. Accordingly, the buyer is responsible for insuring the goods, and the transportation cost is the buyer's expense. In this case, the goods in transit should be included in the buyer's inventory.

If goods are shipped "F.O.B. destination," the goods belong to the seller until they are delivered to the destination point by the shipping agent. In this case, title and the responsibilities of ownership remain with the seller until the goods reach the specified destination, and the goods in transit should be included in the seller's inventory. When goods are shipped F.O.B. destination, the transportation cost is an expense of the seller.

When there is some question as to whether title has passed to the buyer, the accountant must make a judgment about the proper inventory treatment. In doing so, the accountant must consider the intent of the sales agreement, special industry practices, normal accounting policy for the buyer, and similar factors. For example, it is a common practice to treat goods manufactured for a special order as being sold as soon as they are physically separated from the manufacturer's regular inventory. In this case, the goods are not considered to be part of the manufacturer's inventory even though they have not yet been delivered to the buyer. Special-ordered goods are not assets of the manufacturer because the economic benefit embodied in such goods can accrue only to the customer who placed the special order.

CONSIGNED GOODS
A **consignment** is a transaction in which one party, the consignor, ships goods to a second party, the consignee, who attempts to sell the goods for the consignor. The consignee is responsible for exercising due care and protecting the goods from loss or damage, but incurs no liability to the consignor. When goods are sold by the consignee, the sales price less a selling commission is remitted to the consignor. Goods that are not sold are returned to the consignor. Even though consigned goods are in the possession of the consignee, the merchandise should be included in the inventory of the consignor because legal title remains with the consignor. Consigned goods should be included in inventory at cost to

the consignor plus the costs of handling and shipping the goods to the consignee. An artist's agreement to sell paintings on consignment through an art gallery is a typical consignment arrangement. Accounting for consignments is discussed and illustrated in Chapter 6.

SALES ON APPROVAL

Sales on approval are similar to consignment sales, except that the party who owns the goods ships the goods directly to potential buyers "on approval" rather than attempting to sell them through a consignee. For example, companies that sell postage stamps to stamp collectors often send stamps to collectors who might be interested in buying them, and the collectors will return to the seller stamps not purchased plus payment for stamps purchased. Goods sent on approval to potential buyers should remain as inventory on the seller's books until payment is received for items kept by the buyer.

PRODUCT FINANCING ARRANGEMENT

A **product financing arrangement** is a transaction in which a company "sells" inventory items and at the same time agrees to repurchase those items or substantially identical items from the buyer at a specified price over a specified future period. For example, Axle Corporation "sells" inventory to Gilson Company and, as part of the transaction, agrees to repurchase those goods at a specified price within the next three months. Legally, title to the goods passes to Gilson, which makes it possible for Gilson to use the goods as collateral for a bank loan, the proceeds of which can be used as payment for the goods. As a result of the bank loan, Gilson does not have to use existing assets to "purchase" the inventory. When Axle repurchases the goods from Gilson, Gilson can use the proceeds to meet its obligation to the bank.

Transactions such as the one between Axle Corporation and Gilson Company often are called **"parking transactions"** because the "seller" (Axle) in effect "parks" its inventory among the "buyer's" (Gilson's) assets for a short period of time. "Parking" became popular because it enabled the "seller" (Axle) to avoid property taxes in some states, reduce current liabilities, and manipulate income. For the seller, "parking" is an example of off-balance-sheet financing, which was introduced in Chapter 5. The "buyer" might benefit by avoiding reduction of early LIFO inventory layers (discussed later in this chapter).

The FASB concluded that, in some cases, parking transactions should not be recorded as sales because the earnings process is not complete or virtually complete.[1] In particular, when the specified repurchase price can be adjusted as necessary to cover fluctuations in carrying and financing costs, the original seller (Axle in our example) actually bears the risks of ownership even though legal title may have passed to the buyer (Gilson). In such cases, *FASB Statement No. 49* requires that the items "sold" must continue to be reported as inventory of the seller (that is, no sale is recorded), and the seller's obligation to repurchase from the buyer must be reported as a liability on the seller's balance sheet.

INSTALLMENT SALES

Any type of sale agreement in which the buyer makes payments in periodic installments over an extended period of time is called an **installment sale.** When it is expected that the buyer will make all payments due or the seller can reasonably estimate the percentage of bad debts on installment sales, goods sold on the installment basis should be excluded from the seller's inventory, even though legal title has not passed to the buyer.

CONDITIONAL SALES

The extended payment period of an installment sale often increases the seller's risk of not collecting the entire amount due. As a result, goods are often sold on a **conditional** basis, under which the seller retains legal title until all payments have been made. For example,

[1] "Accounting for Product Financing Arrangements," *Statement of Financial Accounting Standards No. 49* (Stamford, Conn.: FASB, 1981).

book publishers often allow bookstores to return unsold books for a refund. In such cases, should all or only part of the books shipped by the publisher to the bookstore be recorded as sold and removed from the publisher's inventory? The answer depends on the degree of certainty about the number of unsold books that may be returned to the publisher. If a reasonable estimate of book returns can be made, then all of the books should be considered as sold and removed from inventory, and an account for estimated sales returns and allowances should be established. If such an estimate cannot be made, the publisher should not remove shipped books from the inventory account until they are sold by the bookstore.[2]

INVENTORY ERRORS AND THEIR EFFECTS ON THE FINANCIAL STATEMENTS

Errors can occur in identifying or counting items that should be included in inventory, and in recording inventory acquisitions or sales. The great variety of goods often found in inventory makes it easy to overlook or misprice items and makes physical counts of inventory items tedious. Extended periods of time required to ship goods from a seller to a buyer may cause several items to be in transit from suppliers or to customers at the end of each accounting period. Individual purchase or sale transactions may erroneously be omitted from the accounting records when there are vast numbers of transactions involving inventory. Errors in accounting for inventory can affect both the balance sheet, because of an incorrect inventory account, and the income statement, because of an incorrect cost of goods sold balance.

Inventory accounting errors can affect both the balance sheet and the income statement.

When analyzing the effects of inventory accounting errors, you should remember:

1. If multiple inventory errors occur in a particular accounting period, the effects of each error should be separately evaluated.

2. The interrelationships shown below can be used to reduce the complexity of the process of analyzing inventory errors.

For a periodic inventory system:

Beginning inventory	+ Purchases	− Ending inventory	= Cost of goods sold
BI	P	EI	CGS

For a perpetual inventory system:

Beginning inventory	+ Purchases	− Cost of goods sold	= Ending inventory
BI	P	CGS	EI

Gross margin is computed as:

Sales revenue	− Cost of goods sold	= Gross margin
SR	CGS	GM

[2] "Revenue Recognition When Right of Return Exists," *Statement of Financial Accounting Standards No. 48* (Stamford, Conn.: FASB, 1981).

All inventory errors affect one or more of the following: beginning inventory, purchases, ending inventory, cost of goods sold, income, and retained earnings. Errors can occur in many combinations. Exhibits 9–4 and 9–5 present two inventory error possibilities simply to demonstrate error effects and error analysis procedures. A full discussion of inventory errors and their correction is presented in Chapter 22.

EXHIBIT 9–4   FAILURE TO RECORD INVENTORY PURCHASE IN CORRECT YEAR

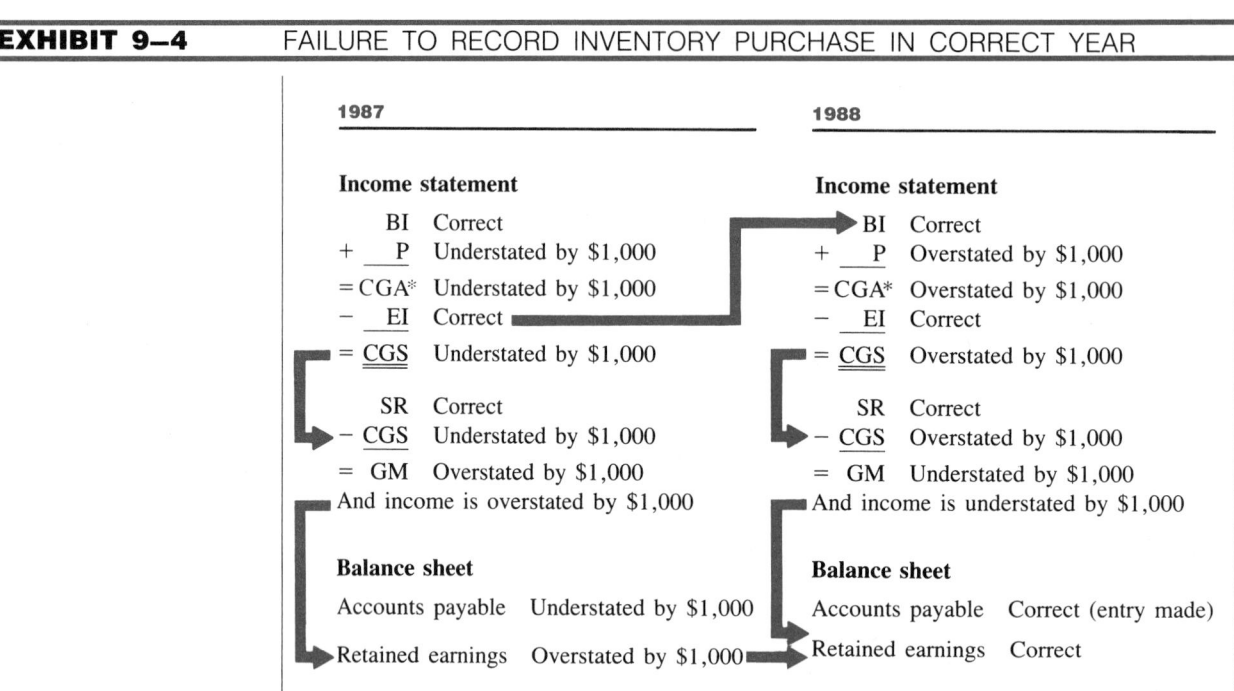

* CGA: Cost of goods available

EXHIBIT 9–5   GOODS INCORRECTLY INCLUDED IN ENDING INVENTORY

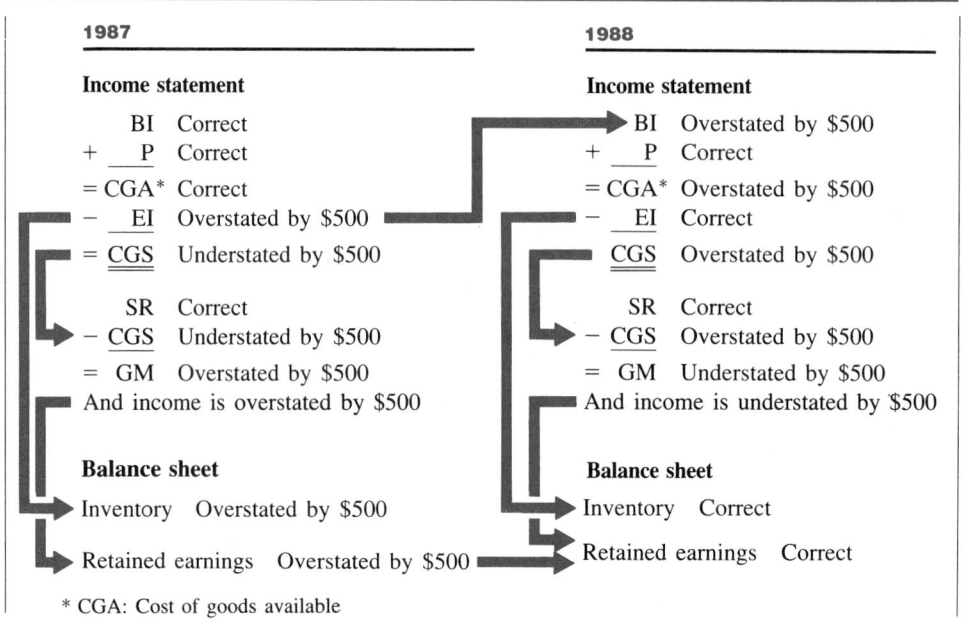

* CGA: Cost of goods available

Both Exhibit 9–4 and Exhibit 9–5 illustrate how inventory and purchases errors can have multiple effects on the financial statements and, of course, on financial data and analyses based on the financial statements. In addition, the exhibits demonstrate that some inventory errors are self-correcting or counterbalancing over two accounting periods. That is, an overstatement or understatement in one period is offset by an error in the opposite direction in the following period. Note that since the ending inventory of one period is the beginning inventory of the next period, errors in ending inventory are carried into the next period. In tracing the effects of the error in Exhibit 9–4, we can see that erroneous recording of a 1987 purchase in 1988 caused 1987 purchases, goods available, and cost of goods sold to be understated, and income and retained earnings to be overstated. On the other hand, 1988 purchases, goods available, and cost of goods sold were overstated, with corresponding understatement of 1988 income. Since 1987 income was overstated and 1988 income was understated by the same amount, retained earnings is correct at the end of 1988. A similar analysis can be made with the data in Exhibit 9–5. We have left that analysis for you to do as a means of developing your error analysis skills.

EXPENDITURES AND COST ALLOCATIONS TO BE INCLUDED IN INVENTORY COST

Inventory cost includes all expenditures needed to get inventory into condition and location for sale.

An important aspect of avoiding inventory errors is to properly determine the expenditures to be included in inventory cost. Inventory, like other assets, generally is accounted for in accordance with the historical cost principle, discussed in Chapter 2, which means that **inventory cost** or **product cost** is the sum of all expenditures required to get inventory items into condition and location for sale. Inventory cost therefore includes the original purchase price plus expenditures for such items as freight in, handling, storage related to goods purchased, applicable insurance and taxes, and materials and labor used in manufactured inventory, because all of the expenditures are made in order to get the inventory into condition and location for sale.

In theory, it also would be appropriate to allocate to inventory a portion of other expenditures, such as expenses of the purchasing department and costs of handling and storing goods before they are sold. Because of the difficulty of allocating such expenditures, however, and because they often are not material in amount in comparison with other expenditures that are included in inventory cost, in practice such expenditures seldom are included. Instead, they are accounted for separately as expenses of the period, or **period costs.**

Other expenditures not directly related to the acquisition or production of inventory normally also are accounted for not as product costs but as expenses of the period. For example, selling costs are accounted for as period costs and are expensed when incurred. They are not included in inventory cost.

Interest costs incurred to finance the purchase of inventory are treated as period costs, even though they seem to be more directly related to inventories than are most other period costs. In fact, some accountants argue that inventory financing expenditures are a direct cost of getting inventory in condition and location for sale, and therefore should be included as part of the cost of the inventory. But others argue that interest expenditures related to inventories are no different from other financing costs, and should be accounted for as a period cost, like other financing costs. In 1979 the FASB took the position that interest costs for inventories that are routinely and continuously manufactured in large quantities, for example, automobiles, should not be included in inventory cost because the value of the information provided by this accounting treatment is outweighed by the cost of providing it. On the other hand, the FASB concluded that material amounts of interest incurred in the construction of assets for the company's own use or as discrete projects for sale or lease, for example, ships, should be capitalized (recorded as part of the cost of the asset), provided that such assets require considerable time to get ready for their intended use. The FASB assumed that the value of the information provided by assigning these interest costs to inventory will exceed the cost of making the assignment.[3] Accounting for interest costs incurred during construction is discussed in more detail in Chapter 11.

THE COSTS OF PURCHASED MERCHANDISE INVENTORY AND COST ADJUSTMENTS

As we indicated earlier and illustrated in Exhibit 9–3, when merchandise is purchased, a debit is made to either inventory (in a perpetual inventory system) or purchases (in a periodic inventory system). The dollar amount debited is the invoice price of the goods purchased. The invoice price, however, is unlikely to be the final recorded acquisition cost for purchased merchandise. Additional costs may be incurred for shipping and handling of the goods, and reductions in acquisition cost may result from purchase discounts, returns of purchased goods, and other allowances or adjustments of the invoice price. Although it would be possible to account for additions to and reductions of the invoice price by directly adjusting the purchases or inventory account, general accounting practice is to use a number of separate accounts for these adjustments. Use of separate accounts provides a breakdown of information that helps management to analyze the elements of the acquisition cost of inventory.

Relative Sales Value Method

Sometimes a company purchases two or more different kinds of inventory items for a single lump-sum amount. In these instances, the company must allocate the single purchase amount among the various items purchased. The procedure that should be used to allocate a lump-sum or ''basket'' purchase price is the **relative sales value method.**

Let us suppose that Wallace Lumber Company purchased 10,000 linear feet of unsorted 2×4 lumber for $8,000. After sorting the 2×4s into grades 1, 2, and 3, Wallace Lumber had 2,000 linear feet of grade 1, 3,000 linear feet of grade 2, and 5,000 linear feet of grade 3. The selling prices of 2×4s were $1.20 per linear foot for grade 1, $1.00 per linear foot for grade 2, and $.80 per linear foot for grade 3.

According to the relative sales value method, the $8,000 lump-sum cost of the lumber would be allocated among the three grades of 2×4s as follows:

$$\text{Grade 1: } \frac{(2{,}000 \text{ ft.} \times \$1.20)}{(2{,}000 \text{ ft.} \times \$1.20) + (3{,}000 \text{ ft.} \times \$1.00) + (5{,}000 \text{ ft.} \times \$.80)} \times \$8{,}000 = \$2{,}043$$

$$\text{Grade 2: } \frac{(3{,}000 \text{ ft.} \times \$1.00)}{(2{,}000 \text{ ft.} \times \$1.20) + (3{,}000 \text{ ft.} \times \$1.00) + (5{,}000 \text{ ft.} \times \$.80)} \times \$8{,}000 = \$2{,}553$$

$$\text{Grade 3: } \frac{(5{,}000 \text{ ft.} \times \$.80)}{(2{,}000 \text{ ft.} \times \$1.20) + (3{,}000 \text{ ft.} \times \$1.00) + (5{,}000 \text{ ft.} \times \$.80)} \times \$8{,}000 = \$3{,}404$$

Note that we use the sales value of each grade of 2×4s as a percentage of the total sales value of all the grades of 2×4s to compute the portion of the lump-sum purchase price that should be allocated to each grade of lumber.

Purchase Discounts

Perhaps the most common adjustment made to the invoice price of goods is for purchase discounts. Purchase discounts are offered by sellers as an incentive to buyers to make prompt payment on purchases. For example, as we saw in Chapter 8, typical sale terms are ''2%/10, net 30,'' which means that a 2 percent discount from invoice price is offered

---

[3] ''Capitalization of Interest Cost,'' *Statement of Financial Accounting Standards No. 34* (Stamford, Conn.: FASB, 1979).

if payment is made within 10 days, and the full invoice price is due within 30 days.

As is true for sales discounts (see Exhibit 8–3), there are basically two methods of accounting for purchase discounts: the gross method and the net method. Under the **gross method,** purchases and accounts payable are recorded at the *full* invoice price, and purchase discounts are recognized only if they are taken. Under the **net method,** purchases and accounts payable are recorded *net* of the purchase discount, and purchase discounts that are not taken are recorded as purchase discounts lost.

Illustrative entries for a company whose fiscal year ends December 31 are shown in Exhibit 9–6 for both the gross method and the net method of accounting for purchase discounts. We assume a full invoice price of $1,000 on a purchase made December 15 and terms of 2%/10, net 30.

Conceptually, the net method is preferable for several reasons. First, on the purchase date, purchases and accounts payable are recorded at the cash equivalent exchange price, which is the invoice price *net* of the purchase discount. Therefore, the cost of the purchased goods and the related liability are correctly stated as of the purchase date, and the purchase discount is recorded when the related purchase is recorded. Second, purchase discounts lost are recorded separately from purchases, which is appropriate because the expense arose from failure to make a timely payment rather than from the purchase transaction itself. Third, accounts payable are adjusted at the end of the year for purchase discounts lost. This adjustment results in proper reporting of the liability. Finally, if the purchase discounts lost account is reported in the income statement as a financing expense or general operating expense, rather than being hidden as an addition to the cost of merchandise purchased, users of the financial statements are made aware of the period expense that arose from failure to pay accounts payable on time. Some users may consider failure to make payments within the discount period to be an important matter, because

---

EXHIBIT 9–6   RECORDING PURCHASE DISCOUNTS BY GROSS
                  AND NET METHODS (TERMS: 2%/10, NET 30)

	GROSS METHOD		**NET METHOD**	
To record purchase on 12/15:				
Purchases (inventory) . . . 1,000		Purchases (inventory) 980		
Accounts payable	1,000	Accounts payable	980	
To record payment within discount period (by 12/25):				
Accounts payable 1,000		Accounts payable 980		
Cash	980	Cash	980	
Purchase discounts . . .	20			
To record payment after discount period but before end of fiscal year (12/16–12/31):				
Accounts payable 1,000		Accounts payable 980		
Cash	1,000	Purchase discounts lost . . . 20		
		Cash	1,000	
Adjusting entry at end of fiscal year (12/31) when invoice is unpaid but discount period has expired:				
No entry required		Purchase discounts lost . . . 20		
		Accounts payable	20	

the *effective* interest rate paid by the buyer, assuming payment is not made until the thirtieth day on a 2%/10, net 30 purchase, is approximately 36 percent or

$$2\% \times \frac{360 \text{ days}}{30 \text{ days} - 10 \text{ days}}.$$

It is almost always better financing policy to borrow money elsewhere and take advantage of the purchase discount than it is to defer payment and lose the purchase discount. Use of the net method provides management with a clear signal of when accounts are not being paid in a timely fashion.

The gross method initially records both purchases and accounts payable at the full invoice price and makes separate note of purchase discounts only if they are taken at the time of payment. The purchase discounts account is deducted from the purchases account at the end of the accounting period. This procedure only *approximates* reporting purchases net of purchase discounts because the adjustment is only for payments made during the period, without regard for the period of purchase. As a result, purchase discounts are not necessarily matched with the period in which the purchase occurs. The gross method misstates the cost of purchases to the extent that purchase discounts on the current period's purchases are *not* taken and discounts on purchases in previous periods *are* taken in the current period. Further, since purchase discounts not taken remain in the purchases account, it is impossible to identify separately what may be an excessive and unnecessary financing expense.

Freight In on Purchases

In accordance with the historical cost principle, the transportation costs, called **transportation in** or **freight in,** as well as the handling costs and other incidental costs, that a company incurs in getting inventory in location and in condition for sale should be included in inventory cost. If it is impractical to identify such costs with specific purchases of goods, however, or if the amounts of such costs are material in comparison with other inventoriable costs, it is common to find them recorded in special separate accounts, such as a freight in account. A typical entry, recording $100 of freight in, is:

Freight in	100	
Accounts payable		100

In practice, freight in increases cost of goods sold when a periodic inventory system is used because it is added to purchases when one computes the goods available for sale, from which ending inventory is subtracted. When a perpetual inventory system is used, freight in should be debited to merchandise inventory at the time of purchase. If freight in is recorded in a separate account, it normally is added to cost of goods sold at the end of the accounting period. Although adjustment of cost of goods sold for freight in during the accounting period is a common practice, it is theoretically unsound because only the freight costs associated with goods sold should be included in cost of goods sold. The remainder of the freight costs should be assigned to the goods still in inventory at the end of the accounting period.

Purchase Returns and Allowances

When the buyer returns goods to the seller, a **purchase return** credit against existing accounts payable or future purchases is given to the buyer. As soon as the amount of the credit is known, it should be recorded on the buyer's books. Assuming the buyer has accounts payable to the seller, a $30 purchase return would be recorded as follows:

Accounts payable 30
    Purchase returns (inventory in a perpetual system)   30

The purchase returns account is a contra-account in relation to the purchases account and is closed along with the purchases account in the year-end adjusting and closing entries in the periodic inventory system.

Damaged or otherwise unsatisfactory goods occasionally are shipped by the seller, and the buyer elects to accept an appropriate adjustment of the purchase price rather than to return the goods. This adjustment of the original purchase price is called a **purchase allowance.** When a periodic inventory system is used, a purchase allowance is credited to a purchase allowances account, which is a contra-account in relation to the purchases account and is closed in the year-end adjusting and closing entries. If a perpetual inventory system is used, purchase allowances are credited directly to inventory. If a $50 purchase allowance is given, it is recorded as follows:

Accounts payable 50
    Purchase allowance (inventory in a perpetual system)   50

THE COSTS OF MANUFACTURED INVENTORIES

Manufacturing companies typically classify their inventories in three major categories: raw materials inventory, work-in-process inventory, and finished goods inventory. As Exhibit 9–2 indicates, work-in-process and finished goods entail three types of costs: raw materials cost, direct labor cost, and allocated manufacturing overhead cost.

The cost of the raw materials inventory purchased by a manufacturing company is calculated exactly as is the cost of purchased merchandise inventory, including adjustments for freight in, purchase discounts, and purchase returns and allowances. Direct labor cost is the cost of labor employed directly in the production process. For example, production supervisors' salaries and the wages of assembly-line workers are included in direct labor. Manufacturing overhead cost includes all manufacturing costs other than the costs of raw materials and direct labor. For example, manufacturing overhead cost would include the salary of the vice-president for manufacturing, indirect materials cost, indirect labor cost, and properly allocated portions of general overhead expenses, such as depreciation, taxes, insurance, and utilities.

The assignment of all manufacturing costs to the product, whether those costs are variable in direct proportion to volume of product output or fixed regardless of volume, is known as **absorption costing.** An alternative approach, advocated by many accountants, and known as **variable (direct) costing,** assigns to the product only those costs that vary directly with the volume of production; fixed manufacturing overhead costs, such as depreciation, taxes, insurance, and the salary of the vice-president for manufacturing, are treated as costs of the accounting period, rather than as product costs. The arguments supporting absorption costing and variable costing are properly topics of a managerial accounting course and are beyond the scope of this book. Only absorption costing is acceptable for external financial statements prepared in conformity with generally accepted accounting principles and for the preparation of income tax returns. Variable costing is used widely for internal reporting, however, because it is so useful in cost control, budget preparation, and management decision making in general.

COST FLOW ASSUMPTIONS

As we have seen, a company usually begins an accounting period with some units of inventory on hand, and it purchases or manufactures additional units during the period. Units on hand plus units acquired constitute the units available for sale. These goods either are sold during the accounting period or remain in inventory at the end of the period. Since the purchases occur at different times during the period, identical units of inventory may be acquired at different costs. The dollar amounts reported for inventory and cost of goods sold at the end of the accounting period depend on the answer to the question "Which of the costs of beginning inventory and purchases should be included in cost of goods sold and which should be included in the cost of ending inventory?"

Generally accepted accounting principles allow several different accounting procedures for assigning costs to ending inventory and to cost of goods sold, and these procedures can produce different amounts for ending inventory and cost of goods sold. In addition, some of these procedures yield one set of answers when they are used in conjunction with a perpetual inventory system and another when they are used with a periodic inventory system. In the next several pages, the cost flows, cost flow assumptions, and corresponding inventory accounting procedures that are most common in current accounting practice are discussed. The data in Exhibit 9–7 will be used to illustrate each accounting procedure.

SPECIFIC IDENTIFICATION

One procedure used to determine the cost of goods sold and cost of ending inventory is known as **specific identification.** When specific identification is used, the flow of costs through goods available for sale into either cost of goods sold or cost of ending inventory is exactly the same as the physical flow of units of inventory. That is, specific identification traces *actual cost flows*. Each unit of inventory obtained, held, and sold, as well as the cost of each unit, must be specifically identified. For example, each of the 100 units sold by Blake Company on May 10 must be specifically identified as being either a $10 unit from beginning inventory or a $12 unit from the March 7 purchase. Since the cost of a unit in the beginning inventory differs from the cost of a unit purchased on March 7, the cost of goods sold on May 10 will depend on which units actually are sold.

The specific identification procedure is easiest to use when inventory consists of a relatively small number of easily distinguishable items; and it is more likely to provide

EXHIBIT 9–7

Blake Company
PHYSICAL INVENTORY FLOWS

	NUMBER OF UNITS	COST PER UNIT	TOTAL COST
Inventory, 1/1	500	$10.00	$ 5,000
Purchase, 3/7	200	12.00	2,400
Purchase, 7/12	100	13.25	1,325
Purchase, 10/24	300	14.00	4,200
Goods available for sale	1,100		$12,925
Sale, 2/5	250		
Sale, 5/10	100		
Sale, 11/7	150		
Goods sold	(500)		
Inventory, 12/31	600		

useful information about inventory flows when those items are relatively costly—high-priced jewelry, for example, or automobiles. Specific identification becomes progressively less practical, and less likely to produce information that justifies the extra bookkeeping effort required, as the number of inventory units increases and inventory cost per unit declines. This is especially true if units of inventory are not easily distinguishable from each other. As an extreme example, consider the relative costs and benefits of using specific identification when the inventory consists of sixteen-penny nails for which the relatively small unit acquisition cost fluctuates substantially and which are sold by the handful.

Some accountants argue that in addition to being impractical in many inventory accounting situations, specific identification allows management to manipulate the cost of ending inventory, cost of goods sold, and net income. That is, by selecting particular goods to be sold, management is able to exercise some control over the cost of goods sold and the cost of inventory remaining on hand. For example, if on May 10 Blake Company selected 100 of the $10 units in beginning inventory to be sold (Exhibit 9–7), cost of goods sold would be $1,000. But if Blake chose to sell 100 of the $12 units purchased on March 7, cost of goods sold would be $1,200. Whether this opportunity for management to influence cost of goods sold and inventory cost by selecting particular units for sale is manipulation or simply the result of reporting actual physical inventory flows, which management certainly is entitled to control, is debatable.

Because of the impracticality of using specific identification of cost flows in most inventory accounting situations, this procedure is not widely used. Instead, most companies use one or more of several generally accepted inventory **cost flow assumptions** in their inventory accounting. These cost flow assumptions, and related accounting procedures, are *not departures from historical cost*. Instead, they are simplifying *assumptions* about the flow of costs through goods available for sale into cost of goods sold and cost of ending inventory. It is important to note that as *cost flow assumptions*, they have no necessary relationship to the actual physical flow of goods through the enterprise. In this sense, cost flow assumptions are fundamentally different from specific identification, which is concerned with *actual,* not assumed, cost flows.

Inventory cost flow assumptions are not necessarily related to the actual physical flow of inventory items.

AVERAGE COST

Under the **average cost** procedure, the costs of goods are equally divided, or averaged, among the units of inventory. The average cost procedure can be applied in either a periodic or a perpetual inventory system. When used in the periodic inventory system, the average cost procedure is known as the weighted average method. When used in the perpetual system, it becomes the moving average method.

Weighted Average Method

The **weighted average method** is the average cost procedure applied in the periodic inventory system. Blake Company's weighted average cost of goods sold for the year and its cost of ending inventory (Exhibit 9–7) would be determined as follows:

$$\text{Average cost of goods available for sale during the period} = \frac{\text{Total } \textit{cost} \text{ of goods available for sale during the period}}{\text{Total } \textit{units} \text{ of goods available for sale during the period}}$$

$$= \frac{\$12,925}{1,100 \text{ units}} = \$11.75$$

$$\text{Cost of goods sold} = 500 \text{ units @ } \$11.75 = \$5,875$$

$$\text{Ending inventory} = 600 \text{ units @ } \$11.75 = \$7,050$$

Moving Average Method

The **moving average method** is the average cost procedure applied in the perpetual inventory system. Because a perpetual system is used, it is necessary to have a continuous, or moving, average unit cost of goods available so that the average cost can be used to determine cost of goods sold at the time of any sale. As a result, the moving average method requires a recomputation of average unit cost after each purchase. The only exception to this rule occurs when the purchase price per unit is the same as the average cost per unit before the purchase in question. When applied to the Blake Company data, the moving average method yields the results shown in Exhibit 9–8.

Notice in Exhibit 9–8 that the average cost per unit of units on hand at the time of each sale is assigned to units sold as well as to units retained in inventory. For example, when 250 units are sold on February 5, they are assigned the $10 average cost per unit that exists at that time. The 250 units that remain in inventory also are assigned a $10 per unit cost. When 200 additional units are purchased on March 7 at a cost of $12 per unit, a new average unit cost must be computed for the 450 units then on hand. Given 250 units with a cost of $10 each and 200 units with a cost of $12 each, the average cost per unit for the 450 units is $10.89, which is shown in the right-hand column of Exhibit 9–8. This average cost per unit is then assigned to the 100 units sold on May 10, as well as to the 350 units remaining in inventory after that sale. The pattern of computations we have just described is followed throughout the remainder of Exhibit 9–8.

EXHIBIT 9–8

Blake Company
COST OF GOODS SOLD AND ENDING
INVENTORY USING THE MOVING AVERAGE METHOD
(AVERAGE COST IN PERPETUAL INVENTORY SYSTEM)

	NUMBER OF UNITS	COST PER UNIT		TOTAL COST	MOVING AVERAGE COST
Beginning inventory, 1/1	500			$5,000	$10.00
Sale, 2/5 (CGS)	(250)		$10.00	(2,500)	
Inventory balance	250	$10.00		$2,500	
Purchase, 3/7	200	$12.00		2,400	
Inventory balance	450			$4,900	$10.89*
Sale, 5/10 (CGS)	(100)		$10.89	(1,089)	
Inventory balance	350	$10.89		$3,811*	
Purchase, 7/12	100	$13.25		1,325	
Inventory balance	450			$5,136	$11.41*
Purchase, 10/24	300	$14.00		4,200	
Inventory balance	750			$9,336	$12.45*
Sale, 11/7 (CGS)	(150)		$12.45	(1,867)*	
Inventory balance	600	$12.45		$7,469*	
Ending inventory	600	$7,469			
Cost of goods sold	250	$2,500			
	100	1,089			
	150	1,867			
	500	$5,456			

* Reflects minor rounding.

FIRST IN, FIRST OUT (FIFO)

The **first in, first out** inventory cost flow assumption, abbreviated **FIFO,** treats the earliest inventory costs of the period as the cost of goods sold and the latest inventory costs as the cost of ending inventory. In other words, regardless of the actual physical flow of goods, cost of goods sold and ending inventory are computed under FIFO as if the goods entering inventory first are sold first and the goods entering inventory last are sold last, or remain in ending inventory. During periods of rising acquisition costs, FIFO yields a lower cost of goods sold and a higher ending inventory cost, as compared with the average cost approach.

Computations of cost of goods sold and ending inventory for Blake Company by the FIFO assumption for both periodic and perpetual inventory systems are shown in Exhibit 9–9. In Exhibit 9–9 you can see that when FIFO is applied in the periodic system, ending

EXHIBIT 9–9

Blake Company

COST OF GOODS SOLD AND ENDING INVENTORY USING FIFO

PERIODIC INVENTORY SYSTEM

Ending inventory: by physical count, 600 units.

UNITS	DATE PURCHASED	COST PER UNIT	TOTAL COST
300	10/24	$14.00	$4,200
100	7/12	13.25	1,325
200	3/7	12.00	2,400
600			$7,925

Cost of goods sold:

	NUMBER OF UNITS	TOTAL COST
Goods available	1,100	$12,925
Less: Ending inventory	(600)	(7,925)
Goods sold	500	$ 5,000

PERPETUAL INVENTORY SYSTEM

Cost of goods sold:

UNITS	COST PER UNIT	TOTAL COST
250	$10	$2,500
100	10	1,000
150	10	1,500
500		$5,000

Ending inventory:

	NUMBER OF UNITS	TOTAL COST
Goods available	1,100	$12,925
Less: Goods sold	(500)	(5,000)
Ending inventory	600	$ 7,925

EXHIBIT 9–10

Blake Company

COST OF GOODS SOLD AND ENDING INVENTORY USING LIFO

PERIODIC INVENTORY SYSTEM

Ending inventory: by physical count, 600 units.

NUMBER OF UNITS	COST PER UNIT	TOTAL COST
500	from beginning inventory $10	$5,000
100	purchased 3/7 12	1,200
600		$6,200

Cost of goods sold:

	NUMBER OF UNITS	TOTAL COST
Goods available	1,100	$12,925
Less: Ending inventory	(600)	(6,200)
Goods sold	500	$6,725

PERPETUAL INVENTORY SYSTEM

DATE	TRANSACTION	COST OF GOODS PURCHASED	COST OF GOODS SOLD	CUMULATIVE BALANCE OF INVENTORY
1/1	Beginning inventory			500 @ $10.00 = $5,000
2/5	Sale		250 @ $10 = $2,500	250 @ $10.00 = 2,500
3/7	Purchase	200 @ $12 = $2,400		250 @ $10.00 ⎱ 200 @ $12.00 ⎰ = 4,900
5/10	Sale		100 @ $12 = $1,200	250 @ $10.00 ⎱ 100 @ $12.00 ⎰ = 3,700
7/12	Purchase	100 @ $13.25 = $1,325		250 @ $10.00 ⎫ 100 @ $12.00 ⎬ = 5,025 100 @ $13.25 ⎭
10/24	Purchase	300 @ $14 = $4,200		250 @ $10.00 ⎫ 100 @ $12.00 ⎪ 100 @ $13.25 ⎬ = 9,225 300 @ $14.00 ⎭
11/7	Sale		150 @ $14 = $2,100	250 @ $10.00 ⎫ 100 @ $12.00 ⎪ 100 @ $13.25 ⎬ = 7,125 150 @ $14.00 ⎭
			Total cost of goods sold $5,800	Ending inventory $7,125

inventory is valued by using the costs of the last goods purchased in the period and then ending inventory cost is subtracted from the cost of goods available to determine the cost of goods sold of $5,000. In contrast, when FIFO is applied in the perpetual system, cost of goods sold is determined at the time of each sale, based on the costs of the earliest purchased goods on hand at the time of the sale. The total cost of goods sold for the period is subtracted from the cost of goods available to get the ending inventory cost of $7,925.

Note that FIFO in the periodic system yields the same cost of goods sold and ending inventory cost as FIFO in the perpetual system. This result occurs because the same goods and costs are first in, and therefore are first out, whether cost of goods sold is determined throughout the accounting period as goods are sold, under the perpetual system, or as a residual amount at the end of the accounting period, under the periodic system.

LAST IN, FIRST OUT (LIFO)

Under the **last in, first out** cost flow assumption, abbreviated **LIFO,** the costs of the most recent purchases are assigned to cost of goods sold first and the costs of the earliest inventory acquisitions are assigned to cost of goods sold last, or remain in the inventory account. Regardless of the actual physical flow of goods, cost of goods sold and the inventory balance are computed under LIFO as if the goods that enter inventory last are sold first, and the goods that enter inventory first are sold last, or remain in inventory. During periods of rising acquisition costs, LIFO yields a higher cost of goods sold and a lower ending inventory, as compared with the average cost approach.

Given the use of LIFO in the periodic and perpetual inventory systems, Blake Company's ending inventory and cost of goods sold are computed as shown in Exhibit 9–10.

As you can see from the top part of Exhibit 9–10, LIFO used in the periodic inventory system requires relatively simple computations. The costs associated with units remaining in ending inventory at the end of the period are assumed to be the costs of the earliest units purchased. The cost of ending inventory is subtracted from the cost of goods available to determine the cost of goods sold.

LIFO in the perpetual system is illustrated in the bottom part of Exhibit 9–10. The computations for the period are relatively complex because the cost of goods sold calculated at the time of each sale is based on the cost of the goods most recently purchased prior to the sale. The total cost of goods sold for the period can be subtracted from the cost of goods available to determine the ending inventory cost.

As Exhibit 9–10 shows, under LIFO, inventory is composed of *layers*. In accounting periods when more units are purchased than sold, the increase in inventory will result in the addition of one or more new layers of inventory. In accounting periods when more units are sold than purchased, layers of inventory added in previous accounting periods will be eliminated, beginning with the most recent layer added. *Once a layer is eliminated, it is never replaced.*

Exhibit 9–10 demonstrates that, in contrast to the FIFO cost flow assumption, during periods of changing prices LIFO does not yield the same results for ending inventory and cost of goods sold when it is used with the perpetual system as it does when it is used with the periodic system. The different results occur because LIFO applied in the periodic system assumes sale of the most recent purchases in the total accounting period, while LIFO applied in a perpetual system assumes sale of the most recent purchases as of the time of each sale.

COMPARATIVE RESULTS OF COST FLOW ASSUMPTIONS

The comparative effects of average cost, FIFO, and LIFO on the amounts reported as Blake Company's cost of goods sold and ending inventory, in both the periodic inventory system and perpetual inventory system, are shown in Exhibit 9–11. The results from using specific identification, which is based on actual cost flows, are not presented because the amounts for cost of goods sold and ending inventory are strictly dependent on the particular inventory items that actually are sold.

EXHIBIT 9–11

Blake Company
COMPARATIVE FINANCIAL STATEMENT EFFECTS OF COST FLOW ASSUMPTIONS

ACCOUNT	PERIODIC INVENTORY SYSTEM			PERPETUAL INVENTORY SYSTEM		
	WEIGHTED AVERAGE	FIFO	LIFO	MOVING AVERAGE	FIFO	LIFO
Cost of goods sold	$5,875	$5,000	$6,725	$5,456	$5,000	$5,800
Ending inventory	7,050	7,925	6,200	7,469	7,925	7,125

As Exhibit 9–11 indicates, whether the periodic or the perpetual inventory system is used, during periods of rising acquisition costs (as is the case for Blake Company) FIFO yields a lower cost of goods sold and LIFO yields a higher cost of goods sold than does the average cost approach. Conversely, the ending inventory figure is higher under FIFO and lower under LIFO. During periods of falling acquisition costs, the results would be the reverse of those reported in Exhibit 9–11, with the average cost procedure continuing to yield cost of goods sold and inventory amounts between those of the FIFO and LIFO cost flow assumptions.

EVALUATION OF THE VARIOUS COST FLOW ASSUMPTIONS

FIFO

Companies normally attempt to sell the oldest goods in inventory first. In fact, perishable goods and goods subject to obsolescence must be handled in a FIFO manner. Although generally accepted accounting principles do not require inventory cost flows to conform to the actual physical flow of goods, cost flow assumptions that do parallel the physical flow of goods are conceptually appealing. One of the advantages claimed for the FIFO cost flow assumption is that it conforms to the actual physical flow of many inventory items. Hence, for many types of inventory, FIFO yields the same cost of goods sold and ending inventory figures as does specific identification.

Another advantage of FIFO is that it is a simple assumption to employ in valuing inventory. FIFO is comparatively inexpensive to use with either the periodic or the perpetual inventory system. In addition, FIFO is systematic and objective, and it is less subject to management manipulation than other inventory cost flow assumptions, particularly LIFO.

When FIFO is used, the cost assigned to ending inventory is based on the most recent inventory acquisition costs. Therefore, FIFO approximates the current replacement cost of inventory on the balance sheet, particularly when inventory turnover is rapid and most of the costs assigned to ending inventory are very recent.

Perhaps the primary disadvantage of FIFO is that, because it assigns the most recent costs to ending inventory, relatively noncurrent or out-of-date costs are assigned to goods sold. This becomes a more severe problem when inventory acquisition costs rise rapidly during the accounting period and the quantity of inventory is stable or increases. Under these conditions, FIFO results in very bad matching on the income statement, because old and comparatively low inventory acquisition costs are matched, as part of cost of goods sold, against current and comparatively high sales revenue. The matching of old, comparatively low inventory acquisition costs against current revenue can yield an income number that is inflated by **inventory holding profits (gains).**

Inventory holding profits occur during periods of rising inventory prices. Inventory holding profits are the difference between old, low inventory costs and current replacement cost of inventory. For example, if a unit of inventory that was purchased at the beginning of the accounting period for $10 would cost $15 to replace at the end of the accounting period, the potential inventory holding profit is $5. If the old cost of $10 is matched against sales revenue, profit will be $5 higher than if the current replacement cost of $15 were matched against sales revenue. When management increases the selling prices for its goods in order to cover increased current acquisition costs of inventory, the inventory holding profit that results from the use of FIFO can cause misleading income and cash flow signals. FIFO ignores the cost of replacing inventory at higher prices (in a period of rising inventory prices), thus resulting in an income number that includes a ''paper profit'' (the inventory holding profit) that is not really available for distribution to owners because it is needed to replace inventory.

LIFO

One of LIFO's most important advantages is that it matches the most recently incurred inventory cost against sales revenue. This matching is especially critical during accounting periods when inventory acquisition costs are rising and inventory turnover is slow. Although the cost of goods sold under LIFO probably will not equal the replacement cost of inventory sold, it may *approximate* replacement cost and thus minimize inventory holding profit. When LIFO is used during periods of rising inventory prices, reported income is more likely to approximate the amount that really is available for distribution to owners.

Because LIFO yields a comparatively low net income during periods when inventory acquisition costs are rising and inventory quantities are not decreasing, it can be used to defer income taxes through reductions in current taxable income. This is perhaps the major advantage of LIFO from management's perspective. In fact, the income tax advantage of LIFO during inflationary periods is considered to be the primary reason for the growth in its use since 1973.

An example of the substantial tax savings that can be realized by companies that use LIFO during inflationary periods appeared in a *New York Times* article: ''The cumulative effect of LIFO in an inflationary era can be striking. Since it switched to LIFO in 1955, G.E. has realized a LIFO tax saving of more than $1 billion, says Thomas O. Thorsen, senior vice president of finance.''[4] Such tax savings can be invested in new plant and equipment, research and development, and other projects that enhance corporate profitability.

The Internal Revenue Service adopted ''LIFO conformity'' regulations requiring companies that use LIFO for tax purposes to also use it in their external financial statements. Therefore, although it is almost always advantageous to defer taxes by reducing taxable income, the use of LIFO to obtain such a deferral results in lower reported income in external financial statements than would be the case if some other cost flow assumption were used. Between 1979 and 1981, the IRS relaxed the LIFO conformity regulations to allow companies that use LIFO to disclose the income or loss that would result if an inventory method other than LIFO were used. These disclosures can be made in notes to the financial statements, in the president's letter, or in other supplementary sections of the annual report. A company that uses LIFO also is allowed to disclose the FIFO value of inventory, adjusted to LIFO, in the balance sheet, but only LIFO may be used for reporting in the income statement.[5] Thus, use of LIFO may be disadvantageous when management would like to avoid reporting low income to external users of financial data. Furthermore, some management compensation plans are tied to reported income, and use of LIFO results in reduced reported income during periods of rising inventory acquisition costs.

[4] Steve Lohr, ''The Question of LIFO vs. FIFO,'' *The New York Times,* February 25, 1981.
[5] *U.S. Treasury Regulation* 1.472-2(e), 1981.

Although LIFO can be used to approximate current replacement cost for cost of goods sold, it does not yield a current cost income. Moreover, during periods of rising inventory acquisition costs, LIFO may yield some very low reported amounts for ending inventory because the oldest acquisition costs remain in the inventory account. To the extent that inventory is reported at a lower amount, financial analysis based on current assets or total assets may be impaired. In addition, because the costs in inventory tend to be outdated when LIFO is used, liquidation of early layers of LIFO inventory can result in the matching of very old and low costs against sales revenue in the income statement. Furthermore, if the inventory is replaced, the new inventory cost would exceed the costs of the LIFO layers liquidated. Hence, liquidation of early layers of LIFO inventory during periods of rising prices can lead to reported income that is distorted simply because inventory replacement did not occur prior to the end of the accounting period.

An example of the effect on cost of goods sold of liquidating early LIFO layers when inventory costs have been increasing is provided by the 1981 annual report of Keystone Consolidated Industries, Inc. In its notes to the consolidated financial statements, Keystone reported that inventory quantities had been reduced, resulting in partial liquidation of the LIFO bases. The liquidation of LIFO layers had the effect of decreasing the cost of goods sold by $2,550,000 in 1981, $3,482,000 in 1980, and $1,089,000 in 1979. The earnings per share effects of the LIFO liquidation were increases of $1.36 in 1981, $.94 in 1980, and $.29 in 1979. These increases reduced Keystone's overall loss per share by 50 percent in 1981 and 34 percent in 1980, and accounted for 73 percent of Keystone's $.40 profit per share in 1979. Clearly, liquidating early LIFO layers resulted in substantial reductions in loss per share or increases in earnings per share for Keystone during the period from 1979 through 1981.

Assuming that the inventory decline causing liquidation of early LIFO layers is temporary, some LIFO users avoid potential distortion of income by debiting cost of goods sold for the current inventory costs even though some of the goods actually sold were carried at older, lower costs. An account such as "excess of replacement cost over LIFO cost of basic inventory temporarily liquidated" is then credited for the excess of the current replacement cost over the LIFO carrying cost for the inventory temporarily liquidated. When the inventory is replenished, the temporary account is removed, and the goods acquired are placed in inventory at their old LIFO costs. While it exists, the temporary account is shown among the current liabilities on the statement of financial position to reflect the expected reduction of reported working capital when the inventory is replaced. In *Statement of Concepts No. 3*, the FASB explicitly states that an account such as the temporary account just described is in fact not a liability as defined in the conceptual framework because the firm is not obligated to sacrifice assets in the future. Of course, *Statements of Concepts* do not establish GAAP.

The increases in net income and related increases in income taxes that can result from liquidation of early LIFO inventory layers during periods of rising acquisition costs may cause management to make economically unsound decisions about purchasing inventory at the end of the accounting period. As suggested above, if unit sales have exceeded unit purchases for the period, management may be faced with the necessity of including some very old and very low inventory costs in cost of goods sold. As a result, management may elect to purchase additional inventory to avoid dipping into the old inventory for LIFO costing purposes. The additional purchase may cause inventory costs to be unusually high or may cause a shortage of liquid assets, and thus may be economically unsound even though it may contribute to a tax saving. In addition, some accountants view management's opportunity to affect the amount of net income by strategic inventory acquisition as manipulation of income.

Finally, the LIFO cost flow assumption seldom conforms to normal physical flow of inventory units. This is not critical, however, because generally accepted accounting principles do not require that cost flow correspond to physical flow, only that a cost flow assumption be systematic, that it be based on cost, and that it appropriately match expense and revenue. LIFO has these characteristics. There are examples of inventories that do have a LIFO physical flow. Piled coal inventory is one: new coal is added to the outside of the pile and inventory withdrawals are from the outside of the pile.

Average Cost

The average cost procedure to determine cost of goods sold and inventory value steers a middle course between FIFO and LIFO. Whether inventory acquisition costs are rising or falling, the average cost approach tends to produce cost of goods sold and ending inventory results that fall between the results produced by FIFO and LIFO. In its effect on the balance sheet, however, average cost is much more like FIFO than LIFO. In fact, when inventory turnover is rapid, the inventory cost figures produced by the average cost method are almost as close to current replacement cost as those produced by FIFO.

The main advantage of the average cost procedure is its practicality. It is a fairly simple procedure that is easy to apply, and it is objective. Average cost does not lend itself so readily to manipulation as do specific identification and LIFO.

PROBLEMS IN USING TRADITIONAL LIFO

Application of LIFO as described to this point in the chapter can be called traditional LIFO. Three problems may arise when traditional LIFO is used. First, LIFO requires a complete record of the unit quantity and unit cost for each purchase during an accounting period, as well as the number of units and the specific unit costs comprising beginning inventory for the period. Compiling such detailed inventory records can be a significant record-keeping task when a company has numerous inventory transactions involving varied inventory acquisition costs.

Second, if it becomes necessary to liquidate early layers of LIFO inventory, and those early layers contain low and out-of-date inventory acquisition costs, LIFO's primary advantage becomes a major disadvantage. That is, matching the low costs against current sales revenue may result in a large reported income and a large tax obligation.

Third, if LIFO is applied to groups of inventory consisting of similar items within total inventory, it is possible that one or more groups may suffer inventory liquidations, which will reduce the overall advantage of using LIFO. For example, the total lumber inventory of a lumberyard may be stable or increasing during an accounting period, but specific types of lumber may be partially or totally liquidated. If this occurs, and LIFO is applied to specific types of lumber, liquidation of some types of lumber will tend to reduce the overall tax benefit of using LIFO. A similar kind of problem occurs as a result of technological or style changes in units of inventory. For example, several style changes in women's dresses may occur within a single accounting period of a women's clothing store. As a result, even though total inventory is stable or increasing in quantity during the period, certain styles of dresses are liquidated. Therefore, if LIFO is applied to each style of dress rather than to total inventory, LIFO liquidation of some styles will have an adverse effect on the overall tax benefit of using LIFO. Because of the problems that may arise when traditional LIFO is used, companies sometimes use a special procedure for applying the LIFO cost flow assumption. This procedure is called dollar-value LIFO.

DOLLAR-VALUE LIFO

Dollar-value LIFO is an inventory valuation procedure that provides the benefits of LIFO, but either avoids or reduces the problems that arise when traditional LIFO is used. Traditional LIFO requires that goods included in the same inventory group or pool be substantially identical. Dollar-value LIFO is less restrictive in that goods in the same pool need only be similar in type or use. A pool should include only goods that are likely to be subject to the same price change pressures. When dollar-value LIFO is used, it can be applied to inventory pools consisting of a greater variety of goods than is possible under traditional LIFO, resulting in fewer pools within total inventory. In fact, the entire inventory can be included in one pool in some cases where dollar-value LIFO is used, although there usually are several pools. Because fewer and larger inventory pools exist, dollar-value LIFO reduces the possibility of liquidating early LIFO layers and also reduces the chance that inventory liquidations of groups within total inventory will diminish the overall advantage of using LIFO.

Dollar-value LIFO calculations are based on the use of period-end acquisition costs and inventory cost indexes for inventory pools to determine reported ending inventory value. The dollar-value LIFO inventory pools consist of *layers of costs* that are related to past and present accounting periods. Dollar-value LIFO does not require detailed records of individual inventory units and unit costs to be maintained. Thus, it completely avoids one of the problems associated with traditional LIFO.

The dollar-value LIFO procedure.

The dollar-value LIFO procedure begins by valuing ending inventory for the accounting period at year-end acquisition cost. Next, any change in inventory acquisition cost during the period is removed from the dollar amount of ending inventory by using an inventory cost index. Then, to determine whether there was a *physical* increase or decrease in inventory for the period, the cost-adjusted ending inventory is compared to beginning inventory for the period. If physical inventory has increased (a layer has been added to inventory), the new layer is valued in terms of current period acquisition cost. If physical inventory has decreased (previously added layers have been taken from inventory), the cost of beginning inventory for the period is reduced accordingly.

To illustrate, assume that a company's beginning inventory had a cost of $1,000. Assume further that the ending inventory was counted, and its price at end-of-year acquisition costs totaled $1,200. Has the company's *physical* level of inventory increased during the year? The answer depends on the amount of increase or decrease in inventory acquisition cost during the year. The increase of $200 in the dollar amount of ending inventory over the dollar amount of beginning inventory may be due to higher acquisition cost, more units of inventory, or both. For example, if acquisition cost has increased 20 percent during the year, the physical level of inventory must be unchanged, because the entire $200 increase in the dollar amount of inventory is the result of the 20 percent increase in acquisition cost. Accordingly, under dollar-value LIFO, ending inventory will be reported as $1,000, because after adjusting for the cost change, the amount of inventory is the same as at the beginning of the year. On the other hand, if there has been no increase in acquisition cost during the year, the entire $200 must be due to additional inventory units on hand at the end of the year. Since these additional units were acquired during the current year, the ending inventory under dollar-value LIFO will consist of beginning inventory plus the layer added in the current year:

Cost of beginning inventory	$1,000
Cost of current layer added	200
Dollar-value LIFO ending inventory	$1,200

If acquisition cost has increased by 10 percent during the current year, the ending inventory under dollar-value LIFO will be $1,100 because only a $100 new layer is added in the current year.

Ending inventory at year-end acquisition cost	$1,200
Less: Beginning inventory at year-end acquisition cost ($1,000 × 1.10)	(1,100)
Cost of layer added at year-end acquisition cost	$ 100
Cost of beginning inventory	$1,000
Plus: Cost of layer added	100
Dollar-value LIFO ending inventory	$1,100

In the preceding computation, we restated the cost of the beginning inventory in terms of end-of-year cost (when we multiplied $1,000 by 1.10) in order to determine the cost of the layer added. In more complex dollar-value LIFO problems, it usually is easier to work backward by restating the ending inventory to determine the cost of the layer added. For example,

Ending inventory at beginning-of-year cost ($1,200 ÷ 1.10)	$1,091
Less: Beginning inventory at beginning-of-year cost	(1,000)
Cost of layer added at beginning-of-year cost	$ 91
Cost of layer added at end-of-year cost ($91 × 1.10)	$ 100
Cost of beginning inventory	$1,000
Plus: Cost of layer added	100
Dollar-value LIFO ending inventory	$1,100

In the following section we shall discuss the application of dollar-value LIFO in more complex situations.

Applying Dollar-Value LIFO

The first year in which the dollar-value LIFO procedure is used is called the **base year.** The inventory at the beginning of the base year, which is equal to the number of units times unit cost at the beginning of the base year, is the **base inventory.** The unit costs of the base inventory are the **base year costs.**

When we introduced the dollar-value LIFO procedure on page 412, we indicated that an inventory cost index is necessary in order to make the dollar-value LIFO calculations. Therefore, an early step in the dollar-value LIFO procedure each year is to calculate or otherwise obtain an inventory cost index. An inventory cost index can be obtained by:

1. calculation, by use of the *double-extension method;*

2. calculation, by use of the *chain-link method;* or

3. use of a published index (the *index method*).

Under the **double-extension method,** the inventory cost index for a particular year is calculated by dividing the cost of a unit of inventory at the end of that year by the cost of that unit at the beginning of the base year (i.e., by the base year cost). For example, assume that the dollar-value LIFO procedure was adopted at the beginning of year 1. Thus, year 1 is the base year. Further assume that at the beginning of year 1 a unit of inventory cost $4 and at the end of the year 1 the same unit of inventory cost $6. Given these facts, the inventory cost index for year 1 would be:

$$\frac{\text{End-of-year 1 inventory units at end-of-year 1 cost}}{\text{End-of-year 1 inventory units at base-year cost}} = \frac{\$6}{\$4} = 1.5 \text{ or } 150\%$$

In other words, the inventory cost at the end of year 1 is 150 percent of the cost at the beginning of year 1. The cost increase for year 1 is 150 percent and the cost index is 1.5. This method of calculating the inventory cost index for a particular year is called the double-extension method because the units in inventory at the end of the year are extended in terms of two costs: the end of the current year cost (the numerator) and the beginning of the base year cost (the denominator).

Now that we have seen a simple example of the double-extension method, let us examine a more complex case. Suppose that Hartley Company adopted dollar-value LIFO on January 1, 1987, and the inventory on that date (the base inventory) was composed of the following:

ITEM	QUANTITY	1/1/87 COST PER UNIT (BASE YEAR COST)	TOTAL BASE INVENTORY
A	500	$10	$ 5,000
B	1,000	5	5,000
C	1,500	3	4,500
			$14,500

The inventory at the end of 1987 consisted of the following quantities and year-end acquisition costs:

ITEM	QUANTITY	12/31/87 COST PER UNIT	12/31/87 INVENTORY AT CURRENT COST
A	600	$11	$ 6,600
B	900	6	5,400
C	1,700	5	8,500
			$20,500

Under the double-extension method, Hartley Company's cost index for 1987 would be:

$$\frac{[(600 \times \$11) + (900 \times \$6) + (1,700 \times \$5)]}{[(600 \times \$10) + (900 \times \$5) + (1,700 \times \$3)]} = \frac{\$20,500}{\$15,600} = 1.314 = 131.4\%$$

Thus, by the end of 1987 the cost of inventory for Hartley had increased approximately 31.4 percent over the base-year cost. In this case, if the dollar value of Hartley's inventory at year-end cost is exactly 131.4 percent greater than that of the same inventory at base year cost, then the physical level of inventory at the end of 1987 is unchanged from the base inventory.

The double-extension method provides an internally calculated inventory cost index that is unique to the particular inventory in question because its calculation is based on the firm's actual costs to acquire the specific inventory units held. For some firms, applying the double-extension method to **all types** of units held in inventory can become burdensome either because of a large number of different types of units or because technological changes make it difficult to compare current and past types of inventory units fairly. If some new type of unit is in the current year-end inventory, it would be necessary to obtain (possibly by ''guesstimate'') a base year cost for that type of inventory even though such units were not held, or may not even have existed, in the base year.

It is possible to reduce the difficulty of the double-extension method arising from the existence of a large variety of inventory items by applying the double-extension method to a **sample group** of inventory items. The sample items can be used to calculate an estimated inventory cost index to be used for all inventory items. When the sample group approach is used, current year-end inventory costs and base year costs are needed only for the sample group items. Of course, since the sample group approach provides only an estimated cost index for all inventory items, it is less precise than the double-extension method applied to all inventory items. Moreover, while the sample group approach to the double-extension method helps a firm cope with having a large number of different types of inventory items, it does not eliminate the possibility that base year costs may have to be estimated for new or technologically changed items.

Because of the potential complexities of the double-extension method, many firms use the **chain-link method** to calculate inventory cost indexes. When the chain-link method is used, an *inventory cost change index for the current year is calculated* by the double-extension method:

$$\frac{\text{Current year cost}}{\text{change index}} = \frac{\text{End-of-year inventory at year-end costs}}{\text{End-of-year inventory at beginning-of-year costs}}$$

Once the current year's inventory cost change index is calculated, it is multiplied by a **linked cost index** that reflects the cumulative change in inventory costs between the beginning of the base year and the beginning of the current year. The linked cost index for each year is the previous year's linked cost index multiplied by the current year's inventory cost change index. The chain-link method requires only (1) the previous year's linked index and (2) beginning and end-of-current year costs (to be used in calculating the current year's cost change index).

The chain-link method can be used to calculate an inventory cost index based on all types of inventory items held at year-end or it can be applied to a sample group of items, thus yielding an *estimated cost* index for all inventory items. Since the chain-link method is commonly used by firms that wish to avoid both the problem of new or technologically changed inventory items as well as the problem of having a large variety of inventory items, use of the sample group approach is common. We shall use the sample group approach to illustrate the chain-link method. Assume the following:

| | TOTAL ENDING INVENTORY AT END-OF-YEAR COSTS | SAMPLE OF ENDING INVENTORY | |
| | | AT END-OF-YEAR COSTS | AT BEGINNING-OF-YEAR COSTS |
YEAR			
1 (base year)	$129,888	$47,500	$45,000
2	149,971	52,500	49,000*
3	169,341	43,000	40,500*

* Beginning-of-year costs differ from the preceding end-of-year costs because the sample group of items is different each year.

We can estimate an inventory cost index for years 1 through 3 as in the two steps shown below:

	YEAR 1	YEAR 2	YEAR 3

STEP 1

Current year's cost change index (based on samples)

$$\frac{\$47,500}{\$45,000} = 1.056 \qquad \frac{\$52,500}{\$49,000} = 1.071 \qquad \frac{\$43,000}{\$40,500} = 1.062$$

STEP 2

Current year's cost change index linked to base index of 1.000

$$1.000 \times 1.056 = 1.056 \quad 1.056 \times 1.071 = 1.131 \quad 1.131 \times 1.062 = 1.201$$

Notice that each year's inventory cost index is linked to the base year by means of the preceding year's linked index.

Now that inventory cost indexes for years 1 through 3 have been estimated, they can be used to restate total ending inventory from current end-of-year costs to beginning-of-year costs, as follows:

	TOTAL ENDING INVENTORY AT END-OF-YEAR COSTS	ESTIMATED COST INDEX		TOTAL ENDING INVENTORY AT BEGINNING-OF-BASE-YEAR COSTS
Year 1	$129,888	÷ 1.056	=	$123,000
Year 2	149,971	÷ 1.131	=	132,600
Year 3	169,341	÷ 1.201	=	141,000

As you will see in the following discussion and in Exhibit 9–12, the current year's total ending inventory stated in terms of base year costs is a key component of the dollar-value LIFO procedure.

Occasionally a firm will choose not to calculate an inventory cost index by either the double-extension method or the chain-link method. Instead, it will use **published price indexes.** For example, a retail store might use the Department Store Price Indexes published by the Bureau of Labor Statistics. Until the early 1980s, the IRS limited the use of external indexes to price indexes for very specific inventory items. Subsequently, the IRS broadened the set of published indexes that could be used to include two general price indexes, the Consumer Price Index and the Producer Price Index. Although use of externally developed indexes, called the **index method,** is certainly the easiest way to obtain inventory cost indexes, it is not used as widely as one might expect. The index method is potentially the least accurate way to obtain inventory cost indexes because published indexes may not be unique to the particular inventory in question.

Under the dollar-value LIFO procedure, the addition of a new LIFO layer as a result of an *increase* in inventory over the period, or the loss of one or more layers as a result of a *decrease* in inventory, is determined by comparing year-end units priced at base year acquisition costs with beginning-of-the-year units priced at base year acquisition costs. Since both beginning and ending inventories are priced at base year costs, any difference between the two must be the result of a change in the quantity of inventory units held.

Once the increase or decrease in inventory quantity at base year cost is determined, it is multiplied by the cost index of the year in which the layer in question was added. In the case of an increase, the LIFO layer in question is the one being added in the current year, and therefore an increase is multiplied by the cost index of the current year. In the case of a decrease, previously added layers are considered to have been sold in the order specified by the LIFO assumption. Then the appropriate portions of the decrease are multiplied by the cost indexes of the years associated with the layers that have been sold.

After the cost of the layer added or sold is determined, it is added to or subtracted from the cost of the beginning inventory for the year to yield the dollar-value LIFO inventory amount to be reported in the financial statements at the end of the year. Use of the dollar-value LIFO method requires the following information: (1) the base year and base inventory cost; (2) an inventory cost index for each year, beginning with the end of the base year; and (3) year-end unit quantities and year-end unit costs for each year, beginning with the end of the base year.

Assume that the base year is 1987 and we have the following information for Ponca Corporation:

DATE	INVENTORY AT CURRENT COST	INVENTORY COST INDEX
1/1/87	$10,000*	1.00
12/31/87	14,000	1.25
12/31/88	16,000	1.50
12/31/89	15,000	1.30
12/31/90	17,000	1.65
12/31/91	20,000	1.70

* Base inventory.

Computations of the amounts of ending inventory that Ponca Corporation would report in its financial statements for the years 1987 through 1991, assuming the use of dollar-value LIFO, are summarized in Exhibit 9–12. Study the computations and procedure carefully. In doing so, you will see that the computations follow the sequence presented in our initial description of the dollar-value LIFO procedure. The essential steps of the dollar-value LIFO procedure are reviewed below:

The essential steps of dollar-value LIFO.

1. Determine the total ending inventory of the current year in terms of current year-end costs. Typically the actual costs of the most recent purchases are used for current year-end costs (col. 1, Exhibit 9–12).

EXHIBIT 9–12

Ponca Corporation
CALCULATION OF ENDING INVENTORY REPORTED IN
FINANCIAL STATEMENTS 1987–91 (DOLLAR-VALUE LIFO)

	(1)	(2)	(3)	(4)	(5)
DATE OF CALCULATING DOLLAR-VALUE LIFO ENDING INVENTORY	INVENTORY STATED IN TERMS OF CURRENT YEAR'S COSTS	INVENTORY STATED IN TERMS OF BASE YEAR COSTS*	INVENTORY LAYERS STATED IN TERMS OF BASE YEAR COSTS (DATE)	INVENTORY LAYERS RESTATED USING THE PROPER INVENTORY COST INDEXES	DOLLAR-VALUE INVENTORY
1/1/87 (base point)	$10,000 (base inventory)	$\dfrac{\$10,000}{1.00} = \$10,000$	$\left\{\$10,000 \text{ (base)}\right.$	$\$10,000 \times 1.00 = \$10,000$	→ $10,000
12/31/87	$14,000	$\dfrac{\$14,000}{1.25} = \$11,200$	$\left\{\begin{array}{l}\$10,000 \text{ (base)} \\ 1,200 \text{ (1987)}\end{array}\right.$	$\begin{array}{l}\$10,000 \times 1.00 = \$10,000 \\ 1,200 \times 1.25 = 1,500\end{array}$	→ $11,500
12/31/88	$16,000	$\dfrac{\$16,000}{1.50} = \$10,667$	$\left\{\begin{array}{l}\$10,000 \text{ (base)} \\ 667 \text{ (1987)}\end{array}\right.$	$\begin{array}{l}\$10,000 \times 1.00 = \$10,000 \\ 667 \times 1.25 = 834\end{array}$	→ $10,834
12/31/89	$15,000	$\dfrac{\$15,000}{1.30} = \$11,538$	$\left\{\begin{array}{l}\$10,000 \text{ (base)} \\ 667 \text{ (1987)} \\ 871 \text{ (1989)}\end{array}\right.$	$\begin{array}{l}\$10,000 \times 1.00 = \$10,000 \\ 667 \times 1.25 = 834 \\ 871 \times 1.30 = 1,132\end{array}$	→ $11,966
12/31/90	$17,000	$\dfrac{\$17,000}{1.65} = \$10,303$	$\left\{\begin{array}{l}\$10,000 \text{ (base)} \\ 303 \text{ (1987)}\end{array}\right.$	$\begin{array}{l}\$10,000 \times 1.00 = \$10,000 \\ 303 \times 1.25 = 379\end{array}$	→ $10,379
12/31/91	$20,000	$\dfrac{\$20,000}{1.70} = \$11,765$	$\left\{\begin{array}{l}\$10,000 \text{ (base)} \\ 303 \text{ (1987)} \\ 1,462 \text{ (1991)}\end{array}\right.$	$\begin{array}{l}\$10,000 \times 1.00 = \$10,000 \\ 303 \times 1.25 = 379 \\ 1.462 \times 1.70 = 2,485\end{array}$	→ $12,864

* Rounded to the nearest dollar.

† Notice that when a decrease occurs, previous layers are "used up" in accordance with the LIFO cost flow assumption.

2. Determine the inventory cost index for the current year, using the double-extension method, the chain-link method, or a price index from an external source. (Inventory cost indexes are given above.)

3. Restate the current year's ending inventory in terms of base year costs (col. 2, Exhibit 9–12).

4. Identify the layers included in inventory stated in terms of base year costs (col. 3, Exhibit 9–12).

5. Restate the inventory layers using the cost index (or indexes) properly associated with the inventory layer(s) in question (col. 4, Exhibit 9–12).

6. Add the restated inventory layers to determine the current year's dollar-value LIFO ending inventory to be reported in the financial statements (col. 5, Exhibit 9–12).

To assist you further in understanding the addition and reduction of layers in dollar-value LIFO, Exhibit 9–13 graphically shows the layers developed in Exhibit 9–12.

Having completed our discussion of dollar-value LIFO and the other historical cost based inventory cost flow assumptions, we direct our attention to the way inventories should be reported in the financial statements.

EXHIBIT 9–13

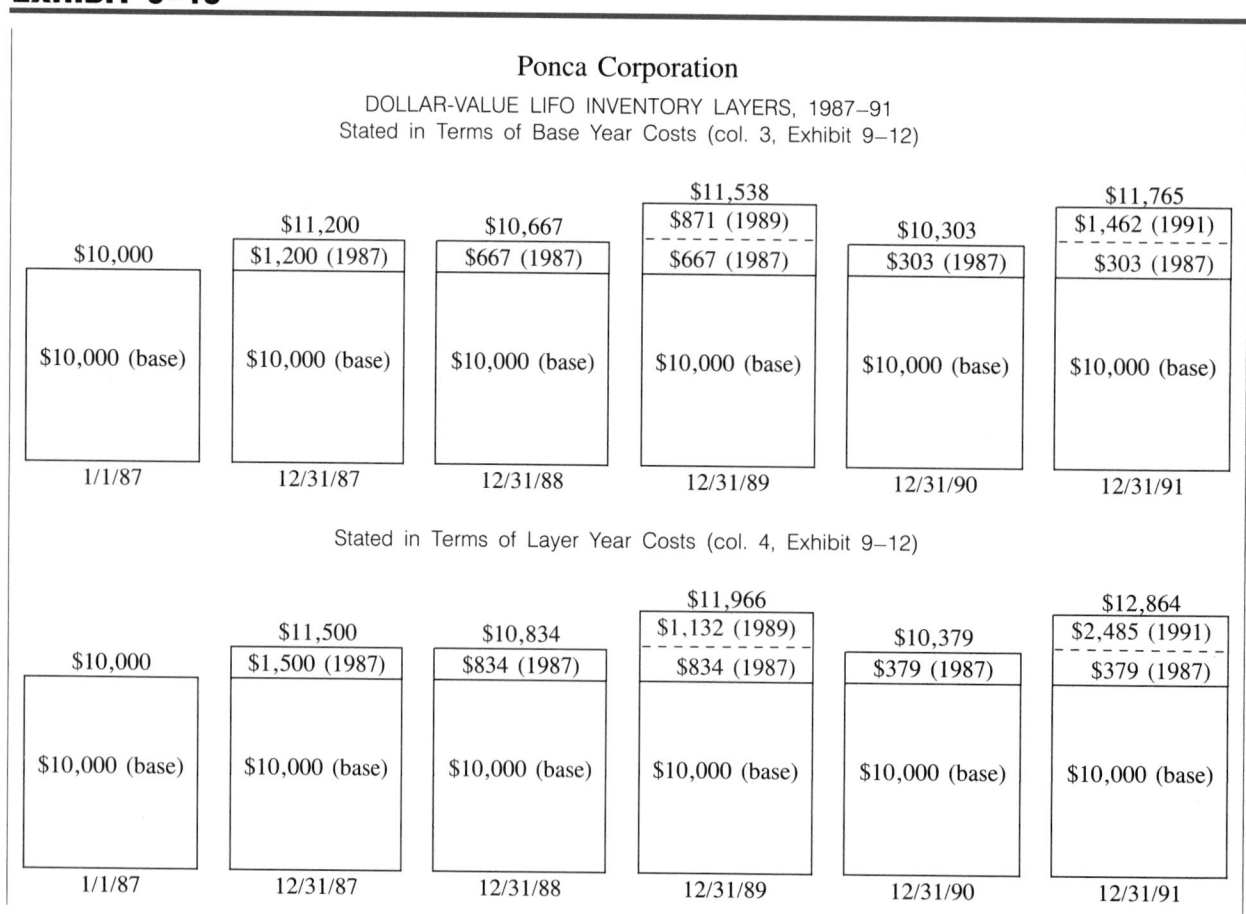

Ponca Corporation

DOLLAR-VALUE LIFO INVENTORY LAYERS, 1987–91
Stated in Terms of Base Year Costs (col. 3, Exhibit 9–12)

Stated in Terms of Layer Year Costs (col. 4, Exhibit 9–12)

REPORTING INVENTORIES IN THE FINANCIAL STATEMENTS

The basis of accounting for inventories should be consistently applied and the basis used should be disclosed in the financial statements. Whenever a significant change in inventory accounting is made, the nature of the change and, if material, the effect on income should be disclosed.

Examples of typical inventory reporting in the balance sheet and related disclosures in the notes to the financial statements are presented in Exhibits 9–14 and 9–15. Exhibit 9–14 shows how inventory might be reported by a manufacturing company, and Exhibit 9–15 shows how inventory might be reported by a merchandising company.

EXHIBIT 9–14   REPORTING OF MANUFACTURING INVENTORIES IN BALANCE SHEET AND NOTES TO FINANCIAL STATEMENTS

Bethlehem Steel Corporation
CONSOLIDATED BALANCE SHEETS
(in millions of dollars)

	DECEMBER 31	
	1984	**1983**
Inventories (Note E)...	$620.1	$529.1

NOTES TO CONSOLIDATED FINANCIAL STATEMENTS

E. INVENTORIES

	DECEMBER 31	
	1984	**1983**
Raw materials and supplies	$ 482.5	$ 578.6
Finished and semi-finished products	844.9	698.6
Contract work in progress less billings rendered of $866.6 and $592.5	28.4	31.6
Total at current cost	$1,355.8	$1,308.8
Less excess of current cost over LIFO values	(735.7)	(779.7)
Total inventories	$ 620.1	$ 529.1

Inventory values are based on the following accounting methods:

	DECEMBER 31	
	1984	**1983**
LIFO	$ 502.0	$ 384.1
FIFO	92.0	119.6
Contract work in progress less billings rendered	26.1	25.4
Total inventories	$ 620.1	$ 529.1

Certain LIFO inventory quantities were lower than their respective year-earlier levels, resulting in liquidations of inventory quantities carried at lower costs prevailing in prior years as compared with current year costs. These liquidations reduced cost of sales by $48.1 million, $103.6 million, and $150.8 million in 1984, 1983, and 1982, respectively.

EXHIBIT 9–15 REPORTING OF MERCHANDISING INVENTORIES IN BALANCE SHEET AND NOTES TO FINANCIAL STATEMENTS

Sears, Roebuck and Company
SEARS MERCHANDISING GROUP
STATEMENTS OF FINANCIAL POSITION
(in millions of dollars)

	DECEMBER 31	
	1984	**1983**
Inventories..	$4,521.8	$3,617.0

NOTES TO SUMMARIZED FINANCIAL STATEMENTS

INVENTORIES

Inventories of the domestic operations are valued at the lower of cost (using the last-in, first-out—LIFO method) or market by application of the Bureau of Labor Statistics price indices to inventories at their selling value. The LIFO method of inventory valuation is used to better match costs and revenues. In 1984, the LIFO adjustment to cost of sales was a credit of $101.3 million, compared with credits of $29.0 and $27.4 million in 1983 and 1982, respectively. If the first-in, first-out (FIFO) method of inventory valuation had been used instead of the LIFO method, inventories would have been $387.1 and $488.4 million higher at December 31, 1984 and 1983, respectively.

Inventories of International operations and Puerto Rico, which represent approximately 11.7 percent of Group inventories, are stated at the lower of cost (FIFO basis) or market as determined by the retail inventory method for store inventories and specific identification for warehouse inventories.

SUMMARY OF IMPORTANT TOPICS AND CONCEPT APPLICATIONS

1. **Inventory** consists of the assets of a company that are intended for sale in the ordinary course of business, are in the process of being produced for sale, or are to be used currently in producing goods to be sold.

2. A merchandising company has one general class of inventory. A manufacturing company normally has three types of inventory: raw materials, work-in-process, and finished goods.

3. The amount of inventory on hand and the cost of inventory sold can be determined by either the **periodic** inventory system or the **perpetual** inventory system.

4. A **product financing arrangement** is a transaction in which a company "sells" inventory items and at the same time agrees to repurchase those items or substantially identical items from the buyer at a specified price over a specified future period. The items that are "sold" must continue to be reported as the seller's inventory, and the obligation to repurchase must be reported as a liability.

5. Inventory errors can affect both the income statement and the balance sheet.

6. Inventory cost includes all expenditures needed to get inventory into condition and location for sale.

7. There are two methods of accounting for purchase discounts: the **gross method** and the **net method.** Under the gross method, purchases and accounts payable are recorded at the full invoice price, and purchase discounts are recognized only if they are taken. Under the net method, purchases and accounts payable are recorded net of the purchase discount, and purchase discounts that are not taken are recorded as purchase discounts lost.

8. The cost of goods sold and cost of ending inventory can be determined by **specific identification.** Alternatively, inventory cost flow assumptions such as **average cost, first in, first out (FIFO),** and **last in, first out (LIFO)** can be used.

9. **Inventory holding profits** are the difference between old, low inventory costs and current replacement cost of inventory.

10. **Dollar-value LIFO** is an inventory valuation procedure that provides the benefits of LIFO, but either avoids or reduces the problems that arise when traditional LIFO is used.

11. The dollar-value LIFO procedure requires an inventory cost index. An inventory cost index can be obtained by using the double-extension method, the chain-link method, or the index method.

APPENDIX 9–1

ADDITIONAL LIFO CONSIDERATIONS

Because of the increasingly widespread use of LIFO and because LIFO is more complex than the other cost flow assumptions, this appendix is devoted to specific issues related to its adoption and use. In particular, we shall discuss accounting for changes to or from LIFO, the LIFO valuation allowance, and the use of LIFO in interim financial statements.

ACCOUNTING FOR CHANGES TO OR FROM LIFO

When changing *to LIFO* from some other procedure for valuing inventory, it is first necessary for the inventory to be stated on a cost basis. Alternatives to the cost basis, such as lower of cost or market, sometimes are used in inventory accounting (we will discuss some of these in Chapter 10). If an alternative to cost has been used and inventory appears in the records at an amount that is less than cost, inventory must be adjusted to the cost basis before LIFO can be used. The amount of the adjustment to increase inventory to cost should be reported as other income on the income statement.

Once the beginning inventory for the year that LIFO is to be adopted is on a cost basis, the change to LIFO is accounted for and reported in accordance with *APB Opinion No. 20,* ''Accounting Changes.'' The details of reporting a change to LIFO are presented in Chapter 22. For our purposes now, it is sufficient to know that when a company initially adopts LIFO, the effect of the change to LIFO on *current* operating results must be disclosed in a footnote to the financial statements, along with an explanation of why no cumulative effect or retroactive adjustment is presented. A footnote from the 1980 financial statements of Rite Aid Corporation illustrates appropriate disclosures:

During the 1980 fiscal year, the Corporation changed its method of accounting for a significant portion of its inventory from the first-in, first-out (FIFO) and retail methods to the last-in, first-out method (LIFO). The change was made in order to more closely match current costs with current revenues, since the LIFO method reduces the effect of cost increases in inventory during periods of rising prices. The effect of the change in fiscal 1980 was to reduce net income by approximately $2,103,000 ($.20 per share). Inventory at March 1, 1980, was lower by $4,168,000 as a result of applying the LIFO method. Pro forma amounts for retroactive application of LIFO are not determinable. There is no cumulative effect on retained earnings at the beginning of the 1980 fiscal year, since the March 3, 1979, inventories, as previously stated, are considered the beginning inventories under the LIFO method.

Accounting for and reporting a change to another inventory accounting method *from LIFO* is one of the exceptions to the general guidelines set forth in *APB Opinion No. 20.* This change, too, is covered in more detail in Chapter 22. Essentially, a change from LIFO must be disclosed by restating the financial statements of prior periods (assuming comparative statements are issued) to reflect the accounting change. In addition, the cumulative effect on the balance sheet and statement of retained earnings of the change from LIFO is recorded by adjusting retained earnings, the inventory account, and any other asset or liability accounts, so that inventory is reported at the amount it would have been had the new inventory method been used in prior years. As an example of the type of footnote that would accompany financial statement restatements and account adjustments required by a switch from LIFO, consider the following note from the 1984 financial statements of The Bethelehem Corporation:

> In the fourth quarter of 1984, the Company changed its method of inventory valuation to the first-in, first-out (FIFO) method from the last-in, first-out (LIFO) method.
>
> The Company believes the changes in valuation method will more fairly present its results of operations and financial condition. The use of the LIFO method has resulted in the reporting of inventories at amounts considerably less than the current replacement cost of inventories, thereby affecting significant financial statement amounts and ratios and understating of the stockholders' investment in the business. In addition, the use of the LIFO method has reduced the Company's comparability with many competitor companies (many of which do not use the LIFO method of inventory valuation) within the industry and the geographic area in which the Company operates. The Company, in its future business plans, is also contemplating the leasing (as well as outright sale) of some of its larger and higher cost units. Under these circumstances, the FIFO method of inventory valuation is the preferable method because inventories are presented in the Company's Statements of Consolidated Financial Condition at cost values that more closely reflect the inventories' current worth.
>
> The new method of accounting has been applied retroactively and financial statements of prior years have been restated.
>
> The accounting change increased the 1984 net loss by approximately $79,000 ($0.06 pre share), decreased the 1983 previously reported net loss by approximately $13,000 ($0.01 per share), and increased the 1982 previously reported net earnings by $90,000 ($0.07 per share).
>
> Inventories consist of the following:

	1984	1983
Raw materials	$2,838,852	$2,459,491
Work in process (net of $54,344 and $874,176 advanced from customers in 1984 and 1983, respectively)	1,416,846	1,192,042
	$4,255,698	$3,651,533

LIFO VALUATION ALLOWANCE

Some companies use LIFO for external reporting and tax purposes, and another inventory accounting procedure, such as FIFO, for internal accounting and reporting purposes. There are several reasons why a company might do this. For example, (1) record keeping is easier with methods other than LIFO because LIFO often does not conform to the physical flow of goods; (2) management and employee compensation plans based on income seldom are based on the LIFO assumption; and (3) LIFO is difficult to use in the preparation of interim financial reports.

Normally there will be a difference between the inventory amount computed under LIFO and the inventory amount resulting from the procedure used for internal purposes. A LIFO valuation allowance account can be used to adjust from the inventory amount calculated for internal purposes to the LIFO inventory needed for external reporting and tax purposes. During periods of rising inventory acquisition costs, the inventory amount computed under LIFO typically is lower than the inventory amount calculated by other procedures. In this case, the LIFO valuation allowance account will be a credit account with a title such as "allowance to reduce inventory to LIFO basis." This account is created and adjusted by making offsetting entries to the cost of goods sold account. For example, assume that Wallace Corporation uses FIFO for internal purposes and LIFO for external and tax purposes. Assume further that in year 4, FIFO inventory exceeded LIFO inventory by $10,000, thus requiring a $10,000 allowance to reduce inventory to LIFO basis. If in year 5 FIFO exceeded LIFO by $15,000, a $5,000 increase in the allowance to reduce inventory to LIFO basis would be required. This increase is illustrated in the following entry:

Cost of goods sold 5,000
    Allowance to reduce inventory to LIFO basis   5,000

The allowance to reduce inventory to LIFO basis account, sometimes inappropriately called the LIFO reserve, must be deducted from the inventory amount computed for internal purposes to get a LIFO inventory amount to be reported on the face of the balance sheet.

USING LIFO IN INTERIM FINANCIAL STATEMENTS

In *Opinion No. 28* the Accounting Principles Board took the position that when interim financial statements, such as quarterly statements, are prepared, each interim period should be treated as an integral part of the annual period. Therefore, the Board concluded, the financial statement results for each interim period should be based on the same accounting principles and practices that are used for annual reporting purposes.[6]

When LIFO and a LIFO valuation allowance account are used, the interim reporting requirement can cause computational problems because of the difficulty of reasonably estimating, before the end of the accounting year, what the year-end LIFO valuation

---

[6] "Interim Financial Reporting," *Opinions of the Accounting Principles Board No. 28* (New York: AICPA, 1973).

allowance account balance will be. Moreover, once the balance is estimated on an annual basis, it is necessary at the time of each interim statement to make an appropriate allocation to the interim period of the estimated annual adjustment of the LIFO valuation allowance account.

An additional problem arises under the requirements of *Opinion No. 28* when LIFO is used, because of the possibility of a temporary interim period liquidation of a LIFO layer. That is, the company may face liquidation of a LIFO layer or base period inventory at an interim date, but expect to replace the liquidated inventory by the end of the annual accounting period. *Opinion No. 28* specifies that when this occurs, the interim period inventory should *not* reflect the LIFO liquidation, and cost of goods sold for the interim period should include the expected replacement cost of the temporarily liquidated LIFO layer.[7] For example, suppose that at the end of the third quarter Staudt Company has a temporary liquidation of a LIFO layer of 500 units costing $100 each, which it expects to replace before the end of the year for $120 per unit. The entry at the end of the third quarter would be:

Cost of goods sold (500 × $120)	60,000	
Inventory (500 × $100)		50,000
Excess replacement cost of temporarily liquidated LIFO layer		10,000

Assuming that replacement cost is in fact $120 per unit when the LIFO layer is replaced later in the fourth quarter, the entry to record replacement would be:

Inventory (500 × $100)	50,000	
Excess replacement cost of temporarily liquidated LIFO layer	10,000	
Accounts payable (or cash)		60,000

If replacement occurs at a price other than the expected $120 per unit, the preceding entry must be appropriately modified. For example, if replacement cost turned out to be $125, the entry when the layer is replaced would be:

Inventory (500 × $100)	50,000	
Excess replacement cost of temporarily liquidated LIFO layer	10,000	
Cost of goods sold (500 × $5)	2,500	
Accounts payable (or cash)		62,500

If replacement cost is less than the expected $120 per unit (for example, $110 per unit), the account "excess replacement cost of temporarily liquidated LIFO layer" is reduced by the amount initially credited and cost of goods sold is reduced as necessary. The required entry would be:

Inventory (500 × $100)	50,000	
Excess replacement cost of temporarily liquidated LIFO layer	10,000	
Cost of goods sold		5,000
Accounts payable (or cash)		55,000

The excess replacement cost of temporarily liquidated LIFO layer account appears *only* in the interim financial statements and is reported as a current liability.

[7] Ibid., para. 14b.

| QUESTIONS | Questions marked with an asterisk (*) refer to Appendix 9–1. |

Q9-1. What are the major inventory classifications that might be reported in the balance sheet of a manufacturing company? of a merchandising company?

Q9-2. How does the periodic inventory system differ from the perpetual inventory system?

Q9-3. What is meant when cost of goods sold is referred to as a *residual* amount under the periodic inventory system?

Q9-4. What disadvantages does the periodic inventory system have?

Q9-5. What should be done if the inventory amount determined by physical count differs from the inventory balance calculated in a perpetual inventory system?

Q9-6. What are some of the factors that should be considered when you determine whether or not a particular item should be included in inventory?

Q9-7. Distinguish between the terms ''F.O.B. shipping point'' and ''F.O.B. destination.''

Q9-8. Describe a consignment arrangement, particularly as it relates to inventory accounting.

Q9-9. What is a product financing arrangement? How does a product financing arrangement affect the inventory of the company that ''sells'' the goods?

Q9-10. How do installment sales affect the seller's inventory accounting?

Q9-11. What is meant by the statement ''Some inventory errors are self-correcting or counterbalancing''?

Q9-12. Describe the differences between the gross method and the net method of accounting for purchase discounts.

Q9-13. Distinguish between purchase returns and purchase allowances, and describe how each would be accounted for *(a)* in a periodic inventory system and *(b)* in a perpetual inventory system.

Q9-14. The cost of manufactured inventory consists of what three types of costs?

Q9-15. Discuss the specific identification method of inventory accounting and comment on the practical and conceptual strengths and weaknesses of the method.

Q9-16. Comment on the argument that the specific identification method of accounting for inventory allows management to manipulate the cost of ending inventory, cost of goods sold, and net income.

Q9-17. Why are FIFO and LIFO called cost flow assumptions?

Q9-18. Compare and contrast the weighted average method and the moving average method of accounting for inventory.

Q9-19. How would the reported amount of ending inventory and cost of goods sold vary under the average cost approach, FIFO, and LIFO during periods of *rising* inventory acquisition costs? during periods of *falling* inventory acquisition costs?

Q9-20. Discuss the advantages and disadvantages of FIFO.

Q9-21. Discuss the advantages and disadvantages of LIFO.

Q9-22. What is an inventory holding profit? Under what conditions do inventory holding profits occur, and how can the use of LIFO help to minimize inventory holding profit?

Q9-23. How is dollar-value LIFO preferable to traditional LIFO with regard to record keeping and the problem of liquidating layers of specific inventories within total inventory?

Q9-24. If you saw a credit balance account called ''excess of replacement cost over LIFO cost of basic inventory temporarily liquidated'' among the current liabilities of a company, what transaction or event would you think might have occurred?

Q9-25. Describe the double-extension method of computing a cost index for use in the dollar-value LIFO inventory method. What purpose is served by the cost index in dollar-value LIFO?

*Q9-26. If you saw a credit balance account with the title ''allowance to reduce inventory to LIFO basis'' in the current asset section of the balance sheet, what do you think that account would represent and under what circumstances would it be used?

*Q9-27. Discuss some problems that may arise in the preparation of interim financial statements when LIFO is used.

| CASES | The case marked with an asterisk (*) refers to Appendix 9–1. |

C9-1. ITEMS AND EXPENDITURES INCLUDED IN INVENTORY As controller of the Wilkins Appliance Company, you have decided to hire an assistant to help with the increasing work load. Because inventory is one of the company's most significant assets and much of your work involves inventory accounting, you plan to select your new assistant on the basis of his or her knowledge of inventory accounting. For purposes of testing applicants, you have listed the following issues for discussion: *(a)* goods in transit, *(b)* consignments, *(c)* inventory financing expenditures, and *(d)* purchase discounts.

REQUIRED

Draft what you would consider to be a good response to this question: "Explain how each of these issues affects inventory accounting and describe the acceptable accounting treatment of each."

C9-2. INVENTORIABLE COSTS Dimmer Company is a retailer and wholesaler of national brand-name household lighting fixtures. Dimmer purchases its inventories from various suppliers.

REQUIRED

1. What criteria should be used to determine which of Dimmer's costs are inventoriable?

2. Are Dimmer's administrative costs inventoriable? Defend your answer.

(AICPA, adapted)

C9-3. PURCHASE DISCOUNTS; FIFO VS. LIFO Taylor Corporation, a household appliances dealer, purchases its inventory from suppliers throughout the United States and uses the FIFO cost flow assumption to account for its inventory.

REQUIRED

1. Taylor is considering alternative methods of accounting for the purchase discounts it takes when it pays its suppliers promptly. From a theoretical standpoint, discuss the acceptability of each of the following approaches for accounting for purchase discounts:
    a) Recording purchase discounts as interest revenue when payments are made.
    b) Reduction of cost of goods sold for the period when payments are made.
    c) Direct reduction of the purchase cost at the time of acquisition.

2. Identify the effects on both the balance sheet and the income statement of using the LIFO inventory method instead of the FIFO inventory method over a substantial time period when purchase prices of household appliances are rising. State why these effects take place.

(AICPA, adapted)

C9-4. ADVANTAGES AND DISADVANTAGES OF LIFO Mr. Jones owns a business enterprise in which inventories of merchandise represent his major investment. He has written you a letter stating that he has heard of an inventory valuation method called LIFO, and understands in part what is meant by the term. He understands, he says, that this method will result in an income tax saving to him. He requests advice as to possible use of LIFO in his business.

REQUIRED

State the factors that you would include in your answer to him, bringing out any advantages or disadvantages related to the use of LIFO. Also briefly explain how the method actually operates.

(AICPA, adapted)

C9-5. LIFO VS. FIFO; LIQUIDATION OF LIFO LAYERS Because you are the senior accountant for your company, the president of the company has asked you to prepare a brief paper comparing the LIFO and FIFO cost flow assumptions. The president is considering a switch from the FIFO assumption currently used to the LIFO assumption and is particularly interested in *(a)* the comparative effects of the two cost flow assumptions on reported income during periods of rising inventory costs and *(b)* how the company might minimize the potential income distortion caused by liquidating early LIFO layers during periods of rising inventory costs.

REQUIRED

In response to the president's request, compare the LIFO and FIFO cost flow assumptions, paying particular attention to their effects on reported income and to the financial statement effects of switching from FIFO to LIFO. In addition, outline an accounting procedure that might be used to avoid distortion of reported income should early LIFO layers be liquidated during periods of rising inventory costs.

(AICPA, adapted)

C9-6. LIFO AND DOLLAR-VALUE LIFO   The CPA sometimes is called upon by clients for advice regarding the appropriateness of valuing inventories by the LIFO method.

REQUIRED

1. List the arguments for and against the use of the LIFO method of valuing inventory.

2. What is the dollar-value method of LIFO inventory valuation? (Confine your discussion to the underlying principles; do not discuss the techniques of developing cost indexes.) What advantages does the dollar-value method have over the traditional method of LIFO inventory valuation?

(AICPA, adapted)

C9-7. COST FLOW ASSUMPTIONS, ESPECIALLY LIFO   Inventory cost should be determined by the method that most clearly reflects periodic income.

REQUIRED

1. Describe the fundamental cost flow assumptions of the average cost, FIFO, and LIFO methods.

2. Discuss the reasons for using LIFO in an inflationary economy.

(AICPA, adapted)

C9-8. THE DOLLAR-VALUE LIFO PROCEDURE   For several years your company has used the LIFO inventory system, but your boss, the senior financial officer, has never really liked LIFO because of the extensive record keeping involved. After much discussion, you have convinced your boss that dollar-value LIFO should be adopted in an effort to reduce record keeping while retaining the benefits of LIFO.

REQUIRED

Explain, in terms your boss can understand and in a step-by-step fashion, how the dollar-value LIFO approach works.

*C9-9. CHANGING TO LIFO; LIFO VALUATION ALLOWANCE

A) Inventory may be computed under one of various cost flow assumptions. Among these assumptions are first in, first out (FIFO) and last in, first out (LIFO). In the past, some companies have changed from FIFO to LIFO to calculate portions or all of their inventory.

REQUIRED

1. Explain the effect of a change from FIFO to LIFO on net income and working capital (current assets less current liabilities). (Ignore income tax.)

2. Explain the difference between the FIFO cost flow assumption and the LIFO cost flow assumption.

B) Companies that use LIFO inventory sometimes establish a ''LIFO valuation allowance.''

REQUIRED

Explain why and how a LIFO valuation allowance account is established and where it should be shown on the statement of financial position.

(AICPA, adapted)

EXERCISES

The exercises marked with an asterisk (*) refer to Appendix 9–1.

E9-1. COMPUTING THE DOLLAR AMOUNT IN INVENTORY   The inventory account of Dallas Lock Company at December 31, 1987, had a balance of $72,300, including the following items:

	INVENTORY AMOUNT
Merchandise out on consignment at sales price (cost = $4,200)	$7,000
Goods purchased, in transit (shipped F.O.B. shipping point)	6,000
Goods held on consignment by Dallas Lock	4,000
Goods out on approval (sales price $2,500, cost $2,000)	2,500

REQUIRED

Calculate the correct inventory account balance at December 31, 1987.

(AICPA, adapted)

E9-2. CALCULATING COST OF GOODS AVAILABLE   The following information is available for Grant, Inc., for 1987:

Freight in	$ 20,000
Purchase returns	80,000
Selling expenses	200,000
Ending inventory	90,000

The cost of goods sold is equal to 700 percent of selling expenses.

REQUIRED

Calculate the cost of goods available for sale.

(AICPA, adapted)

E9-3. DETERMINING COST OF GOODS SOLD   The Sampson Company supplies you with the following available information and asks you to determine in good form the amount of cost of goods sold.

Freight in	$ 3,000
Freight out (selling expense)	2,000
Gross sales	100,000
Merchandise inventory, 1/1/87	12,000
Merchandise inventory, 12/31/87	15,000
Purchases	70,000
Office supplies used	7,000
Purchase discounts	4,000
Purchase returns and allowances	6,000
Sales returns and allowances	10,000
Supplies inventory, 12/31/87	5,000

REQUIRED

Calculate the cost of goods sold for Sampson Company. Make entries to (1) record and (2) close the cost of goods sold.

(CGAA, adapted)

E9-4. ACCOUNTING FOR PURCHASE DISCOUNTS   Martin Company, which has a periodic inventory system, bought $50,000 of inventory on September 10, 1987, at terms of 2%/10, net 30. $35,000 of the inventory was paid for on September 19, 1987, and the remaining $15,000 was paid on October 5, 1987.

REQUIRED

Make the journal entries to record *(a)* the purchase, *(b)* the September 19 payment, and *(c)* the October 5 payment, under each of the following methods of accounting for purchase discounts:

1. The gross method.

2. The net method.

E9-5. EFFECTS OF INVENTORY ERRORS A company that uses a periodic inventory system neglected to record a $3,000 purchase of merchandise on account at the end of the year. This merchandise also was omitted from the year-end physical count.

REQUIRED

Give the dollar amount and direction of effect (overstate, understate, no effect) of these errors on (1) assets, (2) liabilities, (3) stockholders' equity, and (4) net income for the year.

(AICPA, adapted)

E9-6. EFFECTS OF INVENTORY ERRORS The December 31, 1986, year-end physical inventory of Clawson Company was adjusted to include $2,500 worth of goods ordered by Clawson from New Line, Inc., on December 28. New Line shipped the goods F.O.B. destination, and the goods arrived at Clawson's on January 2, 1987, at which time the purchase was recorded.

Clawson's December 31, 1987, physical inventory appropriately included $3,800 of merchandise that was not recorded as purchases until January 1988.

REQUIRED

What effect, in dollar amount and direction of effect (overstate, understate, no effect), will these errors have on (1) assets, (2) liabilities, (3) retained earnings, and (4) net income for 1987?

E9-7. EFFECTS OF INVENTORY ERRORS In examining the books of Careless Company, you discover the following:

a) Incorrect exclusion from the ending inventory of goods costing $5,000 for which the purchase was not recorded.

b) Inclusion in the ending inventory of goods costing $8,000, although the purchase was not recorded. The goods in question were being held on consignment from Alta Company.

c) Incorrect exclusion of $3,000 from the inventory count at the end of the period. The goods were in transit (F.O.B. shipping point); the invoice was received and the purchase was recorded.

d) Items on the receiving dock that were being held for return to the vendor because of damage were incorrectly included in inventory and a purchase of $6,000 was recorded.

The records (uncorrected) showed the following amounts:

e) Purchases, $150,000.

f) Income before tax, $25,000.

g) Accounts payable, $30,000.

h) Inventory at the end of the period, $40,000.

REQUIRED

Determine the corrected amounts for items *e* through *h* (show calculations).

(CGAA, adapted)

E9-8. CORRECTION OF INVENTORY ERRORS During the course of your examination of the financial statements of Power Company, a new client, for the year ended December 31, 1987, you discover the following:

a) Inventory at January 1, 1987, was overstated by $3,000.

b) Inventory at December 31, 1987, was understated by $5,000.

c) During 1987 Power Company received a $1,000 cash advance from a customer for merchandise to be manufactured and shipped during 1988. The $1,000 was credited to sales revenue.

d) Net income reported on the 1987 income statement (before reflecting any adjustments for the above items) was $20,000.

REQUIRED

1. Calculate the correct net income for 1987.

2. Assuming that the 1987 books have not been closed, make the appropriate adjusting entry or entries to correct any errors that you discover in examining your new client's financial statements.

E9-9. WEIGHTED AVERAGE METHOD AND MOVING AVERAGE METHOD   The following information was available from the inventory records of the Jacobson Company for January 1987:

	UNITS	UNIT COST	TOTAL COST
Balance at 1/1/87	2,000	$ 9.775	$19,550
Purchases			
1/6/87	1,500	10.300	15,450
1/26/87	3,400	10.750	36,550
Sales			
1/7/87	(1,800)		
1/31/87	(3,200)		
Balance at 1/31/87	1,900		

REQUIRED

1. Assuming that Jacobson maintains perpetual inventory records, what should be the inventory at January 31, 1987, according to the moving average method, rounded to the nearest dollar?

2. Assuming that Jacobson does *not* maintain perpetual inventory records, what should be the inventory at January 31, 1987, according to the weighted average inventory method, rounded to the nearest dollar?

(AICPA, adapted)

E9-10. CALCULATING INVENTORY UNDER ALTERNATIVE COST FLOW ASSUMPTIONS   The Quilt Company was formed on January 1, 1987. The following information is available from Quilt's inventory records:

	UNITS	UNIT COST
Beginning inventory, 1/1/87	800	$ 9.00
Purchases		
1/5/87	1,500	10.00
1/25/87	1,200	10.50
2/16/87	600	11.00
3/26/87	900	11.50

A physical inventory on March 31, 1987, shows 1,600 units on hand.

REQUIRED

Prepare schedules to calculate the ending inventory at March 31, 1987, under each of the following inventory methods:

1. FIFO.

2. LIFO.

3. Weighted average.

(AICPA, adapted)

E9-11. FIFO, LIFO; PERPETUAL VS. PERIODIC INVENTORY RECORDS   The records of Davis Corporation show the following for the inventory account for 1987:

	UNITS	UNIT COST	UNIT SELLING PRICE	TOTAL
Beginning inventory, 1/1/87	250	$10.00		$2,500.00
Purchase, 3/7/87	200	11.00		2,200.00
Purchase, 7/15/87	275	11.75		3,231.25
Sale, 5/20/87....................	(120)		$14.00	1,680.00
Sale, 6/30/87....................	(75)		15.00	1,125.00
Sale, 9/17/87....................	(285)		16.00	4,560.00
Ending inventory, 12/31/87	245			

REQUIRED

1. Assuming that Davis maintains perpetual inventory records, what is the cost of the ending inventory according to *(a)* FIFO? *(b)* LIFO?

2. Assuming that Davis does *not* maintain perpetual inventory records, what is the cost of the ending inventory according to *(a)* FIFO? *(b)* LIFO?

E9-12. USE OF ALTERNATIVE COST FLOW ASSUMPTIONS   Master Faucets Ltd. sells only one product. During the year just ended, Master sold 155,000 units, generating total sales of $3.1 million. Inventory at the beginning of the year was 30,000 units at a cost of $225,000. During the year purchases were as follows:

February 1 . . . . 40,000 units @ $15.50
April 1 . . . . 57,000 units @ $16.00
June 1 . . . . 42,000 units @ $16.60
September 1 . . . . 31,000 units @ $16.80
    Total . . . . 170,000 units

REQUIRED

1. Calculate the year-end inventory using:
   a) FIFO.
   b) LIFO.
   c) Weighted average cost.

2. Construct a partial income statement (down to gross profit on sales), with separate columns side by side, for each of the above inventory cost flow assumptions.

(CGAA, adapted)

E9-13. USE OF ALTERNATIVE COST FLOW ASSUMPTIONS   The Harrison Product Company had the following inventory transactions during the month of December 1987:

12/1	Inventory of 20 units at $4.60 each
12/8	Purchased 80 units at $5.00 each
12/15	Purchased 40 units at $5.30 each
12/22	Purchased 60 units at $5.60 each
12/29	Purchased 40 units at $5.50 each

By December 31, 1987, 190 units of inventory had been sold by Harrison.

REQUIRED

Calculate the cost of the ending inventory under *(a)* FIFO, *(b)* LIFO, and *(c)* average cost.

E9-14. DOLLAR-VALUE LIFO—DOUBLE-EXTENSION METHOD   Hillford Company sells lawnmowers and began operations on January 1, 1984. From the outset, Hillford has used the dollar-value LIFO method of accounting for its inventory. Over the years Hillford has maintained an inventory consisting of eight types of lawnmowers, quantity and wholesale cost data for which are given below.

LAWNMOWER TYPE	12/31/87 QUANTITY	12/31/87 COST PER UNIT	1/1/84 COST PER UNIT
A	9	$180	$145
B	10	165	150
C	7	210	180
D	5	290	250
E	2	340	300
F	8	275	230
G	6	315	290
H	20	140	110

REQUIRED

1. Using the double-extension method applied to all eight types of lawnmowers, calculate Hillford's inventory cost index as of December 31, 1987.

2. Suppose that Hillford decided to reduce the difficulty of using the double-extension method by basing its calculations on the cost data of a sample of only four lawnmower types—types A, D, F, and H. What estimated inventory cost index would Hillford calculate for December 31, 1987?

E9-15. DOLLAR-VALUE LIFO—CHAIN-LINK METHOD   Masterson Company, which uses the dollar-value LIFO inventory method, has the following information about a sample group of its inventory items for the four years since Masterson began operations:

| | SAMPLE OF ENDING INVENTORY | |
YEAR	AT END-OF-YEAR COSTS	AT BEGINNING-OF-YEAR COSTS
1	$214,000	$200,000
2	233,000	225,000
3	205,000	215,000
4	237,000	230,000

REQUIRED

Using the chain-link method, calculate (1) the cost change index and (2) the cost change index linked to the base index for each of the four years of Masterson's operations.

E9-16. DOLLAR-VALUE LIFO   Hill Company adopted dollar-value LIFO on January 1, 1987, at which time it had $200,000 worth of inventory. On December 31, 1987, the current cost of inventory on hand was $230,000 and the cost index was 1.08, as compared to the January 1, 1987, cost index of 1.00.

REQUIRED

1. Calculate Hill Company's December 31, 1987, ending inventory by the dollar-value LIFO procedure.

2. Assuming that at December 31, 1988, Hill Company had ending inventory with a current cost of $260,000 and the cost index was 1.10, calculate the company's December 31, 1988, ending inventory by dollar-value LIFO.

3. What principal advantages does dollar-value LIFO have over traditional LIFO?

E9-17. DOLLAR-VALUE LIFO   The Bronson Corporation manufactures one product. On December 31, 1986, Bronson adopted the dollar-value LIFO inventory method. The inventory on that date was evaluated by the dollar-value LIFO method at $200,000.

Inventory data are as follows:

YEAR	INVENTORY AT YEAR-END PRICES	PRICE INDEX (1986 = 100)
1987	$231,000	1.05
1988	299,000	1.15
1989	300,000	1.20

REQUIRED

Calculate the inventory at December 31, 1987, 1988, and 1989 by the dollar-value LIFO method.

(AICPA, adapted)

*E9-18. CHANGING FROM FIFO TO LIFO   The Fellwick Company began operations on January 1, 1986, at which time it issued 110,000 shares of common stock. At the present time, Fellwick uses the FIFO method to cost its raw material inventory. Management is contemplating a change to the LIFO method in 1987 and is interested in determining what effect such a change will have on net income. Accordingly, the following information has been developed:

	ENDING INVENTORY	
	1986	**1987**
FIFO	$240,000	$270,000
LIFO	200,000	210,000
Net income (calculated by FIFO)	120,000	170,000

REQUIRED

1. On the basis of the above information, a change to the LIFO method in 1987 would result in net income for 1987 of how much? On a per share basis?

2. Using the answers to part 1, prepare an appropriate footnote disclosure of the change from FIFO to LIFO to be included in the 1987 financial statements.

(AICPA, adapted)

*E9-19. LIFO VALUATION ALLOWANCE   Jackson Company maintains its inventory records for internal purposes on a FIFO basis, but reports inventory on a LIFO basis for external reporting and tax purposes. At the end of 1987 the following inventory information is available:

	ENDING INVENTORY	
	1986	**1987**
FIFO	$180,000	$210,000
LIFO	150,000	170,000

REQUIRED

Assuming the proper adjustment from FIFO to LIFO was made in 1986:

1. Make the necessary 1987 entry to adjust inventory from a FIFO basis to a LIFO basis.

2. Describe how the adjustment would be reported in the external financial statements for 1987.

PROBLEMS   The problem marked with an asterisk (*) refers to Appendix 9–1.

P9-1. PERIODIC VS. PERPETUAL INVENTORY   Wilson Company started year 3 with 100 units of inventory costing $10 per unit. During year 3 the summary transactions listed below affected Wilson's inventory. Wilson uses the FIFO cost flow assumption in accounting for its inventory.

4/30	Purchases (200 × $11)	$2,200
9/20	Purchases (150 × $12)	1,800
5/10	Sales (220 sold for $15 each)	3,300
11/15	Sales (100 sold for $16 each)	1,600
	Ending inventory (physical count).....................	120 units

REQUIRED

1. Make summary journal entries, including adjusting and closing entries, for Wilson Company under (a) the periodic inventory system and (b) the perpetual inventory system.

2. Compare the advantages and disadvantages of the periodic and perpetual inventory systems.

P9-2. MERCHANDISE TO BE INCLUDED IN INVENTORY   As you prepare the December 31, 1987, financial statements for Hastings Electronics, you must decide whether each of several year-end transactions involving inventory requires any further adjustment of the inventory balance. The transactions under consideration are listed below.

a) Merchandise worth $900 was ordered by Hastings Electronics on December 28, 1987, and was shipped to Hastings F.O.B. shipping point on December 30, arriving January 3, 1988. This merchandise was not included in Hastings' 1987 ending inventory.

b) Hastings ordered $500 of goods on December 24, 1987. Those goods, shipped to Hastings F.O.B. destination, arrived on January 2, 1988. They were not included in Hastings' 1987 ending inventory.

c) On December 29, 1987, Hastings received $1,300 of merchandise on consignment from Hooney, Inc. The merchandise was on hand at December 31 and was included in Hastings' physical inventory count.

d) Hastings' December 31 physical inventory count included $400 worth of merchandise set aside for shipment to Paxon's Radio Shop. Paxon had ordered the goods on December 23 and had enclosed a 30 percent down payment with the order.

e) Goods worth $750 were in Hastings' warehouse at December 31, 1987, but were not included in ending inventory. These goods had been ordered by Dekin Company on December 22 and Hastings had billed Dekin $750, although the goods were not shipped until January 1, 1988, because of an error on the shipping dock.

f) Hastings' December 31, 1987, inventory included $1,300 of goods Hastings had shipped on consignment to Larken Electronics on December 20, 1987. It had cost Hastings $120 to ship the goods to Larken.

REQUIRED

Examine each transaction carefully and determine whether it was handled properly in Hastings' December 31, 1987, inventory determination. In each case state what you think is the proper inventory treatment and give your reasons.

P9-3. DETERMINING COSTS TO BE INCLUDED IN INVENTORY The Delta Corporation is a wholesale distributor of automotive replacement parts. At the end of 1987 Delta took a physical count of its inventory and determined its cost to be $1,250,000 at December 31. Accounts payable at that date were as follows:

VENDOR	TERMS	AMOUNT
Biggs Company	2%/10, net 30	$ 265,000
Charlie Company	Net 30	210,000
Dilts Company	Net 30	300,000
Eager Company	Net 30	225,000
Base Company	Net 30	—
Greg Company	Net 30	—
		$1,000,000

Sales in 1987 were $9 million.

Additional information is as follows:

a) Parts held on consignment from Charlie to Delta, the consignee, amounting to $155,000, were included in the physical count of goods in Delta's warehouse on December 31, 1987, and in accounts payable at December 31, 1987.

b) $22,000 of parts that were purchased from Base and paid for in December 1987 were sold in the last week of 1987 and appropriately recorded as sales of $28,000. The parts were included in the physical count of goods in Delta's warehouse on December 31, 1987, because they were on the loading dock waiting to be picked up by the customers.

c) Parts in transit to customers on December 31, 1987, shipped F.O.B. shipping point on December 28, amounted to $34,000. The customers received the parts on January 6, 1988. Sales of $40,000 to the customers for the parts were recorded by Delta on January 2, 1988.

d) On December 31, 1987, retailers were holding goods on consignment from Delta, the consignor, with a value of $210,000 at cost ($250,000 at retail). These goods were not included in Delta's ending inventory.

e) Goods were in transit from Greg to Delta on December 31, 1987. The cost of the goods was $25,000, and they were shipped F.O.B. shipping point on December 29, 1987.

f) A quarterly freight bill in the amount of $2,000, specifically related to merchandise purchased in December 1987, was received on January 3, 1988. All of that merchandise was still in the inventory at December 31, 1987. The freight bill was not included in either the inventory or accounts payable at December 31, 1987.

g) All of the purchases from Biggs occurred during the last seven days of the year. These items have been recorded in accounts payable and accounted for in the physical inventory at cost before discount. Delta's policy is to pay invoices in time to take advantage of all cash discounts, adjust inventory accordingly, and record accounts payable net of cash discounts.

REQUIRED

Prepare a schedule of adjustments to the initial amounts using the format shown below. Show the effect, if any, of each of the transactions separately; if any transaction would have no effect on the amount shown, state "None."

	INVENTORY	ACCOUNTS PAYABLE	SALES
Initial amounts	$1,250,000	$1,000,000	$9,000,000
Adjustments increase (or decrease)			
a................................			
b................................			
c................................			
d................................			
e................................			
f................................			
g................................			
Total adjustments			
Adjusted amounts	$	$	$

(AICPA, adapted)

P9-4. DETERMINING COSTS TO BE INCLUDED IN INVENTORY Layne Corporation, a manufacturer of small tools, provided the following information from its accounting records for the year ended December 31, 1987:

Inventory at December 31, 1987 (based on physical count of goods in Layne's plant at cost on December 31, 1987)	$1,750,000
Accounts payable at December 31, 1987	1,200,000
Net sales (sales less sales returns)	8,500,000

Additional information is as follows:

a) Included in the physical count were tools billed to a customer F.O.B. shipping point on December 31, 1987. These tools had a cost of $28,000 and were billed at $35,000. The shipment was on Layne's loading dock waiting to be picked up by the common carrier.

b) Goods were in transit from a vendor to Layne on December 31, 1987. The invoice cost was $50,000, and the goods were shipped F.O.B. shipping point on December 29, 1987.

c) Work-in-process inventory costing $20,000 was sent to an outside processor for plating on December 30, 1987.

d) Tools returned by customers and held pending inspection in the returned goods area on December 31, 1987, were not included in the physical count. On January 8, 1988, the tools, costing $26,000, were inspected and returned to inventory. Credit memos totaling $40,000 were issued to the customers on the same date.

e) Tools shipped to a customer F.O.B. destination on December 26, 1987, were in transit at December 31, 1987, and had a cost of $25,000. Upon notification of receipt by the customer on January 2, 1988. Layne issued a sales invoice for $42,000.

f) Goods received from a vendor at 5:00 P.M. on December 31, 1987, were recorded on a receiving report dated January 2, 1988. The goods, with an invoice cost of $30,000, were not included in the physical count, but the invoice was included in accounts payable at December 31, 1987.

g) Goods received from a vendor on December 26, 1987, were included in the physical count. However, the related $60,000 vendor invoice was not included in accounts payable at December 31, 1987, because the accounts payable copy of the receiving report was lost.

h) On January 3, 1988, a monthly freight bill in the amount of $4,000 was received. The bill specifically related to merchandise purchased in December 1987, one-half of which was still in the inventory at December 31, 1987. The freight charges were not included either in the inventory or in accounts payable at December 31, 1987.

REQUIRED

Using the format shown below, prepare a schedule of adjustments as of December 31, 1987, to the initial amounts per Layne's accounting records. Show separately the effect, if any, of each of the eight transactions on the December 31, 1987, amounts. If the transactions would have no effect on the initial amount shown, state *NONE*.

	INVENTORY	ACCOUNTS PAYABLE	NET SALES
Intitial amounts.....................	$1,750,000	$1,200,000	$8,500,000
Adjustments—increase (decrease)			
a.................................			
b.................................			
c.................................			
d.................................			
e.................................			
f.................................			
g.................................			
h.................................			
Total adjustments			
Adjusted amounts	$	$	$

(AICPA, adapted)

P9-5. DETERMINING COSTS TO BE INCLUDED IN INVENTORY   The 1987 beginning inventory for Allison Company was $19,200. During 1987 the following inventory-related transactions took place:

a) Allison incurred $3,100 of interest expense related to the manufacture of its primary product. Allison elected to include this interest expense in the cost of its inventory.

b) Allison purchased $10,000 (invoice price) of merchandise inventory at terms of 2%/15, net 30 on July 10, 1987. Allison uses the net method of accounting for purchase discounts. The inventory was recorded at $10,000 on July 10 and payment was made by Allison on July 22. Freight in costs from the inventory acquisition were $200. Allison elected to exclude these costs from the inventory account.

c) Allison purchased $1,700 worth of merchandise inventory for cash from Ellison, Inc., on August 17, 1987. The inventory was recorded at the time of purchase. Upon receipt of the goods, Allison discovered that $550 worth of the merchandise was the wrong model and returned the goods to Ellison for credit.

d) On December 28, 1987, Allison shipped $12,300 worth of merchandise to Wilson Company. The shipping terms were F.O.B. destination and the goods arrived on Wilson's receiving dock on January 4, 1988. The goods were not included in Allison's 1987 ending inventory.

e) Allison's 1987 ending inventory included $4,000 of goods held on consignment from Jackson, Inc., the consignor.

f) Before paying the amount due, Allison received a $400 allowance from Davis Company for part of a $3,000 order received from Davis on November 20, 1987, and recorded on that date. No record of the allowance was made.

g) On December 27, 1987, Allison ordered $6,000 worth of goods from Ellison, Inc.

Those goods were shipped F.O.B. destination by Ellison on December 29, 1987, and were received by Allison on January 2, 1988. Allison included the goods in its 1987 ending inventory.

REQUIRED

1. Comment on Allison's accounting treatment of each transaction, indicating which treatments were correct and which were not; if you consider an entry incorrect, indicate what entry should have been made. Give your reasons.

2. Calculate Allison's correct ending inventory balance.

P9-6. ACCOUNTING FOR PURCHASE DISCOUNTS   Marvis Company uses a periodic inventory system. Its fiscal year ends June 30. The company's purchase transactions for June of the current year are as follows:

June 4	Purchased $10,000 worth of merchandise inventory on account; terms 2%/10, net 20.
June 10	Returned 5% of the June 4 purchase and received a credit on account.
June 15	Purchased $5,000 worth of merchandise on account; terms 2%/10, net 30.
June 20	Paid 90% of the amount due on the June 4 purchase.
June 23	Paid all of the amount due on the June 15 purchase.

REQUIRED

1. Assuming that Marvis uses the *gross method* of accounting for purchase discounts:
a) Make a journal entry to record each of the above transactions. Date each entry.
b) Make any year-end adjusting entry or entries that may be required.
c) Describe how the accounts used in your entries would be reported in the financial statements.

2. Assume that Marvis uses the *net method* of accounting for purchase discounts and repeat requirements *a, b,* and *c* in part 1.

3. Outline the practical and conceptual strengths and weaknesses of the gross method and the net method of accounting for purchase discounts.

P9-7. EFFECTS OF INVENTORY ERRORS   You are the auditor for Gilbert, Incorporated, for the year ended December 31, 1987. In your examination of Gilbert's accounts you discover the following:
a) $1,000 of goods purchased by Gilbert have been shipped F.O.B. shipping point. The goods have not been received, but the invoice has been received. The purchase has been recorded but does not appear in the inventories account.
b) Items costing $3,000 are being held in the receiving department for return as unacceptable. The purchase has been recorded and is included in the inventories account.
c) Goods costing $1,000 are included in the inventories account but the purchase has not been recorded. The goods were shipped F.O.B. destination and were received December 30, 1987.
d) Goods costing $5,000 have been received on consignment but have not been recorded as purchases and do not appear in the inventories account.

REQUIRED

1. What effect, in dollar amount and in direction (overstate, understate, no effect), will each of these errors have on *(a)* assets, *(b)* liabilities, and *(c)* retained earnings?

2. Gilbert reported net income of $40,000 without considering items *a* through *d* above. Starting with the reported net income of $40,000, calculate the correct net income as of December 31, 1987.

(CGAA, adapted)

P9-8. EFFECTS OF INVENTORY ERRORS   During your audit of Farcy Company's ending inventory at December 31, 1987, you find the following inventory accounting errors:

a) On December 29, 1987, Farcy shipped goods costing $5,000 to Browne, F.O.B. destination. Browne received the goods on January 3, 1988. The goods were not included in Farcy's 1987 ending inventory.

b) Goods in Farcy's warehouse on consignment from Trace, Inc., were included in Farcy's ending inventory.

c) Merchandise purchased on account by Farcy on December 30, 1987, and shipped F.O.B. shipping point was excluded from ending inventory and the purchase was not recorded.

d) Some of Farcy's merchandise, on consignment with Allison, Inc., was excluded from Farcy's ending inventory.

e) On December 28, 1987, Farcy received $3,500 worth of inventory, which was included in the 1987 ending inventory. However, the invoice on the shipment was not received by Farcy until January 3, 1988, at which time the purchase was recorded. The purchase should have been recorded in 1987.

REQUIRED

Assume that Farcy uses the periodic inventory system. Indicate the effect (overstate, understate, no effect) each of the above errors would have on:

1. 12/31/87 ending inventory.

2. 12/31/88 ending inventory.

3. 12/31/87 cost of goods sold.

4. 12/31/88 cost of goods sold.

5. 12/31/87 accounts payable.

6. 12/31/88 accounts payable.

P9-9. USE OF ALTERNATIVE COST FLOW ASSUMPTIONS   The inventory records of the Hilson Company showed the following inventory transactions for January:

	UNITS	UNIT COST
Beginning inventory	100	$5.00
Purchases		
1/5	100	5.50
1/9	50	5.75
1/17	120	6.00
1/25	90	6.20
Sales		
1/10	120	
1/15	30	
1/21	110	
1/24	60	
1/27	100	

REQUIRED

1. Assuming that Hilson Company uses a periodic inventory system, calculate cost of goods sold and cost of ending inventory under *(a)* FIFO, *(b)* LIFO, and *(c)* average cost.

2. Assuming that Hilson Company uses a perpetual inventory system, calculate the cost of goods sold and cost of ending inventory under *(a)* FIFO, *(b)* LIFO, and *(c)* average cost.

P9-10. USE OF ALTERNATIVE COST FLOW ASSUMPTIONS   The following data relate to the LMN Company Ltd. for the month of March 1987. There was no beginning inventory.

MERCHANDISE PURCHASED

	UNITS	COST PER UNIT
3/4	2,000	$5.00
3/11	1,600	$5.20
3/23	3,200	$4.60
3/29	1,800	$4.80
	8,600	

MERCHANDISE SOLD

	UNITS
3/5	1,200
3/12	1,000
3/17	1,000
3/27	800
3/30	1,200
	5,200

REQUIRED

1. Calculate the number of units and the cost of the ending inventory using the following methods:

a) First in, first out, periodic basis.

b) Last in, first out, periodic basis.

c) Weighted average method, periodic basis.

2. Assuming a perpetual inventory system is being used, prepare journal entries to record purchases and sales under methods *a* and *b* above. Selling price is $10 per unit.

(CGAA, adapted)

P9-11. CALCULATING INVENTORY UNDER ALTERNATIVE COST FLOW ASSUMPTIONS   The controller of the Davison Corporation, a retail company, made three different schedules of gross margin for the first quarter ended September 30, 1987. These schedules appear below.

	SALES ($10 PER UNIT)	COST OF GOODS SOLD	GROSS MARGIN
Schedule A	$280,000	$118,550	$161,450
Schedule B	280,000	116,900	163,100
Schedule C	280,000	115,750	164,250

The calculation of cost of goods sold in each schedule is based on the following data:

	UNITS	COST PER UNIT	TOTAL COST
Beginning inventory, 7/1	10,000	$4.00	$40,000
Purchase, 7/25	8,000	4.20	33,600
Purchase, 8/15	5,000	4.13	20,650
Purchase, 9/5	7,000	4.30	30,100
Purchase, 9/25	12,000	4.25	51,000

The president of the corporation cannot understand how three different gross margins can be calculated from the same set of data. As controller, you have explained to him that the three schedules are based on three different assumptions concerning the flow of inventory costs: first in, first out; last in, first out; and weighted average. Schedules A, B, and C were not necessarily prepared in this sequence of cost flow assumptions.

REQUIRED

Prepare three separate schedules calculating cost of goods sold and supporting schedules showing the composition of the ending inventory under each of the three cost flow assumptions.

(AICPA, adapted)

P9-12. CALCULATING INVENTORY UNDER ALTERNATIVE COST FLOW ASSUMPTIONS The Sellright Department Store maintains separate inventory records for each type of merchandise it sells. The inventory records for product type *A* show the following for the month of September:

	UNITS	UNIT COST	UNIT SELLING PRICE
Beginning inventory, 9/1	200	$3.00	
Purchase, 9/8	150	3.20	
Sale, 9/13	130		$5.00
Purchase, 9/19	50	3.50	
Sale, 9/22	80		5.25
Purchase, 9/26	100	3.55	
Purchase, 9/29	50	3.60	
Sale, 9/30	75		5.50

REQUIRED

1. Assume that Sellright uses a periodic inventory system and calculate the cost of ending inventory and the cost of goods sold for September under *(a)* FIFO, *(b)* average cost, and *(c)* LIFO.

2. Assume that Sellright uses a perpetual inventory system and calculate the cost of ending inventory and the cost of goods sold for September under *(a)* FIFO, *(b)* average cost, and *(c)* LIFO.

3. September was a month of increasing inventory acquisition cost for Sellright. Will FIFO or LIFO yield the lower net income under these circumstances? Explain why.

P9-13. CALCULATING INVENTORY COST You are engaged in an audit of the Easy Manufacturing Company for the year ended December 31, 1987. To reduce the work load at the end of the year, the company took its annual physical inventory under your observation on November 30, 1987. The company's inventory account, which includes raw material and work in process, is on a perpetual basis, and the first in, first out method of pricing is used. There is no finished goods inventory. The company's physical inventory revealed that the book inventory of $60,570 was understated by $3,000. To avoid distorting the interim financial statements, the company decided not to adjust the book inventory until the end of the year except for obsolete inventory items.

Your audit revealed the following information regarding the November 30 inventory:

a) Pricing tests showed that the physical inventory was overpriced by $2,200.

b) Footing and extension errors resulted in a $150 understatement of the physical inventory.

c) Direct labor included in the physical inventory amounted to $10,000. Overhead was included at the rate of 200 percent of direct labor. You determined that the amount of direct labor was correct and the overhead rate was proper.

d) The physical inventory included obsolete materials recorded at $250. During December these obsolete materials were removed from the inventory account by a charge to cost of sales.

Your audit also disclosed the following information about the December 31 inventory:

e) Total debits to certain accounts during December are listed below:

	DECEMBER
Purchases	$24,700
Direct labor	12,100
Manufacturing expense	25,200
Cost of goods sold	68,600

f) The cost of goods sold of $68,600 included direct labor of $13,800.

g) Normal scrap loss on established product lines is negligible. A special order started and completed during December, however, had excessive scrap loss of $800, which was charged to manufacturing expense.

REQUIRED

1. Calculate the correct amount of the physical inventory at November 30, 1987.

2. Without prejudice to your solution to part 1, assume that the correct amount of the physical inventory at November 30, 1987, was $57,700. Calculate the amount of the inventory at December 31, 1987.

(AICPA, adapted)

P9-14. DETERMINING COST OF GOODS SOLD Leininger Wholesale Company has been growing rapidly, but during this period of rapid growth the accounting records have not been properly maintained. You were recently employed to correct the accounting records and to assist in the preparation of the financial statements for the fiscal year ended February 29, 1987. One of the accounts you have been analyzing is titled ''Merchandise.'' That account, in summary form, follows. Letters following each entry correspond to the lettered explanations and additional information below, which you have accumulated during your analysis.

Merchandise

Balance, 3/1/86	*a*	Merchandise sold *e*
Purchases	*b*	Consigned merchandise *f*
Freight in	*c*	
Insurance	*d*	
Freight out on consigned merchandise	*g*	
Freight out on merchandise sold	*h*	

a) You have satisfied yourself that the March 1, 1986, inventory balance represents the approximate cost of the few units in inventory at the beginning of the year. Leininger employs the FIFO method of accounting for inventories.

b) The merchandise purchased was recorded in the account at the vendors' catalog list price, which is the price that appears on the face of each vendor's invoice. All purchased merchandise is subject to trade (chain) discounts. These discounts have been accounted for as revenue when the merchandise was paid for.

All merchandise purchased was also subject to cash terms of 2%/15, net 30. During the fiscal year Leininger recorded $3,500 in cash discounts as revenue when the merchandise was paid for. Some cash discounts were lost because payment was made after the discount period ended. All purchases of merchandise were paid for in the fiscal year during which they were recorded as purchased.

c) All merchandise is purchased F.O.B. vendors' business locations. The freight in amount is the cost of transporting the merchandise from the vendors' business locations to Leininger.

d) The insurance charge is for an all-perils policy to cover merchandise in transit to Leininger from vendors.

e) The credit to this account for merchandise sold represents the vendors' catalog list price of merchandise sold plus the cost of the beginning inventory; the debit side of the entry was made to the cost of goods sold account.

f) Consigned merchandise represents goods that were shipped to Lee Company during January 1987, priced at the vendors' catalog list price. The offsetting debit was made to accounts receivable when the merchandise was shipped to Lee. Leininger does not account for consigned goods and consignment profits separately; it commingles all consignment inventories, costs, expenses, and revenues with those from nonconsigned goods.

On March 5, 1987, Leininger received a payment from Lee for one-third of the consigned merchandise, the quantity that was sold through February 28, 1987; the payment was recorded as a reduction in accounts receivable. Lee sold the merchandise at the agreed price, deducted its 16 percent sales commission and 4 percent advertising allowance, and remitted the difference. The remaining two-thirds of the consigned merchandise was unsold and held by Lee on February 28, 1987.

g) The freight out on consigned goods is the cost of trucking the consigned goods to Lee from Leininger.

h) Freight out on merchandise sold is the amount paid trucking companies to deliver merchandise sold to Leininger's customers.

REQUIRED

Consider each of the eight lettered items independently and explain specifically how and why each item should have (if correctly accounted for) affected:

1. The amount of cost of goods sold to be included in Leininger's income statement.

2. The amount of any other account to be included in Leininger's February 28, 1987, financial statements.

Organize your answer in the following format:

ITEM	HOW AND WHY THE AMOUNT OF COST OF GOODS SOLD SHOULD HAVE BEEN AFFECTED	HOW AND WHY THE AMOUNT OF ANY OTHER ACCOUNT SHOULD HAVE BEEN AFFECTED

(AICPA, adapted)

P9-15. DOLLAR-VALUE LIFO   On January 1, 1987, Lucas Distributors, Inc., adopted the dollar-value LIFO inventory method for income tax and external financial statements reporting purposes. However, Lucas continued to use the FIFO inventory method for internal accounting and management purposes. In applying the LIFO method, Lucas uses internal conversion price indexes and the multiple-pools approach, under which substantially identical inventory items are grouped into LIFO inventory pools. The following data were available for Inventory Pool No. 1, which is comprised of products A and B, for the two years following the adoption of LIFO:

	FIFO BASIS PER RECORDS		
	UNITS	UNIT COST	TOTAL COST
Inventory, 1/1/87			
Product A	12,000	$30	$360,000
Product B	8,000	25	200,000
			$560,000
Inventory, 12/31/87			
Product A	17,000	35	$595,000
Product B	9,000	28	252,000
			$847,000
Inventory, 12/31/88			
Product A	13,000	40	$520,000
Product B	10,000	32	320,000
			$840,000

REQUIRED

1. Using the double-extension method, prepare a schedule to calculate the cost indexes for 1987 and 1988. Round indexes to three decimal places.

2. Using the chain-link method, calculate the cost change indexes and the linked cost indexes for 1987 and 1988. Round indexes to three decimal places.

3. Prepare a schedule to calculate the inventory amounts at December 31, 1987 and 1988, using the dollar-value LIFO inventory method and the indexes calculated in part 1.

(AICPA, adapted)

P9-16. LIFO VS. FIFO; DOLLAR-VALUE LIFO   The Genie Company is considering a change from the first in, first out (FIFO) method of inventory valuation to the dollar-value last in, first out (LIFO) method for the fiscal year ended May 31, 1987. Genie manufactures two staplers—compact and standard—that would be combined into a single inventory pool if dollar-value LIFO is adopted.

Selected financial data for Genie's two products are presented in the schedule shown below. Pretax income for the 1986–87 fiscal year would be $420,000 under the FIFO method of inventory valuation. Genie is subject to an income tax rate of 40 percent.

| | COMPACT STAPLER | | | STANDARD STAPLER | | | |
	UNITS	COST PER UNIT	TOTAL	UNITS	COST PER UNIT	TOTAL	TOTAL INVENTORY
Ending inventory at May 31, 1986 (FIFO)	65,000	$4.80	$ 312,000	35,000	$8.00	$ 280,000	$592,000
1986–87 fiscal year Production*	500,000	$5.52	$2,760,000	600,000	$9.00	$5,400,000	
Sales	525,000			583,000			
Ending inventory at May 31, 1987 (FIFO)	40,000	$5.52	$ 220,800	52,000	$9.00	$ 468,000	$688,800

* The unit production costs are annual averages.

REQUIRED

1. Discuss the advantages and disadvantages of a switch from the FIFO method of inventory valuation to the LIFO method.

2. Explain the following terms that are commonly used with the LIFO method of inventory valuation:
   a) LIFO pool.
   b) Dollar-value method.
   c) LIFO increment.
   d) LIFO valuation allowance.

3. a) Calculate the ending inventory as of May 31, 1987, for Genie Company using the dollar-value LIFO method of inventory valuation and a single inventory pool.
   b) Calculate the effect the change to the dollar-value LIFO inventory method would have on pretax income and on income taxes.

(IMA, adapted)

P9-17. DOLLAR-VALUE LIFO   On December 31, 1986, the Mitchell Company adopted the dollar-value LIFO inventory method. The company's inventory records provide the following information:

DATE	YEAR-END COST	RELEVANT COST INDEX
12/31/86	$300,000	1.00
12/31/87	363,000	1.10
12/31/88	420,000	1.20
12/31/89	430,000	1.25

REQUIRED

What inventory amounts would be reported in the financial statements at December 31, 1986, 1987, 1988, and 1989, assuming use of the dollar-value LIFO method?

(AICPA, adapted)

P9-18. DOLLAR-VALUE LIFO   The Grayson Company began using dollar-value LIFO on January 1, 1987. The following information is available from the company's records and other sources:

DATE	CURRENT COST OF ENDING INVENTORY	PRICE LEVEL IN ACQUISITION MARKET
1/1/87	$12,000	120
12/31/87	15,000	140
12/31/88	15,800	160
12/31/89	18,000	170

REQUIRED

Calculate the ending inventory for Grayson Company for 1987, 1988, and 1989, using the dollar-value LIFO procedure.

Hint: The cost index for each year, with 1.00 for January 1, 1987, can be obtained by dividing the price level for each year by the price level at January 1, 1987.

*P9-19. CHANGING FROM FIFO TO LIFO   The Thomas Manufacturing Company manufactures two products: New and Old. At December 31, 1986, Thomas used the first in, first out (FIFO) inventory method. Effective January 1, 1987, Thomas changed to the last in, first out (LIFO) inventory method. The cumulative effect of this change is not determinable, and as a result the ending inventory of 1986, for which the FIFO method was used, is also the beginning inventory for 1987, for the LIFO method. Any layers added during 1987 should be costed by reference to the first acquisitions of 1987, and any layers liquidated during 1987 should be considered a permanent liquidation.

The following information is available from Thomas's inventory records for the two years:

	NEW		OLD	
	UNITS	UNIT COST	UNITS	UNIT COST
1986 purchases				
1/7	5,000	$4.00	22,000	$2.00
4/16	12,000	4.50		
11/8	17,000	5.00	18,500	2.50
12/13	10,000	6.00		
1987 purchases				
2/11	3,000	7.00	23,000	3.00
5/20	8,000	7.50		
10/15	20,000	8.00		
12/23			15,500	3.50
Units on hand				
12/31/86	15,000		14,500	
12/31/87	16,000		13,000	

REQUIRED

Calculate the effect on income before income taxes for the year ended December 31, 1987, resulting from the change from the FIFO to the LIFO inventory method.

(AICPA, adapted)

10 INVENTORY VALUATION: DEPARTURES FROM HISTORICAL COST AND METHODS OF ESTIMATING INVENTORY COST

In Chapter 9 we discussed the use of historical cost and cost flow assumptions to value inventory and to determine cost of goods sold. Departures from the historical cost basis of inventory valuation may, however, be appropriate at times. For example, should changes in inventory value after the acquisition date be recognized before the point of sale? Should inventory valuation be based on selling price when production of the inventory, rather than sale, is the critical event? How should inventory be valued when a physical count is not possible, as when inventory is destroyed by a flood? Such questions have led to the development of inventory valuation bases other than historical cost, including techniques for estimating the value of inventory without a physical count. In this chapter we examine methods of inventory valuation other than historical cost.

VALUATION OF INVENTORY AT LOWER OF COST OR MARKET

Generally accepted accounting principles require a departure from the historical cost basis of valuing inventory if revenue-producing ability through sale of inventory falls below its original cost. When physical deterioration, obsolescence, a change in price level, or any other event causes the value of inventory to fall below its cost, a loss should be recognized and the inventory should be reduced in value on the balance sheet. In these circumstances, inventory is valued at the lower of cost or market (LCM), rather than on the basis of historical cost. The reduced utility of the inventory is reported as a loss of the current period, thus matching the loss with the period in which it occurs. If the amount of damaged, obsolete, or otherwise less marketable goods is material, such goods should be segregated from regular inventories on the balance sheet.

What is meant by "cost" and "market" when inventory is valued at LCM? **Cost** is the inventory value calculated by one of the historical-cost-based methods discussed in Chapter 9—specific identification, average cost, FIFO, or LIFO. **Market** generally is the replacement cost of the inventory. For a merchandising firm, replacement cost is the price in the market where the inventory is purchased. For a manufacturing firm, replacement cost is the cost to produce inventory, called the reproduction cost.

GAAP limits the "market" used to value inventory at LCM to an amount that does not exceed **net realizable value,** which is the estimated selling price in the ordinary course of business minus reasonably predictable costs of completion and disposal. For example, the net realizable value of an inventory item that normally sells for $100 and that costs $5 to deliver to the customer is $95. In effect, net realizable value is a *ceiling* on the

EXHIBIT 10–1   DETERMINING "MARKET" TO BE USED IN LOWER OF COST OR MARKET FOR INVENTORY

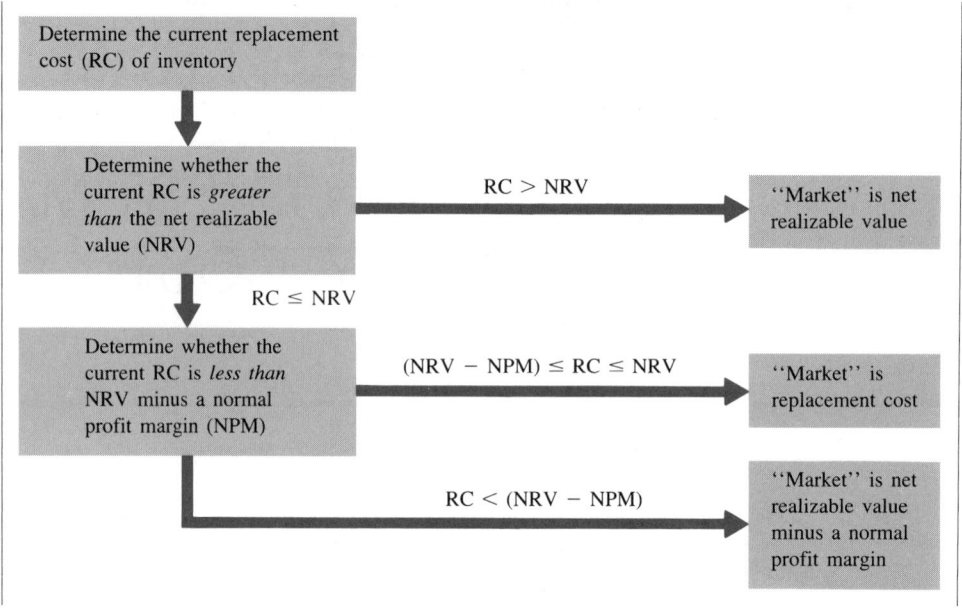

amount used as "market." GAAP also requires that "market" should not be less than net realizable value reduced by an amount approximating a normal profit margin on inventory sales. A **normal profit margin** is the amount by which the net realizable value *normally* exceeds the cost of inventory. For example, if an inventory item normally sells for $100, with a net realizable value of $95, and normally costs $70, then the normal profit margin is $25. In effect, net realizable value minus a normal profit margin is a *floor* on the amount used as "market." Exhibit 10–1 describes how "market" is under GAAP.

Examples of the determination of "market" for use in valuing inventory at LCM are presented in Exhibit 10–2. For our purposes here, we have assumed that net realizable value is $60 and net realizable value minus a normal profit margin is $40.

EXHIBIT 10–2   DETERMINING "MARKET" IN THREE HYPOTHETICAL CASES

CASE	ASSUMED REPLACEMENT COST	CEILING LIMIT	FLOOR LIMIT	AMOUNT TO BE USED AS "MARKET" IN LOWER OF COST OR MARKET
A	$62	$60	$40	The ceiling ($60) should be used as "market" because replacement cost exceeds the ceiling.
B	55	60	40	Replacement cost should be used as "market" because replacement cost is between the ceiling and floor.
C	38	60	40	The floor ($40) should be used as "market" because replacement cost is below the floor.

When the LCM procedure is used to value inventory, the accountant compares inventory cost, as calculated by one of the historical-cost-based methods, with market, which is replacement cost constrained by the ceiling (net realizable value) and the floor (net realizable value minus a normal profit margin). If market is below cost, the inventory value is reduced to market; if cost is equal to or below market, the inventory value remains at cost. The LCM procedure for valuing inventory is outlined in Exhibit 10–3.

RATIONALE FOR CEILING AND FLOOR CONSTRAINTS ON "MARKET"

Replacement cost should not be used in LCM when misleading cash flow signals might result.

In the normal course of business, the selling price of inventory will increase as the replacement cost of that inventory increases. Conversely, the selling price of inventory will decline as the replacement cost declines. This relationship between selling price and replacement cost underlies the use of the LCM procedure for valuing inventory. Accountants accept a decline in replacement cost as evidence of a decline in the sale utility of inventory. It is possible, however, that replacement cost and selling price will not always move together. When this is the case, replacement cost should not be used as the value for inventory because it could result in misleading cash flow signals.

The purpose of the ceiling and floor constraints on the use of replacement cost as "market" is to avoid the use of replacement cost when the normal gross profit relationship between replacement cost and selling price does not exist. Net realizable value is a ceiling, or upper constraint, on the use of replacement cost as "market" because the utility of inventory is no greater than the cash inflow that can be realized through the sale of that inventory. Bear in mind that inventory is useful only because it can be sold. Therefore a company would replace inventory at a cost that exceeds net realizable value only under unusual circumstances, and only for a limited time. Since replacement cost in excess of net realizable value does not reflect the normal relationship between cost and

EXHIBIT 10–3   THE LOWER-OF-COST-OR-MARKET PROCEDURE APPLIED TO INVENTORIES

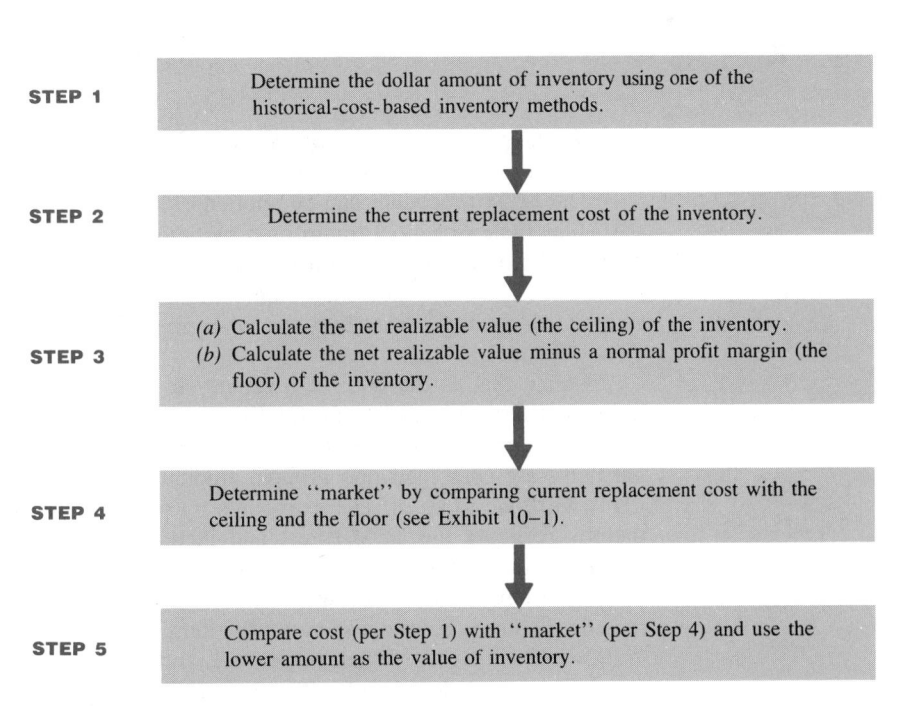

STEP 1   Determine the dollar amount of inventory using one of the historical-cost-based inventory methods.

STEP 2   Determine the current replacement cost of the inventory.

STEP 3   (a) Calculate the net realizable value (the ceiling) of the inventory.
(b) Calculate the net realizable value minus a normal profit margin (the floor) of the inventory.

STEP 4   Determine "market" by comparing current replacement cost with the ceiling and the floor (see Exhibit 10–1).

STEP 5   Compare cost (per Step 1) with "market" (per Step 4) and use the lower amount as the value of inventory.

selling price, and because the utility of inventory cannot exceed its net realizable value, net realizable value serves as an appropriate ceiling on replacement cost as a measure of utility. For example, if the net realizable value of an item of inventory is $60, only under unusual circumstances would more than $60 be paid to replace that inventory. Therefore, $60 is an appropriate upper limit on "market" as a value for inventory.

When the normal relationship between selling price and replacement cost of inventory exists, replacement cost will be below net realizable value by the amount of a normal profit margin. For example, if the normal profit margin is $20 on a particular inventory item that has a net realizable value of $100, then the normal replacement cost of that item is $80. Any replacement cost that is below net realizable value by more than a normal profit margin is below normal replacement cost and should not be used as "market" in valuing inventory. The net realizable value minus a normal profit margin is therefore an appropriate floor, or lower constraint, on replacement cost as a measure of inventory utility.

APPLICATIONS OF THE LCM PROCEDURE

To explore the use of the LCM procedure, consider the Wallace Corporation, a manufacturing firm. The cost of Wallace's inventory is calculated by the FIFO method. The replacement cost of its inventory is current reproduction cost, and the normal profit margins used in pricing inventory are derived from the relationships between net realizable values and replacement costs for the most recent two-year period. The cost to complete each inventory item at the time inventory is valued includes the costs of minor mechanical adjustments and touch-up painting. Detailed data about the five items in Wallace's inventory are as follows:

INVENTORY ITEM	COST	CURRENT REPLACEMENT COST	ESTIMATED SELLING PRICE	COST TO COMPLETE	NORMAL PROFIT MARGIN
1	$100	$110	$130	$-0-	$30
2	95	90	125	5	20
3	110	105	128	3	25
4	115	120	120	6	4
5	80	70	100	10	15

Now suppose that the LCM procedure is *applied separately to each item* of Wallace's inventory to determine a total inventory value, as in Exhibit 10–4.

The LCM procedure can be applied either to individual inventory items, such as a particular model of clock radio or a particular model of portable AM-FM radio, or to *groups* of similar inventory items, or to *total* inventory. Suppose that Wallace's inventory items 1, 2, and 3 are radios and items 4 and 5 are small black-and-white television sets. Exhibit 10–5 shows what happens when the LCM procedure is applied under each of these approaches.

Notice that as the pool of inventory to which LCM is applied is broadened from individual items to groups and finally to total inventory, the dollar amount reported for inventory increases from $489 to $494 to $500. These increases occur because as individual items are combined into groups, amounts by which market is below cost for some items will tend to be offset by amounts by which market is above cost for other items, thereby reducing the LCM effect and increasing the dollar amount of inventory. For example, consider the group of radios (items 1, 2, and 3). When they are considered as individual items, cost is below market by $10 for item 1; cost is below market by $5 for item 2; market is below cost by $5 for item 3; and the LCM inventory amount is $300 ($100 + $95 + $105). When items 1, 2, and 3 are grouped together, the $5 amount by which market is below cost for item 3 is offset by part of the total amount of $15 by which

EXHIBIT 10—4   LCM APPLIED TO INDIVIDUAL INVENTORY ITEMS

Wallace Corporation

INVENTORY ITEM	ANALYSIS	INVENTORY VALUE AT LOWER OF COST OR MARKET
1	Cost is $100. Market is the $110 replacement cost because it is less than the ceiling ($130 − $0) and greater than the floor ($130 − $0 − $30).	$100 (cost)
2	Cost is $95. Market is $100, which is net realizable value minus the normal profit margin (floor = $125 − $5 − $20), because replacement cost is below the floor.	95 (cost)
3	Cost is $110. Market is the $105 replacement cost because it is less than the ceiling ($128 − $3) and greater than the floor ($128 − $3 − $25).	105 (market)
4	Cost is $115. Market is the $114 net realizable value (ceiling = $120 − $6), because replacement cost is above the ceiling.	114 (market)
5	Cost is $80. Market is $75, which is net realizable value minus the normal profit margin (floor = $100 − $10 − $15), because replacement cost is below the floor.	75 (market)
Total		$489

EXHIBIT 10—5   LCM APPLIED TO INDIVIDUAL ITEMS, GROUPS OF ITEMS, AND TOTAL INVENTORY

Wallace Corporation

INVENTORY ITEM	COST	MARKET	LOWER OF COST OR MARKET APPLIED TO: INDIVIDUAL ITEMS	GROUPS OF ITEMS	TOTAL INVENTORY
1	$100	$110	$100		
2	95	100	95		
3	110	105	105		
	$305	$315		$305	
4	$115	$114	114		
5	80	75	75		
	$195	$189		189	
Total	$500	$504	$489	$494	$500

cost is below market for items 1 and 2. Therefore, LCM applied to the group yields an inventory of $305, which is $5 higher than the inventory amount when LCM is applied to individual items ($300). This offsetting effect increases as the number of inventory items combined into a group is increased. Accordingly, the reported dollar amount of inventory will tend to increase as the number of items that are combined is increased.

The most common practice is to apply the LCM procedure to individual items, because as a general rule LCM must be used on an item-by-item basis for income tax purposes. However the LCM procedure is applied, it should be applied consistently over time.

LCM AND CONSERVATISM

When inventory is valued at market, the new inventory value becomes the cost used in the next period's LCM test.

The LCM procedure provides an excellent example of the influence of conservatism on GAAP. When LCM is used to value inventory, if market is below cost, the value of inventory is reduced to market, and this new, lower inventory value is considered to be cost for future comparisons of cost and market. Any recovery in the value of inventory that was previously reduced to market is ignored. These practices cause the LCM procedure to be biased toward the reporting of lower inventory values on the balance sheet. The LCM procedure also has a conservative effect on the income statement of the period in which inventory value is reduced to market, because this reduction makes it necessary to report a loss. In subsequent periods, however, when the inventory is sold, income will be unconservatively higher because of the reduced inventory values that are included in cost of goods sold.

RECORDING THE REDUCTION OF INVENTORY TO "MARKET"

Special accounting and reporting problems arise when the LCM procedure causes inventory to be reduced to "market." The accountant must decide (1) how to record the reduction of inventory value to market, and (2) how to report the inventory holding loss, which is equal to the amount by which market is below cost, in the income statement.

An inventory market value below cost may be accounted for and reported in either of two ways: (1) reduce the inventory account to market value, with a corresponding increase in cost of goods sold for the amount by which market is below cost; or (2) adjust inventory reported in the balance sheet by using a contra-inventory allowance account to reduce inventory to market value, with a corresponding debit to a separate inventory holding loss account, which is reported in the income statement for the period.

The two ways to account for and report market value below inventory cost are illustrated in Exhibits 10–6 and 10–7. These exhibits are based on the following data:

	BEGINNING OF YEAR 1	END OF YEAR 1	END OF YEAR 2	END OF YEAR 3
Sales (net)	—	$ 80,000	$140,000	$150,000
Purchases (net)	—	100,000	120,000	130,000
Inventory (cost)	$–0–	42,000	46,000	48,000
Inventory (market)	–0–	40,000	45,000	50,000
Expenses	–0–	10,000	12,000	14,000

As Exhibits 10–6 and 10–7 indicate, direct reduction of the inventory account to record reduction to market yields the same results for total assets on the balance sheet and net income before taxes as use of a contra-inventory allowance account. The two approaches differ, however, in the manner in which the reduction of inventory to market value is recorded and reported in the financial statements. Under the direct adjustment of inventory approach, inventory is decreased and cost of goods sold is increased for the amount by which the market value of inventory is below cost. In contrast, when a contra-inventory allowance account is used, the amount by which inventory market is below

EXHIBIT 10–6   ACCOUNTING FOR AND REPORTING MARKET BELOW COST

DIRECT ADJUSTMENT OF INVENTORY ACCOUNT: LOSS INCLUDED IN COST OF GOODS SOLD

YEAR	PERPETUAL SYSTEM		PERIODIC SYSTEM	

1	Cost of goods sold 2,000
	    Inventory . . . .
	To record inventory holding loss.
		2,000	Ending inventory (market). 40,000
			Cost of goods sold. 60,000
			    Beginning inventory. . . . .
			    Purchases . . . .
			Year-end adjusting and closing entry.
				–0–
				100,000

2	Cost of goods sold 1,000
	    Inventory . . . .
	To record inventory holding loss.
		1,000	Ending inventory (market). 45,000
			Cost of goods sold. 115,000
			    Beginning inventory. . . . .
			    Purchases . . . .
			Year-end adjusting and closing entry.
				40,000
				120,000

3	No entry because cost is below market.		Ending inventory (cost) 48,000
			Cost of goods sold. 127,000
			    Beginning inventory. . . . .
			    Purchases . . . .
			Year-end adjusting and closing entry.
				45,000
				130,000

	YEAR 1		YEAR 2		YEAR 3	
PARTIAL BALANCE SHEET						
Inventory (at LCM)	$40,000		$ 45,000		$ 48,000	
PARTIAL INCOME STATEMENT						
Sales (net)	$80,000		$140,000		$150,000	
Less: Cost of goods sold						
Beginning inventory			$ 40,000		$ 45,000	
Purchases (net)	$100,000		120,000		130,000	
Goods available	$100,000		$160,000		$175,000	
Ending inventory	(40,000)	(60,000)	(45,000)	(115,000)	(48,000)	(127,000)
Gross margin		$20,000		$ 25,000		$ 23,000
Other expenses		(10,000)		(12,000)		(14,000)
Income before taxes		$10,000		$ 13,000		$ 9,000

inventory cost is recorded as a loss separate from cost of goods sold, and the contra-inventory allowance account is credited for the same amount. Notice that when an inventory allowance account is used (Exhibit 10–7), it is necessary to eliminate the allowance account balance, with a corresponding reduction in the beginning inventory balance for the next period, so that beginning inventory is not misstated.

The entries required under the direct adjustment approach are less complex than

EXHIBIT 10–7 ACCOUNTING FOR AND REPORTING MARKET BELOW COST

INDIRECT ADJUSTMENT OF INVENTORY BY USE OF AN ALLOWANCE ACCOUNT: LOSS REPORTED SEPARATELY

YEAR	PERPETUAL SYSTEM		PERIODIC SYSTEM	
1	Inventory holding loss 2,000		Inventory holding loss 2,000	
	Allowance to adjust		Allowance to adjust	
	inventory to market...	2,000	inventory to market.........	2,000
	To record inventory holding loss.		To record inventory holding loss.	
			Ending inventory (cost) 42,000	
			Cost of goods sold 58,000	
			Purchases...................	100,000
			Year-end adjusting and closing entry.	
2	Allowance to adjust		Allowance to adjust	
	inventory to market... 2,000		inventory to market......... 2,000	
	Beginning inventory	2,000	Beginning inventory	2,000
	To close year 1 allowance balance.		To close year 1 allowance balance.	
	Inventory holding loss 1,000		Inventory holding loss 1,000	
	Allowance to adjust		Allowance to adjust	
	inventory to market...	1,000	inventory to market.........	1,000
	To record inventory holding loss.		To record inventory holding loss.	
			Ending inventory (cost) 46,000	
			Cost of goods sold 114,000	
			Beginning inventory	40,000
			Purchases...................	120,000
			Year-end adjusting and closing entry.	
3	Allowance to adjust		Allowance to adjust	
	inventory to market... 1,000		inventory to market......... 1,000	
	Beginning inventory	1,000	Beginning inventory	1,000
	To close year 2 allowance balance.		To close year 2 allowance balance.	
	No entry to record inventory holding loss because cost is below market.		No entry to record inventory holding loss because cost is below market.	
			Ending inventory (cost) 48,000	
			Cost of goods sold 127,000	
			Beginning inventory	45,000
			Purchases...................	130,000
			Year-end adjusting and closing entry.	

	YEAR 1		YEAR 2		YEAR 3	
PARTIAL BALANCE SHEET						
Inventory (cost)	$42,000		$ 46,000		$ 48,000	
Less: Allowance to adjust						
inventory to market	(2,000)	$40,000	(1,000)	$ 45,000	–0–	$ 48,000
PARTIAL INCOME STATEMENT						
Sales (net)...........................		$80,000		$140,000		$150,000
Less: Cost of goods sold						
Beginning inventory			$ 40,000		$ 45,000	
Purchases (net)	$100,000		120,000		130,000	
Goods available	$100,000		$160,000		$175,000	
Ending inventory	(42,000)	(58,000)	(46,000)	(114,000)	(48,000)	(127,000)
Gross margin		$22,000		$ 26,000		$ 23,000
Other expenses		(10,000)		(12,000)		(14,000)
Less: Inventory holding loss		(2,000)		(1,000)		–0–
Income before taxes		$10,000		$ 13,000		$ 9,000

those required under the allowance approach. The direct adjustment approach can be justified because it directly reduces the inventory account to market value. This treatment is consistent with the LCM practice of using the inventory market value as the cost amount for the next period's LCM analysis.

The weakness of the direct adjustment approach and the strength of the allowance approach result from the fact that an inventory holding loss is not caused by selling goods, but rather by holding them. Hence it is unsound conceptually to include the amount by which inventory market value is below cost in the figure for cost of goods sold. Burying the holding loss in cost of goods sold can be justified only on the basis of materiality. That is, if the holding loss is not material, as compared to the rest of cost of goods sold, then it probably makes no difference if it is included in cost of goods sold.

The allowance approach is also superior to the direct adjustment approach in regard to the way the inventory holding loss is reported in the financial statements. Because the holding loss is buried in cost of goods sold under the direct adjustment approach, cost of goods sold actually is overstated, and it is impossible for a user of the income statement to identify the amount of inventory holding loss. On the other hand, the partial income statements under the allowance approach presented in Exhibit 10–7 show the inventory holding loss as a separate line item and properly report cost of goods sold for each period.

USING LCM IN INTERIM FINANCIAL STATEMENTS

APB Opinion No. 28 specifies that inventory holding losses from market declines should be recognized in the interim reporting period in which the decline occurs, unless the losses are temporary in the sense that they can reasonably be expected to be restored within the current fiscal year by market recovery. If an inventory holding loss is recognized in an interim reporting period, and the loss is subsequently restored in a later interim period of the same fiscal year, an inventory holding gain should be recognized in the later interim reporting period. *Opinion No. 28* specifies that subsequently recognized gains from market recovery cannot exceed inventory holding losses previously recognized in the current fiscal year.[1]

VALUING FIRM PURCHASE COMMITMENTS AT LCM

A business sometimes will enter into a contract to purchase inventory items at a fixed price at a specified date in order to ensure a supply of the goods or as a means of protection against future price increases. Some purchase contracts can be revised or canceled under particular conditions, while others cannot be changed and are noncancelable. Noncancelable purchase commitments, along with other purchase commitments under which performance is probable because of large disincentives for nonperformance, are called **firm purchase commitments.** While a firm purchase commitment protects the buyer from price increases, such commitments also expose the buyer to the risk that future open market prices for the contracted goods will decline below the contract price. Should this happen, the buyer will end up paying a price for the contracted inventory items that is higher than their current market value at the time of purchase.

GAAP requires that goods contracted for under a firm purchase commitment should be accounted for by LCM, just as if those goods were already in inventory.[2] A buyer who enters into and executes a firm purchase commitment within a single fiscal year needs to make no entry until the contract is executed. For example, suppose that Anderson Company, whose fiscal year ends on December 31, signs a firm purchase commitment on April 30 to buy goods from Dorsey Company for $20,000 by September 15 of the same year. If the open market price of the goods at the purchase date (i.e., September 15) is

[1] "Interim Financial Reporting," *Opinions of the Accounting Principles Board No. 28* (New York: AICPA, May 1973), para. 14c.

[2] "Restatement and Revision of Accounting Research Bulletins Nos. 1–42," *Accounting Research Bulletin No. 43* (New York: AICPA, 1953), chap. 4, statements 5 and 10.

equal to or greater than the $20,000 contract price, Anderson simply records the purchase at the contract price:

Inventory (or purchases)	20,000	
Accounts payable (or cash)		20,000

However, if the open market price on the date the contract is executed (September 15) is below the contract price—for example, $18,000—Anderson must record the purchase at the lower market price and show a loss on the purchase:

Inventory (or purchases)	18,000	
Loss on purchase commitment	2,000	
Accounts payable (or cash)		20,000

Accounting for a firm purchase commitment on the buyer's books is somewhat more complicated if the purchase contract period extends beyond the end of the buyer's fiscal year. First, the terms and the amount of the contract should be disclosed, usually in a footnote, in the buyer's financial statements if the contract is for a material dollar amount. Moreover, if the fiscal year-end market price is below the contract price and it appears that this price decline is a reasonable estimate of a probable loss at the time the purchase actually will occur, then a loss on the purchase commitment should be recorded in the period of the price decline. For example, if the $20,000 purchase commitment made by Anderson extends into February of the next fiscal year, and the market price of the contracted goods is $17,000 at the end of Anderson's fiscal year, Anderson will make the following year-end adjusting entry:

Estimated loss on purchase commitment	3,000	
Estimated liability on purchase commitment		3,000

The liability account in the above entry is included in Anderson's current liabilities if the purchase commitment is to be executed within the longer of the next fiscal year or the next operating cycle. In Chapter 15 we discuss the nature of this ''liability'' in greater detail and evaluate it in terms of the FASB's conceptual framework. The estimated loss on purchase commitment account is closed to Anderson's income summary and appears in Anderson's income statement.

When the purchase commitment is executed by Anderson in February, several possibilities exist with respect to the relationship between the open market price and the contract price of the goods:

1. The market price remains exactly $3,000 below the contract price.

2. The market price is more than $3,000 below the contract price.

3. The market price is less than $3,000 below the contract price.

4. The market price is equal to or above the contract price.

If the market price remains $3,000 below the contract price, Anderson will make the following entry at the time of purchase, recording the purchase at the lower market price:

Inventory (or purchases)	17,000	
Estimated liability on purchase commitment	3,000	
Accounts payable (or cash)		20,000

If the market price at the time of purchase is more than $3,000 below the contract price, Anderson will have to recognize an additional loss in the period of the purchase and record the purchase at the lower market price. For example, assume that the open market price is $5,000 below the contract price when the contract is executed:

Inventory (or purchases)	15,000	
Estimated liability on purchase commitment	3,000	
Loss on purchase commitment	2,000	
Accounts payable (or cash)		20,000

If the open market price has recovered and is less than $3,000 below the contract price, is equal to the contract price, or is above the contract price, under the LCM rule Anderson should ignore the market price recovery and record the purchase at the $17,000 market price that existed when the loss was recognized at year-end. In this case, Anderson will make the same purchase entry as if the market price had remained $3,000 below the contract price, namely:

Inventory (or purchases)	17,000	
Estimated liability on purchase commitment	3,000	
Accounts payable (or cash)		20,000

In short, as is the case when the LCM rule is applied to inventories on hand, recovery of the market price of the goods is ignored in the accounting for a firm purchase commitment. This procedure for handling improvement in the market price–contract price relationship when a firm purchase commitment exists has the same theoretical deficiency as does LCM applied to inventory on hand. The increased utility of the contract because of the market price improvement is not reported in the period of the increase, but instead is reported indirectly in the gross margin related to future sales at the time the undervalued inventory passes through cost of goods sold.

A business that is the buyer in a firm purchase commitment may **hedge** against the possibility of market price movements of goods under contract. Hedging can be accomplished through a **futures contract** in which the buyer in the firm purchase commitment simultaneously agrees to sell the same quantity of similar, perhaps identical, goods at a fixed price. A firm that holds a sell position in the futures contract and a buy position in the purchase commitment when the market price of goods changes is better off under one contract by approximately the same amount by which it is worse off under the other contract. (If the goods specified in the two contracts are not identical, some difference in the market price changes may occur, but the difference should be small.) For example, if the market price of the goods drops, the buyer may suffer from having signed the purchase commitment, but may benefit from the fixed selling price in the futures contract.

The widespread use of hedging arrangements resulted in the issuance of FASB *Statement No. 80*. The general principle set forth in *Statement No. 80* is that a change in the market value of a futures contract should be recognized in income in the period in which the change occurs. However, when a futures contract exists as a hedge against a firm purchase commitment, changes in the market value of the futures contract should be recognized in income when the effects of related changes in the market prices of the hedged items are recognized.

VALUATION OF INVENTORY AT REPLACEMENT COST

In addition to LCM, there are other inventory valuation bases that are alternatives to historical cost and that may be used. Some accountants believe that the current value of inventory, as measured by replacement cost, is more useful to decision makers than historical cost as a measure of inventory utility. These accountants prefer to report the replacement cost of inventory in the balance sheet whether it is above or below historical cost. In those situations where the net realizable value of inventory is more clearly determinable than the replacement cost, however, they would report inventory at net realizable value.

A major argument for the valuation of inventories at replacement cost is that if replacement cost measures the utility of inventory when replacement cost is below historical cost (the LCM argument), then replacement cost is also a valid measure of inventory utility when it is above historical cost. This argument is very persuasive unless the LCM use of replacement cost is justified on the basis of conservatism rather than as an effort to report information about future cash flows.

If replacement cost were used as the primary basis of inventory valuation, a gain or loss on holding inventory would be reported in each accounting period in which replacement cost was below or above that of the previous period. Valuation of inventory at replacement cost would result in the reporting of inventory gains and losses in the income statement before the period in which the inventory was sold. Under current GAAP, revenue is reported at the time inventory is sold, except for the holding losses that arise under LCM. If an entity valued inventory at replacement cost, both changes in replacement cost *and* sale of inventory would become events that justify recognition of revenue.

Although there is some support for valuing inventory at replacement cost in the balance sheet, GAAP limits the use of replacement cost in the financial statements to inventory items that have suffered a reduction in value below historical cost (i.e., the LCM procedure). The use of replacement costs that are higher than historical costs to report inventory values in the financial statements is not a generally accepted accounting principle. However, replacement costs, whether below or above historical costs, may be reported as supplementary data to the financial statements.[3]

VALUATION OF INVENTORY AT NET REALIZABLE VALUE

Net realizable value is another alternative to historical cost inventory values. As we saw earlier, net realizable value serves as the upper limit, or the ceiling, on market when the LCM procedure is used. Therefore, net realizable value is used to value inventory under LCM whenever replacement cost is below historical cost but above net realizable value.

It also is acceptable under GAAP to value inventory at net realizable value when two special conditions exist: (1) inventory has a known and reasonably certain selling price and (2) any costs of completing and selling the inventory are known or are not material. In Chapter 2 we stated that revenue should be recognized when the amount and timing of revenue to be received and the costs to be incurred are reasonably determinable, and when the earnings process is virtually complete. Therefore, when the inventory selling price is known and is also reasonably certain, and when the costs of completing and selling the inventory are known or are not material, it is acceptable under GAAP to recognize revenue before the point of sale, and to report inventory at net realizable value.

The two most common types of inventory that meet the conditions for revenue recognition before sale, and therefore for valuation at net realizable value, are (1) inventories of precious metals and minerals, of some agricultural goods, and of some other readily marketable items, and (2) inventories associated with long-term construction contracts that are accounted for by the percentage-of-completion method. For both of these

[3] "Financial Reporting and Changing Prices," *Statement of Financial Accounting Standards No. 33* (Stamford, Conn.: FASB, 1979), as amended by subsequent *Statements*.

types of inventory, the essential conditions are that (1) the selling price is reasonably certain because of ready marketability at an established price (as in the case of wheat) or because of contractual agreement (as in a long-term construction contract), and (2) costs of completion and disposal are reasonably predictable (as they are in some long-term construction contracts) or are not material (as they are once a bushel of wheat is harvested). These revenue recognition criteria were presented and discussed in Chapter 6.

VALUATION OF INVENTORY AT STANDARD COSTS

A third alternative to historical cost inventory value is valuation at standard costs. Many manufacturing companies use a standard cost system, in which the unit costs for material, labor, and manufacturing overhead are predetermined. Standard costs usually are based on the cost of material, labor, and overhead per unit of product when the plant is operating at normal capacity. The standard costs provide management with an ideal or goal against which to compare actual costs. By recording and analyzing variances from the standard costs, management is able to obtain information that is helpful in controlling and managing inventory costs.

Standard costs also are allowed under GAAP for external reporting purposes provided that they are adjusted at reasonable intervals to reflect current conditions, so that at the balance sheet date standard cost reasonably approximates cost determined under one of the recognized cost bases discussed in Chapter 9; namely, specific identification, average cost, FIFO, and LIFO.

METHODS OF ESTIMATING INVENTORY COSTS

In the preceding sections and in Chapter 9 we discussed the valuation of inventory when there is a physical count of inventory. Sometimes it is necessary to *estimate* the dollar amount of ending inventory because it is either not practical or not possible to make a physical count. For example, determination of an inventory figure for interim financial statements normally does not justify the cost and inconvenience of a physical count. Or a corporate executive might want an estimate of ending inventory to use for verification of an inventory figure developed by a subordinate under normal inventory procedures. Occasionally it is necessary to estimate the dollar amount of ending inventory because inventory records and the inventory itself have been lost, stolen, or destroyed by a fire or some other type of catastrophe. The remainder of this chapter is devoted to two methods of estimating the dollar amount of inventory—the gross profit method and the retail inventory method.

THE GROSS PROFIT METHOD

The **gross profit** method of estimating inventory costs, sometimes called the **gross margin** method, converts goods sold during the period from selling price to a cost basis. This cost of goods sold amount is then subtracted from the cost of goods available for sale to yield an estimate of the cost of goods remaining in inventory. The gross profit method relies on the following relationships and assumptions:

1. Cost of beginning inventory + Purchases = Cost of goods available for sale.

2. All goods available for sale are assumed either to have been sold or to be in inventory. That is, it is assumed that there are no inventory shrinkages through theft, loss, or similar occurrences.

3. Selling price − Gross profit = Cost of goods sold.

4. Cost of goods available for sale − Cost of goods sold = Cost of ending inventory.

When the gross profit method is used, it is essential to have a reasonable estimate of the relationship between gross profit and selling price. This estimate is obtained by analyzing the historical relationship between the gross profit and the selling price of the inventory in question. Once this estimate is obtained, the dollar amount of gross profit is estimated by multiplying the gross profit as a percentage of sales by the selling price.

$$\text{Estimated gross profit percentage} \times \text{Selling price in dollars} = \text{Estimated gross profit in dollars}$$

Then the estimated dollar amount of gross profit can be subtracted from the dollar amount of sales to yield an estimate of the dollar amount of cost of goods sold (3 above). Under the assumption that all goods available for sale are either sold or in inventory, the cost of goods sold can be subtracted from the cost of goods available for sale to yield an estimate of the cost of inventory (4 above). Of course, goods available for sale can be determined from beginning inventory and the purchase records for the accounting period.

To illustrate, assume that the following data are available for Willis Company for the current year:

Beginning inventory (at historical cost)	$12,000
Net purchases	68,000
Net sales (retail prices)	90,000
Estimated gross profit as a percentage of net sales (derived from past accounting records)	30%

Under the gross profit method, ending inventory for the current year would be estimated as follows:

Step 1: Estimated gross profit = 30% × $90,000 = $27,000.
Step 2: Estimated cost of goods sold = $90,000 − $27,000 = $63,000.
Step 3: Goods available for sale = $12,000 + $68,000 = $80,000.
Step 4: Estimated ending inventory = Goods available for sale − Estimated cost of goods sold.

$$\text{Estimated ending inventory} = \$80,000 − \$63,000 = \$17,000.$$

As you can see, the gross profit method employs simple calculations. It does, however, require an estimate of gross profit as a percentage of sales. Companies typically maintain records of their gross profit as a percentage of sales, so the required data for the gross profit method calculations usually are readily available. Companies do, however, occasionally compute gross profit as a *percentage of cost*. When this is the company's practice, it is necessary to restate gross profit as a percentage of sales before the gross profit method can be used. This restatement is not difficult, if you use simple logic and remember that cost + gross profit = selling price.

Assume that gross profit is available from company records as a percentage of cost rather than as a percentage of sales. For example, let gross profit be 25 percent of cost, which in effect means that selling price equals cost plus 25 percent of cost. If we remember the relationship in column *A* below, and choose arbitrary numerical values for each element of the relationship in a logical fashion, as in column *B*, it is possible to ascertain the relationship between gross profit and sales.

COLUMN A	COLUMN B*
Sales	5
− Cost of goods sold	−4
= Gross profit	1

* Values are arbitrarily chosen.

We chose the values 1 and 4 in column B for gross profit and cost of goods sold, respectively, because we knew that gross profit was 25 percent, or one-fourth, of cost. The value 5 was assigned to sales in column B, so that the column A relationship holds. It is now possible to inspect the numbers in column B and see that gross profit is one-fifth, or 20 percent, of sales. Hence, we have gross profit as a percentage of sales. This sort of analysis can be used to derive gross profit as a percentage of sales any time it is available only as a percentage of cost.[4]

Weaknesses of the Gross Profit Method

Estimates based on the gross profit method depend on the accuracy of the estimated gross profit percentage. The primary disadvantage of the gross profit method is that the gross profit percentage is based on *past* relationships between gross profit and selling price or gross profit and cost. If past relationships between selling price and cost differ from present relationships, then the gross profit method will not provide accurate estimates.

Because the gross profit method is so dependent on the gross profit percentage, it is essential to make adjustments in the percentage when the relationship between gross profit and sales changes. For example, if increased inventory costs are not fully reflected in increased selling prices, then the gross profit percentage should be adjusted. The gross profit method must be separately applied to different types of inventory that have different relationships between cost and selling price. A single gross profit percentage should be used for all types of inventory only when the relationship of cost to selling price is the same for all types or when the relative amounts of different types of inventory in the overall inventory are stable over time. Finally, the gross profit percentage depends on the cost flow assumption used and on inventory conditions that existed during the period of time over which the percentage is computed. Hence, data for periods in which inventory cost flow assumptions differ from those of the current period, or for periods in which special circumstances existed, such as liquidation of a LIFO layer or use of market values, should not be used for computing the gross profit percentage.

The gross profit method is a comparatively inaccurate method of estimating inventory in most cases because the gross profit percentage used in the method typically is an *average* figure for several prior years. The gross profit method therefore should be relied on to estimate ending inventory only as a last resort. For example, it may provide a reasonable estimate of inventory when the inventory has been destroyed and when the retail inventory method cannot be used.

THE RETAIL INVENTORY METHOD Like the gross profit method, the **retail** inventory method is used to estimate the dollar amount of ending inventory. As compared with the gross profit method, however, the retail inventory method is capable of providing more accurate estimates of inventory. The retail method is acceptable for external reporting if it yields results that reasonably ap-

---

[4] Alternatively, the following formula could be used to arrive at gross profit as a percent of sales, given gross profit as a percent of cost:

$$\text{Gross profit as percent of sales} = \frac{\text{Gross profit as percent of cost}}{1.00 + \text{Gross profit as percent of cost}}$$

proximate the results that would have been obtained under one of the cost flow methods described in Chapter 9.

Whereas the gross profit method relies on *past* relationships between cost and selling price to determine the gross profit percentage, the retail inventory method uses the *current* relationship between cost and selling price to estimate inventory. As a result, the retail inventory method not only is used in circumstances that invite the use of the gross profit method, but also is used widely by retail stores on a daily basis, with at least an annual confirmation of the inventory amount by a physical count valued at retail.

In its simplest form, the retail inventory method requires the following data: (1) beginning inventory expressed in both cost and retail selling prices; (2) the current period's purchases expressed in both cost and retail prices; and (3) the retail sales for the period. Given these data, current purchases are added to beginning inventory to calculate total goods available for sale. Total goods available for sale must be calculated at both cost and retail selling prices. Cost and retail prices are compared, and a cost to retail percentage is calculated by dividing cost by selling price. Sales for the period expressed in retail selling prices are subtracted from goods available for sale expressed in retail selling prices, yielding ending inventory expressed in retail selling prices. Ending inventory expressed in retail selling prices is multiplied by the cost to retail percentage to obtain an estimate of the cost of ending inventory.

Assume the following data for year 2 for Mitchell Corporation:

	COST	RETAIL
Beginning inventory	$ 6,000	$ 8,000
Purchases	40,000	45,000
Sales		47,000

Ending inventory for year 2, estimated by the retail inventory method, is calculated as shown in Exhibit 10–8.

The retail inventory method is most effective when there is a consistent relationship between the cost and retail selling price of inventory items. Therefore, the retail inventory method is particularly appropriate in cases where a consistent markup above acquisition cost is used to establish retail prices. To increase the effectiveness of the retail inventory method, a separate cost to retail percentage should be calculated for each group or type of goods for which there is a relatively uniform markup above cost. For example, if a store

---

EXHIBIT 10–8   ENDING INVENTORY, RETAIL INVENTORY METHOD

Mitchell Corporation

	COST	RETAIL
Beginning inventory	$ 6,000	$ 8,000
Purchases	40,000	45,000
Goods available for sale	$46,000	$53,000
Cost to retail percentage: $\dfrac{\$46,000}{\$53,000} = 87\%$		
Less: Sales		(47,000)
Estimated ending inventory at retail		$ 6,000
Estimated ending inventory at cost ($6,000 × 87%)	$ 5,220	

that uses the retail inventory method sells both tobacco products and toiletry items, and the markup on cost for tobacco products is different than the markup on cost of toiletry items, the store should compute one cost to retail percentage for tobacco products and a separate percentage for toiletry items.

The retail inventory method of estimating inventory has several advantages. It can be used to estimate ending inventory when a physical count is not practical or not possible. Like the gross profit method, it can be used when inventory has been lost, stolen, or destroyed. For this reason it is used often to generate inventory data for insurance purposes. The retail inventory method also provides comparatively accurate figures on inventory and cost of goods sold for use in interim financial statements. When used daily, the retail inventory method simplifies bookkeeping and expedites confirmation of physical inventory counts because the store maintains records of inventory, purchases, and sales expressed in retail selling prices.

Retail Inventory Method Terminology

So far in our discussion of the retail inventory method we have assumed that inventory was purchased and assigned a retail selling price and that the selling price remained constant. In reality the selling prices of goods often change, rising with increases in cost or in demand and falling with decreases in demand and sometimes with decreases in cost. Special terminology is used to describe retail selling price changes. This terminology must be understood if the retail inventory method is to be applied correctly.

When a retail merchant acquires inventory, the sum of all expenditures required to get it into condition and location for sale is known as the **original cost** of the inventory. Each inventory item is assigned an **initial** or **original selling price.** The difference between the initial selling price and the original cost of goods is called the original markup, or sometimes simply the markup. In this text the difference between initial selling price and original cost is called the **original markup.** If the selling price of an item is raised above the initial selling price, the increase is called an additional markup, or simply markup. (We refer to an increase in selling price above the initial selling price as a **markup.**) If the selling price of an item is reduced to an amount below the initial selling price, the difference between the initial selling price and the new, lower selling price is called a **markdown.** If a selling price previously raised above the initial selling price is subsequently lowered, the amount by which it is lowered is called a **markup cancellation** until the price is reduced to the level of the initial selling price; any further lowering of the selling price results in a markdown. If a selling price previously was reduced below the initial selling price (i.e., a markdown) and is subsequently increased, the amount by which it is increased is called a **markdown cancellation** until the price is increased to the level of the initial selling price; any further increases of the selling price result in markups. Markups less markup cancellations are called **net markups,** and markdowns less markdown cancellations are called **net markdowns.** Exhibit 10–9 summarizes the retail inventory method terminology.

Complicating Factors

Markups, markup cancellations, markdowns, and markdown cancellations add to the complexity of the basic retail inventory method. Several other factors, such as freight in and purchase returns and allowances, also complicate the retail inventory calculations. Note that the format used to calculate Mitchell's retail inventory costs in Exhibit 10–8 consists of two columns of data: the *cost column* and the *retail column*. We shall be referring to these two columns as we describe the proper treatment of several factors that complicate the retail inventory method.

Freight in is part of the cost of inventory purchases and should appear in the cost column of retail inventory calculations as an addition to purchases. Freight in is not

EXHIBIT 10—9   TERMINOLOGY APPLIED TO PRICE CHANGES
IN RETAIL INVENTORY METHOD

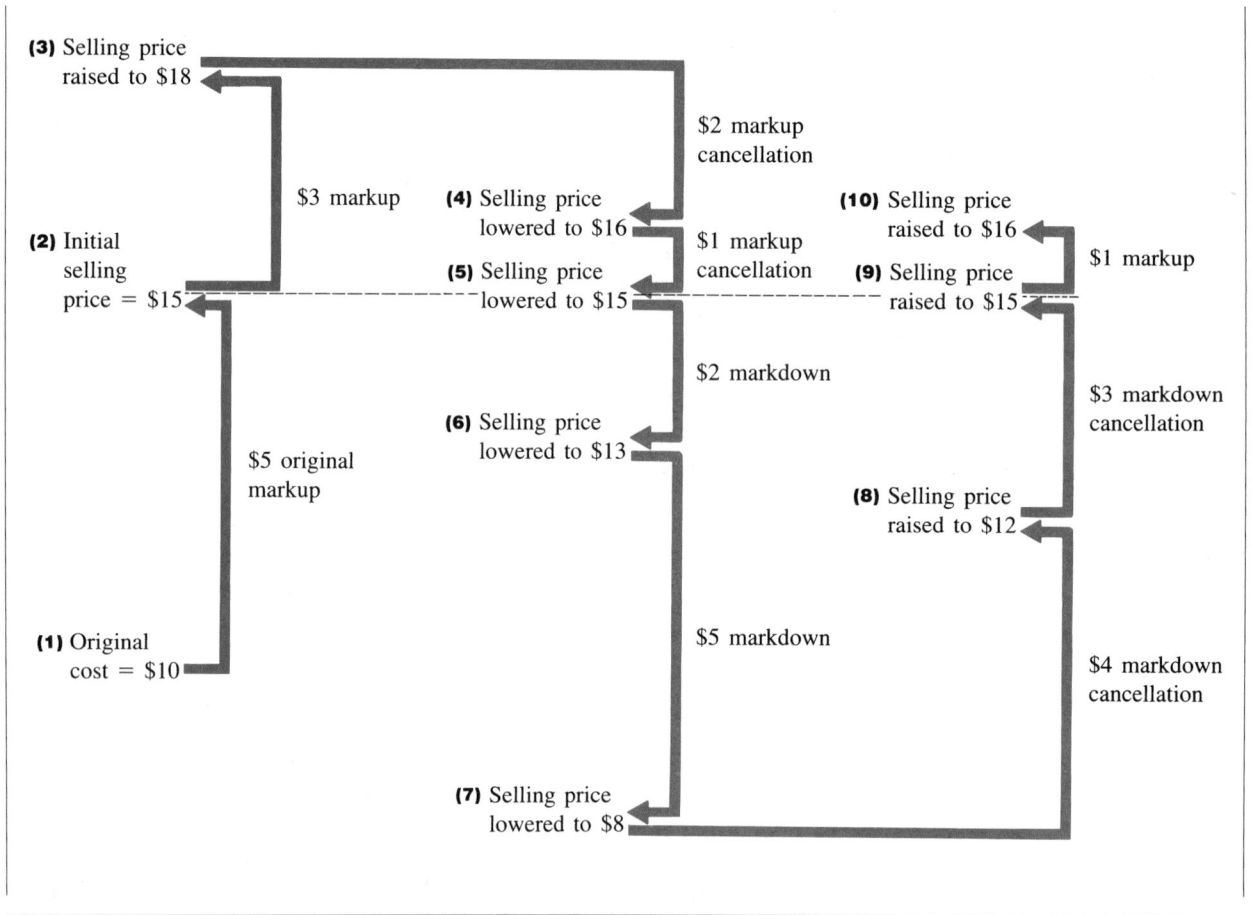

included in the retail column because normal management practice is to establish an initial retail price that will cover incidental costs such as freight in. *Purchase allowances* should be deducted from purchases in the cost column, but not in the retail column, because factors that normally lead to purchase allowances, such as damage, are taken into consideration when the initial selling price is assigned. *Purchase returns* should be deducted from purchases in both the cost column and the retail column because returned goods reduce both the total cost and the total selling price of purchased goods. If purchases are recorded at gross amounts, *purchase discounts taken* should be deducted from purchases in the cost column.

Sales returns and sales allowances should be deducted from sales in the retail column if sales are recorded on a gross basis. *Sales discounts* (e.g., a 2 percent discount if payment is received within 30 days) are not deducted from sales when sales are recorded at their gross amount, however, because they are not an adjustment of the initial markup, but rather are expenses that are incurred to obtain early payment on accounts receivable. When sales to employees are recorded net of employee discounts, *employee discounts* should be deducted from goods available for sale—added to sales—in the retail column. This treatment is necessary to obtain a total sales figure for the current period.

Normal spoilage, such as normal breakage during handling or deterioration in quality of such items as fresh vegetables, should be deducted from goods available in the retail column *after* the cost to retail percentage is calculated. This treatment is appropriate because spoiled goods are not available to be sold, but the cost of *normal* spoilage is relevant to the establishment of the normal cost to retail percentage. *Abnormal spoilage* should be deducted in both cost and retail columns *before* the normal cost to retail percentage is calculated because the goods are not available for sale and the cost of such goods is not relevant to the normal cost to retail percentage.

Variations of the Retail Inventory Method

So far we have discussed the retail inventory method in its most fundamental form. In practice, it can become considerably more complex in application, and several variations of the retail inventory method exist. These variations can be used to provide estimates of inventory expressed in average cost, lower of cost or market, FIFO, and LIFO. Basically, each variation differs from the others with respect to the components included in the calculation of the cost to retail percentage, as follows:

Average cost: The cost to retail percentage includes the cost and retail amounts for both beginning inventory and net purchases, adjusted for net markups and net markdowns.

Lower of cost or market: The net markdowns are included in the retail inventory method format *after* the cost to retail percentage is computed.

FIFO: The cost and retail amounts for beginning inventory are excluded from the calculation of the cost to retail percentage, but are included in determining the cost and retail amounts of goods available for sale. Net markups and net markdowns are included in the cost to retail percentage.

LIFO: Separate cost to retail percentages are computed for beginning inventory and net purchases. Net markups and net markdowns are included in the cost to retail percentage for net purchases. In addition, LIFO layers are identified and accounted for.

We shall use the following data for Mitchell Corporation in our discussion of each of these variations:

	COST	RETAIL
Beginning inventory	$ 6,000	$ 8,000
Net purchases	35,200	43,800
Net markups		3,000
Net markdowns		1,800
Net sales		44,700
Freight in	2,000	

Note that these are *net* amounts for purchases and sales, after adjustments for purchase returns and allowances, purchase discounts, sales returns and allowances, and employee sales discounts. Thus, they differ from the figures in Exhibit 10–8, but are derived from them.

ESTIMATING AVERAGE COST ENDING INVENTORY   When ending inventory is estimated under the average cost method, the cost to retail percentage includes the cost and retail amounts for both beginning inventory and net purchases, adjusted for net markups and net markdowns. The estimation of ending inventory on an average cost basis is illustrated in Exhibit 10–10.

EXHIBIT 10–10   RETAIL INVENTORY METHOD, AVERAGE COST BASIS

Mitchell Corporation

	COST	RETAIL
Beginning inventory	$ 6,000	$ 8,000
Net purchases	35,200	43,800
Freight in	2,000	
Net markups		3,000
Net markdowns		(1,800)
Goods available for sale	$43,200	$53,000

Cost to retail percentage: $\dfrac{\$43,200}{\$53,000} = 82\%$

Net sales		(44,700)
Estimated ending inventory at retail		$ 8,300
Estimated ending inventory at average cost ($8,300 × 82%)	$ 6,806	

Careful examination of the format of the average cost procedure in Exhibit 10–10 reveals why this particular variation of the retail inventory method provides an estimate of ending inventory at average cost. Beginning inventory and net purchases are combined, and net markups and net markdowns are applied to *all* goods available for sale. As a result, the cost to retail percentage is an average percentage, weighted by the dollar value of goods in beginning inventory and net purchases as adjusted by overall retail price changes. This "average" cost to retail percentage is applied to retail ending inventory to yield ending inventory at average cost.

ESTIMATING LOWER-OF-COST-OR-MARKET ENDING INVENTORY   Accountants assume that the retail inventory method yields an estimate of ending inventory on a lower-of-cost-or-market basis when net markdowns are not included in the retail inventory method format until *after* the cost to retail percentage is calculated. Use of the retail inventory method to estimate ending inventory on a lower-of-cost-or-market basis is shown in Exhibit 10–11.

EXHIBIT 10–11   RETAIL INVENTORY METHOD, LOWER-OF-COST-OR-MARKET BASIS ("CONVENTIONAL RETAIL METHOD")

Mitchell Corporation

	COST	RETAIL
Beginning inventory	$ 6,000	$ 8,000
Net purchases	35,200	43,800
Freight in	2,000	
Net markups		3,000
	$43,200	$54,800

Cost to retail percentage: $\dfrac{\$43,200}{\$54,800} = 79\%$

Net markdowns		(1,800)
Goods available for sale	$43,200	$53,000
Net sales		(44,700)
Estimated ending inventory at retail		$ 8,300
Estimated ending inventory at lower of cost or market ($8,300 × 79%)	$ 6,557	

Notice that Mitchell's estimated ending inventory on the lower-of-cost-or-market basis, $6,557, is less than estimated ending inventory on an average cost basis, $6,806 (Exhibit 10–10). This relationship will hold whenever net markdowns exist, because by excluding net markdowns from the cost to retail percentage, the lower-of-cost-or-market format yields a lower cost to retail percentage. If there are no net markdowns, the lower-of-cost-or-market format and the average cost format will yield the same results.

In most cases the lower-of-cost-or-market variation of the retail method only *approximates* the lower-of-cost-or-market valuation of inventory. It is easy to see, however, why the accounting profession has adopted this particular variation of the retail method to estimate lower-of-cost-or-market inventory value. Since the lower-of-cost-or-market variation will yield a lower ending inventory figure than the average cost method only when net markdowns exist, the net markdowns obviously are responsible for the lower inventory figure. Further, as we noted earlier, reductions in retail selling prices (i.e., markdowns) are evidence of a loss of utility. Therefore a net markdown of a selling price from the initial retail selling price implies that the utility of the merchandise is less than its acquisition cost. Thus the merchandise should be reported at a figure below cost. As you can see by comparing the estimate of ending inventory in Exhibit 10–11 with the estimate in Exhibit 10–10, the lower-of-cost-or-market variation of the retail method does report inventory at less than cost when net markdowns exist.

Lower-of-cost-or-market is the "conventional retail method."

The lower-of-cost-or-market variation of the retail method is used widely and is commonly known as the **conventional retail inventory method.**

ESTIMATING FIFO COST ENDING INVENTORY   When a FIFO cost flow is assumed, we can use the retail inventory method to estimate the cost of ending inventory by excluding the cost and retail amounts for beginning inventory from the calculation of the cost to retail percentage. This procedure is consistent with the FIFO assumption that the cost of beginning inventory is included in cost of goods sold and that ending inventory cost comes from purchases unless the cost of goods sold is less than the cost of beginning inventory. The use of the retail inventory method to estimate the Mitchell Corporation's ending inventory under FIFO cost flow is shown in Exhibit 10–12.

EXHIBIT 10–12   RETAIL INVENTORY METHOD, FIFO COST FLOW

Mitchell Corporation	COST	RETAIL
Net purchases	$35,200	$43,800
Freight in	2,000	
Net markups		3,000
Net markdowns		(1,800)
	$37,200	$45,000
Cost to retail percentage: $\dfrac{\$37,200}{\$45,000} = 83\%$		
Beginning inventory	6,000	8,000
Goods available for sale	$43,200	$53,000
Net sales		(44,700)
Estimated ending inventory at retail		$ 8,300
Estimated ending inventory at FIFO cost ($8,300 × 83%)	$ 6,889	

In this example, we assume that all of beginning inventory is sold during the period. If cost of sales during the period was less than the cost of beginning inventory, so that some of beginning inventory was included in ending inventory, the ending inventory would consist of two layers—the net purchases layer and some of the beginning inventory layer. Each layer would have its own cost to retail percentage. For the Mitchell Corporation, it would be 83% for the net purchases layer and 75% ($6,000 ÷ $8,000) for the beginning inventory layer.

ESTIMATING LIFO COST ENDING INVENTORY If the objective is to use the retail inventory method to estimate the cost of ending inventory under the LIFO cost flow assumption, it is necessary to calculate separate cost to retail percentages for beginning inventory and net purchases. Net markups and net markdowns are included when the cost to retail percentage for net purchases is calculated. In addition, it is necessary to identify and account for LIFO layers. Exhibit 10–13 shows how to generate an estimate of ending inventory by the retail inventory method under LIFO cost flow.

Notice that ending inventory in Exhibit 10–13 consists of two layers, the beginning inventory ($6,000 cost and $8,000 retail) and the new layer ($249 cost and $300 retail) from the current year's purchases. If the retail amount of ending inventory had been less than the retail amount of beginning inventory, only the 75 percent cost to retail percentage of the beginning inventory would have been used to calculate the cost of ending inventory. It would not be necessary to calculate a cost to retail percentage for the current year's net purchases because none of those purchases would be included in ending inventory. As the

---

EXHIBIT 10–13   RETAIL INVENTORY METHOD, LIFO COST FLOW

Mitchell Corporation

	COST	RETAIL
Beginning inventory	$ 6,000	$ 8,000
Cost to retail percentage, beginning inventory:		
$\dfrac{\$6,000}{\$8,000} = 75\%$		
Net purchases $35,200		$43,800
Freight in 2,000		
Net markups		3,000
Net markdowns.		(1,800)
	37,200	45,000
Cost to retail percentage, excluding beginning inventory:		
$\dfrac{\$37,200}{\$45,000} = 83\%$		
Goods available for sale	$43,200	$53,000
Net sales		(44,700)
Estimated ending inventory at retail		$ 8,300
Estimated ending inventory at LIFO cost		
Beginning inventory layer ($8,000 × 75%) . . .	$ 6,000	
Current layer ($300 × 83%)	249	
	$ 6,249	

number of years of LIFO use increases, beginning inventory for each year will consist of more layers from prior years' additions to inventory. The normal LIFO cost flow assumption would apply to liquidation of any layers that are included in beginning inventory for each year.

THE DOLLAR-VALUE RETAIL LIFO METHOD

In illustrating retail LIFO (Exhibit 10–13), we assumed that the *same* retail price level existed for (1) beginning inventory, (2) net purchases for the period, and (3) ending inventory. That is, in Exhibit 10–13 we assumed that the selling prices associated with (1) the $8,000 retail beginning inventory, (2) the $43,800 net purchases (adjusted for net markups and net markdowns), and (3) the $8,300 retail ending inventory were the same. Thus, the increase of $300 in inventory at retail prices represents the selling prices of *additional* merchandise on hand at the end of year 2, rather than selling price increases.

Suppose that instead of a constant selling price, the retail selling price had changed during year 2. For example, assume that as a result of inflation, the retail price level for a company's goods rose 3 percent in year 2. This would mean that, as measured by retail prices, the dollar amount of ending inventory could be 3 percent more than the dollar amount of beginning inventory simply as a result of the change in the retail price level, without any *real* increase in the physical level of inventory. If this were the case, the cost of the ending inventory under LIFO would be the same as the cost of the beginning inventory. In the case of the Mitchell Corporation data in Exhibit 10–13, assumption of a 3 percent increase in the retail price level during year 2 would mean that the $8,300 retail ending inventory amount would have to be deflated by the 3 percent increase in retail price level before it could be compared to beginning inventory, at retail, to compute the increase or decrease in inventory at retail for year 2.

Deflating the year-end dollar amounts for inventory to reflect changes in price levels was discussed in Chapter 9. The dollar-value LIFO method was discussed as a technique for adjusting the dollar amount of inventory *cost* for changes in the inventory cost index (or cost price level), so that calculated changes in total inventory on a *cost* basis from period to period would be the result of increases or decreases in the physical level of inventory and not merely the result of changes in costs.

When the retail price level changes during an accounting period, a dollar-value LIFO adjustment to *retail* prices should be used in conjunction with the retail LIFO method. This combination of the retail LIFO method and a dollar-value LIFO adjustment for unstable retail prices is known as the **dollar-value retail LIFO method.**

The effect of a changing retail price level and of the appropriate dollar-value adjustments on retail LIFO calculations can be seen if we add two assumptions to the data in Exhibit 10–13. First, assume that the beginning inventory for year 2 is the base inventory for dollar-value LIFO purposes. Second, assume that during year 2 the retail price level increased by 3 percent, causing the retail price index to rise from 1.00 to 1.03. Given these additional assumptions, the dollar-value retail LIFO method is applied to the Mitchell Corporation data for year 2 in Exhibit 10–14.

Notice that the top part of Exhibit 10–14 is the same as Exhibit 10–13. The only difference between Exhibit 10–14 (dollar-value retail LIFO) and Exhibit 10–13 (retail LIFO) is that when dollar-value retail LIFO is used, the ending inventory at current retail prices ($8,300) is adjusted to base retail prices ($8,058) before it is compared with beginning retail at base retail prices. The result is that in Exhibit 10–14 the increase in inventory measured in retail prices is $58 at base retail value, or $60 at current retail value. Once the increase of $60 at current retail value is determined, it is adjusted to a cost basis by being multiplied by the current year's cost to retail percentage of 83 percent. This percentage, as well as the cost to retail percentage for beginning inventory, is the same as in Exhibit 10–13.

In review, the principal steps of the dollar-value retail LIFO method are as follows:

EXHIBIT 10–14 DOLLAR-VALUE RETAIL LIFO

Mitchell Corporation

	COST	RETAIL
Beginning inventory (cost to retail percentage = 75%)	$ 6,000	$ 8,000
Net purchases $35,200		$43,800
Freight in 2,000		
Net markups		3,000
Net markdowns.........................		(1,800)
	37,200	45,000
Cost to retail percentage, excluding beginning inventory:		
$\dfrac{\$37,200}{\$45,000} = 83\%$		
Goods available for sale	$43,200	$53,000
Net sales		(44,700)
Ending inventory at current retail prices (retail price index = 1.03)		$ 8,300
Ending inventory at retail base prices ($8,300 ÷ 1.03)		$ 8,058
Beginning inventory at retail base prices...............................		(8,000)
Real increase in inventory at retail base prices		$ 58
Real increase in inventory stated in terms of current retail prices ($58 × 1.03)		$ 60
Real increase in inventory stated in terms of current period cost ($60 × 83%)	$ 50	83%
Beginning inventory at cost ($8,000 × 75%)	6,000	
Ending inventory at dollar-value retail LIFO cost	$ 6,050	

1. The cost to retail percentages for beginning inventory and net purchases are calculated by means of the LIFO cost variation of the retail inventory method. In addition, the ending inventory at current retail prices is calculated in accordance with the retail inventory method (Exhibit 10–13 or the top part of Exhibit 10–14).

2. The ending inventory at current retail prices is adjusted to base-year retail prices by means of the current year's retail price index (Exhibit 10–14).

3. The current ending inventory expressed in base-year retail prices (from Step 2) is compared with the current beginning inventory expressed in base-year retail prices to determine the increase or decrease in inventory during the current year expressed in base-year retail prices ($58 in Exhibit 10–14).

4. If an increase is found in Step 3 (as was the case in Exhibit 10–14), the increase is restated in terms of current retail prices by being multiplied by the current year's retail price index. (This restatement yielded $60 in Exhibit 10–14.) If a decrease is found, it is restated in terms of the retail price indexes for the years in which the layers now sold were originally added.

5. Once the increase or decrease has been restated in terms of the appropriate retail price level, the increase or decrease is adjusted to a cost basis by being multiplied by the cost to retail percentage or percentages associated with the increase or decrease. (This calculation yielded $50 in Exhibit 10–14.)

6. The increase (decrease) on a cost basis is added to (deducted from) beginning inventory on a cost basis to yield the ending inventory on a cost basis. (This result was $6,050 in Exhibit 10–14.) The amount calculated in Step 6 is the dollar-value retail LIFO inventory cost figure that would be reported in the current year's financial statements.

If the basic concepts of both the retail LIFO variation and dollar-value LIFO are well understood, dollar-value retail LIFO is not difficult to grasp because it is essentially a combination of retail LIFO and dollar-value LIFO, in which the price index used is for *retail* selling prices. A retail price index must be used because the retail method initially determines ending inventory in terms of retail prices.

As an additional aid to a clear understanding of the dollar-value retail LIFO method, the necessary data for the Mitchell Corporation for years 3 and 4 are added to the data for year 2 in Exhibit 10–15, and are used in Exhibit 10–16 to demonstrate use of the dollar-value retail LIFO method over a three-year period.

EXHIBIT 10–15   COST AND RETAIL DATA FOR YEARS 2–4

MITCHELL CORPORATION

	YEAR 2		YEAR 3		YEAR 4	
	COST	RETAIL	COST	RETAIL	COST	RETAIL
Beginning inventory*	$ 6,000	$ 8,000				
Net purchases	35,200	43,800	$37,500	$45,000	$39,000	$50,000
Freight in	2,000		3,000		3,000	
Net markups		3,000		4,000		3,000
Net markdowns		1,800		2,000		2,000
Net sales		44,700		45,060		50,740

Retail selling price indexes:

1/1, year 2	1.00
12/31, year 2	1.03
12/31, year 3	1.12
12/31, year 4	1.19

* It is assumed that dollar-value retail LIFO was adopted at the beginning of year 2, so that the year 2 beginning inventory is the base inventory and the retail selling price index at January 1, year 2, is the base-year index.

EXHIBIT 10-16 DOLLAR-VALUE RETAIL LIFO METHOD

MITCHELL CORPORATION

	YEAR 2		YEAR 3		YEAR 4	
	COST	RETAIL	COST	RETAIL	COST	RETAIL
Beginning inventory	$ 6,000	$ 8,000¹ →	$ 6,050 →	$ 8,300 →	$ 7,095	→ $10,240
Net purchases	$35,200	$43,800	$37,500	$45,000	$39,000	$50,000
Freight in	2,000		3,000		3,000	
Net markups		3,000		4,000		3,000
Net markdowns		(1,800)		(2,000)		(2,000)
	37,200	45,000²	40,500	47,000³	42,000	51,000⁴
Goods available for sale	$43,200	$53,000	$46,550	$55,300	$49,095	$61,240
Net sales		(44,700)		(45,060)		(50,740)
Ending inventory at current retail		$ 8,300 →		$10,240 →		$10,500
Ending inventory at base retail prices:						
12/31/year 2 ($8,300 ÷ 1.03)		$ 8,058				
12/31/year 3 ($10,240 ÷ 1.12)				$ 9,143		
12/31/year 4 ($10,500 ÷ 1.19)						$ 8,824
Beginning inventory at base retail prices:						
1/1/year 2		(8,000)				
1/1/year 3				(8,058)		
1/1/year 4						(9,143)
Real increase (decrease) in inventory in terms of base retail prices		$ 58		$ 1,085		$ (319)
Real increase (decrease) in inventory in terms of relevant retail prices:						
Year 2 ($58 × 1.03)		$ 60				
Year 3 ($1,085 × 1.12)				$ 1,215		
Year 4 [($319) × 1.12]						$ (357)
Real increase (decrease) in inventory in terms of relevant current cost:						
Year 2 ($60 × 83%)	$ 50		$ 50		$ 50	
Year 3 ($1,215 × 86%)			1,045		1,045	
Year 4 [($357) × 86%]					(307)	
Base inventory	6,000		6,000		6,000	
Ending inventory at cost	$ 6,050		$ 7,095		$ 6,788	

(circled percentages: Year 2 = 83%, Year 3 = 86%, Year 4 = 86%)

¹ Cost to retail percentage for base inventory is 75%.
² Cost to retail percentage for year 2 is 83%.
³ Cost to retail percentage for year 3 is 86%.
⁴ Cost to retail percentage for year 4 is 82%.

In studying Exhibit 10–16, you should note the following:

1. The base inventory, as well as each year's purchases (adjusted for freight, net mark-ups, and net markdowns), has its own cost to retail percentage.

2. Ending inventory expressed in current retail prices for each year is deflated to base retail prices by means of the retail price index for that particular year.

3. The retail price increase or decrease for each year is restated in terms of relevant retail prices by means of the retail price index of the current year for an increase, and the price indexes of the appropriate prior years for a decrease. The appropriate years are determined by the layers sold as a result of the decrease.

4. The relevant cost associated with each increase or decrease is determined by means of the cost to retail percentage that is related to the layer added (in the case of an increase) or deducted (in the case of a decrease). In year 4, for example, Mitchell had a decrease of $357 at retail from the year 3 layer, and the year 3 cost to retail percentage of 86 percent was used to calculate the $307 cost decrease.

5. The cost and retail ending inventories for each year become the cost and retail beginning inventories for the next year.

6. The ending inventory at cost computed for each year is the ending inventory amount that would be reported in the financial statements for that year under dollar-value retail LIFO.

SUMMARY OF IMPORTANT TOPICS AND CONCEPT APPLICATIONS

1. Inventory should be valued at the **lower of cost or market (LCM)** when physical deterioration, obsolescence, a change in price level, or any other event causes the value of inventory to fall below its cost. The ''market'' in LCM is replacement cost, although it cannot be greater than net realizable value or less than net realizable value minus a normal profit margin.

2. The purpose of the ceiling and floor constraints on the use of replacement cost as ''market'' is to avoid the use of replacement cost when the normal gross profit relationship between replacement cost and selling price does not exist.

3. The LCM method can be applied to individual inventory items, to groups of similar inventory items, or to total inventory.

4. The LCM method provides an excellent example of **conservatism** because if market is below cost, the value of inventory is reduced to ''market,'' and this new, lower inventory value is considered to be cost for the next period's LCM test.

5. Reduction of inventory to ''market'' can be accomplished by (1) directly reducing inventory to ''market,'' with a corresponding increase in cost of goods sold, or (2) adjusting reported inventory by using an allowance account, with a corresponding debit to an inventory holding loss account.

6. Noncancelable purchase commitments, along with other purchase commitments under which performance is probable because of large disincentives for nonper-formance, are called **firm purchase commitments.** Goods contracted for under a firm purchase commitment should be accounted for by LCM.

7. The **gross profit method** can be used to estimate inventory costs. In such cases, it is essential to have a reasonable estimate of the historical relationship between gross profit and selling price.

8. Like the gross profit method, the **retail inventory method** can be used to estimate the dollar amount of ending inventory. Whereas the gross profit method relies on past relationships between cost and selling price to determine the gross profit percentage, the retail inventory method uses the current relationship between cost and selling price to estimate inventory.

9. There are several variations of the retail inventory method, including average cost, lower of cost or market (the conventional retail method), FIFO, and LIFO. Each variation differs from the others with respect to the components included in the calculation of the cost to retail percentage.

10. When the retail price level changes during an accounting period, a dollar-value LIFO adjustment to retail prices should be used in conjunction with the retail LIFO method. This combination of the retail LIFO method and a dollar-value LIFO adjustment for unstable retail prices is known as the **dollar-value retail LIFO method.**

QUESTIONS

Q10-1. Define replacement cost and net realizable value as they pertain to inventory.

Q10-2. Define cost and market as these terms are used in lower-of-cost-or-market inventory accounting.

Q10-3. Why is net realizable value an appropriate upper constraint, or ceiling, on market in lower-of-cost-or-market valuation of inventory?

Q10-4. Why is net realizable value less a normal profit margin an appropriate lower constraint, or floor, on market in lower-of-cost-or-market valuation of inventory?

Q10-5. Lower-of-cost-or-market can be applied to individual inventory items, to groups of inventory items, or to total inventory. Which level of application would you expect to yield the highest inventory value? Why?

Q10-6. Direct adjustment of the inventory account and use of a contra-inventory allowance account are two ways to record and report that market is below cost when lower-of-cost-or-market inventory valuation is used. Describe how these two approaches differ with respect to recording and reporting the inventory holding loss that arises when inventory market is below cost.

Q10-7. In what ways is indirect adjustment of inventory (the allowance approach) preferable to direct adjustment of inventory when market is below cost and the LCM method is used?

Q10-8. What is the proper treatment in interim financial statements of an inventory holding loss arising when lower of cost or market is used to value inventory?

Q10-9. What is a firm purchase commitment? Why might a business enter into a firm purchase commitment?

Q10-10. Under GAAP, what is the general accounting treatment for goods contracted for in a firm purchase commitment?

Q10-11. What does it mean to hedge against the possibility of market price movements of goods included in a firm purchase commitment? How can the buyer in a firm purchase commitment hedge against the purchase commitment?

Q10-12. According to *FASB Statement No. 80,* when should a change in market value of a futures contract be recognized if that contract is a hedge against a firm purchase commitment?

Q10-13. Give some examples of situations in which it might be necessary to estimate the dollar amount of ending inventory.

Q10-14. What is the key variable that must be estimated in order to use the gross profit method of estimating inventory cost? Describe the basic steps of the gross profit method.

Q10-15. When the gross profit method of estimating inventory cost is used, available information sometimes includes gross profit as a percentage of cost. In this case, it is necessary to restate gross profit as a percentage of sales. How would you make this restatement?

Q10-16. What are the comparative advantages and disadvantages of the gross profit method and the retail inventory method of estimating ending inventory?

Q10-17. What data are required in order to use the retail inventory method in its simplest form?

Q10-18. Provide examples of what is meant by the following retail inventory method terminology: original markup, markup, markdown, markup cancellation, markdown cancellation, net markup, net markdown.

Q10-19. Explain how and why purchase returns and purchase allowances should be incorporated in retail inventory calculations.

Q10-20. Explain how and why normal and abnormal spoilage should be incorporated in retail inventory calculations.

Q10-21. Distinguish among the computational procedures of the average cost, lower-of-cost-or-market, FIFO, and LIFO variations of the retail inventory method.

Q10-22. Describe the computational procedure for the conventional retail method.

Q10-23. What inventory estimation method would be used if a company chose to use the retail inventory method on a LIFO basis to estimate inventory during a period of changing retail price levels?

Q10-24. What are the principal steps of the dollar-value retail LIFO method?

CASES

C10-1. REPLACEMENT COST AND NET REALIZABLE VALUE The senior vice-president of your company has just attended a seminar on current value accounting at a nearby university. During the seminar, replacement cost and net realizable value were mentioned as types of current value. The senior vice-president is very interested in these concepts, particularly as they might relate to accounting for your company's inventories. The discussion at the seminar, however, left him confused about the nature of replacement cost and net realizable value and their possible applications to inventory accounting.

REQUIRED

Draft a detailed explanation of the meaning of and possible applications of *(a)* replacement cost and *(b)* net realizable value in accounting for inventory.

C10-2. LOWER OF COST OR MARKET Accountants generally follow the lower-of-cost-or-market basis of inventory valuation.

REQUIRED

    1. Define ''cost'' as applied to the valuation of inventories.

    2. Define ''market'' as applied to the valuation of inventories.

    3. Why are inventories valued at the lower of cost or market? Discuss.

    4. List arguments against using the lower-of-cost-or-market method of valuing inventories.
(AICPA, adapted)

C10-3. LOWER OF COST OR MARKET When lower of cost or market is used to value inventories, net realizable value and the normal profit margin play important roles in the calculation of an upper limit (''ceiling'') and a lower limit (''floor'') on the dollar amount of ''market.''

REQUIRED

Assume that you are teaching an accounting class about lower of cost or market applied to inventories, and in the process must explain the underlying logic of the ceiling and the floor. Draft such an explanation and precede your explanation with definitions of both the ceiling and the floor.

C10-4. LOWER OF COST OR MARKET   Lower of cost or market, as applied to inventory, often is mentioned as an example of the impact of conservatism on accounting principles and standards.

REQUIRED

1. Explain why lower of cost or market exemplifies conservatism.

2. Explain why some accountants might argue that it is incorrect to describe lower of cost or market as conservative.

C10-5. FIRM PURCHASE COMMITMENTS   Susan Dale, the vice-president of marketing for your company, is seriously considering a new policy of entering into firm purchase commitments for inventory items as a way of coping with a seemingly endless series of inventory market price increases over the past three years. While recent market prices have only increased, Vice-President Dale is concerned with the ''downside risk'' of market price decreases. She has come to you to learn about the accounting implications of market price decreases when a firm purchase commitment exists.

REQUIRED

1. Discuss the application of the LCM procedure to goods contracted for under firm purchase commitments. Include in your discussion commitments that are both made and executed within one of the buyer's fiscal years and commitments that extend beyond the end of the buyer's fiscal year. Discuss also the impact of additional market price changes between the end of the fiscal year in which the buyer makes the commitment and the time the commitment is met in a subsequent fiscal year. It might be useful to include illustrative journal entries in your discussion.

2. Describe the concept of hedging to Vice-President Dale, indicating how hedging might be accomplished with respect to a firm purchase commitment and briefly commenting on how hedging might reduce the adverse accounting impact of market price decreases when a firm purchase commitment exists.

C10-6. RETAIL INVENTORY METHOD   The Dobson Paint Company, your client, manufactures paint. The company's president, Bill Dobson, has decided to open a retail store to sell Dobson Paint, and also wallpaper and other supplies that he would purchase from other companies. He has asked you for information about the retail method of pricing inventories at the retail store.

REQUIRED

Prepare a report to the president explaining the retail method of pricing inventories. Your report should include the following points:

1. Description and accounting features of the retail method.

2. The conditions that may distort the results under the retail method.

3. The advantages of using the retail method as compared to cost methods of inventory pricing.

4. The accounting theory underlying the treatment of net markdowns and net markups under the retail method.

(AICPA, adapted)

C10-7. RETAIL INVENTORY METHOD   When the retail inventory method is used, markups, markdowns, markup cancellations, and markdown cancellations all must be considered when inventory calculations are made. In addition, several other factors can complicate retail inventory calculations, including freight in, purchase returns, purchase allowances, sales returns, sales allowances, purchase discounts taken, employee discounts, normal spoilage, and abnormal spoilage.

REQUIRED

Explain the proper treatment of each of the complicating factors mentioned above when retail inventory calculations are made.

C10-8. DOLLAR-VALUE RETAIL LIFO   One of your client companies has used the retail inventory method for several years. After reviewing their inventory accounting records and considering the retail price movements of their inventory items, you have concluded that retail prices have been changing enough from year to year to justify the use of dollar-value retail LIFO.

REQUIRED

Prepare a written description of the dollar-value retail LIFO method for your client. You should include the motivation for using dollar-value retail LIFO during periods of changing retail prices and outline the principal steps of the dollar-value retail LIFO method.

EXERCISES

E10-1. LOWER OF COST OR MARKET   Mason Corporation has two products in its ending inventory, each accounted for at lower of cost or market. A profit margin of 30 percent of selling price is considered normal for each product. Specific data with respect to each product follow:

	PRODUCT 1	PRODUCT 2
Historical cost	$17	$ 45
Replacement cost	15	46
Estimated cost to dispose	5	26
Estimated selling price	30	100

REQUIRED

If Mason values its ending inventory by the lower-of-cost-or-market method, what unit values should be used for products 1 and 2, respectively?

(AICPA, adapted)

E10-2. LOWER OF COST OR MARKET   Stanton Company uses the lower-of-cost-or-market method of valuing its inventory. Data for four of its inventory items are:

ITEM	COST	CURRENT REPLACEMENT COST	EXPECTED SELLING PRICE	EXPECTED COST TO COMPLETE AND DISPOSE	NORMAL PROFIT MARGIN (PERCENT OF SELLING PRICE)
1	$25	$23	$30	$3.00	10%
2	32	28	35	2.00	20
3	17	21	22	5.50	5
4	41	46	48	4.00	8

REQUIRED

Calculate unit inventory values for items 1 through 4. As part of your answer, clearly indicate the "ceiling" and "floor" used in determining "market" for each inventory item.

E10-3. LOWER OF COST OR MARKET   The following inventory data are available for Mohr Corporation:

INVENTORY ITEM	COST	CURRENT REPLACEMENT COST	CURRENT SELLING PRICE	COST OF COMPLETION AND DISPOSAL	NORMAL PROFIT MARGIN
A	$1.00	$1.05	$1.10	$-0-	$.05
B	1.50	1.40	1.80	.20	.10
C	2.20	2.50	3.00	.60	.20
D	1.80	1.90	2.00	.25	.10
E	2.40	2.00	2.60	.20	.50

REQUIRED

Using the lower-of-cost-or-market method, calculate the dollar amount of inventory:

1. On an individual item basis.

2. On a group basis, assuming group 1 consists of items *A* and *B*, and group 2 consists of items *C*, *D*, and *E*.

3. On the basis of total inventory.

E10-4. LOWER OF COST OR MARKET Fallon Company has six inventory items, data for which are:

ITEM	COST	CURRENT REPLACEMENT COST	EXPECTED SELLING PRICE	EXPECTED COST TO COMPLETE AND DISPOSE	NORMAL PROFIT MARGIN (PERCENT OF COST)
1	$75.00	$75.00	$80.00	$6.00	5%
2	84.00	85.00	90.00	4.00	5
3	61.00	59.00	70.00	3.00	8
4	68.00	71.00	74.50	2.50	4
5	81.00	80.00	87.00	5.00	10
6	76.00	74.00	81.00	.75	7

REQUIRED

Using the lower-of-cost-or-market method, calculate the dollar amount of inventory:

1. On an individual item basis.

2. On a group basis, assuming group 1 consists of items 2, 5, and 6 and group 2 consists of items 1, 3, and 4.

3. On the basis of total inventory.

E10-5. RECORDING MARKET BELOW COST Assume the following inventory data for the first three years of operation of Gibson Company. Use net purchases from Exercise 10-6.

DATE	COST	MARKET
12/31, year 1	$100,000	$ 98,000
12/31, year 2	125,000	126,000
12/31, year 3	130,000	135,000

REQUIRED

1. Assuming that Gibson Company has a *perpetual* inventory system, record the fact, when it is a fact, that market is below cost, by:
  a) Direct adjustment of the inventory account.
  b) Indirect adjustment of the inventory account by use of an allowance account.

2. Assuming that Gibson Company has a *periodic* inventory system, record the fact, when it is a fact, that market is below cost, by:
  a) Direct adjustment of the inventory account.
  b) Indirect adjustment of the inventory account by use of an allowance account.

E10-6. REPORTING MARKET BELOW COST IN THE FINANCIAL STATEMENTS Given the following additional information for Gibson Company (see Exercise 10-5):

	YEAR 1	YEAR 2	YEAR 3
Net sales	$200,000	$210,000	$225,000
Net purchases	210,000	230,000	240,000
Expenses	43,000	48,000	50,000

Follow the formats of Exhibits 10–6 and 10–7 and use the results obtained in Exercise 10-5 to prepare partial balance sheets and income statements for years 1, 2, and 3 under:

1. The direct adjustment approach of recording market below cost.

2. The indirect adjustment approach of recording market below cost.

E10-7. LOSS ON FIRM PURCHASE COMMITMENT On November 15, 1987, Reilly Company signed a noncancelable contract to purchase 10,000 units of inventory at $5 per unit in six months. On December 31, 1987, the end of Reilly's fiscal year, the same units of inventory could be bought in the open market at $4.80 per unit. By the end of the first quarter of 1988, the open market price per unit of inventory had risen to $5.25.

REQUIRED

Assuming that on December 31, 1987, the open market price appeared to be a reasonable estimate of the open market price that would exist at the time the contract was fulfilled, how should the facts related to this firm purchase commitment be accounted for:

1. At December 31, 1987?

2. At the end of the first quarter of 1988?

E10-8. FIRM PURCHASE COMMITMENT On June 10, 1987, Brink Corporation entered into a noncancelable purchase contract specifying the purchase of 8,000 units of inventory for $4.50 per unit. Brink has a December 31 fiscal year-end. In addition, the following price information is available:

DATE	MARKET PRICE OF GOODS
August 31, 1987	$4.00
September 27, 1987	4.25
November 30, 1987	4.40
December 31, 1987	4.45
January 31, 1988	5.00
February 20, 1988	4.35

REQUIRED

1. Assuming that the contract is executed with a cash purchase on September 27, 1987, what entries (if any) would Brink make on August 31 and September 27, 1987?

2. If the contract is executed on September 27 and the market price at that time is $4.75 rather than $4.25, what entry would Brink make to record the purchase?

3. If the contract is executed on February 20, 1988, with a cash payment, what entries (if any) would Brink make on November 18, 1987; on December 31, 1987; on January 31, 1988; and on February 20, 1988?

4. If the contract is executed on February 20, 1988, but the market price at that time is $4.50 instead of the $4.35 specified above, what entry would Brink make to record the cash purchase?

E10-9. GROSS PROFIT METHOD The following information is available for the Silver Company for the three months ended March 31, 1987:

Merchandise inventory, 1/1/87	$ 900,000
Purchases...	3,400,000
Freight in	200,000
Sales	4,800,000

The gross profit margin was 25 percent of sales.

REQUIRED

What is the cost of merchandise inventory at March 31, 1987?

(AICPA, adapted)

E10-10. GROSS PROFIT METHOD On January 1, 1987, the merchandise inventory of Martin Company was $300,000. During 1987 Martin purchased merchandise costing $1.9 million and recorded sales of $2 million. The gross profit, based on cost, was 25 percent.

REQUIRED

What is the cost of merchandise inventory of Martin at December 31, 1987?

(AICPA, adapted)

E10-11. GROSS PROFIT METHOD   On June 13, 1987, a fire destroyed the entire uninsured merchandise inventory of the Blane Merchandising Company. The following data are available:

Inventory, 1/1/87 .... $ 20,000
Purchases, 1/1/87–6/13/87 (including $20,000 of goods in transit
   on 6/13/87, shipped F.O.B. destination) 160,000
Sales, 1/1/87–6/13/87 194,000
Markup percentage on cost 25%

REQUIRED

Calculate the approximate inventory loss as a result of the fire.

(AICPA, adapted)

E10-12. GROSS PROFIT METHOD   On April 10, 1987, a flood destroyed the entire merchandise inventory on hand of Wilks Wholesale Company. The following information is available:

Sales, 1/1/87–4/10/87 .... $360,000
Inventory, 1/1/87 80,000
Freight in 10,000
Merchandise purchases, 1/1/87–4/10/87 (including $40,000 of goods
   in transit on 4/10, shipped F.O.B. shipping point) 340,000
Purchase returns 20,000

REQUIRED

1. Assuming that the markup percentage on cost is 20 percent, what is the estimated inventory on April 10, 1987, immediately before the flood?

2. Assuming that the gross profit is 30 percent of sales, what is the estimated inventory on April 10, 1987, immediately before the flood?

E10-13. AVERAGE COST; RETAIL INVENTORY METHOD   The Value Department Store uses the retail inventory method. Information related to the calculation of the inventory at December 31, 1987, is as follows:

	COST	RETAIL
Inventory, 1/1/87	$ 16,000	$ 40,000
Sales		290,000
Purchases	135,000	300,000
Freight in	3,800	
Net markups		20,000
Net markdowns		10,000

REQUIRED

What should be the ending inventory in terms of average cost at December 31, 1987, under the retail inventory method?

(AICPA, adapted)

E10-14. LOWER OF COST OR MARKET; RETAIL INVENTORY METHOD   The Klawse Department Store uses the retail inventory method to approximate the lower-of-cost-or-market value of inventory. The following information is available for the month of August 1987:

	COST	RETAIL
Goods available for sale	$180,000	$225,000*
Net markups		25,000
Net markdowns		10,000
Sales		170,000

* Before net markups and net markdowns.

REQUIRED

Using the retail inventory method, calculate the approximate value of inventory, in terms of lower of cost or market, at August 31, 1987.

(AICPA, adapted)

E10-15. LOWER OF COST OR MARKET; RETAIL INVENTORY METHOD   The Vistale Company values its inventory by the retail method (FIFO basis, lower of cost or market). The following information is available for the year 1987:

	COST	RETAIL
Beginning inventory	$ 80,000	$140,000
Purchases	297,000	420,000
Freight in	4,000	
Shortages		8,000
Markups (net)		10,000
Markdowns (net)		2,000
Sales		400,000

REQUIRED

What amount would the Vistale Company report for its ending inventory?

(AICPA, adapted)

E10-16. RETAIL INVENTORY METHOD   The True Sales Company uses the retail inventory method to value its merchandise inventory. The following information is available:

	COST	RETAIL
Beginning inventory	$ 40,000	$ 70,000
Purchases	290,000	400,000
Freight in	2,000	
Markups (net)		3,000
Markdowns (net)		5,000
Employee discounts		1,000
Sales		390,000

REQUIRED

1. Calculate the ending inventory at retail.

2. If the ending inventory is to be valued at the lower of cost or market, what is the cost to retail ratio?

3. If the ending inventory is valued on a LIFO basis, what is the current year's cost to retail ratio?

E10-17. RETAIL INVENTORY METHOD   The following data concerning the retail inventory method are taken from the financial records of the Farley Corporation:

	COST	RETAIL
Beginning inventory	$18,600	$ 30,000
Purchases	91,000	154,000
Freight in	1,400	
Net markups		1,000
Net markdowns		1,740
Sales		156,760

REQUIRED

1. What should be the ending inventory at retail?

2. If the ending inventory is to be valued at approximately the lower of cost or market, what dollar amounts of cost and retail would be used for goods available for sale in calculating the cost to retail percentage?

3. If the ending inventory for the current period at cost amounts to $15,900, how does the gross profit for the current year, as a percentage of sales, compare with the gross profit percentage of the preceding year?

4. If the LIFO inventory method were used, the retail inventory method would provide an estimate of ending inventory of how much?

E10-18. DOLLAR-VALUE RETAIL LIFO METHOD The Herndon Corporation uses the dollar-value retail LIFO method of inventory valuation. Current year inventory and price index data are:

	COST	RETAIL
Beginning inventory (cost to retail = 80%)	$400,000	$?
Net purchases	210,000	250,000
Net markups		13,000
Net markdowns		15,000
Net sales		230,000
Price index at beginning of year: 1.12		
Price index at end of year: 1.15		

REQUIRED

Calculate Herndon Corporation's ending inventory.

E10-19. DOLLAR-VALUE RETAIL LIFO METHOD The following information is available for the Bando Corporation, which uses the dollar-value retail LIFO method in valuing its inventory:

	COST	RETAIL
Beginning inventory	$ 70,000	$ 85,000
Net purchases	110,000	140,000
Freight in	6,000	
Net markups		8,000
Net markdowns		6,000
Net sales		136,000
Normal spoilage		2,000
Price index at beginning of year: 1.10		
Price index at end of year: 1.20		

REQUIRED

Calculate Bando Corporation's ending inventory.

E10-20. DOLLAR-VALUE RETAIL LIFO METHOD Devlin Company adopted the dollar-value retail LIFO inventory method on January 1, 1987. The following information is available for the Devlin Company:

	RETAIL PRICE INDEX	LIFO INVENTORY		COST TO RETAIL PERCENTAGE
		COST	RETAIL	
Inventory, 1/1/87	1.00	$17,000	$20,000	85%
Inventory, 12/31/87	1.12	?	33,000	87
Inventory, 12/31/88	1.23	?	36,000	83

REQUIRED

Using the dollar-value retail LIFO method, calculate the ending inventories on December 31, 1987, and December 31, 1988.

E10-21. DOLLAR-VALUE RETAIL LIFO METHOD   Lattor Corporation adopted the dollar-value retail LIFO method of inventory valuation at the beginning of 1987, at which time the retail price index was 1.05. In addition, the following information is available for Lattor Corporation.

	LIFO INVENTORY		COST TO RETAIL PERCENTAGE	RETAIL PRICE INDEX
	COST	RETAIL		
Inventory, 1/1/87	$18,000	$21,000	?	
Inventory, 12/31/87	?	27,000	91%	1.09
Net purchases, 1988.....	31,000	34,000		
Net markups, 1988......		400		
Net sales, 1988.........		33,500		
Inventory, 12/31/88	?	?		1.12

REQUIRED

Using the dollar-value retail LIFO method, calculate the inventory costs on December 31, 1987, and December 31, 1988.

PROBLEMS

P10-1. LOWER OF COST OR MARKET   Johnson Distributing Company has a perpetual inventory system and uses the lower-of-cost-or-market method of valuing its inventories. The following information is available from the inventory records as of December 31, 1987:

INVENTORY ITEM	NUMBER OF UNITS	UNIT COST	CURRENT REPLACEMENT COST PER UNIT	ESTIMATED SELLING PRICE	UNIT COST TO COMPLETE	NORMAL UNIT PROFIT
A	300	$2.00	$2.50	$3.00	$.25	$1.00
B	500	2.50	3.00	2.75	.15	.50
C	150	5.00	4.80	6.00	.20	1.20
D	450	3.50	3.25	4.50	.40	.75
E	280	2.40	2.40	4.00	.30	.80
F	375	4.30	4.20	4.60	.50	1.25

REQUIRED

1. Calculate the ending inventory on December 31, 1987, using lower of cost or market applied on an individual item basis.

2. If you find that market is below cost in part 1, make the appropriate journal entry to record this fact, assuming:
   a) Direct reduction of the inventory account.
   b) Use of a contra-inventory allowance account.

3. Calculate the ending inventory on December 31, 1987, on a group basis, treating inventory items A, B, and C as Group 1 and items D, E, and F as Group 2.

4. Why might lower of cost or market yield a higher inventory value when applied to groups than when applied to individual items?

P10-2. LOWER OF COST OR MARKET   The Shaner Company manufactures and sells four products. Its inventories are priced at cost or market, whichever is lower. A normal profit margin rate of 30 percent of selling price is maintained on each of the four products.
   The following information was compiled as of December 31, 1987:

PRODUCT	ORIGINAL COST	COST TO REPLACE	ESTIMATED COST TO DISPOSE	EXPECTED SELLING PRICE
A	$35.00	$42.00	$15.00	$ 80.00
B	47.50	45.00	20.50	95.00
C	17.50	15.00	5.00	30.00
D	45.00	46.00	26.00	100.00

REQUIRED

1. Why are expected selling prices important in the application of the lower-of-cost-or-market method?

2. Prepare a schedule containing unit values (including floor and ceiling) for determining the lower-of-cost-or-market value of each of the four products. The last column of the schedule should contain the unit value of each product for the purpose of inventory valuation resulting from the application of the lower-of-cost-or-market method.

3. What effects, if any, do the expected selling prices have on the valuation of products *A, B, C,* and *D* by the lower-of-cost-or-market method?

(AICPA, adapted)

P10-3. LOWER OF COST OR MARKET The Palin Corporation sells a single product and uses the lower-of-cost-or-market inventory method. Application of this method for 1987 and 1988 yielded the following:

	COST	MARKET
1/1/87	$20,000	$20,000
12/31/87	31,000	29,000
12/31/88	30,000	29,000

REQUIRED

1. Assuming Palin has a perpetual inventory system, make the necessary journal entries for 1987 and 1988 to record market value below cost, using:
  a) Direct adjustment of the inventory account.
  b) Indirect adjustment of inventory with an allowance account.

2. Assuming Palin has a periodic inventory system, make the necessary journal entries for 1987 and 1988 to record market value below cost, using:
  a) Direct adjustment of the inventory account.
  b) Indirect adjustment of inventory with an allowance account.

3. Compare and contrast the direct method and the allowance method of accounting for market value below cost with respect to reporting in the financial statements.

P10-4. GROSS PROFIT METHOD On November 21, 1987, a fire at Hanson Company's warehouse caused severe damage to its entire inventory. Hanson estimates that all usable damaged goods can be sold for $8,000. The following information is available from Hanson's accounting records for inventory:

Inventory cost, 11/1/87	$ 80,000
Purchases, 11/1/87–11/21/87	140,000
Net sales, 11/1/87–11/21/87	210,000

In recent periods Hanson had a gross profit margin of 30 percent of net sales.

REQUIRED

1. Prepare a schedule to calculate the estimated loss on the inventory in the fire, using the gross profit method. Show supporting calculations in good form.

2. Discuss the weaknesses of the gross profit method.

(AICPA, adapted)

P10-5. ESTIMATING INVENTORY BY THE GROSS PROFIT METHOD The Cedar Mall housed the premises of the Home Hardware Company. On the morning of November 1, 1987, fire gutted the hardware store and some of the other tenants. Home Hardware had been a popular store and had consistently earned a gross profit equal to about two-thirds of cost.

Appropriate data covering the period from January 1, 1987, until the date of the fire are as follows:

Sales	$1,220,000
Purchases..	700,000
Purchase returns	20,000
Sales returns	16,000
Delivery expense	30,000
Freight in	12,000
Administrative expenses...................................	8,000
Inventory, 1/1/87	100,000
Advertising expense	20,250
Salesmen's salaries.......................................	85,500
Sales discounts	4,000

REQUIRED

Prepare a schedule and calculate Home Hardware's estimated inventory on November 1, 1987.

(CGAA, adapted)

P10-6. ESTIMATING INVENTORY BY THE GROSS PROFIT METHOD On June 30, 1987, a flash flood damaged the warehouse and factory of Flaxon Corporation, completely destroying the work-in-process inventory. There was no damage to either the raw materials or finished goods inventories. A physical inventory count taken after the flood revealed the following valuations:

Raw materials	$ 62,000
Work in process	–0–
Finished goods	119,000

The inventory on January 1, 1987, consisted of the following:

Raw materials	$ 30,000
Work in process	100,000
Finished goods	140,000
	$270,000

A review of the books and records disclosed that the gross profit margin historically approximated 25 percent of sales. The sales for the first six months of 1987 were $340,000. Raw material purchases were $115,000. Direct labor costs for this period were $80,000, and manufacturing overhead historically has been applied at 50 percent of direct labor.

REQUIRED

Calculate the value of the work-in-process inventory lost at June 30, 1987. Show supporting calculations in good form.

(AICPA, adapted)

P10-7. GROSS PROFIT RATIO AND GROSS PROFIT METHOD The Bradshaw Corporation is an importer and wholesaler. Its merchandise is purchased from a number of suppliers and is warehoused by Bradshaw until it is sold to consumers.

In conducting his audit for the year ended June 30, 1987, the company's CPA determined that the system of internal control was good. Accordingly, he observed the physical inventory at an interim date, May 31, 1987, instead of at the end of the year.

The following information was obtained from the general ledger:

Inventory, 7/1/86	$ 87,500
Physical inventory, 5/31/87...	95,000
Sales for eleven months ended 5/31/87	840,000
Sales for year ended 6/30/87......................................	960,000
Purchases for eleven months ended 5/31/87 (before audit adjustments)	675,000
Purchases for year ended 6/30/87 (before audit adjustments).............	800,000

The CPA's audit disclosed the following information:

Shipments received in May and included in the physical
    inventory but recorded as June purchases . . . . $ 7,500
Shipments received in unsalable condition and excluded from
    physical inventory; credit memos not received and
    charge-backs to vendors not recorded
    Total at 5/31/87 1,000
    Total at 6/30/87 (including the May unrecorded charge-backs) 1,500
Deposit made with vendor and charged to purchases in April
    1987; product shipped in July 1987 2,000
Deposit made with vendor and charged to purchases in
    May 1987; product shipped F.O.B. destination 5/29/87
    and included in 5/31/87 physical inventory as goods
    in transit 5,500
Through carelessness of receiving department, June shipment
    damaged by rain; sold later in June at cost 10,000

REQUIRED

When interim physical inventory counts are made, a frequently used auditing procedure is to test the reasonableness of the year-end inventory by the application of gross profit ratios.

    Prepare in good form the following schedules:

1. Calculation of the gross profit ratio for the eleven months ended May 31, 1987.

2. Calculation by the gross profit method of cost of goods sold during June 1987.

3. Calculation by the gross profit method of June 30, 1987, inventory.

(AICPA, adapted)

P10-8. LOWER OF COST OR MARKET; RETAIL INVENTORY METHOD   The Medal Clothing Store values its inventory under the retail inventory method at the lower of cost or market. The following data are available for the month of November 1987:

	COST	SELLING PRICE
Inventory, 11/1/87	$ 53,800	$ 80,000
Markdowns		21,000
Markups		29,000
Markdown cancellations		13,000
Markup cancellations		9,000
Purchases	173,200	223,600
Sales		244,000
Purchase returns and allowances	3,000	3,600
Sales returns and allowances		12,000

REQUIRED

On the basis of the data presented above, prepare a schedule in good form to calculate the estimated inventory at November 30, 1987, at lower of cost or market under the retail inventory method.

(AICPA, adapted)

P10-9. LIFO AND FIFO; RETAIL INVENTORY METHOD   The Jacobson Variety Store uses the retail inventory method. Information related to the calculation of the inventory at December 31, 1987, follows:

	COST	RETAIL
Inventory, 1/1/87	$ 30,600	$ 45,000
Purchases..	120,000	172,000
Freight in	15,000	
Sales		190,000
Net markups		40,000
Net markdowns...................................		12,000

REQUIRED

1. Assuming that there was no change in the price index during the year, calculate the inventory at December 31, 1987, using the LIFO retail inventory method.

2. Assuming that there was no change in the price index during the year, calculate the inventory at December 31, 1987, using the FIFO retail inventory method.

(AICPA, adapted)

P10-10. THE CONVENTIONAL RETAIL METHOD   The Lewis Department Store, Inc., uses the conventional retail inventory method to estimate ending inventory for its monthly financial statements. The following data pertain to a single department for the month of October 1987.

Inventory, 10/1/87	
At cost...	$ 20,000
At retail	30,000
Purchases (exclusive of freight and returns):	
At cost...	100,151
At retail	146,495
Freight in	5,100
Purchase returns	
At cost...	2,100
At retail	2,800
Additional markups	2,500
Markup cancellations	265
Markdowns (net)	800
Normal spoilage and breakage	4,500
Sales	135,730

REQUIRED

1. Prepare a schedule to calculate estimated lower-of-cost-or-market inventory for October 31, 1987.

2. Lewis estimates the cost of the ending inventory of another department as $29,000. An accurate physical count reveals only $22,000 of inventory at lower of cost or market. List the factors that may have caused the difference between the estimated inventory and the physical count.

(AICPA, adapted)

P10-11. LOWER OF COST OR MARKET; RETAIL INVENTORY METHOD   The Zanon Department Store uses the retail inventory method. Information related to the calculation of its inventory at December 31, 1987, is as follows:

	COST	RETAIL
Inventory at 1/1/87................................	$ 32,000	$ 80,000
Sales		600,000
Purchases..	270,000	590,000
Freight in	7,600	
Markups		60,000
Markup cancellations		10,000
Markdowns		25,000
Markdown cancellations............................		5,000
Estimated normal spoilage: 2% of sales		

REQUIRED

1. Prepare a schedule to calculate the estimated ending inventory at the lower of average cost or market at December 31, 1987, using the retail inventory method. Show supporting calculations in good form.

2. What are some of the advantages of the retail inventory method?

(AICPA, adapted)

P10-12. RETAIL INVENTORY METHOD   The following data are available for the Rison Company for 1987:

Sales	$106,000
Sales returns	4,000
Markups	9,000
Markup cancellations	2,500
Markdowns	6,000
Markdown cancellations	1,500
Freight in	5,000
Purchases at cost	75,000
Purchases at retail	100,000
Purchase returns at cost	3,000
Purchase returns at retail	4,000
Beginning inventory at cost	10,000
Beginning inventory at retail	12,000
Employee discounts	3,000
Normal spoilage	1,000

REQUIRED

Using the retail inventory method, estimate ending inventory in terms of:

1. Average cost.

2. Lower of cost or market.

3. FIFO cost flow.

4. LIFO cost flow.

P10-13. LIFO RETAIL METHOD; DOLLAR-VALUE RETAIL LIFO METHOD   Under your guidance, on January 1, 1987, the Huntsman Sporting Goods Store installed the retail method of accounting for its merchandise inventory.

When you undertook the preparation of the store's financial statements at June 30, 1987, the following data were available:

	COST	SELLING PRICE
Inventory, 1/1/87	$26,900	$ 40,000
Markdowns		10,500
Markups		19,500
Markdown cancellations		6,500
Markup cancellations		4,500
Purchases	86,200	111,800
Sales		122,000
Purchase returns and allowances	1,500	1,800
Sales returns and allowances		6,000

REQUIRED

1. Prepare a schedule to calculate the Huntsman Sporting Goods Store's June 30, 1987, inventory under the retail method of accounting for inventories. The inventory is to be valued at cost under the LIFO method.

2. Without prejudice to your solution to part 1, assume that you calculated the June 30, 1987, inventory to be $44,100 at retail and the ratio of cost to retail to be 80 percent. The retail price level has increased from 100 at January 1 to 105 at June 30. Prepare a schedule to calculate the June 30, 1987, inventory at the June 30 price level under the dollar-value retail LIFO method.

(AICPA, adapted)

P10-14. DOLLAR-VALUE RETAIL LIFO METHOD   Accent Company began using the dollar-value retail LIFO method on January 1, 1987. Information related to inventory, purchases, sales, and retail price levels for 1987 and 1988 is as follows:

	1987		1988	
	COST	RETAIL	COST	RETAIL
Beginning inventory	$ 8,000	$10,000	$?	$?
Gross purchases	50,000	56,000	48,000	54,200
Freight in	4,000		3,000	
Purchase allowances	2,500		2,015	
Purchase returns	1,000	1,800	500	1,000
Purchase discounts	3,400		2,400	
Net markups		5,200		4,000
Net markdowns		3,100		2,800
Abnormal spoilage	300	400	100	300
Normal spoilage		600		500
Gross sales		53,500		53,100
Employee discounts		2,300		2,000
Sales returns		1,200		1,100
Sales allowances		1,800		1,700
Retail selling price indexes:				
1/1/87 .... 1.00				
12/31/87 .... 1.02				
12/31/88 .... 1.06				

REQUIRED

Prepare a schedule to calculate the costs of 1987 and 1988 ending inventories under the dollar-value retail LIFO method.

P10-15. CONVENTIONAL RETAIL; LIFO RETAIL; DOLLAR-VALUE RETAIL LIFO   Kelso Department Store converted from the conventional retail method to the LIFO retail method on January 1, 1988, and is now considering converting to the dollar-value retail LIFO inventory method. During your examination of the financial statements for the year ended December 31, 1989, management requested that you furnish a summary showing certain calculations of inventory costs for the past three years. Available information follows:

a) The inventory at January 1, 1987, had a retail value of $45,000 and a cost of $27,500 based on the conventional retail method.

b) Transactions during 1987 were as follows:

	COST	RETAIL
Gross purchases	$282,000	$490,000
Purchase returns	6,500	10,000
Purchase discounts	5,000	
Gross sales		492,000
Sales returns		5,000
Employee discounts		3,000
Freight in	26,500	
Net markups		25,000
Net markdowns		10,000

c) The retail value of the December 31, 1988, inventory was $56,100, the cost ratio for 1988 under the LIFO retail method was 62 percent, and the regional price index was 102 percent of the January 1, 1988, price level.

d) The retail value of the December 31, 1989, inventory was $48,300, the cost ratio for 1989 under the LIFO retail method was 61 percent, and the regional price index was 105 percent of the January 1, 1988, price level.

REQUIRED

1. Prepare a schedule showing the calculation of the cost of inventory on hand at December 31, 1987, based on the conventional retail method.

2. Prepare a schedule showing the calculation of the cost of inventory on hand at the store on December 31, 1987, based on the LIFO retail method. Kelso Department Store does not consider beginning inventories in calculating its LIFO retail cost ratio.

3. Without prejudice to your solution to part 2, assume that you calculated the December 31, 1987, inventory (retail value $50,000) under the LIFO retail method at a cost of $28,000. Prepare a schedule showing the calculations of the cost of the store's 1988 and 1989 year-end inventories under the dollar-value retail LIFO method.

(AICPA, adapted)

P10-16. DOLLAR-VALUE RETAIL LIFO METHOD Norton Corporation has just completed its third year of operations. When it began operations, it adopted the dollar-value retail LIFO method of inventory valuation. Inventory, purchases, sales, and retail price data for the three years Norton has been in existence are provided below.

| | YEAR 1 | | YEAR 2 | | YEAR 3 | |
	COST	RETAIL	COST	RETAIL	COST	RETAIL
Beginning inventory	$ 9,000	$12,000	$?	$?	$?	$?
Gross purchases	30,000	37,000	28,500	35,600	32,170	38,200
Purchase returns	800	1,000	620	1,050	1,012	1,300
Purchase discounts	1,400				800	
Net markdowns........		2,100		2,130		2,200
Net markups				380		600
Gross sales		33,500		38,300		35,400
Sales returns		1,300		1,600		500
Sales allowances		1,100		1,500		1,020

Retail selling price indexes:

1/1/year 1 .... 1.00
12/31/year 1 .... 1.04
12/31/year 2 .... 1.08
12/31/year 3 .... 1.10

REQUIRED

Prepare a schedule to calculate the costs of year 1, year 2, and year 3 ending inventories under the dollar-value retail LIFO method.

11 PLANT ASSETS: ACQUISITION AND DISPOSITION

In this chapter and the next we continue our analysis of accounting for assets by examining plant assets. First we present the financial accounting and reporting issues related to acquiring and disposing of plant assets. In Chapter 12 we describe accounting for and reporting of depreciation. The issues involved in accounting for intangible assets and natural resources, which tend to be quite similar to the issues involving plant assets, are discussed in Chapter 13.

CHARACTERISTICS OF PLANT ASSETS

Virtually all business firms acquire some physical resources, even if only a typewriter or a desk, which they expect to use in operations over an extended period of time. We commonly refer to these resources by one of three terms: *property, plant, and equipment; fixed assets;* or *plant assets.* We generally use the latter term in this text. **Plant assets** may be distinguished from other assets by the following characteristics:

1. *Plant assets are physical objects*. They can be seen and felt. You can stub your toe on them. Because they have a physical existence, we refer to them as tangible assets. In contrast, intangible resources, such as patents, copyrights, and goodwill, which are discussed in Chapter 13, have no physical substance.

2. *Plant assets are acquired to be used in operations*. The value of plant assets results from the services they provide, not from potential resale. A firm acquires plant assets for use in its operations; it considers selling the assets only after they have generated revenue for several periods through the firm's internal use. Assets that are idle, such as those whose service potential has been used up, are not considered to be plant assets for accounting purposes. Land that a firm buys for speculative purposes is another type of idle asset. The firm should classify the land as an investment rather than as a part of plant assets because it is not being used in operations. However, firms should classify land that is used in operations, such as the land on which factories, warehouses, or corporate offices are located, as a plant asset.

3. *Plant assets provide benefits over several accounting periods*. According to the matching principle, the cost of a resource that provides service potential only during the

period in which it is acquired should be expensed entirely in that period. Because plant assets provide benefits over several accounting periods, they are classified as noncurrent assets in the balance sheet.

Typical plant assets include buildings, improvements, machinery, furniture, tools, certain leased property, and leasehold improvements. The **service potential,** that is, the cash generating ability, for most plant assets decreases as they are used in producing revenues. Thus, firms must expense the cost of the service potential embodied in such assets, according to the matching principle, over the periods in which the service potential is consumed. We discuss the process of expensing the initial cost in Chapter 12.

In providing their service benefits, plant assets normally do not deteriorate to the point where they do not physically exist when their service potential has been consumed. In contrast, natural resources—also called wasting assets—such as standing timber and oil and gas reserves, are consumed physically as they are used in the production process. We refer to the process of using up wasting assets as **depletion.** Accounting for natural resources is discussed in Chapter 13.

When a firm receives service potential in the form of plant assets, it must record the plant assets in the accounts. In the next section we describe the guidelines for accounting for the acquisition of plant assets.

VALUATION OF PLANT ASSETS AT ACQUISITION

Plant assets, like other assets, are recorded in the accounts when an exchange transaction occurs, such as when a building is purchased. An entity also may receive service potential in the form of plant assets in the absence of such an exchange transaction, such as when an entity constructs its own plant assets or receives them through donations. In both of these cases, the entity receives service potential, and so an asset must be recorded.

Cost is usually the best estimate of fair market value.

When a firm acquires plant assets, cost usually is the best estimate of an asset's fair market value on the acquisition date. Thus, assets usually should be recorded initially at the cost incurred in a transaction actually entered into by the accounting entity. When a cost is not incurred at acquisition, such as when a firm issues shares of its stock to acquire a plant asset, the asset and the stock should be recorded at the fair market value of what is received or at the fair market value of what is given, whichever is more reasonably determinable. We often refer to this method of valuation as *historical cost* valuation. Keep in mind, however, that we record the asset at cost because, at the date an asset is acquired, cost is our best estimate of its fair market value.

Few accountants disagree with this valuation method *at acquisition*. Nevertheless, there is much disagreement on the appropriate valuation of plant assets after they are acquired. The greater the time that has passed since the acquisition date, the more likely it is that the asset's fair market value will differ from its acquisition cost. Under GAAP, plant assets are reported at depreciated historical cost subsequent to acquisition. But rapid and significant changes in replacement costs as well as in the value of the monetary unit have led the accounting profession to require additional disclosures. We describe these additional disclosures in Chapter 25.

Application of the historical cost principle to plant assets means that all necessary sacrifices made to obtain the asset's service potential and to place the asset in position for its intended use should be recorded in the asset account. This principle should sound familiar, since we discussed it in Chapter 2. Also, it is precisely the same guideline that we use to record inventory acquisitions, discussed in Chapter 9. We will look at how this principle is applied to each of the major types of plant assets.

LAND The cost of obtaining land and readying it for its intended use may include, in addition to the purchase price, closing costs (for example, attorney's fees incurred in connection with the purchase), survey costs, earth-moving costs, and unpaid taxes or mortgages assumed by the purchaser. The purchaser may incur some or all of these costs before the land is put into use to generate revenues. The purchase implies that the buyer believes that the service potential of the land is at least equal to the cost incurred. Thus, the buyer should record all costs incurred in an asset account.

The cost of land improvements that produce permanent benefits, such as landscaping, sewer installation, and special assessments by a government body for paving and street lights, may all be included in the land account. Because these improvements provide benefits indefinitely, depreciation is inappropriate. An outside agency replaces and maintains many such improvements.

On the other hand, the cost of improvements that provide benefits over limited periods, such as fences and parking lots, and those items listed above that are not maintained by an outside agency, should be recorded separately in a land improvements account. The firm then depreciates them over the expected benefit period.

Firms often acquire land with the objective of constructing on it a factory, office building, warehouse, or some other facility. In such circumstances, the firm should record all costs incurred up to the point where construction on the building begins as a part of the cost of the land, because the firm is incurring the costs to get the land ready for its intended use. If the firm must remove old structures, the cost of removing them, net of any salvage value, is a cost of the land. At first glance it may not seem to matter whether such costs are treated as a part of the land cost or as a cost of the building. When you consider, however, that we do not depreciate land but we do depreciate buildings, the importance of proper treatment of these costs becomes apparent.

Recall that a firm must use an asset in operations if it is to be classified as a plant asset. Thus, if a firm acquires land primarily for speculative purposes, even though management considers the possibility of ultimately constructing a plant there, the firm should classify that land as an investment rather than as a plant asset.

The treatment of taxes on land being held for speculation or for future use is subject to some debate. Theoretically, the entity would not incur costs, including taxes, unless it believed that the total service potential of the land was at least equal to the total of the costs incurred. Further, the firm generates no revenue from speculative land against which costs of taxes may be matched. Thus, capitalization (that is, recording as an asset) of taxes is appropriate in these circumstances, although many companies, as a matter of expediency, expense property taxes as they are incurred. In cases in which land generates revenues, the firm should expense the costs of maintaining the land, including periodic taxes, as they are incurred.

MACHINERY AND EQUIPMENT The basic cost of machinery and equipment usually is determined by the amount paid for an item. However, entities often sell machinery and equipment at a price that is subject to a cash discount for prompt payment. Thus, theoretically, the invoice price *net* of the cash discount is the cash equivalent exchange price of the asset. If the purchaser does not pay promptly and thus does not qualify for the discount, the additional cost incurred represented by the discount not taken is not a cost of the asset; instead, it is a financing charge for the use of the seller's cash over the discount period. From a practical standpoint, however, many companies include discounts not taken as a part of the asset cost if they are not material.

Included in the cost of machinery and equipment (and furniture and fixtures) in addition to the net invoice cost are freight charges, in-transit insurance costs, applicable taxes, the cost of special foundations or bases, and assembly, installation, and testing costs. These costs are necessary to obtain the asset and to get it into position for its intended use.

In some instances, entities construct their own machinery or equipment. We discuss valuation problems arising in such circumstances in the section of this chapter headed "Self-Constructed Assets."

BUILDINGS An entity may obtain buildings by purchasing them, by contracting with an outside party to construct them, or by constructing them itself. Regardless of the way a building is obtained, the general valuation guideline remains the same: the firm should capitalize all necessary costs to obtain the building and to get it into position for its intended use as a part of the cost of the building.

When a firm acquires a building from an external party, either through construction by an outside party or through purchase of an existing building, an objective market transaction occurs that establishes a value for the building. Additional costs incidental to the purchase, such as attorneys' fees and building permits, should be capitalized along with the building transaction price. When an entity constructs its own facilities, however, valuation of the facilities is not so simple, as we discuss in the next section.

SELF-CONSTRUCTED ASSETS When an entity constructs its own plant asset, the asset should be recorded at cost. That cost, however, is often difficult to determine, since there is no exchange transaction to provide an objective figure. Instead of a purchase price, a firm incurs material, labor, overhead, and incidental costs for a self-constructed asset. Direct material, direct labor, and direct overhead costs pose no problems in valuation because they clearly are incremental costs associated with the construction of the asset. The treatment of indirect manufacturing costs, however, is not so easily resolved. Also, the firm may incur interest costs from debt financing. If equity (as opposed to debt) financing is involved, is there an implicit cost associated with the use of equity funds for the construction activity? Because the asset generates no revenues during construction, there is some question regarding the appropriate accounting treatment of interest costs (either actual costs from debt financing or implicit costs from equity financing) incurred during construction.

Indirect Manufacturing Costs

Indirect manufacturing costs include such items as electricity, taxes on manufacturing facilities, factory supervisory costs, manufacturing supplies, factory janitorial services, and depreciation on manufacturing facilities. By definition, *indirect* manufacturing costs cannot be attributed *directly* to a self-constructed asset. Instead, if a firm wishes to assign these costs to a self-constructed asset, the costs must be allocated, just as a manufacturing firm allocates indirect costs (factory overhead costs) to inventories. To a large extent, these indirect manufacturing costs will be incurred whether or not the firm is constructing a plant asset, so they are not incremental costs of self-construction. If they were, the firm could trace them directly to the self-constructed asset.

There are three methods for dealing with this issue:

1. Assign none of the indirect manufacturing overhead to self-constructed assets (**direct costing approach**).

2. Assign indirect manufacturing overhead to self-constructed assets on the same basis that is used to assign indirect costs to normal inventory production (**full costing approach**).

3. If the company is operating at full capacity, include in the cost of the self-constructed asset the profit that would have been earned by normal business operations but has been sacrificed to build the asset (**opportunity cost approach**).

The full costing approach is used most commonly for self-constructed assets.

Of the three methods, the *full costing approach* is the most common in practice, and it is consistent with the way in which we apply the historical cost principle to inventories. The *direct costing approach,* while perhaps useful for management purposes, is not acceptable for external reporting under current generally accepted accounting principles.

The *opportunity cost approach* has considerable theoretical appeal, but the subjective ''what if'' nature of the approach (that is, determining the profit that the firm would have earned if it had dedicated its operating capacity to inventory production instead of to the self-construction activity) renders it rather impractical, and so it is infrequently used.

Interest during Construction

In order to place this issue in perspective, recall that we typically treat interest costs as period costs; that is, we expense interest costs when they are incurred. The rationale for this treatment is that the funds for which interest costs are incurred are being used currently to generate revenues. Therefore, proper matching requires that the costs of using the funds be expensed as the costs are incurred. When a firm incurs interest costs in the process of constructing assets that are not yet generating revenues, however, a question arises as to whether treating interest costs as period costs is appropriate.

Three methods have been proposed for accounting for interest costs during construction:

1. Expense interest costs as they are incurred.

2. Capitalize only the interest costs actually incurred during the construction period.

3. Capitalize both interest costs actually incurred and any implicit interest costs on other funds employed.

Advocates of the first method argue that interest costs should not be capitalized because they are a cost of financing, which is a period cost rather than a cost of the asset. Interest costs result from the decision to finance rather than from the decision to construct an asset. Furthermore, if a company were allowed to show a higher cost for an asset simply because it used debt financing, comparability would be lacking between that company and companies that used nondebt sources to finance self-construction. Although this method is consistent with the treatment of interest costs in other circumstances, there is some question about how well matching is achieved in the case of self-construction, since no revenues are generated during construction.

The second method views interest costs incurred during construction as simply another cost of construction, like material and labor costs, which a firm must recover from future operations. Capitalizing only the actual interest costs incurred is consistent with the historical cost principle. The problem with this method is that the means of financing construction is then a determinant of the cost of the asset. The fair value or service potential of an asset, however, conceptually is independent of the means of financing. Further, there is a cost, either explicit or implicit, for all funds employed, whether they are generated from debt issuance, from existing assets, or from the issuance of equity securities. There is a conceptual inconsistency in recording a cost for debt securities but no cost for equity funds or for the use of existing assets.

The third method gives explicit recognition to the costs of all funds employed. The cost of all kinds of financing is considered to be as much a part of the total cost of the self-constructed asset as are the material, labor, and other costs incurred. Under this method, the means of financing does not affect the amount at which self-constructed assets are carried in the accounts. Thus, comparability is enhanced. Opponents of this method argue that any determination of the cost of either equity capital or the use of existing assets is too subjective. They argue further that if implicit interest is added to the asset cost, it also must be credited either to a revenue account or to stockholders' equity, neither of which is conceptually appealing. Also, according to the historical cost principle, we generally record in the accounts only costs actually incurred.

THE BACKGROUND   Historically, only public utilities capitalized interest during construction. Public utilities, regulated by various governmental agencies, argued that the rates established for current customers, which were based largely on capitalized costs, should enable the utilities to recover the full cost of providing services, including the cost of all funds employed. Thus, they felt justified in capitalizing interest costs on all funds used during construction, because the rate-making process assured them of recovering these capitalized costs through revenues.

In the early 1970s, a period when business entities suffered declining profits and cash inflows, a number of nonregulated companies began to capitalize interest costs incurred during construction. Of course, the effect of this practice was to report higher profits in construction periods than would have been reported had interest costs been expensed as incurred.

In 1974 the SEC became concerned over the diversity of practices developing in accounting for interest costs during construction and the resultant lack of comparability of financial reports. Therefore, the SEC prohibited capitalization of interest costs by nonregulated companies that had not previously adopted the practice.[1] Companies that had already begun to capitalize such interest costs were allowed to continue. This SEC moratorium halted the proliferation of practices and provided the FASB with an opportunity to address the problem. The FASB's response to this rather strong encouragement by the SEC to deal with the issue came in 1979, in the form of *FASB Statement No. 34,* "Capitalization of Interest Costs,"[2] which we summarize in the remainder of this section.

FASB Statement No. 34 requirements for interest during construction.

CURRENT REQUIREMENTS   The philosophy underlying *FASB Statement No. 34* is that, in accordance with the historical cost principle, a firm should capitalize all necessary costs incurred in obtaining an asset and getting it in position for its intended use. We then achieve proper matching by allocating these costs as depreciation expense over the periods in which the firm generates revenues by using the asset. Following this philosophy, *Statement No. 34* includes the following basic requirement: interest costs are capitalized for all assets that require a period of time to get them ready for their intended use, that is, all assets that require an *acquisition period.*

The basic requirements of *Statement No. 34* cover three categories:

1. Qualifying assets.

2. Amount to be capitalized.

3. Capitalization period.

Qualifying assets.   A firm should capitalize interest for assets that it constructs for its own use (for example, an office building or machinery) and for assets constructed as discrete projects for sale or lease (for example, a ship or a real estate development). Also included in this category are assets that are constructed for an entity by others and for which progress payments or deposits are required (for example, long-term construction contracts). Specifically excluded from coverage by *FASB Statement No. 34* are routinely manufactured inventories, assets in use or ready for use, and assets that are not ready for use in the earning process and that are not being prepared for use (for example, vacant land being held for possible future expansion).

When land qualifies for interest capitalization, per the preceding discussion, the interest cost capitalized is a cost of the asset resulting from the activities. For example, if a building results from the activities, the interest cost is a cost of the building. If devel-

---

[1] "Capitalization of Interest by Companies Other Than Public Utilities," *Accounting Series Release No. 163* (Washington, D.C.: SEC, 1974).

[2] "Capitalization of Interest Costs," *Statement of Financial Accounting Standards No. 34* (Stamford, Conn.: FASB, 1979). In response to this action, the SEC rescinded its moratorium in November 1979 *(Accounting Series Release No. 272).*

oped land results from the activities, such as lots for sale, the interest cost is a cost of the developed land.

Amount to be capitalized. In determining the amount of interest to be capitalized, *the basic conceptual objective is to capitalize interest that could have been avoided had the qualifying assets not been acquired.* We implement this conceptual objective by considering the entity's actual interest cost incurred, actual borrowings, and actual expenditures for qualifying assets during the period.

The amount of interest to be capitalized is determined by multiplying appropriate interest rate(s) by the average amount of accumulated expenditures for the qualifying asset during the period, referred to as **average accumulated expenditures.** The rationale for using "average" expenditures instead of "total" expenditures can be demonstrated by a simple example.

Assume that three companies, *A*, *B*, and *C*, are undertaking self-construction that qualifies for interest capitalization. All three companies spend $1,000,000 on qualifying expenditures related to the self-construction during the period. However, company *A* incurs the entire expenditure at the beginning of the period, company *B* incurs the expenditure evenly throughout the period, and company *C* incurs the entire expenditure on the last day of the period. The average accumulated expenditures for company *A* for the period is $1,000,000, because the expenditures took place at the beginning of the period. That is, interest *could be* incurred on the entire $1,000,000 for the entire period. The average accumulated expenditures for company *B* is $500,000 ($1,000,000 × 6/12). Because company *B*'s average investment is $500,000, it can incur interest only on $500,000, not on the total expenditures of $1,000,000. Stated another way, spending $1,000,000 evenly throughout the period is equivalent to spending $500,000 on July 1. Company *C* has average accumulated expenditures of $0 ($1,000,000 × 0/12), because the expenditure occurred on the last day of the year. Because company *C* had no investment during the period, it could not incur interest on the self-construction.

Only the interest that could have been avoided had construction not occurred may be capitalized.

If a firm has borrowed specifically to finance a qualifying asset, the interest rate on the specific borrowing should be applied to the average accumulated expenditures up to the amount of the specific borrowing. Continuing the previous example, assume that all three companies borrowed $500,000 at 10 percent at the beginning of the period specifically to finance the self-construction. Companies *A* and *B* could capitalize $50,000 ($500,000 × 10%) as a result of the specific borrowing. Company *C* could capitalize nothing.

Average accumulated expenditures in excess of specific borrowings should be multiplied by the weighted average rate on other outstanding borrowings during the period. Interest rates used generally are the actual rates on borrowings outstanding during the period. However, if some borrowings originated in periods when interest rates were substantially different from the current rates, those interest rates may be excluded from the weighted-average calculation, because the objective is to approximate interest costs that could have been avoided, which implies current borrowing costs. Thus, judgment is required to determine which of the historical rates should be used to approximate avoidable interest costs.

To illustrate the application of the weighted average interest rate to average accumulated expenditures in excess of specific borrowings, we continue our earlier example. Assume that companies *A*, *B*, and *C* all had the following long-term debt outstanding throughout the period:

FACE AMOUNT	INTEREST RATE
$400,000	8%
800,000	12

The weighted average interest rate on these other borrowings is 10.67 percent, calculated as follows:

$$
\begin{array}{rcl}
\$ \ \ 400,000 \times .08 & = & \$ \ 32,000 \\
\underline{\ \ \ \ 800,000 \times .12} & = & \underline{\ \ \ 96,000} \\
\$1,200,000 & & \$128,000
\end{array}
$$

$$\$128,000 \div \$1,200,000 = 10.67\%$$

Thus, company *A* may capitalize additional interest of \$53,350 [(\$1,000,000 − \$500,000) × .1067]. Company *B* may not capitalize any of the additional interest costs incurred, because it had no average accumulated expenditures that were not absorbed by the specific borrowing. Likewise, company *C* cannot capitalize any of the additional interest costs incurred. Note that all three companies incurred total interest costs of \$178,000 during the period, consisting of \$50,000 from the specific borrowing and \$128,000 from other borrowings. Of this amount, company *A* capitalized \$103,350 (\$50,000 + \$53,350), company *B* capitalized \$50,000, and company *C* capitalized nothing.

In calculating average accumulated expenditures, we are attempting to approximate the average amount of expenditures for qualifying assets on which the firm has incurred interest costs during the period. Thus, a simple average of beginning and ending amounts capitalized in the asset account may be acceptable if expenditures have occurred evenly throughout the period and if all expenditures have involved the payment of cash, the transfer of assets, or the incurrence of a liability on which interest is recognized. However, if expenditures have not occurred evenly, a quarterly or monthly average should be calculated. Likewise, if a significant portion of the expenditures were financed by trade payables on which interest is not recognized, this portion of the expenditures should be excluded when average accumulated expenditures are calculated.

The amount of interest capitalized cannot exceed actual interest costs incurred during the period. The firm must disclose both total interest costs incurred during the period and the amount capitalized.

Capitalization period. The capitalization period begins when three things happen: (1) expenditures for the asset have been made; (2) activities necessary to prepare the asset for its intended use (for example, planning, obtaining permits, and physical construction) are in progress; and (3) interest cost is being incurred. As long as all three conditions are met, interest capitalization continues. The capitalization period ends when the asset is substantially complete and ready for its intended use.

Assume that Landry Corporation began construction activity on January 2, 1987, on a new office building. On that date, Landry obtained a construction loan of \$1,600,000 with an 11 percent annual interest rate. Expenditures on the construction project during 1987 and 1988, all of which qualify for inclusion in the calculation of average accumulated expenditures, were as follows:

January 2, 1987	\$300,000
March 1, 1987	400,000
June 1, 1987	600,000
September 1, 1987	400,000
October 1, 1987	600,000
December 31, 1987	500,000
March 1, 1988	400,000
May 1, 1988	300,000
June 30, 1988	500,000

The project was completed on June 30, 1988. Landry's only other outstanding debt during the construction period consisted of two long-term notes in the principal amounts of $500,000 and $1,000,000, bearing interest at the rates of 12 percent and 14 percent, respectively. These notes were outstanding throughout the construction period.

Average accumulated expenditures for 1987 may be calculated as follows:

1/2/87	$ 300,000 × 12/12 =	$ 300,000
3/1/87	400,000 × 10/12 =	333,333
6/1/87	600,000 × 7/12 =	350,000
9/1/87	400,000 × 4/12 =	133,333
10/1/87	600,000 × 3/12 =	150,000
12/31/87	500,000 × 0/12 =	–0–
	$2,800,000	$1,266,666

Average accumulated expenditures amount to $1,266,666. Because this amount is less than $1,600,000 (the amount borrowed specifically for the construction), the capitalized interest is $1,266,666 × .11 = $139,333. The following aggregate journal entry would be made for 1987 expenditures:

Building.	2,939,333	
Cash.		2,939,333
($2,800,000 + $139,333)		

Actual interest costs incurred in 1987 in excess of $139,333 would be expensed.

Average accumulated expenditures in 1988 would be calculated as follows:

1/1/88	$2,939,333 × 6/6 =	$2,939,333
3/1/88	400,000 × 4/6 =	266,667
5/1/88	300,000 × 2/6 =	100,000
6/30/88	500,000 × 0/6 =	–0–
	$4,139,333	$3,306,000

The 1988 interest capitalization consists of two parts: (1) interest of $88,000 on specific borrowing ($1,600,000 × .11 × 1/2 year) plus (2) interest of $113,449 on $1,706,000, the average accumulated expenditures in excess of $1,600,000, calculated as follows:

$ 500,000 × .12 =	$ 60,000
1,000,000 × .14 =	140,000
$1,500,000	$200,000

$200,000 ÷ $1,500,000 = 13.3% weighted average interest rate on other debt
($3,306,000 − $1,600,000) × .133 × 1/2 year = $113,449

Note that, because the capitalization period ended at midyear, the interest is capitalized for only one-half of the year. The balance in the asset account, building, will be increased by $1,401,449 for the six months ending June 30, 1988:

Building.	1,401,449	
Cash.		1,401,449
($400,000 + $300,000 + $500,000 + $88,000 + $113,449)		

Actual interest cost incurred in 1988 [($1,600,000 × .11) + ($500,000 × .12) + ($1,000,000 × .14) = $376,000] exceeds the amount calculated as being capitalizable ($201,449). The noncapitalizable portion of the interest incurred ($376,000 − $201,449 = $174,551) should be recorded as interest expense in 1988.

DEFERRED PAYMENTS

Entities often incur debt in connection with the acquisition of plant assets. That is, rather than use its own cash immediately, an entity may issue bonds, notes, or other debt instruments. When debt is incurred, the total of the actual cash outlays over the term of the loan contract will be greater than the current cash equivalent of the asset, because the lender will charge the borrower interest for the use of the money. The objective in recording a plant asset acquired by incurring debt is to record the asset at the best estimate of its fair market value at the date of acquisition.

If the debt contract specifies a reasonable interest rate, then the face amount of the obligation normally constitutes the best estimate of the fair market value of the asset received. Suppose, for example, that Mullins Company acquired equipment in exchange for a five-year, $10,000 note payable at 12 percent, with the principal to be repaid at the end of the fifth year and the interest to be paid at the end of each year. Assuming that 12 percent is a reasonable cost of borrowing for Mullins, then $10,000 is the present value of the note, calculated as follows:

Present value of principal	= $10,000(.5674)*	=	$ 5,674
Present value of interest payments	= $ 1,200(3.6048)†	=	4,326
			$10,000

* Table B, Appendix 7–1, factor for 5 periods, 12%.

† Table D, Appendix 7–1, factor for 5 periods, 12%.

The transaction would be recorded as follows:

Equipment	10,000	
Notes payable		10,000

Interest of $1,200 (12% × $10,000) is paid and recorded as an expense at the end of each year.

As we described in Chapter 8 in our discussion of receivables, in some instances notes are issued with no stated interest rate (that is, noninterest-bearing debt) or with an unreasonably low rate of interest. In these cases the face amount of the note does not provide a reasonable estimate of the fair market value of the asset received. For example, assume that Mullins issued a five-year noninterest-bearing note with a face amount of $18,000. We could take the simplistic view that the face amount of the note represents the fair market value of the asset received. If Mullins' cost of borrowing is 12 percent, however, a better estimate of fair value is $10,213, which we determine by calculating the present value of the note (.5674 × $18,000).

If the asset acquired also is being offered for cash by the seller, or if the acquired asset's fair market value is otherwise determinable, that fair market value should be assigned to the acquired asset and to the debt. For example, assume that an asset has a cash price of $10,000 and that Mullins purchases it by issuing a noninterest-bearing one-year note in the face amount of $11,500. The face amount of the note is not a reasonable estimate of the fair market value exchanged because the note bears no interest, which merely means that the interest is included in the face amount of the note. The interest is the difference between the face amount of the note and the cash price of the asset. The transaction should be recorded as follows:

Equipment	10,000	
Discount on notes payable	1,500	
Notes payable		11,500

For statement presentation purposes, we deduct the discount on notes payable ($1,500) from the notes payable ($11,500) so that the net liability is $10,000.

When the note is paid at the end of the year, we make the following entry:

Notes payable	11,500	
Interest expense	1,500	
Discount on notes payable		1,500
Cash		11,500

Notice that if we had recorded the asset at $11,500, the face amount of the note, we would have overstated the asset's cost and depreciation expense by $1,500 over the life of the asset. We also would have understated interest expense by $1,500, and the liability (debt) would have been overstated by $1,500.

If the entity cannot determine the fair market value of the acquired asset and the interest rate on the debt is unreasonable, then the fair market value of the asset is estimated by calculating the present value of the obligation exchanged for it. We determine the present value of the debt, and thus the amount to be recorded for the asset, by discounting the cash flows associated with the debt using the prevailing market rate of interest for the entity.

Assume, for example, that an entity acquires machinery in exchange for a three-year $8,000 note, with 6 percent interest payable annually and the face amount payable at the end of three years. The prevailing rate of interest for notes in this risk category is 12 percent, and the fair market value of the machinery is not readily determinable. The present value of the note is:

Present value of principal at 12%:	
$8,000 × .7118*	$5,694
Present value of interest payments at 12%:	
.06 × $8,000 × 2.4018†	1,153
Present value of note	$6,847

* Table B, Appendix 7–1.

† Table D, Appendix 7–1.

The following entry should be made to record the exchange:

Machinery	6,847	
Discount on notes payable	1,153	
Notes payable		8,000

The following entries would be made at the ends of years 1, 2, and 3:

	YEAR 1		YEAR 2		YEAR 3	
Notes payable					8,000	
Interest expense	822*		863§		908¶	
Cash		480†		480		8,480
Discount on notes payable		342‡		383		428

* 12% × $6,847 = $822.

† 6% × $8,000 = $480.

‡ $822 − $480 = $342.

§ 12% × ($6,847 + $342) = $863.

¶ 12% × ($6,847 + $342 + $383) = $908 (rounded).

Acquired assets should be recorded at the best estimate of fair market value.

In summary, when a firm acquires a plant asset in exchange for debt, our objective is to determine the best estimate of its fair market value. In many cases, the face amount of the debt provides this estimate. If the interest rate on the debt is unreasonable, however, the face amount is not a good indicator of value exchanged. In such instances, we should first attempt to value the asset acquired directly at its cash equivalent price as evidenced by the marketplace. Failing this, the debt must be discounted at the prevailing rate of interest to arrive at the amount at which the acquired asset should be recorded.

ACQUIRING PLANT ASSETS BY ISSUING STOCK

Another possible means of acquiring plant assets is by issuing stock. In attempting to determine the amount at which to record the assets, we should use the fair market value of the assets acquired or the fair market value of the stock given up, whichever is more readily determinable. If the stock is actively traded on an organized stock exchange, the market value of the stock provides a good estimate of the fair market value of the assets acquired. If the market value of the stock is not readily determinable, then we must attempt to determine directly the fair market value of the assets acquired, either by analyzing current market activity for those assets or by appraisal. As a last resort, if the market value of neither the stock nor the acquired assets is readily determinable, the board of directors must establish a value for the acquired assets, and thus of the stock. The board of directors normally would seek expert opinion in such a case.

DONATED ASSETS

The conventional system of accounting relies on exchange transactions. Usually something is given up and something is received, thus offering several possibilities for determining what the acquired asset is worth. It may be difficult, however, to determine the value of an asset received in a **nonreciprocal transfer**—the receipt of an asset without a corresponding sacrifice, either at the time of receipt or in the future. A business entity may receive donated property either from the firm's owners or from outsiders, as when a local government donates land to attract industry. Donated property from outsiders often is subject to contingencies, such as a requirement for a certain level of employment for so many years before title passes to the entity. Unless there is substantial doubt that the conditions will be met, the donated assets should be recorded in the accounts at the time of donation, and the financial statements should disclose any contingencies.

Historical cost is not useful in recording donated assets.

When we consider our objective in valuing assets at acquisition, it is apparent that the historical cost principle does not help us to determine the amount at which to record donated assets. The only costs incurred by the recipient (for example, legal fees) are likely to be insignificant in relation to the fair market value of the donated assets. The historical cost to the recipient therefore is not a reasonable estimate of fair market value. Thus, donated assets should be recorded at their fair market value at the date of donation, as determined by appraisal or by current market activity.[3] This is not a violation of the historical cost principle, but rather a recognition that historical cost is used to value assets at acquisition only when such an approach produces a reasonable estimate of the fair market value of the acquired assets. When historical cost does not accomplish this objective, we abandon it in favor of an approach that produces results more in accord with economic reality.

As an example, assume a business entity received a building appraised at $750,000 as a donation. The following entry would be made:

Building 750,000
    Donated capital   750,000

---

[3] ''Accounting for Nonmonetary Transactions,'' *Opinions of the Accounting Principles Board No. 29* (New York: AICPA, 1973), para. 3.

Note that when donated assets are received, the offsetting credit should be to donated capital, an owners' equity account. Depreciation would be recorded subsequently in the same manner as for other depreciable assets.

Some accountants have argued that donated assets represent income to the recipient and thus the credit should be to a gain account rather than to donated capital. This approach, however, seems to violate the realization and matching principles—an entity should recognize the benefits from owning and using an asset not at the point of acquisition but over the periods in which the asset generates revenues. That is, we do not recognize a gain at the time of acquisition.

LUMP-SUM PURCHASES

It is not unusual for an entity to acquire two or more different assets in exchange for a single price. We refer to such a transaction as a **lump-sum** or **basket purchase.** Since the total cost of the assets normally is presumed to be the best evidence of the combined fair market value of all of the assets acquired, we somehow must allocate an appropriate share of this cost to each of them.

The standard practice, as we described in Chapter 9 in discussing inventory accounting, is to allocate the acquisition cost among the assets on the basis of the relative fair market value of each asset. The acquiring entity may have to rely on appraisals, tax assessments, insurance data, and the like to arrive at fair market values for allocation purposes. The seller's book values, which may or may not be known by the buyer, seldom would be realistic indicators of fair market value.

Note that with this method it is quite likely that the sum of the fair market values will not be equal to the total purchase price. It is the *relative* fair market values that are important, however, because it is the fair market value of each asset relative to the total fair market value that we use to allocate the purchase price among the assets.

Assume, for example, that an entity acquires land and a building in a lump-sum purchase for $90,000 cash. Thus, $90,000 is the best estimate of the total fair market value of both the land and the building. Independent appraisals and other information gathered by the purchaser indicate that the land has an estimated fair market value of $25,000 and the building has an estimated fair market value of $75,000. The $90,000 would be allocated as follows:

$$\text{Land: } \frac{\$\ 25,000}{\$100,000} \times \$90,000 = \$22,500$$

$$\text{Building: } \frac{\$\ 75,000}{\$100,000} \times \$90,000 = \$67,500$$

INVESTMENT TAX CREDIT

Since 1962 Congress intermittently has permitted taxpayers to reduce taxes otherwise payable by means of an investment tax credit. The purpose of the investment tax credit is to stimulate investment in qualifying property. The Tax Reform Act of 1986 eliminated this tax credit retroactive to the beginning of 1986. However, because of the possibility that the credit may reappear as an investment incentive, in this section we cover the accounting and reporting alternatives for the investment tax credit.

The effect of the investment tax credit on the entity is a direct reduction in taxes payable in the year in which the qualifying assets are put into service. For example, assume that a company has $1 million of pretax income in a period in which the tax rate is 40 percent. The company also has invested $300,000 in depreciable property during the period that qualifies for a 10 percent investment tax credit. Taxes payable would be calculated as follows:

Taxes payable before investment credit (40% × $1,000,000)	$400,000
Tax credit (10% × $300,000)	(30,000)
Income taxes payable	$370,000

There are two methods of accounting for the benefit from the investment tax credit: the deferral method and the flow-through method.

Deferral Method

In 1962 the APB issued *Opinion No. 2,*[4] which required that the benefit, such as the $30,000 tax credit in the preceding example, be recognized over the life of the asset. The APB maintained that the entity acquiring the property realizes the benefit from the investment as it is used in operations. Under the **deferral method,** also called the **cost-reduction method,** the investment tax credit is perceived to be a reduction in the cost of the asset. The entity realizes the benefit from this cost reduction through *use* of the asset, however, not through the act of *acquiring* it.

Flow-Through Method

The flow-through and deferral methods are both acceptable.

Companies were not pleased with the deferral method because it spread the income statement recognition of the benefit accruing from the investment tax credit over several years, rather than allowing firms to recognize the benefit in the period of acquisition. Companies directed so much criticism at the deferral method that the SEC "encouraged" the APB to permit either the deferral or the flow-through method. In 1964 the APB issued *Opinion No. 4,*[5] which continued to specify a preference for the deferral method, but also permitted the flow-through method. The issue of accounting for the investment tax credit provides an excellent example of the pressures that face the accounting profession as it attempts to narrow the number of accounting alternatives. Owing to political pressure, two alternatives are now acceptable where earlier only one method was permissible.

Under the **flow-through method,** also called the **tax-reduction method,** the investment tax credit is presumed to be earned by the act of purchasing the asset. Therefore, the benefit from the credit is recognized in the income statement entirely in the period of acquisition. Since this method "front-ends" the recognition of the benefit from the investment, most companies prefer the flow-through method. Many accountants argue, however, that the flow-through method violates both the revenue realization principle and the matching principle by recognizing the benefit at acquisition rather than over the periods in which the asset is used.

To illustrate the two methods of accounting for the investment tax credit, assume that a company pays $80,000 for equipment that qualifies for a 10 percent investment tax credit. The useful life of the equipment is estimated to be 10 years. Pretax income is $100,000, and the income tax rate is 40 percent. The entries to record income tax expense and income taxes payable in the first year under the deferral and flow-through methods are as follows:

DEFERRAL METHOD*			FLOW-THROUGH METHOD		
Income tax expense . 39,200			Income tax expense . 32,000		
Income taxes			Income taxes		
payable		32,000	payable		32,000
Deferred invest-					
ment credit		7,200†			

* Assumes 10-year amortization period for investment credit.

† $8,000 − ($8,000 ÷ 10 yrs.) = $7,200

---

[4] "Accounting for the Investment Credit," *Opinions of the Accounting Principles Board No. 2* (New York: AICPA, 1962).

[5] "Accounting for the Investment Credit," *Opinions of the Accounting Principles Board No. 4* (New York: AICPA, 1964).

Under both methods, we reduce income taxes payable immediately by the full amount of the investment credit. That is, we determine income taxes payable by multiplying the tax rate (40 percent) by pretax income ($100,000) and then deducting the investment credit ($8,000). Under the flow-through method, net income is $8,000 higher than it would be without the credit because income tax expense is reduced by the full amount of the credit. Under the deferral method, however, we recognize only $800 ($8,000 ÷ 10 years) of the benefit from the credit each year. We reduce income tax expense, and thus increase net income, by $800 each year for 10 years.

Assuming the same pretax income and tax rate in the second year, the following entries would be required to record taxes at the end of the second year:

DEFERRAL METHOD		FLOW-THROUGH METHOD	
Income tax expense . 39,200		Income tax expense . 40,000	
Deferred invest-		Income taxes	
ment credit	800	payable	40,000
Income taxes			
payable	40,000		

Because the rationale for the deferral method is that the investment tax credit is a reduction in the cost of the asset, conceptually the credit should be reported as a contra-account to the related asset. However, in practice, the deferred investment credit often is reported in the liability section of the balance sheet.

Since 1981 (as a result of the passage of the Economic Recovery Tax Act, known as ERTA), qualifying property has been broken down into two categories: (1) three-year recovery property; and (2) other recovery property. Firms may claim a 6 percent tax credit for three-year property and a 10 percent tax credit for other recovery property. Also, since 1982 and the passage of the Tax Equity and Fiscal Responsibility Act, known as TEFRA, firms must elect either (1) a reduction of 2 percent in the tax credit (making the credit either 4 percent or 8 percent, respectively) and depreciation of the entire cost, or (2) a reduction in the depreciable basis of the qualifying asset for tax purposes by one-half of the investment tax credit. If a firm chooses to reduce the basis, deferred tax issues may arise.

EXCHANGES OF PLANT ASSETS

We have already noted that firms may acquire plant assets in exchange for other plant assets. Such transactions are called **nonmonetary exchanges.**

General Guideline

The accounting guidelines for nonmonetary exchanges are readily understandable if you keep in mind that a fundamental objective in all exchanges involving the acquisition of an asset is to record the acquired asset at its fair market value. In some cases, the value surrendered is the best estimate of the value received (for example, when cash is surrendered). In other exchanges, we record the asset acquired directly at its estimated fair market value (for example, when a firm issues a noninterest-bearing note and the fair market value of the acquired asset is readily determinable). In *all* exchanges, including nonmonetary exchanges, the general guideline is that the assets acquired are recorded at their own fair market value or at the fair market value of the assets sacrificed, whichever is more clearly evident. That is, fair market values govern the recording process. We record the acquired assets at our best estimate of their worth to the entity that acquires them at the time it acquires them, the point at which their earning process begins. Also, gains and losses are recognized on assets surrendered, since their earning process is over when they are given up.

Fair market values generally govern the recording process.

APB Opinion No. 29 provides the accounting and reporting requirements for non-monetary exchanges.[6] That *Opinion* basically implements and reiterates the above general guideline. There are two circumstances, however, in which the general guideline does not apply:

Exceptions to the fair market approach.

1. When the fair market value of neither the asset surrendered nor the asset acquired is determinable.

2. When the exchange results in a gain and involves *similar* assets.

We discuss the first of these two exceptions at the end of the next section. Then we describe the second exception in our discussion of exchanges of similar assets.

Exchanges of Dissimilar Assets

Many nonmonetary exchanges involve assets that have dissimilar functions. For example, a tract of land may be exchanged for a group of machines. We refer to such transactions as **nonmonetary exchanges of dissimilar assets.** Accounting for these exchanges follows the general guideline, and gains or losses are recognized in full at the time of the exchange.

Let us assume that Pamco surrenders a tract of land (book value, $60,000; fair market value, $150,000) to Daveco in exchange for machinery whose fair market value is not readily determinable. Pamco would record the exchange as follows:

Machinery	150,000	
Land		60,000
Gain on exchange		90,000

Modifying the example slightly, if the fair market value of the machinery were determinable, say $100,000, and if that value were more clearly evident than the fair market value of the land, the firm would record the machinery at its fair market value and the gain would be $40,000, the difference between the fair market value of the machinery ($100,000) and the book value of the land ($60,000):

Machinery	100,000	
Land		60,000
Gain on exchange		40,000

Note that when the fair market value of only the land is determinable, the firm recognizes a gain on the disposal of the land and records the machinery at its estimated fair market value, with the estimate based on the fair market value of the land. The earning process for the land has culminated, and the machinery's earning process has just begun. If the fair market value of the land were less than its book value, the firm would recognize a loss.

A small amount of cash, called **boot,** may be included in a dissimilar exchange. Boot is included whenever the fair market values of the assets exchanged are not the same. Cash included in an exchange transaction creates no particular difficulty. If boot is given up, it increases the amount at which the acquired asset is recorded. If boot is received, it decreases the amount at which the acquired asset is recorded. You may think of the boot surrendered along with an asset as increasing the fair market value surrendered in a nonmonetary exchange of dissimilar assets. On the other hand, boot received decreases the net fair market value surrendered.

[6] "Accounting for Nonmonetary Transactions," *Opinions of the Accounting Principles Board No. 29* (New York: AICPA, 1973).

As we stated earlier, the general guideline does not apply when the fair market value of neither the asset surrendered nor the asset acquired is determinable. In such instances, we record the asset acquired at the book value of the asset surrendered and recognize no gain or loss. This situation, caused by an inability to *measure* the exchange, is the only case involving dissimilar assets in which we depart from the fair market value approach and suppress the recognition of gains and losses.

Exchanges of Similar Assets

A departure from the fair market value approach also occurs in some nonmonetary exchanges involving **similar assets,** defined as assets that are of the same general type or that perform the same function. Specific examples of similar asset exchanges provided in *APB Opinion No. 29* are:

1. An exchange of inventory for inventory in the same line of business to facilitate sales to customers other than the parties to the exchange.

2. An exchange of a productive asset normally not held for sale for a similar productive asset. (A productive asset is one that is held for or used in the production of goods or services.)[7]

Consider how these exchanges differ from the exchange of dissimilar assets described earlier. In an exchange of dissimilar assets, an entity gives up one asset for a distinctly different type of asset. Therefore, recognition of a gain or loss on disposal and recording of the acquired asset at fair market value make sense, since we presume that the earning process is culminated for the old asset. In an exchange of similar assets, however, the entity is *trading* one nonmonetary asset for another that performs the same function. Thus, you may view the earning process not as ending for the surrendered asset and beginning for the acquired asset, but simply as continuing; though a new asset has replaced the old, the process goes on. When the exchange is seen from this perspective, it seems logical to transfer the book value of the old asset to the new asset, and in fact this logic underlies the general rule for accounting for exchanges of similar assets.

In exchanges of similar assets, gains are not recognized unless boot is received (and then only partially); losses are recognized fully. When we compare this type of exchange with exchanges of dissimilar assets, we see that we recognize losses fully in both instances. A loss occurs when the asset surrendered has a book value greater than either its own fair market value or the fair market value of the asset received. We recognize gains fully in exchanges of dissimilar assets, but we do not recognize them in an exchange of similar assets unless the entity receives boot, and even then we recognize only a portion of the gain.

When a firm receives boot in an exchange of similar assets, we consider the old asset to be partially sold (and thus the earning process is complete and a gain can be recognized on this portion) and partially exchanged (and thus the earning process is continued rather than ended for this portion).

Let us assume that Ginny Company exchanges old machinery (cost, $100,000; accumulated depreciation, $40,000) for new machinery. Let us assume further that the fair market value of the old machinery is not reasonably determinable and that the fair market value of the new machinery is $64,000. Ginny also pays boot (cash) of $10,000.

Ginny thus gives up assets with a total book value of $70,000 ($60,000 of old machinery net of depreciation, plus $10,000 cash) and receives an asset with a fair market value of $64,000. The difference of $6,000 is a loss, because the old machinery is worth only $54,000—$6,000 less than its book value, as evidenced by the terms of the ex-

---

[7] Ibid., para. 21.

change. Recalling that we recognize losses fully whether the assets exchanged are dissimilar or similar, we record the transaction as follows:

Machinery (new)	64,000	
Accumulated depreciation	40,000	
Loss [($60,000 + $10,000) − $64,000]	6,000	
Machinery (old)		100,000
Cash		10,000

Thus, we record a loss on disposal of the old machinery and record the new machinery at its fair market value. If the fair market value of the old machinery had been more clearly evident than the fair market value of the new machinery, we would have used the old machinery's fair market value to determine the amount of the loss, and we would have recorded the old machinery's fair market value, along with the boot given, as the cost of the new machinery.

Now let us assume that the Varton Corporation surrenders a tract of land (book value, $20,000; fair market value, $24,000) and $8,000 in cash to the Renwick Corporation in exchange for another piece of land whose fair market value is not readily determinable. Because the fair market value of the sacrificed land exceeds its book value ($24,000 − $20,000), a gain of $4,000 is implicit in this transaction. Since Varton receives no cash, however, the exchange is considered to be a continuation of the earning process for the asset land and no gain is recognized. We merely transfer the book value of the old land, along with the boot given, to the new land, as follows:

Land (new)	28,000	
Land (old)		20,000
Cash		8,000

A further implication of this transaction is that the new land is worth $32,000, the sum of the fair values of the assets surrendered to obtain it. The gain of $4,000, however, is suppressed at this point. When the new land is disposed of in a dissimilar exchange, or in a similar exchange involving a loss, the $4,000 will appear as an increase in the gain or as a decrease in the loss.

Consider again for a moment an exchange of similar assets in which no cash is involved. Each entity in such an exchange has neither purchased nor sold anything; each has merely traded an asset. Therefore, neither entity is more or less liquid than it was before the exchange. Also, an entity that gives up boot has moved to a position of less liquidity. Thus, no gain can be recognized in either of these instances, because realization has not occurred.

Now consider a case in which an entity *receives* both cash and a nonmonetary asset in an exchange of similar assets. It has given up a strictly nonmonetary asset partly for cash and partly for a similar nonmonetary asset. Thus, we may conceive of this transaction as consisting of two parts:

1. A portion of the old asset is converted to cash (or sold). The firm may recognize a gain on this part of the transaction since it is a *sale*—that is, the conversion of a nonmonetary asset to cash, which terminated the earning process.

2. The other portion of the old asset simply is replaced by a similar asset. The firm may not recognize a gain on this portion because the company has not completed the earning process for this portion of the asset.

To demonstrate the accounting procedures involved here, consider the exchange between Varton and Renwick from Renwick's point of view. Renwick receives $8,000 cash and land with a fair market value of $24,000 in exchange for similar land. The only additional information we need is the book value of the land that Renwick surrenders. Let us assume that the fair market value of the land is not reasonably determinable, but that the book value is $18,000. The total gain is $14,000, calculated as follows:

Fair market value received:

Cash...	$ 8,000	
Similar asset	24,000	$32,000
Book value surrendered		(18,000)
Total gain		$14,000

Since similar assets are exchanged, only one-fourth of the book value (.25 × $18,000 = $4,500) is presumed to have been sold. Thus, Renwick may recognize a gain only on the portion of the book value that was converted to cash (sold), which we determine by the ratio of cash received to total fair market value received ($8,000 ÷ $32,000 = .25). Since the cash received for this portion of the book value was $8,000, Renwick should recognize a gain of $3,500 ($8,000 − $4,500). It cannot recognize the remainder of the gain ($14,000 − $3,500 = $10,500) because that applies to the portion of the transaction that is considered to be an exchange of similar assets. Renwick must record the acquired land at its fair market value ($24,000) less the unrecognized gain of $10,500, or at $13,500. Stated another way, Renwick records the new asset at the book value of the old asset ($18,000) minus the portion of that book value that was converted to cash ($4,500), or $13,500. The journal entry to record the exchange is as follows:

Land (new)	13,500*	
Cash...	8,000	
Land (old)		18,000
Gain...		3,500†

* Recorded amount for asset acquired = Book value of asset given up − Portion of book value converted to cash
= $18,000 − $4,500
= $13,500

† Recognized gain = Total gain × Ratio of cash received to total fair market value received

$$= (\$24,000 + \$8,000 - \$18,000) \times \frac{\$ 8,000}{\$32,000}$$

$$= \$14,000 \times .25 = \$3,500$$

or

Recognized gain = Cash received − Book value of portion of land converted to cash (sold)

$$= \$8,000 - \left(\frac{\$ 8,000}{\$32,000} \times \$18,000 \right)$$

$$= \$8,000 - \$4,500 = \$3,500$$

Exhibit 11–1 summarizes the accounting requirements for exchanges of nonmonetary assets.

Thus far in this chapter we have been concerned with the appropriate accounting for plant assets when they are acquired. Once a plant asset has been placed in service, additional costs are incurred related to the plant asset. Some of these costs increase service potential whereas others do not increase the service potential of the asset beyond original expectations. In the following section we describe the accounting for these costs.

EXHIBIT 11–1   EXCHANGES OF NONMONETARY ASSETS

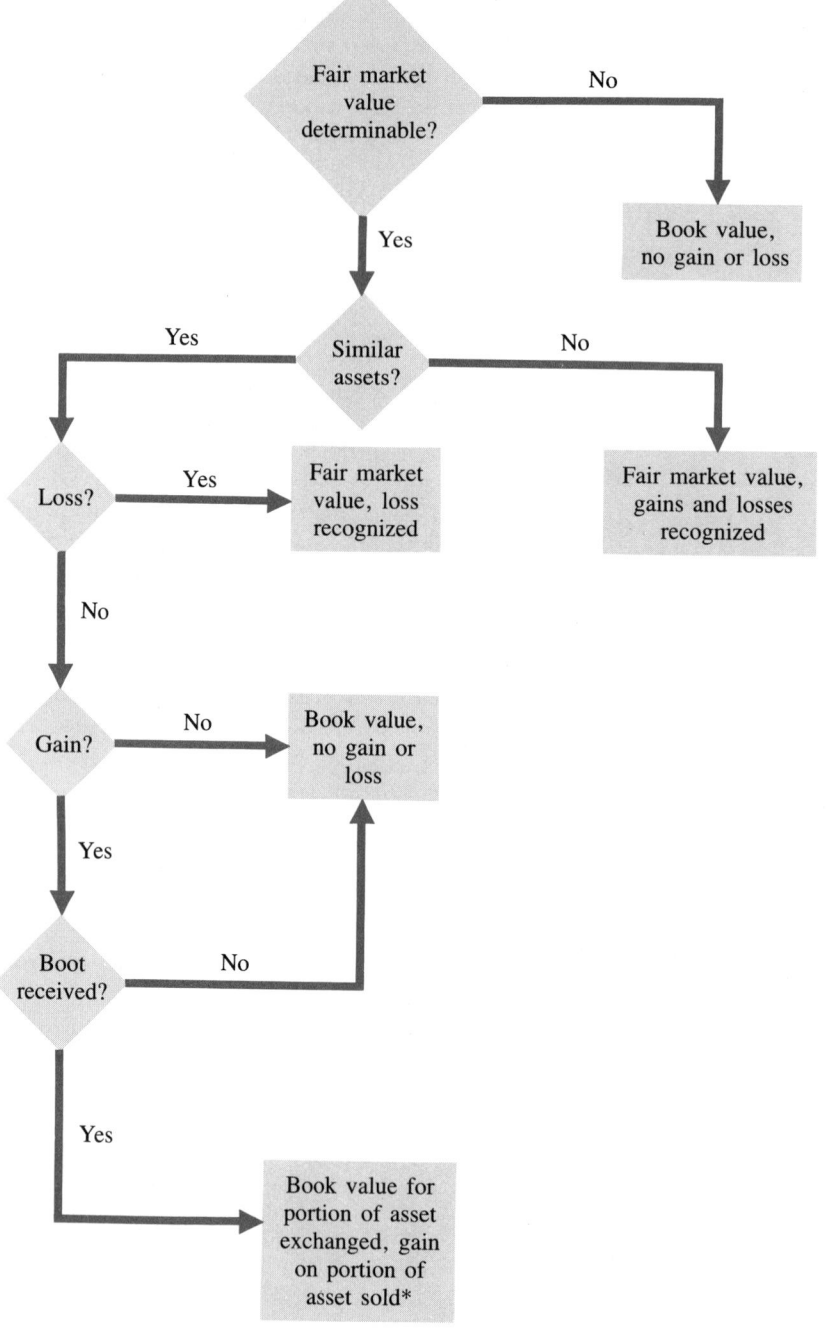

* Asset acquired recorded at book value of asset given up minus portion of book value sold, or fair value minus suppressed (unrecognized) gain. Recognized gain is cash received minus book value of portion of asset sold.

EXPENDITURES AFTER ACQUISITION

Many costs are incurred for plant assets after entities begin to use them. Some of these costs represent normal repair and maintenance activity, whereas other costs represent significant alterations to the assets, such as the addition of several floors to an existing building. Accountants must determine whether these costs should be recorded as an asset (capitalized) or as an expense.

The general guideline for accounting for these costs is that if the expenditures provide material benefits beyond the current period, they should be capitalized; if they do not provide material future benefits, they should be expensed as incurred. We refer to expenditures that provide future benefits as **capital expenditures.** We call expenditures that do not result in a significant increase in future service potential **revenue expenditures,** because we match them against current-period revenues in determining net income.

An entity may benefit future periods by making current expenditures that:

1. Extend the useful life of an asset.

2. Increase the quantity of services provided by the asset.

3. Increase the quality of services provided by the asset.

Capital expenditures benefit future periods; revenue expenditures benefit only the current period.

If an expenditure causes one or more of these results, then, according to the historical cost principle and the matching principle, the entity should debit the expenditure to an asset account. Through depreciation charges, the entity will then match the cost against the revenues generated over the estimated benefit period.

Even though the guideline for distinguishing between capital expenditures and revenue expenditures is conceptually clear-cut, it is not always so straightforward in practice. Many companies, as a matter of expediency, expense all costs incurred below a certain amount (for example, $1,000) on the grounds of materiality. This practice makes it unnecessary to distinguish between capital expenditures and revenue expenditures for these costs. We must still exercise professional judgment, however, to determine what is material and to classify properly those costs that we determine to be material. It often is difficult to determine whether a particular expenditure increases the future benefits provided by an asset, and if so, what the benefit period is. Given this difficulty, it is important that financial statement users, company management, and auditors understand a company's policy in this area, and that the policy be consistently applied.

REPAIRS AND MAINTENANCE

Entities incur many costs to keep plant assets in normal operating condition. Costs are associated, for example, with lubrication of machinery, cleaning of buildings and machinery, replacement of minor parts, and painting. These activities do not add to the benefits provided by the plant asset; they merely enable the asset to provide the benefits originally expected of it. Therefore, these costs should be expensed as they are incurred.

Two situations sometimes exist in practice that complicate the accounting for repairs and maintenance expenditures. First, these expenditures may be seasonal. For example, a manufacturing concern may routinely overhaul machinery at a low point during the year's production activity. If the firm prepares quarterly financial statements, it should accrue the expense evenly over the year, crediting allowance for repairs, a contra-asset account. For interim reporting purposes, the allowance would be reported as a deduction from the asset(s) to which it relates. Any remaining balance at the end of the year must be eliminated by a debit to allowance for repairs and a credit to the repairs and maintenance expense account. As expenditures occur, they should be debited to allowance for repairs. For example, assume that Lewis Company usually incurs $100,000 of repair and maintenance expenditures at the end of the second quarter of each year. Lewis would accrue one-fourth of the amount at the end of each quarter, as follows:

```
Repairs and maintenance expense . . . . . . . . . . . . . . . . . . . . . . . 25,000
    Allowance for repairs . . . . . . . . . . . . . . . . . . . . . . . . . . . . . . .        25,000
```

If Lewis spent $100,000 at the end of the second quarter, it would make the following entry:

```
Allowance for repairs . . . . . . . . . . . . . . . . . . . . . . . . . . . . . . . 100,000
    Cash, payables, etc. . . . . . . . . . . . . . . . . . . . . . . . . . . . . . . .        100,000
```

The other complication arises when a firm incurs a routine repair and maintenance cost only once every few years, as when oil tankers are drydocked for cleaning and repainting. Such activities usually are predictable and the amounts often can be estimated with reasonable accuracy well in advance of their incurrence. Some people argue that these costs should be accrued as an expense in the years preceding the cost incurrence. However, it is difficult to justify the recognition of an expense for an activity that has not yet begun. Further, the credit portion of the entry certainly cannot be classified as a liability, because the firm does not have an obligation as the result of a past transaction. Thus, these costs should not be accrued in advance of their incurrence. Usually, the appropriate treatment is to record the costs as an expense in the period in which they are incurred. However, some major repairs enhance the future service potential of the related asset. Where this is the case, capitalization as a part of the asset cost would be appropriate.

ADDITIONS   **Additions,** as the term implies, are enlargements, expansions, or extensions of existing plant assets—the addition of a wing to an existing building, for example, or the addition of air conditioning to a fleet of cars. Since an addition provides future benefits to the entity, it is a capital expenditure. Thus, an entity should capitalize the cost of an addition and match the cost with the revenues of future periods. The cost of any work required on the existing asset because of the addition, such as the cost of removing walls or strengthening foundations, also should be capitalized as a part of the cost of the addition. If the addition is an integral part of the older asset, the entity should depreciate the addition over the remaining life of the older asset or over its own useful life, whichever is shorter. If the addition has an existence separate from the older asset, it should be depreciated over its own useful life.

REPLACEMENTS AND IMPROVEMENTS   Companies often dispose of and replace major components of existing plant assets. If the new component has virtually the same operating capabilities as its predecessor, we refer to the new component as a **replacement.** For example, the substitution of a new air conditioning system with essentially the same characteristics as the old system is a replacement. If the new component substantially improves the operating capabilities of the asset, we refer to the new component as an **improvement** or **betterment.** For example, the substitution for an old air conditioning system of a new and significantly more powerful, more sophisticated air conditioning system is an improvement or betterment.

Both replacements and improvements provide additional future benefits to the entity, and thus are capital expenditures. In practice, it is often difficult to distinguish repairs from replacements and improvements.

Three methods are used to record replacements and improvements. Each of the three methods is acceptable under certain circumstances, and all produce an increase in the book value of the related asset.

Substitution

If we can identify the cost and accumulated depreciation associated with the old component, we can eliminate its cost from the accounts and record a gain or loss on its disposal.

Then we can debit the cost of the new component to the asset account. This method, called the **substitution method,** recognizes that the entity is disposing of an old component of an asset and acquiring a new component.

Suppose the Truckee Company replaced the air conditioning unit in its manufacturing facility with a new unit at the beginning of 1987. Although the cost of the air conditioning unit is included in the buildings account, Truckee has depreciated the air conditioning unit separately from the building. Through 1986, Truckee recorded accumulated depreciation of $40,000 on the old unit, which cost $45,000. The replacement unit had a cost of $70,000.

Truckee would make the following entries at the beginning of 1987 under the substitution method:

Accumulated depreciation, buildings	40,000	
Loss on disposal	5,000	
Buildings		45,000
Buildings	70,000	
Cash		70,000

This method cannot be used, however, if the firm does not have a record of the cost and accumulated depreciation for the old component. In that case the firm must use one of the following two methods.

Capitalization of New Cost

Under this method, the cost of the new asset is debited to the asset account. The only difference between this approach and the substitution approach is that under this method the entity does not remove the book value of the old asset from the accounts. This method may be appropriate when it is reasonable to assume that the entity has reduced the book value of the old component to an insignificant amount through depreciation charges. Even though this approach may be unrealistic, entities often use it when the book value of the old component is not determinable.

Reduction of Accumulated Depreciation

It may be argued that if a replacement or improvement extends the useful life of an asset, the result is equivalent to a partial recovery or recapture of previously recorded depreciation. Thus, rather than adding the cost to the asset account, the entity debits accumulated depreciation for the cost. This method and the capitalization method both produce the same book value. The cost and accumulated depreciation, however, differ under the two approaches. A debit to accumulated depreciation for the cost of a replacement is acceptable only when the expenditure extends the useful life of the asset. Even then, there is some question about the logic of the method, since it is unlikely that the cost of the new component will be equal to the depreciation previously recorded on the old component.

REARRANGEMENT AND RELOCATION

Entities sometimes rearrange machinery and equipment to achieve greater operating efficiency. Similarly, plants or portions of plants often are relocated with the objective of providing additional future benefits to the entity. If the rearrangement or relocation costs are material and the benefits clearly extend beyond the current period, the entity should capitalize the cost as deferred rearrangement (relocation) costs and amortize them over the estimated benefit period. If it is not possible to determine with reasonable certainty whether significant benefits from the expenditures will extend beyond the current period, then the entity should expense the costs as they are incurred.

We have discussed the guidelines and many of the problems associated with valuing plant assets at acquisition and accounting for expenditures on them subsequent to acquisition. We will now look at the accounting and reporting issues associated with the disposal of these assets.

DISPOSITION OF PLANT ASSETS

Entities may dispose of plant assets voluntarily through sale, abandonment, exchange, or donation. They also may dispose of plant assets involuntarily, through acts of nature (for example, fire, flood, and earthquake) or as a result of condemnation by a governmental body. Regardless of the method of disposal, the objectives in accounting for the disposition are (1) to eliminate the book value of the asset disposed of, (2) to record the consideration received (if any), and (3) to record any resulting gain or loss. If the consideration received exceeds the book value of the asset given up, a gain arises. If the book value of the asset given up is greater than the consideration received, a loss results. The firm must record depreciation expense up to the date of disposal in order to bring accumulated depreciation and book value up to date so that it may calculate the proper amount of gain or loss. Gains and losses from disposal of plant assets enter into the determination of income from continuing operations unless the disposition meets the criteria for treatment as an extraordinary item.

There are a number of ways in which an entity may dispose of plant assets. We will discuss several of them.

SALE Companies often sell plant assets before their service potential is exhausted. Since a plant asset is not carried in the accounts at fair market value after its acquisition, but rather at depreciated historical cost, it is likely that the book value of the asset sold will differ from the amount of consideration received from its sale. Thus, a gain or loss is very likely to arise when the asset is sold. For example, if a company sold a building with a historical cost of $200,000 and accumulated depreciation of $140,000 at the date of disposal for $80,000 cash, the firm would record the sale as follows:

Cash...	80,000	
Accumulated depreciation	140,000	
Buildings...		200,000
Gain on sale of building		20,000

Unless the event is unusual and infrequent, and thus qualifies as an extraordinary item, the firm would include the gain in the income statement as a part of income from continuing operations.[8]

ABANDONMENT A company simply may stop using a plant asset that no longer has service potential. If such an asset is fully depreciated, the entity should debit the accumulated depreciation account and credit the asset account for the historical cost of the asset. No gain or loss arises in this case. If the asset has a nonzero book value when the entity stops using it, however, the company must eliminate the historical cost and accumulated depreciation

---

[8] If the gain or loss relates to the disposal of a segment of the business, the entity must include it as a part of the gain or loss on disposal of the segment. See "Reporting the Results of Operations— Reporting the Effects of Disposal of a Segment of a Business, and Extraordinary, Unusual and Infrequently Occurring Events and Transactions," *Opinions of the Accounting Principles Board No. 30* (New York: AICPA, 1973), para. 16.

from the accounts and recognize a loss equal to the book value. Any salvage value received for the asset decreases the loss, and any disposal costs incurred increase the loss.

Assume that at the end of 1987, Pitt Corporation disposes of office equipment that has a historical cost of $8,000 and on which Pitt has recorded accumulated depreciation of $7,000 through 1987. A local salvage yard operator pays Pitt $200 for the office equipment. Pitt must record the disposal as follows:

Cash	200	
Accumulated depreciation	7,000	
Loss on disposal	800	
Office equipment		8,000

DONATION

A company may also dispose of a plant asset by donating it to an individual or to another organization. Again, it is unlikely that the donated asset's fair market value will be the same as its book value. In an economic sense, the cost of the donation to the company donating the asset is the fair market value of the asset given up. Thus, the donor should recognize this fair market value as donation expense, and record a gain or loss on donation equal to the difference between book value and fair market value.

Assume that Nice Corporation donates five acres of land to a city in which Nice has production facilities. The city will construct a community center on the land. The land had an original cost to Nice Corporation of $25,000 and has a fair market value of $40,000 at the time of donation. Nice would make the following entry to record the donation:

Donation expense	40,000	
Land		25,000
Gain on donated land		15,000

INVOLUNTARY CONVERSION

Not infrequently, plant assets are partially or totally destroyed by fires, floods, and other catastrophes. Governmental bodies may, through their right of eminent domain, force companies to dispose of plant assets in exchange for consideration that may be more or less than the book value of the assets.

When an entity disposes of a plant asset involuntarily, it must record any asset received at its fair market value, eliminate the book value of the old asset, and recognize a gain or loss, just as in voluntary disposals. Suppose a building with a cost of $150,000 and accumulated depreciation of $100,000 is totally destroyed by fire. The building is insured against fire loss and the insurance settlement is $80,000. The entity would make the following entry to record the disposal:

Cash	80,000	
Accumulated depreciation	100,000	
Building		150,000
Gain on disposal of building		30,000

If the gain meets the criteria for treatment as an extraordinary item, the entity would show it as an extraordinary gain on the income statement. Otherwise, it would be a part of income from continuing operations.

Entities sometimes immediately reinvest the proceeds from involuntary conversion in similar assets. Some people argue that since the entity is in the same economic situation as it was before the conversion, the investment amounts to an exchange of similar nonmonetary assets, and therefore the entity should recognize no gain or loss. However, the FASB requires that, even though reinvestment of the proceeds from conversion in nonmonetary assets occurs or is contemplated, entities must recognize fully gains and losses on involuntary conversions.[9]

Many entities carry insurance on plant assets for protection against losses from various casualties. In some instances, a company may insure the plant asset for less than the fair market value of the asset. Also, two or more insurance policies may provide the coverage on a single plant asset. Such situations are called coinsurance situations and are discussed in Appendix 11–1.

SUMMARY OF IMPORTANT TOPICS AND CONCEPT APPLICATIONS

1. **Plant assets** are physical resources acquired for use in operations over several accounting periods. Because these assets benefit several accounting periods, their cost is capitalized and **matched** against revenues over the periods benefited through the process of **depreciation.**

2. In accounting for **self-constructed assets, interest during construction** is capitalized for assets that require an acquisition period to ready them for their intended use. Because no revenues are generated from these assets until they are placed in service, **matching** requires that all costs necessary to get the assets into position for their intended use, including interest costs, should be capitalized and depreciated over their useful lives.

3. Plant assets acquired through a **deferred payment** arrangement should be recorded at their fair market value at the date of acquisition, which may be determined by the face amount of the debt if it is issued at a reasonable interest rate, or at the cash equivalent price of the asset or discounted value of the debt if the debt is not issued at a reasonable interest rate.

4. The **investment tax credit** may be accounted for by either the deferral (cost-reduction) method or the flow-through (tax-reduction) method.

5. Fair market values generally govern the recording of exchanges of plant assets. However, if the exchange involves **similar assets,** gains cannot be recognized except to the extent that a portion of the asset given up is converted to cash through the receipt of boot. In general, the exchange of similar assets is considered to be a continuation of the earning process rather than the culmination of the earning process.

6. Expenditures on plant assets subsequent to acquisition may be either **capital expenditures** or **revenue expenditures.** Capital expenditures provide future benefits beyond the period in which the expenditures are made and should be added to the asset cost. Revenue expenditures benefit only the period in which the expenditures are made and should be expensed as incurred.

7. Plant assets may be disposed of through sale, abandonment, donation, or involuntary conversion. The gain or loss on disposal is the difference between the book value at the date of the disposal and the consideration received, if any.

[9] "Accounting for Involuntary Conversions of Nonmonetary Assets to Monetary Assets," *FASB Interpretation No. 30* (Stamford, Conn.: FASB, 1979).

APPENDIX 11–1

COINSURANCE

Many companies carry insurance to protect their plant and other assets, such as inventories, against losses due to fire, explosion, storms, and similar events. The effect of the insurance coverage is to shift at least a portion of the risk of loss to the insurance company, in exchange for premium payments.

The gain or loss recorded for an insured casualty is the difference between the book value of the asset and the amount recoverable under the insurance policy. The amount recoverable is based on the fair market value of the property at the time of the loss. The amount recoverable is the lesser of the fair market value of the loss or the face amount of the insurance policy. For example, if a fire totally destroys an asset with a book value of $30,000 and a fair market value of $40,000, and the asset is insured for $35,000, the entity would recover $35,000 and record a book gain of $5,000 ($35,000 − $30,000).

Casualty insurance policies usually include a **coinsurance** clause. This clause forces the insured company to share the risk of loss—that is, to become a **coinsurer** with the insurance company—if the insurance coverage is less than a specified percentage of the fair market value of the asset. Coinsurance thus encourages policyholders to insure their assets for close to fair market value. Without coinsurance requirements, management would tend to insure assets for only a portion of fair market value, because casualties often do not totally destroy the assets involved.

A coinsurance clause requires that if an entity carries insurance on an asset for less than a certain percentage of the asset's fair market value at the time of a loss, the entity may recover only a portion of the loss. The amount recoverable is the lowest of (1) the face value of the policy, or (2) the fair market value of the loss, or (3) the coinsurance formula amount. The coinsurance formula amount, also called the **coinsurance indemnity,** is determined as follows:

$$\text{Coinsurance indemnity} = \frac{\text{Face value of policy}}{\text{Coinsurance requirement}} \times \text{Fair market value of loss}$$

We determine the coinsurance requirement, the denominator in the above formula, by multiplying the coinsurance percentage by the fair market value of the property at the time of loss. The formula for computing the coinsurance indemnity may be expressed as follows:

$$\text{Coinsurance indemnity} = \frac{\text{Face value of policy}}{\text{Coinsurance percentage} \times \text{Fair market value of property at time of loss}} \times \text{Fair market value of loss}$$

Assume that the fair market value of a property at the time of loss is $50,000 and that the coinsurance requirement is 80 percent ($40,000), which means that the entity must insure the property for at least $40,000 to recover the full value of any losses up to that amount. The amount recoverable under three different situations is shown on the next page.

	SITUATION 1	SITUATION 2	SITUATION 3
Fair market value of loss	$35,000	$45,000	$30,000
Face value of policy	45,000	35,000	25,000
Amount recoverable	35,000*	35,000†	18,750‡

* Fair market value of loss.

† Face value of policy.

‡ Coinsurance formula amount: $\dfrac{\$25,000}{\$40,000} \times \$30,000 = \$18,750.$

In situation 1, the company recovers the fair market value of the loss because the coverage ($45,000) exceeds the coinsurance requirement ($40,000). In situation 2, the company recovers the face value of the policy because it is lower than both the fair market value of the loss ($45,000) and the coinsurance indemnity [($35,000 ÷ $40,000) × $45,000 = $39,375]. In situation 3, the company recovers the coinsurance indemnity because it is lower than both the fair market value of the loss and the face value of the policy.

In some instances, entities protect themselves against casualty losses by carrying more than one insurance policy on the same asset. When this is the case, the entity determines the amount recoverable under each individual policy by multiplying the fair market value of the loss by a fraction whose numerator is the face value of that particular policy and whose denominator is the *higher* of (1) the coinsurance requirement for that policy or (2) the total face value of all policies:

$$
\begin{array}{l}
\text{Amount recoverable} \\
\text{under an individual} \\
\text{policy}
\end{array}
=
\dfrac{\text{Face value of policy}}{\text{Higher of}\left\{\begin{array}{c}\text{Coinsurance requirement}\\ \text{for policy}\\ or\\ \text{Total face value of}\\ \text{all policies}\end{array}\right.}
\times \text{Fair market value of loss}
$$

Assume that an entity carries three separate insurance policies on a particular asset, in face amounts of $10,000, $15,000, and $15,000, with coinsurance requirements of 70, 80, and 90 percent, respectively. The fair market value of the property at the date of the loss is $50,000, and the fair market value of the loss is $35,000. Calculation of the amount recoverable from each policy is as follows:

POLICY	FACE VALUE OF POLICY	COINSURANCE REQUIREMENT	FRACTION	LOSS	AMOUNT RECOVERABLE
1	$10,000	$35,000	10,000/40,000	$35,000	$ 8,750
2	15,000	40,000	15,000/40,000	35,000	13,125
3	15,000	45,000	15,000/45,000	35,000	11,667
	$40,000				$33,542

The denominator of the fraction for policies 1 and 2 is $40,000, the total face value of all policies, because $40,000 is the coinsurance requirement for policy 1 and the same as the coinsurance requirement for policy 2. The denominator of the fraction for policy 3 is $45,000, because that amount exceeds the total face value of all policies ($40,000).

QUESTIONS	The question marked with an asterisk (*) refers to Appendix 11–1.

Q11-1. What three characteristics distinguish plant assets from other assets?

Q11-2. What is the general guideline governing the amount that an entity should assign to a plant asset at the time it is acquired?

Q11-3. What types of costs do entities typically incur in connection with the acquisition of land?

Q11-4. What is the appropriate accounting and reporting treatment for land improvements that *(a)* produce relatively permanent benefits and *(b)* have a limited life?

Q11-5. What are the two major accounting problems associated with self-constructed assets that are not associated with assets acquired from an external source?

Q11-6. Describe the three possible approaches to accounting for indirect manufacturing costs when a company constructs assets for its own use. Which method is the most common in practice? Why?

Q11-7. What three methods have been proposed for accounting for interest costs during construction?

Q11-8. Describe briefly the current requirements for accounting for interest during construction. In your description, include *(a)* an identification of qualifying assets, *(b)* a discussion of the amount to be capitalized, and *(c)* a definition of the capitalization period.

Q11-9. At what amount should an entity record assets acquired through the incurrence of debt? How should the entity determine this amount when the fair market value of the asset acquired is not determinable and the interest rate on the debt is unreasonable?

Q11-10. When a firm acquires plant assets by issuing its own capital stock, at what amount should the plant assets and the capital stock be recorded?

Q11-11. What is a nonreciprocal transfer? At what amount should an entity record plant assets acquired by donation at acquisition? subsequent to acquisition?

Q11-12. How is the cost of plant assets acquired in a lump-sum purchase allocated to the separate assets?

Q11-13. Describe the two acceptable methods of accounting for an investment tax credit.

Q11-14. What is the general guideline governing the valuation at acquisition of plant assets acquired in a nonmonetary exchange? In what two circumstances does this general guideline not apply?

Q11-15. Give two examples of exchanges of similar assets. Describe the appropriate accounting for exchanges of similar assets in a loss situation. Describe the appropriate accounting for exchanges of similar assets in a gain situation where *(a)* boot is given and *(b)* boot is received.

Q11-16. Explain why entities recognize gains fully in exchanges of dissimilar assets and why they do not recognize, or only partially recognize, gains resulting from exchanges of similar assets.

Q11-17. What is the basic accounting guideline governing costs related to plant assets after they have been acquired? Distinguish between capital expenditures and revenue expenditures.

Q11-18. Describe the appropriate accounting treatment for *(a)* repair and maintenance costs, *(b)* additions, *(c)* replacements and improvements, and *(d)* rearrangement and relocation costs.

Q11-19. List three methods for voluntarily disposing of plant assets. Describe the appropriate accounting treatment for each method of disposal.

Q11-20. How should an entity record involuntary conversions of plant assets? How should an entity report a gain or loss from an involuntary conversion in the financial statements?

*Q11-21. Describe how we determine the amount recoverable from an insurance policy if a loss occurs when *(a)* there is no coinsurance clause, *(b)* a coinsurance clause exists, and *(c)* multiple policies cover the asset, all with coinsurance requirements.

CASES

C11-1. ACQUISITION COST OF PLANT ASSETS A company may acquire plant assets for cash, on a deferred-payment plan, by exchanging other assets, and by a combination of all three, among other ways.

REQUIRED

1. Identify six costs that an entity should capitalize as part of the cost of land. For your answer, assume that an entity acquires land with an existing building in exchange for cash and that the firm plans to remove the building in the immediate future in order to construct a new building on the site.

2. At what amount should a company record a plant asset acquired on a deferred-payment plan?

3. In general, at what amount should an entity record a plant asset received in exchange for other nonmonetary assets? Specifically, at what amount should a company record a new machine acquired in exchange for an older, similar machine plus a cash payment?

C11-2. ACQUISITION COST OF MACHINERY The invoice price of a machine is $10,000. Various other costs related to the acquisition and installation of the machine amount to $2,000 and include such things as transportation, electrical wiring, and a special base. The machine has an estimated life of 10 years, with no residual value at the end of that period.

The owner of the business suggests that the incidental costs of $2,000 be charged to expense immediately, for the following reasons: *(a)* if the machine is sold, the company cannot recover these costs in the sales price; *(b)* the inclusion of the $2,000 in the machinery account on the books will not necessarily result in a closer approximation of the market price of this asset over the years, because of the possibility of changing price levels; and *(c)* charging the $2,000 to expense immediately will reduce federal income taxes.

REQUIRED

Discuss each of the points raised by the owner of the business.

(AICPA, adapted)

C11-3. ACQUISITION COST OF FIXED ASSETS Following are three independent situations involving application of the guidelines for valuing fixed assets. Answer the question(s) posed for each situation. Provide the reasoning underlying your answer(s).

1. Greenberg Corporation entered into a contract to purchase certain plant assets. As part of the transaction, Greenberg received a commission from the real estate broker, who was paid by the seller. Would the commission be considered as income to Greenberg or as a reduction of the cost of the property acquired?

2. Bergevin Corporation acquired a site for the construction of a building 10 years ago. At that time a building on the site had an estimated expected life of 40 years. Currently the building is being demolished because of obsolescence, and a completely new structure is being built. Should the undepreciated cost of the old building be carried forward as part of the cost of the new building, or should it be expensed in the current period?

3. Several years ago, Doherty Corporation entered into an agreement with a customer, Tormey Corporation, whereby Tormey would take the entire output of one of Doherty's plants. As part of the consideration, Doherty gave Tormey an option to purchase the plant at a future date at a price that is adjusted annually for capital additions and depreciation. As the option date approaches, Doherty would now like to negotiate with Tormey for the cancellation of the option. This would require Doherty to make some payment to Tormey. If this transaction occurs, how should the matter be shown in the financial statements? Should the cancellation cost be divided between the land and the plant?

C11-4. SELF-CONSTRUCTED ASSETS Jay Manufacturing, Inc., began operations in 1982 to produce probos, a new type of instrument it hoped to sell to doctors, dentists, and hospitals. The demand for probos far exceeded initial expectations, and the company was unable to produce enough of them to fill its orders.

For a time Jay manufactured its product using equipment that it built at the start of its operations. To meet the demand, it needed more efficient equipment. The company decided to design and build new equipment since the kind available on the market was unsuitable for the production of probos.

In 1987 Jay devoted a section of the plant to development of the new equipment and hired a special staff. Within six months, at a cost of $170,000, a machine was developed which increased production and reduced labor costs substantially. Elated by the success of the new machine, the company built three more machines of the same type at a cost of $80,000 each.

REQUIRED

1. In addition to satisfying a need that outsiders cannot meet within the desired time, why might a firm construct fixed assets for its own use?

2. In general, what costs should an entity capitalize for a self-constructed fixed asset?

3. Discuss the propriety of including in the capitalized cost of self-constructed assets:
  a) The increase in overhead caused by the self-construction of fixed assets.
  b) A proportionate share of overhead on the same basis as that applied to goods manufactured for sale.

4. Discuss the proper accounting treatment of the $90,000 ($170,000 − $80,000) by which the cost of Jay's first machine exceeded the cost of the subsequent machines.

(AICPA, adapted)

C11-5. ACQUISITION OF PROPERTY BY ISSUING DEBT Entities often acquire plant assets by incurring debt. The debt may have a reasonable interest rate or an unreasonable interest rate (including noninterest-bearing notes).

REQUIRED

1. Explain why it is important from a financial reporting standpoint to identify debt issued at an unreasonable interest rate.

2. Describe the appropriate accounting for the acquired assets and debt if *(a)* the debt bears a reasonable rate of interest, and *(b)* the debt bears an unreasonable rate of interest.

C11-6. INVESTMENT TAX CREDIT Two methods of accounting for the investment tax credit are acceptable under GAAP. These methods may produce substantially different results in periodic income.

REQUIRED

1. Explain the purpose of the investment tax credit and its effect on firm cash flows.

2. Identify and describe the two methods of accounting for the investment tax credit. Explain the rationale underlying each method.

C11-7. CAPITAL EXPENDITURES VS. REVENUE EXPENDITURES Conceptually, expenditures may be categorized as capital expenditures or revenue expenditures. However, from a practical standpoint, it is often difficult to determine in which category a particular expenditure belongs.

REQUIRED

1. Explain why these two categories of expenditures exist and why it is important to classify expenditures in these two categories properly.

2. Taylor Corporation treats all expenditures of less than $10,000 as revenue expenditures. Explain why this practice may be acceptable in spite of your reasoning in part 1.

C11-8. CLASSIFICATION OF EXPENDITURES The controller for Alpine, Inc., has asked a member of the staff to review the repair and maintenance expense account to determine if all of the charges are appropriate. The staff member has reviewed this account and has identified the following 10 transactions for further scrutiny. All of these transactions are considered material in amount.

	DATE	**AMOUNT**	**DESCRIPTION**
a)	1-3-87	$10,000	Service contract on office equipment.
b)	3-7-87	10,000	Initial design fee for proposed extension of office building.

	DATE	AMOUNT	DESCRIPTION
c)	4-12-87	$18,500	New condenser for central air conditioning unit located on the roof of office building.
d)	4-20-87	7,000	Purchase of two executive chairs and desks.
e)	5-12-87	40,850	Purchase of storm and screen windows and installation of same on all office windows.
f)	5-18-87	38,450	Sealing of roof leaks over entire production plant.
g)	6-19-87	28,740	Replacement of large door to production area.
h)	7-3-87	11,740	Installation of automatic door opening system on the above door to speed opening.
i)	9-14-87	38,500	Purchase of overhead crane for the Assembly Department to speed up production.
j)	10-18-87	11,000	Replacement of broken gear on machine in the Machining Department.

REQUIRED

For each of the ten transactions identified by the controller's staff member, indicate whether the transaction is properly charged to the repair and maintenance expense account, and if not, indicate the appropriate account to which the transaction should be charged. Explain your reasoning in each case.

(IMA, adapted)

EXERCISES

The exercises marked with an asterisk (*) refer to Appendix 11–1.

E11-1. CLASSIFICATION OF PLANT ASSET EXPENDITURES Burdick Company incurred the following costs in connection with plant assets:

a) Cash paid for land.
b) Attorneys' fees connected with land purchase.
c) Improvements to land—limited life.
d) Survey costs for new building.
e) Architect's fee.
f) Net invoice cost of machinery.
g) Insurance on machinery in transit.
h) Unpaid taxes on land assumed by Burdick.
i) Cost of assembling and installing machinery.
j) Removal costs of old building on land.
k) Landscaping costs—indefinite life.
l) Excavation costs for new building.
m) Freight costs on machinery.
n) Material, labor, and overhead on new building.
o) Foundation for machinery (not usable elsewhere).
p) Interest costs incurred on debt associated with construction of building.
q) Cost of testing new machinery.
r) Mortgage assumed on land.

REQUIRED

Indicate whether each of the items listed should be included in land (L), buildings (B), machinery and equipment (M), or other (O). Where your response is "other," indicate the appropriate treatment of the item in the accounts.

E11-2. BALANCE SHEET CLASSIFICATION OF ASSETS The following types of assets may be held by a company at various times:

a) Land held for investment purposes.
b) Idle machinery awaiting disposal.

c) Land held for future plant site.

d) Leasehold improvements.

e) Fully depreciated assets still in use.

REQUIRED

What is the appropriate balance sheet classification of each of the items listed?

E11-3. ACQUISITION COST On November 1, 1987, Rice Company purchased for $200,000 a tract of land as a factory site. The old building on the property was razed, and salvaged materials resulting from demolition were sold. Additional costs incurred and salvage proceeds realized during November were as follows:

Demolition of old building	$25,000
Legal fees for purchase contract and recording ownership	5,000
Title guarantee insurance	6,000
Proceeds from sale of salvaged materials	4,000

REQUIRED

Prepare a schedule showing the amount that Rice should report for land in its balance sheet at November 30, 1987.

(AICPA, adapted)

E11-4. INTEREST DURING CONSTRUCTION Wilkinson Company is constructing a production facility for an estimated cost of $4 million. Construction began on January 1, 1987, and is expected to take about two years. Also on January 1, 1987, to finance the construction, Wilkinson borrowed $4 million at a 12 percent annual interest rate. For 1987, total construction expenditures were $1.5 million and average accumulated expenditures were $650,000.

REQUIRED

1. Calculate the amount of interest that Wilkinson should capitalize for 1987.

2. Prepare the journal entries to reflect the aggregate construction costs for 1987 and to reflect interest costs incurred. Assume cash was paid for all expenditures.

E11-5. CAPITALIZATION OF INTEREST On January 1, 1987, Sego Corporation borrowed $20 million at 14 percent to finance the construction of a new building complex to be used in its operations. Construction activities began immediately. The loan repayments began after completion of the construction project. Sego had other outstanding debt during the period of $30 million with an average interest rate of 16 percent. During 1987, expenditures of $12 million were incurred evenly throughout the year in connection with the self-construction.

REQUIRED

Calculate the amount of interest that should be capitalized in 1987.

E11-6. CAPITALIZATION OF INTEREST During 1987, Rambo Corporation constructed and manufactured certain assets, and incurred the following interest costs in connection with these activities:

	INTEREST COSTS INCURRED
Warehouse constructed for Rambo's own use	$20,000
Special-order machine for sale to customer, produced according to customer specifications	9,000
Inventories routinely manufactured, produced on a repetitive basis	7,000

All of these assets required an extended period of time for completion.

REQUIRED

Assuming the effect of interest capitalization is material, calculate the amount of interest cost that should be capitalized for 1987.

(AICPA, adapted)

E11-7. DEFERRED PAYMENTS   The Mutt Company bought some machinery from the Jeff Company on January 1, 1987. The sales contract required annual payments of $100,000 over five years. The first payment was due on December 31, 1987.

REQUIRED

Prepare the journal entries for Mutt Company on January 1, 1987, and December 31, 1987, under the following two independent assumptions:

1. The cash selling price of the machinery was $379,080.

2. The cash selling price of the machinery is not available. The market rate of interest at the time the transaction took place was 12 percent.

E11-8. EXCHANGE OF STOCK FOR LAND   On December 1, 1987, Wheat Corporation exchanged 1,000 shares of its $25 par value common stock for a parcel of land to be held for a future plant site. On the exchange date a common share of Wheat Corporation had a fair market value of $55. Wheat received $5,000 for selling scrap when an existing building on the property was removed from the site.

REQUIRED

Prepare the journal entry to record the transaction.

E11-9. LUMP-SUM ACQUISITION   On December 1, 1987, Brooks Corporation purchased for $270,000 a tract of land on which a warehouse and office building were located. The following data were available concerning the property:

	CURRENT APPRAISED VALUE	SELLER'S BOOK VALUE
Land	$ 87,500	$ 70,000
Warehouse.................................	37,500	40,000
Office building	100,000	90,000
	$225,000	$200,000

REQUIRED

Prepare the journal entry to record the property acquisition.

(AICPA, adapted)

E11-10. LUMP-SUM ACQUISITION   The Reif Company made a lump-sum purchase of three pieces of machinery for $130,000. At the time of acquisition, Reif paid $5,000 to determine the appraised value of the machinery. The appraisal disclosed the following values:

Machine 1	$70,000
Machine 2	52,000
Machine 3	23,000

REQUIRED

Calculate the amount that Reif should record in the accounts for each machine.

E11-11. INVESTMENT TAX CREDIT   At the beginning of Year 1, Yuma Company paid $50,000 for machinery that qualified for a 10 percent investment credit. The estimated useful life of the machinery is 10 years. Income before taxes for Year 1 was $200,000 and the income tax rate was 40 percent.

REQUIRED

1. Prepare the journal entry to record income tax expense and income taxes payable for Year 1, assuming that Yuma uses the deferral method to account for the investment credit and that the credit is to be amortized over the useful life of the machinery.

2. Prepare the journal entry to record income tax expense and income taxes payable, assuming Yuma uses the flow-through method to account for the investment credit.

E11-12. INVESTMENT TAX CREDIT   On January 1, Year 1, Reedem & Weep (R&W) purchased for $60,000 a machine that qualified for a 10 percent investment tax credit. The machine had an estimated useful life of five years and a $5,000 estimated salvage value. R&W has an average tax rate of 40 percent, and its pretax income was $120,000 in Year 1 and $150,000 in Year 2.

REQUIRED

1. Assuming R&W uses the flow-through method to account for the investment tax credit, prepare journal entries to record income taxes for Year 1 and Year 2.

2. Assuming R&W uses the deferral method to account for the investment tax credit, prepare journal entries to record income taxes for Year 1 and Year 2.

E11-13. EXCHANGE OF DISSIMILAR NONMONETARY ASSETS   Lawrence Corporation exchanged a building for a special-purpose piece of equipment. The building had cost Lawrence $140,000; the book value at the time of the exchange was $80,000. The equipment could have been purchased for $100,000 cash; the fair market value of the building was not readily determinable.

REQUIRED

Prepare the journal entry to record the exchange.

E11-14. EXCHANGE OF SIMILAR NONMONETARY ASSETS   Minor Baseball Company had a player contract with Doe that was recorded in its accounting records at $145,000. Better Baseball Company had a player contract with Smith that was recorded in its accounting records at $140,000. Minor traded Doe to Better for Smith by an exchange of contracts. The estimated fair market value of each contract was $150,000.

REQUIRED

Prepare the journal entries to record the exchange for both Minor and Better.

(AICPA, adapted)

E11-15. EXCHANGE OF SIMILAR NONMONETARY ASSETS   On January 2, 1987, Dorsett Delivery Company traded in an old delivery truck for a newer model. Data relative to the old and new trucks follow:

OLD TRUCK

Original cost	$ 8,000
Accumulated depreciation as of 1/2/87	6,000
Average published retail value	1,700

NEW TRUCK

List price	10,000
Cash price without trade-in	9,000
Cash paid with trade-in	7,800

REQUIRED

Prepare the appropriate journal entry to record the exchange on Dorsett's books.

E11-16. ACCOUNTING FOR COSTS INCURRED FOR PLANT ASSETS   During 1987, Montgomery Company made the following expenditures:

Jan.   2   Acquired land and building for $300,000 cash. The appraised values of the land and building were $110,000 and $220,000, respectively.

Feb. 15   Acquired machinery for $20,000 cash. Paid freight charges of $2,000 and an insurance premium of $480 to cover goods in transit.

April 10   Completed remodeling of building acquired on January 2 at a cost of $65,000, paid in cash.

July 20   Performed periodic maintenance on machinery at a cost of $2,400.

Aug. 3 Completed new foundation for machinery acquired on February 15 at a cost of $3,700. The original foundation, which was included in the cost of the machinery, was inadequate. Scrap from the old foundation was sold for $400.

Nov. 12 The machinery and equipment in the plant were rearranged to enhance the efficiency of the production process at a cost of $7,200.

REQUIRED

Prepare journal entries to record all of the above transactions.

E11-17. DISPOSAL OF MACHINERY FOR NONINTEREST-BEARING NOTE   Dandy Company sold a plant asset (machinery) in exchange for a noninterest-bearing note to be paid at the rate of $5,000 per year for 10 years, beginning one year from the date of disposal of the machinery. Dandy originally had paid $60,000 for the machinery. At the time it was disposed of, accumulated depreciation equaled $25,000. A fair rate of interest for this transaction is 12 percent.

REQUIRED

Give the necessary journal entries to record the disposal of the machinery and to record the collection of the first installment on the note.

E11-18. DISPOSAL OF PLANT ASSETS   Grogan Company has a machine that is no longer useful. The machine cost $40,000, and on December 31, 1987, accumulated depreciation of $30,000 had been recorded. The fair market value on that date was $6,000.

REQUIRED

Prepare the journal entry to record the disposal of the machine on January 2, 1988, under each of the following *independent* assumptions:

1. Grogan sells the machine for $6,000 cash.
2. Grogan abandons the machine, incurring $400 of removal costs.
3. Grogan donates the machine to a newly formed small business in the community.

*E11-19. COINSURANCE   In 1987 Payton Company incurred a loss when a fire destroyed a building. The book value of the building at the time of the fire was $128,000. The building had an estimated fair market value of $155,000. The loss was covered by an insurance policy with a face value of $120,000 and an 80 percent coinsurance clause.

REQUIRED

Determine the amount collectible as a result of the loss.

*E11-20. COINSURANCE   Assume that four separate carriers have written fire insurance policies totaling $60,000 on a single property with a fair market value of $100,000.

REQUIRED

Calculate the amount collectible from a carrier whose $30,000 policy contains a 90 percent coinsurance clause, assuming that the fair market value of the loss is $20,000.

PROBLEMS

The problem marked with an asterisk (*) refers to Appendix 11–1.

P11-1. ACQUISITION OF PLANT ASSETS   The following transactions are unrelated:

a) Equipment listed at $12,000 was purchased at terms of 2%/10, net 30. To take advantage of the discount, the company borrowed $9,000 of the purchase price by issuing a one-year 12 percent note that was repaid with interest at maturity.

b) Equipment with a list price of $6,000 was purchased under the terms of 2%/10, net 30. Payment was made 20 days after purchase.

c) A machine was purchased on the following terms: cash of $10,000 plus 10 semiannual payments of $2,000 each. The company's borrowing rate is 10 percent.

d) An asset listed at $80,000 was purchased. Settlement was effected by issuance of bonds with a face amount of $80,000 and an 8 percent stated interest rate. The company had identical bonds outstanding which were selling at 96 on the open market when it purchased the asset.

REQUIRED

Prepare journal entries for the above transactions. For item *(c),* record only the acquisition.

(CGAA, adapted)

P11-2. ACQUISITION OF PLANT ASSETS On January 1, 1987, the Examination Corporation acquired from Mr. Stu Dent a truck, equipment, and some land with an old building on it. The company did not want the old building and, according to plan, demolished it during the first week of January to make way for a new building on the site. The net demolition costs were $5,000.

A local garage appraised the truck at $5,500. The *Gold Book of Used Trucks,* a survey of 200 similar trucks in the area in December, estimated the average price of such trucks in similar condition at $5,000.

On the date of acquisition, a local equipment dealer offered to buy the equipment from the Examination Corporation for $7,500. The equipment cost Mr. Dent $9,000 in 1984, and in his opinion it was worth $8,000.

To acquire these assets, the company put $7,000 down and signed a $13,000 interest-bearing note with Mr. Dent on which it agreed to pay $2,000 interest over the next two years. The company also promised to pay the 1986 property tax arrearages of $1,000. Legal fees in the purchase were $1,500.

The property tax assessments for 1986 were as follows:

Land $3,000
Building. 2,000

REQUIRED

Prepare the journal entry or entries required to record the January 1987 plant asset acquisitions by the Examination Corporation.

(CGAA, adapted)

P11-3. ACQUISITION OF PLANT ASSETS Bookston, Inc., needs to acquire additional machine capacity to meet the growing demand for its product. The Machine Supply Company offers to provide the machines to Bookston under any of the options listed below. Each option gives Bookston exactly the same machines and gives Machine Supply approximately the same net present value cash equivalent at 8 percent.

a) Cash purchase, $100,000.
b) Installment purchase, 15 equal payments of $11,700.
c) 10-year lease with right to purchase for $1,000; annual lease payments of $14,800.
d) 15-year rental contract at $11,300 per year.

The expected economic life of these machines to Bookston is 15 years. Salvage value is estimated to be $10,000 at the end of that time.

REQUIRED

For each option, prepare the journal entry (if any) to record the transaction. Assume that all cash flows are at the end of the year.

(IMA, adapted)

P11-4. SELF-CONSTRUCTED ASSETS The Campbell Machine Company manufactures small and large milling machines. Selling prices of these machines range from $35,000 to $200,000. During the five-month period from August 1, 1987, through December 31, 1987, the company manufactured a milling machine for its own use. This machine was built as part of the regular production activities. The project required a large amount of planning and supervisory personnel's time, as well as that of some of the company's officers, because it was a more sophisticated type of machine than their regular production models.

Throughout the five-month period all costs directly associated with the construction of the machine were charged to a special asset construction account. An analysis of the debits to this account as of December 31, 1987, is shown below.

Campbell Machine Company

ASSET CONSTRUCTION ACCOUNT

ITEM DESCRIPTION		COST
Raw materials		
Iron castings:		
Main housing, 3 sections	$37,480	
Movable heads, 2 @ $3,900	7,800	
Machine bed	4,760	
Table, 2 sections @ $5,500	11,000	$ 61,040
Other raw materials:		
Electrical components and wiring	$28,000	
Worm screws and housing	8,600	
Cutter housings	2,700	
Conveyor system	8,400	
Other parts	2,500	50,200
Direct labor costs		
Layout 90 hrs. @ $5.00	$ 450	
Electricians 380 hrs. @ 9.00	3,420	
Machining 1,100 hrs. @ 8.00	8,800	
Heat treatment 100 hrs. @ 7.50	750	
Assembly 450 hrs. @ 7.00	3,150	
Testing 180 hrs. @ 8.00	1,440	18,010
Other direct charges		
Repairs and maintenance during testing period	$ 1,340	
Interest expense from 8/1/87 to 12/31/87 on funds borrowed for construction purposes	4,260	
Additional labor to assist during machine testing period, 180 hrs. @ $5	900	6,500
Balance, 12/31/87		$135,750

Factory overhead is allocated to normal production as a percentage of direct labor dollars, as follows:

DEPARTMENT	FACTORY OVERHEAD RATES (PERCENT OF DIRECT LABOR DOLLARS)		
	VARIABLE	FIXED	TOTAL
Layout and electricians	50%	20%	70%
Machining,* heat treatment, and assembly	50	50	100

* All testing is conducted by employees in the machining department.

Campbell uses a flat rate of 40 percent of direct labor dollars to allocate general and administrative overhead.

During the machine testing period a cutter head malfunctioned and did extensive damage to the machine table and one cutter housing. This damage was the result of an error in the assembly operation. Although no additional raw materials were needed to make the machine operational after the accident, the following labor for rework was required:

DIRECT LABOR HOURS

Electric	80
Machining	200
Assembly..	100
Testing (conducted by machining department)	20

Campbell included all of these labor charges in the asset construction account. In addition, the repairs and maintenance charges of $1,340 included in the account were incurred as a result of the malfunction.

REQUIRED

Calculate in accordance with generally accepted accounting principles the amount that Campbell should capitalize for the milling machine as of December 31, 1987, when the machine was declared operational.

(IMA, adapted)

P11-5. INTEREST CAPITALIZATION

A) At the beginning of 1986, Mona Lisa Corporation signed a construction contract to have a deluxe swimming pool, spa, and club built at its apartment complex. Construction was to begin in late 1986 and was to be completed by the end of 1987. In anticipation of construction expenditures for 1986, on October 1, 1986, Mona Lisa borrowed $1 million by issuing a two-year noninterest-bearing note with a maturity value of $1,266,800. Interest at 3 percent per quarter was implicit in the note.

Because of bad weather, construction did not begin until April 1, 1987; it was completed on December 31, 1987. Construction expenditures during 1987 were as follows:

April 1, 1987	$400,000
May 1, 1987...	100,000
June 1, 1987...	200,000
October 1, 1987	200,000
December 31, 1987	100,000

Mona Lisa's only other debt outstanding was a 10 percent 10-year bond issue sold three years ago at its par value of $3 million. Mona Lisa's fiscal year ends on December 31.

REQUIRED

1. Calculate Mona Lisa's actual interest cost for 1986 and 1987.

2. Calculate the amount of interest that Mona Lisa should capitalize for 1986 and 1987.

B) Refer to part *A* and assume the same facts except that the expenditures in 1987 were as follows:

April 1, 1987	$500,000
June 1, 1987...	800,000
August 1, 1987...	600,000
October 1, 1987	200,000
December 1, 1987	300,000

REQUIRED

Calculate the amount of interest that Mona Lisa should capitalize for 1987.

P11-6. NONMONETARY EXCHANGE Truman Company owns a warehouse with a fair value of $650,000, a recorded cost of $900,000, and accumulated depreciation of $450,000. Clyde Corporation owns an office building with a fair market value of $612,000, a recorded cost of $1,080,000, and accumulated depreciation of $594,000. Truman and Clyde exchange assets. Clyde also gives Truman cash of $38,000 in the exchange.

REQUIRED

1. Assume this is considered an exchange of dissimilar assets. Record the exchange on the books of
  a) Truman.
  b) Clyde.

2. Assume this is considered an exchange of similar assets. Record the exchange on the books of
  a) Truman.
  b) Clyde.

P11-7. NONMONETARY EXCHANGE Two independent companies, Beam and Wall, are in the home building business. Each owns a tract of land that it is holding for development, but each company would prefer to build on the other's land. Accordingly, they agree to exchange their land.

An appraiser is hired, and from his report and the companies' records, the following information is obtained:

	BEAM COMPANY'S LAND	WALL COMPANY'S LAND
Cost and book value	$ 80,000	$50,000
Fair market value based on appraisal	100,000	90,000

The exchange of land is made, and in view of the difference in appraised fair market values, Wall pays $10,000 cash to Beam.

REQUIRED

Prepare the necessary journal entries to record the exchange for both Wall and Beam.

(AICPA, adapted)

P11-8. COMPREHENSIVE You are engaged in the examination of the financial statements of the Saunders Company and are auditing the machinery and equipment account and the related depreciation accounts for the year ended December 31, 1987. Your permanent file contains the schedules shown below.

MACHINERY AND EQUIPMENT

	BALANCE 12/31/85	1986 RETIREMENTS	1986 ADDITION	BALANCE 12/31/86
1976	$ 8,000	$2,100	—	$ 5,900
1977	400	—	—	400
1978	—	—	—	—
1979	—	—	—	—
1980	3,900	—	—	3,900
1981	—	—	—	—
1982	5,300	—	—	5,300
1983	—	—	—	—
1984	4,200	—	—	4,200
1985	—	—	—	—
1986	—	—	$5,700	5,700
	$21,800	$2,100	$5,700	$25,400

ACCUMULATED DEPRECIATION

	BALANCE 12/31/85	1986 RETIREMENTS	1986 PROVISION	BALANCE 12/31/86
1976	$ 7,840	$2,100	$ 160	$ 5,900
1977	340	—	40	380
1978	—	—	—	—
1979	—	—	—	—
1980	2,145	—	390	2,535
1981	—	—	—	—
1982	1,855	—	530	2,385
1983	—	—	—	—
1984	630	—	420	1,050
1985	—	—	—	—
1986	—	—	285	285
	$12,810	$2,100	$1,825	$12,535

Here is a transcript of the machinery and equipment journal for 1987:

1987	MACHINERY AND EQUIPMENT	REF.	DEBIT	CREDIT
1/1	Balance forward		$25,400	
3/1	Burnham grinder	VR	1,200	
5/1	Air compressor	VR	4,500	
6/1	Power lawnmower	VR	600	
6/1	Lift-truck battery	VR	320	
8/1	Rockwood saw	CR		$ 150
11/1	Electric spot welder	VR	5,400	
11/1	Baking oven	VR	2,800	
12/1	Baking oven	VR	236	
			$40,456	$ 150
12/31	Balance			40,306
			$40,456	$40,456

Your examination reveals the following:

a) The company depreciates all machinery and equipment over 10 years. Depreciation is calculated by the straight-line method. Six months' depreciation is recorded in the year of acquisition or retirement. For 1987 the company recorded depreciation of $2,800 on machinery and equipment.

b) The Burnham grinder was purchased for cash from a firm in financial distress. The chief engineer and a dealer in used machinery agreed that the machine, which was practically new, was worth $2,100 in the open market.

c) For production reasons the new air compressor was installed in a small building that was erected in 1987 to house the machine. The building also will be used for general storage. The cost of the building, which has a 25-year life, was $2,000, which is included in the $4,500 voucher for the air compressor.

d) The power lawnmower was delivered to the home of the company president for his personal use.

e) On June 1 the battery in a battery-powered lift truck was accidentally damaged beyond repair. The damaged battery was included at a price of $600 in the $4,200 cost of the lift truck purchased on July 1, 1984. The company decided to rent a replacement battery instead of buying a new one. The $320 expenditure is the annual rental for the battery paid in advance, net of a $40 allowance for the scrap value of the damaged battery, which was returned to the battery company.

f) The Rockwood saw sold on August 1 had been purchased on August 1, 1974, for $1,500. The saw was in use until it was sold.

g) On September 1 the company determined that a production casting machine was no longer needed and advertised it for sale for $1,800 after determining from a dealer in used machinery that this was its market value. The casting machine had been purchased for $5,000 on September 1, 1982.

h) On November 1 a baking oven was purchased for $10,000. A $2,800 down payment was made, and the balance will be paid in monthly installments over a three-year period. The December 1 payment includes interest charges of $36. Legal title to the oven will not pass to the company until the payments are completed.

REQUIRED

Prepare the auditor's adjusting journal entries required on December 31, 1987, for machinery and equipment and the related depreciation. Prepare schedules detailing the effects of additions and retirements on the assets and related accumulated depreciation balances.

(AICPA, adapted)

P11-9.   REPLACEMENTS, IMPROVEMENTS   In your examination of the financial statements of Fess Corporation on December 31, 1987, you observe the contents of certain accounts and other pertinent information as follows:

BUILDING

DATE	EXPLANATION	REF.	DEBIT	CREDIT	BALANCE
12/31/86	Balance		$100,000	—	$100,000
7/1/87	New boiler	CD	16,480	$1,480	115,000
9/1/87	Insurance recovery	CR	—	2,000	113,000

ACCUMULATED DEPRECIATION, BUILDING

12/31/86	Balance: 15 years @ 4% of $100,000 (no salvage value)			$60,000	$60,000
12/31/87	Annual depreciation	GJ		4,440	64,440

You learn that on June 15 the company's old high-pressure boiler exploded and was extensively damaged. Damage to the building was insignificant. The boiler was replaced by a more efficient oil-burning one. The company received $2,000 as an insurance adjustment under the terms of its policy for damage to the boiler. The disbursement voucher charged to the building account on July 1, 1987, is reproduced below:

To: Peacock Heating Company
Fair market value, new oil-burning boiler (including fuel oil
   tank and 5,000 gallons fuel oil) $16,000
Sales tax, 3% of $16,000 480
    Total $16,480
Less: Allowance (fair market value) for old coal-burning
   boiler in building, to be removed at expense of Peacock
   Heating Company .... (1,480)
    Total price $15,000

In vouchering the expenditure you determine that the terms included a 2 percent cash discount that was calculated properly and taken. Neither the sales tax nor the trade-in allowance on the old boiler is subject to discount. Your audit discloses that a voucher for $1,000 was paid to Willis Company on July 2, 1987, and charged to the repair expense account. The voucher is adequately supported and is marked "installation costs for new oil-burning boiler."

The company's fuel oil supplier advises that fuel oil had a market price of 96¢ per gallon on July 1 and 98¢ per gallon on December 31. The fuel oil inventory on December 31 was 2,000 gallons.

A review of subsidiary property records discloses that the replaced coal-burning boiler was installed when the building was constructed and was recorded at a cost of $10,000. According to its manufacturers, the new boiler should be serviceable for the estimated useful life of the building.

In calculating depreciation for retirements, Fess Corporation consistently treats a fraction of a month as a full month.

REQUIRED

Prepare the adjusting journal entries that you would suggest for entry on the books of the Fess Corporation. The books have not been closed. Support your entries with calculations in good form. Assume that the building has no salvage value.

(AICPA, adapted)

P11-10. COMPREHENSIVE   On December 31, 1986, certain accounts included in the property, plant, and equipment section of the Townsand Company's balance sheet had the following balances:

Land	$100,000
Buildings	800,000
Leasehold improvements	500,000
Machinery and equipment	700,000

During 1987 the following transactions occurred:

a) Land site number 621 was acquired for $1 million. In addition, Townsand paid a $60,000 commission to a real estate agent. Costs of $15,000 were incurred to clear the land. During the course of clearing the land, timber and gravel were recovered and sold for $5,000.

b) A second tract of land (site number 622) with a building was acquired for $300,000. The closing statement indicated that the land's value was $200,000 and the building's value was $100,000. Shortly after acquisition, the building was demolished at a cost of $30,000. A new building was constructed for $150,000 plus the following costs:

Excavation fees	$11,000
Architectural design fees	8,000
Building permit fee	1,000
Imputed interest on funds used during construction	6,000

The building was completed and occupied on September 30, 1987.

c) A third tract of land (site number 623) was acquired for $600,000 and was put on the market for resale.

d) Extensive work was done to a building occupied by Townsand under a lease agreement that expires on December 31, 1993. The total cost of the work was $125,000, which consisted of the following:

WORK DONE	COST	ESTIMATED USEFUL LIFE (YEARS)
Ceilings painted	$ 10,000	1
Electrical work	35,000	10
Extension to current work area constructed	80,000	30
Total	$125,000	

The lessor paid one-half of the costs incurred in connection with the extension to the current working area.

e) During December 1987 costs of $65,000 were incurred to improve leased office space. The related lease will terminate on December 31, 1989, and is not expected to be renewed.

f) A group of new machines was purchased under a royalty agreement that provides for payment of royalties based on units of production for the machines. The invoice price of the machines was $75,000, freight costs were $2,000, unloading charges were $1,500, and royalty payments for 1987 were $13,000.

REQUIRED

Prepare a detailed analysis of the changes in each of the following balance sheet accounts for 1987:

1. Land.

2. Buildings.

3. Leasehold improvements.

4. Machinery and equipment.

Disregard the related accumulated depreciation accounts.

(AICPA, adapted)

*P11-11. COINSURANCE Schwartz, Inc., has two fire insurance policies. Policy *A* covers the office building at a face value of $360,000 and the furniture and fixtures at a face value of $108,000. Policy *B* covers only the office building at an additional face value of $140,000. Each policy is issued by a different insurance company. A fire caused losses to both the office building and the furniture and fixtures. The relevant data are summarized below:

	FURNITURE AND FIXTURES	OFFICE BUILDING	
Insurance policy	*A*	*A*	*B*
Fair market value of property *before* fire	$150,000	$700,000	$700,000
Fair market value of property *after* fire	20,000	420,000	420,000
Face value of insurance policy	108,000	360,000	140,000
Coinsurance requirement	80%	80%	80%

REQUIRED

Calculate the amount due from each insurance company for the loss in each asset category.

(AICPA, adapted)

12 PLANT ASSETS: DEPRECIATION

In Chapter 11 we discussed how to account for and report plant assets at acquisition, when subsequent expenditures occur, and at disposal. In this chapter we extend our coverage of plant assets by discussing the process of depreciation, which is the systematic and rational allocation of an asset's cost over its useful life. We then complete our coverage of plant assets by describing circumstances in which write-downs of plant assets may occur in addition to the normal depreciation expense, and by explaining and illustrating the required disclosures for plant assets.

THE NATURE OF DEPRECIATION IN ACCOUNTING

To those who are not familiar with accounting, depreciation often implies a decline in the "value" or "worth" of an asset. For example, you may hear people lament that their car is *depreciating* at the rate of $2,000 per year. What they mean is that the trade-in value, or perhaps the resale value, of the car is declining by $2,000 annually. These people are using "depreciation" to refer to the amount by which the market value of the car is declining each period. In accounting, however, *depreciation is a process of cost allocation rather than a means of valuation*. Depreciation is an application of the matching principle, whereby the cost of plant assets used up during a period is matched with the revenues generated by their use.

COST ALLOCATION VS. VALUATION Recall that when a plant asset is acquired, it usually is recorded at cost, because cost (that is, the sacrifice made to obtain the plant asset) usually is the best estimate of the asset's fair market value. The cost of a plant asset may be thought of as a long-term prepayment, because the entity incurs the cost in one period and realizes the service potential over future periods for as long as it uses the asset in the earning process.

Under generally accepted accounting principles, income determination requires that (1) revenues be recognized according to the realization principle, and (2) expenses then be recorded according to the matching principle. We discussed this process in Chapter 2.

For plant assets, we apply the matching principle by allocating a part of the acquisition cost to a nominal account called depreciation expense during each accounting period in which the asset generates revenues. In other words, we allocate the amount initially invested in the asset (acquisition cost) to the accounting periods in which the entity uses the asset.

Generally, the only market values that are relevant in accounting for a plant asset are (1) the market value at the time the asset is acquired and (2) the estimated market value at the time the asset is disposed of—its salvage value.[1] The difference between these two values becomes **depreciation expense;** it is the part of the acquisition cost that the firm does not expect to recover at the time it disposes of the asset. Thus, in accounting, depreciation may be thought of as a valuation process only when viewed over the entire life of the asset. On a periodic basis it is merely a method of allocating cost.

Consider a plant asset acquired for $40,000 cash, having an estimated useful life of 10 years and an estimated salvage value of $5,000 at the end of the 10 years. The problem appears graphically in Exhibit 12–1. The objective of depreciation accounting is to decrease the book value (which is the acquisition cost minus accumulated depreciation) from $40,000 (point A) to $5,000 (point B) over the 10-year period, with the periodic reduction in book value being shown as depreciation expense. Curves I and II indicate only two of the many depreciation patterns that could be used. Curve I depicts the straight-line depreciation method; curve II depicts an accelerated depreciation method. In either case, the fair market value of the asset is expected to decline by $35,000 over the 10 years. In accounting, we consider this $35,000 depreciation expense to be the cost of the service potential used up over the 10-year life of the asset.

[1] However, as we discuss in more detail later in this chapter, many companies in recent years have reduced the book value of plant assets to recoverable value because of "loss of economic value."

Under GAAP, depreciation expense is a cost allocation.

EXHIBIT 12–1   THE DEPRECIATION PROBLEM

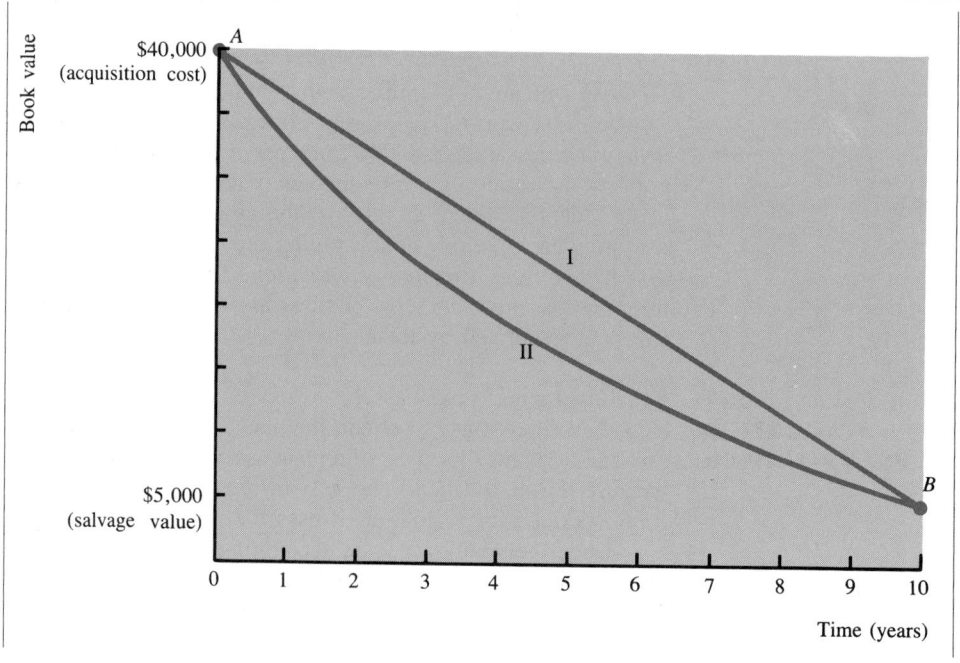

DEPRECIATION AND CASH FLOWS

Some users of financial statements erroneously perceive depreciation to be a source of funds. Although the *acquisition* of the asset does represent a *use* of resources, the subsequent *depreciation is neither a source nor a use of funds.* Depreciation is merely a current allocation of a previously incurred cost. Because depreciation is a deductible expense for income tax purposes, however, the pattern of depreciation expense does affect cash flows through its impact on taxes. For example, using an accelerated depreciation method for tax purposes results in greater tax savings in the earlier years than in later years. The use of straight-line depreciation for tax purposes results in the same tax savings in each year.

In summary, depreciation in accounting is a process of cost allocation. The cost not expected to be recovered on disposal is deducted from revenues during the years in which the firm uses the asset to generate revenues. The only cash flow implications related to depreciation are the tax savings provided because depreciation is deductible for tax purposes. In the next section, we describe the factors that enter into the determination of depreciation expense.

RELEVANT FACTORS IN CALCULATING DEPRECIATION

Estimates are an inherent part of the conventional accounting system. There are many areas of accounting that require well-informed professional judgment. One of the best examples of the lack of certainty in accounting and the resultant need for the exercise of professional judgment is depreciation of plant assets (and, for similar reasons, depletion and amortization of other assets, which are discussed in Chapter 13).

Three factors enter into the determination of depreciation expense for plant assets:

1. Depreciation base.

2. Useful life.

3. Pattern of cost allocation.

Depreciation Base

The term **depreciation base** refers to the difference between the acquisition cost, which is the amount at which the asset is initially recorded, and estimated salvage or residual value. The depreciation base is the amount that we record as the total depreciation expense—that is, the total cost of using the asset—over the accounting periods in which a firm uses an asset.

Usually we can determine the acquisition cost in a reasonably objective manner. In some cases, however, such as when an entity receives plant assets in exchange for noninterest-bearing debt, the determination of acquisition cost becomes more complex (as we discussed in Chapter 11).

Salvage or residual value is the amount that a firm expects to receive for an asset upon disposal. Estimating a plant asset's salvage value is very subjective because of uncertainty about the future. If a firm expects to incur disposal costs it must deduct the estimated amount of these costs from the estimated disposal proceeds; the difference is the net salvage value. Because of uncertainty and immateriality, it is often practical to assume that salvage value is zero. This assumption is quite valid for assets that a firm expects to use until they are virtually worthless. In these cases, any proceeds from disposal are likely to be offset by the costs of disposal, such as dismantling costs. Many companies, however, follow a practice of replacing certain plant assets (for example, a fleet of trucks) long before their utility has expired. The salvage value in such cases usually is relatively large and therefore must be considered in determining the depreciation base.

Salvage value could be negative if the expected costs of disposal exceed the expected proceeds. If this negative salvage value is material, it should be added to the acquisition cost to arrive at the depreciation base. For example, assume a plant asset cost $10,000 and that it is expected that it will be scrapped at the end of its useful life at a net disposal cost of $1,000. The depreciation base would be $11,000. An estimated liability of $1,000 would be established for the excess of disposal costs over proceeds.

After a firm determines the depreciation base, it must estimate the time period over which the asset will generate revenues, referred to as the **useful life** of the asset. The next section describes the factors that must be considered in estimating useful life.

Useful Life

The **useful life** of a plant asset is the period of time during which the firm expects to use the asset in the earning process. It should be clear that the useful life of a plant asset cannot exceed its physical life. The physical life of a building or a machine is merely the upper limit on its useful life. Several different entities may use the same asset over the physical life of the asset.

The cost of maintaining a plant asset in efficient operating condition is usually very high during the latter years of its physical life. This is the main reason that an asset's useful life is often shorter than its physical life. Thus, we must consider both physical and economic factors in estimating the useful life of a plant asset. From a practical standpoint, income tax considerations also often play an important role in determining useful life. Also, a firm's experience with previous plant assets provides some basis for estimating the useful life of a similar asset that is newly acquired.

Physical factors affecting useful life are the normal wear and tear that result from use and the passage of time, and any casualties it may suffer, such as a fire. With the exception of land, the service potential of a plant asset expires as a firm uses the asset in the earning process. Because repair and maintenance policies (which are designed to slow down the "inevitable march of plant assets to the junkyard") vary among companies, so do the estimated useful and physical lives of identical plant assets.

Economic factors often limit useful life.

More often than not, **economic factors** are the limiting factors in the determination of useful life, especially in a highly industrialized, technology-oriented economy. Economic factors include obsolescence, inadequacy, and changing economic conditions.

Obsolescence refers to the process by which an existing plant asset becomes outmoded as improved, more efficient substitutes become available. For example, consider the continuing development of new generations of computers, making the previous generation obsolete. In many cases, to remain competitive a firm must continually replace its assets with the most up-to-date resources available, even though the replaced assets may not be near the end of their physical lives.

Assets may become **inadequate** as a result of growth. A growth company reaches a point where its existing assets simply cannot perform the work required. Therefore the firm must replace them with more efficient assets.

Changing economic conditions can cause an asset to lose its service potential; such economic changes include inflation, energy crises, and changes in consumer tastes. For example, much of the equipment used in the manufacture of large cars, such as the body molds, is no longer useful even though its physical life still may be substantial.

The accelerated cost recovery system provides rapid write-offs of asset costs for tax purposes.

The Economic Recovery Tax Act of 1981 includes a provision requiring firms to use an accelerated cost recovery system (ACRS) for tax purposes.[2] The purpose of the ACRS provision is to encourage capital investment by allowing rapid recovery of capital expenditures through tax deductions. The ACRS abandons the notions of useful life and salvage value and establishes classes of depreciable assets, each with a prescribed life. Firms that invest in these assets may depreciate the cost, for tax purposes, over a prescribed life that is much shorter than the actual useful life.

---

[2] Actually, firms still could elect the straight-line depreciation method over a life at least as long as the ACRS life. (The 1986 Tax Reform Act revised the ACRS guidelines.)

The concept of depreciation under the ACRS provision differs greatly from the traditional financial accounting approach of matching costs with revenues generated over the useful life of a plant asset. Because of the historical influence of taxation on financial accounting, the impact of the ACRS guidelines on the traditional financial accounting approach to depreciation remains to be seen.

Pattern of Cost Allocation

The third factor affecting the determination of periodic depreciation expense is the pattern of cost allocation, or what is more commonly called the depreciation method. GAAP requires only that the depreciation method must be systematic and rational. Given this rather permissive guideline, it is not surprising that a number of depreciation methods exist in practice, as described in the next section.

DEPRECIATION METHODS

It is important to remember that depreciation is a process of cost allocation; it is not a method of valuation. Depreciation methods allocate costs actually incurred. The cost allocation patterns found in practice are:

1. Straight-line method.

2. Production or use method.

3. Accelerated depreciation methods.
   a) Sum-of-the-years'-digits.
   b) Declining balance.

4. Inventory method.

5. Retirement and replacement methods.

6. Group and composite methods.

7. Compound interest methods.

We discuss these methods and some of the issues relating to their use in the sections that follow.

STRAIGHT-LINE METHOD
The **straight-line method** of depreciation is the most common depreciation method for financial reporting purposes. Under this method the amount of depreciation is a linear function of time. The amount of activity during an accounting period has no bearing on the amount of depreciation expense recorded for that period. Depreciation expense is the same amount every period; we determine the depreciation expense allocated to each year by dividing the depreciation base by the estimated useful life of the asset in years.

Assume that on the first day of the year the Duncan Company acquires a plant asset for $70,000 cash. The estimated useful life is five years, and estimated salvage value is $10,000. Depreciation expense under the straight-line method would be $12,000 per year, calculated as follows:

$$\text{Depreciation expense} = \frac{\text{Acquisition cost} - \text{Estimated salvage value}}{\text{Estimated useful life}}$$

$$= \frac{\$70,000 - \$10,000}{5 \text{ years}}$$

$$= \$12,000$$

Note that we also may express the annual depreciation expense as a rate, in this case, $12,000 ÷ $60,000 = 20 percent.

Exhibit 12–2 depicts the decline in book value under the straight-line method, assuming that the firm records depreciation expense only once each year. Note that the firm determines the book value each year by deducting the total (accumulated) depreciation expense from the acquisition cost, not by deducting it from the depreciation base. Thus, the book value at the end of the fifth year, when the asset is fully depreciated, is $70,000 − $60,000 = $10,000, the estimated salvage value.

When approximately the same amount of the asset's service potential is used up each period, straight-line depreciation provides a reasonable estimate of the decline in service potential. The expiration of an equal amount of service potential each period, however, implies that the net cash flows generated by the asset (the difference between the revenues generated and the costs of maintaining the asset) are equal each period, an unrealistic assumption in most cases.

The straight-line method owes its popularity to its simplicity. Also, it often produces results that are reasonable approximations of the depreciation expense that would be calculated under more conceptually appealing but more complex depreciation methods.

Whereas the straight-line method results in a constant amount of depreciation per time period, the production or use method, described in the next section, produces a constant depreciation amount per unit of activity.

PRODUCTION OR USE METHOD

We often refer to the **production** or **use method** of depreciation as an *activity* method because the depreciation expense allocated to a period is based on some measure of the asset's activity during the period. The activity measure used in this depreciation method

---

EXHIBIT 12–2 BOOK VALUE UNDER THE STRAIGHT-LINE DEPRECIATION METHOD

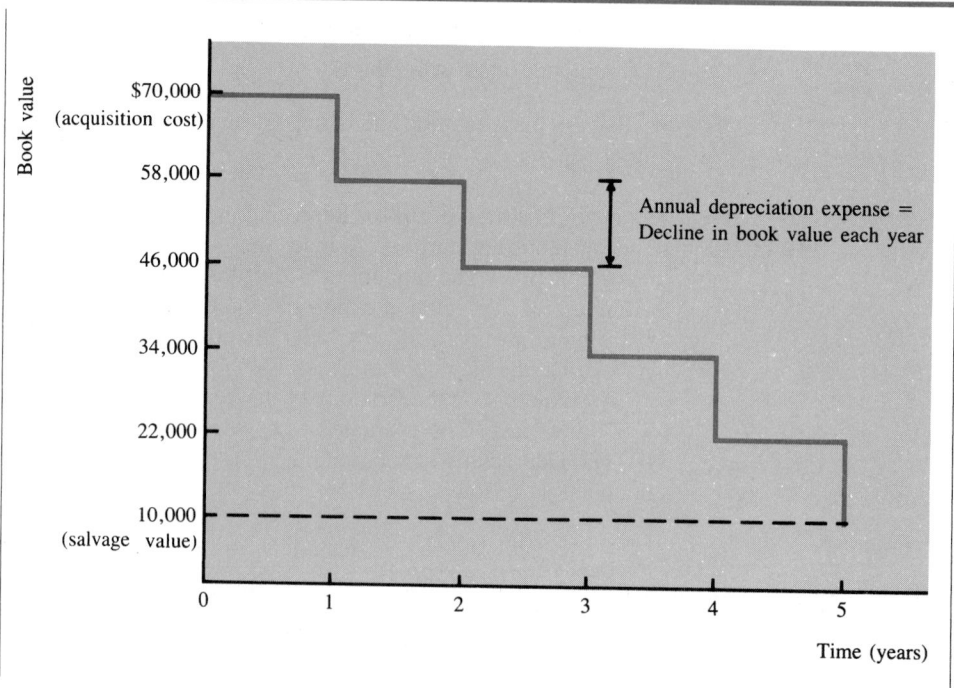

should have some relationship to the actual decline in service potential of the asset. Examples of commonly used activity measures include miles driven (for trucks and cars), number of hours used (for machinery), and number of units produced (also for machinery). Depreciation expense for a particular accounting period is the depreciation per unit of activity times the number of units of activity during that period. Depreciation per unit of activity is calculated as follows:

$$\begin{array}{c} \text{Depreciation} \\ \text{per unit} \\ \text{of activity} \end{array} = \frac{\text{Acquisition cost} - \text{Estimated salvage value}}{\text{Total estimated number of units of activity during useful life}}$$

Continuing with the Duncan Company data, assume that the number of hours that Duncan's new plant asset is used is a reasonable measure of its activity, and that Duncan estimates that the asset may be used for 20,000 hours during its useful life. That implies a depreciation cost per hour of ($70,000 − $10,000) ÷ 20,000 hours = $3. Assume further that during each of the next five years Duncan uses the plant asset as indicated in the following schedule:

YEAR	(1) DEPRECIATION EXPENSE PER HOUR	(2) NUMBER OF HOURS USED	(3) DEPRECIATION EXPENSE PER YEAR (col. 1 × col. 2)
1	$3	3,000	$ 9,000
2	3	6,000	18,000
3	3	4,000	12,000
4	3	5,000	15,000
5	3	2,000	6,000
		20,000	$60,000

This method is a logical approach to determining depreciation expense when (1) actual usage varies substantially over time; (2) the firm can reliably estimate the total units of activity over the useful life of the asset for a reasonable activity measure; and (3) the decline in service potential is related closely to the extent of the asset's use. In such circumstances, matching is best achieved by a production or use method. The production or use depreciation method, however, generally is a bit more difficult to apply than the straight-line method, because it is easier to estimate the useful life of an asset in years than it is to estimate the useful life in total units of activity. The production or use method also requires that a firm keep records of the actual use of the asset during each period.

The production method is a straight-line method per unit of activity.

The production or use depreciation method allocates a fixed depreciation charge per unit used or produced. Hence it may be thought of as a straight-line method per unit of activity. That is, the book value declines in a straight line as a function of activity rather than as a function of time. Exhibit 12–3 compares the activity method with the straight-line depreciation method on the basis of time.

Some depreciation methods are designed to produce decreasing depreciation amounts each period. Because they result in higher depreciation charges in the early years of an asset's life, they are called accelerated depreciation methods. We discuss these methods in the following section.

ACCELERATED DEPRECIATION METHODS

Accelerated depreciation methods provide higher depreciation expense in the early years of an asset's useful life and lower depreciation expense in the later years. That is, they "accelerate" the recognition of depreciation expense to the earlier years of asset life.

EXHIBIT 12–3 ACTIVITY DEPRECIATION METHOD VS. STRAIGHT-LINE DEPRECIATION METHOD BASED ON TIME

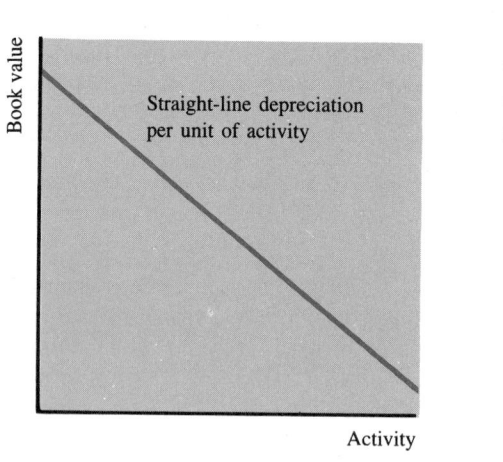
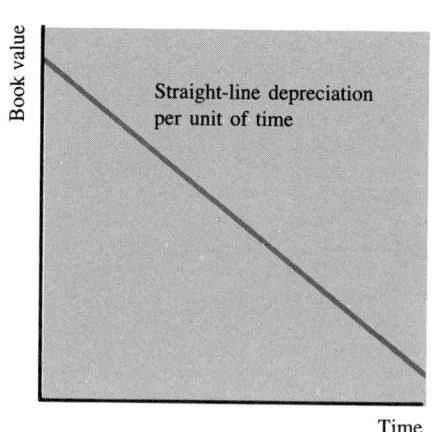

Accelerated depreciation methods provide an excellent example of the impact of income tax regulations on financial reporting practices. Before the IRS accepted accelerated methods for tax purposes in 1954, virtually all companies used straight-line depreciation for financial reporting. After accelerated methods were accepted for tax purposes, many companies began to use them for financial reporting purposes as well as for tax reporting to avoid the necessity of keeping two separate sets of records for the same assets. When firms use accelerated depreciation methods for tax purposes, they are able to defer tax payments. Higher depreciation expense in the early years of an asset's life reduces taxable income in those years. The taxes saved in the early years are paid later, when depreciation expense is lower, so that the *present value* of the total tax obligation is reduced.[3] Hence, the government encourages capital investment by decreasing the cost of owning plant assets through tax savings resulting from accelerated depreciation.

There is also some theoretical basis for the use of accelerated depreciation methods, although the decision to use them usually is based on the tax savings they provide. The amount of service potential obtained from a plant asset may decline each year. When plant assets are new, they are very efficient and require little maintenance. As they age, efficiency declines and maintenance costs rise. Thus, the net cash flows from assets decline as the years pass. As a result, a depreciation expense pattern that recognizes higher depreciation expense in the early years, when the asset is generating larger cash flows, and lower depreciation expense in the later years, when the asset is contributing smaller cash flows, is theoretically supportable.

Sum-of-the-Years'-Digits

One common accelerated depreciation method is the **sum-of-the-years'-digits method.** Under the sum-of-the-years'-digits accelerated depreciation method, we determine the amount of depreciation expense for a period by multiplying the depreciation base by a fraction:

1. The numerator of the fraction is the number of years of useful life remaining at the beginning of the year for which depreciation is being calculated.

[3] Further, if a company is expanding its fixed asset base in a growth situation, the high depreciation on the new assets may offset the lower depreciation on the old assets, so that the taxes are postponed indefinitely.

EXHIBIT 12—4   SUM-OF-THE-YEARS'-DIGITS DEPRECIATION

Duncan Company

YEAR	DEPRECIATION BASE (ACQUISITION COST − SALVAGE VALUE)	REMAINING LIFE (YEARS)	FRACTION	ANNUAL DEPRECIATION EXPENSE
1	$60,000	5	5/15	$20,000
2	60,000	4	4/15	16,000
3	60,000	3	3/15	12,000
4	60,000	2	2/15	8,000
5	60,000	1	1/15	4,000
15 (sum-of-the-years'-digits)				$60,000

2. The denominator of the fraction is the sum of the numbers representing each year of useful life, or the sum of the years' digits.

For example, if the estimated useful life of an asset is five years, the denominator is the sum of the years' digits, or $1 + 2 + 3 + 4 + 5 = 15$. In cases where the useful life is long, we may calculate the denominator by the relationship $\dfrac{n(n + 1)}{2}$, where n is the number of years of useful life. This is an extremely helpful rule to remember. The numerator would be 5 for the first year, 4 for the second year, and so on. Thus, we allocate a decreasing amount of depreciation expense by applying successively smaller fractions to the fixed depreciation base. Exhibit 12–4 illustrates the data and calculations for the Duncan Company.

Declining Balance

With the **declining balance method,** which is also an accelerated depreciation method, depreciation expense each year follows the pattern of the declining book value. We determine a depreciation fraction, or rate, and then multiply that same rate by the declining book value each year to determine the depreciation expense allocated to each year.

A widely used declining balance method is the **double declining balance method,** which historically was the maximum rate acceptable by the IRS for tax purposes. Under the double declining balance method, the rate applied to the book value is twice the straight-line rate. Note that the rate is multiplied by the *book value*, not by the depreciation base. Thus, the salvage value is not deducted initially when calculating depreciation expense under the double declining balance method. Toward the end of an asset's useful life, however, the salvage value must be considered. Otherwise, the asset might be depreciated below its salvage value.

Consider again the Duncan Company, whose asset cost $70,000, had an estimated salvage value of $10,000, and an estimated useful life of five years. Since the straight-line depreciation rate is 20 percent ($12,000 ÷ $60,000), the double declining balance rate would be 40 percent (2 × 20 percent). Exhibit 12–5 illustrates the calculations for the depreciation expense to be allocated each year under the double declining balance method.

Applying the 40 percent rate to the $15,120 book value at the beginning of year 4 would allocate depreciation expense of $6,048 to year 4 and produce a book value of $15,120 − $6,048 = $9,072, which is less than estimated salvage value. One solution to

Under the double declining balance method, the depreciation rate is multiplied by book value, not by the depreciation base.

EXHIBIT 12–5 DOUBLE DECLINING BALANCE DEPRECIATION

Duncan Company

YEAR	BOOK VALUE, BEGINNING OF YEAR	DOUBLE DECLINING DEPRECIATION RATE	ANNUAL DEPRECIATION EXPENSE
1	$70,000	.40	$28,000
2	42,000	.40	16,800
3	25,200	.40	10,080
4	15,120	—	2,560*
5	12,560	—	2,560*
6	10,000		

* ($15,120 − $10,000) ÷ 2.

this problem would be to depreciate the asset down to salvage value in year 4 ($15,120 − $10,000 = $5,120 depreciation). But if that were done, there would be no depreciation expense in year 5, even though the asset still possesses service potential in year 5. The solution commonly found in practice and illustrated in Exhibit 12–5 is to begin depreciating at the straight-line rate in the year in which the double declining balance method would depreciate the asset below its salvage value.[4]

When a firm owns a large number of low-cost plant assets or groups of similar or dissimilar plant assets, the methods that we have described are costly to apply. In these cases, other depreciation methods may be used, such as the inventory method, the retirement and replacement methods, and group or composite methods.

INVENTORY METHOD

Most firms own certain types of plant assets, such as hand tools, patterns, and utensils, which individually may be insignificant but in total may comprise a significant group of assets. As a practical expedient, some firms match the cost of these assets against revenues by using the **inventory method** of depreciation, sometimes called the **appraisal method.** Under the inventory method, the company takes a physical inventory of the

---

[4] It is possible to determine mathematically the rate that, when applied to the book value at the beginning of each period, will reduce the book value to salvage value (ignoring rounding errors) at the end of the asset's useful life. The method, called "constant percent of declining balance," is based on the following formula:

$$r = 1 - \sqrt[n]{\frac{s}{C}}$$

where r = depreciation rate per period
n = number of years of useful life
s = salvage value
C = acquisition cost

Applying this formula to Duncan's asset, we obtain a rate of 32.24 percent:

$$r = 1 - \sqrt[5]{\frac{\$10,000}{\$70,000}} = 1 - .6776 = 32.24\%$$

This method is not commonly found in practice because of its complexity and its lack of acceptability for tax purposes.

assets at the end of the period and assigns a value to them. The difference between the book value of the assets at the beginning of the period and the value assigned at the end of the period is the depreciation expense, representing the cost of the available services consumed from these assets during the period.

Unlike the other methods discussed, the credit to reduce the book value of the asset usually is made directly to the asset account instead of to accumulated depreciation. For example, if a number of tools were purchased for $2,000 at the beginning of the year and the firm determines that the recorded value at the end of the year should be $1,200, then the following journal entry is appropriate:

Depreciation expense—tools	800	
Tools		800

With this depreciation method, it is very difficult to stay within the confines of historical cost and the concept of depreciation as a cost allocation process, rather than as a valuation process. When asset prices are increasing, historical cost as a basis for valuing the assets at the end of the period tends to be downplayed and current market prices tend to dominate the determination of depreciation expense. When this occurs, the method represents a departure from the historical cost principle. In spite of this conceptual inconsistency, the method is used quite commonly because of its simplicity when a large number of items of low unit cost are held.

RETIREMENT AND REPLACEMENT METHODS

Like the inventory depreciation method, the retirement and replacement depreciation methods sometimes are used to depreciate a large group of low-cost items, such as telephone poles and gas meters. These methods differ significantly from the straight-line, production, and accelerated methods in that there is no systematic and rational allocation of acquisition cost. Instead, the firm records depreciation expense either at the time it retires the asset (the retirement depreciation method) or at the time it replaces the asset (the replacement depreciation method).

Under the **retirement depreciation method,** the firm records depreciation expense only once—when the asset is retired from use. Thus, it is the act of *retirement* that triggers the recording of depreciation. The depreciation expense recorded is the acquisition cost of the retired asset less any salvage proceeds. The firm allocates no depreciation expense to years before it retires the asset. When the entity acquires a replacement asset, it records the acquisition cost of the replacement in the asset account.

The retirement method is an application of FIFO cost flow.

The retirement method is an application of the FIFO cost flow concept, because the entity debits the retired asset's cost to depreciation expense and records the new asset's cost in the asset account.

Under the **replacement depreciation method,** the entity debits the acquisition cost of the replacement asset, net of any salvage proceeds from the old asset, to depreciation expense in the year of replacement. Again, there are no intervening depreciation charges with respect to the old asset. Thus, it is the act of *replacement* that triggers the depreciation entry.

The replacement method is an application of LIFO cost flow.

The replacement method is an application of the LIFO cost flow concept, because the firm records the cost of the replacement as depreciation expense and the cost of the retired asset remains in the asset account. If the firm is in a growth situation and acquires additional assets beyond the number needed to replace the old assets, it must debit the cost of the assets acquired in excess of replacement to the asset account, not to depreciation expense.

In periods of changing prices, the replacement method does a better job than the retirement method of matching current costs with current revenues. The balance in the asset account may differ significantly from the fair market value of the assets, however, and may not be useful in assessing future cash flows.

Let's assume that a telephone company retires 5,000 telephone poles that originally cost $250,000 and received salvage proceeds of $50,000. The same number of replacement poles now cost $350,000. The entries to reflect this information under both methods are as follows:

RETIREMENT METHOD			REPLACEMENT METHOD		
To record retirement of old poles:					
Depreciation expense 200,000					
Cash................. 50,000			No entry		
Telephone poles (old)..		250,000			
To record replacement poles:					
Telephone poles (new) ... 350,000			Depreciation expense.. 300,000		
Cash...............		350,000	Cash ($350,000 −		
			$50,000)		300,000

Note that depreciation expense is $250,000 − $50,000 = $200,000 under the retirement method and $350,000 − $50,000 = $300,000 under the replacement method.

These depreciation methods provide acceptable results only for assets that a company continually retires and replaces. In such cases, the pattern of depreciation expense will be comparable to what would result from applying one of the more common methods discussed earlier. A common application of these methods, accounting for track structures by railroads, was eliminated in 1983 when the Interstate Commerce Commission adopted changes requiring depreciation calculations under the conventional methods described earlier.

GROUP AND COMPOSITE METHODS

Many companies find it convenient and logical to group assets to simplify the depreciation process. An average depreciation rate then is applied to depreciate the entire group. If the assets in the group are *similar,* such as a fleet of delivery trucks, we call the method **group depreciation.** If they are *dissimilar,* such as all machinery and equipment in a particular factory, we call the method **composite depreciation.** From an accounting standpoint, the two methods are identical. The primary purpose in using these depreciation methods is to eliminate the clerical work that would be needed if each plant asset were depreciated individually.

Assume that a company acquires three dissimilar assets, *A, B,* and *C,* within the same year, and that they are to be depreciated on a composite basis. Relevant data are as follows:

ASSET	ACQUISITION COST	SALVAGE VALUE	DEPRECIATION BASE	USEFUL LIFE	STRAIGHT-LINE DEPRECIATION PER YEAR
A	$17,000	$2,000	$15,000	6	$2,500
B	11,000	1,000	10,000	5	2,000
C	10,000	1,000	9,000	3	3,000
	$38,000	$4,000	$34,000		$7,500

The *average depreciation rate* for this group may be determined by dividing the straight-line depreciation per year ($7,500) by the acquisition cost ($38,000), or

$7,500 \div \$38,000 = 19.74$ percent.[5] We can determine the *average composite life* of the group by dividing the depreciation base by the straight-line depreciation per year, or $34,000 \div \$7,500 = 4.53$ years. If no changes occur in the composition of the assets in the group, applying the 19.74 percent average depreciation rate to the total group acquisition cost for 4.53 years will reduce the book value of the group to the salvage value of $4,000.[6]

In practice, however, it is likely that during each year the firm will add some new assets to the group and retire others. As these changes occur, the amount of depreciation expense will change; we calculate depreciation expense for the period by multiplying the average depreciation rate by the acquisition cost of assets in use during the period. For example, if asset C were retired as expected at the end of year 3, depreciation expense for year 4 would be $[.1974 \times (\$38,000 - \$10,000)] = \$5,527$. While asset C was in use with the others during years 1, 2, and 3, depreciation expense each year was $(.1974 \times \$38,000) = \$7,500$.

Because depreciation records are not kept on a unit basis, an assumption underlying the method is that the firm disposes of assets at their book value. When a firm retires assets from the group, it recognizes no gain or loss. The firm probably will retire some assets early and use others beyond the originally expected useful lives that it used to determine the average depreciation rate. To record a disposal, we credit the asset account for the acquisition cost of the retired asset, debit cash (or other assets) for the amount received upon disposal, and debit accumulated depreciation for the difference. Thus, we bury any gain or loss in the accumulated depreciation account. For example, if the firm disposes of asset C for $500 at the end of year 3, it must make the following entry:

Accumulated depreciation	9,500	
Cash	500	
Asset C		10,000

We calculate the average depreciation rate when we establish a group, and normally we use this rate throughout the life of the group. If, however, additions to the group have useful lives that differ significantly from the average composite life of the assets initially in the group, it is necessary to calculate a new average depreciation rate for the group. Note that generally it is not necessary to estimate the useful life and salvage value of assets added to the group, since we depreciate them by applying the average depreciation rate to their acquisition cost.

It is also possible to use the declining balance method to depreciate on a group or composite basis. For example, if the double declining balance method were used to depreciate assets A, B, and C, the depreciation rate applied to their book value at the beginning of each period would be 19.74 percent $\times 2 = 39.48$ percent. We cannot use the sum-of-the-years'-digits method because we cannot determine the numerator of the fraction to calculate depreciation expense when we are depreciating multiple assets with different remaining useful lives.

The depreciation methods described in the preceding sections all are commonly found in practice. Compound interest depreciation methods, described in the following section, have considerable theoretical appeal but are used rarely in practice due to their complexity.

---

[5] Other methods of calculating the average depreciation rate occasionally are found in practice, such as basing the rate on the longest-lived asset in the group (here, 1/6 or 16 2/3 percent), or on the average useful life of the assets that make up the group (here, $1/[(6 + 5 + 3)/3]$ or 21.4 percent).

[6] Because the average depreciation rate was rounded to 19.74 percent, the book value after 4.53 years actually would be $[\$38,000 - (4.53 \times .1974 \times \$38,000)] = \$4,019$, rather than $4,000.

COMPOUND INTEREST DEPRECIATION METHODS

Compound interest depreciation methods are based on present values of future cash flows and the time value of money. To illustrate, assume that the Barnes Company acquires a plant asset for $38,500. The asset has an expected useful life of five years, no salvage value, and is expected to produce net cash flows (increased cash revenues or decreased cash expenses) of $11,485 at the end of each year. These cash flows are an ordinary annuity, and the company's rate of return on this investment is 15 percent:

$$\$38,500 = \$11,485(P_{\overline{5}|x\%})$$
$$P_{\overline{5}|x\%} = 3.3522$$

In Table D in Appendix 7–1, we find by interpolation that the interest rate that corresponds to the present value of an annuity factor of 3.3522 for five periods is 15 percent.

Annual depreciation expense is calculated under the compound interest method as follows:

$$\begin{matrix} \text{Annual} \\ \text{depreciation} \\ \text{expense} \end{matrix} = \begin{matrix} \text{Annual} \\ \text{cash} \\ \text{flows} \end{matrix} - \left(\begin{matrix} \text{Rate} \\ \text{of} \\ \text{return} \end{matrix} \times \begin{matrix} \text{Book value} \\ \text{of asset,} \\ \text{beginning of each year} \end{matrix} \right)$$

Note that the expression in parentheses represents the annual income from use of the asset. Exhibit 12–6 shows the calculation of Barnes's depreciation expense by the compound interest method.

As we discussed in Chapter 7, many companies use present value methods in planning and evaluating capital expenditures. For example, Barnes's expected rate of return on the plant asset acquisition was 15 percent. One of the strengths of compound interest depreciation is that this method allocates the asset's cost in such a way as to maintain a constant rate of return on the investment each year, as indicated in column 6 of Exhibit 12–6. The return on investment (ROI) of 15 percent is the same as we found by consulting Table D in Appendix 7–1. Other depreciation methods do not result in a constant rate of

---

EXHIBIT 12–6   COMPOUND INTEREST DEPRECIATION

Barnes Company

(1) YEAR	(2) BOOK VALUE, BEGINNING OF YEAR	(3) NET CASH FLOWS	(4) ANNUAL INCOME (15% × col. 2)	(5) DEPRECIATION EXPENSE (col. 3 − col. 4)	(6) RATE OF RETURN (col. 4 ÷ col. 2)
1	$38,500	$11,485	$ 5,775	$ 5,710	15%
2	32,790	11,485	4,919	6,566	15
3	26,224	11,485	3,934	7,551	15
4	18,673	11,485	2,801	8,684	15
5	9,989	11,485	1,496*	9,989	15
		$57,425	$18,925	$38,500	

* Rounded by $2.

return. For example, the use of straight-line depreciation on Barnes's asset would result in the following rates of return each year.

$$\text{Annual straight-line depreciation} = \frac{\$38,500}{5} = \$7,700$$

$$\text{ROI} = \frac{\text{Cash flows} - \text{Depreciation expense}}{\text{Book value, beginning of year}}$$

$$\text{Year 1: } \frac{\$11,485 - \$7,700}{\$38,500} = 9.83\%$$

$$\text{Year 2: } \frac{\$11,485 - \$7,700}{\$38,500 - \$7,700} = 12.29\%$$

$$\text{Year 3: } \frac{\$11,485 - \$7,700}{\$30,800 - \$7,700} = 16.39\%$$

$$\text{Year 4: } \frac{\$11,485 - \$7,700}{\$23,100 - \$7,700} = 24.58\%$$

$$\text{Year 5: } \frac{\$11,485 - \$7,700}{\$15,400 - \$7,700} = 49.16\%$$

Thus, the use of straight-line depreciation gives the appearance of an increasing rate of return even though the actual rate of return, assuming actual cash flows are as expected at the date the asset was acquired, is 15 percent.[7]

Compound interest depreciation also has conceptual appeal from the standpoint of the cash flow benefits expected from use of the asset. Under compound interest depreciation, the book value of the asset at the beginning of each year is the *present value* of the remaining cash flows associated with use of the asset; annual depreciation expense equals the periodic decline in the present value of these remaining cash flows. For example, the Exhibit 12–6 book values at the beginning of year 2 and year 3—$32,790 and $26,224, respectively—may be derived as follows:

$$\text{Beginning of year 2: } \$11,485(P_{\overline{4}|15\%})$$
$$= \$11,485(2.8550)$$
$$= \$32,790$$

$$\text{Beginning of year 3: } \$11,485(P_{\overline{3}|15\%})$$
$$= \$11,485(2.2832)$$
$$= \$26,224$$

Depreciation expense of $6,566 for year 2 is the difference between the two present values of $32,790 and $26,224. The book value and depreciation expense for each of the remaining years may be derived in a similar fashion.

The compound interest method discussed above is called the **sinking fund method.** Another compound interest method, the **annuity method,** is similar. Under the annuity method, the asset's book value increases each year as interest (column 4 in Exhibit 12–6) is presumed to be earned on the investment. The annual depreciation expense that de-

[7] Accelerated depreciation methods cause even greater distortions. For example, sum-of-the-years'-digits depreciation would result in a negative rate of return in the first year:

$$\frac{\$11,485 - 5/15(\$38,500)}{\$38,500} = -3.5\%$$

creases the book value each year is equal to the cash flow benefits received each year (column 3 in Exhibit 12–6). For example, in year 2 the interest earned on the investment of $32,790 is $4,919, which increases the book value to $37,709. Depreciation expense for year 2 is equal to the cash flow of $11,485, which decreases the book value to $26,224. Thus, although the annual depreciation expense is larger under the annuity method, the annual *net expense* (depreciation expense minus interest revenue) is the same as under the sinking fund method.

Despite the conceptual appeal of compound interest depreciation methods, they are found rarely in practice. Their lack of general use for external reporting is due to the complexity of the methods and the widespread belief that a depreciation method that results in increasing amounts of depreciation each year (see column 5 in Exhibit 12–6) is not rational and thus does not meet the requirements of GAAP. Since managers evaluate and monitor investments on the basis of rate of return, however, compound interest depreciation methods are useful internally.

SELECTING A METHOD

Conceptually, the best depreciation method for an asset is the one that best depicts the decline in the asset's usefulness. To determine which method accomplishes this objective, we must be able to estimate the net cash flows from the asset for each year of its useful life, because an asset's usefulness is determined by its ability to generate cash flows.

From a practical standpoint, the straight-line depreciation method is the most common, not because it best reflects the decline in usefulness, but because it is easy to apply. Many firms use accelerated depreciation methods also. It is not uncommon to find a firm that depreciates some assets by using the straight-line method and depreciates other assets by using one of the accelerated methods.

OTHER DEPRECIATION ISSUES

To complete our discussion of depreciation accounting, we now consider the accounting and reporting requirements for the following issues:

1. Partial-year depreciation.

2. Changes in accounting for depreciation.

Plant assets often are acquired or disposed of at times other than at the beginning of an accounting period. Also, because estimates are inherent in the depreciation process, changes in the useful life or salvage value often occur which require accounting changes. We describe the accounting requirements for these circumstances in the following sections.

PARTIAL-YEAR DEPRECIATION

Often, plant assets are acquired and disposed of at times other than the beginning or end of an accounting period. Therefore, firms must adopt some logical and consistent means of allocating depreciation expense to the period of acquisition and to the period of disposition. Return to the Duncan Company example and assume Duncan acquired its $70,000 plant asset on April 1, and that the company's accounting period coincided with the calendar year. Since the asset provided service potential for only 9 months in the year of acquisition, Duncan should charge only three-fourths of the first year's depreciation on the asset to the first accounting period. If Duncan uses the asset for five years, as it expects to do, each of the next four years will absorb depreciation charges for 12 months, and the fifth year, the year of retirement, Duncan will record only three months of depreciation expense.

Exhibit 12–7 shows how Duncan's plant asset would be depreciated by each of the three basic methods (a) if it were acquired on January 1, and (b) if it were acquired on April 1.

Some companies simplify the accounting for depreciation in the years of acquisition and disposal. One common approach is to take one-half year's depreciation in the year of

---

EXHIBIT 12–7   DEPRECIATION PER YEAR OF PLANT ASSET ACQUIRED JANUARY 1 AND APRIL 1 BY THREE BASIC METHODS

Duncan Company

(COST = $70,000; SALVAGE VALUE = $10,000; USEFUL LIFE = 5 YEARS)

YEAR	STRAIGHT-LINE METHOD*	SUM-OF-THE-YEARS'-DIGITS METHOD†	DOUBLE DECLINING BALANCE METHOD‡
January 1 acquisition			
1	$12,000	$20,000	$28,000
2	12,000	16,000	16,800
3	12,000	12,000	10,080
4	12,000	8,000	2,560
5	12,000	4,000	2,560
April 1 acquisition			
1 (4/1–12/31)	$3/4 \times \$12,000 = \$9,000$	$3/4 \times \$20,000$ $= \$15,000$	$3/4 \times \$28,000$ $= \$21,000$
2	$12,000	$(1/4 \times \$20,000) + (3/4 \times \$16,000)$ $= \$17,000$	$.4 \times (\$70,000 - \$21,000)$ $= \$19,600$ *or* $(1/4 \times \$28,000) + (3/4 \times \$16,800)$ $= \$19,600$
3	$12,000	$(1/4 \times \$16,000) + (3/4 \times \$12,000)$ $= \$13,000$	$.4 \times (\$70,000 - \$21,000$ $- \$19,600) = \$11,760$
4	$12,000	$(1/4 \times \$12,000) + (3/4 \times \$8,000)$ $= \$9,000$	$.4 \times (\$70,000 - \$21,000$ $- \$19,600 - \$11,760)$ $= \$7,056$
5	$12,000	$(1/4 \times \$8,000) + (3/4 \times \$4,000)$ $= \$5,000$	$12/15 \times (\$10,584 - \$10,000)$ $= \$467.20\S$
6 (1/1–3/31)	$1/4 \times \$12,000 = \$3,000$	$1/4 \times \$4,000 = \$1,000$	$3/15 \times (\$10,584 - \$10,000)$ $= \$116.80\S$

* ($70,000 − $10,000) ÷ 5.

† Exhibit 12–4.

‡ Exhibit 12–5.

§ Because continued application of the double declining balance method in year 5 would reduce the book value below the $10,000 estimated salvage value, the firm depreciates the book value at the beginning of year 5 in excess of salvage value, $10,584 − $10,000 = $584, on a straight-line basis over the remaining 15 months.

acquisition and one-half year's depreciation in the year of disposal. Another approach is to record no depreciation in the year of acquisition and a full year's depreciation in the year of disposal. Other companies record a full year's depreciation on assets acquired during the first half of the year and no depreciation on assets acquired during the last half of the year. For problem-solving purposes in this book, unless the problem states otherwise, you should assume that depreciation is to be calculated to the nearest whole month. In large companies that frequently acquire and dispose of plant assets, the results from using one of the simpler approaches tend to approximate the results obtained by depreciating to the nearest whole month.

CHANGES IN ACCOUNTING FOR DEPRECIATION

For various reasons the depreciation schedule anticipated when a firm acquires a plant asset may require alterations later. In this section the accounting and reporting requirements set forth in *APB Opinion No. 20*[8] for the following three events are discussed:

1. Change in estimate.
2. Change in depreciation method.
3. Error correction.

Change in Estimate

To establish a depreciation schedule, an entity must estimate useful life and salvage value at the time it acquires a plant asset. Occasionally the entity must revise these estimates because of events that occur after acquisition. Even though estimates are made in good faith and with the best information available at the time of acquisition, the future cannot be predicted with total accuracy. Estimates of useful life and of salvage value may have to be revised as new events occur and as additional information becomes available.

Entities must account for changes in accounting estimates currently and prospectively, which means that the book value of the plant asset at the time the revision occurs should be depreciated over the new estimated useful life. If the estimated salvage value also has changed, the new salvage estimate should be used as well. Financial statement amounts reported in prior periods should not be altered.

Let's assume that Duncan has depreciated its $70,000 asset, with a salvage value of $10,000 and a five-year useful life, for two years by the straight-line method. In the third year it becomes apparent that the asset will provide service potential for a total of eight years rather than five. Because Duncan has recorded depreciation of $12,000 in each of the first two years, the book value at the time the estimate was changed was $70,000 − $24,000 = $46,000. If Duncan still estimates salvage value to be $10,000, the new depreciation base is $46,000 − $10,000 = $36,000. Therefore, depreciation expense of $6,000 per year would be recorded in each of the last six years.

Thus, changes in estimate are accounted for on a prospective basis. However, a change in depreciation method, as described in the following section, requires a cumulative effect adjustment and pro forma (''as if'') information.

Change in Depreciation Method

Companies sometimes change from one generally accepted depreciation method to another (for example, from the double declining balance method to the straight-line method) after the asset has been in use for some time. An entity that makes such a change must include the cumulative effect of the change (net of tax) in the income statement in the year in which the change occurs. To do so it calculates what net income would have been in the

---

[8] ''Accounting Changes,'' *Opinions of the Accounting Principles Board No. 20* (New York: AICPA, 1971). We discuss accounting changes in detail in Chapter 22.

years in which the old method was used if the new method had been used instead. The firm does not adjust prior period statements. However, it does include pro forma data for income before extraordinary items and net income in the income statements for all prior periods presented for comparative purposes in the current year's annual report. The purpose of this procedure is to show what those figures would have been had the new method been used in those periods.

Let's assume again that Duncan has been depreciating its $70,000 asset for two years by the straight-line method. In the third year the company changes to the sum-of-the-years'-digits method for financial reporting purposes. It determines the cumulative effect of the change as follows:

| | DEPRECIATION | | |
YEAR	STRAIGHT-LINE METHOD	SUM-OF-THE-YEARS'-DIGITS METHOD*	DIFFERENCE
1	$12,000	$20,000	$ 8,000
2	12,000	16,000	4,000
Total	$24,000	$36,000	$12,000

* Exhibit 12–4.

Assume the income tax rate in the first two years was 40 percent and that Duncan used accelerated cost recovery system (ACRS) guidelines to determine depreciation for tax purposes and will continue to do so. During the first two years, depreciation for tax purposes totaled $25,900. As a result of using ACRS for tax purposes and straight-line depreciation for book purposes, Duncan's tax liability for the first two years was less than its tax expense for financial reporting purposes by $760 [.4 × ($25,900 − $24,000)]. This amount would be shown as a credit to an account called deferred taxes.[9] However, if Duncan had used sum-of-the-years'-digits depreciation for book purposes, the deferred taxes account would have a debit balance of $4,040 [.4 × ($36,000 − $25,900)], because tax expense would have been less than the tax liability by that amount for the two years combined.

Thus, the net-of-tax effect of the change in income for the two years combined is $7,200, because income before taxes would have been less by $12,000 and, as a result, income tax expense would have been less by $4,800 (.4 × $12,000). The $7,200 would be shown on the income statement as the last item in arriving at net income. The journal entry to record the accounting change would be as follows:

Cumulative effect of accounting change	7,200	
Deferred income taxes ($4,040 + $760)	4,800	
Accumulated depreciation		12,000

The entry to record depreciation for year 3, using the sum-of-the-years'-digits method, would be:

Depreciation expense	12,000	
Accumulated depreciation		12,000
[3/15 × ($70,000 − $10,000)]		

---

[9] Chapter 19 contains a detailed discussion of accounting for timing differences of this nature between financial accounting and tax accounting.

Another event that requires an entity to alter its accounting for a plant asset is the discovery of an error regarding depreciation in prior periods. We discuss the appropriate accounting for depreciation errors in the next section.

Error Correction

Occasionally errors are discovered in accounting for depreciation in prior periods. When this occurs, the entity must revise the statements for prior periods so that the correct amounts are shown in the financial statements. The entity must make the correction by debiting or crediting accumulated depreciation and retained earnings, according to *FASB Statement No. 16.*[10]

Assume again that Duncan has depreciated its $70,000 asset for two years by the straight-line method. Then during the third year it is discovered that the firm has overlooked salvage value in calculating depreciation expense during each of the first two years (for both financial reporting and income tax purposes). The firm may calculate the effect of the error on the first two years as follows (again assuming a tax rate of 40 percent for both years):

Depreciation actually recorded, first two years ($70,000 ÷ 5) × 2 years	$28,000
Correct depreciation for first two years [($70,000 − $10,000) ÷ 5] × 2 years	(24,000)
Excess depreciation, first two years	$ 4,000
Underpayment of taxes due to error (40%)	(1,600)
Effect of error net of taxes	$ 2,400

Duncan understated net income by $2,400 as a result of the error. The entry to record the error correction would be:

Accumulated depreciation	4,000	
Retained earnings (prior period adjustment)		2,400
Income taxes payable (or cash)		1,600

The firm adds the $2,400 credit to retained earnings at the beginning of year 3 to arrive at a corrected beginning balance. If the year 3 financial statements include the year 1 and year 2 statements for comparative purposes, all items affected by the errors should be corrected. At the end of year 3, Duncan must record depreciation expense of $12,000.

Thus far in Chapter 11 and in this chapter, we have dealt with the primary accounting issues related to plant assets. In the concluding sections of this chapter we describe the accounting for impairment of value of plant assets and required plant asset disclosures.

IMPAIRMENT OF VALUE OF PLANT ASSETS

Philip Morris recently announced that it was reducing the book value of a newly completed $450 million Miller brewery by $280 million because of lack of product demand. Texaco announced a $765 million partial write-down of tankers, refineries, and investments in exploration leases, even though the company is continuing to use the facilities. A motion picture producer wrote down a film library and certain other assets to reflect the new management's evaluation of the value of certain projects. All of the above writedowns are examples of an increasingly common occurrence—the partial write-down of

---

[10] "Prior Period Adjustments," *Statement of Financial Accounting Standards No. 16* (Stamford, Conn.: FASB, 1977), para. 11.

assets that the company intends to continue to use. Why do partial write-downs occur? How does the company decide when and in what amount to record partial write-downs? Unfortunately, authoritative guidance on these questions is lacking. However, in this section we will describe the nature of the issues involved, apply our conceptual knowledge to the resolution of the issues, and analyze how companies seem to be addressing this problem today.

As described in Chapter 4, for several years companies have recognized losses on discontinued operations, which are segments of a business that are disposed of through sale or abandonment. However, the recognition of losses on plant assets that a company is going to continue to use or operate has been rare until recent years. Historically, plant assets have been carried at cost less accumulated depreciation, unless a significant and permanent decline in value below book value occurs. When such a decline in value occurs, the plant asset is written down to its **recoverable value.** The difference between the book value and the recoverable value is recorded as a loss in the period of the write-down. Recoverable value is defined as **net realizable value** if the asset is to be sold, and recoverable value is the **present value of net future cash flows** from the asset if the asset is to be used internally to generate cash flows.

The difficulty arising under the above guidelines has been determining when a recoverable value impairment is ''permanent.'' Only with hindsight can a firm accurately assess the permanence of a decline in recoverable value. For obvious reasons, companies were reluctant to admit a ''permanent'' decline in the value of assets that they were still planning to use or sell. Thus, what seems to have happened in recent years is that the notion of ''permanence'' has been softened somewhat. Companies now seem to be writing down assets when the value decline is ''more than temporary'' but, in many cases, less than ''permanent.'' The effect of these write-downs, of course, is to absorb a current-period loss and to relieve future periods of depreciation charges approximating the amount of the loss.

From a conceptual standpoint, write-downs, either partial or total, to reflect significant declines in the value of plant assets should be recognized as soon as they are objectively determinable, because the write-downs and the resulting lower book values of plant assets provide relevant, reliable information regarding decreased future cash flows. The desire for timely information encourages the recognition of such value declines as soon as they are reasonably certain to exist and when the amount of value decline can be reasonably determined. That is, when we have a high degree of certainty of the existence of a significant value decline, and we can measure the decline with an acceptable level of reliability, we should report it.

Clearly, much judgment is involved in determining whether a value decline is permanent enough to warrant recognition in the accounts. Also, the measurement of the decline is often subject to considerable uncertainty. Thus, the need for guidelines is apparent, both for companies faced with making the decision about whether and when to record a write-down, and in what amount, and for auditors charged with determining whether the value decline has been dealt with properly. In the absence of such guidelines, different accountants will deal with similar circumstances in a different manner, auditors have no basis for assessing the propriety of the accounting, and users cannot reasonably interpret the resulting financial statements with respect to these items.

The Accounting Standards Executive Committee (AcSEC) of the AICPA presented a position paper addressing this topic to the FASB in 1980. The position paper urged the FASB to provide some guidance in this area. However, the FASB did not add the topic to its agenda. More recently, AcSEC again approached the FASB about adding the issue to its agenda, without success. Thus, until more definitive guidelines are forthcoming, the objective of providing timely information regarding cash flows will have to suffice as conceptual guidance for the timing of recognition of such write-downs. Because of the vagueness of this general objective, the opportunity for manipulation of profits is significant. That is, companies may conveniently time the write-downs to occur in a year that is already less than glamorous (the "big bath theory"), or they may time the write-downs to occur in a year that is abnormally profitable, when they can better "afford" the write-down. While manipulative practices such as these may not be commonplace, this "gap in GAAP" provides an excellent example of the reason for the existence of GAAP—to provide assurance that comparable events and circumstances are being accounted for in a comparable manner.

PLANT ASSET DISCLOSURES

Plant assets, measured in dollars invested, represent the most significant resources of many companies. The financial statements must include disclosures about plant assets that will enable users to determine how efficiently management has used these assets and to determine their future cash flow potential. Specifically, firms must disclose the following information in the financial statements or notes:[11]

1. Depreciation expense for the period.

2. Balances of major classes of depreciable assets, by nature or function, on the balance sheet date.

3. Accumulated depreciation, either by major classes of depreciable assets or in total, on the balance sheet date.

4. A general description of the method or methods used to calculate depreciation with respect to major classes of depreciable assets.

Exhibit 12–8 shows information regarding plant assets included in the consolidated balance sheet in the 1984 annual report of Raytheon Company.

All of the disclosure requirements discussed so far are related to the historical cost principle and the view that depreciation is a means of allocating acquisition cost over the periods of benefit. Because of inflation and changes in the supply of and demand for assets, the historical cost approach to valuation and depreciation does not result in account balances that approximate the current value of plant assets, as we described in the preceding section. Thus, the conventional financial accounting and reporting system may not provide adequate information for assessing an entity's investment in plant assets and the cost of resources used up during the period.

The FASB, recognizing the concern over the impact of inflation and changing prices, issued *FASB Statement No. 33*[12] in 1979. This *Statement,* as modified by subsequent statements, requires companies to make supplementary disclosures of either historical cost adjusted for inflation or current cost data for plant assets, among other things. All publicly held companies with inventories and plant assets amounting to $125 million or more or total assets amounting to $1 billion or more are subject to the requirements of *FASB Statement No. 33.* We describe its reporting requirements in detail in Chapter 25.

[11] "Omnibus Opinion—1967," *Opinions of the Accounting Principles Board No. 12* (New York: AICPA, 1967), para. 5.

[12] "Financial Reporting and Changing Prices," *Statement of Financial Accounting Standards No. 33* (Stamford, Conn.: FASB, 1979). A recent FASB *Exposure Draft* would make such disclosures voluntary. ["Financial Reporting and Changing Prices," *Proposed Statement of Financial Accounting Standards* (Stamford, Conn.: FASB, 1986.]

EXHIBIT 12–8

Raytheon Company and Subsidiaries

INFORMATION ON PLANT ASSETS IN 1984 ANNUAL REPORT

(in thousands of dollars)

	DECEMBER 31,	
FROM CONSOLIDATED BALANCE SHEET:	**1984**	**1983**
Property, plant and equipment, net (notes A and E)...................................	$948,249	$936,385
FROM CONSOLIDATED STATEMENT OF CHANGES IN FINANCIAL POSITION:		
Depreciation and amortization of property, plant and equipment..	173,630	148,010

FROM NOTE A (ACCOUNTING POLICIES):

Property, plant and equipment

Property, plant and equipment are stated at cost. Betterments and major renewals are capitalized and included in property, plant and equipment accounts while expenditures for maintenance and repairs and minor renewals are charged to expense. When assets are retired or otherwise disposed of, the assets and related allowances for depreciation and amortization are eliminated from the accounts and any resulting gain or loss is reflected in income.

Provisions for depreciation are computed generally on the sum-of-the-years-digits method, except for certain operations which use the straight-line or declining-balance method. Depreciation provisions are based on estimated useful lives: buildings—20 to 45 years; machinery and equipment including production tooling—3 to 18 years; equipment leased to others—5 to 8 years. Leasehold improvements are amortized over the lesser of the life of the lease or the estimated useful life of the improvement.

FROM NOTE E (PROPERTY, PLANT AND EQUIPMENT):

Property, plant and equipment consist of the following at December 31:

	1984	1983
	(in thousands)	
Land	$ 23,238	$ 26,382
Buildings and leasehold improvements	428,856	423,779
Machinery and equipment	1,236,932	1,203,186
Equipment leased to others	154,789	339,172
	$1,843,815	$1,992,519
Less accumulated depreciation and amortization	(895,566)	(1,056,134)
	$ 948,249	$ 936,385

Accumulated depreciation of equipment leased to others is $23,208,000 at December 31, 1984.

Future minimum lease payments from noncancelable operating leases in Aircraft Products which extend to 1994, amount to $159,019,000, of which $41,120,000 is due from the U.S. Government and $117,899,000 from other lessees, principally commuter airlines. At December 31, 1984, these payments are due as follows:

	(in thousands)
1985	$23,219
1986	21,482
1987	21,495
1988	21,439
1989	18,296
Thereafter	53,088

The 1983 cost and accumulated depreciation amounts for equipment leased to others include $302,145,000 and $177,782,000 respectively, for Raytheon Data Systems, a discontinued operation (see Note O).

SUMMARY OF IMPORTANT TOPICS AND CONCEPT APPLICATIONS

1. In accounting, depreciation is a process of allocating the cost of plant assets to expense over the periods that benefit from the use of the asset. It is an application of the **matching** principle.

2. Depreciation is neither a source nor a use of funds. It is an allocation of a previously incurred cost. The only funds impact of depreciation is the tax savings created by the deduction of depreciation for tax purposes.

3. Determination of depreciation expense involves a depreciation base, an estimate of useful life, and the application of a depreciation method.

4. Commonly used depreciation methods include straight-line, production or use, and accelerated methods such as sum-of-the-years'-digits and double declining balance. Less common methods include the inventory method and the retirement and replacement methods. The group and composite methods often are used to depreciate groups of assets.

5. Compound interest depreciation methods have considerable theoretical appeal, but seldom are found in practice because of their complexity and the belief that they are not rational because they result in increasing amounts of depreciation each year.

6. Partial-year depreciation must be recorded if a plant asset is acquired or disposed of at some time other than the beginning or end of an accounting period.

7. Depreciation calculations may be altered due to a **change in estimate,** a **change in depreciation method,** or an **error correction.** A change in estimate of useful life or salvage value is accounted for prospectively. A change in depreciation method requires the calculation of the cumulative effect on prior periods of the change. The cumulative effect must be reported in the income statement on a net-of-tax basis after extraordinary items and before net income. Error corrections related to depreciation calculations in prior periods require retroactive restatement of prior period financial statements presented currently on a comparative basis. The prior period statements should be corrected to reflect the amounts that would have been reported had the error not occurred.

8. The need for **timely** information regarding the cash flow consequences of owning assets requires that plant assets should be evaluated periodically to determine whether the **recoverable value** is at least as great as the book value. If it is determined that a measurable, permanent decline in recoverable value below book value has occurred, the asset should be written down to recoverable value. Recoverable value is defined as **net realizable value** for assets to be sold and as the **present value of net future cash flows** for assets to be used internally.

9. Required plant asset disclosures include depreciation expense for the period, balances of major classes of depreciable assets, accumulated depreciation, and a general description of depreciation methods.

QUESTIONS

Q12-1. Distinguish between the concept of depreciation in accounting and the use of the term in everyday language.

Q12-2. What role do market prices play in the process of depreciation in accounting?

Q12-3. Describe the relationship between depreciation expense and cash flows. Does depreciation provide funds for replacement of plant assets? Explain.

Q12-4. Name and describe the three relevant factors in calculating depreciation expense.

Q12-5. If, at the time a firm acquires a plant asset, the expected disposal costs exceed the expected proceeds from disposal, what effect does this have on the depreciation base?

Q12-6. Distinguish between estimated useful life and physical life in accounting for plant assets. Discuss the factors that enter into the estimate of useful life.

Q12-7. In general, what would be the effect on a company's financial statements of using the accelerated cost recovery system required for tax purposes by the Economic Recovery Tax Act of 1981 for determining the depreciation period for financial reporting? Explain.

Q12-8. Under what circumstances might it be appropriate to use a depreciation method in which the periodic depreciation charge is a function of (1) the passage of time, or (2) use or productive activity?

Q12-9. What is the practical reason for the popularity of accelerated depreciation methods? What conceptual support exists for accelerated depreciation methods?

Q12-10. Explain the numerator and denominator in the fraction used to calculate depreciation expense under the sum-of-the-years'-digits method.

Q12-11. Describe the inventory method of depreciation and the circumstances in which its use may be appropriate.

Q12-12. Describe the retirement and replacement methods of depreciation and identify the circumstances in which firms commonly use them. Distinguish between the retirement method and the replacement method.

Q12-13. Why would a firm prefer group or composite depreciation rather than depreciation on a unit basis? Distinguish between group depreciation and composite depreciation.

Q12-14. Explain the process for recording retirement or disposal of assets being depreciated by a group or composite depreciation method. What is the rationale for this treatment?

Q12-15. What theoretical flaw existing in other depreciation methods does not exist in compound interest depreciation methods? Explain.

Q12-16. Distinguish between the sinking fund method and the annuity method of compound interest depreciation.

Q12-17. Explain why there is often a conflict between the depreciation method deemed most desirable for financial reporting and the method deemed most desirable for income tax purposes.

Q12-18. How should a firm account for the effect of changes in estimates of useful life and salvage value?

Q12-19. How should a firm account for changes in depreciation methods?

Q12-20. How should a firm account for errors related to depreciation expense?

Q12-21. Explain why a firm may record a write-down in the book value of a plant asset, other than through depreciation expense, even though the firm may not be planning to dispose of the asset.

Q12-22. What theoretical guidance is helpful to a firm in deciding whether a partial write-down is appropriate for a plant asset?

Q12-23. Why would it be useful to have authoritative guidelines for determining the conditions under which partial write-downs are appropriate and for determining the amount of the write-down? Explain how these guidelines would benefit preparers, auditors, and users.

Q12-24. Identify the information that must be disclosed in the financial statements or notes with respect to plant assets.

CASES

C12-1. COST AND DEPRECIATION—PLANT ASSETS Property, plant, and equipment (plant assets) represent a material portion of the total assets of most companies. Accounting for the acquisition and use of such assets is therefore an important part of the financial reporting process.

REQUIRED

1. Distinguish between revenue expenditures and capital expenditures and explain why this distinction is important.

2. Briefly define ''depreciation'' as the term is used in accounting.

3. Identify the factors that are relevant in determining annual depreciation expense and explain whether these factors are determined objectively or are based on judgment.

(AICPA, adapted)

C12-2. DEPRECIATION CONCEPTS Superior Manufacturing Company was organized January 1, 1987. During 1987 it used the straight-line method of depreciating its plant assets in its reports to management.

On November 8 you are having a conference with Superior's officers to discuss the depreciation method to be used for income tax and stockholder reporting. The president of Superior has suggested the use of a new method, which he feels is more suitable than the straight-line method for the company's needs during the period of rapid expansion of production and capacity that he foresees. Following is an example in which the proposed method is applied to a fixed asset with an original cost of $32,000, an estimated useful life of 5 years, and a scrap value of approximately $2,000.

YEAR	YEARS OF LIFE USED	FRACTION	DEPRE- CIATION EXPENSE	ACCUMULATED DEPRECIATION AT END OF YEAR	BOOK VALUE AT END OF YEAR
1	1	1/15	$ 2,000	$ 2,000	$30,000
2	2	2/15	4,000	6,000	26,000
3	3	3/15	6,000	12,000	20,000
4	4	4/15	8,000	20,000	12,000
5	5	5/15	10,000	30,000	2,000

The president favors the new method because he has heard that it will *(a)* increase the funds recovered during the years near the end of the assets' useful lives, when maintenance and replacement disbursements will be high, and *(b)* result in increased write-offs in later years and thereby reduce taxes.

REQUIRED

1. What is the purpose and hence the nature of accounting for depreciation?

2. Is the president's proposal within the scope of generally accepted accounting principles? In making your decision, discuss the circumstances, if any, under which the method would be reasonable, and those, if any, under which it would not be reasonable.

3. The president wants your advice.
  a) Do depreciation charges recover or create funds? Explain.
  b) Assume that the Internal Revenue Service will accept the proposed depreciation method in this particular case. If the proposed method were used for stockholder and tax reporting purposes, how would it affect the availability of funds generated by operations?

(AICPA, adapted)

C12-3. SELECTION OF DEPRECIATION METHOD Tru-Value Corporation sells and erects shell houses—frame structures that are completely finished on the outside but are unfinished on the inside except for flooring, partition studding, and ceiling joists. Shell houses are sold chiefly to customers who are handy with tools and who have time to do the interior wiring, plumbing, wall completion and finishing, and other work necessary to make the houses livable.

Tru-Value buys shell houses from a manufacturer in unassembled packages consisting of all lumber, roofing, doors, windows, and similar materials necessary to complete a shell house. Upon commencing operations in a new area, Tru-Value buys or leases land as a site for its local warehouse, field office, and display houses. Sample display houses are erected at a total cost of from $3,000 to $7,000, including the cost of the unassembled packages. The chief element of cost of the display houses is the unassembled packages, since erection is a short, low-cost operation. Old sample models are torn down or altered into new models every three to seven years. Sample display houses have little salvage value because dismantling and moving costs amount to nearly as much as the cost of an unassembled package.

REQUIRED

Would it be preferable to depreciate the cost of display houses on the basis of *(a)* the passage of time or *(b)* the number of shell houses sold? Explain.

(AICPA, adapted)

C12-4. SELECTION OF A DEPRECIATION METHOD Appleton Corporation recently acquired an apartment building. As chief accountant for Appleton, you have the responsibility of determining the appropriate depreciation method for the appliances (stoves, refrigerators, etc.) that are provided in the apartments.

REQUIRED

Describe the depreciation method that you believe is the most practical for depreciating appliances in the apartment buildings. In addition to describing the method, explain why you believe this method is the most practical and identify any theoretical shortcomings of the method.

C12-5. UNIT VS. GROUP DEPRECIATION The accountant frequently is called on by management for advice regarding methods of calculating depreciation. Although the question arises less frequently, of comparable importance is whether the depreciation method should be based on the consideration of the assets as units, as a group, or as having a composite life.

REQUIRED

1. Briefly describe the depreciation method based on treating assets as
   a) Units.
   b) A group or as having a composite life.
2. Present the arguments for and against the use of each of the two methods.
3. Describe how retirements are recorded under each of the two methods.

(AICPA, adapted)

C12-6. IMPAIRMENT OF VALUE OF PLANT ASSETS Diversified Corporation has just completed construction of a plant facility designed for use in manufacturing a consumer product. However, during the latter stages of construction, the release on the market of a substitute product at a lower cost caused the market potential of Diversified's product to decline considerably. It now appears that Diversified will be unable to recover more than about 60 percent of the cost of the plant unless the market for the product recovers, which appears highly unlikely at this time.

REQUIRED

1. Explain why a firm may record a partial write-down on a plant asset. Include in your explanation a discussion of when the write-down should be recorded and how the amount of the write-down should be determined.
2. Should Diversified write down the book value of the plant? Explain.

EXERCISES

E12-1. CALCULATION OF DEPRECIATION EXPENSE   The Jackson Company acquired machinery on January 2, 1987, for $60,000 in cash. The estimated useful life is 10 years and estimated salvage value is $10,000. Jackson estimates that the machine will produce 10,000 units of product and that 25,000 direct labor hours will be utilized over the useful life of the machine. During 1987 Jackson manufactured 800 units of product and used 1,700 direct labor hours.

REQUIRED

Calculate depreciation expense for 1987 under each of the following methods:

1. Straight-line method.
2. Production method (units of output).
3. Use method (units of input—direct labor hours).
4. Sum-of-the-years'-digits method.
5. Double declining balance method.

E12-2. CALCULATION OF DEPRECIATION EXPENSE   On April 1, 1987, the Pagel Company acquired machinery for $40,000 cash. The estimated useful life is six years and estimated salvage value is $4,000. Pagel estimates that the machine can produce 12,000 units of product. During 1987 and 1988, 2,400 and 1,800 units were produced, respectively. Pagel's reporting year ends on December 31.

REQUIRED

Calculate depreciation expense for 1987 and 1988 under each of the following methods (assuming Pagel calculates depreciation expense to the nearest month in the year of acquisition):

1. Straight-line method.
2. Production method (units of output).
3. Sum-of-the-years'-digits method.
4. Double declining balance method.

E12-3. CALCULATION OF DEPRECIATION EXPENSE   Milton Company bought a machine at the beginning of year 1 for $25,000 cash. The machine has an estimated useful life of six years and an estimated salvage value of $400.

REQUIRED

What is the amount of depreciation expense for year 2 under each of the following methods?

1. Straight-line method.
2. Sum-of-the-years'-digits method.
3. Double declining balance method.

E12-4. CALCULATION OF DEPRECIATION EXPENSE   A machine was purchased on January 1, 1985, for $15,000. Its expected useful life is five years or 9,000 hours of operation, with a $500 salvage value at that time. It is also expected that, over its useful life, the machine can produce 3,500 units of product.

REQUIRED

Calculate depreciation expense for 1987, the third year of use, under each of the following methods:

1. Straight-line method.
2. Sum-of-the-years'-digits method.
3. Double declining balance method.
4. Production method, if 500 units were produced.
5. Use method, if the machine was used 1,450 hours.

E12-5. SUM-OF-THE-YEARS'-DIGITS DEPRECIATION On January 2, 1986, Mogul Company acquired equipment to use in its manufacturing operations. The equipment has an estimated useful life of 10 years and an estimated salvage value of $5,000. The depreciation applicable to this equipment was $24,000 for 1988, calculated under the sum-of-the-years'-digits method.

REQUIRED

Determine the acquisition cost of the equipment.

E12-6. DEFERRED PAYMENTS; DOUBLE DECLINING BALANCE METHOD On January 2, 1987, Pacific Company purchased a machine having an estimated life of 10 years with no salvage value. The terms of the purchase included a $4,000 cash down payment plus three equal annual payments of $10,000 each, which included interest on the unpaid balance at 10 percent per annum. The first payment was due January 2, 1988.

REQUIRED

1. Prepare the January 2, 1987, entry to record the purchase of the machine.

2. Prepare the entry to record depreciation for 1987, assuming Pacific uses the double declining balance method of depreciation.

3. Prepare the entry to record the final $10,000 payment, assuming the effective interest method is used to record interest expense.

(CGAA, adapted)

E12-7. DEFERRED PAYMENTS; PARTIAL-YEAR DEPRECIATION On September 1, 1987, Reno Corporation acquired a machine by paying $10,000 cash and signing a two-year note. The note had a face amount of $30,000 due at the end of the two-year period. The note did not specify interest. The market rate of interest for a note of this type for Reno was 10 percent. Reno's accounting period ends on December 31.

REQUIRED

1. Prepare the entry to record the purchase of the machine.

2. Prepare the entry to record interest expense for 1987, assuming the effective interest method is used.

3. Prepare the entry to record depreciation expense for 1987, assuming the straight-line method is used, the machine has a useful life of five years, and no salvage value is expected.

E12-8. RETIREMENT AND REPLACEMENT METHODS The Hawkeye Utility Company depreciates its poles used for power lines by the retirement depreciation method. In 1987 poles that had an original cost of $120,000 were sold for scrap for $6,000 and replaced with poles costing $160,000.

REQUIRED

1. Prepare the necessary journal entries to record the disposal of the old poles and the acquisition of new ones in 1987.

2. Assume instead that Hawkeye used the replacement method of depreciation. Prepare journal entries for 1987.

E12-9. GROUP DEPRECIATION The Devil Delivery Company began operations in 1987. At the beginning of the year, the company acquired three delivery trucks. An accountant friend told the owners that they could save considerable bookkeeping by treating the trucks as a group for depreciation purposes. Relevant data on the trucks are as follows:

TRUCK	ACQUISITION COST	SALVAGE VALUE	USEFUL LIFE
A	$12,000	$2,000	5
B	11,000	1,500	4
C	13,000	1,000	6

REQUIRED

1. Calculate depreciation expense for 1987 by the group method of depreciation.

2. If truck *A* is sold at the beginning of 1990 for $3,000, what journal entry will be required?

E12-10. COMPOUND INTEREST DEPRECIATION METHODS   The president of Arrington Company is puzzled by the apparent rate of return on machinery acquired two years ago. Although calculations supporting the acquisition of the machinery indicated a 12 percent return on investment, Arrington's financial statements indicate that the rate of return is not 12 percent, and that the return has been increasing each period. The company has been using the straight-line method of depreciation. The machinery cost $60,000 with no salvage value and an estimated useful life of 10 years.

REQUIRED

To satisfy the president's concern, and assuming a 12 percent rate of return, prepare journal entries for the first two years under:

1. The sinking fund method.

2. The annuity method.

E12-11. CHANGE IN ESTIMATED LIFE   The George Company acquired a machine in 1977 for $25,000. George has been depreciating the machine over an estimated useful life of 20 years, assuming no salvage value, by the straight-line method of depreciation. At the beginning of 1987, George overhauled the machine at a cost of $5,000. As a result of the overhaul, George estimated that the useful life of the machine would extend five years beyond the original estimate.

REQUIRED

1. Prepare the journal entry to record the overhaul.

2. Calculate depreciation expense for 1987.

E12-12. CALCULATION OF DEPRECIATION BASE; ADDITIONS; DEPRECIATION EXPENSE   Samson Manufacturing Company, a calendar-year company, purchased a machine for $65,000 on January 1, 1986. At the date of purchase, Samson incurred the following additional items:

Loss on sale of old machinery $1,000
Freight in   500
Installation cost. 2,000
Testing costs prior to regular operation   300

The estimated salvage value of the machine was $5,000 and Samson estimated that the machine would have a useful life of 20 years. Depreciation was calculated by the straight-line method. In January 1988, accessories costing $3,600 were added to the machine in order to reduce its operating costs. These accessories neither prolonged the machine's life nor provided any additional salvage value.

REQUIRED

Calculate depreciation expense for 1988.

E12-13. EXTRAORDINARY REPAIRS; IMPROVEMENTS; DEPRECIATION EXPENSE   On January 2, 1984, Moreland Limited purchases a new machine at a cost of $55,000. Installation costs for the machine are $2,000. The machine has a salvage value of $7,000 and an expected useful life of 10 years. The company uses straight-line depreciation.

On January 2, 1986, an extraordinary repair is made to the machine in the amount of $3,400. The repair extends the machine's life to 16 years but leaves the salvage value unchanged.

On January 2, 1988, an improvement is made to the machine in the amount of $1,200 which increases the machine's productivity and increases the residual value to $9,400 but does not affect the remaining useful life.

REQUIRED

Determine depreciation expense for the years ended December 31, 1984, 1986, and 1988.

(CGAA, adapted)

E12-14. CHANGE IN ESTIMATED LIFE AND SALVAGE VALUE   Brett Company acquires a machine on July 1, 1984, for $85,000. The estimated useful life is 10 years and estimated salvage value is $5,000. In 1987 it is determined that the machine will not be useful beyond the end of 1991 and that there will be no scrap value. Accumulated depreciation on the machine as of December 31, 1986, is $20,000, calculated using the straight-line method.

REQUIRED

Calculate depreciation expense for 1987.

E12-15. DEPRECIATION METHODS; CHANGE IN ESTIMATE   At the beginning of year 1, Poco Corporation purchased for $60,000 cash a machine that will be used to produce an estimated 5,000 units of output over a 10-year period. Salvage value is expected to be $5,000.

REQUIRED

1. Calculate depreciation expense for year 3 under each of the following methods:
   a) Sum-of-the-years'-digits method.
   b) Double declining balance method.
   c) Production method, assuming 1,000 units are produced during year 3.

2. Assume that Poco used the straight-line method of depreciation and that, at the beginning of year 3, Poco changes its estimate of the machine's total useful life from 10 to 12 years.
   a) What entry is necessary at the beginning of year 3 to recognize the change in estimate?
   b) Prepare the entry to record depreciation expense at the end of year 3.

E12-16. CHANGE IN DEPRECIATION METHODS   Gura Company acquires machinery on January 2, 1986, at a cost of $75,000. Gura estimates that the machinery will have an estimated useful life of 10 years and no salvage value. Gura uses the double declining balance method of depreciation until the beginning of 1988, at which time it changes to the straight-line method of depreciation.

REQUIRED

Determine the cumulative effect on prior years' income of the change in depreciation methods. Assume an income tax rate of 40 percent in all years.

E12-17. CHANGE IN DEPRECIATION METHODS   On January 1, 1984, Trail Company purchased a machine (its only depreciable asset) for $150,000. The machine had a five-year life and no salvage value. Trail has been using sum-of-the-years'-digits depreciation for both financial statement reporting and income tax reporting.

Effective January 1, 1987, Trail decided to change to the straight-line method for depreciation of the machine for financial statement reporting but not for income tax reporting.

Trail's income *before* depreciation, *before* income taxes, and *before* the cumulative effect of the accounting change (if any) for the year ended December 31, 1987, is $100,000. The income tax rate for 1987, as well as for the years 1984–86, is 40 percent.

REQUIRED

Determine Trail's net income for 1987.

(AICPA, adapted)

E12-18. CHANGE IN DEPRECIATION METHODS   Before 1987 the Cougar Company used accelerated depreciation methods for plant equipment. In 1987 Cougar changed to the straight-line method for previously acquired plant equipment as well as for new acquisitions. On December 31, 1986, the book value of the plant equipment was $3.5 million. If the straight-line method had been used previously, the book value on December 31, 1986, would have been $3.8 million. For 1987, depreciation for plant equipment under the straight-line method amounted to $120,000, whereas it would have amounted to $150,000 had accelerated depreciation methods still been used. The income tax rate is 40 percent in all years.

REQUIRED

1. Determine the cumulative effect of the change in depreciation methods on prior years.

2. How should the effect of the change be reported in the 1987 financial statements?

(AICPA, adapted)

E12-19. CHANGE IN DEPRECIATION METHODS   Nolan Company began operations in 1984. It calculates depreciation by an accelerated method until January 1, 1988, when it changed to the straight-line method. Depreciation calculated by the accelerated method was reported as follows:

1984	1985	1986	1987
$9,000	$8,000	$8,000	$7,000

Had the straight-line method been used, depreciation would have been as follows:

1984	1985	1986	1987
$5,200	$5,200	$5,800	$5,800

The change to straight-line depreciation was effective January 1, 1988, and the new method was applied both to assets acquired before that date and to those subsequently acquired.

Nolan's income tax rate has been 40 percent throughout the years 1984–87.

Nolan's 1988 income before taxes and before the cumulative effect of the accounting change was $50,000.

REQUIRED

Determine Nolan's net income for 1988.

(AICPA, adapted)

E12-20. ERROR CORRECTION   Carter Corporation acquired a machine in 1985 for $40,000. The estimated useful life of the machine was 10 years and the estimated salvage value was $4,000. Carter depreciated the machine by the sum-of-the-years'-digits method. At the end of 1988, while reviewing the depreciation schedules in preparation for recording the annual depreciation charges, it was discovered that salvage value had been ignored in recording depreciation expense from 1985 through 1987, both for financial reporting and for income tax purposes. The income tax rate for all years was 40 percent.

REQUIRED

Prepare the journal entry to correct the error.

PROBLEMS

P12-1. ACQUISITION, SUBSEQUENT EXPENDITURES, AND DEPRECIATION OF PLANT ASSETS   The following information relates to the purchase and upkeep of machinery of the Cronkite Company during the years 1987 and 1988:

1987

April 1 — Purchased machine *A* for $6,000 cash; paid $500 for installation and $100 for freight. Machine *A* is expected to have a useful life of 8 years from this date and scrap value of $200.

July 1 — Purchased machine *B* for $14,000, including delivery and installation. No scrap value is anticipated, and the machine is expected to have a useful life of 10 years.

Dec. 31 — Recorded depreciation on a straight-line basis.

1988

March 31 — Paid repair bills of $294, of which $80 applied to machine *A*, $100 to machine *B*, and the balance to sundry equipment.

July 1 — Traded in machine *A* plus $4,000 cash for machine *C*. The new machine has a life expectancy of 10 years and no salvage value.

Oct. 1 — Sold machine *B* for $13,000 cash.

Dec. 31 — Recorded depreciation on a straight-line basis.

REQUIRED

Prepare journal entries to record each of the above items.

P12-2. ACQUISITION, SUBSEQUENT EXPENDITURES, AND DEPRECIATION OF PLANT ASSETS   On the first business day of 1983, King Truckers purchased for cash a new truck from its local dealer. The truck was a heavy-duty type and records indicated it should have a 10-year life span and no salvage value. The vehicle cost $12,000. The straight-line depreciation method is used.

During the first week of January 1987, the truck was repaired and rebuilt at a total cost of $3,200: $2,400 for additions and $800 for ordinary repair. The additions increased the efficiency of the vehicle but no change was contemplated in life expectancy or salvage value.

On April 1, 1988, the truck was completely wrecked. Beta Insurance Company settled the claim for $4,000.

REQUIRED

Prepare journal entries for:

1. The purchase of the vehicle.
2. Depreciation during the first year.
3. The 1987 transaction involving the rebuilding.
4. The 1987 depreciation.
5. The 1988 entries.

(CGAA, adapted)

P12-3. CALCULATION OF DEPRECIATION EXPENSE   The Weidle Animal Clinic began operations on September 1, 1987. Before that date, Dr. Weidle acquired a new oxygen unit at a cost of $3,000, which was put into service on September 1. Weidle estimated that the unit would last about seven years and have a salvage value of $200. He also estimated that the unit could be used for about 12,000 hours. It was used for 1,000 hours in 1987 and 1,800 hours in 1988. The estimated rate of return on the unit was 12 percent.

REQUIRED

Calculate depreciation expense for 1987 and 1988 under each of the following methods:

1. Straight-line method.
2. Use method (hours of use).
3. Sum-of-the-years'-digits method.
4. Declining balance method (150% of straight-line rate).

P12-4. EFFECT OF DEPRECIATION METHODS ON INCOME   On January 1, 1985, Ward Company, a small machine-tool manufacturer, acquired for $1 million a piece of new industrial equipment. The new equipment was eligible for a 10 percent investment tax credit. Ward took full advantage of the credit and accounted for the amount by the flow-through method. The new equipment had a useful life of five years and Ward estimated that the salvage value would be $100,000. Ward estimated that the new equipment could produce 10,000 machine tools in its first year. Production would then decline by 1,000 units per year over the remaining useful life of the equipment.

The following depreciation methods may be used:

Double declining balance.
Straight line.
Sum-of-the-years'-digits.
Production (units of output).

REQUIRED

1. Which depreciation method would result in the maximization of profits for financial statement reporting for the three-year period ending December 31, 1987? Prepare a schedule showing the amount of accumulated depreciation as of December 31, 1987, under the method selected. Show supporting calculations in good form. Ignore present value, income tax, and deferred income tax considerations in your answer.

2. Which depreciation method would result in the minimization of profits for financial reporting for the three-year period ending December 31, 1987? Prepare a schedule showing the amount of accumulated depreciation as of December 31, 1987, under the method selected. Show supporting calculations in good form. Ignore present value considerations.

(AICPA, adapted)

P12-5. RETIREMENT AND REPLACEMENT METHODS   Western Communications Company had the following acquisitions and disposals of telephone poles for the years indicated:

	1987	1988
Original cost of poles disposed of	$300,000	$1,180,000
Salvage proceeds	10,000	74,000
Cost of new poles	420,000	2,050,000

REQUIRED

Prepare journal entries for 1987 and 1988 to record depreciation expense and the acquisition of poles, assuming:

1. The retirement method is used.

2. The replacement method is used.

P12-6. COMPREHENSIVE   Selected accounts included in the property, plant, and equipment section of the Wilson Corporation's balance sheet on December 31, 1986, had the following balances:

Land	$175,000
Land improvements	90,000
Buildings	900,000
Machinery and equipment	850,000

During 1987 the following transactions occurred:

a) A tract of land was acquired for $125,000 as a potential future building site.

b) A plant facility consisting of land and building was acquired from the Nostrand Company in exchange for 10,000 shares of Wilson's common stock. On the acquisition date, Wilson's stock had a closing market price of $45 per share on a national stock exchange. The plant facility was carried on Nostrand's books at $89,000 for land and $130,000 for the building on the exchange date. Current appraised values for the land and building, respectively, are $120,000 and $240,000.

c) Items of machinery and equipment were purchased at a total cost of $300,000. Additional costs were incurred as follows:

Freight and unloading	$ 5,000
Sales and use taxes	12,000
Installation	25,000

d) Expenditures totaling $75,000 were made for new parking lots, streets, and sidewalks at the corporation's various plant locations. These expenditures had an estimated useful life of 15 years.

e) A machine costing $50,000 on January 1, 1979, was scrapped on June 30, 1987. Double declining balance depreciation has been recorded on the basis of a 10-year life.

f) A machine was sold for $20,000 on July 1, 1987. Original cost of the machine was $36,000 on January 1, 1984, and it was depreciated on a straight-line basis over an estimated useful life of seven years, with a salvage value of $1,000.

REQUIRED

1. Prepare a detailed analysis of the changes in each of the following balance sheet accounts for 1987:

a) Land.

b) Land improvements.

c) Buildings.

d) Machinery and equipment.

Disregard the related accumulated depreciation accounts.

2. List the lettered items above which were not used to determine the answer to part 1, showing the pertinent amounts and supporting calculations in good form for each item. In addition, indicate where, or if, these items should be included in Wilson's financial statements.

(AICPA, adapted)

P12-7. ANALYSIS OF PLANT ASSET ACCOUNTS Thompson Corporation, a manufacturer of steel products, began operations on October 1, 1987. Thompson's accounting department has started the fixed asset and depreciation schedule presented below. You have been asked to assist in completing this schedule. In addition to ascertaining that the data already on the schedule are correct, you have obtained the following information from the company's records and personnel:

a) Depreciation is calculated from the first of the month of acquisition to the first of the month of disposition.

b) Land A and building A were acquired from the Boatsman Corporation. Thompson paid $812,500 for the land and building together. At the time of acquisition, the land had an appraised value of $72,000 and the building had an appraised value of $828,000.

c) Land B was acquired on October 2, 1987, in exchange for 3,000 newly issued shares of Thompson's common stock. At the date of acquisition, the stock had a par value of $5 per share and a fair market value of $25 per share. During October 1987, Thompson paid $10,400 to demolish an existing building on this land so it could construct a new building.

d) Construction of building B on the newly acquired land began on October 1, 1988. By September 30, 1989, Thompson had paid $210,000 of the estimated total construction costs of $300,000. Estimated completion and occupancy are scheduled for July 1990.

e) Certain equipment was donated to the corporation by a local university. An independent appraisal of the equipment when it was donated placed the fair market value at $16,000 and the salvage value at $2,000.

f) Machinery A's total cost of $110,000 includes installation expense of $550 and normal repairs and maintenance of $11,000. Salvage value is estimated to be $5,500. Machinery A was sold on February 1, 1989.

g) On October 1, 1988, machinery B was acquired with a down payment of $4,000, the remaining payments to be made in 10 annual installments of $4,000 each beginning October 1, 1989. The prevailing interest rate was 8 percent.

FIXED ASSET AND DEPRECIATION SCHEDULE

ASSETS	ACQUISITION DATE	COST	SALVAGE	DEPRECIATION METHOD	ESTIMATED LIFE (YEARS)	DEPRECIATION EXPENSE, YEAR ENDED 9/30 1988	1989
Land A	10/1/87	(1)	N/A	N/A	N/A	N/A	N/A
Building A	10/1/87	(2)	$47,500	Straight line	(3)	$14,000	(4)
Land B	10/2/87	(5)	N/A	N/A	N/A	N/A	N/A
Building B	Under construction	$210,000 to date	—	Straight line	30	—	(6)
Donated equipment	10/2/87	(7)	2,000	150% declining balance	10	(8)	(9)
Machinery A	10/2/87	(10)	5,500	Sum-of-years'-digits	10	(11)	(12)
Machinery B	10/1/88	(13)	—	Straight line	15	—	(14)

N/A = Not applicable.

REQUIRED

For each numbered item in the schedule, calculate the correct amount. Supporting calculations should be in good form.

(AICPA, adapted)

P12-8. MISCELLANEOUS PLANT ASSET TRANSACTIONS   On January 2, 1980, the Northern Construction Company purchased new heavy-duty equipment and placed it in service. The cost to the company was $60,000 cash. The equipment was expected to have no salvage value after a life of 10 years. On January 2, 1983, a device was added to the equipment to increase output by approximately 20 percent. The cost was $2,800. This addition brought no change in either life expectancy or salvage value.

The equipment was overhauled during the first week of January 1987, for $18,000. The salvage value still remained the same, but the life expectancy was increased by three years. On July 1, 1988, the equipment was a total loss following a fire. The insurance company arranged for settlement and paid the company $20,000.

REQUIRED

Prepare journal entries to record:

1. The original purchase.
2. Depreciation for 1980 (straight-line method).
3. The addition to the equipment.
4. The depreciation for 1984.
5. The overhauling of the equipment.
6. The depreciation for 1987.
7. The fire loss and settlement.

(CGAA, adapted)

P12-9. DEPRECIATION; CHANGE IN ESTIMATE; EXCHANGE OF PLANT ASSETS   Hansen Corporation purchased machine *A* at a cost of $12,400 on January 2, 1981. From 1981 through 1984, the machine was depreciated on a straight-line basis, under the assumption that it would have a 10-year useful life and a $2,400 salvage value. After more experience and before recording 1985 depreciation, Hansen revised its estimate of the machine's remaining useful life downward from six years to four years, and revised the estimated salvage value downward to $2,000.

On April 2, 1987, after recording part of a year's depreciation for 1987, the company traded in machine *A* on machine *B*, a newer model, receiving a $4,000 trade-in allowance. Machine *B* cost $15,300, less the trade-in allowance, and the balance of $11,300 was paid in cash. Machine *B* was depreciated on a straight-line basis under the assumption that it would have a six-year useful life and a $2,300 salvage value.

REQUIRED

Prepare journal entries to record:

1. The purchase of machine *A*.
2. 1981 depreciation.
3. 1985 depreciation.
4. The exchange of the machines.
5. 1987 depreciation.

P12-10. CHANGES IN ESTIMATED LIFE AND SALVAGE VALUE   The Winslow Company, which uses the straight-line method of depreciation, purchased three machines on the first day of business in January 1982. Details of the purchase are as follows:

	MACHINE X	**MACHINE Y**	**MACHINE Z**
Cost	$15,000	$15,000	$15,000
Estimated life	5 years	6 years	8 years
Estimated scrap	None	$2,400	$600

During the first week of business in January 1987, machine *X* was sold for $1,000. This prompted management to reexamine not only the useful life expectancy but also the scrap expectancy of machines *Y* and *Z*. They decided that machine *Y* had a remaining life of two years as of

January 1, 1987, and that the scrap evaluation of $2,400 was about right. Machine Z, however, had a remaining life of five years and there probably would be no salvage.

REQUIRED

Prepare journal entries to reflect all of the events and information related to the three machines during 1987, including depreciation expense. Supporting calculations should be in good form.

(CGAA, adapted)

P12-11. CHANGE IN DEPRECIATION METHODS   The Wong Company purchased a machine on January 1, 1984, for $240,000. At the date of acquisition, the machine had an estimated useful life of 10 years and an estimated salvage value of $20,000. The machine is being depreciated on a straight-line basis. On January 1, 1987, Wong appropriately adopted the sum-of-the-years'-digits method of depreciation for this machine.

REQUIRED

1. Prepare a schedule calculating the book value of this machine, net of accumulated depreciation, which would be included in Wong's balance sheet on December 31, 1987. Show supporting calculations in good form.

2. Prepare a schedule calculating the cumulative effect on prior years of changing to a different depreciation method for the year ended December 31, 1987. Assume that the direct effects of this change are limited to the effect on depreciation and the related tax provision, and that the income tax rate was 50 percent in all years. Show supporting calculations in good form.

(AICPA, adapted)

P12-12. COMPREHENSIVE; ERROR CORRECTIONS   The Potter Corporation is in the process of negotiating a loan for expansion purposes. The books and records have never been audited and the bank has requested that an audit be performed. Potter has prepared the following comparative financial statements for the years ended December 31, 1988 and 1987:

BALANCE SHEET
AS OF DECEMBER 31, 1988 AND 1987

ASSETS	1988	1987
Current assets		
Cash	$241,000	$160,000
Accounts receivable	392,000	296,000
Allowance for uncollectible accounts	(37,000)	(18,000)
Merchandise inventory	207,000	202,000
Total current assets	$803,000	$640,000
Fixed assets		
Property, plant, and equipment	$167,000	$169,500
Accumulated depreciation	(121,600)	(106,400)
Total fixed assets	$ 45,400	$ 63,100
Total assets	$848,400	$703,100
LIABILITIES AND STOCKHOLDERS' EQUITY		
Liabilities		
Accounts payable	$121,400	$196,100
Stockholders' equity		
Common stock, par value $10, authorized 50,000 shares, issued and outstanding 26,000 shares	$260,000	$260,000
Retained earnings	467,000	247,000
Total stockholders' equity	$727,000	$507,000
Total liabilities and stockholders' equity	$848,400	$703,100

STATEMENT OF INCOME
FOR THE YEARS ENDED DECEMBER 31, 1988 AND 1987

	1988	**1987**
Sales	$1,000,000	$ 900,000
Cost of sales	(430,000)	(395,000)
Gross profit	$ 570,000	$ 505,000
Operating expenses	$ 210,000	$ 205,000
Administrative expenses	140,000	105,000
Total expenses	$ (350,000)	$(310,000)
Net income	$ 220,000	$ 195,000

During the course of the audit, the following additional facts were determined:

a) An analysis of collections and losses on accounts receivable during the two years indicates a drop in anticipated losses due to bad debts. After consultation with management, it was agreed that the loss experience rate on sales should be reduced from the recorded 2 percent to 1 percent, beginning with the year ended December 31, 1988.

b) The merchandise inventory on December 31, 1987, was overstated by $4,000 and the merchandise inventory on December 31, 1988, was overstated by $6,100.

c) On January 2, 1987, equipment costing $12,000 (estimated useful life of 10 years and residual value of $1,000) was incorrectly charged to operating expenses. Potter records depreciation by the straight-line method. In 1988 fully depreciated equipment (with no residual value) that originally cost $17,500 was sold as scrap for $2,500. Potter credited the proceeds of $2,500 to property and equipment.

d) An analysis of 1987 operating expenses revealed that Potter charged to expense a three-year insurance premium of $2,700 on January 15, 1987.

REQUIRED

1. Prepare the journal entries to correct the books as of December 31, 1988. The books for 1988 have not been closed. Ignore income taxes.

2. Prepare a schedule showing the calculation of corrected net income for the years ended December 31, 1988 and 1987, assuming that any adjustments are to be reported on comparative statements for the two years. The first items on your schedule should be the net income for each year. Ignore income taxes. (Do not prepare financial statements.)

(AICPA, adapted)

13

INTANGIBLE ASSETS AND NATURAL RESOURCES

In Chapters 11 and 12, accounting and reporting issues related to plant assets were examined. Like plant assets, natural resources (also called wasting assets) and intangible assets represent future benefits that are expected to flow from current expenditures. Much greater uncertainty exists, however, about the amount and timing of the future benefits that will flow from current expenditures for intangible assets and natural resources. In this chapter we describe these assets, the reasons for the greater degree of uncertainty surrounding the benefits associated with the assets, and the resulting accounting and reporting requirements. In the last part of the chapter, we address the controversial issue of accounting for exploration costs by oil and gas companies.

INTANGIBLE ASSETS

Plant assets, which also are called tangible fixed assets, are operating resources that have physical substance and that provide benefits for more than one year. There are other types of resources that have no physical substance, but that firms expect also will provide benefits for more than one year; patents, copyrights, trademarks, and goodwill are examples. Such assets are characterized as **intangibles** because of their lack of physical substance. There are certain other assets that lack physical substance (for example, accounts receivable), but they are *current* assets. The term *intangibles* in accounting refers only to those nonphysical assets which are *long term*.

Although there are particular difficulties in accounting for specific intangibles, in general we measure and report each of the various kinds of intangibles in much the same way. *APB Opinion No. 17* summarizes the issues and complications in accounting for intangibles:

> Accounting for an intangible asset involves the same kinds of problems as accounting for other long-lived assets, namely, determining an initial carrying amount, accounting for that amount after acquisition under normal business conditions (amortization), and accounting for that amount if the value declines substantially and permanently. Solving the problems is complicated by the characteristics of an intangible asset: its lack of physical qualities makes evidence of its existence elusive, its value is often difficult to estimate, and its useful life may be indeterminable.[1]

[1] "Intangible Assets," *Opinions of the Accounting Principles Board No. 17* (New York: AICPA, 1970), para. 2.

In other words, the problems of accounting for intangibles are the same as for other noncurrent assets. Analyzing and resolving the problems, however, is more difficult in the case of intangibles. The difficulty lies in identifying intangible assets, valuing them, and estimating the number of periods in which they will provide benefits.

In the next section, we discuss the characteristics of intangibles that provide possible bases for classification for accounting purposes. The accounting guidelines for intangibles rely upon these characteristics.

CLASSIFICATION

Intangible assets vary in their characteristics. They may be classified according to the following characteristics:

1. *Identifiability*. Many intangibles, such as patents, copyrights, trademarks, and franchises, are **separately identifiable.** Goodwill, however, is a combination of several factors that cannot be separately identified and evaluated. Thus, goodwill is referred to as an **unidentifiable intangible asset.**

2. *Manner of acquisition*. Firms may either develop intangible assets internally or acquire them from external sources. A patent, for example, may be developed or purchased. If intangibles are acquired externally, they may be acquired singly, in groups, or as part of a business combination.

3. *Expected period of benefit*. Some intangible assets, such as organization costs, may provide benefits indefinitely. The benefit period of others may be limited by economic factors or by legal or contractual restrictions. Patents, for example, have a legal life of 17 years.

4. *Separability* (exchangeability). Some intangibles, such as patents and franchises, may be sold separately. Others, such as goodwill and organization costs, relate solely to the enterprise as a whole and cannot be sold separately.[2]

Each of these characteristics was considered to some extent by the accounting profession when it established the accounting requirements. You should keep these distinctions in mind as we discuss the accounting for intangibles in the next section, because they are useful in making the accounting guidelines comprehensible.

ACCOUNTING FOR INTANGIBLES

Opinion No. 17 provides the accounting and reporting guidelines for intangibles. *Opinion No. 17* does not, however, apply to research and development costs.[3] The origin of *Opinion No. 17* is an interesting and informative case in the politics of accounting policy making. It actually evolved as a spinoff of *Opinion No. 16*, ''Business Combinations.'' The APB required the approval of two-thirds of its 18 members before issuing an opinion. Fearing that the controversial problem of accounting for goodwill arising in a business combination would put the proposed opinion's passage in jeopardy, the Board dropped the goodwill issue from it. After *Opinion No. 16* was passed, the issue of goodwill was then taken up separately. Not only did the APB decide to provide guidance in accounting for goodwill, it also expanded its consideration to include accounting for all intangibles.

According to *Opinion No. 17*, the costs of intangibles acquired from others, whether specifically identifiable or unidentifiable (that is, goodwill), must be recorded as assets and amortized over the periods benefited. **Amortization** is the process of systematically matching the cost of an intangible against revenues over those periods, a process identical

---

[2] *APB Opinion No. 17*, para. 10.

[3] Guidelines for research and development costs are provided by ''Accounting for Research and Development Costs,'' *Statement of Financial Accounting Standards No. 2* (Stamford, Conn.: FASB, 1974). These guidelines are discussed later in this chapter.

For intangibles, the maximum amortization period is 40 years.

to the recording of *depreciation* of a plant asset. *Opinion No. 17* specifies a *maximum* amortization period of 40 years. If the benefit period is less than 40 years, the firm must amortize the cost over the periods benefited.

The costs of developing intangibles that are not specifically identifiable must be expensed as they are incurred. *APB Opinion No. 17* does not specify how firms should record costs incurred to *develop* specifically identifiable intangibles, such as patents, trademarks, and copyrights. Thus, firms may either (1) record the costs as assets and amortize them over the periods benefited, or (2) expense them as they are incurred. If a firm records them in an asset account, it must amortize them over the shorter of 40 years or the useful life.

In spite of the lack of definitive guidance in the authoritative literature for internally developed intangible assets that can be specifically identified, the conceptual framework assists us in determining the appropriate accounting in particular circumstances. We know that in order to be reported as an asset in the balance sheet, an item must meet the definition of an asset. However, this criterion provides only a ''first cut'' for determining the items to be reported as assets. In order to be reported in the financial statements, items that meet the definition of an asset must have a relevant attribute that is measurable with sufficient reliability. Keeping these criteria in mind, a firm should be able to establish a conceptually acceptable method of accounting for costs incurred in developing specifically identifiable intangibles.

Firms usually credit the asset account directly when they amortize intangible assets. It is acceptable, however, to use an accumulated amortization account, comparable to the accumulated depreciation account used for tangible fixed assets.

Before the issuance of *Opinion No. 17,* most firms amortized the costs of *acquired* intangibles over an arbitrary, short period of time. Some firms, however, retained such costs in an asset account until there was evidence of impairment of value, at which time they recorded a large write-down. Likewise, as indicated earlier, costs incurred to *develop* intangible assets sometimes were recorded as assets and at other times were expensed as they were incurred. *Opinion No. 17* was an attempt to eliminate these inconsistencies and to produce uniform, comparable treatment of intangibles.

Preparers and users of financial statements have severely criticized *Opinion No. 17.* While the *Opinion* accomplished the objective of providing greater uniformity, and eliminated much of the subjectivity in accounting for intangibles, it also produced major theoretical objections. In addition, it left unresolved a significant issue—how to account for the costs of developing specifically identifiable intangibles internally.

Under *Opinion No. 17,* entities must record the cost of purchased intangibles, including the cost of purchased goodwill, as an asset, and must amortize that cost over not more than 40 years. Some accountants argue that when goodwill is purchased, a market transaction occurs, which establishes a value for the goodwill acquired. Thus, we record the goodwill as an asset. Costs incurred internally to generate goodwill, however, must be expensed as they are incurred. The firm may not record the costs incurred in an asset account. Conceptually, however, there is no reason to expect that the benefit period and value will be any greater when goodwill is bought and paid for than when a firm incurs internal costs to generate it. Exhibit 13–1 summarizes the *Opinion No. 17* guidelines.

The requirement that deferred costs of intangibles (that is, costs recorded in an asset account) must be amortized over not more than 40 years is an arbitrary and theoretically unappealing rule. Certain intangibles, such as a copyright in certain circumstances or a perpetual franchise, may provide benefits for more than 40 years. The 40-year limit on the amortization period appears to be a compromise between the view that entities should not amortize certain intangibles unless evidence of a decline in value occurs and the view that all intangibles have a limited life, and thus firms should systematically amortize the costs over the periods benefited. By placing a maximum number of years on the amortization

EXHIBIT 13–1   SUMMARY OF ACCOUNTING REQUIREMENTS
FOR INTANGIBLE ASSETS

TYPE OF INTANGIBLE	METHOD OF ACQUISITION	
	PURCHASED	**INTERNALLY DEVELOPED**
SPECIFICALLY IDENTIFIABLE	Capitalize and amortize over shorter of 40 years or useful life	Expense as incurred *or* Capitalize and amortize over shorter of 40 years or useful life
UNIDENTIFIABLE (GOODWILL)	Capitalize and amortize over shorter of 40 years or useful life	Expense as incurred

period, *Opinion No. 17* requires firms to amortize all intangibles, reflecting the latter view. A maximum amortization period of 40 years, rather than some smaller number, enables a firm to minimize the impact of amortization on net income in each year, thereby appeasing the proponents of the former view.

Opinion No. 17 further requires that entities must use the straight-line method of amortization unless they can demonstrate that some other systematic method is more appropriate. This requirement implies that equal amounts of service potential are being used up each period, and thus that firms should allocate equal amounts of the cost of intangibles to expense each period. Theoretically, there appears to be no more basis for this presumption with respect to intangibles than with respect to depreciable fixed assets.

Opinion No. 17 provides what some accountants regard as the needed uniformity of treatment of intangibles in practice. But the *Opinion* allows little flexibility, although many people believe flexibility is needed to deal with different circumstances.

As is the case with many other accounting issues, the shortcomings that are evident in the accounting standards for intangibles exist primarily because of measurement difficulties. As indicated in Chapter 2, we frequently sacrifice relevance for reliability. If we could improve our ability to assess the value and benefit period of internally generated intangibles, we could then minimize these theoretical inconsistencies. Likewise, an increased emphasis on relevance would minimize theoretical flaws in our standards. The conceptual framework efforts of the FASB may provide the impetus for improved accounting for intangibles.

Specifically Identifiable Intangibles

Many intangibles can be specifically identified. We can account for these intangibles individually using the guidelines of *Opinion No. 17*. In this section we describe the common types of specifically identifiable intangibles and the appropriate accounting for each type.

PATENTS   A **patent,** granted by the U.S. Patent Office, is the exclusive right to use, manufacture, and sell a product or process. Patents are granted for a period of 17 years. Although patents are not renewable, a minor modification may lead to a new patent, effectively extending the useful life of the original patent. The ownership of a patent does not guarantee that an asset exists. If a patent is not expected to increase a firm's future cash flow, then it is not an asset. An entity may defer and amortize the cost of a patent only if that patent confers on the entity measurable future benefits that exceed the cost.

Research and development costs incurred to develop products or processes that become patented must be expensed as they are incurred.[4] Since the actual costs of obtaining a patent from the government are minimal (government processing fees and attorneys' fees), for all practical purposes the only patents that firms capitalize are existing patents that are purchased from another party.

If the estimated benefit period extends beyond the year of acquisition, patent costs should be deferred and amortized over the shorter of its remaining legal life (17 years for a newly issued patent) or its useful life. The amount deferred should include the direct costs of acquiring the patent plus other costs incurred in securing it, such as attorneys' fees.

Often, firms become involved in litigation involving patent infringement. For example, General Motors Corporation (GM) recently filed a suit in federal court against American Motors Corporation (AMC), alleging that AMC is using a mechanism patented by GM that allows a driver to switch from two-wheel drive to four-wheel drive "on the run." GM asked for an injunction prohibiting AMC from using the device in its vehicles. The outcome of litigation involving patents determines the appropriate accounting for the costs of litigation and for the book value of the patent.

If a firm *successfully* defends a patent, costs of litigation should be deferred in the patent account and amortized over the remaining useful life of the patent, along with the previously existing book value. However, if a firm is *unsuccessful* in defending against patent infringement, the costs of litigation should be expensed as incurred. Also, the firm should assess the recoverable value of the patent to determine whether a partial or total write-down of the book value is required, because presumably the reason for the litigation was to attempt to protect the value of the patent.

The useful economic life of a patent is often considerably less than 17 years because of such factors as competing products or processes and changing consumer demand. Assume, for example, that on January 2, 1987, a company pays $20,000 for a patent from another company and that the government issued the patent 5 years previously. Even though the remaining legal life is 12 years, the company acquiring the patent estimates that it will be economically useful for only 4 more years. On December 31, 1987, the company that acquired the patent would record amortization as follows:

Patent amortization expense............................5,000		
Patent..		5,000
($20,000 ÷ 4 years)		

Entities should periodically review the amortization period for their patents. If reviews lead to revised estimates, firms should allocate the unamortized cost over the remaining years of estimated useful life.

COPYRIGHTS A **copyright** is a grant by the federal government providing to the owner the exclusive right to reproduce and sell an artistic or literary work. The government grants copyrights for the life of the creator plus 50 years.[5] The owner of a copyright may assign or sell it to other parties.

Ideally, a firm should capitalize the cost of a copyright and amortize the cost over the periods benefited. From a practical standpoint, it is difficult to estimate the useful life of

---

[4] *FASB Statement No. 2*, para. 12.

[5] In an interesting, related development, the U.S. Copyright Office recently began providing 10-year copyright protection to registrants who manufacture microchips. The penalty for infringement is $250,000 for each "mask work" (circuit pattern) that is reproduced without the copyright owner's permission.

a copyright. Thus, firms generally amortize the costs over some arbitrary, short time period. In no instance may the amortization period exceed 40 years. In accordance with the historical cost principle, we do not record increases in the value of copyrights above the unamortized cost.

TRADEMARKS AND TRADE NAMES **Trademarks** and **trade names** are words, symbols, or other devices that identify particular products. The right of exclusive use of a trademark resides with the original user as long as the original user employs the trademark continuously. Companies may register trademarks with the U.S. Patent Office for a period of 20 years. Registrations are renewable for additional 20-year periods as long as the trademark is used continuously. Thus, from a legal standpoint, we may consider trademarks to have unlimited lives. However, the period over which the exclusive use of the trademark provides benefits to the firm in the form of increased cash flows may be only a few years. Conversely, the trademark benefit may extend indefinitely into the future, as in the case of ''Coke.''

Firms may develop trademarks internally or they may purchase them from outside parties. In both cases, firms should capitalize the cost of trademarks and amortize the cost over the benefit period, not to exceed 40 years. Costs of developed trademarks include attorneys' fees, registration fees, costs incurred in connection with defending trademark rights, and any other direct costs (excluding research and development costs, as discussed later) associated with developing or retaining a trademark.

FRANCHISES A **franchise** is an agreement whereby one party (the franchisor) provides to another party (the franchisee) the exclusive right to market a product or service within a designated area. For example, governmental units often grant franchise rights to utility companies. Likewise, individuals and companies often operate under franchise arrangements with other organizations, such as fast-food operations (for example, Kentucky Fried Chicken and Burger King), motels (for example, TraveLodge), and professional sports teams (for example, the Kansas City Royals). As another recent example, Greyhound lines recently began a bus-route franchising program in an attempt to enhance the profitability of the firm. Under the program, independent carriers operate as part of Greyhound's intercity bus network.

If the franchisee must pay an initial franchise fee, it should record the fee as an intangible asset. The franchisee should amortize the franchise fee over the life of the franchise if the fee is for a specified number of years, or over 40 years if the franchise term exceeds 40 years. If the franchise is indefinite in duration or perpetual, the franchisee should amortize the initial franchise fee over the estimated benefit period, but in no case should the period of amortization exceed 40 years. The periodic payments that are required under a franchise arrangement, such as fees based on periodic operating income, should be expensed by the franchisee when they are incurred, in accordance with the matching principle.

LEASE PREPAYMENTS AND LEASEHOLD IMPROVEMENTS A **lease** is a contractual agreement whereby one party (the lessor) grants to another party (the lessee) the right to use specified property owned by the lessor for a specific period of time in exchange for periodic cash payments.[6] In many instances the lessee must make a lump-sum payment, also called a **prepayment,** to the lessor at the time of signing the lease agreement. The lessee should capitalize this prepayment and amortize it to expense over the lease period, since the prepayment provides benefits over the period of the lease. Because lease prepayments usually relate to tangible property, firms often include them under property, plant, and equipment in the balance sheet.

[6] We describe the detailed accounting and reporting requirements for leases in Chapter 17.

Improvements made to leased property by the lessee, such as buildings, usually revert to the lessor at the termination of the lease. Thus, although the lessee pays for the improvements, the lessee does not own them. Rather, the lessee has the right to use the improvements over the lease term. As explained in Chapter 11, the cost of lease-hold improvements usually is reported under plant assets in the balance sheet. However, some firms include such costs in intangible assets.

Since the lease term establishes a maximum benefit period, the lessee should amortize the cost of the improvements over the lease term or the life of the improvement, whichever is shorter. The lessee should not consider a lease renewal option in determining the lease term for amortization purposes unless there is substantial certainty that the renewal option will be exercised.

ORGANIZATION COSTS   Firms incur costs for a variety of purposes in the process of organizing a company. Legal fees, accounting fees, fees paid to underwriters in connection with bond and stock issuance, state fees and taxes, and promotional costs are common examples of such **organization costs.** An entity usually incurs these costs either before it commences operations or during the early stages of operations.

A firm would not incur organization costs if it did not anticipate that future revenues would be sufficient to cover them and to provide a fair rate of return. Further, if the entity expects to continue in existence indefinitely, conceptually these organization costs should be capitalized and reported as an intangible asset; the rationale is that these costs were incurred to benefit the company over its entire life. However, since *Opinion No. 17* requires that all intangible assets must be amortized over not more than 40 years, this conceptually attractive alternative is not feasible. From a practical standpoint, most companies amortize organization costs over an arbitrary, short period of time on a straight-line basis. For income tax purposes, organization costs must be amortized over five years or more.

DEFERRED CHARGES   Many companies have a balance sheet classification within assets referred to as **deferred charges** or **other assets.** Items in this category include long-term prepayments (such as license fees, rent, insurance, and taxes), plant rearrangement or moving costs, the book value of idle plant assets, and, sometimes, organization costs. The category seems to be a catchall for items that do not fit conveniently into some other asset category and that are not material enough individually to constitute a separate category. Firms must amortize each item in the deferred charges category over its estimated benefit period, not to exceed 40 years.

Goodwill

In 1985 Philip Morris, Inc., acquired General Foods Corporation for about $5.8 billion. As a result of this acquisition, Philip Morris added about $2.8 billion of goodwill to its balance sheet. When General Motors acquired Hughes Aircraft for about $5 billion in 1985, about $4 billion of the purchase price was attributable to goodwill! These two transactions are indicative of an increasingly common phenomenon—the recording of goodwill in connection with corporate takeovers. Goodwill has become so significant as an asset on the books of many companies that it can no longer be ignored. Exhibit 13–2 indicates the significance of goodwill as a percentage of net worth on the books of many companies at the end of 1984. Standard & Poor reported that intangible assets on the books of 5,500 companies rose to $55.3 billion in 1984, 37 percent more than in 1983.[7] Thus, the significance of goodwill today makes the accounting issues more relevant than ever.

[7] Stuart Weiss, "What's Invisible and Worth $55 Billion?" *Business Week,* October 14, 1985, p. 132.

EXHIBIT 13—2   WHERE GOODWILL LOOMS LARGE ON THE BALANCE SHEET

COMPANY	1984 GOODWILL	
	MILLIONS OF DOLLARS	PERCENT OF NET WORTH
Tiger International	$ 57	2,850%
Financial Corp. of America	1,106	570
Rapid-American	234	241
A. H. Belo	453	158
Beatrice	2,607	111
Philip Morris	3,200	78*
Gelco	163	78
Hasbro	178	61
Gannett	629	55
Allis-Chalmers	37	52
Texas Eastern	621	40
Avon	447	39
IC Industries	541	35
American Brands	598	28
Fluor	423	25
GM	5,939	24*
Allied	702	23
Warner-Lambert	282	20
Cooper Industries	232	19
United Technologies	523	13

* Including pending 1985 acquisition.

Source: *Business Week,* October 14, 1985, p. 134.

Goodwill is perhaps the most misunderstood asset in financial accounting and reporting. A primary reason for this misunderstanding is that most discussions of goodwill fail to distinguish clearly between the definition and the measurement of goodwill. Goodwill consists of the favorable characteristics of a business enterprise which are intangible and which cannot be separately identified and valued. Examples of favorable characteristics that often comprise goodwill include the following:

Characteristics comprising goodwill.

1. Superior management team.
2. Outstanding sales manager or organization.
3. Weakness in the management of a competitor.
4. Effective advertising.
5. Secret manufacturing process.
6. Good labor relations.
7. Outstanding credit rating.
8. Top-flight training program for employees.
9. High standing in the community.
10. Unfavorable developments in operations of a competitor.
11. Favorable association with another company.
12. Strategic location.

13. Discovery of talents or resources.

14. Favorable tax conditions.

15. Favorable government regulation.[8]

Unlike inventory, property, and even specifically identifiable intangibles, such as patents and copyrights, the components of goodwill cannot be sold separately because they cannot exist apart from the firm to which they belong. By increasing earning power, these components increase the value of the entity; they are, then, assets. We record goodwill as an asset, however, only when we can identify part of an entity's acquisition cost with goodwill. Certainly a firm may generate goodwill in its normal business operations, such as when it develops resources or gains a favorable image in the community. But to value this goodwill without a market transaction is so difficult, and the results are so subjective, that the firm generating the goodwill cannot record it as an asset. *Only by acquiring another entity may a firm record goodwill as an asset.*

Regardless of the accounting treatment of goodwill, whenever a firm is considering acquiring or disposing of another business entity, it must calculate the value of unrecorded assets (that is, goodwill) as well as recorded assets. We shall describe some common techniques of estimating the value of goodwill—not so much because of their importance in accounting as because of the additional insight they provide into the nature and complexities of accounting for goodwill.

METHODS OF ESTIMATING GOODWILL   Theoretically, the value of goodwill is the present value of the characteristics that comprise it. This conceptual measurement is of little practical significance, however, because the values of the individual characteristics that make up goodwill are not subject to measurement. Often, they are not even identifiable. Thus, we cannot use this direct approach to determine the value of goodwill.

One method of estimating the value of a business enterprise's goodwill is to focus on the earning power of the enterprise. This approach, called the **excess earnings** approach, requires knowledge of (1) the normal rate of return for companies in the industry, (2) the expected earnings of the company, and (3) the fair market value of the company's identifiable net assets. Given this information, expected earnings in excess of a normal rate of return on the fair market value of identifiable net assets are due to and evidence of goodwill. More specifically, we presume that the "excess" earnings reflect the earning power of unrecorded, unidentifiable intangibles, which we call, collectively, goodwill.

Assume that the Sun Company is considering the acquisition of the Moon Company in early 1987. In attempting to determine whether there is goodwill present in the Moon Company, Sun estimates that the fair market value of Moon's identifiable net assets is $10 million. The normal rate of return in the industry in which Moon operates is 10 percent. Thus, Moon's expected average earnings in excess of $1 million (.10 × $10 million) are attributable to goodwill.

As a starting point in estimating Moon's expected average earnings, Sun notes that Moon's net income for the last five years was as follows:

1982	$ 800,000
1983	1,000,000
1984	700,000
1985	1,200,000
1986	1,500,000
	$5,200,000

[8] George R. Catlett and Norman O. Olson, "Accounting for Goodwill," *Accounting Research Study No. 10* (New York: AICPA, 1968), pp. 17–18.

The average annual earnings over the past five years were thus $5,200,000 ÷ 5 years = $1,040,000 per year. This represents a rate of return of 10.4 percent on the current fair market value of the *identifiable* net assets ($10 million).

Sun also must determine whether Moon's past earnings are likely to be representative of its future earnings. Moon's accounting procedures—for example, its depreciation methods—may differ from Sun's. If so, Moon's past earning stream should be adjusted in accordance with Sun's procedures. This change would make the records of the two firms more comparable. Moreover, should the takeover occur, Sun would probably impose its procedures on Moon anyway. In projecting future earnings, Sun also must consider any anticipated changes in Moon's operations and market potential. On the basis of the preceding considerations, Sun projects Moon's expected average annual earnings at $1,300,000. Expected earnings above the industry normal rate of return would be $1,300,000 − $1,000,000 = $300,000. Sun is now in a position to estimate the value of goodwill.

If Sun assumes the excess earnings will continue indefinitely, the value of goodwill is the present value of a perpetual annuity of $300,000, since theoretically the value of any asset is the discounted cash flows produced by the asset. Mathematically, the present value of the perpetual annuity is determined by dividing the annual excess earnings by the discount rate. If Sun determines that a 20 percent discount rate is appropriate, given the risk associated with the goodwill, the estimated value of goodwill would be $1,500,000:

$$\frac{\text{Annual excess earnings}}{\text{Discount rate}} = \frac{\$300,000}{.20} = \$1,500,000$$

We call this process **capitalization of excess earnings,** and we call the discount rate the **capitalization rate.** It should be apparent that the higher the discount rate, the lower will be the capitalized amount of goodwill. The discount rate chosen should reflect the risk associated with the excess earnings. Since goodwill often is subject to greater risk and uncertainty than identifiable assets, the capitalization rate used to value goodwill usually is somewhat higher than the normal rate of return for the industry.

As another approach, Sun might assume that excess earnings resulting from prior management efforts will continue for only a limited number of years. It is assumed that any excess earnings beyond the first few years after acquisition will be due to the efforts of the new management. The estimate of goodwill in this case involves the discounting of an annuity for the number of years in which Sun expects to have excess earnings attributable to prior management.

If Sun expects excess earnings of $300,000 attributable to Moon's management to continue for five years, and deems a discount rate of 20 percent to be appropriate, the estimated value of goodwill would be $300,000 × 2.9906 = $897,180 ($300,000 times the present value factor for an ordinary annuity of 1 for 5 periods at 20 percent).

Sun might use an even simpler approach to obtain a rough approximation of the value of goodwill. Sun could estimate the value of goodwill as the *sum of expected excess earnings for a specified number of years*. This approach ignores the time value of money, and thus is theoretically inferior to the previous methods. If Sun expects excess earnings of $300,000 attributable to prior management to continue for five years, this method would give an estimated value of $300,000 × 5 years = $1,500,000.

In an actual situation involving the acquisition of an entity, both the buyer and the seller probably would use several methods to estimate the value of goodwill in the acquired entity. These estimates, along with many other considerations, such as the bargaining power and persuasiveness of the two parties, would then serve as inputs in the process of negotiating the purchase price of the entity.

Goodwill as a master valuation account.

Another approach is to estimate the value of the entity as a whole, subtract from that the value of the identifiable net assets, and consider the difference to be the value of goodwill. This approach treats goodwill as a **master valuation account**—the assumption being that whatever part of the total value of the entity is not attributable to identifiable assets is associated with goodwill. In the context of the purchase of a business entity, we would value goodwill as the difference between the purchase price of the entity as a whole and the estimated fair market value of the identifiable net assets. The purchase price depends partially on the earning power of the entity and partially on the relative bargaining power of the buyer and seller. Also, the determination of the fair market values of identifiable net assets often involves considerable subjectivity. As a result, this approach produces a figure for goodwill that may or may not be a valid measure of its intrinsic value.

Assume that Easymark Company has the following balance sheet on December 31, 1986 (in thousands of dollars):

ASSETS		LIABILITIES AND STOCKHOLDERS' EQUITY	
Cash.....................	$ 30	Short-term notes payable	$ 147
Receivables	391	Accounts payable	109
Inventory	378	Other current liabilities........	343
Other current assets	270	Long-term debt..............	100
Plant and equipment (net)	490	Stockholders' equity	900
Other assets................	40		$1,599
	$1,599		

Takeover Company wishes to acquire Easymark. In the process of analyzing Easymark's resources and obligations, Takeover determines that the fair market values of Easymark's assets and liabilities are equal to their book values, except for plant and equipment, for which the estimated fair market value exceeds book value by $25,000. Thus, the fair market value of net assets acquired is $925,000 ($900,000 + $25,000).

Following a process of negotiation, Easymark and Takeover agree to a purchase price of $1 million. Takeover records the $75,000 difference between the purchase price and the fair market value of the identifiable net assets of Easymark ($1,000,000 − $925,000) as goodwill. Easymark does not record the $75,000 of goodwill; from an accounting standpoint it is relevant only to Takeover.

In summary, determining the value of goodwill is a very subjective process. Regardless of the method used, the amount to be assigned to goodwill for accounting purposes depends on (1) the purchase price of the entity and (2) the fair market value of the identifiable net assets. Thus, the relative bargaining ability of the buyer and seller often plays a significant role in determining the amount paid for goodwill.

ACCOUNTING AND REPORTING REQUIREMENTS   The difference between an entity's total acquisition price and the fair market value of that entity's identifiable net assets is recorded as goodwill. Goodwill appears on the balance sheet only when an entity has purchased it in connection with the acquisition of another entity. The cost of acquired goodwill must be amortized, like other intangible assets, over not more than 40 years. A firm should use the straight-line method of amortization unless it can demonstrate that another systematic method is more appropriate. Entities must expense costs incurred internally for developing, maintaining, or restoring goodwill as they are incurred. This treatment is comparable to the treatment of repair costs on fixed assets. The cost of goodwill is not a deductible expense for tax purposes.

As an example of goodwill in published financial statements, American Can Company included in its 1984 balance sheet, under noncurrent assets, an item called "Cost of acquired businesses in excess of net assets," in the amount of $70.1 million. The notes to the financial statements included the following: "Substantially all of the cost of acquired businesses in excess of net assets is being amortized on a straight-line basis principally over a forty year period."

It is possible to have a situation in which the fair market value of the identifiable net assets *exceeds* the purchase price of the entity. Conceptually, such a situation makes little sense, because it implies that the seller would be better off to sell the identifiable assets separately rather than to sell the entity in total. As a result of market imperfections and relatively strong bargaining on the part of the buyer, however, such situations do occur. We refer to this negative difference between acquisition price and the fair market value of the identifiable net assets as **negative goodwill** or **badwill.** For example, the fair market value of Easymark's identifiable net assets was $925,000. If the purchase price had been $875,000, Takeover would have recorded negative goodwill of $50,000.

> Negative goodwill arises when the fair market value of net assets exceeds acquisition price.

When negative goodwill arises, the acquiring firm must apply it to reduce the values otherwise assignable to noncurrent (long-term) assets, except long-term investments in marketable securities, *in proportion to their fair market value.*[9] For example, Easymark's noncurrent assets were plant and equipment of $515,000 and other assets of $40,000— $555,000 altogether. If negative goodwill of $50,000 arose in the purchase of Easymark, Takeover would eliminate the negative goodwill against plant and equipment and other assets as follows:

Plant and equipment:

$$\$515,000 - \left(\frac{515}{555} \times \$50,000 \right) = \$468,604$$

Other assets:

$$\$40,000 - \left(\frac{40}{555} \times \$50,000 \right) = \underline{\quad 36,396\quad}$$
$$\$505,000$$

If through this process the firm reduces its noncurrent assets to zero value and an excess of fair market value over cost remains, the firm should establish a deferred credit, excess of assigned value of identifiable assets over cost, and amortize it over the periods benefited, not exceeding 40 years. The firm must disclose the method and period of amortization.

The rationale for the *APB Opinion No. 16* requirements for negative goodwill is that firms should not record assets at more than cost. Also, the measured consideration given up provides a more reliable estimate of fair value of noncurrent assets acquired, except securities, than does direct valuation of the assets. The effect of this approach is to *increase* the reported earnings over the lives of the noncurrent assets by reducing their fair market values, and thus subsequent depreciation, and by amortizing negative goodwill. Thus, firms may increase earnings by acquiring an entity at less than the fair market value of its identifiable assets, but the increase occurs over several periods.

In summary, goodwill is recorded as an asset only when it is "bought and paid for" in connection with the acquisition of another entity. This approach does not deny the existence of goodwill in the absence of a market transaction; instead, it recognizes the lack of verifiability associated with estimating the value of goodwill in the absence of a market transaction.

---

[9] "Business Combinations," *Opinions of the Accounting Principles Board No. 16* (New York: AICPA, 1970), para. 91.

In the following section we discuss accounting for research and development costs (R&D), which many companies historically recorded as intangible assets. However, as described in the next section, GAAP now requires that R&D costs must be expensed as incurred in most circumstances.

Research and Development Costs

Expenditures aimed at developing new products or processes, or modifying existing products or processes, often represent a highly significant portion of the cost of doing business. For many years a substantial lack of uniformity existed in accounting and reporting for these costs, hereafter referred to as **research and development costs,** or simply **R&D.** Two factors caused the accounting profession to tighten up on the flexibility previously allowed in accounting for R&D: (1) R&D costs became a more significant part of the operating costs of many firms; and (2) an increased emphasis on the needs of financial statement users led to a desire for uniform, meaningful information about firms' R&D activities. Thus, the FASB addressed the question and issued *Statement No. 2* in 1974. Before we discuss the requirements of *FASB Statement No. 2,* it might be helpful to consider the environmental complexities that had led to diversity of accounting for R&D in practice and to the need for accounting and reporting guidelines.

ROLE OF RESEARCH AND DEVELOPMENT EXPENDITURES   Entities embark on R&D programs because they believe the benefits will exceed the costs. That is, there is an expectation of benefits sufficient to recover the costs and to provide a fair return on the funds invested. However, there is often considerable uncertainty regarding the profitability of individual R&D projects. Further, the timing of the expected benefits often is projected to occur over several years and also is subject to considerable uncertainty. In many instances, moreover, it is very difficult to associate, even after the fact, specific benefits with specific R&D expenditures. Thus, although one may argue theoretically that an entity creates an intangible asset by investing in an R&D program, the inability to reasonably estimate the amount and timing of the benefits that flow from R&D expenditures makes it difficult, from a practical standpoint, to support any particular pattern of amortization if a firm were to capitalize R&D expenditures. As a result, before *FASB Statement No. 2* was issued, many companies chose to capitalize R&D costs and to amortize them over some arbitrary period (not more than 40 years), whereas other companies expensed R&D costs as incurred, thus avoiding the difficulty of choosing an amortization pattern and period. It was in the midst of this diversity of practices that the FASB issued *Statement No. 2.*

R&D expenditures are
expensed as incurred

SUMMARY OF *FASB STATEMENT NO. 2*   The basic requirement of *Statement No. 2* is that entities must expense research and development costs covered by the *Statement* as they are incurred. To enable accountants to respond to this requirement, it was necessary for the FASB to define research and development activity and the costs to be identified with it. The FASB provided the following definitions of research and development for purposes of applying *Statement No. 2:*

> *Research* is planned search or critical investigation aimed at discovery of new knowledge with the hope that such knowledge will be useful in developing a new product or service (hereinafter ''product'') or a new process or technique (hereinafter ''process'') or in bringing about a significant improvement to an existing product or process.

> *Development* is the translation of research findings or other knowledge into a plan or design for a new product or process or for a significant improvement to an existing product or process whether intended for sale or use.[10]

[10] *FASB Statement No. 2*, para. 8.

To clarify further what constitutes research and development activity, the FASB provided the following examples of activities that typically would constitute research and development activity:

Examples of typical
R&D activity.

1. Laboratory research aimed at discovery of new knowledge.
2. Searching for applications of new research findings or other knowledge.
3. Conceptual formulation and design of possible product or process alternatives.
4. Testing in search for or evaluation of product or process alternatives.
5. Modification of the formulation or design of a product or process.
6. Design, construction, and testing of preproduction prototypes and models.
7. Design of tools, jigs, molds, and dies involving new technology.
8. Design, construction, and operation of a pilot plant that is not of a scale economically feasible to the enterprise for commercial production.
9. Engineering activity required to advance the design of a product to the point where it meets specific functional and economic requirements and is ready for manufacture.[11]

In addition, the FASB provided the following examples of activities that typically are not considered R&D:

1. Engineering follow-through in an early phase of commercial production.
2. Quality control during commercial production, including routine testing of products.
3. Troubleshooting in connection with breakdowns during commercial production.
4. Routine, ongoing efforts to refine, enrich, or otherwise improve upon the qualities of an existing product.
5. Adaptation of an existing capability to a particular requirement or customer's need as part of a continuing commercial activity.
6. Seasonal or other periodic design changes to existing products.
7. Routine design of tools, jigs, molds, and dies.
8. Activity, including design and construction engineering, related to the construction, relocation, rearrangement, or startup of facilities or equipment other than pilot plants and facilities or equipment whose sole use is for a particular research and development project.
9. Legal work in connection with patent applications or litigation, and the sale or licensing of patents.[12]

In general, it appears that the intent of the FASB was to include in R&D those activities related to preproduction efforts, and to exclude from R&D those activities related to existing and ongoing production. *FASB Statement No. 2* does not cover activities that are unique to companies in the extractive industries, such as prospecting, acquisition of mineral rights, exploration, drilling, and mining.[13] *Statement No. 2* does apply, however, to R&D activities of companies in extractive industries where those activities are comparable to such activities in other types of entities, such as the development or improvement of processes and techniques.

[11] Ibid., para. 9.
[12] Ibid., para. 10.
[13] Ibid., para. 3.

The FASB specified five elements of cost that entities should associate with R&D activities encompassed by *Statement No. 2:*

Cost elements associated with R&D activity.

1. *Materials, equipment, and facilities.* Costs of materials, equipment, or facilities that are acquired or constructed for a specific R&D project and that have no alternative future use (and thus no separate economic value) are research and development costs and, therefore, must be expensed as incurred. If, however, the materials, equipment, or facilities have an alternative future use (in other research and development projects or otherwise), the costs should be capitalized as tangible assets. If such materials subsequently are consumed in R&D activities, they must be expensed as R&D costs. Likewise, depreciation on other equipment and facilities used in research and development activities constitutes research and development cost.

2. *Personnel.* Costs of personnel engaged in R&D activities must be expensed as they are incurred as R&D costs.

3. *Purchased intangibles.* Costs of intangibles that are purchased from others for use in a specific R&D project, and that have no alternative future use, must be expensed as they are incurred. If, however, the intangibles have an alternative future use (in R&D activities or otherwise), the costs should be capitalized and amortized as intangible assets. The amortization of those intangibles used in R&D activities constitutes R&D cost.

4. *Contract services.* Costs of services performed by others in connection with the R&D activities of an entity must be expensed as they are incurred as R&D costs.

5. *Indirect costs.* A *reasonable* allocation of indirect costs should be included in R&D costs, and thus expensed as the costs are incurred. General and administrative costs, however, should not be included as R&D costs unless they are clearly related to R&D activity.[14]

FASB Statement No. 2 does not cover the accounting for costs incurred by a company in performing R&D activities under *contractual arrangement.* For example, if company *A* agrees to pay company *B* $100,000 to conduct research, *Statement No. 2* does not govern company *B*'s treatment of costs incurred under the contract. If, however, the activities of company *B* constitute R&D as defined by *Statement No. 2,* company *A* must expense the $100,000 as the cost is incurred. Likewise, accounting for indirect costs that are reimbursable under the terms of a contract are not covered by the *Statement.* For example, a firm that incurs costs for R&D activity conducted under a government contract may capitalize and amortize the costs. Thus, companies that perform R&D both under contract and on their own account (for themselves) may capitalize costs associated with the contract R&D, but must expense the costs incurred in connection with R&D done for themselves.

FASB Statement No. 2 requires that entities must disclose the amount of R&D costs charged to expense for each period for which they present an income statement. This is perhaps the most important requirement of *Statement No. 2,* because many companies previously did not disclose this information. The amount of R&D expenditures would seem to be useful information for assessing an entity's future cash flows. For example, W. R. Grace & Company reported research and development expenses of $78.6 million as a line item in its 1984 income statement, which was 11 percent more than the 1983 amount and 28 percent more than the 1982 amount. Evaluation of these expenditures for R&D within the context of a changing economic environment should be helpful in projecting future cash flows.

[14] Ibid., para. 11.

EVALUATION OF *FASB STATEMENT NO. 2* The FASB considered several alternatives before settling on the requirements of *Statement No. 2:*

1. Charge all costs to expense as they are incurred.

2. Capitalize all costs when they are incurred.

3. Selectively capitalize some costs and charge others to expense as they are incurred.

4. Accumulate all costs in a special category pending determination of the existence of future benefits.[15]

The *Statement No. 2* solution, expensing R&D costs as they are incurred, is a practical solution to a complex problem. The uncertainty with respect to both the amount and the timing of future benefits resulting from specific R&D projects, the inability to demonstrate a cause-and-effect relationship between individual R&D expenditures and specific future benefits, and the lack of evidence demonstrating that capitalization would facilitate the assessment of future returns and risk, all point toward expensing of R&D costs as they are incurred. This approach does not deny that there may be future benefits associated with R&D expenditures. It is merely a practical, conservative way of dealing with the uncertainty and measurement difficulties inherent in research and development programs.

Computer Software

A relatively recent issue on which the accounting profession has had to provide guidance is accounting for the costs of computer software. The FASB chose not to provide specific guidance on accounting for computer software costs in *Statement No. 2*. The Board decided instead to rely upon the general guidelines of that *Statement* to determine whether particular costs of computer software should be included in research and development costs. However, as computer software companies became more prominent, the need for more detailed guidance became apparent. Because the primary activity of these companies is the development and sale of computer software, development and sale costs are highly significant. Most computer software companies were expensing software development and production costs as incurred. However, some firms were capitalizing some of the costs. Among those capitalizing costs, there was considerable variation in terms of the selection of costs to be capitalized and the amortization process for the capitalized costs. In 1985, the FASB issued *Statement No. 86* to produce uniformity in accounting for and reporting these costs.[16]

Statement No. 86 requires that costs incurred to (1) purchase or (2) develop computer software to be sold, leased, or otherwise marketed must be charged to expense as research and development costs until the technological feasibility of the product or process has been established. Technological feasibility is deemed to be established when a firm has completed all planning, designing, coding, and testing activities necessary to determine that a product can be produced to design specifications. This criterion is derived from the example in *Statement No. 2* that includes in research and development activity "engineering activity required to advance the design of a product to the point that it meets specific functional and economic requirements and is ready for manufacture." In defining more specifically when technological feasibility may be deemed to have been established, the FASB states that, at a minimum, a detailed program design must be completed or, in the absence of such a design, a working model of the product must be completed and confirmed by testing.

---

[15] Ibid., para. 37.

[16] "Accounting for the Costs of Computer Software to Be Sold, Leased, or Otherwise Marketed," *Statement of Financial Accounting Standards No. 86* (Stamford, Conn.: FASB, 1985).

Once technological feasibility has been established, costs incurred to produce product masters must be capitalized. Product masters include a completed version of the software product ready for copying, the documentation, and training materials. As soon as the product is available for release to customers, capitalization must cease. Costs of duplicating the software, documentation, and training materials from the product masters and of physically packaging the product for distribution are to be capitalized as inventory, as they are for other products. These costs should be charged to cost of sales when sales revenue from the product is recognized. Maintenance and customer support costs must be charged to expense when the related revenue is recognized or when the costs are incurred, if earlier.

Costs of computer software that have been capitalized must be amortized on a product-by-product basis. The periodic amortization must be *the greater of (a)* the ratio of current gross revenues from the product to total current and anticipated gross revenues from the product or *(b)* the amount determined by the straight-line method over the remaining estimated economic life of the product. For example, assume that HiTec Company appropriately capitalized computer software costs of $120,000 in connection with the production of ABC, version 1.0, a word processing program that is expected to produce revenues for three years. Revenues for the first year were $800,000, and total expected revenues for the three years combined are $2,000,000. Amortization for the first year would be $48,000 [($800,000/$2,000,000) × $120,000], because this amount is greater than the straight-line amortization of $40,000 ($120,000/3 years).

In addition to periodic amortization, at each balance sheet date the unamortized amount of computer software costs must be compared to the estimated net realizable value of the product. Net realizable value is the estimated future gross revenues from the product minus the estimated future costs of completing and disposing of the product, including maintenance and customer support costs. If net realizable value is below unamortized cost, the asset should be written down to net realizable value and a loss equal to the write-down should be recorded. Thus, the asset is carried on the books at the lower of unamortized cost or net realizable value. If the asset is written down to net realizable value, the reduced amount of capitalized cost is considered cost for subsequent accounting purposes, and write-downs cannot be subsequently restored.

> Capitalized software costs are carried at the lower of unamortized cost or net realizable value.

The following disclosures are required for computer software costs:

1. Unamortized computer software costs included in each balance sheet presented.

2. The amount charged to expense in each income statement presented, broken down into amortization and write-downs to net realizable value.

3. For those computer software costs classified as research and development costs, the disclosure requirements of *Statement No. 2*.

Thus, the FASB has provided guidelines for the treatment of costs associated with the development and production of computer software to be sold, leased, or otherwise marketed. A rather high and relatively objective capitalization threshold has been established. *Statement No. 86* has dealt with a significant practice problem and, it is hoped, will help to standardize treatment of computer software costs in the circumstances covered by the *Statement*. However, many significant issues remain unresolved in the area of accounting for computer software. For example, the *Statement* does not cover accounting for the costs of computer software to be used internally. Also, there are no specific guidelines available for revenue recognition from the sale of computer software. As the emphasis in our society continues to shift from tangible, physical outputs to intangible, creative outputs, more guidance is likely to be needed to account for these increasingly important activities.

In summary, the FASB has adopted a rather conservative stance for R&D and computer software because of uncertainty regarding the amount and timing of future cash flows related to these items. There is often significant uncertainty about whether these activities will produce future cash flows sufficient to recover the costs. A similar complexity exists for companies that invest in natural resources—significant expenditures are often incurred before it is possible to determine whether future cash flows will be sufficient to recover the amount invested in the natural resources. In the next section the accounting and reporting standards for natural resources are described.

NATURAL RESOURCES

As a firm consumes the services embodied in plant and equipment and other depreciable assets, the physical characteristics of the assets appear to remain unchanged. On the other hand, **natural resources,** also called **wasting assets,** are consumed physically in the production process. Examples of wasting assets include timberland, oil and gas deposits, and mineral deposits. As in the case of depreciable assets, a major accounting problem is to determine the cost of natural resources and to match that cost with the revenues generated by their sale. The amount of natural resource cost expensed each period is called **depletion,** an appropriate designation because firms physically *deplete* the resource by the production process.

Investments in natural resources are critical to the well-being of our society. Likewise, reliable information regarding such investments is critical to decision makers. Our goals as a society—to increase reliance on our own domestic resources and to use them more efficiently—create a demand for reliable information regarding natural resources and the way we have been using them. Current accounting practice for natural resources is described in the following section.

ACCOUNTING FOR NATURAL RESOURCES

The costs associated with natural resources may be divided into four categories: (1) acquisition costs, (2) exploration costs, (3) development costs, and (4) production costs. **Acquisition costs** include all costs incurred to acquire the property, the rights to search for the natural resources, or the rights to previously discovered resources. **Exploration costs** are costs incurred in the process of searching for natural resources, such as drilling and excavation costs. After a firm discovers a natural resource, it incurs **development costs.** Some of these development costs relate to tangible assets, such as the costs of constructing or purchasing special-purpose equipment, whereas others relate to intangibles, such as costs of drilling wells or digging shafts and tunnels. A firm then incurs **production costs,** such as labor, as it depletes the resource.

Depletion Base

Conceptually, the objective in accounting for the costs of wasting assets, just as in accounting for costs of depreciable assets, is to capitalize those costs that a firm incurs now that are expected to produce benefits over a number of future periods. These capitalized costs, typically including acquisition, exploration, and development costs, should be amortized (recorded as **depletion expense**) over the periods in which the firm realizes the benefits. The **depletion base** is the amount of capitalized cost not expected to be recovered through residual value. Any expected residual value thus reduces the depletion base. If the expected net residual value is negative, it increases the depletion base. For example, additional costs may be required to restore the property containing the resource after the firm has depleted the resource.

Entities also must depreciate the cost of tangible assets used in the exploration, development, or production phase. If the tangible asset can be moved from site to site—a drilling rig, for instance—the firm should depreciate it over its useful life. If a tangible asset is not movable—for example, it is not always economically feasible to move a building—the firm should amortize its cost over the shorter of the asset's expected useful life or the expected life of the natural resource.

Recording Depletion

The most reasonable method for recording depletion for most capitalized natural resource costs is the **units-of-production (activity) approach.** A firm calculates the depletion per unit as follows:

$$\text{Depletion per unit} = \frac{\text{Depletion base}}{\text{Estimated recoverable units}}$$

Assume, for example, that Phelps-Plymouth Corporation, a major copper producer, incurred costs of $2 million in connection with property acquisition, exploration, and development of an open-pit copper mine. Phelps-Plymouth expects the property can be sold for $500,000 after it depletes the copper and spends $300,000 to restore the property. The total estimated recoverable units available in the property are 1 million tons of copper ore. The depletion charge per unit would be calculated as:

$$
\begin{aligned}
\text{Depletion per unit} &= \frac{\text{Depletion base}}{\text{Estimated recoverable units}} \\[6pt]
&= \frac{\$2{,}000{,}000 - (\$500{,}000 - \$300{,}000)}{1{,}000{,}000 \text{ tons}} \\[6pt]
&= \frac{\$1{,}800{,}000}{1{,}000{,}000 \text{ tons}} \\[6pt]
&= \$1.80 \text{ per ton}
\end{aligned}
$$

If Phelps-Plymouth recovered 200,000 tons of copper ore during the first year of production, depletion would be 200,000 × $1.80 = $360,000. The entry to record depletion expense, assuming that Phelps-Plymouth sells all of the copper, would be as follows:

Depletion expense	360,000	
Mining property		360,000

Note that the credit is to an asset account, mining property, rather than to an accumulated depletion account. This approach is the most common. It is acceptable, however, to credit a contra-asset account, accumulated depletion.

Changes in Estimates

There usually is substantial uncertainty regarding the number of recoverable units of a natural resource at the time the firm incurs associated costs. When a firm revises its estimates, as firms frequently do, it must calculate a new depletion rate per unit. Since this is a change in accounting estimate, the firm does not revise prior period depletion charges to reflect this new estimate. It merely spreads the remaining book value over the new estimate of recoverable units. For example, continuing the Phelps-Plymouth illustration into the second year, assume that the company recovered 100,000 tons in the second year. However, the firm now estimates that *total* recoverable units will be only 800,000 units. Thus, the depletion rate in the second year will be $2.40 per ton [($1,800,000 − $360,000)/(800,000 tons − 200,000 tons)]. Depletion expense in the second year will be $240,000.

Statement Presentation

Depletion expense is part of the product cost. Thus, depletion associated with product sold is a part of cost of goods sold. If a firm does not sell all of the production for a period, the depletion on the unsold portion is an inventory cost, along with production costs. A firm includes the unamortized portion of capitalized costs of natural resources under property, plant, and equipment in the balance sheet. For example, Potlatch Corporation reported timber, timberlands, and related logging facilities, net, of $250,882,000 in its December 31, 1984, balance sheet. The notes presented the following information in the Summary of Significant Accounting Policies:

> Timber, timberlands and related logging facilities are valued at cost net of the cost of fee timber harvested and depreciation or amortization. Logging roads and related facilities are depreciated over their useful lives or amortized as related timber is removed. Cost of fee timber harvested and amortization of logging roads are determined annually on the basis of timber removals at rates based on the estimated existing volumes of recoverable timber.

and in Note 3:

> Timber, timberlands and related logging facilities are stated at cost less cost of fee timber harvested and amortization or depreciation (in thousands of dollars):

	1984	1983
Timber and timberlands	$234,922	$228,696
Related logging facilities	15,960	15,246
	$250,882	$243,942

Amortization or depreciation of logging facilities amounted to $.9 million in 1984 ($1.3 million in 1983 and $1.1 million in 1982). Cost of fee timber harvested amounted to $3.3 million in 1984 ($5.2 million in 1983 and $4.1 million in 1982).

An income tax provision regarding the calculation of depletion expense for tax purposes creates a difference between depletion for tax purposes and depletion for financial reporting purposes. We discuss this issue in the next section.

Percentage (Statutory) Depletion

Percentage depletion is acceptable only for tax purposes.

For many years the Internal Revenue Code has permitted taxpayers to deduct the greater of **cost depletion** (as described earlier in this chapter) or **percentage depletion** for oil, gas, and most minerals. A firm calculates percentage depletion, also known as **statutory depletion,** by multiplying a rate specified by the Internal Revenue Service by the gross income from the property for the period. The amount of depletion taken for tax purposes may exceed the amount invested in the property, because the firm bases depletion expense on revenues rather than on costs.

The IRS has changed the percentage depletion rates from time to time; the rates also vary depending on the type of natural resource. (As of 1986, the maximum rate is 15 percent, with a minimum rate of 5 percent, which will reduce significantly the number of firms that use percentage depletion.) Because percentage depletion is calculated as a percentage of gross income instead of on the basis of cost, depletion for tax purposes can exceed cost depletion by a substantial amount on the financial statements. Thus, the use of percentage depletion creates a permanent difference between taxable income and income for financial reporting purposes.[17]

---

[17] We discuss the financial accounting implications of permanent differences in Chapter 19.

So far in our discussion of accounting for natural resources, we have said little about exploration costs. One of the most complex theoretical issues in accounting, however, relates to the appropriate accounting for exploration costs of oil and gas companies. We discuss this issue and the alternative accounting methods in the following section.

THE OIL AND GAS CONTROVERSY

Oil and gas companies are constantly involved in exploration activities. They face significant uncertainties when they incur property acquisition costs, costs for property rights, and exploration costs. These companies typically record acquisition costs in a "suspense" account, undeveloped property. If exploration proves successful, the firm transfers the acquisition cost to a wasting asset account. If exploration proves unsuccessful, the firm records the acquisition cost as a loss.

Oil and gas companies engage in exploration with the expectation that this activity will produce benefits in excess of costs. That is, the firms expect an acceptable return on investment from the exploration program. The difficulty from an accounting standpoint is that, at the time the costs are incurred, it usually is not possible to determine which exploratory efforts are going to be successful and which ones will be unsuccessful. This is precisely the same issue that companies, and accountants, face with respect to research and development expenditures. As we saw earlier, the FASB resolved the R&D controversy by requiring firms to expense R&D costs, other than contract R&D, as they are incurred.

Accounting for Exploration Costs

Historically, firms in the oil and gas industry have used one of two methods to account for exploration costs. Many companies capitalize exploratory costs associated with successful exploration and expense costs associated with unsuccessful exploration. This approach, called the **successful efforts method,** is prevalent among the larger oil companies. Other firms, primarily smaller, exploration-oriented oil companies, capitalize all exploration costs. This approach is called the **full-cost method.**

To illustrate these alternative methods, assume that Explore Company incurs costs of $1 million for each of 10 oil wells during 1987. Nine of the 10 wells are unsuccessful. The journal entry in 1987 to record the cost incurred is as follows under the two approaches:

FULL-COST		SUCCESSFUL EFFORTS	
Oil reserves .. 10,000,000		Oil reserves .. 1,000,000	
Cash	10,000,000	Exploration	
		expense 9,000,000	
		Cash	10,000,000

In subsequent periods, Explore would expense $10 million under the full-cost method as the successful well is depleted; under the successful efforts method, only $1 million remains to be expensed in future periods as the successful well is depleted.

Advocates of the successful efforts method argue that the only exploration costs properly capitalizable are those that provide future benefits. Exploratory costs incurred in an unsuccessful effort to provide future benefits (future cash flows) should be expensed as they are incurred. Capitalization of costs of unsuccessful drilling efforts creates a misleading impression that the firm expects future cash flows from the unsuccessful wells and overstates current net income.

Full-cost advocates argue that the costs of unsuccessful exploration are just as much a part of the cost of the commercially profitable deposits as are the specific costs associated with the successful efforts. Therefore, a firm should capitalize all exploration costs and amortize them against the cash flows generated in future periods by the successful ventures. Note that the arguments made by the full-cost and the successful efforts advocates are precisely the same as those made with respect to research and development expenditures.

A third possible treatment of exploration costs—the treatment now required for R&D costs—is to expense all such costs as they are incurred. This method has not gained favor in practice, probably because it lowers a firm's reported income in the period in which the costs are incurred. Major oil producers can expense costs of unsuccessful ventures as they are incurred without significantly affecting reported earnings. For smaller, exploration-oriented companies, however, exploration costs may be highly significant with respect to revenues and other costs, because, in contrast to the major oil companies, many of these smaller companies are not involved in marketing and refining activities. Thus the smaller, exploration-oriented companies generally prefer to defer and amortize all exploration costs to avoid a significant negative impact on current earnings and to provide some stability to the earnings number. Representatives of smaller companies, including lobbyists and legislators, have argued that if the successful efforts method were required for accounting and reporting purposes, smaller companies would decrease their exploration activities because of the negative effect on earnings and because they would not be able to raise capital. This argument is particularly effective in our current economic environment, because the federal government has announced its intention to encourage the development of domestic energy resources and to decrease dependence on foreign sources.

Currently both the successful efforts and full-cost methods are acceptable. In 1977, as a part of its efforts to narrow acceptable alternatives, the FASB issued *Statement No. 19,* which would have required all oil and gas companies to employ the successful efforts method.[18] However, the extensive pressures brought to bear by the industry, legislators, the Department of Energy, the Justice Department, and the SEC forced the FASB to retreat from its proposed requirement in 1979.[19]

The SEC argued that neither the successful efforts method nor the full-cost method conveyed adequate information to users regarding exploration activities and oil and gas resources. It proposed, as a substitute, a method referred to as **reserve recognition accounting (RRA),** which is a departure from the historical cost model because it requires firms to estimate the discounted net cash flows associated with oil and gas reserves. In 1981, however, the SEC announced that it no longer considers RRA appropriate in the primary financial statements and that it would look to the FASB for comprehensive disclosure requirements for oil and gas companies.[20] The FASB subsequently established such requirements, as we describe in the next section.

The FASB's pronouncement on research and development costs *(Statement No. 2),* its attempted pronouncement on exploration costs of oil and gas companies *(Statement No. 19),* and its pronouncement on computer software *(Statement No. 86)* reflect a stringent approach to capitalization in the face of uncertainty. Further, *Statement No. 7,* issued in 1975, prohibits development stage companies (companies that have not yet commenced

---

[18] "Financial Accounting and Reporting by Oil and Gas Producing Companies," *Statement of Financial Accounting Standards No. 19* (Stamford, Conn.: FASB, 1977).

[19] "Suspension of Certain Accounting Requirements for Oil and Gas Producing Companies," *Statement of Financial Accounting Standards No. 25* (Stamford, Conn.: FASB, 1979).

[20] The SEC issued several *Accounting Series Releases* related to the controversy: "Adoption of Requirements for Financial Accounting and Reporting Practices for Oil and Gas Producing Activities," *Accounting Series Release No. 253* (Washington, D.C.: SEC, 1978); "Requirements for Financial Accounting and Reporting Practices for Oil and Gas Producing Activities," *Accounting Series Release No. 257* (Washington, D.C.: SEC, 1978); "Oil and Gas Producers—Full-Cost Accounting Practices," *Accounting Series Release No. 258* (Washington, D.C.: SEC, 1978); and "Financial Reporting by Oil and Gas Producers," *Accounting Series Release No. 289* (Washington D.C.: SEC, 1981).

their principal operations) from capitalizing costs that cannot be capitalized by other entities.[21] The primary consideration in all of these instances appears to be the uncertainty regarding cost recoverability at the time expenditures occur. As a result of this uncertainty, the FASB requires that the costs be recorded as expenses as they are incurred. These *Statements* indicate that the FASB is emphasizing reliability of information as well as the elements' definitions in admitting items to the balance sheet.

The oil and gas controversy provides another illustration of the rather tenuous relationship between the SEC and the FASB. The SEC has the *authority* to establish financial accounting standards, but it has delegated the *responsibility* for establishing such standards to the FASB. When the FASB attempted to implement its charge of narrowing the number of accounting alternatives and the SEC did not like the choice, the FASB was stymied in its efforts to carry out its responsibilities.

Because of the existence of alternative accounting methods in accounting for exploration costs, significant disclosure is necessary to enable users to make meaningful comparisons among companies. In the last section we describe and illustrate these disclosures.

Disclosures by Oil and Gas Companies

As an example of full-cost disclosures, CSX Corporation, a large transportation and natural resource corporation, employs the full-cost method of accounting for exploration costs. CSX described its accounting policy as follows in the notes to its 1984 financial statements:

> Exploration and production activities adhere to the full-cost method of accounting. Under this method, all costs of exploring for and developing oil and gas reserves, whether productive or nonproductive, are capitalized to the extent that such costs are not in excess of the fair value of proven reserves. Such costs are amortized on the unit-of-production basis over the production of these reserves.

In contrast, W. R. Grace & Company, a large diversified corporation, uses the successful efforts method to account for its exploration costs. Grace disclosed this accounting practice and its depletion policy in its summary of significant accounting and financial reporting policies for 1984 as follows:

> The successful efforts method of accounting is used for oil and gas operations. Depletion of natural resource reserves is determined by the unit-of-production method.

In 1982, in response to the SEC's encouragement, the FASB issued *Statement No. 69,* which requires oil and gas companies to disclose the following *supplementary information:*

1. Proved oil and gas reserve quantities.

2. Capitalized costs relating to oil- and gas-producing activities.

3. Costs incurred for property acquisition, exploration, and development activities.

4. Results of operations for oil- and gas-producing activities.

5. A standardized measure of discounted future net cash flows relating to proved oil and gas reserve quantities.[22]

The last disclosure listed is similar to the RRA method previously proposed by the SEC.

---

[21] ''Accounting and Reporting by Development Stage Enterprises,'' *Statement of Financial Accounting Standards No. 7* (Stamford, Conn.: FASB, 1975).

[22] ''Disclosure about Oil and Gas Producing Activities,'' *Statement of Financial Accounting Standards No. 69* (Stamford, Conn.: FASB, 1982), para. 7.

SUMMARY OF IMPORTANT TOPICS
AND CONCEPT APPLICATIONS

1. Accounting for **intangible assets** involves the same problems as accounting for tangible assets, but solving the problems is more difficult because intangible assets **lack physical substance.**

2. **Amortization** is the process of systematically **matching** the cost of intangibles against revenues over the periods that benefit from the expenditure.

3. The cost of **purchased intangibles,** including **goodwill,** must be capitalized and amortized over the shorter of 40 years or the useful life of the intangible asset.

4. The cost of **internally developed, specifically identifiable intangibles** may be either expensed as incurred or capitalized and amortized over the shorter of 40 years or the useful life of the intangible. However, the cost of **internally developed goodwill** must be expensed as incurred.

5. **Leasehold improvements** should be amortized over the shorter of the lease term or the life of the improvements.

6. **Goodwill** may be estimated either by an excess earnings approach or by a master valuation account approach. Regardless of the estimation techniques used, the amount recorded for purchased goodwill is the difference between the purchase price of the entity and the fair market value of identifiable assets.

7. **Negative goodwill** arises when the fair value of the identifiable assets exceeds the purchase price of the entity. This difference should be applied to reduce the carrying value of noncurrent assets acquired (except long-term investments in marketable securities) in proportion to their fair market value.

8. **Research and development costs** generally must be expensed as incurred. This approach appears to place greater emphasis on **reliability** than on **relevance** in the face of uncertainty regarding future cash flows from the expenditures.

9. **Computer software costs** incurred in the development of software products to be sold, leased, or otherwise marketed must be expensed as incurred up to the point at which technological feasibility is established. This approach is consistent with the required treatment of research and development costs.

10. The cost of natural resources used up each period is referred to as **depletion.** Exploration costs of oil and gas companies may be accounted for by either the **successful efforts** method or the **full cost** method. Because of the perceived lack of **relevance** of the results under both of these methods, oil and gas companies also must disclose the estimated discounted future cash flows related to proved oil and gas reserves.

QUESTIONS

Q13-1. Describe three major differences between tangible and intangible assets.

Q13-2. Describe four criteria by which we may classify intangibles.

Q13-3. What is the appropriate accounting treatment under GAAP for each of the following categories of expenditures related to intangibles?

1. Specifically identifiable, purchased.

2. Unidentifiable, purchased.

3. Specifically identifiable, internally developed.

4. Unidentifiable, internally developed.

Q13-4. How should a firm treat the costs of successfully defending a patent against infringement suits? How should a firm treat costs of unsuccessful defense? Explain.

Q13-5. Describe the following intangibles:

1. Patents.

2. Copyrights.

3. Trademarks and trade names.

4. Franchises.

Q13-6. What is a lease prepayment? How should a firm account for lease prepayments and report them in financial statements?

Q13-7. Over what period should a firm amortize leasehold improvements? Why?

Q13-8. Give some examples of organization costs. What is the appropriate accounting treatment for such costs? Why?

Q13-9. Give several examples of characteristics that might comprise goodwill. Why can we not record these items separately rather than combining them in a category called goodwill?

Q13-10. Why do we capitalize goodwill only when it is acquired in connection with the acquisition of another entity?

Q13-11. How is the value of goodwill estimated when goodwill is viewed as a master valuation account? Discuss the validity of this approach to determining the value of goodwill.

Q13-12. Describe the excess earnings approach to estimating the value of goodwill. What complexities are inherent in this approach?

Q13-13. What assumption is being made when we capitalize excess earnings in an effort to estimate goodwill? Is this assumption likely to be realistic in most circumstances? Explain. What alternatives are available for assigning a value to excess earnings?

Q13-14. What is the appropriate accounting treatment of purchased goodwill?

Q13-15. What is negative goodwill? How should a firm account for it?

Q13-16. How should costs incurred internally for research and development be recorded in the accounts? Describe briefly the justification for this requirement.

Q13-17. What are the five elements of cost that an entity should identify with research and development activities according to *FASB Statement No. 2?* Under certain circumstances, a firm may capitalize two of these cost elements rather than expensing them as incurred as a part of R&D expense. What are the circumstances and which two cost elements are involved?

Q13-18. What is the significance of the *FASB Statement No. 2* requirement that firms must disclose the amount of research and development expenditures charged to expense?

Q13-19. Under what circumstances should costs of developing or purchasing computer software be charged to expense as research and development costs?

Q13-20. When should costs of developing computer software be capitalized? How should the amount of periodic amortization be determined for such costs?

Q13-21. What role does net realizable value play in the valuation of capitalized computer software costs? Explain.

Q13-22. What distinguishes natural resource assets from depreciable assets?

Q13-23. What four types of costs do companies incur in connection with wasting assets (natural resources)? Briefly describe each category.

Q13-24. How do firms usually allocate the capitalized cost of natural resources to expense? Why?

Q13-25. How do companies report depletion costs in financial statements? Distinguish between the treatment of depletion costs associated with product sold and such costs associated with product still unsold at the statement date.

Q13-26. What accounting complexities exist with regard to tangible assets constructed or purchased in connection with wasting assets? What are the accounting requirements for such assets?

Q13-27. What is percentage (statutory) depletion?

Q13-28. Describe the similarity between *(a)* research and development expenditures and *(b)* exploration costs of oil and gas companies.

Q13-29. Distinguish between the successful efforts method and the full-cost method of accounting for exploration costs.

Q13-30. According to many individuals and groups, there are significant public policy implications associated with the standards of accounting for exploratory costs of oil and gas companies. What are these alleged implications?

Q13-31. What are the current accounting guidelines for accounting for the costs of exploration?

CASES

C13-1. PATENTS In examining the books of Long Company, you find on the December 31, 1987, balance sheet the item "Costs of patents, $308,440."

Referring to the ledger accounts, you note the following items regarding one patent acquired in 1984.

1984 Legal costs incurred in defending the validity of the patent	$12,600
1986 Legal costs in prosecuting an infringement suit	18,600
1986 Legal costs (additional expenses) in the infringement suit	6,200
1986 Cost of improvements (unpatented) on the patented device	18,400

There are no credits in the account, and no allowance for amortization has been set up on the books for any of the patents. Three other patents were issued in 1981, 1983, and 1984; all were developed by the staff of your client. The patented articles are currently very marketable, but it is estimated that they will be in demand for only the next few years.

REQUIRED

Discuss the items included in the patent account from an accounting standpoint.

(AICPA, adapted)

C13-2. PATENTS On June 30, 1987, your client, Inventive Corporation, was granted two patents covering plastic cartons that it has been producing and marketing profitably for the past three years. One patent covers the manufacturing process and the other covers the related products.

Inventive executives tell you that these patents represent the most significant breakthrough in the industry in the past 30 years. The products have been marketed under the registered trademarks Safetainer, Duratainer, and Sealrite. Licenses under the patents have already been granted by your client to other manufacturers in the United States and abroad and are producing substantial royalties.

On July 1, Inventive commenced patent-infringement actions against several companies whose names you recognize as those of substantial and prominent competitors. Inventive's management believes that these suits will result in a permanent injunction against the manufacture and sale of the infringing products and collection of damages for loss of profits caused by the alleged infringement.

REQUIRED

1. What basis of valuation for Inventive's patents would be generally accepted in accounting? Give supporting reasons for this basis.

2. Assuming no practical problems of implementation and ignoring generally accepted accounting principles, what is the preferable basis of valuation for patents? Explain.

3. What would be the preferable theoretical basis of amortization? Explain.

4. What recognition, if any, should be made of the patent-infringement litigation in the financial statements for the year ended September 30, 1987? Discuss.

(AICPA, adapted)

C13-3. GOODWILL   Wilson Corporation, a retail fuel oil distributor, has increased its annual sales volume to a level three times that of the dealer it purchased in 1985 in order to begin operations.

Wilson's board of directors recently received an offer to negotiate the sale of Wilson Corporation to a large competitor. The majority of the board wants to increase the stated value of goodwill on the balance sheet to reflect the larger sales volume developed through intensive promotion and the current market price of oil. A few of the board members, however, would prefer to eliminate goodwill from the balance sheet altogether in order to prevent "possible misinterpretations." Goodwill was recorded properly in 1985.

REQUIRED

1. Discuss the meaning of the term "goodwill."

2. List the techniques used to calculate the tentative value of goodwill in negotiations to purchase a going concern.

3. Why does the book value of Wilson's goodwill differ from its market value?

4. Discuss the propriety of:
  a) Increasing the stated value of goodwill before the negotiations.
  b) Eliminating goodwill from the balance sheet before negotiations.

(AICPA, adapted)

C13-4. GOODWILL   Patterson Company acquired Ponsford Corporation, a service business, for an amount in excess of the fair value of identifiable tangible and intangible net assets. The excess purchase price was paid for customer lists, going concern value, and other unidentifiable resources, and was recorded as goodwill on Patterson's balance sheet. The purchase agreement also provided that Patterson would pay Ponsford additional amounts that were dependent upon the earnings of the acquired company during subsequent years. As a result of this agreement, an additional $200,000 became due three years from the date of the original purchase.

Because of the nature of Ponsford's business, Patterson tentatively decided on the date of acquisition to adopt a 10-year life for amortization purposes. The additional $200,000 is payable only because Ponsford has demonstrated continued earning power. Because of this evidence of continued value of the excess purchase price, Patterson would like to write off the unamortized balance of the original goodwill amount and the $200,000 over 15 years from the date of payment of the additional $200,000.

REQUIRED

1. Is Patterson's accounting for the original goodwill amount acceptable? Explain.

2. Is Patterson's proposed change in accounting for goodwill acceptable? Explain.

(AICPA, adapted)

C13-5. TREATMENT OF START-UP COSTS   After securing lease commitments from several major stores, Saline Valley Shopping Center, Inc., was organized and built a shopping center in a growing suburb.

The shopping center would have opened on schedule on January 1, 1988, if it had not been struck by a severe tornado in December 1987; it opened for business on October 1, 1988. All additional construction costs that were incurred as a result of the tornado were covered by insurance.

In July 1987, in anticipation of the scheduled January opening, a permanent staff had been hired to promote the shopping center, obtain tenants for the uncommitted space, and manage the property.

A summary of some of the costs incurred in 1987 and the first nine months of 1988 follows.

	1987	**1/1/88—9/30/88**
Interest on mortgage bonds	$75,000	$70,000
Cost of obtaining tenants	32,000	44,000
Promotional advertising	34,000	38,000

The promotional advertising campaign was designed to familiarize shoppers with the center. Had it been known in time that the center would not open until October 1988, the 1987 expenditure for promotional advertising would not have been made. The advertising had to be repeated in 1988.

All of the tenants who had leased space in the shopping center at the time of the tornado accepted the October occupancy date on condition that the monthly rental charges for the first nine months of 1988 be canceled.

REQUIRED

Explain how each of the costs for 1987 and the first nine months of 1988 should be treated in the accounts of the shopping center corporation. Give the reasons for each treatment.

(AICPA, adapted)

C13-6. RESEARCH AND DEVELOPMENT COSTS   The Patrick Company is in the process of developing a revolutionary new product. A new division of the company was formed to develop, manufacture, and market this new product. As of December 31, 1987, the new product has not been manufactured for resale; however, a prototype unit has been built and is in operation.

Throughout 1987 the new division incurred certain costs. These costs include design and engineering studies, prototype manufacturing costs, administrative expenses (including salaries of administrative personnel), and market research costs. In addition, approximately $500,000 in equipment (estimated useful life, 10 years) was purchased for use in developing and manufacturing the new product. Approximately $200,000 of this equipment was built specifically for the design development of the new product; the remaining $300,000 of equipment was used to manufacture the preproduction prototype and will be used to manufacture the new product once it is in commercial production.

REQUIRED

1. What is the definition of "research" and of "development" as defined in *FASB Statement No. 2?*

2. Briefly indicate the practical and conceptual reasons for the conclusion reached by the FASB on accounting and reporting practices for research and development costs.

3. In accordance with *FASB Statement No. 2,* how should the various costs of Patrick described above be recorded on the financial statements for the year ended December 31, 1987?

(AICPA, adapted)

C13-7. COMPUTER SOFTWARE COSTS   The AtoZ Software Company has recently completed the development and testing of an integrated software package called "Do-It-All." The software has a common command structure that allows a user to perform data base, spreadsheet, and word processing functions. While operating within any one of these programs, the user may integrate data from the other programs.

Because of its past success with stand-alone data base, spreadsheet, and word processing software, AtoZ has never had any doubts about the commercial profitability of Do-It-All. Thus, management believes that the costs of designing, developing, coding, and testing the software package should be capitalized and amortized on a straight-line basis over five years, which is the length of time Do-It-All is expected to produce revenues.

REQUIRED

1. Is AtoZ's proposed accounting for the development costs acceptable? Explain.

2. Explain how the costs incurred to produce product masters, after technological feasibility has been established, should be accounted for.

3. Explain how the costs of duplicating the software, documentation, and training materials should be accounted for.

C13-8. SOFTWARE DEVELOPMENT COSTS During an examination of the financial statements of the Benson Company, your assistant calls attention to significant costs incurred in the development of software programs for major segments of the sales and inventory scheduling systems.

The software program development costs will benefit future periods to the extent that the systems change slowly and the program instructions are compatible with new equipment acquired at three- to six-year intervals. The service value of the software programs is affected almost entirely by changes in the technology of systems and hardware and does not decline with the number of times the program is used. Because many system changes are minor, program instructions can frequently be modified with only minor losses in program efficiency. The frequency of such changes tends to increase with the passage of time.

REQUIRED

1. Discuss the propriety of classifying the unamortized software program development costs as:
   a) A prepaid expense.
   b) An intangible asset.
   c) A tangible fixed asset.

2. Discuss the propriety of amortizing the software program development costs by means of:
   a) The straight-line method.
   b) A decreasing charge method (for example, the sum-of-the-years'-digits method).
   c) A variable charge method (for example, the units-of-production method).

(AICPA, adapted)

C13-9. ACCOUNTING FOR EXPLORATION COSTS Soon after hiring you as the controller of a small oil exploration and production company, the executive vice-president for finance calls you into his office to discuss an issue that has been bothering him for some time. He is concerned about a recent proposal by the FASB that would allow oil and gas companies to capitalize only those exploration costs associated with successful exploration efforts. The executive vice-president is adamantly opposed to the proposed requirement, preferring to capitalize all exploration costs, as is the company's current practice.

After an extended discussion of the issues involved, the executive vice-president decides that the best course of action is to send a letter to the FASB in response to the proposed requirement. As a basis for drafting the letter, he requests that you prepare a memorandum summarizing all arguments supporting the company's current practice.

REQUIRED

1. Why is the executive vice-president so concerned about the method of accounting for exploration costs?

2. Draft a memorandum to the executive vice-president which summarizes the arguments in favor of capitalization and subsequent amortization of all exploration costs.

EXERCISES

E13-1. PATENTS At the beginning of 1987 Seko Company purchases a patent on a product for $300,000. The remaining legal life of the patent is 12 years. The estimated economic life of the patent, however, is 8 years. In January 1988, Seko incurs legal fees of $28,000 in connection with a successful defense of a patent-infringement suit. In 1990, Seko withdraws the product from the market because of a potential health hazard.

REQUIRED

Prepare journal entries related to the patent for 1987, 1988, 1989, and 1990.

E13-2. ORGANIZATION COSTS The Schultz Company was organized in 1987 and began operations on January 1, 1988. Schultz is engaged in conducting market research studies on behalf of manufacturers. Before the start of operations, the following costs were incurred:

Attorneys' fees in connection with organization of Schultz	$ 8,000
Improvements to leased offices prior to occupancy	14,000
Meetings of incorporators, state filing fees, and other organization expenses	10,000
	$32,000

Schultz has elected to record amortization of organization costs over the maximum period allowable under generally accepted accounting principles.

REQUIRED

1. Prepare the journal entry to record amortization of organization costs for 1988.

2. If any of the above items should be excluded from organization costs, explain how they should be accounted for.

(AICPA, adapted)

E13-3. CLASSIFICATION OF INTANGIBLES The following account balances were taken from the general ledger of Sodders Corporation at the end of 1987:

Patents	$ 8,400
Trademark	3,100
Organization costs	24,000
Discount on bonds payable	2,100
Franchise	5,600
Research and development costs	164,000
Excess of cost over fair market value of net assets of acquired business	20,000
Trade accounts receivable (net)	82,000

REQUIRED

Prepare the intangible assets section of the balance sheet for Sodders Corporation as of December 31, 1987.

E13-4. GOODWILL On July 31, 1987, Dark Company purchased for $8 million cash all of the outstanding common stock of Reneau Company when Reneau's balance sheet showed net assets of $6.4 million. The fair market values of Reneau's assets and liabilities differed from their book values, as follows:

	BOOK VALUE	FAIR MARKET VALUE
Property, plant, and equipment (net)	$10,000,000	$11,500,000
Other assets	1,000,000	700,000
Long-term debt	6,000,000	5,600,000

REQUIRED

Calculate the amount paid for goodwill.

(AICPA, adapted)

E13-5. GOODWILL   Baldwin Company is contemplating the purchase of all of the outstanding common stock of Reed Corporation. Reed's recorded assets and liabilities are as follows:

Cash	$ 40,000
Receivables (net)	180,000
Inventory	320,000
Property, plant, and equipment (net)	500,000
Liabilities	(220,000)

Baldwin estimated that the fair market value (net realizable value) of Reed's receivables was $160,000, the fair market value of inventory was $400,000, and the fair market value of property, plant, and equipment was $560,000.

REQUIRED

1. If Baldwin paid $1 million for all of Reed's common stock, what amount would be recorded for goodwill?

2. What should be the minimum amount that Reed would be willing to accept for its net assets? Why?

E13-6. GOODWILL   Growth Company and Ripe Company have agreed to a transaction in which Growth will acquire all of Ripe's outstanding common shares. The agreement stipulates that Growth will pay cash equal to the fair market value of the identifiable net assets plus an amount for goodwill determined by capitalizing at 20 percent annual excess earnings from normal operations for the past 5 years. The following information is available:

Net income of Ripe Company for last 5 years (total)	$2,820,000
Fair market value of Ripe's identifiable net assets	5,000,000
Extraordinary gains during last 5 years	180,000
Normal rate of return for industry	10%

REQUIRED

Calculate the amount to be paid for the common stock of Ripe Company. Show supporting calculations.

E13-7. GOODWILL   Big Company wishes to acquire Little Company. Big projects average annual earnings for Little of $80,000. The estimated fair market value of Little's identifiable net assets is $500,000 and the normal rate of return for the industry in which Little operates is 12 percent. Big estimates that excess earnings attributable to Little's management should continue for 6 years.

REQUIRED

Calculate the estimated amount for goodwill, assuming *(a)* excess annual earnings are discounted at 16 percent, and *(b)* the time value of money is ignored in valuing the excess earnings.

E13-8. GOODWILL   Net income for Sell Company for the years 1984 through 1988 is as follows:

1984	$40,000
1985	20,000
1986	60,000
1987	80,000
1988	90,000

At the beginning of 1989, Buy Company contemplates the acquisition of Sell Company. Buy discovers that 1986 net income reflects an extraordinary loss (net) of $10,000 and that 1987 net income reflects an extraordinary gain (net) of $20,000. Assume that, with the exception of the extraordinary items, Buy expects past earnings to be representative of future earnings. The fair market value of Sell's identifiable net assets is $450,000 at the beginning of 1989. The normal rate of return for Sell's industry is 10 percent.

REQUIRED

Calculate the estimated amount of goodwill, assuming *(a)* annual excess earnings are capitalized at 16 percent, and *(b)* annual excess earnings are expected to continue for 5 years and are discounted at 16 percent.

E13-9. NEGATIVE GOODWILL   During 1987 the Jackson Company purchased the net assets of Bird Corporation for $800,000. On the date of the transaction, Bird had no long-term investments in marketable securities and had $100,000 of liabilities. The fair market value of Bird's assets when they were acquired was as follows:

Current assets	$ 400,000
Noncurrent assets	600,000
	$1,000,000

REQUIRED

1. How should Jackson Company account for the $100,000 excess of fair market value of net assets acquired ($900,000) over the cost ($800,000)?

2. How would your answer to part 1 change if the cost were $200,000?

E13-10. RESEARCH AND DEVELOPMENT COSTS   In 1987 Burton Corporation developed a new product to be marketed in 1988. In connection with the development of this product, the following costs were incurred in 1987:

Research and development departmental costs	$200,000
Materials and supplies consumed	100,000
Compensation paid to research consultants	60,000
	$360,000

It is anticipated that these costs will be recovered in 1990.

REQUIRED

What is the amount of research and development costs that should be expensed in 1987?

(AICPA, adapted)

E13-11. RESEARCH AND DEVELOPMENT COSTS   Pattison Company incurred research and development costs in 1987 as follows:

Materials used in research and development projects	$ 500,000
Equipment acquired that will have alternate uses in future research and development projects	2,000,000
Depreciation for 1987 on above equipment	500,000
Personnel costs of persons involved in research and development projects	1,000,000
Consulting fees paid to outsiders for research and development projects	100,000
Indirect costs reasonably allocable to research and development projects	200,000
	$4,300,000

REQUIRED

Calculate the amount of research and development expense that Pattison Company should record in 1987.

(AICPA, adapted)

E13-12. COMPUTER SOFTWARE COSTS   Softsource, Inc., a computer software company, incurred the following costs in the process of developing and producing a new software program:

Program planning and design	$ 80,000
Production of product masters	20,000
Coding	120,000
Testing to determine consistency with product design	40,000
Duplication of product masters and packaging	30,000

The costs of planning and design, coding, and testing were all incurred before the technological feasibility of the product was determined. Softsource believes that the product will produce revenues for the next three years. Estimated revenues from the product for the next three years are $200,000, $150,000, and $125,000, respectively. Assume all costs were paid in cash.

REQUIRED

1. Prepare journal entries to record the costs incurred by Softsource.

2. Prepare the journal entry to record amortization of capitalized software costs at the end of the first year.

E13-13. DEPLETION   The Gudger Company acquired a tract of land containing an extractable natural resource. Gudger is required by its purchase contract to restore the land to a condition suitable for recreational use after it has extracted the natural resource. Geological surveys estimate that the recoverable reserves will be 4 million tons, and that the land will have a value of $1 million after restoration. Relevant cost information follows:

Land	$9,000,000
Estimated restoration costs	1,200,000

Gudger maintains no inventories of extracted material.

REQUIRED

What should be the depletion expense per ton of extracted material?

(AICPA, adapted)

E13-14. DEPLETION

A) During 1987 Fisher Corporation acquired a mine for $900,000, of which $150,000 was ascribed to land value after the mineral has been removed. Geological surveys have indicated that 15 million units of the mineral could be extracted. During 1987, 1.2 million units were extracted and 800,000 units were sold.

REQUIRED

What is the amount of depletion for 1987?

B) In January 1987, the Mother Lode Corporation purchased for $3.4 million a mine with removable ore estimated at 4 million tons. The property has an estimated value of $200,000 after the ore has been extracted. The company incurred $800,000 of development costs preparing the mine for production. During 1987, 400,000 tons were removed and 375,000 tons were sold.

REQUIRED

What is the amount of depletion that Mother Lode should record for 1987?

(AICPA, adapted)

E13-15. DEPLETION; TANGIBLE ASSETS ACQUIRED FOR PRODUCTION OF NATURAL RESOURCE   On July 1, 1987, Mueller Mining, a calendar-year corporation, purchased the rights to a copper mine. Of the total purchase price, $2.8 million was appropriately allocable to the copper. Estimated reserves were 800,000 tons of copper. Production began immediately. Mueller found it could extract and sell 10,000 tons of copper per month. The selling price was $25 per ton.

To aid production, Mueller also purchased some new equipment on July 1, 1987. The equipment cost $76,000 and had an estimated useful life of eight years. After all the copper was removed from this mine, the equipment would be of no use to Mueller and would be sold for an estimated $4,000.

REQUIRED

1. What was Mueller's depletion expense on this mine for 1987?

2. What was Mueller's depreciation expense on the new equipment for 1987?

(AICPA, adapted)

E13-16. ACCOUNTING FOR EXPLORATION COSTS   Resources, Inc., incurred exploration costs as follows on oil-drilling efforts during 1987:

Well *A*	$40,000
Well *B*	80,000
Well *C*	30,000
Well *D*	50,000
Well *E*	25,000

As a result of these efforts, wells *A*, *B*, and *C* were abandoned, well *D* was determined to be commercially successful, and Resources plans to continue drilling on well *E* during 1988 to determine its feasibility.

REQUIRED

Prepare a summary journal entry to account for the above costs at the end of 1987, assuming that Resources uses *(a)* the full-cost method of accounting for exploration costs, and *(b)* the successful efforts method of accounting for exploration costs.

PROBLEMS

P13-1. ACCOUNTING FOR INTANGIBLES   Toshi Corporation commenced operations at the beginning of 1987. During 1987 the following selected transactions and events took place:

a) During January, Toshi incurred organization costs of $32,000.

b) On January 31, Toshi acquired a patent for $18,000. The remaining legal life at the time of acquisition was 12 years. Toshi estimated, however, that the useful economic life was 6 years.

c) Throughout the year, the firm incurred costs of $22,000 to publicize its products.

d) Toshi acquired a franchise on July 1. The company paid an initial franchise fee on July 1 of $15,000. The franchise term is 5 years.

e) Toshi incurred research and development costs of $54,000. Of this amount, $12,000 relates to equipment acquired on October 1 which Toshi can use for other research and development activities. The estimated useful life of the equipment is 6 years and Toshi anticipates that there will be no salvage value. Toshi depreciates similar equipment on a straight-line basis.

REQUIRED

1. Prepare journal entries to record the above expenditures. Assume that Toshi amortizes organization costs over the minimum period allowable for tax purposes.

2. Prepare the intangible assets section of the balance sheet for December 31, 1987.

P13-2. ACCOUNTING FOR INTANGIBLES   Selected transactions for Reckers Company at the beginning of 1987 were as follows:

a) Reckers acquired a patent for $10,000 cash. The remaining legal life was 15 years; the estimated remaining economic life was 5 years.

b) The firm incurred promotional costs of $21,000 related to existing products. Reckers anticipates that these expenditures will generate additional revenues for approximately 3 years.

c) Reckers paid $6,000 in legal fees for successful defense of a patent-infringement suit. The related patent had a remaining useful life of 3 years and a remaining legal life of 12 years at the beginning of 1987.

d) The company paid $4,000 in legal fees connected with unsuccessful defense of a patent-infringement suit. The related patent, which Reckers subsequently determined was worthless, had a book value of $8,000 at the beginning of 1987 and a remaining legal life of 4 years.

e) Reckers acquired a trademark from another company for $40,000.

f) Reckers paid $2,000 cash for media ads to promote the new trademark.

REQUIRED

Prepare journal entries to record the above transactions, including year-end adjusting entries where appropriate. Unless the information provided indicates otherwise, amortize intangibles over their legal life.

P13-3. INTANGIBLES—STATEMENT PRESENTATION   The Jensen Company has provided information on intangible assets as follows:

a) A patent was purchased from the Johnson Company for $1.5 million on January 1, 1986. Jensen estimated the remaining useful life of the patent to be 10 years. The patent was carried in Johnson's accounting records at net book value of $1.25 million when Johnson sold it to Jensen.

b) During 1987, a franchise was purchased from the Dink Company for $500,000. In addition, 5 percent of revenue from the franchise must be paid to Dink. Revenue from the franchise for 1987 was $2 million. Jensen estimates the useful life of the franchise to be 10 years and takes a full year's amortization in the year of purchase.

c) Jensen incurred research and development costs in 1987 as follows:

Materials and equipment	$220,000
Personnel	140,000
Indirect costs	60,000
	$420,000

Jensen estimates that these costs will be recovered by December 31, 1989.

d) On January 1, 1987, Jensen estimated, on the basis of recent events in the field, that the remaining life of the patent purchased on January 1, 1986, was only 5 years.

REQUIRED

1. Prepare a schedule showing the intangibles section of Jensen's balance sheet on December 31, 1987. Show supporting calculations in good form.

2. Prepare a schedule showing the income statement effect for the year ended December 31, 1987, as a result of the above facts. Show supporting calculations in good form.

(AICPA, adapted)

P13-4. INTANGIBLES—CLASSIFICATION   Pany Corporation began operations in 1987. As the senior accountant assigned to the audit of Pany Corporation for 1987, you discover a ledger account, "intangibles," comprised of the following items:

Jan. 2	Organization costs	$12,000
Feb. 1	Advertising costs	5,300
Mar. 30	Registered a patent to be used in R&D activities ($15,000 of the cost constitutes research and development costs related to development of patent)	17,400
July 1	Operating loss, first six months	7,000
Oct. 1	Acquired copyright, estimated remaining economic life of 5 years	10,000
Oct. 15	Labor costs associated with R&D activities	8,000
Dec. 1	Acquired two patents to be used for R&D activities: patent no. 1 (cost of $6,000), to be used solely for current R&D project, has remaining legal life of 4 years; patent no. 2 (cost of $21,000), to be used for several R&D projects over 3-year period, has remaining legal life of 14 years	27,000

REQUIRED

Prepare correcting entries to eliminate the intangibles account. You should amortize organization costs over the minimum period allowable for tax purposes.

P13-5. GOODWILL The Hunt Company, in assessing the prospects for acquiring Pearce Corporation, makes the following estimates regarding Pearce's earnings and asset valuations:

Estimated average annual earnings................................$ 62,000
Estimated fair market value of identifiable net assets 500,000
Estimated normal rate of return for industry........................ 10%

REQUIRED

1. Calculate the estimated amount of goodwill under the following three independent assumptions:

a) Goodwill is to be valued at 4 years' excess earnings.

b) Goodwill is to be valued at the present value of 5 years' excess earnings, discounted at 16 percent.

c) Goodwill is to be valued at the capitalized amount of excess earnings, calculated at a 20 percent capitalization rate.

2. Under what conditions might each of the three methods of estimating goodwill be appropriate? In general, which method do you prefer? Why?

P13-6. GOODWILL At the beginning of 1988, Holmes Corporation enters into an agreement to acquire the Dukes Company. The agreement stipulates that the purchase price will be the fair market value of the identifiable net assets of Dukes on December 31, 1987, plus an amount for goodwill determined by capitalizing at 16 percent average annual earnings for the last 4 years (1984 through 1987) from normal operations in excess of 12 percent of the fair market value of identifiable net assets at December 31, 1987.

The following information is available for determining the purchase price:

a) Net income of Dukes Company:

1984	$42,000
1985	61,000
1986	54,000
1987	79,000

b) Condensed balance sheet of Dukes Company on December 31, 1987:

Current assets	$150,000	Liabilities	$200,000
Investments	40,000	Stockholders' equity	400,000
Fixed assets (net)	410,000		
	$600,000		$600,000

c) The fair market value of inventory on December 31 exceeds book value by $30,000. The fair market value of fixed assets on December 31 exceeds book value by $20,000.

d) In 1985, Dukes included an extraordinary gain from expropriation of property of $4,000 (net) in net income.

e) In 1986, an extraordinary loss of $8,000 (net) resulting from tornado damage was included in net income.

f) In 1987, a receivable of $1,900 which Dukes had written off in 1984 was collected and credited to "other income."

REQUIRED

Determine the purchase price to be paid by Holmes Corporation for the Dukes Company in accordance with the agreement. Supporting calculations should be in good form.

P13-7. GOODWILL On September 1, 1987, the Deer Company purchased 200,000 shares representing 45 percent of the outstanding stock of Lion Company for cash. Goodwill of $500,000 was appropriately recognized by Deer at the date of the purchase.

On December 1, 1988, Deer purchased 300,000 shares representing 30 percent of the outstanding stock of Bear Company for $2.5 million cash. The stockholders' equity section of Bear's balance sheet at the date of the acquisition was as follows:

Common stock, par value $2 a share	$2,000,000
Contributed capital in excess of par	1,000,000
Retained earnings	4,000,000
	$7,000,000

At the date of acquisition, the fair market value of Bear's property, plant, and equipment (net) was $3.8 million, whereas the book value was $3.5 million. The fair market values of all of Bear's other assets and liabilities were equal to their book values.

Deer amortizes goodwill over the maximum period allowed and takes a full year's amortization in the year of purchase.

REQUIRED

Prepare a schedule calculating the amount of goodwill and accumulated amortization on December 31, 1988, and the goodwill amortization for the year ended December 31, 1988. Show supporting calculations in good form.

(AICPA, adapted)

P13-8. INTANGIBLES—COMPREHENSIVE Empress Tool Corporation was incorporated on January 3, 1986. The corporation's financial statements for its first year's operations were not examined by a CPA. You have been engaged to examine the financial statements for the year ended December 31, 1987, and your examination is substantially completed. The corporation's trial balance is as follows:

	DEBIT	CREDIT
Cash	$ 11,000	
Accounts receivable	42,500	
Allowance for doubtful accounts		$ 500
Inventories	38,500	
Machinery	75,000	
Equipment	29,000	
Accumulated depreciation		10,000
Patents	85,000	
Leasehold improvements	26,000	
Prepaid expenses	10,500	
Organization costs	29,000	
Goodwill	24,000	
Licensing agreement no. 1	50,000	
Licensing agreement no. 2	49,000	
Accounts payable		147,500
Unearned revenue		12,500
Capital stock		300,000
Retained earnings, 1/1/87	27,000	
Sales		668,500
Cost of goods sold	454,000	
Selling and general expenses	173,000	
Interest expense	3,500	
Extraordinary losses	12,000	
Total	$1,139,000	$1,139,000

The following information relates to accounts that may yet require adjustment.

a) Patents for Empress' manufacturing process were acquired January 2, 1987, at a cost of $68,000. An additional $17,000 was spent in December 1987 to improve machinery covered by the patents and debited to the patents account. Depreciation on fixed assets has been properly recorded for 1987 in accordance with Empress' practice, which provides a full year's depreciation for property on hand June 30 and no depreciation otherwise. Empress uses the straight-line method for all depreciation and amortizes patents over their legal life.

b) On January 3, 1986, Empress purchased licensing agreement no. 1, which was believed to have an unlimited useful life. The balance in the licensing agreement no. 1 account includes its purchase price of $48,000 and other costs of $2,000 related to the acquisition. On January 1, 1987, Empress purchased licensing agreement no. 2, which had a life expectancy of 10 years. The balance in the licensing agreement no. 2 account includes its $48,000 purchase price and $2,000 in acquisition expenditures, but it has been reduced by a credit of $1,000 for the advance collection of 1988 revenue from the agreement.

In late December 1986 an explosion caused a permanent 60 percent reduction in the expected revenue-producing value of licensing agreement no. 1, and in January 1988 a flood caused additional damage that rendered the agreement worthless.

c) The balance in the goodwill account includes (1) $8,000 paid December 30, 1986, for an advertising program it was estimated would help to increase Empress' sales over a period of four years following the disbursement, and (2) legal expenses of $16,000 incurred for Empress' incorporation on January 3, 1986.

d) The leasehold improvements account includes (1) the $15,000 cost of improvements, with a total estimated useful life of 12 years, which Empress made to property it leased in January 1986; (2) movable assembly-line equipment costing $8,500 that was installed in the leased premises in December 1987; and (3) real estate taxes of $2,500 paid by Empress in 1987, which under the terms of the lease should have been paid by the landlord. Empress paid its rent in full during 1987. A 10-year nonrenewable lease was signed January 3, 1986, for the leased building, which Empress used in manufacturing operations.

e) The balance in the organization expenses account properly includes costs incurred during the organizational period. The corporation has exercised its option to amortize organization costs over a 60-month period for federal income tax purposes and wishes to amortize them on the same basis for accounting purposes.

REQUIRED

Prepare an eight-column worksheet to adjust accounts that require adjustment and include columns for an income statement and a balance sheet. A separate account should be used for the accumulation of each type of amortization and for each prior period adjustment. Adjusting journal entries and financial statements are *not* required. (Hint: Licensing agreement no. 1 should be amortized over the maximum life required in *APB Opinion No. 17* before the explosion damage loss is determined.)

(AICPA, adapted)

P13-9. RESEARCH AND DEVELOPMENT COSTS During 1985 ARD Company purchased a building site for its proposed research and development laboratory at a cost of $60,000. Construction of the building was started in 1985. The building was completed on December 31, 1986, at a cost of $200,000, and was placed in service on January 2, 1987. The estimated useful life of the building for depreciation purposes was 20 years; the straight-line method of depreciation was to be employed and there was no estimated net salvage value.

Management estimates that about 50 percent of the projects of the research and development group will result in long-term benefits (i.e., at least 10 years) to the corporation. The remaining projects either benefit the current period or are abandoned before completion. A summary of the number of projects and the direct costs incurred in conjunction with the research and development activities for 1987 appears below.

At the recommendation of the research and development group, ARD Company acquired a patent for manufacturing rights at a cost of $100,000. The patent was acquired on April 1, 1986, and has an economic life of 5 years.

	NUMBER OF PROJECTS	SALARIES AND EMPLOYEE BENEFITS	OTHER EXPENSES (EXCLUDING BUILDING DEPRECIATION CHARGES)
Completed projects with long-term benefits	15	$ 75,000	$35,000
Abandoned projects or projects that benefit current period	10	20,000	10,000
Projects in process— results indeterminate	5	25,000	10,000
Total	30	$120,000	$55,000

REQUIRED

How should the above items related to research and development activities be reported:

1. On the company's income statement for 1987?

2. On the company's balance sheet as of December 31, 1987?

Be sure to give account titles and amounts, and briefly justify your presentation.

(IMA, adapted)

P13-10. INTANGIBLES—COMPREHENSIVE   Parker Corporation was founded in 1974 and experienced only moderate growth until the last three years, when it became a pioneer in the field of robotics. Parker has experienced a 30 percent growth rate in revenues during the last three years and is planning several expenditures that would enable it to meet increased demand and continue its excellent growth rate.

Jon Griffith of Parker's accounting department is having some difficulty in determining the appropriate accounting for several transactions that occurred during the first quarter of 1987. These transactions are described below. All amounts are considered to be material.

1. Parker paid $260,000 for land upon which to build a new research facility. The cost to raze and remove an old building on the site of the newly proposed research facility was $50,000. Usable fixtures from the old building were sold for $10,000. Parker paid $4,000 to the architect that designed the new building, $30,000 for excavation of the basement, and $420,000 to a contractor for construction of the building. The new building is expected to be appropriate for the needs of the company for about 20 years.

2. Parker gave a one-year noninterest-bearing note for $165,000 to Roberts Industries in exchange for a conveyor to be installed in the new facility and a temperate monitoring system (TMS). The imputed interest rate on the note is 10 percent per year. The conveyor had an estimated value of $60,000 at the date of the exchange, is expected to last for 30 years, and will be needed as long as the research facility is used by the company. The TMS had an estimated value of $100,000 at the date of the exchange and is expected to last five years.

3. Parker incurred the following costs in developing and securing a trademark:

Design costs $2,000
Registration fees   300
Attorney's fees   700

Parker's marketing manager believes the trademark will be of value to the company for 50 years.

4. Parker incurred $6,000 in legal fees to defend its rights in a patent. The patent was purchased at the beginning of 1985 for $15,000 and is being amortized over 12 years.

5. Parker spent $30,000 searching for practical applications of new research findings that are believed to be of use to the company for the next 20 years.

REQUIRED

As controller for Parker Corporation, you are to review the five items described, summarize the amounts to be capitalized and expensed in 1987, and determine the number of years over which capitalized amounts are to be written off.

(IMA, adapted)

P13-11. NATURAL RESOURCES   Kenny Copper Company purchases a tract of mining property in 1986 for $4.2 million. Kenny constructs buildings on the property during 1986 at a cost of $200,000. Kenny estimates that the buildings will have a physical life of 20 years, but Kenny does not intend to use the buildings after it has depleted the copper ore from the property. Kenny acquires machinery for $120,000 to be used in the mining operation, and estimates that one-third of the machinery (in terms of book value) will be useful throughout the mining of this tract, with no anticipated salvage value. The other two-thirds of the machinery will be useful beyond the current mining operation; only one-half of this portion of the book value should be absorbed by the mining of the tract in question.

Mining operations commence at the beginning of 1987. At that time, Kenny estimates that it will extract 800,000 tons of low-grade ore from the property. Kenny incurs production costs of $220,000 during 1987 to extract 80,000 tons of ore.

In 1988, Kenny extracts 100,000 tons of ore and incurs production costs of $260,000. At the end of 1988, the company estimates that 700,000 tons of ore remain that can be extracted economically.

REQUIRED

Assuming Kenny Copper maintains no inventories, and that restoration costs negate any residual value, calculate depletion expense for 1987 and 1988 by the units-of-production method.

14 INVESTMENTS

The role of cash, receivables, inventories, plant assets, natural resources, and intangibles in most business entities is readily apparent. For example, a manufacturing concern uses cash to acquire raw materials; it uses the raw materials in the production process, creating inventories, and it sells the inventories, thus generating receivables. Ultimately, cash appears at the end of the operating cycle. Plant assets, natural resources, and intangibles are resources that are used up in the production process. In addition to investing in assets used in regular operations, many companies invest in securities, such as stocks and bonds issued by other companies. Such investments are made either (1) to earn a return on temporarily idle cash, or (2) to achieve an economically beneficial business relationship with a customer, supplier, or other business entity. Both types of investment are made to generate future cash flows, either directly or indirectly.

Interest and dividends on temporary investments in commercial paper, U.S. Treasury bills, and similar securities provide relatively low-risk returns on idle cash while maintaining the liquidity of that cash. When investments are made in other securities to establish or strengthen an economic relationship with another entity, they tend to be long-term investments. For example, a company may acquire enough common shares of a major customer to gain influence over the management of the customer and thus guarantee a continuing market for its product. Likewise, a company may invest in shares of a major supplier of a critical raw material, thereby gaining influence over the supplier's management and ensuring a continuing source of raw material.

Both temporary and long-term security investments, other than investments in bonds, are discussed in this chapter. Because bond investments are covered in detail in Chapter 16 (along with bonds payable), we mention them only briefly here. In addition, in this chapter we describe the accounting for and reporting of special-purpose funds and the cash surrender value of life insurance of which the company is the beneficiary.

INVESTMENTS IN COMMON STOCK

Equity securities represent ownership shares in an enterprise (for example, common stock and other capital stock), or the right to acquire ownership shares (for example, stock warrants, stock rights, and call options) or dispose of ownership shares (for example, put options) at fixed or determinable prices.[1] Holders of **common stock** are owners of the entity. They rank behind all other holders of claims against the entity when dividends or assets are distributed in the event the entity liquidates. Thus, we sometimes refer to common stocks as *residual securities* (what is left over after all other claims) and to owners of such securities as residual equity holders. As recipients of dividends and as benefactors of changes in market prices of shares owned, holders of common stock reap the reward of successful operations and bear the greatest risk of loss through business failure.

VALUATION AT ACQUISITION

Acquisition for Cash

Investors buy many common stock issues through an organized stock exchange, such as the New York Stock Exchange or the American Stock Exchange, or "over the counter." Stock also may be acquired directly from the company that issues it, or from a current owner of stock. Regardless of how an investor acquires stock, the historical cost or initial recording principle governs valuation at acquisition. In other words, the stock is recorded at our best estimate of its fair market value. When a firm pays cash for stock, the cash sacrificed is recorded as the value of the stock acquired. Any broker's fees, taxes, or other miscellaneous costs incurred in connection with the acquisition of securities also must be included as part of the cost of the stock.

Historical cost or the initial recording principle governs valuation at acquisition.

Acquisition in Exchange for Noncash Consideration

In transactions involving the sacrifice of cash, the number of dollars given up usually represents the best measure of the fair market value of the securities acquired. When only nonmonetary items are involved in an exchange, however, we must determine fair market value by assessing the values of both the securities acquired and the resources given up. When a firm purchases stock in exchange for noncash resources, it should record the stock either at the fair market value of the securities received or at the fair market value of the resources sacrificed, whichever is more readily determinable.[2] Thus we use *cost,* as measured by the fair market value of the resources sacrificed, to value resources acquired only when that approach produces the best estimate of the fair market value of the resources acquired.[3]

Assume, for example, that Spector Corporation acquires 200 shares of Flyer Corporation common stock in exchange for certain machinery no longer needed in Spector's operations. The machinery originally cost $15,000, has a book value of $8,000 at the time of the exchange, and has an estimated fair market value of $10,000. The fair market value of the Flyer shares is not determinable because the company is "closely held" (that is, Flyer has relatively few stockholders and a limited number of stock transactions), and no recent exchanges of the stock have occurred.

In this case, the more readily determinable fair market value is that of the machinery—$10,000. Therefore, Spector assigns a fair market value of $10,000 to the stock and records the exchange as follows:

Investment in stock of Flyer Corp.	10,000	
Accumulated depreciation—machinery	7,000	
Machinery		15,000
Gain on exchange		2,000

[1] "Accounting for Certain Marketable Securities," *Statement of Financial Accounting Standards No. 12* (Stamford, Conn.: FASB, 1975), para. 7.

[2] "Accounting for Nonmonetary Transactions," *Opinions of the Accounting Principles Board No. 29* (New York: AICPA, 1973), para. 18.

[3] For a related discussion of the historical cost principle, see p. 40.

The gain of $2,000 is the difference between the machinery's book value ($8,000) and its fair market value ($10,000).

As far as Spector's operations are concerned, this transaction marks the culmination of the earning process on its machinery. Consequently, Spector will recognize a gain or a loss on the exchange at this time—in this case a gain, because the machinery's fair market value exceeds its book value. Likewise, Flyer's stock begins its earning process for Spector at this time, and Spector records the stock at the best estimate of its fair market value.[4]

Sometimes a firm acquires two or more types of securities in a single transaction. For example, a company issuing new common shares may include preferred stock as a "sweetener" to enhance the marketability of the common shares. Accounting for these transactions is described in the following section.

Lump-Sum Purchase

Cost allocation is based on relative fair market values.

When a firm acquires two or more types of assets for a single sum (referred to as a *lump-sum* or *basket purchase*), it must allocate the cost among the acquired assets on the basis of the relative fair market values of the assets.[5]

Assume, for example, that Ajax Company pays $25,000 for 500 shares of newly issued $10 par common stock of Best Company, plus 1 share of Best's $5 par preferred stock for every 5 shares of common Ajax purchases. The common stock is traded at $40 per share on the date of the sale and the preferred shares are traded at $60 per share. The $25,000 purchase price is allocated between the common and preferred shares as follows:

Common ($40 × 500 shares) $20,000
Preferred ($60 × 100 shares)   6,000
  Total fair market value $26,000

Purchase price allocated to common shares:

$$\frac{\$20,000}{\$26,000} \times \$25,000 = \$19,231$$

Purchase price allocated to preferred shares:

$$\frac{\$6,000}{\$26,000} \times \$25,000 = \$5,769$$

The journal entry to record the transaction is as follows:

Investment in Best Co. common 19,231
Investment in Best Co. preferred 5,769
  Cash   25,000

If Ajax knew the market value of only one of the securities at the time of the transaction, it would assign that market value to the appropriate security and then allocate the remainder of the $25,000 purchase price to the remaining security. If neither security is actively traded, it may be necessary to record the total purchase price in one account pending the availability of subsequent market data or appraisals.

---

[4] Exchanges of nonmonetary assets are described in detail in Chapter 11.

[5] We described this process with respect to lump-sum purchases of plant assets in Chapter 11.

VALUATION FOLLOWING ACQUISITION

As we have seen, the objective in valuing common stock at acquisition is to approximate its fair market value. While different circumstances require different means of estimating fair market value at acquisition, the basic principle is the same regardless of the circumstances. Accounting for common stock investments after they have been recorded initially becomes more complex. Under GAAP there are three different methods of accounting for common stock investments subsequent to acquisition. Which one to use depends on the current circumstances characterizing the particular stock to be valued. The three methods are: (1) the cost method; (2) the lower-of-cost-or-market method, and (3) the equity method.

Cost Method

Under the **cost method,** the common stock investment is carried at acquisition cost, including brokerage fees and other incidental costs. For example, if Jet Stream Company acquires 1,000 shares of common stock in Atlas Corporation at $35 per share and incurs incidental fees of $500 in connection with the acquisition, Jet Stream records the transaction as follows:

Investment in Atlas Corp. common	35,500	
Cash		35,500

Thus, the book value per share of the common stock held by Jet Stream is $35,500 divided by 1,000 shares, or $35.50 per share.

Dividends received are recognized as revenue under the cost method. For example, if Atlas paid dividends of $2,000 to Jet Stream, Jet Stream would record the dividends as follows:

Cash	2,000	
Dividend revenue		2,000

> Under the cost method, dividends are recognized as revenue.

No recognition is given to the earnings of the *investee* (the company that issues the securities) in the books of the *investor* (the company that owns the securities). The investment carrying value should be reduced only if (1) dividends received exceed the investor's cumulative share of investee earnings since the shares were acquired (a liquidating dividend to the investor), or (2) a significant decline in market value below cost is determined to be other than temporary.

> The cost method is appropriate to value non-marketable, passive common stock investments.

The cost method must be used to value common stock if (1) the investment does not allow the investor to exercise significant influence over the financial and operating policies of the investee (that is, the investment is *passive*), and (2) the investment is nonmarketable. Investments in common stock that constitute less than 20 percent of the outstanding voting common shares are *presumed* to result in a lack of ability to exercise significant influence over the financial and operating policies of the investee. However, if the investor can demonstrate an ability to exercise significant influence, even though the investment constitutes less than 20 percent of the outstanding shares, the presumption is invalid and the equity method should be used to account for the investment. Evidence of significant influence may be indicated by (1) representation on the board of directors, (2) participation in policy making, (3) material intercompany transactions, (4) interchange of managerial personnel, (5) technological dependency, and (6) extent of ownership in relation to concentration of other shareholdings.[6]

[6] "The Equity Method of Accounting for Investments in Common Stock," *Opinions of the Accounting Principles Board No. 18* (New York: AICPA, 1971), para. 17.

An investment of 20 percent or more of the outstanding common shares of an investee carries with it the presumption of an ability to exercise significant influence. If there is predominant evidence to the contrary, however, the cost method should be applied, or if the securities are marketable, the lower-of-cost-or-market method should be used. Examples of evidence of an inability to exercise significant influence include the following situations:

1. The investee, through litigation or regulatory authorities, challenges the investor's ability to exercise significant influence.

2. The investor and investee enter into an agreement whereby the investor surrenders significant rights as a stockholder (such as a "stand-still agreement," in which the investor agrees to limit its percentage of ownership in an investee).

3. Majority ownership of the investee is concentrated in a small group of stockholders who control the investee without regard to the views of the investor.

4. The investor attempts and fails to obtain financial information beyond that normally available to stockholders, to permit application of the equity method.

5. The investor attempts and fails to obtain representation on the investee's board of directors.[7]

This list is illustrative rather than all-inclusive, and the existence of any one of the circumstances does not necessarily overcome the presumption of significant influence. The presence of one or more of these or similar circumstances, however, does require an evaluation of the facts to determine whether the presumption is overcome.

It is important to remember that it is not the percentage of ownership that determines whether the cost method should be applied, but whether the investor is able to exercise significant influence over the financing and operating policies of the investee. The 20 percent cutoff is merely a guideline to establish a basis for beginning to determine whether significant influence exists. All of the facts and circumstances surrounding each investment, not solely the percentage of ownership, must be evaluated to determine whether the ability to exercise significant influence exists, and thus which accounting method is appropriate for the investment.

The second requirement for use of the cost method is that the security must be nonmarketable. A common stock is considered to be *nonmarketable* if it is not being traded on a national securities exchange or in an active over-the-counter market.[8] Without market prices based on the interaction of large numbers of buyers and sellers, it is not feasible to use the lower-of-cost-or-market valuation method. In summary, the cost method is used for nonmarketable common stock investments that do not provide the investor with the ability to exercise significant influence over the investee.

To further illustrate application of the cost method, assume that Johnson Company purchases 1,000 shares of common stock of Kaplan Corporation, a closely held company, at $50 per share on January 3, 1987. Additional costs incidental to the purchase amount to $2,000. Johnson's 1,000 shares constitute 2 percent of Kaplan's outstanding common stock. Johnson's purchase does not enable it to influence the investee. Because of the lack of significant influence and the closely held nature of Kaplan Corporation, the cost method is the appropriate method to account for the investment.

---

[7] "Criteria for Applying the Equity Method of Accounting for Investments in Common Stock," *Interpretation No. 35* (Stamford, Conn.: FASB, 1981), para. 4.

[8] *FASB Statement No. 12,* para. 7(b).

Kaplan's net income and dividend distributions for 1987 and 1988 are as follows:

YEAR	NET INCOME	DIVIDENDS
1987	$150,000	$100,000
1988	50,000	50,000
	$200,000	$150,000

Johnson's journal entries related to the investment are as follows for 1987 and 1988:

1/3/87	Investment in Kaplan Corp. common 52,000	
	Cash	52,000
	To record investment in 1,000 shares at $50 per share plus incidental costs of $2,000.	
12/31/87	Cash 2,000	
	Dividend revenue	2,000
	To record share of dividends received during 1987—2% × $100,000.	
12/31/88	Cash 1,000	
	Dividend revenue	1,000
	To record share of dividends received during 1988—2% × $50,000.	

The investment continues to be carried at its cost of $52,000. Johnson reports the dividends received from the investment in the income statement.

Recall that under the cost method the investment must be reduced if the investee pays dividends to the investor in excess of the investor's share of earnings. Note that Johnson's share of earnings exceeds the dividends received both in 1987 and *in total* for 1987 and 1988:

YEAR	SHARE OF NET INCOME (2%)	SHARE OF DIVIDENDS (2%)
1987	$3,000	$2,000
1987 and 1988	4,000	3,000

Thus, the dividends received represent a distribution of Johnson's share of Kaplan's income earned since the investment was acquired by Johnson.

Assume instead that Kaplan had a net loss of $50,000 in 1988:

YEAR	KAPLAN NET INCOME (LOSS)	KAPLAN DIVIDENDS
1987	$150,000	$100,000
1988	(50,000)	50,000
	$100,000	$150,000

Johnson's journal entries to record the dividends received in 1987 and 1988 would be as follows:

12/31/87	Cash 2,000	
	Dividend revenue	2,000
12/31/88	Cash 1,000	
	Investment in Kaplan Corp. common	1,000

Kaplan's cumulative earnings for 1987 and 1988 are \$100,000 (\$150,000 − \$50,000). Johnson's share of these earnings would be \$2,000 (2% × \$100,000). Therefore, any dividends received in excess of \$2,000 represent a return *of* Johnson's investment rather than a return *on* the investment. Since Johnson received dividends of \$2,000 in 1987, the \$1,000 received in 1988 is a *liquidating dividend* and is thus a reduction in the investment, rather than dividend revenue. In summary, to the extent that Kaplan distributes assets representing earnings before 1987 (when Johnson acquired its interest in Kaplan), the receipt is a return of a portion of Johnson's original investment. That is, a portion of the investment is being converted to cash. Note that we determine whether a particular dividend payment is a liquidating dividend or an ordinary dividend to the investor by comparing *cumulative* earnings since acquisition with *cumulative* dividends since acquisition.

Lower-of-Cost-or-Market Method

The lower-of-cost-or-market method of valuing inventories was described in Chapter 10. For common stocks, the general philosophy is similar, but the specific application of the lower-of-cost-or-market method differs. The lower-of-cost-or-market method is an extension of the cost method. Acquisition of common stocks, disposal of common stocks, and recognition of dividend income are identical under the cost and lower-of-cost-or-market methods. The only difference between the two methods is that changes in market value are not recognized in the accounts under the cost method, whereas changes in market value (as long as market value is less than cost) are recorded in the accounts under the lower-of-cost-or-market method.

Lower of cost or market is appropriate for valuing marketable, passive common stock investments.

The lower-of-cost-or-market method of valuation is required for investments in common stock which (1) are marketable and (2) do not provide the investor with the ability to exercise significant influence over the investee. A common stock investment is deemed marketable if sales prices or bid and ask prices are currently available on a national securities exchange or in an over-the-counter market.[9]

The lower-of-cost-or-market method must be applied to the *portfolio* of marketable equity securities on an *aggregate* basis. If an entity owns both short-term and long-term investments in marketable equity securities, all short-term investments constitute one portfolio and all long-term investments constitute another portfolio. The lower-of-cost-or-market method is applied separately to the short-term and long-term portfolios. The basic rationale for applying the method on an aggregate basis is that businesses tend to view the collection of securities in total as a single resource when they evaluate risk and return characteristics of investments. Accounting for market value and cost differences on an individual-item basis would be inconsistent with this perspective.[10]

Because the lower-of-cost-or-market method is applied on an aggregate basis, the individual accounts that make up the portfolio are not adjusted when the portfolio value changes. Instead, the carrying value of the portfolio is reduced to market value by the use of a valuation account, called allowance for excess of cost over market value of security investments. This contra account is like the allowance for doubtful accounts for receivables. The individual securities that make up the portfolio continue to be carried at acquisition cost. When the balance of the contra account is deducted from the cost of the securities, the portfolio of marketable equity securities is reported at the lower-of-cost-or-market value.

[9] *FASB Statement No. 12*, para. 7(b).

[10] *FASB Statement No. 12*, para. 31. Further support for an aggregate approach is provided by modern portfolio theory, which argues that the relevant variables to an investor are the risk and return characteristics of the portfolio, rather than the risk and return characteristics of the individual securities that make up the portfolio.

To apply the lower-of-cost-or-market method at the end of each reporting period, the firm compares the aggregate market value of the portfolio of securities held at the end of the period with the acquisition cost. If market value exceeds or equals cost, the valuation allowance is adjusted to a zero balance. If cost exceeds market value, the valuation allowance is adjusted to the difference between cost and market value. If the required adjustment to the allowance account is a credit, implying that cost exceeds the market value of the portfolio by a greater amount at the end of the period than at the beginning, the offsetting debit is considered to be an *unrealized* loss on the portfolio. If the required adjustment to the allowance account is a debit, implying that cost exceeds market value by a lesser amount at the end of the period than at the beginning, the offsetting credit is considered to be a *recovery of a previously recorded unrealized loss.*

To illustrate the lower-of-cost-or-market method, assume that Sanders Corporation acquired the following marketable equity securities as short-term investments during 1987, its first year of operations:

SECURITY	NUMBER OF SHARES	ACQUISITION COST
A	200	$4,000
B	100	5,000
C	400	4,000

The following summary journal entry reflects the acquisitions:

Investment in securities 13,000		
Cash...		13,000

At the end of 1987, the market values per share of securities A, B, and C are $24, $40, and $9, respectively. Assuming that the lower-of-cost-or-market method is appropriate for these securities (that is, they are marketable and they do not permit the investor to exercise significant influence over the investee), the balance of the valuation allowance at the end of 1987 should be $600:

Acquisition cost		$13,000
Aggregate market value:		
Security A ($24 × 200 shares) $4,800		
Security B ($40 × 100 shares) 4,000		
Security C ($9 × 400 shares) 3,600		(12,400)
Valuation allowance		$ 600

The following end-of-period adjusting entry recognizes the unrealized loss of $600 and adjusts the carrying value of the securities portfolio to the market value of $12,400:

Unrealized loss on security investments 600	
Allowance for excess of cost over market value of	
security investments	600

The unrealized loss is reported in the income statement.

Now assume that during 1988, Sanders sells its shares of security B for $45 per share and makes the following entry to record the disposal:

Cash ($45 × 100 shares) 4,500	
Loss on security investment 500	
Investment in securities ($50 × 100 shares)..............	5,000

Note that the unrealized loss recorded on the portfolio at the end of 1987 has no relevance when the disposal of security *B* is recorded. The valuation allowance relates to the entire portfolio and not to any particular security. Hence, the gain or loss on the sale of common stock is the difference between the acquisition cost and the sales price—the same approach as that used under the cost method of valuation.

Finally, assume that during 1988 Sanders acquires as a temporary investment 50 shares of security *D* at $30 per share. At the end of 1988 market values per share are $18, $11, and $21 for securities *A, C,* and *D,* respectively. With these values, the required balance in the valuation allowance for the portfolio at the end of 1988 is calculated as follows:

Acquisition cost ($4,000 + $4,000 + $1,500)		$9,500
Aggregate market value:		
Security *A* ($18 × 200 shares)	$3,600	
Security *C* ($11 × 400 shares)	4,400	
Security *D* ($21 × 50 shares)	1,050	(9,050)
Valuation allowance		$ 450

Since the allowance balance for the portfolio at the end of 1987 was $600, and at the end of 1988 a balance of $450 is required, Sanders must reduce the allowance by $150 ($600 − $450):

Allowance for excess of cost over market value of security		
investments 150		
Recovery of unrealized loss on security investments		150

The balance of the account "recovery of unrealized loss on security investments" ($150) is shown in the income statement under "other income (expense)."

Lower of cost or market illustrates conservatism.
The lower-of-cost-or-market method provides an excellent illustration of *conservatism* as a constraint on the application of generally accepted accounting principles. Declines in market value below cost are recognized, but increases in market value are recognized only to the extent of recovery of previously recognized losses.

In the following sections we extend the discussion of the lower-of-cost-or-market method. Because there is a difference between the application of the method to temporary investments and long-term investments, the application of the method to these two types of investments is discussed separately in the next two sections. Accounting for nontemporary declines in market value is then described, followed by a discussion of accounting for a change in classification of investments in marketable equity securities. We conclude our coverage of the lower-of-cost-or-market method by discussing the required financial statement disclosures.

TEMPORARY INVESTMENTS IN MARKETABLE EQUITY SECURITIES   As previously noted, temporary investments in marketable equity securities generally are made to generate a low-risk return on otherwise idle cash. The investor places the funds in assets that can be converted readily back into cash as needed. Thus, the market value of these securities has direct relevance to financial statement users who wish to assess the entity's cash-generating ability; it is relevant because the primary source of cash flow is the market price of the securities. Changes in the valuation allowance are included in the income statement as "unrealized losses" or "recovery of unrealized losses." The losses are considered to be unrealized because uncertainty still exists about the ultimate cash flow from the securities. That is, the market price may change before the securities are sold. Recall from Chapter 2 that *realization* requires, among other things, that the amount and timing of cash inflows must be reasonably determinable. Because a firm intends to convert temporary investments into cash in the near future, and the loss in value thus will be realized in the near future, the valuation adjustments are included in income.

LONG-TERM INVESTMENTS IN MARKETABLE EQUITY SECURITIES   Long-term (noncurrent) investments in marketable equity securities, by definition, are intended to be held for more than one year or one operating cycle, whichever is longer. The purpose of such investments generally is to establish a *continuing,* rather than temporary, economic relationship with the investee. Since the intent of the investor is to *hold* the stock rather than to sell it, the market value of the stock as of the date of the balance sheet may not be as relevant as it is for temporary investments. That is, the amount of cash that could be generated from the sale of long-term investments may not be relevant because there is no intent to sell. The primary source of cash flow from these investments is dividends.

As a result of the above reasoning, changes in the carrying value of the portfolio of long-term investments must be shown directly in stockholders' equity; these changes are not included in the determination of net income.[11] This characteristic is the only difference between accounting and reporting requirements for marketable temporary investments in common stock and long-term common stock investments that are accounted for by the lower-of-cost-or-market method.

The difference in the reporting for changes in the carrying value of temporary and long-term investments came about in the following way: In the *Exposure Draft* preceding *Statement No. 12,* the FASB proposed that all marketable securities should be lumped together into one portfolio and that changes in the carrying value of that portfolio should be reported currently in net income. Many respondents to the *Exposure Draft* pointed out, however, that the inclusion in net income of fluctuations in the market value of long-term investments would distort net income and would not be understood by investors. While the FASB did not agree with these arguments, it decided not to include unrealized gains and losses on long-term assets in the determination of net income because the conceptual question of whether such gains and losses constitute income remained unresolved. The Board settled on the reporting of unrealized gains and losses on long-term marketable securities as a part of stockholders' equity, thus leaving the more general issue of holding gains and losses on long-term assets unresolved.

The Board opted for showing changes in the carrying value of the long-term investment portfolio in the equity section of the balance sheet because current practice at the time *Statement No. 12* was issued would be least affected by this alternative. It appears that the FASB's objective was to introduce a requirement for market value disclosures, but to do so in a way that had a minimal impact on current practice. Further, the FASB justified the treatment on grounds that could not readily support the general use of market values for other long-term assets.

NONTEMPORARY DECLINES IN MARKET VALUE   If a decline below cost in the market value of a marketable equity security investment classified as noncurrent is "nontemporary," the investment account balance must be reduced *directly* to a new cost basis. For example, if the fair market value of an investment in common stock with a book value of $10,000 declines to $6,000, and management determines that the decline is nontemporary, the following entry is required:

Realized loss from decline in market value of investments 4,000
 Investment in common stock 4,000

[11] *FASB Statement No. 12,* para. 11.

The amount of the reduction is accounted for as a *realized* loss on the income statement; the investment balance of $6,000 becomes the new carrying basis for application of the lower-of-cost-or-market method.[12] The loss is considered *realized* because presumably the net cash flow effect can be determined with reasonable certainty.

The FASB has created an area where judgments are difficult. When are market price changes "temporary" and when are they "nontemporary"? Does "nontemporary" mean "permanent"? The ability to make these judgments is rare, and accountants certainly do not appear to have any comparative advantage in this regard over other segments of the population. Nevertheless, this judgment must be made to determine whether declines in market value below cost for noncurrent investments are "unrealized" (and thus reflected in stockholders' equity) or "realized" (and thus included in the determination of net income). The only guidance the FASB provides is the advice that accountants should consider "all available evidence," including (1) realized gains or losses on disposition and (2) changes in market price after the balance sheet date but before the issuance of financial statements.[13]

CHANGE IN CLASSIFICATION   The intent of the investor determines how investments in marketable equity securities should be classified on the balance sheet. Thus, a change in intent with respect to a particular security leads to a change in its classification.[14] The change in classification may be from current to noncurrent or from noncurrent to current. *Statement No. 12* requires that securities transferred in either direction between the current and noncurrent portfolios must be recorded at the lower-of-cost-or-market value at the transfer date. If market value is below cost, the investor must treat the market value as the

Lower of cost or market at date of change in classification becomes the new cost basis.

cost basis for subsequent accounting. The reduction in carrying value is reported as a *realized loss* in the determination of net income. The effect of this treatment is the same as if the firm had sold the stock for cash, realized a loss, and then immediately reacquired the same stock with a different intent.

To illustrate, assume that Reif Company holds common shares that it acquired for $40,000 several years ago as a noncurrent asset. Reif has accounted for the investment under the lower-of-cost-or-market method. The market price is now $34,000, and Reif decides to sell the stock as soon as possible to generate cash. The following entry is required to reflect the change in intent:

Realized loss on reclassification of investments..............	6,000	
Temporary investments (current)..........................	34,000	
Investments (noncurrent)		40,000

The new cost basis for the stock is $34,000. If the market value later increases above $34,000, Reif will not record the increase in the accounts.

The purpose of the accounting requirements for reclassification is to reduce the incentive to transfer stocks between portfolios with the intent of manipulating income. Without the reclassification method demonstrated, the investor could affect income by transferring stock between current and noncurrent portfolios. The opportunity to affect income lies in the different treatment of changes in market value for the current and noncurrent portfolios. For example, assume a company acquires shares of common stock as a temporary investment of idle cash for $10,000; the shares are held for one period and

---

[12] *FASB Statement No. 12*, para. 21.

[13] "Changes in Market Value after the Balance Sheet Date," *Interpretation No. 12* (Stamford, Conn.: FASB, 1976), para. 3.

[14] Entities presenting unclassified balance sheets treat the entire portfolio of stock investments as noncurrent (*FASB Statement No. 12*, para. 9).

the market value at the end of that period is $8,000. If there were no requirement that securities transferred between current and noncurrent must be recorded at the lower of cost or market, this company could conveniently change its intent and reclassify the securities as long-term so that the $2,000 unrealized loss would bypass the income statement and appear in stockholders' equity. With the reclassification requirement, however, the company must include a realized loss of $2,000 in the income statement if it changes the classification. Furthermore, the firm could not increase income in future periods if market value should rise above $8,000, because $8,000 would constitute the new cost basis for the securities.

REQUIRED DISCLOSURES The financial statements and accompanying notes must disclose the following information for investments in marketable equity securities accounted for by the lower-of-cost-or-market method:

1. For *each balance sheet* presented, the aggregate cost and the aggregate market value for both the current and noncurrent portfolios, with identification of the carrying amount for each portfolio.

2. For the *latest balance sheet,* separately for the current and noncurrent portfolios:
   a) Gross unrealized gains (excess of market value over cost for all securities for which market value exceeds cost).
   b) Gross unrealized losses (excess of cost over market value for all securities for which cost exceeds market value).

3. For *each income statement* presented:
   a) Net realized gain or loss included in net income.
   b) The basis for determining cost (average cost, FIFO, etc.) in calculating realized gain or loss.
   c) The change in the valuation allowance(s) that has been included in the equity section of the balance sheet and in the determination of net income.

4. Significant net realized gains and losses and net unrealized gains and losses that occur after the date of the financial statements but before their issuance.[15]

To illustrate these disclosures, assume that the information for Thurston Corporation's investments shown in Exhibit 14–1 is available on December 31, 1988 (all securities were acquired during 1987). During 1988 Thurston made the following sales of stock (it sold no stock in 1987):

SECURITY	NET PROCEEDS OF SALE	COST	REALIZED GAIN (LOSS)
A	$125,000	$100,000	$ 25,000
B	65,000	100,000	(35,000)
	$190,000	$200,000	$(10,000)

The valuation allowances required on December 31, 1988, are as follows:

	DEDUCTED FROM INCOME	DEDUCTED FROM EQUITY
In current assets:		
Cost ($900,000) less market ($850,000)	$50,000	
In noncurrent assets:		
Cost ($650,000) less market ($540,000)		$110,000

[15] *FASB Statement No. 12,* paras. 12 and 13.

EXHIBIT 14–1   MARKETABLE EQUITY SECURITY INVESTMENTS

Thurston Corporation

	DECEMBER 31, 1988			DECEMBER 31, 1987		
	COST	MARKET	UNREALIZED GAIN (LOSS)	COST	MARKET	UNREALIZED GAIN (LOSS)
In current assets:						
Security *A*	$100,000	$100,000	$ —	$200,000	$250,000	$ 50,000
Security *B*	200,000	150,000	(50,000)	300,000	250,000	(50,000)
Security *C*	200,000	175,000	(25,000)	200,000	150,000	(50,000)
Security *D*	150,000	100,000	(50,000)	150,000	200,000	50,000
Security *E*	50,000	100,000	50,000	50,000	75,000	25,000
Security *F*	200,000	225,000	25,000	—	—	—
Total of portfolio	$900,000	$850,000	$ (50,000)	$900,000	$925,000	$ 25,000
Valuation allowance, current			$ (50,000)			$ –0–
In noncurrent assets:						
Security *G*	$300,000	$200,000	$(100,000)	$300,000	$100,000	$(200,000)
Security *H*	100,000	190,000	90,000	100,000	250,000	150,000
Security *I*	250,000	150,000	(100,000)	250,000	150,000	(100,000)
Total of portfolio	$650,000	$540,000	$(110,000)	$650,000	$500,000	$(150,000)
Valuation allowance, noncurrent			$(110,000)			$(150,000)

Source: Adapted from *FASB Statement No. 12*, Appendix B.

The balance sheet and footnote disclosures related to the above information are shown in Exhibit 14–2.

In summary, the lower-of-cost-or-market method must be used to account for investments in marketable equity securities, both temporary and long-term, that do not permit the investor to exercise significant influence over the investee. Adjustments to the valuation allowance are included in the income statement for temporary investments, but are included in stockholders' equity for long-term investments. If a long-term investment in equity securities enables the investor to exercise significant influence over the investee, the investment must be accounted for by the equity method, which is described in the next section.

Equity Method

The equity method is appropriate for common stock investments in which the investor significantly influences the investee.

The equity method of valuation must be used to account for long-term investments in common stock in which the investor exercises significant influence over the investee. Significant influence is *presumed* to exist if the investment constitutes 20 percent or more of the investee's outstanding voting common stock. However, as described in our discussion of the cost method, this presumption may be overcome by predominant evidence to the contrary.

Under the equity method, as income is earned by the investee, a proportionate share of that income is presumed to accrue to the investor. Thus, when the investee's net assets increase as a result of earnings, the investor increases its investment account to record its share of the increase in the investee's net assets:

Investment . . . . *xx*
    Investment revenue (or equity in income of investee) . . . .   *xx*

When the investee declares dividends, the dividend reduces the net assets of the investee, and the investor accordingly reduces its investment account by its share of the decrease in net assets:

Cash (or dividends receivable) .... *xx*
Investment.. *xx*

EXHIBIT 14—2   LOWER-OF-COST-OR-MARKET DISCLOSURES

Thurston Corporation

	12/31/88	12/31/87
Current assets		
Marketable equity securities, carried at market in 1988 and at cost in 1987 (Note 1)	$850,000	$900,000
Noncurrent assets		
Marketable equity securities, carried at market in 1988 and in 1987 (Note 1)	540,000	500,000
Stockholders' equity		
Net unrealized loss on noncurrent marketable equity securities (Note 1)	(110,000)	(150,000)

NOTES TO FINANCIAL STATEMENTS

Note 1—Marketable Equity Securities

The Corporation's current portfolio and noncurrent portfolio of marketable equity securities are carried at their lower-of-cost-or-market values at the balance sheet date. Marketable equity securities included in current and noncurrent assets had costs of $900,000 and $650,000, respectively, at December 31, 1988. Marketable equity securities included in current and noncurrent assets had market values of $925,000 and $500,000, respectively, at December 31, 1987. At December 31, 1988, gross unrealized gains and gross unrealized losses pertaining to the marketable equity securities in the portfolios were as follows:

	GROSS UNREALIZED GAINS	GROSS UNREALIZED LOSSES
Current	$75,000*	$125,000†
Noncurrent	$90,000‡	$200,000§

* Securities *E* and *F:* $50,000 + $25,000.

† Securities *B, C,* and *D:* $50,000 + $25,000 + $50,000.

‡ Security *H:* $90,000.

§ Securities *G* and *I:* $100,000 + $100,000.

A net realized loss of $10,000 on the sale of marketable equity securities was included in the determination of net income for 1988. The cost of the securities sold was based on the average cost of all the shares of each such security held at the time of sale. The Corporation sold no marketable equity securities during 1987. To reduce the carrying amount of the current marketable equity securities portfolio to market, which was lower than cost at December 31, 1988, a valuation allowance in the amount of $50,000 was established with a corresponding charge to net income at that date.

To reduce the carrying amount of the noncurrent marketable equity securities portfolio to market, which was lower than cost at December 31, 1987, a valuation allowance in the amount of $150,000 was established with a corresponding charge to stockholders' equity representing the net unrealized loss.

At December 31, 1988, to reflect a recovery of $40,000 of market value, the valuation allowance related to the noncurrent portfolio was reduced by $40,000 with a corresponding reduction in the previously established charge to stockholders' equity.

Increases (via earnings) and decreases (via losses and dividends) in net assets of the investee are presumed to "flow through" to the investor as they occur. Since the investor presumably can influence the investee's dividend policy, the investor could "realize" (convert to cash) the recorded increase in the investment account by influencing the investee to pay dividends. Conversely, dividends received represent a realization of earnings previously recorded in the investment account. The equity method is thus an extension of accrual accounting to common stock investments.

The following steps are involved in applying the equity method:

Steps in applying the equity method.

1. Record the initial investment at its acquisition cost.

2. Record the investor's share of the investee's net income as an increase in the investment account and as investment revenue. Record the investor's share of the investee's net loss as a decrease in the investment account and as investment loss.

3. Record the investor's share of the investee's dividends as a decrease in the investment account.

4. The acquisition cost may differ from the book value of the underlying interest in the investee's net assets at the date of acquisition. If so, the investor must adjust the earnings recorded by amortizing the excess of cost over book value (or book value over cost) which arises from the following circumstances:

a) An excess of *cost over book value* may arise because:

i. Assets of the investee are *undervalued* in terms of the price paid by the investor.

ii. The investor pays a premium because of *unrecorded goodwill* applicable to the investee.

b) An excess of *book value over cost* may arise because assets of the investee are *overvalued* in terms of the price paid by the investor.

To the extent that these overvaluations or undervaluations would affect the investee's net income *if they were recorded by the investee,* the investor must adjust the investment account and investment revenue. For example, undervalued depreciable assets of the investee understate depreciation expense and thus overstate the investee's net income. Thus, the investor must reduce the amount of investee earnings recorded as investment revenue to reflect depreciation based on the fair market value of the depreciable assets as evidenced by the price paid for the investee's stock. If the overvalued or undervalued assets are not depreciable or amortizable, no adjustment to investment revenue and the investment account is required. As a result of steps 2 through 4, the investor's investment account moves in tandem with changes in the net assets of the investee.

5. The investor's share of the investee's extraordinary items and of the cumulative effect of a change in accounting principle should be reported in a similar fashion in the investor's income statement, if they are material to the investor.

To illustrate the equity method, we will use the same data that we employed in Chapter 13 in our discussion of goodwill. Assume that at the beginning of 1987, Takeover Company acquires 40 percent (10,000 shares), rather than the 100 percent assumed in Chapter 13, of the outstanding common stock of Easymark Corporation at a cost of $400,000, thus gaining significant influence over Easymark's operating and financing policies. The book value of Easymark's net assets at the beginning of 1987 is $900,000. The entry to record the acquisition is:

Investment in Easymark	400,000	
Cash		400,000

Easymark Corporation has net income of $120,000 in 1987:

```
Investment in Easymark ................................ 48,000
    Investment revenue ...................................        48,000
(.40 × $120,000)
```

Dividends declared and paid by Easymark during 1987 amount to $60,000:

```
Cash .................................................. 24,000
    Investment in Easymark ..............................        24,000
(.40 × $60,000)
```

Takeover paid $40,000 [$400,000 − .4($900,000)] more than book value for its 40 percent interest in Easymark Corporation. Of this amount, assume that $10,000 is attributable to undervalued depreciable plant assets with a remaining life of 4 years and that the remainder ($30,000) is attributable to unrecorded goodwill. Recall that in Chapter 13, with a 100 percent acquisition, these amounts were $25,000 and $75,000. It is decided that 30 years is a reasonable period over which to amortize the unrecorded goodwill. Since Takeover's investment account moves in tandem with changes in Easymark's net assets, Takeover must eliminate the excess of cost over book value recorded in the investment account as Easymark's undervalued assets are consumed in operations. Although Easymark does not adjust the carrying value of its assets to reflect their implied fair market values, Takeover must adjust its investment account and investment revenue to reflect Easymark's net income on the basis of the implied fair market values established in Takeover's acquisition of Easymark's stock. Thus, Takeover makes the following adjusting entry:

```
Investment revenue ..................................... 3,500
    Investment in Easymark ..............................        3,500
To record amortization of unrecorded goodwill of $1,000 ($30,000
÷ 30 years) and depreciation on undervalued plant assets of
$2,500 ($10,000 ÷ 4 years).
```

The investment in Easymark Corporation has a balance of $420,500 at the end of 1987:

Acquisition cost	$400,000
Net income, 1987	48,000
Dividends, 1987	(24,000)
Amortization of unrecorded goodwill	(1,000)
Depreciation of undervalued plant assets	(2,500)
Balance, 12/31/87	$420,500

If Takeover sold 4,000 of the 10,000 shares for $200,000 at the beginning of 1988, the following journal entry would be required:

```
Cash .................................................. 200,000
    Investment in Easymark ..............................        168,200*
    Gain on sale of investment ..........................         31,800
```

$$* \$420,500 \times \frac{4,000 \text{ shares}}{10,000 \text{ shares}} = \$168,200.$$

In the remainder of this section we extend our discussion of the equity method. The next two sections describe appropriate accounting for (1) a change from some other method to the equity method, and (2) a change from the equity method. We then discuss the unusual situation in which the investor's share of investee losses exceeds the cost of the investment. The equity method discussion concludes with a description of required financial statement disclosures and a discussion of the concept of "significant influence."

CHANGE TO THE EQUITY METHOD   Circumstances may not permit an investor in common stock to exercise significant influence over the investee. In such cases, the investment does not qualify for the equity method. If the investor subsequently gains significant influence (for example, by increasing the proportion of ownership), the investor must adopt the equity method of accounting for the investment. The change in accounting principle from the cost method to the equity method requires the investor to adjust (1) the investment account, (2) prior period income statements presented currently, and (3) retained earnings, as if the equity method had been applied to the investment in prior years.[16] The objective is to make prior period financial statements appear as they would have had the equity method been applied during those periods, thus making them comparable to current and future statements that are based on the equity method.

Assume, for example, that Tan Corporation acquires 10 percent of the outstanding common shares of Brown Corporation at the beginning of 1987 for $240,000. The 10 percent interest does not permit Tan to gain significant influence over Brown. The book value of Brown's net assets at the acquisition date is $2 million. Net income and dividend payments of Brown Corporation are as follows:

YEAR	NET INCOME	DIVIDENDS
1987	$300,000	$100,000
1988	400,000	150,000
1989	500,000	200,000

At the beginning of 1989, when the book value of Brown's net assets is $2.6 million, Tan acquires an additional 30 percent of the outstanding common shares for $850,000. Acquisition of the additional shares enables Tan to exercise significant influence over Brown's operations. The difference between the acquisition price and the book value of both the initial 10 percent acquisition and the additional 30 percent acquisition is attributed to unrecorded goodwill, which should be amortized over 40 years from the acquisition date.

Tan must use the cost method to account for the investment in Brown for 1987 and 1988 (assuming that the securities are not actively traded, and therefore the lower-of-cost-or-market method is inappropriate) and must change to the equity method at the beginning of 1989. The following journal entries are required to account for the investment in Brown Corporation. At the beginning of 1987:

Investment in Brown Corp. 240,000
  Cash 240,000
To record investment.

---

[16] This retroactive treatment of the effect of the change in accounting principle is an exception to the *general* requirement that the cumulative effect of changes in accounting principles should be reflected in the income statement in the period of change. For further discussion of changes in accounting principles, see Chapter 22.

At the end of 1987:

```
Cash. . . . . . . . . . . . . . . . . . . . . . . . . . . . . . . . . . . . . . . . . . . . . . .  10,000
    Dividend revenue . . . . . . . . . . . . . . . . . . . . . . . . . . . . . . . . . . .           10,000
    To record dividends received (.10 × $100,000).
```

At the end of 1988:

```
Cash. . . . . . . . . . . . . . . . . . . . . . . . . . . . . . . . . . . . . . . . . . . . . . .  15,000
    Dividend revenue . . . . . . . . . . . . . . . . . . . . . . . . . . . . . . . . . . .           15,000
    To record dividends received (.10 × $150,000).
```

At the beginning of 1989:

```
Investment in Brown Corp. . . . . . . . . . . . . . . . . . . . . . . . . . . . . 850,000
    Cash. . . . . . . . . . . . . . . . . . . . . . . . . . . . . . . . . . . . . . . . . . . . .          850,000
    To record additional investment.

Investment in Brown Corp. . . . . . . . . . . . . . . . . . . . . . . . . . . . .  43,000
    Retained earnings . . . . . . . . . . . . . . . . . . . . . . . . . . . . . . . . . . .           43,000
    To adjust investment account and retained earnings to reflect equity
    method applied retroactively, calculated as follows:
```

	1987	1988	TOTAL
Tan's interest (10%) in Brown's earnings	$30,000	$40,000	$70,000
Amortization of unrecorded goodwill {[$240,000 − .10($2,000,000)] ÷ 40 years}	(1,000)	(1,000)	(2,000)
Equity method revenue	$29,000	$39,000	$68,000
Dividends (already recorded as revenue under the cost method)	(10,000)	(15,000)	(25,000)
Increase in investment and retained earnings to reflect the equity method	$19,000	$24,000	$43,000

At the end of 1989:

```
Investment in Brown Corp. . . . . . . . . . . . . . . . . . . . . . . . . . . . . 200,000
    Investment revenue. . . . . . . . . . . . . . . . . . . . . . . . . . . . . . . . . . .          200,000
    To record share of Brown's earnings: (.40 × $500,000).

Investment revenue. . . . . . . . . . . . . . . . . . . . . . . . . . . . . . . . . . .   2,750
    Investment in Brown Corp. . . . . . . . . . . . . . . . . . . . . . . . . . . . .            2,750
    To adjust share of earnings for amortization of unrecorded
    goodwill:
```

1987 acquisition:
  [$240,000 − .10($2,000,000)] ÷ 40 years = $1,000

1989 acquisition:
  [$850,000 − .30($2,600,000)] ÷ 40 years = 1,750
                                            $2,750

```
Cash. . . . . . . . . . . . . . . . . . . . . . . . . . . . . . . . . . . . . . . . . . . . . . .  80,000
    Investment in Brown Corp. . . . . . . . . . . . . . . . . . . . . . . . . . . . .           80,000
    To record dividends received (.4 × $200,000).
```

Note that Tan changes to the equity method at the beginning of 1989 by crediting retained earnings and debiting investment in Brown Corporation for $43,000. This adjustment reflects the fact that retained earnings and the investment account would have been $43,000 greater if Tan had been using the equity method in 1987 and 1988. This adjustment has no effect on reported earnings in 1989, the period of change. The financial statements for 1987 and 1988, if presented at the end of 1989 or later for comparative purposes, must be restated to reflect the retroactive application of the equity method.

CHANGE FROM THE EQUITY METHOD   When circumstances lead the investor to lose significant influence over the investee, either because of reduction in the number of shares held or for other reasons, the investor must change from the equity method of valuation to either the cost method or the lower-of-cost-or-market method. When such a change occurs, the carrying value of the investment at the time of the change becomes the cost basis for subsequent accounting. There is no retroactive calculation to determine what the balance in the investment account would have been had the cost method been used in prior periods. The effect of using the equity method in prior periods remains in the investment account and in retained earnings.

A change from the equity method also means that, at the time of change, the investor discontinues amortization of undervalued or overvalued assets. Since the investor does not record its share of investee earnings under either the cost method or the lower-of-cost-or-market method, there is no need to adjust those earnings for overvalued or undervalued assets.

INVESTEE LOSSES IN EXCESS OF COST   It is possible that an investor's share of investee losses may exceed the carrying value of the investment. Applying the equity method, the investor would record its share of investee losses as a debit to investment revenue (or investment loss) and a credit to the investment account. However, after the investment account has been reduced to zero, the investor normally should not record additional losses. In other words, application of the equity method normally stops when the carrying value of the investment account reaches zero. If operations again become profitable, the equity method should be resumed only when the investor's share of profits exceeds the investor's *unrecorded* share of the investee's losses incurred when the investor was not applying the equity method.

The investor should continue to apply the equity method, thus producing a credit balance in the investment account, in two special circumstances: (1) when the investor is committed to provide further economic support to the investee beyond the amount of the original investment (for example, if the investor has guaranteed certain obligations of the investee), and (2) when the investee's return to profitable operations seems assured in the near future (for example, if the investee's loss is due to an isolated, nonrecurring situation that is not expected to have an adverse effect on future profitability).[17]

---

[17] *APB Opinion No. 18,* para. 19(i). The reason is unclear for these exceptions to the general rule that application of the equity method should cease when the investment account is reduced to zero. Note that continued application of the equity method in such circumstances produces a credit balance in the investment account. The authoritative literature does not discuss the nature of this credit balance for financial reporting purposes. We do not believe the exceptions are justified. If the investor has commitments to the investee beyond the amount of the investment, perhaps a liability exists, but it is unlikely that continued application of the equity method will produce a reasonable estimate of the amount of the liability. When the equity method continues to be applied under the second special circumstance, it is likewise difficult to see how the credit balance in the investment account could be perceived as a liability.

REQUIRED DISCLOSURES   The significance of an investment to the investor is a factor in determining the extent of disclosure required. Generally, the following disclosures are appropriate for equity method investments:

1. The name of each investee and the percentage of ownership of common stock.

2. The accounting policies of the investor with respect to investments in common stock.

3. Any difference between the carrying value of an investment and the underlying equity in the investee's net assets, and the accounting treatment of the difference.

4. The market value of each common stock investment for which a quoted market price is available (except investments in common stock of subsidiaries).

5. When equity method investments are material to the investor, summarized information as to assets, liabilities, and results of operations of the investees may be necessary, either individually or in groups.[18]

The above disclosures may be combined when the investor has investments in common stock of more than one entity. Also, the investor must disclose the reasons for using the equity method for investments of less than 20 percent and for not using the equity method for minority investments of 20 percent or more.

An example of actual disclosures related to equity method investments is provided by a recent annual report of U.S. Steel, presented in Exhibit 14–4, at the end of this chapter.

THE CONCEPT OF SIGNIFICANT INFLUENCE   As has been shown in the discussions about each valuation method, judgment is required to determine whether significant influence exists. This point has been highlighted by some investors who have claimed significant influence even though the circumstances indicated otherwise. For example, during the third quarter of 1979, Curtiss-Wright Corporation changed to the equity method in accounting for its 14.3 percent investment in Kennecott Copper Corporation, which is about six times larger than Curtiss-Wright. In 1978 Curtiss-Wright had failed in an attempt to change Kennecott's board of directors, but subsequently gained representation following court actions. Curtiss-Wright also entered into an agreement with Kennecott limiting Curtiss-Wright's ownership percentage to not more than 21 percent. Curtiss-Wright claimed, and their auditors concurred, that the presence of three Curtiss-Wright directors on Kennecott's 18-member board was adequate evidence of ability to exercise significant influence, and thus justified the use of the equity method. The change from the cost method to the equity method increased Curtiss-Wright's earnings for the first nine months of 1979 from $13.8 million ($1.64 per share) to $21.3 million ($2.55 per share).[19]

Such situations led to *Interpretation No. 35* by the FASB in May 1981. The purpose of this *Interpretation* was to clarify the criteria for use of the equity method. The *Interpretation* reemphasizes the need to evaluate all facts and circumstances surrounding an investment rather than relying solely on percentage of ownership.

Immediately after *Interpretation No. 35* was issued, the SEC filed suit against McLouth Steel Corporation, accusing McLouth of incorrectly using the equity method to account for its 19.87 percent interest in Jewell Coal & Coke Company from 1974 until 1978, when McLouth sold its investment. McLouth, according to the SEC, had tried and failed to obtain representation on Jewell's board of directors. Also, Jewell had ignored McLouth's wishes on several corporate issues. Thus, the SEC argued that McLouth did not have the ability to influence Jewell. Without admitting or denying the charges,

[18] *APB Opinion No. 18,* para. 20.

[19] *The Wall Street Journal,* January 21, 1980, p. 14.

McLouth agreed to a court order barring future violations of both the antifraud section and the periodic reporting section of federal securities laws.[20]

The SEC action against McLouth, coupled with *Interpretation No. 35,* makes it apparent that *all* of the facts and circumstances surrounding minority ownership of common shares must be evaluated to justify the use of the equity method. The 20 percent ownership guideline now appears to be less important than it once was. It is likely that companies will tend to look a little harder even at investments in excess of 20 percent to determine whether use of the equity method is justified.

CONSOLIDATED FINANCIAL STATEMENTS   Some investments accounted for by the equity method convey *control,* rather than merely significant influence, to the investor. Generally, investments of more than 50 percent of the outstanding voting common stock of an investee provide such control. In these situations, referred to as *parent-subsidiary relationships,* it is generally desirable to view the combined entities as one economic entity. Consequently, the investment account is replaced by the individual assets and liabilities of the subsidiary on the balance sheet of the combined entities, and the investment revenue account is replaced by the revenues and expenses of the subsidiary on the income statement of the combined entities. The financial statements of the combined entities are referred to as **consolidated financial statements.**

The point of our discussion is to emphasize that not all equity-method investments are reported in the balance sheet as one amount within the investments category. For those that qualify for consolidation, the investment account is carried on the parent's separate books under the equity method. However, when consolidated financial statements are prepared, the investment account is eliminated for reporting purposes and replaced with the individual assets and liabilities of the subsidiary company. The rationale for this approach is that users should view the combined entities as one economic entity, and that combining the individual financial statement elements is more meaningful than merely showing a ''one-line consolidation''—the investment account.

The process of preparing consolidated financial statements is beyond the scope of our discussion. Likewise, a full understanding of the circumstances in which consolidation is appropriate for equity-method investments is beyond our purposes at this point. Advanced accounting textbooks describe these circumstances and the consolidation process in detail.

OTHER SECURITY INVESTMENTS

So far in this chapter, we have concentrated on the appropriate accounting for common stock investments. In addition to common stock, investors may hold other security investments:

1. Marketable debt securities, such as bonds.

2. Preferred stock.

3. Stock rights and warrants.

To complete our coverage of investments in securities of other companies, we discuss each of these investments in turn in this section.

---

[20] *The Wall Street Journal,* June 18, 1981, p. 10. See also ''A Bit More Equity,'' *Forbes,* August 17, 1981, p. 79.

MARKETABLE DEBT SECURITIES

Temporary Investments

The requirements of *FASB Statement No. 12* apply only to marketable *equity* securities, that is, common stock, nonredeemable preferred stock,[21] and rights to acquire such stocks. Accounting for *temporary* investments in marketable *debt* securities, such as bonds, continues to be governed by *Accounting Research Bulletin No. 43*.[22] *ARB No. 43* requires that such investments be carried at cost unless their market value falls significantly and permanently below cost, in which case the bond investment account balance should be reduced to the market value. The reduction in carrying value to market value is deducted in determining income. The market value at the time of the reduction becomes the new cost basis for the securities. Thus, subsequent recoveries in market value are not recognized in the accounts.

The issuance of *Statement No. 12* provided impetus to an already existing movement toward use of the lower-of-cost-or-market method to value marketable debt securities included in current assets. Thus, in practice, temporary investments in marketable debt securities are carried at *either* cost *or* lower of cost or market through the use of a valuation allowance. If a firm uses the lower-of-cost-or-market method, it should treat the portfolio of marketable debt securities separately from the portfolio of marketable equity securities.

Long-Term Investments

Long-term investments in debt securities (whether marketable or nonmarketable) are accounted for after acquisition by the cost method. Assume, for example, that on July 1, 1987, Avanti Corporation acquires bonds with a stated annual interest rate of 10 percent and a face value of $100,000. For the sake of simplicity, assume that the bonds are purchased at their face value. (Accounting for bonds acquired at more or less than face value is discussed in Chapter 16.) The bonds pay interest on June 30 and December 31 and mature on June 30, 1997. Avanti records the bond purchase as follows:

Bond investment	100,000	
Cash		100,000

Avanti must make the following entry on December 31, 1987, and on each subsequent interest date, to record interest revenue:

Cash	5,000	
Interest revenue		5,000
$(.10 \times 1/2 \times \$100,000)$		

If Avanti holds the bonds until maturity, it will record the receipt of the face value and the final interest payment as follows:

Cash	105,000	
Bond investment		100,000
Interest revenue		5,000

Thus, investments in debt securities are carried at either cost or lower of cost or

---

[21] Nonredeemable preferred stock is preferred stock that is not subject to a mandatory redemption requirement or that is redeemable solely at the option of the issuing entity.

[22] "Restatement and Revision of Accounting Research Bulletins," *Accounting Research Bulletin No. 43* (New York: AICPA, 1953), chap. 3A.

market, depending on the circumstances. Likewise, one of these two accounting methods must be used to account for preferred stock, as we describe in the following section.

PREFERRED STOCK

Nonredeemable preferred stock is an equity security as defined by *Statement No. 12*. Firms must account for investments in marketable, nonredeemable preferred stock by the lower-of-cost-or-market method, applied separately to the current and noncurrent portfolios of such equity securities. These securities are included in the portfolio (current or noncurrent, as appropriate) of marketable equity securities to apply the lower-of-cost-or-market method.

Investments in preferred stocks that are nonmarketable or redeemable must be accounted for by the cost method.[23] Because ownership of preferred shares cannot provide the owner with influence over the investee's operating and financial policies, the equity method is inappropriate.

STOCK RIGHTS

Owners of common or preferred stock often receive a *preemptive right* to purchase additional shares from a pending new issue of stock in proportion to their present holdings. Also, the right to acquire stock in exchange for cash and a warrant, which is a certificate evidencing such a right, may be *purchased* either separately or in conjunction with another security. Stock rights indicate the price at which stock can be acquired (the exercise price), the number of shares that may be acquired for each right, and the expiration date. Since the source of value of such securities is their relationship to a particular equity security, they also are equity securities. They are classified as either current or noncurrent depending on the intent of the investor.

Preemptive Stock Rights

Preemptive rights may be granted to existing stockholders to allow them to maintain their ownership proportion. When preemptive rights exist in a stock contract, the firm must issue stock rights to existing stockholders whenever it is attempting to sell additional shares. The rights provide the current stockholders with an opportunity to purchase additional stock at a specified price. Although one right is issued for each share held, the number of rights required to purchase an additional share depends on the terms of the offering. For example, the warrant evidencing the rights may indicate that a firm requires five rights plus a specified amount of cash for each additional share. Thus, each stockholder would be entitled to one additional share for each five shares held.

When an investor receives stock rights, the *total* book value of the investment remains unchanged. The investee has given up nothing and the investor has invested nothing beyond the original investment in shares to receive the rights. Between the announcement date of the rights and the date the rights are issued, the stock to which the rights relate is bought and sold in the marketplace **rights on,** which means the value of the rights is embedded in the stock price. After the issuance date, the rights trade separately from the stock and the stock is said to trade **ex-rights.** Thus, when a firm receives rights from a corporation, the total investment no longer is represented solely by the original shares held; it is represented by those shares *and* the rights. As a result, the firm must allocate the book value of the investment between the shares held and the new rights received, using the relative fair market value method.

Assume, for example, that Anderson Company owns 1,000 shares of common stock in Harkins Corporation, which it acquired for $20,000. Anderson subsequently receives one right for each share held. Anderson may purchase additional common shares in

[23] Redeemable preferred stock is subject to mandatory redemption requirements or the redemption feature is outside the control of the issuing entity.

exchange for two rights and $15 cash per share. The market price of the common stock is $26 per share immediately before the issuance of the rights (rights on), and $22 immediately after the rights are issued (ex-rights). The market price of the rights upon issuance is $2. Anderson allocates the $20,000 investment between the original shares and the rights as follows:

Market value of stock (ex-rights):
  $22 × 1,000 shares $22,000
Market value of rights:
  $2 × 1,000 rights 2,000
    Total market value of investment $24,000

Portion of cost allocated to stock:

$$\frac{\$22,000}{\$24,000} \times \$20,000 = \$18,333$$

$18,333 ÷ 1,000 shares = $18.333 per share

Portion of cost allocated to rights:

$$\frac{\$2,000}{\$24,000} \times \$20,000 = \$1,667$$

$1,667 ÷ 1,000 rights = $1.667 per right

The investment account still has a carrying value of $20,000. However, $1,667 (1,000 rights × $1.667 per right) of the $20,000 has been allocated to the rights. If desired, the following entry could be made:

Investment in Harkins Corp. rights 1,667
  Investment in Harkins Corp. common 1,667

The *book value* of the common shares for subsequent accounting purposes, such as recognition of gains and losses when the shares are sold, is $18.33 per share. Each right has a book value of $1.67.

The recipient of stock rights may dispose of them in three ways:

1. The rights may be exercised.

2. The rights may be sold. That is, the recipient sells warrants, which evidence the rights, to other investors.

3. The rights may be allowed to expire.

If Anderson exercises all of the rights for additional shares of Harkins, it will record the transaction as follows:

Investment in Harkins Corp. stock 9,167
  Investment in Harkins Corp. rights 1,667
  Cash ($15 × 500) 7,500

The book value per share of the common stock Anderson acquires by exercising the rights is $18.33, consisting of $15 cash and two stock rights with a book value of $1.667 each ($1.667 × 2 = $3.334).

If, instead, Anderson sells all of the rights for $2,000 ($2 each), it will make the following entry:

Cash.. 2,000		
Investment in Harkins Corp. rights........................	1,667	
Gain on sale of rights	333	

Because the rights have a carrying value of $1.667 each and Anderson sells them for $2 each, a gain of $333 [($2.00 − $1.667) × 1,000] results.

Finally, assume instead that Anderson allows the rights to expire. The firm should do that only if the rights have no value. The rights would be valueless if shares could be purchased in the market for less than the price specified by the rights. If the rights expire, Anderson makes the following journal entry:

Loss on expiration of stock rights........................... 1,667		
Investment in Harkins Corp. rights........................	1,667	

Purchased Stock Warrants

Investors who buy warrants, whether from an issuing corporation or from another investor, may either sell them to other investors or exercise them for a specified number of shares of stock at the specified price per share. Warrants generally expire at a particular date, although companies sometimes issue warrants without an expiration date (referred to as ''perpetual'' warrants). The issuing company may sell warrants either separately or as part of a unit with bonds or preferred stock, as a ''sweetener.'' In the latter case, the investor may detach the warrants and either sell them or exercise them.

Investors record stock warrants in the accounts at acquisition cost and account for them by the lower-of-cost-or-market method after acquisition (assuming that they are marketable). If the issuing company sells the warrants as part of a unit with another security, the investor must allocate the total cost of the unit between the warrants and the other security according to the relative fair market value approach. When the investor exercises the warrants, the book value of the warrants plus the cash paid when they are exercised becomes the cost basis for the new shares.

As an illustration, assume that Rook Corporation acquires 500 warrants for $2,500 cash, or $5 per warrant. Each warrant is exchangeable, along with $20 cash, for one share of Forest Products common. Rook makes the following journal entries to record the acquisition of the warrants and their subsequent exercise:

Investment in Forest Products warrants 2,500		
Cash..	2,500	
To record acquisition of warrants.		

Investment in Forest Products common 12,500		
Cash ($20 × 500 warrants)	10,000	
Investment in Forest Products warrants	2,500	
To record exercise of warrants.		

If the investor sells stock warrants rather than exercising them, the difference between the market value and the carrying value of the warrants is recorded as a gain or loss. If the warrants are allowed to expire, their carrying value is eliminated and recorded as a loss on expiration of stock warrants. Expiration should be a rare occurrence, because the exercise period generally is quite long.

In addition to acquiring securities through the types of transactions described up to this point in the chapter, companies also may obtain additional shares of stock as the result of investee stock splits and stock dividends. The accounting requirements for such transactions are described in the following section.

STOCK SPLITS AND STOCK DIVIDENDS

When a company issues a stock split or a stock dividend, current stockholders receive additional shares of stock on a pro rata basis, that is, in proportion to their current holdings. A firm accomplishes a stock split by reducing the par value or stated value per share, whereas a stock dividend involves the distribution of additional shares without a proportionate reduction in the par value or stated value. For example, if a firm has 100,000 shares of $10 par value common stock outstanding, a 2 for 1 stock split would result in the issuance of 100,000 more shares and a reduction of par value to $5 per share. In contrast, a 100 percent stock dividend would result in the issuance of 100,000 more shares without a reduction in the par value per share. While the legal distinction between a stock split and a stock dividend affects the issuer's accounting, the investor's accounting is not affected by this legal distinction.

The *total* carrying value (book value) of the investment is unaffected by the receipt of additional shares via a stock split or stock dividend. This situation is comparable to the receipt of stock rights from an investee. The investor must reduce the *per share* book value in proportion to the increase in the number of shares received. That is, the same investment amount is now represented by, and must be spread over, more shares.

Suppose that Boyd Corporation owns 1,000 shares of common stock in Duncan Company, acquired at a cost of $15,000 ($15 per share) and accounted for by the cost method. If Boyd receives one additional share for each 10 shares held (a 10 percent stock dividend), the book value per share is reduced to $13.64 ($15,000 ÷ 1,100 shares), rounded to the nearest cent. The investor makes no entry upon receipt of the additional shares. The investor must, however, note the change in the cost basis per share for subsequent accounting purposes. If 100 shares are subsequently sold for $2,000 ($20 per share), Boyd records the sale as follows:

Cash 2,000		
Investment in Duncan common	1,364	
Gain on sale of investments	636	
To record sale of 100 shares with a cost basis of $13.64 per share		
for $20 per share.		

In many cases, investors do not hold precisely the number of shares that permits receipt of a whole number of shares. For example, if a 10 percent stock dividend were declared, an investor who owned 95 shares would be entitled to 9.5 additional shares. In such instances, the issuing company either (1) pays cash equal to the market value of the fractional shares, which the investor records as a credit to the investment account because the receipt of cash constitutes a reduction in the cost of the remaining shares, or (2) issues **fractional share warrants,** which may be bought and sold by investors in the marketplace.

SUMMARY OF VALUATION METHODS

Exhibit 14–3 summaries the accounting requirements for investments in securities. If the intent of management is to hold the securities only as a short-term investment, the equity method is inappropriate. Only the cost method (for marketable debt securities) or the lower-of-cost-or-market method may be used. However, if the intent of management is to hold the investment beyond one year or one operating cycle, whichever is longer, and the investor exercises significant influence over the investee, the equity method is appropriate.

Securities of other companies constitute a major portion of the investments category in the balance sheets of many companies. Two other common items in the investments

EXHIBIT 14—3   ACCOUNTING FOR INVESTMENTS IN SECURITIES

INVESTMENT CHARACTERISTICS	ACCOUNTING METHOD
Current:	
Marketable, equity	Lower of cost or market
Marketable, debt	Cost or lower of cost or market
Noncurrent:	
Equity:	
Control (>50% ownership)	Equity*
Significant influence	Equity
No significant influence, marketable	Lower of cost or market
No significant influence, nonmarketable	Cost†
Debt	Cost†

* Consolidated financial statements usually required.

† Reduce to recoverable value if it declines significantly and permanently below cost.

category are special-purpose funds and the cash surrender value of life insurance. Both of these items constitute long-term investments and are discussed in the following two sections.

SPECIAL-PURPOSE FUNDS

We introduced the notion of a special-purpose fund in Chapter 8 with respect to petty cash. Firms use the petty cash fund to make small expenditures for specified purposes without going through the formal, time-consuming procedures required for other expenditures. Companies often establish other short-term funds for such purposes as dividends, payroll, and interest payments. All of these funds constitute short-term segregations of cash for specified operating purposes. These funds are classified as current assets.

Many entities also establish special-purpose funds for long-term use. The purpose of these funds is to accumulate resources systematically to meet specific future objectives. These funds may be required by contractual commitments or they may be voluntary. Common types of special-purpose funds required by contract include:

1. Bond sinking fund to retire long-term debt.

2. Stock redemption fund to retire capital stock, usually preferred stock.

3. Pension fund to meet pension obligations.

An outside trustee usually administers funds required by contract. The trustee invests and accounts for the fund's assets and periodically reports the income and expenses of the fund to the company that established it.

Companies may voluntarily establish long-term funds to accumulate resources for such purposes as plant expansion and environmental improvements. While an outside trustee may administer this type of fund, often the company that establishes the fund also administers it.

Because firms establish long-term funds for purposes that will not require current use of the funds, the cash is invested. These funds are included in the investments section of a classified balance sheet, usually between current assets and property, plant, and equipment.

ACCOUNTING FOR FUNDS

Transactions involving a long-term fund include cash contributions to the fund, investment of fund cash in securities, receipt of income on securities, incurrence of expenses, sale of investments, use of fund assets to fulfill the purpose for which the fund was created, and the transfer of any unused assets back into unrestricted assets.

A firm should account for each fund as a separate entity. Thus, a separate account must be maintained for each type of transaction involving the fund. For example, a bond sinking fund typically would require the use of the following accounts:

Sinking fund cash	Sinking fund expense
Sinking fund investments	Gain on sale of sinking fund investments
Sinking fund revenue	Loss on sale of sinking fund investments

To illustrate a bond sinking fund, assume that the terms of a bond agreement require Beaton Company to establish a bond sinking fund and to contribute $10,000 to it at the end of each year for 10 years. The maturity value of the bonds, due in 10 years, is $200,000. Assuming a 16 percent rate of return, the company must pay $9,380 ($200,000 ÷ 21.3215) into the fund each year in order to accumulate $200,000 at the end of 10 years (see Table C, Appendix 7–1). Thus, if Beaton contributes $10,000 annually, the investments could earn slightly less than 16 percent and still accumulate to $200,000 by the end of the tenth year. Selected transactions over the life of the fund and accompanying journal entries are as follows:

Contribution of $10,000 to fund at end of first year:

Sinking fund cash	10,000	
Cash		10,000

Purchase of securities for $9,500:

Sinking fund investments	9,500	
Sinking fund cash		9,500

Receipt of $1,700 in dividend and interest revenue:

Sinking fund cash	1,700	
Sinking fund revenue		1,700

Incurrence of expenses (for example, trustee's fee for managing the fund) of $400:

Sinking fund expense	400	
Sinking fund cash		400

Sale of securities (several years later) with a cost basis of $36,000 for $44,000:

Sinking fund cash	44,000	
Sinking fund investments		36,000
Gain on sale of sinking fund investments		8,000

At end of tenth year, when the fund balance is $204,000, trustee pays off bonds with sinking fund cash, leaving a balance of $4,000 in the fund:

Bonds payable 200,000		
Sinking fund cash.................................	200,000	

The trustee returns the remaining balance of $4,000 in the fund to Beaton Company:

Cash... 4,000		
Sinking fund cash.................................	4,000	

Beaton reports the nominal (temporary) accounts used in accounting for the sinking fund (revenue, expense, gain, and loss) in its income statement and closes them to retained earnings at the end of each year. The sum of sinking fund cash and sinking fund investments is reported in the investment section of the balance sheet as a trusteed sinking fund. The last entry above eliminates the sinking fund.

PURCHASES OF A COMPANY'S OWN SECURITIES

It is not unusual for a firm with special-purpose funds to invest them in the security that the fund was established to retire. For example, a firm may establish a fund to redeem preferred stock, and before the redemption date of the stock, may acquire shares of the stock with cash in the fund. A firm may do this when the market price of the stock is considerably below the redemption price; thus the company benefits from acquiring the stock before the redemption date. From an economic standpoint, the effect of investing in securities that the fund was created to retire is to retire the acquired securities prematurely, because they no longer are available in the marketplace.

If the firm retires the securities as soon as it acquires them, no particular accounting problems arise. The firm eliminates the carrying value of the securities, credits the fund for the cash paid, and recognizes a gain or loss (or adjustment of additional contributed capital in the case of stock)[24] when it retires the securities.

Assume, for example, that Debt Company establishes a sinking fund for the retirement of an outstanding bond issue, which was originally sold at face value. At the end of 1984, Debt Company purchases for $9,000 some of these bonds with a maturity value of $10,000, even though the bonds do not mature for several years. If Debt Company retires the bonds immediately, it records the transaction as follows:

Bonds payable 10,000		
Sinking fund cash.....................................	9,000	
Gain on retirement of bonds	1,000	

If the firm does not retire the securities as soon as it acquires them, accounting for the transaction is more complex. Resolution of this issue depends on whether the fund is a preferred stock redemption fund or a bond sinking fund.

Stock Redemption Fund

A company pays dividends only on outstanding stock. Thus, a firm should treat the acquisition of its own preferred stock before the redemption date as a retirement, and should declare dividends only on the remaining outstanding shares. The company must deduct the cost of the acquired shares from the balance of the stock redemption fund, and must deduct the amounts originally received for the shares from the appropriate stockholders' equity accounts.

Bond Sinking Fund

A company also may invest sinking fund cash in bonds that the fund was established to

---

[24] We discuss accounting for the retirement of equity securities in Chapter 20.

retire. The company cannot report income from an investment in its own bonds. If the company pays interest on both the bonds outstanding and those acquired, net income is not misstated because the interest revenue recognized on the bonds is offset by interest expense. Interest revenue and expense, however, are overstated by the amount of interest accrued and paid on the company's own bonds held in the fund. To eliminate the overstatement, the company should treat the acquisition of its own bonds as a retirement, as in the case of Debt Company's retirement of its bonds.[25]

CASH SURRENDER VALUE OF LIFE INSURANCE

Many business entities purchase life insurance policies on key executives, naming the company as the beneficiary, so that the company will be compensated for losses resulting from the death of the executive. **Term insurance** policies provide for payment to the beneficiary if the insured dies while the policy is in force. Periodic premium payments constitute insurance expense to the company, because no value accrues to the company.

Whole-life insurance policies provide, in addition to the payment to the beneficiary in the event of death, a **cash surrender value** that the owner of the policy may receive when the policy is canceled or expires. The cash surrender value, which increases each period as the company pays the premiums, is an asset of the company that owns the policy. Since the normal intent is to continue the policies indefinitely, the cash surrender value constitutes a long-term investment and is classified under investments and funds in the balance sheet. In essence, the owner of a whole-life policy is paying premiums (1) to provide protection against losses and disruptions from the untimely death of key executives and (2) to generate cash surrender value.[26]

Accounting for whole-life policies recognizes these two aspects of the investment: (1) the company recognizes the current period protection as insurance expense; and (2) the company records the investment in cash surrender value as an asset. Any dividends received on the policies reduce insurance expense.

Assume that Pioneer Paint Company, a small paint manufacturer, acquires a whole-life insurance policy, with a face amount of $70,000, on its president. The annual premiums, payable at the beginning of each year, are $2,000. There is no cash surrender value until the beginning of year 2, at which time $600 of the $2,000 premium represents an increase in cash surrender value. Pioneer makes the following entry at the beginning of year 1:

Prepaid insurance	2,000	
Cash		2,000

At the end of year 1:

Insurance expense	2,000	
Prepaid insurance		2,000

---

[25] Practice is unsettled in this area because generally accepted accounting principles do not provide clear guidance. While there are a number of alternatives to the remedies suggested above, we believe that the approaches suggested are conceptually preferable.

[26] Whole-life policies also provide the owner with borrowing capacity, because the owner may borrow against the cash surrender value.

At the beginning of year 2:

Prepaid insurance	1,400	
Cash surrender value of life insurance	600	
Cash.		2,000

At the end of year 2:

Insurance expense.	1,400	
Prepaid insurance		1,400

If the president dies at the beginning of year 6, and the cash surrender value of the policy is $3,300, Pioneer records the event as follows:

Cash.	70,000	
Cash surrender value of life insurance		3,300
Gain on life insurance		66,700

Insurance premiums on whole-life policies for which the company is the beneficiary are not tax-deductible by the company, nor are the proceeds taxable as income.

FINANCIAL STATEMENT PRESENTATION

We discussed several types of long-term investments and related accounting issues in this chapter. Exhibit 14–4 illustrates how these investments are reported in actual financial statements. Notice that U.S. Steel combines long-term receivables (an investment, as discussed in Chapter 8) with other long-term investments. The note to the financial statements (Note 5) discloses the amount of the various types of investments included in the balance sheet figures. Also in the notes, U.S. Steel discloses the bases for valuation of the investments. For equity method investments, the company summarizes aggregate assets, liabilities, income, and dividends. For marketable equity securities, the company discloses both cost and market value.

SUMMARY OF IMPORTANT TOPICS AND CONCEPT APPLICATIONS

1. When an investment in common stock is made in exchange for cash, the **historical cost principle** governs the recording process, because historical cost is the best estimate of the fair market value of the stock acquired.

2. Common stock acquired in exchange for noncash consideration should be recorded at the fair value of the stock acquired or the fair value of the consideration given, whichever is more clearly evident.

3. The three different methods of accounting for investments in common stock subsequent to acquisition are (1) the cost method, (2) the lower-of-cost-or-market method, and (3) the equity method.

4. The **cost method** is required for passive, nonmarketable common stock investments. Under the cost method, which may be perceived as a **cash basis** method, dividends received are reported by the investor as revenue. The investor gives no accounting recognition to the earnings of the investee.

EXHIBIT 14—4 FINANCIAL REPORTING OF LONG-TERM INVESTMENTS

United States Steel Corporation
FROM 1984 ANNUAL REPORT
(in millions of dollars)

FROM THE BALANCE SHEET (immediately after current assets):

	DECEMBER 31	
	1984	1983
Long-term receivables and other investments, less estimated losses of $35 and $10 (Note 5)	$846	$1,006

FROM NOTE 1:

    Investments in other entities in which the Corporation has significant influence in the management and control are accounted for using the equity method of accounting. They are carried in the investment account at the Corporation's share of the entity's net assets plus advances. The proportionate share of income from equity investments is included in income from affiliates.

    Investments in marketable equity securities are carried at the lower of cost or market and investments in other companies are carried at cost, with income recognized when dividends are received.

FROM NOTE 5:

5. Long-Term Receivables and Other Investments

	DECEMBER 31	
	1984	1983
Receivables due after one year	$ 81	$ 125
Trusteed funds for environmental improvements	187	203
Other trusteed funds and statutory deposits	6	26
Equity method entities:		
Unconsolidated subsidiaries	195	178
Other partially owned companies	275	324
Partnership interests	62	80
Cost method companies	14	34
Other	26	36
Total	$846	$1,006

5. The **lower-of-cost-or-market method** is required for passive, marketable common stock investments. The method must be applied on an aggregate basis separately to the current portfolio and the noncurrent portfolio. Unrealized losses on the current portfolio are reported in the income statement, whereas unrealized losses on the noncurrent portfolio are reported in a contra account in stockholders' equity. The lower-of-cost-or-market method reflects a **conservative** valuation approach.

6. The **equity method** must be used to account for common stock investments that permit the investor to exercise **significant influence** over the operating and financial policies of the investee. Under the equity method, the investor reports its share of investee earnings as an increase in the investment account and as investment revenue in the income statement. Dividends received reduce the investment account. Because increases and decreases in the net assets of the investee "flow through" to the investor, the equity method may be perceived as an **accrual basis** approach to accounting for an investment.

The following financial data summarize the Corporation's share in equity method entities. Geographic areas and industries of principal unconsolidated affiliates are shown on page 49.

	UNCONSOLIDATED SUBSIDIARIES			50% OR LESS OWNED ENTITIES		
	1984	1983	1982	1984	1983	1982
Balance sheet data, December 31:						
Current assets	$ 22	$ 12	$ 11	$224	$ 224	$ 254
Noncurrent assets	156	294	194	735	823	848
Leasing and finance assets	717	500	529			
Current liabilities	39	126	111	174	200	238
Noncurrent liabilities	30	83	19	448	445	425
Leasing and finance liabilities	631	421	457			
Income data, year:						
Net sales/revenues	$113	$ 93	$ 99	$871	$1,017	$1,086
Gross profit	23	16	27	87	100	104
Net income (loss)	14	14	7	21	(28)	52
Dividends from equity method entities				30	18	26

PRINCIPAL DIRECT AND INDIRECT OWNERSHIP INTERESTS—UNCONSOLIDATED AFFILIATES

COMPANY	COUNTRY	PERCENT OWNERSHIP*	ACTIVITY
U.S. Steel Credit Corporation	United States	100%	Leasing and finance
Emro Land Company	United States	100	Real estate
Marathon Finance Company	United States	100	Finance
Navois Shipholding, Inc.	Liberia	50	Holding company, shipping
RMI Company	United States	50	Titanium products
Terninoss Acciai Inossidabili, S.p.A.	Italy	50	Stainless steel products
Prieska Copper Mines (Pty.) Ltd.	South Africa	46	Copper and zinc concentrates
Feralloys Ltd.	South Africa	45	Ferromanganese and ferrochrome
LOCAP Inc.	United States	37	Pipeline and storage facilities
Compagnie Minière de l'Ogooue	Gabon	36	Manganese ore
Zuari Agro Chemicals, Ltd.	India	36	Fertilizer
CLAM Petroleum Company	Netherlands	33	Oil and gas production
LOOP Inc.	United States	32	Offshore oil port
Associated Manganese Mines of South Africa, Ltd.	South Africa	21	Manganese and iron ores

* As of December 31, 1984.

7. **Significant influence** is presumed to exist if the investor owns 20 percent or more of the outstanding common stock of the investee. However, this presumption may be overcome by predominant evidence to the contrary. Likewise, the presumption that significant influence is lacking if the investor owns less than 20 percent of the outstanding common stock may be overcome by predominant evidence to the contrary.

8. Temporary investments in marketable debt securities may be accounted for by either the cost method or the lower-of-cost-or-market method. Long-term investments in debt securities, whether marketable or nonmarketable, must be accounted for by the cost method.

9. Marketable nonredeemable preferred stock investments must be accounted for by the lower-of-cost-or-market method. Nonmarketable or redeemable preferred stock investments must be accounted for by the cost method.

10. **Special-purpose funds** and the **cash surrender value of life insurance** for which the company is beneficiary are included in long-term investments.

QUESTIONS

Q14-1. Discuss the meaning of the term "equity securities."

Q14-2. Why are common stockholders often referred to as "residual" equity holders?

Q14-3. What is the general principle governing the valuation of common stock at the date of acquisition if *(a)* cash is given up and *(b)* noncash consideration is given up?

Q14-4. If two or more types of securities are acquired as a unit, how is the transaction recorded?

Q14-5. When the cost method is used to account for investments in common stock, what two circumstances require a write-down of the investment account after acquisition?

Q14-6. Why is the lower-of-cost-or-market method applied on an aggregate basis to investments in common stock?

Q14-7. Explain the difference between the cost method and the lower-of-cost-or-market method of accounting for investments in common stock.

Q14-8. Explain how to account for the disposal of common stock investments carried at lower of cost or market. Specifically, what role, if any, does the valuation allowance play in the entry to record the disposal?

Q14-9. What is the difference in the financial statement presentation of unrealized losses (or recoveries) on short-term as opposed to long-term investments in common stock? Explain the rationale for this difference.

Q14-10. What is the appropriate accounting treatment for nontemporary declines in market value of marketable securities below cost?

Q14-11. How is a change in classification of marketable securities accounted for? Why does this special requirement exist?

Q14-12. Why are dividends received accounted for as a reduction in the investment account for equity-method investments and as revenue under the cost method?

Q14-13. Explain why the investor's share of investee earnings must be adjusted for amortization of the excess of cost over book value, or for the excess of book value over cost, for investments accounted for by the equity method.

Q14-14. Describe the procedure required to change *(a) to* the equity method and *(b) from* the equity method of accounting for investments in common stock.

Q14-15. In general, what is the appropriate accounting treatment when the investor's share of investee losses exceeds the carrying value of an investment accounted for by the equity method?

Q14-16. Give four examples that may provide evidence of significant influence by an investor in common stock. How does this evidence relate to the presumption that investments of less than 20 percent do not convey significant influence to the investor?

Q14-17. Give four examples of evidence of an investor's inability to exercise significant influence over an investee. How does this evidence relate to the presumption that investments of 20 percent or more convey to the investor the ability to exercise significant influence over the investee?

Q14-18. How should investments that constitute more than 50 percent of the outstanding voting common stock of the investee usually be reported in the financial statements?

Q14-19. What two methods are commonly found in practice for valuing temporary investments in marketable debt securities?

Q14-20. What is the appropriate method of accounting for long-term investments in debt securities?

Q14-21. What is the appropriate accounting method for preferred stock investments that are *(a)* marketable and nonredeemable, *(b)* nonmarketable, and *(c)* redeemable? Explain.

Q14-22. Distinguish between stock rights and stock warrants and describe the investor's accounting requirement upon receipt of stock rights and stock warrants.

Q14-23. Distinguish between a stock split and a stock dividend. What must the investor do from an accounting standpoint upon the receipt of shares resulting from a stock split or a stock dividend? Explain.

Q14-24. Describe the nature of special-purpose funds. Give three examples of long-term special-purpose funds.

Q14-25. What special problem arises when a company with a fund established to redeem securities invests fund resources in the securities that the fund was established to retire? How could the company resolve the difficulty for *(a)* a preferred stock redemption fund and *(b)* a bond sinking fund?

Q14-26. Explain the relationship between the cash surrender value of a life insurance policy and the periodic premiums on the policy. Where is the cash surrender value reported in the balance sheet of the company that owns the policy?

CASES

C14-1. MARKETABLE EQUITY SECURITIES The following four situations involving marketable equity securities are unrelated.

a) A noncurrent portfolio with an aggregate market value in excess of cost includes one particular security whose market value has declined to less than half of the original cost. The decline in value is not considered to be temporary.

b) The statement of financial position of a company does not classify assets and liabilities as current and noncurrent. The portfolio of marketable equity securities includes securities normally considered current that have a net cost in excess of market value of $2,000. The remainder of the portfolio has a net market value in excess of cost of $5,000.

c) A marketable equity security, whose market value is currently less than cost, is classified as noncurrent but is to be reclassified as current.

d) A company's noncurrent portfolio of marketable equity securities consists of the common stock of one company. At the end of the previous year the market value of the security was 50 percent of original cost, and this effect was properly reflected in a valuation allowance account. At the end of the current year, however, the market value of the security had appreciated to twice the original cost. The security is still considered noncurrent at the year's end.

REQUIRED

What is the effect on classification, carrying value, and earnings of each of the above situations? Complete your response to each situation before proceeding to the next.

(AICPA, adapted)

C14-2. LOWER-OF-COST-OR-MARKET METHOD The president of the company that you serve as controller is looking for a way to maximize reported annual earnings. It is her understanding that one means of accomplishing this task is through the classification of marketable equity securities. That is, she is aware that, in accordance with GAAP, managerial intent determines the appropriate classification of marketable equity securities, and that changes in the valuation allowance related to the current portfolio flow through the income statement, whereas changes in the valuation allowance related to the noncurrent portfolio are taken directly to stockholders' equity. It is her belief that if marketable equity securities are classified in a certain manner at the end of each year, the income effect of the securities portfolio can be maximized. The president comes to you for advice.

REQUIRED

Is the president correct in her analysis? Draft a memo to the president supporting your position.

C14-3. VALUATION OF EQUITY SECURITY INVESTMENTS SUBSEQUENT TO ACQUISITION

A) Business entities often make investments by purchasing the equity securities of other business entities.

REQUIRED

Under what circumstances should equity investments be reported in balance sheets:

1. At cost? Explain.

2. At lower of cost or market? Explain.

B) The Vise Company, a manufacturing company, has invested in equity securities of many corporations. The company buys and sells the securities in small blocks strictly for dividend revenue and appreciation. Although Vise's total investment in equity securities is large, the amount invested in each security is small in terms of both the total amount of its investments and the market for the security. All securities are traded regularly on one or more organized exchanges.

Vise's board of directors is attempting to determine whether to report its investment in these securities at cost or at lower-of-cost-or-market value.

REQUIRED

What would be the conceptual merits of the Vise Company's decision to report its investment in equity securities:

1. At cost? Explain.

2. At lower-of-cost-or-market value? Explain.

(AICPA, adapted)

C14-4. EQUITY METHOD

A) A common method of accounting for long-term investments in common stock is the equity method.

REQUIRED

1. Under what circumstances should the equity method be applied?

2. At what amount should the initial investment be recorded, and what events following the initial investment (if any) would change this amount?

3. How is investment revenue recognized under the equity method, and how is the amount determined?

B) For the past five years Hubert has maintained an investment (properly accounted for and reported) in Brock amounting to a 10 percent interest in Brock's voting common stock. The purchase price was $700,000 and the underlying net equity in Brock at the date of purchase was $620,000. On January 2 of the current year, Hubert purchased an additional 14 percent of Brock's voting common stock for $1.2 million. Now for the first time Hubert is able to exercise significant influence over Brock's operations. The underlying net equity of the additional investment at January 2 was $1 million. Brock has been profitable and has paid dividends annually since Hubert's initial acquisition.

REQUIRED

Discuss how this increase in ownership affects Hubert's accounting for and reporting on the investment in Brock. Include in your discussion any adjustments that might be made to the amount shown before the increase in investment to bring the amount into conformity with generally accepted accounting principles. Also, discuss how the investment would be reported in current and subsequent periods.

(AICPA, adapted)

C14-5. CLASSIFICATION OF SECURITY INVESTMENTS; EQUITY METHOD   Morris Systems, Inc., a chemical processing company, has been operating profitably for many years. On March 1, 1987, Morris purchased 50,000 shares of Diverse Company stock for $2 million. The 50,000 shares represented 25 percent of Diverse's outstanding stock. The fiscal years of both Morris and Diverse end August 31.

For the fiscal year ended August 31, 1987, Diverse reported net income of $800,000 earned evenly throughout the year. During November 1986 and February, May, and August 1987, Diverse paid its regular quarterly cash dividend of $100,000.

REQUIRED

1. What criteria should Morris consider in determining whether its investment in Diverse should be classified as (1) a current asset (marketable security) or (2) a noncurrent asset

(investment) in Morris' August 31, 1987, balance sheet? Confine your discussion to the decision criteria for determining the balance sheet classification of the investment.

2. Assume that the investment should be classified as a long-term investment in Morris' balance sheet. The cost of Morris' investment equaled its equity in the recorded values of Diverse's net assets; recorded values were not materially different from fair values (individually or collectively). For the fiscal year ended August 31, 1987, how did the net income reported and dividends paid by Diverse affect Morris' accounts? Indicate each account affected, whether it increased or decreased, and explain the reason for the change in the account balance (cash, investment in Diverse, etc.).

(AICPA, adapted)

C14-6. LONG-TERM INVESTMENTS   Jody Company acquired 15 percent of the outstanding voting common stock of Erin Company. Jody also made a loan to Erin which is convertible into voting common stock of Erin and is secured by voting common stock of Lisa Company, which is a wholly owned subsidiary of Erin. For as long as the loan is outstanding, Jody will have several seats on Erin's board of directors. Jody also has options to purchase a substantial number of shares of Lisa.

REQUIRED

What method of accounting should Jody Company use to account for its investment in Erin? Explain.

(AICPA, adapted)

C14-7. ACCOUNTING FOR CASH SURRENDER VALUE   At the beginning of 1987, Provence Corporation purchased a $200,000 life insurance policy on the life of the corporation's president. Information relating to this whole-life policy for the first 10 years is as follows:

YEAR	ANNUAL PREMIUM	INCREASE IN CASH SURRENDER VALUE	TOTAL CASH SURRENDER VALUE
1	$6,000	$ –0–	$ –0–
2	6,000	2,000	2,000
3	6,000	3,000	5,000
4	6,000	4,000	9,000
5	6,000	5,500	14,500
6	6,000	6,000	20,500
7	6,000	7,000	27,500
8	6,000	7,500	35,000
9	6,000	8,000	43,000
10	6,000	10,000	53,000

Two employees of Provence's accounting department are discussing the proper method of accounting for the policy, especially in view of the substantial increase in cash surrender value. Mr. Gunn believes that, because the net cost to Provence by the end of the 10th year is only $7,000 ($60,000 − $53,000), this $7,000 should be allocated equally over the 10-year period. For example, the entries to record the insurance expense for years 1 and 2 and for years 9 and 10 would be as follows:

YEAR 1

Insurance expense.....	700	
Deferred charge 5,300		
Cash.............		6,000

YEAR 2

Insurance expense	700	
Cash surrender value..	2,000	
Deferred charge	3,300	
Cash		6,000

YEAR 9

Insurance expense.....	700	
Cash surrender value ..8,000		
Deferred charge		2,700
Cash.............		6,000

YEAR 10

Insurance expense	700	
Cash surrender value..	10,000	
Deferred charge		4,700
Cash		6,000

Mr. Gunn further maintains that this approach would "even out" the cash value increases and would better match insurance expense against the revenues generated (indirectly) by the company's president.

Mr. Hessel believes that the periodic insurance expense should be the difference between the annual premium paid and the periodic increase in cash surrender value. Although Mr. Gunn's idea is attractive to him, something about the idea bothers him.

REQUIRED

Explain why Mr. Hessel's approach is superior to Mr. Gunn's. Be specific in regard to the aspects of Mr. Gunn's proposal that are not in accord with the concepts discussed in Chapter 2 of the text.

C14-8. CASH SURRENDER VALUE   Elmallah Company has secured a short-term loan from an insurance company against the cash surrender value of its life insurance policies. According to generally accepted accounting principles, the cash surrender value is excluded from current assets.

REQUIRED

Discuss the appropriateness of classifying a readily liquid asset (cash surrender value) as noncurrent, while simultaneously showing the related borrowings as a current liability. Include in your discussion any alternative reporting practice(s) that you consider acceptable.

EXERCISES

E14-1. ACQUISITION OF SECURITIES   White Company acquired the following securities during 1987 in exchange for the consideration indicated:

a) 250 shares of *X* Company common at $40 per share. White paid cash for the shares. Brokerage fees of $200 were incurred.

b) 1,000 shares of *Y* Company preferred were acquired in exchange for land. The land had a carrying value of $30,000 and an appraised value of $45,000; the preferred stock had a market price per share (on the New York Stock Exchange) of $42 on the date the shares were acquired. Brokerage fees of $750 were incurred.

REQUIRED

Prepare the journal entries required by White Company to record the securities acquisitions.

E14-2. LUMP-SUM PURCHASE OF SECURITIES   Arnold Corporation invested in 2,000 shares of Quest Corporation's $5 par value common. To increase the marketability of the common shares, Quest issued one share of its $10 par preferred with each 10 shares of common. Arnold paid $35,000 for the securities. The market prices per share of the securities on the date of the transaction were $16 for the common and $25 for the preferred.

REQUIRED

1. Prepare the journal entry to record the acquisition of the securities by Arnold. Show calculations.

2. How would the journal entry in part 1 differ if there were no readily determinable market price for the preferred shares?

E14-3. COST METHOD   At the beginning of 1987, Warren Corporation acquired 500 (4 percent) of the outstanding common shares of Johnston Company for $20,000. Incidental costs incurred in connection with the acquisition amounted to $750. In 1987, Johnston's net income was $40,000 and dividend payments totaled $20,000. In 1988, Johnston's net income was $30,000 and dividend payments totaled $40,000. The Johnston Company common stock was not actively traded and, therefore, market value was not readily determinable. Warren has no ability to influence Johnston's operations.

REQUIRED

1. Prepare all entries required by Warren Corporation in 1987 and 1988 in connection with the investment.

2. How would the entries in part 1 differ if Johnston's net income in 1988 had been $10,000 instead of $30,000? Explain.

E14-4. COST METHOD AND EQUITY METHOD Panich Company made the following investments in the common stock of Strange Company, a closely held concern:

1/2/87	4,000 shares at $20 per share
1/2/88	2,000 shares at $28 per share

Strange has 40,000 shares outstanding and reported net income in 1987 and 1988 of $60,000 and $100,000, respectively. Dividends of $50,000 were paid each year.

REQUIRED

1. Prepare entries for Panich for 1987 and 1988, assuming that the investment does not allow Panich to influence the operating and financial policies of Strange.

2. Prepare entries for Panich for 1987 and 1988, assuming that, as a result of the investment, Panich exercises significant influence over the operating and financial policies of Strange in those years.

E14-5. LOWER-OF-COST-OR-MARKET METHOD Waco Corporation acquired 2,000 shares of Austin Corporation common at $30 per share on January 2, 1987. The purchase, which did not permit Waco to exercise significant influence over Austin, was made as a long-term investment and is the only noncurrent marketable equity security owned by Waco. On November 30, 1987, when the market price per share was $18, Waco determined that there had been a nontemporary decline in market value of the Austin common. On December 31, 1987, the market price per share was $16.

REQUIRED

1. Prepare journal entries required by Waco Corporation in 1987 to account for its investment in Austin.

2. Where would the temporary (nominal) accounts in your answer to part 1 appear in Waco's financial statements? Explain.

E14-6. EQUITY METHOD On January 3, 1987, Limberg Corporation paid $600,000 for 20,000 shares of Greenberg Corporation common. The investment represents a 25 percent interest in the net assets of Greenberg, and gave Limberg the ability to exercise significant influence over Greenberg's operations. Limberg received dividends of $1.50 per share in 1987 and Greenberg reported net income of $320,000 for the year ended December 31, 1987.

REQUIRED

1. Assuming that the book value of Greenberg's net assets was $2.4 million on January 3, 1987, prepare the journal entries required by Limberg for 1987.

2. Assume instead that the book value of Greenberg's net assets was $2 million and that the excess of cost over book value was attributable to unrecorded goodwill, to be amortized over 40 years. How would the entries in part 1 differ?

E14-7. CHANGE FROM THE EQUITY METHOD Grabski Company acquired 40 percent (40,000 shares) of the outstanding common stock of Margheim Corporation for $450,000 at the beginning of 1985, enabling Grabski to exercise significant influence over Margheim. The book value of Margheim's net assets at the date of acquisition was $1 million. The difference between the cost and the book value of Grabski's 40 percent interest in Margheim was attributable to undervalued depreciable assets that were being depreciated on a straight-line basis with a remaining life of 10 years. The investment in Margheim account appeared as follows at the beginning of 1987:

Investment in Margheim

1/2/85	450,000	12/27/85 Dividends	33,000
12/31/85 Income	60,000	12/31/85 Amortization	
12/31/86 Income	70,000	of undervalued	
		assets	5,000
		12/27/86 Dividends	37,000
		12/31/86 Amortization	
		of undervalued	
		assets	5,000

At the beginning of 1987, Grabski sold 30,000 of the Margheim shares for $300,000, thus losing its ability to influence Margheim's operating and financial policies. In 1987 Margheim had net income of $75,000 and paid dividends of $40,000. The market price of the Margheim stock (the only security owned by Grabski) was $8 per share at the end of 1987.

REQUIRED

Prepare the journal entries required by Grabski in 1987 related to its investment in Margheim.

E14-8. MARKETABLE EQUITY SECURITIES Miller Company owned various marketable equity securities. Aggregate cost and market values at the end of 1986 and 1987 were as follows for the temporary and long-term portfolios:

	1987	1986
Temporary portfolio		
Cost	$ 734,000	$ 610,000
Market	720,000	580,000
Long-term portfolio		
Cost	1,530,000	1,200,000
Market	1,480,000	1,240,000

REQUIRED

1. Prepare any journal entries required at the end of 1987 related to the securities portfolios.

2. Assume that on February 15, 1988, Miller decides to dispose of an investment in its long-term portfolio with a cost of $27,000 and a market value on February 15, 1988, of $24,000. The change in intent requires that the securities be reclassified as temporary as of February 15. Miller sells the securities on March 10, 1988, for $26,000. Prepare journal entries to reflect these events.

E14-9. LONG-TERM BOND INVESTMENTS On July 2, 1987, Greer Company acquired 250 of the $1,000 face value, 10 percent bonds of Togo Corporation at face value. The bonds pay interest semiannually on January 1 and July 1. Greer intends to hold the bonds as a long-term investment.

REQUIRED

1. Prepare the journal entry required on July 2, 1987, to record the purchase.

2. Prepare the journal entry required on December 31, 1987, to accrue interest revenue for 1987.

3. Prepare the journal entry required on January 1, 1988, to record the collection of interest revenue. Assume that reversing entries are used by Greer for the end-of-year interest accruals.

E14-10. STOCK RIGHTS Mendoza Corporation purchased 10,000 shares of Tormey Company for $620,000 in 1985. Since then the securities have been properly accounted for by the cost method. At the beginning of 1987, Tormey issued one preemptive right per share to existing stockholders in connection with a new issue of securities. The purchase of each additional common share required five rights and $50. Immediately after the rights were issued, the stock was selling for $70 per share and the market price of each right was $5.

REQUIRED

1. Prepare the journal entry that could be made (optional) by Mendoza on receipt of the rights.

2. Prepare the journal entry to record the disposal of the rights under each of the following alternatives (assuming the entry in part 1 was made):
   a) All of the rights are exercised.
   b) All of the rights are sold for $45,000.
   c) All of the rights are allowed to expire.

E14-11. STOCK WARRANTS   On September 1, 1987, Peterson Company acquired 4,000 shares of Rafferty Corporation's preferred stock for $216,000. Each share had one warrant attached. Warrant holders could acquire one share of Rafferty common in exchange for two warrants and $19. The market price of the preferred stock (without warrant) was $50 per share and the market price of the stock warrants was $10 per warrant on September 1, 1987.

REQUIRED

1. Prepare the journal entry required to record the acquisition of the preferred shares and warrants on September 1, 1987.

2. Prepare the entry required by Peterson under the assumption that Peterson sold the warrants on November 1, 1987, for $39,600.

3. Prepare the entry required by Peterson under the assumption that all of the warrants were exercised on November 1, 1987.

E14-12. SPECIAL-PURPOSE FUNDS   James Corporation established a trusteed fund to accumulate resources over a five-year period to be used for environmental improvements. The following transactions involving the fund took place:
   a) Transferred $100,000 cash to the trustee.
   b) Common stock of Jeffrey Corporation was acquired for $40,000 by the trustee.
   c) Dividends of $3,000 were received on the Jeffrey common.
   d) Trustee's fee of $3,000 was charged against the fund.
   e) At the end of the fifth year, after all fund investments were converted to cash, $725,000 was spent on environmental improvements.
   f) Remaining cash in the fund ($16,000) was returned to unrestricted cash.

REQUIRED

Prepare the journal entries required by James Corporation to reflect the above transactions.

E14-13. CASH SURRENDER VALUE OF LIFE INSURANCE   Cooper Company owns and pays premiums on insurance policies on several of its key executives. Cooper Company is designated as the beneficiary of all of the policies. At the end of 1987 Cooper paid premiums of $4,000 and the cash surrender value of policies owned increased by $1,800. At the beginning of 1988 an executive covered by a $100,000 face value policy with a cash surrender value of $7,600 died and Cooper received the face amount.

REQUIRED

1. Prepare the entry required by Cooper at the end of 1987 to record the premium payments and the increase in cash surrender value.

2. Prepare the entry required by Cooper at the beginning of 1988 to record the collection of the face amount of the $100,000 policy.

PROBLEMS

P14-1. ACQUISITION OF SECURITY INVESTMENTS   During 1987 Wade Corporation acquired the following securities:

a) 6,000 shares of Bailey Corporation's common stock at $16 per share, plus brokerage fees of $3,000.

b) 200 of Prescott Corporation's 10 percent, $1,000 face value bonds maturing in 1997 at 101 (101 percent of face value), plus accrued interest of $5,000.

c) 1,000 shares of Winslow Company's preferred at $26 per share. Included with each preferred share was a warrant that permitted the holder to acquire common shares of Winslow at a specified price. Immediately after the transaction, the preferred shares had a market price of $24 per share (without the warrant), and the market price of the warrants was $4 per warrant.

d) 3,000 shares of Flagstaff Corp. preferred and 300 shares of Flagstaff's common stock in exchange for land with a book value of $120,000 and an appraised value of $165,000. The market prices of the preferred and common shares at the date of the transaction were $56 and $23 per share, respectively. Both securities were actively traded on an organized exchange.

REQUIRED

Prepare the journal entries required by Wade to record the purchases.

P14-2. COST METHOD AND EQUITY METHOD   On January 2, 1986, Lane Company purchased 20 percent of the outstanding shares of Trammell Corporation for $2.4 million. Trammell experienced the following net income (loss) and dividends from 1986 through 1990:

YEAR	NET INCOME (LOSS)	DIVIDENDS
1986	$1,600,000	$ 800,000
1987	(1,200,000)	400,000
1988	2,400,000	1,200,000
1989	1,200,000	800,000
1990	(1,600,000)	400,000

REQUIRED

1. Prepare entries by Lane related to the investment from 1986 through 1990 using the cost method (that is, assuming that the 20 percent investment does not convey to Lane the ability to exercise significant influence over Trammell).

2. Prepare entries by Lane related to the investment for 1986 through 1990 using the equity method (that is, assuming that the 20 percent investment permits Lane to exercise significant influence over Trammell's financial and operating policies).

P14-3. COST METHOD AND EQUITY METHOD   At the beginning of 1986, Wheeler Corporation acquired 30 percent of the outstanding voting common stock of Jackson Company for $6 million. The book value of Jackson's net assets at the acquisition date was $18 million. Any amount paid in excess of book value is attributable to goodwill, to be amortized over 40 years. Jackson's net income (loss) and dividends from 1986 through 1989 were as follows:

YEAR	NET INCOME (LOSS)	DIVIDENDS
1986	$2,400,000	$1,200,000
1987	1,100,000	800,000
1988	(1,000,000)	400,000
1989	500,000	600,000

REQUIRED

1. Prepare entries by Wheeler to account for its investment in Jackson from 1986 through 1989 under the cost method.

2. Prepare entries by Wheeler to account for its investment in Jackson from 1986 through 1989 under the equity method.

3. Summarize the balance sheet amount and the income statement amount reported for the investment for each of the four years (1986–1989) under (*a*) the cost method and (*b*) the equity method.

P14-4. MARKETABLE EQUITY SECURITIES Hock Corporation had the following marketable equity securities on hand at the end of 1986:

	COST	MARKET
A Corporation	$12,000	$15,000
B Corporation	8,000	6,000
C Corporation	24,000	28,000
D Corporation	16,000	10,000
E Corporation	7,000	4,000

All of these securities are classified as current assets at the end of 1986, and Hock has accounted for them by the lower-of-cost-or-market method.

During 1987, Hock engaged in the following transactions involving marketable equity securities:

a) Sold one-half of its shares in *C* Corporation for $13,000.
b) Acquired additional shares of *A* Corporation for $10,000.
c) Acquired shares of *F* Corporation for $18,000.
d) Disposed of its shares of *E* Corporation for $5,500.

At the end of 1987, cost and market data were as follows:

	COST	MARKET
A Corporation	$22,000	$26,000
B Corporation	8,000	5,000
C Corporation	12,000	10,000
D Corporation	16,000	14,000
F Corporation	18,000	19,000

REQUIRED

1. Prepare entries to record the transactions involving marketable securities during 1987.

2. Prepare any end-of-period adjusting entry required to adjust the carrying amount of the marketable equity securities portfolio at December 31, 1987.

3. Assume that the *D* Corporation shares were reclassified as noncurrent in 1987 when the market value was $13,000. Prepare any journal entry required to record the reclassification, and prepare any end-of-period adjusting entries required for the current and noncurrent portfolios.

P14-5. LOWER-OF-COST-OR-MARKET METHOD Blake Company, which began operations in 1987, had the following marketable equity securities appropriately classified as current assets at the end of 1987 and 1988:

	12/31/87		
	COST	MARKET	UNREALIZED GAIN (LOSS)
Altman Corp.	$10,000	$ 8,000	$(2,000)
Baker Corp.	30,000	26,000	(4,000)
Chase Co.	20,000	24,000	4,000
	$60,000	$58,000	$(2,000)

	COST	MARKET	12/31/88 UNREALIZED GAIN (LOSS)
Altman Corp.	$10,000	$10,000	—
Baker Corp.	20,000	15,000	$(5,000)
Chase Co.	25,000	26,000	1,000
Decker Corp.	14,000	12,000	(2,000)
	$69,000	$63,000	$(6,000)

During 1988, Blake sold some of its shares of Baker for a gain of $3,000.

REQUIRED

1. Prepare the adjusting entry, if any, required at the end of 1987 related to the securities portfolio.

2. Prepare the entry required to record the sale of Baker Corporation shares in 1988.

3. Prepare the adjusting entry, if any, required at the end of 1988 related to the securities portfolio.

P14-6. EQUITY METHOD Montvale Corporation has been manufacturing industrial products for over 30 years. Montvale decided to diversify into the home products industry and purchased 60 percent of the outstanding common stock of Arbor Company for $8 million in cash on December 1, 1986, the first day of the 1986–87 fiscal year for both Montvale and Arbor.

Information pertaining to Arbor Company as of December 1, 1986, is presented below:

a) The book value of Arbor's total stockholders' equity was $10 million.

b) Arbor's inventory, valued at lower of cost (determined by the FIFO method) or market, was undervalued by $500,000.

c) Included in Arbor's plant and equipment were some depreciable assets that had a market value of $1.3 million in excess of book value. These undervalued assets had a remaining life of 10 years.

Arbor reported net income of $900,000 for the 1986–87 fiscal year. Dividends in the amount of $300,000 were declared and paid by Arbor in the 1986–87 fiscal year. None of the items in Arbor's inventory on December 1, 1986, were in the inventory on November 30, 1987.

Montvale uses the equity method to account for its investment in Arbor, recognizes only its portion of the undervalued assets for any amortization, and amortizes any goodwill over the maximum period allowed under generally accepted accounting principles.

REQUIRED

1. Prepare a schedule to compute the balance of investment in Arbor common that would appear on the balance sheet of Montvale Corporation at November 30, 1987.

2. Prepare a schedule to compute the amount of equity in subsidiary earnings that would appear on the income statement of Montvale Corporation for the year ended November 30, 1987. Ignore income taxes.

(IMA, adapted)

P14-7. MARKETABLE EQUITY SECURITIES On December 31, 1986, Winsor Corporation properly reported as current assets the following marketable equity securities:

Bea Corporation, 1,000 shares, $2.40 convertible preferred	$ 40,000
Cha, Inc., 6,000 shares, common	60,000
Dey Co., 2,000 shares, common	55,000
Marketable equity securities, at cost	$155,000
Less valuation allowance	(7,000)
Marketable equity securities, at market	$148,000

On January 2, 1987, Winsor paid $1.7 million to purchase 100,000 shares of Eddie Corporation common stock, representing 30 percent of Eddie's outstanding common stock and an underlying equity of $1.4 million in Eddie's net assets at January 2. Winsor, which had no other financial transactions with Eddie during 1987, amortizes goodwill over a 40-year period. As a result of Winsor's 30 percent ownership of Eddie, Winsor has the ability to exercise significant influence over Eddie's financial and operating policies.

During 1987, Winsor disposed of the following securities:

January 18—Sold 2,500 shares of Cha for $13 per share.

June 1—Sold 500 shares of Dey, after a 10 percent stock dividend, for $21 per share.

October 1—Converted 500 shares of Bea's preferred stock into 1,500 shares of Bea's common stock.

The following 1987 dividend information pertains to the stock held by Winsor:

February 14—Dey issued a 10 percent stock dividend, when the market price of Dey's common was $22 per share.

April 5 and October 5—Bea paid dividends of $1.20 per share on its $2.40 preferred stock to stockholders of record on March 9 and September 9, respectively. Bea paid no dividends on its common shares during 1987.

June 30—Cha paid a $1 per share dividend on its common stock.

March 1, June 1, September 1, December 1—Eddie paid quarterly dividends of $0.50 per share on each of these dates. Eddie's net income for the year ended December 31, 1987, was $1.2 million.

At December 31, 1987, Winsor's management intended to hold the Eddie stock as a long-term investment, with the remaining investments being considered as temporary. Market prices per share of the marketable equity securities were as follows:

	DECEMBER 31	
	1987	1986
Bea Corporation preferred	$56	$42
Bea Corporation common	20	18
Cha, Inc., common	11	11
Dey Company common	22	20
Eddie Corporation common	16	18

All of the foregoing stocks are listed on national stock exchanges. Declines in market value from cost are not considered to be permanent declines.

REQUIRED

1. Prepare a schedule of Winsor's *current* marketable equity securities at December 31, 1987, including any information necessary to determine the related valuation allowance and unrealized gross gains and losses.

2. Prepare a schedule to show the carrying amount of Winsor's *noncurrent* marketable equity securities at December 31, 1987.

3. Prepare a schedule showing all income, gains, and losses (realized and unrealized) related to Winsor's investments for the year ended December 31, 1987.

(IMA, adapted)

P14-8. EQUITY METHOD, UNDERVALUED ASSETS On January 2, 1987, Pany Company purchased for cash 60 percent of the 20,000 outstanding common shares of Sentry Corporation at $15 per share. The following additional data were available for Sentry Corporation on January 2, 1987:

	BOOK VALUE	FAIR MARKET VALUE
Assets not subject to depreciation	$160,000	$170,000
Assets subject to depreciation (10-year remaining life)	120,000	134,000
Total	$280,000	$304,000
Liabilities	$ 20,000	
Contributed capital	200,000	
Retained earnings	60,000	
Total	$280,000	

In 1987 Sentry Corporation reported net income of $40,000 (including a $10,000 extraordinary gain) and paid cash dividends of $16,000.

REQUIRED

Prepare journal entries on the books of Pany Company for 1987 related to its investment in Sentry Corporation. Show calculations.

(CGAA, adapted)

P14-9. LONG-TERM INVESTMENTS IN EQUITY SECURITIES   On September 1, 1986, the Horn Company purchased 200,000 shares representing 45 percent of the outstanding stock of Mat Company for cash. As a result of the purchase, Horn has the ability to exercise significant influence over Mat's operating and financial policies. Goodwill of $400,000 was appropriately recognized by Horn at the date of the purchase.

On December 1, 1987, Horn purchased 300,000 shares representing 30 percent of the outstanding stock of Simon Company for $2.5 million cash. The stockholders' equity section of Simon's balance sheet at the date of the acquisition was as follows:

Common stock, par value $2	$2,000,000
Contributed capital in excess of par	1,000,000
Retained earnings	4,000,000
Total	$7,000,000

Furthermore, at the date of acquisition, the fair market value of Simon's property, plant, and equipment, net, was $3.8 million, whereas the book value was $3.5 million. The fair market value and book value of all of Simon's other assets and liabilities were equal. As a result of the transaction, Horn has the ability to exercise significant influence over Simon's operating and financial policies.

Horn amortizes goodwill over the maximum period allowed and takes a full year's amortization in the year of purchase.

REQUIRED

Prepare a schedule calculating the amount of goodwill and accumulated amortization on December 31, 1987, and the goodwill amortization for the year ended December 31, 1987. Show supporting calculations in good form.

(AICPA, adapted)

P14-10. CHANGE TO EQUITY METHOD   On January 1, 1987, Jeffries, Inc., paid $700,000 for 10,000 shares of Wolf Company's voting common stock, which represented a 10 percent interest in Wolf. At that date Wolf's net assets totaled $6 million. The fair market values of all of Wolf's identifiable assets and liabilities were equal to their book values. Jeffries does not have the ability to exercise significant influence over Wolf's operating and financial policies. Jeffries received dividends of $.90 per share from Wolf on October 1, 1987. Wolf reported net income of $400,000 for the year ended December 31, 1987.

On July 1, 1988, Jeffries paid $2.3 million for 30,000 additional shares of Wolf Company's voting common stock, which represents a 30 percent investment in Wolf. The fair market values of all of Wolf's identifiable assets net of liabilities were equal to their book values of $6.5 million. As a result of this transaction, Jeffries has the ability to exercise significant influence over Wolf's operating and financial policies. Jeffries received dividends of $1.10 per share from Wolf on April 1, 1988, and $1.35 per share on October 1, 1988. Wolf reported net income of $500,000 for the year ended December 31, 1988, and $200,000 for the six months ended December 31, 1988. Jeffries amortizes goodwill over 40 years.

REQUIRED

1. Prepare a schedule showing the income or loss before income taxes for the year ended December 31, 1987, which Jeffries should report from its investment in Wolf in its income statement.

2. During March 1989 Jeffries issues comparative financial statements for 1987 and 1988. Prepare schedules showing the income or loss before income taxes for the years ended December 31, 1987 and 1988, which Jeffries should report from its investment in Wolf. Show supporting calculations in good form.

(AICPA, adapted)

P14-11. CHANGE TO EQUITY METHOD   On January 2, 1987, Barton Corporation acquired 15 percent of the outstanding common stock of Taylor Company for $120,000. The book value of Taylor's net assets on that date totaled $700,000. The 15 percent interest did not give Barton the ability to exercise significant influence over Taylor's operating and financial policies. On January 3, 1988, Barton acquired another 10 percent of Taylor's outstanding shares for $80,000. The book value of Taylor's net assets at this date totaled $750,000. As a result of this latter transaction, Barton was able to exercise significant influence over Taylor's operating and financial policies. The difference between Barton's cost and its share of the book value of Taylor at both acquisition dates is attributed to depreciable assets with a remaining estimated life of five years at the date of acquisition.

Taylor's income and dividends for 1987 and 1988 were:

	NET INCOME	DIVIDENDS PAID
1987.................................	$100,000	$ 50,000
1988.................................	200,000	150,000

REQUIRED

1. Prepare the journal entries required by Barton during 1987 to account for its investment in Taylor, assuming that the Taylor shares are not actively traded and therefore a market value is not readily determinable on December 31, 1987.

2. Prepare the journal entries required by Barton during 1988 to account for its investment in Taylor. Show supporting calculations.

P14-12. CHANGE TO EQUITY METHOD   Sterling, Inc., a domestic corporation whose fiscal year ends June 30, has purchased common stock in several other domestic corporations. As of June 30, 1988, the balance in Sterling's investments account was $870,600, the total cost of stock purchased less the cost of stock sold. Sterling wishes to restate the investments account to reflect the provisions of the equity method.

Data concerning the investments are given on the following page.

	TURNER, INC.	GROTEX, INC.	SCOTT, INC.
Shares of common stock outstanding	3,000	32,000	100,000
Shares purchased by Sterling........ *(a)*	300	8,000	30,000
(b)	810		
Date of purchase.................. *(a)*	7/1/85	6/30/86	6/30/87
(b)	7/1/87		
Cost of shares purchased .... *(a)*	$ 49,400	$ 46,000	$ 670,000
(b)	$ 142,000		

Balance sheet at date indicated:

ASSETS	**7/1/87**	**6/30/86**	**6/30/87**
Current assets	$ 362,000	$ 39,600	$ 994,500
Fixed assets, net of depreciation...................	1,638,000	716,400	3,300,000
Patent, net of amortization			148,500
	$2,000,000	$756,000	$4,443,000

LIABILITIES AND EQUITY			
Liabilities	$1,500,000	$572,000	$2,494,500
Common stock	260,000	80,000	1,400,000
Retained earnings	240,000	104,000	548,500
	$2,000,000	$756,000	$4,443,000
Changes in common stock since 7/1/85	None	None	None
Average remaining life of fixed assets at date of balance sheet (above)...................	12 years	9 years	22 years
Analysis of retained earnings:			
Balance, 7/1/85	$234,000		
Net income, 7/1/85–6/30/86	53,400		
Dividend paid, 4/1/86	(51,000)		
Balance, 6/30/86	$236,400	$104,000	
Net income (loss), 7/1/86–6/30/87	55,600	(2,000)	
Dividend paid, 4/1/87	(52,000)		
Balance, 6/30/87	$240,000	$102,000	$548,500
Net income, 7/1/87–6/30/88	25,000	18,000	330,000
Dividends paid			
12/28/87			(150,000)
6/1/88		(5,600)	
Balance, 6/30/88	$265,000	$114,400	$728,500

Sterling's first purchase of Turner's stock was made because of the high rate of return expected on the investment. All later purchases of stock have been made to gain substantial influence over the operations of the various companies.

In December 1987 changing market conditions caused Sterling to reevaluate its relation to Grotex. On December 31, 1987, Sterling sold 6,400 shares of Grotex for $54,400.

For Turner and Grotex, the fair market values of the net assets did not differ materially from the book values as shown in the above balance sheets. For Scott, fair market values exceeded book values only with respect to the patent, which had a fair market value of $300,000 and a remaining life of 15 years as of June 30, 1987.

REQUIRED

Prepare a worksheet to restate Sterling's investments account as of June 30, 1988, and its investment revenue by year for the three years then ended. Transactions should be listed in chronological order and supporting calculations should be in good form. Ignore income taxes. Amortization of goodwill, if any, is to be over a 40-year period. Use the column headings listed below for your worksheet:

		INVESTMENTS			INVESTMENT REVENUE, YEAR ENDED JUNE 30			OTHER ACCOUNTS	
DATE	DESCRIPTION	TURNER	GROTEX	SCOTT	1986	1987	1988	AMOUNT	NAME

(AICPA, adapted)

P14-13. COMPREHENSIVE During the course of your examination of the financial statements of Craig Corporation for the year ended December 31, 1987, you find a new account, Investments. Your examination reveals that during 1987 Craig began a program of investments, and all investment-related transactions were entered in this account. Your analysis of this account for 1987 follows:

ANALYSIS OF INVESTMENTS
FOR THE YEAR ENDED DECEMBER 31, 1987

DATE		DEBIT	CREDIT
Ace Tool Company Common Stock			
3/15/87	Purchased 1,000 shares @ $25 per share.	$ 25,000	
6/28/87	Received 50 shares of Bymore Sales Co. common stock as a dividend on Ace Tool Co. common stock (memorandum entry in general ledger).		
9/30/87	Sold 50 shares of Bymore Sales Co. common stock @ $14 per share.		$ 700
10/31/87	Awarded 500 shares of Ace Tool Co. common stock to selected members of Craig's management as an incentive award and accounted for as employee compensation.		12,500
Mascot, Inc., Common and Preferred Stock			
3/15/87	Purchased 600 units of common and preferred stock @ $36 per unit. Each unit consists of one share of preferred and two shares of common stock.	21,600	
4/30/87	Sold 300 shares of common stock @ $13 per share.		3,900
6/28/87	Received 900 common stock rights. Each right entitles the holder to purchase one share of common stock for $12 (memorandum entry in general ledger).		
9/30/87	Exercised 450 common stock rights to acquire 450 shares of common stock @ $12 per share.	5,400	
9/30/87	Sold remaining 450 common stock rights @ $4 per right.		1,800
Standard Service, Inc., Common Stock			
3/15/87	Purchased 10,000 shares @ $17 per share.	170,000	
10/31/87	Received dividend of $.75 per share.		7,500
Kevin Instruments, Inc., Common Stock			
3/15/87	Purchased 4,000 shares @ $28 per share.	112,000	
4/30/87	Purchased 2,000 shares @ $30 per share.	60,000	
6/28/87	Received dividend of $.40 per share.		2,400

Additional information:

a) The fair market values for each security as of the date of each transaction follow:

SECURITY	3/15/87	4/30/87	6/28/87	9/30/87	10/31/87
Ace Tool Co. common stock.....	$25				$42
Bymore Sales Co. common stock.....			$8	$14	
Mascot, Inc., preferred stock	20				
Mascot, Inc., common stock.....	10	$13	15*	16	
Mascot, Inc., common stock rights				3	4
Standard Service, Inc., common stock	17				
Kevin Instruments, Inc., common stock	28	30			

* Ex-rights.

b) Standard Service, Inc., has only one class of stock authorized, and 30,000 shares of its common stock were outstanding throughout 1987. Craig's cost of its investment in Standard was *not* materially different from its equity in the recorded values of Standard's net assets; recorded values were *not* materially different from fair market values (individually or collectively). Standard's net income from the date of acquisition of Craig's investment to December 31, 1987, was $336,000. There were *no* intercompany transactions requiring elimination.

c) Kevin Instruments, Inc., has only one class of stock authorized and there were 40,000 shares of its common stock outstanding throughout 1987. Craig's cost of its investment in Kevin was *not* materially different from its equity in the recorded values of Kevin's net assets; recorded values were *not* materially different from fair market values (individually or collectively). Kevin's net income from the date of acquisition of Craig's investment to December 31, 1987, was $120,000. There were *no* intercompany transactions requiring elimination.

d) All other investments of Craig are widely held, and Craig's percentage of ownership in each is nominal (5 percent or less).

REQUIRED

Prepare necessary adjusting journal entries classified by each of the securities analyzed to adjust the investments account properly. Identify each security by type (preferred stock, common stock, rights, etc.) as well as by company. Schedules supporting calculations should be in good form and either included as part of the journal entry explanation or properly cross-referenced to the appropriate journal entry. Ignore income taxes.

(AICPA, adapted)

P14-14. COMPREHENSIVE The Putnam Company owned marketable securities on December 31, 1986, which were appropriately recorded as current assets as follows:

Bart Corp., 500 shares of $200 par value 6% cumulative preferred
    stock, at cost (market value, $240,000) $110,000
Behrend Corp., 1,000 shares of $3 no-par convertible preferred stock,
    at cost (market value, $230,000) 225,000
Bella Co., 10,000 shares of common stock, at cost (market value,
    $250,000)... 200,000
Chockey, Inc., 3,000 shares of common stock, at cost (market value,
    $92,000)..   90,000
Dempsey Co., 4,000 shares of common stock, at cost (market value,
    $25,000)..   24,000
       Total marketable securities $649,000

Putnam appropriately recorded $42,000 cash surrender value of life insurance carried on the life of Putnam's president on December 31, 1986.

During 1987 the following transactions occurred:

a) Bart Corporation could not pay dividends on preferred stock because of adverse business conditions. The market value of the stock was $120,000 on December 31, 1987.

b) Behrend Corporation issues cash dividends once a year to stockholders of record on May 31. The cash was received on June 10, 1987. On June 15, 1987, Putnam converted 500 shares of Behrend $3 no-par convertible preferred stock into 1,000 shares of Behrend common stock, which had a market value of $114,000 at the date of the conversion and $116,000 on December 31, 1987. The market value of the remaining $3 no-par convertible preferred stock was $117,000 on December 31, 1987.

c) Bella Company issued a 10 percent stock dividend in 1987. The market value of the common stock on December 31, 1987, was $24 per share.

d) Chockey, Inc., effected a 2-for-1 stock split in 1987. The market value of the stock on December 31, 1987, was $91,000.

e) Dempsey Company issued cash dividends of $.30 per share to stockholders of record on March 31 and June 30, 1987. The cash was received on April 15 and July 15. On July 4, 1987, Putnam sold all of its shares of Dempsey for $7 per share.

f) In January 1987 premiums of $2,500 for the six months ended June 30, 1987, were paid on the president's $100,000 life insurance policy. During this six-month period, the cash surrender value of the policy increased $1,300. The president of Putnam died on July 1, 1987, and Putnam received the proceeds from the insurance policy shortly thereafter.

g) On October 1, 1987, Putnam purchased 100,000 shares representing 40 percent of the outstanding stock of Neville Company for $1.6 million cash; on that date the underlying equity in net assets of 40 percent of Neville was $1.2 million. Putnam amortizes goodwill over a 40-year period and takes a full year's amortization in the year of the purchase. As a result of this transaction, Putnam has the ability to exercise significant influence over Neville's operating and financial policies. Neville's net income for the three months ended December 31, 1987, was $90,000 and for the year ended December 31, 1987, $170,000. On December 1, 1987, Putnam made a long-term loan of $500,000 to Neville. The market value of the stock was $1,605,000 on December 31, 1987. On January 20, 1988, cash dividends of $.20 per share were paid to stockholders of record on December 31, 1987.

REQUIRED

1. Prepare a schedule of the balance in Putnam's current marketable securities as of December 31, 1987. Show supporting calculations in good form.

2. Prepare a schedule of the balance in Putnam's long-term investments as of December 31, 1987. Show supporting calculations in good form.

3. List and calculate the amounts of the above transactions that affect Putnam's income statement. Ignore income tax considerations. Show supporting calculations in good form.

(AICPA, adapted)

15

CURRENT LIABILITIES AND CONTINGENCIES

Until the early 1970s, when the FASB began working on a conceptual framework for financial accounting and reporting, accounting thought and practice were mainly concerned with identifying and measuring assets and expenses. Liabilities often were treated as if they were little more than a credit that was necessary when making an accounting entry to record an asset or an expense. When the FASB set forth the objectives of financial accounting and reporting in *Statement of Financial Accounting Concepts No. 1,* it established the importance of identifying, measuring, and reporting liabilities.[1] According to the FASB, the primary objective of financial accounting and reporting is to provide existing and potential investors, creditors, and others with information about an enterprise that is useful for decision making. The FASB specified that financial reporting should provide information about the amounts, timing, and uncertainty of the entity's prospective net cash flows. Further, the Board specified that the enterprise's obligations to transfer resources to other entities are sources, direct or indirect, of future cash outflows of the enterprise. Later, *Statement of Financial Accounting Concepts Nos. 3* and *6* discussed liabilities as one of the basic elements of financial statements and further emphasized their importance.[2] In this chapter the general characteristics of liabilities are presented, and current liabilities and contingencies are considered in detail.

CHARACTERISTICS OF LIABILITIES

What are liabilities? Traditionally, accountants' responses to this question have been based on one of two views. One view is that liabilities are limited to economic obligations. The other is that in addition to economic obligations, liabilities include certain deferred credits that are not obligations but that are necessary to achieve proper matching

---

[1] "Objectives of Financial Reporting by Business Enterprises," *Statement of Financial Accounting Concepts No. 1* (Stamford, Conn.: FASB, 1978).

[2] "Elements of Financial Statements of Business Enterprises," *Statement of Financial Accounting Concepts No. 3* (Stamford, Conn.: FASB, 1980); "Elements of Financial Statements," *Statement of Financial Accounting Concepts No. 6* (Stamford, Conn.: FASB, 1985).

of expenses and revenues.[3] The definition of liabilities provided by the FASB in *Statement of Financial Accounting Concepts No. 6* is consistent with the first view.

In Chapter 2, liabilities were defined as probable future sacrifices of economic benefits arising from present obligations of a particular entity to transfer assets or provide services to other entities in the future as a result of past transactions or events.[4] According to this definition, a liability has three characteristics:

Three characteristics of a liability.

1. There is a present duty or responsibility to one or more other entities that is expected to be settled by transfer of assets or provision of services in the future.

2. The duty or responsibility obligates a particular entity.

3. The transaction or event that caused the entity to be obligated has already occurred.

Most liabilities can be traced to legal rights and duties, such as those specified in contracts. A **legally enforceable claim,** however, is not a necessary condition for an obligation to qualify as a liability. What is necessary is the expectation of a future transfer of assets to settle the obligation. Some liabilities rest on an **equitable obligation** to another entity to do that which an ordinary sense of justice would deem fair, just, and right. For example, a company may have an equitable obligation to complete and deliver a product to a customer for whom it is the sole supplier, even though the company's only legal obligation would be to return the customer's deposit. Other liabilities arise because of a **constructive obligation** that is created, inferred, or construed from the facts in a particular situation. For example, a company may create a constructive obligation to employees for vacation pay or year-end bonuses by according them those privileges over a period of years even though it is not contractually bound to do so and has not announced a policy to do so.

The line between equitable or constructive obligations and obligations that are legally enforceable is sometimes unclear; the line between equitable or constructive obligations and no obligation may be even less clear. The important point to remember is that under the right circumstances, liabilities that should be reported can arise from equitable or constructive obligations as well as from obligations that are legally enforceable.

CIRCUMSTANCES THAT CAUSE LIABILITIES

There are a variety of transactions and events that give rise to liabilities, in addition to circumstances such as those mentioned above. One of the most common transactions resulting in a liability occurs when a supplier provides goods or services to a firm before the firm has paid for them. The obligation to pay the supplier is a **trade account payable,** or simply an **account payable.**

Another common type of liability arises when customers make deposits or other payments to a firm before the firm delivers goods or services to the customers. The firm has an obligation to the customers to the extent of the advance payments it has received; this obligation is often reported as a liability called **revenue collected in advance** or **unearned revenue.** In this situation the firm has, in effect, borrowed the advance payment from the customer, usually without interest.

Other liabilities arise because one entity borrows resources from another with the understanding that those resources will be repaid with interest in the future. Liabilities can

---

[3] The first of these two views follows from the "asset and liability" view of financial accounting and reporting. The second follows from the "revenue and expense" view. Both views are discussed in "An Analysis of Issues Related to Conceptual Framework for Financial Accounting and Reporting: Elements of Financial Statements and Their Measurement," *Discussion Memorandum* (Stamford, Conn.: FASB, 1976).

[4] *FASB Statement of Financial Accounting Concepts No. 6,* para. 35.

also occur indirectly, as in the case of product warranties that give rise to an obligation to correct product defects or to replace faulty products.

Still other liabilities result from **nonreciprocal transfers,** such as distributions of cash dividends, which are transfers of assets for which the firm receives no identifiable good or service in return. Taxes payable, cash dividends payable, fines, and assessments are examples of liabilities that arise from nonreciprocal transfers.

Liabilities are not valued or recorded in isolation.

Despite their variety, all liabilities are similar in that they are not recorded or valued in isolation. When a liability is valued and recorded there is a simultaneous valuation, recognition, and recording of increases in assets or expenses, or decreases in other liabilities, revenues, or owners' equity.

VALUING LIABILITIES

The theoretical basis for valuing liabilities is the present value of the sacrifice required to settle the obligation.

In theory, a liability should be valued at the present value of the assets or services that must be given up in the future to settle the obligation.[5] This guideline is the same one presented in Chapter 8 for the valuation of receivables. To determine the present value of a receivable we must know the amounts and timing of cash or cash equivalent flows expected in the future. The same information is needed to determine the present value of a liability. It usually is not difficult to value liabilities because the terms of the liability, including amounts and timing of payments, are specified in a contract. When the amounts or timing of payments are not clearly specified, they must be determined by examination of the characteristics of the transaction or event that created the obligation and by a review of the results of similar transactions or events that have occurred in the past. For example, the valuation of a liability arising from a lawsuit against the firm might require consideration of the outcomes of previous similar lawsuits.

Liabilities may arise in transactions where the amount of the obligation is dependent on the value of the other side of the transaction. For example, the fair market value or cash price of an asset acquired in exchange for a future payment or payments often provides the best estimate of the amount of the liability that is incurred by the company that acquires the asset.

Some obligations require estimates of the amounts or timing of payments, or depend on operating results; the very existence of some obligations may be uncertain. For example, warranty liabilities usually must be estimated, income taxes payable depend on the taxable income of the entity, and when a lawsuit filed against the firm is pending, the existence of an obligation may be uncertain.

THE NATURE OF CURRENT LIABILITIES

Liabilities normally are divided into two categories: (1) current liabilities and (2) noncurrent, or long-term, liabilities. The distinction between current and noncurrent liabilities is based on the period of time that will pass before the obligation will be settled. A **current liability** requires the transfer of resources or the incurrence of another liability within the *longer* of one fiscal year or one operating cycle. This means that a current liability is an obligation that is expected to be settled by the use of resources classified as current assets, or by the creation of another current liability. For example, when the payment period is

---

[5] The appropriate interest rate to be used in calculating the present value would incorporate both a risk factor and a factor that reflects expectations about the future purchasing power of the dollar.

extended but remains current, an account payable may be replaced by a short-term note payable. All liabilities that are not classified as current are noncurrent.

Whether an obligation is a current or noncurrent liability depends on the operating cycle of the accounting entity. It is possible for a particular type of obligation to be a current liability for one entity and a noncurrent liability for another. For example, many obligations, such as a note payable in three years, that would be noncurrent liabilities for most businesses might properly be classified as current liabilities for a distiller of seven-year whiskey because of the more than seven-year operating cycle of the distiller.

Theoretically, every liability should be valued at the present value of the future services or goods that must be transferred in order to eliminate it. However, because many current liabilities are due within very short periods of time and the present value is not materially different from the future payment, it has become customary in practice to record current liabilities at their future payment amounts (or face amounts) rather than at their present values. This is a concession to practical considerations, such as expediency and materiality, and results in minor overstatements of current liabilities before their due dates.

TYPES OF CURRENT LIABILITIES

Although all current liabilities must have the three characteristics of liabilities that were presented earlier, other characteristics may vary. As discussed earlier, the existence and amounts of some current liabilities are determined by contracts or by the transactions in which they arise. The amounts of other known current liabilities must be estimated, while either the existence or amount, or both, of some current liabilities depend on operating results. Still other current liabilities, such as those that arise from lawsuits, are uncertain as to existence, amount, or both, and are contingent on the outcome of some future event, such as a court settlement. Because of the differences among current liabilities, our discussion of current liabilities is divided into: (1) determinable current liabilities, (2) current liabilities dependent on operating results, and (3) contingent current liabilities.

DETERMINABLE CURRENT LIABILITIES

Determinable current liabilities are known with certainty to exist as of the balance sheet date, and the amount due is known with certainty or can be reasonably estimated. In the case of some determinable current liabilities, the exact due date of the obligation may be unknown—for example, when advance payments are received from customers. In most cases, however, the existence, amounts due, and due dates of determinable current liabilities are prescribed by written or implied contracts. Therefore, the primary accounting problem related to determinable current liabilities is to be certain that they are recorded.

Determinable current liabilities include trade accounts payable, current notes payable, the current portion of long-term obligations, cash dividends payable, advances from customers, collections for third parties, and accrued liabilities (e.g., accrued wages payable).

TRADE ACCOUNTS PAYABLE **Trade accounts payable,** also known as **accounts payable,** arise when an entity purchases goods, supplies, or services in the normal course of business and there is a time lag between the time of purchase and the time of payment. Because the time lag usually is short, often less than 60 days, accounts payable normally are recorded at their face amount rather than at their present value. Accounts payable should be recorded net of purchase discounts (sometimes called cash discounts), or an allowance for purchase discounts should be deducted from gross accounts payable in the balance sheet to obtain a proper valuation of accounts payable. A typical purchase entry for a firm that has a perpetual inventory system and that uses the net method of accounting for purchase discounts is given below, assuming a gross purchase price of $1,000 and payment terms of 2%/10, net 30.

Inventory	980	
Accounts payable		980

The amount and due date of an account payable liability normally are stated in the invoice from the seller. Since accounts payable and purchases usually are recorded when title passes to the buyer, careful consideration must be given to end-of-period transactions and shipping terms (that is, F.O.B. shipping point or F.O.B. destination) to be sure that purchases are recorded for goods belonging to the buyer and that purchases are not recorded for goods that do not yet belong to the buyer. It is important that purchases and the corresponding account payable are not misstated. Such errors affect both the income statement and the balance sheet of the buyer.

NOTES PAYABLE

Current notes payable are written promissory notes. The maker of the note promises to pay the face amount of the note at the due date, which also is called the maturity date. The note may or may not specify an interest rate, called the stated, nominal, or contract interest rate, to be applied to the face value of the note. If an interest rate is stated, it may or may not be the same as the prevailing interest rate in the money market for notes of similar risk.

In theory, notes payable should be recorded at the present value of the cash outflows associated with the note. If the time value of money is ignored, the liability reported in the balance sheet will be overstated, and the interest expense reported in the income statement will be understated. If notes payable are secured by collateral, that fact, as well as the dollar amount of specific assets pledged as collateral, should be disclosed in the financial statements.

Trade Notes Payable

Trade notes payable are current obligations to suppliers that are evidenced by written promissory notes. Trade notes payable typically arise when the terms of payment include a longer payment period than is normal for trade accounts payable. The due date, the amount of the obligation, and the interest rate, if any, usually are stated in the promissory note. The generally accepted practice is to report a trade note payable at its face amount because the dollar amount and the relatively short duration of such a note make the difference between its face amount and its present value immaterial.

Short-Term Notes Payable

Short-term notes payable typically are issued in exchange for cash or for special purposes, such as the purchase of equipment on short-term credit. Short-term notes payable usually include all current notes payable other than trade notes payable to suppliers.

Sometimes cash is borrowed from a bank or other lending institution in return for a noninterest-bearing note. These short-term notes payable often are referred to as **discounted notes.** Instead of specifying an interest rate in a contract, the bank discounts the note and gives only the proceeds to the borrower. As we described in Chapter 8, the bank applies its discount rate to the face value of the note to calculate the amount of the discount, which is then subtracted from the face value of the note to determine the proceeds. An entry to record such a transaction, involving a $1,000 one-year note and a 9 percent bank discount rate, is as follows:

Cash ($1,000 − $90) 910
Discount on notes payable ($1,000 × .09) 90
    Notes payable   1,000

Because the discount is subtracted from the face value of the note, the effective rate of interest paid by the borrower is greater than the bank's stated discount rate. The effective interest rate on the cash actually received in exchange for the note in the above example is $90 divided by $910, or 9.89 percent. For financial reporting purposes, the discount is deducted from the notes payable account on the balance sheet so that the liability is reported at its present value.

CURRENT MATURITIES OF LONG-TERM OBLIGATIONS

A long-term obligation that will be due within the longer of one year or the firm's operating cycle generally should be reclassified as a current liability. There are three exceptions to this rule: (1) when the currently due portion of the long-term obligation will be retired by the use of assets classified as noncurrent; (2) when the due portion of the long-term obligation will be refinanced on a long-term basis (for example, by use of the proceeds from a long-term debt contract); and (3) when the due portion of the long-term obligation will be retired by issuance of capital stock. In these three cases the currently due portion of the long-term obligation should not be reclassified as a current liability. The effect of these guidelines is that only the portion of long-term obligations requiring the use of a current asset or the incurrence of a current liability should be reclassified as a current obligation.

OBLIGATIONS THAT ARE CALLABLE BY THE CREDITOR

An obligation is **callable** at a given date if the creditor has the right at that date to demand, or to give notice of its intention to demand, repayment of the obligation owed to it by the debtor.[6] Companies must report as current liabilities those obligations that, by their terms, are or will be due on demand within the longer of one year or one operating cycle from the balance sheet date. Long-term obligations that are callable by the creditor because of the debtor's violation of a provision of the debt agreement must be classified as current liabilities. In addition, long-term obligations that will be callable within the longer of one year or one operating cycle, if the debtor's violation of a debt provision is not corrected within a specified grace period, also must be classified as current liabilities, unless it is probable that the violation will be cured within the grace period. The only exception to the above requirements occurs when the creditor has waived or subsequently lost the right to demand repayment for more than the longer of one year or one operating cycle.

SHORT-TERM OBLIGATIONS EXPECTED TO BE REFINANCED

FASB Statement No. 6 specifies how to account for short-term obligations expected to be refinanced.[7] An obligation that must be settled within the longer of one year or one operating cycle normally is classified as a current liability. However, if the debtor intends to refinance a short-term obligation on a long-term basis and can demonstrate the ability to refinance the obligation, the obligation should be classified as a noncurrent liability. The debtor can satisfactorily demonstrate the ability to refinance the obligation by either

---

[6] "Classification of Obligations That Are Callable by the Creditor," *Statement of Financial Accounting Standards No. 78* (Stamford, Conn.: FASB, 1983).

[7] "Classification of Short-Term Obligations Expected to Be Refinanced," *Statement of Financial Accounting Standards No. 6* (Stamford, Conn.: FASB, 1975).

(1) refinancing during the period between the balance sheet date and the date the financial statements are issued[8] or (2) entering into an agreement, before the financial statements are issued, that clearly permits such refinancing on a long-term basis.

If refinancing occurs, the amount of short-term obligation excluded from current liabilities and included in noncurrent liabilities on the balance sheet should not exceed the proceeds from the new long-term obligation that is incurred or capital stock that is issued to retire the short-term obligation. For example, assume that Hicks Company had $5 million of short-term notes payable as of December 31, the end of its fiscal year. Also assume that before issuing its balance sheet Hicks issued $3 million of 10-year bonds, with the intention of using the proceeds of the bond issue to liquidate the short-term notes payable at maturity. Since the bond issue was for $3 million, only that amount of the short-term obligation should be reclassified from current liabilities to noncurrent liabilities on the December 31 balance sheet. The remaining $2 million of the short-term notes payable would continue to be reported as a current liability.

If the ability to refinance is demonstrated by entering into a financing agreement before the balance sheet is issued, the amount of short-term obligation excluded from current liabilities on the balance sheet should not exceed the amount available for refinancing under the financing agreement. If the funds obtainable under the financing agreement fluctuate in proportion to some factor, such as in proportion to the value of collateral, the amount of short-term obligation excluded from current liabilities should be limited to the minimum amount expected to be available for refinancing. For example, assume that the financing agreement limits the amount that can be borrowed to the replacement cost of inventory, which is pledged as collateral and is expected to have a replacement cost ranging from $2 million to $4 million during the period beginning with the maturity date of the refinanced short-term obligation. Since the minimum amount expected to be available for refinancing is $2 million, only $2 million of short-term obligations should be reclassified from current liabilities to noncurrent liabilities on the balance sheet.

In order for a financing agreement to be acceptable as evidence of the ability to refinance, the agreement must meet *all* of the following conditions:

1. The agreement must not expire within the longer of one operating cycle or one year from the date of the balance sheet, and must not be cancelable, except for violation of a provision with which compliance is objectively determinable.

2. There must be no violation or evidence of violation of any provision in the agreement before the balance sheet is issued.

3. The lender or investor is expected to be financially capable of honoring the agreement.

Disclosure of Short-Term Obligations Expected to Be Refinanced

If a short-term obligation is excluded from current liabilities because of refinancing, the notes to the financial statements must include:

1. A general description of the financing agreement.

2. The terms of any new obligation incurred or expected to be incurred.

3. The terms of any equity securities issued or expected to be issued.

Even though equity securities are issued or expected to be issued as the source of funds for refinancing, the short-term obligation excluded from current liabilities should be included

---

[8] There usually is a lapse of several weeks between the balance sheet date (the end of the fiscal year) and the date the financial statements actually are published.

in noncurrent liabilities and should *not* be included in owners' equity. Exhibits 15–1 and 15–2 illustrate the disclosure requirements under *FASB Statement No. 6.*[9]

DIVIDENDS PAYABLE

Most dividends payable are determinable current liabilities. The term **dividend** is generally understood to mean a cash dividend, that is, a distribution of economic resources to existing stockholders in the form of cash. However, three other types of dividends also are

[9] Exhibits 15-1 and 15-2 are adapted from Appendix B of *FASB Statement No. 6.*

EXHIBIT 15–1   DISCLOSURE WHEN AN ACTUAL REFINANCING OCCURS

FOR THE YEAR ENDED DECEMBER 31, 1987

Current liabilities:
Accounts payable and accruals	$ 8,000,000
Income taxes payable	2,000,000
Total current liabilities	$10,000,000

Long-term liabilities:
9% notes payable refinanced in February 1988 (Note A)	$ 3,000,000
8% bonds payable due in March 1989	22,000,000
Total liabilities	$35,000,000

Note A. On February 5, 1988, the Company borrowed $3,000,000 at 10% and liquidated the 9% short-term notes payable that matured on February 10, 1988. Accordingly, the 9% notes payable are reported as long-term obligations in the December 31, 1987, balance sheet.

EXHIBIT 15–2   DISCLOSURE WHEN A FINANCING AGREEMENT EXISTS

FOR THE YEAR ENDED DECEMBER 31, 1987

Current liabilities:
Accounts payable and accruals	$ 8,000,000
Income taxes payable	2,000,000
Total current liabilities	$10,000,000

Long-term liabilities:
9% notes payable refinanced in February 1988 (Note A)	$ 3,000,000
8% bonds payable due in March 1989	22,000,000
Total liabilities	$35,000,000

Note A. The Company has entered into a financing agreement with a major commercial bank that permits the Company to borrow up to $4,000,000 at the bank's prime interest rate at any time through 1988. The Company must pay an annual commitment fee of 1/2 of 1% of the unused portion of the commitment. Borrowings under the financing agreement mature three years after the date of the loan. The agreement prohibits acquisition of treasury stock without prior approval by the bank, requires maintenance of working capital of $10,000,000 exclusive of borrowings under the agreement, and limits annual rental payments under lease agreements to $1,000,000.

recognized: property dividends (dividends in the form of assets other than cash), liability or scrip dividends (promissory notes to pay dividends in the form of assets at some future date), and stock dividends (dividends of shares of the firm's own stock). All of these types of dividends except stock dividends ultimately will require the distribution of economic resources (assets) of the firm and thus result in liabilities on the date the board of directors declares the dividend, which is known as the date of declaration.

A **stock dividend** is a distribution of additional shares of the firm's own stock to existing stockholders in proportion to their relative shareholdings before the dividend is declared. Since stock dividends require the issuance of additional shares of stock rather than the use of assets, stock dividends distributable are not liabilities. Instead, the stock dividends distributable account should be included in the stockholders' equity section of the balance sheet, immediately below the capital stock account of the class of stock that will be issued when the stock dividend is distributed.

Because **cash dividends payable, property dividends,** and **liability** or **scrip dividends** all are obligations that will be met in a relatively short period of time, they normally appear among the current liabilities. Of course, if payment of the dividend is not expected to occur within one year or one operating cycle, whichever is longer, the dividend payable should be classified as a noncurrent liability.

PREPAYMENTS AND DEPOSITS BY CUSTOMERS

A payment received from a customer in advance of the delivery of goods or services creates an obligation either to provide goods or services or to return the **prepayment.** An example of a prepayment is the advance receipt of the $36 price of a one-year subscription to a monthly magazine. Upon receiving the payment, the seller of the magazine should make an entry such as the following:

Cash	36	
Unearned revenue		36

Upon delivery of each magazine the customer has paid for, the seller would make the following entry:

Unearned revenue	3	
Revenue from magazine sales		3

During the interval between receipt of the payment and delivery of the magazines, the unearned revenue account represents an obligation either to deliver magazines or to return the prepayment, and thus is a liability account.

Deposits are payments made by customers to guarantee performance of a contract or delivery of services or to guarantee against damage to or loss of property in the possession of the customer. Examples include deposits made with utility companies, damage deposits on an apartment rental, and deposits on returnable bottles and cans. To see how the recipient of deposits accounts for them, assume that during January Homer's Grocery sells 5,000 cans of soda and receives a 10-cent deposit for each can sold. Homer makes the following entry to record the January deposits:

Cash	500	
Liability for returnable deposits		500
(5,000 × $.10)		

If 4,000 cans are subsequently returned to Homer's Grocery, the following entry is made:

```
Liability for returnable deposits  . . . . . . . . . . . . . . . . . . . . . . . . . . . . . . . 400
    Cash. . . . . . . . . . . . . . . . . . . . . . . . . . . . . . . . . . . . . . . . . . . . . . . . . . .         400
(4,000 × $.10)
```

If the other 1,000 cans are not returned and are not expected to be returned, Homer makes the following entry:

```
Liability for returnable deposits  . . . . . . . . . . . . . . . . . . . . . . . . . . . . . . . 100
    Revenue from unclaimed deposits. . . . . . . . . . . . . . . . . . . . . . . . . . . .         100
```

Classification of an obligation arising from prepayments or deposits as current or noncurrent depends on whether the obligation is expected to be met within the longer of one year or one operating cycle.

COLLECTIONS FOR THIRD PARTIES Another determinable liability arises when an entity collects or withholds assets, usually cash, from one party for the purpose of remitting those assets to a third party. During the period between the time of withholding or collecting the assets and the time of remitting the assets to the third party, the entity withholding or collecting the assets has an obligation to the third party that should be reported as a liability in the withholding entity's balance sheet.

Assets are collected for third parties on many occasions. Perhaps the most common examples are (1) the collection of sales taxes from customers at the time of sale and (2) the withholding of payroll-related taxes, insurance premiums, union dues, and other amounts from employees' paychecks. In these examples, as in all collections for third parties, the withholding entity acts as an agent of the third party, which may be a government unit, an insurance company, or a labor union, and is obligated to remit the collected or withheld amounts to the third party.

Some collecting or withholding responsibilities are established by contract, as in the collection of union dues or insurance premiums. However, many collections for third parties, such as collection of sales taxes and withholding of taxes on wages and salaries, result from compliance with various government requirements.

Sales Taxes Collected

Businesses act as agents for state and local governments in the collection of sales taxes on transfers of tangible personal property and on some services. Between the time of collecting sales taxes from customers and the time of remitting the taxes to the government unit, the business has an obligation that must be recorded and, if financial statements are prepared during the period of obligation, must be reported.

When a sales tax is included in the total amount paid by the customer, the seller should make an entry in the form shown below, where we assume a $100 sales price and a 4 percent sales tax.

```
Cash. . . . . . . . . . . . . . . . . . . . . . . . . . . . . . . . . . . . . . . . . . . . . . . . . . . . . 104
    Sales revenue  . . . . . . . . . . . . . . . . . . . . . . . . . . . . . . . . . . . . . . . . . . .         100
    Sales taxes payable. . . . . . . . . . . . . . . . . . . . . . . . . . . . . . . . . . . . . . .          4
```

Later, remittance of the sales tax to the appropriate governmental taxing unit would be recorded with the entry:

```
Sales taxes payable. . . . . . . . . . . . . . . . . . . . . . . . . . . . . . . . . . . . . . . . . . 4
    Cash. . . . . . . . . . . . . . . . . . . . . . . . . . . . . . . . . . . . . . . . . . . . . . . . . . . .          4
```

If it happens that the sales tax collections shown in the sales taxes payable account are not equal to the tax liability calculated by the governmental unit, then the sales taxes payable account should be adjusted accordingly, with an offsetting gain or loss on sales tax collections.

Some companies do not separate sales and sales taxes payable at the time of sale. They record the sale transactions as:

```
Cash.....................................................104
    Sales revenue .........................................        104
```

When this method of accounting is used, it is necessary to make an adjusting entry at the end of the accounting period.

```
Sales revenue ............................................ 4
    Sales taxes payable........................................        4
```

This entry records the liability for sales taxes collected and due to the governmental taxing unit and adjusts sales revenue to the proper balance.

Payroll Taxes Withheld

The Federal Insurance Contribution Act (FICA) requires that the employer withhold and remit to the federal government 7.15 percent of the first $42,000 of an employee's wages. (This percentage and wage level were effective for 1986; the percentage and wage amount have been increasing regularly.) This tax commonly is referred to as the *social security tax*. In addition, federal tax law, some state tax laws, and some local tax laws require employers to withhold income taxes from employees' paychecks and to remit those taxes to the appropriate governmental taxing unit. Until the withheld payroll tax is conveyed to the proper taxing unit, the employer has a current liability. A hypothetical entry to record liabilities related to payroll taxes withheld from total salaries of $50,000 (assuming that no single employee received more than $42,000 in wages) is:

```
Salaries expense ........................................50,000
    Federal, state, and local income taxes payable
        (amount assumed)...................................        11,000
    Employee FICA taxes payable (7.15% × $50,000)...........         3,575
    Cash or salaries payable ...............................        35,425
```

ACCRUED LIABILITIES
Accrued liabilities arise in conjunction with expenses that have been incurred but not yet paid. For example, if wages of $15,000 normally are paid on the fifteenth of each month, and the accounting period ends on September 30, proper matching of expenses and revenues necessitates the following adjusting entry to recognize accrued wage expense and the related accrued liability for wages payable as of September 30:

```
Wage expense ..........................................7,500
    Wages payable .......................................        7,500
    (1/2 × $15,000)
```

A similar adjusting entry should be made for any expense that has been incurred but has not yet been paid as of the end of the accounting period.

There are several types of accrued liabilities and they should be recorded separately in such accounts as payroll taxes payable, property taxes payable, income taxes payable, and bonuses payable. Although they are recorded in separate ledger accounts, most accrued liabilities—except for taxes payable—usually are combined for reporting purposes under the single heading ''accrued liabilities'' and are shown as current liabilities in the balance sheet. Compensated employee absences, payroll taxes payable, and property taxes payable are discussed in the next three sections; income taxes payable and bonuses payable are discussed later as current liabilities dependent on operating results.

Compensated Future Employee Absences

Compensated future employee absences are future absences from work, such as for vacations, illness, and holidays, for which it is expected that the employee will be paid. An employer must accrue a liability for employees' rights to receive compensation for future absences from work when *all* of the following four conditions are met:[10]

1. The employer's obligation to pay compensation for future absences is attributable to services already rendered by the employee.

2. The employee's right to compensation for future absences is not contingent on the employee's future service (the right is vested), or the employee's right to compensation for future absences can be accumulated over time by the employee.

3. Payment of the compensation by the employer is probable.

4. The amount of compensation that will be paid for future absences is reasonably estimable.

If conditions 1, 2, and 3 are met, but an accrual is not made because condition 4 is not met, that fact should be disclosed.

A modification of the general rule for accounting for compensated future absences exists for sick pay. The employer's actual administration of sick pay benefits determines the appropriate accounting. If employees are allowed to use accumulated sick pay to take compensated time off from work even though they are not ill, or if employees are routinely allowed to receive compensated ''terminal leave'' for nonvested accumulated sick pay benefits prior to retirement, a liability must be accrued. This treatment is appropriate because sick pay will be paid whether or not the employees are absent from work because of illness in the future. If employees receive sick pay only if they are absent from work because of illness in the future, accrual of a liability is not required, although accrual is permitted if all of the four criteria listed above are met.

The expense and accrued liability arising from an employee's right to be compensated for future absences should be recorded in the year in which the right is earned by the employee. For example, if new employees receive vested rights to two weeks' paid vacation at the beginning of their second year of employment, the vacation pay is considered to be earned during their first year of employment. Once the period in which compensated future absences have been earned has been identified, it is necessary to determine the pay rate that should be used to calculate the expense and accrued liability. The issue is whether the current pay rate or an estimated future pay rate should be used. The FASB did not address this issue, but it seems reasonable for employers to use the current pay rate because of uncertainty about future pay rates.

To illustrate accounting for compensated future employee absences, assume that White Manufacturing Company hired 20 new employees at the beginning of fiscal year 1987 to work for $300 per week. White's policy is to give two weeks of paid vacation for each year of work and to allow vacation time to be used only after one full year of employment. All 20 employees took their first two weeks of paid vacation during White's

[10] ''Accounting for Compensated Absences,'' *Statement of Financial Accounting Standards No. 43* (Stamford, Conn.: FASB, 1980).

1988 fiscal year, at which time their rate of pay was \$325 per week. The entry to record the wages expense and accrued vacation wages payable at the end of White's 1987 fiscal year is as follows:

```
Wages expense ......................................  12,000
    Vacation wages payable ..............................          12,000
    (20 × $300 × 2 weeks)
```

The vacation wages payable liability would appear among the current liabilities on White's 1987 balance sheet. (Reporting the obligation as a noncurrent liability would be appropriate to the extent that it is probable that employees will not take paid vacations during the longer of one year or one operating cycle.) When the employees take their paid vacations in fiscal year 1988, payment of vacation wages would be recorded as follows:

```
Vacation wages payable ................................. 12,000
Wages expense ........................................  1,000
    Cash (20 × $325 × 2 weeks) ..........................          13,000
```

Note that additional wages expense must be recorded in 1988 to reflect the fact that the weekly rate of pay increased from \$300 to \$325 between the time vacation wages payable were accrued and the time vacation wages were paid. For the 20 employees, vacation wages actually paid exceeded the accrued liability by \$1,000.

Payroll Taxes Payable

Under the Federal Insurance Contributions Act (FICA) employers must make a contribution matching the employee's share of FICA tax. The employer's share of FICA tax (7.15 percent in 1986) accrues as wages and salaries are earned by employees and must be remitted monthly to the federal government along with the employee's withheld share. Any unremitted portion of the employer's share, as well as any unremitted employee's share withheld, should be recorded as payroll taxes payable.

The Federal Unemployment Tax Act (FUTA) imposes a tax on all employers who either (1) employ one or more individuals for some portion of a day in each of 20 weeks in the current or preceding calendar year, or (2) pay \$1,500 or more wages in a calendar quarter of the current or preceding calendar year.

The FUTA tax for 1986 was 6.2 percent on the first \$7,000 of wages paid to each employee. The employer receives a credit against the FUTA tax rate equal to the standard state tax rate in the state of employment. The credit is limited to 5.4 percent of taxable wages. The result of the state tax credit is that the effective FUTA tax rate normally does not exceed .8 percent (6.2 percent less the 5.4 percent credit).

Hypothetical entries for *employer* payroll tax expense and payroll taxes payable on wages of \$5,000, given the FICA tax (7.15 percent), the FUTA tax (.8 percent after state unemployment tax credit), and a state unemployment tax of 5.4 percent, are:

```
Payroll taxes expense ....................................  667.50
    Employer FICA taxes payable (7.15% × $5,000) ...........          357.50
    FUTA taxes payable (.8% × $5,000) .....................           40.00
    State unemployment taxes payable (5.4% × $5,000) ........          270.00
```

When the taxes are remitted to the proper taxing units, the respective current liability accounts are debited and cash is credited to account for settlement of the obligations.

Property Taxes Payable

Property taxes based on the assessed value of real and personal property are the primary source of revenue for most local governments. There are two basic questions in accounting for property taxes:

1. When should the liability for property taxes be recorded on the books of the taxpayer?
2. When should property tax expense be recognized in the taxpayer's income statement?

A number of responses to each of these questions have evolved in practice. However, we shall discuss only the two most common practices. Both of these practices recognize property tax expense over the fiscal year of the governmental taxing unit. The distinction between the two practices lies in when property taxes payable are recorded. Under one procedure the property taxes payable account is credited on the lien date[11] for the entire year's property tax obligation, while under the alternative procedure property taxes payable are accrued monthly on the taxpayer's books during the fiscal year of the governmental taxing unit.

Assume, for example, that Travis Company's fiscal year ends on December 31 and that it receives its property tax bill for $12,000, based on a January 1 assessment, in February. Assume further that the fiscal year of the governmental taxing unit begins on April 1, which is also the lien date for the property taxes. The property taxes must be paid in equal installments on June 1 and August 1. Accountants who record property taxes payable for the year on the lien date would make the following entry on April 1:

Deferred property tax expense	12,000	
Property taxes payable		12,000

Deferred property tax expense is a current asset and property taxes payable is a current liability.

Accountants using this method would then recognize an equal amount of property tax expense each month over the fiscal year of the taxing unit. For example, beginning at the end of April, Travis Company would make the following entry at the end of each month through the end of March of the next calendar year:

Property tax expense	1,000	
Deferred property tax expense		1,000

Finally, the following entry would be made on June 1 and on August 1 to record Travis' payment of the two equal installments:

Property taxes payable	6,000	
Cash		6,000

Accountants who record monthly accruals of property taxes payable would make the following entry at the end of April and at the end of May:

Property tax expense	1,000	
Property taxes payable		1,000

On June 1, the first payment date, the following entry would be made:

Property taxes payable	2,000	
Deferred property tax expense	4,000	
Cash		6,000

[11] The *lien date* is established by the governmental taxing unit and is the date on which property taxes become a lien or legal claim against the taxed property.

Note that because property taxes payable for only two months are accrued as of June 1, it is necessary to debit an asset account, deferred property tax expense, for the rest of the payment.

On June 30 and July 31, property tax expense for June and July would be recorded with the entry:

Property tax expense	1,000	
Deferred property tax expense		1,000

On August 1 the second cash payment would be recorded as follows:

Deferred property tax expense	6,000	
Cash		6,000

Subsequently, property tax expense would be recognized each month by a $1,000 reduction in the deferred tax expense account and a corresponding debit to property tax expense.

These two procedures are conceptually quite different. They may yield fairly similar results, however, if the cash payment dates closely follow the lien date. Regardless of which procedure is used to account for property taxes, the primary objective should be to report one year's property tax expense on the income statement and the correct liability on the balance sheet.

CURRENT LIABILITIES DEPENDENT ON OPERATING RESULTS

The amounts of some obligations depend on the firm's operating results, which cannot be known with certainty until the end of the accounting period. Although the amounts of these obligations can be determined easily once operating results for the period are known, difficulties sometimes do arise in estimating interim (for example, quarterly) amounts of such liabilities. Perhaps the most common of the current liabilities dependent on operating results are income taxes payable and bonuses payable.

INCOME TAXES PAYABLE

Income taxes payable are common current liabilities of corporations. Income taxes payable are not found on the balance sheets of sole proprietorships or partnerships because individual proprietors and partners are taxed personally for their share of the business entity's profits. The corporate income tax generally is due by the fifteenth day of the third calendar month following the close of the tax year. For example, the income tax for a corporation on the calendar-year basis would be due on March 15 of the following year. A corporation may, however, elect to pay the tax in two equal installments, the first by the fifteenth day of the third month after the close of the tax year, the second by the fifteenth day of the sixth month after the close of the tax year.

Most corporations have to pay income taxes in advance in the form of an estimated tax. The estimated tax is the excess of the anticipated tax liability over any tax credits. The estimated tax is due in equal quarterly installments on the fifteenth day of the fourth, sixth, ninth, and twelfth months of the tax year. Quarterly payments of estimated taxes should be debited to the asset account, prepaid income tax. At the end of the accounting year an adjusting entry should be made to recognize income tax expense and to reduce the prepaid income tax account. Of course, if the total tax obligation for the year exceeds the total estimated tax payments, it will be necessary to debit income tax expense and credit income taxes payable for the additional obligation. Income taxes payable are included among current liabilities because, as indicated earlier, income taxes must be paid in full by the fifteenth day of the sixth month following the end of the tax year.

Accounting for Income Taxes in Interim Periods

Accounting for income taxes in interim periods poses accounting problems because of the progressive nature of business income taxes. For example, effective July 1, 1987, the maximum corporate income tax rate became 34 percent. Special graduated rates of 15 percent and 25 percent were established for the first $75,000 of taxable income. Beginning at $100,000, the graduated rates phase out, so that corporate income of $335,000 or more is taxed at 34 percent.

Preparation of interim financial statements requires interim estimates of the income tax liability. For example, to prepare financial statements for the first quarter requires an estimate of the income tax liability related to the firm's first-quarter operations. The basic question raised because of the progressive tax rate schedule is: What tax rate should be applied to interim taxable income? Should it be (1) the tax rate applicable to the taxable income level that exists as of the interim date or (2) the estimated final tax rate resulting from estimated total annual income? *APB Opinion No. 28* requires use of the estimated final tax rate for the year. (The procedure for determining estimated income taxes payable on an interim basis is illustrated in the section on interim financial reporting in Chapter 26.)

BONUSES PAYABLE

Bonuses payable is another current liability that often is dependent on a company's operating results. It is a common business practice to give key employees compensation bonuses in addition to their basic wage or salary. If these bonuses are based on revenues earned or on output produced, it is not difficult to calculate the bonus due. All that is necessary to calculate the bonus at any point in time is to determine the revenue or output to date that is subject to the bonus and multiply by the bonus factor. (A typical bonus factor might be $.10 per unit produced.)

Other contractual agreements that are similar to this type of bonus arrangement include rent or royalty payments that are conditional on revenues earned or quantity produced. For example, a lease for a local retailer might specify a fixed monthly payment of $1,000 plus an incremental charge of 1 percent of the retailer's sales revenue in excess of $10,000 for the month.

Bonus arrangements based on income make it more difficult to determine the amount of bonus due. From the point of view of the firm, bonuses paid to employees are simply additions to wages or salaries and therefore are accounted for as one of the expenses deducted when income is calculated for the period. Moreover, in most cases bonuses to employees are deductible for tax purposes. Hence bonuses affect taxes, which in turn affect income. But if the bonus is based on income, we have the problem of a circular relationship between bonus and income: the bonus is dependent on the amount of income and the amount of income is dependent on the bonus expense.

A bonus plan based on the firm's income can be formulated in a variety of ways. For example, bonuses could be based on:

Alternative bonus plans.

1. Income before bonus expense and before income taxes.
2. Income after bonus expense but before taxes.
3. Income after income taxes but before deduction of bonus expense.
4. Income after bonus expense and after income taxes.

The procedure for solving income-based bonus problems involves the following steps:

Step 1. Construct an equation that mathematically describes the bonus plan.

Step 2. Construct an equation for calculating income taxes (if the amount of income taxes must be known for the calculation of bonuses).

Step 3. Substitute known data in the equation(s).

Step 4. Solve for any unknown variables.

Equations describing the four bonus plans suggested above would be:

1. $B = bI$

2. $B = b(I - B)$

3. $B = b(I - T)$

4. $B = b(I - B - T)$

where b = the bonus rate

I = income before bonuses and income taxes

B = the bonus in dollars

T = income taxes

Given the applicable tax rate (t) and that a bonus is a tax-deductible expense, income taxes (T) can be determined as follows:

5. $T = t(I - B)$

Equations 1 and 2 have only one unknown variable, B, which can be calculated by simply substituting I, the amount of income (from the corporate records), and b, the bonus rate (from the bonus agreement), in the equation. For example, if under the second bonus plan (equation 2) income before the bonus and income taxes was \$100,000 and the bonus rate was 2 percent, the solution would be:

$$B = b(I - B)$$

$$B = .02(\$100,000 - B)$$

$$B = \$2,000 - .02B$$

$$1.02B = \$2,000$$

$$B = \$2,000/1.02$$

$$B = \$1,960.78$$

Equations 3 and 4 are more difficult to solve because they have two unknown variables, B and T. However, given the tax rate (t) from the corporate income tax rate schedule and the income tax calculation formula in equation 5, we can substitute for T in terms of B in either equation 3 or equation 4 and solve for the B specified by the particular bonus plan under consideration.

For example, continuing the original assumptions of \$100,000 income before bonus and taxes and a bonus rate of 2 percent, we would solve equation 4 as follows, assuming a tax rate of 48 percent:

6. $B = b(I - B - T)$

7. $T = t(I - B)$

Substitution of the right-hand side of equation 7 for T in equation 6 yields:

$$B = b[I - B - t(I - B)]$$

$$B = b(I - B - tI + tB)$$

$$B = .02[\$100,000 - B - .48(\$100,000) + .48B]$$

$$B = \$2,000 - .02B - .0096(\$100,000) + .0096B$$

$$1.0104B = \$1,040$$

$$B = \$1,040/1.0104$$

$$B = \$1,029.30$$

The following adjusting entry should be made to record the bonus expense and the related obligation to pay the bonus:

Bonus expense	1,029.30	
Bonus payable		1,029.30

The bonus expense account should appear on the income statement, probably in combination with other salary and wage expenses, and the accrued bonus payable liability should be included among the current liabilities on the balance sheet until the bonus is paid. When the bonus is paid, the following entry would be made:

Bonus payable	1,029.30	
Cash		1,029.30

CONTINGENT LIABILITIES

A **contingent liability** arises when the existence of an obligation, the amount payable, or the settlement date is uncertain, and the resolution of the uncertainty depends on some future event or events. Accounting for contingencies, including contingent liabilities, is the topic of *FASB Statement No. 5*, which defines a contingency as:

Definition of a contingency.

> an existing condition, situation, or set of circumstances involving uncertainty as to possible gain (hereinafter a ''gain contingency'') or loss (hereinafter a ''loss contingency'') to an enterprise that will ultimately be resolved when one or more future events occur or fail to occur. Resolution of the uncertainty may confirm the acquisition of an asset or the reduction of a liability or the loss or impairment of an asset or the incurrence of a liability.[12]

Three essential elements of a contingency.

The essential elements of this definition are that a contingency is (1) an *existing* condition, situation, or set of circumstances (2) involving *uncertainty* about an outcome (3) that will be resolved by the occurrence or nonoccurrence of some *future* event or events. For example, the loss that may occur as the result of a lawsuit that has been filed against the firm is a contingency because (1) the lawsuit has been filed, (2) there is uncertainty about its outcome, and (3) its resolution will occur in the future.

[12] ''Accounting for Contingencies,'' *Statement of Financial Accounting Standards No. 5* (Stamford, Conn.: FASB, 1975).

Are all accounting uncertainties treated as contingencies? The answer clearly is no. For example, uncertainty is involved in the estimation of depreciation expense, but accounting for depreciation is not considered to be part of accounting for contingencies. What characteristic qualifies accounting uncertainties as contingencies? If you examine the essential elements of the contingency definition, you will observe that occurrence or nonoccurrence of one or more *future* events (such as the resolution of the lawsuit mentioned earlier) is necessary before the outcome in question can be resolved with certainty. This is the characteristic that distinguishes contingencies from other accounting uncertainties. There is uncertainty about the exact amount of depreciation expense, so it is estimated. But there is certainly no question (at least there should be no question) that the service potential of the asset being depreciated is in fact expiring. No future event is required for us to know with certainty that the service potential embodied in a depreciable asset will eventually expire.

In *FASB Statement No. 5,* contingencies are classified as being either *loss contingencies* or *gain contingencies*. Our primary concern here is loss contingencies, because they are the source of contingent liabilities. We shall briefly consider accounting for gain contingencies, which *FASB Statement No. 5* carries forward as prescribed by *Accounting Research Bulletin No. 50,* near the end of the chapter.[13]

LOSS CONTINGENCIES

A **loss contingency** arises when an uncertain existing condition, situation, or set of circumstances will be resolved by the occurrence or nonoccurrence of a future event that may result in the impairment of an asset or the incurrence of a liability. Among the examples of loss contingencies provided by *FASB Statement No. 5* are collectibility of receivables; obligations related to product warranties and product defects; risk of loss or damage of property by fire, explosion, or other hazards; pending or threatened litigation; actual or possible claims or assessments; guarantees of indebtedness of others; and agreements to repurchase receivables that have been sold.

When a loss contingency exists, the likelihood that a future event or events will confirm the impairment of an asset or the incurrence of a liability can range from very likely to very unlikely. Within this range, the FASB has chosen to identify three levels of likelihood:

1. *Probable.* The future event or events are likely to occur.
2. *Reasonably possible.* The chance that the future event or events will occur is more than remote but less than probable.
3. *Remote.* The chance that the future event or events will occur is slight.

The accounting treatment of a particular loss contingency depends in part on whether the related future event has a probable, reasonably possible, or remote chance of confirming impairment of an asset or incurrence of a liability.

There are three basic ways to account for and report loss contingencies:

1. *Accrual* of an estimated loss from the contingency, which should be reported in the body of the financial statements.
2. *Disclosure, but not accrual,* of the loss contingency.
3. *Neither accrual nor disclosure* of the loss contingency.

Loss Contingencies That Should Be Accrued

An estimated loss from a loss contingency should be accrued if *both* of the following conditions are met:

[13] "Contingencies," *Accounting Research Bulletin No. 50* (New York: AICPA, 1958).

1. Information available before issuance of the financial statements indicates that it is *probable* that an asset had been impaired or a liability had been incurred by the date of the financial statements. It is implicit in this condition that it must be *probable* that one or more future events will occur confirming the fact of the loss.

2. The amount of loss can be reasonably estimated.

These two conditions require accrual of losses when they are reasonably estimable and relate to the current or a prior period. The condition that the loss be reasonably estimable prevents accrual of amounts so uncertain as to impair the integrity of the financial statements. As we shall see, disclosure by footnote or other means is preferable to accrual when a reasonable estimate of loss cannot be made. The requirement that it be *probable* that an asset has been impaired or a liability has been incurred *by the financial statement date* ensures that losses that are accrued relate to the current period or a prior period rather than to a future period.

There are some situations when condition 1 is met, but only a *range* of loss can be reasonably estimated in response to condition 2. For example, an unfavorable verdict on a lawsuit against the firm might be probable, but the amount of loss can only be estimated to be in the range of $3 million to $6 million. In these situations, when some amount within the range appears to be a better estimate of the loss than any other amount within the range, that amount should be accrued by a charge to income. If no single amount within the range appears to be a better estimate of loss than any other, the minimum amount in the range should be accrued.[14]

It is interesting to note that since the discussion here is about a potential loss situation, use of the minimum amount in the range of loss is unconservative. That is, a conservative approach would be to report the maximum estimated loss. However, accrual of a minimum loss is better than no accrual at all, which was often the practice before *FASB Statement No. 5* was issued.

In addition to requiring accrual of a loss contingency that meets *both* of the conditions for accrual, *Statement No. 5* states that disclosure of the nature of the accrual and, in "some circumstances," the amount of the accrual "may" be necessary. Unfortunately, the statement provides no guidance as to the meaning of "some circumstances" or the intention of the qualifier "may." As a result, the best disclosure policy for any accrued loss contingency is to report a liability or the reduction of an asset on the balance sheet, and a corresponding estimated expense or loss, depending on the situation, on the income statement, with a footnote describing the circumstances surrounding the contingency accrual.

FASB Statement No. 5 also states that if there is a reasonable possibility of loss in excess of the amount accrued, the additional possible loss should be disclosed. Finally, when the minimum loss in a range of possible losses is used (because there is no better estimate within the range of possible losses), the reporting entity should disclose the difference between the maximum and minimum possible loss as an upper limit on potential additional loss. In the next few paragraphs we discuss various loss contingencies that generally should be accrued. Accruable loss contingencies other than those discussed here should be accounted for by procedures similar to those shown.

GUARANTEES AND PRODUCT WARRANTIES   Most products, and many services as well, are accompanied by a guarantee or a warranty that the product or the service will be as advertised and that it is free of defects. Such guarantees and warranties typically are effective for some limited period of time, such as 90 days or one year, during which the

---

[14] "Reasonable Estimation of the Amount of a Loss: An interpretation of *FASB Statement No. 5*," *Interpretation No. 14* (Stamford, Conn.: FASB, 1976).

seller or manufacturer will repair or replace the product without charge or will refund some, all, or even more than the original purchase price—for example, ''double your money back.'' The seller or manufacturer has to comply with the terms of the guarantee or warranty if two future events occur: (1) failure of the product or service to satisfy the customer because of defect or for some other reason covered by the guarantee or warranty, and (2) a request by the customer for the seller or manufacturer to comply with the guarantee or warranty.

Guarantees or warranties create loss contingencies because there is an existing circumstance—the guarantee—that will be resolved by future events—nonfailure of the product or failure of the product combined with a customer claim—that may result in the impairment of an asset or the incurrence of a liability by the seller or manufacturer.

While normally it is not possible to reasonably estimate the amount of the seller's potential warranty expense and related liability for any particular item sold, the seller can usually estimate, on the basis of past experience, potential warranty expense associated with *total* sales occurring during some period of time, such as a month. For example, suppose that Kinney Manufacturing Company sold 10 drill presses during July for $3,000 cash each and that past experience has been that warranty expense is equal to about 2 percent of sales revenue. In this case, entries to record the aggregate sales and estimated warranty expense and liability for July would be:

Cash..	30,000	
Sales revenue		30,000
(10 × $3,000)		

Estimated warranty expense.............................	600	
Estimated liability under warranties		600
(2% × $30,000)		

If actual costs of $400 are incurred when warranty work is done, these costs are recorded as in the following entry:

Estimated liability under warranties 400		
Wages payable, parts inventory, cash, etc.		400

If warranty expense is reasonably estimated, the difference between estimated and actual warranty expense should approximate zero over time. If not, the basis for estimating warranty expense should be appropriately adjusted.

The procedure used to estimate warranty liabilities for a period is exactly the same procedure as that used in the percentage-of-sales method of estimating uncollectible accounts receivable expense. Accordingly, it is useful to make periodic tests to determine if the percentage used to estimate warranty expense and the corresponding estimated warranty liability are satisfactory, given recent actual warranty expense experience. If the percentage must be changed, a change in accounting estimate will be necessary. The method used to account for the change is described in Chapter 22.

When warranty expense is not a material item or when it is not possible to develop a reasonable estimate of warranty expense and the related liability during the period of sale, it is acceptable to use the cash basis of accounting for warranty expense. That is, warranty expense is debited, with an offsetting credit to cash, materials, wages payable, and so forth, at the time that obligations under the warranty agreement are met. Assuming $400 cost is incurred to settle warranty claims, the cash basis accounting entry would be:

Warranty expense 400		
Wages payable, parts inventory, cash, etc.		400

PREMIUMS, COUPONS, AND TRADING STAMPS It is a fairly common practice for sellers or manufacturers to give premiums such as cash or merchandise to customers in exchange for coupons, labels, wrappers, and so forth that accompany purchased merchandise. Examples include cash refunds in exchange for jar labels, toys given in exchange for cereal boxtops, and household utensils given in exchange for coupons included in boxes of detergent. Since premium offers are made in an effort to increase sales of the product, the matching principle requires that the expense of premium offers be included among the expenses of the period in which the related sales of the product occur. In conjunction with recognition of the premium expense it is also appropriate to record an obligation to provide the premium to those customers who are expected to turn in coupons before the expiration date on the premium offer.

The seller who makes premium offers must (1) purchase any toys, utensils, and the like that are offered as premiums; (2) record premium expense for any premiums given out or expected to be given out as the result of sales for the period; and (3) distribute premiums as customers turn in the required labels, boxtops, or coupons.

In the case of cash refund offers, it is only necessary for the seller to estimate its refund expense for the period and to record the related obligation to make cash refunds to the extent such refunds have not been made before the end of the accounting period.

Assume that the following entries were made by Super Cereal Company with respect to its offer of an official-size football in exchange for 10 Super Cereal boxtops plus $10. Assume that a total of 100,000 boxes of Super Cereal were sold at $1.20 each during the accounting period and that estimates are that 40 percent of the boxtops will be turned in for footballs.

Super Cereal must obtain an inventory of footballs to be given out as premiums. Assume that Super Cereal acquired 5,000 footballs at $12.50 each for this purpose. The entry recording this acquisition would be:

Inventory of premiums	62,500	
Cash		62,500
(5,000 × $12.50)		

The entry to record sales of the 100,000 boxes of Super Cereal at $1.20 per box would be:

Cash	120,000	
Sales revenue		120,000
(100,000 × $1.20)		

In conjunction with the current period's sales, estimated premium expense would be debited for the $2.50 per football cost in excess of the $10 charge to the customer for the 4,000 footballs given out or expected to be given out in exchange for boxtops (100,000 boxtops divided by 10 boxtops per football multiplied by a 40 percent return rate on the boxtops equals 4,000 footballs). Redemption of 30,000 boxtops and receipt of $30,000 in exchange for 3,000 footballs during the accounting period would be recorded as:

Cash	30,000	
Premium expense (3,000 × $2.50)	7,500	
Inventory of premiums (3,000 × $12.50)		37,500

At the end of the accounting period, the adjusting entry to record estimated premium expense and the associated obligation for premiums still outstanding that are related to the current period's sales of Super Cereal would be:

Premium expense 2,500
    Estimated premium obligation   2,500
    (1,000 × $2.50)

For the accounting period, sales of $120,000 and premium expense of $10,000 would appear on the income statement. An inventory of premiums of $25,000 (2,000 footballs costing $12.50 each) would be included in current assets and estimated premium obligation of $2,500 would be reported as a current liability on the balance sheet.

Trading stamps are handled slightly differently. The merchant who issues the trading stamps simply buys them from a trading stamp company, which in turn assumes responsibility for redeeming them. In this situation, the merchant merely records the purchase and the issuance of the stamps. Issued stamps are a selling expense, and stamps still in inventory are a current or noncurrent asset, depending on when the stamps are expected to be issued.

The trading stamp company records (1) the sale of trading stamps to the merchant, (2) the purchase of premiums, (3) the distribution of premiums, and (4) the estimated premium obligation outstanding at the end of the accounting period.

LITIGATION, CLAIMS, AND ASSESSMENTS   When we must determine whether accrual or disclosure is required with respect to threatened litigation (lawsuit not yet filed) or pending litigation (lawsuit filed but not settled) and possible or actual claims and assessments, *FASB Statement No. 5* specifies three factors that must be considered:

1. The period in which the underlying cause (that is, the cause for action) of the pending or threatened litigation or of the actual or possible claim or assessment occurred.

2. The degree of probability of an unfavorable outcome.

3. The ability to make a reasonable estimate of the amount of loss.

Accrual of a loss contingency for litigation, claims, or assessments is appropriate only if:

1. The cause for action occurs by the date of the financial statements.

2. Information available *before* the issuance of the financial statements indicates that it is *probable* that an asset has been impaired or a liability has been incurred as of the date of the financial statements.

3. It is possible to make a reasonable estimate of the amount of loss that may arise from the loss contingency.

Among the factors that should be considered in determining the probability that an asset has been impaired or a liability has been incurred are the nature of the litigation, claim, or assessment; the progress of the case; the opinions or views of management, legal counsel, and other advisers; the experiences of the entity in previous similar cases; the experiences of other entities; and any decision of the entity's management as to how the entity will respond to the lawsuit, claim, or assessment. Legal counsel for the entity may be unable to express an opinion that the outcome will be favorable, but this should not necessarily be interpreted to mean that an unfavorable outcome is probable. As we mentioned earlier, satisfactory disclosure of an accrued loss contingency would include a footnote in the financial statements describing the circumstances surrounding the loss contingency. Note H in Exhibit 15–3 is an example of appropriate disclosure related to accrual of a loss contingency.

Consider now the circumstances surrounding a hypothetical lawsuit filed against Hairston Corporation, a manufacturer of men's hair products. The plaintiff in the case

EXHIBIT 15—3   DISCLOSURE RELATED TO ACCRUAL
OF A LITIGATION LOSS CONTINGENCY

Southern Development, Inc.

PARTIAL BALANCE SHEET, 1987

Current liabilities:
    Liability for legal claims (Note H) $175,000

.
.
.

Note H: On January 5, 1987, Florida Mortgage and Investment Company filed a suit against Southern Development demanding a judgment in the amount of approximately $1,200,000 with regard to alleged loan guarantees by Southern Development for the Sea Side Estates Project in Wallace, Florida. The case is presently in pre-trial discovery. While legal counsel is unable to opine as to the likely resolution, due to the early stage of pre-trial discovery, counsel reported that the plaintiffs have offered to settle the case for $175,000. Although the $175,000 offer was rejected by management, recent conversations with plaintiffs' counsel indicate that a $175,000 settlement is still possible. Thus, while the outcome of any litigation is, at best, uncertain, it appears that this litigation could be resolved for the suggested $175,000 amount. The company has provided an accrual for a loss contingency amounting to the proposed settlement.

---

bought a bottle of Hairston's ''guaranteed to grow hair'' tonic on November 10, 1987. On February 12, 1988, twelve days after the end of Hairston's fiscal year but well before the issuance date of the 1987 financial statements, the plaintiff filed an $80,000 lawsuit against Hairston. Damages were sought because the tonic purchased by the plaintiff caused loss of what little hair he had rather than causing new hair to grow. Hairston's management and legal counsel expect that the company will lose the lawsuit, but estimate that damages will be only $10,000. In this case, the appropriate entry, which should be incorporated in the 1987 financial statements, is:

Estimated loss from pending lawsuit 10,000
    Estimated liability from pending lawsuit   10,000

The estimated loss from pending lawsuit account should be presented in Hairston's income statement in accordance with the criteria presented in *APB Opinion No. 30* for reporting extraordinary, unusual or infrequent, or ordinary items in the income statement (see Chapter 4). If settlement of the lawsuit is expected within the longer of one year or one operating cycle, the estimated liability should be reported as a current liability.

The key point here is that the cause for action—purchase of the tonic and the initial stages of hair loss—occurred by the date of Hairston's financial statements even though Hairston was not aware of the lawsuit until after the end of the fiscal year. A second important point is the relevance of information obtained after the end of the fiscal year but before the issuance date of the financial statements.

LOSSES ON PURCHASE COMMITMENTS   In Chapter 10 we discussed application of the lower-of-cost-or-market procedure to purchase commitments on the same basis as that used to apply the procedure to inventory on hand. In this chapter, we want to discuss purchase commitments once again, but here the emphasis is on the contingent liability that sometimes is recorded when losses on purchase commitments are accounted for.

When a purchase commitment cannot be revised or canceled and a loss on the contract occurs or a *reasonably estimable* material future loss is *probable,* the utility of that purchase commitment is impaired. This loss of utility should be recognized as a deduction from the revenues of the period in which the circumstances giving rise to the loss or probable future loss occur.[15] In Chapter 10 we discussed the recording of an estimated loss on a purchase commitment when that commitment extends beyond the end of the buyer's fiscal year. We assumed that the buyer had a $20,000 purchase commitment that extended into February of the buyer's next fiscal year and that the market price of the contracted goods was $17,000 at the end of the buyer's current fiscal year. Under these circumstances, the buyer would make the following year-end adjusting entry:

```
Estimated loss on purchase commitment ....................3,000
    Estimated liability on purchase commitment ...............          3,000
```

It is the liability account in the above entry that is of interest to us in this chapter.

The estimated liability on purchase commitment is reported among the buyer's current liabilities if the goods are to be purchased within the longer of the next year or the next operating cycle. This liability may be thought of as an estimate of the amount that the buyer would have to pay the seller if the buyer could and did cancel the contract. The liability account is debited for its credit balance in the period in which the purchase commitment is completed. An entry such as the following would be made at the time of purchase (assuming that the market price remained at $17,000):

```
Inventory (or purchases) .................................17,000
Estimated liability on purchase commitment .................  3,000
    Accounts payable (or cash) ...........................         20,000
```

In our opinion, the estimated liability that may be recorded under current GAAP to account for losses on purchase commitments can be justified only as the credit that is necessary to match the estimated loss on the purchase commitment with the period in which the market price falls below the contract price of the goods. The estimated liability on purchase commitment account lacks one of the three essential characteristics of a liability, as defined by the FASB in its conceptual framework project.[16]

Specifically, the estimated liability on purchase commitment does not represent an *existing obligation* that entails settlement by probable future transfer or use of assets. The decline in market price below contract price places no equivalent obligation on the buyer, although it is true that the buyer may suffer a loss because of the contractual commitment. Support for the liability credit rests entirely on the importance of accruing the probable loss. This loss may provide a signal that expected cash flows from future sales may be reduced if inventory selling prices, like acquisition costs, are reduced.[17]

Loss Contingencies That Should Be Disclosed but Not Accrued

FASB Statement No. 5 states that a loss contingency that fails to meet either or both of the two conditions for accrual that we mentioned earlier should not be accrued, but should be

---

[15] The utility of a purchase commitment is *not* impaired and there is no loss when the amounts to be realized from the disposition of the future inventory are adequately protected by sales contracts or when there are other circumstances that reasonably ensure continuing sales without price decline. "Restatement and Revision of Accounting Research Bulletins," *Accounting Research Bulletin No. 43* (New York: AICPA, 1953), chap. 4, statement 10.

[16] "Liability" is defined in "Elements of Financial Statements," *Statement of Financial Accounting Concepts No. 6.*

[17] Current GAAP for losses on purchase commitments provides an example of what might be called an "unrealized *preholding* loss."

disclosed in a footnote or by other means if there is at least a reasonable possibility that a loss may have been incurred. In addition, *remote* loss contingencies that have the characteristics of guarantees should be disclosed. Such remote loss contingencies include direct or indirect guarantees of indebtedness of others[18] and guarantees to repurchase receivables.

Acceptable forms of disclosure include parenthetical notes in the financial statements, showing items "short" in the financial statements, appropriations of retained earnings, and footnotes to the financial statements. By far the most common form of disclosure for loss contingencies is the use of footnotes to the financial statements. Disclosure of a loss contingency should indicate the nature of the contingency and should either (1) give an estimate of the possible loss or range of loss or (2) state that such an estimate cannot be made. For a remote loss contingency with the characteristics of a guarantee, the amount of the guarantee should be disclosed and, if estimable, amounts that are expected to be recovered from outside parties also should be disclosed.

Disclosure is not required for a loss contingency related to an unasserted claim or assessment when there is no evidence that a potential claimant is aware that a claim or assessment is possible. If it is *probable* that a claim will be asserted, however, *and* there is a *reasonable possibility* that the outcome will be unfavorable, a loss contingency should be disclosed. For example, an accident resulting from faulty brakes on a new automobile will probably generate a claim for redress that has a reasonable possibility of an unfavorable outcome for the automobile manufacturer or its insurer. In this case, it would be appropriate for the automobile manufacturer to disclose the loss contingency even though, at the moment, no claim has been asserted.

Sometimes, though, loss contingencies involving unasserted claims *should not* be disclosed. Consider a firm that believes there is a possibility that it has infringed on another firm's patent rights, but the company that owns the patent has not indicated any intention of taking any action or even any awareness of the possible infringement. If the potentially infringing firm believes that the patent owner's assertion of a claim is not probable, then no accrual or disclosure is required. On the other hand, if there is reason to believe that assertion is probable, then the infringing firm must estimate the degree of probability of an unfavorable outcome. If an unfavorable outcome is probable and the amount of loss can be reasonably estimated, accrual of a loss is required. If an unfavorable outcome is probable but the amount of loss cannot be reasonably estimated, accrual is not appropriate but disclosure is required.

Occasionally information becomes available before the financial statements are issued indicating that an asset was impaired or a liability was incurred *after* the date of the financial statements or that there is at least a reasonable possibility that an asset was impaired or a liability was incurred after that date. In such circumstances, the first condition for accrual of a loss contingency is not met because there was no asset impairment or liability incurrence *by* the date of the financial statements. *Disclosure* of losses or loss contingencies of this type may be necessary to keep the financial statements from being misleading. If disclosure is necessary, it should indicate the nature of the loss or loss contingency and give an estimate of the amount or range of loss, or possible loss, or state that such an estimate cannot be made. When the amount of asset impairment or liability incurrence can be reasonably estimated, disclosure may best be made by supplementing the financial statements with pro forma financial data treating the loss as if it had occurred at the date of the financial statements.

---

[18] In a *direct* guarantee of the indebtedness of others, if the debtor fails to make payment to the creditor when the debt is due, the guarantor must pay the creditor. In an *indirect* guarantee, instead of paying the creditor, the guarantor must transfer funds to the debtor.

Loss Contingencies That Are Neither Accrued nor Disclosed

General or unspecified business risks—for example, strikes, wars, and recessions—do not meet the conditions for accrual of loss contingencies, and no accrual or disclosure of loss or possible loss from such risks should be made. *FASB Statement No. 5* does not require disclosure of remote loss contingencies that are not guarantees or for which a reasonable estimate of possible loss cannot be made, but neither does it prohibit such disclosures.

Having considered the proper accounting treatments of all levels of likelihood of loss contingencies, we shall turn our attention briefly to accounting for gain contingencies.

GAIN CONTINGENCIES

A **gain contingency** arises when an uncertain existing condition, situation, or set of circumstances will be resolved with the occurrence or nonoccurrence of a future event that may result in an increase in assets or a decrease in liabilities. Claims against others for patent infringement, upward price redetermination, and claims for reimbursement under condemnation proceedings are examples of gain contingencies.

Both the revenue realization principle and conservatism influence accounting for gain contingencies. *Accounting Research Bulletin No. 50* sets forth two fundamental provisions related to accounting for and reporting of gain contingencies. The first provision is that a contingency that might result in a gain usually should *not* be accrued and reported in the body of the financial statements until the gain is realized. The second provision is that before the gain is realized, a material gain contingency should be given adequate disclosure, provided that care is exercised to avoid misleading implications as to the likelihood of realization. That is, the disclosure should not cause the financial statement reader to become overly optimistic about the possible gain. Given this provision, it is clear that it would be inappropriate to disclose *remote* gain contingencies.

FINANCIAL STATEMENT PRESENTATION OF CURRENT LIABILITIES AND CONTINGENCIES

Current liabilities normally are presented as the first group of items in the liabilities section of the balance sheet. This presentation follows the traditional practice of ordering items in the balance sheet according to liquidity.[19] Occasionally current liabilities are presented immediately below current assets and deducted from them as a group, yielding a working capital balance.

Within the current liability group the accounts may be presented in order of increasing dollar amount, in order of maturity (more liquid accounts first), or in order of creditors' liquidation preferences. Disclosures should identify secured liabilities and the assets pledged as collateral for those liabilities. Current liabilities should not be offset against current assets that may be used to liquidate them. Generally, liabilities are not claims against specific assets but rather are claims against some portion of total assets. If the date for meeting any current liability can be extended, that fact should be disclosed, along with relevant details.

Exhibit 15–4 shows how current liabilities may be reported in the balance sheet. It also presents a litigation contingency note to the financial statements.

---

[19] "Liquidity" of a balance sheet item refers to the item's nearness to providing cash, if an asset, or to requiring the use of cash, if a liability.

EXHIBIT 15—4   CURRENT LIABILITIES AND A CONTINGENCY FOOTNOTE

Abbot Laboratories and Subsidiaries

FROM ANNUAL REPORT, 1984
(in thousands of dollars)

	DECEMBER 31		
LIABILITIES AND SHAREHOLDERS' INVESTMENT	**1984**	**1983**	**1982**
Current Liabilities:			
Short-term borrowings	$ 269,948	$ 145,860	$ 362,003
Trade accounts payable	152,989	169,170	145,787
Other accrued liabilities	186,785	191,868	133,733
Salaries, wages, and commissions	71,876	65,119	57,465
Dividends payable	36,057	30,344	25,642
Income taxes payable	85,954	72,048	160,820
Current portion of long-term debt	2,721	2,360	7,942
Total current liabilities	$ 806,330	$ 676,769	$ 893,392
Long-term debt	470,165	483,929	190,937
Other liabilities and deferrals:			
Deferred income taxes	199,688	157,772	107,548
Other	94,014	87,775	64,146
Total liabilities	$1,570,197	$1,406,245	$1,256,023
Shareholders' investment:			
Common shares, without par value; authorized, 300,000,000 shares; issued at stated capital amount, 1984, 1983, and 1982:			
124,086,672 shares	186,384	183,725	180,683
Earnings employed in the business	1,651,227	1,402,742	1,188,022
Cumulative translation adjustments	(84,232)	(57,504)	—
	$1,753,379	$1,528,963	$1,368,705
Less: common shares held in treasury at cost 1984: 3,852,400 shares; 1983: 2,988,900 shares; 1982: 1,983,006 shares	(150,679)	(111,080)	(57,819)
Total shareholders' investment	$1,602,700	$1,417,883	$1,310,886
Total liabilities and shareholders' investment	$3,172,897	$2,824,128	$2,566,909

NOTE 10—LITIGATION

There are various suits and other legal proceedings and claims against the Company. These include one group of product liability cases brought against the Company and varying numbers of other pharmaceutical companies on behalf of individuals or groups or alleged classes of individuals claiming billions of dollars in damages and other monetary, injunctive, and declaratory relief as a result of injuries alleged to have resulted from the use by their or their spouses' mothers of certain synthetic estrogen drugs, including diethylstilbestrol, during pregnancy. Such use allegedly occurred generally during the period 1946 through 1971. The Company sold diethylstilbestrol products from 1941 through 1961 during which period its total sales of such products approximated $1 million. (These matters are discussed more fully in Item 3, Legal Proceedings, in the Annual Report on Form 10-K, which is available upon request.) While it is not feasible to predict the outcome of these suits and other legal proceedings and claims with certainty, management is of the opinion, with which its General Counsel concurs, that their ultimate disposition should not have a material adverse effect on the Company's consolidated financial position.

SUMMARY OF IMPORTANT TOPICS AND CONCEPT APPLICATIONS

1. A **current liability** requires the transfer of resources or the incurrence of another liability within the longer of one fiscal year or one operating cycle.

2. Current liabilities can be categorized as: (1) determinable current liabilities, (2) current liabilities dependent on operating results, and (3) contingent current liabilities.

3. Short-term obligations expected to be refinanced on a long-term basis should be classified as noncurrent liabilities. The ability to refinance can be demonstrated by either (1) refinancing during the period between the balance sheet date and the date the financial statements are issued or (2) entering into an agreement, before the financial statements are issued, that clearly permits such refinancing on a long-term basis.

4. An employer must accrue a liability for employees' rights to receive compensation for future absences from work when all four of the following conditions are met: (1) the employer's obligation is attributable to services already rendered by the employee; (2) the employee's right to compensation is not contingent on the employee's future service, or the right to compensation can be accumulated over time; (3) payment of the compensation by the employer is probable; and (4) the amount of compensation is reasonably estimable.

5. A **contingent liability** arises when the existence of an obligation, the amount payable, or the settlement date is uncertain, and the resolution of the uncertainty depends on some future event or events. A **loss contingency** arises when an uncertain existing condition, situation, or set of circumstances will be resolved by the occurrence or nonoccurrence of a future event that may result in the impairment of an asset or the incurrence of a liability.

6. A loss contingency may be (1) probable, (2) reasonably possible, or (3) remote. The level of likelihood determines the appropriate accounting treatment.

7. The basic ways to account for and report loss contingencies are: (1) accrual; (2) disclosure, but not accrual; and (3) neither accrual nor disclosure.

8. Accrual of a loss contingency requires that (1) it is probable that an asset has been impaired or a liability has been incurred and (2) the amount of the loss can be reasonably estimated.

9. A loss contingency that fails to meet either or both of the two conditions for accrual should not be accrued, but should be disclosed in a footnote or by other means if there is at least a reasonable possibility that a loss may have been incurred. In addition, remote loss contingencies that have the characteristics of guarantees should be disclosed. Remote loss contingencies that are not guarantees, or for which a reasonable estimate of possible loss cannot be made, need not be disclosed.

QUESTIONS

Q15-1. What three characteristics are common to all liabilities?

Q15-2. What is the theoretically correct valuation of a liability?

Q15-3. Distinguish between current liabilities and noncurrent liabilities.

Q15-4. Why might a liability that is current for one entity be properly classified as noncurrent for another entity?

Q15-5. Give two examples each of *(a)* determinable current liabilities, *(b)* current liabilities dependent on operating results, and *(c)* contingent current liabilities that require accrual.

Q15-6. What are the characteristics of a determinable current liability?

Q15-7. What are the exceptions to the accounting policy of reclassifying as a current liability any portion of long-term obligations that will be due for payment within the longer of one year or one operating cycle?

Q15-8. Under what conditions would a long-term obligation that is callable be classified as a current liability?

Q15-9. What two conditions must be satisfied before a short-term obligation that is expected to be refinanced can be classified as a noncurrent liability?

Q15-10. Explain how a company can satisfactorily demonstrate the ability to refinance a short-term obligation.

Q15-11. Why are stock dividends declared not recognized as liabilities?

Q15-12. How do accrued liabilities arise?

Q15-13. Under what conditions must an employer accrue a liability for employees' rights to receive compensation for future absences from work?

Q15-14. When should the expense and accrued liability arising from an employee's right to be compensated for future absences be recorded?

Q15-15. Briefly describe the two most common practices used to account for property tax expense and property taxes payable.

Q15-16. What is the basic accounting issue related to accounting for income taxes in interim periods? What was the APB's resolution of this issue?

Q15-17. Why is calculation of a bonus on the basis of income after *all* expenses a "circular" problem?

Q15-18. Define a contingency, identifying the three essential elements of the definition.

Q15-19. Define a loss contingency. Give three examples of loss contingencies.

Q15-20. Identify and describe the three levels of likelihood of the occurrence of a future event related to accounting for loss contingencies.

Q15-21. What three ways are available to account for and report loss contingencies?

Q15-22. Identify and explain the two conditions that must be satisfied before it is proper to accrue an estimated loss from a loss contingency.

Q15-23. If it is *probable* that an asset has been impaired or a liability has been incurred by the financial statement date, but only a *range* of loss can be reasonably estimated, what amount should be accrued?

Q15-24. Identify the three factors that must be considered in determining whether accrual or disclosure is required with respect to threatened or pending litigation.

Q15-25. What basis is there for arguing that the estimated liability that may be recorded when purchase commitments are accounted for is not really a liability?

Q15-26. In the case of loss contingencies that should be disclosed but not accrued, what information should be disclosed?

Q15-27. What types of loss contingencies never require disclosure?

Q15-28. What are the two fundamental provisions related to accounting for and reporting gain contingencies?

CASES

C15-1. GENERAL DISCUSSION OF LIABILITIES   One of your distant relatives knows that you have recently graduated from an undergraduate accounting program and soon will be beginning a career in accounting. He spots you at a family reunion and immediately begins asking questions about liabilities. You are surprised by both his sudden interest in you and his questions, and so you ask why he wants to know so much about liabilities. He tells you that he started a new business during the past year and just recently had his first set of financial statements prepared by a public accountant. He had always thought that a liability was a legal debt to another party, but his accountant has included several items in his financial statements as liabilities or contingent liabilities that seem not to be legal debts. Your relative is concerned that the accountant does not know what he is doing, or that the accountant is intentionally misrepresenting the company's liabilities.

REQUIRED

As an aid to your relative, draft responses to the following questions:

1. What are the essential characteristics of a liability?

2. What kinds of circumstances and transactions can cause a liability to arise? Give examples.

3. What is the theoretically correct value of a liability?

4. How can current liabilities be distinguished from noncurrent liabilities?

5. What are the distinctions among determinable current liabilities, current liabilities dependent on operating results, and contingent liabilities?

C15-2. CURRENT AND NONCURRENT LIABILITIES   The following items are listed as liabilities on the balance sheet of Dillard Company on December 31, 1987:

Accounts payable	$ 305,000
Notes payable	310,000
Bonds payable	1,350,000

The accounts payable represent obligations to suppliers that are due in January 1988. The notes payable mature on various dates during 1988. The bonds payable mature on July 1, 1988. These liabilities must be reported on the balance sheet in accordance with generally accepted accounting principles.

REQUIRED

1. What is the general rule for determining whether a liability is classified as current or noncurrent?

2. Under what conditions may any of Dillard Company's liabilities be classified as noncurrent? Explain your answer.

(IMA, adapted)

C15-3. LOSSES ON PURCHASE COMMITMENTS   On March 7, 1987, Norris Company entered into an agreement to purchase 10,000 units of inventory at a fixed price of $8 per unit by June 20, 1988. During 1987, Norris purchased 7,000 units at the agreed price when the market price of the units was $7.50. By December 31, 1987, the end of Norris's fiscal year, the market price of inventory units had dropped to $7 and 1,500 of the purchased units remained in Norris's inventory.

REQUIRED

1. Prepare the journal entry to record Norris's purchase of the 7,000 units.

2. Prepare the journal entry to adjust Norris's December 31 inventory to market.

3. Prepare any year-end adjusting entry that may be necessary to account properly for the purchase commitment.

4. Prepare the necessary entry to record Norris's purchase of the remaining 3,000 units under contract, assuming the market price was $6.75 at the date of purchase.

5. Describe the nature of the estimated liability that may be recorded under current GAAP for accounting for losses on purchase commitments. Is this estimated liability really a liability?

6. Why should a loss on the purchase commitment be recorded on December 31, 1987?

C15-4. LOSS CONTINGENCIES AND LIABILITY ON COUPONS   Branerd Company is a manufacturer of toys. During the year, the following situations arose:

Situation 1: A safety hazard related to one of Branerd's toy products was discovered. It is considered probable that liabilities have been incurred. A reasonable estimate of the amount of loss can be made on the basis of past experience.

Situation 2: One of Branerd's small warehouses is located on the bank of a river and can no longer be insured against flood losses. No flood losses have occurred since the date when the insurance became unavailable.

Situation 3: This year, Branerd began to promote a new toy by including a coupon, redeemable for a movie ticket, in each toy's carton. The movie ticket, which costs Branerd $2, is purchased in advance and then mailed to the customer when the coupon is received by Branerd. Branerd estimated, on the basis of past experience, that 60 percent of the coupons would be redeemed. Forty percent of the coupons were actually redeemed this year, and the remaining 20 percent of the coupons are expected to be redeemed next year.

REQUIRED

1. How should Branerd report the safety hazard? Why?

2. How should Branerd report the noninsurable flood risk? Why?

3. How should Branerd account for the toy promotion campaign this year?

(AICPA, adapted)

C15-5. LOSS CONTINGENCIES   You are employed as an auditor for a regional CPA firm. During the course of the audit of a local manufacturing firm, you discover a set of events and circumstances that the audit client does not intend to include, in any way, in its financial statements. The firm's point of view is that no transaction has occurred and so there is nothing to include in the financial statements. You, on the other hand, have the feeling that a loss contingency may exist.

REQUIRED

Develop for the client responses to the following questions:

1. What conditions should be met for an estimated contingent loss to be accrued and reported in the income statement?

2. When is disclosure required and what disclosure should be made for an estimated contingent loss that need not be accrued?

3. What is the proper procedure when a loss contingency should be accrued, but only a *range* of loss can be reasonably estimated?

C15-6. LOSS CONTINGENCIES

A) The two basic requirements for the accrual of a loss contingency are supported by several basic concepts of accounting. Three of these concepts are periodicity (time periods), measurement, and verifiability.

REQUIRED

Discuss how the two basic requirements for the accrual of a loss contingency relate to the three concepts named above.

B) The following three independent sets of facts relate to the possible accrual of a loss contingency or its possible disclosure by other means.

Situation 1: A company offers a one-year warranty for the product that it manufactures. A history of warranty claims has been compiled and the probable amount of claims related to sales for a given period can be determined.

Situation 2: After the date of a set of financial statements but before they have been issued, a company enters into a contract that will probably result in a significant loss to it. The amount of the loss can be reasonably estimated.

Situation 3: A company has adopted a policy of recording self-insurance for any possible losses resulting from injury to others by its vehicles. The premium for an insurance policy for the same risk from an independent insurance company would have an annual cost of $2,000. During the period covered by the financial statements, there were no accidents involving the company's vehicles which resulted in injury to others.

REQUIRED

For each of the three independent sets of facts above, discuss the accrual or type of disclosure necessary (if any) and the reason why such disclosure is appropriate.

(AICPA, adapted)

C15-7. CLASSIFICATION OF OBLIGATIONS   Under some conditions, current maturities of long-term obligations and obligations that are callable by the creditor should be classified as current liabilities. On the other hand, short-term obligations that are expected to be refinanced sometimes are classified as noncurrent liabilities.

REQUIRED

1. Under what conditions would current maturities of long-term obligations *not* be classified as current liabilities?

2. Under what conditions would long-term obligations that are callable by the creditor or that will be callable within the longer of one year or one operating cycle *not* be classified as current liabilities?

3. Under what conditions would short-term obligations that are expected to be refinanced be classified as noncurrent liabilities? For each condition for classification as a noncurrent liability, what amount of short-term obligation should be classified as a noncurrent liability?

EXERCISES

E15-1. ACCOUNTING FOR SHORT-TERM NOTES PAYABLE   Assume that Susan Smith wishes to obtain $630, after bank charges, from her local bank for the purpose of buying a television set. The note signed by Smith is a noninterest-bearing one-year note, which the bank intends to discount at a 10 percent discount rate.

REQUIRED

1. What is the face value of the note?

2. Prepare the entry on Smith's books to record her transaction with the bank.

3. What is the effective interest rate incurred by Smith on this transaction?

E15-2. ACCOUNTING FOR SHORT-TERM OBLIGATIONS EXPECTED TO BE REFINANCED   Perles Company has a September 30 fiscal year-end, and on September 30, 1987, Perles has $2.3 million of short-term notes payable outstanding. On October 15, 1987, Perles issued 115,000 shares of its $5 par value common stock at $20 per share for the purpose of generating funds to be used to retire short-term notes payable due on November 7, 1987. After paying brokerage fees and other costs of issuing the common stock, Perles received proceeds from the stock sale of $2.15 million, which was used on October 28 to liquidate short-term notes payable. Perles' 1987 financial statements were published on November 15.

REQUIRED

Show how the short-term notes payable that were liquidated on October 28 should be reported on the September 30, 1987, financial statements, including footnote disclosures.

E15-3. DIVIDENDS PAYABLE   Types of dividends payable include cash dividends payable, stock dividends payable, property dividends payable, and scrip dividends payable.

REQUIRED

1. Which of these types of dividends payable require recognition of a liability at the date of declaration?

2. If declaration of any of the above dividends does not result in a liability, why not? Be specific about the type of dividend.

3. How should stock dividends payable be reported in the balance sheet?

E15-4. SALES TAXES COLLECTED   The current fiscal year's sales for Johnson, Inc., totaled $2.5 million, including a 3 percent sales tax. The sales taxes are to be remitted to the proper taxing authority within six months of the end of the fiscal year.

REQUIRED

Prepare the appropriate journal entries *(a)* to record Johnson's total sales revenue and sales tax obligation for the current year and *(b)* to record remittance of the sales taxes collected for each of the following independent cases.

1. Johnson separates sales revenues and sales taxes when recording sales transactions.

2. Johnson does not separate sales revenues and sales taxes when recording sales transactions.

(AICPA, adapted)

E15-5. AMOUNTS WITHHELD FROM PAYROLL   In 1987 Wilson Company paid total wages and salaries of $480,000, of which $350,000 was subject to a 7.15 percent FICA tax rate. Federal, state, and local income taxes withheld from wages and salaries amounted to $185,000, and union dues withheld were $23,500.

REQUIRED

Make the appropriate entry to record wages and salaries expense, the various amounts withheld from employees' wages and salaries, and payment of employees' wages and salaries.

E15-6. ACCOUNTING FOR COMPENSATED FUTURE EMPLOYEE ABSENCES   Osburn Corporation began operations on January 1, 1987, at which time it hired 25 new employees at a wage of $12.50 per hour for a 40-hour workweek. Osburn's vacation policy allows 90 hours of paid vacation to be vested for each full year of employment. No paid vacation can be taken until after one year of employment. All of Osburn's new employees took paid vacations during 1988, with 2,200 total vacation hours taken. All vacation hours were taken when the wage rate was $13 per hour.

REQUIRED

Prepare the necessary entries for 1987 and 1988 to record the accrual and payment of vacation wages.

E15-7. ACCOUNTING FOR EMPLOYER PAYROLL TAX EXPENSE   Total wages and salaries paid by Bill's TV Repair were $173,000 in 1987. Bill has 15 employees, each of whom earns more than $10,000 but less than $16,000 per year. Because of his outstanding record of providing stable employment, Bill is subject to a state unemployment tax rate of only 2.7 percent, although the standard rate in his state is 5.4 percent on the first $7,000 earned by any employee. In 1987 the FUTA tax rate, before credit for state unemployment taxes paid, was 6.2 percent on the first $7,000 paid to each employee.

REQUIRED

Prepare the appropriate journal entry to record the employer's payroll tax expense for 1987.

E15-8. ACCOUNTING FOR PROPERTY TAXES   Maxwell Township assesses property in January, sends out property tax bills in February, and expects payment of property taxes in two equal installments on June 30 and December 31. Maxwell Township's fiscal year begins on March 1, which also is the lien date for property taxes. Ranson Company received a $3,600 property tax bill on February 17.

REQUIRED

1. What two basic questions must be answered in accounting for property taxes?

2. Assuming that all property taxes payable for the year are recorded on the lien date, what entries would be made by Ranson Company on February 17, March 1, June 30, and December 31?

3. Assuming that property taxes payable are accrued monthly, what entries would be made by Ranson Company on February 17, March 31, June 30, and December 31?

E15-9. RECORDING WARRANTY EXPENSE AND LIABILITY   Winson Company estimated its annual warranty expense as 1 percent of annual net sales. The following data relate to the year 1987:

Net sales $6,400,000
Warranty liability account balance at 12/31/87 ....   10,000 debit before
                                                                     adjustment

REQUIRED

Prepare the appropriate entry to record the 1987 estimated warranty expense.

E15-10. CALCULATING AND RECORDING BONUS EXPENSE   W. T. Harvey, president of Harvey Tool Company, receives an annual bonus of 20 percent of income after tax expense. His bonus is deductible for tax purposes and for purposes of bonus calculation. The current year's income before taxes and bonus is $400,000 and the tax rate is 25 percent.

REQUIRED

1. Calculate the tax expense and Mr. Harvey's bonus for the current year. (Round your answer to the nearest dollar.)

2. Prepare the appropriate journal entries to record the bonus and income taxes.

E15-11. CALCULATING BONUS AND TAX EXPENSES   The chief administrative officer of White Cosmetics, Inc., Mary White, receives a bonus of 10 percent of income each year. Assume effective tax rates for 1987 and 1988 of 20 percent and 25 percent, respectively. Income in 1987 before bonus and taxes is $100,000 and the bonus is deductible for tax purposes, but only taxes are deductible for the purpose of calculating the bonus. Income in 1988 before bonus and tax expenses is $200,000, and the 1988 bonus is based on income after bonus expense but before income taxes.

REQUIRED

1. Calculate Mary White's bonus and the corporation's tax expense for 1987.

2. Calculate Mary White's bonus and the corporation's tax expense for 1988.

E15-12. ACCOUNTING FOR A LOSS CONTINGENCY   Clark Corporation, a manufacturer of automobile tires, is preparing annual financial statements as of December 31, 1987. Because of a recently identified flaw in one of its specialty tires, the government has clearly indicated that Clark will be required to recall all of the specialty tires sold in the last six months. Clark's management estimates that this recall will cost $1 million.

REQUIRED

1. What accounting recognition, if any, should be given to this situation?

2. Assume the situation justifies accrual of a loss contingency. Prepare the appropriate accrual entry.

3. Draft a footnote related to the loss contingency recorded in part 2.

E15-13. CALCULATING AND ACCOUNTING FOR A WARRANTY LIABILITY   In 1987 Roth Company began selling a new line of products with a two-year warranty against defects. Industry experience with similar products indicates that estimated warranty costs are 2 percent of sales during the first year of the warranty and 5 percent of sales during the second year of the warranty. Sales and actual warranty expenditures for 1987 and 1988 are:

YEAR	SALES	ACTUAL WARRANTY EXPENDITURES
1987	$300,000	$ 6,000
1988	500,000	18,000

REQUIRED

1. Give entries for 1987 and 1988 to (a) record the sales (on account), (b) record estimated warranty expense, and (c) record actual warranty expenditures.

2. Calculate the balance of the estimated warranty liability account at the end of 1988.

E15-14. CALCULATING ESTIMATED LIABILITY ON PRODUCT PREMIUMS   Cola Corporation has inaugurated a new sales promotional program. For every eight bottle caps from one-liter bottles that are returned to Cola, customers will receive a beachball that costs Cola $.50 per unit. Cola estimates that only 20 percent of the bottle caps in the hands of customers will be redeemed. During the year, 4 million one-liter bottles of Cola are sold at a total retail price of $6 million. Cola has purchased 100,000 beachballs and distributed 80,000 of them to customers. At the end of the year, Cola recognizes a liability equal to the estimated cost of beachballs that may be distributed in the future.

REQUIRED

Calculate the estimated liability for beachballs still to be distributed.

E15-15. ACCOUNTING FOR ESTIMATED LIABILITY ON PRODUCT PREMIUMS   Setter Company includes one coupon in each box of dog food it sells. In return for 10 coupons, customers receive a doggy toy that the company purchases in large quantities for $1 each. Setter's experience indicates that 70 percent of the coupons will be redeemed. During 1987, 8,000 toys were purchased, 100,000 boxes of dog food were sold, and 50,000 coupons were redeemed. During 1988, an additional 5,000 toys were purchased, 90,000 boxes of dog food were sold, and 60,000 coupons were redeemed.

REQUIRED

Prepare the appropriate 1987 and 1988 journal entries to record the following events:

1. The purchase of toys.

2. Premium expense.

3. Coupon redemption.

(CGAA, adapted)

E15-16. CALCULATING AND ACCOUNTING FOR LIABILITY ON COUPONS   Wolf Dog Food Company distributes to consumers coupons that may be presented (on or before a stated expiration date) to grocers for discounts on purchases of Wolf Dog Food. The grocers are reimbursed when they send the coupons to Wolf. Wolf has found that in the past an average of 40 percent of the coupons have been redeemed. During 1987 Wolf issued two separate series of coupons, as follows:

ISSUE DATE	EXPIRATION DATE	TOTAL VALUE ISSUED	AMOUNT DISBURSED ON REDEMPTION AS OF 12/31/87
1/1/87	6/30/88	$50,000	$17,000
7/1/87	12/31/88	60,000	20,000

REQUIRED

1. Calculate the amount of the liability for unredeemed coupons as of December 31, 1987.

2. Prepare the appropriate December 31 adjusting entry, given your answer to part 1 and assuming no liability account existed before December 31.

E15-17. ACCOUNTING FOR LIABILITY ON PURCHASE COMMITMENT   On February 21, 1987, Billings Corporation signed a noncancelable agreement to purchase inventory items for $17,000 by March 25, 1988. Billings, which has a December 31 fiscal year-end, purchased $15,000 of the items prior to the end of its 1987 fiscal year. At the time of purchase, the open market price for the items purchased was $14,250. On December 31, 1987, the remainder of the goods under contract had a market price of $1,800, and when the final purchase was made the goods had a market price of $2,100.

REQUIRED

With respect to the purchase commitment, prepare all journal entries necessary for Billings for 1987 and 1988. A perpetual inventory system is used.

E15-18. REPORTING LIABILITIES   Indicate how each of the following items should be reported in the financial statements.

   1. Discount on note payable.

   2. A short-term obligation that management intends to refinance, but to date has not shown the ability to refinance.

   3. A declared but unpaid cash dividend.

   4. A declared but unpaid stock dividend.

   5. Prepayments by customers.

   6. Employee taxes that have been withheld but not yet remitted.

   7. Employee bonuses payable.

   8. A material gain that is contingent on an event that appears to have only a remote chance of occurring.

   9. A material unusual and infrequent loss that is dependent on a future event that is very likely to occur.

   10. A pending lawsuit that probably will result in a loss whose amount is impossible to estimate reasonably at the present time.

   11. An unasserted claim that probably will be asserted and from which there is a reasonable possibility of loss.

E15-19. CALCULATING LITIGATION LOSS   A truck owned and operated by Baker Company was involved in an accident with an auto driven by Watson on November 15, 1987. Baker received notice on January 10, 1988, of a lawsuit for $750,000 damages for a personal injury suffered by Watson. The company counsel believes it is probable that the company will have to pay Watson $250,000, and perhaps as much as $350,000. Baker's accounting year ends on December 31, and the 1987 financial statements were issued on March 15, 1988.

REQUIRED

   1. What amount of loss, if any, must be accrued by a charge to income in 1987?

   2. What disclosures, if any, should accompany any contingent loss reported in the 1987 income statement?

(AICPA, adapted)

E15-20. LOSS CONTINGENCIES FROM LITIGATION   In May 1987 the Crane Company became involved in litigation. As a result, it is probable that Crane will have to pay $1.4 million. In July 1987 a competitor commenced a suit against Crane alleging violation of antitrust laws and seeking damages of $2.2 million. Crane denies the allegations, and the likelihood that Crane will have to pay any damages is remote. In September 1987 Blane County brought action against Crane for $1.8 million for polluting Bass Lake. It is possible that the county's suit will be successful, but the amount of damages Crane will have to pay is not reasonably determinable.

REQUIRED

1. What amount, if any, should be accrued in 1987?

2. Draft the disclosures, if any, that should appear in Crane Company's 1987 financial statements as the result of the litigation in 1987.

(AICPA, adapted)

PROBLEMS

P15-1. RECORDING TRANSACTIONS INVOLVING LIABILITIES   Selected transactions of Wiley Manufacturing for the fiscal year ended December 31, 1987, are listed below.

a) On December 15, monthly wages and salaries of $290,000 were paid.

b) On December 1, Wiley received a $50,000 deposit from a customer to be applied against a parts delivery scheduled to be made on January 20, 1988.

c) December sales were $435,000, including a 4 percent sales tax that is to be remitted to the state before March 15, 1988. Sales and sales taxes are recorded in separate accounts.

d) On November 1, Wiley borrowed cash from the local bank in exchange for a six-month $90,000 note discounted at 8 percent.

REQUIRED

1. Prepare the appropriate journal entries to record the above transactions.

2. Prepare any 1987 year-end adjusting entries related to interest. Assume straight-line amortization of discounts.

P15-2. RECORDING TRANSACTIONS INVOLVING LIABILITIES   Selected transactions of Brazda Company for the current fiscal year ending December 31 are listed below.

a) On December 3, Brazda received a $3,130 prepayment from a customer for goods that Brazda is to deliver on January 10 of the next year.

b) During December, deposits from customers on returnable containers amounted to $650.

c) During December, cash sales of products totaled $17,344, which included a 5 percent sales tax that must be remitted to the state by February 1 of the next year.

d) Salaries expense for December was $12,500, which included federal, state, and local income taxes payable of $4,350 and employee FICA taxes withheld at the rate of 6 percent.

e) Brazda follows the practice of recording its current property tax liability on the lien date and then recognizing an equal amount of property tax expense each month over the fiscal year of the taxing unit. Property taxes of $11,250 became a lien on March 1, the beginning of the taxing unit's current fiscal year, and were paid in equal amounts on June 30 and December 31.

f) Warranty expense related to the $193,000 of current year sales were estimated to be 3 percent of sales revenue. Actual warranty costs incurred during the current year were $3,270.

REQUIRED

Prepare the necessary journal entries to record the above events and transactions on Brazda's books. For part *d*, prepare only the withholding entry. For part *e*, prepare all necessary entries for events that occurred during the current fiscal year.

P15-3. ACCOUNTING FOR SHORT-TERM OBLIGATIONS TO BE REFINANCED   The fiscal year of Hodges Implement Company ends on June 30 and Hodges normally issues its financial statements about August 15. As of the end of the current fiscal year, Hodges has $280,000 in one-year notes payable that are due within the next six to eight months, but Hodges intends to refinance them by replacing them with a five-year series of guaranteed renewable short-term obligations. On July 20 Hodges signs just the sort of refinancing agreement that it has been looking for, except that the new agreement provides a maximum of only $260,000 worth of refinancing, and the total amount available is limited to 70 percent of the fair market value of the collateral provided by Hodges. Because of restrictive aspects of other financing agreements to which Hodges is a party, it is determined that collateral available for the new agreement is $350,000.

REQUIRED

1. Identify and discuss the circumstances under which a short-term obligation should be reported in the financial statements as other than a current liability.

2. What are the important factors to be considered in determining Hodges' proper accounting for and disclosure of the $280,000 of one-year notes in the current year's financial statements?

3. Demonstrate by balance sheet classification and appropriate footnote disclosure how Hodges should report this situation in its current financial statements.

P15-4. CALCULATING AND ACCOUNTING FOR PAYROLL OBLIGATIONS   Wages for the period January 1 through June 30 and wages for June for the four employees of Delta Concrete Construction are listed below.

EMPLOYEE	WAGES THROUGH 6/30	WAGES FOR JUNE
T. Smith	$42,300	$6,000
R. Jones	32,000	5,500
L. Yoder	21,500	4,000
J. Davis	17,000	3,000

Assume a FICA tax rate of 7.15 percent for both the employee and the employer applicable to the first $42,000 of an employee's wages. Further assume a FUTA tax rate of 6.2 percent (before credit for contributions to state unemployment) and a state unemployment tax rate of 5.4 percent, only two-thirds of which is applicable to Delta because of the company's stable employment record. Both unemployment tax rates are applicable to the first $7,000 of wages paid to each employee. The federal income tax rate for Smith and Jones is 40 percent, while Yoder and Davis are subject to a 20 percent federal tax rate.

REQUIRED

1. Calculate the federal income tax withheld, the employer and employee FICA taxes, and the state and federal unemployment taxes related to each employee's wages for June.

2. Prepare the necessary entry to record wage expense, various payroll liabilities, and payment of June wages to the four employees.

3. Prepare the necessary entry to record Delta's payroll tax expense for June.

P15-5. ACCOUNTING FOR COMPENSATED FUTURE EMPLOYEE ABSENCES   Wright Company's policy is to allow one hour of paid sick leave to accrue for each two weeks of employment. During its first year of operation, Wright's employees accumulated 500 hours of sick leave, 150 hours of sick leave were taken, and hourly wage rates were $15. Wright's employees are allowed to use accumulated sick leave to take compensated time off from work even though they are not ill.

REQUIRED

1. What conditions must exist in order for an employer to accrue a liability for employees' rights to receive compensation for future absences from work?

2. Under what sick pay benefits policy might an employer not accrue a liability for sick pay benefits?

3. Assuming that accrual of a sick leave pay liability is appropriate, prepare any entry(ies) that may be necessary for Wright in its first year of operations.

P15-6. ACCOUNTING FOR PROPERTY TAXES   Arnold Distributing Company, a calendar-year company, receives a property tax bill for $15,000 on February 20. The bill is for one year and is based on an early January assessment of the value of Arnold's business property. Arnold employs two accountants, J. Tightfist and D. Crossfoot, who normally have similar views about accounting issues. Accounting for property taxes, however, is one subject about which the two simply cannot agree. Tightfist believes that property taxes for the year should be recorded as a liability on the lien date, April 30, while Crossfoot thinks that the property tax liability should be accrued on a monthly basis over the taxing authority's fiscal year, which begins on April 30. In any case, the taxes are due in two equal installments on July 1 of the current year and January 1 of the following year.

REQUIRED

1. Present the best argument you can in support of each accountant's view.

2. Assume that Tightfist's opinion is adopted as Arnold's property tax accounting policy. Make the necessary entries (if any) on February 20, April 30, July 1, and December 31 (the end of Arnold's fiscal year).

3. Prepare the necessary entries for the dates given in part 2, assuming that Crossfoot's opinion is adopted as Arnold's property tax accounting policy.

P15-7. CALCULATING BONUSES PAYABLE Rother's Clothing Company has four district sales managers. Each district manager receives a basic salary plus an annual bonus based on income for his or her district. Because the four managers have different levels of experience and have been with the company for different lengths of time, each is compensated under a different bonus arrangement. The four bonus arrangements are described below.

R. Wiston (District 1): 3 percent bonus based on district income before either bonus expense or income taxes are deducted.

B. Atwell (District 2): 3 percent bonus based on district income after deduction of income taxes, but the bonus is not treated as an expense in determining income subject to the bonus.

T. Ritter (District 3): 2 percent bonus based on district income after deduction of both bonus expense and income tax expense.

C. Boyton (District 4): 2 percent bonus based on district income after deduction of bonus expense but before deduction of income taxes.

The income figures for the four districts, before deduction of either bonus expense or income taxes, are as follows for the current year.

DISTRICT	INCOME
1	$72,000
2	67,500
3	79,800
4	59,700

Rother's Clothing Company is subject to a 40 percent income tax rate, and bonus expense is deductible for purposes of calculating income taxes payable.

REQUIRED

Calculate the amount of income taxes payable and the bonus due to each district sales manager for the current year.

P15-8. ACCOUNTING FOR PRODUCT WARRANTIES Zeller is an 18-month-old firm that sells office equipment and supplies. A major part of Zeller's business is sales of a well-known brand of electric typewriter. The marketing arrangement for this particular brand of typewriter requires that the seller, rather than the manufacturer, take total responsibility for any warranty that may be offered in conjunction with the sale of a typewriter. While Zeller has essentially no experience with either the cost or the number of repairs associated with the typewriter it is selling, the typewriter does have a long history of industry-wide performance that is available for Zeller's consideration. With each typewriter sold, Zeller provides a one-year warranty covering all parts and labor. In addition, purchasers of new typewriters have the option of buying an additional two-year service contract at the time the typewriter is purchased. About 80 percent of the customers who buy new typewriters also purchase this contract. The additional two-year service contract costs $50 and provides the owner with free labor on typewriter maintenance and repair for two years beyond the initial one-year warranty. Necessary parts must be paid for by the customer. On the basis of industry experience, Zeller estimates that labor costs under the two-year service contracts will average about $40 per contract, and labor and parts under the warranty given with each typewriter sold will average about $20 and $15, respectively, per unit sold.

REQUIRED

1. Which of the two methods of accounting for product warranties do you think is most appropriate in Zeller's case? Why?

2. Prepare pro forma entries (use account titles, but enter no dollar amounts) for each of the two accounting methods *(a)* at the time a typewriter is sold, *(b)* at the time a service contract is sold, *(c)* at the time warranty work is performed, and *(d)* at the time service contract work is performed.

3. Explain the effect(s) each of the two accounting methods would have on the income statement and balance sheet during the term of a warranty or a service contract.

P15-9. ACCOUNTING FOR PRODUCT WARRANTIES The Compex Company manufactures and sells remote computer terminals. In the current year Compex sold 300 terminals for $4,100 each. The terminals have a two-year warranty on labor and a one-year warranty on parts. Compex estimates that warranty expenses will average about $20 per year for labor and 5 percent of selling price for parts for each terminal sold. During the current year there were 30 warranty claims requiring a total of $6,400 for labor and $5,800 for parts.

REQUIRED

1. Assuming the estimates of warranty expenses are reasonable and that warranty expenses are a material income statement item, prepare the necessary entries to record *(a)* aggregate sales, *(b)* warranty expense, *(c)* warranty work on claims, and *(d)* year-end adjustments (if any).

2. For the current year, what accounts and dollar amounts would be reported in the income statement? in the balance sheet?

P15-10. PREMIUM OFFERS In a massive promotional campaign the Classical Record Club sent coupons to 2 million families in the United States on November 1, 1987. In order to benefit from the coupon, the recipient had to return it along with an order for a $49.95 five-record set within six months of November 1. Each customer who did so would receive, in addition to the five-record set, a free classical record with a retail value of $9.95. Any customer who was not satisfied with the five-record set could return it within 30 days for a full refund and keep the free record without obligation. Classical expected about 35 percent of the families who received coupons to respond to the offer. Of those who responded to the offer, Classical estimated that about 10 percent would return the five-record set within 30 days of receipt. In preparation for the campaign, Classical purchased 700,000 of the records to be given as premiums at a price of $3.95 per record on October 25. As of December 31 (end of the fiscal year), 417,500 coupons had been received by Classical and 22,300 customers had subsequently returned the five-record set for a refund.

REQUIRED

Prepare all journal entries (including year-end adjusting entries) suggested by the above facts.

P15-11. ACCOUNTING FOR PREMIUM OFFERS The Sudsy Detergent Company hopes to stimulate sales by inserting a coupon in each box of Sudsy that can be sent to the Sudsy Company, along with $1.25, to obtain a set of three towels retailing for $6.95. Fifty cents of the $1.25 charge is to cover shipping charges. Sudsy Detergent sells for $1.89 a box and the three-towel sets cost Sudsy $1.50 each. Shipping the towels to customers is expected to cost the Sudsy Company an average of $.35 per set. Data related to the towel promotion in 1987 and 1988 are:

	1987	1988
Towel sets purchased by Sudsy	93,140	97,480
Boxes of Sudsy Detergent sold	178,280	169,340
Coupons redeemed by customers	76,670	83,410
Percent of coupons expected to be redeemed	50%	45%

REQUIRED

1. Prepare any journal entries necessary for 1987 and 1988 to account for the Sudsy Detergent towel promotion.

2. Indicate the account titles, the dollar amounts, and the financial statement classification of accounts arising from the towel promotion that would be reported at the end of fiscal 1987 and 1988, respectively.

P15-12. ACCOUNTING FOR WARRANTIES AND PREMIUMS Tannen Music Emporium carries a wide variety of musical instruments, sound reproduction equipment, recorded music, and sheet music. Tannen uses two sales promotion techniques—warranties and premiums—to attract customers.

Musical instruments and sound equipment are sold with a one-year warranty for replacement of parts and labor. The estimated warranty cost, based on experience, is 1 percent of sales.

The premium is offered on recorded music and on sheet music. Customers receive a coupon for each dollar spent on recorded music or sheet music. Customers may exchange 200 coupons and $20 for a cassette player. Tannen pays $32 for each cassette player and estimates that 60 percent of the coupons given to customers will be redeemed.

Tannen's total sales for 1987 were $7.2 million—$5.4 million from musical instruments and sound reproduction equipment and $1.8 million from recorded music and sheet music. Replacement parts and labor for warranty work totaled $80,000 during 1987. A total of 6,200 cassette players used in the premium program were purchased during the year. There were 1.2 million coupons redeemed in 1987.

Tannen uses the accrual method to account for the warranty and premium costs for financial reporting purposes. The balances in the accounts related to warranties and premiums on January 1, 1987, were as shown below.

Inventory of premium cassette players	$35,200
Estimated premium claims outstanding	40,800
Estimated liability from warranties	66,000

REQUIRED

Tannen Music Emporium is preparing its financial statements for the year ended December 31, 1987. Determine the amounts that will be shown on the 1987 financial statements for the following:

  a) Warranty expense.
  b) Estimated liability from warranties.
  c) Premium expense.
  d) Inventory of premium cassette players.
  e) Estimated premium claims outstanding.

(IMA, adapted)

P15-13. ACCOUNTING FOR LAWSUITS Brake failures on a special run of automobiles manufactured and sold by U.S. Motors Company between November 1 and December 15, 1987, resulted in 73 personal injury lawsuits for damages totaling $14.6 million. Of this amount, $9.2 million related to suits filed before the end of the company's fiscal year, December 31, and the remainder arose from suits filed during January 1988. U.S. Motors' lawyers expect that essentially all of the 73 suits will result in unfavorable outcomes, but that total damages will probably not exceed $10 million. Management expects that about 25 similar additional suits will be filed before the 1987 financial statements are issued on February 20, 1988.

REQUIRED

1. What factors should be considered in determining proper accounting treatment of a threatened or pending lawsuit?

2. What conditions must be met before it is acceptable accounting practice to accrue a loss contingency for litigation, claims, or assessments?

3. Give some factors that must be considered in determining the probability of asset impairment or liability incurrence in litigation loss contingency situations.

4. Prepare any journal entries or 1987 financial statement disclosures called for by the facts given above.

P15-14. ACCOUNTING FOR LOSSES ON PURCHASE COMMITMENTS   In 1986 Long Building Corporation entered into a three-year noncancelable lumber contract with Wise Lumber Company. In late 1987 the market price of lumber dropped sharply, and by December 31, 1987 (the end of Long's fiscal year), the lumber Long had contracted for over the remainder of the three-year contract could be purchased in the open market for about $280,000 less than the contract price. By September 1988, when the balance of the lumber contracted for was finally purchased for $1 million, the open market price had deteriorated so much that Long's management figured that $310,000 was lost because of the noncancelable provision in the contract with Wise.

REQUIRED

1. Prepare any journal entries required in 1987 and 1988 on Long's books to record the above facts. A perpetual inventory system is used.

2. Explain the accounting treatment that would have been appropriate for Long had the open market price been only $200,000 below contract price at the time of the final $1 million purchase.

P15-15. ACCOUNTING FOR PREPAYMENTS AND CONTINGENCIES   Manley, Inc., a publishing company, is preparing its December 31, 1987, financial statements and must determine the proper accounting treatment for each of the following situations:

Situation 1: Manley sells subscriptions to several magazines for a one-year, two-year, or three-year period. Cash receipts from subscribers are credited to magazine subscriptions collected in advance, and this account had a balance of $2.4 million at December 31, 1987. Outstanding subscriptions at December 31, 1987, expire as follows:

During 1988	$600,000
During 1989	900,000
During 1990	400,000

Situation 2: On January 2, 1987, Manley discontinued collision, fire, and theft coverage on its delivery vehicles and became self-insured for these risks. Actual losses of $45,000 during 1987 were charged to delivery expense. The 1986 premium for the discontinued coverage amounted to $100,000. The controller wants to set up a reserve for self-insurance by a debit of $55,000 to delivery expense and a credit of $55,000 to the reserve for self-insurance.

Situation 3: A suit for breach of contract seeking damages of $1 million was filed by an author against Manley on July 1, 1987. The company's legal counsel believes that an unfavorable outcome is probable. A reasonable estimate of the court's award to the plaintiff is in the range between $100,000 and $500,000. No amount within this range is a better estimate of potential damages than any other amount.

Situation 4: During December 1987, a competitor company filed suit against Manley for industrial espionage, claiming $2 million in damages. In the opinion of management and company counsel, it is reasonably possible that damages will be awarded to the plaintiff. However, the amount of damages that might be awarded cannot reasonably be estimated.

REQUIRED

For each of the four situations above, prepare the journal entry that should be recorded as of December 31, 1987. If no entry is required, give your reasoning. Show supporting calculations in good form.

(AICPA, adapted)

P15-16. ACCOUNTING FOR VARIOUS CONTINGENCIES   Walsh Pizza Company, which sells boxed pizza mixes through grocery stores, encountered the following situations during fiscal 1987.

a) On April 30 Walsh filed a lawsuit against Little Italy Pizza Company for infringing on one of Walsh's pizza dough patents. Walsh management believes that the infringement may ultimately cost Walsh as much as $1 million in lost sales. Walsh's legal counsel, however, expects that proving an infringement may be very difficult.

b) During the third week in October, an unhappy employee put small amounts of sand in a number of batches of dry pizza dough mix. Most of the ruined mix was located before it was boxed and shipped, but a few boxes of bad mix did manage to reach customers. While no customer claims have been filed as of the end of the fiscal year, management thinks that it is very likely that one or more lawsuits will be filed, and that an unfavorable outcome is almost certain. However, the nature of the problem is such that a reasonable estimate of any loss that may arise is not yet possible.

c) Jason Jackson, a former Walsh employee, has filed a suit against Walsh for injuries alleged to have occurred on Walsh property after the period of time during which he worked for Walsh. The suit seeks to recover $1.5 million in damages. Walsh is insured for this sort of claim up to $200,000, although the coverage is being contested by the insurance company. Jackson's claim is still pending in the county court and legal counsel has advised Walsh that a favorable outcome is likely.

d) A small overseas division of Walsh with a book value of $250,900 and a current market value of $400,000 was taken over by the new government of the country in which it is located shortly after a bloodless coup in August. At the present time it appears unlikely that any of the company's investment in the division will be recovered.

e) On June 30 Walsh signed a three-year noncancelable agreement to purchase flour from Axle Milling. As the result of a bumper wheat crop in 1987, year-end market prices on flour have dropped $.15 a pound below Walsh's contract price. Given expected flour purchases under the contract, the purchase contract will cause Walsh to spend an average of about $80,000 more per year on flour than if the flour were purchased at the present market price. Walsh is not concerned with the present state of affairs, however, because the market price for flour is notoriously unstable.

REQUIRED

1. Indicate the appropriate 1987 accounting treatment (including journal entries, if any) for each of the above situations. Justify your choices of treatments.

2. Provide appropriate disclosures, including accounts reported, in the balance sheet, income statement, statement of retained earnings, and associated footnotes for each of the above situations.

16

BONDS (INVESTMENTS AND PAYABLES) AND LONG-TERM NOTES PAYABLE

Current liabilities, which usually arise and are extinguished routinely in a firm's operating cycle, were discussed in the previous chapter. Many business firms and not-for-profit entities, such as governments, churches, and hospitals, often issue long-term debt when a large amount of financing, covering several operating cycles, is required. In 1985, for example, as a part of its strategy to thwart Turner Broadcasting's takeover attempt, CBS purchased 21 percent of its own common stock. CBS financed this stock transaction in large part by issuing approximately $700 million in long-term notes.[1]

Historically, accounting for long-term debt has been fairly straightforward. Recently, however, the deregulation of financial institutions, coupled with a federal monetary policy that focuses on managing the supply of money while allowing interest rates to seek their own levels, has increased the complexity of financing instruments and the accounting for them. The following is but one example of how companies are issuing complex debt instruments:

> The ranks of financial felines known as zero-coupon bonds grew larger in April. Merrill Lynch, which in 1982 created the first zero-coupon Treasury bonds (known as Treasury Investment Growth Receipts, or TIGRS), came up with a new breed of cat called a LYON, short for Liquid Yield Option Note. Issued by Waste Management, Inc., an Illinois-based waste disposal company, and underwritten by Merrill Lynch, these zeros are convertible into 4.36 shares of Waste Management stock anytime over their 16-year life.
>
> Like all zero-coupon securities, LYONs pay out no interest until they are redeemed or reach maturity. Instead they initially sell at a deep discount—in this case $250. They pay out their face value upon maturity; LYON holders will collect $1000 in 2001. The difference between the purchase price and the maturity value represents interest accrued over the years. LYONs come with more bells and whistles than a Mississippi steamboat.[2]

These "bells and whistles" include a "put" feature that allows investors to sell the bonds back to Waste Management, a feature that allows Waste Management to call the bonds for cash, and an "automatic escalator" that causes the cost of converting the bonds to stock to rise as the bonds increase in value over time. Such features will be discussed later.

In this chapter we discuss accounting for bonds by both the issuer and the investor. In addition, we discuss accounting for long-term notes payable. We begin our discussion by examining the nature and characteristics of bonds.

[1] "CBS Blunts Turner Bid to Buy Network," *Tulsa World,* July 4, 1985, p. 10.
[2] "A New Convertible with Pros and Cons," *Fortune,* May 27, 1985, p. 152.

NATURE AND CHARACTERISTICS OF BONDS

An issuer of bonds usually incurs two cash flow obligations—one for interest and one for the maturity value.

A **bond** is a borrowing agreement between the bond issuer and the purchaser or investor. The terms of the agreement are specified in writing in the bond **indenture** or contract. Bonds are offered for sale through a **prospectus,** a brochure that sets forth details of the bond issue. A company that issues bonds generally incurs two obligations: an obligation to pay investors a specified amount, called the maturity (par) value, on a specified maturity date, and an obligation to pay investors interest at specified dates to compensate them for the use of their funds. The cash flows on a bond are similar to the cash flows on a note; both forms of debt usually require cash outflows for interest and maturity value.

Bonds often are traded in organized security markets established to facilitate transfers of ownership. Because a bond obligates the issuer to make specified cash payments at future dates, the valuation principle for bonds, as with other monetary items, is based on the present value of the future cash flows on the bond.

A bond that becomes due or matures on the same date as all other bonds in the same issue is called a **term bond,** while a bond issue that matures in installments is said to consist of **serial bonds.** For example, a company may issue 100 $1,000 term bonds with a maturity value of $100,000, all of which mature 10 years from the date of issue. It may also issue 100 $1,000 serial bonds that mature at the rate of 10 bonds per year over a 10-year period.

BOND INTEREST

Bonds often are issued with a fixed or stated contract rate of interest. This stated rate is also called the nominal rate or, if interest coupons are attached, the coupon rate. Bond interest may be payable monthly, quarterly, semiannually, or annually. Historically, bonds have been issued at fixed stated interest rates. Recently, however, the desire of investors to earn returns commensurate with the rate of inflation has forced many borrowers to issue bonds whose stated interest varies in response to inflation and changes in market rates of interest. (Variable-rate debt securities are introduced in Appendix 16–1.)

Many companies, such as General Motors Acceptance Corporation (GMAC), J. C. Penney, BankAmerica Corporation, and Waste Management, Inc., have issued noninterest-bearing bonds, which are called **deep discount** or **zero-coupon bonds.** The Waste Management illustration pointed out that these noninterest-bearing bonds sell for much less than their maturity values, as your knowledge of present value would lead you to suspect. The GMAC bonds, for example, were sold at approximately 25 percent of par; that is, for each $1,000 in maturity value, the buyer paid only $250. This selling price represented a 14.25 percent annual yield to maturity (annual rate of return). As in the case of the Waste Management bonds, the discount represents interest earned over the life of the bonds. This periodic interest is calculated by the effective interest method, discussed in Chapters 7 and 8. Because the investor's amortization of discount is taxable even though no cash is received until maturity, zero-coupon bonds have been most attractive as investments for tax-exempt entities.

SECURITY FOR BONDS ISSUED

Some companies, such as General Motors, are able to issue bonds without any tangible security other than their general financial strength. Such bonds are referred to as **debenture bonds.** Most bond indentures, however, provide that specific assets of the issuer serve as security in case of the issuer's default. When a company has several bond issues outstanding, the priority of the claims of bondholders in case of default is noted by such terms as **senior** (first claim among bondholders) and **subordinated** or **junior** (takes priority after another class of creditors). **Guaranty bonds** are those for which another party guarantees payment of principal and interest in case the original issuer defaults. A parent company, for example, may guarantee bonds issued by a subsidiary.

OWNERSHIP REGISTRATION

Companies that issue **registered bonds** maintain detailed records of all changes in ownership for purposes of paying interest and principal. On the other hand, bonds may be **bearer bonds,** and interest and principal are paid to anyone who demonstrates ownership of the bonds. **Coupon bonds** usually are bearer bonds, and interest is paid to whoever presents the interest coupon for payment on the payment dates.

In practice, many companies appoint an agent or **trustee,** usually a bank or other financing institution, to handle the actual disbursements of cash for interest and principal. The company periodically deposits the necessary funds with the trustee, and the trustee disburses the funds to bondholders on behalf of the company.

SINKING FUND REQUIREMENTS

Bonds are not risk-free investments. Although the timing and amount of cash flows associated with bonds are specified in the indenture, the possibility exists that an issuing company will be unable to pay interest or maturity value when these amounts become due. Furthermore, because the market value of a bond varies inversely with the market rate of interest, an investor incurs a risk that the market value of the bonds held may decline when interest rates rise. This risk can be significant if the investor contemplates selling before maturity.

To ensure that funds will be available to pay interest and principal, many bond indentures require that the issuer periodically set aside or earmark cash in a special fund called a **sinking fund.** (We discussed a bond sinking fund in Chapter 14.) Sinking fund cash is invested in income-earning securities until needed. In this way, adequate cash is available to pay maturing obligations. The following are hypothetical entries to record cash transfers to a sinking fund, earnings on sinking fund investments, and subsequent disbursements from a sinking fund.

TRANSACTION	ENTRY	
To transfer cash to a sinking fund	Sinking fund . . . . *xx*	
	Cash	*xx*
To record revenue earned on investments	Sinking fund . . . . *xx*	
	Interest revenue	*xx*
To record payment of interest and maturing principal from sinking fund cash	Bonds payable . . . . *xx*	
	Interest payable . . . . *xx*	
	Sinking fund	*xx*

OTHER CHARACTERISTICS OF BONDS

Other characteristics of bonds include their method of retirement, whether they can be exchanged for common stock, and whether debt service must be provided from specific revenue sources. A company may retire its bonds before maturity by purchasing them on the open market. Additionally, some bond indentures, such as Waste Management's, include a call provision, which allows the issuer to retire the bonds at a specified price. Bonds with such a provision are known as **callable bonds.** Other methods of retirement or extinguishment are discussed later.

Convertible bonds allow the bondholder to convert or exchange the bonds for shares of capital stock of the issuing company. Convertible bonds have been issued by many companies, including Computervision Corporation, Westinghouse Electric Corporation, and Waste Management, Inc.

Revenue bonds are issued by cities, counties, turnpike authorities, and other governmental units. Interest on revenue bonds is paid from specified revenue sources. For example, a city may issue revenue bonds to obtain financing for construction of an electric utility. Interest is paid solely from utility revenues generated from services rendered to city residents. A university may issue revenue bonds to finance a dormitory or a football stadium. A portion of the revenues generated by these facilities is earmarked to pay interest and principal on the bonds.

DETERMINING BOND SELLING PRICES

In Chapter 7 we saw how present value concepts are used to determine bond prices. Because of the importance of this topic, however, we shall review these concepts at this point before we begin our discussion of accounting for bonds.

PRICING ON DATE OF BOND CONTRACT

A bond's selling price equals the present value of the future cash flows for interest and principal.

The market selling price of a bond is determined by supply and demand of sellers and buyers in the market. In theory, the selling price is equal to the present value of the future cash flows for interest and principal. The discount rate used to determine this present value is the market rate of interest at the date of sale for investments of similar risk.

Assume that on January 2, 1987, Oklahoma Instruments issues five-year term bonds with a maturity value of $100,000. The bonds are dated January 2, 1987 (interest begins to accrue on this date), and have a stated rate of interest of 10 percent, payable annually each December 31. They mature on December 31, 1991.

The selling price of these bonds depends on the market rate of interest on January 2, 1987. Because some time may have elapsed since the issuer made the decision to sell the bonds and proceeded to have them printed and readied for sale, the market rate of interest may have changed and thus may be different from the bonds' stated rate of 10 percent. Exhibit 16–1 presents the calculation of the selling prices of the Oklahoma Instruments bonds under three assumed market rates of interest. The time diagram in Exhibit 16–1 is

EXHIBIT 16–1   DETERMINING SELLING PRICES OF FIVE-YEAR 10 PERCENT BONDS UNDER THREE ASSUMED MARKET RATES OF INTEREST

	PV = ?	$10,000	$10,000	$10,000	$10,000	$100,000 Principal $10,000 Interest
	1/2/87	12/31/87	12/31/88	12/31/89	12/31/90	12/31/91

	MARKET RATE ON 1/2/87		
	10%	**8%**	**12%**
Present value of principal:			
$100,000(p_{\overline{5}|10\%})$			
$100,000(.6209)*$	$ 62,090		
$100,000(p_{\overline{5}|8\%})$			
$100,000(.6806)*$		$ 68,060	
$100,000(p_{\overline{5}|12\%})$			
$100,000(.5674)*$			$56,740
Present value of interest:			
$10,000(P_{\overline{5}|10\%})$			
$10,000(3.7908)†$	37,908		
$10,000(P_{\overline{5}|8\%})$			
$10,000(3.9927)†$		39,927	
$10,000(P_{\overline{5}|12\%})$			
$10,000(3.6048)†$			36,048
Bond selling price	$100,000‡	$107,987	$92,788

* From Table B, Appendix 7–1.

† From Table D, Appendix 7–1.

‡ $2 rounding error.

helpful for visualizing the cash flows associated with the bond issue. The selling price is calculated by discounting the maturity value (a single amount) and the interest payments (an ordinary annuity) at the *market* rate of interest.

If the rate that investors can earn on investments of similar risk is 10 percent, the bonds will sell at par and thus *yield* 10 percent. On the other hand, if the market rate of interest is 8 percent, investors will bid up the price of the bonds to $107,987 because the stated rate of 10 percent is more favorable than the current market rate. Thus, the effective yield will correspond to the market rate of 8 percent, and the bonds will sell at a **premium** of $7,987, or at 107.987 percent of par. Finally, if the market rate of interest is 12 percent, the bond price will be only $92,788 because the stated rate is less than the market rate. The effective rate is 12 percent, and thus the bonds will sell at a **discount** of $7,212, or at 92.788 percent of par. Bond selling prices on any subsequent interest date can be calculated by discounting the remaining cash flows for interest and maturity value at the market rate of interest prevailing on that date.

BOND PRICING BETWEEN INTEREST DATES

Bond issues are not always sold on the date stated in the indenture or on an interest date. Frequently they are sold between interest dates because of time delays in the printing of the bonds, a decision on the part of the issuer to wait until market interest rates are more favorable, or a lack of demand. In addition, subsequent exchanges between investors rarely occur precisely on an interest date.

When bonds are sold between interest dates, the selling price is equal to the present value of the debt on the date of sale. Assume, for example, that the Oklahoma Instruments bonds, dated January 2, 1987, are sold on May 1, 1987, when the market interest rate is 8 percent. The selling price is calculated as follows:

Selling price at 1/2/87 (Exhibit 16–1) $107,987
Growth in bond value for first four months of 1987 at market rate of 8%
   ($107,987 × .08 × 1/3)   2,879
Selling price on 5/1/87 (including interest) $110,866

Notice that because the market rate of interest is 8 percent, interest at 8 percent for four months must be added to the January 2, 1987, selling price of $107,987. Thus, the selling price on May 1, 1987, is $110,866.

Exhibit 16–2 shows the pattern of values or selling prices of the Oklahoma Instruments bonds throughout the bond term at an 8 percent yield. The initial selling price is $107,987. Each year the bond value grows at 8 percent. At the end of the first year, for example, *immediately before the first interest cash flow of $10,000,* the bonds have a value of $116,626 ($107,987 × 1.08). The first interest payment of $10,000 causes the bond value to decrease to $106,626. In Exhibit 16–2, the growth each year is shown by the solid, upward-sloping lines; the annual interest cash flows are shown by the vertical dashed lines. At the end of the fifth year (the maturity date), the bonds have a value of $100,000, which is the maturity value. The May 1, 1987, selling price of $110,866 also is shown in Exhibit 16–2. The selling price at an 8 percent yield at any other date can be determined by reference to the solid, upward-sloping lines.

In practice, bond prices are quoted net of the accrued interest at the *stated rate*. For example, the Oklahoma Instruments bonds would be quoted on May 1, 1987, at $107,533, plus accrued interest from January 2, 1987:

Selling price on 5/1/87 (including interest) $110,866
Less accrued interest from 1/2/87 at 10% stated rate
   ($100,000 × .10 × 1/3) . . . .   (3,333)
Selling price, net of accrued interest $107,533

EXHIBIT 16—2   VALUES OF A FIVE-YEAR 10 PERCENT
$100,000 BOND AT A YIELD OF 8 PERCENT

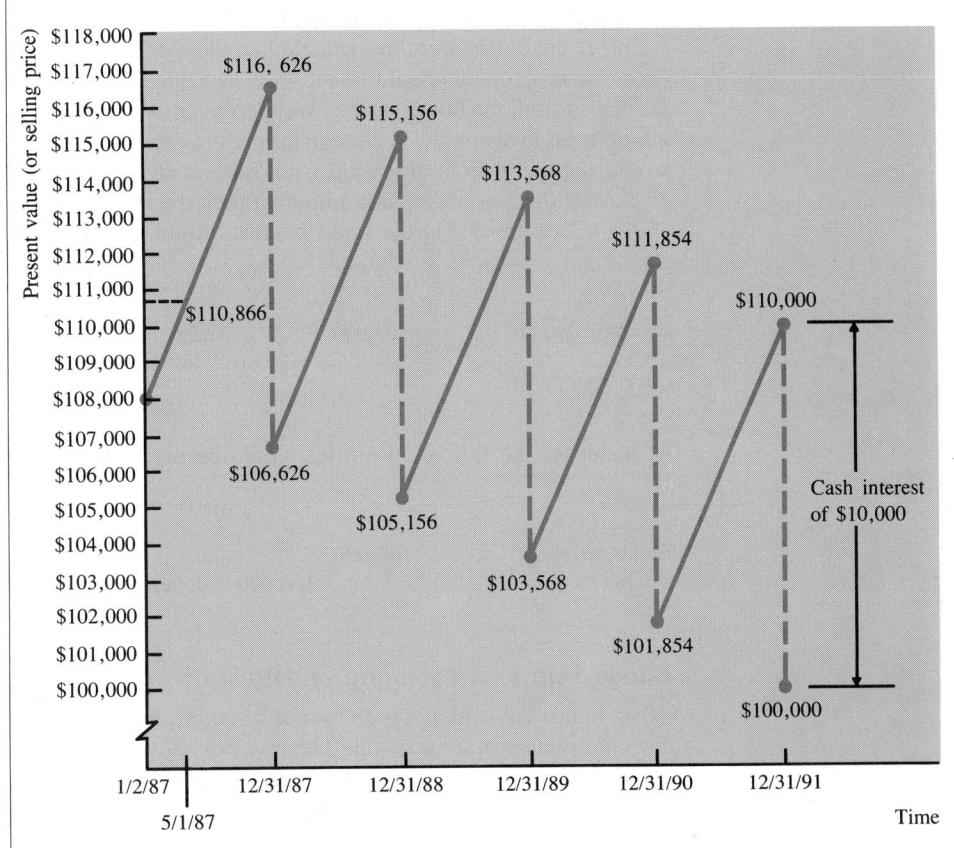

Thus, on May 1, 1987, an investor must pay $107,533 for the bonds and $3,333 for the interest that has accrued between January 2 and May 1 at the stated rate, or a total of $110,866.

ACCOUNTING FOR BONDS—ISSUER AND INVESTOR

We are now ready to discuss accounting for bonds from the standpoints of both issuer and investor. We shall examine the accounting procedures when bonds are sold on interest dates as well as between interest dates. Adjusting entries that are required when a company's fiscal period does not coincide with the interest periods stated on the bonds also will be covered.

ACCOUNTING AT DATE OF ISSUE AND ON SUBSEQUENT INTEREST DATES

Assume that on January 2, 1987, Oklahoma Instruments sells its bonds at par to yield 10 percent. The following entries are necessary for the issuer (Oklahoma Instruments) and the investor:

ISSUER

Cash. 100,000
   Bonds payable . . .   100,000

INVESTOR

Investment in Oklahoma
   Instruments bonds 100,000
      Cash   100,000

If Oklahoma Instruments prepared a balance sheet immediately after this transaction, it would report the bonds payable as a long-term liability. The investor's balance sheet classification would depend on the marketability of the bonds as well as on the investor's intent. If the bonds were marketable and the investor intended to sell them within a short time, the investment should be reported as a current asset. If the investor had no immediate plans to sell the bonds or they were not readily marketable, they should be classified as a long-term investment. A change in intent on the part of the investor at some future date would require a reclassification from current to noncurrent or vice versa.

After the issue date, assuming that both the issuer's and investor's accounting period ends on December 31, the bond interest would be recorded as follows:

ISSUER		**INVESTOR**	
Interest expense 10,000		Cash 10,000	
Cash...............	10,000	Interest revenue	10,000
($100,000 × .10)			

At maturity, the following entries would be made by the issuer and investor:

ISSUER		**INVESTOR**	
Bonds payable 100,000		Cash 100,000	
Cash...............	100,000	Investment in Oklahoma	
		Instruments bonds	100,000

Bonds Sold at a Premium or Discount

When bonds are sold at a premium or discount, the issuer usually records the premium or discount in a separate account. The investor, however, usually records the bonds including the premium or net of the discount. The issuer and investor would make the following entries to record the bonds in Exhibit 16–1:

ISSUER		**INVESTOR**	
Bonds sold at discount:			
Cash................. 92,788		Investment in Oklahoma	
Discount on bonds		Instruments bonds 92,788	
payable 7,212		Cash	92,788
Bonds payable	100,000		
Bonds sold at premium:			
Cash................. 107,987		Investment in Oklahoma	
Bonds payable	100,000	Instruments bonds 107,987	
Premium on bonds		Cash	107,987
payable	7,987		

For balance sheet purposes, a discount is a contra-account to bonds payable and is deducted from the $100,000 maturity value. A premium is added to the maturity value and is part of the long-term liability.

NATURE OF PREMIUM AND DISCOUNT   Over the life of the bonds the issuer must pay interest at the stated rate and the maturity (par) value at maturity. At the date of sale the issuer receives the par value plus the premium (or less the discount), and when the bonds mature the issuer must pay more (in the case of a discount) or less (in the case of a premium) than was received at the time the bonds were sold. The difference between what was received at the date of sale and what must be paid at maturity is the premium or discount and must be recognized in the accounts.

Earlier we pointed out that bonds sell at a premium or discount because of differences between the current market interest rate and the interest rate stated on the bonds. If the market rate at the date of sale exceeds the stated rate, the bonds will sell at a discount; if the market rate is less than the stated rate, the bonds will sell at a premium. In Exhibit 16–1, for example, note that the bonds sold at a discount when the market interest rate was 12 percent and at a premium when the market rate of interest was 8 percent. For bonds sold at a discount, the amount of the discount represents additional interest over the life of the bonds. For bonds sold at a premium, the amount of the premium represents a reduction of interest over the life of the bonds. Therefore, the premium or discount is amortized over the life of the bond issue. These concepts and relationships are summarized in Exhibit 16–3.

> A bond premium reduces interest expense (revenue) over the life of the bond; a bond discount increases interest expense (revenue) over the life of the bond.

There are two methods of amortizing bond premium and discount: the straight-line method and the effective interest method. Each of these methods is discussed below.

STRAIGHT-LINE AMORTIZATION Under the **straight-line method** of amortizing premium or discount, interest expense or revenue is a *constant amount* each year. For bonds sold at a premium, annual interest expense equals the cash interest less the annual premium amortization. For bonds sold at a discount, annual interest expense equals the cash interest plus the annual discount amortization. Assume, for example, that the Oklahoma Instruments bonds in Exhibit 16–1 were sold at a discount of $7,212, that is, for $92,788. Since the bonds mature in five years, the annual amortization of that discount is $1,442.40 ($7,212 ÷ 5). Thus, the annual interest expense is $11,442.40 ($10,000 stated interest plus $1,442.40). Similar reasoning applies to the investor. The entries to record the interest for the first year are as follows:

> Under the straight-line method, periodic interest expense (revenue) is a constant amount each period.

ISSUER			INVESTOR		
Interest expense	11,442.40		Cash	10,000.00	
Cash		10,000.00	Investment in		
Discount on			bonds	1,442.40	
bonds payable . .		1,442.40	Interest revenue . .		11,442.40

The effect of amortizing the discount is to increase the book value (or carrying value) of the bonds each year so that at maturity the book value equals the par value. This effect

---

EXHIBIT 16–3 RELATIONSHIP BETWEEN THE SALE OF BONDS AT A DISCOUNT OR PREMIUM AND INTEREST OVER THE BOND TERM

TRANSACTION	ISSUER	INVESTOR
Bonds sold at par; market rate = stated rate	Interest expense over life of bonds equals cash interest paid	Interest revenue over life of bonds equals cash interest received
Bonds sold at a discount; market rate > stated rate	Interest expense over life of bonds equals cash interest paid plus discount	Interest revenue over life of bonds equals cash interest received plus discount
Bonds sold at a premium; market rate < stated rate	Interest expense over life of bonds equals cash interest paid less premium	Interest revenue over life of bonds equals cash interest received less premium

EXHIBIT 16—4   DISCOUNT AMORTIZATION SCHEDULE, STRAIGHT-LINE AMORTIZATION

YEAR ENDING	(1) CASH*	(2) DISCOUNT AMORTIZATION†	(3) INTEREST EXPENSE/REVENUE‡	(4) BOOK VALUE OF BONDS§
				$ 92,788.00
12/31/87	$10,000.00	$1,442.40	$11,442.40	94,230.40
12/31/88	10,000.00	1,442.40	11,442.40	95,672.80
12/31/89	10,000.00	1,442.40	11,442.40	97,115.20
12/31/90	10,000.00	1,442.40	11,442.40	98,557.60
12/31/91	10,000.00	1,442.40	11,442.40	100,000.00
	$50,000.00	$7,212.00	$57,212.00	

* .10 × $100,000.

† $7,212 ÷ 5.

‡ Col. 1 plus col. 2.

§ Previous book value balance plus col. 2. The *unamortized* discount at the end of each year equals $100,000 less the amounts shown.

is shown in the discount amortization and interest expense schedule in Exhibit 16–4.

Assuming instead that the Oklahoma bonds sold for $107,987, the annual premium amortization would be $1,597.40 ($7,987 ÷ 5); Oklahoma Instruments' annual interest expense and the investor's annual interest revenue would be $8,402.60 ($10,000 − $1,597.40). Entries for the first year appear below, and the premium amortization schedule appears in Exhibit 16–5.

ISSUER

Interest expense 8,402.60	
Premium on bonds	
payable 1,597.40	
Cash.	10,000.00

INVESTOR

Cash 10,000.00	
Investment in	
bonds	1,597.40
Interest revenue	8,402.60

EXHIBIT 16—5   PREMIUM AMORTIZATION SCHEDULE, STRAIGHT-LINE AMORTIZATION

YEAR ENDING	(1) CASH*	(2) PREMIUM AMORTIZATION†	(3) INTEREST EXPENSE/REVENUE‡	(4) BOOK VALUE OF BONDS§
				$107,987.00
12/31/87	$10,000.00	$1,597.40	$8,402.60	106,389.60
12/31/88	10,000.00	1,597.40	8,402.60	104,792.20
12/31/89	10,000.00	1,597.40	8,402.60	103,194.80
12/31/90	10,000.00	1,597.40	8,402.60	101,597.40
12/31/91	10,000.00	1,597.40	8,402.60	100,000.00
	$50,000.00	$7,987.00	$42,013.00	

* .10 × $100,000.

† $7,987 ÷ 5.

‡ Col. 1 minus col. 2.

§ Previous book value balance minus col. 2. The *unamortized* premium at the end of each year equals the amounts shown less $100,000.

Under the effective interest method, periodic interest expense (revenue) is a constant percentage of the beginning-of-period liability (investment).

EFFECTIVE INTEREST METHOD   The **effective interest method** was discussed in Chapter 7 and in Chapter 8, on accounting for interest on receivables. Under this method the issuer's periodic interest expense (the investor's periodic interest revenue) is calculated by multiplying the bonds' book value at the beginning of each period by the effective interest rate, also called the yield rate, at the time the bonds are issued.

The premium or discount amortization for each interest period is the difference between the interest calculated at the stated rate and the interest calculated at the effective rate. The amortization schedules in Exhibits 16–6 and 16–7 illustrate the interest calculations and the discount and premium amortization under the effective interest method. The schedules in both exhibits are based on the data in Exhibit 16–1. In Exhibit 16–6 we assume that the bonds were sold at a discount for $92,788 to yield 12 percent; in Exhibit 16–7 we assume that the bonds were sold at a premium for $107,987 to yield 8 percent.

EXHIBIT 16–6   DISCOUNT AMORTIZATION SCHEDULE, EFFECTIVE INTEREST METHOD

YEAR ENDING	(1) INTEREST EXPENSE/REVENUE*	(2) CASH†	(3) DISCOUNT AMORTIZATION‡	(4) BOOK VALUE OF BONDS§
				$ 92,788.00
12/31/87	$11,134.56	$10,000.00	$1,134.56	93,922.56
12/31/88	11,270.71	10,000.00	1,270.71	95,193.27
12/31/89	11,423.22	10,000.00	1,423.22	96,616.49
12/31/90	11,594.00	10,000.00	1,594.00	98,210.49
12/31/91	11,789.51¶	10,000.00	1,789.51	100,000.00
	$57,212.00	$50,000.00	$7,212.00	

* .12 × book value at beginning of year.

† .10 × $100,000.

‡ Col. 1 minus col. 2.

§ Previous book value balance plus col. 3.

¶ Rounding error of $4.25.

EXHIBIT 16–7   PREMIUM AMORTIZATION SCHEDULE, EFFECTIVE INTEREST METHOD

YEAR ENDING	(1) INTEREST EXPENSE/REVENUE*	(2) CASH†	(3) PREMIUM AMORTIZATION‡	(4) BOOK VALUE OF BONDS§
				$107,987.00
12/31/87	$8,638.96	$10,000.00	$1,361.04	106,625.96
12/31/88	8,530.08	10,000.00	1,469.92	105,156.04
12/31/89	8,412.48	10,000.00	1,587.52	103,568.52
12/31/90	8,285.48	10,000.00	1,714.52	101,854.00
12/31/91	8,146.00¶	10,000.00	1,854.00	100,000.00
	$42,013.00	$50,000.00	$7,987.00	

* .08 × book value at beginning of year.

† .10 × $100,000.

‡ Col. 2 minus col. 1.

§ Previous book value balance minus col. 3.

¶ Rounding error of $2.32.

As we pointed out in our discussion of notes receivable in Chapter 8, *the effective interest method of amortizing premium and discount results in reporting the bond liability or investment at the present value of the future cash flows on the bond, with the discount rate being the effective rate*. This concept can be reinforced by comparing the bond values in Exhibit 16–2 with the book values in Exhibit 16–7. Notice that the end-of-year amounts in Exhibit 16–2 equal the end-of-year amounts in Exhibit 16–7.

Interest on bonds often is paid quarterly or semiannually. To apply the effective interest method in these cases, we must use *interest periods* rather than years in determining selling prices and accounting for the bonds. For example, for a five-year 12 percent bond issue paying 3 percent interest each quarter, we determine the selling price by discounting the quarterly cash interest and maturity value for 20 periods at the effective rate per period. That is, if the quarterly market rate of interest at the date of sale is 2 percent, the cash flows are discounted at 2 percent per quarter for 20 quarters. Furthermore, the premium amortization schedule must be constructed on a quarterly basis covering 20 periods. Under the straight-line method the premium is apportioned equally over 20 periods. Under the effective interest method, the effective interest rate of 2 percent per quarter is used to calculate the issuer's quarterly interest expense and the investor's quarterly interest revenue.

EVALUATION OF STRAIGHT-LINE AND EFFECTIVE INTEREST METHODS   The straight-line method results in a constant *amount* of interest each period. In contrast, the effective interest method employs a constant *rate* of interest each period which is applied to the book value of the bonds at the beginning of each period to determine interest expense. The amount of interest changes each period as the book value of the bonds changes. As bonds sold at a discount increase to maturity value, the periodic interest also increases. As the book value of bonds sold at a premium decreases to maturity value, the periodic interest also decreases. As illustrated in Exhibit 16–8, the interest patterns under the effective interest method conform more closely to economic reality—interest should be a function of the amount of the liability or investment. Both the straight-line method and the effective interest method provide the same amount of *total* interest over the life of the bonds.

The straight-line method is more widely used in practice, probably because of its simplicity. Under GAAP, however, the effective interest method must be used if the results are materially different from those of the straight-line method.[3] Because materiality varies among firms, the amortization method used by the bond issuer may differ from the method used by the investor.

> The effective interest method conforms to economic reality—the amount of interest should be a function of the amount of the liability or the investment.

Bond Issue Costs

A firm incurs many types of expenditures when bonds are issued, such as the cost of printing the bonds, attorneys' fees, the cost of preparing the prospectus, and sales commissions if the bonds are sold through a broker. Under GAAP, the issue costs are recorded as an asset, deferred bond issue costs, and are expensed over the period of time from the issue date to the maturity date. The rationale for this practice is that the company should expense the cost over the periods in which the bond proceeds contribute to the earnings process. Some accountants argue that bond issue costs should be treated as a reduction in the net proceeds from the sale of the bonds. This method either increases the bond discount or decreases the bond premium. Therefore, the issue costs effectively increase interest expense over the life of the bonds.

If the method of amortizing the discount or premium corresponds to the method of amortizing the bond issue costs, the effect on periodic income will be the same under the two methods. The only difference will appear on the balance sheet. Bond issue costs have

---

[3] "Interest on Receivables and Payables," *Opinions of the Accounting Principles Board No. 21* (New York: AICPA, 1971).

EXHIBIT 16–8   INTEREST PATTERNS UNDER THE STRAIGHT-LINE
AND EFFECTIVE INTEREST METHODS OF
AMORTIZING BOND DISCOUNT AND PREMIUM

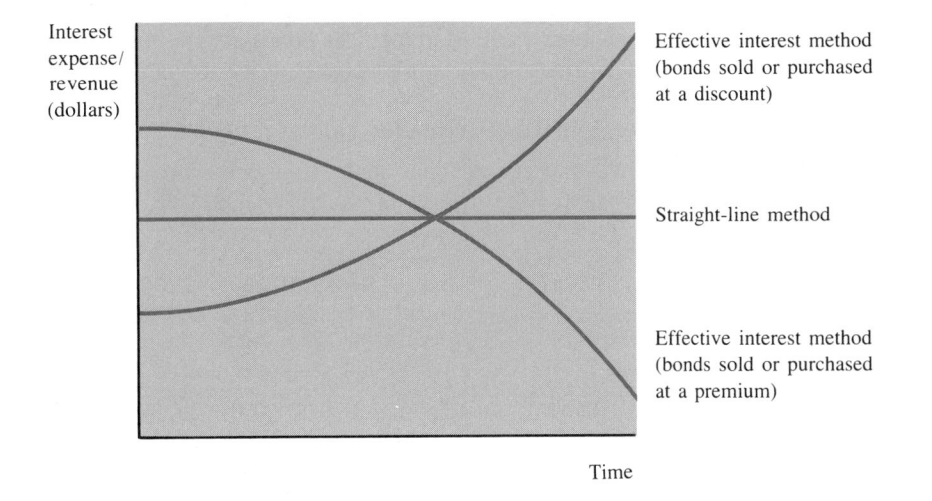

been cited by the FASB in *Statement of Financial Accounting Concepts No. 3* as an expenditure that does not meet the definition of an asset.[4] Thus, the second method appears to be supported by *Statement of Financial Accounting Concepts No 3*.

Short-Term Bond Investments

Premiums and discounts are not amortized on bonds held as short-term investments.

Bond investments should be classified as current assets in the balance sheet if the bonds are marketable and if the purchaser intends to dispose of them within the longer of one year or the operating cycle. Because of materiality, discount or premium is not amortized on bonds held as short-term investments. The primary cash inflows from short-term bond investments are from sales of these securities instead of from interest. Therefore, amortization of discounts or premiums is not relevant in evaluating and assessing cash flows.

Lower-of-cost-or-market procedures generally are not required for bond investments if the market fluctuations are temporary. As with any other asset, however, current or noncurrent bond investments should be reduced to recoverable value (net realizable value) if the market value is below cost and if such declines are expected to be permanent. The loss should be reported in the income statement in accordance with the guidelines for extraordinary items set forth in *APB Opinion No. 30*.

At this point we have discussed the basic concepts in accounting for bonds. We have also seen how bonds and their related interest appear on the financial statements. In the following sections we discuss the accounting procedures necessary when a company's accounting periods differ from the bond interest periods. We also cover accounting for bonds sold between interest periods.

ACCRUALS WHEN INTEREST AND ACCOUNTING PERIODS DO NOT COINCIDE

Although a firm's accounting period seldom coincides with the interest period stated in the bond indenture, this simplifying assumption permitted us to focus on conceptual issues in the previous section. Such a coincidence, however, rarely occurs in practice. Therefore, we need to know how to make adjusting entries for interest expense and revenue when the accounting periods of the firm and the bond interest periods do not coincide.

[4] "Elements of Financial Statements," *Statement of Financial Accounting Concepts No. 3* (Stamford, Conn.: FASB, 1980), para. 161. In Chapter 1, we pointed out that *Concepts Statements* do not constitute or modify generally accepted accounting principles.

In order to provide a basis for discussion, assume that on March 1, 1987, a company issues 10-year term bonds with a maturity value of $300,000. The bonds are dated March 1, 1987, and have a stated interest rate of 12 percent, payable 6 percent semiannually on September 1 and March 1. The bonds are sold for $337,390 to yield 5 percent semiannually.[5] The issuing firm's accounting period ends on December 31.

Straight-Line Amortization

Under the straight-line method the premium amortization is approximately $1,869.48 ($37,390 ÷ 20) every six months, or $311.58 per month. Entries to record the interest expense for 1987 and for the first two months of 1988 appear below:

9/1/87	Interest expense ($18,000 − $1,869.48)	16,130.52	
	Premium on bonds payable ($311.58 × 6)	1,869.48	
	Cash ($300,000 × .12 × 1/2)		18,000.00
	To record interest expense for the first six months.		

12/31/87	Interest expense ($12,000 − $1,246.32)	10,753.68	
	Premium on bonds payable ($311.58 × 4)	1,246.32	
	Interest payable ($300,000 × .12 × 4/12)		12,000.00
	To accrue interest for four months ending 12/31/87.		

3/1/88	Interest expense	5,376.84	
	Interest payable	12,000.00	
	Premium on bonds payable ($311.58 × 2)	623.16	
	Cash		18,000.00
	To record interest expense for two months and payment of interest.[6]		

As shown in Exhibit 16–9, the second interest period encompasses four months in 1987 (September through December) and two months in 1988 (January and February). Therefore, the interest expense of $16,130.52 for the *second interest period* is apportioned $10,753.68 to 1987 and $5,376.84 to 1988. Relevant information would appear on the 1987 income statement as follows:

Interest expense ($16,130.52 + $10,753.68) $26,884.20

The following information would appear on the balance sheet at December 31, 1987:

Current liabilities:
    Interest payable . . . . $ 12,000.00

Noncurrent liabilities
    Bonds payable $300,000.00
    Premium on bonds payable ($37,390 − $1,869.48 − $1,246.32) 34,274.20
                                                                  $334,274.20

[5] The selling price can be calculated as follows:

Present value of principal = $300,000($p_{\overline{20}|\,5\%}$) = $300,000(.3769) = $113,070
Present value of interest = $18,000($P_{\overline{20}|\,5\%}$) = $18,000(12.4622) =   224,320
                                                              $337,390

[6] If reversing entries had been made on January 1, 1988, the following entry would be made on March 1, 1988:

Interest expense 16,130.52
Premium on bonds payable ($311.58 × 6) 1,869.48
    Cash 18,000.00

EXHIBIT 16–9 APPORTIONING INTEREST WHEN THE INTEREST PERIODS AND FISCAL PERIODS DO NOT COINCIDE

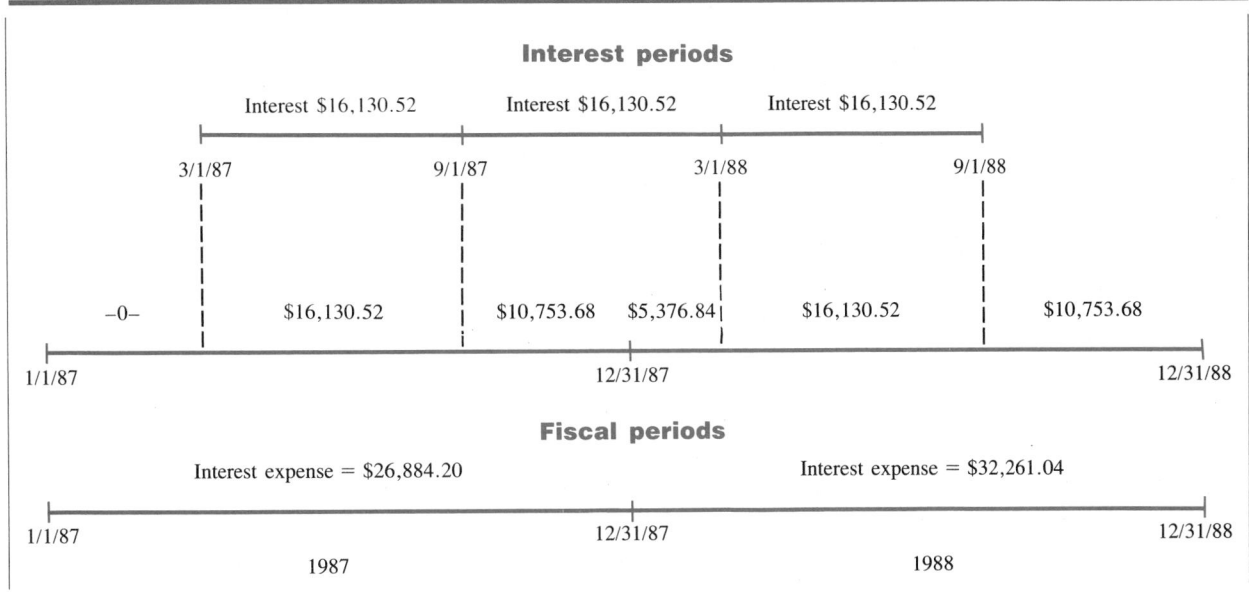

The accrual procedures shown above also apply to the investor. The bond investor would make similar entries for the interest revenue if the investor's accounting period also ended on December 31.

Effective Interest Method

A partial premium amortization schedule under the effective interest method and entries through March 1, 1989, appear in Exhibit 16–10. Notice that the schedule is based on *interest periods,* not on the issuer's accounting periods. When the interest periods do not coincide with a firm's accounting periods, it is necessary to apportion amounts appearing in the schedule to the proper accounting periods. For example, the entries on December 31 and March 1 for the first two years are based on the data for the six months ended March 1, 1988, and March 1, 1989, and assume that the company closes its books on December 31.

SALE OF BONDS BETWEEN INTEREST DATES

As we said earlier, an issuer may not always sell bonds on the date specified in the bond indenture. And because bonds usually are traded on organized markets, investors rarely purchase them on an interest payment date. When bonds are sold between interest dates, the accounting problems are twofold: (1) accounting for accrued interest at the date of sale and (2) amortizing premium or discount if the bonds are not sold at par.

Accrued Interest at the Date of Sale

As we described earlier (pp. 710–11), when bonds are sold between interest dates the exchange price includes any interest accrued to the date of sale. If, for example, a $100,000 five-year bond issue paying interest at 12 percent annually is dated January 1, 1987, and is sold on April 1, 1987, at par plus accrued interest, the selling price is $103,000:

Selling price, exclusive of accrued interest $100,000
Accrued interest ($100,000 × .12 × 3/12) 3,000
Total selling price $103,000

EXHIBIT 16—10   PARTIAL PREMIUM AMORTIZATION SCHEDULE

SIX MONTHS ENDED	(1) INTEREST EXPENSE*	(2) CASH†	(3) PREMIUM AMORTIZATION‡	(4) BOOK VALUE OF BONDS§
				$337,390.00
9/1/87	$16,869.50	$18,000.00	$1,130.50	336,259.50
3/1/88	16,812.98	18,000.00	1,187.02	335,072.48
9/1/88	16,753.62	18,000.00	1,246.38	333,826.10
3/1/89	16,691.31	18,000.00	1,308.69	332,517.41

* .05 × book value at beginning of period.

† .06 × $300,000.

‡ Col. 2 minus col. 1.

§ Previous book value balance minus col. 3.

9/1/87	Interest expense	16,869.50	
	Premium on bonds payable	1,130.50	
	Cash		18,000.00

12/31/87	Interest expense (4/6 × $16,812.98)	11,208.65	
	Premium on bonds payable (4/6 × $1,187.02)	791.35	
	Interest payable (4/6 × $18,000)		12,000.00

3/1/88	Interest payable	12,000.00	
	Interest expense (2/6 × $16,812.98)	5,604.33	
	Premium on bonds payable (2/6 × $1,187.02)	395.67	
	Cash		18,000.00

9/1/88	Interest expense	16,753.62	
	Premium on bonds payable	1,246.38	
	Cash		18,000.00

12/31/88	Interest expense (4/6 × $16,691.31)	11,127.54	
	Premium on bonds payable (4/6 × $1,308.69)	872.46	
	Interest payable (4/6 × $18,000)		12,000.00

3/1/89	Interest payable	12,000.00	
	Interest expense (2/6 × $16,691.31)	5,563.77	
	Premium on bonds payable (2/6 × $1,308.69)	436.23	
	Cash		18,000.00

The entry to record the sale is as follows:

Cash	103,000	
Bonds payable		100,000
Interest payable		3,000

When the first interest payment is made on December 31, 1987, the following entry is appropriate:[7]

[7] Bookkeeping is simplified if, at the date of sale, interest expense, instead of interest payable, is credited. Then when the first interest payment occurs, interest expense can be debited for the full amount of the payment.

To illustrate, assume that the issuer made the following entry to record the sale of bonds:

Cash	103,000	
Bonds payable		100,000
Interest expense		3,000

When the first interest payment is made, the following entry can be made:

Interest expense	12,000	
Cash		12,000

The balance in the interest expense account is $9,000. The same concepts apply to the investor.

```
Interest expense ........................................ 9,000
Interest payable ........................................ 3,000
    Cash .............................................              12,000
```

The interest expense of $9,000, which is reported on the income statement, represents interest incurred from April 1, 1987, through December 31, 1987 ($100,000 × .12 × 3/4), which is the length of time that the bonds have been outstanding during 1987.

Premium and Discount Amortization

When bonds are sold between interest dates, any premium or discount should be amortized over the remaining bond term.

When bonds are sold at a premium or discount between interest dates, the premium or discount must be amortized over the period between the date of sale and the maturity date. To illustrate, assume that Sharkskin Corporation issued two-year 8 percent term bonds with a maturity value of $200,000. The bonds, dated January 1, 1987, pay $8,000 interest semiannually, on July 1 and January 1. They were sold on March 1, 1987, at a market price of $193,456, plus accrued interest from January 1, 1987, to yield 5 percent semiannually. The company's fiscal year ends on December 31.

The entry to record the sale on March 1, 1987, is as follows:

```
Cash ($193,456 + $2,667) ............................. 196,123
Discount on bonds payable ($200,000 − $193,456) ..........   6,544
    Bonds payable ......................................           200,000
    Interest payable ($200,000 × .08 × 2/12) ................             2,667
```

Under the straight-line method, the bond discount of $6,544 is amortized at the rate of $297.45 per month ($6,544 ÷ 22) over the remaining 22 months that the bonds are outstanding. The entry to record interest expense, bond discount amortization, and the cash interest payment on July 1, 1987, is as follows:

```
Interest payable ........................................ 2,667
Interest expense [$1,190 + 4/6($8,000)] ..................... 6,523
    Discount on bonds payable ($297.45 × 4) ..................           1,190
    Cash ($200,000 × .04) ..............................             8,000
```

The entry on December 31, 1987, is:

```
Interest expense ........................................ 9,785
    Discount on bonds payable ($297.45 × 6) ..................           1,785
    Interest payable ....................................             8,000
```

Under the effective interest method, periodic interest expense and discount amortization may be determined by preparing a discount amortization schedule such as the one in Exhibit 16–11.

As shown in Exhibit 16–11, the schedule is constructed under the assumption that the bonds were sold on January 1, 1987, even though the sale occurred on March 1. Thus, the interest expense and the discount amortization for the four months from March 1, 1987, to July 1, 1987, are calculated by multiplying the line entries for the first interest period in Exhibit 16–11 by the fraction of the time that the bonds were outstanding during that period. For example, interest expense for the four months ending July 1, 1987, is $6,430 (4/6 × $9,645), and the discount amortization is $1,097 (4/6 × $1,645). (Interest expense of $6,430 also may be calculated as follows: $192,908 × .05 × 4/6 = $6,430.) The fraction used is 4/6 since the bonds were outstanding for four months of the first six-month interest period.

EXHIBIT 16—11 DISCOUNT AMORTIZATION SCHEDULE

SIX MONTHS ENDING	(1) INTEREST EXPENSE*	(2) CASH†	(3) DISCOUNT AMORTIZATION‡	(4) BOOK VALUE OF BONDS§
				$192,908¶
7/1/87	$ 9,645	$ 8,000	$1,645	194,553
12/31/87	9,728	8,000	1,728	196,281
7/1/88	9,814	8,000	1,814	198,095
12/31/88	9,905	8,000	1,905	200,000
	$39,092	$32,000	$7,092	

* .05 × book value of bonds at beginning of period.

† $200,000 × .04.

‡ Col. 1 minus col. 2.

§ Previous book value balance plus col. 3.

¶ If the sale had been on January 1, 1987, the selling price would have been $192,908:

Present value of principal: $200,000($p_{\overline{4}|\,5\%}$) = $200,000(.8227) = $164,540
Present value of interest: 8,000($P_{\overline{4}|\,5\%}$) = 8,000(3.5460) = 28,368
$$$192,908

The entries to record interest expense for the first two interest periods appear below:

7/1/87	Interest expense 6,430		
	Interest payable 2,667		
	Discount on bonds payable	1,097	
	Cash	8,000	
12/31/87	Interest expense 9,728		
	Discount on bonds payable	1,728	
	Interest payable	8,000	
1/1/88	Interest payable 8,000		
	Cash	8,000	

Our discussion thus far has focused on term bonds, where the entire issue matures on a given date. In the following section we discuss accounting for serial bond issues, which mature at various dates.

SERIAL BONDS

Serial bonds mature in installments and thus have a series of maturity dates. Serial bonds are popular for various reasons. For example, bond investors may insist that a company issuing term bonds maintain a sinking fund for interest and principal payments. Because serial bonds mature in installments, however, the cash flow requirements are spread over time, so a sinking fund may not be required. Furthermore, serial bonds are attractive to investors because of their multiple maturity dates.

DETERMINING SELLING PRICES FOR SERIAL BONDS

The following example will be used to illustrate determining selling prices and accounting for serial bonds. On January 1, 1987, Dowell Corporation issues serial bonds with a maturity value of $40,000, which pay 10 percent interest annually on December 31. The bonds mature in two installments, as follows:

SERIES	DATE	PRINCIPAL AMOUNT MATURING
A	12/31/88	$20,000
B	12/31/89	20,000
		$40,000

Time diagrams showing the cash flows for each series appear in Exhibit 16–12.

When valuing serial bonds, we use the same bond valuation procedures discussed earlier. In theory, the longer the life of each series, the higher the yield demanded by the market to compensate for the increased risk. Investors who bought Dowell's bonds, for example, probably would require a higher rate of return on Series *B* than on Series *A*. Assuming that the market interest rate at the date of sale was 12 percent for Series *A* and 14 percent for Series *B,* the serial bond issue would sell for $37,467, or at a $2,533 discount, as shown in Exhibit 16–13.

ACCOUNTING FOR SERIAL BONDS

Based on the data in Exhibit 16–13, the entry to record the sale of the bonds on January 1, 1987, is as follows:

Cash.	37,467	
Discount on bonds payable	2,533	
Bonds payable		40,000

EXHIBIT 16–12   CASH FLOWS FOR A SERIAL BOND ISSUE

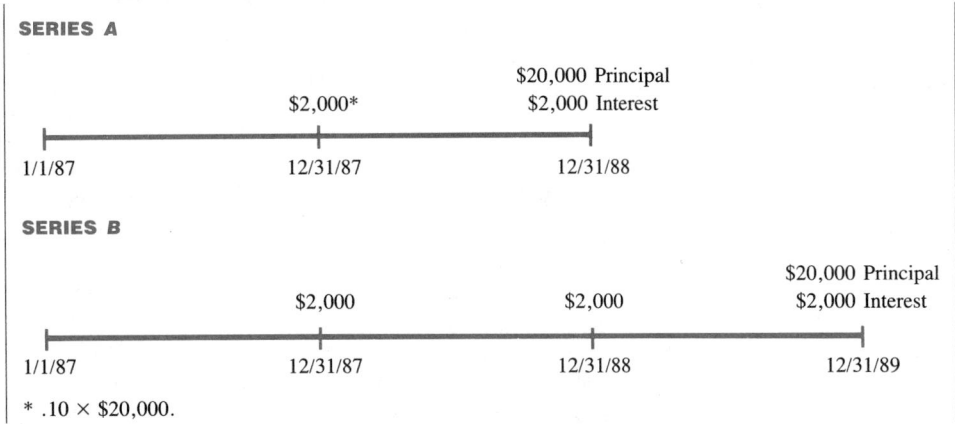

SERIES A

$20,000 Principal
$2,000 Interest

$2,000*

1/1/87   12/31/87   12/31/88

SERIES B

$20,000 Principal
$2,000 Interest

$2,000 $2,000

1/1/87   12/31/87   12/31/88   12/31/89

* .10 × $20,000.

EXHIBIT 16–13   CALCULATING THE SELLING PRICE OF SERIAL BONDS

	SERIES A	SERIES B	TOTAL
Present value of principal:			
$20,000(p$\overline{2}$ 12%) = $20,000(.7972)	$15,944		$15,944
$20,000(p$\overline{3}$ 14%) = $20,000(.6750)		$13,500	13,500
Present value of interest:			
$2,000(P$\overline{2}$ 12%) = $2,000(1.6901)	3,380		3,380
$2,000(P$\overline{3}$ 14%) = $2,000(2.3217)		4,643	4,643
Total	$19,324	$18,143	$37,467
Discount	676	1,857	2,533
Maturity.	$20,000	$20,000	$40,000

As with term bonds, there are two methods of accounting for interest expense and for amortizing the discount or premium on serial bonds: the straight-line method and the effective interest method.

Straight-Line Method

Since we knew the market rate of interest applicable to each series, we were able to determine the discount applicable to each. The schedule in Exhibit 16–14 shows the calculation of interest expense and the discount amortization for the Dowell bonds.

The entries to record the interest expense on the serial bonds for 1988 and the maturity of Series *A* at the end of 1988 are as follows:

Interest expense	4,957	
Discount on bonds payable		957
Cash		4,000
Bonds payable	20,000	
Cash		20,000

In practice, serial bonds, like term bonds, often are sold to an investment banker or broker. Under these circumstances, the issuer receives proceeds from the entire serial issue and may not be able to ascertain the premium or discount applicable to each series. In that case, the periodic amortization can be approximated by the bonds-outstanding method illustrated in Exhibit 16–15. Under this method the total discount or premium is apportioned to each period on the basis of the ratio of the face value of the bonds outstand-

---

EXHIBIT 16–14 STRAIGHT-LINE AMORTIZATION OF DISCOUNT ON SERIAL BONDS

	12/31/87	12/31/88	12/31/89
Series *A*, $676 discount ÷ 2-year life	$ 338	$ 338	
Series *B*, $1,857 discount ÷ 3-year life	619	619	$ 619
Total discount amortization	$ 957	$ 957	$ 619
Cash interest	4,000*	4,000*	2,000†
Interest expense	$4,957	$4,957	$2,619

* $40,000 × .10.

† $20,000 × .10.

EXHIBIT 16–15 PERIODIC DISCOUNT AMORTIZATION, BONDS-OUTSTANDING METHOD

YEAR	(1) FACE VALUE OUTSTANDING	(2) RATIO	(3) AMORTIZED DISCOUNT
1987	$ 40,000	$40,000/$100,000 = .4	.4 × $2,533* = $1,013.20
1988	40,000	$40,000/$100,000 = .4	.4 × $2,533 = 1,013.20
1989	20,000	$20,000/$100,000 = .2	.2 × $2,533 = 506.60
	$100,000	1.0	$2,533.00

* From Exhibit 16–13.

EXHIBIT 16—16   EFFECTIVE INTEREST AMORTIZATION OF
DISCOUNT ON SERIAL BONDS

YEAR ENDING	(1) INTEREST EXPENSE*	(2) CASH†	(3) DISCOUNT AMORTIZATION‡	(4) PAR VALUE OF BONDS MATURING§	(5) BOOK VALUE OF BONDS¶
					$38,364
12/31/87	$4,604	$4,000	$604	—	38,968
12/31/88	4,676	4,000	676	$20,000	19,644
12/31/89	2,356**	2,000	356	20,000	–0–
	$11,636	$10,000	$1,636	$40,000	

* .12 × book value of bonds at beginning of year.

† .10 × par value of bonds outstanding.

‡ Col. 1 minus col. 2.

§ Given.

¶ Previous book value balance plus col. 3 minus col. 4.

** Rounded by $1.

ing each period to the sum of face values outstanding for all the periods in the series. The greater the amount of bonds outstanding in a given year, the larger the discount apportioned to that year. Since the face value of Dowell's bonds outstanding during 1987 and 1988 is twice the face value outstanding in 1989, the discount amortization is twice as great in each of the first two years. If monthly amortization were necessary, the schedule could be constructed on the basis of months outstanding instead of years outstanding.

Effective Interest Method

When the effective inter-est rate for each bond series is known, each series can be treated as a term bond in calculat-ing interest and amorti-zation of premium or discount.

When the effective rate is known for each series, each series can be treated separately as a term bond, and the effective interest method can be applied in the same manner as in Exhibit 16–6. For the Dowell bonds, separate discount amortization schedules under the effective interest method could be constructed for the discounts of $676 and $1,857 for Series *A* and Series *B,* respectively.

When the discount applicable to each series is not determinable, an *average* yield for the entire series must be used to apply the effective interest method. For example, assume that the Dowell Company received $38,364 instead of $37,467 on the sale of the serial bonds. This amount represents an *average* effective rate of 12 percent. A discount amorti-zation schedule under the effective interest method appears in Exhibit 16–16. Notice that when Series *A* matures on December 31, 1988, it is necessary to reduce the book value by the amount of the maturity value of $20,000. Subsequent interest expense and discount amortization calculations are based on this reduced amount.

In the previous sections we have discussed the pricing of and accounting for term bonds and serial bonds under the assumption that they would remain outstanding until maturity. In the next section we discuss the accounting procedures required when they are retired (extinguished) prior to maturity.

EXTINGUISHMENT OF DEBT

Although long-term debt often remains outstanding until maturity, economic conditions sometimes cause companies to extinguish (retire) the debt before maturity. There are several methods of extinguishing debt:

1. The debtor may pay the creditor, thus relieving the debtor of any present and future obligations. A debtor company may accomplish this type of extinguishment in one of several ways. First, a company may retire its debt by purchasing it on the open market at the current market price. Second, if the debt is callable, the debtor may extinguish it by exercising the call privilege and paying the call price. Finally, a new debt issue may be substituted for the original issue through a process called **refunding.**

2. The debtor may be legally released from being the primary obligor for the debt, and it is probable that the debtor will not be required to make any future payments under any guarantees. For example, a parent company may agree to become the primary obligor for the debt of a subsidiary. From the subsidiary company's viewpoint, the debt is extinguished. This process is **defeasance,** meaning release from legal liability.

3. A debtor may place sufficient risk-free assets in an irrevocable trust solely for the purpose of servicing the debt. In addition, the probability that the debtor will be required to make any future payments associated with the debt is remote. This process, which is called **in-substance defeasance,** does not release the debtor from legal liability.[8]

   In addition to the above methods, a debt may be extinguished when a creditor makes a concession to a debtor in financial stress. Accounting for concessions made because of a debtor's financial difficulties is discussed in a later section. Converting bonds to common stock is not considered early extinguishment because the conversion option rests with the investor.[9]

   Several factors may motivate a company to extinguish outstanding debt. First, when market rates of interest are high, bonds sell at a "deep discount." The issuer may be able to retire the debt at a substantial gain because the current market price of the bonds is below the current book value of the bonds. Second, a company that wishes to lower its debt/equity ratio in order to increase its borrowing capacity may exercise the call privilege on callable debt outstanding. Finally, current market interest rates and other economic conditions may be such that the company finds it advantageous to issue refunding bonds at a lower rate of interest than the interest rate on the bonds previously outstanding. In debt refunding, the proceeds of one debt issue are used to retire another debt issue, and in effect, creditors exchange one form of debt for another. Although refunding by the issuer is economically desirable if the present value of the cash savings associated with refunding is greater than zero, management may not always refund under such circumstances.[10] Under GAAP, market values generally are not recorded in the accounts until an exchange occurs. As a result, refunding may cause an *accounting* loss to be recognized although the refunding decision clearly would be desirable from an *economic* standpoint.

EXTINGUISHMENT BY PAYING CREDITOR

When debt is extinguished before maturity, current GAAP requires that *the gain or loss on extinguishment,* if material, *be reported as an extraordinary item, net of related taxes.*[11] The gain or loss is the difference between the book value of the debt, including unamortized bond issue costs, and the amount of cash (or other consideration) given.

---

[8] "Extinguishment of Debt," *Statement of Financial Accounting Standards No. 76* (Stamford, Conn: FASB, 1984).

[9] "Early Extinguishment of Debt," *Opinions of the Accounting Principles Board No. 26* (New York: AICPA, 1972).

[10] The savings from refunding are equal to the difference between the after-tax cash flows, including a possible call premium, associated with the current outstanding issue and the after-tax cash flows associated with the refunding issue when the rate used for discounting is the current market rate of interest.

[11] *FASB Statement No. 76.*

It is interesting, as well as important, to understand the history behind the ''extraordinary item'' classification of gain or loss on debt extinguishments, in view of the fact that many extinguishments do not appear to be unusual and nonrecurring, especially within the context of the environment in which they arose. Inflationary pressures and extremely high interest rates in the 1970s depressed bond prices and motivated many companies to extinguish their debt at huge gains. *FASB Statement No. 4,* issued in 1975, required that gains and losses on early extinguishment be classified as extraordinary items. Many companies were reporting large gains that distorted their income statements, and the objective of the requirement was to ''flag'' these numbers so that users would not get a misleading impression of companies' future cash-generating abilities. *FASB Statement No. 76,* issued in 1984, affirmed this requirement for in-substance defeasance of debt for similar reasons and also for reasons of consistency. In the following paragraphs we shall illustrate accounting for these methods of debt extinguishment.

Assume that on January 1, 1983, Houston Corporation issues $100,000, 10-year, 12 percent bonds for $115,000. Interest is payable annually. On April 1, 1987, because of the high current market rate of interest, Houston retires 60 percent of the bonds outstanding for $59,000 plus accrued interest. Houston uses the straight-line method of amortizing bond premium. Houston's fiscal year ends on December 31.

Before recording the retirement, Houston must record the interest expense and premium amortization for the first three months of 1987 on the bonds retired:

Interest expense ($1,800 − $225) 1,575		
Premium on bonds payable 225*		
Interest payable ($60,000 × .12 × 1/4)		1,800

* Premium amortization per year on 100% of the bonds = $15,000/10 = $1,500. Premium amortization per year on 60% of the bonds = $1,500 × .60 = $900. Premium amortization for 1/4 of a year on 60% of the bonds = $900/4 = $225.

The gain on retirement is $6,175, calculated as follows:

Book value of bonds retired:
  Book value of 100% of bonds on 1/1/87:
    $115,000 less $1,500 amortization per year
      for 4 years ($115,000 − $6,000) = $109,000
  Book value of 60% of bonds on 1/1/87:
  $109,000 × .6 .... $65,400
  Less premium amortization calculated above ....   (225)
  Book value of 60% of bonds on 4/1/87 .... $65,175
Cash paid (*excluding* payment for accrued interest) .... (59,000)
Gain on retirement .... $ 6,175

The April 1 entry to record the retirement is as follows:

Interest payable 1,800		
Bonds payable 60,000		
Premium on bonds payable ($65,175 − $60,000) 5,175		
Cash ($59,000 + $1,800)		60,800
Extraordinary gain on retirement of bonds		6,175

Had Houston used the effective interest method, the gain (or loss) would be calculated in a similar manner. The book value on January 1, 1987, would be determined from a premium amortization schedule. The numbers used in the adjusting entry for the first three months of 1987 would be determined by taking one-fourth of 60 percent of the interest expense, of the premium amortization, and of the cash payment amounts for the interest period ending December 31, 1987.

When serial bonds are extinguished before maturity, the calculations differ slightly, though they are identical conceptually. If serial bonds are accounted for under the effective interest method, the book value of the bonds retired is determined by discounting the remaining cash flows on that series at the effective rate of interest that existed when the series was issued. If the straight-line method of amortizing premium or discount is used, and the discount or premium applicable to each series is known, the unamortized portion can be determined from a schedule similar to the one shown in Exhibit 16–14. For example, assume that Series B in that exhibit is retired at the end of 1988. The unamortized discount applicable to that series is $619, and the book value on December 31, 1988, is $19,381 ($20,000 − $619).

When the bonds-outstanding method is used to amortize premium or discount on serial bonds, a slightly more complex calculation is necessary to determine the unamortized discount or premium applicable to the series retired. To illustrate, refer to Exhibit 16–15 and assume that one-half of the Series B issue is retired at the end of 1987. The annual discount amortization applicable to these bonds is calculated as follows:

$$\frac{\text{Annual}}{\text{amortization}} = \frac{\text{Face value retired}}{\text{Total of column 1, Exhibit 16–15}} \times \frac{\text{Original}}{\text{discount}}$$

$$= \frac{\$10,000}{\$100,000} \times \$2,533 = \$253.30$$

Because these bonds have two years remaining until maturity, the unamortized discount applicable on December 31, 1987, is $506.60 ($253.30 × 2). The gain or loss on extinguishment will be the difference between the amount paid and the book value of $9,493.40 ($10,000 − $506.60). Finally, the annual discount amortization for 1988 and 1989 is reduced by $253.30.

DEFEASANCE AND IN-SUBSTANCE DEFEASANCE

As we discussed at the beginning of this section, debt may be extinguished if the debtor is legally released from liability. This process is called *defeasance* and requires that the debtor debit the liability and credit an extraordinary gain. *In-substance defeasance* occurs when a debtor, instead of obtaining legal release from a liability, irrevocably transfers risk-free assets to a trust and the cash flows from the assets in the trust are sufficient to service the debt. In-substance defeasance may be desirable when a company has sufficient resources to retire its debt but, for legal or other reasons, cannot formally do so. One of the first companies to use in-substance defeasance was Exxon Corporation, which in 1982 extinguished $515 million in debt at a gain of $132 million. As another example, Marine Midland Banks recorded a $30 million gain on a defeasance transaction in 1984.

To illustrate in-substance defeasance, assume that four years ago a company issued at par $100,000 of 10-year bonds with a stated interest rate of 10 percent. At the present date, the current market rate of interest for bonds of similar risk is 14 percent; thus these bonds have a current market value of less than $100,000. The company purchases and places in a trust 10 percent U.S. government bonds with a maturity value of $100,000, maturing in six years. These bonds are currently selling for $91,800 to yield approximately 12 percent. Since the government bonds are essentially risk-free and since the cash flows from interest ($10,000) and principal ($100,000) are sufficient to service the debt outstanding, this transaction represents in-substance defeasance. The entries to record the purchase of government bonds and the defeasance are as follows:

U.S. government bonds (investments) 91,800		
Cash..	91,800	
Bonds payable 100,000		
U.S. government bonds (investments)	91,800	
Extraordinary gain on bond extinguishment	8,200	

An interesting theory question arises in connection with in-substance defeasance: Does this event extinguish the liability? Many people believe that the answer is no and that placing risk-free assets in a trust simply ensures that the debt can be serviced; the placement does not eliminate the liability. Therefore, some people believe that *Statement No. 76* is inconsistent with the definition of a liability. On the other hand, it can be argued that because the company has no further cash flow obligations, recording the event as an extinguishment is consistent with the financial reporting objective of providing information to assist users in assessing and predicting a firm's cash flows.

After *Statement No. 76* was issued, many investment bankers promoted what was called ''instantaneous defeasance,'' whereby a company could issue bonds in one market and concurrently invest in risk-free assets yielding a higher return in another market. The risk-free assets would then be placed in an irrevocable trust, and the ''arbitrage gain'' could be included in income immediately. The FASB ultimately issued a technical bulletin prohibiting companies from accounting for these concurrent transactions in the manner described because of what was perceived to be an attempt to manipulate income.

BONDS ISSUED WITH EQUITY PRIVILEGES

The 1980s appears to be a decade of mergers, as was the 1960s. Also like the 1960s, it is a decade characterized by the issuance of financial securities with both debt and equity features. In the 1960s many companies acquired either the net assets or the common stock of other companies by issuing these ''hybrid'' securities. Two hybrid securities that became popular during this period and that remain popular in the 1980s are (1) convertible bonds and (2) bonds issued with detachable stock warrants that may be used to purchase shares of the issuing company's common stock. Conversion features and detachable warrants are called ''sweeteners'' because they allow securities to command a higher price than securities issued without these features.

CONVERTIBLE BONDS   A **convertible bond** gives the investor the option of converting the bond into a specified number of shares of common stock within a specified time period. Companies issue convertible bonds as a means of raising equity capital, assuming conversion takes place, and also as a means of issuing debt at a lower effective interest cost. Convertible bonds also may be attractive to bond investors because if the market price of the firm's common shares increases, the holder of convertible debt can convert the bonds into common stock, thus realizing increased wealth with no additional cash investment. On the other hand, if the common shares do not increase in price, then conversion does not become attractive, and the investor can continue to hold the bonds and to receive interest. As an illustration of these concepts, each $1,000 Westinghouse Electric Corporation 9 percent convertible bond mentioned at the beginning of the chapter was sold at par in August of 1984 and was convertible into Westinghouse common stock at $31. At the issue date of the bonds, the company's common stock was selling at $26.625 per share. On April 9, 1985, the stock closed at $29.125, and each bond was selling for $1,125.

The accounting problems related to convertible debt are twofold: (1) valuation at the date of issue and (2) accounting for the conversion.

Date of Issue Valuation

If the investor perceives the conversion feature to have value, the convertible bonds can be sold at a higher price than similar bonds issued without a conversion feature. Assume, for example, that Grange Company sold a $1,000 12 percent convertible bond at par at a time when 12 percent bonds of similar risk, but without a conversion privilege, were selling at only 88 percent of par. It therefore appears that the market value of the conversion option is $120 ($1,000 − $880).

There are two views regarding accounting for convertible debt at the time of issuance. Under the first view, the total proceeds received on the sale of convertible debt are allocated between debt and stockholders' equity. The amount assigned to debt is based on the selling price of similar bonds *without* the conversion privilege. The amount assigned to contributed capital is the difference between the total proceeds and the amount assigned to the debt. Under this view, Grange would make the following entry to allocate the proceeds between the liability and equity:

Cash	1,000	
Discount on bonds payable	120	
Bonds payable		1,000
Contributed capital from conversion option		120

Proponents of this view argue that the conversion privilege has economic value, and that the proceeds related to this conversion privilege should be accounted for as contributed capital because the bond investor has paid for the option to become a common stockholder.

Under the second view, no portion of the proceeds is assigned to the conversion option or accounted for as contributed capital; the rationale is that the conversion option is *inseparable* from the debt. That is, exercising the conversion option means surrendering the bond; the bond and the option to convert cannot be separated. Proponents of the second view also argue that practical measurement problems prohibit the splitting of the proceeds between debt and equity. Therefore, subjectivity is introduced, which reduces the reliability of the financial statements.

Under the second view Grange would record the bond issue as follows:

Cash	1,000	
Bonds payable		1,000

Notice that periodic interest expense will be larger under the first view because the initial book value of the bond will be decreased by either a discount or a reduced premium.

The APB opted for the second view in *Opinion No. 14*. The Board placed greater weight on the inseparability of the debt and the conversion option, less weight on practical measurement problems, and concluded that no portion of the proceeds from the issuance of convertible debt should be assigned to the conversion option.

When convertible bonds are issued at a premium or discount, a question arises regarding the time period over which the premium or discount should be amortized, since conversion may occur before the bonds mature. Because there is no way to predict with certainty when conversion will occur, the premium or discount should be amortized as if the bonds will remain outstanding until maturity.

> Convertible bonds are accounted for in the same manner as nonconvertible bonds.

Conversion of Debt into Common Shares

Convertible debt generally is convertible into common shares on or immediately after an interest date. When convertible debt is converted into common shares, it is necessary to remove the debt from the accounts and to record the common shares issued.

To illustrate conversion, assume that Jamie Corporation has convertible bonds outstanding as follows: bonds payable, $300,000; premium on bonds payable, $6,000. Each $1,000 bond is convertible into 10 shares of Jamie's $50 par common stock. The bonds are converted into common shares at a time when the common shares are selling at $125 per share. In practice, the most common method of accounting for bond conversion is the **book value method.** Under this method, no gain or loss is recognized when the bonds are converted, because the conversion occurs under terms of a preexisting contract that already has been recognized in the financial statements. Jamie records the common stock issued at the converted bonds' book value of $306,000:[12]

Bonds payable	300,000	
Premium on bonds payable	6,000	
Common stock		150,000*
Contributed capital in excess of par		156,000†

* $\dfrac{\$300,000}{\$1,000}$ = 300 bonds × 10 common shares per bond = 3,000 shares;

3,000 shares × $50 par value per share = $150,000.

† $306,000 − $150,000 = $156,000.

Assuming an investor also carried the bonds at $306,000, the investor would record the conversion as follows:

Investment in Jamie stock	306,000	
Investment in bonds		306,000

Induced Conversions of Debt

Many companies with outstanding convertible debt offer creditors additional consideration, such as cash, warrants, or a more favorable conversion ratio of debt for common stock, as an inducement for prompt conversion. Companies may be motivated to induce conversion for various reasons, including the desire to reduce interest expense and the desire to improve their debt/equity ratio. The additional consideration usually is offered for a specified time period. *FASB Statement No. 84* requires that when a company induces conversion by using such a sweetener, it must recognize the additional consideration given up as an expense. This expense is measured by the fair value of the additional securities or other consideration issued to induce conversion. Unlike a gain or loss on extinguishment in which an existing contract between the debtor and debt holder is voided, the preexisting conversion contract remains in effect. The inducement is viewed as the sacrifice made to effect conversion.

To illustrate accounting for induced conversion, refer to the Jamie Corporation example but assume that to induce conversion, the corporation offered a more favorable conversion ratio of 12 common shares, instead of 10 common shares, for each $1,000 bond converted within a specified period of time. During the inducement period, 66 bonds, or 22 percent of the total issue, were converted ($300,000 par value divided by $1,000 par value per bond equals 300 bonds; and 66/300 = .22). The entry to record the induced conversion is as follows:

Bonds payable (66 × $1,000)	66,000	
Premium on bonds payable (.22 × $6,000)	1,320	
Conversion expense [66 × (12 − 10) × $125]	16,500	
Common stock (66 × 12 × $50)		39,600
Contributed capital in excess of par		44,220

[12] A less-used method is the **market value method.** Under this method, a gain or loss is recognized equal to the difference between the book value of the bonds and their market value at the time of conversion. The market value of the common shares issued may be used for measurement if it is more easily determinable.

Notice that $16,500 represents the fair value of the additional shares sacrificed. Any bonds converted after the inducement period had lapsed would be accounted for under the original conversion terms of 10 common shares for each $1,000 bond. Therefore, conversion expense applies only to the bonds converted during the inducement period.

DEBT ISSUED WITH DETACHABLE WARRANTS

Some companies sweeten their bond issues by offering bonds with detachable—that is, physically separable—stock purchase warrants. A **warrant** is simply a certificate that gives its holder the right to purchase stock at a specified price within a specified time period. A warrant thus has economic value because the market price of the shares may increase in relation to the specified option price of the shares. *APB Opinion No. 14* requires that the proceeds received from the sale of bonds issued with detachable warrants be allocated between the bonds and the warrants.[13] This allocation may be based on the relative market values of the warrants and bonds of similar risk issued without warrants. If only one of these market values is known, the known market value is subtracted from the total proceeds to determine the amount assigned to the other security.

To illustrate, assume that Wham Corporation issued $150,000 par value 10 percent bonds with 1,500 detachable stock warrants (10 detachable warrants for each $1,000 bond). Each warrant could be used to purchase one share of Wham's $2 par common stock for $25 per share. The bond issue sold for $160,000, and shortly after issuance the warrants sold in the market for $3 each.

The bond issuance would be recorded by Wham as follows:

Cash.. 160,000		
Bonds payable	150,000	
Premium on bonds payable		
($160,000 − $150,000 − $4,500)	5,500	
Contributed capital—stock warrants outstanding		
(1,500 × $3)	4,500	

If 1,200 of the warrants were subsequently exercised when the stock was selling at $30 per share, Wham would make the following entry:

Cash (1,200 × $25) 30,000		
Contributed capital—stock warrants outstanding		
(1,200 × $3) 3,600		
Common stock (1,200 × $2)............................	2,400	
Contributed capital in excess of par	31,200	

Notice that neither the issuer nor the investor recognizes the $30 market price per share because of the $25 fixed price in the warrant contract between the parties. If the warrants expired without being exercised, Wham would debit contributed capital—stock warrants outstanding and credit contributed capital from expired warrants for the carrying value of the expired warrants.

BONDS ISSUED WITH EQUITY PRIVILEGES: A SUMMARY

The accounting procedures required for convertible bonds are not the same as the procedures required for bonds issued with detachable stock warrants, although in substance these types of securities are identical. Is GAAP consistent, then, and are the financial statements representationally faithful? Assume, for instance, that Mr. *A,* a holder of convertible bonds, desires to hold regular term bonds. He can exchange the convertible bonds for term bonds and, assuming that the conversion option does have value, realize a gain in cash. Assume that Ms. *B,* a holder of bonds with detachable warrants, likewise desires to hold term bonds. Ms. *B* can sell the warrants and realize a gain in cash. On the

[13] This approach is similar to the allocation of cost in a ''basket purchase'' of plant equipment.

other hand, assume that Mr. *A* and Ms. *B* both desire stock instead of bonds. Mr. *A* can sell the convertible bonds and buy stock. Ms. *B* can exercise the warrants for common shares, sell the bonds, and buy more stock. Thus, given either convertible bonds or bonds with detachable stock warrants, either a bond position or a common stock position can be attained with, conceptually, the same amount of economic resources.

Some accountants contend that more relevant and useful financial information would result if both convertible bonds and bonds issued with detachable warrants were accounted for in the same way. This issue provides a good illustration of the trade-off between qualitative characteristics that sometimes is necessary in accounting policy making. The APB opted to treat convertible bonds as ''straight debt'' because of the inseparability of the bonds and the conversion privilege and, to a lesser extent, the lack of verifiability associated with measurement of the conversion feature. In other words, comparability may have been sacrificed somewhat because the value of the conversion feature could not be measured in a verifiable manner.

LONG-TERM NOTES PAYABLE

Companies often issue notes as a means of obtaining long-term financing. For example, in 1985 International Harvester issued almost $200 million in 10-year 13¼ percent senior notes with warrants to purchase its common stock. Although accounting for notes payable does not differ in substance from accounting for bonds, there are some differences in characteristics between the two types of debt instruments. For example, a note generally has a shorter maturity than a bond. Notes are not traded in organized securities markets as easily as bonds. Small companies normally issue only long-term notes; large firms generally issue both long-term notes and bonds.

The accounting principles for long-term notes and bonds are conceptually equivalent. That is, the valuation principle is based on the present value of the future cash flows of a note; discounts, and possibly premiums, are amortized over the life of the note. Balance sheet classification of a note and of related discount or premium is similar to that for bonds. Long-term notes receivable were discussed in Chapter 8. Accounting for long-term notes payable parallels accounting for long-term notes receivable.

NOTES ISSUED FOR CASH   When a note is issued for cash, its present value equals the cash received; therefore, the note should be recorded at that amount. The present value of the note will equal its maturity value if the rate of interest stated on the note is equal to the current market rate of interest for notes of similar risk. Noninterest-bearing notes payable or notes with interest at a stated rate below the current market rate of interest will always have a present value less than the maturity amount. If the maturity value of the note is recorded in the accounts, a discount on the note, similar to a discount on a bond, will also be recorded.

Assume that on January 1, 1987, Georgia Company issues a three-year note payable in the amount of $18,000. The note bears interest at a rate of 6 percent, payable annually. If the current market rate of interest is 10 percent, obviously no lender will lend Georgia $18,000 for the right to receive a 6 percent rate of return, since the lender can earn 10 percent on other similar investments. The proceeds of the note would be $16,209:

Present value of principal:
$\quad$ $18,000(p_{\overline{3}|\,10\%}) = \$18,000(.7513) = \$13,523$
Present value of interest:
$\quad$ $1,080*(P_{\overline{3}|\,10\%}) = \$1,080(2.4869) = \underline{\quad 2,686}$
$\qquad\qquad\qquad\qquad\qquad\qquad\qquad\quad \underline{\$16,209}$

* $18,000 × .06.

The entry to record the issuance of the note is as follows:

```
Cash............................................... 16,209
Discount on notes payable..........................  1,791
    Notes payable ........................................        18,000
```

Annual interest expense is calculated by the effective interest method. The annual discount amortization is the difference between interest expense and the annual cash interest payment or interest accrual. For example, the entries to record interest expense for 1987 and 1988 are as follows:

	1987	1988
Interest expense (.10 × $16,209) 1,621		
[.10 × ($16,209 + $541)]		1,675
Discount on notes payable................	541	595
Cash................................	1,080	1,080

NOTES ISSUED FOR NONCASH ASSETS

Occasionally notes may be issued in exchange for assets other than cash. When assets other than cash are received, an exchange price may be more difficult to determine. In theory, however, the assets received should be recorded at their fair market value, which also is the best estimate of the present value of the note issued. That is, when assets are acquired by issuance of notes payable, the transaction is recorded at the fair market value of the asset received or the present value of the note payable, whichever is more clearly evident.

Assume that Debra Company acquires land by issuing a six-year, 8 percent note for $10,000. Interest is payable annually. While the fair market value of the land is not objectively determinable, the current market rate of interest for notes of similar risk is 12 percent.

Since the fair market value of the land is not determinable, the exchange price must. be *imputed* from the present value of the note. The present value of the note and the imputed fair market value of the land are $8,355, as calculated below:

Present value of principal: $10,000(p $\overline{_6|}$ 12%) = $10,000(.5066) = $5,066
Present value of interest: $800(P $\overline{_6|}$ 12%) = $800(4.1114) = $\underline{3,289}$
                                                                $8,355

Debra would record the transaction as follows:

```
Land ...............................................8,355
Discount on notes payable.............................1,645
    Notes payable ........................................        10,000
```

Under the effective interest method, interest expense for the first year would be recorded as follows:

```
Interest expense (.12 × $8,355) ...........................1,003
    Discount on notes payable.............................        203
    Cash (.08 × $10,000) ..................................        800
```

Now assume that Shelby Corporation acquires a machine with a fair market value of $16,967 by issuing a five-year $20,000 note with interest at 6 percent. Shelby's machine would be recorded at its fair market value of $16,967, and this amount is imputed as the present value of the note:

Machine 16,967
Discount on notes payable 3,033
   Notes payable   20,000

This example illustrates two important points. First, recording the machine and the payable at $20,000 would be improper because $20,000 is more than the machine's current fair market value and overstates the present value of the note and presumably the future cash flows associated with the use of the machine. Second, the effective rate of interest on the note must be *imputed* to calculate periodic interest expense. The process of imputing the effective rate of interest requires finding an interest rate that, when applied to the cash flows associated with the note, equates the present value of the cash flows with the fair market value of the machinery acquired. We discussed this concept in connection with annuities in Chapter 7. A time diagram for this situation appears below:

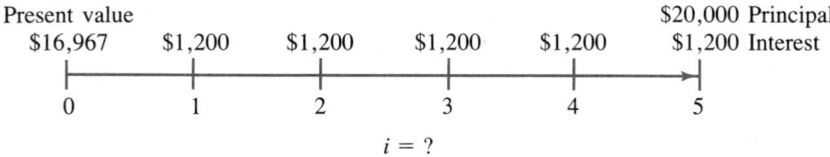

Since we have both an annuity—the five annual $1,200 cash flows—and a single future amount of $20,000, a trial-and-error approach must be used to solve the following equation:[14]

$$\$16,967 = \$1,200(P_{\overline{5}|\,i\%}) + \$20,000(p_{\overline{5}|\,i\%})$$

We know the effective rate is greater than 6 percent because the note was issued at a discount. We might begin our calculations with 8 percent, which produces a present value of $18,403:

**PRESENT VALUE OF
CASH FLOWS AT 8%**

Principal:
   $20,000($p_{\overline{5}|\,8\%}$) = $20,000(.6806) $13,612
Interest:
   $1,200($P_{\overline{5}|\,8\%}$) = $1,200(3.9927)   4,791
                                                                 $18,403

Since $18,403 is larger than $16,967, we know that the effective rate is higher than 8 percent. Using 10 percent, we obtain the present value of $16,967:

**PRESENT VALUE OF
CASH FLOWS AT 10%**

Principal:
   $20,000($p_{\overline{5}|\,10\%}$) = $20,000(.6209) $12,418
Interest:
   $1,200($P_{\overline{5}|\,10\%}$) = $1,200(3.7908)   4,549
                                                                 $16,967

---

[14] Notice that we have one equation and two unknowns, $P_{\overline{5}|\,i\%}$ and $p_{\overline{5}|\,i\%}$. In Chapter 7, our illustrations dealt with either a single amount or an annuity, but not both.

Subsequent use of the effective interest method for interest expense would be based on the effective rate of 10 percent.

NOTES AND OTHER OBLIGATIONS EXCHANGED FOR CASH

Chapter 8 discussed the lending of cash in exchange for a note *and* some right or privilege. Here we shall discuss this type of transaction from the standpoint of the borrower. Assume that Supplier, Inc., borrows $20,000 cash from a customer by issuing a three-year noninterest-bearing note for $20,000 and also agrees to supply the customer with 800 widgets at a discount over some future time period.

Since the note payable bears no interest, the only reason that Supplier's customer would give up $20,000 now for the right to receive $20,000 three years hence would be in order to receive something of value *in addition to* the $20,000, such as the right to purchase widgets at a discount. From Supplier's standpoint, then, two liabilities are incurred in exchange for the cash received: (1) an obligation to pay $20,000 three years hence, and (2) an obligation to sell 800 widgets to the customer at a discount. The difference between the present value of the note, based on the current market rate of interest, and the maturity amount represents the exchange price of the additional obligation implicitly agreed on by the two parties. If the current market rate of interest for notes of similar risk is 12 percent, the following entry would be recorded by Supplier on receipt of the cash:

Cash.	20,000	
Discount on notes payable	5,764*	
Notes payable		20,000
Unearned revenue		5,764

* Present value of note: $20,000(p_{\overline{3}|\,12\%}) = \$20,000(.7118) = \$14,236$.

$$\begin{array}{ccccc} \text{Maturity value} & - & \text{Present value} & = & \text{Discount} \\ \$20,000 & - & \$14,236 & = & \$5,764 \end{array}$$

The exchange price of the additional obligation will always equal the calculated discount. Although the note may bear no interest or a low rate of interest, both parties are presumed to have bargained on the basis of current market rates. The discount is amortized over the life of the note by the effective interest method. Unearned revenue is recognized as earned revenue as the 800 widgets are sold to Supplier's customer. Assume, for example, that the customer purchased 240 widgets the first year at a discount price of $100 per widget. Supplier would make the following entries to recognize the sales and the portion of unearned revenue earned:

Cash.	24,000	
Sales		24,000
Unearned revenue	1,729	
Sales revenue		1,729
(240/800 × $5,764)		

TROUBLED DEBT RESTRUCTURING

Liquidity problems, high interest rates, and other unfavorable economic circumstances in the U.S. economy have forced many debtors to arrange **debt-restructuring** agreements with creditors because of an inability to meet obligations (interest or principal) as they become due. For example, both Cleveland and New York City have effected debt-restructuring arrangements. Many business firms, such as Midland Mortgage Investors Trust and International Harvester, have found it necessary to restructure debt. Creditors often make concessions through restructuring agreements rather than force troubled debtors into bankruptcy proceedings, because a restructure agreement may allow creditors the maximum recovery of their investment.

A **troubled debt restructuring** occurs when a creditor makes a concession that is *favorable* to a debtor and may take either one or a combination of the following forms:

1. The debtor may transfer assets or equity securities in *settlement* of a debt obligation.

2. The terms of the debt agreement may be *modified.*[15]

Each of these forms is discussed in the following paragraphs.

ASSETS OR EQUITY SECURITIES TRANSFERRED IN SETTLEMENT OF OUTSTANDING DEBT

When a debtor sacrifices assets or issues equity securities in settlement of an outstanding debt, the debtor recognizes an *extraordinary gain* equal to the difference between the book value of the debt and the fair market value of assets or securities sacrificed. The extraordinary classification may help users to assess cash flows when a troubled debtor who has experienced continuing losses from operations suddenly shows a gain due to restructuring of an outstanding debt. Since the creditor makes a concession to the debtor, *the restructuring will never result in a loss to the debtor.* Furthermore, when assets are transferred to the creditor, the debtor also recognizes a gain or loss equal to the difference between the book value and the fair market value of the assets transferred. This gain or loss is classified according to the criteria in *APB Opinion No. 30.*

The creditor either recognizes a loss or reduces allowance for doubtful accounts, whichever is applicable, for the difference between the book value of the debtor's receivable and the fair market value of the assets or securities received. If a loss is recognized, it is classified according to the criteria in *APB Opinion No. 30.* Since a concession is made, *there will never be a gain to the creditor.* To illustrate, assume that Creditor Corporation holds a $150,000 note receivable that is currently due with interest payable of $7,500. Debtor Corporation is unable to pay the amounts due. Therefore, Creditor agrees to accept land with a fair market value of $135,000 in full settlement. The carrying value of the land on Debtor's books is $100,000.

The following entries would be made by the debtor and creditor to record the debt restructuring:

CREDITOR

Land 135,000		
Loss on restructuring* 22,500		
Notes receivable	150,000	
Interest receivable......	7,500	

DEBTOR

Notes payable 150,000		
Interest payable 7,500		
Land	100,000	
Extraordinary gain		
on debt restructuring		
($157,500 − $135,000)....	22,500	
Gain on transfer of land		
($135,000 − $100,000)....	35,000	

* Or allowance for doubtful accounts.

If, instead of sacrificing land, the debtor issued stock with a par value of $90,000 and a fair market value of $135,000, the creditor would debit investments instead of land in the above entry. The debtor would make the following entry:

Notes payable 150,000		
Interest payable...................................... 7,500		
Common stock	90,000	
Contributed capital in excess of par ($135,000 − $90,000)	45,000	
Extraordinary gain on debt restructuring	22,500	

[15] "Accounting by Debtors and Creditors for Troubled Debt Restructurings," *Statement of Financial Accounting Standards No. 15* (Stamford, Conn.: FASB, 1977).

MODIFICATION OF DEBT TERMS

As an alternative to restructuring by transferring assets or equity securities, the debtor may receive a concession from the creditor in the form of a modification of the terms of the debt agreement. Modification of the terms may take one or more of the following forms:

1. Forgiveness of interest due currently or forgiveness of a part of the principal amount owed.

2. Deferral of the principal or interest due to a later date.

3. Reduction in the rate of interest on the original debt.

The following example will be used to discuss restructuring debt when the debt terms are modified. Assume that on January 1, 1984, Debtor Company issued a four-year 10 percent $100,000 note with interest payable annually. Debtor made the interest payments for 1984 and 1985 but began to have severe financial difficulties in 1986. At the end of 1986, Debtor was unable to pay the $10,000 interest due. Further, it is unlikely that Debtor will be able to meet the principal obligations under the original debt contract. Creditor Company agrees to forgive the $10,000 interest payable at the end of 1986, to reduce the original principal to $95,770, to extend the due date of the new principal to the end of 1992, and to lower the rate of interest to 5.743 percent beginning in 1987.

The accounting issue centers on what recognition should be given to the restructuring arrangements in the accounts and in the financial statements. Some accountants argue that an exchange has occurred, that new debt has been issued to replace debt currently outstanding, and that a gain or loss should be recognized in the same manner as previously discussed under early extinguishment of debt through debt refunding. Other accountants argue that no exchange of resources or obligations has occurred and that the same debt is still outstanding with modified terms.

Since the ability of a debtor in financial stress to meet future cash flow obligations may be highly uncertain, the FASB opted for the more conservative approach represented by the latter argument. Under *FASB Statement No. 15,* the restructuring effects are treated *prospectively.* That is, the debtor recognizes no gain unless the *total cash flows,* as restructured, are less than the *book value* of the debt *before* restructuring. If the restructured cash flows exceed the current book value of the debt, a new effective interest rate on the debt is imputed by finding the interest rate that equates the present value of the restructured cash flows with the book value of the debt before restructure. Thus, the book value of the debt is considered to be the present value of the restructured cash flows, and an effective interest rate on the debt is imputed for purposes of recording interest expense in future periods.

In the example above, Debtor Company's restructured cash flows exceed the book value of the original debt:

Restructured cash flows:		
Principal (due end of 1992)........................	$ 95,770	
Interest ($95,770 × .05743 for		
six years = $5,500 × 6).........................	33,000	$128,770
Current book value:		
Principal (due end of 1987).......................	$100,000	
Interest due at end of 1986	10,000	(110,000)
Excess of restructured cash flows		
over book value of debt....................		$ 18,770

Since the restructured cash flows exceed the book value of the debt, no gain is recognized.

A time diagram depicting the current book value of the debt, the restructured cash flows, and the new effective interest rate calculations appears in Exhibit 16–17. As the

EXHIBIT 16—17   IMPUTATION OF AN EFFECTIVE
INTEREST RATE FOR RESTRUCTURED DEBT

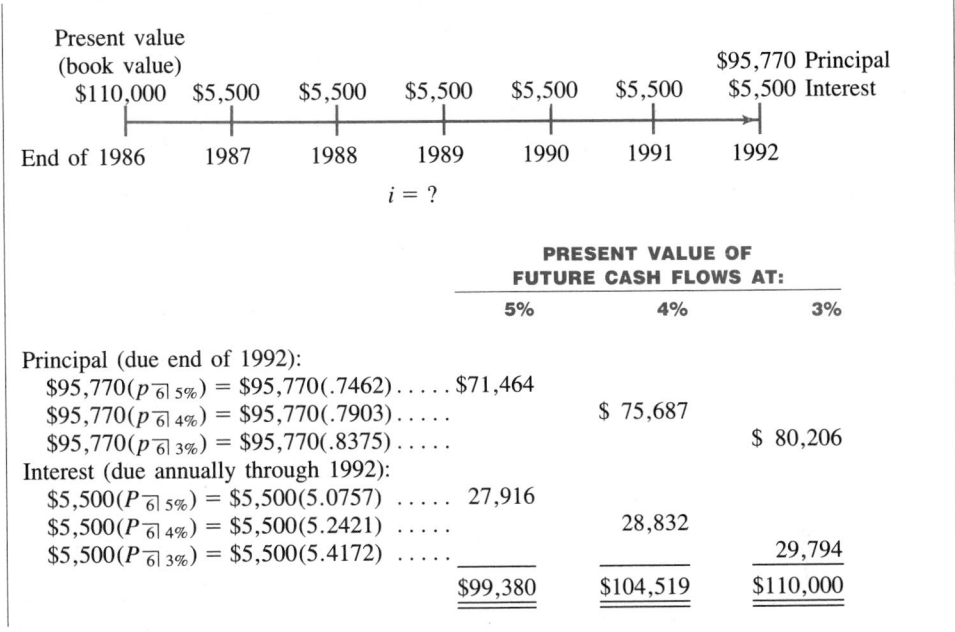

	PRESENT VALUE OF FUTURE CASH FLOWS AT:		
	5%	**4%**	**3%**
Principal (due end of 1992):			
$95,770(p\overline{6}_{\,5\%}) = \$95,770(.7462)\ldots\ldots\$71,464$	$71,464		
$95,770(p\overline{6}_{\,4\%}) = \$95,770(.7903)\ldots\ldots$		\$ 75,687	
$95,770(p\overline{6}_{\,3\%}) = \$95,770(.8375)\ldots\ldots$			\$ 80,206
Interest (due annually through 1992):			
$5,500(P\overline{6}_{\,5\%}) = \$5,500(5.0757)\ \ldots\ldots$ 27,916	27,916		
$5,500(P\overline{6}_{\,4\%}) = \$5,500(5.2421)\ \ldots\ldots$		28,832	
$5,500(P\overline{6}_{\,3\%}) = \$5,500(5.4172)\ \ldots\ldots$			29,794
	$99,380	$104,519	$110,000

calculations in Exhibit 16–17 indicate, the effective rate of interest, determined by a trial-and-error process, is 3 percent. This rate, when applied to the restructured cash flows, equates the present value of the restructured cash flows with the book value of the original debt.

Annual interest expense is calculated by the effective interest method, and the difference between the cash interest paid and interest expense represents a reduction in the carrying value of the debt. A reclassification entry for Debtor at the date of restructure might be as follows:

Notes payable	100,000	
Interest payable	10,000	
Notes payable		110,000

Entries for interest expense for 1987 and 1988 are as follows:

Interest expense (.03 × $110,000)	3,300	
Notes payable ($5,500 − $3,300)	2,200	
Cash		5,500
To record interest for 1987.		

Interest expense [.03 × ($110,000 − $2,200)]	3,234	
Notes payable ($5,500 − $3,234)	2,266	
Cash		5,500
To record interest for 1988.		

Since the interest expense is less than the cash interest paid, the difference represents a reduction in the notes payable balance.[16] By the end of the sixth year, the note will be reduced to $95,770, which is the amount due at that time. Parallel entries also would be made by Creditor.

---

[16] Notice that the effect is identical to amortization of a premium on bonds payable.

In the above example, a trial-and-error approach was necessary because the rate of interest was applied to a single amount and to an annuity. If the restructured cash flows are either a single future amount or an annuity, the effective rate can be determined by the present value concepts discussed in Chapter 7. For example, if we assume that Creditor agreed to permit Debtor to pay a lump-sum amount of $139,183 at the end of 1992 in full settlement, the effective rate could be determined by the formula for the present value of a single amount:

$$p = a(p\,\overline{_{6}}\,_{i\%})$$

$$\$110,000 = \$139,183(p\,\overline{_{6}}\,_{i\%})$$

$$p\,\overline{_{6}}\,_{i\%} = .7903$$

As Table B in Appendix 7–1 indicates, the rate of interest that corresponds to the present value factor of .7903 for six periods is 4 percent. In this situation, periodic interest expense would be calculated by multiplying each beginning-of-year liability by 4 percent. Thus, the liability would increase by 4 percent each year and would total $139,183 at the end of 1992.

If the restructured cash flows are *less* than the book value of the debt, an extraordinary gain on restructure is recognized at the date of restructuring. The gain is the difference between the book value of the debt and the restructured cash flows. Subsequent cash payments are accounted for as reductions in the book value of the debt, and *no periodic interest expense is recorded*. To illustrate, assume that on June 30, 1987, Debtor owes Creditor $50,000 on a note. Interest of $4,500 also has accrued. Because of Debtor's financial difficulties, Creditor agrees to forgive the interest currently due, to reduce the note principal to $40,000, to extend the due date of the note until December 31, 1989, and to reduce the interest rate on the note from 9 percent annually to 2 percent semiannually on the new principal.

The book value of the debt exceeds the restructured cash flows by $10,500:

Book value of debt ($50,000 + $4,500)		$54,500
Restructured cash flows:		
Principal (due at end of 1989)	$40,000	
Semiannual interest (.02 × $40,000 × 5 payments = $800 × 5) ...	4,000	(44,000)
Excess of book value over restructured cash flows		$10,500

Since the restructured cash flows are less than the book value of the original debt, Debtor recognizes a gain of $10,500, and subsequent interest payments are accounted for as reductions in the note balance. At the date of restructure Debtor would make the following entry to recognize the gain and to reclassify the note:

Notes payable 50,000		
Interest payable.. 4,500		
Extraordinary gain on debt restructuring	10,500	
Notes payable	44,000	

At the date of each semiannual interest payment, the following entry would be made:

Notes payable	800	
Cash..		800

At the note's maturity date, the following entry would be made:

Notes payable 40,000
    Cash.   40,000

Creditor makes parallel entries, with one exception. At the restructure date, Creditor debits either a loss or an allowance account for $10,500. If a loss is recorded, it is classified according to the criteria in *APB Opinion No. 30*.

A summary of accounting for debt restructuring agreements appears in Exhibit 16–18. Begin at the top of the figure and follow the arrows for the various types of agreements.

EXHIBIT 16—18   ACCOUNTING FOR TROUBLED DEBT RESTRUCTURING
(FASB STATEMENT NO. 15)

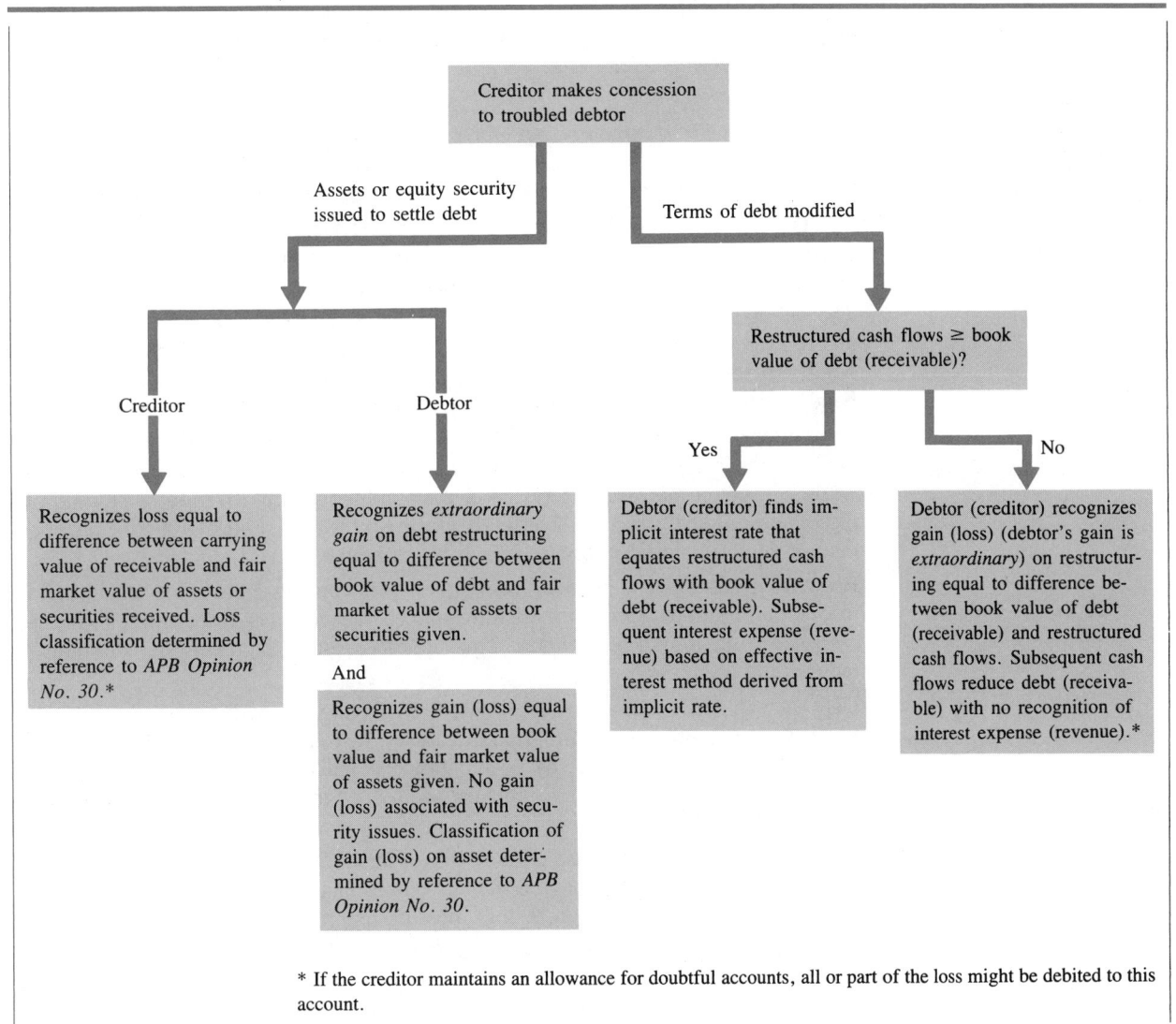

Creditor makes concession to troubled debtor

Assets or equity security issued to settle debt

Terms of debt modified

Restructured cash flows ≥ book value of debt (receivable)?

Creditor

Debtor

Yes

No

Recognizes loss equal to difference between carrying value of receivable and fair market value of assets or securities received. Loss classification determined by reference to *APB Opinion No. 30.**

Recognizes *extraordinary gain* on debt restructuring equal to difference between book value of debt and fair market value of assets or securities given.

And

Recognizes gain (loss) equal to difference between book value and fair market value of assets given. No gain (loss) associated with security issues. Classification of gain (loss) on asset determined by reference to *APB Opinion No. 30*.

Debtor (creditor) finds implicit interest rate that equates restructured cash flows with book value of debt (receivable). Subsequent interest expense (revenue) based on effective interest method derived from implicit rate.

Debtor (creditor) recognizes gain (loss) (debtor's gain is *extraordinary*) on restructuring equal to difference between book value of debt (receivable) and restructured cash flows. Subsequent cash flows reduce debt (receivable) with no recognition of interest expense (revenue).**

* If the creditor maintains an allowance for doubtful accounts, all or part of the loss might be debited to this account.

Many accountants question the economic reality of the accounting requirements of *FASB Statement No. 15*. They argue that when the debt terms are modified in a restructure agreement, the restructured debt should be adjusted and reported at present value based on the market rate of interest at the date of restructuring, like any other debt transaction at an exchange date. Under this approach the debtor would recognize gains even when the restructured cash flows exceeded the book value of the debt. Larger gains would result when the restructured cash flows were less than the book value of the debt. Furthermore, interest expense would be recorded over the life of the new agreement.

Many observers believe that banks and other financial institutions that were holding notes of financially troubled debtors exerted some influence on the outcome of *FASB Statement No. 15*. By threatening to be more conservative in their lending policies, and thus curtailing the economic activities of their clients, they obtained an accounting treatment under *Statement No. 15* that *minimized* their recognition of losses.

On the other hand, the accounting requirements of *Statement No. 15* minimize the debtor's gain. Many accountants support this result because a troubled debtor may continue to have difficulties meeting financial obligations in future periods. Thus, when a creditor makes a concession by modifying debt terms, the required accounting treatment is consistently conservative for the debtor.

SUMMARY OF IMPORTANT TOPICS AND CONCEPT APPLICATIONS

1. Bonds may be classified as term vs. serial, interest-bearing vs. noninterest-bearing (zero-coupon), secured vs. debenture (unsecured), registered vs. bearer, convertible vs. nonconvertible, and callable vs. noncallable.

2. The selling price of a bond is the **present value of the future cash flows** for interest and principal. If the market rate of interest equals the bond's stated interest rate, the bond will sell at par. If the market rate of interest is less than (is greater than) the bond's stated interest rate, the bond will sell at a **premium (discount).**

3. A premium or discount represents an adjustment of interest over the period of time that the bonds are outstanding. A premium decreases interest over the bond term, while a discount increases interest over the bond term. Amortization of premium or discount should be based on the **effective interest method,** unless straight-line amortization is not materially different from the effective interest method.

4. **Bond issue costs** should be recorded as an asset and amortized over the bond term. In theory, an argument exists for treating bond issue costs as a reduction in the net proceeds from the sale of bonds. This approach either increases the discount or reduces the premium.

5. Debt may be **extinguished** in several ways: by paying the creditor and thus relieving the debtor of any present and future obligations, by **defeasance** (the debtor is legally released from obligation), or by **in-substance defeasance** (the debtor places sufficient risk-free assets in an irrevocable trust to render any future cash flow obligations remote).

6. When debt is extinguished, the **gain or loss** is the difference between the book value of the debt (including unamortized bond issue costs) and the amount of cash or other consideration given. This gain or loss must be reported as an **extraordinary** item.

7. At issuance, **convertible bonds** are accounted for in the same manner as nonconvertible bonds. Bond conversions usually are accounted for under the **book value method.** Many companies induce conversion by offering a more favorable conversion ratio or some other consideration for a limited period of time. Any additional consideration given up to induce conversion must be recorded as an expense.

8. When bonds are issued with **detachable warrants,** the proceeds from issue should be allocated between the bonds and the warrants based on their relative fair market values.

9. Notes payable may be issued for cash or for noncash assets. As with bonds payable, notes payable should be recorded at the present value of the future cash flows associated with the notes. The present value may be determined from the cash received or from the fair value of noncash assets received in exchange. When notes payable and other obligations are exchanged for cash, the notes payable are recorded at their present value; the exchange price of the additional obligation will equal the calculated discount on the note. Interest expense is based on the **effective interest method.**

10. A **troubled debt restructuring** occurs when a creditor makes a concession that is favorable to the debtor and may take one or a combination of the following forms: (a) the debtor transfers assets or equity securities in settlement of the debt obligation, or (b) the terms of the debt are modified.

11. A debtor recognizes an **extraordinary gain on restructure** either when assets or equity securities, whose market value is less than the book value of the debt, are transferred in settlement of the debt or when the debt's restructured future cash flows are less than the book value of the debt. A loss, if recognized by the creditor, is classified according to the criteria for extraordinary items. Under these circumstances, interest is not recorded during the period in which the restructured debt is outstanding; cash flows are accounted for as reductions in the debt. If the restructured cash flows exceed the book value of the debt (receivable), no gain (loss) is recognized by the debtor (creditor). A new effective interest rate must be determined and used for calculating periodic interest expense (revenue) over the period in which the modified debt is outstanding.

APPENDIX 16—1

INFLATION-RELATED DEBT INSTRUMENTS

Inflationary pressures in the U.S. economy have led to the devising of many types of debt instruments to protect lenders against loss of purchasing power as a result of holding notes and bonds that have fixed cash flows for interest and principal. At the same time, many borrowers have issued such securities in order to avoid obligating themselves to high interest rates over a long period of time. The use of variable or adjustable interest rate mortgages on real estate is a good example. Other types of inflation-hedging securities include bonds with variable (floating) interest rates, shared-appreciation mortgages, price-indexed notes and bonds, and bonds payable in goods or commodities instead of dollars (commodity bonds).

Accounting for some of these securities is controversial, because official pronouncements do not contain specific guidance on acceptable accounting procedures. Because these securities specifically consider inflation, while the conventional historical cost model does not, practicing accountants have been forced to ''account by analogy''—that is, to use a generally accepted procedure that is considered to be analagous to the issue at hand.[17]

[17] G. Michael Crooch, ''Accounting for Inflation's Stepchild Securities,'' *Papers and Proceedings of the 1981 AAA Convention* (Sarasota, Fla.: American Accounting Association, 1981).

VARIABLE INTEREST RATE DEBT

Variable interest rate mortgages have replaced many conventional, fixed interest rate mortgages on real estate. Financial institutions that lend money under long-term contracts at, say, 8 percent suffer losses when they are forced to pay, say, 18 percent for money because of higher market interest rates. In addition, the current market value of their loan portfolios is much below historical cost. To illustrate a variable interest rate note, assume that at the beginning of 1987 Crabtree Company purchases property with a fair market value of $2,486 and issues a variable rate note to be repaid in end-of-year installments over a three-year period. Further assume that applicable market rates of interest are as follows:

At the beginning of 1987................................10%
During and at the end of 1987 10
During and at the end of 1988 15
During and at the end of 1989 20

The annual installment payment based on the initial 10 percent rate would be determined as follows:

$$\text{Present value} = \text{Periodic payments} \times P\overline{_{3|}}\ _{10\%}$$
$$\$2,486 = \text{Periodic payments} \times P\overline{_{3|}}\ _{10\%}$$

$$\text{Periodic payments} = \frac{\$2,486}{2.486}$$
$$= \$1,000$$

Under a conventional loan, Crabtree would use the effective interest method to amortize the loan balance. Exhibit 16–19 presents amortization schedules that Crabtree would use to make accounting entries under two versions of a variable interest rate note. Under a variable rate loan with fixed payments and a ''balloon'' balance (section *a* of Exhibit 16–19), annual interest expense is calculated on the basis of the interest rate in effect that year. The difference between the cash payment and interest expense is the reduction in the payable. Thus, at the end of 1989, the balloon balance due is $194.

Under the variable rate note with variable payments, the payments must be recalculated each year when the interest rate changes. This procedure is shown in column 2 of part *b* of Exhibit 16–19. The payments for 1988 and 1989 would have been the same as the payment for 1987 if the rate had not changed.

PRICE-INDEXED DEBT

Price-indexed debt requires the issuer to pay at maturity an amount that is tied to a price index—either a general price index, such as the Consumer Price Index, or a price index related to a specific good. The periodic interest, if any, may or may not be indexed. For example, the Mexican development bank (NAFINSA) has sold several ''petro-bond'' issues. The maturity value of these coupon bonds is indexed to the price of oil.

To illustrate a price-indexed debt security, assume that Lynn Corporation issues at par a $1,000, 10 percent, four-year bond whose maturity value is tied to the Consumer Price Index (CPI). At the issue date the CPI is 120, and it increases to 180 at the end of the fourth year. In addition to $100 in interest payments each year, the corporation must pay $1,500 ($1,000 × 180/120) to retire the bond at maturity. These types of securities present some difficult accounting problems:

1. Should the additional $500 premium be considered interest over the life of the bonds or should it be considered a holding loss to be recognized either over the four-year period or at the end of the fourth year?

EXHIBIT 16–19	AMORTIZATION SCHEDULES FOR A VARIABLE INTEREST RATE NOTE

(Interest rate: 1987, 10%; 1988, 15%; 1989, 20%)

(a) Variable rate note with fixed payments and a "balloon" balance

| | (1) INTEREST EXPENSE | (2) | (3) LIABILITY REDUCTION | (4) |
| | (DR)* | CASH | (DR)† | LIABILITY |
YEAR		(CR)		BALANCE‡
				$2,486
1987	$249	$1,000	$751	1,735
1988	260	1,000	740	995
1989	199	1,000	801	194

(b) Variable rate note with variable payments

| | (1) INTEREST EXPENSE | (2) | (3) LIABILITY REDUCTION | (4) |
| | (DR)* | CASH | (DR)† | LIABILITY |
YEAR		(CR)		BALANCE‡
				$2,486
1987	$249	$1,000§	$751	1,735
1988	260	1,068¶	808	927
1989	185	1,112**	927	–0–

* Interest rate times previous balance in col. 4.

† Col. 2 minus col. 1.

‡ Liability balance at beginning of year minus col. 3.

§ $2,486 ÷ $P_{\overline{3}|\,10\%}$ = $2,486 ÷ 2.486 = $1,000.

¶ $1,735 ÷ $P_{\overline{2}|\,15\%}$ = $1,735 ÷ 1.625 = $1,068.

** $927 ÷ $P_{\overline{1}|\,20\%}$ = $927 ÷ .8333 = $1,112.

2. If the premium is to be recognized as interest or as a holding loss over the four-year period, the actual amount of the premium is *unknown* until the maturity date. Should the premium be estimated and allocated over the four-year period or should the liability be adjusted each year according to the change in the CPI?

If Lynn Corporation recognizes the $500 premium as interest over the four-year period by adjusting the liability each year for the change in the CPI, annual interest expense would be determined as shown in Exhibit 16–20.

COMMODITY BONDS

A commodity bond (or note) is payable at maturity in terms of a specified commodity or its cash equivalent. The bond usually is linked to a commodity that is produced by the company that issues the bond. As an example, a few years ago Texas International Company, an Oklahoma City–based oil and gas producer, issued $50 million in 9 percent commodity notes. These notes were redeemable at maturity for 29 times the free market price of one barrel of oil or $1,000, whichever was greater. The company had the option of calling the notes if oil reached $69.86 a barrel, a price that would place each $1,000 note's value at $2,000. Commodity bonds usually are issued at relatively low rates of interest. (Since the Texas International notes had a stated rate of 9 percent, they were issued at a premium.) The value of the bond at maturity usually is guaranteed.

EXHIBIT 16–20 INTEREST EXPENSE ON A PRICE-INDEXED BOND

END OF YEAR	(1) CPI	(2) CASH INTEREST*	(3) BOND LIABILITY	(4) INCREASE IN BOND LIABILITY†	(5) INTEREST EXPENSE‡
	120		$1,000		
1	132	$100	132/120 × $1,000 = $1,100	$100	$200
2	150	100	150/132 × $1,100 = $1,250	150	250
3	160	100	160/150 × $1,250 = $1,333	83	183
4	180	100	180/160 × $1,333 = $1,500	167	267

* $1,000 × .10

† Increase over previous year's amount from col. 3.

‡ Col. 2 plus col. 4.

Several possibilities exist for accounting for commodity bonds, depending on how the debt transaction is viewed. To illustrate, assume that at the beginning of 1987 Esso Oil Company issues a five-year, $2,000, 2 percent bond for $2,000. The maturity value is payable in 100 barrels of oil or its cash equivalent. If Esso views the bond as a debt payable in goods but does not own the oil in which the bond is payable, the accounting may be similar to that of a price-indexed bond. If Esso does own the oil, the obligation and the oil that is to be used to satisfy it can be recorded at their fair market values at the date of exchange. Subsequently, the asset and the liability may or may not be adjusted to their fair market values at the end of each year.

If Esso views the bond as a below-market-interest-rate borrowing, the accounting may follow that prescribed in *Opinion No. 21,* which deals with debt and other obligations exchanged for cash. We discussed this approach on page 736.

Finally, Esso may view the bond as a sale of oil with future delivery. Under this view, the proceeds are recorded as unearned revenue. This unearned revenue is recognized as revenue when the oil is delivered at the end of the fifth year.

Other accounting possibilities may exist. The point here is that in periods of inflation, these types of debt issues may occur. The accounting questions they raise are complex, and proposed solutions can become controversial. The financial reporting objectives and other theory concepts discussed in Chapter 2 can assist in resolving these issues.

QUESTIONS

Q16-1. Identify and discuss at least two similarities and two differences between bonds payable and notes payable.

Q16-2. Listed below are various types of bonds. Briefly describe each.

1. Coupon bonds.
2. Serial bonds.
3. Mortgage bonds (in which assets are pledged).
4. Revenue bonds.
5. Zero-coupon bonds.

6. Registered bonds.
7. Sinking fund bonds.
8. Debenture bonds.
9. Convertible bonds.
10. Bonds with detachable warrants.

Q16-3. **A)** Explain how bond prices are determined in the marketplace.
B) Under what conditions will bonds sell:

    1. At par (principal) value?

    2. At a premium?

    3. At a discount?

C) A $1,000 bond was quoted in the market for ''97½ plus accrued interest.'' Explain the phrase in quotation marks.

D) What effects do risk and inflation have on market prices of bonds?

Q16-4.   **A)** Explain two methods of amortizing bond premium and discount.

    B) What is the relationship between interest expense and cash interest payments for bonds sold at:

    1. A discount?

    2. A premium?

Q16-5.   **A)** From a bond investor's standpoint, what accounting differences arise when bonds are classified as current rather than as long-term, if such bonds are purchased at a discount?

    B) What justification can be given for the accounting differences described in part *A*?

Q16-6. Discuss the accounting and reporting procedures for expenditures made in connection with a sale of bonds (bond issue costs).

Q16-7. How are premiums and discounts on serial bonds amortized under the bonds-outstanding method?

Q16-8. Long-term notes are sometimes issued as a means of obtaining cash. Describe the valuation principles for long-term notes under the following circumstances:

    1. Notes are issued in exchange for cash.

    2. Notes are issued in exchange for fixed assets.

    3. Notes and other obligations are exchanged for cash.

Q16-9.   **A)** When notes are issued, under what circumstances will the amount of cash received be equal to the face (principal) amount of the note?

    B) Under what circumstances will the present value of a note payable be less than the face amount of the note?

Q16-10. Identify three methods of extinguishing (retiring) outstanding debt before maturity.

Q16-11. How are gains and losses on early extinguishment of debt determined and reported?

Q16-12. When long-term debt is retired before maturity, what disposition is made of unamortized bond issue costs associated with such debt?

Q16-13. Incurring long-term debt with an arrangement whereby lenders receive an option to buy common stock during all or a portion of the time the debt is outstanding is a frequent corporate financing practice. In some situations the result is achieved through the issuance of convertible bonds; in other situations, debt is issued with detachable warrants to buy stock.

    1. Describe the differences that exist in current accounting for original proceeds of the issuance of convertible bonds and of debt instruments with separate warrants to purchase common stock.

    2. Discuss the underlying rationale for the differences described in part 1 above.

    3. Summarize the arguments that have been presented for the alternative accounting treatment.

          (AICPA, adapted)

Q16-14.   **A)** Describe accounting for the conversion of bonds into common stock.

    B) Discuss how to account for sweeteners offered to holders of convertible bonds to induce them to exercise a conversion privilege.

Q16-15.   **A)** Identify the accounting procedures necessary to record the exercise of warrants issued in connection with long-term debt.

    B) Why are market values ignored in part *A*?

Q16-16.   **A)** What is meant by ''debt restructuring''?

    B) Describe two methods set forth in *FASB Statement No. 15* that are used to restructure debt.

Q16-17. Debt may be restructured by modifying the terms of the original debt agreement. From the debtor's standpoint, under what circumstances will modification lead to the:

1. Recognition of no gain or loss on restructuring?

2. Recognition of a gain on restructuring?

3. Recognition of a loss on restructuring?

Q16-18. Explain what is meant by "in-substance defeasance" of debt.

Q16-19. On December 31, 1987, Walther Corporation has serial bonds outstanding totaling $2 million. The unamortized premium on the bonds on December 31, 1987, is $120,000, and $200,000 of the bonds are due on January 4, 1988. How would these bonds be presented on Walther Corporation's balance sheet as of December 31, 1987?

CASES

The case marked with an asterisk (*) refers to Appendix 16–1.

C16-1. BOND VALUATION On January 1, 1987, Dowteen Corporation issued for $79,000, three-year, 10 percent bonds that have a maturity value of $100,000 and pay interest annually on December 31. The following are three presentations of the long-term liability section of the balance sheet that might be used for these bonds at the issue date:

a) Bonds payable (maturing 12/31/89)............................ $100,000
   Discount on bonds payable.................................... (21,000)
   Total bond liability .... $ 79,000

b) Bonds payable—principal (face value $100,000, maturing 12/31/89) $ 58,000*
   Bonds payable—interest (annual payment $10,000).............. 21,000†
   Total bond liability .... $ 79,000

c) Bonds payable—principal (maturing 12/31/89) $100,000
   Bonds payable—interest ($10,000 per year for 3 years) 30,000
   Total bond liability $130,000

* The present value of $100,000 due at the end of three years at the yield rate of 20 percent per year.

† The present value of $10,000 per year for 3 years at the yield rate of 20 percent per year.

REQUIRED

1. Discuss the conceptual merits of each of the date-of-issue balance sheet presentations shown above.

2. Explain why investors would pay only $79,000 for bonds that have a maturity value of $100,000.

3. Assuming that a discount rate is needed to calculate the carrying value of the obligations arising from a bond issue at any date during the life of the bonds, discuss the conceptual merits of using for this purpose:
    a) The stated or nominal rate (also calculate the carrying value at the end of each year using the stated rate of 10 percent).
    b) The effective or yield rate at date of issue (also calculate the carrying value at the end of each year using the yield rate of 20 percent).

4. If the obligations arising from these bonds are to be carried at their present value calculated by means of the current market rate of interest, how would the bond valuation at dates subsequent to the date of issue be affected by an increase or a decrease in the market rate of interest?

(AICPA, adapted)

C16-2. CONVERTIBLE DEBT—INITIAL VALUATION AND CONVERSION Supra Company recently issued $1 million face-value 5 percent 30-year debentures at 97. The debentures are callable at 103 by the issuer at any date on 30 days' notice 10 years after the issue. The debentures are convertible into $10 par value common stock of the company at the conversion price of $12.50 per share for each $500 or multiple thereof of the principal amount of the debentures (each $500 bond is convertible into 40 shares of common: $500 ÷ $12.50 = 40).

REQUIRED

1. Explain how the conversion feature of convertible debt has a value to the *(a)* issuer and *(b)* investor.

2. Supra's management has suggested that when the issuance of the debentures is recorded, a portion of the proceeds should be assigned to the conversion feature.

    a) What are the arguments for according separate accounting recognition to the conversion feature of the debentures?

    b) What are the arguments supporting accounting for the convertible debentures as a single element?

3. Assume that no value is assigned to the conversion feature when the debentures are issued. Assume further that five years after issuance, debentures with a face value of $100,000 and book value of $97,500 are tendered for conversion on an interest payment date when the market price of the common stock is $14 per share, and that the company records the conversion as follows:

Bonds payable	100,000	
Bond discount		2,500
Common stock		80,000
Premium on common stock		17,500

Discuss the propriety of the above accounting treatment.

4. Now assume that 12 years after issuance, Supra's management wants to sweeten the conversion rate in order to induce conversion. Therefore, management lowers the conversion price from $12.50 per share for each $500 bond to $10 per share. Management argues that since the inducement did not affect cash or other assets, an expense need not be recognized in connection with conversions during the inducement period. Draft a brief response to the company's management.

(AICPA, adapted)

C16-3. APPLICATIONS OF BOND CONCEPTS WITH A PROSPECTUS Selected portions of an actual bond prospectus appear below.

HIGHLAND PARK METHODIST CHURCH
Stillwater, Oklahoma

$130,000.00 8 1/2% FIRST MORTGAGE COUPON BONDS

$85,000.00 8 1/2% FIRST MORTGAGE COMPOUND INTEREST DISCOUNT BONDS

Dated September 1, 1976; Due Serially through September 1, 1991

PAYING AGENT AND TRUSTEE

Stillwater National Bank
Stillwater, Oklahoma

AMOUNT OF ISSUE	OFFERING PRICE	UNDERWRITING DISCOUNTS AND COMMISSIONS	SERVICE CHARGE AND EXPENSES	PROCEEDS TO ISSUER
$215,000.00	100% (1)	None	$3,225.00	$211,775.00

(1) Plus accrued interest from September 1, 1976.
This offering involves certain risks. See ''Risk factors'' in this Prospectus.

Risk factors

1. Interest on the Compound Interest Discount Bonds will be paid at maturity, so the holder of a bond due in fifteen years will receive no interest income for fifteen years.

2. The Church is solely dependent on contributions to pay these bonds. There is no assurance they will be able to meet these payments on time and retire the bonds and coupons as they mature.

3. Under present law, interest on the bonds offered by this prospectus will be taxable each year for both Federal and Oklahoma income tax purposes even though no interest is paid on the compound interest bonds until maturity.

4. The Church's scheduled weekly sinking fund payments escalate from $310.00 per week the first year to $572.00 per week from the sixth to the fifteenth year. The total annual required payments range from $16,120.00 the first year to $29,744.00 for the sixth through fifteenth years. Based on the 1975 annual receipts of $44,041.00, the Church's debt service requires approximately 37% of the total receipts the first year to approximately 68% of the total for the sixth through the fifteenth years. The Church's total receipts will need to reach approximately $64,766.00 per year to keep its highest debt service requirement to 68% of its annual receipts.

Maturity schedule

8 1/2% COUPON BONDS

YEARS TO MATURITY	MATURITY DATE	INTEREST EARNED ON EACH $1,000	VALUE OF BONDS MATURING	SEMI-ANNUAL INTEREST	TOTAL BONDS & INTEREST
1/2	3/1/77	$ 42.50	$ 2,000.00	$ 5,525.00	$ 7,525.00
1	9/1/77	85.00	3,000.00	5,440.00	8,440.00
1 1/2	3/1/78	127.50	4,000.00	5,312.50	9,312.50
2	9/1/78	170.00	4,000.00	5,142.50	9,142.50
2 1/2	3/1/79	212.50	6,000.00	4,972.50	10,972.50
3	9/1/79	255.00	6,000.00	4,717.50	10,717.50
3 1/2	3/1/80	297.50	8,000.00	4,462.50	12,462.50
4	9/1/80	340.00	8,000.00	4,122.50	12,122.50
4 1/2	3/1/81	382.50	10,000.00	3,782.50	13,782.50
5	9/1/81	425.00	10,000.00	3,357.50	13,357.50
5 1/2	3/1/82	467.50	12,000.00	2,932.50	14,932.50
6	9/1/82	510.00	12,000.00	2,422.50	14,422.50
6 1/2	3/1/83	552.50	13,000.00	1,912.50	14,912.50
7	9/1/83	595.00	14,000.00	1,360.00	15,360.00
7 1/2	3/1/84	637.50	14,000.00	765.00	14,765.00
8	9/1/84	680.00	4,000.00	170.00	4,170.00
			$130,000.00	$56,397.50	$186,397.50

8 1/2% COMPOUND INTEREST DISCOUNT BONDS

YEARS TO MATURITY	MATURITY DATE	BOND COST $1,000	BOND COST $500	ORIGINAL BOND COST	TOTAL BONDS MATURING
8	9/1/84	$513.79	$256.89	$ 5,651.69	$ 11,000.00
8 1/2	3/1/85	492.84	246.42	7,392.60	15,000.00
9	9/1/85	472.75	236.37	6,854.88	14,500.00
9 1/2	3/1/86	453.48	226.74	6,802.20	15,000.00
10	9/1/86	434.99	217.49	6,524.85	15,000.00
10 1/2	3/1/87	417.26	208.63	6,258.90	15,000.00
11	9/1/87	400.25	200.12	5,803.63	14,500.00
11 1/2	3/1/88	383.93	191.96	5,758.95	15,000.00
12	9/1/88	368.28	184.14	5,524.20	15,000.00
12 1/2	3/1/89	353.26	176.63	5,298.90	15,000.00
13	9/1/89	338.86	169.43	4,913.47	14,500.00
13 1/2	3/1/90	325.05	162.52	4,875.75	15,000.00
14	9/1/90	311.80	155.90	4,677.00	15,000.00
14 1/2	3/1/91	299.08	149.54	4,486.20	15,000.00
15	9/1/91	286.89	143.45	3,299.24	14,500.00
				$84,122.46	$219,000.00

REQUIRED

1. Explain what is meant by ''offering price of 100% plus interest from September 1, 1976.''

2. What impact might item 4 under ''Risk factors'' have on the bond issue price?

3. Why is the inclusion of a maturity schedule of interest to prospective investors?

4. Why did the 8 1/2 percent coupon bonds sell at 100 percent?

5. Is the bond interest paid semiannually or annually? Explain how you arrived at your answer.

6. Verify, to the extent possible, that a $1,000 compound discount bond due on September 1, 1991, sold for only $286.89.

C16-4. BOND CONCEPTS   On March 1, 1987, Wesley Company sold its five-year, $1,000 face value, 8% bonds dated March 1, 1987, at an effective semiannual interest rate (yield) of 5 percent. Interest is payable semiannually and the first interest payment date is September 1, 1987. Wesley uses the effective interest method of amortization. Bond issue costs were incurred in preparing and selling the bond issue. The bonds can be called by Wesley at 101 at any time on or after March 1, 1988.

REQUIRED

1. **a)** How would the selling price of the bond be determined?

  b) Specify how all items related to the bonds would be presented in a balance sheet prepared immediately after the bond issue was sold.

2. What items related to the bond issue would be included in Wesley's 1987 income statement, and how would each be determined?

3. Would the amount of bond discount amortization using the effective interest method of amortization be lower in the second or third year of the life of the bond issue? Why?

4. Assuming that the bonds were called in and retired on March 1, 1988, how should Wesley report the retirement of the bonds on the 1988 income statement?

(AICPA, adapted)

C16-5. ZERO-COUPON BONDS; DEFEASANCE   Bruloff Corporation, a multinational company, has experienced declining earnings since the lifting of import quotas in the United States. The board chairman's young nephew has been assigned the task of improving the appearance of the firm's income statement through creative financing techniques. Recently, he entered your office and made the following proposal:

 ''In yesterday's *Wall Street Journal,* I read where the government of Krypton is offering 20-year zero-coupon bonds with a 16 percent yield. What a deal—each $1,000 bond can be bought for $51.40! I have a great idea that will make us some money. First, we issue our own 20-year zeros. Our brokers say that we can issue them for perhaps as low as $148.60 for each $1,000 in maturity value. Next, we use some of the cash to buy the Krypton government bonds. Then we put the government bonds in a trust to service the maturity value of our debt. No one will pay attention to the fact that Krypton has had three revolutions in five years and has borrowed to the hilt over the last ten years. Finally, presto! A defeasance coup! We can report a huge gain on defeasance and have extra cash to boot. You can't beat that! And here's the clincher—the more bonds we issue and the more government bonds we place in the trust, the larger the gain and the more cash we have in the bank. Issuing debt at a gain—creative financing and creative accounting. What a nice pair!''

REQUIRED

1. Verify the 16 percent yield on the Krypton bonds and determine the effective interest cost on the proposed bond issue by Bruloff.

2. Prepare journal entries to record the proposal offered by the board chairman's nephew. Assume that the two bond issues will have maturity values of $1 million.

3. Discuss the propriety of the proposal.

*C16-6. EMERGING DEBT INSTRUMENTS   Wizard Fertilizer Corporation is a manufacturer and distributor of garden fertilizers. The company is considering an expansion program that will require it to raise $10 million for financing purposes. Wizard has decided to issue some form of debt instead of common stock. Since the current market rate of interest is 12 percent, the company is considering one of the following types of emerging debt instruments:

a) Zero-coupon bonds that will mature in 20 years.

b) A $10 million floating-rate bond issue that will mature in 15 years. Wizard predicts future interest rates will fall drastically and desires not to be locked in at 12 percent.

c) A $10 million bond issue whose maturity value is linked to the Consumer Price Index. The company believes that investors would buy this issue at a yield of only 5 percent if the maturity value is linked to an inflation index.

d) A $10 million noninterest-bearing commodity bond payable in 1 million 50-pound sacks of the company's most popular fertilizer. The commodity bond will mature in six years, and at that time Wizard promises to pay the par value or the cash equivalent price of the fertilizer, whichever is higher.

REQUIRED

1. What proceeds are likely to be received if Wizard selects debt instrument *a*?

2. If Wizard finances with debt instrument *b*, explain how the company might account for the bond issue.

3. Assume that Wizard finances with debt instrument *c*. If the CPI has *fallen* 50 percent from the issue date to the maturity date, how might Wizard account for this maturity date discount? (*Note:* The final decrease in the CPI is *not known* until the maturity date.)

4. Assume that Wizard finances with debt instrument *d* and that 1 million 50-pound sacks are immediately transferred to an outside trustee, The Farmer's Bank. Discuss some alternative approaches for accounting for these fertilizer bonds.

EXERCISES

The exercise marked with an asterisk (*) refers to Appendix 16–1.

E16-1. BOND PRICING Calculate the selling prices and prepare entries to record the sale for each of the following bond issues:

ISSUE	PRINCIPAL	STATED INTEREST RATE	INTEREST PAYABLE	LIFE OF ISSUE (YEARS)	MARKET RATE AT ISSUE DATE
1	$250,000	8%	Annually	10	6% per year
2	100,000	10	Quarterly	5	2½% per quarter
3	150,000	10	Semiannually	4	6% semiannually
4	200,000	8	Annually	20	12% per year

E16-2. PREMIUM AND DISCOUNT AMORTIZATION On January 1, 1987, Texas issued $60,000 12 percent five-year term bonds for $64,548. Interest is paid annually on December 31, and Texas' accounting period ends on December 31.

REQUIRED

1. Prepare a premium amortization schedule under the straight-line method.

2. Prepare a premium amortization schedule under the effective interest method. (The effective interest rate on the bonds is 10 percent.)

3. Compare and contrast the interest expense patterns over the five-year period in parts 1 and 2.

4. Prepare the entry to record interest expense on December 31, 1989, under the effective interest method.

E16-3. SERIAL BONDS At the beginning of year 1, Suzuki Corporation issued five-year $100,000 serial bonds at 108. The bonds carry an interest rate of 8 percent, payable annually, and mature as follows:

End of year 2	$10,000
End of year 3	20,000
End of year 4	30,000
End of year 5	40,000

REQUIRED

1. Calculate the annual premium amortization under the bonds-outstanding method.

2. Prepare the entries to record interest expense and payment of the maturing series at the end of *(a)* year 2 and *(b)* year 4.

E16-4. SERIAL BONDS Trivitt Corporation sold a $300,000 serial bond issue at the beginning of 1987. The stated rate on the bond issue was 12 percent, payable annually. The bonds mature at the rate of $100,000 each year, beginning on December 31, 1988. Assume that each series was sold to yield 16 percent.

REQUIRED

1. Calculate the issue price of each series and of the total bond issue.

2. Since you know the discount applicable to each series (from part 1), calculate the total annual discount amortization on the bonds under the straight-line method.

3. Prepare a schedule for interest expense and discount amortization by the effective interest method.

E16-5. BONDS SOLD BETWEEN INTEREST DATES On April 1, 1987, Issod sold a $70,000 6-year bond issue to Pullman for $72,415 plus accrued interest. The bonds were dated January 1, 1987, and the stated interest rate was 7 percent, payable semiannually on June 30 and December 31. The fiscal year of both Issod and Pullman ends December 31, and both use the straight-line method of calculating interest.

REQUIRED

Prepare all required entries on the books of Issod (issuer) and Pullman (purchaser) from April 1, 1987, through December 31, 1988.

E16-6. BOND INVESTMENTS—ACCRUALS
A) On July 1, 1987, Liftwich acquired a long-term bond investment for $48,000 plus accrued interest. The 10 percent bonds have a par value of $50,000, mature on November 1, 1990, and pay interest semiannually on May 1 and November 1. Liftwich's accounting period ends on December 31. Assume straight-line amortization for the discount.

REQUIRED

Prepare the required entries on Liftwich's books on the following dates:

1. July 1, 1987.

2. November 1, 1987.

3. December 31, 1987.

4. May 1, 1988.

B) On November 2, 1988, Liftwich sold a portion of the bonds held as a long-term investment. The par value of the bonds sold was $30,000, and the proceeds from the sale were $51,700.

REQUIRED

Prepare the entry to record the sale.

E16-7. ACCRUALS FOR BOND ISSUES—EFFECTIVE INTEREST METHOD On June 1, 1987, Groogan sold a six-year $200,000 par bond issue for $167,102. The bonds pay interest at 8 percent each May 30 and were sold to yield 12 percent. Groogan's fiscal year ends on December 31. Groogan uses the effective interest method for interest expense and discount amortization.

REQUIRED

Prepare journal entries for the following dates. (*Hint:* You may wish to prepare a discount amortization schedule before making journal entries.)

1. June 1, 1987 (the date of the issue).

2. December 31, 1987 (to accrue interest for 1987).

3. May 30, 1988 (to record interest expense and the interest payment). Prepare this entry under two different assumptions:
   a) Groogan makes reversing entries on January 1.
   b) Groogan does not make reversing entries on January 1.

4. December 31, 1988 (to accrue interest to the end of 1988).

E16-8. INVESTOR AMORTIZATION OF DISCOUNT   On January 1, 1987, Smart Investors, Inc., purchased for $46,171 a $100,000 par value, five-year bond paying 2 percent interest on December 31 of each year. The purchase price represented a 20 percent effective annual yield.

REQUIRED

1. Verify that the annual yield on the bond is 20 percent.

2. Prepare the adjusting entry for interest revenue on December 31, 1987, using:
   a) The effective interest method.
   b) The straight-line method.

3. Calculate the reported rates of return on the bond investment in 2*a* and 2*b* and comment on any differences.

E16-9. LONG-TERM NOTES PAYABLE

A) At the beginning of the current year, Lockes acquired a tract of land with a fair market value of $38,130 by issuing a four-year noninterest-bearing note in the amount of $60,000.

REQUIRED

1. What is the effective (implicit) rate of interest on the note?

2. Prepare the entry at the beginning of the current year to record the acquisition.

3. Prepare the entries to record interest expense for the first and second years.

B) Drake acquired a machine at the beginning of the current year by issuing a noninterest-bearing note with a face value of $100,000. The note is payable in four annual installments of $25,000 beginning at the end of the current year. The current rate of interest for notes of similar risk is 10 percent.

REQUIRED

1. What is the imputed fair market value of the machine?

2. Prepare the entry to record the acquisition at the beginning of the current year.

3. Prepare the entries to record interest expense and the note payable at the end of each of the next four years. (*Hint:* You may wish to prepare an effective interest amortization schedule.)

E16-10. EARLY EXTINGUISHMENT OF DEBT   Several years ago Mason Corporation issued 10 percent, $100,000, 12-year bonds at 108. Bond issue costs totaled $2,000. After the bonds had been outstanding for four years, Mason retired them by issuing $100,000 6 percent refunding bonds at par. Mason uses the straight-line method of amortizing bond premium and bond issue costs.

REQUIRED

Prepare the entry to record the extinguishment through refunding.

E16-11. DEBT EXTINGUISHMENT   On January 1, 1987, Byeback sold five-year 9 percent bonds with a maturity value of $100,000 for $89,186, which represented an effective interest rate of 12 percent. On

January 1, 1989, Byeback extinguished the entire issue on the open market when the bonds were priced to yield 16 percent.

REQUIRED

1. Record Byeback's interest expense for 1987 and 1988. Byeback uses the effective interest method.

2. Record the extinguishment on January 1, 1989.

E16-12. ZERO-COUPON BONDS: ISSUER   At the beginning of the current year, Stresstax Company issued $1.5 million par value, 10-year zero-coupon bonds for $483,000.

REQUIRED

1. Prepare Stresstax's entry to record the bond issue.

2. Prepare Stresstax's entries to record interest expense for the first two years that the bonds are outstanding. Stresstax uses the effective interest method.

3. Prepare Stresstax's entry to record extinguishment at maturity.

E16-13. ZERO-COUPON BONDS: INVESTOR   Refer to Exercise 16-12. Assume that Sanstax purchased 30 percent of the Stresstax bonds on the issue date.

REQUIRED

Repeat the requirements in Exercise 16-12 from the standpoint of Sanstax, the investor, who also uses the effective interest method.

E16-14. CONVERTIBLE BONDS   The Yankee Corporation issued $60,000, 10 percent, 10-year convertible bonds for $63,000. Each $1,000 bond was convertible to eight shares of Yankee common stock (par $100) on any interest date beginning two years from date of issue. Southern Company acquired 40 percent of this issue.

REQUIRED

1. Prepare the entries to record the issuance by Yankee and the acquisition by Southern.

2. Calculate Yankee's annual interest expense under the straight-line method.

3. At the end of the sixth year, when Yankee stock was selling for $130 per share, Southern converted the bonds to Yankee common. Give the entries for Yankee and Southern to record the conversion under both the book value and market value methods.

E16-15. CONVERTIBLE BONDS; INDUCEMENTS   On January 1, 1985, Block Company issued 100 $1,000, 12 percent convertible bonds at par. The maturity date of the bonds was December 31, 1994, and each bond was convertible into 25 shares of Block's $5 par common stock. On January 1, 1987, Block induced conversion by making each bond convertible into 40 shares of its common stock if conversions took place within 90 days of January 1, 1987.

During the inducement period, 80 percent of the bonds were converted when the market price of Block's common stock was $9. The remaining bonds were converted to Block's common stock during 1988 when the market price of the stock was $14.

Block uses the book value method for bond conversion.

REQUIRED

1. Prepare Block's journal entry to record the conversions during the inducement period.

2. Prepare Block's journal entry to record the conversions during 1988.

E16-16. BONDS WITH DETACHABLE WARRANTS

A) Rebel Company sold $100,000, 12 percent, five-year bonds with detachable stock warrants to Northern Corporation for $114,000. Each $1,000 bond included 25 detachable warrants for 25 shares of Rebel common stock ($10 par value). The option price was $30. Shortly after the sale, the warrants were selling for $2 each.

REQUIRED

Prepare the entries for Rebel and Northern at the date of issue.

B) At a later date, when Rebel's shares were selling at $44 per share, Northern exercised 1,000 warrants and acquired 1,000 of Rebel's shares.

REQUIRED

Prepare the entries for Rebel and Northern to record the exercise.

E16-17. DEBT RESTRUCTURING—TRANSFERS OF ASSETS/EQUITY SECURITIES

a) Dan Corporation has bonds payable outstanding that are now due in the amount of $100,000. Accrued interest on the bonds totals $10,000. Since Dan is having financial difficulties, Cranium Corporation, the holder of Dan's bonds, agrees to accept inventory in full settlement of the debt. Dan carries the inventory at historical cost of $85,000, although the fair market value is $87,000.

b) Instead of accepting inventory, Cranium Corporation agrees to accept 1,000 shares of Dan's common stock (par value $10 per share, market value $92.50 per share).

REQUIRED

Prepare the entries to record both of the above restructuring agreements in the books of both debtor and creditor.

E16-18. DEBT RESTRUCTURING—MODIFICATION OF TERMS   The three independent cases below represent situations in which a creditor has made a concession to a debtor in financial difficulty.

a) Book value of debt/receivable at beginning of current year: $58,000. Terms of restructuring agreement: Principal is reduced to $40,000 and due at the end of three years. The interest rate is changed to 8 percent, payable annually at the end of each year.

b) Book value of debt/receivable at beginning of current year: principal, $100,000; accrued interest, $6,950. Terms of restructuring: All payments are deferred until the end of the fourth year, at which time $130,000 will be due and payable.

c) Book value of debt/receivable:

Bonds payable	$100,000
Premium on bonds	2,710
Interest payable	2,000

Terms of restructuring: Accrued interest payable is forgiven; bond principal is deferred to the end of the fifth year; the interest rate on the bonds is changed to 3 percent, payable annually.

REQUIRED

Complete the following requirements for each case:

1. Determine if an entry by the debtor and creditor is required at the date of restructure.

2. If no entry is required, calculate the effective interest rate applicable to the restructure agreement.

3. Prepare any necessary entries at the date of restructure and at the end of the first year on the books of the debtor and creditor.

E16-19. BALANCE SHEET CLASSIFICATION   The following amounts appear in the books of Purcell Corporation:

a) Interest payable, $5,000.
b) Bonds payable ($30,000 due next year), $300,000.
c) Bond sinking fund, $112,500.
d) Interest expense (credit balance), $5,900.
e) Discount on notes payable, $12,500.
f) Unearned revenue (services to be performed over next 10 years), $36,000.
g) Premium on bonds payable, $12,600.
h) Unamortized bond issue costs, $60,000.

    i) Amortization of bond issue costs, $3,000.

    j) Sinking fund revenue, $1,200.

    k) Notes payable (due 10 years hence), $75,000.

    l) Gain on early extinguishment of debt, $4,700.

    m) Notes payable (due next year), $5,400.

    n) Gain on debt restructuring (for a debtor), $14,000.

REQUIRED

Indicate how each of the above accounts would appear in Purcell's financial statements.

*E16-20. VARIABLE INTEREST RATE NOTES   On January 3, 1987, Brothers issued a $12,000 variable interest note to be repaid in three annual installments beginning December 31, 1987. The applicable interest rate was 12 percent on January 3, 1987, and throughout the year; it rose to 16 percent during 1988 and fell to 14 percent during 1989.

REQUIRED

    1. Construct a schedule showing the interest expense and amortization of the liability each year, assuming that the installment payments are fixed (based on the 12 percent rate on January 3, 1987) and that a balloon note, if applicable, will be due on December 31, 1989.

    2. Construct a schedule similar to that in part 1, assuming that the annual installment payments will be recalculated each year on the basis of the applicable interest rate.

PROBLEMS

P16-1. STRAIGHT-LINE AMORTIZATION OF PREMIUM—ISSUER AND INVESTOR   The Sarnia Corporation deposited a deed of trust with the Shensa Trust Company on February 1, 1987. The trust deed entitled Sarnia to issue $2 million of 6 percent 20-year bonds to be dated March 1, 1987. Interest was to be paid March 1 and September 1 each year. Sarnia uses straight-line amortization of bond premium. The following transactions occurred:

1987
May 1	Sold the issue for $2,071,400 plus accrued interest.
Sept. 1	Paid interest on the bonds and recorded premium amortization.
Dec. 31	Accrued interest on the bonds.

1988
Mar. 1	Paid interest on the bonds and amortized premium.
Sept. 1	Paid interest on the bonds and amortized premium.

1991
Sept. 1	Paid interest on the bonds and amortized premium. On the same date $400,000 of the bonds were purchased in the open market at 101, including commission, and retired by the company.

1992
Sept. 1	Paid interest on the bonds and amortized premium.

    Trevino Investments acquired $400,000 (par value) of the Sarnia bonds for $414,280 [($400,000 ÷ $2,000,000) × $2,071,400] plus accrued interest on May 1, 1987. The bonds retired by Sarnia on September 1, 1991, were the bonds held by Trevino.

REQUIRED

    1. Prepare journal entries for Sarnia to record the transactions listed above.

    2. Prepare journal entries for Trevino for all of the applicable dates. Trevino also uses straight-line amortization of bond premium.

(CGAA, adapted)

P16-2. BOND PREMIUM AMORTIZATION   On November 1, 1984, a corporation issued bonds having a maturity value of $100,000 on November 1, 1989. A portion of the amortization table related to the issue appears below:

DATE	(1) INTEREST PAYMENT (CASH)	(2) INTEREST EXPENSE	(3) PREMIUM AMORTIZATION (1 – 2)	(4) CARRYING VALUE (4 – 3)
11/1/84				$102,194.99
11/1/85	$5,000	$4,598.77	$401.23	101,793.76
11/1/86	5,000	4,580.72	419.28	101,374.48
11/1/87	5,000	4,561.85	438.15	100,936.33
11/1/88	5,000	4,542.13	457.87	100,478.46
11/1/89	5,000	4,521.54	478.46	100,000.00

REQUIRED

1. Amortization is calculated by the _____ method.

2. The annual rates of interest are _____ percent nominal and _____ percent effective.

3. The issuing corporation's fiscal year ends on December 31. Prepare entries for its books as indicated below:
   a) Reversing entry on January 1, 1987.
   b) Entries on November 1, 1987.
   c) Entries on December 30, 1987.

P16-3. STRAIGHT-LINE AND EFFECTIVE INTEREST METHODS—ISSUER AND INVESTOR   At the beginning of year 1, a corporation sold a $100,000 term bond issue (dated the beginning of year 1) that matured at the end of year 3. The bonds carried a stated rate of 12 percent, payable annually, and were sold for $104,973 to yield 10 percent.

REQUIRED

1. Prepare a premium amortization schedule under *(a)* the straight-line method and *(b)* the effective interest method.

2. Prepare all entries for the three-year period for the issuer and investor under the straight-line method.

P16-4. BOND INVESTMENTS—CURRENT AND NONCURRENT   On December 31, 1987, Hummer Investments reported the following on its balance sheet:

Long-term investments:
   9% Jaco Corporation bonds (par value, $100,000;
      interest payable semiannually 5/1 and 11/1;
      maturity date, 11/1/ 90) $93,600
Current assets:
   Interest receivable on Jaco bonds 1,500
   10% Silo, Ltd., bonds (par value, $50,000;
      interest payable annually 12/31;
      maturity date, 12/31/95) 53,000

The following transactions took place:

1988
May 1   Recorded interest revenue on receipt of interest on Jaco bonds.
Nov. 1   Recorded interest revenue on receipt of interest on Jaco bonds.
Dec. 31   Recorded interest revenue on receipt of interest from Silo and recorded accrued interest revenue on Jaco bonds.

1989
Mar. 1   Sold Silo bonds for 108 plus accrued interest.
Apr. 1   Sold 10% of Jaco bonds at par plus accrued interest.

Hummer uses the straight-line method to amortize bond premium and discount.

REQUIRED

Prepare entries for Hummer to record the above transactions.

P16-5. SERIAL BONDS

A) At the beginning of year 1, Loving Corporation issued 10 percent serial bonds for $164,600 (interest payable annually at the end of the year). The bonds mature in installments as follows:

	PAR VALUE
End of year 1	$20,000
End of year 2	40,000
End of year 3	40,000
End of year 4	60,000

REQUIRED

1. Calculate the amount of interest expense each year by the bonds-outstanding method.

2. Assume that the $60,000 series maturing at the end of year 4 is retired at the end of year 2 for $61,000. Prepare the entry to record the retirement.

B) At the end of year 2, Care, Inc., issued 9 percent serial bonds in the face amount of $150,000. Interest is payable annually, the bonds were sold to yield 12 percent, and they mature as follows:

	PAR VALUE
End of year 4	$20,000
End of year 5	20,000
End of year 6	30,000
End of year 7	30,000
End of year 8	50,000

REQUIRED

1. Calculate the proceeds of the bond issue.

2. Since the discount applicable to each series is known (or can be determined), calculate the discount to be amortized each year by the straight-line method.

3. Prepare a discount amortization schedule using the effective interest method.

4. Referring to the schedule made for part 3, prepare the entry to record interest expense and maturing bonds at the end of year 6.

P16-6. EFFECTIVE INTEREST METHOD, ACCRUALS, EARLY EXTINGUISHMENT OF DEBT   On May 1, 1987, Argon issues $200,000 in 10 percent term bonds. The bonds are dated March 1, 1987, pay interest semiannually on March 1 and September 1, mature on March 1, 1990, and are sold to yield 6 percent semiannually. On November 1, 1989, Argon retires $100,000 (par value) of the bonds through an open market purchase at $98,000 plus accrued interest. Argon's fiscal year ends on December 31, and the company uses the effective interest method.

REQUIRED

1. Calculate the total cash received on the bond sale on May 1, 1987.

2. Prepare the entries on the following dates:
   a) May 1, 1987 (date of sale).
   b) September 1, 1987 (to record interest expense and the first interest payment).
   c) December 31, 1987 (to record accrued interest expense and interest payable).
   d) March 1, 1988 (to record interest expense and the second interest payment).
   e) November 1, 1989 (to record the bond retirement).

3. Calculate the amount of interest expense to be reported on Argon's 1989 income statement.

P16-7. EARLY EXTINGUISHMENT OF DEBT   In each of the three independent cases below, straight-line amortization of premium or discount is appropriate.

a) Immediately after a semiannual interest payment, Dover retired outstanding debt by purchasing bonds with a par value of $100,000 for $96,680 on the open market. The 20-year bonds had been outstanding for 10½ years and were originally issued at a premium of $9,000.

b) On March 1, 1980, Delcorp issues bonds for $227,153 (including accrued interest). The bonds have a par value of $250,000, are dated January 1, 1980, pay 8 percent interest annually, and mature on December 31, 1999. Expenditures associated with the bond issue total $11,900. The bonds are callable at 103 percent after January 1, 1983. On January 1, 1989, Delcorp exercises the call privilege and retires the bonds.

c) The facts are the same as in part *b*, except that instead of calling the bonds, Delcorp extinguishes them by issuing $260,000 par value refunding bonds with a stated rate of 9 percent. The bonds are issued at par.

REQUIRED

Prepare the entry to record the debt extinguishment in each case. Ignore issue costs on the refunding bonds in part *c*.

P16-8. DEBT EXTINGUISHMENT; IN-SUBSTANCE DEFEASANCE   At the beginning of 1984, Martin Company issued, at 107 percent of par, $100,000 in 10-year, 5 percent term bonds. Interest expense for 1984, 1985, and 1986 was accounted for under the straight-line method. At the beginning of 1987 these bonds were selling in the market to yield 10 percent, and Martin decided to extinguish this debt.

REQUIRED

Prepare the entry to record Martin's debt extinguishment under each of the following independent methods of extinguishment:

1. Martin purchases the 5 percent bonds on the open market and retires them.

2. Martin issues, at par, 10 percent refunding bonds with a maturity value of $100,000 which mature in seven years.

3. Martin purchases 5 percent, seven-year U.S. government bonds with a maturity value of $100,000 and places them in an irrevocable trust. The government bonds were purchased to yield 8 percent.

4. Martin issues, at a discount, seven-year zero-coupon refunding bonds with a maturity value of $120,000. Investors required a 12 percent effective yield to maturity.

P16-9. CONVERTIBLE BONDS AND DETACHABLE WARRANTS

A) On December 1, 1987, the Simpson Company issued 100, 5 percent, $1,000 bonds at 103. Attached to each bond was a detachable stock purchase warrant entitling the holder to purchase 10 shares of Simpson's no-par common stock for $80 per share. On December 1, 1987, the market value of the bonds without the stock purchase warrants was 94% of par and the market value of each stock purchase warrant was $100.

REQUIRED

Prepare the entry to record the issue by Simpson.

B) Several years after buying 20 percent of the Simpson bonds, Timpson exercised the warrants.

REQUIRED

Prepare the entries to record the exercise for both Simpson and Timpson.

C) On April 7, 1987, the Script Corporation sold a 20-year, $1 million, 8 percent bond issue at 103. Each $1,000 bond had a detachable warrant that permitted the purchase of one share of the corporation's $25 par value common stock for $30. Immediately after the sale of the bonds the corporation's securities had the following market values:

Warrants	$10
Common stock	28

Dip acquired the entire bond issue.

REQUIRED

Prepare the entry to record the bond transaction for both Script and Dip.

D) On December 30, 1987, Front issued $10 million of 8 percent convertible bonds. The bonds had a life of 10 years, and each $1,000 bond was convertible into 25 shares of Front's $15 par common stock. Back purchased the entire bond issue for $10.3 million on December 30, 1987, and Back's investment broker estimated that without the conversion feature, the bonds would have sold at 98. On January 1, 1990, Back converted bonds with a par value of $4 million. Both parties used the straight-line method for amortization of bond premium.

REQUIRED

1. Prepare the entries to record the 1987 transaction on the books of Front and Back.

2. Prepare entries for the 1990 conversion for Front and Back under the book value method.

P16-10. CONVERTIBLE DEBT; INDUCEMENTS On January 1, 1987, Penultimate Corporation issued serial bonds with a par value of $120,000. Interest at 8 percent was payable annually each December 31, and the bonds matured at the rate of 25 percent per year beginning on December 31, 1988. The bonds were sold for $113,287, which represented an average effective yield of 10 percent. Each $1,000 par bond was convertible into 20 shares of Penultimate's $5 par common stock at any time after January 1, 1988.

REQUIRED

1. Prepare journal entries to record interest expense for 1987 and 1988 under both the effective interest method and the bonds-outstanding method.

2. Determine what the selling price of the bonds would have been if they had been sold to yield 10 percent on July 1, 1987. Your answer should be expressed net of accrued interest.

3. None of the bonds were converted during 1987, 1988, and 1989. Near the end of 1989, the company announced that for one day only—January 1, 1990—the conversion ratio would be modified such that each $1,000 bond would be convertible into 25 shares of Penultimate common stock. The stock was selling for $24 per share at that date. The entire series scheduled to mature at the end of 1990 was converted on January 1, 1990. Prepare the journal entry to record the conversion, assuming Penultimate uses the effective interest method to record interest expense.

4. The remaining series, scheduled to mature at the end of 1991, was converted on January 1, 1991. Prepare the entry to record the conversion, assuming Penultimate uses the effective interest method of recording interest expense.

P16-11. LONG-TERM NOTES The transactions below are independent.

a) At the beginning of year 2 Longneck acquired a machine by issuing a three-year noninterest-bearing note for $14,400. Although the machine had a cash price of less than $14,400, Longneck was satisfied, since the company would normally have to borrow at 10 percent. The note is to be repaid at the rate of $4,800 per year, beginning at the end of year 2.

b) Barlow Storage acquired some refrigerators with a fair market value of $44,012 by issuing a five-year note for $50,000. Interest on the note is at 5 percent, payable annually.

c) Badger issued a two-year 10 percent note for $20,000 in exchange for a tract of land. The note bears interest at the current market rate.

REQUIRED

Prepare the entries to record the above transactions and to record any related interest expense for the first two years.

P16-12. LONG-TERM NOTES PAYABLE

A) Mandrake purchased equipment by issuing a five-year $50,000 note with interest at 4 percent, payable annually. The current rate of interest for notes of similar risk is 8 percent.

REQUIRED

Prepare entries for Mandrake to record the purchase and interest expense for the first two years.

B) Blondie Supply Corporation borrowed $25,000 from a customer by issuing a three-year 2 percent note for $25,000 (interest payable annually). Blondie also agreed to sell 400 cases of hair coloring to its customer at a discount in exchange for such a favorable rate of interest. The current rate of interest on notes of similar risk is 12 percent.

REQUIRED

1. Calculate the discount, if any, applicable to the note.

2. Prepare the entries to record the original transaction and annual interest expense for the three-year period.

3. Assume that Blondie's customer purchased 140 cases of hair coloring during the first year at the reduced price of $25 per case. Prepare the entry to record the sale and recognition of other revenue on the basis of your answers to parts 1 and 2.

P16-13.   TROUBLED DEBT RESTRUCTURING   Debtor owes $100,000 principal plus $15,000 of accrued interest to Creditor. The debt is a 10-year 15 percent note due today, October 29, 1987. Creditor makes a concession because Debtor is in financial stress.

REQUIRED

Prepare Debtor's entries to record the following restructurings. Consider each one independently.

1. Creditor agrees to accept some of Debtor's real estate in full settlement of the debt. The property cost Debtor $75,000 and has a market value of $103,000.

2. Creditor agrees to forgive the $15,000 accrued interest, extend the maturity date to October 29, 1989, and reduce the interest rate to 6 percent.

3. Creditor agrees to forgive the $15,000 accrued interest and to accept 5,000 shares of Debtor's $10 par common stock in full settlement of the debt. Each share of Debtor's common stock has a market value of $18.

4. Creditor agrees to extend the maturity date to October 29, 1989.

P16-14.   CONVERTIBLE BONDS; TROUBLED DEBT   Selected transactions and events for Wolf Corporation are as follows:

a) On January 1, 1987, the Wolf Corporation issued a five-year, 8 percent, $100,000 bond issue for $92,416, with interest payable annually on December 31. Each $1,000 bond was convertible into 100 shares of Wolf's $5 par common stock on any interest date after December 31, 1988. The bonds were sold to yield 10 percent.

b) On December 31, 1987, Wolf paid the interest and recorded interest expense for 1987. Wolf uses the effective interest method.

c) On January 1, 1989, bondholders converted bonds with a par value of $40,000. The market price of Wolf's stock on this date was $24 per share. Wolf uses the book value method.

d) On December 31, 1989, Wolf recorded the interest payable and recorded interest expense for 1989. Wolf did not pay the interest, as the company was in a severe cash bind.

e) On January 2, 1990, because of Wolf's financial difficulties, holders of the remaining bonds made the following concessions to Wolf in an attempt to maximize their return:

1. Eliminated the conversion feature (Wolf's common stock price had been declining over the last year).

2. Forgave the amount of interest due at the end of 1989.

3. Reduced the stated rate on the remaining $60,000 (par value) bonds to 4.37 percent and deferred their receipt of the interest until the end of 1991 (the maturity date of the bonds). The creditors agreed that interest was not to be compounded.

f) On December 31, 1990, Wolf recorded interest expense using the new effective rate.

g) On December 31, 1991, Wolf recorded interest expense and retired the debt in accordance with the concession made by the creditors on January 2, 1990.

REQUIRED

1. Prepare the entries to record the above transactions in Wolf's books.

2. Prepare the appropriate entries for the bond investors (in the aggregate) for each of the dates shown. Assume the investors also use the effective interest method.

P16-15. RESTRUCTURED DEBT   The following transactions are unrelated.

a) On January 1, 1987, Samuel Corporation issued to Mace Investments at par $100,000 in 8 percent 10-year bonds, with interest payable annually. Samuel began having cash flow problems in early 1988 and was unable to pay the accrued interest on the bonds at the end of 1988. At the beginning of 1989 Mace agreed to defer all interest payments (including the one currently due) until December 31, 1996 (the bond maturity date).

b) Several years ago Patrick Ltd. issued a 10-year 6 percent note to Kim Supply Company in exchange for equipment. Patrick has been in a financial bind recently and at the end of the current year Kim agrees to accept 1,400 shares of Coleman Securities that have a fair market value of $10,000 in exchange for the note and interest payable of $12,200. Patrick Ltd. carries the securities in its investment account at $10,000.

REQUIRED

Prepare the entries to record each transaction for both the debtor and the creditor. If no gain or loss is to be recorded, calculate the effective interest rate to be used to calculate interest in the future.

P16-16. COMPREHENSIVE REVIEW PROBLEM   You are conducting the audit for Gomex for the year ending December 31, 1987, and the transactions below have been called to your attention.

a) On January 1, 1986, Gomex issued a three-year noninterest-bearing note for $40,000 in exchange for equipment with a fair market value of $30,052. Gomex recorded the transaction as follows:

Equipment	40,000	
Notes payable		40,000

Gomex has recorded no interest on the note to date, arguing that the note is interest-free. The equipment is being depreciated at the rate of 20 percent per year.

b) On July 1, 1987, Gomex borrowed $10,000 from a bank by issuing a two-year note with 1 percent interest payable each July 1. In exchange for such a favorable interest rate, Gomex agreed to repair as needed, and without charge, the bank's air conditioning system for two years. No repairs have been necessary to date. The market rate of interest on July 1, 1987, was 10 percent.

c) On January 1, 1981, Gomex acquired IVM bonds with a par value of $30,000 for $28,500. The bonds mature 15 years from January 1, 1981. Gomex sold the bonds on June 30, 1987 for $26,000, including accrued interest of $1,600. The sale was recorded as follows (no discount amortization was recorded by Gomex during the time it held the bonds, although straight-line amortization is proper):

Cash	26,000	
Interest expense	4,000	
Bond investment		30,000

d) Several years ago Gomex issued callable bonds for $190,000 ($200,000 par). In early 1987 Gomex called the bonds and substituted a new $200,000 bond issue with a lower interest rate. The call premium was $12,000, and the unamortized discount on the old issue was $6,000. Gomex reasoned that the call premium and discount applicable to the old issue constituted an additional cost of the new issue and thus recorded the refunding as follows:

Cash	200,000	
Bonds payable		200,000
To record the new issue.		
Bonds payable	200,000	
Discount (new issue)	18,000	
Discount (old issue)		6,000
Cash		212,000
To record retirement of the old issue.		

Interest expense for 1987 was increased by $1,800 through amortization of the $18,000 discount.

e) At the end of 1987 Gomex Company issued $6 million of non-interest bearing notes along with warrants to buy 400,000 shares of its $10 par value common stock at $18 per share. The notes mature over 10 years, starting one year from date of issuance, with annual maturities of $600,000. At the time, Gomex had 3.2 million shares of common stock outstanding and the market price was $23 per share. The company received $6,680,000 for the notes and the warrants. The notes would have been issued at an 8 percent interest rate had they been issued without the warrants. Gomex recorded the transaction as a debit to cash and a credit to notes payable in the amount of $6,680,000.

f) Several years ago Gomex accepted a five-year 10 percent note for $38,000 in exchange for a machine. At the end of 1986, the debtor began to have financial difficulties and now owes Gomex the note principal plus a total of $7,600 in interest. Gomex has agreed to forgive the interest due and to reduce the principal amount to $36,000, which will be due and payable with no interest at the end of 1989. Gomex has made no entries in connection with the agreement.

g) On July 1, 1987, Gomex purchased convertible bonds for $103,000, plus accrued interest of $5,000. The bonds have a 10 percent stated rate of interest and a scheduled maturity date of December 31, 1990. Gomex reasoned that the bonds would have sold for $100,000 (par value) without the conversion privilege and recorded the purchase and interest during 1987 as follows:

July 1	Investment in bonds	105,000	
	Conversion privilege	3,000	
	Cash		108,000
Dec. 31	Cash	10,000	
	Interest revenue		10,000

REQUIRED

For each transaction prepare any adjusting or correcting entry that is necessary.

17 LEASES

A lease is an arrangement whereby one party, called the **lessor,** transfers property and the rights to use it to another party, called the **lessee,** in return for cash lease payments that extend over a given time period. Leasing arrangements extend into many areas of our society and cover many types of property. The grocer's building where you shop is probably leased rather than owned by the grocer. The main-frame computer at your college or university probably is leased from a computer manufacturer or a financial institution. Other commonly leased properties include warehouses, railroad cars, trucks, automobiles, space satellites, land, and airplanes. Even clothing is leased:

> Top Shelf, a Minnesota company, deals in made-to-measure garments for men and women. Last year it got into suit leasing. The company leases custom-made suits to executives with a signed agreement and a down payment of 40 percent of the lease cost. The minimum two-year lease costs $5,000, for which Top Shelf provides 12 to 15 suits costing around $420 apiece. The balance is paid off in monthly payments made over two years. At the end of the two-year lease period, the suits are returned to Top Shelf.
>
> A "direct buy option" also is offered. If interest rates or other factors make leasing unrealistic for a company, the suits can be purchased.
>
> Suit leasing began about four years ago in England, where some companies were embarrassed by the tacky appearance of their executives. Because of Britain's lower wage rates and high taxes, some executives couldn't afford expensive clothes.
>
> In the United States the Internal Revenue Service is thought to be watching for potential abuses. Leased suits are intended for business, but who's going to make sure they're not worn at nonbusiness parties?[1]

Leasing is now the most widely used external method of plant and equipment financing in the United States. An estimated $61 billion of capital equipment was leased in 1983—more than was financed by bank loans, corporate bonds, equities, or commercial mortgages.[2] IBM Corporation, which for many years had to compete with computer leasing companies, recently began to lease its computers through its financing subsidiary, IBM Credit Corporation. In 1984, the corporation's computer leases totaled approximately $1.5 billion.[3]

---

[1] *Tulsa World,* March 22, 1981.

[2] *Equipment Leasing: Clearing the Air* (Pittsburgh: Mellon Bank, 1985).

[3] "IBM Credit Unit Attracts Attention for Fast Start in Computer Leasing," *The Wall Street Journal,* November 20, 1984, p. 33.

Why has there been such an unprecedented growth in leasing in recent years? Proponents of leasing claim many advantages. First, the lessee obtains greater financing without having to make the substantial down payment required under a credit purchase. Second, larger tax deductions may be taken through leasing than with a purchase. Third, the risk of property obsolescence may be reduced. Finally, under some circumstances, the lessee may not be required to report the lease obligation as a liability on its balance sheet; therefore, this method of "off-balance-sheet financing" may increase the lessee's borrowing capacity.

Accounting for leases has been controversial.

Accounting for leases, especially by the lessee, has been controversial for at least 30 years. Many lessees have "window-dressed" their financial statements through leasing arrangements; that is, they have acquired the use of assets through a lease without showing either the assets or the related liability on the balance sheet. They also have opposed disclosing long-term lease obligations in their balance sheets. The motives for window-dressing include a desire to increase apparent return on investment, to obtain a more favorable debt/equity ratio, and to increase borrowing capacity. As a result, accounting for leases ranks high on the list of controversial areas in accounting.

CONCEPTUAL CONSIDERATIONS: RENTAL OR ACQUISITION?

The basic issue in accounting for leases is whether a lease is (1) a *rental of property* or (2) an *acquisition of property by financing*. This distinction is important because accounting for rentals of property is quite different from accounting for the acquisition and financing of property.

LEASES THAT TRANSFER OWNERSHIP RIGHTS, RISKS, AND REWARDS

To determine whether a lease is a rental or an acquisition of property, one must ask the following questions:

Has the lessor transferred substantially all ownership rights, risks, and rewards associated with the property to the lessee? If so, the lessor has either financed property for the lessee or sold property to the lessee and financed the purchase. Otherwise, the lessor is merely renting the property to the lessee.

Does the lease agreement transfer all rights, risks, and rewards of ownership to the lessee? If so, the lessee has acquired an asset—property—and has incurred a liability—the lease obligation. Otherwise, the lessee is merely renting the property.

The following example will be used as a basis for discussing the conceptual issues.

At the beginning of 1987, Lessor Bank, Inc., entered into a noncancelable lease agreement with Lessee Video Marketing Company whereby the bank transferred computer equipment to Lessee Video. The equipment had a fair market value of $2,486, a useful life of three years, and no residual (salvage) value. The term of the lease covered three years—1987, 1988, and 1989. Lessee Video agreed to assume all ownership risks associated with the equipment, such as maintenance, taxes, and insurance. Lessor Bank had recently purchased the equipment for $2,486. Because the bank desired a 10 percent rate of return on its investment, it established the annual lease payments at $1,000 per year, payable at the end of each year,[4] as follows:

---

[4] At this point the lease payments are assumed to be made at the *end* of each period. In practice, lease payments usually are made at the *beginning* of each period. Later in this chapter we will use beginning-of-period payments. End-of-year payments are used here for instructional purposes.

$$\frac{\text{Investment to be}}{\text{recovered}} = \frac{\text{Lease}}{\text{payments}} \times P_{\overline{3|}\,10\%}$$

$$\$2,486 = \text{Lease payments} \times 2.4869^*$$

$$\text{Lease payments} = \frac{\$2,486}{2.4869}$$

$$\text{Lease payments} = \$1,000 \text{ (rounded)}$$

* From Table D, Appendix 7–1.

We can analyze this lease agreement by reference to the theory concepts presented in Chapter 2. There we defined assets as probable future economic benefits obtained or controlled by a particular entity as a result of past transactions or events. Liabilities are probable future sacrifices of economic benefits arising from present obligations of a particular entity to transfer assets or provide services to other entities in the future as a result of past transactions or events. Clearly Lessee Video has acquired an asset and has incurred a liability. As an asset, the computer equipment presumably will provide future economic benefits to Lessee Video by contributing to its revenue-generating activities and thus to its net cash inflows. Lessee Video can obtain these economic benefits by using the computer equipment and can control others' access to those benefits because it possesses the equipment. An exchange transaction has occurred; Lessee Video has the equipment to use as it wishes. It also has incurred a liability. It has a noncancelable obligation to pay $1,000 at the end of each year for three years. The obligation will be discharged in the future, and the exchange transaction that created the obligation has occurred.

Lessee Video will have use of the asset throughout the asset's useful life, agrees to assume responsibility for its maintenance, insurance, and taxes, and essentially is paying Lessor Bank the fair market value of the equipment plus interest at 10 percent over the lease term. In summary, Lessor Bank has transferred all ownership rights, risks, and rewards to Lessee Video. Lessee has purchased the computer equipment from Lessor. Lessor is merely financing the purchase for Lessee.

If the lease terms transfer ownership risk and benefits to the lessee, the lessee has purchased the equipment.

These conclusions also are supportable by other theory concepts presented in Chapter 2. Failure to record and disclose the asset acquired and liability incurred violates the qualitative characteristic of representational faithfulness, the full disclosure concept, and does not provide information about the future cash flows associated with Lessee's economic resources and obligations.

ACCOUNTING FOR A LEASE THAT REPRESENTS A TRANSFER OF OWNERSHIP

Based on our analysis above, on January 1, 1987, Lessor and Lessee would make the following entries to record the lease:

LESSOR

Lease receivable ($1,000 × 3)	3,000	
Equipment		2,486
Unearned interest revenue ($3,000 − $2,486)		514
To record the receivable from financing.		

LESSEE

Leased property	2,486	
Lease liability		2,486
To record the asset acquired and the liability incurred.		

Lessor debits lease receivable for the total lease payments of $3,000, credits equipment for $2,486, and credits unearned interest revenue for $514. Unearned interest reve-

EXHIBIT 17–1   LEASE RECEIVABLE/PAYABLE AMORTIZATION SCHEDULE

YEAR	(1) ANNUAL LEASE PAYMENT	(2) INTEREST REVENUE/ EXPENSE*	(3) REDUCTION IN RECEIVABLE/ PAYABLE†	(4) RECEIVABLE/PAYABLE BALANCE (END OF YEAR)‡
				$2,486
1987	$1,000	$249	$ 751	1,735
1988	1,000	174	826	909
1989	1,000	91	909	–0–
	$3,000	$514	$2,486	

* 10% of beginning-of-period receivable/payable balance.

† Col. 1 minus col. 2.

‡ Beginning balance of receivable/payable minus col. 3.

nue is a contra-account to the lease receivable; thus the net investment in the lease receivable is $2,486 ($3,000 − $514). Notice that **the net investment in the lease receivable equals the fair market value of the equipment** transferred to Lessee. This method of recording the receivable at its gross amount separately from the unearned revenue is sometimes referred to as the **gross method** of recording a lease.[5]

The interest (discount) rate of 10 percent which, when applied to the annual lease payments of $1,000, makes the present value of the lease payments of $2,486 equal to the equipment's fair market value of $2,486 is called the **interest rate implicit in the lease.** Notice that this 10 percent implicit rate also is the rate of return desired by Lessor.

Lessee records an asset, leased property, at its fair market value of $2,486 and credits lease liability for $2,486, which is the present value of the three $1,000 annual lease payments, given the 10 percent implicit rate. For instructional purposes, we have recorded the liability net of the $514 discount in order to illustrate the **net method** of recording a lease obligation.[6]

During 1987, 1988, and 1989, Lessor's only entries are to record the receipt of the annual lease payments and interest revenue. Lessee makes parallel entries for the lease payments and interest expense, and in addition depreciates the leased property over the three-year period on the basis of the services received from the use of the asset.

A schedule showing the amortization of the receivable/payable, suitable for both Lessor and Lessee, appears in Exhibit 17–1. Notice that interest is based on the *effective interest method*. The following entries, based on the information in Exhibit 17–1, are made by Lessor and Lessee at the end of 1987 to record the lease payments and interest:

[5] Under the net method, the entry would be:

Lease receivable 2,486
    Equipment   2,486

[6] Lessee's entry under the gross method is as follows:

Leased property 2,486
Discount on lease liability 514
    Lease liability   3,000

The discount is a contra-liability to the lease liability account and is interpreted in the same manner as a discount on bonds payable.

LESSOR

Cash...	1,000	
Lease receivable		1,000

To record receipt of lease payment.

Unearned interest revenue	249	
Interest revenue		249

To recognize interest for 1987.

LESSEE

Interest expense	249	
Lease liability	751	
Cash..		1,000

To record the lease payment and interest for 1987.

Because Lessee acquires all ownership rights associated with the equipment, the following entry is made at the end of each year to record depreciation on the leased property, assuming that straight-line depreciation is appropriate:

Depreciation expense—leased property	829	
Accumulated depreciation		829

($2,486 ÷ 3)

The following data relative to the lease would appear on Lessor's and Lessee's income statements for the year ended December 31, 1987:

LESSOR

Interest revenue	$249

LESSEE

Interest expense	$249
Depreciation expense—leased property	829

As of December 31, 1987, their balance sheets would contain the following information:

LESSOR

Assets:

Lease receivable	$2,000
Less: Unearned interest revenue	(265)*
	$1,735

LESSEE

Assets:

Leased property	$2,486
Less: Accumulated depreciation	(829)
	$1,657

Liabilities:

Lease liability	$1,735†

* $514 − $249.

† $2,486 − $751.

EXHIBIT 17–2 CLASSIFICATION OF LEASES BY LESSOR AND LESSEE

	LESSOR	LESSEE

Ownership rights, risks, and rewards transferred	Capital lease
	  1. Direct-financing
	  2. Leveraged
	  3. Sales-type
		Capital lease

Ownership rights, risks, and rewards not transferred	Operating lease	Operating lease

If Lessor and Lessee prepare classified balance sheets at the end of 1987, they must allocate the balances of the lease receivable and lease liability between the current and noncurrent classifications. This allocation is made from the data in Exhibit 17–1. The portion of the receivable and payable eliminated in 1988 will be $826; therefore, $826 is the current portion and $909 is the noncurrent portion.

Lessor's receivable and Lessee's payable balance at the end of 1987:	$ 826	classified as current
	909	classified as noncurrent
	$1,735	total

Notice in Exhibit 17–1 that although Lessor will receive $1,000 in cash at the end of 1988, $174 of this amount is interest that will accrue in 1988 and thus is not an asset at the end of 1987. Similar reasoning also applies to Lessee.[7]

The previous example has allowed us to focus on conceptual issues and the accounting procedures for a lease that transfers substantially all ownership rights, risks, and rewards. In the following section we shall discuss how these types of leases, as well as those that do not transfer ownership rights, risks, and rewards, are classified in practice.

CLASSIFICATION OF LEASES

Leases may be classified as either capital leases or operating leases (see Exhibit 17–2). Capital leases are, in effect, purchases of property by the lessee from the lessor; operating leases are similar to rentals of property by the lessee from the lessor.

Capital Leases

Capital leases are, in effect, purchases of property by the lessee.

Capital leases are leases that transfer ownership rights, risks, and rewards from the lessor to the lessee. Lessee Video's lease with Lessor Bank (p. 766) was a capital lease. From the lessee's standpoint, accounting for a capital lease is similar to any other exchange

---

[7] Under GAAP, unanimity is lacking on the current/noncurrent balance sheet classification of lease receivables and lease obligations. As alternatives to the approach shown above, many accountants would classify as the current portion either (1) the next year's lease payment or (2) the *present value* of next year's lease payment and the remainder of the receivable or obligation as the noncurrent portion. In terms of our example, these additional alternatives would lead to the following classifications:

ALTERNATIVE	CURRENT PORTION	+	NONCURRENT PORTION	=	TOTAL
1	$1,000		$735		$1,735
2	$1,000/1.10 = $909		826		1,735

transaction in which an entity acquires an asset and incurs a liability. From the lessor's standpoint, a capital lease may be further classified as either a direct-financing, leveraged, or sales-type lease.

DIRECT-FINANCING LEASE   If the terms of the lease are such that the lessor essentially *finances* the property acquisition for the lessee, the lease is called a **direct-financing lease.** Under a direct-financing lease, no income accrues to the lessor at the inception of the lease, because the present value of the lease payments equals the lessor's net investment in the property. Lessor Bank had a direct-financing lease with Lessee Video. Notice that Lessor Bank's only source of income from the transaction was interest over the lease term. Most direct-financing leases involve financial institutions, which profit by lending money at interest. These institutions do not sell property of the type being leased, but merely finance property acquisitions for a lessee.

LEVERAGED LEASE   A **leveraged lease** is a special type of direct-financing lease and has been attractive to lessors because of tax advantages it offers. Under a leveraged lease, the lessor finances, with nonrecourse debt, a large portion of the property purchased and leased to the lessee. For tax purposes, the lessor ''owns'' the property. Although the lease payments represent taxable income, the lessor experiences tax savings from depreciation and interest deductions on the debt. The pattern of net cash flows to the lessor over the lease term provides a high rate of return on the lessor's investment in the leased property. Because of their technical complexity, leveraged leases are not discussed further in this chapter.

SALES-TYPE LEASE   If the lease terms are such that the lessor has income (gross profit) on the transfer (sale) of property to the lessee *in addition* to providing financing for the lessee, the lease is a **sales-type lease** from the lessor's standpoint. The lessor has two sources of earnings under a sales-type lease:

1. A profit (loss) on the sale of the property to the lessee.

2. Interest revenue over the lease term.

Most sales-type leases involve companies that are in the business of both selling and leasing property, such as an equipment manufacturer or dealer. Under this type of lease, the lessor not only sells property to the lessee but also finances the sale for the lessee's benefit.

　　To illustrate a sales-type lease, go back to the lease between Lessor Bank and Lessee Video, only this time assume that Lessor is an equipment dealer rather than a bank. Lessor normally sells such equipment for $2,486. Assume further that the equipment has a cost to Lessor of $1,800. Lessor would make the following entry to record the sales-type lease (Lessee's entry would be the same as that shown on page 767):

Lease receivable 3,000		
Unearned interest revenue	514	
Sales	2,486	
Cost of goods sold 1,800		
Inventory	1,800	

The gross profit of $686 ($2,486 − $1,800) would appear on Lessor's income statement for 1987, and the remaining items on Lessor's financial statements would appear as shown on page 769.

Operating Leases

Operating leases are similar to rentals.

If the lease does not transfer ownership rights, risks, and rewards from the lessor to the lessee, the lease is called an **operating lease** and is similar to a rental. To illustrate,

EXHIBIT 17–3   TERMS OF OPERATING LEASE BETWEEN
LESSEE VIDEO AND A COMPUTER DISTRIBUTOR

ITEM IN LEASE AGREEMENT	OPERATING LEASE TERMS
Cancelability	Cancelable at Lessee's option
Lease term	3 years
Useful life of leased property	15 years
Residual value of leased property, end of lease term	$6,500
Fair market value of leased property	$8,000
Annual lease payments	$800
Responsibility for maintenance, taxes, insurance, etc.	Lessor

assume that the terms of Lessee's lease with a computer equipment distributor were as shown in Exhibit 17–3. Under these lease terms, which are quite different from our earlier example, the lessor has not transferred any rights, risks, and rewards of ownership to Lessee. First, Lessee can cancel the lease at any time. Second, the future economic benefits accruing to Lessee relative to the total benefits associated with the equipment are small, since the three-year term of the lease is small relative to the life of the property. Third, the lease payments of $800, especially if they are discounted, are small relative to the equipment's fair market value of $8,000. Thus, Lessee is not purchasing the equipment at fair market value, but is renting it. Finally, because the lessor agrees to maintain the equipment and to pay insurance and property taxes, the lessor is retaining the risks of ownership. In summary, the lessor retains the rights to most of the service potential associated with the equipment.

This operating lease agreement is similar to a typical rental agreement on an apartment, with which you are probably familiar. Your landlord assumes responsibility for maintenance (if he or she delivers!), taxes, and insurance. You can cancel the lease at any time but probably forfeit a deposit or a month's advance rent. In any event, under no circumstances would you consider that you have "bought" the apartment and that the landlord is financing the purchase.

Accounting for an operating lease is much less complicated than accounting for a capital lease. The lessor records the annual lease payments as rent revenue. The equipment remains on the books of the lessor as property leased to lessees and is depreciated over its useful life. The lessee records the annual lease payments as rent expense. The following entries, based on the information in Exhibit 17–3, would be made each year by the lessor and lessee under an operating lease:

LESSOR

Cash	800	
Rental revenue		800
Depreciation expense	xx*	
Accumulated depreciation		xx*

LESSEE

Rent expense	800	
Cash		800

* The amount of depreciation each year would depend on the depreciation method used by the lessor.

EXHIBIT 17–4   EFFECTS ON LESSEE'S INCOME OF RECORDING
A CAPITAL LEASE AS AN OPERATING LEASE
(BASED ON DATA ON PAGE 766)

	RECORDED AS A CAPITAL LEASE				RECORDED AS AN OPERATING LEASE	
1987	Interest expense $249			1987	Rent expense	$1,000
	Depreciation expense . . 829	$1,078				
1988	Interest expense $174			1988	Rent expense	1,000
	Depreciation expense . . 829	1,003				
1989	Interest expense . . . . $ 91			1989	Rent expense	1,000
	Depreciation expense . . 828	919				
	Total expenses	$3,000			Total expenses	$3,000

Capital Leases Accounted for as Operating Leases

At the beginning of the chapter, we pointed out that many lessees have resisted reporting leased property and the corresponding lease obligation arising from a capital lease in their financial statements. Refer to the example on page 766. What are the financial statement effects of Lessee Video recording the capital lease as an operating lease? The income statement effects for Lessee Video are shown in Exhibit 17–4. Notice that over the three-year period Lessee reports total expenses of $3,000 under both methods. However, the *timing* of the earnings effect differs between the two methods. While only data applicable to the lessee are shown in Exhibit 17–4, the income effects are similar for a lessor.

Recording a capital lease as an operating lease also has significant balance sheet effects. Under a capital lease, the lessee reports the leased property as an asset and the lease obligation as a liability. Under an operating lease, the lessee's balance sheet shows neither an asset nor a liability. Significant balance sheet differences also apply to the lessor. In terms of financial reporting objectives, these financial statement differences can present quite different cash flow signals.

Difficulties in Classifying Leases

In practice, classifying a lease as a capital lease or an operating lease often is difficult for several reasons. First, the terms of the lease agreement may fall somewhere between the two extremes presented in our earlier capital lease example and in Exhibit 17–3. As a result, it may be difficult to determine the intentions of the lessor and lessee: Was the intent to rent or to purchase? Second, as we have mentioned, many lessees traditionally have attempted to avoid capital leases in order to improve their financial position, and many lease agreements have been structured specifically to avoid capitalization. In the next section of the chapter, we look at how the FASB attempted to apply the conceptual distinctions between a capital lease and an operating lease as we study the lease classification criteria set forth in *FASB Statement No. 13*.

APPLYING THE CONCEPTUAL CONSIDERATIONS

To increase financial statement comparability, to thwart accounting abuses, and to reduce user confusion, the accounting profession has made several attempts to develop criteria for distinguishing between capital leases and operating leases. A brief history of these attempts follows.

HISTORICAL BACKGROUND

Although leases have been used for many years as a means of obtaining the right to use property, lease arrangements have expanded rapidly and have become increasingly complex since the 1960s. Lease contracts now include such complexities as clauses prohibiting cancellation; provisions for insurance, repair, and maintenance; sublease agreements; contingent rental agreements; renewal options; bargain purchase options; sale-and-lease-back provisions; and guarantees of the leased property's residual values. These complexities have made it increasingly difficult for accountants to determine proper lease classification and accounting procedures.

The accounting profession's first attempt to improve lease accounting was *Accounting Research Bulletin No. 38*, "Disclosure of Long-Term Leases in Financial Statements of Lessees," issued in 1949. (This bulletin was restated as Chapter 14 of *ARB No. 43* in 1953.) *ARB No. 38* recommended that leases that were equivalent to installment purchases be accounted for as capital leases. In 1962 the Accounting Research Division of the AICPA issued *Accounting Research Study No. 4*, "Reporting of Leases in Financial Statements." *ARS No. 4* recommended that *all* long-term, noncancelable leases be accounted for as capital leases. Between 1964 and 1973 the Accounting Principles Board attempted to narrow the accounting alternatives for leases by issuing four *Opinions*, two affecting the lessor and two affecting the lessee. Many people were critical of these pronouncements because of the resulting lack of symmetry between lessor accounting and lessee accounting. That is, frequently a lease agreement would be classified and accounted for as a sale (capital lease) by the lessor and as an operating lease by the lessee. As a result, the leased property appeared on the books of neither the lessor nor the lessee. In addition, because of the controversy surrounding lessee accounting, pronouncements affecting lessees primarily dealt with *disclosure* rather than with accounting *recognition*.

The FASB placed the lease issue on its agenda and issued a *Discussion Memorandum* on the subject in 1974. This project culminated two years later in the issuance of *FASB Statement No. 13*. *Statement No. 13*, as amended by and clarified through many additional *Statements, Interpretations*, and *Technical Bulletins*, is now the authoritative document on leases.[8]

FASB STATEMENT NO. 13 LEASE CLASSIFICATION CRITERIA

The Statement No. 13 criteria are applications of the conceptual distinctions discussed earlier.

Criteria for the Lessee

If, at the date of the lease agreement, a lease meets *any one* of the following criteria, it is classified and accounted for as a capital lease. If *none* of the criteria below is met, the lease is classified and accounted for as an operating lease:

1. The lease transfers ownership of the property to the lessee by the end of the lease term.

2. The lease contains a bargain purchase option.

3. The lease term is equal to 75 percent or more of the estimated economic life of the leased property.

4. The present value of the minimum lease payments at the beginning of the lease term (excluding payments representing executory costs) equals or exceeds 90 percent of the excess of the fair market value of the leased property at the date of the lease agreement over any investment tax credit retained and expected to be realized by the lessor.[9]

Let us explain these criteria more fully. The lease term normally includes only the fixed noncancelable term of the lease. However, periods that include a penalty for failure

---

[8] "Accounting for Leases," *Statement of Financial Accounting Standards No. 13* (Stamford, Conn.: FASB, 1976). In May 1980 the FASB issued an amended version that integrates *Statement No. 13* with subsequent amendments and interpretations so that, except for pronouncements issued after May 1980, financial accounting standards for leases are set forth in one document.

[9] *FASB Statement No. 13*, para. 7a–e.

to renew the lease and periods covered by bargain renewal options and, under some conditions, ordinary renewal options also are included in the lease term. A bargain purchase option gives the lessee the option to purchase the property at a price that is substantially below the expected fair market value at the date the option may be exercised, that is, a price that seems so favorable at the date of the lease agreement that the option is reasonably certain to be exercised. If the beginning of the lease term falls within the last 25 percent of the estimated economic life of the property, the third and fourth criteria above are not applicable.[10] The fourth criterion sometimes is called a *fair value recovery criterion.* In the application of the fourth criterion, the minimum lease payments are the amounts that the lessee is obligated to pay under the terms of the lease. Executory costs, such as insurance, maintenance, and taxes on the leased property, are excluded from minimum lease payments because they are period costs rather than part of the acquisition cost of the property.

The lessee uses the interest rate implicit in the lease to determine the present value of the minimum lease payments. As we discussed earlier, this rate of interest equates the present value of the lease payments with the leased property's fair market value.[11] When the lessor expects to retain and realize an investment tax credit on the property, the lessee must compare the present value of the minimum lease payments with the property's fair market value *less any investment credit* retained by the lessor. The fair market value of the leased property is the price at which the leased property could be sold in an exchange transaction. In a sales-type lease, the fair market value of the leased property is the dealer's normal selling price. In a direct-financing lease, the fair market value equals the cost of the leased property to the lessor.

Criteria for the Lessor

For the lessor, a lease is classified as a direct-financing or sales-type capital lease if *all* of the criteria below are met; otherwise the lease is classified as an operating lease.

1. The lease meets *any one* of the four criteria on page 774.

2. Collectibility of the lease payments is reasonably predictable.

3. There is no significant uncertainty related to the amount of unreimbursable costs yet to be incurred by the lessor under the lease.

If the above criteria are met, the lessor classifies the lease as a sales-type lease if a profit arises on the transfer of property. In addition, interest revenue is earned over the lease term. If the above criteria are met and the lessor's only source of earnings is interest over the lease term, the lease is a direct-financing lease. If the above criteria are not met, the lease is an operating lease to the lessor.

Lease Criteria and Conceptual Considerations

We have discussed the conceptual considerations in a lease and have presented the lease classification criteria in *FASB Statement No. 13.* Now let us relate these criteria to the conceptual issue of whether the lessor transfers ownership risks and rewards to the lessee.

---

[10] Excluding the third and fourth criteria in this circumstance thus prevents, for example, a lease of property with a 20-year life under, say, four separate and succeeding five-year leases from being classified as an operating lease at the beginning of each of the first three leases but as a capital lease at the beginning of the last lease.

[11] Later in this chapter we discuss situations where the implicit rate may not be known by the lessee, and the lessee's incremental borrowing rate must be used to determine the present value of the minimum lease payments.

CRITERION 1: PASSAGE OF TITLE   If title to the property passes to the lessee at the end of the lease term, then *all* ownership benefits accrue to the lessee even if the leased property has a useful life that extends beyond the lease term. Furthermore, the property's residual value, if any, will also accrue to the lessee.

CRITERION 2: BARGAIN PURCHASE OPTION   If the lease contains a bargain purchase option, it is assumed that the lessee will exercise the option and obtain title to the leased property. Thus, the conclusions about ownership transfer discussed in the previous paragraph apply here as well.[12]

CRITERION 3: RELATIONSHIP BETWEEN LEASE TERM AND LIFE OF PROPERTY   If the lease term equals the economic life of the property, the lessee will obtain all of the benefits associated with the property, assuming a nominal residual value, throughout its economic life. Notice that a company could avoid classifying a lease as a capital lease if the lease term had to equal *100 percent* of the economic life of the property. Under these circumstances, a lease contract could easily be drafted so that the lease term was slightly less than the life of the property, thereby circumventing this criterion.

The FASB concluded that the lessee obtains essentially all ownership risks and rewards if the lease term is a substantial portion of the life of the leased property. For the lease term, "substantial" was quantified, possibly arbitrarily, as 75 percent of the leased property's estimated economic life. In summary, the third criterion means that if the lease term is at least 75 percent of the useful life of the property, the parties are presumed to have entered into a capital lease agreement.

CRITERION 4: FAIR MARKET VALUE RECOVERY   If the present value of the lease payments equals 100 percent of the property's fair market value, obviously the lessor either has financed the purchase for the lessee (e.g., a direct-financing lease) or has sold the property to the lessee and financed its purchase (e.g., a sales-type lease). In either case the lessee is paying the fair market value (cash-equivalent exchange price) for the leased property plus interest over the lease term. However, a requirement that the present value of the lease payments must equal *100 percent* of the property's fair market value would not allow for any residual value that might accrue to the lessor at the end of the lease term. If residual value accrues to the lessor at the end of the lease term, then the required lease payments can be lowered and still allow the lessor to obtain the desired rate of return. For example, assume that on January 1, 1987, Lessee enters into a ten-year capital lease with Lessor for equipment that on that date has a fair market value of $10,000. The equipment has a useful life of 10 years and an estimated residual value of $3,000. If the $3,000 residual value accrues to Lessor, the lessor need not recover the entire $10,000 in the form of lease payments. (Later we shall see how lease payments are determined when residual values are present.)

In addition, a 100 percent requirement could be abused because a lease contract could be drafted specifically to avoid this criterion. Because of residual value considerations and possible abuses with a 100 percent requirement, the FASB chose 90 percent of the fair market value of the leased property for comparison with the present value of the lease payments. Conceptually, however, the essence of this criterion is that the lessee

---

[12] If a bargain purchase option is the vehicle that transfers ownership risks and rewards to the lessee, the lease payments determined by the lessor should ensure a specified rate of return on the lessor's investment. Thus higher lease payments should be required if a bargain purchase option, as opposed to an ordinary purchase option, is included.

EXHIBIT 17–5   DEPRECIATION (AMORTIZATION) PERIOD
FOR ASSETS ACQUIRED UNDER A CAPITAL LEASE

FASB STATEMENT NO. 13 CRITERION MET	LESSEE DEPRECIATES LEASED PROPERTY OVER:	
	ITS USEFUL LIFE	THE LEASE TERM
Criterion 1: Title passes to lessee by end of lease term	x	
Criterion 2: Lease contains a bargain purchase option	x	
If neither Criterion 1 nor 2 is met:		
Criterion 3: Term of lease at least 75% of property's useful life		x
Criterion 4: Present value of lease payments at least 90% of property's fair market value		x

pays *fair market value* for the leased property plus interest over the lease term, and in return receives substantially all ownership benefits associated with the property.

LESSEE AMORTIZATION OF A CAPITAL LEASE   We already have presented the accounting procedures for the lessee's depreciation (amortization) of the leased property (capital lease). Since the capital lease criteria affect the period over which the leased property is depreciated, *FASB Statement No. 13* requires that if the lease meets either the first or second criterion listed on page 774, the property must be depreciated (amortized) over the life of the leased property (because the lessee will have the use of the property over its entire useful life). If neither of the first two criteria is met, but either criterion 3 or 4 is met, the property must be depreciated (amortized) over the term of the lease. Exhibit 17–5 provides a summary of these depreciation requirements.

The additional lessor criteria are applications of the revenue realization principle.

ADDITIONAL LESSOR CRITERIA   The two additional criteria for the lessor, especially for dealer lessors who also sell property, are merely applications of the revenue realization principle discussed in Chapter 2. Reasonable predictability of the lease payments to be collected is a criterion for revenue recognition at the point of sale and applies to lessors under sales-type leases. This criterion also applies to lessors under direct-financing leases, since most lenders would not finance purchases for lessees unless they could make reasonable estimates of uncollectible amounts. The second criterion, which states that no significant uncertainties exist in regard to nonreimbursable costs to be incurred by the lessor, is another way of saying that the lessor's earnings process must be virtually complete before income can be recognized under sales-type leases.

One objective of *FASB Statement No. 13* is to increase comparability between companies that *buy* their operating assets and companies that *lease* their operating assets. Since lessees often attempt to avoid capitalization of a lease, another objective is to eliminate many of the lease abuses discussed earlier and to close loopholes in previous accounting pronouncements that have allowed lessees to engage in off-balance-sheet financing. At the end of this chapter, we will discuss the apparent success of *Statement No. 13* and also present some of its alleged weaknesses.

ADDITIONAL LEASING ISSUES

To this point, we have presented the basic lease concepts. We now turn to the following technical issues:

1. The composition of minimum lease payments that the lessee may be required to pay.
2. Accounting for residual values and bargain purchase options.
3. A closer examination of the discount rate used by the lessee to calculate the present value of minimum lease payments.
4. Accounting for direct costs of leasing incurred by the lessor.
5. The nature of and accounting for sale-and-leaseback transactions.

Real estate leases and subleases are covered briefly in Appendix 17–1.

MINIMUM LEASE PAYMENTS

As we stated earlier, the minimum lease payments consist of amounts that the lessee is obligated to pay under the terms of the lease agreement. An accountant needs to know what must be included in the minimum lease payments, since they are used to test the fourth lease criterion and to determine the capitalized amount for capital leases.

If the lease agreement contains a bargain purchase option, the minimum lease payments include (1) the periodic lease payments up to the date that the bargain purchase option becomes exercisable and (2) the amount of the bargain purchase option. If the lease agreement does not contain a bargain purchase option, the minimum lease payments include (1) the periodic lease payments over the lease term; (2) the amount of any guaranteed residual value at the end of the lease term (discussed in the following section); and (3) any payment required by the lessee for failure to renew or extend the lease at the end of the lease term.

Lease agreements frequently contain a provision for increases or decreases in lease payments that are contingent on events occurring after the date of the lease agreement, such as revenues generated from the use of the leased property. These payments, called **contingent rentals,** are excluded from the minimum lease payments and are recorded as revenue by the lessor when earned and as expense by the lessee when incurred.

RESIDUAL (SALVAGE) VALUE

When the lease term equals the useful life of the leased property, the property may have some estimated residual (salvage) value at the end of the lease term. When the lease term is less than the estimated economic life of the leased property, the property's estimated residual value at the end of the lease term may be substantial. The lessee may or may not guarantee the property's residual value.

Guaranteed Residual Value

A lease agreement may include a guaranteed residual value (GRV), in which case the lessee assures to the lessor that the lessor will recover at least the guaranteed amount at the end of the lease term. Lessors often include a GRV clause in lease contracts in order to minimize their risk. In essence, the guarantee transfers the risk of a decrease in value to the lessee or, in some cases, to a third-party guarantor. In addition, a residual value guarantee may cause the lessee to make more prudent use of the leased property than might otherwise be the case.

If the actual residual value is below the amount guaranteed at the end of the lease term, the lessee must pay the difference to the lessor. For example, assume that a lessee leases property and guarantees a residual value of $3,000. The amount to be paid to the lessor at the end of the lease term, assuming four different actual residual values, is as follows:

GUARANTEED RESIDUAL VALUE	ACTUAL RESIDUAL VALUE	AMOUNT PAID BY LESSEE TO LESSOR
$3,000	$ 500	$2,500
3,000	2,700	300
3,000	3,000	–0–
3,000	3,800	–0–

Notice that if the actual residual value exceeds $3,000, the lessor has a gain at the end of the lease term. Some lease agreements provide that the gain is to be shared with the lessee.

To illustrate accounting for GRV, assume that on January 1, 1987, Lessor Corporation leased equipment with a six-year useful life to Lessee Corporation. The following data are pertinent:

1. Cost to Lessor and fair market value of equipment, $20,000.

2. Term of lease, four years.

3. Lessee guarantees 100 percent of the expected residual value, $3,000.

4. Implicit rate of interest in the lease payments, 12 percent.

5. Annual lease payments to be made at the beginning of each year (an annuity due) were determined by Lessor as follows:[13]

Cost and fair market value of equipment	$20,000
Present value of guaranteed residual value:	
$3,000($p_{\overline{4}\mid 12\%}$)	
$3,000(.6355)	(1,906)
Amount to be recovered through lease payments	$18,094
Annual lease payments:	
$18,094 \div ($P_{D\overline{4}\mid 12\%}$)	
$18,094 \div 3.4018	$ 5,319

6. Lessee uses straight-line depreciation on the leased asset.

The present value of the minimum lease payments is $20,000 ($5,319 × 3.4018 = $18,094; $3,000 × .6355 = $1,906; $18,094 + $1,906 = $20,000). Because this present value exceeds 90 percent of the fair market value of the equipment at the date of the lease agreement, the lease is a capital lease to the lessee. Assuming that the two additional lessor criteria (p. 775) are met, the lease is a direct-financing lease for the lessor.

The lease receivable/payable amortization schedule, suitable for both lessor and lessee, is shown in Exhibit 17–6. Notice that the schedule is slightly different from the one in Exhibit 17–1. The lease payments in this example occur at the beginning instead of at the end of each year. Notice, too, that the lessor's lease receivable balance and the lessee's lease liability balance both equal the amount of the residual value guarantee at the end of 1990.

---

[13] A time diagram for the cash flows associated with the lease would appear as follows:

Present value	$20,000				
Lease payments	$5,319	$5,319	$5,319	$5,319	$3,000 (GRV)
	1/1/87	1/1/88	1/1/89	1/1/90	12/31/90

EXHIBIT 17–6 LEASE RECEIVABLE/PAYABLE AMORTIZATION
SCHEDULE WITH GUARANTEED RESIDUAL VALUE

YEAR	(1) ANNUAL LEASE PAYMENTS*	(2) RECEIVABLE/ PAYABLE OUTSTANDING DURING YEAR†	(3) INTEREST REVENUE/ EXPENSE‡	(4) REDUCTION IN RECEIVABLE/ PAYABLE§	(5) RECEIVABLE/ PAYABLE BALANCE (END OF YEAR)¶
					(1/1/87) $20,000
1987	$ 5,319	$14,681	$1,762	$ 3,557	16,443
1988	5,319	11,124	1,335	3,984	12,459
1989	5,319	7,140	857	4,462	7,997
1990	5,319	2,678	322**	4,997	3,000
	$21,276		$4,276	$17,000	

* Previously calculated.

† Previous balance in col. 5 minus col. 1.

‡ .12 × col. 2.

§ Col. 1 minus col. 3.

¶ Previous balance minus col. 4 (or col. 2 + col. 3).

** Rounded by $1.

On January 1, 1987, lessor and lessee would make the following entries to record the capital lease:

LESSOR

Lease receivable [($5,319 × 3) + $3,000]	18,957	
Cash	5,319	
Unearned interest revenue		4,276
Equipment		20,000

LESSEE

Leased property	20,000	
Lease liability		14,681
Cash		5,319

Observe that in the lessor's entry, the present value of the guaranteed residual value (GRV) is transferred from the equipment account to the lease receivables account. Furthermore, the unearned interest of $4,276 includes interest to be earned on the present value of (1) the periodic lease payments and (2) the GRV. In other words, the lessor's beginning *net* receivable balance and the lessee's beginning liability balance are the sum of the present value of the lease payments and the present value of the guaranteed residual value.

On December 31, 1987, the following entries would be made by the lessor and the lessee:

LESSOR

Unearned interest revenue	1,762	
Interest revenue		1,762
To record interest earned.		

LESSEE

Interest expense 1,762
    Lease liability (or interest payable)   1,762
To record interest expense.

Depreciation expense 4,250
    Accumulated depreciation   4,250
To record depreciation on the leased equipment for 1987,
assuming that the estimated salvage value equals the guaranteed residual
value [($20,000 − $3,000) ÷ 4].

On January 1, 1988, the following entries would be made to record the lease payment for 1988:

LESSOR

Cash 5,319
    Lease receivable   5,319

LESSEE

Lease liability 5,319
    Cash   5,319

On December 31, 1988, the following entries would be made by the lessor and the lessee:

LESSOR

Unearned interest revenue 1,335
    Interest revenue   1,335

LESSEE

Interest expense 1,335
    Lease liability (or interest payable)   1,335

Depreciation expense 4,250
    Accumulated depreciation   4,250

The entries below would be made at the end of 1990 to record the return of the equipment to the lessor and the final settlement based on the residual value guarantee. First, assume that the *actual* residual value was $2,000:

LESSOR

Cash ($3,000 − $2,000) 1,000
Equipment 2,000
    Lease receivable   3,000

LESSEE

Loss on residual value guarantee 1,000
Accumulated depreciation 17,000
Lease liability 3,000
    Leased property   20,000
    Cash   1,000

Now, assume instead that the *actual* residual value was $3,000:

LESSOR

Equipment 3,000
  Lease receivable   3,000

LESSEE

Accumulated depreciation 17,000
Lease liability 3,000
  Leased property   20,000

If the actual residual value exceeded $3,000, a gain would accrue to the lessor (and perhaps to the lessee, depending on the agreement). Until the lessor sold the asset, however, the equipment would be reported at the amount of the guarantee since the earnings process is not complete. In practice, the leased equipment need not be physically transferred to the lessor. The lessee may sell the equipment and remit the proceeds to the lessor, including any amount required under the guarantee.

Unguaranteed Residual Value

The portion of the leased property's residual value at the end of the lease term that is not guaranteed by the lessee or by another party is called the unguaranteed residual value. When the residual value of leased property is not guaranteed, the lessor still determines the lease payments so as to recover the fair market value of the leased asset plus interest over the lease term. If the estimated residual value of Lessor Corporation's leased equipment is not guaranteed, Lessor will determine the annual lease payments as follows:

Cost (fair market value) of equipment $20,000
Present value of unguaranteed residual value ($3,000 × .6355) . . . . (1,906)
Amount to be recovered (present value) $18,094

Annual lease payments:
  $18,094 ÷ $(P_{D\overline{4}|\ 12\%})$
  $18,094 ÷ 3.4018 . . . . $ 5,319

Notice that even though the residual value is *not* guaranteed by the lessee, the lessor determines the annual lease payments in exactly the same manner as when the residual value is guaranteed.[14]

Because the residual value is not guaranteed, only the lease payments would be included in Lessee's calculation of the present value of the minimum lease payment:

Present value = Lease payments × $(P_{D\overline{4}|\ 12\%})$
         = $5,319 × 3.4018
         = $18,094

Since the present value exceeds 90 percent of the equipment's fair market value [$18,094 ≥ .90($20,000)], the lease still qualifies as a capital lease to Lessee and to Lessor.

---

[14] Although the *method* of determining the lease payments is the same, the lessor's required rate of return (and the implicit interest rate) would be *higher,* to compensate for the increased risk when there is no residual value guarantee.

Lessor's entries to record the lease and subsequent entries for interest would be the same as the entries on pages 780–81. The residual value is unguaranteed, so if the actual residual value at the end of the lease term differs from the $3,000 original estimate, Lessor would record a loss or a gain when the asset is sold.[15]

Because Lessee did not guarantee the residual value, Lessee would record the capital lease as follows:

Leased property 18,094		
Lease liability	12,775	
Cash...	5,319	

This entry is similar to Lessee's entry shown on page 780. The difference of $1,906 in the amount recorded for the asset and liability is the present value of the residual value, which was guaranteed in the entry shown on page 780 but is *not* guaranteed in the present example. Exhibit 17–7 presents the lease liability amortization schedule for Lessee. Subsequent entries for interest expense and the lease payments would be based on the amounts in the exhibit. Since Lessee makes no residual value guarantee, the liability is fully discharged at the beginning of 1990.

When unguaranteed residual value exists in a sales-type lease, the lessor's entry to record the lease is modified slightly. For example, assuming that the equipment leased by Lessee in the example on page 782 had a cost of $15,000, Lessor would make the following entry on January 1, 1987:

[15] A loss might be recognized before the actual sale, whereas a gain would not be recognized until the asset was sold.

EXHIBIT 17–7 LESSEE'S AMORTIZATION OF LEASE LIABILITY—NO RESIDUAL VALUE GUARANTEE

YEAR	(1) ANNUAL LEASE PAYMENTS*	(2) LIABILITY OUTSTANDING DURING YEAR†	(3) INTEREST EXPENSE‡	(4) REDUCTION IN LIABILITY§	(5) LIABILITY BALANCE (END OF YEAR)¶
					(1/1/87) $18,094
1987	$ 5,319	$12,775	$1,533	$ 3,785	14,309
1988	5,319	8,990	1,079	4,240	10,069
1989	5,319	4,750	570	4,749	5,319**
1990	5,319	–0–	–0–	5,319	–0–
	$21,276		$3,182	$18,094**	

* Previously calculated.
† Previous balance in col. 5 minus col. 1.
‡ .12 × col. 2.
§ Col. 1 minus col. 3.
¶ Previous balance minus col. 4 (or col. 2 + col. 3).
** Rounding error of $1.

Lease receivables [($5,319 × 3) + $3,000] 18,957		
Cash.. 5,319		
Cost of goods sold ($15,000 − $1,906) 13,094		
Sales ($20,000 − $1,906)		18,094
Inventory..		15,000
Unearned interest revenue		4,276

Under *FASB Statement No. 13,* the recorded amount of sales in a sales-type lease is the present value of the minimum lease payments. Had the residual value been guaranteed, the present value of the lease payments and corresponding sales price would have been $20,000 (see p. 779). But because the residual value is not guaranteed, the present value of the lease payments and corresponding sales price are only $18,094 ($20,000 − $1,906). Thus when residual value is not guaranteed, the present value of the unguaranteed value is deducted from sales and cost of goods sold. This accounting procedure for unguaranteed residual value has no effect on Lessor's gross profit of $5,000 ($20,000 − $15,000), since $18,094 less $13,094 also equals $5,000.

The rationale for this accounting treatment for unguaranteed residual value under sales-type leases is as follows: When the estimated residual value is guaranteed, the lessor's sacrifice is measured by the entire cost of the property transferred to the lessee, and in return the lessor is assured of the entire sales price (lease payments plus guaranteed residual value) from the lessee. When the estimated residual value is not guaranteed, the *cost* of the property sacrificed is the original cost less the present value of the unguaranteed residual value. Nor does the lessor recover the full sales price *from the lessee* when the estimated residual value is *not* guaranteed.

Leases of property with unguaranteed residual values highlight a potential problem with the fourth criterion in lessee classifications of leases. If the unguaranteed residual value is quite large relative to the fair market value of the leased property, many leases will not qualify as capital leases under the fourth criterion. For example, in the illustration above, the present value of the lease payments was $18,094, which was only slightly more than 90 percent of the equipment's fair market value. In practice, lessees have often circumvented this criterion by paying an unrelated third party to guarantee the residual value. (Interestingly, a whole new industry arose in which an unrelated company would guarantee, for a fee similar to an insurance premium, the residual value to the lessor.) Since the lessor considers residual value in determining the lease payments, but the lessee disregards any residual value not guaranteed by the lessee, the lease may fail the 90 percent test when present values are calculated by the lessee. (Both the lessor and lessee may fail the 90 percent test when the unguaranteed residual value is large.)

Lessors' consideration of residual values is important for determining lease payments, and failure to make realistic estimates can affect their profits from leasing activities. For example, many computer leasing companies have purchased computers from IBM, Honeywell, and other computer manufacturers, then leased the computers to users. The leasing companies have attempted to compete with the computer manufacturers by setting lower lease payments as a consequence of overly optimistic estimates of unguaranteed residual values. Many of these computer leasing companies have experienced huge losses, financial difficulties, and even bankruptcy because of these erroneous estimates of residual value. Earlier in this chapter, we discussed IBM Corporation's computer leases. Interestingly, at least one of IBM's principal competitors has stated that IBM's aggressive pricing structure in computer leasing can be attributed to overoptimism about the residual value of used computers at the end of the terms of the leases.[16]

[16] "IBM Credit Unit Attracts Attention for Fast Start in Computer Leasing," *The Wall Street Journal,* November 20, 1984, p. 33.

BARGAIN PURCHASE OPTIONS Bargain purchase options were discussed briefly on page 775. The lessor's treatment of a bargain purchase option in determining the annual lease payments is similar to the treatment of a residual value guarantee. To illustrate, assume that on January 1, 1987, R. Lessor acquired equipment at a cost of $90,000 and leased it to E. Lessee under a 10-year noncancelable lease agreement. The terms of the lease were as follows:

1. The lease term was 10 years and the useful life of the equipment was 20 years.

2. E. Lessee was given a bargain purchase option of $20,000 at the end of the fourth year.

3. The rate of return required by R. Lessor was 10 percent.

4. Annual lease payments, due at the beginning of each year, were $21,893, determined by Lessor as follows:

Cost and fair market value of property on 1/1/87	$90,000
Less present value of bargain purchase option:	
$20,000 \times p_{\overline{4}|\,10\%} = \$20,000 \times .6830$	(13,660)
Amount to be recovered through annual lease payments	$76,340
Annual lease payments:	
$76,340 \div (P_{D\overline{4}|\,10\%})$	
$76,340 \div 3.4869$	$21,893

5. Collectibility of the lease payments by Lessor was assured.

6. Lessor would not incur any remaining costs associated with the lease.

As shown above, $90,000 needs to be recovered through the bargain purchase option and annual lease payments. Lessee's minimum lease payments include those lease payments for the periods up to the date of the bargain purchase option plus the amount of the bargain purchase option. Because of the bargain purchase option, the lease is a capital lease to Lessee. It is a direct-financing lease to Lessor because the two additional lessor criteria are met and there is no profit at the lease inception date.

A lease receivable/payable amortization schedule appears in Exhibit 17–8. As the exhibit shows, at the end of 1990 the balance of Lessor's receivable and Lessee's payable equals the amount of the bargain purchase option. In addition, Lessee amortizes the equipment over its useful life because the lease contains a bargain purchase option.

A bargain purchase option should be distinguished from an ordinary purchase option. Under a bargain purchase option, the lessee is given the option to purchase the leased property at a price that is substantially below fair market value. An ordinary purchase option allows the lessee to acquire the asset by paying approximately the fair market value at the exercise date.[17]

---

[17] A bargain purchase option should also be distinguished from a **bargain renewal option,** which allows the lessee to renew the lease at below-market lease payments. Bargain renewal options are not included explicitly in the *FASB Statement No. 13* lease criteria, but are included implicitly in the third criterion listed on p. 774.

EXHIBIT 17–8 RECEIVABLE/PAYABLE AMORTIZATION SCHEDULE
FOR A LEASE WITH A BARGAIN PURCHASE OPTION

YEAR	(1) ANNUAL LEASE PAYMENTS*	(2) RECEIVABLE/ PAYABLE OUTSTANDING DURING YEAR†	(3) INTEREST REVENUE/ EXPENSE‡	(4) REDUCTION IN RECEIVABLE/ PAYABLE§	(5) RECEIVABLE/ PAYABLE BALANCE (END OF YEAR)¶
					(1/1/87) $90,000
1987	$21,893	$68,107	$ 6,811	$15,082	74,918
1988	21,893	53,025	5,303	16,590	58,328
1989	21,893	36,435	3,644	18,249	40,079
1990	21,893	18,186	1,819	20,079**	20,000
	$87,572		$17,577	$70,000	

* Previously calculated.

† Previous balance in col. 5 minus col. 1.

‡ .10 × col. 2.

§ Col. 1 minus col. 3.

¶ Previous balance minus col. 4 (or col. 2 + col. 3).

** Rounding error of $5.

LESSEE'S USE OF THE IMPLICIT RATE IN DETERMINING PRESENT VALUE

Up to this point, the lessee has used the interest rate implicit in the lease in calculating the present value of the minimum lease payments. This approach has been appropriate because the interest rate implicit in the lease is that rate which equates the minimum lease payments with the fair market value, net of any applicable investment credit, of the leased property. But what if the lessee is unable to determine the implicit rate either directly or indirectly through knowledge of the fair market value of the property?[18] *FASB Statement No. 13* requires the lessee to use his or her own incremental borrowing rate to calculate the present value of the minimum lease payments unless (1) it is practicable for the lessee to learn the implicit rate calculated by the lessor and (2) the lessor's implicit rate is less than the lessee's incremental borrowing rate.[19] The **incremental borrowing rate** is the interest rate that the lessee would have to pay to borrow the funds necessary to purchase the property. In setting this requirement, the FASB apparently had two concerns related to the lessee's calculation of present values:

1. The higher the interest rate used to discount the minimum lease payments, the lower the present value. Thus, if the lessee's borrowing rate were *higher* than the implicit rate, a lessee might avoid the all-important 90 percent of fair market value (fair value recovery) criterion.

2. Under GAAP, assets are not recorded in excess of their fair market value. If the lessee's borrowing rate were *lower* than the implicit rate, in the absence of a substan-

[18] As long as the unguaranteed residual value is nominal, knowledge of the amount of the lease payments and the fair market value will allow a close approximation of the implicit rate.

[19] *FASB Statement No. 13*, para. 7d.

tial unguaranteed residual value, the present value of the lease payments, when calculated using the incremental borrowing rate, would probably exceed the fair market value of the property.

To see the first concern, refer to the lessee's present value calculations on page 782. There, the present value of the minimum lease payments using the *implicit* rate was $18,094, which barely exceeded 90 percent of the fair market value of the leased property. If the lessee had used a *higher* incremental borrowing rate to discount the lease payments, the present value almost certainly would have been less than 90 percent of the fair market value. As a result, the lease would not have met the fourth lease criterion. Even if the residual value were zero, avoidance of the 90 percent rule would still be possible depending on the difference between the incremental borrowing rate and the implicit rate and on the term of the lease.

As for the second concern, if the lessee's incremental borrowing rate were *lower* than the implicit rate, the present value of the lease payments might exceed the fair market value of the leased property. Refer again to the present value calculations on page 782, but assume that the unguaranteed residual value was only $500. If the lessee's borrowing rate was lower than the implicit rate of 12 percent—say, 10 percent—the present value of the lease payments would exceed the fair market value of the property:

LESSOR'S DETERMINATION OF ANNUAL LEASE PAYMENTS AT 12%

Cost	$20,000
Present value of unguaranteed residual value ($500 × .6355)	(318)
Amount to be recovered through lease payments	$19,682
Annual lease payments ($19,682 ÷ 3.4018)	$ 5,786

LESSEE'S DETERMINATION OF PRESENT VALUE AT A 10% INCREMENTAL BORROWING RATE

$$\text{Present value} = \text{minimum lease payments} \times (P_{D_{\overline{4}|\ 10\%}})$$
$$= \$5,786 \times 3.4868$$
$$= \$20,175$$

The present value of $20,175 exceeds the $20,000 fair market value of the property. The smaller the unguaranteed residual value, the more likely that the fair market value will be exceeded. Because assets are not recorded in excess of their fair market value, *FASB Statement No. 13 limits the amount of the capital lease to be recorded to the fair market value of the leased property.*[20]

In summary, the lessee uses the lower of (1) the incremental borrowing rate, subject to the fair market value limitation, or (2) the rate implicit in the lease to discount the minimum lease payments. This approach means that the lessee will always record a capital lease at the lower of (1) the leased asset's fair market value or (2) the present value of the minimum lease payments. In practice, the number of instances in which the incremental borrowing rate applies would appear to be small, for the following reasons:

1. Most lessors disclose the interest rate implicit in the lease agreement.

---

[20] The lessee would have to calculate an effective interest rate for purposes of amortizing the lease liability:

$$\$20,000 = \$5,786 \ (P_{D_{\overline{4}|\ i\%}})$$

When we solve for i, we find that the interest rate is slightly more than 10 percent.

2. The lessee usually knows virtually as much about the fair market value of the property as the lessor, since the lessee presumably has already made the decision to lease rather than to borrow and buy the asset.

3. Leased property may be subject to a high rate of obsolescence, which makes expected residual values nominal. Furthermore, when the lease term is fairly long, the present value of unguaranteed residual values, obsolescence notwithstanding, is likely to be small. As a result, the lessor's determination of the required lease payments will be based, for the most part, on the fair market value of the property at the date of the lease agreement. Thus, a *lower* incremental borrowing rate will probably cause the present value of the lease payments to exceed the property's fair market value.[21]

INITIAL DIRECT COSTS OF LEASING

Lessors usually incur various costs in negotiating and completing lease transactions. Those costs that can be directly related to the lease are called **initial direct costs** and include commissions, credit investigations, legal fees, and costs associated with preparation of the lease contract. Should these costs incurred by a lessor be expensed or recorded as an asset at the date of the lease agreement? We can answer by recalling the distinction between assets and expenses. *Assets* represent probable future economic benefits resulting in direct or indirect future cash inflows. *Expenses* are sacrifices that contribute to the revenue-generating or earnings process of the current accounting period.

For operating leases, the initial direct costs are recorded as assets and are amortized over the lease term. The amortization pattern should be similar to the pattern of rent revenue recognition, which typically is straight-line. This procedure is consistent with the fact that the lessor incurred these costs in order to earn rental revenue over the lease term and that these direct costs, along with depreciation of the leased asset and other expenses, should therefore be matched against the revenue generated.

For sales-type leases, initial direct costs are expensed and deducted, along with the cost of the property sold, from the revenue reported on the sale. Notice that this treatment is consistent with accounting for direct costs incurred in connection with an outright sale of the property. While an argument could be made for deferring a portion of the costs related to the financing portion of the lease agreement because the lessor also earns interest revenue over the lease term, this treatment is not permitted under *FASB Statement No. 13*.

If the lease qualifies as a direct-financing lease, the initial direct costs should be recorded as assets and amortized over the lease term. In this instance, the lessor incurred the costs in order to finance the property acquisition for the lessee. Since the lessor's only source of revenue under a direct-financing lease is interest, the costs should be matched against interest revenue over the term of the lease. In practice, accounting for initial direct costs in a direct-financing lease differs slightly from this procedure, but the effect on net income is the same. To illustrate, assume that a lessor and lessee enter into a lease agreement that meets the criteria for a direct-financing lease. The terms of the lease and other information are as follows:

1. Cost of leased property to lessor, $2,486.

2. Term of lease, three years.

3. Initial direct costs incurred by lessor, $200.

4. Rate of return desired by lessor, 10 percent.

---

[21] A much stronger case against the use of the incremental borrowing rate was made by John Coughlan, ''Regulation, Rents, and Residuals,'' *Journal of Accountancy,* February 1980, pp. 58–66.

5. Annual lease payments to be made at the end of each year are determined as follows:

Cost of property	$2,486
Direct costs	200
Investment to be recovered	$2,686

Annual lease payments:
$2,686 \div P\overline{3|}\,10\%$
$2,686 \div 2.4869$ $1,080

6. Net income over life of lease:

Lease payments ($1,080 × 3)	$3,240
Investment by lessor ($2,486 + $200)	(2,686)
Net income	$ 554

The entry to record the direct-financing lease is as follows:

Lease receivable ($1,080 × 3)	3,240	
Expenses (direct costs)	200	
Equipment		2,486
Cash		200
Revenue		200
Unearned interest revenue		554

As shown above, the initial direct costs are expensed and an equal amount of revenue is recognized at the date of the lease agreement. Since revenue equals expense, this initial entry has no effect on the lessor's income. The FASB permitted this procedure because it had been a common practice in the leasing industry and thus may have reduced the cost of implementing *Statement No. 13* for many lessors.

A schedule showing the amortization of the lessor's receivable balance appears in Exhibit 17–9. The beginning net receivable balance of $2,686 ($3,240 − $554) is the present value of the three $1,080 annual lease payments. This present value also represents the lessor's investment to be recovered—the cost of the property and the initial

EXHIBIT 17—9 LESSOR'S AMORTIZATION OF LEASE RECEIVABLE WITH INITIAL DIRECT COSTS

YEAR	(1) ANNUAL LEASE PAYMENTS	(2) INTEREST REVENUE*	(3) REDUCTION IN RECEIVABLE BALANCE†	(4) RECEIVABLE BALANCE (END OF YEAR)‡
				$2,686
1	$1,080	$269	$ 811	1,875
2	1,080	187	893	982
3	1,080	98	982	–0–
	$3,240	$554	$2,686	

* Previous balance in col. 4 times .10.

† Col. 1 minus col. 2.

‡ Previous balance in col. 4 minus col. 3.

direct costs. Given that the lease payments provide a 10 percent rate of return for the lessor, the same amount of net income is obtained each year as would be obtained if the lessor had recorded these costs in a separate asset account and had amortized these costs by the effective interest method.[22]

SALE-LEASEBACK TRANSACTIONS

A sale-leaseback transaction occurs when a company sells property and immediately leases it back from the purchaser. This type of transaction became popular after World War II as another means for the seller-lessee to obtain cash through off-balance-sheet financing, but still retain substantially all ownership rights associated with the property sold and leased back. In addition, a sale-leaseback transaction may provide tax advantages to the seller-lessee in the earlier years of the lease if the lease payments, which are tax deductible, exceed depreciation on purchased property and interest on debt, if any, incurred to finance the purchase. Many corporations, such as Ramada Inns, Inc., Crocker National Corporation (a parent of the fourth largest bank in California), and Dr Pepper, recently have engaged in sale-leaseback transactions.

To illustrate a sale-leaseback, assume that the Wilton Transit Authority (WTA) owns a railroad car with a book value of $600,000. The car has a remaining useful life of 10 years and no salvage value. At the beginning of 1987, WTA sells the car to Financial Services for $800,000 (its fair market value), then immediately leases it back under a 10-year noncancelable lease agreement at annual lease payments of $141,588, payable at the end of each year. Financial Services desires a 12 percent rate of return and thus determines the lease payments as follows:

$$\$800,000 \div P_{\overline{10}|\,12\%} = \$800,000 \div 5.6502 = \$141,588$$

Thus, it appears that WTA could record the sale as follows:

Cash	800,000	
Equipment		600,000
Gain on sale of equipment		200,000

In analyzing the substance of the transaction, however, compare WTA's financial position before the sale-leaseback with its financial position after the sale-leaseback. Before the transaction occurred, WTA had equipment with a book value and fair market value of $600,000 and $800,000, respectively. After the sale-leaseback, WTA has all rights to the services of the same equipment, cash of $800,000, and a noncancelable obligation to pay $141,588 each year for 10 years, which has a present value of $800,000. As a result, it appears that WTA has simply borrowed $800,000 and must pay it back over a 10-year period with interest of 12 percent.

A sale-leaseback is a financing transaction.

This line of reasoning underlies accounting for sale-leaseback transactions. First, when the sale-leaseback occurs, the "profit" or "gain" is deferred because the earnings

---

[22] When direct costs are involved in a direct-financing lease, the *interest rate implicit in the lease,* which equates the present value of the lease payments with the fair market value of the leased property, will be higher than the interest rate used by the lessor to calculate the required lease payments. The implicit rate in our example may be determined as follows:

$$\text{Fair market value of equipment} = \text{Lease payments} \times (P_{\overline{3}|\,i\%})$$
$$\$2,486 = \$1,080(P_{\overline{3}|\,i\%})$$
$$P_{\overline{3}|\,i\%} = 2.3018$$

Referring to Table D in Appendix 7–1, we find that the interest rate that corresponds to a present value factor of 2.3018 is between 12 and 16 percent.

process is incomplete and because of the interdependency between the sales price and the lease terms. That is, because the property is sold to the same party from whom it is simultaneously leased back, the terms of the sale and the terms of the lease usually are negotiated as a package. Second, the seller-lessee and the purchaser-lessor apply the *FASB Statement No. 13* lease criteria in classifying and accounting for the lease. Third, the seller-lessee amortizes the deferred gain over the life of the leased property or the lease term, whichever is appropriate. WTA's lease agreement satisfies both the third and the fourth capital lease criteria: the term of the lease exceeds 75 percent of the useful life of the property, and the present value of the lease payments exceeds 90 percent of the fair market value of the property. Therefore, the lease is a capital lease to WTA as seller-lessee. WTA would make the following entries on January 1, 1987:

Cash	800,000	
Equipment		600,000
Deferred gain on sale-leaseback		200,000
To record the sale and deferred gain.		
Leased property	800,000	
Lease liability		800,000
To record the capital lease.		

On December 31, 1987, WTA would make the following entries:

Interest expense (.12 × $800,000)	96,000	
Lease liability ($141,588 − $96,000)	45,588	
Cash		141,588
To record the first lease payment.		
Depreciation expense	80,000	
Accumulated depreciation		80,000
To record depreciation expense on the leased equipment, assuming straight-line depreciation.		
Deferred gain on sale-leaseback	20,000	
Depreciation expense		20,000
To reduce depreciation expense by the amount of the deferred gain recognized in 1987 ($200,000 ÷ 10).		

The effects of the above transactions would appear on WTA's 1987 income statement as follows:

Interest expense	$96,000
Depreciation expense ($80,000 − $20,000)	$60,000

and on its balance sheet as of December 31, 1987:

ASSETS			LIABILITIES	
Leased property		$800,000	Lease liability	$754,412
Less: Accumulated				
depreciation	(80,000)			
Deferred gain	(180,000)			
		$540,000		

Notice that amortizing the deferred gain as a reduction in depreciation expense on the income statement and offsetting the unamortized deferred gain against the leased property on the balance sheet reduce the depreciation expense and the book value of the leased property to the cost basis originally used by WTA.

If a sale-leaseback of *land* qualifies as a capital lease, amortization of the deferred gain is recorded as miscellaneous revenue. If the sale-leaseback transaction does not meet the criteria for a capital lease and therefore is classified as an operating lease, the seller-lessee amortizes the deferred gain as a reduction in rent expense related to the annual lease payments. For example, if WTA's lease had been an operating lease, WTA would make the following entries on January 1, 1987:

Cash..	800,000	
Equipment.......................................		600,000
Deferred gain on sale-leaseback		200,000
To record the sale and deferred gain.		

and on December 31, 1987:

Rent expense......................................	141,588	
Cash..		141,588
To record the lease payment.		
Deferred gain on sale-leaseback	20,000	
Rent expense.....................................		20,000
To amortize the deferred gain for 1987.		

Thus, the gain is realized as WTA uses the equipment over the lease term.

An anomalous situation arises in financial statement presentation of the deferred gain when the seller-lessee classifies the lease as an operating lease. While a deferred gain on a sale-leaseback suggests that a financing transaction instead of a sale has occurred, neither the equipment nor the obligation appears on the seller-lessee's balance sheet. Therefore, the deferred gain cannot be treated as as contra-asset to the leased equipment. In practice, the deferred gain is often reported as a deferred credit.

Occasionally a loss is incurred in a sale-leaseback transaction. A loss occurs if the fair market value of the property is less than the seller-lessee's book value of the asset sold and leased back. Losses are not deferred but are recognized in the current income statement.[23]

In the previous example and discussion, the seller-lessee sold and leased back the entire property over its remaining useful life and thus retained *substantially* all of the ownership rights to use the property. In many sale-leaseback transactions, however, property is sold and only a portion of the property is leased back. For example, in 1984, First National Bank of Boston sold its 37-story headquarters building for $365 million and leased back space to maintain its headquarters.[24] Also, a company may sell property and lease it back for only a *portion* of its useful life. Transactions of this kind are called **sale–partial leaseback** transactions. With two exceptions, any gain on a sale–partial leaseback should be deferred and amortized as previously illustrated.

According to *Statement No. 28,* the two exceptions are the following:

1. When only a *minor* portion of the property is leased back, the sale and leaseback should be considered separate transactions and accounted for separately. "Minor"

---

[23] This treatment is an example of conservatism and is consistent, conceptually, with lower-of-cost-or-market procedures for inventories and short-term marketable equity securities and with the treatment of losses on exchanges of nonmonetary assets.

[24] "Bank of Boston to Sell, Lease Back Its Headquarters," *The Wall Street Journal,* November 15, 1984, p. 10.

means that the present value of the lease payments equals or is less than 10 percent of the fair market value of the leased property. Any gain should be recognized in the income statement for the period that includes the lease inception date, because the sale represents the completion of an earnings process, rather than a financing transaction.

2. When the portion of the property leased back represents *more than a minor part but less than substantially all* of the ownership rights, the gain should be deferred and amortized in the manner previously illustrated. However, if the gain is greater than (*a*) the recorded amount of the leased property (if a capital lease) or (*b*) the present value of the lease payments (if an operating lease), that portion of the gain in excess of *a* or *b* should be recognized in the income statement. The remainder should be deferred and amortized.[25] This procedure is consistent with deferring a gain when substantially all of the ownership rights are retained by the seller-lessee. It prevents a deferred gain from exceeding the amount recorded as a capital lease or from exceeding the present value of the minimum lease payments if the lease is classified as an operating lease.

To illustrate a sale–partial leaseback, refer to the previous illustration and assume that WTA leased back the railroad car for only six months. The monthly lease payments were $11,478, payable at the end of each month. (These payments represent an assumed implicit rate of 1 percent per month.) The present value of these lease payments is $66,521 ($11,478 $\times P_{\overline{6}|1\%}$, which is $11,478 $\times$ 5.7955). This present value is less than 10 percent of the railroad car's fair market value of $800,000. Therefore, the leaseback is minor, and the gain of $200,000 ($800,000 less the $600,000 book value) would be recognized in WTA's income statement. Under these circumstances, the leaseback would be an operating lease and the monthly rentals would be debited to rent expense. The amounts of the $200,000 gain recognized and deferred under several alternative lease terms are as follows:

LEASE TERM	PRESENT VALUE OF LEASE PAYMENTS	PORTION OF $200,000 GAIN	
		RECOGNIZED	DEFERRED
8 months	$ 87,834*	$112,166	$ 87,834
15 months	159,144†	40,856	159,144
24 months	243,832‡	–0–	200,000

* $11,478 $\times P_{\overline{8}|1\%}$.

† $11,478 $\times P_{\overline{15}|1\%}$.

‡ $11,478 $\times P_{\overline{24}|1\%}$.

Notice that as a greater portion of the property rights is leased back, the more the transaction resembles a financing transaction; consequently, the recognized gain becomes smaller.

The Economic Recovery Tax Act of 1981 allowed companies with unusable investment tax credits and depreciation deductions to sell these tax deductions to companies that can use them to lower their taxable income. For example, IBM, which had large amounts of taxable income and an abundance of cash, acquired unused investment tax credits and

---

[25] ''Accounting for Sales with Leasebacks,'' *Statement of Financial Accounting Standards No. 28* (Stamford, Conn.: FASB, 1979). The 10 percent test for the first exception can be related to the 90 percent of fair value recovery criterion for a capital lease. Stated another way, when the present value of the lease payments exceeds 90 percent of the fair market value of the leased property, the lessee is presumed to have acquired substantially all of the ownership rights associated with the property.

EXHIBIT 17–10   LESSEE DISCLOSURES

Wickes Companies, Inc., and Subsidiaries

FROM SUMMARY OF SIGNIFICANT ACCOUNTING POLICIES

Leases—Leases that transfer substantially all the benefits and risks incident to the ownership of property are considered capital leases and are reflected as assets and liabilities in the balance sheet. Other leases are considered operating leases and rental payments are charged to expense.

FROM NOTES TO FINANCIAL STATEMENTS

LONG-TERM LEASES AND LEASE COMMITMENTS:

The Company is lessee under various long-term leases for land and buildings for periods ranging from one to forty years. The majority of these leases contain renewal provisions. Under certain conditions the Company may acquire leased properties. A majority of the store leases provide for a minimum rental plus a percentage of the store's sales in excess of stipulated amounts. Certain of the store leases are sublet to independent dealers. The majority of these subleases are for the same term as the Company's primary leases. In addition, the Company leases transportation, operating and administrative equipment for periods ranging from one to ten years.

Assets recorded under capital leases are included in property, plant and equipment as follows (in thousands):

	JANUARY 26, 1985	JANUARY 28, 1984
Buildings	$111,160	$117,624
Machinery and equipment	2,301	3,970
	$113,461	$121,594
Less accumulated amortization	(44,967)	(50,234)
	$ 68,494	$ 71,360

At January 26, 1985, future minimum lease payments were as follows (in thousands):

FISCAL YEAR ENDING	CAPITAL LEASES	OPERATING LEASES
January 1986	$ 12,825	$ 29,714
January 1987	12,842	27,270
January 1988	12,770	25,625
January 1989	12,604	23,076
January 1990	12,467	21,071
Later years	132,414	118,411
Total minimum lease payments	$195,922	$245,167
Less imputed interest	(109,276)	
Present value of net minimum lease obligations	$ 86,646	
Less current portion	(3,401)	
Long-term capital lease obligations	$ 83,245	

tax depreciation deductions from Ford Motor Company, which could not benefit from these deductions because of losses for tax purposes. These transactions were structured through sale-leaseback arrangements, whereby Ford sold equipment with applicable tax deductions and tax credits to IBM and then immediately leased back the equipment.

LEASE DISCLOSURES

Lease disclosures provide information about future cash flows.

In accordance with the full disclosure principle, *FASB Statement No. 13* requires various types of disclosures for lessors and lessees. These disclosures are designed to help users assess risk as well as the lessor's and lessee's future cash flows. The disclosure requirements also increase comparability among firms and thus increase the usefulness of financial reporting.

Lessee Disclosures

FASB Statement No. 13 requires lessees to disclose information related to leasing activities. For capital leases, the disclosures relate to additional information regarding capital leases and lease liabilities. For noncancelable operating leases, the disclosures relate to future lease payments to be made. Lessees should also provide a general description of leasing arrangements. Exhibit 17–10 illustrates these disclosures for Wickes Companies, Inc., and subsidiaries. Notice that these required lessee disclosures provide information about future cash outflows for minimum lease payments associated with both capital leases and operating leases. In addition, the disclosures also show the types of assets included in the capital leases account on the balance sheet.

Lessor Disclosures

For sales-type and direct-financing leases, the lessor is required to disclose information about the net investment in lease receivables and related income statement information. For noncancelable operating leases, the lessor must disclose information about equipment leased under operating leases and future lease payments to be received under operating leases. The lower part of Exhibit 12-8 on page 555 illustrates a noncancelable operating lease disclosure for a lessor. The lessor must also describe the nature of leasing arrangements. In summary, the required lessor disclosures are very similar to those of lessees.

CONTINUING LEASE CONTROVERSIES

While *FASB Statement No. 13* has resolved many leasing issues, others remain unresolved. Many lessees continue to structure lease agreements to avoid meeting the four capital lease criteria. Thus off-balance-sheet financing continues.[26]

Given the lease criteria which are set forth in *Statement No. 13,* it is often the case that capital leases to the lessor also are capital leases to the lessee. The reverse, however, is not necessarily true. A lease agreement may satisfy one or more of the first four criteria, and thus be a capital lease to the lessee, but may not satisfy both of the additional criteria for the lessor. As a result, a lease may be classified as a capital lease by the lessee and an operating lease by the lessor, in which case the leased property appears on both the lessor's and lessee's balance sheets.

One of the most controversial aspects of *Statement No. 13* has been its alleged economic effects on lessees. Many opponents of *Statement No. 13* have asserted that the *Statement* has increased the number of leasing arrangements that must be accounted for as capital leases, has increased the cost of financing for lessees, and has adversely affected lessees' security prices. An *FASB Research Report* issued in 1981 did not substantiate these assertions. This comprehensive research study examined preparers', users', and auditors' attitudes toward and perceptions of information required by *Statement No. 13.* Although the study concluded that *Statement No. 13* has not adversely affected lessee companies' security prices, the *Statement* apparently has had some effect on economic

[26] However, *FASB Statement No. 13* requires that information about noncancelable operating leases in excess of one year must be disclosed by the lessee. See Exhibit 17–10.

behavior. For example:

1. Many respondents indicated that new lease contracts were drafted and many existing contracts renegotiated to avoid capitalization.

2. There appeared to be an increase in assets purchased instead of leased.

3. In analyzing the financial statements of two identical companies, one of which capitalized its leases while the other did not, many bankers and analysts considered the company that did not capitalize its leases to be more profitable and to have stronger debt-paying ability.[27]

Thus, although *Statement No. 13* appears to have affected the behavior and perceptions of some participants in the *FASB Research Report,* the economic consequences have not been unfavorable in general.

Under present financial accounting and reporting standards for leases, the conceptual distinction between a capital lease and an operating lease is whether the lease transfers substantially all ownership risks and rewards from the lessor to the lessee. Many people believe that this all-or-nothing approach is not in the best interests of society, given the continuing lease abuses in practice. Those who hold this view believe that lease accounting should adopt a property-rights approach whereby the lessee would record the property rights acquired under a noncancelable lease as an asset, and the obligation incurred under a noncancelable lease as a liability, even though the lease agreement may not transfer *substantially all* ownership risks and rewards from the lessor to the lessee. Proponents of the property-rights approach maintain that it would preserve the conceptual aspects of capital leases vs. operating leases when substantially all ownership risks and rewards *are* transferred from the lessor to the lessee and would reduce the amount of lessee resources expended to circumvent the present *Statement No. 13* criteria. Thus, accounting abuses of leases would be reduced and society would be better served. Interestingly, *Accounting Research Study No. 4,* issued in 1962, also stated that noncancelable leases should be considered as transfers of rights to use property and made accounting recommendations similar to those above. Whether the FASB will adopt the property-rights approach remains to be seen. In any event, because many leasing issues remain unresolved, further changes in standards for lease accounting and disclosure are likely.

[27] "The Economic Effect on Leases of *SFAS No. 13:* Accounting for Leases," *FASB Research Report* (Stamford, Conn.: FASB, 1981).

SUMMARY OF IMPORTANT TOPICS AND CONCEPT APPLICATIONS

1. Under a lease, a lessor transfers property and the right to use it to a lessee and receives lease payments extending over a period of time.

2. Leases have become popular among lessees for tax reasons, for financing reasons, and perhaps for purposes of balance sheet "window dressing" (being able to keep debt off of the balance sheet).

3. From an accounting standpoint, the basic issue is whether a lease is a rental of property or a purchase of property by financing. Conceptually, if ownership risks and rewards are transferred from the lessor to the lessee, a **purchase transaction** (a **capital lease**) has occurred. If ownership risks and rewards are retained by the lessor, a **rental transaction** (an **operating lease**) has occurred.

4. Although the financial statement differences between a capital lease and an operating lease "wash out" over the term of the lease, the differences can be significant in the

short run. Therefore, proper classification of and accounting for leases are important in order to provide **relevant** and **reliable** information to financial statement users. Such information can assist them in **predicting, comparing,** and **evaluating cash flows** of lessors and lessees, which, in turn, affect cash flows to these users.

5. The four classification criteria for the lessee and the lessor are means of resolving the basic conceptual issue of whether ownership risks and rewards are transferred from the lessor to the lessee. The two additional lessor criteria are applications of the **revenue recognition criteria** presented in Chapters 2 and 6.

6. Lessee accounting for capital leases is based on the **pervasive measurement principle** of **recording exchanges at exchange prices at the exchange date.** Therefore, at least conceptually, the lessee records property acquired under a capital lease at its **fair market value.** The lease liability is recorded at the **present value of the minimum lease payments.**

7. Lessor accounting for capital leases is based on the same pervasive measurement principle as is lessee accounting. The lessor exchanges property for a lease receivable and measures and records the capital lease at the established **exchange price** (fair market value of the property, which equals the present value of the minimum lease payments). In a sales-type lease, a profit arises on the exchange because the fair market value (normal selling price) of the property exceeds the lessor's cost. In a direct-financing lease, there is no profit on the exchange because only a financing transaction has occurred.

8. In practice, such factors as unguaranteed residual value and lack of lessee knowledge about the implicit rate in the lease (the rate that equates the present value of the minimum lease payments with the fair market value of the leased property) may affect lessee and lessor accounting for a capital lease.

9. The following capital lease journal entries for the lessee and the lessor at the lease inception date illustrate how the recording concepts in 6 and 7 above and the factors referred to in 8 above are applied under *Statement No. 13:*

LESSEE

Leased property .... xx*		
Lease liability		xx*

LESSOR

Lease receivable .... xx†		
Property		xx
(Direct-financing lease)		

Lease receivable .... xx†		
Cost of goods sold .... xx‡		
Sales		xx§
Inventory		xx¶
(Sales-type lease)		

* Amount equals the present value of the minimum lease payments, which, if applicable, include either a bargain purchase option or a residual value guarantee; the discount rate used is the lower of (1) the implicit rate in the lease or (2) the lessee's incremental borrowing rate, subject to the fair market value limitation.

† Amount is the present value of the minimum lease payments plus the present value of any unguaranteed residual value.

‡ Amount is the lessor's cost minus the present value of any unguaranteed residual value.

§ Amount is the present value of the minimum lease payments.

¶ Amount is the lessor's cost.

10. Since a capital lease also represents a financing of property by the lessor for the benefit of the lessee, the periodic lease payments consist of interest and a recovery (reduction) of the lessor's (lessee's) investment (liability). The **effective interest method** is used to allocate the lease payments between interest and investment recovery (liability reduction) because it is more **representationally faithful** than alternative interest methods.

11. Lessor and lessee accounting under an operating lease is identical to accounting for rent revenue and rent expense. In addition, the lessor **matches,** through depreciation, the cost of the property transferred under the operating lease against rent revenue.

12. Initial direct costs incurred by the lessor are expensed under a sales-type lease and **matched,** along with the cost of goods sold, against sales. Under direct-financing and operating leases, initial direct costs are deferred and amortized over the term of the lease.

13. Sale-leaseback transactions generally represent lessee financing transactions. Gains on a sale-leaseback transaction are deferred, because of the nature of a sale-leaseback and because the seller/lessee's continued use of the property leased back does not complete the **earnings process.** The gains are subsequently amortized as a reduction in depreciation expense or rent expense, depending on whether the lessee classifies the leaseback transaction as a capital lease or as an operating lease. Occasionally, a sale may be accompanied by a leaseback of only a minor portion of the property sold. In these instances, the sale and leaseback must be evaluated separately.

APPENDIX 17–1

OTHER TECHNICAL ISSUES RELATED TO LEASES

The material presented in the body of this chapter covered the basic leasing issues and their applications in practice. This appendix deals with some additional technical aspects of leases. As you study real estate leases, subleases, and leveraged leases in the following pages, you should keep in mind that these topics are simply extensions of the issues discussed previously.

REAL ESTATE LEASES Lease agreements often cover land, land and buildings, part of a building—for example, a store in a shopping center—or land and equipment. Leases that cover these types of real estate, especially those that cover two properties jointly, present some additional accounting problems.

Leases Involving Land

In a lease of land, ownership risks and rewards are transferred from the lessor to the lessee only if the lessee obtains title to the land or can do so through a bargain purchase option. Therefore, from the lessee's standpoint, the lease is classified as a capital lease if either one of the first two lease criteria is met; otherwise, it is classified as an operating lease. From the lessor's standpoint, the lease is classified as a direct-financing or sales-type capital lease if title is transferred to the lessee *or* if the lease contains a bargain purchase option *and* if both of the two additional lessor criteria are met. Otherwise, the lease is classified as an operating lease.

Only the first two lease criteria apply to leases of land.

Notice that the third and fourth criteria are not applicable to leases involving land. Land does not have a limited useful life; therefore, the third criterion, which states that the lease term must equal or exceed 75 percent of the useful life of the property, is not meaningful. Furthermore, a lease that meets the fourth (90 percent of fair market value) criterion probably would also have to meet the first criterion. A lessee would not pay the fair market value of the land over a fixed lease term unless title to the land were obtained at the end of that term. In short, *FASB Statement No. 13,* for obvious and practical reasons, excludes the third and fourth criteria for leases of land.

Leases Involving Land and Buildings

When a lease agreement covers both land and buildings, problems arise in applying the third and fourth criteria because of the nature of land. In addition, allocation of the present value of the lease payments between the two types of property can become difficult. Classifying and accounting for leases that involve land and buildings are outlined in Exhibit 17–11.

As section I of Exhibit 17–11 shows, if a land and building lease meets either the first or second criterion, it is a capital lease, and once the lease payments have been allocated to land and buildings, subsequent accounting is straightforward. However, if title is not transferred and a bargain purchase option does not exist, the land element can never be accounted for as a capital lease unless the fair market value of the land is small (less than 25 percent of the total fair market value) relative to the fair market value of the combined property, in which case the land and building are treated as a single unit. This situation is covered in section II of Exhibit 17–11. If the land's fair market value is large relative to the fair market value of the combined property and if title is not transferred or if a bargain purchase option does not exist, the land element is classified as an operating lease. This situation appears in section III of Exhibit 17–11.

Leases Involving Equipment and Real Estate

Some lease agreements cover both real estate and equipment. The lessee and lessor should try to estimate the portion of the lease payments applicable to the equipment. Once this determination has been made, the equipment and real estate should be classified and accounted for separately as a capital or operating lease, according to the lease criteria.

Leases Involving Only Part of a Building

Many leases cover property that is part of a larger tract; for example, individual stores in a shopping center, or offices or floors in a commercial building.

From the lessee's standpoint, if the fair market value of the leased property is objectively determinable, the lease should be classified and accounted for according to the procedures outlined in Exhibit 17–11. If the fair market value is not objectively determinable and if the lease term equals or exceeds 75 percent of the estimated economic life of the building in which the leased property is located, the lease is classified as a capital lease. If this criterion is not met, it is classified as an operating lease.

The lessor should classify and account for the lease according to Exhibit 17–11 if the leased property's cost and fair market value are objectively determinable. Both cost and fair market value must be known before the lessor can determine whether to account for the lease as a direct-financing or a sales-type lease. If either the cost or fair market value of the leased property is not objectively determinable, the lessor should account for the lease as an operating lease.

SUBLEASES Occasionally a lessee may enter into a sublease with a third party, and the original lease between the original lessor and lessee may remain in effect. Alternatively, a new lease

EXHIBIT 17—11 ACCOUNTING FOR LEASES INVOLVING LAND AND BUILDINGS

I. Lease either transfers title or contains a bargain purchase option.
  A. Lessee classifies lease as a capital lease.
    1. Present value of minimum lease payments allocated to land and buildings in proportion to their fair market values.
    2. Building(s) depreciated over estimated useful life.
    3. Land not depreciated.
  B. Lessor.
    1. Direct financing or sales-type lease, as appropriate, if the two additional lessor criteria are met.
    2. Operating lease if two additional criteria are not met.

II. Lease neither transfers title nor contains a bargain purchase option, and the fair market value of the land is less than 25 percent of the total fair market value of the leased property.
  A. Lessee.
    1. Either the third or fourth criterion is met. Lease is classified as a capital lease.
      (a) Land and building recorded as a single unit.
      (b) Single unit amortized over the lease term.
    2. Neither the third nor fourth criterion is met. Lease is classified as an operating lease.
  B. Lessor.
    1. Either the third or fourth criterion and the two additional lessor criteria are met. The single unit (land and building) is classified as a direct-financing or sales-type lease, as appropriate.
    2. Lease meets neither the third nor fourth criterion, or does not meet the two additional lessor criteria. Lease classified as an operating lease.

III. Lease neither transfers title nor contains a bargain purchase option, and the fair market value of the land equals or exceeds 25 percent of the total fair market value of the leased property.
  A. Lessor and lessee consider land and building *separately* for purposes of applying the third and fourth criteria. The allocation of the minimum lease payments to the land and buildings is determined as follows:

Minimum lease payments applicable to both land and building . . . . $*xxx*
Less portion of minimum lease payments allocated to land (fair market value of
  land divided by the appropriate present value factor) . . . . *(xxx)*

Portion of minimum lease payments allocated to buildings . . . . $*xxx*

  B. Lessee.
    1. The building element of the lease meets either the third or fourth criterion. The building is accounted for as a capital lease.
      (a) The building element is amortized over the lease term.
      (b) The land is classified as an operating lease.
    2. The building element meets neither criteria. The lease is classified as an operating lease.
  C. Lessor.
    1. Building element meets either the third or fourth criterion and the two additional lessor criteria are met.
      (a) Building element classified as a direct-financing or sales-type lease, as appropriate.
      (b) Land element classified as an operating lease.
    2. Building element meets neither the third nor fourth criterion, or does not meet the two additional lessor criteria. Building element and land element classified as a single operating lease.

Source: *FASB Statement No. 13* (as amended), para. 26.

with a new lessee may replace the original lease, and the original lessee may or may not be secondarily liable. For example, because of inflation, intense competition, and other factors, many discount store chains that leased their buildings from real estate developers have closed unprofitable outlets and have been forced to sublease the property to other businesses.

If a new lease is substituted and the original lessee's primary obligation is canceled, and if the original lease was a capital lease, the original lessee must remove the leased property and lease liability from the accounts and recognize either a gain or a loss. Any secondary liability should be accounted for as a loss contingency. Assume, for example, that Milsap Corporation, the original lessee, enters into a sublease with Pride Company, that a new lease is substituted for the original lease, and that Milsap Corporation is released from its original obligation. Relevant data taken from the accounts of Milsap Corporation are as follows:

Leased property	$40,000	
Accumulated depreciation	(19,000)	$21,000
Lease liability		14,000

Milsap's entry to recognize the loss on the lease termination is as follows:

Lease liability	14,000	
Loss on lease termination	7,000	
Accumulated depreciation	19,000	
Leased property		40,000

The new lessee (Pride Company) would use the lease classification criteria in classifying and accounting for the new lease.

When the original lessee enters into a sublease by transferring the original lease to a third party, the original lessee generally remains liable under the old lease agreement. The original lessee becomes the sublessor and applies the lessor criteria in classifying and accounting for the sublease. The original lessee continues to account for the original obligation as before, making no accounting changes in regard to the lease, and the new lessee applies the lease criteria discussed in this chapter.

QUESTIONS

Q17-1. Define a lease.

Q17-2. The president of Sneak Corporation stated that his company would prefer to lease rather than purchase property in almost all instances. Explain why the president might have a preference for leasing.

Q17-3. **A)** For a lessor, distinguish between the following types of leases:

    1. Sales-type lease.

    2. Direct-financing lease.

    3. Operating lease.

    4. Leveraged lease.

B) For a lessee, distinguish between the following types of leases:

    1. Capital lease.

    2. Operating lease.

Q17-4. Conceptually, under what circumstances would a lease be equivalent to a purchase or sale of property?

Q17-5. *FASB Statement No. 13* sets forth certain criteria for classifying and accounting for leases as either capital leases or operating leases.

    1. List the criteria for the lessee.

    2. List the criteria for the lessor.

Q17-6. Generally, what items are included in the lessee's minimum lease payments?

Q17-7. Explain how a lessor would calculate the annual lease payments for purposes of a lease agreement.

Q17-8. From the lessor's standpoint, briefly discuss the accounting procedures for:

    1. A sales-type lease.

    2. A direct-financing lease.

    3. An operating lease.

Q17-9. From the lessee's standpoint, briefly discuss the accounting procedures for:

    1. A capital lease.

    2. An operating lease.

Q17-10. What is a bargain purchase option and how does it affect the lessee's minimum lease payments to the lessor?

Q17-11. **A)** What are residual values within a leasing context?
B) Under what circumstances would no residual value accrue to a lessor?
C) Distinguish between unguaranteed and guaranteed residual values.
D) How would a lessor consider residual value (either guaranteed or unguaranteed) in determining the annual lease payments to be paid by the lessee?

Q17-12. **A)** Define the following terms:

    1. Interest rate implicit in the lease.

    2. Incremental borrowing rate.

B) How are the above interest rates used by the lessee in accounting for capital leases?

Q17-13. Although *FASB Statement No. 13* requires the lessee, under certain circumstances, to use the incremental borrowing rate in discounting minimum lease payments, this rate is highly unlikely to be used in most instances. Explain.

Q17-14. Define and give some examples of initial direct costs of leasing.

Q17-15. Summarize the lessor's accounting for initial direct costs for the following types of leases:

    1. Sales-type leases.

    2. Direct-financing leases.

    3. Operating leases.

Q17-16. **A)** Discuss the nature of a sale-leaseback transaction.
B) Explain how the following parties account for a sale-leaseback:

    1. The seller-lessee.

    2. The purchaser-lessor.

Q17-17. Certain lease criteria and other data that pertain to a lessor appear below. For each independent situation, determine whether the lessor should classify the lease as a sales-type lease, a direct-financing lease, or an operating lease.

SITUATION	TITLE TRANSFERRED AT END OF LEASE TERM?	BARGAIN PURCHASE OPTION?	COLLECTIBILITY PREDICTABLE?	UNCERTAINTY REGARDING OTHER COSTS TO BE INCURRED?	DEALER PROFIT?
1	Yes	Yes	Yes	Yes	No
2	No	No	No	Yes	No
3	Yes	No	Yes	No	No
4	No	Yes	Yes	No	Yes
5	Yes	Yes	No	No	No
6	Yes	Yes	Yes	No	Yes
7	Yes	Yes	No	Yes	Yes
8	No	Yes	No	No	No

CASES

C17-1. LEASE CRITERIA, CLASSIFICATION, AND ACCOUNTING Milton Corporation entered into a lease arrangement with James Leasing Corporation for a certain machine. James's primary business is leasing; it is not a manufacturer or dealer. Milton will lease the machine for a period of three years, which is 50 percent of the machine's economic life. James will take possession of the machine at the end of the initial three-year lease and lease it to another, smaller company that does not need the most current version of the machine. Milton does not guarantee any residual value for the machine and will not purchase it at the end of the lease term.

Milton's incremental borrowing rate is 10 percent and the rate implicit in the lease is 8 1/2 percent. Milton has no way of knowing the implicit rate used by James. At either rate, the present value of the minimum lease payments is more than 90 percent of the fair market value of the machine at the date of the lease agreement.

Milton has agreed to pay all executory costs directly, and no allowance for these costs is included in the lease payments.

James is reasonably certain that Milton will pay all lease payments, and because Milton has agreed to pay all executory costs, there are no important uncertainties regarding costs to be incurred by James.

REQUIRED

    1. With respect to Milton (the lessee):
      a) What type of lease has been entered into? Explain the reason for your answer.
      b) How should Milton calculate the appropriate amount to be recorded for the lease or asset acquired?
      c) What accounts will be created or affected by this transaction and how will the lease or asset and other costs related to the transaction be matched with revenue?
      d) What disclosures must Milton make regarding this lease or asset?

    2. With respect to James (the lessor):
      a) What type of leasing arrangement has been entered into? Explain the reason for your answer.
      b) How should James record this lease and how are the appropriate amounts determined?
      c) How should James determine the appropriate amount of income to be recognized from each lease payment?
      d) What disclosures must James make regarding this lease?

(AICPA, adapted)

C17-2. ACCOUNTING FOR LEASES—LESSEE The Davids Corporation is a diversified company with nationwide interests in commercial real estate developments, banking, copper mining, and metal fabrication. The company has offices and operating locations in major cities throughout the United States. Corporate headquarters for Davids Corporation is located in a midwestern metropolitan area, and executives connected with various phases of company operations travel extensively. Corporate management is now evaluating the feasibility of acquiring a business aircraft that can be used by company executives to expedite business travel to areas not adequately served by commercial airlines. Proposals for either leasing or purchasing a suitable aircraft have been analyzed, and the leasing proposal is considered to be more desirable.

The proposed lease agreement involves a twin-engine turboprop Viking that has a fair market value of $900,000. This plane would be leased for a period of 10 years beginning January 1, 1987. The lease agreement is cancelable only upon accidental destruction of the plane. An annual lease payment of $127,600 is due on January 1 of each year; the first payment is to be made on January 1, 1987. Maintenance operations are strictly scheduled by the lessor, and Davids Corporation will pay for these services as they are performed. Estimated annual maintenance costs are $6,200. The lessor will pay all insurance premiums and local property taxes, which amount to a combined total of $3,600 annually and are included in the annual lease payment of $127,600. Upon expiration of the 10-year lease, Davids Corporation can purchase the Viking for $40,000. The estimated useful life of the plane is 15 years, and its salvage value in the used plane market is estimated to be $100,000 after 10 years. The salvage value probably will never be less than $75,000 if the engines are overhauled and maintained as prescribed by the manufacturer. If the purchase option is not exercised, possession of the plane will revert to the lessor, and there is no provision for renewing the lease agreement beyond its termination on December 31, 1996.

Davids Corporation can borrow $900,000 under a 10-year term loan agreement at an annual interest rate of 12 percent. The lessor's implicit interest rate is not expressly stated in the lease agreement, but this rate appears to be approximately 8 percent on the basis of the 10 net rental payments of $124,000 per year and the plane's initial market value of $900,000. On January 1, 1987, the present value of all net rental payments and the purchase option of $40,000 is $800,000 on the basis of the 12 percent interest rate. The present value of all net rental payments and the $40,000 purchase option on January 1, 1987, is $900,000 on the basis of the 8 percent interest rate implicit in the lease agreement. The financial vice-president of Davids Corporation has established that this lease agreement is a capital lease as defined in *FASB Statement No. 13*.

REQUIRED

1. What is the appropriate amount that Davids Corporation should recognize for the leased aircraft on its statement of financial position after the lease is signed?

2. Without prejudice to your answer in part 1, assume that the annual lease payment is still $127,600, that the appropriate capitalized amount for the leased aircraft is $1 million on January 1, 1987, and that the interest rate is 6 percent. How will the lease be reported in the December 31, 1987, statement of financial position and related income statement? (Ignore any income tax implications.)

3. Identify and explain the four criteria that differentiate a capital lease from an operating lease, from the lessee's standpoint.

(IMA, adapted)

C17-3. LEASE CLASSIFICATION AND ACCOUNTING—LESSEE On January 1, Morrow Painters, a lessee, entered into three noncancelable leases for new equipment: lease *T*, lease *E*, and lease *X*. None of the three leases transfers ownership of the equipment to Morrow at the end of the lease term. For each of the three leases, the present value at the beginning of the lease term of the minimum lease payments, excluding that portion of the payments representing executory costs, is 75 percent of the excess of the fair value of the equipment to the lessor at the inception of the lease.

The following information is peculiar to each lease:

a) Lease *T* does not contain a bargain purchase option; the lease term is equal to 80 percent of the estimated economic life of the equipment.

b) Lease *E* contains a bargain purchase option; the lease term is equal to 50 percent of the estimated economic life of the equipment.

c) Lease *X* does not contain a bargain purchase option; the lease term is equal to 50 percent of the estimated economic life of the equipment.

REQUIRED

1. How should Morrow Painters classify each of the three leases above, and why? Discuss your rationale for the classification of each lease.

2. What amount, if any, should Morrow record as a liability at the inception of the lease for each of the three leases?

3. Assuming that the minimum lease payments are made on a straight-line basis, how should Morrow record the minimum lease payment for each of the three leases?

(AICPA, adapted)

C17-4. LEASE CLASSIFICATION; AUTOMOBILE LEASE In early 1986, a Lincoln-Mercury dealer had the following advertising headline in a local newspaper: "Lease a cat with nine lives." The dealer was offering to lease a 1986 Mercury Cougar GS for $265 per month. The car was fully equipped with a V-6 electronic fuel-injected engine, air conditioning, electronic AM/FM four-speaker stereo, LCD digital speedometer, and other options. The information below is reproduced from the advertisement:

THE TERMS:

a) Lessee may have the option to purchase the car at lease end, at a price to be negotiated with the dealer at lease inception; however, lessee has no obligation to purchase the car at lease end.
b) Lessee is responsible for excess wear and tear.
c) Refundable security deposit, cash down payment, and first month's lease payment due at lease inception.

THE ARITHMETIC:

Monthly lease payment	$265
Number of months	48
Refundable security deposit	$275
Cash down payment	$1,500
Total amount due at inception	$1,775
Total amount of payments	$12,720
Total mileage allowed	60,000
Mileage penalty over 60,000	$.06 per mile

REQUIRED

1. Assume that you are a prospective lessee. Based on the above terms, discuss whether the lease is a capital lease or an operating lease.

2. Again, assume that you are a prospective lessee. The actual "window sticker" price of the Cougar was $14,065, which included a manufacturer's discount of $600. Assuming that your incremental borrowing rate was 1 percent per month and applying the *Statement No. 13* criteria, how should you classify the lease? You may want to consider the nature of a "window sticker" price in arriving at your answer. (*Note:* The factor for the present value of an annuity due for 48 rents at 1 percent is 38.3537.)

C17-5. SALE-LEASEBACK You are the controller for Red Rider Transport Company and have been approached by the company president, who has heard that a company can profit and increase cash flow by a device known as a sale-leaseback. Your company recently purchased 20 new tractor-trailers, and the president thinks that Red Rider would be better off by selling the tractor-trailers and leasing them back over their useful lives.

REQUIRED

Draft a response to each of the following questions presented to you by the president:

1. What is the nature of a sale-leaseback transaction?

2. How should any gain on a sale-leaseback be accounted for and reported?

3. Under what circumstances, if any, must Red Rider report the tractor-trailers and the related lease obligation on a sale-leaseback on its financial statements?

EXERCISES

E17-1. LESSOR'S DETERMINATION OF ANNUAL LEASE PAYMENTS Below are four independent cases that deal with the lessor's use of present value and other concepts in determining annual lease payments to be received at the end of each year.

	CASE 1	CASE 2	CASE 3	CASE 4
Cost of equipment to lessor	$54,000	$100,000	$75,000	$ 80,000
Fair market value of equipment	54,000	140,000	75,000	100,000
Residual value				
Guaranteed	—	9,000	—	4,000
Unguaranteed	—	—	10,000	6,000
Life of lease	10 years	8 years	6 years	15 years
Initial direct costs	$ 1,000	—	$ 2,000	$ 2,000
Rate of return required by lessor	12%	12%	10%	12%

REQUIRED

Calculate the lease payments for each case above.

E17-2. ACCOUNTING FOR CAPITAL LEASES On January 1, 1987, Thompson Corporation entered into a lease agreement with Sheree Drilling whereby Thompson would lease drilling equipment to Sheree for a period of four years. Details of the agreement, which qualified as a capital lease for both parties (sales-type to the lessor), were as follows:

Cost of equipment to Thompson	$25,000
Life of lease	4 years
Life of equipment	4 years
Annual lease payments (to be made at end of each year)	$10,000
Rate implicit in lease (and lessee's borrowing rate)	12%
Residual value	–0–

REQUIRED

1. Construct a lease receivable/payable amortization schedule from the above data.

2. In parallel columns, prepare all entries for the lessor and lessee for the first two years of the lease. Sheree uses sum-of-the-years'-digits depreciation on its other drilling equipment.

3. Prepare all balance sheet data related to this problem for both Thompson and Sheree on December 31, 1988.

E17-3. OPERATING LEASES Refer to the data in Exercise 17-2. Assume that the lease qualified as an operating lease rather than as a capital lease (even though the facts indicate otherwise). Thompson uses straight-line depreciation on all depreciable assets.

REQUIRED

In parallel columns, prepare all entries for the lessor and lessee for the first two years of the lease.

E17-4. DIRECT-FINANCING CAPITAL LEASES The following information is available for a truck lease that is classified as a direct-financing lease by the lessor and a capital lease by the lessee.

Cost of truck to lessor .... ?
Initial payment by lessee at date of lease agreement.................... $ 1,000
Present value of remaining 47 end-of-month payments of $1,000 discounted
    at 1% per month... $37,354

REQUIRED

1. Record the lease (including the initial receipt of $1,000) and the receipt of the lease payment at the end of the first month in the accounts of the lessor. The lessor records unearned interest revenue in a separate account.

2. Record the lease (including the initial $1,000 payment) and the $1,000 payment at the end of the second month in the accounts of the lessee. The lessee records the lease obligation net of the discount (the net method).

E17-5. BARGAIN PURCHASE OPTION Terms of a lease agreement between Paul Lessor and Dan Lessee are as follows (the lease is a capital lease to both parties):

Cost (and fair market value) of property to lessor.................... $25,000
Term of lease .... 20 years
Bargain purchase option (exercisable at beginning of fifth year) .... $ 4,000
Annual lease payments made at end of each year.................... $ 7,025
Rate implicit in lease 10%

REQUIRED

Prepare a lease receivable/payable amortization schedule that both parties could use in accounting for the annual lease payments.

E17-6. IMPLICIT RATE IN LEASE Conrad Office Supply has a computer for sale or lease. The cash selling price is $21,741. Under the lease terms, the lessee must sign a noncancelable lease and must make ten annual payments of $3,000 each, beginning on the first day of the lease term. Title passes to the lessee at the end of the lease term.

REQUIRED

Calculate the implicit rate in the above lease.

E17-7. RESIDUAL VALUE GUARANTEE A lessor and lessee enter into a lease agreement whereby a spacecraft with a fair market value of $65,000 will be leased for a period of four years at an annual rental of $17,239, payable at the beginning of each year. The lessee guarantees that at the end of the lease term, the spacecraft's residual value will be at least $10,000. The lessee is aware that a discount rate of 12 percent is used by the lessor to calculate the annual lease payments, although the lessee's incremental borrowing rate is 10 percent. This lease is a direct-financing lease to the lessor and a capital lease to the lessee, and the lessee plans to depreciate the spacecraft by the sum-of-the-years'-digits method. The spacecraft is transferred to the lessor at the end of the lease term.

REQUIRED

1. Explain why the lessee's incremental borrowing rate cannot be used as a basis for recording the capital lease.

2. Record the lease on the books of the lessor and lessee at the date of the lease agreement.

3. Prepare a lease receivable/payable amortization schedule for the lessor and lessee.

4. Prepare all necessary entries on the books of the lessor and lessee at the end of the lease term, assuming that the actual residual value of the spacecraft at that time is:
   a) $10,000.
   b) $2,000.
   c) $16,000 (the lease term provides that all gains shall accrue to the lessor).

E17-8. UNGUARANTEED RESIDUAL VALUE   Refer to Exercise 17-7. Assume that all of the facts in that exercise apply here, except that the residual value is not guaranteed by the lessee.

REQUIRED

1. Verify that the annual lease payments will still be $17,239.

2. Which discount rate will the lessee use to calculate the present value of the annual lease payments? Explain and support your answer with calculations.

3. Prepare a lease payable amortization schedule for the lessee (the lessor's schedule will not change from the schedule in Exercise 17-7).

4. Prepare any entries necessary for the lessor and lessee at the end of the lease term, assuming that the equipment's residual value is $10,000.

E17-9. SALES-TYPE LEASES; RESIDUAL VALUE   The following information relates to a sales-type lease for Maverick, Inc., a dealer-lessor:

Term of lease . . . . 10 years
Cost of leased property $125,000
Normal selling price of leased property $180,000
Residual value, end of lease term . . . .$ 20,000
Lease payments required at end of each year on basis of 12%
   interest rate . . . .$ 30,718

REQUIRED

1. Prepare the lessor's entry to record the sales-type lease under the assumption that the residual value is guaranteed.

2. Prepare the lessor's entry to record the sales-type lease under the assumption that the residual value is not guaranteed but the 12 percent interest rate still applies.

E17-10. INITIAL DIRECT COSTS   The following information pertains to a lease agreement between a lessor and a lessee:

Fair market value of equipment $5,045
Term of lease . . . . 3 years
Initial direct costs incurred by lessor (attorneys' fees, filing fees, and
   contract fees) . . . . $ 150
Discount rate to be used by lessor in calculating annual, end-of-year
   lease payments 10%

REQUIRED

1. Assume that the lease is a sales-type lease and that the lessor calculated the lease payments in order to recover the normal sales price of the equipment as follows:

$$\frac{\text{Sales price}}{P_{\overline{3}|\,10\%}} = \frac{\$5,045}{2.4869} = \$2,029$$

The leased property had a cost of $4,000 to the lessor. Prepare the lessor's entries to record the lease and the receipt of each year's lease payment.

2. Assume that the lease is a direct-financing lease and that the lessor calculated the lease payments in order to recover cost ($5,045) plus the initial direct costs over the lease term as follows:

$$\frac{\$5,045 + \$150}{2.4869} = \$2,089$$

Prepare the lessor's entries to record the lease and receipt of each year's lease payment.

3. Assume that the lease is an operating lease with annual payments of $2,100. Prepare the lessor's entries to record the initial direct costs, the receipt of each year's rental, and each year's amortization of the initial direct costs.

E17-11. LEASE CLASSIFICATION AND ACCOUNTING—LESSEE On July 1, 1987, Dale Mail Service leased a small jet airplane from Vortex Aircraft Corporation. The lease covered a 10-year period and required annual lease payments of $55,000, beginning on July 1, 1987. On July 1, 1987, the airplane had a fair market value of $400,000 and had an estimated life of 16 years. Dale could not determine the implicit rate in the lease, but had an incremental borrowing rate of 10 percent. Dale's fiscal year ends on December 31, and the company depreciates its other equipment on a straight-line basis.

REQUIRED

1. Determine whether Dale should classify the lease agreement with Vortex as a capital lease or as an operating lease.

2. Prepare the appropriate journal entry for Dale on July 1, 1987.

3. Prepare the appropriate journal entries for Dale on the following dates:
a) December 31, 1987.
b) July 1, 1988.
c) December 31, 1988.

E17-12. IMPLICIT RATE AND UNGUARANTEED RESIDUAL VALUE Refer to the data in Exercise 17-11. Notice that the estimated residual value of the aircraft leased by Vortex Aircraft Corporation to Dale Mail Service was not guaranteed by Dale at the end of the lease term.

REQUIRED

Calculate the estimated residual value, assuming that the implicit rate in the lease was:

1. 10 percent.

2. 12 percent.

E17-13. LEASE CLASSIFICATION AND ACCOUNTING—LESSOR Myron Company manufactures electronic synthesizers at a cost of $17,500 and sells them for $30,000. On January 1, 1987, Myron leased a synthesizer with an estimated useful life of 10 years to a rock band. The lease term covered an eight-year period. The annual lease payments were $4,785, payable at the end of each year, in addition to a $2,500 payment to Myron on the date of the lease agreement. At the end of the lease term, the band could purchase the synthesizer for $1. Collectibility of the lease payments was reasonably assured, and Myron expected to incur no other costs during the eight-year lease period, except for expenses of $1,500 in negotiating and closing the lease with the rock band. The implicit rate in the lease was 8 percent.

REQUIRED

1. How should Myron classify the lease with the rock band? Explain.

2. Prepare Myron's journal entry or entries on January 1, 1987.

3. Prepare all necessary journal entries for Myron Company on December 31, 1987, and December 31, 1988.

E17-14. SALE-LEASEBACK On January 1, 1987, Germain sold a concert grand piano to Nashville Piano Company for $32,000, then immediately leased it back under a 15-year noncancelable lease at an annual rental of $4,195, payable at the beginning of each year. Nashville used an implicit rate of 12 percent to determine the annual lease payments. The piano had a carrying value of $20,000 on Germain's books.

REQUIRED

1. Assume the lease qualifies as a capital lease and prepare all necessary entries for 1987 for Germain (seller-lessee) and Nashville Piano Company (purchaser-lessor). Germain will depreciate the piano on a straight-line basis over the lease term.

2. Assume that the lease is an operating lease (though the facts indicate otherwise). Prepare all necessary entries for 1987 for Germain and Nashville Piano Company. Nashville will depreciate the piano on a straight-line basis over its estimated useful life of 25 years.

E17-15. LEASE CRITERIA; INCOME DETERMINATION   The Morn Company leased equipment to the Lizard Company on May 1, 1987. At that time the collectibility of the minimum lease payments was not reasonably predictable. The lease expires on May 1, 1989. Lizard could have bought the equipment from Morn for $900,000 instead of leasing it. Morn's accounting records showed a book value for the equipment on May 1, 1987, of $800,000. Morn's depreciation on the equipment in 1987 was $200,000. During 1987, Lizard paid $240,000 in rentals to Morn, and Morn incurred maintenance and other related costs of $18,000 under the terms of the lease. After the lease with Lizard expires, Morn will lease the equipment to the Cold Company for another two years.

REQUIRED

1. On the basis of the above data, calculate Morn's income from this transaction before taxes for the year ended December 31, 1987.

2. On the basis of the above data, calculate the amount of expense incurred by Lizard from this lease for the year ended December 31, 1987.

(AICPA, adapted)

E17-16. SALE AND SALE–PARTIAL LEASEBACK   On January 1, 1987, Foster Corporation sold a machine to Scribner Company and simultaneously leased it back for two years. Pertinent data are as follows:

Estimated remaining useful life on 1/1/87	10 years
Sales price..	$120,000
Foster's carrying value on 1/1/87	$ 20,000
Monthly rental under leaseback, payable end of month	$ 2,000
Interest rate implicit in lease (per month)	1%

REQUIRED

1. Prepare Foster's entry to record the sale and leaseback on January 1, 1987.

2. Calculate Foster's monthly rental expense under the sale and leaseback.

3. Now assume that Foster leased back the machine for only six months (the other facts remain the same). Calculate the gain Foster should recognize on January 1, 1987.

E17-17. OPERATING LEASES   The Jackson Company manufactured a piece of equipment at a cost of $7 million and held it for resale at a price of $8 million from January 1, 1987, to June 30, 1987. On July 1, 1987, Jackson leased the equipment to the Crystal Company. The lease is appropriately recorded as an operating lease for accounting purposes. The lease is for a three-year period that expires June 30, 1990. Equal monthly payments under the lease are $115,000 and are due on the first of the month. The first payment was made on July 1, 1987. The equipment is being depreciated on a straight-line basis over an eight-year period with no residual value expected.

REQUIRED

1. What expense should Crystal record for the year ended December 31, 1987?

2. What income or loss before income taxes should Jackson record for the year ended December 31, 1987?

(AICPA, adapted)

E17-18. CAPITAL LEASES   The Truman Company leased equipment from the Roosevelt Company on October 1, 1987. For accounting purposes the lease is appropriately recorded as a purchase for Truman and as a sale for Roosevelt. The lease is for an eight-year period that expires September 30, 1995. Equal annual payments under the lease are $600,000 and are due on October 1 of each year. The first payment was made on October 1, 1987. The cost of the equipment on Roosevelt's accounting records was $3 million. The equipment has an estimated useful life of eight years with no residual value expected. Truman uses straight-line depreciation and takes a full year's depreciation in the year of purchase. The implicit rate of interest in the lease is 10 percent.

REQUIRED

1. What expense should Truman record for the year ended December 31, 1987?

2. What income or loss before income taxes should Roosevelt record for the year ended December 31, 1987?

(AICPA, adapted)

E17-19. INCOME EFFECTS OF CAPITAL VS. OPERATING LEASES   On January 1, 1987, Jasper Wholesale entered into a 15-year lease agreement to lease a movable storage building. The annual lease payments are $8,000, payable at the end of each year. Jasper should have accounted for the lease as a capital lease totaling $44,604, because title to the building passed to Jasper at the end of the lease term. Jasper, however, mistakenly accounted for it as an operating lease. The storage building has an estimated life of 20 years with no residual value and should have been depreciated by the straight-line method.

REQUIRED

Calculate the effect of Jasper's error for the years 1987 and 1988.

PROBLEMS   The problems marked with an asterisk (*) refer to Appendix 17–1.

P17-1. LEASE CLASSIFICATION AND ACCOUNTING   A lease agreement between a lessor and a lessee has the following terms:

Term of lease	12 years
Cost of leased property to lessor	$48,000
Normal selling price of leased property	$80,000
Useful life of leased property	20 years
Unguaranteed residual value of property, end of year 12	$25,000
Annual lease payments due at end of each year (including executory costs of $4,000)	$15,879
Interest rate implicit in lease and lessee's incremental borrowing rate	12%

Collectibility of the lease payments is reasonably predictable by the lessor, and the lessor will incur no additional unreimbursable costs subsequent to the date of the lease agreement.

REQUIRED

1. Determine how the lessor and lessee should classify the lease.

2. Prepare the lessor's and lessee's entries to record the lease at the beginning of the lease term.

3. Prepare all entries for the lessor and lessee for the first two years of the lease. (*Hint:* Remember that the lessor's interest revenue will not equal the lessee's interest expense, because the lessor considered unguaranteed residual value but the lessee did not.) The lessee uses straight-line depreciation. Ignore closing entries.

4. What entry would be made by the lessor at the end of year 12 if the leased property had a fair market value of only $16,000 at that time?

5. If the lessee's incremental borrowing rate were 16 percent and if he did not know the implicit rate, would the lease still be classified as a capital lease to the lessee? Explain and show calculations.

6. Assume that the lease qualified as an operating lease. Prepare the entries for the lessor and lessee for the first year. The lessor uses straight-line depreciation.

P17-2. DETERMINING ANNUAL LEASE PAYMENTS Bolivar Savings has been requested by Perkins Transit Corporation to purchase and lease a fleet of buses to Perkins. The cost of the fleet is $1.8 million. The lease term will be for a period of 10 years with annual lease payments due at the beginning of each year. Perkins Transit will guarantee a residual value for the fleet of $100,000 at the end of the lease term, although Bolivar Savings estimates that the residual value will be at least $200,000. Bolivar Savings will incur direct costs of $22,000 in negotiating and closing the lease agreement. Bolivar Savings desires a 12 percent rate of return on the investment. Perkins' incremental borrowing rate is 14 percent; the rate implicit in the lease is unknown to Perkins.

REQUIRED

1. Calculate the annual lease payments that Bolivar Savings would require.

2. Assume that the lease is classified as a direct-financing capital lease for Bolivar Savings and as a capital lease for Perkins Transit. Prepare the entries for both parties to record the lease and to record any adjusting entries at the end of the first year. Perkins uses straight-line depreciation on its other buses. The appropriate present value factors for $n = 10$ and $i = 14\%$ are as follows: present value of 1 = .2697; present value of annuity due of 1 = 5.9464.

P17-3. CAPITAL LEASES Kiger, Inc., was incorporated in 1986 to operate as a computer software service firm with a fiscal year ending August 31. Kiger's primary product is a sophisticated on-line inventory-control system; its customers pay a fixed fee plus a use charge for using the system.

Kiger has leased a large, BIG-I computer system from the manufacturer. The lease calls for a monthly rental of $30,000 for the 144 months (12 years) of the lease term. The estimated useful life of the computer is 15 years.

Each scheduled monthly rental payment includes $5,000 for full-service maintenance on the computer to be performed by the manufacturer. All rentals are payable on the first day of the month beginning with August 1, 1987, the date the computer was installed and the lease agreement was signed. The lease is noncancelable for its 12-year term, and it is secured only by the manufacturer's chattel lien on the BIG-I system. On any anniversary date of the lease after August 1992, Kiger can purchase the BIG-I system from the manufacturer at the then current fair market value of the computer.

This lease is to be accounted for as a capital lease by Kiger, and it will be depreciated by the straight-line method with no expected salvage value. Borrowed funds for this type of transaction would cost Kiger 1 percent per month. Following is a schedule of the present value of $1 for selected periods discounted at 1 percent per period when payments are made at the beginning of each period.

PERIODS (MONTHS)	PRESENT VALUE OF $1 PER PERIOD DISCOUNTED AT 1% PER PERIOD
1	1.000
2	1.990
3	2.970
143	76.658
144	76.899

REQUIRED

1. Why is the lease a capital lease to Kiger?

2. Prepare, in general journal form, all entries Kiger should have made in its accounting records during August 1987 in relation to this lease. Give full explanations and show supporting calculations for each entry. Remember, August 31, 1987, is the end of Kiger's fiscal accounting period and it will be preparing financial statements on that date.

(AICPA, adapted)

P17-4. BARGAIN PURCHASE OPTIONS Flanagan Corporation sells and leases oil tankers. The oil tankers normally sell for $20 million and cost Flanagan $16 million each. At the beginning of 1987, Flanagan leased one of these tankers to Texas Shipping Company with the following terms:

Lease term	10 years
Bargain purchase option (end of 1991)	$5,000,000
Estimated life of tanker	12 years
Lease payments (payable at beginning of each year)	$4,638,908
Interest rate implicit in lease (known to Texas Shipping)	16%
Estimated residual value	
End of lease term	$1,000,000
End of tanker life	$ 400,000

Flanagan expects to collect the lease payments in full from Texas Shipping and does not expect to incur any future costs related to the lease. The fiscal years of both parties coincide with the calendar year.

REQUIRED

1. Show how Flanagan calculated the annual lease payments.

2. Determine whether this lease is a capital or operating lease for each party, and if a capital lease for Flanagan, whether it is a direct-financing lease or a sales-type lease.

3. Give the necessary entries on the books of Flanagan and Texas Shipping on January 1, 1987.

4. Prepare a lease receivable/payable amortization schedule that would be suitable for both Flanagan and Texas Shipping.

5. On the basis of the amortization schedule in part 4, prepare all entries for Flanagan and Texas Shipping relative to any lease receivable/payable accruals and payments on December 31, 1987, and January 1, 1988.

6. Texas Shipping Company uses straight-line depreciation on other oil tankers that it owns. Calculate the annual depreciation expense on the leased oil tanker.

7. Assume that Texas Shipping Company exercised the bargain purchase option at the end of 1991. Prepare the entries to record the exercise on the books of Flanagan and Texas Shipping.

*P17-5. LEASES INVOLVING LAND AND BUILDINGS On July 1, 1987, Wesley leased a tract of land with a building to Dossey Corporation. The lease was for 12 years, and title to the land and building was to be transferred at the end of that time. The annual lease payments were $35,000 and were due on July 1 of each year, beginning July 1, 1987. The annual payments included $5,000 for taxes and insurance on the properties. The land had recently been appraised for $18,131; the building had a fair market value of $190,000 and a remaining useful life of 38 years from July 1, 1987, and was carried on Wesley's books at a cost of $114,000. Any salvage value on the building at the end of its useful life was expected to be approximately equal to the cost of its removal from the land.

Dossey had been paying 10 percent for money recently, and Dossey knew that Wesley used a 12 percent discount rate in determining the lease payments. Wesley was not able to make a reasonable prediction of collectibility because Dossey had recently experienced some difficulties in paying its creditors. Both Wesley's and Dossey's fiscal years end on December 31.

REQUIRED

1. Discuss the nature and classification of this lease agreement from the standpoint of both the lessor and the lessee.

2. Prepare all necessary entries for the lessee and the lessor on July 1, 1987.

3. Prepare all adjusting entries for both parties as of December 31, 1987. Straight-line depreciation is appropriate for the building.

P17-6. CAPITAL LEASES In 1986 the Agudelo Freight Company negotiated and closed a long-term lease contract for newly constructed truck terminals and freight storage facilities. The buildings were erected to the company's specifications on land owned by the company. On January 1, 1987, Agudelo Freight Company took possession of the leased properties. On January 1, 1987 and 1988, the company made cash payments of $1.2 million, which were recorded as rental expenses.

Although the terminals have a composite useful life of 40 years, the noncancelable lease runs for 20 years from January 1, 1987, with a bargain purchase option available at the expiration of the lease. Therefore, you have determined that the leased properties and related obligation should be accounted for as a capital lease.

The 20-year lease is effective for the period January 1, 1987, through December 31, 2006. Advance rental payments of $1 million are payable to the lessor on January 1 of each of the first 10 years of the lease term. Advance rental payments of $300,000 are due on January 1 for each of the last 10 years of the lease. The company has an option to purchase all of these leased facilities for $1 on December 31, 2006. It also must make annual payments to the lessor of $75,000 for property taxes and $125,000 for insurance. The lease was negotiated to assure the lessor a 6 percent rate of return.

REQUIRED

1. Prepare a schedule for Agudelo Freight Company to calculate the discounted present value of the terminal facilities and related obligation on January 1, 1987.

2. Assuming that the discounted present value of terminal facilities and related obligation on January 1, 1987, was $10 million, prepare journal entries for Agudelo Freight Company to record the following:

a) Cash payment to the lessor on January 1, 1989.

b) Depreciation expense for 1989 by the straight-line method and assuming a zero salvage value.

c) Accrual of interest expense on December 31, 1989, using the effective interest method.

(AICPA, adapted)

P17-7. LEASE CLASSIFICATION AND UNGUARANTEED RESIDUAL VALUE   On July 1, 1987, Haworth Corporation, a manufacturer and distributor of video cassette recorders (VCRs), entered into a lease with Boelte Tape Rentals, Inc. Boelte agreed to lease twenty VCRs for a period of six years beginning July 1, 1987. Other lease terms are as follows:

Annual lease payments beginning 7/1/87	$2,003
Manufacturing cost of each VCR	$ 300
Normal selling price of each VCR	$ 525
Estimated economic life for VCRs	9 years
Estimated residual value of each VCR at end of lease term (not guaranteed by Boelte).	$ 80
Implicit rate in lease (not known by Boelte)	10%

Boelte can borrow money at 12 percent and agrees to assume full responsibility for all repairs and maintenance of the machines. At the end of the lease term, Boelte will return the VCRs to Haworth. Since Boelte is a good credit risk, Haworth is certain to collect the lease payments and will not incur any additional costs after the date of the lease agreement.

REQUIRED

1. Determine how Haworth, the lessor, and Boelte, the lessee, should classify the lease.

2. Prepare all required entries for the lessor and the lessee on July 1, 1987.

3. Prepare all required entries for the lessor and the lessee on December 31, 1987 (both firms' fiscal year-end) and July 1, 1988.

4. Assume that when the VCRs are returned to Haworth at the end of the lease term, the residual value of each VCR is only $70. Prepare the entry for Haworth to record the receipt of the machines.

P17-8. UNGUARANTEED RESIDUAL VALUE; IMPLICIT RATE IN LEASE   Space Shuttle, Inc. (SSI), enters into a lease agreement with Murphy Industrial Complex (MIC) whereby MIC agrees to lease 35 shuttle flights from SSI. The cost and fair value of the shuttle is $20 million. The term of the lease is 10 years. MIC must utilize its 35 flights during this 10-year period and has exclusive use during this period. The estimated life of the shuttle is 100 flights, after which its residual value will be zero. At the end of the 10-year lease term, the estimated residual value is $9 million, which is not guaranteed by MIC. SSI sets the lease payments, payable at the beginning of each year, to earn a 16 percent rate of return. MIC's incremental borrowing rate is 10 percent and MIC may purchase the shuttle at the end of the lease term for $10 million. MIC agrees to pay all costs associated with operating the shuttle.

REQUIRED

1. Calculate the annual lease payments required by SSI.

2. What type of a lease is the above to SSI? to MIC? Explain and show calculations.

3. Prepare all necessary entries for SSI and for MIC (*a*) at the inception of the lease and (*b*) for the first year of the lease. MIC made three shuttle flights during the first year. Assume that the appropriate interest (discount) rate for MIC is 12.4 percent and that the company already has recorded operating costs.

P17-9. RESIDUAL VALUES On July 1, 1987, Fast Freight Forwarders leased a fleet of trucks from Lemon Rentals, Inc. Lemon had recently purchased the trucks from Nash Motor Division at a cost of $5 million. Terms of the lease agreement were as follows:

Length of lease	4 years
Semiannual lease payments, beginning 7/1/87	$ 645,224
Estimated life of trucks	6 years
Estimated residual value of trucks at end of lease term (guaranteed by Fast Freight Forwarders)	$1,200,000
Implicit (semiannual) rate in lease (known to Fast Freight Forwarders)	6%

The lessee agreed to assume full responsibility for periodic maintenance and service on the fleet. The full amount of the lease payments was expected to be collectible, and no other costs were expected to be incurred by the lessor. Both the lessor and the lessee have fiscal years that end on December 31.

REQUIRED

1. Determine how Lemon Rentals (the lessor) and Fast Freight Forwarders (the lessee) should classify the lease.

2. Prepare all necessary journal entries for the lessor and the lessee on July 1, 1987.

3. Prepare a lease receivable/payable amortization schedule suitable for the lessor and the lessee.

4. Prepare all necessary journal entries for the lessor and the lessee on December 31, 1987, and on July 1, 1988. Straight-line depreciation is appropriate.

5. At the end of the lease term, the actual residual value of the truck fleet was determined to be $900,000. On behalf of Lemon Rentals, Fast Freight Forwarders sold the trucks at this price and remitted the appropriate amount to Lemon Rentals. Prepare journal entries for the lessor and the lessee to record this transaction.

P17-10. LESSEE ACCOUNTING; RESIDUAL VALUE Refer to the lease data in Problem 17-9, but assume now that Fast Freight Forwarders did not guarantee the residual value, estimated to be $1.2 million at the end of the lease term.

REQUIRED

Repeat requirements 1, 2, 4, and 5 of Problem 17-9 for Fast Freight Forwarders, the lessee.

*P17-11. LAND AND BUILDING LEASES Gordon Discount Center entered into a lease agreement with DeKalb Construction Company for land, recently purchased by DeKalb at a cost of $85,000, and a building that had recently been constructed on the land. Terms of the lease agreement were as follows:

Date of lease agreement	January 1, 1987
Term of lease	15 years
Semiannual lease payments	$40,000, end of each 6 months
Life of building	18 years
Fair market value of land on 1/1/87	$140,000
Semiannual interest rate implicit in lease	6%

DeKalb Construction constructed the building at a cost of $375,000 and expects the residual value at the end of the lease term to be nominal. DeKalb is assured of collecting the lease payments and will incur no further costs related to the lease, as Gordon Discount Center will assume responsibility for maintenance, taxes, insurance, and other costs.

REQUIRED

1. Explain how the lease should be classified by DeKalb and by Gordon.

2. Prepare a lease amortization schedule for the first two years of the lease.

3. Prepare all entries for the lessor and lessee on January 1, 1987; June 30, 1987; and December 31, 1987. The building is to be depreciated by the straight-line method.

4. Assume that at the beginning of 1989 DeKalb agreed to transfer title to the land and building to Gordon under the following condition: For the building Gordon must pay to DeKalb the balance of the net lease receivable; for the land, $150,000 (the current fair market value), reduced by any principal amounts that would have resulted had the land portion of the lease been originally accounted for as a capital lease, with the 6 percent semiannual implicit rate used. Gordon agreed to this condition. Prepare the entries for both parties on January 1, 1989, to record the above agreement.

5. Calculate the amount of depreciation on the building to be recorded by Gordon for 1989.

*P17-12. CAPITAL LEASES FOR PART OF A BUILDING; SUBLEASES   On February 1, 1987, Computers-R-Yours, a national chain, signed a 10-year noncancelable lease with Wegehoft Developers for a 20,000-square-foot space in a shopping mall. Wegehoft determined the lease payments, to be made at the end of each year, as follows:

Fair market value of building (estimated economic life of 12 years)	$ 90,000
Fair market value of land	10,000
Total	$100,000
Less present value of unguaranteed residual value at a 10% discount rate ($30,000 × .3855)	(11,565)
Amount to be recovered through lease payments	$ 88,435
Annual lease payments:	
$88,435 ÷ $P_{\overline{10}|\,10\%}$	
$88,435 ÷ 6.1446	$ 14,392
Plus annual executory costs for maintenance, taxes, insurance	2,000
Annual lease payments, including executory costs	$ 16,392

Computers-R-Yours had an incremental borrowing rate of 12 percent and was not able to determine the implicit rate in the lease.

Computers-R-Yours, whose accounting year ends on January 31, occupied the building through January 31, 1990. On February 2, 1990, Computers-R-Yours ceased operations in the shopping mall. With the permission of Wegehoft Developers, a new lessee, Leroy's Discount Foods, assumed all rights and obligations under the original lease agreement between Computers-R-Yours and Wegehoft Developers. Computers-R-Yours was released from all obligations under the original lease agreement.

REQUIRED

1. Explain why the lease agreement between Computers-R-Yours and Wegehoft Developers is a capital lease to Computers-R-Yours.

2. Prepare Computers-R-Yours' entry to record the lease on February 1, 1987.

3. Prepare a lease payable amortization schedule for Computers-R-Yours for the first four years of the lease.

4. Prepare all entries required by Computers-R-Yours relative to the lease for the year ended January 31, 1988. The company uses straight-line depreciation on the building unit.

5. Prepare the entry required by Computers-R-Yours to record the sublease (lease termination) on February 2, 1990.

P17-13. SALE-LEASEBACK Ransom Construction Company sold a piece of construction equipment with a carrying value of $300,000 to Mowen Finance Company for $400,000, then immediately leased it back under the following lease terms:

Term of lease .... 8 years, beginning 1/1/ 87
Annual lease payments (beginning of each year)....... $68,264
Residual value guarantee, end of 1994.............. $50,000
Interest rate implicit in lease payments
(known by Ransom)........................... 12%

The lease qualified as a capital lease for Ransom and a direct-financing lease for Mowen Finance.

REQUIRED

1. Prepare the entries for Ransom Construction and Mowen Finance on January 1, 1987, to record the sale-leaseback.

2. Prepare all entries, including any adjusting entries, for both parties on December 31, 1987; January 1, 1988; and December 31, 1988. Ransom uses the double declining balance depreciation method.

3. At the end of the lease term, Ransom Construction sold the construction equipment for the benefit of Mowen Finance. Mowen agreed to share equally any proceeds in excess of the guaranteed residual value. Prepare the entries necessary for Ransom and Mowen at the end of the lease term, assuming that the actual residual value of the equipment at that time was:
   a) $30,000.
   b) $50,000.
   c) $70,000.

P17-14. CAPITAL AND OPERATING LEASES; UNEQUAL LEASE PAYMENTS At the beginning of 1987, the Dallas Cowgirls basketball franchise entered into a 12-year noncancelable lease with Texas Underwriters to lease the Queendome basketball arena, which had been constructed on land owned by the basketball franchise. Terms of the lease agreement were as follows:

Cost and fair market value of facility
   to Texas Underwriters $304,738
Annual lease payments to be made at
   the end of each year:
   1987, 1988, and 1989 .... $100,000
   Thereafter .... $ 50,000
Bargain purchase option (end of 1992) .... $ 20,000 (40% of estimated fair
                                                        market value of
                                                        $50,000 at the end
                                                        of 1992)

Interest rate implicit in lease and
   lessee's incremental borrowing
   rate................................ 16%

Collectibility of the lease payments was reasonably predictable. Texas Underwriters agreed to assume all risks and contingencies regarding upkeep of the facility and to protect the basketball franchise from obsolescence of the facility. This agreement was such that significant uncertainties existed in regard to future costs to be incurred by Texas Underwriters.

REQUIRED

1. Discuss the nature of this lease from the standpoint of the lessor and lessee.

2. If necessary, prepare a lease payable amortization schedule for the Dallas Cowgirls.

3. Prepare all entries for the lessor and lessee for 1987 and 1988. Straight-line depreciation is appropriate and the basketball arena has an estimated useful life of 20 years.

4. On December 31, 1992, the end of the lease term, the fair market value of the Queendome facility was $55,000, and the Dallas Cowgirls exercised the bargain purchase option. Prepare the entries to record the exercise on the books of both lessor and lessee.

18 PENSIONS

Vast numbers of people and substantial sums of money are involved in pension plans. At the end of 1984, almost $300 billion was invested in pension assets by the 200 largest U.S. corporations. Late in 1985, *Business Week* reported that among 200 of the nation's largest corporations, total pension benefits based on employee services rendered up to the end of the most recent fiscal year ranged up to $22 billion (for General Motors) and were as much as 7.4 times greater than corporate net worth (for International Harvester). For the entire group of 200 largest corporations, total pension benefits were reportedly equal to more than one-third of corporate net worth. Pension expense in 1984 was reported to have been as much as $1.6 billion (for General Motors).[1] Pension plans continue to grow at such a rate that, in both absolute and relative dollar terms, pension assets, pension obligations, and annual pension expense make accounting for and reporting on private pension plans very significant. Moreover, pension accounting involves many of the conceptual aspects of financial accounting and reporting. Both matching and expense recognition, for example, bear on the issue of when the cost of a pension plan should be recorded as an expense. Also, disagreement about the essential characteristics of a liability underlies the accounting profession's controversy about the amount of pension liability that should be reported by an employer who sponsors a pension plan.

A **pension plan** is essentially an arrangement under which a government unit or a private entity provides income to retired workers. Sometimes pension coverage is required by law, sometimes it is established by an agreement between employer and employees. **Public pension plans** are established by law and are sponsored by a government unit, such as the federal government. The largest and best known public pension plan is Federal Old-Age, Survivors, and Disability Insurance, which is the national program of social insurance. This plan was created by the Social Security Act of 1935 and is generally known as "social security." **Private,** or employer-sponsored, **pension plans,** on the other hand, exist largely at the discretion of the employers who sponsor the plans, and are established by agreements between employers and employees. Private pension plans and related accounting and reporting issues are the subject of this chapter, which is divided into four sections:

[1] "The Huge Pension Overflow Could Make Waves in Washington," *Business Week,* August 12, 1985, pp. 71–75.

PRIVATE PENSION PLANS IN THE UNITED STATES

Private pension plans began to appear in the United States in the late 1800s, but they have become significant sources of financial support for retirees only since about 1950. Under early private pension plans the payment of retirement benefits to employees was regarded by both the employer and employees as a gratuity for long and faithful service. Benefit payments usually were discretionary, and the employer had no legal obligation to provide retirement income. By the late 1940s, organized labor began to demand pensions in lieu of wage increases, and in 1949 a federal court ruled that pensions, like wages, are a bargainable issue.[2] Today pension benefits are an important element in the total compensation package of many employees.

In 1974 Congress passed the Employee Retirement Income Security Act (ERISA) with the intention of strengthening and encouraging the growth of private pension plans in the United States. Before ERISA, statutory law governing pension plans was primarily set forth in the Internal Revenue Code. The Code was essentially silent on such matters as standards for employee participation in the plan, vesting of pension benefits, and funding of the pension obligation. ERISA not only established standards in these and other areas, but also amended the Internal Revenue Code of 1954 by adding those standards to the Code. ERISA applies to virtually all private pension plans in the United States, but does not apply to government, church, or certain special-purpose plans.

In addition to establishing minimum funding, participation, and vesting requirements for pension plans, ERISA created a new agency, the Pension Benefit Guaranty Corporation (PBGC). The PBGC is responsible for ensuring payment of minimum benefits by defined benefit pension plans and for administering defined benefit plans that have been terminated. The PBGC guarantees the payment of covered vested benefits under a defined benefit pension plan in the event of the termination of the plan. (Defined benefit pension plans are described on page 822.)

ACCOUNTING PRONOUNCEMENTS ON PRIVATE PENSION PLANS

From 1966 to 1986, *Accounting Principles Board Opinion No. 8,* "Accounting for the Cost of Pension Plans," served as the primary source of GAAP related to accounting for pension plans by employers. In 1974, however, the FASB added two pension projects to its agenda—(1) accounting and reporting by employee benefit plans and (2) employers' accounting for pensions—in response to the passage of ERISA and to criticisms concerning deficiencies in *APB Opinion No. 8*. Critics of *Opinion No. 8* asserted that pension costs were not comparably measured from company to company and often not even from period to period for the same company, and that *Opinion No. 8* did not adequately portray the effect of a pension plan on a company. There was concern about the ability of users of financial reports to understand and assess net periodic pension cost. Because a variety of measurement methods and assumptions were used under *Opinion No. 8*, financial state-

[2] Inland Steel Company v. National Labor Relations Board, 170 F. 2d 247, 251 (1949).

ment users could not be certain about the funded status of the employer's obligation. Concerns were expressed about the reporting of both unfunded pension obligations and excess pension plan assets.

The first of the two FASB pension projects led to the issuance of *Statement of Financial Accounting Standards No. 35,* "Accounting and Reporting by Defined Benefit Plans," in March 1980. *Statement No. 35,* for the first time, addressed financial reporting by the pension plan itself. We briefly present the more important aspects of *Statement No. 35* in Appendix 18–1.

Although the FASB published some interim *Statements,* the central portion of the second pension project initiated in 1974 ultimately led to the issuance of *Statement No. 87,* "Employers' Accounting for Pensions," and *Statement No. 88,* "Employers' Accounting for Settlements and Curtailments of Defined Benefit Pension Plans and for Termination Benefits." Although pension accounting remains in a transitional stage, these two *Statements* now form the basis for GAAP related to accounting for pension plans by employers and underlie most of the content of this chapter.

The FASB's primary motivation in issuing *Statement No. 87* was to improve the decision usefulness of financial statements of companies that sponsor pension plans for their employees. In its effort to obtain more useful financial reporting, the FASB made three basic changes in pension accounting in *Statement No. 87:*

1. The *Statement* requires a standardized method for measuring net periodic pension cost. This requirement is intended to improve comparability and understandability, as the compensation cost of an employee's pension is recognized over that employee's approximate service period, and that cost is related more directly to the terms of the pension plan.

2. The *Statement* requires immediate recognition of a liability (defined in the *Statement* as the minimum liability) when the accumulated benefit obligation exceeds the fair value of pension plan assets.

3. The *Statement* requires expanded disclosures intended to provide more complete and more current information on employer-sponsored pension plans.

Statement No. 88 is closely related to *Statement No. 87.* The Board decided to issue a separate *Statement* on an employer's accounting for a settlement of a pension obligation, a curtailment of a defined benefit pension plan, or termination benefits so that both the Board and the public could identify and fully consider the underlying issues.

CHARACTERISTICS OF PRIVATE PENSION PLANS

If both the employer and the employees make contributions to the pension fund, whether the employees' contributions are voluntary or required, the pension plan is a **contributory pension plan.** Under a contributory plan the amount contributed by the employees may differ from the amount contributed by the employer. Many private pension plans are **noncontributory,** which means that employees do not contribute to the pension fund. In this chapter, our discussion will focus on *employer* accounting and reporting for noncontributory pension plans for the sake of simplicity and because this text is concerned with financial accounting and reporting by business enterprises—in this case, the employer.

Employees retain a claim to their own contributions to the pension fund under nearly all contributory pension plans. Employees' rights to the employer's contributions to the pension fund, under either a contributory or a noncontributory pension plan, are prescribed by the vesting provisions of the pension plan. An employee's right to receive earned (or accumulated) pension benefits that are funded by employer contributions to the pension fund is **fully vested** when the employee's right is no longer contingent on continued employment by that particular employer. If the employee's right to pension benefits is only **partially vested,** then the employee will lose any nonvested claim to pension benefits if employment with that particular employer should cease. For example, if Joanna Smith's right to pension benefits under a noncontributory pension plan is 40 percent vested at the time she leaves her job with her sponsoring employer, then she will lose her nonvested right to 60 percent of her accumulated pension benefits.

There are essentially two types of private pension plans: defined contribution plans and defined benefit plans. In a **defined contribution plan,** the employer promises to make specified contributions to the pension fund, but there is no specification of the amount of pension benefits that will be paid to retired employees. Employer contributions usually are determined by applying a specific rate against a variable such as labor hours worked or wages earned, or by a formula applied to defined earnings of the employer. An example of a defined contribution pension plan is TIAA-CREF, a retirement benefit program in which faculty and staff members of many United States colleges and universities participate. In this program, the university (employer) contributes a specified amount (say, 10 percent of the employees' academic-year or annual salary) to TIAA-CREF on behalf of each faculty or staff member (employee). The amount that a particular employee will receive at retirement depends on (1) the funds in TIAA-CREF on his or her behalf at the time of retirement, (2) the retirement age, and (3) the salary level of that employee. Defined contribution plans are often encountered in nonprofit organizations and professional associations.

With a defined contribution pension plan, the amount of pension benefits ultimately paid to retired employees depends on how well the pension fund's assets are managed. Since pension benefits are limited to contributions to the pension fund plus earnings on the fund's assets, neither accounting for employer contributions nor accounting for the present value of accumulated pension benefits presents special problems when there is a defined contribution plan. Periodic pension expense simply equals the amount the employer contributes to the pension fund during the period. *Throughout the remainder of this chapter our discussion either assumes or explicitly states that the pension plan in question is a defined benefit pension plan.*

In a **defined benefit pension plan,** the employer promises to make benefit payments in specified amounts during retirement years, but there is no specification of the amount that the employer will contribute to the pension fund. It is necessary only that the employer meet the minimum contribution requirements of ERISA, and that the employer's contributions plus the investment earnings of the pension fund are sufficient to make the specified benefit payments to retired employees when those payments are due. Defined benefit plans are more common than defined contribution plans because defined benefit plans provide employees with greater assurance regarding retirement benefits.

As an example of a defined benefit plan, assume that the employer promises to pay an individual employee an annual retirement benefit equal to 1.5 percent for each year of employee service that qualifies for pension credit, multiplied by the simple average of the employee's five highest annual salaries. The formula for this defined benefit plan is:

$$\text{Pension benefit for each year of retirement} = .015 \times n \times \text{Average of five highest annual salaries}$$

where n is the number of full years of the employee's service that qualify for pension plan coverage. In the case of an employee who has 10 years of employment that qualify for pension credit, and whose five highest salaries during those 10 years average $50,000, the pension benefit that the employee can expect to receive during each year of retirement is:

$$\text{Pension benefit for each year of retirement} = .015 \times 10 \text{ years} \times \$50,000$$

$$= \underline{\$7,500}$$

A **funded pension plan** is one in which the employer sets aside funds for future pension benefits by making payments to some *independent* funding agent, such as a bank or insurance company. The funding agent then invests the employer's payments in stocks, bonds, and other income-yielding assets. An **unfunded pension plan** is one in which the pension fund remains under the control of the sponsoring employer, rather than under the control of an independent funding agent. The employer's act of making cash contributions to an independently controlled pension fund is called **funding** the pension plan.

A defined benefit pension plan controlled by an independent funding agent may be fully funded or partially funded. When a defined benefit plan is fully funded, the employer's cash contributions to the pension fund plus earnings on the fund's assets are at least equal to the present value of accumulated pension benefits (i.e., the present value of all expected future pension benefits earned through employee services to date). If the amount in the pension fund is less than the present value of accumulated pension benefits, the pension plan is partially funded. It is not necessary that a pension plan be fully funded, but it is necessary that pension fund assets be sufficient to meet current pension benefit payments. And, as we shall discuss later, the employer needs to know the present value of accumulated pension benefits because it is a measure of the employer's obligation to provide funds to cover the future pension benefits that employees have earned through their services to date.

A TYPICAL DEFINED BENEFIT PENSION PLAN ARRANGEMENT

A typical defined benefit pension plan arrangement includes an independent funding agent who receives the cash contributions to the fund, manages the pension fund assets, and pays pension benefits. Defined benefit private pension plans therefore usually involve three parties: (1) the employer, who is the plan sponsor; (2) the funding agent; and (3) the employees. The interrelationships and roles of these three parties are shown in Exhibit 18–1.

EXHIBIT 18–1 INTERRELATIONSHIPS OF EMPLOYER, FUNDING AGENT, AND EMPLOYEES: DEFINED BENEFIT PENSION PLAN

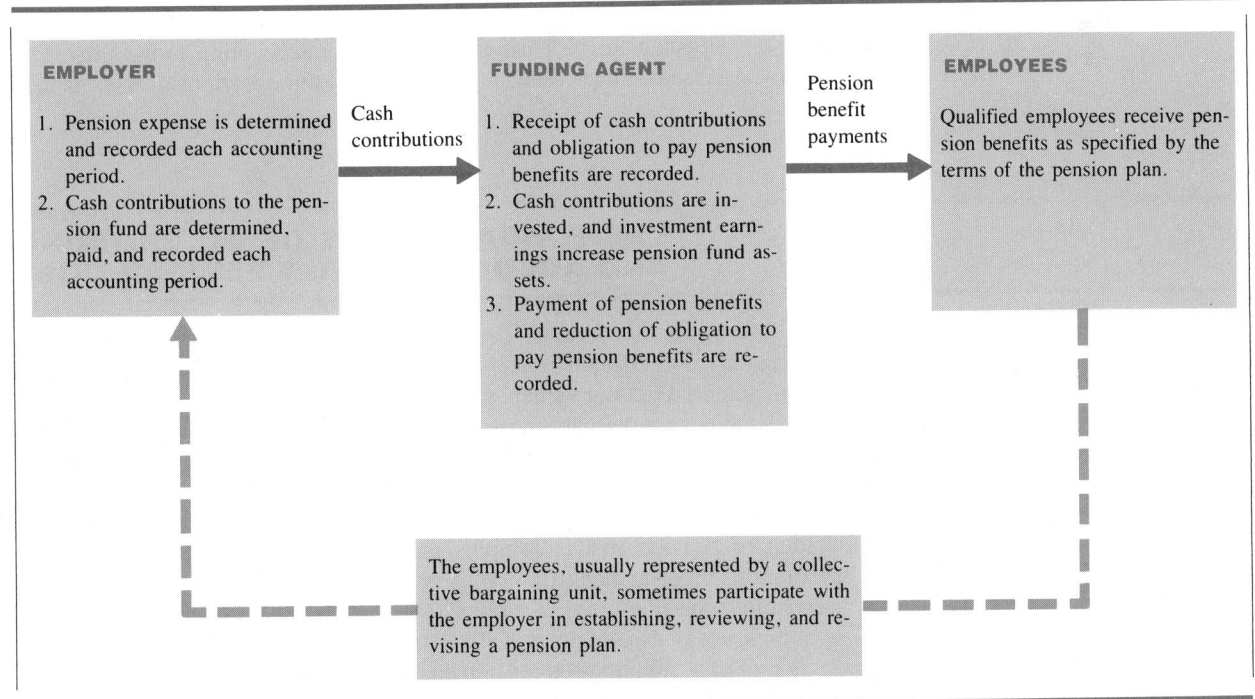

OBJECTIVES IN ACCOUNTING FOR DEFINED BENEFIT PENSION PLANS

In the long run, pension expense equals cash disbursed for pension benefits.

In Chapter 2 we pointed out that, with a given capital maintenance concept and over long periods of time, a company's income equals its net cash flows. Applied to pensions and pension expense, this concept means that, *in the long run, a company's total pension expense must equal the total cash contributions it makes to its pension fund* (or cash payments to its employees for pension benefits, in the absence of a pension fund). As with many other revenues and expenses, however, this equality seldom holds in the short run. As we shall see later, pension cost determination incorporates many estimates of variables and assumptions about future events. Because lengthy periods of time are involved, actual variables and events may not be the same as estimates and assumptions.

Few accounting topics incorporate such pervasive theoretical issues and concepts as does accounting for pensions. For example, the concepts of *present value, asset and liability definition and measurement, recognition versus disclosure, matching,* and *classification and aggregation* all are relevant to accounting for pensions. In addition, because of the importance of pension benefits and the sheer magnitude of pension funds, concerns about the economic consequences of accounting standards as well as political compromises have influenced the standards established for pension accounting.

Acknowledging these issues, the FASB stressed several objectives in its work leading to *Statement Nos. 87* and *88:*

FASB objectives in establishing pension accounting standards.

1. To provide a more *representationally faithful* measure of net periodic pension cost in the sense that it reflects the terms of the pension plan and better approximates the cost of an employee's pension over that employee's service period.

2. To provide a more *understandable,* more *comparable,* and therefore more *useful* measure of net periodic pension cost.

3. To provide pension *disclosures* that help financial statement users to understand the full extent and effect of an employer's commitment to provide pension benefits and to make related financial arrangements.

4. To improve *reporting* of the employer's resources and claims against those resources (financial position).

These objectives are reflected in the pension calculations, accounting procedures, and disclosures that are described and discussed in the remaining three sections of this chapter.

THE FUNDAMENTALS OF DETERMINING AND ACCOUNTING FOR PENSION COST

In this section we discuss and illustrate the concepts of pension accounting and four of the components of pension cost. Pension *concepts* that are discussed and illustrated include actuarial valuation, actuarial present values, projected pension benefits, accumulated pension benefits, projected benefit obligation, pension cost or pension expense, discount rate, rate of return on plan assets, and prior service cost. The four *components* of pension cost that are discussed and illustrated in this section are service cost, interest on the projected benefit obligation, earnings on plan assets, and amortization of prior service cost.

Determination of pension cost is complex and involves several economic issues. During its deliberations on accounting for pension costs, the FASB was faced with political as well as economic considerations. As a result, *Statement No. 87* requirements reflect the need for compromise and sometimes deviate from theoretically sound conclusions. During our discussion of accounting for pension costs, we often will compare what theory might suggest with the accounting requirements of *Statement No. 87.*

Our discussion begins with a fairly simple example, which is subsequently modified in a series of case illustrations to incorporate additional complexities and considerations. This incremental approach should allow you to see how each issue discussed affects calculation of and accounting for pension cost. Before we begin our case illustrations, however, it is important that you understand actuarial valuation and some of the fundamental concepts underlying accounting for pension cost.

ACTUARIAL ASSUMPTIONS AND VALUATION

Determining pension cost requires present value techniques and actuarial assumptions.

An actuarial valuation is only an estimate.

Determination of the employer company's cost of providing pension benefits to employees is based on the use of present value techniques and requires that assumptions be made about such factors as interest rates, mortality rates, employee turnover, future salary levels, and inflationary trends. Pension cost often is determined by **actuaries,** who are individuals trained in the use of present value techniques and in the making of reasonable assumptions about future events, such as the events listed above. The calculation of pension amounts based on present value techniques and on reasonable assumptions about the future is called an **actuarial valuation,** and amounts so calculated are called **actuarial present values.**[3] Because actual future events may not correspond to the assumptions incorporated in the actuarial valuation, an actuarial present value calculated at any point in time is only an estimate.

To illustrate an actuarial valuation, we shall use the data given in Exhibit 18–2 for the Akins Corporation's defined benefit pension plan and one of its employees, Bill

[3] An actuarial present value not only considers the time value of money, but also reflects the probabilities associated with outcomes of actuarial assumptions. We often use the term ''present value'' rather than ''actuarial present value'' in our discussion.

EXHIBIT 18–2   DATA FOR AKINS CORPORATION'S PENSION PLAN AND EMPLOYEE BILL HARDY

PENSION PLAN

1. A defined benefit, noncontributory plan.

2. Retirement benefits are paid at the *end* of each retirement year.

3. No credit toward pension benefits is given for employee service prior to inception of the pension plan.

4. Assumed discount rate is 8%.

5. The pension plan pays annual retirement benefits equal to 1.5% for each year of service that qualifies for pension credit, multiplied by the simple average of the employee's five highest annual salaries. Hence,

$$\begin{matrix} \text{Pension benefit} \\ \text{received each year} \\ \text{of retirement} \end{matrix} = .015 \times n \times \begin{matrix} \text{Average of five} \\ \text{highest annual} \\ \text{salaries} \end{matrix}$$

where n equals the number of years of service that qualify for pension credit.

EMPLOYEE (BILL HARDY)

1. Will retire at age 65.

2. Has an expected retirement period of 15 years.

3. Is 55 years old at the time the pension plan becomes effective.

4. Was employed by Akins Corporation for 20 years before inception of the pension plan.

5. Average of five highest annual salaries before retirement is expected to be $65,000.

Hardy. The data in Exhibit 18–2 and in subsequent illustrations apply to a single employee in order to minimize complexity. In reality, an employer's pension calculations apply to large groups of employees and thus are more complex than the calculations shown in this chapter. In addition, many medium-sized and large firms have more than one pension plan, such as one plan for salaried employees and another for hourly workers.

The relationship between the Akins Corporation's defined benefit pension plan and the employment/retirement life of Bill Hardy can be diagramed as follows:

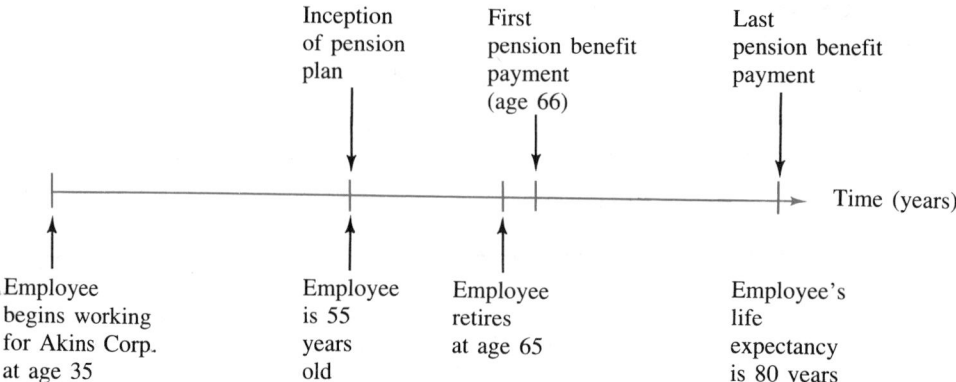

ACCUMULATED BENEFITS VERSUS PROJECTED BENEFITS

Pension benefits based on future compensation levels are called projected benefits.

Depending on the purpose for which the calculation is made, calculation of pension benefits may be based on either *current compensation levels* or *future compensation levels*. The benefit formula for Bill Hardy is based on the average of his five highest annual salaries. Calculation of pension benefits based on the average of Hardy's five highest annual salaries to be received at *any time before retirement* (including estimated future salaries) is called calculation of **projected benefits.** On the other hand, calculation of Hardy's pension benefits based on the average of his five highest actual salaries received *to date,* rather than on the average of his five highest salaries to be received at any time, is called calculation of **accumulated benefits.**

Which of these two methods of calculating pension benefits is more useful in determining pension cost for accounting purposes? This is a difficult question to answer because of the trade-off between relevance and reliability. At any given point in time, the calculation of accumulated benefits is *more reliable* than the calculation of projected benefits because accumulated benefits are based on known salaries to date. However, a projected benefit calculation may be considered to be *more relevant* because it encompasses estimates of future salaries, which affect *future cash flows.* In addition, if the pension benefits calculation is based on future salary levels, the result may be *more representationally faithful* because, under the *going concern assumption,* it is presumed that benefits paid will be based on salaries up to the retirement date. *Statement No. 87 requires that the cost of pension benefits be based on future salary levels if the pension benefit formula incorporates future salary levels.* Thus, Hardy's pension benefits will be based on future salary levels, because Akins's plan benefit formula incorporates future salary levels.

Calculating Projected Benefits

Let us return to our example and to the data in Exhibit 18–2. Since the pension plan specifies that no credit is given for service before the plan inception date, Hardy has only 10 years of service that will qualify for pension credit. Notice that, according to the benefit formula given in Exhibit 18–2, Hardy's first year of service (ending at the end of year 1) earns him an estimated annual retirement benefit of $975 (.015 × 1 × $65,000), which he will receive at the end of each year, beginning one year from his retirement date and continuing for 15 years:

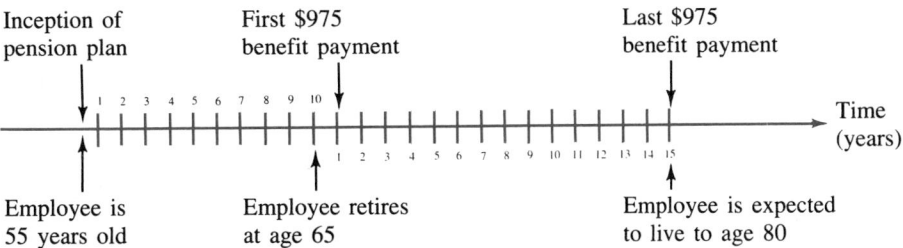

Likewise, Hardy's second year of service will earn him an estimated annual retirement benefit of $975. Thus, at the end of the second year, his *projected* annual retirement benefits total $1,950 ($975 × 2 years). By way of comparison, if Hardy's actual average salary to date, as of the end of the second year, was $40,000, he would have an *accumulated* annual retirement benefit at the end of the second year of only $1,200 (.015 × 2 × $40,000). Based on projected benefits, by the time of his retirement Hardy's ten years of service will entitle him to estimated annual retirement benefits of $9,750 ($975 × 10 years), beginning at age 66 and extending over his expected retirement period of 15 years.

ALLOCATING (ATTRIBUTING) COST OF BENEFITS TO PERIODS

A benefit approach must be used for determining pension cost.

Once we have calculated Hardy's annual retirement benefits, accrual accounting and the time period assumption require that we allocate the cost of the benefits to each of the ten years over which Hardy will provide employee services to Akins Corporation. Actuaries have developed two general approaches for allocating or attributing the cost of benefits to accounting periods—a "cost" approach and a "benefit" approach. Within each of these two general approaches, several actuarial methods, which incorporate different assumptions, have been developed. Although the cost approach and the benefit approach originally were developed as guides for funding a pension plan, these approaches also have been used to determine pension cost for a period. *Statement No. 87* requires that a benefit approach be used. In the following section we will discuss and illustrate the benefit approach for determining pension cost.

SERVICE COST AND INTEREST COST

Determination and Accounting

The cost of pension benefits attributed to a given period is called the service cost of that period.

Akins Corporation's cost of Hardy's retirement benefits earned during a particular year is called the **service cost** for that year. The service cost is equal to the present value of benefits attributed by Akins's pension plan formula to services rendered by Hardy during the current year, measured by expected future salary levels. Calculation of the present value of expected pension benefits requires the use of an assumed discount rate, which should reflect the rate of interest at which pension benefits could be settled. Thus, in selecting a discount rate, it is appropriate to consider available information about rates implicit in current prices of annuity contracts that could be used to settle the pension obligation. Employers may also look to rates of return on high-quality fixed-income investments currently available and expected to be available during the period to maturity of the pension benefits. Assumed discount rates are used in calculations of the projected and accumulated benefit obligations, in calculations of the service and interest cost components of pension cost, and in the calculation of prior service cost.

Given the 8 percent discount rate specified in Exhibit 18–2 and an expected annual retirement benefit of $975 arising from Hardy's work during year 1 of the pension plan, the service cost for year 1 is $4,175, calculated as follows:

Present value at Hardy's *retirement date* of
pension benefits arising from service during $= \$975 \times P_{\overline{15}|\,8\%}$
year 1

$$= \$975 \times 8.5595 \text{ (Table D, Appendix 7–1)}$$
$$= \underline{\underline{\$8,346}}$$

Present value of future retirement benefits of
$\$8,346$ as of the *end of year 1* $= \$8,346 \times p_{\overline{9}|\,8\%}$

$$= \$8,346 \times .5002 \text{ (Table B, Appendix 7–1)}$$
$$= \underline{\underline{\$4,175}} = \text{Service cost for year 1}$$

The present value of benefits attributed to employee service prior to a particular date is the projected benefit obligation at that date.

Based on this calculation, both Akins's pension cost for year 1 and its pension obligation at the end of year 1 are $4,175. The pension obligation is called the **projected benefit obligation (PBO).** *The projected benefit obligation as of a particular date is the present value of all benefits attributed by the plan's benefit formula to employee service rendered prior to that date.* Because Akins's benefit formula gives no credit for service prior to the plan inception date, the projected benefit obligation at the end of year 1 is based only on Hardy's service for year 1.

The $4,175 obligation can be interpreted as the amount that Akins would have to pay to settle its pension obligation to Hardy at the end of year 1. For example, Akins might settle the pension obligation by purchasing an **annuity contract** from an insurance company on Hardy's behalf. Under an annuity contract, an insurance company agrees to pay the retirement benefits during the retirement period in return for a fixed premium. As a result, an annuity contract shifts the risk associated with the pension benefits from the employer to the insurance company. As discussed earlier, the discount rate of 8 percent used to calculate Akins's pension obligation may be interpreted as the interest rate implicit in an annuity contract, if such a contract *were* purchased in order to settle the $4,175 pension obligation at the end of year 1.

To calculate pension cost for year 2 and for subsequent years, another component, **interest on the projected benefit obligation** at the beginning of each year, must be added to the service cost for that year. Conceptually, the interest cost component of pension cost is identical to the interest expense that accrues on any other monetary liability.

Applying the two pension cost components to the Hardy illustration, Exhibit 18–3 shows the calculation of pension cost for each year of Hardy's ten years of service. We have assumed in Exhibit 18–3 that *Akins has not established a pension fund,* that an 8 percent discount rate is used, and that Hardy earns an expected annual pension benefit of $975 for each year of his service that is covered by the pension plan.

The service cost component for each year is calculated as demonstrated earlier, except that each succeeding year's service cost is discounted for one year less as retirement approaches. Each year's service cost component is 8 percent larger than for the preceding year. At the end of the 10th year, the projected benefit obligation is $83,455, which is the present value of the $9,750 retirement benefits ($975 × 10 years) earned by Hardy over the 10-year service period covered by the plan. These $9,750 retirement benefits are expected to be paid to Hardy at the end of each of his 15 retirement years:

Present value of retirement
benefits at age 65 $= \$9,750 \times P_{\overline{15}|\,8\%}$

$$= \$9,750 \times 8.5595 \text{ (Table D, Appendix 7–1)}$$
$$= \underline{\underline{\$83,455}}$$

Each year Akins would record periodic net pension cost by debiting pension expense and crediting a pension liability account (either ''projected benefit obligation'' or ''ac-

EXHIBIT 18–3　SCHEDULE OF NET PENSION COST WITH NO FUNDING OF THE PENSION PLAN

Akins Corporation

END OF YEAR	AGE	(1) SERVICE COST*	(2) INTEREST COST†	(3) NET PENSION COST (PENSION EXPENSE)‡	(4) PROJECTED BENEFIT OBLIGATION (PBO)§
1	56	$4,175	$ 0	$ 4,175	$ 4,175
2	57	4,509	334	4,843	9,018
3	58	4,870	721	5,591	14,609
4	59	5,259	1,169	6,428	21,037
5	60	5,680	1,683	7,363	28,399
6	61	6,134	2,272	8,406	36,805
7	62	6,625	2,944	9,569	46,375
8	63	7,155	3,710	10,865	57,240
9	64	7,727	4,579	12,307	69,546
10	65	8,346	5,564	13,908¶	83,455
				$83,455	

* Present value of $8,346 for 9, 8, . . . , 0 years.

† Previous balance in col. 4 × .08.

‡ Col. 1 + col. 2.

§ Previous PBO + col. 1 + col. 2.

¶ Rounded by $1.

crued pension liability'' would be suitable account titles) for that year's amount in column 3 of Exhibit 18–3.[4] For example, journal entries to record pension expense for years 1 and 2 would be:

	YEAR 1		YEAR 2	
Pension expense	4,175		4,843	
Accrued pension liability		4,175		4,843

Akins's accrued pension liability balance at the end of each year equals the projected benefit obligation shown in column 4 of Exhibit 18–3. If Akins purchased an annuity contract at the end of year 10 for $83,455 in order to settle its obligation to Hardy, the following entry would be required to record the settlement of the pension obligation:

Accrued pension liability	83,455	
Cash..		83,455

[4] *Statement No. 87* uses the term ''net pension cost'' in recognition of the fact that, depending on the circumstances, some of this cost may be capitalized as part of an asset, such as inventory, which is on hand at the balance sheet date. For simplicity, in this chapter we often use the term ''pension expense'' instead of ''net pension cost'' and assume that the entire annual debit amount would be reported as an expense on the income statement.

Relationship Between Service Cost and Projected Benefit Obligation

Notice how the service cost component of pension cost is related to the measurement of Akins's projected benefit obligation. Each year's service cost component is that portion of the projected benefit obligation attributable to employee services rendered *during that year*. Of the projected benefit obligation balance of $9,018 at the end of year 2, for example, $4,509 is attributable to Hardy's service during year 2. The remaining $4,509 consists of service cost for year 1 ($4,175) plus interest that accrued during year 2 on the end-of-year-1 balance of the projected benefit obligation ($334 = .08 × $4,175).

At this point, you should be able to see why the approach we have described for determining pension cost is called a "benefit" approach. In the Bill Hardy example, each year we determined the amount of expected pension benefits attributed to service in that year. We then calculated the service cost component as the present value of those expected benefits. The attribution (allocation) method for a plan benefit formula that defines benefits in terms of years of service sometimes is referred to as a **benefit/years-of-service** approach. Actuarial methods based on this approach are discussed in the next paragraph.

Benefit Attribution Methods

Plans that base pension benefits on future compensation levels, such as Akins Corporation's plan, are called **final-pay** and **career-average-pay** plans. The benefit approach used to attribute cost to periods under these types of plans is called the "projected unit credit" or "unit credit with service prorate" actuarial method. Pension plans that do not define benefits in terms of compensation are called **flat-benefit** plans. For example, during his retirement period an employee may be given a fixed pension benefit of, say, $1,000 for each year of service. The benefit approach used to attribute cost under such a plan is called the "unit credit" actuarial method. Under a non-pay-related plan, the projected benefits equal the accumulated benefits at any point in time because expected future compensation levels are not incorporated in the pension formula or in the pension benefit calculations.

FUNDING AND RETURNS ON PLAN ASSETS

The previous illustration assumed that Akins did not establish a pension fund and thus did not make periodic contributions to the fund to accumulate assets to be used to make retirement payments to Hardy. This assumption allowed us to focus on two components of pension cost: service cost and interest cost. In practice, a company usually establishes a pension fund and makes periodic cash contributions to the fund. *Funding a pension plan is primarily a financial decision, as contrasted with determining pension cost, which is an accounting issue.* The amount contributed to the pension fund each period is a function of many considerations, such as working capital requirements, ERISA funding requirements, and tax deductibility. Contributions to the fund are invested by the funding agent or trustee in a variety of assets, as indicated by a recent study of large U.S. corporations:[5]

TYPE OF INVESTMENT	PENSION FUND PERCENTAGE
Common stocks	49.6%
Marketable bonds	24.5
Cash and short-term investments	8.3
Guaranteed investment contracts	4.6
Equity real estate	4.3
Company's own securities	0.8
Other	7.9
Total	100.0%

[5] Greenwich Associates, *Large Corporate Pensions—1986*, reprinted in *DH&S Review*, March 17, 1986, p. 5.

EXHIBIT 18—4 SCHEDULE OF NET PENSION COST WITH
ANNUAL FUNDING EQUAL TO NET PENSION COST

Akins Corporation

Facts and assumptions:

Annual benefit = $975.

Present value of annual benefits at age 65 = $8,346.

Discount rate = Return on plan assets = 8%.

Annual funding = Annual net pension cost.

END OF YEAR	AGE	(1) SERVICE COST*	(2) INTEREST COST†	(3) RETURN ON PLAN ASSETS‡	(4) NET PENSION COST§	(5) PROJECTED BENEFIT OBLIGATION (PBO)¶	(6) FUNDING**	(7) PLAN ASSETS††
1	56	$4,175	$ 0	$ 0	$ 4,175	$ 4,175	$ 4,175	$ 4,175
2	57	4,509	334	334	4,509	9,018	4,509	9,018
3	58	4,870	721	721	4,870	14,609	4,870	14,609
4	59	5,259	1,169	1,169	5,259	21,037	5,259	21,037
5	60	5,680	1,683	1,683	5,680	28,399	5,680	28,399
6	61	6,134	2,272	2,272	6,134	36,805	6,134	36,805
7	62	6,625	2,944	2,944	6,625	46,375	6,625	46,375
8	63	7,155	3,710	3,710	7,155	57,240	7,155	57,240
9	64	7,727	4,579	4,579	7,727	69,546	7,727	69,546
10	65	8,346	5,564	5,564	8,346	83,455	8,346	83,455
					$60,480		$60,480	

* Present value of $8,346 for 9, 8, 7, . . . , 0 years.

† Preceding balance of col. 5 × .08.

‡ Preceding balance of col. 7 × .08.

§ Col. 1 + col. 2 − col. 3.

¶ Preceding balance of col. 5 + col. 1 + col. 2.

** Given.

†† Preceding balance of col. 7 + col. 3 + col. 6.

The accumulated earnings on pension fund assets increase the amount of assets in the fund over time. In determining the assumed rate of return, appropriate consideration should be given to the returns being earned by the plan assets in the fund and to the rates of return expected to be available for reinvestment. *The rate of return on plan assets may differ from the discount rate that we discussed earlier because the two rates are based on different considerations.*

When Discount Rate for Projected Benefit Obligation Equals Return on Plan Assets

Earnings on the assets in a pension fund increase the net assets of the fund, decrease required contributions, and reduce the employer company's pension cost. To illustrate, return to the data in Exhibit 18–3 and assume that Akins had established a pension fund. Also assume that at the end of each year Akins contributed cash to the pension fund equal to the service cost component for that year, and that both the return on plan assets and the discount rate are 8 percent. In this example, we assume that the rate of return on plan assets equals the discount rate; however, these two rates often differ in practice. Later we will illustrate the effect on pension cost when there is a difference between the rate of return on plan assets and the discount rate.

Exhibit 18–4 demonstrates the calculation of annual pension expense under the above assumptions. Notice that net pension cost now is an aggregation of *three* components: service cost + interest cost − return on plan assets. Over the 10-year period, as in Exhibit 18–3, total net pension cost equals the amount of cash paid to settle the obligation at the end of year 10. In addition, total net pension cost in Exhibit 18–4 ($60,480) is less than total net pension cost in Exhibit 18–3 ($83,455) because, when a pension fund exists, the return on plan assets *reduces* net pension cost. Akins would record pension expense each year by debiting pension expense for the amount in column 4 of Exhibit 18–4 and crediting cash for the amount in column 6.

Let us examine the relationship between the projected benefit obligation and plan assets shown in Exhibit 18–4. The projected benefit obligation is a measure of Akins's pension obligation as determined by the plan's benefit formula. The plan assets figure represents the amount accumulated in the pension fund from contributions and earnings to date. The difference between these two amounts at the end of each year is called the **funded status of the plan.** This difference appears on Akins's balance sheet as *prepaid pension cost* (if plan assets exceed the projected benefit obligation) or as an *accrued pension liability* (if the projected benefit obligation exceeds the plan assets). In Exhibit 18–4, because Akins's periodic pension expense equals the periodic contributions to the fund and because both the discount rate and return on plan assets are 8 percent, the projected benefit obligation and plan assets are equal at the end of each year. As a result, Akins's balance sheet would show no prepaid pension cost or accrued pension liability.

When Discount Rate for Projected Benefit Obligation Is Not Equal to Return on Plan Assets

Exhibit 18–5 illustrates what happens when the rate of return on plan assets differs from the discount rate. In Exhibit 18–5 it is assumed that the plan assets earn a rate of return of 10 percent, that the discount rate is 8 percent, that funding is a level amount ($5,236) each year, and that $83,455 of plan assets exist as of Hardy's retirement date. The annual funding payments can be viewed as the ten rents comprising the ordinary annuity that has a value of $83,455 at Hardy's retirement date, given a 10 percent rate of return on plan assets:

$$\$83,455 = R(A_{\overline{10}|\,10\%})$$
$$\$83,455 = R(15.9374)$$
$$R = \$83,455 \div 15.9374$$
$$= \underline{\underline{\$5,236}} = \text{Annual cash funding}$$

The journal entries for each year can be taken directly from Exhibit 18–5. For example:

Year 1:
Pension expense 4,175
Prepaid pension cost ($5,236 − $4,175) 1,061
   Cash.   5,236

Year 2:
Pension expense 4,319
Prepaid pension cost ($5,236 − $4,319)   917
   Cash.   5,236

Year 9:
Pension expense 6,318
  Prepaid pension cost ($6,318 − $5,236)   1,082
  Cash.   5,236

EXHIBIT 18–5   SCHEDULE OF PENSION COST WHEN ANNUAL
FUNDING IS NOT EQUAL TO NET PENSION COST

Akins Corporation

Facts and assumptions:

Annual benefit = $975.

Present value of annual benefits at age 65 = $8,346.

Discount rate = 8%.

Return on plan assets = 10%.

Funding in equal annual amounts, not equal to net pension cost.

Plan assets are used to settle the projected benefit obligation at the end of year 10.

		(1)	(2)	(3)	(4)	(5)	(6)	(7)
				RETURN	NET	PROJECTED		
END OF		SERVICE	INTEREST	ON PLAN	PENSION	BENEFIT		PLAN
YEAR	AGE	COST*	COST†	ASSETS‡	COST§	OBLIGATION¶	FUNDING**	ASSETS††
1	56	$4,175	$ 0	$ 0	$ 4,175	$ 4,175	$ 5,236	$ 5,236
2	57	4,509	334	524	4,319	9,018	5,236	10,997
3	58	4,870	721	1,100	4,491	14,609	5,236	17,333
4	59	5,259	1,169	1,733	4,695	21,036	5,236	24,302
5	60	5,680	1,683	2,430	4,932	28,399	5,236	31,969
6	61	6,134	2,272	3,197	5,209	36,805	5,236	40,402
7	62	6,625	2,944	4,040	5,529	46,375	5,236	49,679
8	63	7,155	3,710	4,968	5,897	57,239	5,236	59,883
9	64	7,727	4,579	5,988	6,318	69,546	5,236	71,108
10	65	8,346	5,564	7,111	6,795‡‡	83,455	5,236	83,455
					$52,360		$52,360	

* Present value of $8,346 for 9, 8, 7, . . . , 0 years.

† Preceding balance of col. 5 × .08.

‡ Preceding balance of col. 7 × .10.

§ Col. 1 + col. 2 − col. 3.

¶ Preceding balance of col. 5 + col. 1 + col. 2.

** Given.

†† Preceding balance of col. 7 + col. 3 + col. 6.

‡‡ Rounded by $4.

Prepaid pension cost is an asset that increases during years 1 through 6 because annual pension expense is less than the amount funded. In years 7 through 10, prepaid pension cost decreases because the debit to pension expense exceeds the credit to cash. By the end of year 10, prepaid pension cost will be reduced to zero. The balance in the prepaid pension cost account at the end of each year is the difference between the plan assets balance and the projected benefit obligation balance. At the end of year 2, for example, the journal entries above give a prepaid pension cost balance of $1,978. This amount also is the difference between the projected benefit obligation and plan assets at the end of year 2 ($10,997 − $9,018 = $1,979; $1 rounding difference). Over the 10-year period *the total amount of pension expense is equal to the total amount of cash paid to the pension fund.* Note also that when a pension fund exists and there is a positive rate of return on the plan assets, the total pension expense over the 10-year period is less than

EXHIBIT 18—6 PROJECTED BENEFIT OBLIGATION AND PLAN ASSETS

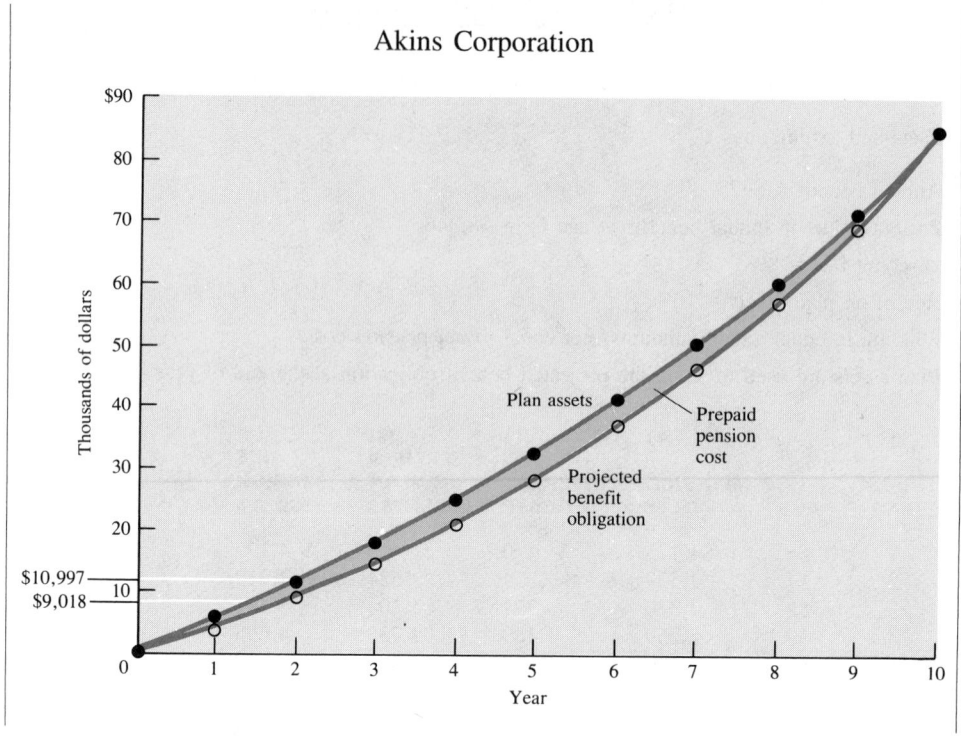

the total expense in Exhibit 18–3, where we assumed that there was no pension fund. Exhibit 18–6 shows the projected benefit obligation and the pension plan assets over the 10-year period based on the data in Exhibit 18–5.

Net Pension Cost over Hardy's Retirement Period

Our discussion of Exhibits 18–3, 18–4, and 18–5 *ignored* net pension cost (pension expense) during Hardy's *retirement period* for the following reasons:

1. Hardy's retirement at the end of year 10 (at age 65) eliminated the service cost component of pension expense.

2. In Exhibit 18–3 we assumed that the projected benefit obligation of $83,455 at the end of year 10 was settled with the purchase of an annuity contract for Hardy.

3. In Exhibit 18–4 we assumed that the discount rate equaled the rate of return on plan assets. Therefore, annual interest on the projected benefit obligation (which increases net pension cost) would equal the annual return on plan assets (which reduces net pension cost). As a result, net pension cost during Hardy's retirement period would be zero each year; thus, calculations for Hardy's retirement years were omitted from Exhibit 18–4.

4. In Exhibit 18–5 we assumed that the rate of return on plan assets was not equal to the discount rate and that Akins settled the projected benefit obligation of $83,455 by using the pension fund balance to purchase an annuity contract on Hardy's behalf.

In Exhibit 18–7 a different schedule is prepared, based on the recognition that both interest cost and return on pension plan assets will continue during Hardy's 15 retirement years. The facts and assumptions are the same as for Exhibit 18–5, except that Akins does

EXHIBIT 18–7 SCHEDULE OF NET PENSION COST WHEN INTEREST COST AND RETURN ON ASSETS CONTINUE DURING RETIREMENT

Akins Corporation

PART I

END OF YEAR	AGE	(1) SERVICE COST*	(2) INTEREST COST†	(3) RETURN ON PLAN ASSETS‡	(4) NET PENSION COST§	(5) PROJECTED BENEFIT OBLIGATION¶	(6) FUNDING**	(7) PLAN ASSETS††
1	56	$4,175	$ 0	$ 0	$4,175	$ 4,175	$ 4,653	$ 4,653
2	57	4,509	334	465	4,377	9,018	4,653	9,772
3	58	4,870	721	977	4,614	14,609	4,653	15,402
4	59	5,259	1,169	1,540	4,888	21,036	4,653	21,595
5	60	5,680	1,683	2,160	5,203	28,399	4,653	28,408
6	61	6,134	2,272	2,841	5,565	36,805	4,653	35,902
7	62	6,625	2,944	3,590	5,979	46,375	4,653	44,145
8	63	7,155	3,710	4,415	6,450	57,239	4,653	53,213
9	64	7,727	4,579	5,321	6,985	69,546	4,653	63,188
10	65	8,346	5,564	6,319	7,590	83,455	4,653	74,160

PART II

END OF YEAR	AGE	RETIREMENT PAYMENTS*	(2)	(3)	(4)	(5)	(6)	(7)
11	66	$9,750	6,676	7,416	(740)	80,381		71,826
12	67	9,750	6,431	7,183	(752)	77,062		69,258
13	68	9,750	6,165	6,926	(761)	73,477		66,434
14	69	9,750	5,878	6,643	(765)	69,605		63,327
15	70	9,750	5,568	6,333	(764)	65,424		59,910
16	71	9,750	5,234	5,991	(757)	60,907		56,151
17	72	9,750	4,873	5,615	(743)	56,030		52,016
18	73	9,750	4,482	5,202	(719)	50,762		47,468
19	74	9,750	4,061	4,747	(686)	45,073		42,464
20	75	9,750	3,606	4,246	(641)	38,929		36,961
21	76	9,750	3,114	3,696	(582)	32,294		30,907
22	77	9,750	2,583	3,091	(507)	25,127		24,248
23	78	9,750	2,010	2,425	(415)	17,387		16,922
24	79	9,750	1,391	1,692	(301)	9,028		8,865
25	80	9,750	722	886	(163)‡‡	–0–		–0–
					$46,530		$46,530	

Part I

* Present value of $8,346 for 9, 8, 7, . . . , 0 years.

† Preceding balance of col. 5 × .08.

‡ Preceding balance of col. 7 × .10.

§ Col. 1 + col. 2 − col. 3.

¶ Preceding balance of col. 5 + col. 1 + col. 2.

** Given.

†† Preceding balance of col. 7 + col. 3 + col. 6.

Part II

* Given.

† Same as in Part I.

‡ Same as in Part I.

§ Col. 2 − col. 3.

¶ Preceding balance of col. 5 + col. 2 − col. 1.

** Not applicable.

†† Preceding balance of col. 7 + col. 3 − col. 1.

‡‡ Rounded by $1.

not settle the projected benefit obligation by acquiring an annuity contract when Hardy reaches age 65.

Exhibit 18–7 shows the periodic pension cost calculations assuming a 10 percent return on plan assets and 10-year funding that is the annuity that would permit the pension fund to pay annual retirement benefits of $9,750, beginning at the end of year 11 (age 66 for Hardy):

Present value of $9,750
annuity at Hardy's $= \$9,750 \times P_{\overline{15}|\,10\%}$
retirement date

$\quad\quad\quad = \$9,750 \times 7.6061$ (Table D, Appendix 7–1)
$\quad\quad\quad = \underline{\underline{\$74,159^*}}$

Periodic funding $= \$74,159 \div A_{\overline{10}|\,10\%}$
$\quad\quad\quad = \$74,159 \div 15.9374$ (Table C, Appendix 7–1)
$\quad\quad\quad = \underline{\underline{\$4,653}} = $ Amount funded each year (in years 1 through 10)

* $74,160 in Exhibit 18–7 (end of year 10) because of rounding.

The periodic net pension cost calculations during Hardy's service period are shown in Part I of Exhibit 18–7. An accrued pension liability ($9,295) will exist at the end of Hardy's service period because the plan assets balance ($74,160) is less than the projected benefit obligation ($83,455). The periodic net pension cost calculations during Hardy's retirement period appear in Part II of Exhibit 18–7. The accrued pension liability will be reduced to zero during the retirement period because the return on plan asset component exceeds the interest cost component. Over the service and retirement periods *combined*, net pension cost (pension expense) and the amount funded both are $46,530.

Selected journal entries, based on the information in Exhibit 18–7, appear below:

End of year 2:
Pension expense 4,377
Prepaid pension cost ($4,653 − $4,377) 276
   Cash. 4,653

End of year 6:
Pension expense 5,565
   Cash. 4,653
   Prepaid pension cost (balance at beginning of year 6:
    $28,408 − $28,399) 9
   Accrued pension liability ($5,565 − $4,653 − $9) 903*

* Also equal to the funded status at the end of year 6 ($36,805 − $35,902 = $903).

End of year 20:
Accrued pension liability 641
   Pension expense (income) 641

Akins makes no entries for the retirement payments to Hardy because these payments are made by the agent who manages the pension fund.

To this point we have introduced three components of periodic pension cost: service cost, interest cost, and return on plan assets. We now turn our attention to a fourth important component of periodic pension cost—cost associated with credit given for services rendered *prior* to the date of inception of a pension plan. This component has created much controversy, both from an accounting theory standpoint and in practice.

RETROACTIVE BENEFITS (PRIOR SERVICE COST)

Many companies establish pension plans that give pension credit for years of service rendered prior to the plan inception date, or amend pension plans to give employees retroactive pension benefits. An employer gives credit for prior years' service because future economic benefits are expected in the form of higher employee productivity and increased employee efficiency, perhaps as a result of higher morale. Prior service credit also may be given in order to provide equity to employees who have long service terms before the establishment of the pension plan. The cost of retroactive benefits arising from prior service credit, whether that credit is given at the plan inception date or at a plan amendment date, is called **prior service cost.** The relationship between prior service cost and the annual service cost component of pension cost can be diagramed as follows:

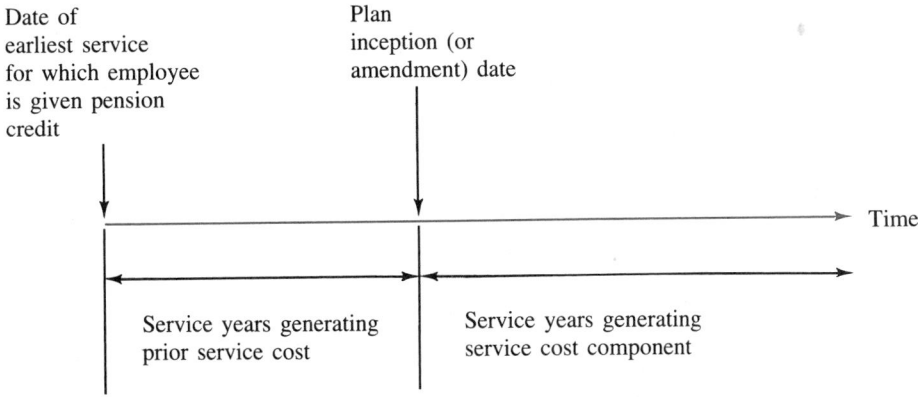

To illustrate prior service cost, let us modify the Bill Hardy example to give him credit for all of his 20 years of service before the plan inception date. Thus, at the beginning of year 1 (the plan inception date), Hardy's service prior to the plan inception had earned him expected annual retirement benefits of $19,500, as calculated below:

$$\text{Expected annual retirement benefits based on credit for 20 years of prior service} = .015 \times 20 \times \$65,000$$
$$= \underline{\underline{\$19,500}}$$

If we assume an 8 percent discount rate, these annual retirement benefits have a present value of $166,910 as of Hardy's retirement date (the end of year 10):

Present value at the end of year 10 of a
$19,500 ordinary annuity for 15 years $= \$19,500 \times P_{\overline{15}|8\%}$
discounted at 8 percent $= \$19,500 \times 8.5595$ (Table D, Appendix 7–1)
$= \underline{\underline{\$166,910}}$

The present value, at the plan inception date, of the benefits attributable to prior service is:

Present value of $166,910 as of $= \$166,910 \times p_{\overline{10}|8\%}$
the plan inception date $= \$166,910 \times .4632$
$= \underline{\underline{\$77,313}} = \text{Prior service cost}$

In terms of a time diagram, the pension obligation and payments to settle the obligation are as follows:

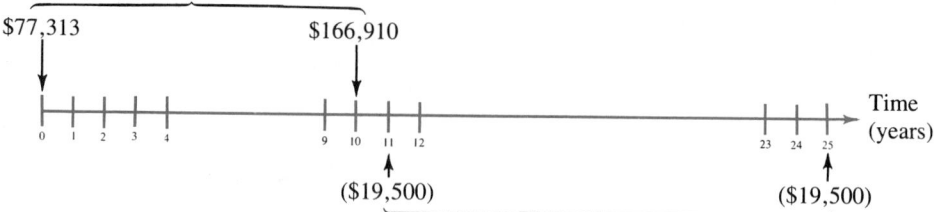

The prior service cost for Bill Hardy is $77,313, which is the present value of Hardy's expected future retirement benefits resulting from services performed for Akins prior to the plan inception date. The procedure used to calculate prior service cost is similar to the procedure followed in our previous calculations of the annual service cost component of pension cost. The prior service cost of $77,313 also is Akins's **projected benefit obligation** at the plan inception date.

Theory Considerations

The prior service cost raises some significant accounting theory questions:

Is the obligation that arises because of credit given for prior service a liability?

If the obligation is a liability, what is the nature of the offsetting debit?

Should the granting of credit for prior service and the related calculation of the projected benefit obligation result in *recognition* in Akins's financial statements?

Let us address the liability issue first. In Chapter 2 we pointed out that, in order for an economic event that affects a firm to be recognized, the following conditions must be satisfied:

1. The item must meet the definition of a financial statement element—in this case, a liability.

2. The item must have a relevant attribute that is measurable with sufficient reliability.

3. Information about the item must be relevant and reliable.

4. Providing information about the item must not be too costly in relation to the benefits to be derived.

We believe that *the granting of prior service credit (resulting in prior service cost and an increase in the projected benefit obligation) meets the definition of a liability.* Akins has a present obligation (estimated to be $77,313) to transfer economic resources to Bill Hardy in the future as a result of a past transaction (Hardy's 20 years of service before the plan was adopted). The prior service cost liability is measurable with as much *reliability* as the service component, and would certainly appear to be *relevant* to financial statement users who wish to assess Akins's *future cash outflows*. Thus, we believe that, in theory, Akins has incurred a liability.

It has been argued that the obligation arising from granting prior service cost should be measured by means of the accumulated benefits approach rather than the projected benefits approach, but we do not agree. Since measurement of annual service cost is based

In theory, the granting of prior service credit creates a liability.

on projected benefits, consistency requires that the projected benefits approach also should be used to measure the prior service cost. However, one could question, at a more fundamental level, whether the determination of any current obligation should be contingent upon future events (such as future salaries), as is the case under the projected benefits approach.

What about the offsetting debit? Has Akins acquired an asset, measured at $77,313? Does the $77,313 represent an additional expense of the current period? Should the amount be deducted from stockholders' equity? We do not believe that the item meets the definition of an expense, because the prior service credits were given in expectation of benefits to the employer in present *and future* years. There appears to be no sound argument for a deduction from stockholders' equity because any benefit the employer may receive will occur in the future, although some practical and political arguments may support this treatment.

As stated earlier, most companies grant retroactive benefits with the expectation that *future* economic benefits will be realized. Accordingly, we believe that, in theory, Akins has acquired an asset, even though there may be some uncertainty about the amount of future economic benefits accruing to Akins as a result of granting credit for prior service. Akins would not incur the obligation for prior services if it did not believe that the benefits exceeded the cost of doing so. Thus, *theoretically*, the following entry would appear to be appropriate to record the prior service cost:

Intangible asset	77,313	
Pension liability		77,313

Amortization of Prior Service Cost

In accordance with the *matching* principle, *Statement No. 87* requires that prior service cost be included in net pension cost over the years in which the employer realizes economic benefits from granting prior service credit. Therefore, prior service cost should be recognized by inclusion in net pension cost during the future service periods of employees who are active at the date of granting prior service credit and who are expected to receive pension benefits because of prior service credit. Akins should amortize prior service cost to pension expense over the time period during which Akins expects to receive economic benefits. The amortization pattern should parallel the manner in which the firm expects to receive benefits from employee service. Since Hardy is expected to work 10 more years at the date prior service credit is granted, 10 years would appear to be a reasonable amortization period for prior service cost. If Akins expects to receive economic benefits *equally* each year during Hardy's remaining 10 years of work, *straight-line* amortization over the 10-year service period should be used.

One additional assumption is necessary for this prior service cost example. Although funding considerations have had no effect on the conceptual nature of our discussion so far, we will assume for now that Akins decides not to fund prior service cost of $77,313 until the end of year 10. Although this assumption probably is not realistic, it will allow us to focus on conceptual issues. We will assume, however, that *some* funding does occur each year—specifically an amount equal to that year's net pension cost, less amortization of prior service cost.

Exhibit 18–8 shows the calculation of annual net pension cost and the projected benefit obligation, the amounts funded, and plan assets at the end of each year under our new assumptions. A graph showing the projected benefit obligation and the plan assets over the 10-year service period appears at the bottom of the exhibit.

As you can see from Exhibit 18–8, introduction of prior service cost results in four components of periodic net pension cost: service cost, interest on the projected benefit obligation, return on plan assets, and amortization of prior service cost.

EXHIBIT 18–8 SCHEDULE OF PENSION COST WHEN PRIOR SERVICE COST IS NOT FUNDED UNTIL THE RETIREMENT DATE

Akins Corporation

Facts and assumptions:

Annual benefit = $975.

Present value of annual benefits at age 65 = $8,346.

Discount rate = Return on plan assets = 8%.

Funding = Net pension cost − amortization of prior service cost.

Prior service cost is not funded until retirement date (end of year 10).

END OF YEAR¶	AGE	(1) SERVICE COST*	(2) INTEREST COST†	(3) RETURN ON PLAN ASSETS‡	(4) AMORTIZATION OF PRIOR SERVICE COST§	(5) NET PENSION COST¶	(6) PROJECTED BENEFIT OBLIGATION (PBO)**	(7) FUNDING††	(8) PLAN ASSETS‡‡
							$77,313	$ 0	$ 0
1	56	$4,175	$ 6,185	$ 0	$7,731	$ 18,091	87,673	10,360	10,360
2	57	4,509	7,014	829	7,731	18,425	99,196	10,694	21,883
3	58	4,870	7,936	1,751	7,731	18,786	112,001	11,055	34,688
4	59	5,259	8,960	2,775	7,731	19,175	126,220	11,444	48,907
5	60	5,680	10,098	3,913	7,731	19,596	141,997	11,865	64,684
6	61	6,134	11,360	5,175	7,731	20,051	159,491	12,319	82,178
7	62	6,625	12,759	6,574	7,731	20,541	178,875	12,810	101,562
8	63	7,155	14,310	8,125	7,731	21,071	200,340	13,340	123,027
9	64	7,727	16,027	9,842	7,731	21,644	224,095	13,912	146,782
10	65	8,346	17,928	11,743	7,731	22,262	250,368	14,530§§	173,055
10								77,313	250,368
					$199,642			$199,642	

* Present value of $8,346 for 9, 8, 7, . . . , 0 years.

† Preceding balance of col. 6 × .08.

‡ Preceding balance of col. 8 × .08.

§ $77,313 ÷ 10.

¶ Col. 1 + col. 2 − col. 3 + col. 4.

** Preceding balance in col. 6 + col. 1 + col. 2.

†† Given (col. 5 − col. 4).

‡‡ Preceding balance of col. 8 + col. 3 + col. 7.

§§ Rounded by $1.

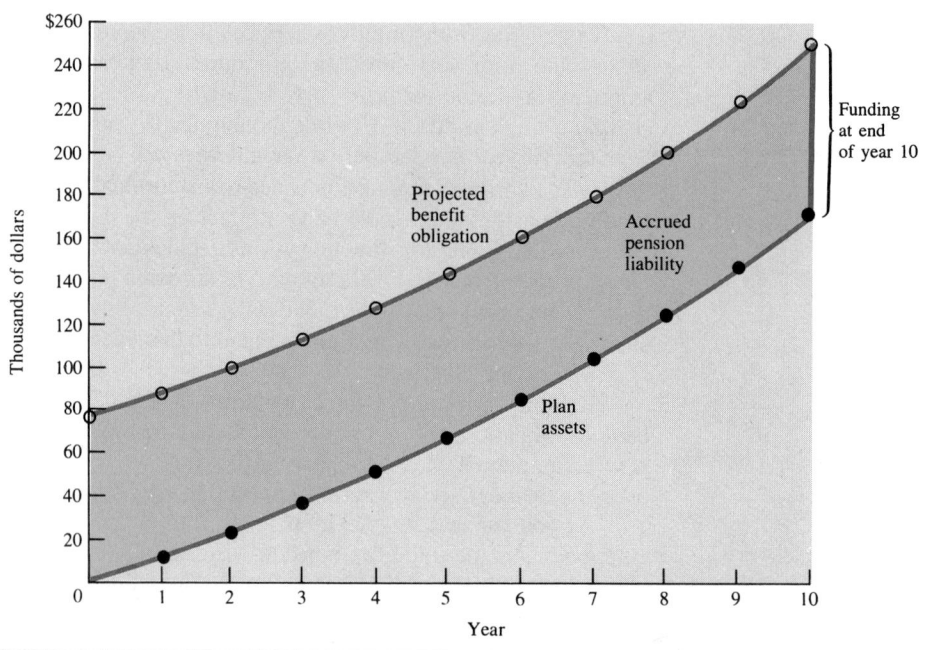

Earlier we concluded that, in theory, Akins had acquired an intangible asset and had incurred a liability at the beginning of year 1 equal to the prior service cost ($77,313). *Statement No. 87*, nevertheless, *does not require that the prior service cost be recognized by the recording of either an asset or a liability in the accounts.*[6] The difference between what theory would suggest (recording of both an asset and a liability) and what is required by *Statement No. 87* can be seen when Akins's journal entry at the beginning of year 1 under a theoretical (recognition) approach is compared with the entry under the nonrecognition (or delayed recognition) approach adopted by *Statement No. 87*:

THEORY

Intangible asset 77,313
    Accrued pension
      liability 77,313

STATEMENT NO. 87

No entry

Journal entries for selected subsequent years both under a theory approach and under the requirements of *Statement No. 87* appear below. These entries coincide with the data in Exhibit 18–8.

THEORY

End of year 1:
Pension expense . . . 18,091
    Cash   10,360
    Intangible asset . .   7,731

End of year 4:
Pension expense . . . 19,175
    Cash   11,444
    Intangible asset . .   7,731

STATEMENT NO. 87

Pension expense 18,091
    Cash   10,360
    Accrued pension
      liability   7,731

Pension expense 19,175
    Cash   11,444
    Accrued pension
      liability   7,731

Notice that in the *Statement No. 87* journal entries, a *liability accrues* during the years before the retirement date. On the other hand, as discussed earlier, theory suggests that both an asset (which subsequently is amortized) and a liability exist on the date that prior service credit is given. Under either *Statement No. 87* requirements or the theoretical approach, however, prior service cost is amortized and included in annual pension expense at the rate of $7,731 per year.

In summary, under the theoretical recognition approach, the funded status of the plan at the end of each year will equal prepaid pension cost or accrued pension liability reported on the employer's balance sheet. Under *Statement No. 87* requirements, however, this relationship will not hold if (1) the intangible is not recognized as an asset and (2) unfunded prior service cost is not recognized as a liability.

Next, we discuss and illustrate the *Statement No. 87* requirements for disclosing the relationship between the funded status of an employer's pension plan and the amounts reported in the employer's balance sheet. These requirements, in effect, provide a connection between the theoretical recognition approach and the delayed recognition approach adopted in *Statement No. 87*.

[6]As we shall see later in the chapter, however, *Statement No. 87* does require companies to record a *minimum liability* under certain circumstances.

Reconciliation of a Plan's Funded Status with the Employer's Balance Sheet Information

Whether a company should be required to recognize an obligation for prior service cost (or for other pension-related obligations that are discussed later in the chapter) was a very controversial issue during the FASB's deliberations on pension accounting. Those who opposed recognition of the prior service cost obligation pointed out that recognition could have an adverse impact on a company's balance sheet and on financial ratios constructed from balance sheet data. In addition, recognition of such obligations could result in the violation of certain contracts by creating sufficient liabilities on the employer's books to put the company in technical default on agreements to keep debt below a certain level.

Even though *Statement No. 87* does not require recognition of the prior service cost obligation in the employer's statement of financial position, the employer is required to disclose, in the notes to the financial statements, a reconciliation of the *funded status* of its pension plan with amounts reported in the balance sheet. As stated earlier, the funded status is the difference between the projected benefit obligation and the fair value of plan assets. A reconciliation schedule for Akins Corporation for selected years appears in Exhibit 18–9.[7] The amounts are taken from Exhibit 18–8. For comparison, we also have indicated how these data would appear on Akins's balance sheet if the theoretical (recognition) approach *were* used. These comparative presentations will help you to understand other *Statement No. 87* disclosure requirements that are discussed later in this chapter.

Reconciliation of the plan's funded status with balance sheet amounts must be disclosed.

[7] Later in the chapter, we discuss other pension cost components that could appear in the reconciliation schedule.

EXHIBIT 18–9 COMPARISON OF RECONCILIATION SCHEDULE UNDER *STATEMENT NO. 87* AND THE THEORY APPROACH (DATA FROM EXHIBIT 18–8)

Akins Corporation
RECONCILIATION SCHEDULE

	END OF YEAR 1	END OF YEAR 5
Projected benefit obligation	$(87,673)	$(141,997)
Plan assets	10,360	64,684
Funded status	$(77,313)	$ (77,313)
Unrecognized prior service cost		
$77,313 − $7,731	69,582	
$77,313 − 5($7,731)		38,658
Prepaid pension cost (accrued pension liability)	$ (7,731)*	$ (38,655)†

* Col. 5 − col. 7 for year 1.
† The sum of col. 5 (years 1 through 5) − the sum of col. 7 (years 1 through 5).

THEORY (RECOGNITION) APPROACH
Balance Sheet Data

	END OF YEAR 1	END OF YEAR 5
Intangible asset (Dr)	$69,582	$38,658
Pension liability (Cr)	$77,313	$77,313

The *Statement No. 87* reconciliation schedule discloses, in "off–balance sheet" form, exactly the same information that would appear in the primary financial statements under the theoretical recognition approach. The unrecognized prior service cost has the same balance as the intangible asset would have and the funded status corresponds to the pension liability. Perhaps those who opposed balance sheet recognition did not object to disclosure of the same information in footnotes.

ADDITIONAL ISSUES IN ACCOUNTING FOR PENSION COST

The primary objective of the previous section was to discuss and illustrate four of the basic components of periodic pension cost:

Service cost

+ Interest on the projected benefit obligation

− Return (earnings) on plan assets

+ Amortization of prior service cost

We made several simplifying assumptions in the illustrations of the previous section. First, we assumed that it was not necessary to change the discount rate assumption over time. Second, we assumed that our estimate of Bill Hardy's future compensation levels was correct. Third, we assumed that the return on plan assets was correctly estimated and stayed constant over time. Fourth, we assumed that Akins made no changes in the pension plan benefit formula during Hardy's service and retirement periods. Finally, because our illustrations dealt with only one employee (Hardy), amortization of prior service cost over his service period was not complicated.

Most of these assumptions would not hold true in reality. For example, the actual return on plan assets in a given year may differ from the expected return. Also, companies that sponsor pension plans for their employees periodically amend the pension plan benefit formula as economic conditions change. These factors and others can affect a company's pension cost over time.

In this section we discuss the impact of the following economic events and additional accounting requirements of *Statement No. 87* on the determination and reporting of pension cost.

1. Gains and losses arising from changes in assumptions or from differences between actual experience and expected interest rates, expected compensation levels, expected retirement patterns, and so on. These gains and losses sometimes are called *actuarial gains and losses,* but we call them *pension gains and losses.*

2. Plan amendments that either increase or decrease the projected benefit obligation at the date of amendment.

3. Alternative methods of amortizing prior service cost when several employees with different service periods are covered by a pension plan.

4. Under certain circumstances, recognition of a *minimum liability* in the statement of financial position of a company sponsoring a pension plan.

5. *Transition rules* required by *Statement No. 87* when a company begins to apply the *Statement* provisions for the first time.

GAINS AND LOSSES

Actuarial valuations made in connection with a pension plan require many assumptions about future events, such as discount rates, returns on plan assets, mortality rates, employees' service periods, and future compensation levels. Obviously, predictions about these events are subject to error. Actual outcomes that differ from predictions or expectations result in "experience gains and losses." In addition, changes in the economic environment in which a company operates necessitate changes in assumptions about the future. These changes in assumptions also give rise to gains and losses. *Gains reduce pension cost* by increasing plan assets, by decreasing the projected benefit obligation, or by a combination of the two. *Losses increase pension cost* because they have the opposite effect on plan assets and on the projected benefit obligation. For example, if the interest rate used to discount an employee's projected benefits is reduced to reflect the current and projected economic environment, a loss results because the lower discount rate *increases* the projected benefit obligation. *Statement No. 87* makes no distinction between experience gains and losses and gains and losses from changes in assumptions. Therefore, our discussion does not distinguish between types of gains and losses, referring to all types as pension gains and losses.

How should pension gains and losses be included in the calculation of periodic pension cost? Many preparers and users of financial statements believe that these gains and losses should be *recognized immediately* and included as a component of pension cost in the accounting period in which they arise. Others disagree, pointing out that immediate recognition creates unacceptable *volatility* in periodic pension cost. Those who oppose immediate recognition also argue that, given the long-run nature of a pension plan agreement, gains and losses in one period may be offset, partially or fully, in following periods. In addition, *because there may be considerable uncertainty about the ultimate cash flow effects of some of these gains and losses, immediate recognition may not provide reliable signals about future cash flows.*

The source of disagreement about the appropriate accounting treatment for pension gains and losses probably can be traced to *accrual accounting* and the *time period assumption.* In the long run, a company's total pension cost equals the outflow of cash for pension funding. Even though the cost of providing retirement benefits to employees can be determined precisely only over a long period of time, information about pension cost must be estimated and provided on a timely basis if it is to be relevant and useful to financial statement readers. As a result, a long-run phenomenon, actual pension cost, must be allocated (attributed) to short-run time periods, such as a year. This, of course, is a fundamental characteristic of accrual accounting and is common to most allocation situations, such as accounting for depreciation.

Delayed recognition of pension gains and losses is required under GAAP.

Statement No. 87 requires that a *delayed recognition* approach be used to account for pension gains and losses. This approach is discussed in the following two illustrations, both based on data for the Akins Corporation and Bill Hardy presented in the previous section.

Calculating and Accounting for a Plan Asset Gain

Before we discuss calculating and accounting for a plan asset gain, the relationship between *expected returns* on assets and *actual returns* on assets should be summarized. Assume that you hold an asset with a fair value of $10,000 at the beginning of the current year. On the basis of the asset's previous return history, you expect it to have a fair value of $12,000 at the end of the year. Thus, the asset's expected return is $2,000, or 20 percent [($12,000 − $10,000) ÷ $10,000]. Suppose, however, that at the end of the current year the asset's actual fair value is $13,000. Thus, the actual return is $3,000, or 30 percent [($13,000 − $10,000) ÷ $10,000]. The actual return can be disaggregated into two parts—an expected return and a gain (or loss) resulting from the difference between expectations and reality:

$$\text{Actual return} = \text{Expected return} + (\text{Gain}/- \text{Loss})$$
$$\$3,000 \quad = \quad \$2,000 \quad + \quad \$1,000$$

This equation can be rearranged as follows:

$$\text{Gain}/- \text{Loss} = \text{Actual return} - \text{Expected return}$$
$$\$1,000 \quad = \quad \$3,000 \quad - \quad \$2,000$$

Familiarity with these relationships will help you understand accounting for pension gains and losses.

Statement No. 87 requires amortization (and inclusion in net pension cost) of a portion of net pension gain or loss if the following condition is met: *as of the beginning of the period,* the net gain or loss exceeds 10 percent of the greater of (1) the market-related value of plan assets (we use fair value)[8] or (2) the projected benefit obligation. The portion to be amortized is the excess of the net gain or loss over 10 percent of the greater of amount (1) or (2). This arbitrary approach for determining the minimum amount of gain or loss to be amortized is called a **corridor approach.** The amortization period is the average remaining service period of active employees expected to participate in the plan. The average remaining service period is recomputed each period and therefore will reflect changes in the employee group from period to period.

Requiring amortization of the amount of gain or loss only outside of the corridor serves to dampen the effect of the gain or loss on net periodic pension cost. The corridor approach establishes the *minimum* amount of gain or loss a company may recognize in a particular accounting period. A larger amount may be recognized each period if a consistent procedure is applied and if there is proper disclosure. Illustrations of the corridor approach are provided in Exhibits 18–10 and 18–11, which are continuations of the Hardy illustration from Exhibit 18–8. The funded status of Akins's pension plan at the end of year 5 and the projected and actual funded status at the end of year 6 appear in Part I of Exhibit 18–10. The facts and assumptions are the same as for Exhibit 18–8 for the first five years. We assume that the 8 percent return on plan assets used in Exhibit 18–10 is the estimated, rather than the actual, return. The projected benefit obligation and plan asset amounts shown in columns 1 and 2 are taken from years 5 and 6 of Exhibit 18–8. For year 6, actual return on plan assets is 25 percent. This rate of return is reflected in column 3 of Exhibit 18–10.

From Part I of Exhibit 18–10, we see that actual fair value of plan assets at the end of year 6 ($93,174) exceeded the estimated fair value ($82,178) by $10,996. This result occurred because the actual return on plan assets of 25 percent exceeded the expected return of 8 percent. Thus, during year 6 there was a gain of $10,996 on plan assets, calculated as follows:

$$\begin{aligned}
\text{Gain} &= \text{Actual return} - \text{Expected return} \\
&= .25(\$64,684) - .08(\$64,684) \\
&= \$16,171 \quad - \$5,175 \text{ (from Exhibit 18–8)} \\
&= \underline{\underline{\$10,996}} = \text{Gain on plan assets in year 6}
\end{aligned}$$

The gain also can be calculated as the difference between the plan's projected funded status and the plan's actual funded status at the end of year 6 ($77,313 − $66,317 = $10,996).

The only new component in the net pension cost calculation shown in the lower portion of Part I of Exhibit 18–10 is the amortization of the net pension gain. Since there

---

[8] The market-related value of plan assets is a balance used to calculate the expected return on plan assets. Market-related value can be either fair market value or a calculated value that recognizes changes in fair value in a systematic and rational manner over not more than five years.

EXHIBIT 18–10   NET PENSION COST: PLAN ASSET GAIN

Akins Corporation

PART I

	(1) ACTUAL END OF YEAR 5	(2) PROJECTED END OF YEAR 6	(3) ACTUAL END OF YEAR 6
Projected benefit obligation	$(141,997)	$(159,491)	$(159,491)
Plan assets (fair value)	64,684	82,178	93,174*
Funded status	$ (77,313)	$ (77,313)	$ (66,317)
Unrecognized prior service cost	38,655	30,924	30,924
Unrecognized (gain)/loss			(10,996)
Prepaid (accrued) pension cost	$ (38,658)	$ (46,389)	$ (46,389)

* $93,174 = $64,684(1.25) + $12,319.

Calculation of pension cost under *Statement No. 87* for year 6:

Service cost (from Exhibit 18–8)	$ 6,134
Interest cost (.08 × $141,997)	11,360
Expected return on plan assets (.08 × $64,684)	(5,175)
Amortization of prior service cost (from Exhibit 18–8)	7,731

Amortization of loss/(gain):

Gain at beginning of year	$ –0–
Corridor (.10 × $141,997)	14,200
Gain subject to amortization	$ –0–
Amount of gain amortized	–0–
Pension cost for year 6	$20,050†

† Rounded by $1 to $20,051 in Exhibit 18–8.

PART II

Statement No. 87 journal entry for year 6:

Pension expense	20,050	
Accrued pension liability		7,731
Cash (from Exhibit 18–8)		12,319

Statement No. 87 footnote disclosures for year 6:

Service cost	$ 6,134
Interest cost	11,360
Actual return on plan assets (.25 × $64,684)	(16,171)
Net prior service cost amortization and gain deferral ($7,731 + $10,996)	18,727
Pension cost	$ 20,050
Projected benefit obligation	$(159,491)
Plan assets (from part I)	93,174
Funded status	$ (66,317)
Unrecognized prior service cost	30,924
Unrecognized net (gain)/loss	(10,996)
Prepaid/(accrued) pension cost¶	$ (46,389)

¶ $38,658 accrued pension cost at the end of year 5 (from Exhibit 18–8) plus $7,731 credit to accrued pension cost for year 6.

was no unrecognized gain or loss at the *beginning* of year 6, no amortization of gain or loss is necessary in year 6.

The journal entry and footnote disclosures required by *Statement No. 87* appear in Part II of Exhibit 18–10. Notice that the *actual return on plan assets* ($16,171) *must be disclosed*. The entire pension gain of $10,996 is added to accrued pension cost (because its recognition has been deferred). The net effect of this procedure is to reduce year 6 pension cost by the $5,175 *expected* return on plan assets ($16,171 − $10,996 = $5,175).

How would Akins's pension cost be calculated for year 6 if the gain on plan assets were recognized under a theoretical recognition approach? Net pension cost for year 6 would be:

PENSION COST COMPONENT	AMOUNT
Service cost (from Exhibit 18–8)	$ 6,134
Interest cost (from Exhibit 18–8)	11,360
Actual return on plan assets (from Exhibit 18–10)	(16,171)*
Amortization of prior service cost (from Exhibit 18–8)	7,731
Net pension cost[9]	$ 9,054†

* Expected return + gain: $5,175 + $10,996 = $16,171.

† $9,055 without rounding effect.

In establishing the *Statement No. 87* requirements, the FASB was sensitive to both sides of the issue of whether pension gains and losses should be included in net pension cost. Because amortization, rather than full recognition of pension gains and losses within the year of occurrence, is a part of actuarial funding techniques and was a part of pension accounting practice under *APB Opinion No. 8,* the FASB concluded that some amortization of pension gains and losses is appropriate when the net gain or loss is significant in relation to the items that determine a company's funded status.

Calculating and Accounting for a Liability Loss

Continuing with the Hardy illustration during year 7, consider Exhibit 18–11. The facts and assumptions for Exhibit 18–11 are the same as for Exhibit 18–10, except that at the end of year 7 the assumed discount rate is reduced from 8 percent to 6 percent. Both the expected return and the actual return on plan assets are 8 percent for year 7. Column 1 is taken from column 3 of Part I of Exhibit 18–10.

Schedules reconciling Akins's funded status with the amounts reported on its balance sheet under *Statement No. 87* are presented in the upper portion of Part I of Exhibit

[9] The year 6 journal entry and resulting balance sheet data for Akins under a *theoretical recognition approach* would be as follows:

Journal entry: Pension expense	9,054	
Pension liability ($7,731 + $12,319 − $9,054)	10,996	
Intangible asset		7,731
Cash		12,319

Balance sheet data: Intangible asset (Dr)	$30,924
Pension liability (Cr)	$66,317

Calculation of pension liability: Balance, end of year 5	$77,313
Debit to pension liability	(10,996)
Pension liability	$66,317

EXHIBIT 18—11   NET PENSION COST: LIABILITY LOSS

Akins Corporation

PART I

	(1) ACTUAL END OF YEAR 6	(2) PROJECTED END OF YEAR 7	(3) ACTUAL END OF YEAR 7
Projected benefit obligation	$(159,491)	$(178,866)	$(214,664)
Plan assets	93,174	113,439	113,439
Funded status	$ (66,317)	$ (65,427)	$(101,225)
Unrecognized prior service cost	30,924	23,193	23,193
Unrecognized net (gain)/loss . . . .·. . .	(10,996)	(10,996)	24,802
Prepaid/(accrued) pension cost	$ (46,389)	$ (53,230)	$ (53,230)

Calculation of pension cost for year 7:		
Service cost		$ 6,625
Interest cost		12,759
Expected return on plan assets (.08 × $93,174)		(7,454)
Amortization of prior service cost		7,731
Amortization of 1/1 gain:		
Gain at 1/1	$10,996	
Corridor (.10 × $159,491)	15,949	
Gain subject to amortization	$ –0–	
Amount of gain amortized		–0–
Pension cost for year 7		$19,661

PART II

Calculation of loss on projected benefit obligation: Annual benefit earned at end of year 7 = 27 × .015 × $65,000 = $26,325.

	DISCOUNT RATE	
	8%	6%
Present value of $26,325 annuity at age 65:		
× 8.5595	$225,329	
× 9.7122		$255,674
Present value of above at end of year 7:		
Projected = $225,329 × .7938	$178,866	
Actual = $255,674 × .8396		$214,664

Loss = $214,664 − $178,866
Loss = $35,798

PART III

Statement No. 87 journal entry for year 7:

Pension expense	19,661	
Accrued pension liability		6,851
Cash (from Exhibit 18–8)		12,810

Statement No. 87 footnote disclosures for year 7:

Service cost	$ 6,625
Interest cost	12,759
Actual return on plan assets (.08 × $93,174)	(7,454)
Net amortization and deferral	7,731
Net pension cost	$19,661
Projected benefit obligation	$(214,664)
Plan assets	113,439
Funded status	$(101,225)
Unrecognized prior service cost	23,193
Unrecognized net (gain)/loss ($35,798 − $10,996)	24,802
Prepaid/(accrued) pension cost	$ (53,230)

18–11. Observe in Part II of Exhibit 18–11 that the reduction in discount rate from 8 percent to 6 percent increased the projected benefit obligation and resulted in a pension loss of $35,798 ($214,664 − $178,866) at the end of year 7.

The calculation of pension cost for year 7 under *Statement No. 87* ($19,661) is shown in the lower portion of Part I of Exhibit 18–11. Notice that the unrecognized pension gain at the beginning of the year ($10,996) is within the corridor for year 7. Therefore, amortization of this gain is not required in year 7. The unrecognized net loss of $24,802 at the end of year 7 is the sum of the unrecognized and unamortized gain at the beginning of the year of $10,996 plus the unrecognized and unamortized loss for year 7 of $35,798. Journal entries for year 7 and the required footnote disclosures at the end of year 7 appear in Part III of Exhibit 18–11.

The following table shows the calculation of net pension cost for years 8 through 10, based on an assumed 6 percent discount rate and assuming no further gains and losses:

END OF YEAR	SERVICE COST	INTEREST COST	RETURN ON PLAN ASSETS	AMORTIZATION OF PRIOR SERVICE COST	NET PENSION COST*	PROJECTED BENEFIT OBLIGATION (PBO)	FUNDING	PLAN ASSETS
7						$214,664		$113,439
8	$8,427	$12,880	$ 9,075	$7,731	$19,963	235,971	$50,000	172,514
9	8,933	14,158	13,801	7,731	17,021	259,062	50,000	236,315
10	9,469	15,544	18,905	7,731	13,839	284,075	28,855	284,075

* Before amortization of any gain or loss.

Changing the discount rate to 6 percent changes the service cost component in years 8 through 10 because the $975 annual pension benefit earned by Hardy for each year of service must be discounted at 6 percent instead of at the 8 percent rate used in Exhibit 18–8. In the funding column of the above table we have assumed that Akins contributed $50,000 to the fund in years 8 and 9, plus the necessary amount in year 10 to fully fund the projected benefit obligation by the end of year 10. The funding amounts for years 8, 9, and 10 are not actuarially determined.

In addition to the cost components shown in the above table, amortization of part of the beginning-of-year-8 unrecognized net pension loss of $24,802 also must be included in pension cost for years 8 and 9. The amount of unamortized net loss outside the corridor each year must be amortized over the remaining period of Hardy's service. Calculation of the amount of loss amortization and the pension costs for years 8 through 10 is shown below:

	YEAR 8	YEAR 9	YEAR 10
Unrecognized net loss, beginning of year (Part III, Exhibit 18–11)	$24,802		
$24,802 − $1,112		$23,690	
$23,690 − $47			$23,643
Corridor:			
.10 × $214,664 (from table above)	(21,466)		
.10 × $235,971 (from table above)		(23,597)	
.10 × $259,062 (from table above)			(25,906)
Amount outside corridor	$ 3,336	$ 93	$ −0−
× 1/average remaining service period	× 1/3	× 1/2	× 1/1
Amount of loss amortized	$ 1,112	$ 47	$ −0−
Pension expense: $19,963 + $1,112	$21,075		
$17,021 + $47		$17,068	
$13,839 + $0			$13,839

At the end of year 10, a reconciliation schedule would be as follows:

Projected benefit obligation	$(284,075)
Plan assets at fair value	284,075
Funded status	$ −0−
Unrecognized prior service cost	−0−
Unrecognized net loss ($24,802 − $1,112 − $47)	23,643
Prepaid pension cost	$ 23,643

What happens to the unrecognized net loss and the asset account "prepaid pension cost" during Hardy's retirement period? If we assume that plan assets are used to purchase an annuity contract on behalf of Hardy for the amount of the projected benefit obligation as of the beginning of Hardy's retirement period, Akins would recognize a settlement loss of $23,643:

Settlement loss	23,643	
Prepaid pension cost		23,643

More is said about pension plan settlements later in the chapter.

ACCOUNTING FOR PLAN AMENDMENTS

Companies often *amend* the provisions of a pension plan as economic conditions change. A plan amendment can either increase or decrease the projected benefit obligation at the amendment date. Refer to Exhibit 18–8 on page 840, but assume that at the beginning of year 6 Akins amended Hardy's plan benefit formula by increasing the annual benefits by $33\frac{1}{3}$ percent:

Original benefit formula = .015 × n × $65,000

Amended benefit formula = .02* × n × $65,000

* .015 × 4/3 = .02.

Part I of Exhibit 18–12 shows how the amendment would increase the projected benefit obligation at the beginning of year 6.[10] Part I also presents the calculation of net periodic pension cost under the amended provisions of the plan. Notice that the prior service cost amortization for years 6 through 10 is comprised of $7,731 plus amortization of the increased projected benefit obligation over Hardy's remaining service period of five years.

Through year 5, the facts and assumptions for Exhibit 18–12 are the same as for Exhibit 18–8. At the beginning of year 6, the benefit formula changes from .015 to .020 and funding changes, as shown in column 7. The funding amounts during years 6 through 10 are not actuarially determined. They are arbitrarily chosen, with the constraint that at the end of year 10 total funding must equal total pension cost for the ten years.

Under a theoretical recognition approach, the plan amendment would be recorded at the end of year 6 by a debit to an intangible asset and a credit to a pension liability for the $47,332 increase in unrecognized prior service cost and projected benefit obligation. In contrast, *Statement No. 87* does *not* require recognition of the increased projected benefit obligation. Therefore, Part II of Exhibit 18–12 shows reconciliation schedules before and after the plan amendment, as well as at the end of year 6. Journal entries for years 6

---

[10] Although we could calculate the present value of these annual retirement benefits, as amended, at the beginning of year 6, an easier approach is simply to increase the original beginning-of-year-6 projected benefit obligation by one-third: $141,997 × 4/3 = $189,329.

EXHIBIT 18–12   PLAN AMENDMENT

Akins Corporation

PART I

END OF YEAR	AGE	(1) SERVICE COST*	(2) INTEREST COST†	(3) RETURN ON PLAN ASSETS‡	(4) AMORTIZATION OF PRIOR SERVICE COST§	(5) NET PENSION COST¶	(6) PROJECTED BENEFIT OBLIGATION (PBO)**	(7) FUNDING††	(8) PLAN ASSETS‡‡
							$ 77,313	$ 0	$ 0
1	56	$ 4,175	$ 6,185	$ 0	$ 7,731	$ 18,091	87,673	10,360	10,360
2	57	4,509	7,014	829	7,731	18,425	99,196	10,694	21,882
3	58	4,870	7,936	1,751	7,731	18,786	112,001	11,055	34,688
4	59	5,259	8,960	2,775	7,731	19,175	126,220	11,444	48,907
5	60	5,680	10,098	3,913	7,731	19,596	141,997	11,865	64,684
		Effect of plan amendment on PBO————————————————→					47,332		
		New PBO ————————————————————————→					189,330§§		
6	61	8,179	15,146	5,175	17,198	35,348	212,655	30,000	99,859
7	62	8,833	17,012	7,989	17,198	35,055	238,501	35,000	142,848
8	63	9,540	19,080	11,428	17,198	34,390	267,121	45,000	199,275
9	64	10,303	21,370	15,942	17,198	32,928	298,793	55,000	270,217
10	65	11,127	23,903	21,617	17,198	30,612§§	333,824	41,988§§	333,824
						$262,406		$262,406	

* Years 1–5, same as in Exhibit 18–8; years 6–10, Exhibit 18–8 amounts increased 33⅓%.

† Interest at 8% on beginning-of-year projected benefit obligation.

‡ Return on plan assets at 8%.

§ Years 1–5, $77,313 ÷ 10; years 6–10, ($77,313 ÷ 10) + ($47,332 ÷ 5).

¶ Col. 1 + col. 2 − col. 3 + col. 4.

** Preceding balance of col. 6 + col. 1 + col. 2.

†† Years 1–5, same as in Exhibit 18–8; years 6–10, assumed (arbitrary selection).

‡‡ Preceding balance of col. 8 + col. 3 + col. 7.

§§ Rounded by $1.

PART II

RECONCILIATION SCHEDULE

	BEGINNING OF YEAR 6 BEFORE AMENDMENT	BEGINNING OF YEAR 6 AFTER AMENDMENT	END OF YEAR 6
Projected benefit obligation	$(141,997)	$(189,329)	$(212,655)
Plan assets...	64,684	64,684	99,859
Funded status	$ (77,313)	$(124,645)	$(112,796)
Unrecognized prior service cost:			
$7,731 × 5	38,657		
$38,657 + $47,332...............................		85,989	
$17,198 × 4			68,792
Accrued pension cost	$ (38,656)	$ (38,656)	$ (44,004)

through 10 would be based on the appropriate row amounts in Part I of Exhibit 18–12. Exhibit 18–13 shows the growth patterns of the plan assets and the projected benefit obligation based on the plan amendment data in Exhibit 18–12. The impact of the plan amendment on the pension benefit obligation at the beginning of year 6 is indicated by the $47,332 increase at the beginning of year 6.

AMORTIZATION OF PRIOR SERVICE COST FOR A GROUP OF EMPLOYEES

In the Akins Corporation example, Bill Hardy was Akins's only employee. Therefore, amortization of prior service cost over Hardy's service period was not difficult. In practice, however, a company may have hundreds or thousands of employees who will either complete their service or leave the company for other reasons at different times.

To illustrate amortization of prior service cost when there is a group of employees, assume that Bond Company has eight employees and has granted them credit for prior service, an action that gives rise to a prior service cost of $66,000. The employees—call them *A* through *H*—are expected to leave the company as follows:

A and *B* will leave after two years.

C, *D*, and *E* will leave after four years.

F will leave after five years.

G and *H* will leave after six years.

EXHIBIT 18–13   PROJECTED BENEFIT OBLIGATION AND PLAN ASSETS UNDER PLAN AMENDMENT

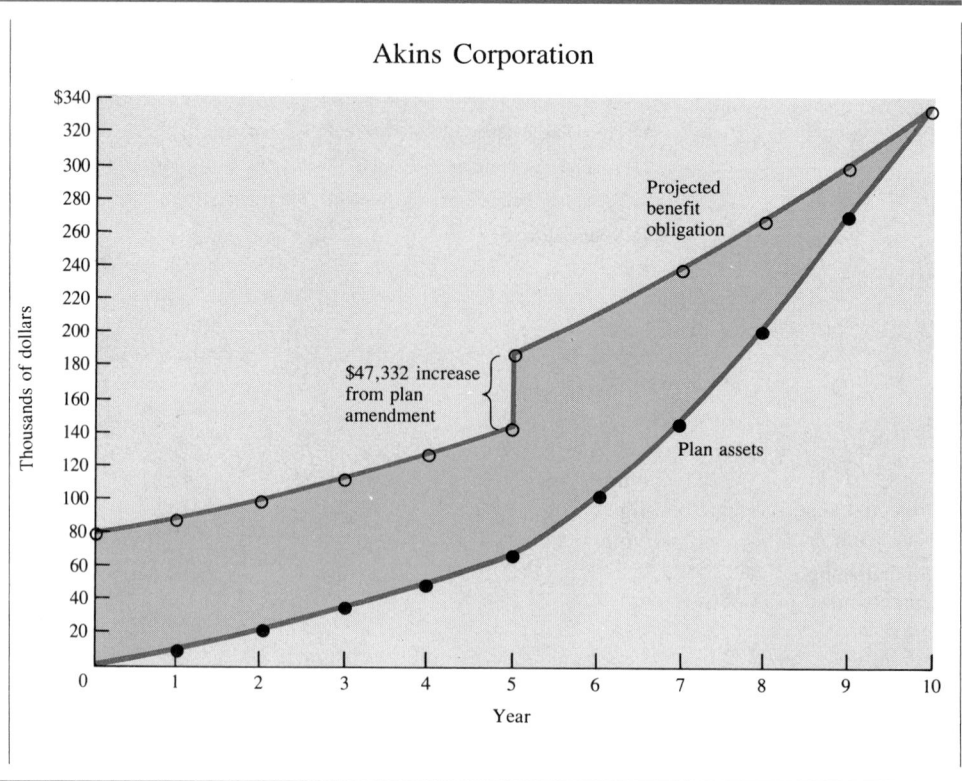

The problem of allocating prior service cost when there is a group of employees is identical to the problem of amortizing premium or discount on serial bonds. As you may recall, one procedure for allocating premium or discount on serial bonds is the bonds-outstanding method. Under *Statement No. 87,* the same procedure can be used to amortize prior service cost for a group of employees. When accounting for prior service cost, we call this method ''service years outstanding.'' This method produces a declining pattern of amortization over time as employees' remaining service years decline through attrition, retirement, or termination:

YEAR	NUMBER OF EMPLOYEES	AMORTIZATION FRACTION	PRIOR SERVICE COST	ANNUAL PRIOR SERVICE COST AMORTIZATION
1	8	8/33	× $66,000	$16,000
2	8	8/33	× 66,000	16,000
3	6	6/33	× 66,000	12,000
4	6	6/33	× 66,000	12,000
5	3	3/33	× 66,000	6,000
6	2	2/33	× 66,000	4,000
	33*			$66,000†

* Total employee years.

† Total prior service cost.

Statement No. 87 also permits the use of other allocation methods as long as they are systematic, rational, and applied consistently over time, and as long as they amortize prior service cost at least as fast as the service years outstanding method. Whatever amortization method is used, the amortization schedule must be based on the existing group of employees at the time the prior service cost develops. For example, *Statement No. 87* permits straight-line amortization of prior service cost over the average remaining service period of a group of employees. A total of 33 service years remain for the 8 employees in the Bond Company example. Thus, the average remaining service period is 4.125 (33 total employee years ÷ 8 employees). Annual prior service cost amortization for years 1 through 4 would be $66,000 ÷ 4.125 = $16,000. Amortization in the fifth year would be .125 × $16,000 = $2,000.

RECOGNIZING A MINIMUM LIABILITY

Employers must record a minimum liability at least equal to the unfunded accumulated benefit obligation.

Thus far we have seen that, in contrast to the theoretical recognition approach, *Statement No. 87* does not require balance sheet recognition of the projected benefit obligation. However, the *Statement* does require recognition of a **minimum liability,** at each balance sheet date, at least equal to a company's unfunded accumulated benefit obligation *(accumulated benefit obligation minus the fair value of plan assets)*. To illustrate this requirement, return to Exhibit 18–8 and assume that Hardy's salary for year 1 was $39,000, which is only 60 percent of the $65,000 expected five-year average annual salary used to calculate projected benefits in Exhibit 18–8. As a result, Akins's *accumulated* benefit obligation at the end of year 1 is $52,604 (.60 × $87,673 from Exhibit 18–8). The *minimum liability* required by *Statement No. 87* is $42,244, which is calculated as follows:

Accumulated benefit obligation	$(52,604)
Plan assets at fair value	10,360
Unfunded accumulated benefits	$(42,244)

Statement No. 87 requires that this $42,244 minimum liability be combined with prepaid pension cost or accrued pension liability, as appropriate, which already appears on the employer company's balance sheet. Since Akins already has recorded a pension liability of $7,731 in year 1 (see p. 841), an additional liability of $34,513 ($42,244 − $7,731) must be recognized in Akins's end-of-year-1 balance sheet. *Statement No. 87* requires that the offsetting debit be to an intangible asset:

Intangible asset 34,513
    Accrued pension liability   34,513

Four other points about the minimum liability adjustment are important:

1. The adjustment affects *only* the employer company's balance sheet. The net pension cost calculations and procedures presented up to this point are not affected. Thus, it is a balance sheet "tack on" procedure.

2. Since the calculation and adjustment, if any, are made at the end of each period and are based on pension data at that date, the amount and form of the journal entry are dependent on the journal entry that was made at the end of the preceding year.

3. Each year's minimum liability journal entry records the amount necessary to *adjust* a company's accrued liability balance or prepaid pension cost balance *to* the minimum liability. As a result, a prepaid pension cost balance must be *added* to unfunded accumulated benefits in order for the adjusted balance to equal the minimum liability.

4. In some instances, the calculated minimum liability may *exceed* unrecognized prior service cost. Since recording the minimum liability may be thought of as recording an intangible asset (prior service cost), based on accumulated benefits rather than on projected benefits, the debit to an intangible cannot exceed unrecognized prior service cost. Any excess must be debited to stockholders' equity.

In summary, recognition of a minimum liability appears to be a compromise between the theoretical recognition approach presented for comparative purposes throughout this chapter and the *Statement No. 87* accounting requirements, under which a liability for prior service cost is not reported. In addition, the minimum liability approach is an interesting, although somewhat inconsistent, compromise in regard to the issue of whether a company's pension obligation should be based on projected benefits or on accumulated benefits. Finally, since a disclosure of this sort was required in companies' footnotes by *Statement No. 36* in 1980, the minimum liability requirement simply brings items previously reported in the footnotes into the balance sheet. In comparison with the *Statement No. 36* disclosures, the minimum liability requirement makes *Statement No. 87* more consistent with *Statement of Financial Accounting Concepts No. 5,* which states that footnote disclosure is not a substitute for recognition in the financial statements, if an economic event meets the criteria for recognition.

TRANSITION REQUIREMENTS AND EFFECTIVE DATE OF STATEMENT NO. 87

Transition Requirements

When a company ceases to apply the provisions of *Opinion No. 8* and begins to apply the provisions of *Statement No. 87,* a change in accounting principle occurs. Should the change in accounting principle be reported as a cumulative effect change in the income statement, as discussed in Chapter 4? Should it be treated retroactively, like a change from the cost method to the equity method of accounting for investments? The FASB chose neither of these approaches because of practical, cost, and political considerations.[11] The

---

[11] These considerations include (1) the infeasibility, in many cases, of obtaining necessary data from prior periods, (2) the cost of obtaining necessary data even when it is feasible to do so, and (3) the possible adverse economic consequences that could result because of the significance of pension amounts.

transition method required by *Statement No. 87* is a "prospective" approach. When the provisions of the *Statement* are applied for the first time, only financial statements of present and future periods are affected.

Under the transition requirements of *Statement No. 87,* an employer must determine, for the beginning of the fiscal year in which the *Statement* is first applied, the amounts of (1) the projected benefit obligation and (2) the fair value of the plan assets. The difference between these two amounts is the funded status of the plan at the transition date. The amount necessary to reconcile the plan's funded status with the employer's prepaid pension cost or pension liability balance at that date is the unrecognized net obligation (or net asset) at the transition date. The unrecognized net obligation (or net asset) at transition must be amortized on a straight-line basis over the average remaining service period of employees who are expected to receive benefits under the plan.[12] This requirement is based, in part, on the assumption that an unrecognized net obligation at transition probably arose from past plan amendments, which were made with the expectation of increased employee productivity in the future.

To illustrate *Statement No. 87* transition requirements, assume that Kim Corporation began to apply the provisions of the *Statement* on January 1, 1987. At that date, the projected benefit obligation was $300,000 and plan assets at fair value were $426,000. In addition, Kim's balance sheet showed a pension liability of $15,000. Thus, the reconciliation schedule on January 1, 1987, would be as follows:

Projected benefit obligation	$(300,000)
Plan assets at fair value	426,000
Funded status	$ 126,000
Unrecognized net asset at transition (reconciling amount)	(141,000)
Pension liability	$ (15,000)

All of the *Statement No. 87* requirements would be applied from January 1, 1987, forward. In addition, the unrecognized net asset at transition ($141,000) would be amortized according to the guidelines set forth above. For example, if the average remaining service period of Kim's active employees was 30 years, annual net pension cost would be reduced by $4,700 ($141,000 ÷ 30 years) each year over the next 30 years. Reconciliation schedules prepared in future years would include the balance of the unamortized net asset (gain) at transition.

Notice that, on the basis of the concepts presented previously, the net asset (gain) of $141,000 represents the aggregation of many pension components applicable to prior periods, such as unrecognized past service cost and unrecognized gains, as well as the cumulative effect of different pension accounting procedures used by Kim prior to the adoption of the *Statement No. 87* provisions.

Effective Date

For most companies, *Statement No. 87* is effective for fiscal years beginning after December 15, 1986. The minimum liability requirement, however, is effective for fiscal years beginning after December 15, 1988. An additional two years was allowed for implementation of the minimum liability recognition in order to give employers time to renegotiate or to obtain waivers of provisions of legal contracts for which liability balances are important.

---

[12] If the average remaining service period is less than 15 years, a company may elect to use 15 years. Furthermore, if all or almost all plan participants are inactive, the amortization period should be the inactive participants' average remaining life expectancy.

DISCLOSURE REQUIREMENTS OF *STATEMENT NO. 87*

In the course of our illustrations and discussion of issues addressed in *Statement No. 87*, we have presented partial disclosures required by the *Statement*. Now we provide an explicit statement of all of the disclosures required by *Statement No. 87* and present an example of such disclosures.

Statement No. 87 requires that an employer sponsoring a defined benefit pension plan shall disclose the following:

1. A description of the plan, including employee groups covered, type of benefit formula, funding policy, types of assets held and significant nonbenefit liabilities, if any, and the nature and effect of significant matters affecting comparability of information for all periods presented.

2. The amount of net periodic pension cost for the period, showing separately the service cost component, the interest cost component, the actual return on assets for the period, and the net total of other components.

3. A schedule reconciling the funded status of the plan with amounts reported in the employer's statement of financial position, showing separately:
   a) The fair value of plan assets.
   b) The projected benefit obligation, identifying the accumulated benefit obligation and the vested benefit obligation.
   c) The amount of unrecognized prior service cost.
   d) The amount of unrecognized net gain or loss.
   e) The amount of any remaining unrecognized net obligation or net asset existing at the date of initial application of *Statement No. 87*.
   f) The amount of any additional liability recognized pursuant to the minimum liability requirement.
   g) The amount of net pension asset or liability recognized in the statement of financial position (which is the net result of items *a* through *f* above).

As you can see, the disclosure requirements of *Statement No. 87* are extensive. To show you what the required disclosures look like in the footnotes to an actual company's financial statements, Exhibit 18–14 presents the 1985 Phillips Petroleum Company footnote disclosures prepared in accordance with *Statement No. 87* requirements. Phillips's early adoption of *Statement No. 87* for 1985 resulted in a negative pension expense (pension income) of $45 million and increased the company's 1985 net income by $31 million.

Many other companies, such as Johnson & Johnson, Du Pont, SeaLand, and Exxon, also elected early adoption of *Statement No. 87*. Because of soaring stock prices in the mid-1980s, most of the early adopters had overfunded pension plans and a net asset when they made the transition to *Statement No. 87*. As a result, the pension expense reported by such companies was significantly less than the amount they would have reported under *APB Opinion No. 8*.

OTHER PENSION AND POSTEMPLOYMENT BENEFIT TOPICS

MULTIEMPLOYER PENSION PLANS

A multiemployer plan is a pension plan to which two or more unrelated employers contribute. A characteristic of multiemployer plans is that assets contributed by one participating employer may be used to provide benefits to employees of other participating employers. *Statement No. 87* states that an employer participating in a multiemployer plan shall recognize as net pension cost the required contribution for the period and shall recognize as a liability any contributions due and unpaid. An employer that participates in

EXHIBIT 18–14 FOOTNOTE DISCLOSURES PREPARED IN
ACCORDANCE WITH *STATEMENT NO. 87* REQUIREMENTS

Phillips Petroleum Company

FROM 1985 ANNUAL REPORT

NOTE 14—RETIREMENT INCOME PLANS

The company elected to adopt FASB Statement No. 87, "Employers' Accounting for Pensions," with respect to its U.S. retirement plans, effective January 1, 1985. Application of FASB Statement No. 87 increased 1985 earnings $31 million ($.11 per common share).

The parent company and its subsidiaries have defined benefit plans covering substantially all employees. The parent company plan is noncontributory and benefits are based on an employee's years of service and average earnings for the three highest consecutive calendar years of compensation during the ten years immediately preceding retirement. Plans of subsidiaries are generally contributory with benefit formulas based on employee earnings. The company's funding policy for U.S. plans is to make, as a minimum contribution, the equivalent of the minimum required by the Employee Retirement Income Security Act of 1974. Plans for the majority of foreign employees are fully insured and premiums are expensed when paid. Pension cost (income) was as follows:

	MILLIONS OF DOLLARS		
	1985	**1984**	**1983**
U.S. Plans			
Service cost—benefits earned during the period	$ 28	$38	$27
Interest cost on projected benefit obligation	101	—	—
Actual return on assets	(300)	—	—
Net amortization and deferral	118	(37)	(2)
Net pension cost (income) for U.S. plans	(53)	1	25
Foreign Plans	8	7	8
Net pension cost (income)	$ (45)	$ 8	$33

**Assumptions Used for U.S. Plans—Weighted
  Average at December 31**

Discount rate	$9\frac{1}{4}$%	8%	8%
Rate of increase in compensation levels	7	6	6
Long-term rate of return on assets	$9\frac{1}{4}$	8	8

For 1984 and 1983, pension cost included current service cost, amortization of unfunded prior service costs and amortization of actuarial gains and losses. Amortization periods ranged from 15 to 40 years. A change in the actuarial cost method from "Entry Age" to "Projected Unit Credit," and substantial actuarial gains for the parent company plan resulting mainly from investments, reduced 1984 pension costs by $13 million and $20 million, respectively.

All of the company's U.S. plans have assets in excess of the accumulated benefit obligation. Plan assets include commingled funds, marketable equity securities, deposit administration insurance contracts, corporate and government debt securities, and real estate. The following table presents a reconciliation of the funded status of the plans at January 1 and December 31, 1985. Prepaid pension cost is included in deferred charges on the company's balance sheet.

	MILLIONS OF DOLLARS			
	DECEMBER 31		**JANUARY 1**	
Plan assets at fair value		$1,454		$1,506
Actuarial present value of benefit obligations:				
Vested benefits	$688		$719	
Nonvested benefits	39		33	
Accumulated benefit obligation	$727		$752	
Effect of projected future salary increases	219		233	
Projected benefit obligation		946		985
Plan assets in excess of projected benefit				
obligation		$ 508		$ 521
Unrecognized net gain		(96)		—
Unrecognized net asset at January 1, 1985		(353)		(495)
Prepaid pension cost		$ 59		$ 26

one or more multiemployer plans shall disclose the following separately from disclosures for a single-employer plan:

1. A description of the multiemployer plan, including the employee groups covered, the type of benefits provided (defined benefit or defined contribution), and the nature and effect of significant matters affecting comparability of information for all periods presented.

2. The amount of cost recognized during the period.

PENSION PLAN TERMINATIONS

Since about 1980, the nation's private corporate pension funds have done very well. Pension fund earnings performance has been good for a variety of reasons, including relatively low inflation rates, healthy bond and stock markets, and the fact that, under ERISA, pension fund assets accumulate tax-free. A majority of the largest pension funds have built up tremendous asset surpluses. In 1985, the nation's 200 largest corporations, ranked by sales, had pension funds with $73 billion in liquid assets that were not needed to provide promised pension benefits.[13]

As a result of the existence of excess pension fund assets, more and more employers terminated asset-rich pension plans and recovered the surplus assets for use in corporate projects unrelated to employee pension benefits. According to the Pension Benefit Guaranty Corporation, the federal insurer of private pension plans, a record 8,674 pension funds were terminated in 1985—more than double the number canceled in 1980. The largest 1985 termination was by United Airlines, which canceled its $962 million plan and targeted the excess money for ''corporate expansion.''[14] *Asset reversions,* such as United's, with replacement of the plan by an annuity contract to cover pension benefits, raise the question of whether any gain or loss should be recognized by the employer at the time the pension assets revert to the corporation.

In 1985, the FASB issued *Statement No. 88,* which established standards for dealing with asset reversions.[15] *Statement No. 88* requirements are based on the pension accounting framework set forth in *Statement No. 87.* In essence, *Statement No. 88* requires recognition in the employer's income statement of any net gain or loss when the employer settles or curtails a pension obligation by either (1) making lump-sum cash payments to plan participants in exchange for the participants' rights to receive specified pension benefits or (2) purchasing nonparticipating annuity contracts to cover vested benefits.

A **settlement** is a transaction that (1) is an irrevocable action, (2) relieves the employer (or the pension plan) of primary responsibility for a pension benefit obligation, and (3) eliminates significant risks related to the obligation and the assets used to effect the settlement.[16] For example, a company might purchase an annuity contract to cover employees' vested benefits or it might make a lump-sum payment to employees in exchange for their rights to receive pension benefits.

A **curtailment** is an event that reduces significantly the expected years of future service of present employees or eliminates for a significant number of employees the accrual of defined benefits for some or all of their future services.[17] For example, a

---

[13] ''The Huge Pension Overflow Could Make Waves in Washington,'' *Business Week,* August 12, 1985, p. 71.

[14] ''The Pension Powder Keg, Whose Pot of Gold Is It?'' *Newsweek,* February 10, 1986, p. 61.

[15] ''Employers' Accounting for Settlements and Curtailments of Defined Benefit Pension Plans and for Termination Benefits,'' *Statement of Financial Accounting Standards No. 88* (Stamford, Conn.: FASB, 1985).

[16] *Statement No. 88,* para. 3.

[17] *Statement No. 88,* para. 6.

company might terminate employees' services earlier than expected or it might terminate or suspend a plan so that its employees would not earn pension benefits for future services. A settlement and a curtailment may occur separately or together.

At a settlement date and/or a curtailment date, the schedule to reconcile the funded status of an employer's pension plan with amounts reported on the company's balance sheet would appear as follows:

Projected benefit obligation	$*(xx)*
Plan assets at fair value	*xx*
Funded status	$*(xx)*
Items not yet recognized in earnings:	
Unrecognized net obligation or (net asset) at transition	*xx*
Unrecognized prior service cost	*xx*
Unrecognized net loss (gain)	*xx*
Prepaid/(accrued) pension cost	$ *xx*

Before the provisions of Statement No. 88 are applied, any net asset arising from transition must be combined with any net gain or loss arising subsequent to the date of transition. In addition, any net obligation arising from transition must be combined with any unrecognized prior service cost. Why are these items combined in this fashion? The FASB reasoned that a transition net asset would be more likely to result from past actuarial gains than from past plan amendments. The Board further reasoned that a transition net obligation would be more likely to result from past plan amendments than from past actuarial losses. Exhibit 18–15 summarizes the accounting requirements for pension plan settlements and curtailments.

Curtailment gains and losses, as well as settlement gains and losses, may be directly related to the disposal of a segment of a business. If they are, the amounts must be included in the calculation of the gain or loss on disposal and must be accounted for under the requirements of *APB Opinion No. 30,* which are discussed in Chapter 4.

Companies often offer special termination benefits to employees who terminate their employment. Phillips Petroleum Company, for example, incurred $62 million in expenses from two early retirement programs in 1985. Phillips reported this event as a noncash accounting transaction because the termination benefits were paid from its pension fund. When termination benefits are offered, a *contingency* arises. Thus, a company must recognize a loss and an associated liability when employees accept such an offer and the amount can be reasonably estimated. The liability is eliminated when the company pays the employees or reimburses the pension fund (if the benefits are paid by the pension fund).

OTHER POSTEMPLOYMENT BENEFITS

Over the years, most of the attention of accounting standard-setters regarding accounting for postemployment benefits has been directed at pension accounting. Other postemployment benefits provided to employees by employers, such as health care or health insurance, life insurance, disability benefits, and several other miscellaneous items, such as company discounts and free tax advice, have received little accounting consideration. In the absence of specific standards, the costs of nonpension postemployment benefits have been accounted for largely on a pay-as-you-go or cash basis.

Seeing the need for standards in the area, in early 1984 the FASB established employers' accounting for postemployment benefits other than pensions as a separate agenda item. A separate agenda item was established because the Board wanted to ensure clear identification and full consideration of the complex measurement and recognition issues

EXHIBIT 18–15 ACCOUNTING FOR PLAN SETTLEMENTS
AND CURTAILMENTS

1. Combine any transition net asset with any unrecognized net loss or gain.

2. Combine any transition net obligation with any unrecognized prior service cost.

SETTLEMENT

3. Maximum gain or loss from settlement is the amount in item 1 above.

4. If the entire projected benefit obligation is settled, the maximum amount is recognized in the income statement.

5. If only part of the projected benefit obligation is settled, a pro rata portion, equal to the percentage reduction in the projected benefit obligation, is recognized in the income statement.

CURTAILMENT

6. The portion of item 2 above associated with reduced future services is recognized as a curtailment loss.

7. The decrease (or increase) in the projected benefit obligation from curtailment is a gain (or loss).

8. If the amount in item 1 is a net loss, the portion of gain in item 7 in excess of the net loss is a curtailment gain; if the amount in item 1 is a net gain, the entire gain in item 7 is a curtailment gain.

9. If the amount in item 1 is a net gain, the portion of loss in item 7 in excess of the net gain is a curtailment loss; if the amount in item 1 is a net loss, the entire loss in item 7 is a curtailment loss.

10. If the sum of item 6 and item 8 (or item 9) is a loss, it is recognized when curtailment is probable and the effects can be estimated. If the sum of item 6 and item 8 (or item 9) is a gain, it is recognized when the related employees terminate or when the plan is suspended or terminated, and is measured at that date.

involved in nonpension postemployment benefits. Because of (1) existing differences in methods of accounting for the cost of health care and life insurance benefits provided to retirees, (2) the lack of disclosures in employers' financial statements about those benefits, and (3) the magnitude of the related costs, the FASB issued *Statement No. 81* as an interim measure, pending completion of the complex overall project.[18] *Statement No. 81* addresses postretirement health care and life insurance benefits provided by individual employers and prescribes only minimum disclosure standards. The minimum disclosures required are as follows:

1. A description of the benefits provided and the employee groups covered.

2. A description of the accounting and funding policies followed for those benefits.

3. The costs of benefits recognized for the period, based on the accounting method described, unless those costs cannot be readily separated from costs for active employees or cannot otherwise be reasonably approximated.

4. The effect of significant matters affecting the comparability of the costs recognized for all periods presented.

[18] "Disclosure of Postretirement Health Care and Life Insurance Benefits," *Statement of Financial Accounting Standards No. 81* (Stamford, Conn.: FASB, 1984).

ACCOUNTING FOR PENSIONS: A SUMMARY

As we stated at the beginning of this chapter, a substantial number of theoretical and pervasive accounting concepts and issues are involved in pension accounting. Moreover, the behavioral implications and economic consequences of a given set of financial accounting standards for pensions make the subject very controversial. Although the pension accounting framework provided by *Statement No. 87* appears to be an improvement over previous accounting standards, several issues remain unresolved, especially when the current pension standards are assessed in the light of the FASB's conceptual framework project. The FASB has acknowledged that, even though the financial reporting standards contained in *Statement No. 87* and *Statement No. 88* represent an improvement over past practices, accounting for pensions remains in a transitional stage. Further changes in pension accounting standards are expected to occur gradually over time.

SUMMARY OF IMPORTANT TOPICS AND CONCEPT APPLICATIONS

1. A private, or employer-sponsored, pension plan is an arrangement under which an employer provides income to retired workers. Such plans exist largely at the discretion of the sponsoring employer and are established by agreements between employers and employees.

2. The Employee Retirement Income Security Act (ERISA), passed by Congress in 1974, established several pension plan requirements, including minimum funding, participation, and vesting requirements. It also created the Pension Benefit Guaranty Corporation (PBGC), which is responsible for ensuring payment of minimum benefits by defined benefit pension plans and for administering defined benefit plans that have been terminated.

3. There are essentially two types of private pension plans: defined contribution plans and defined benefit plans. An employer that institutes a defined benefit plan promises to make benefit payments in specified amounts during retirement years, but the plan does not specify the amount that the employer will contribute to the pension fund. Defined benefit plans are the most difficult to account for and are the subject of this chapter.

4. Determination of employer costs of providing pension benefits is based on the use of present value techniques and requires that assumptions be made about such factors as interest rates, mortality rates, employee turnover, future salary levels, and inflationary trends. Actuaries often are called on to make pension calculations, and amounts calculated are called actuarial present values.

5. Calculation of pension benefits based only on salaries earned to date is called calculation of **accumulated benefits.** Calculation of pension benefits based on salaries that have been earned or may be earned prior to retirement is called calculation of **projected benefits.** The calculation of accumulated benefits is more *reliable,* but calculation of projected benefits may be more *relevant* because it encompasses estimates of future salaries that will affect future cash flows. Also, projected benefits may be more *representationally faithful* because, under the *going concern assumption,* it is presumed that benefits paid will be based on salaries up to the retirement date. *Statement No. 87* requires that the cost of pension benefits be based on *future* salary levels if the pension benefit formula incorporates future salary levels.

6. The *time period assumption* and *accrual accounting* require that the cost of pension benefits be allocated to the years when the employee provides services to the employer. There are two general approaches for allocating pension cost to accounting periods—a cost approach and a benefit approach. *Statement No. 87* requires that a benefit/years-of-service approach be followed and limits the employer to use of the projected unit credit actuarial method in pension calculations.

7. The cost of retirement benefits earned during a particular year is called the **service cost** for that year.

8. The employer's **projected benefit obligation** as of a particular date is the present value of all benefits attributed by the pension plan's benefit formula to employee service rendered prior to that date.

9. Over the term of the pension arrangement between a particular employee and the employer (that is, the credited employee service period plus the retirement period during which benefits are received), the total amount of pension expense recognized is equal to the total amount of cash paid to the pension fund to cover the employer's obligation to the employee in question.

10. Many pension plans give pension benefit credit for years of service rendered before the plan inception date. The cost of benefits arising from credit given for service prior to the plan inception is called **prior service cost.**

11. In theory, the granting of prior service credit results in the incurrence of a liability by the employer—there is a present obligation to transfer economic resources in the future as a result of a past transaction (the prior service). Nevertheless, *Statement No. 87* does not require that the unfunded prior service cost be recorded as a liability.

12. In theory, because prior service credit is given in expectation of future benefits to the employer through employee service, the granting of prior service credit results in acquisition of an asset. The intangible asset representing anticipated future economic benefits to the employer should be amortized to pension expense over the period during which the employer expects to receive the benefits.

13. Pension cost can have six components: (1) service cost, (2) interest on the projected benefit obligation, (3) return on pension assets, (4) amortization of prior service cost, (5) pension gains and losses, and (6) transition gains and losses.

14. The employer is required to disclose, in the notes to the financial statements, a reconciliation of the funded status of its pension plan with amounts reported in the statement of financial position. The funded status is the difference between the projected benefit obligation and the fair value of plan assets.

15. Gains and losses can arise because of (1) differences between actuarial assumptions about the future and what actually occurs or (2) changes in the environment in which the employer operates. *Statement No. 87* requires that a delayed recognition approach be used to account for pension gains and losses. The approach that is to be used in amortizing a net gain or a net loss is the **corridor approach.**

16. *Statement No. 87* requires recognition, at each balance sheet date, of a **minimum liability** at least equal to the employer's unfunded accumulated benefit obligation (accumulated benefit obligation less the fair value of plan assets).

17. **Asset reversions** can be accomplished through **settlements** and/or **curtailments** of pension plans.

APPENDIX 18–1

ACCOUNTING AND REPORTING BY THE PENSION PLAN

The *pension plan* is a separate accounting entity from the *employer* who sponsors the plan. The pension plan has its own accounting records and its own financial statements. Under a defined benefit pension plan, the funding agent receives contributions, invests them in pension assets, incurs obligations to pay pension benefits, and pays pension benefits to qualified employees. All of these transactions and events are recorded in the pension plan's accounts.

As a result of the passage of ERISA, many defined benefit pension plans were required to prepare financial statements in conformity with GAAP. The FASB therefore attempted to establish accounting and reporting standards for the external financial statements of defined benefit pension plans. As we indicated earlier, *Statement of Financial Accounting Standards No. 35,* ''Accounting and Reporting by Defined Benefit Pension Plans'' (1980), is the first authoritative pronouncement issued by the FASB or its predecessor bodies that addresses financial accounting and reporting standards for defined benefit pension plans.

Statement No. 35 applies both to private pension plans and to plans of state and local governmental units. It does not require the preparation, distribution, or attestation of any plan's financial statements. But when external financial statements are prepared, they must meet the requirements of *Statement No. 35*. The disclosure requirements prescribed by the FASB are intended to help pension plan financial statements to provide information that is useful in assessing the plan's present and future ability to pay pension benefits when they are due. The primary reporting and disclosure provisions of *Statement No. 35* are as follows:

1. The annual financial statements of a pension plan shall include:
   a) Information regarding the net assets available to pay benefits as of the end of the plan year. Information regarding net assets must be prepared in accordance with accrual accounting. The fair market value at the reporting date of plan investments (excluding contracts with insurance companies) must be reported.
   b) A statement of changes during the year in net assets available to pay benefits.
   c) The actuarial present value of accumulated plan benefits, calculated in accordance with the accrued benefit actuarial cost method, as of either the beginning or end of the plan year. Presentation as of the end of the year is preferable. If beginning-of-the-year information is presented, the net assets available as of that date as well as the changes in net assets during the preceding year must be given. Accumulated plan benefits are to be presented in three categories: vested benefits of participants currently receiving payments, other vested benefits, and nonvested benefits.
   d) Information regarding the effects, if significant, of factors affecting the year-to-year change in the actuarial present value of accumulated plan benefits, such as plan amendments, changes in the nature of the plan, and changes in actuarial assumptions.

2. Disclosure of a pension plan's accounting policies shall include:
   a) A description of the methods and significant assumptions used to determine the fair market value of investments and the reported value of contracts with insurance companies.
   b) A description of the method and significant assumptions (for example, assumed rates of return, inflation rates, and retirement ages) used to determine the actuarial

present value of accumulated plan benefits. Any significant changes in method or assumptions between benefit information dates shall be described.

c) Several additional disclosures that *may* be applicable, such as a description of the plan agreement, a description of plan amendments during the current year, the funding policy and any changes in that policy during the current year, and the federal income tax status of the plan.

QUESTIONS	The question marked with an asterisk (*) refers to Appendix 18–1.

Q18-1. What is a pension plan? Distinguish between public and private pension plans.

Q18-2. What parties typically are involved in a private pension plan arrangement, and what role does each party play in the arrangement?

Q18-3. Distinguish between contributory and noncontributory pension plans.

Q18-4. What is the purpose of vesting provisions in a pension plan? What does it mean to say that contributions to the pension are fully vested?

Q18-5. Distinguish between a fully funded and partially funded pension plan.

Q18-6. Private pension plans are of essentially two types: defined contribution plans and defined benefit plans. Describe each of these two types of pension plans.

*Q18-7. Discuss and contrast accounting for pensions by the employer (sponsor) and accounting by the pension plan.

Q18-8. What objectives were stressed by the FASB in its work leading to *Statement Nos. 87* and *88?*

Q18-9. What is an actuarial valuation?

Q18-10. Why is an actuarial present value calculated at any point in time only an estimate?

Q18-11. Distinguish between projected pension benefits and accumulated pension benefits.

Q18-12. Why may the calculation of accumulated benefits be more reliable than the calculation of projected benefits?

Q18-13. Why may the calculation of projected benefits be more relevant and more representationally faithful than the calculation of accumulated benefits?

Q18-14. What general approach for allocating the cost of pension benefits to accounting periods is required by *Statement No. 87?*

Q18-15. What is meant by the concept of service cost?

Q18-16. What is included in the projected benefit obligation as of any particular date?

Q18-17. List the potential components of pension cost.

Q18-18. Name the allocation method for a plan benefit formula that defines benefits in terms of years of service.

Q18-19. Distinguish between a final-pay pension benefit plan and a flat-benefit plan.

Q18-20. How do earnings on pension plan assets affect each of the following: net assets of the pension fund, required contributions to the fund, and employer's pension cost?

Q18-21. Define prior service cost.

Q18-22. Why may prior service cost be considered to be a liability? Does current GAAP require that unfunded prior service cost be recorded as a liability?

Q18-23. How can gains and losses arise in the accounting for an ongoing pension plan?

Q18-24. Under GAAP, how are we to account for actuarial gains and losses in measuring periodic pension cost?

Q18-25. When is the corridor approach used?

Q18-26. What is the minimum liability that must be recognized at each balance sheet date under *Statement No. 87?*

Q18-27. Outline the disclosures required for a defined benefit pension plan under *Statement No. 87.*

Q18-28. What is an asset reversion?

Q18-29. List the minimum disclosures required by *Statement No. 81,* ''Disclosure of Postretirement Health Care and Life Insurance Benefits.''

Q18-30. With respect to pension plans, what is a settlement? a curtailment?

CASES

C18-1. PENSION COST COMPONENTS; DISCLOSURE   You are the controller for Beverly Corporation. Several years ago, the company initiated a noncontributory defined benefit pension plan for its employees. At the beginning of 1987, Beverly began to apply the provisions of *Statement Nos. 87* and *88.* At that time, the funded status of its pension plan was a deficiency of $600,000 because the projected benefit obligation of $1.5 million exceeded the fair value of its plan assets of $900,000. In addition, the unrecognized net obligation at the date of transition was $1 million. In accordance with the requirements of *Statement No. 87,* Beverly used a "benefit/years-of-service" approach to measure the projected benefit obligation and will use this approach, in conjunction with a discount rate of 8 percent, to measure the service component of periodic pension cost. The expected return on plan assets is 7 percent. Finally, Beverly decided to use the straight-line method to amortize the unrecognized net obligation over the 20-year remaining period of service of employees expected to receive benefits under the plan.

Pension expense for 1987 was $307,000, and the company contributed $280,000 to the pension fund in 1987. No benefits were paid by the pension fund during 1987. At the end of fiscal 1987, the accumulated benefit obligation equaled 80 percent of the projected benefit obligation.

You have prepared the following footnote information for the fiscal year 1987 annual report (amounts shown are in thousands of dollars):

COMPONENTS OF NET PENSION COST		**RECONCILIATION OF PLAN FUNDED STATUS WITH AMOUNT SHOWN ON ENDING BALANCE SHEET**	
Service cost	$200	Projected benefit obligation	$(1,820)
Interest cost	120	Plan assets at fair value	1,017
Actual return on plan assets (loss)	163	Funded status	$ (803)
		Items not yet recognized in earnings:	
Net amortization and deferral	(176)	Unrecognized net obligation	950
		Unrecognized net loss	226
Total	$307	Prepaid pension cost	$ 373

The president of Beverly Corporation is very confused about the pension information for the annual report and has prepared the following questions for you to answer:

a) Why is interest included as a part of net pension cost instead of being reported as interest expense?

b) What caused the unrecognized net loss and what justification is there for deferring it, rather than recognizing it in the 1987 income statement?

c) What is the rationale for amortizing the unrecognized net obligation over the remaining service period of employees expected to receive benefits under the pension plan?

d) What makes up the "net amortization and deferral" portion of net pension cost?

e) *Statement No. 87* requires the recording of a minimum liability under certain circumstances. Will Beverly be required to record one? If so, what journal entry will be necessary?

The president also says that she does not quite understand why the reconciliation schedule is necessary. She recently has read *Concepts Statement No. 5* and believes that if the information in the reconciliation schedule is useful, disclosure should not be a substitute for recognition in the financial statements.

REQUIRED

1. Prepare a brief response to each of the five questions raised by Beverly Corporation's president. Support your responses with calculations where necessary.

2. Prepare a response to the president's concern about the reconciliation schedule both from a theoretical standpoint and from the standpoint of the standards-setting environment.

3. Refer to requirement 2. Indicate what the effects on the fiscal 1987 financial statements would be if accounting recognition were given to items in the reconciliation schedule presented above.

C18-2. PENSION PLAN SETTLEMENTS   This case is a continuation of Case 18-1. Assume that early in fiscal 1988, Beverly Corporation settled the vested portion of the projected benefit obligation and appropriately recognized a settlement loss of $40,000. Near the end of 1988, Beverly's president comes to you even more confused than she was at the end of 1987. She cannot understand what portion of the projected benefit obligation was settled. Furthermore, she fails to see why recognition of the loss is appropriate in 1988 if recognition was not appropriate in 1987, especially when viewed in terms of conservatism.

REQUIRED

Prepare a brief response to the president's questions and concerns.

C18-3. PRIOR SERVICE COST   Checkerboard Corporation's board of directors recently approved a noncontributory defined benefit plan for the corporation's 3,000 employees. Checkerboard has been in existence for over 30 years, and the Board of Directors decided to grant retroactive pension benefits to the employees. The benefit formula is not based on future compensation levels, but rather provides a fixed-dollar retirement benefit for each year of service. In addition, employees are given credit for prior service up to a maximum of 20 years prior to the plan inception date.

Checkerboard's president majored in accounting in college and is curious about the nature of the retroactive pension benefits, which he also calls *prior service cost*. He has asked you, the controller, the following questions:

a) From a theoretical standpoint, does the obligation arising from the granting of retroactive benefits represent a liability to Checkerboard?

b) If so, has Checkerboard also incurred an expense or a loss, acquired an asset, or suffered a reduction in stockholders' equity?

c) Under the accounting requirements of *Statement No. 87,* what are the financial statement effects of prior service cost during the first year of the plan's existence?

REQUIRED

Prepare a brief answer to each of the president's questions.

C18-4. MINIMUM LIABILITY   Your friend recently attended an accounting conference that featured a round-table discussion of pervasive accounting concepts. One participant discussed "financial statement articulation." He said that articulation meant that "two classes of financial statement elements include statement of financial position elements and income statement elements. They are related in such a way that elements of the former class are changed by elements of the latter class, and, at any time, are their cumulative result." He also stated that "articulation results in financial statements that are fundamentally related. Thus, information appearing on the balance sheet is related to information appearing on the income statement, and vice versa."

Upon returning home, your friend began to study *Statement No. 87,* "Employers' Accounting for Pensions." She noticed that the *Statement* requires that future compensation levels be used to calculate the service cost component of pension expense and to determine the projected benefit obligation for disclosure purposes. (The projected benefit obligation also is used to calculate the interest component of pension expense.) However, she also noticed that the *Statement* requires that a minimum liability, equal to the unfunded accumulated benefit obligation, be recorded and presented in an employer's statement of financial position. Since the projected benefit obligation and some components of pension expense are based on *future* compensation, whereas the accumulated benefit obligation and the minimum liability are based on *current* compensation levels, she was puzzled about whether these requirements are consistent with the accounting concepts (especially articulation) presented at the conference.

REQUIRED

Prepare a brief response to your friend's comments, explaining the apparent inconsistency.

EXERCISES

E18-1. CALCULATING ANNUAL PENSION EXPENSE   The Hudson Company sponsors a contributory pension plan. In 1987 a total of $200,000 was withheld from employees' paychecks and deposited in the pension fund. In addition, Hudson deposited $400,000 of its own money in the fund in 1987.

Actuarial calculations as of the end of 1987 indicated that net pension cost for 1987 was $640,000, including $140,000 of prior service cost amortization. As a result of this information, Hudson contributed an additional $40,000 of its own money to the pension fund in early 1988.

REQUIRED

1. Distinguish between contributory and noncontributory pension plans.

2. Calculate the amount of pension expense that Hudson should report for 1987.

(AICPA, adapted)

E18-2. CALCULATING AND RECORDING PENSION EXPENSE AND FUND CONTRIBUTIONS The Miller Company adopted a pension plan at the beginning of 1987 on a funded, noncontributory basis. Miller amortizes prior service cost over 17 years (the remaining service period of employees granted retroactive benefits) and funds prior service cost over 10 years. The service cost component of pension expense is funded as it is incurred each year. The following schedule shows amortization and funding of prior service cost for 1987 and 1988:

	1987	1988
17-year amortization of prior service cost	$100,000	$100,000
Interest on projected benefit obligation	136,000	162,880
10-year funding of prior service cost (each year-end)	253,349	253,349
Return on plan assets	–0–	36,268
Prepaid pension cost (on balance sheet):		
Balance as of 12/31	17,349	44,086
Increase for year	17,349	26,737

Both the discount rate and the rate of return on plan assets are 8 percent.

REQUIRED

1. If the service component of pension cost in 1987 was $200,000, what was Miller Company's pension expense for 1987?

2. If the service component of pension cost in 1988 was $220,000, what entries would Miller make in 1988 to record pension expense and funding?

E18-3. FUNDED STATUS OF PENSION PLAN Refer to Exercise 18-2. Calculate the funded status of Miller's plan on December 31, 1988, and prepare a schedule that reconciles the funded status of the plan with the pension amounts reported on Miller's balance sheet on December 31, 1988.

E18-4. PENSION EXPENSE AND PREPAID PENSION COST McMahon adopted a pension plan for its employees at the beginning of 1987. An actuary provided the following information:

a) The pension service cost component for 1987 is $10,000.

b) Prior service cost at the beginning of 1987 is $70,000.

Management decided to fund prior service cost in full at the beginning of 1987 and to fund the service cost component in full at the end of each year. Prior service cost will be amortized over the remaining service period (10 years) for employees given retroactive benefits. Both the discount rate and the rate of return on plan assets are 12 percent.

REQUIRED

1. Calculate pension expense for 1987.

2. What is the balance in the prepaid pension cost account at the end of 1987?

3. Prepare a schedule that reconciles the funded status of McMahon's pension plan with the amounts reported in the company's balance sheet at the end of 1987.

E18-5. PENSION COST COMPONENTS Darlene Corporation adopted a defined benefit pension plan for its employees. At the plan inception date the projected benefit obligation, arising from credit for prior service and based on a 6 percent discount rate, was $40,000. The annual service cost components for the first five years were as follows (the amounts follow no specific pattern because of newly hired employees, attrition, and other factors, but were calculated in accordance with a benefits approach): year 1, $20,000; year 2, $27,000; year 3, $34,000; year 4, $40,000; year 5, $48,000.

Darlene decided to fund an amount each year equal to net pension cost less amortization of prior service cost and to fund prior service cost with three equal year-end payments of $13,333, beginning at the end of year 1. The expected return on plan assets was 10 percent. Prior service cost is to be amortized over a five-year period, which is the remaining service period for employees granted retroactive benefits.

REQUIRED

1. Prepare a schedule, similar to the one in Exhibit 18–8, which shows the calculation of net pension cost for years 1 through 5.

2. Using data from the schedule prepared in part 1, make all necessary journal entries for years 1 and 4.

3. Reconcile the funded status of Darlene's pension plan at the end of year 3 with the amounts reported on the corporation's balance sheet at that date.

E18-6. PENSION GAINS AND LOSSES Sandmeyer began to apply the provisions of *Statement No. 87* on January 1, 1987. At the transition date, the unrecognized net obligation (asset) was not material. The table below shows the projected benefit obligation (PBO) and the market-related value (fair value) of plan assets for the years 1987–1992:

YEAR ENDING 12/31	PROJECTED		ACTUAL		REASONS FOR DIFFERENCE
	PBO	PLAN ASSETS	PBO	PLAN ASSETS	
1987	$100,000	$ 60,000	$100,000	$ 60,000	—
1988	130,000	76,000	130,000	96,000	Actual return > expected return
1989	173,000	123,600	173,000	107,000	Actual return < expected return
1990	225,300	146,960	180,000	180,000	Increased discount rate; actual return > expected return
1991	210,000	220,000	210,000	200,000	Actual return < expected return
1992	245,000	233,000	260,000	233,000	Decreased discount rate

REQUIRED

1. Calculate the pension gain or loss for each year.

2. Determine the amount of pension gain or loss amortization for each year, assuming that at the transition date, the average remaining service period for employees expected to receive retirement benefits was 12 years.

3. Calculate the accumulated benefit obligations as of the benefit information date.

E18-7. RECORDING PENSION EXPENSE Buzby, Inc., a calendar-year corporation, adopted a noncontributory pension plan at the beginning of 1987. Buzby used a benefit approach actuarial method to determine the service cost component of pension cost for 1987 and 1988 of $30,000 and $33,000, respectively. These amounts were funded at the end of each of those years.

The granting of retroactive benefits gave rise to a projected benefit obligation at the beginning of 1987. Buzby funded this amount, plus accrued interest, in full on December 31, 1987, by contributing $110,000 to the pension fund. Prior service cost is being amortized over a 10-year period, based on the provisions of *Statement No. 87*. The assumed discount rate is 10 percent, as is the expected rate of return on plan assets.

REQUIRED

Prepare journal entries to record the funding of prior service cost on December 31, 1987, and the pension expense for the years 1987 and 1988. Assume actual experience equaled expectations.

E18-8. NET ASSET OR OBLIGATION AT TRANSITION At the beginning of 1987, Roderick Corporation began to apply the provisions of *Statement No. 87*. At that date the projected benefit obligation was $1 million and the fair value of plan assets was $910,000. Roderick's balance sheet showed an accrued pension liability with a balance of $30,000 at the beginning of 1987.

REQUIRED

Calculate the unrecognized net obligation or net asset at the transition date.

E18-9. CALCULATING PENSION EXPENSE Early in 1987, Bradley Company adopted a noncontributory defined benefit pension plan. Using a 6 percent discount rate, an actuary calculated a $100,000 prior service cost at the plan inception date. The service cost components of net pension cost for the years ended December 31, 1987, 1988, and 1989 were $15,000, $18,000, and $22,000, respectively. The rate of return on plan assets is 8 percent. At the beginning of 1989, the pension plan was amended, resulting in an increase of $30,000 in the projected benefit obligation.

Bradley contributed an amount equal to the service cost component to the pension fund at the end of each year, but did not fund any of the prior service cost during the three-year period. At the plan inception date, the average remaining years of service for employees expected to receive benefits under the plan was 20 years.

REQUIRED

Determine Bradley Company's annual pension expense for 1987, 1988, and 1989.

E18-10. RECONCILIATION SCHEDULE Refer to Exercise 18-9. Prepare a schedule to reconcile the funded status of Bradley's pension plan with amounts reported on the company's balance sheet at December 31, 1989.

E18-11. CALCULATING PENSION VARIABLES The following information relates to the status of a pension plan. For simplicity, assume that only a single employee is covered by the plan.

    a) Benefit formula: Annual year-end payment of 2.5 percent of highest year's salary for each year of service (up to a maximum of 100 percent).

    b) Retirement date: December 31, 1989.

    c) Expected date of death: December 31, 1991.

    d) Projected benefit obligation as of January 1, 1987: $19,396.

    e) Fair value of plan assets as of January 1, 1987: $10,000.

    f) Unamortized prior service cost as of January 1, 1987: $9,396.

    g) Interest rate used to compute benefit obligations: 10 percent.

    h) Employee's years of service as of January 1, 1987: 17.

    i) Salary during 1987: $25,000.

    j) Expected salary during 1989: $35,000.

    k) Earnings on plan assets during 1987: $1,200.

    l) Cash contribution to plan on December 31, 1987: $3,000.

REQUIRED

    1. Calculate the projected benefit obligation as of December 31, 1987.

    2. Calculate the accumulated benefit obligation as of December 31, 1987.

    3. Determine the fair value of the plan assets as of December 31, 1987 (after the $3,000 contribution on December 31, 1987).

    4. Calculate pension expense for 1987.

    5. Calculate the minimum liability to be reported on the balance sheet as of December 31, 1987.

E18-12. CALCULATING NET GAIN OR LOSS FROM CURTAILMENT Listed below are four cases involving curtailment of a pension plan:

	CASE			
ITEM	1	2	3	4
Projected benefit obligation decrease (increase) from transition . .	$100,000	$80,000	$(65,000)	$90,000
Unrecognized net asset at transition plus unrecognized gain (loss)	60,000	(55,000)	(20,000)	(95,000)
Loss from reduced prior service cost (including net obligation at transition)	(30,000)	(36,000)	(20,000)	(30,000)

REQUIRED

For each case, calculate the net gain or loss from curtailment.

E18-13. PENSION SETTLEMENT, CURTAILMENT, TERMINATION Teagarden sponsors a noncontributory defined benefit plan for its employees. Teagarden had the following pension disclosure in the notes to its financial statements for the year ending December 31, 1989:

Accumulated benefit obligation:	
Vested	$ (90,000)
Nonvested	(60,000)
Effects of future compensation levels	(30,000)
Projected benefit obligation	$(180,000)
Plan assets at fair value	120,000
Unrecognized net asset at transition	(20,000)
Unrecognized prior service cost	50,000
Unrecognized net loss	40,000
Prepaid pension cost...	$ 10,000

Consider each situation below separately.

A) Assume that on January 1, 1990, Teagarden settled the vested portion of the accumulated benefit obligation by using plan assets to purchase annuity contracts for employees covered by the plan.

REQUIRED

Prepare the journal entry to record the settlement.

B) Assume that on January 1, 1990, Teagarden terminated several of its employees. The termination resulted in the following:

   a) Nonvested accumulated benefits were reduced by $20,000.
   b) Projected benefits from future compensation levels were reduced by $12,000.
   c) Unrecognized prior service cost associated with the terminated employees was $15,000.

REQUIRED

Prepare the journal entry to record the plan curtailment.

C) Assume that on January 1, 1990, Teagarden terminated its pension plan. Nonvested accumulated benefits became vested upon termination. Pension plan assets and Teagarden's cash were used to pay a lump-sum settlement to employees covered by the plan. The plan then ceased to exist and was not replaced with another plan.

REQUIRED

Prepare the journal entry to record termination of the pension plan.

PROBLEMS

Problems 18-1 through 18-4 are intended to increase your familiarity with and understanding of serveral important pension concepts. The employee data used in Problems 18-1 through 18-4 (see below) are single-employee data so that complexity does not interfere with the learning process. Problems 18-1 through 18-4 can be worked as a group or as independent problems.

PENSION PLAN DATA AND EMPLOYEE DATA
FOR PROBLEMS 18-1 THROUGH 18-4

PENSION PLAN DATA

   a) Defined benefit, noncontributory pension plan.
   b) Retirement benefits paid at year-end, with the first payment one year after retirement.
   c) Assumed discount rate is 6 percent.
   d) Pension plan formula is:

Annual retirement benefit = $.016 \times n \times$ Highest salary level

where n equals the number of years of service that qualify for pension credit, subject to a maximum of 30 years.

DATA FOR A PARTICULAR EMPLOYEE

 e) Retirement age of 62.

 f) Expected retirement period of 18 years.

 g) Employee is 40 years old when the plan is adopted.

 h) Employee began working for the company at age 38.

 i) Various salary levels for the employee:

AGE	SALARY LEVEL
38	$12,000
40	15,000
44	18,000
45	20,000
62	60,000

P18-1.   PENSION COST COMPONENTS; SERVICE COST AND INTEREST   Assume the pension plan and employee data given above and assume that no credit is given for service before adoption of the plan.

REQUIRED

 1. Draw a diagram similar to the one on page 826 to show the relationship between the pension plan and the employment and retirement life of the employee.

 2. Calculate the estimated annual retirement benefit at the time of retirement.

 3. Calculate the projected benefit obligation at the time of retirement.

 4. Calculate the service cost and interest cost components of pension cost for years 1 and 2.

 5. Calculate net pension cost for years 1 and 2, assuming $1,200 contributions to the pension fund at the end of each year. The pension fund earns a 10 percent rate of return.

P18-2.   PENSION COST COMPONENTS; PRIOR SERVICE COST   Using the pension plan and employee data given before Problem 18-1, assume that pension credit is given for up to five years of service before adoption of the pension plan.

REQUIRED

 1. Explain how prior service cost is related to the service cost component of periodic net pension cost.

 2. Calculate the expected annual retirement benefit arising from prior service credit.

 3. Calculate the projected benefit obligation at the plan inception date.

 4. Calculate the amount of prior service cost amortization that would be included in net pension cost for each year.

P18-3.   PLAN AMENDMENTS   Assume *(a)* the pension plan and employee data that are given before Problem 18-1, *(b)* that pension credit is given for up to five years of service before adoption of the plan, and *(c)* that five years after adoption, the plan benefit formula was amended to:

Annual retirement benefit $= .02 \times n \times$ Highest salary level

REQUIRED

 1. Discuss the impact of the plan amendment on *(a)* the annual expected retirement benefit and *(b)* the projected benefit obligation at the amendment date.

 2. Calculate the projected benefit obligation at the amendment date based on the amended plan formula.

 3. Calculate the amount of prior service cost amortization that would be included in net pension cost for each year following the amendment date.

P18-4. ACCUMULATED BENEFIT OBLIGATION AND MINIMUM LIABILITY   Both *Statement No. 87* (employers' accounting for pensions) and *Statement No. 35* (accounting and reporting by the pension plan) require information about accumulated plan benefits. Therefore, an understanding of accumulated plan benefits, sometimes called the accumulated benefit obligation, and of the relationship between the accumulated benefit obligation and the projected benefit obligation is very important.

Assume *(a)* the pension plan and employee data given prior to Problem 18-1, *(b)* that credit is given for a maximum of five years of service before the plan's adoption, and *(c)* a benefit information (actuarial valuation) date four years after adoption of the plan.

REQUIRED

1. Distinguish between the accumulated benefit obligation and the projected benefit obligation.

2. Calculate the accumulated plan benefit per year of retirement, as of the benefit information date.

3. Calculate the accumulated benefit obligation, as of the benefit information date.

4. *Statement No. 87* requires the recording, at the balance sheet date, of a minimum liability at least equal to the unfunded accumulated benefit obligation. Calculate the minimum liability, as of the benefit information date, assuming that the fair value of plan assets was $3,000 at that date.

5. Refer to part 4. Prepare the journal entry, if any, to record the minimum liability, assuming that at the benefit information date the employer's balance sheet showed prepaid pension cost of $800.

P18-5. PENSION COST COMPONENTS; NON-PAY-RELATED PLAN   On January 1, 1987, Zebra Corporation initiated a noncontributory defined benefit pension plan for all five employees in its word processing department. (Employees in other departments already were covered by a pension plan.) The plan benefit formula provides that each year of service earns each employee an annual retirement benefit of $3,000. The benefits are payable at the end of each retirement year. All five employees are expected to retire on December 31, 1991, and each is expected to live for four years following retirement.

Zebra also provided retroactive benefits for employee services rendered prior to January 1, 1987. Total years of service for which retroactive benefits were granted equaled 25 years. Arrangements were made for an outside trustee to administer all aspects of the plan on Zebra's behalf.

The following additional data are pertinent:

   a) Expected return on plan assets, 10 percent.
   b) Discount rate applicable to the projected benefit obligation, 8 percent.
   c) Zebra will contribute a level amount each year to the pension fund, which, together with earnings at 10 percent, will fully fund the projected benefit obligation by December 31, 1991. Zebra will make five annual contributions, beginning on January 1, 1987. Zebra will purchase an annuity contract on December 31, 1991, to settle its pension obligation.

Assume that actual results equal the original estimates and assumptions, and that Zebra's fiscal year ends on December 31.

REQUIRED

1. Draw a time diagram, similar to the one on page 827, to show the relationship between the pension plan and the employment and retirement life of Zebra's employees. (Be sure to show the total amount of benefits expected to be paid each year over the employees' retirement period.)

2. Calculate the amount that Zebra should contribute to the pension fund each year.

3. Calculate prior service cost on January 1, 1987.

4. Prepare a schedule, similar to Exhibit 18-8, which shows the annual calculation of pension expense.

5. Prepare all necessary entries for 1987, 1989, and 1991 (ignore the minimum liability).

6. Prepare a schedule that reconciles the funded status of Zebra's pension plan with Zebra's pension-related balance sheet amounts at the end of 1987.

7. Calculate the minimum liability for 1987 and 1988.

P18-6. PENSION COST COMPONENTS; PLAN AMENDMENTS   Refer to Problem 18-5. Assume that on January 1, 1990, Zebra amended the plan by increasing the annual retirement benefits to $3,450 for each year of service. Zebra made no changes in the contributions to the pension fund. All other problem data remain the same.

REQUIRED

1. Prepare a schedule that shows the annual calculation of pension expense.

2. Prepare *(a)* all necessary journal entries for 1990 (ignore the minimum liability) and *(b)* a schedule reconciling funded status with Zebra's balance sheet amounts at December 31, 1990.

3. Calculate the amount that Zebra would need to contribute to the pension fund at the end of 1991 in order to fully fund the projected benefit obligation at that time.

P18-7. PENSION COST COMPONENTS; PLAN ASSET GAIN   Refer to Problem 18-5. Assume that on December 31, 1989, the fair value of the pension plan assets was $390,000. During 1990 and 1991, however, the plan assets continued to earn a 10 percent rate of return. All other problem data remain the same.

REQUIRED

1. Calculate the gain or loss on plan assets for the year ending December 31, 1989.

2. Calculate Zebra's pension expense for 1989 and 1990.

3. Prepare schedules to reconcile the funded status of Zebra's pension plan with Zebra's pension-related balance sheet amounts at December 31, 1989 and 1990.

P18-8. PENSION COST COMPONENTS; JOURNAL ENTRIES   When Wintersteen Corporation adopted its defined benefit pension plan, the projected benefit obligation arising from the grant of retroactive benefits to employees was $165,000, based on a benefit approach and an 8 percent discount rate. The service cost component of pension cost was $25,000 for year 1 and $30,000 for year 2. The following amounts were contributed to the pension fund at the end of each year: year 1, $40,000; year 2, $40,000. The rate of return on plan assets is 8 percent.

Since the average remaining period of service for employees expected to receive benefits under the plan was less than 15 years, Wintersteen decided to use 15 years as the amortization period, in accordance with *Statement No. 87.*

REQUIRED

1. Make the necessary journal entries in Wintersteen Corporation's books for years 1 and 2.

2. Indicate the accounts and amounts related to the pension plan that would appear on Wintersteen's balance sheet and income statement for year 1.

3. Prepare a schedule to reconcile the funded status of Wintersteen's pension plan with the amounts reported on the corporation's balance sheet at the end of year 2.

P18-9. GAINS AND LOSSES; MINIMUM LIABILITY   Cook Corporation, a calendar-year company, adopted a noncontributory defined benefit pension plan on January 1, 1987. The pension plan granted retroactive benefits for prior service. On the basis of the plan benefit formula, Cook's actuarial consultants used a "benefit/years-of-service" method and a 10 percent discount rate, and determined that the projected benefit obligation at the plan inception date was $300,000. This amount is to be amortized over a 16-year period, which is the average remaining service period for employees expected to receive benefits under the plan.

Management decided to fund the service cost component of pension cost at the end of each year. Prior service cost would be funded by a $100,000 contribution to the pension fund's trustee at the beginning of 1987, followed by equal payments at the end of each year for 20 years for the $200,000 balance. The rate of return on plan assets is expected to be 10 percent. The actuarial consultants and Cook's accountants provided the following information related to the pension plan for the years ending December 31, 1987 and 1988:

	1987	1988
Pension service cost component	$80,000	$85,000
Amortization of prior service cost	18,750	18,750
Funding of prior service cost	23,491	23,491

No changes in assumptions were necessary during the first two years. Experience results equaled the original estimates, except that during 1987 there was a $50,000 loss on the sale of plan assets and on write-downs of plan assets to market value.

REQUIRED

1. Calculate net pension cost for 1987 and 1988.

2. Prepare all necessary journal entries for Cook Corporation for both years.

3. Show how Cook's footnote disclosure of net pension cost would appear for 1987.

4. Prepare a schedule that reconciles the funded status of Cook's pension plan with amounts appearing on the corporation's balance sheet at December 31, 1988.

5. Assume that on December 31, 1988, employees' accumulated plan benefits equaled 60 percent of the projected benefit obligation. Prepare any necessary entry for Cook Corporation to record the minimum liability at that date.

P18-10. PENSION COMPONENTS; PLAN TERMINATION   Several years ago, McVay Company initiated a non-contributory defined benefit plan for its employees. A schedule that reconciles the funded status of its plan with the amount reported on the company's balance sheet at the beginning and end of the current year appears below:

	BEGINNING	END
Projected benefit obligation	$(400,000)	$(478,000)
Plan assets at fair value	285,000	397,800
Funded status	$(115,000)	$ (80,200)
Unrecognized net obligation at transition	60,000	54,000
Unrecognized net gain	(50,000)	(49,000)
Accrued pension liability	$(105,000)	$ (75,200)

McVay recorded pension expense for the current year as follows:

Pension expense	60,200	
Accrued pension liability	29,800	
Cash		90,000

No retirement payments were made during the year. Actual results for the current year equaled expectations, and there were no changes in assumptions. The service cost component of pension cost equaled 95 percent of the interest cost component.

REQUIRED

1. Calculate the following for the current year:
   a) Rate of return on plan assets.
   b) Discount rate used.
   c) Service cost component of pension cost.
   d) Interest cost component of pension cost.

2. Assume that at the end of the current year McVay terminated its pension plan, which defined benefits in terms of a flat benefit per year. Plan assets and the necessary amount of cash were used to purchase nonparticipating annuity contracts equal to the projected benefit obligation, which was fully vested. Prepare the journal entry to record the termination of the plan.

P18-11. SETTLEMENT OF A PENSION OBLIGATION   Refer to Problem 18-10. Assume that the plan benefit formula was based on future compensation levels. At the end of the current year, McVay settled a $382,400 portion of the fully vested accumulated benefit obligation by using plan assets to purchase annuity contracts on its employees' behalf.

REQUIRED

Prepare the entry to record the settlement.

P18-12. COMPREHENSIVE   Several years ago, Groff Company initiated a noncontributory defined benefit pension plan for its employees. On December 31, 1986, Groff's statement of financial position showed an accrued pension liability of $65,000.

On January 1, 1987, Groff began to apply the provisions of *Statement No. 87,* and the funded status of the plan at that date was as follows:

Projected benefit obligation . . . . $(1,400,000)
Plan assets at fair value   1,800,000
Funded status . . . . $ 400,000

Financial data relating to the pension plan for the years 1987–1990 are as follows:

	1987	1988	1989	1990
Service cost component	$ 80,000	$ 86,400	$111,974	$120,932
Fund contributions (beginning of each year)	75,000	90,000	160,000	100,000
Retirement payments by fund (end of each year)	155,000	180,000	240,000	260,000
Plan asset loss	–0–	225,000	–0–	–0–
Liability gain (decrease in projected benefit obligation)	–0–	–0–	90,000	–0–

The expected return on plan assets was 10 percent, and the discount rate applicable to the projected benefit obligation was 8 percent. These estimates and assumptions were realized, except for the gain and loss above. On December 31, 1989, an amendment to the plan increased the projected benefit obligation by 20 percent. As of January 1, 1987, the average remaining service period for employees expected to receive plan benefits was 20 years.

REQUIRED

1. Reconcile the funded status of Groff's pension plan with the company's pension liability on January 1, 1987, the transition date.

2. Calculate the projected benefit obligation and the plan assets on December 31 for each of the four years above.

3. Prepare all necessary journal entries for Groff Company for each year.

4. Prepare the footnote disclosure for fiscal years 1988 and 1989, showing the components of net pension cost (pension expense) reported on Groff's income statement.

5. Prepare the footnote disclosure that reconciles the funded status of Groff's pension plan with amounts reported on the company's December 31, 1990, balance sheet.

6. Assume that the accumulated benefit obligation at December 31, 1990, is $1.5 million. Will Groff be required to record a minimum liability? Explain.

19 INCOME TAXES

A recent study of 275 major corporations reported that in 1984, 40 of these firms, with combined profits of more than $10 billion, paid no federal income taxes.[1] In fact, 36 of the 40 corporations received tax refunds. American Telephone & Telegraph Company (AT&T) reported net income of $1.9 billion, yet received a tax refund of $241.6 million. During the period covered by the study, 1981–1984, Boeing Company had net income of more than $2 billion but received $285 million in tax refunds. General Electric Company had no federal tax liability from 1981 through 1983, and in 1984 paid only $185 million in taxes on income of $3 billion. Even though the statutory corporate tax rate was 46 percent during the period of the study, the average effective tax rate for the corporations surveyed was 15 percent.

Another recent study reported that major companies in the oil and gas industry had an effective tax rate in 1984 of 8.4 percent.[2] Publishing and broadcasting companies paid an average tax of 30.5 percent of pretax earnings while aerospace manufacturers paid just 15.3 percent of pretax earnings, even though these two industries reported about the same average pretax profits as a percentage of sales in 1984—about 6.5 percent.

How is it that corporations faced with a statutory tax rate of 46 percent can pay little or no taxes, or get a tax refund, even though they are highly profitable? The answer is that a number of allowable deductions and credits enable corporations to minimize their tax burden while reporting substantial profits for financial accounting purposes. Companies in capital-intensive industries often achieve substantial tax savings by using accelerated depreciation methods for tax purposes. For example, CSX Corporation, the owner of the Chessie System Railroad and the Seaboard Coast Line Railroad, had an effective tax rate in 1984 of 3 percent, attributable primarily to accelerated depreciation. Also, defense contractors often defer profit recognition for tax purposes until the contracts are completed, although they recognize income as progress occurs for financial accounting purposes. For example, Boeing Company had pretax income of $569 million in 1984 but paid taxes of only $5 million, owing largely to tax deferrals of $298 million from completed contract accounting.

The investment tax credit has enabled many firms to reduce their tax bills. AT&T reduced its taxes by $372 million in 1984 by this means. The investment tax credit constituted about 27 percent of AT&T's 1984 net income. To put the magnitude of invest-

[1] "No U.S. Income Taxes Were Paid in '84 by 40 Big, Profitable Firms, Study Says," *The Wall Street Journal,* August 29, 1985, p. 8.

[2] "What Makes Corporate Taxes a Target for Tax Reform?" *Business Week,* June 10, 1985, pp. 96–99.

ment tax credits in perspective, consider that the U.S. Treasury estimated that federal receipts from corporate taxes in 1985 would be about $66 billion, and that the investment tax credit would reduce corporations' 1985 tax bills by $26 billion!

To summarize, it should not be surprising that *taxable income* may differ considerably from *pretax accounting income*. The government's basic objective in levying taxes is to provide revenues for its operations. At the same time, Congress designs tax laws to encourage some types of economic and social activity and to discourage others. Corporations' objectives in measuring accounting income, on the other hand, are to provide the users of financial reports with information to help them in decision-making and, as a result, to promote the efficient allocation of scarce resources.

In this chapter we address the issues associated with accounting for income taxes. As this text goes to press, an *Exposure Draft* of a *Proposed Statement of Financial Accounting Standards,* titled ''Accounting for Income Taxes,'' is being considered by the Financial Accounting Standards Board.[3] Because any *Statement* resulting from the *Exposure Draft* is not likely to be issued until well into 1987 at the earliest, our presentation is based on existing generally accepted accounting principles. However, at the end of the chapter, we provide a glimpse of the possible changes by summarizing the general proposals contained in the *Exposure Draft*.

DIFFERENCES BETWEEN PRETAX ACCOUNTING INCOME AND TAXABLE INCOME

Differences between pretax accounting income and taxable income can be classified as *timing differences* and *permanent differences*. We shall examine each in turn.

TIMING DIFFERENCES

Many differences between taxable income and pretax accounting income are caused by **timing differences** in the recognition of revenues and expenses for financial accounting purposes and tax return purposes. Although over the life of an entity exactly the same *amount* of revenue or expense is recognized for certain items for both accounting and tax purposes, the amount of revenue or expense recognized in each period differs. In other words, timing differences originate in one period and are reversed in one or more later periods. Exhibit 19–1 provides some common examples of timing differences. Because of timing differences, a company's tax liability in a given period differs from the amount of taxes implied by the revenues and expenses reported for accounting purposes.

In addition to the examples in Exhibit 19–1, significant additional timing differences have resulted from the Economic Recovery Tax Act of 1981. The purpose of the Act was to stimulate capital investment and to increase productivity. It accomplishes these goals by shifting the emphasis in determining depreciation expense for tax purposes from the useful life concept to recovery of capital invested. The Act provides for five classes of depreciable property, with each class having a specified predetermined depreciation schedule for tax purposes. This system, called the **accelerated cost recovery system (ACRS),** represents a radical departure from the concept of depreciation used for financial reporting. The ACRS guidelines result in additional timing differences because depreciation for tax purposes is recorded over fewer years and in different amounts than depreciation for financial reporting. The 1986 Tax Reform Act revised the ACRS guidelines. Under this act there are eight classes of depreciable property, and in general, the depreciation schedules are longer.

The accelerated cost recovery system results in significant timing differences.

[3] ''Accounting for Income Taxes,'' *Proposed Statement of Financial Accounting Standards* (Stamford, Conn.: FASB, 1986).

EXHIBIT 19—1   EXAMPLES OF TIMING DIFFERENCES

I. Items recognized earlier for accounting purposes than for tax purposes.
  A. Revenues (or gains).
    1. Percentage-of-completion method used for accounting purposes in accounting for long-term contracts, but completed-contract method used for tax purposes.
    2. Profit (loss) on installment sales recognized at time of sale for accounting purposes, but installment method used for tax purposes.
    3. Earnings of foreign subsidiaries recognized currently for accounting purposes, but recognized when remitted for tax purposes.
  B. Expenses (or losses).
    1. Estimated warranty costs deducted on an accrual basis for accounting purposes, but expensed as incurred for tax purposes.
    2. Costs of bonus plans and deferred compensation accrued for accounting purposes, but deducted when paid for tax purposes.
    3. Pension costs deducted on an accrual basis for accounting purposes, but deducted when paid to trustee for tax purposes.
    4. Estimated inventory losses recognized when reasonably anticipated for accounting purposes, but deducted only when goods are disposed of for tax purposes.
    5. Estimated losses from litigation recorded when probable and amount reasonably determinable for accounting purposes, but recognized when actually incurred for tax purposes.
    6. Estimated losses from discontinued operations accrued for accounting purposes when reasonably determinable, but recognized on disposal for tax purposes.

II. Items recognized later for accounting purposes than for tax purposes.
  A. Revenues (or gains).
    1. Unearned revenue recognized when received for tax purposes, but deferred and recognized when earned for accounting purposes.
    2. Gain on sale in connection with sale-leaseback transaction recognized at date of sale for tax purposes, but deferred and recognized over life of lease for accounting purposes.
    3. Customer deposits on sale contracts recognized when received for tax purposes, but deferred until goods are delivered for accounting purposes.
  B. Expenses (or losses).
    1. Depreciation expense recognized on an accelerated basis for tax purposes, but deducted on a straight-line basis for accounting purposes.
    2. Depreciable assets depreciated over a shorter life for tax purposes than for accounting purposes.
    3. Sales commissions paid on signing of sales contract recognized when paid for tax purposes, but deferred and recognized when goods are shipped for accounting purposes.
    4. Interest incurred during construction deducted as incurred for tax purposes, but capitalized as part of cost of asset for accounting purposes.

Source: Adapted from Homer A. Black, ''Interperiod Allocation of Corporate Income Taxes,'' *Accounting Research Study No. 6* (New York: AICPA, 1966), pp. 8–10.

The Accounting Issue Resulting from Timing Differences

The existence of timing differences has created a dilemma for accountants. The basic issue is whether the periodic provision for income taxes in the income statement, also called income tax expense, should be based on pretax accounting income or on taxable income. Further, if income tax expense is based on pretax accounting income, how should the difference between income tax expense and the tax liability be reported in the financial statements?

Assume that Reliable Company has annual revenues of $100,000 and annual expenses (excluding depreciation) of $50,000 for 1987, 1988, and 1989. With the exception

EXHIBIT 19–2   CALCULATION OF TAX LIABILITY

Reliable Company

	1987	1988	1989	TOTAL
Revenues...	$100,000	$100,000	$100,000	$300,000
Expenses (excluding depreciation)	(50,000)	(50,000)	(50,000)	(150,000)
Income before depreciation and income taxes	$ 50,000	$ 50,000	$ 50,000	$150,000
Depreciation expense	(30,000)	(20,000)	(10,000)	(60,000)
Taxable income......................................	$ 20,000	$ 30,000	$ 40,000	$ 90,000
Tax liability at 40% (taxes payable)	$ 8,000	$ 12,000	$ 16,000	$ 36,000

EXHIBIT 19–3   INCOME STATEMENTS WHEN TIMING
DIFFERENCES ARE IGNORED

Reliable Company

	1987	1988	1989	TOTAL
Revenues...	$100,000	$100,000	$100,000	$300,000
Expenses (excluding depreciation)	(50,000)	(50,000)	(50,000)	(150,000)
Income before depreciation and income taxes	$ 50,000	$ 50,000	$ 50,000	$150,000
Depreciation expense	(20,000)	(20,000)	(20,000)	(60,000)
Income before income taxes	$ 30,000	$ 30,000	$ 30,000	$ 90,000
Provision for income taxes (per tax return, from Exhibit 19–2)	(8,000)	(12,000)	(16,000)	(36,000)
Net income	$ 22,000	$ 18,000	$ 14,000	$ 54,000

of depreciation, revenues and expenses are the same for accounting and tax purposes. At the beginning of 1987, Reliable purchases a fixed asset for $60,000 cash. The estimated useful life is three years and no salvage value is anticipated. Reliable uses the straight-line method of depreciation for accounting purposes, but uses sum-of-the-years'-digits for tax purposes. Thus, annual depreciation expense for accounting purposes is $20,000 ($60,000 ÷ 3 years), but for tax purposes is $30,000 for 1987 (3/6 × $60,000), $20,000 for 1988 (2/6 × $60,000), and $10,000 for 1989 (1/6 × $60,000). Assuming a 40 percent tax rate, Exhibit 19–2 shows the calculation of Reliable's tax liability for each of the three years.

For accounting purposes, if Reliable reports income tax expense equal to the tax liability calculated in the tax return, the income statements for the three years would appear as in Exhibit 19–3. On the other hand, if Reliable bases its calculation of income tax expense on pretax accounting income, the income statements for the three years would appear as in Exhibit 19–4.

As the exhibits indicate, depreciation expense included in the determination of pretax accounting income for 1987 and 1989 differs from depreciation expense included in the determination of taxable income for those years. If one ignores the timing difference in 1987, as in Exhibit 19–3, the effective tax rate for 1987 is 26.7 percent ($8,000 ÷ $30,000). The reason for the relatively low effective tax rate in 1987 is the *temporary* tax

EXHIBIT 19—4 INCOME STATEMENTS WHEN TIMING DIFFERENCES ARE RECOGNIZED

Reliable Company

	1987	1988	1989	TOTAL
Revenues	$100,000	$100,000	$100,000	$300,000
Expenses (excluding depreciation)	(50,000)	(50,000)	(50,000)	(150,000)
Income before depreciation and income taxes	$ 50,000	$ 50,000	$ 50,000	$150,000
Depreciation expense	(20,000)	(20,000)	(20,000)	(60,000)
Income before income taxes	$ 30,000	$ 30,000	$ 30,000	$ 90,000
Provision for income taxes (at 40%)	(12,000)	(12,000)	(12,000)	(36,000)
Net income	$ 18,000	$ 18,000	$ 18,000	$ 54,000

advantage provided by use of accelerated depreciation for tax purposes. The temporary advantage is offset by a 53.3 percent effective tax rate ($16,000 ÷ $30,000) when the timing difference is reversed in 1989. If timing differences are ignored, however, the provision for income taxes may be misleading if the figures are used to project future cash flows for income taxes. If one observed the 26.7 percent effective tax rate in 1987 and assumed that this relationship was indicative of future tax burdens, erroneous decisions could result.

To avoid misleading inferences, the accounting profession has adopted the process of **interperiod income tax allocation** to deal with situations in which pretax accounting income and taxable income differ as a result of timing differences. The income statements in Exhibit 19–4 reflect interperiod tax allocation. In each year, the provision for income taxes is 40 percent of pretax accounting income. In other words, the temporary postponement of taxes in 1987 does not reduce the 1987 income tax expense. Likewise, the payment of the postponed taxes of $4,000 in 1989 does not increase the 1989 income tax expense.

Reasons for Interperiod Tax Allocation

Interperiod tax allocation is the generally accepted accounting practice for dealing with the tax effects of timing differences in the recognition of revenues, expenses, gains, and losses. Under interperiod tax allocation, the tax effect of income statement items affects income tax expense in the period in which the items are reported in pretax accounting income, regardless of when the items are included in taxable income. In *Opinion No. 11,* the APB identified four specific underlying ideas that support interperiod tax allocation:

1. The going-concern assumption is adopted, in the absence of evidence to the contrary.

2. Income taxes are an expense.

3. Accounting for income taxes involves accrual, deferral, and estimation, just like other expenses.

4. The matching principle is fundamental to income determination.[4]

The assumption of a going concern implies that the business entity will continue to exist long enough to carry out its present commitments. In the context of our depreciation

[4] "Accounting for Income Taxes," *Opinions of the Accounting Principles Board No. 11* (New York: AICPA, 1967), para. 14.

case, this means that, in the absence of evidence to the contrary, we assume the business will operate and earn income long enough for the temporary tax advantage to be reversed.

The other three ideas enunciated in *Opinion No. 11* are closely related to each other. First, the APB adopted the view that income taxes are an expense of doing business, like cost of goods sold, salaries, depreciation, rent, and interest expense. Expenses are actual or expected cash outflows resulting from major operations during a period.[5]

The adoption of the position that income taxes are an expense implies that *accrual accounting* is appropriate for expenses (and other elements) if the measurement and recognition criteria are satisfied.[6] Accrual accounting requires that firms recognize the cash consequences of transactions, events, and circumstances in the periods when they occur, rather than in the periods when cash is received or paid. The use of accrual accounting, and the associated *matching principle,* implies that income tax expense should be determined on the basis of revenues and expenses reported for accounting purposes during the period, regardless of the timing of revenue and expense recognition for tax purposes. That is, income tax expense is matched (reported in the same period) with the pretax accounting income that gives rise to the tax obligation, regardless of the timing of tax payments.

Note that Reliable's total income tax expense over the three-year period is $36,000 (Exhibits 19–3 and 19–4), whether or not timing differences are recognized for accounting purposes. Thus, the issue being addressed is the *timing* of recognition of the tax benefits from the depreciable asset. Over the three-year period, Reliable Company deducts $60,000 of depreciation expense. Since depreciation is deductible for tax purposes, the tax obligation over the three years is $24,000 (.40 × $60,000) *less* than it would have been without the depreciation deduction. That is, the depreciation provides a reduction in taxes or a "tax shield" of $24,000. Without interperiod tax allocation, Reliable would distribute this tax benefit over the three years in accordance with the timing of the depreciation deductions for tax purposes (see Exhibit 19–2): $12,000 in 1987 (.4 × $30,000); $8,000 in 1988 (.4 × $20,000); and $4,000 in 1989 (.4 × $10,000). Using interperiod tax allocation procedures, Reliable would recognize the tax benefit evenly over the three years in accordance with the recognition of depreciation expense for accounting purposes (see Exhibit 19–4): $8,000 (.4 × $20,000) in 1987, 1988, and 1989.

The Basic Process of Interperiod Tax Allocation

In the absence of timing differences, the tax liability and the provision for income taxes in the income statement would be identical. The entry to record the expense and the liability (assuming for simplicity that no taxes have been paid on the accrued amount during the period) would take the following form:

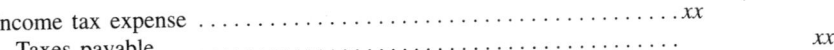

Income tax expense . . . . *xx*
    Taxes payable . . . .   *xx*

However, if timing differences exist and income tax expense is based on pretax accounting income, income tax expense will differ from taxes payable. The account *deferred income taxes* is used to account for the tax effect of timing differences.

---

[5] See "Elements of Financial Statements," *Statement of Financial Accounting Concepts No. 6* (Stamford, Conn.: FASB, 1980), para. 81.

[6] Identification as an expense is a necessary but not a sufficient condition for recognition of income taxes in the income statement. Income taxes also must meet the other recognition criteria. They must be measurable, relevant, and reliable, and they are subject to a cost-benefit constraint and a materiality threshold ("Recognition and Measurement in Financial Statements of Business Enterprises," *Statement of Financial Accounting Concepts No. 5* [Stamford, Conn.: FASB, 1984], para. 63).

To see how the deferred income taxes account is used when pretax accounting income initially exceeds taxable income because of a timing difference, consider the following journal entries for 1987 through 1989 to record Reliable's tax expense and tax liability and the difference between these two amounts:

```
1987 Income tax expense (.4 × $30,000) ................... 12,000
        Taxes payable (.4 × $20,000) ......................        8,000
        Deferred income taxes (.4 × $10,000) ...............        4,000

1988 Income tax expense (.4 × $30,000) ................... 12,000
        Taxes payable (.4 × $30,000) ......................       12,000

1989 Income tax expense (.4 × $30,000) ................... 12,000
     Deferred income taxes (.4 × $10,000) ................  4,000
        Taxes payable (.4 × $40,000) ......................       16,000
```

Income tax expense is calculated by multiplying the tax rate by pretax accounting income. Taxes payable is calculated by multiplying the tax rate by taxable income. Deferred income taxes is calculated by multiplying the tax rate by the difference between pretax accounting income and taxable income. The deferred income taxes ledger account would appear as follows at the end of 1989:

Deferred income taxes			
12/31/89	4,000	12/31/87	4,000

The account is credited in 1987 because pretax accounting income (and income tax expense) is greater than taxable income (and taxes payable). The timing difference in 1987 is called an **originating difference.** In 1989, taxable income exceeds pretax accounting income and so we must debit the deferred income taxes account. The 1989 timing difference is called a **reversing difference.** Over the three-year period, income tax expense and taxes payable both total $36,000. The deferred income taxes account absorbs the *temporary* differences between these two items. Thus, deferred income taxes increases when originating differences occur (1987) and decreases when reversing differences occur (1989). The zero balance at the end of 1989 indicates that the timing difference has been completely reversed.

Originating differences increase deferred taxes; reversing differences decrease deferred taxes.

To understand the process when taxable income initially exceeds pretax accounting income, consider Albrecht Company, which receives rent revenue of $40,000 cash at the end of 1987. For financial reporting purposes, Albrecht recognizes the rent revenue in 1988, when it is earned. For tax purposes, Albrecht includes the $40,000 in taxable income in 1987. The income tax rate is 40 percent, and there are no other differences between taxable income and pretax accounting income. Income before consideration of the $40,000 and before income taxes is $200,000 in both 1987 and 1988. Journal entries for 1987 and 1988 are as follows:

```
1987 Income tax expense (.4 × $200,000) ................... 80,000
     Deferred income taxes (.4 × $40,000) ................. 16,000
        Taxes payable (.4 × $240,000) ......................       96,000

1988 Income tax expense (.4 × $240,000) ................... 96,000
        Taxes payable (.4 × $200,000) ......................       80,000
        Deferred income taxes (.4 × $40,000) ...............       16,000
```

Taxes payable exceeds income tax expense in 1987 by $16,000, which is the tax rate (40 percent) times the originating timing difference of $40,000. Income tax expense exceeds taxes payable in 1988 by $16,000 because the timing difference of $40,000 is reversed in

1988. The deferred income taxes account would appear as follows at the end of 1988:

Deferred income taxes			
12/31/87	16,000	12/31/88	16,000

In contrast to the previous example, here the originating difference produced a debit to deferred income taxes and the reversing difference produced a credit to deferred income taxes.

**ALTERNATIVE
APPROACHES TO
INTERPERIOD TAX
ALLOCATION**

Conceptually, there are alternative ways to apply interperiod tax allocation. These alternatives may be categorized as (1) partial versus comprehensive allocation and (2) methods of interperiod tax allocation.

Partial vs. Comprehensive Allocation

There are two basic views about the extent to which interperiod tax allocation procedures should be applied. One of these views advocates partial allocation and the other supports comprehensive allocation. The two views reflect fundamental differences of opinion about the nature of income tax expense. Each view is presented below.

PARTIAL ALLOCATION   Proponents of **partial allocation** believe that, generally, income tax expense should be the same as the taxes payable for the period. They argue that interperiod tax allocation should not be used for recurring timing differences when they give rise to an *indefinite postponement* or prepayment of taxes. The tax effects of recurring timing differences are *remote contingencies*. Thus, the application of interperiod tax allocation procedures may overstate or understate the cash flow consequences.

Taxes are assessed on an aggregate income measure rather than on individual revenues and expenses. Thus, if a growing company uses accelerated depreciation for tax purposes and straight-line depreciation for accounting purposes, the company may indefinitely postpone the tax effect of the timing difference, especially in periods of inflation. While the timing differences on *individual* assets would be reversed, the *aggregate timing difference* would not be reversed so long as the company continued at least to maintain its operating capacity. In essence, because originating differences on new plant assets offset reversing differences on older plant assets, the aggregate net timing difference continues to grow. Further, the amount of deferred taxes is not anticipated to require cash outflows in the foreseeable future. Thus, it is argued that no liability exists and interperiod tax allocation is inappropriate.

For the tax effect of recurring depreciation timing differences to have potential relevance, plant acquisitions must be declining, which means that the company may be incurring losses and so may not be paying taxes. Thus, even when the going concern assumption seems questionable, the relevance of interperiod tax allocation for recurring timing differences is debatable. Since future cash flows resulting from the timing difference are not reasonably predictable, current income tax expense should not include the tax effect of the reversal of the timing difference. Rather, the best estimate of future cash outlays for taxes is the amount of taxes payable currently.

Partial allocation advocates believe interperiod tax allocation is appropriate only for nonrecurring timing differences expected to reverse in the near term.

Proponents of partial allocation argue that interperiod tax allocation is appropriate only when timing differences are not recurring and when they are expected to be reversed in a relatively short time. For example, a company may own only one depreciable asset, which it depreciates on an accelerated schedule for tax purposes and by the straight-line method for accounting purposes. Tax allocation is appropriate in this instance because the timing difference is not expected to recur and because the tax effect of the difference is reasonably certain to affect cash flows in the near future. In this case, interperiod tax allocation provides better cash flow signals than would be provided in the absence of interperiod tax allocation.

COMPREHENSIVE ALLOCATION   Proponents of **comprehensive allocation** argue that taxes payable for the period do not necessarily provide the best measure of the tax consequences of the transactions that enter into the determination of pretax accounting income. Instead, income tax expense should include the tax effects of all transactions included in pretax accounting income for the period. Income tax expense accrues as transactions are included in the determination of pretax accounting income, regardless of the timing of recognition of items for tax purposes. In accordance with accrual accounting, income tax expense is *matched* with the items that give rise to it. Partial allocation, because of its emphasis on cash flows, is considered to be a departure from accrual accounting.

> Comprehensive alloca-
> tion advocates believe
> all timing differences
> should lead to inter-
> period tax allocation.

Advocates of comprehensive allocation argue that individual timing differences, both recurring and nonrecurring, are expected to be reversed, that their tax effects are measurable, and therefore that tax allocation procedures are appropriate. The fact that originating timing differences on new plant assets may offset the tax effect of reversing differences on older plant assets is irrelevant—the timing differences on individual assets are reversed. Accounting principles should not rely on the assumption that offsets will continue indefinitely.

GAAP   The APB concluded in *Opinion No. 11* that ''comprehensive interperiod tax allocation is an integral part of the determination of income tax expense.''[7] Although the APB did not state explicitly why it adopted the comprehensive approach, the *Opinion* implies acceptance of the arguments related to accrual accounting, the matching principle, and the revolving nature of timing differences. Acceptance of the comprehensive approach also is more objective, because it avoids the problem of distinguishing between recurring and nonrecurring timing differences.

Methods of Interperiod Tax Allocation

Three methods of interperiod tax allocation have received some support: the deferred method, the liability method, and the net-of-tax method.

DEFERRED METHOD   Under the **deferred method,** deferred (or prepaid) taxes are recorded at the amount of taxes postponed (or prepaid) as a result of a timing difference. For example, Reliable Company postponed the payment of $4,000 of income taxes in 1987 as a result of the timing difference. The deferred amount was calculated by multiplying the 1987 tax rate of 40 percent by the timing difference of $10,000.[8]

In general, the deferred amount is based on the tax rate in effect in the period in which timing differences originate. Future tax rates have no relevance under the deferred method, because this method emphasizes the tax effect of originating differences rather than that of reversing differences. When timing differences later are reversed, income tax

---

[7] *APB Opinion No. 11,* para. 34.

[8] This ''shortcut'' approach to determining the tax effect of the timing difference cannot be used when there are certain complications, such as a capital gain or loss or a surtax exemption. In such cases, the ''with-without'' technique must be used. Under this technique, the deferred tax adjustment is the difference between (1) the amount of taxes actually payable (the *with* calculation) and (2) the amount of taxes that would be payable if all revenue and expense items entering into pretax accounting income also were reported at the same amount for tax purposes (the *without* calculation). In both of these calculations, special rates and surtax exemptions are applied as appropriate. Under the *Exposure Draft,* which is summarized at the end of the chapter, the with-without technique would no longer be applicable, because it relates only to the deferred method.

expense is adjusted for the same amount that was deferred when the timing difference originated.

Advocates of the deferred method are divided as to whether a deferred tax credit constitutes a liability and whether a deferred tax debit constitutes an asset. Also, many advocates of this method do not consider valuation of the deferred amount in terms of anticipated future cash flows to be a major consideration. *The deferred method emphasizes the income statement, and does not look forward in terms of what tax rates are expected to be when the differences reverse.*

LIABILITY METHOD   Under the **liability method,** the objective is to record as income tax expense the *expected* tax consequences of items that enter into the determination of pretax accounting income. Thus, the tax effects of originating differences are calculated at the tax rate expected to be in effect when the timing differences are reversed. If an originating difference causes pretax accounting income to exceed taxable income, the tax effect of the timing difference is a *liability for taxes payable* in the future. If the originating difference causes taxable income to exceed pretax accounting income, the tax effect of the timing difference is an *asset for prepaid taxes*. *The liability method emphasizes the balance sheet impact of timing differences.*

The emphasis is on the ultimate cash consequences of the items that have a tax effect. Current tax rates have no relevance to the recording of the tax effect of originating timing differences, except insofar as current rates are indicative of rates expected to exist when the timing differences are reversed. Since future cash flows related to the tax effect of timing differences receive primary emphasis in this method, changes in tax rates which were unanticipated when the tax effects of originating differences were recorded would cause an adjustment in the liability for taxes payable or in the asset for prepaid taxes. Theoretically, any long-term liability for taxes payable or asset for prepaid taxes should be discounted and recorded at its present value to be consistent with the treatment of other long-term monetary liabilities and assets.

NET-OF-TAX METHOD   The **net-of-tax method** is related to both the deferred method and the liability method because it requires the application of one of these two methods. The issue under the net-of-tax method is the appropriate balance sheet and income statement presentation of the tax effect of timing differences. The net-of-tax method treats the tax effect of timing differences—that is, the deferred amount—as an adjustment to the valuation of the asset or liability that gives rise to the timing difference and to related revenues or expenses. This method recognizes that taxability of revenues and tax deductibility of expenses are relevant factors in the valuation of assets and liabilities. For example, if a firm depreciates an asset more rapidly for tax purposes than for accounting purposes, the tax effect of the timing difference reduces the value of the related asset because of the loss of future tax deductibility of the excess depreciation. Under the net-of-tax method, the firm reduces the carrying value of the asset by the tax effect of the timing difference and includes in depreciation expense an amount for the tax effect of the timing difference. Because the tax effect of timing differences is used to adjust related revenue and expense accounts rather than to adjust income tax expense, income tax expense and taxes payable for the period are equal under the net-of-tax method.

GAAP   *APB Opinion No. 11* requires the deferred method. The APB provided little rationale for the choice of the deferred method, stating only that it ''provides *the most useful and practical approach* to interperiod tax allocation and the presentation of income taxes in financial statements.''[9]

---

[9]*APB Opinion No. 11,* para. 35 (emphasis added).

The deferred method is probably the least objectionable of the three possible methods. It is more *verifiable* because it does not require estimates of future tax rates or of the timing of reversals. It emphasizes current tax savings or prepayments. It does not require one to take a position regarding the liability status of deferred credits or the asset status of deferred charges. It discloses the effects of tax allocation, whereas the net-of-tax method may bury such effects.

We believe, however, that the liability method is more consistent with the objective of providing information useful in predicting cash flows. Future cash flows related to income taxes can best be predicted when the tax effects of originating timing differences are deferred at the tax rate expected to be in effect when the difference is reversed. Such a procedure emphasizes the ultimate cash consequences of the aggregate timing differences rather than the current tax savings. The tax effect of the timing difference, discounted if the term is long, would constitute a liability (assuming a credit difference) valued at the cash payment required to eliminate the obligation. Income measured under this approach would provide more meaningful cash flow signals.

The main weakness of this argument is related to the definition of a liability as a "probable future sacrifice of economic benefits arising from present obligations."[10] While the taxes deferred as a result of originating timing differences may constitute a "probable future sacrifice of economic benefits" (just as planned capital expenditures do, for example), it is not clear that there is a "present obligation." Taxes become payable in the future only when a firm has *future* taxable income. Until it does so, it has no obligation to anyone. The federal government does not have a legal claim against entities when deferred tax credits originate. Resolution of this issue seems to hinge on whether an originating timing difference constitutes a past transaction or event that creates a present obligation, or whether future taxable income must occur to create the obligation. If the former is determined to be the case, the liability method is conceptually sound, even though measurement problems may exist. If the latter is determined to be the case, then the entire process of interperiod tax allocation would appear to be inappropriate.

GAAP requires comprehensive allocation using the deferred method.

In summary, GAAP currently requires the application of interperiod tax allocation procedures on a comprehensive basis using the deferred method. (The FASB's September 1986 *Exposure Draft* requires use of the liability method.) Within this framework, additional refinements often are necessary to apply GAAP to actual situations. We discuss the practical application of the deferred method in the next section.

PRACTICAL APPLICATIONS OF THE DEFERRED METHOD

Only one timing difference caused Reliable Company's pretax accounting income to differ from its taxable income. In reality, a number of timing differences may affect a business in an accounting period. Some of these differences may be originating differences and others may be reversing differences. Keeping track of the tax effect of these timing differences on an item-by-item basis can become fairly complicated. Thus, in practice the individual-item basis is used only when a small number of significant timing differences exist. In all other instances, the **group basis** is used.

When it becomes impractical to account for timing differences on an individual-item basis, firms may group *similar* timing differences to determine the tax effect of timing differences. For example, a company may group fixed assets being depreciated on an accelerated basis for tax purposes and on a straight-line basis for accounting purposes. Likewise, all installment sales for which a firm recognizes gross profit for accounting purposes in the period of sale and on a cash collection basis for tax purposes may constitute a group.

If a firm uses the group basis, it may calculate the tax effect under either the gross change method or the net change method. Once a firm selects a method for a particular

[10] *Statement of Financial Accounting Concepts No. 6*, para. 35.

group of timing differences, it must apply that method consistently unless it can demonstrate that the other method is preferable.

Gross Change Method

Under the **gross change method,** the adjustment to deferred income taxes for the period for a group of similar timing differences is the *net* of two calculations:

1. The tax effect of *originating timing differences* for the group, based on the *current period tax rate,* which increases deferred taxes. (Note that the originating difference may cause either a debit or a credit to deferred taxes.)

2. The tax effect of *reversing timing differences* for the group, based on appropriate *prior period tax rates* when the originating differences occurred, which decreases deferred taxes.

The difference between the results of these two calculations is the change in deferred income taxes for the group of timing differences.

The tax rates may not be the same in all years in which originating differences occur. Therefore, some assumption must be made regarding the year of origination when the tax effect of reversing differences is calculated. When it is not practical or possible to associate specific reversing differences with specific originating differences, a firm may adopt either a FIFO or average rate assumption to amortize (reduce) deferred taxes when reversing differences occur. All of the examples in this chapter assume, for the sake of simplicity, that reversing differences can be identified with specific originating differences.

To illustrate the gross change method, assume the following tax rates for Tompkins Company:

YEAR	TAX RATE
1987	30%
1988	40
1989	40
1990	45

Further, assume the following timing differences on depreciable fixed assets from the use of ACRS depreciation for tax purposes and the straight-line method for accounting purposes:

YEAR	AMOUNT	ORIGINATING (O) OR REVERSING (R)
1987	$10,000	*O*
1988	12,000	*O*
1989	14,000	*O*
1990	12,000	*O*
	4,000	*R**

* Reversal of portion of 1987 originating difference.

Pretax accounting income for 1990 is $200,000. Taxable income for 1990 is $192,000. The deferred income taxes account at the beginning of 1990 is as follows:

Deferred income taxes		
	12/31/87	3,000
	12/31/88	4,800
	12/31/89	5,600

Under the gross change method, the change in deferred income taxes at the end of 1990 is as follows:

Tax effect of *originating* timing differences (.45 × $12,000)............. $5,400
Tax effect of *reversing* timing differences (.30 × $4,000) .... (1,200)
Net increase in deferred income taxes $4,200

The journal entry to record income tax expense and taxes payable and to adjust deferred taxes is as follows:

Income tax expense ($86,400 + $4,200) 90,600
    Taxes payable (.45 × $192,000)   86,400
    Deferred income taxes (per above)   4,200

Note that income tax expense cannot be calculated directly from pretax accounting income because the income tax effect of reversing timing differences is recognized at prior period tax rates. Taxes payable is calculated directly from the tax return and the net change in deferred taxes is calculated by the gross change method. Income tax expense is a *residual calculation,* the amount required to balance the journal entry.

Net Change Method

For any group of similar timing differences for which a firm uses the **net change method,** it nets originating timing differences against reversing timing differences for the group and applies the current period tax rate to the net timing difference. The resulting amount is the increase or decrease in deferred taxes.

If Tompkins Company used the net change method, the change in deferred taxes for 1990 would be as follows:

Originating timing differences $12,000
Reversing timing differences ....   (4,000)
Net *originating* difference .... $ 8,000

Net increase in deferred income
    taxes (.45 × $8,000) .... $ 3,600

The journal entry to record tax expense and taxes payable and to adjust deferred taxes would be as follows:

Income tax expense (.45 × $200,000) 90,000
    Taxes payable   86,400
    Deferred income taxes   3,600

The gross change method and the net change method differ in the tax rate applied to reversing differences.

In contrast to the gross change method, under the net change method income tax expense can be calculated from pretax accounting income because both originating and reversing differences are accounted for at the current period rate. That is, the tax effects of reversing timing differences are not recognized at prior period rates as they are under the gross change method. Stated another way, *under the gross change method we look back at prior period rates for reversing differences, but under the net change method we do not look back.*

Taxes payable is unaffected by the choice of the net change or gross change method ($86,400 in both instances). Taxes payable is calculated by multiplying the current period tax rate by taxable income. This calculation is *independent* of any accounting procedures employed to calculate deferred taxes. Likewise, if tax rates do not change over time, the gross change and net change methods produce the same results for income tax expense and for the change in deferred taxes. In the more realistic situation of tax rate changes, however, the two methods produce different results for income tax expense and for the change in deferred taxes.

The primary advantages of the net change method usually are simplicity and understandability. It is not necessary to keep track of specific originating differences. Under the net change method, however, we record the tax effects of originating timing differences at one rate and, assuming tax rate changes, we record the tax effects of reversing timing differences at another rate. Thus the deferred income taxes account balance related to a particular group of similar timing differences may not be a reasonable representation of the actual tax effects of the timing differences. It is possible that a deferred tax balance could remain after all reversing timing differences of a particular type have occurred.[11]

The gross change method is logically superior to the net change method. Reversals take place at the same rate as the originating deferrals, thus producing a zero balance in deferred taxes when all timing differences have been reversed. From a practical standpoint, however, the more complex gross change method may not be justified in the common situation where companies are expanding and, thus, originating differences continually overwhelm reversing differences. Recall that the only way in which the methods differ is in the tax rate applied to reversing differences. Thus, despite the theoretical deficiency of the net change method, its popularity and general acceptance can be expected to continue.

PERMANENT DIFFERENCES

Certain revenue and expense items are included in *either* pretax accounting income *or* taxable income, but not both. Those items that are not included in taxable income are said to be **tax-exempt.** Other items are recognized as expenses in the determination of pretax accounting income but are not deductible in the calculation of taxable income. For example, a firm deducts goodwill amortization for accounting purposes but cannot deduct it for tax purposes. Such items are called **permanent differences** between pretax accounting income and taxable income.

Permanent differences arise because the income tax laws afford special treatment to certain items which enter into the determination of accounting income. This special tax treatment exists because of certain goals sought at the time the laws were passed and reflects differences in the underlying objectives of financial reporting and taxation. Exhibit 19–5 provides some common examples of permanent differences.

Accounting and Reporting Issues

Tax-exempt income must be excluded from the figure from which we calculate income tax expense for accounting purposes. Likewise, we must add back to pretax accounting income accounting expenses that are not tax-deductible to arrive at the figure for calculating income tax expense.

Suppose that Raider Corporation has pretax accounting income of $200,000, which includes $30,000 of interest income on municipal bonds and goodwill amortization of $20,000. Assuming a 40 percent tax rate, income tax expense would be calculated as follows:

[11] If a deferred tax balance does remain, it must be amortized (written off) in the period in which all timing differences have been reversed. See Donald J. Bevis and Raymond E. Perry, "Accounting for Income Taxes," *An Interpretation of APB Opinion No. 11* (New York: AICPA, 1969), sec. 10.

EXHIBIT 19–5   EXAMPLES OF PERMANENT DIFFERENCES

A. Items included in pretax accounting income but never in taxable income (tax exempt).
  1. Interest received on state and local government obligations.
  2. Life insurance proceeds received by a company as beneficiary of a policy on officers or employees.
  3. Gains arising from involuntary conversions and condemnation of property (to the extent they are reinvested in similar property within a specified time period).
  4. 80 percent of dividends received by one corporation from another corporation (100 percent of dividends received from a wholly owned subsidiary).

B. Items recognized as expenses in determining pretax accounting income that are never deductible in calculating taxable income.
  1. Interest expense on debt incurred to acquire tax-exempt securities.
  2. Premiums paid for life insurance on officers and employees when the company is the beneficiary.
  3. Amortization of goodwill.
  4. Fines and expenses resulting from violations of law.

C. Percentage (statutory) depletion for tax purposes in excess of cost depletion for accounting purposes.

Pretax accounting income	$200,000
Add: Goodwill amortization	20,000
Deduct: Interest on municipal bonds	(30,000)
Adjusted pretax accounting income	$190,000
Income tax expense (.40 × $190,000)	$ 76,000

The journal entry to record income taxes, assuming no timing differences, would be as follows:

Income tax expense	76,000	
Taxes payable		76,000

The accounting treatment of permanent differences is not controversial. As the APB has stated, "Since permanent differences do not affect other periods, interperiod tax allocation is not appropriate to account for such differences."[12] In summary, although at times it may be difficult to determine whether a difference is a permanent difference or a timing difference, permanent differences do not require interperiod tax allocation.

FINANCIAL STATEMENT PRESENTATION
Under *APB Opinion No. 11,* companies must apply interperiod tax allocation procedures to timing differences on a comprehensive basis by the deferred method. As a result, many companies have numerous deferred tax accounts. Also, income tax expense usually differs from taxes payable when companies apply interperiod tax allocation procedures. Further, the relationship between income tax expense and pretax accounting income may differ significantly from the relationship expected on the basis of current tax rates, owing to such items as permanent differences and investment tax credits. These issues raise questions about the requirements for (1) balance sheet classification of deferred income taxes and (2) income statement disclosures. The required balance sheet classification and income statement disclosures are discussed in the next two sections.

[12] *APB Opinion No. 11,* para. 34.

Balance Sheet Classification of Deferred Income Taxes

APB Opinion No. 11 requires firms to categorize their deferred income tax accounts as a *net current* amount and a *net noncurrent* amount.[13] If the net current amount has a debit balance, the firm must classify it as a current asset. If the net current amount has a credit balance, the firm must classify it as a current liability. Likewise, the noncurrent amount is a noncurrent asset if it has a debit balance and it is a noncurrent liability if it has a credit balance. Thus, at most, two deferred tax amounts may appear on the balance sheet: (1) a current asset or current liability, and (2) a noncurrent asset or noncurrent liability.

If a deferred tax amount *relates to* an asset or liability, the firm classifies the deferred tax the same way it classifies the related asset or liability. According to *FASB Statement No. 37*, "a deferred charge or credit is related to an asset or liability if reduction of the asset or liability causes the timing difference to reverse."[14] For example, if a company uses accelerated depreciation on fixed assets for tax purposes and straight-line depreciation for accounting purposes, the deferred tax credits *relate to* the fixed assets, because the reduction of fixed assets, by either sale or depreciation, causes the timing difference to be reversed. Since the fixed assets are noncurrent, the deferred tax credit is a noncurrent liability.

Deferred or prepaid taxes are not *related to* an asset or liability if (1) no asset or liability is associated with the deferred or prepaid taxes, or (2) an associated asset or liability exists, but its reduction does not reverse the timing difference. For example, a company may use the percentage-of-completion method for accounting purposes and the completed-contract method for tax purposes to account for construction contracts. There is no *single* asset or liability related to the deferred tax credits. For these situations, the deferred tax balance must be classified as current or noncurrent on the basis of the estimated time of reversal of the timing differences, in accordance with the same criteria used for classifying other assets and liabilities.[15]

The net-of-tax method of presenting the tax effects of timing differences is prohibited for financial reporting.[16] The reason is not readily apparent in the authoritative literature. It appears, however, that the profession did not want the interperiod tax allocation issue to lead to a debate about the valuation of specific assets and liabilities, which is what the net-of-tax method entails. Further, if firms adopted the net-of-tax method of presentation, information regarding the tax effects of timing differences might not be so visible.

Income Statement Disclosures

Companies must disclose the following components of income tax expense:

1. Taxes currently payable.

2. Tax effects of timing difference (that is, the adjustment to deferred taxes).[17]

In addition, income tax expense must be separated into (1) U.S. federal taxes, (2) foreign taxes, and (3) state and local taxes, if all of these components are material. For example, CSX Corporation, which reported income tax expense of $344 million for 1984, provided the disclosures shown in Exhibit 19–6 in its financial statement notes.

[13] Ibid., para. 57.

[14] "Balance Sheet Classification of Deferred Income Taxes," *Statement of Financial Accounting Standards No. 37* (Stamford, Conn.: FASB, 1980), para. 4.

[15] Ibid., para. 4. Chapter 6 includes a discussion of the methods of accounting for long-term construction contracts.

[16] *APB Opinion No. 11*, para. 64.

[17] Ibid., para. 60.

EXHIBIT 19—6 DISCLOSURES RELATED TO INCOME TAXES

CSX Corporation

(IN MILLIONS OF DOLLARS)

NOTE 4: INCOME TAXES

	1984	1983	1982
Current			
United States	$ 25	$ (3)	$ 19
State and Foreign	14	3	2
Total current	$ 39	—	$ 21
Deferred			
United States	$283	$149	$103
State	22	16	14
Total deferred	$305	$165	$117
Total	$344	$165	$138

The income tax provision reconciled to the tax computed at statutory rates was:

	1984		1983		1982	
Tax at statutory rate	$386	46%	$214	46%	$266	46%
Investment tax credits	(52)	(6)	(39)	(8)	(49)	(8)
Capital gains rate differential	(19)	(2)	(11)	(2)	(46)	(8)
State income taxes	15	2	11	2	10	2
Adjustment for prior years' income taxes	4	—	(4)	(1)	(34)*	(6)
Other items	10	1	(6)	(2)	(9)	(2)
Total	$344	41%	$165	35%	$138	24%

* Includes $23 million ($.18 per share) in the fourth quarter of 1982, primarily related to estimated investment tax credits and frozen asset base adjustments.

Cumulative investment tax credits of approximately $253 million have been recognized for financial reporting purposes as a reduction of deferred taxes, and are being carried forward for Federal tax return purposes. The earliest investment tax credit carryforwards begin to expire in 1994.

The deferred income tax provision, which represents the tax effect of timing differences between earnings for income tax and financial reporting purposes, was:

	1984	1983	1982
Depreciation	$237	$230	$122
Investment tax credits	27	(78)	12
Costs recoverable through gas rate adjustments	(11)	(22)	—
Interest on prior years' taxes	—	19	(4)
Other timing differences	52	16	(13)
Total	$305	$165	$117

The Federal income tax returns of certain CSX subsidiaries have been examined for various periods and proposed adjustments are being contested. Management believes adequate provision has been made for adjustments which might be assessed.

Companies also must reconcile the actual income tax expense with the amount that would be expected based on current tax rates.[18] Note the reconciliation provided by CSX Corporation in Exhibit 19–6.

NET OPERATING LOSSES

If, when taxable income is calculated, deductions exceed revenues, a **net operating loss** (NOL) exists. Federal tax laws provide that companies may use net operating losses to offset *taxable income* of other years to reduce taxes otherwise payable in those years. Specifically, a company must elect one of two options, as Exhibit 19–7 demonstrates.

Under the **loss carryback** election, shown above the time line in Exhibit 19–7, the company carries the loss back to the third year preceding the loss year to offset taxable income of that year and to claim a refund for all or a portion of the taxes paid in that year. If taxable income of year −3 is inadequate to absorb the entire NOL, the firm may apply the remainder of the loss against taxable income of years −2, −1, +1, +2, . . . , +15, respectively, until the loss has been absorbed. Under the **loss carryforward** election, shown below the time line in Exhibit 19–7, the company carries the NOL forward to offset taxable income, and to reduce taxes that would otherwise be payable, in the 15 carryforward years.

Under normal circumstances, a company with a NOL elects the loss carryback, because the company then has an immediate claim for refund of taxes already paid, rather than having to depend on taxable income to be generated in the carryforward years to realize the benefit of the net operating loss. If, however, a firm expects to have taxable income in the 15 carryforward years *and* expects tax rates to increase significantly, the firm may benefit from electing the loss carryforward. Or special tax credits may have resulted in nominal tax payments in the carryback years. The time value of money might be a factor in the decision. A claim for refund of taxes previously paid results in an

[18] Ibid., para. 63.

EXHIBIT 19–7   NET OPERATING LOSS CARRYBACK AND CARRYFORWARD OPTIONS

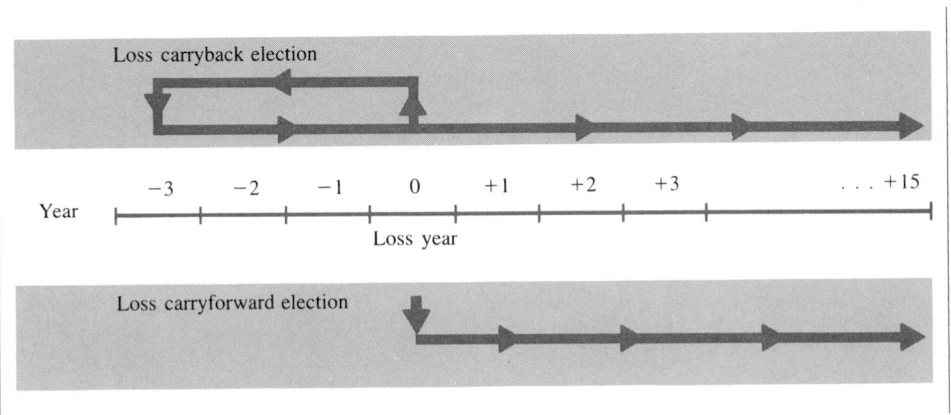

immediate cash inflow, whereas the cash flow benefit from reducing taxes otherwise payable in carryforward years does not take place until earnings occur in future periods.

The objective of the net operating loss provision of the tax law is to equalize the tax burden between companies that experience loss years in the midst of profitable years and companies that have more stable earning patterns. Assume, for example, that Brett Company's taxable income, tax rate, and tax liability for the years 1985 through 1987 are as follows:

YEAR	TAXABLE INCOME	TAX RATE	TAX LIABILITY
1985	$100,000	40%	$40,000
1986	100,000	40	40,000
1987	100,000	40	40,000

There is no difference between pretax accounting income and taxable income for the three years.

In 1988, however, Brett incurs a net operating loss of $300,000. Brett calculates the tax refund claim by applying the $300,000 NOL against the taxable income of 1985, 1986, and 1987, and claiming a refund for the taxes paid in those years. The $300,000 NOL exactly offsets total taxable income in the three years preceding the loss. Therefore, the tax refund claim is for all income taxes paid during the preceding three years, or $120,000. This results in a *net* tax payment over the four years of zero, which is reasonable because the aggregate taxable income over the four years was zero.

ACCOUNTING FOR LOSS CARRYBACKS

In the above example, Brett's tax rate was the same each period and the amount of Brett's NOL was exactly the same as total taxable income for the three years preceding the loss. As a more realistic example, assume the following figures for Patek Corporation:

YEAR	TAXABLE INCOME	TAX RATE	TAX LIABILITY
1985	$100,000	40%	$ 40,000
1986	130,000	40	52,000
1987	160,000	45	72,000
	$390,000		$164,000

In 1988 Patek experiences a $300,000 NOL. The tax rate in 1988 is 50 percent. There are no differences between pretax accounting income and taxable income in any of the years.

Calculation of the tax refund claim in 1988 would be as follows:

YEAR	INCOME	TAX RATE	TAX REFUND
1985	$100,000	40%	$ 40,000
1986	130,000	40	52,000
1987	70,000	45	31,500
	$300,000		$123,500

Patek first carries the loss back to 1985, leaving $200,000 to be carried to 1986 and 1987, resulting in a refund of all 1985 and 1986 income taxes and a refund of taxes paid on $70,000 of taxable income in 1987. The 50 percent tax rate in 1988, the year of the loss, has no bearing on the calculation of the tax refund. The loss carryback does not absorb the remaining $90,000 of taxable income in 1987. Therefore, the related taxes of $40,500 ($90,000 × .45) are not refundable.

The following journal entry at the end of 1988 records the effect of the loss carryback in the accounts of Patek Corporation:

Income tax refund receivable 123,500		
Refund of taxes due to loss carryback		123,500

APB Opinion No. 11 requires that firms include the tax benefits from loss carrybacks in the determination of income in the loss period.[19] Patek shows the tax benefit in its 1987 income statement as follows:

Operating loss before tax benefit of carryback	$(300,000)
Refund of taxes due to loss carryback	123,500
Net loss	$(176,500)

As a result of the NOL provision, Patek's net loss has been reduced from $300,000 to $176,500.[20] The receivable arising from a loss carryback should be recognized as a current asset, because it will be realized currently.

ACCOUNTING FOR LOSS CARRYFORWARDS

Tax benefits of loss carryforwards generally are not recognized until future taxable income occurs.

If taxable income in the three years preceding a NOL is less than the amount of the loss, or if a company elects the loss carryforward, the company may use the NOL to reduce taxes otherwise payable in the years following the loss year, up to a maximum of 15 years. Since *carrybacks* result in legal claims for amounts previously paid, there is no accounting question regarding the realization of the claim. To realize the tax benefit of a loss carryforward, in contrast, a company must have future earnings. Otherwise, there will be no future taxes to be reduced by the NOL carryforward. Recognizing this uncertainty, the APB required that "the tax benefits of loss carry*forwards* should not be recognized until they are actually realized, except in unusual circumstances when realization is *assured beyond any reasonable doubt* at the time the loss carry*forwards* arise."[21] Thus, the *general rule* is to delay recognition of the tax benefits of loss carryforwards until future taxable income occurs; the *exception* is to recognize the benefit in the loss year. When a firm delays the recognition of the tax benefits, it must report the tax benefits of the carryforward as an extraordinary item in the carryforward periods.

Assume that White Corporation experiences the following income (loss) for the years indicated:

---

[19] Ibid., para. 44.

[20] If a company has a difference between pretax accounting income and taxable income, it could report a NOL for tax purposes and report positive pretax accounting income and income tax expense for accounting purposes. In such instances, the credit in the above entry would be to the income tax expense account. The company must explain the reduction in tax expense resulting from the tax refund claim.

[21] *APB Opinion No. 11,* para. 45.

YEAR	TAXABLE INCOME (LOSS)	TAX RATE	CURRENT TAX*
1985	$ 50,000	40%	$20,000
1986	70,000	40	28,000
1987	40,000	40	16,000
1988	(200,000)	45	–0–
1989	20,000	48	9,600
1990	40,000	48	19,200

* Excludes carryback or carryforward effect, if any.

If, at the end of 1988, White is not virtually assured of future earnings to provide tax benefits from the loss carryforward, it will make the following journal entry:

```
Income tax refund receivable ............................ 64,000
    Refund of taxes due to loss carryback ...................        64,000
    [.4($50,000 + $70,000 + $40,000)]
```

Thus, $40,000 of the $200,000 NOL remains after the carryback [$200,000 − ($50,000 + $70,000 + $40,000)]. This amount is available to use as a carryforward. At the end of 1989, White can apply $20,000 of the remaining NOL of $40,000 to eliminate the 1989 tax liability of $9,600. White will make the following journal entry at the end of 1989:

```
Income tax expense ..................................... 9,600
    Tax reduction due to loss carryforward (extraordinary item) ..        9,600
```

At the end of 1990 White can use the remaining loss carryforward of $20,000 to reduce 1990 taxes by $9,600 (.48 × $20,000), and will make the following entry:

```
Income tax expense (.48 × $40,000) ...................... 19,200
    Taxes payable [.48 × ($40,000 − $20,000)] ..............        9,600
    Tax reduction due to loss carryforward (extraordinary item) ..        9,600
```

The bottom portion of White's income statements for 1988, 1989, and 1990 will appear as follows:

	1990	1989	1988
Income (loss) before taxes	$40,000	$20,000	$(200,000)
Income tax expense	(19,200)	(9,600)	
Refund of taxes due to loss carryback			64,000
Income (loss) before extraordinary item	$20,800	$10,400	$(136,000)
Extraordinary item: Tax reduction due to loss carryforward	9,600	9,600	
Net income (loss)	$30,400	$20,000	$(136,000)

White does not recognize any benefits from the loss carryforwards in its accounts in 1988. Companies must, however, disclose the amount and expiration dates of unrecognized loss carryforwards in the notes to the financial statements.

We have assumed that there was no assurance in the loss year of White Corporation's ability to realize the benefit of the carryforward. When the benefit is assured beyond reasonable doubt in the loss year, accounting for the benefit differs. The tax benefit of loss carryforwards is "assured beyond any reasonable doubt" when *both* of the following conditions are met:[22]

1. The loss results from an identifiable, isolated, and nonrecurring cause.

2. Taxable income during the carryforward period is virtually certain to be adequate to offset the loss carryforward.

If both of these conditions are met in the period in which the loss occurs, the firm recognizes the tax benefit from the loss carryforward in determining the results of operations for the loss period.

Assume that in 1988 White Corporation is assured of realizing the tax benefit from the loss carryforward. White will then recognize in 1988 the claim for refund of taxes previously paid ($64,000), plus the expected tax benefit of the loss carryforward. Assuming that in 1988 White is aware of the pending change in tax rates, White uses the tax rates expected to be in effect in future periods when the NOL is absorbed to determine the tax benefit. White records the effect of the NOL as follows at the end of 1988:

```
Income tax refund receivable ........................... 64,000
Expected reduction in future taxes due to
    loss carryforward (.48 × $40,000) .................... 19,200
    Reduction of loss due to loss carryback and
        loss carryforward ..................................      83,200
```

At the end of 1989 and 1990, White makes the following entries:

```
1989 Income tax expense ............................. 9,600
    Expected reduction in future taxes
        due to loss carryforward ........................      9,600

1990 Income tax expense ............................. 19,200
    Expected reduction in future taxes
        due to loss carryforward ........................      9,600
        Taxes payable ..................................      9,600
```

Comparative income statements for 1988, 1989, and 1990 (beginning with income before taxes) appear as follows:

	1990	1989	1988
Income (loss) before taxes	$40,000	$20,000	$(200,000)
Income tax expense	(19,200)	(9,600)	
Reduction of loss due to NOL carryback and carryforward ($64,000 + $19,200)			83,200
Net income (loss)	$20,800	$10,400	$(116,800)

A comparison of White's income statements on page 896 and immediately above demonstrates the results under the two different treatments of the carryforward tax benefits. The difference between the two treatments lies in *when* firms recognize the carryforward tax benefits. The effect of applying the exception treatment to White's loss carryfor-

---

[22] Ibid., para. 47.

ward is to recognize the entire tax benefit from the NOL in the period in which the loss occurs. When the carryforward benefit is recognized in the loss year, reported income in the carryforward years is unaffected by the net operating loss in 1988.

The expected reduction in future taxes due to loss carryforward account is an asset, and companies should classify it as current or noncurrent according to the anticipated time of realization. If the actual future tax rate differs from the tax rate used to record the asset and to record the benefit, the firm should adjust the account and include the effect on income as a change in estimate in the period in which the actual rate becomes known. When a firm recognizes the tax benefit of loss carryforwards in the loss period, it does *not* classify the tax benefit as an extraordinary item, in contrast to the treatment when recognition of the tax benefit is deferred to the carryforward years.

OVERVIEW OF PROPOSED CHANGES IN ACCOUNTING FOR INCOME TAXES

As we indicated at the beginning of the chapter, in September 1986 the FASB issued an *Exposure Draft* of a *Proposed Statement of Financial Accounting Standards. APB Opinion No. 11* and related pronouncements that require the deferred method would be superseded by the proposed *Statement.* In this section we provide an overview of the proposed changes.

The proposed *Statement* would require recognition of an asset or liability to account for the tax consequences of income taxes resulting from events and transactions. That is, an asset or liability approach would be required, rather than an income statement approach as required under current GAAP (the deferred method). The emphasis is on the *future tax consequences,* rather than on the amount of taxes saved or prepaid currently, as a result of current period *temporary* differences. *Temporary differences* include both timing differences (as discussed in the chapter) and differences between the tax bases of assets and the amounts reported in the financial statements.

Consistent with the asset/liability view, the asset or liability that recognizes the tax consequences of temporary differences would be based on enacted tax rates for the future years in which the temporary differences are expected to produce taxable or tax deductible amounts. *That is, the liability method would be required.* The deferred tax liability or asset would not be discounted. Tax planning strategies that meet specified criteria would be used to determine the years in which the temporary differences would result in taxable or tax deductible amounts.

If a change in tax rates were enacted, any deferred tax liability or asset would be adjusted as of the date of enactment of the change. The adjustment, which represents the effect of a *change in accounting estimate,* would be reported as a part of continuing operations.

Balance sheet classification of a deferred tax liability or asset would be based on the expectations regarding when temporary differences would result in taxable or tax deductible amounts. Deferred tax consequences that would result in taxable or deductible amounts within the next year would be classified as current; all other deferred tax consequences would be classified as noncurrent.

The proposed *Statement* would not permit the anticipation of the tax consequences of earning income or incurring losses in future years when recognizing and measuring a deferred tax liability or asset. Operating loss or tax credit carryforwards from prior years may be available to reduce a deferred tax liability, subject to limitations of the tax law. However, the tax benefit of an operating loss or tax credit carryforward that cannot be recognized as a reduction of a deferred tax liability may not be recognized as an asset, because to do so would be anticipating future earnings.

The cumulative effect of the change in accounting principle to apply the proposed *Statement* could be treated either as a cumulative effect change in determining net income for the year of change or as a restatement of previously issued financial statements.

In summary, the FASB has proposed that the liability method, without discounting, should be applied on a comprehensive basis. It has proposed further that net operating loss carryforwards may not be anticipated except to reduce a deferred tax liability as permitted by tax law. The proposed transition approach allows companies to include the cumulative effect of the change in net income for the period of change.

Because of the newly lowered corporate tax rates, many companies have urged the FASB to make the proposed *Statement* effective as soon as possible so that net income could be enhanced sooner by writing down the deferred tax liabilities to reflect the newly enacted lower tax rates. However, FASB representatives indicated that the Board would not shortcut its usual and often lengthy procedures, which include an exposure period, public hearings, and subsequent deliberations.

Thus, at the time of this writing, significant changes in accounting for income taxes are on the horizon. The exact nature of those changes probably will be known sometime in 1987.

SUMMARY OF IMPORTANT TOPICS AND CONCEPT APPLICATIONS

1. **Taxable income** is determined from a firm's tax return. **Pretax accounting income** is determined in a firm's income statement prepared for financial reporting purposes. Many legitimate differences between these two measures exist within an accounting period.

2. Timing differences are items of revenue and expense that are reported for both tax and accounting purposes, but the amount recognized in each period differs for the two purposes. The accelerated cost recovery system (ACRS) resulting from the Economic Recovery Tax Act of 1981, and revised by the 1986 Tax Act, accentuated timing differences.

3. The income tax burden is perceived to be an **expense** from an accounting standpoint, which is subject to accrual, deferral, and estimation just like other expenses. Also, the assumption of a **going concern** implies that a firm will continue in existence long enough for timing differences to reverse. Therefore, the existence of timing differences gives rise to the process of **interperiod tax allocation** and to **deferred taxes.**

4. Originating timing differences cause the deferred tax account balance to increase; reversing timing differences cause the deferred tax account balance to decrease.

5. Currently, GAAP requires that interperiod tax allocation procedures be applied on a comprehensive basis using the deferred method. However, substantial controversy exists regarding the appropriate approach. **Matching** is a primary objective under the comprehensive approach. Many believe that **cash flow projections** would be enhanced if the liability method applied on a partial basis were required.

6. The gross change method and the net change method are practical applications of the deferred method to groups of similar assets. While the gross change method is conceptually superior, most firms use the net change method because of its simplicity.

7. Permanent differences are items of revenue and expense that are included in either pretax accounting income or taxable income, but not both. Permanent differences do not affect deferred taxes. Nontaxable revenues and non–tax-deductible expenses that are included in pretax accounting income must be excluded from the base for calculating income tax expense.

8. At most, two deferred tax amounts are required to be reported on the balance sheet: (1) a net current amount; and (2) a net noncurrent amount. In the income statement or notes, companies must disclose the portion of income tax expense that is currently payable and the tax effects of timing differences (change in deferred taxes).

9. The net operating loss (NOL) provision of the tax law is designed to equalize the tax burden between those companies with stable earnings patterns and those with erratic earnings and loss patterns.

10. The tax benefit of a NOL **carryback** is assured of realization because it represents a refund of taxes previously paid. The tax benefit is recognized in the income statement in the period in which the loss occurs as a reduction in the reported loss.

11. The tax benefit of a NOL **carryforward** is a **gain contingency.** Thus, the carryforward benefit generally is not recorded in the accounts until **realization** occurs in the carryforward periods. The benefit of the carryforward is reported as an extraordinary gain when it is recognized in the carryforward periods. In the rare circumstances in which realization of the carryforward is assured beyond any reasonable doubt in the loss year, it may be accrued at that time as an asset and as a reduction in the loss in the income statement. The income statement effect is not classified as extraordinary in the latter case.

QUESTIONS

Q19-1. Without identifying specific items that are treated differently for tax purposes than for accounting purposes, explain briefly and in a general way why taxable income and accounting income often differ.

Q19-2. Identify the four categories of timing differences and provide two examples in each category.

Q19-3. What is the basic accounting issue resulting from timing differences?

Q19-4. Identify four underlying concepts that support the process of interperiod tax allocation. Explain these notions, their relationship to each other, and how they support interperiod tax allocation.

Q19-5. Is a company's tax liability affected by the adoption or nonadoption of interperiod tax allocation procedures? Explain.

Q19-6. Describe originating timing differences and reversing timing differences. Explain the circumstances under which originating differences cause a credit to deferred income taxes and a debit to deferred income taxes. Which type of originating difference would you expect to appear most frequently? Why?

Q19-7. Explain the meanings of partial allocation and comprehensive allocation. Describe the arguments for and against each of these approaches to interperiod tax allocation. What is the accounting profession's current authoritative position on these two approaches?

Q19-8. Identify and briefly describe three basic methods of interperiod tax allocation. What is the nature of deferred income taxes under each of these three methods? Which of the three methods is required by the accounting profession?

Q19-9. Conceptually, would you expect the deferred method or the liability method to produce better cash flow signals? Explain.

Q19-10. Briefly describe the with–without technique for calculating the change in deferred taxes. In what circumstances is this technique useful?

Q19-11. Give an example of *similar* timing differences for purposes of using the group basis for determining the tax effect of timing differences. What benefit is derived from grouping similar timing differences?

Q19-12. Explain the process of determining the required adjustment to deferred income taxes under *(a)* the gross change method and *(b)* the net change method. Describe the merits and shortcomings of each method from both a conceptual and a practical viewpoint.

Q19-13. Describe the process of classifying deferred income taxes *(a)* related to an asset or liability and *(b)* not related to an asset or liability.

Q19-14. What income-statement-related disclosures are required with respect to income tax expense and the tax effect of timing differences?

Q19-15. Distinguish between permanent differences and timing differences. Why are interperiod tax allocation procedures inappropriate for permanent differences?

Q19-16. Give five examples of permanent differences.

Q19-17. Describe how permanent differences can distort the customary relationship between income tax expense and pretax accounting income. What financial statement disclosures, if any, are required with respect to permanent differences?

Q19-18. Define a net operating loss. Describe the two alternatives available to a company for obtaining a tax benefit from a net operating loss. Which alternative would you expect to be chosen most frequently? Why?

Q19-19. Explain the fundamental distinction between the tax benefit of a loss carryback and the tax benefit of a loss carryforward.

Q19-20. Describe the accounting and reporting requirements for tax benefits associated with *(a)* net operating loss carrybacks and *(b)* net operating loss carryforwards.

Q19-21. Under what circumstances is the tax benefit associated with a net operating loss reported as an extraordinary item? How is the tax benefit of a net operating loss reported when it is not reported as an extraordinary item?

Q19-22. Assess the accounting and reporting requirements for loss carrybacks and loss carryforwards from the viewpoint of providing information regarding cash flows.

CASES

C19-1. THEORETICAL ANALYSIS OF INTERPERIOD TAX ALLOCATION   Corporations must use interperiod tax allocation procedures. Even though generally accepted accounting principles require comprehensive allocation using the deferred method, other approaches to interperiod tax allocation are conceptually possible.

REQUIRED

1. Discuss the theoretical justification for interperiod tax allocation.

2. Describe and discuss the pros and cons of the partial approach and the comprehensive approach to interperiod tax allocation.

3. Describe the deferred method, the liability method, and the net-of-tax method of interperiod tax allocation. Explain the rationale underlying each method.

C19-2. DEFERRED INCOME TAXES

A) For the current year, Lorac Company has the following items in its income statement:

· **1.** Gross profits on installment sales.

2. Revenues on long-term construction contracts.

3. Estimated costs of product warranty contracts.

4. Premiums on officers' life insurance with Lorac as beneficiary.

REQUIRED

1. Under what conditions would deferred income taxes need to be reported in the financial statements?

2. Specify when deferred income taxes would need to be recognized for each of the items above, and indicate the rationale for such recognition.

B) Eneri Company's president has heard that deferred income taxes can be variously classified in the balance sheet.

REQUIRED

Identify the conditions under which deferred income taxes would be classified as a noncurrent item in the balance sheet. What justification exists for such classification?

(AICPA, adapted)

C19-3. THEORETICAL BASIS FOR AND FINANCIAL REPORTING OF DEFERRED TAXES   The Primrose Company appropriately uses the deferred method for interperiod tax allocation. To report depreciation expense for certain machinery purchased this year, Primrose uses the accelerated cost recovery system (ACRS) for income tax purposes and the straight-line basis for accounting purposes. The tax deduction is the larger amount this year. Also, Primrose received rent revenues in advance this year. These revenues are included in this year's taxable income. For accounting purposes, however, these revenues are reported as unearned revenues, a current liability.

REQUIRED

1. What is the theoretical basis for deferred income taxes?

2. How should Primrose determine and account for the income tax effect of depreciation and rent? Why?

3. How should Primrose classify the income tax effect of the depreciation and rent on its balance sheet and income statement? Why?

(AICPA, adapted)

C19-4. PERMANENT VS. TIMING DIFFERENCES   The following differences enter into the reconciliation of accounting income and taxable income of W. Nelson Corporation for the current year.

a) Tax depreciation exceeds book depreciation by $30,000.

b) Estimated warranty costs of $6,000 applicable to the current year's sales have not been paid.

c) Percentage depletion deducted on the tax return exceeds cost depletion by $45,000.

d) Unearned rent revenue of $25,000 was deferred on the books but appropriately included in taxable income.

e) A book expense of $2,000 for life insurance premiums on officers' lives is not allowed as a deduction on the tax return.

f) A $7,000 tax deduction resulted from expensing research and development costs for tax purposes which were capitalized for financial reporting.

g) Gross profit of $80,000 was excluded from taxable income because Nelson had appropriately elected the installment sale method for tax reporting while recognizing all gross profit from installment sales at the time of the sale for financial reporting.

REQUIRED

Consider each reconciling item independently of all others and explain whether each item would enter into the calculation of income taxes to be allocated. For any that are included in the income tax allocation calculation, explain the effect of the item on the current year's income tax expense and how the amount would be reported on the balance sheet. (Tax allocation calculations are not required.)

(AICPA, adapted)

EXERCISES

E19-1. PERMANENT VS. TIMING DIFFERENCES   The following items are treated differently for tax purposes than for accounting purposes:

a) Installment sales recognized at time of sale for accounting purposes, recognized as sales revenue is collected for tax purposes.

b) Insurance premiums paid on policies on officers' lives for which company is beneficiary.

c) Warranty expenses accrued for accounting purposes, deducted as incurred for tax purposes.

d) Rent revenue recognized when received for tax purposes, deferred and recognized as earned for accounting purposes.

e) Goodwill amortization.

f) ACRS depreciation used for tax purposes, straight-line depreciation used for accounting purposes.

g) Life insurance proceeds received by company as beneficiary of policy on officer.

h) Interest income on municipal bonds.

i) Pension costs expensed as incurred for accounting purposes, expensed when remitted to trustee for tax purposes. (Expense is greater than funding.)

j) In accounting for construction contracts, percentage-of-completion method used for accounting purposes, completed-contract method used for tax purposes.

k) Assets depreciated over a shorter life for tax purposes than for accounting purposes.

l) Interest expense incurred to acquire municipal bonds.

m) Interest during construction capitalized as part of cost of asset for accounting purposes, deducted as incurred for tax purposes.

n) Sales deposits recognized when received for tax purposes, deferred until goods shipped for accounting purposes.

o) Fines paid as a result of law violations.

REQUIRED

Indicate whether each of the above items is a permanent difference or a temporary timing difference. For timing differences, indicate whether deferred income taxes would be debited or credited for the tax effect of originating differences.

E19-2. CALCULATION OF DEFERRED TAXES   For financial statement reporting, the Concord Corporation recognizes royalty income in the period earned. For income tax reporting, royalties are taxed when they are collected. As of December 31, 1987, unearned royalties of $400,000 are included in Concord's balance sheet. All of these royalties were collected in 1987. During 1988, royalties of $600,000 are collected. Unearned royalties in Concord's December 31, 1988, balance sheet amounted to $350,000.

REQUIRED

Assuming that the income tax rate was 45 percent, what should be the change in deferred income taxes at the end of 1988? Show calculations.

(AICPA, adapted)

E19-3. CALCULATION OF DEFERRED TAXES   Lynn Company uses an ACRS method to depreciate its machinery for income tax reporting and the straight-line method for financial statement reporting. For the 1987 calendar year, depreciation on machinery amounted to $900,000 under the ACRS method and $550,000 under the straight-line method. Also, in 1987 Lynn received interest on municipal obligations of $150,000.

REQUIRED

Assuming a 45 percent income tax rate, by what amount should the deferred income tax account change? Show calculations.

E19-4. CALCULATION OF DEFERRED TAXES   Dugan Corporation, which began operations on January 1, 1985, recognizes income from long-term construction contracts under the percentage-of-completion method in its financial statements, but uses the completed-contract method for income tax reporting. Reported income from long-term contracts under each method is as follows:

YEAR	PERCENTAGE OF COMPLETION	COMPLETED CONTRACT
1985	$400,000	$ –0–
1986	650,000	350,000
1987	950,000	750,000

For all years, the income tax rate was 40 percent, and there are no other timing differences.

REQUIRED

Calculate the balance of the deferred tax account related to the timing difference at the end of 1987.

(AICPA, adapted)

E19-5. INTERPERIOD TAX ALLOCATION For the year ended December 31, 1987, Rex Corporation reported pretax accounting income of $1,000,000. Selected information for 1987 from Rex's records is as follows:

> Interest income on municipal bonds—$80,000
>
> Depreciation claimed on tax return in excess of depreciation per books—$140,000
>
> Warranty expense on the accrual basis—$65,000
>
> Actual warranty expenditures—$35,000

Rex's income tax rate for 1987 is 40 percent. There were no other differences between Rex's pretax accounting income and taxable income.

REQUIRED

Prepare the journal entry to record income taxes for Rex Corporation for the year ended December 31, 1987.

(AICPA, adapted)

E19-6. BASIC PROCESS OF INTERPERIOD TAX ALLOCATION Pretax accounting income and taxable income are as follows for Parton Corporation for the years indicated:

YEAR	PRETAX ACCOUNTING INCOME	TAXABLE INCOME
1987	$ 90,000	$ 80,000
1988	100,000	100,000
1989	85,000	90,000

The tax rate in all years is 40 percent. The differences between pretax accounting income and taxable income are caused by the fact that a different depreciation method is used for tax purposes than for accounting purposes.

REQUIRED

Prepare the journal entry required at the end of each year to record income tax expense, taxes payable, and deferred taxes.

E19-7. BASIC PROCESS OF INTERPERIOD TAX ALLOCATION Income tax returns of Desert Corporation reflect the following:

	1987	1988	1989
Royalty income......................	$ 60,000		
Investment income	30,000	$20,000	$40,000
Rent income	10,000	10,000	10,000
	$100,000	$30,000	$50,000
Deductible expenses	(20,000)	(10,000)	(10,000)
Taxable income......................	$80,000	$20,000	$40,000

The tax rate for each year is 40 percent.

The only differences between taxable income and pretax accounting income relate to royalty income. For accounting purposes, royalty income is recognized equally over the three-year period.

REQUIRED

Give journal entries at the end of each year to reflect income tax expense, taxes payable, and deferred taxes.

(CGAA, adapted)

E19-8. BASIC PROCESS OF INTERPERIOD TAX ALLOCATION; PERMANENT DIFFERENCES E. L. Harris Company has the following pretax accounting income and taxable income for the years indicated:

YEAR	PRETAX ACCOUNTING INCOME	TAXABLE INCOME
1987	$200,000	$160,000
1988	240,000	210,000
1989	300,000	250,000

Interest income on tax-exempt municipal bonds of $10,000, $15,000, and $20,000 is included in pretax accounting income in 1987, 1988, and 1989, respectively. Also, goodwill amortization of $30,000 is recorded each year for accounting purposes. Installment sales are recognized at the time of sale for accounting purposes and are recognized under the installment method for tax purposes. The tax rate in all periods is 40 percent.

REQUIRED

Prepare journal entries for each year to record income tax expense, taxes payable, and deferred taxes.

E19-9. DEFERRED METHOD   W. Jennings Company uses the same methods of accounting for financial reporting and tax accounting with the exception of depreciation, which is calculated by the sum-of-the-years'-digits method for tax purposes and on a straight-line basis for financial reporting. Pretax accounting income, taxable income, and tax rates are as follows for 1987, 1988, and 1989:

YEAR	PRETAX ACCOUNTING INCOME	TAXABLE INCOME	TAX RATE
1987	$100,000	$ 90,000	40%
1988	100,000	100,000	45
1989	100,000	110,000	50

Jennings has several depreciable assets, all of which were acquired at the beginning of 1987 with estimated useful lives of three years.

REQUIRED

1. Determine the amount of depreciation expense each year for *(a)* accounting purposes and *(b)* tax purposes.

2. Jennings uses the deferred method. Prepare the journal entry at the end of each of the three years to record income tax expense, assuming:
    a) Jennings uses the gross change method.
    b) Jennings uses the net change method.

E19-10. LIABILITY METHOD   Assume the same facts as in Exercise 19-9 *except* assume that Jennings uses the liability method to recognize deferred taxes.

REQUIRED

Prepare the journal entry at the end of each of the three years under two different assumptions:
    a) Future tax rates are known with certainty.
    b) Future tax rates are unknown.

E19-11. WITH–WITHOUT TECHNIQUE   Gayle Corporation has pretax accounting income of $72,000 and taxable income of $60,000 in 1987. Included in both figures is a capital gain of $10,000 on the sale of investments. Pretax accounting income and taxable income differ because installment sales are recognized at the time of sale for accounting purposes but are recognized on the basis of cash collections for tax purposes. Applicable tax rates are 22 percent on the first $25,000 of income, 48 percent on income in excess of $25,000, and 25 percent for capital gains.

REQUIRED

Prepare the journal entry to record income tax expense, using the with–without technique.

E19-12. GROSS CHANGE AND NET CHANGE METHODS Pretax accounting income and taxable income for the Spring Corporation over a two-year period are as follows:

YEAR	PRETAX ACCOUNTING INCOME	TAXABLE INCOME
1987	$100,000	$122,000
1988	100,000	88,000

The difference between pretax accounting income and taxable income is explained as follows:

a) Taxable income in 1987 includes $24,000 of rental revenue, which for financial reporting purposes was recorded as earned at the rate of $12,000 per year for 1987 and 1988.

b) Amortization of goodwill at the rate of $10,000 per year is recorded for financial reporting purposes but is not deductible in arriving at taxable income.

c) In 1988 depreciation for tax purposes exceeds depreciation for financial accounting purposes by $10,000. Spring acquired the asset at the beginning of 1988 and uses ACRS depreciation for tax purposes and straight-line depreciation for financial accounting purposes.

REQUIRED

1. Prepare entries required for 1987 and 1988 to allocate income taxes properly. Assume a tax rate of 40 percent in 1987 and 50 percent in 1988. Use the gross change method.

2. Repeat part 1, but use the net change method.

E19-13. GROSS CHANGE AND NET CHANGE METHODS Pretax accounting income and taxable income for Hound Dog, Inc., appear below:

YEAR	PRETAX ACCOUNTING INCOME	TAXABLE INCOME
1987	$ 80,000	$ 48,000
1988	100,000	87,000
1989	120,000	112,000

Differences between pretax accounting income and taxable income are as follows:

a) Pretax accounting income in 1987 includes $30,000 that for tax purposes is recognized in accordance with the installment method in amounts of $10,000 each year for 1987, 1988, and 1989.

b) Percentage depletion on a mine deposit is allowed for tax purposes although the mine has been fully depleted for financial reporting purposes. The amount of depletion allowed for tax purposes is $12,000, $8,000, and $6,000 for 1987, 1988, and 1989, respectively.

c) In 1988 and 1989, depreciation for tax purposes exceeds depreciation for financial accounting purposes in the following amounts: 1988, $15,000; 1989, $12,000. Hound Dog acquired the depreciable asset at the beginning of 1988.

REQUIRED

1. Prepare the journal entries related to income taxes at the end of 1987, 1988, and 1989 using the gross change method, assuming tax rates of 40, 45, and 50 percent in the three years.

2. Repeat part 1, except use the net change method.

E19-14. CLASSIFICATION OF DEFERRED TAXES Haggard Corporation, an installment seller of furniture, records sales on the accrual basis for financial reporting purposes but on the installment method for tax purposes. As a result, $50,000 of deferred income taxes has been accrued as of December 31, 1987. In accordance with trade practice, installment accounts receivable from customers are shown as current assets, although the average collection period is approximately three years.

As of December 31, 1987, Haggard Corporation has recorded a $20,000 deferred income tax debit arising from a book accrual of noncurrent deferred compensation expense that is *not* currently tax deductible.

Also as of December 31, 1987, Haggard has accrued $15,000 of deferred income taxes resulting from the use of ACRS depreciation for tax purposes and straight-line depreciation for financial reporting purposes.

REQUIRED

How should the deferred income taxes be classified on Haggard's December 31, 1987, balance sheet?

(AICPA, adapted)

E19-15. NET OPERATING LOSS CARRYBACK   Daniels Corporation experiences the following pretax accounting income (loss) for the years indicated:

YEAR	PRETAX ACCOUNTING INCOME (LOSS)	TAX RATE
1985	$20,000	40%
1986	30,000	40
1987	40,000	45
1988	(70,000)	45
1989	10,000	45
1990	50,000	45

There were no differences in the above years between pretax accounting income and taxable income.

REQUIRED

1. Prepare the journal entry required at the end of 1988 to recognize the tax benefit of the net operating loss (assuming the carryback option is elected).

2. How should the tax benefit be shown in the 1988 income statement?

E19-16. NET OPERATING LOSS CARRYBACK AND CARRYFORWARD   Assume the same facts as presented in Exercise 19-15 except that the loss in 1988 is $110,000 instead of $70,000.

REQUIRED

1. Prepare the journal entry required at the end of 1988 to recognize the tax benefit of the loss, assuming *(a)* future earnings sufficient to obtain the carryforward benefit are *not* assured beyond a reasonable doubt at the end of 1988, and *(b)* future earnings sufficient to obtain the carryforward benefit *are* assured beyond a reasonable doubt at the end of 1988.

2. Prepare the appropriate journal entries related to taxes at the end of 1989 and 1990 under assumptions *a* and *b* in part 1.

3. Prepare partial income statements for 1988, 1989, and 1990 under assumptions *a* and *b* in part 1. Begin with income (loss) before taxes.

E19-17. NET OPERATING LOSS   Bishop Corporation began operations in 1985 and had operating losses of $200,000 in 1985 and $150,000 in 1986. For the year ended December 31, 1987, Bishop had pretax accounting income of $300,000. For the three-year period 1985 to 1987, assume an income tax rate of 40 percent and no permanent or timing differences.

REQUIRED

1. Prepare the journal entry to accrue income taxes at the end of 1987.

2. Prepare the bottom part of the income statement for Bishop for the year ending December 31, 1987, beginning with pretax accounting income.

(AICPA, adapted)

PROBLEMS

P19-1. BASIC PROCESS OF INTERPERIOD TAX ALLOCATION Swan Company has pretax accounting income of $84,000 and $110,000 in 1987 and 1988, respectively. In both years the tax rate on ordinary income is 40 percent and the capital gains tax rate is 25 percent. Included in the determination of 1987 accounting income is $4,000 of interest income on municipal bonds which is not taxable. Also, goodwill amortization of $10,000 is deducted in the calculation of pretax accounting income in both years. Owing to the use of ACRS depreciation for tax purposes and straight-line depreciation for book purposes, depreciation for tax purposes exceeds book depreciation by $6,000 in 1987 and book depreciation exceeds tax depreciation by $2,000 in 1988. A capital gain (before taxes) of $8,000 is recognized in 1988 for both book and tax purposes.

REQUIRED

1. Calculate taxable income for 1987 and 1988.

2. Prepare journal entries to record income tax expense for 1987 and 1988. Show your calculations.

P19-2. DIFFERENCES BETWEEN PRETAX ACCOUNTING INCOME AND TAXABLE INCOME; CALCULATION OF DEFERRED TAXES The Brazos Valley Corporation reports taxable income of $250,000 for the year ended December 31, 1987. To determine pretax accounting income, the following information may be relevant:

a) Interest income earned on tax-exempt securities is $14,000 in 1987.

b) Depreciation expense for tax purposes exceeds book depreciation by $10,000 in 1987 because of the use of different depreciation methods for the two purposes.

c) Installment sales revenue of $35,000 is recognized in 1987 for tax purposes on the basis of cash collections, whereas $50,000 of installment sales revenue is recognized for book purposes on the accrual basis.

d) Goodwill amortization of $8,000 is recorded in 1987.

e) Royalty income of $74,000 is recognized for tax purposes on the basis of cash receipts, while $86,000 is recognized on the accrual basis for book purposes.

f) Estimated inventory losses of $16,000 are recorded for book purposes, but can be deducted for tax purposes only upon disposal.

g) Brazos Valley paid a $10,000 fine as a result of violation of a pollution law.

The income tax rate is 40 percent.

REQUIRED

1. Determine pretax accounting income for 1987.

2. Prepare the journal entry to record income taxes for 1987.

P19-3. CALCULATION OF TIMING DIFFERENCES AND DEFERRED TAX ADJUSTMENT Chuckwagon Corporation has pretax accounting income and income tax liability (at 40 percent) as follows:

YEAR	PRETAX ACCOUNTING INCOME	TAX LIABILITY
1986	$160,000	$80,000
1987	140,000	64,000
1988	190,000	60,000
1989	80,000	72,000

The only differences between pretax accounting income and taxable income are timing differences.

REQUIRED

1. Calculate the amount of timing difference for each year.

2. Prepare the journal entry to record income taxes for each year.

P19-4. DEFERRED METHOD AND LIABILITY METHOD The Green Company commenced operations in 1986. It uses the same accounting methods for both financial reporting and tax purposes with the exception of depreciation, which it determines by the sum-of-the-years'-digits method for tax purposes and by the straight-line method for book purposes. Green's depreciable assets were acquired at the beginning of 1986 at a cost of $220,000 with an estimated salvage value of $20,000 and a useful life of four years. Pretax accounting income and tax rates are as follows:

YEAR	PRETAX ACCOUNTING INCOME	TAX RATE
1986	$190,000	40%
1987	230,000	45
1988	160,000	50
1989	210,000	50

REQUIRED

1. Construct the deferred income taxes account in T-account form and enter the appropriate amounts for each of the four years. Use the gross change method, assuming a FIFO flow for reversing differences.

2. Prepare journal entries to record income taxes at the end of each year using the deferred method.

3. Prepare journal entries to record income taxes at the end of each year using the liability method. Assume that future tax rates are known when timing differences occur.

P19-5. GROSS CHANGE AND NET CHANGE METHODS The Carter Corporation accounts for installment sales on the accrual basis for accounting purposes and on the basis of cash collections for tax purposes. Data regarding originating and reversing timing differences for installment sales follow:

YEAR	TAX RATE	ORIGINATING DIFFERENCES	REVERSING DIFFERENCES 1987	1988	1989
1986	40%	$ 80,000	$30,000	$40,000	$10,000
1987	45	120,000	—	48,000	60,000
1988	48	200,000	—	—	60,000
1989	50	160,000	—	—	—

Carter began operations in 1986. Pretax accounting income is $500,000 in all years. There are no other timing differences and no permanent differences.

REQUIRED

1. Prepare the journal entry to record income taxes for each year from 1986 through 1989 using the gross change method.

2. Prepare the journal entry to record income taxes for each year from 1986 through 1989 using the net change method.

P19-6. GROSS CHANGE AND NET CHANGE METHODS Coulter Company, which commenced operations in 1987, follows the same accounting methods for book and tax purposes with the exception of accounting for depreciation expense and royalty income. ACRS depreciation is taken for tax purposes and the straight-line basis is used for accounting purposes. Royalty income is recognized when received for tax purposes and later when earned for accounting purposes. Originating and reversing timing differences related to these two groups of items are shown below:

	ORIGINATING DIFFERENCES	REVERSING DIFFERENCES 1988	1989	1990
Depreciation				
1987	$ 30,000	$ 5,000	$10,000	$ 8,000
1988	20,000	—	3,000	7,000
1989	50,000	—	—	6,000
Royalty income				
1987	60,000	40,000	20,000	—
1988	100,000	—	80,000	20,000
1989	30,000	—	—	26,000

The tax rates are 40, 44, and 48 percent in 1987, 1988, and 1989, respectively. Pretax accounting income for the three years is $420,000, $500,000, and $380,000, respectively.

REQUIRED

1. Using the gross change method, calculate income tax expense, taxes payable, and the change in deferred taxes for 1987, 1988, and 1989.

2. Using the net change method, calculate income tax expense, taxes payable, and the change in deferred taxes for 1987, 1988, and 1989.

P19-7. TIMING DIFFERENCES—COMPREHENSIVE REVIEW   In January, 1989, you begin the examination of the financial statements of Snow Corporation, a new audit client, for the year ended December 31, 1988. During your examination the following information is disclosed:

a) Federal tax liabilities reported on tax returns were:

YEAR	AMOUNT DUE PER TAX RETURN
1986	$33,850
1987	77,020
1988	51,966

b) On January 2, 1986, packaging equipment was purchased at a cost of $225,000. The equipment had an estimated useful life of five years and a salvage value of $15,000. The sum-of-the-years'-digits method was used for income tax reporting and the straight-line method was used on the financial statements.

c) On January 8, 1987, $60,000 was collected in advance rental of a building for a three-year period. The $60,000 was reported as taxable income in 1987, but $40,000 was reported as deferred revenue in 1987 in the financial statements. The building will continue to be rented for the foreseeable future.

d) On February 12, 1988, the corporation sold land with a book and tax basis of $150,000 for $200,000. The gain, reported in full in 1988 on the financial statements, is being reported in equal installments on the income tax returns over a period of 10 years and is taxable as a capital gain.

e) On March 15, 1988, a patent developed at a cost of $34,000 was granted to Snow. The corporation is amortizing the patent over a period of seventeen years on the financial statements and over four years on its income tax return. The corporation elected to record a full year's amortization in 1988 on both its financial statements and its income tax return.

f) The income tax rates for 1986, 1987, and 1988 were:

	RATE
Ordinary income	48%
Long-term capital gains	25

REQUIRED

1. Prepare a schedule calculating the amount of the total net deferred tax debits and credits for each year ended December 31, 1986, 1987, and 1988.

2. Prepare a schedule calculating the total amount of income tax expense for financial reporting purposes for each year ended December 31, 1986, 1987, and 1988.

(AICPA, adapted)

P19-8. COMPREHENSIVE REVIEW—PERMANENT AND TIMING DIFFERENCES   The Gatlin Company has supplied you with information regarding its 1987 income tax expense for financial statement reporting as follows:

a) The provision for current income taxes was $600,000 for the year ended December 31, 1987. Gatlin made estimated tax payments of $550,000 during 1987.

b) Gatlin generally depreciates fixed assets by the straight-line method for financial statement reporting and by various ACRS methods for income tax reporting. During 1987, depreciation on fixed assets amounted to $900,000 for financial statement reporting and

$950,000 for income tax reporting. Commitments for the purchase of fixed assets amounted to $450,000 on December 31, 1987.

c) For financial statement reporting, Gatlin has accrued estimated losses from product warranty contracts prior to their occurrence. For income tax reporting, no deduction is taken until payments are made. As of December 31, 1986, accrued estimated losses of $200,000 were included in the liability section of Gatlin's balance sheet. On the basis of the latest available information, Gatlin estimates that this figure should be 30 percent higher on December 31, 1987. Payments of $250,000 were made in 1987.

d) In 1983 Gatlin acquired another company for cash. Goodwill resulting from this transaction was $800,000 and is being amortized over a 40-year period for financial statement reporting. The amortization is not deductible for income tax reporting.

e) Premiums paid on officers' life insurance amounted to $80,000 in 1987. These premiums are not deductible for income tax reporting.

f) The income tax rate was 48 percent.

REQUIRED

1. What amounts should be shown for *(a)* provision for current income taxes; *(b)* provision for deferred income taxes recognized in Gatlin's income statement for the year ended December 31, 1987? Show supporting calculations in good form.

2. Identify any information given that you did not use to determine your answer to part 1 and explain why you did not use this information.

(AICPA, adapted)

P19-9. COMPREHENSIVE REVIEW—INTERPERIOD TAX ALLOCATION   You have been retained to help the office manager of Lynn Corporation to develop certain year-end financial information for the corporation. Lynn is a domestic corporation, files its tax return on the accrual basis, and is engaged in the manufacture of office supplies and furniture. Lynn's accounts had been adjusted properly as of December 31, 1986.

Lynn's trial balance before adjustment as of December 31, 1987, the close of its fiscal year, follows:

	DEBIT	CREDIT
Cash	$ 45,120	
Inventory	70,000	
Installment accounts receivable	85,000	
Accounts receivable	20,000	
Deferred income tax	37,880	
Fixed assets (net of depreciation)	178,000	
Investment in Mash Corporation stock	260,000	
Accounts payable		$ 31,000
Note payable		100,000
Rental fees received in advance		6,000
Capital stock		250,000
Retained earnings		135,000
Sales		600,000
Cost of goods sold	360,000	
Operating expenses	105,000	
Dividend revenue, Mash Corporation		15,000
Rental revenue		24,000
Total	$1,161,000	$1,161,000

The following information has been gathered from the accounting records and verified to be correct.

a) *Installment accounts receivable* Gross profit on installment sales is included in the income tax return in the period of collection rather than in the period of sale.

| | GROSS-PROFIT | INSTALLMENT RECEIVABLES | |
SALES	PERCENTAGE	12/31/86	12/31/87
1985	25%	$10,000	—
1986	30	41,000	$25,000
1987	40	—	60,000

b) *Deferred income tax* The only entry charged to this account during 1987 is a debit of $43,000 representing payments on the 1987 estimated tax liability.

c) *Investment in Mash Corporation stock* On January 2, 1987, Lynn purchased 80 percent of the outstanding common stock of Mash for $260,000 cash.

On the date of acquisition, Mash's recorded net assets had a fair market and book value of $230,000. Any goodwill arising from the acquisition is to be amortized over 20 years by the straight-line method.

The 1987 calendar-year earnings according to Mash's income statement were $55,000. Dividend revenue represents actual cash distributions received in 1987. (*Hint:* Lynn should be using the equity method.)

d) *Note payable* The note is noninterest-bearing and was issued in exchange for cash borrowed from a supplier. It matures five years from October 1, 1987. The loan was negotiated in connection with a $100,000 purchase contract for the supplier's product, at prices above the prevailing market rate. An appropriate rate of interest on this note would have been six percent.

Seventy-five percent of the merchandise purchased under this contract is included in cost of goods sold, and 25 percent is included in the ending inventory.

e) *Rental fees received in advance* This figure represents rent received in advance from a tenant who occupies a portion of the building owned by Lynn Corporation. The use of the funds is not restricted. The rent is $2,000 per month, and one month's rent was received in advance at the end of 1986 for January 1987.

REQUIRED

1. Prepare a comparative schedule for pretax accounting income and taxable income, including supporting schedules. Discounts and/or premiums should be amortized on the straight-line basis. Do not impute any interest in your calculation of taxable income.

2. Independent of your answer to part 1, prepare a schedule analyzing deferred income taxes for the year ended December 31, 1987, showing the amount of deferred tax attributable to each variation between pretax accounting income and taxable income, including the reversal of any timing differences that originated in a prior period. Assume that the effective tax rate is 40 percent for all calculations.

(AICPA, adapted)

P19-10. COMPREHENSIVE REVIEW Your firm has been appointed to examine the financial statements of Cash Engineering, Inc. (CEI), for the two years ended December 31, 1987, in conjunction with an application for a bank loan. CEI was formed on January 2, 1986, by the nontaxable incorporation of the Cash family partnership.

Early in the engagement you learn that the controller is unfamiliar with income tax accounting and that no tax allocations have been recorded. During your examination you gather considerable information from the accounting records and client employees regarding interperiod tax allocation. This information has been audited and is as follows (with dollar amounts rounded to the nearest $100):

a) CEI uses a bad debt write-off method for tax purposes and a full accrual method for book purposes. The balance of the allowance for doubtful receivables account as of December 31, 1985, was $62,000. Following is a schedule of accounts written off and the corresponding years in which the related sales were made.

YEARS IN WHICH	AMOUNTS WRITTEN OFF	
SALES WERE MADE	**1987**	**1986**
1985 and before	$19,800	$29,000
1986..	7,200	
1987..		
	$27,000	$29,000

The following is a schedule of changes in the allowance for doubtful receivables account for the two years ended December 31, 1987:

	1987	**1986**
Balance at beginning of year........................	$66,000	$62,000
Accounts written off during year	(27,000)	(29,000)
Bad debt expense for year.........................	38,000	33,000
Balance at end of year............................	$77,000	$66,000

b) Following is a reconciliation between net income per books and taxable income:

		1987	**1986**
a)	Net income per books........................	$333,100	$262,800
b)	Federal income tax payable	182,300	236,800
c)	Taxable income not recorded on books:		
	Deferred sales commissions	10,000	
d)	Expenses recorded on books not deducted on tax return:		
	Allowance for doubtful receivables	11,000	4,000
	Amortization of goodwill	8,000	8,000
e)	Total of lines *a* through *d*	$544,400	$511,600
f)	Income recorded on books not included on tax return:		
	Tax-exempt interest—Watertown 5% municipal bonds	$ 5,000	
g)	Deductions on tax return not charged against book income: depreciation	83,700	$ 38,000
h)	Total of lines *f* and *g*	$(88,700)	$(38,000)
i)	Taxable income (line *e* less line *h*)	$455,700	$473,600

c) The effective tax rates are as follows:

1985 and prior years	60%
1986	50
1987	40

d) In December, 1987, CEI entered into a contract to serve as distributor for Black Manufacturing's engineering products. The contract became effective December 31, 1987, and $10,000 of advance commissions on the contract were received and deposited on December 31, 1987. Since the commissions had not been earned, they were accounted for as a deferred credit on the balance sheet as of December 31, 1987.

e) Goodwill represents the excess of cost over fair market value of the net tangible assets of a retiring competitor that were acquired for cash on January 2, 1982. The original balance was $80,000.

f) Depreciation on plant assets transferred at incorporation and acquisitions through December 31, 1985, have been accounted for on a straight-line basis for both financial and tax reporting. Beginning in 1986, all additions of machinery and equipment have been depreciated by an ACRS method for tax reporting but by the straight-line method for financial reporting. Company policy is to take a full year's depreciation in the year of acquisition and none in the year of retirement. There have been no sales, trade-ins, or retirements since incorporation. Following is a schedule disclosing significant information about depreciable property and related depreciation:

ASSET	COST	LIFE (YEARS)	ANNUAL STRAIGHT-LINE AMOUNT*	ACRS DEPRECIATION 1987	ACRS DEPRECIATION 1986	DEPRECIATION TAKEN THROUGH 12/31/85
Buildings	$1,190,000	20 & 50	$31,000			$380,000
Machinery and equipment:						
Transferred at incor- poration or acquired through 12/31/85	834,000	Various	45,900			495,800
Acquisitions since 12/31/85						
1986.	267,000	6	38,000	$ 63,700	$76,000	
1987.	395,000	6	58,000	116,000		
Total asset cost	$2,686,000					

* After appropriate consideration is given to salvage value.

	TOTAL DEPRECIATION EXPENSE		
	1987	1986	THROUGH 12/31/85
For book purposes	$172,900	$114,900	$875,800
For tax purposes.	$256,600	$152,900	$875,800

REQUIRED

1. Prepare a schedule calculating *(a)* the balance of deferred income taxes as of December 31, 1986 and 1987, and *(b)* the amount of the timing differences between income tax payable and income tax expense for 1986 and 1987. Round all calculations to the nearest $100.

2. Independent of your solution to part 1 and assuming data shown below, prepare the section of the income statement beginning with pretax accounting income to disclose properly income tax expense for the years ended December 31, 1987 and 1986.

	1987	1986
Pretax accounting income	$480,400	$465,600
Taxes payable currently	182,300	236,800
Net change in deferred taxes—Dr. (Cr.)	(28,100)	24,500
Balance of deferred tax at end of year—Dr. (Cr.)	(44,200)	(16,100)

(AICPA, adapted)

P19-11. NET OPERATING LOSS CARRYBACK AND CARRYFORWARD   Pretax accounting income (loss) for Axton Mining Company is as follows for the years indicated:

YEAR	PRETAX ACCOUNTING INCOME	TAX RATE
1984	$(20,000)	30%
1985	30,000	35
1986	40,000	40
1987	(60,000)	45
1988	20,000	50
1989	30,000	50
1990	10,000	50

1984 was Axton's first year of operations. Pretax accounting income in 1986 includes $10,000 of tax-exempt municipal bond income. Percentage depletion of mining property (for tax purposes) exceeds cost depletion (for book purposes) by $4,000, $3,000, $5,000, and $5,000 in 1987, 1988, 1989, and 1990, respectively. There are no other differences between pretax accounting income and taxable income for the years indicated. Axton elects the loss carryback option in 1987.

REQUIRED

1. Prepare the journal entry required at the end of 1987 to recognize the tax benefit of the net operating loss, assuming that there is no assurance at the end of 1987 that future earnings will be sufficient to obtain the carryforward benefit.

2. Repeat part 1, assuming instead that future earnings sufficient to obtain the carryforward benefit are assured at the end of 1987.

3. Describe how the tax benefit associated with the carryback should be shown in the 1987 financial statements.

4. Describe how the tax benefit of the carryforward should be shown in the financial statements under parts 1 and 2.

P19-12. NET OPERATING LOSS CARRYBACK AND CARRYFORWARD   Revenues and expenses of Milsap Company and applicable tax rates for its first five years of operations are as follows:

YEAR	REVENUES	EXPENSES	TAX RATE
1986	$100,000	$110,000	30%
1987	160,000	120,000	40
1988	130,000	170,000	45
1989	195,000	190,000	50
1990	210,000	195,000	48

REQUIRED

1. Prepare journal entries required at the end of each year related to income taxes, assuming that Milsap elects the loss carryback option where possible.

2. Prepare a summarized income statement for each year from 1986 through 1990.

P19-13. COMPREHENSIVE   Included in Bristol Corporation's liability account balances at December 31, 1986, were the following:

Note payable, bank $2,800,000
Liability under capital lease...................................... 430,000
Deferred income taxes 360,000

Transactions during 1987 and other information relating to Bristol's liabilities were as follows:
    a) The principal amount of the note payable is $2,800,000 and it bears interest at 15 percent. The note is dated April 1, 1986, and is payable in four equal installments of $700,000 beginning April 1, 1987. The first payment of principal and interest was made on April 1, 1987.
    b) The capitalized lease is for a 10-year period beginning December 31, 1984. Equal annual payments of $100,000 are due on December 31 of each year, and the 14 percent interest rate implicit in the lease is known by Bristol. At December 31, 1986, the present value of the seven remaining lease payments (due December 31, 1987, through December 31, 1993) discounted at 14 percent was $430,000.
    c) Deferred income taxes are provided in recognition of timing differences between financial statement and income tax reporting of depreciation. For the year ended December 31, 1987, depreciation per tax return exceeded book depreciation by $90,000. Bristol's effective income tax rate for 1987 was 40 percent.

d) On July 1, 1987, Bristol issued 10 percent $1,000 bonds with a face amount of $2,000,000. The bonds, issued for $1,774,000 to yield 12 percent, are dated July 1, 1987, and mature on July 1, 1997. Interest is payable annually on July 1. Bristol uses the interest method to amortize bond discount.

REQUIRED

1. Prepare the long-term liabilities section of Bristol's balance sheet at December 31, 1987.

2. Prepare a schedule showing the current portion of the long-term liabilities and accrued interest payable that would appear in Bristol's balance sheet at December 31, 1987.

3. Prepare a schedule showing interest expense from the long-term liabilities and deferred income tax expense that would appear in Bristol's income statement for the year ended December 31, 1987.

(AICPA, adapted)

20 STOCKHOLDERS' EQUITY: CONTRIBUTED CAPITAL

In previous chapters we discussed generally accepted accounting principles underlying the accounting and reporting for various assets and liabilities. These guidelines for assets and liabilities are applicable to the three legal forms of business organization: sole proprietorships, partnerships, and corporations. However, accounting and reporting for the **owners' equity of corporations,** often called **stockholders' equity** or **shareholders' equity,** differ significantly from accounting and reporting for the owners' equity of partnerships and sole proprietorships, primarily because of legal requirements and complex terminology associated with corporations.

Stockholders' equity consists of (1) **contributed capital,** which arises from investments by stockholders, and (2) **retained earnings,** which is the amount of capital earned by profitable operations and retained in the business. In this chapter we concentrate primarily on transactions that affect contributed capital; in Chapter 21 we address the accounting and reporting issues that affect retained earnings.

CORPORATE FORM OF ORGANIZATION

There are many more sole proprietorships and partnerships than corporations in the United States. The corporation, however, is the dominant form of business organization in our economy, whether the measurement is total revenue, assets, number of employees, or any other characteristic. This dominance is due to certain characteristics unique to corporations, such as the limited liability of owners and the system of capital accumulation.

Corporations may be classified as follows:

I. Private: privately owned corporations.
    A. Stock: private corporations that issue stock as evidence of ownership interest, and seek profits and increased wealth for the owners.
        1. Open: stock corporations whose stock is widely held and is available for purchase by the general public.
            (a) Listed: stock is traded on an organized stock exchange, such as the New York Stock Exchange.
            (b) Unlisted: stock is traded over the counter through securities dealers.

2. Closed: stock corporations whose stock is held by a few individuals and is not available for purchase by the general public.

B. Nonstock: private corporations that do not seek profits or issue stock, such as churches and charities.

II. Public: corporations owned by governmental units.

In this chapter we are concerned primarily with private corporations that issue stock.

STATE LAWS GOVERNING CORPORATIONS

Each state has its own laws governing the incorporation of businesses. Individuals who want to incorporate a business must apply to the appropriate governmental unit in the state in which they want to incorporate. The application typically includes the names of the individuals who desire to incorporate, the name and address of the proposed corporation, the nature of the business, and the types of stock to be issued. Upon approval by the state, a **corporate charter,** also called the **articles of incorporation,** is granted. The charter is an agreement between the state and the corporation whereby the state grants to the corporation the right to operate and to raise capital according to the terms of the charter. Each state recognizes the corporation as a legal entity separate from its owners. Thus, the corporation can enter into contracts, can sue and be sued, and can buy and sell property.

To accountants, the fact that laws govern both the incorporation process and the subsequent business activity of corporations is quite important. Corporate management must abide by state law regarding such items as terminology, permissible transactions, distributions of profits, and the treatment of proceeds from stock issuances. These laws create complexity that would not exist if the accountant's only requirement were to distinguish between contributed capital and retained earnings.

It is not necessary for you to learn the various states' laws governing corporations in order to understand the accounting for stockholders' equity. It is necessary only to recognize that because state laws are so diverse, there are exceptions to any generalizations we may make in regard to stockholders' equity. You can learn about these exceptions more effectively as you are required to know them in the practice of accounting.

In addition to state laws, the characteristics of corporations themselves affect the accounting for stockholders' equity. Those characteristics include:

1. The system of capital accumulation.

2. Limited liability.

3. Different classes of stock (e.g., preferred stock).

We analyze the impact of each of these characteristics in the following sections.

THE SYSTEM OF CAPITAL ACCUMULATION

Corporations obtain assets primarily by borrowing, by issuing capital stock, and by operating at a profit. Of these three sources, only the issuance of capital stock is unique to corporations. We discuss the characteristics of stock, the rights of stockholders, and classes of stock in this section.

Stock

The issuance of ownership units in the form of capital stock enables corporations to accumulate large amounts of assets. Individual investments may range from one share of stock and only a few dollars to many shares of stock and millions of dollars. The proportion of ownership of individual investors is equal to the proportion of outstanding shares of stock owned by each investor. For example, if an investor owns 300,000 shares out of 1,000,000 outstanding shares, that investor has a 30 percent (300,000 ÷ 1,000,000) ownership interest in the net assets of the corporation.

Individual investors may buy and sell outstanding shares of capital stock in listed or over-the-counter markets. The transfer of ownership shares between investors affects neither the corporation's assets nor the continuity of corporate operations. On the other hand, an ownership change in a sole proprietorship or partnership generally terminates the entity's legal existence. The fact that the corporation continues despite frequent ownership changes makes it possible for corporate management to plan and control operations to achieve long-run objectives.

Since investors buy and sell shares of capital stock frequently, corporations must periodically update their list of stockholders, called a **stockholders' ledger.** The stockholders' ledger provides a reference for allocating dividend payments and stock rights and for communicating with stockholders on other issues. Many companies employ a **transfer agent** when they issue new shares. In addition, major corporations often employ a **registrar** to provide a current list of owners of stock.

Rights of Stockholders

Ownership of stock in a corporation conveys certain rights and privileges to the owner. A **stock contract** enumerates the rights of each class of stock issued by a corporation. In the absence of specific provisions to the contrary, each class of stock generally conveys the following rights:

1. The right to share in profits, as declared and distributed as dividends, in proportion to the number of shares held.
2. The right to vote for directors and on management policy issues.
3. The right to maintain ownership proportion by sharing proportionately in new issues of the same class of stock. We refer to this right as the **preemptive right.**
4. The right to share proportionately in corporate assets in the event of liquidation.

If the stock contract is silent with respect to the preceding four rights, common law presumes that these rights exist. Thus, if the corporation wants to deny one or more of the rights, the stock contract must state specifically that the right does not exist. For example, because of difficulties associated with raising substantial amounts of additional capital in the presence of a preemptive right, many corporations exclude the preemptive right of stockholders. Because most stockholders do not own enough shares to be concerned about their proportion of ownership, the absence of the preemptive right usually is not a significant factor in the evaluation of a particular stock's attractiveness.

Classes of Stock

A **class of stock** is a homogeneous group of shares of stock. That is, all shares within a class have the same rights and restrictions. When two or more classes of stock exist in a corporation, the stockholders of one class of stock control the management of the corporation, reap the rewards of success, and bear the ultimate risk of failure. We call the stock owned by this class of stockholders **common stock.** Common stock usually has the four rights listed previously, except perhaps the preemptive right.

By excluding selected rights and conveying additional privileges, a corporation may create special classes of stock called **preferred stock.** The objective of creating two or more classes of stock with different risks and privileges is to appeal to a broader spectrum of investors. For example, corporations often eliminate the voting privilege from a particular class of stock in exchange for a preference over common stockholders in dividend or asset distributions if the firm is liquidated. The corporation may promise preferred stockholders dividends at a specified rate (for example, $6 per share) before common stockholders are entitled to dividends. Likewise, in the event of liquidation, the corporation must pay preferred stockholders their stated liquidation value per share before common stockholders receive anything. In exchange for a dividend preference or a preference claim on assets upon liquidation, the preferred stockholders give up their rights to participate in management policy decisions and to share in profits beyond the specified return.

Investors and creditors require information about the rights and privileges of the various classes of stock. Dividend preferences and liquidation preferences for classes of stock may be relevant to users in assessing future cash flows. Thus, accounting reports must include such information.

In summary, the issuance of capital stock enables corporations to generate large amounts of capital and to continue operating indefinitely even though ownership of the stock may change. From the stockholders' viewpoint, a major advantage to stock ownership is the limited liability feature, as discussed in the next section.

LIMITED LIABILITY

Investors in corporate stock generally may not lose more than the amount invested.

The corporate form of organization limits the liability of stockholders. Investors have no responsibility for corporate debt because the corporation, as a separate legal entity, incurs debt and has the responsibility for its repayment. The personal assets of investors are not available for the satisfaction of corporate liabilities. Generally, the maximum loss that an individual stockholder can incur is the amount he or she has invested. Investors in stock may lose their investment because the amount invested becomes a part of corporate assets, and therefore is subject to the claims of creditors. They may not, however, lose more than the amount they have invested.

The limited liability feature is an advantage of the corporate form of business over partnerships and sole proprietorships. In the latter two organizational forms, creditors have a legal claim not only to business assets but also to the personal assets of the owners to satisfy business debts. That is, the obligations of the business likewise are obligations of the owners, and therefore creditors may claim both business and personal assets to eliminate business obligations.

Issuance of Stock at Discount

There is one exception to the generalization that a stockholder's loss is limited to the amount invested. In order to understand this exception, it is necessary to understand some additional terminology related to capital stock.

In many states, corporations issue **par value stock,** either by choice or because state corporation laws require that a corporation designate a par value. The par value is an arbitrary dollar amount assigned by the corporation to each share. There is no necessary relationship between the price at which a corporation issues stock, or the price at which the stock trades in the marketplace, and the par value of the stock. If a corporation issues par value stock at a price in excess of par, it is issuing the stock at a **premium.** If a corporation issues stock at a price below par value, it is issuing the stock at a **discount.** The issuance of stock at a discount results in the exception to the limited liability rule for stockholders.

A corporation may incur losses of such magnitude that the resulting decrease in corporate assets exceeds the total of contributed capital and retained earnings. If creditors' claims exceed the assets available to meet them, and the corporation has issued stock at a discount, creditors may force stockholders who bought stock at a discount to pay them the amount of the discount. Shares of stock are not fully paid until the corporation receives at least the par value. Thus, a *contingent liability* exists for stockholders who acquire stock from a corporation at a price below par value. The contingent liability becomes an actual liability only if a corporation's liabilities exceed its assets and creditors then enforce their legal claim to the discount. The contingent liability is to the creditors, not to the corporation. It is a liability of the original purchaser of shares unless a contractual arrangement transfers the liability to subsequent stockholders.

In summary, the limited liability feature means that investors in par value stock who purchase shares from a corporation at a price equal to or exceeding par value cannot lose more than their investment. Investors who acquire shares at a discount may lose their original investment plus an amount equal to the discount.

Impairment of Contributed Capital

Creditors' claims to corporate assets take priority over the claims of stockholders. Although operating losses may result in the impairment of all or a portion of contributed capital, corporations may not distribute assets to stockholders voluntarily if prior claims exist (i.e., claims of creditors and preferred stockholders) and if the dollar amount of contributed capital would be impaired as a result of the distribution.[1] Corporations have a responsibility for maintaining assets equal to the dollar amount of contributed capital as long as the business is in existence. Upon dissolution, corporations must maintain assets equal to contributed capital until all prior claims have been settled.

To demonstrate the significance to creditors of this requirement, assume that, just as it commences operations, the Malone Corporation has assets valued at $100,000, liabilities of $80,000, and contributed capital from issuance of capital stock of $20,000, as shown in Exhibit 20–1. If Malone were permitted to distribute $20,000 of assets to stockholders, creditors would have no protection against any asset shrinkage that might result from unprofitable operations or from other events and transactions. By requiring Malone to retain assets equivalent to contributed capital, the state protects creditors against losses to the extent of contributed capital. The contributed capital may be thought of as a buffer against losses for the protection of creditors.

The requirement that a firm must retain capital contributions from owners is unique to corporations. The owners of sole proprietorships and partnerships may withdraw assets up to the amount of their capital balance whenever they desire. Because of the legal restrictions on distributions of corporate assets, the board of directors of a corporation must formally approve dividend distributions to stockholders, and must maintain records

---

[1] Technically, the dollar amount that a corporation must maintain is called **legal capital.** The definition of legal capital is not the same in all states. At a minimum, the par value of shares issued is included in legal capital, and in some states premiums paid in when a corporation issues shares also are included. Corporations cannot distribute assets to shareholders if the distribution would impair legal capital, however defined.

EXHIBIT 20–1   MALONE CORPORATION'S INITIAL FINANCIAL POSITION

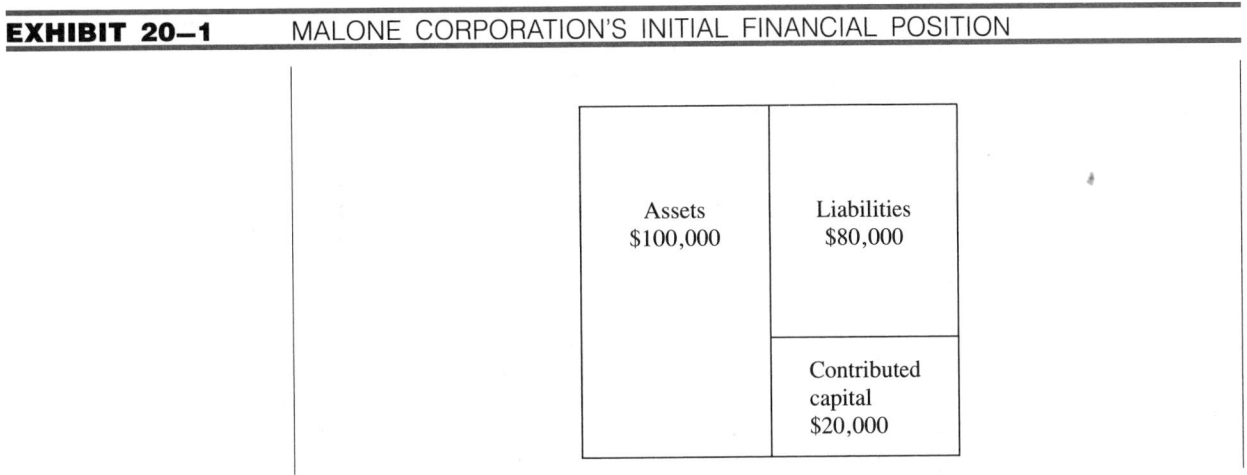

of dividend declarations and distributions. Dividend distributions must be in accord with the stock contract and with the appropriate state corporation laws. If a corporation cannot pay creditors because illegal distributions have been made to stockholders, the board of directors may be legally liable to the creditors.

PREFERRED STOCK

Preferred stock has characteristics of both debt and equity.

As mentioned earlier in this chapter, corporations often issue stock, called preferred stock, that has different terms than common stock. We discuss the characteristics of preferred stock in this section.

Preferred stock occupies a position between long-term debt and common stock in terms of its characteristics. It is similar to long-term debt because corporations usually pay preferred dividends at a specified rate per share, just as they make interest payments on long-term debt at a specified rate. The corporation does not, however, have an obligation to repay the preferred stockholders' investment at a specified date. Thus, preferred stock tends to be a relatively permanent source of assets. Preferred stock, like common stock, generally is classified as a part of stockholders' equity.

In addition to the normal preferences with respect to dividends and assets upon liquidation, preferred stock may possess one or more of the following features:

1. **Cumulative feature:** dividends not paid in any year must be paid subsequently to holders of preferred stock before holders of common shares can receive dividends.

2. **Participation feature:** holders of preferred shares may receive dividends beyond the specified dividend rate.

3. **Call feature:** the corporation may redeem the stock at a specified price.

4. **Conversion feature:** stockholders may convert preferred shares to shares of another class of stock.

The stock contract must specify whether these features apply to a particular issue of preferred stock.

Cumulative Feature

Preferred stock is *cumulative* if dividends not paid on preferred shares in any year must be paid before holders of common shares may receive dividends. The failure to declare dividends at the specified rate on cumulative preferred stock creates **passed dividends,** also called **dividends in arrears.** Holders of common shares cannot receive a dividend until the corporation has paid both dividends in arrears and current dividends on preferred stock. Dividends in arrears, however, do not constitute a liability to the corporation until the board of directors formally declares the dividend. Corporations must disclose the amount of dividends in arrears in the footnotes to the financial statements because they represent a probable future outflow of cash and a potential constraint on dividends to common stockholders. If preferred stock is *noncumulative,* dividends in arrears can never exist, because the corporation is not obligated to pay passed dividends. Most preferred stock issues are cumulative. This feature appeals to many investors.

Participation Feature

Preferred stock is **participating** if holders of preferred and common stock share dividends paid after the corporation has paid both groups a dividend equal to the preferred dividend rate. For example, if a corporation had 9 percent $100 par value participating preferred stock outstanding, any dividends paid would go first to meet the preferred requirement, at $9 per share. The corporation would allocate additional dividends to the common stockholders up to 9 percent of the par value of the common stock. If additional dividends were paid and the preferred stock was **fully participating,** the corporation would allocate the remainder to preferred and common shares in proportion to the total par value of each class of stock as compared to the total par value of both classes of stock.

Preferred stock also may be **partially participating,** which means the stock contract limits the participation to a maximum amount per share. For example, the stock contract could specify that the 9 percent participating preferred stock may participate up to a maximum of 12 percent, or $12 per share.

Although the participation feature was once common, we rarely find it in practice today. Thus, dividends for a particular class of preferred stock tend to remain constant over time. If total dividends paid increase as a result of higher corporate earnings, the increased dividends accrue to the common stockholders. We illustrate the effect of the cumulative and participating features on dividend distributions in Chapter 21.

Call Feature

Many preferred stock issues are **callable.** A corporation may call, or redeem, callable preferred stock at a specified price. The firm must pay any dividends in arrears when it redeems the stock. For example, several years ago Castle & Cooke, Inc., issued preferred stock that it could call beginning in 1985 at $110 per share, decreasing to $100 per share in 1990, plus accumulated dividends.

The call feature is advantageous to a corporation because it permits some flexibility in the timing of the retirement of the preferred stock. A call privilege is likely to be exercised when market interest rates have declined below the dividend rate on the outstanding preferred issue. At such a time, the corporation can replace the outstanding issue with a new issue with lower dividend requirements.

The call feature generally is not attractive to investors. The call price tends to put a ceiling on the market price of the preferred stock, and a corporation is most likely to exercise the call privilege when retiring (calling) the stock is more attractive than alternative uses of cash. Because the call feature is disadvantageous to investors, a **call premium,** an excess of the call price paid by the corporation above the original issuance price, usually exists to increase the attractiveness of the stock.

Some preferred stock issues have mandatory redemption (retirement) terms, requiring redemption at specified times, usually in 5 to 10 years, and in specified amounts. In recent years, many corporations have resorted to this type of financing in order to improve existing debt to equity ratios. Preferred stock with required redemption terms is much more like debt than equity, because the issuing corporation commits itself to reacquire the shares at a definite date. Thus, the investment is temporary, like debt, rather than permanent, like equity capital.

Recognizing the similarity of redeemable preferred stock to debt, the SEC requires that corporations must exclude from stockholders' equity amounts received from the issuance of redeemable preferred stock in corporate financial statements filed with the SEC.[2] The corporation must describe the redemption feature and must present a redemption schedule for the five years ahead.

GAAP does not require corporations to exclude redeemable preferred stock from stockholders' equity in annual reports to stockholders. Because a redemption feature affects future cash flows, however, the issuing corporation must disclose the redemption terms in the notes to the financial statements. Exhibit 20–2 illustrates a recent annual report's disclosure of redeemable preferred stock by CP National Corporation.

---

[2] "Presentation in Financial Statements of Redeemable Preferred Stocks," *Accounting Series Release No. 268* (Washington, D.C.: SEC, July 1979). The excluded amount should be reported immediately before stockholders' equity.

EXHIBIT 20–2   FOOTNOTE DISCLOSURE REGARDING REDEEMABLE PREFERRED STOCK

CP National Corporation
1984 ANNUAL REPORT

NOTE 8. PREFERRED STOCK WITH MANDATORY REDEMPTION REQUIREMENTS

Three series of preferred stock have mandatory redemption requirements. Activity in such preferred stock in 1984, 1983, and 1982 is summarized as follows (in thousands):

	8.4% CUMULATIVE	9.75% CUMULATIVE	10.8% CUMULATIVE	TOTAL
Balance, December 31, 1981	$2,400	$1,400	$3,484	$7,284
Sinking fund purchases	(120)	(60)	(137)	(317)
Balance, December 31, 1982	$2,280	$1,340	$3,347	$6,967
Sinking fund purchases	(120)	(60)	(268)	(448)
Balance, December 31, 1983	$2,160	$1,280	$3,079	$6,519
Sinking fund purchases	(120)	(60)	(79)	(259)
Balance, December 31, 1984	$2,040	$1,220	$3,000	$6,260
Current sinking fund redemption requirements	(120)	(60)	(200)	(380)
Net.................................	$1,920	$1,160	$2,800	$5,880

The preferred stock with mandatory redemption requirements is redeemable at the option of the Company at the following prices plus accrued dividends as of December 31, 1984 (in thousands except per share amounts):

	PER SHARE	TOTAL
8.4% cumulative.............................	$21.18	$2,160
9.75% cumulative.............................	21.43	1,307
10.8% cumulative.............................	21.51	3,238

Aggregate annual sinking fund redemption requirements at par for each of the four years 1986 through 1989 are $380,000. At the option of the Company, $200,000 of additional sinking fund redemptions at par of the 10.8% cumulative preferred may be made each year. The Company may make purchases in the open market and apply such purchases against the annual sinking fund requirements.

Conversion Feature

If preferred stock is **convertible,** holders of preferred stock may, at their option, exchange their preferred shares for common shares according to a specified ratio. The conversion privilege may be advantageous to both the issuing corporation and the investor. The investor in convertible preferred stock has the dividend preferences of a holder of preferred stock and, at the same time, has the opportunity to convert the investment into common shares if conversion becomes attractive. When the option of conversion is available, preferred stock prices tend to rise with common stock price increases. On the other hand, the fixed-return aspect of preferred shares tends to keep the price of the preferred stock from following major price declines in the common stock.

A company usually issues convertible preferred stock as an indirect means of issuing additional common stock. The attractiveness of the conversion privilege enables the issuing corporation to pay a lower dividend rate than it would otherwise have to pay.

ACCOUNTING FOR
THE ISSUANCE OF STOCK

The issuance of capital stock constitutes a primary asset source for corporations. Exhibit 20–3 shows that corporations generate huge sums of money through the issuance of stock. In 1980 alone, corporations generated $13.3 billion through the issuance of capital stock. We describe the various processes by which corporations issue stock and the associated accounting procedures in this section.

Before issuing capital stock, a corporation must receive authorization to do so from the state in which it is incorporated. Once the company receives authorization, it offers stock for sale, the investors enter into a contract with the corporation to acquire the shares, the investors pay the corporation for the shares, and the corporation issues the stock.

ISSUANCE FOR CASH

Corporations may issue capital stock as par value stock, no-par stock with a stated value, or no-par stock with no stated value (also called true no-par stock).

Par Value Stock

When a corporation issues **par value stock,** it usually establishes par value at an amount well below the issuance price so that no discount occurs when the stock is issued. Most states now prohibit the issuance of capital stock at a discount. The issuing corporation records any premium, which is the excess of the proceeds over the par value, in the account contributed capital in excess of par value.

To illustrate, if George Corporation issues 10,000 shares of $10 par value common stock for cash at $50 per share, the journal entry to record the issuance is as follows:

Cash... 500,000		
Common stock		100,000
Contributed capital in excess of par—common		400,000

EXHIBIT 20–3   ASSETS GENERATED BY 13 U.S. CORPORATIONS THROUGH ISSUANCE OF CAPITAL STOCK, 1980

COMPANY	NUMBER OF SHARES (MILLIONS)	SHARE PRICE	MILLIONS OF DOLLARS RAISED
AT&T	16.5	$57.00	$940
United Technologies	5	53.625	268
Digital Equipment	2.5	99.25	248
Monsanto	3	71.00	213
Southern California Edison	8	24.375	195
Deere & Company	4	43.00	172
American Electric Power	9	16.25	146
Long Island Lighting	9	14.25	128
Southern Companies	11	11.55	127
Cetus*	5.2	23.00	120
Mexico Fund*	10	12.00	120
Global Marine	2	54.75	109
Mitel	2.9	35.25	102

* Initial public offering.

Source: Merrill Lynch, in *New York Times,* June 22, 1981, p. D1.

Other terms for contributed capital in excess of par—common include additional paid-in capital—common, paid-in capital in excess of par—common, or premium on common stock.

Stated Value Stock

In many states corporations may issue capital stock without par value. Some of these states require that the issuing corporation assign such shares a **stated value** per share. The stated value serves the same purpose as par value—to distinguish between legal (stated) capital and amounts paid in above legal capital. Thus, corporations account for no-par stock with a stated value in the same way that they account for par value stock.

True No-Par Stock

When a corporation issues no-par capital stock with no stated value, also called **true no-par stock,** it credits the entire amount received for the stock to the capital stock account. There are no premiums or discounts associated with true no-par capital stock. For example, if a corporation issues 1,000 shares of true no-par common stock for $50 per share, it makes the following journal entry:

Cash.	50,000	
Common stock		50,000

The valuation of capital stock issued for cash is straightforward because the number of dollars of cash received provides a basis for recording the transaction. That is, the corporation records the number of dollars of cash received at the date of acquisition, and then assigns this amount to the shares issued. However, when a corporation issues stock in exchange for noncash consideration, such as property or services, accounting for the transaction becomes more complex.

ISSUANCE FOR NONCASH CONSIDERATION   When a corporation issues stock for assets other than cash, or for services, the general rule is that the company should record both the assets or services received and the stock issued at the fair market value of the consideration received or the fair market value of the stock issued, whichever is more readily determinable. In virtually all cases, the fair market value of either the consideration received or the stock issued will clearly be more easily determinable. If the two parties to the transaction are independent, the two fair market values should be about the same.

If it is not possible to determine the fair market value of either the noncash consideration received or the capital stock issued, the board of directors must assign a value to record the transaction. The board of directors often uses independent appraisals in such circumstances. Note that the board's assignment of value is acceptable *only* if neither the fair market value of the noncash consideration nor the fair market value of the capital stock is readily determinable.

To illustrate, assume that the Mustang Corporation acquires a piece of equipment in exchange for 500 shares of its $5 par common stock. Mustang records the transaction as follows, given the stated alternatives:

1. The fair market value of the equipment is $10,000; the fair market value of the common stock is not readily determinable.

Equipment	10,000	
Common stock		2,500
Contributed capital in excess of par—common		7,500

2. The fair market value of the equipment is not readily determinable; the fair market value of the common stock is $18 per share.

Equipment ($18 × 500 shares) 9,000
    Common stock   2,500
    Contributed capital in excess of par—common   6,500

3. Neither the fair market value of the equipment nor the fair market value of the stock is readily determinable. The board of directors assumes responsibility for assigning a value to record the transaction. The board obtains three independent appraisals to value the equipment, and accepts the average appraisal value of $9,600 as a reasonable estimate of the value exchanged.

Equipment 9,600
    Common stock   2,500
    Contributed capital in excess of par—common   7,100

Some companies have used this provision incorrectly to overstate or understate assets, with a corresponding overstatement or understatement of stockholders' equity. If a company receives noncash consideration and overvalues the assets received, with a corresponding overvaluation of capital stock, it is said to have **watered stock.** If a company undervalues assets received and capital stock issued, it is said to have **secret reserves.** The company should eliminate an overstatement or understatement by restating the assets and the capital stock to the best estimate of fair market value. With conscientious and informed use of all available evidence, firms should be able to avoid watered stock and secret reserves.

In summary, a corporation should use the best evidence available to record the transaction when it issues stock in exchange for noncash consideration. Occasionally the corporation may have to rely on the board of directors to assign a value, pending better evidence regarding the value exchanged.

STOCK SUBSCRIPTIONS

Corporations sometimes issue capital stock by **subscription,** which means that the purchasers of the stock, also called **subscribers,** make a down payment in cash and pay the remainder of the purchase price later, according to the terms of the subscription agreement. The corporation does not issue the shares of stock until it receives full payment for the shares. Newly formed companies, companies issuing capital stock to the public for the first time, and companies issuing stock to employees often use subscriptions to issue capital stock.

Issuance of capital stock on a subscription basis is equivalent to a credit sale of stock. The issuing firm receives a down payment in cash and receives a promise to be paid cash, a receivable, in the amount of the deferred purchase price. The receivable, called subscriptions receivable, is the amount that the company must collect before it issues the stock.

Suppose that Long Corporation receives subscriptions for 5,000 shares of $5 par common stock at $40 per share. The subscription terms require a down payment of 20 percent, with the remainder of the purchase price to be paid in two equal installments, at the end of three months and six months from the subscription date. The entry to record the subscriptions is as follows:

Cash.. 40,000
Subscriptions receivable. 160,000
    Common stock subscribed   25,000
    Contributed capital in excess of par—common   175,000

Long credits common stock subscribed for the par value of the subscribed shares ($5 × 5,000 shares = $25,000) and credits contributed capital in excess of par—common for the excess of the purchase price over par value ($35 × 5,000 shares = $175,000).

At the end of three months, Long records the collection of the first installment of the receivable as follows:

Cash	80,000	
Subscriptions receivable		80,000

At the end of six months, Long records the collection of the remaining balance of the receivable and the issuance of the shares:

Cash	80,000	
Subscriptions receivable		80,000
Common stock subscribed	25,000	
Common stock		25,000

Defaults on Stock Subscriptions

Whenever a firm issues capital stock on a subscription basis, the possibility exists that the company will not collect all or a portion of the receivable. If a subscriber to capital stock is unable or unwilling to pay the full purchase price of the subscribed shares, the subscriber is said to be in **default.**

State corporation laws govern the issuing corporation's treatment of amounts paid in by defaulting subscribers. According to the applicable state laws, the corporation may (1) return the amount paid in, (2) keep the amount paid in without issuing shares, (3) return the amount paid in less any deficiency in amount realized on reissue compared to subscription price, or (4) keep the amount paid in and issue shares to the defaulting subscriber based on the amount paid in.

Continuing the above example, assume instead that a subscriber to 50 shares of Long Corporation's stock at $40 per share defaults on the last installment of the subscription. The account balances related to the defaulting subscriber are:

Subscriptions receivable ($16 × 50 shares)	$ 800
Common stock subscribed ($5 × 50 shares)	250
Contributed capital in excess of par—common ($35 × 50 shares)	1,750

Long Corporation has already received cash of $400 (down payment) plus $800 (first installment) or a total of $1,200 ($24 × 50 shares) for the shares.

Accounting for the alternative treatments that might be available to Long Corporation for the $1,200 of cash paid in before the default is as follows:

1. Return amount paid in to defaulting subscriber.

Common stock subscribed	250	
Contributed capital in excess of par—common	1,750	
Subscriptions receivable		800
Cash		1,200

2. Retain amount paid in.

Common stock subscribed	250	
Contributed capital in excess of par—common	1,750	
Subscriptions receivable		800
Contributed capital from defaulted stock subscriptions		1,200

3. Return amount paid in, less any deficiency in amount realized on reissue compared to the original subscription price. Assume that the company subsequently reissues the 50 shares for $38 per share, thereby suffering a deficiency of $2 per share:

Common stock subscribed	250	
Contributed capital in excess of par—common	1,750	
Subscriptions receivable		800
Payable to defaulting subscriber		1,200
Cash ($38 × 50 shares)	1,900	
Common stock		250
Contributed capital in excess of par—common		1,650
Payable to defaulting subscriber	1,200	
Cash		1,100
Contributed capital in excess of par—common		100

4. Issue shares to defaulting subscriber based on amount paid in. Because the defaulting subscriber has paid $1,200 and the subscription price was $40 per share, the corporation would issue 30 shares to the defaulting subscriber.

Common stock subscribed	250	
Contributed capital in excess of par—common ($35 × 20 shares)	700	
Common stock ($5 × 30 shares)		150
Subscriptions receivable		800

Keep in mind that the laws of the state of incorporation determine which one of these treatments is appropriate in a given situation.

Balance Sheet Presentation

The only new accounts associated with stock subscriptions, in the absence of default, are common stock subscribed or preferred stock subscribed and subscriptions receivable. Companies must include common stock subscribed in the contributed capital section of stockholders' equity, along with common stock. Likewise, they must include preferred stock subscribed with preferred stock in stockholders' equity. In most states, subscribers to common or preferred stock have the same status as stockholders who hold fully paid shares. Subscribers can vote and, in general, operate as though they owned fully paid shares. Thus, it is logical to include the capital accounts associated with subscribed shares along with the accounts related to fully paid shares.

There is some disagreement among accountants regarding the appropriate balance sheet presentation of subscriptions receivable. In most cases, companies include subscriptions receivable in the current asset section of the balance sheet, reported separately from trade receivables. Some accountants, however, believe that in certain circumstances it is more appropriate to show subscriptions receivable as a deduction from the contributed capital account to which it relates, which is the method of presentation required by the SEC in reports filed with the Commission. For example, if the firm has no intention of collecting the receivable in the foreseeable future, some accountants prefer the latter treatment. Under this treatment, contributed capital does not increase until the corporation receives cash for the shares. Although we find both methods of presentation in practice, presentation of subscriptions receivable as a current asset is theoretically preferable and more common.

Subscriptions receivable generally should be reported as a current asset.

LUMP-SUM STOCK ISSUANCES   To increase the attractiveness of its stock and to generate additional capital, a corporation sometimes issues two or more types of stock as a unit—for example, one share of common stock and one share of preferred stock. The company must allocate the amount received between the two classes of securities issued on the basis of the relative market values of the securities at the time of issuance. If the company knows the market value of only one of the securities issued, it must assign the known market value to the appropriate security and then allocate the remainder of the amount received to the security whose market value is not determinable.

Assume that Jensen Corporation offers a package consisting of one share of $10 par common stock and one share of $100 par preferred stock for $150. Jensen issues 1,000 of the units. At the time of issuance, the market price of the common stock is $50 per share, and the market price of the preferred stock is $130 per share. Jensen allocates the $150,000 ($150 × 1,000 units) to the common and preferred stock as follows:

Fair market value of common ($50 × 1,000 shares)	$ 50,000
Fair market value of preferred ($130 × 1,000 shares)	130,000
Total fair market value	$180,000

Allocation to common:

$$\frac{\$\ 50,000}{\$180,000} \times \$150,000 = \$\ 41,667$$

Allocation to preferred:

$$\frac{\$130,000}{\$180,000} \times \$150,000 = \ 108,333$$

Total allocated	$150,000

The required journal entry is:

Cash	150,000	
Common stock		10,000
Contributed capital in excess of par—common		31,667
Preferred stock		100,000
Contributed capital in excess of par—preferred		8,333

If, instead, the market price of the preferred stock is not determinable, and the market price of the common stock is known to be $50 per share, Jensen allocates the $150,000 as follows:

Cash received	$150,000
Allocated to common stock ($50 × 1,000 shares)	(50,000)
Allocated to preferred stock	$100,000

Note that the approach to valuing a lump-sum issuance of securities is comparable to the problem of valuing two or more assets received in a lump-sum exchange. In both cases, we base the allocation on market values.

STOCK ISSUE COSTS

Regardless of the method of issuance, corporations incur legal, accounting, administrative, and promotional costs when they issue capital stock. For example, a company might announce a proposed offering of capital stock in *The Wall Street Journal*. The cost of the advertisement is a cost of the stock issue. Stock issue costs are a reduction of the contributed capital associated with the shares. The net amount of capital generated is the selling price of the securities minus the stock issue costs. Because stock issue costs do not relate to operations, they should not affect reported earnings. Corporations incur these costs in association with capital transactions rather than earnings activities.

CONVERSION OF PREFERRED INTO COMMON

Companies sometimes issue common stock through conversion of debt or preferred stock. As described in Chapter 16, when debt is converted into common stock, the book value method or, less frequently, the market value method may be used to record the transaction. However, when preferred stock is converted into common stock, only the book value method is acceptable. Because the conversion of preferred into common is a capital transaction, no gains and losses may be recognized. Thus, the amount recorded for the converted preferred is simply reclassified to the common stock that is issued in its place.

As an example, assume that Brett Company has $50 per value convertible preferred outstanding, issued at an average price of $70 per share. The conversion ratio is two shares of preferred for one share of common. If 20,000 shares of preferred are converted into common stock, and the par value of the common is $5 per share, the following entry would be made to record the conversion:

Preferred stock ($50 × 20,000)	1,000,000	
Contributed capital in excess of par—		
preferred ($20 × 20,000)	400,000	
Common stock ($5 × 10,000)		50,000
Contributed capital in excess of		
par—common ($135 × 10,000)		1,350,000

STOCK RIGHTS

So far in this chapter we have discussed accounting for transactions in which corporations issue capital stock in exchange for cash, for noncash consideration, and by subscription. Many corporations also issue **stock rights** as a preliminary step to issuing additional shares of stock. A stock right entitles the holder to acquire shares of the issuing corporation's stock according to specified terms. The most common situations in which companies issue stock rights are:

1. To satisfy the preemptive right of existing stockholders in connection with the issuance of additional shares of stock.

2. To enhance the marketability of another type of security, such as bonds or preferred stock. We discussed this situation in Chapter 16.

3. To give executives and employees an opportunity to acquire shares of stock in connection with company stock plans.

The accounting procedures for stock rights depend on the circumstances under which the company issues the rights.

Rights to Existing Stockholders

If existing stockholders have a preemptive right, the corporation must give the stockholders an opportunity to keep their proportion of ownership whenever it issues additional shares. The corporation issues stock rights to stockholders as evidence of this privilege. The certificate that verifies this right is called a **warrant.** The rights, which usually expire in a relatively short time, permit stockholders to purchase more shares at a price generally below the current market price of the stock. Normally, the longer the time period before the rights expire, the less the difference between exercise price and market price when the rights are issued. In fact, in some cases the exercise price may exceed the market price at the time the company issues the rights, as the following news story indicates:

> American Express Co. will issue to holders about 930,000 five-year warrants to purchase a common share at $55 each.
>
> The warrants will be distributed to stock of record Feb. 11 at the rate of one warrant for each 100 shares held. These warrants would expire Feb. 28, 1987, but American Express said it reserves the right to move up the expiration date if the common rises to at least $95 a share for 10 consecutive days. Cash will be given in lieu of fractional warrants.
>
> American Express common closed on the New York Stock Exchange composite tape yesterday at $39.625, down $2. The company currently has about 93 million shares outstanding.[3]

When a company issues warrants as evidence of preemptive rights, it does not need to make a formal accounting entry. The company should record a memorandum entry, however, specifying the number of rights issued. The memorandum entry appears in the general journal and provides a description of the agreement. The corporation must be certain that enough unissued shares are available to permit exercise of the rights.

Stockholders can either exercise the stock rights, sell them, or let them expire. The issuing company must account for only the exercise of stock rights. For example, if a stockholder exercises preemptive rights to acquire 100 shares of $10 par common at $25 per share, the company must make the following journal entry:

Cash ($25 × 100 shares)	2,500	
Common stock		1,000
Contributed capital in excess of par—common		1,500

Stock Option Plans

Many companies issue stock rights to officers and employees under stock option plans. A **stock option plan** is an agreement to issue stock to employees, either individually or as a group, according to the terms of the plan. Accountants classify plans as *noncompensatory* or *compensatory*.

NONCOMPENSATORY PLANS Many corporations adopt stock option plans to raise capital or to spread ownership of corporate shares among employees. Compensating employees is not the primary purpose of such plans, hence the title **noncompensatory.** A noncompensatory plan must have all four of the following characteristics:

1. Substantially all full-time employees who meet limited employment qualifications may participate.

2. Stock is offered to eligible employees equally or on the basis of a uniform percentage of salary or wages.

3. The time permitted for exercise of an option is limited to a reasonable period.

4. The discount from the market price of the stock is no greater than would be reasonable in an offer of stock to stockholders or others.[4]

Because a noncompensatory plan is not designed to provide compensation to em-

---

[3] *The Wall Street Journal,* January 27, 1982, p. 37.

[4] "Accounting for Stock Issued to Employees," *Opinions of the Accounting Principles Board No. 25* (New York: AICPA, 1972), para. 7.

ployees, the company makes no journal entry until employees exercise their warrants and the company issues shares. At that time, the company records the cash received and the issuance of shares in the normal manner.

COMPENSATORY PLANS Accountants classify any plan that does not have all four characteristics of a noncompensatory plan as a **compensatory plan.** Because the primary purpose of a compensatory plan is to compensate employees, the employer's accounting issues include:

1. Determination of compensation expense, if any.
2. Allocation of compensation expense to appropriate accounting periods.
3. Disclosure requirements.

Compensation expense. Compensation expense for a compensatory plan is measured by the excess of the quoted market price of the stock over its option price at the measurement date.[5] If a quoted market price is unavailable, we must use the best estimate of fair market value to measure compensation expense. The **measurement date** is the earliest date on which the corporation knows both (1) the option price and (2) the number of shares that an individual employee can receive. For many plans, the measurement date is the **date of grant,** which is the date when the company offers an option to an individual employee. On this date the corporation usually knows for the first time both the option price and the number of shares under option. In recent years, however, companies increasingly have adopted plans with variable terms that depend on events after the date of grant, such as future market prices. For these plans, the measurement date may be later than the date of grant.

Note that compensation expense is recorded only if the market price exceeds the option price on the measurement date. If the option price is equal to or greater than the market price on the measurement date, we do not recognize compensation expense, even though the plan is compensatory.

Theoretically, there are several alternative methods of measuring compensation expense. We could measure it by the fair market value of the employee services received for the options. The APB rejected this method because of the subjectivity involved in determining the fair market value of services received. Alternatively, we could use the market value of the stock option to measure compensation expense. From a practical standpoint, however, this method is not feasible, because generally there is no market for stock options issued under a compensatory plan. Employees usually cannot trade such options in the marketplace; they must either exercise them or allow them to expire.

Controversy also remains regarding the appropriate date for measuring compensation expense. *APB Opinion No. 25* requires that we use the difference between the quoted market price and the option price at the measurement date to measure compensation expense. Other dates that some accountants have proposed for measuring compensation expense include (1) the date on which the employee completes the performance of all services required to exercise the option, (2) the date on which the option becomes exercisable, and (3) the date on which the employee exercises the option. The objective, however, is to determine the cost to the employer rather than to determine the ultimate value of the option to the employee. The APB argued that the quoted market price at the date of grant provides the best evidence of the value that the employer presumably had in mind. Further, the only condition for exercising the options typically is continuance in the employment of the granting corporation. A primary objective of a compensatory plan is to

---

[5] *APB Opinion No. 25,* para. 10.

encourage officers and employees to stay with the firm. Although the market price may change substantially after the date of grant, the market price on that date still provides the best measure of the compensation expense that both parties to the agreement had in mind.

The Economic Recovery Tax Act of 1981 encourages companies to compensate executives with incentive stock option plans. Basically, stock options that meet the criteria for classification as an incentive stock option plan have no tax implications at either the grant date or exercise date. One of the criteria for classification as an incentive stock option is that the option price must be at least equal to the fair market value of the stock on the date of grant. Employees receive favorable long-term capital gain tax treatment when the stock received is subsequently sold if the employee (1) holds the stock for at least two years after the date of grant and at least one year after the date of exercise, and (2) is employed by the company that grants the option continuously from the date of grant until three months before the date of exercise. The employer cannot deduct compensation expense under such plans. The favorable tax treatment of the employee, however, lowers the effective cost to the employer of providing compensation. Thus, the 1981 Act makes stock option plans a more attractive way to compensate executives.

Allocation of compensation expense to accounting periods. If we determine that compensation expense exists, we must recognize the expense when the employees perform services to earn the compensation, which we call the **service period.** The grant may specify the service period, or in some cases we can infer the service period from the past pattern of grants. If the grant does not specify the service period and we cannot infer it from the past pattern of grants, any systematic and rational allocation of compensation expense is acceptable.

Assume, for example, that Shriver Company has adopted a stock option plan for key executives. The plan permits the executives to purchase shares of Shriver's $1 par common stock at $15 per share. On January 2, 1987, Shriver grants to the company president options to acquire 5,000 shares. The grant specifies that the president cannot exercise the options before January 2, 1989, and that the options will expire at the end of 1993. The president must still be employed by Shriver when she exercises the options. The quoted market price of Shriver's common on January 2, 1987, is $25 per share.

The terms of the grant imply that the service period includes 1987 and 1988, because the president must work for Shriver during those two years in order to exercise the options. Thus, Shriver makes the following journal entry on January 2, 1987:

Deferred compensation expense 50,000		
Contributed capital—stock options		50,000
[($25 − $15) × 5,000 shares]		

Shriver makes the following entry at the end of 1987 and 1988:

Compensation expense 25,000		
Deferred compensation expense		25,000

If the president exercises all of the stock options early in 1989, Shriver records the transaction as follows:

Cash ($15 × 5,000 shares) 75,000		
Contributed capital—stock options 50,000		
Common stock		5,000
Contributed capital in excess of par—common		120,000

If instead the president allows the options to expire, Shriver makes the following entry at the end of 1993:

Contributed capital—stock options 50,000
    Contributed capital—expired stock options   50,000

As this entry indicates, failure to exercise the options does not affect the recording of compensation expense if the employee performs all services for which the option is granted. However, if the employee fails to perform the services for which the option is granted, estimated compensation expense must be adjusted. For example, assume that Shriver's president leaves the company at the beginning of 1988. Shriver would make the following entry to record this *change in accounting estimate:*

Contributed capital—stock options 50,000
    Deferred compensation expense   25,000
    Compensation expense   25,000

The deferred compensation expense account is a contra-account to the contributed capital—stock options account in the additional contributed capital section of stockholders' equity. For example, at the end of 1987, Shriver Company's stockholders' equity section might appear as follows:

Stockholders' equity		
Common stock, $1 par, 500,000		
shares issued and outstanding		$ 500,000
Additional contributed capital		
Contributed capital in excess of par—common		3,000,000
Contributed capital—stock options	$50,000	
Less: Deferred compensation expense	(25,000)	25,000
Total contributed capital		$ 3,525,000
Retained earnings		7,341,000
Total stockholders' equity		$10,866,000

Thus, the increase in contributed capital is recognized at the same time that we recognize compensation expense in the income statement.

Note that the total amount recorded for shares issued under a stock option plan is the quoted market price at the measurement date, consisting of the option price plus the excess of the quoted market price over the option price. We reclassify the excess of the quoted market price over the option price when the option is exercised.

If the measurement date is later than the date of grant, the employer must recognize compensation expense each period from the date of grant to the measurement date on the basis of the quoted market price of the stock at the end of each period. Compensation expense is the excess of the quoted market price over the option price at the end of the period. Thus, changes in the quoted market price at the end of successive years result in changes in total estimated compensation expense.

Under one common type of stock plan in which the measurement date is later than the date of grant, the company grants **stock appreciation rights (SARs)** to selected employees. The stock appreciation rights allow the employee to receive cash, stock, or a combination of cash and stock based on the difference between a specified amount per share of stock and the quoted market price per share at some future date. We must account for SAR plans in the same manner as traditional stock plans.[6] However, the amount of compensa-

[6] "Accounting for Stock Appreciation Rights and Other Variable Stock Option or Award Plans," *FASB Interpretation No. 28* (Stamford, Conn.: FASB, 1978).

Stock appreciation rights create accounting measurement difficulties.

tion expense is not determinable with certainty between the date of grant and the measurement date. Instead, we must estimate it based upon the quoted market price of the stock at the end of each period between the date of grant and the measurement date. At the measurement date, we can determine compensation expense with certainty. At that time, we record any difference between estimated compensation expense and actual compensation expense as a change in estimate in the period in which the measurement date falls.

Assume that at the beginning of 1986, Heber Corporation grants stock appreciation rights to certain key executives. Under the terms of the SAR plan, the executive may receive either cash, Heber Corporation $5 par common stock, or a combination of cash and common stock, with the amount to be determined by the difference between the quoted market price of the stock and a price of $20 per SAR. Heber granted a total of 20,000 SARs. The SARs are exercisable after January 1, 1989, and they expire on December 31, 1993. The per share market price of Heber Corporation common at the end of 1986, 1987, and 1988 was $35, $38, and $29, respectively.

Under this plan, the service period appears to be 1986 through 1988, since the executives cannot exercise the SARs until 1989. The calculation of compensation expense for the years 1986 through 1988 is shown below.

| | ENDING | | COMPENSATION | | | COMPENSATION | EXPENSE | | |
YEAR	MARKET PRICE	OPTION PRICE	PER SHARE	AGGREGATE	ACCRUED PERCENTAGE	ACCRUED TO DATE	1986	1987	1988
1986	$35	$20	$15	$300,000	33⅓%	$100,000	$100,000		
1987	38	20	18	360,000	66⅔	240,000		$140,000	
1988	29	20	9	180,000	100	180,000			$(60,000)

If it is likely that Heber will pay the obligation in cash, journal entries at the end of each year are as follows:

12/31/86 Compensation expense	100,000	
Liability under stock plan		100,000
12/31/87 Compensation expense	140,000	
Liability under stock plan		140,000
12/31/88 Liability under stock plan	60,000	
Compensation expense		60,000

Note that compensation expense must be *credited* in 1988 because estimated total compensation expense at the end of 1988 is $180,000, whereas a total of $240,000 was recorded in the two previous years.

If the executives exercise all of the SARs in 1989, when the quoted market price is $36 per share, total compensation expense is $320,000 [($36 − $20) × 20,000 shares]. Because Heber recognized compensation expense of $180,000 in prior periods, an additional $140,000 arises in 1989 at the measurement date, which in this case is also the date of exercise:

Liability under stock plan	180,000	
Compensation expense	140,000	
Cash..		320,000

If Heber were likely to meet the obligation by the issuance of stock instead of by the payment of cash, Heber would credit an additional contributed capital account, contributed capital—stock appreciation rights, instead of crediting the liability.

Disclosures for stock option plans.   Disclosures are necessary so that financial statement users can assess the potential effect of stock option plans on cash flow. Companies that have stock option plans must include in their financial statements, or in the accompanying notes, the status of the plan at the end of the period, including the number of shares under option and the option price. For options exercised during the period, the company also must disclose the number of shares issued and the option price. Exhibit 20–4 shows how the Potlatch Corporation described its stock option plan in a recent annual report.

EXHIBIT 20–4   FOOTNOTE DISCLOSURES RELATED TO STOCK OPTION PLAN

Potlatch Corporation
1984 ANNUAL REPORT

NOTE 10. STOCK OPTIONS

Under the company's stock option plans, options for shares of the company's common stock have been issued to certain key personnel. Options outstanding include options from two existing plans, the 1976 stock option plan and the 1983 stock option plan, and options granted previously under a plan that has since been terminated.

Terms and provisions of the 1976 and 1983 stock option plans are substantially the same. Options granted may be either nonqualified or incentive stock options and may include a stock appreciation right. Nonqualified options are exercisable for a period of 10 years from date of grant with certain restrictions. Incentive stock options granted on or after December 4, 1981, are exercisable for a period of seven years from date of grant with certain restrictions.

Information with respect to the company's stock options for the years ended December 31, 1984 and 1983, follows:

	NON-QUALIFIED	NONQUALIFIED WITH SARS†	INCENTIVE	INCENTIVE WITH SARS†	TOTAL
Option price range*	$10.5625 to $39.75	$25.875 to $39.75	$25.875 to $36.75	$25.875 to $36.75	
Options outstanding at December 31, 1982	100,761	379,188	231,131	100,563	811,643
Granted	2,300	22,892	44,750	30,608	100,550
Options exercised	(9,618)	(1,700)	(11,558)	(3,207)	(26,083)
SARs exercised	—	(33,128)	—	(6,501)	(39,629)
Canceled or expired	(5,947)	(2,800)	(10,550)	(900)	(20,197)
Other	8,855	(8,855)	650	(650)	—
Options outstanding at December 31, 1983	96,351	355,597	254,423	119,913	826,284
Granted	65,400	80,652	1,300	3,448	150,800
Options exercised	(5,625)	(1,050)	(1,714)	(113)	(8,502)
SARs exercised	—	(4,112)	—	(4,939)	(9,051)
Canceled or expired	(7,086)	(14,105)	(18,276)	(9,271)	(48,738)
Other	12,594	(12,594)	1,420	(1,420)	—
Options outstanding at December 31, 1984	161,634	404,388	237,153	107,618	910,793
Options exercisable:					
December 31, 1983	58,940	183,103	153,669	70,580	466,292
December 31, 1984	80,276	230,797	215,403	90,339	616,815
Shares reserved for future grants:					
December 31, 1983					600,925
December 31, 1984					495,663

* Option price at 100 percent of fair market value at date of grant.

† Stock appreciation rights (an appropriate accrual has been made for related compensation).

DONATED CAPITAL

The issuance of stock is the primary method that corporations use to generate contributed capital. A less common source of capital consists of donations from stockholders or other parties. For example, a city may donate land to a corporation to induce it to locate there. As indicated in Chapter 11 (p. 500) in our discussion of donated assets, the corporation records the asset acquired at its fair market value, with a corresponding credit to donated capital. Accountants view this as an event affecting capital rather than earnings, and thus no gain or loss arises. The donated capital account usually appears in the balance sheet in the additional contributed capital section of stockholders' equity. Alternatively, some companies report donated capital as a separate category between contributed capital from investments by stockholders and retained earnings.

ACCOUNTING FOR ACQUIRED CAPITAL STOCK

The "merger mania" of recent years has encouraged more and more companies to join the trend toward engaging in transactions in their own common stock. These transactions often are entered into in an attempt to prop up the price of the outstanding shares in a firm whose shares are viewed by potential suitors as underpriced. For example, in May 1985, Litton Industries, Inc., announced that it was planning to buy up to about 36 percent of its own outstanding common stock. Litton was to accomplish the acquisition by issuing debt securities in exchange for the common stock. The announced reason for the planned acquisition of its own shares was that its stock was "undervalued." However, there was some speculation that Litton, one of the largest defense contractors in the nation, was attempting to decrease its attractiveness as a takeover target by increasing the share price.

Exhibit 20–5, based on a recent study by *Fortune,* indicates the extent to which several companies reduced their outstanding shares during 1984. Teledyne, which acquired 42.5 percent of its shares during 1984, has acquired 85 percent of its shares over the last few years at a total cost of about $2.7 billion! The *Fortune* study reported that the average annual return to shareholders from 1974 to 1983 for companies that bought significant amounts of their own shares during that period was 22.6 percent. During that same period, the average annual return for Standard & Poor's 500-stock index, an indicator of the general market activity, was only 14.1 percent.[7] Thus, it appears that stockholders in companies that engaged in significant acquisitions of their own shares fared much better during this time period.

To complete our discussion of accounting for stock transactions, in this section we describe the appropriate accounting and reporting for acquired shares of a company's own capital stock.

When a corporation acquires shares of its own common stock, it may either retire them or hold them for subsequent reissue. If the company does not formally retire or cancel the shares, we call the acquired shares **treasury shares** or **treasury stock.** After a brief look at accounting for the retirement of capital stock, we shall discuss the accounting procedures for treasury stock.

ACCOUNTING FOR RETIREMENT OF CAPITAL STOCK

When a corporation acquires and retires its own capital stock, net assets and stockholders' equity of the company are reduced. Since the selling price of shares varies over time, companies usually calculate an average paid-in price per share as a basis for determining

[7] Carol J. Loomis, "Beating the Market by Buying Back Stock," *Fortune,* April 29, 1985, p. 42.

EXHIBIT 20–5 BIG BUYBACKS OF 1984

COMPANY	DECLINE IN SHARES OUTSTANDING	COMPANY	DECLINE IN SHARES OUTSTANDING
Teledyne	42.5%	Bandag	13.4%
Resorts International	31.4	Color Tile	13.3
Iroquois Brands	27.3	SCOA	13.2
Integrated Resources	23.9	Pennzoil	13.2
FMC	23.9	Crown Cork & Seal	12.8
Houston Natural Gas	21.4	Dart & Kraft	12.7
Ethyl	18.9	Pioneer	12.6
General Dynamics	18.0	International Controls	12.5
Colt Industries	17.7	Levi Strauss	11.9
Mark Controls	17.0	Crane	11.6
Tandy	15.1	Ralston Purina	11.3
Celanese	13.8	Brown-Forman Distillers	11.2

Source: *Fortune,* April 29, 1985, p. 48.

the reduction in contributed capital. If the amount paid to retire the shares exceeds the average paid-in price per share, the company must debit the difference to retained earnings. If the amount paid to retire the shares is less than the average paid-in price per share, the firm credits the difference to contributed capital from retirement of stock.

To illustrate, assume that Jackson Corporation has the following stockholders' equity account balances on December 31, 1987:

Common stock (1,000 shares, $10 par)	$ 10,000
Contributed capital in excess of par—common	140,000
Retained earnings	500,000

Thus, the average paid-in price per share is $150 ($150,000 ÷ 1,000). Assuming that the following three independent transactions occurred at the beginning of 1988, the required journal entries would be as follows:

1. Jackson acquires and retires 100 shares at $150 per share:

Common stock	1,000	
Contributed capital in excess of par—common	14,000	
Cash		15,000

2. Jackson acquires and retires 100 shares at $170 per share:

Common stock	1,000	
Contributed capital in excess of par—common	14,000	
Retained earnings ($20 × 100 shares)	2,000	
Cash		17,000

3. Jackson acquires and retires 100 shares at $135 per share:

Common stock	1,000	
Contributed capital in excess of par—common	14,000	
Cash		13,500
Contributed capital from retirement of stock ($15 × 100 shares)		1,500

Note that a company may *decrease* retained earnings when it retires shares, but it cannot *increase* retained earnings through transactions in its own stock. The retained earnings reduction may be viewed as an additional dividend paid to the stockholders whose shares are being retired.

ACCOUNTING FOR TREASURY STOCK

State laws, federal agencies, and stock exchanges carefully regulate transactions by a corporation involving its own capital stock. Such transactions must be for legitimate corporate purposes. Corporations may want to acquire treasury stock for several purposes:

1. To meet stock needs in connection with stock option plans.
2. To eliminate the ownership interests of a particular stockholder.
3. To possibly increase earnings per share by decreasing the number of shares outstanding.
4. To meet stock needs in connection with convertible bonds or convertible preferred stock.
5. To prop up the market price, as indicated at the beginning of this section.
6. To make shares available for a pending merger.
7. To make shares available for the issuance of a stock dividend.
8. To reduce the size of the entity's operations.

Treasury stock is not an asset.

Regardless of the purpose of acquiring treasury shares, the accounting effect is the same as when stock is retired: *net assets and stockholders' equity are reduced*. When a corporation issues capital stock, net assets and stockholders' equity increase; when a corporation acquires its own shares, the effect is the opposite. Treasury stock is not an asset; it constitutes a reduction in stockholders' equity. That a company can reissue the treasury shares to generate additional resources is irrelevant, because the same can be said about authorized but unissued shares, which are not assets.

The amount of the retained earnings of a firm usually restricts the amount that the firm can pay for treasury stock, so that such acquisitions do not affect legal capital. Also, retained earnings available for dividends usually is restricted by the cost of treasury shares held so that subsequent dividends will not reduce contributed capital. Since a company cannot own a portion of itself, treasury shares obviously do not confer voting rights, do not receive dividends, and confer no liquidation rights.

Two methods of accounting for treasury stock are acceptable in practice: the cost method and the par value method.

The Cost Method

Under the cost method, treasury stock is viewed as a temporary item awaiting ultimate disposition.

Under the **cost method,** we view the purchase of treasury stock as a *temporary* reduction in stockholders' equity. The corporation eliminates the temporary reduction when it reissues the treasury shares. We look upon the purchase and subsequent reissue of treasury stock as two parts of one transaction. The purchase temporarily reduces stockholders' equity, and the reissue increases it.

To record the acquisition of treasury shares under the cost method, the treasury stock account is debited for the *cost* of the acquired shares. Upon the reissuance of treasury shares, treasury stock is credited for the cost basis of the reissued shares. If acquisitions of treasury shares take place at different prices, we must adopt a cost flow assumption, such as average cost, FIFO, or specific identification, to record the reissuance of shares. Under the cost method, the amount originally received for shares has no influence on the entries to record the acquisition and reissuance of treasury shares.

If a company reissues treasury shares for more than their cost, it should credit an additional contributed capital account, contributed capital from treasury stock transactions, for the amount received in excess of cost. If a company reissues treasury shares for less than the cost, the difference between the proceeds and the cost reduces any additional contributed capital credit balance arising from earlier reissuances or retirements of treasury stock of the same class. If a difference remains after this additional contributed capital balance is reduced to zero, the company should debit retained earnings for the remainder. Note that retained earnings may be decreased, but not increased, as a result of treasury stock transactions. Accountants view any debit to retained earnings as a result of treasury stock transactions as an additional dividend paid to retiring stockholders.

Assume that Lewis Corporation receives authorization to issue 1 million shares of $10 par common stock. To date, Lewis has issued 300,000 shares at various prices. The balances of the contributed capital accounts are as follows:

Common stock	$3,000,000
Contributed capital in excess of par—common	9,000,000

Thus, the average price paid per share is $12,000,000 ÷ 300,000 shares = $40.

Now assume the following transactions occur in the sequence indicated. Journal entries accompany each transaction.

1. Lewis acquires 10,000 shares of common at a price of $53 per share.

Treasury stock	530,000	
Cash		530,000

2. Lewis reissues 2,000 treasury shares at $56 per share.

Cash	112,000	
Treasury stock (2,000 × $53)		106,000
Contributed capital from treasury stock transactions—common		6,000

3. Lewis reissues 3,000 treasury shares at $48 per share.

Cash	144,000	
Contributed capital from treasury stock transactions—common	6,000	
Retained earnings	9,000	
Treasury stock (3,000 × $53)		159,000

4. Lewis formally retires the remaining 5,000 treasury shares.

Common stock	50,000	
Contributed capital in excess of par—common	150,000	
Retained earnings	65,000	
Treasury stock (5,000 × $53)		265,000

In transaction 3, the cost of the reissued treasury shares is $159,000, and the proceeds upon reissuance are only $144,000. Of the $15,000 difference, Lewis debits $6,000 against the additional contributed capital created in transaction 2, and debits retained earnings for the remaining $9,000. Upon retirement in transaction 4, the excess of the cost of the treasury shares ($265,000) over the amount originally paid in ($40 average price per share × 5,000 shares = $200,000) is $65,000. Lewis debits the difference to retained earnings. If the cost of treasury shares retired were less than the amount originally received, the company should credit the difference to an additional contributed capital account, called contributed capital from retirement of common stock.

The Par Value Method

Under the par value method, treasury stock is viewed as equivalent to retired shares.

Under the **par value method,** the acquisition of a company's own shares is viewed as equivalent to a retirement of the acquired shares. Thus treasury stock is debited for the par or stated value of the acquired shares, the appropriate additional contributed capital account is debited for the amount originally received in excess of par or stated value, and cash is credited. If the cash paid to acquire the shares exceeds the amount originally received, we debit retained earnings for the difference. As mentioned earlier in the example of stock retirement, the difference may be viewed as a dividend to retiring stockholders. If the cash paid to acquire the shares is less than the amount originally received, the difference is credited to contributed capital from treasury stock transactions. You may view this difference as a contribution from the retiring stockholders.

Upon reissuance of treasury shares accounted for by the par value method, cash is debited for the proceeds, treasury stock is credited for the par value of the reissued shares, and contributed capital in excess of par—common is credited for the excess of the proceeds over par value. The only difference between this entry and the entry to record the sale of previously unissued shares is that, in the latter case, common stock, rather than treasury stock, is credited for the par value of the shares issued.

To illustrate the par value method, assume that Lewis Corporation has 300,000 shares of $10 par common stock outstanding with the following account balances, implying an average price paid per share of $40:

Common stock	$3,000,000
Contributed capital in excess of par—common	9,000,000

1. Lewis acquires 10,000 shares of common stock at $53 per share.

Treasury stock	100,000	
Contributed capital in excess of par—common	300,000	
Retained earnings ($13 × 10,000 shares)	130,000	
Cash		530,000

2. Lewis reissues 2,000 shares at $56 per share.

Cash	112,000	
Treasury stock (2,000 × $10)		20,000
Contributed capital in excess of par—common		92,000

3. Lewis reissues 3,000 shares at $48 per share.

Cash	144,000	
Treasury stock (3,000 × $10)		30,000
Contributed capital in excess of par—common		114,000

4. Lewis formally retires the remaining 5,000 treasury shares.

Common stock	50,000	
Treasury stock (5,000 × $10)		50,000

The cost method is more popular than the par value method because of its simplicity. The corporation does not have to keep track of original premiums and discounts arising from the original issuance of the reacquired shares. The par value method is conceptually preferable because when a firm acquires shares under the par value method, it eliminates the amounts originally received, and upon reissuance replaces these amounts with the proceeds from resale. In addition, there is no economic difference between a formal retirement of shares and the acquisition of treasury stock. Because of the additional record keeping required, however, companies seldom use the par value method.

Donated Treasury Stock

Stockholders occasionally donate shares of stock to the issuing corporation, usually for their personal tax benefit. If a company uses the cost method to account for treasury stock, it does not make a journal entry when it receives donated shares, because there is no cost to the corporation. The company should, however, make a memorandum entry indicating the number of donated shares. When the company reissues the donated shares, it should credit the entire proceeds to the account donated capital from treasury stock.

If a company uses the par value method to record donated treasury stock, it should debit treasury stock for the par value, debit contributed capital in excess of par for the amount paid in excess of par at the time of issuance, and credit donated capital from treasury stock. When the shares are reissued, the company debits cash for the proceeds, credits treasury stock for the par value of the reissued shares, and credits contributed capital in excess of par for the difference. For example, if Kneer Corporation receives 1,000 shares of its $10 par common stock, originally issued at $15 per share, from a stockholder donation, Kneer would make the following entry:

Treasury stock	10,000	
Contributed capital in excess of par—common	5,000	
Donated capital from treasury stock		15,000

If Kneer subsequently reissues the shares at $30 per share, the company records the reissuance as follows:

Cash ($30 × 1,000 shares)	30,000	
Treasury stock		10,000
Contributed capital in excess of par—common		20,000

Note that under both the cost method and the par value method, contributed capital ultimately is increased by the amount received when the shares are reissued.

Balance Sheet Presentation of Treasury Stock

There are two acceptable methods of reporting treasury stock in the balance sheet, corresponding to the two methods of accounting for treasury stock. If a company uses the cost method, it reports the treasury stock account balance as a lump-sum reduction of total stockholders' equity. Under the cost method, the acquisition of treasury stock does not affect the individual contributed capital accounts. The unallocated reduction in stockholders' equity is consistent with the view that treasury stock is only a temporary account.

If a company uses the par value method, it deducts the treasury stock account balance from the par value of the issued shares of stock of the same class. Recall that when a company uses the par value method to account for treasury shares, it debits the additional contributed capital account for the excess over par received when the shares were originally issued. Thus the treasury stock account balance is deducted from the common stock account. This deduction, combined with the reduction of additional contributed capital,

EXHIBIT 20—6 REPORTING OF TREASURY STOCK
CONSISTENT WITH COST METHOD

Lewis Corporation

Stockholders' equity:	
Common stock—$10 par value, authorized	
1,000,000 shares, issued 300,000 shares	$ 3,000,000
Contributed capital in excess of par	9,000,000
	$12,000,000
Retained earnings ($265,000 restricted for cost of treasury	
stock held)	17,991,000
	$29,991,000
Less: Cost of 5,000 treasury shares	(265,000)
Total stockholders' equity	$29,726,000

EXHIBIT 20—7 REPORTING OF TREASURY STOCK
CONSISTENT WITH PAR VALUE METHOD

Lewis Corporation

Stockholders' equity:	
Common stock—$10 par value, authorized 1,000,000 shares, issued	
300,000 (of which 5,000 shares are held in the treasury)	$ 2,950,000
Contributed capital in excess of par	8,906,000
	$11,856,000
Retained earnings ($265,000 restricted for cost of treasury	
stock held)	17,870,000
Total stockholders' equity	$29,726,000

results in a reduction of contributed capital by the amount originally received for the shares. This reporting method is consistent with the view that the acquisition of treasury shares is equivalent to a retirement of the shares.

Exhibits 20–6 and 20–7 are based on the Lewis Corporation's transactions, with the following modifications: (1) retained earnings before the treasury stock transactions was $18 million; and (2) transaction 4 has not yet occurred, and Lewis Corporation therefore has 5,000 treasury shares at the end of the period. Exhibit 20–6 illustrates the reporting method that is consistent with the cost method of accounting for treasury stock, and Exhibit 20–7 illustrates the reporting method consistent with the par value method.

Total stockholders' equity is the same under the two methods. In Exhibit 20–6 the cost of treasury stock is deducted as an unallocated amount, whereas in Exhibit 20–7 the reduction from treasury stock acquisitions is allocated among the appropriate equity accounts. Note that each reporting method relates logically to an accounting method. As you would expect, given the popularity of the cost method, the reporting method demonstrated in Exhibit 20–6 is by far the most common. In most states, corporations also must restrict the amount of retained earnings available for dividends by the cost of treasury shares held. Companies must disclose this restriction either parenthetically, as we have illustrated, or in a footnote to the financial statements.

Remember that corporations cannot "create earnings" through transactions in its own capital stock. In general, such transactions increase and decrease contributed capital. A company may occasionally *reduce* retained earnings through treasury stock transactions, but it cannot increase retained earnings through such transactions.

SUMMARY OF IMPORTANT TOPICS
AND CONCEPT APPLICATIONS

1. The two primary components of stockholders' equity are (1) contributed capital, which reflects investments by owners, and (2) retained earnings, which comprise the cumulative earnings that have not been distributed as dividends to shareholders.

2. Ownership in a corporation is evidenced by shares of stock. In the absence of contrary provisions in the stock contract, stockholders have the right to share in profits, to vote on management issues, to maintain their proportion of ownership through the preemptive right, and to share proportionately in corporate assets in the event of liquidation.

3. Generally, the maximum loss that an investor in corporate stock can incur is the amount paid in. Thus, investors in corporate stock are said to have **limited liability.**

4. In addition to a preference with respect to dividends and assets upon liquidation, preferred stock also sometimes possesses other characteristics, such as the cumulative feature, a participation feature, a call provision, and a conversion privilege.

5. When capital stock is issued, the best available evidence should be used to record the exchange. If cash is received, the amount of cash received is recorded for the stock. If noncash assets are received, the fair value of either the assets received or the stock issued, whichever is more clearly evident, should be assigned to both the assets and the stock. If two or more classes of stock are issued as a package, the consideration received should be allocated to the classes of stock issued in proportion to their relative fair values.

6. When stock is issued on a subscription basis, the receivable usually should be classified as a current asset. The amounts attached to the stock that will be issued upon final payment of the receivable should be included in contributed capital. State law governs the treatment of amounts paid in on defaulted shares of subscribed stock.

7. When preferred stock is converted into common stock, the book value of the preferred stock being converted should be assigned to the common stock issued in place of the preferred.

8. Stock rights are issued to provide evidence that the holder of the right is entitled to acquire shares of a corporation's stock according to specified terms. Where such rights are issued in connection with stock option plans, no accounting is required for the rights unless the plan is **compensatory** and the market price of the stock exceeds the option price at the measurement date. If the latter situation exists, compensation expense should be recognized over the service period of the employees holding the stock rights.

9. Measurement difficulties often exist in stock option plans for which the terms are variable and depend upon future events, such as stock appreciation right (SAR) plans. However, the need for **timely** information regarding future **cash flows** requires that periodic estimates be made of the expected cost to a firm under these plans.

10. When a company acquires and retires its own capital stock, the amounts originally received for the retired shares should be eliminated from the contributed capital accounts. If the shares are retired for less than the amount originally received (or the average paid-in per share), the difference should be credited to contributed capital from retirement of stock. If the shares are retired for more than the amount received, retained earnings should be debited for the difference.

11. Treasury stock is a company's own capital stock that has been issued, acquired by the company, but not retired. Treasury stock is not an asset; it is a reduction of stockholders' equity. The two common methods of accounting for treasury stock are (1) the cost method and (2) the par value method.

12. Under the **cost method,** treasury stock is viewed as a suspense item awaiting ultimate disposition. The shares are accounted for at cost and reported in the balance sheet as a lump-sum reduction of stockholders' equity.

13. Under the **par value method,** the acquisition of treasury shares is viewed as equivalent to the retirement of the shares. The treasury stock is debited for the par value of the shares acquired, contributed capital in excess of par is debited for the average (or actual) amount originally received in excess of par, and any difference between these two amounts and the cash paid is either debited to retained earnings or credited to contributed capital from treasury stock transactions. In the balance sheet, contributed capital is reduced directly as a result of the accounting procedures under the par value method.

QUESTIONS

Q20-1. Identify and describe the two primary components of stockholders' equity.

Q20-2. Describe the following types of corporations:

1. Private	**4.** Stock	**7.** Listed
2. Public	**5.** Open	**8.** Unlisted
3. Nonstock	**6.** Closed	

Q20-3. How do state corporation laws affect the accounting and reporting for stockholders' equity?

Q20-4. How does the system of capital accumulation for corporations differ from the system for partnerships and sole proprietorships?

Q20-5. What are the usual rights of corporate stockholders?

Q20-6. What is the difference between preferred stock and common stock?

Q20-7. What is the limited liability feature and why is it advantageous to corporations?

Q20-8. Under what conditions might an investor in corporate stock be liable for more than the amount invested?

Q20-9. Why are corporations required to retain assets equivalent to contributed capital?

Q20-10. Describe the following features of preferred stock:

1. Cumulative

2. Participation

3. Call

4. Conversion

Q20-11. What are dividends in arrears? Do they constitute a liability? Explain.

Q20-12. Why does the SEC require corporations to exclude redeemable preferred stock from stockholders' equity?

Q20-13. What is the difference in accounting for the issuance of par value stock, stated value stock, and true no-par stock?

Q20-14. At what amount should a corporation record stock issued for noncash assets or services?

Q20-15. What is watered stock? What are secret reserves?

Q20-16. In what ways may a corporation treat amounts paid in by defaulting subscribers?

Q20-17. How should subscriptions receivable be reported in the financial statements? How should common stock subscribed be reported in the financial statements?

Q20-18. When two or more types of stock are issued as a unit, how does a corporation determine the amount to be assigned to each type of stock?

Q20-19. What is the acceptable method of accounting for stock issue costs? Why?

Q20-20. Describe the accounting for the conversion of preferred stock into common stock.

Q20-21. Identify three circumstances in which corporations commonly issue stock rights.

Q20-22. What are the four characteristics of a noncompensatory stock option plan? Why would a company have a noncompensatory stock option plan?

Q20-23. How is compensation expense measured for a compensatory stock option plan?

Q20-24. Over what time period should compensation expense associated with a compensatory stock option plan be recognized?

Q20-25. What are stock appreciation rights? Why do these rights create accounting difficulties?

Q20-26. How should a company record donations of assets from stockholders or other parties?

Q20-27. Explain why retained earnings may decrease, but not increase, when a firm retires its own capital stock.

Q20-28. What are some reasons that corporations acquire their own shares? What is the effect on a corporation of acquiring its own shares?

Q20-29. Describe the cost method and the par value method of accounting for treasury stock.

Q20-30. What is the difference between the cost method and the par value method in terms of their effect on (a) total stockholders' equity and (b) the components of stockholders' equity?

Q20-31. How does a corporation account for donated treasury stock under (a) the cost method and (b) the par value method?

CASES

C20-1. COMPONENTS OF STOCKHOLDERS' EQUITY   Stockholders' equity is an important part of a corporation's balance sheet. Also, because of legal requirements and reporting objectives, it is considerably more complex than the capital section of a partnership or sole proprietorship balance sheet.

REQUIRED

1. Identify the components of stockholders' equity.

2. Describe the contents of each component.

C20-2. CHARACTERISTICS OF EQUITY SECURITIES; TERMINOLOGY
A) Capital stock is an important area of a corporation's equity section. Generally the term ''capital stock'' embraces both the common and preferred stock issued by a corporation.

REQUIRED

1. What are the basic rights inherent in ownership of common stock, and how are they exercised?

2. What is preferred stock? Discuss the various preferences afforded preferred stock.

B) In dealing with the various equity securities of a corporate entity, it is important to understand certain terminology related thereto.

REQUIRED
Define the following terms:

1. Treasury stock.

2. Legal capital.

3. Stock right.

4. Stock warrant.

(AICPA, adapted)

C20-3. ISSUANCE OF STOCK FOR NONCASH CONSIDERATION   You have been engaged to examine the financial statements of Custer Corporation for the year ending December 31, 1987. Custer was organized in January 1987 by Moses and Price, original owners of options to acquire for $350,000 oil leases on 5,000 acres of land. They contemplated that, first, the oil leases would be acquired by the corporation, and subsequently 180,000 shares of the corporation's common stock would be issued to the public at $6 per share. In February 1987 they exchanged their options, $150,000 cash, and $50,000 of other assets for 75,000 shares of Custer's common stock. Custer's board of directors appraised the leases at $600,000, on the basis of leases recently issued for other acreage in the same area. The options were therefore recorded at $250,000 ($600,000 − $350,000 option price).

The options were exercised by Custer in March 1987, prior to the issuance of common stock to the public in April 1987. Leases on approximately 500 acres of land were abandoned as worthless during the year.

REQUIRED

1. Why is the valuation of assets acquired by a corporation in exchange for its own common stock sometimes difficult?

2. What reasoning might Custer Corporation use to support its valuation of the leases at $600,000, the amount of the appraisal by the board of directors?

3. Assuming the board's appraisal was sincere, what steps might Custer have taken to strengthen its position to use the $600,000 value and to provide additional information if questions are raised about possible overvaluation of the leases?

4. Discuss the propriety of charging one-tenth of the recorded value of the leases against income in 1987 because leases on 500 acres of land were abandoned during the year.

(AICPA, adapted)

C20-4. STOCK OPTIONS   Stock option plans may be either compensatory or noncompensatory. The accounting requirements differ for these two types of plans.

REQUIRED

1. Describe the accounting requirements at the date stock is issued under (*a*) a noncompensatory plan and (*b*) a compensatory plan.

2. When is compensation expense measured for a compensatory plan? Explain why it is often difficult to measure compensation expense and to match it with the services received.

C20-5. ACCOUNTING FOR TREASURY STOCK   For numerous reasons a corporation may acquire shares of its own capital stock. When a company purchases treasury stock, it has two options as to how to account for the shares: *(a)* the cost method, and *(b)* the par value method.

REQUIRED

Compare and contrast the cost method with the par value method for each of the following:

1. Acquisition of shares at a price less than par value.

2. Acquisition of shares at a price greater than par value.

3. Subsequent reissue of treasury shares at a price less than purchase price, but more than par value.

4. Subsequent reissue of treasury shares at a price greater than both purchase price and par value.

5. Effect on net income.

(AICPA, adapted)

EXERCISES

E20-1. CAPITAL STOCK TRANSACTIONS   The Kaneer Corporation was incorporated on January 1, 1987, with the following authorized capitalization:

a) 100,000 shares of common stock, par value $10 per share.

b) 20,000 shares of 9 percent cumulative preferred stock, par value $5 per share.

During 1987 Kaneer issued 15,000 shares of common stock at $40 per share and 2,500 shares of preferred stock at $12 per share. Also, on December 10, 1987, subscriptions for 1,000 shares of preferred stock were taken at a purchase price of $15 per share. These subscribed shares were paid for on January 10, 1988.

REQUIRED

> **1.** Prepare journal entries for Kaneer to record each of the events described above.
>
> **2.** Prepare the contributed capital section of stockholders' equity at December 31, 1987.

E20-2. ISSUANCE OF STOCK FOR NONCASH CONSIDERATION Reckers Corporation issued 10,000 shares of its own previously unissued $10 par common stock for land to be used as a future plant site.

REQUIRED

Record the transaction under each of the following independent assumptions:

> **1.** The land was appraised at $900,000; the stock, which was actively traded on a national stock exchange, had a market value at the time of the transaction of $800,000.
>
> **2.** The land was appraised at $600,000; the stock, which was closely held, did not have a readily determinable market value.
>
> **3.** Neither the fair market value of the land nor the fair market value of the stock was readily determinable.

E20-3. STOCK SUBSCRIPTIONS On October 10, 1987, 100,000 shares of Erin Corporation's $5 par value common stock were sold at a subscription price of $35 per share. A down payment of $5 per share was received, with the remainder of the subscription price payable in three equal installments on November 10, 1987, December 10, 1987, and January 10, 1988.

REQUIRED

> **1.** Prepare journal entries on the books of Erin Corporation to record:
> **a)** The subscription and collection of the down payment.
> **b)** Collection of the three installments from all subscribers.
> **c)** Issuance of the subscribed shares.
>
> **2.** Assume, instead, that a subscriber to 10,000 shares made the down payment and then defaulted. Assuming further that the cash paid in by the defaulting subscriber was returned, record the default.

E20-4. STOCK SUBSCRIPTIONS Pepper Corporation issued 100,000 shares of its $10 par common stock on March 1, 1987, on a subscription basis for $60 per share. The subscription terms called for a 20 percent down payment and for the remainder of the subscription price to be paid in two equal installments in 30 and 60 days from the subscription date. All of the subscribed amount was collected except for the last installment from a subscriber to 1,000 shares. Applicable state law requires that Pepper return amounts paid in by defaulting subscribers less any loss on reissue. The defaulted shares were reissued for $56 per share.

REQUIRED

Prepare all the journal entries required in connection with this stock subscription.

E20-5. LUMP-SUM ISSUES OF STOCK Arrington Corporation issued 100,000 shares of its $1 par common stock for $1,000,000. One share of Arrington's $5 par preferred stock was issued with every 10 shares of common stock.

REQUIRED

Record the issuance of the common and preferred stock under each of the following independent assumptions:

1. The market price per share for the common stock was $6; the market price per share for the preferred stock was $50.

2. The market price per share for the common stock was $8; the market price per share for the preferred stock was not readily determinable because it was not actively traded.

E20-6. CONVERTIBLE PREFERRED STOCK   At the beginning of 1987, McRae Corporation issued 10,000 shares of $10 par convertible preferred stock at $30 per share. The stock is convertible into $5 par common shares on a share-for-share basis. During 1987, 2,000 of the preferred shares were converted into common. The market price of the preferred at the time of conversion was $42 per share; the market price of the common was $44 per share.

REQUIRED

1. Prepare the entry to record the issuance of the preferred stock at the beginning of 1987.

2. Prepare the entry to record the conversion of preferred into common.

E20-7. STOCK WARRANTS   On July 1, 1987, Round Company issued for $525,000 a total of 5,000 shares of $100 par value, 7 percent noncumulative preferred stock along with one detachable warrant for each share issued. Each warrant contains a right to purchase one share of Round's $10 par value common stock for $15. The market price of the rights on July 1, 1987, was $2.25 per right. On October 31, 1987, when the market price of the common stock was $19 per share and the market value of the rights was $3.00 per right, 4,000 rights were exercised.

REQUIRED

Prepare journal entries for Round Company to record:

1. The issuance of the preferred stock and rights.

2. The exercise of the rights.

(AICPA, adapted)

E20-8. STOCK OPTIONS   On January 2, 1987, Woods Company granted Roger Gordon, the president, an option to purchase 4,000 shares of Woods's $10 par value common stock at $50 per share. The option becomes exercisable on January 2, 1989, after Gordon has completed two years of service.

REQUIRED

Prepare journal entries for Woods Company relative to the stock option agreement for the year ended December 31, 1987, under each of the following independent assumptions:

1. The quoted market price of Woods' common stock was as follows:

January 2, 1987	$45
December 31, 1987	60

2. The quoted market price of Woods' common stock was as follows:

January 2, 1987	$60
December 31, 1987	70

E20-9. STOCK APPRECIATION RIGHTS   At the beginning of 1986, Kristin Corporation granted stock appreciation rights (SARs) to three of its key executives. Under the terms of the SAR plan, each executive was entitled to receive either cash, shares of Kristin's $1 par value common stock, or a combination of both cash and stock. The amount to be received was to be determined by the difference between the quoted market price of Kristin's common stock at the date of exercise and a predetermined price of $10 per SAR.

Kristin granted a total of 30,000 SARs, which were exercisable after January 1, 1989, and the executives were required to be in the employ of the company at the date of exercise. The per share market price of Kristin's common stock at the end of 1986, 1987, and 1988 was $24, $32, and $28, respectively. When the plan was adopted, it was assumed that the executives would select the option to receive cash. All of the SARs were exercised on January 2, 1989, and the appropriate amount of cash was paid.

REQUIRED

Prepare all journal entries required in connection with the SAR plan for 1986 through 1989.

E20-10. RETIREMENT OF CAPITAL STOCK Simmons Company acquired 20,000 shares of its $5 par value common stock and immediately retired the shares. The average paid-in capital for Simmons' common shares was $35 per share.

REQUIRED

Prepare the journal entry required to record the acquisition and retirement of the shares assuming:

1. The shares were acquired for $30 per share.

2. The shares were acquired for $43 per share.

E20-11. TREASURY STOCK The stockholders' equity accounts of Mendoza Company appeared as follows as of January 1, 1987:

Common stock, par value $10; authorized 200,000 shares;
    issued and outstanding 140,000 shares $1,400,000
Contributed capital in excess of par value   700,000
Retained earnings 1,100,000
      Total $3,200,000

During 1987, Mendoza entered into the following transactions:
    a) Acquired 10,000 shares of its stock for $200,000.
    b) Reissued 4,000 treasury shares at $16 per share.
    c) Retired the remaining treasury shares.

REQUIRED

Prepare the journal entries to record the treasury stock transactions using:

1. The cost method.

2. The par value method.

E20-12. TREASURY STOCK At the end of 1986, Eberhardt Corporation had the following balances in its stockholders' equity accounts:

Common stock, par value $5; authorized 500,000 shares;
    issued and outstanding 300,000 shares . . . . $ 1,500,000
Contributed capital in excess of par value   4,500,000
Retained earnings 17,400,000
      Total $23,400,000

The following transactions occurred during 1987:
    a) 10,000 shares were acquired for $360,000.
    b) 12,000 shares were acquired for $240,000.
    c) 15,000 shares of treasury stock were reissued at $26 per share.

REQUIRED

Prepare journal entries to record the treasury stock transactions using:

1. The cost method, assuming a FIFO cost flow.

2. The par value method.

E20-13. DONATED TREASURY STOCK On September 5, 1987, a stockholder of the Rodgers Corporation donated 6,000 shares of Rodgers' $1 par common stock to the corporation. The average price paid in per share was $15. At the time of the donation the quoted market price of the stock was $46. On December 10, 1987, the shares were reissued for $52 per share.

REQUIRED

Record the donation and subsequent reissue using:

1. The cost method.

2. The par value method.

PROBLEMS

P20-1. ACCOUNTING FOR STOCK ISSUANCE   Ward Corporation engaged in the following stock transactions during the year:

a) Issued 10,000 shares of $1 par value common stock for cash at $20 per share.

b) Issued 4,000 shares of $1 par common stock in exchange for a land site. The common stock, which was actively traded on a national stock exchange, had a market price per share of $24 at the time of the exchange. The appraised value of the land, based on the average appraisal from three independent appraisers, was $100,000. The appraisals ranged from $75,000 to $140,000.

c) Received subscriptions for 20,000 shares of $5 par preferred stock. The subscription price was $100; 25 percent was paid in cash as a down payment and the remainder was due in three equal installments in 30, 60, and 90 days.

d) Collected the deferred portion of the subscription price as scheduled and issued the preferred stock.

e) Issued as a combination 32,000 shares of $1 par common stock and 4,000 shares of $5 par preferred stock for $1,250,000. The market prices per share of the common and preferred stock at the date of issuance were $30 and $120, respectively.

REQUIRED

Prepare journal entries to record the stock transactions.

P20-2. STOCK ISSUANCE AND CONTRIBUTED CAPITAL PRESENTATION   Schultz Company began the 1987 calendar year with the following balances in its contributed capital accounts:

Preferred stock, $100 par value, authorized 1 million
  shares, issued and outstanding 200,000 shares $20,000,000
Common stock, $5 par value, authorized 5 million shares,
  issued and outstanding 1,500,000 shares   7,500,000
Contributed capital in excess of par—preferred.   2,000,000
Contributed capital in excess of par—common 10,500,000

During 1987 the following stock transactions occurred:

a) Issued 100,000 shares of common at $15 per share. Incurred stock issue costs of $80,000.

b) Issued 20,000 shares of preferred for $2,400,000. As a sweetener, Schultz included one share of common stock with each five shares of preferred. The market prices of the common and preferred at the time of issuance were $15 and $120 per share, respectively. Stock issue costs were $140,000.

c) Received subscriptions for 200,000 shares of common at $18 per share. Subscribers paid one-third of the subscription price as a down payment, with the remainder due in two equal installments in 30 and 60 days. (The installments are due in 1988.)

REQUIRED

1. Prepare journal entries to record the stock transactions.

2. Prepare the contributed capital section of Schultz Company's balance sheet at December 31, 1987.

P20-3. PRESENTATION OF STOCKHOLDERS' EQUITY   You have been provided with the following accounts and balances from the general ledger of the General Manufacturing Company as of December 31, 1987:

Capital from land site donation $200,000
Cash dividend payable—common   20,000
Common stock dividend distributable   20,000

Retained earnings	600,000
Preferred stock	100,000
Subscriptions receivable—common stock...........................	12,000
Common stock	200,000
Contributed capital in excess of par—preferred......................	16,000
Common stock subscribed	50,000
Loan payable to stockholders	300,000
Treasury stock—common	20,000

Additional information is as follows:

a) Common stock is $10 par value; authorization 400,000 shares.

b) There are 2,000 common shares held as treasury stock.

c) Preferred stock is $100 par value, 6 percent cumulative and nonparticipating. The authorization is 4,000 shares.

REQUIRED

Prepare in good form the stockholders' equity section of the balance sheet for General Manufacturing Company as of December 31, 1987.

P20-4. VARIOUS STOCK TRANSACTIONS During May 1986, Gilroy, Inc., was organized with 3,000,000 authorized shares of $10 par value common stock, and 300,000 shares of its common stock were issued for $3,300,000. Net income through December 31, 1986, was $125,000.

On July 3, 1987, Gilroy issued 500,000 shares of its common stock for $6,250,000. Gilroy's net income for the year ended December 31, 1987, was $350,000.

During 1988 Gilroy had the following transactions:

a) In February, Gilroy acquired 30,000 shares of its common stock for $9 per share. Gilroy uses the cost method to account for treasury stock.

b) In June, Gilroy reissued 15,000 shares of its treasury stock for $12 per share.

c) In September, each stockholder was issued (for each share held) one stock right to purchase two additional shares of common stock for $13 per share. The rights expire on December 31, 1988.

d) In October, 250,000 stock rights were exercised when the market value of the common stock was $14 per share.

e) In November, 400,000 stock rights were exercised when the market value of the common stock was $15 per share.

f) On December 15, 1988, Gilroy declared its first cash dividend to stockholders of $.20 per share, payable on January 10, 1989, to stockholders of record on December 31, 1988.

g) On December 21, 1988, in accordance with the applicable state law, Gilroy formally retired 10,000 shares of its treasury stock. The market value of the common stock was $16 per share on this date.

h) Net income for 1988 was $750,000.

REQUIRED

Prepare a schedule of all transactions affecting the capital stock (shares and dollar amounts), additional paid-in capital, retained earnings, the treasury stock (shares and dollar amounts), and the amounts that would be included in Gilroy's balance sheet at December 31, 1986, 1987, and 1988, as a result of the above facts. Show supporting computations in good form.

(AICPA, adapted)

P20-5. STOCK OPTIONS At the beginning of 1987, Weinhaur Corporation had the following account balances:

Common stock, $10 par, authorized 5 million shares.................	$5,000,000
Contributed capital in excess of par—common	2,000,000

Selected transactions during 1987 were as follows (in chronological order):

a) Stock option plan A was adopted. The plan covers all employees and allows employees to purchase up to 100 shares of Weinhaur's common stock at $16 per share, the market price at the date of grant. The options expire on December 31, 1987.

b) Options were granted to five key executives under stock option plan B. Under the grant the executives may purchase up to 3,000 shares each. The shares may be acquired between January 1, 1989, and December 31, 1998, at $18 per share; the market price at the date of grant was $20. The executives must be in the employ of Weinhaur when they exercise the options.

c) 4,000 shares were issued during 1987 under option plan A.

d) One of the five executives covered under option plan B left Weinhaur Corporation at the end of 1987.

REQUIRED

1. Prepare journal entries for 1987 related to the above information.

2. Prepare the contributed capital section of Weinhaur's balance sheet for 1987.

P20-6. STOCK OPTIONS On January 1, 1986, Holt, Inc., granted stock options to officers and key employees for the purchase of 30,000 shares of the company's $10 par common stock at $25 per share. The options were exercisable within a four-year period beginning January 1, 1988, by grantees still in the employ of the company, and expiring December 31, 1992. The market price of Holt's common stock was $33 per share at the date of grant.

On April 1, 1987, 2,000 option shares were terminated when two employees resigned from the company. The market value of the common stock was $35 per share on this date. On March 31, 1988, 12,000 option shares were exercised when the market price of the common stock was $40 per share.

REQUIRED

Prepare journal entries to record issuance of the stock options, termination of the stock options, exercise of the stock options, and charges to compensation expense, for 1986, 1987, and 1988.

(AICPA, adapted)

P20-7. STOCK APPRECIATION RIGHTS Kaylee Company granted stock appreciation rights (SARs) to certain key executives at the beginning of 1987. The plan provides that the executives may receive either cash, Kaylee's $5 par value common stock, or a combination of cash and stock, with the amount to be received determined by the difference between the quoted market price at the date of exercise and a predetermined price of $20 per SAR.

Kaylee granted a total of 50,000 SARs in 1987, exercisable after January 1, 1990, and before January 1, 1999, by executives still employed by the company at the date of exercise. Kaylee assumed that the executives would choose to receive common stock. The per share market price of Kaylee's common stock was as follows:

DATE	QUOTED MARKET PRICE
12/31/87	$34
12/31/88	39
12/31/89	49
12/31/90	45
12/31/91	48

On December 31, 1990, 40,000 of the SARs were exercised and the appropriate amount of common stock was issued. The remaining 10,000 SARs were still outstanding at the end of 1991.

REQUIRED

Prepare all journal entries required in connection with the SAR plan from 1987 through 1991.

P20-8. TREASURY STOCK, COST METHOD Presented below is the stockholders' equity section of Caper Corporation at December 31, 1986:

Common stock, par value $20; authorized 50,000 shares;
  issued and outstanding 30,000 shares $600,000
Contributed capital in excess of par value 150,000
Retained earnings 230,000
                                                                                                    $980,000

During 1987 the following transactions occurred relating to stockholders' equity:

a) 1,000 shares were acquired at $28 per share.

b) 900 shares were acquired at $30 per share.

c) 1,500 shares of treasury stock were reissued at $32 per share.

d) 200 shares of treasury stock were reissued at $27 per share.

Caper accounts for treasury stock using the cost method, assuming a FIFO cost flow. For the year ended December 31, 1987, Caper reported net income of $110,000.

REQUIRED

1. Prepare journal entries for the treasury stock transactions.

2. Prepare the stockholders' equity section of Caper's balance sheet at December 31, 1987.

(AICPA, adapted)

P20-9. TREASURY STOCK, PAR VALUE METHOD Jenny Corporation was organized on January 1, 1987, with an authorization of 500,000 shares of common stock with a par value of $5 per share. During 1987 the corporation had the following equity transactions:

a) 1/5/87: Issued 100,000 shares at $5 per share.

b) 4/6/87: Issued 50,000 shares at $7 per share.

c) 6/8/87: Issued 15,000 shares at $10 per share.

d) 7/28/87: Acquired 25,000 shares at $4 per share.

e) 12/31/87: Reissued the 25,000 treasury shares at $8 per share.

Jenny uses the par value method to account for treasury shares. Net income for 1987 was $94,000.

REQUIRED

1. Prepare journal entries to record the stock transactions during 1987.

2. Prepare the stockholders' equity section of Jenny Corporation's balance sheet at December 31, 1987.

(AICPA, adapted)

P20-10. TREASURY STOCK Sliwicki Company had the following stockholders' equity account balances at the beginning of 1987:

Common stock, $1 par, 2 million shares authorized	$ 500,000
Contributed capital in excess of par—common	3,500,000
Retained earnings	6,200,000
	$10,200,000

Treasury stock transactions for Sliwicki were as follows for 1987:

a) Acquired 22,000 of its own shares at $10 per share.

b) Acquired 8,000 of its own shares at $7 per share.

c) Reissued 18,000 treasury shares for $12 per share.

d) Reissued 6,000 treasury shares for $10 per share.

e) Retired 3,000 treasury shares.

REQUIRED

1. Prepare journal entries to record the treasury stock transactions assuming that Sliwicki Company uses the cost method and a FIFO cost flow.

2. Prepare the stockholders' equity section of Sliwicki's balance sheet at the end of 1987 assuming use of the cost method and 1987 net income of $320,000.

3. Prepare journal entries to record the treasury stock transactions assuming that Sliwicki Company uses the par value method.

4. Prepare the stockholders' equity section of the balance sheet at the end of 1987 assuming use of the par value method and 1987 net income of $320,000.

21 STOCKHOLDERS' EQUITY: RETAINED EARNINGS AND DIVIDENDS

Stockholders' interest in a firm's assets derives from two sources—contributed capital and retained earnings. Contributed capital, the amount of capital invested by stockholders, was introduced in Chapter 20. This chapter discusses retained earnings. First, we discuss the nature of retained earnings and transactions that affect it. Second, we discuss corporate dividend policy and accounting for various types of dividends. Third, we cover restrictions or appropriations of retained earnings. Because retained earnings is affected by quasi-reorganizations, the chapter concludes with a discussion of this topic.

THE NATURE OF RETAINED EARNINGS

In Chapter 2 stockholders' equity was defined as a residual interest in the assets of a corporation that remains after its liabilities are deducted. In Chapter 20 we pointed out that stockholders' equity may be further subdivided into contributed capital and retained earnings. This subdivision provides useful financial information by indicating the portion of a company's net assets that has arisen from stockholder investments and other capital transactions and the portion that has arisen from profitable operating activities—**retained earnings.** If a corporation operates at a profit, net assets increase. If it operates at a loss, net assets decrease. This increase or decrease is recorded in the retained earnings account. Thus, retained earnings is the balance sheet account that is debited or credited for these changes in net assets resulting from earnings activities.

TRENDS IN TERMINOLOGY

While "retained earnings" is probably the most often used term for earnings that have been retained in the business, terminology varies somewhat in practice. Synonymous terms include "earnings retained in the business," "accumulated earnings," "earnings employed in the business," and "retained income." The accounting profession has discouraged the use of "earned surplus" to describe retained earnings and "capital surplus" to describe contributed capital in excess of par. The use of the term *surplus* can cause two possible misconceptions: (1) if a company has a "surplus," it has something it does not need; and (2) assets generated from earnings are in a form available for distribution.

EXHIBIT 21–1   TRANSACTIONS AND OTHER ECONOMIC EVENTS
AFFECTING RETAINED EARNINGS

ECONOMIC EVENT	EFFECT ON RETAINED EARNINGS
Net income (loss)	Increase (decrease)
Prior period adjustments, e.g., error corrections	Increase or decrease
Some changes in accounting principle (discussed in Chapters 4 and 22)	Increase or decrease
Dividends (discussed later in this chapter)	Decrease
Some treasury stock transactions (discussed in Chapter 20)	Decrease
Quasi-reorganizations (discussed later in this chapter)	Increase

TRANSACTIONS AFFECTING RETAINED EARNINGS

There are several types of transactions and other economic events that affect retained earnings. These transactions and other events appear in Exhibit 21–1. In addition to net income or net loss, which is transferred to the retained earnings account, corrections of errors affecting prior periods are recorded in retained earnings. Furthermore, some changes in accounting principle, which we shall discuss in Chapter 22, also affect retained earnings. Dividends, which are distributions of earnings, decrease the retained earnings account. Some treasury stock transactions, which we discussed in Chapter 20, decrease retained earnings. Finally, when a corporation initiates a quasi-reorganization, retained earnings is increased to eliminate a deficit.

Under the all-inclusive form of the income statement which we discussed in Chapter 4, extraordinary, unusual, or infrequently occurring items are reported in the income statement and are not recorded directly in the retained earnings account.

Retained earnings makes up a significant portion of the stockholders' equity of most companies. Rockwell International's stockholders' equity, for example, totaled approximately $2.9 billion at the end of 1985. Retained earnings made up approximately $2.8 billion, or 96 percent, of this total. At the end of 1985, Dow Chemical's stockholders' equity was approximately $4.8 billion, of which 85 percent, or approximately $4.1 billion, represented earnings retained in the company.

Retained earnings makes up a significant portion of many companies' stockholders' equity.

Retained earnings may also represent a significant source of financing for many companies. Companies may "expand internally" by retaining assets that have arisen from profitable operations and using these assets for growth. Also, retained earnings is the basis for dividends, which we will now discuss.

DIVIDENDS

Dividends, other than stock dividends, are *nonreciprocal transfers* between a company and its stockholders and represent a distribution of earnings in the form of assets. In this section we explain the various types of dividends, but first we provide a general description of the dividend policies of corporations.

CORPORATE DIVIDEND POLICIES

Corporations generally maintain stable dividend patterns over time. Periodic dividends usually are considerably less than periodic net income for one or more of the following reasons:

1. As we mentioned earlier, a corporation may desire to retain assets arising from profitable operations for internal expansion or growth.

2. A corporation and its creditors may agree that the corporation must retain assets arising from earnings activities in order to provide additional protection to creditors if operations cease to be profitable.

3. A corporation may wish to smooth dividends over time by retaining assets arising from earnings in profitable years so that these accumulated assets can be used for dividends in less profitable years. Empirical evidence indicates that corporations are reluctant to lower dividends in less profitable years.[1] For example, Coca-Cola's dividends have increased steadily for many years, and the company has paid a dividend *every* year since 1893.[2] Some companies even *borrow* money to pay dividends when their cash balances are low temporarily.

4. State law may require that retained earnings equal to the cost of treasury stock purchases be restricted from use as a basis for dividends. As we saw in Chapter 20, such a requirement prevents a distribution of assets that would cause legal capital to be impaired.

One important financial statistic that captures dividend policy is the **dividend payout ratio:** annual dividends divided by annual net income. Historically, this ratio has varied among companies in different industries as well as among companies in the same industry.

While dividends represent distributions of income from a corporation to its stockholders and therefore are not expenses, dividends paid to preferred stockholders may be viewed as an expense *from the standpoint of common stockholders*. This view underlies the calculation of *earnings per share*, which was introduced in Chapter 4 and will be discussed in more detail in Chapter 24. In practice, many companies, especially in the utility industry, deduct preferred dividends from net income in the income statement to arrive at net income available to common stockholders. Exhibit 21–2 is a partial income statement that illustrates this practice.

> Dividends are not expenses, but are distributions of earnings; preferred dividends may be viewed, however, as expenses from the standpoint of common stockholders.

[1] Thomas Copeland and J. Fred Weston, *Financial Theory and Corporate Policy* (Reading, Mass.: Addison-Wesley, 1980), chap. 14.

[2] *Barron's*, March 9, 1981, p. 56.

EXHIBIT 21–2 PREFERRED DIVIDENDS TREATED AS EXPENSES FROM THE STANDPOINT OF COMMON STOCKHOLDERS

Oklahoma Gas and Electric Company

	1985	(in thousands) 1984	1983
Net income	$108,554	$113,268	$117,661
Preferred dividend requirements	(11,916)	(11,916)	(11,916)
Earnings available for common	$ 96,638	$101,352	$105,745

Source: OG&E 1985 Annual Report, p. 25.

ABILITY TO PAY DIVIDENDS

A company may distribute, as a dividend, assets equal to the credit balance in retained earnings unless retained earnings is legally restricted. In some cases, if a deficit (debit balance) in retained earnings exists, a corporation must eliminate the deficit by profitable operations or by a quasi-reorganization (discussed later in this chapter) before subsequent dividends can be declared. A corporation's financial position and financial strategies also influence its ability and inclination to pay dividends. A dividend, other than a stock dividend, results ultimately in a decrease in assets. Therefore, the amount and composition of cash and other assets, the amount of liabilities that require settlement in cash, and the need for future cash and future asset acquisitions all are factors that may affect dividend distributions.

To illustrate, assume the following balance sheet for Michelite Corporation:

Cash	$ 30,000	Current liabilities	$ 20,000
Plant assets	90,000	Capital stock	30,000
		Other contributed capital	20,000
		Retained earnings	50,000
Total	$120,000	Total	$120,000

We can draw some generalizations about dividends from this balance sheet:

1. Assuming that there are no legal restrictions against retained earnings, the corporation could distribute dividends equal to the retained earnings balance of $50,000. A dividend of this amount would represent a return on capital to the stockholders. Since dividends are paid with assets, however, the corporation would have to either sell some plant assets or borrow money, since the amount of cash on hand is only $30,000.

2. The maximum *cash* dividend that could be paid, given the current balance sheet, is $30,000.

3. Assuming that legal capital is equal to $30,000—the par value of the shares issued—the corporation could pay dividends of $70,000, which is equal to the sum of the balances in the retained earnings and other contributed capital accounts. Again, since the cash balance is only $30,000, the corporation would have to sell some plant assets or borrow to make such a cash distribution. If $70,000 were distributed, $50,000 would be considered a *distribution of earnings* (a return on capital), and the other $20,000 would be a *return of a portion of the stockholders' original investment* (a return of capital). The $20,000 distribution would be a *liquidating dividend*, and the stockholders should be so informed.[3] (Liquidating dividends will be discussed in more detail later in this chapter.) In summary, the maximum legal distribution of assets that could be paid to stockholders is:

$$\text{Maximum distribution (including liquidating dividends)} = \text{Stockholders' equity} - \text{Legal capital}$$

TYPES OF DIVIDENDS

While cash dividends are the most popular type of dividend distributions, there are also other types of dividends as well: scrip dividends, property dividends, dividends that are liquidating, and stock dividends.

---

[3] An individual stockholder who receives a portion of the $70,000 distribution may or may not consider the receipt to be partially liquidating. Liquidating dividends were discussed from the standpoint of the investor in Chapter 14.

Cash Dividends

Cash dividends represent a distribution of income in the form of cash. The *net effect* of a cash dividend is to reduce retained earnings and cash, as shown in the entry below:[4]

Retained earnings	xx	
Cash		xx

Three dates are important with respect to cash, property, and scrip dividends: the declaration date, the date of record, and the payment date. To illustrate how these dates are important, assume that on December 10, 1987, CD Corporation has 10,000 shares of common stock outstanding and declares a $1.50 per share cash dividend payable on January 10, 1988, to stockholders of record on December 30, 1987. The **declaration date** is December 10, the date on which the corporation's board of directors formally announces that a dividend is to be paid. Since dividends do not accrue with the passage of time, the declaration date is the date on which the corporation incurs an obligation (a liability) to pay the dividend. Except for stock dividends, dividends normally are not revocable once they have been declared.

On December 10, 1987, the following entry would be made to record the dividend declaration:

Retained earnings	15,000	
Dividends payable		15,000
(10,000 × $1.50)		

If a balance sheet were prepared on December 31, 1987, dividends payable would be reported as a current liability.

Dividends are not declared on treasury shares. The notion of a company distributing a dividend on shares of its own stock that it holds is illogical; furthermore, this practice would convey misleading cash flow signals to financial statement users.

The **date of record** is a date chosen by the corporation's board of directors to establish to whom the dividend will be paid on the payment date. Generally, the date of record is several days after the declaration date. No accounting entry is required at the date of record, since this date simply serves as a point in time to establish stock ownership.

Stockholders who have purchased shares in the market before the **ex-dividend date** (which, on the New York Stock Exchange, is four trading days before the date of record) receive the dividend whether or not they own the shares at the declaration date or payment date. In theory, however, the market price of the shares traded between the declaration date and the ex-dividend date will increase by the amount of the dividend. From the declaration date to the ex-dividend date, the common shares sell in the market "dividends on," which means that the market price of the shares includes the dividend. Thus, investors who purchased shares before the ex-dividend date will receive the dividend declared. After the ex-dividend date the shares sell "ex-dividend," which means that the price of the shares does not include the dividend. A stockholder who purchases shares after this date will not receive the dividend.

The **payment date** is the date when the dividend is paid and the liability is discharged. CD Corporation would make the following entry on January 10, 1988:

Dividends payable	15,000	
Cash		15,000

---

[4] In Chapter 3 a temporary account, dividends declared, was debited for dividend declarations. This account was then closed to retained earnings at the end of the accounting period. For simplicity, this account is not used in this chapter.

Scrip Dividends

Occasionally a corporation will declare a dividend several months before it is to be paid. For example, the corporation may be temporarily short of cash but may expect inflows of cash in a few months. In this instance, the corporation declares a **scrip** or **liability dividend** and issues promissory notes—pieces of paper, or "scrip"—as evidence of the intention to pay the dividend. Because of the waiting period, scrip dividends usually bear interest. Any interest that accrues on scrip dividends should be recorded as interest expense, since the interest has accrued on a *liability,* scrip dividends payable. To illustrate a scrip dividend, assume that Proctor Corporation declares a scrip dividend of $1.20 per share on 30,000 shares of its outstanding common stock and issues 10 percent 90-day promissory notes to its stockholders. The following entries are necessary to record the dividend declaration and payment of the dividend and interest:

Retained earnings	36,000	
Scrip dividends payable		36,000
To record the dividend declaration (30,000 × $1.20).		
Scrip dividends payable	36,000	
Interest expense ($36,000 × .10 × 1/4)	900	
Cash		36,900
To record payment of dividend and interest of $900.		

Property Dividends

A **property dividend** is a distribution of income in the form of assets other than cash. For example, company *X* may declare as a property dividend some shares of company *Z*'s stock that it holds as an asset. Several years ago, Ranchers Exploration and Development Corporation, a New Mexico mining company, announced plans to pay its quarterly dividend in gold—a specified quantity of gold per share. The company made the decision in recognition of "shareholders' concerns about inflation and the resultant loss of purchasing power or intrinsic value represented by paper currency and stock certificates." [5]

A property dividend may be any asset or group of assets. Most property dividends, however, are other companies' shares that are being held as investments by the dividend-issuing company. These shares are used as property dividends because their market value is readily determinable. Furthermore, shares of stock can be allocated easily among stockholders in proportion to their holdings. In accordance with the initial recording principle discussed in Chapter 2, assets distributed to stockholders as a property dividend should be adjusted to fair market value and a gain or loss should be recognized on the distribution. [6]

> Property dividends are measured and recorded at fair market value.

Assume that Spinet Corporation holds 5,800 shares of TV Industries' common stock, which it acquired at $10 per share. Spinet declares a property dividend of 500 shares of TV Industries' stock when the shares are selling at $38 per share. The following entries are necessary to record the declaration of the property dividend:

Investment in TV common	14,000	
Gain on disposition of investments		14,000
To record gain on 500 shares to be distributed		
[500 × ($38 − $10)].		
Retained earnings	19,000	
Property dividend payable		19,000
To record property dividend (500 × $38).		

[5] *Arizona Republic,* May 19, 1981.

[6] "Accounting for Nonmonetary Transactions," *Opinions of the Accounting Principles Board No. 29* (New York: AICPA, 1973).

At the payment date the following entry is made:

```
Property dividend payable .............................. 19,000
    Investment in TV common ...........................          19,000
To record payment of dividend.
```

An interesting type of "property" dividend was proposed by Eastern Airlines a few years ago. Eastern planned to allow stockholders to apply for travel vouchers good for 25 cents of travel for each common share owned. (Eastern had not paid a cash dividend on its common stock for many years.) We placed quotation marks around the word "property" because one might question whether the travel vouchers represent property dividends or merely sales discounts. The rationale for treating the travel vouchers as a property dividend is that Eastern obligated itself to deliver asset *services*—the services of the planes—in a nonreciprocal transfer between the company and its stockholders.[7]

Liquidating Dividends

Distributions of assets to stockholders in amounts greater than the dollar balance in retained earnings are called **liquidating dividends.** Stockholders should be informed if any portion of a dividend is liquidating, because the distribution results in both a return *on* capital (the portion that represents the earnings distribution) and a return *of* capital (the portion that represents a return of contributed capital). Other things being equal, a return of capital to shareholders may result in decreased future cash flows to the company and to its shareholders, because of a reduction in the asset base that generates cash flows. Liquidating dividends usually are paid by companies that are ceasing operations or reducing their level of operations. Also, companies with wasting assets often pay dividends equal to *earnings before depletion* if they have no plans to acquire other wasting assets. The liquidating portion of the dividend is equal to the amount of depletion.

Liquidating dividends should be recorded by debiting retained earnings for the portion of the dividend that represents an earnings distribution, debiting other contributed capital for the liquidating portion of the dividend, and crediting the asset (usually cash) that is distributed.

Stock Dividends

Stock dividends represent a distribution of additional shares of a corporation's own stock to its stockholders on a pro rata basis, that is, in proportion to the percentage of shares held. For stock dividends, the word "dividend" is somewhat misleading because dividends that we have discussed thus far have been distributions of cash, property, or other assets. A company's own stock, however, is not an asset to that company. Nevertheless, since the term commonly is used in practice, we will use it here.

Historically, corporations have issued stock dividends for one or more of the following reasons:

1. A stock dividend increases the number of shares outstanding without decreasing the corporation's assets; therefore, the stock dividend may cause the market price of the shares to fall, thus making the lower-priced stock accessible to a greater number of investors.

2. Some corporations may wish to retain assets which have arisen from profitable operations, and to distribute something to stockholders in lieu of a cash or property dividend. A stockholder may be willing to accept stock in lieu of cash or other property

[7] Also, the IRS indicated that the travel vouchers applied for would be considered as taxable income to the stockholders.

since the shares may be sold for cash (with a resulting decrease in the stockholder's interest). Thus, stock may be issued to satisfy stockholders' demands for dividends.

3. Management may desire to reduce the retained earnings available for future dividends by declaring a stock dividend. As we shall see, the recording of a stock dividend reduces retained earnings and increases contributed capital.

Small stock dividends are measured at fair market value; large stock dividends are measured, at a minimum, at par.

ACCOUNTING FOR STOCK DIVIDENDS   Under present GAAP, accounting for a stock dividend depends on whether the dividend is considered large or small. Small stock dividends, which are less than approximately 20 to 25 percent of the shares outstanding, are recorded at the fair market value of the shares distributed; large stock dividends, which are greater than 20 to 25 percent of the shares outstanding, are recorded, at a minimum, at the legal requirement, which usually is par value (stock dividends increase legal capital). Alternatively, large stock dividends may be measured at the average contributed amount per share. The Committee on Accounting Procedure (CAP) justified this accounting treatment as follows:

> A stock dividend does not, in fact, give rise to any change whatsoever in either the corporation's assets or its respective shareholders' proportionate interests therein. However, it cannot fail to be recognized that, merely as a consequence of the expressed purpose of the transaction and its characterization as a *dividend* in related notices to shareholders and the public at large, many recipients of stock dividends look upon them as distributions of corporate earnings and usually in an amount equivalent to the fair value of the additional shares received. Furthermore, it is to be presumed that such views of recipients are materially strengthened in those instances, which are by far the most numerous, where the issuances are so small in comparison with the shares previously outstanding that they do not have any apparent effect upon the share market price, and consequently, the market value of the shares previously held remains substantially unchanged. The committee therefore believes that where these circumstances exist, the corporation should in the public interest account for the transaction by transferring from earned surplus to the category of permanent capitalization (represented by the capital stock and capital surplus accounts) an amount equal to the fair value of the additional shares issued. Unless this is done, the amount of earnings which the shareholder may believe to have been distributed to him will be left, except to the extent otherwise dictated by legal requirements, in earned surplus subject to possible further similar stock issuances or cash distributions.
>
> Where the number of additional shares issued as a stock dividend is so great that it has, or may reasonably be expected to have, the effect of materially reducing the share market value, the committee believes that the implications and possible constructions discussed in the preceding paragraph are not likely to exist. Consequently, the committee considers that under such circumstances there is no need to capitalize earned surplus, other than to the extent occasioned by legal requirements.[8]

In summary, the CAP's rationale was as follows: Since market prices of shares may not be affected by small stock dividends, small stock dividends may produce extra value to stockholders. Therefore, accounting for small stock dividends should be based on the fair market value of shares distributed. Retained earnings should be debited for this extra value. Large stock dividends do not produce extra value because the market price declines proportionately. Therefore, retained earnings should be debited only to the extent of legal requirements.

To illustrate accounting for stock dividends, assume that Lacy Industries has the following stockholders' equity balances:

[8] "Restatement and Revision of Accounting Research Bulletins," *Accounting Research Bulletin No. 43* (New York: AICPA, 1953), chap. 7, paras. 10–11.

Common stock ($10 par, 10,000 shares issued and outstanding) $100,000
Contributed capital in excess of par 80,000
Retained earnings 160,000
    Total $340,000

If Lacy declares and distributes a 10 percent stock dividend when the fair market value of its shares is $32 per share, the following entry is made:

Retained earnings (.10 × 10,000 × $32) 32,000
    Common stock (.10 × 10,000 × $10) 10,000
    Contributed capital in excess of par ($32,000 − $10,000) 22,000

If the shares were no-par, the common stock account would be credited for $32,000.

If Lacy declares and distributes a 50 percent stock dividend, the following entry is required if par value is used as the basis of measurement:

Retained earnings 50,000
    Common stock 50,000
    (.50 × 10,000 × $10)

Alternatively, if the 50 percent stock dividend is to be recorded at the average contributed capital per share of $18 [($100,000 + $80,000) ÷ 10,000], the entry to record the dividend is as follows:

Retained earnings (5,000 × $18) 90,000
    Common stock (5,000 × $10) 50,000
    Contributed capital in excess of par (5,000 × $8) 40,000

Note that this measurement approach for large stock dividends maintains the average contributed capital per share.

The effects of the stock dividend on total stockholders' equity in these three situations may be summarized as follows:

	BEFORE STOCK DIVIDEND	AFTER STOCK DIVIDEND		
		SMALL STOCK DIVIDEND RECORDED AT FAIR MARKET VALUE	LARGE STOCK DIVIDEND RECORDED AT PAR VALUE	LARGE STOCK DIVIDEND RECORDED AT AVERAGE CONTRIBUTED CAPITAL PER SHARE
Common stock	$100,000	$110,000	$150,000	$150,000
Contributed capital in excess of par	80,000	102,000	80,000	120,000
Retained earnings	160,000	128,000	110,000	70,000
Total	$340,000	$340,000	$340,000	$340,000

Notice that in all three cases the stock dividend has no effect on *total* stockholders' equity of $340,000. Accounting for the stock dividend merely results in a reclassification within the elements of stockholders' equity.

Up to this point we have assumed that the stock dividends are declared and issued on the same date. If the issue date follows the declaration date, the following entries are required to account for the small stock dividend on the declaration date:

```
Retained earnings ........................................ 32,000
    Stock dividends distributable ...........................         10,000
    Contributed capital in excess of par .....................         22,000
```

and on the issue date:

```
Stock dividends distributable ............................. 10,000
    Common stock ........................................         10,000
```

Stock dividends distributable is not a liability, since there is no obligation to transfer assets to stockholders. If a balance sheet were prepared between the declaration date and the issue date, stock dividends distributable would be classified as a part of contributed capital and would be shown immediately below common stock issued and outstanding.

FRACTIONAL SHARE WARRANTS FROM STOCK DIVIDENDS   Frequently stock dividend transactions result in **fractional share warrants** being issued when some stockholders would otherwise receive less than a whole share of stock. Assume, for example, that FSW Corporation declares a 10 percent stock dividend on 1,000 shares of $5 par stock outstanding which are held by five FSW stockholders. The shares and warrants to be issued are as follows:

STOCKHOLDER	SHARES HELD	SHARES ISSUED	WARRANTS ISSUED
A	600	60	—
B	240	24	—
C	60	6	—
D	58	5	8
E	42	4	2
	1,000	99	10

While stockholders A, B, and C receive whole shares of 60, 24, and 6 shares, respectively, stockholders D and E are entitled to 5.8 and 4.2 shares, respectively. Since D and E cannot receive part of a share, fractional share warrants would be issued to these two stockholders. Stockholders D and E would receive eight warrants and two warrants, respectively. Ten warrants could be turned in to FSW Corporation in exchange for one share.

Stockholders D and E could sell their warrants either to the other or to someone else, and one party could then exchange the ten warrants for a share of stock. Since warrants have an expiration date, the stockholders also might allow the warrants to expire. If the fair market value of FSW Corporation's stock is $12 at the date of declaration, FSW will record the stock dividend and issuance of fractional share warrants as follows:

```
Retained earnings (.10 × 1,000 × $12) ....................... 1,200
    Common stock (99 × $5) ..................................         495
    Contributed capital—stock warrants outstanding (10 warrants
        for 1 share, par $5) ...................................           5
    Contributed capital in excess of par .......................         700
```

When the warrants are presented in exchange for the share, the following entry is made:

Contributed capital—stock warrants outstanding	5	
Common stock		5

If the warrants are allowed to expire, the following entry might be made to adjust the stockholder equity accounts to reflect the actual stock dividend of 99 shares rather than 100:[9]

Contributed capital—stock warrants outstanding	5	
Contributed capital in excess of par	7	
Retained earnings		12

Instead of issuing fractional share warrants, many corporations pay these fractional share dividends in cash. If FSW Corporation followed this policy, the following entry would be made to record the stock dividend declaration and distribution:

Retained earnings	1,200	
Common stock		495
Cash (1 equivalent share × $12)		12
Contributed capital in excess of par		693

Stockholder D would receive $9.60 in cash for her fractional share (.8 × $12), and stockholder E would receive $2.40 (.2 × $12).

From the standpoint of the stockholders, stock dividends are not considered to be income, since a stockholder has the same ownership in the company after receipt of the additional shares as before. (Accounting for stock dividends from the standpoint of the stockholder was discussed in Chapter 14.)

Stock Splits

In addition to stock dividends, another way of increasing outstanding shares is through stock splits. Many corporations that have operated profitably and whose stock has appreciated in market value over a period of time **split** their stock in order to make the market price more attractive to investors. For example, in 1985 Borden Company split its stock 2-for-1, causing the market price to fall from approximately $80 per share to approximately $40 per share.

Conceptually, stock dividends are identical to stock splits.

Conceptually, there is no difference between a stock dividend and a stock split, since both result in an increased number of shares outstanding with no effect on a corporation's net assets. Legally, however, there is a difference. As we saw earlier, a stock dividend results in an increased number of shares outstanding with no change in the par or stated value per share. As a result, the common stock account and legal capital are increased. A stock split, however, results in an increased number of shares outstanding and also a proportional decrease in the par or stated value per share, but the total dollar amount of the capital stock account is unchanged.[10]

---

[9] An acceptable alternative would be to credit contributed capital from expired stock warrants for the rights not exercised:

Contributed capital—stock warrants outstanding	5	
Contributed capital from expired stock warrants		5

[10] Corporations occasionally effect a *reverse* stock split by decreasing the shares outstanding. This strategy increases the market price of the (fewer) shares outstanding. For example, in 1985 Unicorp American effected a 15-for-1 reverse stock split designed to increase the market price of its stock, which sold for $.75 per share before the split.

EXHIBIT 21–3 EFFECTS OF LARGE STOCK DIVIDENDS
AND STOCK SPLITS ON STOCKHOLDERS' EQUITY

Stockholders' equity before stock dividend or stock split:

Common stock (par $10, 10,000 shares issued)	$100,000
Contributed capital in excess of par	100,000
Retained earnings	350,000
	$550,000

	STOCKHOLDERS' EQUITY AFTER	
	2-FOR-1 STOCK SPLIT	100% STOCK DIVIDEND
Common stock (par $5, 20,000 shares)	$100,000	
(par $10, 20,000 shares)		$200,000*
Contributed capital in excess of par	100,000	100,000
Retained earnings	350,000	250,000†
	$550,000	$550,000

* $100,000 + $100,000 (par value of shares issued in stock dividend).

† $350,000 − $100,000 (reduction from stock dividend, assuming that the dividend is measured at par).

No formal accounting entry is necessary to record a stock split. The corporation simply makes a memorandum entry to indicate the new shares outstanding with the lowered par value. As an alternative to a memorandum entry, if a corporation declared a 3-for-1 stock split on its 10,000 shares of $6 par common stock outstanding, the following formal entry could be made:

Common stock (10,000 shares, $6 par)	60,000	
Common stock (30,000 shares, $2 par)		60,000

The effects on stockholders' equity of a large stock dividend and of a stock split are shown in Exhibit 21–3.

Since the usual objective of a large stock dividend is to lower the market price of a company's shares, and since the market impact is identical to a stock split, the Committee on Accounting Procedure suggested that a large stock dividend should be described as a "split-up effected in the form of a dividend." [11] When Murphy Oil Corporation declared a 200 percent stock dividend, the event was described in the financial statements as follows:

The shareholders approved an increase in the Company's authorized Common Stock to 40,000,000 shares and the Board of Directors declared a 200% stock dividend to effect a three-for-one stock split. Net income and dividends per share, average shares outstanding, shares subject to options and the related option prices have been adjusted to reflect the stock distribution.

Evaluation of Accounting for Stock Dividends

Although reporting a corporation's capital by source is a primary objective of accounting for stockholders' equity, the accounting procedures for stock dividends are inconsistent with that objective. Furthermore, the argument that accounting should be based on the fair market value of shares distributed—because the dividends produce extra value to stock-

[11] *Accounting Research Bulletin No. 43*, para. 11.

holders—does not appear to have empirical support.[12] From the standpoint of the issuing company, stock dividends merely increase the number of shares outstanding and correspondingly reduce the market price of the shares. Any *increases* in market price are due to investors' expectations about the level of future cash dividends and not to the stock dividends per se. Except for legal requirements, we believe that a logical accounting approach for all stock dividends would be merely to decrease proportionately the par value of the increased shares outstanding, which is the procedure used for stock splits. This approach appears to meet the qualitative characteristics of consistency and representational faithfulness, which were discussed in Chapter 2.

Interestingly, the United States is one of the few countries, if not the only one, in which small stock dividends must be measured at fair market value. From an examination of historical events in the late 1930s and early 1940s, Stephen Zeff concluded that "evidently the New York Stock Exchange and a majority of the Committee on Accounting Procedure (of the AICPA) regarded periodic stock dividends as objectionable, and the CAP acted to make it more difficult for corporations to sustain a series of stock dividends out of their accumulated earnings."[13] Since market values typically are much greater than par values, the requirement that a stock dividend be recorded at fair market value causes a much greater debit to (decrease in) retained earnings. This line of reasoning may partially explain the CAP's position on small stock dividends and shows how accounting standards can affect the economic environment, in this case by influencing corporate policy for stock dividends.

THE EFFECT OF DIVIDEND PREFERENCES ON DIVIDEND DISTRIBUTIONS

In Chapter 20 we discussed the characteristics of preferred and common stock. We pointed out that one characteristic of preferred stock is its preference with respect to dividends. If a company has both preferred stock and common stock issued and outstanding, preferred stockholders' claims to dividends must be satisfied before dividends are paid to common stockholders. If the preferred stock is *cumulative, dividends in arrears* must be paid before earnings distributions can be made to common stockholders. Preferred stock that is *participating* allows preferred stockholders to share proportionately in dividends with common stockholders over and above the stated dividend rate on the preferred shares. Participation may be either *full,* such that the preferred stockholders are paid dividends at the same rate as payments to common stockholders, or *partial,* up to a maximum total rate. Under partial participation, if a preferred share has, for example, a 10 percent stated dividend rate and is participating up to an additional 5 percent, the maximum total dividend rate is 15 percent.

To illustrate dividend preferences, assume that Comanche Industries has the following capital stock outstanding:

Common ($10 par, 30,000 shares issued and outstanding) $300,000
8% preferred ($100 par, 2,000 shares issued and outstanding) 200,000

Comanche plans to distribute $80,000 in cash dividends during the current year. The distribution of dividends to each class of stock under six independent assumptions appears in Exhibit 21–4.

---

[12] Sherman Chottiner and Allan Young, "A Test of the AICPA Differentiation Between Stock Dividends and Stock Splits," *Journal of Accounting Research,* Autumn 1971, pp. 367–74; Eugene Fama, Lawrence Fisher, Michael Jensen, and Richard Roll, "The Adjustment of Stock Prices to New Information," *International Economic Review,* February 1969, pp. 1–21; Taylor Foster and Don Vickrey, "The Information Content of Stock Dividend Announcements," *Accounting Review,* April 1978, pp. 360–70.

[13] Stephen Zeff, "The Rise of Economic Consequences," *Journal of Accountancy,* December 1978, pp. 57–58.

EXHIBIT 21–4   DISTRIBUTION OF DIVIDENDS TO COMMON AND PREFERRED STOCKHOLDERS UNDER SIX INDEPENDENT ASSUMPTIONS

Comanche Industries

Assumption 1: The preferred stock is noncumulative and nonparticipating.

	PREFERRED	COMMON	TOTAL
8% of $200,000 (par value of preferred) to preferred stockholders	$16,000		$16,000
Remainder ($80,000 − $16,000) to common stockholders		$64,000	64,000
Total	$16,000	$64,000	$80,000

Assumption 2: The preferred stock is cumulative and nonparticipating; dividends are in arrears for the three preceding years.

	PREFERRED	COMMON	TOTAL
Dividends in arrears, $16,000 (8% of $200,000) for 3 years	$48,000		$48,000
Current year's dividend	16,000		16,000
Remainder ($80,000 − $64,000) to common stockholders		$16,000	16,000
Total	$64,000	$16,000	$80,000

Assumption 3: The preferred stock is noncumulative and fully participating.

	PREFERRED	COMMON	TOTAL
Current year's dividend (8% of $200,000)	$16,000		$16,000
Ratable dividend to common (8% of $300,000)		$24,000	24,000
Amount available for participation: $80,000 − $40,000 = $40,000			
Participation rate:			

$$\frac{\$40,000*}{(\$200,000 + \$300,000)\dagger} = 8\%$$

	PREFERRED	COMMON	TOTAL
Participating dividend:			
To preferred, 8% of $200,000.................	16,000		16,000
To common, 8% of $300,000		24,000	24,000
Total	$32,000	$48,000	$80,000

* Amount available for participation.
† Par value of preferred plus par value of common.

Assumption 4: The preferred stock is cumulative and fully participating; dividends are in arrears for the preceding year.

	PREFERRED	COMMON	TOTAL
Dividends in arrears	$16,000		$16,000
Current year's dividend, including ratable dividend to common	16,000	$24,000	40,000
Amount available for participation: $80,000 − $56,000 = $24,000			
Participation rate:			

$$\frac{\$24,000}{\$500,000} = 4.8\%$$

	PREFERRED	COMMON	TOTAL
Participating dividend:			
To preferred, 4.8% of $200,000	9,600		9,600
To common, 4.8% of $300,000		14,400	14,400
Total	$41,600	$38,400	$80,000

EXHIBIT 21—4 DISTRIBUTION OF DIVIDENDS TO COMMON AND PREFERRED STOCKHOLDERS UNDER SIX INDEPENDENT ASSUMPTIONS (CONTINUED)

Assumption 5: The preferred stock is cumulative and participating up to an additional 3%; dividends are in arrears for the two preceding years.

	PREFERRED	COMMON	TOTAL
Dividends in arrears:			
$16,000 × 2 years	$32,000		$32,000
Current year's dividend, including			
ratable dividend to common	16,000	$24,000	40,000
Amount available for participation:			
$80,000 − $72,000 = $8,000			
Participation rate:			
Participating dividend:*			
To preferred, 1.6% of $200,000	3,200		3,200
To common, 1.6% of $300,000		4,800	4,800
Total	$51,200	$28,800	$80,000

* Since the amount available for participation is less than 3%, the participating dividend in the current year is only 1.6%.

Assumption 6: The preferred stock is cumulative and participating up to an additional 3%; no dividends are in arrears.

	PREFERRED	COMMON	TOTAL
Current year's dividend, including			
ratable dividend to common	$16,000	$24,000	$40,000
Amount available for participation:			
$80,000 − $40,000 = $40,000			
Participation rate.*			

$$\frac{\$40,000}{\$500,000} = 8\%$$

	PREFERRED	COMMON	TOTAL
Participating dividend:			
To preferred, 3% of $200,000.................	6,000		6,000
Remainder ($40,000 − $6,000) to common		34,000	34,000
Total	$22,000	$58,000	$80,000

* The participation rate should be calculated in order to determine if it exceeds 3%. If so, it is ignored in the participating dividend calculation, since preferred stock is limited to an additional 3%. Notice that the *actual* additional participation rate is as follows:

Preferred, 3%

Common, $\dfrac{\$34,000}{\$300,000} = 11.33\%$

APPROPRIATIONS (RESTRICTIONS) OF RETAINED EARNINGS

Corporations often find it necessary or desirable to restrict the payment of dividends to amounts considerably less than the credit balance in retained earnings. Restrictions may arise because of one or more of the following circumstances:

1. *Legal restrictions.* A corporation that purchases its treasury stock may be required to restrict retained earnings equal to the cost of the treasury stock. (This type of restriction was discussed earlier in this chapter and in Chapter 20.)

2. *A desire to retain assets for expansion.* A corporation may wish to retain assets that have arisen from profitable operations for internal expansion purposes.

3. *Contractual restrictions.* A bond indenture, for example, may require a corporation to maintain not less than a specified amount of working capital, thus restricting the amount of liquid assets available for dividends. The indenture also may require that a portion of retained earnings be restricted from availability for dividends during the life of the bond issue. (This type of restriction was discussed in Chapter 16.)

4. *Possibility of future losses.* Corporations often restrict all or a portion of retained earnings from availability for dividends because of expected or possible losses arising from such contingencies as inventory price declines, lawsuits, or risk of uninsured losses from casualties.[14]

These restrictions, if incorporated in the accounts, are referred to as **retained earnings appropriations.** These appropriations communicate to stockholders that there are dividend restrictions. As we shall see below, formal accounting entries are optional. But whether entries are made or not, the restriction may be communicated either by a disaggregation of retained earnings or by a parenthetical or footnote disclosure.

When a corporation's board of directors approves a retained earnings restriction and it is to be recorded in the accounts, the following entry is made:

Retained earnings	*xx*	
Retained earnings appropriated for (given purpose)............		*xx*

The retained earnings appropriation is still a part of the total retained earnings balance since the entry merely subdivides or disaggregates the retained earnings account balance. When the appropriation is no longer necessary, the entry is reversed.

Four types of appropriations are illustrated below:

1. A corporation purchases treasury stock at a cost of $125,000. State law requires that retained earnings available for dividends be restricted by the cost of treasury stock purchased. The entry to record the appropriation is:

Retained earnings	125,000	
Retained earnings appropriated for cost of treasury stock		125,000

When the treasury stock is sold, the entry is reversed.

2. A corporation desires to retain assets for the purpose of expanding a building to

---

[14] The practice of not insuring against possible losses sometimes is described, quite incorrectly, as "self-insurance."

increase its manufacturing capability, and decides to appropriate $25,000 annually for 10 years. Each year it makes the following entry:

Retained earnings	25,000	
Retained earnings appropriated for building expansion		25,000

A retained earnings appropriation does not set aside assets or earmark funds; it is merely a communication device.

Notice that this entry does *not* set aside or earmark assets to be used in building construction. It simply communicates to stockholders that assets that have arisen from profitable operations will be retained and used for expansion purposes.

At the end of 10 years, the appropriation, if no longer needed, is reversed as follows:

Retained earnings appropriated for building expansion	250,000	
Retained earnings		250,000
(10 × $25,000)		

Also, the company may choose to establish a special fund for building expansion and periodically transfer cash to it. As we saw in Chapter 14, the following entry is required if a special fund is created:

Building fund cash	*xx*	
Cash		*xx*

3. A bond indenture requires a company to make annual deposits of $10,000 to a sinking fund designed to retire the debt at maturity. Additionally, retained earnings of $10,000 are to be appropriated each year, since the sinking fund assets are specifically earmarked to retire the bonds. The bonds mature 10 years from the issue date. The yearly entries to record the transfer of assets to the sinking fund and the retained earnings appropriation are as follows:

Sinking fund cash	10,000	
Cash		10,000
Retained earnings	10,000	
Retained earnings appropriated for bond sinking fund		10,000

When the bonds mature, the entries to record the retirement of the debt and the reversal of the appropriation are as follows:

Bonds payable	100,000	
Sinking fund cash*		100,000
Retained earnings appropriated for bond sinking fund	100,000	
Retained earnings		100,000

* Income on assets in the sinking fund are ignored here.

4. A company decides to appropriate $85,000 of retained earnings because of a possible loss due to a decline in inventory prices. If the loss materializes, dividends may be reduced because of the decrease in the value of the company's assets and the accompanying reduction in earnings. The entry to record the appropriation is as follows:

Retained earnings	85,000	
Retained earnings appropriated for possible inventory losses		85,000

Recognition of the possible loss is inappropriate at this point because the economic event giving rise to the loss has not occurred. Under accrual accounting, transactions and other economic events are recognized when they occur. This situation is an example of a contingency. Accounting for contingencies was discussed in Chapter 15. Notice that the above analysis is consistent with the criteria for accruing loss contingencies; that is, loss contingencies are accrued only if it is highly probable that the loss has occurred and if the loss can be reasonably estimated.

When retained earnings are appropriated for future specified contingencies, losses that may subsequently materialize should not be debited to the appropriation account. These losses are a component of net income and must be reported on the income statement. To illustrate, refer to the fourth appropriation above and assume that the realizable value of the company's inventory declines the following year, resulting in a loss of $60,000. No further price declines are expected. The entries to record the loss and reversal of the appropriation are as follows:

Loss on write-down of inventory to realizable value 60,000

    Inventory 60,000

Retained earnings appropriated for possible inventory losses 85,000

    Retained earnings 85,000

A NOTE ON ACCOUNT TITLES

Despite discouragement from the accounting profession, the term "reserve" sometimes is used to refer to appropriations of retained earnings and to other financial statement items, such as those listed below. The suggested titles more accurately describe the accounts.

TITLE SOMETIMES USED	SUGGESTED TITLE
Reserve for bad debts	Allowance for uncollectible accounts
Reserve for depreciation	Accumulated depreciation
Reserve for income taxes	Estimated income taxes payable
Reserve for plant expansion	Retained earnings appropriated for plant expansion

These suggested titles enhance statement users' understanding because they are more representationally faithful.

DISCLOSURE OF RETAINED EARNINGS RESTRICTIONS

As an alternative to formal appropriation entries, retained earnings restrictions can be communicated to stockholders in footnotes. Disclosures may appear directly on the balance sheet in parentheses following the retained earnings account, in notes to the financial statements, or both. For example, the treasury stock appropriation (p. 971) could be disclosed on the company's balance sheet as follows:

Formal journal entries for a retained earnings appropriation are optional, never necessary.

Retained earnings ($125,000 restricted for cost

    of treasury stock purchased—see Note *X*) . . . .*xx*

Note *X*: State law restricts retained earnings available for dividends in an amount equal to the cost of treasury stock purchased by the corporation. In accordance with state law, $125,000 of retained earnings are so restricted and are not available for dividends.

In our opinion, disclosure by note is preferable, since it is less confusing than a formal appropriation, and in many cases a formal appropriation still may require additional commentary in the financial statement notes. Furthermore, because companies generally do not intend to pay dividends equal to the unappropriated retained earnings balance, subdividing the account balance appears to add little information.

STATEMENT OF STOCKHOLDERS' EQUITY

Under the full disclosure principle, financial reports include a statement that shows the changes in retained earnings during the accounting period. When such a statement includes changes in contributed capital, it is usually referred to as a statement of stockholders' equity. Such a statement for Shoney's, Inc., appears in Exhibit 21–5. Notice that the statement discloses all significant transactions that affected the stockholders' equity accounts during the accounting period—dividends declared, acquisitions and issuances of common stock, and other capital transactions. This statement complements the other required financial statements by disclosing information not found directly in the other statements and thus increases usefulness.

QUASI-REORGANIZATIONS

A corporation that experiences continued losses may accumulate a debit balance—a deficit—in retained earnings. A deficit may also arise if assets—currently overstated because a change in economic conditions has diminished their value—are adjusted to fair market value. In many states the deficit may prevent the corporation from paying dividends until

EXHIBIT 21–5   STATEMENT OF STOCKHOLDERS' EQUITY

Shoney's, Inc., and Subsidiaries

	COMMON STOCK	ADDITIONAL PAID-IN CAPITAL	RETAINED EARNINGS	TOTAL STOCKHOLDERS' EQUITY
Balances at October 30, 1983	$20,197,253	$19,768,365	$ 98,026,177	$137,991,795
Net income			30,180,460	30,180,460
Tax benefits related to nonqualified stock options		834,331		834,331
Exercise of employee stock options	89,052	435,825		524,877
Deferred compensation agreement	9,480	40,520		50,000
Conversion of debentures	954,609	13,335,287		14,289,896
Cash dividends—$.12 a share			(3,315,476)	(3,315,476)
Four-for-three stock split	7,083,465	(7,083,465)		
Balances at October 28, 1984	$28,333,859	$27,330,863	$124,891,161	$180,555,883
Net income			37,211,104	37,211,104
Tax benefits related to nonqualified stock options		1,737,053		1,737,053
Exercise of employee stock options	149,692	566,575		716,267
Deferred compensation agreement	14,220	48,030		62,250
Cash dividends—$.15 a share			(4,265,710)	(4,265,710)
Sale of stock by unconsolidated affiliate		1,272,201		1,272,201
Other	7,253	(15,541)		(8,288)
Balances at October 27, 1985	$28,505,024	$30,939,181	$157,836,555	$217,280,760

Source: Shoney's, Inc., 1985 Annual Report, p. 23.

it is fully eliminated by future net income. Even though the operating activities of the corporation may be capable of generating future cash flows and the corporation may have what appears to be a promising future, it may have difficulty obtaining capital to improve profitability if potential investors are aware of its inability to pay dividends as long as a retained earnings deficit exists. Furthermore, an inability to obtain capital may result in future losses and eventual insolvency or bankruptcy.

Under these circumstances, many states allow a company to eliminate its retained earnings deficit, revalue its assets, and proceed as a going concern without legally reorganizing. Such an arrangement is called a **quasi-reorganization.** A quasi-reorganization may be preferable to a legal reorganization because of the time and money required for legal reorganization. Quasi-reorganization initially became popular in the 1930s as a result of companies' upward appraisals of assets before that time. These appraised values turned out to be much greater than realizable values.

A quasi-reorganization allows a company to make a fresh start from an accounting standpoint, as if the company were being started at the date of the quasi-reorganization by acquiring assets and recording them at fair market value.

The following procedures take place in a quasi-reorganization:

1. Assets are revalued to current fair market value. While some individual assets may be written up to fair market value, generally there is a write-down of assets in the aggregate.[15] This revaluation process increases the deficit in retained earnings.

2. The retained earnings deficit is eliminated (the balance is reduced to zero) by reducing the balances in the contributed capital accounts and increasing (crediting) retained earnings. In some instances, contributed capital may be decreased through stockholder donations of capital stock or by reducing the par value of the shares outstanding.

3. In subsequent financial statements, retained earnings is dated for a reasonable number of years to show that a quasi-reorganization has been effected.

To illustrate a quasi-reorganization, assume that Indy Corporation has incurred operating losses for many years and decides, with the approval of stockholders, to undergo a quasi-reorganization. The balance sheet as of December 31, 1987, is as follows:

> The accounting characteristics of a quasi-reorganization are a write-down of assets and the elimination of a retained earnings deficit.

ASSETS		LIABILITIES AND STOCKHOLDERS' EQUITY	
Current assets	$ 70,000	Current liabilities	$ 30,000
Plant and equipment, net	100,000	Common stock (par $5, 40,000 shares outstanding)	200,000
Other assets	30,000	Contributed capital in excess of par	20,000
		Retained earnings	(50,000)
	$200,000		$200,000

[15] We believe that a net *write-up* of assets is inconsistent with the economic conditions that originally led to the use of quasi-reorganizations. A sustained series of operating losses implies that an operating asset's (or group of operating assets') present (fair market) value is less than book value. An exception might occur when a *nonoperating* asset, such as land, is written up in an amount that exceeds the write-down of the *operating* assets in the aggregate.

The quasi-reorganization is carried out as follows:

1. Inventories, included in current assets, are written down by $10,000 to net realizable value.

2. Plant and equipment are written down by $20,000 to fair market value.

3. Other assets are decreased by $10,000 to fair market value.

4. Stockholders agree to donate 5,000 shares of stock to Indy Corporation.

5. The par value of the remaining shares outstanding is reduced to $3 per share.

Indy would record the quasi-reorganization as follows:

Retained earnings	40,000	
Inventories (current assets)		10,000
Plant and equipment.		20,000
Other assets.		10,000
To revalue assets to fair market value.		
Common stock	25,000	
Contributed capital in excess of par		25,000
To record donations (5,000 × $5).		
Common stock	70,000	
Contributed capital in excess of par		70,000
To record the reduction of par value from $5 per share to $3 per share on the remaining shares outstanding (35,000 × $2).		
Contributed capital in excess of par	90,000	
Retained earnings		90,000
To eliminate the deficit in retained earnings. The sum of the initial deficit of $50,000 in retained earnings plus the $40,000 debit to that account.		

Before a quasi-reorganization is effected, stockholders must approve it. Furthermore, the revaluation of assets must be based on reliable estimates of fair market values.

Indy's balance sheet after the quasi-reorganization appears below. The dating of retained earnings is shown parenthetically in the stockholders' equity section of the balance sheet.

ASSETS		LIABILITIES AND STOCKHOLDERS' EQUITY	
Current assets	$ 60,000	Current liabilities.	$ 30,000
Plant and equipment.	80,000	Common stock ($3 par, 35,000 shares outstanding)	105,000
Other assets.	20,000	Contributed capital in excess of par	25,000
		Retained earnings (quasi-reorganization effected 12/31/87)	–0–
	$160,000		$160,000

STOCKHOLDERS' EQUITY: AN OVERVIEW

As we have seen in the last two chapters, under current accounting practice it is customary to disaggregate stockholders' equity into many subclassifications. These classifications have as their objective the disclosure of capital by source. Based on the transactions presented in these chapters, the common classifications are as follows:

Contributed capital:	
Capital stock: Preferred (at par)	$*xxx*
Common (at par)	*xxx*
Common (preferred) stock subscribed	*xxx*
Stock dividends (common or preferred) distributable	*xxx*
Treasury stock (par value method)	(*xxx*)
Other contributed capital:	
Contributed capital in excess of par	*xxx*
Donated capital	*xxx*
Contributed capital from treasury stock transactions	*xxx*
Contributed capital from retirement of stock	*xxx*
Contributed capital—stock options	*xxx*
Contributed capital—stock warrants outstanding	*xxx*
	$*xxx*
Retained earnings:	
Appropriated for (specific reason)	$*xxx*
Unappropriated	*xxx*
Less:[16] Treasury stock (cost method)	(*xxx*)
Unrealized losses on noncurrent marketable equity securities	(*xxx*)
Total stockholders' equity	$*xxx*

In practice, companies often combine any other contributed capital accounts that may exist and present them as a single amount.

Since we defined stockholders' equity in Chapter 2 as a residual amount—the difference between total assets and total liabilities—conceptually there is no reason why we could not aggregate the various classifications shown above into one single amount for balance sheet reporting. This approach has many positive implications from an instructional standpoint. First, accounting for many of the stockholders' equity transactions would be simplified. To illustrate, several transactions from Chapter 20 and this chapter appear in Exhibit 21–6. Beside each page reference is the entry that would be made under the above suggestion. You should compare each original entry with the one shown in Exhibit 21–6. Second, this approach provides a precise conceptual overview of the effects of various transactions on stockholders' equity. Finally, if stockholders' equity were presented as a single amount, detailed information about its components—par values, shares outstanding, shares and cost of shares held in treasury, retained earnings, retained earnings restrictions, and other information—could be disclosed in the notes to the financial statements.

---

[16] Foreign currency translation adjustments, discussed in advanced accounting, also appear here as additions or subtractions.

EXHIBIT 21—6   SELECTED STOCKHOLDERS' EQUITY TRANSACTIONS
WITH AGGREGATION

TEXT PAGE NUMBER	AGGREGATED ENTRY		
925	Cash 500,000		
	Stockholders' equity		500,000
928 (fourth entry)	Stockholders' equity 2,000		
	Subscriptions receivable		800
	Cash		1,200
934 (first entry)	No entry; no effect on net assets		
939 (first entry)	Stockholders' equity 15,000		
	Cash		15,000
942 (first entry)	Stockholders' equity 530,000		
	Cash		530,000
942 (transactions 2,3,4)	Cash	xx	
	Stockholders' equity		xx
	2: $112,000; 3: $144,000;		
	4: no entry		
964	No entries required		
971	No entries required		

SUMMARY OF IMPORTANT TOPICS AND CONCEPT APPLICATIONS

1. Contributed capital and retained earnings are the two major subdivisions of stockholders' equity. Contributed capital is that portion of equity arising from stockholder investments. Retained earnings include the portion of equity that has arisen from a company's profitable operations.

2. Retained earnings may be increased or decreased by net income or net loss, prior period adjustments, and some changes in accounting principle. Dividends and some capital stock transactions decrease retained earnings. A quasi-reorganization increases retained earnings.

3. Corporations distribute many types of dividends—cash, scrip, property, liquidating, and stock. Except for stock dividends, all of these types of dividends are recorded at the **fair market value** of the assets given up.

4. Stock dividends and stock splits do not affect net assets or total stockholders' equity, but rather are distributions of additional shares of a company's stock to existing shareholders. The effects of these share distributions are as follows:

		EFFECT ON		
TYPE	RECORDED AT	RETAINED EARNINGS	PAR VALUE PER SHARE	TOTAL PAR VALUE OF SHARES
Small stock dividend	Fair market value	Decreased	Unchanged	Increased
Large stock dividend	Legal requirements (usually par value)	Decreased	Unchanged	Increased
Stock split	Not recorded	No effect	Decreased	Unchanged

5. Preferred stock has preference over common stock in dividend distributions and may be cumulative and/or participating. A cumulative feature means that all dividend arrearages on preferred stock must be satisfied before common shareholders can receive any dividends. A participating feature allows preferred shareholders to participate with common shareholders in receiving dividends, if declared, in excess of the stated dividend rate on preferred.

6. Companies often find it necessary to restrict dividends. Dividend restrictions may be communicated to shareholders and other financial statement users through the footnotes or through formal retained earnings appropriations.

7. A statement of stockholders' equity is a summary of changes in the various stockholders' equity accounts during an accounting period.

8. A quasi-reorganization may occur when a company has overvalued net assets and has experienced continued losses over a period of time. The accounting characteristics of a quasi-reorganization are (1) a downward revaluation of assets to fair market value, (2) elimination of a retained earnings deficit, and (3) dating of retained earnings for a reasonable period of time in order to disclose that a quasi-reorganization has occurred.

QUESTIONS

Q21-1. List the types of transactions that affect retained earnings.

Q21-2. What considerations influence a corporate board of directors' decisions regarding dividends?

Q21-3. Comment on the following statement: ''A corporation pays dividends out of retained earnings.''

Q21-4. Define the following dates related to cash dividends:

1. Declaration date.

2. Date of record.

3. Payment date.

Q21-5. **A)** What is a property dividend?
B) Describe the proper accounting for property dividends.

Q21-6. **A)** Why do corporations initiate stock splits?
B) Why is the distinction between large and small stock dividends important from an accounting standpoint?

Q21-7. Compare a stock split and a large stock dividend in the following areas:

1. Par value of shares after issuance.

2. Shares outstanding after issuance.

3. Balance in the common stock account after issuance.

4. Effect on legal capital.

5. Market price of shares after issuance.

6. Effect on retained earnings.

Q21-8. **A)** What is a scrip dividend?
B) Why do corporations occasionally issue scrip dividends?

Q21-9. Discuss the purpose of an appropriation of retained earnings and give some examples of circumstances that may give rise to appropriations.

Q21-10. Discuss the use of fractional share warrants in connection with issuances of small stock dividends.

Q21-11. Why do corporations sometimes initiate quasi-reorganizations?

Q21-12. Describe the procedures involved in accounting for a quasi-reorganization.

Q21-13. **A)** Give some examples of the misuse of the term ''reserve'' in financial statements.
B) What position has the accounting profession taken in regard to the use of the term ''reserve''?

Q21-14. Why is it important that liquidating dividends be identified as such in financial statements?

Q21-15. What transactions and events could appear on a statement of changes in stockholders' equity?

Q21-16. Indicate where the following items would appear in a corporation's financial statements:

1. Cash dividends declared.

2. Property dividends payable.

3. Warrants outstanding as a result of a stock dividend.

4. An appropriation of retained earnings for a purchase of treasury stock.

5. Stock dividends distributable.

6. A 4-for-1 stock split.

Q21-17. **A)** What is meant by a stock split effected in the form of a dividend?

B) From an accounting viewpoint, how does a stock split effected in the form of a dividend differ from an ordinary stock dividend?

C) How should a stock dividend that has been declared but not yet issued be classified in a statement of financial position? Why?

(AICPA, adapted)

CASES

C21-1. DIVIDEND PAYING ABILITY: ALTERNATIVE DIVIDEND PROPOSALS   The board of directors of Classic Autos has met to discuss dividends for 1987 and has asked you to evaluate various proposals. Classic Auto's December 31, 1987, balance sheet appears below:

ASSETS			LIABILITIES AND EQUITY		
Cash		$ 125,000	Current liabilities		$ 140,000
Short-term investments			Long-term notes payable		60,000
(market value, $90,000)		210,000	Common stock ($10 par,		
Long-term investments		595,000	40,000 shares outstanding)		400,000
Plant and equipment, net		60,000	Contributed capital in		
Other assets		40,000	excess of par		80,000
			Reserve for investment losses		120,000
			Reserve for plant expansion		20,000
			Retained earnings		
			(unappropriated)		210,000
		$1,030,000			$1,030,000

The following alternative dividend proposals have been made by board members:

a) Mr. Cord proposes that a cash dividend be paid equal to the unappropriated balance in retained earnings.

b) Mr. Studebaker proposes that the reserves be used to pay dividends.

c) Mr. Leeacoca proposes that all of the retained earnings be distributed.

d) Mr. De Soto proposes that dividends be paid equal to the cash balance of $125,000.

e) Mr. Edsel proposes that the short-term investments be distributed as a dividend and that the dividend be measured at $210,000.

f) Mr. Ferrari proposes that short-term and long-term investments be sold and that dividends be paid equal to total stockholders' equity less the par value of shares outstanding.

g) Mr. Saturn proposes that a 10 percent stock dividend be distributed and that the dividend be measured at par value.

h) Mr. Hudson proposes that 40,000 additional shares be distributed to the shareholders on a pro rata basis and that the dividend be measured at par value.

REQUIRED

1. Draft a response to each of the board members' proposals.

2. Draft a response outlining a recommendation for the payment of a cash dividend.

C21-2. STOCK DIVIDENDS The Wiz Corporation, a client, is considering the authorization of a 5 percent common stock dividend. The financial vice-president of Wiz wishes to discuss the accounting implications of such an authorization with you before the next meeting of the board of directors.

REQUIRED

1. The first topic he wishes to discuss is the nature of the stock dividend to the recipient.
   a) Discuss the case *for* considering the stock dividend as income to the recipient.
   b) Discuss the case *against* considering the stock dividend as income to the recipient. (*Hint:* You may want to review this discussion in Chapter 14.)

2. The other topic for discussion is the propriety of issuing the stock dividend to all ''stockholders of record'' or to ''stockholders of record exclusive of shares held in the name of the Corporation as treasury stock.''
   a) Discuss the case *for* issuing stock dividends on treasury shares.
   b) Discuss the case *against* issuing stock dividends on treasury shares.

(AICPA, adapted)

C21-3. STOCK DIVIDENDS VS. STOCK SPLITS The directors of Shirley Corporation are considering the issuance of a stock dividend. They have asked you to discuss the proposed action by answering the questions below.

REQUIRED

1. What is a stock dividend? How is a stock dividend distinguished from a stock split *(a)* from a legal standpoint? *(b)* from an accounting standpoint?

2. For what reasons does a corporation usually declare a stock dividend? a stock split?

3. Discuss the amount, if any, of retained earnings to be capitalized in connection with a stock dividend.

(AICPA, adapted)

C21-4. RETAINED EARNINGS RESTRICTIONS: APPROPRIATIONS VS. FOOTNOTE DISCLOSURES The stockholders' equity section of Jerrold Corporation's balance sheet as of December 31, 1987, appears below:

Preferred stock (no par, 5,000 shares outstanding)	$ 20,000
Common stock ($5 par, 10,000 shares outstanding)	50,000
Contributed capital in excess of par—common	25,000
Retained earnings	
Appropriated for plant expansion	5,000
Appropriated for inventory losses	2,500
Appropriated for treasury stock	3,000
Appropriated for bonded indebtedness	5,000
Unappropriated	10,000
Treasury stock (par value method)	(3,000)
Total	$117,500

Additional information:
   a) The plant expansion appropriation represents an estimate of the cost of enlarging the plant. The expansion will begin next year.
   b) The inventory appropriation represents a write-down of inventory to net realizable value, recorded as follows:

Loss on inventory	2,500	
Retained earnings appropriated for inventory losses		2,500

c) State law requires that retained earnings be restricted equal to the cost of treasury stock purchases. Cost of purchases to date totals $5,000.

d) Jerrold issued bonds several years ago. The bond indenture requires that retained earnings restrictions be in effect until the bonds mature. The bonds were extinguished before maturity during the 1987 fiscal year.

Jerrold's management has asked you to reconstruct the stockholders' equity section of the balance sheet as of December 31, 1987, under the assumption that formal appropriations are to be eliminated and that restrictions of retained earnings are to be disclosed in notes to the financial statements.

REQUIRED

Prepare the stockholders' equity section of Jerrold's balance sheet and draft the notes to its financial statements to disclose the appropriate restrictions of retained earnings.

C21-5. STOCK DIVIDENDS The board of directors of Glenn, Inc., declared an "ordinary stock dividend" equal to 5 percent of the corporation's outstanding common stock, to be issued to common stockholders of record as of April 15, 1988. The corporation's treasury stock was to be used for this purpose to the extent available. The market value of the common stock just before the declaration was $64 per share, and it remained at substantially that figure for more than a month after the dividend shares were issued.

The corporation's equity accounts at the dates of declaration and record included the following balances:

Preferred stock, $5 cumulative (no par): authorized, 25,000 shares; in treasury, 130 shares; outstanding, 10,402 shares	$1,053,200
Common stock (par $50): authorized, 50,000 shares; in treasury, 880 shares; outstanding, 27,780 shares	1,433,000
Additional contributed capital—amounts contributed in excess of par value of common shares	251,464
Retained earnings	963,425
Treasury stock, $5 cumulative preferred (at cost)	14,922
Treasury stock, common (at cost)	40,920

At the time of declaration, the board directed that retained earnings in the amount of the aggregate par value of the dividend shares be transferred to the appropriate permanent capital accounts.

REQUIRED

1. Prepare an entry to record the net effect of the board's actions.

2. Discuss the Glenn board's action in regard to the retained earnings transfer in the light of generally accepted accounting principles.

3. Assuming that the entry in part 1 had not been made and that the board had followed GAAP, prepare an entry that will give effect to the issuance of the stock dividend in accordance with the recommendations.

4. Assume the same facts as set forth above, except that the dividend declaration equaled 40 percent (instead of 5 percent) of the outstanding common shares and resulted in a substantial reduction in the market value of the common shares of Glenn, Inc.

a) Discuss the generally accepted method of accounting in these circumstances.

b) Does the board's transfer of retained earnings on a par value basis conflict with or conform to the generally accepted method? Explain.

(AICPA, adapted)

C21-6. QUASI-REORGANIZATIONS The Aaron Company, a medium-sized manufacturer, has been experiencing losses for the five years that it has been doing business. Although the operations for the year just ended resulted in a loss, several important changes resulted in a profitable fourth quarter, and the future operations of the company are expected to be profitable.

The treasurer suggests that there be a quasi-reorganization to (1) eliminate the accumulated deficit of $423,620, (2) write up the $493,100 cost of operating land and buildings to their fair market value, and (3) set up an asset of $203,337 representing the estimated future tax benefit of the losses accumulated to date.

REQUIRED

1. What are the characteristics of a quasi-reorganization? That is, of what does it consist?

2. List the conditions under which a quasi-reorganization generally would be justified.

3. Discuss the propriety of the treasurer's proposals to:
   a) Eliminate the deficit of $423,620.
   b) Write up the cost of the operating land and buildings to their fair market value.
   c) Set up an asset of $203,337 representing the future tax benefit of the losses accumulated to date.

(AICPA, adapted)

EXERCISES

E21-1. TRANSACTIONS AFFECTING RETAINED EARNINGS For each of the transactions below, indicate the effect on retained earnings, using + for increase, − for decrease, or 0 for no effect. Consider each transaction separately.

_____ 1. Declaration of a scrip dividend.

_____ 2. Correction of an error involving an asset acquired two years ago. The asset had a 10-year useful life but was expensed when it was purchased.

_____ 3. An appropriation for contingencies.

_____ 4. A net loss for the year.

_____ 5. Distribution of a previously declared stock dividend.

_____ 6. A sale of treasury stock in excess of cost.

_____ 7. A 2-for-1 stock split.

_____ 8. Reversal of a previously recorded appropriation.

_____ 9. Declaration of a cash dividend.

_____ 10. Net income for the year.

_____ 11. Receipt of land as a donation.

_____ 12. An extraordinary loss from a flood.

_____ 13. Declaration and payment of a property dividend.

_____ 14. Purchase of goodwill in the acquisition of another company.

_____ 15. A quasi-reorganization.

E21-2. CASH AND SCRIP DIVIDENDS Jay Corporation's stockholders' equity accounts at the end of 1987 appear below:

8% preferred stock ($10 par, 50,000 shares issued)	$ 500,000
Common stock ($2 par, 90,000 shares issued)	180,000
Contributed capital in excess of par	
Preferred	125,000
Common	180,000
Retained earnings ($64,000 restricted for cost of treasury stock).......	400,000
Treasury stock (8,000 shares of common, at cost)	(64,000)
Total	$1,321,000

The following transactions occurred during 1988:

1/15/88   Declared the annual preferred stock dividend, payable on 2/10, to stockholders of record on 2/1.

1/20/88   Sold 1,000 shares of treasury stock for $11,000.

2/10/88   Paid the preferred dividend.

3/1/88   Declared a $1 per share cash dividend on outstanding common shares, payable 4/15 to stockholders of record on 3/25.

4/15/88   Paid the common stock dividend.

9/1/88   Declared a scrip dividend of $1 per share to common stockholders payable 11/30 to stockholders of record on 10/1. The scrip notes bear interest at 8%.

11/30/88 Recorded interest on the scrip dividend and paid the interest and dividend to common stockholders.

12/31/88 Closed the net income of $226,000 for 1988 to retained earnings.

REQUIRED

1. Record the above transactions.

2. Prepare Jay Corporation's stockholders' equity section of the balance sheet at the end of 1988.

E21-3.   PROPERTY DIVIDENDS; STOCK DIVIDENDS

A) Raulo Corporation owned 1 million shares of marketable equity securities of Sub Corporation. On December 31, 1987, when Raulo's account, investment in common stock of Sub Corporation, had a carrying value of $8 per share, Raulo distributed these shares to its stockholders as a dividend. Raulo originally paid $10 for each share. Sub has 2 million shares issued and outstanding, which are traded on a national stock exchange. The quoted market price for a Sub share was $4 on the declaration date and $3 on the distribution date.

REQUIRED

Prepare the entry or entries to record the property dividend.

B) The stockholders' equity of Slumber Company on July 31, 1987, is presented below:

Common stock, par value $20: authorized, 400,000 shares;
   issued and outstanding, 150,000 shares $3,000,000
Contributed capital in excess of par   140,000
Retained earnings   390,000
                                                             $3,530,000

On August 1, 1987, the board of directors of Slumber declared a 4 percent stock dividend on common stock, to be distributed on September 15. The market price of Slumber's common stock was $35 on August 1, 1987, and $40 on September 15, 1987.

REQUIRED

Prepare the entries to record the declaration on August 1, 1987, and the distribution on September 15, 1987.

(AICPA, adapted)

E21-4.   DIVIDENDS Using the format shown below, indicate the effect on assets, liabilities, and stockholders' equity of the items set forth below. For no change write 0, for an increase +, and for a decrease −.

	ASSETS	LIABILITIES	STOCKHOLDERS' EQUITY
1. Declaration of a stock dividend.			
2. Declaration of a cash dividend.			
3. Issuance of new shares in place of old shares associated with a stock split.			
4. Distribution of stock dividend in part 1.			
5. Payment of cash dividend in part 2.			

(CGAA, adapted)

E21-5. STOCK DIVIDENDS; STOCK SPLITS   Stockholders' equity account balances for Douglas, Inc., are as follows:

Common stock ($5 par, 40,000 shares issued and outstanding) $200,000
Contributed capital in excess of par 200,000
Retained earnings 400,000
$800,000

REQUIRED

1. Prepare all entries to record the transactions and events for the four cases below. Consider each case separately.

  a) Douglas declares and issues a 10 percent stock dividend when the fair market value of its stock is $20 per share.
  b) Douglas declares and issues a 100 percent stock dividend. The dividend is to be measured at par value.
  c) Douglas declares and issues a 40 percent stock dividend. The dividend is to be measured at the average contributed capital per share.
  d) Douglas declares and effects a 4-for-1 stock split.

2. For each case in part 1, prepare the resulting stockholders' equity section of Douglas' balance sheet.

E21-6. DIVIDEND PREFERENCES ON PREFERRED STOCK   Bobo Corporation has the following capital stock outstanding:

Common ($5 par, 50,000 shares outstanding) $250,000
10% preferred ($50 par, 1,000 shares outstanding) 50,000

Bobo has decided to declare and issue a cash dividend of $50,000 during the current year.

REQUIRED

Determine how the $50,000 dividend would be distributed among the common and preferred stockholders under the following independent situations:

1. The preferred stock is cumulative and nonparticipating; dividends are in arrears for the two preceding years.

2. The preferred stock is noncumulative and fully participating.

3. The preferred stock is noncumulative and participating up to an additional 4 percent.

4. The preferred stock is cumulative and participating up to an additional 3 percent. Dividends are in arrears for the preceding two years.

5. The preferred stock is cumulative and fully participating. Dividends are in arrears for the preceding year.

E21-7. DIVIDEND PREFERENCES ON PREFERRED STOCK During the current year Twang paid the following cash dividends to common and preferred stockholders:

Common $39,000
Preferred 27,000

Par value of the outstanding preferred stock is $100,000, and the par value of the outstanding common stock is $300,000. The dividend distribution includes an additional 6 percent participating dividend, as the preferred stock is fully participating. The preferred stock is cumulative, and dividends were in arrears for the two preceding years.

REQUIRED

Calculate the stated dividend rate on the preferred shares.

E21-8. DIVIDENDS; FRACTIONAL SHARE WARRANTS Ross Corporation had the following balances in its stockholders' equity accounts at the beginning of 1987:

10% preferred stock ($2 par, 20,000 shares issued) . . . . $ 40,000
Common stock (no-par, 50,000 shares issued) 125,000
Contributed capital in excess of par—preferred. 80,000
Retained earnings
   Appropriated for the cost of treasury stock 9,000
   Unappropriated 316,000
Treasury stock (1,000 shares of preferred, at cost) . . . . (9,000)
     Total $561,000

During 1987 the following transactions occurred:

1/10/87   Declared the annual preferred stock dividend.

2/15/87   Declared and distributed a 15% common stock dividend to common stockholders when the fair market value of Ross's shares was $12 per share. Six thousand shares and fractional share warrants for 1,500 shares were issued.

2/25/87   Paid the preferred stock dividend.

3/1/87   Sold the treasury shares for $8 per share.

3/10/87   Split the preferred stock, 2 for 1.

3/25/87   Fractional share warrants for 1,200 shares were received by Ross, and the shares were issued. The remaining warrants expired.

6/1/87   Declared and issued a 100% stock dividend on outstanding common shares. The dividend was measured at the average contributed capital per share.

REQUIRED

1. Record the above transactions in journal form.

2. Prepare Ross Corporation's stockholders' equity section of the balance sheet after the above transactions have taken place.

E21-9. STOCKHOLDERS' EQUITY TRANSACTIONS The following transactions occurred during the current year for Hodge Industries:

a) Declared and issued as a property dividend 600 shares of Charley Company held as a long-term investment. Information about the investment in Charley appears below:

SHARES HELD	COST	MARKET VALUE AT DIVIDEND DATE
3,600	$21,600	$32,400

b) Established a retained earnings appropriation of $20,000 for possible future losses on a contract to purchase minerals.

c) Purchased at a cost of $10,000 its own no-par common shares to be held as treasury stock. Hodge uses the par value method, and the issue price associated with the shares purchased was $8,800. State law requires that retained earnings equal to the cost of treasury shares held be appropriated.

d) Established a retained earnings appropriation of $100,000 for future building expansion.

e) Incurred a $16,000 loss on the mineral contract.

f) Sold the treasury shares for $11,500.

g) Hodge has a bond sinking fund (and a retained earnings appropriation) established to retire long-term bonds payable. During the year Hodge transferred $15,000 in cash to the sinking fund.

h) At the end of the year Hodge eliminated all previous retained earnings appropriations, except for the sinking fund, and established an appropriation for possible litigation totaling $130,000.

REQUIRED

Prepare the journal entries to record the above transactions.

E21-10. TRANSACTIONS AFFECTING STOCKHOLDERS' EQUITY   Using the format shown below, indicate the effect in terms of assets, liabilities, and stockholders' equity of the items set forth below. For no change write 0, for an increase +, and for a decrease −.

| | | | STOCKHOLDERS' EQUITY | | |
	ASSETS	LIABILITIES	CAPITAL STOCK	OTHER CONTRIBUTED CAPITAL	RETAINED EARNINGS
1. Net income for period					
2. Cash dividends declared					
3. Payment of dividend in part 2					
4. Declaration and distribution of small stock dividend					
5. Declaration of large stock dividend					
6. Distribution of stock dividend in part 5					
7. 2-for-1 stock split					
8. Prior period adjustment—correction of asset understatement					
9. Prior period adjustment—correction of liability overstatement					
10. Retained earnings appropriation					
11. Reversal of appropriation in part 10					
12. Declaration of a scrip dividend					
13. Declaration and payment of a property dividend					
14. Liability canceled as a donation					
15. Expiration of previously issued fractional share warrants					
16. Purchase of treasury stock at less than original issue price—par value method used					
17. Resale of treasury stock in part 16 at more than par value					
18. A change in accounting principle that increases liabilities					
19. Acquisition of another company's common stock through an issuance of previously unissued preferred stock					
20. Net loss for period					

E21-11. SCRIP AND PROPERTY DIVIDENDS   On March 1, 1987, Patrick Company declared a scrip dividend of $2 per share on 30,000 outstanding shares of common stock. The scrip notes carried a 10 percent rate of interest until such time as the dividend was paid. Patrick's fiscal year ends June 30, and on June 30, 1987, Patrick accrued the interest on the scrip dividend. On December 1, 1987, Patrick distributed 1,000 shares of Ireland Corporation stock held as an investment in settlement of the dividend due. Patrick had paid $20 per share for the Ireland stock, which had a market price of $58 per share on December 1, 1987. Patrick also paid scrip holders cash for the amount due in excess of the market value of the Ireland shares distributed.

REQUIRED

Prepare the entries required by Patrick Company on the following dates:

1. March 1, 1987.
2. June 30, 1987.
3. December 1, 1987.

E21-12. STOCKHOLDERS' EQUITY TRANSACTIONS   For each of the following numbered items you are to select the corresponding lettered effect or effects on the corporation's statements. If there is no appropriate response among the effects listed, leave the item blank. If more than one effect is applicable to a particular item, list *all* applicable letters.

ITEM

1. Declaration of a cash dividend due in one month on noncumulative preferred stock.
2. Declaration and distribution of an ordinary stock dividend.
3. Receipt of a cash dividend, not previously recorded, on stock of another corporation.
4. Passing of a dividend on cumulative preferred stock.
5. Receipt of preferred shares as a dividend on stock held as a temporary investment.
6. Payment of dividend in part 1.
7. Issue of new common shares in a 5-for-1 stock split.

EFFECT

a) Reduces working capital.
b) Increases working capital.
c) Reduces the dollar amount of total capital stock.
d) Increases the dollar amount of total capital stock.
e) Reduces total retained earnings.
f) Increases total retained earnings.
g) Reduces equity per share of common stock.
h) Reduces equity of each common stockholder.

(AICPA, adapted)

E21-13. RETAINED EARNINGS TRANSACTIONS   The retained earnings account for Sheree Company had a credit balance of $100,000 at the end of 1987. Selected transactions affecting stockholders' equity during 1988 were as follows:

a) Net income for 1988, $62,000.
b) Cash dividends declared, $28,000.
c) Purchased treasury stock (par value, $6,000) at a cost of $10,000. Sheree uses the par value method, and the stock was originally sold at par.
d) Stock dividends were declared and measured at $3,200.
e) Sold treasury stock in part *c* for $8,900.
f) Sheree Company made a retained earnings appropriation of $4,500 for possible investment losses.
g) Declared and distributed a 3-for-1 stock split on 10,000 shares of $3 par common stock.
h) Corrected an error made in 1983. The correcting entry was as follows:

Plant and equipment............................12,000
    Accumulated depreciation   4,000
    Prior period adjustment   8,000

REQUIRED

Calculate Sheree's retained earnings balance as of December 31, 1988.

E21-14. APPROPRIATIONS: STOCK DIVIDENDS On January 15, 1987, the directors of Western Company voted to appropriate $80,000 of retained earnings and to retain assets equal to the appropriation for use in expanding the corporation's plant. This was the fifth such appropriation of $80,000. On January 16 the company had the following stockholders' equity accounts:

Common stock, $10 par value: 400,000 shares
    authorized, 300,000 issued $3,000,000
Contributed capital in excess of par   75,000
Retained earnings appropriated for plant expansion................... 400,000
Unappropriated retained earnings 120,000

    Total stockholders' equity $3,595,000

On February 15 Western contracted for the construction of the plant addition for which appropriations had been made. On October 15, when the addition was completed, Western paid Acme Builders, the contractor, $387,000, the amount of the contract.

On November 15 the directors returned the balance of the retained earnings appropriated for plant expansion account to unappropriated retained earnings. At the same time a stock dividend was declared capitalizing the amount previously carried in the appropriation account. The stock at that time was trading at $12.50 per share. The dividend was distributed December 15.

REQUIRED

1. Prepare the journal entries on:
   a) January 15, 1987.
   b) October 15, 1987.
   c) November 15, 1987.
   d) December 15, 1987.

2. Prepare the stockholders' equity section of the balance sheet as of December 15, 1987.

(CGAA, adapted)

E21-15. QUASI-REORGANIZATION Current conditions warrant a quasi-reorganization of the Austin Company on December 31, 1987. Selected balance sheet items before the quasi-reorganization are as follows:
    a) Inventory was recorded in the accounting records on December 31, 1987, at its fair market value of $3 million.
    b) Property, plant, and equipment was recorded in the accounting records on December 31, 1987, at $6 million net of accumulated depreciation.
    c) Stockholders' equity consisted of:

Common stock, par value $10 per share; authorized, issued,
    and outstanding, 350,000 shares $3,500,000
Contributed capital in excess of par 800,000
Retained earnings (deficit) .... (450,000)

    Total stockholders' equity $3,850,000

    d) Inventory cost on December 31, 1987, was $3.25 million.
    e) Property, plant, and equipment had a fair market value of $4 million.
    f) The par value of the common stock is to be reduced from $10 per share to $5 per share.

REQUIRED

Prepare the stockholders' equity section of the Austin Company's balance sheet as of December 31, 1987, as it should appear after the quasi-reorganization has been accomplished.

(AICPA, adapted)

E21-16. QUASI-REORGANIZATION For the last several years Dykes Lumber Company has suffered losses. The company's controller believes that a quasi-reorganization will allow the company to get on its feet, secure additional credit, operate profitably, and pay dividends in the near future.

The balance sheet prepared before the reorganization showed the following:

ASSETS		LIABILITIES AND STOCKHOLDERS' EQUITY	
Cash	$ 5,000	Current liabilities	$144,000
Receivables, net	38,000	Long-term liabilities	300,000
Inventories	126,000	Common stock (par $100)	250,000
Plant and equipment, net	300,000	Preferred stock (par $50)	50,000
Prepaid expenses	5,000	Other contributed capital	60,000
Goodwill	70,000	Retained earnings (deficit)	(225,000)
Deferred charges	35,000		
	$579,000		$579,000

Stockholders and creditors have approved the following quasi-reorganization arrangement:
a) Receivables are to be reduced to $10,000.
b) Inventories are undervalued and are to be revalued to $150,000.
c) Plant and equipment is to be written down to $200,000 because of obsolescence factors.
d) Goodwill and all deferred charges are to be written off.
e) Short-term creditors have agreed to reduce all amounts owed to them by $40,000.
f) Long-term creditors have agreed to reduce amounts owed to them by $100,000.
g) The other contributed capital is to be closed (eliminated).
h) The par value of preferred is to be changed to $10 with no change in the number of shares outstanding.
i) Common stockholders have agreed to relinquish their shares and accept new no-par shares. The common stock account will be reduced in an amount necessary to reduce the retained earnings deficit to zero.

REQUIRED

1. Prepare separate entries for items *a* through *i* to record the quasi-reorganization agreement.

2. Prepare the balance sheet immediately after the quasi-reorganization.

PROBLEMS

P21-1. STOCKHOLDERS' EQUITY TRANSACTIONS; BALANCE SHEET REPORTING At the end of 1987, Valentine's stockholders' equity was as follows:

Common stock ($5 par, 100,000 shares authorized)		$250,000
Treasury stock (par value method)		(50,000)
Other contributed capital		
Contributed capital in excess of par	$50,000	
Donated capital (receipt of land)	60,000	110,000
Retained earnings appropriated for self-insurance		50,000
Unappropriated retained earnings		150,000
Total		$510,000

During 1988 the following transactions and events occurred:
a) Net income, $70,000; cash dividends, $10,000.
b) Sold 6,000 treasury shares at $7 per share.
c) Reversed retained earnings appropriation.
d) Subsequent to sale of treasury stock in part *b*, declared and distributed a 30 percent stock dividend when the market price of the common was $10 per share.
e) Issued convertible bonds with a par value of $100,000 for $110,000. It was estimated that, had the bonds not been convertible, they would have been issued for $90,000.
f) Sold previously donated land for a gain of $10,000; the gain was included in net income.

REQUIRED

Prepare, in good form, the stockholders' equity section of the balance sheet for Valentine as of December 31, 1988.

P21-2. DIVIDENDS The Red River Company presented the following stockholders' equity section of its balance sheet to the stockholders on December 31, 1987:

Capital stock
Preferred: 6% cumulative, nonparticipating,
    par value $100; authorized, 10,000
    shares; issued, 4,000 shares................ $ 400,000
Common: par value, $10; authorized,
    400,000 shares; issued, 200,000 shares ...._2,000,000_ $2,400,000
Contributed capital in excess of par 300,000
Retained earnings .... _900,000_
    $3,600,000

During the 1988 fiscal year the following transactions took place:

2/20/88 Declared the regular 3% semiannual dividend on the preferred stock and a $.50 per share dividend on the common stock to holders of record 3/5/88, payable 4/1/88.

4/1/88 Dividends were paid.

4/5/88 Accepted subscriptions for 40,000 shares of common stock at $35 per share. The subscriptions were accompanied by a 25% down payment on the shares.

5/30/88 Issued stock subscribed on 4/5/88 on basis of receipt of balance of cash.

7/2/88 Issued $1 million 8% first mortgage bonds to Regional Trust at face value. The bonds have a 10-year maturity. Interest is payable semiannually on 12/31 and 6/30.

8/20/88 Declared the regular 3% semiannual dividend on preferred and a dividend of $.50 per share on the common to stockholders of record 8/31/88, payable 10/1/88.

10/1/88 Paid dividends declared.

12/1/88 Declared a 10% stock dividend to the common stockholders of record 12/20/88 to be issued on 1/15/89. The common stock was actively traded on this date at $40 per share. This price was designated as the fair market value for record purposes.

12/31/88 Paid bond interest.

12/31/88 Closed to retained earnings net income of $1,444,600.

REQUIRED

    1. Prepare the journal entries to record the above transactions.

    2. Prepare the stockholders' equity section of the balance sheet as of December 31, 1988.
                                      (CGAA, adapted)

P21-3. DIVIDENDS AND STOCK SPLITS The stockholders' equity accounts for Carson, Inc., are as follows:

12% preferred stock: $50 par, 5,000 shares issued ....$ 250,000
Common stock: $20 par, 10,000 shares issued 200,000
Contributed capital in excess of par
    Preferred 50,000
    Common 200,000
Donated capital from receipt of securities 100,000
Retained earnings .... _700,000_
    $1,500,000

The following dividend declaration and distribution alternatives are being considered:

a) Declaration of the 12 percent preferred cash dividend and a $3 per share cash dividend on common.

b) Declaration of a 10 percent preferred stock dividend when the preferred shares are selling for $80 per share.

c) Declaration of a 40 percent common stock dividend when the common shares are selling for $60 per share.

d) Declaration of a 100 percent common and 100 percent preferred stock dividend. Both stock dividends are to be measured at par.

e) Same as part *d* except that the stock dividends are to be measured at the average contributed capital per share.

f) Declaration of a 4-for-1 stock split on common.

g) Declaration of a 2-for-1 reverse stock split on preferred.

h) Declaration of a dividend from donated capital. Investment securities with a carrying value of $100,000 and a fair market value of $215,000 will be distributed to common stockholders.

i) Declaration of a $2 per share scrip dividend to common stockholders.

j) Declaration of a special stock dividend to common stockholders. Each common stockholder will receive one share of preferred for each share of common held. The market values of the shares are as follows:

Common $60
Preferred 80

REQUIRED

Prepare the journal entries and the resulting stockholders' equity section of the balance sheet under each alternative.

P21-4. DIVIDENDS Tomasco, Inc., began operations in January 1983 and had the following reported net income or loss for each of its five years of operations:

1983	$ 150,000 loss
1984	130,000 loss
1985	120,000 loss
1986	250,000 income
1987	1,000,000 income

On December 31, 1987, the Tomasco capital accounts were as follows:

Common stock, par value $10 per share: authorized, 100,000 shares; issued and outstanding, 50,000 shares	$ 500,000
4% nonparticipating noncumulative preferred stock, par value $100 per share: authorized, issued, and outstanding, 1,000 shares	100,000
8% fully participating cumulative preferred stock, par value $100 per share: authorized, issued, and outstanding, 10,000 shares	1,000,000

Tomasco has never paid a cash or stock dividend. There has been no change in the capital accounts since Tomasco began operations. The appropriate state law permits dividends only from retained earnings.

REQUIRED

Prepare a schedule showing the maximum amount available for cash dividends on December 31, 1987, and how it would be distributable to the holders of the common shares and each class of preferred shares.

(AICPA, adapted)

P21-5. APPROPRIATIONS; STOCKHOLDERS' EQUITY Below are some of the accounts appearing in the trial balance of ATV Corporation, as of December 31, 1987:

	DR	CR
Common stock (no par, issued at $8 per share)		80,000
Preferred stock ($10 par)		30,000
Treasury stock (common, 1,000 shares at cost).............. 13,000		
Contributed capital in excess of par		10,000
Stock dividends distributable (common)....................		16,000
Scrip dividends payable on preferred		2,700
Reserve for treasury stock		13,000
Reserve for bond sinking fund		26,000
Donated capital		21,000
Prior period adjustment—error correction 14,000		
Prior period adjustment—inventory write-down 6,000		
Loss on fire at warehouse 20,000		
Reserve for contingencies		60,000
Retained earnings, 1/1/87		87,000
1987 net income		18,000
Suspense—debits recorded for dividends above 18,700		

REQUIRED

1. Prepare a statement of changes in unappropriated retained earnings for 1987.

2. Prepare the stockholders' equity section of the balance sheet as of December 31, 1987. Use preferred account titles in this statement.

P21-6. STATEMENT OF STOCKHOLDERS' EQUITY   Stockholders' equity as of December 31, 1987, for Racquet Corporation was as follows:

8% preferred stock, $100 par value: 10,000 shares issued	$1,000,000
Common stock, $5 par value: 100,000 shares issued	500,000
Contributed capital in excess of par	
Preferred	500,000
Common	500,000
Treasury stock, 10,000 shares of common at par value	(50,000)
Retained earnings	
Appropriated for cost of treasury stock	75,000
Unappropriated	750,000
	$3,275,000

The following events, listed in chronological order, affected stockholders' equity during 1988:

a) Dividends declared: preferred, 8% of par; common, $1 per share.

b) Sold 5,000 treasury shares for $12 per share.

c) Declared and issued a 10 percent stock dividend on common shares outstanding. The fair market value of the shares on the declaration date was $20 per share.

d) The preferred stock was split 5 for 1.

e) Land with a fair market value of $60,000 was donated to Racquet Corporation.

f) The directors appropriated $100,000 of retained earnings for a possible loss as a result of a lawsuit filed against Racquet Corporation.

g) Declared and issued a property dividend in the form of Tame, Inc., shares held as an investment. Fair market value of shares distributed, $40,000; historical cost, $21,000.

h) 5,000 preferred shares were donated to Racquet Corporation by preferred stockholders.

i) Corrected an error that occurred two years earlier. At that time Racquet decided to record internally generated goodwill of $44,000. The credit was made to miscellaneous income. No amortization had been recorded.

j) Net income for 1988, $300,000.

REQUIRED

Prepare a statement of changes in stockholders' equity using the following headings and format:

| | PREFERRED STOCK | COMMON STOCK | CONTRIBUTED CAPITAL IN EXCESS OF PAR (COMMON AND PREFERRED) | OTHER CONTRIBUTED CAPITAL (OMIT DETAILS) | TREASURY STOCK | RETAINED EARNINGS | | TOTAL |
						APPROPRIATED	UNAPPROPRIATED	
End of 1987	$1,000,000	$500,000	$1,000,000	—	($50,000)	$75,000	$750,000	$3,275,000
1988 transactions:								
End of 1988								

P21-7. PREFERRED DIVIDEND PREFERENCES   The Rambo Company has a capitalization of 2,000 shares of 6 percent $100 par value preferred stock and 5,000 shares of $100 par value common stock. On December 31, 1987, there were no dividends in arrears. During the five following years the company's dividend declarations were as follows:

1988	$70,000	1991	$12,000
1989	42,000	1992	54,000
1990	6,000		

REQUIRED

Under the following assumptions, complete the schedule below, which shows the amount of dividends for each of the two classes of stock:

1. The preferred is cumulative and fully participating.

2. The preferred is noncumulative and fully participating.

3. The preferred is cumulative and nonparticipating.

4. The preferred is noncumulative and nonparticipating.

YEAR	STOCK	CUMULATIVE AND FULLY PARTICIPATING	NONCUMULATIVE AND FULLY PARTICIPATING	CUMULATIVE AND NON-PARTICIPATING	NONCUMULATIVE AND NON-PARTICIPATING
1988	Preferred				
	Common				
1989	Preferred				
	Common				
1990	Preferred				
	Common				
1991	Preferred				
	Common				
1992	Preferred				
	Common				

P21-8. STOCKHOLDERS' EQUITY RELATIONSHIPS   On December 31, 1988, Newtwist Corporation's stockholders' equity appeared as follows:

Common stock ($10 par value)	$26,400,000
Contributed capital in excess of par	25,610,000
Retained earnings appropriated for plant expansion	600,000
Retained earnings, unappropriated	12,380,000
Less: Treasury cost (at cost)	(260,000)
Total stockholders' equity	$64,730,000

During the year ended December 31, 1988, Newtwist had the following transactions and events (in chronological order):

1. Convertible debt holders converted $10 million par value of bonds to Newtwist's common stock. Each $1,000 bond was convertible into 40 shares of Newtwist common stock. The bonds originally were issued at par, and Newtwist uses the book value method of recording bond conversions.

2. Newtwist declared and distributed a 10 percent stock dividend when the market price of its common stock was $25 per share.

3. Newtwist acquired 20,000 shares of its common stock for $26 per share; shortly after the acquisition, the company issued 10,000 of these shares for $27 per share.

4. The company made a retained earnings appropriation of $600,000, the first in the company's history.

5. Cash dividends of $1 per share were declared and paid on the common shares.

6. Newtwist's net income for 1988 was $7,210,000.

REQUIRED

Prepare the stockholders' equity section of Newtwist's balance sheet on December 31, 1987.

P21-9. STOCKHOLDERS' EQUITY CLASSIFICATION DiPanni Corporation's post-closing trial balance at December 31, 1987, was as follows:

	DR	CR
Accounts payable		$ 290,000
Accounts receivable	$ 550,000	
Accumulated depreciation— building and equipment		200,000
Additional paid-in capital— common		
In excess of par value		1,660,000
From sale of treasury stock		250,000
Allowance for doubtful accounts		30,000
Allowance to reduce long-term		
equity securities to market		25,000
Bonds payable		400,000
Building and equipment	1,100,000	
Cash	270,000	
Common stock ($1 par value)		150,000
Common stock subscribed		10,000
Dividends payable on preferred stock—cash		4,000
Inventories	620,000	
Land	380,000	
Long-term equity securities at cost	310,000	
Marketable equity securities at cost (short-term)	215,000	
Net unrealized loss on long-term equity securities	25,000	
Preferred stock ($50 par value)		500,000
Prepaid expenses	40,000	
Retained earnings		231,000
Treasury stock—common, at cost	180,000	
Subscriptions receivable	60,000	
Total	$3,750,000	$3,750,000

At December 31, 1987, DiPanni had the following number of common and preferred shares:

	COMMON	PREFERRED
Authorized	500,000	50,000
Issued	150,000	10,000
Outstanding	140,000	10,000
Subscribed	10,000	–0–

The dividends on preferred stock are $4 cumulative. In addition, the preferred stock has a preference in liquidation of $50 per share. Subscriptions are expected to be collected.

REQUIRED

Prepare the stockholders' equity section of DiPanni's balance sheet at December 31, 1987.

(AICPA, adapted)

P21-10. DIVIDENDS Superior Products, Inc., for the first time is including a five-year summary of earnings and dividends per share in its 1988 annual report to stockholders. On January 1, 1984, the corporation issued 7,000 shares of 4 percent cumulative, nonparticipating $100 par preferred stock and 40,000 shares of $10 par common stock. Of these shares, 108 shares of preferred and 4,000 shares of common were held in the treasury.

Dividends were declared and paid semiannually on the last day of June and December. Cash dividends paid per share of common stock and net income for each year were as shown.

	1984	1985	1986	1987	1988
Net income (loss)	$126,568	$(11,812)	$47,148	$115,824	$193,210
Dividend on common					
6/30	0.40	0.11	0.10	0.40	0.60
12/31	0.48	0.11	0.30	0.40	0.40

In addition, a 10 percent stock dividend was declared and distributed on all common stock (including treasury shares) on April 1, 1986, and common was split 5-for-1 on October 1, 1988. The corporation has met a sinking fund requirement to purchase and retire 140 shares of its preferred stock on October 1 of each year, beginning in 1987, using any available treasury stock. On July 1, 1985, the corporation purchased 400 shares of its common stock and placed them in the treasury, and on April 1, 1987, it issued 5,000 shares of common stock to officers, using treasury stock to the extent available.

REQUIRED

1. Prepare a schedule showing the calculation of preferred stock dividends paid semiannually and annually for the five years. Use the following column headings:

		NUMBER OF SHARES		DIVIDENDS PAID	
YEAR	HALF (1ST OR 2ND)	PURCHASED AND RETIRED	OUTSTANDING	SEMIANNUALLY	ANNUALLY

2. Prepare a schedule that shows for each of the five years the cash dividends paid to common stockholders and the average number of shares of common stock outstanding after adjustment for the stock dividend and split. Use the following format.

DIVIDEND DATE	SHARES OF COMMON STOCK		TOTAL DIVIDENDS PAID PER SHARE	COMMON STOCK ADJUSTED FOR	
	IN TREASURY	OUTSTANDING		10% STOCK DIVIDEND	5-FOR-1 STOCK SPLIT
6/30/84					
12/31/84					
Total for year					
Average for year					

(Continue this format for the remaining four years.)

3. Prepare a five-year financial summary, presenting for each year:
   a) Net income and dividends paid.
   b) Earnings and dividends per share on common stock.

(AICPA, adapted)

P21-11. STOCKHOLDERS' EQUITY REVIEW The Shlee Company was formed on July 1, 1985. It was authorized to issue 200,000 shares of $5 par value common stock and 50,000 shares of 6 percent, $10 par cumulative and nonparticipating preferred stock. Shlee Company's fiscal year ends June 30.

The following information relates to the stockholders' equity accounts of Shlee Company:

COMMON STOCK

Before the 1987–88 fiscal year, Shlee Company had 105,000 shares of outstanding common stock issued as follows:

a) 95,000 shares were issued for cash on July 1, 1985, at $20 per share.

b) On July 24, 1985, 5,000 shares were exchanged for a plot of land that cost the seller $70,000 in 1979 and had an estimated fair market value of $102,000 on July 24, 1985.

c) 5,000 shares were issued on March 1, 1987; the shares had been subscribed for $32 per share on October 31, 1986.

d) During the 1987–88 fiscal year, the following common stock transactions took place:

10/1/87 Subscriptions were received for 10,000 shares at $40 per share. Cash of $80,000 was received in full payment for 2,000 shares and stock certificates were issued. The remaining subscriptions for 8,000 shares were to be paid in full by 9/30/88, at which time the certificates were to be issued.

11/30/87 Shlee purchased 2,000 shares of its own stock on the open market at $38 per share. Shlee uses the cost method for treasury stock.

12/15/87 Shlee declared a 2 percent stock dividend for stockholders of record on 1/15/88, to be issued on 1/31/88. Shlee was having a liquidity problem and could not afford a cash dividend at the time. Shlee's common stock was selling at $43 per share on 12/15/87.

6/20/88 Shlee issued 500 shares of its own common stock that it had purchased on 11/30/87 for $21,000.

PREFERRED STOCK

e) Shlee issued 30,000 shares of preferred stock at $15 per share on July 1, 1986.

CASH DIVIDENDS

f) Shlee has followed a schedule of declaring cash dividends in December and June, with payment being made to stockholders of record in the following month. The cash dividends that have been declared through June 30, 1988, are shown below.

DECLARATION DATE	COMMON STOCK, PER SHARE	PREFERRED STOCK, PER SHARE
12/15/86	$.10	$.30
6/15/87	$.10	$.30
12/15/87	—	$.30

No cash dividends were declared in June 1988 because of Shlee's liquidity problems.

RETAINED EARNINGS

g) As of June 30, 1987, Shlee's retained earnings account had a balance of $370,000. For the fiscal year ended June 30, 1988, Shlee reported net income of $20,000.

h) In March 1987, Shlee received a term loan from Union National Bank. The bank requires Shlee to establish a sinking fund and restrict retained earnings in an amount equal to the sinking fund deposit. The annual sinking fund payment of $40,000 is due on April 30 each year; the first payment was made on schedule on April 30, 1988.

REQUIRED

Prepare the stockholders' equity section of the statement of financial position, including appropriate notes, for Shlee Company as of June 30, 1988.

(IMA, adapted)

P21-12. STOCKHOLDERS' EQUITY REVIEW   Howard Corporation is a publicly owned company whose shares are traded on a national stock exchange. On December 31, 1987, Howard had 25 million shares of $10 par value common stock authorized, of which 15 million shares were issued and 10 million shares were outstanding.

The stockholders' equity accounts had the following balances on December 31, 1987:

Common stock	$150,000,000
Contributed capital in excess of par	80,000,000
Retained earnings	50,000,000
Treasury stock	18,000,000

During 1988 Howard had the following transactions:

a) On February 1 a secondary distribution of 2 million shares of $10 par value common stock was completed. The stock was sold to the public at $18 per share, net of offering costs.

b) On February 15 Howard issued at $110 per share 100,000 shares of $100 par 8 percent cumulative preferred stock with 100,000 detachable warrants. Each warrant contained one right that could be exchanged, with $20, for one share of $10 par value common stock. On February 15 the market price for one stock right was $1.

c) On March 1 Howard acquired 20,000 shares of its common stock for $18.50 per share. Howard uses the cost method to account for treasury stock.

d) On March 15, when the common stock was trading for $21 per share, a major stockholder donated 10,000 shares, which are appropriately recorded as treasury stock.

e) On March 31 Howard declared a semiannual cash dividend on common stock of $.10 per share, payable on April 30, 1988, to stockholders of record on April 10, 1988. The appropriate state law prohibits cash dividends on treasury stock.

f) On April 15, when the market price of the stock rights was $2 each and the market price of the common stock was $22 per share, 30,000 stock rights were exercised. Howard issued new shares to settle the transaction.

g) On April 30 employees exercised 100,000 options that were granted in 1986 under a noncompensatory stock option plan. When the options were granted, each option had a preemptive right and entitled the employee to purchase one share of common stock for $20 per share. On April 30 the market price of the common stock was $23 per share. Howard issued new shares to settle the transaction.

h) On May 31, when the market price of the common stock was $20 per share, Howard declared a 5 percent stock dividend distributable on July 1, 1988, to stockholders of record on June 1, 1988. The appropriate state law prohibits stock dividends on treasury stock.

i) On June 30 Howard sold the 20,000 treasury shares acquired on March 1 and an additional 280,000 treasury shares costing $5.6 million which were on hand at the beginning of the year. The selling price was $25 per share.

j) On September 30 Howard declared a semiannual cash dividend of $.10 per share on common stock and the yearly dividend on preferred stock, both payable on October 30 to stockholders of record on October 10. The appropriate state law prohibits cash dividends on treasury stock.

k) On December 31 the remaining outstanding rights expired.

l) Net income for 1988 was $25 million.

REQUIRED

Prepare a worksheet to be used to summarize, for each transaction, the changes in Howard's stockholders' equity accounts for 1988. The columns on the worksheet should have the following headings:

Date of transaction (or beginning date)
Common stock, number of shares
Common stock, amount
Preferred stock, number of shares
Preferred stock, amount
Common stock warrants, number of rights

Common stock warrants, amount
Additional paid-in capital
Retained earnings
Treasury stock, number of shares
Treasury stock, amount

(AICPA, adapted)

P21-13.   MISCELLANEOUS STOCKHOLDERS' EQUITY   You are a senior accountant responsible for the annual audit of Lemon, Inc., for the year ended December 31, 1987. The information available to you is presented below. You may assume that any pertinent information not presented below has already been checked and found satisfactory.

a) Excerpts from trial balance, December 31, 1987:

	CREDIT
Retained earnings	$40,000
Inventory reserve (appropriation)	7,500
Capital stock (600 shares)	60,000

b) The books have not been closed, but all adjusting entries that the company expects to make have been posted. The trial balance shows $15,000 net income for the year.

c) Selected ledger accounts:

Retained earnings

8/6/87	CD 62	160	12/31/86	Balance	52,960
10/10/87	J 34	10,000	4/29/87	CR 8	200
12/31/87	J 40	3,000			

(Note: The balance at 12/31/86 agrees with last year's working papers and represents the net difference over the years between credits from the income summary account and debits for dividends.)

Inventory reserve (appropriation)

9/26/87	CD 78	500	6/30/87	J 19	5,000
			12/31/87	J 40	3,000

d) Analysis of selected cash receipts (CR):

DATE	PAGE	ACCOUNT CREDITED	EXPLANATION	AMOUNT
4/29/87	8	Capital stock	Sold $100 par stock @ $102	10,000
		Retained earnings		200
10/10/87	20	Building	See J 34	20,000

e) Analysis of selected cash disbursements (CD):

DATE	PAGE	ACCOUNT DEBITED	EXPLANATION	AMOUNT
8/6/87	62	Retained earnings	Freak accident to company truck not covered by insurance; repair by Doe & Co.	160
9/26/87	78	Inventory reserve	Purchase of materials (X Co.) to be used on orders taken prior to 6/30/87. $500 is price increase since 6/30/87.	500
		Purchases		6,300

f) Selected entries in general journal (J):

DATE	PAGE	ENTRY AND EXPLANATION	DEBIT	CREDIT
6/30/87	19	Inventory loss	5,000	
		Inventory reserve (appropriation)		5,000
		Provision voted by board of directors for estimated future price increases in materials needed to complete orders on hand. (Note: Orders do not represent contractual obligations.)		
10/10/87	34	Accumulated depreciation	50,000	
		Retained earnings	10,000	
		Building		60,000
		Sale of main office building, moved to rental quarters downtown. (See CR 20.)		
12/31/87	40	Retained earnings	3,000	
		Inventory reserve (appropriation)		3,000
		Provision to value materials inventory at lower of cost or market in accordance with company pricing policy.		

Cost	$30,000
Market	(27,000)
	$ 3,000

REQUIRED

Prepare the following:

1. A schedule of recommended adjusting entries to be placed on the books to state the stockholders' equity accounts in accordance with generally accepted accounting principles.

2. A statement of retained earnings for 1987.

3. The stockholders' equity section of the balance sheet as of December 31, 1987.

(AICPA, adapted)

P21-14. STOCKHOLDERS' EQUITY: COMPREHENSIVE   At the beginning of the current year, Barney Corporation had the following stockholders' equity balances:

Common stock ($10 par value)	$5,000,000
Contributed capital in excess of par	1,875,000
Retained earnings	1,625,000

During the current year, Barney engaged in the following transactions, listed in chronological order:

1. Purchased 5,000 shares of its common stock for $20 per share. The company uses the cost method of accounting for treasury shares.

2. Issued 25,000 shares of $20 par convertible preferred stock, convertible 1-for-1 with its common, for $48 per share.

3. Issued 90,000 shares of previously unissued $10 par common stock for $22 per share.

4. Declared a cash dividend of $2 per share on the common shares outstanding.

5. Sold 4,000 shares of treasury stock for $25 per share.

6. Declared a cash dividend of $1 per share on the preferred shares.

7. Converted 10,000 preferred shares into common shares at stockholders' request.

8. Declared and distributed a 1 percent stock dividend on common when the market price of its common stock was $28 per share.

9. Corrected an error made several years ago. At that time, a purchase of land for $275,000 was incorrectly expensed.

10. Recorded net income of $1,500,000 for the year.

REQUIRED

1. Indicate the dollar effect of each transaction listed above on total stockholders' equity.

2. Prepare a statement of retained earnings for the current year.

3. Prepare the stockholders' equity section of Barney's balance sheet at the end of the current year.

P21-15. QUASI-REORGANIZATION   The Khartoum Corporation has $105,000 of dividends in arrears on its preferred stock as of March 31, 1987. While retained earnings are adequate to meet the accumulated dividends, the company's management does not wish to weaken its working capital position. It also realizes that a portion of the fixed assets are no longer used or useful in the firm's operation. Therefore, the following reorganization is proposed and approved by stockholders, effective April 1, 1987:

a) The preferred stock is to be exchanged for $300,000 of 5 percent debenture bonds. Dividends in arrears are to be settled by the issuance of $120,000 of $10 par value 5 percent noncumulative preferred stock.

b) Common stock is to be assigned a value of $50 per share.

c) Goodwill is to be written off.

d) Property, plant, and equipment is to be written down, on the basis of appraisal and estimates of useful value, by a total of $103,200, consisting of $85,400 increase in accumulated depreciation and $17,800 decrease in certain assets.

e) Current assets are to be written down by $10,460 to reduce certain items to expected realizable values.

The condensed balance sheet as of March 31, 1987, is as shown below.

ASSETS

Cash		$ 34,690
Other current assets		252,890
Property, plant, and equipment	$1,458,731	
Accumulated depreciation	(512,481)	946,250
Goodwill		50,000
		$1,283,830

LIABILITIES AND STOCKHOLDERS' EQUITY

Current liabilities	$ 136,860
7% cumulative preferred stock ($100 par)*	300,000
Common stock (9,000 shares, no-par)	648,430
Premium on preferred stock	22,470
Retained earnings	176,070
	$1,283,830

* $105,000 dividends in arrears.

REQUIRED

1. Prepare the journal entries to give effect to the reorganization as of April 1, 1987. Give complete explanations with each entry and comment as to any possible options in recording the reorganization.

2. Prepare a balance sheet as of April 30, 1987, assuming that net income for April is $10,320 after provision for taxes. The operations result in $5,290 increase in cash, $10,660 increase in other current assets, $2,010 increase in current liabilities, and $3,620 increase in accumulated depreciation.

(AICPA, adapted)

22 ACCOUNTING CHANGES AND ERROR ANALYSIS

Changing economic circumstances often cause a company to change its methods of accounting. For example, rising prices may motivate a firm to switch from FIFO to LIFO. External conditions may also bring about revisions in estimates, as when a firm revises its estimate of the useful life of a depreciable asset. Whatever their cause, accounting changes are made to meet the financial reporting objective of providing information useful for decision making.

Although accounting changes may increase decision usefulness in one way, the qualitative characteristics of comparability and consistency may suffer. Comparability helps users make comparisons across firms; however, if firms use different accounting methods, comparability is impaired. Consistency helps users evaluate a particular firm over time; if the firm changes accounting methods, consistency may be sacrificed. An accounting change may materially affect a company's reported earnings, even though it may not affect its cash flows. To illustrate, consider the following accounting changes made by U.S. corporations:

> In 1980, Union Carbide extended the estimated lives of its depreciable assets, switched from the deferred method to the flow-through method of accounting for investment tax credits, and began capitalizing interest during construction. These changes increased the firm's net income for 1980 by approximately $380 million, but none of the changes affected Union Carbide's cash flows.
>
> When Tenneco switched to LIFO inventory accounting, the change reduced earnings approximately $75 million. The change to LIFO increased Tenneco's cash flow by lowering its income taxes.
>
> In 1983, Bethlehem Steel Corporation began depreciating its steel-producing facilities over 18 years instead of 12. This change, and others, reduced Bethlehem's net loss by almost $269 million.[1]

Although a significant body of empirical research indicates that the securities market is not fooled by accounting changes that do not affect the value of the firm, accounting for these types of changes remains controversial, because capital market efficiency has its skeptics. In addition, accounting information is used in many types of resource allocation decisions other than those in securities markets.

[1] *Business Week*, March 5, 1984, p. 81.

Accounting changes may affect reported earnings, but may or may not affect cash flows.

Another problem arises when accounting errors are discovered. How should they be corrected and disclosed in order to make the financial statements as useful as possible? Meaningful disclosure of the effects of both accounting changes and error corrections increases the usefulness of financial statements by allowing users to distinguish between changes in resources and obligations and changes in the method of accounting for them.

In this chapter we discuss the various types of accounting changes and how to account for them and disclose them in the financial statements. Then we examine the nature of accounting errors, their effect on the financial statements, and their correction and disclosure.

ACCOUNTING CHANGES

To illustrate the possible diversity in financial reporting of accounting changes, consider the following hypothetical situation:[2] At the beginning of 1983, four competing commuter airlines—Transtate, Southeast, Northern, and Alpha—acquired identical planes at a cost of $12 million to each airline. The companies, which operate in very similar business and economic environments, estimated that the planes would have a useful life of six years, with no salvage value. All four companies estimated that the planes' services would be received equally each year, so all four companies decided to use straight-line depreciation.

In early 1987, after four years' experience with the planes, it became obvious that they still had a remaining useful life of six years. That is, the total useful life of the planes now appeared to be 10 years. All four airlines decided to change the total estimated life from six years to 10 years. At the date of the accounting change, the book value of the planes for each airline was $4 million:

Airplanes (original cost)...................................	$12,000,000
Accumulated depreciation ($12,000,000 ÷ 6 = $2,000,000; $2,000,000 × 4 years = $8,000,000)	(8,000,000)
Book value	$ 4,000,000

Transtate's controller reasoned that since the total useful life of the planes was now estimated to be 10 years, depreciation to date should be reduced to show the (now) smaller depreciation each year for the four years already passed. Since four years of the 10 years had elapsed, the planes should be depreciated by 40 percent. Transtate therefore made the following entries to record the accounting change and the 1987 depreciation:

Accumulated depreciation	3,200,000	
Miscellaneous income from accounting change		3,200,000

To record the change in estimate: 40 percent × original cost of $12,000,000 = $4,800,000 (new accumulated depreciation balance); $8,000,000 (accumulated depreciation before the change) − $4,800,000 = $3,200,000 (adjustment required).

Depreciation expense	1,200,000	
Accumulated depreciation		1,200,000

To record 1987 depreciation based on the revised 10-year life: $12,000,000 × .10 = $1,200,000.

[2] For simplicity, taxes are ignored. In addition, as we shall see later, not all of the alternatives considered here are acceptable under generally accepted accounting principles. This example does, however, illustrate the issues involved in accounting changes.

Southeast's controller reasoned in a similar manner. He argued, however, that the credit should be to retained earnings, since the adjustment applied to prior years and not the current year. Southeast therefore recorded the change and 1987 depreciation as follows:

Accumulated depreciation	3,200,000	
Retained earnings		3,200,000
Depreciation expense	1,200,000	
Accumulated depreciation		1,200,000

Southeast's controller also decided that comparative income statements for the years 1983 through 1986 should be restated by reducing depreciation expense for each prior period by $800,000 ($3,200,000 ÷ 4). He thought that this approach would help users to analyze trends and also would be more consistent because prior years' depreciation expense would be the same as the current and future years' depreciation expense. (From a bookkeeping standpoint, the reduced depreciation expense each year would increase net income each year by $800,000 and over four years would equal the $3.2 million increase in retained earnings.)

Northern's controller reasoned the same as Southeast's, and made the same entries for the accounting change and for 1987 depreciation. However, he decided not to restate the prior periods' statements. The controller argued that "what is past is water over the dam." So Northern simply reported the $3.2 million increase in retained earnings in the retained earnings statement for 1987 and did not restate the comparative income statements for 1983 through 1986.

Alpha's controller took a different approach. She felt that, because the original estimate was based on the best information available at the time the planes were purchased, no adjustment should be made to the accumulated depreciation account. The net book value of $4 million should be allocated over the (new) remaining life of six years. The controller also concluded that since estimates are inherent in accounting, adjustments to income or retained earnings arising from revisions of estimates might cause users to lose confidence in and place less reliability on the financial statements. Alpha therefore made the following entry to record 1987 depreciation:

Depreciation expense	666,667	
Accumulated depreciation		666,667
($4,000,000 ÷ 6 years)		

Alpha, however, did disclose the change in estimate and its impact on depreciation and net income for 1987 in the footnotes to the 1987 financial statement.

Information from the four airlines' comparative financial statements for 1983–87 is shown in Exhibit 22–1. Obviously, the financial statements for the four companies are not comparable. For example, Transtate's 1987 net income is $3.2 million more than Southeast's and Northern's. Alpha's 1987 net income is $533,333 more than Southeast's and Northern's. Although all four airlines have identical planes with identical useful lives, there is considerable variation in the asset carrying values on the balance sheets. In addition, some of the companies' statements are not consistent over time. For example, Transtate, Northern, and Alpha report different amounts of depreciation in 1987 than they reported in previous years, since only 1987 depreciation was based on the new estimate. While Southeast's reported depreciation expenses for 1983–87 are consistent, the amounts reported in the 1983–86 comparative statements are *different* from the amounts *originally* reported in those years.

The financial statements of these four hypothetical companies, then, may not permit

EXHIBIT 22-1 INFORMATION FROM INCOME STATEMENTS AND BALANCE SHEETS, 1983–87, REFLECTING ACCOUNTING CHANGES

Transtate, Southeast, Northern, and Alpha Airlines

	INCOME STATEMENTS FOR THE YEARS ENDED DECEMBER 31				
	1987	1986	1985	1984	1983
Transtate					
Depreciation expense	$(1,200,000)	$(2,000,000)	$(2,000,000)	$(2,000,000)	$(2,000,000)
Accounting change	3,200,000				
Southeast					
Depreciation expense (restated) ...	(1,200,000)	(1,200,000)	(1,200,000)	(1,200,000)	(1,200,000)
Northern					
Depreciation expense	(1,200,000)	(2,000,000)	(2,000,000)	(2,000,000)	(2,000,000)
Alpha					
Depreciation expense	(666,667)	(2,000,000)	(2,000,000)	(2,000,000)	(2,000,000)

	BALANCE SHEETS, DECEMBER 31				
	1987	1986	1985	1984	1983
Transtate					
Airplanes	$12,000,000	$12,000,000	$12,000,000	$12,000,000	$12,000,000
Accumulated depreciation	(6,000,000)	(8,000,000)	(6,000,000)	(4,000,000)	(2,000,000)
	$ 6,000,000	$ 4,000,000	$ 6,000,000	$ 8,000,000	$10,000,000
Southeast					
Airplanes	$12,000,000	$12,000,000	$12,000,000	$12,000,000	$12,000,000
Accumulated depreciation					
(after restatement)	(6,000,000)	(4,800,000)	(3,600,000)	(2,400,000)	(1,200,000)
	$ 6,000,000	$ 7,200,000	$ 8,400,000	$ 9,600,000	$10,800,000
Northern					
Airplanes	$12,000,000	$12,000,000	$12,000,000	$12,000,000	$12,000,000
Accumulated depreciation	(6,000,000)	(8,000,000)	(6,000,000)	(4,000,000)	(2,000,000)
	$ 6,000,000	$ 4,000,000	$ 6,000,000	$ 8,000,000	$10,000,000
Alpha					
Airplanes	$12,000,000	$12,000,000	$12,000,000	$12,000,000	$12,000,000
Accumulated depreciation	(8,666,667)	(8,000,000)	(6,000,000)	(4,000,000)	(2,000,000)
	$ 3,333,333	$ 4,000,000	$ 6,000,000	$ 8,000,000	$10,000,000

users to make intelligent investment decisions, because four different approaches were used to account for and disclose the same accounting change. Which of the above approaches results in the most useful financial statements when relevance, reliability, comparability, and consistency are considered? A definitive answer to this question is difficult because, as we said in Chapter 2, a trade-off must be made between some qualitative characteristics and others.

For many years, companies had considerable latitude in reporting accounting changes. APB *Opinion No. 20,* ''Accounting Changes,'' was issued in 1971 to reduce the widespread diversity in the reporting of accounting changes. The next several sections of this chapter are based on this pronouncement. First, we will describe the three types of accounting changes set forth in *Opinion No. 20* and give some examples of each. Second, we will discuss alternative approaches for recording and reporting accounting changes. Then, for each of the three types of accounting changes, we will discuss the accounting and reporting requirements of *Opinion No. 20.*

TYPES OF ACCOUNTING CHANGES

There are three types of accounting changes: (1) a change in accounting principle; (2) a change in accounting estimate; and (3) a change in reporting entity. We will discuss each type below.

Change in Accounting Principle

A **change in accounting principle** occurs when a company adopts a generally accepted accounting principle that is different from a generally accepted accounting principle that it previously used. Some examples of such changes include:

1. A change in the method of inventory pricing (e.g., a change from FIFO to LIFO).
2. A change in depreciation methods for previously recorded assets (e.g., from straight-line to accelerated depreciation).
3. A change in the method of accounting for long-term construction contracts (e.g., from the completed-contract method to the percentage-of-completion method).

A change in accounting principle also includes a change in the method of applying the principle, for example, a change from the aggregate approach to the individual item approach in applying lower of cost or market to inventories. However, a change from an accounting principle that is *not* generally accepted to one that *is* generally accepted is not a change in accounting principle. Changes of this type are classified as error corrections.

Change in Accounting Estimate

Estimates are inherent in the accounting process. For example, estimation is necessary for uncollectible receivables, the salvage values and useful lives of depreciable assets, the number of periods that will be benefited by a particular expenditure, and inventory obsolescence. Occasionally accountants must revise estimates as time passes, as circumstances change, or as additional information is obtained. The case of the four airlines discussed earlier is an example of a **change in accounting estimate.** As another example, you probably continually revise your estimate of your grade in a class as you move through a semester and are exposed to new material and obtain feedback on your examinations. Your original grade estimate should not be considered *wrong,* since it was based on all the facts you knew at the time. As additional information becomes available, however, your revised estimates probably become more accurate.

Under certain circumstances, it may be difficult to distinguish between a change in accounting principle and a change in accounting estimate. For example, because of a change in estimated future benefits, a company may change to a practice of recording certain costs as assets and amortizing these costs over future periods instead of expensing them as they are incurred. Since the change in principle arises as a result of a change in estimated future benefits, it is difficult to separate the two types of changes. *APB Opinion No. 20* requires that in these circumstances the change be classified as a change in estimate.[3]

Change in Reporting Entity

An accounting change that involves the preparation of financial statements for a new accounting entity is called a **change in the reporting entity.** Changes of this type include:

1. Presenting consolidated or combined statements in place of statements of individual companies.

---

[3] "Accounting Changes," *Opinions of the Accounting Principles Board No. 20* (New York: AICPA, 1971), para. 10.

2. Changing specific subsidiaries comprising the group of companies for which consolidated statements are presented.

3. Changing the companies included in combined financial statements.

APPROACHES TO RECORDING AND REPORTING ACCOUNTING CHANGES

Three approaches have been suggested for reporting accounting changes: report the total financial statement effects of the change in the *current period,* report them *retroactively,* and report them *prospectively.* We shall discuss each in turn.

Current Period Approach

Under the **current period approach,** one calculates the *cumulative effect* of the change on the financial statements—that is, the cumulative effect on assets or liabilities—at the beginning of the period in which the change is made. The cumulative effect is the difference between the present carrying value of the asset or liability and what the carrying value would have been if the accounting change had been in effect in all previous periods of the asset's or liability's existence. The cumulative effect of the change is recorded by adjusting the asset or liability; the offsetting debit or credit is made to the account, cumulative effect of change in accounting principle, which is reported on the income statement. Revenues or expenses affected by the accounting change for the period in which the change is made are based on the new accounting method. The financial statements of prior periods reported currently for comparative purposes are not restated. In the airline example discussed earlier, notice that Transtate used the current period approach to record and report the change.

The rationale for the current period approach is that by recording and reporting the effect of the change in the current period, the credibility of the prior period statements and of financial reporting in general is maintained. Many accountants believe that if prior period statements are *continually* restated for comparative purposes, users may begin to question the reliability and credibility of financial reporting.

Retroactive Approach

The **retroactive approach** is similar to the current period approach, since one calculates the cumulative effect of the change at the beginning of the period in which the change is made. In recording and disclosure, however, this approach differs from the current period approach in that the cumulative effect is recorded by adjusting the asset or liability, with an offsetting debit or credit to *retained earnings.* The change is disclosed by restating the financial statements of prior periods for comparative purposes. In the earlier example, Southeast used the retroactive approach to record and report the accounting change.

Support for the retroactive approach is based on interperiod comparability or consistency. Prior period financial statements are consistent with present and future statements when accounting changes are treated retroactively.

Prospective Approach

As its name implies, the **prospective approach** is "forward looking"; that is, prior period financial statements are not restated under this approach. The accounting effect of the change is reported in the current period if future periods are not affected. If the change affects current and future periods, the financial effects of the change are reported in those periods. The argument for this approach is similar to that for the current period approach—it maintains financial statement credibility. Another argument is that since previously reported results have affected past decisions and behavior, mathematical reconstruction of what already has happened may not be meaningful. The prospective approach was used by Alpha in the hypothetical example earlier.

Now that we have introduced accounting changes and some approaches for recording and reporting them, we will discuss how each type must be recorded and disclosed under *Opinion No. 20*. Additionally, the rationale underlying the reporting requirements will be presented.

CHANGES IN ACCOUNTING PRINCIPLE

For **changes in accounting principle,** there is a general accounting and reporting requirement, as well as two groups of exceptions to the general requirement. These accounting and reporting requirements are presented on the next several pages.

The cumulative effect of changes in accounting principle appears in the income statement.

General Requirement—Current Period Approach

Generally, changes in accounting principle are accounted for under the current period approach, in which the cumulative effect of the change, as of the beginning of the period in which the change is made, is reported in the current period income statement. As we stated earlier, the cumulative effect of the change means that the asset or liability affected is adjusted to the amount it would have been if the new principle had been used in previous periods. This approach is also sometimes referred to as a **catch-up** approach. The *new* accounting principle is applied to the asset or liability in the current period and in future periods.

To illustrate the general accounting and reporting requirements for changes in accounting principle using the current approach, assume that in late 1987 Bowie Corporation decides to change the depreciation method on its plant and equipment from sum of the years' digits to straight line. The assets were purchased at the beginning of 1983 for $110,000, have a useful life of 10 years, and have no salvage value. Bowie will continue to use the sum-of-the-years'-digits method for tax purposes, and the tax rate is 40 percent. The cumulative effect of the change in accounting principle is determined as shown in Exhibit 22–2. Notice that the cumulative effect is calculated as of the end of 1986 (or the beginning of 1987). This approach is logical because presumably the economic conditions that justify the change apply to 1987 and the following years. Therefore, depreciation expense for 1987 will be based on the new accounting principle and will be a better financial representation of the currently expiring service potential of the asset.

Using the data in Exhibit 22–2, the entry to record the change in accounting principle is as follows:

Accumulated depreciation 24,000		
Deferred income taxes		9,600
Cumulative effect of change in accounting principle.........		14,400

The accumulated depreciation is reduced by $24,000 so that the balance in the account of $44,000 ($68,000 − $24,000), after adjustment, is the total depreciation that would have been recorded on the plant assets as of the beginning of 1987 if the straight-line method had been used in previous periods. The deferred income taxes credit of $9,600 is the tax effect of the cumulative timing difference between the depreciation under the straight-line method and the depreciation that has been deducted for tax purposes. At some future point, the deferred income taxes account will decrease because the timing difference between depreciation expense for tax purposes and for financial accounting purposes will begin to reverse. The deferred income taxes will have a balance of zero when the asset is fully depreciated.

Depreciation expense for 1987, based on the new method, is recorded as follows:

Depreciation expense 11,000		
Accumulated depreciation		11,000

EXHIBIT 22–2   CALCULATION OF CUMULATIVE EFFECT
OF CHANGE IN ACCOUNTING PRINCIPLE

Bowie Corporation

| | DEPRECIATION UNDER | | | | |
| | (1) SUM-OF-THE-YEARS'-DIGITS METHOD | (2) STRAIGHT-LINE METHOD | (3) DIFFERENCE | (4) TAX AT 40% | (5) DIFFERENCE, NET OF TAX (3 – 4) |
YEAR					
1983	10/55 × $110,000 = $20,000	$110,000/10 = $11,000	$ 9,000	$3,600	$ 5,400
1984	9/55 × $110,000 = 18,000	11,000	7,000	2,800	4,200
1985	8/55 × $110,000 = 16,000	11,000	5,000	2,000	3,000
1986	7/55 × $110,000 = 14,000	11,000	3,000	1,200	1,800
	$68,000	$44,000	$24,000	$9,600	$14,400

At the end of 1987 the plant assets are 50 percent depreciated, and the accumulated depreciation account balance is now $55,000:

Accumulated depreciation			
Accounting change adjustment	24,000	Balance, 12/31/86	68,000
Balance, 12/31/87	55,000	Depreciation, 1987	11,000
	79,000		79,000
		Balance, 12/31/87	55,000

The change in accounting principle is disclosed by reporting the cumulative effect in the 1987 income statement as shown in the following comparative income statement data (figures assumed) for Bowie Corporation:

	1987	1986	1985
Revenues	$50,000	$50,000	$50,000
Depreciation	(11,000)	(14,000)	(16,000)
Other expenses	(10,000)	(10,000)	(10,000)
Income before taxes and accounting change	$29,000	$26,000	$24,000
Income tax expense	(11,600)	(10,400)	(9,600)
Income before accounting change	$17,400	$15,600	$14,400
Cumulative effect of change in accounting principle (net of tax)	14,400		
Net income	$31,800	$15,600	$14,400
Earnings per share*	$3.18	$1.56	$1.44

* Assuming 10,000 common shares outstanding.

The cumulative effect is disclosed in the income statement between extraordinary items and net income. The cumulative effect is not an extraordinary item but should be reported in a similar manner.[4]

At this point one might argue that the income statements are not comparable since the depreciation method used in 1986 and 1985, before the change, differs from the method used in 1987, after the change. Even though revenues and expenses, except for depreciation, are the same for each of the three years, net income and earnings per share are much greater for 1987 than for 1985 and 1986, solely because of the difference in depreciation methods. In order to make the income statements more comparable, *Opinion No. 20* also requires that the cumulative effect of the change in accounting principle be applied *retroactively* on a pro forma (''as if'') basis and that income before extraordinary items, net income, and related earnings per share amounts be disclosed on the retroactive pro forma basis. This requirement means that net income and earnings per share must be disclosed for all prior periods presented, as if the new method had been in effect during those periods. This pro forma information is an *additional* disclosure requirement that increases the interperiod comparability of the disclosures. The previously reported income statement and earnings per share numbers for earlier periods are still presented within the body of the primary statements.

The comparative statements for Bowie Corporation shown in Exhibit 22–3 illustrate the basic reporting requirements under *Opinion No. 20*. A footnote is included to describe the accounting change and its effects for financial statement users.[5] Notice that in the primary statements, the cumulative effect of the change in depreciation methods is shown in the 1987 income statement, and depreciation expense for 1987 is based on the new depreciation method. The additional pro forma disclosures show that if the straight-line method had been used in previous periods, net income and earnings per share would have been equal for all three years, since revenues were $50,000 and other expenses were $10,000 for each of the three years.

Pro forma disclosures of changes in accounting principle on a retroactive basis increase comparability.

Exceptions to the General Requirement

There are two classes of exceptions to the general requirement of reporting the cumulative effect of a change in accounting principle in the current period income statement:

1. Retroactive reporting of *some* changes in accounting principle.

2. Changes in accounting principle whose cumulative effect is not determinable.

Some changes in accounting principle are reported in the primary financial statements on a retroactive basis.

RETROACTIVE REPORTING OF CHANGES IN ACCOUNTING PRINCIPLE Even though most changes in accounting principle are not reported retroactively except on the pro forma basis discussed above, the following changes in accounting principle must be reported retroactively:

[4] *APB Opinion No. 20*, para. 20. The cumulative effect of a change in accounting principle is an example of an item that would be reported between ''earnings'' and ''comprehensive income'' under the reporting format in *Statement of Concepts No. 5*.

[5] *APB Opinion No.* 20 specifies that when the cumulative effect is calculated for inclusion in the primary financial statements, only *direct effects* of the change and the related income tax should be considered. The direct effect of the change in Bowie Corporation's depreciation methods, for example, was calculated in Exhibit 22-2. The direct effect involved only two items—depreciation and taxes. In the pro forma presentation, however, *indirect effects* also should be considered. For example, if the Bowie Corporation had a bonus agreement with employees which was tied to net income, the indirect effect should also be considered in the pro forma disclosures. If the straight-line method had been used in previous periods, net income excluding the bonus would have been greater. When the hypothetical bonus is considered, the pro forma net income and earnings per share numbers would be less than those shown in Exhibit 22-3.

EXHIBIT 22–3 DISCLOSURE OF A CHANGE IN ACCOUNTING PRINCIPLE, CURRENT PERIOD APPROACH

Bowie Corporation

COMPARATIVE INCOME STATEMENTS

	1987	1986	1985
Revenues	$50,000	$50,000	$50,000
Depreciation (Note A)	(11,000)	(14,000)	(16,000)
Other expenses	(10,000)	(10,000)	(10,000)
Income taxes	(11,600)	(10,400)	(9,600)
Income before change in accounting principle	$17,400		
Cumulative effect of change in accounting principle (Note A)	14,400		
Net income	$31,800	$15,600	$14,400
Earnings per share	$3.18	$1.56	$1.44

PRO FORMA (NOTE A)			
Net income	$17,400*	$17,400†	$17,400‡
Earnings per share	$1.74	$1.74	$1.74

Note A: Prior to 1987 Bowie used sum-of-the-years'-digits depreciation on its plant assets. In 1987 Bowie changed to the straight-line method of depreciation, which management felt better represented the service expiration of its plant assets. The cumulative effect of the change in accounting principle of $14,400 (net of tax) has been included in 1987 net income. The pro forma data report what net income would have been had the straight-line method been used prior to 1987.

* $31,800 − $14,400, since the straight-line method was used in 1987.

† $15,600 + $1,800 (from Exhibit 22–2).

‡ $14,400 + $3,000 (from Exhibit 22–2).

1. A change *from* LIFO to another inventory valuation method.

2. A change in the method of accounting for long-term construction contracts (e.g., from completed contract to percentage of completion).

3. A change to or from the full cost method of accounting for exploration costs in the extractive industries.

4. A change in accounting principle made by a company issuing comparative financial statements for the first time in order to effect a business combination, to register securities, or to obtain equity financing.

5. A retroactive change in accounting principle that is required by an authoritative pronouncement. As examples, we pointed out in Chapter 14 that *APB Opinion No. 18* requires that a change from the cost method to the equity method be treated retroactively; *FASB Statement No. 13* requires retroactive treatment of changes in accounting for leases.

In the first three situations and possibly the fifth, retroactive application of a change in accounting principle is thought to be a more meaningful approach. For these items, the cumulative effect can be quite material; thus, retroactive application prevents a large catch-up amount from distorting the current period income statement. In the fourth situation, retroactive application is more relevant to users since the company is issuing financial statements for the first time, and thus interperiod comparisons are enhanced.

Interestingly, many of the *FASB Statements* have required retroactive application when a company begins following a *Statement's* provisions. These mandatory accounting changes and disclosure requirements are called **transition rules** and should be distinguished from *voluntary changes* in accounting principle. A voluntary change is one that results from a freely made decision to substitute one generally accepted accounting principle for another that also is generally accepted.

To illustrate retroactive application of a change in accounting principle, assume that Crane Company uses the completed-contract method to account for long-term construction contracts. The company changes to the percentage-of-completion method in 1987 because its management believes that reliable construction costs and completion estimates can be made, and that therefore the financial statements will provide more useful cash flow signals under the new method. The company plans to continue to use the completed-contract method for tax purposes, and the tax rate is 40 percent. Crane issues comparative statements that cover a three-year period. The comparative income statements originally issued for 1984, 1985, and 1986 under the completed-contract method contain the following information:

	1986	1985	1984
Construction revenue	$500,000	$450,000	$400,000
Cost of construction revenue	(400,000)	(355,000)	(330,000)
Income before taxes	$100,000	$ 95,000	$ 70,000
Income tax expense (40% rate)	(40,000)	(38,000)	(28,000)
Net income	$ 60,000	$ 57,000	$ 42,000

The comparative statements of retained earnings originally issued for the same three years contain the following information:

	1986	1985	1984
Retained earnings, beginning	$867,000	$828,000	$800,000
Net income	60,000	57,000	42,000
Dividends	(20,000)	(18,000)	(14,000)
Retained earnings, ending	$907,000	$867,000	$828,000

The cumulative effect of the change from the completed-contract method to the percentage-of-completion method is calculated in Exhibit 22–4.

The entry to record the change, as of the beginning of 1987, is:

Construction in progress	155,000	
Deferred income taxes		62,000
Retained earnings		93,000

As we saw in Chapters 6 and 10, income from construction activity is recorded as an increase in construction in progress under the percentage-of-completion method. The debit to construction in progress increases this account balance to what it would have been if the percentage-of-completion method had been used in prior years. The credit to deferred income taxes is the cumulative tax effect of timing differences that would have

EXHIBIT 22–4   CUMULATIVE EFFECT OF A CHANGE IN ACCOUNTING METHOD FOR LONG-TERM CONSTRUCTION CONTRACTS

Crane Company

	PRETAX ACCOUNTING INCOME				
	(1)	**(2)**	**(3)**	**(4)**	**(5)**
	PERCENTAGE-OF-COMPLETION METHOD*	**COMPLETED-CONTRACT METHOD**		**TAX EFFECT**	**EFFECT ON INCOME, NET OF TAX**
YEAR			**DIFFERENCE**	**(40%)**	**(3 – 4)**
Before 1984	$300,000	$180,000*	$120,000	$48,000	$72,000
1984	100,000	70,000	30,000	12,000	18,000
1985	90,000	95,000	(5,000)	(2,000)	(3,000)
1986	110,000	100,000	10,000	4,000	6,000
Total (as of 1/1/87)	$600,000	$445,000	$155,000	$62,000	$93,000
1987	$ 80,000	$ 72,000*	$ 8,000	$ 3,200	$ 4,800
Tax at 40%	(32,000)				
Net income for 1987	$ 48,000				

* Numbers assumed.

existed at the end of 1986 (beginning of 1987) had the percentage-of-completion method been used in prior years for financial reporting purposes and the completed-contract method been used for tax purposes. The credit to retained earnings represents the cumulative increase in income, net of taxes, that would have resulted under the percentage-of-completion method.

The comparative statements that incorporate the retroactive application of the accounting change are shown in Exhibit 22–5. The $93,000 credit to retained earnings in the formal journal entry above is a credit to the retained earnings account as of the *beginning* of 1987 and affects the restated comparative statements as follows:

```
      $72,000  increase in beginning 1984 retained earnings, which is the cumulative effect
                  (net of taxes) for years prior to 1984
  +     18,000  increase in 1984 net income ($60,000 as restated less $42,000 originally reported)
  =   $90,000  increase in 1985 beginning retained earnings
  −      3,000  decrease in 1985 net income ($54,000 as restated less $57,000 originally reported)
  =   $87,000  increase in beginning 1986 retained earnings
  +      6,000  increase in 1986 net income ($66,000 as restated less $60,000 originally reported)
      $93,000  cumulative increase in retained earnings at the beginning of 1987.
```

The following 1985 and 1986 balance sheet effects of the retroactive accounting change for Crane Company are based on Exhibit 22–4:

	1986	1985*	TOTAL†
Assets: Construction in progress	$10,000	$145,000‡	$155,000
Liabilities: Deferred income taxes	4,000	58,000§	62,000
Retained earnings	6,000	87,000	93,000

* Includes cumulative effect of prior years.

† See journal entry, p. 1012.

‡ Exhibit 22–4, col. 3: $120,000 + $30,000 − $5,000.

§ Exhibit 22–4, col. 4: $48,000 + $12,000 − $2,000.

The following journal entries that were made to record construction costs, construction revenue, and related taxes in 1987 are based on the data in Exhibit 22–5. Notice that the percentage-of-completion method is used for 1987 construction activities.

Construction in progress	420,000	
Miscellaneous credits		420,000
To record construction costs.		

Cost of construction revenue	420,000	
Construction in progress	80,000	
Construction revenue		500,000
To record construction revenue and related expense under the percentage-of-completion method.		

Income tax expense	32,000	
Deferred income taxes (Exhibit 22–4, col. 4)		3,200
Income taxes payable (.4 × $72,000 in		
Exhibit 22–4, col. 2)		28,800
To record income taxes for 1987.		

CUMULATIVE EFFECT NOT DETERMINABLE   Occasionally the cumulative effect of a change in accounting principle cannot be determined. In these cases, disclosure is limited to showing the effect of the change on the operating results of the period of change and explaining the reason for omitting accounting for the cumulative effect and disclosure of pro forma amounts for prior periods.[6]

One type of change in accounting principle whose cumulative effect generally cannot be calculated is a change *to* the LIFO method of inventory. Companies often change to LIFO in a period of inflation in order to obtain a better matching of current cost and current revenue and to reduce income taxes. Under LIFO, as we pointed out in Chapter 10, "layers" are added as the physical inventory increases through time. If a company is changing to LIFO, however, it is unlikely that information is available when the change is made to allow the company to calculate the LIFO layers that would have existed had LIFO been used in prior periods. Therefore, the beginning inventory for the period in which the change is made is designated as the initial LIFO layer or base inventory, no cumulative effect is calculated, and no adjusting entry is required.[7]

The SEC requires that when a company filing with it makes a voluntary change in accounting principle, the company's auditors must state, in the audit opinion, that the new principle is the *preferable* one. This requirement has come under severe criticism from many accountants because an auditor may be placed in the uncomfortable position of stating that, say, accounting procedure *X* is preferable for one client when another client with similar operations is using accounting procedure *Y*, both of which are generally accepted.

CHANGES IN ACCOUNTING ESTIMATES

Changes in accounting estimates are accounted for prospectively.

As we have seen, estimates are an inherent part of the accounting process. Even though estimates may be made in good faith and may be based on all known facts and circumstances at a point in time, subsequent experience may indicate a need to revise the original estimates. Estimates that are not made in good faith represent errors and are discussed later in this chapter.

Opinion No. 20 requires that changes in accounting estimates must be accounted for prospectively. Thus, the effect of a change in estimate is accounted for and reported in the current period if the change affects that period only. If a change in estimate affects both current and future periods, it is accounted for and reported in those periods.

[6] *APB Opinion No. 20,* para. 26.

[7] As we saw in Chapter 10, an entry may be required to adjust the beginning inventory to cost if it is carried at the lower of cost or market.

EXHIBIT 22–5 | RETROACTIVE DISCLOSURE OF A CHANGE IN ACCOUNTING PRINCIPLE

Crane Company
COMPARATIVE INCOME STATEMENTS, 1985–87

	1987	1986	1985
Construction revenue	$500,000	$510,000	$445,000
Cost of construction revenue	(420,000)	(400,000)	(355,000)
Income before taxes	$ 80,000	$110,000	$ 90,000
Income tax expense	(32,000)	(44,000)	(36,000)
Net income	$ 48,000	$ 66,000	$ 54,000

COMPARATIVE STATEMENTS OF RETAINED EARNINGS*

	1987	1986	1985
Retained earnings, beginning (as previously reported)	$ 907,000	$ 867,000	$828,000
Cumulative effect of change in accounting principle, applied retroactively (Note A)	93,000	87,000	90,000
Balance, as adjusted.....................	$1,000,000	$ 954,000	$918,000
Net income	48,000	66,000	54,000
Dividends	(22,000)	(20,000)	(18,000)
Retained earnings, ending	$1,026,000	$1,000,000	$954,000

Note A: In 1987 the company changed to the percentage-of-completion method to account for long-term construction contracts. The completed-contract method was used in previous years. The change was made because management determined that estimates of construction costs could be made with a high degree of reliability. The new method therefore provides more useful information to users. The completed-contract method is continued for tax purposes. The effect of the accounting change on 1987 net income was an increase of $4,800 after related taxes, and net income for 1984, 1985, and 1986 (as previously reported) increased (decreased) by $18,000, ($3,000), and $6,000, respectively, net of related taxes. The retained earnings balances (as previously reported) have been adjusted for retroactive application of the change in accounting principle.

* An alternative presentation is as follows:

	1987	1986	1985
Retained earnings, beginning	$1,000,000	$954,000	$828,000
Prior period adjustment to apply change in accounting principle retroactively (see analysis for years prior to 1985) (Note A).........			90,000
Net income	48,000	66,000	54,000
Dividends (assumed)	(22,000)	(20,000)	(18,000)
Retained earnings, ending	$1,026,000	$1,000,000	$954,000

To illustrate the prospective application of a change in estimate, assume that Zero Corporation uses the allowance method of accounting for uncollectible accounts and has previously calculated its periodic uncollectible accounts expense as 3 percent of net credit sales. In 1987, after a review of its collection experience, Zero revises its estimate to 2 percent of net credit sales, and sales in 1987 were $150,000. The new estimate is used to calculate the expense for 1987 and in subsequent periods. The entry to record the 1987 expense is as follows:

Uncollectible accounts expense	3,000	
Allowance for doubtful accounts		3,000
(.02 × $150,000)		

The effect of the change in estimate on 1987 income would be disclosed in a footnote, as follows:

> Note *X:* In 1987 the company revised its estimate of uncollectible accounts expense. The revised estimate is thought to provide better matching of uncollectible accounts expense with sales. The effect of the change in estimate was to increase 1987 net income by $1,500.[8]

For another illustration, assume that W. Nelson, Inc., acquired plant assets at the beginning of 1983 at a cost of $100,000. The assets were expected to have a useful life of 10 years with no salvage value. Straight-line depreciation was used. During 1987 the estimated useful life was revised downward to eight years. The book value of the assets at the beginning of 1987 was $60,000:

Original cost	$100,000
Accumulated depreciation ($10,000 × 4)	(40,000)
Book value	$ 60,000

Since the change in estimate is applied prospectively, depreciation for 1987 is based on the new estimate. The net book value at the beginning of 1987 is depreciated over the revised remaining useful life of four years. The depreciation expense for 1987 and subsequent years is $15,000, calculated as follows:

$$\frac{\text{Book value at beginning of 1987 ($60,000)}}{\text{Remaining life based on new estimate (4 years)}} = \$15,000$$

The entry to record 1987 depreciation expense is as follows:

Depreciation expense	15,000	
Accumulated depreciation		15,000

Disclosure is limited to showing the effect of the change on 1987 income; the change decreased income by $5,000 ($15,000 − $10,000).

Notice that in both of these examples, the changes in estimate affected both current and future periods (1987 and subsequent years). Occasionally, a change in estimate affects the current period only. To illustrate, recall how losses on construction contracts were calculated under the percentage-of-completion method (p. 249). Since future periods

---

[8] (.03 − .02) × $150,000.

were not affected by the change in estimate, the accounting effects of the change were recognized in the period of change. As another example, refer to the stock appreciation rights (SARs) illustration on page 936. There, at the end of the second year, the change in estimated compensation (from $300,000 to $360,000) affected expenses for the second *and* third years. At the end of the third year, however, *another* change in estimated compensation (from $360,000 to $180,000) affected only the third year because no future years were involved.

CHANGES IN REPORTING ENTITY

A change in reporting entity is disclosed by restating the prior period financial statements for the new reporting entity. Accounting and reporting for a change in reporting entity are not discussed further here, since this subject normally is covered in advanced accounting texts on business combinations and consolidations.

Accounting Changes: Summary and Evaluation

The intent of *APB Opinion No. 20* was to increase the usefulness of financial information by increasing comparability in the manner in which accounting changes are recorded and reported. A brief summary of the accounting requirements of *APB Opinion No. 20* appears in Exhibit 22–6.

The objective of *APB Opinion No. 20* was to increase comparability in accounting for and disclosing accounting changes.

EXHIBIT 22–6 ACCOUNTING CHANGES: A SUMMARY OF ACCOUNTING AND REPORTING REQUIREMENTS

TYPE OF ACCOUNTING CHANGE	BASIC ACCOUNTING REQUIREMENT	OTHER DISCLOSURE REQUIREMENTS
Change in accounting principle:		
Generally	Cumulative effect included in current period income statement; comparative statements not restated	Effects of change on current period income disclosed; also, on a pro forma basis, cumulative effect applied retroactively to selected income and per share data
Exceptions: Some changes in accounting principle	Cumulative effect applied retroactively by restating prior period statements presented for comparative purposes	Effects of change on current period income disclosed
Cumulative effect not determinable	No cumulative effect calculated	Effects of change on current period income disclosed
Change in accounting estimate	Applied prospectively in current period or in current and future periods	Effects of change on current period income disclosed
Change in reporting entity	Cumulative effect applied retroactively by restating prior period statements presented for comparative purposes	

As we stated at the beginning of the chapter, arguments can be made for the various methods of reporting an accounting change. For example, many accountants believe that retroactive application is preferable for all accounting changes because it increases the comparability of financial statements. Others agree with this argument but are concerned about the effect of retroactive application on the credibility and reliability of financial statements. As a result, these accountants prefer prospective application, since continued retroactive application over time might cast doubt on the reliability of the original data and on the reliability of financial reporting in general. Notice that trade-offs must be made among the qualitative characteristics discussed in Chapter 2.

In another vein, some accountants believe that almost *all* changes in accounting principle are necessitated by changes in estimates. According to this view, there is no such thing as a change in accounting principle that is not inextricably tied to a change in estimate. Presumably a company should not change from, say, the completed-contract to percentage-of-completion method (or vice versa) unless estimates of construction completion costs have become more or less accurate. Is this not a change in principle necessitated by a change in estimate? Presumably a company should not change depreciation methods unless there has been a change in the *estimated* pattern of future benefits received from use of the asset. Is this not a change in principle necessitated by a change in estimate?

Finally, the transition rules for many of the *FASB Statements* require retroactive application of the *Statements'* provisions. As a result, critics point out, current accounting practice lacks consistency in the manner of accounting and reporting for changes in accounting principle, because the current period approach is used for some changes while the retroactive approach is used for many others.

As we pointed out in Chapters 1 and 2, accounting standard-setting cannot be perfect and free of criticism. Individual preferences differ, choices are necessary, and compromises are made. Any pronouncement will invariably please some constituents and displease others. While certain aspects of *Opinion No. 20* are subject to criticism, on balance it appears to have improved financial reporting.

ANALYSIS AND CORRECTION OF ERRORS

This part of the chapter covers the analysis and correction of errors. Occasionally a company will make an error in recording a transaction. For example, a company may purchase a long-lived asset, such as a machine, and improperly record the acquisition as an expense. In such a situation, the accountant must be able to assess the error's impact on the financial statements, correct the error in the accounts, and disclose the correction in the financial statements.

In the remaining sections of this chapter, we will discuss the nature and types of errors, how errors are corrected in the accounts and disclosed in the financial statements, and how errors are analyzed in terms of their effects on the financial statements. The chapter concludes with a discussion of how a worksheet can be used to facilitate error analysis.

NATURE AND TYPES OF ERRORS A listing of all possible accounting errors that could be made is almost impossible. Errors generally arise, however, as a result of one or more of the following:

1. Mathematical mistakes in the calculation of quantities and amounts of inventory, depreciation, salary expense, and other items.

2. Use of an incorrect accounting principle in a given economic circumstance (e.g., use of the installment method in revenue recognition when estimates of uncollectible receivables can be made).

3. Oversight or misuse of facts available (e.g., failure to expense an item when no future benefits exist).

4. Incorrect classification in the income statement or balance sheet, intentionally or through oversight.

CORRECTION AND DISCLOSURE OF ERRORS

As soon as an error is discovered, it should be corrected.[9] An error may be discovered in the same accounting period in which it was made. If so, the incorrect entry should be reversed and the correct entry should be made. When an error is discovered after the period in which it was made, *APB Opinion No. 20* and *FASB Statement No. 16* require that it be corrected *as of the beginning of the period* in which the discovery is made and that prior period statements presented for comparative purposes be restated to correct for the error. Also, prior period statements affected by an error discovered in the current period should be restated for comparative purposes to correct for the error, even though a correcting entry may not be necessary in the current period.

Because of the many types of errors that can be made, it is difficult to formulate any specific rules or procedures that always can be relied on to correct errors. However, four steps are helpful:

1. Determine the entry that *was made* or *omitted* and that gave rise to the error.

2. Determine the entry that *should have been made*.

3. Determine the effect of the error on the current and previous (if applicable) financial statements.

4. Determine the entry, if any, that is necessary to correct the error and determine how the prior period statements should be restated, if necessary.

To illustrate these steps, assume that on January 2, 1983, Edd Corporation purchased a machine at a cost of $100,000. The machine had an expected life of 10 years with no salvage value, and was to be depreciated on a straight-line basis. When the bookkeeper recorded the purchase, he erred by expensing the entire cost of the machine. The error also was made for tax purposes, and a 40 percent tax rate is applicable. The error was discovered during the audit for the year ending December 31, 1987. Edd Corporation issues three-year comparative financial statements, and the 1987 income statement and statement of retained earnings, with the 1986 and 1985 statements shown for comparative purposes, appear below (before correction for the error):

INCOME STATEMENTS FOR YEAR ENDED 12/31

	1987	1986	1985
Revenues	$200,000	$180,000	$150,000
Expenses, including depreciation	(120,000)	(100,000)	(90,000)
Income tax expense	(32,000)	(32,000)	(24,000)
Net income	$ 48,000	$ 48,000	$ 36,000

STATEMENTS OF RETAINED EARNINGS FOR YEAR ENDED 12/31

	1987	1986	1985
Retained earnings, 1/1	$300,000	$274,000	$250,000
Net income	48,000	48,000	36,000
Dividends	(24,000)	(22,000)	(12,000)
Retained earnings, 12/31	$324,000	$300,000	$274,000

[9] All errors discussed in this text are assumed to be material. In practice, auditors often do not insist on correction of immaterial errors.

EXHIBIT 22–7 EFFECTS OF ERROR ON FINANCIAL STATEMENTS

Edd Corporation
INCOME STATEMENT FOR YEAR ENDED 12/31

	1987	1986	1985	1984	1983
Depreciation expense	$10,000 *U*	$10,000 *U*	$10,000 *U*	$10,000 *U*	$ 10,000 *U*
Other expenses	—	—	—	—	100,000 *O*
Tax expense	4,000 *O*	4,000 *O*	4,000 *O*	4,000 *O*	36,000 *U*
Net income	6,000 *O*	6,000 *O*	6,000 *O*	6,000 *O*	54,000 *U*

BALANCE SHEET, 12/31

	1987	1986	1985	1984	1983
Assets					
Machinery (net of accumulated depreciation)	$50,000 *U*	$60,000 *U*	$70,000 *U*	$80,000 *U*	$90,000 *U*
Liabilities					
Taxes payable	20,000 *U*	24,000 *U*	28,000 *U*	32,000 *U*	36,000 *U*
Owners' equity					
Retained earnings	30,000 *U*	36,000 *U*	42,000 *U*	48,000 *U*	54,000 *U*

Note: *U* = understated; *O* = overstated.

The entry that was made to record the equipment purchase on January 2, 1983, was:

Other expenses 100,000

    Cash.. 100,000

The entry that should have been made is:

Machinery 100,000

    Cash.. 100,000

The entry for each year's depreciation expense should have been:

Depreciation expense 10,000

    Accumulated depreciation, machinery 10,000

Exhibit 22–7 shows the financial statement effects of the error for the years 1983–87. In 1983 the company recorded other expenses of $100,000 instead of depreciation expense of $10,000. Therefore, 1983 income before taxes and taxable income are understated by $90,000 ($100,000 − $10,000). Income tax expense is understated by $36,000 (.4 × $90,000), and net income is understated by $54,000 ($90,000 − $36,000). On the balance sheet at the end of 1983, machinery, net of accumulated depreciation, is understated by $90,000 ($100,000 original cost less $10,000 accumulated depreciation), and taxes payable is understated by $36,000.[10] Retained earnings is understated by $54,000 because of the $54,000 understatement of 1983 net income which was closed to retained earnings.

On the 1984 income statement, depreciation expense is understated by $10,000. Tax expense is overstated by $4,000 ($10,000 × .4), and net income is overstated by $6,000

[10] In practice, an error for tax purposes may give rise to a tax deficiency penalty, plus interest, if the error is in the taxpayer's favor (as in this example). For simplicity, this deficiency is ignored.

($10,000 understatement of depreciation expense less $4,000 overstatement of tax expense). On the ending 1984 balance sheet, the machinery is now understated by $80,000 ($100,000 cost minus *two* years' depreciation of $10,000 per year). Taxes payable is understated by $32,000, since the previous year's understatement of $36,000 is reduced by the 1984 overstatement of taxes of $4,000. Retained earnings is understated by $48,000, which is the cumulative effect of the error as of the end of 1984. (The beginning 1984 retained earnings is *understated* by $54,000, and 1984 net income is *overstated* by $6,000.) The effects of the error on the 1985, 1986, and 1987 financial statements can be analyzed in a similar manner.

If the error was discovered before the books were closed for 1987, it should be corrected *as of the beginning of 1987,* as shown below. Also, depreciation expense and income tax expense for 1987 are recorded as shown below:

Machinery	100,000	
Accumulated depreciation, machinery		40,000
Taxes payable		24,000
Retained earnings		36,000
To correct the error as of 1/1/87.		
Depreciation expense	10,000	
Accumulated depreciation, machinery		10,000
To record depreciation for 1987.		
Taxes payable	4,000	
Tax expense		4,000
To reduce taxes payable and 1987 tax expense as a result of the $10,000 additional 1987 depreciation expense.		

In the error correction entry above, a temporary account, prior period adjustment—error correction, could be credited instead of retained earnings. This temporary account would be closed to retained earnings at the end of the accounting period. And instead of three separate entries, one compound correcting entry could be made. The corrections and adjustments, when posted to the appropriate accounts, will bring the accounts up to date at the end of 1987.

Comparative income statements, statements of retained earnings, and partial balance sheet increases for Edd Corporation, restated to show the effect of the error correction, appear in Exhibit 22–8. On the restated income statements, net income is $6,000 lower each year as a result of the $10,000 depreciation expense less the $4,000 reduction in tax expense. On the retained earnings statements, the $48,000 increase in retained earnings as of January 1, 1985, is the cumulative effect of the error as of that date:

Error (overstatement of expense) when machine was purchased	$100,000
Understatement of 1983 depreciation	(10,000)
	$ 90,000
Error at 12/31/83, net of tax [$90,000 − .4($90,000)]	$ 54,000
Overstatement of 1984 net income	(6,000)
Cumulative error at 12/31/84 (1/1/85)	$ 48,000

Finally, the correcting entry to retained earnings shown above can be reconciled to the comparative retained earnings statements as follows:

Cumulative error as of 12/31/84	$48,000
Overstatement of 1985 income	(6,000)
Overstatement of 1986 income	(6,000)
Correction of retained earnings required as of 1/1/87	$36,000

EXHIBIT 22—8   COMPARATIVE FINANCIAL STATEMENTS
RESTATED FOR ERROR CORRECTION

Edd Corporation

INCOME STATEMENTS FOR YEAR ENDED 12/31

	1987	1986	1985
Revenues	$200,000	$180,000	$150,000
Expenses, including depreciation	(130,000)	(110,000)	(100,000)
Income tax expense	(28,000)	(28,000)	(20,000)
Net income	$ 42,000	$ 42,000	$ 30,000

STATEMENTS OF RETAINED EARNINGS FOR YEAR ENDED 12/31*

	1987	1986	1985
Retained earnings, 1/1, as previously reported	$300,000	$274,000	$250,000
Prior period adjustment—cumulative effect of error	36,000	42,000	48,000
Retained earnings, 1/1, as corrected	$336,000	$316,000	$298,000
Net income	42,000	42,000	30,000
Dividends	(24,000)	(22,000)	(12,000)
Retained earnings, 12/31	$354,000	$336,000	$316,000

PARTIAL BALANCE SHEET INCREASES, 12/31

	1987	1986	1985
Assets			
Machinery, net of accumulated depreciation	$ 50,000	$ 60,000	$ 70,000
Liabilities			
Income taxes payable	20,000	24,000	28,000
Owners' equity			
Retained earnings	30,000	36,000	42,000

* Alternatively, these statements could be presented as follows:

	1987	1986	1985
Retained earnings, 1/1	$336,000	$316,000	$250,000
Prior period adjustments to beginning retained earnings for correction of error (net of tax)			48,000
Net income	42,000	42,000	30,000
Dividends	(24,000)	(22,000)	(12,000)
Retained earnings, 12/31	$354,000	$336,000	$316,000

One final point should be made about the tax effect of errors. We have assumed that Edd Corporation's error was made for both book and tax purposes, and thus resulted in an additional tax liability. If an error results in an overstatement of taxable income, a tax refund can be claimed. On the other hand, occasionally a company may make an error in its books but not on its tax return. In this case, there is no effect on its tax liability or claim. The difference between pretax accounting income and taxable income that results from this type of error is a result of one of the following occurrences:

1. In error, the company considers the difference to be one of timing, which affects deferred income taxes. In this case, correction of the error involves correction of the deferred taxes account.

2. In error, the company ignores the difference and reports as tax expense the amount due on the tax return. In this case, correction of the error is limited to correction of the affected real and nominal accounts, excluding any current or deferred tax accounts.

ANALYSIS OF ERRORS

Various types of errors, their effects on financial statements, and the procedures for correcting them are discussed in this section. We also discuss the use of a worksheet when numerous errors must be analyzed.

Classification Errors That Have No Effect on Income

Occasionally a company will make a classification error in its balance sheet or income statement that has no effect on net income. For example, a company may sell common stock at a price in excess of par and credit the excess to common stock instead of to contributed capital in excess of par. This error is simply a **classification error** on the balance sheet and has no effect on income. When errors of this kind are discovered, they should be corrected. In addition, prior period statements issued for comparative purposes should be corrected to show the proper classification. As another example, if a company's accounting system is computerized, salary expense may be recorded as cost of goods sold because of an error in coding. Again net income is not affected, although a classification error exists in the income statement. If the error is discovered in the period in which it is made, it should be corrected. If the error is discovered in a subsequent period, no correcting entry can be made, since these nominal accounts already have been closed. If comparative statements are presented, however, the income statement data (here cost of goods sold and salary expense) for the period in which the error was made should be corrected to show the proper classification.

Errors That Affect Both Income Statement and Balance Sheet

While classification errors can be misleading to users, a far more serious error is one that affects net income. For net income to be misstated, an error must affect both the income statement and the balance sheet. Accountants sometimes categorize these errors as counterbalancing and noncounterbalancing errors.

Counterbalancing Errors

Counterbalancing errors are defined as those that are automatically corrected through the recording process over a two-year period. Net income in one year, and a corresponding asset or liability, may be overstated or understated, but net income for the following year, and the corresponding asset or liability, will be misstated equally in the opposite direction. Thus, for the two years together, there is no cumulative effect on net income, assets, or liabilities. Counterbalancing errors usually involve the following types of accounts:

1. Inventories.

2. Prepayments—prepaid expenses and unearned revenue.

3. Accruals—accrued expenses and accrued revenues.

Whether a correcting entry is required when one of these types of errors is discovered depends on when the error is discovered, as the examples which follow demonstrate.

INVENTORY ITEMS The following hypothetical situations illustrate the analysis and correction of inventory errors. In all cases we have assumed that the errors made in one period are not discovered until a subsequent accounting period, and we have ignored taxes.

Assume that Waco failed to record a merchandise purchase in transit at the end of 1987 (title passed to Waco at the point of shipment). The merchandise, which cost $20,000, was excluded from the 1987 ending inventory. The purchase was recorded in early 1988, when the merchandise was received. An analysis reveals the following errors of overstatement and understatement:

INCOME STATEMENT FOR YEAR ENDED 12/31

	1988	1987
Beginning inventory	$20,000 *U*	*N*
+ Purchases	20,000 *O*	$20,000 *U*
− Ending inventory	*N*	20,000 *U*
= Cost of goods sold	*N*	*N*
Net income	*N*	*N*

BALANCE SHEET, 12/31

	1988	1987
Assets (inventory)	*N*	$20,000 *U*
− Liabilities	*N*	20,000 *U*
= Owners' equity	*N*	*N*

If the books for 1988 have *not* been closed, the correcting entry is:

Inventory (beginning)	20,000	
Purchases		20,000

If the 1988 books have been closed, no correcting entry is made.

The error has no effect on 1987 income, since both purchases and ending inventory are understated by equal amounts. The error is counterbalanced in 1988 by an understatement of the beginning 1988 inventory and an overstatement of 1988 purchases. Since the liability has been paid by the end of 1988, no correcting entry is necessary for the liability.

If only 1988 statements are issued, no disclosure is required, since the errors in both the beginning inventory and purchases are components of cost of goods sold.

If 1987 and 1988 comparative statements are issued, no disclosure is required for 1988. On the balance sheet at the end of 1987, inventory and accounts payable are increased by $20,000.

Now assume that Waco correctly included the merchandise in the ending 1987 inventory. An error analysis would show the following:

INCOME STATEMENT FOR YEAR ENDED 12/31

	1988	1987
Beginning inventory	*N*	*N*
+ Purchases	$20,000 *O*	$20,000 *U*
− Ending inventory	*N*	*N*
= Cost of goods sold	20,000 *O*	20,000 *U*
Net income	20,000 *U*	20,000 *O*

BALANCE SHEET, 12/31

	1988	1987
Assets (inventory)	*N*	*N*
− Liabilities	*N*	$20,000 *U*
= Owners' equity	*N*	20,000 *O*

If the books for 1988 have *not* been closed, the correcting entry is:

Retained earnings (beginning) 20,000
    Purchases   20,000

If the books for 1988 have been closed, no correcting entry is necessary.

If only 1988 statements are issued, beginning retained earnings is decreased by $20,000; cost of goods sold is stated correctly after the correcting entry.

If 1987 and 1988 comparative statements are issued, cost of goods sold is increased and net income decreased by $20,000 on the 1987 income statement. On the balance sheet at the end of 1987, liabilities and owners' equity are increased and decreased, respectively, by $20,000. On the 1988 income statement, cost of goods sold and net income are stated correctly after the correcting entry.

In Chapter 9, we discussed and illustrated some additional types of inventory errors. You may wish to review these at this point.

ERRORS INVOLVING PREPAYMENTS   Prepayments involve transactions in which the cash flows precede the earnings activities; that is, a cash inflow or outflow precedes the earning of revenue or the incurring of expenses. Since a company's internal control system normally is effective in controlling cash receipts and disbursements, errors involving prepayments usually do not affect the cash account. Rather, these types of errors result from failure to allocate the prepaid expense or unearned revenue to the correct period.

To illustrate an error involving a prepayment, assume that on January 1, 1987, Candy Company purchased a two-year insurance policy on its building and paid the two $900 annual premiums in advance. The prepaid insurance account was debited for $1,800. The company failed to expense the portion of the prepayment that applied to 1987 and expensed the entire $1,800 in 1988. This error causes the following amounts of overstatement and understatement on Candy's financial statements for 1987 and 1988:

INCOME STATEMENT FOR YEAR ENDED 12/31

	1988	1987
Insurance expense	$900 *O*	$900 *U*
Net income	900 *U*	900 *O*

BALANCE SHEET, 12/31

	1988	1987
Assets (prepaid insurance)	*N*	$900 *O*
− Liabilities	*N*	*N*
= Owners' equity	*N*	900 *O*

If the books for 1988 have *not* been closed, the correcting entry is:

Retained earnings (beginning) 900
    Insurance expense   900

If the books for 1988 have been closed, no correcting entry is made.

If only 1988 statements are presented, beginning retained earnings is decreased by $900; insurance expense (after the correction) is properly stated.

If 1987 and 1988 comparative statements are presented, insurance expense and net income are increased and decreased, respectively, by $900 on the 1987 income statement.

On the ending 1987 balance sheet, prepaid insurance and retained earnings are decreased by $900. The 1988 financial data are correct after the correcting entry is made.

As another illustration, assume that on September 1, 1987, Edwards, Inc., received $1,200 rent for one year in advance on a building that it owned. Edwards credited rent revenue when the cash was received and failed to make an adjusting entry on December 31, 1987, the end of the accounting period. An error analysis reveals the following amounts of overstatement and understatement on Edwards's financial statements:

INCOME STATEMENT FOR YEAR ENDED 12/31

	1988	1987
Rent revenue	$800 *U*	$800 *O* *
Net income	800 *U*	800 *O*

* [$1,200 − 1/3 ($1,200)].

BALANCE SHEET, 12/31

	1988	1987
Assets	*N*	*N*
− Liabilities (unearned rent)	*N*	$800 *U*
= Owners' equity	*N*	800 *O*

If the books for 1988 have *not* been closed, the correcting entry is:

| Retained earnings (beginning) | 800 | |
| Rent revenue | | 800 |

If the books for 1988 have been closed, no correcting entry is made.

If only 1988 statements are issued, beginning retained earnings is decreased by $800; 1988 income statement data are correct after the correcting entry.

If 1987 and 1988 comparative statements are issued, rent revenue and net income are decreased $800 on the 1987 income statement. On the ending 1987 balance sheet, liabilities are increased and retained earnings is decreased by $800. The 1988 statements are correct as a result of the correcting entry.

ERRORS INVOLVING ACCRUALS Accruals involve transactions in which the earnings activities precede the cash flows. Accrued revenues arise when revenues have been earned but cash has not yet been collected. Revenue accruals increase assets on the balance sheet and revenue on the income statement. Accrued expenses arise when an expense has been incurred but has not yet been paid. Expense accruals increase expenses on the income statement and liabilities on the balance sheet. Errors involving accruals probably constitute one of the most frequent types of errors, because the accrual transactions, which in error are not recorded, occur before the related cash inflow or outflow.

To illustrate an error with an accrual, assume that Irene Company failed to record accrued interest revenue of $1,800 on a note receivable at the end of 1987. The company recorded the interest as revenue in 1988, when the cash was received. Analysis of the effects of this error on Irene's financial statements would reveal the following:

INCOME STATEMENT FOR YEAR ENDED 12/31

	1988	1987
Interest revenue	$1,800 *O*	$1,800 *U*
Net income	1,800 *O*	1,800 *U*

BALANCE SHEET, 12/31

	1988	1987
Assets (interest receivable)	*N*	$1,800 *U*
− Liabilities	*N*	*N*
= Owners' equity	*N*	1,800 *U*

If the books for 1988 have *not* been closed, the correcting entry is:

Interest revenue	1,800	
Retained earnings (beginning)		1,800

If the books for 1988 have been closed, no correcting entry is required.

If only 1988 statements are issued, beginning retained earnings are increased by $1,800. Other 1988 financial data are correct after the correction.

If 1987 and 1988 comparative statements are issued, interest revenue and net income are increased $1,800 on the 1987 income statement. On the ending 1987 balance sheet, interest receivable and retained earnings are increased $1,800. The 1988 financial data are correct after the correcting entry.

The previous illustration dealt with an error involving accrued revenues. A similar analysis would apply to an error involving accrued expenses.

One point should be made about counterbalancing errors when income taxes are considered. Unless the income tax rate changes from period to period, ignoring interest and penalties, there is no additional tax liability or claim after the errors have been counterbalanced. However, when the accounts are corrected and the error correction is disclosed, the tax effects of the error must also be considered. The expense or revenue account affected by the error is still corrected by the full amount of the error. The tax effect of the error affects tax expense, and the net of tax effect of the error is an adjustment to net income or retained earnings, as appropriate.

Noncounterbalancing Errors

Whereas counterbalancing errors automatically correct themselves over a two-year period, **noncounterbalancing errors** do not. Noncounterbalancing errors require several periods to self-correct. Generally, errors involving long-lived assets and long-term liabilities are noncounterbalancing. The earlier case of Edd Corporation, which expensed the cost of a new machine, provides a good example of a noncounterbalancing error. The net income understatement of $54,000 in 1983 (see Exhibit 22–7) was gradually offset (counterbalanced) by the net income overstatements of $6,000 in subsequent years as the machine was being used during its useful life. By the end of 1992 when the machine's service potential has expired, the original error of $54,000 will have been completely counterbalanced.

As another illustration, assume that at the beginning of 1986, Kimbrell Corporation sold five-year 10 percent term bonds with a maturity value of $100,000 for $90,000. Interest is payable annually at the end of each year. The discount of $10,000 should have been amortized on a straight-line basis over the five-year period but was expensed when the bonds were sold. The error was not discovered until late in 1988, before the books were closed. The amortization error was not made for tax purposes, and the difference between interest expense for tax purposes and for book purposes was treated, in error, as a timing difference. The tax rate is 40 percent. An analysis and correction are as follows:

1. Compare the entry actually made and the resulting tax effect with the entry that should have been made and the resulting tax effect.

Entries made in error
Cash 90,000
Interest expense . . . 10,000
   Bonds payable . .   100,000

Deferred income
     taxes 3,200*
    Tax expense 3,200*

Correct entry
Cash 90,000
Discount on bonds
   payable 10,000
   Bonds payable   100,000

* Interest expense for:

	TAX PURPOSES	BOOK PURPOSES
Cash interest ($100,000 × .10)	$10,000	$10,000
Amortization of bond discount ($10,000 ÷ 5)	2,000	10,000
	$12,000	$20,000

The tax effect of the difference [.4 ($20,000 − $12,000) = $3,200] was treated as a timing difference.

2. Determine the financial statement effects of the error from 1986 to the end of 1988:

INCOME STATEMENT FOR YEAR ENDED 12/31

	1988	1987	1986
Interest expense	$2,000 *U*	$2,000 *U*	$8,000 *O*
Tax expense	800 *O*	800 *O*	3,200 *U*
Net income	1,200 *O*	1,200 *O*	4,800 *U*

BALANCE SHEET, 12/31

	1988	1987	1986
Assets			
Deferred income taxes	$1,600 *O*	$2,400 *O*	$3,200 *O*
Liabilities			
Discount on bonds payable*	4,000 *U*	6,000 *U*	8,000 *U*
Owners' equity			
Retained earnings	2,400 *U*	3,600 *U*	4,800 *U*

* This account is a contra liability account to bonds payable.

3. Correct the error as of the beginning of 1988:

Discount on bonds payable 6,000
   Deferred income taxes   2,400
   Retained earnings   3,600

4. Record the interest expense for 1988:

Interest expense 12,000
   Discount on bonds payable   2,000
   Cash   10,000

5. If financial statements are being presented for 1988 only, the income statement and balance sheet items affected by the error already have been corrected as a result of entries 3 and 4 above. On the retained earnings statement, the beginning 1988 retained

earnings is increased by $3,600, which is the cumulative effect of the error for 1986 and 1987, or as of January 1, 1988.

If comparative statements for 1987 and 1988 are being presented, the misstated income statement and balance sheet items for 1987 are corrected. On the retained earnings statement, beginning 1987 retained earnings is increased by $4,800.

Finally, if comparative statements for 1986, 1987, and 1988 are presented, the income statement and balance sheet items are corrected for the misstatements as shown in step 2 on page 1028. Since the statements presented include 1986, the year in which the error was made, no cumulative adjustment is necessary in the retained earnings statement because the amounts in the income statements correct for the error.

Worksheet Analysis for Numerous Errors

The use of a worksheet facilitates the analysis of errors. While it is unlikely that a company would have as many errors as we assume in the following illustration, the worksheet is helpful for analytical and instructional purposes. Additionally, the illustration provides a good summary of error correction and analysis.

Assume that Dandy Don Corporation reported the following amounts of net income for the years ended December 31, 1985, 1986, and 1987:

1985	$127,000
1986	110,000
1987	98,500

You are performing the audit for the year ended December 31, 1987. During your examination you discover the following errors:

a) As a result of errors in the physical count, ending inventories were misstated as follows:

12/31/86	$14,000 overstated
12/31/87	22,000 understated

b) On December 29, 1987, Dandy Don recorded as a purchase, merchandise in transit that cost $10,000. The merchandise was shipped F.O.B. destination and had not arrived by December 31. The merchandise was not included in the ending inventory.

c) Dandy Don records sales on the accrual basis, but failed to record sales on account made near the end of each year as follows:

1985	$3,500
1986	5,500
1987	2,000

The sales were recorded in each of the following years, when the cash was received.

d) On December 30, 1985, Dandy Don purchased the net assets of Jamey Company and paid $40,000 in excess of the fair market value of Jamey's assets. This excess, which should have been recorded as goodwill and amortized over a 10-year period, was expensed on December 30, 1985. Goodwill amortization is not deductible for tax purposes.

e) The company failed to record accrued office salaries as follows:

12/31/85	$10,000
12/31/86	12,000

f) On March 1, 1986, a small stock dividend was declared and distributed; the par value of the shares distributed was $10,000, and the fair market value was $13,000. The stock dividend was recorded as follows:

Miscellaneous expense	13,000	
Common stock		10,000
Retained earnings		3,000

g) Dandy Don rents an office building to a CPA firm. The company records rent revenue as the cash is received and failed to record unearned rent at the end of each year as follows (for tax purposes, rent is taxable when cash is received):

12/31/85	$15,000
12/31/86	12,000

h) On July 1, 1986, Dandy Don acquired a three-year insurance policy. The three-year premium of $4,800 was paid on that date, and the entire premium was recorded as insurance expense.

i) On January 1, 1987, Dandy Don retired bonds with a book value of $120,000 for $106,000. The gain was incorrectly deferred and is being amortized over 10 years as a reduction of interest expense on other outstanding obligations.

j) On December 30, 1986, Dandy Don exchanged similar machines as follows:

	MACHINE *O* SACRIFICED	MACHINE *N* RECEIVED
Book value	$2,000	
Fair market value	5,000	$4,000
Cash received		1,000

For tax purposes, gains arising from machine trade-ins are recognized to the extent that cash is received. Dandy Don incorrectly recorded the exchange for financial reporting purposes at the same amounts that were correctly reported for tax purposes, as follows:

Cash	1,000	
Machine (new)	2,000*	
Machine		2,000
Gain on exchange		1,000†

* Fair market value less unrecognized gain ($4,000 − $2,000 [see below]).

† Portion of gain recognized: $3,000 ($5,000 − $2,000) is the total gain; since $1,000 was received in cash, only $1,000 of the gain is recognized. The unrecognized gain is $2,000.

Dandy Don depreciates all machinery for both book and tax purposes on the basis of a useful life of 10 years.

k) Unless otherwise indicated, all errors made for financial reporting purposes were also made for tax purposes. The tax rate each year was 40 percent.

A worksheet to correct the errors appears in Exhibit 22–9. Each item in the worksheet is explained below. The tax effect of all errors is considered in part *k*.

a) *Errors in physical count of inventories.* Since the ending 1986 inventory is overstated by $14,000, net income for 1986 is also overstated by $14,000 because of the $14,000 understatement in cost of goods sold. The overstatement of 1986 net income is counterbalanced, however, by an understatement of 1987 income. The counterbalancing error comes about because the beginning 1987 inventory overstatement of $14,000 causes 1987 cost of goods sold to be overstated by $14,000. The ending inventory for 1987 is understated by $22,000, which causes cost of goods sold for 1987 to be overstated and net income to be understated by $22,000.

The correcting entry for the two inventory errors appears to the right in Exhibit 22–9. Beginning retained earnings is debited for $14,000 to correct the overstatement of 1986 net income. Ending inventory for 1987 is debited for $22,000, since assets are understated. The two errors, in the aggregate, cause 1987 cost of goods sold to be overstated by $36,000. Therefore, cost of goods sold is credited for $36,000, which reduces cost of goods sold and increases 1987 income by $36,000, as shown in the 1987 net income column.

b) *Error in merchandise shipment.* Since the company recorded the purchase and liability in error, cost of goods sold is overstated and net income is understated by $10,000. Thus, the entry in the right-hand column of Exhibit 22–9 corrects the error, and 1987 net income is increased by $10,000. The ending inventory is not affected, since the company correctly excluded the shipment in transit from the ending inventory.

c) *Errors on unrecorded sales.* The sales that were made near the end of 1985, 1986, and 1987 were not recorded until the year immediately following. For example, failure to record the sales of $3,500 made in 1985 until 1986 causes 1985 net income to be understated by $3,500 and 1986 net income to be overstated by $3,500.

The entry to correct the accounts at the end of 1987 is shown in the right-hand column of Exhibit 22–9. The debit of $3,500 to sales is the difference between the $5,500 overstatement of sales made in 1986 but recorded in 1987 and the $2,000 understatement of sales for 1987. Accounts receivable is debited for $2,000 and beginning retained earnings is credited for $5,500. The $5,500 credit to retained earnings corrects 1986 net income, which was understated because of failure to record 1986 sales.

d) *Error in recording goodwill.* When goodwill was purchased, it was expensed. To correct for the error, net income for 1985 is increased by $40,000, while net income for 1986 and 1987 is decreased by $4,000, which is the goodwill amortization for these years. The debit of $32,000 to goodwill is the unamortized goodwill at the end of 1987 ($40,000 − $4,000 − $4,000). Goodwill amortization is debited for the current year's amortization, and the credit to beginning retained earnings corrects for the cumulative effect of the error as of the beginning of 1987.

e) *Error in recording accrued salaries.* This error may be analyzed in much the same way as the unrecorded sales in transaction *c*. The only difference between the two is that since no error was made in salary accruals at the end of 1987, a real account, salaries payable, is not misstated at the end of 1987.

EXHIBIT 22—9 WORKSHEET ANALYSIS OF ERRORS

	1985	1986	1987	CORRECTING ENTRY, 12/31/87	
a) Error in physical count of ending inventories					
End of 1986, overstated . . .		(14,000)	14,000	Retained earnings 14,000	
End of 1987, understated . .			22,000	Inventory 22,000	
				Cost of goods sold	36,000
b) Error on in-transit					
merchandise shipment . . .			10,000	Accounts payable 10,000	
				Cost of goods sold	10,000
c) Error on unrecorded sales					
End of 1985	3,500	(3,500)		Sales ($5,500 − $2,000) 3,500	
End of 1986		5,500	(5,500)	Accounts receivable 2,000	
End of 1987			2,000	Retained earnings	5,500
d) Error in recording goodwill . .	40,000	(4,000)	(4,000)	Goodwill 32,000	
				Goodwill amortization 4,000	
				Retained earnings	36,000
e) Error in recording accrued salaries					
1985	(10,000)	10,000		Retained earnings 12,000	
1986		(12,000)	12,000	Salary expense	12,000
f) Error in recording					
stock dividend		13,000		Retained earnings 3,000	
				Contributed capital	
				in excess of par	3,000
g) Error in recording unearned rent					
End of 1985	(15,000)	15,000		Retained earnings 12,000	
End of 1986		(12,000)	12,000	Rent revenue	12,000
h) Error in recording prepaid insurance					
End of 1986		4,000		Insurance expense 1,600	
End of 1987			(1,600)	Prepaid insurance 2,400	
				Retained earnings	4,000
i) Error in recording gain on					
debt retirement			12,600	Deferred gain 12,600	
				Interest expense 1,400	
				Gain on bond retirement . .	14,000

f) *Error in recording stock dividend.* This error may be analyzed most efficiently by comparing the erroneous entry with the entry that should have been made:

Entry made in error		*Correct entry*	
Expense 13,000		Retained earnings 13,000	
Common stock	10,000	Common stock	10,000
Retained		Contributed	
earnings	3,000	capital in	
		excess of par . . .	3,000

In the 1986 worksheet column, $13,000 is added to net income because 1986 expenses are overstated and net income is understated by $13,000. Since net income is closed to retained earnings, however, the net debit to retained earnings in

j) Error on machine exchange and subsequent depreciation

1986	(400)		Accumulated depreciation. . . .	40		
1987		40	Retained earnings	400		
			Depreciation expense			40
			Machinery			400

k) Tax effect (see below) . . . . . . (7,400) (2,240) (31,016)

Retained earnings
($7,400 + $2,240) 9,640
Tax expense. 31,016
Deferred income taxes 144

Adjustment to net income
(after taxes) 11,100   (640)   42,524

Income taxes payable
(see below)   40,800

Net income as previously
reported 127,000 110,000   98,500

Net income (corrected) 138,100 109,360 141,024

TAX EFFECT OF ERRORS

	1985	1986	1987
Effect of errors, before taxes (summation of errors *a* through *j*)	$18,500	$ 1,600	$73,540
Permanent difference on goodwill amortization		4,000	4,000
Increase in pretax accounting income	$18,500	$ 5,600	$77,540

Additional tax expense:
1985 $18,500 × .4 = $ 7,400
1986 $ 5,600 × .4 =   2,240
1987 $77,540 × .4 = 31,016

Timing difference on rent	15,000	(15,000)	
		12,000	(12,000)
Timing difference on machine gain and subsequent depreciation on carrying value.		400	(40)
Increase in taxable income	$33,500	$ 3,000	$65,500

Additional taxes payable:
1985 $33,500 × .4 = $13,400
1986 $ 3,000 × .4 =   1,200
1987 $65,500 × .4 = 26,200
         $40,800

the error entry is $10,000 ($13,000 − $3,000). Since retained earnings should have been debited for $13,000, it is overstated by $3,000. The correcting entry reduces retained earnings by $3,000 and increases contributed capital in excess of par by $3,000.

g) *Error in recording unearned rent.* This error is similar to the sales and salaries errors in transactions *c* and *e*, except that it involves a prepayment rather than an accrual. The company recorded rent revenue when cash was received and failed to make appropriate adjusting entries at the end of 1985 and 1986. The failure to adjust for unearned rent of $15,000 at the end of 1985 overstates 1985 net income by $15,000. This error, however, is counterbalanced by an understatement of rent revenue of $15,000, which was earned in 1986 instead of 1985. The $15,000 error is counterbalanced at the end of 1986, so no correcting entry is necessary in 1987.

h) *Error in recording prepaid insurance*. This error is not a counterbalancing one. The error will not automatically correct itself over two consecutive years because the premium covers a three-year period. The annual premium expense is $1,600 ($4,800 ÷ 3). The $4,000 addition to 1986 income is the amount of insurance expense overstated at the end of 1986 [$4,800 − ($1,600 ÷ 2)]. Net income for 1987 is reduced by $1,600 for the insurance expense understatement for 1987.

The correcting entry at the end of 1987 appears in the right-hand column of Exhibit 22–9. Insurance expense is debited for $1,600 (the expense for 1987). Prepaid insurance is debited for $2,400, which is the unexpired insurance at the end of 1987 (at the end of 1987 the policy has a remaining life of 1 1/2 years). The credit to beginning retained earnings corrects for the 1986 net income understatement of $4,000.

i) *Error on debt retirement*. The gain on retirement should have been included in 1987 net income but was incorrectly deferred and is being amortized as a reduction of interest expense over a 10-year period. Thus, net income for 1987 is understated by $12,600 ($14,000 − $1,400). The correcting entry removes the balance of the deferred gain, increases interest expense by $1,400, and records the gain on retirement of $14,000.

j) *Error on machine exchange*. The effects of the machine error can be analyzed most efficiently by comparing the entry incorrectly made with the entry that should have been made. (Transactions involving exchanges of similar assets were discussed in Chapter 11.)

Entry made in error		Correct entry	
Cash 1,000		Cash 1,000	
Machine (new) 2,000		Machine (new) 1,600*	
Machine (old)	2,000	Machine (old)	2,000
Gain on exchange . . .	1,000	Gain on exchange . .	600†

* $4,000 (fair market value) less deferred gain of $2,400 (see below).

$$\text{† Gain recognized} = \text{Total gain} \times \frac{\text{Cash received}}{\text{Fair market value of assets received}}$$

$$= \$3,000 \times \frac{\$1,000}{\$1,000 + \$4,000}$$

$$= \$600$$

$$\text{Deferred gain} = \$3,000 - \$600 = \$2,400$$

Since the gain is overstated by $400, $400 is subtracted from the 1986 net income column. The machine is overstated by $400, and annual depreciation is overstated by $40. Therefore $40 is added to the 1987 net income column.

In the correcting entry accumulated depreciation is debited for $40, which is the amount of overstatement of this account at the end of 1987. Beginning retained earnings is debited for $400 to correct for the 1986 net income overstatement, depreciation expense is credited for $40, and machinery is credited for $400.

k) *Tax effects of all errors*. The tax effects of the errors are calculated at the bottom of Exhibit 22–9. We have assumed that, unless otherwise indicated, errors made for book purposes were also made for tax purposes. In calculating the tax effects of the errors, however, we must adjust the before-tax effect of errors for permanent and timing differences between pretax accounting income and taxable income. As we saw in Chapter 19, goodwill is *not* deductible for tax purposes. The $4,000 annual amortization that was included in transaction *d* must therefore be added back to the 1986 and 1987 income adjustments so that we can calculate the additional tax expense and tax payable applicable to the net income increases for those years.

Since rent is taxable when it is received, a timing difference arises for the portion of the rent that is unearned at the end of 1985 and 1986. These timing differences are reversed in the following years, when the rent is earned. The timing differences have been completely reversed by the end of 1987, and there is no effect on the company's income tax liability at the end of 1987.

On the machine exchange, an originating timing difference of $400 should arise between the tax gain of $1,000 and the book gain of $600. This timing difference is reversed in subsequent periods because of differences in depreciation for book purposes and for tax purposes. For tax purposes, a larger gain is recognized initially. A larger depreciation expense, however, will be recognized in subsequent years for tax purposes:

Annual depreciation for tax purposes: $2,000 ÷ 10 = $200

Annual depreciation for book purposes: $1,600 ÷ 10 = $160

Thus, the $400 originating difference, in the form of a gain, is reversed over the next 10 years by higher depreciation for tax purposes than for book purposes. We must consider the timing difference in arriving at the additional tax liability associated with the net income for 1985, 1986, and 1987, as is shown at the bottom of Exhibit 22–9.

The entry to record the tax effects of the errors is shown in the right-hand column of the worksheet. Beginning retained earnings is debited for $9,640, which is the additional tax expense arising from the increased income for 1985 and 1986. Tax expense is debited for the tax expense related to the 1987 income adjustments. Deferred income taxes is debited for the tax effect of the cumulative timing difference at the end of 1987 [.4($400 − $40)], and taxes payable is credited for the additional tax liability of $40,800. Finally, the net income adjustments are added to the previously reported net income amounts to arrive at the corrected net income amounts for the three years.

SUMMARY OF IMPORTANT TOPICS AND CONCEPT APPLICATIONS

1. A change in economic circumstances may cause a company to change its methods of accounting.

2. The three types of accounting changes are: (1) a change in accounting principle, (2) a change in accounting estimate, and (3) a change in reporting entity.

3. With two exceptions, a change in accounting principle is accounted for under the **current period approach.** Under this approach, the cumulative effect of the change is reported in the current period income statement and the new principle is used in the current period. Comparative statements for prior periods are not restated. In addition, net income and earnings per share for all periods presented are restated on a pro forma basis to show what these amounts would have been if the new principle had been used in previous periods.

4. The two exceptions for reporting a change in accounting principle are: (1) some changes are reported **retroactively,** that is, the cumulative effect is debited or credited to retained earnings, and comparative statements for prior periods are restated to reflect the new method; (2) when the cumulative effect of a change cannot be determined, the new principle is applied to the carrying value of the asset or liability as of the beginning of the period in which the change is made.

5. A change in accounting estimate is applied **prospectively;** that is, in the current period and, if applicable, in future periods. A cumulative effect is not calculated, and comparative statements for prior periods are not restated.

6. A change in reporting entity is applied **retroactively** by restating comparative statements for prior periods.

7. An error made and discovered in the current period is corrected either by reversing the erroneous entry and making the correct entry or by making the correct entry if the error was an omission of an entry. An error made in a prior period and discovered in the current period is corrected as of the beginning of the current period, assuming that the error still remains in a balance sheet account. Prior period statements, presented for comparative purposes, should be **restated** to reflect the error correction.

8. An error may be one of several types: classification errors, which have no effect on net income; errors that affect both the balance sheet and income statement and that cause net income for a period to be overstated or understated; and counterbalancing errors, which correct themselves automatically through the recording process over a two-year period.

9. Accountants must understand how to analyze the effects of an error on the financial statements, how to correct an error once it has been discovered, and how to prepare financial statements that reflect an error correction.

QUESTIONS

Q22-1. What prompted the issuance of *APB Opinion No. 20*, ''Accounting Changes,'' and what improvements in financial reporting occurred after the *Opinion* was issued?

Q22-2. Define a change in accounting principle, give an example of such a change, and describe the *general rule* of accounting for and disclosing changes in accounting principles.

Q22-3. State the advantages and disadvantages of the following approaches to accounting for and reporting of accounting changes:

1. Retroactive approach.
2. Prospective approach.
3. Current period approach.

Q22-4. Identify the exceptions to the general rule of reporting the cumulative effect of a change in accounting principle in the income statement for the period in which the change is made.

Q22-5. What are pro forma data and how do these data relate to changes in accounting principle?

Q22-6. Distinguish between a voluntary change in accounting principle and one arising from transition rules.

Q22-7. Define a change in accounting estimate and give an example of such a change.

Q22-8. Give some examples of a change in reporting entity.

Q22-9. How are the following accounting changes recorded in the accounts and reported in financial statements for the current year?

1. A change in the estimated salvage value of machinery.
2. A change in the estimated useful life of machinery.
3. A change from LIFO to FIFO for merchandise inventories.
4. A change from FIFO to LIFO for merchandise inventories.
5. A change from the cash basis to the accrual basis of accounting.
6. A change in the composition of companies included in consolidated statements.

7. A change from the direct write-off method to the allowance method for uncollectible receivables.

8. A change in depreciation methods for plant and equipment.

9. A change in the estimated amount recoverable from investments.

10. A change from deferring and amortizing marketing costs to expensing these costs as incurred because of increased uncertainty regarding future benefits.

11. A change from the percentage-of-completion to the completed-contract method for long-term construction contracts.

12. A change from recognizing revenue at the point of sale to recognition prior to sale because of an improved ability to estimate the amount of revenue to be received prior to the point of sale. Assume the earnings process is deemed complete before the point of sale.

Q22-10. Explain what is meant by a change in accounting principle necessitated by a change in accounting estimate.

Q22-11. Describe how an error discovered in the current period which affects previously issued financial statements should be corrected and disclosed.

Q22-12. Why must an error that affects net income affect both the balance sheet and the income statement?

Q22-13. Give an example of each of the following types of errors:

1. An error that affects the balance sheet only.

2. An error that affects the income statement only.

3. An error that affects both the balance sheet and the income statement.

Q22-14. Distinguish between counterbalancing and noncounterbalancing errors and give an example of each.

Q22-15. "All errors sooner or later correct themselves." Discuss.

Q22-16. Assume that a company fails to record depreciation in a given accounting period. When the impact of the error on net income *after taxes* is considered, it is possible that income taxes payable or deferred income taxes may also be affected by the depreciation error.

1. Under what circumstances would income taxes payable be affected?

2. Under what circumstances would deferred income taxes be affected?

3. Under what circumstances would a related tax account not be affected?

CASES

C22-1. ACCOUNTING CHANGES   Sometimes a business entity may change its method of accounting for certain items. The change may be classified as a change in accounting principle, a change in accounting estimate, or a change in reporting entity.

The following sets of facts related to accounting changes are independent and unrelated.

a) A company determined that the depreciable lives of its fixed assets are now too long to match fairly the cost of the fixed assets with the revenue produced. The company decided at the beginning of the current year to reduce the depreciable lives of all of its existing fixed assets by five years.

b) A company decides in January 1987 to adopt the straight-line method of depreciation for plant equipment. The straight-line method will be used for new acquisitions as well as for previously acquired plant equipment that has been depreciated on an accelerated basis.

REQUIRED

For each of the situations described above, provide the information indicated below. Complete your discussion of each situation before going on to the next.

1. Type of accounting change.

2. Manner of reporting the change under current generally accepted accounting principles, including a discussion, where applicable, of how amounts are calculated.

3. Effect of the change on the balance sheet and income statement.

4. Footnote disclosures that are necessary.

(AICPA, adapted)

C22-2. ACCOUNTING CHANGES; ERRORS   D. L. Roth Manufacturing is preparing its year-end financial statements. The controller is confronted with several decisions about statement presentation with regard to the following items:

1. When the year-end physical inventory adjustment was made for the current year, the prior year's physical inventory sheets for an entire warehouse were discovered to have been misplaced and excluded from last year's count.

2. The method of accounting used for financial reporting purposes for certain receivables has been approved for tax purposes during the current tax year by the IRS. This change for tax purposes will cause both deferred and current taxes payable to change substantially.

3. Management has decided to switch from the FIFO method to the LIFO method for all inventories.

4. Roth's Custom Division manufactures large-scale, custom-designed machinery on a contract basis. Management decided to switch from the completed-contract method to the percentage-of-completion method of accounting for long-term contracts.

5. The vice-president of sales indicated that one product line has lost its customer appeal and will be phased out over the next three years. Therefore, a decision has been made to lower the estimated lives of related production equipment from the remaining five years to three years.

6. Estimating the lives of new products in the Leisure Products Division has become very difficult because of the highly competitive conditions in this market. Therefore, the practice of deferring and amortizing preproduction costs has been abandoned in favor of expensing such costs as they are incurred.

7. The MTV Building was converted from a sales office to offices for the accounting department at the beginning of this year. Therefore, the expense related to this building will now appear as an administrative expense rather than as a selling expense on current and future years' income statements.

REQUIRED

1. *APB Opinion No. 20* identifies three types of accounting changes—changes in accounting principle, changes in estimates, and changes in the reporting entity; and there are error corrections. For each of these types of accounting changes and for error corrections:
  a) Define the type of change or error.
  b) Explain the general accounting treatment required according to *APB Opinion No. 20* with respect to the current year and prior years' financial statements.

2. For each of the seven changes or errors D. L. Roth Manufacturing has made in the current year, identify and explain whether the change is a change in accounting principle, in estimate, or in reporting entity, or an error. If any of the changes is not one of these items, explain why.

(IMA, adapted)

C22-3. METHODS OF DISCLOSING ACCOUNTING CHANGES   You are discussing the audit and financial statements of Compare Corporation with the company's board of directors. During the course of the discussion, three board members begin to debate the merits of various approaches to accounting for and disclosure of accounting changes. (Compare Corporation changed an accounting principle during the current year.)

Board Member Mr. Lorne: ''I don't understand why all accounting changes shouldn't be accounted for on a prospective basis. What's past is past!''

Board Member Mr. Green: ''It seems to me that accounting changes should be made retroactively. Just because a previous year's statements have already been issued doesn't mean we shouldn't clean up spilled milk!''

Board Member Mr. Cartright: "You're both wrong. Why mess up previous and future years' statements because of an accounting change? Changes are made all the time. Report the effect of the change in the period in which it's made!"

REQUIRED

1. Discuss the positive and negative features of the following approaches to the reporting of accounting changes:
  a) Prospective approach.
  b) Retroactive approach.
  c) Current period approach (catch-up shown in current period).

2. Which of the above approaches generally is required under *APB Opinion No. 20* for the following types of accounting changes?
  a) A change in accounting principle.
  b) A change in accounting estimate.
  c) A change in reporting entity.

C22-4. ERROR CORRECTION AND DISCLOSURE   Momota, Inc., is a high-flying conglomerate and has shown tremendous growth over the past 10 years through acquisitions of smaller companies. These acquisitions have always been made for cash, since Momota's operating activities have generated tremendous inflows of cash.

Momota is considering going public, and you have been engaged to audit the company's financial statements for 1987. During the course of your work you discover that on several occasions Momota has paid a substantial premium above the fair market value of net assets acquired from smaller companies it has acquired.

Momota's accounting policy has been to write off the excess against stockholders' equity on the date of acquisition. Momota's management is aware that this practice is in violation of GAAP and has agreed to change its policy to conform to GAAP.

REQUIRED

1. Discuss the nature of the decision to change the procedure to conform with GAAP and discuss the disclosures Momota must make in its comparative statements so as to conform to GAAP.

2. Given that the amounts involved are material, discuss the effect that the company's write-off procedures have had on the following financial statement elements:
  a) Assets.
  b) Liabilities.
  c) Stockholders' equity.
  d) Expenses.
  e) Net income.

3. What entries must Momota make in order to conform with GAAP?

C22-5. ERROR CORRECTION; ACCOUNTING CHANGES   In reviewing the working papers for the audit of Von Erich Corporation for the year ended December 31, 1987, you find the following adjusting and correcting entries that were made, without explanations, by the controller:

a) Machinery	100,000	
Depreciation expense	10,000	
Retained earnings		30,000
Accumulated depreciation		80,000
b) Cumulative effect (to income)	52,000	
Depreciation expense	12,000	
Accumulated depreciation		64,000
c) Retained earnings, cumulative effect	136,000	
Construction in progress		136,000
d) Retained earnings	14,000	
Wages payable		14,000

e) Rent revenue 10,000
    Retained earnings.............................   10,000
f) Retained earnings............................... 36,000
    Premium on bonds payable.....................   33,000
    Interest expense   3,000
g) Inventory 18,000
    Cost of goods sold   18,000
h) Cumulative effect............................... 90,000
    Deferred investment credit   90,000
i) Prepaid insurance............................... 4,000
    Insurance expense 1,000
    Retained earnings.............................   5,000
j) Gain on donation.............................. 15,000
    Donated capital   15,000

REQUIRED

Describe the event that probably gave rise to each of the above working paper entries. If errors are involved, state when the error was probably made.

EXERCISES

E22-1. ACCOUNTING CHANGES: DEPRECIABLE ASSETS AND INVENTORY

a) During 1987 the management of Ray Corporation decided to change from sum-of-the-years'-digits to straight-line depreciation for equipment that was acquired at the beginning of 1984 at a cost of $220,000. The equipment has a useful life of 10 years from the date of purchase and no salvage value. Net income for the years involved, before consideration of the cumulative effect of the change, was as follows:

1984	$60,000
1985	64,000
1986	68,000
1987	78,000 (depreciation expense for this year is based on the new method)

b) At the beginning of 1985, Tiger acquired a building at a cost of $240,000. At that time the estimated life of the building was 10 years, with an estimated salvage value of $20,000. Tiger uses straight-line depreciation on all buildings.

Near the end of 1987, management revised the estimated life of the building to five years and the salvage value to $30,000.

Net income numbers were as follows:

1985	$59,000
1986	64,500
1987	70,000 (depreciation expense for this year is based on the new estimates)

c) During 1987 Allman, Inc., which was formed at the beginning of 1983, decided to change its inventory pricing methods from FIFO to average cost. Net income for the pertinent years under each method was as follows:

YEAR	FIFO	AVERAGE COST
1983	$64,000	$61,000
1984	58,000	59,000
1985	69,000	62,000
1986	72,000	72,000
1987	75,000	70,000

REQUIRED

For each of the three independent cases above, perform the following for the fiscal year ended December 31, 1987 (ignore taxes):

1. Describe the type of accounting change involved.
2. Prepare the entry, if any, to record the accounting change.
3. Show how the changes would be disclosed for the years indicated.

E22-2. ACCOUNTING CHANGES: TAX EFFECTS   Refer to the data in Exercise 22-1 and repeat requirement 2, assuming the income tax rate is 45 percent. With respect to the tax effects, assume the following for each case:
   a) Ray Corporation made the change described for book purposes but not for tax purposes.
   b) Tiger made the change for both book purposes and tax purposes.
   c) Allman, Inc., made the change for both book purposes and tax purposes.

E22-3. ERROR ANALYSIS   Certain errors listed below were made by Atchley Window Corporation. Indicate the effects of the errors on the company's statements by inserting in the spaces *O* to indicate overstatement, *U* to indicate understatement, and *N* to indicate no effect.

	TOTAL REVENUE	TOTAL EXPENSE	TOTAL ASSETS	TOTAL LIABILITIES	OWNERS' EQUITY
a)					
b)					
c)					
d)					
e)					

   a) Failed to accrue revenue on bond investments.
   b) Failed to amortize discount on bonds payable.
   c) Declared but failed to record a 3 percent stock dividend.
   d) Recorded the receipt of cash on an account receivable by a debit to cash and a credit to accounts payable.
   e) Failed to record the purchase of land by issuance of common stock.

E22-4. ERROR CORRECTION: INVENTORIES   In 1987 the Butler Company ordered merchandise that had a cost of $8,000. The merchandise was shipped in 1987 but was still in transit on December 31. The following inventory errors related to this merchandise are independent.
   a) The merchandise was shipped F.O.B. shipping point. Butler failed to record as a purchase the merchandise in transit at the end of 1987 and excluded it from ending 1987 inventory.
   b) The merchandise was shipped F.O.B. shipping point. Butler failed to record as a purchase the merchandise in transit at the end of 1987, but the manager of the receiving warehouse noticed the shipping terms on his copy of the purchase order and included the merchandise in the ending 1987 inventory.
   c) The merchandise was shipped F.O.B. destination. Butler recorded as a purchase the merchandise in transit at the end of 1987 and included it in the ending 1987 inventory.
   d) The merchandise was shipped F.O.B. destination. Butler recorded as a purchase the merchandise in transit at the end of 1987 but excluded it from ending 1987 inventory.

REQUIRED

For each case prepare the entry, if any, to correct the accounts (ignore taxes), assuming that the errors were discovered:

1. At the end of 1987, before the books for 1987 were closed.

2. At the end of 1988, before the books for 1988 were closed.

E22-5. ERROR ANALYSIS: INVENTORIES AND PURCHASES Listed below are four accounting errors. Using the format shown below, indicate the effect, if any, of each error on the items shown. The company uses a periodic inventory method. Use *O* to indicate that an item is too high as a result of the error (overstated), *U* to indicate that it is too low (understated), and *N* to indicate no effect.

| | 1986 STATEMENTS | | | 1987 STATEMENTS | | |
ERROR	COST OF GOODS SOLD	TOTAL ASSETS	NET INCOME	COST OF GOODS SOLD	TOTAL ASSETS	NET INCOME
1. Goods bought in 1986 were included in 12/31/86 inventory. In error, the purchase and liability were recorded in early 1987.						
2. Goods received in 1987 were incorrectly included in 12/31/86 inventory and the purchase and liability were incorrectly recorded in 1986.						
3. Goods were bought in 1986 and the purchase was recorded in that year, but the goods were not included in 12/31/86 inventory.						
4. Goods received in 1986 were incorrectly excluded from 12/31/86 inventory and the purchase was recorded early in 1987.						

(CGAA, adapted)

E22-6. ACCOUNTING CHANGES: ERRORS Oleta Company purchased a plant asset at a cost of $55,000. The asset had an estimated useful life of 10 years and no salvage value. Three independent situations related to the plant asset acquisition appear below.

Situation A: At the end of the fifth year, an audit revealed that no depreciation on the plant asset had ever been recorded. Straight-line depreciation is appropriate.

Situation B: At the end of the fifth year, the total estimated life was revised from 10 years to 15 years.

Situation C: At the end of the fifth year, Oleta changed from straight-line to sum-of-the-years'-digits depreciation.

REQUIRED

For each situation, perform the following:

1. Indicate whether an error correction or an accounting change (specify the type of accounting change) is involved.

2. Prepare the journal entry to correct the error or to record the accounting change. For each situation, assume that Oleta's books have not been closed.

3. Calculate the appropriate amount of depreciation expense for the fifth year.

E22-7. ACCOUNTING CHANGES: LONG-TERM CONSTRUCTION CONTRACTS   In 1987 German Construction Company switched from the completed-contract to the percentage-of-completion method of accounting for long-term construction contracts. The company continued to use the completed-contract method for tax purposes, and the tax rate was 45 percent. Before-tax net income under the two methods was as follows:

YEAR	COMPLETED CONTRACT	PERCENTAGE OF COMPLETION
Before 1985	$160,000	$240,000
1985	40,000	20,000
1986	40,000	60,000
1987	50,000	55,000

REQUIRED

1. Prepare the entry to record the change in accounting principle.

2. Assuming that German's retained earnings at the beginning of 1985 was $200,000 and that German prepares three-year comparative statements, indicate how the net income numbers and statement of retained earnings would appear. Use the following format:

INCOME STATEMENT

	1987	1986	1985
Income before taxes			
Income tax expense			
Net income			

STATEMENT OF RETAINED EARNINGS

	1987	1986	1985
Beginning retained earnings..........			$200,000
Cumulative effect of change in accounting principle, applied retroactively			
Beginning retained earnings, as adjusted			
Net income			
Dividends (assumed)	(25,000)	(22,000)	(16,000)
Ending retained earnings			

E22-8. ERROR ANALYSIS   Your employer approaches you for help regarding the financial statements prepared for the years ending December 31, 1986 and 1987. The owner is not satisfied with the previous accountant's work and has asked you to check on the accuracy of the statements prepared. Your examination reveals the following:

a) An invoice for a $2,000 shipment of goods was received and the purchase recorded on December 26, 1986. The goods were shipped F.O.B. destination, did not arrive until January 3, 1987, and were not included in the December 31, 1986, inventory count.

b) A three-year insurance policy was purchased for $1,200 on June 30, 1986, and the full amount was expensed at that time.

c) Accrued wages at the end of 1986 and 1987 amounted to $500 and $400, respectively. The accountant did not make the necessary year-end adjustments.

d) On October 1, 1986, the company purchased at par $10,000 of 8 percent corporate bonds. The bonds were dated October 1, 1986, and paid interest semiannually. The accountant recorded interest revenue when the cash was received.

e) Depreciation was not recorded in 1986 and 1987. The amounts were $800 for 1986 and $1,200 for 1987.

REQUIRED

Indicate the amount of the understatement *(U)* or overstatement *(O)* of each of the above errors. Indicate no effect by *N*. Treat each item independently. Ignore taxes.

	NET INCOME		TOTAL ASSETS, 12/31		TOTAL LIABILITIES, 12/31	
	1986	1987	1986	1987	1986	1987
a)						
b)						
c)						
d)						
e)						

(CGAA, adapted)

E22-9. ACCOUNTING CHANGES: INVENTORY METHODS   The numbers below represent what net income would be (excluding any cumulative effects of changes in inventory methods) under various inventory pricing methods.

	FIFO	AVERAGE COST	LIFO
1985	$100,000	$94,000	$83,000
1986	102,000	95,000	82,000
1987	106,000	97,000	85,000

REQUIRED

For each independent case below, determine the appropriate net income number that would appear on the 1987 income statements, and show the net income for 1986 and 1985 for comparative purposes (ignore pro forma data).

   1. Change from FIFO to average cost.

   2. Change from average cost to LIFO. (Assume that the cumulative effect is not determinable.)

   3. Change from LIFO to FIFO.

E22-10. ERROR CORRECTION: ACCRUALS, PREPAYMENTS   Below are several errors made by Roderick Corp. in 1987.

   a) 12/1/87: Purchased a two-year fire insurance policy on equipment. The two-year premium of $3,600 was paid in advance and the company expensed the entire $3,600 premium.

   b) 12/10/87: Purchased supplies at a cost of $1,500. Failed to record supplies used during 1987 costing $300. The remaining supplies were used in 1988.

   c) 12/31/87: Failed to record $300 of dividends declared on preferred stock held as an investment. Dividend revenue was recorded in March 1988, when the dividend was received.

   d) 12/31/87: Failed to record accrued salaries payable of $500. The monthly salary payments of $1,200 were paid on January 15, 1988, and recorded as an expense at that time.

   e) 12/31/87: Received $400 advance on a sales contract. The receipt was recorded as sales revenue, although performance of the contract began in March 1988 and was completed in May 1988.

REQUIRED

For each error outlined above, prepare the correcting entry required, if any (ignore taxes), assuming that the error was discovered:

1. Before the 1987 books were closed and before any 1988 transactions related to the errors occurred.

2. After the 1987 books were closed but before any 1988 transactions related to the errors occurred.

3. At the end of 1988, before the books for 1988 were closed.

E22-11. ERROR CORRECTION: NONCURRENT ASSETS AND LIABILITIES In the course of your audit of Rin, Inc., for the year ended December 31, 1987, you discover the following errors:

a) On July 1, 1984, Rin issued 10-year 10 percent bonds with a maturity value of $50,000. The bonds were dated April 1, 1984, pay interest annually each April 1, and were sold on July 1, 1984, for $56,000 plus accrued interest. The company recorded the issuance as follows:

Cash 57,250		
Bonds payable		50,000
Miscellaneous revenue		6,000
Contributed capital—prepaid interest		1,250

Interest expense reported for the years 1984–87 was as follows:

1984	$–0–
1985	$5,000 ($50,000 × .10) recorded when interest was paid on 4/1/85
1986	$5,000 ($50,000 × .10) recorded when interest was paid on 4/1/86
1987	$5,000 ($50,000 × .10) recorded when interest was paid on 4/1/87

Assume that straight-line premium amortization is applicable.

b) On December 31, 1986, Rin purchased the net assets of Tin, including goodwill of $40,000. The goodwill should have been amortized over the maximum period set forth in *APB Opinion No. 17* but was debited to contributed capital in excess of par.

c) On January 1, 1985, Rin acquired a machine at a cost of $12,000. The machine had a useful life of five years with no salvage value, and was to be depreciated by the sum-of-the-years'-digits method. No depreciation has been recorded since acquisition.

d) On July 1, 1984, Rin began a research and development program. Expenditures since July 1, 1984, were as follows:

7/1/84	$10,000
1985	–0–
1/3/86	10,000
1/3/87	10,000

Rin has deferred all research and development expenditures and has amortized the deferred amounts over a five-year period.

e) On September 15, 1986, Rin received land with a fair market value of $5,500 as a donation from a stockholder. Rin reported the transaction as a gain in the 1986 income statement.

REQUIRED

For each error cited above, prepare the entry or entries required to correct the accounts at December 31, 1987 (before the 1987 books are closed). Ignore taxes.

E22-12. ERROR ANALYSIS AND CORRECTION Unaudited comparative income statements for Errorprone, Inc., appear below:

	1988		1987	
	UNCORRECTED	**CORRECTED**	**UNCORRECTED**	**CORRECTED**
Sales	$100,000	_____	$80,000	_____
Cost of sales	(60,000)	_____	(50,000)	_____
Depreciation	(2,000)	_____	(5,000)	_____
Net income	$ 38,000	_____	$25,000	_____

In your audit you discover the following errors:

   a) Errorprone failed to record sales of $2,000 on account made near the end of 1988.

   b) Ending inventory for 1987 was overstated by $1,000 as a result of an error in the physical count.

   c) At the beginning of 1987, Errorprone purchased a fixed asset for $4,000. Although the estimated life of the asset was five years, the entire cost was expensed in 1987. Errorprone uses straight-line depreciation on all fixed assets.

REQUIRED

   1. Prepare the entry to correct Errorprone's books at the end of 1988, assuming the books have not been closed. Ignore taxes.

   2. Fill in the blanks above to show the correct income statement items for 1988 and 1987.

E22-13. ERROR ANALYSIS Following is a list of 14 accounting errors. Using the format shown, indicate the effect, if any, on each of the six items indicated by the column headings. If the error would cause an item to be too high, write a +; if too low, write −; if it has no effect, write 0. You may assume the business has been operating for a number of years and has adjusted and closed its books annually each December 31. Each case is independent. The first two items serve as examples.

ERROR	1987 INCOME STATEMENT			BALANCE SHEET, 12/31/87		
	NET INCOME	**COST OF GOODS SOLD**	**OTHER EXPENSE**	**ASSETS**	**LIABILITIES**	**OWNERS' EQUITY**
1. Failed to amortize discount on bonds payable.	+	0	−	0	−	+
2. Inventory on 12/31/86 was overstated.	−	+	0	0	0	0
3. Recorded too much depreciation in 1987.						
4. Failed to adjust for unexpired insurance. Debits during 1987 were made to insurance expense.						
5. Inventory on 12/31/87 was overstated.						
6. Office supplies inventory at the end of 1987 was overstated. Purchases during the year were debited to supplies expense.						

	1987 INCOME STATEMENT			BALANCE SHEET, 12/31/87		
ERROR	**NET INCOME**	**COST OF GOODS SOLD**	**OTHER EXPENSE**	**ASSETS**	**LIABILITIES**	**OWNERS' EQUITY**
7. Failed to accrue interest on notes receivable at the end of 1986.						
8. Inventory on 12/31/86 was overstated.						
9. Failed to add to bad debt allowance at the end of 1987.						
10. Failed to adjust for accrued wages at the end of 1986.						
11. Failed to record dividends declared at the end of 1987.						
12. Debited a discount on capital stock to land.						
13. Failed to replenish petty cash on 12/31/87. The petty cash fund contained a number of vouchers for miscellaneous expenses.						
14. Recorded December 1987 bank service charge as an expense for January 1988.						

PROBLEMS

P22-1. ACCOUNTING CHANGES: INVENTORIES, RECEIVABLES, INVESTMENT CREDIT   Near the end of 1987, before the books were closed, management of Classic Corporation decided to make the following accounting changes.

a) Management decided to change from LIFO to FIFO in accounting for inventories. The resulting effect on net income was as follows:

YEAR	INCREASE IN INCOME
Before 1986	$164,000
1986	38,000
1987	26,000

b) The company has always used the deferral (cost reduction) method of accounting for the investment credit but has adopted the flow-through method. Income effects are as follows:

YEAR	INCREASE (DECREASE) IN INCOME
Before 1986	$75,000
1986	(6,000)
1987	(8,000)

c) The company uses the allowance method of accounting for uncollectible accounts and has previously calculated annual uncollectible accounts expense as 3 percent of net credit sales. On the basis of past experience, the company decided that 2 percent would provide a better estimate. Net credit sales were $400,000 in 1986 and $480,000 in 1987.

d) Net income for 1986 was $125,000.

e) Net income for 1987 before any accounting changes (i.e., under the previous accounting procedures) was $140,000.

f) Ignore all income tax effects.

REQUIRED

1. Prepare all necessary journal entries related to the above accounting changes at the end of 1987.

2. Prepare comparative income statements for 1986 and 1987. Start with net income before cumulative effects of changes in accounting principle.

3. Prepare comparative statements of retained earnings for 1986 and 1987. Classic declared no dividends in 1986 and 1987, and retained earnings at the end of 1985 were $600,000.

P22-2.   ACCOUNTING CHANGES AND ERROR CORRECTIONS: DEPRECIABLE ASSETS   Boomer Railway Leasing owns three locomotives that it leases to grain companies to move grain cars to market. During December 1987, management made the following discoveries and decisions:

a) Locomotive CAP was acquired at the beginning of 1984 at a cost of $1 million. The estimated life of the locomotive was 10 years with no estimated salvage value. Double declining balance depreciation was used for book and tax purposes. During December 1987, management decided to change to the straight-line method for book purposes, although the double declining balance method would be continued for tax purposes.

b) Locomotive ERC was acquired at the beginning of 1985 at a cost of $750,000. This locomotive has an estimated useful life of eight years with an estimated salvage value of $30,000. Straight-line depreciation is appropriate for book purposes. Management discovered that no depreciation had been recorded on this locomotive for either book or tax purposes. ACRS depreciation is appropriate for tax purposes, and the following assumed percentages are applicable for an assumed three-year recovery period: 1985, 50 percent; 1986, 30 percent; 1987, 20 percent.

c) Locomotive CAE was purchased at the beginning of 1981 at a cost of $820,000. The firm has depreciated this locomotive on a straight-line basis for book and tax purposes, using an estimated useful life of 10 years and $20,000 salvage value. Based on company experience, it was decided that the remaining useful life as of January 1, 1987, should be eight years and that the estimated salvage value should be $40,000. The changes apply for both book and tax purposes.

Additional data:

d) The applicable income tax rate for all years is 40 percent.

e) Boomer's only source of revenue is from the leasing of the locomotives, and revenues for 1987 totaled $800,000. Boomer's only expenses are depreciation, income taxes, and administrative expenses. Administrative expenses for 1987 totaled $80,000. No depreciation has been recorded for 1987.

REQUIRED

1. Prepare all necessary entries related to items *a* through *c* at the end of 1987.

2. Prepare the income statement for 1987. Ignore pro forma data.

P22-3.   DISCLOSURE OF ACCOUNTING CHANGES AND ERRORS   Refer to Problem 22-2. Assume that Boomer wishes to issue a 1987 income statement with 1985 and 1986 income statements presented for comparative purposes. Net income previously reported for 1985 and 1986 is as follows:

1985	$220,000
1986	240,000

REQUIRED

Calculate the amounts of net income for 1985, 1986, and 1987 that would appear on the three-year comparative income statements. Include pro forma data where applicable.

P22-4. ACCOUNTING CHANGES: DISCLOSURE Condensed statements of income and retained earnings of the Diego Company for the years ended December 31, 1987, and December 31, 1986, appear below:

	1987	1986
Sales	$3,000,000	$2,400,000
Cost of goods sold	(1,300,000)	(1,150,000)
Gross margin	$1,700,000	$1,250,000
Selling, general, and administrative expenses	(1,200,000)	(950,000)
Income before extraordinary item	$ 500,000	$ 300,000
Extraordinary item	(400,000)	—
Net income	$ 100,000	$ 300,000
Retained earnings, 1/1	750,000	450,000
Retained earnings, 12/31	$ 850,000	$ 750,000

The following three unrelated situations involve accounting changes and classification of certain items as ordinary or extraordinary. Each situation is based on the condensed statements of income and retained earnings of the Diego Company shown above and requires revisions in these statements.

a) On January 1, 1985, Diego acquired machinery at a cost of $150,000. The company adopted the double declining balance method of depreciation for this machinery and had been recording depreciation over an estimated life of 10 years, with no residual value. At the beginning of 1987, a decision was made to adopt the straight-line method of depreciation for this machinery. Owing to an oversight, however, the double declining balance method was used for 1987. For financial reporting purposes, depreciation is included in selling, general, and administrative expenses.

The extraordinary item in the condensed statement of income and retained earnings for 1987 relates to shutdown expenses incurred by the company during a major strike by its operating employees during 1987.

b) At the end of 1987, Diego's management decided that the estimated loss rate on uncollectible accounts receivables was too low. The loss rate used for the years 1986 and 1987 was 1 percent of total sales, and owing to an increase in the write-off of uncollectible accounts, the rate has been raised to 3 percent of total sales. The amount recorded as bad debt expense under selling, general, and administrative expenses for 1987 was $30,000; for 1986 it was $24,000.

The extraordinary item in the condensed statement of income and retained earnings for 1987 relates to a loss incurred in the abandonment of outmoded equipment formerly used in the business.

c) The extraordinary item appearing in the condensed statement of income and retained earnings for 1987 relates to a settlement agreement between Diego and the Internal Revenue Service, according to which Diego agreed to pay additional income taxes of $60,000 for 1986 and $340,000 for the years 1982–1985.

REQUIRED

For each of the three *unrelated* situations, prepare revised condensed statements of income and retained earnings for the years ended December 31, 1987, and December 31, 1986. Each answer should recognize the appropriate accounting changes and other items outlined in the situation. Ignore income tax considerations unless the contrary is indicated. Ignore all earnings per share and pro forma calculations.

(AICPA, adapted)

P22-5. ACCOUNTING CHANGES: INVENTORY METHODS AND TAX EFFECTS Annie Corporation has used the LIFO inventory method since its organization at the beginning of 1983. Near the end of 1987, management decides to switch to the FIFO inventory method. The switch will also be made for tax purposes. Inventory data for the two methods, net income under the LIFO method, and tax rates are as follows:

YEAR	ENDING INVENTORY LIFO	ENDING INVENTORY FIFO	AFTER TAX NET INCOME UNDER LIFO	TAX RATE
1983	$10,000	$14,500	$60,000	35%
1984	11,000	16,000	62,500	35
1985	11,200	18,800	74,000	40
1986	14,000	20,800	80,000	40
1987	14,600	22,200	81,000	45

REQUIRED

1. Prepare the entry to record the change in accounting principle. (*Hint:* In calculating the income effect of the change, remember that the ending inventory for a given year becomes the beginning inventory for the following year.)

2. Assume that Annie issues five-year comparative statements and that no dividends have been declared since the company was organized. Prepare all necessary disclosures to show the change in accounting principle.

P22-6. ERROR CORRECTION   Early in January 1988 you assume your new post as controller of Poole Corporation. Your predecessor has prepared the following preliminary financial statements:

INCOME STATEMENT
FOR THE YEAR ENDED DECEMBER 31, 1987

Sales		$586,700
Cost of goods sold	$362,300	
Depreciation	5,400	
Wages and salaries	68,000	
Interest, insurance, and property taxes	11,600	
Advertising	35,000	(482,300)
Income before taxes and extraordinary items		$104,400
Income taxes		(26,100)
Income before extraordinary items		$ 78,300
Extraordinary items (net of tax)		
Settlement of lawsuit	$ 25,000	
Sales office relocation expenses	20,000	(45,000)
Net income		$ 33,300

STATEMENT OF RETAINED EARNINGS
FOR THE YEAR ENDED DECEMBER 31, 1987

Retained earnings, 1/1/87	$158,200
Add: Net income less dividends of $20,000	13,300
	$171,500
Less: Loss on disposal of manufacturing division, net of tax	(50,000)
Retained earnings, 12/31/87	$121,500

In the course of examining the records, you discover the following:

a) A $1,000 purchase invoice dated December 27 was received December 31 and recorded. The goods were shipped F.O.B. shipping point, were in transit, and were not included in the inventory.

b) A $700 purchase of merchandise was received on December 31 and included in the inventory. The invoice did not arrive until after the trial balance was prepared, and therefore the merchandise was not recorded among the December purchases.

c) A sales invoice for $2,700 dated December 27 had been properly recorded. The goods, which cost $1,800, had not been shipped and were included in inventory on December 30, the date of the physical inventory count. The goods were shipped to the customer on December 31.

d) A $1,200 item of office equipment, received on December 31, was erroneously recorded as a purchase of merchandise. The company depreciates office equipment on a straight-line basis over a five-year service life.

e) The $68,000 of wages and salaries represented debits to this account during the year. Your predecessor failed to recognize $800 of accrued wages and salaries expense at December 31, 1986, and $1,200 at December 31, 1987.

REQUIRED

1. Determine the correct cost of goods sold (periodic inventory method was used).

2. Determine the correct depreciation expense.

3. Determine the correct wages and salaries expense.

4. Prepare, in proper form, a corrected income statement. The income tax rate is 25 percent.

(CGAA, adapted)

P22-7. ACCOUNTING CHANGES; ERROR CORRECTION You are conducting the audit of Judy, Inc., for 1988. The books for 1988 have not been closed. For each of the accounting changes and errors below, indicate the effects on 1987 and 1988 income by placing the amount in the proper columns. If income is understated because of the error, write *U* and the amount of understatement; if income is overstated because of the error, write *O* and the amount of overstatement; if income is not affected by the error, write *N* (no effect); for accounting changes, indicate the income effect of the change by + or − and the amount. In the last column, give the entry or entries, if any, to correct the books or to record the accounting change.

ITEM	1987 INCOME	1988 INCOME	ENTRY AT 12/31/88
1. Failed to record depreciation expense of $2,000 in 1987.			
2. Failed to record merchandise purchased on account totaling $1,000 near the end of 1987. The merchandise was properly included in the ending inventory at the end of 1987.			
3. The firm bases uncollectible accounts expense (allowance method) on sales and has used 2% of sales as the amount in the past. In 1988 management decided that 3% of sales would provide better matching. Sales for 1987 and 1988 were $400,000 and $440,000, respectively.			
4. A machine costing $2,000 (useful life of 10 years, no salvage) was expensed when purchased at the end of 1986. Straight-line depreciation is proper.			
5. A building costing $15,000 (5-year life, no salvage) was acquired at the beginning of 1985. The building has been depreciated on a straight-line basis. In 1988, management decided to change to sum-of-the-years'-digits depreciation.			

ITEM	1987 INCOME	1988 INCOME	ENTRY AT 12/31/88
6. Judy failed to record interest accrued on bonds payable at the end of 1987. The interest totaled $1,400 and was paid early in 1988.			
7. In 1988, treasury stock costing $300 was issued for $500. The difference of $200 was included in revenue.			
8. Inventory at the end of 1987 was understated by $1,200 because of an error in the physical count.			

P22-8. ACCOUNTING CHANGES: INVENTORY METHODS   The data below apply to inventory purchases and sales of the Granger Company, which uses a periodic inventory system.

YEAR	TRANSACTION	UNITS	PRICE PER UNIT
1985	Purchase 1	20,000	$2.00
	Purchase 2	15,000	2.25
	Purchase 3	20,000	3.00
	Sales	25,000	
1986	Purchase 1	4,000	4.00
	Purchase 2	16,000	4.50
	Sales	20,000	
1987	Purchase 1	5,000	5.00
	Purchase 2	10,000	5.20
	Purchase 3	12,000	6.00
	Sales	30,000	

REQUIRED

1. Assume that Granger has used FIFO in 1985 and 1986 and switches to average cost in 1987. Prepare the entry to record the accounting change in 1987 and explain all necessary disclosures related to the change.

2. Assume that Granger has used FIFO in 1985 and 1986 and switches to LIFO in 1987. Prepare the entry to record the accounting change in 1987 and explain all necessary disclosures related to the change.

3. Assume that Granger has used LIFO in 1985 and 1986 and switches to FIFO in 1987. Prepare the entry to record the change and explain all necessary disclosures related to the change.

P22-9. ERROR ANALYSIS AND CORRECTION   You have been engaged by the Robust Heat Company to adjust its financial statements for the years ended June 30, 1987, and June 30, 1988. The company manufactures, sells, and services forced-air heating systems for the home. The company's financial statements for the year ended June 30, 1986, were audited by another CPA, who gave an unqualified opinion on them.

The company's financial statements as prepared by its controller for the years ended June 30, 1987, and June 30, 1988, are presented below:

BALANCE SHEET

	JUNE 30	
ASSETS	**1988**	**1987**
Current assets		
Cash..	$ 120,000	$ 103,000
Accounts receivable (less allowance for doubtful accounts of $95,000 at 6/30/88 and 6/30/87)	824,000	602,000
Inventory, heating systems	1,801,000	1,604,000
Inventory, spare parts.........................	198,000	137,000
Prepaid expenses	144,000	144,000
Total current assets......................	$3,087,000	$2,590,000
Property and equipment		
Land	$ 113,000	—
Machinery and equipment (less accumulated depreciation of $923,000 at 6/30/88 and $751,000 at 6/30/87)	1,561,150	$1,522,000
Leasehold improvements (less accumulated amortization of $1,050)	82,950	—
Total property and equipment	$1,757,100	$1,522,000
Total assets	$4,844,100	$4,112,000
LIABILITIES AND STOCKHOLDERS' EQUITY		
Current liabilities		
Accounts payable	$ 449,000	$ 462,000
Accrued liabilities...........................	82,000	46,000
Total current liabilities	$ 531,000	$ 508,000
Stockholders' equity		
Common stock, authorized 100,000 shares, par value $10 per share; issued and outstanding, 53,300 shares at 6/30/88, and 53,000 shares at 6/30/87	$ 533,000	$ 530,000
Retained earnings	3,780,100	3,074,000
Total stockholders' equity	$4,313,100	$3,604,000
Total liabilities and stockholders' equity.............................	$4,844,100	$4,112,000

INCOME STATEMENT

	YEAR ENDED 6/30	
	1988	**1987**
Sales of heating systems	$ 4,907,000	$ 4,265,000
Revenues from service and repairs	73,000	49,000
Total revenues...........................	$ 4,980,000	$ 4,314,000
Cost of sales	$ 3,121,000	$ 2,650,000
Cost of service and repairs	41,000	27,000
Total	$(3,162,000)	$(2,677,000)
Gross margin	$ 1,818,000	$ 1,637,000
Selling, general, and administrative expenses	(1,111,900)	(1,004,000)
Net income	$ 706,100	$ 633,000

The following additional information regarding the company is available:

a) Your review of accounts receivable discloses that the following items are included in the accounts receivable account balance on June 30, 1988:

Receivables from officers (1988) $11,800
Customer trade accounts receivable known
  to be uncollectible on sales recorded in
  fiscal year 1987 80,000

b) Historical data indicate that 2 percent of heating system sales for the year ended June 30, 1988, will prove uncollectible. No accounts receivable have been written off during the year ended June 30, 1988.

c) On June 30, 1987, spare parts costing $17,280 were on hand but had *not* been included in the physical inventory on that date, although the liability for them had been recorded. In addition, the inventory on June 30, 1988, included spare parts sold during April 1988 for $5,000 and returned on June 17, 1988. No entry had been made to adjust the customer's account for the return, and the merchandise was included in the inventory at selling price, which was 125 percent of cost.

d) Annual service contracts are sold to homeowners for $70, covering labor charges on all service or repair calls during the year as well as an annual inspection and cleaning of the heating system. All contracts commence on January 1 of each year. Almost all repair calls occur between September 1 and June 30; during this period, the number of calls remains stable from month to month. During the months of July and August, the company performs its annual inspection and cleaning service for contract holders. The charge for a similar inspection and cleaning service to customers who do not have contracts is $10. The company had 400 contracts in the calendar year 1987 and 600 contracts in the calendar year 1988. The company had $10,200 of unearned service contract revenue on its June 30, 1986, balance sheet.

e) On June 2, 1988, the company issued 300 shares of common stock having a fair market value of $27 per share and paid $110,000 cash for a parcel of property consisting of land and an unused building. The property was acquired in order to secure a building site for a new warehouse. At the date of transfer, the company assumed and paid property taxes in arrears of $2,000. On June 18 the building was demolished at a cost of $20,000. Scrap materials recovered from the demolition yielded $16,000.

f) The payment of the property taxes and the net cost of demolishing the building were recorded as selling, general, and administrative expenses.

g) On April 1, 1987, the company leased a building to be used as its corporate headquarters. The lease, which was appropriately not capitalized, was for 15 years at an annual rental of $96,000, payable in advance each April 1. On that date the company paid the landlord the sum of $144,000 and charged this amount to prepaid expenses. This payment covered the first year's rent and a refundable security deposit to be held in escrow by the landlord. On April 1, 1988, the annual rental of $96,000 was paid.

h) On April 1, 1988, the company had an interoffice communications system installed in its offices at a cost of $84,000. This system has an estimated useful life of 20 years, but it will have to be abandoned if the company's lease is not renewed.

i) The company has an incentive commission plan for its salesmen entitling them to an additional commission when quarterly sales exceed budgeted estimates. An analysis of the incentive commission expense account as of June 30, 1988, follows:

AMOUNT	FOR QUARTER ENDING	DATE PAID
$18,000	6/30/87	7/10/87
21,000	9/30/87	10/11/87
26,000	12/31/87	1/9/88
17,000	6/30/88	7/11/88
$82,000		

Note: No payment was made for the first quarter of the calendar year 1988, as quarterly sales did not meet the requirements of the plan.

REQUIRED

Prepare a worksheet showing the adjustments required to correct the financial statements of the Robust Heat Company for the years ended June 30, 1988, and June 30, 1987. Though these entries may be used later to prepare entries to adjust the books, their purpose on this worksheet is to adjust the amounts shown in the financial statements. Show supporting calculations in good form. Ignore income taxes and deferred tax considerations. The columns of your worksheet should have the following headings:

	6/30/88			6/30/87		
	INCOME STATEMENT	**BALANCE SHEET**		**INCOME STATEMENT**	**BALANCE SHEET**	
EXPLANATION	**DR (CR)**	**DR (CR)**	**ACCOUNT**	**DR (CR)**	**DR (CR)**	**ACCOUNT**

(AICPA, adapted)

P22-10. ERROR ANALYSIS AND CORRECTION   On January 1, 1985, Harley paid $40,000 for 40 percent interest in Suzuki, which had net assets of $100,000 on that date.

You are conducting Harley's audit for the year ended December 31, 1988, and discover that Harley has, in error, been using the cost method instead of the equity method to account for its investment in Suzuki. Suzuki's net income and dividends paid since 1/1/85 are as follows:

YEAR	NET INCOME (LOSS)	DIVIDENDS
1985	$10,000	$4,000
1986	3,000	1,000
1987	(2,000)	1,000
1988	5,000	2,000

Harley has recorded the dividends received each year in the investment revenue account.

REQUIRED

1. Calculate the error made by Harley with respect to the investment revenue account for 1988.

2. Prepare the entry to correct Harley's books as of December 31, 1988. The books have not been closed for 1988.

3. Assume that Harley plans to issue comparative income statements for 1986, 1987, and 1988. Using the format below, indicate the correct amounts to be reported.

	1988	**1987**	**1986**
INCOME STATEMENT			
Investment revenue..................	_____	_____	_____
RETAINED EARNINGS STATEMENT			
Beginning balance, as originally reported	xx	xxx	xxx
Prior period adjustment	_____	_____	_____
Beginning balance, as adjusted	_____	_____	_____
Net income	_____	_____	_____
Ending balance	xx	xxx	xxx

P22-11. ERROR CORRECTION   Byron Corporation was incorporated on December 1, 1987, and began operations one week later. Byron is a nonpublic enterprise. Before closing the books for the fiscal year ended November 30, 1988, Byron's controller prepared the following financial statements:

BALANCE SHEET
NOVEMBER 30, 1988

ASSETS:

Current assets

Cash	$	150,000
Marketable securities, at cost		60,000
Accounts receivable		450,000
Less allowance for doubtful accounts		(59,000)
Inventories		430,000
Prepaid insurance		15,000
Total current assets		$ 1,046,000
Property, plant, and equipment		426,000
Less accumulated depreciation		(40,000)
Research and development costs		120,000
Total assets		$ 1,552,000

LIABILITIES & STOCKHOLDERS' EQUITY:

Current liabilities

Accounts payable and accrued expenses	$	592,000
Income taxes payable		224,000
Total current liabilities	$	816,000
Stockholders' equity		
Common stock, $10 par value	$	400,000
Retained earnings		336,000
Total stockholders' equity	$	736,000
Total liabilities and stockholders' equity	$	1,552,000

INCOME STATEMENT
FOR THE YEAR ENDED NOVEMBER 30, 1988

Net sales		$ 2,950,000
Operating expenses		
Cost of sales	$	1,670,000
Selling and administrative		650,000
Depreciation		40,000
Research and development		30,000
		$(2,390,000)
Income before income taxes	$	560,000
Provision for income taxes		(224,000)
Net income	$	336,000

Byron is in the process of negotiating a loan for expansion purposes and the bank has requested audited financial statements. During the course of the audit, the following additional information was obtained:

1. The investment portfolio consists of short-term investments in marketable equity securities with a total market valuation of $55,000 as of November 30, 1988.

2. Based on an aging of the accounts receivable as of November 30, 1988, it was estimated that $36,000 of the receivables will be uncollectible.

3. Inventories at November 30, 1988, did not include work-in-process inventory costing $12,000 sent to an outside processor on November 29, 1988.

4. A $3,000 insurance premium paid on November 30, 1988, on a policy expiring one year later, was charged to insurance expense.

5. Byron adopted a pension plan on June 1, 1988, for eligible employees, to be administered by a trustee. Based on actuarial computations, the first 12 months' pension expense was estimated at $45,000. None of this amount was funded. Byron has made no entry for pension expense. Assume Byron's minimum liability, calculated under *Statement No. 87,* was $10,000.

6. On June 1, 1988, a production machine purchased for $24,000 was charged to repairs and maintenance. Byron depreciates machines of this type on the straight-line method over a five-year life, with no salvage value, for financial and tax purposes.

7. Research and development costs of $150,000 were incurred in the development of a patent that Byron expects to be granted during the fiscal year ending November 30, 1989. Byron initiated a five-year amortization of the $150,000 total cost during the fiscal year ended November 30, 1988.

8. During December 1988 a competitor company filed suit against Byron for patent infringement, claiming $200,000 in damages. Byron's legal counsel believes that an unfavorable outcome is probable. A reasonable estimate of the court's award to the plaintiff is $50,000.

9. A 40 percent effective tax rate was determined to be appropriate for calculating the provision for income taxes for the fiscal year ended November 30, 1988. Ignore computation of deferred portion of income taxes.

REQUIRED

Prepare a four-column worksheet for Byron to correct the November 30, 1988, balance sheet and the income statement for the year ended November 30, 1988. Use the same format for account titles as appears in the problem data. Your worksheet should have the following column headings:

ACCOUNT	UNADJUSTED BALANCE	ADJUSTMENTS		CORRECTED BALANCE
		DR	CR	

Supporting calculations should be in good form.

(AICPA, adapted)

P22-12. ERROR CORRECTION AND ANALYSIS Bougnot has been in business since January 1, 1983, but has never had an audit. In the course of the first audit for the year ended December 31, 1987, the errors listed below were discovered.

a) Because of an error in the physical count, the December 31, 1983, inventory was overstated by $4,000.

b) In 1984 a purchase of $9,000 was not recorded as a purchase or included in the December 31, 1984, inventory. Title to the goods passed to Bougnot when they were shipped. The overstatement of the December 31, 1983, inventory was not discovered in 1984.

c) In 1985 the goods in transit on December 31, 1984, were received and recorded as a purchase in 1985, and payment was made to the seller. In addition, a sale on account on December 30, 1985, totaling $1,000 was not recorded.

d) The $1,000 sale on December 30, 1985, was recorded as a sale in 1986, when the cash payment was received. In addition, inventory for December 31, 1986, was understated by $12,000, and accrued wages of $1,500 were not recorded on that date.

e) The accrued wages in item *d* were paid and expensed in early 1987. The December 31, 1987, inventory was overstated by $10,200, and the 1986 inventory error was not discovered. In the end-of-the-year adjustments for 1987, depreciation was overstated by $1,000 and accrued interest expense was overstated by $900.

REQUIRED

1. Indicate the effects that the above errors have on all items in the financial statements on the next page. Indicate the effects as *O* = overstatement and *U* = understatement, and the amounts (e.g., $12,000 *U*). If there is no effect, leave blank. Assume that items not mentioned are correct unless a counterbalancing error is involved. Ignore taxes. The 12/31/83 column has been completed as a guide.

2. Assuming that the books are not closed, prepare the entry to correct Bougnot's books as of December 31, 1987. Ignore taxes.

	12/31/83	12/31/84	12/31/85	12/31/86	12/31/87
Income statement for year ended					
Sales...............					
Beginning inventory					
Purchases					
Goods available for sale .					
Ending inventory.......	4,000 O				
Cost of goods sold	4,000 U				
Gross margin..........	4,000 O				
Operating expenses					
Net income	4,000 O				
Balance sheet, 12/31					
Current assets	4,000 O				
Total assets	4,000 O				
Current liabilities.......					
Total liabilities.........					
Stockholders' equity	4,000 O				

P22-13. WORKSHEET FOR ERRORS For three years Sticker failed to recognize accruals, prepayments, and other transactions in its accounts. Reported net income and a listing of the errors appear below.

	1986	1987	1988
Reported net income (loss)....................	$12,000	$4,000	$(1,000)
a) Failed to record accrued revenues	2,000	2,500	4,800
b) Failed to record uncollectible accounts expense ...	600	800	200
c) Failed to record accrued salaries	1,300	1,800	—
d) Understated depreciation expense	1,200	1,500	1,500
e) Goodwill purchased and expensed (should be amortized over 10 years)...............	5,000	—	1,000
f) Overstated ending inventories	3,600	2,800	—
g) Failed to record purchase on account; merchandise properly included in ending inventory...	—	—	4,000
h) Failed to recognize unused supplies as an asset (expensed them instead)........................	300	—	400
i) Failed to recognize gain on sale of land; land credited for amount of proceeds	600	—	—
j) Failed to recognize unearned revenue at end of year	—	500	900

REQUIRED

Prepare a four-column worksheet to correct the reported net income for each year. In the fourth column prepare the entry, if necessary, to correct the books at the end of 1988, assuming that the books have not been closed. Ignore taxes.

P22-14. ACCOUNTING CHANGES; ERROR CORRECTION The Hooks Corporation is in the process of negotiating a loan for expansion purposes. The books and records have never been audited and the bank has requested that an audit be performed. Hooks has prepared the following comparative financial statements for the years ended December 31, 1987 and 1986:

BALANCE SHEET
AS OF DECEMBER 31

ASSETS	1987	1986
Current assets		
Cash...	$163,000	$ 82,000
Accounts receivable	392,000	296,000
Allowance for uncollectible accounts	(37,000)	(18,000)
Marketable securities, at cost	78,000	78,000
Merchandise inventory	207,000	202,000
Total current assets........................	$803,000	$640,000
Fixed assets		
Property, plant, and equipment	$167,000	$169,500
Accumulated depreciation	(121,600)	(106,400)
Total fixed assets	$ 45,400	$ 63,100
Total assets	$848,400	$703,100

LIABILITIES AND STOCKHOLDERS' EQUITY

	1987	1986
Liabilities		
Accounts payable	$121,400	$196,100
Stockholders' equity		
Common stock, par value $10; authorized,		
50,000 shares; issued and outstanding,		
20,000 shares	$260,000	$260,000
Retained earnings	467,000	247,000
Total stockholders' equity	$727,000	$507,000
Total liabilities and		
stockholders' equity	$848,400	$703,100

INCOME STATEMENT
FOR THE YEAR ENDED DECEMBER 31

	1987	1986
Sales	$1,000,000	$ 900,000
Cost of sales	(430,000)	(395,000)
Gross profit....................................	$ 570,000	$ 505,000
Operating expenses.............................	$ 210,000	$ 205,000
Administrative expenses.........................	140,000	105,000
Total expenses	$ (350,000)	$(310,000)
Net income	$ 220,000	$ 195,000

During the course of the audit, the following additional facts were determined:

a) An analysis of collections and losses on accounts receivable during 1986 and 1987 indicated a drop in anticipated losses due to bad debts. After consultation with management, it was agreed that the loss experience rate on sales should be reduced from the recorded 2 percent to 1 percent, beginning with the year ended December 31, 1987.

b) An analysis of marketable securities revealed that this investment portfolio consisted entirely of short-term investments in marketable equity securities that were acquired in 1986. The total market valuation for these investments as of the end of each year was as follows:

12/31/86	$81,000
12/31/87	62,000

c) The merchandise inventory as of December 31, 1986, was overstated by $4,000 and the merchandise inventory as of December 31, 1987, was overstated by $6,100.

d) On January 2, 1986, equipment costing $12,000 (estimated useful life of 10 years and residual value of $1,000) was incorrectly charged to operating expenses. Hooks records depreciation by the straight-line method. In 1987 fully depreciated equipment (with no residual value) that originally cost $17,500 was sold as scrap for $2,500. Hooks credited the proceeds of $2,500 to property and equipment.

e) An analysis of 1986 operating expenses revealed that Hooks recorded as an expense a three-year insurance premium of $2,700 on January 3, 1986.

REQUIRED

1. Prepare the journal entries to correct the books as of December 31, 1987. The books for 1987 have not been closed. Ignore income taxes.

2. Prepare a schedule showing the calculation of corrected net income for the years ended December 31, 1987 and 1986, assuming that any adjustments are to be reported on comparative statements for the two years. The first items on your schedule should be the net income for each year. Ignore income taxes.

(AICPA, adapted)

P22-15. WORKSHEET ANALYSIS OF ERRORS   Vandy Corporation reported the following amounts of net income for the years ending January 31, 1986, 1987, and 1988:

1986	$100,000
1987	150,000
1988	180,000

During your audit for the year ending January 31, 1988, you discover the following errors:

a) Vandy failed to record a $4,000 purchase of merchandise on account on January 27, 1987. The merchandise, shipped F.O.B. factory, was in transit at year-end, and was properly included in the ending inventory. The purchase was recorded on February 4, 1987, when the merchandise was received.

b) In the physical count of inventory on January 30, 1988, Vandy failed to include merchandise totaling $5,750 which had been shipped to a dealer to be sold on a consignment basis.

c) Vandy failed to record accrued interest revenue of $1,000 at the end of fiscal 1986 (ending January 31, 1987) and fiscal 1987 (ending January 31, 1988). The interest was recorded when the cash was received, early in each following year.

d) At the beginning of fiscal 1985, Vandy purchased machinery with a cost of $12,000. Vandy's depreciation policy for book and tax purposes is to depreciate all machinery over a five-year period by the double declining balance method. No depreciation has been recorded to date for book purposes.

e) On January 30, 1987, Vandy leased equipment under a 10-year lease. The equipment cost Vandy $15,000, and the present value of the lease payments was $18,985. The lessee's annual lease payments were $3,000. Vandy received the first lease payment on January 30, 1987. The lease was a sales-type lease, but Vandy has been accounting for it as an operating lease and has been using straight-line depreciation for the leased asset over its estimated 10-year life.

f) On February 2, 1987, Vandy purchased a four-year casualty insurance policy at a cost of $8,000. Vandy expensed the entire amount at the date of purchase.

REQUIRED

1. Prepare and complete a worksheet similar to the one presented in Exhibit 22-9. Your worksheet should show the effects of the errors on Vandy's net income for the fiscal years ending January 31, 1986, 1987, and 1988. For each error, the worksheet also should show the correcting entry at January 31, 1988 (assume the books have not been closed). At the bottom of the worksheet, you should calculate the correct amount of net income for each year. Ignore taxes in this requirement.

2. Assume that the above errors were made only on Vandy's books (the tax return was correct) and that differences between income per books and taxable income were considered timing differences. Prepare a summary adjusting entry at January 31, 1988, which incorporates the tax effect of the errors. Vandy's tax rate is 40 percent.

P22-16. COMPREHENSIVE: ACCOUNTING CHANGES, ERRORS, DISCLOSURE   You are conducting the audit for the Xing Company for the year ended December 31, 1987. The company has never been audited, and the financial statements appearing below have been presented to you for review in connection with the audit.

During the audit examination, five items come to your attention.

a) During 1987 management decided to change from average cost to FIFO for inventory valuation purposes. The change will also be made for tax purposes. Cost of goods sold under each of the methods is as follows:

	COST OF GOODS SOLD	
YEAR	**AVERAGE COST**	**FIFO**
Before 1985	$760,000	$720,000
1985	120,000	110,000
1986	145,000	142,000
1987	150,000	140,000

b) Xing's products are warranted against defects for two years. The company accrues estimated warranty expenses. Before 1987 the annual warranty expenses were estimated at 5 percent of sales. In 1987 the company wishes to revise the estimate to 8 percent of sales because the previous years' estimates appeared to be lower than actual warranty claims. Warranty expenses are included in other expenses on the income statement. For tax purposes, warranty expenses are not deductible until costs are actually incurred. Warranty expenditures, deductible for tax purposes, totaled $24,800 in 1987.

c) The company owns several machines. On June 30, 1986, the company acquired a machine at a cost of $120,000. The asset had a 10-year life with no salvage value, and was to be depreciated by the straight-line method. Your examination reveals that the machine acquired was debited to land. No depreciation has been recorded for book or tax purposes since the acquisition date.

d) The company failed to record accrued salaries of $10,000 at the end of 1986. The salaries were recorded as expenses in 1987, when the cash was paid. The error was also made for tax purposes.

e) The company has failed to record a cash dividend in the amount of $15,000 declared near the end of 1987.

Additional data:

f) The income tax rate is 45 percent.

g) None of the above accounting changes or errors has been reflected or corrected in the financial statements below and on the next page.

COMPARATIVE FINANCIAL STATEMENTS
(unaudited)

	INCOME STATEMENTS FOR THE YEAR		
	1987	**1986**	**1985**
Sales	$310,000	$280,000	$260,000
Cost of goods sold	(150,000)	(145,000)	(120,000)
Depreciation expense	(35,000)	(36,000)	(30,000)
Other expenses	(45,000)	(42,000)	(40,000)
Income tax expense	(36,000)	(25,650)	(31,500)
Net income	$ 44,000	$ 31,350	$ 38,500

	BALANCE SHEET, DECEMBER 31		
	1987	**1986**	**1985**
ASSETS			
Cash and receivables	$165,000	$148,000	$125,000
Inventories (average cost)	95,000	83,000	70,000
Property, plant, and equipment (net).....................	438,000	440,000	350,000
Other assets.................	32,000	40,000	44,000
Total	$730,000	$711,000	$589,000
LIABILITIES AND OWNERS' EQUITY			
Accounts payable	$170,150	$176,650	$109,000
Taxes payable	52,000	58,000	40,000
Other liabilities	81,500	85,000	60,000
Common stock (no par)	200,000	200,000	200,000
Retained earnings	226,350	191,350	180,000
Total	$730,000	$711,000	$589,000

	STATEMENT OF RETAINED EARNINGS FOR THE YEAR		
	1987	**1986**	**1985**
Retained earnings, 1/1	$191,350	$180,000	$165,500
Net income	44,000	31,350	38,500
Dividends	(9,000)	(20,000)	(24,000)
Retained earnings, 12/31	$226,350	$191,350	$180,000

REQUIRED

1. Prepare all necessary entries for items *a* through *e*.

2. Prepare new financial statements giving effect to the adjusting entries in part 1. Prepare pro forma data as necessary.

3. Draft any footnotes that are appropriate for the above items.

23 THE STATEMENT OF CASH FLOWS

Since the early 1980s, many companies have acquired substantial amounts of economic resources through merger activities financed with cash, as well as with long-term borrowing and capital stock issues. How did Du Pont finance its acquisition of Conoco? And how did General Motors finance the acquisitions of Electronic Data Systems and Hughes Aircraft? Information about merger activities is of interest to investors. U.S. automobile companies have spent billions of dollars in efforts to compete with foreign automobile makers. How much did Ford Motor Company spend to retool and modify its operating assets in order to meet the shift in consumer demand to smaller cars? Investors need answers to questions of this type. Furthermore, investors may want to know how a company can report large profits, yet face severe shortages of cash.

Answers to questions like those in the preceding paragraph generally are not found by examining only a company's income statement or its statement of financial position (balance sheet). Another important financial statement—the **statement of cash flows**—also may be useful to investors and other financial statement users who seek answers to such questions. The statement of cash flows, which shows the cash generated and the cash used by the operating, investing, and financing activities of a company during an accounting period, was introduced in Chapter 5. In this chapter we discuss the background and purpose of the statement of cash flows and examine its preparation in more detail.

HISTORICAL BACKGROUND

"Funds flow" reporting has been of interest to accounting theorists and practitioners for decades. During the 1960s, both the AICPA and the Accounting Principles Board issued documents recommending that a funds flow statement be included in companies' financial reports. In 1970 the SEC issued *Accounting Series Release No. 117* (now *Financial Reporting Release No. 1*), which required companies registered with the SEC to include a funds flow statement in their annual SEC filings. As a result of the AICPA, APB, and SEC pronouncements, most companies began to include a funds flow statement in their annual reports. There were variations in practice, however, regarding the concept of funds used as the focus of the statement, and the presentation of a funds flow statement in the annual report remained optional under GAAP.

Historically, the term "funds" usually has meant cash or working capital, but other concepts of funds, such as cash plus temporary investments or net current monetary assets, also have been used.[1] Because of the apparent usefulness of funds flow information and because of the diversity in practice, in 1971 the APB issued *Opinion No. 19*, "Reporting Changes in Financial Position."[2] This *Opinion* required the inclusion of a funds flow statement among the primary financial statements of a company and recommended that the title of the statement be "Statement of Changes in Financial Position." *Opinion 19* allowed flexibility in the focus and form of the statement and permitted companies to report cash flow information.

Since *Opinion No. 19* was issued, the significance of a company's cash flow information has been increasingly recognized. For example, in *Statement of Concepts No. 5*, the FASB stated that a full set of financial statements for an accounting period should show *cash flows* during the period. Moreover, *Opinion 19* created problems through the use of ambiguous terms, such as "funds" rather than descriptive terms such as "cash" or "cash and cash equivalents," lack of comparability arising from variation in the focus of the statement (cash, cash and cash equivalents, net monetary assets, or working capital), differences in the statement formats used by companies, variation in the way funds flows are classified, and the reporting of net changes in amounts of assets and liabilities rather than funds flows. The lack of clear objectives for the statement of changes in financial position has been suggested as a cause of this diversity.

Acknowledging the importance now placed on cash flow information and attempting to reduce variations in practice, the FASB has issued an *Exposure Draft* of a proposed *Statement of Financial Accounting Standards* titled "Statement of Cash Flows."[3] If issued, this *Statement* would supersede *APB Opinion No. 19* and would require that a statement of cash flows replace the statement of changes in financial position. We believe that opinion favoring cash flow information is strong enough that, by the time this text is published, or shortly thereafter, the FASB very likely will issue a *Statement* that is substantially the same as the *Exposure Draft*. Therefore, while we shall briefly describe several concepts of funds and provide a simple illustration of funds flow analysis using the working capital concept of funds in the chapter (and present a more detailed working capital illustration in an appendix), most of the technical material in the chapter is based on the *Exposure Draft*.

CONCEPTS OF FUNDS

As indicated earlier, the term "funds" usually has been defined in one of four ways, with cash and working capital being the most commonly used definitions:

1. Net current monetary assets—current monetary assets minus current monetary liabilities.

2. Working capital—current assets minus current liabilities.

3. Cash and cash equivalents—cash and highly liquid short-term investments.

4. Cash.

[1] The use of the term "funds" in this chapter should not be confused with accounting for various funds (e.g., assets restricted for certain purposes), which was discussed in Chapter 14.

[2] "Reporting Changes in Financial Position," *Opinions of the Accounting Principles Board No. 19* (New York: AICPA, 1971).

[3] "Statement of Cash Flows," *Proposed Statement of Financial Accounting Standards* (Stamford, Conn.: FASB, 1986).

EXHIBIT 23–1   INFLOWS AND OUTFLOWS OF CASH

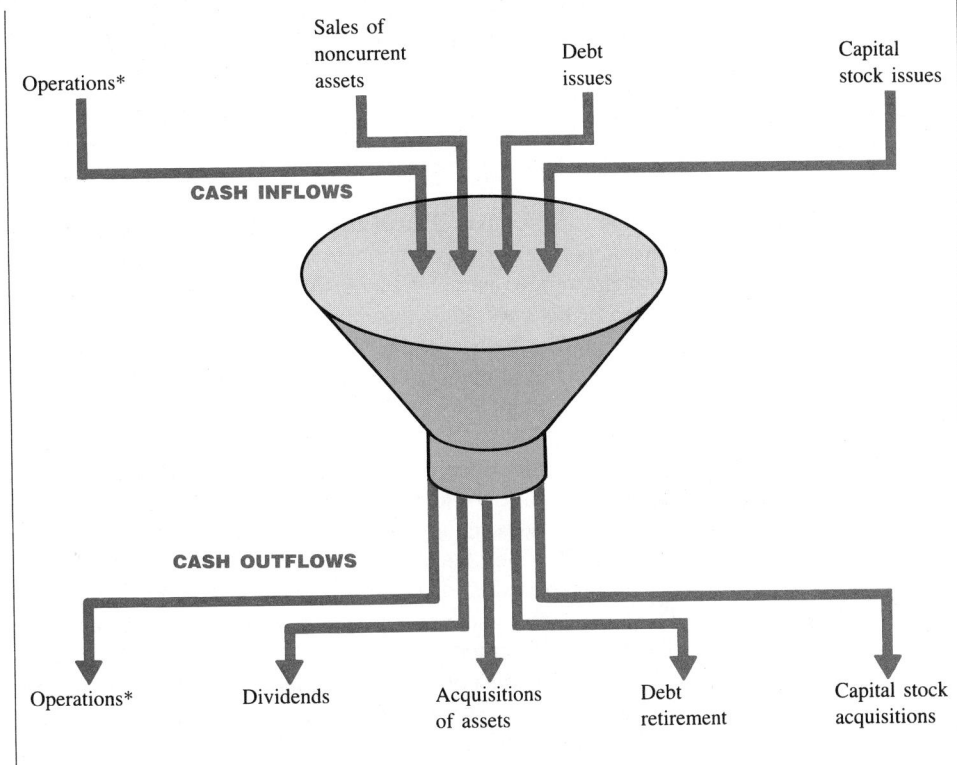

* Generally, operations represent a net cash inflow if revenues exceed expenses. If expenses exceed revenues, a net cash outflow from operations usually results.

A company's funds flows, however funds are defined, result from many types of economic events. Exhibit 23–1, reproduced from Chapter 5 and based on a cash concept, illustrates the major inflows and outflows of cash for most companies. It depicts funds as a pool of cash. Economic events that *increase* cash represent **inflows (sources)** and economic events that *decrease* cash represent **outflows (uses).**

FUNDS DEFINED AS NET CURRENT MONETARY ASSETS

Funds have been defined as **net current monetary assets**—current monetary assets less current monetary liabilities. A funds flow statement prepared on the basis of this concept of funds discloses transactions that result in increases or decreases in the pool of net current monetary assets. Because such nonmonetary items as inventories, prepaid expenses, and unearned revenue are excluded from this definition of funds, this pool is composed of cash, short-term claims to fixed amounts of cash, and short-term obligations to pay fixed amounts of cash. This concept of funds flow is closer to the cash concept of funds than to the working capital concept.

FUNDS DEFINED AS WORKING CAPITAL

Working capital equals current assets less current liabilities. This concept of funds focuses on flows of working capital and the resulting funds statement summarizes and reports those transactions that caused working capital to increase and decrease during the accounting period. This concept of funds is important because many of the current assets and current liabilities that comprise working capital are relatively liquid and usually arise from a company's primary operating activities.

Historically, the working capital concept of funds has been the most widely used in practice. Recently, however, preparers and users of financial statements have questioned the relevance of the working capital concept since positive working capital does not necessarily indicate liquidity nor does negative working capital necessarily indicate lack of liquidity. As a result, cash or cash and cash equivalents have become more widely used funds concepts.

FUNDS DEFINED AS CASH AND CASH EQUIVALENTS

Next to cash, **cash and cash equivalents** (cash plus highly liquid short-term investments) constitutes the narrowest concept of funds. Under this concept, funds are a pool of highly liquid resources and the funds flow statement focuses on transactions that increase or decrease this pool. This concept of funds is useful because companies usually attempt to minimize cash balances in periods of inflation by temporarily investing idle cash in highly liquid short-term investments, such as Treasury bills, commercial paper, and money market funds.

FUNDS DEFINED AS CASH

Under the **cash** concept of funds, only cash on hand or on deposit comprises the pool of funds. The funds flow statement summarizes those operating, investing, and financing activities of the company that result in inflows and outflows of cash. The cash concept and the related cash and cash equivalents concept are superior to the other concepts of funds because investors' and creditors' decisions are based on assessments of future cash flows. Thus, these concepts are more consistent with the financial reporting objectives that were discussed in Chapter 2.

The cash concept of funds has increased in popularity and now appears in funds flow statements more frequently than the working capital concept. A recent study of *Fortune's* top 100 industrials for the period 1979–83 revealed that, whereas 98 of 100 companies were using the working capital concept in 1979, 76 of 100 companies were using either the cash concept or the cash and cash equivalents concept in 1983.[4]

COMPARISON OF WORKING CAPITAL AND CASH CONCEPTS OF FUNDS

Because working capital and cash have been the most often used concepts of funds, we shall briefly compare and illustrate these two concepts. As you might expect, if the working capital concept and the cash concept are applied to the same transaction, different amounts of funds flow are possible. To illustrate, assume that a firm purchases a fixed asset with a fair market value of $10,000, paying $8,000 cash and issuing a short-term note payable for the balance of $2,000. The journal entry to record the transaction and the effects on working capital and cash are as follows:

ORIGINAL JOURNAL ENTRY			WORKING CAPITAL USED	CASH USED
Equipment 10,000				
Cash		8,000	$ 8,000	$8,000
Notes payable		2,000	2,000	
			$10,000	$8,000

If funds are defined as working capital, this transaction results in a decrease in working capital (an outflow of funds) of $10,000, because the note payable is a current liability

---

[4] Richard Kochanek and Corine Norgaard, "Reporting and Using Cash Flow from Operations Information," *Proceedings of the American Accounting Association 1986 Southwest Regional Meeting,* Dallas, Texas, March 12–15, 1986, pp. 233–34.

which is a part of the pool of funds. On the other hand, if funds are defined as cash, there is an outflow of funds of only $8,000.

Now assume that a firm sells a parcel of land, with an original cost of $10,000, for $25,000. A 50 percent down payment is received, and the balance is due at the end of six months. The journal entry to record the transaction and the effects on working capital and cash are as follows:

ORIGINAL JOURNAL ENTRY			WORKING CAPITAL PROVIDED	CASH PROVIDED
Cash	12,500		$12,500	$12,500
Receivable	12,500		12,500	
Land		10,000		
Gain on sale of land		15,000		
			$25,000	$12,500

If funds are defined as working capital, there is an inflow of funds of $25,000, because the receivable is a current asset and is part of the pool of funds. If funds are defined as cash, the inflow of funds is $12,500.

As a final example of how various transactions can have different effects on working capital and cash, Exhibit 23–2 shows the income statement for XYZ Corporation for its

---

EXHIBIT 23–2   DIFFERENCES BETWEEN INCOME FLOWS, WORKING CAPITAL FLOWS, AND CASH FLOWS

XYZ Corporation

	INCOME STATEMENT		WORKING CAPITAL PROVIDED (USED) BY OPERATIONS	CASH PROVIDED (USED) BY OPERATIONS
Revenues				
Sales for cash	$78,000			$78,000
Sales on account...................	20,000	$98,000	$98,000	
Expenses				
Cost of goods sold				
Purchases: cash...................	$44,000			(44,000)
Ending inventory	(10,000)	(34,000)	(34,000)	
Salaries				
Paid in cash	$20,000			(20,000)
Accrued, end of year	12,000	(32,000)	(32,000)	
Rent: paid in cash		(6,000)	(6,000)	(6,000)
Depreciation expense		(4,000)	—	—
Other expenses				
Paid in cash	$ 3,000			(3,000)
Accrued, end of year	6,000	(9,000)	(9,000)	
Net income		$13,000		
Total			$17,000	$ 5,000

EXHIBIT 23–3   COMPARISON OF INCOME FLOWS, WORKING
CAPITAL FLOWS, AND CASH FLOWS

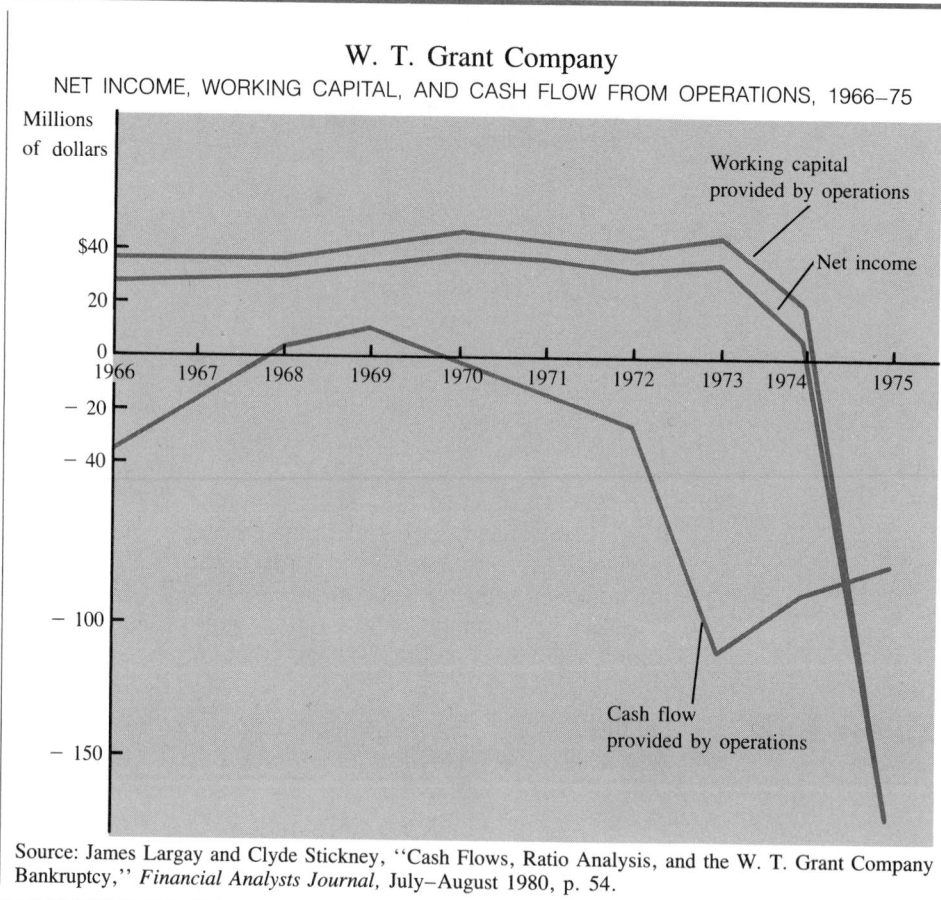

W. T. Grant Company
NET INCOME, WORKING CAPITAL, AND CASH FLOW FROM OPERATIONS, 1966–75

Source: James Largay and Clyde Stickney, "Cash Flows, Ratio Analysis, and the W. T. Grant Company Bankruptcy," *Financial Analysts Journal,* July–August 1980, p. 54.

first year of operations. XYZ Corporation's net income is $13,000; the amount of working capital provided by operations is $17,000; but the amount of cash provided by operations is only $5,000. The $4,000 difference between net income and working capital provided by operations occurs because depreciation expense reduces net income but does not affect working capital. The $12,000 difference between working capital flows and cash flows occurs because some revenues and expenses that affect working capital do not affect cash.

A significant difference between working capital flows and cash flows can be seen in Exhibit 23–3, which graphically demonstrates the flows of W. T. Grant, a department/ variety store chain, that went bankrupt in the 1970s. Grant's inability to generate cash from operating activities was not revealed in its statement of changes prepared under a working capital approach:

> Grant's profitability, turnover and liquidity ratios had trended downward over the 10 years preceding bankruptcy. But the most striking characteristic of the company during that decade was that it generated no cash internally. Although working capital provided by operations remained fairly stable through 1973, this figure (which constitutes net income plus depreciation and is frequently referred to in the financial press as "cash flow") can be a very poor indicator of a company's ability to generate cash. Through 1973, the W. T. Grant Company's operations were a net user, rather than provider, of cash.

For W. T. Grant, the working capital concept of funds was not a good surrogate for its cash flows.

Grant's continuing inability to generate cash from operations should have provided investors with an early signal of problems. Yet, as recently as 1973, Grant stock was selling at nearly 20 times earnings. Investors placed a much higher value on Grant's prospects than an analysis of the company's cash flow from operations would have warranted.[5]

Exhibit 23–4 contrasts the general strengths and weaknesses of the working capital and cash concepts of funds.

[5] James Largay and Clyde Stickney, ''Cash Flows, Ratio Analysis, and the W. T. Grant Company Bankruptcy,'' *Financial Analysts Journal,* July–August 1980, p. 51.

EXHIBIT 23–4   STRENGTHS AND WEAKNESSES OF WORKING CAPITAL AND CASH CONCEPTS OF FUNDS

WORKING CAPITAL CONCEPT

STRENGTHS

1. Many components of working capital are fairly close to cash.

2. Working capital is not affected by timing of collections of receivables or payments of payables, which may be subject to chance variations.

3. Allocation problems associated with some items on the income statement (e.g., depreciation) are avoided.

4. Is closely related to earnings activities, because the time needed to convert many current assets to cash is fairly short.

WEAKNESSES

1. Investors' and creditors' primary interests are in cash flows.

2. May be significant differences over time between working capital flows and cash flows.

3. Some allocation problems still remain in working capital accounts (e.g., inventories, prepaid expenses).

4. Affected by criteria for distinguishing between current and noncurrent assets and liabilities.

5. Aggregates many important transactions (e.g., short-term borrowings, cash purchases of inventory).

CASH CONCEPT

STRENGTHS

1. Usefulness to investors and creditors.

2. Most objective, since it is entirely free from accounting allocations and accruals.

3. Comparability is increased (related to 2).

4. Reveals increased cash requirements when volume, output, and prices are increasing.

WEAKNESSES

1. Influenced by variations in timing of collections of receivables and payments of liabilities that may be due to chance.

2. Short-run cash flows may be poor predictors of long-run cash flows and profitability.

REPORTING ALL INVESTING AND FINANCING ACTIVITIES

Many investing and financing activities are of interest to financial statement users, yet have no effect on any of the concepts of funds that we have discussed. Assume, for instance, that a company acquires plant and equipment by issuing long-term debt. Should this economic event be disclosed in, or as a supplement to, a funds flow statement? Although most users would consider the acquisition of plant and equipment to be a significant investing activity and the issuing of long-term debt to be a significant financing activity, these transactions have no effect on funds flow under any of the previous definitions.

The usefulness of providing information about this type of investing and financing transaction was recognized by the APB in *Opinion No. 19*. *Opinion 19* required that an ''all financial resources'' approach must be used in preparing the statement of changes in financial position, resulting in the reporting of investing and financing transactions that do not affect funds. The FASB advocates a similar approach by requiring that *the cash flow statement, or supplementary disclosures, report the effects of investing and financing transactions that do not directly affect cash.*

To this point we have discussed how the reporting of funds flows evolved and how user interests have shifted to a preference for a statement of cash flows, which, when presented in conjunction with an income statement, a statement of financial position (balance sheet), and a statement of stockholders' equity, assists financial statement users in decision making. In the next section we present a thorough discussion of the statement of cash flows. After a brief overview of the statement, we discuss and illustrate how to prepare it. We also discuss and illustrate the more important technical aspects of reporting cash flows. Finally, we summarize the major user-oriented objectives of the statement.

THE STATEMENT OF CASH FLOWS

BRIEF OVERVIEW OF THE STATEMENT

Purpose of the statement of cash flows.

Under the FASB's proposed *Statement of Financial Accounting Standards,* a statement of cash flows replaces the statement of changes in financial position as one of the financial statements that must be provided when a company presents a set of financial statements purporting to report both financial position and results of operations. The primary purpose of the statement of cash flows is to provide information regarding a company's cash receipts and cash payments during an accounting period. In addition, the statement should provide information about a company's investing and financing activities. In an effort to be responsive to the common practice of investing idle cash in highly liquid assets, the proposed *Statement* requires that companies should combine cash and cash equivalents in a single pool (the cash and cash equivalents concept of funds).

Statement of cash flows format.

The statement of cash flows should be based on an **activity format,** which classifies cash inflows and outflows in terms of operating, investing, and financing activities. *Operating activities* relate to a company's primary revenue-generating activities, and cash flows from operating activities are generally the cash effects of transactions and economic events included in the determination of income. *Investing activities* include lending money and collecting on those loans, buying and selling productive assets that are expected to generate revenues over long periods, and buying and selling securities not classified as cash equivalents. *Financing activities* include borrowing money from creditors and repaying the amounts borrowed, and obtaining resources from owners and providing them with both a return on their investment (through dividends) and a return of their investment. Investing and financing transactions not affecting cash must be reported either in the statement itself or in a supplementary schedule. If these noncash transactions are reported directly in the statement, the noncash aspects should be clearly identified.

EXHIBIT 23–5

Second Serve, Inc.
COMPARATIVE BALANCE SHEETS

| | | | NET CHANGE | |
	12/31/86	12/31/87	DR	CR
Assets				
Cash..........................	$ 50,000	$ 90,000	$40,000	
Accounts receivable	70,000	60,000		$10,000
Inventories.....................	100,000	75,000		25,000
Plant and equipment.............	200,000	190,000		10,000
Accumulated depreciation	(40,000)	(35,000)	5,000	
Land	30,000	38,000	8,000	
Total	$410,000	$418,000		
Liabilities and stockholders' equity				
Accounts payable	$ 70,000	$ 80,000		10,000
Salaries payable	10,000	15,000		5,000
Bonds payable (12% stated rate)....	100,000	100,000		
Premium on bonds payable	10,000	8,000	2,000	
Common stock	80,000	60,000	20,000	
Contributed capital in excess				
of par.......................	40,000	30,000	10,000	
Retained earnings	100,000	125,000		25,000
Total	$410,000	$418,000	$85,000	$85,000

INCOME STATEMENT
FOR THE YEAR ENDED
DECEMBER 31, 1987

Revenues	$250,000
Cost of goods sold	(120,000)
Depreciation expense	(25,000)
Salaries expense	(40,000)
Interest expense.....................	(10,000)
Gain on sale of equipment	10,000
Net income	$ 65,000

PREPARING THE STATEMENT OF CASH FLOWS

In this section we discuss how to prepare the statement of cash flows. For instructional purposes, we present the completed statement first and then we analyze how each inflow and outflow of cash was determined.

Financial statements for Second Serve, Inc., appear in Exhibit 23–5. The following information further describes events and transactions affecting the company during 1987:

1. Machinery with an original cost of $50,000 and accumulated depreciation of $30,000 was sold for $30,000.

2. Common stock with a book value of $30,000 was purchased for $35,000 and retired; the $5,000 difference was debited to retained earnings.

3. Dividends declared and paid during 1987 totaled $35,000.

The following steps are necessary in order to prepare the statement of cash flows:

1. Determine the net increase or decrease in cash for the period. By referring to Exhibit 23–5, we can see that Second Serve's cash balance increased by $40,000 during 1987. This amount serves as a control figure in that once we have completed the statement of cash flows, the net cash inflow or outflow must agree with the net change in the cash account on the comparative balance sheets.

2. Analyze any available income statement data, changes in the noncash balance sheet accounts, and any additional information provided in order to determine the transactions that caused inflows and outflows of cash during the period.

3. Prepare the statement of cash flows on the basis of the two previous steps.[6]

Exhibit 23–6 presents a statement of cash flows for Second Serve, Inc. Notice that the statement is divided into three sections—operating, investing, and financing—which correspond to the three major cash-generating activities discussed in Chapter 5 and earlier in this chapter. This reporting format is called an **activity format.** Under each activity, the sources and uses (inflows and outflows) of cash are summarized. As we proceed through the analysis below, refer to Exhibit 23–6 to see how each transaction that affected cash is reported.

[6] In Chapter 3, we prepared the statement of cash flows directly from the cash ledger account. Although that approach appears to be a logical one, in practice the volume of cash transactions could make that approach inefficient.

EXHIBIT 23–6   STATEMENT OF CASH FLOWS

Second Serve, Inc.

STATEMENT OF CASH FLOWS
FOR THE YEAR ENDED DECEMBER 31, 1987

Cash flows from operating activities:		
Operations: Net Income	$ 65,000	
Add (deduct) items not affecting cash:		
Depreciation expense	25,000	
Amortization of bond premium	(2,000)	
Gain on sale of equipment	(10,000)	
Decrease in accounts receivable	10,000	
Decrease in inventories	25,000	
Increase in accounts payable	10,000	
Increase in salaries payable	5,000	
Net cash provided by operating activities		$128,000
Cash flows from investing activities:		
Sale of equipment	$ 30,000	
Purchase of equipment	(40,000)	
Purchase of land	(8,000)	
Net cash used by investing activities		(18,000)
Cash flows from financing activities:		
Retire common stock	$(35,000)	
Dividends	(35,000)	
Net cash used by financing activities		(70,000)
Net increase in cash		$ 40,000

EXHIBIT 23—7 CASH FLOWS FROM OPERATING ACTIVITIES—INDIRECT APPROACH

Second Serve, Inc.

Cash flows from operating activities:	
Operations: Net income	$ 65,000
Add (deduct) items not affecting cash:	
Depreciation expense	25,000
Amortization of bond premium	(2,000)
Gain on sale of equipment	(10,000)
Decrease in accounts receivable	10,000
Decrease in inventories	25,000
Increase in accounts payable	10,000
Increase in salaries payable	5,000
Net cash provided by operating activities	$128,000

Cash Flows from Operating Activities

This section of the statement of cash flows summarizes the cash flows generated from a company's operating activities. As you probably suspect, the major recurring inflow of cash for most companies is from sales of their primary products or services, or, stated another way, *cash inflows from customer collections. Operating cash outflows* include payments to suppliers, payments to employees for wages and salaries, payments to creditors for interest, and payments to government agencies for taxes. Two approaches may be used to determine and report a company's cash flows from operating activities—the indirect approach and the direct approach. Each is discussed and illustrated below.

Under the indirect approach, net income is adjusted for revenues, expenses, gains, and losses that do not affect cash.

Depreciation is not a source of cash; rather, it is an expense that does not require the use of cash.

INDIRECT APPROACH Under the indirect approach, we determine cash flows from operating activities by adding back to or deducting from net income those income statement items that do not affect cash. We also must adjust net income for cash operating receipts and payments not reported on the accrual basis income statement. For Second Serve, Inc., the adjustments to net income are shown in Exhibit 23–7. Notice that Exhibit 23–7 is identical to the "cash flows from operating activities" section of Exhibit 23–6.

Depreciation expense. Depreciation expense did not result in an outflow of cash but was included in the calculation of net income. Therefore, it is added back to determine net cash provided by operating activities. This "add-back" procedure for depreciation often is interpreted to mean that depreciation provides funds, in this case, cash. Nothing could be more incorrect—a bookkeeping entry cannot provide anything! Depreciation is added back to net income because it is an expense that does not require the use of cash.

Amortization of bond premium. The bond premium amortization of $2,000 is subtracted because it reduced interest expense for 1987, but did not affect cash (the premium on bonds payable account was reduced). Thus, the outflow of cash for interest was $2,000 greater than the related interest expense.

Gain on sale of equipment. The gain on sale of equipment is subtracted for two reasons. First, the dollar amount of the gain is not a measure of the cash provided by the sale; the amount of cash provided by the sale is $30,000. Second, the gain does not relate to operating activities. Revenues relate to the company's *primary* operating activities, whereas gains relate to *peripheral* activities, in this case an investing activity. In addition, revenues occur more regularly and more continuously than gains. It follows that more accurate measurement and better signals about future cash flows from operating activities result when gains are excluded. To summarize, because we are reporting the

EXHIBIT 23–8   SOURCE OF DIFFERENCES IN SALES REVENUES UNDER ACCRUAL BASIS AND CASH BASIS

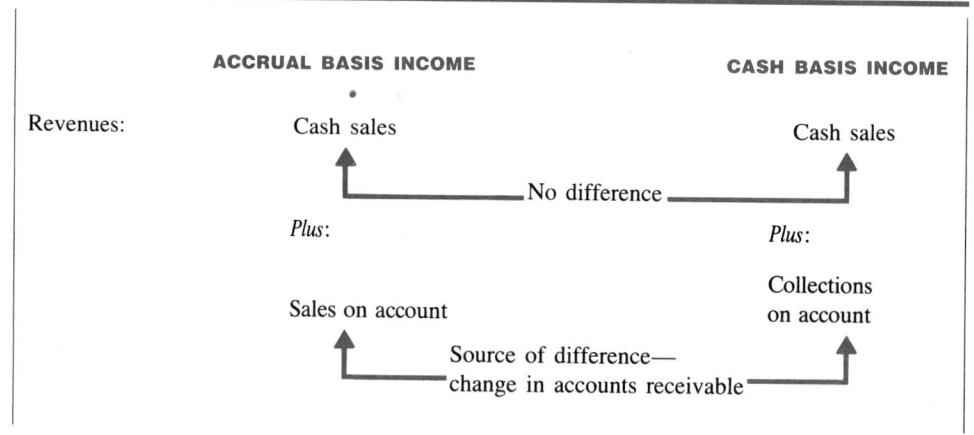

amount of cash flows from operating activities, we deduct the gain from net income. The cash provided by the equipment sale will be reported under cash flows from investing activities.

To summarize what we have discussed so far, *any amounts entering into the determination of net income that do not have a corresponding and equal effect on cash will require an adjustment to net income in arriving at net cash provided (used) by operating activities.* In addition to the above adjustments, a company's operating cash flows also may include transactions not appearing on the income statement because the income statement is based on accrual accounting. For example, a company may collect, in the current period, cash arising from credit sales made in a previous period. As another example, current period cash payments to employees may be for settlement of salary expense accrued in a previous period. Because most current asset and current liability accounts arise from and are affected by transactions related to a company's operating activities, *additional adjustments to net income result from analysis of the current asset and current liability accounts other than cash.* These adjustments, along with the three adjustments discussed and illustrated above, are necessary to convert the accrual basis net income to cash flows from operating activities. These additional adjustments are explained below.

Decrease in accounts receivable. The net dollar decrease of $10,000 in accounts receivable during the year represents cash collections from customers in excess of revenues reported on the income statement. This amount must be added to net income to arrive at net cash provided by operating activities. We can see why this figure must be added by examining the source of differences in sales revenue under the accrual basis and the cash basis, as shown in Exhibit 23–8. The difference between accrual basis revenue and cash basis revenue arises because cash collections on account exceeded sales on account by $10,000 during the year.

Decrease in inventories. If there had been no change in inventories during the year, the cost of goods sold would have equaled purchases for the year. However, the decrease in inventories increased cost of goods sold and decreased net income; but this inventory decrease included in the calculation of cost of goods sold had no effect on cash. Because the inventory decrease of $25,000 is included in the calculation of cost of goods sold and net income and does not represent a cash outflow, it must be added back to net income.

Increase in accounts payable. The $10,000 increase in accounts payable represents additional purchases on credit over and above the cash payments made to creditors during

EXHIBIT 23–9	SOURCE OF DIFFERENCES BETWEEN COST OF GOODS SOLD UNDER ACCRUAL BASIS AND CASH OUTFLOWS TO SUPPLIERS UNDER CASH BASIS

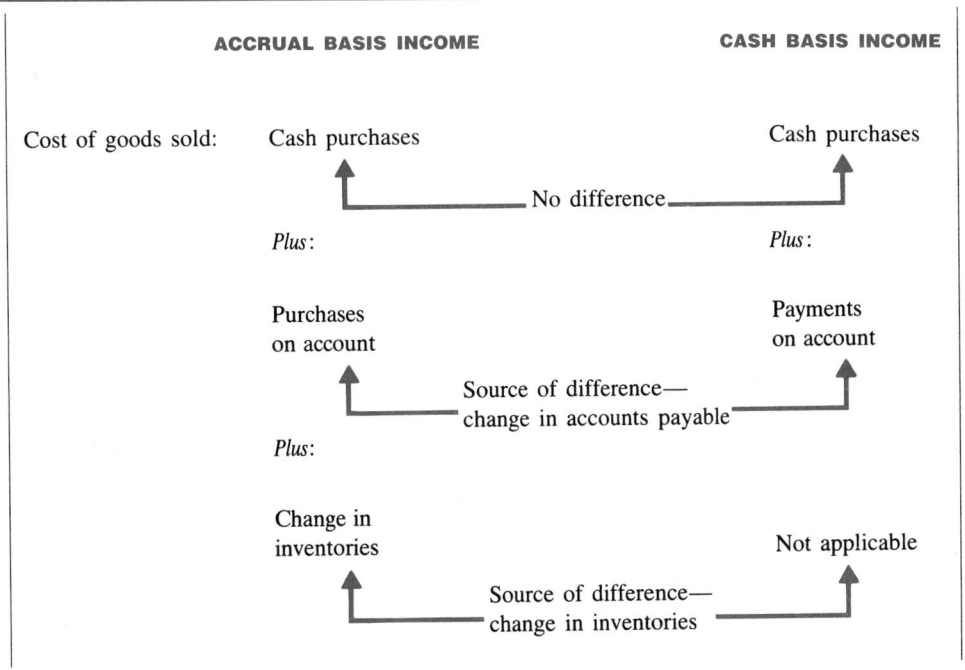

the year. Because these additional credit purchases increased goods available for sale but did not cause an outflow of cash, this $10,000 increase is added back to net income.

Notice that both the inventory and accounts payable adjustments are necessary to convert cost of goods sold from an accrual basis to a cash basis. The source of differences between the accrual basis cost of goods sold and the cash outflows to suppliers of merchandise is shown in Exhibit 23–9.

Increase in salaries payable. The increase of $5,000 in salaries payable may be explained in exactly the same manner as the increase in accounts payable. Exhibit 23–10 makes the reason clear. Since the $5,000 increase in salaries payable is included in salaries expense, which reduces net income but does not cause an outflow of cash, it is added back to net income.

Once we have adjusted net income for the items that appear on the income statement that have no effect on cash flows, and have analyzed the effect on cash flows of the changes in the current asset and current liability accounts related to operations, we arrive at net cash provided by operating activities. Notice that although Second Serve's net income for 1987 was $65,000, the net cash provided by operating activities was $128,000.

DIRECT APPROACH   Under the **direct approach,** cash flows from operating activities is determined and reported as the difference between operating cash receipts and cash payments. This approach is illustrated in Exhibit 23–11. The first column shows the income statement items and the third column shows the operating cash receipts and payments. The middle column is used to adjust the accrual basis income statement to a cash basis. The logic underlying these adjustments is identical to the discussion of Exhibits 23–8 through 23–10. As shown in Exhibit 23–11, adjusting revenues for the decrease in accounts

EXHIBIT 23–10　SOURCE OF DIFFERENCES IN SALARIES
UNDER ACCRUAL BASIS AND CASH BASIS

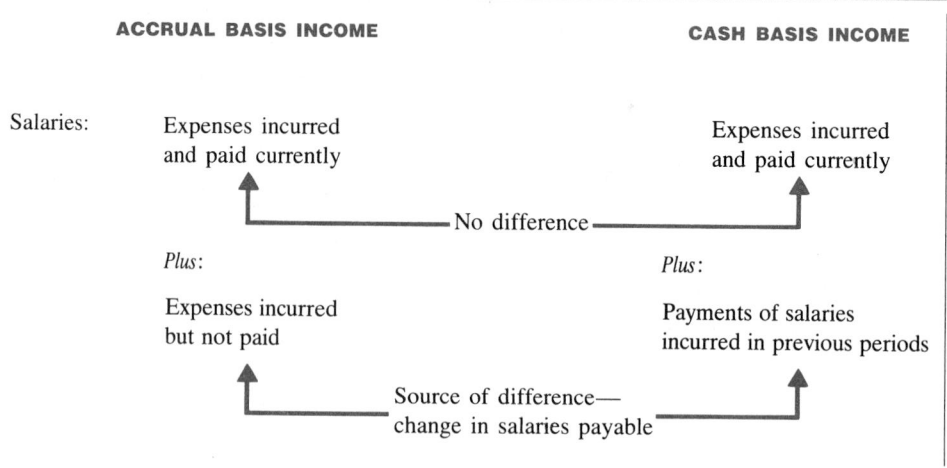

EXHIBIT 23–11　CASH FLOWS FROM OPERATING ACTIVITIES—DIRECT APPROACH

Second Serve, Inc.

	INCOME STATEMENT	ADJUSTMENTS	CASH FLOWS
Revenues	$250,000	$10,000*	$260,000
Cost of goods sold	(120,000)	25,000†	
		10,000‡	(85,000)
Depreciation expense	(25,000)	25,000	—
Salary expense	(40,000)	5,000§	(35,000)
Interest expense	(10,000)	(2,000)¶	(12,000)
Gain on sale of equipment	10,000	(10,000)	—
Net income	$ 65,000		
Net cash provided by operating activities			$128,000

* Decrease in accounts receivable.

† Decrease in inventories.

‡ Increase in accounts payable.

§ Increase in salaries payable.

¶ Amortization of bond premium.

receivable gives the *amount of cash collected from customers*. Similarly, adjusting the cost of goods sold for the decrease in inventories and the increase in accounts payable gives the *amount of cash paid to Second Serve's suppliers* during 1987. Because depreciation expense is a noncash expense, it does not appear in the cash flow column. Adjusting salary expense for the increase in salaries payable gives the *amount of cash paid to employees during the year.* Interest expense is adjusted for the amortization of bond premium, which reduced interest expense by $2,000, compared with the amount of cash paid to creditors. This effect may be seen more clearly if we reconstruct the original entry made by Second Serve to record interest expense for 1987:

Interest expense	10,000	
Premium on bonds payable	2,000	
Cash		12,000

The gain is removed because (1) the sale of equipment is an investing activity, rather than an operating activity, and (2) $10,000 is not the amount of cash received. On the formal statement, the four amounts in the third column of Exhibit 23–11 would be reported as follows:

Cash flows from operating activities:	
Cash collected from customers	$260,000
Cash paid to merchandise suppliers	(85,000)
Cash paid for salaries	(35,000)
Cash interest paid	(12,000)
Net cash provided by operating activities	$128,000

COMPARING THE TWO APPROACHES   As you can see by comparing Exhibit 23–7 with Exhibit 23–11 (and the schedule above), the indirect approach and the direct approach are *equivalent methods* of reporting the same information. Whereas the indirect approach arrives at net cash provided by operating activities by adjusting the final net income number, the direct approach directly converts the items making up the accrual basis income statement to a cash basis. In addition, the direct approach provides more detailed information about the major sources of operating cash receipts and payments, whereas the indirect approach nets some cash receipts and payments because its calculation begins with net income.

Even though the direct approach is somewhat more straightforward than the indirect approach, the indirect approach has been much more popular in practice. One argument supporting the indirect approach is that by adjusting net income for noncash items and adjusting for other cash flows related to operations, but not reported on the income statement, financial statement users can link operating cash flows with a company's net income. As a result, they are able to make a better assessment of a company's "earnings quality"—that is, how closely income flows are correlated with cash flows. The direct approach, on the other hand, probably is less confusing and clearly shows that cash inflows are from customers and that cash outflows are for merchandise, salaries, taxes, and other operating items.[7] Under the FASB *Exposure Draft,* either approach may be used to determine and report cash flows from operating activities.

Cash Flows from Investing and Financing Activities

As shown in Exhibit 23–6, the two other major activities that result in cash inflows and outflows are investing and financing activities. Investing activities include purchases and sales of productive assets that are expected to generate revenues over long periods of time, purchases and sales of securities that are not classified as cash equivalents, and lending money and collecting interest on the loans. Financing activities include borrowing money from creditors and repaying the amounts borrowed, and obtaining resources from owners

---

[7] A similar point has been made by Loyd C. Heath. See Loyd C. Heath, "Let's Scrap the Funds Statement," *Journal of Accountancy,* October 1978, pp. 94–103.

and providing them with both a return on their investment (through dividends) and a return of their investment.

An analysis of Second Serve's investing and financing activities appears below. You should refer to Exhibit 23–6 in order to see how each transaction is reported on the statement of cash flows.

SALE OF EQUIPMENT   Equipment with a book value of $20,000 (original cost of $50,000 less accumulated depreciation of $30,000) was sold for $30,000 cash. This investing transaction would appear as follows:

> Cash provided by sale of equipment. $30,000

RETIREMENT OF COMMON STOCK   Common stock with a book value of $30,000 was purchased and retired for $35,000; the $5,000 difference was debited to retained earnings. An examination of the contributed capital accounts in the balance sheets in Exhibit 23–5 suggests that the following entry was made to record the retirement:

> Common stock 20,000
> Contributed capital in excess of par 10,000
> Retained earnings 5,000
> Cash.   35,000

On the statement of cash flows, this financing transaction would be reported as follows:

> Cash used to retire common stock $35,000

DIVIDENDS   Cash dividends for the year totaled $35,000. This financing transaction would be reported as follows:

> Cash used to pay dividends $35,000

At this point we have analyzed the income statement data and the additional information provided for Second Serve, Inc. Each of Second Serve's noncash balance sheet accounts must now be inspected and reconciled to ensure that all transactions affecting cash have been considered. Changes in some of these noncash accounts already have been reconciled as a result of the analysis to this point. Information about changes in other noncash accounts, however, has not been considered, and this information has not been given directly. When this information is not directly available, we must make an *inference* about the transaction that caused the change. For example, we must make an inference about the equipment purchase.

PURCHASE OF EQUIPMENT   From the comparative balance sheets in Exhibit 23–5, we can see that the plant and equipment account decreased by $10,000. Since the equipment that was sold had an original cost of $50,000, which was removed from the account at the date of sale, additional equipment costing $40,000 must have been purchased for cash:

> Beginning balance + Purchases −   Sales   = Ending balance
> $200,000   + $40,000 − $50,000 = $190,000

Thus, the purchase of equipment decreased cash by $40,000. This investing transaction appears on the statement of cash flows as follows:

> Cash used to purchase equipment $40,000

ACCUMULATED DEPRECIATION ACCOUNT   The accumulated depreciation account decreased by $5,000. The change in this account balance can be reconciled by summarizing the transactions we already have considered that affected this account:

	EFFECT ON ACCUMULATED DEPRECIATION ACCOUNT
Depreciation expense (Exhibit 23–6)	$25,000 Cr
Accumulated depreciation on equipment sold (p. 1071)..	30,000 Dr
Net change	$ 5,000 Dr

We considered the $25,000 credit to the accumulated depreciation account when we added back depreciation to net income to determine net cash provided by operating activities. We considered the $30,000 debit when we analyzed the gain on the sale of equipment and the cash proceeds received on the sale.

PURCHASE OF LAND   We have no information about this transaction. By inspecting the comparative balance sheets in Exhibit 23–5, however, we can see that the land account increased by $8,000 during 1987. Therefore, we must infer that land was purchased at a cost of $8,000. This investing transaction appears on the statement of cash flows as follows:

> Cash used to purchase land $8,000

BONDS PAYABLE AND PREMIUM ON BONDS   There was no change in the bonds payable account. The $2,000 decrease in the premium on bonds payable account was reconciled earlier.

CONTRIBUTED CAPITAL ACCOUNTS   The $20,000 decrease in the common stock account and the $10,000 decrease in the contributed capital in excess of par account already have been reconciled in the common stock retirement transaction.

RETAINED EARNINGS   As shown in Exhibit 23–5, the retained earnings account increased by $25,000 during the year. This increase can be reconciled by summarizing the transactions that affected retained earnings, which we already have analyzed:

Net income	$65,000 Cr
Dividends	35,000 Dr
Amount paid in excess of book value of common stock retired	5,000 Dr
Net change	$25,000 Cr

We have now completed the statement of cash flows for Second Serve, Inc. The net cash provided by operating activities was $128,000, net cash used by investing activities totaled $18,000, and net cash used by financing activities was $70,000. These three activities and the inflows and outflows of cash within each activity summarize how Second Serve's cash balance increased by $40,000 during 1987.

CASH AND CASH EQUIVALENTS   At the beginning of the chapter we discussed the cash and cash equivalents concept of funds. For several years many companies have used this concept instead of a pure cash concept. Under the *FASB Exposure Draft*, companies that invest cash in excess of immediate needs in highly liquid investments as part of their overall cash management must use the cash and cash equivalents concept in their cash flow statement. Some examples of cash equivalents include Treasury bills, commercial paper, and money market funds. Purchases and sales of these investments would *not* be reported as investing activities in the statement of cash flows, because they are included as *part of cash*.

To illustrate, assume that at the beginning of the current year, Patz Company invested $20,000 of its $50,000 cash balance in three-month Treasury bills that paid 2 percent per quarter. The Treasury bills were converted to cash at the end of the first quarter. At the beginning of the fourth quarter, Patz invested $30,000 in three-month money market funds paying $1\frac{1}{2}$ percent per quarter. At the end of the year, this investment was renewed for three months at $1\frac{1}{4}$ percent. These transactions were Patz's only transactions during the year. Since these investments are cash equivalents, the $850 cash inflow from interest [($20,000 × .02) + ($30,000 × .015)] would be the only transaction reported on Patz's statement of cash flows for the current year (as a part of net income under the indirect approach or as interest collected under the direct approach). Even though Patz's actual cash balance is $29,150 less at the end of the year than at the beginning of the year ($850 increase from interest less $30,000 investment made at the end of the year), the increase in cash and cash equivalents is $850 because the money market funds are considered equivalents to cash.

The cash and cash equivalents approach is preferable to a "pure" cash approach for at least two reasons:

1. Users' assessments of future cash flows probably are unaffected by whether cash is on hand, on deposit, or invested in highly liquid assets of a short-term nature.

2. Reporting numerous purchases and sales ("rollovers") of highly liquid investments, which are a common cash management practice, could present information about a company's investing activities that is not representationally faithful.

INVESTING AND FINANCING ACTIVITIES NOT AFFECTING CASH

As discussed earlier, *Opinion No. 19* required that significant investing and financing activities not affecting funds must be disclosed in the statement of changes in financial position. The *FASB Exposure Draft* continues this requirement for the statement of cash flows, but specifies that these types of transactions must be disclosed in one of two ways:

1. Noncash investing and financing activities may be disclosed in a *supplementary schedule*. Cash and noncash aspects of transactions involving similar items should be clearly identified.

2. Noncash investing and financing activities may be reported in the *body of the statement of cash flows*. If this approach is followed, the noncash aspects of a transaction must be identified and deducted from the cash aspects in order to preserve the focus on cash flows.

To illustrate, assume that a company acquired plant and equipment with a fair market value of $100,000 by paying $30,000 cash and issuing common stock for the $70,000 balance. Exhibit 23–12 shows how this transaction would be reported on the statement of cash flows under each alternative listed above. We favor the first approach on conceptual grounds: The first approach preserves the focus on reporting inflows and outflows of cash on a statement *entitled* the statement of cash flows. Thus, we believe that the first approach is less confusing and is more representationally faithful than the second approach.[8]

---

[8] One reason that the FASB issued the *Exposure Draft* on the statement of cash flows was that the statement of changes in financial position under *Opinion No. 19* was criticized for compressing too much information into one statement with meaningless results. See Loyd C. Heath, "Financial Reporting and the Evaluation of Solvency," *Accounting Research Monograph No. 3* (New York: AICPA, 1978).

SUMMARY OF CASH FLOW REPORTING OBJECTIVES

Our examples and discussion to this point have illustrated most of the basic concepts and procedures related to preparing the statement of cash flows. As we said earlier, information reported in the statement of cash flows, when used with other financial statement information, helps users to assess a company's future cash flow potential. The information also helps users to assess a company's ability to pay its debts and to pay dividends, and to meet its external financing needs. Finally, the statement of cash flows helps users to understand differences between a company's income flows and cash flows and to assess both cash and noncash aspects of the company's investing and financing activities during a period.

The next section of the chapter addresses some additional concepts associated with the statement of cash flows. Some of these concepts relate to statement preparation while others relate to disclosure issues.

EXHIBIT 23–12   REPORTING NONCASH TRANSACTIONS ON THE STATEMENT OF CASH FLOWS

NONCASH TRANSACTION DISCLOSED IN A SUPPLEMENTARY SCHEDULE

Operating activities:

   ⋮

Investing activities:
  Purchased plant and equipment .... $ (30,000)
Financing activities:

   ⋮

Net increase (decrease) in cash .... $ *xx*

Noncash investing and financing activities:
  Acquisition of plant and equipment $100,000
  Less: Common stock issued in acquisition .... (70,000)
  Cash paid for plant and equipment .... $ 30,000

NONCASH TRANSACTION DISCLOSED IN THE BODY OF THE STATEMENT

Operating activities:

   ⋮

Investing activities:
  Acquired plant and equipment... $(100,000)
  Less: Common stock issued 70,000
  Cash outflows for plant and equipment .... $ (30,000)
Financing activities:

   ⋮

Net increase (decrease) in cash .... $ *xx*

OTHER CASH FLOW STATEMENT PREPARATION AND DISCLOSURE ISSUES

ADJUSTMENTS TO NET INCOME TO DETERMINE CASH PROVIDED BY OPERATIONS

Refer to Exhibit 23–6 and notice how we adjusted Second Serve's net income to determine cash flows from operating activities. Under the indirect approach, the more common revenue, expense, gain, and loss adjustments to net income to determine cash flows from operating activities are as follows:

ADDITIONS TO NET INCOME

Depreciation expense

Depletion expense

Amortization of goodwill

Amortization of deferred charges

Amortization of discount on bonds payable, long-term notes payable, and lease obligations

Increases (decreases) in noncurrent deferred income tax credits (debits)

Pension expense not funded currently

Compensation expense from executive stock option plans

Investment losses under the equity method

Losses on retirement of long-term debt

Increases in deferred investment credits

Common adjustments to net income to determine net cash flows from operations.

Losses on sales of plant and equipment, investments, or other noncurrent assets

Minority interests in net income of subsidiaries (discussed in advanced accounting)

DEDUCTIONS FROM NET INCOME

Investment revenue from use of the equity method

Amortization of premium on bonds payable

Increases (decreases) in noncurrent deferred tax debits (credits)

Decreases in deferred investment credits

Gains on sales of plant and equipment, investments, or other noncurrent assets

Gains on retirement of long-term debt

All of the additions and deductions listed above enter into the calculation of net income as revenue, expense, gain, or loss. However, they affect *noncash* accounts rather than *cash*.

CURRENT ASSETS AND CURRENT LIABILITIES NOT RELATED TO OPERATIONS

When we used the indirect approach to report cash flows from the operating activities of Second Serve, Inc., we adjusted net income for those revenues, expenses, gains, and losses that appeared on the company's income statement but that had no effect on cash. We also adjusted the company's net income for the changes in the current asset and current liability accounts, other than the cash account, in order to complete the conversion of the accrual basis income statement to a cash basis. This procedure was proper, because transactions affecting Second Serve's current accounts—accounts receivable, inventories, accounts payable, and salaries payable—related to the company's primary operating activities.

In some cases, a current asset account or a current liability account may be affected by a financing or an investing transaction, rather than by a transaction related to operations. For example, a company might borrow money on a short-term basis (a financing transaction), or it might acquire plant and equipment on account or by issuing a short-term note (an investing and financing transaction). On the statement of cash flows, the first transaction would be reported as a financing activity; the second transaction would be reported as a noncash investing and financing activity. As another example, a company might declare dividends but not pay them until the following accounting period. Although dividends paid would be reported as a financing activity, dividends declared but not paid would be reported as a noncash financing activity.

NET LOSSES Just as we adjusted net income, we must also adjust net losses for items that enter into the determination of the net loss but which have no effect on cash. Four possible relationships between reported net income or net loss and net cash provided (used) by operating activities are shown in the following table.

CASE	NET INCOME (LOSS)	ASSUMED ADDITIONS TO (DEDUCTIONS FROM) NET INCOME (LOSS) FOR NONCASH ITEMS	NET CASH PROVIDED (USED) BY OPERATING ACTIVITIES
A	$65,000	$63,000	$128,000
B	(60,000)	85,000	25,000
C	25,000	(55,000)	(30,000)
D	(10,000)	(25,000)	(35,000)

Case A is based on the statement of cash flows for Second Serve. In case B, although there is a net loss, a positive amount of cash is provided by operating activities. In case C there is a use or an outflow of cash from operating activities even though net income is reported. Finally, in case D there is a loss and a decrease in cash. If operations cause a *decrease* in cash, this decrease is reported as net cash used by operating activities.

EXTRAORDINARY ITEMS *Opinion No. 19* required that funds flows associated with extraordinary items on the income statement should be reported immediately below funds provided (used) by operations. The *FASB Exposure Draft* does not address extraordinary items directly. However, it does require that cash flows from transactions and other events whose effects are included in income, but which are not related to operations, be reported either as investing activities or as financing activities. For example, assume that a company extinguished debt by paying debtholders $50,000 and recognized an extraordinary gain on extinguishment of $8,000. In the statement of cash flows, the $8,000 gain would be excluded from operating cash flows, and the $50,000 cash outflow would be reported as a financing activity (and perhaps labeled extraordinary).

TRANSACTIONS AND EVENTS NOT DISCLOSED ON THE STATEMENT OF CASH FLOWS Many transactions and events, such as stock dividends, stock splits, retained earnings appropriations, and reversals of appropriations, affect only stockholders' equity accounts. Since these economic events are reclassifications within stockholders' equity, they are not shown on the statement of cash flows. They have no effect on cash and are not significant investing and financing activities. However, a conversion of preferred stock to common stock would be disclosed as a noncash financing activity on the statement of cash flows, in a manner similar to the illustration in Exhibit 23–12.

USE OF A WORKSHEET TO PREPARE THE STATEMENT OF CASH FLOWS

A worksheet is a useful tool for preparing a statement of cash flows. The primary advantage of the worksheet is that all of the data for analysis appear in one place, so that the analysis can be performed in a well-organized and efficient manner. The worksheet does not take the place of the formal statement. However, the formal statement can be prepared very easily by copying data from the completed worksheet. The following example will be used to prepare a worksheet.

Assume that comparative balance sheets for the Three Strikes Company appear as in Exhibit 23–13. Assume further that additional information about the company's transactions in 1987 is as follows:

1. Net income for 1987, $30,000; cash dividends declared and paid, $10,000.

2. Plant and equipment, with an original cost of $35,000 and accumulated depreciation of $10,000, was sold at a loss of $10,000. The loss, not extraordinary, was included in other expenses. Equipment was also purchased at a cost of $20,000.

3. Land costing $60,000 was sold at book value. In addition, land with a fair market value of $30,000 was acquired by issuing common stock with a par value of $15,000.

4. Three Strikes uses the equity method in accounting for its long-term investment in Claud common stock. No dividends were declared by the investee.

5. Bonds payable, with a carrying value of $46,000, were retired at the end of 1987. The extraordinary gain was $9,000, net of taxes of $6,000.

6. During 1987 preferred stock was converted to common stock. The book value method was used, and the common stock issued had a par value of $30,000.

7. A stock dividend of 5,000 shares was declared and distributed during 1987. The shares distributed had a fair market value of $4 per share.

8. The retained earnings appropriation for inventory losses was reversed in 1987.

9. Uncollectible accounts expense for 1987 was $16,000; receivables of $10,000 were written off against the allowance account in 1987.

10. Three Strikes' condensed income statement was as follows:

Sales	$300,000
Investment revenue	80,000
Cost of goods sold	(250,000)
Other expenses (including taxes)	(109,000)
Income before extraordinary gain	$ 21,000
Extraordinary gain: debt extinguishment, net of tax	9,000
Net income	$ 30,000

A worksheet for Three Strikes Company's statement of cash flows appears in Exhibit 23–14. The worksheet is divided into two sections. The upper section contains the amount of cash at the beginning and end of the period and also shows the beginning and ending balances in the noncash accounts. The bottom section, as completed, contains the cash flows that will appear on the formal statement. Notice that the major headings in the bottom section correspond to the activity format in the formal statement. The two middle

EXHIBIT 23—13

Three Strikes Company

COMPARATIVE BALANCE SHEETS, 1986 AND 1987

	12/31/86	12/31/87	NET CHANGE DR	NET CHANGE CR
Assets				
Cash	$ 60,000	$117,000	$ 57,000	
Accounts receivable	50,000	64,000	14,000	
Allowance for doubtful accounts	(10,000)	(16,000)		$ 6,000
Inventory	126,000	100,000		26,000
Plant and equipment	120,000	105,000		15,000
Accumulated depreciation	(40,000)	(50,000)		10,000
Land	60,000	30,000		30,000
Investment in Claud common stock	250,000	330,000	80,000	
Goodwill	30,000	28,000		2,000
Total	$646,000	$708,000		
Liabilities and stockholders' equity				
Accounts payable	$ 75,000	$ 50,000	25,000	
Other current liabilities	16,000	20,000		4,000
Deferred income taxes (noncurrent)	40,000	18,000	22,000	
Bonds payable (8 percent stated rate)	50,000	–0–	50,000	
Discount on bonds payable	(5,000)	–0–		5,000
Preferred stock (no par)	70,000	35,000	35,000	
Common stock ($2 par)	100,000	205,000		105,000
Contributed capital in excess of par	100,000	180,000		80,000
Retained earnings appropriated for inventory losses	40,000	–0–	40,000	
Retained earnings, unappropriated	160,000	200,000		40,000
Total	$646,000	$708,000	$323,000	$323,000

columns are used to record, in summary form, the transactions that caused the changes in cash during the period.

As a general rule, the debits made to noncash accounts in the upper portion of the worksheet are associated with the credits made in the lower portion. The credits in the lower portion represent either (1) adjustments to net income to determine cash flows from operating activities or (2) other outflows of cash. Similarly, the credits made to noncash accounts in the upper portion of the worksheet are associated with the debits made in the lower portion. These debits in the lower portion represent either (1) adjustments to net income to determine cash flows from operating activities or (2) other inflows of cash.

The explanations that follow show how various transactions were recorded originally in the company's books and also show the worksheet entries in a journal format. You should study each entry and trace it into the worksheet. Notice how each worksheet entry is grouped under the appropriate activity.

EXHIBIT 23—14 WORKSHEET FOR THE STATEMENT OF CASH FLOWS

Three Strikes Company

	BALANCE SHEET, 12/31/86	ANALYSIS OF TRANSACTIONS		BALANCE SHEET, 12/31/87
		DR	CR	
ASSETS				
Cash	$ 60,000	(23) $57,000		$117,000
Accounts receivable (net)	40,000	(19) 8,000		48,000
Inventory	126,000		(20) $26,000	100,000
Plant and equipment	120,000	(4) 20,000	(3) 35,000	105,000
Accumulated depreciation	(40,000)	(3) 10,000	(14) 20,000	(50,000)
Land	60,000	(6) 30,000	(5) 60,000	30,000
Investment in Claud common stock	250,000	(8) 80,000		330,000
Goodwill	30,000		(15) 2,000	28,000
Total	$646,000			$708,000
LIABILITIES AND STOCKHOLDERS' EQUITY				
Accounts payable	$ 75,000	(21) 25,000		$ 50,000
Other current liabilities	16,000		(22) 4,000	20,000
Deferred income taxes	40,000	(16) 22,000		18,000
Bonds payable	50,000	(9) 50,000		–0–
Discount on bonds payable	(5,000)		(9) 4,000	
			(17) 1,000	–0–
Preferred stock	70,000	(11) 35,000		35,000
Common stock	100,000		(7) 15,000	
			(10) 30,000	
			(12) 10,000	
			(18) 50,000	205,000
Contributed capital in excess of par	100,000		(7) 15,000	
			(10) 5,000	
			(12) 10,000	
			(18) 50,000	180,000
Retained earnings appropriated for inventory losses	40,000	(13) 40,000		–0–
Retained earnings, unappropriated	160,000	(2) 10,000	(1) 30,000	
		(12) 20,000	(13) 40,000	200,000
Total	$646,000			$708,000
CASH FLOWS FROM OPERATING ACTIVITIES				
Operations: Net income		(1) 30,000		
Loss on equipment sale		(3) 10,000		
Investment revenue			(8) 80,000	
Gain on bond retirement (extraordinary)			(9) 9,000	
Depreciation expense		(14) 20,000		Net cash used by operating activities, $51,000
Amortization of goodwill		(15) 2,000		
Change in deferred income taxes			(16) 22,000	
Amortization of bond discount		(17) 1,000		
Increase in accounts receivable (net)			(19) 8,000	
Decrease in inventory		(20) 26,000		
Decrease in accounts payable			(21) 25,000	
Increase in other current liabilities		(22) 4,000		
CASH FLOWS FROM INVESTING ACTIVITIES				
Sale of equipment		(3) 15,000		
Purchase of equipment			(4) 20,000	
Sale of land		(5) 60,000		
CASH FLOWS FROM FINANCING ACTIVITIES				
Pay dividends			(2) 10,000	
Retire debt—extraordinary item (net of tax)			(9) 37,000	
Issue common stock		(18) 100,000		
INVESTING AND FINANCING ACTIVITIES NOT AFFECTING CASH				
Land acquired by issuing common stock		(7) 30,000	(6) 30,000	
Conversion of preferred stock to common stock		(10) 35,000	(11) 35,000	
Net increase in cash			(23) 57,000	

EXPLANATION OF THE WORKSHEET

Each explanation is keyed to the additional information given for Three Strikes Company.

Entry 1: Additional information item 1; net income for 1987, $30,000 (operating activity)

Original entry			*Worksheet entry*		
Income summary ... 30,000			Cash flows from		
Retained			operating		
earnings		30,000	activities:		
			net income 30,000		
			Retained		
			earnings		30,000

The net income for 1987 is entered on the worksheet as a debit to cash flows from operating activities: net income and a credit to retained earnings.

Entry 2: Additional information item 1; dividends, $10,000 (financing activity)

Original entry			*Worksheet entry*		
Retained earnings ... 10,000			Retained earnings ... 10,000		
Cash...........		10,000	Cash used to		
			pay dividends ..		10,000

Entry 3: Additional information item 2; sale of equipment (investing activity)

Original entry			*Worksheet entry*		
Cash............. 15,000			Cash provided		
Accumulated			by sale of		
depreciation.... 10,000			equipment 15,000		
Loss on sale of			Accumulated		
equipment 10,000			depreciation.... 10,000		
Equipment		35,000	Operations: net		
			income—		
			adjustment for		
			loss on sale of		
			equipment 10,000		
			Equipment		35,000

Cash provided by sale of equipment is entered on the worksheet as a $15,000 debit under investing activities, since the sale generated cash of $15,000. Accumulated depreciation is debited for $10,000 because this account was debited for $10,000 when the sale was originally recorded. Since the loss did not affect cash, it is added back to net income by entering the $10,000 in the debit to "Operations: net income." Finally, the equipment account is credited for $35,000.

Entry 4: Additional information item 2; equipment purchase, $20,000 (investing activity)

Original entry			*Worksheet entry*		
Equipment 20,000			Equipment 20,000		
Cash...........		20,000	Cash used		
			to purchase		
			equipment		20,000

The equipment account is debited for $20,000 in the upper portion of the worksheet.

In the lower portion of the worksheet, cash used to purchase equipment is credited for $20,000.

Entry 5: Additional information item 3; sale of land at book value, $60,000 (investing activity)

Original entry
Cash 60,000
   Land 60,000

Worksheet entry
Cash provided
  by sale of
   land 60,000
  Land 60,000

Entries 6 and 7: Additional information item 3; issued stock for land with a fair market value of $30,000 (noncash investing and financing activity)

Original entry
Land 30,000
  Common stock . . . 15,000
  Contributed
   capital in
   excess of par . . . 15,000

Worksheet entries
(6) Land 30,000
  Land acquired
   by issuing
   common
   stock 30,000
(7) Land acquired
   by issuing
   common
   stock 30,000
  Common
   stock 15,000
  Contributed
   capital in
   excess of
   par 15,000

This entry records a transaction that is a noncash investing and financing activity. On the worksheet, two entries are made. In entry 6, land is debited for $30,000 while the credit is entered under "investing and financing activities not affecting cash." In entry 7, the debit is entered under "investing and financing activities not affecting cash." The credits are made to common stock for the par value of the shares issued and to contributed capital in excess of par for the difference between the fair market value of the land and the par value of the shares issued. From the standpoint of the accounts in the upper portion of the worksheet, entry 6 is similar to the one that would have been made if the land had been acquired with cash. Entry 7 is similar to one that would have been made if the stock had been issued for cash.

Entry 8: Additional information item 4; investment revenue from use of equity method, $80,000 (operating activity)

Original entry
Investment in
  Claud common . 80,000
  Investment
   revenue 80,000

Worksheet entry
Investment in
  Claud common . 80,000
  Operations: net
   income—
   adjustment for
   investment
   revenue 80,000

Since the investment revenue reported on Three Strikes' income statement has no effect on cash, reported net income must be adjusted to determine cash flows from operating activities. This adjustment is accomplished on the worksheet by crediting "Operations: net income."

Entry 9: Additional information item 5; early extinguishment of debt at a gain, net of tax, of $9,000 (financing activity)

Original entries

Bonds payable	50,000	
Discount on bonds payable		4,000
Cash		31,000
Extraordinary gain		15,000
To record before-tax gain.		
Extraordinary gain	6,000	
Cash		6,000
To record payment of taxes on gain and to show gain net of tax.		

Worksheet entry

Bonds payable	50,000	
Discount on bonds payable		4,000
Retire debt—extraordinary item (net of tax)		37,000*
Operations: net income—gain on bond retirement		9,000

* $31,000 (cash used in retirement)
   6,000 (cash paid in taxes)
  $37,000 (total cash outflow)

For instructional purposes, two original entries are shown above. The first entry is to record the bond retirement before taxes are considered. The second entry is to record the income taxes on the gain. Since the gain must be shown net of tax, in accordance with intraperiod tax allocation procedures discussed in Chapter 4, the tax of $6,000 is shown as a reduction of the gain. In the worksheet entry, bonds payable is debited for $50,000. The discount is credited for $4,000 because the book value of the debt at the time of retirement was $46,000 ($50,000 − $4,000). Cash used to retire bonds is credited for $37,000, which is the total outflow of cash associated with the early extinguishment.

Entries 10 and 11: Additional information item 6; conversion of preferred stock to common stock, $35,000 (noncash financing activity)

Original entry

Preferred stock	35,000	
Common stock		30,000
Contributed		
capital in		
excess of		
par		5,000

Worksheet entries

(10) Conversion of		
preferred stock		
to common		
stock	35,000	
Common stock		30,000
Contributed		
capital in		
excess of par		5,000
(11) Preferred stock	35,000	
Conversion of		
preferred stock		
to common		
stock		35,000

This transaction is a financing activity that has no effect on cash. It is recorded on the worksheet in a manner similar to worksheet entries 6 and 7.

Entry 12: Additional information item 7; stock dividend of $20,000

Original entry			*Worksheet entry*
Retained earnings ...	20,000		(Same as original entry)
Common stock ...		10,000	
Contributed capital in excess of par ...		10,000	

A stock dividend has no effect on cash and constitutes neither an investing activity nor a financing activity. As we discussed earlier, the stock dividend is merely a reclassification within stockholders' equity. Therefore, it does not appear in the bottom portion of the worksheet.

Entry 13: Additional information item 8; reversal of retained earnings appropriation of $40,000

Original entry			*Worksheet entry*
Retained earnings appropriated for inventory losses	40,000		(Same as original entry)
Retained earnings ..		40,000	

This event is similar to the previous entry and can be explained in the same manner.

Additional information item 9; uncollectible accounts expense for 1987, $16,000; write-off of receivables during 1987, $10,000

The recording of uncollectible accounts expense is included in other expenses and appears on Three Strikes' income statement. Since this expense has no effect on cash but is included as an expense in the determination of net income, a worksheet entry is necessary and will be made when we consider the change in accounts receivable below.

The write-off of uncollectible accounts against the allowance account has no effect on cash. The allowance account and the receivable account are reduced by the same amount, and there is no effect on the net receivable balance.

Now that each item of additional information has been analyzed, we must inspect each noncash account to determine whether we have included all cash transactions.

Entry 14: Accumulated depreciation account; depreciation for 1987, $20,000 (operating activity)

Original entry			*Worksheet entry*		
Depreciation expense	20,000		Operations: net income— adjustment for depreciation....	20,000	
Accumulated depreciation....		20,000	Accumulated depreciation....		20,000

The first noncurrent account that has not been fully reconciled is accumulated depreciation. The net increase in this account was $10,000. To this point, however, we have recorded only a debit of $10,000 (entry 3), which represented the accumulated depreciation on the equipment sold. Entry 14 is the $20,000 credit necessary to reconcile this account, and is the depreciation expense for 1987. Since this expense has no effect on cash, it is added to net income.

Entry 15: Goodwill account; amortization of goodwill for 1987, $2,000 (operating activity)

Original entry			*Worksheet entry*		
Amortization of			Operations: net		
goodwill	2,000		income—		
Goodwill		2,000	adjustment for		
			goodwill		
			amortization	2,000	
			Goodwill		2,000

The decrease of $2,000 in the goodwill account is for the amortization of goodwill. The worksheet entry shown above adds this noncash expense back to net income to determine cash flows from operating activities.

Entry 16: Deferred income taxes account; reduction of tax expense for 1987, $22,000 (operating activity)

Original entry			*Worksheet entry*		
Income tax expense	*xx*		Deferred income		
Deferred income taxes ...22,000			taxes	22,000	
Cash..............		*xx*	Operations: net		
			income—		
			adjustment for		
			change in		
			deferred tax		
			account		22,000

Deferred income taxes was debited for $22,000 when income tax expense and cash paid for taxes were recorded. Although the amounts of tax expense and cash were not given, we know that the cash outflow exceeded the amount of tax expense recorded in the income statement because of the $22,000 debit to deferred income taxes. Therefore, the $22,000 change in deferred taxes is deducted from net income.

Entry 17: Discount on bonds payable account; amortization of discount for 1987, $1,000 (operating activity)

Original entry			*Worksheet entry*		
Interest expense	1,000		Operations: net		
Discount on bonds ..		1,000	income—		
			adjustment for		
			amortization		
			of discount	1,000	
			Discount on bonds ..		1,000

When the worksheet entry to retire the bonds was made, the discount was credited for $4,000 because the book value of the bonds at the retirement date was $46,000 ($50,000 par value less $4,000 unamortized discount). The unreconciled amount of the change in the discount account is $1,000. This $1,000 represents amortization of the discount for 1987. (Amortization of the discount for 1987 in the amount of $1,000 is the reason that the bonds had a book value of $46,000 at the date of retirement.) On the worksheet, the $1,000 is added back to net income, because amortization of the discount increased interest expense and decreased net income but had no effect on cash.

Entry 18: Common stock and contributed capital in excess of par accounts; issuance of stock for $100,000 (financing activity)

The contributed capital accounts that have not been reconciled are common stock and contributed capital in excess of par:

	BEGINNING BALANCE	+ PREVIOUS CREDITS	− ENDING BALANCE	= UNRECONCILED DEBIT (CREDIT)
Common stock	$100,000 +	$15,000		
	+	30,000		
	+	10,000 −	$205,000 =	$(50,000)
Contributed capital in excess of par	$100,000 +	$15,000		
	+	5,000		
	+	10,000 −	$180,000 =	$(50,000)

These unreconciled credits (increases) must represent an issuance of common stock, as shown in the entries below.

Original entry
Cash............ 100,000
    Common stock ..   50,000
    Contributed
      capital in
      excess of par..   50,000

Worksheet entry
Cash provided
    by issuance of
    common stock . 100,000
    Common stock...   50,000
    Contributed
      capital in
      excess of par ..   50,000

Entry 19: Increase in accounts receivable, net of allowance, $8,000 (operating activity)

As we discussed in item 9 on page 1090, uncollectible accounts expense of $16,000 decreased net income but had no effect on cash, and the write-off of customers' accounts had no effect on either net income or cash. Although the $16,000 expense could have been added back to the net income to determine cash flows from operating activities, we consider it here because the increase in accounts receivable is given *net* of the changes in the allowance account. (If the two accounts had been listed separately, accounts receivable would have been a $14,000 increase [$64,000 − $50,000 from Exhibit 23–13] and allowance for doubtful accounts would have been a $6,000 increase [see Exhibit 23–13], for a *net* increase of $8,000).

Original entries			*Worksheet entry*		
Accounts receivable	24,000		Accounts receivable		
Sales		24,000	(net)	8,000	
Allowance for			Operations: net		
doubtful accounts ..	10,000		income—		
Accounts receivable ..		10,000	adjustment for		
Uncollectible			increase in		
accounts expense ..	16,000		accounts		
Allowance for			receivable (net)		8,000
doubtful					
accounts..........		16,000			

The $8,000 deduction from net income thus is the difference between a $24,000 deduction representing noncash revenues and a $16,000 addition representing noncash expenses.

Entry 20: Decrease in inventory, $26,000 (operating activity)

As shown in Exhibit 23–9, the decrease in inventory increased cost of goods sold but had no effect on cash. Therefore, the $26,000 is added back to net income.

Entry 21: Decrease in accounts payable, $25,000 (operating activity)

This type of item also was shown in Exhibit 23–9. The decrease in accounts payable represents additional cash payments in excess of purchases that enter into the calculation of cost of goods sold reported on the income statement. As a result, this $25,000 is deducted from net income. Notice that if the inventory decrease and the accounts payable decrease are considered jointly, the net addition to net income is $1,000 ($26,000 − $25,000). This $1,000 is the amount by which cost of goods sold (a component of net income) exceeded the amount of cash paid to creditors for merchandise purchases during the year.

Entry 22: Increase in other current liabilities, $4,000 (operating activity)

This $4,000 represents expenses that were accrued during the year. Because cash was not affected, the amount is added back to net income to determine net cash flows from operating activities.

Entry 23: Net increase in cash, $57,000

By inspecting the worksheet, you can see that all changes in the noncash account balances have been reconciled, and all transactions that caused the increase in cash have been listed in the lower portion of the worksheet. Therefore, this entry records the increase in cash by debiting cash for $57,000 and crediting increase in cash for $57,000.

PREPARING THE STATEMENT OF CASH FLOWS FROM THE WORKSHEET

The statement of cash flows for Three Strikes Company, based on the data in the bottom portion of the worksheet, appears in Exhibit 23–15. Notice that Three Strikes' operations for 1987 resulted in a net use of cash. In addition, the noncash investing and financing activities are disclosed in a supplementary schedule below the formal statement.

USING T-ACCOUNTS TO PREPARE THE STATEMENT OF CASH FLOWS

An alternative to the worksheet for analyzing data to prepare the statement of cash flows is T-accounts. Under this approach, instead of making summary worksheet entries to develop data for preparing the formal statement, one makes these entries in T-accounts.

Exhibit 23–16 illustrates the T-account approach, based on the data for Second Serve on page 1071. Under the T-account approach, the net change in cash and the net change in

EXHIBIT 23—15   STATEMENT OF CASH FLOWS

Three Strikes Company

STATEMENT OF CASH FLOWS
FOR THE YEAR ENDED DECEMBER 31, 1987

CASH FLOWS FROM OPERATING ACTIVITIES

Net income	$ 30,000	
Add (deduct) items not affecting cash:		
Investment revenue	(80,000)	
Depreciation expense	20,000	
Amortization of goodwill	2,000	
Amortization of bond discount	1,000	
Decrease in deferred income taxes	(22,000)	
Loss on sale of equipment	10,000	
Gain on bond retirement	(9,000)	
Increase in accounts receivable (net)	(8,000)	
Decrease in inventory	26,000	
Decrease in accounts payable	(25,000)	
Increase in other current liabilities	4,000	
Net cash used by operating activities		$(51,000)

CASH FLOWS FROM INVESTING ACTIVITIES

Sale of equipment	$ 15,000	
Sale of land	60,000	
Purchase of equipment	(20,000)	
Net cash provided by investing activities		55,000

CASH FLOWS FROM FINANCING ACTIVITIES

Issuance of common stock	$100,000	
Extraordinary item—retirement of debt (including taxes of $6,000 on gain)	(37,000)	
Dividends	(10,000)	
Net cash provided by financing activities		53,000
Net increase in cash		$ 57,000

INVESTING AND FINANCING ACTIVITIES NOT AFFECTING CASH

Conversion of preferred stock to common stock	$ 35,000
Land acquired by issuing common stock	30,000
	$ 65,000

EXHIBIT 23—16   PREPARATION OF THE STATEMENT OF CASH
FLOWS BY THE T-ACCOUNT APPROACH

Second Serve, Inc.

Cash

Net change	40,000			
Inflows:				
Operations and adjustments to operations		Adjustment to operations		
		(3) Premium amortization	2,000	
(1) Net income	65,000	(4) Gain on sale of equipment	10,000	
(2) Depreciation	25,000			
(5) Change in receivables	10,000			
(6) Change in inventories	25,000			
(7) Change in accounts payable	10,000			
(8) Change in salaries payable	5,000			
	140,000		12,000	
		Outflows:		
(4) Sale of equipment	30,000	(9) Purchase of equipment	40,000	
		(10) Purchase of land	8,000	
		(11) Retirement of common stock	35,000	
		(12) Dividends	35,000	

Plant and equipment

		Net change	10,000
(9)	40,000	(4)	50,000

Accumulated depreciation

Net change	5,000		
(4)	30,000	(2)	25,000

Land

Net change	8,000		
(10)	8,000		

Premium on bonds payable

Net change	2,000		
(3)	2,000		

Common stock

Net change	20,000		
(11)	20,000		

Contributed capital in excess of par

Net change	10,000		
(11)	10,000		

Retained earnings

		Net change	25,000
(11)	5,000	(1)	65,000
(12)	35,000		

Accounts receivable

Net change	10,000		
(5)	10,000		

Inventories

Net change	25,000		
(6)	25,000		

Accounts payable

		Net change	10,000
		(7)	10,000

Salaries payable

		Net change	5,000
		(8)	5,000

Explanation of T-account entries:
(1) To record net income.
(2) To add back depreciation to net income.
(3) To deduct bond premium amortization from net income.
(4) To deduct gain on sale of equipment from net income and show sale of equipment as an inflow of cash. Note: T-account entries under operations, when aggregated, equal net cash provided by operating activities: $140,000 − $12,000 = $128,000.
(5) Additional cash collections from customers.

(6) Increase in cost of goods sold (no cash effect).
(7) Additional purchases on account (no cash effect).
(8) Accrued salaries (no cash effect).
(9) To record and show sale of equipment as an inflow of cash.
(10) To record and show purchase of land as an outflow of cash.
(11) To record and show retirement of common stock as an outflow of cash.
(12) To record and show dividends paid as an outflow of cash.

each of the noncash accounts are first entered in the appropriate T-accounts. Cash inflows are entered on the debit side of the cash T-account, and cash outflows are entered on the credit side. For each debit or credit entry made in the cash T-account, an offsetting debit or credit is made in the appropriate noncash T-account. Entries are made until all of the net changes in the noncash accounts have been reconciled.

The idea behind the T-account approach is the same as for the worksheet approach. The only difference is that the debits and credits made in the "analysis of transactions" columns of the worksheet are entered on the debit and credit sides of the T-accounts.

Once the cash inflows and outflows have been summarized in the cash T-account, we must classify and group these cash flows as operating, investing, and financing activities for inclusion on the formal statement of cash flows.

SUMMARY OF IMPORTANT TOPICS AND CONCEPT APPLICATIONS

1. Funds flow reporting has been part of generally accepted accounting principles for many years. The term "funds" has been defined in one of four ways: net current monetary assets, working capital, cash and cash equivalents, and cash.

2. For many years, *APB Opinion No. 19* required the preparation of a statement of changes in financial position, based on a working capital, cash, or cash and cash equivalents concept of funds, as a primary financial statement.

3. A recent *FASB Exposure Draft* of a *Proposed Statement of Financial Accounting Standards* titled "Statement of Cash Flows," if issued, would supersede *Opinion No. 19* and would require that a **statement of cash flows** replace the statement of changes in financial position.

4. The primary purpose of the statement of cash flows is to provide information regarding a company's **cash inflows and outflows** during an accounting period. A secondary purpose is to provide information about the **investing and financing activities** of a company.

5. Information presented in a statement of cash flows, when used with information presented in the other financial statements and other information, can help users predict, assess, and evaluate a company's **present cash flows and future cash flow potential.**

6. Firms that invest excess idle cash in highly liquid short-term investments as part of their overall cash management should prepare the statement of cash flows on a **cash and cash equivalents basis.** Purchases and sales of these highly liquid investments should not be reported on the statement of cash flows because these investments are considered part of the pool of cash.

7. The statement of cash flows should be based on an **activity format** and should report the net cash inflow or outflow from each of three major activities—operating, investing, and financing.

8. **Operating activities** refer to a company's primary revenue-generating activities, and cash flows from operating activities are generally the cash effects of transactions and economic events that are included in the determination of income.

9. **Investing activities** include lending money and collecting on those loans, buying and selling productive assets that are expected to generate revenues over long periods of time, and buying and selling securities not classified as cash equivalents.

10. **Financing activities** include obtaining resources from owners and providing them with a return on their investment and a return of their investment. Financing activities also include obtaining resources from creditors and repaying amounts borrowed.

11. Two equivalent approaches may be used to determine cash flows from operating activities—the direct approach and the indirect approach. The **direct approach** summarizes directly the major operating inflows and outflows of cash—cash collected from customers and cash interest and dividends received, cash paid to merchandise suppliers, cash paid for salaries, cash paid to government agencies, and other operating cash outflows. Under the **indirect approach,** net income is adjusted for items entering into the determination of net income that do not affect cash and for other operating cash inflows and outflows.

12. The statement of cash flows should provide information about all investing and financing activities, including **noncash investing and financing transactions.** Noncash investing and financing transactions should be reported in a **separate supplementary schedule** or **directly in the statement.** If noncash transactions are reported directly in the statement of cash flows, the noncash aspects should be clearly identified.

13. Two tools that are useful in preparing the statement of cash flows are the worksheet and T-accounts. These tools provide an efficient means of analyzing information in order to prepare the formal statement.

APPENDIX 23–1

THE STATEMENT OF CHANGES IN FINANCIAL POSITION AND THE WORKING CAPITAL CONCEPT OF FUNDS

This appendix is included because, at the time that this chapter was written, *Opinion No. 19* was still in force and the statement of changes in financial position (SCFP) prepared under either a cash concept or a working capital concept of funds was acceptable in practice. In addition, those of you who may become financial analysts and who may utilize historical financial data in trend analysis and other types of analysis need to understand funds flows reporting under the working capital concept.

The statement of changes in financial position under the working capital concept of funds may be prepared using the same three steps discussed for the statement of cash flows:

1. Calculate the change in working capital during the accounting period—ending working capital minus beginning working capital.

2. Referring to the income statement (if available), the changes in the noncurrent accounts, and any additional available information, determine the specific transactions that caused working capital to increase or decrease.

3. Prepare the SCFP on the basis of the analysis in step 2.

Notice that, in the preparation of the statement of cash flows, we analyzed *noncash* accounts to determine the causes of cash flows. Since working capital equals current assets minus current liabilities, we analyze *noncurrent* accounts in order to determine the causes of working capital flows.

In the following two sections we discuss how to prepare the SCFP based on the working capital concept of funds. We use the data for Second Serve presented in Exhibit 23–5.

CALCULATING THE CHANGE IN WORKING CAPITAL

Distinguishing between the change in working capital and transactions that caused changes in working capital.

At the outset, it is important to distinguish between the changes in working capital and the events and transactions that *caused* those changes. As we saw earlier, the purpose of the SCFP is to disclose the sources and uses of funds. Under the working capital concept of funds, the SCFP discloses those transactions and events that *caused* working capital to increase or decrease during the accounting period. As an analogy, if you suddenly began to gain weight, you might be concerned about what caused the weight gain. Calculation of the change in working capital in step 1 is analogous to your stepping on the scales and measuring a gain in your weight. Step 2, which isolates the causes of the change, is analogous to determining what factors, such as too little exercise, too many sweets, or too many snacks, caused your weight gain.

A schedule of the changes in working capital for Second Serve appears in Exhibit 23–17. This schedule is constructed from the data in Exhibit 23–5. Since working capital equals current assets less current liabilities, only the current asset and current liability accounts from Exhibit 23–5 are included in the schedule. Current liabilities are subtracted from current assets in order to determine the amount of working capital at the beginning and end of the year (see columns 1 and 2). Working capital changed from $140,000 on December 31, 1986, to $130,000 on December 31, 1987, a decrease of $10,000.

Alternatively, the change in working capital can be determined by calculating the increase or decrease in *each* current asset and current liability account, adding each of the increases, and subtracting each of the decreases (see column 3). For example, cash increased from $50,000 at the end of 1986 to $90,000 at the end of 1987, an increase in working capital of $40,000. As another example, salaries payable increased from $10,000

EXHIBIT 23–17   CALCULATING THE CHANGE IN WORKING CAPITAL

Second Serve, Inc.

SCHEDULE OF CHANGES IN COMPONENTS
OF WORKING CAPITAL

| | WORKING CAPITAL | | |
| | DECEMBER 31 | | |
	1986	1987	INCREASE (DECREASE)
Cash	$ 50,000	$ 90,000	$ 40,000
Accounts receivable	70,000	60,000	(10,000)
Inventories	100,000	75,000	(25,000)
Accounts payable	(70,000)	(80,000)	(10,000)
Salaries payable	(10,000)	(15,000)	(5,000)
Total	$140,000	$130,000	$(10,000)

EXHIBIT 23–18   SCFP—WORKING CAPITAL APPROACH

Second Serve, Inc.

STATEMENT OF CHANGES IN FINANCIAL POSITION
FOR THE YEAR ENDED DECEMBER 31, 1987

Working capital was provided by:		
Operations: Net income		$ 65,000
Add (deduct) items not affecting working capital:		
Depreciation	25,000	
Amortization of premium on bonds payable	(2,000)	
Gain on sale of equipment............................	(10,000)	
Working capital provided by operations		$ 78,000
Sale of equipment....................................		30,000
Total working capital provided		$108,000
Working capital was used to:		
Purchase equipment	$ 40,000	
Purchase land	8,000	
Retire common stock	35,000	
Pay dividends	35,000	
Total working capital applied		(118,000)
Decrease in working capital		$(10,000)

Note: Under *Opinion No. 19*, the schedule of changes in the components of working capital (Exhibit 23–17) would appear here or in a footnote.

---

at the end of 1986 to $15,000 at the end of 1987. Since current liabilities are deducted from current assets when working capital is calculated, the increase in salaries payable decreased working capital by $5,000. The other current asset and current liability accounts can be analyzed in a similar manner.

PREPARATION OF THE STATEMENT OF CHANGES IN FINANCIAL POSITION

Exhibit 23–18 presents the SCFP for Second Serve, Inc. The following points are pertinent to its preparation and to its similarity to the statement of cash flows:

1. Accounts receivable and inventories are current assets, and accounts payable and salaries payable are current liabilities. These items are part of the *pool of working capital*, rather than adjustments to net income to determine working capital provided by operations. Thus, the only income statement items that do not have an equal and corresponding effect on working capital are depreciation expense, amortization of bond premium, and the gain on sale of equipment.

2. The remaining working capital flows shown in Exhibit 23–18 are analyzed in the same manner as on pages 1077–79, except that the focus is on working capital instead of cash.

3. The format of Exhibit 23–18 is a "sources and uses format," in contrast to the "activity format" presented in the chapter. In practice, both formats have been used for the SCFP.

4. To the extent that a given transaction affects working capital in the same manner in which it affects cash, the additional statement preparation problems that were discussed on pages 1082–83 also apply to the SCFP.

In summary, the SCFP, prepared under a cash concept, a cash and cash equivalents concept, or a working capital concept has constituted GAAP since the issuance of *Opinion No. 19.* However, if the *FASB Exposure Draft* becomes a *Statement of Financial Accounting Standards,* perhaps with some modification, the statement of cash flows will replace the SCFP as a required financial statement.

QUESTIONS

Questions marked with an asterisk (*) refer to Appendix 23–1.

Q23-1. What is the purpose of the statement of cash flows?

Q23-2. How does the statement of cash flows relate to *Statement of Financial Accounting Concepts No. 1,* "Objectives of Financial Reporting"?

Q23-3. List and briefly discuss the various concepts of funds discussed in the chapter.

Q23-4. Distinguish among a company's operating activities, investing activities, and financing activities.

Q23-5. List three examples of investing activities and three examples of financing activities.

Q23-6. How can the statement of cash flows provide information related to the "quality" of earnings?

Q23-7. Give an example of each of the following transactions:

1. A transaction that increases working capital and cash.

2. A transaction that increases working capital but has no effect on cash.

3. A transaction that has no effect on either working capital or cash.

Q23-8. **A)** What is meant by the all financial resources approach to the funds flow statement?
B) List three types of transactions that have no effect on cash, but that must be disclosed on the statement of cash flows.

Q23-9. Briefly summarize the strengths and weaknesses of:

1. The working capital concept of funds.

2. The cash concept of funds.

Q23-10. Two approaches that may be used to determine the amount of cash flows from operating activities are the "direct" approach and the "indirect" approach. What are the differences between the two approaches?

Q23-11. **A)** When cash flows from operating activities is calculated, why must net income be adjusted for certain items on the income statement?
B) Indicate whether each item listed below should be added to or deducted from net income to determine cash flows from operating activities. If the item should be neither added nor deducted, so indicate.

1. Depreciation expense.

2. Amortization of goodwill.

3. Gain on sale of equipment.

4. Increase in accounts payable.

5. Loss on sale of an investment classified as a cash equivalent.

6. Decrease in noncurrent deferred income taxes payable.

7. Stock dividends distributed.

8. Amortization of discount on long-term capital lease.

9. Uncollectible accounts expense.

10. Unrealized losses on long-term marketable equity securities.

11. Write-off of uncollectible accounts (allowance method used).

12. Decrease in deferred investment credit classified as noncurrent.

*Q23-12. Refer to Question 23-11, part *B*. Indicate whether each item should be added to or deducted from net income to determine working capital provided by operations. If the item should be neither added nor deducted, so indicate.

Q23-13. A company acquired a tract of land with a fair market value of $300,000 by paying $125,000 cash and issuing a 10-year note for the balance. Explain how this transaction would be reported on the statement of cash flows.

Q23-14. During 1987 Snow Corporation, which uses the allowance method of accounting for doubtful accounts, recorded $15,000 of uncollectible accounts expense and wrote off $8,000 of uncollectible accounts. What effect did these combined transactions have on:

   1. Working capital?

   2. Cash?

Q23-15. Explain how a company could report a net loss for the year and still have cash flows generated from operations.

Q23-16. A partial statement of cash flows for Halliburton Company appears below. What changes would you suggest for improving this statement?

Cash flows from operating activities
Net income	$360,352
Depreciation charged to income	196,159
Net book value of property, plant, and equipment retired	18,730
Other noncash items.......................................	(44,881)
Net cash provided by operating activities.....................	$530,360

Q23-17. Indicate how the following transactions would appear on a statement of cash flows. Use the following key for your answers:
   a) Added to net income.
   b) Deducted from net income to determine cash from operations.
   c) Investing activity.
   d) Financing activity.
   e) None of the above.

   1. Declaration (but not payment) of a cash dividend.

   2. Gain on disposal of equipment.

   3. Interest accrued on short-term notes receivable.

   4. Interest accrued on long-term notes receivable.

   5. Issuance of long-term notes for cash.

   6. Issuance of short-term notes for cash.

   7. Amortization of patents.

   8. Proceeds from sale of land.

   9. Investment revenue from use of the equity method.

   10. Dividends received from investee under the cost method.

   11. Loss on sale of marketable equity securities classified as current assets.

   12. Appropriation of retained earnings for cost of treasury stock purchased.

   13. Issue of treasury stock in excess of cost.

   14. Issue of treasury stock at less than cost.

   15. Interest expense on bonds issued at par.

*Q23-18. Distinguish between the SCFP prepared under the working capital approach and a schedule that shows the changes in the composition of working capital.

CASES

The case marked with an asterisk (*) refers to Appendix 23–1.

C23-1. ALL FINANCIAL RESOURCES APPROACH AND THE STATEMENT OF CASH FLOWS For many years the statement of changes in financial position was a required basic financial statement for each period for which an income statement was presented. The reporting entity had flexibility in the form, content, and terminology of this statement. For example, the concept of "funds" could be interpreted to mean, among other things, cash or working capital. The statement was prepared, however, on the basis of the all financial resources approach.

REQUIRED

1. What is the all financial resources approach?

2. What are two types of financial transactions that would be disclosed under the all financial resources approach that would not be disclosed otherwise?

3. What effect, if any, would each of the following seven items have on the preparation of a statement of cash flows?
  a) Accounts receivable—trade.
  b) Inventory.
  c) Depreciation.
  d) Deferred income tax credit from interperiod tax allocation.
  e) Issuance of long-term debt in payment for a building.
  f) Payoff of current portion of debt.
  g) Sale of a fixed asset resulting in a loss.

(AICPA, adapted)

C23-2. OBJECTIVES OF CASH FLOW STATEMENT; WEAKNESSES IN STATEMENT PREPARATION The following statement was prepared by the accountant for the Dingell Corporation:

Statement of Source and Application of Cash
FOR THE YEAR ENDED SEPTEMBER 30, 1987

Sources of cash:	
Net income	$ 52,000
Depreciation and depletion	59,000
Increase in long-term debt	178,000
Common stock issued under employee option plans	5,000
Changes in current receivables and inventories, less current liabilities (excluding current maturities of long-term debt)	3,000
	$297,000
Uses of cash:	
Cash dividends	$ 33,000
Expenditures for property, plant, and equipment	202,000
Investments and other uses	9,000
Change in cash	53,000
	$297,000

The following additional information is available for Dingell Corporation for the year ended September 30, 1987:

a) Depreciation expense	$58,000
Depletion expense	1,000
	$59,000

b) Increase in long-term debt $600,000
Retirement of debt .... (422,000)

Net increase $178,000

c) The corporation received $5,000 in cash from its employees on its employee stock option plan, and wage and salary expense attributable to the shares issued under the option plan was an additional $22,000.

d) Expenditures for property, plant, and equipment $212,000
Proceeds from retirements of property, plant, and equipment...... (10,000)

Net expenditures $202,000

e) A stock dividend of 10,000 shares of Dingell Corporation common stock was distributed to common stockholders on April 1, 1987, when the market price was $6 per share and par value was $1.

f) On July 1, 1987, when its market price was $5 per share, 16,000 shares of Dingell Corporation common stock were issued in exchange for 4,000 shares of preferred stock.

REQUIRED

1. In general, what are the objectives of a statement of the type shown above for the Dingell Corporation? Explain.

2. Identify the weaknesses in the form and format of the Dingell Corporation's statement of source and application of cash without reference to the additional information.

3. For each of the seven items of additional information, indicate the preferable treatment and explain why the treatment you suggest is preferable.

(AICPA, adapted)

C23-3. ANALYSIS OF CASH FLOWS   Clayton Instruments Corporation, a scientific research and production company, has decided to expand its operations and is preparing a registration statement for the SEC in connection with a new stock offering. The company has never prepared a statement of cash flows and must include one in the registration statement. The controller is puzzled about how several items should be reported. You have agreed to assist the controller in determining how the following events that occurred during the current year should be reported on the statement of cash flows:

a) Used research equipment, which was secured by a mortgage of $80,000, was sold for $300,000 cash. The mortgage was canceled, and a gain of $25,000 was recorded on this transaction. Depreciation of $100,000 had been recorded on the equipment since acquisition.

b) During the year, the company borrowed $400,000 for plant expansion. The funds are being held by a bank under a trust arrangement, and $36,000 was unexpended at the end of the year. The debt matures in five years.

c) The company holds, as a long-term investment, common stock of Biotech Corporation. During the current year, the investment account increased by $100,000:

Additional stock purchased (financed in
part by a $15,000 three-year note) .... $ 65,000
Stock dividend distributed by Biotech (the
offsetting credit was made to miscellaneous
revenue)... 8,000
Share of Biotech's reporting earnings....................... 40,000
Dividends received from Biotech .... (13,000)

$100,000

d) Cash proceeds from the sale of assets of discontinued operations amounted to $10,000. The loss on sale was $90,000; $82,000 of this amount had been accrued in the previous year, when management made the decision to dispose of the segment.

e) The company wrote off $12,000 in uncollectible receivables during the year and accrued uncollectible accounts expense of $20,000 at the end of the year.

f) A stock option plan was made available to key executives during the current year. This compensatory plan resulted in deferred compensation expense of $50,000, of which $10,000 was expensed. The remainder will be amortized over the next four years.

g) Near the end of the current year, the company acquired the assets of Mighty Mite Services by issuing preferred stock. The fair market value of the assets acquired was $60,000:

Inventories	$25,000
Land	10,000
Plant and equipment	20,000
Supplies	5,000

h) During the current year, the company's long-term bonds payable decreased by $125,000: A gain of $20,000 was recorded on an open-market purchase and retirement of bonds with a book value of $75,000. Bonds with a book value of $10,000 were reclassified as a current liability, as they are due next year. Convertible bonds with a book value of $15,000 were converted to common stock. The remaining bonds were extinguished through an in-substance defeasance, whereby U.S. government securities were purchased for $20,000 and placed in an irrevocable trust. The securities' cash flows are sufficient to service the debt.

i) The company wishes to calculate cash flows from operating activities by adjusting net income for income statement items that do not affect cash. One of these adjustments, depreciation expense, amounted to $15,000 for the current year. Of the $15,000, $8,000 represented depreciation on manufacturing facilities (a part of factory overhead). At the end of the year, $3,000 of this $8,000 factory overhead was applied as part of the cost of the ending inventory.

j) A stock dividend, measured at $30,000, was distributed during the year. The controller believes that this event should be reported as both a use of cash (similar to a cash dividend from the standpoint of the decrease in retained earnings) and a source of cash (similar to an issuance of shares from the standpoint of the increase in contributed capital).

REQUIRED

Discuss how each of the ten items above should be reported in Clayton's statement of cash flows.

C23-4. CONCEPTS OF FUNDS AND REPORTING ON THE STATEMENT OF CASH FLOWS

A) Funds flow reporting has been of interest to accountants and financial statement users for some time. *APB Opinion No. 19* required the issuance of a statement of changes in financial position based on an "all financial resources" approach. A recent *FASB Exposure Draft,* if issued as a *Statement of Financial Accounting Standards,* would replace the statement of changes in financial position with a statement of cash flows.

REQUIRED

1. Compare the statement of changes in financial position with the statement of cash flows in terms of the concepts of funds used in each statement.

2. What is meant by the "all financial resources" approach required by *Opinion No. 19?*

3. Compare the "all financial resources" approach required by *Opinion No. 19* with any similar requirements set forth in the *FASB Exposure Draft* on the statement of cash flows.

B) Chen Engineering Company is a young and growing producer of electronic measuring instruments and technical equipment. You have been retained by Chen to advise it in the preparation of a statement of cash flows. You have obtained the following information concerning certain events and transactions of Chen during the fiscal year ended October 31, 1987.

a) The amount of reported income for the fiscal year was $800,000, which included a deduction for an extraordinary loss of $93,000 (see item *e* below).

b) Depreciation expense of $240,000 was included in the income statement.

c) Uncollectible accounts receivable of $30,000 were written off against the allowance for uncollectible accounts. Also, $37,000 of bad debts expense was included in the determination of income for the fiscal year, and the same amount was added to the allowance for uncollectible accounts.

d) A gain of $4,700 was realized on the sale of a machine; it originally cost $75,000, of which $25,000 was undepreciated on the date of sale.

e) On April 1, 1987, a freak storm caused an uninsured inventory loss of $93,000 ($180,000 loss, less reduction in income taxes of $87,000). This extraordinary loss was included in the determination of income, as indicated in *a* above.

f) On July 3, 1987, building and land were purchased for $600,000; Chen gave in payment $100,000 cash, $200,000 market value of its unissued common stock, and a $300,000 mortgage note.

g) On August 3, 1987, $700,000 face value of Chen's 6 percent convertible debentures was converted into $140,000 par value of its common stock. The bonds were originally issued at face value.

h) The board of directors declared a $320,000 cash dividend on October 20, 1987, payable on November 15, 1987, to stockholders of record on November 5, 1987.

REQUIRED

Explain whether each of the items above provided or used cash and explain how each item should be disclosed in Chen's statement of cash flows for the fiscal year ended October 31, 1987. If any item is neither an inflow nor an outflow of cash, explain why it is not and indicate how the item should be disclosed, if at all, in Chen's statement of cash flows. Chen reports cash from operating activities under the indirect approach.

(AICPA, adapted)

*C23-5. PURPOSE AND CONTENT OF THE SCFP A statement of changes in financial position for IBM Corporation appears below and on the next page. Your father-in-law is considering investing in IBM's stock and has asked you, as a serious student of accounting, various questions about this statement.

Statement of Changes in Financial Position

(IN THOUSANDS OF DOLLARS)

Sources of working capital:	
Net earnings	$ 3,011,259
Items not requiring the current use of working capital:	
Depreciation	1,970,248
Net book value of rental machines and other property	
retired or sold	778,863
Other	352,385
Total from operations	$ 6,112,755
Proceeds from stock sold or issued under employee plans	416,314
Long-term borrowings	1,449,505
Total sources	$ 7,978,574
Uses of working capital:	
Investment in plant and other property	$ 1,779,250
Investment in rental machines	4,211,732
	$ 5,990,982
Less: Depreciation of manufacturing facilities	
capitalized in rental machines	(351,080)
	$ 5,639,902
Increase in deferred charges and other assets	337,955
Cash dividends paid or payable	1,505,962
Reduction of long-term debt	145,681
Treasury stock purchased for employee plan	453,986
Total uses	$(8,083,486)
Decrease in working capital	$ (104,912)

Changes in working capital:

Cash	$ (259,463)
Notes and accounts receivable	536,857
Inventories and prepaid expenses	252,460
U.S. Federal and non-U.S. income taxes	(257,924)
Accounts payable and accruals	(187,207)
Loans payable	(691,245)
Dividend payable	501,610
Decrease in working capital	$ (104,912)
Working capital at beginning of year	4,510,789
Working capital at end of year	$ 4,405,877

REQUIRED

Draft a brief response to each of the following questions for your father-in-law.

1. What is meant by working capital?

2. What does the statement of changes disclose that IBM's comparative balance sheets and income statement do not?

3. Why are certain items added to net income under "sources of working capital"?

4. Why was "depreciation of manufacturing facilities capitalized in rental machines" deducted from working capital applications?

5. How is "increase in deferred charges and other assets" a use of working capital? Provide an example.

6. Can the amount of cash provided by operating activities be derived from the above statement? If so, explain how.

EXERCISES

Exercises marked with an asterisk (*) refer to Appendix 23–1.

E23-1. CALCULATING CASH FLOWS An income statement and comparative balance sheets for Armadillo, Inc., appear below and on the next page.

Armadillo, Inc.

COMPARATIVE BALANCE SHEETS

	12/31/86	12/31/87
Assets		
Cash	$ 19,000	$ 60,000
Receivables	24,000	15,000
Inventory	31,000	59,000
Plant and equipment	48,000	72,000
Accumulated depreciation	(12,000)	(24,000)
Land	20,000	4,000
Total	$130,000	$186,000
Liabilities and stockholders' equity		
Accounts payable	$ 16,000	$ 20,000
Notes payable (short-term)	7,000	–0–
Bonds payable	–0–	20,000
Common stock (no-par)	80,000	102,000
Retained earnings	27,000	44,000
Total	$130,000	$186,000

INCOME STATEMENT
FOR THE YEAR ENDED DECEMBER 31, 1987

Revenues	$200,000
Cost of goods sold	(130,000)
Depreciation	(12,000)
Other expenses	(18,000)
Loss on sale of land	(8,000)
Net income	$ 32,000

The notes were issued in 1986 for the acquisition of plant and equipment.

REQUIRED

Calculate the following for Armadillo, Inc., for 1987:

1. Cash flows from operating activities under the:
   a) Direct approach.
   b) Indirect approach.

2. Proceeds received on the sale of land.

3. Amount of cash received from issuing the bonds.

4. Dividends paid during the year.

5. Proceeds received on the issuance of common stock.

*E23-2. WORKING CAPITAL PROVIDED BY (USED IN) OPERATIONS   An income statement for 1987 for Pitt Company appears below:

Revenues—sale of products		$300,000
Investment revenue from use of equity method		44,000
Interest revenue		
Short-term investments		6,000
Long-term investments		12,500
Cost of goods sold		(160,000)
Salary expense		(20,000)
Depreciation expense		(36,000)
Interest expense on bonds payable (including discount amortization of $3,000)		(18,000)
Income tax expense		
Current	$110,000	
Deferred	(26,000)	(84,000)
Extraordinary loss on hurricane damage to inventory (net of $10,000 tax credit)		(25,000)
Net income		$ 19,500

REQUIRED

Calculate the working capital provided by (or used in) operations for 1987 under the indirect approach.

E23-3. FUNDS FLOW FROM OPERATIONS—WORKING CAPITAL AND CASH APPROACHES

REQUIRED

Using the data on page 1108, calculate the amounts of *(a)* working capital provided by (used in) operations and *(b)* cash provided by (used in) operations.

ITEM	(a) WORKING CAPITAL	(b) CASH
1. Net income for the period	$80,000	$80,000
2. Depreciation expense, $36,000	_____	_____
3. Salary expense, $25,000...........................	_____	_____
4. Amortization of bond premium, $5,500	_____	_____
5. Gain on sale of investments (net of taxes of $4,000), $8,000	_____	_____
6. Purchase of land, $12,000	_____	_____
7. Uncollectible accounts expense, $3,200	_____	_____
8. Amortization of discount on long-term notes, $2,000...	_____	_____
9. Issuance of long-term notes for cash, $30,000	_____	_____
10. Dividends of $4,000 received from investees (equity method)	_____	_____
11. Increase in inventories, $5,000	_____	_____
12. Decrease in noncurrent deferred income taxes, $4,000	_____	_____
13. Decrease in accounts receivable, $10,000............	_____	_____
14. Issued stock for equipment, $34,000...............	_____	_____
15. Dividends declared but not paid, $13,000	_____	_____
Total	_____	_____

E23-4. CALCULATING CASH FLOWS FROM OPERATING ACTIVITIES   An income statement for the Dallas Corporation appears below:

Revenues from sales of product		$250,000
Cost of goods sold		
Beginning inventory	$ 50,000	
Purchases.....................................	140,000	
Ending inventory	(90,000)	(100,000)
Depreciation expense		(30,000)
Uncollectible accounts expense		(3,000)
Amortization of goodwill.........................		(10,000)
Salary expense		(50,000)
Insurance expense................................		(5,000)
Equity in losses of investee		(8,000)
Income tax expense		
Current	$ 20,000	
Deferred	6,000	(26,000)
Cumulative effect of change from accelerated to straight-line depreciation (net of deferred tax credits of $8,000)		12,000
Extraordinary gain on retirement of bonds (net of taxes of $10,000).........................		40,000
Net income		$ 70,000

Additional information related to Dallas Corporation's operations:
a) Decrease in accounts receivable (net of allowance for doubtful accounts), $25,000.
b) The change in accounting principle was made for financial reporting purposes but not for tax purposes.
c) The prepaid insurance account increased by $4,000 during the year.
d) Included in salary expenses are salaries of $4,000 accrued at the end of the year; there were no unpaid salaries at the beginning of the year.
e) At the date of retirement, the bonds payable had a book value of $64,000.

REQUIRED

Prepare a schedule showing the net cash flows generated by the operating activities of Dallas Corporation.

E23-5.   CASH FLOWS; EXTRAORDINARY ITEMS   Michelle began operating at the beginning of the current year with the following balance sheet:

Land .... $100,000   Capital stock $100,000

During the year, Michelle leased the land for $5,000 per month. At the end of the year, federal authorities condemned the land because of carcinogenic materials discovered by the lessee. Michelle received $60,000 from authorities as a condemnation award. The company's income statement for the year and its balance sheet at the end of the year appeared as follows:

INCOME STATEMENT FOR THE YEAR

Rental revenues	$60,000
Operating expenses...	(2,000)
Income before taxes and extraordinary item	$58,000
Income tax expense	(23,200)
Income before extraordinary item	$34,800
Extraordinary item:	
Loss on condemnation of land (net of $16,000 tax benefit)	(24,000)
Net income	$10,800

BALANCE SHEET, END OF YEAR

Cash.........................	$110,800	Capital stock	$100,000
		Retained earnings.....	10,800
	$110,800		$110,800

REQUIRED

Prepare the statement of cash flows for Michelle for the current year.

E23-6.   WORKING CAPITAL AND CASH FLOWS   Indicate whether each item in the following chart represents a flow of working capital and/or a flow of cash and whether it is an inflow, an outflow, or neither.

	WORKING CAPITAL			CASH		
	OUTFLOW	INFLOW	NEITHER	OUTFLOW	INFLOW	NEITHER
1. Net income from operations.						
2. Purchase of treasury stock.						
3. Issued bonds payable at a discount.						
4. Issuance of bonds payable at par for tract of land.						
5. Sale of delivery equipment at a gain.						
6. Declaration (but not payment) of dividend payable in cash.						
7. Reclassification of currently maturing portion of serial bonds issue from noncurrent to current liability.						
8. Payment of a dividend during current period which had been declared in a prior period.						

(CGAA, adapted)

E23-7. CASH FLOWS Kristin Company reported a net loss of $5,000 for the fiscal year just ended. In arriving at the net loss, the company included the following items:

Loss on sale of equipment	$ 3,000
Amortization of bond discount	500
Depreciation expense	15,000
Bad debts expense	200

Changes (Dr or Cr) in the current accounts were as follows:

Accounts receivable	$2,000 Dr
Allowance for doubtful accounts	200 Cr
Inventories	1,000 Cr
Accounts payable	3,000 Dr

REQUIRED

Calculate the amount of net cash provided by operating activities.

E23-8. RELATIONSHIPS BETWEEN BALANCE SHEET AND STATEMENT OF CASH FLOWS Selected financial statements for WTA, Inc., appear below:

BALANCE SHEET
DECEMBER 31, 1986

Assets		Equities	
Cash	$26,000	Capital stock (no-par)	$27,000
Buildings and equipment	48,000	Retained earnings	37,000
Accumulated deprecia-tion—buildings and equipment	(15,000)		
Patents	5,000		
	$64,000		$64,000

STATEMENT OF CASH FLOWS
FOR THE YEAR ENDED DECEMBER 31, 1987

Cash flows from operating activities		
Net income	$24,000	
Add (deduct) noncash items:		
Gain on sale of buildings	(4,000)	
Depreciation: buildings and equipment	10,000	
Amortization of patents	1,000	
Net cash provided by operating activities		$31,000
Cash flows from investing activities		
Sale of buildings	$ 7,000	
Purchase of land	(14,000)	
Purchase of buildings and equipment	(30,000)	
Net cash used by investing activities		(37,000)
Cash flows from financing activities		
Issue of capital stock	$13,000	
Dividends	(12,000)	
Net cash flows from financing activities		1,000
Net decrease in cash		$(5,000)

Other information:
  a) Total assets on the balance sheet as of December 31, 1987, $89,000.
  b) Accumulated depreciation on the building sold, $6,000.

REQUIRED

On the basis of the above data, prepare the balance sheet for WTA, Inc., as of December 31, 1987.

(AICPA, adapted)

E23-9. WORKSHEET ENTRIES FOR A STATEMENT OF CASH FLOWS The information shown below was taken from the ledger accounts of Erin Company.

a)

Accounts receivable			
Beginning balance	70,000	Customer collections	120,000
Credit sales	100,000	Sale of receivables to ABC Factors (without recourse)	30,000
		Write-off of customer accounts	7,500

Allowance for doubtful accounts			
Write-off of customer accounts	7,500	Beginning balance	8,000
		Expense for period	11,000

b)

Land			
Beginning balance	65,000	Sale of unused tract (loss on sale was $7,000)	38,000
Purchased by issuing long-term notes	50,000		

c)

Plant and equipment			
Beginning balance	200,000	Obsolete machine written off	20,000
Acquisitions	130,000	Sale of building (proceeds received, $50,000)	60,000

Accumulated depreciation			
Accumulated depreciation on obsolete machine	17,000	Beginning balance	50,000
Accumulated depreciation on building sold	30,000	Depreciation for period	36,000

d)

Investment in Ricky Corp.			
Beginning balance	60,000	Ricky dividends received	5,000
Share of Ricky Corp. earnings	10,000		

e)

Bond sinking fund			
Beginning balance	80,000	Retirement of maturing bonds	100,000
Additions	20,000		

Bonds payable			
Bonds retired	100,000	Beginning balance	300,000
Bonds to be retired next year	20,000		

Premium on bonds payable			
Amortization for period	15,000	Beginning balance	75,000

f)

Retained earnings			
Net loss for period	30,000	Beginning balance	110,000
Cash dividends paid	10,000		
Stock dividend distributed	20,000		

REQUIRED

On the basis of the data provided, prepare, in journal form, all relevant worksheet entries necessary to prepare the statement of cash flows.

E23-10. ANALYSIS OF CHANGES IN ACCOUNT BALANCES IN PREPARATION OF STATEMENT OF CASH FLOWS
In preparing the worksheet for the statement of cash flows for Yamahaw Corporation, you find the following data related to the equipment and bonds payable accounts:

a) Account balances and information related to equipment during the year:

	BALANCE, BEGINNING OF YEAR	BALANCE, END OF YEAR
Equipment	$66,000	$210,000
Accumulated depreciation	30,000	38,000

Equipment with an original cost of $22,000 and a book value of $9,000 was sold at a gain of $8,000.

b) Account balances and information relating to bonds payable during the year:

	BALANCE, BEGINNING OF YEAR	BALANCE, END OF YEAR
Bonds payable	$80,000	$60,000
Premium on bonds payable	12,000	9,000

Bonds with a par value of $20,000 were issued at a 10 percent premium for land. Bonds with a par value of $40,000 were retired; the amount paid was $50,000, and the loss of $6,000 was extraordinary.

REQUIRED

In journal form, prepare all worksheet entries related to the above information necessary to prepare the statement of cash flows for Yamahaw Corporation.

E23-11. STATEMENT OF CASH FLOWS Thornton Racquet Club is applying for a bank loan and furnishes you with the trial balances below:

	12/31/86, POSTCLOSING DR	12/31/86, POSTCLOSING CR	12/31/87, PRECLOSING DR	12/31/87, PRECLOSING CR
Cash.	$ 35,000		$ 20,000	
Accounts receivable (net).	71,000		118,000	
Dividends receivable	20,000		–0–	
Inventories.	6,000		20,000	
Plant and equipment.	180,000		250,000	
Accumulated depreciation		$ 22,000		$ 70,000
Land	40,000		20,000	
Investment in Head Co. (cost method)	38,000		24,000	
Accounts payable		80,000		44,000
Estimated warranty obligations . . .		8,000		9,000
Salaries payable		5,000		3,000
Other current liabilities		7,000		28,000
Long-term serial notes payable . . .		50,000		40,000
B. Thornton, capital.		118,000		98,000
P. Arterbury, capital.		100,000		90,000
Membership and court revenues . .				94,000
Sales of racquets, racquetballs, etc.				84,000
Dividend revenue				10,000
Cost of goods sold			30,000	
Depreciation expense			48,000	
Salaries and other expenses			26,000	
Loss on sale of land.			14,000	
	$390,000	$390,000	$570,000	$570,000

Additional information:

a) Investments were sold at book value.
b) There were no sales of plant and equipment.
c) There were no purchases of land.
d) The partners share income equally. Their cash withdrawals during 1987 were as follows: Thornton, $20,000; Arterbury, $10,000.

REQUIRED

Prepare Thornton Racquet Club's statement of cash flows for 1987.

*E23-12.   CALCULATING WORKING CAPITAL FROM OPERATIONS

REQUIRED

Referring to Exercise 23-11, calculate the working capital provided by operations for Thornton Racquet Club.

E23-13.   WORKSHEET FOR THE STATEMENT OF CASH FLOWS   The records of Jogger, Inc., showed the following data:

	BALANCE SHEET		CHANGE DR (CR)
	12/31/86	12/31/87	
Cash..............................	$148,300	$185,200	$ 36,900
Plant and equipment..................	96,000	100,500	4,500
Accumulated depreciation	(30,000)	(34,000)	(4,000)
Investments	35,000	32,000	(3,000)
Goodwill	25,000	–0–	(25,000)
Total	$274,300	$283,700	$ 9,400
Accounts payable	$ 43,300	$ 58,800	$(15,500)
Bonds payable	50,000	–0–	50,000
Discount on bonds payable	(1,250)	–0–	(1,250)
Common stock	155,000	165,000	(10,000)
Contributed capital in excess of par	–0–	40,000	(40,000)
Retained earnings	27,250	19,900	7,350
Total	$274,300	$283,700	$ (9,400)

Additional data for 1987:

a) Net income for year, $11,150; dividends paid, $18,500.
b) Fully depreciated equipment (original cost, $10,500) was sold for $1,500. The remaining changes in the plant and equipment and accumulated depreciation accounts represent equipment purchases and depreciation expense.
c) Investments purchased with cash totaled $17,000. Other investments were sold at a loss of $2,500.
d) On July 1, Jogger retired the bonds outstanding at a price of $52,500. Discount amortization on the bonds from January to July totaled $250.
e) The equipment purchased was acquired by issuing common stock (par value of shares issued, $2,000). The remaining common stock was issued for cash.
f) Goodwill was written off during the year.

REQUIRED

Prepare a worksheet for the statement of cash flows for Jogger, Inc.

E23-14.   WORKSHEET ENTRIES FOR STATEMENT OF CASH FLOWS   The following information relates to 1987 financial data for Presley Corporation.

a) During 1987 Presley sold its only holding in the preferred stock of Parker Enterprises.

The stock, which had a book value of $120,000, was sold for $180,000. The gain was considered extraordinary, and taxes of $25,000 were paid on the gain.

b) In early 1987 bonds with a par value of $100,000 were sold at a 10 percent discount. The discount amortization for 1987 was $1,000.

c) Presley holds a 30 percent interest in the common stock of Dubois, Inc. During 1987 the investment account reflected the following transactions:

Balance, 1/1/87	$65,000
Equity in 1987 earnings of Dubois	10,000
Dividends received from Dubois in 1987	(2,000)
Balance, 12/31/87	$73,000

d) Income tax expense for 1987:

Paid and accrued during 1987	$46,000
Deferred (noncurrent)	23,000
	$69,000

e) Near the end of 1987 Presley issued common stock with a par value of $30,000 for land with a fair market value of $120,000.

f) On December 30, 1987, Presley declared a 100 percent stock dividend on 50,000 shares of $10 par common stock.

g) Inventory purchases on account during 1987 totaled $200,000.

h) For the past two years, Presley has been engaged in self-construction of an energy-saving device designed to recirculate heat exhaust through its manufacturing facilities. Construction expenditures for 1987 were $64,000.

REQUIRED

For each transaction above, prepare the appropriate worksheet entry or entries necessary to prepare the statement of cash flows.

E23-15. PREPARATION OF WORKSHEET FOR STATEMENT OF CASH FLOWS Comparative balance sheets for Larry Hugh, Inc., are as follows:

	12/31/86	12/31/87
Assets		
Cash	$ 9,000	$ 7,000
Accounts receivable	3,000	5,000
Inventories	12,000	12,000
Prepaid expenses	500	200
Capital leases (long-term)	38,000	33,000
Long-term investments	12,000	15,000
Total	$74,500	$72,200
Liabilities and stockholders' equity		
Accounts payable	$ 3,000	$10,100
Interest payable	400	500
Notes payable (short-term)	4,000	4,000
Obligations under capital leases	30,000	20,000
Discount on lease obligations	(5,000)	(4,000)
Common stock	30,000	25,000
Contributed capital in excess of par	3,000	2,500
Retained earnings	9,100	14,100
Total	$74,500	$72,200

Additional data:
   a) Net income for 1987, $10,000; dividends declared and paid, $4,500.

b) Investments purchased during the year, $3,000.

c) During the year common stock was retired; the excess of the amount paid over the original issue price was debited to retained earnings.

REQUIRED

Prepare a worksheet for the statement of cash flows.

E23-16. CONVERSION OF STATEMENT OF CASH FLOWS TO ACCRUAL BASIS INCOME STATEMENT   The statement of cash flows for the fiscal year ended November 30, 1987, and other data for Backward Corporation are shown below:

Cash flows from operating activities		
Cash collections from customers	$300,000	
Dividends received	15,000	
Cash outflows for:		
Merchandise	(100,000)	
Salaries	(50,000)	
Taxes	(25,000)	
Other operating expenses	(25,000)	
Net cash provided by operating activities		$115,000
Cash flows from investing activities		
Sales of investments (extraordinary gain, $5,000)	$ 30,000	
Purchased machinery	(100,000)	
Net cash used by investing activities		(70,000)
Cash flows from financing activities		
Issue of capital stock		75,000
Net increase in cash		$120,000

Additional data:

a) Backward uses the equity method of accounting for investments. During 1987 the net increase in the investment account was $10,000.

b) The machinery account, net of accumulated depreciation, increased by $70,000 during the year. The only other transaction, exclusive of depreciation, was the write-off on May 1, 1987, of obsolete machinery that had a book value of $5,000.

c) Accounts receivable increased by $40,000 during 1987; the allowance account increased by $5,000. There were no write-offs of uncollectible accounts.

d) Salaries payable at the beginning of the year were $6,000; at the end of the year, $9,000.

e) Inventories decreased $24,000 during 1987.

f) Taxes payable decreased $6,000 during the year.

REQUIRED

On the basis of the above data, prepare Backward Corporation's income statement for the year ended November 30, 1987.

PROBLEMS

Problems marked with an asterisk (*) refer to Appendix 23–1.

P23-1. PREPARATION OF STATEMENT OF CASH FLOWS   The balance sheets of Sauna Corporation provided the information shown below and on the next page.

	12/31/86	12/31/87
Debits		
Cash	$ 80	$ 220
Accounts receivable (net)	180	240
Inventory	160	100
Long-term investments	40	–0–
Plant and equipment	1,000	1,040
Land	200	800
Patents	160	140
	$1,820	$2,540

	12/31/86	12/31/87
Credits		
Accumulated depreciation—plant and equipment	$ 340	$ 360
Accounts payable	160	40
Accrued wages payable	20	–0–
Notes payable, long-term	200	380
Common stock (no-par)	1,000	1,500
Retained earnings	100	260
	$1,820	$2,540

Additional data:

a) Net income for 1987, $240.

b) Depreciation of plant and equipment, $100.

c) Amortization of patents, $20.

d) Sales on account, $1,340.

e) Purchases on account, $700.

f) Other expenses paid in cash, $300.

g) At the end of the year, sold plant and equipment costing $160 (50 percent depreciated) for $60 cash.

h) Purchased land costing $200; paid $40; gave long-term note for the balance.

i) Paid $80 on long-term notes.

j) Issued common stock for $200 cash.

k) Purchased plant and equipment costing $200; paid one-half cash, gave a long-term note for the balance due.

l) Issued 300 shares of common stock for land with a fair market value of $400 and paid the balance in cash. The shares were actively traded at $1 per share.

m) Collections on accounts receivable, $1,280.

n) Payment of accounts payable, $820.

o) Sold the long-term investments for $140.

p) Paid dividends, $80.

q) There were no extraordinary items.

REQUIRED

1. Calculate the cash flows from operating activities, using:

  a) The direct approach.

  b) The indirect approach.

2. Prepare the statement of cash flows.

*P23-2.   PREPARATION OF SCFP—WORKING CAPITAL APPROACH   Refer to the data in Problem 23-1.

REQUIRED

Prepare the SCFP under the working capital concept of funds. Use a sources and uses format.

P23-3.   STATEMENT OF CASH FLOWS   The records of Vantage Machine Works showed the following information related to the balance sheet accounts.

Debits	12/31/86	12/31/87
Cash	$ 1,000	$ 1,100
Accounts receivable (net)	1,900	2,400
Inventory	5,200	5,000
Prepaid expenses	300	400
Long-term investments	1,000	–0–
Buildings	9,000	12,000
Machinery	4,000	6,200
Patents	500	400
	$22,900	$27,500

Credits

Accounts payable	$ 1,200	$ 800
Notes payable—short-term (operating)	900	1,300
Accrued wages	300	200
Accumulated depreciation	4,000	3,900
Notes payable—long-term	3,000	3,500
Common stock	12,000	15,000
Retained earnings	1,500	2,800
	$22,900	$27,500

Additional data for 1987:

a) Net income for the year, $2,600.
b) Sales of $12,000 on account.
c) Amortization of patents, $100.
d) Purchased machinery costing $1,500; paid one-third in cash and gave a five-year interest-bearing note for the balance.
e) Purchased machinery costing $2,500 by issuing common stock.
f) Collections on accounts receivable, $11,500.
g) Made addition to building costing $3,000; paid cash.
h) Paid a $500 long-term note by issuing common stock.
i) Sold investment for $1,200 cash.
j) Paid cash dividends.
k) Depreciation recorded on fixed assets, $800.
l) Sold for $700 old machinery that originally cost $1,800 and that was one-half depreciated.

REQUIRED

Prepare the statement of cash flows.

*P23-4.   WORKING CAPITAL PROVIDED BY (USED IN) OPERATIONS   Refer to Problem 23-3.

REQUIRED

Calculate the amount of working capital provided by or used in Vantage's operations.

P23-5.   STATEMENT OF CASH FLOWS; DIRECT AND INDIRECT APPROACH   The financial data given below and on the next page were furnished to you by Beetlebaum Company:

Beetlebaum Company

COMPARATIVE TRIAL BALANCES
AT BEGINNING AND END OF FISCAL YEAR
ENDED JANUARY 31, 1988

DEBITS	FEBRUARY 1, 1987	INCREASE	DECREASE	JANUARY 31, 1988
Cash.........................	$ 5,000	$17,600		$ 22,600
Accounts receivable	10,000	4,800		14,800
Inventories....................	30,000		$ 900	29,100
Prepaid insurance	200	50		250
Long-term investments	4,000		3,000	1,000
Sinking fund	8,000	1,000		9,000
Plant and equipment............	28,500	12,500		41,000
Treasury stock (at cost)	1,000		500	500
Cost of goods sold				53,900
Other expenses				32,200
Loss on sale of equipment.......				100
Total	$86,700			$204,450

CREDITS	FEBRUARY 1, 1987	INCREASE	DECREASE	JANUARY 31, 1988
Allowance for doubtful accounts....................	$ 500	300		$ 800
Accumulated depreciation	5,000	1,600		6,600
Accounts payable	8,000		500	7,500
Note payable—current	–0–	5,000		5,000
Accrued expenses payable	2,500	2,800		5,300
Unearned revenue.............	900		800	100
Note payable—long-term........	6,000		2,000	4,000
Bonds payable (net of unamortized discount)	24,100	50		24,150
Common stock	20,000	10,000		30,000
Contributed capital in excess of par	500	11,100		11,600
Retained earnings appropriated for bond sinking fund	8,000	1,000		9,000
Retained earnings, unappropriated	11,200		1,800	9,400
Sales				89,800
Gain on sale of investments				1,200
Total	$86,700			$204,450

The following additional information was available:

    a) All purchases and sales were on account.

    b) The bonds payable will be retired from the sinking fund.

    c) Equipment with an original cost of $1,500 was sold for $700.

    d) Other expenses included the following:

Insurance expired	$ 200
Depreciation expense	2,300
Bad debt expense	400
Interest expense	1,800

    e) Treasury stock was issued for $100 more than cost.

    f) All dividends declared were paid in cash.

    g) New equipment was purchased; cash and a six-month note payable in the amount of $5,000 were issued.

    h) The long-term note payable requires the payment of $2,000 per year plus interest until paid.

REQUIRED

    1. Prepare a schedule showing the cash flows from operating activities under each of the following approaches:

        a) The direct approach.

        b) The indirect approach.

    2. Prepare a statement of cash flows for Beetlebaum Company. Use your answer to part 1 for the cash flows from operating activities.

P23-6. STATEMENT OF CASH FLOWS   The Salem Furniture Company is an established firm specializing in the manufacture of wood furniture. The company is well known nationally for its high-quality furnishings.

    The company's accounting department is in the process of preparing the financial statements for the fiscal year just completed on December 31, 1987. The comparative statements of income and financial position for 1986 and 1987 appear on the next page.

Salem Furniture Company

INCOME STATEMENT
FOR THE YEARS ENDED DECEMBER 31, 1986 AND 1987
(in thousands of dollars)

	1986	1987
Revenue		
Sales (net)	$ 5,850	$ 6,320
Interest and dividends	20	8
Total revenue	$ 5,870	$ 6,328
Costs and expenses		
Cost of goods sold	$ 4,330	$ 4,740
Selling expenses	610	620
Administrative expenses	510	515
Interest expense	90	83
Loss on sale of investments	–0–	10
Total costs and expenses	$(5,540)	$(5,968)
Net income	$ 330	$ 360

Salem Furniture Company

STATEMENT OF FINANCIAL POSITION
DECEMBER 31, 1986 AND 1987
(in thousands of dollars)

	1986	1987
Assets		
Cash	$ 220	$ 46
Marketable securities	80	40
Accounts receivable (net)	960	1,152
Inventories	1,580	1,802
Current assets	$2,840	$3,040
Investments	320	135
Property, plant, and equipment (net)	1,320	1,370
Total assets	$4,480	$4,545
Liabilities and equities		
Short-term notes payable (nontrade)	$ 350	$ 430
Accounts payable	450	450
Cash dividends payable	–0–	30
Accrued and other liabilities	120	130
Current portion of long-term debt	200	200
Current liabilities	$1,120	$1,240
Serial bonds payable	1,000	800
Convertible bonds payable	150	95
Total liabilities	$2,270	$2,135
Common stock, $4 par	$1,120	$1,164
Paid-in capital	280	291
Retained earnings	810	1,020
	$2,210	$2,475
Less treasury stock	–0–	(65)
Total stockholders' equity	$2,210	$2,410
Total liabilities and equities	$4,480	$4,545

The following additional data regarding Salem's operations have been assembled by the accounting department:

1. The allowance for uncollectible accounts had a balance of $50,000 on December 31, 1986, and a balance of $63,000 on December 31, 1987. A total of $52,000 in accounts receivable was written off as uncollectible during 1987. Provisions for uncollectible accounts amounting to $60,000 in 1986 and $65,000 in 1987 were included in the selling expenses.

2. The company liquidated some of its investments during 1987 in order to raise cash. Marketable securities were sold at their recorded cost of $40,000. In addition, Salem sold its interest in Nova Products Co. for $175,000.

3. Equipment costing $215,000 was purchased during 1987, and used equipment was sold at its book value of $25,000. Annual depreciation on plant and equipment included in the operating expenses amounted to $130,000 and $140,000 for 1986 and 1987 respectively.

4. At the end of the current year, holders of Salem's short-term notes agreed to extend the maturities through 1988. The serial bonds are being retired on schedule at the rate of $200,000 per year. A total of 55 convertible bonds were exchanged for common stock during 1987.

5. The company purchased $65,000 of its own common stock; the cost method was used to record this purchase of treasury stock.

6. Salem declared cash dividends of $150,000 during 1987: a total of $120,000 was actually paid during 1987.

REQUIRED

Using the data provided, prepare a statement of cash flows for the year. Include marketable securities as cash equivalents.

(IMA, adapted)

P23-7. CASH FLOWS; FINANCIAL STATEMENT RELATIONSHIPS   Cadillac Corporation's ending balance sheet and its statement of cash flows appear below and on the next page.

Cadillac Corporation

BALANCE SHEET
DECEMBER 31, 1987

Assets

Cash	$ 54,100
Accounts receivable	58,500
Marketable securities	–0–
Inventories	89,500
Land	35,000
Plant and equipment	106,000
Accumulated depreciation	(29,500)
Leased property	15,800
Investment in Berritz	18,000
Total	$347,400

Liabilities and Equity

Accounts payable and accrued expenses	$ 76,000
Current portion of long-term debt	15,900
Notes payable, long-term	30,000
Lease liability	12,400
Bonds payable	50,000
Premium on bonds payable	1,600
Deferred income taxes	6,000
Common stock ($20 par)	64,000
Contributed capital in excess of par	30,400
Retained earnings	61,100
Total	$347,400

Cadillac Corporation

STATEMENT OF CASH FLOWS
FOR THE YEAR ENDED DECEMBER 31, 1987

Cash flows from operating activities

Net income	$25,300	
Add (deduct) items not affecting cash:		
Depreciation	14,900	
Amortization of bond premium	(200)	
Deferred income taxes	1,500	
Gain on sale of equipment.......................	(500)	
Change in accounts receivable....................	(9,000)	
Change in inventories...........................	(11,500)	
Change in accounts payable and accrued expenses	(6,300)	
Payment of tax assessment	(2,000)	
Net cash provided by operating activities..........		$12,200
Cash flows from investing activities		
Sale of equipment................................	$ 3,300	
Purchases of equipment	(39,200)	
Net cash used by investing activities		(35,900)
Cash flows from financing activities		
Issuance of long-term notes	$45,000	
Payments under capital lease	(2,500)	
Dividends	(3,000)	
Net cash provided by financing activities..........		39,500
Net increase in cash and cash equivalents		$15,800
Noncash investing and financing activities		
Acquired land by issuing common stock		$10,000
Acquired equipment through capital lease		15,800
		$25,800

Additional information:

a) At the beginning of 1987, Cadillac sold all of its marketable securities, which were cash equivalents carried at $7,500, for $9,500 cash.

b) In April of 1987, Cadillac issued 200 shares of its common stock for land with a fair market value of $10,000.

c) On May 20, 1987, Cadillac borrowed $45,000. The note is payable in three equal annual installments of $15,000 and bears interest at 15 percent. The first payment is due on May 20, 1988.

d) During 1987, Cadillac purchased equipment for $39,200 cash. The company also sold equipment with an original cost of $5,200 and accumulated depreciation of $2,400 for $3,300 cash.

e) In September of 1987, Cadillac paid a $2,000 additional tax assessment because of an error on its 1985 tax return. The payment was recorded as an error correction (prior period adjustment).

f) On December 31, 1987, Cadillac entered into a capital lease for equipment. The present value of the lease payments was $15,800 on December 31, 1987. Equal annual payments of $2,500 were required. The first payment was made on December 31, 1987, and the $2,500 lease payment due on December 31, 1988, will consist of $900 principal and $1,600 interest.

g) Cadillac owns a 10 percent interest in Berritz, which is accounted for under the cost method.

h) Cadillac's net income for 1987 was $25,300. The only entries in retained earnings were for net income, dividends declared, and the error correction.

REQUIRED

On the basis of the information provided above, prepare the balance sheet for Cadillac Corporation on December 31, 1986.

P23-8. USE OF WORKSHEET FOR STATEMENT OF CASH FLOWS   A worksheet for a statement of cash flows appears below. Additional information is as follows:

    a) Equipment with a cost of $20,000 and accumulated depreciation of $5,000 was sold for $25,000; the gain is not extraordinary. Equipment costing $40,000 was purchased during the year.

    b) Land was purchased at a cost of $30,000.

    c) Preferred stock was retired during the year; the liquidation premium of $5,000 was debited to retained earnings.

    d) Common stock was issued during the year.

    e) Net income for the year was $40,000.

    f) Dividends declared and paid, $18,000.

REQUIRED

Complete the worksheet below. You may need to make inferences about some transactions not otherwise explicitly stated.

	BEGINNING BALANCES	ANALYSIS OF TRANSACTIONS DR	CR	ENDING BALANCES
Debits				
Cash....................	$ 70,000		(x) 26,000	$ 44,000
Plant and equipment.......	100,000			120,000
Land	60,000			90,000
Deferred charges..........	20,000			10,000
Total	$250,000			$264,000
Credits				
Accumulated depreciation ..	$ 40,000			$ 50,000
Bonds payable	60,000			60,000
Premium on bonds payable	8,000			4,000
Preferred stock	20,000			–0–
Common stock	60,000			70,000
Contributed capital in excess of par:				
Preferred	2,000			–0–
Common	12,000			15,000
Retained earnings appropriated for contingencies.........	–0–			10,000
Unappropriated retained earnings......	48,000			55,000
Total	$250,000			$264,000

Operating activities

    ⋮

Investing activities

    ⋮

Financing activities

    ⋮

Net decrease in cash ....   (x) 26,000

P23-9. STATEMENT OF CASH FLOWS   The net changes in the balance sheet accounts of X Company for the year 1987 are shown on the next page.

	DEBIT	CREDIT
Investments		$ 25,000
Land	$ 3,200	
Buildings	35,000	
Machinery	6,000	
Office equipment		1,500
Accumulated depreciation		
Buildings		2,000
Machinery		900
Office equipment	600	
Dividends payable		18,000
Discount on bonds	2,000	
Bonds payable		40,000
Common stock		12,400
Preferred stock	10,000	
Contributed capital in excess of par–common		5,600
Retained earnings		6,800
Cash.	55,400	
	$112,200	$112,200

Additional information:

a) Cash dividends of $18,000 were declared December 15, 1987, payable January 15, 1988. A 2 percent stock dividend was issued March 31, 1987, when the market value was $12.50 per share.

b) The investments were sold for $27,500.

c) A building that cost $45,000 and had a depreciated basis of $40,500 was sold for $50,000.

d) The following entry was made to record an exchange of an old machine for a new one:

Machinery	13,000	
Accumulated depreciation—machinery	5,000	
Machinery		7,000
Cash.		11,000

e) A fully depreciated office machine that cost $1,500 was written off.

f) Preferred stock of $10,000 par value was redeemed for $10,200.

g) The company issued 1,000 shares of its common stock (par value $10) on June 15, 1987, for $15 a share. There were 13,240 shares outstanding on December 31, 1987.

REQUIRED

Prepare the statement of cash flows for the year ended December 31, 1987.

(AICPA, adapted)

P23-10. STATEMENT OF CASH FLOWS Presented below and on the next page are comparative statements of financial position of Kenwood Corporation as of December 31, 1987, and December 31, 1986.

STATEMENT OF FINANCIAL POSITION

	12/31/87	12/31/86	INCREASE (DECREASE)
Assets			
Cash.	$ 100,000	$ 90,000	$ 10,000
Accounts receivable (net of allowance			
for uncollectible accounts)	210,000	140,000	70,000
Inventories.	260,000	220,000	40,000
Land	325,000	200,000	125,000
Plant and equipment.	580,000	633,000	(53,000)
Less: Accumulated			
depreciation.	(90,000)	(100,000)	10,000
Patents	30,000	33,000	(3,000)
Total assets	$1,415,000	$1,216,000	$199,000

	12/31/87	12/31/86	INCREASE (DECREASE)
Liabilities and stockholders' equity			
Liabilities			
Accounts payable	$ 260,000	$ 200,000	$ 60,000
Accrued expenses	200,000	210,000	(10,000)
Deferred income taxes	140,000	100,000	40,000
Long-term bonds			
(due 12/15/93)	130,000	180,000	(50,000)
Total liabilities	$ 730,000	$ 690,000	$ 40,000
Stockholders' equity			
Common stock, par value $5, authorized, 100,000 shares; issued and outstanding, 50,000 and 42,000 shares, respectively	$ 250,000	$ 210,000	$ 40,000
Additional paid-in capital	233,000	170,000	63,000
Retained earnings	202,000	146,000	56,000
Total stockholders' equity	$ 685,000	$ 526,000	$159,000
Total liabilities and stockholders' equity	$1,415,000	$1,216,000	$199,000

Presented below is the income statement of Kenwood Corporation for the year ended December 31, 1987.

INCOME STATEMENT
FOR THE YEAR ENDED DECEMBER 31, 1987

Sales	$1,000,000
Expenses	
Cost of sales	$ 560,000
Salary and wages	190,000
Depreciation	20,000
Amortization	3,000
Loss on sale of equipment	4,000
Interest	16,000
Miscellaneous	8,000
Total expenses	$ (801,000)
Income before income taxes and extraordinary item	$ 199,000
Income taxes	
Current	$ 50,000
Deferred	40,000
Provision for income taxes	$ (90,000)
Income before extraordinary item	$ 109,000
Extraordinary item—gain on extinguishment of debt (net of $10,000 income tax)	12,000
Net income	$ 121,000

Additional information:

a) On February 2, 1987, Kenwood issued a 10 percent stock dividend to stockholders of record on January 15, 1987. The market price per share of the common stock on February 2, 1987, was $15.

b) On March 1, 1987, Kenwood issued 3,800 shares of common stock for land. The common stock and land had current market values of approximately $40,000 on March 1, 1987.

c) On April 15, 1987, Kenwood extinguished long-term bonds with a face value of $50,000. The gain was reported as an extraordinary item on the income statement.

d) On June 30, 1987, Kenwood sold equipment costing $53,000, with a book value of $23,000, for $19,000 cash.

e) On September 30, 1987, Kenwood declared and paid a $.04 per share cash dividend to stockholders of record on August 1, 1987.

f) On October 10, 1987, Kenwood purchased land for $85,000 cash.

g) Deferred income taxes represent timing differences relating to the use of ACRS for income tax reporting and straight-line depreciation for financial statement reporting.

REQUIRED

Prepare the statement of cash flows for the year ended December 31, 1987.

(AICPA, adapted)

P23-11. STATEMENT OF CASH FLOWS   The manager of the Thomas Manufacturing Company has reviewed the annual financial statements for the year 1987 and is unable to determine the reasons for the changes in cash from a reading of the balance sheet. He asks you for assistance and presents the following balance sheets of the Thomas Manufacturing Company.

	12/31/87	12/31/86	INCREASE (DECREASE)
Debits			
Goodwill	$ –0–	$ 200,000	$(200,000)
Buildings	810,000	560,000	250,000
Land	140,000	150,000	(10,000)
Machinery	330,000	200,000	130,000
Tools	40,000	70,000	(30,000)
Bond investment (long-term)	18,000	15,000	3,000
Inventories.....................	210,000	218,000	(8,000)
Accounts receivable	180,000	92,000	88,000
Notes receivable—trade	21,000	27,000	(6,000)
Cash in bank....................	–0–	8,000	(8,000)
Cash on hand	2,000	1,000	1,000
Unexpired insurance—machinery	1,200	1,400	(200)
Discount on bonds payable	2,100	2,500	(400)
	$1,754,300	$1,544,900	$ 209,400
Credits			
Capital stock	$ 700,000	$ 400,000	$ 300,000
Bonds payable	150,000	100,000	50,000
Accounts payable	58,000	52,000	6,000
Bank overdraft	4,000	–0–	4,000
Notes payable—trade.............	9,000	10,000	(1,000)
Bank loans—short-term	5,500	6,800	(1,300)
Accrued interest	10,000	6,000	4,000
Accrued taxes	5,000	3,000	2,000
Allowance for doubtful accounts.....	4,500	2,300	2,200
Accumulated depreciation	271,200	181,000	90,200
Retained earnings	537,100	783,800	(246,700)
	$1,754,300	$1,544,900	$ 209,400

You are advised that the following transactions took place during the year:

a) A 2 percent cash dividend was declared and paid on the capital stock outstanding at the beginning of the year.

b) There were no purchases or sales of tools.

c) Stock was sold during the year at 90 percent of par value; the discount was debited to the goodwill account.

d) Old machinery that cost $4,500 was scrapped and written off the books. Accumulated depreciation on the equipment was $3,300. The loss was debited to retained earnings.

e) The income statement for the year 1987 was as follows:

Sales (net)		$1,250,000
Operating expenses		
Material and supplies	$250,000	
Direct labor...........................	440,000	
Manufacturing overhead.................	181,500	
Depreciation	123,500	
Selling expenses	245,000	
Goodwill write-off	230,000	
Interest expense (net)	7,500	
Total expenses		(1,477,500)
Net loss..........................		$ (227,500)

f) Land costing $10,000 was donated to the Moose Club. The donation was debited to retained earnings.

REQUIRED

Prepare a statement of cash flows for Thomas for 1987. Use the direct approach to determine cash flows from operating activities.

(AICPA, adapted)

*P23-12. SCFP—WORKING CAPITAL BASIS The following schedule showing *net changes* in balance sheet accounts as of December 31, Year 12, compared to December 31, Year 11, was prepared from the records of the Sodium Company. The statement of changes in financial position for the year ended December 31, Year 12, has not yet been prepared.

	NET INCREASE (DECREASE)
Assets	
Cash...	$ 50,000
Accounts receivable, net	76,000
Inventories...	37,000
Prepaid expenses	1,000
Property, plant, and equipment, net	64,000
Total assets	$ 228,000
Liabilities	
Accounts payable	$ (55,500)
Notes payable—current	(15,000)
Accrued expenses..	33,000
Bonds payable	(28,000)
Less: Unamortized bond discount	(1,200)
Total liabilities	$ (64,300)
Stockholders' equity	
Common stock, $10 par value	$ 500,000
Capital contributed in excess of par value	200,000
Retained earnings	(437,700)
Appropriation of retained earnings for possible future inventory price decline...............................	30,000
Total stockholders' equity	$ 292,300
Total liabilities and stockholders' equity	$ 228,000

Additional information:

a) The net income for the year ended December 31, Year 12, was $172,300. There were no extraordinary items.

b) During the year ended December 31, Year 12, uncollectible accounts receivable of $26,400 were written off by a debit to allowance for doubtful accounts.

c) A comparison of property, plant, and equipment as of the end of each year follows:

	END OF YEAR 12	END OF YEAR 11	NET INCREASE (DECREASE)
Property, plant, and equipment	$570,500	$510,000	$60,500
Less: Accumulated depreciation	(224,500)	(228,000)	(3,500)
Property, plant, and equipment, net	$346,000	$282,000	$64,000

During Year 12 machinery was purchased at a cost of $45,000. In addition, machinery that was acquired in Year 1 at a cost of $48,000 was sold for $3,600. At the date of sale the machinery had an undepreciated cost of $4,200. The remaining increase in property, plant, and equipment resulted from the acquisition of a tract of land for a new plant site.

d) The bonds payable mature at the rate of $28,000 every year.

e) In January of Year 12 the company issued an additional 10,000 shares of its common stock at $14 per share upon the exercise of outstanding stock options held by key employees. In May of Year 12 the company declared and issued a 5 percent stock dividend on its outstanding stock. During the year a cash dividend was paid on the common stock. On December 31, Year 12, there were 840,000 shares of common stock outstanding.

f) The appropriation of retained earnings for possible future inventory price decline was made by debiting retained earnings, in anticipation of an expected future drop in the market related to goods in inventory.

REQUIRED

1. Prepare a schedule of changes in working capital for Year 12.

2. Prepare the SCFP for the year ended December 31, Year 12, based on the information presented above. The statement should be prepared under the working capital concept of funds.

(AICPA, adapted)

P23-13. STATEMENT OF CASH FLOWS The management of Garfield Corporation, concerned over a decrease in working capital and cash, has provided you with a comparative analysis of changes in account balances between December 31, 1986, and December 31, 1987, shown below and on the next page.

	12/31/87	12/31/86	INCREASE (DECREASE)
Debit balances			
Cash	$ 145,000	$ 186,000	$(41,000)
Accounts receivable	253,000	273,000	(20,000)
Inventories	483,000	538,000	(55,000)
Securities held for plant expansion purposes	150,000	–0–	150,000
Machinery and equipment	927,000	647,000	280,000
Leasehold improvements	87,000	87,000	–0–
Patents	27,800	30,000	(2,200)
	$2,072,800	$1,761,000	$311,800

	12/31/87	12/31/86	INCREASE (DECREASE)
Credit balances			
Allowance for uncollectible accounts receivable . . . .$	14,000	$ 17,000	$ (3,000)
Accumulated depreciation of machinery and equipment	416,000	372,000	44,000
Allowance for amortization of leasehold improvements	58,000	49,000	9,000
Accounts payable	232,800	105,000	127,800
Cash dividends payable	40,000	–0–	40,000
Current portion of 6% serial bonds payable	50,000	50,000	–0–
6% serial bonds payable	250,000	300,000	(50,000)
Preferred stock	90,000	100,000	(10,000)
Common stock	500,000	500,000	–0–
Retained earnings	422,000	268,000	154,000
Total . . . .$	2,072,800	$1,761,000	$311,800

During 1987 the following transactions occurred:

a) New machinery was purchased for $386,000. In addition, obsolete machinery having a book value of $61,000 was sold for $48,000. No other entries were recorded in machinery and equipment or related accounts other than for depreciation.

b) Garfield paid $2,000 legal costs in a successful defense of a new patent. Amortization of patents amounting to $4,200 was recorded.

c) Preferred stock, par value $100, was purchased at $110 and subsequently retired. The premium paid was debited to retained earnings.

d) On December 10, 1987, the board of directors declared a cash dividend of $.20 per share payable to holders of common stock on January 10, 1988.

e) A comparative analysis of retained earnings as of December 31, 1987 and 1986, is presented below:

	12/31/87	12/31/86
Balance, January 1	$268,000	$131,000
Net income	195,000	172,000
	$463,000	$303,000
Dividends declared	(40,000)	(35,000)
Premium on preferred stock purchased	(1,000)	–0–
	$422,000	$268,000

REQUIRED

Prepare a statement of cash flows for Garfield Corporation for the year ended December 31, 1987.

(AICPA, adapted)

P23-14. STATEMENT OF CASH FLOWS; DIRECT APPROACH Wright Corporation's income statement for the year ended December 31, 1987, and comparative balance sheets at December 31, 1986 and 1987, appear on the next page. Wright Corporation has previously prepared the statement of changes in financial position under the working capital concept of funds, but will switch to a statement of cash flows for 1987 and following years.

Wright Corporation

INCOME STATEMENT
FOR THE YEAR ENDED DECEMBER 31, 1987

Revenues		$2,410,655
Other revenue, primarily dividends and interest		21,708
		$2,432,363
Expenses and losses:		
Materials and supplies used	$870,531	
Salaries expense	906,387	
Depreciation expense	114,079	
State and local taxes	26,221	
Interest expense	1,297	
Loss on sale of investments....................	6,016	
Miscellaneous expenses	33,762	
Income tax expense	284,442	(2,242,735)
Net income		$ 189,628

Wright Corporation

COMPARATIVE STATEMENTS OF FINANCIAL POSITION
FOR THE YEARS ENDED DECEMBER 31, 1987 AND 1986

	1987	1986	INCREASE (DECREASE) IN NET ASSETS
Current assets:			
Cash..............................	$ 215,221	$ 225,351	$ (10,130)
Marketable securities	180,767	251,388	(70,621)
Receivables, net	266,559	195,991	70,568
Inventories, at cost..................	322,438	359,175	(36,737)
Prepaid expenses	15,209	17,894	(2,685)
Total current assets...............	$1,000,194	$1,049,799	
Less current liabilities:			
Accounts payable	(108,623)	(254,181)	145,558
Salaries payable	(12,602)	(11,495)	(1,107)
Taxes payable	(295,580)	(299,466)	3,886
Dividends payable	(23,726)	(25,591)	1,865
Interest payable....................	(750)	(296)	(454)
Other payables	(12,622)	(14,942)	2,320
Working capital	$ 546,291	$ 443,828	$102,463
Plant and equipment, net	1,356,132	1,200,816	155,316
Less long-term debt	(50,000)	–0–	(50,000)
Net assets	$1,852,423	$1,644,644	$207,779
Stockholders' equity:			
Preferred stock, 6%, $100 par.........	$ 260,200	$ 265,200	$ (5,000)
Common stock, par value, $100	1,272,400	1,092,300	180,100
Contributed capital in excess of par	61,524	42,043	19,481
Retained earnings	258,299	245,101	13,198
Total stockholders' equity	$1,852,423	$1,644,644	$207,779

Additional information:

a) During the year, marketable securities (not considered cash equivalents) were purchased at a cost of $24,692.

b) The allowance for uncollectible accounts increased $11,448, despite the write-off of $2,605 in customers' accounts. During the year, an account of $2,000, written off in a prior year, was recovered; the credit was made to (netted against) miscellaneous expenses.

c) During the year, 50 shares of preferred stock were retired at a 9 percent premium. The shares originally were sold for $105 per share. The difference between the issue price and the amount paid was debited to retained earnings.

d) The only entries in retained earnings were for net income, dividend declarations, and the retirement of preferred stock.

e) There were no sales or retirements of plant and equipment during the year.

REQUIRED

Prepare the statement of cash flows using an activity format. Use the direct approach to calculate the cash flows from operating activities. Prepare a supporting schedule showing the conversion of the income statement to a cash basis, item by item. Use the following format for this schedule:

PER INCOME STATEMENT	ADJUSTMENTS TO CASH BASIS		CASH BASIS
	ADD	DEDUCT	

(AICPA, adapted)

*P23-15. WORKING CAPITAL FLOWS AND CASH FLOWS   The officers of Henke Brothers are reviewing the preliminary drafts of the financial statements for the 1987–88 fiscal year. The statement of changes in financial position prepared on a working capital concept and the related schedule of working capital changes appear on page 1131. Henke's management prefers to use a direct approach to determine sources from operations rather than start with net income from operations (an indirect approach).

Fred Henke, chairman of the board and chief executive officer, commented, "The company is doing well considering the sour economy. Our net income was $495,000 even after the loss on the subsidiary we sold. The important thing is that our working capital increased over $950,000."

George Henke, vice-president of sales, stated, "We fought hard to obtain that income in this stagnant economy. We reduced our profit margins to meet the increased competition. I don't think these financial statements represent all of the economic facts. I would like to see more data."

Jan Kranz, vice-president of finance, has suggested that a statement of cash flows might be required in the near future. The officers agreed that Kranz should have her staff prepare such a statement.

Additional facts regarding the company's operations for the 1987–88 fiscal year are as follows:

a) Henke Brothers sold a subsidiary during the year for $590,000. The basis of the property was $740,000. The loss on the sale of the subsidiary ($90,000 net of taxes) was reflected as discontinued operations on the income statement.

b) Bad debt expense of $94,000 was recorded for the fiscal year. Write-offs of bad accounts totaled $102,500.

c) Goodwill arising from a company Henke Brothers purchased is being amortized over 20 years. The annual amortization is $15,600.

d) The premium on the bonds payable is being amortized at the rate of $9,500 per year.

e) Depreciation expense for the fiscal year was $173,700.

REQUIRED

1. Using Henke Brothers' SCFP, determine the firm's cash inflows and outflows for the year ended May 31, 1988.

2. Explain how the cash flow data reveal important factors regarding Henke Brothers' operations for the current fiscal year.

Henke Brothers

STATEMENT OF CHANGES IN FINANCIAL POSITION
FOR THE YEAR ENDED MAY 31, 1988
(in thousands of dollars)

Working capital provided by:		
Operations		
Sales		$7,520.0
Operating expenses:		
Merchandise purchases	$3,675.0	
Salaries and wages	1,459.0	
Utilities, insurance, and other expenses	655.5	
Selling and administrative	361.7	
Interest	120.0	
Income taxes	390.0	(6,661.2)
Working capital provided by operations		$ 858.8
Other sources of working capital:		
Issuance of preferred stock	$ 300.0	
Issuance of long-term note payable for building	885.0	
Sale of subsidiary (including $60,000 tax benefit)	650.0	1,835.0
Total sources of working capital		$2,693.8
Working capital used for:		
Purchase of building	$ 885.0	
Purchase of machinery	640.0	
Purchase of Henke Brothers' common stock	150.0	
Cash dividends declared	65.0	
Total uses of working capital		(1,740.0)
Increase in working capital		$ 953.8

Henke Brothers

SCHEDULE OF WORKING CAPITAL CHANGES
FOR THE YEAR ENDED MAY 31, 1988
(in thousands of dollars)

ACCOUNT	INCREASE (DECREASE) IN WORKING CAPITAL
Cash	$100.5
Accounts receivable (net)	354.0
Inventory	300.5
Prepaid expenses	(25.0)
Accounts payable (trade)	270.8
Accrued wages	(7.5)
Accrued liabilities	39.7
Cash dividends payable	(25.0)
Income taxes payable	(54.2)
Increase in working capital	$953.8

(IMA, adapted)

P23-16. COMPREHENSIVE REVIEW OF FINANCIAL STATEMENT RELATIONSHIPS The following information concerns the Flutie Company for the year ended December 31, 1987. The omitted balances, numbered from 1 through 16, can be calculated from the other information given.

STATEMENT OF CASH FLOWS

Cash flows from operating activities
Net loss for 1987 .... $ (2,885)
　Add (deduct) items not affecting cash:
　　Depreciation 3,000
　　Amortization of bond premium .... (500)
　　Deferred income taxes .... (200)
　　Goodwill amortization for 1987 2,000
　　Gain on sale of equipment........................ (2,000)
　　Increase in current liabilities 3,200
　　　Net cash provided by operating activities　　　　　　 $ 2,615
Cash flows from investing activities
　Sale of equipment................................. $12,000
　Purchase of land.................................. (14,715)
　　Net cash used by investing activities ....　　 (2,715)
Cash flows from financing activities
　Sale of treasury stock............................. $11,400
　Retirement of debt at maturity .... (7,200)
　　Net cash provided by financing activities...........　　 4,200
Net increase in cash ....　　　　 $ 4,100

Noncash investing and financing activities
　Retired preferred stock by issuing common stock ....　 $ 7,500

INFORMATION FROM INCOME STATEMENT

Uncollectible accounts expense ....　 $ 750

Bond interest expense (net of amortization
　of bond premium)................................　 $ 3,500

Loss before tax adjustment ....　 $(3,900)
Add:
　Income tax adjustment (refund due) $815
　Deferred income taxes .... 200　 1,015
Net loss ....　 $(2,885)

BALANCE SHEETS

	1/1/87 (BEFORE RESTATEMENT)	12/31/87
Cash....................................	$22,000	$ (5)
Building and equipment	92,000	(6)
Accumulated depreciation	(25,000)	(7)
Land	(1)	(8)
Goodwill	12,000	(9)
Total assets	$ (?)	$ (?)
Current liabilities (operating)...............	(2)	(10)
Bonds payable (8%)	(3)	(11)
Bond premium	(?)	(12)
Deferred income taxes	(4)	$1,700
Common stock	$66,000	(13)
Paid-in capital...........................	13,000	(14)
Preferred stock	16,000	(15)
Retained earnings (deficit)	(6,000)	(16)
Treasury stock (at cost)	(9,000)	–0–
Total liabilities and stockholders' equity	$ (?)	$ (?)

Additional information:

  a) The book value of the equipment sold was two-thirds of the cost of that equipment.

  b) Selected ratios of accounts in the January 1 and December 31 balance sheets are as follows:

	1/1/87 (BEFORE RESTATEMENT)	12/31/87
Current ratio	?	3:1
Total stockholders' equity divided by total liabilities	4:3	?

  c) Flutie Company had neglected to amortize $2,000 of goodwill in 1986. The correction of this material error has been appropriately made in 1987.

REQUIRED

    Calculate the correct balance for each balance sheet account or group of accounts. (One account balance and the totals are shown as question marks. Calculation of these amounts may be necessary to calculate the numbered balances.) Do not restate the January 1 balance sheet for the error.

(AICPA, adapted)

24 CALCULATING AND REPORTING EARNINGS PER SHARE

Earnings per share (EPS) on outstanding common stock probably is the most often mentioned and reported measure of a company's performance. Its popularity stems from the importance placed on income by investors, creditors, and others, and from the fact that as a measure *per share* of common stock, EPS is meaningful to individual stockholders. EPS figures appear in prospectuses, in proxy statements, in annual reports to stockholders, in reports filed with the SEC, and in the financial press, and are published by investment services. Investors, creditors, and other external decision makers use EPS to evaluate the past and present performance of a company and to predict future performance.

Before the late 1960s, companies were not required by GAAP to calculate and disclose EPS. Although they often did so, the figures typically were presented only as supplementary data in annual reports to stockholders and other reports of summarized financial data. Moreover, both the procedure for calculating EPS and the disclosure of EPS varied widely among companies. By the mid-1960s the APB had concluded that EPS figures would be most useful to decision makers if they were calculated consistently and disclosed in the income statement. As a result, the APB issued *Opinion No. 9* (1966), which provided guidance for calculating EPS, provided a format for EPS presentation in the income statement, and strongly recommended that EPS be disclosed in the income statement.[1]

In 1969 the APB changed its recommendation to a requirement by issuing *Opinion No. 15*, which *requires* at a minimum that EPS for income before extraordinary items and EPS for net income must be disclosed on the face of the income statement.[2] *Opinion No. 15* also provides complex guidelines for calculating EPS. Because of the complexity of *Opinion No. 15*, the AICPA soon issued an unofficial interpretation of *Opinion No. 15*, which is more than 100 pages long.[3] In 1973 the APB amended *Opinion No. 15* in *Opinion No. 30*, which clarifies the presentation and calculation of EPS for continuing and discontinued operations.[4]

[1] "Reporting the Results of Operations," *Opinions of the Accounting Principles Board No. 9* (New York: AICPA, 1966).

[2] "Earnings per Share," *Opinions of the Accounting Principles Board No. 15* (New York: AICPA, 1969).

[3] *Computing Earnings per Share: Unofficial Accounting Interpretations of APB Opinion No. 15* (New York: AICPA, 1970).

[4] "Reporting the Results of Operations," *Opinions of the Accounting Principles Board No. 30* (New York: AICPA, 1973).

In 1978 the FASB suspended the EPS requirements of *Opinion No. 15* for any entity other than one whose securities are traded publicly or which is required to file financial statements with the SEC.[5] *Statements No. 55* (1982) and *No. 85* (1985) change the *Opinion No. 15* rules for incorporating convertible securities into the EPS calculations.[6] The intent of this chapter is to discuss, illustrate, and summarize the rules and adjustments that comprise GAAP for computing and reporting EPS.

AN OVERVIEW OF THE CALCULATION OF EPS

If the concept of earnings per share is taken literally, then the calculation of EPS is obvious:

$$EPS = \frac{\text{Income (or loss) for period}}{\text{Number of shares of common stock outstanding at end of period}}$$

However, the complexities of a corporation's capital structure and changes in that structure often require that the calculation of EPS be adjusted to give a better reflection of economic reality and to improve the consistency and comparability of EPS figures. Some of the adjustments that are required are straightforward and objective. Others represent an effort to account for economic events and circumstances that are difficult to quantify with certainty, and therefore must be "hypothetically quantified" (quantified on an "as if" basis). For example, as you will soon see, several hypothetical events underlie the procedure for incorporating stock options, stock purchase rights, warrants, and their equivalents in the EPS calculation.

DETERMINING INCOME APPLICABLE TO COMMON STOCK

If we examine the basic formulation of the EPS calculation above, we can see a possible deficiency in the numerator of the ratio. How do we account for the claims of owners of outstanding securities that are senior to—must be paid before—the claims of the common stockholders? Senior claims, such as dividends declared on nonconvertible preferred stock, must be deducted from income (or added to a loss) for the period in order to determine the income (or loss) applicable to shares of common stock. Hence we must adjust the basic EPS formula to:

$$EPS = \frac{\text{Income (or loss) for period} - \text{Income applicable to senior securities}}{\text{Number of shares of common stock outstanding at end of period}}$$

To illustrate, assume that Janson Corporation earned $100,000 after taxes during fiscal year 1987 and that during the entire period 10,000 shares of common stock and 5,000 shares of nonconvertible preferred stock with a dividend rate of $2 per share were outstanding. In this case, net income must be adjusted for the income applicable to the nonconvertible preferred stock. Hence,

---

[5] "Suspension of the Reporting of Earnings per Share and Segment Information by Nonpublic Enterprises," *Statement of Financial Accounting Standards No. 21* (Stamford, Conn.: FASB, 1978).

[6] "Determining Whether a Convertible Security Is a Common Stock Equivalent," *Statement of Financial Accounting Standards No. 55* (Stamford, Conn.: FASB, 1982); "Yield Test for Determining Whether a Convertible Security Is a Common Stock Equivalent," *Statement of Financial Accounting Standards No. 85* (Stamford, Conn.: FASB, 1985).

$$\text{EPS for } 1987 = \frac{\$100,000 - \$2(5,000 \text{ shares})}{10,000 \text{ common shares}} = \frac{\$90,000}{10,000 \text{ shares}} = \$9$$

We must adjust income by the amount of dividends on *noncumulative* preferred stock outstanding any time those dividends for the current period have been paid or declared. Also, *cumulative* preferred dividends *for the current period,* even when not paid or declared, must be deducted from income when income applicable to common stock is determined. However, preferred dividends that are cumulative only if they are earned are deducted from income only to the extent that they are earned. Dividends declared or accumulated during a prior period are not deducted when EPS is calculated for the current period, even though they may have been paid during the current period. These dividends would have been deducted from income when EPS was calculated for the particular prior period in which they were declared or accumulated.

We also may need to adjust income for dividend claims of *convertible* preferred stock. The need for such an adjustment depends on whether the rules for calculating EPS specify that the convertible preferred stock should be treated as a preferred stock or as the common stock into which it can be converted. If the convertible preferred stock is treated as a preferred stock, its dividends should be handled in the same way as we described earlier for nonconvertible preferred stock. The rules for incorporating convertible preferred stock into the EPS calculations are discussed in more detail later.

CALCULATION OF THE WEIGHTED AVERAGE NUMBER OF COMMON SHARES

Having adjusted the numerator of the EPS formulation to yield income applicable to common stock, we can turn our attention to the denominator. If we divide income applicable to common stock by the number of shares of common stock outstanding *at the end of the accounting period,* we are, in effect, saying that the income that was generated *during* the accounting period was generated from the amount of equity that corresponds to the common shares outstanding at the *end* of the period. This statement is true only if there is no change in the number of common shares outstanding during the period.

Since the earning process occurs continuously throughout the accounting period, we must recognize that the income for the period was generated from the capital available *during* the period, rather than from the amount of capital represented by the common stock at the end of the period. That is, we must adjust the denominator to reflect the lengths of time during the period that different amounts of capital (or net assets), from different numbers of common shares outstanding, were available to generate income. More specifically, we must ''weight'' the number of shares outstanding at any time during the accounting period by the length of time (e.g., the number of months) those shares were outstanding:

$$\text{EPS} = \frac{\text{Income (or loss) for period} - \text{Income applicable to senior securities}}{\text{Weighted average number of shares of common stock outstanding during period}}$$

We can demonstrate the weighting procedure by using a simple case where 3,000 shares of common stock are outstanding for an entire year and 1,000 additional shares are issued and outstanding for the last three months of the year. In this case, at the end of the year the 3,000 shares would be multiplied by a weighting factor of 12/12, which means that the 3,000 shares were outstanding for 12 of the 12 months in the year. The 1,000 shares would be multiplied by a weighting factor of 3/12, which means that the 1,000 shares were outstanding for 3 of the 12 months in the year. As a result of our calculations, we determine that the weighted average number of shares in this case is 3,250 [3,000(12/12) + 1,000(3/12)]. If the number of shares of common stock changes frequently during the year, we may need to calculate the weighted average number of common shares on the basis of days outstanding rather than months outstanding.

To further illustrate the weighted average procedure, assume that Adams, Inc., earned $100,000 after taxes during fiscal year 1987 and that Adams started 1987 with 6,000 common shares outstanding, issued 6,000 new common shares at the end of three months, and retired 2,000 common shares at the end of six months. In this case it is necessary for us to calculate the *weighted average* number of common shares outstanding during the year because the number of shares changed during the year. The calculation of the weighted average number of common shares outstanding during 1987 is as follows:

PERIOD OF TIME	SHARES OUTSTANDING	WEIGHTING FACTOR	WEIGHTED SHARES
First 3 months	6,000	3/12	1,500
Second 3 months	12,000	3/12	3,000
Last 6 months	10,000	6/12	5,000
Weighted average common shares			9,500

Alternatively, we could calculate the weighted average number of shares as we did in the simple case discussed earlier by treating 6,000 shares as outstanding for the entire 12 months, 6,000 shares as outstanding for nine months, and 2,000 shares as *not* outstanding for six months. If we take this approach, we calculate the weighted average number of shares as follows:

$$6,000(12/12) + 6,000(9/12) - 2,000(6/12) = 6,000 + 4,500 - 1,000$$
$$= 9,500 \text{ weighted average common shares}$$

Using the adjusted equation for EPS, we find:

$$\text{EPS for 1987} = \frac{\$100,000}{9,500 \text{ shares}} = \$10.53$$

It should be noted that, for purposes of calculating EPS, acquisition of treasury stock is treated the same as a retirement of shares, since net assets decrease when treasury stock is acquired. Correspondingly, reissue of treasury stock is treated the same as an issuance of new shares of stock.

If convertible securities, such as convertible preferred stock or convertible bonds, are converted into common stock during the period, we must adjust the weighted average number of common shares outstanding to reflect the shares of common stock that are issued upon conversion. When making the EPS calculation, we must be careful *also* to reduce income by any dividend claims of convertible preferred stock that arose during the current period *before* the conversion date. On the other hand, when a convertible bond is converted to common stock during the current period, we must consider the conversion when we determine the weighted average number of common shares, but we need not adjust income for bond interest expense incurred during the current period before the conversion date. The bond interest expense incurred before conversion of the bond would already have been deducted when net income was calculated for the period.

To illustrate the incorporation of stock conversion into the EPS calculation, assume that Benson, Inc., earned $50,000 after taxes for the fiscal year 1987. Further assume that as of the beginning of the fiscal year, Benson had two classes of stock outstanding— 2,500 shares of common stock and 5,000 shares of a convertible preferred stock that pays a $1 dividend per share at the end of the year. The conversion rate of the preferred stock is 2 preferred shares for 1 common share.

Assume that at the end of the ninth month of the fiscal year, 3,200 of the preferred shares were converted to common shares. With respect to calculation of EPS, there are two problems to be dealt with in this situation. First, we must determine the income applicable to the common stock. Second, we must determine the weighted average number of common shares to be used to calculate EPS.

Since only 1,800 preferred shares (5,000 shares − 3,200 shares converted) remain outstanding at the end of fiscal year 1987, the senior claim on income, preferred stock dividends, is $1,800 (1,800 shares × $1). Income applicable to the common stock, therefore, equals $48,200 ($50,000 − $1,800).

With 2,500 common shares outstanding for the entire accounting period and 1,600 (3,200 ÷ 2) new common shares outstanding for the final three months of the period as a result of the conversion of preferred stock, the weighted average number of common shares is:

$$2,500(12/12) + 1,600(3/12) = 2,500 + 400 = 2,900 \text{ shares}$$

Therefore, in this case, the EPS for fiscal year 1987 is:

$$\frac{\$50,000 - \$1,800}{2,900 \text{ shares}} = \frac{\$48,200}{2,900 \text{ shares}} = \$16.62 \text{ per share}$$

Exercise of stock options, stock purchase rights, and stock warrants increases the number of common shares outstanding. When exercise occurs during the accounting period for which EPS is being calculated, the weighted average number of common shares outstanding must be adjusted to reflect the issuance of new common shares.

For example, assume that Carson Corporation earned $80,000 after taxes for the fiscal year ended December 31, 1987. Also assume that on January 1, 1987, 3,300 shares of Carson common stock and 730 stock purchase warrants were outstanding. The warrants specified that the purchase of one share of Carson common stock required the exercise of a warrant and the payment of $50.

Suppose that all of the stock purchase warrants were exercised on January 16, 1987. In order to calculate EPS, we must determine the weighted average number of common shares outstanding during the period, given exercise of the warrants.

$$\begin{aligned}\text{Weighted average number} \\ \text{of common shares}\end{aligned} \begin{aligned}&= [3,300 \text{ shares} \times (365/365)] + [730 \text{ shares} \times (350/365)] \\ &= 3,300 \text{ shares} + 700 \text{ shares} = 4,000 \text{ shares}\end{aligned}$$

In this calculation, we weight the 3,300 shares by 365/365 because those shares were outstanding for all 365 days of the year. The 730 shares issued because of the exercise of the stock purchase warrants are weighted by 350/365 because they were outstanding only after January 15, 1987, or for 350 days of the year.

On the basis of the information provided, the entire $80,000 income is applicable to the common stock. Therefore,

$$\text{EPS for 1987} = \frac{\$80,000}{4,000 \text{ shares}} = \$20$$

ADJUSTING THE WEIGHTED AVERAGE FOR STOCK DIVIDENDS, STOCK SPLITS, OR REVERSE SPLITS

Calculation of the weighted average number of common shares also may require adjustment for stock dividends, stock splits, or reverse splits. When a stock dividend or stock split occurs, a stockholder has more shares of stock (fewer shares in the case of a reverse split) but no greater *proportionate* interest in the corporation. Therefore, when a stock dividend or stock split occurs during the year for which EPS is being calculated, the resulting number of shares must be treated in the EPS calculation as if the shares were outstanding for the *entire* year. This retroactive-to-the-first-of-the-fiscal-year treatment of a stock split or stock dividend is required because, even though the number of shares changes as a result of the split or dividend, the invested capital represented by the new number of shares is exactly the same as the capital represented by the old number of shares. That is, there is no change in corporate assets as a result of a stock split or stock dividend. The effect of the retroactive treatment is to generate an EPS figure after the stock split or stock dividend that results in the same earnings *per investor* as would have been calculated had there been no stock split or stock dividend.

To illustrate, assume that Lawson, Inc., earned $90,000 after income taxes during fiscal year 1987. Also assume that at the end of fiscal year 1987 Lawson had 10,000 shares of common stock outstanding after giving effect to a 2-for-1 stock split at the end of the fourth month of the fiscal year.

Recognizing that the 10,000 end-of-the-year shares represent no more invested capital than that represented by the 5,000 old shares, we should treat the stock split as if the total ownership of the entity remained unchanged during 1987; that is, the EPS calculation should be made as if the 10,000 shares existed throughout the 1987 fiscal year. Therefore,

$$\text{EPS for 1987} = \frac{\$90,000}{10,000 \text{ shares}} = \$9$$

Stock dividends and stock splits require a retroactive-to-the-first-of-the-accounting-period treatment when EPS is calculated.

When stock dividends, stock splits, or reverse splits occur, EPS calculation rules require the retroactive-to-the-first-of-the-accounting-period adjustment just demonstrated. In addition, the weighted average number of common shares of all prior periods that are presented for comparative purposes also must be retroactively adjusted and EPS recalculated to reflect the stock dividend or stock split. The important point to remember is that stock dividends, stock splits, or reverse splits *are not weighted* by the length of time the dividend or split is outstanding during the period, because there is no change in assets as a result of a stock dividend or stock split.

If a stock dividend or stock split occurs after the end of the accounting period but before the financial statements are issued, the weighted average number of common shares for the period for which EPS is being calculated must be restated and EPS recalculated to reflect the stock dividend or split. In addition, the weighted average number of common shares for any prior periods presented for comparative purposes also must be restated and EPS adjusted accordingly. When EPS figures are adjusted for stock dividends or stock splits occurring after the date of the balance sheet, pertinent facts about the adjustment and its effect on EPS should be disclosed in a note to the financial statements.

THE CONCEPT OF DILUTION

In the preceding section we saw how the conversion of convertible securities and the exercise of stock purchase warrants must be handled when calculating the weighted average number of common shares outstanding. These securities are not actually common stock, but they do enable the holder to obtain common stock through conversion or exercise. Thus, in discussions of EPS calculations, they are called **potentially dilutive securities.** Potentially dilutive securities include convertible preferred stock, convertible bonds, stock purchase rights, stock warrants, and contingent shares.

Dilutive securities reduce the earnings per share of common stock.

The exercise or conversion of a potentially dilutive security increases the number of shares of common stock outstanding. Dilutive securities reduce (or dilute) the earnings per share of common stock. Conservatism influences the rules for the calculation of EPS in that we are required to include the effect of dilutive securities in EPS calculations only when a corporation has net income. Such securities are antidilutive when a corporation has a net loss, and therefore must be excluded from EPS calculations. Only the weighted average number of common shares actually outstanding is considered when calculating net loss per share. The purpose of including dilutive securities in EPS calculations is to place substance over form and to provide a reasonably conservative measure of corporate profitability per share of common stock outstanding. In addition, the inclusion of dilutive securities in EPS calculations provides relevant and timely information about the effect that exercise or conversion of the securities *could* have on EPS.

Inclusion of dilutive securities in EPS calculations increases the denominator of the EPS ratio. Inclusion of dilutive securities may also increase income applicable to common stock, which is the numerator of the EPS ratio. However, because the rules for calculation of EPS require that a potentially dilutive security be included in EPS calculations only when it causes a reduction in EPS, any increase in income per share applicable to common stock must be less than EPS for outstanding common shares before inclusion of the security.

To demonstrate the impact of a dilutive security on EPS computations, assume that Dawson, Inc., earned $25,000 after taxes for fiscal year 1987 and had 10,000 shares of common stock outstanding throughout 1987. In addition, Dawson had convertible bonds outstanding throughout 1987, which resulted in interest expense of $500 per year and which the bondholders could convert into 2,000 shares of common stock.

Ignoring Dawson's convertible bonds for a moment, we can calculate EPS for 1987 as follows:

$$\frac{\$25{,}000}{10{,}000 \text{ shares}} = \$2.50 \text{ per share}$$

A dilutive security is included in EPS calculations by assuming exercise or conversion of the security.

Under the rules for calculation of EPS, we include a dilutive security in EPS calculations by *assuming* exercise or conversion of the security. The hypothetical exercise or conversion of a dilutive security allows us to determine what EPS would have been if the dilutive security actually had been exercised or converted. In the case of Dawson, Inc., hypothetical conversion of the convertible bonds into common stock at the beginning of 1987 requires two adjustments of the EPS calculation. Assume the 1987 tax rate was 40 percent. Income applicable to common stock must be increased by $500 because the interest on the bonds would not have been paid if the bonds had been converted at the beginning of the period. Because tax-deductible expenses would be reduced by $500, however, income applicable to common stock also must be decreased by 40 percent × $500, which is the increased tax that would have been paid had the bonds been converted at the beginning of the period. Hence, income applicable to common stock would be:

$$\$25{,}000 + \$500 - .4(\$500) = \$25{,}300$$

Second, conversion of the bonds would require issuance of 2,000 shares of common stock, thereby raising the number of common shares outstanding to 12,000. As a result, conversion of the bonds would make 1987 EPS:

$$\frac{\$25{,}300}{12{,}000 \text{ shares}} = \$2.11$$

Notice that although conversion of the convertible bonds would result in adjustments to both the numerator and the denominator of the EPS fraction, the EPS effect resulting from conversion,

$$\frac{\$300 \text{ additional after-tax income applicable to common stock}}{2{,}000 \text{ additional shares of common stock}} = \$.15$$

is well below EPS before inclusion of the dilutive security ($2.50). Therefore, EPS after inclusion of the dilutive security ($2.11) is below EPS before inclusion of the dilutive security ($2.50). Later in the chapter we will discuss how the EPS effect of potentially dilutive securities is used to determine the order of entry of such securities into the EPS calculations.

An **antidilutive security** is a security that increases EPS or decreases loss per share if it is included in EPS calculations. For example, convertible debt is antidilutive if the assumed or actual conversion of the security causes income applicable to common stock to increase (because of the after-tax interest adjustment) by a greater amount per additional common share (because of the conversion) than EPS was before conversion of the security.

Let us modify the facts given in the previous example for Dawson, Inc. Assume now that the annual interest expense related to Dawson's convertible bonds is $3,000 and that the bonds are convertible into only 700 common shares. We shall continue to assume $25,000 income after taxes for 1987, 10,000 shares of common stock outstanding if the bonds are not converted, and a 40 percent tax rate.

In this case hypothetical conversion of the convertible bonds into common stock at the beginning of 1987 requires that income applicable to common stock be adjusted as follows:

$$\$25,000 + \$3,000 - .4(\$3,000) = \$26,800$$

Given the incremental 700 common shares issuable upon conversion of the bonds, Dawson's EPS after inclusion of the convertible bonds would be:

$$\frac{\$26,800}{10,700 \text{ shares}} = \$2.51$$

The convertible bonds are antidilutive.

We could also have identified the convertible bonds as antidilutive because the incremental EPS resulting from assumed conversion,

$$\frac{\$1,800 \text{ additional after-tax income applicable to common stock}}{700 \text{ additional shares of common stock}} = \$2.57$$

is greater than EPS before assumed conversion of the bonds ($2.50). Antidilutive securities, such as Dawson's convertible bonds, should not be included in EPS calculations.

The existence of dilutive securities is important when determining whether a corporation has a simple or complex capital structure.

> Antidilutive securities should not be included in EPS calculations.

SIMPLE VS. COMPLEX CAPITAL STRUCTURES

For purposes of EPS calculations, *Opinion No. 15* classifies corporations as having either a simple capital structure or a complex capital structure. A corporation has a **simple capital structure** if during the period it had no securities outstanding, or agreements to issue securities, which in the *aggregate* could dilute EPS by 3 percent or more, as compared to EPS based strictly on the weighted average number of common shares actually outstanding during the period. A corporation has a **complex capital structure** if it has issued, in addition to common stock, securities that in the *aggregate* could dilute EPS by 3 percent or more. The 3 percent dilution test is noteworthy because it is one of the few situations in accounting where a quantitative materiality guideline exists. Aggregate dilution of less than 3 percent is not considered to be material.

As part of EPS calculations, each period a corporation is required to determine whether its capital structure is simple or complex. A corporation could have a simple capital structure one period and a complex capital structure the next, or vice versa.

Consider Dawson, Inc., once again. Given the initial set of facts, we determined that Dawson's convertible bonds were dilutive securities. Having calculated a potential dilution of EPS from $2.50 to $2.11, we can now say that Dawson had a complex capital structure in 1987. That is, because the revised EPS figure ($2.11) was only 84.4 percent of the original EPS figure ($2.50), the potential dilutive effect of the convertible bonds was 3 percent or more.

Suppose we modify our earlier assumptions about Dawson, Inc., slightly and assume that the bonds are convertible into 320 shares of common stock. In this case, the adjusted income available to common stock if the bonds were converted remains $25,300. Only 320 additional shares of common stock would be issued in the conversion, however, raising the total number of outstanding common shares to 10,320. Therefore, with our new assumption, EPS for 1987 would be:

$$\frac{\$25,300}{10,320 \text{ shares}} = \$2.45$$

We would now classify Dawson as having a simple capital structure in 1987 for EPS purposes. Specifically, $2.45 is 98 percent of $2.50, so the potential dilutive effect of the convertible bonds is less than 3 percent. (Remember that the 3 percent test is an *aggregate* test—a test to be applied to the combination of all dilutive securities. In the Dawson case, however, the convertible bonds are the only dilutive securities.) Because aggregate dilution is less than 3 percent, conversion of the convertible bonds should not be hypothesized in the calculation of Dawson's EPS, and we would report Dawson's 1987 EPS as $2.50. This treatment is consistent with the view that dilution of less than 3 percent implies a simple capital structure.

CLASSIFICATION OF POTENTIALLY DILUTIVE SECURITIES FOR EPS CALCULATIONS

As we have seen, securities that provide the holder with the right to obtain common stock through exercise or conversion of the security can be either dilutive or antidilutive, depending on the circumstances of the exercise or conversion. We therefore refer to such securities as *potentially dilutive securities. APB Opinion No. 15* requires that, for purposes of calculating EPS, we classify all outstanding potentially dilutive securities of a corporation as either **common stock equivalents** or **other potentially dilutive securities.**

Description of primary and fully diluted EPS.

Including common stock equivalents and other potentially dilutive securities in the EPS calculations allows us to determine what EPS would have been if common stock actually had been issued to replace the common stock equivalent or other dilutive security. If we assume the replacement of all dilutive common stock equivalents with shares of common stock, we can calculate an amount called **primary EPS.** If we assume the replacement of both dilutive common stock equivalents *and* other potentially dilutive securities with shares of common stock, we calculate an amount called **fully diluted EPS.** *Primary EPS* is based on the weighted average number of common shares outstanding *plus* the weighted average number of common shares that would be issued in the event of the exercise or conversion of securities that are in substance equivalent to common stock. *Fully diluted EPS* is a more conservative EPS figure, because it reflects the *maximum dilutive effect* of common stock equivalents and all other potentially dilutive securities. The differences between primary EPS and fully diluted EPS are (1) the additional dilution that results from slightly different treatment of some common stock equivalents when fully diluted EPS is calculated, and (2) the inclusion of other potentially dilutive securities outstanding in the fully diluted calculation.

In the next few pages we discuss common stock equivalents and other potentially dilutive securities, together with the rules and assumptions set forth by the APB for their inclusion in EPS calculations. Keep in mind that even though the events and transactions comprising the assumptions underlying EPS calculations might not actually occur, the APB's assumptions and rules do provide a practical means of ensuring consistent and comparable EPS calculations. Remember, too, that accounting for securities, presentation of securities in the financial statements, and determination of book value per share are not affected by the way we classify securities for EPS calculations.

> Accounting for securities, presentation of securities in the financial statements, and determination of book value per share are not affected by the way securities are classified for EPS calculations.

COMMON STOCK EQUIVALENTS

APB Opinion No. 15 defines a **common stock equivalent** as ''a security which, because of its terms or the circumstances under which it was issued, is in substance equivalent to common stock.''[7] A common stock equivalent is not a common stock in form, but it does enable its holder to become a common stockholder, and therefore its market value tends to change with changes in the market value of the common stock for which it can be exchanged. Common stock equivalents include:

1. Stock options and warrants and their equivalents.
2. Contingently issuable shares of common stock.
3. Convertible securities for which the effective yield rate is less than two-thirds of the average Aa corporate bond yield at the time the convertible securities are issued.[8]

Stock Options and Warrants and Their Equivalents

Stock options and warrants and their equivalents are *always* classified as common stock equivalents. However, options and warrants are included in EPS calculations only if they are dilutive. Stock purchase contracts, stock subscriptions not fully paid, deferred compensation plans providing for the issuance of common stock, and convertible debt and convertible preferred stock allowing or requiring the payment of cash at conversion, regardless of the effective yield of such convertible securities at the time of issuance, are considered the equivalents of stock options and warrants.

THE TREASURY STOCK METHOD   The **treasury stock method** is the procedure used to include the dilutive effect of stock options, stock purchase rights, warrants, and their equivalents in EPS calculations. Use of the treasury stock method results in an increase in the number of common shares *assumed* to be outstanding when the exercise price of a stock option or its equivalent is below the market price of the common stock.

Even though stock options, stock purchase rights, warrants, and their equivalents are always classified as common stock equivalents, they are not always included in EPS calculations. Under the treasury stock method, if the market price of the common stock has been greater than the exercise price of the stock options or equivalents under consideration for *substantially all* (at least 11 weeks) of the quarter preceding the end of the accounting period for which EPS data are being calculated, then the options or equivalents are assumed to have been exercised and must be included in EPS calculations. The exercise date is assumed to be the beginning of the accounting period, or the issue date of

---

[7] *APB Opinion No. 15,* app. D.

[8] For convertible securities issued before March 1, 1982, common stock equivalency requires that the effective yield rate be less than 66 2/3 percent of the *bank prime interest rate* at the time the convertible security was issued.

the options or their equivalents if they were issued during the period. When we use the treasury stock method, we also assume that any cash that would be received by the corporation upon exercise of the options or their equivalents would be used to purchase shares of the corporation's own common stock in the open market.[9]

Using the treasury stock method to calculate primary EPS.

When the treasury stock method is used to calculate *primary EPS,* we assume that the corporation would use the cash proceeds it would receive when the options or their equivalents are exercised to purchase ("buy back") shares of its own common stock at the *average market price* for the accounting period. When *fully diluted EPS* is calculated, the *higher of the end-of-the-period market price or the average market price* is used as the assumed buy-back price to determine incremental shares. Use of the *higher* of the end-of-the-period market price or the average market price for the period in the calculation of fully diluted EPS generates maximum potential dilution from stock options, stock purchase rights, warrants, and their equivalents under the treasury stock method.

Using the treasury stock method to calculate fully diluted EPS.

To illustrate the treasury stock method, assume that the current year's income for Ace Company was $270,000 and that during the year Ace had an average of 45,000 shares of common stock outstanding. In addition, throughout the year there were options outstanding to purchase 10,000 shares of Ace's common stock at $10 per share. During the year, the average price of Ace's common stock was $12 and the year-end closing price of the common stock was $13. Ace's primary and fully diluted EPS would be calculated as follows:

	PRIMARY EPS	FULLY DILUTED EPS
Shares issued under assumed exercise of options ..	10,000	10,000
Proceeds from assumed exercise of options ($10 × 10,000 shares): $100,000		
Shares purchased with proceeds:		
Primary EPS ($100,000 ÷ $12)	(8,333)	
Fully diluted EPS ($100,000 ÷ $13)		(7,692)
Incremental equivalent shares	1,667	2,308
Average shares outstanding during year	45,000	45,000
Common shares plus equivalent shares.	46,667	47,308
Primary EPS ($270,000 ÷ 46,667 shares)	$5.79	
Fully diluted EPS ($270,000 ÷ 47,308 shares)		$5.71

In this example, without considering the options, EPS is $6.00 ($270,000 ÷ 45,000 shares). Thus, potential dilution is in excess of 3 percent (.97 × $6.00 = $5.82), which means that for the current year Ace has a complex capital structure. Therefore, both primary and fully diluted EPS should be reported. Had only fully diluted EPS resulted in dilution equal to or in excess of 3 percent, a complex capital structure also would have

[9] Technically, the treasury stock method should be applied on a quarter-by-quarter basis within the accounting period (normally a year) for which EPS data are being calculated. The "substantially all" test is a one-time test within each accounting period. Therefore, ideally, the treasury stock method should be applied to any quarter within the year for which EPS data are required, beginning with the first quarter for which the market price has exceeded the exercise price for substantially all of the quarter. Of course, if application of the treasury stock method for a particular quarter results in antidilution, then that quarter must be excluded from the primary or fully diluted EPS calculations for the year.

existed and the dual presentation of EPS would have been required. Had neither primary EPS nor fully diluted EPS been equal to or less than $5.82, Ace would have had a simple capital structure for the current year. In this case, the stock options would have been ignored in the EPS calculation and a single EPS figure of $6.00 would have been reported.

Stock options, stock purchase rights, warrants, and their equivalents are included in EPS calculations only when the "substantially all" test for assumed exercise under the treasury stock method is met *and* when they are dilutive. This requirement means that options, warrants, and their equivalents are included in primary EPS calculations only when the average market price of the common stock for the period is above the exercise price of the option, warrant, or equivalent. Stock options, warrants, and their equivalents would be included in the calculation of fully diluted EPS when they are included in the primary calculation or when the end-of-period market price of common stock exceeds the exercise price. Hence, stock options, warrants, and equivalents might be included in fully diluted EPS because end-of-period stock price exceeds exercise price, but excluded from primary EPS because the average stock price for the period is below the exercise price.

THE 20 PERCENT TEST   If the number of common shares issuable under the exercise agreements of *all* stock options, stock purchase rights, warrants, and their equivalents *in the aggregate* exceeds 20 percent of the number of common shares outstanding at the end of the accounting period, then the buy-back portion of the treasury stock method is modified. Under the modified approach, the cash proceeds from the exercise of options, warrants, and their equivalents in the aggregate (including antidilutive ones) are assumed to be used in the following order:

1. To purchase common shares, not to exceed 20 percent of the common shares outstanding *at the end of the accounting period*.
2. To reduce any short-term debt or long-term debt of the corporation.
3. To acquire U.S. government securities or commercial paper.

The rationale for the 20 percent limit on stock assumed to be purchased with the cash proceeds is that purchase of more than this amount of stock probably would have a significant effect on the market price of the stock, making use of the treasury stock method questionable.

Note that any assumed reduction of debt or assumed acquisition of government securities or commercial paper probably will require adjustments to both the numerator and the denominator of the EPS ratio. The numerator will have to be adjusted for any after-tax reductions in interest expense or increases in interest revenue. The denominator will have to be adjusted for changes in the number of shares of common stock that are assumed to be outstanding. The results of applying steps 1 through 3 above should be *aggregated* and, if the net effect on EPS is dilutive, the results of all three steps should enter the EPS calculations. If the net aggregate effect is antidilutive, the options and their equivalents under consideration should be omitted from the EPS calculations.

We can illustrate the impact of the 20 percent limit on the buy-back portion of the treasury stock method by adding a few additional facts to the Ace Company example. Assume that there were also warrants outstanding to purchase 4,000 shares of Ace common stock at $8 per share. Ace had no short-term or long-term debt, and U.S. government securities currently are yielding 7 percent. Finally, at year-end Ace had 48,000 common shares outstanding. Ace is subject to a 40 percent tax rate. Given these new facts, Ace's primary EPS and fully diluted EPS are calculated as follows:

	PRIMARY EPS	FULLY DILUTED EPS
Proceeds from exercise of:		
Options ($10 × 10,000 shares) $100,000		
Warrants ($8 × 4,000 shares) 32,000		
Total proceeds................................ $132,000		
Average shares outstanding during year	45,000	45,000
Shares issued under assumed exercise of options	10,000	10,000
Shares issued under assumed exercise of warrants	4,000	4,000
Shares assumed to be purchased with proceeds of issues— limited to 20 percent of 48,000 year-end outstanding shares.....................................	(9,600)	(9,600)
Common shares plus equivalent shares...........	49,400	49,400
Reported net income for year	$270,000	$270,000
Plus after-tax interest revenue on assumed purchase of U.S. government securities:		
Primary EPS: $(1 - .4) \times [.07 \times (\$132,000 - \$115,200*)]$	706	
Fully diluted EPS: $(1 - .4) \times [.07 \times (\$132,000 - \$124,800\dagger)]$		302
Adjusted net income for year	$270,706	$270,302
Primary EPS ($270,706 ÷ 49,400 shares)	$5.48	
Fully diluted EPS ($270,302 ÷ 49,400 shares)		$5.47

* 9,600 shares × $12 = $115,200.

† 9,600 shares × $13 = $124,800.

In the example above, both primary EPS and fully diluted EPS result in dilution well in excess of 3 percent ($.18), so Ace has a complex capital structure this year and both primary and fully diluted EPS should be reported.

Contingently Issuable Shares of Common Stock

Contingently issuable shares of common stock are common stock equivalents. Contingently issuable shares of common stock are shares of common stock that will be issued when some specified future event occurs—attainment of a specified level of income, perhaps, or simply the passage of time. Shares of common stock that are to be issued after the mere passage of time should be classified as common stock equivalents and should be considered as outstanding shares when both primary EPS and fully diluted EPS are calculated. Shares of common stock that are issuable for little or no consideration when specified conditions are met should be considered to be outstanding stock for both primary and fully diluted EPS calculations when the specified conditions are met. For example, if attainment or maintenance of a particular level of income is the specified condition, and if that level of income is currently being attained, the contingently issuable shares of stock should be considered as outstanding shares when both primary and fully diluted EPS are calculated.

To illustrate, assume that Mead, Inc., purchased Atkinson Company and, as part of the purchase agreement, is to give Atkinson's stockholders 10,000 additional shares of Atkinson common stock if Atkinson's 1988 income after taxes is $100,000 or more. If Atkinson earns $100,000 in 1987, the 10,000 contingently issuable shares should be included in both primary and fully diluted EPS calculations for 1987, just as if the contingently issuable shares were outstanding in 1987.

Contingently issuable shares of common stock that are issuable only if a level of income higher than the current level is attained or maintained over a period of years should be considered as outstanding shares only for fully diluted EPS, and then only if the contingent shares are dilutive. In this case, current income applicable to common stock should be adjusted to give effect to the increased income that is required in order to reach the higher specified income level.

Suppose, for example, that the 10,000 shares of Atkinson Company are issuable in 1988 provided that Atkinson earns 10 percent more in 1988 than it earned in 1987. In this case, the 10,000 contingently issuable shares are included in the 1987 EPS calculations *only* when fully diluted EPS is calculated. In addition, the 1987 income used in the fully diluted EPS calculation is increased by the 10 percent ($10,000) necessary to meet the conditions of the agreement.

Convertible Securities

Convertible securities may or may not be common stock equivalents. Whether a convertible bond or a convertible preferred stock is a common stock equivalent must be determined at the time the security is issued and, with one exception, the classification should not be changed while the security remains outstanding.[10]

A convertible security that, at the time of issuance, has terms that make it substantially equivalent to a common stock should be regarded as a common stock equivalent. Whether the security is substantially equivalent to a common stock depends on its **effective yield.** If the effective yield to the holder of a convertible security at the time of issuance is significantly below what would be a reasonable yield for a similar security without the conversion feature, then the convertible security must have been acquired because it provided the option of converting to common stock. Therefore, the convertible security should be classified as a common stock equivalent.

The effective yield is based on the security's stated annual interest or dividend payments, any original issuance premium or discount, any call premium or discount, and is the lowest of the yield to maturity and the yields to all call dates. Effective yield for a security that does not have a stated maturity date—for example, a convertible preferred stock—is calculated by dividing the security's stated annual interest or dividend payments by its market price at issuance.

A convertible security is a common stock equivalent if, at the time of issuance, it has an effective yield of less than two-thirds of the then current average Aa corporate bond yield. For purposes of the yield test, the average Aa corporate bond yield is based on bond yields for a brief period of time—for example, one week—including or immediately preceding the date of issuance of the security being tested. If stated annual interest or

---

[10] The single exception to the general rule of permanent classification occurs when a convertible security is issued with terms (market price is not a term) identical to the terms of a previously issued convertible security. If the previously issued security is a common stock equivalent, then the new issue is a common stock equivalent, whether or not it passes the test for common stock equivalency at its issuance. Alternatively, if the newly issued security meets the test for common stock equivalent status, then the previously issued security also should be classified as a common stock equivalent, regardless of its classification when it was originally issued. Thus, for example, if a material portion of a previously issued convertible preferred stock that was not a common stock equivalent at its issuance is reacquired by the corporation as treasury stock and is later reissued, the reissue is treated as a new issue and common stock equivalent status must be tested. If the reissue qualifies as a common stock equivalent, then the remaining outstanding portion of the original issue must be reclassified as a common stock equivalent.

dividend payments on the security are scheduled to change within the first five years after issuance, then the lowest scheduled payments during those five years should be used to determine the effective yield at issuance.

To illustrate the effective yield test, assume that West, Inc., purchased a 5-year convertible bond for $1,126.42. The bond had a face value of $1,000 and a 9 percent stated interest rate. The effective yield to West would be 6 percent.[11] If the average Aa corporate bond yield was 11 percent when the convertible bond was issued, the convertible bond would be a common stock equivalent because the effective yield is less than 7.33 percent (two-thirds of 11 percent).

Convertible securities that have an effective yield equal to or exceeding two-thirds of the average Aa corporate bond yield at the time the securities are issued should be classified as other potentially dilutive securities and should be considered only when fully diluted EPS is calculated. In the case of the West, Inc., convertible bond, an effective yield of 7.33 percent or more would make the stock an other potentially dilutive security rather than a common stock equivalent.

THE IF-CONVERTED METHOD   The **if-converted method** is used to include the dilutive effect of convertible securities in EPS calculations. Conversion is assumed, and the if-converted method is applied, only when the result is dilutive unless (1) the security is included in an aggregate calculation that has a net dilutive effect or (2) fully diluted EPS is being calculated and an actual conversion has occurred during the period. In the second situation, conversion is assumed at the beginning of the period, regardless of whether the result is dilutive or antidilutive.

When we use the if-converted method, we assume that convertible securities are converted into common stock as of the beginning of the accounting period or as of the issue date of the convertible securities, if they are issued during the period. Furthermore, we must adjust income applicable to common stock for the effects of interest expense (after taxes) on convertible bonds and for dividends on convertible preferred stock that would not have to be paid if the securities were converted. For example, if convertible bonds actually were converted into common stock at the beginning of the period, there would be no interest expense for the period related to those bonds. Since interest expense would have been deducted when income was determined, and tax expense would have been based on that income, assumed conversion of the bonds would mean that

(Related cash interest − Premium amortization or + Discount amortization) × (1 − Tax rate)

must be added back to after-tax income applicable to common stock.

In the case of convertible preferred stock, assumed conversion would mean that any dividends that were deducted in the determination of income applicable to common stock must be added back, because such dividends would not exist if the preferred stock actually had been converted. Because dividends paid are not deductible for tax purposes, there is no tax effect for the dividend adjustment.

Assumed conversion of convertible securities, whether bonds or preferred stocks, also requires adjustment of the weighted average number of common shares to reflect the additional shares that would be issued upon conversion of the securities. For convertible securities issued during the accounting period, the assumed new shares must be weighted for the length of time from the convertible security issue date to the end of the period.

[11] $1,126.42 = \left[\frac{1}{(1+i)^5} \times \$1,000\right] + \left[\frac{1 + \frac{1}{(1+i)^5}}{i} \times \$90\right]$. Using a trial-and-error approach

to solve for i results in an effective yield of 6 percent.

If the conversion privilege provided by a convertible security is not effective during the period for which EPS is being calculated, the length of time before the privilege becomes effective determines when the security is eligible for assumed conversion in EPS calculations. We should *not* assume conversion for either primary or fully diluted EPS calculations if the conversion privilege is not effective within 10 years from the end of the period for which EPS is being calculated. We should assume conversion only for fully diluted EPS calculations if the conversion privilege is effective after 5 years but within 10 years. If the conversion privilege is effective within 5 years from the end of the period for which EPS is being calculated, we should assume conversion for both primary and fully diluted EPS calculations.

To illustrate the if-converted method, assume that Waldo Company had net income of $320,000 for the year and had an average of 20,000 shares of common stock outstanding during the year. Waldo also had two types of convertible securities outstanding. One was 2,500 shares of convertible preferred stock that were issued in a prior year at a market price of $30 per share when the average Aa corporate bond yield was 10 percent. The convertible preferred stock pays an annual dividend of $1.50 and is convertible into 5,000 shares of common stock. The second was a $50,000, 7 percent convertible bond issue sold at face value at the beginning of the fifth month of the current fiscal year, when the average Aa corporate bond yield was 9 percent. The bond issue is convertible into 2,400 shares of common stock. Waldo is taxed at a 40 percent rate.

The convertible preferred stock is a common stock equivalent because it had an effective yield of 5 percent ($1.50 ÷ $30.00) when issued, at which time two-thirds of the average Aa corporate bond yield was 6 2/3 percent. The convertible bond issue is an other potentially dilutive security, rather than a common stock equivalent, because its effective yield at the time of issuance was 7 percent, while two-thirds of the average Aa corporate bond yield at the time was 6 percent. Thus, only the convertible preferred stock will be included in the calculation of primary earnings per share. Both the convertible preferred stock and the convertible bond issue will be included in the calculation of fully diluted earnings per share.

Primary earnings per share is calculated as follows:

Net income for the year *before* adjustment for preferred dividends	$320,000
Average number of shares outstanding during the year 20,000	
Shares assumed to be issued upon conversion of the preferred stock 5,000	
Common shares plus equivalent shares 25,000	

$$\text{Primary EPS} = \frac{\$320,000}{25,000 \text{ shares}} = \$12.80$$

Fully diluted earnings per share is calculated as follows:

Net income for the year	$320,000
Add: adjustment for interest expense (net of tax) on the bond issue for the last eight months of the current year [$50,000 × .07 × 2/3 × (1 − .40 tax rate)]	1,400
Adjusted net income	$321,400
Average number of shares outstanding during the year 20,000	
Shares assumed to be issued upon conversion of the preferred stock 5,000	
Weighted shares assumed to be issued upon conversion of the convertible bond issue (2,400 shares × 2/3 year) 1,600	
Common shares plus equivalent shares 26,600	

$$\text{Fully diluted EPS} = \frac{\$321,400}{26,600 \text{ shares}} = \$12.08$$

Notice that when primary EPS was calculated, preferred stock dividends were not subtracted from net income to determine income available for common stockholders because we assumed that the common stock equivalent preferred shares were converted into 5,000 common shares at the beginning of the year. In calculating fully diluted EPS we further assumed conversion of the convertible bond issue into 2,400 shares of common stock. Because the bonds were issued at the beginning of the fifth month of the year, the common shares were weighted by two-thirds. Similarly, only two-thirds of a year's interest expense, net of tax, was added back to net income for the year. This interest expense would not have been incurred had the bond issue been converted on the date of issuance.

Since fully diluted EPS reflects dilution in excess of 3 percent, Waldo has a complex capital structure for the current year, and a dual presentation of primary and fully diluted EPS would appear in the financial statements.

OTHER POTENTIALLY DILUTIVE SECURITIES

Other potentially dilutive securities are *not* in substance equivalent to common stock, but, through exercise or conversion, allow the holder to obtain shares of common stock. For example, in the case of Waldo Company, we saw convertible bonds that were classified as other potentially dilutive securities because the 7 percent effective yield exceeded two-thirds of the average Aa corporate bond yield at the time the convertible bonds were issued. A security that allows its holder to obtain shares of common stock and that does not meet the definitions and rules for classification as a common stock equivalent, which we discussed earlier, should be included among **other potentially dilutive securities.**

As we indicated earlier, common stock equivalents are included when both primary and fully diluted EPS are calculated, while other potentially dilutive securities are included only in fully diluted EPS calculations. Therefore, including the dilutive effects on EPS of other potentially dilutive securities allows us to determine the dilution of EPS that would occur if *all* potential issuances of common stock had taken place during the period.

ORDER OF ENTRY INTO EPS CALCULATIONS

If several potentially dilutive securities are to be considered for inclusion in the EPS calculations at the same time, whether for primary or fully diluted EPS, the first step is to calculate the "income per incremental common share effect" embodied in each potentially dilutive security under consideration. Next, the securities should be ranked from the smallest income per incremental share effect (most dilutive) to the largest income per incremental share effect (least dilutive). The smallest income per incremental share effect should be compared to the EPS figure just before the inclusion of the security under consideration, and if the previous EPS is larger, the security should be included in the EPS calculation because it will be dilutive. A new EPS figure should be calculated, including the security just tested, and the new EPS figure should be compared with the next lowest income per incremental share effect. Once again, if the income per incremental share effect is smaller than the newly calculated EPS, the security under consideration is dilutive and should be included in the calculation of another EPS figure. This process should continue, testing each increasing income per incremental share effect in turn and including the security under consideration in a new EPS calculation, until an income per incremental share effect is reached that exceeds the previous EPS figure. At that point, antidilutive securities have been encountered and the potentially dilutive securities remaining in the list should not be included in the EPS calculations.

To illustrate the process of ordering potentially dilutive securities for entry into EPS calculations, assume that Wixom Company has three potentially dilutive securities outstanding, all of which meet the criteria for classification as common stock equivalents. It is necessary to order the securities for possible entry into Wixom's primary EPS calculations. The three potentially dilutive securities are:

1. Stock options, which, if exercised, would not change the numerator of EPS but would add 1,000 incremental common shares to the denominator. Hence, the income per incremental share effect would be $0 \div 1,000$ shares $= \$0$.

2. Six percent convertible bonds, which, if converted, would reduce after-tax interest expense by \$500, thus increasing the numerator of EPS, and would add 1,500 incremental common shares to the denominator of EPS. Hence, the income per incremental share effect would be $\$500 \div 1,500$ shares $= \$.33$.

3. Eight percent convertible bonds, which, if converted, would reduce after-tax interest expense by \$750, thus increasing the numerator of EPS, and would add 1,000 incremental common shares to the denominator of EPS. Hence, the income per incremental share effect would be $\$750 \div 1,000$ shares $= \$.75$.

These three securities would be considered for entry into Wixom's primary EPS calculations on the basis of their income per incremental share effects, from the smallest income per incremental share effect (the stock options' effect of \$0) to the largest income per incremental share effect (the 8 percent convertible bonds' effect of \$.75). As each security is considered for inclusion in the EPS calculations, its income per incremental share effect would be compared with the most recently calculated EPS and the security would be included in the EPS calculations only if its income per incremental share effect is lower than the previous EPS figure, that is, if the security is dilutive.

REPORTING EPS AND MAKING RELATED DISCLOSURES

Earlier we discussed the capital structures of corporations as being either simple or complex for purposes of calculating EPS. A corporation with a simple capital structure must present only EPS based on the weighted average number of common shares *outstanding* during the period, both for income before extraordinary items and for net income. This is called a **single presentation** of EPS and is often expressed as "earnings per common share" on the face of the income statement, as in Exhibit 24–1. A corporation with a complex capital structure (aggregate dilution of 3 percent or more) is required to make a **dual presentation** of primary and fully diluted EPS, both for income before extraordinary items and for net income, as in Exhibit 24–2.

EXHIBIT 24–1	PARTIAL INCOME STATEMENT AND PRESENTATION OF EPS FOR A SIMPLE CAPITAL STRUCTURE

	1987	1986
Income before extraordinary item	$18,300,000	$15,300,000
Extraordinary item—gain on sale of property less applicable income taxes	1,800,000	
Net income	$20,100,000	$15,300,000
Earnings per common share:*		
Income before extraordinary item	$5.54	$4.64
Extraordinary item	.56	
Net income	$6.10	$4.64

* Assuming that the weighted average number of common shares is 3.3 million.

EXHIBIT 24–2   PARTIAL INCOME STATEMENT AND PRESENTATION
OF EPS FOR A COMPLEX CAPITAL STRUCTURE

	1987	1986
Income before extraordinary item	$25,800,000	$20,600,000
Extraordinary item—gain on sale of property less applicable income taxes	1,800,000	
Net income	$27,600,000	$20,600,000
Earnings per common share and common equivalent share (primary EPS):		
Income before extraordinary item	$6,40	$5.50
Extraordinary item	.44	
Net income	$6.84	$5.50
Earnings per common share, assuming maximum dilution (fully diluted EPS):		
Income before extraordinary item	$6.22	$5.32
Extraordinary item	.42	
Net income	$6.64	$5.32

Whether a single or dual presentation is required, the per share amount of the cumulative effect of a change in accounting principle must be shown on the face of the income statement. In addition, when the disposal of a segment of the business is reported on the income statement, income from continuing operations must be reported on a per share basis. The EPS disclosure would be accompanied by a footnote describing the components of the weighted average number of common shares, the common stock equivalents and other potentially dilutive securities, and how each entered into the EPS calculations.

EPS amounts that must be reported.

Whether a single or dual presentation of EPS is required, EPS amounts for (1) income before extraordinary items, (2) net income, (3) income from continuing operations (when disposal of a segment of the business is reported), and (4) the cumulative effect of a change in accounting principle must be shown for all accounting periods for which an income statement is presented. The EPS figures for all previous periods presented, as well as those of the current period, should reflect adjustments for stock dividends and stock splits. If the results of operations for previous periods have been adjusted and restated because of a prior period adjustment or retroactive treatment of an accounting change, then the EPS figures for those previous periods also must be restated.

In addition, the following disclosures must accompany EPS figures:[12]

1. A summary explanation of the pertinent rights and privileges of the various securities outstanding.

2. A schedule or footnote explaining the bases on which both primary EPS and fully diluted EPS are calculated. Information disclosed should include:
   a) Identification of any securities regarded as common stock equivalents.
   b) Identification of securities included in the calculation of fully diluted EPS.
   c) Descriptions of all assumptions and resulting adjustments used in the derivation of the EPS figures.
   d) The number of shares issued upon conversion, exercise, or satisfaction of required conditions.

[12] *APB Opinion No. 15,* paras. 19–23. An analysis of the extent of compliance with these requirements is provided by R. E. Flaherty and B. N. Schwartz, "Earnings per Share: Compliance and Understandability," *Journal of Accounting, Auditing, and Finance,* Fall 1980, pp. 47–56.

3. Calculations and/or reconciliations, if necessary, to provide a clear understanding of how the EPS figures were derived.

4. Supplementary information about the effects of conversions after the balance sheet date but before issuance of the financial statements.

In the next section we illustrate the calculation and reporting of EPS for a corporation with a simple capital structure and for a corporation with a complex capital structure.

ILLUSTRATIONS OF CALCULATING AND REPORTING EARNINGS PER SHARE

EPS FOR A SIMPLE CAPITAL STRUCTURE

A corporation with a simple capital structure either has no dilutive securities outstanding or has outstanding dilutive securities with less than 3 percent (i.e., immaterial) aggregate dilutive effect on EPS, as calculated without considering dilutive securities.

Assume, for example, that Rex, Inc., began 1987 with 8,000 shares of common stock outstanding, acquired 2,000 of the outstanding common shares for treasury stock at the beginning of April, and reissued 1,200 of the treasury shares at the beginning of November. In addition, assume:

1. Rex had 1,000 shares of $20 par, 8 percent nonconvertible cumulative preferred stock outstanding during all of 1987.

2. At the end of 1987, Rex had stock options outstanding for 1,012 shares of common stock, with an exercise price of $20 per share. Options on 460 shares were outstanding during the entire year and options on 552 shares were issued on May 1, 1987.

3. The average common stock price for the year was $23, and the end-of-the-year market price was $24 per share. During the last three months of the year, the stock price ranged from $20.50 to $25.

4. During 1987 Rex earned $75,000 after income taxes.

The first step in calculating and reporting Rex's EPS is to determine whether Rex has a simple or complex capital structure. In order for Rex to have a simple capital structure, the aggregate dilutive effect of all outstanding dilutive securities must be less than 3 percent. The stock options are Rex's only outstanding dilutive securities because the preferred stock is nonconvertible, so we must assess the dilutive effect of the stock options as the basis for determining Rex's capital structure.

$$\text{Income applicable to common stock} = \$75,000 - \$1.60(1,000 \text{ preferred shares})^*$$
$$= \$75,000 - \$1,600$$
$$= \$73,400$$

* Because the preferred stock is cumulative, the dividends would be deducted whether they had been declared or not for the current year. If the preferred stock had *not* been cumulative, dividends would not be deducted unless declared for the current year.

$$\begin{aligned}\text{Weighted average number of common shares} &= 8,000(12/12) - 2,000(9/12) + 1,200(2/12) \\ &= 8,000 - 1,500 + 200 \\ &= 6,700 \text{ shares}\end{aligned}$$

$$\text{EPS based strictly on weighted average common shares outstanding} = \frac{\$73,400}{6,700 \text{ shares}}$$

$$= \$10.96$$

Since the common stock price during the last three months of the accounting period was above the $20 exercise price of the stock options, it is appropriate to assume exercise of the options, as prescribed by the treasury stock method.

For purposes of calculating primary EPS, the weighted average common share equivalents of the stock options would be:

	SHARES
Common share equivalents for options outstanding on 1/1/87	460
Weighted average common share equivalents for options issued 5/1/87: 552 shares × (8/12).	368
Weighted average treasury shares *assumed purchased at average market price:* [($20 × 460 shares)/$23] + [(8/12) × ($20 × 552 shares)/$23]	(720)
Net weighted average number of common share equivalents of stock options for primary EPS	108

For fully diluted EPS, however, we must assume purchase of weighted average treasury shares at the higher end-of-period market price.

	SHARES
Common share equivalents for options outstanding on 1/1/87	460
Weighted average common share equivalents for options issued 5/1/87: 552 shares × (8/12).	368
Weighted average treasury shares *assumed purchased at end-of-period market price:* [($20 × 460 shares)/$24] + [(8/12) × ($20 × 552 shares)/$24]	(690)
Net weighted average number of common share equivalents of stock options for fully diluted EPS.	138

Using the maximum net weighted average number of common shares that would be added to the EPS calculation under the treasury stock method applied to the stock options, we calculate EPS as:

$$\frac{\$73,400}{6,700 \text{ shares} + 138 \text{ shares}} = \frac{\$73,400}{6,838 \text{ shares}} = \$10.73$$

Rex, Inc., has a simple capital structure because the maximum dilution of EPS caused by the stock options is $.23 ($10.96 − $10.73), which is only 2.1 percent ($.23 ÷ $10.96) dilution. Since Rex has a simple capital structure, the dilutive effect of the stock options can be ignored, and Rex can make a single presentation of EPS at the bottom of the 1987 income statement, as follows:

Earnings per common share:
  Net income ($73,400/6,700 shares) $10.96

EPS FOR A COMPLEX CAPITAL STRUCTURE

A corporation with a complex capital structure has dilutive securities outstanding that, in the aggregate, reduce EPS by 3 percent or more as compared to EPS calculated without considering dilutive securities.

Suppose that, in addition to the data provided earlier, the following information applies to Rex, Inc.:

5. Rex had two different issues of convertible bonds outstanding at the end of fiscal year 1987:
   a) $20,000 of $1,000, 7 percent, 10-year bonds, each convertible into 50 shares of common stock. These bonds were issued at 107.4, which provided an effective yield of 6 percent. At the time the bonds were issued, the average Aa corporate bond yield was 11 percent. For tax purposes, the bond premium is amortized on a straight-line basis.
   b) $25,000 of $1,000, 8 percent, 10-year bonds, each convertible into 50 shares of common stock. These bonds were issued at 100 when the average Aa corporate bond yield was 11 percent.

6. The average income tax rate applicable to Rex, Inc., is 40 percent.

With the additional assumptions 5 and 6, Rex has a complex capital structure. In fact, the 7 percent convertible bonds alone are sufficient to cause 3 percent or more dilution of EPS. Under the if-converted method, income applicable to common stock would be increased by the add-back of after-tax interest expense of $751: [($70 × 20 bonds) − $148 premium amortization] × (1 − .4). In addition, 1,000 equivalent common shares (20 bonds × 50 shares per bond) arising from assumed conversion must be added to the denominator of the EPS ratio. Therefore, EPS after inclusion of the effect of the 7 percent convertible bonds is:

$$\frac{\$73,400 + \$751}{6,700 \text{ shares} + 1,000 \text{ shares}} = \frac{\$74,151}{7,700 \text{ shares}} = \$9.63$$

Since the dilution caused by the 7 percent convertible bonds is well in excess of 3 percent [($10.96 − $9.63) ÷ $10.96 = 12.1%], and both the stock options and the 8 percent convertible bonds also are dilutive, we can safely conclude that aggregate dilution is 3 percent or more, and therefore that Rex, Inc., has a complex capital structure. Rex is required to make a dual presentation of EPS.

The process of calculating and reporting primary and fully diluted EPS for Rex, Inc., consists of the following steps:

1. Determination of the basic income applicable to common stock. We did this earlier, when Rex was assumed to have a simple capital structure.

Net income	$75,000
Less: Cumulative preferred dividends	(1,600)
Income applicable to common stock	$73,400

2. Detailed analysis of all outstanding securities.
   a) *Common stock.* Earlier (p. 1153) we calculated the basic weighted average number of common shares to be 6,700.

b) *$20 par, 8 percent nonconvertible cumulative preferred stock.* Being nonconvertible, this security cannot be dilutive. We know that these preferred shares have a senior claim on income of $1,600 (p. 1153), which we deducted in step 1 to calculate income applicable to common stock.

c) *Stock options.* The stock options are common stock equivalents by definition and, if dilutive, must be considered when both primary and fully diluted EPS are calculated. Earlier we used the treasury stock method to determine that:

   i. Net weighted average number of common share equivalents of stock options *for primary EPS* = 108.

   ii. Net weighted average number of common share equivalents of stock options *for fully diluted EPS* = 138.

   Since the number of common shares issuable under the exercise agreement of the stock options (460 shares + 368 shares from p. 1154) is less than 20 percent of the number of common shares outstanding at the end of fiscal year 1987 (20% × 7,200 shares = 1,440 shares), the modified treasury stock method is not applicable.

d) *Convertible securities.* Rex, Inc., has two convertible securities, both of which are convertible bonds. The 7 percent bonds were issued at 107.4 to provide an effective yield of 6 percent when the average Aa corporate bond yield was 11 percent. The effective yield (6 percent) was less than two-thirds of the 11 percent average Aa corporate bond yield when the bonds were issued. These bonds are therefore common stock equivalents and, if dilutive, will be included in the calculation of both primary and fully diluted EPS.

   Rex's 8 percent convertible bonds were issued at 100 when the average Aa corporate bond yield was 11 percent. These bonds have an effective yield of 8 percent, which is greater than two-thirds of the average Aa corporate bond yield (11 percent). Hence, these bonds are other potentially dilutive securities and, if dilutive, will be considered only when we calculate fully diluted EPS.

Deciding whether each potentially dilutive security has a dilutive or an antidilutive effect on primary or fully diluted EPS requires that, as each security is considered for entry into the EPS calculations, we compare its "income per incremental common share effect" with the EPS figure that applies just before the possible entry of the security in question. If the security's income per incremental share effect is less than the previous EPS figure, then the security is dilutive and should be included in the EPS calculations. Otherwise, the security is antidilutive and is not included in the EPS calculations.

As discussed earlier, the "income per incremental common share effect" for each potentially dilutive security also is important because it is the basis for deciding the order in which dilutive securities will enter the EPS calculations. Potentially dilutive securities enter the EPS calculations beginning with the security having the smallest income per incremental share effect and proceeding to securities with increasingly larger income per incremental share effects, until an antidilutive security is encountered. In preparation for calculating Rex's primary and fully diluted EPS, we determine the income per incremental share effect for each of Rex's potentially dilutive securities as follows:

1. Stock options:

   a) For primary EPS: Exercise of the options would not change the numerator of EPS, but 108 incremental common shares would be added to the denominator. Income per incremental share is $0 ÷ 108 shares = $0.

   b) For fully diluted EPS: Exercise of the options would not change the numerator of EPS, but 138 incremental common shares would be added to the denominator. Income per incremental share is $0 ÷ 138 shares = $0.

2. Seven percent convertible bonds: If converted as of the beginning of the year, these bonds would increase the numerator of EPS by the after-tax interest expense savings of $751: [($70 × 20 bonds) − $148 premium amortization] × (1 − .4) and would add 1,000 incremental common shares to the denominator of EPS. Income per incremental share is $751 ÷ 1,000 shares = $.751.

3. Eight percent convertible bonds: If converted as of the beginning of the year, these bonds would increase the numerator of EPS by the after-tax interest savings of $1,200 [($80 × 25 bonds) × (1 − .4)] and would add 1,250 incremental common shares to the denominator of EPS. Income per incremental share is $1,200 ÷ 1,250 shares = $.96.

Given the income per incremental common share effect of each security, we can see that the securities will enter the EPS calculations in the following order: stock options, 7 percent convertible bonds, and 8 percent convertible bonds. Because the 8 percent convertible bonds are not common stock equivalents, they enter the EPS calculations only when fully diluted EPS is calculated.

a) We now must calculate primary EPS. At this point we want to include all dilutive common stock equivalents in the calculation. Our earlier analysis revealed that Rex, Inc., has two common stock equivalents—stock options and the 7 percent convertible bonds. Using the order of entry guidelines discussed above, we will begin our primary EPS calculations by first considering the stock options. For purposes of calculating primary EPS, assumed exercise of the stock options has no effect on the numerator of EPS and increases the denominator by a net 108 shares. Therefore, we have the following tentative primary EPS figure:

$$\frac{\$73,400}{6,700 \text{ shares} + 108 \text{ shares}} = \$10.78$$

Next, we consider inclusion of the 7 percent convertible bonds. These bonds are dilutive because their income per incremental common share effect is $.751, which is well below the previously calculated EPS figure of $10.78. Including the 7 percent convertible bonds in the calculations increases the numerator of EPS by the $751 after-tax interest expense savings and increases the denominator by 1,000 shares, yielding a primary EPS figure of

$$\frac{\$73,400 + \$751}{6,700 \text{ shares} + 1,000 \text{ shares} + 108 \text{ shares}} = \$9.50$$

Thus, Rex, Inc., would report primary EPS of $9.50 for the current year.

b) We are now ready to begin calculating fully diluted EPS. *We do not calculate fully diluted EPS by building on the primary EPS calculations presented above. Instead, we must return to the basic EPS figure and start over when we calculate fully diluted EPS.* We start over because the basis on which some securities are included in the fully diluted EPS calculations may differ from the basis on which they are included in the primary EPS calculations.[13] It also is possible for a security to be

---

[13] For example, as we saw in the Rex illustration, stock options are included in fully diluted EPS by using the *higher* of the end-of-the-period market price or the average market price of the stock for the period as the buy-back price, whereas the average market price for the period is used as the buy-back price in the primary EPS calculations.

dilutive for purposes of calculating primary EPS, but to be antidilutive when fully diluted EPS is calculated.[14]

In calculating fully diluted EPS, we have three potentially dilutive securities to consider: the stock options, the 7 percent convertible bonds, and the 8 percent convertible bonds. We shall include these securities in the fully diluted EPS calculations beginning with the security having the smallest income per incremental share effect (the stock options) and ending with the security having the largest income per incremental share effect (the 8 percent convertible bonds), provided that each security included in the calculations is dilutive.

For purposes of calculating fully diluted EPS, assumed exercise of the stock options has no effect on the numerator of EPS and increases the denominator by a net 138 shares. Tentatively, fully diluted EPS is

$$\frac{\$73,400}{6,700 \text{ shares} + 138 \text{ shares}} = \$10.73$$

We next consider the 7 percent convertible bonds. These bonds are dilutive because their $.751 income per share effect is below the previous EPS figure of $10.73. Including the 7 percent convertibles in the EPS calculations results in an increase in the numerator of $751 from the after-tax interest expense savings and an increase in the denominator of 1,000 shares. Consequently, fully diluted EPS is now

$$\frac{\$73,400 + \$751}{6,700 \text{ shares} + 138 \text{ shares} + 1,000 \text{ shares}} = \$9.50$$

[14] For example, assume that a company has 10,000 shares of common stock and two potentially dilutive securities outstanding: 1,000 shares of convertible preferred stock that convert to 1,250 shares of common stock and receive $10,000 annual dividends; and bonds issued at face value, which convert into 5,000 shares of common stock and result in $15,000 (net of tax savings) interest expense. Assume further that the convertible preferred stocks qualify as common stock equivalents and are dilutive when included in the primary EPS calculations. The convertible bonds are not common stock equivalents. Thus, they are not included in the primary EPS calculations, but are included in the fully diluted EPS calculations. If net income for the year is $100,000, assumed conversion of the preferred stocks would yield primary EPS as follows:

$$\frac{\$100,000 - \$10,000 + \$10,000}{10,000 \text{ common shares} + 1,250 \text{ equivalent shares}} = \$8.89$$

If, when fully diluted EPS is calculated, it is determined that the convertible bonds have a greater dilutive effect than the convertible preferred stock, then the bonds would enter the calculations first, as shown below:

$$\frac{\$100,000 \text{ net income} - \$10,000 \text{ preferred dividends} + \$15,000 \text{ after-tax interest}}{10,000 \text{ common shares} + 5,000 \text{ equivalent shares}} = \$7.00$$

If the convertible preferred stock enters the fully diluted EPS calculations, it would be necessary to add back the preferred dividends, resulting in the following:

$$\frac{\$100,000 - \$10,000 + \$15,000 + \$10,000}{10,000 \text{ common shares} + 5,000 \text{ equivalent shares} + 1,250 \text{ equivalent shares}} = \$7.08$$

Under the given assumptions, the convertible preferred stock is antidilutive in the fully diluted EPS calculations. Hence, even though the convertible preferred stock was included in the primary EPS calculations, it is not included in the fully diluted EPS calculations. Fully diluted EPS would be reported as $7.00.

The 8 percent convertible bonds, with an income per share effect of $.96, are dilutive when compared to the previous EPS figure of $9.50. Including the 8 percent convertible bonds in the calculations causes the numerator of EPS to increase by a $1,200 after-tax interest expense savings and the denominator to increase by 1,250 additional shares. After the 8 percent convertible bonds are included, the fully diluted EPS figure that would be reported by Rex in the current year is

$$\frac{\$73,400 + \$751 + \$1,200}{6,700 \text{ shares} + 138 \text{ shares} + 1,000 \text{ shares} + 1,250 \text{ shares}} = \$8.29$$

Now that the primary and fully diluted EPS for Rex, Inc., have been calculated, the next step is to make the dual presentation of the EPS figures in Rex's income statement.

4. Presentation of EPS figures on the face of the income statement. One possible dual presentation, with accompanying footnote, is as follows:

	1987
Net income	$75,000
Income per common share and common share equivalent (Note A)	
Net income	$9.50
Income per common share, assuming maximum dilution (Note A)	
Net income	$8.29

Note A. During 1987, 2,000 shares of common stock were acquired as treasury stock. Twelve hundred of those shares were subsequently reissued.

One thousand shares of $20 par, 8 percent nonconvertible cumulative preferred stock were outstanding throughout 1987.

Options are outstanding for 1,012 shares of common stock at an option price of $20. Options on 460 shares were outstanding during all of 1987 and options on 552 shares were granted on May 1, 1987. The $1,000, 7 percent convertible bonds are each convertible into 50 shares of common stock. The $1,000, 8 percent convertible bonds are each convertible into 50 shares of common stock. For EPS purposes, the 7 percent bonds are common stock equivalents and the 8 percent bonds are other potentially dilutive securities.

Income per common share and common share equivalent was calculated by dividing income applicable to common stock plus net interest expense savings from hypothetical conversion of the 7 percent bonds by the weighted average number of shares of common stock and common stock equivalents outstanding during 1987. The weighted average number of common shares was 6,700 shares. The number of common shares was increased by the shares issuable upon the assumed exercise of the stock options (828 shares), less the number of shares assumed to have been purchased (720 shares) with the exercise proceeds. These purchases were assumed to have been made at the average market price of the common stock for 1987. The number of common share equivalents was further increased by the 1,000 shares issuable upon the hypothetical beginning-of-the-year conversion of the 7 percent bonds.

Income per common share, assuming maximum dilution, was determined by assuming that the 8 percent convertible bonds were converted at the beginning of 1987 and assuming that the proceeds from exercise of the stock options were used to purchase common shares at the year-end market price. The hypothetical conversion of the bonds resulted in an increase in income applicable to common stock of $1,200, which would be the after-tax interest expense savings from conversion of the bonds. The hypothetical bond conversion also yielded an additional 1,250 shares of common stock. The assumption that the proceeds from assumed exercise of the stock options were used to purchase shares of common stock at the year-end market price resulted in the addition of 30 equivalent shares of common stock, as compared to the number of equivalent shares used in the primary EPS calculation.

EXHIBIT 24–3 SUMMARY OF CALCULATING EPS

Collect the necessary data for EPS calculations, including:
- □ Income before extraordinary items.
- □ Extraordinary items.
- □ Income from continuing operations.
- □ Cumulative effect of changes in accounting principles.
- □ Income tax expense.
- □ Market prices of common stock.
- □ Data on various securities outstanding.
- □ Relevant average Aa corporate bond yields.

Calculate income applicable to common stock, after adjusting for senior claims, if any, on income.
Calculate weighted average number of common shares outstanding.

Simple capital structure (single presentation of EPS)

Complex capital structure (dual presentation of EPS)

$$\frac{\text{Basic}}{\text{EPS}} = \frac{\text{Income applicable to common stock}}{\text{Weighted average number of shares of common stock outstanding during period}}$$

PRIMARY EPS

(assume replacement of all dilutive common stock equivalents (CSE) with shares of common stock)*

1. *Stock options, warrants, and equivalents* are always CSE. If dilutive, use the *treasury stock method* (and average market price) for assumed conversion.
2. *Contingently issuable shares of common stock* are CSE if based on passage of time or on conditions currently being met.
3. *Convertible securities* are CSE if effective yield is less than ⅔ of average Aa corporate bond yield. If dilutive, include in EPS calculation using the *if-converted method*.

FULLY DILUTED EPS

(assume replacement of both dilutive common stock equivalents (CSE) and other potentially dilutive securities with shares of common stock)*

1. *Stock options, warrants, and equivalents.* If dilutive, use the *treasury stock method* (and higher of average market price or period-end market price) for assumed conversion.
2. *Contingently issuable shares of common stock.* If dilutive, include in EPS calculation.
3. *Convertible securities.* If dilutive, include in EPS calculation using the *if-converted method*.

$$\frac{\text{Primary}}{\text{EPS}} = \frac{\text{Income applicable to common stock adjusted for after-tax interest expense on convertible bonds and for dividends on convertible preferred stock, when those securities are CSE}}{\text{Weighted average number of shares of common stock outstanding and common stock equivalents}}$$

$$\frac{\text{Fully diluted}}{\text{EPS}} = \frac{\text{Income applicable to common stock adjusted for after-tax interest expense on dilutive convertible bonds and for dividends on dilutive convertible preferred stock}}{\text{Weighted average number of shares of common stock outstanding, assuming maximum dilution from CSE and other potentially dilutive securities}}$$

3 PERCENT TEST

When fully diluted EPS is not at least 3 percent less than basic EPS, a dual presentation is not required and only EPS based on the weighted average number of common shares outstanding is reported.

* Multiple potentially dilutive securities enter the EPS calculations beginning with the smallest income per incremental share effect security and proceeding to the next largest income per incremental share effect security, until an antidilutive security is encountered.

SUMMARY OF CALCULATING EPS

Exhibit 24–3 summarizes the process of calculating EPS. As you have seen, while the concept of EPS is simple, its calculation under GAAP can be complex. You should become very familiar with Exhibit 24–3 and use it as a format for organizing your solutions to the exercises and problems at the end of the chapter.

SUMMARY OF IMPORTANT TOPICS AND CONCEPT APPLICATIONS

1. Earnings per share (EPS) on outstanding common stock probably is the most often mentioned and reported measure of a company's performance. EPS must be disclosed in the income statement.

2. When determining income applicable to common stock, total income must be reduced by income applicable to senior securities, including cumulative preferred dividends for the current period, even when those dividends have not been paid or declared.

3. The weighted average number of common shares outstanding during the period is the basis for calculating EPS. Shares issued or retired during the period are weighted by the fraction of the period during which they were outstanding. Stock dividends and stock splits are assumed to have occurred at the beginning of the year for the purpose of calculating the weighted average number of common shares outstanding.

4. When a corporation has income, dilutive securities reduce the earnings per share of common stock. Including dilutive securities in EPS calculations provides **relevant** and **timely** information about the effect that exercise or conversion of the securities could have on EPS.

5. Antidilutive securities should not be included in EPS calculations.

6. A **common stock equivalent** is a security that, because of its terms or the circumstances under which it was issued, is equivalent in substance to common stock.

7. **Primary EPS** is calculated by assuming that all dilutive common stock equivalents are replaced with shares of common stock. **Fully diluted EPS** is calculated by assuming that both dilutive common stock equivalents and other potentially dilutive securities are replaced with shares of common stock.

8. A corporation has a **simple capital structure** if during the accounting period it had no dilutive securities outstanding or the aggregate dilutive effect of outstanding dilutive securities on EPS was 3 percent or less, as compared to EPS based strictly on the weighted average number of common shares actually outstanding during the period. A corporation with a simple capital structure is required to make only a **single presentation** of EPS.

9. A corporation has a **complex capital structure** if it has issued, in addition to common stock, securities that could have an aggregate dilutive effect on EPS of 3 percent or more. A corporation with a complex capital structure is required to make a **dual presentation** of primary and fully diluted EPS.

10. The **treasury stock method** is the procedure used to include the dilutive effect of stock options, stock purchase rights, warrants, and their equivalents in EPS calculations.

11. A convertible security that, at the time of issuance, has terms that make it substantially equivalent to common stock should be regarded as a common stock equivalent. A convertible security is substantially equivalent to a common stock if its **effective yield** at the time of issuance is less than two-thirds of the then-current Aa corporate bond yield.

12. The **if-converted method** is used to include the dilutive effect of convertible securities in EPS calculations.

13. If several convertible securities are being considered for inclusion in the EPS calculations at the same time: (1) the income per incremental common share effect for each security is calculated; (2) the securities are ranked from the smallest effect to the largest effect; (3) beginning with the security having the smallest effect, the securities are added to the EPS calculation and EPS is recalculated after each security is added, until a security is encountered that is antidilutive.

QUESTIONS

Q24-1. What does the term "senior securities" refer to in the context of corporate capital structure?

Q24-2. Why are senior claims on income important in EPS calculations?

Q24-3. For purposes of calculating income applicable to common stock, how do dividends on cumulative preferred stock differ from dividends on noncumulative preferred stock?

Q24-4. What is the reasoning behind calculation of a weighted average number of common shares for an accounting period?

Q24-5. For purposes of EPS calculations, how should the acquisition and reissue of treasury stock be treated?

Q24-6. How do annual interest expense and dividends on preferred stock affect income applicable to common stock?

Q24-7. Describe the nature of a stock split or stock dividend with respect to the total ownership of a corporation.

Q24-8. Explain how a stock split or stock dividend should be handled in calculating the weighted average number of common shares.

Q24-9. Is a stock dividend or stock split that occurs after the end of the accounting period relevant to EPS calculations for the accounting period? If so, what treatment should they be given?

Q24-10. What does the term "dilution" mean in the context of EPS calculations?

Q24-11. What does the term "antidilution" mean in the context of EPS calculations?

Q24-12. What are the characteristics of a common stock equivalent?

Q24-13. Distinguish between common stock equivalents and other potentially dilutive securities.

Q24-14. What is the purpose of classifying a corporation's dilutive securities as either common stock equivalents or other potentially dilutive securities when making EPS calculations?

Q24-15. What is the exception to the general rule that a convertible bond or a convertible preferred stock should be classified as a common stock equivalent or other potentially dilutive security only at the time the security is issued?

Q24-16. What is the basis for determining whether a convertible security is a common stock equivalent?

Q24-17. What types of securities are always common stock equivalents? Does this mean that they always will be included in EPS calculations? Explain.

Q24-18. For purposes of calculating EPS, what does it mean to say that a corporation has a simple capital structure? A complex capital structure?

Q24-19. Is it possible for a corporation to have a simple capital structure in one accounting period and a complex capital structure in the next? Explain.

Q24-20. Distinguish between a single presentation and a dual presentation of EPS.

Q24-21. Distinguish between primary and fully diluted EPS.

Q24-22. What is the difference between the treasury stock method applied in calculating primary EPS and the treasury stock method applied in calculating fully diluted EPS?

Q24-23. Explain the 20 percent test as applied in the treasury stock method.

Q24-24. What role does the if-converted method play in EPS calculations?

Q24-25. Are premiums or discounts on outstanding convertible bonds relevant to EPS calculations? If so, how?

Q24-26. Explain what is meant by the ''income per additional common share effect'' as it applies to convertible securities in EPS calculations.

Q24-27. What disclosures must accompany EPS figures reported in the income statement?

CASES

C24-1. EPS CONCEPTS AND PROCEDURES *APB Opinion No. 15* discusses the concept of common stock equivalents and prescribes the reporting of primary EPS and fully diluted EPS.

REQUIRED

1. Discuss the reasons why securities other than common stock may be considered common stock equivalents for the calculation of primary EPS.

2. Define the term ''senior security'' and explain how senior securities that are not convertible enter into the determination of EPS.

3. Explain how convertible securities are determined to be common stock equivalents and how those convertible senior securities that are not considered to be common stock equivalents enter into the determination of EPS.

4. Explain the treasury stock method as it applies to options and warrants in the calculation of primary EPS.

(AICPA, adapted)

C24-2. EPS CONCEPTS AND PROCEDURES Earnings per share is the most widely featured single financial statistic issued in regard to modern corporations. Daily published quotations of stock prices have been expanded to include a ''times earnings'' figure (based on EPS) for many securities. Often the focus of analysts' discussions will be on the EPS of the corporations that receive their attention.

REQUIRED

1. Explain how dividends or dividend requirements on any class of preferred stock that may be outstanding affect the calculation of EPS.

2. One of the technical procedures applicable in EPS calculations is the treasury stock method.
a) Briefly describe the circumstances under which it might be appropriate to apply the treasury stock method.
b) There is a limit to the extent to which the treasury stock method is applicable. Indicate what this limit is and give a succinct indication of the procedures that should be followed beyond the treasury stock method limits.

3. Under some circumstances convertible debentures may be considered common stock equivalents while under other circumstances they are not.
a) When is it proper to treat convertible debentures as common stock equivalents? What is the effect on calculations of EPS in such cases?
b) In case convertible debentures are not considered to be common stock equivalents, explain how they are handled for purposes of EPS calculations.

(AICPA, adapted)

C24-3. COMMON STOCK EQUIVALENTS; CAPITAL STRUCTURE The EPS data required of a company depend on the nature of its capital structure. A corporation may have a simple capital structure and calculate only earnings per common share, or it may have a complex capital structure and have to calculate primary EPS and fully diluted EPS.

REQUIRED

1. Define the term ''common stock equivalent'' and describe what securities would be considered common stock equivalents in the calculation of EPS.

2. Define the term ''complex capital structure'' and discuss the disclosures (both financial and explanatory) necessary for EPS when a corporation has a complex capital structure.

(AICPA, adapted)

C24-4. PRIMARY AND FULLY DILUTED EPS Publicly held corporations are required to present EPS data on the face of the income statement.

REQUIRED

Compare and contrast primary EPS with fully diluted EPS for each of the following:

1. The effect of common stock equivalents on the number of shares used in the calculation of EPS.

2. The effect of convertible securities that are *not* common stock equivalents on the number of shares used in the calculation of EPS.

3. The effect of antidilutive securities.

(AICPA, adapted)

EXERCISES

E24-1. WEIGHTED AVERAGE NUMBER OF SHARES Warton Corporation had 900,000 common shares outstanding on January 1, issued 600,000 shares on May 1, and had income applicable to common stock of $2.6 million for the year ended December 31, 1987.

REQUIRED

Calculate Warton's EPS for 1987.

E24-2. WEIGHTED AVERAGE NUMBER OF SHARES Art Company's net income for the year ended December 31, 1987, was $10,000. During 1987 Art declared and paid $1,000 cash dividends on preferred stock and $1,750 cash dividends on common stock.

On December 31, 1987, 12,000 shares of common stock were issued and outstanding, 10,000 of which had been issued and outstanding throughout the year and 2,000 of which were issued on July 1, 1987. There were *no* other common stock transactions during the year, and there is *no* potential dilution of earnings per share.

REQUIRED

Calculate Art Company's 1987 EPS, rounded to the nearest penny.

(AICPA, adapted)

E24-3. WEIGHTED AVERAGE NUMBER OF SHARES; INCOME APPLICABLE TO COMMON STOCK On December 31, 1986, the Marlin Company had 50,000 shares of common stock issued and outstanding. On April 1, 1987, an additional 10,000 shares of common stock were issued. Marlin's net income for the year ended December 31, 1987, was $172,500. During 1987 Marlin declared and paid $100,000 cash dividends on its nonconvertible preferred stock.

REQUIRED

What are Marlin's earnings per common share for the year ended December 31, 1987?

(AICPA, adapted)

E24-4. WEIGHTED AVERAGE NUMBER OF SHARES; EXTRAORDINARY ITEM   Anderson Company had 100,000 shares of common stock outstanding on December 31, 1986. During 1987, Anderson issued 20,000 new shares on April 1 and retired 10,000 shares on September 1. Anderson's after-tax income for 1987 was $275,000 before an extraordinary loss of $50,000 (net of tax).

REQUIRED

Give the EPS figures that should appear at the bottom of Anderson's income statement. Provide schedules showing the calculations leading to the EPS figures.

E24-5. WEIGHTED AVERAGE NUMBER OF SHARES; CONVERTIBLE BONDS   Spray, Inc., had 5 million shares of common stock outstanding on December 31, 1986. An additional 1 million shares of common stock were issued on April 1, 1987, and 500,000 more shares were issued on July 1, 1987. On October 1, 1987, Spray issued 10,000, $1,000 face-value, 7 percent convertible bonds. Each bond is convertible into 40 shares of common stock. The bonds were *not* considered common stock equivalents at the time of their issuance and *no* bonds were converted into common stock in 1987.

REQUIRED

What is the number of shares to be used in calculating primary EPS and fully diluted EPS, respectively? Assume that the convertible bonds are dilutive.

(AICPA, adapted)

E24-6. WEIGHTED AVERAGE NUMBER OF SHARES; STOCK SPLIT   Wagner, Inc., earned $700,000 after taxes in 1987. Wagner began 1987 with 200,000 shares of common stock outstanding. On May 1, 25,000 new shares were issued and on October 31, 20,000 shares were acquired as treasury stock. On December 1, Wagner split its common stock 2 for 1.

In addition to common stock, Wagner had 50,000 shares of $100 par 8 percent cumulative nonconvertible preferred stock outstanding during all of 1987. The average Aa corporate bond yield was 13 percent during 1987.

REQUIRED

Calculate Wagner's EPS for 1987. Provide a schedule showing determination of the weighted average number of common shares used in the EPS calculation.

E24-7. PRIMARY EPS; FULLY DILUTED EPS

A) On December 31, 1986, the Back Company had 400,000 shares of common stock outstanding. On October 1, 1987, an additional 100,000 shares of common stock were issued. In addition, Back had $10 million of 8 percent convertible bonds outstanding on December 31, 1986, which were issued at face value and are convertible into 225,000 shares of common stock. The bonds were considered common stock equivalents at the time of their issuance and *no* bonds were converted into common stock in 1987. The net income for the year ended December 31, 1987, was $3.5 million and the tax rate was 50 percent.

REQUIRED

Calculate Back Company's primary EPS for the year ended December 31, 1987.

B) On December 31, 1986, the Front Company had 350,000 shares of common stock outstanding. On September 1, 1987, an additional 150,000 shares of common stock were issued. In addition, Front had $10 million of 8 percent convertible bonds outstanding on December 31, 1986, which are convertible into 200,000 shares of common stock. The bonds were *not* considered common stock equivalents at the time of their issuance and *no* bonds were converted into common stock in 1987. The net income for the year ended December 31, 1987, was $3 million and the income tax rate was 50 percent.

REQUIRED

Calculate fully diluted EPS for the Front Company for the year ended December 31, 1987.

(AICPA, adapted)

E24-8. STOCK OPTIONS AND EPS CALCULATIONS On January 1, 1987, Sage Corporation granted options to purchase 9,000 of its common shares at $7 each. The market price of common was $10.50 per share on March 31, 1987, and averaged $9 per share during the quarter then ended. There was no change in the 50,000 shares of outstanding common stock during the quarter ended March 31, 1987. Net income for the quarter was $8,268.

REQUIRED

1. What number of shares should be used in calculating primary EPS for the quarter?

2. What number of shares should be used in calculating fully diluted EPS for the quarter?

(AICPA, adapted)

E24-9. TREASURY STOCK METHOD; 20 PERCENT TEST Dixon Company earned $320,000 and had an average of 80,000 shares of common stock outstanding during the current year. In addition, throughout the entire year there were options outstanding to purchase 20,000 shares of Dixon's common stock at $15 per share. The average market price of Dixon's common stock for the year was $16. At year-end, the market price of the common stock was $20 per share, there were 90,000 common shares outstanding, and Dixon's total outstanding debt consisted of $100,000 of 10 percent short-term notes. Dixon is subject to a 40 percent tax rate.

REQUIRED

1. How many common and common equivalent shares should be used to calculate Dixon's primary EPS and fully diluted EPS for the current year?

2. Calculate Dixon's primary EPS and fully diluted EPS for the current year. Show all calculations.

E24-10. TREASURY STOCK METHOD; 20 PERCENT TEST Gilson Company had net income of $260,000 for the current year. During the year, Gilson had an average of 50,000 common shares outstanding and there were 45,000 shares outstanding at year-end. The average market price per share of Gilson common during the year was $10 and the year-end price was $11.50. In addition to common stock, Gilson had stock options outstanding throughout the year to purchase 12,000 common shares at $9 per share. Gilson's total debt at year-end consisted of $5,000 of 5 percent notes. The tax rate applicable to Gilson is 40 percent. Recently, when funds have been available for investment, Gilson has been purchasing 7 percent U.S. government securities.

REQUIRED

Calculate Gilson's primary and fully diluted EPS for the current year. Show your calculations.

E24-11. CONTINGENTLY ISSUABLE COMMON SHARES In 1986, Jacobs Company purchased Wild Company. As part of the purchase agreement, Jacobs is to give Wild stockholders 5,000 additional shares of Wild common stock if Wild's income after taxes is at least $100,000 in 1989. In 1987, Wild earned $103,000 and had an average of 15,000 common shares outstanding. Wild also had $4,000 of 6 percent bonds outstanding throughout 1987. These bonds are convertible into 2,000 shares of common stock and were issued to yield 6 percent at a time when the average Aa corporate bond yield was 10 percent. Wild is subject to a 35 percent tax rate.

REQUIRED

Calculate primary EPS and fully diluted EPS for Wild Company for 1987. Show your calculations.

E24-12. CONTINGENTLY ISSUABLE COMMON SHARES During the current year, Mio, Inc., earned $125,000. An average of 12,000 shares of Mio's common stock were outstanding during the year and 10,000 shares were outstanding at year-end. The average price of Mio common stock for the year was $5 per share, and the year-end price was $6. Throughout the year, there were stock options outstanding to purchase 1,000 shares of Mio common stock for $4.50 per share.

In an effort to stimulate management, Mio's board of directors established a contingent issuance agreement stating that management would receive 800 shares of common stock if Mio's annual after-tax income next year is 5 percent more than was earned in the current year.

REQUIRED

Calculate the primary EPS and fully diluted EPS for Mio, Inc., for the current year. Show your calculations. Would both primary EPS and fully diluted EPS be reported for the current year?

E24-13. CONVERTIBLE SECURITIES AND EPS CALCULATIONS   Information concerning the capital structure of the Wetrock Corporation is as follows:

	12/31/86	12/31/87
Common stock	90,000 shares	90,000 shares
Convertible preferred stock	10,000 shares	10,000 shares
8% convertible bonds......................	$1,000,000	$1,000,000

During 1987 Wetrock paid dividends of $1.00 per share on its common stock and $2.40 per share on its preferred stock. The preferred stock is convertible into 20,000 shares of common stock, but is *not* considered a common stock equivalent. The 8 percent convertible bonds are convertible into 30,000 shares of common stock and are considered common stock equivalents. The net income for the year ended December 31, 1987, was $285,000. The income tax rate was 50 percent.

REQUIRED

Calculate the primary EPS and the fully diluted EPS for Wetrock for the year ended December 31, 1987.

(AICPA, adapted)

E24-14. IF-CONVERTED METHOD   The Mason Company is preparing EPS data for 1987. Net income for 1987 was $200,000, and there were 60,000 shares of common stock outstanding during the entire year. Mason has the following two convertible securities outstanding:

10% convertible bonds (each $1,000 bond is convertible into 25 shares
    of common stock)... $100,000
4% convertible $100 par value preferred stock (each share is
    convertible into two shares of common stock)...................... $ 50,000

Both convertible securities were issued at face value in 1984. At the time of issuance, the convertible bonds met the yield test for common stock equivalency, but the preferred stock did not. There were no conversions during 1987, and Mason's income tax rate is 40 percent. The preferred stock is cumulative and the dividends are paid quarterly (1 percent per quarter).

REQUIRED

1. Calculate Mason Company's primary and fully diluted EPS for 1987.

2. Recalculate Mason Company's primary and fully diluted EPS for 1987, assuming instead that the preferred stock pays an 8 percent dividend (2 percent per quarter).

E24-15. IF-CONVERTED METHOD WHEN ACTUAL CONVERSIONS OCCUR   Assume the same facts as are given in Exercise 24-14 (exclusive of requirement 2).

REQUIRED

1. Calculate primary and fully diluted EPS for Mason Company, assuming that $20,000 par value of the preferred stock actually was converted into common stock on October 1, 1987.

2. Ignoring the conversion assumption made in part 1, calculate primary and fully diluted EPS for Mason Company, assuming instead that 40 percent of the convertible bonds were converted to common stock on April 1, 1987.

3. What is the impact on EPS calculations of actual conversions during the year? Are EPS figures any different than if no conversions had occurred?

E24-16. IF-CONVERTED METHOD WITH BOND DISCOUNT   Grey Company has 10,000 shares of common stock and $30,000 of $1,000, 8 percent, 20-year convertible bonds outstanding. Each bond is convertible into 100 shares of common stock. The bonds were issued at 98 in 1980, with an effective yield such that they qualify as common stock equivalents. The bond discount is being amortized by the straight-line method. Ignoring bond interest expense, Grey earned $100,000 before taxes in 1987 and is subject to a 40 percent income tax rate.

REQUIRED

1. What is the rule for determining whether the Grey Company bonds are common stock equivalents?

2. Assume that the bonds are dilutive.
a) Determine earnings applicable to common stock for purposes of calculating primary EPS for 1987.
b) Determine the weighted average number of common shares and common equivalent shares to be used in calculating primary EPS for 1987.

E24-17. ORDER OF ENTRY INTO EPS CALCULATIONS   Larson, Inc., had income after taxes of $500,000 for the current year. An average of 125,000 shares of Larson's common stock were outstanding for the entire year, and 130,000 shares were outstanding at year-end. In addition, options were outstanding throughout the year to buy 12,000 shares of Larson common stock at $7.50 per share. During the year, Larson's common stock had an average market price of $9 per share. The stock was selling for $10 per share at year-end. Larson is subject to a 25 percent tax rate.

Larson had the following convertible securities outstanding throughout the current year:
a) 6% cumulative convertible preferred stock. Each $10 par value share is convertible into two common shares. A total of $100,000 par value is outstanding. This security did not qualify as a common stock equivalent at the time of issuance.
b) 8%, 10-year, $1,000 par convertible bonds that were issued at 105. Total par value outstanding is $100,000. Each bond converts into 90 shares of common stock. At the time they were issued, the bonds qualified as common stock equivalents.
c) 13%, 5-year, $1,000 par convertible bonds that were issued at 97. Total par value outstanding is $30,000. Each bond converts into 25 shares of common stock. At the time they were issued, the bonds did not qualify as common stock equivalents.
d) 7%, 8-year, $1,000 par convertible bonds that were issued at 95. Total par value outstanding is $60,000. Each bond converts into 20 shares of common stock. At the time they were issued, the bonds qualified as common stock equivalents.
Any bond premium or discount is amortized on a straight-line basis.

REQUIRED

1. Determine the income per incremental common share for each of Larson's convertible securities. Order the securities from lowest per share effect to highest per share effect. Show your calculations.

2. Calculate Larson's primary EPS and fully diluted EPS for the current year. Show your calculations.

PROBLEMS

P24-1. WEIGHTED AVERAGE NUMBER OF COMMON SHARES   Brown Company had the following account titles on its December 31, 1987, trial balance:

6% cumulative convertible preferred stock, $100 par value

Contributed capital in excess of par, preferred stock

Common stock, $1 stated value

Contributed capital in excess of stated value, common stock

Retained earnings

The following additional information about the Brown Company is available for the year ended December 31, 1987:

a) There were 2 million shares of preferred stock authorized, of which 1 million were outstanding. All 1 million shares outstanding were issued on January 2, 1984, for $120 a share. The average Aa corporate bond yield was 8.5 percent on January 2, 1984, and was 10 percent on December 31, 1987. The preferred stock is convertible into common stock on a one-for-one basis until December 31, 1993; then the preferred stock ceases to be convertible and is callable at par value by the company. No preferred stock has been converted into common stock, and there were no dividends in arrears on December 31, 1987.

b) The common stock has been issued at amounts above stated value per share since incorporation in 1969. Of the 5 million shares authorized, 3.5 million shares were outstanding on January 1, 1987. The market price of the outstanding common stock has increased slowly but consistently since 1982.

c) The company has an employee stock option plan whereby certain key employees and officers may purchase shares of common stock at 100 percent of the market price at the date of the option grant. All options are exercisable in installments of one-third each year, commencing one year after the date of the grant, and expire four years after the grant date if they have not been exercised by that date. On January 1, 1987, options for 70,000 shares were outstanding at prices ranging from $47 to $83 a share. Options for 20,000 shares were exercised at $47 to $79 a share during 1987. No options expired during 1987 and additional options for 15,000 shares were granted at $86 a share during the year. The 65,000 options outstanding on December 31, 1987, were exercisable at $54 to $86 a share; of these options, 30,000 were exercisable at that date at prices ranging from $54 to $79 a share.

d) The company also has an employee stock purchase plan whereby the company pays one-half and the employee pays one-half of the market price of the stock at the date of the subscription. During 1987, employees subscribed to 60,000 shares at an average price of $87 a share. All 60,000 shares were paid for and issued late in September 1987.

e) On December 31, 1987, 355,000 shares of common stock were set aside for the granting of future stock options and for future purchases under the employee stock purchase plan. The only changes in the stockholders' equity for 1987 were those described above, 1987 net income, and cash dividends paid.

REQUIRED

1. Prepare the stockholders' equity section of the balance sheet of Brown Company as of December 31, 1987; where appropriate, substitute *x*'s for unknown dollar amounts. Use good form and provide full disclosure. Write appropriate footnotes as they should appear in the published financial statements.

2. Explain how the amount of the denominator should be determined to calculate *primary* EPS for presentation in the financial statements. Be specific as to the handling of each item. If additional information is needed to determine whether an item should be included or excluded or the extent to which an item should be included, identify the information needed and how the item would be handled if the information were known. Assume Brown Company had substantial net income for the year ended December 31, 1987.

(AICPA, adapted)

P24-2. COMMON STOCK EQUIVALENTS; WEIGHTED AVERAGE NUMBER OF SHARES   The following schedule sets forth the short-term debt, long-term debt, and stockholders' equity of Hayes Company as of December 31, 1987. The president of Hayes has requested that you assist the controller in preparing figures for earnings per share calculations.

Short-term debt
Notes payable—banks .... $ 4,000,000
Current portion of long-term debt 10,000,000
Total short-term debt .... $ 14,000.000

Long-term debt
    4% convertible debentures due 4/15/2000 .... $ 30,000,000
    Other long-term debt less current portions   20,000,000
        Total long-term debt .... $ 50,000,000
Stockholders' equity
    $4 cumulative convertible preferred stock, par value $20 per
        share: authorized, 2,000,000 shares; issued and outstanding,
        1,200,000 shares; liquidation preference, $30 per share,
        aggregating $36,000,000 .... $ 24,000,000
    Common stock, par value $1 per share: authorized, 20,000,000
        shares; issued, 7,500,000 shares, including 600,000 shares
        held in treasury   7,500,000
    Contributed capital in excess of par   4,200,000
    Retained earnings 76,500,000
        Total $112,200,000
        Less: Cost of 600,000 shares of common stock held in
          treasury (acquired prior to 1987).....................   (900,000)
            Total stockholders' equity $111,300,000
            Total long-term debt and stockholders' equity $161,300,000

a) The other long-term debt and the related amounts due within one year are amounts due on unsecured promissory notes that require payments each year to maturity. The effective interest rates on these borrowings range from 6 percent to 7 percent. At the time that this money was borrowed, the average Aa corporate bond yield was 7 percent.

b) The 4 percent convertible debentures were issued at their face value of $30 million in 1985, when the average Aa corporate bond yield was 5 percent. The debentures are due in 2015 and until then are convertible into the common stock of Hayes at the rate of 25 shares for each $1,000 debenture.

c) The $4 cumulative convertible preferred stock was issued in 1986. The stock had a market value of $75 at the time of issuance, when the average Aa corporate bond yield was 9 percent. On July 1, 1987, and on October 1, 1987, holders of the preferred stock converted 80,000 and 20,000 preferred shares, respectively, into common stock. Each share of preferred stock is convertible into 1.2 shares of common stock.

d) On April 1, 1987, Hayes acquired the assets and business of Davis Industries by the issuance of 800,000 shares of Hayes common stock.

e) On October 1, 1986, the company granted options to its officers and selected employees to purchase 100,000 shares of Hayes's common stock at a price of $33 per share. The options are not exercisable until 1989.

f) Both the average and ending market prices of Hayes common stock during 1987 were $34.

g) Dividends on the preferred stock have been paid through December 31, 1987. Dividends paid on the common stock were $.50 per share for each quarter.

h) The net income of Hayes Company for the year ended December 31, 1987, was $8.6 million. There were *no* extraordinary items. The provision for income taxes was calculated at a rate of 48 percent.

REQUIRED

1. Prepare a schedule that shows the adjusted number of shares for 1987 to calculate:
  a) Primary EPS.
  b) Fully diluted EPS.

2. Prepare a schedule that shows the adjusted net income for 1987 to calculate:
  a) Primary EPS.
  b) Fully diluted EPS.

(AICPA, adapted)

P24-3. COMMON STOCK EQUIVALENCY; WEIGHTED AVERAGE NUMBER OF SHARES; CALCULATING EPS **The** stockholders' equity section of High Company's balance sheet as of December 31, 1987, contains the following:

$1 cumulative convertible preferred stock, par value $25 a share: authorized, 1,600,000 shares; issued, 1,400,000; converted to common, 750,000; outstanding, 650,000 shares; involuntary liquidation value, $30 a share, aggregating $19,500,000	$16,250,000
Common stock, par value $.25 a share: authorized, 15,000,000 shares; issued and outstanding, 8,800,000 shares	2,200,000
Contributed capital in excess of par	32,750,000
Retained earnings	40,595,000
Total stockholders' equity	$91,795,000

a) On January 1, 1987, High Company acquired the business and assets and assumed the liabilities of Dawn Corporation. For each of Dawn Corporation's 2.4 million shares of $.25 par value common stock outstanding, the owner received one share of common stock of High Company.

b) Included in the liabilities of High Company are 5 1/2 percent convertible subordinated debentures issued at their face value of $20 million in 1986. The debentures are due in 2006 and until then are convertible into the common stock of High Company at the rate of five shares of common stock for each $100 debenture. To date none of these debentures have been converted.

c) On April 2, 1987, High Company issued 1.4 million shares of convertible preferred stock at $40 per share. Quarterly dividends to December 31, 1987, have been paid on these shares. The preferred stock is convertible into common stock at the rate of two shares of common for each share of preferred. On October 1 and November 1, 1987, 150,000 and 600,000 shares, respectively, were converted into common stock.

d) During July 1986 High Company granted options to its officers and key employees to purchase 500,000 shares of the company's common stock at a price of $20 a share. The options do not become exercisable until 1988.

e) During 1987 dividend payments were $.50 per share and the average market price of the High common stock was $25. On December 31, 1987, the closing price of the common stock was $25 a share.

f) The average Aa corporate bond yield was 7 percent throughout 1986 and 1987.

g) High Company's consolidated net income for the year ended December 31, 1987, was $9.2 million.

h) The provision for income taxes was calculated at a rate of 48 percent.

REQUIRED

1. Prepare a schedule that shows the evaluation of the common stock equivalency status of:
   a) The convertible debentures.
   b) The convertible preferred stock.
   c) The employee stock options.

2. Prepare a schedule that shows for 1987 the calculation of:
   a) The weighted average number of shares for calculating primary EPS.
   b) The weighted average number of shares for calculating fully diluted EPS.

3. Prepare a schedule that shows for 1987 the calculation to the nearest cent of:
   a) Primary EPS.
   b) Fully diluted EPS.

(AICPA, adapted)

P24-4. CALCULATING WEIGHTED AVERAGE NUMBER OF SHARES AND EPS   Marshall Corporation's capital structure is as follows:

	12/31/87	12/31/86
Outstanding shares		
Common stock	336,000	300,000
Nonconvertible preferred stock	10,000	10,000
8% convertible bonds........................	$1,000,000	$1,000,000

The following additional information is available:

a) On September 1, 1987, Marshall sold 36,000 additional shares of common stock.

b) Net income for the year ended December 31, 1987, was $750,000.

c) During 1987 Marshall paid dividends of $3 per share on its nonconvertible preferred stock.

d) The 8 percent convertible bonds are convertible into 40 shares of common stock for each $1,000 bond, and were not considered common stock equivalents at the date of issuance.

e) Unexercised stock options to purchase 30,000 shares of common stock at $22.50 per share were outstanding at the beginning and end of 1987. The average market price of Marshall's common stock was $36 per share during 1987. The market price was $33 per share on December 31, 1987.

f) Warrants to purchase 20,000 shares of common stock at $38 per share were attached to the preferred stock at the time of issuance. The warrants, which expire on December 31, 1992, were outstanding on December 31, 1987.

g) Mason's effective income tax rate was 40 percent for 1986 and 1987.

REQUIRED

1. Calculate the number of shares that should be used for the calculation of primary EPS for the year ended December 31, 1987.

2. Calculate the primary EPS for the year ended December 31, 1987.

3. Calculate the number of shares that should be used for the calculation of fully diluted EPS for the year ended December 31, 1987.

4. Calculate the fully diluted EPS for the year ended December 31, 1987.

(AICPA, adapted)

P24-5. WEIGHTED AVERAGE NUMBER OF SHARES; CALCULATING EPS   The controller of Langley Corporation has requested assistance in determining income, primary earnings per share, and fully diluted earnings per share for presentation in the company's income statement for the year ended September 30, 1987. As currently calculated, the company's net income is $400,000 for fiscal year 1986–87. The controller has indicated that the income figure might be adjusted for the following transactions, which were recorded by debits or credits directly to retained earnings (the amounts are net of applicable income taxes):

a) The sum of $375,000, applicable to a breached 1983 contract, was received as a result of a lawsuit. Before the award, legal counsel was uncertain about the outcome of the suit.

b) A gain of $300,000 was realized on the sale of a subsidiary.

c) A gain of $80,000 was realized on the reissue of treasury stock.

d) A special inventory write-off of $160,000 was made, of which $125,000 applied to goods manufactured before October 1, 1986.

Your working papers disclose the following opening balances and transactions in the company's capital stock accounts during the year:

e) Common stock (on October 1, 1986, stated value $10, authorized 300,000 shares; effective December 1, 1986, stated value $5, authorized 600,000 shares):

Balance, 10/1/86—issued and outstanding, 60,000 shares

12/1/86—60,000 shares issued in 2-for-1 stock split

12/1/86—280,000 shares (stated value $5) issued at $39 per share

f) Treasury stock, common:

3/1/87—purchased 40,000 shares at $38 per share

4/1/87—reissued 40,000 shares at $40 per share

g) On October 1, 1986, 25,000 stock purchase warrants, Series A, were issued at $6 each. Initially, each warrant was exchangeable with $60 for one common share; effective December 1, 1986, each warrant became exchangeable for two common shares at $30 per share.

h) On April 1, 1987, 20,000 stock purchase warrants, Series B, were authorized and issued at $10 each. Each warrant is exchangeable with $40 for one common share.

i) As of October 1, 1986, $1.4 million face value of 5 1/2 percent first mortgage bonds were authorized, issued, and outstanding. The bonds are due in 2002 and are not convertible. When they were issued they were priced to yield 5 percent.

j) On October 1, 1986, $2.4 million of 7 percent convertible debentures, due 2006, were authorized and issued at face value (no premium or discount). Initially each $1,000 bond was convertible at any time until maturity into 12 1/2 common shares, but effective December 1, 1986, the conversion rate became 25 shares for each bond.

The following table shows market prices for the company's securities and the average Aa corporate bond yield during 1986–87:

	PRICE OR RATE			AVERAGE FOR YEAR ENDED 9/30/87
	10/1/86	4/1/87	9/30/87	
Common stock	66	40	36 1/4	37 1/2*
First mortgage bonds	88 1/2	87	86	87
Convertible debentures	100	120	119	115
Series A warrants	6	22	19 1/2	15
Series B warrants	—	10	9	9 1/2
Current average Aa corporate bond yield....	8%	7 3/4%	7 1/2%	7 3/4%

* Adjusted for stock split.

REQUIRED

1. Prepare a schedule calculating net income as it should be presented in the company's income statement for the year ended September 30, 1987.

2. Assuming that net income after income taxes for the year was $540,000 and that there were no extraordinary items, prepare a schedule calculating *(a)* the primary EPS and *(b)* the fully diluted EPS which should be presented in the company's income statement for the year ended September 30, 1987. A supporting schedule calculating the numbers of shares to be used in these calculations should also be prepared. Because of the relative stability of the market price for its common shares, the annual average market price may be used where appropriate in your calculations. Assume an income tax rate of 48 percent.

(AICPA, adapted)

P24-6. CALCULATING EPS; QUARTERLY CALCULATIONS   The Rip M. Off Record Company had 100,000 shares of common stock outstanding on January 1, 1987. On July 1, 1987, the company acquired 5,000 of its common shares for the treasury. On April 1, 1987, the company issued $400,000 worth of convertible bonds at par. The bonds carry a 6 percent interest rate and interest is due each April 1 and October 1 until April 1, 1998, when the bonds mature. Each $1,000 bond is convertible into 30 shares of common stock.

In 1986 the company issued 4,000 shares of convertible preferred stock for $60 per share. The preferred has a par value of $50 per share and pays $3 per share in dividends. A $3 dividend was declared and paid in 1987. Each share of preferred is convertible into two shares of common stock.

In 1986 the company issued 6,000 stock options to its key executives. Each option entitles the holder to purchase one share of common stock for $10. The following price information relates to the price per share for Rip M. Off's common stock in 1987:

QUARTER	AVERAGE PRICE	END-OF-QUARTER PRICE
1	$15	$20
2	12	11
3	10	9
4	9	8

The average Aa corporate bond yield in 1986 and 1987 was 8 percent. All convertible securities and the stock options are currently exercisable. The company's tax rate is 45 percent. Rip M. Off's retained earnings on January 1, 1987, were $420,000. Retained earnings at the end of 1987 were $608,000. Assume that convertible securities are dilutive.

REQUIRED

1. Calculate primary EPS for 1987. With regard to the stock options, apply the treasury stock method on a quarter-by-quarter basis only in those quarters in which exercise price is below average market price. (See footnote 9, page 1144).

2. Calculate fully diluted EPS for 1987. With regard to the stock options, apply the treasury stock method on a quarter-by-quarter basis only in those quarters in which exercise price is below average market price. (See footnote 9, page 1144).

P24-7. WEIGHTED AVERAGE NUMBER OF SHARES; INCOME APPLICABLE TO EPS CALCULATIONS   The Drake Company had 19,000 shares of common stock outstanding on December 31, 1987. No dividends were paid on the common stock in 1987. On October 1, 1987, Drake acquired 1,000 shares of its common for use as treasury stock.

The company issued 5,000 shares of 8 percent convertible preferred stock in 1986 at the $100 par value. Each share of preferred stock is convertible into two shares of common stock. Holders of the preferred stock converted 2,000 shares into common stock on July 1, 1987. Dividends have been paid on the preferred stock at the end of each quarter.

Drake issued 20, 20-year bonds ($1,000 face) on April 1, 1987, at $1,100 per bond. Each bond is convertible into 50 shares of common stock. Interest is payable at 7 percent of face value. The bonds are common stock equivalents.

Drake issued options in 1986 to its executives to purchase 3,000 shares of common stock. Each option entitles the holder to buy one share of common at $20. None of the options have been exercised.

The average Aa corporate bond yield was 10 percent in 1986 and 1987. The average and year-end market prices per share of common stock during 1987 were $25 and $26, respectively.

Drake's fiscal year ends December 31 and its effective income tax rate for 1987 is 40 percent. January 1, 1987, retained earnings were $122,000 and December 31, 1987, retained earnings are $150,000.

REQUIRED

1. Calculate the 1987 weighted average number of shares for:
a) Primary EPS.
b) Fully diluted EPS.

2. Calculate the 1987 net income applicable to:
a) Primary EPS.
b) Fully diluted EPS.

P24-8. WEIGHTED AVERAGE NUMBER OF SHARES; INCOME APPLICABLE TO EPS CALCULATIONS   The Wilson Company had 51,000 shares of common stock outstanding on December 31, 1987, after acquiring 2,000 shares of common as treasury stock on April 1, 1987. No dividends were declared on the common stock in 1987.

Wilson issued 3,000 shares of 7 percent cumulative convertible preferred stock in 1985. The shares were issued at their par value of $50 per share. Each share of preferred is convertible into 3 shares of common stock. Holders of the preferred stock converted 2,500 shares on July 1, 1987. Dividends were paid on the preferred stock at the end of each of the first three quarters of 1987. In order to conserve cash, the company's board of directors did not declare a dividend for the fourth quarter of 1987. The average Aa corporate bond yield in 1985 was 10 percent.

On July 15, 1985, Wilson Company issued 100 convertible debentures. The bonds were dated July 15, 1985, and were sold for their face value of $1,000 per bond. The bonds have a stated interest rate of 10 percent, with interest payable each January 15 and July 15. Each bond is convertible into 15 shares of common stock. The bonds mature on July 15, 2005. None of the bonds were converted as of December 31, 1987.

On July 1, 1987, Wilson Company issued 200 convertible debentures. The bonds were dated July 1, 1987, and were sold at 110. Each bond has a face value of $1,000 and a nominal interest rate of 6.5 percent. Interest is payable each January 1 and July 1. Each bond is convertible into 30 shares of common stock. The bonds mature on July 1, 2007 and are common stock equivalents. None of the bonds have been converted.

In 1986 the company issued options for the purchase of 9,000 shares of common stock to its key executives. Each option entitles the holder to buy one share of common stock at $20. None of the options have been exercised as of December 31, 1987.

The average and ending market prices per share of common stock for 1987 were $24 and $25, respectively.

Wilson's fiscal year ends on December 31 and its effective income tax rate for 1987 was 40 percent. Retained earnings were $211,575 and $310,075 on January 1, 1987, and December 31, 1987, respectively.

REQUIRED

1. Calculate the 1987 weighted average number of shares for:
   a) Primary EPS.
   b) Fully diluted EPS.

2. Calculate the 1987 net income applicable to:
   a) Primary EPS.
   b) Fully diluted EPS.

P24-9. EPS PROCEDURES AND TREND ANALYSIS Gemini Products Corporation was formed on January 1, 1983, to manufacture and supply the National Aeronautics and Space Administration (NASA) with high-quality precision instruments to be used on the space shuttle. Because of the nature of the agreement with NASA, Gemini was assured of earning a 10 percent annual rate of return on stockholders' equity. Stockholders' equity was $100,000 on January 1, 1983, which represented 10,000 shares of common stock issued at $10 per share. Since its formation, Gemini has declared and paid a cash dividend each year equal to that year's net income (10 percent return on beginning stockholders' equity).

No common stock transactions occurred during 1983 and 1984. On July 1, 1985, Gemini issued 1,000 shares of common stock for $10,000, and at the end of 1986, the company effected a 2-for-1 stock split. On April 1, 1987, Gemini issued 1,000 shares of common stock for $5 per share (the market price of the stock declined after the stock split). Gemini also declared and distributed a 20 percent stock dividend on October 1, 1987.

Gemini's net income each year, based on the assured 10 percent rate of return, was as follows:

$$
\begin{aligned}
1983: \quad & .10 \times \$100,000 & = \$10,000 \\
1984: \quad & .10 \times \$100,000 & = 10,000 \\
1985: \quad & .10 \times \$100,000 + \tfrac{1}{2}(.10 \times \$\,10,000) = & 10,500 \\
1986: \quad & .10 \times \$110,000 & = 11,000 \\
1987: \quad & .10 \times \$110,000 + \tfrac{3}{4}(.10 \times \$\,\,5,000) = & 11,375
\end{aligned}
$$

Gemini reported the following EPS numbers for the years ending December 31, 1983 through 1987:

1983: $\dfrac{\$10,000}{10,000} = \$1.00$

1984: $\dfrac{\$10,000}{10,000} = \$1.00$

1985: $\dfrac{\$10,500}{11,000} = \$.955$
(11,000 shares outstanding, end of 1985)

1986: $\dfrac{\$11,000}{22,000} = \$.50$
$(22,000 = 11,000 \times 2)$

1987: $\dfrac{\$11,375}{27,600} = \$.4121$
$[22,000 + 1,000 + .20(22,000 + 1,000) = 27,600]$

The above EPS numbers also were reported in Gemini's 5-year comparative statements for the year ending December 31, 1987.

Gemini's president was very disturbed when she was provided with the five-year EPS data. She was concerned about the effect that the declining EPS numbers would have on investors' evaluations and assessments of the company's earnings trend. She could not understand how EPS could show a downward trend, especially since the company's profitability had not declined (a 10 percent return on stockholders' equity has been realized since the company was formed). In addition, she pointed out that the stock split and stock dividend had not caused a reduction in the company's net assets available for earnings.

REQUIRED

1. Recalculate the EPS numbers that should have been reported for each year.

2. Prepare the EPS data as they should have appeared on the 5-year comparative statements for the year ending December 31, 1987.

3. Prepare a brief response to the president's concern about the declining earnings trend and explain how the presentation in part 2 will alleviate her concern.

P24-10. EARNINGS PER SHARE; DILUTION AND ANTIDILUTION   Holtz Corporation has gathered the following information for purposes of presenting EPS data for the year ending December 31, 1987:

a) Net income for 1987 was $200,000.

b) Common shares outstanding at December 31, 1987, 60,000 shares. There were no common stock transactions during 1987.

c) Several years ago, Holtz issued at par, $200,000 in 10 percent convertible bonds. Each $1,000 bond is convertible into 20 shares of common stock.

d) At the beginning of 1987, Holtz Corporation issued for $58,000, 10 percent preferred stock with a par value of $50,000. These shares are convertible into 1,000 shares of common shares.

e) During 1985, Holtz issued options to purchase 4,000 common shares. The option price was $5 per share. The average market price of Holtz's shares was $8 per share during 1987, and the market price on December 31, 1987, was $12.50 per share. No options have been exercised since they were issued.

f) The income tax rate is 40 percent.

REQUIRED

1. Assume that the preferred stock meets the effective yield test but that the convertible bonds do not. Calculate primary and fully diluted EPS for Holtz for 1987.

2. Assume that the convertible bonds meet the effective yield test and that the preferred stock does not. Assume also that the preferred shares are convertible into 10,000 rather than 1,000 shares of common. Calculate primary and fully diluted EPS for Holtz for 1987.

P24-11. EARNINGS PER SHARE RELATIONSHIPS Figaro Corporation presented the following EPS data for the year ending December 31, 1987:

Primary EPS $7.50
Fully diluted EPS 2.25

These numbers were based on 225,000 shares of common outstanding on December 31, 1987, of which 50,000 were issued during 1987. In addition, the above amounts reflected the assumed exercise of options and convertible bonds for primary EPS and the assumed exercise of options, convertible bonds, and convertible preferred stock for fully diluted EPS.

You are conducting the audit of Figaro for the year ending December 31, 1987, and have requested verification of the EPS amounts. Figaro's accountant was fired on January 5, 1988, and in retaliation destroyed the computer diskette that contained the detailed calculations. The accountant has confessed, under oath, that although the fully diluted EPS amount is correct, the primary EPS amount was inflated in an attempt to secure personal gain.

As a result, you must rely on the following fragmented data in order to reconstruct and verify the fully diluted EPS amount and to calculate the correct primary EPS amount.

a) Options to purchase 75,000 shares of common stock at an option price of $2 were outstanding during 1987. Both the average and ending market price of Figaro's stock was $6 per share. No options were exercised during 1987.

b) Figaro's net income applicable to common stock was $680,000 for 1987.

c) The convertible bonds were issued in 1985 at par and are convertible into 100,000 shares of common stock. Annual interest expense is $208,333. No bonds were converted during the year.

d) The convertible preferred stock was issued on October 1, 1987, and is convertible into 100,000 shares of common stock. You have determined that the income per incremental common share effect of the convertible preferred stock was $1.55. No preferred stock conversions occurred during the last quarter of 1987, and preferred dividends were declared and paid near the end of the year.

e) The income tax rate is 40 percent.

REQUIRED

1. Reconstruct and verify the fully diluted EPS amount of $2.25. Indicate the date on which the additional 50,000 common shares were issued.

2. Calculate the correct primary EPS amount.

25 ACCOUNTING FOR PRICE CHANGES

"Whatever catastrophe inflation may be to the country as a whole, it shakes the very foundation of accountancy."[1] This statement expresses one of the most serious and controversial issues in accounting: How should changing prices be disclosed in financial reporting? In this chapter we discuss the nature of price changes and examine various approaches that can be used to account for different types of price changes. In addition, we examine how companies disclose the effects of changing prices as supplementary information in their financial reports.[2]

WEAKNESSES OF THE CONVENTIONAL SYSTEM IN PERIODS OF CHANGING PRICES

NATURE OF PRICE CHANGES

Inflation causes a decline in the general purchasing power of money.

Economists define **inflation** as a sustained upward movement in the average price of all goods and services or as a continued rise in the general level of prices. Notice that these definitions include, conceptually at least, *all* goods and services in the economy. During a period of inflation, prices of some goods may be rising faster than prices of other goods, and prices of some goods may even be falling. On the average, however, prices in general are rising. Because money is a medium of exchange, inflation also may be defined as a continual decrease in the general purchasing power of money—that is, a decrease in the ability of money to command goods and services in general.

Price indexes are used to measure and report price changes from period to period. A price index is a percentage relationship among the weighted average prices of a group of goods and services at various points in time and thus provides a price history for those items. Two indexes that are used in the United States to measure general price level changes are the Gross National Product Implicit Price Deflator (GNP Deflator) and the Consumer Price Index (CPI). The GNP Deflator measures changes in the prices of goods and services included in the gross national product. The CPI is somewhat narrower and measures changes in the prices of a "market basket" of goods and services purchased by urban consumers.

Exhibit 25–1 shows the CPI for selected years from 1913 through 1985. Except for

[1] Lloyd Paxton, "How a Large Oil Company Adjusted Its Accounts during Postwar Inflation behind the Iron Curtain," *Journal of Accountancy,* August 1951, pp. 190–98.

[2] "Financial Reporting and Changing Prices," *Statement of Financial Accounting Standards No. 33* (Stamford, Conn.: FASB, 1979), as amended by several subsequent *Statements.*

EXHIBIT 25–1   CONSUMER PRICE INDEX (CPI) AND GENERAL PURCHASING POWER OF THE DOLLAR, SELECTED YEARS, 1913–85

YEAR	AVERAGE ANNUAL CPI (1967 = 100)	PURCHASING POWER OF THE DOLLAR (1967 = $1.00)
1913	29.7	$3.36
1918	45.1	2.22
1923	51.1	1.96
1928	51.3	1.95
1933	38.8	2.58
1938	42.2	2.37
1943	51.8	1.93
1948	72.1	1.39
1953	80.1	1.25
1958	86.6	1.15
1963	91.7	1.09
1967	100.0	1.00
1969	109.8	.91
1971	121.3	.82
1973	133.1	.75
1975	161.2	.62
1977	181.5	.55
1979	217.4	.46
1981	272.4	.37
1982	289.1	.35
1983	298.4	.34
1984	311.1	.32
1985	322.2	.31

Source: U.S. Department of Labor, Bureau of Labor Statistics.

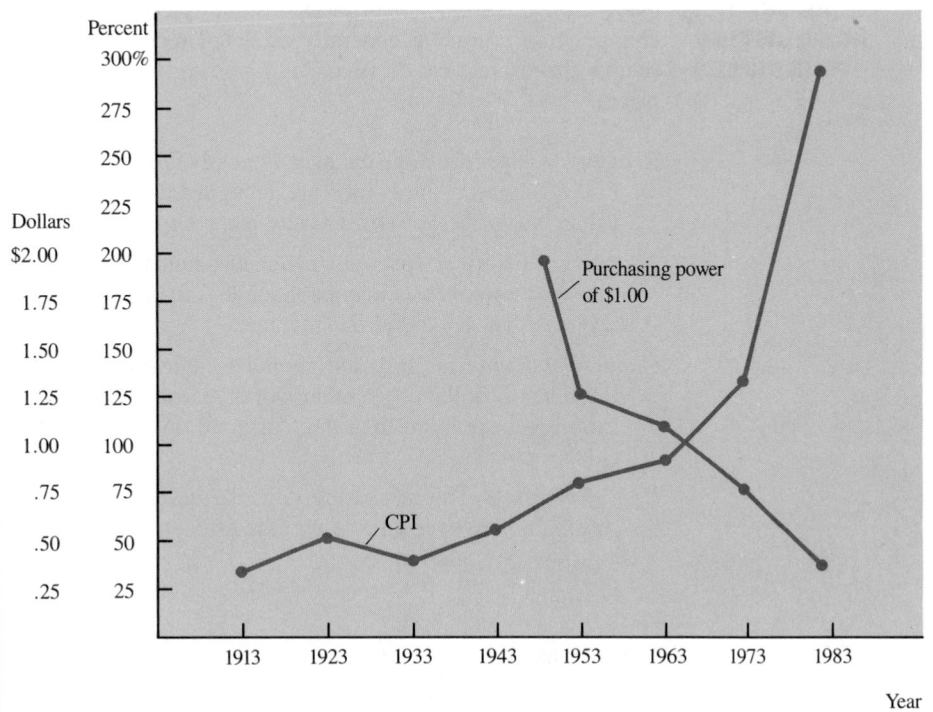

the depression years of the 1930s, the CPI has risen steadily since 1913, although the *rate* of increase was more pronounced during the 1970s. Several other aspects of Exhibit 25–1 are worth noting. First, 1967 is arbitrarily designated as the *base period* to serve as a reference point for measuring comparative price changes. Second, the base period index of 100 is read 100 percent; thus, the consumer price level in 1975 was 161.2 percent of the price level in 1967, or an increase of 61.2 percent $[(161.2 \div 100.0) - 1]$. Third, the CPI rose from 161.2 in 1975 to 322.2 in 1985, which is an increase in *percentage points* of 161.0 $(322.2 - 161.2)$ but is a *percentage increase* of 99.9 percent $[(322.2 \div 161.2) - 1]$. Thus, the general price level, as measured by the CPI, almost doubled from 1975 to 1985. Exhibit 25–1 also shows that the purchasing power of the dollar has declined dramatically during these years. For example, $1.00 of purchasing power in 1967 had only $.31 of equivalent purchasing power in 1985.

In contrast to general price level changes, another type of price change is a change in the *specific* price of a good or service. For example, owing to changes in supply and demand, the price of a barrel of oil or the price of a loaf of bread may vary from one year to the next, regardless of the change in the level of prices in general. A change in the price of a specific good or service may occur not only during a period of inflation but also during a period when prices in general are fairly stable or are falling. For example, even though the CPI changed little from 1918 to 1928, automobile prices decreased quite drastically during that period. More recently, although the CPI has increased substantially, prices of microcomputers, digital watches, and video cassette recorders have declined, whereas housing prices have increased at a much greater rate than the CPI.[3] In summary, the distinction between general and specific price changes is very important and is crucial to understanding much of the material in this chapter.

PRICE CHANGES AND GENERALLY ACCEPTED ACCOUNTING PRINCIPLES

In periods of changing prices, the conventional historical cost model that underlies GAAP can cause a company's net income and financial position to be distorted. As we shall see, even though GAAP incorporates some piecemeal procedures that recognize price changes, the following generally accepted recognition and measurement principles can reduce the usefulness of financial reporting during periods of inflation and changing prices:

Realization: Specific price changes typically are not recognized until a transaction occurs. Price decreases sometimes are recognized if an asset has experienced a decline in value, but price *increases* rarely are recognized.

Matching: Historical costs are matched against current revenue to determine earnings. These historical costs may be much less than the costs required to replace the goods or services that generated the revenue.

Capital maintenance: Invested capital is perceived as "originally invested dollars" or "number of dollars." In other words, earnings arise as long as a company can recover from revenues more than the "original dollar investment" associated with a sale of goods or services.

Unit of measure: The measuring unit, the dollar, is assumed to have stable general purchasing power over time. Thus, the effect of inflation on the dollar's general purchasing power is ignored.

---

[3] The CPI has been criticized as being an ineffective measure of inflation. See, for example, "The Confounded Price Index," *The Wall Street Journal,* May 13, 1981, p. 22.

Effects of Inflation on Financial Statements

A vivid illustration of the effects of inflation on financial reporting is the experience of the Standard Oil Company with a Hungarian subsidiary immediately after World War II.[4] Before August 1, 1946, the Hungarian monetary unit was the pengo. In 1938, five pengos could be exchanged for one U.S. dollar (i.e., the pengo was worth $.20). As we have noted, periods of inflation in a country cause its currency to lose purchasing power, and in foreign exchange markets, more and more of the country's currency units are needed to exchange for a unit of foreign currency. Hungary experienced *hyperinflation* shortly after the war. As shown in Exhibit 25–2, in slightly over one year the exchange rate of pengos for dollars increased from 635 to $1 on July 1, 1945, to 405 *septillion* to $1 on July 15, 1946.

Obviously, the stable monetary unit assumption was called into question. What were some of the accounting results under the conventional historical cost, transaction-based, stable monetary assumption system that comprises GAAP? First, the historical cost balance sheet of Standard Oil's Hungarian subsidiary at July 30, 1946, showed current assets to be 45,446 *septillion* (45,446,000,000,000,000,000,000,000,000) times as great as the company's capital stock. Second, the work-in-progress construction account was 165 times the entire plant and equipment account, but the physical construction represented a small addition to plant and equipment. Finally, the rate of return for a seven-month period was about 3.7 *nonillion* percent (3,705,300,000,000,000,000,000,000,000,000%)! As Lloyd Paxton stated, "It should be evident that any profit figures such as the above are meaningless."[5]

The Hungarian experience highlights the kinds of problems that can arise when generally accepted accounting principles are used in a hyperinflationary economic environment, especially (1) the principle of matching of historical cost in dollars against revenue and (2) the stable monetary unit assumption. Although the United States has not experienced and we hope will not experience such inflation, the Hungarian experience illustrates forcefully that the conventional system may not effectively meet financial accounting and reporting objectives in an inflationary environment.

[4] The following discussion is based on Paxton, "How a Large Oil Company Adjusted Its Accounts . . . ."

[5] To cope with inflation, the government of Hungary instituted stabilization policies, including regulations, controls, and a new currency unit. After stabilization had been put into effect, one Hungarian accountant remarked, "It will be a pleasure to work again with figures we can understand. It is like awakening from a bad dream in which one was being drowned in figures."

EXHIBIT 25–2	EXCHANGE RATE OF PENGOS TO DOLLARS, 1938–JULY 30, 1946

1938	5
July 1, 1945	635
January 1, 1946	280,000
April 1, 1946	17,000,000
July 1, 1946	45,000,000,000,000,000
July 15, 1946	405,000,000,000,000,000,000,000,000
July 30, 1946	4,600,000,000,000,000,000,000,000,000,000

Several studies have examined the impact of inflation on companies' income and financial position.[6] Although many companies have been affected adversely, the impact varies by industry and even among companies in the same industry. Factors that determine how companies are affected by price changes include:

1. The rate of inflation.
2. The type of business (e.g., product vs. service).
3. The degree of capital intensity (e.g., amounts of long-lived assets).
4. Technological improvements that offset increased input prices.
5. The extent to which selling prices can be increased in response to inflation.
6. The extent to which price changes can be anticipated or predicted.
7. Whether a company is a net debtor or net creditor. (More will be said about this factor later.)

Piecemeal Approaches to Accounting for Changing Prices

Within the conventional historical cost system, two procedures partially recognize the effects of specific price changes on income determination:

1. The LIFO method of inventory valuation.
2. Accelerated depreciation of plant and equipment.

The LIFO inventory method attempts to achieve a better matching of current cost against current revenues by using the most recent cost of inventory acquisitions in the calculation of cost of goods sold, thus eliminating "paper profits" from ending inventories. The use of accelerated depreciation is an attempt to correct for the understatement of depreciation expense in a period of rising plant and equipment prices.

Both methods are based on costs actually incurred, and both have shortcomings as methods of dealing with the effects of price changes. First, they focus only on two financial statement elements—cost of goods sold and depreciation expense. Second, liquidation of a LIFO inventory layer may cause very old costs to be matched against revenue. Third, accelerated depreciation calculations are higher than, say, straight-line figures only in the early years of an asset's useful life. Finally, neither method considers the effect of changing prices on the balance sheet.

Alleged Deficiencies of GAAP and Corrective Proposals

Although those who have an interest in financial reports agree that these reports, as prepared under GAAP, may not provide relevant information during periods of inflation, there is little agreement on what should be done to make them more useful:

1. Many people consider the conventional historical cost system to be useful, but believe that the stable monetary assumption is unrealistic. Under this view, the conventional system should be retained, but the measuring unit should be changed from units of money to *units of general purchasing power*. Stated another way, the capital maintenance concept used to measure earnings should be the maintenance of the general purchasing power equivalent of invested capital instead of maintenance of originally

[6] See, for example, *FASB Inflation Accounting: The First Year* (Cleveland: Ernst & Whinney, 1980); *Financial Reporting and Changing Prices: A Survey of How 300 Companies Complied with SFAS No. 33* (New York: Arthur Young, 1980). Also, the FASB has compiled a computer tape that contains *Statement No. 33* data for several hundred companies.

invested (nominal) dollars. This proposed system has various names—historical cost in units of general purchasing power, general price level accounting, general purchasing power accounting, historical cost/constant dollar accounting, historical cost/constant purchasing power accounting, and, somewhat cynically, pu-pu (*pu*rchasing *p*ower *u*nits) accounting.

2. Others contend that inflation is not the problem, but rather is a factor that merely magnifies weaknesses in the historical cost system. Proponents of this view would abandon historical cost and would substitute some form of current value (e.g., exit value, present value, or current cost). Alternatively, some form of current value might be used to supplement historical cost financial reports.

3. Still others feel that more useful information would result from supplementing or replacing our present historical cost system with some form of current value. In addition, the measuring unit should be changed from units of money (nominal dollars) to units of general purchasing power (constant dollars).

> To correct deficiencies in the conventional system, one may change the measuring unit, shift to current value, or both.

Thus, some people favor historical cost but would change the measuring unit from dollars to general purchasing power units. Others favor some form of current value over historical cost. Still others favor some form of current value expressed in general purchasing power units instead of nominal dollars.

In the following section we will discuss and illustrate these proposals. The discussion will be based on the concepts of capital maintenance and asset valuation that were introduced in Chapter 2.

CAPITAL MAINTENANCE AND ASSET VALUATION

As discussed in Chapter 2, any one of several capital maintenance concepts uniquely determines a company's income over long periods of time. An asset (and perhaps liability) valuation method, however, *must* be used in conjunction with a capital maintenance concept in order to determine a company's periodic net income. Several accounting systems, including the historical cost system, combine a capital maintenance concept with an asset valuation method and can be used for financial reporting purposes.

To illustrate, assume that Clark Company begins business on January 2, 1986, by selling common stock for $3,000 and investing the $3,000 in an inventory of 100 stereo headsets. The company sells 60 sets for $3,600 at the end of 1986 and 40 sets for $2,400 at the end of 1987. The cash received in 1986 is held during 1987, and earns no interest. Price changes during the two-year period are as follows:

DATE	GENERAL PRICE INDEXES	CURRENT (REPLACEMENT) COST PER SET
1/2/86	100	$30
12/31/86	110	45
12/31/87	121	45

Before income for the two-year period can be determined, it is necessary to specify a concept of capital maintenance.

CONCEPTS OF CAPITAL MAINTENANCE

A company's profitability depends on its ability to recover, through revenues, the capital invested in the asset or assets used to generate revenue. As discussed in Chapter 2, three concepts of **capital maintenance** that might be used for measuring investment recovery are:

1. Financial capital maintenance: maintaining capital in units of money (nominal dollars).

2. General purchasing power capital maintenance: maintaining capital in units of general purchasing power (constant dollars, also called constant purchasing power).

3. Physical capital maintenance: maintaining capital in terms of productive capacity (physical units).

The capital maintenance concept also can be stated as follows: Since income represents a return *on* invested capital, what portion of a company's cash flows should be considered a return *of* capital (investment recovery) and what portion should be considered a return *on* capital (income)?

Maintaining Capital in Units of Money

Under GAAP the capital maintenance concept used is maintenance of original invested (nominal) dollars. Income arises if the company can recover from revenues more dollars than it invested in the asset that generated the related revenues.

If capital is to be maintained in nominal dollars, Clark's income for the two-year period can be calculated as follows:

Cash on hand, end of 1987 ($3,600 + $2,400)	$6,000
Original investment in nominal dollars (return *of* capital)	($3,000)
Income (return *on* capital)	$3,000

Maintaining Capital in Units of General Purchasing Power

Because a greater number of dollars is required to preserve general purchasing power in periods of inflation, many people believe that income should be measured not in units of money (nominal dollars) but rather in units of general purchasing power. Thus, income arises only if revenues exceed an equivalent amount of general purchasing power invested in assets sold. Under this capital maintenance concept, Clark's income for the two-year period is calculated as follows:

Cash on hand, end of 1987	$6,000
Original investment stated in units of general purchasing power at the end of 1987: $3,000 × (121 ÷ 100)	(3,630)
Income (in units of ending 1987 general purchasing power)	$2,370

When Clark invested $3,000 in the headsets at the beginning of 1986, it invested **general purchasing power** of $3,000, since this amount could have been spent or invested in a variety of alternative goods and services. To be as well off at the end of 1987 as it was at the beginning of 1986 in general purchasing power, Clark would need to have $3,630 at the end of 1987, because the general level of prices has risen 21 percent [(121 ÷ 100) − 1] over this period. Since Clark's cash balance at the end of 1987 is $6,000, income is $2,370.

Comparing the two concepts at this point, we might say that even though Clark has 3,000 more *dollars* than before, the improvement or increase in general purchasing power at the end of 1987 is only $2,370 when we consider inflation at a rate of 21 percent over the two-year period.

Maintaining Physical Capital

A third capital maintenance concept is that of maintaining the productive capacity of the company's assets or physical units of production. This capital concept means that Clark must be able to replace the assets—100 headsets—that it has sold.[7] Since the specific price (current cost) per set is $45 at the end of 1987, income for the two-year period is:

Cash on hand, end of 1987 . . . . $6,000
Return of capital (amount needed to replace physical units):
    100 headsets × $45 per set . . . . (4,500)
Income $1,500

Stated another way, if Clark wishes to restore the headset inventory to its original level, $4,500 of the cash inflows must be considered investment recovery or return of capital, and $1,500 is income. Note that if Clark considers $3,000 to be income, as we did earlier, the remaining $3,000 in cash will purchase only 67 sets ($3,000/45), which is a *reduction* in the inventory level. Thus, its physical capital has been impaired, which may affect its ability to generate future cash flows.

In summary, a concept of capital maintenance is the only requirement for determining lifetime income or, perhaps more realistically, income for long periods of time. Because users of financial statements need timely financial information for decision making, however, we now turn to the process of determining periodic income.

MEASURING ATTRIBUTES AND CAPITAL MAINTENANCE— PERIODIC EARNINGS

If we attempt to determine Clark's 1986 income, we immediately encounter a problem. In order to prepare an income statement, we must value the inventory sold to match against revenue of $3,600. Alternatively, if we decide to use a balance-sheet approach to determine 1986 income, we must value the 40 sets on hand at the end of 1986. Either way, we must value the inventory to determine periodic income.

Measuring Attributes—Valuing Assets and Liabilities

In accounting, **valuation** means the assignment of dollar amounts to assets and liabilities. In Chapter 2 we discussed several attributes or valuation methods for assigning a dollar amount to a company's economic resources and obligations in financial reporting. We briefly review these attributes below.

HISTORICAL COST   Under the historical cost method, assets are recorded on the date of acquisition at an amount equal to the cash or cash equivalent paid to acquire them. Liabilities are recorded on the date an obligation is incurred at an amount equal to the cash or cash equivalent received. After the date the asset is acquired or the obligation incurred, the historical amount may be adjusted for amortization.

CURRENT COST   Under the current cost method, assets are reported at the end of each accounting period at the amount of cash or cash equivalent that would have to be paid if the same asset were acquired currently. Some people consider the "same asset" to be an identical asset, while others consider the term to refer to an asset with equivalent productive capacity. Liabilities are reported at the end of each accounting period at the amount of cash or cash equivalent that would be received if the same obligation were incurred currently.

CURRENT EXIT VALUE   Under current exit value, assets are reported at the end of each accounting period at the amount of cash or cash equivalent that would be received cur-

---

[7] We have assumed a two-year period for analytical purposes only. If Clark were to liquidate at the end of 1987, obviously it would not replace the assets sold. Thus a two-year period serves as an analytical device.

rently if the asset were sold in orderly liquidation, or current market selling price when an asset is sold in the ordinary course of business. Liabilities are reported at the end of each accounting period at the amount of cash or cash equivalent that would have to be paid currently in order to eliminate the liability.

EXPECTED EXIT VALUE   Under expected exit value, assets are reported at the end of each accounting period at the amount of cash or cash equivalent into which the asset is expected to be converted in the ordinary course of business, less direct costs necessary to make the conversion. This attribute, when applied to accounts receivable and inventories, typically is referred to as *net realizable value*. Liabilities are reported at the end of each accounting period at the amount of cash or cash equivalent expected to be paid to eliminate the liability in the ordinary course of business, including direct costs necessary to make the payment.

PRESENT VALUE OF EXPECTED CASH FLOWS   Under present value of expected cash flows, assets are reported at the end of each accounting period at the present value of the future cash inflows into which the asset is expected to be converted in the ordinary course of business, less the present value of cash outflows necessary to obtain the cash inflows. Liabilities are reported at the end of each accounting period at the present value of the future cash outflows expected to be necessary to eliminate the liability in the ordinary course of business.

In theory, all of the above attributes or valuation methods yield identical dollar amounts on the date that an asset is acquired or an obligation incurred. After that date, however, such factors as transaction costs, supply and demand, technological change, changes in expectations, the adding of utility through operations, or inflation may change the amount of a measured attribute for an asset or liability.

Combining Attribute Measurement with Capital Maintenance

Earlier we demonstrated how a company's lifetime income is uniquely determined by a particular capital maintenance concept. In Chapter 2, we also pointed out that periodic income is determined by measuring asset attributes *in conjunction with* a concept of capital. Alternative attributes that could be measured for assets and liabilities may be combined with any of the previously discussed capital maintenance concepts, as shown in Exhibit 25–3. Each attribute/capital maintenance combination yields a unique accounting system for periodic income measurement.

Each row in the matrix of Exhibit 25–3 is an attribute of (valuation method for) assets and liabilities, and each column is a capital maintenance concept. The intersection of each row and column in the matrix (a "cell") is an income determination system. Some of the cells in the matrix have been left blank because these attribute/capital maintenance combinations either have not received great support in the accounting literature or do not appear to be logical. Additionally, there is no reason why a system that uses a particular capital maintenance concept could not measure some assets at current cost, other assets at, say, exit value, and still other assets at, say, historical cost.

Because of space limitations, we discuss only the following income determination systems presented in Exhibit 25–3:

SYSTEM

A	Historical cost/nominal dollars (HC/N$)
B	Historical cost/constant dollars (HC/C$)
C	Current cost/nominal dollars (CC/N$)
D	Current cost/constant dollars (CC/C$)
E	Current cost/physical capacity (CC/PC)

EXHIBIT 25–3 ALTERNATIVE INCOME-DETERMINATION SYSTEMS RESULTING FROM COMBINING ASSET VALUATION METHODS (ATTRIBUTE MEASUREMENTS) AND CAPITAL MAINTENANCE CONCEPTS

	CONCEPT OF CAPITAL MAINTENANCE		
ATTRIBUTE MEASURED	ORIGINAL INVESTED (NOMINAL) DOLLARS	GENERAL PURCHASING POWER (CONSTANT DOLLARS)	PHYSICAL CAPACITY (PHYSICAL UNITS)
Historical cost:			
Number of dollars	A		
Restated in units of general purchasing power		B	
Current cost	C	D	E
Current exit value	F	G	

We assume that the present historical cost/nominal dollar system will continue to be used to accumulate financial information in the accounts. Thus, the alternative income systems are supplementary disclosures, and bookkeeping procedures will not be illustrated.

The manner in which an entity is affected by inflation depends on the type of asset or liability it holds. For example, are you more adversely affected by inflation if you hold cash as an asset or if you hold land? Regardless of your answer, you probably are aware that inflation may affect some assets differently than others. Because a company may have several types of assets and liabilities, we must examine how inflation affects these assets and liabilities before we can discuss the income determination systems identified above.

CLASSIFYING ASSETS AND LIABILITIES ON THE BASIS OF CASH CLAIMS   Assets and liabilities are classified as monetary or nonmonetary depending on the nature of cash claims. **Monetary assets** include cash and claims to fixed amounts of cash to be received in the future. Some examples of monetary assets are accounts receivable, notes receivable, interest receivable, and rent receivable. Because monetary assets represent claims to *fixed* amounts of cash, holders of monetary assets suffer a *general purchasing power loss* in periods of inflation. This loss arises because the dollars held or dollars to be received in the future have command over fewer goods and services when the general price level rises. For example, if you hold $100 in cash during a period in which the general price index increases 10 percent, you suffer a loss in general purchasing power of $10 ($100 × .10). That is, you would need $110 in cash at the end of the period in order to have the same general purchasing power that your $100 in cash had at the beginning of the period. If a company has an account receivable of $200 that is outstanding during a period in which the general price level increases 20 percent, the company suffers a loss in general purchasing power of $40 since the $200 claim to cash at the end of the period has command over fewer goods and services than it had at the beginning of the period.

> Holders of monetary assets suffer general purchasing power losses in periods of inflation.

Monetary liabilities are obligations to pay a fixed number of dollars in the future. Monetary liabilities include accounts payable, notes payable, interest payable, bonds payable, and wages payable. Because most liabilities are obligations to pay fixed amounts of money, almost all liabilities are monetary. In periods of inflation, monetary liabilities owed by a company result in *general purchasing power gains* since the dollars repaid have less general purchasing power (the debtor is able to pay the debt with ''cheaper'' dollars).[8]

> General purchasing power gains result from owing monetary liabilities in periods of inflation.

[8] Creditors usually protect themselves by charging higher rates of interest to compensate for inflation. Thus, whether a debtor has a real gain from borrowing depends on the relationship between the anticipated rate of inflation that is built into the interest rate charged and the actual rate of inflation on which the purchasing power gain is calculated.

Various terms have been used to describe these losses and gains in general purchasing power. In addition to "general purchasing power losses and gains," other terms include "general price-level losses and gains," "inflation gains and losses," "losses and gains from holding net monetary items," and simply "*pu*rchasing *p*ower *u*nit (pu-pu) gains and losses."

Nonmonetary assets include all assets not classified as monetary. Examples of nonmonetary assets are inventories, prepaid expenses (e.g., a claim to future insurance protection), plant and equipment, and land. Whereas prices of monetary assets are fixed, prices of nonmonetary assets may change during inflation. Thus, holders of nonmonetary assets *may* experience an increase in general purchasing power during periods of inflation if the asset's specific price increase is greater than the general price level increase. For example, assume that land is purchased for $1,000 at the beginning of 1987 and has a selling price of $1,500 at the end of 1987. If the general price level increases 20 percent during 1987, the amount of general purchasing power embodied in the land is $300 greater at the end of 1987 than at the beginning [$1,500 − $1,000(1.20)]. If the land has a selling price of $1,200 at the end of the year, however, general purchasing power has simply been maintained. Notice that the increase in general purchasing power is not due to the change in the general price level per se, but rather to the relationship between the change in the *specific* price of the land and the change in the *general* price level.

Nonmonetary liabilities represent obligations to deliver goods and services. As with nonmonetary assets, the specific prices of these obligations may change in periods of inflation. Nonmonetary liabilities include unearned rent (an obligation to permit an occupant to use a building for a specified time period), a warranty obligation (an obligation to repair damaged goods when the repair costs may rise as other prices rise), and an advance on a sales contract (an obligation to deliver goods or services).

Capital stock is classified as monetary or nonmonetary depending on the type and nature of the stock. For example, common stock is nonmonetary since common stockholders' claims to cash flows are not fixed in amount. On the other hand, nonparticipating preferred stock is monetary because dividends are fixed by the contract dividend rate, and preferred stock generally has a fixed liquidation amount.

To summarize, monetary assets and liabilities have prices that are fixed in terms of dollars to be received and paid. All other assets and liabilities are nonmonetary. Holding *monetary* assets during a period of inflation gives rise to losses in general purchasing power; conversely, holding monetary liabilities during a period of inflation gives rise to gains in general purchasing power. On the other hand, holding *nonmonetary* assets (liabilities) during a period of inflation may or may not give rise to general purchasing power gains and losses.[9] (In practice, classification can be difficult because under GAAP, asset and liability recognition and measurement are not always based on theory considerations alone. A comprehensive classification of assets and liabilities as monetary and nonmonetary is provided in *FASB Statement No. 33*.)

We are now ready to use the data for the Clark Company to prepare financial statements under the five alternative income determination systems introduced on page 1186. In the following sections we will discuss and illustrate these systems.

HISTORICAL COST/NOMINAL DOLLARS   The historical cost/nominal dollar system is the conventional one underlying GAAP. Historical cost/nominal dollar financial statements

---

[9] People often seek "hedges against inflation" during periods of inflation. For example, an individual may withdraw cash from a savings account and invest in the stock market. While stock prices generally keep up with inflation, there are exceptions; witness many stock price movements in the 1970s. Many investors took quite a beating on stock investments in the 1970s because the stock prices failed to keep up with the general price level. In some cases, stock prices actually decreased.

EXHIBIT 25–4   FINANCIAL STATEMENTS IN HISTORICAL COST/NOMINAL DOLLARS

Clark Company
BALANCE SHEETS

	12/31/86	12/31/87
Cash..	$3,600	$6,000
Inventory ($30 × 40 sets)	1,200	–0–
	$4,800	$6,000
Contributed capital	$3,000	$3,000
Retained earnings (1986 net income)	1,800	
(1986 net income + 1987 net income)		3,000
	$4,800	$6,000

INCOME STATEMENTS
FOR THE YEAR ENDED DECEMBER 31

	1986	1987
Revenue ($60 × 60 sets)	$3,600	
($60 × 40 sets)		$2,400
Cost of sales ($30 × 60 sets)	(1,800)	
($30 × 40 sets)		(1,200)
Net income	$1,800	$1,200

for 1986 and 1987 based on the data for Clark Company appear in Exhibit 25–4. If the 1986 income is added to the 1987 income, the total is the lifetime income calculated earlier under the units of money or nominal dollar concept of capital maintenance. Note, however, that in determining *periodic income,* both an asset valuation method (historical cost) and a capital maintenance concept (nominal dollars) were used.

HISTORICAL COST/CONSTANT DOLLARS Under the historical cost/constant dollar system— system *B* in Exhibit 25–3—the attribute measured for assets is historical cost, and the capital maintenance concept is maintenance of equivalent units of general purchasing power. Historical cost, however, is restated in units of equivalent general purchasing power (constant dollars). This system often is characterized as being identical to the historical cost/nominal dollar system except for a different measuring unit. The measuring unit is changed from units of money (nominal dollars) to units of general purchasing power (constant dollars). Because the general purchasing power of money decreases in a period of inflation, a general purchasing power unit is simply a dollar that is *dated* in terms of its purchasing power.[10] Although it is possible to use the general purchasing power of the dollar at *any* point in time as the measuring unit, we will use general purchasing power units at each current balance sheet date.[11] This approach will conform more closely to the Clark Company data and to most of the extant accounting literature.

[10] The dollar is the term in which purchasing power units are *measured* or *expressed*. Money is the form in which purchasing power units are *held*.

[11] In contrast, Exhibit 25–1 uses the annual average general purchasing power of the dollar in 1967 as the "measuring unit" for comparison purposes.

EXHIBIT 25—5 1986 FINANCIAL STATEMENTS IN HISTORICAL COST/CONSTANT DOLLARS

Clark Company
BALANCE SHEET

	12/31/86 HISTORICAL COST/ NOMINAL DOLLARS	RESTATE FACTOR	12/31/86 HISTORICAL COST/ CONSTANT DOLLARS (end-of-1986 general purchasing power units)
Cash..	$3,600		$3,600
Inventory.....................................	1,200	110/100	1,320
	$4,800		$4,920
Contributed capital............................	$3,000	110/100	$3,300
Retained earnings (1986 net income).............	1,800		1,620
	$4,800		$4,920

INCOME STATEMENT
FOR THE YEAR ENDED DECEMBER 31

	12/31/86 HISTORICAL COST/ NOMINAL DOLLARS	RESTATE FACTOR	12/31/86 HISTORICAL COST/ CONSTANT DOLLARS (end-of-1986 general purchasing power units)
Revenue.......................................	$3,600		$3,600
Cost of sales..................................	(1,800)	110/100	(1,980)
Net income	$1,800		$1,620

The historical cost/constant dollar balance sheet at the end of 1986 and the income statement for 1986 appear in Exhibit 25–5. Since the objective is to restate the historical cost financial statements to historical cost in units of ending 1986 general purchasing power, a ''restate factor'' column allows us to restate the necessary balance sheet and income statement items. The restate factor is constructed as follows:

$$\text{Restate factor} = \frac{\text{General price index, end of current year}}{\text{General price index, transaction date}}$$

The numerator is the general price index at the end of the current year, and the denominator is the general price index on the date that the transaction giving rise to the particular financial statement item occurred.

As you know, assets and liabilities generally are reported on the historical cost/nominal dollar balance sheet at exchange prices established at the transaction date. Similarly, revenues and expenses reported on the historical cost/nominal dollar income statement also are measured at exchange prices prevailing at the time of exchange. For example, revenue is measured at the exchange price prevailing at the date of the revenue transaction. Expenses are measured at the exchange price that prevailed at the date of acquisition of the asset whose service potential has expired. These exchange prices represent dollars of current general purchasing power at the date of exchange; however, they do not represent dollars of current general purchasing power at a later balance sheet date if the general price level has changed between the exchange date and the later balance sheet date. Therefore, multiplying the historical cost/nominal dollar financial statement item by the appropriate restate factor adjusts the historical cost/nominal dollar amount for the percentage increase or decrease in the general price level from the transaction date to the current balance sheet date. Thus, historical cost is preserved, but it is expressed in terms of a *constant* measuring unit—dollars of current general purchasing power.

On the balance sheet cash is a monetary item, and it already is stated in units of ending 1986 general purchasing power; that is, the cash on hand at the end of 1986 has command over any and all combinations of goods and services priced at $3,600. Inventory is a nonmonetary item and is restated by multiplying the historical cost of the ending inventory by 1.10 (110/100) because the general price level has increased 10 percent since the inventory was acquired.

Notice that the numerator of the restate factor of 110/100 is the general price index at the end of 1986, since our objective is to restate the financial statements in constant (end of 1986) dollars. The denominator is the general price index at the time the inventory was acquired. The $1,320 restated amount does *not* represent a "current value," that is, what the inventory could be sold for or what it would now cost to replace it. The restated amount is simply the historical cost, which represented an investment of general purchasing power when the inventory was acquired, restated for the 10 percent increase in the general price level. The restated amount can be interpreted as the amount needed from the sale of the inventory in order for Clark to be as well off in general purchasing power as it was when it invested in the inventory.[12]

Contributed capital is a nonmonetary item and is restated with the factor 110/100, because the general price index was 100 when the stock was issued. The restated amount of $3,300 can be interpreted as the dollar amount of net assets necessary at the end of 1986 for Clark Company to be as well off in units of general purchasing power as it was when the original $3,000 was invested. Since restated total assets equal $4,920, income for 1986 (shown in retained earnings) is $1,620 ($4,920 − $3,300). This net income amount also can be derived on the income statement.

On the income statement in Exhibit 25–5, revenue needs no restatement. The sale was made at the end of 1986; therefore, revenue already is measured in end-of-1986 general purchasing power units. If the headsets had been sold, for example, at the beginning of 1986, revenue would have been restated with the following factor:

$$\frac{\text{General price index, end of 1986}}{\text{General price index, beginning of 1986}}$$

For cost/benefit and materiality reasons, an average-for-the-year index may be used in the denominator of the restate factor if revenues are earned evenly during the year and if the general price index changes fairly evenly during the year.

Cost of goods sold is restated by the factor 110/100, because the inventory that was sold was acquired at the beginning of 1986. The restated amount of $1,980 can be interpreted as the amount that must be recovered from revenue in order for the company to maintain its general purchasing power investment in the inventory sold. The $1,980 also can be interpreted as that portion of 1986 revenues that represents a return *of* capital, when

---

[12] Notice that the historical cost/nominal dollar amount of $1,200 can be interpreted in a similar way. It can be interpreted as the amount the company would have to receive from the inventory in order to be as well off in *units of money,* or number of dollars, as it was when it invested in the inventory.

capital is measured in general purchasing power units. Had Clark Company incurred other expenses during the year, they would be restated with the appropriate restate factors. In practice, services that are acquired evenly during the year (e.g., salaries expense) are restated in the same manner as revenue.

Summarizing the 1986 income statement restatements, when the restated cost of goods sold of $1,980 is deducted from revenue of $3,600, net income is $1,620. The $1,620 income figure also represents the return *on* capital for 1986.

The 1987 historical cost/constant dollar financial statements appear in Exhibit 25–6. Cash is not restated on the balance sheet since it already is stated in units of end-of-1987 general purchasing power.[13] Since the general price index was 100 when the stock was sold and is 121 at the end of 1987, the restate factor for contributed capital is 121/100. Although retained earnings can be derived as a balancing figure, it also is the sum of the incomes for the two years. *The 1986 income of $1,620, however, was in units of end-of-1986 purchasing power and must be restated in end-of-1987 general purchasing power before it can be added meaningfully to 1987 income. The restatement of 1986 income in end-of-1987 purchasing power units is called a "roll-forward" procedure.* We will say more about this important concept later.

On the 1987 income statement, revenue needs no restatement since the sale was made at the end of 1987 and already is measured in units of end-of-1987 general purchasing power. Cost of goods sold is restated by the factor 121/100, because the general price level has risen 21 percent since the inventory was purchased. The restated cost of goods sold for 1987 may be interpreted in exactly the same manner as the 1986 restatement. The other income statement element is the general purchasing power loss on cash. The company held $3,600 in cash during the year and suffered a loss in general purchasing power of $360 on the cash held because the general price level increased 10 percent in 1987 $[(121/110) - 1]$. The general purchasing power loss also can be calculated as shown in Exhibit 25–7.

The calculation in Exhibit 25–7 starts with the beginning net monetary items (cash) and shows the increases and decreases resulting from the 1987 transactions that affected cash, which was Clark's only monetary item. The beginning cash balance is restated because Clark would need $3,960 at the end of 1987 to have the same general purchasing power as it had with cash of $3,600 at the beginning of 1987. The $2,400 inflow of cash from sales needs no restatement because it was received at the *end* of 1987. Thus, the restated ending balance of cash is the number of dollars needed at the end of 1987 to maintain the same general purchasing power as the cash had (1) at the beginning of 1987 for the beginning cash balance and (2) at the time the additional $2,400 in cash was received. At the end of 1987 Clark has only $6,000 in units of current general purchasing power; therefore a general purchasing power loss of $360 results.

If the 1986 income is rolled forward to units of end-of-1987 general purchasing power and is added to the 1987 income, which already is measured in units of end-of-1987 general purchasing power, we obtain the same two-year income total that we obtained earlier (p. 1184):

1986 income (in units of end-of-1987 general purchasing power):
$$\$1,620 \times 121/110 \dots \dots \dots \dots \dots \dots \dots \dots \dots \dots \dots \dots \dots \dots \$1,782$$
1987 income $\dots \dots \dots \dots \dots \dots \dots \dots \dots \dots \dots \dots \dots \dots \dots \quad \underline{588}$

Two-year (lifetime) income $\dots \dots \dots \dots \dots \dots \dots \dots \dots \dots \dots \underline{\underline{\$2,370}}$

---

[13] The cash held during 1987 cannot command the same amount of goods and services at the end of 1987 as it did at the beginning of 1987 because the general price level increased another 10 percent $[(121/110) - 1]$. This general loss of purchasing power will appear on the 1987 income statement.

EXHIBIT 25—6   1987 FINANCIAL STATEMENTS IN
HISTORICAL COST/CONSTANT DOLLARS

Clark Company
BALANCE SHEET

	12/31/87 HISTORICAL COST/ NOMINAL DOLLARS	RESTATE FACTOR	12/31/87 HISTORICAL COST/ CONSTANT DOLLARS (end-of-1987 general purchasing power units)
Cash	$6,000		$6,000
Contributed capital	$3,000	121/100	$3,630
Retained earnings ($1,800 + $1,200)	3,000		
[$1,620(121/110) + $588]			2,370
	$6,000		$6,000

INCOME STATEMENT
FOR THE YEAR ENDED DECEMBER 31

	12/31/87 HISTORICAL COST/ NOMINAL DOLLARS	RESTATE FACTOR	12/31/87 HISTORICAL COST/ CONSTANT DOLLARS (end-of-1987 general purchasing power units)
Revenues	$2,400		$2,400
Cost of sales	(1,200)	121/100	(1,452)
General purchasing power loss ($3,600 × .10)			(360)
Net income	$1,200		$ 588

EXHIBIT 25—7   CALCULATION OF 1987 GENERAL PURCHASING POWER LOSS

Clark Company

	HISTORICAL COST/ NOMINAL DOLLARS	RESTATE FACTOR	HISTORICAL COST/ CONSTANT DOLLARS (end-of-1987 general purchasing power units)
Beginning net monetary items:	$3,600	121/110	$3,960
Add: Inflows of monetary items:			
Revenue	2,400		2,400
Less: Outflow of monetary items	—		—
Ending net monetary items	$6,000		$6,360
General purchasing power loss			(360)
	$6,000		$6,000

"Rolling forward" earnings of prior periods is necessary for comparison.

The **"roll-forward" procedure** is necessary because income for each year must be stated in terms of the same measuring unit for addition or comparison (apples plus oranges equal fruit!). To better understand why the roll-forward procedure is important, assume that your annual salary for your first two years as a professional is $25,000 and $27,500 in year 1 and year 2, respectively. If the general price index is 10 percent higher at the end of year 2 than at the end of year 1, *your annual salary and your command over goods and services are the same each year.* Your salary for the two-year period may be measured in end-of-year-2 general purchasing power units: ($25,000 × 1.10) + $27,500 = $55,000; or in end-of-year-1 general purchasing power units: $25,000 + ($27,500 ÷ 1.10) = $50,000, since $50,000 × 1.10 = $55,000.

Other aspects of historical cost/constant dollar reporting are examined in more detail later. To sum up at this point, remember that this reporting system may be described in two equivalent ways:

1. It is a reporting system identical to the historical cost/nominal dollar system, except for a changed unit of measure. The measuring unit is general purchasing power units (constant dollars) instead of units of money (nominal dollars).

2. It is a reporting system in which the attribute measured is historical cost, restated for general price level changes, and the capital maintenance concept is maintaining general purchasing power of invested capital.

CURRENT COST/NOMINAL DOLLARS   Under the current cost/nominal dollar system represented by cell *C* in Exhibit 25–3, assets sold during an accounting period and assets on hand at the end of an accounting period are measured at current cost. The capital maintenance concept is maintenance of capital in units of money or (nominal dollars). Clark Company's balance sheets and income statements for 1986 and 1987 under this system are shown in Exhibit 25–8.

On the balance sheet as of December 31, 1986, inventory is measured at its current cost of $45 per set. Since the capital maintenance concept is original invested dollars, the difference between total assets of $5,400 and contributed capital of $3,000 represents 1986 income of $2,400. At the end of 1987, retained earnings are $3,000, which consists of 1986 income of $2,400 and 1987 income of $600. These income numbers may be added since both are stated in nominal dollars. Income can also be determined from the income statements in the lower portion of Exhibit 25–8.

Under the current cost/nominal dollar system, income arises from two activities— operating activities and holding activities. Operating activities encompass the company's sale of its primary products. Holding activities include those activities associated with the purchase of products for resale or the acquisition of inputs for use in production, such as productive plant and equipment. In both instances, holding activities encompass the timely acquisition of these products or productive assets in advance of specific price increases. Income or loss from operating activities is called **current operating income** or **loss,** and income or loss from holding activities is called **holding gain** or **loss.**

Current operating income. Clark's income from operating activities is determined by matching current cost and current revenues. Cost of goods sold is the current cost of the inventory sold at the sale date (end of 1986). This amount is $45 per headset. Thus, cost of goods sold is $2,700, and current operating income is $900.

Holding gains (losses) occur when an asset is held during a period in which its current cost increases (decreases).

Holding gains and losses. Another element of income under the current cost/nominal dollar system is the gain or loss arising from the *specific* price change of the inventory. A holding gain occurs when an asset is held during a period in which its current cost increases. A holding loss occurs if the asset's current cost decreases. Since Clark Company held 100 headsets during the period and the current cost of each set increased during

EXHIBIT 25—8 FINANCIAL STATEMENTS FOR 1986 AND 1987 IN CURRENT COST/NOMINAL DOLLARS

Clark Company

BALANCE SHEETS

	12/31/86 CURRENT COST/ NOMINAL DOLLARS	12/31/87 CURRENT COST/ NOMINAL DOLLARS
Cash...............................	$3,600	$6,000
Inventory (40 × $45)	1,800	–0–
	$5,400	$6,000
Contributed capital	$3,000	$3,000
Retained earnings		
1986 net income....................	2,400	
1986 net income + 1987 net income		3,000
	$5,400	$6,000

INCOME STATEMENTS FOR THE YEAR ENDED

	12/31/86 CURRENT COST/ NOMINAL DOLLARS	12/31/87 CURRENT COST/ NOMINAL DOLLARS
Revenues...........................	$3,600	$2,400
Cost of goods sold: 60 × $45	(2,700)	
40 × $45		(1,800)
Current operating income..............	$ 900	$ 600
Holding gain or specific price		
increase [100 × ($45 − $30)]	1,500	–0–
Net income	$2,400	$ 600

1986 by $15 ($45 − $30), it experienced a holding gain of $1,500 (100 × $15). An equivalent approach to calculation of a holding gain or loss is as follows:

Beginning inventory at *beginning-of-period* current cost (100 × $30) ...	$ 3,000
+ Purchases during period at *historical* cost	–0–
− Cost of goods sold during period at *ending* current cost (60 × $45)	(2,700)
− Ending inventory at *ending* current cost (40 × $45).................	(1,800)
= Holding loss (gain) recognized during period[14]....................	$(1,500)

Although we generally refer to the $30 cost at the beginning of the period as the historical cost, it is also the current cost, because historical cost and current cost are equal at the acquisition date. The logic of the above calculation may be strengthened if the numbers and relationships are analyzed in a T-account:

Inventory			
Beginning (at beginning current cost)	3,000	Cost of goods sold (current cost at sale date)	2,700
Purchases (at historical cost)	–0–	Ending (at ending current cost)	1,800
Holding gain recognized during period	1,500		
	4,500		4,500

[14] The holding gain recognized sometimes is called a **realizable holding gain.**

The holding gain is the number necessary to balance the debits and credits in the T-account. Stated another way, the holding gain is recognized on the beginning inventory and current purchases. The sum of the dollar amount of beginning inventory plus purchases plus the holding gain recognized must equal the sum of cost of goods sold plus the ending inventory. As we shall see later, this "back-door" approach for calculating holding gains is much easier to apply in more complicated situations, such as when assets are purchased during a period and when holding gains are calculated on depreciable assets.

On the 1987 income statement, cost of goods sold is $1,800 (40 sets times $45 per set), and current operating income is $600. Income for 1987 is $600. A holding gain did not arise in 1987 because there was no change in the current cost of the inventory during the year.

Realized and unrealized holding gains (losses). Holding gains and losses recognized during a period may be further subdivided into a realized component and an unrealized component. The holding gain *realized* during a period applies to specific price changes for assets *sold* or *used* during the period, while *unrealized* holding gains apply to assets *on hand* at the *end of the period*. More specifically, the **realized holding gain** is the difference between the *current cost* and *historical cost* of expenses reported on the income statement, whereas an **unrealized holding gain** is the difference between the *current cost* and *historical cost* of assets on hand at the balance sheet date. The relationship between recognized, realized, and unrealized holding gains is as follows:

> Realized holding gains (losses) apply to assets sold; unrealized holding gains (losses) apply to assets on hand at a balance sheet date.

HOLDING GAIN	HOW CALCULATED
Unrealized holding gain at the beginning of a period	Current cost of asset on hand less historical cost of assets on hand at beginning of period
+ Holding gain *recognized* during the period	See above.
− Holding gain *realized* during the period	Current cost of assets sold less historical cost of assets sold during period
= Unrealized holding gain at the end of a period	Current cost of assets on hand less historical cost of assets on hand at end of period

The holding gains recognized, realized, and unrealized by Clark Company are shown in Exhibit 25–9.

As Exhibit 25–9 indicates, the unrealized holding gain at the end of 1986, $600, is the difference between the historical cost and current cost of the inventory on hand. Because the inventory was sold in 1987, this holding gain was *realized* in 1987. Notice, however, that this holding gain does not appear in the 1987 current cost/nominal dollar income statement (see Exhibit 25–8) because it was part of the $1,500 holding gain *recognized* in 1986.

Theories underlying the current cost/nominal dollar system may be summarized as follows:

> Theories underlying the current cost/nominal dollar system.

1. The use of current cost permits users to evaluate a company's current operating activities as measured by current operating income and holding activities as measured by holding gains or specific price increases.

2. Users base predictions on financial reports, and current operating income may be a better predictor of future operating income and future dividend distributions than income under the conventional historical cost/nominal dollar system.

3. Under certain circumstances, holding gains may signal increased future cash flows to

EXHIBIT 25—9   SCHEDULE OF RECOGNIZED, REALIZED, AND UNREALIZED
HOLDING GAINS IN CURRENT COST/NOMINAL DOLLARS

Clark Company

1986	HISTORICAL COST/ NOMINAL DOLLARS	CURRENT COST/ NOMINAL DOLLARS	UNREALIZED HOLDING GAIN
Beginning inventory	$3,000	$3,000	$ –0–
Purchases at historical cost	–0–	–0–	
Cost of goods sold	(1,800)	(2,700)	(900) realized
Holding gain recognized (see p. 1195)	–0–	1,500	1,500 recognized
Ending inventory	$1,200	$1,800	$ 600 unrealized
1987			
Beginning inventory	$1,200	$1,800	$ 600 unrealized
Purchases at historical cost	–0–	–0–	
Cost of goods sold	(1,200)	(1,800)	(600) realized
Holding gain recognized	–0–	–0–	–0–
Ending inventory	$ –0–	$ –0–	$ –0–

the firm. Although a detailed discussion of the circumstances is beyond the scope of this book, the underlying rationale is that if future cash inflows associated with use of an asset are expected to increase, the current cost of the asset will also increase because of market demand for the asset. This concept is similar to the rationale for LCM discussed in Chapter 10 on pages 445–48, except that it applies to price increases as well as price decreases.

When the 1986 and 1987 current cost/nominal dollar income numbers are added together, the two-year total of $3,000 is exactly the same amount as the two-year total under the historical cost/nominal dollar system:

	1986	1987	TOTAL
Historical cost/nominal dollar (Exhibit 25–4)	$1,800	$1,200	$3,000
Current cost/nominal dollar (Exhibit 25–8)	2,400	600	3,000

Since the nominal dollar concept of capital maintenance is used for both systems, we would expect income for the two-year period to be the same. We can conclude that the use of different asset attributes or valuation methods in conjunction with a given capital maintenance concept leads to *timing* differences in the amount of periodic income, but lifetime income (or income for long periods of time) will be the same under both of these systems.

CURRENT COST/CONSTANT DOLLARS   The current cost/constant dollar system—system *D* in Exhibit 25–3—incorporates *both* specific and general price changes in the determination of income. The measured asset attribute is current cost, and the capital maintenance concept is maintaining general purchasing power. The theory or rationale underlying this system is similar to that underlying the current cost/nominal dollar system, except that the measurements are in constant dollars.

EXHIBIT 25—10 FINANCIAL STATEMENTS FOR 1986 IN
CURRENT COST/CONSTANT DOLLARS

Clark Company

(end-of-1986 general purchasing power units)

BALANCE SHEET
AS OF DECEMBER 31, 1986

Cash.	$3,600
Inventory (40 × $45)	1,800
	$5,400
Contributed capital ($3,000 × 110/100)	$3,300
Retained earnings (1986 net income)	2,100
	$5,400

INCOME STATEMENT
FOR THE YEAR ENDED DECEMBER 31, 1986

Revenue.	$3,600
Cost of goods sold (60 × $45)	(2,700)
Current operating income	$ 900
Holding gain, net of inflation [100($45 − $30) − $3,000(.10)]	1,200
Net income	$2,100

Clark Company's current cost/constant dollars financial statements for 1986 appear in Exhibit 25–10. Cash is not restated because it is a monetary item and already is in units of ending 1986 general purchasing power. Inventory is reported at its current cost at the end of 1986. Even though the measuring unit is end-of-1986 general purchasing power units, the inventory needs no further restatement because current cost already is expressed in end-of-1986 dollars (the $45 per headset price is end-of-1986 current cost). Contributed capital is restated by the general price-level restate factor of 110/100, and the restated amount has the same interpretation as discussed earlier in connection with Exhibit 25–5. The retained earnings amount is 1986 income, as shown in the income statement in the lower portion of Exhibit 25–10.

Current operating income Revenue needs no restatement, because the sale was made at the end of 1986. Cost of goods sold is stated at current cost at the end of 1986, which already is in end-of-1986 constant dollars. Current operating income is $900.

Holding gain The holding gain is calculated by deducting from the nominal holding gain of $1,500 the impact of inflation (the 10 percent increase in the general price level) *on the beginning carrying value of the inventory* ($3,000 × .10). After the inflation effect is deducted, the holding gain is $1,200.[15] The holding gain of $1,200 also may be calculated as follows:

$$\begin{matrix} \text{Beginning inventory} \\ \text{carrying-value} \end{matrix} \times \left(\begin{matrix} \text{Percentage increase} \\ \text{in specific price} \end{matrix} - \begin{matrix} \text{Percentage increase} \\ \text{in general price index} \end{matrix} \right) = \begin{matrix} \text{Holding gain,} \\ \text{net of inflation} \end{matrix}$$

$$\$3,000 \quad \times \quad (.50 - .10) \quad = \quad \$1,200$$

[15] Some accountants and economists refer to the inflation element as a fictitious holding gain. Once the fictitious element of $300 is deducted from the nominal holding gain of $1,500, the resulting $1,200 is referred to as the real holding gain.

EXHIBIT 25—11 | FINANCIAL STATEMENTS FOR 1987 IN CURRENT COST/CONSTANT DOLLARS

Clark Company

(end-of-1987 general purchasing power units)

BALANCE SHEET
AS OF DECEMBER 31, 1987

Cash..	$6,000
Contributed capital ($3,000 × 121/100)	$3,630
Retained earnings [($2,100 × 121/110) + $60]	2,370
	$6,000

INCOME STATEMENT
FOR THE YEAR ENDED DECEMBER 31, 1987

Revenue...	$2,400
Cost of goods sold (40 × $45)	(1,800)
Current operating income...............................	$ 600
Holding loss, net of inflation [$0 − .10($1,800)]	(180)
General purchasing power loss ($3,600 × .10)	(360)
Net income	$ 60

Financial statements for 1987 are shown in Exhibit 25–11. On the balance sheet, cash needs no restatement because it is already stated in end-of-1987 general purchasing power units. Contributed capital is restated to $3,630 because the general price index has increased 21 percent since the stock was issued. Since the measuring unit for 1987 is end-of-1987 general purchasing power units, 1986 income is rolled forward to end-of-1987 dollars with the restate factor 121/110. The ending retained earnings of $2,370 is the sum of the restated 1986 income and the 1987 income.

On the income statement in Exhibit 25–11, the current cost of goods sold is $1,800 (remember that the current cost already is in end-of-1987 dollars and needs no further restatement), and current operating income is $600. Clark Company experienced a *holding loss* on inventory in 1987 because when the impact of inflation on the beginning current cost of the inventory is subtracted from the nominal holding gain of $0, a holding loss of $180 results. This holding loss arises because the general price level increase *exceeded* the specific price increase. Finally, the general purchasing power loss on cash is $360.

The holding gains and losses recognized in the 1986 and 1987 income statements also can be derived by the back-door approach that was illustrated earlier. However, in calculating the holding gain or loss, the beginning carrying value and current purchases, if any, must be restated in end-of-year general purchasing power units, as illustrated in Exhibit 25–12. Moreover, the holding gains and losses may be disaggregated into their realized and unrealized components, as shown in Exhibit 25–13. Because our measuring unit is *units of general purchasing power*, we determine the realized and unrealized components by using the *historical cost/constant dollar* amounts calculated earlier.

EXHIBIT 25–12 CALCULATION OF HOLDING GAINS AND LOSSES, 1986 AND 1987, IN CURRENT COST/CONSTANT DOLLARS

Clark Company

1986	CURRENT COST/ NOMINAL DOLLARS	RESTATE FACTOR	CURRENT COST CONSTANT (EOY) DOLLARS
Beginning inventory at beginning-of-period current cost	$ 3,000	110/100	$ 3,300
Purchases at historical cost (zero in our example)	–0–		–0–
Cost of goods sold at ending current cost	(2,700)		(2,700)
Ending inventory at ending current cost	(1,800)		(1,800)
Holding loss (gain)	$(1,500)		$(1,200)
1987			
Beginning inventory at beginning-of-period current cost (above)	$ 1,800	121/110	$ 1,980
Purchases at historical cost	–0–		–0–
Cost of goods sold at ending current cost	(1,800)		(1,800)
Ending inventory at ending current cost	–0–		–0–
Holding loss (gain)	$ –0–		$ 180

EXHIBIT 25–13 SCHEDULE OF RECOGNIZED, REALIZED, AND UNREALIZED HOLDING GAINS, 1986 AND 1987, IN CURRENT COST/CONSTANT DOLLARS

Clark Company

1986*	HISTORICAL COST/ CONSTANT DOLLARS	CURRENT COST/ CONSTANT DOLLARS	UNREALIZED HOLDING GAIN (LOSS)
Beginning inventory carrying value	$3,000 × $\frac{110}{100}$ = $3,300	$3,000 × $\frac{110}{100}$ = $3,300	$ –0–
Purchases	–0–	–0–	–0–
Cost of goods sold	(1,980)†	(2,700)‡	(720) realized
Holding gain (loss) recognized	–0–	1,200‡	1,200 recognized
Ending inventory carrying value	$1,320†	$1,800‡	$ 480 unrealized
1987§			
Beginning inventory carrying value	$1,320 × $\frac{121}{110}$ = $1,452	$1,800 × $\frac{121}{110}$ = $1,980	$480 × $\frac{121}{110}$ = $ 528 unrealized
Purchases	–0–	–0–	–0–
Cost of goods sold	(1,452)¶	(1,800)**	(348) realized
Holding gain (loss) recognized	–0–	(180)**	(180) recognized
Ending inventory carrying value	$ –0–	$ –0–	$ –0–

* In end-of-1986 general purchasing power units. § In end-of-1987 general purchasing power units.
† From Exhibit 25–5. ¶ From Exhibit 25–6.
‡ From Exhibit 25–10. ** From Exhibit 25–11.

CURRENT COST/CONSTANT DOLLARS VS. HISTORICAL COST/CONSTANT DOLLARS The two-period income of $2,370 under the current cost/constant dollar system is identical to the lifetime income calculated on page 1184 and to the two-period income under the historical cost/constant dollar system on page 1192. Since the capital maintenance concept of general purchasing power underlies *both* the historical cost/constant dollar system and the current cost/constant dollar system, these two systems lead only to *timing* differences in periodic income:

	1986*	1987	TOTAL
Historical cost/constant dollars ..... $1,620(121/110) = $1,782		$588	$2,370
Current cost/constant dollars .... $2,100(121/110) = $2,310		60	2,370

* In units of end-of-1987 general purchasing power.

Current cost/physical capital is based on the distributable earnings theory.

CURRENT COST/PHYSICAL CAPITAL The current cost/physical capital system—system *E* in Exhibit 25–3—has received support in many foreign countries, especially in Germany and the Netherlands. Current cost is the measured asset attribute, and physical capacity (productive capacity) is the capital maintenance concept used. The theory or rationale underlying this system is based on **distributable income,** defined as the maximum amount that can be distributed to stockholders each period while allowing the company to maintain its productive capacity (the ability to replace the assets or equivalent asset services that generate revenues). Clark's financial statements for 1986 and 1987 prepared under this system appear in Exhibit 25–14.

EXHIBIT 25–14 FINANCIAL STATEMENTS, 1986 AND 1987, CURRENT COST/PHYSICAL CAPITAL

Clark Company
BALANCE SHEET

	12/31/86	12/31/87
Cash..........	$3,600	$6,000
Inventory (40 × $45)	1,800	–0–
Total	$5,400	$6,000
Contributed capital	$3,000	$3,000
Capital maintenance adjustment	1,500	1,500
Retained earnings		
(1986 net income)	900	
(1986 net income + 1987 net income)		1,500
Total	$5,400	$6,000

INCOME STATEMENT
FOR THE YEAR ENDED DECEMBER 31

	1986	1987
Revenue........	$3,600	$2,400
Cost of goods sold		
60 × $45	(2,700)	
40 × $45		(1,800)
Net income	$ 900	$ 600

On the income statement for 1986, current cost of goods sold is $2,700, and this figure is subtracted from revenues of $3,600, leaving income of $900. This $900 represents the maximum amount that could be distributed in dividends and still allow Clark to replace the inventory sold in 1986. Since the company had an inflow of cash of $3,600 in 1986, a dividend of $900 would allow replacement of the inventory that has been sold, and that now has a current cost of $2,700.

Notice that the 1986 income of $900 under this approach corresponds with the 1986 current operating income of $900 that was obtained under the current cost/nominal dollar and current cost/constant dollar systems. Since the objective of the current cost/physical capacity system is to measure income based on maintaining productive capacity, however, the holding gain of $1,500, which is calculated the same way as it was under the current cost/nominal dollar system, is considered a *capital maintenance adjustment* to contributed capital and is *not* considered a component of income.[16] This point may be seen by examining the balance sheet in Exhibit 25–14. The capital maintenance adjustment is reported as part of stockholders' equity. The 1987 income shown in Exhibit 25–14 may be interpreted in the same way as 1987 income. If the 1986 income is added to the 1987 income, the total of $1,500 corresponds to Clark's lifetime (two-period) income shown on page 1185.

We have now presented five approaches for determining periodic income during periods of changing prices. The Clark Company example showed how price changes affect some of the major items in the financial statements, such as cash, inventory, net income, and owners' equity. Before providing a brief summary of how large U.S. companies disclose, as supplementary information, the effects of changing prices in their financial reports, we will examine how depreciable assets are accounted for under the five systems illustrated for the Clark Company.

CHANGING PRICES AND DEPRECIABLE ASSETS

Because depreciable assets contribute to the generation of revenues and cash flows over several accounting periods, changing prices can have a significant impact on a firm's income and financial position when these types of assets are used in the earnings process. Our objective in this section is to illustrate how to determine depreciation expense and the carrying value of depreciable assets under historical cost/constant dollars and current cost.

As an example, assume that Bobo Company acquires a depreciable asset at the beginning of year 1 for $60,000. The asset is to be depreciated on a straight-line basis over its 10-year useful life, and no salvage value is anticipated. General price indexes and current cost figures for the asset during the first two years are as follows:

	GENERAL PRICE INDEX	CURRENT COST (NEW)
Beginning of year 1	120	$60,000
End of year 1	130	70,000
End of year 2	150	85,000

Under the historical cost/constant dollar system, depreciation expense for the first two years and the asset carrying value at the end of those years would be calculated as follows:

[16] This holding gain interpretation is similar to the one that many homeowners have applied to investments in homes, whose current costs have increased in recent years. Most homeowners do not regard these holding gains or current cost increases as income. Since they wish to maintain the same standard of living and have the same kind of home, they are aware that selling their houses would make them no better off if the entire proceeds from the sale must be reinvested to purchase a similar house.

YEAR 1	HISTORICAL COST/NOMINAL DOLLARS	RESTATE FACTOR	HISTORICAL COST/CONSTANT DOLLARS
Depreciation expense ($60,000 × .10)	$ 6,000	130/120	$ 6,500
Plant and equipment..........	$60,000	130/120	$65,000
Less accumulated depreciation..............	(6,000)	130/120	(6,500)
Plant and equipment (net)	$54,000		$58,500
YEAR 2			
Depreciation expense	$ 6,000	150/120	$ 7,500
Plant and equipment..........	$60,000	150/120	$75,000
Less accumulated depreciation..............	(12,000)	150/120	(15,000)
Plant and equipment (net)	$48,000		$60,000

Recall that when current cost data were calculated for Clark Company, cost of goods sold was based on current cost at the date of sale. If the inventory had been sold periodically throughout the year, it would have been necessary to determine the current cost at each sale date. Alternatively, an average-for-the-year current cost figure could have been used if it did not differ materially from current cost at the sale date or if it was not feasible to determine the current cost of goods sold at each sale date. These concepts also apply to depreciable assets. Because the services of plant and equipment usually are provided continuously over time, many accountants advocate that current cost depreciation should be based on average-for-the-year current cost, rather than on current cost at the balance sheet date.[17]

When the current cost data for Bobo's depreciable assets are used, depreciation expense, based on ending and average current cost, is calculated as follows:

DEPRECIATION EXPENSE

YEAR	ENDING CURRENT COST	AVERAGE CURRENT COST
1	$70,000 × .10 = $7,000	$\frac{\$60,000 + \$70,000}{2}$ = $65,000 × .10 = $6,500
2	$85,000 × .10 = $8,500	$\frac{\$70,000 + \$85,000}{2}$ = $77,500 × .10 = $7,750

Exhibit 25–15 shows the calculation of the holding gain (increase in specific price) recognized each period and the realized and unrealized components. The annual depreciation expense and the holding gain realized each year differ under the two methods, but the unrealized holding gain at the end of each year is the same for both methods since the ending carrying value of the asset is based on *ending* current cost. Also, although annual depreciation expense is based on either ending or average current cost for that year, the ending carrying value of the asset (cost less accumulated depreciation) is based on *ending*

[17] Both approaches are supportable in theory. For example, end-of-year current cost would be more consistent with the concept of distributable income, which underlies the current cost/physical capital system.

EXHIBIT 25—15   HOLDING GAINS CALCULATED ON THE BASIS OF ENDING AND AVERAGE CURRENT COST

HOLDING GAINS BASED ON ENDING CURRENT COST
(in nominal dollars)

	YEAR 1	YEAR 2
Beginning carrying value at beginning current cost	$ 60,000	$ 63,000
+ Additions (purchases) at historical cost	–0–	–0–
− Depreciation expense at ending current cost	(7,000)	(8,500)
− Ending carrying value at ending current cost		
($70,000 − $7,000)	(63,000)	
($85,000 − $17,000)		(68,000)
= Holding loss (gain) recognized	$(10,000)	$(13,500)
Unrealized holding gain at beginning of year	$ –0–	$ 9,000
+ Holding gain recognized during year (above)	10,000	13,500
− Holding gain realized during year (current cost depreciation − historical cost depreciation of $6,000)	(1,000)	(2,500)
= Unrealized holding gain at end of year	$ 9,000	$ 20,000

HOLDING GAINS BASED ON AVERAGE CURRENT COST
(in nominal dollars)

	YEAR 1	YEAR 2
Beginning carrying value at beginning current cost	$ 60,000	$ 63,000
+ Additions (purchases) at historical cost	–0–	–0–
− Depreciation expense at average current cost	(6,500)	(7,750)
− Ending carrying value at ending current cost		
($70,000 − $7,000)	(63,000)	
($85,000 − $17,000)		(68,000)
= Holding loss (gain) recognized	$(9,500)	$(12,750)
Unrealized holding gain at beginning of year	$ –0–	$ 9,000
+ Holding gain recognized during year (above)	9,500	12,750
− Holding gain realized during year (current cost depreciation − historical cost depreciation of $6,000)	(500)	(1,750)
= Unrealized holding gain at end of year	$ 9,000	$ 20,000

current cost. For example, when depreciation is based on ending current cost, the expense for years 1 and 2 is $7,000 and $8,500, respectively. Since the asset is 20 percent depreciated at the end of year 2, however, the asset is reported at the end of year 2 as $85,000 less two years' depreciation of $17,000, or $68,000.

Notice that for illustration purposes, the current cost calculations in Exhibit 25–15 are in nominal dollars. The holding gains recognized, realized, and unrealized in terms of current cost/constant dollars could be calculated by the procedures presented in Exhibits 25–12 and 25–13.

THE PROFESSION'S CURRENT RESPONSE TO FINANCIAL REPORTING IN PERIODS OF CHANGING PRICES

The alternative income determination systems presented in this section were developed over many years and have been discussed by practitioners and educators for decades. High rates of inflation in the United States in the 1970s forced the accounting profession to issue *Statement of Financial Accounting Standards No. 33,* which requires certain large companies to disclose, as supplementary information, the impact of price changes in their financial reports. These supplementary disclosures encompass, conceptually, the historical cost/constant dollar and the current cost/constant dollar systems. In addition, the current cost/constant dollar disclosure format allows users to derive information pertaining to the other two current cost systems.

Experience with *Statement No. 33* has led to several modifications in the required disclosures. For example, several companies now present only current cost/constant dollar disclosures, while others now present only historical cost/constant dollar disclosures. The modifications have resulted from considerations of perceived usefulness and understandability of the disclosures and from cost/benefit and materiality considerations. A recent *FASB Statement of Financial Accounting Standards* (No. 89) makes these disclosures *voluntary,* rather than mandatory. A discussion and an illustration of the *Statement No. 33* disclosures appear at the end of the chapter.

ACCOUNTING FOR PRICE CHANGES— A CLOSER LOOK

The use of the hypothetical data of the Clark Company and the depreciable asset example allowed us to present the essential concepts underlying income determination under alternative methods of asset valuation and alternative capital maintenance concepts. From a theoretical as well as from a practical standpoint, other issues have not been addressed. These issues are raised below and are discussed in this part of the chapter.

Under the historical cost/constant dollar system:

What impact do alternative inventory valuation methods have on the restatement procedures?

How are gains and losses on sales of assets restated?

If a company issues comparative financial statements, what restatement procedures are necessary to achieve comparability?

How are general purchasing power gains and losses calculated when many monetary assets and liabilities exist and when several transactions affecting monetary assets and liabilities occur?

What are the perceived advantages and disadvantages of historical cost/constant dollar accounting?

Under the current cost systems:

How are current costs determined?

What impact do price changes have on a firm's effective income tax rate?

What are the perceived advantages and disadvantages of current cost?

HISTORICAL COST/CONSTANT DOLLARS

As we stated earlier, the historical cost/constant dollar system is similar to the historical cost/nominal dollar system but uses a different measuring unit. Units of general purchasing power or constant dollars are used instead of units of money or nominal dollars. Alternatively, the system may be described as one in which the attribute measured is historical cost restated in units of general purchasing power, and the capital maintenance concept adopted is maintaining general purchasing power.

Historical Background

Development of this method in the United States is credited to Henry Sweeney.[18] Accounting practitioners became interested in this approach to inflation accounting following World War II, when the United States experienced a period of inflation. Both the APB and its Accounting Research Division studied the problem and issued two documents in the 1960s.[19] *APB Statement No. 3* encouraged, but did not require, companies to disclose supplementary historical cost/constant dollar data. Few companies chose to follow these recommendations and, when inflation leveled off in the late 1960s, public interest in these disclosures declined.

Because of double-digit inflation in the early 1970s, the FASB issued an *Exposure Draft* in 1974 on historical cost/constant dollar accounting. However, because the FASB also had undertaken the conceptual framework project, which incorporated the issue of accounting for changing prices, it decided to defer a final statement on this topic until more progress had been made on the conceptual framework project. In 1979, however, because of continuing inflation and public pressure, the FASB issued *Statement No. 33*.

Additional Historical Cost/Constant Dollar (HC/C$) Restatement Procedures

We illustrated the basic HC/C$ restatement procedures earlier in this chapter. We shall discuss some additional conceptual considerations and practical problems in the following sections.

COST OF GOODS SOLD RESTATEMENT   When a company acquires inventory at varying costs, a cost flow assumption such as FIFO or LIFO must be adopted. As a result, the components of cost of goods sold must be restated because of the different amounts of general purchasing power invested in the inventory sold. Assume that on January 1, 1987, Kromm Company had 2,000 units of inventory acquired at the end of 1986 at a cost of $2 per unit. During April 1987, 5,000 units were purchased at a cost of $3.50 per unit. Sales of 3,000 units were made in November 1987 at a sales price of $6 per unit. The company's fiscal year ends on December 31. Applicable general price indexes are as follows: December 31, 1986, 110; April 1987, 125; November 1987, 140; December 31, 1987, 160. The restatement procedure for cost of goods sold is shown in Exhibit 25–16 under two different cost flow assumptions—FIFO and LIFO.

We restate beginning inventory and purchases by using 160 in the numerator and the index when the inventory was acquired in the denominator. Under FIFO, 160/125 is the restate factor used for ending inventory, since the inventory on hand on December 31, 1987, is assumed to have been acquired in April. Under LIFO, since the ending inventory is assumed to consist of the beginning inventory plus the layer added in April, it is restated accordingly.

GAINS AND LOSSES FROM SALES OF ASSETS   If a company reports a HC/N$ gain or loss from the sale of an asset or from other transactions, the HC/C$ gain or loss is calculated by restating the components of the gain or loss. For example, assume that a company sells

---

[18] Henry W. Sweeney, *Stabilized Accounting* (New York: Holt, Rinehart & Winston, 1964). Originally published by Harper in 1936.

[19] "Reporting the Financial Effects of Price-Level Changes," *Accounting Research Study No. 6* (New York: AICPA, 1963); "Financial Statements Restated for General Price-Level Changes," *Statement of the Accounting Principles Board No. 3* (New York: AICPA, 1969).

EXHIBIT 25—16 COST OF GOODS SOLD RESTATED IN HISTORICAL
COST/CONSTANT DOLLARS UNDER FIFO AND LIFO

FIFO

	HC/N$	RESTATE FACTOR	HC/C(EOY)$
Beginning inventory (2,000 @ $2)	$ 4,000	160/110	$ 5,818
Purchases (5,000 @ $3.50)	17,500	160/125	22,400
Ending inventory (4,000 @ $3.50)	(14,000)	160/125	(17,920)
Cost of goods sold	$ 7,500		$10,298

LIFO

	HC/N$	RESTATE FACTOR	HC/C(EOY)$
Beginning inventory	$ 4,000	160/110	$ 5,818
Purchases	17,500	160/125	22,400
Ending inventory: 2,000 @ $2	(4,000)	160/110	(5,818)
2,000 @ $3.50	(7,000)	160/125	(8,960)
Cost of goods sold	$10,500		$13,440

Note: Under either assumption, revenues of $18,000 (3,000 × $6) would be restated by the restate factor of 160/140.

---

land at the end of the current year for $2,000 when the general price level index is 200. The land was purchased for $1,000 when the general price level index was 125. The gain is restated as follows:

	HISTORICAL COST/NOMINAL DOLLARS	RESTATE FACTOR	HISTORICAL COST/CONSTANT (EOY) DOLLARS
Proceeds from sale .	$2,000	200/200	$2,000
Cost	(1,000)	200/125	(1,600)
Gain on sale	$1,000		$ 400

CALCULATION OF GAIN OR LOSS IN PURCHASING POWER When several monetary transactions occur in an accounting period, a schedule similar to the one presented in Exhibit 25–7 is helpful in calculating the purchasing power gain or loss on monetary items. Assume, for example, that a company starts operating at the beginning of the current year by issuing a $2,000 note and $3,000 in common stock for $1,000 cash and land with a fair market value of $4,000. The company leases the land for $100 per month. Interest on the note is 12 percent. Additional land is acquired in April at a cost of $400. Relevant general price level indexes are as follows:

Beginning of year	120
Average for year	135
End of year	150
Index for April	130

EXHIBIT 25—17 CALCULATING PURCHASING POWER GAINS AND LOSSES FOR HISTORICAL COST/CONSTANT DOLLAR FINANCIAL STATEMENTS

BALANCE SHEET,
BEGINNING OF YEAR
(HC/N$)

Cash........................	$1,000	12% notes payable	$2,000
Land........................	4,000	Contributed capital	3,000
	$5,000		$5,000

INCOME STATEMENT
FOR THE YEAR

	HC/N$	RESTATE FACTOR	HC/C(EOY)$
Revenues................................	$1,200	150/135	$1,333
Interest expense	(240)	150/135	(267)
Purchasing power gain....................		Schedule 1	206
Net income	$ 960		$1,272

SCHEDULE 1. CALCULATION OF GAIN IN GENERAL PURCHASING POWER

	HC/N$	RESTATE FACTOR	HC/C(EOY)$
Beginning monetary items:			
Cash − Notes payable: ($1,000 − $2,000)..	$(1,000)	150/120	$(1,250)
Add: Revenues	1,200	150/135	1,333
Deduct: Interest expense	(240)	150/135	(267)
Purchase of land.................	(400)	150/130	(462)
Ending monetary items:			
Cash − Notes payable ($1,560 − $2,000) ..	$ (440)		$ (646)
General purchasing power gain			206
	$ (440)		$ (440)

BALANCE SHEET,
END OF YEAR

	HC/N$	RESTATE FACTOR	HC/C(EOY)$
Cash....................................	$1,560		$1,560
Land	4,400	Schedule 2	5,462
	$5,960		$7,022
Notes payable	$2,000		$2,000
Contributed capital	3,000	150/120	3,750
Retained earnings	960		1,272
	$5,960		$7,022

SCHEDULE 2. RESTATEMENT OF LAND

Purchased at beginning of year	$4,000 × 150/120 = $5,000
Purchased in April	400 × 150/130 = 462
	$5,462

Calculation of the purchasing power gain or loss appears in Exhibit 25–17. For purposes of illustration, the beginning historical cost/nominal dollar balance sheet, the restatement of the current year's income statement, and the ending balance sheet restatement also appear in Exhibit 25–17. Schedule 1 in Exhibit 25–17 shows the calculation of the general purchasing power gain. Since the company was in a net monetary *liability* position at the beginning of the period (monetary liabilities exceeded monetary assets), a purchasing power gain of $250 ($1,250 − $1,000) resulted on the beginning balance. In addition, a purchasing power loss of $133 ($1,333 − $1,200) resulted on the monetary inflows from sales, while purchasing power gains of $27 and $62 resulted on the monetary outflows for interest expense and the land purchase, respectively. At the end of the year the company's actual net monetary liability position is $440, as compared with the $646 restated amount. In other words, if the company's net debt *did* increase because of inflation, the firm would be in a $646 net debt position. Because prices of monetary items are fixed and do not fluctuate with inflation, however, a gain results.

Only transactions that affect *net* monetary items are included in the calculation of gains and losses in purchasing power. Transactions *within* the monetary item classification are excluded. For example, a sale on account is included but collection of the account is excluded because the collection increases cash and decreases accounts receivable with no effect on *net* monetary items. A cash dividend declaration is included but actual payment of the dividend is excluded because payment decreases both cash and dividends payable with no effect on *net* monetary items. Whether a purchasing power gain or loss arises on monetary items in a period of inflation is indicated by the following end-of-period relationships:

Purchasing power loss (gain) if actual net monetary assets are less than (exceed) restated net monetary assets.

Purchasing power loss (gain) if actual net monetary liabilities exceed (are less than) restated net monetary liabilities.

Comparative financial statements must be based on a constant measuring unit.

COMPARATIVE STATEMENTS Companies issue comparative financial statements in accordance with the **disclosure principle,** and under the HC/C$ system, these statements must be based on a constant measuring unit. The logic of expressing comparative income statements in terms of a constant purchasing power unit was demonstrated by the example of your hypothetical salary over a two-year period (see page 1194). There, we were explaining why the Clark Company's historical cost/constant dollar net income figure for 1986 must be rolled forward to end-of-1987 dollars. Additionally, if Clark were to issue comparative income statements and balance sheets for 1986 and 1987, the statements must be reported in the same general purchasing power (measuring) unit. Exhibit 25–18 shows the comparative financial statements for the Clark Company in end-of-1987 dollars. Notice that each item on Clark's 1986 historical cost/constant dollar statements is restated to end-of-1987 dollars with the following restate factor:

$$\frac{\text{General price index, end of 1987}}{\text{General price index, end of 1986}} = \frac{121}{110}$$

In Exhibit 25–18, the statements shown in the first column would have been issued at the end of 1986. The statements in the last two columns would be issued at the end of 1987. Notice that historical cost/constant dollar income for 1986 of $1,620 becomes $1,782 once the income statement items have been restated to end-of-1987 dollars. This amount is the same as we obtained when we rolled forward Clark's income number on page 1192.

Because constant dollar accounting is based on a constant measuring unit, these same restatement procedures apply to current cost/constant dollar comparative statements. For

EXHIBIT 25—18   HISTORICAL COST/CONSTANT DOLLAR COMPARATIVE STATEMENTS

Clark Company

INCOME STATEMENTS
FOR THE YEARS ENDED DECEMBER 31

	1986*	1986	1987†
	(constant, end-of-1986 dollars)	(constant, end-of-1987 dollars)	
Revenue.......................................	$3,600	$3,960	$2,400
Cost of sales	(1,980)	(2,178)	(1,452)
Purchasing power loss			(360)
Net income	$1,620	$1,782	$ 588

BALANCE SHEETS
DECEMBER 31

	1986*	1986	1987†
	(constant, end-of-1986 dollars)	(constant, end-of-1987 dollars)	
Cash...	$3,600	$3,960	$6,000
Inventory	1,320	1,452	–0–
	$4,920	$5,412	$6,000
Contributed capital	$3,300	$3,630	$3,630
Retained earnings	1,620	1,782	2,370
	$4,920	$5,412	$6,000

* From Exhibit 25–5. These statements would have been issued at the end of 1986.

† From Exhibit 25–6. These statements and the restated 1986 statements would be issued at the end of 1987.

example, Clark's 1986 current cost/constant dollar statements in Exhibit 25–10 would be restated to end-of-1987 dollars if they were issued for comparative purposes in 1987.

In summary, restatement of prior period financial statements is necessary so that the comparative statements will be expressed in the same measuring unit. This procedure improves the comparability of the statements.

Advantages and Disadvantages of Historical Cost/Constant Dollar Reporting

The historical cost/constant dollar system has received both staunch support and strong criticism. The most common arguments for and against the system are listed below.

Arguments *for* historical cost/constant dollar accounting:

1. Except for a different measuring unit, the underlying principles are the same as those that underlie the historical cost/nominal dollar system. Therefore, the data are objective, verifiable, and thus reliable.

2. Comparability among companies is enhanced because the procedures are applied in the same way by all companies.

3. Interperiod comparability for a single firm is enhanced, since a constant measuring unit is used to report financial data.

Arguments *against* historical cost/constant dollar accounting:

1. The use of a general price index is not representative of price changes that face a particular company. For example, if a company acquires assets whose price changes are not similar to general price level changes, the company is not affected by those general price changes. Specific price changes that affect a firm are more meaningful.

2. Some users are confused and do not understand the objectives of historical cost/constant dollar accounting.

3. Many surveys show that users neither demand nor use historical cost/constant dollar information; several empirical studies have shown that historical cost/constant dollar information has little ''information content'' in its impact on stock prices. Thus, the cost of preparing such data exceeds the benefits derived.

4. The system is based on the same principles as the historical cost/nominal dollar system and suffers the same weaknesses.

5. Published general price indexes used in historical cost/constant dollar restatement have weaknesses in their construction. They overstate or distort the true inflation rate, thus rendering the data meaningless.

**CURRENT COST—
ADDITIONAL
ISSUES**

Current cost accounting has received strong theoretical and practical support in many foreign countries for many years.[20] Until recently, however, authoritative accounting bodies in the United States have not been overly receptive to current cost, partly because of the rich history of historical cost and partly because of the perceived lack of reliability of current cost data. What interest there has been in the United States, and the more recent use of current cost accounting methods for decision making are due, in part, to a book by Edwards and Bell.[21] Interest in current cost increased tremendously with the onset of double-digit inflation of the early 1970s. In 1976 the SEC began requiring large U.S. companies to disclose certain current replacement cost data in 10-K filings. These requirements were rescinded after *FASB Statement No. 33* was issued.

We introduced three current cost accounting systems in the Clark Company illustration, and we examine some additional issues in this section. First, we discuss some methods of determining current cost. Second, we discuss the problem of maintaining physical capital when current costs continually increase over time. Next, we briefly illustrate how current cost highlights an increased effective tax rate in inflationary periods. Finally, we summarize the advantages and disadvantages of current cost.

Determining Current Cost

Some accountants would calculate the current cost of replacing assets currently owned by a company, while others would measure the current cost of equivalent productive capacity or equivalent service potential of the asset. The first approach would focus on either a used asset or a new asset, adjusted for accumulated depreciation. Under the latter ap-

---

[20] For example, for many years Phillips Industries of the Netherlands has used a variation of the current cost/physical capital model in its financial reports.

[21] Phillip Edwards and Edgar Bell, *The Theory and Measurement of Business Income* (Berkeley: University of California Press, 1961).

proach the effects of technological change, greater service potential, longer life, or increased operating efficiency should be included. For example, an airline using Boeing 707s probably would not replace such planes with Boeing 707s. As an alternative, modified Boeing 727s or 767s might be preferred replacements. Even though the current cost of a Boeing 767 exceeds that of a 707, the Boeing 767 is much more efficient to operate. Thus, although current cost depreciation based on the cost of a 767 is higher than the historical cost depreciation of a 707, fuel savings and maintenance costs may be much less if replacement is assumed.

In practice, current cost may be determined by use of one or a combination of the following methods:

1. *Indexation.* Specific price indexes may be used to adjust the historical cost of an asset to current cost. These indexes may be obtained from government sources or developed internally.

2. *Direct pricing.* Under this approach current cost is obtained from current invoice prices, vendors' price lists, or standard costs that reflect current cost.[22]

Backlog Depreciation

When the current cost of a long-lived asset continually increases over time, a company may be unable to replace the asset and to maintain productive capacity, even though each year's depreciation is based on current cost for that year. For example, assume a company purchases a fixed asset for $1,500 at the beginning of year 1. The asset has an expected life of four years with no salvage value, and straight-line depreciation is used. Each year's current cost depreciation, based on assumed current cost figures, is shown below:

YEAR	ASSUMED CURRENT COST, END OF YEAR	CURRENT COST DEPRECIATION EXPENSE
1	$2,000	$2,000/4 = $ 500
2	2,500	2,500/4 = 625
3	2,800	2,800/4 = 700
4	3,000	3,000/4 = 750
Total		$2,575

At the end of year 4, while the current cost of the new asset is $3,000, only $2,575 has been deducted from revenues over the four-year period; the result is a cumulative *backlog* amount of $425 ($3,000 − $2,575). Some accountants would reduce retained earnings each year for the backlog, and others would record the backlog as additional depreciation expense. Some argue that backlog can be ignored if funds equal to each year's current cost depreciation can be invested at a rate that approximates the rate of increase in current cost.

Current Cost and Taxation

Under present U.S. income tax laws, taxes are calculated on the basis of historical cost.[23] Many supporters of current cost argue that the current cost/physical capital system dramatically highlights the high effective tax rate suffered by companies in periods of changing prices. The following anecdote appeared in the *Journal of Accountancy:*

---

[22] *Statement of Financial Accounting Standards No. 33,* para. 60.

[23] Indexation proposals represent a step toward the adjustment of historical cost to take into consideration the effects of price changes in taxation.

Two merchants had an identical item in their shops; each had paid $1 for it. One sunny morning, one of the merchants opened his shop for business while the other closed his shop and went fishing. The merchant who opened his shop sold his item for $2, making a profit of $1. On this profit, he paid a tax of $.50. During the day, the wholesale cost of the item rose to $2. The hard-working merchant who had sold his item for $2 and had paid $.50 in taxes now had only $1.50 with which to replace the same item of inventory. He was forced to go to the bank to borrow the additional $.50 he needed. At the end of the day, he assessed his results. He had made a profit of $1, he had the same item in stock, and he owed the bank $.50:

| | NET INCOME UNDER | |
	CONVENTIONAL ACCOUNTING	CURRENT COST
Sales	$2.00	$2.00
Cost	(1.00)	(2.00)
Income before tax	$1.00	$-0-
Tax expense	(.50)	(.50)
Net income (loss)	$ .50	$(.50)

Meanwhile, the other merchant had thoroughly enjoyed his day fishing, had done no work and made no profit—but he had the same item in stock and owed the bank nothing. Apart from the obvious social message on work ethics, this little anecdote demonstrates the important and basic dilemma in deciding what is income during times of inflation.[24]

In practice, effective tax rates increase dramatically during periods of changing prices. Exhibit 25–19 shows the average effective tax rates experienced by almost 700 U.S. companies that applied *Statement No. 33* for the first time in 1979.

[24] Adapted from a speech by Michael Alexander, Director of Research and Technical Activities of the Financial Accounting Standards Board. Reprinted in *Journal of Accountancy,* February 1980, pp. 75–78.

EXHIBIT 25–19   CHANGING PRICES AND EFFECTIVE TAX RATES

	EFFECTIVE TAX RATE
Constant dollar companies*	
Historical	39.6%
Adjusted for general inflation	53.6
Current cost companies*	
Historical	39.7
Adjusted for specific prices	53.0

* *Excludes* companies that reported historical cost/nominal dollar profits but constant dollar and/or current cost losses.

Source: Ernst & Whinney, *FASB Inflation Accounting: The First Year* (1980), p. 22.

Advantages and Disadvantages of Current Cost

The advantages of the current cost systems are as follows:

1. Current operating income provides information about a company's ability to operate efficiently under current economic conditions.

2. Under the current cost/nominal dollar and current cost/constant dollar systems, income or loss is disaggregated into two components—current operating income or loss and holding gains or losses. Current operating income or loss, which also is synonymous with income or loss under the current cost/physical capacity system, may help users to predict future income or loss. Holding gains or losses in the current cost/nominal dollar system may help users to assess future cash flows if input and output prices change in the same direction.

3. The current cost/constant dollar system considers the effects of both changes in specific prices and changes in the general level of prices. Thus, under certain conditions, this system contains the same current cost information as the current cost/nominal dollar and current cost/physical capital systems, in addition to information about the effects of general price level changes.

4. Current cost disclosures are more relevant than historical cost/constant dollar disclosures because current cost is based on specific price changes that affect a particular company rather than on general price level changes.

The disadvantages of the current cost systems are as follows:

1. The use of current cost introduces subjectivity into financial reporting, thus reducing the disclosures' reliability. First, a market for used assets may not exist. Second, assets may not be replaced with identical assets; therefore the assumptions necessary to consider replacement with an improved asset make the replacement calculation too hypothetical. The difficulty in quantifying other cost reductions because of efficiency or technology may cause current cost to be misstated.

2. Current cost may not approximate an asset's potential to generate future cash flows.

3. The current cost/physical capital system is too restrictive, as it assumes that a company *must* maintain its productive capacity. The theory underlying the system also ignores or suppresses the possibility of maintaining productive capacity through issues of debt or equity securities.

4. When input and output prices do not move in the same direction, current operating income and holding gains may not be good predictors of future cash flows.

5. Empirical evidence indicates that current cost data have little information content. (This is discussed in more detail at the end of the chapter.)

DISCLOSURES ON CHANGING PRICES

A summary of the disclosures specified by FASB *Statement of Financial Accounting Standards No. 33,* ''Financial Reporting and Changing Prices,'' appears in Exhibit 25–20. In this section we illustrate these disclosures.

Assume that CFO Corporation was formed at the beginning of the current year with the balance sheet shown below:

CFO Corporation
BALANCE SHEET,
BEGINNING OF YEAR

Cash....................	$10,000	Accounts payable	$ 5,000
Inventories (2,000 @ $10)....	20,000	Stockholders' equity........	75,000
Plant and equipment........	50,000		
	$80,000		$80,000

Additional information:

1. Cash sales made evenly during the year, 2,500 at $25 = $62,500.

2. Purchases on account, 1,500 units at $12.50 per unit, made evenly during year.

3. The company uses the FIFO method of pricing inventory. The ending inventory of 1,000 units was acquired evenly during the last three quarters. For restatement purposes, it is assumed that this is equivalent to acquiring the units, on the average, at the end of the third quarter.

4. Plant and equipment have a useful life of five years with no salvage value, and straight-line depreciation is used.

5. Other expenses, incurred evenly during the year and paid in cash, $12,000.

6. Cash payments on account, $15,750.

7. Consumer price indexes (general price indexes):

Beginning of year	120
End of year	160
Average for year	140
End of 3rd quarter	150

8. Current cost of inventory, per unit:

Beginning of year	$10.00
End of year	15.00
Average for year	12.50

9. Specific price index for plant and equipment to be used in determining current cost:

Beginning of year	140
End of year	224
Average for year	182

10. On the basis of the specific price indexes in item 9, current cost of plant and equipment is determined as follows:

Current cost, end of year: $50,000 \times \dfrac{224}{140} = \$80,000$

Average current cost: $\$50,000 \times \dfrac{182}{140} = \$65,000*$

* Or alternatively, $\dfrac{\$50,000 + \$80,000}{2} = \$65,000.$

11. CFO Corporation's historical cost/nominal dollar income statement is shown in Exhibit 25–21.

EXHIBIT 25—20 *STATEMENT OF FINANCIAL ACCOUNTING STANDARDS NO. 33 DISCLOSURES**

1. *Statement No. 33* applies to public enterprises that prepare financial statements in accordance with GAAP and that have either *(a)* inventories and gross property, plant, and equipment exceeding $125 million or *(b)* total gross assets exceeding $1 billion. Other companies are encouraged to present the disclosures.

2. No changes are made in the traditional historical cost/nominal dollar statements. The disclosures are to be presented as supplementary information.

3. Unless a company has specialized assets (e.g., mineral resources, timberlands and growing timber, income-producing real estate, and motion picture films), it should disclose information on income from continuing operations on a current cost/constant dollar basis. The purchasing power gain or loss is disclosed, but not as a part of income from continuing operations. The current cost of inventory and property, plant, and equipment at the current balance sheet date also is disclosed. Increases or decreases in the current cost of inventory and property, plant, and equipment (holding gains), net of inflation, are disclosed but are not to be included in income from continuing operations.

4. A company with specialized assets should disclose information on income from continuing operations on a historical cost/constant dollar basis. The purchasing power gain or loss is disclosed, but not as a part of income from continuing operations.

5. In connection with items 3 and 4 above, *partial restatement* (i.e., restatement of only inventories, property, plant, and equipment, cost of goods sold, and depreciation expense) is permitted as a minimum, although comprehensive restatement (restatement of all nonmonetary assets and liabilities in historical cost/constant dollars or current cost/constant dollars) also is permitted. If partial restatement is used, the information must be disclosed in terms of constant *average-for-the-year* (AFY) dollars. If comprehensive restatement is used, constant (AFY) dollars or constant end-of-year (EOY) dollars may be used.

6. Historical cost/constant dollar data may be substituted for current cost/constant data in part 3 if the difference in income from continuing operations calculated by the two methods is not material.

EXHIBIT 25—21 HISTORICAL COST/NOMINAL DOLLAR INCOME STATEMENT

CFO Corporation
INCOME STATEMENT
FOR THE YEAR

		HC/N$
Sales (2,500 × $25)		$62,500
Cost of goods sold		
Beginning inventory	$20,000	
Purchases	18,750	
Ending inventory	(12,500)	
Cost of goods sold		(26,250)
Depreciation expense		(10,000)
Other expenses		(12,000)
Net income		$14,250

7. The general price index to be used for constant dollar restatements is the Consumer Price Index (CPI).

8. An enterprise should disclose the following additional items for each of its five most recent years:
  a) Net sales and other operating revenues.
  b) If appropriate (see item 3), current cost/constant dollar:
    i. Income from continuing operations.
    ii. Income per common share from continuing operations.
    iii. Net assets at year end.
    iv. Increases or decreases in current cost (net of inflation) for inventories and property, plant, and equipment.
  If appropriate (see item 4), historical cost/constant dollar:
    i. Income from continuing operations.
    ii. Income per common share from continuing operations.
    iii. Net assets at year end.
  c) Other information:
    i. Purchasing power gain or loss on net monetary items.
    ii. Cash dividends declared per common share.
    iii. Market price per common share at year end.
Companies should disclose the AFY or EOY Consumer Price Index (whichever applies) in the five-year summary. Also, the five-year summary may be stated in terms of the CPI base period dollars.

9. The upper limit on historical cost/constant dollar and current cost/constant dollar restatement is recoverable value. Write-downs to recoverable value are required, if applicable.

10. Interperiod income tax allocation is not permitted for timing differences (which might be deemed to arise from disclosure of current cost). No intraperiod tax allocation is permitted for allocation of income tax expense between income from continuing operations and holding gains or losses.

* As amended by several subsequent *Statements.*

Exhibit 25–22 illustrates reporting formats recommended by *Statement No. 33* using partial restatement. The first column shows the primary historical cost/nominal dollar numbers. The supplementary historical cost/constant dollar and current cost/constant dollar disclosures are shown in the second and third columns. For instructional purposes, we show both disclosures; in practice, a company would disclose one or the other. Each category of disclosures described in *Statement No. 33* is explained in the sections that follow.

HISTORICAL COST/CONSTANT DOLLAR DISCLOSURES

Sales and other expenses need no restatement because these transactions are assumed to have occurred evenly during the year. Thus, they already are measured in terms of constant average-for-the-year dollars.

Cost of goods sold is restated in constant dollars, as shown below.

	HC/N$	RESTATE FACTOR	HC/C(AFY)$
Beginning inventory.	$20,000	140/120	$23,333
+ Purchases	18,750	*	18,750
− Ending inventory	(12,500)	140/150	(11,667)
= Cost of goods sold.	$26,250		$30,416

* Already stated in C(AFY)$.

EXHIBIT 25—22 *STATEMENT NO. 33* SUPPLEMENTARY DISCLOSURES ON CHANGING PRICES

CFO Corporation

	FROM PRIMARY STATEMENTS	SUPPLEMENTARY INFORMATION*	
	HC/N$	HC/C(AFY)$	CC/C(AFY)$
Sales	$62,500	$62,500	$62,500
Cost of goods sold	(26,250)	(30,416)	(31,250)
Depreciation expense	(10,000)	(11,667)	(13,000)
Other expenses	(12,000)	(12,000)	(12,000)
Income from continuing operations.......	$14,250	$ 8,417	$ 6,250
Purchasing power loss on monetary items .		$ 5,427	$ 5,427
Increase in current cost of inventory, plant, and equipment			$34,500
Inflation component			(21,541)
Increase in current cost of inventory, plant, and equipment (net of inflation)			$12,959

Note: At the end of the current year, the current cost of inventory was $15,000, and the current cost of plant and equipment, net of accumulated depreciation, was $64,000.

* An individual company would present only one of these two disclosures.

Because average-for-the-year dollars (average general purchasing power for the year) is the measuring unit used, the average-for-the-year index rather than the end-of-year index appears in the numerator of the restate factor.

Depreciation expense is restated as follows:

	HC/N$	RESTATE FACTOR	HC/C(AFY)$
Depreciation expense	$10,000	140/120	$11,667

The *purchasing power loss* is calculated as shown below.

	HC/N$	RESTATE FACTOR	HC/C(AFY)$
Beginning monetary items:			
Cash − Payables ($10,000 − $5,000) ..	$ 5,000	140/120	$ 5,833
Increase during year	31,750	*	31,750
			$37,583
Ending monetary items:			
Cash − Payables ($44,750 − $8,000) ..	$36,750	140/160	(32,156)
Purchasing power loss			$ 5,427

* Assumed to have occurred evenly during the period and stated in C(AFY)$.

The beginning monetary items are restated in average-for-the-year dollars. The ending monetary items, which are stated in end-of-year dollars, must be restated in average-for-the-year dollars.

CURRENT COST/CONSTANT DOLLAR DISCLOSURES

Because *sales* and *other expenses* already are in average-for-the-year dollars, no restatement is necessary.

Cost of goods sold on a current cost basis is calculated as follows:

$$2,500 \text{ units} \times \$12.50 = \$31,250$$

Because average current cost is more consistent with average-for-the-year dollars, *Statement No. 33* recommends that current cost be based on *average* current cost, which already is stated in average-for-the-year dollars.

Depreciation expense is based on average current cost, which already is in terms of average-for-the-year dollars:

$$\text{Average current cost} = \frac{\$50,000 + \$80,000}{2} = \$65,000$$

$$\text{Depreciation expense} = \$65,000 \times \frac{1}{5} = \$13,000$$

The *purchasing power loss* has been explained previously.

The *increase in specific prices* (holding gains, net of inflation) is calculated below.

INVENTORY

	CC/N$	RESTATE FACTOR	CC/C(AFY)$
Beginning carrying value (at beginning current cost)	$20,000	140/120	$23,333
+ Purchases (at historical cost)........	18,750		18,750
− Cost of goods sold (at average current cost)	(31,250)		(31,250)
− Ending carrying value (at ending current cost)	(15,000)	140/160	(13,125)
= Holding loss (gain) (or specific price increase)	$(7,500)		$(2,292)

PLANT AND EQUIPMENT

	CC/N$	RESTATE FACTOR	CC/C(AFY)$
Beginning carrying value (at beginning current cost)	$ 50,000	140/120	$ 58,333
− Depreciation expense (at average current cost)	(13,000)		(13,000)
− Ending carrying value (at ending current cost) ($80,000 − $16,000) .	(64,000)	140/160	(56,000)
= Holding loss (gain) (or specific price increase)	$(27,000)		$(10,667)

HOLDING GAINS

	CC/N$	CC/C(AFY)$
Inventory	$ 7,500	$ 2,292
Plant and equipment	27,000	10,667
Total	$34,500	$12,959

Because purchases occur evenly during the year and because cost of goods sold and depreciation are based on average current cost, which is in average-for-the-year dollars, no constant dollar restatements are necessary for purchases, cost of goods sold, and depreciation expense.

RECOVERABLE VALUE

Recoverable value is the exit value (exchange value) or present value (value in use) expected to be received from the sale or use of an asset. Under the historical cost/nominal dollar system, if an asset's recoverable value is less than its historical cost, the asset generally is written down to recoverable value. The same concept applies in the historical cost/constant dollar system. Recoverable value is the maximum amount of accessible purchasing power available at the balance sheet date and should be reported if it is less than the historical cost/constant dollar amount. For example, assume that a company purchased inventory for $1,000 when the general price index was 130. At the current balance sheet date, the general price index is 170, and the inventory's exit value is $1,200. Since the historical cost/constant dollar inventory amount is $1,307 [$1,000 × (170/130)], which is greater than the inventory's recoverable value of $1,200, the inventory would be reported at $1,200, and a loss or cost of goods sold adjustment should be reported in the historical cost/constant dollar income statement.

The concept of recoverable value also applies to current cost. Thus, assets are measured and reported at current cost or recoverable value, whichever is lower. Since the maximum amount that a company would be willing to pay for an asset is either its exchange value (exit value) or its value in use (present value), recoverable value establishes an upper limit on the asset's carrying value. Therefore, a modification should be made when current cost is higher than the value of the asset to the business; the asset should be valued at the **lower** of current cost or recoverable value.

STATEMENT NO. 33 DISCLOSURES IN PRACTICE

Exhibit 25–23 shows Union Pacific Corporation's current cost/constant dollar disclosures for 1985. Although Union Pacific reported income from continuing operations of $501 million in historical cost/nominal dollars, the company reported a loss from continuing operations of $147 million when expenses were measured at current cost. Notice that Union Pacific reported a purchasing power gain of $188 million in 1985 because of its net monetary liability position. Notice also that, because the company's current cost increases exceeded the increase in the Consumer Price Index in 1985, there was a holding gain, net of inflation, of $695 million. You might also wish to refer to page 216 in Appendix 5–1, which shows the changing prices disclosures for Coca-Cola.

CHANGING PRICES DISCLOSURES: EVALUATION OF DECISION USEFULNESS

Several empirical studies have assessed the usefulness (in terms of information content) of the FASB required disclosures on the effects of changing prices. Almost all of these studies have concluded that the supplementary disclosures provide little, if any, incremental usefulness (over and above that provided by the primary statements). Possible explanations for the apparent lack of usefulness include the following:

1. Users do not understand the disclosures.

2. The information is useful, but is not being used because the data are being obtained from other sources.

EXHIBIT 25—23   CHANGING PRICES DISCLOSURES

Union Pacific Corporation

FROM THE 1985 ANNUAL REPORT

MEASURING INFLATIONARY IMPACTS

The following experimental disclosures of certain financial information, adjusted for changes in specific price levels (current cost data), are intended to supplement the traditional financial statements.

Properties have been restated to current cost through engineering estimates and application of industry indices, except for railroad equipment costs which were developed from recent purchase prices and quotations, and oil and gas exploration and production properties which were developed by using the consumer price index. Crude oil and gas and refined products inventories have been restated to a FIFO basis, while the costs of crude oil and refined products sales are determined on a LIFO basis.

Railroad track structure and related right of way have been reflected in net assets at book value ($2,596 million at December 31, 1985) since the rate-regulated and competitive environment of the industry does not in general contemplate recovery of inflation-adjusted costs (at December 31, 1985, $5,562 million current cost) for these assets. Income has been adjusted so that the cost of replacing track in kind is expensed currently rather than capitalized and depreciated over the useful life of the track. Since track is being replaced on a planned programmed basis, this charge to income approximates the current cost of operations.

1985

The following current cost amounts are stated in average 1985 dollars.

MILLIONS OF DOLLARS	HISTORICAL AMOUNTS	CURRENT COST
Revenues	$7,908	$7,908
Depreciation	(546)	(955)
Other costs and expenses	(6,613)	(6,852)
Income before Federal income taxes	$ 749	$ 101
Federal income taxes[a]	(248)	(248)
Income (loss) from continuing operations	$ 501	$ (147)

[a] Federal income taxes have not been adjusted since the additional depreciation and other inflationary costs and expenses are not deductible under current tax law.

Current cost of inventories and properties, net of accumulated depreciation, depletion and amortization are $540 million and $16,251 million, respectively, at December 31, 1985. During 1985, specific prices for these assets increased $1,367 million, of which $672 million was attributable to general inflation.

Operating results on a current cost basis are substantially below historical amounts. This results primarily from the significant increase in depreciation expense caused by the inflation adjustment of the historical asset base, which is particularly pronounced because of the Corporation's capital-intensive businesses and further because of the long-lived railroad assets, together with the adjustment for the cost of replacing track in kind.

(EXHIBIT CONTINUES ON NEXT PAGE)

EXHIBIT 25—23 CHANGING PRICES DISCLOSURES (CONTINUED)

THE PAST FIVE YEARS

The following amounts are stated in average 1985 dollars, in millions except per share amounts.

	1985	1984	1983	1982	1981
Revenues	$ 7,908	$ 8,198	$ 9,196	$ 6,603	$ 7,598
Current Cost Data:					
Income from continuing operations	(147)	(64)	(60)	2	168
Per share	(1.23)	(.52)	(.49)	.02	1.74
Net assets at year end	12,213	12,355	11,934	13,571	8,929
Cash from operations	1,317	1,264	1,291	1,392	1,227
Dividends declared per share	1.80	1.86	1.95	2.02	1.97
Purchasing power gain	188	161	249	202	270
Excess of increase in specific prices over general inflation	695	424	540	581	327
Market price at year end	$53.02	$41.74	$53.90	$51.78	$59.52
Average CPI-U	322.2	311.1	298.4	289.1	272.4

Economic and competitive conditions in recent years have exerted downward pressure on earnings and revenues; however, cash from operations, after eliminating the effects of inflation, has remained strong. The Corporation has not been limited in its access to capital markets and it has been able to continue a strong commitment to capital investment programs.

Purchasing power gains reflect the year-to-year impact of the declining purchasing power of the dollar on net amounts owed, representing principally the excess of long-term financing and deferred tax credits over working capital. While these gains do not represent receipt of cash and, therefore, do not provide funds for reinvestment in the business or dividend distribution, they do provide an economic advantage to the Corporation of paying fixed current obligations in the future with dollars having less purchasing power.

3. The disclosures have potential incremental information content, but may contain measurement error, thus reducing the perceived reliability and usefulness of the data.

The third explanation was suggested in an empirical study by William Beaver and Wayne Landsman.[25] They pointed out that measurement error may arise when companies fail to apply the recoverable value concept. Another source of measurement error is "double-counting" of the effects of inflation. That is, if companies already have made an adjustment for anticipated inflation in their primary statements (e.g., accelerated depreciation or a shortened depreciation life for plant and equipment), a "double-counting" effect may occur when current cost or constant dollar adjustments are made to these data in the primary statements.

Because the *Statement No. 33* disclosures are experimental, the FASB has continued to monitor and assess the disclosure requirements. Since 1979, many modifications have been made in the required disclosures. For example, several subsequent *Statements* have

[25] William Beaver and Wayne Landsman, "Incremental Information Content of *Statement 33* Disclosures," *FASB Research Report* (Stamford, Conn.: FASB, 1983).

either permitted or required companies with specialized assets such as mineral resources, growing timber, motion picture films, and income-producing real estate to disclose historical cost/constant dollar data instead of current cost/constant dollar data, because current cost data probably are not meaningful for these types of assets. In addition, *FASB Statement No. 82,* issued in 1985, eliminated the historical cost/constant dollar disclosures for companies that were presenting current cost/constant dollar disclosures, because of user confusion and because of the apparent lack of usefulness of historical cost/constant dollar data for these companies. This *Statement* also allowed companies to substitute historical cost/constant dollar data for current cost/constant dollar data under certain circumstances (see part 6 of Exhibit 25–20).

Many individuals and groups have argued for the elimination of all changing prices disclosures, now that the rate of inflation has declined. Opponents of this position maintain that from a cost/benefit standpoint, the disclosures should be continued because of the difficulties of implementation should the rate of inflation increase in the future. In an attempt to be responsive to its constituents and to the current economic environment, in December 1986, the FASB issued a *Statement of Financial Accounting Standards* that makes the changing prices disclosure voluntary, rather than mandatory.[26] Companies that chose to present changing prices disclosures generally would follow the requirements of *Statement No. 33,* as amended.

[26] ''Financial Reporting and Changing Prices,'' *Statement of Financial Accounting Standards No. 89* (Stamford, Conn.: FASB, 1986).

SUMMARY OF IMPORTANT TOPICS AND CONCEPT APPLICATIONS

1. There are two types of price changes: (1) changes in the **general level of prices,** also called inflation or deflation; and (2) changes in **specific prices**—changes in prices of specific goods and services.

2. Proposals on accounting for the effects of price changes include: (1) report the effects of general price level changes only—retain the historical cost/nominal dollar system that comprises GAAP, but change the measuring unit from units of money to **units of general purchasing power;** (2) report **current values**—substitute some form of current value for historical costs; and (3) incorporate both **specific and general price changes** in financial reports—report **current values** but measure these amounts in **units of general purchasing power.**

3. **Capital maintenance** is a concept that distinguishes investment recovery from profitability. Whether a company has maintained its capital during an accounting period is determined by one of three alternative capital maintenance concepts: (1) maintaining capital in units of money **(nominal dollars),** (2) maintaining capital in units of general purchasing power (**constant dollars** or **constant purchasing power**), and (3) maintaining **physical capital.**

4. Attributes (methods) used to measure (value) assets and liabilities include **historical cost, current cost, current exit value, expected exit value,** and **present value.**

5. Over the life of a company, its aggregate (lifetime) income is uniquely determined by a specified capital maintenance concept. However, both a **capital maintenance concept** and a **measured attribute** for assets and liabilities are necessary to determine **periodic income.**

6. There are four major alternative systems to the historical cost/nominal dollar income determination system that comprises GAAP. Each alternative combines an asset attribute with a capital maintenance concept, as follows: **historical cost/constant dollars**

or **constant purchasing power, current cost/nominal dollars, current cost/ constant dollars,** and **current cost/physical capital.**

7. The effect of general price changes is a function of the type of asset (liability) held (owed). **Monetary assets and liabilities** represent claims to and obligations to pay fixed amounts of cash at a future date. Assets and liabilities not possessing these characteristics are **nonmonetary.** Whereas prices of monetary items are fixed in terms of dollars and do not change during periods of inflation or deflation, prices of nonmonetary items can change during an inflationary or deflationary period.

8. Holders (issuers) of monetary assets (liabilities) suffer **losses (gains) in general purchasing power** during a period of inflation. On the other hand, holders (issuers) of nonmonetary assets (liabilities) may experience either gains or losses in general purchasing power during a period of inflation, depending on the relationship between the specific price change of the asset (liability) held (owed) and the general price level change.

9. Under the historical cost/constant dollar system, nonmonetary items, which appear on the balance sheet at historical exchange prices, are restated to reflect the percentage change in the general price level from the exchange date to the current balance sheet date. Thus, the restated amounts are reported in constant end-of-year units of general purchasing power. (*Statement No. 33* permits, as an alternative, restatement to constant average-for-the-year dollars.) Revenues and expenses, which appear on the income statement at historical exchange prices, are restated in a similar manner. Monetary items appearing on the balance sheet at current exchange prices (and which already are expressed in end-of-year dollars) are not restated and thus give rise to general purchasing power gains and losses.

10. Income statement characteristics of the historical cost/constant dollar system are:
    a) Expenses, measured at historical exchange prices, are restated for general price level changes and are matched against revenues, which also are restated for general price level changes.
    b) General purchasing power gains (losses)—the gain (loss) in general purchasing power that results from owing (holding) monetary liabilities (assets) during a period of inflation.
    c) Net income (loss)—the sum of items *a* and *b*.

11. Under the three current cost systems, nonmonetary assets are valued at current cost on the balance sheet. Expenses, which appear on the income statement, also are measured at current cost. Additional characteristics of each current cost system are:

    CURRENT COST/NOMINAL DOLLARS
    a) **Current operating income (loss)**—the difference between revenues and current cost expenses.
    b) **Holding gains (losses)**—the increase (decrease) in the current cost of assets held during a period of time.
    c) Net income (loss)—the sum of items *a* and *b*.

    CURRENT COST/CONSTANT DOLLARS
    a) **Current operating income (loss)**—the difference between revenues and current cost expenses. Income statement items are also stated in constant dollars.
    b) **Holding gains (losses), net of inflation**—the increase (decrease) in the current cost of assets held during a period of time in excess of the general price level increase (decrease) during this same period.
    c) **General purchasing power gains (losses)**—the gain (loss) in general purchasing power that results from owing (holding) monetary liabilities (assets) during a period of inflation.
    d) Net income (loss)—the sum of items *a* through *c*.

CURRENT COST/PHYSICAL CAPITAL

    a) Current operating income (loss), which also equals net income (loss)—the difference between revenues and current cost expenses.

    b) Holding gains are not considered as components of income, but rather as **capital adjustments.**

12. Under *Statement No. 33,* large companies disclose, as supplementary information, the effects of inflation in their financial reports. Generally, companies disclose current cost/constant dollar information. Some companies, however, disclose historical cost/constant dollar information, instead of current cost/constant dollar information. A recent FASB *Statement of Standards* makes *Statement No. 33* disclosures voluntary, rather than mandatory.

QUESTIONS

Q25-1. Explain the meaning of the term "inflation."

Q25-2. What is the relationship between inflation and the general purchasing power of the dollar?

Q25-3. **A)** Distinguish between general price level changes and specific price changes.
B) Give some examples of specific price changes.

Q25-4. Briefly explain a price index and list two types of government-constructed price indexes.

Q25-5. There are at least three perceptions of the financial reporting problems caused by changing prices. Discuss these three perceptions.

Q25-6. **A)** What is meant by "capital maintenance"?
B) Discuss the following concepts of capital maintenance:

    1. Maintenance of original invested (nominal) dollars.

    2. Maintenance of general purchasing power.

    3. Maintenance of productive capacity.

Q25-7. **A)** What is meant by "measuring asset attributes"?
B) Explain the following attributes that might be measured for assets:

    1. Historical cost.

    2. Current cost.

    3. Current exit value.

    4. Present value of expected cash flows.

    5. Expected exit value.

Q25-8. **A)** Distinguish between monetary items and nonmonetary items.
B) Give some examples of monetary assets, monetary liabilities, nonmonetary assets, and nonmonetary liabilities.
C) Should preferred and common stock be considered as monetary or nonmonetary? Give reasons for your answers.

Q25-9. Company *A* classifies its bond investments as monetary, while company *B* classifies its bond investments as nonmonetary. What justification can you offer for these apparently inconsistent classifications?

Q25-10. Explain the logic of the "roll forward" procedure for preparing comparative statements under the historical cost/constant dollar system.

Q25-11. Can a company experience an increase in its command over goods and services during a period of inflation? Discuss.

Q25-12. **A)** What is a holding gain?
B) Distinguish between recognized, realized, and unrealized holding gains.

Q25-13. A company has prepared historical cost/constant end-of-year dollar statements. What adjustments are necessary to restate the amounts in constant average-for-the-year dollars?

Q25-14. Some accountants, in applying the attribute of current cost, substitute recoverable value when this amount is below current cost. Explain the concept of recoverable value and the rationale behind the practice.

Q25-15. ''In the final analysis, the use of supplementary disclosures about the effects of changing prices must be evaluated in terms of cost-benefit analysis.'' Explain.

Q25-16. A company earned revenues of $10,000 in 1987 and $11,000 in 1988. At the beginning of 1987, the general price index was 120. The index was 130 and 150 at the end of 1987 and 1988, respectively. Revenues were earned evenly during the two years. Assuming that the same number of units was sold each year, what conclusions can you draw from the historical cost/constant dollar restatements of revenue?

CASES

C25-1. HISTORICAL COST/CONSTANT DOLLAR THEORY AND RESTATEMENT   Classic Corporation, a manufacturer with large investments in plant and equipment, began operations in 1964. The company's history has been one of expansion in sales, production, and physical facilities. Recently some concern has been expressed that the conventional financial statements do not provide sufficient information for decisions by investors. After consideration of proposals for various types of supplementary financial statements to be included in the 1987 annual report, management has decided to present a balance sheet as of December 31, 1987, and a statement of income and retained earnings for 1987, both restated for changes in the general price level.

REQUIRED

1. On what basis can it be contended that Classic's conventional statements should be restated for changes in the general price level?

2. Distinguish between financial statements restated for general price level changes and current value financial statements.

3. Distinguish between monetary and nonmonetary assets and liabilities, as the terms are used in general price level accounting. Give examples of each.

4. Outline the procedures Classic should follow in preparing the proposed supplementary statements.

5. Indicate the major similarities and differences between the proposed supplementary statements and the corresponding conventional statements.

6. Assuming that in the future Classic will want to present comparative supplementary statements, can the 1987 supplementary statements be presented in 1988 without adjustment? Explain.

(AICPA, adapted)

C25-2. HISTORICAL COST/CONSTANT DOLLAR THEORY   Published financial statements of United States companies are currently prepared on a stable dollar assumption even though the general purchasing power of the dollar has declined considerably because of inflation in recent years. To account for this changing value of the dollar, many accountants suggest that financial statements should be adjusted for general price level changes. Three independent, unrelated statements regarding financial statements so adjusted follow. Each statement contains some fallacious reasoning.

   a) The accounting profession has not seriously considered price-level-adjusted financial statements before because the rate of inflation usually has been so small from year to year that the adjustments would have been immaterial in amount. Price-level-adjusted financial statements represent a departure from the historical cost basis of accounting. Financial statements should be prepared from facts, not estimates.

   b) If financial statements were adjusted for general price level changes, depreciation charges in the income statement would permit the recovery of dollars of current purchasing power and thereby equal the cost of new assets to replace the old ones. General price-level-adjusted data would yield amounts closely approximating current values in statements of financial position. Furthermore, management can make better decisions if general price-level-adjusted financial statements are published.

c) When financial data are adjusted for general price level changes, a distinction must be made between monetary and nonmonetary assets and liabilities, which under the historical cost basis of accounting have been identified as "current" and "noncurrent." When the historical cost basis of accounting is used, no gain or loss in purchasing power is recognized in the accounting process, but when financial statements are adjusted for general price level changes, a gain or loss in purchasing power will be recognized on monetary and nonmonetary items.

REQUIRED

Evaluate each of the independent statements; identify the areas of fallacious reasoning in each and explain why the reasoning is incorrect.

(AICPA, adapted)

C25-3. CONSTANT DOLLAR RESTATEMENTS FOR HISTORICAL COST AND MARKET VALUE   You are requested to advise two clients on how to restate certain items on their financial statements for the effects of changes in the general price level. Client *A* is a manufacturer of gold necklaces and has substantial raw material inventories of gold, which are accounted for at cost (under GAAP). Client *B* is a gold speculator and has accumulated substantial quantities of gold coins, bars, and so on for investment and speculative purposes. Because of the price variability of gold in recent months and because of the nature of client *B*'s business, client *B* carries the gold at market value.

REQUIRED

Advise both clients on the proper restatement procedures for their inventories, given the valuation methods used. Explain and give reasons for your recommendations.

C25-4. MONETARY VS. NONMONETARY ITEMS   Hunan Realty Investments Ltd. is considering using a new type of debt instrument to finance a proposed expansion of its land purchase activities. The instrument will be called a "price-indexed bond." Each bond will promise to pay each year 3 percent of the par value times the ratio of the price index in that year to the price index in the year the security was issued, and to repay at the end of 10 years the par value times the ratio of the price index in that year to the price index in the year the security was issued. The GNP Implicit Price Deflator is specified as the index to be used.

REQUIRED

1. Discuss briefly the advantages and disadvantages of such a debt instrument for the issuing company.

2. Discuss two possible methods of accounting for these price-indexed bonds under historical cost/nominal dollar accounting (ignore historical cost/constant dollar restatement).

3. Discuss the accounting effects of such an issue if historical cost/constant dollar accounting is used. Consider that the GNP Deflator may not be the index specified for restatement purposes.

(CCA, adapted)

C25-5. MAINTENANCE OF GENERAL PURCHASING POWER   Charles G. Adam, a prominent accountant, left the local university $500,000 at his death in 1986. His will stipulated that the university was to invest the money at its discretion and that the income was to be used to provide scholarships for worthy students studying in the field of accounting. The will further stipulated that not all the income need be distributed in any one year and that no distributions could be made when the scholarship fund was below the general purchasing power equivalent of the initial bequest. The following information relates to the C.G.A. Scholarship Fund:

FINANCIAL POSITION	GENERAL PRICE INDEX	NET ASSETS (MARKET)	NET ASSETS (COST)
1/1/87 opening of fund	100	$500,000	$500,000
12/31/87	110	520,000	530,000
12/31/88	120	550,000	610,000

CASH FLOWS	1987	1988
Cash received from interest and dividends	$60,000	$70,000
Cash distributed to students	30,000	40,000

REQUIRED

1. Write a brief report to the Board of Trustees of the university explaining whether or not the intent of Mr. Adams has been carried out.

2. The change in assets at cost during 1988 took the following form. Construct the traditional measures of income for 1987 and 1988. Comment on the distribution decisions.

	12/31/87	TRANSACTIONS	12/31/88
Cash	$ 5,000	$(170,000)* 150,000† (40,000)‡ 70,000§	$ 15,000
Securities at cost	525,000	(100,000)† 170,000*	595,000
	$530,000		$610,000
Capital	$500,000		$500,000
Accumulated effect of operations	30,000	50,000† 70,000§ (40,000)‡	110,000
	$530,000		$610,000

* Purchase of additional securities.

† Sale of securities at a gain of $50,000.

‡ Cash distributions.

§ Interest and dividends received.

(CGAA, adapted)

C25-6. *FASB STATEMENT NO. 33* DISCLOSURES   As controller for Finer Corporation, you have prepared and delivered to the company president the supplementary current cost/constant dollar disclosures shown on page 1229, as specified by *Statement No. 33*. While the president is aware of the intent of the disclosures, to provide information about the effects of changing prices on a company's operating activities, he is both confused about the disclosures and somewhat upset by the additional costs involved in preparing them.

Two days later you receive a memorandum from the president requesting your responses to the following questions and comments:

a) Why do some companies present historical cost/constant dollar disclosures while others present current cost/constant dollar disclosures?

b) What is the difference between "partial" and "comprehensive" restatement?

c) The use of average-for-the-year dollars is confusing, yet at the same time may simplify restatement. State whether you agree or disagree and explain your position.

d) If purchasing power gains are not distributable in dollars, why disclose such a number?

e) Isn't it folly to refer to increases in specific prices as "holding gains," since we will have to expend more resources if and when these assets are replaced? It seems as if increased prices make us worse off, not better off!

f) What is this "recoverable value" notion?

g) The financial press states that the current cost disclosures contain information common to many current cost systems. Use the current cost disclosures to calculate earnings under the following systems:

1. Current cost in nominal dollars when holding gains are included in income.

2. Current cost in constant dollars when inflation effects are removed from holding gains. These holding gains and "purchasing power" gains (or something like that) are included in earnings.

3. Current cost when capital is maintained in terms of productive capacity.

h) There seem to be so many income numbers that it is almost like "pick and choose" or "as you like it"!

	REPORTED IN PRIMARY STATEMENTS	SUPPLEMENTARY DISCLOSURES, CURRENT COST/CONSTANT DOLLARS
Sales	$1,200,000	$1,200,000
Cost of sales	(700,000)	(900,000)
Depreciation	(200,000)	(210,000)
Other expenses	(50,000)	(50,000)
Income from continuing operations	$ 250,000	$ 40,000
Purchasing power gain on net monetary items		$ 140,000
Increase in specific prices		$ 320,000
Inflation component		(195,000)
Increase in specific prices (net of inflation)		$ 125,000

REQUIRED

Prepare a memorandum to the president responding to each of his points.

EXERCISES

E25-1. CAPITAL MAINTENANCE CONCEPTS; LIFETIME INCOME   Tulsa Company was organized at the end of 1984 and invested $36,000 in soybeans. Cash sales and price indexes over the next three years were as follows:

	SALES	GENERAL PRICE INDEXES (END OF YEAR)	SPECIFIC PRICE INDEXES FOR SOYBEANS (END OF YEAR)
1984		80	120
1985	$21,000	90	130
1986	18,000	110	165
1987	27,000	130	200

REQUIRED

Calculate the three-year income for Tulsa Company under the following capital maintenance concepts:

1. Nominal dollars (original invested dollars).

2. Constant (end of 1987) dollars (units of general purchasing power at the end of 1987).

3. Physical units (based on end-of-1987 current cost).

E25-2. MONETARY VS. NONMONETARY ITEMS; RESTATE FACTORS   Listed below are various account balances for Eastex Corporation. The general price index in effect when the transaction that gave rise to each item occurred is indicated beside the account. At the end of the current year the general price index is 225.

ITEM	INDEX
a) Accounts receivable	200
b) Prepaid expenses	175
c) Inventory	230
d) Notes payable	190
e) Plant and equipment	150
f) Preferred stock	165
g) Retained earnings	various
h) Sales	195
i) Purchases	195
j) Depreciation of plant and equipment	various
k) Cost of goods sold	various
l) Interest expense	195
m) Income tax expense	195
n) Bond investment	164
o) Estimated warranty obligations	195

REQUIRED

If historical cost/constant end-of-year dollar statements are to be prepared by Eastex Corporation, indicate what restate factor (if any) would be applied to each item. Explain your answers.

E25-3. HISTORICAL COST/CONSTANT DOLLAR RESTATEMENTS   The Bradford Electric Utility purchased buildings and equipment in the following years:

YEAR	COST	ESTIMATED LIFE (YEARS)	GENERAL PRICE INDEX
1963	$ 50,000	40	50
1971	120,000	25	100
1980	200,000	20	150
1986	300,000	25	250
1988	80,000	10	300

Bradford uses straight-line depreciation and no salvage value is expected. The general price index at the end of 1988 is 330.

REQUIRED

1. Calculate the historical cost/constant dollar depreciation expense for 1988 in end-of-1988 dollars. Assume that all acquisitions occurred at the beginning of the year.

2. Restate the plant and equipment and accumulated depreciation balances at the end of 1988 in historical cost/constant end-of-1988 dollars.

(CGAA, adapted)

E25-4. ALTERNATIVE ATTRIBUTES/CAPITAL MAINTENANCE CONCEPTS   Matrix, Inc., was organized at the beginning of 1985 and at that time had the following balance sheet:

Cash.....................	$10,000	Contributed capital	$65,000
Land.....................	55,000		$65,000
	$65,000		

Matrix held the cash and land during 1985 and 1986, and sold the land for $90,000 at the end of 1987. Other pertinent data are as follows:

	GENERAL PRICE INDEXES	CURRENT COST OF LAND
Beginning of 1985	110.0	$55,000
End of 1985	121.0	65,000
End of 1986	127.0	75,000
End of 1987	139.7	90,000

Applicable accounting systems are as follows:

SYSTEM	ASSET ATTRIBUTE/ CAPITAL MAINTENANCE CONCEPT
1	Current value/nominal dollars
2	Historical cost/constant dollars
3	Current value/constant dollars
4	Historical cost/nominal dollars

REQUIRED

Calculate the following (use end-of-year dollars, as applicable):

1. Lifetime income under system 2.

2. 1985 income under system 1.

3. 1986 income under system 2.

4. 1986 income under system 3.

5. 1987 income under system 2.

6. 1987 income under system 3.

7. 1987 income under system 4.

8. Lifetime income under system 3.

E25-5. GENERAL PURCHASING POWER GAINS, LOSSES   At the beginning and end of the current year a company had the following monetary assets and liabilities:

	BEGINNING	END
Cash	$10,000	$ 6,000
Accounts receivable	5,000	3,000
Notes receivable	3,000	–0–
Accounts payable	4,000	10,000
Bonds payable	8,000	–0–

Transactions affecting monetary items are assumed to have occurred evenly during the year, except for the sale of a machine for $12,000 at the end of the year.

General price level indexes are as follows:

Beginning of year	80
Average for year	105
End of year	130

REQUIRED

1. Prepare a schedule calculating the gain or loss in general purchasing power for the year in constant EOY dollars.

2. Assume the machine was sold in the middle of the year. Prepare a schedule calculating the gain or loss in general purchasing power in constant EOY dollars. Explain why your answer differs from your answer in part 1.

E25-6. GENERAL PURCHASING POWER GAINS, LOSSES For each case below calculate the gain or loss in general purchasing power using average-for-the-year dollars. Assume that all changes in monetary items occur evenly during the year. Consumer Price Indexes are as follows:

Beginning of year	150
Average for year	175
End of year	200

CASE	BEGINNING	END
1	Net monetary assets, $15,000	Net monetary assets, $30,000
2	Net monetary liabilities, $12,000	Net monetary assets, $50,000
3	Net monetary assets, $60,000	Net monetary liabilities, $10,000
4	Net monetary liabilities, $40,000	Net monetary liabilities, $65,000
5	Net monetary assets, $0	Net monetary assets, $36,000

E25-7. RESTATING COST OF GOODS SOLD IN HISTORICAL COST/CONSTANT DOLLARS The historical cost/ nominal dollar cost of goods sold for Beverly Company appears below:

Beginning inventory	$120,000
Purchases	238,000
Ending inventory	(80,000)
Cost of goods sold	$278,000

The beginning inventory was acquired when the general price index was 95. Purchases were made evenly during the year, when the general price index was 110. The company uses FIFO. Assume that the ending inventory was acquired when the general price index was 115. The general price index at the end of the year was 120.

REQUIRED

1. Calculate the historical cost/constant EOY dollar cost of goods sold.

2. Calculate the historical cost/constant AFY dollar cost of goods sold.

E25-8. RESTATING COST OF GOODS SOLD IN HISTORICAL COST/CONSTANT DOLLARS Complete the requirements in Exercise 25-7, but this time assume that the company uses the LIFO inventory method.

E25-9. BALANCE SHEET HISTORICAL COST/CONSTANT DOLLAR RESTATEMENT; COMPARATIVE STATEMENTS At the end of 1985 the land account for McNew, Inc., consisted of the following:

Purchased 1/1/77	$32,000
Purchased 12/31/79	40,000
Purchased in 3rd quarter, 1983	10,000
Balance, 12/31/85	$82,000

On December 31, 1986, land costing $6,000 was purchased, and on June 30, 1987, the parcel that was purchased in 1979 was sold at a historical cost/nominal dollar gain of $16,000. Relevant general price indexes are as follows:

1/1/77	90
12/31/79	100
3rd quarter, 1983	125
12/31/85	140
12/31/86	150
6/30/87	160
12/31/87	170

REQUIRED

1. Calculate the historical cost/constant EOY dollar carrying amount for the land at the end of 1985.

2. Calculate the historical cost/constant EOY dollar carrying amount for the land at the end of 1986 with the historical cost/constant EOY dollar carrying amount at the end of 1985 presented for comparative statement purposes.

3. Calculate the gain or loss on the sale of land which would appear on the 1987 historical cost/constant EOY dollar income statement.

E25-10. HISTORICAL COST/CONSTANT DOLLAR RESTATEMENT—MACHINERY AND DEPRECIATION At the beginning of 1984 Selry Corporation purchased a machine for $60,000. The machine had a useful life of five years with an expected salvage value of $5,000. Selry uses the straight-line method of calculating depreciation. Relevant general price indexes are as follows:

Beginning of 1984	80
End of 1984	95
End of 1985	115
End of 1987	130

REQUIRED

1. At what amounts would the machine, accumulated depreciation, and depreciation expense appear on the historical cost/constant EOY dollar financial statements for:
   a) 1984?
   b) 1985?

2. How would the amounts in 1*a* appear on the 1985 historical cost/constant EOY dollar statements for comparative purposes?

3. Calculate the gain or loss that Selry would show on the historical cost/constant EOY income statement for 1987 if it sold the machine at the end of 1987 for $22,000.

E25-11. CURRENT COST—INVENTORIES AND COST OF GOODS SOLD At the beginning of 1987 Vern's inventory of antifreeze consisted of 14,000 gallons acquired at the beginning of 1987 at a cost of $2 per gallon. During 1987 Vern purchased 90,000 gallons (evenly during the year) at a cost of $2.70 per gallon. At the end of 1987 the antifreeze inventory totaled 35,000 gallons purchased, on average, in the third quarter of 1987. Vern uses the FIFO method for inventory pricing. General price indexes and current cost data appear below:

	GENERAL PRICE INDEX	CURRENT COST
Beginning of 1987	100	$2.00
Average during 1987	110	2.70
3rd quarter of 1987	116	—
End of 1987	121	3.20

REQUIRED

1. Restate Vern's historical cost/nominal dollar cost of goods sold for 1987 in historical cost/constant EOY dollars.

2. Calculate the current cost/nominal dollar and the current cost/constant EOY dollar cost of goods sold for 1987 on the basis of ending current cost.

3. Calculate the current cost/nominal dollar and the current cost/constant EOY dollar holding gain or loss for 1987.

4. What portion of the holding gain or loss under each approach in part 3 is realized in 1987?

E25-12. CURRENT COST—INVENTORIES AND COST OF GOODS SOLD   Repeat requirements 1 through 4 of Exercise 25-11, except use average-for-the-year dollars and average current cost to calculate cost of goods sold.

E25-13. CURRENT COST—FIXED ASSETS AND DEPRECIATION EXPENSE   Earnest acquired a fixed asset for $75,000 at the beginning of 1987. The asset had a five-year life with no salvage value, and was to be depreciated by the sum-of-the-years'-digits method. General price level and current cost data appear below:

	GENERAL PRICE INDEX	CURRENT COST (NEW)
Beginning of 1987	120	$75,000
Average for 1987	140	82,500
End of 1987	160	90,000

REQUIRED

1. Calculate the depreciation expense for 1987 and the carrying value of the asset at the end of 1987 using ending current cost.

2. Calculate the holding gain or loss in current cost/nominal dollars and in current cost/ constant dollars for 1987 using ending current cost in end-of-year dollars.

3. What portion of each gain or loss in part 2 is realized during 1987?

E25-14. CURRENT COST—FIXED ASSETS AND DEPRECIATION EXPENSE   Repeat requirements 1 through 3 of Exercise 25-13, but this time use average current cost for depreciation expense and average-for-the-year dollars.

E25-15. HISTORICAL COST/CONSTANT DOLLAR RESTATEMENTS   The following schedule lists the general price level index at the end of each of the six indicated years and is to be used to answer questions 1 through 4:

19A	100
19B	110
19C	115
19D	120
19E	140
19F	160

1. In December 19D Harper Corporation purchased land for $300,000. The land was held until December 31, 19E, when it was sold for $400,000. Calculate the historical cost/constant end-of-19E dollar gain or loss on the sale.

2. On January 1, 19B, West Company purchased equipment for $300,000. The equipment was being depreciated over a 10-year period on a straight-line basis, with no salvage value. On December 31, 19E, the equipment was sold for $200,000. Calculate the historical cost/ constant end-of-19E dollar gain or loss on the sale.

3. An analysis of Forsman Corporation's machinery and equipment account as of December 31, 19E, follows:

Machinery and equipment	
Acquired in December 19B	$400,000
Acquired in December 19D	100,000
	$500,000
Accumulated depreciation	
On equipment acquired in December 19B	$160,000
On equipment acquired in December 19D	20,000
	$180,000

Calculate the amount of machinery and equipment net of accumulated depreciation that would appear on a historical cost/constant end-of-19E dollar balance sheet prepared at the end of 19E.

4. Assume that Forsman Corporation's depreciation expense for 19F was $50,000; $40,000 represented depreciation on machinery acquired in December 19B and $10,000 represented depreciation on machinery acquired in December 19D. Calculate the amount of machinery and equipment net of accumulated depreciation that would appear on a historical cost/constant end-of-19F dollar balance sheet prepared at the end of 19F. Also calculate the amount of machinery and equipment net of accumulated depreciation that would appear on a historical cost/constant end-of-19F dollar balance sheet for December 19E, disclosed, for comparative purposes, with the end-of-19F balance sheet.

(AICPA, adapted)

E25-16. CURRENT COST/NOMINAL DOLLAR AND CURRENT COST/CONSTANT DOLLAR HOLDING GAINS— INVENTORIES Magic, Inc., was formed at the beginning of 1987 and had the following purchases and sales of inventory during 1987 and 1988:

1987	Purchases	20,000 units @ $5
	Sales	12,000 units
1988	Purchases	15,000 units @ $8
	Sales	10,000 units

Magic uses the FIFO method of inventory pricing. For simplicity, assume that purchases were made evenly during each year and that the ending inventories were also acquired evenly during each year.

General price indexes and current cost data are as follows (Magic's supplier raises prices at the end of each year):

	GENERAL PRICE INDEX	CURRENT COST
Beginning of 1987	100.0	$ 5
Average for 1987	105.0	–0–
End of 1987	110.0	8
Average for 1988	115.5	–0–
End of 1988	121.0	12

REQUIRED

1. Calculate the holding gain (loss) on inventory for 1987 and 1988 in current cost/nominal dollars and current cost/constant EOY dollars. Use end-of-year current cost.

2. Prepare schedules showing the holding gains realized each year and the unrealized holding gain at the end of each year in current cost/nominal dollars and current cost/constant EOY dollars.

E25-17. HOLDING GAINS ON FIXED ASSETS; BACKLOG At the beginning of 1987 Panama purchased a fixed asset at a cost of $300,000. The fixed asset had an estimated life of 25 years with no salvage value, and was to be depreciated on a straight-line basis. The specific price index (applicable to the fixed asset) and general price index are as follows:

	GENERAL PRICE INDEX	SPECIFIC PRICE INDEX
Beginning of 1987	100	100
End of 1987	110	150
End of 1988	121	175

REQUIRED

Calculate the following for 1987 and 1988 (use end-of-year current cost):

1. Depreciation expense in current cost/nominal dollars and current cost/constant (EOY) dollars.

2. Balance sheet carrying value for the fixed asset in current cost/nominal dollars and current cost/constant (EOY) dollars.

3. Holding gains recognized each year in current cost/nominal dollars and current cost/constant (EOY) dollars.

4. A schedule showing the realized holding gain each year and the unrealized holding gain at the end of each year in current cost/nominal dollars.

5. The amount of backlog depreciation, if any, at the end of each year.

E25-18. HISTORICAL COST/CONSTANT DOLLAR EARNINGS; TWO-PERIOD INCOME   An auto dealer purchased three identical used cars for $1,000 each at the beginning of 1987. Two cars were sold at the end of 1987 for $1,800 each, and the third car was sold in mid-1988 for $2,200. General price indexes during 1987 and 1988 are as follows (assume prices increased evenly):

Beginning of 1987	120
End of 1987	150
End of 1988	165

Cash that became available during those periods was not invested.

REQUIRED

1. Calculate the dealer's 1988 income in units of general purchasing power at the end of 1988.

2. At the end of 1988 the auto dealer has $5,800 in cash ($3,600 inflow in 1987, $2,200 inflow in 1988). In units of end-of-1988 general purchasing power, what portion of this cash represents a return *of* investment and what portion represents a return *on* investment for the two years combined?

E25-19. CURRENT COST/NOMINAL DOLLAR FINANCIAL STATEMENTS   Given the facts below, complete the financial statements that appear below the factual information:

Cost of machine: $1,000	Current cost of machine (new):
Life: 2 years	End of year 1: $1,200
Salvage: $0	End of year 2: 1,500

   a) Depreciation: straight-line, based on average current cost.
   b) Revenues less expenses (except depreciation): $2,000.
   c) Dividends paid each year equal to current operating income.
   d) Attribute to be measured for fixed machine: current cost.
   e) Capital maintenance concept: original invested (nominal) dollars.

INCOME STATEMENTS

	YEAR 1	YEAR 2
Revenues less expenses	$2,000	$2,000
Depreciation	(_____)	(_____)
Current operating income	_____	_____
Holding gains	_____	_____
Net income	======	======

BALANCE SHEETS

	YEAR 1	YEAR 2
Cash	_____	_____
Equipment	_____	_____
Accumulated depreciation	(_____)	(_____)
Total	======	======
Contributed capital	$1,000	$1,000
Retained earnings	_____	_____
Total	======	======

E25-20. HISTORICAL COST/CONSTANT DOLLAR AND CURRENT COST SYSTEMS   Several transactions concerning one asset of a calendar-year company are summarized as follows:

1985 Purchased land for $40,000 cash on 12/31.
Replacement cost at year end was $40,000.

1986 Held the land all year.
Replacement cost at year end was $52,000.

1987 Sold the land for $68,000 on 10/31. Its current cost on that date was $68,000.

General price index:

12/31/85	100
12/31/86	110
10/31/87	120
12/31/87	125

REQUIRED

On the basis of the transactions above, complete the schedule below:

VALUATION OF LAND ON BALANCE SHEET	HISTORICAL COST/NOMINAL DOLLARS	HISTORICAL COST/CONSTANT DOLLARS*	CURRENT COST/ NOMINAL DOLLARS	CURRENT COST/ CONSTANT DOLLARS*	CURRENT COST/ PHYSICAL CAPITAL
12/31/85	_____	_____	_____	_____	_____
12/31/86	_____	_____	_____	_____	_____
GAIN OR LOSS (HOLDING OR FROM SALE) ON INCOME STATEMENT					
1985	_____	_____	_____	_____	_____
1986	_____	_____	_____	_____	_____
1987	_____	_____	_____	_____	_____

* Use constant end-of-year dollars for each year.

(AICPA, adapted)

E25-21. RECOVERABLE VALUE   For each independent situation below, first determine (1) the historical cost/ constant dollar amount and (2) the current cost amount of the asset, then indicate whether the asset would be carried at the calculated amount under each system or at its recoverable value.

a) Inventory of $100,000 was acquired when the CPI was 80. The CPI is currently 100. Current cost of the inventory is $120,000, while its net realizable value is $115,000.

b) Equipment with a net carrying value of $230,000 was acquired when the CPI was 60. The CPI is currently 130. The current cost of a similar used asset is $500,000. Management estimates that the asset's value in use (present value) is at least $525,000.

c) A machine was acquired at a cost of $70,000 when the CPI was 125. At the end of the current year the CPI is 160 and the machine is 40 percent depreciated. The current cost of a new machine is $62,500, while the estimated value in use (present value) and exchange value are $57,500.

PROBLEMS

P25-1. INCOME DETERMINATION UNDER VARIOUS ATTRIBUTE/CAPITAL MAINTENANCE ALTERNATIVES   At the beginning of year 1, a company was organized with a single asset, a machine acquired at a cost of $10,000. The machine had a useful life of two years with no salvage value, and straight-line depreciation was used. The company immediately rented the machine to another company at an annual rental of $12,000 per year (earned evenly throughout each year). The cash received from the rentals was held idle each year. General price indexes and current cost (new) for the machine are as follows:

	GENERAL PRICE INDEX	CURRENT COST
Beginning of year 1	100.0	$10,000
Average, year 1	105.0	
End of year 1	110.0	10,500
Average, year 2	115.5	
End of year 2	121.0	14,000

REQUIRED

1. Calculate the two-year income under the following concepts of capital maintenance:
   a) Nominal dollars.
   b) Constant end-of-year-2 dollars.
   c) Physical capacity (based on end-of-year-2 current cost).

2. Calculate income for each year under the following attribute/capital maintenance combinations. For the current cost systems, use end-of-year current cost for depreciation.
   a) Historical cost/nominal dollars.
   b) Historical cost/constant end-of-year dollars.
   c) Current cost/nominal dollars.
   d) Current cost/constant end-of-year dollars.
   e) Current cost/physical capacity.

3. For each capital maintenance concept, compare your answers in part 1 with the totals for the two years in part 2.

P25-2. HISTORICAL COST/CONSTANT DOLLAR FINANCIAL STATEMENTS   The Constant Corporation Ltd. has prepared the following historical cost/nominal dollar comparative balance sheets:

	12/31/86	12/31/87
Cash	$ 20,000	$ 19,500
Accounts receivable	25,000	72,250
Inventories	42,000	85,000
Total current assets	$ 87,000	$176,750
Plant and equipment	78,000	78,000
Less accumulated depreciation	(26,000)	(28,200)
Total assets	$139,000	$226,550
Current liabilities	$ 40,000	$105,500
Stockholders' equity	99,000	121,050
Total equities	$139,000	$226,550

The income statement for 1987 was as follows:

Sales		$108,500
Less: Cost of goods sold	$88,000	
Depreciation	2,200	(90,200)
Net income		$ 18,300

Transactions for the year included the following:
   a) Sales of $108,500 (all on account) evenly during year.
   b) Cost of goods sold, $88,000.
   c) Collections on accounts receivable, $61,250.
   d) Purchases of inventory (on account), $131,000, evenly during year.
   e) Payments on accounts payable, $65,500.
   f) Depreciation, $2,200.
   g) On December 30, 1987, common stock was issued for cash, $3,750.
The plant and equipment were purchased on January 1, 1976.

The Constant Corporation uses a FIFO procedure to account for inventories. The beginning inventory was acquired at the end of 1986 and the ending inventory was acquired at the end of 1987. An index of general price levels is as follows:

DATE	INDEX
1/1/76	55
12/31/86	100
12/31/87	110
Average for 1987	105

REQUIRED

1. Prepare comparative balance sheets for December 31, 1986, and December 31, 1987, in historical cost/constant end-of-1987 dollars.

2. Calculate the gain or loss in general purchasing power during 1987.

3. Restate the income statement in historical cost/constant end-of-1987 dollars.

4. Prepare a statement of changes in stockholders' equity in historical cost/constant end-of-1987 dollars.

(CGAA, adapted)

P25-3. HISTORICAL COST/CONSTANT DOLLAR AND CURRENT COST/CONSTANT DOLLAR INCOME STATEMENTS
Jane Fashion Mart began operations on December 31, 1987. Its historical cost/nominal dollar comparative balance sheets at December 31, 1987, and December 31, 1988, and income statement for the year ending December 31, 1988, are presented below:

COMPARATIVE BALANCE SHEETS

	DECEMBER 31	
ASSETS	**1987**	**1988**
Cash	$20,000	$ 24,000
Accounts receivable	–0–	40,000
Inventory (FIFO)	40,000	60,000
Furniture and fixtures (net)	20,000	18,000
Land (held for future expansion)	10,000	10,000
Total	$90,000	$152,000

LIABILITIES AND EQUITY		
Accounts payable	$30,000	$ 80,000
Common stock	60,000	60,000
Retained earnings	–0–	12,000
Total	$90,000	$152,000

INCOME STATEMENT
FOR THE YEAR ENDING DECEMBER 31, 1988

Sales		$110,000
Cost of goods sold		(80,000)
Gross margin		$ 30,000
Other expenses:		
Rent expense	$3,600	
Depreciation	2,000	
Other (paid in cash)	4,400	
Income taxes	8,000	(18,000)
Net income		$ 12,000

Other information:

a) Jane rents its facilities at a cost of $300 per month, which equals current cost.

b) Purchases during 1988 were $100,000. Sales, purchases, income taxes, and other cash expenses were incurred evenly during 1988.

c) For simplicity, assume that the ending inventory was acquired on October 1, 1988.

d) Current cost data for 1988:

i) Inventory at current cost on December 31, 1988, was $70,000.

ii) Cost of goods sold at current cost at the dates of sale was $87,500. Assume that this amount also equaled average current cost of goods sold.

iii) Current cost of the land on December 31, 1988, was $15,000.

iv) The current cost (new) of furniture and fixtures on December 31, 1988, was $25,000. Assume that the average current cost of furniture and fixtures was $22,500.

e) Consumer price indexes were as follows:

December 31, 1987	200
October 1, 1988	216
December 31, 1988	220
Average for 1988	212

REQUIRED

1. Calculate Jane Fashion Mart's general purchasing power gain or loss for 1988 in terms of December 31, 1988, dollars.

2. Prepare a historical cost/constant dollar income statement for 1988 for Jane Fashion Mart in terms of December 31, 1988, dollars.

3. Prepare a current cost/constant dollar income statement for 1988 for Jane Fashion Mart in terms of average-for-1988 dollars. Use average current cost.

P25-4. CURRENT COST FINANCIAL STATEMENTS   A firm began operations at the beginning of 1986 with 10,000 racquet balls (its only asset) purchased at that time for $.60 each. Operating activities during 1986 and 1987 were as follows:

	1986	1987
Purchases for cash (evenly during year)	10,000 @ $.80	12,000 @ $1.00
Sales for cash (evenly during year)	15,000 @ $1.50	10,000 @ $1.65
Other expenses	none	none
Current cost: Average	$ .80	$1.00
Ending	1.00	1.25
General price level indexes		
Beginning	110.0	121.0
Average	115.5	130.1
Ending	121.0	139.2

All cash that became available each year was invested at the rate of inflation for the time period involved.

REQUIRED

1. Prepare income statements for 1986 and 1987 in current cost/nominal dollars. Use end-of-year current cost.

2. Prepare income statements for 1986 and 1987 in current cost/constant average-for-the-year dollars. Use average current cost.

3. Prepare income statements for 1986 and 1987 under the current cost/physical capacity model. Use end-of-year current cost.

P25-5. HISTORICAL COST/CONSTANT DOLLAR RESTATEMENTS   Beaver, Inc., a retailer, was organized during 1984. Beaver's management has decided to supplement its December 31, 1987, historical dollar financial statements with general price level financial statements. The following general ledger trial balance (HC/N$) and additional information have been furnished.

	DEBIT	CREDIT
Cash and receivables (net)	$ 540,000	
Marketable securities (common stock)	400,000	
Inventory	440,000	
Equipment	650,000	
Equipment—accumulated depreciation		$ 164,000
Accounts payable		300,000
6% first mortgage bonds, due 1991		500,000
Common stock, $10 par		1,000,000
Retained earnings, 12/31/86		2,000
Sales		1,900,000
Cost of sales	1,508,000	
Depreciation	65,000	
Other operating expenses, interest, and losses	263,000	
	$3,866,000	$3,866,000

a) Monetary assets (cash and receivables) exceeded monetary liabilities (accounts payable and bonds payable) by $445,000 at December 31, 1986.

b) Purchases ($1,840,000 in 1987) and sales are made uniformly throughout the year.

c) Depreciation is calculated on a straight-line basis, with a full year's depreciation being taken in the year of acquisition and none in the year of retirement. The depreciation rate is 10 percent and no salvage value is anticipated. Acquisitions and retirements have been made fairly evenly over each year and the retirements in 1987 consisted of assets purchased during 1985 which were scrapped. An analysis of the equipment account reveals the following:

YEAR	BEGINNING BALANCE	ADDITIONS	RETIREMENTS	ENDING BALANCE
1985	—	$550,000	—	$550,000
1986	$550,000	10,000	—	560,000
1987	560,000	150,000	$60,000	650,000

d) The bonds were issued in 1985 and the marketable securities were purchased evenly during 1987. Other operating expenses and interest were incurred evenly throughout the year.

e) The Consumer Price Indexes were as follows:

YEAR	ANNUAL AVERAGE INDEX
1984	113.9
1985	116.8
1986	121.8
1987	126.7

YEAR		QUARTERLY AVERAGE INDEX
1986	4th	123.5
1987	1st	124.9
	2nd	126.1
	3rd	127.3
	4th	128.5

REQUIRED

1. Prepare a schedule to restate the equipment account balance as of December 31, 1987, in historical cost/constant end-of-1987 dollars.

2. Prepare a schedule to analyze in historical cost/nominal dollars the equipment—accumulated depreciation account for the year 1987.

3. Prepare a schedule to analyze in historical cost/constant end-of-1987 dollars the equipment—accumulated depreciation account for the year 1987.

4. Prepare a schedule to calculate Beaver's general purchasing power gain or loss on its net holdings of monetary assets for 1987.

(AICPA, adapted)

P25-6. HISTORICAL COST/CONSTANT DOLLAR RESTATEMENTS Refer to Problem 25–5. Prepare the historical cost/constant end-of-year dollar income statement for 1987 and the December 31, 1987, balance sheet for Beaver, Inc. Assume that the beginning inventory (which you must calculate) was acquired during the fourth quarter of 1986 and that the ending inventory was acquired during the third quarter of 1987.

P25-7. CONSTANT DOLLAR COMPARATIVE STATEMENTS Superclean Products, a manufacturer of household soaps and detergents, was established on January 1, 1986. Superclean has shown impressive growth in sales and operating income, but its board of directors has questioned whether these increases are due to real growth or to changes in specific and general prices. You have been asked to address this question at the next board meeting.

Condensed income statements of Superclean for the years 1986, 1987, and 1988 are as follows (in thousands of dollars):

	1986	1987	1988
Sales	$ 8,000	$ 9,600	$ 11,500
Cost of goods sold			
Raw materials	$ 1,410	$ 1,720	$ 2,070
Direct labor and overhead other than			
depreciation	2,300	2,850	3,450
Depreciation	940	940	940
Total	$(4,650)	$(5,510)	$ (6,460)
Gross profit	$ 3,350	$ 4,090	$ 5,040
Selling and administrative expenses	(1,800)	(1,880)	(1,940)
Operating income	$ 1,550	$ 2,210	$ 3,100

Additional information:

a) Assume that raw materials included in each year's cost of goods sold were purchased at the beginning of that year and that direct labor and overhead other than depreciation were incurred evenly during each year.

b) Selling and administrative expenses include $100,000 of depreciation per year. The remaining selling and administrative expenses were incurred evenly during each year.

c) All property, plant, and equipment used by Superclean through 1988 was acquired when the business was established.

d) Price indexes were as follows:

	RAW MATERIALS SPECIFIC PRICE INDEX	PROPERTY, PLANT, AND EQUIPMENT SPECIFIC PRICE INDEX	CONSUMER PRICE INDEX
Beginning of 1986	90	100	260
Average for 1986	100	110	264
End of 1986	110	115	270
Average for 1987	120	120	275
End of 1987	122	125	290
Average for 1988	125	130	300
End of 1988	150	135	330

Except for raw materials and property, plant, and equipment, assume that current cost was not materially different from historical cost.

REQUIRED

1. Restate Superclean's income statements for the years 1986, 1987, and 1988 in current cost/constant (end-of-1988) dollars. In calculating current cost expenses each year, use end-of-year current cost for that year.

2. Comment briefly on what the restated comparative statements reveal about the effects of price changes on Superclean's operations for the past three years.

(IMA, adapted)

P25-8. HISTORICAL COST/CONSTANT DOLLAR FINANCIAL STATEMENTS Financial statements for Antle Corporation appear below:

BALANCE SHEET
DECEMBER 31, 1987

Cash	$ 60,000	Current liabilities	$ 80,000
Accounts receivable	50,000	Bonds payable (12%)	100,000
Inventories (LIFO)	90,000	Stockholders' equity	190,000
Equipment	100,000		
Accumulated depreciation	(20,000)		
Building	100,000		
Accumulated depreciation	(40,000)		
Land	30,000		
	$370,000		$370,000

INCOME STATEMENT
FOR YEAR ENDED DECEMBER 31, 1987

Sales	$550,000
Cost of goods sold	(340,000)
Selling expenses	(30,000)
Depreciation	(12,000)
Interest	(12,000)
Income taxes	(35,000)
Net income	$121,000

Additional information:

a) The beginning inventory cost was $80,000, and was acquired when the Consumer Price Index (CPI) was 120. For simplicity, assume that the inventory increase of $10,000 during 1987 occurred at the end of 1987.

b) Purchases, sales, selling expenses, interest expense, and income taxes occurred evenly during the year.

c) Half of the equipment was acquired when the CPI was 80, and the other half was acquired when the CPI was 100. The equipment has a 10-year life.

d) The building and land were acquired when the CPI was 75. The building has a 50-year life.

e) The bonds were issued to acquire the buildings.

f) All revenues and expenses (except depreciation and cost of goods sold) were in cash.

g) Dividends of $23,000 were declared and paid at the end of 1987.

h) At the beginning of 1987, monetary liabilities exceeded monetary assets by $170,000.

i) Other CPI indexes are as follows:

Beginning of year	160
Average for year	175
End of year	190

REQUIRED

Restate the 1987 income statement and the December 31, 1987, balance sheet in historical cost/constant end-of-year dollars. (Restated stockholders' equity will be a balancing amount.)

P25-9. HISTORICAL COST/CONSTANT DOLLAR STATEMENT NO. 33 DISCLOSURES   Refer to Problem 25-8. Prepare the historical cost/constant dollar income statement disclosures using the partial restatement approach illustrated on pages 1215–20. Remember that the measuring unit is constant average-for-the-year dollars.

P25-10. FINANCIAL STATEMENTS BASED ON CURRENT COST SYSTEMS   Mitchell began operations at the beginning of 1987 with the following assets and stockholders' equity:

Cash.....................	$10,000	Stockholders' equity........	$90,000
Inventory (5,000 @ $6)......	30,000		
Buildings*................	50,000		
	$90,000		$90,000

* Twenty-year life, no salvage value, straight-line depreciation used.

Transactions during 1987 were as follows:
   a) Purchases on account made evenly during year, 20,000 @ $11.
   b) Sales for cash made evenly during year, 22,000 @ $18.
   c) Assume that the ending inventory was acquired, on the average, in the third quarter of 1987.
   d) Current cost of the building increased 50 percent during the year.
   e) Current cost of ending inventory, end of year, $16 per unit.
   f) Paid creditors $100,000 at end of year.
   g) Consumer Price Index:

Beginning of year	90
Average for year	100
3rd quarter	108
End of year	115

REQUIRED

   1. Prepare the 1987 income statements (use end-of-year current cost) under the following accounting systems:
      a) Current cost/nominal dollars.
      b) Current cost/constant end-of-1987 dollars.
      c) Current cost/physical capacity.

   2. For parts 1a and 1b, calculate the realized holding gains on the inventory and buildings.

P25-11. FASB STATEMENT NO. 33 CURRENT COST DISCLOSURES   Refer to Problem 25-10. Prepare the current cost/constant dollar income statement disclosures using the partial restatement approach illustrated on pages 1215–20. Current cost should be based on average current cost ($11 per unit for inventory and $62,500 for the building) and the measuring unit should be constant average-for-the-year dollars.

P25-12. CALCULATING SELECTED HC/C$ AND CC/C$ AMOUNTS.   Wilburn and Kilpatrick, CPAs, prepared financial statements for OSU Corporation under four different income systems: historical cost/nominal dollars, current cost/nominal dollars, historical cost/constant dollars, and current cost/constant dollars. These four sets are presented below. OSU was incorporated on January 1, 1987, and commenced operations shortly thereafter.

OSU Corporation

BALANCE SHEETS
DECEMBER 31, 1987

ASSETS	HC/N$	CC/N$	HC/C$	CC/C$
Cash........................	$ 840,000	$ 840,000	$ 840,000	$ 840,000
Inventories..................	20,000	28,000	25,000	28,000
Land	75,000	80,000	(A) 102,273	80,000
Building....................	225,000	315,000	306,818	315,000
Less: Accumulated depreciation..............	(9,000)	(12,600)	(B) (12,273)	(12,600)
Equipment...................	250,000	300,000	280,000	300,000
Less: Accumulated depreciation..............	(25,000)	(30,000)	(28,000)	(30,000)
Total	$1,376,000	$1,520,400	$1,513,818	$1,520,400

LIABILITIES AND EQUITY				
Current liabilities (all monetary)	$ 210,000	$ 210,000	$ 210,000	$ 210,000
Contributed capital	1,000,000	1,000,000	1,500,000	(C) 1,500,000
Retained earnings	166,000	310,400	(196,182)	(189,600)
Total	$1,376,000	$1,520,400	$1,153,818	$1,520,400

INCOME STATEMENTS
FOR THE YEAR ENDED DECEMBER 31, 1987

	HC/N$	CC/N$	HC/C$	CC/C$
Sales	$350,000	$350,000	(F) $437,500	$437,500
Cost of goods sold*	(100,000)	(140,000)	(125,000)	(140,000)
Depreciation	(34,000)	(42,600)	(G) (40,273)	(J) (42,600)
Other expenses	(50,000)	(60,000)	(H) (60,000)	(60,000)
Purchasing power loss			(I) (408,409)	(408,409)
Holding gains: Realized		(D) 58,600		(K) 17,327
Unrealized		(E) 144,400		(L) 6,582
Net income (loss)	$166,000	$310,400	$(196,182)	$(189,600)

*COST OF GOODS SOLD
FOR THE YEAR ENDED DECEMBER 31, 1987

	HC/N$	CC/N$	HC/C$	CC/C$
Inventories, January 1, 1987	—	—	—	—
Purchases, 12,000 units	$120,000	$168,000	$150,000	$168,000
	$120,000	$168,000	$150,000	$168,000
Less: Inventories, December 31, 1987, 2,000 units	(20,000)	(28,000)	(25,000)	(28,000)
Cost of goods sold	$100,000	$140,000	$125,000	$140,000

a) The general price index at the beginning of the year was 100.

b) Land and building were acquired on January 15, 1987, and the general price index at that date was 110. The general price index on December 31, 1987, and the average index for 1987 were 150 and 120, respectively. Assume also that the average index (120) applies to merchandise unsold at the end of the year.

c) The monetary assets as of January 1, 1987, amounted to $1 million. This amount represents the cash invested by the shareholders. There were no monetary liabilities on January 1, 1987.

REQUIRED

1. Calculate how each item indicated by a letter, e.g., (A), on OSU Corporation's financial statement was determined.

2. Assume that OSU Corporation's president would like a measure of "distributable income" under the physical capital concept. Calculate this number.

P25-13. COMPREHENSIVE REVIEW PROBLEM ON PRICE CHANGES CA has recently completed the audit of *X* Company Ltd., which commenced operations on January 1, 1986. CA's firm was appointed auditors at the inception of the company.

The company is a wholesaler of a highly specialized line of electrical components. The rate of technical obsolescence in the industry is high. The company operates in a competitive market and bases its selling prices on incurred costs. The shares of *X* Company Ltd. are traded on a major stock exchange.

CA is currently meeting with the audit committee to discuss the audited financial statements. During the meeting the committee chairman presents to CA the following current cost financial statements, prepared in accordance with the *productive capacity* definition of capital maintenance. The chairman indicates that he wishes to publish such statements in the company's annual report, in order to show the company's employees and stockholders (as well as the government) the "true" income of the company. The chairman believes this practice would help avoid what he considers to be excessive demands for salary increases and management bonuses based on historical cost net income, and an unfair income tax burden.

X Company Ltd.

INCOME STATEMENTS
FOR THE YEAR ENDING

	HISTORICAL COST		CURRENT COST	
	12/31/87	**12/31/86**	**12/31/87**	**12/31/86**
Sales	$24,000,000	$20,000,000	$ 24,000,000	$20,000,000
Cost of goods sold	(12,400,000)	(10,000,000)	(14,000,000)	(13,000,000)
Gross margin	$11,600,000	$10,000,000	$ 10,000,000	$ 7,000,000
Depreciation	$ 4,000,000	$ 4,000,000	$ 5,334,000	$ 4,666,000
Interest on bonds	400,000	400,000	400,000	400,000
Other expenses	4,800,000	3,600,000	4,800,000	3,600,000
Total	$(9,200,000)	$(8,000,000)	$(10,534,000)	$(8,666,000)
Net income (loss) for the year	$ 2,400,000	$ 2,000,000	$ (534,000)	$(1,666,000)

BALANCE SHEETS

	HISTORICAL COST		CURRENT COST	
	12/31/87	**12/31/86**	**12/31/87**	**12/31/86**
Assets				
Cash..................	$ 6,400,000	$ 3,000,000	$ 6,400,000	$ 3,000,000
Inventory (FIFO)	2,600,000	2,000,000	2,800,000	2,600,000
Plant and				
equipment (net)........	4,000,000	8,000,000	5,332,000	9,334,000
	$13,000,000	$13,000,000	$14,532,000	$14,934,000
Liabilities and				
stockholders' equity				
10% bonds payable	$ 4,000,000	$ 4,000,000	$ 4,000,000	$ 4,000,000
Contributed				
capital	9,000,000	9,000,000	9,000,000	9,000,000
	$13,000,000	$13,000,000	$13,000,000	$13,000,000
Capital maintenance				
adjustment, current.....$	–0–	$ –0–	$ 2,532,000	$ 5,600,000
Balance at beginning				
of year..............	–0–	–0–	5,600,000	–0–
Balance at end of year....$	–0–	$ –0–	$ 8,132,000	$ 5,600,000
Retained earnings				
(deficit)				
Balance at beginning				
of year..............$	–0–	$ –0–	$(3,666,000)	$ –0–
Net income (loss)				
for year	2,400,000	2,000,000	(534,000)	(1,666,000)
Dividends	(2,400,000)	(2,000,000)	(2,400,000)	(2,000,000)
Balance at end				
of year.............. $	–0–	$ –0–	$(6,600,000)	$(3,666,000)
	$13,000,000	$13,000,000	$14,532,000	$14,934,000

NOTES TO THE CURRENT
COST FINANCIAL STATEMENTS

Principles of Valuation

The current costs of inventories and of plant and equipment are shown on the balance sheet and income is determined by matching current costs with current revenues. Adjustments of the historical cost of physical assets to their current costs are considered as restatements of stockholders' equity and are shown on the balance sheet as a capital maintenance adjustment.

Current cost is the lowest amount that would have to be incurred in the normal course of business to obtain an asset of *equivalent operating capacity*.

CA was also given the following additional data related to the preparation of the current cost financial statements:

a) Inventory is valued at current cost at the end of the year at the following prices per unit as of December 31: 1986, $650; 1987, $700. There are 4,000 units on hand at the end of years 1986 and 1987.

b) Used plant and equipment were bought on January 1, 1986, for $12 million and had a remaining useful life of only three years. For the historical cost financial statements, *X* Company Ltd. is depreciating the cost on a straight-line basis over three years commencing January 1, 1986. Land is rented and the rental cost is included in other expenses. The current cost (new) of plant and equipment is based on independent appraisals, and the amounts, as of December 31, 1986 and 1987, are $14 million and $16 million, respectively. Depreciation in the current cost financial statements is taken on *end-of-year* replacement costs.

c) There is no change in the market rate of interest on the bonds over the two-year period. The bond interest accrues evenly during the year.

d) Stockholders contributed capital of $9 million on January 1, 1986, when *X* Company Ltd. was formed.

e) Sales occur evenly throughout the year. In 1986 and 1987, 20,000 units were sold at the following prices per unit (all sales are made at prices prevailing at the beginning of each year): as of January 1, 1986, $1,000; as of January 1, 1987, $1,200.

f) Purchases are made evenly throughout the year, at prices prevailing at the beginning of each year. The supplier changes his prices on January 1 of each year. The following purchases were made:

1986	24,000 @ $500 =	$12,000,000
1987	20,000 @ $650 =	$13,000,000

The ending inventory was acquired evenly during the year.

g) For simplicity, cost of goods sold reported in the current cost financial statements is based on the current cost at the *end of the year*.

h) "Other expenses" accrue evenly during the year.

i) Dividends are declared and paid at the end of each year.

j) General price indexes:

	1986	**1987**
Beginning	90.0	95
Average	92.5	100
End	95.0	105

REQUIRED

1. A member of the audit committee of *X* Company Ltd. has suggested that an alternative to the *productive capacity capital maintenance concept* in the above current cost financial statements would be to use the *general purchasing power concept of capital maintenance*. In that case it would be necessary to:

a) Restate the current cost financial statements in terms of end-of-year general purchasing power units (current cost/constant dollars).

b) Include holding gains, net of inflation, in the income statement.

Prepare the 1987 income statement for *X* Company Ltd. under the current cost/constant EOY dollar approach.

2. Another member of the audit committee suggested that a second alternative would be to restate the 1987 historical cost/nominal dollar income statement in historical cost/constant dollars. Prepare an income statement under this approach, using comprehensive restatement and end-of-year dollars.

3. Prepare the 1987 supplemental income statement disclosures as set forth in *Statement No. 33*. Because *X* Company Ltd. is not sure which disclosure will be presented, prepare both historical cost/constant dollar and current cost/constant dollar disclosures. Use partial restatement, average-for-the-year dollars, and the format appearing on page 1218 of this text.

(CCA, adapted)

26 SOURCES OF FINANCIAL INFORMATION AND ANALYSIS OF FINANCIAL STATEMENTS

General-purpose external financial statements report a firm's financial position, results of operations, and changes in financial position (cash flows), and are analyzed by a variety of decision makers. *Creditors* and *potential creditors* evaluate the firm's ability to meet its obligations, including interest payments. Since short-term obligations are likely to be paid with cash on hand or cash generated by the sale of inventory or the collection of receivables, *short-term creditors* are particularly interested in the composition of current assets and the relationship between current assets and current liabilities. On the other hand, because long-term obligations and related interest expense are paid primarily with assets generated by profitable operations, *long-term creditors* are interested in the profit potential of the firm and the financial structure that is expected to support future profits. Present and potential *stockholders* expect returns on their stock investments from dividends and increases in the market value of their investments. Because both dividends and increases in investment market value largely depend on the future profitability of the firm, profitability, financial stability, and corporate capital structure are important to present and potential stockholders. *Management* is interested in the cost, amounts, and types of external financing available to the firm. Management closely monitors profits and profit trends and pays close attention to the capital structure of the firm because both profitability and capital structure influence the decisions of potential investors and creditors.

Financial accountants need to know about financial analysis.

Financial accountants often are called upon by management and external users of financial statements to provide financial information that supplements the basic financial statements or to provide analyses of published financial information. Moreover, a financial accountant's ability to prepare useful financial statements should be enhanced by an understanding of (1) sources of financial information other than annual financial statements, (2) who uses external financial reports, and (3) how external financial reports may be analyzed. The objectives of this chapter are:

1. To identify and discuss some sources of financial information about a firm and its environment.
2. To discuss and illustrate the analysis and interpretation of information contained in financial statements.

In Chapter 4 we mentioned reports on the operations of industry segments of a firm and financial statements issued between annual report dates. In this chapter we discuss segment reporting and interim reporting in more detail. In addition, we describe and illustrate the analysis of financial statements.

SOURCES OF FINANCIAL INFORMATION
FOR EXTERNAL USERS

The first step in financial analysis is to obtain the financial information to be analyzed. We summarized the available financial information in Exhibit 1–1 (p. 6). Many sources of financial information about a company are available to external users. Some of the more important of these sources are described below. Special attention is given to segment reports and interim reports as sources of useful financial information.

FINANCIAL PUBLICATIONS

Financial publications, such as *The Wall Street Journal* and *Barron's,* provide a substantial amount and variety of general financial information as well as information about specific firms. Other publications provide annual summary financial data for numerous industries. These publications are available from Robert Morris Associates and Dun & Bradstreet, among others, and from several government agencies. Many trade associations and most security brokerage houses provide financial data about individual firms, industries, and the economy as a whole.

ADVISORY SERVICES

Organizations that provide advisory services to investors compile financial information about companies and aid investors in summarizing, analyzing, and evaluating available financial information. An organization that offers complete advisory services can provide economic forecasts for individual firms, industries, and the general economy.

FORMS AND REPORTS FILED WITH THE SEC

Companies that want to issue securities to the general public or that already have issued securities to the public are required to file a variety of forms and financial reports with the SEC.[1] Prior to the early 1980s, each form arising from the Securities Act of 1933 and the Securities Exchange Act of 1934 contained its own specific, detailed financial and nonfinancial statement disclosure requirements. In 1980, the SEC initiated an integrated disclosure program with the objectives of uniform disclosure and interchangeable document parts, consistent reporting under the 1933 and 1934 acts, and more concise disclosure documents, relying on disclosure by reference wherever possible. In 1983, the SEC completed its efforts to integrate the disclosure requirements of the 1933 and 1934 acts. The specific disclosures were centralized in either *Regulation S-K* or *Regulation S-X*. All nonfinancial statement disclosure requirements are included in *Regulation S-K* and all financial statement disclosure requirements are included in *Regulation S-X*. Now, each form provided for under the 1933 and 1934 acts merely specifies the disclosures contained in *Regulations S-K* and *S-X* that are to be made for that form.

The 1933 act prohibits sales of, or offers to sell, securities to the public in interstate commerce or through the use of the mail unless those securities have been registered with the SEC. The SEC has adopted two categories of registration forms—general forms and special forms.

Three general forms—Forms S-1, S-2, and S-3—serve as the primary registration forms. These three forms are set up on a tier system based on the issuer's "following" in the stock market. All three forms require essentially the same information, but the method of providing the information varies. Form S-1, the most widely used of the forms, requires complete disclosure of all financial and nonfinancial information to be included in the prospectus and permits no incorporation of information by reference to other reports filed with the SEC. Form S-2 streamlines disclosure and reporting requirements and allows some incorporation by reference to other SEC reports. Form S-3 allows the most use of incorporation by reference and is used by large companies having a wide following in the stock market.

---

[1] You may want to review the Chapter 1 discussion about the SEC and its role in the development of financial accounting and reporting.

The 11 special registration forms of the SEC are used in special circumstances, such as when securities are offered to employees under stock option plans, or when small dollar amounts of securities are being offered by small initial registrants.

The SEC has approximately 20 reporting forms to be used by companies that have securities registered under the 1934 act. Most of these forms are used in very specialized circumstances and will not be discussed here. However, three of the forms (Forms 8-K, 10-K, and 10-Q) are commonly used and deserve mention.

Form 8-K is used to report significant, unusual events that occur between annual report dates. Form 8-K must be filed within 15 days after the occurrence of any of the following events: a change in control of the registrant; significant acquisitions or dispositions of assets; bankruptcy or receivership; a change in the registrant's certifying accountant; resignation of a director; or any other event that the registrant considers to be important to its security holders.

Within 90 days after the registrant's fiscal year-end, an annual report must be filed with the SEC. Unless some other form is prescribed, Form 10-K is used for this purpose. Although it must be furnished to stockholders on request, Form 10-K is not a substitute for the registrant's annual report to stockholders. Form 10-K includes substantially all of the nonfinancial statement disclosure requirements set forth in *Regulation S-K* as well as the financial statement information specified in *Regulation S-X*. As a result of the SEC's integrated disclosure program, companies may omit information from the 10-K report if that information is included in the annual report to stockholders. In this case, a copy of the annual report to stockholders must be filed with Form 10-K, and the 10-K must indicate that the omitted information is included in the annual report.

Form 10-Q provides a quarterly report of interim financial statement information, and must be filed within 45 days of the end of each of the first three quarters of each fiscal year. Form 10-Q also requires a management discussion and analysis of the financial condition and results of operations, as specified in *Regulation S-K*. Form 10-Q is not required for the fourth quarter. As is true of Form 10-K, information may be omitted from Form 10-Q if that information is contained in a quarterly report to the stockholders and a copy of that quarterly report is filed with Form 10-Q.

ANNUAL STATEMENTS, SEGMENT REPORTING, AND INTERIM REPORTS

Most of the financial information that is generally available for a company can be found in the annual financial statements (which usually include industry segment information), interim financial reports (e.g., quarterly financial reports), footnotes to the financial statements, schedules and commentary that supplement the financial statements, and the external auditor's report. (As an example, a complete set of consolidated financial statements for The Coca-Cola Co. is presented in Appendix 5–1.) In the next few pages we will discuss segment reporting and interim financial reports because they are very important sources of information about the operations of a company.

Segment Reporting

A company's financial statements usually are prepared on a consolidated basis, such as the consolidated financial statements of The Coca-Cola Co., shown in Appendix 5–1. In consolidated financial statements the revenues, expenses, assets, liabilities, and other financial statement elements of the controlling (parent) firm and its subsidiaries are combined for reporting purposes, and a consolidated dollar amount for each account is reported. For example, the amount of cash reported in the consolidated financial statements is the total of all the cash of the various operating components of the firm and its subsidiaries.

In **segment reporting,** the consolidated accounts are broken down into amounts related to particular industry segments of the firm or amounts related to firm operations in specific geographic areas. For example, in Exhibit 26–1 you will find that General Mills,

EXHIBIT 26–1

General Mills, Inc., and Subsidiaries

SEGMENT INFORMATION FOR THE YEARS ENDED MAY 27, 1979–84

NOTE FOURTEEN: SEGMENT INFORMATION (a)

(In Millions)

	CONSUMER FOODS	RESTAURANTS	TOYS	FASHION	SPECIALTY RETAILING AND OTHER	UNALLOCATED CORPORATE ITEMS (b)	CONSOLIDATED TOTAL
Sales							
1984	$2,713.4	$1,079.7	$782.7	$587.4	$437.6		$5,600.8 (c)
1983	2,792.6	984.5	728.3	616.3	429.1		5,550.8 (c)
1982	2,707.4	839.4	654.8	657.3	453.2		5,312.1
1981	2,514.6	704.0	674.3	580.5	379.0		4,852.4
1980	2,218.8	525.7	647.0	422.5	356.3		4,170.3
1979	2,062.4	436.3	583.9	360.4	302.0		3,745.0
Operating Profits before Redeployments							
1984	275.3	70.0	72.0	48.8	25.4	$(100.5)	391.0 (c)
1983	269.4	80.0	104.6	75.9	12.2	(135.1)	407.0 (c)
1982	274.0	79.2	81.2	105.1	5.5	(104.5)	440.5
1981	217.7	75.3	70.6	87.5	13.2	(89.9)	374.4
1980	210.5	52.7	60.1	43.7	26.4	(76.8)	316.6
1979	188.8	41.5	55.7	20.3	19.7	(66.5)	259.5
Operating Profits after Redeployments							
1984	383.0	37.3	51.0	37.9	(10.9)	(99.6)	398.7
1983	268.2	80.0	104.6	75.9	16.1	(135.1)	409.7
1982	263.0	79.2	79.2	101.7	(11.9)	(104.5)	406.7
1981	217.7	75.3	70.6	87.5	13.2	(89.9)	374.4
1980	210.5	52.7	60.1	43.7	26.4	(76.8)	316.6
1979	193.2	41.5	55.7	20.3	19.7	(66.5)	263.9
Identifiable Assets							
1984	934.1	585.3	545.2	391.9	210.3	191.3	2,858.1
1983	983.8	572.7	450.9	346.7	238.8	351.0	2,943.9
1982	918.4	495.6	403.6	361.1	259.9	263.1	2,701.7
1981	841.1	379.0	401.8	323.9	239.3	116.2	2,301.3
1980	761.1	269.1	441.2	231.2	181.6	128.2	2,012.4
1979	686.5	217.3	367.9	241.2	154.7	167.6	1,835.2
Capital Expenditures							
1984	130.3	82.3	36.3	16.3	14.3	2.9	282.4
1983	123.8	107.6	39.3	17.3	17.1	2.9	308.0
1982	96.2	122.4	30.6	13.4	21.8	2.9	387.3
1981	95.7	85.1	28.6	14.4	19.2	3.6	246.6
1980	80.6	49.8	34.7	5.2	19.3	6.9	196.5
1979	68.9	31.0	25.8	9.8	13.1	5.5	154.1
Depreciation Expense							
1984	53.9	34.7	22.2	7.3	9.2	1.7	129.0
1983	51.9	30.6	22.8	6.2	9.1	1.7	122.3
1982	46.6	24.4	20.7	6.0	7.7	1.6	107.0
1981	40.6	19.7	22.9	5.0	5.2	1.7	95.1
1980	33.6	14.3	19.2	3.9	4.1	2.8	77.9
1979	31.9	11.9	18.8	3.7	3.2	1.0	70.5

(In Millions)	U.S.A.	OTHER WESTERN HEMISPHERE	EUROPE	OTHER	UNALLOCATED CORPORATE ITEMS (b)	CONSOLI-DATED TOTAL
Sales (d)						
1984	$5,094.5	$195.3	$291.1	$19.9		$5,600.8 (c)
1983	5,068.6	200.5	262.6	19.1		5,550.8 (c)
1982	4,808.4	223.4	259.1	21.2		5,312.1
1981	4,300.6	223.3	307.9	20.6		4,852.4
1980	3,649.2	191.9	308.5	20.7		4,170.3
1979	3,187.5	161.8	377.8	17.9		3,745.0
Operating Profits before Redeployments (d)						
1984	446.9	19.4	20.8	4.4	$(100.5)	391.0 (c)
1983	490.3	34.3	15.4	2.1	(135.1)	407.0 (c)
1982	494.0	41.0	7.4	2.6	(104.5)	440.5
1981	422.3	31.6	7.0	3.4	(89.9)	374.4
1980	366.5	20.4	3.9	2.6	(76.8)	316.6
1979	298.3	16.6	9.8	1.3	(66.5)	259.5
Operating Profits after Redeployments (d)						
1984	460.7	16.0	17.2	4.4	(99.6)	398.7
1983	493.0	34.3	15.4	2.1	(135.1)	409.7
1982	462.2	39.0	7.4	2.6	(104.5)	406.7
1981	422.3	31.6	7.0	3.4	(89.9)	374.4
1980	366.5	20.4	3.9	2.6	(76.8)	316.6
1979	298.3	16.6	14.2	1.3	(66.5)	263.9
Identifiable Assets (d)						
1984	2,362.8	93.5	199.4	11.1	191.3	2,858.1
1983	2,323.9	91.9	165.6	11.5	351.0	2,943.9
1982	2,156.3	112.4	157.6	12.3	263.1	2,701.7
1981	1,886.2	114.3	176.0	8.6	116.2	2,301.3
1980	1,571.4	108.6	189.6	14.6	128.2	2,012.4
1979	1,393.2	88.6	172.6	13.2	167.6	1,835.2

(a) Both inter-segment sales and export sales are immaterial.

(b) Corporate expenses include interest expense, profit sharing, employee stock ownership plan, balance sheet related foreign currency effects and general corporate expenses. Corporate assets consist mainly of cash and short-term investments, investments in tax leases and other miscellaneous investments.

(c) Comparable year to year results from continuing operations (dollars in millions):

	1984	1983	PERCENT CHANGE
Sales	$5,540.7	$5,183.6	6.9%
Consolidated Operating Profits after Corporate Items	389.3	383.4	1.5

(d) Certain amounts for years prior to 1984 have been reclassified to conform to 1984 presentation.

Inc., reports that consolidated sales of $5,600.8 million (in 1984) came from industry segments of the firm as follows: consumer foods, $2,713.4 million; restaurants, $1,079.7 million; toys, $782.7 million; fashion, $587.4 million; and specialty retailing and other, $437.6 million. General Mills also reports that its 1984 consolidated sales of $5,600.8 million were made in the following geographic areas: U.S.A., $5,094.5 million; other Western Hemisphere, $195.3 million; Europe, $291.1 million; and other areas, $19.9 million.

Since both consolidated financial statements and segment reporting normally are studied in detail in an advanced accounting course, we will discuss only the fundamental aspects of segment reporting.

THE BASIS FOR SEGMENT REPORTING   When a company's operations take place in several different industries or are located in different geographic areas, the difficulty of analyzing its financial condition, operating trends, and financial ratios can be greatly increased. The various industry segments or geographic areas of operation of the company can have different rates of profitability, different levels and types of risk, and different opportunities for growth. Such differences may be difficult to identify when only consolidated financial data are available for analysis. As a result, financial statement users believe that consolidated data are more useful when supplemented by disaggregated financial information to help them analyze the amounts, timing, and uncertainties of expected cash flows and risks associated with an investment or loan to a company that operates in different industries or different geographic areas. Providing this disaggregated information is the objective of segment reporting.

> Segment reporting provides disaggregated financial information.

In 1976, *FASB Statement No. 14*, ''Financial Reporting for Segments of a Business Enterprise,'' was issued to provide guidelines for the reporting of disaggregated financial data for a firm.[2] Several additional *Statements of Standards* have been issued as amendments to *Statement No. 14*.[3] *Statement No. 18* (November 1977) states that segment information is not required in interim financial statements. *Statement No. 21* (April 1978) specifies that segment data are not required for a nonpublic company. *Statement No. 24* (December 1978) eliminates the requirement to disclose segment information in the separate financial statements of a parent company or affiliated companies when those statements accompany consolidated or combined financial statements. *Statement No. 30* (August 1979) requires disclosure of the amount of sales to an individual domestic government or foreign government when those revenues are 10 percent or more of the firm's revenues.

Statement No. 14 requires that when a company issues a fiscal year-end balance sheet, income statement, and statement of changes in financial position in conformity with GAAP, those financial statements must include information about the company's operations in different industries, its foreign operations and export sales, and its major customers. A firm that operates predominantly or exclusively in a single industry is not required to provide industry segment information, but it must identify the industry in which it operates.

---

[2] ''Financial Reporting for Segments of a Business Enterprise,'' *Statement of Financial Accounting Standards No. 14* (Stamford, Conn.: FASB, 1976).

[3] ''Financial Reporting for Segments of a Business Enterprise—Interim Financial Statements,'' *Statement of Financial Accounting Standards No. 18* (Stamford, Conn.: FASB, 1977); ''Suspension of the Reporting of Earnings per Share and Segment Information by Nonpublic Enterprises,'' *Statement of Financial Accounting Standards No. 21* (Stamford, Conn.: FASB, 1978); ''Reporting Segment Information in Financial Statements That Are Presented in Another Enterprise's Financial Report,'' *Statement of Financial Accounting Standards No. 24* (Stamford, Conn.: FASB, 1978); ''Disclosure of Information about Major Customers,'' *Statement of Financial Accounting Standards No. 30* (Stamford, Conn.: FASB, 1979).

REPORTING ON OPERATIONS IN DIFFERENT INDUSTRIES   An **industry segment** is a component of the company that is engaged in providing a product or service or a group of related products and services, primarily to unaffiliated customers (customers outside the company), for a profit. For example, consumer foods is an industry segment of General Mills, Inc. Identification of industry segments depends largely on the judgment of the firm's management. Revenue and expense information often is accumulated for internal planning and control purposes for each of the firm's components that sells primarily to outside markets. These components of the firm sometimes are called profit centers. Existing profit centers are logical starting points for determining industry segments. Other aids in determining industry segments are the Standard Industrial Classification system and the Enterprise Standard Industrial Classification system.[4]

Factors that should be considered in identifying industry segments include: (1) the nature of the product, (2) the nature of the production process, and (3) markets and marketing methods. Related products or services may have similar purposes or end uses; may share production or sales facilities or use the same or similar raw materials; or may have similar geographic marketing areas, types of customers, or marketing methods.

A company is not required to provide financial information for all identified industry segments. Financial information is required only for those industry segments that meet *Statement No. 14* requirements for classification as reportable segments. **Reportable segments** are determined on the basis of the significance, or materiality, of the industry segment to the company. Hence, *Statement No. 14* provides us with an example of the influence of materiality on the development of useful accounting information.

An industry segment is reportable if it satisfies *one or more* of the following three materiality tests:

Tests for identifying a reportable segment.

1. *Revenue test*. The industry segment's revenue, including both sales to unaffiliated customers and intersegment sales or transfers, must be 10 percent or more of the combined revenue of all the firm's industry segments.

2. *Operating profit or loss test*. The operating profit or loss of the industry segment must be 10 percent or more of the greater, in absolute amount, of:
   a) The combined operating profit of all industry segments with operating profits.
   b) The combined operating loss of all industry segments with operating losses.
   To illustrate, assume that a company has six industry segments with operating profits and losses as shown below.

INDUSTRY SEGMENT	OPERATING PROFIT (LOSS)	
A	$200	
B	50	$650
C	400	
D	(100)	
E	(40)	$(640)
F	(500)	

The absolute amount of the combined operating profits of all profitable industry segments is $650 and the absolute amount of the combined operating losses of all industry segments with losses is $640. The greater of these two absolute amounts is $650. Therefore, all industry segments with operating profits or losses having an absolute

---

[4] Both of these systems are prepared by the Statistical Policy Division of the U.S. Office of Management and Budget.

amount equal to or greater than $65 (10% × $650) meet the operating profit or loss test. Industry segments *A, C, D,* and *F* are reportable segments because they meet the operating profit or loss test.

3. *Identifiable assets test.* The identifiable assets of the industry segment must be 10 percent or more of the combined identifiable assets of all industry segments.

In addition to the three materiality tests for identifying reportable segments, *Statement No. 14* requires that the combined reportable segments of a company represent a material portion of the company's total operations. Specifically, the combined revenue from sales of all reportable segments to unaffiliated customers must be at least 75 percent of the combined revenue from all industry segment sales to unaffiliated customers. If the industry segments identified as reportable by the three materiality tests do not satisfy the 75 percent of revenue test, additional industry segments of the firm must be classified as reportable segments until the 75 percent test is met. For example, if the reportable segments identified by the materiality tests account for only 73 percent of all industry segment revenue from unaffiliated customers, one or more additional industry segments must be included among reportable segments so that at least 75 percent of all industry segment revenue is accounted for by the reported segments. On the other hand, it is possible to present overly detailed segment information, so *Statement No. 14* suggests reporting a maximum of ten industry segments.

SEGMENT INFORMATION TO BE REPORTED   Companies are required to report the following information for each reportable segment and in the aggregate for their industry segments that are not classified as reportable:

Information required for reportable segments.

1. *Revenue information.* Revenue from sales to unaffiliated customers and from intersegment sales or transfers must be disclosed. The basis of accounting for intersegment sales or transfers must be described and consistently applied.

2. *Profitability information.* Disclosure of operating profit or loss of each reportable segment is required. In addition, it is acceptable, but not required, to report other measures or components of reportable segment profitability, such as cost of goods sold.

When the operating profit or loss of a reportable segment is calculated, the following are to be excluded: general corporate expenses, interest expense, income taxes, equity income or loss from unconsolidated subsidiaries and other unconsolidated investees, gain or loss on discontinued operations, extraordinary items, minority interest, and the cumulative effect of a change in accounting principle.

3. *Identifiable assets information.* The identifiable assets of a reportable segment must be disclosed, and must include those tangible and intangible assets that are used exclusively by the segment plus an allocated portion of any assets used jointly with other industry segments. The identifiable assets of a reportable segment do not include either assets used only for general corporate purposes or intersegment loans and advances (unless the reportable segment is a financial segment).

4. *Other related disclosures.* Additional disclosures required for each reportable segment are:
   a) The segment's aggregate depreciation, depletion, and amortization expense.
   b) The segment's additions to property, plant, and equipment.
   c) The company's equity in the net income from investment in unconsolidated subsidiaries or other equity-method investees whose operations are vertically integrated with the operations of the reportable segment.[5]

---

[5] ''Vertical integration'' refers to a situation in which one entity—e.g., an unconsolidated subsidiary—supplies inputs to another related entity, such as a reportable segment of the parent company.

d) The geographic areas of operations of equity-method investees who are vertically integrated with the reportable segment.

e) The effect of any change in accounting principle on the operating profit or loss of the reportable segment in the period of change.

The information presented for each reportable segment and in the aggregate for industry segments that are not classified as reportable must be reconciled to related amounts in the consolidated financial statements of the company.

METHODS OF PRESENTING SEGMENT INFORMATION   Information about the reportable segments of a company can be included in the company's financial statements in any of three ways:

1. Within the body of the financial statements, with supporting footnote disclosures.

2. Entirely in the footnotes to the financial statements.

3. In a separate schedule that is included as an integral part of the financial statements.

Most companies report industry segment information in separate schedules included as part of the financial statements. Exhibit 26–2 presents the consolidated income statement of the hypothetical Multi-Segment Company. Exhibit 26–3 shows a schedule that could be prepared to report segment information for Multi-Segment.

EXHIBIT 26–2

Multi-Segment Company

CONSOLIDATED INCOME STATEMENT
FOR THE YEAR ENDED DECEMBER 31, 1987

Sales		$6,750
Cost of sales	$4,410	
Selling and general and administrative expenses	950	(5,360)
Operating profit before taxes		$1,390
Other revenues and expenses		
Interest expense	$ (120)	
Equity in net income of Acme Company (25% owned)	100	(20)
Income from continuing operations before taxes		$1,370
Income taxes		(500)
Income from continuing operations		$ 870
Discontinued operations		
Loss from operations of discontinued West Coast division (net of $50 income tax effect)	$ (90)	
Loss on disposal of West Coast division (net of $100 income tax effect)	(110)	(200)
Income before extraordinary gain and before cumulative effect of change in accounting principle		$ 670
Extraordinary gain (net of $80 income tax effect)		90
Cumulative effect on prior years of change from straight-line to accelerated depreciation (net of $60 income tax effect)		(70)
Net income		$ 690

Source: ''Financial Reporting for Segments of a Business Enterprise,'' *Statement of Financial Accounting Standards No. 14* (Stamford, Conn.: FASB, 1976), Exhibit A, app. F.

EXHIBIT 26–3

Multi-Segment Company

INFORMATION ABOUT OPERATIONS IN DIFFERENT INDUSTRIES FOR THE YEAR ENDED DECEMBER 31, 1987

	REPORTABLE INDUSTRY SEGMENTS			OTHER INDUSTRY SEGMENTS	ADJUST- MENTS AND ELIMINA- TIONS	CONSOL- IDATED
	A	B	C			
Sales to unaffiliated customers	$ 2,350	$ 3,500	$ 700	$ 200		$ 6,750
Intersegment sales		775			$(775)*	
Total sales revenue	$ 2,350	$ 4,275	$ 700	$ 200	$(775)	$ 6,750
Operating expenses						
Cost of sales	$ 1,500	$ 2,260	$ 500	$ 150		$ 4,410
Selling and general and administrative expenses	225	350	75	100		750
Total operating expenses	$(1,725)	$(2,610)	$(575)	$ (250)		$(5,160)
Operating profit before taxes	$ 625	$ 1,665	$ 125	$ (50)	$(775)	$ 1,590
General company expenses						(200)†
Equity in net income of Acme Company						100
Interest expense						(120)
Income from continuing operations before taxes.................						$ 1,370
Identifiable assets, 12/31/87‡	$ 4,000	$ 7,000	$ 900	$1,000	$(300)	$12,600
Investment in net assets of Acme Company						400
Corporate assets						1,400
Total assets, 12/31/87						$14,400

* Intersegment sales must be eliminated to reconcile industry and consolidated sales revenue.

† General company expenses total $200. These expenses are deducted as a separate line item in the calculation of consolidated income from continuing operations.

‡ The amounts reported for identifiable assets are based on balance sheet data. One hundred dollars of intersegment profit in inventory and $200 of assets used for general corporate purposes were eliminated.

Note to schedule: The Company operates principally in three industries, *A, B,* and *C.* Operations in industry *A* involve production and sale of [describe types of products and services]. Operations in industry *B* involve production and sale of [describe types of products and services]. Operations in industry *C* involve production and sale of [describe types of products and services]. Total revenue by industry includes both sales to unaffiliated customers, as reported in the Company's consolidated income statement, and intersegment sales, accounted for by [describe the basis of accounting for intersegment sales].

Operating profit is total revenue less operating expenses. When operating profit is calculated, none of the following items has been added or deducted: general corporate expenses, interest expense, income taxes, equity in income from unconsolidated investee, loss from discontinued operations of the West Coast division (which was a part of the Company's operations in industry *B*), extraordinary gain (which relates to the Company's operations in industry *A*), and the cumulative effect of the change from straight-line to accelerated depreciation (of which $30 relates to the Company's operations in industry *A,* $20 to industry *B,* and $20 to industry *C*). Depreciation for industries *A, B,* and *C* was $160, $180, and $40, respectively. Capital expenditures for the three industries were $200, $40, and $50, respectively.

The effect of the change from straight-line to accelerated depreciation was to reduce the 1987 operating profit of industries *A, B,* and *C* by $40, $30, and $20, respectively. Identifiable assets by industry are those assets that are used in the Company's operations in each industry. Corporate assets are principally cash and marketable securities.

The Company has a 25 percent interest in Acme Co., whose operations in the U.S. are vertically integrated with the Company's operations in industry *A.* Equity in net income of Acme Co. was $100; investment in net assets of Acme Co. was $400.

Contracts with a U.S. government agency account for $1,100 of the sales to unaffiliated customers of industry *B.*

Source: ''Financial Reporting for Segments of a Business Enterprise,'' *Statement of Financial Accounting Standards No. 14* (Stamford, Conn.: FASB, 1976), Exhibit B, app. F.

INFORMATION ABOUT FOREIGN OPERATIONS AND EXPORT SALES   In addition to industry segment information, *Statement No. 14* requires companies to disclose information about foreign operations and export sales. **Foreign operations** include any revenue-producing operations that are located outside a company's home country and that generate revenue from sales to unaffiliated customers or from intracompany sales or transfers between geographic areas. **Domestic operations,** on the other hand, include revenue-producing operations of the company that are located in the company's home country and that generate sales revenue from unaffiliated customers or from intracompany sales or transfers between geographic areas.

A company is required to disclose revenue, operating profit or loss, and identifiable assets separately for its foreign operations and domestic operations if either:

1. Foreign operations produce revenue from sales to unaffiliated customers that is 10 percent or more of consolidated revenue, or

2. The identifiable assets of foreign operations are 10 percent or more of consolidated total assets.

If foreign operations are conducted in more than one foreign geographic area, revenue, operating profit or loss, and identifiable assets must be reported separately for each geographic area whose sales to unaffiliated customers are 10 percent or more of consolidated sales revenue. The same information must be reported in the aggregate for all other foreign geographic areas. Export sales to unaffiliated customers by a company's domestic operations that are 10 percent or more of consolidated sales revenue must be reported separately. Exhibit 26–4, which is based on the Multi-Segment Company data, presents an illustrative schedule of information about operations in different geographic areas.

INFORMATION ABOUT MAJOR CUSTOMERS   *Statement No. 14* requires companies to disclose information about the extent of reliance on major customers. If 10 percent or more of the revenue of a company is derived from sales to any single customer, including a governmental body, that fact and the amount of revenue from each customer must be disclosed. In addition, the industry segment or segments that make the sales must be disclosed.

In summary, companies that publish annual financial statements in conformity with GAAP also must provide information about operations in reportable industry segments, foreign operations and export sales, and major customers. In the next section we shall discuss reporting another type of useful information—interim financial information.

Interim Financial Reporting

The length of time between annual financial statements may be too long to permit timely evaluation of a company's financial position, operating results, and cash flows. Financial reports issued between the dates of annual financial statements are called **interim financial reports** and are another, more timely source of financial information about a company. Interim financial reports most often are issued externally on a quarterly basis. Interim financial reports, which must be prepared in accordance with *APB Opinion No. 28,*[6] need not be audited. Thus, each page of an unaudited interim report should be clearly labeled "Unaudited" to avoid misleading inferences.

Several inherent difficulties complicate interim reporting. For example, the revenues of some companies fluctuate widely from one interim period to the next because of seasonal factors, while in other companies heavy fixed costs incurred in one interim period may benefit other interim periods. In other situations, costs and expenses related to

---

[6] "Interim Financial Reporting," *Opinions of the Accounting Principles Board No. 28* (New York: AICPA, 1973).

EXHIBIT 26—4

Multi-Segment Company

INFORMATION ABOUT OPERATIONS IN DIFFERENT
GEOGRAPHIC AREAS FOR THE YEAR ENDED DECEMBER 31, 1987

	UNITED STATES	GEOGRAPHIC AREA A	GEOGRAPHIC AREA B	ADJUSTMENTS AND ELIMINATIONS	CONSOL- IDATED
Sales to unaffiliated customers	$ 4,000	$1,750	$1,000		$ 6,750
Transfers between geographic areas	1,000			$(1,000)*	
Total revenue	$ 5,000	$1,750	$1,000	$(1,000)	$ 6,750
Operating expenses					
Cost of sales	$ 3,010	$ 900	$ 500		$ 4,410
Selling and general and administrative expenses	600	90	60		750
Total operating expenses	$(3,610)	$ (990)	$ (560)		$(5,160)
Operating profit, before taxes	$ 1,390	$ 760	$ 440	$(1,000)	$ 1,590
General company expenses					(200)†
Equity in net income of Acme Co.					100
Interest expense					(120)
Income from continuing operations, before taxes					$ 1,370
Identifiable assets, 12/31/87‡	$ 7,500	$3,500	$1,800	$ (200)	$12,600
Investment in net assets of Acme Co.					400
Corporate assets					1,400
Total assets, 12/31/87					$14,400

* Transfers between geographic areas must be eliminated to reconcile geographic area revenue with consolidated revenue.

† General company expenses total $200. These expenses are deducted as a separate line item in the calculation of consolidated income from continuing operations.

‡ The amounts reported for identifiable assets are based on balance sheet data. Two hundred dollars of assets used for general corporate purposes were eliminated.

Note to schedule: Transfers between geographic areas are accounted for by [describe the basis of accounting for such transfers]. Operating profit is total revenue less operating expenses. In the calculation of operating profit, none of the following items has been added or deducted: general corporate expenses, interest expense, income taxes, equity in income from unconsolidated investee, loss from discontinued operations of West Coast division (which was part of the Company's U.S. operations), extraordinary gain (which relates to the Company's operations in geographic area *B*), and the cumulative effect of the change from straight-line to accelerated depreciation (which relates entirely to the Company's operations in the United States).

Identifiable assets are those assets of the Company that are identified with the operations in each geographic area. Corporate assets are principally cash and marketable securities.

Of the $4,000 U.S. sales to unaffiliated customers, $1,200 were export sales, principally to geographic area *A*.

Source: "Financial Reporting for Segments of a Business Enterprise," *Statement of Financial Accounting Standards No. 14* (Stamford, Conn.: FASB, 1976), Exhibit C, app. F.

a full year's activities are incurred at irregular intervals during the year and must be allocated to products in process or to other interim periods to avoid distortion of interim financial results. In addition, because of the limited time available to develop interim information, many costs and expenses must be estimated for interim reports. For example, it may not be practical to review each type of inventory item or to accurately determine costs incurred on individual long-term contracts. Precise income tax calculations for each interim period may not be possible. Subsequent refinement of interim estimates may distort the results of operations of later interim periods.

Interim reporting also is complicated by the existence of two fundamentally different views of the relationship between interim report periods and the annual report period. One view is that each interim period is a basic accounting period that stands on its own, and therefore the results of operations for each interim period should be determined in essentially the same manner as if the interim period were an annual accounting period. In this view, the same principles employed for annual reports should be used to report deferrals, accruals, and estimations at the end of each interim period.

The second view is that each interim period is an integral part of the annual period. Under the second view, deferrals, accruals, and estimations at the end of each interim period depend on judgments made at each interim date about the results of operations for the entire annual period. Thus, under the second view, an expense occurring within the fiscal year could be allocated among interim periods on the basis of the passage of time, sales volume, production volume, or some other activity factor.

The APB issued *Opinion No. 28* in 1973 in an effort to (1) reduce the variety of approaches to interim reporting, (2) reduce the inconsistencies caused by the difficulties inherent in interim reporting, and (3) focus attention on only one view of interim reporting. The guidelines set forth in *Opinion No. 28* reflect the APB's view that each interim period should be considered an integral part of the annual period. In general, the Board felt that the results for each interim period should be based on the accounting principles and practices used to prepare the company's most recent annual financial statements. The Board also concluded, however, that certain accounting principles and practices followed in preparing the annual report might require modification at interim report dates so that interim financial information would better relate to the information in the annual report and thus would be more useful.

GAAP for interim reporting, as prescribed by *Opinion No. 28* and amended by *FASB Statements of Financial Accounting Standards Nos. 3* and *18,* are summarized in the next few sections.[7] Each section presents interim reporting requirements for a different type of financial data.

REVENUE   Revenue from products sold or services rendered should be recognized for interim periods on the same basis that is used for the annual period. For example, if the completed-contract method to recognize revenue from long-term construction contracts is used for the annual period, the same method must be used in each interim period. Companies engaged in seasonal business activities must disclose that fact. Such companies should provide supplemental information for the current and preceding twelve-month periods ending at the interim date so that users will not be misled by the seasonally influenced interim results. Any losses projected under revenue recognition bases should be recognized in full in the interim period in which the existence of such losses becomes evident.

---

[7] "Reporting Accounting Changes in Interim Financial Statements," *Statement of Financial Accounting Standards No. 3* (Stamford, Conn.: FASB, 1974); "Financial Reporting for Segments of a Business Enterprise—Interim Financial Statements," *Statement of Financial Accounting Standards No. 18* (Stamford, Conn.: FASB, 1977).

For reporting purposes, each interim period should be considered an integral part of the annual period.

EXPENSES ASSOCIATED WITH REVENUE Expenses that can be associated directly with or allocated to products sold or services rendered should be matched against interim revenue on the same basis or bases as those used for annual reporting purposes. Such expenses include costs of materials used, wages and salaries and related fringe benefits, manufacturing overhead, and warranty expense.

Companies generally should use the same cost flow assumptions (e.g., FIFO, LIFO, average cost) for interim reporting as are used for annual reporting in determining inventory costs and cost of goods sold. Some exceptions, however, are appropriate for interim reporting purposes:

1. Companies may use the gross profit method or some other estimation method for interim valuation of inventory. However, disclosure of the method used at the interim date and any significant adjustments needed to reconcile interim figures with those for the annual inventory are required.

2. Companies that use LIFO may have a liquidation of base period inventories at an interim date that is expected to be replaced by the end of the annual period. This temporary LIFO liquidation should be ignored when interim inventory is determined, and cost of goods sold for the interim period should include the expected replacement cost of the liquidated LIFO base.

3. An apparently *permanent* inventory loss from market price declines should be recognized in the interim period in which the decline occurs. If that inventory loss is recovered as a result of market price increases in a later interim period within the same fiscal year, a gain should be recognized in the interim period in which the loss is recovered. The gain from price recovery cannot exceed the previously recognized loss. *Temporary* market price declines need not be recognized in interim periods because no loss is expected for the annual period.

4. Companies that use standard cost accounting systems to determine inventory and product costs should, at interim report dates, defer recognition of *planned* price, volume, or cost variances that are expected to be absorbed by the end of the annual period. *Unplanned* or unanticipated variances, however, should be recognized in interim periods in accordance with the same procedures used at the end of the annual period.

OTHER EXPENSES Expenses other than those associated directly with or allocated to products sold or services rendered should be accounted for in interim periods as follows:

1. Expenses should be deducted in calculating interim period income as they are incurred, or be allocated among interim periods on the basis of an estimate of time expired, benefit received, or activity associated with the periods. Allocation procedures used should be consistent with those used for annual reporting purposes. For example, utility expense, rent expense, and interest expense should be recognized in the interim periods in which they are incurred. On the other hand, such expenses as insurance premiums and property taxes should be allocated among the interim periods.

2. Expenses incurred in an interim period which cannot be readily identified with the activities or benefits of other interim periods should be recognized in the interim period in which they are incurred and should not be arbitrarily assigned to other interim periods.

3. Gains and losses that occur in an interim period and that are similar to those that would not be deferred at year end, such as a gain or loss on sale of property, plant, or equipment, should be recognized in the interim period in which they occur.

INCOME TAX EXPENSE   In order to determine the income tax expense at the end of each interim period, the company must estimate the effective tax rate for the full fiscal year. The estimated effective annual tax rate is equal to the expected annual income tax expense divided by expected annual pretax income. The estimated effective annual tax rate should include the effects of foreign tax rates, percentage depletion, capital gains rates, and other available tax planning alternatives, but should *not* include significant unusual, infrequent, or extraordinary items that will be reported separately or net of income tax effects for the interim period or for the annual period. The estimated effective annual tax rate should be used to calculate estimated year-to-date taxes on income from continuing operations at the end of each interim period. The income tax expense for the current interim period is equal to the estimated year-to-date tax on income from continuing operations minus the income tax expense for all previous interim periods within the fiscal year.

To illustrate, assume that ORS Company reported taxable income from continuing operations of $40,000 in the first quarter and $35,000 in the second quarter of the current year. The estimated income tax expenses on each of these amounts, as calculated at the end of each quarter, were reported as $12,000 and $10,000, respectively. ORS is now in the process of determining its income tax expense for the third-quarter interim report.

ORS has calculated its third-quarter taxable income from continuing operations as $25,000 and anticipates earnings of $30,000 in the fourth quarter. The company has a tax rate of 22 percent on the first $25,000 of taxable income and 34 percent on any taxable income over $25,000. At the end of the third quarter ORS would estimate its effective annual tax rate as follows:

Estimate of annual taxable income:

Actual 1st-quarter income	$ 40,000
Actual 2nd-quarter income	35,000
Actual 3rd-quarter income	25,000
Estimated 4th-quarter income	30,000
Estimated annual income	$130,000

Estimate of effective annual tax rate:

22% of first $25,000	$ 5,500
34% of remaining $105,000	35,700
Estimated total annual tax expense	$ 41,200

$$\text{Estimated effective annual tax rate} = \frac{\$41,200 \text{ estimated total annual taxes}}{\$130,000 \text{ estimated total annual income}} = 32\%$$

The estimated effective annual tax rate can be used to calculate the estimated year-to-date income tax expense and the income tax expense for the current quarter:

32% × ($40,000 + $35,000 + $25,000)
= $32,000 estimated income tax expense
on income of first three quarters

Estimated third-quarter income tax expense:

Estimated taxes on income of first three quarters		$32,000
Actual tax expense for 1st quarter	$12,000	
Actual tax expense for 2nd quarter	10,000	(22,000)
Estimated 3rd-quarter income tax expense		$10,000

EARNINGS PER SHARE   Companies must report primary and fully diluted earnings per share (EPS) related to net income, income from continuing operations, extraordinary items, and discontinued operations in interim reports, following the guidelines of *APB Opinion No. 15.* (The calculation of EPS was discussed in detail in Chapter 24.)

Several precautions should be noted in interpreting interim EPS. Use of the treasury stock method of *Opinion No. 15* to calculate EPS may change EPS from one interim period to another simply because of stock price changes. In addition, the weighted average number of shares outstanding may change from one interim period to another because shares issued in one interim period have been outstanding longer in a subsequent period or were not outstanding at all in a prior interim period. As a result, the summation of all interim EPS figures may not equal the annual EPS figure. It also should be noted that the base period for determining the weighted average number of shares to be used in interim EPS calculations is the interim period, not the annual period.

DISCLOSURES IN INTERIM FINANCIAL REPORTS   In addition to the interim financial data described above, *APB Opinion No. 28* requires companies to disclose the following information, as a minimum, in interim financial reports:

Minimum interim financial report disclosures.

1. Sales or gross revenues, income tax expense, extraordinary items, cumulative effect of a change in accounting principles, and net income.

2. Primary and fully diluted earnings per share data for each period presented, determined in accordance with *APB Opinion No. 15*.

3. Seasonal revenues, costs, or expenses.

4. Significant changes in estimated or actual income tax expense.

5. Disposal of a segment of the company and extraordinary, unusual, or infrequent items.

6. Contingent items.

7. Changes in accounting principles or accounting estimates.

8. Significant changes in financial position. (This requirement will be modified if the FASB requires a statement of cash flows.)

When disclosing the above information for an interim period, the company should present data for the current year to date or the last 12 months to date along with comparable data for the preceding year. Companies also are encouraged, but are not required, to publish a balance sheet and a statement of changes in financial position (cash flows) at interim dates. When a balance sheet and a statement of changes in financial position (cash flows) are not presented, the company must disclose material changes in liquid assets, net working capital, long-term liabilities, and stockholders' equity since the last reporting period. The third-quarter consolidated interim financial statements of General Mills, Inc., presented in Exhibit 26–5, illustrate interim disclosures.

DISCLOSURES OF SPECIAL ITEMS   How should special items such as disposal of a segment of a business, contingencies, and changes in accounting principles or accounting estimates be presented in interim reports? Extraordinary items that are material in relation to annual net income should be disclosed separately and included in the determination of net income for the interim period in which they occur. Likewise, companies must disclose separately the effects of disposal of a business segment and unusual or infrequently occurring transactions and events that are material with respect to net income of the interim period. Contingencies that are judged to be material with respect to the annual financial statements and that might affect the fairness of interim reports should be disclosed in interim reports in the same manner required for annual reports.

Interim financial reports should indicate any change in accounting principles or accounting estimates from those used in (1) the comparable interim period of the prior

EXHIBIT 26–5

General Mills, Inc., and Subsidiaries
INTERIM FINANCIAL STATEMENTS FOR THE QUARTER AND
THIRTY-NINE WEEKS ENDED FEBRUARY 24, 1985, AND FEBRUARY 26, 1984
(in millions of dollars, except per share data)

CONSOLIDATED STATEMENTS OF EARNINGS

	THIRTEEN WEEKS ENDED		THIRTY-NINE WEEKS ENDED	
(Unaudited) (In Millions, Except Per Share Data)	FEB. 24, 1985	FEB. 26, 1984[1]	FEB. 24, 1985	FEB. 26, 1984[1]
Sales	$ 1,098.1	$1,051.7	$ 3,300.6	$ 3,188.9
Costs and expenses:				
Cost of sales, exclusive of items below	639.8	618.3	1,913.1	1,853.2
Selling, general and administrative expenses	345.4	325.7	1,052.2	992.4
Depreciation and amortization expenses	27.5	24.4	80.1	78.7
Interest expense	18.9	6.5	48.5	24.5
Total costs and expenses	$(1,031.6)	$ (974.9)	$(3,093.9)	$(2,948.8)
Earnings from continuing operations, pretax[2]	$ 66.5	$ 76.8	$ 206.7	$ 240.1
Gain (loss) from redeployments[3]	(21.2)	(5.0)	(22.9)	57.9
Earnings from continuing operations after redeployments, pretax...	$ 45.3	$ 71.8	$ 183.8	$ 298.0
Income taxes	(14.1)	(29.9)	(71.2)	(129.0)
Earnings from continuing operations after redeployments	$ 31.2	$ 41.9	$ 112.6	$ 169.0
Earnings per share—continuing operations after redeployments	$ .71	$ .91	$ 2.51	$ 3.58
Discontinued operations after tax[4]	$ (105.3)	$ (3.2)	$ (77.0)	$ 23.9
Net earnings (loss)	$ (74.1)	$ 38.7	$ 35.6	$ 192.9
Earnings per share—net earnings (loss)...................................	$ (1.64)	$ .85	$ .79	$ 4.08
Dividends per share	$ .56	$ .51	$ 1.68	$ 1.53
Average number of common shares	44.3	46.4	44.9	47.3

[1] Prior year amounts have been restated to reflect the discontinued Toy and Fashion operations separately

[2] Consumer Foods, Restaurants & Specialty Retailing exclusive of redeployment program

[3] Redeployment program for continuing operations (Consumer Foods, Restaurants and Specialty Retailing)

[4] Toy and Fashion operations including estimated loss on disposal

See accompanying notes to consolidated condensed financial statements.

EXHIBIT 26–5 (CONTINUED)

CONSOLIDATED CONDENSED BALANCE SHEETS

(In Millions)	(Unaudited) FEBRUARY 24, 1985	(Unaudited) FEBRUARY 26, 1984	MAY 27, 1984
Assets			
Current assets:			
Cash and short-term investments..........................	$ 93.3	$ 88.0	$ 66.0
Receivables and prepaid expenses........................	302.3	597.1	594.2
Inventories:			
Valued primarily at FIFO	251.4	401.6	399.1
Valued at LIFO (FIFO value exceeds LIFO by $54.9, $83.6, and $79.7, respectively)................	166.8	230.2	262.6
Investments in tax leases	—	84.5	49.6
Net assets of discontinued operations	634.5	—	—
Net assets held for disposal under redeployment program	14.6	16.0	18.4
Total current assets.................................	$1,462.9	$1,417.4	$1,389.9
Land, buildings and equipment, at cost	$1,642.8	$1,785.0	$1,829.2
Less accumulated depreciation	(549.9)	(581.6)	(599.8)
Net land, buildings and equipment	$1,092.9	$1,203.4	$1,229.4
Other Assets:			
Intangible assets, principally goodwill	$ 65.2	$ 146.8	$ 146.0
Investments and miscellaneous assets	159.2	85.4	92.8
Total other assets	$ 224.4	$ 232.2	$ 238.8
Total assets	$2,780.2	$2,853.0	$2,858.1
Liabilities and Stockholders' Equity			
Current liabilities:			
Accounts payable	$ 357.5	$ 472.3	$ 477.8
Current portion of long-term debt........................	52.5	67.7	60.3
Notes payable..	416.8	223.8	251.0
Accrued taxes and other current liabilities	197.5	376.5	356.3
Total current liabilities	$1,024.3	$1,140.3	$1,145.4
Long-term debt, excluding current portion....................	$ 445.9	$ 361.3	$ 362.6
Deferred income taxes	130.5	87.9	76.5
Other liabilities and deferred credits	45.6	42.7	49.0
Total liabilities	$1,646.3	$1,632.2	$1,633.5
Stockholders' equity:			
Common stock	$ 214.2	$ 215.0	$ 215.4
Retained earnings	1,335.2	1,334.4	1,375.0
Less common stock in treasury, at cost	(339.8)	(253.9)	(291.8)
Cumulative foreign currency adjustment....................	(75.7)	(74.7)	(74.0)
Total stockholders' equity	$1,133.9	$1,220.8	$1,224.6
Total liabilities and stockholders' equity	$2,780.2	$2,853.0	$2,858.1

See accompanying notes to consolidated condensed financial statements.

EXHIBIT 26–5 (CONTINUED)

CONSOLIDATED CONDENSED STATEMENTS OF CHANGES IN FINANCIAL POSITION*

	THIRTY-NINE WEEKS ENDED	
(Unaudited) (In Millions)	FEBRUARY 24, 1985	FEBRUARY 26, 1984
Funds provided from (used for) operations:		
Working capital provided from continuing operations[1]	$ 202.6	$ 213.2
Increase in working capital used in continuing operations	(212.0)	(54.9)
Cash provided from (used for) continuing operations	$ (9.4)	$ 158.3
Cash provided from discontinued operations[2]	30.1	42.4
Cash provided from operations	$ 20.7	$ 200.7
Funds provided from (used for) investment activities:		
Purchase of land, buildings and equipment	$(164.0)	$(219.9)
Proceeds from completed dispositions	12.3	264.2
Other, net	1.3	16.0
Net cash provided from (used for) investments	$(150.4)	$ 60.3
Funds used for dividends	$ (75.4)	$ (72.6)
Funds provided from (used for) financing activities:		
Increase (decrease) in notes payable	$ 168.2	$(170.4)
Issuance of long-term debt	183.3	11.6
Issuance of debt warrants	4.0	—
Investment of certain debt proceeds	(65.5)	—
Reduction of long-term debt	(97.2)	(48.9)
Net cash flows from tax leases	88.8	142.8
Purchase of treasury stock	(53.8)	(102.9)
Common stock issued	4.6	9.4
Net cash provided from (used for) financing	$ 232.4	$(158.4)
Net increase in cash and short-term investments	$ 27.3	$ 30.0)
Cash and short-term investments at beginning of period	66.0	58.0
Cash and short-term investments at end of period	$ 93.3	$ 88.0

[1] Consumer Foods, Restaurants & Specialty Retailing including redeployments

[2] Toy and Fashion operations

See accompanying notes to consolidated condensed financial statements.

*When issued, these statements of changes in financial position were consistent with GAAP. Under the FASB's 1986 *Exposure Draft,* the statement of changes in financial position would be replaced by a statement of cash flows.

EXHIBIT 26–5 (CONTINUED)

NOTES TO CONSOLIDATED CONDENSED FINANCIAL STATEMENTS (UNAUDITED)

1. Background: These financial statements do not include certain information and footnotes required by generally accepted accounting principles for complete financial statements. However, in the opinion of management, all adjustments considered necessary for a fair presentation have been included. Our business is seasonal. Operating results for the thirty-nine weeks ended February 24, 1985 are not necessarily indicative of the results that may be expected for the fiscal year ending May 26, 1985.

These statements should be read in conjunction with the financial statements and footnotes included in our annual report for the year ended May 27, 1984. The accounting policies used in preparing these financial statements are the same as those described in our annual report.

2. Discontinued Operations: In the third quarter of fiscal 1985, the Board of Directors authorized disposition of the Toy and Fashion segments of our business. A reserve was established in the third quarter for the estimated loss on disposal of the two segments. The amount of the reserve, net of income tax benefit of $46.8 million, was $105.3 million ($2.35 per share). The earnings from operations for these two segments for the first two quarters of fiscal 1985, net of income tax expense of $17.8 million, were $28.3 million ($.63 per share).

The Consolidated Statements of Earnings have been restated to show continuing operations for the periods presented. The Toy and Fashion discontinued segments are shown separately from continuing operations, and include both operating results and the estimated reserve for loss upon disposal of these activities.

Sales for the discontinued segments were $220.1 million and $290.1 million for the third quarter and $963.5 million and $1,050.8 million for the nine months of fiscal 1985 and 1984, respectively.

The net assets of the discontinued segments presented on the balance sheet as of February 24, 1985 represent their estimated net realizable value upon disposition. The assets consist primarily of receivables, inventory, fixed assets, and certain intangibles.

3. Effect of LIFO: We use the LIFO method of accounting for valuing portions of our inventories. If these inventories had been valued using the FIFO method, net earnings from continuing operations would have been decreased by $1.0 million ($.02 per share) and increased by $1.2 million ($.02 per share) in the third quarters of fiscal 1985 and 1984, respectively, and decreased by $.6 million ($.01 per share) and increased by $3.5 million ($.07 per share) for the respective year-to-date periods.

4. Long-Term Debt: In the first quarter of fiscal 1985, we filed a shelf registration statement with the Securities and Exchange Commission for the issuance of up to $150 million net proceeds in unsecured debt securities to reduce short-term debt and for other general corporate purposes. In addition, $50 million net proceeds in unsecured debt securities is still available for issuance under a previously filed shelf registration statement.

In the second quarter of fiscal 1985, we issued outside of the United States $250 million face amount, $26.3 million net value, of zero coupon notes yielding 11.73% that will mature on August 15, 2004, and $1 billion face amount, $45.4 million net value of zero coupon notes yielding 11.14% that will mature on August 15, 2013.

In the third quarter of fiscal 1985, we issued outside of the United States $100 million principal amount of 12% notes maturing on December 19, 1991. In the same offering we issued 100,000 warrants, net value $4 million which expire on December 19, 1989, to purchase an additional $100 million principal amount of 12% notes maturing on December 19, 1991.

In the second quarter of fiscal 1985, we satisfied the future requirements of certain sinking fund debentures through the deposit of U.S. obligations in an irrevocable trust. This transaction increased second quarter 1985 net earnings by $6.7 million ($.15 per share).

In the second quarter of fiscal 1984, we satisfied the future requirements of certain sinking fund debentures primarily through the deposit of U.S. obligations in an irrevocable trust. This transaction increased second quarter 1984 net earnings by $4.0 million ($.09 per share).

5. Redeployment Program: Net earnings for the first three quarters of fiscal 1985 includes a net after-tax charge of $9.4 million ($.21 per share) resulting from adjustments to previously established redeployment items and a decision to sell We Are Sportswear, a Specialty Retailing operation. This includes an $8.5 million ($.19 per share) charge in the third quarter.

Net earnings for the first three quarters of fiscal 1984 included a net after-tax gain of $30.8 million ($.65 per share). The most significant item was the sale of the net assets of Tom's Foods which resulted in an after-tax gain of $73.7 million. This was offset by losses associated with the disposition of assets that did not fit the company's ongoing strategy as well as the closing of certain low volume or marginal Specialty Retailing and Restaurant operations. This included a $2.3 million ($.05 per share) charge in the third quarter.

The above redeployment results relate to continuing operations and exclude the items from the Toy and Fashion segments prior to their being discontinued. Redeployment program charges for the Toy and Fashion segments are included in the discontinued operations amount in the statement of earnings.

annual period, (2) the preceding interim periods in the current annual period, or (3) the prior annual report. If a change in accounting principle that requires the cumulative effect treatment (discussed in Chapter 22) is made in the first interim period of a company's fiscal year, the cumulative effect of the change on retained earnings at the beginning of that fiscal year should be included in the net income of the first interim period. If a cumulative effect change in accounting principle is made in other than the first interim period, no cumulative effect should be included in the net income of the period of change. Instead, financial data of prechange interim periods within the current fiscal year should be restated by applying the new accounting principle. In addition, the cumulative effect of the change on the retained earnings at the beginning of the fiscal year should be included in the restated net income of the first interim period.[8] The effect of a change in an accounting estimate should be accounted for in the interim period in which the change in estimate is made.

Having completed our discussion of interim reporting and our overall discussion of sources of financial information, we turn our attention to analysis of financial statements.

ANALYSIS OF FINANCIAL STATEMENTS

Definition of market efficiency.

The relationship between security prices and information such as is contained in financial statements is called **market efficiency**.[9] As discussed in Chapter 1, the securities market is efficient with respect to some specified information system, such as a company's financial statements, if and only if the company's security prices act *as if* everyone observes the information system.[10] There is considerable evidence that security prices *do* react in a fashion that is consistent with the hypothesis that the securities market is efficient with respect to published financial statement data.

The securities market's efficiency with respect to financial statement information means that security prices *fully reflect* financial statement information. This suggests that little, if anything, is to be gained by analyzing financial statements in an attempt to discover over- or undervalued securities. Rather than engaging in such an activity when the securities market is efficient, an investor generally would be better off to decide on an acceptable level of risk and invest in a well-diversified securities portfolio that yields returns commensurate with the selected risk level. Individual securities would be evaluated with respect to their effect on the entire portfolio's risk and return distributions. Investors who cannot afford to buy well-diversified personal portfolios should invest in something, such as a mutual fund, with the desired risk-return level.

Since there is considerable evidence supporting the existence of an efficient securities market with respect to financial statement information, it is reasonable to ask, "Why bother to explain financial statement analysis techniques?" Some of the reasons why financial accountants should have some understanding of financial statement analysis are:

Some reasons that financial accountants should understand financial statement analysis.

1. Many investors are not aware of or do not believe in securities market efficiency and do not behave in a manner consistent with market efficiency. Therefore, regardless of the evidence of market efficiency, financial statements are analyzed by many decision makers. Knowledge of the techniques of financial statement analysis may help accountants prepare more useful financial statements.

---

[8] "Reporting Accounting Changes in Interim Financial Statements," *Statement of Financial Accounting Standards No. 3* (Stamford, Conn.: FASB, 1974), paras. 9 and 10.

[9] William A. Beaver, *Financial Reporting: An Accounting Revolution* (Englewood Cliffs, N.J.: Prentice-Hall, 1981), p. 142.

[10] Ibid., p. 147.

2. The securities of many companies are not traded in organized markets. When these securities are made available to the public, it is necessary to determine the appropriate offering price. This determination usually is made by underwriters and is based partially on analysis of financial statement data.

3. Lending institutions often require prospective borrowers to submit financial statements for analysis before they extend loans. In addition, many loan covenants require that certain financial relationships, or ratios, be maintained by the borrower. These ratios must be monitored by the lender.

4. In order for the securities market to be efficient, someone, such as a professional financial analyst, must be analyzing available data, including financial statement data, and reacting to those data.

5. The relative risk of a given security may change over time. Changes in risk may be related to changes in the company's capital structure, product mix, industry, or other relevant variables. Careful assessment of such factors, as disclosed in financial statements and other sources of financial information, may enable an investor to forecast expected returns more accurately.

THE FINANCIAL ANALYSIS PROCESS

Evaluation of investment or lending alternatives typically consists of a three-step analysis process: (1) analysis of general economic conditions, (2) analysis of industries, and (3) analysis of individual companies. The remainder of this chapter is concerned with techniques often used in step 3—the analysis of individual companies.

Much of the information considered when one evaluates a company's financial strength and future prospects is derived from interim and annual financial statements, schedules and commentary that supplement the financial statements, notes to the financial statements, and the external auditors' report. Many of these sources of information are illustrated by the annual report of The Coca-Cola Co., which is presented in Appendix 5–1. Specific sections of that annual report are referenced as relevant in our discussion of financial analysis.

Financial analysis of a company should include, as a minimum, consideration of the following sources of information:

1. *The auditors' report* (for Coca-Cola, see p. 215). The auditors' report informs the reader that the financial statements have been audited in accordance with generally accepted auditing standards. In addition, the auditors' report indicates whether the financial statements fairly present the company's financial position and changes in its financial position in accordance with generally accepted accounting principles. In general, the auditors' report provides the user of the financial statements with some guidance as to the amount of confidence the user should place in the data reported in the statements and the related footnotes. The auditors' report also alerts financial statement users about special accounting practices followed by the company and about special conditions within the company or in its operating environment. Interim financial statements usually are not audited; if they are not audited, they must be so labeled, as General Mills' third-quarter statements are (Exhibit 26–5).

2. *Notes to the financial statements* (for Coca-Cola, see pp. 209–14). The notes to the financial statements explain the accounting policies of the company and often provide detailed explanations of how those policies were applied. As discussed in Chapter 5, companies often make supplementary disclosures elaborating on specific amounts reported in the financial statements. For example, in Note 7 (p. 210), Coca-Cola discusses its pension plans. Sometimes the notes are used to explain specific management actions and the reasons for those actions. The notes to the financial statements must be read carefully if the statements are to be understood fully.

3. *The financial statements* (for Coca-Cola, see pp. 204–8). The basic financial statements are, of course, the balance sheet, the income statement, the statement of changes in financial position (1986 *FASB Exposure Draft* requires a statement of cash flows), and the statement of retained earnings (or statement of stockholders' equity).

FINANCIAL ANALYSIS TECHNIQUES Analysis of financial statements often involves some transformation of the reported data. It is difficult to assess how well a company is doing merely by examining the dollar amounts reported for individual items in the financial statements. Techniques such as ratio analysis and percentage analysis make it possible to identify, highlight, and summarize significant relationships in a company's financial data. These analysis techniques are most effective when they are applied to data for several accounting periods, which usually is possible because most companies report two or three years of comparative financial statement data at each report date. In fact, it is not uncommon for a company to provide a five- or even ten-year summary of selected financial data as a supplement to its annual financial statements. We have provided an example of five-year summary data for the hypothetical Commex Company in Exhibit 26–6.

Percentage Analysis

Percentage analysis is a technique in which particular accounts or line items in the financial statements, such as cost of goods sold or net earnings, are evaluated *over time* as a percentage of their value as of a designated base period, or are evaluated *within a particular time period* as a percentage of some designated account (line item), such as net sales. Percentage analysis is useful for highlighting trends in individual line items of the financial statements. The two most common versions of percentage analysis are horizontal analysis and vertical analysis.

HORIZONTAL ANALYSIS **Horizontal analysis** expresses financial data from two or more accounting periods in terms of a single designated base period, or expresses data in each succeeding period as compared to the amount for the preceding period. We illustrate these two types of horizontal analysis in Exhibits 26–7 and 26–8, using the summary data for Commex Company that are presented in Exhibit 26–6.

Examination of Exhibits 26–7 and 26–8 raises at least three questions about the operations of Commex Company that might cause an analyst to conduct further research, depending on the analyst's reasons for studying the Commex data:

1. Why does the overall level of operations, as measured by net sales, drop off in 1987 after several years of growth?

2. Why is there such great deterioration of net income in 1987?

3. Why has interest expense increased so much in 1986 and 1987?

Some additional information related to these questions is provided by the notes that accompany Commex's five-year summary data in Exhibit 26–6. These notes mention charges to income for plant closings in 1985 and 1987, and a credit to income in 1985 for a gain on sale of securities.

When we use percentage analysis, we must remember that percentages are relative to the designated base. If the base amount is small, only a comparatively small change in dollar amount is necessary to yield a substantial percentage change. For example, in Exhibit 26–7 the 1987 interest expense is 261 percent of the 1983 interest expense, partially because the 1983 interest expense was a comparatively small dollar amount. Also, when the period-to-period type of horizontal analysis is used, as in Exhibit 26–8, the changes in percentage for a particular item are partially the result of the period-

EXHIBIT 26–6

Commex Company

FIVE-YEAR SUMMARY OF SELECTED CONSOLIDATED FINANCIAL DATA

	1987	1986	1985	1984	1983
	(Dollars in thousands, except per share data)				
Operations					
Net sales	$1,159,863	$1,208,061	$1,107,128	$978,692	$871,505
Cost of products sold	952,176	966,568	882,362	760,312	663,840
Interest expense	21,891	16,038	9,526	8,151	8,400
Income taxes	6,300	35,300	42,300	43,900	46,600
Net earnings	28,831*	58,078	65,800†	58,944	58,864
Dividends on series A preferred stock	4,817	4,817	4,818	4,830	4,992
Earnings attributable to common stock	24,014	53,261	60,982	54,114	53,872
Per share data:					
Primary:					
Average shares outstanding§	11,088	11,093	11,084	11,084	10,958
Per share amount	2.17	4.80	5.50	4.88	4.92
Fully diluted:					
Average shares outstanding§	12,609	12,615	12,605	12,608	12,542
Per share amount	2.17	4.60	5.22	4.67	4.69
Cash dividends per share:					
Preferred	4.75	4.75	4.75	4.75	4.75
Common	1.70	2.30	2.30	2.20	2.00
Financial position					
Cash, short-term investments, and marketable securities	$ 38,951	$ 39,064	$ 49,410	$ 26,331	$ 64,126
Receivables (net)	162,521	138,459	129,221	117,632	92,931
Inventories	267,663	270,592	242,558	233,380	196,770
Plants and properties (cost)	834,743	805,408	689,113	637,041	599,660
Plants and properties (net)	361,949	347,581	260,194	231,308	224,973
Total assets‡	903,841	846,010	726,588	653,632	627,556
Current assets‡	494,961	457,525	427,931	384,070	363,419
Current liabilities‡	181,308	163,453	148,279	121,021	129,882
Working capital‡	313,653	294,072	279,652	263,049	233,537
Long-term debt	190,521	165,033	90,916	83,834	81,816
Stockholders' equity‡	509,992	504,716	476,807	441,238	410,072
Book value per common share‡	36.84	36.38	33.88	30.68	28.10
Other data					
Expenditures for plants and properties (includes properties of businesses acquired)	$ 58,840	$128,398	$ 64,032	$ 39,618	$ 24,233
Depreciation	42,551	37,172	33,262	31,298	32,352
Employee compensation and benefits	453,502	463,037	430,046	384,020	340,740
Return on average stockholders' equity‡	5.7%	11.8%	14.3%	13.8%	14.9%
Shares outstanding at December 31§					
Preferred	1,014	1,014	1,014	1,014	1,017
Common	11,090	11,085	11,080	11,077	10,973
Number of employees at December 31	17,817	19,916	20,997	20,578	19,417

* Includes charge for provision for plant closing costs ($11,000 pretax, $5,850 net, equal to $.53 per share).

† Includes charge for provision for plant closing costs ($12,000 pretax, $5,952 net, equal to $.53 per share) and credit for gain on sale of securities ($16,885 pretax, $11,820 net, equal to $1.07 per share).

‡ Amounts for years prior to 1987 restated for a change in accounting method.

§ 000 omitted.

EXHIBIT 26–7 HORIZONTAL ANALYSIS USING 1983 AS A BASE

Commex Company

HORIZONTAL ANALYSIS OF 1984–87 SUMMARY DATA
(as percent of 1983 amount)

	1983		1984		1985		1986		1987	
	THOUSANDS OF DOLLARS	% OF 1983	THOUSANDS OF DOLLARS	% OF 1983	THOUSANDS OF DOLLARS	% OF 1983	THOUSANDS OF DOLLARS	% OF 1983	THOUSANDS OF DOLLARS	% OF 1983
Net sales	$871,505	100%	$978,692	112%	$1,107,128	127%	$1,208,061	139%	$1,159,863	133%
Cost of products sold	663,840	100	760,312	115	882,362	133	966,568	146	952,176	143
Interest expense	8,400	100	8,151	97	9,526	113	16,038	191	21,891	261
Income taxes..............	46,600	100	43,900	94	42,300	91	35,300	76	6,300	14
Net income	58,864	100	58,944	100	65,800	112	58,078	99	28,831	49

EXHIBIT 26–8 HORIZONTAL ANALYSIS ON A YEAR-TO-YEAR BASIS

Commex Company

HORIZONTAL ANALYSIS OF 1984–87 SUMMARY DATA
(as percent of preceding year's amount)

	1983		1984		1985		1986		1987	
	THOUSANDS OF DOLLARS	% OF 1983	THOUSANDS OF DOLLARS	% OF 1983	THOUSANDS OF DOLLARS	% OF 1984	THOUSANDS OF DOLLARS	% OF 1985	THOUSANDS OF DOLLARS	% OF 1986
Net sales	$871,505	100%	$978,692	112%	$1,107,128	113%	$1,208,061	109%	$1,159,863	96%
Cost of products sold	663,840	100	760,312	115	882,362	116	966,568	110	952,176	99
Interest expense	8,400	100	8,151	97	9,526	117	16,038	168	21,891	136
Income taxes..............	46,600	100	43,900	94	42,300	96	35,300	83	6,300	18
Net income	58,864	100	58,944	100	65,800	112	58,078	88	28,831	50

to-period change in the base. Finally, changes in percentages from period to period for a particular item are meaningful when the base period remains the same, as in Exhibit 26–7; changes in percentages from period to period are not as meaningful when the base changes from period to period, as in Exhibit 26–8.

VERTICAL ANALYSIS In **vertical analysis** all of the data in a particular financial statement are presented as a percentage of a single designated line item of that financial statement. For example, we might report income statement items as a percentage of net sales, balance sheet items as a percentage of total assets, and the statement of changes in financial position items as a percentage of the change in working capital. Vertical analysis is illustrated in Exhibit 26–9, based on the Commex Company data in Exhibit 26–6.

The vertical analysis in Exhibit 26–9 adds further concerns about the questions raised earlier by the analyses in Exhibits 26–7 and 26–8. For example, we can see from Exhibit 26–9 that net income as a percentage of net sales fell to only 2 percent in 1987. This decline is partly explained by increases in both cost of products sold and interest expense as a percentage of net sales. We also observe that the relative amount of income taxes is falling; but this is not surprising, given the apparent drop in taxable income.

If more than one year's data are used in vertical analysis, as is the case in Exhibit 26–9, care must be exercised when percentages are compared from period to period. For example, although interest expense in Exhibit 26–9 is 1 percent of net sales in 1986 and 2 percent of net sales in 1987, it would be incorrect to say that interest expense was twice as much in 1987 as in 1986. The purpose of vertical analysis is to highlight relationships between components of the financial statements and not to assess trends in individual components over time.

EXHIBIT 26—9 VERTICAL ANALYSIS AS A PERCENT OF NET SALES

Commex Company
VERTICAL ANALYSIS OF 1983–87 SUMMARY DATA
(as percent of net sales)

	1983		1984		1985		1986		1987	
	THOUSANDS OF DOLLARS	% OF NET SALES	THOUSANDS OF DOLLARS	% OF NET SALES	THOUSANDS OF DOLLARS	% OF NET SALES	THOUSANDS OF DOLLARS	% OF NET SALES	THOUSANDS OF DOLLARS	% OF NET SALES
Net sales	$871,505	100%	$978,692	100%	$1,107,128	100%	$1,208,061	100%	$1,159,863	100%
Cost of products sold....	663,840	76	760,312	78	882,362	80	966,568	80	952,176	82
Interest expense	8,400	1	8,151	1	9,526	1	16,038	1	21,891	2
Income taxes...........	46,600	5	43,900	4	42,300	4	35,300	3	6,300	1
Net income	58,864	7	58,944	6	65,800	6	58,078	5	28,831	2

EXHIBIT 26—10

Commex Company
CONSOLIDATED BALANCE SHEETS AS OF DECEMBER 31, 1987 AND 1986

	DECEMBER 31	
	1987	**1986**
	(in thousands)	
Assets		
Current assets		
Cash and short-term investments, at cost (approximate market)	$ 38,951	$ 39,064
Receivables, less allowances of $8,511,000 and $7,672,000 respectively	162,521	138,459
Inventories..	267,663	270,592
Federal income tax refund receivable	14,700	
Deferred income taxes and other current assets	11,126	9,410
Total current assets	$494,961	$457,525
Investments and other assets		
Investments in and advances to affiliates	$ 17,037	$ 13,760
Other assets.......................................	7,562	4,812
	$ 24,599	$ 18,572
Plants and properties		
Land	$ 13,500	$ 13,316
Land improvements	22,998	19,941
Buildings..	215,208	206,343
Machinery and equipment	567,901	494,824
Construction in progress	15,136	70,984
	$834,743	$805,408
Less accumulated depreciation	(472,794)	(457,827)
	$361,949	$347,581
Excess of cost of investments in subsidiaries over net assets acquired	$ 22,332	$ 22,332
Total assets	$903,841	$846,010

Ratio Analysis

Probably the most widely used financial analysis technique is **ratio analysis,** the analysis of relationships between two or more line items on the financial statements. For example, a commonly used financial ratio is the **current ratio,** which is the relationship between current assets and current liabilities.

Generally, financial ratios are calculated for the purpose of evaluating four aspects of a company's operations: (1) liquidity, (2) activity or turnover of assets, (3) leverage, and (4) profitability. **Liquidity ratios** help users to assess the company's ability to meet currently maturing or short-term obligations. **Activity** or **turnover ratios** are useful for evaluating the effectiveness with which the company uses its assets. **Leverage ratios** provide information about the company's ability to meet both current and long-term obligations. **Profitability ratios** are helpful for evaluating management's success in generating returns for those who provide capital to the company. Each of these types of financial ratios is discussed in the following sections. Ratio calculations are illustrated by using the Commex Company data in Exhibits 26–10, 26–11, and 26–12.

Generally, financial ratios are calculated to evaluate:
(1) liquidity
(2) asset activity or turnover
(3) leverage
(4) profitability

	DECEMBER 31	
	1987	**1986**
	(in thousands)	
Liabilities and stockholders' equity		
Current liabilities		
Notes payable to banks	$ 25,540	$ 18,428
Accounts payable	41,079	40,248
Employees' compensation and amounts		
withheld therefrom	39,731	37,683
Taxes, other than federal and foreign income taxes	16,700	18,134
Accrued product warranty expense	19,250	16,250
Other accrued liabilities	26,561	22,846
United States and foreign income taxes	9,536	8,900
Current maturities of long-term debt	911	964
Total current liabilities	$181,308	$163,453
Deferred income taxes	13,468	6,663
Unfunded pension costs of closed plants	8,552	6,145
Long-term debt (9% promissory notes)	190,521	165,033
Total liabilities	$393,849	$341,294
Stockholders' equity		
Serial preferred stock, authorized 4,000,000 shares:		
$4.75 cumulative convertible, Series A, upon liquidation		
entitled to $100 per share, $101,414,500 in the		
aggregate at December 31, 1987; outstanding, 1,014,145		
shares, stated value	$ 39,074	$ 39,074
Common stock (par value $5.00 a share)		
Authorized, 20,000,000 shares		
Outstanding, 11,089,956 and 11,084,938 shares		
respectively (after deducting 80,772 and 85,790		
shares respectively, in treasury)	55,450	55,425
Contributed capital in excess of par	10,499	10,415
Retained earnings	404,969	399,802
Total stockholders' equity	$509,992	$504,716
Total liabilities and stockholders' equity	$903,841	$846,010

EXHIBIT 26–11

Commex Company

STATEMENT OF CONSOLIDATED NET INCOME FOR THE YEARS ENDED DECEMBER 31, 1985–87
(in thousands, except per share data)

	1987	1986	1985
Revenues and gains:			
Net sales	$ 1,159,863	$ 1,208,061	$ 1,107,128
Royalties and interest	7,562	7,127	5,259
Gain on sale of securities			16,885
Other revenues	4,019	2,569	5,791
Total revenues	$ 1,171,444	$ 1,217,757	$ 1,135,063
Costs and expenses:			
Cost of products sold	$ 952,176	$ 966,568	$ 882,362
General and administrative, selling, advertising, and other expenses	128,176	120,880	104,651
Engineering, research and development	23,070	20,893	18,424
Interest expense	21,891	16,038	9,526
Provision for plant closing costs	11,000		12,000
Total costs and expenses	$(1,136,313)	$(1,124,379)	$(1,026,963)
Income before income taxes	$ 35,131	$ 93,378	$ 108,100
Income taxes	(6,300)	(35,300)	(42,300)
Net income	$ 28,831	$ 58,078	$ 65,800
Dividends on preferred stock	(4,817)	(4,817)	(4,818)
Income attributable to common stock	$ 24,014	$ 53,261	$ 60,982
Net income per share of common stock:			
Primary	$ 2.17	$ 4.80	$ 5.50
Assuming full dilution	2.17	4.60	5.22

Liquidity Ratios

Liquidity ratios are used to evaluate the short-term financial strength of a company. The most common liquidity ratios are described in this section.

CURRENT RATIO   The **current ratio,** also called the **working capital ratio,** is calculated by dividing current assets by current liabilities. It is an indicator of a company's ability to meet its short-term obligations with current assets. For example, Commex Company's 1987 current liabilities equal $181,308. Can these current obligations be met when they are due? Since noncash current assets are, in theory, expected to be converted into cash in the near term, the ratio of current assets to current liabilities should provide an indication of Commex Company's ability to satisfy short-term creditors.

The 1987 Commex current ratio is calculated as follows:

$$\text{Current ratio} = \frac{\text{Current assets}}{\text{Current liabilities}} = \frac{\$494,961}{\$181,308} = 2.73$$

This current ratio indicates that Commex's short-term creditors can feel reasonably secure about receiving payment when due from Commex. Analysts view a low current ratio with concern because short-term cash flow problems could force a company into bankruptcy.

EXHIBIT 26–12

Commex Company

STATEMENT OF CONSOLIDATED STOCKHOLDERS' EQUITY FOR THE YEARS ENDED DECEMBER 31, 1985–87
(in thousands)

	PREFERRED STOCK	COMMON STOCK	ADDITIONAL PAID-IN CAPITAL	RETAINED EARNINGS
Balance at January 1, 1985	$39,074	$55,384	$10,246	$338,904
Cumulative effect of change in accounting principle				(2,370)
Balance at January 1, 1985, as restated	$39,074	$55,384	$10,246	$336,534
Issuance of 3,220 common shares under employee				
stock option plans		16	53	
Net income for the year				65,800
Cash dividends paid:				
Common stock ($2.30 a share)				(25,482)
Preferred stock ($4.75 a share)				(4,818)
Balance at December 31, 1985	$39,074	$55,400	$10,299	$372,034
Issuance of 4,856 common shares under employee				
stock option plans		25	116	
Net income for the year				58,078
Cash dividends paid:				
Common stock ($2.30 a share)				(25,493)
Preferred stock ($4.75 a share)				(4,817)
Balance at December 31,1986	$39,074	$55,425	$10,415	$399,802
Issuance of 5,018 common shares under employee				
stock option plan		25	84	
Net income for the year				28,831
Cash dividends paid:				
Common stock ($1.70 a share)				(18,847)
Preferred stock ($4.75 a share)				(4,817)
Balance at December 31, 1987	$39,074	$55,450	$10,499	$404,969

For example, lack of liquidity was supposedly one of the causes of the collapse of the Penn Central Railroad. On the other hand, a current ratio that is too high may indicate bad management of liquid resources. Excessive current assets might be better used to pay dividends, to retire long-term debt, or as investment capital. The current ratio should be evaluated in light of the company's circumstances, including management plans, as well as industry and general economic conditions.

The current ratio can be manipulated by such techniques as irregular dividend payments. The possibility of such activity, known as **window dressing,** makes it important to keep in perspective the information that is derived from any single financial ratio.

QUICK RATIO AND DEFENSIVE INTERVAL   One problem with the current ratio is that current assets have varying degrees of liquidity. To avoid this problem, analysts often calculate other liquidity ratios that more directly consider degrees of liquidity of current assets than does the current ratio. Two of these ratios are the quick, or acid-test, ratio and the defensive interval ratio.

We calculate the **quick ratio** by dividing the most liquid assets—generally, the total of cash, short-term marketable securities, and net short-term receivables—by total current liabilities. Exclusion of inventories, prepaid items, and similar comparatively nonliquid assets from the numerator of the quick ratio might provide short-term creditors with better information about a company's liquidity than does the current ratio. When we calculate and evaluate the quick ratio, however, we must consider the particular circumstances of the company we are studying. Some companies, such as a jewelry store, may have very liquid inventories, while other normally liquid current assets, such as short-term receivables, may be comparatively nonliquid.

The 1987 quick ratio for Commex Company is calculated as follows:

$$\text{Quick ratio} = \frac{\text{Cash} + \text{Short-term marketable securities*} + \text{Net short-term receivables}}{\text{Current liabilities}}$$

$$= \frac{\$38,951 + \$162,521}{\$181,308} = 1.11$$

* Commex has no short-term marketable securities.

Although Commex's quick ratio is substantially lower than the current ratio, it is greater than 1.0, which means that Commex can meet all of its current obligations with only its most liquid current assets.

The **defensive interval ratio** is equal to **defensive assets** (cash, short-term marketable securities, and net short-term receivables) divided by average daily expenditures for operations. The defensive interval ratio addresses a company's survivability in the absence of external cash flows. This ratio measures the length of time that a company could carry on its daily operations with only its liquid assets. The defensive interval ratio is useful because it directly considers the size and timing of average daily cash flows.

In theory, the average daily expenditures for operations (the denominator of the defensive interval ratio) should be based on the company's cash budget for the coming period. In practice, the cash budget is not available to external analysts and they therefore must estimate average daily expenditures for operations by adding together cost of goods sold, selling and administrative expenses, and all other ordinary daily cash expenditures, and dividing the total by 365 days. If total expense is used in the denominator, noncash expenses, such as tax expense for which payment is deferred and depreciation, must be subtracted from total expenses.

The 1987 defensive interval for Commex is:

$$\frac{\text{Defensive}}{\text{interval}} = \frac{\text{Defensive assets}}{\text{Average daily expenditures for operations}}$$

$$= \frac{\text{Cash} + \text{Short-term marketable securities} + \text{Net short-term receivables}}{(\text{Cost of goods sold} + \text{Selling and administrative expenses} + \text{Other ordinary expenses} - \text{Depreciation}) \div 365 \text{ days}}$$

$$= \frac{\$38,951 + \$162,521}{(\$952,176 + \$128,176 + \$23,070 + \$21,891 - \$42,551) \div 365 \text{ days}}$$

$$= \frac{\$201,472}{\$1,082,762 \div 365 \text{ days}} = \frac{\$201,472}{\$2,966 \text{ per day}}$$

$$= 67.9 \text{ days}$$

Thus, based on the defensive interval, it appears that Commex could carry on its normal operations for more than two months by using its most liquid assets to finance operating expenses.

Activity or Turnover Ratios

Turnover ratios are used to measure the relative efficiency with which a company uses its assets. Both current and long-term aspects of asset management can be analyzed.

INVENTORY TURNOVER   **Inventory turnover** is cost of goods sold divided by average inventory for the period. Cost of goods sold is used as the numerator instead of sales because sales include profit, and inventory is a cost figure. The *average* inventory is used as the denominator because the ratio is a measure of inventory activity *during* the period.

Commex's inventory turnover for 1987 is calculated as follows:

$$\text{Inventory turnover} = \frac{\text{Cost of goods sold}}{\text{Average inventory}}$$

$$= \frac{\text{Cost of goods sold}}{(\text{Beginning inventory} + \text{Ending inventory}) \div 2}$$

$$= \frac{\$952,176}{(\$270,592 + \$267,663) \div 2}$$

$$= 3.54 \text{ times per year, or every 103 days}$$

Low values for the inventory turnover ratio may indicate sluggish sales or too much inventory on hand, with resultant increases in inventory carrying costs. In addition, the amount of time it takes to turn over inventory is a good indicator of a company's cash inflow prospects. High inventory turnover ratios may mean that there are problems with stockouts and disgruntled customers. Such problems would necessitate an increase in inventory levels.

ACCOUNTS RECEIVABLE TURNOVER   In theory, the **accounts receivable turnover ratio** is net credit sales divided by average net accounts receivable outstanding during the period. In practice, however, the numerator is often net total sales, since most companies do not report credit sales. This practice will not adversely affect the information provided by the ratio if the relationship between credit sales and cash sales is fairly stable.

The Commex Company's 1987 accounts receivable turnover is calculated as follows:

$$\begin{aligned}\text{Accounts receivable} \atop \text{turnover} &= \frac{\text{Net sales}}{\text{Average accounts receivable}}\end{aligned}$$

$$= \frac{\text{Net sales}}{(\text{Beginning net accounts receivable} + \text{Ending net accounts receivable}) \div 2}$$

$$= \frac{\$1,159,863}{(\$138,459 + \$162,521) \div 2}$$

$$= 7.71 \text{ times per year, or every 47 days}$$

Commex's average dollar balance of accounts receivable is outstanding for a little more than 47 days before being converted to cash. When the accounts receivable turnover period is combined with Commex's inventory turnover period of 103 days, it can be inferred that each credit sale (including the inventory holding period) ties up cash for about 150 days. If credit sales are a substantial part of total sales, 150 days is a good estimate of the length of Commex's operating cycle. If most sales are for cash, then the inventory turnover period of 103 days is a good estimate of the length of the operating cycle. An excessively long accounts receivable turnover period would suggest a need to investigate and perhaps modify the company's policy for granting credit to customers or its accounts receivable collection practices.

TOTAL ASSETS TURNOVER   The **total assets turnover ratio** is net sales divided by the average total assets for the period. This ratio emphasizes how productive total assets were during the period.

Commex's 1987 total assets turnover is calculated as follows:

$$\text{Total assets turnover} = \frac{\text{Net sales}}{\text{Average total assets}}$$

$$= \frac{\text{Net sales}}{(\text{Beginning total assets} + \text{Ending total assets}) \div 2}$$

$$= \frac{\$1,159,863}{(\$846,010 + \$903,841) \div 2}$$

$$= 1.33 \text{ times per year, or every 274 days}$$

An excessively low total assets turnover suggests the existence of high opportunity costs for asset use, or at least inefficient use of assets. In such cases, reduction of the asset base may be called for, and in extreme cases liquidation of the company may be economically preferable to existing inefficient uses of company assets. As we suggested earlier, however, no ratio should be analyzed without also examining other measures of financial strength.

Leverage Ratios

Leverage ratios indicate to investors and long-term creditors the riskiness of the firm as an investment or lending alternative. These ratios provide information to investors about the relative emphasis on debt in the capital structure of the company. As debt increases and debt servicing requirements grow, there is greater uncertainty about the return on an investment in the company's common stock. Leverage ratios also are useful for evaluating a company's ability to service both current and long-term debt, whether on a continuing basis or a liquidation basis.

TOTAL LIABILITIES TO TOTAL ASSETS   The **total liabilities to total assets ratio** provides information about the company's ability to absorb asset reductions arising from losses without jeopardizing the interests of creditors. High values of the total liabilities to total assets ratio indicate increased risk to creditors because of the possibility that the company will become insolvent before all creditors' claims are met. Investors prefer that the total liabilities to total assets ratio not be too high because of the interest charges that accompany debt. Loan covenants often require companies not to exceed specified levels of the total liabilities to total assets ratio. Desired levels of this ratio usually vary with the stability of company income. Generally, the more stable the historical income, the greater the likelihood that investors and creditors will tolerate increased debt.

The 1987 total liabilities to total assets ratio for Commex is calculated as follows:

$$\text{Total liabilities to total assets} = \frac{\text{Total liabilities}}{\text{Total assets}}$$

$$= \frac{\$393,849}{\$903,841} = .44$$

Since less than half of Commex's financing comes from debt, further but limited growth through debt may be possible. Given the increase in this ratio from .40 in 1986 to .44 in

1987, however, stockholders may oppose further debt financing, especially if there are restrictions on cash dividends that are part of Commex's existing debt arrangements.

TIMES INTEREST EARNED   The **times interest earned ratio** is ordinary income before interest expense and taxes divided by the interest expense. Ordinary income before interest and taxes is used as the numerator of the ratio because this is the income that is available for interest payments. This ratio is useful for assessing a company's ability to make annual interest payments using only ongoing income.

The 1987 times interest earned ratio for Commex is calculated as follows:

$$\text{Times interest earned} = \frac{\begin{array}{c}\text{Income before taxes + Interest expense}\\ \text{+ Provision for plant closings}\end{array}}{\text{Interest expense}}$$

$$= \frac{\$35,131 + \$21,891 + \$11,000}{\$21,891}$$

$$= 3.1 \text{ times}$$

In calculating the times interest earned ratio for Commex, we added the $11,000 special provision for plant closings to income before taxes and interest expense in order to obtain a normal operating income figure. Both investors and creditors prefer a high value for times interest earned because a high value indicates a margin of safety for their investments or loans. That is, normal operating income available to pay interest will be well in excess of annual interest expense.

Sometimes the times interest earned ratio is modified to include all fixed expenses (e.g., interest payments, lease payments, and pension payments) in the denominator. Fixed expenses usually do not include preferred dividends because declaration of dividends is a management prerogative. When the times interest earned ratio is modified to include all fixed expenses, the ratio is called a **fixed expenses** (or **fixed charges**) **coverage ratio.** This ratio provides a more severe test of the company's ability to meet its obligations from ongoing income.

Profitability Ratios

Management's ultimate goal should be to maximize the return to stockholders, and the net income number probably is the best single measure under management's control of how well that goal has been achieved. Thus, investors are quite interested in net income and consider profitability ratios to be among the most important financial ratios.

PROFIT MARGIN ON SALES   The **profit margin on sales** is net income divided by net sales. This ratio indicates the return a company receives for each dollar of sales. The most obvious weakness of this ratio is that many items included in net income, such as financing costs, are not related directly to the company's sales activity.

Commex's profit margin on sales in 1987 is calculated as follows:

$$\text{Profit margin on sales} = \frac{\text{Net income}}{\text{Net sales}}$$

$$= \frac{\$28,831}{\$1,159,863} = .025$$

Commex's profit margin on sales is fairly low, but this ratio does not provide the best evidence of profitability in 1987. Better evidence is provided by the net operating margin and the return on total assets.

NET OPERATING MARGIN The **net operating margin** is operating income divided by net sales. Nonoperating items, such as interest income and interest expense, royalties, and gains or losses on disposals of assets, are excluded from operating income. Since operating income is the numerator of the net operating margin ratio, this ratio is better than profit margin on sales as a measure of the effectiveness with which a company produces and sells its products.

Commex's 1987 net operating margin is calculated as follows:

$$\text{Net operating margin} = \frac{\text{Operating income}}{\text{Net sales}}$$

$$= \frac{\text{Net sales} - (\text{Cost of goods sold} + \text{Operating expenses})}{\text{Net sales}}$$

$$= \frac{\$1,159,863 - (\$952,176 + \$128,176 + \$23,070)}{\$1,159,863}$$

$$= \frac{\$56,441}{\$1,159,863} = .049$$

Commex's net operating margin is almost twice as large as the profit margin on sales, indicating that Commex has large nonoperating charges. Remember that we first saw this with interest expense in our earlier percentage analyses—for example, see Exhibits 26–7 and 26–8.

RETURN ON TOTAL ASSETS The **return on total assets** equals net income divided by average total assets. This ratio is a better measure of profitability than either profit margin on sales or net operating margin because it indicates management's effectiveness at using company assets to generate net income.

Commex's 1987 return on total assets is calculated as follows:

$$\text{Return on total assets} = \frac{\text{Net income}}{\text{Average total assets}}$$

$$= \frac{\text{Net income}}{(\text{Beginning total assets} + \text{Ending total assets}) \div 2}$$

$$= \frac{\$28,831}{(\$846,010 + \$903,841) \div 2}$$

$$= \frac{\$28,831}{\$874,925} = .03$$

The denominator is *average* total assets because the return on total assets is earned during the entire period.

Some analysts contend that the numerator should be net income before interest expense (net of tax savings resulting from interest expense), because interest expense is a cost of obtaining additional assets and therefore should not be considered as a deduction in determining return on assets. If we follow this reasoning, Commex's return on total assets is calculated as follows:

$$\text{Return on total assets} = \frac{\text{Net income} + \text{Interest expense}(1 - \text{Tax rate})}{\text{Average total assets}}$$

$$= \frac{\$28,831 + (\$21,891)\left(1 - \dfrac{\$6,300}{\$35,131}\right)}{(\$846,010 + \$903,841) \div 2}$$

$$= \frac{\$28,831 + (\$21,891)(.82)}{\$874,925}$$

$$= \frac{\$46,782}{\$874,925} = .05$$

RETURN ON STOCKHOLDERS' EQUITY   **Return on stockholders' equity** is net income minus preferred dividends divided by average common stockholders' equity. Since dividends on common stock are paid after preferred dividends are paid, only net income minus preferred dividends is available for distribution to common stockholders.

Commex Company's 1987 return on stockholders' equity is calculated as follows:

$$\text{Return on stockholders' equity} = \frac{\text{Net income} - \text{Preferred dividends}}{\text{Average common stockholders' equity}}$$

$$= \frac{\text{Net income} - \text{Preferred dividends}}{(\text{Beginning common stockholders' equity} + \text{Ending common stockholders' equity}) \div 2}$$

$$= \frac{\$28{,}831 - \$4{,}812}{(\$465{,}642 + \$470{,}918) \div 2}$$

$$= \frac{\$24{,}014}{\$468{,}280} = .05$$

Return on stockholders' equity summarizes management's success at maximizing the return to common stock investors. When we compare Commex's return on stockholders' equity to profit margin on sales, net operating margin, and return on total assets, it appears that the interests of common stockholders have been reasonably well served. That is, the return on stockholders' equity is greater than or equal to all these measures of company profitability. As we shall see shortly, however, the return on stockholders' equity for Commex still may be less than satisfactory.

TRADING ON THE EQUITY   **Trading on the equity** and the use of **financial leverage** describe the practice of borrowing money at fixed interest rates or issuing preferred stock with fixed dividend rates with the expectation of using the money received to invest in assets that will yield a return that exceeds the interest and preferred dividends paid. Because the claims of creditors and preferred stockholders come before the claims of common stockholders, common stockholders benefit from trading on the equity only when the yield on assets exceeds the fixed returns due to creditors and preferred stockholders. In this case, the margin of excess return will accrue to the benefit of the common stockholders, and trading on the equity is *favorable* to them. But when the cost of non-equity capital is greater than the return on assets, trading on the equity is *unfavorable* to the common stockholders.

One way of writing the accounting equation is:

Total assets = Creditors' equity + Preferred stockholders' equity
+ Common stockholders' equity

We know from earlier calculations that Commex Company's 1987 return on total assets was 3 percent. Therefore, based on the accounting equation, *aggregate return* on creditors', preferred stockholders', and common stockholders' equities, which together equal total assets, also was 3 percent. Since the return on common stockholders' equity was 5 percent, we can conclude that the combined returns to creditors and preferred stockholders must have been less than 3 percent because the return on *all* equity was 3 percent. On this basis, trading on the equity by Commex was favorable to the common stockholders. On the other hand, by examining Commex's balance sheet (see Exhibit 26–10), we see that a substantial portion of Commex's creditors' equity is short-term and is essentially interest-free. The 9 percent long-term debt and the preferred stock (4.75 percent cumulative) both have returns exceeding 3 percent, and the long-term debt return exceeds the 5 percent return on Commex's common stockholders' equity. Viewed from this perspective, Commex's return on common stockholders' equity might not be satisfactory to some investors.

EARNINGS PER SHARE Investors often are interested in measures of profitability on a per share of stock basis. There are several such measures, perhaps the most widely used being earnings per share. When a company has no potentially dilutive securities outstanding, the **earnings per share ratio** is calculated by dividing net income minus senior claims on earnings, such as dividends on preferred stock, by the weighted average number of common stock shares outstanding during the period. When potentially dilutive securities, such as stock options, stock warrants, and convertible securities, are outstanding, it may be necessary to calculate two earnings per share figures: (1) primary earnings per share and (2) fully diluted earnings per share.[11] Commex Company has potentially dilutive securities outstanding—for example, the $4.75 cumulative convertible preferred stock—and reports both primary earnings per share and fully diluted earnings per share for 1987 (see Exhibit 26–11).

Care must be exercised in relying on the earnings per share figure because it is possible to increase earnings per share by simply reducing the number of shares outstanding. If potentially dilutive securities exist, earnings per share can be manipulated by adding to or reducing the dilutive securities outstanding. In addition, like all per share figures, earnings per share may cause an analyst to place too much emphasis on company performance with respect to a single share of stock and not give sufficient consideration to total company operations and profitability.

PRICE-EARNINGS RATIO The **price-earnings ratio** (P/E) is the market price of a share of company stock divided by earnings per share. Assuming that *The Wall Street Journal* reported a December 31, 1987, closing common stock price for Commex of 22 7/8 ($22.875), Commex's price-earnings ratio is calculated as follows:

$$\text{Price-earnings ratio} = \frac{\text{Market price per share}}{\text{Earnings per share}}$$

$$= \frac{\$22.875}{\$2.17} = 10.54$$

The trend of the price-earnings ratio is indicative of the long-term growth potential of the company. A rising price-earnings ratio reflects a favorable investor view of growth potential and a steadily declining price-earnings ratio indicates investor doubt about growth potential.

DIVIDEND YIELD The **dividend yield** is the ratio of dividend per common share to market price per common share. Commex's 1987 dividend yield is calculated as follows:

$$\text{Dividend yield} = \frac{\text{Dividend per common share}}{\text{Market price per common share}}$$

$$= \frac{\$1.70}{\$22.875} = .07$$

When dividend yield is added to the percentage change in stock price for the period, we derive a reasonable measure of a common stockholder's total return for the period.

[11] Chapter 24 contains a thorough discussion of earnings per share.

The **dividend payout ratio** is closely related to the dividend yield. The dividend payout ratio is total cash dividends paid divided by net income available to common stockholders. Commex's dividend payout ratio for common stock in 1987 is calculated as follows:

$$\text{Dividend payout ratio} = \frac{\text{Cash dividends}}{\text{Net income} - \text{Preferred dividends}}$$

$$= \frac{\$18,847}{\$24,014} = .79$$

BOOK VALUE PER SHARE **Book value per share** equals common stockholders' equity divided by the number of common shares outstanding at the end of the period. Common stockholders' equity is total stockholders' equity minus any preferred stockholder claims, such as a redemption or liquidation value, dividends in arrears on cumulative preferred stock, or preferred stock participation rights.

Commex's 1987 book value per share is calculated as follows:

$$\text{Book value per share} = \frac{\text{Common stockholders' equity}}{\text{Number of common shares outstanding}}$$

$$= \frac{\text{Total stockholders' equity} - \text{Preferred stockholder claims}}{\text{Number of common shares}}$$

$$= \frac{\$509,992,000 - \$101,414,500^*}{11,089,956 \text{ shares}}$$

$$= \frac{\$408,577,500}{11,089,956 \text{ shares}} = \$36.84 \text{ per share}$$

* As of 12/31/87, Commex's preferred shares had an aggregate liquidation value of $101,414,500 (see Exhibit 26–10).

Although book value per share often is quoted for common stock and can be found regularly in supplementary schedules to annual financial statements (for example, see Commex's five-year summary data in Exhibit 26–6), it normally is not a good measure of the economic or market value of a share of common stock. Because modified historical cost accounting practices typically do not yield market-based values for net assets, only under unusual circumstances will book value per share be a reasonable approximation of the economic value of a share of stock. Only when a company has just started operations or is being accounted for on a liquidation basis is it likely that book value may be close to economic or market value.

THE DU PONT METHOD Financial ratios can be combined in a series to assess return on investment. Use of ratios in a system of interrelationships is known as the **Du Pont method** because E. I. Du Pont de Nemours & Company was one of the first to use the system of ratios approach to financial control and management. The system of ratios approach can yield several forms of equations, one of which is:

$$\frac{\text{Return on}}{\text{investment}} = \frac{\text{Net sales}}{\text{Total assets}} \times \frac{\text{Total assets}}{\text{Stockholders' equity}} \times \frac{\text{Net income} - \text{Preferred dividends}}{\text{Net sales}}$$

The benefit of the Du Pont method is that it can be used to consider simultaneously several responses to a single question. For example, the question "How can return on

EXHIBIT 26–13 SUMMARY OF FINANCIAL RATIOS

EVALUATING FINANCIAL STRENGTH

RATIO	FORMULA FOR CALCULATION
Liquidity ratios	
Current ratio	$\dfrac{\text{Current assets}}{\text{Current liabilities}}$
Quick ratio	$\dfrac{\text{Cash + Short-term marketable securities + Net short-term receivables}}{\text{Current liabilities}}$
Defensive interval	$\dfrac{\text{Cash + Short-term marketable securities + Net short-term receivables}}{\text{Average daily expenditures for operations}}$
Activity or turnover ratios	
Inventory turnover	$\dfrac{\text{Cost of goods sold}}{\text{Average inventory}}$
Accounts receivable turnover	$\dfrac{\text{Net sales}}{\text{Average net accounts receivable}}$
Total assets turnover	$\dfrac{\text{Net sales}}{\text{Average total assets}}$
Leverage ratios	
Total liabilities to total assets	$\dfrac{\text{Total liabilities}}{\text{Total assets}}$
Times interest earned	$\dfrac{\text{Income before taxes + Interest expense}}{\text{Interest expense}}$

investment be increased?'' might be answered in several ways—such as by increasing asset turnover through increased sales, or by increasing net income through cost-cutting policies, or by a combination of changes.

Exhibit 26–13 provides a summary of the financial ratios we have discussed. Financial ratios are often evaluated by using time series analysis or cross-section analysis, which we discuss in the next two sections.

Time Series Analysis

Time series analysis is the study of increases and decreases in variables over time. Knowledge of trends or other relationships should permit future levels of variables to be estimated with increased precision, provided past relationships continue into the future. Time series analysis can be applied to many of the ratios discussed in this chapter, as well as to net earnings and cash flow measures. Time series analysis often is combined with cross-section analysis in the development of investment strategies.

Cross-Section Analysis

Analysts often compare the operating results or financial condition of one company with the operating results of other companies in the same industry, or of companies in different industries during the same period of time. This type of analysis is known as **cross-section analysis,** or **comparative analysis.** Although cross-section analysis is widely used, the

EVALUATING PROFITABILITY

RATIO	FORMULA FOR CALCULATION
Profitability ratios	
Profit margin on sales	$\dfrac{\text{Net income}}{\text{Net sales}}$
Net operating margin	$\dfrac{\text{Operating income}}{\text{Net sales}}$
Return on total assets	$\dfrac{\text{Net income}}{\text{Average total assets}}$
Return on total assets (income before interest expense)	$\dfrac{\text{Net income} + \text{Interest expense}(1 - \text{Tax rate})}{\text{Average total assets}}$
Return on stockholders' equity	$\dfrac{\text{Net income} - \text{Preferred dividends}}{\text{Average common stockholders' equity}}$
Earnings per share	$\dfrac{\text{Net income} - \text{Senior claims on earnings}}{\text{Weighted average number of common shares}}$
Price-earnings ratio	$\dfrac{\text{Market price per share of stock}}{\text{Earnings per share}}$
Dividend yield	$\dfrac{\text{Cash dividend per common share}}{\text{Market price per share of stock}}$
Dividend payout ratio	$\dfrac{\text{Cash dividends}}{\text{Net income} - \text{Preferred dividends}}$
Book value per share	$\dfrac{\text{Common stockholders' equity}}{\text{Number of common shares outstanding}}$

technique has several potential problems. For example, operating results of companies may be interdependent, especially when those companies are in the same industry. Or similar companies may use different accounting techniques, making comparisons difficult. Additionally, economies of scale or other economic factors may affect companies differently.

Another problem with cross-section analysis arises when industry average ratios are used for comparative purposes. First, this practice implies that the industry level of performance is desirable. Although this may be true, it is also true that entire industries sometimes do poorly, as mid-1980s experiences in the oil and gas industry show. However, such comparisons do provide a benchmark for assessing how well a particular company's management has performed in relation to others in the industry. Second, many enterprises operate in several industries, and it may be difficult or impossible to decide which industry is the appropriate one for comparisons. For example, the Commex Company has operations in several industries, and thus we have not presented industry ratios for comparison with Commex ratios. A company should be compared to other companies that have the same general characteristics, such as products, markets, and size. Care also should be taken to ensure that companies that are compared are as similar as possible in terms of accounting techniques employed, capital structure, and other variables. While it is virtually impossible to match companies perfectly for comparative purposes, reasonably valid conclusions necessitate that companies be reasonably matched. Third, it is important to remember that many industry ratios are not weighted for size of member companies; a large multinational company may be equally weighted with a regional company when industry ratios are calculated. Very likely, the requirements for success of a multinational company differ substantially from those of a regional company. Analysts must consider issues such as these in order to maximize the value of cross-section analysis, especially when industry average ratios are used for comparison.

LIMITATIONS OF RATIO ANALYSIS

Ratio analysis is a popular technique for analyzing financial statements because ratios are simple to calculate, convenient to use, and widely published. In addition, ratios provide some types of financial information much more effectively than does study of the line item amounts reported in the financial statements. However, users of financial statements must be aware of the limitations of ratio analysis so that financial ratios are not inappropriately emphasized and other types of financial information overlooked or underutilized.

As we indicated earlier, one factor that limits the usefulness of ratio analysis is that not all companies use the same accounting principles and practices. A variety of accounting practices are used in several areas, such as:

1. Inventory accounting (LIFO, FIFO, average cost, etc.).
2. Depreciation methods (double declining balance, straight-line, etc.).
3. Capitalizing vs. expensing of various expenditures.
4. Different bases for accounting for investments in stocks (cost, equity, market value).

Differences among companies in accounting for these and other items make it essential that users exercise care when making intercompany ratio comparisons, and require that accounting data be adjusted for differences in accounting practices among companies whenever possible.

The potentially significant influence of different accounting practices on financial data and ratio analysis results is illustrated by a footnote to the General Mills, Inc., 1984 financial statements in which it is stated that 1984 inventories would have been $79.7 million higher if the FIFO method of inventory accounting had been used in place of LIFO. The effect of a $79.7 million larger inventory amount on the 1984 current ratio would be an increase in the current ratio of 7 percent.

Because ratios can be calculated so precisely, it is tempting to attach greater precision to financial ratios than exists in the data used in the ratio calculation. We must remember that ratios can be no more precise than the accounting data used in their calculation. As you know, accounting data often are based on judgments, estimations, and allocations. Ratios based on accounting data will be affected by these same factors. In addition, ratios are sensitive to management policies, and are affected by the particular accounting practices used by a company.

The accounting data used in ratios generally are not based on current values. In the modified historical cost system, judgments, estimations, and allocations cause amounts for many items, particularly assets, to differ significantly from current values in many cases.

Some financial ratios provide information about different aspects of a company and its operations *at a point in time*. Since companies operate in a changing environment and are continuously active, these ratios have the same deficiencies in describing a company as snapshots have in describing a running event in a track meet.

Individual financial ratios should not be used in isolation. We need a broader perspective on a company than we can gain by evaluating individual ratios in isolation. In addition, many financial ratios are correlated with other ratios, and a change in one accounting variable may affect several ratios.

Finally, ratio analysis is only one of several types of financial statement analysis, and a company's annual financial statements are only one of several sources of information about that company. Proper evaluation of a company's economic status and potential for future success must include attention to all available sources of information.

SUMMARY OF IMPORTANT TOPICS AND CONCEPT APPLICATIONS

1. Among the users of external financial statements are creditors and potential creditors, present and potential stockholders, and management.

2. Companies which wish to issue securities to the general public or which already have issued securities to the public are required to file a variety of forms and financial reports with the Securities and Exchange Commission (SEC).

3. A company's financial statements usually are prepared on a consolidated basis. In **segment reporting,** the consolidated accounts are broken down into amounts related to particular industry segments of the firm or amounts related to firm operations in specific geographic areas.

4. Financial reports issued between the dates of annual financial statements are called **interim financial reports** and are another, more **timely,** source of financial information about a company.

5. For reporting purposes, each interim period should be considered an integral part of the annual period.

6. **Percentage analysis** is a technique in which particular accounts or line items in the financial statements are evaluated over time as a percentage of their value as of a designated base period, or are evaluated within a particular time period as a percentage of some designated account or line item.

7. **Horizontal analysis** expresses financial data from two or more accounting periods in terms of a single designated base period, or expresses data in each succeeding period as compared to the amount for the preceding period.

8. In **vertical analysis** all of the data in a particular financial statement are presented as a percentage of a single designated line item of that financial statement.

9. Probably the most widely used financial analysis technique is **ratio analysis,** the analysis of relationships between two or more line items on the financial statements.

10. Generally, financial ratios are calculated to evaluate: (1) liquidity, (2) asset activity or turnover, (3) leverage, or (4) profitability. A summary of financial ratios is provided by Exhibit 26–13 on pages 1286–87.

11. **Time series analysis** is the study of increases and decreases in variables over time.

12. **Cross section** or **comparative analysis** is the comparison of operating results or financial condition of one company with the operating results or financial conditions of other companies in the same industry, or of companies in different industries during the same period of time.

QUESTIONS

Q26-1. Name three groups of decision makers who analyze financial statements and briefly indicate what each group is interested in learning about the financial affairs of a company.

Q26-2. Identify five sources of financial information about companies that are available to decision makers outside the company.

Q26-3. Distinguish between the subject matter of SEC *Regulations S-X* and *S-K*.

Q26-4. What forms are most commonly used for SEC reporting by registrants?

Q26-5. Why might an analyst wish to have segment information when attempting to evaluate the financial condition and profitability of a company that has operations in different industries or different geographic areas?

Q26-6. Define an industry segment.

Q26-7. Briefly indicate the circumstances under which an industry segment is a reportable segment.

Q26-8. Under GAAP, what information must a company report for each reportable segment?

Q26-9. Describe the different presentation methods that can be used by a company to report segment information in its financial statements.

Q26-10. Under what conditions must a company disclose revenue, operating profit or loss, and identifiable assets separately for its foreign operations and domestic operations?

Q26-11. Discuss some of the circumstances that may complicate interim reporting.

Q26-12. What general guideline should be followed when GAAP is applied to interim financial reporting?

Q26-13. What is the proper procedure for dealing with a temporary liquidation of base period inventories at an interim reporting date?

Q26-14. Describe the proper treatment of *(a)* permanent and *(b)* temporary inventory losses from market price declines during an interim reporting period.

Q26-15. What information must companies disclose, as a minimum, in interim financial reports?

Q26-16. Explain what it means to say that the securities market is efficient. If the securities market is efficient, and given that a financial accountant's traditional role is to prepare external financial reports, what reasons can you give for a financial accountant to be familiar with analysis of financial statements?

Q26-17. What information about a company and its financial statements can be found in the CPA's audit report?

Q26-18. Describe the percentage analysis technique.

Q26-19. Distinguish between horizontal and vertical percentage analysis.

Q26-20. What is the primary objective of vertical analysis?

Q26-21. Most financial ratios can be classified as one of four types of ratios. What are the four general types of financial ratios, and what sort of information is provided by each general type of ratio?

Q26-22. Name, and write the formulas for, financial ratios that can be used to evaluate the short-term liquidity of a company.

Q26-23. What information is provided by turnover ratios? Name three commonly used turnover ratios.

Q26-24. Explain how the accounts receivable turnover ratio and the inventory turnover ratio can be used to estimate a company's operating cycle.

Q26-25. What information is provided by leverage ratios?

Q26-26. Explain why creditors and investors usually prefer that the total debt to total assets ratio not be too high.

Q26-27. Write the formulas for at least four profitability ratios. Explain what an analyst might learn from each of the ratios you have listed.

Q26-28. What is meant by the term "trading on the equity"?

Q26-29. Explain the Du Pont method.

Q26-30. Describe some of the problems that may be associated with cross-section analysis.

Q26-31. Discuss the limitations of ratio analysis.

CASES

C26-1. SEC REPORTING Companies that want to issue securities to the general public or that already have issued securities to the public are required to file a variety of forms and financial reports with the SEC. There are three general forms that can be used to register securities to be offered for sale, and there are three forms that are commonly used for reporting by companies that have securities already registered with the SEC.

REQUIRED

1. Identify and briefly describe the three general forms that can be used to register securities to be offered for sale to the general public.

2. Identify and briefly describe the three forms that are commonly used by companies that have securities registered with the SEC.

C26-2. SEGMENT REPORTING Many accountants and financial analysts contend that companies should report financial data for segments of the enterprise.

REQUIRED

1. What does financial reporting for segments of a business enterprise involve?

2. Identify the reasons for the requirement that financial data be reported by segments.

3. Identify the possible disadvantages of requiring financial data to be reported by segments.

4. Identify the accounting difficulties inherent in segment reporting.

(AICPA, adapted)

C26-3. SEGMENT REPORTING An organization composed of financial officers and senior accounting officials of firms that recently have become multiproduct, multidivision, or multigeographic area firms has asked you to present a seminar on GAAP for segment reporting. The members of this organization either know that segment reporting soon will be required for their firms or are trying to determine whether it will be required. Although the organization's representatives have indicated that you should emphasize those aspects of GAAP for segment reporting that you consider the most important, they have asked that, as a minimum, you address the following questions:

    a) Why is segment reporting important to users of financial statements?

    b) What is an industry segment and how can it be identified?

    c) Must financial information be reported for all industry segments? If not, for which industry segments is financial information required and how should these reportable segments be identified?

    d) What financial information should be reported for each reportable segment?

    e) What are the acceptable methods of presenting financial information for reportable industry segments?

REQUIRED

Prepare a brief draft of the comments you think should be made at the seminar. Be sure that you include responses to each of the specific questions presented to you.

C26-4. SEGMENT REPORTING

A) In order to understand current generally accepted accounting principles for reporting on segments of a business enterprise, as stated by the Financial Accounting Standards Board in *Statement No. 14,* it is necessary to be familiar with certain unique terminology.

REQUIRED

With respect to segments of a business enterprise, explain the following terms:

1. Industry segment.

2. Revenue.

3. Operating profit and loss.

4. Identifiable assets.

B) A central issue in reporting on industry segments of a business enterprise is the determination of which segments are reportable.

REQUIRED

1. What are the tests to determine whether or not an industry segment is reportable?

2. What is the test to determine if enough industry segments have been separately reported upon and what is the guideline on the maximum number of industry segments to be shown?

(AICPA, adapted)

C26-5. INTERIM FINANCIAL REPORTING Interim financial reporting has become an important topic in accounting. There has been considerable discussion of the proper way to reflect results of operations at interim dates. Accordingly, the Accounting Principles Board issued an opinion clarifying some aspects of interim financial reporting.

REQUIRED

1. Discuss generally how revenue should be recognized at interim dates and specifically how revenue should be recognized for industries subject to large seasonal fluctuations in revenue and for long-term contracts that are reported by the percentage-of-completion method at annual reporting dates.

2. Discuss generally how product and period costs should be recognized at interim dates. Also discuss how inventory and cost of goods sold may be afforded special accounting treatment at interim dates.

3. Discuss how income tax expense is calculated and reflected in interim financial statements.

(AICPA, adapted)

C26-6. FINANCIAL STATEMENT ANALYSIS You and a close friend, who is about to graduate from the accounting program at another university, are planning to take the next CPA examination. As part of preparing for the exam, the two of you have wisely decided to study several recent CPA examinations and suggested question answers, which you have purchased from the AICPA.

After receiving the questions and answers, you and your friend take an evening to analyze them superficially for the purpose of identifying general topic areas covered. Your friend expresses surprise about the number of questions, especially multiple-choice questions, dealing with financial statement analysis. He notes, with concern, that his accounting professor decided to skip the chapter on financial statement analysis in the intermediate accounting textbook because of a shortage of time and because "financial statement analysis really isn't accounting." Your friend asks you what you know about financial statement analysis and wonders "why accountants need to know anything about that stuff."

REQUIRED

Explain to your friend why it might be important for a financial accountant to know something about financial statement analysis.

C26-7. INFORMATION PROVIDED BY FINANCIAL RATIOS Information provided by several financial ratios is given below:

a) Primary test of solvency.
b) A more severe test of immediate solvency.
c) Measures efficiency of collection of accounts receivable.
d) Indicates liquidity of inventory.
e) Measures use of total assets.
f) Indicates ability to protect creditor interests.
g) Indicates net productivity of each sales dollar.
h) Measures success at maximizing common stockholders' return.

    i) Indicates the long-term growth potential of the firm.

    j) Useful for determining the firm's ability to make annual interest payments.

REQUIRED

1. Name the financial ratio that provides each of the above pieces of information and give the formula for calculating that ratio.

2. For each ratio named in part 1, indicate what a high or low value of the ratio may mean.

C26-8. FINANCIAL STATEMENT CONTENT AND ANALYSIS   Selected information from the financial statements of the Dell Company follows:

Dell Company

CURRENT ASSETS SECTION OF
BALANCE SHEETS
(in thousands of dollars)

	DECEMBER 31	
	1987	**1986**
Cash..	$ 7,000	$ 7,200
Marketable securities at cost, which approximates		
market	26,000	22,000
Accounts receivable, net of allowance for doubtful		
accounts.....................................	210,000	190,000
Inventories......................................	252,000	308,000
Prepaid expenses	5,000	4,800
Total current assets..........................	$500,000	$532,000

STATEMENTS OF INCOME
(in thousands of dollars)

	YEAR ENDED DECEMBER 31	
	1987	**1986**
Net sales	$ 1,200,000	$1,000,000
Costs and expenses:		
Cost of goods sold	$ 960,000	$ 800,000
Selling, general, and administrative expenses	147,000	120,000
Other, net	24,000	18,300
Total costs and expenses	$(1,131,000)	$ (938,300)
Income from continuing operations before		
income taxes	$ 69,000	$ 61,700
Income taxes.................................	(26,900)	(25,300)
Income from continuing operations.........	$ 42,100	$ 36,400
Cumulative effect of change in estimates of		
salvage values of property, plant, and		
equipment, less applicable income taxes of		
$1,500,000	—	(3,000)
Net income	$ 42,100	$ 33,400
Earnings per share of common stock:		
Income from continuing operations.............	$4.21	$3.64
Cumulative effect of change in estimates of		
salvage values of property, plant, and		
equipment, less applicable income taxes	—	(.30)
Net income	$4.21	$3.34

Selected information from the summary of significant accounting policies in the notes to the financial statements of the Dell Company is as follows:

Inventories: Inventories are stated at the lower of cost (FIFO) or market.

Deferred income taxes: Deferred income taxes arise from timing differences when profits or expenses are included in taxable income on the income tax return later or earlier than they are included in the statement of income. Such timing differences relate principally to depreciation. A provision for deferred income taxes of $6,700,000 in 1987 and $6,300,000 in 1986 is included in the statements of income in "Other, net."

Selected information from other notes to the financial statements of the Dell Company is as follows:

Inventories: Inventories are comprised of the following:

	DECEMBER 31	
	1987	1986
	(in thousands of dollars)	
Finished goods	$176,000	$215,000
Goods in process	13,000	14,000
Raw materials	63,000	79,000
	$252,000	$308,000

Inventories at December 31, 1987, were reduced from a cost of $292,000,000 to a market value of $252,000,000 under the direct inventory reduction method. The cost of inventories at December 31, 1986, approximated their market value.

Accounting change: During the third quarter of 1986, Dell Company revised earlier estimates of salvage values for its property, plant, and equipment. This change in accounting reduced the 1986 net income by $3,000,000 ($0.30 per share).

REQUIRED

1. Are inventories and the related cost of goods sold presented appropriately? Explain why or why not. If the presentation is not appropriate, specify the appropriate presentation and explain why.

2. a) What are the components of the quick (acid-test) ratio?
b) How should the quick ratio be used?

3. Is the provision for deferred income taxes presented appropriately? Explain why or why not. If the presentation is not appropriate, specify the appropriate presentation and explain why.

4. Is the accounting change presented appropriately? Explain why or why not. If the presentation is not appropriate, specify the appropriate presentation and explain why. Assume that the accounting change did not involve deferred income taxes.

(AICPA, adapted)

EXERCISES

E26-1. DETERMINING SEGMENT OPERATING PROFIT Neuaxton, Inc., engages in three lines of business, each of which is considered to be a significant industry segment. In 1987 Neuaxton's sales aggregated $1.8 million, of which segment 3 contributed 60 percent. Traceable costs were $600,000 for segment 3 out of a total of $1.2 million for the company as a whole. In addition, $350,000 of common costs are allocated on the basis of the ratio of a segment's income before common costs to the total income before common costs.

REQUIRED

What should Neuaxton report as operating profit for segment 3 in 1987?

(AICPA, adapted)

E26-2. IDENTIFYING REPORTABLE SEGMENTS   Balen Company has seven industry segments. Summary financial data for the past year for the seven segments are as follows:

SEGMENT	REVENUE	OPERATING PROFIT (LOSS)	IDENTIFIABLE ASSETS
1	$ 350,000	$ 90,000	$ 800,000
2	1,200,000	500,000	4,200,000
3	620,000	270,000	1,850,000
4	500,000	(50,000)	2,050,000
5	1,800,000	(370,000)	3,800,000
6	175,000	(290,000)	750,000
7	810,000	125,000	1,200,000

REQUIRED

Analyze the data for each industry segment and identify the reportable segments. In each case in which the segment is reportable, give the reason or reasons that the segment qualifies.

E26-3. PREPARING SEGMENT INFORMATION   The 1987 consolidated income statement for Miller, Inc., is presented below:

Sales		$485,000
Less: Operating expenses		
Cost of goods sold	$275,000	
Selling and administrative expenses	110,000	
Depreciation expense	75,000	
Other operating expenses	5,000	(465,000)
Operating profit before taxes		$ 20,000
Other revenues and expenses		
Equity in income of unconsolidated subsidiary	$ 7,500	
Interest expense	(3,500)	4,000
Income before taxes		$ 24,000
Income taxes		(9,600)
Net income		$ 14,400
Earnings per share (288,000 shares)		$ .05

Miller, Inc., has two reportable industry segments, *A* and *B*. There are no intersegment sales in the company. Selling and administrative expenses include $10,000 of general corporate expense, and depreciation expense includes $5,000 depreciation on general corporate assets. All other operating revenues and expenses are directly allocable to industry segments as follows:

	SEGMENT A	SEGMENT B	OTHER SEGMENTS
Sales	50%	40%	10%
Cost of goods sold	46	45	9
Selling and administrative expense	44	44	12
Depreciation expense	55	30	15
Other operating expenses	43	50	7

REQUIRED

1. Prepare a schedule reporting financial information about the operations of the segments of

Miller, Inc., during 1987. Industry segment amounts should be reconciled with consolidated amounts.

2. Prepare a footnote describing the calculation of operating income before taxes for segments A and B.

E26-4. REPORTING IN INTERIM FINANCIAL STATEMENTS   The following information is available for Hunter Corporation for 1987:

a) On January 1, 1987, Hunter paid property taxes amounting to $40,000 on its plant for the calendar year 1987. In late March 1987, Hunter made annual major repairs to its machinery amounting to $120,000. These repairs will benefit the remainder of the calendar year's operations.

b) An inventory loss of $420,000 from market decline occurred in April 1987. Hunter recorded this loss in April 1987 after its March 31 quarterly report was issued. None of this loss had been recovered by the end of 1987.

REQUIRED

State the dollar amounts that should appear in Hunter Corporation's March 31, June 30, September 30, and December 31, 1987, quarterly financial statements to report:

1. Property taxes.

2. Major repairs to machinery.

3. Inventory loss from market decline.

(AICPA, adapted)

E26-5. REPORTING IN INTERIM FINANCIAL STATEMENTS   On January 1, 1987, Davis Construction Company, a calendar-year firm, entered into a $1 million, long-term, fixed-price contract to construct a bridge for the state of Washington. Davis accounts for this contract by the percentage-of-completion method. At the end of each quarter of 1987, the estimated percentage of completion and estimated total costs related to the bridge construction were:

QUARTER	ESTIMATED PERCENTAGE OF COMPLETION	ESTIMATED TOTAL COSTS AT COMPLETION
1	10%	$750,000
2*	10	750,000
3	25	960,000
4*	25	960,000

* No work performed in the second and fourth quarters.

In January 1987, Davis paid $80,000 in property taxes on its plant for 1987. In the same month Davis estimated that its year-end bonus to executives for 1987 would be $320,000. And in August 1987, Davis sold machinery with a book value of $80,000 for $65,000.

REQUIRED

What amounts should be reported in Davis Construction Company's first- through fourth-quarter income statements for:

1. The construction contract?

2. The property taxes?

3. The bonus?

4. The sale of machinery?

E26-6. DETERMINING INTERIM TAX PROVISION   Wildlife Publications, Inc., has the following income before income tax provision and estimated effective annual income tax rates for the first three quarters of 1987:

QUARTER	INCOME BEFORE INCOME TAX PROVISION	ESTIMATED EFFECTIVE ANNUAL TAX RATE AT END OF QUARTER
1st	$60,000	40%
2nd	70,000	40
3rd	40,000	45

REQUIRED

What should be Wildlife Publications' income tax provision in the third-quarter interim income statement?

(AICPA, adapted)

E26-7. HORIZONTAL AND VERTICAL ANALYSIS Halverson, Inc., manufactures and sells portable radios. Condensed comparative income statements for 1986 and 1987 are presented below:

Halverson, Inc.

COMPARATIVE INCOME STATEMENTS

	1987	1986
Sales	$486,100	$305,200
Sales returns	(24,300)	(6,100)
Beginning inventories	131,250	110,100
Cost of manufactured radios	291,600	137,300
Ending inventories	(160,400)	(131,250)
Cost of goods sold	262,450	116,150
Selling expenses	102,100	91,500
Administrative expenses	48,600	45,750
Income before tax	48,650	45,700

REQUIRED

1. Prepare a horizontal percentage analysis using 1986 as the base year. Round each figure to the nearest percentage point.

2. Prepare a vertical percentage analysis for both 1986 and 1987, using sales as the basis for comparison. Round each figure to the nearest percentage point.

3. Halverson is concerned with its 1987 profit. On the basis of your analysis in parts 1 and 2, identify those financial statement items that appear to be problem areas for Halverson. Give reasons for your choices.

(CGAA, adapted)

E26-8. CALCULATING LIQUIDITY RATIOS Information from Green Company's income statement and balance sheet is as follows:

Loss on sale of building	$ 10,000,000
Cost of goods sold	565,500,000
Selling and administrative expense	121,000,000
Depreciation expense	280,000,000
Current assets	
Cash	$ 2,400,000
Marketable securities	7,500,000
Accounts receivable	57,600,000
Inventories	66,300,000
Prepaid expenses	1,200,000
Total current assets	$135,000,000

Current liabilities

Notes payable	$ 1,500,000
Accounts payable	19,500,000
Accrued expenses	12,500,000
Income taxes payable	500,000
Payments due within one year on long-term debt	3,500,000
Total current liabilities	$ 37,500,000

REQUIRED

Calculate the current ratio, quick ratio, and defensive interval for Green Company.

E26-9. TURNOVER RATIOS Selected information from the accounting records of the Valor Company is as follows:

Net accounts receivable, 12/31/86	$ 900,000
Net accounts receivable, 12/31/87	$1,000,000
Accounts receivable turnover	5:1
Inventories, 12/31/86	$1,100,000
Inventories, 12/31/87	$1,200,000
Inventory turnover	4:1

REQUIRED

1. Calculate Valor's gross margin for 1987.

2. Assuming a business year consisting of 300 days, what was the number of days' sales in average receivables for 1987 and the number of days' sales in average inventories for 1987?

(AICPA, adapted)

E26-10. CALCULATING RATIOS THAT MEASURE FINANCIAL STRENGTH The following selected financial data are taken from the financial statements of Federal Corporation:

	12/31/87	12/31/86
Cash	$ 10,000	$ 80,000
Accounts receivable (net)	50,000	150,000
Merchandise inventory	90,000	150,000
Short-term marketable securities	30,000	10,000
Land and buildings (net)	340,000	360,000
Mortgage payable (noncurrent)	270,000	280,000
Accounts payable (trade)	70,000	110,000
Short-term notes payable	20,000	40,000

	YEAR ENDED	
	12/31/87	12/31/86
Cash sales	$1,800,000	$1,600,000
Credit sales	500,000	800,000
Cost of goods sold	1,000,000	1,400,000

REQUIRED

Calculate, for 1987, Federal Corporation's:

1. Quick ratio.

2. Receivable turnover.

3. Merchandise inventory turnover.

4. Current ratio.

(AICPA, adapted)

E26-11. DETERMINING LENGTH OF OPERATING CYCLE   Selected information for 1987 for the Price Company is as follows:

Cost of goods sold	$5,400,000
Average inventory	1,800,000
Net sales	7,200,000
Average receivables	960,000
Net income	720,000

REQUIRED

Assuming a business year consisting of 360 days, what was the average number of days in Price's operating cycle for 1987? What were Price's accounts receivable turnover (in days) and inventory turnover (in days) for 1987?

(AICPA, adapted)

E26-12. CALCULATING PROFITABILITY RATIOS   Selected information for Irvine Corporation is as follows:

	12/31/86	12/31/87
Preferred stock, 8%, par $100, nonconvertible, noncumulative	$ 125,000	$ 125,000
Common stock	300,000	400,000
Retained earnings	75,000	185,000
Dividends paid on preferred stock	10,000	10,000
Net income	60,000	120,000
Total assets	1,000,000	1,400,000

REQUIRED

Calculate Irvine's return on total assets and return on common stockholders' equity, rounded to the nearest percentage point, for 1987.

(AICPA, adapted)

E26-13. CALCULATING PROFITABILITY RATIOS   As of December 31, 1986, Rich Company had 100,000 shares of $10 par value common stock issued and outstanding. There was no change in the number of shares outstanding during 1987. Total stockholders' equity as of December 31, 1987, was $2.8 million. The net income for the year ended December 31, 1987, was $800,000. During 1987 Rich Company paid $3 per share in dividends on its common stock. The quoted market price of Rich's common stock on a national stock exchange was $20 on December 31, 1986, and $24 on December 31, 1987.

REQUIRED

Calculate the price-earnings ratio, dividend yield, dividend payout, and estimated common stockholders' return for 1987.

(AICPA, adapted)

E26-14. CALCULATING BOOK VALUE PER SHARE OF COMMON STOCK   Elm Corporation's stockholders' equity as of June 30, 1987, consisted of the following:

Preferred stock, 10%, $50 par value: liquidating value, $55 per share; 20,000 shares issued and outstanding	$1,000,000
Common stock, $10 par value: 500,000 shares authorized; 150,000 shares issued and outstanding	1,500,000
Retained earnings	500,000

REQUIRED

What is Elm Corporation's book value per share of common stock at June 30, 1987?

(AICPA, adapted)

E26-15. COMPONENTS OF FINANCIAL RATIOS The following information has been taken from the financial statements of the Talston Company:

Current assets	$200,000
Current liabilities	100,000
Common stock	100,000
Retained earnings	100,000
Long-term debt to stockholders' equity	.5:1
Inventory turnover	9 times per year
Gross margin	.10
Acid-test ratio	1:1
Average collection period	18 days
Sales	$1,000,000

REQUIRED

Assuming a 360-day year and that all sales are on credit, determine the amounts of the following balance sheet accounts:

1. Cash.

2. Accounts receivable.

3. Inventory.

4. Long-term debt.

(CGAA, adapted)

E26-16. COMPONENTS OF FINANCIAL RATIOS The December 31, 1987, balance sheet of Realty, Inc., is presented below. These are the only accounts in Realty's balance sheet. Amounts indicated by a question mark (?) can be calculated from the additional information given.

Assets	
Cash..	$ 25,000
Accounts receivable (net).................................	?
Inventory	?
Property, plant, and equipment (net)	294,000
	$432,000
Liabilities and stockholders' equity	
Accounts payable (trade)	$?
Income taxes payable (current)	25,000
Long-term debt	?
Common stock	300,000
Retained earnings	?
	$?
Additional information	
Current ratio (at year end)................................	1.5:1
Total liabilities divided by total stockholders' equity	.8
Inventory turnover based on sales and ending inventory.............	15 times
Inventory turnover based on cost of goods sold and ending inventory	10.5 times
Gross margin, 1987	$315,000

REQUIRED

1. What was Realty's December 31, 1987, balance in accounts payable?

2. What was Realty's December 31, 1987, balance in retained earnings?

3. What was Realty's December 31, 1987, balance in the inventory account?

(AICPA, adapted)

PROBLEMS

P26-1. SEGMENT REPORTING The 1987 consolidated income statement for Wallace Corporation is presented below:

Sales revenue		$3,100,000
Less: Operating expenses		
Cost of goods sold	$1,741,000	
Selling expenses	320,000	
Depreciation expense	712,000	
General administrative expense	210,000	(2,983,000)
Operating profit before taxes....................		$ 117,000
Income taxes.................................		(43,000)
Net income		$ 74,000

Wallace Corporation has five industry segments. There are no intercompany sales. Cost of goods sold, selling expense, and depreciation expense are traceable to each segment according to the percentages indicated below. The general administrative expense is a common cost that is allocated among the segments on the basis of each segment's income or loss before common costs as a percentage of consolidated income or loss before common costs. For example, if a segment had a $10,000 loss before common costs and the consolidated profit for the year was $100,000, then one-tenth of the common costs would be *deducted* (because the segment had a loss) from the segment's loss before common costs to arrive at the segment's operating profit or loss for the year.

ASSIGNMENT OF TRACEABLE REVENUES, COSTS, AND IDENTIFIABLE ASSETS

	SEGMENT 1	SEGMENT 2	SEGMENT 3	SEGMENT 4	SEGMENT 5
Sales revenue .	$800,000	$270,000	$600,000	$290,000	$1,140,000
Cost of goods sold	20%	7%	26%	3%	44%
Selling expense	24%	20%	25%	3%	28%
Depreciation expense	26%	9%	24%	5%	36%
Identifiable assets	$2,700,000	$1,200,000	$2,150,000	$820,000	$3,430,000

REQUIRED

1. According to *FASB Statement No. 14,* what is the definition of an industry segment?

2. What is the before-tax operating profit or loss of each of Wallace Corporation's five industry segments?

3. Which of the five industry segments qualifies as a reportable segment? Give the materiality tests that are met by each industry segment that qualifies as reportable.

4. Prepare segment information for the reportable segments of Wallace Corporation. Use the format shown in Exhibit 26–3.

P26-2. INTERIM REPORTING The Alexander Manufacturing Company, a California corporation listed on the Pacific Coast Stock Exchange, budgeted activities for 1987 as follows:

	AMOUNT
Net sales (1,000,000 units)	$6,000,000
Cost of goods sold	(3,600,000)
Gross margin	$2,400,000
Selling and general and administrative expenses	(1,400,000)
Operating income	$1,000,000
Nonoperating revenues and expenses	–0–
Income before income taxes	$1,000,000
Estimated income taxes (current and deferred)	(550,000)
Net income	$ 450,000
Earnings per share of common stock	$4.50

Alexander has operated profitably for many years and has experienced a seasonal pattern of sales volume and production similar to the following patterns forecast for 1987.

Sales volume is expected to follow a pattern of 10, 20, 35, and 35 percent for the four quarters, because of the seasonality of the industry. Also, because of production and storage capacity limitations, it is expected that production will follow a pattern of 20, 25, 30, and 25 percent per quarter.

At the conclusion of the first quarter of 1987, Alexander's controller has prepared and issued the following interim report for public release:

	AMOUNT
Net sales (100,000 units)	$ 600,000
Cost of goods sold	(360,000)
Gross margin	$ 240,000
Selling and general and administrative expenses	(275,000)
Operating loss	$ (35,000)
Loss from warehouse fire	(175,000)
Loss before income taxes	$(210,000)
Estimated income taxes	–0–
Net loss	$(210,000)
Loss per share of common stock	$(2.10)

The following additional information is available for the first quarter just completed, but was not included in the public information released:

a) The company uses a standard cost system in which standards are set at currently attainable levels on an annual basis. At the end of the first quarter, underapplied fixed factory overhead (volume variance) of $50,000 was treated as an asset. Production during the quarter was 200,000 units, of which 100,000 were sold.

b) The selling, general, and administrative expenses were budgeted on a basis of $900,000 fixed expenses for the year plus $.50 variable expenses per unit of sales.

c) The warehouse fire loss met the conditions of an extraordinary loss. The warehouse had an undepreciated cost of $320,000; $145,000 was recovered from insurance on the warehouse. No other gains or losses are anticipated this year from similar events or transactions, nor has Alexander had any similar losses in preceding years; thus the full loss will be deductible as an ordinary loss for income tax purposes.

d) The effective income tax rate, for federal and state taxes combined, is expected to average 55 percent of income before income taxes during 1987. There are no permanent differences between pretax accounting income and taxable income.

e) Earnings per share were calculated on the basis of 100,000 shares of capital stock outstanding. Alexander has only one class of stock issued, no long-term debt outstanding, and no stock option plan.

REQUIRED

1. Without reference to the specific situation described above, what are the standards of disclosure for interim financial data (published interim financial reports) for publicly traded companies? Explain.

2. Identify the weaknesses in form and content of Alexander's interim report without reference to the additional information.

3. Indicate the preferable treatment for each of the five items of additional information for interim-reporting purposes and explain why that treatment is preferable.

(AICPA, adapted)

P26-3. FINANCIAL STATEMENT CONTENT Shown below and on page 1304 are the financial statements issued by Bellon Corporation for its fiscal year ended October 31, 1987.

STATEMENT OF FINANCIAL POSITION
OCTOBER 31, 1987

Assets		
Cash		$ 15,000
Accounts receivable, net		150,000
Inventory		120,000
Total current assets		$285,000
Trademark (Note 3)		250,000
Land		125,000
Total assets		$660,000
Liabilities and stockholders' equity		
Accounts payable		$ 80,000
Accrued expenses		20,000
Total current liabilities		$100,000
Deferred income tax payable (Note 4)		80,000
Total liabilities		$180,000
Common stock, par $1 (Note 5)	$100,000	
Contributed capital in excess of par	180,000	
Retained earnings	200,000	480,000
Total liabilities and stockholders' equity		$660,000

INCOME STATEMENT
FOR THE FISCAL YEAR ENDED OCTOBER 31, 1987

Sales		$1,000,000
Cost of goods sold		(750,000)
Gross margin		$ 250,000
Expenses		
Bad debt expense	$ 7,000	
Insurance	13,000	
Lease expenses (Note 1)	40,000	
Repairs and maintenance	30,000	
Pensions (Note 2)	12,000	
Salaries	60,000	(162,000)
Income before provision for income tax		$ 88,000
Provision for income tax		(28,740)
Net income		$ 59,260
Earnings per common share outstanding		$0.5926

STATEMENT OF RETAINED EARNINGS
FOR THE FISCAL YEAR ENDED OCTOBER 31, 1987

Retained earnings, 11/1/86	$150,000
Extraordinary gain, net of income tax	25,000
Net income for fiscal year ended 10/31/87	59,260
	$234,260
Dividends ($0.3426 per share)	(34,260)
Retained earnings, 10/31/87	$200,000

FOOTNOTES

Note 1. Long-Term Lease

Under the terms of a five-year noncancelable lease for buildings and equipment, the Company is obligated to make annual rental payments of $40,000 in each of the next four fiscal years. At the conclusion of the lease period, the Company has the option of purchasing the leased assets for $20,000 (a bargain purchase option) or entering into another five-year lease of the same property at an annual rental of $5,000.

Note 2. Pension Plan

Substantially all employees are covered by the Company's pension plan. Pension expense is equal to the total of pension benefits paid to retired employees during the year.

Note 3. Trademark

The Company's trademark was purchased from Barron Corporation on January 1, 1985, for $250,000.

Note 4. Deferred Income Tax Payable

The entire balance in the deferred income tax payable account arose from tax-exempt municipal bonds that were held during the previous fiscal year, giving rise to a difference between taxable income and reported net income for the fiscal year ended October 31, 1986. The deferred liability amount was calculated on the basis of expected tax rates in future years.

Note 5. Warrants

On January 1, 1986, one common stock warrant was issued to stockholders of record for each common share owned. An additional share of common stock is to be issued upon exercise of 10 stock warrants and receipt of an amount equal to par value. For the six months ended October 31, 1987, the average market value for the Company's common stock was $5 per share and no warrants had yet been exercised.

Note 6. Contingent Liability

On October 31, 1987, the Company was contingently liable for product warranties in an amount estimated to aggregate $75,000.

REQUIRED

Review the preceding financial statements and related footnotes. Identify any inclusions or exclusions from them that are in violation of generally accepted accounting principles, and indicate corrective action to be taken. Do *not* comment on format or style. Respond in the following order:

1. Statement of financial position.

2. Footnotes.

3. Income statement.

4. Statement of retained earnings.

5. General.

(AICPA, adapted)

P26-4. FINANCIAL STATEMENT CONTENT AND ANALYSIS The Harrison Company is listed on the New York Stock Exchange. The market value of its common stock was quoted at $18 per share on both December 31, 1987, and December 31, 1986. Harrison's balance sheets as of December 31, 1987, and December 31, 1986, and statements of income and retained earnings for the years then ended are presented below and on page 1306 (in thousands of dollars):

BALANCE SHEETS

	12/31/87	12/31/86
Assets		
Current assets		
Cash	$ 3,500	$ 3,600
Marketable securities, at cost that approximates market	13,000	11,000
Accounts receivable, net of allowance for doubtful accounts	105,000	95,000
Inventories at lower of cost or market	126,000	154,000
Prepaid expenses	2,500	2,400
Total current assets	$250,000	$266,000
Property, plant, and equipment, net of accumulated depreciation	311,000	308,000
Other assets	29,000	34,000
Total assets	$590,000	$608,000
Liabilities and stockholders' equity		
Current liabilities		
Notes payable	$ 5,000	$ 15,000
Accounts payable and accrued expenses	62,500	74,500
Income taxes payable	1,000	1,000
Payments due within one year on long-term debt	6,500	7,500
Total current liabilities	$ 75,000	$ 98,000
Long-term debt	169,000	180,000
Deferred income taxes	74,000	67,000
Other liabilities	9,000	8,000
Total liabilities	$327,000	$353,000
Stockholders' equity		
Common stock, par value $1 per share: authorized, 20,000,000 shares; issued and outstanding, 10,000,000 shares	$ 10,000	$ 10,000
Contributed capital in excess of par	111,000	111,000
Retained earnings	142,000	134,000
Total stockholders' equity	$263,000	$255,000
Total liabilities and stockholders' equity	$590,000	$608,000

STATEMENTS OF INCOME AND RETAINED EARNINGS

	YEAR ENDED			
	12/31/87		**12/31/86**	
Net sales		$600,000		$500,000
Costs and expenses				
Cost of goods sold	$480,000		$400,000	
Selling, general, and				
administrative expenses	66,000		60,000	
Other expenses, net	17,000		6,000	
Total costs and expenses . .		(563,000)		(466,000)
Income before income taxes		$ 37,000		$ 34,000
Income taxes		(16,800)		(15,800)
Net income		$ 20,200		$ 18,200
Retained earnings at beginning				
of period, as previously				
reported	$141,000		$132,000	
Adjustment required for				
correction of error	(7,000)		(6,000)	
Retained earnings at beginning				
of period, as restated		134,000		126,000
Dividends on common stock		(12,200)		(10,200)
Retained earnings at end of				
period		$142,000		$134,000

Additional facts are as follows:

a) Selling, general, and administrative expenses for 1987 included a usual but infrequently occurring loss of $9 million.

b) Other expenses, net, for 1987 included an extraordinary item (loss) of $10 million. If the extraordinary item (loss) had not occurred, income taxes for 1987 would have been $21.8 million instead of $16.8 million.

c) Adjustment required for correction of error was a result of a change from an accounting principle that is not generally accepted to one that is generally accepted.

d) Harrison Company has a simple capital structure and has disclosed earnings per common share for net income in the notes to the financial statements.

REQUIRED

1. Determine from the additional facts above whether or not the presentation of those facts in Harrison Company's statements of income and retained earnings is appropriate. If the presentation is appropriate, discuss the theoretical rationale for the presentation. If the presentation is not appropriate, describe the appropriate presentation and discuss its theoretical rationale. Do not discuss disclosure requirements for the notes to the financial statements.

2. Describe the general significance of the following financial analysis tools:
   a) Quick (acid-test) ratio.
   b) Inventory turnover.
   c) Return on stockholders' equity.

3. On the basis of the Harrison Company balance sheets, statements of income and retained earnings, and additional information, describe how to determine each of the above financial analysis tools (for the year 1987 only).

(AICPA, adapted)

P26-5. CALCULATING FINANCIAL RATIOS

REQUIRED

Using the information given for Harrison Company in Problem 26-4, calculate (for 1987 only) the following:

1. Current (working capital) ratio.

2. Profit margin on sales.

3. Number of days' sales in average receivables, assuming a business year of 300 days and all sales on account.

4. Inventory turnover.

5. Book value per share of common stock.

6. Earnings per share on common stock.

7. Price-earnings ratio on common stock.

8. Dividend payout ratio on common stock.

Show supporting calculations in good form.

(AICPA, adapted)

P26-6. CALCULATING FINANCIAL RATIOS Comparative statements of financial position and income covering the last two fiscal years for Sage Corporation are reproduced below and on the next page. The market price of Sage's common stock was $20 per share on May 31, 1987.

Sage Corporation

STATEMENTS OF FINANCIAL POSITION
MAY 31, 1986 AND 1987
(in thousands of dollars)

	1987	1986
Assets		
Current assets		
Cash	$ 3,000	$ 2,000
Short-term marketable securities	1,000	1,000
Accounts receivable (net)	14,000	11,000
Merchandise inventory	24,000	16,000
Total current assets	$ 42,000	$ 30,000
Property, plant, and equipment (net)	68,000	60,000
Long-term investments	10,000	10,000
Total assets	$120,000	$100,000
Liabilities and stockholders' equity		
Current liabilities		
Accounts payable	$ 5,000	$ 4,000
Wages payable	1,000	1,000
Total current liabilities	$ 6,000	$ 5,000
Bonds payable, 10%, due 1994	20,000	20,000
Total liabilities	$ 26,000	$ 25,000
Stockholders' equity		
Common stock, 10,000,000 shares, no-par	$ 25,000	$ 25,000
Retained earnings	69,000	50,000
Total stockholders' equity	$ 94,000	$ 75,000
Total liabilities and stockholders' equity	$120,000	$100,000

Sage Corporation

COMPARATIVE STATEMENTS OF INCOME
FOR THE YEARS ENDED MAY 31, 1986 AND 1987
(in thousands of dollars)

	1987	1986
Sales (all made on credit)	$200,000	$140,000
Cost of goods sold	(120,000)	(80,000)
Gross profit	$ 80,000	$ 60,000
Selling and administrative expenses	(38,000)	(30,000)
Income before interest and income taxes	$ 42,000	$ 30,000
Interest expense	(2,000)	(2,000)
Income before income taxes	$ 40,000	$ 28,000
Income tax expense	(15,000)	(11,000)
Net income	$ 25,000	$ 17,000

REQUIRED

Calculate the ratios specified below. Average balance sheet account balances should be used in calculating ratios involving income statement accounts. Ending balance sheet account balances should be used in calculating ratios involving only balance sheet items.

1. Calculate the following as of May 31, 1987:
   a) Current ratio.
   b) Quick (acid-test) ratio.
   c) Book value per share of common stock.

2. Calculate the following for the year ended May 31, 1987:
   a) Accounts receivable turnover.
   b) Merchandise inventory turnover.
   c) Times interest earned.
   d) Dividend yield.
   e) Return on stockholders' equity.

(IMA, adapted)

P26-7. SOLVENCY RATIOS   As the CPA responsible for an "opinion" audit engagement, you are requested by the client to organize the work to provide him at the earliest possible date with some key ratios based on the final figures appearing on the comparative financial statements. This information is to be used to convince creditors that the client business is solvent and to support the use of going-concern valuation procedures in the financial statements. The client wishes to save time by concentrating on only these key data.

The data requested and the calculations taken from the financial statements follow:

	LAST YEAR	THIS YEAR
Current ratio	2.0:1	2.5:1
Quick (acid-test) ratio	1.2:1	.7:1
Property, plant, and equipment to owners' equity	2.3:1	2.6:1
Sales to owners' equity	2.8:1	2.5:1
Net income	Down 10%*	Up 30%*
Earnings per common share	$2.40	$3.12
Book value per common share	Up 8%*	Up 5%*

*As compared to the previous year.

REQUIRED

1. The client asks that you prepare a list of brief comments stating how each of these items supports the solvency and going-concern potential of his business. He wishes to use these comments to support his presentation of data to his creditors. Prepare the comments as requested, giving the implications and the limitations of each item separately and then the collective inference one may draw from them about the client's solvency and going-concern potential.

2. Having done as the client requested in part 1, prepare a brief listing of additional ratio-analysis data for this client which you think his creditors are going to ask for to supplement the data provided in part 1. Explain why you think the additional data will help these creditors to evaluate this client's solvency.

3. What warnings should you offer these creditors about the limitations of ratio analysis for the purpose stated here?

(AICPA, adapted)

P26-8. CALCULATING FINANCIAL RATIOS

REQUIRED

Calculate as many of the financial ratios summarized in Exhibit 26–13 (pp. 1286–87) as you can for Coca-Cola in 1985, using the financial statements and supporting data presented in Appendix 5–1. State any assumptions you make in calculating the ratios.

INDEX